Peterson's®
Scholarships, Grants & Prizes
2019

 PETERSON'S®

About Peterson's®

Peterson's® has been your trusted educational publisher for over 50 years. It's a milestone we're quite proud of, as we continue to offer the most accurate, dependable, high-quality educational content in the field, providing you with everything you need to succeed. No matter where you are on your academic or professional path, you can rely on Peterson's for its books, online information, expert test-prep tools, the most up-to-date education exploration data, and the highest quality career success resources—everything you need to achieve your education goals. For our complete line of products, visit **www.petersons.com.**

For more information about Peterson's range of educational products, contact Peterson's, 8740 Lucent Blvd., Suite 400, Highlands Ranch, CO 80129, or find us online at **www.petersons.com.**

ISBN 978-0-7689-4230-9

Printed in the United States of America

10 9 8 7 6 5 4 3 2 1   20 19 18

Twenty-third Edition

OTHER RECOMMENDED TITLES

Peterson's *The "C" Students Guide to Scholarships,* by Felecia Hatcher
Peterson's *How to Get Money for College: Go Beyond Federal Aid—Get Money from Your School and State*
Peterson's *Plan and Finance Your Family's College Dreams,* by John A. Hupalo and Peter Mazareas, Ph.D.

Peterson's Four-Year Colleges
Peterson's Two-Year Colleges

Contents

CONTENTS

INDEXES

A Note from the Peterson's® Editors

Billions of dollars in financial aid are made available by private donors and governmental agencies to students and their families every year to help pay for college. Yet, to the average person, the task of finding financial aid awards in this huge network of scholarships, grants, and prizes appears to be nearly impossible.

For nearly forty years, Peterson's® has given students and parents the most comprehensive, up-to-date information on how to get their fair share of the financial aid pie. *Peterson's® Scholarships, Grants & Prizes* was created to help students and their families pinpoint those specific private financial aid programs that best match students' backgrounds, interests, talents, or abilities.

In *Peterson's® Scholarships, Grants & Prizes,* you will find nearly 3,500 award programs and resources that are providing financial awards to undergraduates in the 2017–18 academic year. Foundations, fraternal and ethnic organizations, community service clubs, churches and religious groups, philanthropies, companies and industry groups, labor unions and public employees' associations, veterans' groups, and trusts and bequests are all possible sources.

For those seeking to enter college, *Peterson's® Scholarships, Grants & Prizes* includes information needed to make financing a college education as seamless as possible.

The **How to Find an Award That's Right for You** section paints a complete picture of the financial aid landscape, discusses strategies for finding financial awards, provides important tips on how to avoid scholarship scams, and offers insight into how to make scholarship management organizations work for you.

Also found in **How to Find an Award That's Right for You** is the "How to Use This Guide" article, which describes how the nearly 3,500 awards in the guide are profiled, along with information on how to search for an award in one of eleven categories.

If you would like to compare awards quickly, refer to the **Quick-Reference Chart.** Here you can search through the "Scholarships, Grants & Prizes At-a-Glance" chart and select awards by the highest dollar amount.

In the **Profiles of Scholarships, Grants & Prizes** section you'll find updated award programs, along with information about award sponsors. The profile section is divided into three categories: *Academic Fields/Career Goals, Nonacademic/Noncareer Criteria,* and *Miscellaneous Criteria.* Each profile provides all of the need-to-know information about available scholarships, grants, and prizes.

Finally, the back of the book features thirteen **Indexes** listing scholarships, grants, and prizes based on award name; sponsor; academic fields/career goals; civic, professional, social, or union affiliation; corporate affiliation; employment/volunteer experience; impairment; military service; nationality or ethnic background; religious affiliation; residence; location of study; and talent/interest area.

Peterson's® publishes a full line of books—financial aid, career preparation, test prep, and education exploration. Peterson's® publications can be found at high school guidance offices, college libraries and career centers, and your local bookstore and library. Peterson's® books are also available at www.petersonsbooks.com. To search for scholarships online, check out www.petersons.com/college-search/scholarship-search.aspx.

We welcome any comments or suggestions you may have about this publication. Your feedback will help us make educational dreams possible for you—and others like you.

HOW TO FIND AN AWARD THAT'S RIGHT FOR YOU

All About Scholarships

Dr. Gary M. Bell
Former Academic Dean, Honors College, Texas Tech University

During the next four (or more) years you will spend your time earning your college baccalaureate degree, think of the learning task as your primary employment. It is helpful to think of a scholarship as part of the salary for undertaking your job of learning. One of your first inquiries as you examine a potential college setting is about the type of assistance it might provide given your interests, academic record, and personal history. Talk to a financial aid officer or a scholarship coordinator at the school. At most schools, these are special officers—people specifically employed to assist you in your quest for financial assistance. Virtually all schools also have brochures or publications and specific information on their website that show the scholarship opportunities at their institution. Take a close look at this scholarship information.

Also, high school counselors often have keen insight into resources available at colleges, especially for the schools in your area. These people are the key points of contact between institutions of higher education and you.

In general, it is not a good idea to use a private company that promises to provide you with a list of scholarships for which you might be eligible. Such lists are often very broad, and you can secure the same results by using available high school, university, web-based, and published information. The scholarship search you perform online will probably be more fruitful than what any private company can do for you.

What do we mean by the word *scholarship*, anyway? In the very broadest sense, scholarships consist of outright grants of monetary assistance to eligible students to help them attend college. The money is applied to tuition or the cost of living while in school. Scholarships do not need to be repaid. They do, however, often carry stringent criteria for maintaining them, such as the achievement of a certain grade point average, the carrying of a given number of class hours, matriculation in a specific program, or membership in a designated group. Scholarships at many schools may be combined with college work-study programs, in which some work is also required. Often, scholarships are combined with other forms of financial aid so that collectively they provide you with a truly attractive financial aid package. This may include low-interest loan programs to make the school of your choice financially feasible.

Scholarships generally fall into three major categories: *need-based scholarships*, predicated on income; *merit-based scholarships*, based on your academic and sometimes extracurricular achievements; and *association-based scholarships*, which are dependent on as many different associations as you can imagine (for instance, your home county, your identification with a particular group, fraternal and religious organizations, or the company for which a parent may work). The range of reasons for which scholarships are given is almost infinite.

Most schools accommodate students who have financial need. The largest and best grant programs are the U.S. government-sponsored Federal Pell Grants and the Federal Supplemental Educational Opportunity Grants, which you might want to explore with your financial aid counselor. Also inquire about state-sponsored scholarship and grant programs.

Merit-based scholarships come from a variety of sources—the university, individual departments or colleges within the university, state scholarship programs, or special donors who want to assist worthy students. Remember this as you meet with your financial aid officer because he or she knows that different opportunities may be available for you as a petroleum engineering, agriculture, accounting, pre-veterinary, or performing arts major. Merit-based scholarships are typically designed to reward the highest performers on such precollege measures as standardized tests (the SAT® or ACT®) and high school grades. Because repeated performance on standardized tests often leads to higher scores, it may be financially advantageous for you to take these college admission tests several times.

Inquire about each of the three categories of scholarships. The association-based scholarships can sometimes be particularly helpful and quite surprising. Employers of parents, people from specific geographic locations, or organizations (churches, civic groups, unions, special interest clubs, and even family name associations) may provide assistance for college students. Campus scholarship literature is the key to unlocking the mysteries of association-based financial assistance (and the other two categories as well), but personal interviews with financial officers are also crucial.

There are several issues to keep in mind as you seek scholarship assistance. Probably the most important is to determine deadlines that apply to a scholarship for which you may be eligible. It's wise to begin your search early, so that your eligibility is not nullified by missing a published deadline. Most scholarship opportunities require that you complete an application form, and it is time well spent to make sure your answers are neat (if using a paper application), grammatically correct, and logical. Correct spelling is essential. Have someone proofread your application. Keep in mind that if applications require essays, fewer students typically take the time to complete these essays, and this gives those students who do so a better chance of winning that particular scholarship. Always be truthful in these applications, but at the same time provide the most positive self-portrayal to enhance your chances of being considered. Most merit-based and association-based scholarships are awarded competitively.

Finally, let the people who offer you assistance know whether you will accept their offer. Too many students simply assume that a scholarship offer means automatic acceptance. This is not the case! In most instances, you must send a letter of acknowledgement and acceptance. Virtually all schools have agreed that students must make up their minds about scholarship acceptance no later than May 1, but earlier deadlines may apply.

As you probably know, tuition at private schools is typically higher than tuition at state colleges and universities. Scholarships can narrow this gap. Many private institutions have a great deal of money to spend on scholarship assistance, so you may find that with a scholarship, going to a private college will cost no more than attending a state-supported college or university. **Note:** A substantial scholarship from a private school may still leave you with a very large annual bill to cover the difference between the scholarship amount and the actual cost of tuition, fees, and living expenses.

When you evaluate a scholarship, take into account your final out-of-pocket costs. Also consider the length of time for which the school extends scholarship support. Be cautious about schools that promise substantial assistance for the first year to get you there, but then provide little or nothing in subsequent years. The most attractive and meaningful scholarships are offered for four to five years. Do not abandon the scholarship search once you are enrolled at the school of your choice. Often, a number of additional scholarship opportunities are available for you once you're enrolled, especially as you prove your ability and interest in a given field.

It's Never Too Early to Look for College Scholarships

Many high school students make the mistake of thinking that their race to the top of the scholarship mountain begins during their senior year. Some have the forethought to begin their hunt for college money in their junior year. But even that may be too late. Rising costs of college tuition, the increasing number of people attending college for the first time, and the reduction in federal, state, and local grants for college goers have made paying for college without student loan debt a competitive sport. And only those who are prepared are coming out unscathed and debt free.

The importance of securing scholarships and grants to help pay for college cannot be overestimated. The nation is currently in the midst of a student-loan debt crisis that is crippling the earning power of millions of college graduates. If you need any further convincing to get serious about finding money for college other than student loans, check out these sobering statistics:*

- In recent years, college students borrowed more than $100 billion to pay for college, the highest amount of student borrowing ever.

- In 2018, the outstanding balance of student loan debt reached nearly $1.48 trillion (yes, that's with a "T"), surpassing credit card debt of $620 billion.

- Nearly every student who earns a four-year degree graduates with student loan debt, which currently averages about $28,000.

Student loan debt may be inevitable, but it doesn't have to be crippling. And the more money you can get that doesn't require repayment, the better your financial future will be once you do get your college degree. Here are some tips on how to get ahead of the college money rat race and come out a winner:

1. **Make a Family College Payment Plan.** While 70 percent of parents surveyed by an investment group said their students are so brilliant that they will win enormous amounts of scholarships to pay for college, the reality is paying for college without student loans doesn't happen by chance. Paying for college takes planning, and the sooner you begin the better off you'll be. But a student cannot plan for college payments alone. Parents must meet with their children to develop a college payment plan. In their discussions, they need to discuss all family college payment plan options, including parental tax credits, college saving accounts, trusts, savings bonds, and even stock options. At the meeting, parents and their children should do the following:

- Calculate the real costs of attending college.

- Decide who is going to pay and how much.

- Develop a strategy to meet those payment commitments.

Making a family college payment plan is an essential first step. The outcome of this plan gives students a clear scholarship money goal and provides an excellent starting point for your scholarship sojourn.

2. **Start scholarship research on day one.** While most scholarships and grants require you to be a junior or senior in high school, this does not preclude you from creating an application strategy the day you enter high school—or even before! In truth, the minute you decide to go to college you should start researching the best ways to pay for it. Talk to guidance counselors, do research online, learn what the scholarship requirements are, and develop a plan to apply when ready. By searching for scholarships as early as possible, you will be able to zero in on the ones that match with your skills, abilities, characteristics, and passions. In addition to finding scholarships, use this preliminary time to learn the scholarship rules. Build a checklist of all the accompanying documents you're going to need to

---

* Statistics are derived from the Student Loan Report's "Student Loan Debt Statistics 2018." www.studentloans.net/student-loan-debt-statistics

accompany your scholarship application. Save items that you think would work well in your personal statement or essay. Develop a list of people who could be references or write letters of recommendations. Organize, organize, organize—the more organized you are, the easier it will be to apply for multiple scholarships.

3. **Be Your Guidance Counselor's Best Friend.** Long the butt of jokes, guidance counselors are the most maligned members of a high school system. But they can be your best ally when it comes to securing scholarships and grants for college. Get to know your guidance counselor well. Offer your counselor a proactive strategy for getting money for college. Your guidance counselor is more apt to help you with planning your high school career if he or she knows you are serious about going to college.

4. **Rack up scholarships as you go along.** College savings bonds may seem like a blast from the 1950s, but believe it or not there are still essay, speech, and music contests all over the nation that offer them to winners. You can earn these types of rewards as well as cold hard cash at anytime—even before you get into high school. Check out contests such as the Ayn Rand Institute's Anthem and Atlas Shrugged Essay Contests or the American Legion National High School Oratorical Contest. These are open to all high school-age students.

5. **Plan Your High School Years with College in Mind.** As you do your research on college scholarships, you will see that many have academic requirements. You need to start early on developing a course of study to help you hit those necessary academic marks. Few students wake up one day and score 31 on the ACT or start a charity out of the blue. So plan your classes, extracurricular events, and charity activities with college in mind. To be sure, you need to do what appeals to you, but keep in mind that every class you attend, every test you take, and every club you join can be an asset to your scholarship hunt. Be deliberate about your school choices, and start with the end goal in mind.

Filling out a scholarship application is the end, not the beginning of a long process to earn money for college. Fortunately, you can begin all the organization and planning necessary to secure scholarship money well before the scholarship is due. Do not wait. It's never too early to start your scholarship journey. The earlier you begin, the better your journey will be!

A Strategy for Finding Awards

rivate scholarships and awards can be characterized by unpredictable, sometimes seemingly bizarre, criteria. Before you begin your award search, write a personal profile of yourself to help establish as many criteria as possible that might form a basis for your scholarship award. Here is a basic checklist of fifteen questions you should consider:

1. **What are your career goals?**

   Be both narrow and broad in your designations. If, for example, you aim to be a TV news reporter, you will find many awards specific to this field in the *TV/Radio Broadcasting* section. However, collegiate broadcasting courses are offered in departments or schools of communication. So, be sure that you consider *Communications* as a relevant section for your search. Consider *Journalism,* too, for the same reasons. Then look under other broadly inclusive but possibly relevant areas, such as *Trade/Technical Specialties.* Or check a related but different field, such as *Performing Arts.* Finally, look under marginally related basic academic fields, such as *Humanities, Social Sciences,* or *Political Science.* Peterson's makes every attempt to provide the best cross-reference aids, but the nuances of specific awards can be difficult to capture even with the most flexible cross-referencing systems. You will need to be broadly associative in your thinking to get the most out of this wealth of information.

   If you have no clear career goal, browsing the huge variety of academic/career awards may well spark new interest in a career path. Be open to imagining yourself filling different career roles that you previously may not have considered.

2. **In what academic fields might you major?**

   Your educational experiences or your sense about your personal talents or interests may have given you a good idea of what academic discipline you wish to pursue. Again, use both broad and narrow focuses in designing your search, and look at related subject fields. For example, if you want to major in history, check the *History* section, but be sure to check out *Social Sciences* and *Humanities* as well, and maybe *Area/Ethnic Studies. Education,* for example, could suggest the perfect scholarship for a future historian.

3. **In which jobs, industries, or occupations have your parents or other members of your immediate family been employed? What employment experiences do you have?**

   Individual companies, employee organizations, trade unions, government agencies, and industry associations frequently establish scholarships for workers, children of workers, or other relatives of workers from specific companies or industries. These awards might require that you stay in the same career field, but most are offered regardless of the field of study you wish to undertake. Also, if one of your parents is a public service employee, especially a firefighter or police officer, you have many relevant awards from which to choose.

4. **Do you have any hobbies or special interests? Have you ever been an officer or leader of a group? Do you possess special skills or talents? Have you won any competitions? Are you a good writer?**

   From gardening to clarinet playing, from caddying to playing basketball, your special interests can win awards for you from groups that wish to promote and/or reward these pursuits. Many scholarships are targeted to "student leaders," including sports team captains; yearbook or newspaper editors; student government officers; and club, organization, and community activists.

5. **Where do you live? Where have you lived? Where will you go to college?**

   Residence criteria are among the most common qualifications for scholarship aid. Local clubs and companies provide millions of dollars in scholarship aid to students who live in a particular state, province, region, or section of a state. This means that your residential identity puts you at the head of the line for these grants. State of residence can—depending on the sponsor's criteria—include the place of your official residence, the place you attend college, the place you were born, or anywhere you have lived for more than a year.

6. **What is your family's ethnic heritage?**

   Hundreds of scholarships have been endowed for students who can claim a particular nationality or racial or ethnic descent. Partial ethnic descent frequently qualifies, so don't be put off if you do not think of your identity as a specific "ethnic" entity. Awards are available for Colonial American,

English, Polish, Welsh, Scottish, European, and other backgrounds that students may not consider especially "ethnic." One is even available for descendants of the signers of the Declaration of Independence, whatever ethnicity that might have turned out to be some ten generations later.

7. **Do you have a physical disability?**
Many awards are available to individuals with physical disabilities. Of course, commonly recognized impairments of mobility, sight, communication, and hearing are recognized, but learning disabilities and chronic diseases, such as asthma and epilepsy, are also criteria for some awards.

8. **Do you currently or have you ever served in the Armed Forces? Did one of your parents serve in a war? Was one of your parents lost or disabled while serving in the Armed Forces?**
Hundreds of awards use these qualifications.

9. **Do you belong to a civic association, union, or religious organization? Do your parents belong to such groups?**
Hundreds of clubs and religious groups provide scholarship assistance to members or children of members.

10. **Are you male or female?**

11. **What is your age?**

12. **Do you qualify for need-based aid?**

13. **Did you graduate in the upper one-half, upper one-third, or upper one-quarter of your class?**

14. **Do you plan to attend a two-year college, a four-year college, or a trade/technical school?**

15. **In what academic year will you be entering?**

Be expansive when considering your possible qualifications. Although some awards may be small, you may qualify for more than one award—and these can add up to significant amounts in the end.

Who Wants to Be a College Scholarship Millionaire?

There are high school seniors around the country who are becoming rich beyond their wildest dreams even before stepping inside the hallowed halls of higher education. These college upstarts are not start-up kings and queens, á la Mark Zuckerberg of Facebook fame. But they may be just as innovative. They're a part of small, but growing, elite—the College Scholarship Millionaire Club.

The concept of earning a million dollars for college sounds like the premise of a television game show. And to be honest, such a goal remains incredibly lofty for some and downright impossible for others. But what was once a fantasy of every would-be college student is now fast becoming a reality for those willing to work incredibly hard to make it happen.

So just what is the College Scholarship Millionaire Club? It's a group of students who have won $1 million or more in scholarship commitments from universities and colleges and private scholarship funds. The definition should clue you in on at least one prerequisite for joining this club—you have to apply for scholarships—a LOT of them. Still, a quick analysis of some college scholarship millionaires and how they secured their awards can offer any pre-college student great advice on how to get the most out of their scholarship application season.

While there is no sure-fire way to ensure that you earn big bucks in the college scholarship process—anyone promising that is just running a scam—there are steps you can take to increase your odds of having a big scholarship haul. Here are some valuable tips.

Make High-Achieving a Group Sport

More than a decade ago James Ralph Sparks, a calculus teacher at Whitehaven High School (WHS) in Memphis, Tennessee, wanted to find a way to get more of his students into college. Back in 2002, the public school located on Elvis Presley Blvd. wasn't exactly known for its academic aptitude. Back then, graduating seniors were bringing in less than $5 million in scholarship offers for the entire school. But Sparks felt the school could do better. So he created a competition. The 30+ club was the first weapon in the battle to get students more money for college. There was only one criterion for membership: a score of 30 or higher on the ACT. By encouraging students to score high on the national standardized test, Sparks ensured that his students would be in the running for top scholarships. Students who achieved entrance into the club had their scholarship offer letters and scores posted on bulletin boards in the school.

But Sparks wasn't finished. He created the Fortune 500 club, providing exclusive membership only to students who could achieve more than $100,000 in scholarships. The combination of the 30+ club and the Fortune 500 club helped to spur students to achieve. The WHS graduating senior class brought in more than $30 million in scholarship offers in 2010–11.

Apply, Apply, and Apply Again

Another facet of the Whitehaven High School's scholarship program was playing the odds. Anyone who has guided students through a college scholarship application understands that the process can become a numbers game. The more applications you complete, the better your chances of securing a scholarship. While the average high school student applies for two to three scholarships, WHS' millionaire club members applied for ten times that number—about thirty or forty.

Become a Super College Candidate

By now everyone applying to college knows you have to do more than get good grades to stand out. If you want to rise to the top of the scholarship heap, you're going to have to be extraordinary. You can't just volunteer at your local soup kitchen—that's a given. You might have to start your *own* soup kitchen to be considered above your peers. To be a part of the million-dollar scholarship club, you're going to have to go above and beyond to pull down that six-figure college gift.

So let's break down what it takes to be a million-dollar scholar:

- **Start early.** It's never too early to research scholarship opportunities as well as plan your scholarship strategy. Practice writing your personal statement, essay, interviewing skills, and so on to get yourself acquainted with the scholarship process.

- **Make applying a group activity.** Everyone loves a good competition, and it seems earning scholarship money is no exception. At Whitehaven High School, teachers publicly listed the scholarship earnings of students with more than $100,000. WHS also had a scoreboard in front of its school that highlighted scholarship amounts, not just football scores.

- **Don't forget the academics.** Many scholarships have an academic threshold, so you want to make sure to get above that to open more opportunities.

- **Keep Your Options Open.** There are critics who say that applying for scholarships you have no intention of using is not appropriate. But how do you know where you want to go until you figure out how to pay for it? Don't pigeon-hole yourself into one option. If you don't get your first-choice, you'll at least have something to fall back upon.

- **Be sincere.** You may think it's all about the numbers, but you become a million-dollar scholar through authenticity not fakery. Apply to scholarships that fit your passion, purpose, and educational prowess. And apply to schools you actually want to attend. Applying for scholarships and grants take time, and you don't want to waste it on pipe dreams.

Snap and Chat: Use Your Fingertips and Social Media to Pay for College

Felecia Hatcher

Author of *The C Student's Guide to Scholarships* **and** *Start Your Business on a Ramen Noodle Budget*

Snapchat, Instagram, Facebook, Twitter—every day a new social media platform is being launched to suck more of our precious time away. As a prospective college student trying to snag scholarship dollars, every second counts. But what if I told you that you don't have to sacrifice your time on social media and that you could find thousands of scholarship dollars and opportunities by using your smartphone and your thumbs!

It's said that more than $1 billion in scholarships goes un-awarded each year. You may think that this money is being hidden on purpose. I promise you that colleges and scholarship committees are not trying to hide the money from you; they are actually starting to use social media more and more to get the information directly to you. Currently, there are thousands of social media sites on the Internet, and these sites could possibly bring you one step closer to paying for college. Keep reading to find out how you can use social media and crowd funding sites to get creative with your search and not only think outside the box, but also think outside the application.

TWITTER

Twitter allows you to send and receive short messages of 280 characters or less in real time. The one thing that is great about Twitter is that it has a search bar that allows you to search for tweets from anyone or any entity that belongs to the social network. By using special keywords in the search bar, you should be able to find scholarship information the organization tweeted about and direct links to scholarship applications.

Go to the search bar in Twitter and type in the following keywords:

"Scholarship Deadline"

"Scholarship + [Your State]"

"Scholarship PDF"

"Scholarship Deadline http"

GOOGLE IT!

I jokingly tell people that I feel like I can rule the world with my smartphone, 2 safety pins, a rubber band, and Google. Need a restaurant recommendation? Google it! Need to research the best place to get school supplies for a project? Google it! Need to find money for your college education? Google it! Yes, believe it or not, it may be just that simple. But in order to not be bombarded with thousands of useless results, you must use the right keywords. Here is a short list of some keyword combinations that will yield great results in your scholarship search.

You can use the same search terms previously used for your Twitter searches for Google, as well as the following:

Scholarship + 2018

Scholarship + 2019

Scholarship + Deadline + Current Month

Scholarship + [your city/hometown]

Scholarship + [your race/ethnicity/religion]

Scholarship + [your talent]

You can also replace the word *scholarship* with *grant* or *fellowship*.

CROWD FUNDING

So, you applied but didn't win that big $25,000 scholarship. Don't despair—put the power of your network of family, friends, and social media followers to work, and create your own scholarship through crowd funding! With crowd funding, you can get 5,000 strangers to donate $5 each, which equals $25,000 . . . right?

No, I'm not talking about standing on a busy corner and playing your guitar. The following websites allow you to reach out to your friends and family or total strangers; pitch your need through a profile, pictures, and compelling video; and creatively fundraise your way to funding your college education.

Paypal.com
YouCaring.com
Indiegogo.com
PeerBackers.com

Gofundme.com
blog.zerobound.com
ScholarMatch.org

TIPS TO HELP YOU MAXIMIZE YOUR CHANCES OF GETTING FUNDING

Tell a compelling story through video: Writing an essay is one way to let your personality shine through, but nothing is better than seeing you! Use social media platforms like Instagram and YouTube to create short videos that showcase who you are and why you deserve the scholarships, and get as many people as you can to share them. Scholarship committees know that you need money, that's a given. But you want to captivate the committee with an exciting story that will keep them viewing and opening up their wallets with each word. Tell them who you are and what makes you and your needs different from other students. Most importantly, tell them why they should care enough to part with their money. Get creative!

Create an exciting profile: Photos and video go a long way when you are creating profiles on crowd-funding sites, or even on an application that asks for additional information. Take the time to capture great pictures that really let your personality show through. There are an increasing number of applications asking for video submissions. This is your time to shine, so take out your camera and start shooting testimonials from teachers, coaches, and guidance counselors raving about how fabulous you are instead of (or in addition to) submitting the traditional recommendation letter. Capture video when you are doing community service work, working at your part-time job, playing sports, or engaging in your hobbies. Remember photos and video paint the best picture and make the need *real*.

Tip: Use WordPress.com to create a portfolio that not only showcases your education and your resume but also your talents and hobbies. Colleges and Scholarship committees are always searching for well-rounded students!

Don't be afraid to ask for help: Let me put it frankly: The truth is you only get what you ask for! Networks like Facebook, Twitter, LinkedIn, and YouCaring.com allow you to amplify your message, so put the message out there. If you don't ask for the help and let everyone know, then you can't expect anyone to assist you.

So, the next time your parents tell you to get off Facebook or Twitter or to put down your phone, tell them that you are tweeting or searching for scholarship dollars.

CLEAN UP YOUR ACT: SPRUCE UP YOUR INTERNET AND SOCIAL MEDIA PRESENCE

Social media is a huge part of today's social realm. There is a good chance that you probably communicate with your friends on Facebook and Twitter more then you do in person. While these social networks are great for connecting with friends and family, and even meeting new people, they can hurt your scholarship efforts if you are not careful. Having this information in mind, set aside some time before, or directly after, you mail out that first scholarship application to investigate and (if necessary) clean up your online presence.

Are you wondering why this is necessary? I bet you think that your Facebook page has nothing to do with your scholarship application. Well, if these are your thoughts, you are unfortunately very wrong. There's an excellent chance that a scholarship organization will spend time searching for you on the Internet. If you're shuddering at the thought of the scholarship committee members seeing anything on your page, I recommend you follow these tips for "scrubbing" your web reputation squeaky clean.

1. **Google yourself.**
   Search for every possible variation of your name on Google. If anything unbecoming pops up in the search results, do what you can to have it taken down.

2. **Check your social media sites.**
   This includes Facebook, LinkedIn, Twitter, Flickr, Instagram, Tumblr, WordPress, and so on. Make sure all the content on these sites is dignified and academic, meaning that it's serious and grammatically correct. It would be wise to include blog posts about social issues, quotes from famous people you admire, poetry you've written (not including dirty limericks), and so on. Your social media pages need to present you as being smart, mature, and hardworking. If they don't do those things, then clean up your pages, and replace them with content that does. I am not saying that you have to be boring; just be cautious of how everything you post on the Internet *looks* because it's like a tattoo—once it is posted, it's difficult to remove.

3. **Web pages that can't be scrubbed should be hidden.**
   Try to use nicknames when creating your social profiles, and always use the highest privacy settings so that people must be approved in order to see the page. After doing these things, you should still log

out and check what information appears on your default profile page. If a picture that depicts you partying or anything else that would be unflattering to a scholarship committee appears, log back in and replace it with something else.

4. **Take those videos off YouTube.**
   Do this right now. You know which ones I mean.

5. **Remain vigilant.**
   Just because you cleaned up your web presence today doesn't mean it will be clean as a whistle next week. Be aware of what others are posting and tagging with your name. Some search engines even allow you to set up "alerts" to warn you every time your name shows up on the web. I would recommend taking advantage of these helpful alerts.

6. **Check your voicemail.**
   This is very important. If you have an inappropriate ring-back tone or voicemail greeting, you need to either replace it with something professional and appropriate, or kiss your scholarship chances goodbye.

ABOUT THE AUTHOR

Felecia Hatcher-Pearson is a trailblazing social entrepreneur with an authentic voice for change. For the past decade, Felecia has dedicated her life to inspiring a new generation of leaders through her conversational talks on entrepreneurship, college funding, and personal branding.

As an author and social entrepreneur, Felecia Hatcher-Pearson has been honored by the White House as a 2014 Champion of Change for STEM Access & Diversity, Black Enterprise Innovator of the Week, and featured *Essence Magazine* Tech Master. She has been featured on NBC's *Today Show*, MSNBC, The Cooking Channel, and Grio's "100 African American's Making History" for her very successful company, Feverish Ice Cream & Gourmet Pops, where she is former Chief Popsicle.

As a "C" student in high school, Felicia beat the odds and won over $100,000 in scholarships to attend college by getting creative. She used her experience and knack for personal marketability to start her first business called Urban Excellence as a freshman in college. She built and ran innovative college-prep programs for DeVry University and companies such as MECA, AMPS Institute, the YMCA, the TED Center, and the Urban League.

In 2008, after falling flat on her face while attempting to chase an ice cream truck in heels, Felecia started her own gourmet ice pops and dessert catering company, Feverish Pops. Felecia has presented engaging talks on Embracing Failure at Google London and Entrepreneurship and Managing Investor Relations at SXSW. She has spoken as part of the White House Young America Series, at Coca-Cola's headquarters, and at TEDxMiami and TEDxJamaica. Felecia is also the author of three books, *Start Your Business on a Ramen Noodle Budget*, *The C Students Guide to Scholarships*, and *Focused*.

Aside from being a successful entrepreneur and author, Felecia Hatcher-Pearson has dedicated her life to turning kids and young adults from undeserved communities into entrepreneurs and exposing them to careers and entrepreneurial opportunities in technology with her Code Fever program and Black Tech Week initiatives that help to increase tech entrepreneurship funding and training to underserved Florida communities.

Ask the Experts: College Scholarships

Here are some frequently asked scholarship-related questions of college planning and admissions experts. You may have some of the same questions too.

Q: When college representatives visit high schools, do they offer a certain amount of scholarships to students who may be interested in attending that institution?

College reps do visit many high schools on recruiting trips, usually in the early to mid-fall and sometimes in the late spring. Watch your guidance office bulletin board or school website to see when representatives from the colleges you might be interested in are visiting your school or a location near your home. Colleges do not offer a limited amount of scholarships based on where you go to high school. School representatives will discuss both need-based and, often, merit-based financial awards their college may provide. Scholarships might be available to students from your area for one reason or another, but, generally there aren't a specific number based on a particular high school. You should apply to the colleges in which you are interested, and apply for both need-based financial aid and possible additional merit (non-need-based) scholarships for which you might qualify.

Q: How do I get a scholarship through the PSAT/NMSQT®?

The "NMSQT" in "PSAT/NMSQT" stands for the National Merit Scholarship Qualifying Test. About 55,000 of the more than 1.3 million students taking that test each year will be selected as National Merit Commended Students. Going into senior year, in September, smaller proportions of students will be selected as Semi-finalists, then Finalists, and, finally, Merit Scholars (who can earn $2,500 awards). See www.nationalmerit.org for more information on these programs.

Q: I am a 4.0 student and I'm in the National Honor Society. Do you know the level of difficulty of getting an NHS scholarship?

The National Honor Society (www.NHS.us) awards 200 scholarships of $1,000 each year. Your NHS chapter can nominate two students to compete for the scholarships, so the first hurdle is to get one of your chapter's nominations. It's pretty competitive after that, since some highly talented students across the country are in the pool for these merit-based awards. But go for it—you could be one of the lucky winners.

Q: What do I need to do to qualify for a merit scholarship?

It is important to research the colleges you are interested in and determine their merit scholarship criteria. For example, a school might state that it will guarantee a scholarship as long as the student has a certain grade point average, minimum SAT®/ACT® scores, and a specific rank in high school. It is critical to make an in-person appointment with an admissions representative to find out all of the details and requirements for obtaining any of the institution's scholarships. You can also search for merit-based scholarships online.

Q: What are some requirements for athletic scholarships?

The website www.ncaa.org is a good place to look into the differences between Division I, II, and III colleges and universities, and recruiting prospects. Division I and II schools (except the Ivies) offer athletic scholarships. Division III colleges do not. Minimum requirements for scholarships are actually quite low on the whole. However, particular colleges and universities have their own admission and scholarship requirements that you'll need to meet in order to be recruited and admitted.

As you begin the athletic recruiting process and talk with coaches, ask them about their college's recruiting and admission requirements, as well as typical scholarship packages for athletes. If you visit a school's campus on an "official visit," talk with other players about their recruiting experiences and scholarship packages. There are typically minimum college GPA and "reasonable academic progress" requirements that you must meet in order to maintain your eligibility to play college sports and keep your scholarship.

If you want to scope out some athletic scholarships, you can take a look through the scholarship search tool at www.petersons.com and also in this book.

Q: Are grants better than scholarships?

Grants and scholarships are both "free money," in the sense that you don't need to repay them. Grants are usually need-based, while scholarships are based on merit of some kind, or they are a basic discounting of tuition. They are equal, though a hitch with scholarships is that sometimes you have to meet conditions, such as participation in a sport or another activity or maintaining a certain GPA, in order to renew the scholarship. Always read the fine print when evaluating scholarship offers to see how long they last, if they are annually renewable, and what the conditions are that are associated with them.

Q: Will my SAT® or ACT® score qualify me for a scholarship?

It's possible that a high score on these college admission tests will qualify you for a scholarship, though typically colleges like to see the score plus a certain GPA in combination for many of their merit-based scholarship opportunities. Sometimes colleges will elaborate on award criteria on their websites and in their informational materials, explaining that a certain SAT, or SAT/GPA, or GPA level will qualify all or a selection of students for certain levels of awards. Other times, it will be apparent that if your scores are in the top third or so of a college's range, you will likely qualify for a merit-based award (aka a discount on tuition) if that institution has a non-need-based aid program. Most do.

Winning the Scholarship with a Winning Essay

W ho knew it was going to be this hard? You've already dealt with SO much: the SAT®, doing community service, excelling in your AP® class, etc. Convincing your parents that you will be fine 1,500 miles from home and that each and every one of those college application fees are, yes, absolutely necessary! You even learned calculus for goodness sake!

And now in front of you—yet, for right now, somehow out of reach—the golden ticket to make it all come true. Just 500 words (more or less) separate you from those hallowed halls: It's the scholarship essay.

IT HAS TO BE EASY, RIGHT?

Much as you may feel like, c'mon, I'm worth it, just give me the scholarship money, we all know it just doesn't work like that. Because you know what—lots of students are worth it! And lots of students are special, just like you! And where does that leave a scholarship selection committee in deciding to whom their money should be awarded? Yes, now you are catching on—they will pore over *everyone*'s scholarship essay.

So, first and foremost, write your scholarship essay in a way that makes it EASY for the scholarship-awarding committees to do their job! It's almost like a partnership—you show them (in 500 words, more or less) why YOU ARE THE MOST WORTHY RECIPIENT, and they say, thank you, you're right, here is a scholarship for you, and everyone wins! Easy, right?

SORRY—IT REALLY ISN'T THAT EASY

What? You are still sitting there in front of a blank computer screen with nary a thought or sentence? Understood. It's really not that easy. That, too, is part of the point.

No doubt that your GPA, SAT scores, volunteer efforts, leadership roles, and community service are immensely important, but again, you must remember that, during the process of selecting an award recipient, pretty much all the applicants are going to be stellar on some level. And so the scholarship-awarding committee uses your essay to see what sets you apart from the crowd. They are looking for a reason to select you over everyone else.

Your scholarship essay serves many purposes. You have to convince the scholarship-awarding committee you are able to do the following:

- Effectively communicate through the written word
- Substantiate your merit and unique qualities
- Follow directions and adhere to guidelines

A winning scholarship essay can mean up to tens of thousands of dollars for your college education, so let's get started on putting that money in YOUR hands!

EFFECTIVE WRITTEN COMMUNICATION

Be Passionate

Let's face it—you have already written lots of essays. And, we won't tell, but most were probably about topics that were as interesting to you as watching paint dry, right? But you plowed through them and even managed to get some good grades along the way. You may think about just "plowing through" your scholarship essay the same way—mustering up the same amount of excitement you feel when you have to watch old videos of your Aunt Monica on her summer camping trips. But that would be a huge mistake!

An important feature of all winning essays is that they are written on subjects about which the author is truly passionate. Think about it—it actually takes a good bit of effort to fake passion for a subject. But when you are genuinely enthusiastic about something, the words and thoughts flow much more easily, and your passion and energy naturally shine through in your writing. Therefore, when you are choosing your scholarship essay topic, be sure it is something about which you truly care and for which you can show affinity—keeping both you and your reader interested and intrigued!

Be Positive

You've probably heard the expression: "If you don't have anything nice to say, don't say anything at all." Try to steer clear of essays that are too critical, pessimistic, or antagonistic. This doesn't mean that your essay shouldn't acknowledge a serious problem or that everything has to have a happy ending. But it does mean that you should not just write about the negative. If you are writing about a problem, present solutions. If your story doesn't have a happy ending, write about what you learned from the experience and how you would do things differently if faced with a similar situation in the future. Your optimism is what makes the scholarship-awarding committee excited about giving you money to pursue your dreams. Use positive language and be proud to share yourself and your accomplishments. Everyone likes an uplifting story, and even scholarship judges want to feel your enthusiasm and zest for life.

Be Clear and Concise

Don't fall into the common essay-writing trap of using general statements instead of specific ones. All scholarship judges read at least one essay that starts with "Education is the key to success." And that means nothing to them. What does mean something is writing about how your tenth-grade English teacher opened your eyes to the understated beauty and simplicity of haiku—how less can be more—and how that then translated into you donating some of your old video games to a homeless shelter where you now volunteer once a month. That's powerful stuff! It's a very real story, clearly correlating education to a successful outcome. Focusing on a specific and concise example from your life helps readers relate to you and your experiences. It also guarantees you bonus points for originality!

Edit and Proofread and Then Edit and Proofread

There is an old saying: "Behind every good writer is an even better editor." Find people (friends, siblings, coaches, teachers, guidance counselors) to read your essay, provide feedback on how to make it better, and edit it for silly, sloppy mistakes. Some people will read your essay and find issues with your grammar. Others will read your essay and point out how one paragraph doesn't make sense in relation to another paragraph. Some people will tell you how to give more examples to better make your point. All of those people are giving you great information, and you need to take it all in and use it to your advantage! However, don't be overwhelmed by it, and don't let it become all about what everyone else thinks. It's your essay and your thoughts—the goal of editing and proofreading is to clean up the rough edges and make the entire essay shine!

And when you do get to that magical point where you think "DONE!"—instead, just put the essay aside for a few days. Come back to it with an open mind and read, edit, and proofread it one last time. Check it one last time for spelling and grammar fumbles. Check it one last time for clarity and readability (reading it out loud helps!). Check it one last time to ensure it effectively communicates why you are absolutely the winning scholarship candidate.

YOUR UNIQUE QUALITIES

It's one thing to help out at the local library a few hours a week; it's a completely different thing if you took it upon yourself to suggest, recruit, organize, and lead a fundraising campaign to buy 10 new laptops for kids to use at the library!

And don't simply rattle off all your different group memberships. Write about things you did that demonstrate leadership and initiative within those groups. Did you recruit new members or offer to head up a committee? Did you find a way for the local news station to cover your event or reach out to another organization and collaborate on an activity? Think about your unique qualities and how you have used them to bring about change.

A SLICE OF YOUR LIFE

While one goal of your essay is surely to explain why you should win the scholarship money, an equally important goal is to reveal something about you, something that makes it easy to see why you should win. Notice we said to reveal "something" about you and not "everything" about you. Most likely, the rest of the scholarship application gathers quite a bit of information about you. The essay is where you need to hone in on just one aspect of your unique talents, one aspect of an experience, one aspect of reaching a goal. It's not about listing all your accomplishments in your essay (again, you probably did that on the application). It's about sharing a slice of your life—telling your story and giving your details about what makes YOU memorable.

YOUR ACCOMPLISHMENTS, LOUD AND PROUD

Your extracurricular activities illustrate your personal priorities and let the scholarship selection committee know what's important to you. Being able to elaborate on your accomplishments and awards within those activities certainly bolsters your chances of winning the scholarship. Again, though, be careful to not just repeat what is already on the application itself. Use your essay to focus on a specific accomplishment (or activity or talent or award) of which you are most proud.

Did your community suffer through severe flooding last spring? And did you organize a clothing drive for neighbors who were in need? How did that make you feel? What feedback did you get? How did it inspire your desire to become a climatologist?

Were school budget cuts going to mean the disbanding of some afterschool clubs? Did you work with teachers and parents to write a proposal to present to the school board, addressing how new funds could be raised in order to save the clubs? How did that make you feel? What feedback did you get? How did it inspire you to start a writing lab for junior high kids?

You have done great things—think about that one special accomplishment and paint the picture of how it has made you wiser, stronger, or more compassionate to the world around you. Share the details!

But Don't Go Overboard

A five-hanky story may translate into an Oscar-worthy movie, but rarely does it translate into winning a scholarship. If your main reason for applying for the scholarship is that you feel you deserve the money because of how much suffering you have been through, you need a better reason. Scholarship selection committees are not really interested in awarding money to people with problems; they want to award money to people who solve problems. While it's just fine to write about why you need the scholarship money to continue your education, it's not fine for your essay to simply be a laundry list of family tragedies and hardships.

So, instead of presenting a sob story, present how you have succeeded and what you have accomplished despite the hardships and challenges you faced. Remember that everyone has faced difficulties. What's unique about you is how YOU faced your difficulties and overcame them. That is what makes your essay significant and memorable.

FOLLOWING DIRECTIONS

Does Your Essay Really Answer the Question?

Have you ever been asked one question but felt like there was another question that was really being asked? Maybe your dad said something like, "Tell me about your new friend Logan." But what he really meant to ask you was, "Tell me about your new friend Logan. Do his lip rings and tattoos mean he's involved in things I don't want you involved in?"

The goal of every scholarship judge is to determine the best applicant out of a pool of applicants who are all rather similar. Pay attention and you'll find that the essay question is an alternate way for you to answer the real question the scholarship-awarding committee wants to ask. For instance, an organization giving an award to students who plan to study business might ask, "Why do you want to study business?" But their real underlying question is, "Why are you the best future business person to whom we should give our money?" If there is a scholarship for students who want to become doctors, you can bet that 99 percent of the students applying want to become doctors. And if you apply for that scholarship with an essay simply delving into your lifelong desire to be a potter, well, that doesn't make you unique, it makes you pretty much unqualified for that opportunity. Be sure to connect your personal skills, characteristics, and experiences with the objectives of the scholarship and its awarding organization.

Does Your Essay Theme Tie In?

Let's say that you are applying for a community service-based award and, on the application, you go ahead and list all the community service groups you belong to and all the awards you have won. But in your essay, you write about how homeless people should find a job instead of sitting on street corners begging for money. Hey—everyone is entitled to their opinion, but would you agree that there is some sort of disconnect between your application and your essay? And no doubt you have made the scholarship-awarding committee wonder the same thing.

So how do you ensure your essay doesn't create a conflicting message? You need to examine the theme of your essay and how it relates both to your application and the reason the scholarship exists in the first place. If the scholarship-funding organization seeks to give money to someone who wants a career in public relations and your essay focuses on how you are not really a "people person," well, you can see how that sends a mixed message to your reader.

Think about it this way: The theme of your essay should naturally flow around the overarching purpose or goal of the organization awarding the scholarship money. Once you have clarified this nugget, you can easily see if and how your words tie in to the organization's vision of whom their scholarship winner is.

Three More Pieces of Advice

1. **Follow the essay length guidelines closely.** You certainly don't want your essay disqualified simply because it was too long or too short!

2. **The deadline is the deadline.** A day late and you could certainly be more than a dollar short in terms of the award money that isn't going to be awarded to you if your application is not received by the due date. Begin the essay writing process well in advance of the scholarship deadline. Writing and editing and rewriting takes time so you should probably allow yourself at least 2 weeks to write your scholarship essay.

3. **Tell the truth.** No need to say anything further on that, right? Right.

Getting in the Minority Scholarship Mix

Did you know that a great duck call can win you scholarship money in the Chick and Sophie Major Memorial Duck Calling Contest?

Website: http://www.stuttgartarkansas.org/scholarship-contest.html

Perhaps duck-calling is not your calling but creativity with Duck® brand duct tape is. If so, the "Stuck at Prom" scholarship may be just for you—design promware for you and your date and win some moola!

Website: http://www.stuckatprom.com

How about this tall order? Tall Clubs International awards scholarships to men who are taller than 6'2" or women who are taller than 5'10".

Website: http://www.tallclubfoundation.org/scholarship-program.html

Oh? Not necessarily the minority group you had in mind? That's OK because guess what? In this day and age, just about everyone is a minority of some sort. It all depends on a scholarship benefactor's definition of minority.

In the college realm, the word "minority" takes on a myriad of meanings. One definition of a minority that often springs to mind is of someone of an underrepresented ethnicity, such as Native Americans, African Americans, or Hispanic Americans. No question there. Similarly though, a minority can be someone pursuing an underrepresented college major, such as paranormal research. Think that all scholarships for minorities target United States–specific groups? Think again. For example, Canadian students, whether they plan to study at home or abroad, can qualify for scholarships for aboriginals. Getting the picture? The key is to use your own unique qualities as you search for scholarships. Think about your gender, your family's economic status, your religious background, and your geographic locale just to start the ball rolling. Once you broadly frame your search along

those lines, you'll quickly see how easily you can qualify for a scholarship!

AM I REALLY A MINORITY?

No matter the source—federal, state, professional organization, private endowment, corporate donor, college, or university—they all offer minority scholarships, looking to create diversity and inclusion in an increasingly global marketplace.

It's more than probable that you fit into at least one of the ever-expanding minority scholarship categories—nearly everyone does—by some broadly based definition of minority. Some of the niche scholarship "minorities" have already been mentioned. Now let's take a look at some of the broader categories—one of which likely fits you!

African American Students

While African Americans make up a large U.S. minority group, they are still met with one of the biggest barriers to college enrollment—money. To combat that challenge, scholarships for African American students have grown over the years, with some of the best sources of funding found within partnerships between minority organizations and corporate sponsors.

As the nation's largest minority education organization, the United Negro College Fund (UNCF) provides operating funds for 38-member historically black colleges and universities (HBCUs), along with scholarships and internships for students at about 900 institutions. The UNCF has helped more than 400,000 students attend and graduate college with the more than $3.3 billion it has raised—more funds helping minorities attend college than any other entity outside of the U.S. government.

United Negro College Fund
8260 Willow Oaks Corporate Drive
P.O. Box 10444
Fairfax, VA 22031-8044
Phone: 800-331-2244
Website: www.uncf.org

Hispanic American Students

Fortunately, over the years, the U.S. government has contributed millions of dollars toward startup costs for the development of Hispanic universities and colleges and toward already established Hispanic universities and colleges. The effort has been paying off with dramatic increases in college enrollment by Hispanic American students. Scholarship programs for Hispanic American students look to increase the number of Hispanic students studying in subject areas most underrepresented by them, for instance, the sciences, engineering, math, and technology.

As the nation's leading Hispanic higher-education fund, the Hispanic Scholarship Fund (HSF) works to remove the barriers keeping many Hispanic American students from earning a college degree. Over the past 35 years, HSF has awarded more than $430 million in scholarships (over 150 types of scholarships) and supported a wide range of outreach and education programs for both college students and their families.

Hispanic Scholarship Fund
55 Second Street, Suite 1500
San Francisco, CA 94105
Phone: 877-HSF-INFO (877-473-4636)
E-mail: scholar1@hsf.net
Website: www.hsf.net

Asian American Students

Identifying yourself as Asian American means you probably consider yourself Cambodian, Hmong, Laotian, Malaysian, Okinawan, Tahitian, or Thai—just to name a few possibilities. As a somewhat smaller, yet growing, minority group, Asian Americans attend college more than any other minority group and tend to stay in college once they have enrolled. Excellent merit-based aid sources for Asian American students include cultural organizations, university departments such as law and journalism, and professional organizations.

The Asian & Pacific Islander American Scholarship Fund (APIASF), founded in 2003, has provided more than $50 million in scholarships to Asian and Pacific Islander Americans with financial need.

The Asian & Pacific Islander American
    Scholarship Fund
2025 M Street NW, Suite 610
Washington, DC 20036

Phone: 202-986-6892
Phone (toll-free): 877-808-7032
Fax: 202-530-0643
E-mail: info@apiasf.org
Website: http://www.apiasf.org/

Native American Students

Native American (inclusive of American Indians and Native Alaskans) students make up the smallest minority population on college campuses. As you explore scholarship opportunities for Native Americans, you may find that you'll need proof of your Native American status, which means your Certificate of Indian Blood (CIB), as well as belonging to a well-recognized tribe. If you are like most Native American descendants, though, you will probably not have this proof, as many tribes change names and have nonexistent documentation records. If somehow you do have a CIB and belong to a tribe, you may have an upper hand in qualifying for some more esoteric scholarship and grant programs.

American Indian College Fund

Located in Denver, Colorado, the mission of the American Indian College Fund (AICF) is threefold: to spread awareness of the Fund and of tribal colleges and universities; to raise college scholarship funds for American Indian students attending tribal and mainstream colleges; and to raise money for other needs and projects of the tribal schools.

The AICF awards approximately 5,000 college scholarships a year. Monies given to individual schools are used to award Tribal College Scholarships to candidates of each school's choosing. Other undergraduate scholarships are awarded directly from the AICF to American Indian students attending both tribal and mainstream colleges and universities.

The American Indian College Fund
8333 Greenwood Boulevard
Denver, CO 80221
Phone: 303-426-8900
Phone (toll-free): 800-776-3863
Website: www.collegefund.org

American Indian Graduate Center

Another large source of student scholarships and financial aid for Native Americans is the American Indian

Graduate Center (AIGC), which provides monies to both undergraduate and graduate students.

The mission of the AIGC is to improve the cultural and economic well-being of American Indians and Native Alaskans both individually and tribally. Their efforts focus on developing educated and forward-thinking leaders who will steer their communities into an era of prosperity, productivity, and self-reliance.

The AIGC, with the generous support of the Tommy Hilfiger Corporation Foundation, also administers the All Native American High School Academic Team, a program recognizing Native American/Alaska Native students who demonstrate superior success in academics, leadership, and American Indian community service.

As part of the AIGC's overall mission, this program promotes academic excellence and the pursuit of higher education among Native American and Alaska Native students, with the goal of preparing them for future roles as community leaders and role models. All of the students recognized by this program receive financial awards to pay for the cost of attending the college or university of their choice.

The American Indian Graduate Center
3701 San Mateo Boulevard NE #200
Albuquerque, NM 87110
Phone: 505-881-4584
Website: www.aigcs.org/aigc-scholarship-fellowship-
  opportunities

Other Opportunities

In addition to the AICF and the AIGC, there are several other organizations that provide various student scholarships to Native Americans:

- **American Indian Science and Engineering Society (AISES):** With the goal of substantially increasing "the representation of American Indian and Alaskan Natives in engineering, science and other related technology disciplines," the AISES awards university scholarships to Native American undergraduate and graduate students pursuing degrees in various areas of engineering and science. (www.aises.org/scholarships)
- **Association on American Indian Affairs (AAIA):** Offers college scholarship opportunities to both undergraduate and graduate students demonstrating financial need. (https://www.indian-affairs.org/scholarships.html)

- **Indian Health Service (IHS):** As an arm of the U.S. Department of Health and Human Services, the IHS awards university scholarships to pay for the education and training of undergraduate, graduate, and doctoral students pursuing degrees in healthcare related areas. (https://www.ihs.gov/scholarship/)
- **Intertribal Timber Council (ITC):** Dedicated to improving the management of natural resources that are important to Native American communities, the ITC sponsors a variety of different undergraduate scholarships and fellowship opportunities each year. (www.itcnet.org/about_us/scholarships.html)

Interracial Students

There is an interesting trend in minority scholarships where scholarship-funding organizations seek to include students of mixed heritage, blended cultures, and students whose ethnic backgrounds don't fit neatly into one particular category. Search for prizes tagged as "interracial scholarships," "multicultural scholarships," or "multiethnic scholarships."

Lesbian, Gay, Bisexual, and Transgender Students

Lesbian, gay, bisexual, and transgender (LGBT) students are recognized as a legitimate minority, and many colleges and organizations offer scholarships to this group. As an LGBT student, also be on the lookout for scholarship opportunities for sons and daughters of gay and lesbian parents, as well as friends and allies of the LGBT community.

Since its inception in 2001, the Point Foundation has invested more than $3 million in outstanding gay, lesbian, bisexual, and transgender students. An average Point Scholarship is about $13,600 and covers tuition, books, supplies, room and board, transportation, and living expenses.

Point Foundation
5055 Wilshire Boulevard, Suite 501
Los Angeles, CA 90036
Phone: 323-933-1234
Fax: 866-397-6468
E-mail: info@pointfoundation.org
Website: www.pointfoundation.org

EVERYONE NEEDS A GOOD RESOURCE

From specialized databases to award programs serving as umbrella organizations for numerous other organizations and awards, many resources are out there for criteria-based scholarships, all with one goal—to help you find the money you need to get you on your college path.

CHCI (Congressional Hispanic Caucus Institute)

CHCI provides a free, comprehensive list of scholarships, internships, and fellowships for Hispanic students.

Congressional Hispanic Caucus Institute
1128 16th Street NW
Washington, DC 20036
Phone: 202-543-1771
Phone: (toll-free) 800-EXCEL-DC (392-3532)
Fax: 202-548-8799
Websites: www.chci.org
www.chcinextopp.net

Gates Millennium Scholars

The Gates Millennium Scholars program was founded by a grant from the Bill and Melinda Gates Foundation with the intention of increasing the number of African Americans, Native Americans, Asian Americans, and Hispanic Americans enrolling in and completing undergraduate and graduate degree programs.

Gates Millennium Scholars
P.O. Box 10500
Fairfax, VA 22031-8044
Phone (toll-free): 877-690-4677
Website: www.gmsp.org

GETTING CREATIVE WITH MINORITY SCHOLARSHIPS

Now that you are really thinking outside of the box, you may consider one or more of your outstanding features as the conduit to classifying yourself as a minority. And if you still need some more inspiration:

- Juniata College in Pennsylvania offers a scholarship for left-handed students.
- Little People of America offers a scholarship to adult students who are 4'10" or shorter.
- There are even scholarships for white males offered by The Former Majority Association for Equality, a nonprofit group in Texas.

Be creative and get in the mix! To which minority groups do *you* belong?

What to Do If You Don't Win a Scholarship, Grant, or Prize

More than 20 million students will enroll in the nation's colleges and universities this year, and you can bet nearly all of them will be vying for the more than $4 billion in private scholarship money that's available. In fact, 85 percent of all first-time undergraduate students attending a four-year college receive some type of financial aid—including scholarships, grants, awards, and student loans.

Yet, even though billions of dollars are out there for the grasping, the average scholarship award may just be a few thousand dollars. That's only going to put a minor dent in the more than $20,000 annual price tag for in-state tuition, room, and board at a public four-year institution (over $40,000 for private). So, unless you started working as a toddler you're going to have to do something spectacular to avoid buckling under a mountain of student loan debt to get your degree.

Applying for grants and private scholarships is a given. But what if your living room table is filling up with denial letters? What do you do then? Well, the first thing is not to panic. There are plenty of ways to pay for college without going into an enormous amount of debt. Here are some tips and suggestions that will help you to formulate a back-up plan if you miss out on the college scholarship lottery.

IF AT FIRST YOU DON'T SUCCEED

A rejection letter doesn't mean no, it really means, "Not right now." There is nothing wrong with applying for a private scholarship, fellowship, or grant again, even if you've been rejected. Just think, you'll have a leg up on everyone who is coming to the competition cold, as you've been there before. Before you dust off your essay from last year and shove it into an envelope this year, be sure to contact the organization and ask for feedback.

Sure, some may not be willing to speak to you, but you won't lose any sleep by trying. Often the best advice comes from the unlikeliest places, and asking pointed, mature questions about why your first application failed can only serve you in your college money hunt. In addition, the counsel might help you to improve an application for another organization. So follow up on those who've said no—you never know what kind of great tips and suggestions they will have for you. Here are some questions you may ask when you seek feedback:

- Did my application get rejected because of a procedural mistake? Did I mess up the application process? Did I meet the deadline? Were all my documents included?
- Was my personal statement/essay well done? How could it have been improved?
- Could you give me suggestions on how best to apply for your scholarship again?

Note: You, of course, can't do any of this if you waited until the last minute to fill out your scholarship application, so it pays to start your quest for college treasure early.

YOU CAN APPLY FOR SCHOLARSHIPS WHILE IN COLLEGE

Even if you've already started your college career with your scholarship coffers empty and your student loan debt toppling over, do not fret. You can still apply for grants, scholarships, and programs that do not require you go into debt while you're attending school. Many scholarships are not automatically renewed, and if students do not apply for them, there may be more cash for you. Create an application cycle for every year you attend school. You never know what opportunity you may be missing if you do not at least try to apply while attending school.

WORK NOW, NOT LATER

It used to be that flipping burgers at the local fast-food joint was the way most college students paid for college. And to be sure that option is still open. But the recent technology boom fueled by the monetization of the Internet has allowed even the youngest among us to become entrepreneurs. From teenage search engine app maker Nick D'Alosio, who has raised capital from one of China's billionaires, to the pre-adolescent Mallory Kiveman, who invented a lollipop to cure the hiccups, the spirit of innovation runs deep among the young. Use technology to start your version of a lemonade stand, and you may make enough in your senior year to pay for college and beyond. Technology has allowed people to think better, smarter, and bigger than ever before. As you're working on that latest science project, think about ways to monetize it. It could be your ticket to a full-ride to college.

DON'T LEAVE MONEY ON THE TABLE

Did you know that only 1 in 10 undergraduate students receive a scholarship award? This isn't because there aren't enough scholarships available. On the contrary, millions of dollars in scholarship money go unclaimed because students do not apply for them.

Yes, that's right. College students, desperate to incur massive amounts of debts forget to apply for grants, miss deadlines, and sloppily fill out scholarship applications to ensure they get rejected and leave money on the table. You, of course, would never do that. But some people will.

Do not be one of those people. Make sure you are taking advantage of all your opportunities to gain debt-free money for college. In addition to applying for private scholarships, make sure you go beyond the Federal Pell Grant. Remember, there are state grants, local grants, need-based grants, merit grants, and college university grants that are available for students. Be sure to check with your admitting institution to make sure you haven't overlooked grants—many of which are automatically offered to students regardless of income.

PRACTICE SOME ALTRUISM

Though it may seem to have gone the way of milkshakes and quaint small-town post offices, there are still some programs that will help pay for your college education as long as you commit to performing public service. From AmeriCorps, which defrays college costs for students who work for nonprofits, or in high-need areas to the Public Service Loan Forgiveness Program, in which borrowers may qualify for forgiveness of the remaining balance of their Direct Loans after they make 120 qualifying payments on those loans while employed full time by certain public service employers, there are dozens of programs that will lower your college costs in exchange for public service. Even top-tier universities such as Harvard and Princeton are offering free tuition (Harvard for just one

year) for students who choose to work in public service careers. There are loan forgiveness programs for virtually every public service profession from state-appointed prosecutors, teachers, primary care doctors, and law enforcement officers; members of the armed forces; nurses and healthcare workers; and even Peace Corps volunteers. But beware—the programs have strict guidelines; one misstep and you could end up footing the bill for your entire college dream. And, as always, consult your tax advisor as current law categorizes the loan amount that is forgiven as income.

Here are some contacts for programs that pay down college costs for volunteerism or public service:

AmeriCorps

More than 75,000 adults work with thousands of nonprofits around the country providing tutoring, mentoring, housing management, and a host of other services to the disadvantaged through AmeriCorps. In exchange they receive money to pay for college or graduate school, or they obtain forgiveness on student loans plus a paycheck.

AmeriCorps
1201 New York Avenue, NW
Washington, DC 20525
Phone: 202-606-5000
TTY: 800-833-3722 (toll-free)
Website: www.nationalservice.gov/programs/
americorps

National Health Service Corps

The National Health Service Corps awards scholarships to students who are pursuing careers in primary care. Students must be pursuing degrees in medicine, dentistry, nursing, and physician assistant studies.

National Health Corps
Phone: 800-221-9393 (toll-free)
Website: http://nhsc.hrsa.gov

Public Service Loan Forgiveness

Congress created the Public Service Loan Forgiveness Program in 2007 as an incentive for people to enter fields that focused on public service. The beneficial program offers qualified borrowers the opportunity to have their federal loans forgiven if they work in certain public service areas.

Website: www.studentaid.gov.

How to Use This Guide

The more than 3,500 award programs described in this book are organized into eleven broad categories that represent the major factors used to determine eligibility for scholarships, awards, and prizes. To build a basic list of awards available to you, look under the broad category or categories that fit your particular academic goals, skills, personal characteristics, or background. The categories are:

- Academic Fields/Career Goals
- Civic, Professional, Social, or Union Affiliation
- Corporate Affiliation
- Employment/Volunteer Experience
- Impairment
- Military Service
- Nationality or Ethnic Heritage
- Religious Affiliation
- Residence/Location of Study
- Talent/Interest Area
- Miscellaneous Criteria

The **Academic Fields/Career Goals** category is subdivided into 131 subject areas that are organized alphabetically by award sponsor. The **Military Service** category is subdivided alphabetically by branch of service. All other categories are organized alphabetically by the name of the award sponsor.

Full descriptive profiles appear in only one location in the book. Cross-references to the name and page number of the full descriptive profile appear at other locations under the other relevant categories for the award. The full description appears in the first relevant location in the book and cross-references later locations, so you will always be redirected toward the front of the book.

Your major field of study and career goals have central importance in college planning. As a result, we have combined these into a single category and have given this category precedence over the others. The **Academic Fields/Career Goals** section appears first in the book. If an academic major or career area is a criterion for a scholarship, the description of this award will appear in this section.

Within the **Academic Fields/Career Goals** section, cross-references are only from and to other academic fields or career areas. You will be able to locate relevant awards from nonacademic or noncareer criteria through the indexes in the back of this book.

For example, the full descriptive profile of a scholarship for any type of engineering student who resides in Ohio might appear under *Aviation/Aerospace*, which is the first engineering category heading in the **Academic Fields/Career Goals** section. Cross-references to this first listing may occur from any other relevant engineering or technological academic field subject area, such as *Chemical Engineering, Civil Engineering, Electrical Engineering/Electronics, Engineering-Related Technologies, Engineering/Technology, Mechanical Engineering,* or *Nuclear Science.* There would not be a cross-reference from the *Residence* category. However, the name of the award will appear in the Residence index under Ohio.

Within the major category sections, descriptive profiles are organized alphabetically by the name of the sponsoring organization. If more than one award from the same organization appears in a particular section, the awards are listed alphabetically under the sponsor name, which appears only once, by the name of the first award.

HOW THE PROFILES ARE ORGANIZED

Here are the elements of a full profile:

Name of Sponsoring Organization

These appear alphabetically under the appropriate category. In most instances, acronyms are given as full names. However, occasionally a sponsor will refer to itself by an acronym. In these instances, we present the sponsor's name as an acronym.

Website Address

Award Name

Brief Textual Description of the Award

Academic Fields/Career Goals (only in the Academic Fields/Career Goals section of the book)

This is a list of all academic or career subject terms that are assigned to this award.

Award

Is it a scholarship? A prize for winning a competition? A forgivable loan? For what type and for what years of college can it be used? Is it renewable or is it for only one year?

Eligibility Requirements

Application Requirements
What information do you need to supply to be considered? What are the deadlines?

Contact
If provided by the sponsor, this element includes the name, mailing address, phone and fax numbers, and e-mail address of the person to contact for information about a specific award.

USING THE INDEXES
The alphabetical indexes in the back of the book are designed to aid your search. Two are name indexes. One lists scholarships alphabetically by academic fields and career goals. The other ten indexes supply access by nonacademic and noncareer criteria. The indexes give you the page number of the descriptions of relevant awards regardless of the part of the book in which they appear.

These are the indexes:

- **Award Name**
- **Sponsor**
- **Academic Fields/Career Goals**
  [131 subject areas, from Academic Advising to Women's Studies]
- **Civic, Professional, Social, or Union Affiliation**
- **Corporate Affiliation**
- **Employment/Volunteer Experience**
- **Impairment**
- **Military Service**
- **Nationality or Ethnic Heritage**
- **Religious Affiliation**
- **Residence**
- **Location of Study**
- **Talent/Interest Area**

In general, when using the indexes, writing down the names and page numbers of the awards that you are interested in is an effective technique.

DATA COLLECTION PROCEDURES
Peterson's takes its responsibility to its readers, as a provider of trustworthy information, very seriously. Peterson's administered an electronic survey between November 2017 and April 2018 in order to update information from all programs listed within this guide. All collected data was updated between November 2017 and April 2018. Additional award program data was obtained between January 2013 and April 2018. Peterson's research staff makes every effort to verify unusual figures and resolve discrepancies. Nonetheless, errors and omissions are possible in a data collection endeavor of this scope. Also, facts and figures, such as number and amount of awards, can suddenly change, or awards can be discontinued by a sponsoring organization. Therefore, readers should verify data with the specific sponsoring agency responsible for administering these awards before applying.

CRITERIA FOR INCLUSION IN THIS BOOK
The programs listed in this book have the primary characteristics of legitimate scholarships: verifiable sponsor addresses and phone numbers, appropriate descriptive materials, and fees that, if required, are not exorbitant. Peterson's assumes that these fees are used to defray administrative expenses and are not major sources of income.

QUICK REFERENCE CHART

Scholarships, Grants & Prizes At-a-Glance

This chart lists award programs that indicate that their largest award provides $2000 or more. The awards are ranked in descending order on the basis of the dollar amount of the largest award. Because the award criteria in the Academic Fields/Career Goals and Nonacademic/Noncareer Criteria column may represent only some of the criteria or limitations that affect eligibility for the award, you should refer to the full description in the award profiles to ascertain all relevant details.

Award Name	Page Number	Highest Dollar Amount	Lowest Dollar Amount	Number of Awards	Academic Fields/Career Goals and Nonacademic/Noncareer Criteria
Regeneron Science Talent Search	964	$250,000	$25,000	40	Must be in high school.
U.S. Army ROTC Four-Year College Scholarship	610	$150,000	$9000	1,000–2,500	Military Service: Army; Army National Guard. Residence: Alabama; Alaska; Arizona; Arkansas; California; Colorado; Connecticut; Delaware; District of Columbia; Florida; Georgia; Guam; Hawaii; Idaho; Illinois; Indiana; Iowa; Kansas; Kentucky; Louisiana; Maine; Maryland; Massachusetts; Michigan; Minnesota; Mississippi; Missouri; Montana; Nebraska; Nevada; New Hampshire; New Jersey; New Mexico; New York; North Carolina; North Dakota; Ohio; Oklahoma; Oregon; Pennsylvania; Puerto Rico; Rhode Island; South Carolina; South Dakota; Tennessee; Texas; Utah; Vermont; Virginia; Washington; West Virginia; Wisconsin; Wyoming. Studying in Alabama; Alaska; Arizona; Arkansas; California; Colorado; Connecticut; Delaware; District of Columbia; Florida; Georgia; Guam; Hawaii; Idaho; Illinois; Indiana; Iowa; Kansas; Kentucky; Louisiana; Maine; Maryland; Massachusetts; Michigan; Minnesota; Mississippi; Missouri; Montana; Nebraska; Nevada; New Hampshire; New Jersey; New Mexico; New York; North Carolina; North Dakota; Ohio; Oklahoma; Ontario; Oregon; Pennsylvania; Puerto Rico; Rhode Island; South Carolina; South Dakota; Tennessee; Texas; Utah; Vermont; Virginia; Washington; West Virginia; Wisconsin; Wyoming. Must be in high school.

Award Name	Page Number	Highest Dollar Amount	Lowest Dollar Amount	Number of Awards	Academic Fields/Career Goals and Nonacademic/Noncareer Criteria
Army (ROTC) Reserve Officers Training Corps Two-, Three-, Four-Year Campus-Based Scholarships	610	$120,000	$10,000	2,000–3,500	Military Service: Army. Residence: Alabama; Alaska; Arizona; Arkansas; California; Colorado; Connecticut; Delaware; District of Columbia; Florida; Georgia; Guam; Hawaii; Idaho; Illinois; Indiana; Iowa; Kansas; Kentucky; Louisiana; Maine; Maryland; Massachusetts; Michigan; Minnesota; Mississippi; Missouri; Montana; Nebraska; Nevada; New Hampshire; New Jersey; New Mexico; New York; North Carolina; North Dakota; Ohio; Oklahoma; Ontario; Oregon; Pennsylvania; Puerto Rico; Rhode Island; South Carolina; South Dakota; Tennessee; Texas; Utah; Vermont; Virginia; Washington; West Virginia; Wisconsin; Wyoming. Studying in Alabama; Alaska; Arizona; Arkansas; California; Colorado; Connecticut; Delaware; District of Columbia; Florida; Georgia; Guam; Hawaii; Idaho; Illinois; Indiana; Iowa; Kansas; Kentucky; Louisiana; Maine; Maryland; Massachusetts; Michigan; Minnesota; Mississippi; Missouri; Montana; Nebraska; Nevada; New Hampshire; New Jersey; New Mexico; New York; North Carolina; North Dakota; Ohio; Oklahoma; Oregon; Pennsylvania; Puerto Rico; Rhode Island; South Carolina; South Dakota; Tennessee; Texas; Utah; Vermont; Virginia; Washington; West Virginia; Wisconsin; Wyoming.

Award Name	Page Number	Highest Dollar Amount	Lowest Dollar Amount	Number of Awards	Academic Fields/Career Goals and Nonacademic/Noncareer Criteria
U.S. Army ROTC Guaranteed Reserve Forces Duty (GRFD), (ARNG/USAR) and Dedicated ARNG Scholarships	611	$120,000	$10,000	1,000–3,000	Military Service: Army National Guard. Residence: Alabama; Alaska; Arizona; Arkansas; California; Colorado; Connecticut; Delaware; District of Columbia; Florida; Georgia; Guam; Hawaii; Idaho; Illinois; Indiana; Iowa; Kansas; Kentucky; Louisiana; Maine; Maryland; Massachusetts; Michigan; Minnesota; Mississippi; Missouri; Montana; Nebraska; Nevada; New Hampshire; New Jersey; New Mexico; New York; North Carolina; North Dakota; Ohio; Oklahoma; Oregon; Pennsylvania; Puerto Rico; Rhode Island; South Carolina; South Dakota; Tennessee; Texas; Utah; Vermont; Virginia; Washington; West Virginia; Wisconsin; Wyoming. Studying in Alabama; Alaska; Arizona; Arkansas; California; Colorado; Connecticut; Delaware; District of Columbia; Florida; Georgia; Guam; Hawaii; Idaho; Illinois; Indiana; Iowa; Kansas; Kentucky; Louisiana; Maine; Maryland; Massachusetts; Michigan; Minnesota; Mississippi; Missouri; Montana; Nebraska; Nevada; New Hampshire; New Jersey; New Mexico; New York; North Carolina; North Dakota; Ohio; Oklahoma; Oregon; Pennsylvania; Puerto Rico; Rhode Island; Saskatchewan; South Carolina; South Dakota; Tennessee; Texas; Utah; Vermont; Virginia; Washington; West Virginia; Wisconsin; Wyoming.
Careers Through Culinary Arts Program Cooking Competition for Scholarships	246	$90,000	$1000	50–70	Culinary Arts; Hospitality Management. Residence: Arizona; California; Illinois; Maryland; New York; Pennsylvania; Virginia. Must be in high school.
SME Family Scholarship	328	$80,000	$5000	1–10	Engineering/Technology.
Intel International Science and Engineering Fair	964	$75,000	$500	1–600	Must be in high school.
Indian Health Service Health Professions Pre-graduate Scholarships	125	$63,500	$23,000	50–100	Applied Sciences; Biology; Health and Medical Sciences. Residence: Alabama; Alaska; Arizona; Arkansas; California; Colorado; Connecticut; Delaware; District of Columbia; Florida; Georgia; Hawaii; Idaho; Illinois; Indiana; Iowa; Kansas; Kentucky; Louisiana; Maine; Maryland; Massachusetts; Michigan; Minnesota; Mississippi; Missouri; Montana; Nebraska; Nevada; New Hampshire; New Jersey; New Mexico; New York; North Carolina; North Dakota; Ohio; Oklahoma; Oregon; Pennsylvania; Rhode Island; South Carolina; South Dakota; Tennessee; Texas; Utah; Vermont; Virginia; Washington; West Virginia; Wisconsin; Wyoming. Limited to American Indian/Alaska Native students.
Tang Scholarship	760	$60,000	$1000	1–4	Residence: California. Talent/Interest Area: LGBT issues. Limited to Asian/Pacific Islander students.

Award Name	Page Number	Highest Dollar Amount	Lowest Dollar Amount	Number of Awards	Academic Fields/Career Goals and Nonacademic/Noncareer Criteria
Health Professions Preparatory Scholarship Program	165	$52,600	$13,250	25–50	Behavioral Science; Biology; Health and Medical Sciences; Nursing; Optometry; Pharmacy; Psychology; Social Sciences. Residence: Alabama; Alaska; Arizona; Arkansas; California; Colorado; Connecticut; Delaware; District of Columbia; Florida; Georgia; Hawaii; Idaho; Illinois; Indiana; Iowa; Kansas; Kentucky; Louisiana; Maine; Maryland; Massachusetts; Michigan; Minnesota; Mississippi; Missouri; Montana; Nebraska; Nevada; New Hampshire; New Jersey; New Mexico; New York; North Carolina; North Dakota; Ohio; Oklahoma; Oregon; Pennsylvania; Rhode Island; South Carolina; South Dakota; Tennessee; Texas; Utah; Vermont; Virginia; Washington; West Virginia; Wisconsin; Wyoming. Limited to American Indian/Alaska Native students.
Tuition Exchange Scholarships	676	$52,140	$4190	7,000–9,000	Employment/Volunteer Experience: teaching/education.
U.S. Army ROTC Military Junior College (MJC) Scholarship	611	$52,000	$5600	110–150	Military Service: Army; Army National Guard. Residence: Alabama; Alaska; Arizona; Arkansas; California; Colorado; Connecticut; Delaware; District of Columbia; Florida; Georgia; Guam; Hawaii; Idaho; Illinois; Indiana; Iowa; Kansas; Kentucky; Louisiana; Maine; Maryland; Massachusetts; Michigan; Minnesota; Mississippi; Missouri; Montana; Nebraska; Nevada; New Hampshire; New Jersey; New Mexico; New York; North Carolina; North Dakota; Ohio; Oklahoma; Oregon; Pennsylvania; Puerto Rico; Rhode Island; South Carolina; South Dakota; Tennessee; Texas; Utah; Vermont; Virginia; Washington; West Virginia; Wisconsin; Wyoming. Studying in Alabama; Alaska; Arizona; Arkansas; California; Colorado; Connecticut; Delaware; District of Columbia; Florida; Georgia; Guam; Hawaii; Idaho; Illinois; Indiana; Iowa; Kansas; Kentucky; Louisiana; Maine; Maryland; Massachusetts; Michigan; Minnesota; Mississippi; Missouri; Montana; Nebraska; Nevada; New Hampshire; New Jersey; New Mexico; New York; North Carolina; North Dakota; Ohio; Oklahoma; Oregon; Pennsylvania; Puerto Rico; Rhode Island; South Carolina; South Dakota; Tennessee; Texas; Utah; Vermont; Virginia; Washington; West Virginia; Wisconsin; Wyoming.
Kentucky Transportation Cabinet Civil Engineering Scholarship Program	209	$51,200	$12,400	15–30	Civil Engineering. Residence: Kentucky. Studying in Kentucky.
Cameron Impact Scholarship	601	$50,000	$20,000	10–15	Must be in high school.
Clara Lionel Foundation Global Scholarship Program	605	$50,000	$5000	5–10	Nationality: Hispanic; Latin American/ Caribbean.

Award Name	Page Number	Highest Dollar Amount	Lowest Dollar Amount	Number of Awards	Academic Fields/Career Goals and Nonacademic/Noncareer Criteria
Davidson Fellows Scholarship Program	124	$50,000	$10,000	15–20	Applied Sciences; Engineering/Technology; Literature/English/Writing; Mathematics; Music; Philosophy; Science, Technology, and Society.
Elks National Foundation Most Valuable Student Scholarship Contest	893	$50,000	$4000	500	Talent/Interest Area: leadership. Must be in high school.
Miss America Organization Competition Scholarships	899	$50,000	$2000	70	Talent/Interest Area: beauty pageant.
U.S. Army ROTC Four-Year Nursing Scholarship	475	$50,000	$5000	100	Nursing. Military Service: Army; Army National Guard. Residence: Alabama; Alaska; Arizona; Arkansas; California; Colorado; Connecticut; Delaware; District of Columbia; Florida; Georgia; Guam; Hawaii; Idaho; Illinois; Indiana; Iowa; Kansas; Kentucky; Louisiana; Maine; Maryland; Massachusetts; Michigan; Minnesota; Mississippi; Missouri; Montana; Nebraska; Nevada; New Hampshire; New Jersey; New Mexico; New York; North Carolina; North Dakota; Ohio; Oklahoma; Ontario; Oregon; Pennsylvania; Puerto Rico; Rhode Island; South Carolina; South Dakota; Tennessee; Texas; Utah; Vermont; Virginia; Washington; West Virginia; Wisconsin; Wyoming. Studying in Alabama; Alaska; Arizona; Arkansas; California; Colorado; Connecticut; Delaware; District of Columbia; Florida; Georgia; Guam; Hawaii; Idaho; Illinois; Indiana; Iowa; Kansas; Kentucky; Louisiana; Maine; Maryland; Massachusetts; Michigan; Minnesota; Mississippi; Missouri; Montana; Nebraska; Nevada; New Hampshire; New Jersey; New Mexico; New York; North Carolina; North Dakota; Ohio; Oklahoma; Ontario; Oregon; Pennsylvania; Puerto Rico; Rhode Island; South Carolina; South Dakota; Tennessee; Texas; Utah; Vermont; Virginia; Washington; West Virginia; Wisconsin; Wyoming.
Veterans United Foundation Scholarship	682	$50,000	N/A	1–10	Military Service: General.
Boettcher Foundation Scholarship	814	$40,000	$13,000	42	Residence: Colorado. Studying in Colorado. Talent/Interest Area: leadership. Must be in high school.
Krishnan-Shah Family Scholarship	866	$40,000	$1000	1–5	Residence: California.
LEADS! Scholarship	856	$40,000	$1500	200–250	Residence: Michigan; Ohio. Studying in Michigan; Ohio. Must be in high school.
Mas Family Scholarship Award	181	$40,000	$8000	5–10	Business/Consumer Services; Chemical Engineering; Civil Engineering; Communications; Economics; Electrical Engineering/Electronics; Engineering-Related Technologies; International Studies; Journalism; Materials Science, Engineering, and Metallurgy; Mechanical Engineering. Limited to Hispanic students.

Award Name	Page Number	Highest Dollar Amount	Lowest Dollar Amount	Number of Awards	Academic Fields/Career Goals and Nonacademic/Noncareer Criteria
Ron Brown Scholar Program	665	$40,000	$10,000	10–20	Must be in high school. Limited to Black (non-Hispanic) students.
U.S. Army ROTC Four-Year Historically Black College/ University Scholarship	610	$40,000	$9000	20–200	Military Service: Army; Army National Guard. Residence: Alabama; Alaska; Arizona; Arkansas; California; Colorado; Connecticut; Delaware; District of Columbia; Florida; Georgia; Guam; Hawaii; Idaho; Illinois; Indiana; Iowa; Kansas; Kentucky; Louisiana; Maine; Maryland; Massachusetts; Michigan; Minnesota; Mississippi; Missouri; Montana; Nebraska; Nevada; New Hampshire; New Jersey; New Mexico; New York; North Carolina; North Dakota; Ohio; Oklahoma; Ontario; Oregon; Pennsylvania; Puerto Rico; Rhode Island; South Carolina; South Dakota; Tennessee; Texas; Utah; Vermont; Virginia; Washington; West Virginia; Wisconsin; Wyoming. Studying in Alabama; Alaska; Arizona; Arkansas; California; Colorado; Connecticut; Delaware; District of Columbia; Florida; Georgia; Guam; Hawaii; Idaho; Illinois; Indiana; Iowa; Kansas; Kentucky; Louisiana; Maine; Maryland; Massachusetts; Michigan; Minnesota; Mississippi; Missouri; Montana; Nebraska; Nevada; New Hampshire; New Jersey; New Mexico; New York; North Carolina; North Dakota; Ohio; Oklahoma; Ontario; Oregon; Pennsylvania; Puerto Rico; Rhode Island; South Carolina; South Dakota; Tennessee; Texas; Utah; Vermont; Virginia; Washington; West Virginia; Wisconsin; Wyoming.
Science, Mathematics, and Research for Transformation Defense Scholarship for Service Program	121	$39,000	$22,000	200	Applied Sciences; Engineering-Related Technologies; Engineering/Technology; Mathematics; Physical Sciences.
Huang Leadership Development Scholarship	668	$34,000	$1000	1–10	N/A
Master's Scholarship Program	195	$32,000	$25,000	1–15	Chemical Engineering; Computer Science/Data Processing; Electrical Engineering/Electronics; Engineering/Technology; Materials Science, Engineering, and Metallurgy. Limited to American Indian/Alaska Native; Black (non-Hispanic); Hispanic students.
Baer Reintegration Scholarship	604	$30,000	$1000	20–30	N/A
The Frank M. and Gertrude R. Doyle Foundation, Inc.	937	$30,000	$500	N/A	N/A
Latinos in Technology Scholarship	760	$30,000	$1000	60–100	Residence: California. Limited to Hispanic students.
National Security Agency Stokes Educational Scholarship Program	232	$30,000	$1000	15–20	Computer Science/Data Processing; Electrical Engineering/Electronics. Must be in high school.
St. Andrews Scholarship	758	$30,000	$20,000	2	N/A
Voice of Democracy Program	917	$30,000	$1000	54	Talent/Interest Area: public speaking; writing. Must be in high school.

Award Name	Page Number	Highest Dollar Amount	Lowest Dollar Amount	Number of Awards	Academic Fields/Career Goals and Nonacademic/Noncareer Criteria
National FFA Collegiate Scholarship Program	570	$29,000	$500	1,700–1,800	Civic Affiliation: Future Farmers of America.
Florida Space Research Program	156	$25,000	$12,500	13–15	Aviation/Aerospace; Earth Science; Education; Electrical Engineering/Electronics; Engineering/Technology; Marine/Ocean Engineering; Materials Science, Engineering, and Metallurgy; Mathematics; Mechanical Engineering; Meteorology/Atmospheric Science; Physical Sciences. Residence: Florida. Studying in Florida.
Ford Opportunity Program	830	$25,000	$1000	30–50	Residence: California; Oregon. Studying in California; Oregon.
Ford ReStart Program	830	$25,000	$1000	46	Residence: California; Oregon. Studying in California; Oregon.
Ford Scholars Program	830	$25,000	$1000	100–120	Residence: California; Oregon. Studying in California; Oregon.
General Study Scholarships	669	$25,000	$4000	6–12	N/A
Henry Salvatori Scholarship for General Study	669	$25,000	$4000	1	Must be in high school.
Horatio Alger Association Scholarship Programs	940	$25,000	$7000	1,009	Must be in high school.
Italian Language Scholarship	215	$25,000	$4000	1	Classics; Foreign Language.
Princess Grace Awards in Dance, Theater, and Film	347	$25,000	$5000	15–25	Filmmaking/Video; Performing Arts.
The Purpose Challenge	622	$25,000	$5000	6	Must be in high school.
Young Entrepreneur Awards	907	$25,000	$2000	100	Talent/Interest Area: entrepreneurship. Must be in high school.
Montana University System Honor Scholarship	848	$24,000	$16,000	200	Residence: Montana. Studying in Montana. Must be in high school.
Pride Foundation Scholarship Program	662	$24,000	$1000	85–125	Residence: Alaska; Idaho; Montana; Oregon; Washington. Talent/Interest Area: LGBT issues.
B. Bradford Barnes Memorial Scholarship	823	$20,000	$15,000	1	Residence: Delaware. Studying in Delaware. Must be in high school.
Charles L. Hebner Memorial Scholarship	823	$20,000	$15,000	2	Residence: Delaware. Studying in Delaware. Must be in high school.
Christian A. Herter Memorial Scholarship	642	$20,000	$500	25–100	Residence: Massachusetts. Studying in Illinois; Indiana; Iowa; Kansas; Kentucky; Louisiana; Maine; Manitoba; Maryland; Massachusetts. Must be in high school.
Coca-Cola Scholars Program	929	$20,000	$10,000	250	Must be in high school.
Herman M. Holloway, Sr. Memorial Scholarship	823	$20,000	$15,000	1	Residence: Delaware. Studying in Delaware. Must be in high school.
Jesse Brown Memorial Youth Scholarship Program	612	$20,000	$5000	8	Employment/Volunteer Experience: community service; helping people with disabilities.
Los Alamos Employees' Scholarship	842	$20,000	$1000	100	Residence: New Mexico.
Marie A. Calderilla Scholarship	866	$20,000	$1000	1–30	Residence: California. Studying in California.

Award Name	Page Number	Highest Dollar Amount	Lowest Dollar Amount	Number of Awards	Academic Fields/Career Goals and Nonacademic/Noncareer Criteria
Milton Fisher Scholarship for Innovation and Creativity	862	$20,000	$250	1–8	Residence: Alabama; Alaska; Arizona; Arkansas; California; Colorado; Connecticut; Delaware; District of Columbia; Florida; Georgia; Hawaii; Idaho; Illinois; Indiana; Iowa; Kansas; Kentucky; Louisiana; Maine; Maryland; Massachusetts; Michigan; Minnesota; Mississippi; Missouri; Montana; Nebraska; Nevada; New Hampshire; New Jersey; New Mexico; New York; North Carolina; North Dakota; Ohio; Oklahoma; Oregon; Pennsylvania; Rhode Island; South Carolina; South Dakota; Tennessee; Texas; Utah; Vermont; Virginia; Washington; West Virginia; Wisconsin; Wyoming. Studying in Alabama; Alaska; Arizona; Arkansas; California; Colorado; Connecticut; Delaware; District of Columbia; Florida; Georgia; Hawaii; Idaho; Illinois; Indiana; Iowa; Kansas; Kentucky; Louisiana; Maine; Maryland; Massachusetts; Michigan; Minnesota; Mississippi; Missouri; Montana; Nebraska; Nevada; New Hampshire; New Jersey; New Mexico; New York; North Carolina; North Dakota; Ohio; Oklahoma; Oregon; Pennsylvania; Rhode Island; South Carolina; South Dakota; Tennessee; Texas; Utah; Vermont; Virginia; Washington; West Virginia; Wisconsin; Wyoming.
National Security Education Program (NSEP) David L. Boren Undergraduate Scholarships	139	$20,000	$8000	130–170	Area/Ethnic Studies; Business/Consumer Services; Economics; Engineering-Related Technologies; Environmental Science; Foreign Language; International Studies; Peace and Conflict Studies; Social Sciences.
NIH Undergraduate Scholarship Program for Students from Disadvantaged Backgrounds	116	$20,000	$2000	10–15	Animal/Veterinary Sciences; Behavioral Science; Biology; Environmental Health; Environmental Science; Health and Medical Sciences; Neurobiology; Nuclear Science; Nursing; Physical Sciences; Public Health; Women's Studies.
RARE Scholars	685	$20,000	$2500	1–5	Disability: learning disabled; physically disabled.
American Legion Department of Kansas High School Oratorical Contest	805	$18,000	$150	4	Residence: Kansas. Talent/Interest Area: public speaking. Must be in high school.
Georgia Public Safety Memorial Grant	621	$18,000	$2000	20–40	Employment/Volunteer Experience: police/firefighting. Residence: Georgia. Studying in Georgia.
Stephen Phillips Memorial Scholarship Fund, Inc.	869	$18,000	$3000	125–135	Residence: Connecticut; Maine; Massachusetts; New Hampshire; Rhode Island; Vermont.
5 Strong Scholars Scholarship	719	$16,000	$10,000	25	Residence: Georgia. Studying in Georgia. Must be in high school. Limited to ethnic minority students.
Massachusetts Public Service Grant Program	643	$15,411	$6360	N/A	Employment/Volunteer Experience: police/firefighting. Residence: Massachusetts. Studying in Massachusetts.

Award Name	Page Number	Highest Dollar Amount	Lowest Dollar Amount	Number of Awards	Academic Fields/Career Goals and Nonacademic/Noncareer Criteria
Air Force ROTC College Scholarship	695	$15,000	$9000	2,000–4,000	Military Service: Air Force.
Barnes Scholarship	870	$15,000	$1000	1–4	Residence: Florida. Must be in high school.
First in Family Scholarship	839	$15,000	$12,500	10	Residence: Alabama. Studying in Alabama. Must be in high school.
Francis Ouimet Scholarship	830	$15,000	$1000	N/A	Residence: Massachusetts. Talent/Interest Area: golf.
Jeffrey L. Esser Career Development Scholarship	85	$15,000	$5000	1–2	Accounting; Finance; Public Policy and Administration.
Life Lessons Scholarship Program	945	$15,000	$5000	20–50	N/A
Margaret McNamara Education Grants	945	$15,000	$7000	27–35	N/A
National Beta Club Scholarship	570	$15,000	$1000	221	Civic Affiliation: National Beta Club. Must be in high school.
National Black MBA Association Graduate Scholarship Program	947	$15,000	$2500	10–25	N/A
ODKF General Scholarship Award	657	$15,000	$1450	30–50	Residence: Hawaii. Talent/Interest Area: athletics/sports.
St. Andrew's Society of Washington DC Scholarships	665	$15,000	$500	1–8	Residence: Delaware; District of Columbia; Maryland; New Jersey; North Carolina; Pennsylvania; Virginia; West Virginia.
Sallie Mae® Make College Happen Challenge	602	$15,000	$1000	10	N/A
Samsung@First Scholars	233	$15,000	$1000	1–3	Computer Science/Data Processing; Electrical Engineering/Electronics; Energy and Power Engineering; Engineering-Related Technologies; Engineering/Technology; Marine/Ocean Engineering; Materials Science, Engineering, and Metallurgy; Mathematics; Mechanical Engineering; Science, Technology, and Society; Statistics. Residence: California. Studying in California.
Saul T. Wilson, Jr., Scholarship Program (STWJS)	118	$15,000	$7500	N/A	Animal/Veterinary Sciences; Biology.
Scholarship America Dream Award	960	$15,000	$5000	8–10	N/A

Award Name	Page Number	Highest Dollar Amount	Lowest Dollar Amount	Number of Awards	Academic Fields/Career Goals and Nonacademic/Noncareer Criteria
Scholarship for Students Pursuing a Business or STEM Degree	91	$15,000	$2500	35–120	Accounting; Advertising/Public Relations; Agribusiness; Agriculture; Animal/Veterinary Sciences; Applied Sciences; Archaeology; Architecture; Audiology; Aviation/Aerospace; Biology; Business/Consumer Services; Chemical Engineering; Civil Engineering; Computer Science/Data Processing; Dental Health/Services; Earth Science; Economics; Electrical Engineering/Electronics; Energy and Power Engineering; Engineering-Related Technologies; Engineering/Technology; Environmental Science; Finance; Food Science/Nutrition; Geography; Health Administration; Health and Medical Sciences; Health Information Management/Technology; Hospitality Management; Human Resources; Insurance and Actuarial Science; Marine Biology; Marine/Ocean Engineering; Marketing; Materials Science, Engineering, and Metallurgy; Mathematics; Mechanical Engineering; Meteorology/Atmospheric Science; Natural Sciences; Neurobiology; Nuclear Science; Nursing; Oceanography; Oncology; Optometry; Osteopathy; Pharmacy; Physical Sciences; Sports-Related/Exercise Science; Therapy/Rehabilitation. Residence: Tennessee.
The Soroptimist Live Your Dream: Education and Training Awards for Women	965	$15,000	$500	N/A	N/A
Sterbenz-Ryan Scholarship	866	$15,000	$5000	44	Residence: Minnesota; Wisconsin.
Tailhook Educational Foundation Scholarship	704	$15,000	$2500	100	Military Service: Coast Guard.
Texas 4-H Opportunity Scholarship	871	$15,000	$1500	225	Residence: Texas. Studying in Texas. Talent/Interest Area: animal/agricultural competition.
Tribal Priority Award	739	$15,000	$2500	1–5	Limited to American Indian/Alaska Native students.
Paul Tsongas Scholarship Program	643	$14,850	$11,500	20–45	Residence: Massachusetts. Studying in Massachusetts. Must be in high school.
Howard P. Rawlings Educational Excellence Awards Guaranteed Access Grant	844	$14,800	$400	1,000	Residence: Maryland. Studying in Maryland.
American Angus Auxiliary Scholarship	948	$14,000	$1000	10	Must be in high school.
Safety Officers' Survivor Grant Program	646	$13,840	N/A	1–10	Employment/Volunteer Experience: police/firefighting. Residence: Minnesota. Studying in Minnesota.
Entitlement Cal Grant B	816	$13,665	$700	61,340	Residence: California. Studying in California.
Law Enforcement Personnel Dependents Scholarship	602	$13,665	$100	N/A	Employment/Volunteer Experience: police/firefighting. Residence: California. Studying in California.

Award Name	Page Number	Highest Dollar Amount	Lowest Dollar Amount	Number of Awards	Academic Fields/Career Goals and Nonacademic/Noncareer Criteria
National Space Grant Consortium Scholarships	127	$13,333	$1250	1–50	Applied Sciences; Aviation/Aerospace; Chemical Engineering; Civil Engineering; Computer Science/Data Processing; Earth Science; Engineering/Technology; Mathematics; Mechanical Engineering; Natural Sciences; Physical Sciences. Residence: Nevada. Studying in Nevada.
The Elizabeth Greenshields Foundation Grant	614	$13,000	$10,500	40–70	N/A
Environmental Protection Scholarship	172	$13,000	$10,000	1–4	Biology; Chemical Engineering; Civil Engineering; Earth Science; Environmental Science; Hydrology; Mechanical Engineering; Natural Sciences. Residence: Kentucky. Studying in Kentucky.
GSBA Scholarship Fund	834	$13,000	$2000	40–45	Residence: Washington. Talent/Interest Area: LGBT issues.
Law Enforcement Officers/Firemen Scholarship	646	$12,854	$2010	18–30	Employment/Volunteer Experience: police/firefighting. Residence: Mississippi. Studying in Mississippi.
Competitive Cal Grant A	816	$12,192	$5472	1,000–2,000	Residence: California. Studying in California.
Tuition Aid Grant	851	$12,190	$1012	N/A	Residence: New Jersey. Studying in New Jersey.
Vermont Incentive Grants	875	$12,050	$850	N/A	Residence: Vermont.
Airline Pilots Association Scholarship Program	549	$12,000	$1000	1–3	Civic Affiliation: Airline Pilots Association.
Educational Benefits for Children of Deceased Veterans	609	$12,000	$10,000	N/A	Employment/Volunteer Experience: police/firefighting. Military Service: General. Residence: Delaware.
Herman O. West Foundation Scholarship Program	589	$12,000	$3000	1–14	Corporate Affiliation: West Pharmaceuticals. Must be in high school.
Humane Studies Fellowships	219	$12,000	$2000	140–180	Communications; Economics; History; Humanities; Law/Legal Services; Literature/English/Writing; Political Science; Social Sciences.
Kappa Alpha Theta Foundation Scholarship Program	567	$12,000	$1000	N/A	Civic Affiliation: Greek Organization.
National Italian American Foundation Category II Scholarship	139	$12,000	$2500	N/A	Area/Ethnic Studies. Talent/Interest Area: Italian language.
Police Officers and Firefighters Survivors Education Assistance Program-Alabama	798	$12,000	$1600	15–30	Residence: Alabama. Studying in Alabama.
North Dakota Scholars Program	654	$11,666	$3462	1–140	Residence: North Dakota. Studying in North Dakota. Must be in high school.
Kentucky National Guard Tuition Award	699	$11,500	$100	1,000–1,500	Military Service: Air Force National Guard; Army National Guard. Residence: Kentucky. Studying in Kentucky.
Minnesota State Grant Program	847	$11,334	$100	71,000–120,000	Residence: Minnesota. Studying in Minnesota.
Global Study Awards	966	$11,215	$11,215	1–9	N/A

Award Name	Page Number	Highest Dollar Amount	Lowest Dollar Amount	Number of Awards	Academic Fields/Career Goals and Nonacademic/Noncareer Criteria
SPIE Educational Scholarships in Optical Science and Engineering	126	$11,000	$2000	100–150	Applied Sciences; Chemical Engineering; Electrical Engineering/Electronics; Engineering-Related Technologies; Engineering/Technology; Materials Science, Engineering, and Metallurgy; Mechanical Engineering.
Frank O'Bannon Grant Program	838	$10,992	$200	48,408–70,239	Residence: Indiana. Studying in Indiana.
Academy of Nutrition and Dietetics Foundation Scholarship Program	351	$10,000	$500	200–250	Food Science/Nutrition. Civic Affiliation: American Dietetic Association.
AFE Floriculture Scholarships	923	$10,000	$500	2–25	N/A
AIAA Foundation Undergraduate Scholarships	121	$10,000	$500	11	Applied Sciences; Aviation/Aerospace; Electrical Engineering/Electronics; Engineering-Related Technologies; Engineering/Technology; Materials Science, Engineering, and Metallurgy; Mechanical Engineering; Physical Sciences; Science, Technology, and Society. Civic Affiliation: American Institute of Aeronautics and Astronautics.
Air Traffic Control Association Scholarship	593	$10,000	$2000	7–12	Employment/Volunteer Experience: air traffic control. Talent/Interest Area: aviation.
Anne Ford and Allegra Ford Thomas Scholarship	689	$10,000	$2500	2	Disability: learning disabled. Must be in high school.
AREMA Graduate and Undergraduate Scholarships	204	$10,000	$1000	30–40	Civil Engineering; Computer Science/Data Processing; Construction Engineering/Management; Electrical Engineering/Electronics; Engineering-Related Technologies; Engineering/Technology; Mechanical Engineering.
Arkansas Governor's Scholars Program	810	$10,000	$4000	75–375	Residence: Arkansas. Studying in Arkansas. Must be in high school.
Association of State Dam Safety Officials (ASDSO) Senior Undergraduate Scholarship	168	$10,000	$5000	1–3	Biology; Civil Engineering; Computer Science/Data Processing; Construction Engineering/Management; Earth Science; Electrical Engineering/Electronics; Energy and Power Engineering; Engineering-Related Technologies; Engineering/Technology; Environmental Science; Geography; Materials Science, Engineering, and Metallurgy; Mechanical Engineering; Natural Resources; Natural Sciences; Science, Technology, and Society; Surveying, Surveying Technology, Cartography, or Geographic Information Science; Urban and Regional Planning.
Atlas Shrugged Essay Contest	600	$10,000	$50	236	N/A
Automotive Aftermarket Scholarships	177	$10,000	$1000	N/A	Business/Consumer Services; Marketing; Mechanical Engineering; Trade/Technical Specialties.
Buckingham Memorial Scholarship	593	$10,000	$2000	1–4	Employment/Volunteer Experience: air traffic control.
California Junior Miss Scholarship Program	815	$10,000	$500	25	Residence: California. Talent/Interest Area: beauty pageant; leadership; public speaking. Must be in high school.

Award Name	Page Number	Highest Dollar Amount	Lowest Dollar Amount	Number of Awards	Academic Fields/Career Goals and Nonacademic/Noncareer Criteria
Center for Architecture, Women's Auxiliary Eleanor Allwork Scholarship	132	$10,000	$4000	1–5	Architecture. Residence: New York. Studying in New York.
Christianson Grant	942	$10,000	$2500	9	N/A
CTIA Wireless Foundation Drive Smart Digital Short Contest	928	$10,000	$1000	6	N/A
Cystic Fibrosis Scholarship	686	$10,000	$1000	40–50	Disability: physically disabled.
DC Tuition Assistance Grant Program (DCTAG)	824	$10,000	$2500	5,999–6,000	Residence: District of Columbia.
Director's Scholarship Award	327	$10,000	$1000	1–5	Engineering/Technology. Talent/Interest Area: leadership.
Duck Brand Duct Tape "Stuck at Prom" Scholarship Contest	625	$10,000	$1000	1–11	Residence: Alabama; Alaska; Alberta; Arizona; Arkansas; British Columbia; California; Connecticut; Delaware; District of Columbia; Florida; Georgia; Guam; Hawaii; Idaho; Illinois; Indiana; Iowa; Kansas; Kentucky; Louisiana; Maine; Manitoba; Massachusetts; Michigan; Minnesota; Mississippi; Missouri; Montana; Nebraska; Nevada; New Brunswick; Newfoundland; New Hampshire; New Jersey; New Mexico; New York; North Carolina; North Dakota; Northwest Territories; Nova Scotia; Ohio; Oklahoma; Ontario; Oregon; Pennsylvania; Prince Edward Island; Puerto Rico; Rhode Island; Saskatchewan; South Carolina; South Dakota; Tennessee; Texas; Utah; Virginia; Washington; West Virginia; Wisconsin; Wyoming; Yukon. Must be in high school.
ESA Youth Scholarship Program	614	$10,000	$500	N/A	Employment/Volunteer Experience: police/firefighting. Must be in high school.
E. Wayne Kay Community College Scholarship Award	327	$10,000	$1000	1–20	Engineering/Technology; Trade/Technical Specialties.
Executive Women International Scholarship Program	935	$10,000	$1000	75–100	Must be in high school.
ExploraVision Science Competition	915	$10,000	$5000	N/A	Talent/Interest Area: science.
Family Scholarship Fund	597	$10,000	$5000	1–2	N/A
Federation of American Consumers and Travelers Educational Grant Program	563	$10,000	$250	4–10	Civic Affiliation: Federation of American Consumers and Travelers.
Gabriel A. Hartl Scholarship	150	$10,000	$2000	1–4	Aviation/Aerospace. Studying in Arkansas.
Hellenic Times Scholarship Fund	737	$10,000	$500	30–40	N/A

Award Name	Page Number	Highest Dollar Amount	Lowest Dollar Amount	Number of Awards	Academic Fields/Career Goals and Nonacademic/Noncareer Criteria
HENAAC Scholarship Program	115	$10,000	$500	100–120	Animal/Veterinary Sciences; Applied Sciences; Architecture; Audiology; Aviation/Aerospace; Biology; Chemical Engineering; Civil Engineering; Computer Science/Data Processing; Construction Engineering/Management; Earth Science; Electrical Engineering/Electronics; Energy and Power Engineering; Engineering-Related Technologies; Engineering/Technology; Entomology; Environmental Health; Environmental Science; Food Science/Nutrition; Horticulture/Floriculture; Hydrology; Industrial Design; Marine Biology; Marine/Ocean Engineering; Materials Science, Engineering, and Metallurgy; Mathematics; Mechanical Engineering; Meteorology/Atmospheric Science; Natural Resources; Natural Sciences; Neurobiology; Nuclear Science; Nursing; Oceanography; Oncology; Optometry; Osteopathy; Paper and Pulp Engineering; Pharmacy; Physical Sciences; Statistics. Studying in Alabama; Alaska; Arizona; Arkansas; California; Colorado; Connecticut; Delaware; District of Columbia; Florida; Georgia; Hawaii; Idaho; Illinois; Indiana; Iowa; Kansas; Kentucky; Louisiana; Maine; Maryland; Massachusetts; Michigan; Minnesota; Mississippi; Missouri; Montana; Nebraska; Nevada; New Hampshire; New Jersey; New Mexico; New York; North Carolina; North Dakota; Ohio; Oklahoma; Oregon; Pennsylvania; Puerto Rico; Rhode Island; South Carolina; South Dakota; Tennessee; Texas; Utah; Vermont; Virginia; Washington; West Virginia; Wisconsin; Wyoming. Limited to Hispanic students.
The Hirsch Family Scholarship	932	$10,000	$2000	N/A	N/A
HORIZONS Scholarship	451	$10,000	$500	5–6	Military and Defense Studies.
Illinois Restaurant Association Educational Foundation Scholarships	246	$10,000	$1000	50–70	Culinary Arts; Food Science/Nutrition; Food Service/Hospitality; Hospitality Management. Employment/Volunteer Experience: food service; hospitality/hotel administration/operations. Residence: Illinois.
James R. Hoffa Memorial Scholarship Fund	565	$10,000	$1000	1–100	Civic Affiliation: International Brotherhood of Teamsters. Must be in high school.
Janet L. Hoffmann Loan Assistance Repayment Program	272	$10,000	$1500	700	Education; Law/Legal Services; Nursing; Social Services; Therapy/Rehabilitation. Employment/Volunteer Experience: government/politics. Residence: Maryland. Studying in Maryland.
John Lennon Scholarships	888	$10,000	$3000	3–5	Talent/Interest Area: music.

Award Name	Page Number	Highest Dollar Amount	Lowest Dollar Amount	Number of Awards	Academic Fields/Career Goals and Nonacademic/Noncareer Criteria
Jules Cohen Scholarship	284	$10,000	$5000	1–13	Electrical Engineering/Electronics; Engineering-Related Technologies; Science, Technology, and Society. Studying in Alabama; Alaska; Arizona; Arkansas; California; Colorado; Connecticut; Delaware; District of Columbia; Florida; Georgia; Guam; Hawaii; Idaho; Illinois; Indiana; Iowa; Kansas; Kentucky; Louisiana; Maine; Maryland; Massachusetts; Michigan; Minnesota; Mississippi; Missouri; Montana; Nebraska; Nevada; New Hampshire; New Jersey; New Mexico; New York; North Carolina; North Dakota; Ohio; Oklahoma; Oregon; Pennsylvania; Puerto Rico; Rhode Island; South Carolina; South Dakota; Tennessee; Texas; Utah; Vermont; Virginia; Washington; West Virginia; Wisconsin; Wyoming.
J. Wood Platt Caddie Scholarship Trust	840	$10,000	$1000	N/A	Residence: Delaware; New Jersey; Pennsylvania.
Lawrence C. Fortier Memorial Scholarship	150	$10,000	$2000	1–5	Aviation/Aerospace.
Lee-Jackson Educational Foundation Scholarship Competition	841	$10,000	$1000	27	Residence: Virginia. Talent/Interest Area: writing. Must be in high school.
Louie Family Foundation Scholarship	944	$10,000	$1000	25–35	N/A
MaleSense Pro Internet Marketing Scholarship	945	$10,000	$1000	1–10	N/A
Marine Corps Scholarship Foundation	586	$10,000	$1500	2,000–2,300	Civic Affiliation: American Legion or Auxiliary.
Medicus Student Exchange	763	$10,000	$2000	1–10	Talent/Interest Area: foreign language.
Nancy Lorraine Jensen Memorial Scholarship	202	$10,000	$2500	1–6	Chemical Engineering; Electrical Engineering/Electronics; Mechanical Engineering. Talent/Interest Area: science.
National Italian American Foundation Category I Scholarship	751	$10,000	$2500	40–45	N/A

Award Name	Page Number	Highest Dollar Amount	Lowest Dollar Amount	Number of Awards	Academic Fields/Career Goals and Nonacademic/Noncareer Criteria
National Restaurant Association Educational Foundation Undergraduate Scholarships for College Students	109	$10,000	$2500	150–300	Agriculture; Business/Consumer Services; Culinary Arts; Food Science/Nutrition; Food Service/Hospitality; Horticulture/Floriculture; Hospitality Management; Marketing. Residence: Alabama; Alaska; Alberta; Arizona; Arkansas; British Columbia; California; Colorado; Connecticut; Delaware; District of Columbia; Florida; Georgia; Guam; Hawaii; Idaho; Illinois; Indiana; Iowa; Kansas; Kentucky; Louisiana; Maine; Manitoba; Maryland; Massachusetts; Michigan; Minnesota; Mississippi; Missouri; Montana; Nebraska; Nevada; New Brunswick; Newfoundland; New Hampshire; New Jersey; New Mexico; New York; North Carolina; North Dakota; Northwest Territories; Nova Scotia; Ohio; Oklahoma; Ontario; Oregon; Pennsylvania; Prince Edward Island; Puerto Rico; Quebec; Rhode Island; Saskatchewan; South Carolina; South Dakota; Tennessee; Texas; Utah; Vermont; Virginia; Washington; West Virginia; Wisconsin; Wyoming; Yukon. Studying in Alabama; Alaska; Alberta; Arizona; Arkansas; British Columbia; California; Colorado; Connecticut; Delaware; District of Columbia; Florida; Georgia; Guam; Hawaii; Idaho; Illinois; Indiana; Iowa; Kansas; Kentucky; Louisiana; Maine; Manitoba; Maryland; Massachusetts; Michigan; Minnesota; Mississippi; Missouri; Montana; Nebraska; Nevada; New Brunswick; Newfoundland; New Hampshire; New Jersey; New Mexico; New York; North Carolina; North Dakota; Northwest Territories; Nova Scotia; Ohio; Oklahoma; Ontario; Oregon; Pennsylvania; Prince Edward Island; Puerto Rico; Quebec; Rhode Island; Saskatchewan; South Carolina; South Dakota; Tennessee; Texas; Utah; Vermont; Virginia; Washington; West Virginia; Wisconsin; Wyoming; Yukon.
Needham and Company September 11th Scholarship Fund	949	$10,000	$7000	8–15	N/A
New York Women in Communications Scholarships	652	$10,000	$2500	18–22	Residence: Connecticut; New Jersey; New York; Pennsylvania. Studying in New York.
PanHellenic Scholarship Awards	657	$10,000	$2500	40	N/A
Peninsula Regent Charitable Foundation Educational Grant Program	867	$10,000	$1000	1–30	Residence: California.
PFund Foundation Scholarship Program	861	$10,000	$2000	15–30	Residence: Iowa; Minnesota; North Dakota; South Dakota; Wisconsin. Studying in Iowa; Minnesota; North Dakota; South Dakota; Wisconsin.

Award Name	Page Number	Highest Dollar Amount	Lowest Dollar Amount	Number of Awards	Academic Fields/Career Goals and Nonacademic/Noncareer Criteria
PG&E Better Together STEM Scholarship Program	233	$10,000	$1000	40	Computer Science/Data Processing; Electrical Engineering/Electronics; Environmental Science; Mechanical Engineering. Residence: California. Studying in California.
Profile in Courage Essay Contest	632	$10,000	$500	7	Must be in high school.
Prompt's $20,000 Scholarship	663	$10,000	$2000	14	Must be in high school.
Ralph Hale and Martha L. Ruppert Educational Scholarship	867	$10,000	$1000	1–30	Residence: California.
Roadway Worker Memorial Scholarship Program	597	$10,000	$5000	2–5	Employment/Volunteer Experience: construction; roadway work; transportation industry.
Sabre Passport to Freedom Survivor Scholarship	962	$10,000	$1000	1–5	N/A
Scholastic Art and Writing Awards	594	$10,000	$500	89	Must be in high school.
SHRM Foundation Student Scholarships	394	$10,000	$2500	44	Human Resources. Civic Affiliation: Society for Human Resource Management.
Sons of Italy Foundation's National Leadership Grant Competition	761	$10,000	$4000	9–10	N/A
Sons of Italy National Leadership Grants Competition Language Scholarship	361	$10,000	$4000	1	Foreign Language.
Spencer Educational Foundation Scholarship	398	$10,000	$5000	30–40	Insurance and Actuarial Science.
State Tuition Assistance	697	$10,000	N/A	1–200	Military Service: Air Force National Guard; Army National Guard. Studying in Delaware.
Swanson Scholarship	362	$10,000	$1000	1–10	Funeral Services/Mortuary Science. Residence: Nebraska.
Technical Minority Scholarship	203	$10,000	$1000	128	Chemical Engineering; Computer Science/Data Processing; Electrical Engineering/Electronics; Engineering-Related Technologies; Engineering/Technology; Materials Science, Engineering, and Metallurgy; Mechanical Engineering; Physical Sciences. Limited to ethnic minority students.
Teletoon Animation Scholarship	145	$10,000	$5000	9	Arts; Filmmaking/Video. Residence: Alberta; British Columbia; Manitoba; New Brunswick; Newfoundland; Northwest Territories; Nova Scotia; Ontario; Prince Edward Island; Quebec; Saskatchewan.
Television Academy Foundation	671	$10,000	$2000	16	N/A
Theodore R. and Vivian M. Johnson Scholarship Program for Children of UPS Employees or UPS Retirees	591	$10,000	$1000	1–205	Corporate Affiliation: Universal American Financial Corporation. Residence: Florida. Studying in Florida.
Thermo Fisher Scientific Antibody Scholarship Program	522	$10,000	$5000	6	Science, Technology, and Society.
UCB Family Epilepsy Scholarship	677	$10,000	$5000	32	Disability: physically disabled.
United States Society on Dams Scholarship Award	214	$10,000	$2000	1–4	Civil Engineering; Engineering/Technology; Environmental Science. Civic Affiliation: United States Society on Dams.

Award Name	Page Number	Highest Dollar Amount	Lowest Dollar Amount	Number of Awards	Academic Fields/Career Goals and Nonacademic/Noncareer Criteria
Vectorworks Design Scholarship	137	$10,000	$3000	15–18	Architecture; Arts; Civil Engineering; Construction Engineering/Management; Drafting; Engineering-Related Technologies; Engineering/Technology; Graphics/Graphic Arts/Printing; Industrial Design; Interior Design; Landscape Architecture; Urban and Regional Planning.
The Vegetarian Resource Group Scholarship	972	$10,000	$5000	N/A	Must be in high school.
The Walter A. Hunt, Jr. Scholarship	132	$10,000	$7500	1–2	Architecture. Residence: New York. Must be in high school.
Wine Group Scholarships	867	$10,000	$1000	1–10	Residence: California.
Young American Creative Patriotic Art Awards Program	901	$10,000	$500	8	Talent/Interest Area: art. Must be in high school.
Vermont Part-Time Student Grants	875	$9040	$425	N/A	Residence: Vermont.
Canadian Nurses Foundation Scholarships	474	$9000	$1500	50–60	Nursing. Employment/Volunteer Experience: nursing. Nationality: Canadian.
Edward T. Conroy Memorial Scholarship Program	642	$9000	$7200	121	Employment/Volunteer Experience: police/firefighting. Military Service: General. Residence: Maryland. Studying in Maryland.
Delegate Scholarship Program-Maryland	843	$8650	$200	3,500	Residence: Maryland. Studying in Maryland.
Undergraduate STEM Research Scholarships	127	$8500	$3000	1–35	Applied Sciences; Aviation/Aerospace; Biology; Chemical Engineering; Computer Science/Data Processing; Electrical Engineering/Electronics; Engineering-Related Technologies; Materials Science, Engineering, and Metallurgy; Mathematics; Mechanical Engineering; Physical Sciences; Science, Technology, and Society. Studying in Virginia.
CBC Spouses Education Scholarship	730	$8200	$500	250–350	Studying in Alabama; Alaska; Arizona; Arkansas; California; Colorado; Connecticut; Delaware; District of Columbia; Florida; Georgia; Guam; Hawaii; Idaho; Illinois; Indiana; Iowa; Kansas; Kentucky; Louisiana; Maine; Maryland; Massachusetts; Michigan; Minnesota; Mississippi; Missouri; Montana; Nebraska; Nevada; New Hampshire; New Jersey; New Mexico; New York; North Carolina; North Dakota; Ohio; Oklahoma; Oregon; Pennsylvania; Puerto Rico; Rhode Island; South Carolina; South Dakota; Tennessee; Texas; Utah; Vermont; Virginia; Washington; West Virginia; Wisconsin; Wyoming. Limited to Black (non-Hispanic) students.
AACE International Competitive Scholarship	130	$8000	$2000	10–20	Architecture; Aviation/Aerospace; Business/Consumer Services; Chemical Engineering; Civil Engineering; Construction Engineering/Management; Electrical Engineering/Electronics; Engineering-Related Technologies; Engineering/Technology; Mechanical Engineering.

Award Name	Page Number	Highest Dollar Amount	Lowest Dollar Amount	Number of Awards	Academic Fields/Career Goals and Nonacademic/Noncareer Criteria
AIFS-HACU Scholarships	723	$8000	$6000	1	Talent/Interest Area: international exchange. Limited to Hispanic students.
AQHF Racing Scholarships	558	$8000	$4000	1–5	Civic Affiliation: American Quarter Horse Association. Employment/Volunteer Experience: designated career field; harness racing.
California Wine Grape Growers Foundation Scholarship	815	$8000	$2000	6–7	Residence: California. Studying in California. Must be in high school.
Hispanic Metropolitan Chamber Scholarships	626	$8000	$2000	45–50	Residence: Oregon. Limited to Hispanic students.
Jewish Federation of Metropolitan Chicago Academic Scholarship Program	742	$8000	$1000	100–125	Religion: Jewish.
Texas Educational Opportunity Grant (TEOG)	872	$8000	N/A	N/A	Residence: Texas. Studying in Texas.
Toward EXcellence, Access, and Success (TEXAS) Grant	872	$8000	N/A	N/A	Residence: Texas. Studying in Texas.
Vocational Nurse & Licensed Vocational Nurse to Associate Degree Nursing Scholarship Program	480	$8000	$4000	N/A	Nursing. Residence: California.
AGC Education and Research Foundation Undergraduate Scholarships	207	$7500	$2500	100–150	Civil Engineering; Construction Engineering/Management.
American Legion Department of Pennsylvania High School Oratorical Contest	808	$7500	$4000	3	Residence: Pennsylvania. Talent/Interest Area: public speaking. Must be in high school.
Civil Air Patrol Academic Scholarships	562	$7500	$1000	40	Civic Affiliation: Civil Air Patrol.
Epsilon Sigma Alpha Foundation Scholarships	733	$7500	$350	125–175	Limited to ethnic minority students.
E. Wayne Kay Scholarship	327	$7500	$2500	10–30	Engineering/Technology; Trade/Technical Specialties.
FSCNY Young Leaders Scholarship	618	$7500	$2000	1–10	Residence: New York. Talent/Interest Area: leadership. Must be in high school.
International Violoncello Competition	917	$7500	$2500	3	Talent/Interest Area: music.
IP Video Contest	838	$7500	$2000	5	Residence: Alabama; Alaska; Arizona; Arkansas; California; Colorado; Connecticut; Delaware; District of Columbia; Florida; Georgia; Hawaii; Idaho; Illinois; Indiana; Iowa; Kansas; Kentucky; Louisiana; Maine; Maryland; Massachusetts; Michigan; Minnesota; Mississippi; Missouri; Montana; Nebraska; Nevada; New Hampshire; New Jersey; New Mexico; New York; North Carolina; North Dakota; Ohio; Oklahoma; Oregon; Pennsylvania; Rhode Island; South Carolina; South Dakota; Tennessee; Texas; Utah; Vermont; Virginia; Washington; West Virginia; Wisconsin; Wyoming.
Military Order of the Purple Heart Scholarship	712	$7500	$2500	84–87	Military Service: General.

Award Name	Page Number	Highest Dollar Amount	Lowest Dollar Amount	Number of Awards	Academic Fields/Career Goals and Nonacademic/Noncareer Criteria
Palmetto Fellows Scholarship Program	868	$7500	$6700	4,846	Residence: South Carolina. Studying in South Carolina. Must be in high school.
Paraprofessional Teacher Preparation Grant Program	273	$7500	$250	N/A	Education. Residence: Massachusetts. Studying in Massachusetts.
TELACU Education Foundation	825	$7500	$500	350–600	Residence: California; Illinois; New York; Texas.
William Faulkner-William Wisdom Creative Writing Competition	440	$7500	$250	8	Mathematics. Employment/Volunteer Experience: human services. Talent/Interest Area: English language; writing.
Choose Ohio First Scholarship	655	$7368	$1500	2,643	Residence: Ohio. Studying in Ohio.
Higher Education Legislative Plan (HELP)	847	$7344	$340	2,912	Residence: Mississippi. Studying in Mississippi.
Teaching Assistant Program in France	113	$7280	$1040	1,120	American Studies; Art History; Education; European Studies; Foreign Language; History; Humanities; International Studies; Literature/English/Writing; Political Science; Social Sciences. Talent/Interest Area: English language; foreign language; French language; international exchange.
Indiana National Guard Supplemental Grant	698	$7110	$20	503–925	Military Service: Air Force National Guard; Army National Guard. Residence: Indiana. Studying in Indiana.
Charles and Lucille King Family Foundation Scholarships	218	$7000	$3500	10–20	Communications; Filmmaking/Video; TV/Radio Broadcasting.
Colorado Masons Benevolent Fund Scholarships	606	$7000	$1000	6–8	Residence: Colorado. Studying in Colorado. Must be in high school.
Freeman Awards for Study in Asia	970	$7000	$3000	N/A	N/A
Jane M. Klausman Women in Business Scholarships	185	$7000	$1000	30–32	Business/Consumer Services.
Myrtle and Earl Walker Scholarship Fund	305	$7000	$1000	1–25	Engineering-Related Technologies; Engineering/Technology; Mechanical Engineering.
Northern Cheyenne Tribal Education Department	753	$7000	$100	90	Limited to American Indian/Alaska Native students.
Selby Scholar Program	877	$7000	$1000	40	Residence: Florida. Talent/Interest Area: leadership.
Senatorial Scholarships-Maryland	844	$7000	$400	7,000	Residence: Maryland. Studying in Maryland.
Women's jewelry association student scholarship	146	$7000	$500	5–12	Arts; Trade/Technical Specialties. Employment/Volunteer Experience: fine arts. Talent/Interest Area: art.
Taylor Opportunity Program for Students Honors Level	842	$6736	$836	9,661	Residence: Louisiana. Studying in Louisiana.
Armenian Students Association of America Inc. Scholarships	724	$6700	$3300	35	N/A
Charles W. Riley Fire and Emergency Medical Services Tuition Reimbursement Program	349	$6500	N/A	1–150	Fire Sciences; Health and Medical Sciences; Trade/Technical Specialties. Employment/Volunteer Experience: police/firefighting. Residence: Maryland. Studying in Maryland.
New Jersey World Trade Center Scholarship	851	$6500	N/A	N/A	Residence: New Jersey.

Award Name	Page Number	Highest Dollar Amount	Lowest Dollar Amount	Number of Awards	Academic Fields/Career Goals and Nonacademic/Noncareer Criteria
Pennsylvania Burglar and Fire Alarm Association Youth Scholarship Program	658	$6500	$500	6–8	Employment/Volunteer Experience: police/firefighting. Residence: Pennsylvania. Must be in high school.
Taylor Opportunity Program for Students Performance Level	842	$6336	$636	11,928	Residence: Louisiana. Studying in Louisiana.
AHLEF Annual Scholarship Grant Program	244	$6000	$500	N/A	Culinary Arts; Food Service/Hospitality; Hospitality Management; Recreation, Parks, Leisure Studies; Travel/Tourism.
American Legion Department of New York High School Oratorical Contest	807	$6000	$2000	N/A	Residence: New York. Talent/Interest Area: public speaking. Must be in high school.
American Meteorological Society Minority Scholarships	448	$6000	$3000	3	Meteorology/Atmospheric Science. Must be in high school. Limited to ethnic minority students.
Conditional Grant Program	212	$6000	$3000	10–20	Civil Engineering; Computer Science/Data Processing; Occupational Safety and Health. Residence: Texas. Studying in Texas.
Contemporary Record Society National Competition for Performing Artists	891	$6000	$2000	1	Talent/Interest Area: music/singing.
Don't Mess With Texas Scholarship Program	825	$6000	$2000	2–3	Residence: Texas. Studying in Texas. Must be in high school.
Elements Behavioral Health College Tuition Scholarship	935	$6000	$1000	3	N/A
Foster Care to Success Scholarship Program	937	$6000	$1000	100	N/A
Friends of 440 Scholarship Fund, Inc.	831	$6000	$500	1–60	Residence: Florida.
GCSAA Scholars Competition	387	$6000	$500	N/A	Horticulture/Floriculture. Civic Affiliation: Golf Course Superintendents Association of America.
Golden Gate Restaurant Association Scholarship Foundation	246	$6000	$1000	9–15	Culinary Arts; Hospitality Management. Residence: California.
International Foodservice Editorial Council Communications Scholarship	96	$6000	$250	1–8	Advertising/Public Relations; Agribusiness; Agriculture; Communications; Culinary Arts; Food Science/Nutrition; Food Service/Hospitality; Graphics/Graphic Arts/Printing; Home Economics; Hospitality Management; Journalism; Literature/English/Writing; Marketing; Photojournalism/Photography. Talent/Interest Area: photography/photogrammetry/filmmaking; writing.
Jackie Robinson Scholarship	631	$6000	$6000	40–60	Employment/Volunteer Experience: community service. Talent/Interest Area: leadership. Must be in high school. Limited to ethnic minority students.
Jo Anne J. Trow Scholarships	922	$6000	$1000	1–36	N/A
Marion Huber Learning Through Listening Awards	568	$6000	$2000	6	Civic Affiliation: Learning Ally. Disability: learning disabled. Must be in high school.
Mary P. Oenslager Scholastic Achievement Awards	568	$6000	$1000	3–9	Civic Affiliation: Learning Ally. Disability: visually impaired.

Award Name	Page Number	Highest Dollar Amount	Lowest Dollar Amount	Number of Awards	Academic Fields/Career Goals and Nonacademic/Noncareer Criteria
National Competition for Composers' Recordings	891	$6000	$2000	1	Talent/Interest Area: music/singing.
New Jersey State Golf Association Caddie Scholarship	652	$6000	$3500	145	Employment/Volunteer Experience: private club/caddying. Residence: New Jersey.
Office and Professional Employees International Union Howard Coughlin Memorial Scholarship Fund	572	$6000	$2400	18	Civic Affiliation: Office and Professional Employees International Union.
RehabCenter.net	664	$6000	$3000	1–3	Residence: Alabama; Alaska; Alberta; Arizona; Arkansas; California; Colorado; Connecticut; Delaware; District of Columbia; Florida; Georgia; Hawaii; Idaho; Illinois; Indiana; Iowa; Kansas; Kentucky; Louisiana; Maine; Manitoba; Maryland; Massachusetts; Michigan; Minnesota; Mississippi; Missouri; Montana; Nebraska; Nevada; New Brunswick; Newfoundland; New Hampshire; New Jersey; New Mexico; New York; North Carolina; North Dakota; Ohio; Oklahoma; Oregon; Pennsylvania; Prince Edward Island; Puerto Rico; Rhode Island; South Carolina; South Dakota; Tennessee; Texas; Utah; Vermont; Virginia; Washington; West Virginia; Wisconsin; Wyoming.
Society of Plastics Engineers Scholarship Program	196	$6000	$1000	35–40	Chemical Engineering; Electrical Engineering/Electronics; Engineering/ Technology; Industrial Design; Materials Science, Engineering, and Metallurgy; Trade/Technical Specialties.
Texas Mutual Insurance Company Scholarship Program	674	$6000	$600	1–25	N/A
Twin Towers Orphan Fund	968	$6000	$1500	N/A	N/A
Taylor Opportunity Program for Students Opportunity Level	842	$5936	$436	24,633	Residence: Louisiana. Studying in Louisiana.
UNCF/Travelers Insurance Scholarship	185	$5850	$3000	N/A	Business/Consumer Services; Insurance and Actuarial Science. Residence: California; Colorado; Florida; Georgia; Illinois; Massachusetts; Missouri; North Carolina; Texas; Washington. Limited to Black (non-Hispanic) students.
Iowa Tuition Grant Program	839	$5650	$100	16,500–19,000	Residence: Iowa. Studying in Iowa.
Kansas Teacher Service Scholarship	272	$5536	$2214	N/A	Education. Residence: Kansas. Studying in Kansas.
Academic Scholars Program	951	$5500	$1800	N/A	Studying in Oklahoma. Must be in high school.
Marion A. and Eva S. Peeples Foundation Trust Scholarship	481	$5500	$1000	5–20	Nursing. Residence: Indiana. Studying in Indiana.
Pine Cone Foundation Scholarship	660	$5500	$500	1–5	Disability: learning disabled. Residence: California. Studying in California. Must be in high school. Limited to ethnic minority students.
Governor's Scholarship Program—Need/Merit Scholarship	607	$5250	$2275	1,967	Residence: Connecticut. Studying in Connecticut.

Award Name	Page Number	Highest Dollar Amount	Lowest Dollar Amount	Number of Awards	Academic Fields/Career Goals and Nonacademic/Noncareer Criteria
Tuition Equalization Grant (TEG) Program	967	$5046	N/A	N/A	Studying in Texas.
Zell Miller Scholarship Program	621	$5004	$534	200,000	Residence: Georgia. Studying in Georgia.
1-800-HANSONS Scholarship Program	592	$5000	$500	8	N/A
Academy of Motion Picture Arts and Sciences Student Academy Awards	345	$5000	$2000	3–15	Filmmaking/Video.
AG Bell College Scholarship Program	594	$5000	$1500	20–40	Disability: hearing impaired. Residence: Alabama; Alaska; Alberta; American Samoa; Arizona; Arkansas; British Columbia; California; Colorado; Connecticut; Delaware; District of Columbia; Florida; Georgia; Guam; Hawaii; Idaho; Illinois; Indiana; Iowa; Kansas; Kentucky; Louisiana; Maine; Manitoba; Maryland; Massachusetts; Michigan; Minnesota; Mississippi; Missouri; Montana; Nebraska; Nevada; New Brunswick; Newfoundland; New Hampshire; New Jersey; New Mexico; New York; North Carolina; North Dakota; Northern Mariana Islands; Northwest Territories; Nova Scotia; Ohio; Oklahoma; Ontario; Oregon; Pennsylvania; Prince Edward Island; Puerto Rico; Quebec; Rhode Island; Saskatchewan; South Carolina; South Dakota; Tennessee; Texas; Utah; Vermont; Virginia; Washington; West Virginia; Wisconsin; Wyoming; Yukon. Studying in Alabama; Alaska; Alberta; American Samoa; Arizona; Arkansas; British Columbia; California; Colorado; Connecticut; Delaware; District of Columbia; Florida; Georgia; Guam; Hawaii; Idaho; Illinois; Indiana; Iowa; Kansas; Kentucky; Louisiana; Maine; Manitoba; Maryland; Massachusetts; Michigan; Minnesota; Mississippi; Missouri; Montana; Nebraska; Nevada; New Brunswick; Newfoundland; New Hampshire; New Jersey; New Mexico; New York; North Carolina; North Dakota; Northern Mariana Islands; Northwest Territories; Nova Scotia; Ohio; Oklahoma; Ontario; Oregon; Pennsylvania; Prince Edward Island; Puerto Rico; Quebec; Rhode Island; Saskatchewan; South Carolina; South Dakota; Tennessee; Texas; Utah; Vermont; Virginia; Washington; West Virginia; Wisconsin; Wyoming; Yukon.
Alabama Student Assistance Program	798	$5000	$300	3,500–4,500	Residence: Alabama. Studying in Alabama.
Alabama Student Assistance Program	798	$5000	$300	3,500–4,500	Residence: Alabama. Studying in Alabama.
Albert E. Wischmeyer Memorial Scholarship Award	325	$5000	$1000	1–10	Engineering/Technology. Residence: New York. Studying in New York.
All-Ink.com College Scholarship Program	921	$5000	$1000	5–10	N/A

Award Name	Page Number	Highest Dollar Amount	Lowest Dollar Amount	Number of Awards	Academic Fields/Career Goals and Nonacademic/Noncareer Criteria
American Chemical Society Scholars Program	187	$5000	$1000	100–130	Chemical Engineering; Environmental Science; Materials Science, Engineering, and Metallurgy; Natural Sciences; Paper and Pulp Engineering; Trade/Technical Specialties. Limited to American Indian/Alaska Native; Black (non-Hispanic); Hispanic students.
AMPCUS Hallmark Scholarship	769	$5000	$2000	N/A	Must be in high school. Limited to Asian/Pacific Islander students.
AMS Freshman Undergraduate Scholarship	448	$5000	$2500	14	Meteorology/Atmospheric Science. Must be in high school.
Anchor Scholarship Foundation	598	$5000	$2000	35–43	Military Service: Navy.
Angus Foundation Scholarships	570	$5000	$250	75–90	Civic Affiliation: American Angus Association.
Anthony Narigi Hospitality Scholarship Fund	391	$5000	$1000	1–5	Hospitality Management. Residence: California.
Arc of Washington Trust Fund Stipend Program	599	$5000	$4000	4–5	Employment/Volunteer Experience: community service; designated career field; helping people with disabilities; human services; medicine (physician/surgeon); nursing; physical therapy/rehabilitation; teaching/education. Residence: Washington. Studying in Washington.
Arkansas Academic Challenge Scholarship Program	810	$5000	$1000	30,000–35,000	Residence: Arkansas. Studying in Arkansas.
Armed Forces Communications and Electronics Association ROTC Scholarship Program	151	$5000	$2000	20	Aviation/Aerospace; Computer Science/Data Processing; Electrical Engineering/Electronics; Engineering-Related Technologies; Engineering/Technology; Materials Science, Engineering, and Metallurgy; Mathematics; Physical Sciences.
ARTBA-TDF Lanford Family Highway Workers Memorial Scholarship Program	599	$5000	$1000	N/A	Employment/Volunteer Experience: construction; roadway work; transportation industry.
Arthur and Gladys Cervenka Scholarship Award	325	$5000	$1000	1–10	Engineering/Technology.
Ashby B. Carter Memorial Scholarship Fund Founders Award	568	$5000	$2000	3	Civic Affiliation: National Alliance of Postal and Federal Employees. Must be in high school.
Associated General Contractors NYS Scholarship Program	207	$5000	$1500	15–25	Civil Engineering; Construction Engineering/Management; Surveying, Surveying Technology, Cartography, or Geographic Information Science; Transportation. Residence: New York.
Audria M. Edwards Scholarship Fund	658	$5000	$1000	8–15	Residence: Oregon; Washington.
Baltimore Ravens Scholarship Program	817	$5000	N/A	1–5	Residence: Maryland. Must be in high school.
BMI Student Composer Awards	141	$5000	$500	6–12	Arts; Music. Talent/Interest Area: music; music/singing.
Bruce Lee Scholarship	971	$5000	$2000	1	Must be in high school.
BURGER KING Scholars Program	928	$5000	$1000	N/A	Must be in high school.

Award Name	Page Number	Highest Dollar Amount	Lowest Dollar Amount	Number of Awards	Academic Fields/Career Goals and Nonacademic/Noncareer Criteria
Caterpillar Scholars Award Fund	325	$5000	$1000	1–15	Engineering/Technology.
Center for Architecture Design Scholarship	132	$5000	$2000	1–2	Architecture; Civil Engineering; Electrical Engineering/Electronics; Industrial Design; Interior Design; Landscape Architecture; Mechanical Engineering. Residence: New York. Studying in New York.
Chapter 198-Downriver Detroit Scholarship	325	$5000	$1000	1–5	Engineering/Technology; Industrial Design; Mechanical Engineering; Trade/Technical Specialties. Studying in Michigan.
Chapter 23-Quad Cities Iowa/Illinois Scholarship	325	$5000	$1000	5	Engineering/Technology. Studying in Illinois; Iowa.
Chapter 31-Tri City Scholarship	326	$5000	$1000	5	Engineering/Technology. Studying in Michigan.
Chapter 3-Peoria Endowed Scholarship	326	$5000	$1000	5	Engineering/Technology. Residence: Illinois. Studying in Illinois.
Chapter 4-Lawrence A. Wacker Memorial Scholarship	326	$5000	$1000	1–10	Engineering/Technology; Mechanical Engineering. Studying in Wisconsin.
Chapter 63-Portland James E. Morrow Scholarship	326	$5000	$1000	5	Engineering/Technology. Residence: Oregon; Washington. Studying in Oregon; Washington.
Chapter 63-Portland Uncle Bud Smith Scholarship	326	$5000	$1000	5	Engineering/Technology. Residence: Oregon; Washington. Studying in Oregon; Washington.
Chapter 67-Phoenix Scholarship	326	$5000	$1000	1–5	Engineering/Technology; Industrial Design; Mechanical Engineering; Trade/Technical Specialties. Studying in Arizona.
Chapter 6-Fairfield County Scholarship	326	$5000	$1000	4	Engineering/Technology.
Chapter 93-Albuquerque Scholarship	326	$5000	$1000	1–5	Engineering/Technology. Studying in New Mexico.
Clarence and Josephine Myers Scholarship	326	$5000	$1000	5	Engineering/Technology. Studying in Indiana.

Award Name	Page Number	Highest Dollar Amount	Lowest Dollar Amount	Number of Awards	Academic Fields/Career Goals and Nonacademic/Noncareer Criteria
Classic Scholarships	874	$5000	$2500	300–350	Residence: Alabama; Alaska; Arizona; Arkansas; California; Colorado; Connecticut; Delaware; Florida; Georgia; Hawaii; Idaho; Illinois; Indiana; Iowa; Kansas; Kentucky; Louisiana; Maine; Maryland; Massachusetts; Michigan; Minnesota; Mississippi; Missouri; Montana; Nebraska; Nevada; New Hampshire; New Jersey; New Mexico; New York; North Carolina; North Dakota; Ohio; Oklahoma; Oregon; Pennsylvania; Puerto Rico; Rhode Island; South Carolina; South Dakota; Tennessee; Texas; Utah; Vermont; Virginia; Washington; West Virginia; Wisconsin; Wyoming. Studying in Alabama; Alaska; Arizona; Arkansas; California; Colorado; Connecticut; Delaware; Florida; Georgia; Hawaii; Idaho; Illinois; Indiana; Iowa; Kansas; Kentucky; Louisiana; Maine; Maryland; Massachusetts; Michigan; Minnesota; Mississippi; Missouri; Montana; Nebraska; Nevada; New Hampshire; New Jersey; New Mexico; New York; North Carolina; North Dakota; Ohio; Oklahoma; Oregon; Pennsylvania; Puerto Rico; Rhode Island; South Carolina; South Dakota; Tennessee; Texas; Utah; Vermont; Virginia; Washington; West Virginia; Wisconsin; Wyoming.
Clinton J. Helton Manufacturing Scholarship Award Fund	327	$5000	$1000	1–5	Engineering/Technology; Trade/Technical Specialties. Studying in Colorado.
College Photographer of the Year Competition	502	$5000	$600	10	Photojournalism/Photography.
CollegeWeekLive.com Scholarship	891	$5000	$1000	1–15	Talent/Interest Area: writing.
Colorado Student Grant	819	$5000	$300	N/A	Residence: Colorado. Studying in Colorado.
Common Scholarship Application	865	$5000	$500	95–110	Residence: California.
Connie and Robert T. Gunter Scholarship	327	$5000	$1000	1–5	Engineering/Technology. Studying in Georgia.
Course Hero $5,000 Monthly Scholarship	931	$5000	$1000	1	N/A
Crain Educational Grants Program	866	$5000	$1000	10	Residence: California.
Culinary Trust Scholarship Program for Culinary Study and Research	246	$5000	$1000	21	Culinary Arts; Food Science/Nutrition; Food Service/Hospitality.
Cynthia H. Kuo Scholarship	759	$5000	$1000	1–5	Religion: Christian. Limited to Asian/Pacific Islander students.
Darooge Family Scholarship for Construction Trades	133	$5000	$1000	1–5	Architecture; Trade/Technical Specialties. Employment/Volunteer Experience: construction. Residence: Michigan. Studying in Michigan.
Daughters of the Cincinnati Scholarship	933	$5000	$3000	4–5	Must be in high school.
Doran/Blair Scholarships	563	$5000	$1000	1–20	Civic Affiliation: Fleet Reserve Association/Auxiliary. Military Service: Coast Guard.

Award Name	Page Number	Highest Dollar Amount	Lowest Dollar Amount	Number of Awards	Academic Fields/Career Goals and Nonacademic/Noncareer Criteria
EDSF Board of Directors Scholarships	364	$5000	$1000	1–40	Graphics/Graphic Arts/Printing.
Edward S. Roth Manufacturing Engineering Scholarship	327	$5000	$1000	1–10	Engineering/Technology. Studying in California; Florida; Illinois; Massachusetts; Minnesota; Ohio; Texas; Utah.
Elie Wiesel Prize in Ethics Essay Contest	893	$5000	$500	5	Talent/Interest Area: writing.
Environmental Litigation Group, P.C. Asbestos Scholarship	615	$5000	$2000	3	N/A
Eric J. Gennuso and LeRoy D. (Bud) Loy, Jr. Scholarship Program	187	$5000	$2500	1–3	Chemical Engineering; Civil Engineering; Construction Engineering/Management; Electrical Engineering/Electronics; Energy and Power Engineering; Engineering-Related Technologies; Engineering/Technology; Environmental Science; Marine/Ocean Engineering; Materials Science, Engineering, and Metallurgy; Mechanical Engineering; Surveying, Surveying Technology, Cartography, or Geographic Information Science; Transportation. Residence: Pennsylvania.
Esther R. Sawyer Research Award	87	$5000	$3000	1–3	Accounting; Business/Consumer Services.
E. Wayne Kay Co-op Scholarship	327	$5000	$1000	1–10	Engineering/Technology.
Explosive Ordnance Disposal Memorial Scholarship	615	$5000	$1000	25–75	Employment/Volunteer Experience: explosive ordnance disposal. Military Service: General.
Federated Garden Clubs of Connecticut Inc. Scholarships	170	$5000	$1000	2–5	Biology; Horticulture/Floriculture; Landscape Architecture. Residence: Connecticut. Studying in Connecticut.
Fleet Reserve Association Education Foundation Scholarships	704	$5000	$1000	1–10	Military Service: Coast Guard.
Foreclosure.com Scholarship Program	936	$5000	$1000	5	N/A
Fort Wayne Chapter 56 Scholarship	328	$5000	$1000	1–10	Engineering/Technology; Industrial Design; Mechanical Engineering; Trade/Technical Specialties. Studying in Indiana.
Foundation for Seacoast Health Scholarships	373	$5000	$1000	2–6	Health and Medical Sciences. Residence: Maine; New Hampshire.
Foundation Fund Scholarship	112	$5000	$1000	1–100	Agriculture. Residence: Washington.
Frame My Future Scholarship Contest	605	$5000	$500	1–3	N/A
Franz Stenzel M.D. and Kathryn Stenzel Scholarship Fund	376	$5000	$2000	70	Health and Medical Sciences; Nursing. Residence: Oregon.
General John Ratay Educational Fund Grants	946	$5000	$4000	1–5	N/A
Georgia Engineering Foundation Scholarship Program	318	$5000	$1000	45	Engineering/Technology. Residence: Georgia.
Geraldo Rivera Scholarship	406	$5000	$1000	N/A	Journalism; TV/Radio Broadcasting.
Gilman Scholarship	970	$5000	$1000	1,000–1,100	N/A
Girls Impact the World Scholarship Program	930	$5000	$1000	12	N/A

Award Name	Page Number	Highest Dollar Amount	Lowest Dollar Amount	Number of Awards	Academic Fields/Career Goals and Nonacademic/Noncareer Criteria
GM Genius	941	$5000	$1000	1–3	N/A
Graduate and Professional Scholarship Program-Maryland	256	$5000	$1000	584	Dental Health/Services; Health and Medical Sciences; Law/Legal Services; Nursing; Social Services. Residence: Maryland. Studying in Maryland.
Great Falls Broadcasters Association Scholarship	544	$5000	$2000	1	TV/Radio Broadcasting. Residence: Montana. Studying in Montana.
Greenhouse Scholars	736	$5000	$1000	15–25	Residence: Colorado; Georgia; Illinois; North Carolina. Studying in Alabama; Alaska; Arizona; Arkansas; California; Colorado; Connecticut; Delaware; District of Columbia; Florida; Georgia; Hawaii; Idaho; Illinois; Indiana; Iowa; Kansas; Kentucky; Louisiana; Maine; Maryland; Michigan; Mississippi; Missouri; Montana; Nebraska; Nevada; New Hampshire; New Jersey; New Mexico; New York; North Carolina; North Dakota; Ohio; Oklahoma; Oregon; Pennsylvania; Rhode Island; South Carolina; South Dakota; Tennessee; Texas; Utah; Vermont; Virginia; Washington; West Virginia; Wisconsin; Wyoming. Must be in high school.
Guiliano Mazzetti Scholarship Award	328	$5000	$1000	1–10	Engineering/Technology.
Harold Johnson Law Enforcement Scholarship	243	$5000	$1000	1–7	Criminal Justice/Criminology. Residence: California.
Harry A. Applegate Scholarship	83	$5000	$1000	20–25	Accounting; Business/Consumer Services; Education; Fashion Design; Finance; Food Service/Hospitality; Hospitality Management; Marketing. Civic Affiliation: Distribution Ed Club or Future Business Leaders of America.
Harry Ludwig Scholarship Fund	692	$5000	$500	1–3	Disability: visually impaired.
Hazel Reed Baumeister Scholarship Program	668	$5000	$1000	1–15	Residence: California.
Herbert Hoover Uncommon Student Award	627	$5000	$1500	15	Residence: Iowa. Must be in high school.
Houston Symphony Ima Hogg Competition	454	$5000	$300	5	Music. Talent/Interest Area: music.
HSF/General College Scholarship Program	739	$5000	$500	2,200–5,000	Limited to Hispanic students.
IAAO Academic Partnership Program	942	$5000	$1000	1–5	N/A
IABA Scholarship	740	$5000	$3000	25–35	Limited to Black (non-Hispanic) students.
IFMA Foundation Scholarships	135	$5000	$1500	25–35	Architecture; Construction Engineering/Management; Engineering-Related Technologies; Engineering/Technology; Interior Design; Urban and Regional Planning.
Indiana Health Care Policy Institute Nursing Scholarship	480	$5000	$750	1–5	Nursing. Residence: Indiana. Studying in Illinois; Indiana; Kentucky; Michigan; Ohio.

Award Name	Page Number	Highest Dollar Amount	Lowest Dollar Amount	Number of Awards	Academic Fields/Career Goals and Nonacademic/Noncareer Criteria
Indian American Scholarship Fund	740	$5000	$500	3	Residence: Georgia. Must be in high school. Limited to Asian/Pacific Islander students.
Ingersoll Rand Scholarship	769	$5000	$2000	N/A	Must be in high school. Limited to Asian/Pacific Islander students.
ISA Educational Foundation Scholarships	301	$5000	$500	15–16	Engineering-Related Technologies.
ISF National Scholarship	119	$5000	$2000	1–40	Anthropology; Filmmaking/Video; History; International Studies; Journalism; Law Enforcement/Police Administration; Law/Legal Services; Near and Middle East Studies; TV/Radio Broadcasting. Religion: Muslim faith.
Jerry McDowell Fund	301	$5000	$1500	1–3	Engineering-Related Technologies; Engineering/Technology.
John Kimball Memorial Trust Scholarship Program for the Study of History	383	$5000	$3000	10–12	History. Residence: Massachusetts. Studying in Massachusetts.
John L. Dales Scholarship Program	960	$5000	$1000	1–16	N/A
John M. Azarian Memorial Armenian Youth Scholarship Fund	742	$5000	$500	1–5	N/A
Joseph Shinoda Memorial Scholarship	388	$5000	$1000	8–15	Horticulture/Floriculture.
Judith McManus Price Scholarship	547	$5000	$2000	N/A	Urban and Regional Planning. Limited to American Indian/Alaska Native; Black (non-Hispanic); Hispanic students.
JVS Scholarship Program	741	$5000	$750	150–200	Residence: California. Religion: Jewish.
Kappa Alpha Theta Foundation Non-Degree Educational Grant Program	567	$5000	$100	1	Civic Affiliation: Greek Organization.
Louis F. Wolf Jr. Memorial Scholarship	224	$5000	$1000	1	Communications; Electrical Engineering/Electronics; Engineering-Related Technologies; Engineering/Technology; Filmmaking/Video; Science, Technology, and Society; TV/Radio Broadcasting. Civic Affiliation: Society of Motion Picture and Television Engineers.
L. Ron Hubbard's Illustrators of the Future Contest	887	$5000	$500	12	Talent/Interest Area: art.
L. Ron Hubbard's Writers of the Future Contest	887	$5000	$500	12	Talent/Interest Area: writing.
Lucile B. Kaufman Women's Scholarship	328	$5000	$1000	1–5	Engineering/Technology.
Making the Turn Against Parkinson's Scholarship	843	$5000	$500	1–4	Residence: Michigan.
Marion Barr Stanfield Art Scholarship	145	$5000	$1500	5–8	Arts. Religion: Unitarian Universalist. Talent/Interest Area: art.
Mary McMillan Scholarship Award	267	$5000	$3000	1–6	Education; Health and Medical Sciences; Therapy/Rehabilitation. Employment/Volunteer Experience: physical therapy/rehabilitation.

Award Name	Page Number	Highest Dollar Amount	Lowest Dollar Amount	Number of Awards	Academic Fields/Career Goals and Nonacademic/Noncareer Criteria
Masonic Range Science Scholarship	103	$5000	$1000	1	Agribusiness; Agriculture; Animal/Veterinary Sciences; Environmental Science; Natural Resources.
Math, Engineering, Science, Business, Education, Computers Scholarships	178	$5000	$500	180	Business/Consumer Services; Computer Science/Data Processing; Education; Engineering/Technology; Humanities; Physical Sciences; Science, Technology, and Society; Social Sciences. Limited to American Indian/Alaska Native students.
Minority Teacher Incentive Grant Program	269	$5000	$2500	87	Education. Residence: Connecticut. Studying in Connecticut. Limited to ethnic minority students.
MOAA American Patriot Scholarship	946	$5000	$2500	1–60	N/A
NADONA Stephanie Carroll Memorial Scholarship	482	$5000	$1000	1–13	Nursing. Employment/Volunteer Experience: nursing.
National Asphalt Pavement Association Research and Education Foundation Scholarship Program	209	$5000	$500	51	Civil Engineering; Construction Engineering/Management.
Native American Leadership in Education (NALE)	178	$5000	$500	30	Business/Consumer Services; Education; Humanities; Physical Sciences; Science, Technology, and Society. Limited to American Indian/Alaska Native students.
New England Employee Benefits Council Scholarship Program	89	$5000	$1000	1–3	Accounting; Business/Consumer Services; Economics; Health Administration; Human Resources; Insurance and Actuarial Science; Law/Legal Services; Public Health; Public Policy and Administration. Residence: Connecticut; Maine; Massachusetts; New Hampshire; Rhode Island; Vermont. Studying in Connecticut; Maine; Massachusetts; New Hampshire; Rhode Island; Vermont.
New York State Tuition Assistance Program	853	$5000	$500	350,000–360,000	Residence: New York. Studying in New York.
NGWA Foundation's Len Assante Scholarship	262	$5000	$1000	1–10	Earth Science; Environmental Science; Hydrology.
Norm Manly—YMTA Maritime Educational Scholarships	425	$5000	$1000	6–7	Marine Biology; Marine/Ocean Engineering; Oceanography; Trade/Technical Specialties. Residence: Washington. Must be in high school.
North Carolina Association of CPAs Foundation Scholarships	88	$5000	$1000	50–60	Accounting. Residence: North Carolina. Studying in North Carolina.
North Carolina Education and Training Voucher Program	950	$5000	N/A	N/A	N/A
North Central Region 9 Scholarship	328	$5000	$1000	1–10	Engineering/Technology; Industrial Design; Mechanical Engineering; Trade/Technical Specialties. Studying in Iowa; Michigan; Minnesota; Nebraska; North Dakota; South Dakota; Wisconsin.
NSCS Scholar Abroad Scholarship	571	$5000	$2500	3	Civic Affiliation: National Society of Collegiate Scholars.
NurseRecruiter.com Scholarship	655	$5000	$1000	1–10	N/A

Award Name	Page Number	Highest Dollar Amount	Lowest Dollar Amount	Number of Awards	Academic Fields/Career Goals and Nonacademic/Noncareer Criteria
Osage Nation Higher Education Scholarship	657	$5000	$150	1–1,200	Limited to American Indian/Alaska Native students.
Outdoor Writers Association of America - Bodie McDowell Scholarship Award	222	$5000	$1000	2–6	Communications; Environmental Science; Filmmaking/Video; Journalism; Literature/English/Writing; Natural Resources; Photojournalism/Photography; TV/Radio Broadcasting. Talent/Interest Area: amateur radio; art; athletics/sports; photography/photogrammetry/filmmaking; writing.
Pellegrini Scholarship Grants	763	$5000	$500	50	Residence: Connecticut; Delaware; New Jersey; New York; Pennsylvania.
PepsiCo Hallmark Scholarships	769	$5000	$2000	1	Must be in high school. Limited to Asian/Pacific Islander students.
Peter and Alice Koomruian Armenian Education Fund	755	$5000	$1000	4–10	Nationality: Armenian.
PHCC Educational Foundation Scholarship Program	182	$5000	$2500	1–4	Business/Consumer Services; Engineering-Related Technologies; Engineering/Technology; Heating, Air-Conditioning, and Refrigeration Mechanics; Mechanical Engineering; Trade/Technical Specialties.
Phoenix Pride Scholarship Program	659	$5000	$1000	9	Residence: Arizona. Studying in Arizona.
Plan New Hampshire Scholarship and Fellowship Program	129	$5000	$1200	5–10	Archaeology; Architecture; Civil Engineering; Construction Engineering/Management; Energy and Power Engineering; Engineering/Technology; Environmental Science; Historic Preservation and Conservation; Interior Design; Landscape Architecture; Mechanical Engineering; Natural Resources; Transportation; Urban and Regional Planning. Residence: New Hampshire.
Print and Graphics Scholarships Foundation	222	$5000	$1500	150–200	Communications; Graphics/Graphic Arts/Printing.
Promise of Nursing Scholarship	478	$5000	$1000	N/A	Nursing. Studying in California; Florida; Georgia; Illinois; Massachusetts; Michigan; New Jersey; Tennessee; Texas.
Regional and Restricted Scholarship Award Program	821	$5000	$2000	200–300	Residence: Connecticut.
The Risk Management Association Foundation Scholarship Program	664	$5000	$2000	40	N/A
Roshan Rahbari Scholarship Fund	867	$5000	$1000	1–4	Residence: California.
Samuel Robinson Award	791	$5000	$250	16	Religion: Presbyterian.
Scholarship Program for Sons and Daughters of Employees of Roseburg Forest Products Co.	588	$5000	$3000	30–47	Corporate Affiliation: Roseburg Forest Products.
Screen Actors Guild Foundation/John L. Dales Scholarship Fund (Standard)	961	$5000	$1000	100–135	N/A

Award Name	Page Number	Highest Dollar Amount	Lowest Dollar Amount	Number of Awards	Academic Fields/Career Goals and Nonacademic/Noncareer Criteria
SEMA Memorial Scholarship Fund	92	$5000	$2000	50–60	Accounting; Advertising/Public Relations; Business/Consumer Services; Communications; Computer Science/Data Processing; Electrical Engineering/Electronics; Engineering/Technology; Finance; Marketing; Mechanical Engineering; Trade/Technical Specialties; Transportation. Talent/Interest Area: automotive.
Sigma Delta Chi Scholarships	409	$5000	$3000	4–7	Journalism. Studying in District of Columbia; Maryland; Virginia.
Sigma Xi Grants-In-Aid of Research	110	$5000	$1000	400	Agriculture; Animal/Veterinary Sciences; Anthropology; Biology; Chemical Engineering; Civil Engineering; Computer Science/Data Processing; Earth Science; Electrical Engineering/Electronics; Energy and Power Engineering; Engineering/Technology; Environmental Science; Geography; Health and Medical Sciences; Hydrology; Marine Biology; Marine/Ocean Engineering; Materials Science, Engineering, and Metallurgy; Mathematics; Mechanical Engineering; Meteorology/Atmospheric Science; Natural Sciences; Nuclear Science; Physical Sciences; Psychology; Science, Technology, and Society; Social Sciences.
Society of Physics Students Leadership Scholarships	508	$5000	$2000	17–22	Physical Sciences. Civic Affiliation: Society of Physics Students.
Straus Scholarship Program for Undergraduate Education	604	$5000	$2500	5–8	Residence: Maryland.
TAC Foundation Scholarships	213	$5000	$2500	30–45	Civil Engineering; Construction Engineering/Management; Economics; Engineering-Related Technologies; Engineering/Technology; Urban and Regional Planning. Nationality: Canadian. Residence: Alberta; British Columbia; Manitoba; New Brunswick; Newfoundland; Northwest Territories; Nova Scotia; Ontario; Prince Edward Island; Quebec; Saskatchewan; Yukon.
Taylor Michaels Scholarship Fund	641	$5000	$1000	N/A	Employment/Volunteer Experience: community service. Must be in high school. Limited to ethnic minority students.
Theta Delta Chi Educational Foundation Inc. Scholarship	967	$5000	$1000	15	N/A
TLMI 4 Year College Degree Scholarship Program	307	$5000	$2500	1–6	Engineering-Related Technologies; Flexography; Graphics/Graphic Arts/Printing.
Tribal Business Management Program (TBM)	82	$5000	$500	35	Accounting; Business/Consumer Services; Computer Science/Data Processing; Economics; Electrical Engineering/Electronics; Engineering-Related Technologies. Limited to American Indian/Alaska Native students.

Award Name	Page Number	Highest Dollar Amount	Lowest Dollar Amount	Number of Awards	Academic Fields/Career Goals and Nonacademic/Noncareer Criteria
Two Ten Footwear Foundation Scholarship	676	$5000	$2500	300–350	Employment/Volunteer Experience: leather/footwear industry. Residence: Alabama; Alaska; Arizona; Arkansas; California; Colorado; Connecticut; Delaware; Florida; Georgia; Hawaii; Idaho; Illinois; Indiana; Iowa; Kansas; Kentucky; Louisiana; Maine; Maryland; Massachusetts; Michigan; Minnesota; Mississippi; Missouri; Montana; Nebraska; Nevada; New Hampshire; New Jersey; New Mexico; New York; North Carolina; North Dakota; Ohio; Oklahoma; Ontario; Oregon; Pennsylvania; Puerto Rico; Rhode Island; South Carolina; South Dakota; Tennessee; Texas; Utah; Vermont; Virginia; Washington; West Virginia; Wisconsin; Wyoming. Studying in Alabama; Alaska; Arizona; Arkansas; California; Colorado; Connecticut; Delaware; Florida; Georgia; Hawaii; Idaho; Illinois; Indiana; Iowa; Kansas; Kentucky; Louisiana; Maine; Maryland; Massachusetts; Michigan; Minnesota; Mississippi; Missouri; Montana; Nebraska; Nevada; New Hampshire; New Jersey; New Mexico; New York; North Carolina; North Dakota; Ohio; Oklahoma; Oregon; Pennsylvania; Puerto Rico; Rhode Island; South Carolina; South Dakota; Tennessee; Texas; Utah; Vermont; Virginia; Washington; West Virginia; Wisconsin; Wyoming.
Udall Undergraduate Scholarship	947	$5000	N/A	50	N/A
UPS Hallmark Scholarships	770	$5000	$2000	N/A	Must be in high school. Limited to Asian/Pacific Islander students.
Vermont Space Grant Consortium	104	$5000	$2500	6–9	Agribusiness; Applied Sciences; Aviation/Aerospace; Biology; Civil Engineering; Computer Science/Data Processing; Earth Science; Electrical Engineering/Electronics; Energy and Power Engineering; Engineering-Related Technologies; Engineering/Technology; Materials Science, Engineering, and Metallurgy; Mathematics; Mechanical Engineering; Physical Sciences; Science, Technology, and Society; Trade/Technical Specialties. Residence: Vermont. Studying in Vermont.
Vertical Flight Foundation Scholarship	148	$5000	$1500	10–19	Aviation/Aerospace; Electrical Engineering/Electronics; Engineering-Related Technologies; Engineering/Technology; Mechanical Engineering. Talent/Interest Area: aviation.
VSCPA Educational Foundation Accounting Scholarships	95	$5000	$1000	26	Accounting. Residence: Virginia. Studying in Virginia.
Warner Norcross and Judd LLP Scholarship for Students of Color	415	$5000	$1000	1–3	Law/Legal Services. Residence: Michigan. Studying in Michigan. Limited to ethnic minority students.
Washington Crossing Foundation Scholarship	511	$5000	$500	N/A	Political Science; Public Policy and Administration. Must be in high school.

Award Name	Page Number	Highest Dollar Amount	Lowest Dollar Amount	Number of Awards	Academic Fields/Career Goals and Nonacademic/Noncareer Criteria
Watson-Brown Foundation Scholarship	877	$5000	$3000	200	Residence: Georgia; South Carolina.
William E. Weisel Scholarship Fund	287	$5000	$1000	1–10	Electrical Engineering/Electronics; Engineering/Technology; Mechanical Engineering; Trade/Technical Specialties.
WinWin Products, Inc. Scholarship	770	$5000	$2000	N/A	Must be in high school. Limited to Asian/Pacific Islander students.
Women in Defense HORIZONS-Michigan Scholarship	879	$5000	$1500	1–4	Residence: Michigan. Studying in Michigan.
Worldstudio AIGA Scholarships	146	$5000	$1000	10–25	Arts; Graphics/Graphic Arts/Printing.
Young Artist Competition	620	$5000	$500	8	Talent/Interest Area: music.
Young Patriots Essay Contest	947	$5000	$2000	3	Must be in high school.
Youth Activity Fund	463	$5000	$500	10–30	Natural Sciences; Science, Technology, and Society.
ASCSA Summer Session and Summer Seminars Scholarships	118	$4900	$500	10–13	Anthropology; Archaeology; Architecture; Art History; Arts; Classics; Education; Foreign Language; Historic Preservation and Conservation; History; Humanities; Landscape Architecture; Museum Studies; Philosophy; Religion/Theology; Science, Technology, and Society; Urban and Regional Planning.
Alaska Performance Scholarship	798	$4755	$500	N/A	Residence: Alaska. Studying in Alaska.
AIA West Virginia Scholarship	138	$4500	$3500	N/A	Architecture. Residence: West Virginia.
American Council of the Blind Scholarships	595	$4500	$1000	16–20	Disability: visually impaired.
Brook Hollow Golf Club Scholarship	932	$4500	$2000	N/A	Must be in high school.
Ernest Alan and Barbara Park Meyer Scholarship Fund	857	$4500	$1000	5	Residence: Oregon.
Glenn Miller Instrumental Scholarship	896	$4500	$1000	3	Talent/Interest Area: music/singing. Must be in high school.
Greater Washington Society of CPAs Scholarship	86	$4500	$2000	3–5	Accounting. Residence: District of Columbia. Studying in District of Columbia.
Hawaii Association of Broadcasters Scholarship	543	$4500	$500	20–30	TV/Radio Broadcasting.
Roberta B. Willis Scholarship Program—Need-Based Grant	607	$4500	N/A	N/A	Residence: Connecticut. Studying in Connecticut.
Tennessee HOPE Scholarship	673	$4500	$2000	N/A	Residence: Tennessee. Studying in Tennessee.
Pennsylvania State Grant Program	658	$4340	$200	N/A	Residence: Pennsylvania.
Nebraska Opportunity Grant	651	$4139	$100	N/A	Residence: Nebraska. Studying in Nebraska.
Actuarial Diversity Scholarship	397	$4000	$1000	N/A	Insurance and Actuarial Science; Mathematics. Limited to ethnic minority students.

Award Name	Page Number	Highest Dollar Amount	Lowest Dollar Amount	Number of Awards	Academic Fields/Career Goals and Nonacademic/Noncareer Criteria
AFIO Undergraduate and Graduate Scholarships	113	$4000	$1000	10	American Studies; Aviation/Aerospace; Computer Science/Data Processing; Criminal Justice/Criminology; Foreign Language; History; International Studies; Law Enforcement/Police Administration; Military and Defense Studies; Natural Sciences; Near and Middle East Studies; Peace and Conflict Studies; Political Science; Public Policy and Administration.
Alask Education Grant	798	$4000	$500	N/A	Residence: Alaska. Studying in Alaska.
Alexander and Maude Hadden Scholarship	684	$4000	$2500	96–108	Employment/Volunteer Experience: community service. Residence: Yukon.
American Legion Auxiliary Department of California Past Presidents' Parley Nursing Scholarships	471	$4000	$4000	1–2	Nursing. Military Service: General. Residence: California.
American Society for Enology and Viticulture Scholarships	105	$4000	$500	30	Agriculture; Chemical Engineering; Food Science/Nutrition; Horticulture/Floriculture.
American Society of Civil Engineers-Maine High School Scholarship	206	$4000	$1000	1–4	Civil Engineering. Residence: Maine. Must be in high school.
American Society of Naval Engineers Scholarship	122	$4000	$3000	8–14	Applied Sciences; Aviation/Aerospace; Civil Engineering; Electrical Engineering/Electronics; Energy and Power Engineering; Engineering/Technology; Marine/Ocean Engineering; Materials Science, Engineering, and Metallurgy; Mechanical Engineering; Nuclear Science; Physical Sciences.
Bridging Scholarship for Study Abroad in Japan	595	$4000	$2500	70–120	N/A
C.A.R. Scholarship Foundation Award	516	$4000	$2000	10–25	Real Estate. Residence: California. Studying in California.
College Now Greater Cleveland Adult Learner Program Scholarship	606	$4000	$1000	100–200	Residence: Ohio.
Community Bankers Assoc. of IL Essay Contest	607	$4000	$500	12–24	Residence: Illinois. Must be in high school.
Elks Emergency Educational Grants	563	$4000	$1000	N/A	Civic Affiliation: Elks Club.
Fifth/Graduate Year Student Scholarship	88	$4000	$2000	16–25	Accounting. Studying in Michigan.
Fresh Start Scholarship	830	$4000	$1000	25–30	Residence: Delaware. Studying in Delaware.
General Henry H. Arnold Education Grant Program	695	$4000	$500	3,000	Military Service: Air Force; Air Force National Guard.
GMP Memorial Scholarship Program	564	$4000	$2000	10	Civic Affiliation: Glass, Molders, Pottery, Plastics and Allied Workers International Union. Must be in high school.
Governors' Scholarship for Foster Youth Program	818	$4000	$2000	30–50	Residence: Washington. Studying in Washington. Must be in high school.
Harvard Travellers Club Permanent Fund	939	$4000	$1000	1–4	N/A
Higher Education Success Stipend Program	875	$4000	$300	1,000–5,000	Residence: Utah. Studying in Utah.

Award Name	Page Number	Highest Dollar Amount	Lowest Dollar Amount	Number of Awards	Academic Fields/Career Goals and Nonacademic/Noncareer Criteria
Illinois CPA Society Accounting Scholarship Program	86	$4000	$500	12–35	Accounting. Residence: Illinois. Studying in Illinois.
John F. and Anna Lee Stacey Scholarship Fund	900	$4000	$1000	3–5	Talent/Interest Area: art.
Minority Student Summer Scholarship	130	$4000	$1500	2	Archaeology; Arts; Classics; Foreign Language; History. Limited to ethnic minority students.
Mississippi Press Association Education Foundation Scholarship	404	$4000	$1000	1	Journalism. Residence: Mississippi.
New Mexico Vietnam Veteran Scholarship	853	$4000	$3500	100	Residence: New Mexico. Studying in New Mexico.
New Mexico Wartime Veterans Scholarship	713	$4000	$3500	100	Military Service: General. Residence: New Mexico. Studying in New Mexico.
NGPA Education Fund, Inc.	159	$4000	$3000	3–4	Aviation/Aerospace. Employment/ Volunteer Experience: community service. Talent/Interest Area: aviation; LGBT issues.
Part-Time Grant Program	838	$4000	$20	4,680–6,700	Residence: Indiana. Studying in Indiana.
Sikh Education Aid Fund	925	$4000	$400	N/A	N/A
South Florida Fair College Scholarship	869	$4000	$1000	10	Residence: Florida.
SSPI International Scholarships	160	$4000	$2500	1–4	Aviation/Aerospace; Communications; Law/Legal Services; Meteorology/ Atmospheric Science; Military and Defense Studies.
Student-View Scholarship program	966	$4000	$500	13	Must be in high school.
Tennessee Student Assistance Award	673	$4000	$1000	N/A	Residence: Tennessee. Studying in Tennessee.
Texas Gridiron Club Scholarships	226	$4000	$500	10–15	Communications; Journalism; Photojournalism/Photography; TV/Radio Broadcasting.
Union Plus Credit Card Scholarship Program	550	$4000	$500	N/A	Civic Affiliation: American Federation of State, County, and Municipal Employees.
Union Plus Education Foundation Scholarship Program	584	$4000	$500	100–120	Civic Affiliation: AFL-CIO. Studying in Alabama; Alaska; Arizona; Arkansas; California; Colorado; Connecticut; Delaware; District of Columbia; Florida; Georgia; Hawaii; Idaho; Illinois; Indiana; Iowa; Kansas; Kentucky; Louisiana; Maine; Maryland; Massachusetts; Michigan; Minnesota; Mississippi; Missouri; Montana; Nebraska; Nevada; New Hampshire; New Jersey; New Mexico; New York; North Carolina; North Dakota; Ohio; Oklahoma; Oregon; Pennsylvania; Rhode Island; South Carolina; South Dakota; Tennessee; Texas; Utah; Vermont; Virginia; Washington; West Virginia; Wisconsin; Wyoming.
Union Plus Scholarship Program	569	$4000	$500	3	Civic Affiliation: National Association of Letter Carriers. Must be in high school.
University Film and Video Association Carole Fielding Student Grants	347	$4000	$1000	2–5	Filmmaking/Video.

Award Name	Page Number	Highest Dollar Amount	Lowest Dollar Amount	Number of Awards	Academic Fields/Career Goals and Nonacademic/Noncareer Criteria
Veterans Education (VetEd) Reimbursement Grant	694	$4000	$1340	N/A	Disability: hearing impaired; learning disabled; physically disabled; visually impaired. Military Service: Air Force; Air Force National Guard; Army; Army National Guard; Coast Guard; General. Residence: Wisconsin. Studying in Minnesota; Wisconsin.
Wenderoth Undergraduate Scholarship	575	$4000	$1750	1–4	Civic Affiliation: Phi Sigma Kappa.
William L. Cullison Scholarship	461	$4000	$2000	1–2	Natural Resources; Paper and Pulp Engineering.
WRI Foundation College Scholarship Program	214	$4000	$2000	2–5	Civil Engineering; Construction Engineering/Management.
Taylor Opportunity Program for Students Tech Level	843	$3985	$436	1,671	Residence: Louisiana. Studying in Louisiana.
LAGRANT Foundation Scholarship for Graduates	97	$3750	$3250	N/A	Advertising/Public Relations; Business/Consumer Services; Communications; Graphics/Graphic Arts/Printing; Marketing. Limited to ethnic minority students.
Early Childhood Educators Scholarship Program	203	$3600	$150	N/A	Child and Family Studies; Education. Residence: Massachusetts. Studying in Massachusetts.
Stella Blum Student Research Grant	138	$3600	$2000	1	Area/Ethnic Studies; Art History; Arts; Historic Preservation and Conservation; History; Home Economics; Museum Studies; Performing Arts. Civic Affiliation: Costume Society of America.
American Legion Auxiliary National President's Scholarship	706	$3500	$2500	15	Military Service: General. Must be in high school.
American Legion Department of Arkansas High School Oratorical Contest	803	$3500	$1250	4	Residence: Arkansas. Talent/Interest Area: public speaking. Must be in high school.
Annual Award Program	779	$3500	$800	6–8	Religion: Muslim faith.
California Council of the Blind Scholarships	602	$3500	$1000	6–20	Disability: visually impaired. Residence: California. Studying in California.
Changemaker In Your Community Documentary Competition	921	$3500	$3100	1	N/A
Freedom Alliance Scholarship Fund	620	$3500	$500	250–326	N/A
Hispanic Heritage Foundation Youth Awards	738	$3500	$1000	190–200	Must be in high school. Limited to Hispanic students.
Idaho Opportunity Scholarship	836	$3500	N/A	700–2,000	Residence: Idaho. Studying in Idaho.
National Defense Transportation Association, Scott Air Force Base-St. Louis Area Chapter Scholarship	849	$3500	$2000	6	Residence: Illinois; Missouri. Studying in Colorado; Illinois; Indiana; Iowa; Kansas; Michigan; Minnesota; Missouri; Montana; Nebraska; North Dakota; South Dakota; Wisconsin; Wyoming.
OAB Foundation Scholarship	221	$3500	$2500	4	Communications; Journalism; TV/Radio Broadcasting. Residence: Oregon.
Order Of The Golden Rule Foundation Awards of Excellence Scholarship Program	362	$3500	$2000	2	Funeral Services/Mortuary Science.

Award Name	Page Number	Highest Dollar Amount	Lowest Dollar Amount	Number of Awards	Academic Fields/Career Goals and Nonacademic/Noncareer Criteria
Robert Guthrie PKU Scholarship and Awards	691	$3500	$500	4–8	Disability: physically disabled.
Unmet NEED Grant Program	651	$3500	$1000	10–500	Residence: Pennsylvania. Limited to Black (non-Hispanic) students.
North Carolina National Guard Tuition Assistance Program	700	$3440	$100	N/A	Military Service: Air Force National Guard; Army National Guard. Residence: North Carolina. Studying in North Carolina.
American Legion Department of Indiana High School Oratorical Contest	804	$3400	$200	N/A	Residence: Indiana. Talent/Interest Area: public speaking. Must be in high school.
Dolphin Scholarships	613	$3400	$2000	25–30	N/A
Peter Kong-Ming New Student Prize	964	$3350	$750	3	N/A
South Carolina Tuition Grants Program	669	$3200	$100	N/A	Residence: South Carolina. Studying in South Carolina.
Virginia Tuition Assistance Grant Program (Private Institutions)	876	$3200	$800	N/A	Residence: Virginia. Studying in Virginia.
Cal Grant C	816	$3168	$576	7,761	Residence: California. Studying in California.
Adelante Fund Scholarships	175	$3000	$1000	30–52	Business/Consumer Services; Science, Technology, and Society. Studying in Arizona; California; Colorado; Florida; Illinois; New Mexico; New York; Texas. Talent/Interest Area: leadership. Limited to Hispanic students.
The Alexander Foundation Scholarship Program	800	$3000	$300	6–35	Residence: Colorado. Studying in Colorado. Talent/Interest Area: LGBT issues.
AMBUCS Scholars-Scholarships for Therapists	148	$3000	$500	275	Audiology; Therapy/Rehabilitation.
American Hotel & Lodging Educational Foundation Pepsi Scholarship	244	$3000	$500	N/A	Culinary Arts; Food Service/Hospitality; Hospitality Management; Recreation, Parks, Leisure Studies; Travel/Tourism. Residence: District of Columbia.
American Legion Department of Tennessee High School Oratorical Contest	808	$3000	$1000	1–3	Residence: Tennessee. Talent/Interest Area: public speaking. Must be in high school.
American Montessori Society Teacher Education Scholarship Fund	267	$3000	$1000	12–20	Education.
American Physical Society Corporate-Sponsored Scholarship for Minority Undergraduate Students Who Major in Physics	506	$3000	$2000	N/A	Physical Sciences. Limited to ethnic minority students.
American Water Ski Educational Foundation Scholarship	560	$3000	$1500	5	Civic Affiliation: USA Water Ski.
Arizona Nursery Association Foundation Scholarship	385	$3000	$500	12–16	Horticulture/Floriculture.
Astrid G. Cates and Myrtle Beinhauer Scholarship Funds	578	$3000	$1000	2–7	Civic Affiliation: Mutual Benefit Society.
A.T. Cross Scholarship	591	$3000	$1000	N/A	Corporate Affiliation: A.T. Cross. Residence: Rhode Island.

Award Name	Page Number	Highest Dollar Amount	Lowest Dollar Amount	Number of Awards	Academic Fields/Career Goals and Nonacademic/Noncareer Criteria
AWG Ethnic Minority Scholarship	260	$3000	$500	1–5	Earth Science; Education; Environmental Science; Gemology; Geography; Hydrology; Meteorology/Atmospheric Science; Museum Studies; Natural Resources; Natural Sciences; Oceanography; Physical Sciences. Limited to American Indian/Alaska Native; Black (non-Hispanic); Hispanic students.
Blackfeet Nation Higher Education Grant	726	$3000	$2800	180	Limited to American Indian/Alaska Native students.
Calcot-Seitz Scholarship	106	$3000	$500	1–30	Agriculture. Residence: Arizona; California; New Mexico; Texas.
Chief Master Sergeants of the Air Force Scholarship Program	696	$3000	$500	30	Military Service: Air Force; Air Force National Guard.
CollegeBound Foundation Last Dollar Grant	817	$3000	$500	60–70	Residence: Maryland. Must be in high school.
Developmental Disabilities Scholastic Achievement Scholarship for College Students who are Lutheran	254	$3000	$500	2–3	Dental Health/Services; Education; Health Administration; Health and Medical Sciences; Health Information Management/Technology; Humanities; Religion/Theology; Social Services; Special Education; Therapy/Rehabilitation. Religion: Lutheran.
The Donaldson Company, Inc. Scholarship Program	588	$3000	$2000	N/A	Corporate Affiliation: Donaldson Company.
E. B Miller Memorial Scholarship	460	$3000	$1000	1–2	Natural Resources. Residence: Ohio.
Edward J. and Virginia M. Routhier Nursing Scholarship	487	$3000	$500	N/A	Nursing. Studying in Rhode Island.
Edwards Scholarship	826	$3000	$2500	136	Residence: Massachusetts.
Freedom From Religion Foundation Michael Hakeem Memorial Ongoing College Essay Competition	780	$3000	$200	6–20	Talent/Interest Area: writing.
Freedom From Religion Foundation William J. Schulz Memorial College-bound High School Senior Essay Competition	780	$3000	$200	6–20	Talent/Interest Area: writing. Must be in high school.
GAPA Scholarships	895	$3000	$1000	3–5	Talent/Interest Area: leadership; LGBT issues.
Hubertus W.V. Wellems Scholarship for Male Students	194	$3000	$2000	1	Chemical Engineering; Engineering-Related Technologies; Engineering/Technology; Physical Sciences. Civic Affiliation: National Association for the Advancement of Colored People. Limited to ethnic minority students.
Humana Foundation Scholarship Program	628	$3000	$1500	74–75	N/A
Illinois PTA Scholarship	271	$3000	$2000	2	Education. Residence: Illinois. Must be in high school.
Joseph S. Rumbaugh Historical Oration Contest	906	$3000	$1000	1–3	Talent/Interest Area: public speaking.
Kildee Scholarships	108	$3000	$1000	1–2	Agriculture; Animal/Veterinary Sciences.

Award Name	Page Number	Highest Dollar Amount	Lowest Dollar Amount	Number of Awards	Academic Fields/Career Goals and Nonacademic/Noncareer Criteria
LabRoots STEM Scholarship	116	$3000	$1000	3	Animal/Veterinary Sciences; Applied Sciences; Audiology; Aviation/Aerospace; Behavioral Science; Biology; Chemical Engineering; Civil Engineering; Computer Science/Data Processing; Construction Engineering/Management; Dental Health/Services; Earth Science; Electrical Engineering/Electronics; Energy and Power Engineering; Engineering-Related Technologies; Engineering/Technology; Entomology; Environmental Health; Environmental Science; Food Science/Nutrition; Health and Medical Sciences; Health Information Management/Technology; Horticulture/Floriculture; Marine Biology; Marine/Ocean Engineering; Materials Science, Engineering, and Metallurgy; Mathematics; Mechanical Engineering; Meteorology/Atmospheric Science; Natural Sciences; Neurobiology; Nuclear Science; Nursing; Oceanography; Oncology; Optometry; Osteopathy; Physical Sciences; Psychology; Public Health; Radiology; Science, Technology, and Society; Statistics; Surveying, Surveying Technology, Cartography, or Geographic Information Science.
Lone Star Rising Career Scholarship	260	$3000	N/A	1–2	Earth Science; Education; Environmental Science; Gemology; Hydrology; Meteorology/Atmospheric Science; Museum Studies; Natural Resources; Natural Sciences; Oceanography; Physical Sciences; Science, Technology, and Society. Employment/Volunteer Experience: physical or natural sciences.
Millie Brother Scholarship for Children of Deaf Adults	605	$3000	$1000	2–5	N/A
Minnesota GI Bill Program	846	$3000	$50	N/A	Residence: Minnesota. Studying in Minnesota.
Missouri Higher Education Academic Scholarship (Bright Flight)	848	$3000	$1000	N/A	Residence: Missouri. Studying in Missouri.
Moody Research Grants	114	$3000	$600	10–15	American Studies; History; International Studies; Military and Defense Studies; Museum Studies; Political Science.
MRCA Foundation Scholarship Program	135	$3000	$500	40	Architecture; Civil Engineering; Construction Engineering/Management; Drafting; Engineering/Technology; Industrial Design; Materials Science, Engineering, and Metallurgy; Trade/Technical Specialties. Employment/Volunteer Experience: construction.

Award Name	Page Number	Highest Dollar Amount	Lowest Dollar Amount	Number of Awards	Academic Fields/Career Goals and Nonacademic/Noncareer Criteria
NASA Idaho Space Grant Consortium Scholarship Program	126	$3000	$500	1–50	Applied Sciences; Biology; Chemical Engineering; Civil Engineering; Computer Science/Data Processing; Earth Science; Electrical Engineering/Electronics; Energy and Power Engineering; Engineering-Related Technologies; Engineering/Technology; Environmental Science; Fire Sciences; Geography; Materials Science, Engineering, and Metallurgy; Mathematics; Mechanical Engineering; Meteorology/Atmospheric Science; Natural Resources; Natural Sciences; Nuclear Science; Physical Sciences; Science, Technology, and Society. Studying in Idaho.
National Federation of Paralegal Associates Inc. Thomson Reuters Scholarship	418	$3000	$2000	2	Law/Legal Services.
National High School Journalist of the Year/Sister Rita Jeanne Scholarships	944	$3000	$850	1–7	Must be in high school.
NMCRS Education Assistance Program	949	$3000	$500	1–300	N/A
Ohio American Legion Scholarships	556	$3000	$2000	15–18	Civic Affiliation: American Legion or Auxiliary. Military Service: General.
OSCPA Educational Foundation Scholarship Program	90	$3000	$500	45–75	Accounting. Studying in Oregon.
Overseas Press Club Foundation Scholar Awards	407	$3000	$2000	16	Journalism. Talent/Interest Area: writing.
Pennsylvania Masonic Youth Foundation Educational Endowment Fund Scholarships	574	$3000	$1000	25–75	Civic Affiliation: Freemasons.
Rama Scholarship for the American Dream	245	$3000	$1000	N/A	Culinary Arts; Food Service/Hospitality; Hospitality Management; Recreation, Parks, Leisure Studies; Travel/Tourism. Limited to ethnic minority students.
Rockefeller State Wildlife Scholarship	172	$3000	$2000	20–30	Biology; Marine Biology; Marine/Ocean Engineering; Natural Resources; Oceanography. Residence: Louisiana. Studying in Louisiana.
Roothbert Fund Inc. Scholarship	864	$3000	$2000	50–60	Residence: Connecticut; Delaware; District of Columbia; Maine; Maryland; Massachusetts; New Hampshire; New Jersey; New York; North Carolina; Ohio; Pennsylvania; Rhode Island; Virginia; West Virginia. Studying in Connecticut; Delaware; District of Columbia; Maryland; Massachusetts; New Hampshire; New Jersey; New York; Ohio; Pennsylvania; Rhode Island; Vermont; Virginia; West Virginia.
Scholar Serve Awards	666	$3000	$500	5–10	N/A
Scholarships for Education, Business and Religion	178	$3000	$500	N/A	Business/Consumer Services; Education; Religion/Theology. Residence: California.

Award Name	Page Number	Highest Dollar Amount	Lowest Dollar Amount	Number of Awards	Academic Fields/Career Goals and Nonacademic/Noncareer Criteria
Seol Bong Scholarship	693	$3000	$2000	21	Disability: learning disabled. Residence: Connecticut; Delaware; Maine; Massachusetts; New Hampshire; New Jersey; New York; Pennsylvania; Rhode Island; Vermont. Studying in Connecticut; Delaware; Maine; Massachusetts; New Hampshire; New Jersey; New York; Pennsylvania; Rhode Island; Vermont. Limited to Asian/Pacific Islander students.
Simplilearn Student Ambassador Scholarship	962	$3000	$1000	1–3	N/A
Society of Louisiana CPAs Scholarships	91	$3000	$500	N/A	Accounting. Residence: Louisiana. Studying in Louisiana.
Sonne Scholarship	480	$3000	$1000	2–4	Nursing. Residence: Illinois. Studying in Illinois.
Student Design Competition	119	$3000	$1000	6	Anthropology.
Tortoise Young Entrepreneurs Scholarship	873	$3000	$1000	3	Residence: Kansas; Missouri. Studying in Kansas; Missouri.
Traub-Dicker Rainbow Scholarship	670	$3000	$1000	3–4	N/A
Undergraduate Marketing Education Merit Scholarships	177	$3000	$500	7	Business/Consumer Services; Marketing. Studying in Maryland.
William P. Willis Scholarship	856	$3000	$2000	N/A	Residence: Oklahoma. Studying in Oklahoma.
Wisconsin Higher Education Grants (WHEG)	878	$3000	$250	N/A	Residence: Wisconsin. Studying in Wisconsin.
WMA Memorial Scholarships	683	$3000	$1500	N/A	Must be in high school.
Women in Logistics Scholarship	185	$3000	$1000	1–3	Business/Consumer Services; Trade/Technical Specialties; Transportation. Civic Affiliation: Women in Logistics. Residence: California. Studying in California.
Women's Independence Scholarship Program	973	$3000	$500	350–500	N/A
Writer's Digest Annual Writing Competition	919	$3000	$100	501	Talent/Interest Area: writing.
Writer's Digest Self-Published Book Awards	919	$3000	$1000	45	Talent/Interest Area: writing.
North Dakota State Student Incentive Grant Program	654	$2925	N/A	1–7,000	Residence: North Dakota. Studying in North Dakota.
Kentucky Tuition Grant (KTG)	841	$2920	$200	10,000–12,500	Residence: Kentucky. Studying in Kentucky.
Ohio College Opportunity Grant	655	$2832	$1056	N/A	Residence: Ohio. Studying in Ohio; Pennsylvania.
Postsecondary Child Care Grant Program-Minnesota	847	$2800	$100	1–3,500	Residence: Minnesota. Studying in Minnesota.
Tennessee HOPE Access Grant	673	$2750	$1750	N/A	Residence: Tennessee. Studying in Tennessee.
Howard P. Rawlings Educational Excellence Awards Educational Assistance Grant	844	$2700	$400	15,000–30,000	Residence: Maryland. Studying in Maryland.
West Virginia Higher Education Grant Program	877	$2700	$300	18,000–21,000	Residence: West Virginia. Studying in Pennsylvania; West Virginia.

Award Name	Page Number	Highest Dollar Amount	Lowest Dollar Amount	Number of Awards	Academic Fields/Career Goals and Nonacademic/Noncareer Criteria
Florida Postsecondary Student Assistance Grant	828	$2610	$200	N/A	Residence: Florida. Studying in Florida.
Florida Private Student Assistance Grant	828	$2610	$200	N/A	Residence: Florida. Studying in Florida.
Florida Public Student Assistance Grant	828	$2610	$200	N/A	Residence: Florida. Studying in Florida.
Florida Student Assistance Grant-Career Education	828	$2610	$200	N/A	Residence: Florida. Studying in Florida.
NJ Student Tuition Assistance Reward Scholarship	851	$2600	$500	N/A	Residence: New Jersey. Studying in New Jersey.
ACES Education Fund Scholarships	920	$2500	$1500	5	N/A
Adult Students in Scholastic Transition	935	$2500	$250	100–150	N/A
Agnes Jones Jackson Scholarship	569	$2500	$1500	1	Civic Affiliation: National Association for the Advancement of Colored People. Limited to ethnic minority students.
AHIMA Foundation Student Merit Scholarship	378	$2500	$1000	1	Health Information Management/Technology. Civic Affiliation: American Health Information Management Association.
Alaska Geological Society Scholarship	259	$2500	$500	3–8	Earth Science. Studying in Alaska.
American Board of Funeral Service Education Scholarships	361	$2500	$1500	5–10	Funeral Services/Mortuary Science.
American Legion Auxiliary Department of North Dakota National President's Scholarship	596	$2500	$1000	3	Employment/Volunteer Experience: community service. Military Service: General. Residence: North Dakota. Studying in North Dakota. Must be in high school.
American Legion Auxiliary Department of Oregon National President's Scholarship	802	$2500	$1000	3	Residence: Oregon. Must be in high school.
American Legion Auxiliary Department of Utah National President's Scholarship	552	$2500	$1000	15	Civic Affiliation: American Legion or Auxiliary. Military Service: General. Residence: Utah. Must be in high school.
American Legion Baseball Scholarship	882	$2500	$500	1–51	Talent/Interest Area: athletics/sports. Must be in high school.
American Legion Department of North Carolina High School Oratorical Contest	807	$2500	$1000	5	Residence: North Carolina. Talent/Interest Area: public speaking. Must be in high school.
American Legion Department of Washington Children and Youth Scholarships	557	$2500	$1500	2	Civic Affiliation: American Legion or Auxiliary. Residence: Washington. Must be in high school.
American-Scandinavian Foundation Translation Prize	421	$2500	$2000	2	Literature/English/Writing. Talent/Interest Area: Scandinavian language.
American Welding Society District Scholarship Program	296	$2500	$100	150–200	Engineering-Related Technologies; Trade/Technical Specialties.
ASCPA Educational Foundation Scholarship	593	$2500	$1500	34–38	Residence: Alabama. Studying in Alabama.
Assured Life Association Endowment Scholarship Program	600	$2500	$500	65–75	N/A

Award Name	Page Number	Highest Dollar Amount	Lowest Dollar Amount	Number of Awards	Academic Fields/Career Goals and Nonacademic/Noncareer Criteria
BAC Local 3 Sullivan Kraw Scholarship	866	$2500	$1000	1–19	Residence: California.
BIA Higher Education Grant	739	$2500	$50	1–150	Limited to American Indian/Alaska Native students.
Breakthrough to Nursing Scholarships for Racial/Ethnic Minorities	477	$2500	$1000	N/A	Nursing. Limited to ethnic minority students.
Career Journalism Scholarship	225	$2500	$1000	1–3	Communications; Journalism; Photojournalism/Photography; TV/Radio Broadcasting. Residence: Florida. Must be in high school.
Clem Judd, Jr. Memorial Scholarship	390	$2500	$1000	2	Hospitality Management. Residence: Hawaii. Limited to Asian/Pacific Islander students.
CrossLites Scholarship Award	892	$2500	$100	33	Talent/Interest Area: writing.
Delaware Solid Waste Authority John P. "Pat" Healy Scholarship	316	$2500	$1500	2	Engineering/Technology; Environmental Science. Residence: Delaware. Studying in Delaware. Talent/Interest Area: leadership.
Distinguished Raven FAC Memorial Scholarship	614	$2500	$1000	10	Limited to Asian/Pacific Islander students.
E. Wayne Kay High School Scholarship	327	$2500	$1000	1–20	Engineering/Technology.
Excellence in Accounting Scholarship	92	$2500	$1000	5–15	Accounting. Studying in South Dakota.
Feeding Tomorrow Undergraduate General Education Scholarships	899	$2500	$1000	N/A	N/A
Feeding Tomorrow Undergraduate General Education Scholarships	899	$2500	$1000	N/A	N/A
Foundation for Accounting Education Scholarship	90	$2500	$500	1–60	Accounting. Residence: New York. Studying in New York.
Foundation of the National Student Nurses' Association Career Mobility Scholarship	477	$2500	$1000	N/A	Nursing.
Foundation of the National Student Nurses' Association General Scholarships	478	$2500	$1000	N/A	Nursing.
Foundation of the National Student Nurses' Association Specialty Scholarship	478	$2500	$1000	N/A	Nursing.
Friends of Bill Rutherford Education Fund	857	$2500	$1000	1–2	Residence: Oregon.
Fulfilling Our Dreams Scholarship Fund	759	$2500	$500	50–60	Residence: California. Studying in California. Limited to Hispanic students.
Graphic Communications Scholarship Fund of New England	365	$2500	$1350	16–35	Graphics/Graphic Arts/Printing. Residence: Connecticut; Maine; Massachusetts; New Hampshire; Rhode Island; Vermont.
HBCUConnect.com Minority Scholarship Program	624	$2500	$1000	1	Limited to ethnic minority students.
High School Scholarship	317	$2500	$1500	6	Engineering/Technology. Employment/Volunteer Experience: engineering/technology. Residence: Florida. Must be in high school.

Award Name	Page Number	Highest Dollar Amount	Lowest Dollar Amount	Number of Awards	Academic Fields/Career Goals and Nonacademic/Noncareer Criteria
Hopi Education Award	739	$2500	$50	1–400	Limited to American Indian/Alaska Native students.
Hungry To Lead Scholarship	249	$2500	$500	4	Culinary Arts; Food Science/Nutrition; Food Service/Hospitality.
Institute of Management Accountants Memorial Education Fund Scholarships	87	$2500	$1000	6–15	Accounting; Business/Consumer Services.
International Association of Fire Chiefs Foundation Scholarship Award	349	$2500	$500	20–30	Fire Sciences.
Jackson-Stricks Scholarship	689	$2500	$1500	1–2	Disability: physically disabled. Studying in New York.
Joseph S. Garske Collegiate Grant Program	564	$2500	$500	1–5	Civic Affiliation: Golf Course Superintendents Association of America. Must be in high school.
Josiah E. DuBois, Jr. College Scholarship Essay Contest	609	$2500	$1000	1–3	Must be in high school.
Kentucky Educational Excellence Scholarship (KEES)	840	$2500	$125	70,500	Residence: Kentucky. Studying in British Columbia.
Kentucky Society of Certified Public Accountants College Scholarship	87	$2500	$1000	10–40	Accounting. Residence: Kentucky. Studying in Kentucky.
Korean-American Scholarship Foundation Northeastern Region Scholarships	744	$2500	$1000	60	Studying in Connecticut; Maine; Massachusetts; New Hampshire; New Jersey; New York; Rhode Island; Vermont. Limited to Asian/Pacific Islander students.
LAGRANT Foundation Scholarship for Undergraduates	97	$2500	$2000	N/A	Advertising/Public Relations; Business/Consumer Services; Communications; Graphics/Graphic Arts/Printing; Marketing. Limited to ethnic minority students.
LEAGUE Foundation Academic Scholarship	639	$2500	$1500	4–8	Talent/Interest Area: LGBT issues. Must be in high school.
Legislative Endowment Scholarships	852	$2500	$1000	1	Residence: New Mexico. Studying in New Mexico.
Leveraging Educational Assistance Partnership	810	$2500	$100	N/A	Residence: Arizona. Studying in Arizona.
Literacy Grant Competition	565	$2500	$300	18	Civic Affiliation: Phi Kappa Phi.
Maine State Society Foundation Scholarship	641	$2500	$1000	5–10	Residence: Maine. Studying in Maine.
Massachusetts Cash Grant Program	643	$2500	$200	N/A	Residence: Massachusetts. Studying in Massachusetts.
Massachusetts Gilbert Matching Student Grant Program	643	$2500	$200	8,000–9,500	Residence: Massachusetts. Studying in Massachusetts.
Minnesota Space Grant Consortium Scholarship Program	156	$2500	$500	40–70	Aviation/Aerospace; Computer Science/Data Processing; Earth Science; Electrical Engineering/Electronics; Engineering/Technology; Environmental Science; Mathematics; Mechanical Engineering; Meteorology/Atmospheric Science; Natural Sciences; Nuclear Science; Oceanography; Physical Sciences. Studying in Minnesota.

Award Name	Page Number	Highest Dollar Amount	Lowest Dollar Amount	Number of Awards	Academic Fields/Career Goals and Nonacademic/Noncareer Criteria
Minority Undergraduate Retention Grant-Wisconsin	771	$2500	$250	N/A	Residence: Wisconsin. Studying in Wisconsin. Limited to ethnic minority students.
Mississippi Eminent Scholars Grant	847	$2500	$1157	2,726	Residence: Mississippi. Studying in Mississippi.
Missouri Broadcasters Association Scholarship Program	544	$2500	$1000	3–5	TV/Radio Broadcasting. Residence: Missouri. Studying in Missouri.
Missouri Insurance Education Foundation Scholarship	398	$2500	$2000	6	Insurance and Actuarial Science. Residence: Missouri. Studying in Missouri.
National Federation of the Blind of Missouri Scholarship Program for Legally Blind Students	691	$2500	$500	1–3	Disability: visually impaired. Residence: Missouri. Studying in Missouri.
National Presbyterian College Scholarship	791	$2500	$1000	25–100	Religion: Presbyterian.
New Hampshire Society of Certified Public Accountants Scholarship Fund	89	$2500	$500	1–7	Accounting. Residence: New Hampshire.
New Jersey Association of Realtors Educational Foundation Scholarship Program	516	$2500	$1000	20–32	Real Estate. Civic Affiliation: New Jersey Association of Realtors. Residence: New Jersey. Must be in high school.
New Mexico Student Incentive Grant	852	$2500	$200	1	Residence: New Mexico. Studying in New Mexico.
Noplag Scholarship Essay Contest	653	$2500	$300	3	N/A
Norma Ross Walter Scholarship	422	$2500	$1250	1–3	Literature/English/Writing. Residence: Nebraska. Must be in high school.
North Carolina Hispanic College Fund Scholarship	752	$2500	$500	N/A	Residence: North Carolina. Limited to Hispanic students.
Ohio Environmental Science & Engineering Scholarships	343	$2500	$1250	18	Environmental Science. Studying in Ohio.
Optimist International Oratorical Contest	908	$2500	$1000	90–115	Talent/Interest Area: public speaking.
Polish Heritage Scholarship	756	$2500	$1500	1–9	Residence: Maryland.
Raymond W. Miller, PE Scholarship	317	$2500	$1500	1	Engineering/Technology. Residence: Florida. Studying in Florida.
Richard B. Gassett, PE Scholarship	317	$2500	$1500	1	Engineering/Technology. Residence: Florida. Studying in Florida.
Robert P. Sheppard Leadership Award for NSHSS Members	572	$2500	$1000	5	Civic Affiliation: National Society of High School Scholars. Talent/Interest Area: leadership. Must be in high school.
Robert T. Kenney Scholarship Program at the American Savings Foundation	597	$2500	$1000	400	Residence: Connecticut.
Samuel Fletcher Tapman ASCE Student Chapter Scholarship	205	$2500	$2000	1–12	Civil Engineering. Civic Affiliation: American Society of Civil Engineers.
SCACPA Educational Fund Scholarships	92	$2500	$500	19–25	Accounting. Residence: South Carolina. Studying in South Carolina.
Scholarships for Orphans of Veterans	714	$2500	$1000	1	Military Service: General. Residence: New Hampshire. Studying in New Hampshire.
Simon Youth Foundation Community Scholarship Program	962	$2500	$1400	100–200	Must be in high school.

Award Name	Page Number	Highest Dollar Amount	Lowest Dollar Amount	Number of Awards	Academic Fields/Career Goals and Nonacademic/Noncareer Criteria
Society of Physics Students Outstanding Student in Research	508	$2500	$500	1–2	Physical Sciences. Civic Affiliation: Society of Physics Students.
South Carolina Need-Based Grants Program	868	$2500	$1250	1–26,730	Residence: South Carolina. Studying in South Carolina.
South Carolina Tourism and Hospitality Educational Foundation Scholarships	250	$2500	$750	5–16	Culinary Arts; Food Service/Hospitality; Hospitality Management. Residence: South Carolina. Studying in South Carolina.
Sussman-Miller Educational Assistance Fund	800	$2500	$500	25–30	Residence: New Mexico.
Swiss Benevolent Society of Chicago Scholarships	762	$2500	$500	30	Residence: Illinois; Wisconsin.
Tennessee Society of CPA Scholarship	92	$2500	$250	120–130	Accounting. Residence: Tennessee.
Tilford Field Studies Scholarship	258	$2500	$500	4–5	Earth Science. Civic Affiliation: Association of Engineering Geologists.
Truman D. Picard Scholarship	341	$2500	$2000	15–30	Environmental Science; Fire Sciences; Natural Resources. Limited to American Indian/Alaska Native students.
U.S. Scholarship Program	645	$2500	$600	100–150	N/A
WIFLE Scholarship	244	$2500	$1000	1–4	Criminal Justice/Criminology; Law Enforcement/Police Administration; Law/Legal Services; Social Sciences.
Women in Accounting Scholarship	84	$2500	$2500	3–4	Accounting. Residence: Massachusetts.
Women in Cybersecurity Scholarships	231	$2500	$1000	3	Computer Science/Data Processing.
Women in Technology Scholarship (WITS)	236	$2500	$500	1–20	Computer Science/Data Processing; Earth Science; Engineering/Technology.
Writer's Digest Popular Fiction Awards	919	$2500	$500	7	Talent/Interest Area: writing.
South Dakota Opportunity Scholarship	869	$2300	$1300	1,000–4,100	Residence: South Dakota. Studying in South Dakota. Must be in high school.
Crush The CPA Exam Scholarship	83	$2295	$1000	1	Accounting.
North Dakota Academic Scholarship	654	$2250	$500	1–3,000	Residence: North Dakota. Studying in North Dakota. Must be in high school.
North Dakota Career and Technical Education Scholarship	654	$2250	$500	1–3,000	Residence: North Dakota. Studying in North Dakota. Must be in high school.
South Dakota Retailers Association Scholarship Program	104	$2250	$500	10–15	Agribusiness.
Menominee Indian Tribe Adult Vocational Training Program	747	$2200	$100	50–70	Limited to American Indian/Alaska Native students.
Menominee Indian Tribe of Wisconsin Higher Education Grants	747	$2200	$100	136	Limited to American Indian/Alaska Native students.

PROFILES OF SCHOLARSHIPS, GRANTS & PRIZES

Academic Fields/Career Goals

ACADEMIC ADVISING

NATIONAL ASSOCIATION FOR CAMPUS ACTIVITIES

http://www.naca.org/

NATIONAL ASSOCIATION FOR CAMPUS ACTIVITIES NORTHERN PLAINS REGION STUDENT LEADERSHIP SCHOLARSHIP

Scholarships will be awarded to undergraduate or graduate students in good standing and enrolled in the equivalent of at least six academic credits at the time of the application and during the academic term in which the scholarship is awarded. Must be currently enrolled in or received a degree from a college or university within the NACA Northern Plains region, including the upper peninsula of Michigan (area code 906) and have demonstrated leadership skill and significant service to their campus community.

Academic Fields/Career Goals: Academic Advising; Campus Activities.

Award: Scholarship for use in freshman, sophomore, junior, senior, or graduate years; not renewable. *Number:* 1. *Amount:* $300.

Eligibility Requirements: Applicant must be enrolled or expecting to enroll full- or part-time at a two-year or four-year institution or university; studying in Alberta, Manitoba, Michigan, Ontario, Saskatchewan, Wisconsin and must have an interest in leadership. Applicant or parent of applicant must have employment or volunteer experience in community service. Available to U.S. citizens.

Application Requirements: Application form, essay. *Deadline:* June 30.

Contact: Executive Assistant
    E-mail: scholarships@naca.org

ACCOUNTING

ALASKA SOCIETY OF CERTIFIED PUBLIC ACCOUNTANTS

http://www.akcpa.org/

PAUL HAGELBARGER MEMORIAL FUND SCHOLARSHIP

Scholarships open to all junior, senior, and graduate students who are majoring in accounting and attending institutions in Alaska.

Academic Fields/Career Goals: Accounting.

Award: Scholarship for use in junior, senior, or graduate years; not renewable. *Number:* 2–3. *Amount:* $2000.

Eligibility Requirements: Applicant must be enrolled or expecting to enroll full-time at a four-year institution or university and studying in Alaska. Available to U.S. citizens.

Application Requirements: Application form, recommendations or references, resume, transcript. *Deadline:* November 15.

Contact: Linda Plimpton, Executive Director
    Alaska Society of Certified Public Accountants
    341 West Tudor Road, Suite 105
    Anchorage, AK 99503
    Phone: 907-562-4334
    Fax: 907-562-4025
    E-mail: akcpa@ak.net

AMERICAN SOCIETY OF WOMEN ACCOUNTANTS

http://www.afwa.org/

AMERICAN SOCIETY OF WOMEN ACCOUNTANTS UNDERGRADUATE SCHOLARSHIP

Scholarship awards are presented to students who have completed their sophomore year of college and are majoring in accounting or finance. Candidates will be reviewed on leadership, character, communication skills, scholastic average, and financial need.

Academic Fields/Career Goals: Accounting.

Award: Scholarship for use in junior, senior, or graduate years; not renewable.

Eligibility Requirements: Applicant must be enrolled or expecting to enroll full- or part-time at a four-year institution or university and must have an interest in leadership. Available to U.S. and non-U.S. citizens.

Application Requirements: Application form, essay, financial need analysis, recommendations or references, transcript. *Deadline:* varies.

Contact: Kristin Edwards, Administrator
    Phone: 703-506-3265
    Fax: 703-506-3266
    E-mail: kedwards@aswa.org

ASSOCIATION OF CERTIFIED FRAUD EXAMINERS

http://www.acfe.com/

RITCHIE-JENNINGS MEMORIAL SCHOLARSHIP

Applicant must be an undergraduate or graduate student, currently enrolled full-time (12 semester hours undergraduate; 9 semester hours graduate, or equivalent) at an accredited four-year college or university (or equivalent) with a declared major or minor in accounting or criminal justice.

Academic Fields/Career Goals: Accounting; Criminal Justice/Criminology.

Award: Scholarship for use in freshman, sophomore, junior, or senior years; not renewable. *Number:* up to 30. *Amount:* $1000.

Eligibility Requirements: Applicant must be enrolled or expecting to enroll full-time at a four-year institution or university. Available to U.S. and non-U.S. citizens.

Application Requirements: Application form, essay, recommendations or references, transcript. *Deadline:* April 16.

Contact: Keely Miers, Scholarship Coordinator
    Association of Certified Fraud Examiners
    The Gregor Building, 716 West Avenue
    Austin, TX 78701
    Phone: 800-245-3321
    Fax: 512-478-9297
    E-mail: scholarships@acfe.com

AUTOMOTIVE WOMEN'S ALLIANCE FOUNDATION

http://awafoundation.org/index.php

AUTOMOTIVE WOMEN'S ALLIANCE FOUNDATION SCHOLARSHIPS

Scholarships are the root of our purpose in Automotive Women's Alliance Foundation (AWAF). As an active professional foundation dedicated to supporting the advancement of automotive professionals, AWAF strives to motivate current and future students studying an automotive related field. Scholarships are selected by the Scholarship Committee and awarded quarterly to the women that solicit passion and drive for the automotive industry. It is our hope that with these scholarships, we can lessen the burden on students and allow them to focus on gaining knowledge and development in automotive related fields and thus enhance their potential career path and the future of the industry. Scholarships are awarded to female, North American citizens, with a passion for a career or advancement in the automotive and its related industries. While AWAF members and family members are encouraged to apply for scholarships, we encourage applicants who are not affiliated with the organization to apply as well. In order to be eligible for a scholarship applicants should be already accepted to or enrolled in an accredited collegiate program, with a 3.0 or higher GPA.

Academic Fields/Career Goals: Accounting; Advertising/Public Relations; Applied Sciences; Business/Consumer Services; Chemical Engineering; Civil Engineering; Communications; Computer Science/Data Processing; Economics; Electrical Engineering/Electronics; Energy and Power Engineering; Engineering-Related Technologies; Engineering/Technology; Environmental Science; Finance; Graphics/Graphic Arts/Printing; Human Resources; Industrial Design; International Studies; Law/Legal Services; Marketing; Materials Science, Engineering, and Metallurgy; Mathematics; Mechanical Engineering; Meteorology/Atmospheric Science; Science, Technology, and Society; Statistics; Transportation.

Award: Scholarship for use in freshman, sophomore, junior, senior, graduate, or postgraduate years; not renewable. *Number:* 15–24. *Amount:* $2500.

Eligibility Requirements: Applicant must be Canadian, Latin American/Caribbean, Mexican citizen; enrolled or expecting to enroll full- or part-time at a two-year or four-year institution or university; female and resident of Mississippi. Applicant must have 3.0 GPA or higher. Available to U.S. and Canadian citizens.

Application Requirements: Application form. *Deadline:* continuous.

Contact: Administrator
Automotive Women's Alliance Foundation
AWAF Scholarships
Box 4305
Troy, MI 48099
E-mail: admin@AWAFoundation.org

CATCHING THE DREAM

http://www.catchingthedream.org/

TRIBAL BUSINESS MANAGEMENT PROGRAM (TBM)

Renewable scholarships available for Native American and Alaska Native students to study business administration, economic development, and related subjects, with the goal to provide experts in business management to Native American tribes in the U.S. Must be at least one-quarter Native American from a federally recognized, state recognized, or terminated tribe. Must demonstrate high academic achievement, depth of character, leadership, seriousness of purpose, and service orientation.

Academic Fields/Career Goals: Accounting; Business/Consumer Services; Computer Science/Data Processing; Economics; Electrical Engineering/Electronics; Engineering-Related Technologies.

Award: Scholarship for use in freshman, sophomore, junior, senior, graduate, or postgraduate years; renewable. *Number:* 35. *Amount:* $500–$5000.

Eligibility Requirements: Applicant must be American Indian/Alaska Native and enrolled or expecting to enroll full-time at a four-year institution or university. Applicant must have 3.0 GPA or higher. Available to U.S. citizens.

Application Requirements: Application form, essay, financial need analysis, personal photograph.

Contact: Joy Noll, Student Services
Catching the Dream
8200 Mountain Road, NE, Suite 103
Albuquerque, NM 87110
Phone: 505-262-2351
E-mail: nscholarsh@aol.com

COLORADO SOCIETY OF CERTIFIED PUBLIC ACCOUNTANTS EDUCATIONAL FOUNDATION

http://www.cocpa.org/

COLORADO COLLEGE AND UNIVERSITY SCHOLARSHIPS

Award available to declared accounting majors at Colorado colleges and universities with accredited accounting programs. Must have completed at least 8 semester hours of accounting courses. Overall GPA and accounting GPA must be at least 3.0. Must be Colorado resident.

Academic Fields/Career Goals: Accounting.

Award: Scholarship for use in junior, senior, graduate, or postgraduate years; not renewable. *Number:* 15–20. *Amount:* $2500.

Eligibility Requirements: Applicant must be enrolled or expecting to enroll full- or part-time at a four-year institution or university; resident of Colorado and studying in Colorado. Applicant must have 3.0 GPA or higher. Available to U.S. citizens.

Application Requirements: Application form, recommendations or references, transcript. *Deadline:* June 1.

Contact: Gena Mantz, Membership Coordinator
Phone: 303-741-8613
Fax: 303-773-6344
E-mail: gmantz@cocpa.org

CONNECTICUT SOCIETY OF CERTIFIED PUBLIC ACCOUNTANTS

http://www.ctcpas.org/

CT SOCIETY OF CPAS RISING SOPHOMORE ACCOUNTING SCHOLARSHIP

The Educational Trust Fund of the Connecticut Society of CPAs (CTCPA) has established this scholarship to assist Connecticut accounting majors entering into their sophomore year of study at a four-year college or university in financing their education.

Academic Fields/Career Goals: Accounting.

Award: Scholarship for use in sophomore year; not renewable. *Number:* 1–4. *Amount:* $1500.

Eligibility Requirements: Applicant must be enrolled or expecting to enroll full-time at a four-year institution or university; resident of Connecticut and studying in Connecticut. Applicant must have 3.0 GPA or higher. Available to U.S. citizens.

Application Requirements: Application form, driver's license, essay. *Deadline:* April 17.

Contact: Mrs. Jill Brightman, Program Coordinator
Connecticut Society of Certified Public Accountants
716 Brook Street, Suite 100
Rocky Hill, CT 06067
Phone: 860-258-0329
E-mail: jillb@ctcpas.org

EDUCATIONAL TRUST FUND OF THE CTCPA - CANDIDATE'S SCHOLARSHIP

Scholarship of $5000 that assists students in complying with the 150-hour requirement of the Connecticut State Board of Accountancy to sit for the Uniform Certified Public Accountant Examination. An overall GPA of 3.0.

Academic Fields/Career Goals: Accounting.

Award: Scholarship for use in senior or graduate years; not renewable. *Number:* 1. *Amount:* $5000.

Eligibility Requirements: Applicant must be enrolled or expecting to enroll full- or part-time at a four-year institution or university; resident of Connecticut and studying in Connecticut. Applicant must have 3.0 GPA or higher. Available to U.S. citizens.

Application Requirements: Application form, driver's license, essay. *Deadline:* April 17.

Contact: Mrs. Jill Brightman, Program Coordinator
Connecticut Society of Certified Public Accountants
716 Brook Street, Suite100
Rocky Hill, CT 06067
Phone: 860-258-0239
E-mail: jillb@ctcpas.org

CRUSH THE CPA EXAM

https://crushthecpaexam.com

CRUSH THE CPA EXAM SCHOLARSHIP

Crush The CPA Exam is very excited to tell you that we have created an annual scholarship program to help one accounting student become a Certified Public Accountant. The winner will receive $1,000 to pay for their CPA exam fees and also a complete CPA review course from Wiley CPAexcel worth $2,295.

Academic Fields/Career Goals: Accounting.

Award: Scholarship for use in senior or graduate years; renewable. *Number:* 1. *Amount:* $1000–$2295.

Eligibility Requirements: Applicant must be enrolled or expecting to enroll full- or part-time at a four-year institution or university. Applicant must have 3.0 GPA or higher. Available to U.S. and non-U.S. citizens.

Application Requirements: Application form, driver's license. *Deadline:* November 30.

Contact: Bryce Welker, CEO
Crush The CPA Exam
10505 Roselle St
San Diego, CA 92121
Phone: 858-888-9063
E-mail: crushthecpaexam@gmail.com

DECA (DISTRIBUTIVE EDUCATION CLUBS OF AMERICA)

http://www.deca.org/

HARRY A. APPLEGATE SCHOLARSHIP

Scholarship available to current DECA or Collegiate DECA members for undergraduate study in marketing education, marketing, entrepreneurship, finance, hospitality or management. Nonrenewable merit-based award for current DECA members based on DECA activities, grades, and leadership.

Academic Fields/Career Goals: Accounting; Business/Consumer Services; Education; Fashion Design; Finance; Food Service/Hospitality; Hospitality Management; Marketing.

Award: Scholarship for use in freshman, sophomore, junior, or senior years; not renewable. *Number:* 20–25. *Amount:* $1000–$5000.

Eligibility Requirements: Applicant must be enrolled or expecting to enroll full-time at a two-year or four-year institution or university. Applicant or parent of applicant must be member of Distribution Ed Club or Future Business Leaders of America. Available to U.S. and non-U.S. citizens.

Application Requirements: Application form. *Deadline:* January 19.

Contact: Cameron Brown, Corporate and External Affairs Assistant
DECA (Distributive Education Clubs of America)
1908 Association Drive
Reston, VA 20191
Phone: 703-860-5000 Ext. 303
E-mail: cameron_burrell@deca.org

DIVERSITYCOMM, INC.

http://www.diversitycomm.net/

DIVERSITY IN STEAM MAGAZINE SCHOLARSHIP

For the 2018 Fall Semester, Diversity in STEAM will be offering a $500 scholarship that is available to students entering a STEAM (Science, Technology, Engineering, Arts, & Math) related field. The Diversity in STEAM Magazine brings science, technology, education, mathematics, educational, business and employment opportunities to all minorities and diverse cultures. We firmly believe that in order to have a successful company, Diversity & Inclusion must be implemented in all departments. STEM and the arts are critical for our future and innovation. Diversity in STEAM Magazine brings you the best combinations of science and technology with arts, creativity and entrepreneurship. Requirements: We would like you to tell your story in a brief narrative, starting with an introduction about who you are, your interests, and anything else you feel we should know about you. Then, please provide your entry in a 300-500 word essay about your college experience so far, and your future career plans in your respective STEAM related field. Graphic or creative

presentations are welcome as well. Judging Criteria: The scholarship will be awarded to the applicant who best demonstrates a genuine desire and goal of using the scholarship to advance in their field, and an overall passion for knowledge.

Academic Fields/Career Goals: Accounting; Applied Sciences; Arts; Aviation/Aerospace; Behavioral Science; Computer Science/Data Processing; Construction Engineering/Management; Earth Science; Economics; Electrical Engineering/Electronics; Energy and Power Engineering; Engineering-Related Technologies; Engineering/Technology; Environmental Science; Filmmaking/Video; Finance; Fire Sciences; Food Science/Nutrition; Geography; Graphics/Graphic Arts/Printing; Library and Information Sciences; Literature/English/Writing; Marine Biology; Marine/Ocean Engineering; Materials Science, Engineering, and Metallurgy; Mathematics; Mechanical Engineering; Meteorology/Atmospheric Science; Music; Natural Sciences; Neurobiology; Nuclear Science; Oceanography; Physical Sciences; Science, Technology, and Society; Statistics.

Award: Scholarship for use in freshman, sophomore, junior, or senior years; renewable. *Number:* 1. *Amount:* $500.

Eligibility Requirements: Applicant must be enrolled or expecting to enroll full- or part-time at a four-year institution or university. Available to U.S. citizens.

Application Requirements: Application form, essay. *Deadline:* August 15.

EDUCATIONAL FOUNDATION FOR WOMEN IN ACCOUNTING (EFWA)

http://www.efwa.org/

MICHELE L. MCDONALD SCHOLARSHIP

Individuals eligible for this award will be women who are returning to college from the workforce or after raising children. Scholarship recipients will be awarded $1000 to begin their studies in pursuit of a college degree in accounting.

Academic Fields/Career Goals: Accounting.

Award: Scholarship for use in freshman, sophomore, junior, or senior years; not renewable. *Amount:* $1000.

Eligibility Requirements: Applicant must be enrolled or expecting to enroll full- or part-time at a four-year institution or university and married female. Available to U.S. citizens.

Application Requirements: Application form, financial need analysis, transcript. *Deadline:* April 15.

Contact: Cynthia Hires, Foundation Administrator
Phone: 610-407-9229
Fax: 610-644-3713
E-mail: info@efwa.org

ROWLING, DOLD & ASSOCIATES LLP SCHOLARSHIP

One year $1000 scholarship award for minority women enrolled in an accounting program at an accredited college or university. Women returning to school with undergraduate status; incoming, current, or reentry juniors or seniors; or minority women are all eligible.

Academic Fields/Career Goals: Accounting.

Award: Scholarship for use in junior, senior, or graduate years; not renewable. *Amount:* $1000.

Eligibility Requirements: Applicant must be American Indian/Alaska Native, Asian/Pacific Islander, Black (non-Hispanic), Hispanic; enrolled or expecting to enroll full- or part-time at a four-year institution or university and female. Available to U.S. citizens.

Application Requirements: Application form, financial need analysis, transcript. *Deadline:* April 15.

Contact: Cynthia Hires, Foundation Administrator
Phone: 610-407-9229
Fax: 610-644-3713
E-mail: info@efwa.org

SEATTLE AMERICAN SOCIETY OF WOMEN ACCOUNTANTS CHAPTER SCHOLARSHIP

Scholarship for an amount up to $2000 to be awarded to a women attending an accredited school within the State of Washington. The scholarship will be renewable for one additional year upon satisfactory completion of course requirements. Must pursue a degree in accounting.

Academic Fields/Career Goals: Accounting.

Award: Scholarship for use in freshman, sophomore, junior, or senior years; renewable. *Amount:* up to $2000.

Eligibility Requirements: Applicant must be enrolled or expecting to enroll full- or part-time at a four-year institution or university; female and studying in Washington. Available to U.S. citizens.

Application Requirements: Application form, financial need analysis, transcript. *Deadline:* April 15.

Contact: Cynthia Hires, Foundation Administrator
Phone: 610-407-9229
Fax: 610-644-3713
E-mail: info@efwa.org

WOMEN IN NEED SCHOLARSHIP

Scholarship provides financial assistance to female reentry students who wish to pursue a degree in accounting. Scholarship is available to incoming, current, or reentry juniors.

Academic Fields/Career Goals: Accounting.

Award: Scholarship for use in junior year; renewable. *Number:* 1. *Amount:* $2000.

Eligibility Requirements: Applicant must be enrolled or expecting to enroll full- or part-time at a four-year institution or university and female. Available to U.S. citizens.

Application Requirements: Application form, financial need analysis, transcript. *Deadline:* April 15.

Contact: Cynthia Hires, Foundation Administrator
Phone: 610-407-9229
Fax: 610-644-3713
E-mail: info@efwa.org

WOMEN IN TRANSITION SCHOLARSHIP

Renewable award available to incoming or current freshmen and women returning to school with a freshman status. Scholarship value may be up to $16,000 over four years.

Academic Fields/Career Goals: Accounting.

Award: Scholarship for use in freshman year; renewable. *Number:* 1. *Amount:* up to $4000.

Eligibility Requirements: Applicant must be enrolled or expecting to enroll full- or part-time at a four-year institution or university and female. Available to U.S. citizens.

Application Requirements: Application form, financial need analysis, transcript. *Deadline:* April 15.

Contact: Cynthia Hires, Foundation Administrator
Phone: 610-407-9229
Fax: 610-644-3713
E-mail: info@efwa.org

EDUCATIONAL FOUNDATION OF THE MASSACHUSETTS SOCIETY OF CERTIFIED PUBLIC ACCOUNTANTS

http://MSCPAonline.org

KATHLEEN M. PEABODY, CPA, MEMORIAL SCHOLARSHIP

Scholarship available for Massachusetts resident who has completed sophomore year. Must be accounting major with plans to seek an accounting career in Massachusetts. Must demonstrate academic excellence and financial need. Information on website at http://www.cpatrack.com.

Academic Fields/Career Goals: Accounting.

Award: Scholarship for use in junior or senior years; not renewable. *Number:* 1. *Amount:* $2500.

Eligibility Requirements: Applicant must be enrolled or expecting to enroll full-time at a four-year institution or university and resident of Massachusetts. Applicant must have 3.0 GPA or higher. Available to U.S. citizens.

Application Requirements: Application form, application form may be submitted online (http://ThisWayToCPA.com/MSCPA), essay, financial need analysis, recommendations or references, transcript. *Deadline:* April 1.

Contact: Barbara Iannoni, Senior Academic Specialist
Educational Foundation of the Massachusetts Society of Certified Public Accountants
105 Chauncy Street
Boston, MA 02111
Phone: 617-303-2415
Fax: 617-556.4126
E-mail: biannoni@mscpaonline.org

MSCPA FIRM SCHOLARSHIP

Scholarship to encourage individuals who have demonstrated academic excellence and financial need to pursue a career in public accounting in Massachusetts.

Academic Fields/Career Goals: Accounting.

Award: Scholarship for use in junior, senior, or graduate years; not renewable. *Number:* 12–16. *Amount:* $2500.

Eligibility Requirements: Applicant must be enrolled or expecting to enroll full-time at a four-year institution or university and resident of Massachusetts. Applicant must have 3.0 GPA or higher. Available to U.S. citizens.

Application Requirements: Application form, essay, financial need analysis, recommendations or references, transcript. *Deadline:* April 1.

Contact: Barbara Iannoni, Senior Academic Specialist
Educational Foundation of the Massachusetts Society of Certified Public Accountants
105 Chauncy Street
Boston, MA 02111
Phone: 617-303-2415
Fax: 617-556.4126
E-mail: biannoni@mscpaonline.org

WOMEN IN ACCOUNTING SCHOLARSHIP

The purpose of these scholarships is to encourage women who have demonstrated academic excellence and financial need to pursue a career as a CPA in Massachusetts.

Academic Fields/Career Goals: Accounting.

Award: Scholarship for use in junior, senior, or graduate years; not renewable. *Number:* 3–4. *Amount:* $2500–$2500.

Eligibility Requirements: Applicant must be enrolled or expecting to enroll full-time at a four-year institution; female and resident of Massachusetts. Applicant must have 3.5 GPA or higher. Available to U.S. citizens.

Application Requirements: Application form, application form may be submitted online (http://ThisWayToCPA.com/MSCPA), essay, financial need analysis, transcript. *Deadline:* April 1.

Contact: Barbara Iannoni, Senior Academic Specialist
Educational Foundation of the Massachusetts Society of Certified Public Accountants
105 Chauncy Street
Boston, MA 02111
Phone: 617-303-2415
Fax: 617-556.4126
E-mail: biannoni@mscpaonline.org

FLORIDA INSTITUTE OF CERTIFIED PUBLIC ACCOUNTANTS SCHOLARSHIP FOUNDATION, INC.

http://www.ficpa.org/

1040K RUN/WALK SCHOLARSHIPS

Applicant(s) must be a citizen of the United States or hold permanent residency status and be a resident of Miami-Dade County, Broward County, Monroe County, or Palm Beach Count. The Lewis Davis scholarship is to be awarded to an African-American student. One scholarship is to be awarded to a minority student (may or not be African-American). One scholarship is to be awarded to a student based on need (may or not be African-American). See website for details.

Academic Fields/Career Goals: Accounting.

Award: Scholarship for use in senior or graduate years; not renewable. *Number:* up to 3. *Amount:* up to $3000.

Eligibility Requirements: Applicant must be Black (non-Hispanic); enrolled or expecting to enroll full-time at a four-year institution or university; resident of Florida and studying in Florida. Applicant must have 3.0 GPA or higher. Available to U.S. citizens.

Application Requirements: Application form, must be recommended by accounting faculty committee at Florida college or university attended, recommendations or references, transcript. *Deadline:* February 15.

Contact: Mrs. Betsy Wilson, Educational Foundation Assistant
Florida Institute of Certified Public Accountants Scholarship
Foundation, Inc.
325 West College Avenue, PO Box 5437
Tallahassee, FL 32314
Phone: 850-224-2727
Fax: 850-222-8190
E-mail: wilsonb@ficpa.org

FICPA EDUCATIONAL FOUNDATION SCHOLARSHIPS

Scholarship for full-time or part-time (minimum of six credit hours), fourth- or fifth-year accounting major at participating Florida colleges or universities. Must be a member of the Florida Institute of CPAs, a Florida resident and plan to practice accounting in Florida. See website for list of institutions
http://www1.ficpa.org/ficpa/Visitors/Careers/EdFoundation/Scholarships
.

Academic Fields/Career Goals: Accounting.

Award: Scholarship for use in senior or graduate years; not renewable. *Number:* up to 63. *Amount:* $1000–$2000.

Eligibility Requirements: Applicant must be enrolled or expecting to enroll full- or part-time at a four-year institution or university; resident of Florida and studying in Florida. Applicant must have 3.0 GPA or higher. Available to U.S. citizens.

Application Requirements: Application form, must be recommended by faculty committee at school attended, recommendations or references, transcript. *Deadline:* April 15.

Contact: Mrs. Betsy Wilson, Educational Foundation Assistant
Florida Institute of Certified Public Accountants Scholarship
Foundation, Inc.
325 West College Avenue, PO Box 5437
Tallahassee, FL 32314
Phone: 850-224-2727
Fax: 850-222-8190
E-mail: wilsonb@ficpa.org

FUKUNAGA SCHOLARSHIP FOUNDATION

http://fukunagascholarship.com

FUKUNAGA SCHOLARSHIP FOUNDATION

Renewable scholarships available only to U.S. citizens/Hawaii residents pursuing a business degree at the undergraduate level at an accredited institution. Minimum 3.0 GPA required.

Academic Fields/Career Goals: Accounting; Advertising/Public Relations; Agribusiness; Business/Consumer Services; Economics; Finance; Health Administration; Hospitality Management; Human Resources; Marketing; Travel/Tourism.

Award: Scholarship for use in freshman, sophomore, junior, or senior years; renewable. *Number:* 10–15. *Amount:* $5000.

Eligibility Requirements: Applicant must be enrolled or expecting to enroll full-time at a four-year institution or university and resident of Hawaii. Applicant must have 3.0 GPA or higher. Available to U.S. citizens.

Application Requirements: Application form, essay, financial need analysis, interview. *Deadline:* March 1.

Contact: Mrs. Sandy Wong, Foundation Director
Fukunaga Scholarship Foundation
PO Box 2788
Honolulu, HI 96803-2788
Phone: 808-564-1386
E-mail: fukunagascholarship@servco.com

GEORGIA GOVERNMENT FINANCE OFFICERS ASSOCIATION

http://www.ggfoa.org/

GGFOA ANNUAL COLLEGE SCHOLARSHIP

The scholarship recognizes outstanding performance in the study of public finance at the undergraduate and graduate level and encourages careers in state and local government. The GGFOA Scholarship is awarded to undergraduate or graduate students who meet the eligibility requirements and are preparing for a career in public finance. Must have nomination by the head of the applicable program (e.g., public administration, accounting, finance). Preference will be given to GGFOA members and employees of GGFOA governmental entities who are eligible for in-state tuition.

Academic Fields/Career Goals: Accounting; Business/Consumer Services; Finance; Public Policy and Administration.

Award: Scholarship for use in freshman, sophomore, junior, senior, or graduate years; not renewable. *Number:* 1–2. *Amount:* $1–$1500.

Eligibility Requirements: Applicant must be enrolled or expecting to enroll full- or part-time at a four-year institution or university; resident of Georgia and studying in Georgia. Available to U.S. citizens.

Application Requirements: Application form, essay. *Deadline:* August 1.

Contact: Jennifer Fricks, Scholarship Selection Committee, GGFOA
Georgia Government Finance Officers Association
117 Putnam Drive
Eatonton, GA 31024
Phone: 706-485-1882
E-mail: jfricks@putnamcountyga.us

GOVERNMENT FINANCE OFFICERS ASSOCIATION

http://www.gfoa.org/

FRANK L. GREATHOUSE GOVERNMENT ACCOUNTING SCHOLARSHIP

Two scholarships awarded to undergraduate or graduate students enrolled full-time, preparing for a career in state or local government finance.

Academic Fields/Career Goals: Accounting; Finance.

Award: Scholarship for use in junior, senior, or graduate years; not renewable. *Number:* 2. *Amount:* $10,000.

Eligibility Requirements: Applicant must be enrolled or expecting to enroll full-time at a four-year institution or university. Applicant must have 3.0 GPA or higher. Available to U.S. and Canadian citizens.

Application Requirements: Application form, essay. *Deadline:* January 26.

Contact: Mr. Robert Kotchen, Administrative Assistant
Government Finance Officers Association
203 North Lasalle Street
Suite 2700
Chicago, IL 60601
Phone: 312-977-9700
E-mail: rkotchen@gfoa.org

JEFFREY L. ESSER CAREER DEVELOPMENT SCHOLARSHIP

Award for part-time student pursuing an Associate's degree or Bachelor's degree in public administration, (governmental) accounting, finance or business administration, and a career plan in state/provincial or local government finance. Must be currently employed at least 3 years by one or more state or local governments.

Academic Fields/Career Goals: Accounting; Finance; Public Policy and Administration.

Award: Scholarship for use in freshman, sophomore, junior, or senior years; not renewable. *Number:* 1–2. *Amount:* $5000–$15,000.

Eligibility Requirements: Applicant must be enrolled or expecting to enroll part-time at a two-year or four-year institution or university. Applicant must have 3.0 GPA or higher. Available to U.S. and Canadian citizens.

Application Requirements: Application form, essay. *Deadline:* January 26.

Contact: Peg Hartnett
Government Finance Officers Association
203 N. LaSalle ST, Suite 2700
Chicago, IL 60601-1210
Phone: 312-977-9700
E-mail: phartnett@gfoa.org

MINORITIES IN GOVERNMENT FINANCE SCHOLARSHIP

Awards upper-division undergraduate or graduate students of public administration, governmental accounting, finance, political science, economics, or business administration to recognize outstanding performance by minority students preparing for a career in state and local government finance.

Academic Fields/Career Goals: Accounting; Business/Consumer Services; Economics; Political Science; Public Policy and Administration.

Award: Scholarship for use in junior, senior, or graduate years; not renewable. *Number:* 1. *Amount:* $10,000.

Eligibility Requirements: Applicant must be American Indian/Alaska Native, Asian/Pacific Islander, Black (non-Hispanic), Hispanic and enrolled or expecting to enroll full- or part-time at a four-year institution or university. Applicant must have 3.0 GPA or higher. Available to U.S. and Canadian citizens.

Application Requirements: Application form, essay. *Deadline:* January 26.

Contact: Mr. Robert Kotchen, Administrative Assistant
Government Finance Officers Association
203 North Lasalle Street
Suite 2700
Chicago, IL 60601
Phone: 312-977-9700
E-mail: rkotchen@gfoa.org

GREATER WASHINGTON SOCIETY OF CPAS

http://www.gwscpa.org/

GREATER WASHINGTON SOCIETY OF CPAS SCHOLARSHIP

Scholarship available to accounting students. School must offer an accounting degree that qualifies graduates to sit for the CPA exam (must meet the 150-hour rule). Minimum 3.0 GPA in major courses required. Application details on our website http://www.gwscpa.org.

Academic Fields/Career Goals: Accounting.

Award: Scholarship for use in junior, senior, or graduate years; not renewable. *Number:* 3–5. *Amount:* $2000–$4500.

Eligibility Requirements: Applicant must be enrolled or expecting to enroll full-time at a four-year institution or university; resident of District of Columbia and studying in District of Columbia. Applicant must have 3.0 GPA or higher. Available to U.S. citizens.

Application Requirements: Application form, essay, financial need analysis, recommendations or references, resume, transcript. *Deadline:* February 15.

Contact: Mr. Brian Calvary, Membership Director
Greater Washington Society of CPAs
1140 Connecticut Ave, NW
Suite 606
Washington, DC 20036
Phone: 202-601-0569
E-mail: info@gwscpa.org

HAWAIIAN LODGE, F&AM

http://www.hawaiianlodgefreemasons.org

HAWAIIAN LODGE SCHOLARSHIPS

The Hawaiian Lodge, Free and Accepted Masons Scholarship Program is dedicated to worthy High School seniors who wish to pursue a degree in the areas of Engineering, the Sciences, Hawaiian Studies, or Education - who may otherwise not be able to attend college. First and foremost, we look for a consistently good GPA throughout High School - with an eye towards the difficulty of the classes attended. Applicants will be asked to submit with their application, a written (or typed) essay which will enlighten the committee on the applicant's views and opinions on a selected topic or philosophy. Also requested will be recommendation letters from the applicant's mentors and role models. An applicant's (family) financial need will be judged by the submission of a (sanitized) IRS Form 1040 showing their household income. Hawaiian Lodge encourages awardees to maintain good study habits, and rewards steadfast follow-on applicants with continuing awards throughout their

Baccalaureate studies. Hawaiian Lodge reserves the right to choose their awardees based on the above criteria, with GPA being important, the Essay being essential and financial need being a strong driver towards the Scholarship selection. Masonic Membership or Affiliation through family is noted by the committee.

Academic Fields/Career Goals: Accounting; Anthropology; Architecture; Civil Engineering; Computer Science/Data Processing; Dental Health/Services; Education; Health Administration; Health and Medical Sciences; Health Information Management/Technology; History; Marine Biology; Marine/Ocean Engineering; Mathematics; Mechanical Engineering; Nuclear Science; Nursing; Occupational Safety and Health; Oceanography; Pharmacy; Public Health; Science, Technology, and Society.

Award: Scholarship for use in freshman, sophomore, junior, or senior years; not renewable. *Number:* 10–16. *Amount:* $1500.

Eligibility Requirements: Applicant must be age 18-25; enrolled or expecting to enroll full-time at a two-year or four-year institution or university and resident of Hawaii. Applicant must have 3.0 GPA or higher. Available to U.S. citizens.

Application Requirements: Application form, essay, financial need analysis, interview. *Deadline:* June 1.

Contact: Mr. Robert Schultz, Chairman, Scholarship Committee
Hawaiian Lodge, F&AM
94-1002 Lauwi Place
Waipahu, HI 96797
Phone: 808-220-3859
E-mail: robert.schultz@icloud.com

HAWAII SOCIETY OF CERTIFIED PUBLIC ACCOUNTANTS

http://www.hscpa.org/

HSCPA SCHOLARSHIP PROGRAM FOR ACCOUNTING STUDENTS

Scholarship for Hawaii resident currently attending an accredited Hawaii college or university. Minimum 3.0 GPA required. Must be majoring, or concentrating, in accounting with the intention to sit for the CPA exam, and have completed an intermediate accounting course. Number of awards vary from year to year.

Academic Fields/Career Goals: Accounting.

Award: Scholarship for use in freshman, sophomore, junior, or senior years; not renewable. *Amount:* $500–$1500.

Eligibility Requirements: Applicant must be enrolled or expecting to enroll full-time at a four-year institution or university; resident of Hawaii and studying in Hawaii. Applicant must have 3.0 GPA or higher. Available to U.S. citizens.

Application Requirements: Application form, community service, recommendations or references, test scores, transcript. *Deadline:* January 31.

Contact: Kathy Castillo, Executive Director
Hawaii Society of Certified Public Accountants
900 Fort Street Mall, Suite 850
Honolulu, HI 96813
Phone: 808-537-9475
Fax: 808-537-3520
E-mail: info@hscpa.org

ILLINOIS CPA SOCIETY/CPA ENDOWMENT FUND OF ILLINOIS

http://www.icpas.org/

ILLINOIS CPA SOCIETY ACCOUNTING SCHOLARSHIP PROGRAM

The Illinois CPA Society has numerous scholarships available to support accounting students who are studying accounting and planning to become a CPA. Candidates must demonstrate a course of study which reflects a goal to sit for the CPA exam in Illinois. The scholarship program supports diversity of students, investing in their success and helping them to realize their dream of becoming CPAs. Scholarship recipients have studied at a variety of schools throughout the state, from large state universities to small private schools to community colleges. Some scholarships have supported students with their graduate studies, while others support a fifth year of undergraduate education.

Academic Fields/Career Goals: Accounting.

Award: Scholarship for use in junior, senior, graduate, or postgraduate years; not renewable. *Number:* 12–35. *Amount:* $500–$4000.

Eligibility Requirements: Applicant must be enrolled or expecting to enroll full- or part-time at a four-year institution or university; resident of Illinois and studying in Illinois. Applicant must have 3.0 GPA or higher. Available to U.S. citizens.

Application Requirements: Application form, essay. *Deadline:* April 1.

Contact: Ms. Devin Payne
E-mail: scholarship@icpas.org

INSTITUTE OF MANAGEMENT ACCOUNTANTS

https://www.imanet.org/students/scholarships-and-awards/scholarships?ssopc=1

INSTITUTE OF MANAGEMENT ACCOUNTANTS MEMORIAL EDUCATION FUND SCHOLARSHIPS

Scholarships for IMA undergraduate or graduate student members studying at accredited institutions in the U.S. and Puerto Rico. Must be pursuing a career in management accounting, financial management, or information technology, and have a minimum GPA of 3.0. Awards based on academic merit, IMA participation, strength of recommendations, and quality of written statements.

Academic Fields/Career Goals: Accounting; Business/Consumer Services.

Award: Scholarship for use in sophomore, junior, senior, or graduate years; not renewable. *Number:* 6–15. *Amount:* $1000–$2500.

Eligibility Requirements: Applicant must be enrolled or expecting to enroll full- or part-time at a two-year or four-year institution or university. Applicant must have 3.0 GPA or higher. Available to U.S. citizens.

Application Requirements: Application form, essay. *Deadline:* February 15.

Contact: Kerry Butkera, Research & Academic Relations Administrator
Institute of Management Accountants
IMA
10 Paragon Drive, Suite 1
Montvale, NJ 07628
Phone: 800-638-4427 Ext. 1546
E-mail: kbutkera@imanet.org

STUART CAMERON AND MARGARET MCLEOD MEMORIAL SCHOLARSHIP

Scholarships for IMA undergraduate or graduate student members studying at accredited institutions in the U.S. and Puerto Rico and carrying 12 credits per semester. Must be pursuing a career in management accounting, financial management, or information technology, and have a minimum GPA of 3.0. Awards based on academic merit, IMA participation, strength of recommendations, and quality of written statements.

Academic Fields/Career Goals: Accounting; Business/Consumer Services.

Award: Scholarship for use in junior, senior, or graduate years; not renewable. *Number:* 1. *Amount:* $5000.

Eligibility Requirements: Applicant must be enrolled or expecting to enroll full- or part-time at a two-year or four-year institution or university. Applicant must have 3.0 GPA or higher. Available to U.S. citizens.

Application Requirements: Application form, essay, resume, transcript. *Deadline:* February 15.

Contact: Kerry Butkera, Research & Academic Relations Administrator
Institute of Management Accountants
IMA
10 Paragon Drive, Suite 1
Montvale, NJ 07628
Phone: 800-638-4427 Ext. 1546
E-mail: kbutkera@imanet.org

INTERNAL AUDIT FOUNDATION

http://www.theiia.org/

ESTHER R. SAWYER RESEARCH AWARD

Awarded to a student entering or currently enrolled in an Internal Auditing Education Partnership (IAEP) program at an IIA-affiliated school. Awarded based on submission of an original manuscript on a specific topic related to modern internal auditing.

Academic Fields/Career Goals: Accounting; Business/Consumer Services.

Award: Prize for use in freshman, sophomore, junior, senior, or graduate years; not renewable. *Number:* 1–3. *Amount:* $3000–$5000.

Eligibility Requirements: Applicant must be enrolled or expecting to enroll full-time at a four-year institution or university. Available to U.S. and non-U.S. citizens.

Application Requirements: Application form, essay. *Deadline:* March 1.

Contact: Benjamin Bouchillon, Director of Publishing and Retail
Internal Audit Foundation
1035 Greenwood Blvd., Suite 401
Lake Mary, FL 32746
Phone: 407-937-1352
E-mail: foundation@theiia.org

KENTUCKY SOCIETY OF CERTIFIED PUBLIC ACCOUNTANTS

http://www.kycpa.org/

KENTUCKY SOCIETY OF CERTIFIED PUBLIC ACCOUNTANTS COLLEGE SCHOLARSHIP

Nonrenewable award for accounting majors at a Kentucky college or university. Must rank in upper third of class or have a minimum 3.0 GPA. Must be a Kentucky resident.

Academic Fields/Career Goals: Accounting.

Award: Scholarship for use in sophomore, junior, or senior years; not renewable. *Number:* 10–40. *Amount:* $1000–$2500.

Eligibility Requirements: Applicant must be enrolled or expecting to enroll part-time at a two-year or four-year institution or university; resident of Kentucky and studying in Kentucky. Applicant must have 3.0 GPA or higher. Available to U.S. citizens.

Application Requirements: Application form, essay. *Deadline:* February 18.

Contact: Julie Salvaggio, Educational Foundation Manager
Kentucky Society of Certified Public Accountants
1735 Alliant Avenue
Louisville, KY 40299-6326
Phone: 502-736-1360
E-mail: jsalvaggio@kycpa.org

MARYLAND ASSOCIATION OF CERTIFIED PUBLIC ACCOUNTANTS EDUCATIONAL FOUNDATION

https://www.macpa.org/for-students/

MACPA EDUCATIONAL FOUNDATION SCHOLARSHIP AWARD

Award for Maryland residents who will have completed at least 60 credit hours at a Maryland college or university by the time of the award. Must have 3.0 GPA, demonstrate commitment to 150 semester hours of education, and intend to pursue a career as a certified public accountant. Number of awards varies. Must be a student member with the Maryland Association of CPAs. U.S. citizenship required. See website at for further details. https://www.macpa.org/for-students/

Academic Fields/Career Goals: Accounting.

Award: Scholarship for use in junior, senior, or graduate years; renewable. *Number:* 10–12. *Amount:* $500–$1500.

Eligibility Requirements: Applicant must be enrolled or expecting to enroll full-time at a four-year institution or university; resident of Maryland and studying in Maryland. Applicant must have 3.0 GPA or higher. Available to U.S. citizens.

Application Requirements: Application form, financial need analysis. *Deadline:* April 15.

Contact: Margaret DeRoose, Staff Accountant
Maryland Association of Certified Public Accountants
Educational Foundation
901 Dulaney Valley Road
Suite 800
Towson, MD 21204
Phone: 443-632-2327
E-mail: margaret@macpa.org

MICHIGAN ASSOCIATION OF CPAS

http://www.michcpa.org/

FIFTH/GRADUATE YEAR STUDENT SCHOLARSHIP

Scholarship for a full-time student in senior year, or a student with a combination of education and employment (defined as a minimum of two classes per term and 20 hours per week of employment). Must be majoring in accounting, and a U.S. citizen.

Academic Fields/Career Goals: Accounting.

Award: Scholarship for use in senior year; not renewable. *Number:* 16–25. *Amount:* $2000–$4000.

Eligibility Requirements: Applicant must be enrolled or expecting to enroll full- or part-time at a four-year institution or university and studying in Michigan. Available to U.S. citizens.

Application Requirements: Application form, application form may be submitted online (http://www.mafonline.org), essay, financial need analysis, recommendations or references, transcript. *Deadline:* January 31.

Contact: MACPA Academic Services Specialist
Michigan Association of CPAs
5480 Corporate Drive, Suite 200
Troy, MI 48007-5068
Phone: 248-267-3700
Fax: 248-267-3737
E-mail: macpa@michcpa.org

MONTANA SOCIETY OF CERTIFIED PUBLIC ACCOUNTANTS

http://www.mscpa.org/

MONTANA SOCIETY OF CERTIFIED PUBLIC ACCOUNTANTS SCHOLARSHIP

Scholarship available to one student in each of the following five schools: Montana State University Billings, MSU Bozeman, Carroll College, Montana Tech and University of Montana. Must be: 1. Accounting Major 2. At least a junior standing with at least one semester of coursework remaining 3. Minimum GPA of 3.0 4. Graduate students eligible 5. Must be a student member of the MSCPA 6. Graduate of a Montana high school and currently a Montana resident. Two additional scholarships are awarded through our Endowment Fund and may be applied for through the Montana Community Foundation.

Academic Fields/Career Goals: Accounting.

Award: Scholarship for use in junior, senior, or graduate years; not renewable. *Number:* 7. *Amount:* $1000.

Eligibility Requirements: Applicant must be enrolled or expecting to enroll full-time at a four-year institution or university; resident of Montana and studying in Montana. Applicant must have 3.0 GPA or higher. Available to U.S. citizens.

Application Requirements: Application form, essay. *Deadline:* March 17.

Contact: Mrs. Margaret Herriges, Communications Director
Montana Society of Certified Public Accountants
1534 9th Avenue
Helena, MT 59601
Phone: 406-442-7301
E-mail: mscpa@mscpa.org

NATIONAL SOCIETY OF ACCOUNTANTS

http://www.nsacct.org/

NATIONAL SOCIETY OF ACCOUNTANTS SCHOLARSHIP

One-time award of $500 to $1000 available to undergraduate students. Applicants must maintain a 3.0 GPA and have declared a major in accounting. Must submit an appraisal form and transcripts in addition to application. Must be U.S. or Canadian citizen attending an accredited U.S. school.

Academic Fields/Career Goals: Accounting.

Award: Scholarship for use in freshman, sophomore, junior, or senior years; not renewable. *Number:* up to 40. *Amount:* $500–$1000.

Eligibility Requirements: Applicant must be enrolled or expecting to enroll full- or part-time at a two-year or four-year institution or university. Applicant must have 3.0 GPA or higher. Available to U.S. and Canadian citizens.

Application Requirements: Application form, appraisal form, financial need analysis, transcript. *Deadline:* March 10.

Contact: Susan Noell, Director of Education Programs
National Society of Accountants
1010 North Fairfax Street
Alexandria, VA 22314-1574
Phone: 703-549-6400 Ext. 1312
Fax: 703-549-2984 Ext. 1312
E-mail: snoell@nsacct.org

STANLEY H. STEARMAN SCHOLARSHIP

One award for accounting major who is a relative of an active, retired, or deceased member of National Society of Accountants. Must be citizen of the United States or Canada and attend school in the United States. Minimum GPA of 3.0 required. Not available for freshman year. Submit application, appraisal form, and letter of intent.

Academic Fields/Career Goals: Accounting.

Award: Scholarship for use in freshman, sophomore, junior, senior, or graduate years; renewable. *Number:* 1. *Amount:* up to $2000.

Eligibility Requirements: Applicant must be enrolled or expecting to enroll full- or part-time at a two-year or four-year institution or university. Applicant or parent of applicant must be member of National Society of Accountants. Applicant must have 3.0 GPA or higher. Available to U.S. and Canadian citizens.

Application Requirements: Application form, appraisal form, essay, financial need analysis, transcript. *Deadline:* March 10.

Contact: Sally Brasse, Director of Education Programs
National Society of Accountants
1010 North Fairfax Street
Alexandria, VA 22314-1574
Phone: 703-549-6400 Ext. 1307
Fax: 703-549-2984
E-mail: sbrasse@nsacct.org

NC CPA FOUNDATION INC.

http://www.ncacpa.org/ncacpa-foundation/

NORTH CAROLINA ASSOCIATION OF CPAS FOUNDATION SCHOLARSHIPS

Scholarship available for North Carolina residents enrolled in a program leading to a degree in accounting or its equivalent in a North Carolina college or university. Must have completed at least one college or university level accounting course and have completed at least 36 semester hours (or equivalent) by the start of the spring semester of the year of application. The applicant must be sponsored by one accounting faculty members. Application and information at http://csbapp.csb.uncw.edu/nccpa.

Academic Fields/Career Goals: Accounting.

Award: Scholarship for use in sophomore, junior, senior, or graduate years; not renewable. *Number:* 50–60. *Amount:* $1000–$5000.

Eligibility Requirements: Applicant must be enrolled or expecting to enroll full- or part-time at a two-year or four-year institution or university; resident of North Carolina and studying in North Carolina. Applicant must have 3.0 GPA or higher. Available to U.S. citizens.

Application Requirements: Application form, application form may be submitted online (http://www.ncacpa.org/Member_Connections/Students/Foundation.aspx), essay, transcript. *Deadline:* February 10.

Contact: Mr. Jim Ahler, Chief Executive Officer
NC CPA Foundation Inc.
PO Box 80188
Raleigh, NC 27623
Phone: 919-469-1040 Ext. 130
E-mail: jtahler@ncacpa.org

NEBRASKA SOCIETY OF CERTIFIED PUBLIC ACCOUNTANTS

http://www.nescpa.org/

THE FOUNDATION OF THE NEBRASKA SOCIETY OF CERTIFIED PUBLIC ACCOUNTANTS 150-HOUR SCHOLARSHIP

The scholarship is for accounting majors who have completed their junior year and are enrolled in a fifth-year (150-hour) program at a Nebraska college or university; accounting students who plan to sit for the CPA exam; accounting students who have the interest and capabilities of becoming a successful accountant and who are considering an accounting career in Nebraska. When candidates are reviewed, scholarship, personality, leadership and character should be considered by the accounting instructional staff at each college or university. Scholarship criteria & applications are available through the qualifying college or university's Accounting Department's Chair.

Academic Fields/Career Goals: Accounting.

Award: Scholarship for use in senior or graduate years; not renewable.

Eligibility Requirements: Applicant must be enrolled or expecting to enroll full-time at a four-year institution or university and studying in Nebraska. Available to U.S. citizens.

Application Requirements: Application form. *Deadline:* April 1.

NEBRASKA SOCIETY OF CPAS GENERAL ACCOUNTING SCHOLARSHIP

Scholarship awards are presented to accounting students who have completed their junior year; accounting majors who plan to sit for the CPA exam; students who have the interest and capabilities of becoming a successful accountant and who are considering an accounting career in Nebraska are to be considered. Recipients need not necessarily have the highest scholastic average. Amounts vary every year. Scholarship criteria & applications are available through the qualifying college or university's Accounting Department's Chair.

Academic Fields/Career Goals: Accounting.

Award: Scholarship for use in senior year; not renewable.

Eligibility Requirements: Applicant must be enrolled or expecting to enroll full-time at a four-year institution or university and studying in Nebraska. Available to U.S. citizens.

Application Requirements: Application form. *Deadline:* August 1.

NEW ENGLAND EMPLOYEE BENEFITS COUNCIL

http://www.neebc.org/

NEW ENGLAND EMPLOYEE BENEFITS COUNCIL SCHOLARSHIP PROGRAM

Renewable award designed to encourage undergraduate or graduate students to pursue a course of study leading to a bachelor's degree or higher in the employee benefits field. Must be a resident of/or studying in Maine, Massachusetts, New Hampshire, Rhode Island, Connecticut or Vermont. Must have demonstrated interest in the fields of employee benefits, human resources, business law.

Academic Fields/Career Goals: Accounting; Business/Consumer Services; Economics; Health Administration; Human Resources; Insurance and Actuarial Science; Law/Legal Services; Public Health; Public Policy and Administration.

Award: Scholarship for use in freshman, sophomore, junior, senior, graduate, or postgraduate years; renewable. *Number:* 1–3. *Amount:* $1000–$5000.

Eligibility Requirements: Applicant must be enrolled or expecting to enroll full- or part-time at a two-year or four-year institution or

university; resident of Connecticut, Maine, Massachusetts, New Hampshire, Rhode Island, Vermont and studying in Connecticut, Maine, Massachusetts, New Hampshire, Rhode Island, Vermont. Applicant must have 3.0 GPA or higher. Available to U.S. citizens.

Application Requirements: Application form, essay. *Deadline:* April 1.

Contact: Ms. Linda Viens, Manager of Operations and Member Services
New England Employee Benefits Council
240 Bear Hill Road
Suite 102
Waltham, MA 02451
Phone: 781-684 Ext. 8700
E-mail: linda@neebc.org

NEW HAMPSHIRE SOCIETY OF CERTIFIED PUBLIC ACCOUNTANTS

http://www.nhscpa.org/

NEW HAMPSHIRE SOCIETY OF CERTIFIED PUBLIC ACCOUNTANTS SCHOLARSHIP FUND

Applicant must be a U.S. citizen, a New Hampshire resident, and an accounting or business major entering their senior year at an accredited four-year college or university; a graduate student pursuing a Master's degree in accounting or business in an accredited program; or those seeking the additional 30 hours of education to become eligible for a CPA license in New Hampshire. Must be recommended by a teacher or person responsible for the accounting or business program where the applicant is presently enrolled. Complete and return the application provided by the New Hampshire Society of Certified Public Accountants by the due date. Must have at least 90 credits or have senior- standing. Must have taken at least 3 courses of upper level accounting courses which would exclude introductory financial and managerial classes or the first 6 credits in accounting courses.

Academic Fields/Career Goals: Accounting.

Award: Scholarship for use in senior or graduate years; not renewable. *Number:* 1–7. *Amount:* $500–$2500.

Eligibility Requirements: Applicant must be enrolled or expecting to enroll full-time at a four-year institution or university and resident of New Hampshire. Available to U.S. citizens.

Application Requirements: Application form, recommendations or references, transcript. *Deadline:* November 30.

Contact: Roberta Daly, CPE and Events Manager
Phone: 603-622-1999 Ext. 201

NEW JERSEY SOCIETY OF CERTIFIED PUBLIC ACCOUNTANTS

http://www.njcpa.org/

NEW JERSEY SOCIETY OF CERTIFIED PUBLIC ACCOUNTANTS COLLEGE SCHOLARSHIP PROGRAM

Award for college juniors or those entering an accounting-related graduate program. Must be a New Jersey resident attending a four-year New Jersey institution. Must be nominated by accounting department chair or submit application directly. Minimum 3.2 GPA required. Award values at $6,000

Academic Fields/Career Goals: Accounting.

Award: Scholarship for use in junior or senior years; not renewable. *Number:* 40–50. *Amount:* $6000.

Eligibility Requirements: Applicant must be enrolled or expecting to enroll full- or part-time at a four-year institution or university; resident of New Jersey and studying in New Jersey. Applicant must have 3.0 GPA or higher. Available to U.S. citizens.

Application Requirements: Application form, essay, interview. *Deadline:* January 5.

Contact: Ms. Pam Isenburg, Membership Coordinator, NextGen Outreach
New Jersey Society of Certified Public Accountants
425 Eagle Rock Avenue, Suite 100
Roseland, NJ 07068-1723
Phone: 973-226-4494 Ext. 241
E-mail: pisenburg@njcpa.org

NEW JERSEY SOCIETY OF CERTIFIED PUBLIC ACCOUNTANTS HIGH SCHOOL SCHOLARSHIP PROGRAM

Renewable scholarship for New Jersey high school seniors who wish to pursue a degree in accounting. Must be resident of New Jersey. Scholarship value is $7,000. Deadline is in December.

Academic Fields/Career Goals: Accounting.

Award: Scholarship for use in freshman, sophomore, junior, or senior years; renewable. *Number:* 15–20. *Amount:* $7000.

Eligibility Requirements: Applicant must be high school student; planning to enroll or expecting to enroll full-time at a four-year institution or university and resident of New Jersey. Applicant must have 3.0 GPA or higher. Available to U.S. citizens.

Application Requirements: Application form, essay, interview. *Deadline:* December 8.

Contact: Ms. Pam Isenburg, Membership Coordinator, NextGen
    Outreach
    New Jersey Society of Certified Public Accountants
    425 Eagle Rock Avenue, Suite 100
    Roseland, NJ 07068-1723
    Phone: 973-226-4494 Ext. 241
    E-mail: pisenburg@njcpa.org

NEW YORK STATE SOCIETY OF CERTIFIED PUBLIC ACCOUNTANTS FOUNDATION FOR ACCOUNTING EDUCATION

http://www.nysscpa.org/page/future-cpas/college-students

FOUNDATION FOR ACCOUNTING EDUCATION SCHOLARSHIP

Awards up to $500 to $2500 scholarships to college students to encourage them to pursue a career in accounting. Must be a New York resident studying in New York and maintaining a 3.0 GPA.

Academic Fields/Career Goals: Accounting.

Award: Scholarship for use in junior, senior, or graduate years; not renewable. *Number:* 1–60. *Amount:* $500–$2500.

Eligibility Requirements: Applicant must be enrolled or expecting to enroll full- or part-time at a four-year institution or university; resident of New York and studying in New York. Applicant must have 3.0 GPA or higher. Available to U.S. citizens.

Application Requirements: Application form, application form may be submitted online (http://www.nysscpa.org), essay, financial need analysis, recommendations or references, transcript. *Deadline:* April 1.

Contact: Ms. Lisa Axisa, Associate Director, Recruitment and Retention
    New York State Society of Certified Public Accountants
    Foundation for Accounting Education
    3 Park Avenue, 18th Floor
    New York, NY 10016
    Phone: 212-719-8362
    E-mail: laxisa@nysspca.org

OREGON ASSOCIATION OF PUBLIC ACCOUNTANTS SCHOLARSHIP FOUNDATION

http://www.oaia.net/

OAIA SCHOLARSHIP

Scholarships of $1000 to $2000 are awarded to full-time students. Must be a resident of the state of Oregon and major in accounting studies at an accredited school in the state of Oregon. The scholarship may be used for tuition, fees, books or other academic expenses incurred during the term.

Academic Fields/Career Goals: Accounting.

Award: Scholarship for use in freshman, sophomore, junior, or senior years; not renewable. *Number:* 5. *Amount:* $1000–$2000.

Eligibility Requirements: Applicant must be enrolled or expecting to enroll full-time at a two-year or four-year institution or university; resident of Oregon and studying in Oregon. Available to U.S. citizens.

Application Requirements: Application form, financial need analysis. *Deadline:* April 1.

Contact: Sue Robertson, Treasurer
    Oregon Association of Public Accountants Scholarship
      Foundation
    1804 NE 43rd Ave.
    Portland, OR 97213
    Phone: 503-282-7247
    E-mail: srobertson4oaia@aol.com

OREGON STUDENT ASSISTANCE COMMISSION

https://oregonstudentaid.gov/

OREGON ASSOCIATION OF CERTIFIED FRAUD EXAMINERS SCHOLARSHIP

Scholarship for students who will enroll as college senior or above for fall term/semester at an Oregon public or nonprofit college. Majoring in accounting, business, criminal justice, finance, law, law enforcement, or risk management. Minimum GPA 3.25.

Academic Fields/Career Goals: Accounting; Business/Consumer Services; Criminal Justice/Criminology; Finance; Law Enforcement/Police Administration; Law/Legal Services.

Award: Scholarship for use in senior or graduate years; not renewable.

Eligibility Requirements: Applicant must be enrolled or expecting to enroll at a four-year institution or university and studying in Oregon. Applicant must have 3.0 GPA or higher. Available to U.S. citizens.

Application Requirements: Application form. *Deadline:* March 1.

Contact: Melissa Adams, Scholarship Processing Coordinator
    Phone: 541-687-7409
    E-mail: melissa.adams@state.or.us

OSCPA EDUCATIONAL FOUNDATION

http://www.orcpa.org/

OSCPA EDUCATIONAL FOUNDATION SCHOLARSHIP PROGRAM

Full-time Oregon college/university undergraduate accounting majors, post baccalaureate and master's program students are eligible to apply. Scholarships will be awarded based on student's academic performance, intent to pursue a CPA career and work within the state of Oregon. Scholarships are for tuition and books. Minimum required GPA is 3.2 in accounting/business classes and an overall cumulative 3.2 GPA.

Academic Fields/Career Goals: Accounting.

Award: Scholarship for use in sophomore, junior, senior, or graduate years; not renewable. *Number:* 45–75. *Amount:* $500–$3000.

Eligibility Requirements: Applicant must be enrolled or expecting to enroll full-time at a two-year or four-year or technical institution or university and studying in Oregon. Applicant must have 3.0 GPA or higher. Available to U.S. citizens.

Application Requirements: Application form. *Deadline:* January 15.

Contact: Tonna Hollis, Senior Manager - Member Services &
    Professional Development
    OSCPA Educational Foundation
    PO Box 4555
    Beaverton, OR 97076-4555
    Phone: 503-641-7200 Ext. 29
    E-mail: thollis@orcpa.org

RHODE ISLAND FOUNDATION

http://www.rifoundation.org/

CARL W. CHRISTIANSEN SCHOLARSHIP

$1000 scholarship for Rhode Island residents pursuing full-time study in accounting or related fields. Must maintain a minimum 3.0 GPA.

Academic Fields/Career Goals: Accounting.

Award: Scholarship for use in freshman, sophomore, junior, senior, or graduate years; not renewable. *Amount:* $1000.

Eligibility Requirements: Applicant must be enrolled or expecting to enroll full-time at a two-year or four-year institution or university and resident of Rhode Island. Applicant must have 3.0 GPA or higher. Available to U.S. citizens.

Application Requirements: Application form. *Deadline:* January 11.

Contact: Denise Jacobson
E-mail: djacobson@riscpa.org

CHERYL A. RUGGIERO SCHOLARSHIP

Award for female Rhode Island residents pursuing full-time study in public accounting. Must maintain a minimum 3.0 GPA.

Academic Fields/Career Goals: Accounting.

Award: Scholarship for use in freshman, sophomore, junior, senior, or graduate years; not renewable. *Amount:* $1000.

Eligibility Requirements: Applicant must be enrolled or expecting to enroll full-time at a two-year or four-year institution or university; female and resident of Rhode Island. Applicant must have 3.0 GPA or higher. Available to U.S. citizens.

Application Requirements: Application form, essay, interview, proof of U.S. citizenship, proof of RI residency, recommendations or references, transcript. *Deadline:* January 11.

Contact: Denise Jacobson
E-mail: djacobson@riscpa.org

RHODE ISLAND SOCIETY OF CERTIFIED PUBLIC ACCOUNTANTS

http://www.riscpa.org/

RHODE ISLAND SOCIETY OF CERTIFIED PUBLIC ACCOUNTANTS SCHOLARSHIP

Annual scholarship for graduates and undergraduates majoring in accounting, who are legal residents of Rhode Island and U.S. citizens. Must have interest in a career in public accounting, and submit one-page memo outlining that interest. Minimum GPA of 3.0 required. For more information, see website http://www.riscpa.org.

Academic Fields/Career Goals: Accounting.

Award: Scholarship for use in freshman, sophomore, junior, senior, or graduate years; not renewable.

Eligibility Requirements: Applicant must be enrolled or expecting to enroll full-time at a four-year institution or university and resident of Rhode Island. Applicant must have 3.0 GPA or higher. Available to U.S. citizens.

Application Requirements: Application form, recommendations or references, resume, test scores, transcript. *Deadline:* January 15.

Contact: Robert Mancini, Executive Director
Phone: 401-331-5720
Fax: 401-454-5780
E-mail: rmancini@riscpa.org

SCARLETT FAMILY FOUNDATION SCHOLARSHIP PROGRAM

http://www.scarlettfoundation.org/

SCHOLARSHIP FOR STUDENTS PURSUING A BUSINESS OR STEM DEGREE

Each year, the Scarlett Family Foundation will award scholarships in varying amounts based on financial need and merit, that is directly tied to the cost of the college the student attends. The minimum scholarship award is $2,500 per academic year. The maximum award is $15,000 per academic year. The scholarship is applied to tuition, books and fees. Scholarships are renewable awards for up to 4 years or until the recipient completes their undergraduate degree, whichever comes first. The scholarships are open to high school seniors and college freshmen, sophomores, and juniors who will graduate or have graduated from a public, independent or homeschool association high school in 40 Middle Tennessee counties. Also eligible are individuals who have obtained a GED.

Academic Fields/Career Goals: Accounting; Advertising/Public Relations; Agribusiness; Agriculture; Animal/Veterinary Sciences; Applied Sciences; Archaeology; Architecture; Audiology; Aviation/Aerospace; Biology; Business/Consumer Services; Chemical Engineering; Civil Engineering; Computer Science/Data Processing; Dental Health/Services; Earth Science; Economics; Electrical Engineering/Electronics; Energy and Power Engineering; Engineering-Related Technologies; Engineering/Technology; Environmental Science; Finance; Food Science/Nutrition; Geography; Health Administration; Health and Medical Sciences; Health Information Management/Technology; Hospitality Management; Human Resources; Insurance and Actuarial Science; Marine Biology; Marine/Ocean Engineering; Marketing; Materials Science, Engineering, and Metallurgy; Mathematics; Mechanical Engineering; Meteorology/Atmospheric Science; Natural Sciences; Neurobiology; Nuclear Science; Nursing; Oceanography; Oncology; Optometry; Osteopathy; Pharmacy; Physical Sciences; Sports-Related/Exercise Science; Therapy/Rehabilitation.

Award: Scholarship for use in freshman, sophomore, junior, or senior years; renewable. *Number:* 35–120. *Amount:* $2500–$15,000.

Eligibility Requirements: Applicant must be enrolled or expecting to enroll full-time at a four-year institution or university and resident of Tennessee. Applicant must have 2.5 GPA or higher. Available to U.S. citizens.

Application Requirements: Application form, driver's license, essay, financial need analysis. *Deadline:* December 15.

Contact: Tom Parrish, Chief Operating Officer
Scarlett Family Foundation Scholarship Program
4117 Hillsboro Pike
Suite 103255
Nashville, TN 37215-2728
E-mail: TomParrish@ScarlettFoundation.org

SOCIETY OF AUTOMOTIVE ANALYSTS

http://saaauto.com/

SOCIETY OF AUTOMOTIVE ANALYSTS SCHOLARSHIP

A scholarship of $1500 awarded to students in economics, finance, business administration or marketing management. Minimum 3.0 GPA required. Must submit two letters of recommendation.

Academic Fields/Career Goals: Accounting; Business/Consumer Services; Economics.

Award: Scholarship for use in freshman, sophomore, junior, or senior years; not renewable. *Number:* 2. *Amount:* $1500.

Eligibility Requirements: Applicant must be enrolled or expecting to enroll full-time at a two-year or four-year or technical institution or university. Applicant must have 3.0 GPA or higher. Available to U.S. and non-U.S. citizens.

Application Requirements: Application form, recommendations or references, transcript. *Deadline:* June 1.

Contact: Lynne Hall, Awards and Scholarships
Phone: 313-240-4000
Fax: 313-240-8641

SOCIETY OF LOUISIANA CERTIFIED PUBLIC ACCOUNTANTS

http://www.lcpa.org/

SOCIETY OF LOUISIANA CPAS SCHOLARSHIPS

One-time award for accounting majors. Applicant must be a Louisiana resident attending a four-year college or university in Louisiana. For full-time undergraduates entering their junior or senior year, or full-time graduate students. Minimum 2.5 GPA required. Deadline varies. Must be U.S. citizen.

Academic Fields/Career Goals: Accounting.

Award: Scholarship for use in junior, senior, or graduate years; not renewable. *Amount:* $500–$3000.

Eligibility Requirements: Applicant must be enrolled or expecting to enroll full-time at a four-year institution or university; resident of Louisiana and studying in Louisiana. Applicant must have 2.5 GPA or higher. Available to U.S. citizens.

Application Requirements: Application form, essay, recommendations or references, transcript. *Deadline:* varies.

Contact: Lisa Richardson, Member Services Manager
Society of Louisiana Certified Public Accountants
2400 Veterans Boulevard, Suite 500
Kenner, LA 70062-4739
Phone: 504-904-1139
Fax: 504-469-7930
E-mail: lrichardson@lcpa.org

SOUTH CAROLINA ASSOCIATION OF CERTIFIED PUBLIC ACCOUNTANTS

http://www.scacpa.org

SCACPA EDUCATIONAL FUND SCHOLARSHIPS

These scholarships are awarded to South Carolina residents who are rising juniors or seniors majoring in accounting, or master's degree students at a South Carolina college or university. Applicants must have a GPA of no less than 3.25 overall and a GPA in accounting no less than 3.5 (on a 4.0 scale).

Academic Fields/Career Goals: Accounting.

Award: Scholarship for use in junior, senior, or graduate years; not renewable. *Number:* 19–25. *Amount:* $500–$2500.

Eligibility Requirements: Applicant must be enrolled or expecting to enroll full-time at a four-year institution or university; resident of South Carolina and studying in South Carolina. Applicant must have 3.0 GPA or higher. Available to U.S. citizens.

Application Requirements: Application form, essay, financial need analysis. *Deadline:* May 31.

Contact: Ms. Jacque Curtin, COO/CFO
South Carolina Association of Certified Public Accountants
1300 12th Street, Suite D
Cayce, SC 29033
Phone: 803-791-4181 Ext. 408
Fax: 803-791-4196
E-mail: jcurtin@scacpa.org

SOUTH DAKOTA CPA SOCIETY

http://www.sdcpa.org/

EXCELLENCE IN ACCOUNTING SCHOLARSHIP

Scholarships available for senior undergraduate and graduate students majoring in accounting. Must have completed 90 credit hours, demonstrated excellence in academics and leadership potential. Application available online at http://www.sdcpa.org.

Academic Fields/Career Goals: Accounting.

Award: Scholarship for use in senior or graduate years; not renewable. *Number:* 5–15. *Amount:* $1000–$2500.

Eligibility Requirements: Applicant must be enrolled or expecting to enroll full-time at a four-year institution or university and studying in South Dakota. Applicant must have 3.0 GPA or higher. Available to U.S. citizens.

Application Requirements: Application form, personal photograph. *Deadline:* April 30.

Contact: Laura Coome, Executive Director
South Dakota CPA Society
5024 S Bur Oak Pl #108
Sioux Falls, SD 57108
Phone: 605-334-3848
E-mail: laura@sdcpa.org

SPECIALTY EQUIPMENT MARKET ASSOCIATION

http://www.sema.org/

SEMA MEMORIAL SCHOLARSHIP FUND

Scholarships for college students pursuing careers in or related to the automotive industry. All applicants must be U.S. citizens who are currently attending U.S. institutions. Minimum 2.5 GPA required. For more information and to apply, please visit: http://www.SEMA.org/scholarships.

Academic Fields/Career Goals: Accounting; Advertising/Public Relations; Business/Consumer Services; Communications; Computer Science/Data Processing; Electrical Engineering/Electronics; Engineering/Technology; Finance; Marketing; Mechanical Engineering; Trade/Technical Specialties; Transportation.

Award: Scholarship for use in junior, senior, graduate, or postgraduate years; not renewable. *Number:* 50–60. *Amount:* $2000–$5000.

Eligibility Requirements: Applicant must be enrolled or expecting to enroll full-time at a two-year or four-year or technical institution or university and must have an interest in automotive. Applicant must have 2.5 GPA or higher. Available to U.S. citizens.

Application Requirements: Application form, essay. *Deadline:* March 1.

Contact: Ms. Juliet Marshall, Education Manager
Phone: 909-978-6655
Fax: 909-860-0184
E-mail: julietm@sema.org

STRAIGHT NORTH

https://www.straightnorth.com/

STRAIGHT NORTH STEM SCHOLARSHIP

With Internet marketing becoming more complex and challenging by the day, successful execution requires a solid education. As an industry leader, Straight North supports students pursuing degrees in science, technology, engineering and math (STEM) disciplines.

Academic Fields/Career Goals: Accounting; Applied Sciences; Aviation/Aerospace; Biology; Chemical Engineering; Civil Engineering; Computer Science/Data Processing; Construction Engineering/Management; Earth Science; Electrical Engineering/Electronics; Energy and Power Engineering; Engineering-Related Technologies; Engineering/Technology; Environmental Health; Environmental Science; Finance; Flexography; Gemology; Health and Medical Sciences; Health Information Management/Technology; Heating, Air-Conditioning, and Refrigeration Mechanics; Hydrology; Insurance and Actuarial Science; Marine Biology; Marine/Ocean Engineering; Marketing; Materials Science, Engineering, and Metallurgy; Mathematics; Mechanical Engineering; Meteorology/Atmospheric Science; Natural Resources; Natural Sciences; Neurobiology; Nuclear Science; Nursing; Occupational Safety and Health; Oncology; Optometry; Osteopathy; Paper and Pulp Engineering; Physical Sciences; Science, Technology, and Society.

Award: Scholarship for use in freshman, sophomore, junior, senior, graduate, or postgraduate years; not renewable. *Number:* 3. *Amount:* $250–$1000.

Eligibility Requirements: Applicant must be enrolled or expecting to enroll full- or part-time at a two-year or four-year institution or university. Available to U.S. and non-U.S. citizens.

Application Requirements: Application form, autobiography. *Deadline:* August 1.

Contact: Tammy Barry, Director of Human Resources
E-mail: tbarry@straightnorth.com

TENNESSEE SOCIETY OF CPAS

http://www.tscpa.com/

TENNESSEE SOCIETY OF CPA SCHOLARSHIP

Scholarships are available only to full-time students who have completed introductory courses in accounting and/or students majoring in accounting. Applicants must be legal residents of Tennessee.

Academic Fields/Career Goals: Accounting.

Award: Scholarship for use in freshman, sophomore, junior, senior, or graduate years; not renewable. *Number:* 120–130. *Amount:* $250–$2500.

Eligibility Requirements: Applicant must be enrolled or expecting to enroll full-time at a four-year institution or university and resident of Tennessee. Available to U.S. citizens.

Application Requirements: Application form, financial need analysis, recommendations or references, transcript. *Deadline:* June 1.

Contact: Wendy Garvin, Member Services Manager
Phone: 615-377-3825
Fax: 390-377-3904
E-mail: wgarvin@tscpa.com

TKE EDUCATIONAL FOUNDATION

http://www.tke.org/

HARRY J. DONNELLY MEMORIAL SCHOLARSHIP

One-time award of $500 given to a member of Tau Kappa Epsilon pursuing an undergraduate degree in accounting or a graduate degree in law. Applicant should have demonstrated leadership ability within his chapter, campus, or community. Minimum 3.0 GPA required.

Academic Fields/Career Goals: Accounting; Law/Legal Services.

Award: Scholarship for use in sophomore, junior, senior, or graduate years; not renewable. *Number:* 1. *Amount:* $500.

Eligibility Requirements: Applicant must be enrolled or expecting to enroll full-time at a four-year institution or university; male and must have an interest in leadership. Applicant or parent of applicant must be member of Tau Kappa Epsilon. Applicant must have 3.0 GPA or higher. Available to U.S. and non-U.S. citizens.

Application Requirements: Application form, application form may be submitted online (http://www.tke.org/member_resources/scholarships/apply_online), essay, narrative summary of how TKE membership has benefited applicant, personal photograph, transcript. *Deadline:* March 15.

Contact: Offices of the Grand Chapter
TKE Educational Foundation
7439 Woodland Drive, Suite 100
Indianapolis, IN 46278
E-mail: tkeogc@tke.org

TRIANGLE PEST CONTROL

http://www.trianglepest.com

TRIANGLE PEST CONTROL SCHOLARSHIP

riangle Pest Control has been a trusted name in pest control in the Raleigh and Charlotte areas for the past ten years. In 2017, Triangle Pest Control completed an expansion to serve pest control to residents of Greenville, SC, and to celebrate, they created a merit-based scholarship fund for individuals seeking education in business management and business administration studies. With this goal in mind, Donnie Shelton, the CEO of Triangle Pest Control, has created a scholarship fund for the 2018 fall academic semester. The $500 scholarship will be awarded to an individual who has displayed academic excellence, in addition to a passionate pursuit of furthered business education at an accredited college or university in North or South Carolina. The purpose of The Triangle Pest Control Scholarship Fund is to encourage commitment by students to a career in business administration, management, marketing or other business-related fields. Entrepreneurship and small business ownership are important principles in the pest control industry, as well as the local community. Triangle Pest Control is constantly seeking new ways to be a leading voice in the pest control industry and to foster growth and opportunity in the communities they serve. This scholarship offers financial assistance to individuals with proven merit and serves to reward students pursuing a degree in business in North or South Carolina schools.

Academic Fields/Career Goals: Accounting; Business/Consumer Services; Marketing.

Award: Scholarship for use in freshman, sophomore, junior, or senior years; not renewable. *Number:* 1. *Amount:* $500.

Eligibility Requirements: Applicant must be enrolled or expecting to enroll full-time at a four-year institution or university and studying in North Carolina, South Carolina. Available to U.S. citizens.

Application Requirements: Application form. *Deadline:* August 31.

Contact: Mr. Frank Andolina, Triangle Pest Control
Triangle Pest Control
131 S. Wilmington St.
Raleigh, NC 27601

UNITED NEGRO COLLEGE FUND

http://www.uncf.org/

BASF/ALFRED CHISHOLM ENDOWED MEMORIAL SCHOLARSHIP

Scholarship of up to $2000 for a student who has a relative employed by the BASF Corporation. Must attend an historically black college or university and have minimum GPA of 3.0. Eligible majors include accounting, biology, business, chemistry, computer science, electrical engineering, engineering, finance, mathematics, supply chain management, and logistics.

Academic Fields/Career Goals: Accounting; Biology; Business/Consumer Services; Computer Science/Data Processing; Electrical Engineering/Electronics; Engineering/Technology; Finance; Mathematics; Physical Sciences.

Award: Scholarship for use in sophomore, junior, or senior years; not renewable.

Eligibility Requirements: Applicant must be Black (non-Hispanic) and enrolled or expecting to enroll full- or part-time at a four-year institution or university. Applicant must have 3.0 GPA or higher. Available to U.S. citizens.

Application Requirements: Application form, essay, financial need analysis. *Deadline:* December 1.

Contact: Mary Williams, Director of Outreach and Recruitment
Phone: 800-331-2244

DISCOVER FINANCIAL SERVICES SCHOLARSHIP

Scholarship and internship opportunities to students who are first semester sophomores enrolled at any UNCF member institution or other accredited HBCU, major in Computer Engineering, Computer Information System, Computer Science, Computer Science/MIS, Engineering Technology, Information Management System, Information Technology, Software Engineering, System Engineering, Finance, Accounting, Marketing, Analytics Risk Management, Supply Chain Logistics, Economics or other STEM related majors. The selected finalists are required to accept internship positions located in Riverwoods, IL.

Academic Fields/Career Goals: Accounting; Applied Sciences; Computer Science/Data Processing; Economics; Engineering-Related Technologies; Engineering/Technology; Finance; Marketing.

Award: Scholarship for use in sophomore year; renewable. *Amount:* $7500.

Eligibility Requirements: Applicant must be Black (non-Hispanic) and enrolled or expecting to enroll full-time at a four-year institution or university. Applicant must have 3.0 GPA or higher. Available to U.S. citizens.

Application Requirements: Application form, essay. *Deadline:* September 21.

Contact: Mary Williams, Director of Outreach and Recruitment
Phone: 800-331-2244

HCN/APRICITY RESOURCES SCHOLARS PROGRAM

Scholarship and internship at TN Apricity Resources, the intent of the internship program is to hire exceptional talent in hopes of converting to full-time hires upon graduation based on performance and business need. The focus is on African American undergraduates at HBCU(s) available during the summer before their senior year. Targeted majors: Accounting, Business, Business (Sales Interest),, Computer Engineering, Computer Science, Counseling, English, Finance, Healthcare Administration, Healthcare Management, Management Information Systems, Marketing, Nursing, Pre-Nursing, Psychology, Social Work, Sociology.

Academic Fields/Career Goals: Accounting; Business/Consumer Services; Computer Science/Data Processing; Finance; Health Administration; Literature/English/Writing; Marketing; Nursing; Psychology; Social Sciences; Social Services; Therapy/Rehabilitation.

Award: Scholarship for use in senior year.

Eligibility Requirements: Applicant must be enrolled or expecting to enroll at a four-year institution or university. Applicant must have 3.0 GPA or higher. Available to U.S. citizens.

Application Requirements: Application form. *Deadline:* February 22.

Contact: Mary Williams, Director of Outreach and Recruitment
Phone: 800-331-2244

MUFG UNION BANK SCHOLARSHIP PROGRAM

The MUFG Union Bank Scholarship Program was established by the Union Bank Foundation in partnership with the UNCF. The Union Bank Scholarship Program is available to Juniors, Seniors or Graduate students who enroll full-time at a four year accredited colleges or universities. Eligible applicants must pursue a degree in Accounting, Banking, Business, Economics, Finance Information Technology; and maintain a minimum cumulative GPA of 3.30 on a 4 point scale. In addition, preference or priority will be given to candidates who are permanent residents of California, New York, New Jersey, or Arizona and first-generation college students. Selected students may be contacted by Union Bank for a potential internship opportunity.

Academic Fields/Career Goals: Accounting; Business/Consumer Services; Computer Science/Data Processing; Economics; Finance.

Award: Scholarship for use in junior, senior, or graduate years; not renewable. *Amount:* $5400.

Eligibility Requirements: Applicant must be Black (non-Hispanic) and enrolled or expecting to enroll full-time at a four-year institution or university. Applicant must have 3.0 GPA or higher. Available to U.S. citizens.

Application Requirements: Application form, essay. *Deadline:* November 1.

Contact: Mary Williams, Director of Outreach and Recruitment
Phone: 800-331-2244

NATIONAL BLACK MCDONALD'S OWNERS ASSOCIATION HOSPITALITY SCHOLARS PROGRAM

Scholarship of up to $5000 for a student majoring in restaurant/hotel/hospitality management, accounting, business, or marketing as full-time students at an accredited Historically Black College or University (HBCU) that have an interest in hospitality management. Minimum 2.8 GPA required. Dependents of either McDonald's executives or NBMOA owners are ineligible for this opportunity as are former recipients of the NBMOA scholarship.

Academic Fields/Career Goals: Accounting; Business/Consumer Services; Food Service/Hospitality; Hospitality Management; Marketing.

Award: Scholarship for use in sophomore, junior, or senior years; not renewable.

Eligibility Requirements: Applicant must be Black (non-Hispanic) and enrolled or expecting to enroll full-time at a two-year or four-year institution or university. Applicant must have 2.5 GPA or higher. Available to U.S. citizens.

Application Requirements: Application form. *Deadline:* June 16.

Contact: Mary Williams, Director of Outreach and Recruitment
Phone: 800-331-2244

PROCTER & GAMBLE GENERAL SCHOLARSHIP

Up to $5000 scholarship for academically achieving undergraduate students at any accredited four-year colleges or universities within the United States. The scholarship is focused on majors in business, information technology and public relations.

Academic Fields/Career Goals: Accounting; Advertising/Public Relations; Business/Consumer Services; Computer Science/Data Processing; Finance; Human Resources; Marketing.

Award: Scholarship for use in freshman, sophomore, junior, or senior years.

Eligibility Requirements: Applicant must be Black (non-Hispanic) and enrolled or expecting to enroll at a four-year institution. Applicant must have 3.0 GPA or higher. Available to U.S. citizens.

Application Requirements: Application form. *Deadline:* June 15.

Contact: Mary Williams, Director of Outreach and Recruitment
Phone: 800-331-2244

RICOH SCHOLARSHIP PROGRAM

Up to $2500 scholarship for a college junior at an HBCU who is majoring in accounting, business, business operations, computer engineering, computer science, finance, information technology, mechanical engineering, or marketing. Must be a U.S. citizen or permanent legal resident; demonstrate leadership abilities through participation in community service, extracurricular or other activities, and/or work history; have an unmet financial need and have a minimum 2.5 GPA.

Academic Fields/Career Goals: Accounting; Business/Consumer Services; Computer Science/Data Processing; Engineering/Technology; Finance; Marketing.

Award: Scholarship for use in sophomore or junior years; renewable.

Eligibility Requirements: Applicant must be Black (non-Hispanic); enrolled or expecting to enroll full-time at a four-year institution or university and must have an interest in leadership. Applicant must have 2.5 GPA or higher. Available to U.S. citizens.

Application Requirements: Application form, financial need analysis. *Deadline:* October 6.

Contact: Mary Williams, Director of Outreach and Recruitment
Phone: 800-331-2244

SUEZ CORPORATE SCHOLARS PROGRAM

$5000 scholarship and paid internship. Applicant must be college sophomore or junior at the time of application. Major in Accounting, Business Administration, Civil Engineering, Communications, Computer Science, Electrical Engineering, English, Environmental Engineering, Environmental Science(s), Health and Safety (Select Environmental Science), Finance, Human Resources, Marketing, Mechanical Engineering, Political Science, Pre-law or Sociology.

Academic Fields/Career Goals: Accounting; Business/Consumer Services; Civil Engineering; Communications; Computer Science/Data Processing; Electrical Engineering/Electronics; Environmental Science; Finance; Human Resources; Law/Legal Services; Marketing; Mechanical Engineering; Political Science; Social Sciences.

Award: Scholarship for use in sophomore, junior, or senior years. *Amount:* $5000.

Eligibility Requirements: Applicant must be Black (non-Hispanic) and enrolled or expecting to enroll at a four-year institution or university. Applicant must have 3.0 GPA or higher. Available to U.S. citizens.

Application Requirements: Application form. *Deadline:* May 1.

Contact: Mary Williams, Director of Outreach and Recruitment
Phone: 800-331-2244

UBS/PAINEWEBBER SCHOLARSHIP

The UBS/PaineWebber Scholarship will be directed to current sophomores or juniors, who demonstrated outstanding academics within the various business disciplines at the targeted UNCF Institutions. Majors can include Accounting, Business, Business-related, Economics, Finance, International Business, Management, Marketing.

Academic Fields/Career Goals: Accounting; Business/Consumer Services; Economics; Finance; Marketing.

Award: Scholarship for use in sophomore or junior years.

Eligibility Requirements: Applicant must be Black (non-Hispanic) and enrolled or expecting to enroll at a four-year institution or university. Applicant must have 3.0 GPA or higher. Available to U.S. citizens.

Application Requirements: Application form, essay. *Deadline:* December 8.

Contact: Mary Williams, Director of Outreach and Recruitment
Phone: 800-331-2244

UNCF/KOCH SCHOLARS PROGRAM FOR UNDERGRADUATES

Scholarships of up to $5,000 each available to African-American high school students planning to attend HBCU colleges and universities on a full-time basis. Must major in accounting, business, economics, engineering, history, philosophy, or political science. Minimum 2.7 GPA required. Must be committed to learning about how entrepreneurship, innovation, and economics contribute to well-being through participation in an online community and Annual Summit.

Academic Fields/Career Goals: Accounting; Business/Consumer Services; Economics; Engineering/Technology; History; Philosophy; Political Science.

Award: Scholarship for use in freshman year; not renewable. *Number:* 200.

Eligibility Requirements: Applicant must be Black (non-Hispanic); high school student and planning to enroll or expecting to enroll full-time at a four-year institution or university. Applicant must have 2.5 GPA or higher. Available to U.S. citizens.

Application Requirements: Application form, financial need analysis. *Deadline:* May 1.

Contact: Mary Williams, Director of Outreach and Recruitment
Phone: 800-331-2244

VOYA SCHOLARS

Award for current juniors who are enrolled full-time at a UNCF member college or university in a restricted major in accounting, actuarial science, business/business management, finance/investment, marketing, mathematics, or quants/quantitative. Preference will be given to students with a home residence in Atlanta, GA; Hartford, CT; Jackson, Mississippi; Minneapolis, MN New York City; and Philadelphia, PA.

Academic Fields/Career Goals: Accounting; Business/Consumer Services; Finance; Insurance and Actuarial Science; Marketing; Mathematics; Statistics.

Award: Scholarship for use in junior year; not renewable.

Eligibility Requirements: Applicant must be enrolled or expecting to enroll full-time at a four-year institution or university. Applicant must have 3.0 GPA or higher. Available to U.S. citizens.

Application Requirements: Application form, essay, financial need analysis. *Deadline:* November 30.

Contact: Mary Williams, Director of Outreach and Recruitment
Phone: 800-331-2244

WILLIAM WRIGLEY FOUNDATION SCHOLARSHIP

The Wm Wrigley scholarship provides financial assistance to junior and seniors attending a UNCF college/university. Candidates for this scholarship should be majoring in engineering (chemical, mechanical, electrical, industrial), business, finance, accounting, chemistry, economics, computer science or marketing. The scholarship will provide an award up to $5,000 depending on the financial need of the student as verified by the attending University or College.

Academic Fields/Career Goals: Accounting; Business/Consumer Services; Chemical Engineering; Computer Science/Data Processing; Economics; Electrical Engineering/Electronics; Engineering/Technology; Finance; Marketing; Mechanical Engineering.

Award: Scholarship for use in junior or senior years; not renewable.

Eligibility Requirements: Applicant must be Black (non-Hispanic) and enrolled or expecting to enroll at a four-year institution or university. Applicant must have 2.5 GPA or higher. Available to U.S. citizens.

Application Requirements: Application form, essay, financial need analysis. *Deadline:* October 6.

Contact: Mary Williams, Director of Outreach and Recruitment
Phone: 800-331-2244

VIRCHOW, KRAUSE & COMPANY, LLP

http://www.virchowkrause.com/

VIRCHOW, KRAUSE AND COMPANY SCHOLARSHIP

One-time scholarship for students enrolled either full-time or part-time in accredited colleges or universities of Wisconsin, majoring in accounting.

Academic Fields/Career Goals: Accounting.

Award: Scholarship for use in freshman, sophomore, junior, or senior years; not renewable. *Number:* up to 3. *Amount:* up to $1000.

Eligibility Requirements: Applicant must be enrolled or expecting to enroll full- or part-time at a two-year or four-year institution or university and studying in Wisconsin. Available to U.S. citizens.

Application Requirements: Application form, transcript. *Deadline:* varies.

Contact: Darbie Miller, Human Resources Coordinator
Virchow, Krause & Company, LLP
4600 American Parkway, PO Box 7398
Madison, WI 53707-7398
Phone: 608-240-2474
Fax: 608-249-1411
E-mail: dmiller@virchowkrause.com

VIRGINIA SOCIETY OF CERTIFIED PUBLIC ACCOUNTANTS EDUCATIONAL FOUNDATION

http://www.vscpa.com/

VSCPA EDUCATIONAL FOUNDATION ACCOUNTING SCHOLARSHIPS

All applicants must be U.S. citizens; successfully complete 3 credit hours of accounting prior to the fall semester; be currently enrolled in an accredited Virginia college or university with the intent to pursue a degree in accounting; and enrollment in an accredited Virginia college or university accounting program in the fall semester.

Academic Fields/Career Goals: Accounting.

Award: Scholarship for use in sophomore, junior, senior, graduate, or postgraduate years; not renewable. *Number:* up to 26. *Amount:* $1000–$5000.

Eligibility Requirements: Applicant must be enrolled or expecting to enroll full- or part-time at a two-year or four-year institution or university; resident of Virginia and studying in Virginia. Applicant must have 2.5 GPA or higher. Available to U.S. citizens.

Application Requirements: Application form, application form may be submitted online (http://www.vscpa.com/Scholarships), essay, recommendations or references, resume, transcript. *Deadline:* April 1.

Contact: Tracey Zink, Academic and Career Development Coordinator
Phone: 800-612-9427
E-mail: tzink@vscpa.com

WASHINGTON SOCIETY OF CERTIFIED PUBLIC ACCOUNTANTS

http://www.wscpa.org/

WA CPA FOUNDATION SCHOLARSHIPS

The Washington CPA Foundation is a 501(c)(3) not-for-profit foundation committed to ensuring that Washington's diverse communities have awareness of and access to both high quality accounting education and the resources required to make sound financial decisions. In order to make our vision a reality, the Foundation funds education and research in the field of accountancy, scholarships for accounting students, programs designed to improve accounting education and expand knowledge within the profession, and initiatives designed to improve the public's skills in personal financial management.

Academic Fields/Career Goals: Accounting.

Award: Scholarship for use in sophomore, junior, senior, graduate, or postgraduate years; not renewable. *Number:* 70. *Amount:* $5000.

Eligibility Requirements: Applicant must be enrolled or expecting to enroll full- or part-time at a four-year institution or university and studying in Washington. Applicant must have 3.0 GPA or higher. Available to U.S. and non-U.S. citizens.

Application Requirements: Application form, essay. *Deadline:* February 14.

Contact: Ms. Monette Anderson, Manager of Student Initiatives
Washington Society of Certified Public Accountants
902 140th Ave NE
Bellevue, WA 98005
Phone: 425-586-1118
E-mail: manderson@wscpa.org

WYOMING TRUCKING ASSOCIATION SCHOLARSHIP FUND TRUST

http://www.wytruck.org/

WYOMING TRUCKING ASSOCIATION SCHOLARSHIP TRUST FUND

To qualify, students must (1) be a graduate of a Wyoming high school; (2) plan to pursue a course of study which will lead to a career in the Highway Transportation Industry with the following approved courses of study: business management, computer skills, accounting, office procedures and management, safety, diesel mechanics and truck driving; (3) attend a Wyoming school (University, Community College or trade school) approved by the WTA Scholarship Committee.

Academic Fields/Career Goals: Accounting; Business/Consumer Services; Communications; Computer Science/Data Processing; Marketing; Trade/Technical Specialties; Transportation.

Award: Scholarship for use in freshman, sophomore, junior, or senior years; not renewable. *Number:* 4–8. *Amount:* $500–$1500.

Eligibility Requirements: Applicant must be enrolled or expecting to enroll full-time at a two-year or four-year or technical institution or university; resident of Wyoming and studying in Wyoming. Available to U.S. citizens.

Application Requirements: Application form, community service, essay, financial need analysis. *Deadline:* March 5.

Contact: Kathy Cundall, Administrative Assistant
Phone: 307-234-1579
E-mail: khcundall@aol.com

ADVERTISING/PUBLIC RELATIONS

ASIAN AMERICAN JOURNALISTS ASSOCIATION, SEATTLE CHAPTER

http://www.aajaseattle.org/

NORTHWEST JOURNALISTS OF COLOR SCHOLARSHIP

One-time award for Washington state high school and college students seeking careers in journalism. Awardees are also paired with a mentor, expected to join AAJA, and participate in AAJA activities. The program also offers The Founder's Scholarship, which pays for registration and airfare so a student may attend the AAJA National Convention.

Academic Fields/Career Goals: Advertising/Public Relations; Communications; Filmmaking/Video; Journalism; Photojournalism/Photography; TV/Radio Broadcasting.

Award: Scholarship for use in freshman, sophomore, junior, or senior years; not renewable. *Number:* 1–5. *Amount:* $250–$1000.

Eligibility Requirements: Applicant must be of African, Chinese, Hispanic, Indian, Japanese, Korean, Lao/Hmong, Latin American/Caribbean, Lebanese, Mexican, Mongolian, Sub-Saharan African, Syrian, Turkish, Vietnamese, Yemeni heritage; American Indian/Alaska Native, Asian/Pacific Islander, Black (non-Hispanic); enrolled or expecting to enroll full- or part-time at a two-year or four-year or technical institution or university and resident of Washington. Applicant or parent of applicant must have employment or volunteer experience in journalism/broadcasting. Available to U.S. citizens.

Application Requirements: Application form, community service, essay, financial need analysis. *Deadline:* May 1.

Contact: Ms. Mai Hoang, AAJA Chapter Treasurer
Asian American Journalists Association, Seattle Chapter
Yakima Herald Republic
114 North Fourth Street
Yakima, WA 98909
Phone: 509-577-7724
E-mail: mhoang@yakimaherald.com

AUTOMOTIVE WOMEN'S ALLIANCE FOUNDATION

http://awafoundation.org/index.php

AUTOMOTIVE WOMEN'S ALLIANCE FOUNDATION SCHOLARSHIPS
• *See page 81*

DIGITAL THIRD COAST I NTERNET MARKETING

http://www.digitalthirdcoast.net/

DIGITAL MARKETING SCHOLARSHIP

In a 500+ word essay, share how you think digital marketing will develop in the next five to ten years, and what you think the industry will be like when you're out of school and working in the marketing industry. You may focus on how one aspect of digital marketing will change, or you can address how each branch of digital marketing will grow to interact with the others.

Academic Fields/Career Goals: Advertising/Public Relations; Business/Consumer Services; Marketing.

Award: Scholarship for use in freshman, sophomore, junior, or senior years; not renewable. *Number:* 1. *Amount:* $500.

Eligibility Requirements: Applicant must be enrolled or expecting to enroll full-time at a four-year institution. Applicant must have 2.5 GPA or higher. Available to U.S. citizens.

Application Requirements: Application form may be submitted online (http://www.digitalthirdcoast.net/blog/dtc-digital-marketing-scholarship), essay, personal photograph. *Deadline:* March 1.

Contact: Barry Dyke, Account Manager
Digital Third Coast Internet Marketing
2035 West Wabansia Avenue
Chicago, IL 60647
Phone: 773-897-0572
E-mail: bdyke@digitalthirdcoast.net

FUKUNAGA SCHOLARSHIP FOUNDATION

http://fukunagascholarship.com

FUKUNAGA SCHOLARSHIP FOUNDATION
• *See page 85*

HOUSE OF BLUES MUSIC FORWARD FOUNDATION

https://hobmusicforward.org/

TIFFANY GREEN OPERATOR SCHOLARSHIP AWARD

Established in the memory of Tiffany Green, US Concerts division supports women pursuing careers in live event operations, production and music engineering related fields of study. The $10,000 scholarship will expand the student's training and professional interactions through participation in educational opportunities.

Academic Fields/Career Goals: Advertising/Public Relations; Audiology; Business/Consumer Services; Communications; Economics; Hospitality Management; Human Resources; Marketing; Music.

Award: Scholarship for use in junior or senior years; not renewable. *Number:* 1. *Amount:* $10,000.

Eligibility Requirements: Applicant must be enrolled or expecting to enroll full-time at a four-year institution or university; female and must have an interest in music or music/singing. Applicant must have 3.0 GPA or higher.

Application Requirements: Application form, essay. *Deadline:* March 31.

Contact: Ms. Nazanin Fatemian, House of Blues Music Forward Foundation
House of Blues Music Forward Foundation
7060 Hollywood Boulevard, Floor 2
Los Angeles, CA 90028
Phone: 323-821-3946
E-mail: nfatemian@hobmusicforward.org

INTERNATIONAL FOODSERVICE EDITORIAL COUNCIL

http://www.ifeconline.com/

INTERNATIONAL FOODSERVICE EDITORIAL COUNCIL COMMUNICATIONS SCHOLARSHIP

Applicant must be a full-time student enrolled in an accredited postsecondary educational institution working toward an associate, Bachelor's, or Master's degree. Must demonstrate financial need, academic achievement, service orientation, and writing ability. Must have background, education, and interests indicating preparedness for entering careers in editorial or public relations within the foodservice industry.

Academic Fields/Career Goals: Advertising/Public Relations; Agribusiness; Agriculture; Communications; Culinary Arts; Food Science/Nutrition; Food Service/Hospitality; Graphics/Graphic Arts/Printing; Home Economics; Hospitality Management; Journalism; Literature/English/Writing; Marketing; Photojournalism/Photography.

Award: Scholarship for use in sophomore, junior, senior, graduate, or postgraduate years; not renewable. *Number:* 1–8. *Amount:* $250–$6000.

Eligibility Requirements: Applicant must be enrolled or expecting to enroll full-time at a two-year or four-year or technical institution or university and must have an interest in photography/photogrammetry/filmmaking or writing. Available to U.S. and non-U.S. citizens.

Application Requirements: Application form, essay. *Deadline:* March 15.

Contact: Jen Mac Kay, Executive Director
International Foodservice Editorial Council
PO Box 581
Pleasant Valley, NY 12569
Phone: 845-723-4434
E-mail: ifec@ifeconline.com

THE LAGRANT FOUNDATION

http://www.lagrantfoundation.org/

LAGRANT FOUNDATION SCHOLARSHIP FOR GRADUATES

Awards are for graduate minority students who are attending accredited four-year institutions and are pursuing careers in the fields of advertising, graphic design, marketing, and public relations. Must have a minimum of two academic semesters or one year left to complete his/her Master's degree from the time the scholarship is awarded. The applicant must make a one-year commitment to maintain contact with TLF to receive professional guidance and academic support. Minimum 3.2 GPA required.

Academic Fields/Career Goals: Advertising/Public Relations; Business/Consumer Services; Communications; Graphics/Graphic Arts/Printing; Marketing.

Award: Scholarship for use in sophomore, junior, senior, graduate, or postgraduate years; not renewable. *Amount:* $3250–$3750.

Eligibility Requirements: Applicant must be American Indian/Alaska Native, Asian/Pacific Islander, Black (non-Hispanic), Hispanic and enrolled or expecting to enroll full-time at an institution or university. Available to U.S. citizens.

Application Requirements: Application form, essay. *Deadline:* February 28.

Contact: Programs & Communications Associate
The LAGRANT Foundation
633 W. 5th Street, 48th Floor
Los Angeles, CA 90071
Phone: 323-469-8680 Ext. 223
E-mail: tlfinfo@lagrant.com

LAGRANT FOUNDATION SCHOLARSHIP FOR UNDERGRADUATES

Awards are for undergraduate minority students who are attending accredited four-year institutions and are pursuing careers in the fields of advertising, graphic design, marketing, and public relations. Must have at least one year to complete his/her degree from the time the scholarships are awarded. The applicant must make a one-year commitment to maintain contact with TLF to receive professional guidance and academic support. Minimum 3.0 GPA required.

Academic Fields/Career Goals: Advertising/Public Relations; Business/Consumer Services; Communications; Graphics/Graphic Arts/Printing; Marketing.

Award: Scholarship for use in freshman, sophomore, junior, or senior years; not renewable. *Amount:* $2000–$2500.

Eligibility Requirements: Applicant must be American Indian/Alaska Native, Asian/Pacific Islander, Black (non-Hispanic), Hispanic and enrolled or expecting to enroll full-time at a four-year institution or university. Available to U.S. citizens.

Application Requirements: Application form, essay. *Deadline:* February 28.

Contact: Programs & Communications Associate
The LAGRANT Foundation
633 W. 5th Street, 48th Floor
Los Angeles, CA 90071
Phone: 323-469-8680 Ext. 223
E-mail: tlfinfo@lagrant.com

NATIONAL ACADEMY OF TELEVISION ARTS AND SCIENCES, MICHIGAN CHAPTER

http://natasmichigan.org

DR. LYNNE BOYLE/JOHN SCHIMPF UNDERGRADUATE SCHOLARSHIP

This scholarship is for tuition for undergraduate school. Only Michigan residents are eligible for the scholarship. The university or college attended does not have to be a Michigan institution. Work submitted must be that done by the student which is representative of the students ability. Scholarships are awarded on the basis of merit. Student must be enrolled in a undergraduate program of an accredited 4-year college or university for their Junior and Senior years of study.

Academic Fields/Career Goals: Advertising/Public Relations; Communications; Filmmaking/Video; Journalism; Performing Arts; TV/Radio Broadcasting.

Award: Scholarship for use in junior or senior years; not renewable. *Number:* 1. *Amount:* $5000.

Eligibility Requirements: Applicant must be enrolled or expecting to enroll full- or part-time at a four-year institution or university and resident of Michigan. Applicant must have 3.0 GPA or higher. Available to U.S. citizens.

Application Requirements: Application form, essay. *Deadline:* April 8.

Contact: Adm. Stacia Mottley, Executive Director
National Academy of Television Arts and Sciences, Michigan Chapter
24903 Lois Lane
Southfield, MI 48075
Phone: 248-827-0931
E-mail: smottley@comcast.net

NATIVE AMERICAN JOURNALISTS ASSOCIATION

http://www.naja.com/

NATIVE AMERICAN JOURNALISTS ASSOCIATION SCHOLARSHIPS

One-time award for undergraduate study leading to journalism career at accredited colleges and universities. Applicants must be current members of Native-American Journalists Association or may join at time of application. Applicants must have proof of tribal association. Send cover letter, letters of reference, and work samples with application. Financial need considered.

Academic Fields/Career Goals: Advertising/Public Relations; Journalism; Photojournalism/Photography.

Award: Scholarship for use in freshman, sophomore, junior, senior, or graduate years; renewable. *Number:* 1–10. *Amount:* $500–$2000.

Eligibility Requirements: Applicant must be American Indian/Alaska Native; enrolled or expecting to enroll full-time at a two-year or four-year institution or university and must have an interest in writing. Applicant or parent of applicant must be member of Native American Journalists Association. Available to U.S. and Canadian citizens.

Application Requirements: Application form, community service, essay, financial need analysis, interview, personal photograph, portfolio. *Deadline:* June 30.

Contact: Jeffrey Palmer, Education Director
Phone: 405-325-9008
Fax: 866-325-7565
E-mail: jeffrey.p.palmer@ou.edu

NEBRASKA PRESS ASSOCIATION

http://www.nebpress.com/

NEBRASKA PRESS ASSOCIATION FOUNDATION SCHOLARSHIP

Award for graduates of Nebraska high schools who have a minimum GPA of 2.5. Preference will be given to students who will be pursuing community journalism education at a Nebraska college or university.

Academic Fields/Career Goals: Advertising/Public Relations; Communications; Graphics/Graphic Arts/Printing; Journalism; Marketing; Photojournalism/Photography.

Award: Scholarship for use in freshman, sophomore, or junior years; not renewable. *Number:* 2–4. *Amount:* $2000.

Eligibility Requirements: Applicant must be enrolled or expecting to enroll full-time at a four-year institution or university; resident of Nebraska and studying in Nebraska. Applicant must have 2.5 GPA or higher. Available to U.S. citizens.

Application Requirements: Application form, essay. *Deadline:* February 20.

Contact: Allen Beermann, Executive Director
Phone: 402-476-2851
Fax: 402-476-2942
E-mail: abeermann@nebpress.com

OHIO NEWS MEDIA FOUNDATION

http://www.ohionews.org

HAROLD K. DOUTHIT SCHOLARSHIP

$1500 scholarship for student enrolled as a sophomore, junior or senior at an Ohio college or university. Must be majoring in journalism, marketing, communications, or advertising. Minimum 3.0 GPA required.

Academic Fields/Career Goals: Advertising/Public Relations; Communications; Journalism; Marketing.

Award: Scholarship for use in sophomore, junior, or senior years; not renewable. *Number:* 1. *Amount:* $1500.

Eligibility Requirements: Applicant must be enrolled or expecting to enroll full-time at a four-year institution or university; resident of Ohio and studying in Ohio. Applicant must have 3.0 GPA or higher. Available to U.S. citizens.

Application Requirements: Application form, autobiography, financial need analysis. *Deadline:* March 31.

Contact: Ms. Michelle Widner, Administrative Assistant
Ohio News Media Foundation
1335 Dublin Road, Suite 216B
Columbus, OH 43215
Phone: 614-486-6677 Ext. 1010
E-mail: mwidner@ohionews.org

OHIO NEWS MEDIA FOUNDATION MINORITY SCHOLARSHIP

One scholarship for a minority high school senior in Ohio who plans to major in a field relevant to the newspaper industry, particularly journalism, advertising, marketing, or a communications degree program. Applicants must plan to enroll for fall classes at an accredited college or university within the United States. Must be African-American, Hispanic, Asian-American or American-Indian. A minimum high school GPA of 2.5 required.

Academic Fields/Career Goals: Advertising/Public Relations; Communications; Journalism; Marketing.

Award: Scholarship for use in freshman year; not renewable. *Number:* 1. *Amount:* $1500.

Eligibility Requirements: Applicant must be American Indian/Alaska Native, Asian/Pacific Islander, Black (non-Hispanic), Hispanic; high school student; planning to enroll or expecting to enroll full-time at a four-year institution or university and resident of Ohio. Applicant must have 2.5 GPA or higher. Available to U.S. citizens.

Application Requirements: Application form, autobiography. *Deadline:* March 31.

Contact: Ms. Michelle "Mike" Widner, Admin. Asst.
Ohio News Media Foundation
1335 Dublin Road, Suite 216B
Columbus, OH 43215
Phone: 614-486-6677 Ext. 1010
E-mail: mwidner@ohionews.org

OHIO NEWS MEDIA FOUNDATION UNIVERSITY JOURNALISM SCHOLARSHIP

The Foundation will award 2 scholarships of $2,000 each for a student currently enrolled in an Ohio college or university and majoring in a field relevant to the newspaper industry, particularly journalism, advertising, marketing, or communications degree program. Preference will be given to students demonstrating a career commitment to newspaper journalism. A minimum GPA of 2.5 required.

Academic Fields/Career Goals: Advertising/Public Relations; Communications; Journalism; Marketing.

Award: Scholarship for use in sophomore, junior, or senior years; not renewable. *Number:* 2. *Amount:* $2000.

Eligibility Requirements: Applicant must be enrolled or expecting to enroll full-time at a four-year institution or university; resident of Ohio and studying in Ohio. Applicant must have 2.5 GPA or higher. Available to U.S. citizens.

Application Requirements: Application form, autobiography. *Deadline:* March 31.

Contact: Ms. Michelle Widner, Administrative Assistant
Ohio News Media Foundation
1335 Dublin Road, Suite 216B
Columbus, OH 43215
Phone: 614-486-6677 Ext. 1010
E-mail: mwidner@ohionews.org

ONWA ANNUAL SCHOLARSHIP

One-time scholarship. Applicant may be a male or female student enrolled as a junior or senior in an Ohio college or university and majoring in a field relevant to the newspaper industry, particularly journalism, advertising, marketing, or communications degree program. Must be U.S. citizen.

Academic Fields/Career Goals: Advertising/Public Relations; Communications; Journalism; Marketing.

Award: Scholarship for use in junior or senior years; not renewable. *Number:* 1. *Amount:* $2000.

Eligibility Requirements: Applicant must be enrolled or expecting to enroll full-time at a four-year institution or university; resident of Ohio and studying in Ohio. Applicant must have 2.5 GPA or higher. Available to U.S. citizens.

Application Requirements: Application form, essay, financial need analysis. *Deadline:* March 31.

Contact: Ms. Michelle "Mike" Widner, Admin. Asst.
Ohio News Media Foundation
1335 Dublin Road, Suite 216B
Columbus, OH 43215
Phone: 614-486-6677 Ext. 1010
E-mail: mwidner@ohionews.org

PUBLIC RELATIONS STUDENT SOCIETY OF AMERICA

http://www.prssa.org/

PUBLIC RELATIONS SOCIETY OF AMERICA MULTICULTURAL AFFAIRS SCHOLARSHIP

Two, one-time $1500 awards for members of a principal minority group who are in their junior or senior year at an accredited four-year college or university. Must have at least a 3.0 GPA and be preparing for career in public relations or communications. Must be a full-time student and U.S. citizen.

Academic Fields/Career Goals: Advertising/Public Relations; Communications.

Award: Scholarship for use in freshman, sophomore, junior, or senior years; not renewable. *Number:* 2. *Amount:* $1500.

Eligibility Requirements: Applicant must be American Indian/Alaska Native, Asian/Pacific Islander, Black (non-Hispanic), Hispanic and enrolled or expecting to enroll full-time at a four-year institution or university. Applicant must have 3.0 GPA or higher. Available to U.S. citizens.

Application Requirements: Application form, essay, financial need analysis. *Deadline:* April 18.

Contact: Dora Tovar, Chair, Multicultural Communications Section
Public Relations Student Society of America
33 Maiden Lane, 11th Floor
New York, NY 10038-5150
Phone: 212-460-1476
E-mail: jeneen.garcia@prsa.org

RHODE ISLAND FOUNDATION

http://www.rifoundation.org/

J. D. EDSAL SCHOLARSHIP

Award to benefit Rhode Island residents studying advertising (public relations, marketing, graphic design, film, video, television, or broadcast production) with the expectation of pursuing a career in one of more of these fields. Applicants must be college undergraduates, sophomore or above.

Academic Fields/Career Goals: Advertising/Public Relations; Communications; Filmmaking/Video; Graphics/Graphic Arts/Printing; Marketing; TV/Radio Broadcasting.

Award: Scholarship for use in sophomore, junior, or senior years; renewable. *Amount:* $500–$1000.

Eligibility Requirements: Applicant must be enrolled or expecting to enroll full-time at a four-year institution or university and resident of Rhode Island. Available to U.S. citizens.

Application Requirements: Application form, essay, financial need analysis, recommendations or references, self-addressed stamped envelope with application, transcript.

Contact: Libby Monahan, Funds Administrator
Phone: 401-274-4564 Ext. 3117
E-mail: libbym@rifoundation.org

SCARLETT FAMILY FOUNDATION SCHOLARSHIP PROGRAM

http://www.scarlettfoundation.org/

SCHOLARSHIP FOR STUDENTS PURSUING A BUSINESS OR STEM DEGREE
• *See page 91*

SPECIALTY EQUIPMENT MARKET ASSOCIATION

http://www.sema.org/

SEMA MEMORIAL SCHOLARSHIP FUND
• *See page 92*

STRAIGHTFORWARD MEDIA

http://www.straightforwardmedia.com/

STRAIGHTFORWARD MEDIA BUSINESS SCHOOL SCHOLARSHIP

Scholarship of $500 for undergraduate and graduate students pursuing a business-related degree, including but not limited to economics, finance, marketing, and management. Students pursuing an online business degree are also eligible. Awarded four times per year. Deadlines: March 31, June 30, September 30, and December 31.

Academic Fields/Career Goals: Advertising/Public Relations; Business/Consumer Services; Economics; Finance; Marketing.

Award: Scholarship for use in freshman, sophomore, junior, senior, or graduate years; not renewable. *Number:* 4. *Amount:* $500.

Eligibility Requirements: Applicant must be enrolled or expecting to enroll full- or part-time at a two-year or four-year or technical institution or university. Available to U.S. and non-U.S. citizens.

Application Requirements: Essay. *Deadline:* varies.

Contact: Scholarship Committee
Phone: 605-348-3042

STRAIGHTFORWARD MEDIA MEDIA & COMMUNICATIONS SCHOLARSHIP

Scholarship of $500 available to students of media and communications. Must be majoring in programs such as journalism, broadcasting, advertising, speech, mass communications, or marketing. Awarded four times per year. Deadlines are March 31, June 30, September 30, and

December 31. For more information, visit website at http://www.straightforwardmedia.com/media/form.php.

Academic Fields/Career Goals: Advertising/Public Relations; Communications; Journalism; Marketing; Photojournalism/Photography; TV/Radio Broadcasting.

Award: Scholarship for use in freshman, sophomore, junior, or senior years; not renewable. *Number:* 4. *Amount:* $500.

Eligibility Requirements: Applicant must be enrolled or expecting to enroll full- or part-time at a two-year or four-year or technical institution or university. Available to U.S. and non-U.S. citizens.

Application Requirements: Essay. *Deadline:* varies.

Contact: Scholarship Committee
Phone: 605-348-3042

TAMPA BAY TIMES FUND, INC.

http://www.tampabay.com/fund

TAMPA BAY TIMES FUND CAREER JOURNALISM SCHOLARSHIPS

Scholarship to high school seniors in the Tampa Bay Times' audience area who have a demonstrated interest in pursuing journalism/media major in college and career after graduation.

Academic Fields/Career Goals: Advertising/Public Relations; Communications; Journalism; Marketing; Photojournalism/Photography; TV/Radio Broadcasting.

Award: Scholarship for use in freshman, sophomore, junior, or senior years; renewable. *Number:* 3. *Amount:* $2500.

Eligibility Requirements: Applicant must be high school student; age 18-22; planning to enroll or expecting to enroll full-time at a four-year institution or university; single and resident of Florida. Applicant must have 3.0 GPA or higher. Available to U.S. citizens.

Application Requirements: Application form, essay, portfolio. *Deadline:* January 23.

Contact: Nancy Waclawek, Scholarship Administrator
Phone: 813-340-4125
E-mail: tbtschls@gmail.com

UNITED NEGRO COLLEGE FUND

http://www.uncf.org/

PROCTER & GAMBLE GENERAL SCHOLARSHIP
• *See page 94*

UNCF/ALLIANCE DATA SCHOLARSHIP AND INTERNSHIP PROGRAM

Up to $5000 scholarship; summer internship; stipend and travel expenses to the UNCF Student Leadership Conference. Applicant must be an under-represented minority college student enrolled at an accredited four-year college or university with preference given to students attending private or public historically black colleges and universities. (Students residing in/or attending school near Plano, TX and Atlanta, GA will receive priority consideration for internships designated in those locations). Must be classified as sophomores (rising juniors) or juniors (rising seniors) at time of application and demonstrate unmet financial need.

Academic Fields/Career Goals: Advertising/Public Relations; Business/Consumer Services; Communications; Computer Science/Data Processing; Human Resources; Marketing.

Award: Scholarship for use in junior or senior years.

Eligibility Requirements: Applicant must be American Indian/Alaska Native, Asian/Pacific Islander, Black (non-Hispanic), Hispanic and enrolled or expecting to enroll at a four-year institution or university. Applicant must have 3.0 GPA or higher. Available to U.S. citizens.

Application Requirements: Application form, essay, financial need analysis. *Deadline:* February 10.

Contact: Mary Williams, Director of Outreach and Recruitment
Phone: 800-331-2244

AFRICAN STUDIES

ABO CAPITAL
http://www.abocapital.net/

CHANGE AFRICA IMPROVE THE WORLD SCHOLARSHIP

Africa is a continent bursting with economic opportunities. Under the right circumstances, it could become a global leader across industries including technology, sustainability, and agriculture. Show us how you can change Africa to change the world. In 500 words or less, demonstrate your knowledge of Africa and explain your deep conceptual ideas for tapping into its economic potential and bettering the continent. These ideas could be your own or showcase your support of projects already in development. The Grand Prize essay will win a scholarship for one full semester of college, up to $30,000. The top three essays will win a 5-night all-expenses paid trip to Angola. Entries will be due February 28, 2018. Finalists will be notified by March 31, 2018. Participants can submit their essays to scholarship@abocapital.net. Must be 18 years or older and currently enrolled in undergraduate, graduate, or university program to enter. Please attach the essay as a word document. Include contact information, proof of enrollment, declared major, and age.

Academic Fields/Career Goals: African Studies.

Award: Prize for use in freshman, sophomore, junior, senior, graduate, or postgraduate years; not renewable. *Number:* 3. *Amount:* $30,000.

Eligibility Requirements: Applicant must be enrolled or expecting to enroll full-time at a four-year institution or university. Available to U.S. and Canadian citizens.

Application Requirements: Application form, essay. *Deadline:* February 28.

Contact: Meghan Busch, Senior Account Executive
New York, NY
E-mail: scholarship@abocapital.net

AGRIBUSINESS

ABBIE SARGENT MEMORIAL SCHOLARSHIP INC.
http://www.nhfarmbureau.org/

ABBIE SARGENT MEMORIAL SCHOLARSHIP

Up to three awards between $400 and $700 will be provided to deserving New Hampshire residents, planning to attend an institution of higher learning. Must be a U.S. citizen.

Academic Fields/Career Goals: Agribusiness; Agriculture; Animal/Veterinary Sciences; Environmental Science; Home Economics; Horticulture/Floriculture.

Award: Scholarship for use in freshman, sophomore, junior, senior, graduate, or postgraduate years; not renewable. *Number:* 1–5. *Amount:* $400–$700.

Eligibility Requirements: Applicant must be enrolled or expecting to enroll full- or part-time at a two-year or four-year or technical institution or university and resident of New Hampshire. Applicant or parent of applicant must have employment or volunteer experience in agriculture. Available to U.S. citizens.

Application Requirements: Application form, driver's license, financial need analysis, personal photograph. *Deadline:* March 15.

Contact: Diane Clary, Administrator
Abbie Sargent Memorial Scholarship Inc.
Abbie Sargent Scholarship
295 Sheep Davis Road
Concord, NH 03301
Phone: 603-224-1934
E-mail: dianec@nhfarmbureau.org

CHS FOUNDATION
http://www.chsfoundation.org/

CHS FOUNDATION HIGH SCHOOL SCHOLARSHIPS

Scholarships available to graduating high school seniors who plan to enroll in an agricultural-related program of study in a two-year or four-year college or university. Student must be a U.S. citizen. For additional information and an application, see website http://www.chsfoundation.org.

Academic Fields/Career Goals: Agribusiness; Agriculture; Horticulture/Floriculture.

Award: Scholarship for use in freshman year; not renewable. *Number:* 50. *Amount:* $1000.

Eligibility Requirements: Applicant must be high school student and planning to enroll or expecting to enroll full- or part-time at a two-year or four-year or technical institution or university. Available to U.S. citizens.

Application Requirements: Application form, essay, recommendations or references, transcript. *Deadline:* April 1.

Contact: Scholarship Committee
Phone: 800-814-0506
E-mail: info@chsfoundation.org

CHS FOUNDATION TWO-YEAR COLLEGE SCHOLARSHIPS

Non-renewable scholarship available to first-year agricultural students at a two-year college. Must be studying an agricultural-related major; scholarship is intended for the second year of study. Must be a U.S. citizen. For additional information and application, see website http://www.chsfoundation.org.

Academic Fields/Career Goals: Agribusiness; Agriculture; Horticulture/Floriculture.

Award: Scholarship for use in sophomore year; not renewable. *Number:* 25. *Amount:* $1000.

Eligibility Requirements: Applicant must be enrolled or expecting to enroll full- or part-time at a two-year or technical institution. Available to U.S. citizens.

Application Requirements: Application form, essay, recommendations or references, transcript. *Deadline:* April 1.

Contact: Scholarship Committee
Phone: 800-814-0506
E-mail: info@chsfoundation.org

CHS FOUNDATION UNIVERSITY SCHOLARSHIPS

Renewable scholarship available for students in sophomore, junior, or senior year currently studying agriculture at select universities around the nation. Preference given to students interested in a career in or studying agricultural-based cooperatives and working towards a degree in agribusiness or production agriculture. Students apply to the School of Agriculture or Financial Aid Office at one of the participating universities and follow individual procedures and deadlines for that institution. For additional information and a list of participating universities, see website http://www.chsfoundation.org.

Academic Fields/Career Goals: Agribusiness; Agriculture.

Award: Scholarship for use in sophomore, junior, or senior years; not renewable. *Number:* up to 150. *Amount:* $1000.

Eligibility Requirements: Applicant must be enrolled or expecting to enroll full- or part-time at a four-year institution or university. Available to U.S. citizens.

Application Requirements: Application form, essay, recommendations or references, transcript.

Contact: Scholarship Committee
Phone: 800-814-0506
E-mail: info@chsfoundation.org

FUKUNAGA SCHOLARSHIP FOUNDATION
http://fukunagascholarship.com

FUKUNAGA SCHOLARSHIP FOUNDATION
• *See page 85*

HERB SOCIETY OF AMERICA, WESTERN RESERVE UNIT

http://www.westernreserveherbsociety.org/

HORTICULTURE SCHOLARSHIP FROM FRANCIS SYLVIA ZVERINA

Awards are given to needy Ohio students who plan a career in horticulture or related field. Preference will be given to applicants whose horticultural career goals involve teaching, research, or work in the public or nonprofit sector, such as public gardens, botanical gardens, parks, arboreta, city planning, public education, and awareness. Students must be America citizens. Applications are only accepted online.

Academic Fields/Career Goals: Agribusiness; Agriculture; Biology; Environmental Science; Horticulture/Floriculture; Landscape Architecture; Natural Sciences.

Award: Scholarship for use in junior or senior years; not renewable. *Number:* 1. *Amount:* $9000.

Eligibility Requirements: Applicant must be enrolled or expecting to enroll full-time at a four-year institution or university; resident of Ohio and studying in Ohio. Applicant must have 3.0 GPA or higher. Available to U.S. citizens.

Application Requirements: Application form, essay. *Deadline:* February 28.

Contact: Ms. Carla Linn—WRHS Scholarship Committee
Herb Society of America, Western Reserve Unit
Cleveland Botanical Garden
11030 East Boulevard
Cleveland, OH 44106
E-mail: scholarship@westernreserveherbsociety.org

HORTICULTURE SCHOLARSHIP OF THE WESTERN RESERVE HERB SOCIETY

Awards are given to needy students who plan a career in horticulture or related field. Preference will be given to applicants whose horticultural career goals involve teaching, research, or work in the public or nonprofit sector, such as public gardens, botanical gardens, parks, arboreta, city planning, public education and awareness.

Academic Fields/Career Goals: Agribusiness; Agriculture; Biology; Environmental Science; Horticulture/Floriculture; Landscape Architecture.

Award: Scholarship for use in junior or senior years; not renewable. *Number:* 1. *Amount:* $7500.

Eligibility Requirements: Applicant must be enrolled or expecting to enroll full-time at a four-year institution or university. Applicant must have 3.0 GPA or higher. Available to U.S. citizens.

Application Requirements: Application form, essay. *Deadline:* February 28.

Contact: Ms. Carla Linn—WRHS Scholarship Committee
Herb Society of America, Western Reserve Unit
c/o Cleveland Botanical Garden
11030 East Blvd.
Cleveland, OH 44106
E-mail: scholarship@westernreserveherbsociety.org

HOLSTEIN ASSOCIATION USA INC.

http://www.holsteinusa.com/

ROBERT H. RUMLER SCHOLARSHIP

Awards to encourage deserving and qualified persons with an established interest in the dairy field, who have demonstrated leadership qualities and managerial abilities to pursue a master's degree in business administration.

Academic Fields/Career Goals: Agribusiness; Business/Consumer Services.

Award: Scholarship for use in freshman, sophomore, junior, senior, or graduate years; not renewable. *Number:* 1. *Amount:* $3000.

Eligibility Requirements: Applicant must be enrolled or expecting to enroll full-time at an institution or university and must have an interest in leadership. Applicant must have 3.0 GPA or higher. Available to U.S. and non-U.S. citizens.

Application Requirements: Application form, essay, personal photograph, recommendations or references, transcript. *Deadline:* April 15.

Contact: John Meyer, Chief Executive Officer
Holstein Association USA Inc.
One Holstein Place, PO Box 808
Brattleboro, VT 05302-0808
Phone: 802-254-4551
Fax: 802-254-8251
E-mail: jmeyer@holstein.com

HORTICULTURAL RESEARCH INSTITUTE

http://www.hriresearch.org/

BRYAN A. CHAMPION MEMORIAL SCHOLARSHIP

On November 10, 2011, Bryan A. Champion, president of Herman Losely and Son, Inc. located in Perry, Ohio, passed away at the age of 47. Champion was diagnosed with cancer in 2007, and fought a courageous 4-year battle to try to beat the devastating disease. Champion was a 5th generation nurseryman with a passion for the nursery and landscape industry. During his career he was involved with local, state and national associations that represent the industry. He sought to advance the industry through sound leadership, volunteer participation, and peer-to-peer networking and education events. He was a Buckeye, and graduated from Ohio State University (OSU) in 1987. Champion understood the value of a quality education and the importance of industry research. During his career at Herman Losely and Son, Inc., he worked with OSU and the United States of America- Agricultural Research Service to successfully solve industry issues. In honor of Champion's legacy and dedication to the nursery and landscape industry, donations have been received from his peers to establish The Bryan A. Champion Memorial Scholarship Fund. Each year, Champion's legacy will be remembered when the fund provides a student scholarship to a deserving horticultural student. It is our hope that each recipient will show a similar passion for the industry as Champion exhibited throughout his life. Applicant must be enrolled in an accredited undergraduate or graduate: landscape, horticulture or related discipline at a two or four-year institution. Students in vocational agriculture programs will also be considered. Undergraduate: Applicant must have at least a sophomore standing in a four-year curriculum or senior standing in a two-year curriculum as of the fall semester of scholarship application year. Graduate: All applicants in graduate school regardless of year in school may apply.

Academic Fields/Career Goals: Agribusiness; Entomology; Horticulture/Floriculture; Landscape Architecture.

Award: Scholarship for use in sophomore, junior, senior, or graduate years; not renewable. *Number:* 1. *Amount:* $1000.

Eligibility Requirements: Applicant must be enrolled or expecting to enroll full-time at a two-year or four-year institution or university and studying in Ohio. Available to U.S. citizens.

Application Requirements: Application form, application form may be submitted online (http://hriresearch.org/index.cfm?page=Content&categoryID=168&ID=7), essay, financial need analysis, recommendations or references, resume, transcript. *Deadline:* May 31.

Contact: Teresa Jodon, Executive Director
Horticultural Research Institute
1200 G Street, NW
Suite 800
Washington, DC 20005
Phone: 202-695-2474
Fax: 888-761-7883
E-mail: scholarships@hriresearch.org

TIMOTHY AND PALMER W. BIGELOW JR, SCHOLARSHIP

Award for students who are enrolled in accredited undergraduate or graduate landscape/horticulture program. Must be resident of Connecticut, Maine, Massachusetts, New Hampshire, Rhode Island, or Vermont. Undergraduates must have a GPA of 2.25. Financial need, desire to work in nursery industry are factors. For more information, visit website http://www.hriresearch.org. Application must be completed on the HRI website.

Academic Fields/Career Goals: Agribusiness; Entomology; Horticulture/Floriculture; Landscape Architecture.

Award: Scholarship for use in junior or senior years; not renewable. *Number:* 1. *Amount:* $3000.

Eligibility Requirements: Applicant must be enrolled or expecting to enroll full-time at a four-year institution or university and resident of Connecticut, Maine, Massachusetts, New Hampshire, Rhode Island, Vermont. Available to U.S. citizens.

Application Requirements: Application form, application form may be submitted online (http://www.hriresearch.org/index.cfm?page=Content&categoryID=168&ID=4), essay, financial need analysis, recommendations or references, resume, transcript. *Deadline:* May 31.

Contact: Ms. Teresa Jodon, Executive Director
Horticultural Research Institute
1200 G Street, NW, Suite 800
Washington, DC 20005
Phone: 202-695-2474
Fax: 888-761-7883
E-mail: scholarships@hriresearch.org

INTERNATIONAL FOODSERVICE EDITORIAL COUNCIL

http://www.ifeconline.com/

INTERNATIONAL FOODSERVICE EDITORIAL COUNCIL COMMUNICATIONS SCHOLARSHIP
• *See page 96*

MAINE DEPARTMENT OF AGRICULTURE, FOOD AND RURAL RESOURCES

http://www.maine.gov/agriculture

MAINE RURAL REHABILITATION FUND SCHOLARSHIP PROGRAM

One-time scholarship open to Maine residents enrolled in or accepted by any school, college, or university. Must be full-time and demonstrate financial need. Those opting for a Maine institution given preference. Major must lead to an agricultural career. Minimum 3.0 GPA required.

Academic Fields/Career Goals: Agribusiness; Agriculture; Animal/Veterinary Sciences.

Award: Scholarship for use in freshman, sophomore, junior, senior, graduate, or postgraduate years; not renewable. *Number:* 10–20. *Amount:* $800–$2000.

Eligibility Requirements: Applicant must be enrolled or expecting to enroll full-time at a two-year or four-year or technical institution or university and resident of Maine. Applicant must have 3.0 GPA or higher. Available to U.S. citizens.

Application Requirements: Application form, driver's license, financial need analysis, transcript. *Deadline:* June 15.

Contact: Jane Aiudi, Director of Marketing
Phone: 207-287-7628
Fax: 207-287-5576
E-mail: jane.aiudi@maine.gov

NATIONAL CATTLEMEN'S FOUNDATION

http://www.nationalcattlemensfoundation.org/

CME BEEF INDUSTRY SCHOLARSHIP

Ten $1500 scholarships will be awarded to students who intend to pursue a career in the beef industry, including areas such as agricultural education, communications, production, or research. Must be enrolled as an undergraduate student in a four-year institution.

Academic Fields/Career Goals: Agribusiness; Agriculture; Communications.

Award: Scholarship for use in freshman, sophomore, junior, or senior years; not renewable. *Number:* 10. *Amount:* $1500.

Eligibility Requirements: Applicant must be enrolled or expecting to enroll full-time at a four-year institution or university. Available to U.S. citizens.

Application Requirements: Application form, essay, recommendations or references, transcript. *Deadline:* varies.

Contact: RoxAnn Johnson, Executive Director
Phone: 303-850-3388
Fax: 303-694-7372
E-mail: mcf@beef.org

NATIONAL DAIRY SHRINE

http://www.dairyshrine.org/

NATIONAL DAIRY SHRINE/MAURICE E. CORE SCHOLARSHIP

Available to college freshman who are majoring in a dairy/animal industry related field with interest in working in the dairy industry in the future. Scholarship is based on leadership abilities, volunteerism, activities and plans for the future.

Academic Fields/Career Goals: Agribusiness; Agriculture.

Award: Scholarship for use in sophomore year; not renewable. *Number:* 1–4. *Amount:* $1000.

Eligibility Requirements: Applicant must be enrolled or expecting to enroll full-time at a four-year institution or university. Applicant must have 2.5 GPA or higher. Available to U.S. citizens.

Application Requirements: Application form, personal photograph. *Deadline:* April 15.

Contact: Executive Director
E-mail: info@dairyshrine.org

NDS STUDENT RECOGNITION AWARD

Awards available to college seniors enrolled in dairy science courses. Applicants must be nominated by their college or university professor and must intend to continue in the dairy field. A college or university may nominate up to 2 applicants.

Academic Fields/Career Goals: Agribusiness; Agriculture; Animal/Veterinary Sciences; Food Science/Nutrition.

Award: Scholarship for use in senior year; not renewable. *Number:* 2–9. *Amount:* $1000–$2000.

Eligibility Requirements: Applicant must be enrolled or expecting to enroll full-time at a four-year institution or university. Applicant must have 3.0 GPA or higher. Available to U.S. and Canadian citizens.

Application Requirements: Application form, personal photograph. *Deadline:* April 15.

Contact: Executive Director
E-mail: info@dairyshrine.org

NATIONAL POULTRY AND FOOD DISTRIBUTORS ASSOCIATION

http://www.npfda.org/

NATIONAL POULTRY AND FOOD DISTRIBUTORS ASSOCIATION SCHOLARSHIP FOUNDATION

The scholarships are awarded to full-time students in their junior or senior years at a U.S. college pursuing degrees in poultry science, food science, Food Marketing, agricultural business, or other related areas of study pertaining to the poultry and food industries. Dietetics does not qualify. Must attend U.S. College or university full time.

Academic Fields/Career Goals: Agribusiness; Agriculture; Animal/Veterinary Sciences; Food Science/Nutrition; Food Service/Hospitality.

Award: Scholarship for use in junior or senior years; not renewable. *Number:* 5. *Amount:* $4000.

Eligibility Requirements: Applicant must be enrolled or expecting to enroll full-time at a four-year institution or university. Available to U.S. citizens.

Application Requirements: Application form, essay. *Deadline:* May 31.

Contact: Kristin McWhorter, Executive Director
National Poultry and Food Distributors Association
2014 Osborne Road
Saint Marys, GA 31558
Phone: 770-535-9901
E-mail: kkm@npfda.org

NEW YORK STATE ASSOCIATION OF AGRICULTURAL FAIRS

http://www.nyfairs.org/

NEW YORK STATE ASSOCIATION OF AGRICULTURAL FAIRS AND NEW YORK STATE SHOWPEOPLE'S ASSOCIATION ANNUAL SCHOLARSHIP

Scholarship of $1000 given to New York high school seniors and students attending college and planning to pursue, or already pursuing a degree in an agricultural field, a fair management related field or an outdoor amusement related field.

Academic Fields/Career Goals: Agribusiness; Agriculture.

Award: Scholarship for use in freshman, sophomore, junior, senior, or graduate years; not renewable. *Number:* 6. *Amount:* $1000.

Eligibility Requirements: Applicant must be enrolled or expecting to enroll full-time at a two-year or four-year institution or university and resident of New York. Available to U.S. citizens.

Application Requirements: Application form, essay, recommendations or references, transcript. *Deadline:* April 9.

Contact: Mark St. Jacques, President
Phone: 518-692-2464
E-mail: markwashfair@aol.com

OHIO FARMERS UNION

http://www.ohfarmersunion.org/

VIRGIL THOMPSON MEMORIAL SCHOLARSHIP CONTEST

Award available to members of Ohio Farmers Union who are enrolled as full-time college sophomores, juniors or seniors. Awards of $1000 to winner and $500 each to two runners-up.

Academic Fields/Career Goals: Agribusiness; Agriculture.

Award: Scholarship for use in sophomore, junior, or senior years; not renewable. *Number:* 1–3. *Amount:* $500–$1000.

Eligibility Requirements: Applicant must be enrolled or expecting to enroll full-time at a four-year institution or university and resident of Ohio. Applicant or parent of applicant must be member of Ohio Farmers Union. Available to U.S. citizens.

Application Requirements: Application form, entry in a contest, essay. *Deadline:* December 31.

Contact: Ms. Linda Borton, Executive Director
Ohio Farmers Union
PO Box 363
Ottawa, OH 45875
Phone: 419-523-5300
E-mail: lborton@ohfarmersunion.org

SCARLETT FAMILY FOUNDATION SCHOLARSHIP PROGRAM

http://www.scarlettfoundation.org/

SCHOLARSHIP FOR STUDENTS PURSUING A BUSINESS OR STEM DEGREE

• *See page 91*

SOCIETY FOR RANGE MANAGEMENT

http://www.rangelands.org/

MASONIC RANGE SCIENCE SCHOLARSHIP

Renewable award for undergraduate students pursuing degree in agribusiness, agriculture, animal/veterinary sciences, earth science, natural resources and range science. Must maintain minimum 2.5 GPA for eligibility. Award amount varies each year.

Academic Fields/Career Goals: Agribusiness; Agriculture; Animal/Veterinary Sciences; Environmental Science; Natural Resources.

Award: Scholarship for use in freshman or sophomore years; renewable. *Number:* 1. *Amount:* $1000–$5000.

Eligibility Requirements: Applicant must be enrolled or expecting to enroll full-time at a four-year institution or university. Applicant must have 2.5 GPA or higher. Available to U.S. citizens.

Application Requirements: Application form, essay. *Deadline:* January 6.

Contact: Vicky Trujillo, Offices Services Manager
Society for Range Management
6901 South Pierce Street, Suite 230
Littleton, CO 80128
Phone: 303-986-3309
Fax: 303-986-3892
E-mail: info@rangelands.org

SOIL AND WATER CONSERVATION SOCIETY

http://www.swcs.org

DONALD A. WILLIAMS SCHOLARSHIP SOIL CONSERVATION SCHOLARSHIP

The scholarship provides financial assistance to members who are employed but wish to improve their technical or administrative competence in a conservation-related field. Applicants must be an SWCS member for at least 1 year and has completed at least one year of full-time employment in a natural resource conservation endeavor.

Academic Fields/Career Goals: Agribusiness; Agriculture; Biology; Earth Science; Environmental Science; Food Science/Nutrition; Hydrology; Natural Resources; Natural Sciences; Science, Technology, and Society.

Award: Scholarship for use in freshman, sophomore, junior, senior, graduate, or postgraduate years; not renewable. *Number:* 1–3. *Amount:* $700–$1000.

Eligibility Requirements: Applicant must be enrolled or expecting to enroll full- or part-time at a two-year or four-year or technical institution or university. Applicant or parent of applicant must be member of Soil and Water Conservation Society. Applicant or parent of applicant must have employment or volunteer experience in agriculture, environmental-related field. Available to U.S. and non-U.S. citizens.

Application Requirements: Application form, essay, recommendations or references. *Deadline:* February 13.

Contact: SWCS Scholarships Program Coordinator
Soil and Water Conservation Society
945 SW Ankeny Road
Ankeny, IA 50023-9723
Phone: 515-289-2331 Ext. 114
E-mail: scholarships@swcs.org

SOIL AND WATER CONSERVATION SOCIETY-NEW JERSEY CHAPTER

http://www.geocities.com/njswcs

EDWARD R. HALL SCHOLARSHIP

Two $500 scholarships awarded annually to students attending a New Jersey accredited college or New Jersey residents attending any out-of-state college. Undergraduate students, with the exception of freshmen, are eligible. Must be enrolled in a curriculum related to natural resources. Other areas related to conservation may qualify.

Academic Fields/Career Goals: Agribusiness; Agriculture; Animal/Veterinary Sciences; Biology; Earth Science; Environmental Science; Horticulture/Floriculture; Natural Resources; Natural Sciences.

Award: Scholarship for use in sophomore, junior, or senior years; not renewable. *Number:* 2. *Amount:* $500.

Eligibility Requirements: Applicant must be enrolled or expecting to enroll full-time at a two-year or four-year institution or university and resident of New Jersey. Available to U.S. and non-U.S. citizens.

Application Requirements: Application form, essay, financial need analysis, list of clubs and organizations related to natural resources of which applicant is a member, recommendations or references, transcript. *Deadline:* April 15.

Contact: Fireman E. Bear Chapter, c/o USDA-NRCS
Soil and Water Conservation Society-New Jersey Chapter
220 Davidson Avenue, Fourth Floor
Somerset, NJ 08873
Phone: 732-932-9295
E-mail: njswcs@yahoo.com

SOUTH DAKOTA BOARD OF REGENTS

http://www.sdbor.edu/

SOUTH DAKOTA BOARD OF REGENTS BJUGSTAD SCHOLARSHIP

Scholarship for graduating North or South Dakota high school senior who is a Native American. Must demonstrate academic achievement, character and leadership abilities. Must submit proof of tribal enrollment. One-time award of $500. Must rank in upper half of class or have a minimum 2.5 GPA. Must be pursuing studies in agriculture, agribusiness, or natural resources.

Academic Fields/Career Goals: Agribusiness; Agriculture; Natural Resources.

Award: Scholarship for use in freshman year; not renewable. *Number:* 2. *Amount:* $500.

Eligibility Requirements: Applicant must be American Indian/Alaska Native; high school student; planning to enroll or expecting to enroll full-time at a four-year institution or university; resident of North Dakota, South Dakota and must have an interest in leadership. Available to U.S. citizens.

Application Requirements: Application form. *Deadline:* February 23.

Contact: Kerri Richards, Student Services Coordinator
South Dakota Board of Regents
306 E. Capital Ave.
Suite 200
Pierre, SD 57501
Phone: 605-773-3455
E-mail: kerri.richards@sdbor.edu

SOUTH DAKOTA RETAILERS ASSOCIATION

http://www.sdra.org

SOUTH DAKOTA RETAILERS ASSOCIATION SCHOLARSHIP PROGRAM

Scholarships for students studying for a career in retailing. See application for eligible fields of study. Applicants must have graduated from a South Dakota high school or be enrolled in postsecondary school in South Dakota. Must complete required number of college or vocational school prior to receiving award, or have work experience in lieu of education.

Academic Fields/Career Goals: Agribusiness.

Award: Scholarship for use in sophomore, junior, senior, graduate, or postgraduate years; not renewable. *Number:* 10–15. *Amount:* $500–$2250.

Eligibility Requirements: Applicant must be enrolled or expecting to enroll full- or part-time at a two-year or four-year or technical institution or university. Available to U.S. and non-U.S. citizens.

Application Requirements: Application form, essay. *Deadline:* April 17.

Contact: Donna Leslie, Communications Director
South Dakota Retailers Association
SDRA
PO Box 638
Pierre, SD 57501
Phone: 800-658-5545
Fax: 605-224-2059
E-mail: donna@sdra.org

VERMONT SPACE GRANT CONSORTIUM

http://www.cems.uvm.edu/vsgc

VERMONT SPACE GRANT CONSORTIUM

Applicant must be a U.S. citizen, Vermont resident, graduating senior in a Vermont high school, or current undergraduate with a minimum 3.0 GPA enrolled full-time for the following academic year in a degree program in a Vermont institution of higher education. Must plan to pursue a professional career which has direct relevance to the U.S. aerospace industry and the goals of NASA. Three awards will be given to students enrolled in the Burlington Technical College Aviation Technology Program.

Academic Fields/Career Goals: Agribusiness; Applied Sciences; Aviation/Aerospace; Biology; Civil Engineering; Computer Science/Data Processing; Earth Science; Electrical Engineering/Electronics; Energy and Power Engineering; Engineering-Related Technologies; Engineering/Technology; Materials Science, Engineering, and Metallurgy; Mathematics; Mechanical Engineering; Physical Sciences; Science, Technology, and Society; Trade/Technical Specialties.

Award: Scholarship for use in freshman, sophomore, junior, or senior years; not renewable. *Number:* 6–9. *Amount:* $2500–$5000.

Eligibility Requirements: Applicant must be enrolled or expecting to enroll full-time at a two-year or four-year or technical institution or university; resident of Vermont and studying in Vermont. Applicant must have 3.0 GPA or higher. Available to U.S. citizens.

Application Requirements: Application form, essay. *Deadline:* March 1.

Contact: Ms. Debra Fraser, Program Coordinator
Vermont Space Grant Consortium
University of Vermont -Vermont Space Grant Consortium
210 Colchester Avenue, Room 120
Burlington, VT 05405-0156
Phone: 802-656-1429
E-mail: dfraser1@uvm.edu

AGRICULTURE

ABBIE SARGENT MEMORIAL SCHOLARSHIP INC.

http://www.nhfarmbureau.org/

ABBIE SARGENT MEMORIAL SCHOLARSHIP

• See page 100

ALABAMA GOLF COURSE SUPERINTENDENTS ASSOCIATION

http://www.agcsa.org/

ALABAMA GOLF COURSE SUPERINTENDENT'S ASSOCIATION'S DONNIE ARTHUR MEMORIAL SCHOLARSHIP

One-time award for students majoring in agriculture with an emphasis on turf-grass management. Must have a minimum 2.0 GPA. Applicant must be a full-time student. High school students not considered. Award available to U.S. citizens.

Academic Fields/Career Goals: Agriculture; Horticulture/Floriculture.

Award: Scholarship for use in freshman, sophomore, junior, or senior years; not renewable. *Number:* 1. *Amount:* $2000.

Eligibility Requirements: Applicant must be enrolled or expecting to enroll full-time at a two-year or four-year institution or university. Applicant must have 2.5 GPA or higher. Available to U.S. citizens.

Application Requirements: Application form, essay. *Deadline:* October 15.

Contact: Melanie Bonds, Secretary
Phone: 205-967-0397
E-mail: agcsa@charter.net

ALBERTA HERITAGE SCHOLARSHIP FUND

http://www.alis.alberta.ca/

ALBERTA BARLEY COMMISSION-EUGENE BOYKO MEMORIAL SCHOLARSHIP

Award of CAN$500 to recognize and encourage students entering the field of crop production and/or crop processing technology studies. Must be a Canadian citizen or landed immigrant attending an Alberta postsecondary institution. Students must be enrolled in the second or subsequent year of postsecondary study and taking courses that have an emphasis on crop production and/or crop processing technology. Awarded on basis of academic achievement. For additional information, see website http://alis.alberta.ca.

Academic Fields/Career Goals: Agriculture.

Award: Scholarship for use in sophomore, junior, or senior years; not renewable. *Number:* 1.

Eligibility Requirements: Applicant must be enrolled or expecting to enroll full-time at a four-year institution or university and resident of Alberta. Available to Canadian citizens.

Application Requirements: Application form, transcript. *Deadline:* August 1.

Contact: Scholarship Committee
          Phone: 780-427-8640
          E-mail: scholarships@gov.ab.ca

AMERICAN NATIONAL CATTLE WOMEN INC.

https://ancw.org

COLLEGIATE BEEF ADVOCACY PROGRAM

Award's purpose is to train young spokespersons in the beef industry. Applicant must be fully prepared to answer questions and debate focusing on topic related to beef consumption and distribution, as well as social factors related to the industry. The prize value is $2,000. Details and tools for preparation are available on the website https://ancw.org

Academic Fields/Career Goals: Agriculture.

Award: Scholarship for use in freshman, sophomore, junior, or senior years; not renewable. *Number:* 3. *Amount:* $2000.

Eligibility Requirements: Applicant must be hearing impaired, learning disabled, physically disabled, or visually impaired; of English heritage; age 18-24; enrolled or expecting to enroll full-time at a two-year or four-year institution or university and single. Applicant or parent of applicant must have employment or volunteer experience in agriculture, farming, food service. Applicant must be hearing impaired, learning disabled, physically disabled, or visually impaired. Applicant must have 2.5 GPA or higher. Available to U.S. citizens.

Application Requirements: Application form, community service, driver's license, personal photograph, portfolio. *Deadline:* October 31.

Contact: Evelyn Greene, Manager
          American National Cattle Women Inc.
          5802 Lee Rd 27
          Auburn, AL 36803
          Phone: 256-708-4833
          E-mail: ancw.cbap@gmail.com

AMERICAN OIL CHEMISTS' SOCIETY

http://www.aocs.org/

AOCS BIOTECHNOLOGY STUDENT EXCELLENCE AWARD

Award to recognize an outstanding paper in the field of biotechnology presented by a student at the AOCS Annual Meeting and Expo. Graduate students presenting within the Biotechnology Division technical program are eligible for the award.

Academic Fields/Career Goals: Agriculture; Chemical Engineering; Food Science/Nutrition.

Award: Prize for use in junior, senior, or graduate years; not renewable. *Number:* 1–3. *Amount:* $100–$300.

Eligibility Requirements: Applicant must be enrolled or expecting to enroll full- or part-time at a four-year institution or university. Available to U.S. and non-U.S. citizens.

Application Requirements: Essay, extended abstract, recommendations or references. *Deadline:* February 1.

Contact: Barbara Semeraro, Area Manager, Membership
          American Oil Chemists' Society
          AOCS
          PO Box 17190
          Urbana, IL 61803
          Phone: 217-693-4804
          Fax: 217-693-4849
          E-mail: awards@aocs.org

AMERICAN SOCIETY FOR ENOLOGY AND VITICULTURE

http://www.asev.org/

AMERICAN SOCIETY FOR ENOLOGY AND VITICULTURE SCHOLARSHIPS

One-time award for college juniors, seniors, and graduate students residing in North America and enrolled in a program studying viticulture, enology, or any field related to the wine and grape industry. Minimum 3.0 GPA for undergraduates; minimum 3.2 GPA for graduate students. Must be a resident of the United States, Canada, or Mexico.

Academic Fields/Career Goals: Agriculture; Chemical Engineering; Food Science/Nutrition; Horticulture/Floriculture.

Award: Scholarship for use in junior, senior, or graduate years; not renewable. *Number:* up to 30. *Amount:* $500–$4000.

Eligibility Requirements: Applicant must be enrolled or expecting to enroll full-time at a four-year institution or university. Applicant must have 3.0 GPA or higher. Available to U.S. and non-U.S. citizens.

Application Requirements: Application form, essay, financial need analysis, recommendations or references, transcript. *Deadline:* March 1.

Contact: Karli Kolb, Administrative Assistant
          Phone: 530-753-3142
          Fax: 530-753-3318
          E-mail: society@asev.org

AMERICAN SOCIETY OF AGRICULTURAL AND BIOLOGICAL ENGINEERS

http://www.asabe.org/

WILLIAM J. ADAMS, JR. AND MARIJANE E. ADAMS SCHOLARSHIP

One-time award for a full-time U.S. or Canadian undergraduate who is a student member of the American Society of Agricultural Engineers and a declared major in biological or agricultural engineering. Must be at least a sophomore and have minimum 2.5 GPA. Must be interested in agricultural machinery product design or development. Application procedures can be found on http://www.asabe.org website.

Academic Fields/Career Goals: Agriculture; Biology.

Award: Scholarship for use in sophomore, junior, or senior years; not renewable. *Number:* 1. *Amount:* $1200.

Eligibility Requirements: Applicant must be enrolled or expecting to enroll full-time at a four-year institution or university. Applicant or parent of applicant must be member of Other Student Academic Clubs. Applicant must have 2.5 GPA or higher. Available to U.S. and Canadian citizens.

Application Requirements: Application form, essay, financial need analysis, recommendations or references, resume. *Deadline:* March 15.

Contact: Carol Flautt, Scholarship Program
          American Society of Agricultural and Biological Engineers
          2950 Niles Road
          St. Joseph, MI 49085-9659
          Phone: 269-932-7036
          Fax: 269-429-3852
          E-mail: flautt@asabe.org

AMERICAN SOCIETY OF AGRONOMY, CROP SCIENCE SOCIETY OF AMERICA, SOIL SCIENCE SOCIETY OF AMERICA

http://www.agronomy.org

J. FIELDING REED SCHOLARSHIP

Scholarship of $1000 to honor an outstanding undergraduate senior pursuing a career in soil or plant sciences. Must have GPA of 3.0, or above, and nominations should contain a history of community and campus leadership activities, specifically in agriculture. For more information on nomination and eligibility criteria, visit website https://www.agronomy.org/awards

Academic Fields/Career Goals: Agriculture; Earth Science; Entomology; Environmental Science; Natural Resources; Natural Sciences.

Award: Scholarship for use in senior year; not renewable. *Number:* 1. *Amount:* up to $1000.

Eligibility Requirements: Applicant must be enrolled or expecting to enroll full-time at a four-year institution or university and must have an interest in leadership. Applicant or parent of applicant must have employment or volunteer experience in community service. Applicant must have 3.0 GPA or higher. Available to U.S. and non-U.S. citizens.

Application Requirements: Application form, application form may be submitted online (http://www.agronomy.org/awards), letter of interest, recommendations or references, resume. *Deadline:* February 26.

Contact: Sara Uttech, Communications Manager
American Society of Agronomy, Crop Science Society of America, Soil Science Society of America
5585 Guilford Road
Madison, WI 53711
Phone: 608-268-4948
Fax: 608-273-2021
E-mail: awards@sciencesocieties.org

ASSOCIATION ON AMERICAN INDIAN AFFAIRS, INC.

http://www.indian-affairs.org/

ELIZABETH AND SHERMAN ASCHE MEMORIAL SCHOLARSHIP FUND

Scholarship of up to $1500 available for undergraduate and graduate students seeking a Bachelor's or Master's degree in science or public health. Students must apply each year. Must be a Native American. See website for details http://www.indian-affairs.org. Must be seeking an Associate's degree or higher at an accredited school.

Academic Fields/Career Goals: Agriculture; Animal/Veterinary Sciences; Biology; Chemical Engineering; Dental Health/Services; Earth Science; Health and Medical Sciences; Marine Biology; Natural Sciences; Nursing; Physical Sciences; Public Health.

Award: Scholarship for use in freshman, sophomore, junior, senior, or graduate years; not renewable. *Number:* 6–8. *Amount:* up to $1500.

Eligibility Requirements: Applicant must be American Indian/Alaska Native and enrolled or expecting to enroll full-time at a two-year or four-year or technical institution or university. Available to U.S. citizens.

Application Requirements: Application form, essay, Tribal Enrollment. *Deadline:* June 1.

Contact: Lisa Wyzlic, Director of Scholarship Programs
Association on American Indian Affairs, Inc.
966 Hungerford Drive, Suite 12-B
Rockville, MD 20850
Phone: 240-314-7155
Fax: 240-314-7159
E-mail: lw.aaia@indian-affairs.org

CALCOT-SEITZ FOUNDATION

http://www.calcot.com/

CALCOT-SEITZ SCHOLARSHIP

Scholarship for young students from Arizona, New Mexico, Texas, and California who plan to attend a college or are attending a college offering at least a four-year degree in agriculture.

Academic Fields/Career Goals: Agriculture.

Award: Scholarship for use in freshman, sophomore, junior, senior, or graduate years; not renewable. *Number:* 1–30. *Amount:* $500–$3000.

Eligibility Requirements: Applicant must be enrolled or expecting to enroll full-time at a four-year institution or university and resident of Arizona, California, New Mexico, Texas. Available to U.S. and non-U.S. citizens.

Application Requirements: Application form, community service, essay, interview, personal photograph. *Deadline:* March 31.

Contact: Marci Cunningham, Scholarship Committee
Calcot-Seitz Foundation
PO Box 259
Bakersfield, CA 93302
Phone: 661-327-5961
E-mail: mcunningham@calcot.com

CHS FOUNDATION

http://www.chsfoundation.org/

CHS FOUNDATION HIGH SCHOOL SCHOLARSHIPS
• *See page 100*

CHS FOUNDATION TWO-YEAR COLLEGE SCHOLARSHIPS
• *See page 100*

CHS FOUNDATION UNIVERSITY SCHOLARSHIPS
• *See page 100*

COUPONBIRDS

https://www.couponbirds.com/

HELP TO SAVE SCHOLARSHIP

To assist students in reducing their tuition fee burden and collect their smart ways of saving money, couponbirds starts the Couponbirds "Help to Save" Scholarship program. The most sparkling idea and response will be drawn to present at our site and rewarded with prize. Please be free to contact us if you have any further questions about the site or the scholarship.

Academic Fields/Career Goals: Agriculture.

Award: Scholarship for use in freshman, sophomore, junior, or senior years; renewable. *Amount:* $1–$1000.

Eligibility Requirements: Applicant must be Disciple of Christ; Armenian citizen; American Indian/Alaska Native or Asian/Pacific Islander; enrolled or expecting to enroll full- or part-time at a two-year or four-year or technical institution or university; resident of Montana; studying in Utah and must have an interest in art. Applicant or parent of applicant must have employment or volunteer experience in computer science. Applicant must have 3.0 GPA or higher. Available to U.S. and non-U.S. citizens.

Application Requirements: Application form, autobiography, community service, essay, interview, personal photograph, portfolio. *Deadline:* October 10.

Contact: couponbirds. Steven Ruff, COUPONBIRDS "HELP TO SAVE" SCHOLARSHIP
Couponbirds
2443 Fillmore St #380-3240
San Francisco, CA 94115
Phone: 6164269997
E-mail: scholarship@couponbirds.com

FOUNDATION FOR SCIENCE AND DISABILITY

http://stemd.org/

GRANTS FOR DISABLED GRADUATE STUDENTS IN THE SCIENCES

Available to graduate students who are disabled. Awards are given for an assistive device or as financial support for scientific research. Undergraduate seniors may apply. One-time award. Electronic application is available.

Academic Fields/Career Goals: Agriculture; Anthropology; Applied Sciences; Aviation/Aerospace; Behavioral Science; Biology; Chemical Engineering; Civil Engineering; Computer Science/Data Processing; Electrical Engineering/Electronics; Energy and Power Engineering; Engineering-Related Technologies; Engineering/Technology; Entomology; Environmental Health; Environmental Science; Health and Medical Sciences; Health Information Management/Technology; Mathematics; Mechanical Engineering; Meteorology/Atmospheric Science; Natural Resources; Natural Sciences; Neurobiology; Nuclear Science; Physical Sciences; Science, Technology, and Society.

Award: Grant for use in senior or graduate years; not renewable. *Number:* 1–3. *Amount:* $1000.

Eligibility Requirements: Applicant must be hearing impaired, learning disabled, physically disabled, or visually impaired and enrolled or expecting to enroll full-time at an institution or university. Applicant must be hearing impaired, learning disabled, physically disabled, or visually impaired. Available to U.S. citizens.

Application Requirements: Application form, essay. *Deadline:* December 1.

Contact: Dr. Richard Mankin, Grants Committee Chair
Foundation for Science and Disability
503 NW 89th Street
Gainesville, FL 32607
Phone: 352-374-5774
E-mail: Richard.Mankin@ars.usda.gov

GARDEN CLUB OF AMERICA

http://www.gcamerica.org/

ELIZABETH GARDNER NORWEB SUMMER ENVIRONMENTAL STUDIES SCHOLARSHIP

Award for college students who wish to pursue summer studies doing field work, research, or classroom work in the environmental field following their freshman, sophomore, or junior years. Work may award academic credit but should be in addition to required courses.

Academic Fields/Career Goals: Agriculture; Earth Science; Environmental Science; Natural Resources.

Award: Scholarship for use in freshman, sophomore, or junior years; not renewable. *Number:* 1. *Amount:* $3000.

Eligibility Requirements: Applicant must be enrolled or expecting to enroll full-time at a four-year institution or university. Available to U.S. citizens.

Application Requirements: Application form, essay. *Deadline:* February 5.

Contact: Garden Club of America
Garden Club of America
14 East 60th Street
New York, NY 10022-1006
Phone: 212-753-8287
E-mail: scholarshipapplications@gcamerica.org

HERB SOCIETY OF AMERICA, WESTERN RESERVE UNIT

http://www.westernreserveherbsociety.org/

HORTICULTURE SCHOLARSHIP FROM FRANCIS SYLVIA ZVERINA

• See page 101

HORTICULTURE SCHOLARSHIP OF THE WESTERN RESERVE HERB SOCIETY

• See page 101

INSTITUTE OF FOOD TECHNOLOGISTS

http://www.ift.org/

EVAN TUREK MEMORIAL SCHOLARSHIP AND INTERNSHIP

Applicant must be enrolled as a full-time rising sophomore, junior, or senior university student pursuing a food science degree at an IFT-approved undergraduate program. Major in agricultural engineering, biochemistry, chemical engineering, dairy science, food chemistry, food engineering, food packaging, non-thermal processing or related discipline. Applicant must demonstrate exceptional leadership experience. Applicant be a member of IFT at time of application. Mondelz International will conduct phone and video interviews for top candidates in November. Scholarship recipient will begin a (10-12 week) internship with Mondelz International beginning in mid-May/June.

Academic Fields/Career Goals: Agriculture; Food Science/Nutrition.

Award: Scholarship for use in sophomore, junior, or senior years; not renewable. *Number:* 1. *Amount:* $1000.

Eligibility Requirements: Applicant must be enrolled or expecting to enroll full-time at a four-year institution or university. Applicant must have 3.0 GPA or higher. Available to U.S. and non-U.S. citizens.

Application Requirements: Application form, interview. *Deadline:* September 30.

Contact: IFT Foundation Coordinator
Institute of Food Technologists
525 West Van Buren, Suite 1000
Chicago, IL 60607
Phone: 312-782-8424
E-mail: info@ift.org

INTERNATIONAL FOODSERVICE EDITORIAL COUNCIL

http://www.ifeconline.com/

INTERNATIONAL FOODSERVICE EDITORIAL COUNCIL COMMUNICATIONS SCHOLARSHIP

• See page 96

JAPANESE AMERICAN CITIZENS LEAGUE (JACL)

http://www.jacl.org/

NATIONAL JACL HEADQUARTERS SCHOLARSHIP

Scholarship offers over 30 awards to qualified students nationwide. Scholarships are provided to students at the entering freshman, undergraduate, graduate, law, financial need and creative & performing arts. All scholarships are one-time awards. Every applicant must be an active National JACL member at either an Individual or Student/Youth Level.

Academic Fields/Career Goals: Agriculture; Journalism; Law/Legal Services; Literature/English/Writing; Public Policy and Administration.

Award: Scholarship for use in freshman, sophomore, junior, senior, or graduate years; not renewable. *Number:* 30.

Eligibility Requirements: Applicant must be of Japanese heritage; Asian/Pacific Islander and enrolled or expecting to enroll full-time at a two-year or four-year institution or university. Available to U.S. and non-U.S. citizens.

Application Requirements: Application form, financial need analysis, recommendations or references, transcript. *Deadline:* varies.

Contact: Scholarship Committee
Phone: 415-921-5225
E-mail: jacl@jacl.org

LES DAMES D'ESCOFFIER INTERNATIONAL, COLORADO CHAPTER

http://www.lesdamescolorado.org

LES DAMES D'ESCOFFIER INTERNATIONAL, COLORADO CHAPTER SCHOLARSHIP

Les Dames d'Escoffier International, Colorado Chapter, will award two $1,000 scholarships each year to qualified female students in food-related fields and attending schools in Colorado. The awards are based on financial need, academic performance, and personal/professional accomplishments.

Academic Fields/Career Goals: Agriculture; Animal/Veterinary Sciences; Culinary Arts; Food Science/Nutrition; Food Service/Hospitality; Home Economics.

Award: Scholarship for use in freshman, sophomore, junior, senior, or graduate years; not renewable. *Number:* 2. *Amount:* $1000.

Eligibility Requirements: Applicant must be enrolled or expecting to enroll full- or part-time at a two-year or four-year or technical institution or university; female and studying in Colorado. Available to U.S. and non-U.S. citizens.

Application Requirements: Essay, financial need analysis. *Deadline:* March 23.

Contact: Carol Fenster
Les Dames d'Escoffier International, Colorado Chapter
5397 E Mineral Circle
Centennial, CO 80122
Phone: 303-741-5408
E-mail: info@savorypalate.com

MAINE DEPARTMENT OF AGRICULTURE, FOOD AND RURAL RESOURCES

http://www.maine.gov/agriculture

MAINE RURAL REHABILITATION FUND SCHOLARSHIP PROGRAM

• *See page 102*

MICHIGAN STATE HORTICULTURAL SOCIETY

http://www.mihortsociety.com

FRUITS INDUSTRIES SCHOLARSHIPS

This scholarship is only for students who intend to pursue careers in or connected to the Midwest fruit industry.

Academic Fields/Career Goals: Agriculture.

Award: Scholarship for use in junior, senior, or graduate years; not renewable. *Number:* 4–7. *Amount:* $1500.

Eligibility Requirements: Applicant must be enrolled or expecting to enroll full-time at a two-year or four-year institution or university. Applicant or parent of applicant must have employment or volunteer experience in agriculture. Available to U.S. citizens.

Application Requirements: Application form. *Deadline:* September 30.

Contact: Ben Smith

NATIONAL CATTLEMEN'S FOUNDATION

http://www.nationalcattlemensfoundation.org/

CME BEEF INDUSTRY SCHOLARSHIP

• *See page 102*

NATIONAL COUNCIL OF STATE GARDEN CLUBS INC. SCHOLARSHIP

http://www.gardenclub.org/

NATIONAL COUNCIL OF STATE GARDEN CLUBS INC. SCHOLARSHIP

Scholarship to students for study in agriculture education, horticulture, floriculture, landscape design, botany, biology, plant pathology/science, forestry, agronomy, environmental concerns.

Academic Fields/Career Goals: Agriculture; Biology; Environmental Science; Horticulture/Floriculture.

Award: Scholarship for use in sophomore, junior, senior, or graduate years; not renewable. *Number:* 34. *Amount:* $3500.

Eligibility Requirements: Applicant must be enrolled or expecting to enroll full-time at a two-year or four-year institution or university. Applicant must have 3.0 GPA or higher. Available to U.S. citizens.

Application Requirements: Application form, financial need analysis, recommendations or references, transcript. *Deadline:* March 1.

Contact: Kathy Romine, National Headquarters
Phone: 314-776-7574 Ext. 15
Fax: 314-776-5108
E-mail: headquarters@gardenclub.org

NATIONAL DAIRY SHRINE

http://www.dairyshrine.org/

KILDEE SCHOLARSHIPS

Top 25 contestants in the three most recent national intercollegiate dairy cattle judging contests or the top ranking team members from the North American Intercollegiate Dairy Challenge are eligible to apply for two $3000 one-time scholarships for graduate study in the field related to dairy cattle production or vet school at the university of their choice. Also the top 25 contestants in the most recent National 4-H & National FFA Dairy Judging contests are eligible to apply for one $1000 scholarship for undergraduate study in the field related to dairy cattle production at the university of their choice.

Academic Fields/Career Goals: Agriculture; Animal/Veterinary Sciences.

Award: Scholarship for use in junior, senior, or postgraduate years; not renewable. *Number:* 1–2. *Amount:* $1000–$3000.

Eligibility Requirements: Applicant must be enrolled or expecting to enroll full-time at a four-year institution or university. Applicant must have 3.0 GPA or higher. Available to U.S. and Canadian citizens.

Application Requirements: Application form, personal photograph. *Deadline:* April 15.

Contact: Executive Director
National Dairy Shrine
PO Box 725
Denmark, WI 54208
Phone: 920-863-6333
E-mail: info@dairyshrine.org

KLUSSENDORF / MCKOWN SCHOLARSHIP

The scholarship will be granted to a student successfully completing the first, second or third years at a two-year or four-year college or university. To be eligible, students must major in a dairy science (animal science) curriculum with plans to enter the dairy cattle field as a breeder, owner, herdsperson, or fitter.

Academic Fields/Career Goals: Agriculture; Animal/Veterinary Sciences.

Award: Scholarship for use in freshman, sophomore, or junior years; not renewable. *Number:* 1–7. *Amount:* $1500.

Eligibility Requirements: Applicant must be enrolled or expecting to enroll full-time at a two-year or four-year institution or university. Available to U.S. and Canadian citizens.

Application Requirements: Application form, personal photograph. *Deadline:* April 15.

Contact: Executive Director
E-mail: info@dairyshrine.org

MARSHALL E. MCCULLOUGH-NATIONAL DAIRY SHRINE SCHOLARSHIPS

Scholarship for high school seniors planning to enter a four-year college or university with an intent to major in dairy/animal science with a communications emphasis, or agricultural journalism with a dairy/animal science emphasis.

Academic Fields/Career Goals: Agriculture; Communications; Journalism; TV/Radio Broadcasting.

Award: Scholarship for use in freshman year; not renewable. *Number:* 2. *Amount:* $1500–$2000.

Eligibility Requirements: Applicant must be high school student and planning to enroll or expecting to enroll full-time at a four-year institution or university. Applicant must have 3.0 GPA or higher. Available to U.S. citizens.

Application Requirements: Application form, personal photograph. *Deadline:* April 15.

Contact: Executive Director
E-mail: info@dairyshrine.org

NATIONAL DAIRY SHRINE/DAIRY MARKETING INC. MILK MARKETING SCHOLARSHIPS

One-time awards for undergraduate students pursuing careers in marketing of dairy products. Major areas can include: dairy science, animal science, agricultural economics, agricultural communications, agricultural education, general education, food and nutrition, home economics and journalism. For more information, visit website http://www.dairyshrine.org.

Academic Fields/Career Goals: Agriculture; Food Science/Nutrition; Marketing.

Award: Scholarship for use in sophomore or junior years; not renewable. *Number:* 5–9. *Amount:* $1000–$1500.

Eligibility Requirements: Applicant must be enrolled or expecting to enroll full-time at a four-year institution or university. Applicant must have 2.5 GPA or higher. Available to U.S. citizens.

Application Requirements: Application form, personal photograph. *Deadline:* April 15.

Contact: Executive Director
E-mail: info@dairyshrine.org

NATIONAL DAIRY SHRINE/IAGER DAIRY SCHOLARSHIP

$1000 annual scholarship to encourage qualified second-year dairy students in a two-year agricultural school to pursue careers in the dairy industry. Scholarships will be awarded based on academic standing, leadership ability, interest in the dairy industry, and plans for the future. Cumulative 2.5 GPA required.

Academic Fields/Career Goals: Agriculture.

Award: Scholarship for use in sophomore year; not renewable. *Number:* 1–2. *Amount:* $1000.

Eligibility Requirements: Applicant must be enrolled or expecting to enroll full-time at a two-year or technical institution. Applicant must have 2.5 GPA or higher. Available to U.S. citizens.

Application Requirements: Application form, personal photograph. *Deadline:* April 15.

Contact: Executive Director
E-mail: info@dairyshrine.org

NATIONAL DAIRY SHRINE/MAURICE E. CORE SCHOLARSHIP
• See page 102

NDS STUDENT RECOGNITION AWARD
• See page 102

NATIONAL GARDEN CLUBS INC.

http://www.gardenclub.org/

NATIONAL GARDEN CLUBS INC. SCHOLARSHIP PROGRAM

One-time award for full-time students in plant sciences, agriculture and related or allied subjects. Applicants must have at least a 3.25 GPA.

Academic Fields/Career Goals: Agriculture; Biology; Earth Science; Environmental Science; Horticulture/Floriculture; Landscape Architecture.

Award: Scholarship for use in junior, senior, or graduate years; not renewable. *Number:* 41. *Amount:* $4000.

Eligibility Requirements: Applicant must be enrolled or expecting to enroll full-time at a four-year institution or university. Available to U.S. citizens.

Application Requirements: Application form, financial need analysis, personal photograph. *Deadline:* February 1.

Contact: Sandra Robinson, Vice President for Scholarship
Phone: 606-878-7281
E-mail: sandyr@kayandkay.com

NATIONAL POULTRY AND FOOD DISTRIBUTORS ASSOCIATION

http://www.npfda.org/

NATIONAL POULTRY AND FOOD DISTRIBUTORS ASSOCIATION SCHOLARSHIP FOUNDATION
• See page 102

NATIONAL RESTAURANT ASSOCIATION EDUCATIONAL FOUNDATION

http://www.chooserestaurants.org

NATIONAL RESTAURANT ASSOCIATION EDUCATIONAL FOUNDATION UNDERGRADUATE SCHOLARSHIPS FOR COLLEGE STUDENTS

Merit-based scholarship awards for students pursuing degrees related to the restaurant/foodservice/hospitality industry.

Academic Fields/Career Goals: Agriculture; Business/Consumer Services; Culinary Arts; Food Science/Nutrition; Food Service/Hospitality; Horticulture/Floriculture; Hospitality Management; Marketing.

Award: Scholarship for use in freshman, sophomore, junior, or senior years; not renewable. *Number:* 150–300. *Amount:* $2500–$10,000.

Eligibility Requirements: Applicant must be enrolled or expecting to enroll full- or part-time at a two-year or four-year or technical institution or university; resident of Alabama, Alaska, Alberta, Arizona, Arkansas, British Columbia, California, Colorado, Connecticut, Delaware, District of Columbia, Florida, Georgia, Guam, Hawaii, Idaho, Illinois, Indiana, Iowa, Kansas, Kentucky, Louisiana, Maine, Manitoba, Maryland, Massachusetts, Michigan, Minnesota, Mississippi, Missouri, Montana, Nebraska, Nevada, New Brunswick, Newfoundland, New Hampshire, New Jersey, New Mexico, New York, North Carolina, North Dakota, Northwest Territories, Nova Scotia, Ohio, Oklahoma, Ontario, Oregon, Pennsylvania, Prince Edward Island, Puerto Rico, Quebec, Rhode Island, Saskatchewan, South Carolina, South Dakota, Tennessee, Texas, Utah, Vermont, Virginia, Washington, West Virginia, Wisconsin, Wyoming, Yukon and studying in Alabama, Alaska, Alberta, Arizona, Arkansas, British Columbia, California, Colorado, Connecticut, Delaware, District of Columbia, Florida, Georgia, Guam, Hawaii, Idaho, Illinois, Indiana, Iowa, Kansas, Kentucky, Louisiana, Maine, Manitoba, Maryland, Massachusetts, Michigan, Minnesota, Mississippi, Missouri, Montana, Nebraska, Nevada, New Brunswick, Newfoundland, New Hampshire, New Jersey, New Mexico, New York, North Carolina, North Dakota, Northwest Territories, Nova Scotia, Ohio, Oklahoma, Ontario, Oregon, Pennsylvania, Prince Edward Island, Puerto Rico, Quebec, Rhode Island, Saskatchewan, South Carolina, South Dakota, Tennessee, Texas, Utah, Vermont, Virginia, Washington, West Virginia, Wisconsin, Wyoming, Yukon. Applicant must have 2.5 GPA or higher. Available to U.S. citizens.

Application Requirements: Application form, community service, essay. *Deadline:* April 1.

Contact: Matt Rosales, Program Manager
National Restaurant Association Educational Foundation
2055 L St NW Suite 700
Washington, DC 20036
Phone: 202-9733672
E-mail: scholars@nraef.org

NEW YORK STATE ASSOCIATION OF AGRICULTURAL FAIRS

http://www.nyfairs.org/

NEW YORK STATE ASSOCIATION OF AGRICULTURAL FAIRS AND NEW YORK STATE SHOWPEOPLE'S ASSOCIATION ANNUAL SCHOLARSHIP
• See page 103

NEW YORK STATE GRANGE

http://www.nysgrange.org/

HOWARD F. DENISE SCHOLARSHIP

Awards for undergraduates under 21 years old to pursue studies in agriculture. Must be a New York resident with a minimum 3.0 GPA. One-time award of $1000.

Academic Fields/Career Goals: Agriculture.

Award: Scholarship for use in freshman, sophomore, junior, or senior years; not renewable. *Number:* 1–6. *Amount:* $1000.

Eligibility Requirements: Applicant must be enrolled or expecting to enroll full-time at a two-year or four-year institution and resident of New York. Applicant must have 3.0 GPA or higher. Available to U.S. citizens.

Application Requirements: Application form, financial need analysis. *Deadline:* April 15.

Contact: Scholarship Committee
New York State Grange
100 Grange Place
Cortland, NY 13045
Phone: 607-756-7553
E-mail: nysgrange@nysgrange.org

OHIO FARMERS UNION

http://www.ohfarmersunion.org/

JOSEPH FITCHER SCHOLARSHIP CONTEST

Scholarship available to member of Ohio Farmers Union who is a high school junior or senior, or enrolled as a college freshman. Participants are to submit an application obtained from OFU and a typed essay. Essay subject matter changes annually. Award of $1000 to winner and $250 to two runners-up.

Academic Fields/Career Goals: Agriculture.

Award: Scholarship for use in freshman year; not renewable. *Number:* 1–3. *Amount:* $250–$1000.

Eligibility Requirements: Applicant must be high school student; planning to enroll or expecting to enroll full-time at a four-year institution or university and resident of Ohio. Applicant or parent of applicant must be member of Ohio Farmers Union. Available to U.S. citizens.

Application Requirements: Application form, entry in a contest, essay. *Deadline:* December 31.

Contact: Ms. Linda Borton, Executive Director
Ohio Farmers Union
PO Box 363
Ottawa, OH 45875
Phone: 419-523-5300
E-mail: lborton@ohfarmersunion.org

VIRGIL THOMPSON MEMORIAL SCHOLARSHIP CONTEST
• *See page 103*

OREGON SHEEP GROWERS ASSOCIATION

http://www.sheeporegon.com

OREGON SHEEP GROWERS ASSOCIATION MEMORIAL SCHOLARSHIP

Award is for those individuals interested in agricultural sciences, pre-veterinary medicine, or an agriculture-related subject area that would be supportive of production agriculture, particularly in the state of Oregon.

Academic Fields/Career Goals: Agriculture; Animal/Veterinary Sciences; Trade/Technical Specialties.

Award: Scholarship for use in sophomore, junior, or senior years; not renewable. *Number:* 1. *Amount:* $1000–$1500.

Eligibility Requirements: Applicant must be enrolled or expecting to enroll full-time at a four-year institution or university and resident of Oregon. Available to U.S. citizens.

Application Requirements: Application form, essay. *Deadline:* July 15.

Contact: Scholarship Committee
Oregon Sheep Growers Association
1270 Chemeketa St. NE
Salem, OR 97301
Phone: 503-364-5462
Fax: 503-585-1921
E-mail: info@sheeporegon.com

OREGON STUDENT ASSISTANCE COMMISSION

https://oregonstudentaid.gov/

OREGON HORTICULTURE SOCIETY SCHOLARSHIP

Award for college sophomore or above for fall term/semester in agriculture science or a related field, with a preference to those students majoring in horticulture. To be used at Oregon public and nonprofit colleges and universities only. Minimum 2.5 GPA preference. Financial need may or may not be considered.

Academic Fields/Career Goals: Agriculture.

Award: Scholarship for use in sophomore, junior, or senior years; not renewable.

Eligibility Requirements: Applicant must be enrolled or expecting to enroll full-time at a four-year institution or university and studying in Oregon. Applicant must have 2.5 GPA or higher. Available to U.S. citizens.

Application Requirements: Application form. *Deadline:* March 1.

Contact: Melissa Adams, Scholarship Processing Coordinator
Phone: 541-687-7409
E-mail: melissa.adams@state.or.us

SCARLETT FAMILY FOUNDATION SCHOLARSHIP PROGRAM

http://www.scarlettfoundation.org/

SCHOLARSHIP FOR STUDENTS PURSUING A BUSINESS OR STEM DEGREE
• *See page 91*

SIGMA XI, THE SCIENTIFIC RESEARCH SOCIETY

http://www.sigmaxi.org/

SIGMA XI GRANTS-IN-AID OF RESEARCH

Award to undergraduate and graduate students currently enrolled in degree seeking programs. Applications are accepted through an online form only. Deadlines for all application material are March 15 and October 11 annually and are available online two months prior to the deadline (January 15 and August 1 respectively).

Academic Fields/Career Goals: Agriculture; Animal/Veterinary Sciences; Anthropology; Biology; Chemical Engineering; Civil Engineering; Computer Science/Data Processing; Earth Science; Electrical Engineering/Electronics; Energy and Power Engineering; Engineering/Technology; Environmental Science; Geography; Health and Medical Sciences; Hydrology; Marine Biology; Marine/Ocean Engineering; Materials Science, Engineering, and Metallurgy; Mathematics; Mechanical Engineering; Meteorology/Atmospheric Science; Natural Sciences; Nuclear Science; Physical Sciences; Psychology; Science, Technology, and Society; Social Sciences.

Award: Grant for use in freshman, sophomore, junior, senior, or graduate years; not renewable. *Number:* 400. *Amount:* $1000–$5000.

Eligibility Requirements: Applicant must be enrolled or expecting to enroll full-time at a four-year institution or university. Available to U.S. and non-U.S. citizens.

Application Requirements: Application form.

Contact: Janelle Simmons, Manager of Programs
Sigma Xi, The Scientific Research Society
3200 Chapel Hill Nelson Hwy
P.O. Box 13975
Research Triangle Park, NC 27709
Phone: 800-243-6534 Ext. 206
E-mail: giar@sigmaxi.org

SOCIETY FOR RANGE MANAGEMENT

http://www.rangelands.org/

MASONIC RANGE SCIENCE SCHOLARSHIP
• *See page 103*

SOIL AND WATER CONSERVATION SOCIETY

http://www.swcs.org

DONALD A. WILLIAMS SCHOLARSHIP SOIL CONSERVATION SCHOLARSHIP

• See page 103

SOIL AND WATER CONSERVATION SOCIETY-MISSOURI SHOW-ME CHAPTER

http://www.moswcs.org/

MO SHOW-ME CHAPTER SWCS SCHOLARSHIP

The SWCS Scholarship provides financial assistance to students wishing to pursue studies with a natural resource conservation orientation at properly accredited colleges or universities. This scholarship is for students who attend/graduated from an approved program of study in Missouri. Applicants must major in a conservation or natural resource-related field. Due date is the Monday after Thanksgiving.

Academic Fields/Career Goals: Agriculture; Biology; Earth Science; Entomology; Environmental Health; Environmental Science; Hydrology; Natural Resources; Natural Sciences; Recreation, Parks, Leisure Studies; Science, Technology, and Society; Surveying, Surveying Technology, Cartography, or Geographic Information Science.

Award: Scholarship for use in freshman, sophomore, junior, or senior years; not renewable. *Number:* 1. *Amount:* $2000.

Eligibility Requirements: Applicant must be enrolled or expecting to enroll full-time at a two-year or four-year institution or university and resident of Missouri. Available to U.S. citizens.

Application Requirements: Application form, essay.

Contact: Kim Vinson
          Soil and Water Conservation Society-Missouri Show-Me
              Chapter
          7005 SE Ketchem Rd
          Cameron, MO 64429
          Phone: 816-632-0735
          E-mail: soilsgal78@gmail.com

SOIL AND WATER CONSERVATION SOCIETY-NEW JERSEY CHAPTER

http://www.geocities.com/njswcs

EDWARD R. HALL SCHOLARSHIP

• See page 103

SOUTH DAKOTA BOARD OF REGENTS

http://www.sdbor.edu/

SOUTH DAKOTA BOARD OF REGENTS BJUGSTAD SCHOLARSHIP

• See page 104

SOUTH FLORIDA FAIR AND PALM BEACH COUNTY EXPOSITIONS INC.

http://www.southfloridafair.com/

SOUTH FLORIDA FAIR AGRICULTURAL COLLEGE SCHOLARSHIP

Renewable award of $2000 for students pursuing a degree in agriculture. Must be a permanent resident of Florida.

Academic Fields/Career Goals: Agriculture.

Award: Scholarship for use in freshman, sophomore, junior, or senior years; renewable. *Number:* 2. *Amount:* $2000.

Eligibility Requirements: Applicant must be enrolled or expecting to enroll full- or part-time at a four-year institution or university and resident of Florida. Available to U.S. and non-U.S. citizens.

Application Requirements: Application form, community service, essay, recommendations or references, test scores, transcript. *Deadline:* October 15.

Contact: Agriculture Committee
          South Florida Fair and Palm Beach County Expositions Inc.
          PO Box 210367
          West Palm Beach, FL 33421-0367
          Phone: 561-790-5245

TAILOR MADE LAWNS

http://www.tailormadelawns.com

TAILOR MADE LAWNS SCHOLARSHIP FUND

This $1,000 scholarship will be awarded to a student based on merit and passion for the enhancement of their local and global environment. Candidates will be evaluated according to letters of recommendation, academic records, and their passion for the environment. These qualifications will be demonstrated through faculty references, academic transcripts, SAT/ACT scores, and most importantly, a letter of intent written by the student. All eligible North Carolina students are encouraged to apply online or through the mail.

Academic Fields/Career Goals: Agriculture; Environmental Science; Nuclear Science; Physical Sciences.

Award: Scholarship for use in freshman, sophomore, junior, or senior years; not renewable. *Number:* 1. *Amount:* $1000.

Eligibility Requirements: Applicant must be enrolled or expecting to enroll full-time at a four-year institution or university; resident of North Carolina and studying in North Carolina. Applicant must have 3.0 GPA or higher. Available to U.S. citizens.

Application Requirements: Application form, essay. *Deadline:* May 31.

Contact: Damon Milotte, General Manager & Vice President
          Tailor Made Lawns
          1003 1st St W
          Conover, NC 28613
          Phone: 828-465-4070
          E-mail: scholarship@tailormadelawns.com

TURF AND ORNAMENTAL COMMUNICATORS ASSOCIATION

http://www.toca.org/

TURF AND ORNAMENTAL COMMUNICATORS ASSOCIATION SCHOLARSHIP PROGRAM

One-time award for undergraduate students majoring or minoring in technical communications or in a green industry field such as horticulture, plant sciences, botany, or agronomy. The applicant must also demonstrate an interest in using this course of study in the field of communications. An overall GPA of 3.0 is required in major area of study.

Academic Fields/Career Goals: Agriculture; Communications; Horticulture/Floriculture.

Award: Scholarship for use in freshman, sophomore, junior, or senior years; not renewable. *Number:* 1. *Amount:* $2500.

Eligibility Requirements: Applicant must be enrolled or expecting to enroll full-time at a two-year or four-year institution or university. Applicant must have 3.0 GPA or higher. Available to U.S. and non-U.S. citizens.

Application Requirements: Application form, essay, portfolio, recommendations or references, resume, transcript. *Deadline:* March 1.

Contact: Den Gardner, Executive Director
          Phone: 952-758-6340
          E-mail: toca@gardnerandgardnercommunications.com

UNITED STATES DEPARTMENT OF AGRICULTURE

http://www.usda.gov/

USDA/1994 TRIBAL SCHOLARS PROGRAM

Scholarships for applicants attending 1994 Land Grant Tribal Colleges and Universities seeking careers in food, agriculture, and natural resource sciences, and/or other related disciplines. The program offers support for an Associate's degree (up to 2 Years of support) or Bachelor's of Science Degree (up to 4 Years of support).

Academic Fields/Career Goals: Agriculture; Food Science/Nutrition; Natural Resources.

Award: Scholarship for use in freshman, sophomore, junior, or senior years; renewable.

Eligibility Requirements: Applicant must be American Indian/Alaska Native and enrolled or expecting to enroll full- or part-time at an institution or university. Available to U.S. citizens.

Application Requirements: *Deadline:* February 1.

WILLIAM HELMS SCHOLARSHIP PROGRAM (WHSP)

The USDA APHIS is the agency responsible for safeguarding America's agricultural and natural resources from exotic plant and animal pests and diseases. APHIS' PPQ program deals specifically with plant health issues. Scholarship benefits include: financial aid while pursuing a degree; mentoring; paid work experience during school breaks; possible permanent employment upon graduation. Applicants must be enrolled in programs related to agriculture or the biological sciences and must maintain at least a 2.5 GPA.

Academic Fields/Career Goals: Agriculture; Biology.

Award: Scholarship for use in junior or senior years; renewable. *Number:* up to 5000.

Eligibility Requirements: Applicant must be enrolled or expecting to enroll full- or part-time at a four-year institution or university. Available to U.S. citizens.

Application Requirements: *Deadline:* March 1.

Contact: United States Department of Agriculture
United States Department of Agriculture
1400 Independence Avenue, SW, Room 1710
Attention: HR/Recruitment
Washington, DC 20250
Phone: 202-690-4759

WASHINGTON WINE INDUSTRY FOUNDATION

http://washingtonwinefoundation.org/

FOUNDATION FUND SCHOLARSHIP

The Foundation Fund was endowed in June 2013 by the Board of Directors. Several family funds, including the Charles Lill, Michael Manz, Glenn Coogan and John Farmer funds, plus the Industry Need and Rainy Day Funds, were combined to create the initial endowment. With this larger endowed fund, WWIF can make a bigger impact on the industry's need for an educated workforce. Individual gifts and dedicated auction revenues continue to grow the endowment. The number of awards is determined annually, ranging from $1,000 to $5,000.

Academic Fields/Career Goals: Agriculture.

Award: Scholarship for use in freshman, sophomore, junior, senior, graduate, or postgraduate years; not renewable. *Number:* 1–100. *Amount:* $1000–$5000.

Eligibility Requirements: Applicant must be enrolled or expecting to enroll full-time at a two-year or four-year institution or university and resident of Washington. Applicant must have 3.0 GPA or higher. Available to U.S. and non-U.S. citizens.

Application Requirements: Application form, essay, financial need analysis, personal photograph. *Deadline:* March 31.

Contact: Lacey Price, Program Manager
Washington Wine Industry Foundation
PO Box 716
Cashmere, WA 98815
Phone: 540-7821108
E-mail: lacey@washingtonwinefoundation.org

GEORGE & SUSAN CARTER SCHOLARSHIP

The George & Susan Carter Scholarship was established in 2017 as an endowed fund in honor of WSU researcher and winemaker George Carter and his wife, Susan. George Carter worked side by side with Dr. Walter Clore and the two were close friends. As part of his day-to-day activities, Carter developed a system for classifying American, European and hybrid grape varietals. In recognition of his wine making accomplishments, Carter was elevated to a Supreme Knight in the

International Brotherhood of the Knights of the Vine. This scholarship was established to assist students of limited means to attain associates, bachelors and graduate level degrees in viticulture and enology and will offer one (1) $1,000 auto-renewing scholarship per year.

Academic Fields/Career Goals: Agriculture.

Award: Scholarship for use in freshman, sophomore, junior, senior, graduate, or postgraduate years; renewable. *Number:* 1. *Amount:* $1000.

Eligibility Requirements: Applicant must be enrolled or expecting to enroll full-time at a two-year or four-year institution or university; resident of Washington and studying in Washington. Applicant must have 3.0 GPA or higher. Available to U.S. citizens.

Application Requirements: Application form, essay, financial need analysis. *Deadline:* March 31.

Contact: Lacey Price, Program Manager
Washington Wine Industry Foundation
PO Box 716
Cashmere, WA 98815
Phone: 509-782-1108
E-mail: lacey@washingtonwinefoundation.org

WALTER J. CLORE SCHOLARSHIP

The Walter J. Clore Scholarship was established in 1997 by the Washington Winegrowers Association in honor of Dr. Clore's grape research and lifetime achievements in the field of viticulture and enology. Working with growers, Dr. Clore and his colleagues published information on grape varieties, diseases, insects, mineral nutrition, irrigation, cover crops, weed control and climatological effects, including winter injury. He tested various trellis designs, which eventually led to the widespread adoption of mechanical harvesting. More than any other individual, Dr. Clore has had a profound and lasting impact on the Washington wine industry. The number of awards is determined annually and scholarships range from $500–$2000.

Academic Fields/Career Goals: Agriculture; Food Science/Nutrition.

Award: Scholarship for use in freshman, sophomore, junior, senior, or graduate years; not renewable. *Number:* 1–100. *Amount:* $500–$2000.

Eligibility Requirements: Applicant must be enrolled or expecting to enroll full- or part-time at a two-year or four-year institution or university; resident of Washington and studying in Washington. Applicant must have 3.0 GPA or higher. Available to U.S. and non-U.S. citizens.

Application Requirements: Application form, essay, financial need analysis. *Deadline:* March 31.

Contact: Lacey Price, Program Manager
Washington Wine Industry Foundation
PO Box 716
Cashmere, WA 98815
Phone: 509-782-1108
E-mail: lacey@washingtonwinefoundation.org

WOMEN GROCERS OF AMERICA

http://www.nationalgrocers.org/

MARY MACEY SCHOLARSHIP

Award for students intending to pursue a career in the independent sector of the grocery industry. One-time award for students who have completed freshman year. Submit statement and recommendation from sponsor in the grocery industry. Applicant should have a minimum 2.0 GPA.

Academic Fields/Career Goals: Agriculture; Business/Consumer Services; Food Service/Hospitality.

Award: Scholarship for use in sophomore, junior, senior, graduate, or postgraduate years; not renewable. *Number:* 2–7. *Amount:* $1000.

Eligibility Requirements: Applicant must be enrolled or expecting to enroll full-time at a two-year or four-year institution or university. Available to U.S. citizens.

Application Requirements: Application form, personal statement, recommendations or references, transcript. *Deadline:* May 15.

Contact: Kristen Comley, Director of Administration
Women Grocers of America
1005 North Glebe Road, Suite 250
Arlington, VA 22201-5758
Phone: 703-516-0700
Fax: 703-516-0115
E-mail: kcomley@nationalgrocers.org

AMERICAN STUDIES

AMERICAN FEDERATION OF STATE, COUNTY, AND MUNICIPAL EMPLOYEES

http://www.afscme.org/

AFSCME/UNCF UNION SCHOLARS PROGRAM

One-time award for a sophomore or junior majoring in ethnic studies, women's studies, labor studies, American studies, sociology, anthropology, history, political science, psychology, social work or economics. Must be African-American, Hispanic-American, Asian Pacific Islander, or American-Indian/Alaska Native. Minimum 2.5 GPA.

Academic Fields/Career Goals: American Studies; Anthropology; History; Political Science; Psychology; Social Sciences; Social Services; Women's Studies.

Award: Scholarship for use in sophomore or junior years; not renewable. *Number:* 10. *Amount:* up to $5000.

Eligibility Requirements: Applicant must be American Indian/Alaska Native, Asian/Pacific Islander, Black (non-Hispanic), Hispanic and enrolled or expecting to enroll full-time at a four-year institution or university. Applicant must have 2.5 GPA or higher. Available to U.S. citizens.

Application Requirements: Application form, essay, recommendations or references, transcript. *Deadline:* February 28.

Contact: Philip Allen, Scholarship Coordinator
Phone: 202-429-1250
Fax: 202-429-1293
E-mail: pallen@asscme.org

ASSOCIATION OF FORMER INTELLIGENCE OFFICERS

http://www.afio.com

AFIO UNDERGRADUATE AND GRADUATE SCHOLARSHIPS

The type of institution attended is less important than the clarity that the course of study being undertaken leads to a career in the U.S. Intelligence Community. So this covers law enforcement, foreign policy, intelligence analysis, counterterrorism, homeland security, foreign language mastery (Farsi, Tagalog, Pashto, Urdu, Mandarin, Arabic, Hindi, etc.—not Spanish or French), and related disciplines. Applicants seeking funding for law or medical school are placed in a third tier as a currently overabundant category inessential to current needs of the I.C. which already suffers from too many lawyers. Applicants must be a U.S. citizen studying at a U.S. Institution. Advanced knowledge and corroboration of claims of near-native performance in one of the mission-critical languages mentioned above puts applicants at top of consideration. Applicants going to online-only schools are acceptable but only institutions that are on a nationally accredited list maintained by the U.S. Dept. of Education. Costly, for-profit and non-profit institutions suspected of gaming the college-loan system, and those with no national accreditation or with fake, odd, bogus, or foreign accreditations, are not considered and cause a student application for support to be set aside.

Academic Fields/Career Goals: American Studies; Aviation/Aerospace; Computer Science/Data Processing; Criminal Justice/Criminology; Foreign Language; History; International Studies; Law Enforcement/Police Administration; Military and Defense Studies; Natural Sciences; Near and Middle East Studies; Peace and Conflict Studies; Political Science; Public Policy and Administration.

Award: Scholarship for use in junior, senior, graduate, or postgraduate years; not renewable. *Number:* 10. *Amount:* $1000–$4000.

Eligibility Requirements: Applicant must be age 19-35 and enrolled or expecting to enroll full-time at a four-year institution or university. Available to U.S. citizens.

Application Requirements: Application form, essay, personal photograph. *Deadline:* July 1.

Contact: Mrs. Eileen Doughty, Director, AFIO Scholarship Program
Association of Former Intelligence Officers
7700 Leesburg Pike, Suite 324
Falls Church, VA 22043
Phone: 703-790-0320
E-mail: scholarships@afio.com

CULTURAL SERVICES OF THE FRENCH EMBASSY

http://www.frenchculture.org/

TEACHING ASSISTANT PROGRAM IN FRANCE

Grants support American students as they teach English for 7 months in the French school system. Monthly stipend of about 790 euros (net) supports recipient in the life-style of a typical French student. Must be U.S. citizen or a permanent resident (not a French citizen). Proficiency in French is required. May not have received a similar grant from the French government for the last three years. For additional information and application, visit website http://highereducation.frenchculture.org/teach-in-france.

Academic Fields/Career Goals: American Studies; Art History; Education; European Studies; Foreign Language; History; Humanities; International Studies; Literature/English/Writing; Political Science; Social Sciences.

Award: Grant for use in junior, senior, graduate, or postgraduate years; not renewable. *Number:* 1120. *Amount:* $1040–$7280.

Eligibility Requirements: Applicant must be age 20-30; enrolled or expecting to enroll full- or part-time at a four-year institution or university and must have an interest in English language, foreign language, French language, or international exchange. Available to U.S. citizens.

Application Requirements: Application form, application form may be submitted online, essay, passport, personal photograph, recommendations or references, transcript. *Fee:* $40. *Deadline:* January 15.

Contact: Ms. Carolyn Collins, Educational Affairs Program Officer
Cultural Services of the French Embassy
Embassy of France
4101 Reservoir Road, NW
Washington, DC 20007
Phone: 202-944-6011
Fax: 202-944-6268
E-mail: assistant.washington-amba@diplomatie.gouv.fr

THE GEORGIA TRUST FOR HISTORIC PRESERVATION

http://www.georgiatrust.org/

B. PHINIZY SPALDING, HUBERT B. OWENS, AND THE NATIONAL SOCIETY OF THE COLONIAL DAMES OF AMERICA IN THE STATE OF GEORGIA ACADEMIC SCHOLARSHIPS

The Georgia Trust annually awards two $1000 and two $1,500 scholarships to encourage the study of historic preservation and related fields. Recipients are chosen on the basis of leadership and academic achievement. Applicants must be residents of Georgia enrolled in an accredited Georgia institution.

Academic Fields/Career Goals: American Studies; Historic Preservation and Conservation; History; Landscape Architecture.

Award: Scholarship for use in sophomore, junior, senior, or graduate years; not renewable. *Number:* 4. *Amount:* $1000–$1500.

Eligibility Requirements: Applicant must be enrolled or expecting to enroll full-time at a four-year institution or university; resident of Georgia and studying in Georgia. Applicant must have 3.0 GPA or higher. Available to U.S. citizens.

Application Requirements: Application form, essay. *Deadline:* February 9.

Contact: Mr. Neale Nickels, Director of Preservation
The Georgia Trust for Historic Preservation
1516 Peachtree Street, NW
Atlanta, GA 30309
Phone: 404-885-7817
E-mail: nnickels@georgiatrust.org

THE LYNDON BAINES JOHNSON FOUNDATION

http://www.lbjlibrary.org/page/foundation/

MOODY RESEARCH GRANTS

Grants to defray travel and other expenses incurred while conducting research at LBJ Library. September 15 deadline for spring term (January 1 - August 31), March 15 deadline for fall term (June 1 - December 31). Must contact Archives regarding availability of material. Should state clearly how Library's holdings will contribute to completion of project.

Academic Fields/Career Goals: American Studies; History; International Studies; Military and Defense Studies; Museum Studies; Political Science.

Award: Grant for use in senior, graduate, or postgraduate years; not renewable. *Number:* 10–15. *Amount:* $600–$3000.

Eligibility Requirements: Applicant must be enrolled or expecting to enroll full- or part-time at an institution or university. Available to U.S. and non-U.S. citizens.

Application Requirements: Application form. *Deadline:* March 15.

Contact: Mrs. Samantha Stone, Deputy Director
Phone: 512-721-0265
Fax: 512-721-0220
E-mail: samantha@lbjfoundation.org

SOUTHERN BAPTIST HISTORICAL LIBRARY AND ARCHIVES

http://www.sbhla.org/

LYNN E. MAY JR. STUDY GRANT

Grants to assist researchers (graduate students, college and seminary professors, historians, and other writers) with travel and research costs related to research in the Southern Baptist Historical Library and Archives.

Academic Fields/Career Goals: American Studies; History; Religion/Theology.

Award: Grant for use in freshman, sophomore, junior, senior, graduate, or postgraduate years; renewable. *Number:* 10–12. *Amount:* $250–$750.

Eligibility Requirements: Applicant must be enrolled or expecting to enroll full- or part-time at a two-year or four-year institution or university. Available to U.S. and non-U.S. citizens.

Application Requirements: Application form. *Deadline:* April 1.

Contact: Taffey Hall, Director
Southern Baptist Historical Library and Archives
901 Commerce Street, Suite 400
Nashville, TN 37203-3630
Phone: 615-244-0344
E-mail: taffey@sbhla.org

ANIMAL/VETERINARY SCIENCES

101ST AIRBORNE DIVISION ASSOCIATION

http://www.screamingeaglefoundation.org/

AL & WILLIAMARY VISTE SCHOLARSHIP

Scholarship to provide financial assistance to students who have the potential to become assets to our nation. The major factors to be considered in the evaluation and rating of applicants are eligibility, career objectives, academic record, and insight gained from the letter requesting consideration and letters of recommendation. Preference will be given, but is not limited, to obtaining a degree in one of the physical sciences, medical, or scientific research fields. Must be an upperclassman and have a minimum 3.75 GPA. Applicants parents, grandparent, husband or wife is (or if deceased was) a regular or life (not Associate) member of the 101st Airborne Division Association.

Academic Fields/Career Goals: Animal/Veterinary Sciences; Applied Sciences; Audiology; Behavioral Science; Biology; Chemical Engineering; Dental Health/Services; Environmental Science; Food Science/Nutrition; Mathematics; Neurobiology; Nursing; Pharmacy; Physical Sciences; Radiology; Sports-Related/Exercise Science; Therapy/Rehabilitation.

Award: Scholarship for use in junior, senior, or graduate years; not renewable. *Number:* 1–2. *Amount:* $1000–$2000.

Eligibility Requirements: Applicant must be enrolled or expecting to enroll full-time at a four-year institution or university. Applicant must have 3.5 GPA or higher. Available to U.S. citizens.

Application Requirements: Application form, essay, personal photograph. *Deadline:* May 11.

Contact: Mr. Randal Underhill, Executive Director
101st Airborne Division Association
P.O. Box 929
Fort Campbell, KY 42223
Phone: 931-431-0199
E-mail: 101exec@comcast.net

ABBIE SARGENT MEMORIAL SCHOLARSHIP INC.

http://www.nhfarmbureau.org/

ABBIE SARGENT MEMORIAL SCHOLARSHIP

• *See page 100*

AMERICAN PHYSIOLOGICAL SOCIETY

http://www.the-aps.org

BARBARA A. HORWITZ AND JOHN M. HOROWITZ UNDERGRADUATE RESEARCH AWARDS

These awards recognize excellence in undergraduate physiology research. The applicant must be the first author on an abstract submitted to the Experimental Biology meeting and must be working with an APS member who attests that the student is deserving of the first authorship. The student must be enrolled as an undergraduate student at the time of abstract submission. There are two types of awards: 1) Barbara A. Horwitz and John M. Horowitz Outstanding Undergraduate Abstract Award for best abstract and student letter. This award provides $100, a certificate and a two-year complimentary APS membership; and 2) Barbara A. Horwitz and John M. Horowitz Excellence in Undergraduate Research Award for the best poster and presentation. Recipient receives $400 and a certificate. The candidate must be an Outstanding Undergraduate Abstract awardee. The top ranked Excellence in Undergraduate Research awardee receives an additional $250. For more information, go to http://www.the-aps.org/EB-undergrad

Academic Fields/Career Goals: Animal/Veterinary Sciences; Biology; Environmental Science; Health and Medical Sciences; Marine Biology; Natural Sciences; Neurobiology; Sports-Related/Exercise Science.

Award: Prize for use in freshman, sophomore, junior, or senior years; not renewable. *Number:* 12–30. *Amount:* $100–$500.

Eligibility Requirements: Applicant must be enrolled or expecting to enroll full-time at a two-year or four-year institution or university. Available to U.S. and non-U.S. citizens.

Application Requirements: Application form, essay. *Deadline:* January 12.

Contact: Jessica Taylor, Senior Program Manager, Higher Education Programs
American Physiological Society
9650 Rockville Pike
Bethesda, MD 20814
Phone: 301-634-7787
E-mail: jtaylor@the-aps.org

AMERICAN QUARTER HORSE FOUNDATION (AQHF)

http://www.aqha.com/foundation

JAY PUMPHREY ANIMAL SCIENCES SCHOLARSHIP

Ideal candidate is an AQHA or AQHYA member from Texas with a rural farming and or ranching background who wishes to pursue a major in animal science or a large animal related degree from Tarleton State University or Texas A&M University.

Academic Fields/Career Goals: Animal/Veterinary Sciences.

Award: Scholarship for use in freshman, sophomore, junior, or senior years; renewable. *Number:* 1. *Amount:* $6000.

Eligibility Requirements: Applicant must be high school student; planning to enroll or expecting to enroll full-time at a four-year institution or university; resident of Texas and studying in Texas. Applicant or parent of applicant must be member of American Quarter Horse Association. Applicant or parent of applicant must have employment or volunteer experience in agriculture, farming. Applicant must have 3.0 GPA or higher. Available to U.S. citizens.

Application Requirements: Application form, financial need analysis. *Deadline:* December 1.

Contact: Scholarship Office
American Quarter Horse Foundation (AQHF)
2601 East Interstate 40
Amarillo, TX 79104
Phone: 806-378-5029
E-mail: foundation@aqha.org

APPALOOSA HORSE CLUB-APPALOOSA YOUTH PROGRAM

http://www.appaloosayouth.com/

LEW AND JOANN EKLUND EDUCATIONAL SCHOLARSHIP

One-time award for college juniors and seniors and graduate students studying a field related to the equine industry. Must be member or dependent of member of the Appaloosa Horse Club.

Academic Fields/Career Goals: Animal/Veterinary Sciences.

Award: Scholarship for use in junior, senior, or graduate years; not renewable. *Number:* 1. *Amount:* $2000.

Eligibility Requirements: Applicant must be enrolled or expecting to enroll full-time at a four-year institution or university. Applicant or parent of applicant must be member of Appaloosa Horse Club/Appaloosa Youth Association. Applicant must have 2.5 GPA or higher. Available to U.S. and non-U.S. citizens.

Application Requirements: Application form, entry in a contest, essay, personal photograph, recommendations or references, transcript. *Deadline:* June 1.

Contact: Anna Brown, AYF Coordinator
Appaloosa Horse Club-Appaloosa Youth Program
2720 West Pullman Road
Moscow, ID 83843
Phone: 208-882-5578 Ext. 264
Fax: 208-882-8150
E-mail: youth@appaloosa.com

ARRL FOUNDATION INC.

http://www.arrl.org/

MEDICAL AMATEUR RADIO COUNCIL (MARCO) SCHOLARSHIP

One $1000 award for a student with an active Technical Class or higher amateur radio license. Field of study must be leading to a career in the healing arts, including, but not necessarily leading to medicine, dentistry, veterinary medicine, nursing, pharmacy, EMT, or radiology technician. Preference will be given to undergraduate students and those in certificate programs, but graduate students may apply. Applicants should be able to describe how they have engaged in volunteer and/or public service activities making use of Amateur Radio. If possible, applicants should show a desire to encourage others in the healing arts to become licensed hams.

Academic Fields/Career Goals: Animal/Veterinary Sciences; Dental Health/Services; Health and Medical Sciences; Nursing; Pharmacy.

Award: Scholarship for use in freshman, sophomore, junior, senior, or graduate years; not renewable. *Number:* 1. *Amount:* $1000.

Eligibility Requirements: Applicant must be enrolled or expecting to enroll full- or part-time at a two-year or four-year institution or university and must have an interest in amateur radio. Available to U.S. citizens.

Application Requirements: Application form, essay. *Deadline:* January 31.

Contact: Ms. Mary Hobart, Secretary
Phone: 860-594-0397
E-mail: k1mmh@arrl.org

ASSOCIATION ON AMERICAN INDIAN AFFAIRS, INC.

http://www.indian-affairs.org/

ELIZABETH AND SHERMAN ASCHE MEMORIAL SCHOLARSHIP FUND

• *See page 106*

AVACARE MEDICAL

https://avacaremedical.com

AVACARE MEDICAL SCHOLARSHIP

The AvaCare Medical Scholarship recognizes those who are working to better the lives of our customers, students who are pursuing a degree in the medical field, with a prize of $1000 toward college tuition. This scholarship is awarded annually to one submission that tells about a truly inspiring act of kindness. AvaCare Medical judges will choose five to ten finalists, whose work will then be posted on our website. Voting will be open on our website, and the scholarship winner will be chosen based on a combination of judges' scores and the number of votes.

Academic Fields/Career Goals: Animal/Veterinary Sciences; Behavioral Science; Cosmetology; Dental Health/Services; Food Science/Nutrition; Health Administration; Health and Medical Sciences; Health Information Management/Technology; Neurobiology; Nursing; Oncology; Optometry; Osteopathy; Pharmacy; Psychology; Public Health; Therapy/Rehabilitation.

Award: Scholarship for use in freshman, sophomore, junior, senior, graduate, or postgraduate years; not renewable. *Number:* 1. *Amount:* $1000.

Eligibility Requirements: Applicant must be enrolled or expecting to enroll full- or part-time at a two-year or four-year institution or university. Applicant must have 3.0 GPA or higher. Available to U.S. citizens.

Application Requirements: *Deadline:* December 15.

Contact: AvaCare Medical Judges
AvaCare Medical
1665 Corporate Road West
Lakewood, NJ 08701
Phone: 877-813-7799
E-mail: scholarship@avacaremedical.com

GREAT MINDS IN STEM

http://www.greatmindsinstem.org

HENAAC SCHOLARSHIP PROGRAM

Scholarships available to Hispanic students maintaining a 3.0 GPA. Must be studying science, technology, engineering or math-related discipline in the United States or Puerto Rico. Some health-related fields qualify.

Academic Fields/Career Goals: Animal/Veterinary Sciences; Applied Sciences; Architecture; Audiology; Aviation/Aerospace; Biology; Chemical Engineering; Civil Engineering; Computer Science/Data Processing; Construction Engineering/Management; Earth Science; Electrical Engineering/Electronics; Energy and Power Engineering; Engineering-Related Technologies; Engineering/Technology; Entomology; Environmental Health; Environmental Science; Food Science/Nutrition; Horticulture/Floriculture; Hydrology; Industrial Design; Marine Biology; Marine/Ocean Engineering; Materials Science, Engineering, and Metallurgy; Mathematics; Mechanical Engineering; Meteorology/Atmospheric Science; Natural Resources; Natural Sciences; Neurobiology; Nuclear Science; Nursing; Oceanography; Oncology; Optometry; Osteopathy; Paper and Pulp Engineering; Pharmacy; Physical Sciences; Statistics.

Award: Scholarship for use in freshman, sophomore, junior, senior, or graduate years; not renewable. *Number:* 100–120. *Amount:* $500–$10,000.

Eligibility Requirements: Applicant must be of Hispanic heritage; enrolled or expecting to enroll full-time at a two-year or four-year institution or university and studying in Alabama, Alaska, Arizona, Arkansas, California, Colorado, Connecticut, Delaware, District of Columbia, Florida, Georgia, Hawaii, Idaho, Illinois, Indiana, Iowa, Kansas, Kentucky, Louisiana, Maine, Maryland, Massachusetts, Michigan, Minnesota, Mississippi, Missouri, Montana, Nebraska, Nevada, New Hampshire, New Jersey, New Mexico, New York, North Carolina, North Dakota, Ohio, Oklahoma, Oregon, Pennsylvania, Puerto Rico, Rhode Island, South Carolina, South Dakota, Tennessee, Texas, Utah, Vermont, Virginia, Washington, West Virginia, Wisconsin, Wyoming. Applicant must have 3.0 GPA or higher. Available to U.S. and non-U.S. citizens.

Application Requirements: Application form, community service, essay, personal photograph. *Deadline:* April 30.

Contact: Dr. Gary Cruz
Great Minds in STEM
2465 Whittier Blvd, Suite 202
Montebello, CA 90640
Phone: 323-262-0997 Ext. 775
E-mail: scholars@greatmindsinstem.org

LABROOTS INC.

http://www.LabRoots.com

LABROOTS STEM SCHOLARSHIP

The program welcomes applications from students seeking support for to cover expenses associated with their academic pursuits in a STEM field. The scholarship will fund one undergraduate or graduate student for one year, providing $1,000–$3,000 in direct costs. The scholarship is merit-based, and applicants can show their qualifications and need in the application process. LabRoots supports undergraduate and graduate students pursuing degrees in Science, Technology, Engineering and Mathematics (STEM) disciplines. This program is open to students both in, and outside the US; there are no geographical limits for applicants. LabRoots wishes to encourage all students to stay in science and aims to help students work towards their research and educational goals. Applicants must be enrolled or accepted for a graduate or undergraduate degree (BSc or higher) for the next academic year at a recognized university. The degree program/research area must be in a STEM field. Open worldwide. Include academic status and institution name, resume/CV, GPA, essay proposal (Your proposal will be limited to 4000 characters, including spaces. You must enter a minimum of 250 words). Selection is based on academic achievement and on the written proposal. No fee is required for the scholarship application. There are no restrictions on how the award can be used by the recipient. Proof of identity may be required. It is the recipient's responsibility to inform the appropriate academic office that you have received the award (often outside awards must be disclosed to your admissions office). The award can be paid to your institute or department for disbursement to you.

Academic Fields/Career Goals: Animal/Veterinary Sciences; Applied Sciences; Audiology; Aviation/Aerospace; Behavioral Science; Biology; Chemical Engineering; Civil Engineering; Computer Science/Data Processing; Construction Engineering/Management; Dental Health/Services; Earth Science; Electrical Engineering/Electronics; Energy and Power Engineering; Engineering-Related Technologies; Engineering/Technology; Entomology; Environmental Health; Environmental Science; Food Science/Nutrition; Health and Medical Sciences; Health Information Management/Technology; Horticulture/Floriculture; Marine Biology; Marine/Ocean Engineering; Materials Science, Engineering, and Metallurgy; Mathematics; Mechanical Engineering; Meteorology/Atmospheric Science; Natural Sciences; Neurobiology; Nuclear Science; Nursing; Oceanography; Oncology; Optometry; Osteopathy; Physical Sciences; Psychology; Public Health; Radiology; Science, Technology, and Society; Statistics; Surveying, Surveying Technology, Cartography, or Geographic Information Science.

Award: Scholarship for use in freshman, sophomore, junior, senior, or graduate years; not renewable. *Number:* 3. *Amount:* $1000–$3000.

Eligibility Requirements: Applicant must be enrolled or expecting to enroll full- or part-time at a two-year or four-year or technical institution or university. Available to U.S. and non-U.S. citizens.

Application Requirements: Application form, essay. *Deadline:* May 1.

Contact: Ms. Karen Sorenson
LabRoots Inc.
18340 Yorba Linda Boulvard
Yorba Linda, CA 92886
Phone: 619-861-0590
E-mail: karen.sorenson@labroots.com

LES DAMES D'ESCOFFIER INTERNATIONAL, COLORADO CHAPTER

http://www.lesdamescolorado.org

LES DAMES D'ESCOFFIER INTERNATIONAL, COLORADO CHAPTER SCHOLARSHIP

• *See page 107*

MAINE DEPARTMENT OF AGRICULTURE, FOOD AND RURAL RESOURCES

http://www.maine.gov/agriculture

MAINE RURAL REHABILITATION FUND SCHOLARSHIP PROGRAM

• *See page 102*

NATIONAL DAIRY SHRINE

http://www.dairyshrine.org/

KILDEE SCHOLARSHIPS

• *See page 108*

KLUSSENDORF / MCKOWN SCHOLARSHIP

• *See page 108*

NDS STUDENT RECOGNITION AWARD

• *See page 102*

NATIONAL INSTITUTES OF HEALTH

https://www.training.nih.gov/programs/ugsp

NIH UNDERGRADUATE SCHOLARSHIP PROGRAM FOR STUDENTS FROM DISADVANTAGED BACKGROUNDS

Awarded to financially disadvantaged students who come from a family with an annual income at or below a level based on low-income thresholds according to family size, as published by the U.S. Bureau of the Census. Must be enrolled full-time at a postsecondary institution and have a GPA of 3.3 or higher. Visit website https://www.training.nih.gov/programs/ugsp for more details.

Academic Fields/Career Goals: Animal/Veterinary Sciences; Behavioral Science; Biology; Environmental Health; Environmental Science; Health and Medical Sciences; Neurobiology; Nuclear Science; Nursing; Physical Sciences; Public Health; Women's Studies.

Award: Scholarship for use in freshman, sophomore, or junior years; renewable. *Number:* 10–15. *Amount:* $2000–$20,000.

Eligibility Requirements: Applicant must be enrolled or expecting to enroll full-time at a four-year institution or university. Applicant must have 3.5 GPA or higher. Available to U.S. citizens.

Application Requirements: Application form, essay, financial need analysis. *Deadline:* March 15.

Contact: Adrian Warren, Administrative Assistant
National Institutes of Health
Two Center Drive, Room 2W11A, MSC 0230
Bethesda, MD 20892-0230
Phone: 301-402-3831
E-mail: wardron@mail.nih.gov

NATIONAL POULTRY AND FOOD DISTRIBUTORS ASSOCIATION

http://www.npfda.org/

NATIONAL POULTRY AND FOOD DISTRIBUTORS ASSOCIATION SCHOLARSHIP FOUNDATION
• *See page 102*

OREGON SHEEP GROWERS ASSOCIATION

http://www.sheeporegon.com

OREGON SHEEP GROWERS ASSOCIATION MEMORIAL SCHOLARSHIP
• *See page 110*

OREGON STUDENT ASSISTANCE COMMISSION

https://oregonstudentaid.gov/

OREGON FOUNDATION FOR BLACKTAIL DEER SCHOLARSHIP

Scholarship for students majoring in forestry, biology, wildlife science, or related fields indicating serious commitment to careers in wildlife management. Must attend Oregon public or nonprofit colleges. Based on financial need.

Academic Fields/Career Goals: Animal/Veterinary Sciences; Biology.

Award: Scholarship for use in freshman, sophomore, junior, or senior years; not renewable.

Eligibility Requirements: Applicant must be enrolled or expecting to enroll at a four-year institution or university and studying in Oregon. Available to U.S. citizens.

Application Requirements: Application form, essay. *Deadline:* March 1.

Contact: Melissa Adams, Scholarship Processing Coordinator
Phone: 541-687-7409
E-mail: melissa.adams@state.or.us

WESTERN VETERINARY SCHOLARSHIP

Award for students who will enroll as college juniors or above. Grad students attending veterinary school preferred. Must be majoring in veterinarian medicine or pre-vet studies with the intent of becoming a DMV. For study at four-year public or nonprofit colleges and universities. Automatically renewable if renewal criteria are met. Based on financial need.

Academic Fields/Career Goals: Animal/Veterinary Sciences.

Award: Scholarship for use in junior, senior, or graduate years; renewable.

Eligibility Requirements: Applicant must be enrolled or expecting to enroll full-time at a four-year institution or university. Available to U.S. citizens.

Application Requirements: Application form, essay, financial need analysis. *Deadline:* March 1.

Contact: Melissa Adams, Scholarship Processing Coordinator
Phone: 541-687-7409
E-mail: melissa.adams@state.or.us

PLATINUM EDUCATIONAL GROUP

http://www.platinumed.com

PLATINUM EDUCATIONAL GROUP SCHOLARSHIPS PROGRAM FOR EMS, NURSING, AND ALLIED HEALTH

Applicant must be attending a state approved or accredited EMS, nursing, or Allied Health Program. Provide a copy of student ID and state identification card; letter of recommendation form from program instructor (form provided); and a brief essay (500 words maximum).

Academic Fields/Career Goals: Animal/Veterinary Sciences; Dental Health/Services; Nursing; Pharmacy; Public Health; Radiology.

Award: Scholarship for use in freshman, sophomore, junior, senior, graduate, or postgraduate years; not renewable. *Number:* 3. *Amount:* $1000.

Eligibility Requirements: Applicant must be enrolled or expecting to enroll full- or part-time at a two-year or four-year or technical institution or university. Available to U.S. and non-U.S. citizens.

Application Requirements: Application form, driver's license, essay. *Deadline:* July 16.

Contact: Jeremy Johnson, Director of Marketing
Platinum Educational Group
4370 Chicago Dr SW
Ste B#205
Grandville, MI 49418
Phone: 616-818-7877 Ext. 2904
E-mail: jeremy@platinumed.com

RKT PUBLISHING

http://www.rktpublishing.com/

EMPATHY FOR ANIMALS (EFA) SCHOLARSHIP AWARD FOR VETERINARY STUDENTS

This is a new scholarship that will be awarded annually in the amount of $500 to undergraduate students enrolled in veterinary or animal science studies, who are in good academic standing and have demonstrated a passion for animal advocacy and fighting animal cruelty. Applicants in good academic standing, with extracurricular community experience or demonstrated passion for animal advocacy and an interest in working to fight animal cruelty. We are looking for applicants with an educational and personal history of working to educate the public about the mistreatment of animals in today's society and a commitment to reshaping the treatment of animals in local communities across the nation. To be eligible, you must meet the following criteria: 1. Currently enrolled, and in good standing, in an accredited pre-veterinary or animal sciences undergraduate program in the United States, 2. Minimum GPA of 3.0, 3. Proven history of advocacy for animals, 4. Demonstrated community involvement, 5. Demonstrated financial need.

Academic Fields/Career Goals: Animal/Veterinary Sciences.

Award: Scholarship for use in freshman, sophomore, junior, or senior years; not renewable. *Number:* 1. *Amount:* $500.

Eligibility Requirements: Applicant must be enrolled or expecting to enroll full-time at a four-year institution and must have an interest in wildlife conservation/animal rescue. Applicant must have 3.0 GPA or higher. Available to U.S. and non-U.S. citizens.

Application Requirements: Essay. *Deadline:* December 31.

Contact: Ken Lyons, Co-Founder
E-mail: efascholarship@petlifetoday.com

SCARLETT FAMILY FOUNDATION SCHOLARSHIP PROGRAM

http://www.scarlettfoundation.org/

SCHOLARSHIP FOR STUDENTS PURSUING A BUSINESS OR STEM DEGREE
• *See page 91*

SIGMA XI, THE SCIENTIFIC RESEARCH SOCIETY

http://www.sigmaxi.org/

SIGMA XI GRANTS-IN-AID OF RESEARCH
• *See page 110*

SOCIETY FOR RANGE MANAGEMENT

http://www.rangelands.org/

MASONIC RANGE SCIENCE SCHOLARSHIP
• *See page 103*

SOIL AND WATER CONSERVATION SOCIETY-NEW JERSEY CHAPTER

http://www.geocities.com/njswcs

EDWARD R. HALL SCHOLARSHIP
• *See page 103*

STRAIGHTFORWARD MEDIA

http://www.straightforwardmedia.com/

STRAIGHTFORWARD MEDIA VOCATIONAL-TECHNICAL SCHOOL SCHOLARSHIP

Scholarship of $500 available to students enrolled in vocational and technical education programs. Awarded four times per year. Deadlines: November 30, February 28, May 31, and August 31. To apply, visit http://www.straightforwardmedia.com/votech/form.php.

Academic Fields/Career Goals: Animal/Veterinary Sciences; Cosmetology; Culinary Arts; Dental Health/Services; Fire Sciences; Heating, Air-Conditioning, and Refrigeration Mechanics; Pharmacy; Real Estate; Sports-Related/Exercise Science; Trade/Technical Specialties.

Award: Scholarship for use in freshman, sophomore, junior, or senior years; not renewable. *Number:* 4. *Amount:* $500.

Eligibility Requirements: Applicant must be enrolled or expecting to enroll full- or part-time at a two-year or four-year or technical institution or university. Available to U.S. and non-U.S. citizens.

Application Requirements: Essay. *Deadline:* varies.

Contact: Scholarship Committee
Phone: 605-348-3042

UNITED STATES DEPARTMENT OF AGRICULTURE

http://www.usda.gov/

SAUL T. WILSON, JR, SCHOLARSHIP PROGRAM (STWJS)

Undergraduate student applicants must have completed at least 2 years (60 semester or 90 quarter hours) of a 4-year pre-veterinary medicine or other biomedical science curriculum. Graduate student applicants must have completed not more than 1 full academic year of study in veterinary medicine. Awards up to $7500 per year for undergraduate studies, up to $15000 for graduate studies. Benefits include paid employment during summers and school breaks, possible full-time employment with APHIS upon successful completion of the program with a D.V.M. degree, training and other work requirements.

Academic Fields/Career Goals: Animal/Veterinary Sciences; Biology.

Award: Scholarship for use in junior, senior, or graduate years; renewable. *Amount:* $7500–$15,000.

Eligibility Requirements: Applicant must be enrolled or expecting to enroll full-time at a four-year institution or university. Available to U.S. citizens.

Application Requirements: *Deadline:* March 10.

Contact: Lin Chambers, Saul T. Wilson, Jr. Scholarship
United States Department of Agriculture
USDA, APHIS, Human Resources Division/Office of Recruitment
1400 Independence Avenue, SW, Room 1710
Washington, DC 20250
Phone: 202-690-4759
E-mail: Lin.S.Chambers@usda.gov

WILSON ORNITHOLOGICAL SOCIETY

http://www.wilsonsociety.org/

GEORGE A. HALL/HAROLD F. MAYFIELD AWARD

One-time award for scientific research on birds. Available to independent researchers without access to funds or facilities at a college or university. Must be a nonprofessional to apply. Submit research proposal.

Academic Fields/Career Goals: Animal/Veterinary Sciences; Biology; Natural Resources.

Award: Grant for use in freshman, sophomore, junior, or senior years; not renewable. *Number:* 1. *Amount:* $1000.

Eligibility Requirements: Applicant must be enrolled or expecting to enroll full- or part-time at a four-year institution or university. Available to U.S. and non-U.S. citizens.

Application Requirements: Application form. *Deadline:* February 1.

Contact: Dr. Jameson Chace, Research Grants Coordinator
Wilson Ornithological Society
Salve Regina University
Newport, RI 02840
Phone: 401-341-3204
E-mail: wos@salve.edu

PAUL A. STEWART AWARDS

One-time award for studies of bird movements based on banding, analysis of recoveries, and returns of banded birds, or research with an emphasis on economic ornithology. Submit research proposal.

Academic Fields/Career Goals: Animal/Veterinary Sciences; Biology; Natural Resources.

Award: Grant for use in freshman, sophomore, junior, or senior years; not renewable. *Number:* 1–4. *Amount:* up to $500.

Eligibility Requirements: Applicant must be enrolled or expecting to enroll full- or part-time at a four-year institution or university. Available to U.S. and non-U.S. citizens.

Application Requirements: Application form, proposal, recommendations or references. *Deadline:* February 1.

Contact: Dr. Jameson Chace, Research Grants Coordinator
Wilson Ornithological Society
Salve Regina University
Newport, RI 02840
Phone: 401-341-3204
E-mail: wos@salve.edu

ANTHROPOLOGY

AMERICAN FEDERATION OF STATE, COUNTY, AND MUNICIPAL EMPLOYEES

http://www.afscme.org/

AFSCME/UNCF UNION SCHOLARS PROGRAM
• *See page 113*

AMERICAN SCHOOL OF CLASSICAL STUDIES AT ATHENS

http://www.ascsa.edu.gr/

ASCSA SUMMER SESSION AND SUMMER SEMINARS SCHOLARSHIPS

Funding for ASCSA Summer Session and Seminars participants only. Awards for graduate students, high school teachers, and college teachers. One award (Charles Edwards for $500) at the undergraduate level used only for participation in the ASCSA Summer Session. The six-week session in Greece is conducted to become acquainted with Greece and its antiquities. Funding cannot be used for home institution in U.S.

Academic Fields/Career Goals: Anthropology; Archaeology; Architecture; Art History; Arts; Classics; Education; Foreign Language; Historic Preservation and Conservation; History; Humanities; Landscape Architecture; Museum Studies; Philosophy; Religion/Theology; Science, Technology, and Society; Urban and Regional Planning.

Award: Scholarship for use in senior or graduate years; not renewable. *Number:* 10–13. *Amount:* $500–$4900.

Eligibility Requirements: Applicant must be enrolled or expecting to enroll part-time at a four-year institution or university. Available to U.S. and non-U.S. citizens.

Application Requirements: Application form. *Deadline:* January 15.

Contact: Chair, Committee on the Summer Sessions
American School of Classical Studies at Athens
ASCSA, 6-8 Charlton Street
Princeton, NJ 08540
Phone: 609-683-0800
E-mail: ssapplication@ascsa.org

FOUNDATION FOR SCIENCE AND DISABILITY

http://stemd.org/

GRANTS FOR DISABLED GRADUATE STUDENTS IN THE SCIENCES
• *See page 106*

HAWAIIAN LODGE, F&AM

http://www.hawaiianlodgefreemasons.org

HAWAIIAN LODGE SCHOLARSHIPS
• *See page 86*

INTERNATIONAL HOUSEWARES ASSOCIATION

http://www.housewares.org

STUDENT DESIGN COMPETITION

Industrial design students invent a new product and must submit user research, market research, concept drawings, exploded views and narrative.

Academic Fields/Career Goals: Anthropology.

Award: Prize for use in freshman, sophomore, junior, or senior years; not renewable. *Number:* 6. *Amount:* $1000–$3000.

Eligibility Requirements: Applicant must be enrolled or expecting to enroll full- or part-time at an institution or university. Available to U.S. and non-U.S. citizens.

Application Requirements: Application form. *Deadline:* December 15.

Contact: MS. Victoria Matranga, Design Programs Coordinator
International Housewares Association
6400 Shafer Court
Suite 650
Rosemont, IL 60302
Phone: 847-692-0136
Fax: 847-292-4200
E-mail: vmatranga@housewares.org

ISLAMIC SCHOLARSHIP FUND

http://islamicscholarshipfund.org/

ISF NATIONAL SCHOLARSHIP

ISF is a non profit 501 (c)(3) organization with the mission to improve the understanding and acceptance of Islam by supporting students and increasing Muslim American representation in the professions that influence public policy and public opinion through academic scholarships, film grants and networking opportunities. Award is available to both U.S. citizens and green card holders and may be renewed if reapplying. Minimum 3.0 GPA required.

Academic Fields/Career Goals: Anthropology; Filmmaking/Video; History; International Studies; Journalism; Law Enforcement/Police Administration; Law/Legal Services; Near and Middle East Studies; TV/Radio Broadcasting.

Award: Scholarship for use in sophomore, junior, senior, graduate, or postgraduate years; not renewable. *Number:* 1–40. *Amount:* $2000–$5000.

Eligibility Requirements: Applicant must be Muslim faith and enrolled or expecting to enroll full-time at a two-year or four-year institution or university. Applicant must have 3.0 GPA or higher. Available to U.S. citizens.

Application Requirements: Application form, essay. *Deadline:* March 21.

Contact: Ms. Somayeh Nikooei, Director of Operations
Islamic Scholarship Fund
540 Shattuck Avenue
Suite 706
Berkeley, CA 94704
Phone: 650-995-6782
E-mail: admin@islamicscholarshipfund.org

LAMBDA ALPHA NATIONAL ANTHROPOLOGY HONOR SOCIETY

https://laanthro.org/

LAMBDA ALPHA NATIONAL ANTHROPOLOGY HONOR SOCIETY SCHOLARSHIP AWARD

Award to give academic recognition to undergraduate students and to encourage the pursuit of careers in anthropology. Must submit statement of future plans. Must include four copies of complete application packet. Minimum 3.00 GPA. For further information applicant should contact their department's Lambda Alpha faculty sponsor or visit the web page laanthro.org.

Academic Fields/Career Goals: Anthropology.

Award: Scholarship for use in senior year; not renewable. *Number:* 1–3. *Amount:* $5000.

Eligibility Requirements: Applicant must be enrolled or expecting to enroll full-time at a four-year institution or university. Applicant or parent of applicant must be member of Lambda Alpha National Collegiate Honor Society for Anthropology. Applicant must have 3.0 GPA or higher. Available to U.S. citizens.

Application Requirements: Application form, driver's license, essay. *Deadline:* March 15.

Contact: Dr. Mark Groover, National Executive Secretary
Lambda Alpha National Anthropology Honor Society
Department of Anthropology, Ball State University
2000 W University Avenue
Muncie, IN 47306-0435
Phone: 765-285-3567
E-mail: mdgroover@bsu.edu

LA-PHILOSOPHIE.COM

http://la-philosophie.com

LA-PHILOSOPHIE.COM SCHOLARSHIP

Since 2008, the mission of La-Philosophie.com is the democratisation of the philosophical knowledge. That is why we want to support a student every year to help him/her by a $200 fund to pursue his/her studies in social sciences. An essay on the interest of philosophy today will have to show their motivation. This essay will attempt to answer the following question: Why Philosophy Matters in Today's World. Your essay should include at least 2,000 words and a maximum of 5,000 words. The essay selected by the editors will be published on the site la-philosophie.com. Applications open December 1st. Deadline for registration is December 31st. Review of applications by the editorial committee takes place from January 1st to 15th. Announcement of the winner takes place January 16th. Application should include your full name, a few words about your course (diploma in progress, etc.), the school of your choice (may be private or public), your essay (2000 to 5000 words) in word or pdf format. Send your application before December 31st to laphilosophie.com@gmail.com. Official page: http://la-philosophie.com/bourse-detudes-la-philosophie-com

Academic Fields/Career Goals: Anthropology; History; Humanities; Journalism; Philosophy; Political Science; Psychology; Religion/Theology; Social Sciences.

Award: Scholarship for use in freshman, sophomore, junior, senior, graduate, or postgraduate years; renewable. *Number:* 1. *Amount:* $200.

Eligibility Requirements: Applicant must be enrolled or expecting to enroll full- or part-time at a four-year institution or university. Available to U.S. and non-U.S. citizens.

Application Requirements: Essay. *Deadline:* December 31.

Contact: Mr. Julien Josset
La-Philosophie.com
139 rue de saussure
Paris
E-mail: laphilosophie.com@gmail.com

MEDICAL SCRUBS COLLECTION

http://medicalscrubscollection.com

MEDICAL SCRUBS COLLECTION SCHOLARSHIP

Medical Scrubs Collection is dedicated to recognizing the individuals who go above and beyond to help others every day. To show our appreciation for these hard working individuals, MSC has decided to Pay it Forward by creating an annual scholarship opportunity for students studying in any health or medical-related field. MSC's scholarship will provide each applicant with a chance to win $1000 towards their college tuition by answering one question: What Inspired You To Pursue A Career In Helping Others? The Medical Scrubs Collection Scholarship will be awarded to the applicant with the winning submission for the thousand dollar question. When the deadline has passed, Medical Scrubs Collection judges will choose five to ten submissions that best fit the criteria for the MSC Scholarship question: What inspired you to pursue a career in helping others? The submissions of these finalists will be posted on Medical Scrubs Collection's website, https://medicalscrubscollection.com/scholarship-program where voting will be open to the public. The final winner will be determined by a combination of judges' scores and the number of votes.

Academic Fields/Career Goals: Anthropology; Applied Sciences; Archaeology; Audiology; Behavioral Science; Biology; Chemical Engineering; Cosmetology; Dental Health/Services; Earth Science; Entomology; Food Science/Nutrition; Health Administration; Health and Medical Sciences; Health Information Management/Technology; Marine Biology; Materials Science, Engineering, and Metallurgy; Natural Sciences; Neurobiology; Nursing; Oncology; Optometry; Osteopathy; Pharmacy; Physical Sciences; Psychology; Public Health; Radiology; Therapy/Rehabilitation.

Award: Scholarship for use in freshman, sophomore, junior, senior, graduate, or postgraduate years; renewable. *Number:* 1. *Amount:* $1000.

Eligibility Requirements: Applicant must be enrolled or expecting to enroll full- or part-time at a two-year or four-year or technical institution or university. Applicant must have 3.0 GPA or higher. Available to U.S. citizens.

Application Requirements: Application form. *Deadline:* December 15.

Contact: Program Manager
Medical Scrubs Collection
1665 Corporate Road West
Lakewood, NJ 08701
Phone: 888-567-2782
E-mail: scholarships@medicalscrubscollection.com

NEXTSTEPU

http://www.nextstepu.com/

$1,500 STEM SCHOLARSHIP

NextStepU.com will award one $1,500 scholarship to one randomly selected winner three times a year. Applicants must enter online at http://www.nextstepu.com/nextstepu-scholarships. Winner must be enrolled in college within 3 years from the time the prize is awarded. 3 Awards: deadline (1): January 31 deadline (2): May 31 deadline (3) September 30

Academic Fields/Career Goals: Anthropology; Applied Sciences; Architecture; Aviation/Aerospace; Behavioral Science; Biology; Chemical Engineering; Civil Engineering; Computer Science/Data Processing; Construction Engineering/Management; Earth Science; Electrical Engineering/Electronics; Energy and Power Engineering; Engineering-Related Technologies; Engineering/Technology; Environmental Health; Environmental Science; Food Science/Nutrition; Health and Medical Sciences; Health Information Management/Technology; Marine Biology; Marine/Ocean Engineering; Materials Science, Engineering, and Metallurgy; Mathematics; Mechanical Engineering; Meteorology/Atmospheric Science; Natural Sciences; Neurobiology; Nuclear Science; Nursing; Oceanography; Oncology; Optometry; Osteopathy; Paper and Pulp Engineering; Pharmacy; Physical Sciences; Radiology; Science, Technology, and Society; Sports-Related/Exercise Science; Statistics; Surveying, Surveying Technology, Cartography, or Geographic Information Science; Trade/Technical Specialties.

Award: Scholarship for use in freshman, sophomore, junior, senior, or graduate years; not renewable. *Number:* 2–3. *Amount:* $1500.

Eligibility Requirements: Applicant must be enrolled or expecting to enroll full- or part-time at a two-year or four-year or technical institution or university. Available to U.S. and Canadian citizens.

Application Requirements: Application form, essay. *Deadline:* continuous.

Contact: Web Department
E-mail: webcopy@nextstepu.com

SIGMA XI,
THE SCIENTIFIC RESEARCH SOCIETY

http://www.sigmaxi.org/

SIGMA XI GRANTS-IN-AID OF RESEARCH

• *See page 110*

THE SOCIETY FOR THE SCIENTIFIC STUDY OF SEXUALITY

http://www.sexscience.org/

THE SOCIETY FOR THE SCIENTIFIC STUDY OF SEXUALITY STUDENT RESEARCH GRANT

Award to support students doing scientific research related to sexuality. Purpose of research can be master's thesis or doctoral dissertation, but this is not a requirement. Must be enrolled in degree-granting program. Deadlines: February 1 and June 1. All applicants must be a member of the SSSS organization. A one-time award of $1000.

Academic Fields/Career Goals: Anthropology; Behavioral Science; Biology; Education; Health and Medical Sciences; Nursing; Psychology; Public Health; Religion/Theology; Social Sciences; Women's Studies.

Award: Grant for use in freshman, sophomore, junior, senior, or graduate years; not renewable. *Number:* 2. *Amount:* $1000.

Eligibility Requirements: Applicant must be enrolled or expecting to enroll full- or part-time at a four-year institution or university. Available to U.S. and non-U.S. citizens.

Application Requirements: Application form, essay.

Contact: Mandy Peters, Executive Director
The Society for the Scientific Study of Sexuality
881 Third Street, Suite B5
Whitehall, PA 18052
Phone: 610-443-3100
E-mail: thesociety@sexscience.org

APPLIED SCIENCES

101ST AIRBORNE DIVISION ASSOCIATION

http://www.screamingeaglefoundation.org/

AL & WILLIAMARY VISTE SCHOLARSHIP

• *See page 114*

AMERICAN CHEMICAL SOCIETY, RUBBER DIVISION

http://www.rubber.org/

AMERICAN CHEMICAL SOCIETY, RUBBER DIVISION UNDERGRADUATE SCHOLARSHIP

Candidate must be majoring in a technical discipline relevant to the rubber industry with a "B" or better overall academic average. Two scholarships are awarded to juniors and seniors enrolled in an accredited college or university in the United States, Canada, Mexico, India or Brazil.

Academic Fields/Career Goals: Applied Sciences; Aviation/Aerospace; Chemical Engineering; Electrical Engineering/Electronics; Energy and Power Engineering; Engineering-Related Technologies; Engineering/Technology; Materials Science, Engineering, and Metallurgy; Mechanical Engineering; Nuclear Science.

Award: Scholarship for use in junior or senior years; not renewable. *Number:* 3. *Amount:* $5000.

Eligibility Requirements: Applicant must be enrolled or expecting to enroll full-time at a four-year institution or university. Applicant must have 3.0 GPA or higher. Available to U.S. and non-U.S. citizens.

Application Requirements: Application form, essay, interview. *Deadline:* March 1.

Contact: Christie Robinson, Training and Development Director
American Chemical Society, Rubber Division
411 Wolf Ledges Pwky
Suite 201
Akron, OH 44311
Phone: 330-595-7602
E-mail: crobinson@rubber.org

AMERICAN INDIAN SCIENCE AND ENGINEERING SOCIETY

http://www.aises.org/

A.T. ANDERSON MEMORIAL SCHOLARSHIP PROGRAM

Award for full-time students majoring in Mathematics, Medical Sciences, Physical Science, Technology, Science, Engineering, or Natural Resources. Must be a member of the AISES and an enrolled member/citizen or a decedent of an enrolled member/citizen of a federally or state recognized American Indian Tribe or Alaskan Native Village (or be Native Hawaiian or decedent from a Native Hawaiian). Must have minimum 3.0 GPA.

Academic Fields/Career Goals: Applied Sciences; Biology; Business/Consumer Services; Chemical Engineering; Civil Engineering; Computer Science/Data Processing; Construction Engineering/Management; Dental Health/Services; Earth Science; Electrical Engineering/Electronics; Energy and Power Engineering; Engineering-Related Technologies; Engineering/Technology; Entomology; Environmental Health; Environmental Science; Food Science/Nutrition; Gemology; Geography; Health and Medical Sciences; Heating, Air-Conditioning, and Refrigeration Mechanics; Horticulture/Floriculture; Hydrology; Marine Biology; Marine/Ocean Engineering; Materials Science, Engineering, and Metallurgy; Mathematics; Mechanical Engineering; Meteorology/Atmospheric Science; Natural Resources; Natural Sciences; Neurobiology; Nuclear Science; Nursing; Occupational Safety and Health; Oceanography; Oncology; Optometry; Osteopathy; Paper and Pulp Engineering; Pharmacy; Physical Sciences; Radiology; Science, Technology, and Society; Social Sciences; Sports-Related/Exercise Science; Statistics; Surveying, Surveying Technology, Cartography, or Geographic Information Science; Therapy/Rehabilitation; Transportation.

Award: Scholarship for use in freshman, sophomore, junior, or graduate years; not renewable. *Amount:* $1000–$2000.

Eligibility Requirements: Applicant must be American Indian/Alaska Native and enrolled or expecting to enroll full-time at a two-year or four-year institution or university. Applicant must have 3.0 GPA or higher. Available to U.S. citizens.

Application Requirements: Application form, essay. *Deadline:* May 1.

Contact: Kyle Coulon, Program Officer
Phone: 720-552-6123 Ext. 108
E-mail: kcoulon@aises.org

AMERICAN INSTITUTE OF AERONAUTICS AND ASTRONAUTICS

http://www.aiaafoundation.org/

AIAA FOUNDATION UNDERGRADUATE SCHOLARSHIPS

Available to college students that will be sophomores, juniors, and seniors enrolled full-time in an accredited college/university. Must be AIAA student member to apply. Course of study must provide entry into some field of science or engineering encompassed by an AIAA technical committee. Minimum 3.3 GPA required.

Academic Fields/Career Goals: Applied Sciences; Aviation/Aerospace; Electrical Engineering/Electronics; Engineering-Related Technologies; Engineering/Technology; Materials Science, Engineering, and Metallurgy; Mechanical Engineering; Physical Sciences; Science, Technology, and Society.

Award: Scholarship for use in sophomore, junior, or senior years; not renewable. *Number:* 11. *Amount:* $500–$10,000.

Eligibility Requirements: Applicant must be enrolled or expecting to enroll full-time at a two-year or four-year institution or university. Applicant or parent of applicant must be member of American Institute of Aeronautics and Astronautics. Applicant must have 3.5 GPA or higher. Available to U.S. and non-U.S. citizens.

Application Requirements: Application form, essay. *Deadline:* January 31.

Contact: Felicia Livingston
American Institute of Aeronautics and Astronautics
12700 Sunrise Valley Drive
Suite 200
Reston, VA 20191
Phone: 703-2647502
E-mail: felicial@aiaa.org

LEATRICE GREGORY PENDRAY SCHOLARSHIP

Available to female college students that will be sophomores, juniors, and seniors enrolled full-time in an accredited college/university. Must be AIAA student member to apply. Course of study must provide entry into some field of science or engineering encompassed by AIAA. Minimum 3.3 GPA required.

Academic Fields/Career Goals: Applied Sciences; Aviation/Aerospace; Electrical Engineering/Electronics; Engineering-Related Technologies; Engineering/Technology; Materials Science, Engineering, and Metallurgy; Mechanical Engineering; Physical Sciences; Science, Technology, and Society.

Award: Scholarship for use in sophomore, junior, or senior years; not renewable. *Number:* 1. *Amount:* $1250.

Eligibility Requirements: Applicant must be enrolled or expecting to enroll full-time at a two-year or four-year institution or university and female. Applicant or parent of applicant must be member of American Institute of Aeronautics and Astronautics. Applicant must have 3.5 GPA or higher. Available to U.S. and non-U.S. citizens.

Application Requirements: Application form, essay. *Deadline:* January 31.

Contact: Felicia Livingston, Foundation Program Coordinator
American Institute of Aeronautics and Astronautics
12700 Sunrise Valley Drive
Suite 200
Reston, VA 20191-5807
Phone: 703-264-7502
E-mail: felicial@aiaa.org

AMERICAN SOCIETY FOR ENGINEERING EDUCATION

http://www.asee.org/

SCIENCE, MATHEMATICS, AND RESEARCH FOR TRANSFORMATION DEFENSE SCHOLARSHIP FOR SERVICE PROGRAM

Award established by the Department of Defense to support the education, recruitment, and retention of undergraduate and graduate students in the fields of science, technology, engineering, and mathematics. Available only to full-time undergraduate or graduate students with 3.0 GPA or above.

Academic Fields/Career Goals: Applied Sciences; Engineering-Related Technologies; Engineering/Technology; Mathematics; Physical Sciences.

Award: Scholarship for use in sophomore, junior, or senior years; renewable. *Number:* 200. *Amount:* $22,000–$39,000.

Eligibility Requirements: Applicant must be enrolled or expecting to enroll full-time at a two-year or four-year institution or university. Applicant must have 3.0 GPA or higher. Available to U.S. citizens.

Application Requirements: Application form, essay, recommendations or references, transcript. *Deadline:* December 14.

Contact: Evan Gaines, Project Coordinator
American Society for Engineering Education
1818 North Street, NW, Suite 600
Washington, DC 20036
Phone: 202-331-3544
Fax: 202-265-8504
E-mail: smart@asee.org

AMERICAN SOCIETY OF NAVAL ENGINEERS

http://www.navalengineers.org/

AMERICAN SOCIETY OF NAVAL ENGINEERS SCHOLARSHIP

Award for naval engineering students or students in related disciplines in the final year of an undergraduate program or for one year of graduate study at an accredited institution. Must be full-time student and a U.S. citizen. Award of $3000 for undergraduates and $4000 for graduate students.

Academic Fields/Career Goals: Applied Sciences; Aviation/Aerospace; Civil Engineering; Electrical Engineering/Electronics; Energy and Power Engineering; Engineering/Technology; Marine/Ocean Engineering; Materials Science, Engineering, and Metallurgy; Mechanical Engineering; Nuclear Science; Physical Sciences.

Award: Scholarship for use in senior or graduate years; not renewable. *Number:* 8–14. *Amount:* $3000–$4000.

Eligibility Requirements: Applicant must be enrolled or expecting to enroll full-time at a four-year institution or university. Applicant must have 2.5 GPA or higher. Available to U.S. citizens.

Application Requirements: Application form, personal photograph. *Deadline:* February 15.

Contact: Erica Cox, Senior Manager for Education and Business Development
American Society of Naval Engineers
1452 Duke St
Alexandria, VA 22314
Phone: 703-836-6727
Fax: 703-836-7491
E-mail: asnehq@navalengineers.org

ARMED FORCES COMMUNICATIONS AND ELECTRONICS ASSOCIATION, EDUCATIONAL FOUNDATION

http://www.afcea.org/site/?q=foundation/scholarships

AFCEA STEM MAJORS SCHOLARSHIPS FOR UNDERGRADUATE STUDENTS

Scholarships of $2,500 for full-time students currently working toward a undergraduate degree in the following STEM majors related to the mission of AFCEA include: Biometry/Biometrics, Computer Engineering, Computer Forensics Science, Computer Programming, Computer Science, Computer Systems, Cybersecurity, Electrical Engineering, Electronics Engineering, Geospatial Science, Information Science, Information Technology, Information Resource, Management, Intelligence, Mathematics, Network Engineering, Network Security, Operations, Research, Physics, Robotics Engineering, Robotics Technology, Statistics, Strategic Intelligence, and Telecommunications Engineering at an accredited college or university in the United States.

Academic Fields/Career Goals: Applied Sciences; Computer Science/Data Processing; Electrical Engineering/Electronics; Engineering-Related Technologies; Engineering/Technology; Materials Science, Engineering, and Metallurgy; Mathematics; Military and Defense Studies; Physical Sciences; Statistics.

Award: Scholarship for use in sophomore or junior years; not renewable. *Number:* 1–8. *Amount:* $2500.

Eligibility Requirements: Applicant must be enrolled or expecting to enroll full-time at a four-year institution or university. Applicant must have 3.0 GPA or higher. Available to U.S. citizens.

Application Requirements: Application form, community service, essay, financial need analysis. *Deadline:* April 23.

Contact: Mrs. Casmere Kistner, Scholarships, Awards and Grants
Armed Forces Communications and Electronics Association, Educational Foundation
4400 Fair Lakes Court
Fairfax, VA 22033
Phone: 703-631-6147
E-mail: edfoundation@afcea.org

ARRL FOUNDATION INC.

http://www.arrl.org/

CHARLES N. FISHER MEMORIAL SCHOLARSHIP

One-time award available to amateur radio operators in any class. Applicant must be majoring in electronics, communications, or a related field. Preference is given to those in the ARRL Southwestern Division (residents of Arizona and Los Angeles, Orange County, San Diego, or Santa Barbara, California). Must attend a regionally accredited institution.

Academic Fields/Career Goals: Applied Sciences; Communications; Electrical Engineering/Electronics; Engineering/Technology.

Award: Scholarship for use in freshman, sophomore, junior, or senior years; not renewable. *Number:* 1. *Amount:* $1000.

Eligibility Requirements: Applicant must be enrolled or expecting to enroll full-time at a four-year institution or university; resident of Arizona, California and must have an interest in amateur radio. Available to U.S. citizens.

Application Requirements: Application form. *Deadline:* January 31.

Contact: Ms. Mary Hobart, Secretary
Phone: 860-594-0397
E-mail: k1mmh@arrl.org

MISSISSIPPI SCHOLARSHIP

Available to students pursuing a degree in electronics, communications, or related fields. Must be licensed in any class of amateur radio operators. Must be a resident of Mississippi attending college in Mississippi and be under 30 years of age.

Academic Fields/Career Goals: Applied Sciences; Communications; Electrical Engineering/Electronics; Engineering/Technology.

Award: Scholarship for use in freshman, sophomore, junior, senior, or graduate years; not renewable. *Number:* 1. *Amount:* $500.

Eligibility Requirements: Applicant must be enrolled or expecting to enroll full-time at a four-year institution or university; resident of Mississippi; studying in Mississippi and must have an interest in amateur radio. Available to U.S. citizens.

Application Requirements: Application form. *Deadline:* January 31.

Contact: Ms. Mary Hobart, Secretary
Phone: 860-594-0397
E-mail: k1mmh@arrl.org

PAUL AND HELEN L. GRAUER SCHOLARSHIP

One award available to students licensed as amateur radio operators. Applicant must be majoring in electronics, communications, or a related field at the Baccalaureate level or higher. Preference given to residents of Iowa, Kansas, Missouri, and Nebraska or those attending institutions in Iowa, Kansas, Missouri, or Nebraska.

Academic Fields/Career Goals: Applied Sciences; Communications; Electrical Engineering/Electronics; Engineering/Technology.

Award: Scholarship for use in freshman, sophomore, junior, senior, or graduate years; not renewable. *Number:* 1. *Amount:* $1000.

Eligibility Requirements: Applicant must be enrolled or expecting to enroll full-time at a four-year institution or university; resident of Iowa, Kansas, Missouri, Nebraska; studying in Iowa, Kansas, Missouri, Nebraska and must have an interest in amateur radio. Available to U.S. citizens.

Application Requirements: Application form. *Deadline:* January 31.

Contact: Ms. Mary Hobart, Secretary
Phone: 860-594-0397
E-mail: k1mmh@arrl.org

WIFDR SCHOLARSHIP

One $1000 scholarship for a student with active general class or higher amateur radio license who is studying at any accredited 4-year college or university. Must be studying science, math, engineering, or technology.

Academic Fields/Career Goals: Applied Sciences; Chemical Engineering; Civil Engineering; Electrical Engineering/Electronics; Energy and Power Engineering; Engineering/Technology; Environmental Science; Health and Medical Sciences; Marine/Ocean Engineering; Materials Science, Engineering, and Metallurgy; Mathematics; Mechanical Engineering; Natural Sciences; Nuclear Science; Paper and Pulp Engineering; Physical Sciences.

Award: Scholarship for use in freshman, sophomore, junior, or senior years; not renewable. *Number:* 1. *Amount:* $1000.

Eligibility Requirements: Applicant must be enrolled or expecting to enroll full- or part-time at a four-year institution or university and must have an interest in amateur radio. Available to U.S. citizens.

Application Requirements: Application form. *Deadline:* January 31.

Contact: Ms. Mary Hobart, Secretary
Phone: 860-594-0397
E-mail: k1mmh@arrl.org

ASSOCIATION FOR WOMEN GEOSCIENTISTS (AWG)

http://www.awg.org/

AWG UNDERGRADUATE EXCELLENCE IN PALEONTOLOGY AWARD

The Association for Women Geoscientists is pleased to announce the AWG Undergraduate Paleontology Award. The award, which consists of a $1000 cash prize and membership in the Paleontological Society and AWG for the tenure of the awardee's schooling, will be presented to an outstanding female undergraduate student pursuing a career in paleontology.

Academic Fields/Career Goals: Applied Sciences; Archaeology; Biology; Earth Science; Marine Biology; Natural Sciences.

Award: Scholarship for use in freshman, sophomore, junior, or senior years; not renewable. *Number:* 1. *Amount:* $1000.

Eligibility Requirements: Applicant must be enrolled or expecting to enroll full- or part-time at a two-year or four-year institution or university and female. Available to U.S. and non-U.S. citizens.

Application Requirements: Application form, essay. *Deadline:* April 15.

Contact: Dr. Erin Saupe, Co-Chair
E-mail: goldring@awg.org

ASSOCIATION OF CALIFORNIA WATER AGENCIES

http://www.acwa.com/

ASSOCIATION OF CALIFORNIA WATER AGENCIES SCHOLARSHIPS

Two $3500 awards available to juniors and seniors who are California residents attending California universities. Must be in a water-related field of study. Community college transfers are also eligible as long as they will hold junior class standing as of the fall.

Academic Fields/Career Goals: Applied Sciences; Biology; Civil Engineering; Environmental Science; Hydrology; Natural Resources; Natural Sciences; Surveying, Surveying Technology, Cartography, or Geographic Information Science.

Award: Scholarship for use in junior or senior years; not renewable. *Number:* 2. *Amount:* $3500.

Eligibility Requirements: Applicant must be enrolled or expecting to enroll full-time at a four-year institution or university; resident of California and studying in California. Available to U.S. citizens.

Application Requirements: Application form, essay. *Deadline:* March 1.

Contact: Marie Meade, Outreach Specialist
Association of California Water Agencies
901 K Street, Suite 100
Sacramento, CA 95814
Phone: 916-441-4545
E-mail: mariem@acwa.com

CLAIR A. HILL SCHOLARSHIP

Scholarship is administered by a different member agency each year and guidelines vary based on the administrator. Contact ACWA for current information. Applicants must be in a water-related field of study and must be a resident of California enrolled in a California four-year college or university.

Academic Fields/Career Goals: Applied Sciences; Biology; Civil Engineering; Environmental Science; Hydrology; Natural Resources; Natural Sciences; Surveying, Surveying Technology, Cartography, or Geographic Information Science.

Award: Scholarship for use in junior or senior years; not renewable. *Number:* 1. *Amount:* $5000.

Eligibility Requirements: Applicant must be enrolled or expecting to enroll full-time at a four-year institution or university; resident of California and studying in California. Available to U.S. citizens.

Application Requirements: Application form, essay. *Deadline:* February 1.

Contact: Marie Meade, Outreach Specialist
Association of California Water Agencies
910 K Street, Suite 100
Sacramento, CA 95814
Phone: 916-441-4545
E-mail: mariem@acwa.com

ASTRONAUT SCHOLARSHIP FOUNDATION

http://www.astronautscholarship.org/

ASTRONAUT SCHOLARSHIP FOUNDATION

Scholarship candidates must be nominated by the faculty members. Students may not apply directly for the scholarship. Must be U.S. citizens. Scholarship nominees must be engineering or natural or applied science students.

Academic Fields/Career Goals: Applied Sciences; Aviation/Aerospace; Biology; Chemical Engineering; Computer Science/Data Processing; Earth Science; Electrical Engineering/Electronics; Engineering-Related Technologies; Materials Science, Engineering, and Metallurgy; Mechanical Engineering; Meteorology/Atmospheric Science.

Award: Scholarship for use in sophomore, junior, senior, or graduate years; renewable. *Number:* 19. *Amount:* $10,000.

Eligibility Requirements: Applicant must be enrolled or expecting to enroll full-time at a four-year institution or university. Available to U.S. citizens.

Application Requirements: Financial need analysis, recommendations or references, transcript. *Deadline:* varies.

Contact: Linn LeBlanc, Executive Director
Astronaut Scholarship Foundation
6225 Vectorspace Boulevard
Titusville, FL 32780
Phone: 321-269-6101 Ext. 6176
Fax: 321-264-9176
E-mail: linnleblanc@astronautscholarship.org

AUTOMOTIVE WOMEN'S ALLIANCE FOUNDATION

http://awafoundation.org/index.php

AUTOMOTIVE WOMEN'S ALLIANCE FOUNDATION SCHOLARSHIPS
• See page 81

BARRY GOLDWATER SCHOLARSHIP AND EXCELLENCE IN EDUCATION FOUNDATION

https://goldwater.scholarsapply.org

BARRY M. GOLDWATER SCHOLARSHIP AND EXCELLENCE IN EDUCATION PROGRAM

One-time award to college juniors and seniors who will pursue advanced degrees in mathematics, natural sciences, or engineering. Students planning to study medicine are eligible if they plan a career in research.

Candidates must be nominated by their college or university. Minimum 3.0 GPA required. Nomination deadline: February 1.

Academic Fields/Career Goals: Applied Sciences; Biology; Chemical Engineering; Computer Science/Data Processing; Earth Science; Electrical Engineering/Electronics; Energy and Power Engineering; Engineering-Related Technologies; Engineering/Technology; Entomology; Environmental Science; Hydrology; Marine Biology; Marine/Ocean Engineering; Materials Science, Engineering, and Metallurgy; Mathematics; Mechanical Engineering; Meteorology/Atmospheric Science; Natural Sciences; Neurobiology; Nuclear Science; Oceanography; Pharmacy; Physical Sciences.

Award: Scholarship for use in junior or senior years; renewable. *Number:* 300. *Amount:* $7500.

Eligibility Requirements: Applicant must be enrolled or expecting to enroll full-time at a two-year or four-year institution or university. Applicant must have 3.0 GPA or higher. Available to U.S. citizens.

Application Requirements: Application form, essay. *Deadline:* January 31.

Contact: Ms. Lucy Decher, Executive Administrator
Phone: 703-756-6012
Fax: 703-756-6015
E-mail: goldh2o@vacoxmail.com

BHW GROUP

https://thebhwgroup.com/

BHW WOMEN IN STEM SCHOLARSHIP

The Women In STEM Scholarship is available to undergraduate and graduate female students. You must be pursuing a degree in science, technology, engineering, or mathematics to be eligible for this award.

Academic Fields/Career Goals: Applied Sciences; Archaeology; Architecture; Aviation/Aerospace; Behavioral Science; Biology; Chemical Engineering; Civil Engineering; Computer Science/Data Processing; Construction Engineering/Management; Dental Health/Services; Earth Science; Electrical Engineering/Electronics; Energy and Power Engineering; Engineering-Related Technologies; Engineering/Technology; Entomology; Environmental Health; Environmental Science; Food Science/Nutrition; Gemology; Geography; Health Administration; Health and Medical Sciences; Health Information Management/Technology; Heating, Air-Conditioning, and Refrigeration Mechanics; Horticulture/Floriculture; Hydrology; Industrial Design; Insurance and Actuarial Science; Landscape Architecture; Marine/Ocean Engineering; Materials Science, Engineering, and Metallurgy; Mathematics; Mechanical Engineering; Meteorology/Atmospheric Science; Military and Defense Studies; Natural Resources; Natural Sciences; Near and Middle East Studies; Neurobiology; Nuclear Science; Nursing; Occupational Safety and Health; Oceanography; Oncology; Optometry; Osteopathy; Paper and Pulp Engineering; Pharmacy; Physical Sciences; Psychology; Science, Technology, and Society; Social Sciences.

Award: Scholarship for use in freshman, sophomore, junior, senior, graduate, or postgraduate years; not renewable. *Number:* 1. *Amount:* $3000.

Eligibility Requirements: Applicant must be enrolled or expecting to enroll full-time at a two-year or four-year or technical institution or university and female. Available to U.S. and non-U.S. citizens.

Application Requirements: Essay. *Deadline:* April 15.

Contact: Mr. Paul Francis, Partner
BHW Group
6011 W. Courtyard Dr
Suite 410
Austin, TX 78730
Phone: 512-2200035
E-mail: scholarship@thebhwgroup.com

CARDS AGAINST HUMANITY

https://cardsagainsthumanity.com/

SCIENCE AMBASSADOR SCHOLARSHIP

The Science Ambassador Scholarship is a full-ride scholarship for undergraduate women studying science, technology, engineering, or math, funded by Cards Against Humanity. To apply, applicants must submit a three minute video explaining a scientific topic they're passionate about. Applications are now open! Apply now at ScienceAmbassadorScholarship.org. If you have questions, you're welcome to email SAS@CardsAgainstHumanity.com.

Academic Fields/Career Goals: Applied Sciences; Aviation/Aerospace; Biology; Chemical Engineering; Civil Engineering; Computer Science/Data Processing; Dental Health/Services; Earth Science; Electrical Engineering/Electronics; Energy and Power Engineering; Engineering-Related Technologies; Engineering/Technology; Environmental Science; Insurance and Actuarial Science; Mathematics; Mechanical Engineering; Meteorology/Atmospheric Science; Natural Sciences; Neurobiology; Nuclear Science; Oceanography; Oncology; Optometry; Osteopathy; Paper and Pulp Engineering; Physical Sciences.

Award: Scholarship for use in freshman, sophomore, junior, or senior years; renewable. *Number:* 1.

Eligibility Requirements: Applicant must be enrolled or expecting to enroll full-time at a four-year institution or university and female. Available to U.S. and non-U.S. citizens.

Application Requirements: Application form. *Deadline:* December 11.

Contact: Maria Ranahan, Community Manager
E-mail: maria@cardsagainsthumanity.com

DAVIDSON INSTITUTE FOR TALENT DEVELOPMENT

http://www.davidsongifted.org/

DAVIDSON FELLOWS SCHOLARSHIP PROGRAM

One-time award to recognize outstanding achievements of young people. Must be 18 or younger as of October 1, 2019. Must have completed a significant piece of work in one of the following areas: science, technology, engineering, mathematics, humanities (music, literature or philosophy) or outside the box. Must be a U.S. citizen or a permanent resident.

Academic Fields/Career Goals: Applied Sciences; Engineering/Technology; Literature/English/Writing; Mathematics; Music; Philosophy; Science, Technology, and Society.

Award: Scholarship for use in freshman, sophomore, junior, senior, or graduate years; not renewable. *Number:* 15–20. *Amount:* $10,000–$50,000.

Eligibility Requirements: Applicant must be enrolled or expecting to enroll full- or part-time at a two-year or four-year or technical institution or university. Available to U.S. citizens.

Application Requirements: Application form, essay, portfolio. *Deadline:* February 13.

Contact: Tacie Moessner, Davidson Fellows Program Manager
Davidson Institute for Talent Development
9665 Gateway Drive, Suite B
Reno, NV 89521
Phone: 775-852-3483 Ext. 423
E-mail: davidsonfellows@davidsongifted.org

DISTIL NETWORKS

http://www.distilnetworks.com

WOMEN FORWARD IN TECHNOLOGY SCHOLARSHIP PROGRAM

The Woman Forward in Technology scholarship is to empower women entering the STEM field. The STEM career field workforce is currently only 24% women. Our mission is to help women who are pursuing undergraduate and graduate degrees in STEM programs to achieve their education goals, an objective which has the added long-term benefit of improving the diversity in STEM careers at large. Women, both U.S. citizen and non-citizen, who are attending at U.S. accredited university are encouraged to apply for a number of $3,000 scholarships being given out. Applicants can be either undergraduate or graduate students with a minimum GPA of 3.5 and a major in a STEM field.

Academic Fields/Career Goals: Applied Sciences; Biology; Chemical Engineering; Civil Engineering; Computer Science/Data Processing; Economics; Electrical Engineering/Electronics; Energy and Power Engineering; Engineering-Related Technologies; Engineering/Technology; Environmental Science; Finance; Marine Biology; Marine/Ocean Engineering; Materials Science, Engineering, and Metallurgy; Mathematics; Mechanical Engineering; Meteorology/Atmospheric Science; Natural Resources; Natural Sciences;

Neurobiology; Nuclear Science; Oceanography; Pharmacy; Physical Sciences; Science, Technology, and Society.

Award: Scholarship for use in freshman, sophomore, junior, senior, graduate, or postgraduate years; not renewable. *Number:* 15–25. *Amount:* $3000.

Eligibility Requirements: Applicant must be enrolled or expecting to enroll full- or part-time at a two-year or four-year institution or university and female. Applicant must have 3.5 GPA or higher. Available to U.S. and non-U.S. citizens.

Application Requirements: Application form, essay. *Deadline:* June 15.

Contact: Ms. Laura Leatherman, Operations Manager
Phone: 703-9979674
E-mail: laura.leatherman@distilnetworks.com

DIVERSITYCOMM, INC.

http://www.diversitycomm.net/

DIVERSITY IN STEAM MAGAZINE SCHOLARSHIP
• *See page 83*

THE ELECTROCHEMICAL SOCIETY

http://www.electrochem.org/

H.H. DOW MEMORIAL STUDENT ACHIEVEMENT AWARD OF THE INDUSTRIAL ELECTROLYSIS AND ELECTROCHEMICAL ENGINEERING DIVISION OF THE ELECTROCHEMICAL SOCIETY INC.

Award to recognize promising young engineers and scientists in the field of electrochemical engineering and applied electrochemistry. Applicant must be enrolled or accepted for enrollment in a college or university as a graduate student. Must submit description of proposed research project and how it relates to the field of electrochemistry, a letter of recommendation from research supervisor, and biography or resume.

Academic Fields/Career Goals: Applied Sciences; Chemical Engineering; Electrical Engineering/Electronics; Energy and Power Engineering; Engineering-Related Technologies; Engineering/Technology; Physical Sciences.

Award: Prize for use in freshman, sophomore, junior, senior, or graduate years; not renewable. *Number:* 1. *Amount:* $1000.

Eligibility Requirements: Applicant must be enrolled or expecting to enroll full-time at a four-year institution or university. Available to U.S. and non-U.S. citizens.

Application Requirements: Abstract of research project, statement of relationship of the project to the field of electrochemical engineering or applied electrochemistry, application form, recommendations or references, resume, transcript. *Deadline:* September 15.

Contact: Ms. Marcelle Austin, Board Relations Specialist
The Electrochemical Society
The Electrochemical Society
65 S Main Street, Building D
Pennington, NJ 08534
Phone: 609-737-1902 Ext. 124
Fax: 609-737-2743
E-mail: marcelle.austin@electrochem.org

STUDENT RESEARCH AWARDS OF THE BATTERY DIVISION OF THE ELECTROCHEMICAL SOCIETY INC.

Award to recognize promising young engineers and scientists in the field of electrochemical power sources. Student must be enrolled or must have been accepted for enrollment at a college or university.

Academic Fields/Career Goals: Applied Sciences; Chemical Engineering; Electrical Engineering/Electronics; Energy and Power Engineering; Engineering-Related Technologies; Engineering/Technology; Materials Science, Engineering, and Metallurgy; Mechanical Engineering; Natural Sciences; Physical Sciences.

Award: Prize for use in freshman, sophomore, junior, senior, or graduate years; not renewable. *Number:* 1. *Amount:* $1000.

Eligibility Requirements: Applicant must be enrolled or expecting to enroll full-time at a four-year institution or university. Available to U.S. and non-U.S. citizens.

Application Requirements: Application form, recommendations or references, resume, transcript, written summary of research accomplished. *Deadline:* March 15.

Contact: Ms. Marcelle Austin, Board Relations Specialist
The Electrochemical Society
The Electrochemical Society
65 S Main Street, Building D
Pennington, NJ 08534
Phone: 609-737-1902 Ext. 124
Fax: 609-737-2743
E-mail: marcelle.austin@electrochem.org

FOUNDATION FOR SCIENCE AND DISABILITY

http://stemd.org/

GRANTS FOR DISABLED GRADUATE STUDENTS IN THE SCIENCES
• *See page 106*

GREAT MINDS IN STEM

http://www.greatmindsinstem.org

HENAAC SCHOLARSHIP PROGRAM
• *See page 115*

INDIAN HEALTH SERVICES, UNITED STATES DEPARTMENT OF HEALTH AND HUMAN SERVICES

http://www.ihs.gov/scholarship

INDIAN HEALTH SERVICE HEALTH PROFESSIONS PRE-GRADUATE SCHOLARSHIPS

Scholarship for American Indian/Alaska Native students who are enrolled part-time or full-time in courses leading to a bachelor degree in the areas of pre-medicine, pre-dentistry, pre-optometry, or pre-podiatry. Minimum 2.0 GPA required to apply. Must intend to serve AI/AN people upon completion of professional healthcare education.

Academic Fields/Career Goals: Applied Sciences; Biology; Health and Medical Sciences.

Award: Scholarship for use in junior or senior years; not renewable. *Number:* 50–100. *Amount:* $23,000–$63,500.

Eligibility Requirements: Applicant must be of English heritage; American Indian/Alaska Native; enrolled or expecting to enroll full- or part-time at a four-year institution or university and resident of Alabama, Alaska, Arizona, Arkansas, California, Colorado, Connecticut, Delaware, District of Columbia, Florida, Georgia, Hawaii, Idaho, Illinois, Indiana, Iowa, Kansas, Kentucky, Louisiana, Maine, Maryland, Massachusetts, Michigan, Minnesota, Mississippi, Missouri, Montana, Nebraska, Nevada, New Hampshire, New Jersey, New Mexico, New York, North Carolina, North Dakota, Ohio, Oklahoma, Oregon, Pennsylvania, Rhode Island, South Carolina, South Dakota, Tennessee, Texas, Utah, Vermont, Virginia, Washington, West Virginia, Wisconsin, Wyoming. Available to U.S. citizens.

Application Requirements: Application form, essay. *Deadline:* March 28.

Contact: Ms. Reta Brewer, Branch Chief
Indian Health Services, United States Department of Health and Human Services
5600 Fishers Lane
Mail Stop: OHR 11E53A
Rockville, MD 20857
Phone: 301-443-6197
Fax: 301-443-6048
E-mail: reta.brewer@ihs.gov

INTERNATIONAL SOCIETY FOR OPTICAL ENGINEERING-SPIE

http://www.spie.org/scholarships

SPIE EDUCATIONAL SCHOLARSHIPS IN OPTICAL SCIENCE AND ENGINEERING

Scholarships for high school seniors, undergraduate and graduate students who are SPIE student member. High school students will receive a one-year complimentary student membership. Undergraduate and graduate students must be enrolled in an optics, photonics, imaging, optoelectronics program or related discipline for the full year. More details on eligibility and application requirements/forms can be found at http://spie.org/scholarships.

Academic Fields/Career Goals: Applied Sciences; Chemical Engineering; Electrical Engineering/Electronics; Engineering-Related Technologies; Engineering/Technology; Materials Science, Engineering, and Metallurgy; Mechanical Engineering.

Award: Scholarship for use in freshman, sophomore, junior, senior, or graduate years; not renewable. *Number:* 100–150. *Amount:* $2000–$11,000.

Eligibility Requirements: Applicant must be enrolled or expecting to enroll full- or part-time at a two-year or four-year or technical institution or university. Available to U.S. and non-U.S. citizens.

Application Requirements: Application form, essay, recommendations or references. *Deadline:* January 15.

Contact: Scholarship Committee
International Society for Optical Engineering-SPIE
PO Box 10
Bellingham, WA 98227-0010
Phone: 360-676-3290 Ext. 5452
Fax: 360-647-1445
E-mail: scholarships@spie.org

THE JACKSON LABORATORY

https://www.jax.org

THE JACKSON LABORATORY COLLEGE SCHOLARSHIP PROGRAM

The Jackson Laboratory, through the JAX College Scholarship Program, will award a $10,000 scholarship to three students from underserved backgrounds who will pursue a college degree and aspire to a career in biomedicine. This program is open to graduating high school seniors who reside in Connecticut, Maine, or in Sacramento County, California. One student from each location will be awarded this scholarship. The mission of The Jackson Laboratory is to discover precise genomic solutions for disease, and the scholarships will be awarded to students who share this goal by pursuing a career in research or medicine. In addition to the financial award, JAX will facilitate internship programs for scholarship recipients throughout their college career and sponsor annual campus visits to Bar Harbor, Maine and Farmington, CT. Scholarship recipients are expected to maintain strong academic performance and provide periodic updates on their college experience through blog posts and presentations.

Academic Fields/Career Goals: Applied Sciences; Behavioral Science; Biology; Computer Science/Data Processing; Environmental Health; Health and Medical Sciences; Nursing; Pharmacy; Public Health; Science, Technology, and Society.

Award: Scholarship for use in freshman or sophomore years; not renewable. *Number:* 3. *Amount:* $10,000.

Eligibility Requirements: Applicant must be high school student; planning to enroll or expecting to enroll full-time at a two-year or four-year institution or university and resident of California, Connecticut, Maine. Applicant must have 3.5 GPA or higher. Available to U.S. and non-U.S. citizens.

Application Requirements: Application form, essay, financial need analysis. *Deadline:* February 1.

Contact: Michael McKernan, Program Director, STEM and
Undergraduate Education
The Jackson Laboratory
The Jackson Laboratory
600 Main St.
Bar Harbor, ME 04609
Phone: 207-288-6000
E-mail: scholarship@jax.org

LABROOTS INC.

http://www.LabRoots.com

LABROOTS STEM SCHOLARSHIP
• See page 116

MEDICAL SCRUBS COLLECTION

http://medicalscrubscollection.com

MEDICAL SCRUBS COLLECTION SCHOLARSHIP
• See page 120

NASA IDAHO SPACE GRANT CONSORTIUM

http://www.idahospacegrant.org

NASA IDAHO SPACE GRANT CONSORTIUM SCHOLARSHIP PROGRAM

Applicants must attend an Idaho accredited institution and maintain a 3.0 GPA. Major/career interest in engineering, mathematics, science or secondary education in math or science. Applicants must be a U.S. citizen. Specifics of the program change from year to year. Please check our website for the most up to date information.

Academic Fields/Career Goals: Applied Sciences; Biology; Chemical Engineering; Civil Engineering; Computer Science/Data Processing; Earth Science; Electrical Engineering/Electronics; Energy and Power Engineering; Engineering-Related Technologies; Engineering/Technology; Environmental Science; Fire Sciences; Geography; Materials Science, Engineering, and Metallurgy; Mathematics; Mechanical Engineering; Meteorology/Atmospheric Science; Natural Resources; Natural Sciences; Nuclear Science; Physical Sciences; Science, Technology, and Society.

Award: Scholarship for use in freshman or sophomore years; not renewable. *Number:* 1–50. *Amount:* $500–$3000.

Eligibility Requirements: Applicant must be enrolled or expecting to enroll full-time at a two-year institution and studying in Idaho. Applicant must have 3.0 GPA or higher. Available to U.S. citizens.

Application Requirements: Application form, essay. *Deadline:* March 5.

Contact: Susie Johnson, Program Manager
NASA Idaho Space Grant Consortium
875 Perimeter Dr
Moscow, ID 83844-1026
Phone: 208-885-4934
Fax: 208-885-1399
E-mail: susiej@uidaho.edu

NASA'S VIRGINIA SPACE GRANT CONSORTIUM

http://www.vsgc.odu.edu/

COMMUNITY COLLEGE STEM SCHOLARSHIPS

This scholarship is designated for Virginia community college students studying STEM fields involving science, technology, engineering and math with aerospace relevance. Applicant must be U.S. citizen with a minimum GPA of 3.0 currently enrolled full-time with at least one semester of coursework (minimum of 12 credit hours) completed.

Academic Fields/Career Goals: Applied Sciences; Biology; Computer Science/Data Processing; Construction Engineering/Management; Drafting; Electrical Engineering/Electronics; Engineering/Technology; Environmental Science; Industrial Design; Materials Science, Engineering, and Metallurgy; Mathematics; Mechanical Engineering.

Award: Scholarship for use in sophomore year; not renewable. *Number:* 1–12. *Amount:* $2000–$2000.

Eligibility Requirements: Applicant must be enrolled or expecting to enroll full-time at a two-year institution and studying in Virginia. Applicant must have 3.0 GPA or higher. Available to U.S. citizens.

Application Requirements: Application form, essay, recommendations or references, resume, transcript. *Deadline:* March 17.

Contact: Mr. Chris Carter, Deputy Director
NASA's Virginia Space Grant Consortium
VSGC ODU, PHEC 600 Butler Farm Road
Hampton, VA 23666
Phone: 757-766-5210
Fax: 757-766-5205
E-mail: cxcarter@odu.edu

UNDERGRADUATE STEM RESEARCH SCHOLARSHIPS

Scholarships designated for undergraduate students pursuing any field of study with aerospace relevance. Must attend one of the five Virginia Space Grant colleges and universities. Must have minimum 3.0 GPA. Please refer to website for further details http://www.vsgc.odu.edu.

Academic Fields/Career Goals: Applied Sciences; Aviation/Aerospace; Biology; Chemical Engineering; Computer Science/Data Processing; Electrical Engineering/Electronics; Engineering-Related Technologies; Materials Science, Engineering, and Metallurgy; Mathematics; Mechanical Engineering; Physical Sciences; Science, Technology, and Society.

Award: Scholarship for use in junior or senior years; not renewable. *Number:* 1–35. *Amount:* $3000–$8500.

Eligibility Requirements: Applicant must be enrolled or expecting to enroll full-time at a four-year institution or university and studying in Virginia. Applicant must have 3.0 GPA or higher. Available to U.S. citizens.

Application Requirements: Application form, essay, recommendations or references, resume, transcript. *Deadline:* February 10.

Contact: Mr. Chris Carter, Deputy Director
NASA's Virginia Space Grant Consortium
VSGC PHEC 600 Butler Farm Road
Hampton, VA 23666
Phone: 757-766-5210
Fax: 757-766-5205

NEVADA NASA SPACE GRANT CONSORTIUM

https://nasa.epscorspo.nevada.edu/

NATIONAL SPACE GRANT CONSORTIUM SCHOLARSHIPS

Scholarships provide financial support to undergraduate and graduate students pursuing science, technology, engineering, and mathematics (STEM) degrees and provide the opportunity for students to deepen their inquiry within STEM through a myriad of channels including research experience, technical collaborations and professional development.

Academic Fields/Career Goals: Applied Sciences; Aviation/Aerospace; Chemical Engineering; Civil Engineering; Computer Science/Data Processing; Earth Science; Engineering/Technology; Mathematics; Mechanical Engineering; Natural Sciences; Physical Sciences.

Award: Scholarship for use in freshman, sophomore, junior, senior, or graduate years; not renewable. *Number:* 1–50. *Amount:* $1250–$13,333.

Eligibility Requirements: Applicant must be enrolled or expecting to enroll full-time at a two-year or four-year institution or university; resident of Nevada and studying in Nevada. Applicant must have 3.0 GPA or higher. Available to U.S. citizens.

Application Requirements: Application form, essay. *Deadline:* continuous.

Contact: Leone Thierman, Program Coordinator
Nevada NASA Space Grant Consortium
2601 Enterprise Way
Reno, NV 89512
Phone: 775-784-3476
Fax: 775-784-1127
E-mail: nvspacegrant@nshe.nevada.edu

NEXTSTEPU

http://www.nextstepu.com/

$1,500 STEM SCHOLARSHIP
• *See page 120*

OREGON STUDENT ASSISTANCE COMMISSION

https://oregonstudentaid.gov/

ANDY AITKENHEAD SCHOLARSHIP

Award for college sophomore or above for fall term/semester of undergraduate study. Must be studying science, mathematics, or engineering. Minimum 3.8 GPA and FAFSA are required.

Academic Fields/Career Goals: Applied Sciences; Earth Science; Engineering/Technology; Environmental Science; Health and Medical Sciences; Mathematics; Natural Sciences; Nuclear Science; Physical Sciences.

Award: Scholarship for use in sophomore, junior, or senior years; not renewable.

Eligibility Requirements: Applicant must be enrolled or expecting to enroll full- or part-time at a four-year institution or university. Applicant must have 3.5 GPA or higher. Available to U.S. citizens.

Application Requirements: Application form, essay, financial need analysis. *Deadline:* March 1.

Contact: Melissa Adams, Scholarship Processing Coordinator
Phone: 541-687-7409
E-mail: melissa.adams@state.or.us

SEHAR SALEHA AHMAD AND ABRAHIM EKRAMULLAH ZAFAR FOUNDATION SCHOLARSHIP

Scholarship available to female graduating seniors of Oregon high schools (including GED recipients and home schooled students). Minimum 3.8 GPA. Must be a mathematics or science major at a 4-year public or nonprofit college or university. Scholarship is automatically renewable if renewal criteria met.

Academic Fields/Career Goals: Applied Sciences; Biology; Earth Science; Natural Sciences; Physical Sciences.

Award: Scholarship for use in freshman year; renewable.

Eligibility Requirements: Applicant must be high school student; planning to enroll or expecting to enroll full-time at a four-year institution or university; female and resident of Oregon. Applicant must have 2.5 GPA or higher. Available to U.S. citizens.

Application Requirements: Application form, financial need analysis. *Deadline:* March 1.

Contact: Melissa Adams, Scholarship Processing Coordinator
Phone: 541-687-7409
E-mail: melissa.adams@state.or.us

SCARLETT FAMILY FOUNDATION SCHOLARSHIP PROGRAM

http://www.scarlettfoundation.org/

SCHOLARSHIP FOR STUDENTS PURSUING A BUSINESS OR STEM DEGREE
• *See page 91*

SINO-AMERICAN PHARMACEUTICAL PROFESSIONALS ASSOCIATION

http://www.sapaweb.org

SAPA SCHOLARSHIP AND EXCELLENCE IN EDUCATION PROGRAM

$1000 award for a high school senior who is planning to attend a full-time undergraduate program at an accredited four-year college/university with a major related to life sciences. Must have a minimum GPA of 3.3, a minimum SAT score of 2000 out of 2400 (or 1400 out of 1600 for new SAT) or ACT score of 30, and be a United States citizen or a legal resident alien.

Academic Fields/Career Goals: Applied Sciences.

Award: Scholarship for use in freshman year; not renewable. *Number:* 2. *Amount:* $1000.

Eligibility Requirements: Applicant must be high school student and planning to enroll or expecting to enroll full-time at a four-year institution or university. Available to U.S. citizens.

Application Requirements: Application form, essay. *Deadline:* June 30.

STRAIGHT NORTH
https://www.straightnorth.com/

STRAIGHT NORTH STEM SCHOLARSHIP
• *See page 92*

TKE EDUCATIONAL FOUNDATION
http://www.tke.org/

CARROL C. HALL MEMORIAL SCHOLARSHIP
One-time award of $400 given to a full-time undergraduate member of Tau Kappa Epsilon, who is earning a degree in education or science and has plans to become a teacher or pursue a profession in science. Applicant should have a demonstrated record of leadership within his chapter, on campus and in the community. Minimum 3.0 GPA required.

Academic Fields/Career Goals: Applied Sciences; Biology; Earth Science; Education; Meteorology/Atmospheric Science; Physical Sciences.

Award: Scholarship for use in sophomore, junior, or senior years; not renewable. *Number:* 1. *Amount:* $400.

Eligibility Requirements: Applicant must be enrolled or expecting to enroll full-time at a four-year institution or university; male and must have an interest in leadership. Applicant or parent of applicant must be member of Tau Kappa Epsilon. Applicant must have 3.0 GPA or higher. Available to U.S. and non-U.S. citizens.

Application Requirements: Application form, application form may be submitted online (http://www.tke.org/member_resources/scholarships/apply_online), essay, personal photograph, transcript. *Deadline:* March 15.

Contact: Offices of the Grand Chapter
TKE Educational Foundation
7439 Woodland Drive, Suite 100
Indianapolis, IN 46278
E-mail: tkeogc@tke.org

UNITED NEGRO COLLEGE FUND
http://www.uncf.org/

DISCOVER FINANCIAL SERVICES SCHOLARSHIP
• *See page 93*

PROCTER & GAMBLE STEM SCHOLARSHIP
Up to $5000 for academically achieving undergraduate students at accredited four-year colleges or universities within the United States. Focus on providing financial assistance to ensure students have access to quality education toward a successful career in the STEM industry.

Academic Fields/Career Goals: Applied Sciences; Chemical Engineering; Civil Engineering; Computer Science/Data Processing; Electrical Engineering/Electronics; Engineering-Related Technologies; Engineering/Technology; Materials Science, Engineering, and Metallurgy; Mathematics; Mechanical Engineering; Natural Sciences; Nuclear Science; Science, Technology, and Society.

Award: Scholarship for use in freshman, sophomore, junior, or senior years.

Eligibility Requirements: Applicant must be Black (non-Hispanic) and enrolled or expecting to enroll at a four-year institution or university. Applicant must have 3.0 GPA or higher. Available to U.S. citizens.

Application Requirements: Application form. *Deadline:* June 15.

Contact: Mary Williams, Director of Outreach and Recruitment
Phone: 800-331-2244

UNIVERSITIES SPACE RESEARCH ASSOCIATION
http://www.usra.edu/

UNIVERSITIES SPACE RESEARCH ASSOCIATION SCHOLARSHIP AWARD PROGRAM
Award for full-time undergraduate students who are within two years of earning a B.A. or B.S. by time award is received. Must be majoring in the physical sciences or engineering, with career interest in fields of space science, aerospace engineering, or space science education. Eligible majors may include, but are not limited to, aerospace engineering, astronomy, astrobiology, biophysics, chemical engineering, computer science, electrical engineering, geophysics, geology, mathematics, mechanical engineering, physics, and space science education. Must be U.S. citizen or permanent resident. Minimum 3.5 GPA required.

Academic Fields/Career Goals: Applied Sciences; Aviation/Aerospace; Chemical Engineering; Computer Science/Data Processing; Earth Science; Electrical Engineering/Electronics; Engineering/Technology; Mathematics; Mechanical Engineering; Nuclear Science; Physical Sciences; Science, Technology, and Society.

Award: Scholarship for use in junior or senior years; not renewable. *Number:* 4–6. *Amount:* $4000.

Eligibility Requirements: Applicant must be enrolled or expecting to enroll full-time at a four-year institution or university. Applicant must have 3.5 GPA or higher. Available to U.S. citizens.

Application Requirements: Application form, community service, essay. *Deadline:* August 8.

Contact: Dr. James Lochner, Director of University Relations
Universities Space Research Association
7178 Columbia Gateway Drive
Columbia, MD 21046
Phone: 410-740-6253
E-mail: jlochner@usra.edu

VERMONT SPACE GRANT CONSORTIUM
http://www.cems.uvm.edu/vsgc

VERMONT SPACE GRANT CONSORTIUM
• *See page 104*

ARCHAEOLOGY

AMERICAN SCHOOL OF CLASSICAL STUDIES AT ATHENS
http://www.ascsa.edu.gr/

ASCSA SUMMER SESSION AND SUMMER SEMINARS SCHOLARSHIPS
• *See page 118*

ARCHAEOLOGICAL INSTITUTE OF AMERICA
http://www.archaeological.org/

JANE C. WALDBAUM ARCHAEOLOGICAL FIELD SCHOOL SCHOLARSHIP
Scholarship available to support participation in an archaeological excavation or survey project. Open to junior and senior undergraduates and first-year graduate students who are currently enrolled in a U.S. or Canadian college or university. Applicants cannot have previously participated in an archaeological excavation, and must be at least a junior at time of application. Applicants must be at least 18 years of age.

Academic Fields/Career Goals: Archaeology.

Award: Scholarship for use in junior, senior, or graduate years; not renewable. *Number:* 5–20. *Amount:* $1000.

Eligibility Requirements: Applicant must be enrolled or expecting to enroll full- or part-time at a four-year institution or university. Available to U.S. and non-U.S. citizens.

Application Requirements: Application form, essay. *Deadline:* March 1.

Contact: Laurel Sparks, Coordinator, Lecture and Fellowship
Phone: 857-305-9360
Fax: 857-233-4270
E-mail: lsparks@archaeology.org

ASSOCIATION FOR WOMEN GEOSCIENTISTS (AWG)

http://www.awg.org/

AWG MARIA LUISA CRAWFORD FIELD CAMP SCHOLARSHIP

The Crawford Scholarship encourages promising young women to pursue geoscience careers through attendance at field camp. Two $750 scholarships are awarded annually through a competitive process.

Academic Fields/Career Goals: Archaeology; Earth Science; Education; Energy and Power Engineering; Environmental Science; Gemology; Hydrology; Meteorology/Atmospheric Science; Natural Resources; Natural Sciences; Oceanography; Physical Sciences.

Award: Scholarship for use in freshman, sophomore, junior, or senior years; not renewable. *Number:* 2. *Amount:* $750.

Eligibility Requirements: Applicant must be enrolled or expecting to enroll full-time at a four-year institution or university and female. Applicant must have 3.0 GPA or higher. Available to U.S. citizens.

Application Requirements: Application form, essay. *Deadline:* February 14.

Contact: Sarah Hunt, Crawford Scholarship Coordinator
E-mail: crawford@awg.org

AWG SALT LAKE CHAPTER (SLC) RESEARCH SCHOLARSHIP

Offered by AWG's Salt Lake Chapter, this scholarship will help defray the costs of presenting geoscience research results at national, or regional, science conventions and meetings. It is awarded based upon the quality and importance of the research being conducted and reported.

Academic Fields/Career Goals: Archaeology; Earth Science; Education; Environmental Science; Geography; Hydrology; Meteorology/Atmospheric Science; Museum Studies; Natural Resources; Natural Sciences; Oceanography; Physical Sciences.

Award: Scholarship for use in freshman, sophomore, junior, senior, or graduate years; not renewable. *Number:* 1. *Amount:* $1–$1000.

Eligibility Requirements: Applicant must be enrolled or expecting to enroll full- or part-time at a two-year or four-year institution or university; female and studying in Utah. Applicant must have 3.0 GPA or higher. Available to U.S. citizens.

Application Requirements: Application form, letter from applicant summarizing research, purpose and importance of research, recommendations or references. *Deadline:* March 12.

Contact: Janae Wallace, AWG Salt Lake Chapter Scholarship Coordinator
Association for Women Geoscientists (AWG)
AWG Salt Lake Chapter
PO Box 58691
Salt Lake City, UT 84152
Phone: 801-537-3387
E-mail: janaewallace@utah.gov

AWG UNDERGRADUATE EXCELLENCE IN PALEONTOLOGY AWARD

• *See page 123*

JANET CULLEN TANAKA GEOSCIENCES UNDERGRADUATE SCHOLARSHIP

This scholarship is for undergraduate women who are committed to completing a Bachelor's degree and pursuing a career or graduate work in the geosciences.

Academic Fields/Career Goals: Archaeology; Earth Science; Environmental Science; Hydrology; Meteorology/Atmospheric Science; Natural Resources; Natural Sciences; Oceanography; Physical Sciences.

Award: Scholarship for use in sophomore, junior, or senior years; not renewable. *Number:* 1–2. *Amount:* $1–$1500.

Eligibility Requirements: Applicant must be enrolled or expecting to enroll full-time at a two-year or four-year institution or university; female and studying in Oregon, Washington. Applicant must have 3.0 GPA or higher. Available to U.S. citizens.

Application Requirements: Essay, financial need analysis, recommendations or references, transcript. *Deadline:* December 15.

Contact: Jenny Saltonstall, AWG PNW Scholarship Chair
Association for Women Geoscientists (AWG)
AWG Pacific Northwest Chapter
PO Box 28391
Seattle, WA 98118
Phone: 425-827-7701
Fax: 425-827-5424
E-mail: scholarship@awg-ps.org

OSAGE CHAPTER UNDERGRADUATE SERVICE SCHOLARSHIP

This Service Scholarship provides an undergraduate student in the geosciences with funding for research, tuition or books. The recipient will be required to participate in two service events (e.g. AWG outreach activities) within a year following receipt of the award.

Academic Fields/Career Goals: Archaeology; Earth Science; Environmental Science; Gemology; Geography; Hydrology; Meteorology/Atmospheric Science; Museum Studies; Natural Resources; Oceanography; Physical Sciences.

Award: Scholarship for use in freshman, sophomore, junior, or senior years; not renewable. *Number:* 1. *Amount:* $500.

Eligibility Requirements: Applicant must be enrolled or expecting to enroll full-time at a four-year institution or university and studying in Kansas, Missouri, Nebraska. Available to U.S. citizens.

Application Requirements: Application form, personal statement, transcript. *Deadline:* April 15.

Contact: Sarah Morton, AWG Osage Chapter President
Association for Women Geoscientists (AWG)
University of Kansas
1475 Jayhawk Boulevard, Room 120
Lawrence, KS 66045
E-mail: awgosage@gmail.com

BHW GROUP

https://thebhwgroup.com/

BHW WOMEN IN STEM SCHOLARSHIP

• *See page 124*

MEDICAL SCRUBS COLLECTION

http://medicalscrubscollection.com

MEDICAL SCRUBS COLLECTION SCHOLARSHIP

• *See page 120*

PLAN NEW HAMPSHIRE

http://www.plannh.org

PLAN NEW HAMPSHIRE SCHOLARSHIP AND FELLOWSHIP PROGRAM

Plan NH, in partnership with the NH Charitable Foundation, offers scholarships and fellowships to students who call New Hampshire home and are studying a field related to planning, design and/or development of the built environment in an accredited school anywhere in the world. Applicants must have at least one semester of college or equivalent completed before application. Scholarships are available for colleges, universities and tech schools; fellowships are available for grad students of architecture. This is a competitive process for funding from several sources.

Academic Fields/Career Goals: Archaeology; Architecture; Civil Engineering; Construction Engineering/Management; Energy and Power Engineering; Engineering/Technology; Environmental Science; Historic Preservation and Conservation; Interior Design; Landscape Architecture;

Mechanical Engineering; Natural Resources; Transportation; Urban and Regional Planning.

Award: Scholarship for use in sophomore, junior, senior, graduate, or postgraduate years; not renewable. *Number:* 5–10. *Amount:* $1200–$5000.

Eligibility Requirements: Applicant must be enrolled or expecting to enroll full-time at a two-year or four-year or technical institution or university and resident of New Hampshire. Available to U.S. citizens.

Application Requirements: Application form, essay, interview, portfolio. *Fee:* $10. *Deadline:* April 12.

Contact: Robin LeBlanc, Executive Director
Plan New Hampshire
PO Box 1105
21 Daniel Street 2nd floor c/o GPI
Portsmouth, NH 03801
Phone: 603-452-7526
E-mail: r_leblanc@plannh.org

SCARLETT FAMILY FOUNDATION SCHOLARSHIP PROGRAM

http://www.scarlettfoundation.org/

SCHOLARSHIP FOR STUDENTS PURSUING A BUSINESS OR STEM DEGREE
• *See page 91*

SOCIETY FOR CLASSICAL STUDIES

http://www.classicalstudies.org/

MINORITY STUDENT SUMMER SCHOLARSHIP

Award to minority undergraduate students for a scholarship to further an undergraduate's preparation for graduate work in classics or archaeology. Applicants should be current students of classics. Eligible proposals might include (but are not limited to) participation in summer programs or field schools in Italy, Greece, Egypt, or language training at institutions in the U.S, Canada, or Europe. Amount of the award will range from $1,500 to $4,000. Application must be supported by a member of the SCS.

Academic Fields/Career Goals: Archaeology; Arts; Classics; Foreign Language; History.

Award: Scholarship for use in freshman, sophomore, junior, or senior years; not renewable. *Number:* 2. *Amount:* $1500–$4000.

Eligibility Requirements: Applicant must be American Indian/Alaska Native, Asian/Pacific Islander, Black (non-Hispanic), Hispanic and enrolled or expecting to enroll full-time at a four-year institution or university. Available to U.S. and non-U.S. citizens.

Application Requirements: Application form, application form may be submitted online (http://www.classicalstudies.org), essay, financial need analysis, recommendations or references, transcript. *Deadline:* December 15.

Contact: Dr. Adam Blistein, Executive Director
Phone: 215-898-4975
Fax: 215-573-7874
E-mail: scsclassics@sas.upenn.edu

ARCHITECTURE

AACE INTERNATIONAL

http://www.aacei.org/

AACE INTERNATIONAL COMPETITIVE SCHOLARSHIP

AACE International scholarships are available in amounts ranging from $2000 to $8000. Specific awards will be determined based on overall scholarship and collegiate accomplishments. Applications are only available on line and are accepted from mid-December through February 7th. Applicants should attach an unofficial transcript in a PDF format to their application.

Academic Fields/Career Goals: Architecture; Aviation/Aerospace; Business/Consumer Services; Chemical Engineering; Civil Engineering; Construction Engineering/Management; Electrical Engineering/Electronics; Engineering-Related Technologies; Engineering/Technology; Mechanical Engineering.

Award: Scholarship for use in freshman, sophomore, junior, senior, or graduate years; not renewable. *Number:* 10–20. *Amount:* $2000–$8000.

Eligibility Requirements: Applicant must be enrolled or expecting to enroll full-time at a two-year or four-year institution or university. Applicant must have 3.0 GPA or higher. Available to U.S. and non-U.S. citizens.

Application Requirements: Application form, application form may be submitted online (http://www.aacei.org/awards/scholarships/application.shtml), essay, recommendations or references, transcript. *Deadline:* February 7.

Contact: Mr. John Hines, Manager, Education
AACE International
1265 Suncrest Towne Centre Drive
Morgantown, WV 26505-1876
Phone: 304-296-8444 Ext. 119
E-mail: jhines@aacei.org

ACI FOUNDATION

http://www.acifoundation.org

ACI FOUNDATION SCHOLARSHIP PROGRAM

Awards available for full-time graduate students in their first or second year of study in a concrete-related field. Must be enrolled in a program in a U.S. or Canadian institution. For more details visit http://www.concrete.org.

Academic Fields/Career Goals: Architecture; Civil Engineering; Engineering/Technology; Materials Science, Engineering, and Metallurgy.

Award: Scholarship for use in freshman, sophomore, junior, senior, or graduate years; not renewable. *Number:* 5. *Amount:* $5000.

Eligibility Requirements: Applicant must be enrolled or expecting to enroll full-time at a four-year institution or university. Available to U.S. and non-U.S. citizens.

Application Requirements: Application form, essay. *Deadline:* continuous.

Contact: Ashley Mayra, Scholarship Coordinator
ACI Foundation
38800 Country Club Drive
Farmington Hills, MI 48331
Phone: 248-848-3737
E-mail: scholarships@concrete.org

AMERICAN SCHOOL OF CLASSICAL STUDIES AT ATHENS

http://www.ascsa.edu.gr/

ASCSA SUMMER SESSION AND SUMMER SEMINARS SCHOLARSHIPS
• *See page 118*

AMERICAN SOCIETY OF HEATING, REFRIGERATING, AND AIR CONDITIONING ENGINEERS, INC.

http://www.ashrae.org/

ASHRAE REGION IV BENNY BOOTLE SCHOLARSHIP

One-year scholarship available to an undergraduate engineering or architecture student enrolled full-time in a program accredited by ABET or NAAB and attending a school located within the geographic boundaries of ASHRAE Region IV (North Carolina, South Carolina, Georgia). See Website for application and additional information, http://www.ashrae.org.

Academic Fields/Career Goals: Architecture; Engineering/Technology.

Award: Scholarship for use in freshman, sophomore, junior, or senior years; not renewable. *Number:* 1. *Amount:* $5000.

Eligibility Requirements: Applicant must be enrolled or expecting to enroll full-time at a four-year institution or university and studying in Georgia, North Carolina, South Carolina. Applicant must have 3.0 GPA or higher. Available to U.S. and non-U.S. citizens.

Application Requirements: Application form, financial need analysis. *Deadline:* December 1.

Contact: Lois Benedict, Scholarship Administrator
Phone: 404-636-8400 Ext. 1120
E-mail: lbenedict@ashrae.org

ARCHITECTS FOUNDATION

https://architectsfoundation.org/

ARCHITECTS FOUNDATION DIVERSITY ADVANCEMENT SCHOLARSHIP

Maybe you chose architecture because you want to design a better world. Or you can't imagine doing anything else. One thing's for certain: You love this work. And we'd love to help fund your college experience with a multiyear scholarship, up to $20,000. We created the Diversity Advancement Scholarship to help more minority students pursue a successful career in architecture. Multiple scholarships are available. We're looking for minority students whose imagination and design thinking will influence the future of the built environment and the architecture profession. Eligible students must be a U.S. citizen, have a minimum 3.0 GPA, and be a high school student planning to enroll in a NAAB-accredited architecture degree program; or, a rising second-year college student in a NAAB-accredited architecture degree program; or a technical school or community college student who has completed high school or its equivalent and intends to transfer to a NAAB-accredited architecture program. NAAB-accredited degree programs may be a five-year Bachelor of Architecture degree, or a four-year pre-professional bachelor degree followed by a Master of Architecture degree. Scholarships may be renewed for up to 5 years (up to a $20,000 total award–multiple scholarships are available).

Academic Fields/Career Goals: Architecture.

Award: Scholarship for use in freshman, sophomore, junior, senior, or graduate years; renewable. *Number:* 3–10. *Amount:* $4000.

Eligibility Requirements: Applicant must be American Indian/Alaska Native, Asian/Pacific Islander, Black (non-Hispanic), Hispanic and enrolled or expecting to enroll full-time at a two-year or four-year or technical institution or university. Applicant must have 3.0 GPA or higher. Available to U.S. citizens.

Application Requirements: Application form, essay, financial need analysis, portfolio. *Deadline:* January 17.

Contact: Amanda Malloy, Development Manager
Architects Foundation
The Architects Foundation
1735 New York Avenue, NW
Washington, DC 20006-5292
Phone: 202-626-7577
E-mail: scholarships@architectsfoundation.org

ARCHITECTS FOUNDATION PAYETTE SHO-PING CHIN MEMORIAL ACADEMIC SCHOLARSHIP

The Payette Sho-Ping Chin Memorial Academic Scholarship was established with the architecture firm Payette to support a woman studying architecture within a NAAB-accredited Bachelor's or Master's degree program. Sho-Ping, a fellow and leader in the AIA, was a long-time principal and healthcare practice leader at Payette. She was a talented and compassionate architect who was fiercely determined to design healthcare architecture of the highest caliber for those in need. Sho-Ping was a wonderful mentor and instilled in her teams a sense of camaraderie and commitment to design. As a founder of the AIA Women's Leadership Summit, held biennially, Sho-Ping was instrumental in defining the national discourse for Women in Design. The $10,000 scholarship will be awarded to a student who will be entering at least their third year of undergraduate or any level of graduate study within an accredited architecture program. Previous Payette Sho-Ping Chin Memorial Academic Scholarship recipients are eligible to reapply in subsequent years. To help the scholarship recipient establish contacts within the profession, she will be assigned a senior mentor from Payette for the scholarship year.

Academic Fields/Career Goals: Architecture.

Award: Scholarship for use in junior, senior, graduate, or postgraduate years; not renewable. *Number:* 1. *Amount:* $10,000.

Eligibility Requirements: Applicant must be enrolled or expecting to enroll full-time at a four-year institution or university and female. Applicant must have 3.0 GPA or higher. Available to U.S. citizens.

Application Requirements: Application form, essay, financial need analysis, portfolio. *Deadline:* January 17.

Contact: Amanda Malloy, Development Manager
Architects Foundation
1735 New York Avenue NW
Washington, DC 20006
Phone: 202-626-7577
E-mail: scholarships@architectsfoundation.org

ASSOCIATION FOR WOMEN IN ARCHITECTURE FOUNDATION

http://www.awa-la.org/

ASSOCIATION FOR WOMEN IN ARCHITECTURE FOUNDATION SCHOLARSHIP

Must be a California resident or attend school in California. Open to women only. Must major in architecture or a related design field (landscape architecture, urban and land planning, interior design and environmental design) and have completed 18 units in that major by the application date. Recipients may reapply. Applications and further details are available for download on Website http://www.awaplusd.org/scholarships.

Academic Fields/Career Goals: Architecture; Interior Design; Landscape Architecture.

Award: Scholarship for use in sophomore, junior, senior, or graduate years; not renewable. *Number:* 3. *Amount:* $2500.

Eligibility Requirements: Applicant must be enrolled or expecting to enroll full-time at a four-year institution or university and female. Available to U.S. and non-U.S. citizens.

Application Requirements: Application form, essay, portfolio. *Deadline:* March 23.

Contact: Ms. Lise Bornstein, Scholarship Chair
Association for Women in Architecture Foundation
AWAF Scholarships/ Association for Women in Architecture Foundation
1315 Storm Parkway
Torrance, CA 90501-5034
Phone: 310-534-8466
E-mail: scholarships@awaplusd.org

BHW GROUP

https://thebhwgroup.com/

BHW WOMEN IN STEM SCHOLARSHIP
• *See page 124*

BRASKEM ODEBRECHT

http://www.odebrechtaward.com

ODEBRECHT AWARD FOR SUSTAINABLE DEVELOPMENT

Award for undergraduate students in all engineering fields, architecture, building and construction management, and chemistry. By submitting a paper that outlines contributions to sustainability, students have an opportunity to win $65,000 in cash prizes for themselves, their faculty advisors and their universities. Ideas can be related to efficient, real-world uses of sustainable materials, new chemical and petrochemical processes or new building techniques. Must register at website to enter.

Academic Fields/Career Goals: Architecture; Chemical Engineering; Civil Engineering; Construction Engineering/Management; Electrical Engineering/Electronics; Energy and Power Engineering; Mechanical Engineering.

Award: Prize for use in freshman, sophomore, junior, or senior years; not renewable.

Eligibility Requirements: Applicant must be enrolled or expecting to enroll full- or part-time at a four-year institution or university. Available to U.S. citizens.

Application Requirements: Application form, application form may be submitted online, recommendations or references, university identification. *Deadline:* May 31.

CENTER FOR ARCHITECTURE

http://www.centerforarchitecture.org

CENTER FOR ARCHITECTURE DESIGN SCHOLARSHIP

Merit-based scholarships that support deserving students studying architecture, design, engineering, planning or a related discipline in an accredited program within New York State.

Academic Fields/Career Goals: Architecture; Civil Engineering; Electrical Engineering/Electronics; Industrial Design; Interior Design; Landscape Architecture; Mechanical Engineering.

Award: Scholarship for use in freshman, sophomore, junior, senior, or graduate years; not renewable. *Number:* 1–2. *Amount:* $2000–$5000.

Eligibility Requirements: Applicant must be enrolled or expecting to enroll full-time at a two-year or four-year or technical institution or university; resident of New York and studying in New York. Available to U.S. and non-U.S. citizens.

Application Requirements: Application form, essay, portfolio. *Deadline:* March 15.

Contact: Ms. Elana Grossman, Manager, Foundation & Government
　　　　　Relations
　　　　Center for Architecture
　　　　Center for Architecture Attn: CFA Design Scholarship
　　　　536 LaGuardia Place
　　　　New York, NY 10012
　　　　Phone: 212-358-6134
　　　　E-mail: scholarships@cfafoundation.org

CENTER FOR ARCHITECTURE, DOUGLAS HASKELL AWARD FOR STUDENT JOURNALS

Any journal (online or print) published by a school of architecture, landscape architecture or planning in the United States that is edited by students is eligible. The publication must have been produced in the current or previous school year.

Academic Fields/Career Goals: Architecture; Engineering/Technology; Landscape Architecture; Urban and Regional Planning.

Award: Prize for use in freshman, sophomore, junior, or graduate years; not renewable. *Number:* 1–3. *Amount:* $1000–$2000.

Eligibility Requirements: Applicant must be enrolled or expecting to enroll full- or part-time at a two-year or four-year or technical institution or university and must have an interest in writing. Available to U.S. citizens.

Application Requirements: Application form, essay, portfolio. *Deadline:* May 1.

Contact: Ms. Elana Grossman, Manager, Foundation & Government
　　　　　Relations
　　　　Center for Architecture
　　　　Center for Architecture, ATTN: Haskell Award
　　　　536 LaGuardia Place
　　　　New York, NY 10012
　　　　Phone: 212-358-6134
　　　　E-mail: scholarships@cfafoundation.org

CENTER FOR ARCHITECTURE, WOMEN'S AUXILIARY ELEANOR ALLWORK SCHOLARSHIP

Students seeking their first degree in architecture from an NAAB accredited school within the State of New York are eligible. The Dean or Chair of the architectural school shall nominate up to three students from their respective college or university to apply. Nominated students will have a high level of academic performance and evidence of financial need. The financial need of each student shall be determined by the guidelines of the Financial Aid Officer of the school nominating the candidate. Students need not be U.S. citizens.

Academic Fields/Career Goals: Architecture.

Award: Scholarship for use in freshman, sophomore, junior, senior, or graduate years; not renewable. *Number:* 1–5. *Amount:* $4000–$10,000.

Eligibility Requirements: Applicant must be enrolled or expecting to enroll full-time at a four-year institution or university; resident of New York and studying in New York. Available to U.S. and non-U.S. citizens.

Application Requirements: Application form, portfolio. *Deadline:* March 15.

Contact: Ms. Elana Grossman, Manager, Foundation & Government
　　　　　Relations
　　　　Center for Architecture
　　　　Center for Architecture, ATTN: Allwork Scholarship
　　　　536 LaGuardia Place
　　　　New York, NY 10012
　　　　Phone: 212-358-6134
　　　　E-mail: scholarships@cfafoundation.org

THE WALTER A. HUNT, JR. SCHOLARSHIP

To promote and encourage the study of architecture by New York City public high school students through a two-year scholarship to supplement tuition and related costs during their freshman and sophomore years at Architecture School in the U.S.

Academic Fields/Career Goals: Architecture.

Award: Scholarship for use in freshman or sophomore years; not renewable. *Number:* 1–2. *Amount:* $7500–$10,000.

Eligibility Requirements: Applicant must be high school student; planning to enroll or expecting to enroll full-time at a four-year institution or university and resident of New York. Available to U.S. and non-U.S. citizens.

Application Requirements: Application form, essay, interview, portfolio. *Deadline:* May 15.

Contact: Ms. Elana Grossman, Manager, Foundation & Government
　　　　　Relations
　　　　Center for Architecture
　　　　Center for Architecture, ATTN: Walter A. Hunt, Jr. Scholarship
　　　　536 LaGuardia Place
　　　　NY, NY 10012
　　　　Phone: 212-358-6134
　　　　E-mail: scholarships@cfafoundation.org

CONGRESSIONAL BLACK CAUCUS FOUNDATION, INC.

http://www.cbcfinc.org/

CBC SPOUSES VISUAL ARTS SCHOLARSHIP

The CBC Spouses Visual Arts Scholarship was established in 2006. This program provides financial awards to students who have a passion for and plan on pursuing a career in the visual arts.

Academic Fields/Career Goals: Architecture; Arts; Fashion Design; Filmmaking/Video; Graphics/Graphic Arts/Printing.

Award: Scholarship for use in freshman, sophomore, junior, or senior years; not renewable. *Number:* 10. *Amount:* $3000.

Eligibility Requirements: Applicant must be enrolled or expecting to enroll full-time at a two-year or four-year institution or university and studying in Alabama, Alaska, Arizona, Arkansas, California, Colorado, Connecticut, Delaware, District of Columbia, Florida, Georgia, Guam, Hawaii, Idaho, Illinois, Indiana, Iowa, Kansas, Kentucky, Louisiana, Maine, Maryland, Massachusetts, Michigan, Minnesota, Mississippi, Missouri, Montana, Nebraska, Nevada, New Hampshire, New Jersey, New Mexico, New York, North Carolina, North Dakota, Ohio, Oklahoma, Oregon, Pennsylvania, Puerto Rico, Rhode Island, South Carolina, South Dakota, Tennessee, Texas, Utah, Vermont, Virginia, Washington, West Virginia, Wisconsin, Wyoming. Applicant must have 2.5 GPA or higher. Available to U.S. citizens.

Application Requirements: Application form, essay, financial need analysis, personal photograph. *Deadline:* April 21.

Contact: Ms. Katrina Finch, Program Administrator, Scholarships
　　　　　Phone: 202-263-2800
　　　　　E-mail: scholarships@cbcfinc.org

CONNECTICUT BUILDING CONGRESS SCHOLARSHIP FUND, INC.

http://www.cbc-ct.org

CBC SCHOLARSHIP FUND

The Connecticut Building Congress Scholarship Fund (CBCSF) announces that it will once again be offering scholarships to graduating Connecticut high school students entering college-level programs in architecture, construction-related engineering, construction management, surveying, planning or other courses of study leading to Associate, Baccalaureate, or Masters degrees in the construction field. The awards will be given for academic merit, extracurricular activities, potential and financial need. The scholarships may be renewable each year based on performance in school and available resources. The number of awards as well as the amounts may vary at the discretion of the CBCSF Board of Directors. In the past, scholarships have ranged from $500 to $2,000 per year.

Academic Fields/Career Goals: Architecture; Civil Engineering; Construction Engineering/Management; Engineering-Related Technologies; Engineering/Technology; Landscape Architecture; Mechanical Engineering.

Award: Scholarship for use in freshman, sophomore, junior, or senior years; renewable. *Number:* 2–4. *Amount:* $500–$2000.

Eligibility Requirements: Applicant must be high school student; planning to enroll or expecting to enroll full-time at a four-year institution or university and resident of Connecticut. Available to U.S. citizens.

Application Requirements: Application form, essay, financial need analysis. *Deadline:* March 9.

Contact: Mr. Thomas DiBlasi, President
Connecticut Building Congress Scholarship Fund, Inc.
500 Purdy Hill Road
Monroe, CT 06468
Phone: 203-452-1331 Ext. 108
Fax: 203-268-8103
E-mail: TomD@DiBlasi-Engrs.com

THE DALLAS FOUNDATION

http://www.dallasfoundation.org/

DALLAS CENTER FOR ARCHITECTURE FOUNDATION—HKS/JOHN HUMPHRIES SCHOLARSHIP

The scholarship must be used in the year it is awarded. If the funds are not used in this time period, they will be forfeited. The funds are intended to be used for college tuition towards a degree in architecture, and as such, will be routed directly to the appropriate college office for credit towards tuition. Must be a Dallas city resident.

Academic Fields/Career Goals: Architecture.

Award: Scholarship for use in freshman year; not renewable. *Amount:* $2000.

Eligibility Requirements: Applicant must be high school student; planning to enroll or expecting to enroll full-time at a four-year institution or university and resident of Texas.

Application Requirements: Application form, essay, portfolio, recommendations or references, transcript. *Deadline:* March 31.

Contact: Rachel Lasseter, Program Associate
Phone: 214-741-9898
E-mail: scholarships@dallasfoundation.org

WHITLEY PLACE SCHOLARSHIP

Established in 2009, the Whitley Place Scholarship seeks to provide aid to graduating seniors in Prosper ISD who plan to study civil engineering, construction science, construction management, architecture, landscape architecture, planning, public administration, mechanical engineering or other math/science related fields.

Academic Fields/Career Goals: Architecture; Civil Engineering; Engineering/Technology; Landscape Architecture; Mathematics; Mechanical Engineering; Physical Sciences; Public Policy and Administration.

Award: Scholarship for use in freshman, sophomore, junior, or senior years; renewable. *Amount:* $2500.

Eligibility Requirements: Applicant must be high school student; planning to enroll or expecting to enroll full-time at a two-year or four-year institution or university and resident of Texas. Applicant must have 3.0 GPA or higher.

Application Requirements: Application form, driver's license, financial need analysis, recommendations or references, resume, transcript. *Deadline:* March 31.

Contact: Rachel Lasseter, Program Associate
Phone: 214-741-9898
E-mail: scholarships@dallasfoundation.org

FLORIDA EDUCATIONAL FACILITIES PLANNERS' ASSOCIATION

http://www.fefpa.org/

FEFPA ASSISTANTSHIP

Renewable scholarship for full-time sophomores, juniors, seniors and graduate students enrolled in an accredited four-year Florida university or community college, majoring in facilities planning or a field related to facilities planning. Must be a resident of Florida with a 3.0 GPA.

Academic Fields/Career Goals: Architecture; Construction Engineering/Management.

Award: Scholarship for use in sophomore, junior, senior, or graduate years; renewable. *Number:* 2. *Amount:* $3000.

Eligibility Requirements: Applicant must be enrolled or expecting to enroll full-time at a four-year institution or university; resident of Florida and studying in Florida. Applicant must have 3.0 GPA or higher. Available to U.S. and non-U.S. citizens.

Application Requirements: Application form, essay, financial need analysis, recommendations or references, test scores, transcript. *Deadline:* June 1.

Contact: Robert Griffith, Selection Committee Chair
Phone: 305-348-4070 Ext. 4002
Fax: 305-341-3377
E-mail: griffith@fiu.edu

THE GEORGIA TRUST FOR HISTORIC PRESERVATION

http://www.georgiatrust.org/

J. NEEL REID PRIZE

A $4000 fellowship is given to an architecture student, architecture intern or a recently-registered architect residing, studying or working in Georgia. Proposed projects should involve the study of an aspect of classic architecture.

Academic Fields/Career Goals: Architecture; Historic Preservation and Conservation; Landscape Architecture.

Award: Prize for use in sophomore, junior, senior, graduate, or postgraduate years; not renewable. *Number:* 1. *Amount:* $4000.

Eligibility Requirements: Applicant must be enrolled or expecting to enroll full- or part-time at a four-year institution or university and resident of Georgia. Available to U.S. and non-U.S. citizens.

Application Requirements: Application form, essay, portfolio. *Deadline:* February 9.

Contact: Mr. Neale Nickels, Director of Preservation
The Georgia Trust for Historic Preservation
1516 Peachtree Street, NW
Atlanta, GA 30309
Phone: 404-885-7817
E-mail: nnickels@georgiatrust.org

GRAND RAPIDS COMMUNITY FOUNDATION

http://www.grfoundation.org/

DAROOGE FAMILY SCHOLARSHIP FOR CONSTRUCTION TRADES

Student is a high school senior residing in Kent County Michigan pursuing an undergrad degree in a construction-related field at an accredited 2 or 4 year college/university/trade school in Michigan. Must have financial need.

Academic Fields/Career Goals: Architecture; Trade/Technical Specialties.

Award: Scholarship for use in freshman, sophomore, junior, or senior years; not renewable. *Number:* 1–5. *Amount:* $1000–$5000.

Eligibility Requirements: Applicant must be enrolled or expecting to enroll full-time at a two-year or four-year or technical institution; resident of Michigan and studying in Michigan. Applicant or parent of applicant must have employment or volunteer experience in construction. Applicant must have 2.5 GPA or higher. Available to U.S. citizens.

Application Requirements: Application form, essay, financial need analysis, *Deadline:* April 1.

Contact: Ms. Ruth Bishop, Education Program Officer
Grand Rapids Community Foundation
185 Oakes SW
Grand Rapids, MI 49503
Phone: 616-454-1751 Ext. 103
E-mail: rbishop@grfoundation.org

GREAT MINDS IN STEM

http://www.greatmindsinstem.org

HENAAC SCHOLARSHIP PROGRAM
• *See page 115*

HAWAIIAN LODGE, F&AM

http://www.hawaiianlodgefreemasons.org

HAWAIIAN LODGE SCHOLARSHIPS
• *See page 86*

HELLENIC UNIVERSITY CLUB OF PHILADELPHIA

http://www.hucphiladelphia.org/

DIMITRI J. VERVERELLI MEMORIAL SCHOLARSHIP FOR ARCHITECTURE AND/OR ENGINEERING

$2000 award for full-time student enrolled in an architecture or engineering degree program at an accredited four-year college or university. High school seniors accepted for enrollment in such a degree program may also apply. Must be a U.S. citizen of Greek descent and a resident of particular counties in NJ or PA.

Academic Fields/Career Goals: Architecture; Engineering/Technology.

Award: Scholarship for use in freshman, sophomore, junior, or senior years; not renewable. *Amount:* up to $2000.

Eligibility Requirements: Applicant must be of Greek heritage; enrolled or expecting to enroll full-time at a four-year institution or university and resident of New Jersey, Pennsylvania. Available to U.S. citizens.

Application Requirements: Application form, financial need analysis, transcript. *Deadline:* April 3.

Contact: Anna Hadgis, Scholarship Chairman
Phone: 610-613-4310
E-mail: www.hucphiladelphia.org

HOUZZ

http://houzz.com

RESIDENTIAL DESIGN SCHOLARSHIP

Houzz has been connecting homeowners with home industry professionals for years and we are dedicated to supporting and strengthening our growing community. We are looking for residential design students who share our passion. Open to students studying interior design, architecture or landscape architecture at the undergraduate or graduate level who want to pursue residential design professionally.

Academic Fields/Career Goals: Architecture; Interior Design; Landscape Architecture.

Award: Scholarship for use in freshman, sophomore, junior, or graduate years; not renewable. *Number:* 1. *Amount:* $2500.

Eligibility Requirements: Applicant must be enrolled or expecting to enroll full- or part-time at a two-year or four-year or technical institution or university and studying in Alabama, Alaska, Arizona, Arkansas, California, Colorado, Connecticut, Delaware, District of Columbia, Florida, Georgia, Hawaii, Idaho, Illinois, Indiana, Iowa, Kansas, Kentucky, Louisiana, Maine, Maryland, Massachusetts, Michigan, Minnesota, Mississippi, Missouri, Montana, Nebraska, Nevada, New Hampshire, New Jersey, New Mexico, New York, North Carolina, North Dakota, Ohio, Oklahoma, Oregon, Pennsylvania, Puerto Rico, Rhode Island, South Carolina, South Dakota, Tennessee, Texas, Utah, Vermont, Virginia, Washington, West Virginia, Wisconsin, Wyoming. Available to U.S. and non-U.S. citizens.

Application Requirements: Application form, essay. *Deadline:* continuous.

Contact: Emily Hurley, Community Manager
E-mail: scholarships@houzz.com

SUSTAINABLE RESIDENTIAL DESIGN SCHOLARSHIP

Sustainability and green design are part of our core values at Houzz. We want to encourage practices that will reduce negative impacts on the environment by supporting students passionate about green building initiatives. Open to students studying architecture, interior design or landscape architecture at the undergraduate or graduate level who want to pursue sustainable residential design professionally.

Academic Fields/Career Goals: Architecture; Interior Design; Landscape Architecture.

Award: Scholarship for use in freshman, sophomore, junior, senior, or graduate years; not renewable. *Number:* 1. *Amount:* $2500.

Eligibility Requirements: Applicant must be enrolled or expecting to enroll full- or part-time at a two-year or four-year or technical institution or university and studying in Alabama, Alaska, Arizona, Arkansas, California, Colorado, Connecticut, Delaware, District of Columbia, Florida, Georgia, Hawaii, Idaho, Illinois, Indiana, Iowa, Kansas, Kentucky, Louisiana, Maine, Maryland, Massachusetts, Michigan, Minnesota, Mississippi, Missouri, Montana, Nebraska, Nevada, New Hampshire, New Jersey, New Mexico, New York, North Carolina, North Dakota, Ohio, Oklahoma, Oregon, Pennsylvania, Puerto Rico, Rhode Island, South Carolina, South Dakota, Tennessee, Texas, Utah, Vermont, Virginia, Washington, West Virginia, Wisconsin, Wyoming. Available to U.S. and non-U.S. citizens.

Application Requirements: Application form, essay. *Deadline:* continuous.

Contact: Emily Hurley, Community Manager
E-mail: scholarships@houzz.com

WOMEN IN ARCHITECTURE SCHOLARSHIP

Houzz is committed to supporting and encouraging women architecture students as they pursue their educational endeavors and enter the world of residential design. Open to female students studying architecture/architectural engineering at the undergraduate or graduate level.

Academic Fields/Career Goals: Architecture.

Award: Scholarship for use in freshman, sophomore, junior, senior, or graduate years; not renewable. *Number:* 1. *Amount:* $2500.

Eligibility Requirements: Applicant must be enrolled or expecting to enroll full- or part-time at a two-year or four-year or technical institution or university; female and studying in Alabama, Alaska, Arizona, Arkansas, California, Colorado, Connecticut, Delaware, District of Columbia, Florida, Georgia, Hawaii, Idaho, Illinois, Indiana, Iowa, Kansas, Kentucky, Louisiana, Maine, Maryland, Massachusetts, Michigan, Minnesota, Mississippi, Missouri, Montana, Nebraska, Nevada, New Hampshire, New Jersey, New Mexico, New York, North Carolina, North Dakota, Ohio, Oklahoma, Oregon, Pennsylvania, Rhode Island, South Carolina, South Dakota, Tennessee, Texas, Utah, Vermont, Virginia, Washington, West Virginia, Wisconsin, Wyoming. Available to U.S. and non-U.S. citizens.

Application Requirements: Application form, essay. *Deadline:* continuous.

Contact: Emily Hurley, Community Manager
E-mail: scholarships@houzz.com

IFDA EDUCATIONAL FOUNDATION

http://www.ifdaef.org/

TRICIA LEVANGIE GREEN/SUSTAINABLE SCHOLARSHIP

The student applying for this scholarship is planning to become an educated participant in the green movement. Paying equal attention to both sustainability factors and design aesthetics, the student should be demonstrating creative use of green products and eco-friendly furnishings in class projects. The student is familiar with current information in the green/sustainable field, is applying this knowledge in class work and has a goal of seeking a future LEED accreditation.

Academic Fields/Career Goals: Architecture; Interior Design.

Award: Scholarship for use in sophomore, junior, or senior years; not renewable. *Number:* 1. *Amount:* $1500.

Eligibility Requirements: Applicant must be enrolled or expecting to enroll full- or part-time at a four-year or technical institution or university. Available to U.S. and non-U.S. citizens.

Application Requirements: Application form, essay. *Deadline:* March 31.

Contact: Earline Feldman, IFDA Director of Scholarships and Grants
IFDA Educational Foundation
112 Hidden Lake Circle
Canton, GA 30114
Phone: 770-378-7221
E-mail: ef.ifda@tapestries.org

ILLUMINATING ENGINEERING SOCIETY OF NORTH AMERICA

http://www.ies.org/

ROBERT W. THUNEN MEMORIAL SCHOLARSHIPS

One-time award for juniors, seniors, or graduate students enrolled at four-year colleges and universities in northern California, Nevada, Oregon, or Washington pursuing lighting career. Must submit statement describing proposed lighting course work or project and three recommendations, at least one from someone involved professionally or academically with lighting. Curriculum must be accredited by ABET, ACSA, or FIDER.

Academic Fields/Career Goals: Architecture; Engineering-Related Technologies; Engineering/Technology; Interior Design; Performing Arts; TV/Radio Broadcasting.

Award: Scholarship for use in junior, senior, or graduate years; not renewable. *Number:* 2. *Amount:* $2500.

Eligibility Requirements: Applicant must be enrolled or expecting to enroll full-time at a four-year institution or university and studying in California, Nevada, Oregon, Washington. Available to U.S. and non-U.S. citizens.

Application Requirements: Application form, recommendations or references, transcript. *Deadline:* April 1.

Contact: Phil Hall, Chairman
Phone: 510-864-0204
Fax: 510-248-5017
E-mail: mrcatisbac@aol.com

ILLUMINATING ENGINEERING SOCIETY OF NORTH AMERICA– GOLDEN GATE SECTION

http://www.iesgg.org/

ALAN LUCAS MEMORIAL EDUCATIONAL SCHOLARSHIP

Scholarship available to full-time student for pursuit of lighting education or research as part of undergraduate, graduate, or doctoral studies. Scholarships may be made by those who will be a junior, senior, or graduate student in an accredited four-year college or university located in Northern California. The scholarships to be awarded will be at least $1500.

Academic Fields/Career Goals: Architecture; Electrical Engineering/Electronics; Filmmaking/Video; Interior Design.

Award: Scholarship for use in junior, senior, or graduate years; not renewable. *Number:* 1. *Amount:* $1500.

Eligibility Requirements: Applicant must be enrolled or expecting to enroll full-time at a four-year institution or university and studying in California. Available to U.S. citizens.

Application Requirements: Application form, recommendations or references, statement of purpose, description of work in progress, scholar agreement form, transcript. *Deadline:* April 1.

Contact: Phil Hall, Scholarship Committee
Phone: 510-864-0204
Fax: 510-864-8511
E-mail: iesggthunenfund@aol.com

INTERNATIONAL FACILITY MANAGEMENT ASSOCIATION FOUNDATION

http://www.ifmafoundation.org/

IFMA FOUNDATION SCHOLARSHIPS

One-time scholarships of up to $5000 awarded to students currently enrolled in full-time facility management programs or related programs. Minimum 3.2 GPA required for undergraduates and 3.5 for graduate students.

Academic Fields/Career Goals: Architecture; Construction Engineering/Management; Engineering-Related Technologies; Engineering/Technology; Interior Design; Urban and Regional Planning.

Award: Scholarship for use in junior, senior, graduate, or postgraduate years; not renewable. *Number:* 25–35. *Amount:* $1500–$5000.

Eligibility Requirements: Applicant must be enrolled or expecting to enroll full-time at a four-year institution or university. Applicant must have 3.5 GPA or higher. Available to U.S. and non-U.S. citizens.

Application Requirements: Application form. *Deadline:* April 20.

Contact: Amy Arnold, Foundation Administrator
International Facility Management Association Foundation
800 Gessner
Suite 900
Houston, TX 77024
Phone: 713-623-4362
E-mail: amy.arnold@ifma.org

MIDWEST ROOFING CONTRACTORS ASSOCIATION

http://www.mrca.org/

MRCA FOUNDATION SCHOLARSHIP PROGRAM

Renewable scholarships for full-time students enrolled or intending to enroll in an accredited university, college, community college, or trade school. Applicant must be pursuing a curriculum leading to a career in the construction industry or related. Award amount ranges from $500 to $3000.

Academic Fields/Career Goals: Architecture; Civil Engineering; Construction Engineering/Management; Drafting; Engineering/Technology; Industrial Design; Materials Science, Engineering, and Metallurgy; Trade/Technical Specialties.

Award: Scholarship for use in freshman, sophomore, junior, or senior years; not renewable. *Number:* up to 40. *Amount:* $500–$3000.

Eligibility Requirements: Applicant must be enrolled or expecting to enroll full-time at a two-year or four-year or technical institution or university. Applicant or parent of applicant must have employment or volunteer experience in construction. Applicant must have 3.0 GPA or higher. Available to U.S. citizens.

Application Requirements: Application form, community service, essay, financial need analysis, recommendations or references, transcript. *Deadline:* June 20.

Contact: Ms. Peggy Doherty, Operations Manager
Midwest Roofing Contractors Association
4700 West Lake Avenue
Glenview, IL 60025
Phone: 847-375-6378
Fax: 847-375-6473

NATIONAL ASSOCIATION OF WOMEN IN CONSTRUCTION

http://www.nawic.org/

NAWIC UNDERGRADUATE SCHOLARSHIPS

One-time award for any student having at least one year of study remaining in a construction-related program leading to an Associate or higher degree. Awards range from $500 to $2000. Submit application and transcript of grades.

Academic Fields/Career Goals: Architecture; Civil Engineering; Drafting; Electrical Engineering/Electronics; Engineering-Related

Technologies; Engineering/Technology; Interior Design; Landscape Architecture; Mechanical Engineering; Trade/Technical Specialties.

Award: Scholarship for use in sophomore or junior years; not renewable. *Number:* 40–50. *Amount:* $500–$2000.

Eligibility Requirements: Applicant must be enrolled or expecting to enroll full-time at a two-year or four-year or technical institution or university. Applicant must have 3.0 GPA or higher. Available to U.S. and Canadian citizens.

Application Requirements: Application form, essay, financial need analysis, interview, transcript. *Deadline:* March 15.

Contact: Scholarship Committee
National Association of Women in Construction
327 South Adams Street
Fort Worth, TX 76104
Phone: 817-877-5551
Fax: 817-877-0324

NEXTSTEPU

http://www.nextstepu.com/

$1,500 STEM SCHOLARSHIP
• See page 120

OREGON STUDENT ASSISTANCE COMMISSION

https://oregonstudentaid.gov/

HOME BUILDERS FOUNDATION JIM IRVINE STATEWIDE SCHOLARSHIP

One-time award for first-year freshmen or other undergraduates studying architecture, construction, engineering (civil, electrical, industrial, management), interior design/architecture, or landscape architecture. Must be enrolled at least half time. Minimum 3.0 GPA preferred. Financial need may or may not be considered.

Academic Fields/Career Goals: Architecture; Civil Engineering; Electrical Engineering/Electronics; Engineering/Technology; Interior Design; Landscape Architecture.

Award: Scholarship for use in freshman, sophomore, junior, or senior years; not renewable.

Eligibility Requirements: Applicant must be enrolled or expecting to enroll full- or part-time at a two-year or four-year institution or university and studying in Oregon. Applicant must have 3.0 GPA or higher. Available to U.S. citizens.

Application Requirements: Application form, essay, financial need analysis. *Deadline:* March 1.

Contact: Melissa Adams, Scholarship Processing Coordinator
Phone: 541-687-7409
E-mail: melissa.adams@state.or.us

PLAN NEW HAMPSHIRE

http://www.plannh.org

PLAN NEW HAMPSHIRE SCHOLARSHIP AND FELLOWSHIP PROGRAM
• See page 129

RCI FOUNDATION

http://www.rcifoundation.org/

LEWIS W. NEWLAN AWARD

RCI Foundation has established a scholarship program to assist students currently enrolled in a architecture, engineering, construction or building sciences postsecondary program. This program is administered by Scholarship America, the nation's largest designer and manager of scholarship, tuition assistance and other education support programs for corporations, foundations, associations, and individuals. Awards are granted without regard to race, color, creed, religion, sexual orientation, age, gender, disability, or national origin. Applicants to the RCI Foundation Scholarship Program must be a current undergraduate or graduate student who has completed a minimum of 24 credit hours and is planning to enroll full-time at an accredited college, university or vocational-technical school for the entire 2018-19 academic year in an accredited program of architecture, engineering, construction or building sciences leading to a career in the construction or building envelope industry. Must have a minimum grade point average of 2.75 on a 4.0 scale (or the equivalent) and be a citizen of the United States or Canada. Up to ten (10) awards of $2,500 each will be granted to undergraduate and graduate students. This award is not renewable; however recipients may re-apply up to four times in four years provided they meet eligibility requirements. Maximum lifetime award for any recipient is $12,500. Awards can be used for tuition, fees, books and supplies only. Awards may not be deferred.

Academic Fields/Career Goals: Architecture; Civil Engineering; Construction Engineering/Management.

Award: Scholarship for use in junior, senior, graduate, or postgraduate years; not renewable. *Number:* 1–10. *Amount:* $2500.

Eligibility Requirements: Applicant must be enrolled or expecting to enroll full-time at a four-year or technical institution or university. Applicant must have 2.5 GPA or higher. Available to U.S. and Canadian citizens.

Application Requirements: Application form, financial need analysis. *Deadline:* February 28.

Contact: Program Manager
RCI Foundation
Scholarship America
Phone: 507-931-1682
E-mail: rcif@scholarshipamerica.org

ROBERT W. LYONS AWARD

RCI Foundation has established a scholarship program to assist students currently enrolled in a architecture, engineering, construction or building sciences postsecondary program.This program is administered by Scholarship America, the nation's largest designer and manager of scholarship, tuition assistance and other education support programs for corporations, foundations, associations, and individuals. Awards are granted without regard to race, color, creed, religion, sexual orientation, age, gender, disability, or national origin. Applicants to the RCI Foundation Scholarship Program must be a current undergraduate student who has completed a minimum of 24 credit hours and is planning to enroll full-time at an accredited college, university or vocational-technical school for the entire 2018-19 academic year in an accredited program of architecture, engineering, construction or building sciences leading to a career in the construction or building envelope industry. Must have a minimum grade point average of 2.75 on a 4.0 scale (or the equivalent) and be a citizen of the United States or Canada. Up to two (2) awards of $5,000 each will be granted to undergraduate students only. This award is not renewable; past recipients may not re-apply. Maximum lifetime award for any recipient is $12,500. Awards can be used for tuition, fees, books and supplies only. Awards may not be deferred.

Academic Fields/Career Goals: Architecture; Construction Engineering/Management.

Award: Scholarship for use in junior or senior years; not renewable. *Number:* 1–2. *Amount:* $5000.

Eligibility Requirements: Applicant must be enrolled or expecting to enroll full-time at a four-year or technical institution or university. Applicant must have 2.5 GPA or higher. Available to U.S. and Canadian citizens.

Application Requirements: Application form, essay. *Deadline:* February 28.

Contact: Program Manager
RCI Foundation
Scholarship America
Phone: 507-931-1682
E-mail: rcif@scholarshipamerica.org

RHODE ISLAND FOUNDATION

http://www.rifoundation.org/

NORTON E. SALK SCHOLARSHIP

Scholarship for a student enrolled in an accredited school in Rhode Island and pursuing the study of architecture. Must have completed at least one academic year and demonstrate financial need.

Academic Fields/Career Goals: Architecture.

Award: Scholarship for use in sophomore, junior, or senior years; not renewable.

Eligibility Requirements: Applicant must be enrolled or expecting to enroll full-time at a four-year institution or university and studying in Rhode Island. Available to U.S. citizens.

Application Requirements: Application form, essay, financial need analysis, letter of eligibility for financial aid, recommendations or references. *Deadline:* June 15.

Contact: Executive Director, Rhode Island AIA Architectural Forum
Phone: 401-272-6418
E-mail: execdir@aia-ri.org

SCARLETT FAMILY FOUNDATION SCHOLARSHIP PROGRAM

http://www.scarlettfoundation.org/

SCHOLARSHIP FOR STUDENTS PURSUING A BUSINESS OR STEM DEGREE

• *See page 91*

SUPPORT CREATIVITY

http://wesupportcreativity.org

SUPPORT CREATIVITY SCHOLARSHIP

The Support Creativity Scholarship is for (but not limited to) passionate designers, animators, editors, photographers, artists, illustrators, and painters, who wish to develop their skills at higher education institutions. The student must submit a project that illustrates their passion for their specific creative field in any medium. The student must also submit an essay describing their project as well as any financial hardships.

Academic Fields/Career Goals: Architecture; Art History; Arts; Communications; Culinary Arts; Drafting; Fashion Design; Filmmaking/Video; Graphics/Graphic Arts/Printing; Industrial Design; Interior Design; Landscape Architecture; Marketing; Photojournalism/Photography.

Award: Scholarship for use in freshman, sophomore, junior, senior, or graduate years; not renewable. *Number:* 3. *Amount:* $1000.

Eligibility Requirements: Applicant must be enrolled or expecting to enroll full- or part-time at a two-year or four-year institution or university and studying in Connecticut, New Jersey, New York. Available to U.S. and non-U.S. citizens.

Application Requirements: Application form, essay. *Deadline:* May 1.

Contact: Steve Lucin, Founder
Support Creativity
244 West 54th Street, Suite 800
New York, NY 10019
E-mail: lucin@wesupportcreativity.org

TURNER CONSTRUCTION COMPANY

http://www.turnerconstruction.com/

YOUTHFORCE 2020 SCHOLARSHIP PROGRAM

The scholarship will be awarded to five graduating high school seniors from New York City schools and in the amount of $2000 per year; totaling $8000 after the completion of four years in college. As a scholarship recipient, students must maintain a 2.80 GPA and complete a four-year summer internship at Turner Construction that begins immediately following their first full year of college.

Academic Fields/Career Goals: Architecture; Civil Engineering; Construction Engineering/Management; Electrical Engineering/Electronics; Engineering-Related Technologies; Engineering/Technology; Interior Design; Landscape Architecture; Materials Science, Engineering, and Metallurgy; Mechanical Engineering.

Award: Scholarship for use in freshman, sophomore, junior, or senior years; renewable. *Number:* 5. *Amount:* $8000.

Eligibility Requirements: Applicant must be American Indian/Alaska Native, Asian/Pacific Islander, Black (non-Hispanic), Hispanic; high school student; planning to enroll or expecting to enroll full-time at a four-year institution or university; resident of New York and studying in New York. Applicant must have 3.0 GPA or higher. Available to U.S. citizens.

Application Requirements: Application form, community service, essay, financial need analysis, interview, personal photograph, recommendations or references, resume, test scores, transcript. *Deadline:* April 30.

Contact: Stephanie Burns, Community Affairs Director
Turner Construction Company
375 Hudson Street
6th Floor
New York, NY 10014
Phone: 212-229-6000 Ext. 6480
Fax: 212-229-6083
E-mail: yf2020@tcco.com

VECTORWORKS, INC.

http://www.vectorworks.net

VECTORWORKS DESIGN SCHOLARSHIP

Nemetschek Vectorworks is inviting talented students across all design disciplines to submit their best individual or group work to the Vectorworks Design Scholarship for the chance to win up to $10,000! Additionally, winners' schools receive free Vectorworks design software, as well as free in-person or virtual training for faculty and students. Submissions can be created in any software, and can even be a project previously completed for school. Entering is simple. Answer three short questions by August 31.

Academic Fields/Career Goals: Architecture; Arts; Civil Engineering; Construction Engineering/Management; Drafting; Engineering-Related Technologies; Engineering/Technology; Graphics/Graphic Arts/Printing; Industrial Design; Interior Design; Landscape Architecture; Urban and Regional Planning.

Award: Scholarship for use in freshman, sophomore, junior, senior, or graduate years; not renewable. *Number:* 15–18. *Amount:* $3000–$10,000.

Eligibility Requirements: Applicant must be enrolled or expecting to enroll full- or part-time at a two-year or four-year or technical institution or university. Available to U.S. and non-U.S. citizens.

Application Requirements: Application form, application form may be submitted online (http://www.vectorworks.net/scholarship/en), CAD or Drawn Design submission, entry in a contest. *Deadline:* August 31.

Contact: Marissa Diehl, Marketing Intern
Vectorworks, Inc.
7150 Riverwood Drive
Columbia, MD 21046
Phone: 443-542-0275 Ext. 275
E-mail: mdiehl97@vectorworks.net

THE WALTER J. TRAVIS SOCIETY

http://www.travissociety.com

THE WALTER J. TRAVIS MEMORIAL SCHOLARSHIP AND THE WALTER J. TRAVIS-RUDY ZOCCHI MEMORIAL SCHOLARSHIP

This scholarship is awarded to students who are pursuing a career in one of the following golf-related professions: golf course architecture, golf course superintendent/turfgrass manager, sports journalism, or professional golf management. Also, any college student who is an outstanding amateur golfer is eligible. Awards based on academic record, extracurricular activities including volunteer service, work experience, and golf-related interests and accomplishments. Award may be used for any educational expenses.

Academic Fields/Career Goals: Architecture; Landscape Architecture; Recreation, Parks, Leisure Studies; Sports-Related/Exercise Science.

Award: Scholarship for use in freshman, sophomore, junior, senior, or graduate years; not renewable. *Number:* 1–5. *Amount:* $1000.

Eligibility Requirements: Applicant must be enrolled or expecting to enroll full-time at a four-year or technical institution or university and must have an interest in athletics/sports or golf. Applicant must have 2.5 GPA or higher. Available to U.S. and non-U.S. citizens.

Application Requirements: Application form, community service, essay. *Deadline:* June 1.

Contact: Mr. Edward Homsey, Scholarship Chairman
The Walter J. Travis Society
24 Sandstone Drive
Rochester, NY 14616
Phone: 585-663-6120
E-mail: TravisSociety@yahoo.com

WEST VIRGINIA SOCIETY OF ARCHITECTS/AIA

http://www.aiawv.org/

AIA WEST VIRGINIA SCHOLARSHIP

Award for a West Virginia resident who has completed at least their sixth semester of an NAAB-accredited undergraduate architectural program or accepted to a NAAB-accredited graduate architectural program by application deadline. Must submit resume and letter stating need, qualifications, and portfolio of work.

Academic Fields/Career Goals: Architecture.

Award: Scholarship for use in junior, senior, graduate, or postgraduate years; not renewable. *Amount:* $3500–$4500.

Eligibility Requirements: Applicant must be enrolled or expecting to enroll full-time at an institution or university and resident of West Virginia. Available to U.S. citizens.

Application Requirements: Application form, portfolio. *Deadline:* October 16.

Contact: William Yoke, Scholarship Committee Chair
West Virginia Society of Architects/AIA
P.O. Box 813
Charleston, WV 25323
Phone: 304-344-9872
E-mail: aiawv@aiawv.org

AREA/ETHNIC STUDIES

CANADIAN INSTITUTE OF UKRAINIAN STUDIES

http://www.cius.ca/

LEO J. KRYSA UNDERGRADUATE SCHOLARSHIP

One-time award for a Canadian citizen or a landed immigrant to enter their final year of undergraduate study in pursuit of a degree with emphasis on Ukrainian and/or Ukrainian-Canadian studies in the disciplines of education, history, humanities, or social sciences. To be used at any Canadian university for an eight-month period of study.

Academic Fields/Career Goals: Area/Ethnic Studies; Education; History; Humanities; Social Sciences.

Award: Scholarship for use in senior year; not renewable. *Number:* 1.

Eligibility Requirements: Applicant must be Canadian citizen; enrolled or expecting to enroll full-time at a four-year institution or university; resident of Alberta, British Columbia, Manitoba, New Brunswick, Newfoundland, Northwest Territories, Nova Scotia, Ontario, Prince Edward Island, Quebec, Saskatchewan, Yukon and studying in Alberta, British Columbia, Manitoba, New Brunswick, Newfoundland, Nova Scotia, Ontario, Prince Edward Island, Quebec, Saskatchewan.

Application Requirements: Application form. *Deadline:* March 1.

Contact: Iryna Fedoriw, Administrative Assistant
Phone: 780-492-2972
E-mail: cius@ualberta.ca

COSTUME SOCIETY OF AMERICA

http://www.costumesocietyamerica.com/

ADELE FILENE STUDENT PRESENTER GRANT

Adele Filene Student Presenter Grants provide financial assistance to students who have been selected to present oral research papers or research exhibits at the CSA National Symposium. These grants of up to $500 award, $100 travel stipend and a day-of-presentation registration fee, funded by the CSA Endowment, are intended to encourage student participation in both the symposium and CSA.

Academic Fields/Career Goals: Area/Ethnic Studies; Art History; Arts; Historic Preservation and Conservation; History; Home Economics; Museum Studies; Performing Arts.

Award: Grant for use in freshman, sophomore, junior, senior, or graduate years; not renewable. *Number:* 2. *Amount:* $500–$600.

Eligibility Requirements: Applicant must be enrolled or expecting to enroll full-time at a two-year or four-year or technical institution or university. Applicant or parent of applicant must be member of Costume Society of America. Available to U.S. and non-U.S. citizens.

Application Requirements: Application form, essay. *Deadline:* October 15.

Contact: Michelle Finamore
E-mail: MFinamore@mfa.org

STELLA BLUM STUDENT RESEARCH GRANT

The Stella Blum Student Research Grant is intended to assist the research of a current undergraduate or graduate student who is a member of the Costume Society of America and conducting original research in the field of North American costume. This $3,000 grant, funded by the CSA Endowment, is awarded annually to provide a student with financial assistance with research. An additional stipend of up to $600 and a day-of-presentation registration fee, also funded by the CSA Endowment, is awarded to allow the recipient to present the completed research at a CSA National Symposium.

Academic Fields/Career Goals: Area/Ethnic Studies; Art History; Arts; Historic Preservation and Conservation; History; Home Economics; Museum Studies; Performing Arts.

Award: Grant for use in freshman, sophomore, junior, senior, or graduate years; not renewable. *Number:* 1. *Amount:* $2000–$3600.

Eligibility Requirements: Applicant must be enrolled or expecting to enroll full- or part-time at a two-year or four-year or technical institution or university. Applicant or parent of applicant must be member of Costume Society of America. Available to U.S. and non-U.S. citizens.

Application Requirements: Application form, essay. *Deadline:* May 1.

Contact: Ann Wass
Costume Society of America
5903 60th Avenue
Riverdale, MD 20737
E-mail: annbwass@aol.com

KOSCIUSZKO FOUNDATION

http://www.thekf.org

YEAR ABROAD PROGRAM IN POLAND

Grants for upper division and graduate students who wish to study language and culture at the Center for Polish Language and Culture in the World, Jagiellonian University in Cracow, Poland. U.S. citizens who are undergraduate sophomores, juniors, seniors and graduate students may apply. Scholarship is given towards junior, senior or graduate year of studies. Graduate students receive priority. Must have letters of recommendation, personal statement, and transcript. Covers tuition fees and provides stipend for housing. Application fee: $50. Minimum 3.0 GPA required. Restricted to U.S. citizens.

Academic Fields/Career Goals: Area/Ethnic Studies; Foreign Language.

Award: Scholarship for use in junior, senior, or graduate years; not renewable. *Number:* 5–11. *Amount:* $900–$1800.

Eligibility Requirements: Applicant must be enrolled or expecting to enroll full-time at a four-year institution or university and must have an interest in Polish language. Applicant must have 3.0 GPA or higher. Available to U.S. citizens.

Application Requirements: Application form, application form may be submitted online (http://www.thekf.org/kf/scholarships/exchange-poland/year-abroad/), essay, interview, personal photograph, personal statement, recommendations or references, transcript. *Fee:* $50. *Deadline:* January 15.

Contact: Ms. Addy Tymczyszyn, Scholarship and Grant Officer for
Americans
Kosciuszko Foundation
15 East 65th Street
New York, NY 10065
Phone: 212-734-2130 Ext. 210
E-mail: Addy@thekf.org

NATIONAL ITALIAN AMERICAN FOUNDATION

http://www.niaf.org/

NATIONAL ITALIAN AMERICAN FOUNDATION CATEGORY II SCHOLARSHIP

Award available to students majoring or minoring in Italian language,
Italian Studies, Italian-American Studies or a related field who have
outstanding potential and high academic achievements. Minimum 3.5
GPA required. Must be a U.S. citizen and be enrolled in an accredited
institution of higher education. Application can only be submitted online.
For further information, deadlines, and online application visit website
http://www.niaf.org/scholarships/index.asp.

Academic Fields/Career Goals: Area/Ethnic Studies.

Award: Scholarship for use in freshman, sophomore, junior, senior, or
graduate years; not renewable. *Amount:* $2500–$12,000.

Eligibility Requirements: Applicant must be enrolled or expecting to
enroll full-time at a two-year or four-year institution or university and
must have an interest in Italian language. Applicant must have 3.5 GPA
or higher. Available to U.S. citizens.

Application Requirements: Application form, essay, recommendations
or references, transcript. *Deadline:* March 6.

Contact: Serena Cantoni, Director, Culture and Education
National Italian American Foundation
The National Italian American Foundation
1860 19th Street, NW
Washington, DC 20009
Phone: 202-939-3107
E-mail: serena@niaf.org

NATIONAL SECURITY EDUCATION PROGRAM

http://www.iie.org/

NATIONAL SECURITY EDUCATION PROGRAM (NSEP) DAVID L. BOREN UNDERGRADUATE SCHOLARSHIPS

The Boren Scholarships provide funding to American undergraduate
students for study abroad in regions critical to U.S. national interests.
Emphasized world areas include Africa, Asia, Central and Eastern
Europe, the NIS, Latin America and the Caribbean, and the Middle East.
NSEP scholarship recipients incur a federal service agreement. Must be a
U.S. citizen. Program must have a foreign language component.

Academic Fields/Career Goals: Area/Ethnic Studies;
Business/Consumer Services; Economics; Engineering-Related
Technologies; Environmental Science; Foreign Language; International
Studies; Peace and Conflict Studies; Social Sciences.

Award: Scholarship for use in freshman, sophomore, junior, or senior
years; not renewable. *Number:* 130–170. *Amount:* $8000–$20,000.

Eligibility Requirements: Applicant must be enrolled or expecting to
enroll full- or part-time at a two-year or four-year institution or
university. Available to U.S. citizens.

Application Requirements: Application form, essay, financial need
analysis. *Deadline:* February 8.

Contact: Boren Awards Program
Phone: 800-618-6737
E-mail: boren@iie.org

SONS OF NORWAY FOUNDATION

http://www.sonsofnorway.com/foundation

KING OLAV V NORWEGIAN-AMERICAN HERITAGE FUND

Scholarship available to American students interested in studying
Norwegian heritage or modern Norway, or Norwegian students 18 or
older interested in studying North American culture. Selection of
applicants is based on a 500-word essay, educational and career goals,
community service, work experience, and GPA. Must have minimum 3.0
GPA.

Academic Fields/Career Goals: Area/Ethnic Studies.

Award: Scholarship for use in freshman, sophomore, junior, or senior
years; not renewable. *Number:* 4–8. *Amount:* $1000–$1500.

Eligibility Requirements: Applicant must be of Norwegian heritage and
Norwegian citizen; age 18-30 and enrolled or expecting to enroll full-
time at a two-year or four-year or technical institution or university.
Applicant must have 3.0 GPA or higher. Available to U.S. and non-
Canadian citizens.

Application Requirements: Application form, application form may be
submitted online (http://www.sonsofnorway.com/foundation),
community service, essay, recommendations or references, transcript.
Deadline: March 1.

Contact: Scholarship Coordinator
Sons of Norway Foundation
1455 West Lake Street
Minneapolis, MN 55408-2666
Phone: 612-827-3611
Fax: 612-827-0658

STRAIGHTFORWARD MEDIA

http://www.straightforwardmedia.com/

STRAIGHTFORWARD MEDIA LIBERAL ARTS SCHOLARSHIP

Scholarship of $500 available exclusively to liberal arts students.
Awarded four times per year. For more information, see web
http://www.straightforwardmedia.com/liberal-arts/form.php.

Academic Fields/Career Goals: Area/Ethnic Studies; Art History;
Classics; Economics; Foreign Language; History; Humanities;
Literature/English/Writing; Philosophy; Political Science; Psychology;
Social Sciences.

Award: Scholarship for use in freshman, sophomore, junior, or senior
years; not renewable. *Number:* 4. *Amount:* $500.

Eligibility Requirements: Applicant must be enrolled or expecting to
enroll full- or part-time at a two-year or four-year or technical institution
or university. Available to U.S. and non-U.S. citizens.

Application Requirements: Essay. *Deadline:* varies.

Contact: Scholarship Committee
Phone: 605-348-3042

WILLIAMS LAW GROUP

https://familylawyersnewjersey.com/

WILLIAMS LAW GROUP OPPORTUNITY TO GROW SCHOLARSHIP

Are you a New Jersey student who will be enrolled in a New Jersey two-
year to five-year institution in 2018-2019? Do you need help paying for
schooling or supplies? You are not alone. College is not cheap, but we
don't want that to stop you from pursuing this irreplaceable experience.
At Williams Law Group, we have experienced the benefits of higher
education. That is why we are offering a $1500 scholarship to help one
New Jersey student go to college, law school, or other institute of higher
education. To apply for this scholarship, you must be a New Jersey high
school or college student and are enrolled in a two-year to five-year
institution in New Jersey in 2018-2019. Additionally, the student must
want to pursue their Juris Doctor, a degree in Social Work or a closely
related field. The student must be well-rounded and demonstrate a
commitment to their school and community. A minimum GPA is not
required. To apply, create a short (30-120 second) video and essay, telling
us the following things: 1. What does your community mean to you?, and
2. How have you demonstrated a commitment to both your school and

larger community? Upload your video to YouTube. Fill out the application, and include a link to your video on YouTube. Applications are due May 11, 2018.

Academic Fields/Career Goals: Area/Ethnic Studies; Behavioral Science; Child and Family Studies; Criminal Justice/Criminology; Law/Legal Services; Political Science; Psychology; Social Sciences; Social Services; Women's Studies.

Award: Scholarship for use in freshman, sophomore, junior, senior, or graduate years; not renewable. *Number:* 1. *Amount:* $1500.

Eligibility Requirements: Applicant must be enrolled or expecting to enroll full- or part-time at a two-year or four-year institution or university; resident of New Jersey and studying in New Jersey. Available to U.S. citizens.

Application Requirements: Application form, essay. *Deadline:* May 11.

Contact: Scholarship Coordinator
Phone: 513-444-2016
E-mail: coordinator@ourscholarship.io

ART HISTORY

AMERICAN SCHOOL OF CLASSICAL STUDIES AT ATHENS

http://www.ascsa.edu.gr/

ASCSA SUMMER SESSION AND SUMMER SEMINARS SCHOLARSHIPS
• *See page 118*

COSTUME SOCIETY OF AMERICA

http://www.costumesocietyamerica.com/

ADELE FILENE STUDENT PRESENTER GRANT
• *See page 138*

STELLA BLUM STUDENT RESEARCH GRANT
• *See page 138*

CULTURAL SERVICES OF THE FRENCH EMBASSY

http://www.frenchculture.org/

TEACHING ASSISTANT PROGRAM IN FRANCE
• *See page 113*

QUALITY BATH

http://www.qualitybath.com

QUALITYBATH.COM SCHOLARSHIP PROGRAM
Convey the beauty of humanity, e.g. a good deed you witnessed or envision, in a way that will inspire others. Original, unpublished content only. Submit one of the following: Essay up to 1,500 words; image up to 8.5 x 11, with description; video up to 90 seconds long, in one of the following formats:.mov,.mp4,.m4v,.flv,.3gp,.avi,.wmv. Submissions containing grammatical or spelling errors, or any inappropriate language or content, may be disqualified. Save a digital copy in case we decide to publish your work. Must be a U.S. citizen or permanent resident alien, high school senior or enrolled in accredited U.S. college or university, achieved minimum cumulative GPA of 3.0, currently pursuing a degree in the arts or design field. Applicant must not have a professional or familial relation with QualityBath.com and its management. Email to scholarships@qualitybath.com or mail to Scholarship Contest, c/o Quality Bath, 1144 East County Line Road, Unit 200, Lakewood, NJ 08701. Include submission; copy of transcript; your name, email address, phone number; degree you are pursuing; proof of citizenship/alien status. Deadline: March 1.

Academic Fields/Career Goals: Art History; Arts; Fashion Design; Filmmaking/Video; Graphics/Graphic Arts/Printing; Interior Design; Landscape Architecture; Music; Performing Arts; Photojournalism/Photography.

Award: Prize for use in freshman, sophomore, junior, senior, or graduate years; not renewable. *Number:* 1. *Amount:* $1500.

Eligibility Requirements: Applicant must be enrolled or expecting to enroll full- or part-time at a two-year or four-year or technical institution or university. Applicant must have 3.0 GPA or higher. Available to U.S. citizens.

Application Requirements: Application form. *Deadline:* April 9.

Contact: Fay Friedman, Director of SEO/Marketing
Quality Bath
1144 East County Line Road
Lakewood, NJ 08701
Phone: 800-554-3210
E-mail: scholarships@qualitybath.com

ROBERT H. MOLLOHAN FAMILY CHARITABLE FOUNDATION, INC.

http://www.mollohanfoundation.org/

MARY OLIVE EDDY JONES ART SCHOLARSHIP
Scholarship awarded to a rising sophomore or junior seriously interested in pursuing an art-related degree. Applicant must be a West Virginia resident attending a West Virginia college or university.

Academic Fields/Career Goals: Art History; Arts; Graphics/Graphic Arts/Printing.

Award: Scholarship for use in sophomore or junior years; not renewable. *Number:* 1–3. *Amount:* up to $1000.

Eligibility Requirements: Applicant must be enrolled or expecting to enroll full- or part-time at a four-year institution or university; resident of West Virginia and studying in West Virginia. Available to U.S. citizens.

Application Requirements: Application form, essay, portfolio, recommendations or references, resume, transcript. *Deadline:* February 9.

Contact: Aime Shaffer, Program Manager
Robert H. Mollohan Family Charitable Foundation, Inc.
1000 Technology Drive, Suite 2000
Fairmont, WV 26554
Phone: 304-333-6783
Fax: 304-333-3900
E-mail: ashaffer@wvhtf.org

STRAIGHTFORWARD MEDIA

http://www.straightforwardmedia.com/

STRAIGHTFORWARD MEDIA LIBERAL ARTS SCHOLARSHIP
• *See page 139*

SUPPORT CREATIVITY

http://wesupportcreativity.org

SUPPORT CREATIVITY SCHOLARSHIP
• *See page 137*

UNITED NEGRO COLLEGE FUND

http://www.uncf.org/

CATHERINE W. PIERCE SCHOLARSHIP
Up to $5000 scholarship for full-time students at UNCF member colleges and universities majoring in the arts or history. Minimum 2.5 GPA required. Open to U.S. citizens, nationals and permanent residents.

Academic Fields/Career Goals: Art History; Arts; History.

Award: Scholarship for use in freshman, sophomore, junior, senior, or graduate years; not renewable.

Eligibility Requirements: Applicant must be American Indian/Alaska Native, Asian/Pacific Islander, Black (non-Hispanic), Hispanic and enrolled or expecting to enroll full-time at a four-year institution or university. Applicant must have 2.5 GPA or higher. Available to U.S. and non-U.S. citizens.

Application Requirements: Application form, essay. *Deadline:* September 29.

Contact: Mary Williams, Director of Outreach and Recruitment
Phone: 800-331-2244

ARTS

AMERICAN INSTITUTE OF POLISH CULTURE INC.

http://www.ampolinstitute.org/

HARRIET IRSAY SCHOLARSHIP GRANT

Merit-based $1000 scholarships for students studying communications, public relations, and/or journalism. All U.S. citizens may apply, but preference will be given to U.S. citizens of Polish heritage. Must submit three letters of recommendation on appropriate letterhead with application mailed directly to AIPC. For study in the United States only. Non-refundable fee of $10 will be collected.

Academic Fields/Career Goals: Arts; Communications; Education; Foreign Language; Journalism; Public Policy and Administration.

Award: Scholarship for use in freshman, sophomore, junior, senior, or graduate years; not renewable. *Number:* 10–15. *Amount:* $1000.

Eligibility Requirements: Applicant must be enrolled or expecting to enroll full-time at a two-year or four-year institution or university. Available to U.S. citizens.

Application Requirements: Application form, recommendations or references, resume, self-addressed stamped envelope with application, transcript. *Fee:* $10. *Deadline:* April 20.

Contact: Scholarship Committee
Phone: 305-864-2349
Fax: 305-865-5150
E-mail: info@ampolinstitute.org

AMERICAN SCHOOL OF CLASSICAL STUDIES AT ATHENS

http://www.ascsa.edu.gr/

ASCSA SUMMER SESSION AND SUMMER SEMINARS SCHOLARSHIPS
• *See page 118*

BMI FOUNDATION, INC.

http://www.bmifoundation.org/

BMI STUDENT COMPOSER AWARDS

One-time awards for original compositions in the classical genre for young student composers who are under age 28 and citizens of the Western Hemisphere. Must submit application and original musical score. Online application available: bmifoundation.org/sca

Academic Fields/Career Goals: Arts; Music.

Award: Prize for use in freshman, sophomore, junior, senior, graduate, or postgraduate years; not renewable. *Number:* 6–12. *Amount:* $500–$5000.

Eligibility Requirements: Applicant must be enrolled or expecting to enroll full- or part-time at a two-year or four-year or technical institution or university and must have an interest in music or music/singing. Available to U.S. and non-U.S. citizens.

Application Requirements: Application form. *Deadline:* February 1.

Contact: Ms. Deirdre Chadwick, Director
BMI Foundation, Inc.
7 World Trade Center
250 Greenwich Street
New York, NY 10007-0030
Phone: 212-220-3103
E-mail: info@bmifoundation.org

BULKOFFICESUPPLY.COM

http://www.bulkofficesupply.com

OFFICE SUPPLY SCHOLARSHIP

If you have an interest in teaching, art or owning your own business you are eligible to apply for our scholarship program. The program is open to all high school students as well as College Freshmen and Sophomores.

Academic Fields/Career Goals: Arts; Business/Consumer Services; Education.

Award: Scholarship for use in freshman or sophomore years; not renewable. *Number:* 1. *Amount:* $1000.

Eligibility Requirements: Applicant must be enrolled or expecting to enroll full- or part-time at a two-year or four-year or technical institution or university. Available to U.S. and non-U.S. citizens.

Application Requirements: Application form may be submitted online (http://www.bulkofficesupply.com/scholarships-in-new-york), entry in a contest, essay. *Deadline:* February 1.

Contact: Mr. Harrison Blackhurst, Online Marketing Manager
BulkOfficeSupply.com
1614 Hereford Road
Hewlett, NY 11557
Phone: 800-658 -1488
E-mail: webteam.bulkofficesupply@gmail.com

CONGRESSIONAL BLACK CAUCUS FOUNDATION, INC.

http://www.cbcfinc.org/

CBC SPOUSES VISUAL ARTS SCHOLARSHIP
• *See page 132*

COSTUME SOCIETY OF AMERICA

http://www.costumesocietyamerica.com/

ADELE FILENE STUDENT PRESENTER GRANT
• *See page 138*

STELLA BLUM STUDENT RESEARCH GRANT
• *See page 138*

DIVERSITYCOMM, INC.

http://www.diversitycomm.net/

DIVERSITY IN STEAM MAGAZINE SCHOLARSHIP
• *See page 83*

FLORIDA PTA/PTSA

http://www.floridapta.org/

FLORIDA PTA/PTSA FINE ARTS SCHOLARSHIP

Renewable award of $1000 to a graduating Florida high school senior who plans to attend a fine arts program within the State of Florida. Must have a least a two-year attendance in a Florida PTA/PTSA high school. Minimum 3.0 GPA.

Academic Fields/Career Goals: Arts.

Award: Scholarship for use in freshman year; renewable. *Number:* 3. *Amount:* $1000.

Eligibility Requirements: Applicant must be high school student; planning to enroll or expecting to enroll full-time at a four-year institution or university; resident of Florida and studying in Florida. Applicant must have 3.0 GPA or higher. Available to U.S. citizens.

Application Requirements: Application form, essay, recommendations or references. *Deadline:* March 1.

Contact: Scholarship Chair, Scholarship Chair
Florida PTA/PTSA
1747 Orlando Central Parkway
Orlando, FL 32809
Phone: 407-855-7604
Fax: 407-240-9577
E-mail: scholarship@floridapta.org

GOLDEN KEY INTERNATIONAL HONOUR SOCIETY

http://www.goldenkey.org/

VISUAL AND PERFORMING ARTS ACHIEVEMENT AWARDS

Award of $500 will be given to winners in each of the following nine categories: painting, drawing, photography, sculpture, computer-generated art/graphic design/illustration, mixed media, instrumental performance, vocal performance, and dance.

Academic Fields/Career Goals: Arts; Graphics/Graphic Arts/Printing.

Award: Prize for use in freshman, sophomore, junior, senior, graduate, or postgraduate years; not renewable. *Number:* 9. *Amount:* $500.

Eligibility Requirements: Applicant must be enrolled or expecting to enroll full- or part-time at a four-year institution or university and must have an interest in art. Available to U.S. and non-U.S. citizens.

Application Requirements: Application form, artwork, cover letter, entry in a contest. *Deadline:* April 1.

Contact: Scholarship Program Administrators
Golden Key International Honour Society
PO Box 23737
Nashville, TN 37202
Phone: 800-377-2401

GRAND RAPIDS COMMUNITY FOUNDATION

http://www.grfoundation.org/

ARTS COUNCIL OF GREATER GRAND RAPIDS MINORITY SCHOLARSHIP

Scholarship is for students of color (African American, Asian, Hispanic, Native American, Pacific Islander) attending a non-profit public or private college/university majoring in Fine Arts including all visual and performing art forms. Must have financial need, be a Kent County resident, and have a minimum 2.5 GPA.

Academic Fields/Career Goals: Arts.

Award: Scholarship for use in freshman, sophomore, junior, or senior years; not renewable. *Number:* 2. *Amount:* $5000.

Eligibility Requirements: Applicant must be American Indian/Alaska Native, Asian/Pacific Islander, Black (non-Hispanic), Hispanic; enrolled or expecting to enroll full-time at a two-year or four-year institution or university; resident of Michigan; studying in Michigan and must have an interest in art, music, photography/photogrammetry/filmmaking, or theater. Applicant must have 2.5 GPA or higher. Available to U.S. citizens.

Application Requirements: Application form, essay, financial need analysis. *Deadline:* April 1.

Contact: Ms. Ruth Bishop, Education Program Officer
Grand Rapids Community Foundation
185 Oakes SW
Grand Rapids, MI 49503
Phone: 616-454-1751 Ext. 103
E-mail: rbishop@grfoundation.org

HEMOPHILIA FOUNDATION OF SOUTHERN CALIFORNIA

http://www.hemosocal.org/

EARL JAMES FAHRINGER PERFORMING ARTS SCHOLARSHIP

Due to the extreme generosity of the late Dr. Earl James Fahringer, the Hemophilia Foundation of Southern California is thrilled to have a scholarship fund known as the Dr. Earl James Fahringer Performing Arts Scholarship, which will be awarded each year to 1-2 students pursuing a major in music, arts, drama, or dance. Dr. Fahringer was a lifelong musician, and music educator in the Pomona School District and served as a violinist, violist, percussionist, Assistant Conductor, Music Director, and Co-Conductor of the Claremont Symphony Orchestra. We hope to provide the means for young musicians and artists to pursue their education through this scholarship.

Academic Fields/Career Goals: Arts; Filmmaking/Video; Music; Performing Arts.

Award: Scholarship for use in freshman, sophomore, junior, senior, graduate, or postgraduate years; not renewable. *Number:* 1–2. *Amount:* $500–$1000.

Eligibility Requirements: Applicant must be physically disabled; enrolled or expecting to enroll full- or part-time at a two-year or four-year or technical institution or university and resident of California. Applicant must be physically disabled. Available to U.S. citizens.

Application Requirements: Application form, essay. *Deadline:* June 29.

Contact: Laura Desai, Operations Manager
Hemophilia Foundation of Southern California
959 E Walnut St Suite 114
Pasadena, CA 91106
Phone: 626-765-6656
Fax: 626-765-6657
E-mail: info@hemosocal.org

IFDA EDUCATIONAL FOUNDATION

http://www.ifdaef.org/

RUTH CLARK FURNITURE DESIGN SCHOLARSHIP

Scholarship available to students studying design at an accredited college or design school with a focus on residential furniture design. Applicant must submit five examples of original designs, three of which must be residential furniture examples. (pdf format only), Include design examples with a short description of each illustration.

Academic Fields/Career Goals: Arts; Industrial Design; Interior Design.

Award: Scholarship for use in sophomore, junior, senior, or graduate years; not renewable. *Number:* 1. *Amount:* $3000.

Eligibility Requirements: Applicant must be enrolled or expecting to enroll full- or part-time at a four-year institution or university. Available to U.S. and non-U.S. citizens.

Application Requirements: Application form, essay, portfolio. *Deadline:* March 31.

Contact: Earline Feldman, Director of Scholarships and Grants
IFDA Educational Foundation
112 Hidden Lake Circle
Canton, GA 30114
Phone: 770-378-7221
E-mail: ef.ifda@tapestries.org

NATIONAL ACADEMY OF TELEVISION ARTS AND SCIENCES

http://www.emmyonline.tv/

DOUGLAS W. MUMMERT SCHOLARSHIP

Awarded to a student pursuing a career in any aspect of the television industry, who has made a positive impact through community service.

Academic Fields/Career Goals: Arts; Communications; Filmmaking/Video; Journalism; Music; Performing Arts; Photojournalism/Photography; Public Policy and Administration; TV/Radio Broadcasting.

Award: Scholarship for use in freshman year; not renewable. *Number:* 1. *Amount:* $10,000.

Eligibility Requirements: Applicant must be high school student and planning to enroll or expecting to enroll full-time at a two-year or four-year institution or university. Available to U.S. citizens.

Application Requirements: Application form, community service, essay, portfolio. *Deadline:* February 26.

Contact: Mr. Adam Sharp, Chair, Scholarship Committee
Phone: 212-586-8424
Fax: 212-246-8129
E-mail: scholarship@emmyonline.tv

NATIONAL OPERA ASSOCIATION

http://www.noa.org/

NOA VOCAL COMPETITION/LEGACY AWARD PROGRAM

Awards granted based on competitive audition to support study and career development. Singers compete in Scholarship and Artist Division. Legacy Awards are granted for study and career development in any opera-related career to those who further NOA's goal of increased minority participation in the profession.

Academic Fields/Career Goals: Arts; Performing Arts.

Award: Prize for use in freshman, sophomore, junior, senior, graduate, or postgraduate years; not renewable. *Number:* 3–8. *Amount:* $500–$2000.

Eligibility Requirements: Applicant must be age 18-24; enrolled or expecting to enroll full- or part-time at a two-year or four-year or technical institution or university and must have an interest in music or music/singing. Available to U.S. and non-U.S. citizens.

Application Requirements: Application form, audition tape/proposal, driver's license, entry in a contest, personal photograph, recommendations or references. *Fee:* $25. *Deadline:* October 15.

Contact: Robert Hansen, Executive Secretary
National Opera Association
2403 Russell Long Boulevard, PO Box 60869
Canyon, TX 79016-0001
Phone: 806-651-2857
Fax: 806-651-2958
E-mail: hansen@mail.wtamu.edu

ONLINE LOGO MAKER

http://onlinelogomaker.com

OLM MALALA YOUSAFZAI SCHOLARSHIP

Online Logo Maker is proud to announce its own Scholarship named after the great activist from the actual time: Malala Yousafzai, known for fighting for education. And from now on, we are going to provide an annual scholarship for minorities as an act for education. Acknowledging the difficulty that women face on a sexist society, the scholarship will provide a $1000 scholarship to a woman. All women, from all over the world, who has 30 years old or more and want the opportunity to go back to school to start or continue interrupted studies in the Arts and Design field can apply. The OLM Malala Yousafzai Scholarship application requires a 500–1000 words essay written in English about a challenge you have faced and how you overcame it. Fill out the online form including your essay and good luck! For more info, see website http://www.onlinelogomaker.com/scholarships-for-women

Academic Fields/Career Goals: Arts; Drafting; Industrial Design; Interior Design; Performing Arts.

Award: Scholarship for use in freshman, sophomore, junior, senior, graduate, or postgraduate years; not renewable. *Number:* 1. *Amount:* $1000.

Eligibility Requirements: Applicant must be Baha'i faith, Baptist, Brethren, Buddhist faith, Christian, Disciple of Christ, Eastern Orthodox, Episcopalian, Friends, Hindu faith, Jewish, Latter-day Saints, Lutheran, Methodist, Muslim faith, Pentecostal, Presbyterian, Protestant, Roman Catholic, Seventh-Day Adventist, Unitarian Universalist; of African, Albanian, Arab, Armenian, Arumanian/Ulacedo-Romanian, Australian, Belgian, Bulgarian, Canadian, Central European, Chinese, Croatian/Serbian, Cypriot, Danish, Dutch, Eastern European, English, European Union, Finnish, former Soviet Union, French, German, Greek, Haitian, Hispanic, Hungarian, Icelandic, Indian, Irish, Israeli, Italian, Japanese, Jewish, Korean, Lao/Hmong, Latin American/Caribbean, Latvian, Lebanese, Lithuanian, Mexican, Mongolian, New Zealander, Nicaraguan, Norwegian, Polish, Portuguese, Rumanian, Russian, Scandinavian, Scottish, Slavic/Czech, Spanish, Sub-Saharan African, Swedish, Swiss, Syrian, Turkish, Ukrainian, Vietnamese, Welsh, Yemeni heritage and African, Albanian, Arab, Armenian, Arumanian/Ulacedo-Romanian, Australian, Belgian, Bulgarian, Canadian, Central European, Chinese, Croatian/Serbian, Cypriot, Danish, Dutch, Eastern European, English, European Union, Finnish, former Soviet Union, French, German, Greek, Haitian, Hispanic, Hungarian, Icelandic, Indian, Irish, Israeli, Italian, Japanese, Jewish, Korean, Lao/Hmong, Latin American/Caribbean, Latvian, Lebanese, Lithuanian, Mexican, Mongolian, New Zealander, Nicaraguan, Norwegian, Polish, Portuguese, Rumanian, Russian, Scandinavian, Scottish, Slavic/Czech, Spanish, Sub-Saharan African, Swedish, Swiss, Syrian, Turkish, Ukrainian, Vietnamese, Welsh, Yemeni citizen; American Indian/Alaska Native, Asian/Pacific Islander, Black (non-Hispanic); age 30-70; enrolled or expecting to enroll full- or part-time at a two-year or four-year or technical institution or university and female. Available to U.S. and non-U.S. citizens.

Application Requirements: Application form, essay. *Deadline:* December 1.

Contact: OLM Malala Yousafzai Scholarship
E-mail: scholarship@onlinelogomaker.com

OREGON STUDENT ASSISTANCE COMMISSION

https://oregonstudentaid.gov/

KERDRAGON SCHOLARSHIP

Scholarships for students who are graduates (including GED recipients) of Oregon high schools who have not yet attended college and are planning to study fine arts, graphic arts, or photography. Minimum GPA of 3.0 preferred for high school students, 2.75 GPA required for prior recipients. Semifinalists will be required to submit nonreturnable slides of photos of art samples or film/video of other artistic endeavors. Financial need may or may not be considered.

Academic Fields/Career Goals: Arts; Graphics/Graphic Arts/Printing; Photojournalism/Photography.

Award: Scholarship for use in freshman year; not renewable.

Eligibility Requirements: Applicant must be enrolled or expecting to enroll full- or part-time at a four-year institution or university and resident of Oregon. Available to U.S. citizens.

Application Requirements: Application form, portfolio. *Deadline:* March 1.

Contact: Melissa Adams, Scholarship Processing Coordinator
Phone: 541-687-7409
E-mail: melissa.adams@state.or.us

KIRCHHOFF FAMILY FINE ARTS SCHOLARSHIP

Award available to students studying fine art or graphic art at an Oregon nonprofit college or university. Preference will be given to upper-level undergraduates and MFA students. Semifinalists may be asked to submit non-returnable slides or photos of art samples. Recipients may apply for one additional year of funding. Financial need may or may not be considered.

Academic Fields/Career Goals: Arts; Graphics/Graphic Arts/Printing.

Award: Scholarship for use in freshman, sophomore, junior, senior, or graduate years; not renewable.

Eligibility Requirements: Applicant must be enrolled or expecting to enroll full-time at a four-year institution or university and studying in Oregon. Available to U.S. citizens.

Application Requirements: Application form, portfolio. *Deadline:* March 1.

Contact: Melissa Adams, Scholarship Processing Coordinator
Phone: 541-687-7409
E-mail: melissa.adams@state.or.us

TECHNICAL TRAINING FUND SCHOLARSHIP

Award is available to graduates (including GED recipients and home-schooled graduates) of Oregon high schools. Preference given to students who will enroll as a junior, senior, or graduate-level student for fall term/semester at a traditional four-year institution; then applicants at any class level enrolled at a special vocational/trade school. Applicants must demonstrate extraordinary technical or artistic potential in areas such as craftsmanship, manual skills, art, music, or culinary arts. Recipient must enroll at least half-time. Financial need may or may not be considered.

Academic Fields/Career Goals: Arts; Culinary Arts; Music; Trade/Technical Specialties.

Award: Scholarship for use in sophomore, junior, senior, or graduate years; not renewable.

Eligibility Requirements: Applicant must be enrolled or expecting to enroll full- or part-time at a four-year or technical institution or university and resident of Oregon. Available to U.S. citizens.

Application Requirements: Application form, essay. *Deadline:* March 1.

Contact: Melissa Adams, Scholarship Processing Coordinator
Phone: 541-687-7409
E-mail: melissa.adams@state.or.us

P. BUCKLEY MOSS FOUNDATION FOR CHILDREN'S EDUCATION

http://www.mossfoundation.org

MOSS ENDOWED SCHOLARSHIP

The Moss Endowed Scholarship is an up-to-$1,000.00 financial award given annually to one high school senior with a verified financial need, a verified language-related learning difference, visual arts talent, acceptance to an accredited 4-year college or university and the intent to pursue a career in the visual arts field. Art classes must be taken each semester to continue the award renewal.

Academic Fields/Career Goals: Arts.

Award: Scholarship for use in freshman year; renewable. *Number:* 1. *Amount:* $1000.

Eligibility Requirements: Applicant must be high school student; planning to enroll or expecting to enroll full-time at a four-year institution; resident of Alabama, Arizona, Arkansas, California, Colorado, Connecticut, Delaware, District of Columbia, Florida, Georgia, Hawaii, Idaho, Illinois, Indiana, Iowa, Kansas, Kentucky, Louisiana, Maine, Maryland, Massachusetts, Michigan, Minnesota, Mississippi, Missouri, Montana, Nebraska, Nevada, New Hampshire, New Jersey, New York, North Carolina, North Dakota, Ohio, Oklahoma, Oregon, Pennsylvania, Rhode Island, South Carolina, South Dakota, Tennessee, Texas, Utah, Vermont, Virginia, Washington, West Virginia, Wisconsin, Wyoming and must have an interest in art. Applicant must have 2.5 GPA or higher. Available to U.S. citizens.

Application Requirements: Application form, essay, financial need analysis, portfolio. *Deadline:* March 31.

POLISH ARTS CLUB OF BUFFALO SCHOLARSHIP FOUNDATION

http://www.pacb.bfn.org/

POLISH ARTS CLUB OF BUFFALO SCHOLARSHIP FOUNDATION TRUST

Provides educational scholarships to students of Polish background who are legal residents of New York. Must be enrolled at the junior level or above in an accredited college or university in NY during the upcoming year of application. Must be a U.S. citizen. For application and additional information, visit website http://www.pacb.bfn.org.

Academic Fields/Career Goals: Arts; Communications; Filmmaking/Video; Music; Performing Arts; TV/Radio Broadcasting.

Award: Scholarship for use in junior, senior, graduate, or postgraduate years; not renewable. *Number:* 1–3. *Amount:* $1000.

Eligibility Requirements: Applicant must be of Polish heritage; enrolled or expecting to enroll full- or part-time at a four-year institution or university and resident of New York. Available to U.S. citizens.

Application Requirements: Application form, essay, interview, portfolio. *Deadline:* April 14.

Contact: Anne Flansburg, Selection Chair
Polish Arts Club of Buffalo Scholarship Foundation
24 Amherston Drive
Williamsville, NY 14221-7002
Phone: 716-863-3631
E-mail: anneflanswz@aol.com

QUALITY BATH

http://www.qualitybath.com

QUALITYBATH.COM SCHOLARSHIP PROGRAM
• See page 140

RHODE ISLAND FOUNDATION

http://www.rifoundation.org/

MJSA EDUCATION FOUNDATION JEWELRY SCHOLARSHIP

Scholarships ranging from $500 to $2000 are available for students enrolled in tool making, design, metals fabrication or other jewelry-related courses of study at colleges, universities or non-profit technical schools on the post-secondary level in the United States. Renewable up to four years if the student maintains good academic standing.

Academic Fields/Career Goals: Arts.

Award: Scholarship for use in freshman year; renewable. *Amount:* $500–$2000.

Eligibility Requirements: Applicant must be enrolled or expecting to enroll full-time at a two-year or four-year or technical institution or university and must have an interest in art. Available to U.S. citizens.

Application Requirements: Application form, essay, financial need analysis, self-addressed stamped envelope with application, transcript. *Deadline:* June 14.

Contact: Libby Monahan, Funds Administrator
Phone: 401-274-4564 Ext. 3117
E-mail: libbym@rifoundation.org

PATRICIA W. EDWARDS MEMORIAL ART SCHOLARSHIP

Award to further education of young Rhode Island artists (such as art lessons for high school students in two-dimensional art) and/or scholarships for Rhode Island art students (freshmen, sophomores, and juniors) at Rhode Island institutions.

Academic Fields/Career Goals: Arts.

Award: Scholarship for use in freshman year; not renewable. *Amount:* up to $425.

Eligibility Requirements: Applicant must be high school student; planning to enroll or expecting to enroll full- or part-time at a two-year or four-year institution or university; resident of Rhode Island and studying in Rhode Island. Available to U.S. citizens.

Application Requirements: Application form. *Deadline:* March 4.

Contact: Libby Monahan, Funds Administrator
Phone: 401-274-4564 Ext. 3117
E-mail: libbym@rifoundation.org

ROBERT H. MOLLOHAN FAMILY CHARITABLE FOUNDATION, INC.

http://www.mollohanfoundation.org/

MARY OLIVE EDDY JONES ART SCHOLARSHIP
• See page 140

SERVICE EMPLOYEES INTERNATIONAL UNION (SEIU)

http://www.seiu.org/

SEIU MOE FONER SCHOLARSHIP PROGRAM FOR VISUAL AND PERFORMING ARTS

Scholarship for students pursuing a degree or training full-time in the visual or performing arts. Scholarship funding must be applied to tuition at a two- or four-year college, university, or an accredited community college, technical or trade school in an arts-related field.

Academic Fields/Career Goals: Arts; Performing Arts.

Award: Scholarship for use in freshman, sophomore, junior, or senior years; not renewable. *Number:* 1. *Amount:* $5000.

Eligibility Requirements: Applicant must be enrolled or expecting to enroll full-time at a two-year or four-year or technical institution or university. Applicant or parent of applicant must be member of Service Employees International Union. Available to U.S. citizens.

Application Requirements: 6 copies of a single original creative work, application form, essay, transcript. *Deadline:* March 1.

Contact: c/o Scholarship Program Administrators, Inc.
Phone: 615-320-3149
Fax: 615-320-3151
E-mail: info@spaprog.com

SOCIETY FOR CLASSICAL STUDIES
http://www.classicalstudies.org/

MINORITY STUDENT SUMMER SCHOLARSHIP
• *See page 130*

SOUTHEASTERN THEATRE CONFERENCE
http://www.setc.org

POLLY HOLLIDAY SCHOLARSHIP
The Polly Holliday Scholarship is awarded each year to a qualified High School Senior planning to major in Theatre Arts at an accredited college or university within the 10 SETC regional states (Alabama, Florida, Georgia, Kentucky, Mississippi, North Carolina, South Carolina, Tennessee, Virginia, West Virginia). All applicants must reside in the SETC region as well as attend college there. Applicant criteria for the Polly Holliday Award is based on financial need, talent, and the potential for academic success in college. https://www.setc.org/scholarships-awards/undergraduate-studies/polly-holliday-award/

Academic Fields/Career Goals: Arts; Performing Arts.

Award: Scholarship for use in freshman year; not renewable. *Number:* 1. *Amount:* $1000.

Eligibility Requirements: Applicant must be high school student; planning to enroll or expecting to enroll full-time at a two-year or four-year or technical institution or university; resident of Alabama, Florida, Georgia, Kentucky, Mississippi, North Carolina, South Carolina, Tennessee, Virginia, West Virginia; studying in Alabama, Florida, Georgia, Kentucky, Mississippi, North Carolina, South Carolina, Tennessee, Virginia, West Virginia and must have an interest in theater. Available to U.S. citizens.

Application Requirements: Application form. *Deadline:* April 1.

Contact: Claire Wisniewski, Educational Services Manager
Phone: 336-272-3645
E-mail: info@setc.org

STRAIGHTFORWARD MEDIA
http://www.straightforwardmedia.com/

STRAIGHTFORWARD MEDIA ART SCHOOL SCHOLARSHIP
Award of $500 for students pursuing a degree in any art-related field. May be used for full- or part-time study. Scholarship is awarded four times per year. Deadlines: November 30, February 28, May 31, and August 31. For more information, visit website http://www.straightforwardmedia.com/art/form.php.

Academic Fields/Career Goals: Arts.

Award: Scholarship for use in freshman, sophomore, junior, or senior years; not renewable. *Number:* 4. *Amount:* $500.

Eligibility Requirements: Applicant must be enrolled or expecting to enroll full- or part-time at a two-year or four-year or technical institution or university. Available to U.S. and non-U.S. citizens.

Application Requirements: Essay. *Deadline:* varies.

Contact: Scholarship Committee
Phone: 605-348-3042

SUPPORT CREATIVITY
http://wesupportcreativity.org

SUPPORT CREATIVITY SCHOLARSHIP
• *See page 137*

TELETOON
http://www.teletoon.com/

TELETOON ANIMATION SCHOLARSHIP
Scholarship competition created by TELETOON to encourage creative, original, and imaginative animation by supporting Canadians studying in the animation field or intending to pursue studies in animation. One-time award. Must submit portfolio.

Academic Fields/Career Goals: Arts; Filmmaking/Video.

Award: Scholarship for use in freshman, sophomore, junior, senior, graduate, or postgraduate years; not renewable. *Number:* 9. *Amount:* $5000–$10,000.

Eligibility Requirements: Applicant must be enrolled or expecting to enroll full-time at a two-year or four-year or technical institution or university and resident of Alberta, British Columbia, Manitoba, New Brunswick, Newfoundland, Northwest Territories, Nova Scotia, Ontario, Prince Edward Island, Quebec, Saskatchewan. Available to Canadian citizens.

Application Requirements: 5-minute film, application form, driver's license, essay, portfolio, transcript. *Deadline:* June 15.

Contact: Denise Vaughan, Senior Coordinator, Public Relations
Phone: 416-956-2060
Fax: 416-956-2070
E-mail: denisev@teletoon.com

UNICO FOUNDATION INC.
http://www.unico.org/

RALPH J. TORRACO FINE ARTS SCHOLARSHIP
The UNICO Foundation will grant two scholarships valued at $2,500 each, to students enrolled full-time in an accredited college/university program in the United States pursuing a degree in Fine Arts. A nominee must hold United States citizenship. This program is open to applicants of all ethnicities. Candidates must reside in the home state of an active UNICO Chapter. Applications must be submitted online. Candidates are to go to the UNICO National website (http://www.unico.org), and click on the Scholarship tab. There they will find complete information and submission instructions. Preference is given to candidates demonstrating financial need.

Academic Fields/Career Goals: Arts.

Award: Scholarship for use in sophomore, junior, senior, or graduate years; not renewable. *Number:* 2. *Amount:* $2500.

Eligibility Requirements: Applicant must be enrolled or expecting to enroll full-time at a four-year institution or university and resident of California, Connecticut, Delaware, Florida, Illinois, Maryland, Massachusetts, Minnesota, Missouri, New Jersey, New York, Pennsylvania, Tennessee, Vermont, Wisconsin. Applicant must have 3.0 GPA or higher. Available to U.S. citizens.

Application Requirements: Application form, essay, financial need analysis. *Deadline:* April 15.

Contact: Joan Tidona, Scholarship Director
Phone: 973-808-0035
Fax: 973-808-0043
E-mail: uniconational@unico.org

UNITARIAN UNIVERSALIST ASSOCIATION
http://www.uua.org/

MARION BARR STANFIELD ART SCHOLARSHIP
Scholarship for graduate or undergraduate students preparing for a career in fine arts. Eligibility is limited to those in the study of painting, drawing, photography, and/or sculpture. Performing arts majors are not eligible. Applicants must be members of or affiliated with a Unitarian Universalist congregation.

Academic Fields/Career Goals: Arts.

Award: Scholarship for use in freshman, sophomore, junior, senior, or graduate years; not renewable. *Number:* 5–8. *Amount:* $1500–$5000.

Eligibility Requirements: Applicant must be Unitarian Universalist; enrolled or expecting to enroll full-time at a four-year institution or university and must have an interest in art. Available to U.S. citizens.

Application Requirements: Application form, essay, financial need analysis, portfolio. *Deadline:* March 1.

Contact: Ms. Hillary Goodridge, Program Director
    Phone: 617-971-9600
    Fax: 617-971-0029
    E-mail: uufp@aol.com

PAULY D'ORLANDO MEMORIAL ART SCHOLARSHIP

Scholarship for graduate or undergraduate students preparing for a career in fine arts. Student must be studying painting, drawing, photography, and/or sculpture. Performing arts majors are not eligible.

Academic Fields/Career Goals: Arts; Photojournalism/Photography.

Award: Scholarship for use in freshman, sophomore, junior, senior, or graduate years; not renewable.

Eligibility Requirements: Applicant must be Unitarian Universalist and enrolled or expecting to enroll full-time at a four-year institution or university. Available to U.S. citizens.

Application Requirements: Application form, essay, financial need analysis, list of works, personal tax information, recommendations or references. *Deadline:* varies.

Contact: Ms. Hillary Goodridge, Program Director
    Phone: 617-971-9600
    Fax: 617-971-0029
    E-mail: uufp@aol.com

STANFIELD AND D'ORLANDO ART SCHOLARSHIP

Scholarships for both Master's and undergraduate Unitarian Universalist students studying the fields of art and law.

Academic Fields/Career Goals: Arts; Law/Legal Services.

Award: Scholarship for use in freshman, sophomore, junior, senior, or graduate years; not renewable.

Eligibility Requirements: Applicant must be Unitarian Universalist and enrolled or expecting to enroll full- or part-time at a four-year institution or university. Available to U.S. citizens.

Application Requirements: Application form. *Deadline:* February 15.

Contact: Ms. Hillary Goodridge, Program Director
    Phone: 617-971-9600
    Fax: 617-971-0029
    E-mail: uufp@aol.com

UNITED NEGRO COLLEGE FUND

http://www.uncf.org/

CATHERINE W. PIERCE SCHOLARSHIP

• See page 140

OSSIE DAVIS ENDOWMENT SCHOLARSHIP PROGRAM

Need-based scholarship of up to $6800 for a high school senior planning to attend a four-year HBCU. Applicants must demonstrate the ability and desire to use artistic activism to proactively address the concerns of humanity. Eligible majors include African American studies, communications, fine arts, humanities, performing arts, political science, social sciences, and theater arts/drama. The scholarship is renewable for up to 4 years, provided that students continue to meet the scholarship criteria. Minimum 3.0 GPA required.

Academic Fields/Career Goals: Arts; Communications; Humanities; Performing Arts; Political Science; Social Sciences.

Award: Scholarship for use in freshman year; renewable.

Eligibility Requirements: Applicant must be Black (non-Hispanic); high school student and planning to enroll or expecting to enroll full-time at a four-year institution or university. Applicant must have 3.0 GPA or higher. Available to U.S. citizens.

Application Requirements: Application form, essay, financial need analysis, portfolio. *Deadline:* October 15.

Contact: Mary Williams, Director of Outreach and Recruitment
    Phone: 800-331-2244

VECTORWORKS, INC.

http://www.vectorworks.net

VECTORWORKS DESIGN SCHOLARSHIP

• See page 137

WARNER BROS. ENTERTAINMENT

http://www.warnerbros.com/

WARNER BROS. ANIMATION/HANNA-BARBERA HONORSHIP

The Honorship will be awarded annually to a graduating high school senior enrolling in a college, university, or trade school to study animation. Applicants must have (1) a passion and talent for a career in animation; (2) a minimum GPA of 3.0 upon graduation; and (3) demonstrate financial need. Each cash scholarship will be for $10,000, disbursed annually in equal amounts over the course of enrollment. In addition, the winner will have the opportunity to receive (4) consecutive, paid summer internships at Warner Bros. Studios in Burbank while at university.

Academic Fields/Career Goals: Arts.

Award: Scholarship for use in freshman, sophomore, junior, or senior years; renewable. *Number:* 1. *Amount:* $10,000.

Eligibility Requirements: Applicant must be high school student and planning to enroll or expecting to enroll full- or part-time at a four-year or technical institution or university. Applicant must have 3.0 GPA or higher. Available to U.S. citizens.

Application Requirements: *Deadline:* March 1.

WOMEN'S JEWELRY ASSOCIATION

http://www.womensjewelryassociation.com

WOMEN'S JEWELRY ASSOCIATION STUDENT SCHOLARSHIP

This is a student scholarship for a woman studying in the jewelry, gem and watch fields.

Academic Fields/Career Goals: Arts; Trade/Technical Specialties.

Award: Scholarship for use in freshman, sophomore, junior, senior, graduate, or postgraduate years; renewable. *Number:* 5–12. *Amount:* $500–$7000.

Eligibility Requirements: Applicant must be enrolled or expecting to enroll full-time at a two-year or four-year or technical institution or university; female and must have an interest in art. Applicant or parent of applicant must have employment or volunteer experience in fine arts. Available to U.S. and non-U.S. citizens.

Application Requirements: Application form, essay, personal photograph, portfolio. *Fee:* $10. *Deadline:* April 1.

Contact: Jenny Calleri
    E-mail: Jennyo@tbirdjewels.com

WORLDSTUDIO FOUNDATION

http://www.aiga.org/

WORLDSTUDIO AIGA SCHOLARSHIPS

Scholarships available for minority and economically disadvantaged students who are pursuing degrees in the design/arts disciplines in colleges and universities in the United States.

Academic Fields/Career Goals: Arts; Graphics/Graphic Arts/Printing.

Award: Scholarship for use in freshman, sophomore, junior, senior, or graduate years; not renewable. *Number:* 10–25. *Amount:* $1000–$5000.

Eligibility Requirements: Applicant must be enrolled or expecting to enroll full-time at a two-year or four-year or technical institution or university. Available to U.S. citizens.

Application Requirements: Application form, application form may be submitted online (http://www.aiga.org/content.cfm/worldstudio-scholarship), essay, portfolio, recommendations or references, transcript. *Deadline:* April 1.

Contact: Tiia Schurig, Web Production Manager
    Worldstudio Foundation
    164 Fifth Avenue
    New York, NY 10010
    Phone: 212-807-1990
    Fax: 212-807-1799
    E-mail: scholarship@aiga.org

ASIAN STUDIES

UNITED NATIONS ASSOCIATION OF CONNECTICUT

http://www.unausa.org

UNITED NATIONS ASSOCIATION OF CONNECTICUT SCHOLARSHIP

Scholarship to encourage and support students with a demonstrated interest in promoting world peace through work in international relations and diplomatic service to cultivate an understanding of and support for the work of the UN in the United States. At least one award of $1000 will be made in the Spring of each year to assist the selected student with his or her college expenses. Applicants must be graduating seniors of a public high school in Connecticut. The scholarship is based on demonstrated academic excellence, evidence of engagement in international issues, progress in developing proficiency in a foreign language, commitment to social advancement as documented through community service or related activities, and participation in a Model UN or similar intercultural program. The e-mail application (postmarked not later than March 31) must be sent to UNACT.studentfund@gmail.com.

Academic Fields/Career Goals: Asian Studies; Foreign Language; Health and Medical Sciences; International Migration; International Studies; Natural Sciences; Near and Middle East Studies; Nuclear Science; Peace and Conflict Studies; Political Science; Women's Studies.

Award: Scholarship for use in freshman year; not renewable. *Number:* 1–3. *Amount:* $1000.

Eligibility Requirements: Applicant must be high school student; planning to enroll or expecting to enroll full-time at a two-year or four-year institution or university and resident of Connecticut. Available to U.S. and non-U.S. citizens.

Application Requirements: Application form, essay. *Deadline:* March 31.

Contact: Ms. Barbara Bacewicz
Phone: 860-9274333
E-mail: jjbaxer@icloud.com

AUDIOLOGY

101ST AIRBORNE DIVISION ASSOCIATION

http://www.screamingeaglefoundation.org/

AL & WILLIAMARY VISTE SCHOLARSHIP
• See page 114

AMERICAN LEGION AUXILIARY DEPARTMENT OF COLORADO

http://www.alacolorado.com

AMERICAN LEGION AUXILIARY DEPARTMENT OF COLORADO PAST PRESIDENTS' PARLEY HEALTH CARE PROFESSIONAL SCHOLARSHIPNURSES SCHOLARSHIP

Open to children, spouses, grandchildren, and great-grandchildren of American Legion veterans, and veterans who served in the armed forces during eligibility dates for membership in the American Legion. Must be Colorado residents who have been accepted by an accredited health care professional school in Colorado.

Academic Fields/Career Goals: Audiology; Dental Health/Services; Health Administration; Health and Medical Sciences; Health Information Management/Technology; Nursing; Oncology; Optometry; Osteopathy; Pharmacy; Therapy/Rehabilitation.

Award: Scholarship for use in freshman, sophomore, junior, senior, or graduate years; not renewable. *Number:* 3–5. *Amount:* $500–$1500.

Eligibility Requirements: Applicant must be enrolled or expecting to enroll full- or part-time at a two-year or four-year institution or university; resident of Colorado and studying in Colorado. Available to U.S. citizens.

Application Requirements: Application form, essay, financial need analysis. *Deadline:* March 15.

Contact: Rhonda Larkowski, Department Secretary and Treasurer
American Legion Auxiliary Department of Colorado
7465 East First Avenue, Suite D
Denver, CO 80230
Phone: 303-367-5388
E-mail: www.dept-sec@alacolorado.com

GREAT MINDS IN STEM

http://www.greatmindsinstem.org

HENAAC SCHOLARSHIP PROGRAM
• See page 115

HOUSE OF BLUES MUSIC FORWARD FOUNDATION

https://hobmusicforward.org/

TIFFANY GREEN OPERATOR SCHOLARSHIP AWARD
• See page 96

INTERMOUNTAIN MEDICAL IMAGING

https://www.aboutimi.com/

INTERMOUNTAIN MEDICAL IMAGING SCHOLARSHIP

Intermountain Medical Imaging (IMI) provides outpatient radiology services such as x-ray, computed tomography (CT), magnetic resonance imaging (MRI), ultrasound, and interventional radiology procedures that are competitively priced and generally far less expensive than the average hospital price. Providing excellence in both quality and experience, with locations in Boise, Meridian, and Eagle Idaho.

Academic Fields/Career Goals: Audiology; Behavioral Science; Dental Health/Services; Health Administration; Health and Medical Sciences; Health Information Management/Technology; Neurobiology; Occupational Safety and Health; Oncology; Optometry; Osteopathy; Psychology; Public Health; Therapy/Rehabilitation.

Award: Scholarship for use in freshman year; not renewable. *Number:* 1. *Amount:* $1000.

Eligibility Requirements: Applicant must be enrolled or expecting to enroll full-time at a four-year institution or university and resident of Idaho. Applicant must have 3.0 GPA or higher. Available to U.S. citizens.

Application Requirements: Essay. *Deadline:* April 30.

Contact: Rachel Bergmann
E-mail: community@aboutimi.com

LABROOTS INC.

http://www.LabRoots.com

LABROOTS STEM SCHOLARSHIP
• See page 116

MEDICAL SCRUBS COLLECTION

http://medicalscrubscollection.com

MEDICAL SCRUBS COLLECTION SCHOLARSHIP
• See page 120

NATIONAL AMBUCS INC.

http://www.ambucs.org/

AMBUCS SCHOLARS-SCHOLARSHIPS FOR THERAPISTS

Scholarships are open to students who are U.S. citizens at a junior level or above in college. Must be enrolled in an accredited program by the appropriate health therapy profession authority in physical therapy, occupational therapy, speech-language pathology, or audiology and must demonstrate a financial need. Application available on website at http://www.ambucs.org. Paper applications are not accepted.

Academic Fields/Career Goals: Audiology; Therapy/Rehabilitation.

Award: Scholarship for use in junior, senior, graduate, or postgraduate years; not renewable. *Number:* 275. *Amount:* $500–$3000.

Eligibility Requirements: Applicant must be enrolled or expecting to enroll full-time at a four-year institution or university. Available to U.S. citizens.

Application Requirements: Application form, enrollment certification form, essay, financial need analysis. *Deadline:* April 15.

Contact: Janice Blankenship, Scholarship Coordinator
National AMBUCS Inc.
PO Box 5127
High Point, NC 27262
Phone: 336-852-0052 Ext. 10
Fax: 336-852-6830
E-mail: janiceb@ambucs.org

NEW YORK STATE GRANGE

http://www.nysgrange.org/

CAROLINE KARK AWARD

Award available to a Grange member who is preparing for a career working with the deaf, or a deaf individual who is furthering his or her education beyond high school. The recipient must be a New York State resident. The award is based on funds available.

Academic Fields/Career Goals: Audiology.

Award: Scholarship for use in freshman year; not renewable. *Number:* 1.

Eligibility Requirements: Applicant must be hearing impaired; high school student; planning to enroll or expecting to enroll full- or part-time at a four-year institution or university and resident of New York. Applicant or parent of applicant must be member of Grange Association. Applicant must be hearing impaired. Available to U.S. citizens.

Application Requirements: Application form. *Deadline:* April 15.

Contact: Program Manager
New York State Grange
100 Grange Place
Cortland, NY 13045
Phone: 607-756-7553
E-mail: nysgrange@nysgrange.com

SCARLETT FAMILY FOUNDATION SCHOLARSHIP PROGRAM

http://www.scarlettfoundation.org/

SCHOLARSHIP FOR STUDENTS PURSUING A BUSINESS OR STEM DEGREE

• See page 91

AVIATION/AEROSPACE

AACE INTERNATIONAL

http://www.aacei.org/

AACE INTERNATIONAL COMPETITIVE SCHOLARSHIP

• See page 130

AHS INTERNATIONAL—THE VERTICAL FLIGHT TECHNICAL SOCIETY

http://www.vtol.org/

VERTICAL FLIGHT FOUNDATION SCHOLARSHIP

This award is available for undergraduate (must be at least a second semester freshman), graduate, or doctoral study in aerospace, electrical, or mechanical engineering. Applicants must demonstrate an interest in vertical flight technology through contribution to the vertical flight technical community such as technical papers presented at technical meetings, submission to technical journals, participating in aerospace engineering design competitions, etc. All students must attend for the entire year following acceptance of the scholarship.

Academic Fields/Career Goals: Aviation/Aerospace; Electrical Engineering/Electronics; Engineering-Related Technologies; Engineering/Technology; Mechanical Engineering.

Award: Scholarship for use in sophomore, junior, senior, graduate, or postgraduate years; not renewable. *Number:* 10–19. *Amount:* $1500–$5000.

Eligibility Requirements: Applicant must be enrolled or expecting to enroll full-time at a four-year institution or university and must have an interest in aviation. Applicant must have 3.5 GPA or higher. Available to U.S. and non-U.S. citizens.

Application Requirements: Application form, essay, recommendations or references, resume, transcript. *Deadline:* February 1.

Contact: Ms. Holly Cafferelli, VFF Scholarship Coordinator
AHS International—The Vertical Flight Technical Society
217 North Washington Street
Alexandria, VA 22314
Phone: 703-684-6777 Ext. 100
Fax: 703-739-9279
E-mail: hcafferelli@vtol.org

AIRCRAFT ELECTRONICS ASSOCIATION EDUCATIONAL FOUNDATION

http://www.aea.net/

CHUCK PEACOCK MEMORIAL SCHOLARSHIP

Scholarship of $1000 for high school seniors or college students who plan to attend or are attending an aviation management program in an accredited school. Minimum 2.5 GPA required.

Academic Fields/Career Goals: Aviation/Aerospace.

Award: Scholarship for use in freshman, sophomore, junior, or senior years; not renewable. *Number:* 1. *Amount:* $1000.

Eligibility Requirements: Applicant must be enrolled or expecting to enroll full- or part-time at a two-year or four-year or technical institution or university. Applicant must have 2.5 GPA or higher. Available to U.S. citizens.

Application Requirements: Application form, essay, transcript. *Deadline:* February 15.

Contact: Mike Adamson, Executive Director
Phone: 816-373-6565
E-mail: info@aea.net

DAVID ARVER MEMORIAL SCHOLARSHIP

Scholarship of $1000 available to high school seniors and college students who plan to or are attending an avionics or aircraft repair program in an accredited school. Restricted to use for study in the following states: Iowa, Illinois, Indiana, Kansas, Michigan, Minnesota, Mississippi, North Dakota, Nebraska, South Dakota, and Wisconsin. Minimum 2.5 GPA required.

Academic Fields/Career Goals: Aviation/Aerospace.

Award: Scholarship for use in freshman, sophomore, junior, or senior years; not renewable. *Number:* 1. *Amount:* $1000.

Eligibility Requirements: Applicant must be enrolled or expecting to enroll full- or part-time at a two-year or four-year or technical institution or university. Applicant must have 2.5 GPA or higher. Available to U.S. and non-U.S. citizens.

Application Requirements: Application form, essay, recommendations or references, test scores, transcript. *Deadline:* February 15.

Contact: Mike Adamson, Executive Director
Phone: 816-373-6565
E-mail: info@aea.net

DUTCH AND GINGER ARVER SCHOLARSHIP

Scholarship available to high school seniors or college students who plan to attend or are attending an avionics or aircraft repair program in an accredited school. Minimum 2.5 GPA required.

Academic Fields/Career Goals: Aviation/Aerospace; Trade/Technical Specialties.

Award: Scholarship for use in freshman, sophomore, junior, or senior years; not renewable. *Number:* 1. *Amount:* $1000.

Eligibility Requirements: Applicant must be enrolled or expecting to enroll full- or part-time at a two-year or four-year or technical institution or university. Applicant must have 2.5 GPA or higher. Available to U.S. citizens.

Application Requirements: Application form, essay, recommendations or references, test scores, transcript. *Deadline:* February 15.

Contact: Mike Adamson, Executive Director
Phone: 816-373-6565
E-mail: info@aea.net

FIELD AVIATION COMPANY INC. SCHOLARSHIP

Scholarship for high school seniors and college students who plan to or are attending an avionics or aircraft repair program in an accredited college/university. The educational institution must be located in Canada.

Academic Fields/Career Goals: Aviation/Aerospace.

Award: Scholarship for use in freshman, sophomore, junior, or senior years; not renewable. *Number:* 1. *Amount:* $1000.

Eligibility Requirements: Applicant must be enrolled or expecting to enroll full-time at a two-year or four-year or technical institution or university. Applicant must have 2.5 GPA or higher. Available to Canadian citizens.

Application Requirements: Application form, essay, recommendations or references, test scores, transcript. *Deadline:* February 15.

Contact: Mike Adamson, Executive Director
Phone: 816-373-6565
E-mail: info@aea.net

GARMIN-JERRY SMITH MEMORIAL SCHOLARSHIP

Scholarship available for high school, college, or vocational or technical school students who plan to attend or are attending an avionics or aircraft repair program in an accredited vocational or technical school. Minimum 2.5 GPA required.

Academic Fields/Career Goals: Aviation/Aerospace; Trade/Technical Specialties.

Award: Scholarship for use in freshman or sophomore years; not renewable. *Number:* 1. *Amount:* $1000.

Eligibility Requirements: Applicant must be enrolled or expecting to enroll full-time at a two-year or technical institution. Applicant must have 2.5 GPA or higher. Available to U.S. and non-U.S. citizens.

Application Requirements: Application form, community service, essay, transcript. *Deadline:* February 15.

Contact: Mike Adamson, Executive Director
Phone: 816-373-6565
E-mail: info@aea.net

GARMIN SCHOLARSHIP

Scholarship available to high school seniors and college students who plan to attend or are attending an avionics or aircraft repair program in an accredited school. Minimum 2.5 GPA required.

Academic Fields/Career Goals: Aviation/Aerospace; Trade/Technical Specialties.

Award: Scholarship for use in freshman, sophomore, junior, or senior years; not renewable. *Number:* 1. *Amount:* $2000.

Eligibility Requirements: Applicant must be enrolled or expecting to enroll full- or part-time at a two-year or four-year or technical institution or university. Applicant must have 2.5 GPA or higher. Available to U.S. citizens.

Application Requirements: Application form, essay, recommendations or references, test scores, transcript. *Deadline:* February 15.

Contact: Mike Adamson, Executive Director
Phone: 816-373-6565
E-mail: info@aea.net

JOHNNY DAVIS MEMORIAL SCHOLARSHIP

Scholarship of $1000 available to high school seniors and college students who plan to or are attending an avionics or aircraft repair program in an accredited school. Minimum 2.5 GPA required.

Academic Fields/Career Goals: Aviation/Aerospace.

Award: Scholarship for use in freshman, sophomore, junior, or senior years; not renewable. *Number:* 1. *Amount:* $1000.

Eligibility Requirements: Applicant must be enrolled or expecting to enroll full- or part-time at a two-year or four-year or technical institution or university. Applicant must have 2.5 GPA or higher. Available to U.S. citizens.

Application Requirements: Application form, essay, transcript. *Deadline:* February 15.

Contact: Mike Adamson, Executive Director
Phone: 816-373-6565
E-mail: info@aea.net

L-3 AVIONICS SYSTEMS SCHOLARSHIP

Scholarship of $2500 available to high school seniors and college students who plan to attend or are attending an avionics or aircraft repair program in an accredited school. Minimum 2.5 GPA required.

Academic Fields/Career Goals: Aviation/Aerospace.

Award: Scholarship for use in freshman, sophomore, junior, or senior years; not renewable. *Number:* 1. *Amount:* $2500.

Eligibility Requirements: Applicant must be enrolled or expecting to enroll full- or part-time at a two-year or four-year or technical institution or university. Applicant must have 2.5 GPA or higher. Available to U.S. citizens.

Application Requirements: Application form, essay, transcript. *Deadline:* February 15.

Contact: Mike Adamson, Executive Director
Phone: 816-373-6565
E-mail: info@aea.net

LEE TARBOX MEMORIAL SCHOLARSHIP

Scholarship available to high school seniors or college students who plan to attend or are attending an avionics or aircraft repair program in an accredited school.

Academic Fields/Career Goals: Aviation/Aerospace; Trade/Technical Specialties.

Award: Scholarship for use in freshman, sophomore, junior, or senior years; not renewable. *Number:* 1. *Amount:* $2500.

Eligibility Requirements: Applicant must be enrolled or expecting to enroll full- or part-time at a two-year or four-year or technical institution or university. Applicant must have 2.5 GPA or higher. Available to U.S. citizens.

Application Requirements: Application form, essay, recommendations or references, test scores, transcript. *Deadline:* February 15.

Contact: Mike Adamson, Executive Director
Phone: 816-373-6565
E-mail: info@aea.net

LOWELL GAYLOR MEMORIAL SCHOLARSHIP

Scholarship for high school seniors and college students who plan to attend or are attending an avionics or aircraft repair program in an accredited school. Minimum 2.5 GPA required.

Academic Fields/Career Goals: Aviation/Aerospace; Trade/Technical Specialties.

Award: Scholarship for use in freshman, sophomore, junior, or senior years; not renewable. *Number:* 1. *Amount:* $1000.

Eligibility Requirements: Applicant must be enrolled or expecting to enroll full- or part-time at a two-year or four-year or technical institution or university. Applicant must have 2.5 GPA or higher. Available to U.S. and non-U.S. citizens.

Application Requirements: Application form, essay, recommendations or references, test scores, transcript. *Deadline:* February 15.

Contact: Mike Adamson, Executive Director
Phone: 816-373-6565
E-mail: info@aea.net

MID-CONTINENT INSTRUMENT SCHOLARSHIP

Scholarship available to high school seniors or college students who plan to attend or are attending an avionics or aircraft repair program in an accredited school. Minimum 2.5 GPA required.

Academic Fields/Career Goals: Aviation/Aerospace; Trade/Technical Specialties.

Award: Scholarship for use in freshman, sophomore, junior, or senior years; not renewable. *Number:* 1. *Amount:* $1000.

Eligibility Requirements: Applicant must be enrolled or expecting to enroll full- or part-time at a two-year or four-year or technical institution or university. Applicant must have 2.5 GPA or higher. Available to U.S. citizens.

Application Requirements: Application form, essay, recommendations or references, test scores, transcript. *Deadline:* February 15.

Contact: Mike Adamson, Executive Director
Phone: 816-373-6565
E-mail: info@aea.net

MONTE R. MITCHELL GLOBAL SCHOLARSHIP

Scholarship of $1000 available to European students pursuing a degree in aviation maintenance technology, avionics, or aircraft repair at an accredited school located in Europe or the United States.

Academic Fields/Career Goals: Aviation/Aerospace.

Award: Scholarship for use in freshman, sophomore, junior, or senior years; not renewable. *Number:* 1. *Amount:* $1000.

Eligibility Requirements: Applicant must be enrolled or expecting to enroll full- or part-time at a two-year or four-year or technical institution or university. Applicant must have 2.5 GPA or higher. Available to citizens of countries other than the U.S. or Canada.

Application Requirements: Application form, essay, recommendations or references, transcript. *Deadline:* February 15.

Contact: Mike Adamson, Executive Director
Phone: 816-373-6565
E-mail: info@aea.net

AIRPORT MINORITY ADVISORY COUNCIL EDUCATIONAL AND SCHOLARSHIP PROGRAM

http://www.amac-org.com/

AMACESP STUDENT SCHOLARSHIPS

Applicant must be seeking a BS or BA with interest and desire to pursue a career in the aviation/airport industry and seeking a degree in Aviation, Business Administration, Accounting, Architecture, Engineering or Finance and admitted by an accredited school or university for the current school term in which you are applying for a scholarship. Demonstration of a cumulative 3.0 GPA and involvement in community activities and extracurricular activities. Applicants must be a U.S. citizen. A commitment to involvement in furthering the mission of the Airport Minority Advisory Council (AMAC) by participating in the AMAC Student Program. AMAC Member Scholarship Awards are offered to Airport Minority Advisory Council (AMAC) members, their spouses, and their children. The AMAC Aviation & Professional Development Committee grant four $2000 scholarships each year to a number of students who are enrolled in an aviation related program and have a grade point average 3.0 or higher.

Academic Fields/Career Goals: Aviation/Aerospace.

Award: Scholarship for use in sophomore, junior, or senior years; not renewable. *Number:* 1–3. *Amount:* $2000.

Eligibility Requirements: Applicant must be enrolled or expecting to enroll full-time at a four-year institution or university. Applicant must have 3.0 GPA or higher. Available to U.S. citizens.

Application Requirements: Application form, autobiography, essay, personal photograph, recommendations or references, transcript. *Deadline:* May 18.

Contact: Miss. Jennifer Ibe, AMACESP Intern
Airport Minority Advisory Council Educational and
Scholarship Program
2345 Crystal Drive, Suite 902
Arlington, VA 22202
Phone: 703-414-2622 Ext. 1
Fax: 703-414-2686
E-mail: gene.roth@amac-org.com

AIR TRAFFIC CONTROL ASSOCIATION INC.

http://www.atca.org/

GABRIEL A. HARTL SCHOLARSHIP

Awarded to students enrolled in an two-year or greater air traffic control program at an institution approved and/or listed by the FAA as supporting the FAA's college training initiative.

Academic Fields/Career Goals: Aviation/Aerospace.

Award: Scholarship for use in freshman, sophomore, junior, or senior years; not renewable. *Number:* 1–4. *Amount:* $2000–$10,000.

Eligibility Requirements: Applicant must be enrolled or expecting to enroll full- or part-time at a two-year or four-year institution or university and studying in Arkansas. Available to U.S. and non-U.S. citizens.

Application Requirements: Application form, community service, essay, financial need analysis, personal photograph. *Deadline:* May 1.

Contact: Tim Wagner, Membership Manager
Air Traffic Control Association Inc.
1101 King Street
Suite 300
Alexandria, VA 22314
Phone: 703-299-2430 Ext. 314
E-mail: info@atca.org

LAWRENCE C. FORTIER MEMORIAL SCHOLARSHIP

Awarded to students enrolled in an aviation related program of study leading to a Bachelor's degree.

Academic Fields/Career Goals: Aviation/Aerospace.

Award: Scholarship for use in freshman, sophomore, junior, or senior years; not renewable. *Number:* 1–5. *Amount:* $2000–$10,000.

Eligibility Requirements: Applicant must be enrolled or expecting to enroll full- or part-time at a two-year or four-year institution or university. Available to U.S. and non-U.S. citizens.

Application Requirements: Application form, community service, essay, financial need analysis, personal photograph. *Deadline:* May 1.

Contact: Tim Wagner, Membership Manager
Air Traffic Control Association Inc.
1101 King Street
Suite 300
Alexandria, VA 22314
Phone: 703-299-2430 Ext. 314
E-mail: info@atca.org

ALASKAN AVIATION SAFETY FOUNDATION

http://www.aasfonline.org

ALASKAN AVIATION SAFETY FOUNDATION MEMORIAL SCHOLARSHIP FUND

Scholarships for undergraduate or graduate study in aviation. Must be a resident of Alaska and a U.S. citizen. Write for deadlines and details.

Academic Fields/Career Goals: Aviation/Aerospace.

Award: Scholarship for use in freshman, sophomore, junior, senior, or graduate years; not renewable. *Number:* 1–3. *Amount:* $500–$750.

Eligibility Requirements: Applicant must be enrolled or expecting to enroll full- or part-time at a two-year or four-year or technical institution or university; resident of Alaska and must have an interest in aviation. Available to U.S. citizens.

Application Requirements: Application form, driver's license, financial need analysis, recommendations or references, test scores, transcript. *Deadline:* May 30.

Contact: Scholarship Committee
Alaskan Aviation Safety Foundation
c/o Aviation Technology Division UAA
2811 Merril Field Drive
Anchorage, AK 99501
Phone: 907-243-7237

AMERICAN ASSOCIATION OF AIRPORT EXECUTIVES-SOUTHWEST CHAPTER

http://www.swaaae.org/

SWAAAE ACADEMIC SCHOLARSHIPS

A scholarship of $1500 for students pursuing an undergraduate or graduate degree in airport management may apply annually for an academic scholarship. Applicant must attend a college in Arizona, California, Nevada, Utah, or Hawaii.

Academic Fields/Career Goals: Aviation/Aerospace.

Award: Scholarship for use in sophomore, junior, senior, or graduate years; not renewable. *Number:* 5. *Amount:* $500–$1500.

Eligibility Requirements: Applicant must be enrolled or expecting to enroll full- or part-time at a four-year institution or university and studying in Arizona, California, Hawaii, Nevada, Utah. Available to U.S. and non-U.S. citizens.

Application Requirements: Application form. *Deadline:* September 29.

Contact: Charles Mangum, Scholarship Committee
American Association of Airport Executives-Southwest
Chapter
8565 North Sand Dune Place
Tucson, AZ 85743
Phone: 520-682-9565
E-mail: cman2122@comcast.net

AMERICAN CHEMICAL SOCIETY, RUBBER DIVISION

http://www.rubber.org/

AMERICAN CHEMICAL SOCIETY, RUBBER DIVISION UNDERGRADUATE SCHOLARSHIP
• *See page 120*

AMERICAN INSTITUTE OF AERONAUTICS AND ASTRONAUTICS

http://www.aiaafoundation.org/

AIAA FOUNDATION UNDERGRADUATE SCHOLARSHIPS
• *See page 121*

LEATRICE GREGORY PENDRAY SCHOLARSHIP
• *See page 121*

AMERICAN SOCIETY OF NAVAL ENGINEERS

http://www.navalengineers.org/

AMERICAN SOCIETY OF NAVAL ENGINEERS SCHOLARSHIP
• *See page 122*

ARMED FORCES COMMUNICATIONS AND ELECTRONICS ASSOCIATION, EDUCATIONAL FOUNDATION

http://www.afcea.org/site/?q=foundation/scholarships

ARMED FORCES COMMUNICATIONS AND ELECTRONICS ASSOCIATION ROTC SCHOLARSHIP PROGRAM

Award for ROTC students in their sophomore or junior years enrolled in four-year accredited colleges or universities in the United States. Eligible C4I-related fields of study or majors that align with the mission statement of AFCEA Educational Foundation. The list of acceptable majors can be found on the website. Must exhibit academic excellence and potential to serve as an officer in the armed forces of the United States. Nominations are submitted by professors of military science, naval science, or aerospace studies.

Academic Fields/Career Goals: Aviation/Aerospace; Computer Science/Data Processing; Electrical Engineering/Electronics; Engineering-Related Technologies; Engineering/Technology; Materials Science, Engineering, and Metallurgy; Mathematics; Physical Sciences.

Award: Scholarship for use in sophomore or junior years; not renewable. *Number:* 20. *Amount:* $2000–$5000.

Eligibility Requirements: Applicant must be enrolled or expecting to enroll full-time at a four-year institution or university. Applicant must have 3.0 GPA or higher. Available to U.S. citizens.

Application Requirements: Application form, community service, financial need analysis. *Deadline:* February 15.

Contact: Mrs. Casmere Kistner, Scholarships, Awards and Grants
Armed Forces Communications and Electronics Association,
Educational Foundation
4400 Fair Lakes Court
Fairfax, VA 22015
Phone: 703-631-6147
E-mail: edfoundation@afcea.org

ASSOCIATION OF FORMER INTELLIGENCE OFFICERS

http://www.afio.com

AFIO UNDERGRADUATE AND GRADUATE SCHOLARSHIPS
• *See page 113*

ASTRONAUT SCHOLARSHIP FOUNDATION

http://www.astronautscholarship.org/

ASTRONAUT SCHOLARSHIP FOUNDATION
• *See page 123*

AVIATION COUNCIL OF PENNSYLVANIA

http://www.acpfly.com/

AVIATION COUNCIL OF PENNSYLVANIA SCHOLARSHIP PROGRAM

Sponsored by the Aviation Council of Pennsylvania, awards for Pennsylvania residents are available in the following categories: Aviation Technology, Aviation Management, and Aviation Pilot.

Academic Fields/Career Goals: Aviation/Aerospace.

Award: Scholarship for use in freshman, sophomore, junior, or senior years; not renewable. *Number:* 3–4. *Amount:* $500–$1000.

Eligibility Requirements: Applicant must be enrolled or expecting to enroll full- or part-time at a two-year or four-year or technical institution or university and studying in Pennsylvania. Available to U.S. citizens.

Application Requirements: Application form, financial need analysis. *Deadline:* July 8.

Contact: Debra Bowman, Executive Director
Aviation Council of Pennsylvania
3915 Union Deposit Road, #935
Harrisburg, PA 17109
Phone: 717-850-0227
Fax: 717-850-0228
E-mail: dbowman@acpfly.com

AVIATION DISTRIBUTORS AND MANUFACTURERS ASSOCIATION INTERNATIONAL

ADMA SCHOLARSHIP

Scholarship to provide assistance to students pursuing careers in the aviation field. Those enrolled in an accredited Aviation program may be eligible.

Academic Fields/Career Goals: Aviation/Aerospace.

Award: Scholarship for use in junior or senior years; not renewable. *Number:* 1. *Amount:* up to $2000.

Eligibility Requirements: Applicant must be enrolled or expecting to enroll full-time at a two-year or four-year institution or university and must have an interest in aviation. Applicant must have 3.0 GPA or higher. Available to U.S. citizens.

Application Requirements: Application form, essay, financial need analysis, recommendations or references, transcript. *Deadline:* March 28.

Contact: Scholarship Committee
    Aviation Distributors and Manufacturers Association
       International
    100 North 20th Street, Fourth Floor
    Philadelphia, PA 19103-1443
    Phone: 215-564-3484
    Fax: 215-963-9785
    E-mail: adma@fernley.com

BHW GROUP

https://thebhwgroup.com/

BHW WOMEN IN STEM SCHOLARSHIP
• *See page 124*

CARDS AGAINST HUMANITY

https://cardsagainsthumanity.com/

SCIENCE AMBASSADOR SCHOLARSHIP
• *See page 124*

CHARLIE WELLS MEMORIAL SCHOLARSHIP FUND

http://www.wellsscholarship.com/

CHARLIE WELLS MEMORIAL AVIATION SCHOLARSHIP

Scholarship(s) of varying amounts will be awarded each year when funds are available. The applicant must be a resident of the United States or one of its territories. Must be a full-time student majoring in an aviation-oriented curriculum.

Academic Fields/Career Goals: Aviation/Aerospace.

Award: Scholarship for use in freshman, sophomore, junior, senior, or graduate years; not renewable.

Eligibility Requirements: Applicant must be enrolled or expecting to enroll full-time at a four-year institution or university. Available to U.S. citizens.

Application Requirements: Application form, recommendations or references, transcript. *Deadline:* April 30.

Contact: Roger Thompson, Manager
    Phone: 217-899-3263
    E-mail: rog@wellsscholarship.com

CHICAGO AREA BUSINESS AVIATION ASSOCIATION

http://www.cabaa.com

CABAA/FLIGHTSAFETY CITATION EXCEL PROFESSIONAL PILOT TRAINING AWARD

The CABAA Education Foundation, along with FlightSafety, will award a 2018 applicant with advanced training to enhance the individual's progress toward a career in Business Aviation. The award will only be available for students who will have graduated with a pilot degree Spring 2018, or graduated Spring/Summer/Winter 2017. This year, the award will be a Citation Excel/XLS Series Course. With completion of this course the pilot will obtain skills to operate a Citation Excel/XLS as an SIC. The retail value of this award is approximately $22,200. CABAA and FlightSafety have teamed up to offer this award to promote professional development for a career in Business Aviation. The winner will be notified by phone and presented the award at the annual CABAA Golf Classic held on August 6th, 2018. The recipient's presence is required at the time of award presentation. For more information about

the course please visit resources.flightsafety.com. For information about CABAA membership, please visit http://www.cabaa.com.

Academic Fields/Career Goals: Aviation/Aerospace.

Award: Scholarship for use in senior year; not renewable. *Number:* 1. *Amount:* $22,000.

Eligibility Requirements: Applicant must be enrolled or expecting to enroll full- or part-time at a two-year or four-year or technical institution or university and resident of Illinois, Indiana, Iowa, Michigan, Missouri, Wisconsin. Applicant must have 3.0 GPA or higher. Available to U.S. citizens.

Application Requirements: Application form, essay, interview. *Deadline:* May 1.

Contact: Brian Zankowski
    Lake Villa, IL 60046
    Phone: 224-931-8064
    E-mail: scholarships@cabaa.com

CABAA MAINTENANCE COMMITTEE FINANCIAL AWARD

One scholarship will be awarded in the amount of $7500 to a student seeking a degree in Aviation Maintenance. This scholarship is open to both high school seniors graduating in 2018 and college level students. Scholarship funds will be paid to the student and college or university of which the recipient is enrolled. The scholarship funds are to be used to pay tuition or fees for aviation specific programs. CABAA and the CABAA Maintenance Committee offer this award to promote professional development for a career in business aviation maintenance. The winner will be notified by phone and presented the award at the annual CABAA Golf Classic held in August. The recipient's presence is required at the time of the award presentation. For more information about CABAA, Including membership, please visit http://www.cabaa.com.

Academic Fields/Career Goals: Aviation/Aerospace.

Award: Scholarship for use in freshman, sophomore, junior, or senior years; not renewable. *Number:* 1. *Amount:* $7500.

Eligibility Requirements: Applicant must be enrolled or expecting to enroll full- or part-time at a two-year or four-year or technical institution or university and resident of Illinois, Indiana, Iowa, Michigan, Missouri, Wisconsin. Applicant must have 2.5 GPA or higher. Available to U.S. citizens.

Application Requirements: Application form, essay. *Deadline:* May 1.

Contact: Brian Zankowski
    Lake Villa, IL 60046
    Phone: 224-931-8064
    E-mail: scholarships@cabaa.com

CABAA SCHOLARSHIP

Up to four (4) scholarships will be awarded in the amount of $7500 per recipient. These scholarships are open to both high school seniors graduating in 2018 and college level students. Scholarship funds will be paid to the student and college or university of which the recipient is enrolled and are to be used to pay tuition or fees for aviation specific programs. CABAA offers this award to promote professional development for a career in business aviation. The winner will be notified by phone and presented the award at the annual CABAA Golf Classic held in August each year. The recipient's presence is required at the time of award presentation. For more information about CABAA, including membership visit http://www.cabaa.com.

Academic Fields/Career Goals: Aviation/Aerospace.

Award: Scholarship for use in freshman, sophomore, junior, or senior years; not renewable. *Number:* 4. *Amount:* $7500.

Eligibility Requirements: Applicant must be enrolled or expecting to enroll full- or part-time at a two-year or four-year or technical institution or university and resident of Illinois, Indiana, Iowa, Michigan, Missouri, Wisconsin. Applicant must have 3.0 GPA or higher. Available to U.S. citizens.

Application Requirements: Application form, essay. *Deadline:* May 1.

Contact: Brian Zankowski
    Lake Villa, IL 60046
    Phone: 224-931-8064
    E-mail: scholarships@cabaa.com

KEN JOHNSON MEMORIAL SCHOLARSHIP

One scholarship will be awarded in the amount of $7500 to a 2018 graduating high school student seeking a degree in aviation. Scholarship funds will be paid to the student and college or university of which the recipient is enrolled and are to be used to pay tuition or fees for aviation specific programs. CABAA offers this award to promote professional development for a career in business aviation. The winner will be notified by phone and presented the award at the annual CABAA Golf Classic held on August 7th, 2018. Recipient presence is required at the time of award presentation. For more information about CABAA, including membership visit http://www.CABAA.com.

Academic Fields/Career Goals: Aviation/Aerospace.

Award: Scholarship for use in freshman year; not renewable. *Number:* 1. *Amount:* $7500.

Eligibility Requirements: Applicant must be high school student; planning to enroll or expecting to enroll full- or part-time at a two-year or four-year or technical institution or university and resident of Illinois, Indiana, Iowa, Michigan, Missouri, Wisconsin. Applicant must have 3.0 GPA or higher. Available to U.S. citizens.

Application Requirements: Application form, essay. *Deadline:* May 1.

Contact: Brian Zankowski
Lake Villa, IL 60046
Phone: 224-931-8064
E-mail: scholarships@cabaa.com

CIVIL AIR PATROL, USAF AUXILIARY

http://www.gocivilairpatrol.com/

MAJOR GENERAL LUCAS V. BEAU FLIGHT SCHOLARSHIPS SPONSORED BY THE ORDER OF DAEDALIANS

One-time scholarships for active cadets of the Civil Air Patrol who desire a career in military aviation. Award is to be used toward flight training for a private pilot license. Must be 15 1/2 to 18 1/2 years of age on April 1st of the year for which applying. Must be an active CAP cadet officer. Not open to the general public.

Academic Fields/Career Goals: Aviation/Aerospace.

Award: Scholarship for use in freshman year; not renewable. *Number:* 5. *Amount:* $2100.

Eligibility Requirements: Applicant must be high school student; planning to enroll or expecting to enroll full- or part-time at a four-year institution or university; single and must have an interest in aviation. Applicant or parent of applicant must be member of Civil Air Patrol. Available to U.S. citizens.

Application Requirements: Application form, essay, interview, personal photograph, recommendations or references, test scores, transcript. *Deadline:* March 1.

Contact: Kelly Easterly, Assistant Program Manager
Civil Air Patrol, USAF Auxiliary
105 South Hansell Street, Building 714
Maxwell Air Force Base, AL 36112-6332
Phone: 334-953-8640
Fax: 334-953-6699
E-mail: cpr@capnhq.gov

DAEDALIAN FOUNDATION

http://www.daedalians.org/

DAEDALIAN FOUNDATION MATCHING SCHOLARSHIP PROGRAM

Scholarship program, wherein the foundation matches amounts given by flights, or chapters of the Order of Daedalians, to deserving college and university students who are pursuing a career as a military aviator.

Academic Fields/Career Goals: Aviation/Aerospace.

Award: Scholarship for use in freshman, sophomore, junior, senior, or graduate years; not renewable. *Number:* 75–80. *Amount:* up to $2500.

Eligibility Requirements: Applicant must be enrolled or expecting to enroll full-time at a four-year institution or university. Available to U.S. citizens.

Application Requirements: Application form, flight/ROTC/CAP recommendation, personal photograph, test scores. *Deadline:* December 31.

Contact: Kristi Cavenaugh, Program Executive Secretary
Daedalian Foundation
55 Main Circle, Building 676
Randolph AFB, TX 78148
Phone: 210-945-2111
Fax: 210-945-2112
E-mail: kristi@daedalians.org

DIVERSITYCOMM, INC.

http://www.diversitycomm.net/

DIVERSITY IN STEAM MAGAZINE SCHOLARSHIP

• *See page 83*

EAA AVIATION FOUNDATION, INC.

http://www.eaa.org/

HANSEN SCHOLARSHIP

Renewable scholarship of $1000 for a student enrolled in an accredited institution and pursuing a degree in aerospace engineering or aeronautical engineering. Student must be in good standing; financial need not a requirement. Must be an EAA member. Applications may be downloaded from the website http://www.youngeagles.org.

Academic Fields/Career Goals: Aviation/Aerospace.

Award: Scholarship for use in freshman, sophomore, junior, or senior years; not renewable. *Number:* up to 1. *Amount:* up to $1000.

Eligibility Requirements: Applicant must be enrolled or expecting to enroll full-time at a two-year or four-year or technical institution or university. Applicant or parent of applicant must be member of Experimental Aircraft Association. Available to U.S. and non-U.S. citizens.

Application Requirements: Application form. *Deadline:* February 28.

Contact: Jane Smith, Scholarship Coordinator
EAA Aviation Foundation, Inc.
PO Box 3086
Oshkosh, WI 54903-3086
Phone: 920-426-6823
Fax: 920-426-4873
E-mail: jsmith@eaa.org

PAYZER SCHOLARSHIP

Scholarship for a student accepted or enrolled in an accredited college, university, or postsecondary school with an emphasis on technical information. Awarded to an individual who is seeking a major and declares an intention to pursue a professional career in engineering, mathematics, or the physical/biological sciences. Visit http://www.youngeagles.org for criteria and to download official application. Must be an EAA member or recommended by an EAA member.

Academic Fields/Career Goals: Aviation/Aerospace; Biology; Engineering/Technology; Physical Sciences.

Award: Scholarship for use in freshman, sophomore, junior, or senior years; not renewable. *Number:* up to 1. *Amount:* up to $5000.

Eligibility Requirements: Applicant must be enrolled or expecting to enroll full-time at a two-year or four-year or technical institution or university. Applicant or parent of applicant must be member of Experimental Aircraft Association. Available to U.S. and non-U.S. citizens.

Application Requirements: Application form. *Deadline:* February 28.

Contact: Jane Smith, Scholarship Coordinator
EAA Aviation Foundation, Inc.
PO Box 3086
Oshkosh, WI 54903-3086
Phone: 920-426-6823
Fax: 920-426-4873
E-mail: jsmith@eaa.org

FABRICATORS AND MANUFACTURERS ASSOCIATION FOUNDATION

http://www.nutsandboltsfoundation.org/scholarships/

COLLEGE AND TRADE/TECHNICAL SCHOOL SCHOLARSHIPS

Nuts, Bolts & Thingamajigs®, The Foundation of the Fabricators & Manufacturers Association, Intl. (NBT) Through its manufacturing summer camps and scholarships, NBT is inspiring the next generation of manufacturers, inventors and entrepreneurs.

Academic Fields/Career Goals: Aviation/Aerospace; Electrical Engineering/Electronics; Engineering-Related Technologies; Engineering/Technology; Industrial Design; Materials Science, Engineering, and Metallurgy; Mechanical Engineering; Trade/Technical Specialties.

Award: Scholarship for use in freshman, sophomore, junior, senior, or graduate years; not renewable. *Amount:* $2500.

Eligibility Requirements: Applicant must be enrolled or expecting to enroll full-time at a two-year or four-year or technical institution or university. Applicant must have 2.5 GPA or higher. Available to U.S. and non-U.S. citizens.

Application Requirements: Application form, essay. *Deadline:* March 31.

Contact: Daunel Czarnecki, FMA & NBT Assistant
Fabricators and Manufacturers Association Foundation
2135 Point Boulevard
Elgin, IL 60123
Phone: 815-227-8222
Fax: 815-844-1270
E-mail: Foundation@fmanet.org

FOUNDATION FOR SCIENCE AND DISABILITY

http://stemd.org/

GRANTS FOR DISABLED GRADUATE STUDENTS IN THE SCIENCES
• *See page 106*

GENERAL AVIATION MANUFACTURERS ASSOCIATION

http://www.gama.aero/

EDWARD W. STIMPSON "AVIATION EXCELLENCE" AWARD

One-time scholarship award for students who are graduating from high school and have been accepted to attend aviation college or university in the upcoming year. See website at http://www.gama.aero for more details.

Academic Fields/Career Goals: Aviation/Aerospace.

Award: Scholarship for use in freshman year; not renewable. *Number:* 1. *Amount:* $500.

Eligibility Requirements: Applicant must be high school student; planning to enroll or expecting to enroll full-time at a four-year institution or university and must have an interest in aviation. Applicant must have 3.0 GPA or higher. Available to U.S. citizens.

Application Requirements: Application form, essay, recommendations or references, transcript. *Deadline:* April 28.

Contact: Katie Pribyl, Director, Communications
Phone: 202-393-1500
Fax: 202-842-4063
E-mail: kpribyl@gama.aero

HAROLD S. WOOD AWARD FOR EXCELLENCE

One-time scholarship award for an university student who is attending a National Intercollegiate Flying Association (NIFA) school. Must have completed at least one semester of coursework. See website at http://www.gama.aero for additional details.

Academic Fields/Career Goals: Aviation/Aerospace.

Award: Scholarship for use in freshman, sophomore, junior, or senior years; not renewable. *Number:* 1. *Amount:* $1000.

Eligibility Requirements: Applicant must be enrolled or expecting to enroll full-time at a four-year institution or university. Applicant must have 3.0 GPA or higher. Available to U.S. citizens.

Application Requirements: Application form, nomination, recommendations or references, transcript. *Deadline:* February 24.

Contact: Katie Pribyl, Director, Communications
Phone: 202-393-1500
Fax: 202-842-4063
E-mail: kpribyl@gama.aero

GRAND RAPIDS COMMUNITY FOUNDATION

http://www.grfoundation.org/

JOSHUA ESCH MITCHELL AVIATION SCHOLARSHIP

For students pursuing studies in the field of professional pilot with an emphasis on general aviation, flight engineer, or airway science. Applicant must be a U.S. citizens enrolled in a full- or part-time program at a college or university in the United States providing an accredited flight science curriculum. Applicant should have a minimum GPA of 2.75. A valid pilot's certificate (not to include a Student Certificate) is required. A letter of recommendation from a professional in the aviation field is required.

Academic Fields/Career Goals: Aviation/Aerospace.

Award: Scholarship for use in sophomore, junior, or senior years; not renewable. *Number:* 1–4. *Amount:* $1000.

Eligibility Requirements: Applicant must be enrolled or expecting to enroll full-time at a four-year institution and must have an interest in aviation. Applicant or parent of applicant must have employment or volunteer experience in transportation industry. Applicant must have 2.5 GPA or higher. Available to U.S. citizens.

Application Requirements: Application form, financial need analysis. *Deadline:* April 1.

Contact: Ms. Ruth Bishop, Education Program Officer
Grand Rapids Community Foundation
185 Oakes SW
Grand Rapids, MI 49503
Phone: 616-454-1751 Ext. 103
E-mail: rbishop@grfoundation.org

GREAT MINDS IN STEM

http://www.greatmindsinstem.org

HENAAC SCHOLARSHIP PROGRAM
• *See page 115*

ILLINOIS PILOTS ASSOCIATION

http://www.illinoispilots.com/

ILLINOIS PILOTS ASSOCIATION MEMORIAL SCHOLARSHIP

Recipient must be a resident of Illinois established in an Illinois postsecondary institution in a full-time aviation-related program. Applicants will be judged by the scholarship committee, and the award (usually $2000 annually) will be sent directly to the recipient's school. For further details visit website http://www.illinoispilots.com.

Academic Fields/Career Goals: Aviation/Aerospace.

Award: Scholarship for use in sophomore, junior, or senior years; not renewable. *Number:* 1. *Amount:* $500–$2000.

Eligibility Requirements: Applicant must be enrolled or expecting to enroll full-time at a two-year or four-year or technical institution or university; resident of Illinois; studying in Illinois and must have an interest in aviation. Available to U.S. citizens.

Application Requirements: Application form, essay, personal photograph, recommendations or references, transcript. *Deadline:* March 1.

Contact: Ruth Frantz, Scholarship Committee Chairman
Illinois Pilots Association
40W297 Apache Lane
Huntley, IL 60142
Phone: 847-669-3821
E-mail: landings8e@aol.com

INTERNATIONAL SOCIETY OF WOMEN AIRLINE PILOTS (ISA+21)

http://www.iswap.org/

INTERNATIONAL SOCIETY OF WOMEN AIRLINE PILOTS AIRLINE SCHOLARSHIPS

Scholarships are available to women who are pursuing careers as airline pilots. Applicants must demonstrate financial need. Must have an U.S. FAA Commercial Pilot Certificate with an Instrument Rating and First Class Medical Certificate. Must have flight time in a fixed wing aircraft commensurate with the rating sought.

Academic Fields/Career Goals: Aviation/Aerospace.

Award: Scholarship for use in freshman, sophomore, junior, or senior years; not renewable. *Number:* up to 5.

Eligibility Requirements: Applicant must be enrolled or expecting to enroll full-time at a four-year institution or university and female. Available to U.S. and non-U.S. citizens.

Application Requirements: Application form, driver's license, financial need analysis, income tax forms, logbook pages, pilot licenses, medical certificates, interview, personal photograph, recommendations or references, resume, transcript. *Deadline:* December 10.

Contact: Ms. Julie Clippard, Scholarship Chairwoman
E-mail: scholarshipsponsor@iswap.org

INTERNATIONAL SOCIETY OF WOMEN AIRLINE PILOTS FINANCIAL SCHOLARSHIP

Scholarships are available to women who are pursuing careers as airline pilots. Must have flight time in a fixed wing aircraft commensurate with the rating sought. Must have flight time in a fixed wing aircraft commensurate with the rating sought.

Academic Fields/Career Goals: Aviation/Aerospace.

Award: Scholarship for use in freshman, sophomore, junior, or senior years; not renewable. *Number:* 1.

Eligibility Requirements: Applicant must be enrolled or expecting to enroll full-time at a four-year institution or university and female. Available to U.S. and non-U.S. citizens.

Application Requirements: Application form, copies of income tax forms, logbook pages, pilot licenses, medical certificates, driver's license, financial need analysis, interview, personal photograph, recommendations or references, resume, transcript. *Deadline:* December 10.

Contact: Ms. Julie Clippard, Scholarship Chairwoman
E-mail: scholarshipsponsor@iswap.org

INTERNATIONAL SOCIETY OF WOMEN AIRLINE PILOTS FIORENZA DE BERNARDI MERIT SCHOLARSHIP

Financial award will aid those pilots endeavoring to fill some of the basic squares, i.e. a CFI, CFII, MEI or any international equivalents. Must have flight time in a fixed wing aircraft commensurate with the rating sought. Must have flight time in a fixed wing aircraft commensurate with the rating sought.

Academic Fields/Career Goals: Aviation/Aerospace.

Award: Scholarship for use in freshman, sophomore, junior, or senior years; not renewable. *Number:* 1.

Eligibility Requirements: Applicant must be enrolled or expecting to enroll full- or part-time at a four-year institution or university and female. Available to U.S. and non-U.S. citizens.

Application Requirements: Application form, copies of income tax forms, logbook pages, pilot licenses, medical certificates, driver's license, financial need analysis, interview, personal photograph, recommendations or references, resume, transcript. *Deadline:* December 10.

Contact: Ms. Julie Clippard, Scholarship Chairwoman
E-mail: scholarshipsponsor@iswap.org

INTERNATIONAL SOCIETY OF WOMEN AIRLINE PILOTS GRACE MCADAMS HARRIS SCHOLARSHIP

Scholarship may fund any ISA scholarship if the applicant has demonstrated an exceptionally spirited and ingenious attitude under difficult circumstances in the field of aviation. Applicants must have an U.S. FAA Commercial Pilot Certificate with an Instrument Rating and First Class Medical Certificate. Visit website http://www.iswap.org for more details.

Academic Fields/Career Goals: Aviation/Aerospace.

Award: Scholarship for use in freshman, sophomore, junior, or senior years; not renewable. *Number:* 1.

Eligibility Requirements: Applicant must be enrolled or expecting to enroll full-time at a four-year institution or university; female and must have an interest in aviation. Available to U.S. and non-U.S. citizens.

Application Requirements: Application form, copies of income tax forms, logbook pages, pilot licenses, medical certificates, driver's license, financial need analysis, interview, personal photograph, recommendations or references, transcript. *Deadline:* December 10.

Contact: Ms. Julie Clippard, Scholarship Chairwoman
E-mail: scholarshipsponsor@iswap.org

INTERNATIONAL SOCIETY OF WOMEN AIRLINE PILOTS HOLLY MULLENS MEMORIAL SCHOLARSHIP

Financial award is reserved for that applicant who is a single mother. Applicants must have an U.S. FAA Commercial Pilot Certificate with an Instrument Rating and First Class Medical Certificate. Visit website, http://www.iswap.org, for more details.

Academic Fields/Career Goals: Aviation/Aerospace.

Award: Scholarship for use in freshman, sophomore, junior, or senior years; not renewable. *Number:* 1.

Eligibility Requirements: Applicant must be enrolled or expecting to enroll full-time at a four-year institution or university and single female. Available to U.S. and non-U.S. citizens.

Application Requirements: Application form, copies of income tax forms, logbook pages, pilot licenses, medical certificates, driver's license, financial need analysis, interview, recommendations or references, transcript. *Deadline:* December 10.

Contact: Ms. Julie Clippard, Scholarship Chairwoman
E-mail: scholarshipsponsor@iswap.org

INTERNATIONAL SOCIETY OF WOMEN AIRLINE PILOTS NORTH CAROLINA FINANCIAL SCHOLARSHIP

Scholarships for a woman pilot from North Carolina interested in a career in the airline world. Must have flight time in a fixed wing aircraft commensurate with the rating sought. Must have flight time in a fixed wing aircraft commensurate with the rating sought.

Academic Fields/Career Goals: Aviation/Aerospace.

Award: Scholarship for use in freshman, sophomore, junior, or senior years; not renewable. *Number:* 1.

Eligibility Requirements: Applicant must be enrolled or expecting to enroll full-time at a four-year institution or university; female and resident of North Carolina. Available to U.S. and non-U.S. citizens.

Application Requirements: Application form, copies of income tax forms, logbook pages, pilot licenses, medical certificates, driver's license, financial need analysis, interview, personal photograph, recommendations or references, resume, transcript. *Deadline:* December 10.

Contact: Ms. Julie Clippard, Scholarship Chairwoman
E-mail: scholarshipsponsor@iswap.org

LABROOTS INC.

http://www.LabRoots.com

LABROOTS STEM SCHOLARSHIP

• *See page 116*

MANUFACTURERS ASSOCIATION OF MAINE

http://www.mainemfg.com/

MAINE MANUFACTURING CAREER AND TRAINING FOUNDATION SCHOLARSHIP

Maine Manufacturing Career and Training Foundation offers scholarship awards to individuals seeking education in the manufacturing field of study. Any Maine student or worker can apply for tuition assistance at any Maine institute of higher learning. All applicants must be full-time students and maintain a minimum of a C average.

Academic Fields/Career Goals: Aviation/Aerospace; Engineering-Related Technologies; Engineering/Technology; Industrial Design; Marine/Ocean Engineering; Materials Science, Engineering, and Metallurgy; Mechanical Engineering; Trade/Technical Specialties.

Award: Scholarship for use in freshman, sophomore, junior, senior, graduate, or postgraduate years; not renewable. *Number:* 5–25. *Amount:* $250–$1000.

Eligibility Requirements: Applicant must be enrolled or expecting to enroll full- or part-time at a two-year or four-year or technical institution or university; resident of Maine and studying in Maine. Available to U.S. citizens.

Application Requirements: Application form, essay. *Deadline:* April 30.

Contact: Marion Sprague, Outreach Communications Director
Manufacturers Association of Maine
101 Mcalister Farm Raod
Portland, ME 04103
Phone: 207-747-4406
E-mail: marion@mainemfg.com

NASA FLORIDA SPACE GRANT CONSORTIUM

http://www.floridaspacegrant.org/

FLORIDA SPACE RESEARCH PROGRAM

Grants for faculty researchers from Florida public and private universities and community colleges. One-time award for aerospace and technology research. Submit research proposal with budget.

Academic Fields/Career Goals: Aviation/Aerospace; Earth Science; Education; Electrical Engineering/Electronics; Engineering/Technology; Marine/Ocean Engineering; Materials Science, Engineering, and Metallurgy; Mathematics; Mechanical Engineering; Meteorology/Atmospheric Science; Physical Sciences.

Award: Grant for use in junior, senior, graduate, or postgraduate years; not renewable. *Number:* 13–15. *Amount:* $12,500–$25,000.

Eligibility Requirements: Applicant must be enrolled or expecting to enroll full- or part-time at a two-year or four-year institution or university; resident of Florida and studying in Florida. Available to U.S. citizens.

Application Requirements: Application form. *Deadline:* May 17.

Contact: Dr. Jaydeep Mukherjee, FSGC Director
NASA Florida Space Grant Consortium
PO Box 160650, 12354 Research Parkway, Room 218
Orlando, FL 32826
Phone: 407-823-6177
E-mail: fsgc@ucf.edu

NASA/MARYLAND SPACE GRANT CONSORTIUM

http://www.mdspacegrant.org/

NASA MARYLAND SPACE GRANT CONSORTIUM UNDERGRADUATE SCHOLARSHIPS

Scholarship for full-time student majoring in the biological and life sciences, chemistry, geological sciences, physics, astronomy, engineering, computer science, or other related fields. Must be a U.S. citizen and a Maryland resident. Enrollment in an affiliate institution of the Maryland Space Grant Consortium is necessary. Award amounts vary.

Academic Fields/Career Goals: Aviation/Aerospace; Biology; Chemical Engineering; Computer Science/Data Processing; Earth Science; Engineering/Technology; Environmental Science; Materials Science, Engineering, and Metallurgy; Mathematics; Physical Sciences.

Award: Scholarship for use in freshman, sophomore, junior, or senior years; not renewable.

Eligibility Requirements: Applicant must be enrolled or expecting to enroll full-time at a four-year institution or university; resident of Maryland and studying in Maryland. Applicant must have 3.0 GPA or higher. Available to U.S. citizens.

Application Requirements: Application form, essay. *Deadline:* May 15.

Contact: Richard Henry, Director
Phone: 410-516-7350
Fax: 410-516-4109
E-mail: henry@jhu.edu

NASA MINNESOTA SPACE GRANT CONSORTIUM

https://www.mnspacegrant.org/

MINNESOTA SPACE GRANT CONSORTIUM SCHOLARSHIP PROGRAM

Scholarships for full-time undergraduates attending institutions belonging to the Minnesota Space Grant Consortium—institution list on the website. Preference given to students studying aerospace engineering, space science, and NASA-related math, science, or engineering fields. Minimum 3.0 GPA required. Must be U.S. citizen. For more details go tohttps://www.mnspacegrant.org/ then explore Opportunities menu.

Academic Fields/Career Goals: Aviation/Aerospace; Computer Science/Data Processing; Earth Science; Electrical Engineering/Electronics; Engineering/Technology; Environmental Science; Mathematics; Mechanical Engineering; Meteorology/Atmospheric Science; Natural Sciences; Nuclear Science; Oceanography; Physical Sciences.

Award: Scholarship for use in freshman, sophomore, junior, or senior years; not renewable. *Number:* 40–70. *Amount:* $500–$2500.

Eligibility Requirements: Applicant must be enrolled or expecting to enroll full-time at a two-year or four-year institution or university and studying in Minnesota. Applicant must have 3.0 GPA or higher. Available to U.S. citizens.

Application Requirements: Application form. *Deadline:* continuous.

Contact: Minnesota Space Grant, Department of Aerospace Engineering
NASA Minnesota Space Grant Consortium
107 Akerman Hall, 110 Union Street, SE
Minneapolis, MN 55455
Phone: 612-626-9295
E-mail: mnsgc@umn.edu

NASA MONTANA SPACE GRANT CONSORTIUM

http://www.spacegrant.montana.edu/

MONTANA SPACE GRANT SCHOLARSHIP PROGRAM

Awards are made on a competitive basis to students enrolled in fields of study relevant to the aerospace sciences and engineering. Must be U.S. citizen enrolled as full-time student at a Montana Consortium campus.

Academic Fields/Career Goals: Aviation/Aerospace; Biology; Chemical Engineering; Civil Engineering; Computer Science/Data Processing; Electrical Engineering/Electronics; Engineering/Technology; Mathematics; Mechanical Engineering.

Award: Scholarship for use in freshman, sophomore, junior, or senior years; not renewable. *Number:* 15–20. *Amount:* $1000–$2000.

Eligibility Requirements: Applicant must be enrolled or expecting to enroll full-time at a two-year or four-year institution or university and studying in Montana. Available to U.S. citizens.

Application Requirements: Application form, application form may be submitted online (http://spacegrant.montana.edu), essay, recommendations or references, transcript. *Deadline:* April 1.

Contact: Chris Harmon, Program Coordinator
Phone: 406-994-4223
Fax: 406-994-4452

NASA RHODE ISLAND SPACE GRANT CONSORTIUM

http://brown/initiatives/ri-space-grant

NASA RHODE ISLAND SPACE GRANT CONSORTIUM UNDERGRADUATE RESEARCH SCHOLARSHIP

Scholarship for undergraduate students for study and/or outreach related to NASA and space sciences, engineering and/or technology. Must attend a Rhode Island Space Grant Consortium participating school. Recipients are expected to devote a maximum of 4 hours per week in science education for K-12 children and teachers. See website for additional information http://www.spacegrant.brown.edu.

Academic Fields/Career Goals: Aviation/Aerospace; Engineering/Technology; Meteorology/Atmospheric Science.

Award: Scholarship for use in sophomore, junior, or senior years; not renewable. *Number:* up to 2. *Amount:* up to $4000.

Eligibility Requirements: Applicant must be enrolled or expecting to enroll full-time at a four-year institution or university and studying in Rhode Island. Applicant must have 3.0 GPA or higher. Available to U.S. citizens.

Application Requirements: Application form, essay, recommendations or references, resume, transcript. *Deadline:* varies.

Contact: Nancy Ciminelli, Program Manager
NASA Rhode Island Space Grant Consortium
Brown University
Box 1846, Lincoln Field
Providence, RI 02912
Phone: 401-863-1151
Fax: 401-863-3978
E-mail: nancy_ciminelli@brown.edu

NASA RISGC SCIENCE EN ESPANOL SCHOLARSHIP FOR UNDERGRADUATE STUDENTS

Award for undergraduate students attending a Rhode Island Space Grant Consortium participating school and studying in any space-related field of science, math, engineering, or other field with applications in space study. Recipients are expected to devote a maximum of 8 hours per week in outreach activities, supporting ESL teachers with science instruction.

Academic Fields/Career Goals: Aviation/Aerospace; Engineering/Technology; Mathematics.

Award: Scholarship for use in sophomore, junior, or senior years; not renewable. *Number:* 2. *Amount:* up to $4000.

Eligibility Requirements: Applicant must be enrolled or expecting to enroll full-time at a four-year institution or university and studying in Rhode Island. Applicant must have 3.0 GPA or higher. Available to U.S. citizens.

Application Requirements: Application form, essay, resume, transcript. *Deadline:* varies.

Contact: Nancy Ciminelli, Program Manager
NASA Rhode Island Space Grant Consortium
Brown University
Box 1846, Lincoln Field
Providence, RI 02912
Phone: 401-863-1151
Fax: 401-863-3978
E-mail: nancy_ciminelli@brown.edu

NASA RISGC SUMMER SCHOLARSHIP FOR UNDERGRADUATE STUDENTS

Scholarship for full-time summer study. Students are expected to devote 75 percent of their time to a research project with a faculty adviser and 25 percent to outreach activities in science education for K-12 students and teachers. Must attend a Rhode Island Space Grant Consortium participating school. See website for additional information http://www.spacegrant.brown.edu.

Academic Fields/Career Goals: Aviation/Aerospace; Education.

Award: Scholarship for use in sophomore, junior, or senior years; not renewable. *Number:* up to 2. *Amount:* up to $4000.

Eligibility Requirements: Applicant must be enrolled or expecting to enroll full-time at a four-year institution or university and studying in Rhode Island. Applicant must have 3.0 GPA or higher. Available to U.S. citizens.

Application Requirements: Application form, letter of interest, recommendations or references, resume. *Deadline:* varies.

Contact: Nancy Ciminelli, Program Manager
NASA Rhode Island Space Grant Consortium
Brown University
Box 1846, Lincoln Field
Providence, RI 02912
Phone: 401-863-1151
Fax: 401-863-3978
E-mail: nancy_ciminelli@brown.edu

NASA'S VIRGINIA SPACE GRANT CONSORTIUM

http://www.vsgc.odu.edu/

UNDERGRADUATE STEM RESEARCH SCHOLARSHIPS
• *See page 127*

NASA WISCONSIN SPACE GRANT CONSORTIUM

https://spacegrant.carthage.edu/

WISCONSIN SPACE GRANT CONSORTIUM UNDERGRADUATE SCHOLARSHIP PROGRAM

Scholarship of up to $2000 for a U.S. citizen enrolled full-time in, admitted to, or applying to any undergraduate program at a Wisconsin Space Grant Consortium college or university. Awards will be given to students with outstanding potential in programs of aerospace, space science, or other interdisciplinary space-related studies. Minimum 3.0 GPA required. Refer to website for more information https://spacegrant.carthage.edu/funding-programs/undergraduate/scholarship/.

Academic Fields/Career Goals: Aviation/Aerospace.

Award: Scholarship for use in freshman, sophomore, junior, or senior years; not renewable. *Number:* 15. *Amount:* $2000.

Eligibility Requirements: Applicant must be enrolled or expecting to enroll full-time at a two-year or four-year institution or university; resident of Wisconsin and studying in Wisconsin. Applicant must have 3.0 GPA or higher. Available to U.S. citizens.

Application Requirements: Application form, essay. *Deadline:* February 5.

Contact: Christine Bolz, Assistant Director
NASA Wisconsin Space Grant Consortium
2001 Alford Park Drive
Kenosha, WI 53140
Phone: 262-551-2120
E-mail: cthompson2@carthage.edu

NATIONAL AIR TRANSPORTATION FOUNDATION

http://www.nata.aero

DAN L. MEISINGER, SR. MEMORIAL LEARN TO FLY SCHOLARSHIP

Scholarship established in the honor and memory of Dan L. Meisinger Sr., whose career in aviation spanned 63 years. He was founder of Executive Beechcraft, headquartered in Kansas City, Mo., and was twice named Beech Aircraft's Man of the Year. Purpose of fund is to provide an annual flight training scholarship to a qualified individual. For more information, visit website http://www.nata.aero/Scholarships/Dan-L.-Meisinger,-Sr.-Memorial-Scholarship.aspx.

Academic Fields/Career Goals: Aviation/Aerospace.

Award: Scholarship for use in freshman, sophomore, junior, or senior years; not renewable. *Number:* 1. *Amount:* $2500.

Eligibility Requirements: Applicant must be enrolled or expecting to enroll full-time at a two-year or four-year institution or university. Applicant must have 3.0 GPA or higher. Available to U.S. citizens.

Application Requirements: Application form, essay, recommendations or references, test scores, transcript. *Deadline:* November 28.

Contact: Ms. Elizabeth Nicholson, Manager, Safety 1st Programs
Phone: 703-845-9000
E-mail: safety1st@nata.aero

NATA BUSINESS SCHOLARSHIP

Scholarship available for education or training to establish a career in the business aviation industry. Applicable education includes any aviation-related two-year, four-year or graduate degree program at an accredited college or university. Must be 18 years of age or older, be nominated and endorsed by a representative of a regular or associate member company of the NATA. Applicable training includes any aviation maintenance program under the aegis of Part 147 or 65, any pilot certificate or rating under Part 61 or 141, and any aviation-related two-year, four-year or graduate degree program at an accredited college or university. Visit website for more information http://www.nata.aero/Scholarships/NATA-Business-Scholarship.aspx.

Academic Fields/Career Goals: Aviation/Aerospace.

Award: Scholarship for use in freshman, sophomore, junior, senior, graduate, or postgraduate years; not renewable. *Number:* 1. *Amount:* $2500.

Eligibility Requirements: Applicant must be enrolled or expecting to enroll full- or part-time at a two-year or four-year or technical institution or university. Available to U.S. citizens.

Application Requirements: Application form, essay, recommendations or references, resume, transcript. *Deadline:* December 26.

Contact: Ms. Elizabeth Nicholson, Manager, Safety 1st Programs
Phone: 703-845-9000
E-mail: safety1st@nata.aero

NAVIGATE YOUR FUTURE SCHOLARSHIP

$2500 scholarship for a high school senior planning a career in the general aviation field. Must be enrolled or accepted into an aviation-related program at an accredited college or university and be able to demonstrate an interest in pursuing a career in general aviation.

Academic Fields/Career Goals: Aviation/Aerospace.

Award: Scholarship for use in freshman year; not renewable. *Number:* 1. *Amount:* $2500.

Eligibility Requirements: Applicant must be high school student and planning to enroll or expecting to enroll full-time at a four-year institution or university. Applicant must have 3.0 GPA or higher. Available to U.S. citizens.

Application Requirements: Application form, essay, personal statement, recommendations or references, transcript. *Deadline:* June 29.

Contact: Ms. Elizabeth Nicholson, Manager, Safety 1st Programs
Phone: 703-845-9000
E-mail: safety1st@nata.aero

PIONEERS OF FLIGHT SCHOLARSHIP

Scholarship recipients will be notified in writing by the end of April. Interested students must complete the attached application and submit it along with a complete transcript of grades, a letter of recommendation, an essay on general aviation and a paper indicating career goals in general aviation postmarked no later than the last Friday in December. For more information, visit website http://www.nata.aero/Scholarships/Pioneers-of-Flight-Scholarship-Program.aspx

Academic Fields/Career Goals: Aviation/Aerospace.

Award: Scholarship for use in sophomore or junior years; not renewable. *Number:* 2. *Amount:* $1000.

Eligibility Requirements: Applicant must be enrolled or expecting to enroll full-time at a four-year institution or university. Applicant must have 3.0 GPA or higher. Available to U.S. citizens.

Application Requirements: Application form, essay, recommendations or references, test scores, transcript. *Deadline:* December 26.

Contact: Ms. Elizabeth Nicholson, Manager, Safety 1st Programs
Phone: 703-845-9000
E-mail: safety1st@nata.aero

RICHARD L. TAYLOR FLIGHT TRAINING SCHOLARSHIP

The Richard L. Taylor Flight Training Scholarship applicant must be enrolled in an accredited college/university, be enrolled in a flight program through the college/university with aspirations to become a pilot (general or commercial aviation), and have a private pilot's license (a copy must be included in application the packet). Must also have a GPA of 3.0 or greater. Show junior and senior grade point averages from high school if applying as an incoming freshman. Submit an essay about aviation, your goals and dreams and why you should receive this scholarship. Complete the official application.

Academic Fields/Career Goals: Aviation/Aerospace.

Award: Scholarship for use in freshman, sophomore, junior, or senior years; not renewable. *Number:* 1. *Amount:* $1500.

Eligibility Requirements: Applicant must be enrolled or expecting to enroll full- or part-time at a two-year or four-year institution or university. Applicant must have 3.0 GPA or higher. Available to U.S. citizens.

Application Requirements: Application form, essay, pilot's license, transcript. *Deadline:* March 29.

Contact: Ms. Elizabeth Nicholson, Manager, Safety 1st Programs
Phone: 703-845-9000
E-mail: safety1st@nata.aero

NATIONAL BUSINESS AVIATION ASSOCIATION INC.

http://www.nbaa.org/

AL CONKLIN AND BILL DE DECKER BUSINESS AVIATION MANAGEMENT SCHOLARSHIP

$5000 scholarship for students pursuing a career in business aviation management at NBAA and UAA institutions. Minimum 3.0 GPA required. Must be a U.S. citizen.

Academic Fields/Career Goals: Aviation/Aerospace.

Award: Scholarship for use in sophomore, junior, or senior years; not renewable. *Amount:* $5000.

Eligibility Requirements: Applicant must be enrolled or expecting to enroll full-time at a four-year institution or university. Applicant must have 3.0 GPA or higher. Available to U.S. citizens.

Application Requirements: Application form, essay. *Deadline:* June 31.

Contact: Tyler Austin, Project Manager, Professional Development
Phone: 202-783-9267
Fax: 202-331-8364
E-mail: taustin@nbaa.org

NBAA INTERNATIONAL OPERATORS SCHOLARSHIP

One-time $5000 scholarship offered to one or more recipients. Include with application 500-word essay explaining how this scholarship will help the applicant achieve their international aviation career goals, statement of the funds required to achieve these goals, and at least one professional letter of recommendation, preferably from an NBAA member company employee.

Academic Fields/Career Goals: Aviation/Aerospace.

Award: Scholarship for use in freshman, sophomore, junior, senior, or graduate years; not renewable. *Number:* 1. *Amount:* $5000.

Eligibility Requirements: Applicant must be enrolled or expecting to enroll full- or part-time at a two-year or four-year or technical institution or university. Applicant must have 3.0 GPA or higher. Available to U.S. and non-U.S. citizens.

Application Requirements: Application form, essay. *Deadline:* November 30.

Contact: Tyler Austin, Project Manager, Professional Development
Phone: 202-783-9267
Fax: 202-331-8364
E-mail: taustin@nbaa.org

NBAA JANICE K. BARDEN SCHOLARSHIP

One-time $1000 scholarships for students officially enrolled in NBAA/UAA programs. Must be U.S. citizen, officially enrolled in an aviation-related program with 3.0 minimum GPA. Include with application a 250-word essay describing the applicant's interest and goals for a career in the business aviation industry, and a letter of recommendation from member of aviation department faculty at institution where applicant is enrolled.

Academic Fields/Career Goals: Aviation/Aerospace.

Award: Scholarship for use in sophomore, junior, senior, graduate, or postgraduate years; not renewable. *Number:* 5. *Amount:* $1000.

Eligibility Requirements: Applicant must be enrolled or expecting to enroll full-time at a two-year or four-year institution or university. Applicant must have 3.0 GPA or higher. Available to U.S. citizens.

Application Requirements: Application form, essay. *Deadline:* October 30.

Contact: Tyler Austin, Project Manager, Professional Development
Phone: 202-783-9267
Fax: 202-331-8364
E-mail: taustin@nbaa.org

NBAA LAWRENCE GINOCCHIO AVIATION SCHOLARSHIP

One-time $4500 scholarship for students officially enrolled in NBAA/UAA programs. Must be officially enrolled in aviation-related program with 3.0 minimum GPA. Include with application a 500- to 1000-word essay describing interest in and goals for a career in the business aviation industry while demonstrating strength of character. Must also have two letters of recommendation, including one from member of aviation department faculty at institution where applicant is enrolled.

Academic Fields/Career Goals: Aviation/Aerospace.

Award: Scholarship for use in sophomore, junior, or senior years; not renewable. *Number:* 5. *Amount:* $4500.

Eligibility Requirements: Applicant must be enrolled or expecting to enroll full-time at a four-year institution or university. Applicant must have 3.0 GPA or higher. Available to U.S. and Canadian citizens.

Application Requirements: Application form, essay. *Deadline:* August 1.

Contact: Tyler Austin, Project Manager, Professional Development
Phone: 202-783-9267
Fax: 202-331-8364
E-mail: taustin@nbaa.org

NBAA WILLIAM M. FANNING MAINTENANCE SCHOLARSHIP

One-time award given to two students pursuing careers as maintenance technicians. One award will benefit a student who is currently enrolled in an accredited Airframe and Power-plant (A&P) program at an approved FAR Part 147 school. The second award will benefit an individual who is not currently enrolled but has been accepted into an A&P program. Include with application a 250-word essay describing applicant's interest in and goals for a career in the aviation maintenance field. A letter of recommendation from an NBAA Member Company representative is encouraged.

Academic Fields/Career Goals: Aviation/Aerospace.

Award: Scholarship for use in freshman, sophomore, junior, or senior years; not renewable. *Number:* 2. *Amount:* $2500.

Eligibility Requirements: Applicant must be enrolled or expecting to enroll full-time at a two-year or four-year or technical institution or university. Available to U.S. citizens.

Application Requirements: Application form, essay. *Deadline:* August 1.

Contact: Tyler Austin, Project Manager, Professional Development
Phone: 202-783-9267
Fax: 202-331-8364
E-mail: taustin@nbaa.org

NATIONAL GAY PILOTS ASSOCIATION EDUCATION FUND

http://www.ngpa.org/

NGPA EDUCATION FUND, INC.

Scholarship for candidates pursuing a career as a professional pilot. Funds cannot be used to pay for the basic private certificate; they must be applied towards advanced fight training at a government certified flight school or to college tuition if enrolled in an accredited aviation degree program. Applicants must provide evidence of their contribution to the gay and lesbian community.

Academic Fields/Career Goals: Aviation/Aerospace.

Award: Scholarship for use in freshman, sophomore, junior, or senior years; not renewable. *Number:* 3–4. *Amount:* $3000–$4000.

Eligibility Requirements: Applicant must be enrolled or expecting to enroll full- or part-time at a two-year or four-year or technical institution or university and must have an interest in aviation or LGBT issues. Applicant or parent of applicant must have employment or volunteer experience in community service. Available to U.S. and non-U.S. citizens.

Application Requirements: Application form, copies of the applicant's pilot certificate, medical certificate, recent logbook page, essay, recommendations or references, transcript. *Deadline:* March 31.

Contact: David Pettet, Executive Director
National Gay Pilots Association Education Fund
PO Box 11313
Norfolk, VA 23517
E-mail: ExecDir@ngpa.org

NEVADA NASA SPACE GRANT CONSORTIUM

https://nasa.epscorspo.nevada.edu/

NATIONAL SPACE GRANT CONSORTIUM SCHOLARSHIPS

• See page 127

NEXTSTEPU

http://www.nextstepu.com/

$1,500 STEM SCHOLARSHIP

• See page 120

PALWAUKEE AIRPORT PILOTS ASSOCIATION

http://www.pwkpilots.org

PAPA SCHOLARSHIP & SAFETY FOUNDATION

Scholarship offered to Illinois residents who are attending accredited programs at Illinois institutions. Must be pursuing a course of study in an aviation-related program. Minimum GPA of 2.0. Applications available on website http://www.pwkpilots.org.

Academic Fields/Career Goals: Aviation/Aerospace.

Award: Scholarship for use in freshman, sophomore, junior, or senior years; not renewable. *Number:* 2. *Amount:* $1000.

Eligibility Requirements: Applicant must be enrolled or expecting to enroll full- or part-time at a two-year or four-year or technical institution or university; resident of Illinois and studying in Illinois. Applicant must have 2.5 GPA or higher. Available to U.S. citizens.

Application Requirements: Application form, driver's license, essay, personal photograph. *Deadline:* May 1.

Contact: Jason Simpson, Chairman, Scholarship Committee
Palwaukee Airport Pilots Association
1005 South Wolf Road Suite 106
Wheeling, IL 60090
Phone: 773-842-5088
E-mail: scholarship@pwkpilots.org

RHODE ISLAND PILOTS ASSOCIATION

http://www.ripilots.com/

RHODE ISLAND PILOTS ASSOCIATION SCHOLARSHIP

A scholarship open to Rhode Island residents to begin or advance a career in aviation. Must be age 16 or above.

Academic Fields/Career Goals: Aviation/Aerospace.

Award: Scholarship for use in freshman, sophomore, junior, or senior years; not renewable. *Number:* 2–4. *Amount:* $500–$1500.

Eligibility Requirements: Applicant must be enrolled or expecting to enroll full- or part-time at a two-year or four-year or technical institution; resident of Rhode Island and must have an interest in aviation. Available to U.S. citizens.

Application Requirements: Application form, essay, financial need analysis. *Deadline:* February 28.

Contact: Marilyn Biagetti, Scholarship Chair
Phone: 401-568-3497
E-mail: biagettim@aol.com

ROBERT H. MOLLOHAN FAMILY CHARITABLE FOUNDATION, INC.

http://www.mollohanfoundation.org/

MID-ATLANTIC AEROSPACE SCHOLARSHIP

The Mid-Atlantic Aerospace Complex Scholarship provides scholarship opportunities to students who wish to pursue one of the following aerospace programs offered at the Robert C. Byrd National Aerospace Education Center which awards degrees through Fairmont State University and Pierpont Community and Technical College: BS in Aviation Administration Management, BS in Aviation Administration-Professional Flight, BS in Aviation Maintenance Management, AAS in Airframe & Aerospace Electronics Technology, AAS in Aviation Maintenance Technology. The student must have at least a 2.5 GPA, and will be expected to remain actively involved in an aviation program upon receipt of the scholarship.

Academic Fields/Career Goals: Aviation/Aerospace.

Award: Scholarship for use in freshman, sophomore, junior, or senior years. *Amount:* $1000.

Eligibility Requirements: Applicant must be high school student; planning to enroll or expecting to enroll full-time at a four-year institution or university; resident of West Virginia and studying in West Virginia. Applicant must have 2.5 GPA or higher. Available to U.S. citizens.

Application Requirements: Application form, essay, recommendations or references, resume, test scores, transcript.

Contact: Aime Shaffer, Program Manager
  Phone: 304-333-6783
  E-mail: ashaffer@wvhtf.org

SCARLETT FAMILY FOUNDATION SCHOLARSHIP PROGRAM

http://www.scarlettfoundation.org/

SCHOLARSHIP FOR STUDENTS PURSUING A BUSINESS OR STEM DEGREE

• *See page 91*

SOCIETY OF AUTOMOTIVE ENGINEERS

https://www.sae.org/participate

BMW/SAE ENGINEERING SCHOLARSHIP

Scholarship is provided by BMW AG in recognition of its commitment to excellence in engineering. This scholarship is in support of the SAE Foundation to ensure an adequate supply of well-trained engineers for the future. One scholarship will be awarded at $1500 per year, renewable for four years. Must have a 3.75 GPA, rank in the 90th percentile in both math and critical reading on SAT or composite ACT scores. A 3.0 GPA must be maintained to renew the scholarship.

Academic Fields/Career Goals: Aviation/Aerospace; Chemical Engineering; Electrical Engineering/Electronics; Engineering-Related Technologies; Engineering/Technology; Mechanical Engineering.

Award: Scholarship for use in freshman year; renewable. *Number:* 1. *Amount:* $1500.

Eligibility Requirements: Applicant must be high school student and planning to enroll or expecting to enroll full-time at a four-year institution or university. Available to U.S. citizens.

Application Requirements: Application form, essay, test scores, transcript. *Deadline:* December 15.

Contact: Claudia Tremmelling, Scholarship Program Administrator
  Phone: 208-388-2200
  E-mail: ctremmelling@idahopower.com

EDWARD D. HENDRICKSON/SAE ENGINEERING SCHOLARSHIP

Scholarship of $4000 awarded at $1000 per year for four years. A 3.0 GPA and continued engineering enrollment must be maintained to renew the scholarship. Applicants must have a 3.75 GPA, rank in the 90th percentile in both math and critical reading on SAT or composite ACT scores, and pursue an engineering degree accredited by ABET.

Academic Fields/Career Goals: Aviation/Aerospace; Chemical Engineering; Electrical Engineering/Electronics; Engineering-Related Technologies; Engineering/Technology; Mechanical Engineering.

Award: Scholarship for use in freshman year; renewable. *Number:* 1. *Amount:* $1000.

Eligibility Requirements: Applicant must be high school student and planning to enroll or expecting to enroll full-time at a four-year institution or university. Available to U.S. citizens.

Application Requirements: Application form, essay, test scores, transcript. *Deadline:* December 15.

Contact: Connie Harnish, SAE Educational Relations
  Society of Automotive Engineers
  400 Commonwealth Drive
  Warrendale, PA 15096-0001
  Phone: 724-772-4047
  Fax: 724-776-0890
  E-mail: connie@sae.org

TMC/SAE DONALD D. DAWSON TECHNICAL SCHOLARSHIP

One scholarship of $1500 a year for up to four years. Minimum 3.0 GPA and continuing engineering enrollment must be maintained to remain qualified. High school seniors must have a 3.25 or higher GPA, SAT math 600 or above and critical reading 550 or above and/or an ACT composite score 27 or above. Transfer students from accredited four-year colleges/universities must have a 3.0 GPA. Students from postsecondary technical/vocational schools must have a 3.5 GPA.

Academic Fields/Career Goals: Aviation/Aerospace; Chemical Engineering; Electrical Engineering/Electronics; Engineering-Related Technologies; Engineering/Technology; Materials Science, Engineering, and Metallurgy; Mechanical Engineering.

Award: Scholarship for use in freshman, sophomore, junior, or senior years; renewable. *Number:* 1. *Amount:* $1500.

Eligibility Requirements: Applicant must be enrolled or expecting to enroll full-time at a two-year or four-year or technical institution or university. Available to U.S. citizens.

Application Requirements: Application form, essay, test scores, transcript. *Deadline:* December 15.

Contact: Connie Harnish, SAE Educational Relations
  Society of Automotive Engineers
  400 Commonwealth Drive
  Warrendale, PA 15096-0001
  Phone: 724-772-4047
  Fax: 724-776-0890
  E-mail: connie@sae.org

SOCIETY OF SATELLITE PROFESSIONALS INTERNATIONAL

http://www.sspi.org/

SSPI INTERNATIONAL SCHOLARSHIPS

Scholarship open to students majoring or planning to major in fields related to satellite communications. Selection is based on academic and leadership achievement, commitment to pursue education and career opportunities in the satellite industry or a field making direct use of satellite technology. Available to members of SSPI.

Academic Fields/Career Goals: Aviation/Aerospace; Communications; Law/Legal Services; Meteorology/Atmospheric Science; Military and Defense Studies.

Award: Scholarship for use in freshman, sophomore, junior, senior, or graduate years; not renewable. *Number:* 1–4. *Amount:* $2500–$4000.

Eligibility Requirements: Applicant must be enrolled or expecting to enroll full- or part-time at a two-year or four-year institution or university. Available to U.S. and non-U.S. citizens.

Application Requirements: Essay, financial need analysis. *Deadline:* April 15.

Contact: Ms. Tamara Bond-Williams, Membership Director
  Society of Satellite Professionals International
  250 Park Avenue, 7th Floor
  New York, NY 10177
  Phone: 212-809-5199 Ext. 103
  Fax: 212-825-0075
  E-mail: tbond-williams@sspi.org

SOCIETY OF WOMEN ENGINEERS-ROCKY MOUNTAIN SECTION

http://www.swe-rms.org/

SOCIETY OF WOMEN ENGINEERS-ROCKY MOUNTAIN SECTION SCHOLARSHIP PROGRAM

One-time award for graduating female high school seniors and female college students in Colorado and Wyoming (except zip codes 80800 and 81599). Eligibility: 1. Applicant must be a woman enrolled or planning to enroll as an undergraduate or graduate student in an ABET accredited engineering, computing, or engineering technology program (see http://www.abet.org/ for a list of eligible schools and majors) or other approved program. 2. Applicant must meet minimum GPA requirements. 3. Applicant must be able to accept the scholarship for the academic year starting in the Fall and must not already be receiving full funding from another source. For more information visit the website: http://www.swe-rms.org/scholarships.html.

Academic Fields/Career Goals: Aviation/Aerospace; Chemical Engineering; Civil Engineering; Computer Science/Data Processing; Construction Engineering/Management; Electrical Engineering/Electronics; Energy and Power Engineering; Engineering-Related Technologies; Engineering/Technology; Hydrology; Marine/Ocean Engineering; Materials Science, Engineering, and Metallurgy; Mechanical Engineering.

Award: Scholarship for use in freshman, sophomore, junior, senior, or graduate years; not renewable. *Number:* 3–8. *Amount:* $500–$2000.

Eligibility Requirements: Applicant must be enrolled or expecting to enroll full-time at a four-year institution or university; female and resident of Colorado, Wyoming. Applicant must have 3.5 GPA or higher. Available to U.S. citizens.

Application Requirements: Application form, community service, essay. *Deadline:* February 1.

Contact: Christi Wisleder, Scholarship Chair
Society of Women Engineers-Rocky Mountain Section
PO Box 260692
Lakewood, CO 80226-0692
E-mail: christi.wisleder@gmail.com

STRAIGHT NORTH

https://www.straightnorth.com/

STRAIGHT NORTH STEM SCHOLARSHIP
• See page 92

TUSKEGEE AIRMEN SCHOLARSHIP FOUNDATION

http://www.taisf.org/

TUSKEGEE AIRMEN SCHOLARSHIP

Each year the Foundation grants scholarship awards to deserving young men and women. The number of available scholarship awards is directly related to income received from investments. The selection committee uses academic achievement, extracurricular and community activities, relative financial need, recommendations, and two essays in order to competitively rank applicants.

Academic Fields/Career Goals: Aviation/Aerospace.

Award: Scholarship for use in freshman year; not renewable. *Number:* 40. *Amount:* $1500.

Eligibility Requirements: Applicant must be high school student and planning to enroll or expecting to enroll full-time at a two-year or four-year institution or university. Applicant must have 3.0 GPA or higher. Available to U.S. citizens.

Application Requirements: Application form, autobiography, community service, essay, financial need analysis, personal photograph. *Deadline:* January 26.

Contact: Mr. Errol Lewis
E-mail: lewisei@aol.com

UNIVERSITIES SPACE RESEARCH ASSOCIATION

http://www.usra.edu/

UNIVERSITIES SPACE RESEARCH ASSOCIATION SCHOLARSHIP AWARD PROGRAM
• See page 128

UNIVERSITY AVIATION ASSOCIATION

http://www.uaa.aero/

CAE SIMUFLITE CITATION TYPE RATING SCHOLARSHIP

Scholarship open to undergraduate seniors and post-Baccalaureate graduates of aviation degree programs up to two years after graduation. Must have a minimum 3.25 GPA. Students must attend, or must have graduated from, a University Aviation Association member institution. The application is posted at the University Aviation Association website at http://www.uaa.aero. There are extensive aviation flight certification and flight time requirements for this application so please consult the application directly for more details.

Academic Fields/Career Goals: Aviation/Aerospace.

Award: Scholarship for use in senior year; not renewable. *Number:* 6. *Amount:* $10,500.

Eligibility Requirements: Applicant must be enrolled or expecting to enroll full-time at a four-year institution or university and must have an interest in aviation. Available to U.S. citizens.

Application Requirements: Application form, essay, FAA first class medical certificate, recommendations or references, resume, transcript. *Deadline:* March 31.

Contact: Dr. David NewMyer, Professor and Department Chair, Aviation Management and Flight
University Aviation Association
Transportation Education Center, 545 North Airport Road
Southern Illinois University Carbondale
Murphysboro, IL 62966
Phone: 616-453-8898
Fax: 618-453-5230
E-mail: newmyer@siu.edu

CHICAGO AREA BUSINESS AVIATION ASSOCIATION SCHOLARSHIP

One-time awards of $2500 for U.S. citizens who are Illinois residents. Minimum GPA of 2.5. Priority given to Chicagoland residents followed by Illinois residents who are attending, or will attend, a postsecondary aviation degree program in such fields as Aerospace Engineering, Air Traffic Control, Aircraft Charter, Aircraft Maintenance, Aviation Administration/Management, Aviation Flight, Avionics/Aviation Electronics, etc. At least three letters of recommendation required; at least one of these must be from a person currently employed in the field of Business Aviation. The financial statement that is included in the CABAA Scholarship Application must be completed and attached to the application. Application is posted at the website of the University Aviation Association at http://www.uaa.aero.

Academic Fields/Career Goals: Aviation/Aerospace.

Award: Scholarship for use in freshman, sophomore, junior, senior, graduate, or postgraduate years; not renewable. *Number:* 8. *Amount:* $4000.

Eligibility Requirements: Applicant must be enrolled or expecting to enroll full-time at a two-year or four-year or technical institution or university and resident of Illinois. Applicant must have 2.5 GPA or higher. Available to U.S. citizens.

Application Requirements: Application form, essay, recommendations or references. *Deadline:* April 20.

Contact: Dr. David Newmyer, Department Chair, Aviation Management
and Flight
University Aviation Association
Southern Illinois University at Carbondale, College of Applied
Sciences and Arts
1365 Douglas Drive
Carbondale, IL 62901-6623
Phone: 618-453-8898
Fax: 618-453-7286
E-mail: newmyer@siu.edu

JOSEPH FRASCA EXCELLENCE IN AVIATION SCHOLARSHIP

Established to encourage those who demonstrate the highest level of commitment to and achievement in aviation studies. Applicant must be a junior or senior currently enrolled in a University Aviation Association member institution. Must be FAA certified/qualified in either aviation maintenance or flight, have membership in at least one aviation organization (such as National Intercollegiate Flying Association flying team, Alpha Eta Rho, Warbirds of America, Experimental Aircraft Association, etc.), and be involved in aviation activities, projects, and events. Minimum 3.0 GPA required. Application is posted at http://www.uaa.aero and applications are due on the second Monday of April each year.

Academic Fields/Career Goals: Aviation/Aerospace.

Award: Scholarship for use in junior or senior years; not renewable. *Number:* 2. *Amount:* $2000.

Eligibility Requirements: Applicant must be enrolled or expecting to enroll full- or part-time at a four-year institution or university and must have an interest in aviation. Applicant must have 3.0 GPA or higher. Available to U.S. and non-U.S. citizens.

Application Requirements: Application form, essay, FAA certification as a pilot or mechanic or both, financial need analysis, recommendations or references, transcript. *Deadline:* April 10.

Contact: Dr. David Newmyer, Department Chair, Aviation Management
and Flight
University Aviation Association
1365 Douglas Drive
Carbondale, IL 62901-6623
Phone: 618-453-8898
Fax: 618-453-4850
E-mail: newmyer@siu.edu

PAUL A. WHELAN AVIATION SCHOLARSHIP

One-time award of $2000 given to sophomore, junior, senior or graduate. Must be a U.S. citizen. Must be enrolled in University Aviation Association member institution. 2.5 GPA required. Current or past military service (active duty, reserves or national guard, FAA certification, membership in aviation-related association preferred. Application is posted at the University Aviation Association website at http://www.uaa.aero

Academic Fields/Career Goals: Aviation/Aerospace.

Award: Scholarship for use in sophomore, junior, senior, or graduate years; not renewable. *Number:* 1. *Amount:* $2000.

Eligibility Requirements: Applicant must be enrolled or expecting to enroll full-time at a two-year or four-year institution or university and must have an interest in aviation. Applicant must have 2.5 GPA or higher. Available to U.S. citizens.

Application Requirements: Application form, essay, FAA certification, recommendations or references, transcript. *Deadline:* May 15.

Contact: David Newmyer, Department Chair, Aviation Management and
Flight
University Aviation Association
Southern Illinois University at Carbondale, College of Applied
Sciences and Arts
1365 Douglas Drive
Carbondale, IL 62901-6623
Phone: 618-453-8898
Fax: 618-453-7268
E-mail: newmyer@siu.edu

VERMONT SPACE GRANT CONSORTIUM

http://www.cems.uvm.edu/vsgc

VERMONT SPACE GRANT CONSORTIUM

• *See page 104*

VIRGINIA AVIATION AND SPACE EDUCATION FORUM

http://www.doav.virginia.gov/

JOHN R. LILLARD VIRGINIA AIRPORT OPERATORS COUNCIL SCHOLARSHIP PROGRAM

Scholarship of $3000 offered to high school seniors planning a career in the field of aviation. Must be enrolled or accepted into an aviation-related program at an accredited college. Minimum 3.75 unweighted GPA.

Academic Fields/Career Goals: Aviation/Aerospace.

Award: Scholarship for use in freshman year; not renewable. *Number:* 1. *Amount:* $3000.

Eligibility Requirements: Applicant must be high school student; planning to enroll or expecting to enroll full-time at a four-year institution or university and must have an interest in aviation. Available to U.S. and non-U.S. citizens.

Application Requirements: Application form, essay, financial need analysis, recommendations or references, transcript. *Deadline:* February 20.

Contact: Betty Wilson, Program Coordinator
Phone: 804-236-3624
Fax: 804-236-3636
E-mail: betty.wilson@doav.virginia.gov

WILLARD G. PLENTL AVIATION SCHOLARSHIP PROGRAM

Scholarship of $1000 awarded to a high school senior who is planning an aviation career in a non-engineering area.

Academic Fields/Career Goals: Aviation/Aerospace.

Award: Scholarship for use in freshman year; not renewable. *Number:* 1. *Amount:* $1000.

Eligibility Requirements: Applicant must be high school student; planning to enroll or expecting to enroll full-time at a four-year institution or university and must have an interest in aviation. Applicant must have 3.5 GPA or higher. Available to U.S. and non-U.S. citizens.

Application Requirements: Application form, essay, financial need analysis, recommendations or references, transcript. *Deadline:* February 20.

Contact: Betty Wilson, Program Coordinator
Virginia Aviation and Space Education Forum
5702 Gulfstream Road
Richmond, VA 23250-2422
E-mail: betty.wilson@doav.virginia.gov

WOMEN IN AEROSPACE FOUNDATION

http://www.womeninaerospace.org/index.html

WIA FOUNDATION SCHOLARSHIP

The WIA Foundation is pleased to provide scholarships to women interested in a career in the aerospace field to pursue higher education degrees in engineering, math or science. One or more awards will be given each year to a rising junior or senior in college, to be applied during the upcoming academic year. To be eligible for the WIA Foundation Scholarship, an applicant must be interested in pursuing a career in the aerospace field and be a rising junior or senior working towards a Bachelor's degree in engineering, math or science. An applicant must have completed at least two and a half academic years of full-time college work at the time of application and must be currently enrolled in an accredited college or university in the United States or its territories, and plan to be enrolled in the subsequent academic year. Each applicant must have a college grade point average of at least 3.0 on a 4.0 scale. Applicants must be female of any nationality. Applications will be available on or about mid-November to mid-December for the subsequent academic year.

Academic Fields/Career Goals: Aviation/Aerospace; Engineering-Related Technologies; Engineering/Technology; Mathematics; Science, Technology, and Society.

Award: Scholarship for use in junior or senior years; not renewable. *Number:* 4. *Amount:* $2000.

Eligibility Requirements: Applicant must be enrolled or expecting to enroll full-time at an institution or university and female. Applicant must have 3.0 GPA or higher. Available to U.S. and non-U.S. citizens.

Application Requirements: Application form, essay. *Deadline:* June 20.

Contact: Ms. Torrie Nickerson, Program and Event Specialist
Women in Aerospace Foundation
204 E Street NE
Washington, DC 20002
Phone: 202-547-0229
E-mail: tnickerson@womeninaerospace.org

WOMEN IN AVIATION, INTERNATIONAL

http://www.wai.org/

AIRBUS LEADERSHIP GRANT

One scholarship to a college sophomore or higher level student who is pursuing a degree in an aviation-related field. Must have a minimum GPA of 3.0 and must exhibit leadership potential. Must be a WAI member.

Academic Fields/Career Goals: Aviation/Aerospace.

Award: Scholarship for use in sophomore, junior, or senior years; not renewable. *Number:* 1. *Amount:* $5000.

Eligibility Requirements: Applicant must be enrolled or expecting to enroll full- or part-time at a four-year institution or university and must have an interest in leadership. Applicant or parent of applicant must be member of Women in Aviation, International. Applicant must have 3.0 GPA or higher. Available to U.S. and non-U.S. citizens.

Application Requirements: Application form, essay, recommendations or references, resume. *Deadline:* November 12.

Contact: Donna Wallace, Scholarships Committee
Women in Aviation, International
3647 State Route 503 South
West Alexandria, OH 45381
Phone: 937-839-4647
Fax: 937-839-4645
E-mail: dwallace@wai.org

BOEING COMPANY CAREER ENHANCEMENT SCHOLARSHIP

Scholarship is available for a woman who wishes to advance her career in aerospace industry in the fields of engineering, technology development or management. The award is to be used for educational purposes only and may not be applied toward flight hours. Applicants may be full-time or part-time employees currently in the aerospace industry or related field. Students pursuing aviation-related degrees that are at the junior level with a minimum GPA of 2.5 (on a 4.0 scale) are also eligible.

Academic Fields/Career Goals: Aviation/Aerospace.

Award: Scholarship for use in junior or senior years; not renewable. *Number:* 2. *Amount:* $2500.

Eligibility Requirements: Applicant must be enrolled or expecting to enroll full- or part-time at a four-year institution or university and female. Applicant or parent of applicant must be member of Women in Aviation, International. Available to U.S. and non-U.S. citizens.

Application Requirements: Application form, essay, recommendations or references, resume. *Deadline:* November 12.

Contact: Donna Wallace, Scholarships Committee
Women in Aviation, International
3647 State Route 503 South
West Alexandria, OH 45381
Phone: 937-839-4647
Fax: 937-839-4645
E-mail: dwallace@wai.org

DELTA AIR LINES AIRCRAFT MAINTENANCE TECHNOLOGY SCHOLARSHIP

Scholarship of $5000 available to a student currently enrolled in an Aviation Maintenance Technician Program (A&P) or a degree in Aviation Maintenance Technology. Applicant must be a full-time student with a minimum of two semesters left (as of February March 2016, with a minimum GPA of 3.0 or better (on a 4.0 scale). Must be a member of WAI. Must be an U.S. citizen or eligible non-citizen.

Academic Fields/Career Goals: Aviation/Aerospace.

Award: Scholarship for use in freshman, sophomore, or junior years; not renewable. *Number:* 1. *Amount:* $5000.

Eligibility Requirements: Applicant must be enrolled or expecting to enroll full-time at a two-year or four-year or technical institution or university. Applicant or parent of applicant must be member of Women in Aviation, International. Applicant must have 3.0 GPA or higher. Available to U.S. and non-U.S. citizens.

Application Requirements: Application form, essay, recommendations or references, resume. *Deadline:* November 12.

Contact: Donna Wallace, Scholarships Committee
Women in Aviation, International
3647 State Route 503 South
West Alexandria, OH 45381
Phone: 937-839-4647
Fax: 937-839-4645
E-mail: dwallace@wai.org

DELTA AIR LINES ENGINEERING SCHOLARSHIP

Student must be currently enrolled in a Baccalaureate degree in Aerospace / Aeronautical, Electrical, or Mechanical Engineering. Applicants must be full-time students at the junior or senior level with a minimum of two semesters left (as of February 2016), with a cumulative GPA of 3.0 (on a 4.0 scale) or better. Must be a member of WAI and be U.S. citizen or eligible non-citizen.

Academic Fields/Career Goals: Aviation/Aerospace; Electrical Engineering/Electronics; Mechanical Engineering.

Award: Scholarship for use in junior or senior years; not renewable. *Number:* 1. *Amount:* $7000.

Eligibility Requirements: Applicant must be enrolled or expecting to enroll full-time at a four-year institution or university. Applicant or parent of applicant must be member of Women in Aviation, International. Applicant must have 3.0 GPA or higher. Available to U.S. and non-U.S. citizens.

Application Requirements: Application form, essay, recommendations or references, resume. *Deadline:* November 12.

Contact: Donna Wallace, Scholarships Committee
Women in Aviation, International
3647 State Route 503 South
West Alexandria, OH 45381
Phone: 937-839-4647
Fax: 937-839-4645
E-mail: dwallace@wai.org

DELTA AIR LINES MAINTENANCE MANAGEMENT/AVIATION BUSINESS MANAGEMENT SCHOLARSHIP

Scholarship to a student currently enrolled in an Associate or Baccalaureate degree in Aviation Maintenance Management or Aviation Business Management. Applicant must be a full-time college student, with a minimum of two semesters left (as of February 2016). Must have a minimum GPA of 3.0 (on a 4.0 scale) or better. Must be a member of WAI and be a U.S. citizen or eligible non-citizen.

Academic Fields/Career Goals: Aviation/Aerospace.

Award: Scholarship for use in freshman, sophomore, or junior years; not renewable. *Number:* 1. *Amount:* $5000.

Eligibility Requirements: Applicant must be enrolled or expecting to enroll full-time at a two-year or four-year institution or university. Applicant or parent of applicant must be member of Women in Aviation, International. Applicant must have 3.0 GPA or higher. Available to U.S. and non-U.S. citizens.

Application Requirements: Application form, essay, recommendations or references, resume. *Deadline:* November 12.

Contact: Donna Wallace, Scholarships Committee
Women in Aviation, International
3647 State Route 503 South
West Alexandria, OH 45381
Phone: 937-839-4647
Fax: 937-839-4645
E-mail: dwallace@wai.org

KEEP FLYING SCHOLARSHIP

One scholarship of up to $3000 will be awarded to an individual working on an instrument or multi engine rating, commercial or initial flight instructor certificate. Flight training must be completed within one year. Minimum requirements: private pilot certificate, 100 hours of flight time, and a copy of a current written test (with passing grade) for the certificate/rating sought. One letter of recommendation must be from a pilot that you have flown with. Finalist will only be interviewed at the annual Women in Aviation Conference. Must be a member of WAI.

Academic Fields/Career Goals: Aviation/Aerospace.

Award: Scholarship for use in freshman year; not renewable. *Number:* 1. *Amount:* $3000.

Eligibility Requirements: Applicant must be enrolled or expecting to enroll full- or part-time at a technical institution. Applicant or parent of applicant must be member of Women in Aviation, International. Available to U.S. and non-U.S. citizens.

Application Requirements: Application form, essay, recommendations or references, resume. *Deadline:* November 12.

Contact: Donna Wallace, Scholarships Committee
Women in Aviation, International
3647 State Route 503 South
West Alexandria, OH 45381
Phone: 937-839-4647
Fax: 937-839-4645
E-mail: dwallace@wai.org

WOMEN IN AVIATION, INTERNATIONAL ACHIEVEMENT AWARDS

One scholarships will be awarded to a full-time college or university student pursuing any type of aviation or aviation related career. A second scholarship will be awarded to an individual, not required to be a student, pursuing any type of aviation interest. Include in your essay how you plan to use the scholarship if awarded and what you have accomplished to date to reach your goals. Must be a member of WAI.

Academic Fields/Career Goals: Aviation/Aerospace.

Award: Scholarship for use in freshman, sophomore, junior, or senior years; not renewable. *Number:* 2. *Amount:* $1000.

Eligibility Requirements: Applicant must be enrolled or expecting to enroll full-time at a two-year or four-year institution or university. Applicant or parent of applicant must be member of Women in Aviation, International. Available to U.S. and non-U.S. citizens.

Application Requirements: Application form. *Deadline:* November 12.

Contact: Donna Wallace, Scholarships Committee
Women in Aviation, International
3647 State Route 503 South
West Alexandria, OH 45381
Phone: 937-839-4647
Fax: 937-839-4645
E-mail: dwallace@wai.org

WOMEN IN CORPORATE AVIATION CAREER SCHOLARSHIPS

Scholarship will be given to a person pursuing professional development or career advancement in any job classification in corporate/business aviation. Applicants should be actively working toward their goal and show financial need. Award can be used toward a specific program of education, flight training, dispatcher training, or upgrades in aviation education, and so forth, but cannot include general business course work. If you are a pilot please submit copies of pilot licenses, medical and the last three pages of logbook with your application. Must be a member of WAI.

Academic Fields/Career Goals: Aviation/Aerospace.

Award: Scholarship for use in freshman, sophomore, junior, or senior years; not renewable. *Number:* 1. *Amount:* $2000.

Eligibility Requirements: Applicant must be enrolled or expecting to enroll full- or part-time at a two-year or four-year or technical institution or university and female. Applicant or parent of applicant must be member of Women in Aviation, International. Available to U.S. and non-U.S. citizens.

Application Requirements: Application form, essay, financial need analysis, recommendations or references, resume, transcript. *Deadline:* November 12.

Contact: Donna Wallace, Scholarships Committee
Women in Aviation, International
3647 State Route 503 South
West Alexandria, OH 45381
Phone: 937-839-4647
Fax: 937-839-4645
E-mail: dwallace@wai.org

WOMEN MILITARY AVIATORS DREAM OF FLIGHT SCHOLARSHIP

This will be awarded to a woman pursuing her flight ratings at an accredited institution or FAA Part 141 approved flight school. Must demonstrate persistence and determination to flight. Training must be completed within one year of the award and be a member of WAI.

Academic Fields/Career Goals: Aviation/Aerospace.

Award: Scholarship for use in freshman, sophomore, junior, or senior years; not renewable. *Number:* 1. *Amount:* $2000.

Eligibility Requirements: Applicant must be enrolled or expecting to enroll full- or part-time at a two-year or four-year or technical institution or university. Applicant or parent of applicant must be member of Women in Aviation, International. Available to U.S. and non-U.S. citizens.

Application Requirements: Application form, financial need analysis, recommendations or references, resume. *Deadline:* November 12.

Contact: Donna Wallace, Scholarships Committee
Women in Aviation, International
3647 State Route 503 South
West Alexandria, OH 45381
Phone: 937-839-4647
Fax: 937-839-4645
E-mail: dwallace@wai.org

WRIGHT CHAPTER, WOMEN IN AVIATION, INTERNATIONAL, ELISHA HALL MEMORIAL SCHOLARSHIP

Scholarship offered to a woman seeking to further the aviation career in flight training, aircraft scheduling or dispatch, aviation management, aviation maintenance, or avionics. Preference will be given to applicants from Cincinnati Ohio/Tri-State area, but all applicants will be considered based upon character, need, community involvement, and accomplishments. Must be a member of WAI, but does not have to be member of Cincinnati Chapter.

Academic Fields/Career Goals: Aviation/Aerospace.

Award: Scholarship for use in freshman, sophomore, junior, or senior years; not renewable. *Number:* 1. *Amount:* $1000.

Eligibility Requirements: Applicant must be enrolled or expecting to enroll full- or part-time at a two-year or four-year or technical institution or university and female. Applicant or parent of applicant must be member of Women in Aviation, International. Available to U.S. and non-U.S. citizens.

Application Requirements: Application form, essay, recommendations or references, resume. *Deadline:* November 12.

Contact: Donna Wallace, Scholarships Committee
Women in Aviation, International
3647 State Route 503 South
West Alexandria, OH 45381
Phone: 937-839-4647
Fax: 937-839-4645
E-mail: dwallace@wai.org

BEHAVIORAL SCIENCE

101ST AIRBORNE DIVISION ASSOCIATION

http://www.screamingeaglefoundation.org/

AL & WILLIAMARY VISTE SCHOLARSHIP

• See page 114

AVACARE MEDICAL
https://avacaremedical.com

AVACARE MEDICAL SCHOLARSHIP
• *See page 115*

BHW GROUP
https://thebhwgroup.com/

BHW WOMEN IN STEM SCHOLARSHIP
• *See page 124*

DIVERSITYCOMM, INC.
http://www.diversitycomm.net/

DIVERSITY IN STEAM MAGAZINE SCHOLARSHIP
• *See page 83*

FOUNDATION FOR SCIENCE AND DISABILITY
http://stemd.org/

GRANTS FOR DISABLED GRADUATE STUDENTS IN THE SCIENCES
• *See page 106*

HEALTH PROFESSIONS EDUCATION FOUNDATION
http://www.healthprofessions.ca.gov/

ALLIED HEALTHCARE SCHOLARSHIP PROGRAM
One-time award available to students enrolled in, or accepted to California accredited allied health education programs. Scholarship worth up to $4000. Deadlines: check website http://oshpd.ca.gov/HPEF. Must be resident of California.

Academic Fields/Career Goals: Behavioral Science; Dental Health/Services; Health and Medical Sciences; Pharmacy; Psychology; Radiology; Social Services; Therapy/Rehabilitation.

Award: Scholarship for use in freshman, sophomore, junior, senior, graduate, or postgraduate years; not renewable. *Number:* 5–40. *Amount:* up to $4000.

Eligibility Requirements: Applicant must be enrolled or expecting to enroll full- or part-time at a two-year or four-year or technical institution or university; resident of California and studying in California. Available to U.S. citizens.

Application Requirements: Application form, application form may be submitted online (http://calreach.oshpd.ca.gov), community service, driver's license, financial need analysis, recommendations or references, Student Aid Report (SAR) or tax return with W2, transcript. *Deadline:* varies.

Contact: Meaghan Harrington, Program Officer
Health Professions Education Foundation
400 R Street
Sacramento, CA 95811
Phone: 800-773-1669
Fax: 916-324-6585
E-mail: HPEF-EMail@oshpd.ca.gov

INDIAN HEALTH SERVICES, UNITED STATES DEPARTMENT OF HEALTH AND HUMAN SERVICES
http://www.ihs.gov/scholarship

HEALTH PROFESSIONS PREPARATORY SCHOLARSHIP PROGRAM
Scholarship for undergraduate American Indian/Alaska Native students enrolled part-time or full-time in programs related to health and allied health professions. Minimum 2.0 GPA required to apply. Applicant must demonstrate a desire to serve AI/AN people when their health or allied health profession education/ training is complete. The dollar amount and number of awards varies annually.

Academic Fields/Career Goals: Behavioral Science; Biology; Health and Medical Sciences; Nursing; Optometry; Pharmacy; Psychology; Social Sciences.

Award: Scholarship for use in junior, senior, or graduate years; not renewable. *Number:* 25–50. *Amount:* $13,250–$52,600.

Eligibility Requirements: Applicant must be of English heritage; American Indian/Alaska Native; enrolled or expecting to enroll full- or part-time at a four-year institution or university and resident of Alabama, Alaska, Arizona, Arkansas, California, Colorado, Connecticut, Delaware, District of Columbia, Florida, Georgia, Hawaii, Idaho, Illinois, Indiana, Iowa, Kansas, Kentucky, Louisiana, Maine, Maryland, Massachusetts, Michigan, Minnesota, Mississippi, Missouri, Montana, Nebraska, Nevada, New Hampshire, New Jersey, New Mexico, New York, North Carolina, North Dakota, Ohio, Oklahoma, Oregon, Pennsylvania, Rhode Island, South Carolina, South Dakota, Tennessee, Texas, Utah, Vermont, Virginia, Washington, West Virginia, Wisconsin, Wyoming. Available to U.S. citizens.

Application Requirements: Application form, essay. *Deadline:* March 28.

Contact: Ms. Reta Brewer, Branch Chief
Indian Health Services, United States Department of Health and Human Services
5600 Fishers Lane
Mail Stop: OHR 11E53A
Rockville, MD 20857
Phone: 301-443-6197
Fax: 301-443-6048
E-mail: reta.brewer@ihs.gov

INTERMOUNTAIN MEDICAL IMAGING
https://www.aboutimi.com/

INTERMOUNTAIN MEDICAL IMAGING SCHOLARSHIP
• *See page 147*

THE JACKSON LABORATORY
https://www.jax.org

THE JACKSON LABORATORY COLLEGE SCHOLARSHIP PROGRAM
• *See page 126*

KETAMINE CLINICS OF LOS ANGELES
http://www.ketamineclinics.com/

KETAMINE CLINICS OF LOS ANGELES SCHOLARSHIP PROGRAM
To be eligible, students must be planning to enroll in medical school, or a degree program that leads to medical school, in the following academic year, or already be enrolled in a medical degree program and plan to return in the next academic year. The scholarship is available to all students ages 18 and over, at all levels from high school to graduate school.

Academic Fields/Career Goals: Behavioral Science; Biology; Health and Medical Sciences; Neurobiology; Nursing; Optometry; Psychology; Therapy/Rehabilitation.

Award: Scholarship for use in freshman, sophomore, junior, senior, graduate, or postgraduate years; renewable. *Number:* 1. *Amount:* $1000.

Eligibility Requirements: Applicant must be enrolled or expecting to enroll full-time at a two-year or four-year or technical institution or university. Available to U.S. and non-U.S. citizens.

Application Requirements: Essay. *Deadline:* December 1.

Contact: Mr. Sam Mandel, Chief Operating Officer
Ketamine Clinics of Los Angeles
11645 Wilshire Blvd. STE 852
Los Angeles, CA 90025
Phone: 310-270-0625
E-mail: scholarship@ketamineclinics.com

LABROOTS INC.

http://www.LabRoots.com

LABROOTS STEM SCHOLARSHIP
• *See page 116*

LAW OFFICES OF PROSPER SHAKED

https://www.prosperlaw.com/

PROSPER SHAKED SCHOLARSHIP FOR FUTURE MEDICAL PROFESSIONALS

The Law Offices of Prosper Shaked is a Miami law firm devoted to representing victims of serious personal injury in South Florida. Through his practice with car accident injury victims and the victims of other catastrophic injuries. After working with these victims, Prosper Shaked found a new appreciation for the work of skilled doctors, nurses, and other healthcare professionals. Therefore, he created this $1,500 scholarship to benefit those who choose these demanding careers.

Academic Fields/Career Goals: Behavioral Science; Biology; Child and Family Studies; Dental Health/Services; Food Science/Nutrition; Health and Medical Sciences; Health Information Management/Technology; Natural Sciences; Neurobiology; Nursing; Occupational Safety and Health; Oncology; Optometry; Osteopathy; Pharmacy; Public Health; Therapy/Rehabilitation.

Award: Scholarship for use in freshman, sophomore, junior, senior, graduate, or postgraduate years; not renewable. *Number:* 1. *Amount:* $1500.

Eligibility Requirements: Applicant must be enrolled or expecting to enroll full-time at a two-year or four-year institution or university. Applicant must have 3.0 GPA or higher. Available to U.S. citizens.

Application Requirements: Application form, essay, transcript. *Deadline:* August 15.

Contact: Mr. Prosper Shaked, Personal Injury Attorney
Law Offices of Prosper Shaked
1160 Kane Concourse
Bay Harbor Islands, FL 33154
Phone: 305-6900244
E-mail: scholarships@prosperlaw.com

MEDICAL SCRUBS COLLECTION

http://medicalscrubscollection.com

MEDICAL SCRUBS COLLECTION SCHOLARSHIP
• *See page 120*

MENTAL HEALTH ASSOCIATION IN NEW YORK STATE INC.

http://www.MHANYS.org

EDNA AIMES SCHOLARSHIP

The Edna Aimes Scholarship is awarded annually by the Mental Health Association in New York State, Inc (MHANYS). The purpose of this scholarship is to encourage the education of individuals to assist in the prevention and treatment of mental illnesses, the promotion of mental health, and the empowerment of adults, children, and families whose lives have been affected by mental illnesses.

Academic Fields/Career Goals: Behavioral Science.

Award: Scholarship for use in junior, senior, or graduate years; not renewable. *Number:* 1. *Amount:* $2500.

Eligibility Requirements: Applicant must be enrolled or expecting to enroll full- or part-time at a four-year institution or university; resident of New York and studying in New York.

Application Requirements: *Deadline:* June 30.

Contact: Awards Committee
E-mail: scholarship@mhanys.org

MICHAEL MOODY FITNESS

http://www.michaelmoodyfitness.com/

MICHAEL MOODY FITNESS SCHOLARSHIP

The Michael Moody Fitness Scholarship offers a college scholarship of $1,500 to a high school senior, undergraduate, or graduate student who has demonstrated outstanding achievement, participation and leadership in school activities and work experience, and interest in pursuing a career in the health and fitness related fields. She or he may apply and use the money for education-related expenses, including tuition, fees, books, supplies, room, and board. The scholarship is sponsored by Michael Moody Fitness. The program will be accepting scholarship applications from August 2nd, 2017 until 1,000 scholarship applications are submitted or July 15th, 2018, whichever comes first. Your scholarship application must be one of the first 1,000 submitted by the deadline date. Please visit http://www.michaelmoodyfitness.com/student-scholarship-chicago/ for more details.

Academic Fields/Career Goals: Behavioral Science; Biology; Child and Family Studies; Dental Health/Services; Education; Environmental Health; Environmental Science; Food Science/Nutrition; Food Service/Hospitality; Health Administration; Health and Medical Sciences; Health Information Management/Technology; Humanities; Neurobiology; Nursing; Occupational Safety and Health; Oncology; Optometry; Osteopathy; Physical Sciences; Psychology; Public Health; Public Policy and Administration; Recreation, Parks, Leisure Studies; Science, Technology, and Society; Social Sciences; Social Services; Special Education; Sports-Related/Exercise Science; Therapy/Rehabilitation.

Award: Scholarship for use in freshman, sophomore, junior, senior, or graduate years; not renewable. *Number:* 1. *Amount:* $1500.

Eligibility Requirements: Applicant must be enrolled or expecting to enroll full-time at a two-year or four-year institution or university. Available to U.S. and non-U.S. citizens.

Application Requirements: Application form. *Deadline:* July 15.

Contact: Mr. Michael Moody, Owner/Personal Trainer
Michael Moody Fitness
900 North North Branch Street
Chicago, IL 60642
Phone: 773-484-8094
E-mail: michael@michaelmoodyfitness.com

NATIONAL INSTITUTES OF HEALTH

https://www.training.nih.gov/programs/ugsp

NIH UNDERGRADUATE SCHOLARSHIP PROGRAM FOR STUDENTS FROM DISADVANTAGED BACKGROUNDS
• *See page 116*

NEXTSTEPU

http://www.nextstepu.com/

$1,500 STEM SCHOLARSHIP
• *See page 120*

THE SOCIETY FOR THE SCIENTIFIC STUDY OF SEXUALITY

http://www.sexscience.org/

THE SOCIETY FOR THE SCIENTIFIC STUDY OF SEXUALITY STUDENT RESEARCH GRANT
• *See page 120*

WILLIAMS LAW GROUP

https://familylawyersnewjersey.com/

WILLIAMS LAW GROUP OPPORTUNITY TO GROW SCHOLARSHIP
• *See page 139*

BIOLOGY

101ST AIRBORNE DIVISION ASSOCIATION

http://www.screamingeaglefoundation.org/

AL & WILLIAMARY VISTE SCHOLARSHIP
• *See page 114*

AIST FOUNDATION

http://www.aistfoundation.org/

ASSOCIATION FOR IRON AND STEEL TECHNOLOGY OHIO VALLEY CHAPTER SCHOLARSHIP
Scholarship of $1000 per year for up to four years provided that applicant continues to meet requirements and reapplies for scholarship. Applicant must be a dependent of Ohio Valley Chapter member, or student or Young Professional member. Must attend or plan to attend an accredited school full-time and pursue a degree in any technological field, including engineering, physics, computer sciences, chemistry or other fields approved by the scholarship committee.
Academic Fields/Career Goals: Biology; Computer Science/Data Processing; Electrical Engineering/Electronics; Engineering-Related Technologies; Engineering/Technology; Materials Science, Engineering, and Metallurgy; Physical Sciences.
Award: Scholarship for use in freshman, sophomore, junior, or senior years; not renewable. *Number:* 1–2. *Amount:* $1000.
Eligibility Requirements: Applicant must be enrolled or expecting to enroll full-time at a four-year institution or university. Applicant or parent of applicant must be member of Association for Iron and Steel Technology. Applicant must have 3.0 GPA or higher. Available to U.S. and non-U.S. citizens.
Application Requirements: Application form, essay, recommendations or references, resume, test scores, transcript. *Deadline:* March 31.
Contact: Jeff McKain, Scholarship Chairman
AIST Foundation
11451 Reading Road
Cincinnati, OH 45241
Phone: 724-776-6040
E-mail: jeff.mckain@xtek.com

ALBERTA HERITAGE SCHOLARSHIP FUND

http://www.alis.alberta.ca/

ABORIGINAL HEALTH CAREERS BURSARY
Award between CAN$2000 and CAN$11,000 for aboriginal students in Alberta, entering their second or subsequent year of postsecondary education in a health field. Must be Indian, Inuit, or Metis students who have been living in Alberta for at least the last three years, and are enrolled full-time at the technical, college, or university level. Students are selected on the basis of financial need, previous academic record, program of study, involvement in the aboriginal community, and experience in the health care field. For additional information and an application, visit website http://alis.alberta.ca.
Academic Fields/Career Goals: Biology; Dental Health/Services; Health Administration; Health and Medical Sciences; Nursing; Therapy/Rehabilitation.
Award: Scholarship for use in sophomore, junior, or senior years; not renewable.

Eligibility Requirements: Applicant must be Canadian citizen; American Indian/Alaska Native; enrolled or expecting to enroll full-time at a two-year or four-year or technical institution or university and resident of Alberta.
Application Requirements: Application form, essay, financial need analysis, proof of Aboriginal status, recommendations or references, transcript. *Deadline:* May 1.
Contact: Scholarship Committee
Phone: 780-427-8640
E-mail: scholarships@gov.ab.ca

AMERICAN ASSOCIATION OF BLOOD BANKS-SBB SCHOLARSHIP AWARDS

http://www.aabb.org/

AABB-FENWAL SCHOLARSHIP AWARD
Scholarship for an individual enrolled, accepted for enrollment in, or having recently completed a program leading to Specialist in Blood Banking certification in an AABB-accredited institution.
Academic Fields/Career Goals: Biology.
Award: Scholarship for use in freshman, sophomore, junior, senior, or graduate years; not renewable. *Number:* 2.
Eligibility Requirements: Applicant must be enrolled or expecting to enroll full- or part-time at an institution or university. Available to U.S. citizens.
Application Requirements: Application form. *Deadline:* June 1.
Contact: Scholarship Coordinator
E-mail: rsinger@aabb.org

AMERICAN INDIAN SCIENCE AND ENGINEERING SOCIETY

http://www.aises.org/

A.T. ANDERSON MEMORIAL SCHOLARSHIP PROGRAM
• *See page 121*

AMERICAN PHYSIOLOGICAL SOCIETY

http://www.the-aps.org

BARBARA A. HORWITZ AND JOHN M. HOROWITZ UNDERGRADUATE RESEARCH AWARDS
• *See page 114*

AMERICAN SOCIETY OF AGRICULTURAL AND BIOLOGICAL ENGINEERS

http://www.asabe.org/

WILLIAM J. ADAMS, JR. AND MARIJANE E. ADAMS SCHOLARSHIP
• *See page 105*

AMERICAN SOCIETY OF ICHTHYOLOGISTS AND HERPETOLOGISTS

http://www.asih.org/

GAIGE FUND AWARD
Funds are used to provide support to young herpetologists for museum or laboratory study, travel, fieldwork, or any other activity that will effectively enhance their professional careers and their contributions to the science of herpetology. Applicants must be members of ASIH and be enrolled for an advanced degree. Visit website at http://www.asih.org for additional information.
Academic Fields/Career Goals: Biology.
Award: Grant for use in freshman, sophomore, junior, senior, or graduate years; not renewable. *Number:* 5–10. *Amount:* $400–$1000.

Eligibility Requirements: Applicant must be enrolled or expecting to enroll full-time at a four-year institution or university. Applicant or parent of applicant must be member of American Society of Ichthyologists and Herpetologists. Available to U.S. and non-U.S. citizens.

Application Requirements: Application form, financial need analysis, recommendations or references. *Deadline:* March 1.

Contact: Maureen Donnelly, Secretary
Phone: 305-348-1235
Fax: 305-348-1986
E-mail: asih@fiu.edu

RANEY FUND AWARD

Applications are solicited for grants awarded from the Raney Fund for ichthyology. Funds are used to provide support for young ichthyologists for museums or laboratory study, travel, fieldwork, or any activity that will effectively enhance their professional careers and their contributions to the sciences of ichthyology. Must be a member of ASIH and be enrolled for an advanced degree. Visit website at http://www.asih.org for additional information.

Academic Fields/Career Goals: Biology.

Award: Grant for use in freshman, sophomore, junior, senior, or graduate years; not renewable. *Number:* 5–10. *Amount:* $400–$1000.

Eligibility Requirements: Applicant must be enrolled or expecting to enroll full-time at a four-year institution or university. Applicant or parent of applicant must be member of American Society of Ichthyologists and Herpetologists. Available to U.S. and non-U.S. citizens.

Application Requirements: Application form, financial need analysis, recommendations or references. *Deadline:* March 1.

Contact: Maureen Donnelly, Secretary
Phone: 305-348-1235
Fax: 305-348-1986
E-mail: asih@fiu.edu

ARRL FOUNDATION INC.

http://www.arrl.org/

YASME FOUNDATION SCHOLARSHIP

Multiple awards available to students who have been licensed for at least two years and currently hold a general class or higher amateur radio license. Preference given to high school applicants ranked in top 5-10% of class and college students ranked in top 10% of class who are active in their local amateur radio club and community service activities. Must be studying sciences or engineering at an accredited four-year college or university. Previous awardees seeking renewal must submit a new application and transcript each year.

Academic Fields/Career Goals: Biology; Engineering-Related Technologies; Engineering/Technology; Natural Sciences; Science, Technology, and Society.

Award: Scholarship for use in freshman, sophomore, junior, or senior years; not renewable. *Amount:* $3000.

Eligibility Requirements: Applicant must be enrolled or expecting to enroll full- or part-time at a four-year institution or university and must have an interest in amateur radio. Applicant must have 3.5 GPA or higher. Available to U.S. citizens.

Application Requirements: Application form. *Deadline:* January 31.

Contact: Ms. Mary Hobart, Secretary
Phone: 860-594-0397
E-mail: k1mmh@arrl.org

ASSOCIATION FOR WOMEN GEOSCIENTISTS (AWG)

http://www.awg.org/

AWG UNDERGRADUATE EXCELLENCE IN PALEONTOLOGY AWARD
• *See page 123*

ASSOCIATION OF CALIFORNIA WATER AGENCIES

http://www.acwa.com/

ASSOCIATION OF CALIFORNIA WATER AGENCIES SCHOLARSHIPS
• *See page 123*

CLAIR A. HILL SCHOLARSHIP
• *See page 123*

ASSOCIATION OF STATE DAM SAFETY OFFICIALS (ASDSO)

http://www.DamSafety.org

ASSOCIATION OF STATE DAM SAFETY OFFICIALS (ASDSO) SENIOR UNDERGRADUATE SCHOLARSHIP

Scholarships will be awarded for the 2018/2019 school year and have ranged from $5,000 to $10,000 in recent years. Successful recipients must be U.S. citizens and enrolled full-time at the senior level (during the 2018/2019 school year) in an accredited civil engineering program, or in a related field as determined by ASDSO, and must demonstrate an interest in pursuing a career in hydraulics, hydrology or geotechnical disciplines, or in another discipline related to the design, construction and operation of dams. Undergraduate students planning to graduate in May/December 2019 will be eligible for the scholarship. Applicants must have a cumulative grade point average of 2.5 for the first three years of college and be recommended by their academic advisor. The basis for selection will generally follow these guidelines: academic scholarship, financial need, work experience/activities, essay. Announcement of successful candidates will be made in July 2018.
https://damsafety.org/apply-scholarship

Academic Fields/Career Goals: Biology; Civil Engineering; Computer Science/Data Processing; Construction Engineering/Management; Earth Science; Electrical Engineering/Electronics; Energy and Power Engineering; Engineering-Related Technologies; Engineering/Technology; Environmental Science; Geography; Materials Science, Engineering, and Metallurgy; Mechanical Engineering; Natural Resources; Natural Sciences; Science, Technology, and Society; Surveying, Surveying Technology, Cartography, or Geographic Information Science; Urban and Regional Planning.

Award: Scholarship for use in senior year; not renewable. *Number:* 1–3. *Amount:* $5000–$10,000.

Eligibility Requirements: Applicant must be enrolled or expecting to enroll full-time at a four-year institution or university. Available to U.S. citizens.

Application Requirements: Application form, essay, financial need analysis. *Deadline:* March 30.

Contact: Student Outreach Coordinator
Association of State Dam Safety Officials (ASDSO)
239 S Limestone
Lexington, KY 40508
Phone: 859-550-2788
Fax: 859-550-2795
E-mail: info@damsafety.org

ASSOCIATION ON AMERICAN INDIAN AFFAIRS, INC.

http://www.indian-affairs.org/

ELIZABETH AND SHERMAN ASCHE MEMORIAL SCHOLARSHIP FUND
• *See page 106*

ASTRONAUT SCHOLARSHIP FOUNDATION

http://www.astronautscholarship.org/

ASTRONAUT SCHOLARSHIP FOUNDATION
• *See page 123*

BARRY GOLDWATER SCHOLARSHIP AND EXCELLENCE IN EDUCATION FOUNDATION

https://goldwater.scholarsapply.org

BARRY M. GOLDWATER SCHOLARSHIP AND EXCELLENCE IN EDUCATION PROGRAM
• *See page 123*

BHW GROUP

https://thebhwgroup.com/

BHW WOMEN IN STEM SCHOLARSHIP
• *See page 124*

B.O.G. PEST CONTROL

http://www.bogpestcontrol.com/

B.O.G. PEST CONTROL SCHOLARSHIP FUND

B.O.G. Pest Control has established a merit-based scholarship fund for individuals seeking undergraduate or graduate level education in chemistry, chemical engineering, biology, environmental studies or related fields. The winner of the scholarship will be a person who demonstrates academic excellence, as well as a passion for the pursuit of further study in environmental education at an accredited college or university.

Academic Fields/Career Goals: Biology; Chemical Engineering; Earth Science; Environmental Science; Natural Resources; Natural Sciences.

Award: Scholarship for use in freshman, sophomore, junior, senior, or graduate years; not renewable. *Number:* 1. *Amount:* $1000.

Eligibility Requirements: Applicant must be enrolled or expecting to enroll full-time at a four-year institution or university. Available to U.S. citizens.

Application Requirements: Application form, essay. *Deadline:* March 15.

Contact: Angela Hieronimus
B.O.G. Pest Control
645 Central Ave E
Edgewater, MD 21037
Phone: 410-867-1002
E-mail: ahieronimus@bladesofgreen.com

BROWN AND CALDWELL

http://www.brownandcaldwell.com

ECKENFELDER SCHOLARSHIP

Dr. Wesley Eckenfelder, Jr.'s career as an environmental trailblazer spanned more than 50 years, during which time he trained thousands of graduate students and professionals in the science and art of industrial wastewater treatment. To honor his dedication to the environmental industry, we offer a $5,000 Dr. Wesley Eckenfelder, Jr. Scholarship to support students who are interested in pursuing a career in the environmental profession. Applicant must be a United States citizen or permanent resident; a full-time student enrolled in his/her junior, senior, or graduate program at an accredited college/university; must have declared a major in civil, chemical or environmental engineering, or one of the environmental sciences (e.g. geology, hydrogeology, ecology); must have a cumulative GPA of 3.0 or higher on a 4.0 scale (or equivalent on a 5.0 scale). All candidates must submit with a completed application; resume; an essay of 250 words minimum, "Tell us about a personal experience that influenced your decision to focus on environmental studies"; two written recommendations, with at least one from a university official (e.g. advisor, professor); and an official transcript of your academic record. Scholarship funds my only be used for university/college billed expenses such as tuition. We will be accepting 2018 applications starting at the end of March 2018. Applications will closed and materials must be postmarked by April 30th 2018 to be considered for our 2018 scholarships.

Academic Fields/Career Goals: Biology; Chemical Engineering; Civil Engineering; Construction Engineering/Management; Earth Science; Electrical Engineering/Electronics; Energy and Power Engineering; Engineering-Related Technologies; Engineering/Technology; Environmental Health; Environmental Science; Geography; Hydrology; Marine/Ocean Engineering; Mechanical Engineering; Meteorology/Atmospheric Science; Natural Resources; Natural Sciences; Oceanography; Paper and Pulp Engineering; Science, Technology, and Society; Surveying, Surveying Technology, Cartography, or Geographic Information Science.

Award: Scholarship for use in junior, senior, graduate, or postgraduate years; not renewable. *Number:* 1. *Amount:* $5000.

Eligibility Requirements: Applicant must be enrolled or expecting to enroll full-time at a four-year institution or university. Applicant must have 3.0 GPA or higher. Available to U.S. citizens.

Application Requirements: Application form, essay. *Deadline:* April 30.

Contact: BC Scholarships Committee
Brown and Caldwell
1527 Cole Boulevard
Suite 300
Lakewood, CO 80401
E-mail: Scholarships@brwncald.com

MINORITY SCHOLARSHIP PROGRAM

At Brown and Caldwell, we value diversity in the workplace, supporting organizations like the National Society of Black Engineers and the Society for Hispanic Professional Engineers. We also offer a $5,000 Minority Scholarship to support students who identify as minorities and are interested in pursuing a career in the environmental profession. Applicant must be a United States citizen or permanent resident; a full-time student enrolled in his/her junior, senior, or graduate program at an accredited college/university; declared a major in civil, chemical, or environmental engineering or one of the environmental sciences (e.g. geology, hydrogeology, ecology); have a cumulative GPA of 3.0 or higher on a 4.0 scale (or equivalent on a 5.0 scale); identify as a member of a minority group (e.g. African American, Hispanic, Asian or Pacific American or Alaska Native). All candidates must submit with a completed application; resume; an essay of 250 words minimum, "Tell us about a personal experience that influenced your decision to focus on environmental studies"; two written recommendations, with at least one from a university official (e.g. advisor, professor); and an official transcript of your academic record. Scholarship funds my only be used for university/college billed expenses such as tuition. We will be accepting 2018 applications starting at the end of March 2018. Applications will closed and materials must be postmarked by April 30th 2018 to be considered for our scholarships

Academic Fields/Career Goals: Biology; Chemical Engineering; Civil Engineering; Construction Engineering/Management; Earth Science; Electrical Engineering/Electronics; Energy and Power Engineering; Engineering-Related Technologies; Engineering/Technology; Environmental Health; Environmental Science; Geography; Hydrology; Marine/Ocean Engineering; Materials Science, Engineering, and Metallurgy; Mechanical Engineering; Meteorology/Atmospheric Science; Natural Resources; Natural Sciences; Oceanography; Paper and Pulp Engineering; Surveying, Surveying Technology, Cartography, or Geographic Information Science.

Award: Scholarship for use in junior, senior, graduate, or postgraduate years; not renewable. *Number:* 1. *Amount:* $5000.

Eligibility Requirements: Applicant must be American Indian/Alaska Native, Asian/Pacific Islander, Black (non-Hispanic), Hispanic and enrolled or expecting to enroll full-time at a four-year institution or university. Applicant must have 3.0 GPA or higher. Available to U.S. citizens.

Application Requirements: Application form, essay. *Deadline:* April 30.

Contact: BC Scholarships Committee
Brown and Caldwell
1527 Cole Boulevard
Suite 300
Lakewood, CO 80401
E-mail: scholarships@brwncald.com

CALAVERAS BIG TREES ASSOCIATION

https://bigtrees.org/

EMILY M. HEWITT MEMORIAL SCHOLARSHIP

Scholarship to provide a monetary award of $1,500 for a promising upper division or graduate student who shows a commitment to communicate and interpret a love of nature and an understanding of the need to practice conservation. Eligibility for application is extended to any student or graduate student enrolled full-time in an accredited California post-secondary educational institution whose educational career goals clearly coincide with Emily Hewitt's interest in communicating and interpreting nature's wonder. Students pursuing degrees in environmental protection, forestry, wildlife and fisheries, biology, parks and recreation, park management, environmental law and public policy, environmental art, and California history are encouraged to apply. Dedication to the ideals of the scholarship's honoree will be considered at least as important as financial need in making the award.

Academic Fields/Career Goals: Biology; Earth Science; Environmental Science; Fire Sciences; Marine Biology; Marine/Ocean Engineering; Natural Resources; Natural Sciences; Oceanography; Recreation, Parks, Leisure Studies.

Award: Scholarship for use in freshman, sophomore, junior, senior, graduate, or postgraduate years; renewable. *Number:* 5. *Amount:* $1500.

Eligibility Requirements: Applicant must be enrolled or expecting to enroll full-time at a two-year or four-year institution or university and studying in California. Available to U.S. and non-U.S. citizens.

Application Requirements: Application form, essay, portfolio. *Deadline:* April 15.

Contact: Sue Hoffmann, Administrative Officer
Calaveras Big Trees Association
PO Box 1196
Arnold, CA 95223
Phone: 209-795-1196
Fax: 209-795-6680
E-mail: cbta@bigtrees.org

CARDS AGAINST HUMANITY

https://cardsagainsthumanity.com/

SCIENCE AMBASSADOR SCHOLARSHIP

• *See page 124*

CUSHMAN FOUNDATION FOR FORAMINIFERAL RESEARCH

http://www.cushmanfoundation.org/index.php

LOEBLICH AND TAPPAN STUDENT RESEARCH AWARD

Research award given to both graduate and undergraduates interested in foraminiferal research. The maximum dollar value for the award is $2000.

Academic Fields/Career Goals: Biology; Marine Biology.

Award: Grant for use in freshman, sophomore, junior, senior, or graduate years; not renewable. *Number:* 1–57. *Amount:* $100–$2000.

Eligibility Requirements: Applicant must be enrolled or expecting to enroll full- or part-time at a four-year institution or university. Available to U.S. and non-U.S. citizens.

Application Requirements: Proposal for research, recommendations or references, resume. *Deadline:* September 15.

Contact: Jennifer Jett, Secretary and Treasurer
Cushman Foundation for Foraminiferal Research
MRC-121 Department of Paleobiology
PO Box 37012
Washington, DC 20013-7012
E-mail: jettje@si.edu

DISTIL NETWORKS

http://www.distilnetworks.com

WOMEN FORWARD IN TECHNOLOGY SCHOLARSHIP PROGRAM

• *See page 124*

EAA AVIATION FOUNDATION, INC.

http://www.eaa.org/

PAYZER SCHOLARSHIP

• *See page 153*

THE EXPERT INSTITUTE

https://www.theexpertinstitute.com

ANNUAL HEALTHCARE AND LIFE SCIENCES SCHOLARSHIP

The scholarship is available to students who are interested in or are already pursuing an undergraduate or graduate-level degree in healthcare or the life sciences. Applicants must have a 3.0 GPA or higher, and must also submit a 1,000-2,000 word essay on how their specialized knowledge could be applied to improving the practice of law.

Academic Fields/Career Goals: Biology; Dental Health/Services; Health and Medical Sciences; Marine Biology; Neurobiology; Nursing; Oncology; Optometry; Public Health; Therapy/Rehabilitation.

Award: Scholarship for use in freshman, sophomore, junior, senior, or graduate years; not renewable. *Number:* 1. *Amount:* $1000.

Eligibility Requirements: Applicant must be enrolled or expecting to enroll full- or part-time at a two-year or four-year or technical institution or university. Applicant must have 3.0 GPA or higher. Available to U.S. and non-U.S. citizens.

Application Requirements: Essay. *Deadline:* December 31.

Contact: Mr. Joseph O'Neill, Associate Director, Marketing
The Expert Institute
48 Wall Street
32nd Floor
New York, NY 10005
Phone: 646-216-2339
E-mail: joe@theexpertinstitute.com

FEDERATED GARDEN CLUBS OF CONNECTICUT

http://www.ctgardenclubs.org/

FEDERATED GARDEN CLUBS OF CONNECTICUT INC. SCHOLARSHIPS

One-time award for Connecticut residents entering his or her junior, senior, or graduate year at a Connecticut college or university and pursuing studies in gardening, landscaping, or biology. Minimum 3.0 GPA. Ph.D. candidates are not eligible.

Academic Fields/Career Goals: Biology; Horticulture/Floriculture; Landscape Architecture.

Award: Scholarship for use in junior, senior, or graduate years; not renewable. *Number:* 2–5. *Amount:* $1000–$5000.

Eligibility Requirements: Applicant must be enrolled or expecting to enroll full-time at a four-year institution or university; resident of Connecticut and studying in Connecticut. Applicant must have 3.0 GPA or higher. Available to U.S. citizens.

Application Requirements: Application form, driver's license, financial need analysis, recommendations or references, self-addressed stamped envelope with application, test scores, transcript. *Deadline:* July 1.

Contact: Barbara Bomblad, Office Manager
Phone: 203-488-5528
Fax: 203-488-5528 Ext. 51
E-mail: fgcctoff@hotmail.com

FOUNDATION FOR SCIENCE AND DISABILITY

http://stemd.org/

GRANTS FOR DISABLED GRADUATE STUDENTS IN THE SCIENCES
• *See page 106*

GARDEN CLUB OF AMERICA

http://www.gcamerica.org/

ZELLER SUMMER SCHOLARSHIP IN MEDICINAL BOTANY

One $3,000 award open to undergraduate students enrolled in an accredited U.S. college or university for study or work during the summer following the freshman, sophomore, junior, or senior year. Program aims to encourage students to expand their knowledge of medicinal botany by pursuing summer study in various projects, courses, and/or internship with supervision and structure.

Academic Fields/Career Goals: Biology.

Award: Scholarship for use in sophomore, junior, or senior years; not renewable. *Number:* 1. *Amount:* $3000.

Eligibility Requirements: Applicant must be enrolled or expecting to enroll full-time at a four-year institution or university. Available to U.S. citizens.

Application Requirements: Application form, essay. *Deadline:* February 1.

Contact: Garden Club of America
Garden Club of America
14 East 60th Street
New York, NY 10022-1006
Phone: 212-753-8287
E-mail: scholarshipapplications@gcamerica.org

GREATER KANAWHA VALLEY FOUNDATION

http://www.tgkvf.org/

MATH AND SCIENCE SCHOLARSHIP

Renewable scholarship for students pursuing a degree in math, science, or engineering at any accredited college or university. For purposes of this fund, science shall include chemistry, physics, biology, and other scientific fields. Must be a resident of West Virginia.

Academic Fields/Career Goals: Biology; Engineering/Technology; Mathematics; Physical Sciences.

Award: Scholarship for use in freshman, sophomore, junior, or senior years; renewable. *Amount:* $1000.

Eligibility Requirements: Applicant must be enrolled or expecting to enroll full-time at a four-year institution or university and resident of West Virginia. Available to U.S. citizens.

Application Requirements: Application form, essay, recommendations or references, transcript. *Deadline:* January 15.

Contact: Susan Hoover, Scholarship Program Officer
Greater Kanawha Valley Foundation
900 Lee Street East, 16th Floor
Charleston, WV 25301
Phone: 304-346-3620
E-mail: shoover@tgkvf.org

GREAT MINDS IN STEM

http://www.greatmindsinstem.org

HENAAC SCHOLARSHIP PROGRAM
• *See page 115*

HERB SOCIETY OF AMERICA, WESTERN RESERVE UNIT

http://www.westernreserveherbsociety.org/

HORTICULTURE SCHOLARSHIP FROM FRANCIS SYLVIA ZVERINA
• *See page 101*

HORTICULTURE SCHOLARSHIP OF THE WESTERN RESERVE HERB SOCIETY
• *See page 101*

INDEPENDENT LABORATORIES INSTITUTE SCHOLARSHIP ALLIANCE

http://www.acil.org/

INDEPENDENT LABORATORIES INSTITUTE SCHOLARSHIP ALLIANCE

Scholarships are given to full-time undergraduate juniors or seniors, or graduate students majoring in the physical sciences: physics, chemistry, geology, engineering, biology or environmental science.

Academic Fields/Career Goals: Biology; Chemical Engineering; Civil Engineering; Earth Science; Electrical Engineering/Electronics; Engineering-Related Technologies; Engineering/Technology; Environmental Science; Fire Sciences; Materials Science, Engineering, and Metallurgy; Mechanical Engineering; Physical Sciences.

Award: Scholarship for use in freshman, sophomore, junior, senior, or graduate years; not renewable. *Number:* 1–2. *Amount:* $1000–$2000.

Eligibility Requirements: Applicant must be enrolled or expecting to enroll full-time at a four-year institution or university. Available to U.S. citizens.

Application Requirements: Application form, recommendations or references, resume, transcript. *Deadline:* April 7.

Contact: Janet Allen, Senior Administrator
Independent Laboratories Institute Scholarship Alliance
1629 K Street, NW, Suite 400
Washington, DC 20006-1633
Phone: 202-887-5872 Ext. 204
Fax: 202-887-0021
E-mail: jallen@acil.org

INDIAN HEALTH SERVICES, UNITED STATES DEPARTMENT OF HEALTH AND HUMAN SERVICES

http://www.ihs.gov/scholarship

HEALTH PROFESSIONS PREPARATORY SCHOLARSHIP PROGRAM
• *See page 165*

INDIAN HEALTH SERVICE HEALTH PROFESSIONS PRE-GRADUATE SCHOLARSHIPS
• *See page 125*

THE JACKSON LABORATORY

https://www.jax.org

THE JACKSON LABORATORY COLLEGE SCHOLARSHIP PROGRAM
• *See page 126*

KENTUCKY ENERGY AND ENVIRONMENT CABINET

http://dep.ky.gov

ENVIRONMENTAL PROTECTION SCHOLARSHIP

Renewable awards for college juniors, seniors, and graduate students for in-state tuition, fees, room and board, and a book allowance at a Kentucky public university. Minimum 3.0 GPA required. Must work full-time for the Kentucky Department for Environmental Protection upon graduation (six months for each semester of scholarship support received). Interview required. Program not generally appropriate for non-residents.

Academic Fields/Career Goals: Biology; Chemical Engineering; Civil Engineering; Earth Science; Environmental Science; Hydrology; Mechanical Engineering; Natural Sciences.

Award: Scholarship for use in junior, senior, or graduate years; renewable. *Number:* 1–4. *Amount:* $10,000–$13,000.

Eligibility Requirements: Applicant must be enrolled or expecting to enroll full-time at a four-year institution or university; resident of Kentucky and studying in Kentucky. Applicant must have 3.0 GPA or higher. Available to U.S. citizens.

Application Requirements: Application form, essay, interview. *Deadline:* February 15.

Contact: James Kipp, Scholarship Program Coordinator
Kentucky Energy and Environment Cabinet
233 Mining/Mineral Resources Building
Lexington, KY 40506-0107
Phone: 859-257-1299
E-mail: kipp@uky.edu

KETAMINE CLINICS OF LOS ANGELES

http://www.ketamineclinics.com/

KETAMINE CLINICS OF LOS ANGELES SCHOLARSHIP PROGRAM

• See page 165

LABROOTS INC.

http://www.LabRoots.com

LABROOTS STEM SCHOLARSHIP

• See page 116

THE LAND CONSERVANCY OF NEW JERSEY

http://www.tlc-nj.org/

ROGERS FAMILY SCHOLARSHIP

The Scholarship Program is administered by the Board of Trustees of The Land Conservancy of New Jersey and is awarded annually to deserving individuals who plan careers in environmental science, natural resource management, conservation, horticulture, park administration, or a related field. An applicant must be a student in good standing with at least 15 credits completed, have an academic average equivalent to a 3.0 or higher, be a resident of New Jersey and considering a career in New Jersey that is consistent with the goals of the Conservancy. Selected finalists will have to attend an interview in late May or early June. Scholarship funds are paid only directly to the institution in which the recipient is enrolled, not to the individual.

Academic Fields/Career Goals: Biology; Earth Science; Environmental Science; Geography; Horticulture/Floriculture; Hydrology; Marine Biology; Meteorology/Atmospheric Science; Natural Resources; Oceanography; Physical Sciences; Recreation, Parks, Leisure Studies; Surveying, Surveying Technology, Cartography, or Geographic Information Science; Urban and Regional Planning.

Award: Scholarship for use in sophomore, junior, senior, or graduate years; not renewable. *Number:* 1. *Amount:* $7500.

Eligibility Requirements: Applicant must be enrolled or expecting to enroll full-time at a four-year institution or university and resident of New Jersey. Applicant must have 3.0 GPA or higher. Available to U.S. citizens.

Application Requirements: Application form, essay. *Deadline:* April 1.

Contact: Scholarship Program
The Land Conservancy of New Jersey
19 Boonton Avenue
Boonton, NJ 07005
Phone: 973-541-1010 Ext. 10
E-mail: info@tlc-nj.org

RUSSELL W. MYERS SCHOLARSHIP

The Scholarship Program is administered by the Board of Trustees of The Land Conservancy of New Jersey and is awarded annually to deserving individuals who plan careers in environmental science, natural resource management, conservation, horticulture, park administration, or a related field. An applicant must be a student in good standing with at least 15 credits completed, have an academic average equivalent to a 3.0 or higher, be a resident of New Jersey and considering a career in New Jersey that is consistent with the goals of the Conservancy. Selected finalists will have to attend an interview with The Committee in late May or early June. Scholarship funds are paid only directly to the institution where the recipient is enrolled, not to the individual.

Academic Fields/Career Goals: Biology; Earth Science; Environmental Science; Hydrology; Landscape Architecture; Marine Biology; Natural Resources; Oceanography; Recreation, Parks, Leisure Studies; Surveying, Surveying Technology, Cartography, or Geographic Information Science; Urban and Regional Planning.

Award: Scholarship for use in sophomore, junior, senior, or graduate years; not renewable. *Number:* 1. *Amount:* $7500.

Eligibility Requirements: Applicant must be enrolled or expecting to enroll full-time at a four-year institution or university and resident of New Jersey. Applicant must have 3.0 GPA or higher. Available to U.S. citizens.

Application Requirements: Application form, essay. *Deadline:* April 1.

Contact: Scholarship Program
The Land Conservancy of New Jersey
19 Boonton Avenue
Boonton, NJ 07005
Phone: 973-541-1010

LAW OFFICES OF PROSPER SHAKED

https://www.prosperlaw.com/

PROSPER SHAKED SCHOLARSHIP FOR FUTURE MEDICAL PROFESSIONALS

• See page 166

LOUISIANA OFFICE OF STUDENT FINANCIAL ASSISTANCE

http://www.osfa.la.gov/

ROCKEFELLER STATE WILDLIFE SCHOLARSHIP

For college undergraduates with a minimum of 60 credit hours who are majoring in Forestry, Wildlife, or Marine Science, and for college graduate students who are majoring in Forestry, Wildlife, or Marine Science. College undergraduates must have a grade point average of at least 2.50 to apply. College graduate students must have a grade point average of at least 3.00 in order to apply. Renewable up to three years as an undergraduate and two years as a graduate student.

Academic Fields/Career Goals: Biology; Marine Biology; Marine/Ocean Engineering; Natural Resources; Oceanography.

Award: Scholarship for use in freshman, sophomore, junior, senior, graduate, or postgraduate years; renewable. *Number:* 20–30. *Amount:* $2000–$3000.

Eligibility Requirements: Applicant must be enrolled or expecting to enroll full-time at a four-year institution or university; resident of Louisiana and studying in Louisiana. Applicant must have 2.5 GPA or higher. Available to U.S. citizens.

Application Requirements: Application form, application form may be submitted online (http://www.osfa.la.gov for Rockefeller app), FAFSA, test scores, transcript. *Deadline:* July 1.

Contact: Bonnie Lavergne, Public Information
Louisiana Office of Student Financial Assistance
PO Box 91202
Baton Rouge, LA 70821-9202
Phone: 800-259-5626 Ext. 7714
Fax: 225-612-6508
E-mail: custserv@osfa.la.gov

MEDICAL SCRUBS COLLECTION

http://medicalscrubscollection.com

MEDICAL SCRUBS COLLECTION SCHOLARSHIP
• *See page 120*

MICHAEL MOODY FITNESS

http://www.michaelmoodyfitness.com/

MICHAEL MOODY FITNESS SCHOLARSHIP
• *See page 166*

NASA IDAHO SPACE GRANT CONSORTIUM

http://www.idahospacegrant.org

NASA IDAHO SPACE GRANT CONSORTIUM SCHOLARSHIP PROGRAM
• *See page 126*

NASA/MARYLAND SPACE GRANT CONSORTIUM

http://www.mdspacegrant.org/

NASA MARYLAND SPACE GRANT CONSORTIUM UNDERGRADUATE SCHOLARSHIPS
• *See page 156*

NASA MONTANA SPACE GRANT CONSORTIUM

http://www.spacegrant.montana.edu/

MONTANA SPACE GRANT SCHOLARSHIP PROGRAM
• *See page 156*

NASA'S VIRGINIA SPACE GRANT CONSORTIUM

http://www.vsgc.odu.edu/

COMMUNITY COLLEGE STEM SCHOLARSHIPS
• *See page 126*

UNDERGRADUATE STEM RESEARCH SCHOLARSHIPS
• *See page 127*

NATIONAL COUNCIL OF STATE GARDEN CLUBS INC. SCHOLARSHIP

http://www.gardenclub.org/

NATIONAL COUNCIL OF STATE GARDEN CLUBS INC. SCHOLARSHIP
• *See page 108*

NATIONAL GARDEN CLUBS INC.

http://www.gardenclub.org/

NATIONAL GARDEN CLUBS INC. SCHOLARSHIP PROGRAM
• *See page 109*

NATIONAL INSTITUTES OF HEALTH

https://www.training.nih.gov/programs/ugsp

NIH UNDERGRADUATE SCHOLARSHIP PROGRAM FOR STUDENTS FROM DISADVANTAGED BACKGROUNDS
• *See page 116*

NEXTSTEPU

http://www.nextstepu.com/

$1,500 STEM SCHOLARSHIP
• *See page 120*

OREGON STUDENT ASSISTANCE COMMISSION

https://oregonstudentaid.gov/

OREGON FOUNDATION FOR BLACKTAIL DEER SCHOLARSHIP
• *See page 117*

ROBERTS SCHOLARSHIP

One-time award for graduates of Oregon public high schools attending four-year public and nonprofit colleges at least half-time. This award is not open to graduating high school seniors. Preference given to Oregon state residents majoring in the biological and chemical sciences and pursing careers in environmental toxicology and chemistry. Must have completed 1+ year of college-level science by the March scholarship deadline. Financial need may or may not be considered.

Academic Fields/Career Goals: Biology; Environmental Science; Natural Sciences.

Award: Scholarship for use in freshman, sophomore, junior, or senior years; not renewable.

Eligibility Requirements: Applicant must be enrolled or expecting to enroll full- or part-time at a four-year institution. Applicant must have 2.5 GPA or higher. Available to U.S. citizens.

Application Requirements: Application form. *Deadline:* March 1.

Contact: Melissa Adams, Scholarship Processing Coordinator
Phone: 541-687-7409
E-mail: melissa.adams@state.or.us

SEHAR SALEHA AHMAD AND ABRAHIM EKRAMULLAH ZAFAR FOUNDATION SCHOLARSHIP
• *See page 127*

ROBERT H. MOLLOHAN FAMILY CHARITABLE FOUNDATION, INC.

http://www.mollohanfoundation.org/

HIGH TECHNOLOGY SCHOLARS PROGRAM

Scholarship for West Virginia students pursuing a technology-related career and residing in one of the following counties: Barbour, Brooke, Calhoun, Doddridge, Gilmer, Grant, Hancock, Harrison, Marion, Marshall, Mineral, Monongalia, Ohio, Pleasants, Preston, Ritchie, Taylor, Tucker, Tyler, Wetzel, Wood. Scholarship recipients become eligible for a paid internship with a West Virginia business. Students may also apply for debt-forgiveness loans up to $2000 per year.

Academic Fields/Career Goals: Biology; Chemical Engineering; Computer Science/Data Processing; Electrical Engineering/Electronics; Energy and Power Engineering; Engineering-Related Technologies; Engineering/Technology; Mechanical Engineering; Physical Sciences.

Award: Scholarship for use in freshman year; not renewable. *Number:* 1–60. *Amount:* $500–$2000.

Eligibility Requirements: Applicant must be high school student; planning to enroll or expecting to enroll full-time at a four-year institution or university and resident of West Virginia. Applicant must have 3.0 GPA or higher. Available to U.S. citizens.

Application Requirements: Application form, essay, recommendations or references, resume, test scores, transcript. *Deadline:* February 9.

Contact: Aime Shaffer, Program Manager
Robert H. Mollohan Family Charitable Foundation, Inc.
1000 Technology Drive, Suite 2000
Fairmont, WV 26554
Phone: 304-333-6783
Fax: 304-333-3900
E-mail: ashaffer@wvhtf.org

SCARLETT FAMILY FOUNDATION SCHOLARSHIP PROGRAM

http://www.scarlettfoundation.org/

SCHOLARSHIP FOR STUDENTS PURSUING A BUSINESS OR STEM DEGREE

• *See page 91*

SIGMA XI, THE SCIENTIFIC RESEARCH SOCIETY

http://www.sigmaxi.org/

SIGMA XI GRANTS-IN-AID OF RESEARCH

• *See page 110*

SOCIETY FOR INTEGRATIVE AND COMPARATIVE BIOLOGY

http://www.sicb.org/

LIBBIE H. HYMAN MEMORIAL SCHOLARSHIP

Scholarship provides assistance to students to take courses or to carry on research on invertebrates at a marine freshwater or terrestrial field station. For more information and/or an application see website, http://www.sicb.org.

Academic Fields/Career Goals: Biology; Marine Biology.

Award: Scholarship for use in senior year; not renewable. *Number:* 1. *Amount:* $750–$1200.

Eligibility Requirements: Applicant must be enrolled or expecting to enroll full- or part-time at a four-year institution or university. Available to U.S. and non-U.S. citizens.

Application Requirements: Application form, essay, financial need analysis, recommendations or references, transcript. *Deadline:* March 6.

Contact: Bruno Pernet, Chair, Scholarship Committee
Society for Integrative and Comparative Biology
California State University
Long Beach, CA 90840
Phone: 562-985-5378
Fax: 562-985-8878
E-mail: bpernet@csulb.edu

THE SOCIETY FOR THE SCIENTIFIC STUDY OF SEXUALITY

http://www.sexscience.org/

THE SOCIETY FOR THE SCIENTIFIC STUDY OF SEXUALITY STUDENT RESEARCH GRANT

• *See page 120*

SOIL AND WATER CONSERVATION SOCIETY

http://www.swcs.org

DONALD A. WILLIAMS SCHOLARSHIP SOIL CONSERVATION SCHOLARSHIP

• *See page 103*

SOIL AND WATER CONSERVATION SOCIETY-MISSOURI SHOW-ME CHAPTER

http://www.moswcs.org/

MO SHOW-ME CHAPTER SWCS SCHOLARSHIP

• *See page 111*

SOIL AND WATER CONSERVATION SOCIETY-NEW JERSEY CHAPTER

http://www.geocities.com/njswcs

EDWARD R. HALL SCHOLARSHIP

• *See page 103*

STRAIGHT NORTH

https://www.straightnorth.com/

STRAIGHT NORTH STEM SCHOLARSHIP

• *See page 92*

TKE EDUCATIONAL FOUNDATION

http://www.tke.org/

CARROL C. HALL MEMORIAL SCHOLARSHIP

• *See page 128*

UNICO FOUNDATION INC.

http://www.unico.org/

LOUISE TORRACO MEMORIAL SCHOLARSHIP FOR SCIENCE

The UNICO Foundation will grant two scholarships valued at $2,500 each, to students currently enrolled, full-time, in an accredited college/university program in the United States pursuing study of the Physical Sciences or Life Sciences. A nominee must hold United States citizenship. This program is open to applicants of all ethnicities. Candidates must reside in the home state of an active UNICO chapter. Applications must be submitted online. Candidates are to go to the UNICO National website (http://www.unico.org), and click on the Scholarship tab. There they will find complete information and submission instructions. Preference is given to candidates demonstrating financial need.

Academic Fields/Career Goals: Biology; Earth Science; Environmental Science; Marine Biology; Natural Sciences; Physical Sciences.

Award: Scholarship for use in sophomore, junior, senior, or graduate years; not renewable. *Number:* 2. *Amount:* $2500.

Eligibility Requirements: Applicant must be enrolled or expecting to enroll full-time at a four-year institution or university and resident of California, Connecticut, Delaware, Florida, Illinois, Maryland, Massachusetts, Minnesota, Missouri, New Jersey, New York, Pennsylvania, Tennessee, Virginia, Wisconsin. Applicant must have 3.0 GPA or higher. Available to U.S. citizens.

Application Requirements: Application form, essay, financial need analysis. *Deadline:* April 15.

Contact: Joan Tidona, Scholarship Director
Phone: 973-808-0035
Fax: 973-808-0043
E-mail: uniconational@unico.org

UNITED NEGRO COLLEGE FUND

http://www.uncf.org/

BASF/ALFRED CHISHOLM ENDOWED MEMORIAL SCHOLARSHIP
• *See page 93*

KIA MOTORS AMERICA STEM/SUSTAINABILITY SCHOLARSHIP

Up to $3,000 need-based scholarship for students majoring in: biology, chemistry, computer science, mathematics, statistics, physics, biomedical Science, engineering, or sustainability/environmental science. Must be a Junior or Senior enrolled full-time at a UNCF member institution and have an unmet financial need. Preference will be given to student who are permanent residents of California.

Academic Fields/Career Goals: Biology; Computer Science/Data Processing; Engineering/Technology; Environmental Science; Mathematics; Physical Sciences; Statistics.

Award: Scholarship for use in junior or senior years.

Eligibility Requirements: Applicant must be Black (non-Hispanic) and enrolled or expecting to enroll full-time at a four-year institution or university. Applicant must have 3.0 GPA or higher. Available to U.S. citizens.

Application Requirements: Application form, essay. *Deadline:* January 26.

Contact: Mary Williams, Director of Outreach and Recruitment
Phone: 800-331-2244

UNCF STEM SCHOLARS PROGRAM

Tiered tuition scholarship for talented African-American high school students who aspire to earn STEM (science, technology, engineering and mathematics) degrees and pursue careers in STEM fields. $2,500 per academic year for freshmen and sophomores, $5,000 for juniors and seniors, and an additional $5,000 for students whose academic programs require a fifth year. Must have demonstrated unmet financial need.

Academic Fields/Career Goals: Biology; Chemical Engineering; Civil Engineering; Computer Science/Data Processing; Construction Engineering/Management; Electrical Engineering/Electronics; Energy and Power Engineering; Engineering-Related Technologies; Engineering/Technology; Health and Medical Sciences; Materials Science, Engineering, and Metallurgy; Mathematics; Mechanical Engineering; Physical Sciences.

Award: Scholarship for use in freshman, sophomore, junior, or senior years; renewable. *Number:* 100.

Eligibility Requirements: Applicant must be Black (non-Hispanic) and enrolled or expecting to enroll at a four-year institution or university. Applicant must have 3.0 GPA or higher. Available to U.S. citizens.

Application Requirements: Application form, essay, financial need analysis. *Deadline:* January 16.

Contact: Mary Williams, Director of Outreach and Recruitment
Phone: 800-331-2244

UNITED STATES DEPARTMENT OF AGRICULTURE

http://www.usda.gov/

SAUL T. WILSON, JR, SCHOLARSHIP PROGRAM (STWJS)
• *See page 118*

WILLIAM HELMS SCHOLARSHIP PROGRAM (WHSP)
• *See page 112*

VERMONT SPACE GRANT CONSORTIUM

http://www.cems.uvm.edu/vsgc

VERMONT SPACE GRANT CONSORTIUM
• *See page 104*

WILSON ORNITHOLOGICAL SOCIETY

http://www.wilsonsociety.org/

GEORGE A. HALL/HAROLD F. MAYFIELD AWARD
• *See page 118*

PAUL A. STEWART AWARDS
• *See page 118*

BUSINESS/CONSUMER SERVICES

AACE INTERNATIONAL

http://www.aacei.org/

AACE INTERNATIONAL COMPETITIVE SCHOLARSHIP
• *See page 130*

THE ACTUARIAL FOUNDATION

http://www.actuarialfoundation.org

ACTUARY OF TOMORROW—STUART A. ROBERTSON MEMORIAL SCHOLARSHIP

The Actuary of Tomorrow—Stuart A. Robertson Memorial Scholarship recognizes and encourages the academic achievements of undergraduate students pursuing a career in actuarial science. Applicants must be full-time students entering as a sophomore, junior or senior, must have a minimum cumulative GPA of 3.0 (on 4.0 scale) and must have successfully completed two actuarial exams. The Actuarial Foundation will provide an award of $9,000 for education expenses at any accredited U.S. educational institution.

Academic Fields/Career Goals: Business/Consumer Services; Economics; Finance; Insurance and Actuarial Science; Mathematics; Statistics.

Award: Scholarship for use in sophomore, junior, or senior years; not renewable. *Amount:* $9000.

Eligibility Requirements: Applicant must be enrolled or expecting to enroll full-time at a four-year institution. Applicant must have 3.0 GPA or higher. Available to U.S. and non-U.S. citizens.

Application Requirements: Application form, essay. *Deadline:* June 1.

Contact: Actuary of Tomorrow, Stuart A. Robertson Memorial
Scholarship
The Actuarial Foundation
475 North Martingale Road, Suite 600
Schaumburg, IL 60173
Phone: 847-706-3535
E-mail: scholarships@actfnd.org

ADELANTE! U.S. EDUCATION LEADERSHIP FUND

http://www.adelantefund.org/

ADELANTE FUND SCHOLARSHIPS

Awards are primarily created to enhance the leadership qualities of the recipients for transition into postgraduate education, business and/or corporate America. Financial need is a factor for these awards. Minimum 3.0 GPA is required for most scholarships. Main awards are available for colleges located in the states of California, New Mexico, Arizona, Texas, Florida, Illinois, and New York. Applicants should view website for all award criteria and for scholarship application forms.

Academic Fields/Career Goals: Business/Consumer Services; Science, Technology, and Society.

Award: Scholarship for use in sophomore, junior, or senior years; renewable. *Number:* 30–52. *Amount:* $1000–$3000.

Eligibility Requirements: Applicant must be of Hispanic heritage; enrolled or expecting to enroll full-time at a two-year or four-year institution or university; studying in Arizona, California, Colorado, Florida, Illinois, New Mexico, New York, Texas and must have an interest in leadership. Applicant must have 3.0 GPA or higher. Available to U.S. citizens.

Application Requirements: Application form, application form may be submitted online (http://www.adelantefund.org), essay, financial need analysis, personal photograph, recommendations or references, resume, transcript. *Deadline:* May 30.

Contact: Miss. Sarah Ramos, Assistant Director of Student Services
Adelante! U.S. Education Leadership Fund
8415 Datapoint Drive, Suite 400
San Antonio, TX 78229
Phone: 210-692-1971
Fax: 210-692-1951
E-mail: sramos@adelantefund.org

ALICE L. HALTOM EDUCATIONAL FUND

http://www.alhef.org/

ALICE L. HALTOM EDUCATIONAL FUND

Award for students pursuing a career in information and records management. Up to $1000 for those in an associate degree program, and up to $2000 for students in a baccalaureate or advanced degree program. Students must be citizens of the United States or Canada.

Academic Fields/Career Goals: Business/Consumer Services; Computer Science/Data Processing; Health Administration; Health Information Management/Technology; Library and Information Sciences.

Award: Scholarship for use in freshman, sophomore, junior, senior, graduate, or postgraduate years; not renewable. *Number:* 5–15. *Amount:* $1000–$2000.

Eligibility Requirements: Applicant must be Canadian citizen and enrolled or expecting to enroll full- or part-time at a two-year or four-year institution or university. Available to U.S. and Canadian citizens.

Application Requirements: Application form, essay, financial need analysis. *Deadline:* May 1.

Contact: Executive Director
E-mail: contact@alhef.org

AMERICAN CONGRESS ON SURVEYING AND MAPPING

http://landsurveyorsunited.com/acsm

TRI-STATE SURVEYING AND PHOTOGRAMMETRY KRIS M. KUNZE MEMORIAL SCHOLARSHIP

One-time award of $1000 for students pursuing college-level courses in business administration or business management. Candidates, in order of priority, include professional land surveyors and certified photogrammetrists, land survey interns and students enrolled in a two- or four-year program in surveying and mapping. Must be ACSM member.

Academic Fields/Career Goals: Business/Consumer Services; Surveying, Surveying Technology, Cartography, or Geographic Information Science.

Award: Scholarship for use in freshman, sophomore, junior, or senior years; not renewable. *Number:* 1. *Amount:* $1000.

Eligibility Requirements: Applicant must be enrolled or expecting to enroll full- or part-time at a two-year or four-year institution or university. Applicant or parent of applicant must be member of American Congress on Surveying and Mapping. Available to U.S. citizens.

Application Requirements: Application form, essay, membership proof, recommendations or references, transcript. *Deadline:* October 1.

Contact: Ilse Genovese, Communications Director
American Congress on Surveying and Mapping
6 Montgomery Village Avenue, Suite 403
Gaithersburg, MD 20879
Phone: 240-632-9716 Ext. 113
Fax: 240-632-1321
E-mail: ilse.genovese@acsm.net

AMERICAN INDIAN SCIENCE AND ENGINEERING SOCIETY

http://www.aises.org/

A.T. ANDERSON MEMORIAL SCHOLARSHIP PROGRAM
• *See page 121*

AMERICAN PUBLIC TRANSPORTATION FOUNDATION

http://www.apta.com/

DAN REICHARD JR. SCHOLARSHIP

Scholarship for study towards a career in the business administration/management area of the transit industry. Must be sponsored by APTA member organization and complete internship with APTA member organization. Minimum GPA of 3.0 required.

Academic Fields/Career Goals: Business/Consumer Services; Transportation.

Award: Scholarship for use in sophomore, junior, senior, or graduate years; renewable. *Number:* 1. *Amount:* $2500.

Eligibility Requirements: Applicant must be enrolled or expecting to enroll full-time at a two-year or four-year institution or university. Applicant must have 3.0 GPA or higher. Available to U.S. and Canadian citizens.

Application Requirements: Application form, essay, financial need analysis, recommendations or references, transcript, verification of enrollment for the current semester, copy of fee schedule from the college/university. *Deadline:* June 16.

Contact: Pamela Boswell, Vice President of Program Management
American Public Transportation Foundation
1666 K Street, NW
Washington, DC 20006-1215
Phone: 202-496-4803
Fax: 202-496-2323
E-mail: pboswell@apta.com

AMERICAN WELDING SOCIETY

http://www.aws.org/

JAMES A. TURNER, JR. MEMORIAL SCHOLARSHIP

Award for a full-time student pursuing minimum four-year bachelor's degree in business that will lead to a management career in welding store operations or a welding distributorship. Applicant must be working in this field at least 10 hours per week. Submit verification of employment, a copy of proposed curriculum, and acceptance letter.

Academic Fields/Career Goals: Business/Consumer Services.

Award: Scholarship for use in freshman, sophomore, junior, or senior years; renewable.

Eligibility Requirements: Applicant must be enrolled or expecting to enroll full-time at a four-year institution or university. Available to U.S. citizens.

Application Requirements: Application form, financial need analysis. *Deadline:* February 15.

Contact: Mr. John Douglass, Associate Director, Foundation
American Welding Society
8669 NW 36 Street, Suite 130
Miami, FL 33166
Phone: 800-443-9353 Ext. 212
E-mail: jdouglass@aws.org

RICHARD J. SEIF TECHNICAL SALES AND MARKETING SCHOLARSHIP

Awarded to a college junior or senior, with a minimum 2.5 overall GPA. Applicant may be a citizen of the U.S. or Canada, and attend a U.S. or Canadian university. The recipient must be pursuing a Bachelor's degree in engineering or business with a sales or marketing emphasis. The annual award is $3,000.

Academic Fields/Career Goals: Business/Consumer Services; Engineering-Related Technologies; Engineering/Technology.

Award: Scholarship for use in junior or senior years; not renewable.

Eligibility Requirements: Applicant must be enrolled or expecting to enroll full- or part-time at a four-year institution or university. Applicant must have 3.5 GPA or higher. Available to U.S. and Canadian citizens.

Application Requirements: Application form, financial need analysis. *Deadline:* February 15.

Contact: Mr. John Douglass, Associate Director, AWS Foundation
American Welding Society
8669 NW 36 Street, #130
Miami, FL 33187
Phone: 305-443-9363 Ext. 212
E-mail: jdouglass@aws.org

AMERICAN WHOLESALE MARKETERS ASSOCIATION

http://www.awmanet.org/

RAY FOLEY MEMORIAL YOUTH EDUCATION FOUNDATION SCHOLARSHIP

Scholarship program annually offers two $5000 scholarships to deserving students. Awards are based on academic merit and a career interest in the candy/tobacco/ convenience-products wholesale industry. Must be employed by an AWMA wholesaler distributor member or be an immediate family member. Must be enrolled full-time in an undergraduate or graduate program. For details visit website http://www.awmanet.org/.

Academic Fields/Career Goals: Business/Consumer Services.

Award: Scholarship for use in freshman, sophomore, junior, senior, or graduate years; not renewable. *Number:* 2. *Amount:* $5000.

Eligibility Requirements: Applicant must be enrolled or expecting to enroll full-time at a four-year institution or university. Available to U.S. citizens.

Application Requirements: Application form, essay, recommendations or references. *Deadline:* May 21.

Contact: Kathy Trost, Manager of Education
American Wholesale Marketers Association
2750 Prosperity Avenue, Suite 530
Fairfax, VA 22031
Phone: 800-482-2962 Ext. 648
Fax: 703-573-5738
E-mail: kathyt@awmanet.org

ARRL FOUNDATION INC.

http://www.arrl.org/

WILSE MORGAN, WX7P, MEMORIAL ARRL NORTHWESTERN DIVISION SCHOLARSHIP

$1000 scholarship for a student with a General Class radio license or higher who is a resident in the ARRL Northwestern Division (Alaska, Idaho, Montana, Oregon or Washington). Must be studying engineering, medicine, science, or business. Preference given to applicants with 3.0 GPA or higher for the academic year immediately prior to application (high school or college).

Academic Fields/Career Goals: Business/Consumer Services; Engineering-Related Technologies; Engineering/Technology; Science, Technology, and Society.

Award: Scholarship for use in freshman, sophomore, junior, or senior years; not renewable. *Number:* 1. *Amount:* $1000.

Eligibility Requirements: Applicant must be enrolled or expecting to enroll full- or part-time at a two-year or four-year or technical institution or university; resident of Alaska, Idaho, Montana, Oregon, Washington and must have an interest in amateur radio. Applicant must have 3.0 GPA or higher. Available to U.S. citizens.

Application Requirements: Application form. *Deadline:* January 31.

Contact: Ms. Mary Hobart, Secretary
Phone: 860-594-0397
E-mail: k1mmh@arrl.org

AUTOMOTIVE AFTERMARKET SCHOLARSHIPS

http://www.automotivescholarships.com/

AUTOMOTIVE AFTERMARKET SCHOLARSHIPS

To receive a scholarship, applicants must be a high school graduate enrolled in a full time college-level program or an ASE/NATEF certified postsecondary automotive technical program, and planning a career in the automotive aftermarket.

Academic Fields/Career Goals: Business/Consumer Services; Marketing; Mechanical Engineering; Trade/Technical Specialties.

Award: Scholarship for use in freshman, sophomore, junior, senior, graduate, or postgraduate years; not renewable. *Amount:* $1000–$10,000.

Eligibility Requirements: Applicant must be enrolled or expecting to enroll full-time at a two-year or four-year or technical institution or university. Available to U.S. and non-U.S. citizens.

Application Requirements: Application form, essay. *Deadline:* March 31.

Contact: Jennifer Hollar, Scholarship Committee Chairman
Automotive Aftermarket Scholarships
PO Box 13966
Research Triangle Park, NC 27709-3966
Phone: 919-406-8811
E-mail: media@mema.org

AUTOMOTIVE WOMEN'S ALLIANCE FOUNDATION

http://awafoundation.org/index.php

AUTOMOTIVE WOMEN'S ALLIANCE FOUNDATION SCHOLARSHIPS

• *See page 81*

BALTIMORE CHAPTER OF THE AMERICAN MARKETING ASSOCIATION

http://www.amabaltimore.org/

UNDERGRADUATE MARKETING EDUCATION MERIT SCHOLARSHIPS

Scholarship of $3000 awarded for first place, two $1000 second place, and four $500 third place awards for full-time students in marketing. Must be attending a 4-year college or university in Maryland with credits equivalent to the status of a junior or senior as of September. Minimum 3.0 GPA required.

Academic Fields/Career Goals: Business/Consumer Services; Marketing.

Award: Scholarship for use in sophomore or junior years; not renewable. *Number:* 7. *Amount:* $500–$3000.

Eligibility Requirements: Applicant must be enrolled or expecting to enroll full-time at a four-year institution or university and studying in Maryland. Applicant must have 3.0 GPA or higher. Available to U.S. and non-U.S. citizens.

Application Requirements: Application form, test scores. *Deadline:* February 16.

Contact: Marisa O'Brien, Scholarship Committee
Phone: 410-467-2529
E-mail: scholarship@amabaltimore.org

BULKOFFICESUPPLY.COM

http://www.bulkofficesupply.com

OFFICE SUPPLY SCHOLARSHIP

• *See page 141*

CATCHING THE DREAM

http://www.catchingthedream.org/

MATH, ENGINEERING, SCIENCE, BUSINESS, EDUCATION, COMPUTERS SCHOLARSHIPS

Renewable scholarships for Native American students planning to study math, engineering, science, business, education, and computers, or presently studying in these fields. Study of social science, humanities and liberal arts also funded. Scholarships are awarded on merit and on the basis of likelihood of recipient improving the lives of Native American people. Scholarships are available nationwide.

Academic Fields/Career Goals: Business/Consumer Services; Computer Science/Data Processing; Education; Engineering/Technology; Humanities; Physical Sciences; Science, Technology, and Society; Social Sciences.

Award: Scholarship for use in freshman, sophomore, junior, senior, graduate, or postgraduate years; renewable. *Number:* 180. *Amount:* $500–$5000.

Eligibility Requirements: Applicant must be American Indian/Alaska Native and enrolled or expecting to enroll full-time at a two-year or four-year institution or university. Applicant must have 3.0 GPA or higher. Available to U.S. citizens.

Application Requirements: Application form, essay, financial need analysis, personal photograph. *Deadline:* continuous.

Contact: Joy Noll, Student Services
Catching the Dream
8200 Mountain Road, NE, Suite 103
Albuquerque, NM 87110
Phone: 505-262-2351
E-mail: nscholarsh@aol.com

NATIVE AMERICAN LEADERSHIP IN EDUCATION (NALE)

Renewable scholarships available for Native American and Alaska Native students. Must be at least one-quarter Native American from a federally recognized, state recognized, or terminated tribe. Must be U.S. citizen. Must demonstrate high academic achievement, depth of character, leadership, seriousness of purpose, and service orientation.

Academic Fields/Career Goals: Business/Consumer Services; Education; Humanities; Physical Sciences; Science, Technology, and Society.

Award: Scholarship for use in freshman, sophomore, junior, senior, graduate, or postgraduate years; renewable. *Number:* 30. *Amount:* $500–$5000.

Eligibility Requirements: Applicant must be American Indian/Alaska Native and enrolled or expecting to enroll full-time at a four-year institution or university. Applicant must have 3.0 GPA or higher. Available to U.S. citizens.

Application Requirements: Application form, essay, financial need analysis, personal photograph.

Contact: Joy Noll, Student Services
Catching the Dream
8200 Mountain Road, NE, Suite 103
Albuquerque, NM 87110
Phone: 505-262-2351
E-mail: nscholarsh@aol.com

TRIBAL BUSINESS MANAGEMENT PROGRAM (TBM)
• *See page 82*

DECA (DISTRIBUTIVE EDUCATION CLUBS OF AMERICA)

http://www.deca.org/

HARRY A. APPLEGATE SCHOLARSHIP
• *See page 83*

DELTA SIGMA PI LEADERSHIP FOUNDATION

http://www.dsp.org/

DELTA SIGMA PI UNDERGRADUATE SCHOLARSHIP

Applicant must be a member of Delta Sigma Pi in good standing with at least one full semester or quarter of college remaining in the fall following application.

Academic Fields/Career Goals: Business/Consumer Services.

Award: Scholarship for use in sophomore, junior, or senior years; not renewable. *Number:* 1–8. *Amount:* $1000.

Eligibility Requirements: Applicant must be enrolled or expecting to enroll full-time at a four-year institution or university. Applicant or parent of applicant must be member of Greek Organization. Available to U.S. and non-U.S. citizens.

Application Requirements: Application form, community service, essay, financial need analysis. *Deadline:* June 15.

Contact: Tyler Wash, Executive Vice President
Delta Sigma Pi Leadership Foundation
330 South Campus Avenue
Oxford, OH 45056
Phone: 513-523-1907
E-mail: foundation@dsp.org

DIGITAL THIRD COAST INTERNET MARKETING

http://www.digitalthirdcoast.net/

DIGITAL MARKETING SCHOLARSHIP
• *See page 96*

EASTERN STAR-GRAND CHAPTER OF CALIFORNIA

http://www.oescal.org/

SCHOLARSHIPS FOR EDUCATION, BUSINESS AND RELIGION

Scholarship of $500 to $3000 awarded to students residing in California for post-secondary study. These scholarships are awarded for the study of business, education or religion.

Academic Fields/Career Goals: Business/Consumer Services; Education; Religion/Theology.

Award: Scholarship for use in freshman, sophomore, junior, or senior years; renewable. *Amount:* $500–$3000.

Eligibility Requirements: Applicant must be enrolled or expecting to enroll full-time at a two-year or four-year or technical institution or university and resident of California. Applicant must have 3.0 GPA or higher. Available to U.S. citizens.

Application Requirements: Application form, financial need analysis, personal photograph, proof of acceptance to college or university, recommendations or references, self-addressed stamped envelope with application, transcript. *Deadline:* March 8.

Contact: Maryann Barrios, Grand Secretary
Eastern Star-Grand Chapter of California
16960 Bastanchury Road, Suite E
Yorba Linda, CA 92886-1711
Phone: 714-986-2380
Fax: 714-986-2385
E-mail: gsecretary@oescal.org

ELECTRONIC DOCUMENT SYSTEMS FOUNDATION

http://www.edsf.org/

LYNDA BABOYIAN MEMORIAL SCHOLARSHIP

$2000 award for full-time students whose academic focus includes all document management and graphic communications careers. Minimum 3.0 GPA required.

Academic Fields/Career Goals: Business/Consumer Services; Computer Science/Data Processing; Graphics/Graphic Arts/Printing.

Award: Scholarship for use in freshman, sophomore, junior, or senior years; not renewable. *Number:* 1. *Amount:* $2000.

Eligibility Requirements: Applicant must be enrolled or expecting to enroll full-time at a two-year or four-year institution or university. Applicant must have 3.0 GPA or higher. Available to U.S. and non-U.S. citizens.

Application Requirements: Application form, community service, essay. *Deadline:* May 1.

Contact: Ms. Brenda Kai, Executive Director
Phone: 817-849-1145
E-mail: brenda.kai@edsf.org

FAMILY, CAREER AND COMMUNITY LEADERS OF AMERICA-TEXAS ASSOCIATION

http://www.texasfccla.org/

FCCLA REGIONAL SCHOLARSHIPS

One-time award for graduating high school seniors enrolled in full-time program in family and consumer sciences. Must be Texas resident and should study in Texas. Must have minimum GPA of 2.5.

Academic Fields/Career Goals: Business/Consumer Services; Home Economics.

Award: Scholarship for use in freshman year; not renewable. *Number:* up to 5. *Amount:* $1000.

Eligibility Requirements: Applicant must be high school student; planning to enroll or expecting to enroll full-time at a four-year institution or university; single; resident of Texas and studying in Texas. Applicant or parent of applicant must be member of Family, Career and Community Leaders of America. Applicant must have 2.5 GPA or higher. Available to U.S. citizens.

Application Requirements: Application form, essay, recommendations or references, test scores, transcript. *Deadline:* March 1.

Contact: Staff
Family, Career and Community Leaders of America-Texas Association
1107 West 45 th
Austin, TX 78756
Phone: 512-306-0099
Fax: 512-442-7100
E-mail: fccla@texasfccla.org

FCCLA TEXAS FARM BUREAU SCHOLARSHIP

One-time award for a graduating high school senior enrolled in full-time program in family and consumer sciences. Must be a Texas resident and must study in Texas. Must have minimum GPA of 2.5. The award value is $5000.

Academic Fields/Career Goals: Business/Consumer Services; Home Economics.

Award: Scholarship for use in freshman year; not renewable. *Number:* 1. *Amount:* $1000.

Eligibility Requirements: Applicant must be high school student; planning to enroll or expecting to enroll full-time at a four-year institution or university; single; resident of Texas and studying in Texas. Applicant or parent of applicant must be member of Family, Career and Community Leaders of America. Applicant must have 2.5 GPA or higher. Available to U.S. citizens.

Application Requirements: Application form, driver's license, essay, recommendations or references, test scores, transcript. *Deadline:* March 1.

Contact: Staff
Family, Career and Community Leaders of America-Texas Association
1107 West 45th
Austin, TX 78756
Phone: 512-306-0099
Fax: 512-442-7100
E-mail: fccla@texasfccla.org

FUKUNAGA SCHOLARSHIP FOUNDATION

http://fukunagascholarship.com

FUKUNAGA SCHOLARSHIP FOUNDATION

• *See page 85*

GEORGIA GOVERNMENT FINANCE OFFICERS ASSOCIATION

http://www.ggfoa.org/

GGFOA ANNUAL COLLEGE SCHOLARSHIP

• *See page 85*

GOLDEN KEY INTERNATIONAL HONOUR SOCIETY

http://www.goldenkey.org/

BUSINESS ACHIEVEMENT AWARD

Award to members who excel in the study of business. Applicants will be asked to respond to a problem posed by an honorary member within the discipline. The response will be in the form of a professional business report. One winner will receive a $1000 award. The second place winner will receive $750 and the third place winner will receive $500.

Academic Fields/Career Goals: Business/Consumer Services.

Award: Prize for use in freshman, sophomore, junior, senior, graduate, or postgraduate years; not renewable. *Number:* 3. *Amount:* $500–$1000.

Eligibility Requirements: Applicant must be enrolled or expecting to enroll full- or part-time at a four-year institution or university. Available to U.S. and non-U.S. citizens.

Application Requirements: Application form, business-related report, entry in a contest, essay, recommendations or references, transcript. *Deadline:* March 3.

Contact: Scholarship Program Administrators
Golden Key International Honour Society
PO Box 23737
Nashville, TN 37202-3737
Phone: 800-377-2401
E-mail: scholarships@goldenkey.org

GOVERNMENT FINANCE OFFICERS ASSOCIATION

http://www.gfoa.org/

MINORITIES IN GOVERNMENT FINANCE SCHOLARSHIP

• *See page 86*

GREATER KANAWHA VALLEY FOUNDATION

http://www.tgkvf.org/

WILLARD H. ERWIN JR. MEMORIAL SCHOLARSHIP FUND

Award of $600 for West Virginia residents who are starting their junior or senior year of undergraduate or graduate studies in a business or health-care finance degree program. Must be enrolled at a college in West Virginia. Scholarships are awarded on the basis of financial need and scholastic ability.

Academic Fields/Career Goals: Business/Consumer Services; Health Administration.

Award: Scholarship for use in junior, senior, or graduate years; renewable. *Number:* 1. *Amount:* $600.

Eligibility Requirements: Applicant must be enrolled or expecting to enroll full- or part-time at a four-year institution or university; resident of West Virginia and studying in West Virginia. Available to U.S. citizens.

Application Requirements: Application form, essay, financial need analysis, recommendations or references, self-addressed stamped envelope with application, test scores, transcript. *Deadline:* January 15.

Contact: Susan Hoover, Scholarship Program Officer
Greater Kanawha Valley Foundation
900 Lee Street East, 16th Floor
Charleston, WV 25301
Phone: 304-346-3620
E-mail: shoover@tgkvf.org

GREENPAL

GREENPAL BUSINESS SCHOLARSHIP

$2000 scholarship open to any high school senior, college freshman, or sophomore who owns and operates his/her own small business, or has put together a business plan to start a business while in college. The student must enter their freshman year at an accredited two- or four-year university, college or vocational/technical institute. Must be graduating high school senior or currently enrolled in a college of business with a 3.0 or higher GPA.

Academic Fields/Career Goals: Business/Consumer Services.

Award: Scholarship for use in freshman or sophomore years; not renewable. *Amount:* $2000.

Eligibility Requirements: Applicant must be enrolled or expecting to enroll full-time at a four-year or technical institution or university. Applicant must have 3.0 GPA or higher. Available to U.S. citizens.

Application Requirements: Application form, essay, recommendations or references, transcript. *Deadline:* February 28.

HOLSTEIN ASSOCIATION USA INC.

http://www.holsteinusa.com/

ROBERT H. RUMLER SCHOLARSHIP
• *See page 101*

HOUSE OF BLUES MUSIC FORWARD FOUNDATION

https://hobmusicforward.org/

STEVEN J. FINKEL SERVICE EXCELLENCE SCHOLARSHIP

Established in the memory of Steven J. Finkel, Live Nation's US Concerts division seeks to support the ever growing customer service expectation within the entertainment industry. The $10,000 scholarship will award students who are passionate about improving the live music customer experience for fans, artists, and employees.

Academic Fields/Career Goals: Business/Consumer Services; Communications; Economics; Hospitality Management; Music.

Award: Scholarship for use in junior or senior years; not renewable. *Number:* 1. *Amount:* $10,000.

Eligibility Requirements: Applicant must be enrolled or expecting to enroll full-time at a four-year institution or university and must have an interest in music or music/singing. Applicant must have 3.0 GPA or higher.

Application Requirements: Application form, essay. *Deadline:* March 31.

Contact: Ms. Nazanin Fatemian, House of Blues Music Forward Foundation
House of Blues Music Forward Foundation
7060 Hollywood Boulevard, Floor 2
Los Angeles, CA 90028
Phone: 323-821-3946
E-mail: nfatemian@hobmusicforward.org

TIFFANY GREEN OPERATOR SCHOLARSHIP AWARD
• *See page 96*

IDAHO STATE BROADCASTERS ASSOCIATION

http://www.idahobroadcasters.org/

WAYNE C. CORNILS MEMORIAL SCHOLARSHIP

Scholarship for students enrolled in an Idaho school on a full-time basis. Must be majoring in a broadcasting related field. Must have minimum GPA of 2.0 if in the first two years of school or 2.5 in the last two years of school.

Academic Fields/Career Goals: Business/Consumer Services; Communications; Engineering/Technology; Journalism; Marketing; TV/Radio Broadcasting.

Award: Scholarship for use in sophomore, junior, or senior years; not renewable. *Number:* 3. *Amount:* $1000.

Eligibility Requirements: Applicant must be enrolled or expecting to enroll full-time at a four-year institution or university; resident of Idaho and studying in Idaho. Applicant must have 2.5 GPA or higher. Available to U.S. citizens.

Application Requirements: Application form, essay. *Deadline:* March 15.

Contact: Connie Searles, President and CEO
Idaho State Broadcasters Association
1674 Hill Road
Suite 3
Boise, ID 83702
Phone: 208-345-3072
E-mail: isba@qwestoffice.net

INSTITUTE FOR OPERATIONS RESEARCH AND THE MANAGEMENT SCIENCES

http://www.informs.org/

GEORGE NICHOLSON STUDENT PAPER COMPETITION

Honors outstanding papers in the field of operations research and the management sciences. Entrant must be student on or after the year of application. Research papers present original results and be written by student. Electronic submission of paper required.

Academic Fields/Career Goals: Business/Consumer Services.

Award: Prize for use in junior, senior, graduate, or postgraduate years; not renewable. *Number:* up to 6. *Amount:* $100–$600.

Eligibility Requirements: Applicant must be enrolled or expecting to enroll full- or part-time at a four-year institution or university. Available to U.S. and non-U.S. citizens.

Application Requirements: Application form, application form may be submitted online (https://www.informs.org/Recognize-Excellence/INFORMS-Prizes-Awards/George-Nicholson-Student-Paper-Competition/George-Nicholson-Student-Paper-Competition-Application-Process), entry in a contest, recommendations or references. *Deadline:* June 5.

Contact: Melissa Moore, Executive Director
Institute for Operations Research and the Management Sciences
5521 Research Park Drive
Catonsville, MD 21228
Phone: 443-757-3500
Fax: 443-757-2505
E-mail: informs@informs.org

INSTITUTE OF MANAGEMENT ACCOUNTANTS

https://www.imanet.org/students/scholarships-and-awards/scholarships?ssopc=1

INSTITUTE OF MANAGEMENT ACCOUNTANTS MEMORIAL EDUCATION FUND SCHOLARSHIPS
• *See page 87*

STUART CAMERON AND MARGARET MCLEOD MEMORIAL SCHOLARSHIP
• *See page 87*

INTERNAL AUDIT FOUNDATION

http://www.theiia.org/

ESTHER R. SAWYER RESEARCH AWARD
• *See page 87*

JORGE MAS CANOSA FREEDOM FOUNDATION

http://masscholarships.org/

MAS FAMILY SCHOLARSHIP AWARD

Scholarship for Cuban American student who is a direct descendant of those who left Cuba or was born in Cuba. Minimum 3.5 GPA in college. Scholarships available only in the fields of engineering, business, international relations, economics, communications and journalism.

Academic Fields/Career Goals: Business/Consumer Services; Chemical Engineering; Civil Engineering; Communications; Economics; Electrical Engineering/Electronics; Engineering-Related Technologies; International Studies; Journalism; Materials Science, Engineering, and Metallurgy; Mechanical Engineering.

Award: Scholarship for use in freshman, sophomore, junior, senior, or graduate years; renewable. *Number:* 5–10. *Amount:* $8000–$40,000.

Eligibility Requirements: Applicant must be of Latin American/Caribbean heritage; Hispanic and enrolled or expecting to enroll full-time at a two-year or four-year institution or university. Applicant must have 3.5 GPA or higher. Available to U.S. and non-U.S. citizens.

Application Requirements: Application form, essay, financial need analysis, proof of Cuban descent, recommendations or references, test scores, transcript. *Deadline:* April 15.

Contact: Mr. Daniel Lafuente, Mas Scholarship Coordinator
Jorge Mas Canosa Freedom Foundation
1312 SW 27th Avenue
Miami, FL 33145
Phone: 305-592-7768
E-mail: dlafuente@canf.org

THE LAGRANT FOUNDATION

http://www.lagrantfoundation.org/

LAGRANT FOUNDATION SCHOLARSHIP FOR GRADUATES
• *See page 97*

LAGRANT FOUNDATION SCHOLARSHIP FOR UNDERGRADUATES
• *See page 97*

LEAGUE OF UNITED LATIN AMERICAN CITIZENS NATIONAL EDUCATIONAL SERVICE CENTERS INC.

http://www.lnesc.org/

GE/LULAC SCHOLARSHIP

The scholarship for business and engineering students offers outstanding minority or low-income students entering their sophomore year in pursuit of an undergraduate degree a renewable scholarship up to 3 years.

Academic Fields/Career Goals: Business/Consumer Services; Engineering/Technology.

Award: Scholarship for use in sophomore, junior, or senior years; renewable. *Number:* up to 9. *Amount:* up to $5000.

Eligibility Requirements: Applicant must be American Indian/Alaska Native, Asian/Pacific Islander, Black (non-Hispanic), Hispanic and enrolled or expecting to enroll full-time at a four-year institution or university. Applicant must have 3.0 GPA or higher. Available to U.S. citizens.

Application Requirements: Application form, personal statement with career goals, recommendations or references, transcript. *Deadline:* July 15.

Contact: Scholarship Administrator
League of United Latin American Citizens National
Educational Service Centers Inc.
2000 L Street, NW, Suite 610
Washington, DC 20036
Phone: 202-835-9646 Ext. 10
Fax: 202-835-9685

MAINE COMMUNITY FOUNDATION, INC.

http://www.mainecf.org/

PATRIOT EDUCATION SCHOLARSHIP FUND

Please go to the Maine Community Foundation, Inc. website for application requirements.

Academic Fields/Career Goals: Business/Consumer Services.

Award: Scholarship for use in freshman, sophomore, junior, or senior years; not renewable.

Eligibility Requirements: Applicant must be enrolled or expecting to enroll full- or part-time at a two-year or four-year institution or university; resident of Maine and studying in Maine. Available to U.S. citizens.

Application Requirements: Application form.

Contact: Ms. Amy Pollien, Grants Administration
Phone: 207-667-9735 Ext. 1109
E-mail: apollien@mainecf.org

NATIONAL RESTAURANT ASSOCIATION EDUCATIONAL FOUNDATION

http://www.chooserestaurants.org

NATIONAL RESTAURANT ASSOCIATION EDUCATIONAL FOUNDATION UNDERGRADUATE SCHOLARSHIPS FOR COLLEGE STUDENTS
• *See page 109*

NATIONAL SECURITY EDUCATION PROGRAM

http://www.iie.org/

NATIONAL SECURITY EDUCATION PROGRAM (NSEP) DAVID L. BOREN UNDERGRADUATE SCHOLARSHIPS
• *See page 139*

NEBRASKA DECA

http://www.nedeca.org/

NEBRASKA DECA LEADERSHIP SCHOLARSHIP

Awards applicants who intend to pursue a full-time two- or four-year course of study in a marketing or business-related field. Applicant must be active in DECA and involved in community service activities.

Academic Fields/Career Goals: Business/Consumer Services.

Award: Scholarship for use in freshman year; not renewable. *Number:* 2–9. *Amount:* $250–$1000.

Eligibility Requirements: Applicant must be high school student; planning to enroll or expecting to enroll full-time at a two-year or four-year or technical institution or university and resident of Nebraska. Applicant or parent of applicant must be member of Distribution Ed Club or Future Business Leaders of America. Applicant must have 2.5 GPA or higher. Available to U.S. citizens.

Application Requirements: Application form, DECA participation and accomplishment documents, essay, recommendations or references, resume, test scores, transcript. *Deadline:* February 1.

Contact: Scholarship Review Committee
Nebraska DECA
301 Centennial Mall South, PO Box 94987
Lincoln, NE 68509-4987
Phone: 402-471-4803
Fax: 402-471-0117
E-mail: nedeca@nedeca.org

NEW ENGLAND EMPLOYEE BENEFITS COUNCIL

http://www.neebc.org/

NEW ENGLAND EMPLOYEE BENEFITS COUNCIL SCHOLARSHIP PROGRAM
• *See page 89*

NEW ENGLAND WATER WORKS ASSOCIATION

http://www.newwa.org/

FRANCIS X. CROWLEY SCHOLARSHIP

Scholarships are awarded to eligible civil engineering, environmental and business management students on the basis of merit, character, and need. Preference given to those students whose programs are considered by a committee as beneficial to water works practice in New England. NEWWA student membership is required to receive a scholarship award. Applicants for scholarships should be residents or attend school in New England. (Maine, New Hampshire, Vermont, Massachusetts, Rhode Island and Connecticut).

Academic Fields/Career Goals: Business/Consumer Services; Civil Engineering; Environmental Science.

Award: Scholarship for use in freshman, sophomore, junior, senior, or graduate years; not renewable. *Number:* 1. *Amount:* up to $3000.

Eligibility Requirements: Applicant must be enrolled or expecting to enroll full-time at a four-year institution or university. Applicant or parent of applicant must be member of New England Water Works Association. Available to U.S. citizens.

Application Requirements: Application form, essay, recommendations or references, transcript. *Fee:* $25. *Deadline:* July 1.

Contact: Thomas MacElhaney, Chair, Scholarship Committee
Phone: 631-231-8100
Fax: 978-418-9156
E-mail: tmacelhaney@preloadinc.com

OREGON STUDENT ASSISTANCE COMMISSION

https://oregonstudentaid.gov/

FRED FIELDS SCHOLARSHIP

For students enrolled at least half-time in Oregon two-year public schools. Must be majoring in industrial mechanics/maintenance, industrial/mechanical engineering, manufacturing technology, business administration, commerce, entrepreneurship, management or career and technology (in order of preference). Automatically renewable if renewal criteria is met. Based on financial need.

Academic Fields/Career Goals: Business/Consumer Services; Engineering-Related Technologies; Mechanical Engineering.

Award: Scholarship for use in freshman, sophomore, junior, or senior years; renewable.

Eligibility Requirements: Applicant must be enrolled or expecting to enroll full- or part-time at a two-year institution and studying in Oregon. Available to U.S. citizens.

Application Requirements: Application form, financial need analysis. *Deadline:* March 1.

Contact: Melissa Adams, Scholarship Processing Coordinator
Phone: 541-687-7409
E-mail: melissa.adams@state.or.us

INSURANCE PROFESSIONALS OF PORTLAND LEGACY SCHOLARSHIP

Scholarship for full-time students enrolled in public or non-profit colleges in Oregon or Washington. Major in business. Minimum high school GPA 3.5, college GPA 3.2. Based on financial need.

Academic Fields/Career Goals: Business/Consumer Services.

Award: Scholarship for use in freshman, sophomore, junior, or senior years; not renewable.

Eligibility Requirements: Applicant must be enrolled or expecting to enroll full-time at a four-year institution or university and studying in Oregon, Washington. Applicant must have 3.0 GPA or higher. Available to U.S. citizens.

Application Requirements: Application form. *Deadline:* March 1.

Contact: Melissa Adams, Scholarship Processing Coordinator
Phone: 541-687-7409
E-mail: melissa.adams@state.or.us

OREGON ASSOCIATION OF CERTIFIED FRAUD EXAMINERS SCHOLARSHIP
• *See page 90*

PLUMBING-HEATING-COOLING CONTRACTORS EDUCATION FOUNDATION

http://www.phccfoundation.org/scholarships

DELTA FAUCET COMPANY SCHOLARSHIP PROGRAM

Applicants must be sponsored by a member of the National Association of Plumbing-Heating-Cooling Contractors. Must pursue studies in a major related to the plumbing-heating-cooling industry. Visit website for additional information.

Academic Fields/Career Goals: Business/Consumer Services; Engineering-Related Technologies; Engineering/Technology; Heating, Air-Conditioning, and Refrigeration Mechanics; Mechanical Engineering; Trade/Technical Specialties.

Award: Scholarship for use in freshman, sophomore, junior, or senior years; not renewable. *Number:* 6. *Amount:* $2500.

Eligibility Requirements: Applicant must be enrolled or expecting to enroll full-time at a two-year or four-year or technical institution or university. Applicant must have 2.5 GPA or higher. Available to U.S. and Canadian citizens.

Application Requirements: Application form, community service, essay, interview. *Deadline:* May 1.

Contact: John Zink, Scholarship Coordinator
Phone: 800-533-7694
E-mail: scholarships@naphcc.org

PHCC EDUCATIONAL FOUNDATION NEED-BASED SCHOLARSHIP

Need-based scholarship worth $2500 to a student enrolled in an approved four-year PHCC apprenticeship program, or at an accredited two-year technical college, community college, or an accredited four-year college or university.

Academic Fields/Career Goals: Business/Consumer Services; Engineering-Related Technologies; Engineering/Technology; Heating, Air-Conditioning, and Refrigeration Mechanics; Mechanical Engineering; Trade/Technical Specialties.

Award: Scholarship for use in freshman, sophomore, junior, or senior years; renewable. *Number:* 1. *Amount:* $2500.

Eligibility Requirements: Applicant must be enrolled or expecting to enroll full-time at a two-year or four-year or technical institution or university. Applicant must have 2.5 GPA or higher. Available to U.S. and Canadian citizens.

Application Requirements: Application form, community service, essay, financial need analysis, interview. *Deadline:* May 1.

Contact: John Zink, Scholarship Coordinator
Phone: 800-533-7694
E-mail: scholarships@naphcc.org

PHCC EDUCATIONAL FOUNDATION SCHOLARSHIP PROGRAM

Applicants must be sponsored by a member of the National Association of Plumbing-Heating-Cooling Contractors. Must pursue studies in a major related to the plumbing-heating-cooling industry. Visit website for additional information.

Academic Fields/Career Goals: Business/Consumer Services; Engineering-Related Technologies; Engineering/Technology; Heating, Air-Conditioning, and Refrigeration Mechanics; Mechanical Engineering; Trade/Technical Specialties.

Award: Scholarship for use in freshman, sophomore, junior, or senior years; not renewable. *Number:* 1–4. *Amount:* $2500–$5000.

Eligibility Requirements: Applicant must be enrolled or expecting to enroll full-time at a two-year or four-year or technical institution or

university. Applicant must have 2.5 GPA or higher. Available to U.S. and Canadian citizens.

Application Requirements: Application form, community service, essay, interview. *Deadline:* May 1.

Contact: John Zink, Scholarship Coordinator
Phone: 800-533-7694
E-mail: scholarships@naphcc.org

ROBERT H. MOLLOHAN FAMILY CHARITABLE FOUNDATION, INC.

http://www.mollohanfoundation.org/

TEAMING TO WIN BUSINESS SCHOLARSHIP

Scholarship for a rising college sophomore or junior pursuing a degree in business administration at a West Virginia college or university.

Academic Fields/Career Goals: Business/Consumer Services.

Award: Scholarship for use in sophomore or junior years; not renewable. *Number:* 2. *Amount:* up to $1000.

Eligibility Requirements: Applicant must be enrolled or expecting to enroll full- or part-time at a four-year institution or university; resident of West Virginia; studying in West Virginia and must have an interest in leadership. Applicant must have 3.0 GPA or higher. Available to U.S. citizens.

Application Requirements: Application form, essay, interview, recommendations or references, resume, test scores, transcript. *Deadline:* February 9.

Contact: Aime Shaffer, Program Manager
Robert H. Mollohan Family Charitable Foundation, Inc.
1000 Technology Drive, Suite 2000
Fairmont, WV 26554
Phone: 304-333-6783
Fax: 304-333-3900
E-mail: ashaffer@wvhtf.org

SALES PROFESSIONALS-USA

http://www.salesprofessionals-usa.com/

SALES PROFESSIONALS-USA SCHOLARSHIP

Scholarships are awarded to students furthering their degree or obtaining a degree in business or marketing. The scholarships are initiated and awarded by the individual Sales Pros Clubs (located in Colorado, Kansas and Missouri) and are not nationally awarded. A listing of local clubs can be found at http://www.salesprofessionals-usa.com.

Academic Fields/Career Goals: Business/Consumer Services.

Award: Scholarship for use in freshman, sophomore, junior, or senior years; not renewable. *Number:* 3–5. *Amount:* $600–$1000.

Eligibility Requirements: Applicant must be enrolled or expecting to enroll full- or part-time at a two-year or four-year institution or university; resident of Colorado, Indiana, Kansas and studying in Colorado, Kansas, Missouri. Applicant must have 3.0 GPA or higher. Available to U.S. citizens.

Application Requirements: Application form, essay. *Deadline:* varies.

Contact: Jay Berg, National President
Sales Professionals-USA
2870 North Speer Boulevard
Denver, CO 80001
Phone: 303-433-1051
E-mail: jberg@spacelogic.net

SCARLETT FAMILY FOUNDATION SCHOLARSHIP PROGRAM

http://www.scarlettfoundation.org/

SCHOLARSHIP FOR STUDENTS PURSUING A BUSINESS OR STEM DEGREE
• *See page 91*

SOCIETY OF AUTOMOTIVE ANALYSTS

http://saaauto.com/

SOCIETY OF AUTOMOTIVE ANALYSTS SCHOLARSHIP
• *See page 91*

SPECIALTY EQUIPMENT MARKET ASSOCIATION

http://www.sema.org/

SEMA MEMORIAL SCHOLARSHIP FUND
• *See page 92*

STRAIGHTFORWARD MEDIA

http://www.straightforwardmedia.com/

STRAIGHTFORWARD MEDIA BUSINESS SCHOOL SCHOLARSHIP
• *See page 99*

TED ROLLINS AND VALEO GROUPE

http://valeogroupe.us/

TED ROLLINS ECO SCHOLARSHIP

Are you a high school graduate or undergraduate looking to offset the cost of your business, sustainability or marketing degree? Ted Rollins and Valeo Partners award a $1,000 scholarship twice each year to one talented student who is majoring in a field related to sustainability. This money may be used to pay for tuition, books or living expenses.

Academic Fields/Career Goals: Business/Consumer Services; Environmental Health; Environmental Science; Natural Sciences.

Award: Scholarship for use in freshman, sophomore, junior, or senior years; not renewable. *Number:* 1. *Amount:* $1000.

Eligibility Requirements: Applicant must be enrolled or expecting to enroll full- or part-time at a two-year or four-year or technical institution or university. Available to U.S. and non-U.S. citizens.

Application Requirements: Application form, essay. *Deadline:* June 1.

Contact: Caroline Davis
Phone: 864-9184534
E-mail: caroline@tedrollinsecoscholars.com

TKE EDUCATIONAL FOUNDATION

http://www.tke.org/

JOHN C. FITZGERALD, JR. SCHOLARSHIP

One-time award of $300 given to an undergraduate member of Tau Kappa Epsilon who has demonstrated leadership ability within his chapter, campus, or community. Must be a full-time student in good standing with a GPA of 2.5 or higher and pursuing a degree in business administration. Preference will first be given to a member of Theta-Upsilon Chapter, but if there is no qualified applicant, the scholarship will be open to any other qualified Teke

Academic Fields/Career Goals: Business/Consumer Services.

Award: Scholarship for use in sophomore, junior, or senior years; not renewable. *Number:* 1. *Amount:* $300.

Eligibility Requirements: Applicant must be enrolled or expecting to enroll full-time at a four-year institution or university; male and must have an interest in leadership. Applicant or parent of applicant must be member of Tau Kappa Epsilon. Applicant must have 2.5 GPA or higher. Available to U.S. and non-U.S. citizens.

Application Requirements: Application form, application form may be submitted online (http://www.tke.org/member_resources/scholarships/apply_online), essay, personal photograph, transcript. *Deadline:* March 15.

Contact: Offices of the Grand Chapter
TKE Educational Foundation
7439 Woodland Drive, Suite 100
Indianapolis, IN 46278
E-mail: tkeogc@tke.org

TRIANGLE PEST CONTROL

http://www.trianglepest.com

TRIANGLE PEST CONTROL SCHOLARSHIP
• *See page 93*

UNITED DAUGHTERS OF THE CONFEDERACY

http://www.hqudc.org/

WALTER REED SMITH SCHOLARSHIP

Award for full-time female undergraduate students who are descendant of a Confederate soldier, studying nutrition, home economics, nursing, business administration, or computer science in accredited college or university. Minimum 3.0 GPA required. Submit application and letter of endorsement from sponsoring chapter of the United Daughters of the Confederacy.

Academic Fields/Career Goals: Business/Consumer Services; Computer Science/Data Processing; Food Science/Nutrition; Home Economics; Nursing.

Award: Scholarship for use in freshman, sophomore, junior, or senior years; renewable. *Number:* 1–2. *Amount:* $800–$1000.

Eligibility Requirements: Applicant must be enrolled or expecting to enroll full-time at a four-year institution or university and female. Applicant or parent of applicant must be member of United Daughters of the Confederacy. Applicant must have 3.0 GPA or higher. Available to U.S. citizens.

Application Requirements: Application form, copy of applicant's birth certificate, copy of confederate ancestor's proof of service, essay, financial need analysis, personal photograph, recommendations or references, self-addressed stamped envelope with application, test scores, transcript. *Deadline:* March 15.

Contact: Ms. Jamie Davis, Second Vice President General
Phone: 804-355-1636
E-mail: hqudc@rcn.com

UNITED NEGRO COLLEGE FUND

http://www.uncf.org/

BASF/ALFRED CHISHOLM ENDOWED MEMORIAL SCHOLARSHIP
• *See page 93*

EDWARD M. NAGEL ENDOWED SCHOLARSHIP

The Edward M Nagel Scholarship is open to undergraduate students pursuing studies in business (and business related majors). Up to $3000. Requires full time enrollment at an accredited 4-year college or university and demonstrated financial need.

Academic Fields/Career Goals: Business/Consumer Services.

Award: Scholarship for use in freshman, sophomore, junior, or senior years; renewable.

Eligibility Requirements: Applicant must be Black (non-Hispanic) and enrolled or expecting to enroll full-time at a four-year institution or university. Applicant must have 3.0 GPA or higher. Available to U.S. citizens.

Application Requirements: Application form, essay, financial need analysis. *Deadline:* September 18.

Contact: Mary Williams, Director of Outreach and Recruitment
Phone: 800-331-2244

HCN/APRICITY RESOURCES SCHOLARS PROGRAM
• *See page 93*

MUFG UNION BANK SCHOLARSHIP PROGRAM
• *See page 93*

NATIONAL BLACK MCDONALD'S OWNERS ASSOCIATION HOSPITALITY SCHOLARS PROGRAM
• *See page 94*

ORACLE CORPORATE SCHOLARS PROGRAM

African American student scholars who are majoring in computer science, computer engineering, mathematics, business, marketing, or human resources. Candidates must be a U.S. citizen, African American college student, have a minimum 3.0 GPA, and attend a four-year, accredited college or university located in the U.S. Successful candidates will be offered internships during the summer.

Academic Fields/Career Goals: Business/Consumer Services; Computer Science/Data Processing; Human Resources; Marketing; Mathematics.

Award: Scholarship for use in sophomore, junior, or senior years; not renewable.

Eligibility Requirements: Applicant must be Black (non-Hispanic) and enrolled or expecting to enroll full-time at a four-year institution or university. Applicant must have 3.0 GPA or higher. Available to U.S. citizens.

Application Requirements: Application form. *Deadline:* January 12.

Contact: Mary Williams, Director of Outreach and Recruitment
Phone: 800-331-2244

PROCTER & GAMBLE GENERAL SCHOLARSHIP
• *See page 94*

RICOH SCHOLARSHIP PROGRAM
• *See page 94*

SUEZ CORPORATE SCHOLARS PROGRAM
• *See page 94*

UBS/PAINEWEBBER SCHOLARSHIP
• *See page 94*

UNCF/ALLIANCE DATA SCHOLARSHIP AND INTERNSHIP PROGRAM
• *See page 99*

UNCF/ANTHEM CORPORATE SCHOLARS PROGRAM

Up $5000 scholarship for an underrepresented minority student that is a college sophomore and a resident of or enrolled in an accredited higher education institution in one of the following states: California, Virginia, Georgia, Indiana, Missouri, New York, or Ohio. Minimum 3.0 GPA required. Must major in business, communications, marketing, finance, health care administration, information systems, management information systems, computer technology or computer science and possess strong analytical problem solving, interpersonal, written and oral communication skills. Must be proficient in Microsoft Office Suite (Excel, Word, and Outlook) and social media platforms. All applicants for the UNCF/Anthem Corporate Scholars Program can apply and may be eligible for internship opportunities at the Anthem Corporation.

Academic Fields/Career Goals: Business/Consumer Services; Communications; Computer Science/Data Processing; Finance; Health Administration; Marketing.

Award: Scholarship for use in senior year; not renewable.

Eligibility Requirements: Applicant must be American Indian/Alaska Native, Asian/Pacific Islander, Black (non-Hispanic), Hispanic and enrolled or expecting to enroll full-time at a four-year institution or university. Applicant must have 3.0 GPA or higher. Available to U.S. citizens.

Application Requirements: Application form, essay, financial need analysis. *Deadline:* February 17.

Contact: Mary Williams, Director of Outreach and Recruitment
Phone: 800-331-2244

UNCF/CARNIVAL CORPORATE SCHOLARS PROGRAM

Up to $5000 scholarship and paid summer internship for minority college sophomores and juniors with an interest in pursuing a career in the hospitality industry and whose experience in their first two years of college demonstrates leadership and strategic and analytical ability. Minimum 3.0 GPA. Open to transfer students from community colleges that have been accepted into an accredited four-year college or university. Majoring in business, communications, culinary arts, hospitality management and/or administration, tourism, finance, marketing, information technology, statistics or other related field.

Academic Fields/Career Goals: Business/Consumer Services; Communications; Culinary Arts; Finance; Hospitality Management; Marketing; Travel/Tourism.

Award: Scholarship for use in sophomore or junior years; renewable.

Eligibility Requirements: Applicant must be American Indian/Alaska Native, Asian/Pacific Islander, Black (non-Hispanic), Hispanic and enrolled or expecting to enroll full-time at a four-year institution or university. Applicant must have 3.0 GPA or higher. Available to U.S. citizens.

Application Requirements: Application form, essay. *Deadline:* January 19.

Contact: Mary Williams, Director of Outreach and Recruitment
Phone: 800-331-2244

UNCF/KOCH SCHOLARS PROGRAM FOR UNDERGRADUATES
• *See page 94*

UNCF/NISSAN SCHOLARSHIP PROGRAM
Scholarship for high school senior who plan to be enrolled at any HBCU. Total award of $10,000 over 4 years ($2,500 per academic year) and an opportunity to participate in Nissan's Internship Program or enrichment opportunities. Must be majoring in engineering, business, marketing, information technology and/or finance. Minimum 3.0 GPA required.

Academic Fields/Career Goals: Business/Consumer Services; Computer Science/Data Processing; Engineering/Technology; Finance; Marketing.

Award: Scholarship for use in freshman, sophomore, junior, or senior years; not renewable. *Number:* 10. *Amount:* $2500.

Eligibility Requirements: Applicant must be Black (non-Hispanic); high school student and planning to enroll or expecting to enroll full-time at a four-year institution or university. Applicant must have 3.0 GPA or higher. Available to U.S. citizens.

Application Requirements: Application form, financial need analysis. *Deadline:* July 28.

Contact: Mary Williams, Director of Outreach and Recruitment
Phone: 800-331-2244

UNCF/TRAVELERS INSURANCE SCHOLARSHIP
Scholarship for African-American students with unmet financial need. Selected Scholars shall be expected to participate in Travelers-sponsored online and/or on site career readiness opportunities. Applicants must be pursuing a major in a business-related field, risk management or insurance.

Academic Fields/Career Goals: Business/Consumer Services; Insurance and Actuarial Science.

Award: Scholarship for use in sophomore, junior, or senior years. *Amount:* $3000–$5850.

Eligibility Requirements: Applicant must be Black (non-Hispanic); enrolled or expecting to enroll at a four-year institution or university and resident of California, Colorado, Florida, Georgia, Illinois, Massachusetts, Missouri, North Carolina, Texas, Washington. Applicant must have 3.0 GPA or higher. Available to U.S. citizens.

Application Requirements: Application form, essay, financial need analysis. *Deadline:* September 30.

Contact: Mary Williams, Director of Outreach and Recruitment
Phone: 800-331-2244

VOYA SCHOLARS
• *See page 94*

WILLIAM WRIGLEY FOUNDATION SCHOLARSHIP
• *See page 95*

WOMEN GROCERS OF AMERICA
http://www.nationalgrocers.org/

MARY MACEY SCHOLARSHIP
• *See page 112*

WOMEN IN LOGISTICS, NORTHERN CALIFORNIA
http://www.womeninlogistics.org/

WOMEN IN LOGISTICS SCHOLARSHIP
Award for students (undergraduate/graduate, male/female) studying and eventually planning careers in logistics/supply chain management. Applicants must be enrolled in a degree program at an institution within the 9 counties comprising the San Francisco Bay Area and have at least one semester left, as this award goes directly to the institution towards tuition/fees. Deadlines typically fall on November 1st. While student need may considered, awards are based primarily on merit, work experience and demonstrated interest in the field.

Academic Fields/Career Goals: Business/Consumer Services; Trade/Technical Specialties; Transportation.

Award: Scholarship for use in freshman, sophomore, junior, senior, or graduate years; not renewable. *Number:* 1–3. *Amount:* $1000–$3000.

Eligibility Requirements: Applicant must be enrolled or expecting to enroll full- or part-time at a two-year or four-year institution or university; resident of California and studying in California. Applicant or parent of applicant must be member of Women in Logistics. Available to U.S. and non-U.S. citizens.

Application Requirements: Application form, essay. *Deadline:* November 1.

Contact: Dr. Susan Cholette, Scholarship Director
Phone: 415-405-2173
E-mail: cholette@sfsu.edu

WYOMING TRUCKING ASSOCIATION SCHOLARSHIP FUND TRUST
http://www.wytruck.org/

WYOMING TRUCKING ASSOCIATION SCHOLARSHIP TRUST FUND
• *See page 95*

Y'S MEN INTERNATIONAL
http://www.ysmen.org/

ALEXANDER SCHOLARSHIP LOAN FUND
The purpose of the fund is to promote the training of staff of the YMCA and/or those seeking to become members or staff of the YMCA. Deadlines are May 30 for fall semester and October 30 for spring semester.

Academic Fields/Career Goals: Business/Consumer Services; Child and Family Studies; Education; Human Resources; Social Sciences; Social Services; Sports-Related/Exercise Science.

Award: Scholarship for use in freshman, sophomore, junior, or senior years; renewable.

Eligibility Requirements: Applicant must be enrolled or expecting to enroll full- or part-time at a two-year or four-year institution or university. Available to U.S. citizens.

Application Requirements: Application form. *Fee:* $1. *Deadline:* varies.

Contact: Dean Currie, Area Service Director
Phone: 908-753-9493
Fax: 602-935-6322
E-mail: kidcurrie@adelphia.net

ZONTA INTERNATIONAL FOUNDATION
http://www.zonta.org/

JANE M. KLAUSMAN WOMEN IN BUSINESS SCHOLARSHIPS
Any woman undertaking a business and/or business-related program at an accredited university/college/institute, in at least the second year of an undergraduate program through the final year of a Masters program at the time the application is submitted, is eligible to apply. Applicants must contact their local Zonta club for deadlines.

Academic Fields/Career Goals: Business/Consumer Services.

Award: Scholarship for use in junior, senior, or graduate years; not renewable. *Number:* 30–32. *Amount:* $1000–$7000.

Eligibility Requirements: Applicant must be enrolled or expecting to enroll full-time at a four-year institution or university and female. Available to U.S. and non-U.S. citizens.

Application Requirements: Application form, essay.

Contact: Programs Department
    Fax: 630-928-1559
    E-mail: programs@zonta.org

CAMPUS ACTIVITIES

NATIONAL ASSOCIATION FOR CAMPUS ACTIVITIES

http://www.naca.org/

MARKLEY SCHOLARSHIP

Scholarship available to students who are strongly involved in the field of student activities and/or student activities employment, and who have made significant contributions to NACA Central. Must be classified as a junior, senior or graduate student at a four-year school/university, or a sophomore at a two-year school in the NACA Central region. Must have minimum 2.5 GPA.

Academic Fields/Career Goals: Campus Activities.

Award: Scholarship for use in sophomore, junior, senior, or graduate years; not renewable. *Number:* 1–2. *Amount:* $300.

Eligibility Requirements: Applicant must be enrolled or expecting to enroll full- or part-time at a two-year or four-year institution or university and studying in Arkansas, Colorado, Kansas, Louisiana, Missouri, New Mexico, Oklahoma, Texas. Applicant or parent of applicant must have employment or volunteer experience in community service. Applicant must have 2.5 GPA or higher. Available to U.S. citizens.

Application Requirements: Application form, essay. *Deadline:* September 30.

Contact: Executive Assistant
    E-mail: scholarships@naca.org

NATIONAL ASSOCIATION FOR CAMPUS ACTIVITIES MID ATLANTIC HIGHER EDUCATION RESEARCH SCHOLARSHIP

Scholarships will be given for research that will add to the college student personnel knowledge base, particularly campus activities, or address issues challenging student affairs practitioners or higher education as they relate to campus activities.

Academic Fields/Career Goals: Campus Activities; Education.

Award: Scholarship for use in freshman, sophomore, junior, senior, graduate, or postgraduate years; not renewable. *Number:* 1. *Amount:* $50–$500.

Eligibility Requirements: Applicant must be enrolled or expecting to enroll full- or part-time at a two-year or four-year institution or university and studying in Delaware, Maryland, New Jersey, New York, Ontario, Pennsylvania. Available to U.S. citizens.

Application Requirements: Application form, essay. *Deadline:* September 30.

Contact: Executive Assistant
    E-mail: scholarships@naca.org

NATIONAL ASSOCIATION FOR CAMPUS ACTIVITIES NORTHERN PLAINS REGION STUDENT LEADERSHIP SCHOLARSHIP

• *See page 81*

NATIONAL ASSOCIATION FOR CAMPUS ACTIVITIES SCHOLARSHIPS FOR STUDENT LEADERS

Scholarships will be awarded to undergraduate students in good standing at the time of the application and who, during the academic term in which the scholarship is awarded, hold a significant leadership position on their campus. Must make significant contributions to their campus communities and demonstrate leadership skills and abilities.

Academic Fields/Career Goals: Campus Activities.

Award: Scholarship for use in freshman, sophomore, junior, or senior years; not renewable. *Number:* 1–7. *Amount:* $300.

Eligibility Requirements: Applicant must be enrolled or expecting to enroll full- or part-time at a two-year or four-year institution or university; studying in Alabama, Alaska, Alberta, Arizona, Arkansas, British Columbia, California, Colorado, Connecticut, Delaware, District of Columbia, Florida, Georgia, Hawaii, Idaho, Illinois, Indiana, Iowa, Kansas, Kentucky, Louisiana, Maine, Manitoba, Maryland, Massachusetts, Michigan, Minnesota, Mississippi, Missouri, Montana, Nebraska, Nevada, New Brunswick, New Hampshire, New Jersey, New Mexico, New York, North Carolina, North Dakota, Ohio, Oklahoma, Ontario, Oregon, Pennsylvania, Quebec, Rhode Island, Saskatchewan, South Carolina, South Dakota, Tennessee, Texas, Utah, Vermont, Virginia, Washington, West Virginia, Wisconsin, Wyoming and must have an interest in leadership. Applicant or parent of applicant must have employment or volunteer experience in community service. Available to U.S. citizens.

Application Requirements: Application form, essay. *Deadline:* December 31.

Contact: Executive Assistant
    E-mail: scholarships@naca.org

CHEMICAL ENGINEERING

101ST AIRBORNE DIVISION ASSOCIATION

http://www.screamingeaglefoundation.org/

AL & WILLIAMARY VISTE SCHOLARSHIP

• *See page 114*

AACE INTERNATIONAL

http://www.aacei.org/

AACE INTERNATIONAL COMPETITIVE SCHOLARSHIP

• *See page 130*

AIST FOUNDATION

http://www.aistfoundation.org/

ASSOCIATION FOR IRON AND STEEL TECHNOLOGY BENJAMIN F. FAIRLESS SCHOLARSHIP (AIME)

Scholarship for full-time students of metallurgy, materials science, chemical, mechanical, electrical, environmental, computer science, and industrial engineering. Students must have an interest in a career in the steel industry as demonstrated by an internship or related experience, or who have plans to pursue such experiences during college. Student may apply after first term of freshman year of college. Applications are accepted from 1 Sep through 31 Dec each year. Note: High school students do not qualify but are encouraged to learn about the steel industry and the career opportunities available therein, during their freshman year.

Academic Fields/Career Goals: Chemical Engineering; Electrical Engineering/Electronics; Engineering-Related Technologies; Materials Science, Engineering, and Metallurgy; Mechanical Engineering.

Award: Scholarship for use in sophomore, junior, or senior years; not renewable. *Number:* 2. *Amount:* $3000.

Eligibility Requirements: Applicant must be enrolled or expecting to enroll full-time at a four-year institution or university. Applicant must have 2.5 GPA or higher. Available to U.S. and non-U.S. citizens.

Application Requirements: Application form, essay, recommendations or references, resume, transcript. *Deadline:* December 31.

Contact: Lori Wharrey, AIST Manager, Board Services
AIST Foundation
186 Thorn Hill Road
Warrendale, PA 15086
Phone: 724-814-3044
E-mail: lwharrey@aist.org

ASSOCIATION FOR IRON AND STEEL TECHNOLOGY DAVID H. SAMSON CANADIAN SCHOLARSHIP

Scholarship for full-time students of metallurgy, materials science, chemical, mechanical, electrical, environmental, computer science, and industrial engineering. Students must have an interest in a career in the steel industry as demonstrated by an internship or related experience, or who have plans to pursue such experiences during college. Student may apply after first term of freshman year of college. Applications are accepted from 1 Sep through 31 Dec each year. Note: High school students do not qualify but are encouraged to learn about the steel industry and the career opportunities available therein, during their freshman year.

Academic Fields/Career Goals: Chemical Engineering; Civil Engineering; Electrical Engineering/Electronics; Engineering/Technology; Materials Science, Engineering, and Metallurgy.

Award: Scholarship for use in sophomore, junior, or senior years; not renewable. *Number:* 1. *Amount:* $3000.

Eligibility Requirements: Applicant must be Canadian citizen and enrolled or expecting to enroll full-time at a four-year institution or university. Applicant must have 2.5 GPA or higher.

Application Requirements: Application form, essay, recommendations or references, resume, transcript. *Deadline:* December 31.

Contact: Lori Wharrey, AIST Manager, Board Services
AIST Foundation
186 Thorn HIll Road
Warrendale, PA 15086
Phone: 724-814-3044
E-mail: lwharrey@aist.org

ASSOCIATION FOR IRON AND STEEL TECHNOLOGY WILLY KORF MEMORIAL SCHOLARSHIP

Scholarships are available for full-time students of metallurgy, chemical, materials science, mechanical, electrical, computer science, industrial and environmental engineering who have a genuine demonstrated interest in a career in the steel industry as demonstrated by an internship or related experience, or who have plans to pursue such experiences during college. Student may apply first during the freshman year of college. Applications are accepted 1 Sep through 31 Dec each year. Note: High school seniors are not eligible though are encouraged to learn and investigate the steel industry and the career opportunities available, during their freshman year.

Academic Fields/Career Goals: Chemical Engineering; Computer Science/Data Processing; Electrical Engineering/Electronics; Environmental Science; Industrial Design; Materials Science, Engineering, and Metallurgy; Mechanical Engineering.

Award: Scholarship for use in sophomore, junior, senior, or graduate years; not renewable. *Number:* 2. *Amount:* $3000.

Eligibility Requirements: Applicant must be enrolled or expecting to cnroll full-timc at a four-ycar institution or university. Applicant or parent of applicant must have employment or volunteer experience in engineering/technology. Applicant must have 2.5 GPA or higher. Available to U.S. and non-U.S. citizens.

Application Requirements: Application form, essay, recommendations or references, resume, transcript. *Deadline:* December 31.

Contact: Lori Wharrey, AIST Manager, Board Services
AIST Foundation
186 Thorn Hill Road
Warrendale, PA 15086
Phone: 724-814-3044 Ext. 621
E-mail: lwharrey@aist.org

AMERICAN CHEMICAL SOCIETY

http://www.acs.org/

AMERICAN CHEMICAL SOCIETY SCHOLARS PROGRAM

Renewable award for minority students pursuing studies in chemistry, biochemistry, chemical technology, chemical engineering, or chemical sciences. Must be U.S. citizen or permanent resident and have minimum 3.0 GPA. Must be Native American, African-American, or Hispanic.

Academic Fields/Career Goals: Chemical Engineering; Environmental Science; Materials Science, Engineering, and Metallurgy; Natural Sciences; Paper and Pulp Engineering; Trade/Technical Specialties.

Award: Scholarship for use in freshman, sophomore, or junior years; renewable. *Number:* 100–130. *Amount:* $1000–$5000.

Eligibility Requirements: Applicant must be American Indian/Alaska Native, Black (non-Hispanic), Hispanic and enrolled or expecting to enroll full-time at a two-year or four-year or technical institution or university. Applicant must have 3.0 GPA or higher. Available to U.S. citizens.

Application Requirements: Application form, essay, financial need analysis. *Deadline:* March 1.

Contact: Dr. Racquel Jemison, Manager, ACS Scholars Program
American Chemical Society
1155 16th Street, NW
Washington, DC 20036
Phone: 202-872-6048
E-mail: scholars@acs.org

AMERICAN CHEMICAL SOCIETY, RUBBER DIVISION

http://www.rubber.org/

AMERICAN CHEMICAL SOCIETY, RUBBER DIVISION UNDERGRADUATE SCHOLARSHIP
• *See page 120*

AMERICAN COUNCIL OF ENGINEERING COMPANIES OF PENNSYLVANIA (ACEC/PA)

http://www.acecpa.org/

ERIC J. GENNUSO AND LEROY D. (BUD) LOY, JR. SCHOLARSHIP PROGRAM

Scholarship for full-time engineering students enrolled in accredited colleges or universities. Must be a Must be a United States Citizen. Must be a full-time sophomore or junior student as of the school year in which the scholarship is awarded, pursuing a bachelor degree in engineering or environmental sciences. Must meet at least one of these criteria: Attend a college or university located in Pennsylvania or be a Pennsylvania Resident. Up to three awards are granted annually.

Academic Fields/Career Goals: Chemical Engineering; Civil Engineering; Construction Engineering/Management; Electrical Engineering/Electronics; Energy and Power Engineering; Engineering-Related Technologies; Engineering/Technology; Environmental Science; Marine/Ocean Engineering; Materials Science, Engineering, and Metallurgy; Mechanical Engineering; Surveying, Surveying Technology, Cartography, or Geographic Information Science; Transportation.

Award: Scholarship for use in sophomore or junior years; not renewable. *Number:* 1–3. *Amount:* $2500–$5000.

Eligibility Requirements: Applicant must be enrolled or expecting to enroll full-time at a four-year institution or university and resident of Pennsylvania. Available to U.S. citizens.

Application Requirements: Application form, community service, essay. *Deadline:* May 15.

Contact: Jenna Earley, Director of Marketing
American Council of Engineering Companies of Pennsylvania
(ACEC/PA)
800 N. 3rd Street
Suite 301
Harrisburg, PA 17102
Phone: 800-651-1946
E-mail: jearley@acecpa.org

AMERICAN INDIAN SCIENCE AND ENGINEERING SOCIETY

http://www.aises.org/

A.T. ANDERSON MEMORIAL SCHOLARSHIP PROGRAM
• *See page 121*

AMERICAN INSTITUTE OF CHEMICAL ENGINEERS

http://www.aiche.org/

CHEME-CAR NATIONAL LEVEL COMPETITION

Each student chapter region may send their first and second place winners to the design competition. Multiple entries from a single school may be permitted at the regional competitions, but only one entry per school is allowed at the national competition. Students majoring in chemical engineering can participate.

Academic Fields/Career Goals: Chemical Engineering.

Award: Prize for use in freshman, sophomore, junior, or senior years; not renewable. *Number:* up to 3. *Amount:* $200–$2000.

Eligibility Requirements: Applicant must be enrolled or expecting to enroll full-time at a four-year institution or university. Available to U.S. and non-U.S. citizens.

Application Requirements: Application form, entry in a contest, student chapter name, team contact, list of team members, title of entry, description of chemical reaction/drive system, list of chemicals to be used and estimated quantity needed. *Fee:* $100. *Deadline:* June 30.

Contact: Prof. David Dixon, Department of Chemistry and Chemical
Engineering
American Institute of Chemical Engineers
South Dakota School of Mines and Technology
501 East Saint Joseph Street
Rapid City, SD 57701
Phone: 605-394-1235
Fax: 605-394-1232
E-mail: david.dixon@sdsmt.edu

DONALD F. AND MILDRED TOPP OTHMER FOUNDATION-NATIONAL SCHOLARSHIP AWARDS

Awards for 15 national AICHE student members, a scholarship of $1000. Awards are presented on the basis of academic achievement and involvement in student chapter activities. The student chapter advisor must make nominations. Only one nomination will be accepted from each AICHE student chapter or chemical engineering club.

Academic Fields/Career Goals: Chemical Engineering.

Award: Scholarship for use in freshman, sophomore, junior, senior, or graduate years; not renewable. *Number:* 15. *Amount:* $1000.

Eligibility Requirements: Applicant must be enrolled or expecting to enroll full-time at a four-year institution or university. Available to U.S. and non-U.S. citizens.

Application Requirements: Application form, essay, recommendations or references, statement of long-range career plans, transcript. *Deadline:* May 11.

Contact: AIChE Awards Administrator
American Institute of Chemical Engineers
Three Park Avenue
New York, NY 10016-5901
Phone: 212-591-7107
Fax: 212-591-8882
E-mail: awards@aiche.org

ENVIRONMENTAL DIVISION UNDERGRADUATE STUDENT PAPER AWARD

Cash prizes awarded to full-time undergraduate students who prepare the best original papers based on the results of research or an investigation related to the environment. The work must be performed during the student's undergraduate enrollment, and the paper must be submitted prior to or within six months of graduation. Student must be the sole author of the paper, but faculty guidance is encouraged. Student must be a member of the American Institute of Chemical Engineers Student Chapter.

Academic Fields/Career Goals: Chemical Engineering; Environmental Science.

Award: Prize for use in freshman, sophomore, junior, or senior years; not renewable. *Number:* 3. *Amount:* $100–$300.

Eligibility Requirements: Applicant must be enrolled or expecting to enroll full-time at a four-year institution or university. Available to U.S. and non-U.S. citizens.

Application Requirements: 5 copies of the nomination package, entry in a contest, essay, recommendations or references. *Deadline:* May 15.

Contact: Tapas Das, Environmental Division Awards Committee
American Institute of Chemical Engineers
125 Mandy Place, NE
Olympia, WA 98516
Phone: 360-456-0573
E-mail: shivaniki@comcast.net

JOHN J. MCKETTA UNDERGRADUATE SCHOLARSHIP

A $5000 scholarship will be awarded to a junior or senior student member of AICHE who is planning a career in the chemical engineering process industries. Must maintain a 3.0 GPA. Applicant should show leadership or activity in either the school's AICHE student chapter or other university sponsored campus activities. Must attend ABET-accredited school in the United States, Canada, or Mexico.

Academic Fields/Career Goals: Chemical Engineering.

Award: Scholarship for use in junior or senior years; not renewable. *Number:* 1. *Amount:* $5000.

Eligibility Requirements: Applicant must be enrolled or expecting to enroll full-time at a four-year institution or university and must have an interest in leadership. Applicant must have 3.0 GPA or higher. Available to U.S. and non-U.S. citizens.

Application Requirements: Application form, essay, recommendations or references. *Deadline:* May 25.

Contact: AIChE Awards Administrator
American Institute of Chemical Engineers
Three Park Avenue
New York, NY 10016
Phone: 212-591-7107
Fax: 212-591-8882
E-mail: awards@aiche.org

MINORITY AFFAIRS COMMITTEE AWARD FOR OUTSTANDING SCHOLASTIC ACHIEVEMENT

Award recognizing the outstanding achievements of a chemical engineering student who serves as a role model for minority students. Offers $1000 award and $500 travel allowance to attend AICHE meeting. Must be nominated.

Academic Fields/Career Goals: Chemical Engineering.

Award: Scholarship for use in freshman, sophomore, junior, senior, or graduate years; not renewable. *Number:* 1. *Amount:* $1500.

Eligibility Requirements: Applicant must be American Indian/Alaska Native, Asian/Pacific Islander, Black (non-Hispanic), Hispanic and enrolled or expecting to enroll full-time at a four-year institution or university. Applicant must have 3.0 GPA or higher. Available to U.S. and non-U.S. citizens.

Application Requirements: Application form. *Deadline:* May 15.

Contact: Dr. Emmanuel Dada, Scholarship Administrator
American Institute of Chemical Engineers
PO Box 8
Princeton, NJ 08543
Phone: 212-591-7107
E-mail: emmanuel_dada@fmc.com

MINORITY SCHOLARSHIP AWARDS FOR COLLEGE STUDENTS

Award for college undergraduates who are studying chemical engineering. Must be a member of a minority group that is underrepresented in chemical engineering. Must be an AICHE national student member at the time of application. Recipients of this scholarship are eligible to reapply.

Academic Fields/Career Goals: Chemical Engineering.

Award: Scholarship for use in freshman, sophomore, junior, or senior years; renewable. *Number:* up to 10. *Amount:* $1000.

Eligibility Requirements: Applicant must be American Indian/Alaska Native, Asian/Pacific Islander, Black (non-Hispanic), Hispanic and enrolled or expecting to enroll full-time at a two-year or four-year institution or university. Applicant must have 3.0 GPA or higher. Available to U.S. and non-U.S. citizens.

Application Requirements: Application form, career objective, essay, financial need analysis, recommendations or references, transcript. *Deadline:* May 15.

Contact: Dr. Emmanuel Dada, FMC Corporation
American Institute of Chemical Engineers
PO Box 8
Princeton, NJ 08543
Phone: 212-591-7107
E-mail: emmanuel_dada@fmc.com

MINORITY SCHOLARSHIP AWARDS FOR INCOMING COLLEGE FRESHMEN

Up to ten awards of $1000 for high school graduates who are members of a minority group that is underrepresented in chemical engineering. Students must be high school seniors planning to enroll during the next academic year in a four-year college or university offering a science/engineering degree.

Academic Fields/Career Goals: Chemical Engineering.

Award: Scholarship for use in freshman year; not renewable. *Number:* up to 10. *Amount:* $1000.

Eligibility Requirements: Applicant must be American Indian/Alaska Native, Asian/Pacific Islander, Black (non-Hispanic), Hispanic; high school student and planning to enroll or expecting to enroll full-time at a four-year institution or university. Applicant must have 3.0 GPA or higher. Available to U.S. and non-U.S. citizens.

Application Requirements: Application form, confirmation of minority status, essay, financial need analysis, recommendations or references, transcript. *Deadline:* May 15.

Contact: Dr. Emmanuel Dada, Minority Affairs Committee
American Institute of Chemical Engineers
PO Box 8
Princeton, NJ 08543
Phone: 212-591-7107
E-mail: emmanuel_dada@fmc.com

NATIONAL STUDENT DESIGN COMPETITION-INDIVIDUAL

Three cash prizes for student contest problem that typifies a real, working, chemical engineering design situation. Competition statements are distributed online to student chapter advisors and department heads.

Academic Fields/Career Goals: Chemical Engineering.

Award: Prize for use in freshman, sophomore, junior, senior, or graduate years; not renewable. *Number:* 3. *Amount:* $200–$500.

Eligibility Requirements: Applicant must be enrolled or expecting to enroll full-time at a four-year institution or university. Available to U.S. and non-U.S. citizens.

Application Requirements: Entry in a contest, essay. *Deadline:* June 6.

Contact: AIChE Awards Administrator
American Institute of Chemical Engineers
Three Park Avenue
New York, NY 10016
Phone: 212-591-7107
Fax: 212-591-8882
E-mail: awards@aiche.org

NATIONAL STUDENT PAPER COMPETITION

First place winners from each of the nine regional student paper competitions present their prize-winning papers during the American Institute of Chemical Engineers meeting held in the current calendar year. First prize is $500, second prize is $300, and third prize is $200.

Academic Fields/Career Goals: Chemical Engineering.

Award: Prize for use in freshman, sophomore, junior, senior, or graduate years; not renewable. *Number:* 3. *Amount:* $200–$500.

Eligibility Requirements: Applicant must be enrolled or expecting to enroll full-time at a four-year institution or university. Available to U.S. and non-U.S. citizens.

Application Requirements: Entry in a contest, student paper. *Deadline:* varies.

Contact: AIChE Awards Administrator
American Institute of Chemical Engineers
Three Park Avenue
New York, NY 10016-5901
Phone: 212-591-7107
Fax: 212-591-8882
E-mail: awards@aiche.org

OUTSTANDING STUDENT CHAPTER ADVISOR AWARD

Award for service and leadership in guiding the activities of an AIChE student chapter in accordance with AIChE principles. Must be advisor of a chartered AIChE student chapter for at least the last three years. Award winners cannot be renominated.

Academic Fields/Career Goals: Chemical Engineering.

Award: Prize for use in freshman, sophomore, junior, or senior years; not renewable. *Number:* 1. *Amount:* up to $1000.

Eligibility Requirements: Applicant must be enrolled or expecting to enroll full-time at a four-year institution or university. Available to U.S. and non-U.S. citizens.

Application Requirements: 4 copies of the nomination, application form, recommendations or references. *Deadline:* June 1.

Contact: Marvin Borgmeyer, Scholarship Committee
American Institute of Chemical Engineers
PO Box 1607
Baton Rouge, LA 70821-1607
Phone: 225-977-6206
Fax: 225-977-6396

PROCESS DEVELOPMENT DIVISION STUDENT PAPER AWARD

Award presented to a full-time graduate or undergraduate student who prepares the best technical paper to describe the results of process development related studies within chemical engineering. Must be carried out while the student is enrolled at a university with an accredited chemical engineering program. Student must be the primary author. Paper must be suitable for publication in a refereed journal. Must be a member of AIChE.

Academic Fields/Career Goals: Chemical Engineering.

Award: Prize for use in freshman, sophomore, junior, senior, or graduate years; not renewable. *Number:* 1. *Amount:* $200.

Eligibility Requirements: Applicant must be enrolled or expecting to enroll full-time at a four-year institution or university. Available to U.S. and non-U.S. citizens.

Application Requirements: Original and five copies of the nomination form, recommendations or references. *Deadline:* June 15.

Contact: A.R. Cartolano, Awards Committee Chair
American Institute of Chemical Engineers
7201 Hamilton Boulevard
Allentown, PA 18195-1501
Phone: 610-481-4262
E-mail: cartolar@airproducts.com

REGIONAL STUDENT PAPER COMPETITION

Students present technical papers at the student regional conferences which are held during spring. Deadlines for regional conferences vary. First prize is $200, second prize is $100, and third prize is $50. First place winner from each region present their paper at the regional competition.

Academic Fields/Career Goals: Chemical Engineering.

Award: Prize for use in freshman, sophomore, junior, or senior years; not renewable. *Number:* 3. *Amount:* $50–$200.

Eligibility Requirements: Applicant must be enrolled or expecting to enroll full-time at a four-year institution or university. Available to U.S. and non-U.S. citizens.

Application Requirements: Entry in a contest, student paper. *Deadline:* varies.

Contact: AIChE Awards Administrator
American Institute of Chemical Engineers
Three Park Avenue
New York, NY 10016-5901
Phone: 212-591-7107
Fax: 212-591-8882
E-mail: awards@aiche.org

SAFETY AND CHEMICAL ENGINEERING EDUCATION (SACHE) STUDENT ESSAY AWARD FOR SAFETY

Awards individuals or a team submitting the best essays on the topic of chemical process safety. Essays may focus on process safety in education, relevance of safety in undergraduate education, or integrating safety principles into the undergraduate chemical engineering curriculum.

Academic Fields/Career Goals: Chemical Engineering.

Award: Prize for use in freshman, sophomore, junior, or senior years; not renewable. *Number:* up to 4. *Amount:* $500.

Eligibility Requirements: Applicant must be enrolled or expecting to enroll full-time at a four-year institution or university. Available to U.S. and non-U.S. citizens.

Application Requirements: Entry in a contest, essay. *Deadline:* June 5.

Contact: AIChE Awards Administrator
American Institute of Chemical Engineers
Three Park Avenue
New York, NY 10016
Phone: 212-591-7107
Fax: 212-591-8880
E-mail: awards@aiche.org

SAFETY AND HEALTH NATIONAL STUDENT DESIGN COMPETITION AWARD FOR SAFETY

Four $600 awards available for each of the teams or individuals who apply one or more of the following concepts of inherent safety in their designs: design the plant for easier and effective maintainability; design the plant with less waste; design the plant with special features that demonstrate inherent safety; include design concepts regarding the entire life cycle. The school must have a student chapter of AIChE.

Academic Fields/Career Goals: Chemical Engineering; Industrial Design.

Award: Prize for use in freshman, sophomore, junior, senior, or graduate years; not renewable. *Number:* 4. *Amount:* $600.

Eligibility Requirements: Applicant must be enrolled or expecting to enroll full- or part-time at a four-year institution or university. Available to U.S. and non-U.S. citizens.

Application Requirements: Application form, design. *Deadline:* June 6.

Contact: AIChE Awards Administrator
American Institute of Chemical Engineers
Three Park Avenue
New York, NY 10016
Phone: 212-591-7478
Fax: 212-591-8882
E-mail: awards@aiche.org

AMERICAN OIL CHEMISTS' SOCIETY

http://www.aocs.org/

AOCS ANALYTICAL DIVISION STUDENT AWARD

$250 prize, $500 travel funding and certificate to recognize an outstanding graduate student's presentation in the field of lipid analytical chemistry at the Society's annual meeting.

Academic Fields/Career Goals: Chemical Engineering; Food Science/Nutrition.

Award: Prize for use in junior, senior, or graduate years; not renewable. *Number:* 1–2. *Amount:* $250–$750.

Eligibility Requirements: Applicant must be enrolled or expecting to enroll full- or part-time at a four-year institution or university. Available to U.S. and non-U.S. citizens.

Application Requirements: Abstract, application form, essay, recommendations or references. *Deadline:* October 15.

Contact: Barbara Semeraro, Area Manager, Membership
American Oil Chemists' Society
AOCS
PO Box 17190
Urbana, IL 61803
Phone: 217-693-4804
Fax: 217-693-4849
E-mail: awards@aocs.org

AOCS BIOTECHNOLOGY STUDENT EXCELLENCE AWARD

• *See page 105*

AOCS PROCESSING DIVISION AWARDS

Award and certificate to recognize graduate students presenting an outstanding paper at the Society's annual meeting. All graduate students presenting a paper at any of the AOCS Annual Meeting Processing Division sessions are eligible for the award.

Academic Fields/Career Goals: Chemical Engineering; Food Science/Nutrition.

Award: Prize for use in junior, senior, or graduate years; not renewable. *Number:* 1. *Amount:* $1000.

Eligibility Requirements: Applicant must be enrolled or expecting to enroll full-time at a four-year institution or university. Available to U.S. and non-U.S. citizens.

Application Requirements: Essay, extended abstract, recommendations or references. *Deadline:* February 1.

Contact: Barbara Semeraro, Area Manager, Membership
American Oil Chemists' Society
AOCS
PO Box 17190
Urbana, IL 61803
Phone: 217-693-4804
Fax: 217-693-4849
E-mail: awards@aocs.org

AMERICAN PUBLIC POWER ASSOCIATION

https://www.publicpower.org/grants-scholarships

DEED EDUCATIONAL SCHOLARSHIP

This scholarship targets students who are pursuing a major that could lead to an electric utility career. Applicants must be sponsored by a DEED member utility and attend an accredited university/college full-time in the U.S. Email DEED@publicpower.org for access to the application. Application deadline: Feb. 15 and Oct. 15 annually.

Academic Fields/Career Goals: Chemical Engineering; Civil Engineering; Construction Engineering/Management; Electrical Engineering/Electronics; Energy and Power Engineering; Engineering-Related Technologies; Engineering/Technology; Environmental Science; Mechanical Engineering; Natural Resources.

Award: Scholarship for use in freshman, sophomore, junior, or senior years; not renewable. *Number:* 20. *Amount:* $2000.

Eligibility Requirements: Applicant must be enrolled or expecting to enroll full-time at a two-year or four-year or technical institution or university. Available to U.S. and non-U.S. citizens.

Application Requirements: Application form, essay.

Contact: Jack Miller, DEED and Engineering Services Assistant
E-mail: DEED@publicpower.org

DEED STUDENT INTERNSHIP

The Student Internships are paid and provide work experience at a DEED member electric utility. Applicants must be sponsored by a DEED member utility and attend an accredited university/college full-time in the U.S. Email DEED@publicpower.org for access to the application. Application deadline is Feb. 15 and Oct. 15 annually.

Academic Fields/Career Goals: Chemical Engineering; Civil Engineering; Construction Engineering/Management; Electrical Engineering/Electronics; Energy and Power Engineering; Engineering-Related Technologies; Engineering/Technology; Environmental Science; Mechanical Engineering; Natural Resources.

Award: Scholarship for use in freshman, sophomore, junior, senior, graduate, or postgraduate years; not renewable. *Number:* 10. *Amount:* $5000.

Eligibility Requirements: Applicant must be enrolled or expecting to enroll full-time at a two-year or four-year or technical institution or university. Available to U.S. and non-U.S. citizens.

Application Requirements: Application form. *Deadline:* continuous.

Contact: Jack Miller, DEED and Engineering Services Assistant
E-mail: DEED@publicpower.org

DEED TECHNICAL DESIGN PROJECT

The Technical Design Project (TDP) provides funding to support students working on a technical project of interest to electric utilities. Applicants must attend an accredited university/college full-time in the U.S. Email DEED@publicpower.org for access to the application. Application deadline is Oct. 15 annually.

Academic Fields/Career Goals: Chemical Engineering; Civil Engineering; Construction Engineering/Management; Electrical Engineering/Electronics; Energy and Power Engineering; Engineering-Related Technologies; Engineering/Technology; Environmental Science; Mechanical Engineering; Natural Resources.

Award: Scholarship for use in junior, senior, or graduate years; not renewable. *Number:* 1. *Amount:* $8000.

Eligibility Requirements: Applicant must be enrolled or expecting to enroll full-time at a two-year or four-year or technical institution or university. Available to U.S. and non-U.S. citizens.

Application Requirements: Application form. *Deadline:* continuous.

Contact: Jack Miller, DEED and Engineering Services Assistant
E-mail: DEED@publicpower.org

AMERICAN SOCIETY FOR ENOLOGY AND VITICULTURE

http://www.asev.org/

AMERICAN SOCIETY FOR ENOLOGY AND VITICULTURE SCHOLARSHIPS
• *See page 105*

AMERICAN SOCIETY OF HEATING, REFRIGERATING, AND AIR CONDITIONING ENGINEERS, INC.

http://www.ashrae.org/

ASHRAE REGION III BOGGARM SETTY SCHOLARSHIP

One $3,000 scholarship for an undergraduate pre-engineering or engineering student enrolled full time in a post-secondary educational institution within the geographic boundaries of ASHRAE Region III (Delaware, Maryland, Pennsylvania, Virginia, Washington, DC). Minimum 3.0 GPA required.

Academic Fields/Career Goals: Chemical Engineering; Construction Engineering/Management; Electrical Engineering/Electronics; Energy and Power Engineering; Engineering-Related Technologies; Engineering/Technology; Mechanical Engineering; Paper and Pulp Engineering.

Award: Scholarship for use in freshman, sophomore, junior, or senior years; not renewable. *Number:* 1. *Amount:* $3000.

Eligibility Requirements: Applicant must be enrolled or expecting to enroll full-time at a four-year institution or university and studying in Delaware, District of Columbia, Maryland, Pennsylvania, Virginia. Applicant must have 3.0 GPA or higher. Available to U.S. citizens.

Application Requirements: Application form, financial need analysis. *Deadline:* December 1.

Contact: Lois Benedict, Scholarship Administrator
Phone: 404-636-8400 Ext. 1120
E-mail: lbenedict@ashrae.org

ARRL FOUNDATION INC.

http://www.arrl.org/

ALFRED E. FRIEND JR., W4CF, MEMORIAL SCHOLARSHIP

One $5000 scholarship for a student with active Amateur Radio license who is studying any field in engineering.

Academic Fields/Career Goals: Chemical Engineering; Civil Engineering; Construction Engineering/Management; Electrical Engineering/Electronics; Energy and Power Engineering; Engineering/Technology; Marine/Ocean Engineering; Materials Science, Engineering, and Metallurgy; Mechanical Engineering; Paper and Pulp Engineering.

Award: Scholarship for use in freshman, sophomore, junior, or senior years; not renewable. *Number:* 1. *Amount:* $5000.

Eligibility Requirements: Applicant must be enrolled or expecting to enroll full- or part-time at a two-year or four-year or technical institution or university and must have an interest in amateur radio. Available to U.S. citizens.

Application Requirements: Application form. *Deadline:* January 31.

Contact: Ms. Mary Hobart, Secretary
Phone: 860-594-0397
E-mail: k1mmh@arrl.org

GARY WAGNER, K3OMI, SCHOLARSHIP

One $1000 award available to student who possesses a novice class or higher amateur radio license and who is or will be attending a four-year college or university. Must be a U.S. citizen and resident of North Carolina, Virginia, West Virginia, Maryland, or Tennessee and studying toward a Bachelor of Science degree in any field of engineering. Financial need must be demonstrated.

Academic Fields/Career Goals: Chemical Engineering; Civil Engineering; Construction Engineering/Management; Electrical Engineering/Electronics; Energy and Power Engineering; Engineering-Related Technologies; Engineering/Technology; Materials Science, Engineering, and Metallurgy; Mechanical Engineering; Paper and Pulp Engineering.

Award: Scholarship for use in freshman, sophomore, junior, or senior years; not renewable. *Number:* 1. *Amount:* $1000.

Eligibility Requirements: Applicant must be enrolled or expecting to enroll full- or part-time at a four-year institution or university; resident of Maryland, North Carolina, Tennessee, Virginia, West Virginia and must have an interest in amateur radio. Available to U.S. citizens.

Application Requirements: Application form, financial need analysis. *Deadline:* January 31.

Contact: Ms. Mary Hobart, Secretary
Phone: 860-594-0397
E-mail: k1mmh@arrl.org

WIFDR SCHOLARSHIP
• *See page 122*

ASSOCIATION ON AMERICAN INDIAN AFFAIRS, INC.

http://www.indian-affairs.org/

ELIZABETH AND SHERMAN ASCHE MEMORIAL SCHOLARSHIP FUND
• *See page 106*

ASTRONAUT SCHOLARSHIP FOUNDATION

http://www.astronautscholarship.org/

ASTRONAUT SCHOLARSHIP FOUNDATION
• *See page 123*

AUTOMOTIVE WOMEN'S ALLIANCE FOUNDATION

http://awafoundation.org/index.php

AUTOMOTIVE WOMEN'S ALLIANCE FOUNDATION SCHOLARSHIPS
• *See page 81*

BARRY GOLDWATER SCHOLARSHIP AND EXCELLENCE IN EDUCATION FOUNDATION

https://goldwater.scholarsapply.org

BARRY M. GOLDWATER SCHOLARSHIP AND EXCELLENCE IN EDUCATION PROGRAM
• *See page 123*

BHW GROUP

https://thebhwgroup.com/

BHW WOMEN IN STEM SCHOLARSHIP
• *See page 124*

B.O.G. PEST CONTROL

http://www.bogpestcontrol.com/

B.O.G. PEST CONTROL SCHOLARSHIP FUND
• *See page 169*

BRASKEM ODEBRECHT

http://www.odebrechtaward.com

ODEBRECHT AWARD FOR SUSTAINABLE DEVELOPMENT
• *See page 131*

BROWN AND CALDWELL

http://www.brownandcaldwell.com

ECKENFELDER SCHOLARSHIP
• *See page 169*

MINORITY SCHOLARSHIP PROGRAM
• *See page 169*

CARDS AGAINST HUMANITY

https://cardsagainsthumanity.com/

SCIENCE AMBASSADOR SCHOLARSHIP
• *See page 124*

DISTIL NETWORKS

http://www.distilnetworks.com

WOMEN FORWARD IN TECHNOLOGY SCHOLARSHIP PROGRAM
• *See page 124*

THE ELECTROCHEMICAL SOCIETY

http://www.electrochem.org/

H.H. DOW MEMORIAL STUDENT ACHIEVEMENT AWARD OF THE INDUSTRIAL ELECTROLYSIS AND

ELECTROCHEMICAL ENGINEERING DIVISION OF THE ELECTROCHEMICAL SOCIETY INC.
• *See page 125*

STUDENT RESEARCH AWARDS OF THE BATTERY DIVISION OF THE ELECTROCHEMICAL SOCIETY INC.
• *See page 125*

FLORIDA ENGINEERING SOCIETY

http://www.fleng.org/scholarships.cfm

DAVID F. LUDOVICI SCHOLARSHIP
One-time scholarship of $1000 given to students in their junior or senior year in any Florida university engineering program, with at least 3.0 GPA. Applicants must be interested in civil, structural, or consulting engineering.

Academic Fields/Career Goals: Chemical Engineering; Civil Engineering; Construction Engineering/Management; Electrical Engineering/Electronics; Energy and Power Engineering; Engineering-Related Technologies; Engineering/Technology.

Award: Scholarship for use in junior or senior years; not renewable. *Number:* 1. *Amount:* $1000.

Eligibility Requirements: Applicant must be enrolled or expecting to enroll full-time at an institution or university; resident of Florida and studying in Florida. Applicant must have 3.0 GPA or higher. Available to U.S. citizens.

Application Requirements: Application form. *Deadline:* February 1.

Contact: Amanda Hudson, Director of Information Technology
Florida Engineering Society
125 South Gadsden Street
Tallahassee, FL 32301
Phone: 850-224-7121
E-mail: ahudson@fleng.org

FOUNDATION FOR SCIENCE AND DISABILITY

http://stemd.org/

GRANTS FOR DISABLED GRADUATE STUDENTS IN THE SCIENCES
• *See page 106*

GREATER KANAWHA VALLEY FOUNDATION

http://www.tgkvf.org/

STEVEN ENGINEERING SCHOLARSHIP
Renewable award for a West Virginia resident pursuing full-time postsecondary studies in engineering. Preference given to students at West Virginia University Institute of Technology or West Virginia University. Minimum 2.5 GPA required.

Academic Fields/Career Goals: Chemical Engineering; Construction Engineering/Management; Electrical Engineering/Electronics; Energy and Power Engineering; Engineering/Technology; Marine/Ocean Engineering; Materials Science, Engineering, and Metallurgy; Mechanical Engineering; Paper and Pulp Engineering.

Award: Scholarship for use in freshman, sophomore, junior, or senior years; renewable. *Amount:* $550.

Eligibility Requirements: Applicant must be enrolled or expecting to enroll full-time at a four-year institution or university and resident of West Virginia. Applicant must have 2.5 GPA or higher. Available to U.S. citizens.

Application Requirements: Application form, recommendations or references, transcript. *Deadline:* January 15.

Contact: Susan Hoover, Scholarship Program Officer
Greater Kanawha Valley Foundation
900 Lee Street East, 16th Floor
Charleston, WV 25301
Phone: 304-346-3620
E-mail: shoover@tgkvf.org

GREAT MINDS IN STEM

http://www.greatmindsinstem.org

HENAAC SCHOLARSHIP PROGRAM
• *See page 115*

INDEPENDENT LABORATORIES INSTITUTE SCHOLARSHIP ALLIANCE

http://www.acil.org/

INDEPENDENT LABORATORIES INSTITUTE SCHOLARSHIP ALLIANCE
• *See page 171*

INTERNATIONAL SOCIETY FOR OPTICAL ENGINEERING-SPIE

http://www.spie.org/scholarships

SPIE EDUCATIONAL SCHOLARSHIPS IN OPTICAL SCIENCE AND ENGINEERING
• *See page 126*

JORGE MAS CANOSA FREEDOM FOUNDATION

http://masscholarships.org/

MAS FAMILY SCHOLARSHIP AWARD
• *See page 181*

KENTUCKY ENERGY AND ENVIRONMENT CABINET

http://dep.ky.gov

ENVIRONMENTAL PROTECTION SCHOLARSHIP
• *See page 172*

LABROOTS INC.

http://www.LabRoots.com

LABROOTS STEM SCHOLARSHIP
• *See page 116*

LOS ANGELES COUNCIL OF BLACK PROFESSIONAL ENGINEERS

http://www.lablackengineers.org/

AL-BEN SCHOLARSHIP FOR ACADEMIC INCENTIVE

One-time scholarship for students enrolled full-time with scholastic achievements in the academic pursuits of engineering, math, computer or scientific studies. Must be from a minority group. Scholarship value is $500 to $1000. Two scholarships are granted annually. Preference given to residents of Southern California.

Academic Fields/Career Goals: Chemical Engineering; Civil Engineering; Computer Science/Data Processing; Electrical Engineering/Electronics; Engineering-Related Technologies; Engineering/Technology; Materials Science, Engineering, and Metallurgy; Mechanical Engineering; Physical Sciences.

Award: Scholarship for use in freshman, sophomore, junior, or senior years; not renewable. *Number:* 2. *Amount:* $500–$1000.

Eligibility Requirements: Applicant must be American Indian/Alaska Native, Asian/Pacific Islander, Black (non-Hispanic), Hispanic and enrolled or expecting to enroll full-time at a four-year institution or university. Available to U.S. citizens.

Application Requirements: Application form, essay, recommendations or references, transcript. *Deadline:* April 2.

Contact: Leroy Freelon, President
Phone: 310-635-7734
E-mail: lfreelonjr@aol.com

AL-BEN SCHOLARSHIP FOR PROFESSIONAL MERIT

One-time scholarship for students enrolled full-time with scholastic achievements in the academic pursuits of engineering, math, computer or scientific studies. Must be from a minority group. Scholarship value is $500 to $1000. Two scholarships are granted annually. Preference given to residents of Southern California.

Academic Fields/Career Goals: Chemical Engineering; Civil Engineering; Computer Science/Data Processing; Electrical Engineering/Electronics; Engineering-Related Technologies; Engineering/Technology; Materials Science, Engineering, and Metallurgy; Mechanical Engineering; Physical Sciences.

Award: Scholarship for use in freshman, sophomore, junior, or senior years; not renewable. *Number:* 2. *Amount:* $500–$1000.

Eligibility Requirements: Applicant must be American Indian/Alaska Native, Asian/Pacific Islander, Black (non-Hispanic), Hispanic and enrolled or expecting to enroll full-time at a four-year institution or university. Available to U.S. citizens.

Application Requirements: Application form, essay, recommendations or references, transcript. *Deadline:* April 2.

Contact: Leroy Freelon, President
Phone: 310-635-7734
E-mail: lfreelonjr@aol.com

AL-BEN SCHOLARSHIP FOR SCHOLASTIC ACHIEVEMENT

Scholarships for students enrolled full-time with scholastic achievements in the academic pursuits of engineering, math, computer or scientific studies. Must be from a minority group.

Academic Fields/Career Goals: Chemical Engineering; Civil Engineering; Computer Science/Data Processing; Electrical Engineering/Electronics; Engineering-Related Technologies; Engineering/Technology; Materials Science, Engineering, and Metallurgy; Mechanical Engineering; Physical Sciences.

Award: Scholarship for use in freshman, sophomore, junior, or senior years; not renewable. *Number:* 2. *Amount:* $500–$1000.

Eligibility Requirements: Applicant must be American Indian/Alaska Native, Asian/Pacific Islander, Black (non-Hispanic), Hispanic and enrolled or expecting to enroll full-time at a four-year institution or university. Available to U.S. citizens.

Application Requirements: Application form, essay, recommendations or references, transcript. *Deadline:* April 2.

Contact: Leroy Freelon, President
Phone: 310-635-7734
E-mail: lfreelonjr@aol.com

MEDICAL SCRUBS COLLECTION

http://medicalscrubscollection.com

MEDICAL SCRUBS COLLECTION SCHOLARSHIP
• *See page 120*

NASA IDAHO SPACE GRANT CONSORTIUM

http://www.idahospacegrant.org

NASA IDAHO SPACE GRANT CONSORTIUM SCHOLARSHIP PROGRAM
• *See page 126*

NASA/MARYLAND SPACE GRANT CONSORTIUM

http://www.mdspacegrant.org/

NASA MARYLAND SPACE GRANT CONSORTIUM UNDERGRADUATE SCHOLARSHIPS
• *See page 156*

NASA MONTANA SPACE GRANT CONSORTIUM

http://www.spacegrant.montana.edu/

MONTANA SPACE GRANT SCHOLARSHIP PROGRAM
• See page 156

NASA'S VIRGINIA SPACE GRANT CONSORTIUM

http://www.vsgc.odu.edu/

UNDERGRADUATE STEM RESEARCH SCHOLARSHIPS
• See page 127

NATIONAL ASSOCIATION FOR THE ADVANCEMENT OF COLORED PEOPLE

http://www.naacp.org/

HUBERTUS W.V. WELLEMS SCHOLARSHIP FOR MALE STUDENTS

Scholarship for a male, full-time student, majoring in engineering, chemistry, physics, or mathematical sciences. Graduate student may be full- or part-time and have 2.5 minimum GPA. Graduating high school seniors and undergraduates must have 3.0 minimum GPA. Must demonstrate financial need. Undergraduate scholarship is $2000; and graduate scholarship is $3000.

Academic Fields/Career Goals: Chemical Engineering; Engineering-Related Technologies; Engineering/Technology; Physical Sciences.

Award: Scholarship for use in freshman, sophomore, junior, senior, or graduate years; not renewable. *Number:* 1. *Amount:* $2000–$3000.

Eligibility Requirements: Applicant must be American Indian/Alaska Native, Asian/Pacific Islander, Black (non-Hispanic), Hispanic; enrolled or expecting to enroll full- or part-time at a two-year or four-year institution or university and male. Applicant or parent of applicant must be member of National Association for the Advancement of Colored People. Applicant must have 3.0 GPA or higher. Available to U.S. citizens.

Application Requirements: Application form, financial need analysis, recommendations or references, transcript. *Deadline:* March 7.

Contact: Victor Goode, Attorney
Phone: 410-580-5760
E-mail: info@naacp.org

NATIONAL BOARD OF BOILER AND PRESSURE VESSEL INSPECTORS

http://www.nationalboard.org/

NATIONAL BOARD TECHNICAL SCHOLARSHIP

Two $6000 scholarships to selected students meeting eligibility standards, who are pursuing a Bachelor's degree in certain engineering or related studies. Must be a child, step-child, grandchild, or great-grandchild of a past or present National Board member (living or deceased), or of a past or present Commissioned Inspector (living or deceased), employed by a member jurisdiction, or of a past or present National Board employee (living or deceased).

Academic Fields/Career Goals: Chemical Engineering; Electrical Engineering/Electronics; Mechanical Engineering.

Award: Scholarship for use in freshman, sophomore, junior, or senior years; not renewable. *Number:* 2. *Amount:* $6000.

Eligibility Requirements: Applicant must be enrolled or expecting to enroll full-time at a four-year or technical institution or university. Applicant or parent of applicant must be member of National Board of Boiler and Pressure Vessel Inspectors. Applicant must have 3.0 GPA or higher. Available to U.S. and Canadian citizens.

Application Requirements: Application form, essay, recommendations or references, transcript. *Deadline:* February 28.

Contact: Donald Tanner, Executive Director
Phone: 614-888-8320
Fax: 614-888-0750
E-mail: dtanner@nationalboard.org

NATIONAL SOCIETY OF PROFESSIONAL ENGINEERS

http://www.nspe.org/

MAUREEN L. AND HOWARD N. BLITMAN, PE SCHOLARSHIP TO PROMOTE DIVERSITY IN ENGINEERING

Award of $5000 in two disbursements of $2500 to a high school senior from an ethnic minority who has been accepted into an ABET-accredited engineering program at a four-year college or university.

Academic Fields/Career Goals: Chemical Engineering; Civil Engineering; Electrical Engineering/Electronics; Engineering-Related Technologies; Engineering/Technology; Materials Science, Engineering, and Metallurgy; Mechanical Engineering.

Award: Scholarship for use in freshman year; not renewable. *Number:* 1. *Amount:* $5000.

Eligibility Requirements: Applicant must be American Indian/Alaska Native, Black (non-Hispanic), Hispanic; high school student and planning to enroll or expecting to enroll full-time at a four-year institution or university. Applicant must have 2.5 GPA or higher. Available to U.S. citizens.

Application Requirements: Application form, community service, essay, recommendations or references, test scores, transcript. *Deadline:* March 1.

Contact: Cindy Simpson, Director of Education
Phone: 703-684-2833
E-mail: csimpson@nspe.org

PAUL H. ROBBINS HONORARY SCHOLARSHIP

Awarded annually to a current engineering undergraduate student entering the junior year in an ABET-accredited engineering program and attending a college/university that participates in the NSPE Professional Engineers in Higher Education (PEHE) Sustaining University Program(SUP).

Academic Fields/Career Goals: Chemical Engineering; Civil Engineering; Electrical Engineering/Electronics; Engineering-Related Technologies; Engineering/Technology; Materials Science, Engineering, and Metallurgy; Mechanical Engineering.

Award: Scholarship for use in junior year; renewable. *Number:* 1. *Amount:* $5000.

Eligibility Requirements: Applicant must be enrolled or expecting to enroll full-time at a four-year institution or university. Applicant or parent of applicant must be member of National Society of Professional Engineers. Available to U.S. citizens.

Application Requirements: Application form, essay, recommendations or references, test scores, transcript. *Deadline:* March 1.

Contact: Cindy Simpson, Director of Education
Phone: 703-684-2833
E-mail: csimpson@nspe.org

PROFESSIONAL ENGINEERS IN INDUSTRY SCHOLARSHIP

Applicants must be sponsored by an NSPE/PEI member. Students must have completed a minimum of two semesters or three quarters of undergraduate engineering studies (or be enrolled in graduate study) accredited by ABET.

Academic Fields/Career Goals: Chemical Engineering; Civil Engineering; Electrical Engineering/Electronics; Engineering-Related Technologies; Engineering/Technology; Materials Science, Engineering, and Metallurgy; Mechanical Engineering.

Award: Scholarship for use in sophomore, junior, or senior years; not renewable. *Number:* 1. *Amount:* $2500.

Eligibility Requirements: Applicant must be enrolled or expecting to enroll full-time at a four-year institution or university. Applicant must have 3.5 GPA or higher. Available to U.S. citizens.

Application Requirements: Application form, community service, essay, recommendations or references, resume, transcript, work experience certificates. *Deadline:* April 1.

Contact: Erin Reyes, Practice Division Manager
National Society of Professional Engineers
1420 King Street
Alexandria, VA 22314
Phone: 703-684-2884
E-mail: egarcia@nspe.org

NEVADA NASA SPACE GRANT CONSORTIUM

https://nasa.epscorspo.nevada.edu/

NATIONAL SPACE GRANT CONSORTIUM SCHOLARSHIPS

• *See page 127*

NEXTSTEPU

http://www.nextstepu.com/

$1,500 STEM SCHOLARSHIP

• *See page 120*

OREGON STUDENT ASSISTANCE COMMISSION

https://oregonstudentaid.gov/

SOCIETY OF AMERICAN MILITARY ENGINEERS PORTLAND POST SCHOLARSHIP

Award for a student who will enroll as college sophomore or above for fall term/semester in undergraduate study at a public college. Preference given to ROTC reservist, National Guard reservist, or prior service veteran. Must major in aeronautical, biomedical, chemical, civil, electrical, or mechanical engineering. Financial need may or may not be considered.

Academic Fields/Career Goals: Chemical Engineering; Civil Engineering; Electrical Engineering/Electronics; Engineering/Technology; Mechanical Engineering.

Award: Scholarship for use in sophomore, junior, or senior years; not renewable.

Eligibility Requirements: Applicant must be enrolled or expecting to enroll full-time at a four-year institution or university and resident of Oregon. Applicant must have 3.0 GPA or higher. Available to U.S. citizens.

Application Requirements: Application form, essay. *Deadline:* March 1.

Contact: Melissa Adams, Scholarship Processing Coordinator
Phone: 541-687-7409
E-mail: melissa.adams@state.or.us

ROBERT H. MOLLOHAN FAMILY CHARITABLE FOUNDATION, INC.

http://www.mollohanfoundation.org/

HIGH TECHNOLOGY SCHOLARS PROGRAM

• *See page 173*

SCARLETT FAMILY FOUNDATION SCHOLARSHIP PROGRAM

http://www.scarlettfoundation.org/

SCHOLARSHIP FOR STUDENTS PURSUING A BUSINESS OR STEM DEGREE

• *See page 91*

SEMICONDUCTOR RESEARCH CORPORATION (SRC)

http://www.src.org/

MASTER'S SCHOLARSHIP PROGRAM

Scholarship given to women or members of an under represented minority category (African-American, Hispanic, Native American). Scholarships are for study in disciplines related to microelectronics at U.S.-based universities having research funded by the Semiconductor Research Corporation and require U.S. citizenship or permanent resident status.

Academic Fields/Career Goals: Chemical Engineering; Computer Science/Data Processing; Electrical Engineering/Electronics; Engineering/Technology; Materials Science, Engineering, and Metallurgy.

Award: Scholarship for use in senior or graduate years; renewable. *Number:* 1–15. *Amount:* $25,000–$32,000.

Eligibility Requirements: Applicant must be American Indian/Alaska Native, Black (non-Hispanic), Hispanic and enrolled or expecting to enroll full-time at a four-year institution or university. Applicant must have 3.0 GPA or higher. Available to U.S. citizens.

Application Requirements: Application form, recommendations or references, resume, test scores, transcript. *Deadline:* February 15.

Contact: Virginia Wiggins, Student Relations Manager
Phone: 919-941-9453
E-mail: students@src.org

SIGMA XI, THE SCIENTIFIC RESEARCH SOCIETY

http://www.sigmaxi.org/

SIGMA XI GRANTS-IN-AID OF RESEARCH

• *See page 110*

SOCIETY OF AUTOMOTIVE ENGINEERS

https://www.sae.org/participate

BMW/SAE ENGINEERING SCHOLARSHIP

• *See page 160*

EDWARD D. HENDRICKSON/SAE ENGINEERING SCHOLARSHIP

• *See page 160*

TMC/SAE DONALD D. DAWSON TECHNICAL SCHOLARSHIP

• *See page 160*

SOCIETY OF PLASTICS ENGINEERS FOUNDATION (SPE)

http://www.4spe.org/

FLEMING/BLASZCAK SCHOLARSHIP

Award available for a full-time undergraduate student, with a demonstrated interest in the plastics industry. Must be a U.S. citizen and provide documentation of Mexican heritage.

Academic Fields/Career Goals: Chemical Engineering; Electrical Engineering/Electronics; Engineering/Technology; Industrial Design; Materials Science, Engineering, and Metallurgy; Trade/Technical Specialties.

Award: Scholarship for use in freshman, sophomore, junior, or senior years; not renewable. *Number:* 1. *Amount:* $2000.

Eligibility Requirements: Applicant must be of Mexican heritage; Hispanic and enrolled or expecting to enroll full-time at a two-year or four-year institution or university. Available to U.S. citizens.

Application Requirements: Application form, community service, essay. *Deadline:* April 1.

Contact: Mr. Gene Havel, Scholarships Program Administrator
Society of Plastics Engineers Foundation (SPE)
6 Berkshire Blvd., Suite 306
Bethel, CT 06801-1065
Phone: 203-740-5457
E-mail: foundation@4spe.org

GULF COAST HURRICANE SCHOLARSHIP

One $6,000 scholarship for a student at a 4-year college. One $2,000 scholarship for a student at a 2-year junior college or technical institute. Must be a resident of and attending school in FL, AL, MS, LA or TX.

Academic Fields/Career Goals: Chemical Engineering; Engineering-Related Technologies; Engineering/Technology; Industrial Design; Materials Science, Engineering, and Metallurgy; Mechanical Engineering; Science, Technology, and Society; Trade/Technical Specialties.

Award: Scholarship for use in freshman, sophomore, junior, senior, or graduate years; not renewable. *Number:* 1. *Amount:* $2000.

Eligibility Requirements: Applicant must be enrolled or expecting to enroll full-time at a two-year or four-year or technical institution or university; resident of Alabama, Florida, Louisiana, Mississippi, Texas and studying in Alabama, Florida, Louisiana, Mississippi, Texas. Available to U.S. citizens.

Application Requirements: Application form, community service, essay. *Deadline:* April 1.

Contact: Mr. Gene Havel, Scholarships Program Administrator
Society of Plastics Engineers Foundation (SPE)
6 Berkshire Blvd., Suite 306
Bethel, CT 06801-1065
Phone: 203-740-5457
E-mail: foundation@4spe.org

SOCIETY OF PLASTICS ENGINEERS SCHOLARSHIP PROGRAM

Scholarships awarded to full-time students who have demonstrated or expressed an interest in the plastics industry. Major or course of study must be beneficial to a career in the plastics industry.

Academic Fields/Career Goals: Chemical Engineering; Electrical Engineering/Electronics; Engineering/Technology; Industrial Design; Materials Science, Engineering, and Metallurgy; Trade/Technical Specialties.

Award: Scholarship for use in freshman, sophomore, junior, senior, or graduate years; not renewable. *Number:* 35–40. *Amount:* $1000–$6000.

Eligibility Requirements: Applicant must be enrolled or expecting to enroll full-time at a two-year or four-year or technical institution or university. Available to U.S. and non-U.S. citizens.

Application Requirements: Application form, community service, essay. *Deadline:* April 1.

Contact: Mr. Gene Havel, Scholarship Program Administrator
Society of Plastics Engineers Foundation (SPE)
6 Berkshire Boulevard, Suite 306
Bethel, CT 06801-1065
Phone: 203-740-5457
E-mail: foundation@4spe.org

SOCIETY OF WOMEN ENGINEERS

http://societyofwomenengineers.swe.org/

ADA I. PRESSMAN MEMORIAL SCHOLARSHIP

$5000 renewable scholarship for women pursuing ABET-accredited baccalaureate or graduate programs in preparation for careers in engineering, engineering technology, and computer science in the United States and Mexico. Must be a U.S. citizen and have a minimum 3.0 GPA.

Academic Fields/Career Goals: Chemical Engineering; Construction Engineering/Management; Electrical Engineering/Electronics; Energy and Power Engineering; Engineering/Technology; Marine/Ocean Engineering; Mechanical Engineering; Paper and Pulp Engineering.

Award: Scholarship for use in sophomore, junior, senior, or graduate years; renewable. *Number:* 9. *Amount:* $5000.

Eligibility Requirements: Applicant must be enrolled or expecting to enroll full-time at a four-year institution or university and female. Applicant must have 3.0 GPA or higher. Available to U.S. citizens.

Application Requirements: Application form. *Deadline:* February 15.

Contact: Scholarship Committee
Phone: 800-793-4636
E-mail: scholarships@swe.org

AMERICAN TRANSMISSION CO. SCHOLARSHIP

$1500 renewable scholarship for women pursuing ABET-accredited baccalaureate or graduate programs in preparation for careers in engineering, engineering technology, and computer science in the United States and Mexico. Must be a U.S. citizen and have a minimum 3.0 GPA. First choice college and home address must be in Illinois, Indiana, Iowa, Michigan, Minnesota, or Wisconsin.

Academic Fields/Career Goals: Chemical Engineering; Civil Engineering; Construction Engineering/Management; Electrical Engineering/Electronics; Energy and Power Engineering; Engineering/Technology; Marine/Ocean Engineering; Materials Science, Engineering, and Metallurgy; Mechanical Engineering; Paper and Pulp Engineering.

Award: Scholarship for use in sophomore, junior, or senior years; renewable. *Number:* 2. *Amount:* $1500.

Eligibility Requirements: Applicant must be enrolled or expecting to enroll full-time at a four-year institution or university; female; resident of Illinois, Indiana, Iowa, Michigan, Minnesota, Wisconsin and studying in Illinois, Indiana, Iowa, Michigan, Minnesota, Wisconsin. Applicant must have 3.0 GPA or higher. Available to U.S. citizens.

Application Requirements: Application form. *Deadline:* February 15.

Contact: Scholarship Committee
Phone: 800-793-4636
E-mail: scholarships@swe.org

ANNE MAUREEN WHITNEY BARROW MEMORIAL SCHOLARSHIP

$7000 award for women pursuing ABET-accredited baccalaureate programs in preparation for careers in engineering or engineering technology in the United States and Mexico. One award, renewable up to 5 years.

Academic Fields/Career Goals: Chemical Engineering; Construction Engineering/Management; Electrical Engineering/Electronics; Energy and Power Engineering; Engineering/Technology; Marine/Ocean Engineering; Mechanical Engineering; Paper and Pulp Engineering.

Award: Scholarship for use in freshman, sophomore, junior, or senior years; renewable. *Number:* 1. *Amount:* $7000.

Eligibility Requirements: Applicant must be enrolled or expecting to enroll full-time at a four-year institution or university and female. Available to U.S. citizens.

Application Requirements: Application form. *Deadline:* February 15.

Contact: Scholarship Committee
Phone: 800-793-4636
E-mail: scholarships@swe.org

ANNE SHEN SMITH ENDOWED SCHOLARSHIP

$1000 scholarship for women pursuing ABET-accredited Baccalaureate programs in preparation for careers in engineering, engineering technology, and computer science in the United States and Mexico. U.S. citizenship and minimum 3.0 GPA required; under-represented groups preferred. Must be studying at a California college or university.

Academic Fields/Career Goals: Chemical Engineering; Civil Engineering; Construction Engineering/Management; Electrical Engineering/Electronics; Energy and Power Engineering; Engineering/Technology; Marine/Ocean Engineering; Materials Science, Engineering, and Metallurgy; Mechanical Engineering; Paper and Pulp Engineering.

Award: Scholarship for use in sophomore, junior, or senior years; not renewable. *Number:* 1. *Amount:* $1000.

Eligibility Requirements: Applicant must be enrolled or expecting to enroll full-time at a four-year institution or university; female and studying in California. Applicant must have 3.0 GPA or higher. Available to U.S. citizens.

Application Requirements: Application form, essay. *Deadline:* February 15.

Contact: Scholarship Committee
Phone: 800-793-4636
E-mail: scholarships@swe.org

BETTY LOU BAILEY SWE REGION F SCHOLARSHIP

$1500 award for women pursuing ABET-accredited Baccalaureate or graduate programs in preparation for careers in engineering, engineering technology, and computer science in the United States and Mexico. U.S. citizenship, SWE membership, minimum 3.0 GPA, and financial need required. First choice is for the applicant to attend a college/university within the Region F boundaries of Connecticut, Maine, Massachusetts, New Hampshire, New York (upstate), Rhode Island, and Vermont. Second choice would be for the applicant's home address to be within the Region F boundaries.

Academic Fields/Career Goals: Chemical Engineering; Civil Engineering; Construction Engineering/Management; Electrical Engineering/Electronics; Energy and Power Engineering; Engineering/Technology; Marine/Ocean Engineering; Materials Science, Engineering, and Metallurgy; Mechanical Engineering; Paper and Pulp Engineering.

Award: Scholarship for use in sophomore, junior, senior, or graduate years; not renewable. *Number:* 1. *Amount:* $1500.

Eligibility Requirements: Applicant must be enrolled or expecting to enroll full-time at a four-year institution or university and female. Applicant or parent of applicant must be member of Society of Women Engineers. Applicant must have 3.0 GPA or higher. Available to U.S. citizens.

Application Requirements: Application form, financial need analysis. *Deadline:* February 15.

Contact: Scholarship Committee
Phone: 800-793-4636
E-mail: scholarships@swe.org

B.J. HARROD SCHOLARSHIP

Two $1500 scholarships for women pursuing ABET-accredited Baccalaureate programs in preparation for careers in engineering, engineering technology, and computer science in the United States and Mexico. Minimum 3.5 GPA required.

Academic Fields/Career Goals: Chemical Engineering; Civil Engineering; Construction Engineering/Management; Electrical Engineering/Electronics; Energy and Power Engineering; Engineering/Technology; Marine/Ocean Engineering; Materials Science, Engineering, and Metallurgy; Mechanical Engineering; Paper and Pulp Engineering.

Award: Scholarship for use in freshman year; not renewable. *Number:* 2. *Amount:* $1500.

Eligibility Requirements: Applicant must be enrolled or expecting to enroll full-time at a four-year institution or university and female. Applicant must have 3.5 GPA or higher. Available to U.S. citizens.

Application Requirements: Application form, essay. *Deadline:* May 1.

Contact: Scholarship Committee
Phone: 800-793-4636
E-mail: scholarships@swe.org

BK KRENZER MEMORIAL REENTRY SCHOLARSHIP

One $2500 award for women pursuing ABET-accredited Baccalaureate or graduate programs in preparation for careers in engineering, engineering technology, and computer science in the United States and Mexico. Must have been out of school and the engineering or technology workforce for a minimum of two years prior to beginning the current course of study. The student is not required to have prior engineering experience or education.

Academic Fields/Career Goals: Chemical Engineering; Construction Engineering/Management; Electrical Engineering/Electronics; Energy and Power Engineering; Engineering/Technology; Marine/Ocean Engineering; Materials Science, Engineering, and Metallurgy; Mechanical Engineering; Paper and Pulp Engineering.

Award: Scholarship for use in freshman, sophomore, junior, senior, or graduate years; not renewable. *Number:* 1. *Amount:* $2500.

Eligibility Requirements: Applicant must be enrolled or expecting to enroll full- or part-time at a four-year institution or university and female. Available to U.S. citizens.

Application Requirements: Application form. *Deadline:* February 15.

Contact: Scholarship Committee
Phone: 800-793-4636
E-mail: scholarships@swe.org

CAROL STEPHENS SWE REGION F SCHOLARSHIP

One $1250 scholarship for women pursuing ABET-accredited Baccalaureate or graduate programs in preparation for careers in engineering, engineering technology, and computer science in the United States and Mexico. Must attend a college/university within the Region F boundaries or home address must be within the Region F boundaries. U.S. citizenship, SWE membership and minimum 3.0 GPA required. Students with financial need preferred.

Academic Fields/Career Goals: Chemical Engineering; Civil Engineering; Construction Engineering/Management; Electrical Engineering/Electronics; Energy and Power Engineering; Engineering/Technology; Marine/Ocean Engineering; Materials Science, Engineering, and Metallurgy; Mechanical Engineering; Paper and Pulp Engineering.

Award: Scholarship for use in sophomore, junior, senior, or graduate years; not renewable. *Number:* 1. *Amount:* $1250.

Eligibility Requirements: Applicant must be enrolled or expecting to enroll full-time at a four-year institution or university and female. Applicant or parent of applicant must be member of Society of Women Engineers. Applicant must have 3.0 GPA or higher. Available to U.S. citizens.

Application Requirements: Application form, financial need analysis. *Deadline:* February 15.

Contact: Scholarship Committee
Phone: 800-793-4636
E-mail: scholarships@swe.org

CUMMINS SCHOLARSHIP

Two $2500 awards for women pursuing ABET-accredited Baccalaureate or graduate programs in preparation for careers in engineering, engineering technology, and computer science in the United States and Mexico. Preference given to under-represented groups and those willing to intern. Minimum 3.0 GPA required.

Academic Fields/Career Goals: Chemical Engineering; Computer Science/Data Processing; Electrical Engineering/Electronics; Engineering/Technology; Materials Science, Engineering, and Metallurgy; Mechanical Engineering.

Award: Scholarship for use in sophomore, junior, senior, or graduate years; not renewable. *Number:* 2. *Amount:* $2500.

Eligibility Requirements: Applicant must be enrolled or expecting to enroll full- or part-time at a four-year institution or university and female. Applicant must have 3.0 GPA or higher. Available to U.S. citizens.

Application Requirements: Application form. *Deadline:* February 15.

Contact: Scholarship Committee
Phone: 800-793-4636
E-mail: scholarships@swe.org

DR. IVY M. PARKER MEMORIAL SCHOLARSHIP

$1500 scholarship for a woman pursuing an ABET-accredited Baccalaureate program in preparation for a career in engineering, engineering technology, and computer science in the United States and Mexico. Must demonstrate financial need and have a minimum 3.0 GPA.

Academic Fields/Career Goals: Chemical Engineering; Civil Engineering; Construction Engineering/Management; Electrical Engineering/Electronics; Energy and Power Engineering; Engineering/Technology; Marine/Ocean Engineering; Materials Science, Engineering, and Metallurgy; Mechanical Engineering; Paper and Pulp Engineering.

Award: Scholarship for use in junior or senior years; renewable. *Number:* 1. *Amount:* $1500.

Eligibility Requirements: Applicant must be enrolled or expecting to enroll full-time at a four-year institution or university and female. Applicant must have 3.0 GPA or higher. Available to U.S. citizens.

Application Requirements: Application form, financial need analysis. *Deadline:* February 15.

Contact: Scholarship Committee
Phone: 800-793-4636
E-mail: scholarships@swe.org

DOROTHY LEMKE HOWARTH MEMORIAL SCHOLARSHIP

Six scholarships of $3000 awarded to sophomore women pursuing ABET-accredited Baccalaureate programs in preparation for careers in engineering, engineering technology, and computer science in the United States and Mexico. Must be a U.S. citizen and have a minimum 3.0 GPA.

Academic Fields/Career Goals: Chemical Engineering; Civil Engineering; Electrical Engineering/Electronics; Energy and Power Engineering; Engineering/Technology; Marine/Ocean Engineering; Materials Science, Engineering, and Metallurgy; Mechanical Engineering; Paper and Pulp Engineering.

Award: Scholarship for use in sophomore year; not renewable. *Number:* 6. *Amount:* $3000.

Eligibility Requirements: Applicant must be enrolled or expecting to enroll full-time at a four-year institution or university and female. Applicant must have 3.0 GPA or higher. Available to U.S. citizens.

Application Requirements: Application form. *Deadline:* February 15.

Contact: Scholarship Committee
Phone: 800-793-4636
E-mail: scholarships@swe.org

DOROTHY P. MORRIS SCHOLARSHIP

One $1500 scholarship for a woman pursuing an ABET-accredited Baccalaureate program in preparation for a career in engineering, engineering technology, or computer science in the United States and Mexico. Must be a U.S. citizen and have a minimum 3.0 GPA. Selection also based on financial need.

Academic Fields/Career Goals: Chemical Engineering; Civil Engineering; Construction Engineering/Management; Electrical Engineering/Electronics; Energy and Power Engineering; Engineering/Technology; Marine/Ocean Engineering; Materials Science, Engineering, and Metallurgy; Mechanical Engineering; Paper and Pulp Engineering.

Award: Scholarship for use in sophomore, junior, or senior years; not renewable. *Number:* 1. *Amount:* $1500.

Eligibility Requirements: Applicant must be enrolled or expecting to enroll full-time at a four-year institution or university and female. Applicant must have 3.0 GPA or higher. Available to U.S. citizens.

Application Requirements: Application form, financial need analysis. *Deadline:* February 15.

Contact: Scholarship Committee
Phone: 800-793-4636
E-mail: scholarships@swe.org

DUPONT COMPANY SCHOLARSHIP

Two $1000 awards for women pursuing ABET-accredited Baccalaureate programs in preparation for careers in engineering and engineering technology in the United States and Mexico. Minimum 3.0 GPA required. Limited to schools in the following states: AL, AR, CT, DC, DE, FL, GA, IA, IL, IN; KY, LA, MA, MD, ME, MI, MN, MO, MS, NC, NH, NJ, NY,OH, OK, PA, PR, RI, SC, TN, TX, VA, VT, WI and WV.

Academic Fields/Career Goals: Chemical Engineering; Engineering/Technology; Mechanical Engineering.

Award: Scholarship for use in sophomore, junior, or senior years; not renewable. *Number:* 2. *Amount:* $1000.

Eligibility Requirements: Applicant must be enrolled or expecting to enroll full-time at a four-year institution or university and female. Applicant must have 3.0 GPA or higher. Available to U.S. citizens.

Application Requirements: Application form. *Deadline:* February 15.

Contact: Scholarship Committee
Phone: 800-793-4636
E-mail: scholarships@swe.org

EXELON SCHOLARSHIP

Five awards of $1000 for freshmen, sophomore, and junior women pursuing ABET-accredited Baccalaureate programs in preparation for careers in electrical and mechanical engineering in the United States and Mexico. U.S. citizenship, under-represented groups, disabled, and veteran candidates preferred. Inquire for preferred list of schools.

Academic Fields/Career Goals: Chemical Engineering; Civil Engineering; Construction Engineering/Management; Electrical Engineering/Electronics; Energy and Power Engineering; Engineering/Technology; Marine/Ocean Engineering; Materials Science, Engineering, and Metallurgy; Mechanical Engineering; Paper and Pulp Engineering.

Award: Scholarship for use in freshman, sophomore, or junior years; not renewable. *Number:* 5. *Amount:* $1000.

Eligibility Requirements: Applicant must be enrolled or expecting to enroll full-time at a four-year institution or university and female. Available to U.S. citizens.

Application Requirements: Application form, essay. *Deadline:* February 15.

Contact: Scholarship Committee
Phone: 800-793-4636
E-mail: scholarships@swe.org

HONEYWELL SCHOLARSHIP

Three $5000 scholarships for women pursuing ABET-accredited Baccalaureate programs in preparation for careers in engineering, engineering technology, and computer science in the United States and Mexico. College or home residence must be located in AZ, CA, FL, IN, KS, MN, NM, PR, TX, or WA. U.S. citizenship, 3.5 GPA, and SWE membership required. Financial need and underrepresented students preferred.

Academic Fields/Career Goals: Chemical Engineering; Computer Science/Data Processing; Electrical Engineering/Electronics; Engineering/Technology; Materials Science, Engineering, and Metallurgy; Mechanical Engineering.

Award: Scholarship for use in sophomore, junior, or senior years; not renewable. *Number:* 3. *Amount:* $5000.

Eligibility Requirements: Applicant must be enrolled or expecting to enroll full-time at a four-year institution or university and female. Applicant or parent of applicant must be member of Society of Women Engineers. Applicant must have 3.5 GPA or higher. Available to U.S. citizens.

Application Requirements: Application form, financial need analysis. *Deadline:* February 15.

Contact: Scholarship Committee
Phone: 800-793-4636
E-mail: scholarships@swe.org

IBM LINDA SANFORD WOMEN'S TECHNICAL ADVANCEMENT SCHOLARSHIP

$1000 renewable scholarship for women pursuing ABET-accredited Baccalaureate or graduate programs in preparation for careers in engineering, engineering technology, and computer science in the United States and Mexico. Must be a U.S. citizen and have a minimum 3.5 GPA. Re-entry/nontraditional students preferred.

Academic Fields/Career Goals: Chemical Engineering; Civil Engineering; Construction Engineering/Management; Electrical Engineering/Electronics; Energy and Power Engineering; Engineering/Technology; Marine/Ocean Engineering; Materials Science, Engineering, and Metallurgy; Mechanical Engineering; Paper and Pulp Engineering.

Award: Scholarship for use in freshman, sophomore, junior, senior, or graduate years; not renewable. *Number:* 1. *Amount:* $1000.

Eligibility Requirements: Applicant must be enrolled or expecting to enroll full- or part-time at a four-year institution or university and female. Applicant must have 3.5 GPA or higher. Available to U.S. citizens.

Application Requirements: Application form. *Deadline:* February 15.

Contact: Scholarship Committee
Phone: 800-793-4636
E-mail: scholarships@swe.org

LILLIAN MOLLER GILBRETH MEMORIAL SCHOLARSHIP

One award of $14,500 for a woman pursuing an ABET-accredited Baccalaureate program in preparation for a career in engineering, engineering technology, and computer science in the United States and Mexico. Renewable for continuing undergraduate study only. Availability dependent upon renewal. Minimum 3.0 GPA required.

Academic Fields/Career Goals: Chemical Engineering; Civil Engineering; Computer Science/Data Processing; Construction Engineering/Management; Electrical Engineering/Electronics; Energy and Power Engineering; Engineering/Technology; Marine/Ocean Engineering; Materials Science, Engineering, and Metallurgy; Mechanical Engineering; Paper and Pulp Engineering.

Award: Scholarship for use in junior or senior years; not renewable. *Number:* 1. *Amount:* $14,500.

Eligibility Requirements: Applicant must be enrolled or expecting to enroll full-time at a four-year institution or university and female. Applicant must have 3.0 GPA or higher. Available to U.S. citizens.

Application Requirements: Application form. *Deadline:* February 15.

Contact: Scholarship Committee
Phone: 800-793-4636
E-mail: scholarships@swe.org

MARY V. MUNGER MEMORIAL SCHOLARSHIP

Two $2750 award for women pursuing an ABET-accredited Baccalaureate program in preparation for a career in engineering, engineering technology, or computer science in the United States and Mexico. Must be a U.S. citizen and a member of SWE. For use by college junior or senior or a re-entry/nontraditional student. Re-entry/nontraditional students must have been out of school and the engineering or technology workforce for a minimum of two years prior to beginning the current course of study. Minimum 3.0 GPA required.

Academic Fields/Career Goals: Chemical Engineering; Civil Engineering; Construction Engineering/Management; Electrical Engineering/Electronics; Energy and Power Engineering; Engineering/Technology; Marine/Ocean Engineering; Materials Science, Engineering, and Metallurgy; Mechanical Engineering; Paper and Pulp Engineering.

Award: Scholarship for use in junior or senior years; not renewable. *Number:* 2. *Amount:* $2750.

Eligibility Requirements: Applicant must be enrolled or expecting to enroll full-time at a four-year institution or university and female. Applicant or parent of applicant must be member of Society of Women Engineers. Applicant must have 3.0 GPA or higher. Available to U.S. citizens.

Application Requirements: Application form. *Deadline:* February 15.

Contact: Scholarship Committee
Phone: 800-793-4636
E-mail: scholarships@swe.org

OLIVE LYNN SALEMBIER MEMORIAL REENTRY SCHOLARSHIP

One $1500 scholarship for a women pursuing an ABET-accredited Baccalaureate or graduate program in preparation for a career in cngineering and cngineering tcchnology in the United States and Mexico. Must have been out of the engineering work force and out of school for a minimum of two years prior to re-entry. Minimum 3.0 GPA except for first year of reentry.

Academic Fields/Career Goals: Chemical Engineering; Civil Engineering; Construction Engineering/Management; Electrical Engineering/Electronics; Energy and Power Engineering; Engineering/Technology; Marine/Ocean Engineering; Materials Science, Engineering, and Metallurgy; Mechanical Engineering; Paper and Pulp Engineering.

Award: Scholarship for use in freshman, sophomore, junior, senior, or graduate years; not renewable. *Number:* 1. *Amount:* $1500.

Eligibility Requirements: Applicant must be enrolled or expecting to enroll full-time at a four-year institution or university and female. Available to U.S. citizens.

Application Requirements: Application form. *Deadline:* February 15.

Contact: Scholarship Committee
Phone: 800-793-4636
E-mail: scholarships@swe.org

PAULA LORING SIMON SCHOLARSHIP

One $1000 scholarship for a woman pursuing an ABET-accredited Baccalaureate program in preparation for a career in engineering, engineering technology, and computer science in the United States and Mexico. Must have a minimum 3.0 GPA.

Academic Fields/Career Goals: Chemical Engineering; Civil Engineering; Electrical Engineering/Electronics; Engineering/Technology.

Award: Scholarship for use in freshman year; not renewable. *Number:* 1. *Amount:* $1000.

Eligibility Requirements: Applicant must be enrolled or expecting to enroll full-time at a four-year institution or university and female. Applicant must have 3.0 GPA or higher. Available to U.S. citizens.

Application Requirements: Application form. *Deadline:* May 1.

Contact: Scholarship Committee
Phone: 800-793-4636
E-mail: scholarships@swe.org

ROBERTA BANASZAK GLEITER ENGINEERING ENDEAVOR SCHOLARSHIP

One $1250 award for women pursuing ABET-accredited Baccalaureate programs in preparation for careers in engineering, engineering technology, and computer science in the United States and Mexico. Must be U.S. citizen, have a minimum 3.0 GPA, and have SWE membership. Under-represented groups, reentry candidates, and financial need preferred. Renewal dependent on continued eligibility.

Academic Fields/Career Goals: Chemical Engineering; Computer Science/Data Processing; Construction Engineering/Management; Electrical Engineering/Electronics; Energy and Power Engineering; Engineering-Related Technologies; Engineering/Technology; Marine/Ocean Engineering; Materials Science, Engineering, and Metallurgy; Mechanical Engineering; Paper and Pulp Engineering.

Award: Scholarship for use in sophomore or junior years; not renewable. *Number:* 1. *Amount:* $1250.

Eligibility Requirements: Applicant must be enrolled or expecting to enroll full-time at a four-year institution or university and female. Applicant or parent of applicant must be member of Society of Women Engineers. Applicant must have 3.0 GPA or higher. Available to U.S. citizens.

Application Requirements: Application form, essay, financial need analysis. *Deadline:* February 15.

Contact: Scholarship Committee
Phone: 800-793-4636
E-mail: scholarships@swe.org

SUSAN MISZKOWICZ SEPTEMBER 11 MEMORIAL SCHOLARSHIP

$1500 award for a woman pursuing an ABET-accredited Baccalaureate program in preparation for a career in engineering, engineering technology, or computer science in the United States and Mexico. Minimum 3.0 GPA required.

Academic Fields/Career Goals: Chemical Engineering; Civil Engineering; Construction Engineering/Management; Electrical Engineering/Electronics; Energy and Power Engineering; Engineering/Technology; Marine/Ocean Engineering; Materials Science, Engineering, and Metallurgy; Mechanical Engineering; Paper and Pulp Engineering.

Award: Scholarship for use in sophomore, junior, or senior years; not renewable. *Number:* 1. *Amount:* $1500.

Eligibility Requirements: Applicant must be enrolled or expecting to enroll full-time at a four-year institution or university and female. Applicant must have 3.0 GPA or higher. Available to U.S. citizens.

Application Requirements: Application form. *Deadline:* February 15.

Contact: Scholarship Committee
Phone: 800-793-4636
E-mail: scholarships@swe.org

SWE BALTIMORE-WASHINGTON SECTION SCHOLARSHIP

One $2000 award for a woman pursuing an ABET-accredited Baccalaureate or graduate program in preparation for a career in engineering, engineering technology, or computer science in the United States and Mexico. For use at a school in DC, MD, or VA. U.S. citizenship and SWE membership required.

Academic Fields/Career Goals: Chemical Engineering; Civil Engineering; Construction Engineering/Management; Electrical Engineering/Electronics; Energy and Power Engineering; Engineering/Technology; Marine/Ocean Engineering; Materials Science, Engineering, and Metallurgy; Mechanical Engineering; Paper and Pulp Engineering.

Award: Scholarship for use in sophomore, junior, senior, or graduate years; not renewable. *Number:* 1. *Amount:* $2000.

Eligibility Requirements: Applicant must be enrolled or expecting to enroll full-time at a four-year institution or university; female and studying in District of Columbia, Maryland, Virginia. Applicant or parent of applicant must be member of Society of Women Engineers. Applicant must have 3.0 GPA or higher. Available to U.S. citizens.

Application Requirements: Application form. *Deadline:* February 15.

Contact: Scholarship Committee
Phone: 800-793-4636
E-mail: scholarships@swe.org

SWE CENTRAL NEW MEXICO PIONEERS SCHOLARSHIP

Renewable $1500 scholarship for a woman pursuing an ABET-accredited Baccalaureate program in preparation for a career in engineering, engineering technology, or computer science in the United States and Mexico. Must attend a NM university or 4-year engineering/technology school. U.S. citizenship, SWE membership, and minimum 3.0 GPA required. Renewable up to three years. Availability dependent upon renewal.

Academic Fields/Career Goals: Chemical Engineering; Civil Engineering; Construction Engineering/Management; Electrical Engineering/Electronics; Energy and Power Engineering; Engineering/Technology; Marine/Ocean Engineering; Materials Science, Engineering, and Metallurgy; Mechanical Engineering; Paper and Pulp Engineering.

Award: Scholarship for use in sophomore, junior, or senior years; renewable. *Number:* 1. *Amount:* $1500.

Eligibility Requirements: Applicant must be enrolled or expecting to enroll full-time at a four-year institution or university; female and studying in New Mexico. Applicant or parent of applicant must be member of Society of Women Engineers. Applicant must have 3.0 GPA or higher. Available to U.S. citizens.

Application Requirements: Application form. *Deadline:* February 15.

Contact: Scholarship Committee
        Phone: 800-793-4636
        E-mail: scholarships@swe.org

SWE CENTRAL NEW MEXICO REENTRY SCHOLARSHIP

$1500 scholarship for a woman pursuing an ABET-accredited Baccalaureate or graduate program in preparation for a career in engineering, engineering technology, or computer science in the United States and Mexico. Must be a U.S. citizen, have SWE membership, and have a minimum 3.0 GPA. Must attend a university located in New Mexico. Reentry for undergraduate sophomore, junior, senior, or graduate student. If there is no qualified candidate, the Scholarship Committee can award a second CNM-Pioneers Scholarship. Renewable up to 6 years.

Academic Fields/Career Goals: Chemical Engineering; Civil Engineering; Construction Engineering/Management; Electrical Engineering/Electronics; Energy and Power Engineering; Engineering/Technology; Marine/Ocean Engineering; Materials Science, Engineering, and Metallurgy; Mechanical Engineering; Paper and Pulp Engineering.

Award: Scholarship for use in sophomore, junior, senior, or graduate years; renewable. *Number:* 1. *Amount:* $1500.

Eligibility Requirements: Applicant must be enrolled or expecting to enroll full-time at a four-year institution or university; female and studying in New Mexico. Applicant or parent of applicant must be member of Society of Women Engineers. Applicant must have 3.0 GPA or higher. Available to U.S. citizens.

Application Requirements: Application form. *Deadline:* February 15.

Contact: Scholarship Committee
        Phone: 800-793-4636
        E-mail: scholarships@swe.org

SWE MID-HUDSON SECTION SCHOLARSHIP

$1250 scholarship for a woman pursuing an ABET-accredited Baccalaureate or graduate program in preparation for a career in engineering, engineering technology, or computer science in the United States and Mexico. New York is the preferred state for home residence and study. Minimum 3.0 GPA required.

Academic Fields/Career Goals: Chemical Engineering; Civil Engineering; Construction Engineering/Management; Electrical Engineering/Electronics; Energy and Power Engineering; Engineering/Technology; Marine/Ocean Engineering; Materials Science, Engineering, and Metallurgy; Mechanical Engineering; Paper and Pulp Engineering.

Award: Scholarship for use in sophomore, junior, senior, or graduate years; not renewable. *Number:* 1. *Amount:* $1250.

Eligibility Requirements: Applicant must be enrolled or expecting to enroll full-time at a four-year institution or university; female; resident of New York and studying in New York. Applicant must have 3.0 GPA or higher. Available to U.S. citizens.

Application Requirements: Application form. *Deadline:* February 15.

Contact: Scholarship Committee
        Phone: 800-793-4636
        E-mail: scholarships@swe.org

SWE PHOENIX SECTION SCHOLARSHIP

$3000 scholarship for a woman pursuing an ABET-accredited Baccalaureate program in preparation for a career in engineering, engineering technology, or computer science in the United States and Mexico. Must attend a school in Arizona. SWE membership and minimum 3.0 GPA required.

Academic Fields/Career Goals: Chemical Engineering; Civil Engineering; Construction Engineering/Management; Electrical Engineering/Electronics; Energy and Power Engineering; Engineering/Technology; Marine/Ocean Engineering; Materials Science, Engineering, and Metallurgy; Mechanical Engineering; Paper and Pulp Engineering.

Award: Scholarship for use in sophomore, junior, or senior years; not renewable. *Number:* 1. *Amount:* $3000.

Eligibility Requirements: Applicant must be enrolled or expecting to enroll full-time at à four-year institution or university; female and studying in Arizona. Applicant or parent of applicant must be member of Society of Women Engineers. Applicant must have 3.0 GPA or higher. Available to U.S. citizens.

Application Requirements: Application form. *Deadline:* February 15.

Contact: Scholarship Committee
        Phone: 800-793-4636
        E-mail: scholarships@swe.org

SWE REGION E SCHOLARSHIP

One $1500 award for women pursuing ABET-accredited Baccalaureate or graduate programs in preparation for careers in engineering, engineering technology, and computer science in the United States and Mexico. SWE membership and minimum 3.0 GPA required. Must be attending school within the Region E boundaries: Delaware, District of Columbia, Eastern Pennsylvania, Maryland, New Jersey, New York, and Virginia.

Academic Fields/Career Goals: Chemical Engineering; Civil Engineering; Computer Science/Data Processing; Construction Engineering/Management; Electrical Engineering/Electronics; Energy and Power Engineering; Engineering-Related Technologies; Engineering/Technology; Marine/Ocean Engineering; Mechanical Engineering; Paper and Pulp Engineering.

Award: Scholarship for use in sophomore, junior, senior, or graduate years; not renewable. *Number:* 1. *Amount:* $1500.

Eligibility Requirements: Applicant must be enrolled or expecting to enroll full-time at a four-year institution or university; female and studying in Delaware, District of Columbia, Maryland, New Jersey, New York, Pennsylvania, Virginia. Applicant or parent of applicant must be member of Society of Women Engineers. Applicant must have 3.0 GPA or higher. Available to U.S. citizens.

Application Requirements: Application form, essay. *Deadline:* February 15.

Contact: Scholarship Committee
        Phone: 800-793-4636
        E-mail: scholarships@swe.org

SWE REGION G JUDY SIMMONS MEMORIAL SCHOLARSHIP

One $1250 award for women pursuing ABET-accredited Baccalaureate or graduate programs in preparation for careers in engineering, engineering technology, and computer science in the United States and Mexico. May attend any colleges and universities with an active SWE section within Region G, which includes all of Kentucky, Ohio, West Virginia, and the western half of Pennsylvania. SWE membership and minimum 3.0 GPA required.

Academic Fields/Career Goals: Chemical Engineering; Civil Engineering; Computer Science/Data Processing; Construction Engineering/Management; Electrical Engineering/Electronics; Energy and Power Engineering; Engineering-Related Technologies; Engineering/Technology; Marine/Ocean Engineering; Materials Science, Engineering, and Metallurgy; Paper and Pulp Engineering.

Award: Scholarship for use in sophomore, junior, senior, or graduate years; not renewable. *Number:* 1. *Amount:* $1250.

Eligibility Requirements: Applicant must be enrolled or expecting to enroll full-time at a four-year institution or university; female and studying in Kentucky, Ohio, Pennsylvania, West Virginia. Applicant or parent of applicant must be member of Society of Women Engineers. Applicant must have 3.0 GPA or higher. Available to U.S. citizens.

Application Requirements: Application form, essay. *Deadline:* February 15.

Contact: Scholarship Committee
Phone: 800-793-4636
E-mail: scholarships@swe.org

SWE REGION H SCHOLARSHIPS

Two awards ranging from $1250 to $1500 for women pursuing ABET-accredited Baccalaureate or graduate programs in preparation for careers in engineering, engineering technology, and computer science in the United States and Mexico. SWE membership and minimum 3.0 GPA required. Must attend a school within Region H boundaries, which includes ND, SD, MN, IA, WI, IL, MI, and IN. Level of involvement in SWE should be high, as well as the amount of time spent volunteering, level of commitment, and years of service.

Academic Fields/Career Goals: Chemical Engineering; Civil Engineering; Construction Engineering/Management; Electrical Engineering/Electronics; Energy and Power Engineering; Engineering/Technology; Marine/Ocean Engineering; Materials Science, Engineering, and Metallurgy; Mechanical Engineering; Paper and Pulp Engineering.

Award: Scholarship for use in sophomore, junior, senior, or graduate years; not renewable. *Number:* 2. *Amount:* $1250–$1500.

Eligibility Requirements: Applicant must be enrolled or expecting to enroll full-time at a four-year institution or university; female and studying in Illinois, Indiana, Iowa, Michigan, Minnesota, North Dakota, South Dakota, Wisconsin. Applicant or parent of applicant must be member of Society of Women Engineers. Applicant must have 3.0 GPA or higher. Available to U.S. citizens.

Application Requirements: Application form. *Deadline:* February 15.

Contact: Scholarship Committee
Phone: 800-793-4636
E-mail: scholarships@swe.org

SWE REGION J SCHOLARSHIP

$1000 scholarship available to women pursuing ABET-accredited Baccalaureate or graduate programs in preparation for careers in engineering, engineering technology, and computer science in the United States and Mexico. SWE membership required. Must be attending school in the Region J boundaries: Alaska, Washington, Oregon, Montana, and Idaho. Renewable for 5 years. Availability dependent upon renewals.

Academic Fields/Career Goals: Chemical Engineering; Civil Engineering; Construction Engineering/Management; Electrical Engineering/Electronics; Energy and Power Engineering; Engineering/Technology; Marine/Ocean Engineering; Materials Science, Engineering, and Metallurgy; Mechanical Engineering; Paper and Pulp Engineering.

Award: Scholarship for use in sophomore, junior, senior, or graduate years; renewable. *Number:* 1. *Amount:* $1000.

Eligibility Requirements: Applicant must be enrolled or expecting to enroll full-time at a four-year institution or university; female and studying in Alaska, Idaho, Montana, Oregon, Washington. Applicant or parent of applicant must be member of Society of Women Engineers. Applicant must have 3.0 GPA or higher. Available to U.S. citizens.

Application Requirements: Application form, essay. *Deadline:* February 15.

Contact: Scholarship Committee
Phone: 800-793-4636
E-mail: scholarships@swe.org

TE CONNECTIVITY EXCELLENCE IN ENGINEERING SCHOLARSHIP

20 scholarships of $5000 for women pursuing ABET-accredited Baccalaureate programs in preparation for careers in engineering, engineering technology, and computer science in the United States and Mexico. Must be a U.S. citizen and have a minimum 3.0 GPA. Preference given to students who are from underrepresented backgrounds in STEM and/or those who demonstrate financial need.

Academic Fields/Career Goals: Chemical Engineering; Civil Engineering; Construction Engineering/Management; Electrical Engineering/Electronics; Engineering-Related Technologies; Engineering/Technology; Marine/Ocean Engineering; Materials Science, Engineering, and Metallurgy; Mechanical Engineering; Paper and Pulp Engineering.

Award: Scholarship for use in junior or senior years; not renewable. *Number:* 20. *Amount:* $5000.

Eligibility Requirements: Applicant must be enrolled or expecting to enroll full-time at a four-year institution or university and female. Applicant must have 3.0 GPA or higher. Available to U.S. citizens.

Application Requirements: Application form. *Deadline:* February 15.

Contact: Scholarship Committee
Phone: 800-793-4636
E-mail: scholarships@swe.org

TURNER CONSTRUCTION SCHOLARSHIP

Two $2500 scholarships available to sophomore women pursuing ABET-accredited Baccalaureate programs in preparation for careers in engineering, engineering technology, and computer science in the United States and Mexico. U.S. citizenship, 3.0 GPA, and SWE membership required.

Academic Fields/Career Goals: Chemical Engineering; Construction Engineering/Management; Engineering/Technology; Mechanical Engineering; Paper and Pulp Engineering.

Award: Scholarship for use in sophomore year; not renewable. *Number:* 2. *Amount:* $2500.

Eligibility Requirements: Applicant must be enrolled or expecting to enroll full-time at a four-year institution or university and female. Applicant or parent of applicant must be member of Society of Women Engineers. Applicant must have 3.0 GPA or higher. Available to U.S. citizens.

Application Requirements: Application form, essay. *Deadline:* February 15.

Contact: Scholarship Committee
Phone: 800-793-4636
E-mail: scholarships@swe.org

WANDA MUNN SCHOLARSHIP

One $1500 award for a woman pursuing an ABET-accredited Baccalaureate or graduate program in preparation for a career in engineering, engineering technology, or computer science in the United States and Mexico. Must have satisfactorily completed of a minimum of two years full-time equivalent credits at an ABET-accredited school. Home or school must be in Alaska, Idaho, Montana, Oregon, or Washington.

Academic Fields/Career Goals: Chemical Engineering; Civil Engineering; Construction Engineering/Management; Electrical Engineering/Electronics; Energy and Power Engineering; Engineering/Technology; Marine/Ocean Engineering; Materials Science, Engineering, and Metallurgy; Mechanical Engineering; Paper and Pulp Engineering.

Award: Scholarship for use in sophomore, junior, senior, or graduate years; not renewable. *Number:* 1. *Amount:* $1500.

Eligibility Requirements: Applicant must be enrolled or expecting to enroll full- or part-time at a four-year institution or university and female. Available to U.S. citizens.

Application Requirements: Application form. *Deadline:* February 15.

Contact: Scholarship Committee
Phone: 800-793-4636
E-mail: scholarships@swe.org

SOCIETY OF WOMEN ENGINEERS-ROCKY MOUNTAIN SECTION

http://www.swe-rms.org/

SOCIETY OF WOMEN ENGINEERS-ROCKY MOUNTAIN SECTION SCHOLARSHIP PROGRAM

• *See page 161*

SONS OF NORWAY FOUNDATION

http://www.sonsofnorway.com/foundation

NANCY LORRAINE JENSEN MEMORIAL SCHOLARSHIP

Scholarship available for full-time undergraduate study in chemistry, physics, or in chemical, electrical, or mechanical engineering by a female student who is a U.S. citizen, and a current member, daughter, or granddaughter of a current member of Sons of Norway. The annual award will be at least 50 percent of the tuition for one semester and no more than 100 percent of the tuition for one year. Must have attained a SAT score of at least 1800, a math score of 600 or better, or an ACT score of at least 26. Applicant must have completed at least one term of studies in the above fields. The award will be made jointly payable to the student and her institution. The award is renewable two times during undergraduate study.

Academic Fields/Career Goals: Chemical Engineering; Electrical Engineering/Electronics; Mechanical Engineering.

Award: Scholarship for use in sophomore, junior, or senior years; not renewable. *Number:* 1–6. *Amount:* $2500–$10,000.

Eligibility Requirements: Applicant must be of Norwegian heritage; age 17-35; enrolled or expecting to enroll full-time at a four-year institution or university; female and must have an interest in science. Applicant must have 3.5 GPA or higher. Available to U.S. citizens.

Application Requirements: Application form, essay, personal photograph, recommendations or references, test scores, transcript. *Deadline:* April 1.

Contact: Scholarship Coordinator
Sons of Norway Foundation
1455 West Lake Street
Minneapolis, MN 55408-2666
Phone: 612-827-3611
Fax: 612-827-0658
E-mail: foundation@sofn.com

STRAIGHTFORWARD MEDIA

http://www.straightforwardmedia.com/

STRAIGHTFORWARD MEDIA ENGINEERING SCHOLARSHIP

Scholarship of $500 to students attending or planning to enroll in a postsecondary engineering program in the United States or abroad. Scholarship is awarded four times per year. Deadlines: March 31, June 30, September 30, and December 31. For more information, see web http://www.straightforwardmedia.com/engineering/form.php.

Academic Fields/Career Goals: Chemical Engineering; Civil Engineering; Electrical Engineering/Electronics; Energy and Power Engineering; Engineering-Related Technologies; Engineering/Technology; Materials Science, Engineering, and Metallurgy; Mechanical Engineering; Paper and Pulp Engineering.

Award: Scholarship for use in freshman, sophomore, junior, or senior years; not renewable. *Number:* 4. *Amount:* $500.

Eligibility Requirements: Applicant must be enrolled or expecting to enroll full- or part-time at a two-year or four-year or technical institution or university. Available to U.S. and non-U.S. citizens.

Application Requirements: Essay. *Deadline:* varies.

Contact: Scholarship Committee
Phone: 605-348-3042

STRAIGHT NORTH

https://www.straightnorth.com/

STRAIGHT NORTH STEM SCHOLARSHIP

• See page 92

TAU BETA PI ASSOCIATION

https://www.tbp.org/

TAU BETA PI SCHOLARSHIP PROGRAM

One-time award for initiated members of Tau Beta Pi for their senior year of full-time undergraduate engineering study.

Academic Fields/Career Goals: Chemical Engineering; Civil Engineering; Electrical Engineering/Electronics; Engineering-Related Technologies; Engineering/Technology; Materials Science, Engineering, and Metallurgy; Mechanical Engineering.

Award: Scholarship for use in senior year; not renewable. *Number:* 200–300. *Amount:* $1000–$2000.

Eligibility Requirements: Applicant must be enrolled or expecting to enroll full- or part-time at a four-year institution or university. Applicant or parent of applicant must be member of Tau Beta Pi Association. Available to U.S. and non-U.S. citizens.

Application Requirements: Application form, essay, personal photograph. *Deadline:* April 1.

Contact: Dylan Lane, Communications Specialist
Knoxville, TN 37996
Phone: 865-546-4578
E-mail: dylan@tbp.org

UNITED NEGRO COLLEGE FUND

http://www.uncf.org/

DAVIS SCHOLARSHIP FOR WOMEN IN STEM

One-time award of up to $5000 for minority female students to pursue a future career in the STEM fields. Must be at least sophomore standing. Preference will be given to students from Massachusetts, although all eligible students are encouraged to apply. Must be a U.S. citizen or permanent resident and have a minimum 3.0 GPA.

Academic Fields/Career Goals: Chemical Engineering; Computer Science/Data Processing; Electrical Engineering/Electronics; Energy and Power Engineering; Engineering/Technology; Mathematics; Mechanical Engineering.

Award: Scholarship for use in sophomore, junior, or senior years; not renewable. *Number:* 2.

Eligibility Requirements: Applicant must be Black (non-Hispanic); enrolled or expecting to enroll full-time at a four-year institution or university and female. Applicant must have 3.0 GPA or higher. Available to U.S. citizens.

Application Requirements: Application form, essay, financial need analysis. *Deadline:* June 9.

Contact: Mary Williams, Director of Outreach and Recruitment
Phone: 800-331-2244

GALACTIC UNITE BYTHEWAY SCHOLARSHIP

Scholarship of up to $7500 for a first-year female college student pursuing STEM degrees at any accredited four-year college or university in the United States. Minimum 3.2 GPA required. The selected recipients will be required to participate in the Galactic Unite mentorship program.

Academic Fields/Career Goals: Chemical Engineering; Computer Science/Data Processing; Energy and Power Engineering; Engineering/Technology; Materials Science, Engineering, and Metallurgy; Mathematics; Mechanical Engineering.

Award: Scholarship for use in freshman year; renewable.

Eligibility Requirements: Applicant must be Black (non-Hispanic); high school student; planning to enroll or expecting to enroll full-time at a four-year institution or university and female. Applicant must have 3.0 GPA or higher. Available to U.S. citizens.

Application Requirements: Application form. *Deadline:* June 30.

Contact: Mary Williams, Director of Outreach and Recruitment
Phone: 800-331-2244

PROCTER & GAMBLE STEM SCHOLARSHIP

• See page 128

UNCF STEM SCHOLARS PROGRAM

• See page 175

WILLIAM WRIGLEY FOUNDATION SCHOLARSHIP

• See page 95

UNIVERSITIES SPACE RESEARCH ASSOCIATION

http://www.usra.edu/

UNIVERSITIES SPACE RESEARCH ASSOCIATION SCHOLARSHIP AWARD PROGRAM

• See page 128

XEROX

http://www.xerox.com//

TECHNICAL MINORITY SCHOLARSHIP

Scholarships are made available to minority students enrolled in technical degree programs at the Bachelor's degree level or above. Eligible students must have a GPA of 3.0 or higher and show financial need. Refer to website http://www.studentcareers-xerox-com.tmpqa.com/ for details.

Academic Fields/Career Goals: Chemical Engineering; Computer Science/Data Processing; Electrical Engineering/Electronics; Engineering-Related Technologies; Engineering/Technology; Materials Science, Engineering, and Metallurgy; Mechanical Engineering; Physical Sciences.

Award: Scholarship for use in freshman, sophomore, junior, senior, graduate, or postgraduate years; not renewable. *Number:* up to 128. *Amount:* $1000–$10,000.

Eligibility Requirements: Applicant must be American Indian/Alaska Native, Asian/Pacific Islander, Black (non-Hispanic), Hispanic and enrolled or expecting to enroll full-time at a four-year institution or university. Applicant must have 3.0 GPA or higher. Available to U.S. citizens.

Application Requirements: Application form, financial need analysis, resume. *Deadline:* September 30.

Contact: Stephanie Michalowski
Xerox
150 State Street
Rochester, NY 14614
Fax: 585-482-3095
E-mail: xtmsp@rballiance.com

CHILD AND FAMILY STUDIES

CALIFORNIA STUDENT AID COMMISSION

http://www.csac.ca.gov/

CHILD DEVELOPMENT TEACHER AND SUPERVISOR GRANT PROGRAM

Award is for those students pursuing an approved course of study leading to a Child Development Permit issued by the California Commission on Teacher Credentialing. In exchange for each year funding is received, recipients agree to provide one year of service in a licensed childcare center.

Academic Fields/Career Goals: Child and Family Studies; Education.

Award: Grant for use in freshman, sophomore, junior, senior, or graduate years; renewable. *Number:* up to 300. *Amount:* $1000–$2000.

Eligibility Requirements: Applicant must be enrolled or expecting to enroll full- or part-time at a two-year or four-year institution or university; resident of California and studying in California. Applicant or parent of applicant must have employment or volunteer experience in teaching/education. Available to U.S. citizens.

Application Requirements: Application form, financial need analysis, GPA verification, recommendations or references. *Deadline:* April 16.

Contact: Catalina Mistler, Chief, Program Administration and Services Division
California Student Aid Commission
PO Box 419026
Rancho Cordova, CA 95741-9026
Phone: 916-464-7268
Fax: 916-526-8004
E-mail: studentsupport@csac.ca.gov

LAW OFFICES OF PROSPER SHAKED

https://www.prosperlaw.com/

PROSPER SHAKED SCHOLARSHIP FOR FUTURE MEDICAL PROFESSIONALS

• See page 166

MASSACHUSETTS OFFICE OF STUDENT FINANCIAL ASSISTANCE

http://www.osfa.mass.edu/

EARLY CHILDHOOD EDUCATORS SCHOLARSHIP PROGRAM

Scholarship to provide financial assistance for currently employed early childhood educators and providers who enroll in an associate or bachelor degree program in Early Childhood Education or related programs. Awards are not based on financial need. Individuals taking their first college-level ECE course are eligible for 100 percent tuition, while subsequent ECE courses are awarded at 50 percent tuition. Can be used for one class each semester.

Academic Fields/Career Goals: Child and Family Studies; Education.

Award: Scholarship for use in freshman, sophomore, junior, or senior years; not renewable. *Amount:* $150–$3600.

Eligibility Requirements: Applicant must be enrolled or expecting to enroll full- or part-time at a two-year or four-year institution or university; resident of Massachusetts and studying in Massachusetts. Available to U.S. citizens.

Application Requirements: Application form. *Deadline:* June 1.

Contact: Ms. Jean Szymaniak, Senior Program Assistant
Massachusetts Office of Student Financial Assistance
75 Pleasant Street
Malden, MA 02148
Phone: 617-391-6083
E-mail: jszymaniak@dhe.mass.edu

MICHAEL MOODY FITNESS

http://www.michaelmoodyfitness.com/

MICHAEL MOODY FITNESS SCHOLARSHIP

• See page 166

SOCIETY OF PEDIATRIC NURSES

http://www.pedsnurses.org/

SOCIETY OF PEDIATRIC NURSES EDUCATIONAL SCHOLARSHIP

Award to a member engaged in a BSN completion program or a graduate program that will advance the health of children. Nominee must be a current Society of Pediatric Nurses member.

Academic Fields/Career Goals: Child and Family Studies; Health and Medical Sciences; Nursing.

Award: Scholarship for use in freshman, sophomore, junior, senior, or graduate years; not renewable. *Number:* 1. *Amount:* $500.

Eligibility Requirements: Applicant must be enrolled or expecting to enroll full-time at a four-year institution or university. Applicant or parent of applicant must be member of Society of Pediatric Nurses. Applicant or parent of applicant must have employment or volunteer experience in nursing. Available to U.S. citizens.

Application Requirements: Application form, essay, recommendations or references, resume. *Deadline:* November 14.

Contact: Scholarship Committee
Phone: 800-723-2902
Fax: 850-484-8762
E-mail: spn@puetzamc.com

WILLIAMS LAW GROUP

https://familylawyersnewjersey.com/

WILLIAMS LAW GROUP OPPORTUNITY TO GROW SCHOLARSHIP
• *See page 139*

Y'S MEN INTERNATIONAL

http://www.ysmen.org/

ALEXANDER SCHOLARSHIP LOAN FUND
• *See page 185*

CIVIL ENGINEERING

AACE INTERNATIONAL

http://www.aacei.org/

AACE INTERNATIONAL COMPETITIVE SCHOLARSHIP
• *See page 130*

ACI FOUNDATION

http://www.acifoundation.org

ACI FOUNDATION SCHOLARSHIP PROGRAM
• *See page 130*

AIST FOUNDATION

http://www.aistfoundation.org/

ASSOCIATION FOR IRON AND STEEL TECHNOLOGY DAVID H. SAMSON CANADIAN SCHOLARSHIP
• *See page 187*

AMERICAN COUNCIL OF ENGINEERING COMPANIES OF PENNSYLVANIA (ACEC/PA)

http://www.acecpa.org/

ERIC J. GENNUSO AND LEROY D. (BUD) LOY, JR. SCHOLARSHIP PROGRAM
• *See page 187*

AMERICAN INDIAN SCIENCE AND ENGINEERING SOCIETY

http://www.aises.org/

A.T. ANDERSON MEMORIAL SCHOLARSHIP PROGRAM
• *See page 121*

AMERICAN PUBLIC POWER ASSOCIATION

https://www.publicpower.org/grants-scholarships

DEED EDUCATIONAL SCHOLARSHIP
• *See page 190*

DEED STUDENT INTERNSHIP
• *See page 190*

DEED STUDENT RESEARCH GRANTS
Student Research Grants are awarded to students who are majoring in a field that could lead to a career in the public power industry. Applicants must be sponsored by a DEED member utility and attend an accredited university/college full-time in the U.S. Email DEED@publicpower.org for access to the application.

Academic Fields/Career Goals: Civil Engineering; Construction Engineering/Management; Electrical Engineering/Electronics; Energy and Power Engineering; Engineering-Related Technologies; Engineering/Technology; Environmental Science; Mechanical Engineering; Natural Resources.

Award: Scholarship for use in freshman, sophomore, junior, senior, graduate, or postgraduate years; not renewable. *Number:* 10. *Amount:* $5000.

Eligibility Requirements: Applicant must be Hispanic and enrolled or expecting to enroll full-time at a two-year or four-year or technical institution or university. Available to U.S. and non-U.S. citizens.

Application Requirements: Application form. *Deadline:* continuous.

Contact: Jack Miller, DEED and Engineering Services Assistant
E-mail: DEED@publicpower.org

DEED TECHNICAL DESIGN PROJECT
• *See page 191*

AMERICAN PUBLIC TRANSPORTATION FOUNDATION

http://www.apta.com/

TRANSIT HALL OF FAME SCHOLARSHIP AWARD PROGRAM
Renewable award for sophomores, juniors, seniors or graduate students studying transportation or rail transit engineering. Must be sponsored by APTA member organization and complete an internship program with a member organization. Must have a minimum 3.0 GPA and be a U.S. or Canadian citizen.

Academic Fields/Career Goals: Civil Engineering; Electrical Engineering/Electronics; Engineering-Related Technologies; Engineering/Technology; Mechanical Engineering; Transportation.

Award: Scholarship for use in sophomore, junior, senior, or graduate years; renewable. *Number:* 1. *Amount:* $2500.

Eligibility Requirements: Applicant must be enrolled or expecting to enroll full-time at a two-year or four-year institution or university. Applicant must have 3.0 GPA or higher. Available to U.S. and Canadian citizens.

Application Requirements: Application form, essay, financial need analysis, nomination by APTA member, verification of enrollment, copy of fee schedule from the college/university for the academic year, recommendations or references, transcript. *Deadline:* June 16.

Contact: Pamela Boswell, Vice President of Program Management
American Public Transportation Foundation
1666 K Street, NW
Washington, DC 20006-1215
Phone: 202-496-4803
Fax: 202-496-4323

AMERICAN RAILWAY ENGINEERING AND MAINTENANCE OF WAY ASSOCIATION

http://www.aremafoundation.org/

AREMA GRADUATE AND UNDERGRADUATE SCHOLARSHIPS
Railroad interest - Applicants must be enrolled as a student in a Graduate or Undergraduate program leading to a degree in Engineering or Engineering Technology in a curriculum which has been accredited by the Accreditation Board of Engineering and Technology (or comparable accreditation in Canada and Mexico). The applicant must have at least a 2.00 GPA (out of 4.00).

Academic Fields/Career Goals: Civil Engineering; Computer Science/Data Processing; Construction Engineering/Management;

Electrical Engineering/Electronics; Engineering-Related Technologies; Engineering/Technology; Mechanical Engineering.

Award: Scholarship for use in freshman, sophomore, junior, senior, or graduate years; not renewable. *Number:* 30–40. *Amount:* $1000–$10,000.

Eligibility Requirements: Applicant must be enrolled or expecting to enroll full- or part-time at a four-year institution or university. Available to U.S. and Canadian citizens.

Application Requirements: Application form. *Deadline:* December 9.

Contact: Alayne Bell, Manager, Committees & Technical Services
Phone: 301-459-3200 Ext. 708
E-mail: abell@arema.org

AMERICAN SOCIETY OF CERTIFIED ENGINEERING TECHNICIANS

http://www.ascet.org/

KURT H. AND DONNA M. SCHULER SMALL GRANT

The small Cash Grant program was suggested by students and faculty advisors who recommended that several grants be awarded to deserving students and that these awards carry as few restrictions as possible. Each award shall be in the amount of $400 to be used to offset the cost of educational expenses as desired. Such grants may be awarded to one or more students each year. Must be either a student, certified, regular, registered or associate member of ASCET, or be a high school senior in the last five months of the academic year who will be enrolled in an Engineering Technology curriculum no later than six months following selection for award. Must also achieve passing grades in present curriculum.

Academic Fields/Career Goals: Civil Engineering; Construction Engineering/Management; Drafting; Electrical Engineering/Electronics; Energy and Power Engineering; Engineering-Related Technologies; Engineering/Technology; Fire Sciences; Landscape Architecture; Marine/Ocean Engineering; Materials Science, Engineering, and Metallurgy; Mechanical Engineering; Surveying, Surveying Technology, Cartography, or Geographic Information Science; Trade/Technical Specialties; Transportation.

Award: Grant for use in freshman, sophomore, junior, or senior years; not renewable. *Number:* 1–4. *Amount:* $400.

Eligibility Requirements: Applicant must be enrolled or expecting to enroll full- or part-time at a two-year or four-year or technical institution or university. Applicant must have 2.5 GPA or higher. Available to U.S. citizens.

Application Requirements: Application form, financial need analysis. *Deadline:* February 28.

Contact: Mr. Jimmy Killer, Financial Aid Committee Chair
American Society of Certified Engineering Technicians
15621 West 87th Street Parkway, #205
Lenexa, KS 66219
Phone: 773-242-7238
E-mail: financialaid@ascet.org

AMERICAN SOCIETY OF CIVIL ENGINEERS

http://www.asce.org/

EUGENE C. FIGG JR. CIVIL ENGINEERING SCHOLARSHIP

Applicant must be a member of the Society in good standing and be enrolled in an ABET-accredited program who will be registered as an undergraduate in the fall term of the year of award, is a U.S. citizen, and have a passion for bridges.

Academic Fields/Career Goals: Civil Engineering.

Award: Scholarship for use in sophomore, junior, or senior years; not renewable. *Number:* 1. *Amount:* $2500.

Eligibility Requirements: Applicant must be enrolled or expecting to enroll full-time at a four-year institution or university. Applicant or parent of applicant must be member of American Society of Civil Engineers. Available to U.S. citizens.

Application Requirements: Application form, essay, financial need analysis. *Deadline:* February 10.

Contact: Ms. Jane Alspach, Senior Manager, Honors and Awards
American Society of Civil Engineers
1801 Alexander Bell Drive
Reston, VA 20191
Phone: 703-295-6300 Ext. 6382
E-mail: awards@asce.org

JOHN LENARD CIVIL ENGINEERING SCHOLARSHIP

For students engaged in the study of civil engineering with a focus on water supply or environmental engineering. Applicant must be a Society member in good standing, enrolled in an ABET-accredited program.

Academic Fields/Career Goals: Civil Engineering.

Award: Scholarship for use in sophomore, junior, or senior years; not renewable. *Number:* 1–2.

Eligibility Requirements: Applicant must be enrolled or expecting to enroll full-time at a four-year institution or university. Applicant or parent of applicant must be member of American Society of Civil Engineers. Available to U.S. and non-U.S. citizens.

Application Requirements: Application form, essay, financial need analysis. *Deadline:* February 10.

Contact: Ms. Jane Alspach, Senior Manager, Honors and Awards
American Society of Civil Engineers
1801 Alexander Bell Drive
Reston, VA 20191
Phone: 703-295-6300 Ext. 6382
E-mail: awards@asce.org

LAWRENCE W. AND FRANCIS W. COX SCHOLARSHIP

Applicants must be Society members in good standing, enrolled in an ABET-accredited program in civil engineering.

Academic Fields/Career Goals: Civil Engineering.

Award: Scholarship for use in sophomore, junior, or senior years; not renewable. *Number:* 1.

Eligibility Requirements: Applicant must be enrolled or expecting to enroll full-time at a four-year institution or university. Applicant or parent of applicant must be member of American Society of Civil Engineers. Available to U.S. and non-U.S. citizens.

Application Requirements: Application form, essay, financial need analysis. *Deadline:* February 10.

Contact: Ms. Jane Alspach, Senior Manager, Honors and Awards
American Society of Civil Engineers
1801 Alexander Bell Drive
Reston, VA 20191
Phone: 703-295-6300 Ext. 6382
E-mail: awards@asce.org

ROBERT B.B. AND JOSEPHINE N. MOORMAN SCHOLARSHIP

Applicant must be Society member in good standing, enrolled in an ABET-accredited program in civil engineering.

Academic Fields/Career Goals: Civil Engineering.

Award: Scholarship for use in sophomore, junior, or senior years; not renewable. *Number:* 1.

Eligibility Requirements: Applicant must be enrolled or expecting to enroll full-time at a four-year institution or university. Applicant or parent of applicant must be member of American Society of Civil Engineers. Available to U.S. and non-U.S. citizens.

Application Requirements: Application form, essay. *Deadline:* February 10.

Contact: Ms. Jane Alspach, Senior Manager, Honors and Awards
American Society of Civil Engineers
1801 Alexander Bell Drive
Reston, VA 20191
Phone: 703-295-6300 Ext. 6382
E-mail: awards@asce.org

SAMUEL FLETCHER TAPMAN ASCE STUDENT CHAPTER SCHOLARSHIP

Not more than one application may be submitted from the membership of any one ASCE Student Chapter. Awards available to currently enrolled undergraduates. Must be a member of local ASCE Student Chapter and an ASCE Student Member in good standing. Selection is based on the applicant's justification of award, educational plan, academic performance and standing, potential for development, leadership capacity, ASCE activities, and financial need.

Academic Fields/Career Goals: Civil Engineering.

Award: Scholarship for use in sophomore, junior, or senior years; not renewable. *Number:* 1–12. *Amount:* $2000–$2500.

Eligibility Requirements: Applicant must be enrolled or expecting to enroll full-time at a four-year institution or university. Applicant or parent of applicant must be member of American Society of Civil Engineers. Available to U.S. and non-U.S. citizens.

Application Requirements: Application form, essay, financial need analysis. *Deadline:* February 10.

Contact: Ms. Jane Alspach, Senior Manager, Honors and Awards
American Society of Civil Engineers
1801 Alexander Bell Drive
Reston, VA 20191
Phone: 703-295-6300 Ext. 6382
E-mail: awards@asce.org

Y.C. YANG CIVIL ENGINEERING SCHOLARSHIP

Applicants must be student members in good standing of the Society. Currently enrolled civil engineering students at an institution with an ABET-accredited program and an interest in structural engineering may apply.

Academic Fields/Career Goals: Civil Engineering.

Award: Scholarship for use in sophomore, junior, or senior years; not renewable. *Number:* 1–2. *Amount:* $2000.

Eligibility Requirements: Applicant must be enrolled or expecting to enroll full-time at a four-year institution or university. Applicant or parent of applicant must be member of American Society of Civil Engineers. Available to U.S. and non-U.S. citizens.

Application Requirements: Application form, essay, financial need analysis. *Deadline:* February 10.

Contact: Ms. Jane Alspach, Senior Manager, Honors and Awards
American Society of Civil Engineers
1801 Alexander Bell Drive
Reston, VA 20191
Phone: 703-295-6300 Ext. 6382
E-mail: awards@asce.org

AMERICAN SOCIETY OF CIVIL ENGINEERS-MAINE SECTION

http://www.maineasce.org/

AMERICAN SOCIETY OF CIVIL ENGINEERS-MAINE HIGH SCHOOL SCHOLARSHIP

One-time award available to a high school student in senior year, pursuing a course of study in civil engineering. Must be enrolled in a four year ABET accredited Civil Engineering program at the time of award. Must be a resident of Maine. Essay, references and transcript required with application.

Academic Fields/Career Goals: Civil Engineering.

Award: Scholarship for use in freshman year; not renewable. *Number:* 1–4. *Amount:* $1000–$4000.

Eligibility Requirements: Applicant must be high school student; planning to enroll or expecting to enroll full-time at a four-year institution or university and resident of Maine. Available to U.S. citizens.

Application Requirements: Application form, essay. *Deadline:* January 31.

Contact: Ms. Leslie Corrow, Senior Engineer P.E.
American Society of Civil Engineers-Maine Section
141 Main Street, PO Box 650
Pittsfield, ME 04967
Phone: 207-487-3328 Ext. 243
E-mail: leslie.corrow@kleinschmidtgroup.com

AMERICAN SOCIETY OF NAVAL ENGINEERS

http://www.navalengineers.org/

AMERICAN SOCIETY OF NAVAL ENGINEERS SCHOLARSHIP

• See page 122

AMERICAN WELDING SOCIETY

http://www.aws.org/

ARSHAM AMIRIKIAN ENGINEERING SCHOLARSHIP

Awarded to an undergraduate pursuing a minimum four-year degree in civil engineering or welding-related program at an accredited university. Applicant must be a minimum of 18 years of age, have a minimum 3.0 GPA and be a citizen of the United States.

Academic Fields/Career Goals: Civil Engineering; Materials Science, Engineering, and Metallurgy; Trade/Technical Specialties.

Award: Scholarship for use in freshman, sophomore, junior, or senior years; not renewable. *Number:* 1.

Eligibility Requirements: Applicant must be enrolled or expecting to enroll full- or part-time at a four-year institution or university. Applicant must have 3.0 GPA or higher. Available to U.S. citizens.

Application Requirements: Application form, financial need analysis. *Deadline:* February 15.

Contact: Mr. John Douglass, Associate Director, Foundation
American Welding Society
8669 NW 36 Street, Suite 130
Miami, FL 33166
Phone: 800-443-9353 Ext. 212
E-mail: jdouglass@aws.org

MATSUO BRIDGE COMPANY LTD. OF JAPAN SCHOLARSHIP

Awarded to a college junior or senior, or graduate student pursuing a minimum four-year degree in civil engineering, welding engineering, welding engineering technology, or related discipline. Applicant must have a minimum 3.0 overall GPA. Financial need is not required to apply. Must be U.S. citizen.

Academic Fields/Career Goals: Civil Engineering; Engineering-Related Technologies; Engineering/Technology; Materials Science, Engineering, and Metallurgy.

Award: Scholarship for use in junior or senior years; not renewable.

Eligibility Requirements: Applicant must be enrolled or expecting to enroll full- or part-time at a two-year or four-year institution or university. Applicant must have 3.0 GPA or higher. Available to U.S. citizens.

Application Requirements: Application form, financial need analysis. *Deadline:* February 15.

Contact: Mr. John Douglass, Associate Director, AWS Foundation
American Welding Society
8669 NW 36 Street, Suite 130
Miami, FL 33166
Phone: 800-443-9353 Ext. 212
E-mail: jdouglass@aws.org

ARRL FOUNDATION INC.

http://www.arrl.org/

ALFRED E. FRIEND JR, W4CF, MEMORIAL SCHOLARSHIP

• See page 191

GARY WAGNER, K3OMI, SCHOLARSHIP

• See page 191

LOIS MANLEY, K7LMZ, AND RANDALL PITCHFORD, WW7ZZ, SCHOLARSHIP

One $1000 scholarship for a student with active Technical Class amateur radio license who is studying science, technology, engineering, or mathematics at any accredited 2- or 4-year college or university. Must reside in ARRL Northwestern Division (Washington, Oregon, Idaho, Montana, Alaska), with preference given to residents of Oregon.

Academic Fields/Career Goals: Civil Engineering; Electrical Engineering/Electronics; Energy and Power Engineering; Engineering-Related Technologies; Engineering/Technology; Marine/Ocean Engineering; Materials Science, Engineering, and Metallurgy; Mathematics; Natural Sciences; Nuclear Science; Physical Sciences.

Award: Scholarship for use in freshman, sophomore, junior, or senior years; not renewable. *Number:* 1. *Amount:* $1000.

Eligibility Requirements: Applicant must be enrolled or expecting to enroll full- or part-time at a two-year or four-year institution or university; resident of Alaska, Idaho, Montana, Oregon, Washington and must have an interest in amateur radio. Available to U.S. citizens.

Application Requirements: Application form. *Deadline:* January 31.

Contact: Ms. Mary Hobart, Secretary
  Phone: 860-594-0397
  E-mail: k1mmh@arrl.org

WIFDR SCHOLARSHIP
• *See page 122*

ASSOCIATED GENERAL CONTRACTORS EDUCATION AND RESEARCH FOUNDATION

http://www.agcfoundation.org/

AGC EDUCATION AND RESEARCH FOUNDATION UNDERGRADUATE SCHOLARSHIPS

College sophomores and juniors enrolled or planning to enroll in a full-time, four or five-year ABET or ACCE-accredited construction management or construction-related engineering program are eligible to apply. High school seniors and college freshmen are not eligible.

Academic Fields/Career Goals: Civil Engineering; Construction Engineering/Management.

Award: Scholarship for use in sophomore, junior, or senior years; renewable. *Number:* 100–150. *Amount:* $2500–$7500.

Eligibility Requirements: Applicant must be enrolled or expecting to enroll full-time at a four-year institution or university. Available to U.S. citizens.

Application Requirements: Application form, essay, interview. *Deadline:* November 1.

Contact: Courtney Bishop, Associate Director
  Associated General Contractors Education and Research
    Foundation
  2300 Wilson Boulevard, Suite 300
  Arlington, VA 22201
  Phone: 703-837-5356
  E-mail: courtney.bishop@agc.org

JAMES L. ALLHANDS ESSAY COMPETITION

The competition is open to any senior–level student in a four or five–year ABET or ACCE–accredited university construction management or construction–related engineering program. The First Place essay author receives $1,000. His/her faculty sponsor receives $500. Second place wins $500 and third place, $300. Both the recipient and sponsor are invited as guests of the Foundation to the AGC Annual Convention.

Academic Fields/Career Goals: Civil Engineering; Construction Engineering/Management.

Award: Prize for use in senior year; not renewable. *Number:* 3. *Amount:* $300–$1000.

Eligibility Requirements: Applicant must be enrolled or expecting to enroll full-time at a four-year institution or university. Available to U.S. citizens.

Application Requirements: Application form, essay. *Deadline:* November 15.

Contact: Melinda Patrician, Director
  Associated General Contractors Education and Research
    Foundation
  2300 Wilson Boulevard, Suite 300
  Arlington, VA 22201
  Phone: 703-837-5342
  E-mail: patricianm@agc.org

ASSOCIATED GENERAL CONTRACTORS OF NEW YORK STATE, LLC

https://www.agcnys.org/programs/scholarship/

ASSOCIATED GENERAL CONTRACTORS NYS SCHOLARSHIP PROGRAM

Scholarship for students enrolled full-time study in civil engineering, construction management and construction technology and diesel technology. Must have minimum GPA of 2.5. Scholarship value is from $1500 to $5000. Must be resident of New York.

Academic Fields/Career Goals: Civil Engineering; Construction Engineering/Management; Surveying, Surveying Technology, Cartography, or Geographic Information Science; Transportation.

Award: Scholarship for use in sophomore, junior, senior, or graduate years; not renewable. *Number:* 15–25. *Amount:* $1500–$5000.

Eligibility Requirements: Applicant must be enrolled or expecting to enroll full-time at a two-year or four-year institution or university and resident of New York. Applicant must have 2.5 GPA or higher. Available to U.S. citizens.

Application Requirements: Application form, financial need analysis. *Deadline:* May 15.

Contact: Mr. Brendan Manning, Vice President, Education and
    Environment
  Associated General Contractors of New York State, LLC
  10 Airline Drive
  Suite 203
  Albany, NY 12205
  Phone: 518-456-1134
  E-mail: bmanning@agcnys.org

ASSOCIATION OF CALIFORNIA WATER AGENCIES

http://www.acwa.com/

ASSOCIATION OF CALIFORNIA WATER AGENCIES SCHOLARSHIPS
• *See page 123*

CLAIR A. HILL SCHOLARSHIP
• *See page 123*

ASSOCIATION OF STATE DAM SAFETY OFFICIALS (ASDSO)

http://www.DamSafety.org

ASSOCIATION OF STATE DAM SAFETY OFFICIALS (ASDSO) SENIOR UNDERGRADUATE SCHOLARSHIP
• *See page 168*

AUTOMOTIVE WOMEN'S ALLIANCE FOUNDATION

http://awafoundation.org/index.php

AUTOMOTIVE WOMEN'S ALLIANCE FOUNDATION SCHOLARSHIPS
• *See page 81*

BHW GROUP

https://thebhwgroup.com/

BHW WOMEN IN STEM SCHOLARSHIP
• *See page 124*

BRASKEM ODEBRECHT

http://www.odebrechtaward.com

ODEBRECHT AWARD FOR SUSTAINABLE DEVELOPMENT
• See page 131

BROWN AND CALDWELL

http://www.brownandcaldwell.com

ECKENFELDER SCHOLARSHIP
• See page 169

MINORITY SCHOLARSHIP PROGRAM
• See page 169

CARDS AGAINST HUMANITY

https://cardsagainsthumanity.com/

SCIENCE AMBASSADOR SCHOLARSHIP
• See page 124

CENTER FOR ARCHITECTURE

http://www.centerforarchitecture.org

CENTER FOR ARCHITECTURE DESIGN SCHOLARSHIP
• See page 132

CONNECTICUT BUILDING CONGRESS SCHOLARSHIP FUND, INC.

http://www.cbc-ct.org

CBC SCHOLARSHIP FUND
• See page 132

THE DALLAS FOUNDATION

http://www.dallasfoundation.org/

JERE W. THOMPSON, JR, SCHOLARSHIP FUND
Renewable scholarships awarded to full-time undergraduate juniors or seniors with disadvantaged backgrounds, who are pursuing a degree in civil engineering and closely related disciplines at Texas colleges and universities. Up to $2000 awarded each semester, beginning with junior year. Must maintain 2.5 GPA. Special consideration given to students from Collin, Dallas, Denton, and Tarrant Counties, Texas.

Academic Fields/Career Goals: Civil Engineering.

Award: Scholarship for use in junior or senior years; renewable. *Number:* 1–2. *Amount:* up to $4000.

Eligibility Requirements: Applicant must be enrolled or expecting to enroll full-time at a four-year institution or university; resident of Texas and studying in Texas. Available to U.S. citizens.

Application Requirements: Application form, essay, financial need analysis, recommendations or references, test scores, transcript. *Deadline:* April 1.

Contact: Rachel Lasseter, Program Associate
The Dallas Foundation
900 Jackson Street, Suite 705
Dallas, TX 75202
Phone: 214-741-9898
Fax: 214-741-9848
E-mail: scholarships@dallasfoundation.org

WHITLEY PLACE SCHOLARSHIP
• See page 133

DISTIL NETWORKS

http://www.distilnetworks.com

WOMEN FORWARD IN TECHNOLOGY SCHOLARSHIP PROGRAM
• See page 124

FLORIDA ENGINEERING SOCIETY

http://www.fleng.org/scholarships.cfm

DAVID F. LUDOVICI SCHOLARSHIP
• See page 192

FECON SCHOLARSHIP
One-time scholarship of $1000 given to Florida citizens in their junior or senior year, who are enrolled or accepted into a Florida university engineering program. Minimum 3.0 GPA required. Applicant must be interested in pursuing a career in the field of construction.

Academic Fields/Career Goals: Civil Engineering; Construction Engineering/Management.

Award: Scholarship for use in junior or senior years; not renewable. *Number:* 1. *Amount:* $1000.

Eligibility Requirements: Applicant must be enrolled or expecting to enroll full-time at an institution or university; resident of Florida and studying in Florida. Applicant must have 3.0 GPA or higher. Available to U.S. citizens.

Application Requirements: Application form, essay. *Deadline:* February 1.

Contact: Amanda Hudson, Director of Information Technology
Florida Engineering Society
125 South Gadsden Street
Tallahassee, FL 32301
Phone: 850-224-7121
E-mail: ahudson@fleng.org

FOUNDATION FOR SCIENCE AND DISABILITY

http://stemd.org/

GRANTS FOR DISABLED GRADUATE STUDENTS IN THE SCIENCES
• See page 106

GREAT MINDS IN STEM

http://www.greatmindsinstem.org

HENAAC SCHOLARSHIP PROGRAM
• See page 115

HAWAIIAN LODGE, F&AM

http://www.hawaiianlodgefreemasons.org

HAWAIIAN LODGE SCHOLARSHIPS
• See page 86

INDEPENDENT LABORATORIES INSTITUTE SCHOLARSHIP ALLIANCE

http://www.acil.org/

INDEPENDENT LABORATORIES INSTITUTE SCHOLARSHIP ALLIANCE
• See page 171

JORGE MAS CANOSA FREEDOM FOUNDATION

http://masscholarships.org/

MAS FAMILY SCHOLARSHIP AWARD
• *See page 181*

KENTUCKY ENERGY AND ENVIRONMENT CABINET

http://dep.ky.gov

ENVIRONMENTAL PROTECTION SCHOLARSHIP
• *See page 172*

KENTUCKY TRANSPORTATION CABINET

http://transportation.ky.gov/Education/Pages/Scholarships.aspx

KENTUCKY TRANSPORTATION CABINET CIVIL ENGINEERING SCHOLARSHIP PROGRAM

Scholarships awarded to qualified Kentucky residents who wish to study civil engineering at University of Kentucky, Western Kentucky University, University of Louisville or Kentucky State University. Applicant should be a graduate of an accredited Kentucky high school or a Kentucky resident. Scholarship recipients are given opportunities to work for the Cabinet during summers and job opportunities upon graduation within the state of KY.

Academic Fields/Career Goals: Civil Engineering.

Award: Scholarship for use in freshman, sophomore, junior, or senior years; renewable. *Number:* 15–30. *Amount:* $12,400–$51,200.

Eligibility Requirements: Applicant must be enrolled or expecting to enroll full-time at a four-year institution or university; resident of Kentucky and studying in Kentucky. Applicant must have 2.5 GPA or higher. Available to U.S. and non-U.S. citizens.

Application Requirements: Application form, essay, interview. *Deadline:* February 1.

Contact: Cherie Mertz, Scholarship Program Coordinator
Kentucky Transportation Cabinet
200 Mero Street, 6th Floor East
Frankfort, KY 40622
Phone: 502-564-3730
E-mail: Cherie.Mertz@ky.gov

LABROOTS INC.

http://www.LabRoots.com

LABROOTS STEM SCHOLARSHIP
• *See page 116*

LOS ANGELES COUNCIL OF BLACK PROFESSIONAL ENGINEERS

http://www.lablackengineers.org/

AL-BEN SCHOLARSHIP FOR ACADEMIC INCENTIVE
• *See page 193*

AL-BEN SCHOLARSHIP FOR PROFESSIONAL MERIT
• *See page 193*

AL-BEN SCHOLARSHIP FOR SCHOLASTIC ACHIEVEMENT
• *See page 193*

MIDWEST ROOFING CONTRACTORS ASSOCIATION

http://www.mrca.org/

MRCA FOUNDATION SCHOLARSHIP PROGRAM
• *See page 135*

NASA IDAHO SPACE GRANT CONSORTIUM

http://www.idahospacegrant.org

NASA IDAHO SPACE GRANT CONSORTIUM SCHOLARSHIP PROGRAM
• *See page 126*

NASA MONTANA SPACE GRANT CONSORTIUM

http://www.spacegrant.montana.edu/

MONTANA SPACE GRANT SCHOLARSHIP PROGRAM
• *See page 156*

NATIONAL ASPHALT PAVEMENT ASSOCIATION RESEARCH AND EDUCATION FOUNDATION

http://www.asphaltpavement.org

NATIONAL ASPHALT PAVEMENT ASSOCIATION RESEARCH AND EDUCATION FOUNDATION SCHOLARSHIP PROGRAM

Our Scholarship program provides funding for undergraduate and graduate students who are U.S. citizens enrolled in a full time civil engineering, construction management, or construction engineering curriculum at an accredited four year college/university or two-year technical institution. The NAPAREF Scholarship Program was initiated in 1994 to encourage young people to take elective courses in asphalt technology and management and to encourage institutions to make such courses available. The Scholarship Program is the keystone for assuring the future of the Asphalt industry through the education of tomorrow's industry leaders and the establishment of opportunities to expand knowledge and training in asphalt technology. Our scholarships provide an incentive for engineering students to select courses in asphalt technology; a workforce with training in asphalt technology; and an incentive for colleges/universities to offer training in asphalt technology. The NAPAREF Scholarship Program ensures the future of the asphalt industry and that of asphalt as America's leading choice in paving materials.

Academic Fields/Career Goals: Civil Engineering; Construction Engineering/Management.

Award: Scholarship for use in freshman, sophomore, junior, senior, graduate, or postgraduate years; not renewable. *Number:* 51. *Amount:* $500–$5000.

Eligibility Requirements: Applicant must be enrolled or expecting to enroll full-time at a two-year or four-year or technical institution or university. Available to U.S. citizens.

Application Requirements: Application form, essay. *Deadline:* continuous.

Contact: Mrs. Carolyn Wilson, Vice President, Finance and Operations
National Asphalt Pavement Association Research and Education Foundation
5100 Forbes Boulevard, Suite 200
Lanham, MD 20706
Phone: 301-731-4748 Ext. 127
Fax: 301-731-4621
E-mail: cwilson@asphaltpavement.org

NATIONAL ASSOCIATION OF WOMEN IN CONSTRUCTION

http://www.nawic.org/

NAWIC UNDERGRADUATE SCHOLARSHIPS
• See page 135

NATIONAL SOCIETY OF PROFESSIONAL ENGINEERS

http://www.nspe.org/

MAUREEN L. AND HOWARD N. BLITMAN, PE SCHOLARSHIP TO PROMOTE DIVERSITY IN ENGINEERING
• See page 194

PAUL H. ROBBINS HONORARY SCHOLARSHIP
• See page 194

PROFESSIONAL ENGINEERS IN INDUSTRY SCHOLARSHIP
• See page 194

NEVADA NASA SPACE GRANT CONSORTIUM

https://nasa.epscorspo.nevada.edu/

NATIONAL SPACE GRANT CONSORTIUM SCHOLARSHIPS
• See page 127

NEW ENGLAND WATER WORKS ASSOCIATION

http://www.newwa.org/

ELSON T. KILLAM MEMORIAL SCHOLARSHIP

Scholarships are awarded to eligible civil and environmental engineering students on the basis of merit, character, and need. Preference given to those students whose programs are considered by a committee as beneficial to water works practice in New England. NEWWA student membership is required to receive a scholarship award. Applicants for scholarships should be residents or attend school in New England. (Maine, New Hampshire, Vermont, Massachusetts, Rhode Island and Connecticut).

Academic Fields/Career Goals: Civil Engineering; Environmental Science.

Award: Scholarship for use in freshman, sophomore, junior, senior, or graduate years; not renewable. *Number:* 1. *Amount:* up to $1500.

Eligibility Requirements: Applicant must be enrolled or expecting to enroll full-time at a four-year institution or university. Applicant or parent of applicant must be member of New England Water Works Association. Available to U.S. citizens.

Application Requirements: Application form, essay, recommendations or references, transcript. *Fee:* $25. *Deadline:* July 1.

Contact: Thomas MacElhaney, Chair, Scholarship Committee
Phone: 631-231-8100
Fax: 978-418-9156
E-mail: tmacelhaney@preloadinc.com

FRANCIS X. CROWLEY SCHOLARSHIP
• See page 182

JOSEPH MURPHY SCHOLARSHIP

Scholarships are awarded to eligible civil or environmental engineering students on the basis of merit, character, and need. Preference given to those students whose programs are considered by a committee as beneficial to water works practice in New England. NEWWA student membership is required to receive a scholarship award.

Academic Fields/Career Goals: Civil Engineering; Environmental Science.

Award: Scholarship for use in freshman, sophomore, junior, senior, or graduate years; not renewable. *Number:* 1. *Amount:* up to $1500.

Eligibility Requirements: Applicant must be enrolled or expecting to enroll full-time at a four-year institution or university. Applicant or parent of applicant must be member of New England Water Works Association. Available to U.S. citizens.

Application Requirements: Application form, essay, recommendations or references, transcript. *Fee:* $25. *Deadline:* July 1.

Contact: Thomas MacElhaney, Chair, Scholarship Committee
Phone: 631-231-8100
Fax: 978-418-9156
E-mail: tmacelhaney@preloadinc.com

WORKS GEORGE E. WATTERS MEMORIAL SCHOLARSHIP.

Scholarships are awarded to eligible Civil Engineering students on the basis of merit, character, and need. Preference given to those students whose programs are considered by a committee as beneficial to water works practice in New England. NEWWA student membership is required to receive a scholarship award. Applicants for scholarships should be residents or attend school in New England. (Maine, New Hampshire, Vermont, Massachusetts, Rhode Island and Connecticut).

Academic Fields/Career Goals: Civil Engineering.

Award: Scholarship for use in freshman, sophomore, junior, senior, or graduate years; not renewable. *Number:* 1. *Amount:* up to $5000.

Eligibility Requirements: Applicant must be enrolled or expecting to enroll full-time at a four-year institution or university. Available to U.S. citizens.

Application Requirements: Application form, essay, recommendations or references, transcript. *Fee:* $25. *Deadline:* July 1.

Contact: Thomas MacElhaney, Chair, Scholarship Committee
Phone: 631-231-8100
Fax: 978-418-9156
E-mail: tmacelhaney@preloadinc.com

NEXTSTEPU

http://www.nextstepu.com/

$1,500 STEM SCHOLARSHIP
• See page 120

OREGON STUDENT ASSISTANCE COMMISSION

https://oregonstudentaid.gov/

AMERICAN COUNCIL OF ENGINEERING COMPANIES OF OREGON SCHOLARSHIP

Applicant must be either a graduating high school senior (including GED students and home-schooled seniors) or have had no previous college education. GPA 3.30+. SAT score: 1800+ combined or ACT composite of 28+. Majoring in civil, electrical, environmental, or mechanical engineering; excludes computer and biomedical engineering. Any Oregon four-year college that offers Accreditation Board for Engineering and Technology accredited programs in the major field of study.

Academic Fields/Career Goals: Civil Engineering; Electrical Engineering/Electronics; Engineering/Technology; Mechanical Engineering.

Award: Scholarship for use in freshman year; renewable.

Eligibility Requirements: Applicant must be enrolled or expecting to enroll at a four-year institution or university and studying in Oregon. Applicant must have 3.0 GPA or higher. Available to U.S. citizens.

Application Requirements: Application form, essay. *Deadline:* March 1.

Contact: Melissa Adams, Scholarship Processing Coordinator
Phone: 541-687-7409
E-mail: melissa.adams@state.or.us

HOME BUILDERS FOUNDATION JIM IRVINE STATEWIDE SCHOLARSHIP
• See page 136

SOCIETY OF AMERICAN MILITARY ENGINEERS PORTLAND POST SCHOLARSHIP
• *See page 195*

PLAN NEW HAMPSHIRE

http://www.plannh.org

PLAN NEW HAMPSHIRE SCHOLARSHIP AND FELLOWSHIP PROGRAM
• *See page 129*

PROFESSIONAL CONSTRUCTION ESTIMATORS ASSOCIATION

http://www.pcea.org/

TED G. WILSON MEMORIAL SCHOLARSHIP FOUNDATION

Amount up to $1000 to a deserving student (high school senior, college freshman, sophomore, or junior) based on their academic ability, need, and desire to enter the construction industry.

Academic Fields/Career Goals: Civil Engineering; Construction Engineering/Management; Drafting; Electrical Engineering/Electronics; Engineering/Technology; Heating, Air-Conditioning, and Refrigeration Mechanics; Landscape Architecture; Mechanical Engineering; Surveying, Surveying Technology, Cartography, or Geographic Information Science; Trade/Technical Specialties.

Award: Scholarship for use in freshman, sophomore, junior, or senior years; not renewable. *Number:* 5. *Amount:* up to $1000.

Eligibility Requirements: Applicant must be enrolled or expecting to enroll full-time at a two-year or four-year or technical institution or university; resident of Florida, Georgia, North Carolina, South Carolina, Virginia and studying in Florida, Georgia, North Carolina, South Carolina, Virginia. Available to U.S. and non-U.S. citizens.

Application Requirements: Application form, financial need analysis, interview, recommendations or references, transcript. *Deadline:* March 15.

Contact: Kim Lybrand, National Office Manager
Professional Construction Estimators Association
PO Box 680336
Charlotte, NC 28216-0336
Phone: 704-987-9978
Fax: 704-987-9979
E-mail: pcea@pcea.org

RCI FOUNDATION

http://www.rcifoundation.org/

LEWIS W. NEWLAN AWARD
• *See page 136*

ROCKY MOUNTAIN COAL MINING INSTITUTE

http://www.rmcmi.org/

ROCKY MOUNTAIN COAL MINING INSTITUTE SCHOLARSHIP

Must be full-time college sophomore or junior at time of application, pursuing a degree in mining-related fields or engineering disciplines such as mining, geology, mineral processing, or metallurgy. For residents of Arizona, Colorado, Montana, New Mexico, North Dakota, Texas, Utah, and Wyoming. Scholarship value is $2500 per year for two-years sent directly to school for tuition.

Academic Fields/Career Goals: Civil Engineering; Earth Science; Engineering-Related Technologies; Engineering/Technology; Materials Science, Engineering, and Metallurgy.

Award: Scholarship for use in junior or senior years; renewable. *Number:* 8. *Amount:* $2500.

Eligibility Requirements: Applicant must be enrolled or expecting to enroll full-time at a four-year institution or university and resident of Arizona, Colorado, Montana, New Mexico, North Dakota, Texas, Utah, Wyoming. Available to U.S. citizens.

Application Requirements: Application form, interview, recommendations or references. *Deadline:* February 1.

Contact: Karen Inzano, Executive Director
Phone: 303-948-3300
E-mail: mail@rmcmi.org

SCARLETT FAMILY FOUNDATION SCHOLARSHIP PROGRAM

http://www.scarlettfoundation.org/

SCHOLARSHIP FOR STUDENTS PURSUING A BUSINESS OR STEM DEGREE
• *See page 91*

SIGMA XI, THE SCIENTIFIC RESEARCH SOCIETY

http://www.sigmaxi.org/

SIGMA XI GRANTS-IN-AID OF RESEARCH
• *See page 110*

SOCIETY OF WOMEN ENGINEERS

http://societyofwomenengineers.swe.org/

AMERICAN TRANSMISSION CO. SCHOLARSHIP
• *See page 196*

ANNE SHEN SMITH ENDOWED SCHOLARSHIP
• *See page 196*

BETTY LOU BAILEY SWE REGION F SCHOLARSHIP
• *See page 197*

B.J. HARROD SCHOLARSHIP
• *See page 197*

CAROL STEPHENS SWE REGION F SCHOLARSHIP
• *See page 197*

DR. IVY M. PARKER MEMORIAL SCHOLARSHIP
• *See page 197*

DOROTHY LEMKE HOWARTH MEMORIAL SCHOLARSHIP
• *See page 197*

DOROTHY P. MORRIS SCHOLARSHIP
• *See page 198*

ELIZABETH MCLEAN MEMORIAL SCHOLARSHIP

$1500 scholarship for a woman pursuing an ABET-accredited Baccalaureate program in preparation for a career in civil engineering in the United States and Mexico. Minimum 3.0 GPA required.

Academic Fields/Career Goals: Civil Engineering; Engineering/Technology.

Award: Scholarship for use in sophomore, junior, or senior years; not renewable. *Number:* 1. *Amount:* $1500.

Eligibility Requirements: Applicant must be enrolled or expecting to enroll full-time at a four-year institution or university and female. Applicant must have 3.0 GPA or higher. Available to U.S. citizens.

Application Requirements: Application form. *Deadline:* February 15.

Contact: Scholarship Committee
Phone: 800-793-4636
E-mail: scholarships@swe.org

EXELON SCHOLARSHIP
• *See page 198*

GENERAL ELECTRIC WOMEN'S NETWORK SCHOLARSHIP

Scholarships for women pursuing ABET-accredited Baccalaureate programs in preparation for a careers in engineering, engineering technology, or computer science in the United States and Mexico. U.S. citizenship, and minimum 3.0 GPA required. Applicant should have leadership roles outside of academics and involvement in engineering professional organizations, discipline related internships, and presentation skills. Recipients should be willing to intern at GE. Inquire for list of preferred schools.

Academic Fields/Career Goals: Civil Engineering; Electrical Engineering/Electronics; Engineering/Technology; Mechanical Engineering.

Award: Scholarship for use in sophomore or junior years; not renewable. *Number:* 43. *Amount:* $5000.

Eligibility Requirements: Applicant must be enrolled or expecting to enroll full-time at a four-year institution or university; female and must have an interest in leadership. Applicant must have 3.0 GPA or higher. Available to U.S. citizens.

Application Requirements: Application form. *Deadline:* February 15.

Contact: Scholarship Committee
    Phone: 800-793-4636
    E-mail: scholarships@swe.org

IBM LINDA SANFORD WOMEN'S TECHNICAL ADVANCEMENT SCHOLARSHIP

• See page 198

INVENERGY WOMEN'S NETWORK SCHOLARSHIP

One $5000 scholarship for a woman pursuing an ABET-accredited Baccalaureate program in preparation for a career in engineering, engineering technology, or computer science in the United States and Mexico. Must be a U.S. citizen, be a student member of SWE, and have a minimum 3.0 GPA.

Academic Fields/Career Goals: Civil Engineering; Computer Science/Data Processing; Electrical Engineering/Electronics; Engineering/Technology; Mechanical Engineering.

Award: Scholarship for use in sophomore or junior years; not renewable. *Number:* 1. *Amount:* $5000.

Eligibility Requirements: Applicant must be enrolled or expecting to enroll full-time at a four-year institution or university and female. Applicant or parent of applicant must be member of Society of Women Engineers. Applicant must have 3.0 GPA or higher. Available to U.S. citizens.

Application Requirements: Application form. *Deadline:* February 15.

Contact: Scholarship Committee
    Phone: 800-793-4636
    E-mail: scholarships@swe.org

LILLIAN MOLLER GILBRETH MEMORIAL SCHOLARSHIP

• See page 198

MARY V. MUNGER MEMORIAL SCHOLARSHIP

• See page 199

OLIVE LYNN SALEMBIER MEMORIAL REENTRY SCHOLARSHIP

• See page 199

PAULA LORING SIMON SCHOLARSHIP

• See page 199

SUSAN MISZKOWICZ SEPTEMBER 11 MEMORIAL SCHOLARSHIP

• See page 199

SWE BALTIMORE-WASHINGTON SECTION SCHOLARSHIP

• See page 199

SWE CENTRAL NEW MEXICO PIONEERS SCHOLARSHIP

• See page 200

SWE CENTRAL NEW MEXICO REENTRY SCHOLARSHIP

• See page 200

SWE MID-HUDSON SECTION SCHOLARSHIP

• See page 200

SWE PHOENIX SECTION SCHOLARSHIP

• See page 200

SWE REGION E SCHOLARSHIP

• See page 200

SWE REGION G JUDY SIMMONS MEMORIAL SCHOLARSHIP

• See page 200

SWE REGION H SCHOLARSHIPS

• See page 201

SWE REGION J SCHOLARSHIP

• See page 201

TE CONNECTIVITY EXCELLENCE IN ENGINEERING SCHOLARSHIP

• See page 201

WANDA MUNN SCHOLARSHIP

• See page 201

SOCIETY OF WOMEN ENGINEERS-ROCKY MOUNTAIN SECTION

http://www.swe-rms.org/

SOCIETY OF WOMEN ENGINEERS-ROCKY MOUNTAIN SECTION SCHOLARSHIP PROGRAM

• See page 161

STRAIGHTFORWARD MEDIA

http://www.straightforwardmedia.com/

STRAIGHTFORWARD MEDIA ENGINEERING SCHOLARSHIP

• See page 202

STRAIGHT NORTH

https://www.straightnorth.com/

STRAIGHT NORTH STEM SCHOLARSHIP

• See page 92

TAU BETA PI ASSOCIATION

https://www.tbp.org/

TAU BETA PI SCHOLARSHIP PROGRAM

• See page 202

TEXAS DEPARTMENT OF TRANSPORTATION

http://www.txdot.gov/

CONDITIONAL GRANT PROGRAM

Renewable award to students who are considered economically disadvantaged based on federal guidelines. The maximum amount awarded per semester is $3,000 not to exceed $6000 per academic year. Students already enrolled in an undergraduate program should have minimum GPA 2.5 and students newly enrolling should have minimum GPA 3.0.

Academic Fields/Career Goals: Civil Engineering; Computer Science/Data Processing; Occupational Safety and Health.

Award: Grant for use in freshman, sophomore, junior, or senior years; renewable. *Number:* 10–20. *Amount:* $3000–$6000.

Eligibility Requirements: Applicant must be enrolled or expecting to enroll full-time at a four-year institution or university; resident of Texas and studying in Texas. Available to U.S. citizens.

Application Requirements: Application form, essay, financial need analysis, interview. *Deadline:* March 1.

Contact: Sheila Brooks, Program Coordinator
Texas Department of Transportation
125 East 11th Street
Austin, TX 78701-2483
Phone: 512-416-4979
E-mail: hrd_recruitment@txdot.gov

TIMOTION

http://www.timotion.com/

TIMOTION ENGINEERING AND EXCELLENCE SCHOLARSHIP

In 2005, TiMOTION entered the world of electric linear actuators, quickly becoming the premier global designer and manufacturer of complete motion system solutions. Since its inception, the company has earned a reputation for reliable, high quality, competitively priced products that satisfy the needs of worldwide medical, furniture, ergonomic, and industrial markets. TiMOTION established this annual scholarship opportunity for aspiring engineers, ergonomists, or technology students to continue their education in hopes of powering the worlds towards a better future. Must be a full-time student enrolled in an engineering, ergonomics, or technology-focused program at an accredited undergraduate university or college. Must provide transcripts indicating strong academic performance with a GPA of 3.0 or higher. Must provide information regarding extracurricular activities, volunteering opportunities, or other community-involvement experience. We advise reading all information listed on our website prior to submitting your application, so that you can be better prepared. You will need to submit: 1. a transcript. You will need this as a record of proof to the course level and grades that you received since your freshman year in high school; 2. contact information. You must be prepared to provide us with your name, email address, and phone number so that we may contact you if your application is selected; 3. a school profile. We have an area of the application that asks you to give us the details of the university or college you will attend; 4.the essay. In 500-700 words, you will need to provide us with a comprehensive look into what inspired you to pursue your field of study. Check out sample applications for ideas.

Academic Fields/Career Goals: Civil Engineering; Electrical Engineering/Electronics; Energy and Power Engineering; Engineering-Related Technologies; Engineering/Technology; Industrial Design; Mechanical Engineering.

Award: Scholarship for use in freshman, sophomore, junior, senior, or postgraduate years; renewable. *Number:* 5. *Amount:* $2000.

Eligibility Requirements: Applicant must be enrolled or expecting to enroll full-time at a four-year institution or university. Applicant must have 3.0 GPA or higher. Available to U.S. and non-U.S. citizens.

Application Requirements: Application form, essay. *Deadline:* December 1.

Contact: Samantha Rosenfeld, Senior Marketing Associate
TiMOTION
1535 Center Park Drive
Charlotte, NC 28217
Phone: 704-708-6924 Ext. 914
E-mail: scholarships@timotion.com

TRANSPORTATION ASSOCIATION OF CANADA FOUNDATION

http://www.tac-foundation.ca

TAC FOUNDATION SCHOLARSHIPS

The TAC Foundation's primary focus for educational support (scholarships) is on the planning, design, construction, operations, maintenance and program management of transportation infrastructure, including urban transit. Scholarships are supported through annual donations to the TAC Foundation from donor organizations and individuals that support the Foundation's mandate. Candidates must be Canadian citizens or permanent residents; enrolled at a post-secondary institution (university or college) in an academic program related to the planning, design, construction, operations, maintenance and program management of transportation infrastructure, including urban transit; are limited to being awarded one TAC Foundation scholarship at each stage of their education (community college, university undergraduate, graduate. TAC Foundation entrance scholarships are not included in this restriction); must have achieved an overall B average or equivalent average mark in their previous academic year; may apply for and receive scholarships from other sources.

Academic Fields/Career Goals: Civil Engineering; Construction Engineering/Management; Economics; Engineering-Related Technologies; Engineering/Technology; Urban and Regional Planning.

Award: Scholarship for use in senior or graduate years; not renewable. *Number:* 30–45. *Amount:* $2500–$5000.

Eligibility Requirements: Applicant must be Canadian citizen; enrolled or expecting to enroll full-time at a two-year or four-year institution or university and resident of Alberta, British Columbia, Manitoba, New Brunswick, Newfoundland, Northwest Territories, Nova Scotia, Ontario, Prince Edward Island, Quebec, Saskatchewan, Yukon. Applicant must have 3.0 GPA or higher.

Application Requirements: Application form. *Deadline:* February 28.

Contact: Ms. Erica Andersen, Secretary-Treasurer
Phone: 613-736-1350 Ext. 235
Fax: 613-736-1395
E-mail: foundation@tac-atc.ca

TURNER CONSTRUCTION COMPANY

http://www.turnerconstruction.com/

YOUTHFORCE 2020 SCHOLARSHIP PROGRAM
• See page 137

UNITED NEGRO COLLEGE FUND

http://www.uncf.org/

DELL CORPORATE SCHOLARS PROGRAM

Scholarship of up to $2500 for a student majoring or having an academic focus in Engineering, Supply Chain Management, Computer Science or Information Technology. Must be a minority student enrolled full-time at a U.S. located accredited four year institution as a junior during the application and interview process. Must possess a demonstrated unmet financial need as verified by their institution/college (for scholarship award) and have a minimum 3.0 GPA. All applicants for the UNCF/Dell Corporate Scholars Program may be considered for summer internship opportunities at Dell HQ in Round Rock TX.

Academic Fields/Career Goals: Civil Engineering; Computer Science/Data Processing; Electrical Engineering/Electronics; Energy and Power Engineering; Engineering-Related Technologies; Engineering/Technology.

Award: Scholarship for use in junior year; not renewable.

Eligibility Requirements: Applicant must be American Indian/Alaska Native, Asian/Pacific Islander, Black (non-Hispanic), Hispanic and enrolled or expecting to enroll full-time at a four-year institution or university. Applicant must have 3.0 GPA or higher. Available to U.S. citizens.

Application Requirements: Application form, essay, financial need analysis. *Deadline:* September 22.

Contact: Mary Williams, Director of Outreach and Recruitment
Phone: 800-331-2244

PROCTER & GAMBLE STEM SCHOLARSHIP
• See page 128

SUEZ CORPORATE SCHOLARS PROGRAM
• See page 94

UNCF STEM SCHOLARS PROGRAM
• See page 175

UNITED STATES SOCIETY ON DAMS

http://www.ussdams.org/

UNITED STATES SOCIETY ON DAMS SCHOLARSHIP AWARD

USSD annually awards scholarships to USSD Student Members whose academic program has a potential for developing practical solutions to dam-related issues. Applicants must be U.S. citizens enrolled full-time in U.S. academic institutions.

Academic Fields/Career Goals: Civil Engineering; Engineering/Technology; Environmental Science.

Award: Prize for use in senior or graduate years; not renewable. *Number:* 1–4. *Amount:* $2000–$10,000.

Eligibility Requirements: Applicant must be enrolled or expecting to enroll full-time at a four-year institution or university. Applicant or parent of applicant must be member of United States Society on Dams. Available to U.S. citizens.

Application Requirements: Application form. *Deadline:* February 28.

Contact: Tina Stanard, Awards Committee Chair
Phone: 512-617-3120
E-mail: ces@freese.com

VECTORWORKS, INC.

http://www.vectorworks.net

VECTORWORKS DESIGN SCHOLARSHIP
• See page 137

VERMONT SPACE GRANT CONSORTIUM

http://www.cems.uvm.edu/vsgc

VERMONT SPACE GRANT CONSORTIUM
• See page 104

WIRE REINFORCEMENT INSTITUTE EDUCATION FOUNDATION

http://www.wirereinforcementinstitute.org/

WRI FOUNDATION COLLEGE SCHOLARSHIP PROGRAM

Academic scholarships for qualified current undergraduate and graduate level students officially declared as or presently pursuing four-year or graduate-level degrees in structural and/or civil engineering at accredited four-year universities or colleges in the U.S. or Canada. Scholarship recipients will also participate in the WRI Mentor Program for the year in which the scholarship is awarded.

Academic Fields/Career Goals: Civil Engineering; Construction Engineering/Management.

Award: Scholarship for use in sophomore, junior, senior, or graduate years; not renewable. *Number:* 2–5. *Amount:* $2000–$4000.

Eligibility Requirements: Applicant must be enrolled or expecting to enroll full-time at a four-year institution or university. Available to U.S. and non-U.S. citizens.

Application Requirements: Application form, essay. *Deadline:* April 15.

Contact: Scholarship Selection Committee
Wire Reinforcement Institute Education Foundation
942 Main Street
Hartford, CT 06103
Phone: 860-240-9545
E-mail: wrischolar@wirereinforcementinstitute.org

CLASSICS

ACL/NJCL NATIONAL LATIN EXAM

http://www.nle.org/

NATIONAL LATIN EXAM SCHOLARSHIP

Scholarships to high school seniors who are gold medal winners in Latin III, III-IV Prose, III-IV Poetry, or Latin V-VI their senior year. Applicants must agree to take at least one year of Latin or classical Greek language in college.

Academic Fields/Career Goals: Classics; Foreign Language.

Award: Scholarship for use in freshman, sophomore, junior, or senior years; renewable. *Number:* 21. *Amount:* $2000.

Eligibility Requirements: Applicant must be high school student; planning to enroll or expecting to enroll full-time at a four-year institution or university and must have an interest in Greek language or Latin language. Available to U.S. and non-U.S. citizens.

Application Requirements: Application form, essay. *Deadline:* May 16.

Contact: Mrs. Ephy Howard, Scholarship Chairperson
Phone: 888-378-7721

AMERICAN CLASSICAL LEAGUE/NATIONAL JUNIOR CLASSICAL LEAGUE

http://www.aclclassics.org/

NATIONAL JUNIOR CLASSICAL LEAGUE SCHOLARSHIP

A one-time award available to graduating high school seniors, who are members of the Junior Classical League. Preference is given to students who plan to major in the classics.

Academic Fields/Career Goals: Classics; Foreign Language; Humanities.

Award: Scholarship for use in freshman year; not renewable. *Number:* 7. *Amount:* $1000–$2000.

Eligibility Requirements: Applicant must be high school student; planning to enroll or expecting to enroll full-time at a two-year or four-year institution or university and must have an interest in foreign language. Applicant or parent of applicant must be member of Junior Classical League. Available to U.S. and non-U.S. citizens.

Application Requirements: Application form, essay. *Deadline:* April 1.

Contact: Sherwin Little, Executive Director
American Classical League/National Junior Classical League
860 NW Washington Boulevard
Suite A
Hamilton, OH 45013
Phone: 513-529-7741
E-mail: info@aclclassics.org

AMERICAN SCHOOL OF CLASSICAL STUDIES AT ATHENS

http://www.ascsa.edu.gr/

ASCSA SUMMER SESSION AND SUMMER SEMINARS SCHOLARSHIPS
• See page 118

SOCIETY FOR CLASSICAL STUDIES

http://www.classicalstudies.org/

MINORITY STUDENT SUMMER SCHOLARSHIP
• See page 130

SONS OF ITALY FOUNDATION

http://www.osia.org/sif

ITALIAN LANGUAGE SCHOLARSHIP

Through the Sons of Italy Foundation (SIF), and hundreds of thousands of family members located in all fifty states and the District of Columbia, the Order Sons and Daughters of Italy in America (OSDIA) has awarded nearly $61 million in scholarships to date. In past years, the SIF has offered 10 to 12 merit-based scholarships (National Leadership Grants), ranging from $4,000 to $25,000, in a nationwide competition. These figures and the number of scholarships may vary according to funding each year. U.S. citizens of Italian descent in their junior or senior year of undergraduate study for the fall 2018 term, majoring or minoring in Italian language studies at an accredited academic institution are eligible for this award.

Academic Fields/Career Goals: Classics; Foreign Language.

Award: Scholarship for use in junior or senior years; not renewable. *Number:* 1. *Amount:* $4000–$25,000.

Eligibility Requirements: Applicant must be of Italian heritage and enrolled or expecting to enroll full-time at a four-year institution or university. Available to U.S. citizens.

Application Requirements: Application form, essay. *Fee:* $35. *Deadline:* February 28.

Contact: Carly Jerome, Director of Programming
Sons of Italy Foundation
219 E Street NE
Washington, DC 20002
Phone: 202-547-2900
E-mail: scholarships@osia.org

STRAIGHTFORWARD MEDIA

http://www.straightforwardmedia.com/

STRAIGHTFORWARD MEDIA LIBERAL ARTS SCHOLARSHIP

• *See page 139*

COMMUNICATIONS

ADC RESEARCH INSTITUTE

http://www.adc.org/

JACK SHAHEEN MASS COMMUNICATIONS SCHOLARSHIP AWARD

Awarded to Arab-American students who excel in the mass communications field (journalism, radio, television or film). Must be a junior or senior undergraduate or graduate student. Must be U.S. citizen. Minimum 3.0 GPA required.

Academic Fields/Career Goals: Communications; Filmmaking/Video; Journalism; TV/Radio Broadcasting.

Award: Scholarship for use in junior, senior, or graduate years; not renewable. *Number:* 4. *Amount:* $2500.

Eligibility Requirements: Applicant must be of Arab heritage and enrolled or expecting to enroll full-time at a four-year institution or university. Applicant must have 3.0 GPA or higher. Available to U.S. citizens.

Application Requirements: Application form, essay. *Deadline:* June 15.

Contact: Mr. Nabil Mohamad, Vice President
ADC Research Institute
1705 Desales street NW, 5th Floor
Washington, DC 20036
Phone: 202-244-2990
E-mail: nmohamad@adc.org

ALPHA OMEGA COUNCIL OF NEW ENGLAND

http://www.alphaomegacouncil.org/

ALPHA OMEGA SCHOLARSHIP IN MEMORY OF PETER AGRIS

Prerequisites for the scholarship include: Greek American heritage; U.S. citizenship; current full-time enrollment as a journalism or communications major at the graduate or undergraduate level in an accredited college or university in the United States; active participation in school, community, church organizations; a minimum of a 3.0 GPA and demonstrated financial need. Interested candidates should visit http://www.alphaomegacouncil.com or write to The Peter Agris Memorial Scholarships Committee, c/o Nancy Agris Savage, 9 Nonesuch Drive, Natick, MA 01760. Any questions may be directed to: nancyasavage@gmail.com. Applications, transcripts, the required essay and any published work that might enhance the application must be returned by email to nancyasavage@gmail.com, or by mail to the above address, no later than March 1.

Academic Fields/Career Goals: Communications; Journalism.

Award: Scholarship for use in freshman, sophomore, junior, senior, graduate, or postgraduate years; not renewable. *Number:* 6. *Amount:* $5000.

Eligibility Requirements: Applicant must be Eastern Orthodox; of Lithuanian heritage and enrolled or expecting to enroll full-time at a four-year institution or university. Applicant or parent of applicant must have employment or volunteer experience in journalism/broadcasting. Applicant must have 3.0 GPA or higher. Available to U.S. citizens.

Application Requirements: Application form, essay. *Deadline:* March 1.

Contact: Mrs. Nancy Savage, Executive Director
Alpha Omega Council of New England
Peter Agris Memorial Journalism Scholarships
9 Nonesuch Drive
Natick, MA 01760
Phone: 508-733-6883
E-mail: nancyasavage@gmail.com

AMERICAN INSTITUTE OF POLISH CULTURE INC.

http://www.ampolinstitute.org/

HARRIET IRSAY SCHOLARSHIP GRANT

• *See page 141*

AMERICAN LEGION AUXILIARY DEPARTMENT OF ARIZONA

http://wwwaladeptaz.org

AMERICAN LEGION AUXILIARY DEPARTMENT OF ARIZONA WILMA HOYAL-MAXINE CHILTON MEMORIAL SCHOLARSHIP

Annual scholarship to a student in second year or higher in one of the three state universities in Arizona. Must be enrolled in a program of study in political science, public programs, or special education. Must be a citizen of United States and of Arizona for at least one year. Honorably discharged veterans or immediate family members are given preference.

Academic Fields/Career Goals: Communications; Public Policy and Administration; Social Services; Special Education.

Award: Scholarship for use in freshman, sophomore, junior, senior, graduate, or postgraduate years; not renewable. *Number:* 3. *Amount:* $1000.

Eligibility Requirements: Applicant must be enrolled or expecting to enroll full- or part-time at a four-year institution or university; resident of Arizona and studying in Arizona. Available to U.S. citizens.

Application Requirements: Application form, essay, financial need analysis, personal photograph. *Deadline:* May 15.

Contact: Barbara Matteson, Department Secretary/Treasurer
American Legion Auxiliary Department of Arizona
4701 North 19th Avenue, Suite 100
Phoenix, AZ 85015
Phone: 602-241-1080
E-mail: secretary@aladeptaz.org

AMERICAN QUARTER HORSE FOUNDATION (AQHF)

http://www.aqha.com/foundation

AQHF JOURNALISM OR COMMUNICATIONS SCHOLARSHIP

Ideal candidate is an AQHA or AQHYA member pursuing a college degree in journalism or communications. Recipient must pursue a career in news, editorial or print journalism, photojournalism or a related field.

Academic Fields/Career Goals: Communications; Journalism; Photojournalism/Photography.

Award: Scholarship for use in freshman, sophomore, junior, senior, or graduate years; renewable. *Number:* 1. *Amount:* $8000.

Eligibility Requirements: Applicant must be enrolled or expecting to enroll full-time at a two-year or four-year institution or university and must have an interest in animal/agricultural competition or writing. Applicant or parent of applicant must be member of American Quarter Horse Association. Applicant must have 2.5 GPA or higher. Available to U.S. and non-U.S. citizens.

Application Requirements: Application form, financial need analysis. *Deadline:* December 1.

Contact: Scholarship Office
American Quarter Horse Foundation (AQHF)
2601 East Interstate 40
Amarillo, TX 79104
Phone: 806-378-5029
E-mail: foundation@aqha.org

ARAB AMERICAN SCHOLARSHIP FOUNDATION

http://www.lahc.org/

LEBANESE AMERICAN HERITAGE CLUB'S SCHOLARSHIP FUND

Scholarship for high school, undergraduate, or graduate students who are of Arab descent. Minimum 3.0 GPA required for high school and undergraduate applicants, 3.5 GPA for graduate student applicants. Must be U.S. citizens.

Academic Fields/Career Goals: Communications; Political Science.

Award: Scholarship for use in freshman, sophomore, junior, senior, or graduate years; not renewable. *Number:* 1. *Amount:* $1000.

Eligibility Requirements: Applicant must be of Arab heritage; enrolled or expecting to enroll full-time at a four-year institution or university and resident of Michigan. Applicant must have 3.0 GPA or higher. Available to U.S. citizens.

Application Requirements: Application form, essay, financial need analysis, recommendations or references, Student Aid Report (SAR), transcript. *Deadline:* April 6.

Contact: Suehalia Amen, Communications Chair
Phone: 313-846-8480
Fax: 313-846-2710
E-mail: sueamen@lahc.org

ARRL FOUNDATION INC.

http://www.arrl.org/

CHARLES CLARKE CORDLE MEMORIAL SCHOLARSHIP

One-time award for licensed amateur radio operators. Must have minimum GPA of 2.5. Preference to students studying electronics, communications, or related fields. Preference given to residents of Georgia or Alabama attending institutions in those states.

Academic Fields/Career Goals: Communications; Electrical Engineering/Electronics.

Award: Scholarship for use in freshman, sophomore, junior, or senior years; not renewable. *Number:* 1. *Amount:* $1000.

Eligibility Requirements: Applicant must be enrolled or expecting to enroll full-time at a four-year institution or university; resident of Alabama, Georgia; studying in Alabama, Georgia and must have an interest in amateur radio. Applicant must have 2.5 GPA or higher. Available to U.S. citizens.

Application Requirements: Application form. *Deadline:* January 31.

Contact: Ms. Mary Hobart, Secretary
Phone: 860-594-0397
E-mail: k1mmh@arrl.org

CHARLES N. FISHER MEMORIAL SCHOLARSHIP
• See page 122

DR. JAMES L. LAWSON MEMORIAL SCHOLARSHIP

One-time award of $500 available to general amateur radio operators. For Baccalaureate or higher course of study in electronics, communications, or a related field. Preference given to residents of New England states (ME, NH, VT, CT, RI, MA) and New York state and attending college in any of those states.

Academic Fields/Career Goals: Communications; Electrical Engineering/Electronics.

Award: Scholarship for use in freshman, sophomore, junior, senior, or graduate years; not renewable. *Number:* 1. *Amount:* $500.

Eligibility Requirements: Applicant must be enrolled or expecting to enroll full-time at a four-year institution or university; resident of Connecticut, Maine, Massachusetts, New Hampshire, New York, Rhode Island, Vermont; studying in Connecticut, Maine, Massachusetts, New Hampshire, New York, Rhode Island, Vermont and must have an interest in amateur radio. Available to U.S. citizens.

Application Requirements: Application form. *Deadline:* January 31.

Contact: Ms. Mary Hobart, Secretary
Phone: 860-594-0397
E-mail: k1mmh@arrl.org

FRED R. MCDANIEL MEMORIAL SCHOLARSHIP

One $500 award is available to students who possess a general class or higher amateur radio license. Must be studying electronics, communications, or related fields at a Bachelor's level. Preference will be given to applicants with a 3.0 GPA or higher who are residents of FCC 5th call district (TX, OK, AR, LA, MS, NM).

Academic Fields/Career Goals: Communications; Electrical Engineering/Electronics.

Award: Scholarship for use in freshman, sophomore, junior, or senior years; not renewable. *Number:* 1. *Amount:* $500.

Eligibility Requirements: Applicant must be enrolled or expecting to enroll full- or part-time at a four-year institution or university; resident of Arkansas, Louisiana, Mississippi, New Mexico, Oklahoma, Texas and must have an interest in amateur radio. Applicant must have 3.0 GPA or higher. Available to U.S. citizens.

Application Requirements: Application form. *Deadline:* January 31.

Contact: Ms. Mary Hobart, Secretary
Phone: 860-594-0397
E-mail: k1mmh@arrl.org

IRVING W. COOK, WA0CGS, SCHOLARSHIP

One-time award of $1000 to students pursuing a Baccalaureate or higher degree in communications, electronics, or related fields. Must be a amateur radio operator. Preference to Kansas resident but may attend school in any state.

Academic Fields/Career Goals: Communications; Electrical Engineering/Electronics.

Award: Scholarship for use in freshman, sophomore, junior, senior, or graduate years; not renewable. *Number:* 1. *Amount:* $1000.

Eligibility Requirements: Applicant must be enrolled or expecting to enroll full-time at a four-year institution or university; resident of Kansas and must have an interest in amateur radio. Available to U.S. citizens.

Application Requirements: Application form. *Deadline:* January 31.

Contact: Ms. Mary Hobart, Secretary
Phone: 860-594-0397
E-mail: k1mmh@arrl.org

L. PHIL AND ALICE J. WICKER SCHOLARSHIP

One-time award available to a licensed general amateur radio operator. Preference given to residents in the ARRL Roanoke Division (North Carolina, South Carolina, Virginia, West Virginia) and attending school in that division. Preference to Baccalaureate or higher degree studies in electronics, communications, or related fields.

Academic Fields/Career Goals: Communications; Electrical Engineering/Electronics.

Award: Scholarship for use in freshman, sophomore, junior, senior, or graduate years; not renewable. *Number:* 1. *Amount:* $500.

Eligibility Requirements: Applicant must be enrolled or expecting to enroll full-time at a four-year institution or university; resident of North Carolina, South Dakota, Virginia, West Virginia; studying in North Carolina, South Carolina, Virginia, West Virginia and must have an interest in amateur radio. Available to U.S. citizens.

Application Requirements: Application form. *Deadline:* January 31.

Contact: Ms. Mary Hobart, Secretary
Phone: 860-594-0397
E-mail: k1mmh@arrl.org

MAGNOLIA DX ASSOCIATION SCHOLARSHIP

One $500 award is available to a student majoring in electronics, communications, computer science, engineering, or a related field. Preference is given to graduating high school seniors who are residents of Mississippi or Delta division planning to study in Mississippi. Must have obtained a technical class or higher amateur radio license.

Academic Fields/Career Goals: Communications; Computer Science/Data Processing; Electrical Engineering/Electronics; Engineering/Technology.

Award: Scholarship for use in freshman, sophomore, junior, or senior years; not renewable. *Number:* 1. *Amount:* $500.

Eligibility Requirements: Applicant must be enrolled or expecting to enroll full- or part-time at a two-year or four-year or technical institution or university; resident of Mississippi; studying in Mississippi and must have an interest in amateur radio. Available to U.S. citizens.

Application Requirements: Application form. *Deadline:* January 31.

Contact: Ms. Mary Hobart, Secretary
Phone: 860-594-0397
E-mail: k1mmh@arrl.org

MISSISSIPPI SCHOLARSHIP
• *See page 122*

ORLANDO HAMCATION SCHOLARSHIP

One $1000 scholarship for U.S. citizen studying a technical field that supports the radio art at an accredited four-year college or university. Applicant may have any class of active amateur radio license. Must be a resident of Florida, with preference given to residents of Central Florida (Orange, Seminole, Osceola, Lake, Volusia, Brevard and Polk Counties).

Academic Fields/Career Goals: Communications; Electrical Engineering/Electronics.

Award: Scholarship for use in freshman, sophomore, junior, or senior years; not renewable. *Number:* 1. *Amount:* $1000.

Eligibility Requirements: Applicant must be enrolled or expecting to enroll full-time at a four-year institution or university; resident of Florida and must have an interest in amateur radio. Available to U.S. citizens.

Application Requirements: Application form. *Deadline:* January 31.

Contact: Ms. Mary Hobart, Secretary
Phone: 860-594-0397
E-mail: k1mmh@arrl.org

PAUL AND HELEN L. GRAUER SCHOLARSHIP
• *See page 122*

ASIAN AMERICAN JOURNALISTS ASSOCIATION

http://www.aaja.org/

CIC/ANNA CHENNAULT SCHOLARSHIP

$5,000 is available to current high school seniors or college students committed to and/or interested in the field of journalism as a career or area of study. The selected student will receive travel, lodging and registration to attend the 2018 AAJA national annual convention August 8-11 in Houston. Depending on the winner's area of study, the student will also be paired with a professional print, online or broadcast mentor at the convention to help them network.

Academic Fields/Career Goals: Communications; Filmmaking/Video; Journalism; Photojournalism/Photography; TV/Radio Broadcasting.

Award: Scholarship for use in freshman, sophomore, junior, senior, or graduate years; not renewable. *Number:* 1. *Amount:* $5000.

Eligibility Requirements: Applicant must be American Indian/Alaska Native, Asian/Pacific Islander, Black (non-Hispanic), Hispanic and enrolled or expecting to enroll full-time at a two-year or four-year institution or university. Available to U.S. citizens.

Application Requirements: Application form, essay, financial need analysis. *Deadline:* April 8.

Contact: Justin Seiter, Program Coordinator
Asian American Journalists Association
5 Third Street
Suite 1108
San Francisco, CA 94103
Phone: 415-346-2051 Ext. 107
E-mail: justins@aaja.org

MARY QUON MOY ING MEMORIAL SCHOLARSHIP AWARD

One-time award of up to $2000 for a deserving high school senior or current undergraduate or graduate student. Must intend to pursue a journalism career and must show a commitment to the Asian-American community. Visit website http://www.aaja.org for application and details.

Academic Fields/Career Goals: Communications; Journalism; Photojournalism/Photography; TV/Radio Broadcasting.

Award: Scholarship for use in freshman, sophomore, junior, senior, or graduate years; not renewable. *Number:* 1. *Amount:* $2000.

Eligibility Requirements: Applicant must be Asian/Pacific Islander and enrolled or expecting to enroll full-time at a two-year or four-year institution or university. Available to U.S. and non-U.S. citizens.

Application Requirements: Application form, essay, financial need analysis. *Deadline:* April 8.

Contact: Justin Seiter, Program Coordinator
Asian American Journalists Association
5 Third Street
Suite 1108
San Francisco, CA 94103
Phone: 415-346-2051 Ext. 107
E-mail: justins@aaja.org

VINCENT CHIN MEMORIAL SCHOLARSHIP

$500 award to a journalism student committed to keeping Vincent Chin's memory alive. Minimum GPA of 2.5.

Academic Fields/Career Goals: Communications; Journalism; Photojournalism/Photography; TV/Radio Broadcasting.

Award: Scholarship for use in freshman, sophomore, junior, senior, or graduate years; not renewable. *Number:* 1. *Amount:* $500.

Eligibility Requirements: Applicant must be Asian/Pacific Islander and enrolled or expecting to enroll full-time at a two-year or four-year or technical institution or university. Applicant must have 2.5 GPA or higher. Available to U.S. and non-U.S. citizens.

Application Requirements: Application form, essay, financial need analysis. *Deadline:* April 8.

Contact: Justin Seiter, Program Coordinator
Asian American Journalists Association
5 Third Street
Suite 1108
San Francisco, CA 94103
Phone: 415-346-2051 Ext. 107
E-mail: justins@aaja.org

ASIAN AMERICAN JOURNALISTS ASSOCIATION, SEATTLE CHAPTER

http://www.aajaseattle.org/

NORTHWEST JOURNALISTS OF COLOR SCHOLARSHIP
• *See page 96*

AUTOMOTIVE WOMEN'S ALLIANCE FOUNDATION

http://awafoundation.org/index.php

AUTOMOTIVE WOMEN'S ALLIANCE FOUNDATION SCHOLARSHIPS

• *See page 81*

BIOCOMMUNICATIONS ASSOCIATION

http://www.bca.org

ENDOWMENT FUND FOR EDUCATION GRANT

The EFFE Scholarship supports educational opportunities for students pursuing a career in scientific/biomedical visual communications.

Academic Fields/Career Goals: Communications; Health and Medical Sciences.

Award: Scholarship for use in sophomore, junior, senior, graduate, or postgraduate years; not renewable. *Number:* 2. *Amount:* $500.

Eligibility Requirements: Applicant must be enrolled or expecting to enroll full-time at a two-year or four-year or technical institution or university. Available to U.S. and non-U.S. citizens.

Application Requirements: Application form, essay, portfolio. *Deadline:* February 1.

Contact: EFFE Chair
BioCommunications Association
389 Newport Ave.
Attleboro, MA 02703
E-mail: office@bca.org

BMI FOUNDATION, INC.

http://www.bmifoundation.org/

BMI FOUNDERS AWARD FOR RADIO BROADCASTING

The BMI Founders Award competition is open to radio broadcasting students age 17 - 24 nationwide. A $5,000 scholarship will be awarded for the best original essay response. The program was established in 2015 to recognize future innovators in broadcast radio, and commemorates the group of radio industry leaders who founded Broadcast Music, Inc. in 1939.

Academic Fields/Career Goals: Communications; Journalism.

Award: Scholarship for use in freshman, sophomore, junior, senior, graduate, or postgraduate years; not renewable. *Number:* 1. *Amount:* $5000.

Eligibility Requirements: Applicant must be age 17-24 and enrolled or expecting to enroll full- or part-time at a two-year or four-year or technical institution or university. Applicant must have 3.0 GPA or higher. Available to U.S. and non-U.S. citizens.

Application Requirements: Application form, essay. *Deadline:* February 1.

Contact: Dan Spears, Director
BMI Foundation, Inc.
7 World Trade Center
250 Greenwich Street
New York, NY 10007
Phone: 212-2203103
E-mail: info@bmifoundation.org

CCNMA: LATINO JOURNALISTS OF CALIFORNIA

http://www.ccnma.org/

CCNMA SCHOLARSHIPS

Scholarships for Latinos interested in pursuing a career in journalism. Awards based on scholastic achievement, financial need, and cultural awareness. Submit sample of work. Award limited to California residents or those attending school in California.

Academic Fields/Career Goals: Communications; Graphics/Graphic Arts/Printing; Journalism; Photojournalism/Photography; TV/Radio Broadcasting.

Award: Scholarship for use in freshman, sophomore, junior, senior, or graduate years; not renewable. *Number:* 5–10. *Amount:* $500–$1000.

Eligibility Requirements: Applicant must be of Latin American/Caribbean heritage; Hispanic; enrolled or expecting to enroll full-time at a two-year or four-year institution or university and resident of California. Applicant must have 2.5 GPA or higher. Available to U.S. and non-U.S. citizens.

Application Requirements: Application form, application form may be submitted online (http://www.ccnma.org), essay, financial need analysis, interview, portfolio, recommendations or references, resume, transcript. *Deadline:* April 1.

Contact: Mr. Julio Moran, Executive Director
CCNMA: Latino Journalists of California
ASU Walter Cronkite School of Journalism and Mass Communication
725 Arizona Avenue, Suite 406
Santa Monica, CA 90401-1723
Phone: 424-229-9482
Fax: 424-238-0271
E-mail: ccnmainfo@ccnma.org

CHARLES AND LUCILLE KING FAMILY FOUNDATION, INC.

http://www.kingfoundation.org/

CHARLES AND LUCILLE KING FAMILY FOUNDATION SCHOLARSHIPS

Renewable award for college undergraduates at junior or senior level pursuing television, film, or communication studies to further their education. Must attend a four-year undergraduate institution. Minimum 3.0 GPA required to renew scholarship. Must have completed at least two years of study and be currently enrolled in a U.S. college or university. Application may be downloaded on website.

Academic Fields/Career Goals: Communications; Filmmaking/Video; TV/Radio Broadcasting.

Award: Scholarship for use in junior or senior years; renewable. *Number:* 10–20. *Amount:* $3500–$7000.

Eligibility Requirements: Applicant must be enrolled or expecting to enroll full-time at a four-year institution or university. Applicant must have 3.0 GPA or higher. Available to U.S. and non-U.S. citizens.

Application Requirements: Application form, financial need analysis. *Deadline:* April 15.

Contact: Mr. Michael Donovan, Educational Director, The Charles and Lucille King Family Foundation
Charles and Lucille King Family Foundation, Inc.
400 Madison Avenue - Room 8D
New York, NY 10017
Phone: 212-682-2913
E-mail: info@kingfoundation.org

CONNECTICUT CHAPTER OF SOCIETY OF PROFESSIONAL JOURNALISTS

http://www.ctspj.org/

CONNECTICUT SPJ BOB EDDY SCHOLARSHIP PROGRAM

One-time awards of $250 to $2000 for college juniors or seniors planning a career in journalism. Must be a Connecticut resident attending a four year college or any student attending a four year college in Connecticut.

Academic Fields/Career Goals: Communications; Journalism; Photojournalism/Photography.

Award: Scholarship for use in junior or senior years; not renewable. *Number:* 5. *Amount:* $250–$2000.

Eligibility Requirements: Applicant must be enrolled or expecting to enroll full-time at a four-year institution or university; resident of Connecticut; studying in Connecticut and must have an interest in writing. Available to U.S. and non-U.S. citizens.

Application Requirements: Application form, entry in a contest, essay, financial need analysis, transcript. *Deadline:* April 4.

Contact: Debra Estock, Scholarship Committee Chairman
Connecticut Chapter of Society of Professional Journalists
71 Kenwood Avenue
Fairfield, CT 06824
Phone: 203-255-2127
E-mail: debae@optonline.net

HOUSE OF BLUES MUSIC FORWARD FOUNDATION

https://hobmusicforward.org/

STEVEN J. FINKEL SERVICE EXCELLENCE SCHOLARSHIP

• *See page 180*

TIFFANY GREEN OPERATOR SCHOLARSHIP AWARD

• *See page 96*

IDAHO STATE BROADCASTERS ASSOCIATION

http://www.idahobroadcasters.org/

WAYNE C. CORNILS MEMORIAL SCHOLARSHIP

• *See page 180*

INSTITUTE FOR HUMANE STUDIES

http://www.theihs.org/

HUMANE STUDIES FELLOWSHIPS

Renewable award for undergraduate and graduate students in selected disciplines. Applicants should have demonstrated interest in classical liberal or libertarian ideas and must intend to pursue a scholarly career. Minimum 3.5 GPA required. Application fee: $25.

Academic Fields/Career Goals: Communications; Economics; History; Humanities; Law/Legal Services; Literature/English/Writing; Political Science; Social Sciences.

Award: Scholarship for use in junior or senior years; not renewable. *Number:* 140–180. *Amount:* $2000–$12,000.

Eligibility Requirements: Applicant must be enrolled or expecting to enroll full-time at a two-year or four-year institution or university. Applicant must have 3.5 GPA or higher. Available to U.S. and Canadian citizens.

Application Requirements: Application form, essay, recommendations or references, resume, test scores, transcript. *Fee:* $25. *Deadline:* December 31.

Contact: Director, Humane Studies Fellowship
E-mail: HSF@TheIHS.org

INTERNATIONAL COMMUNICATIONS INDUSTRIES FOUNDATION

http://www.infocomm.org/scholarships

ICIF SCHOLARSHIP FOR EMPLOYEES AND DEPENDENTS OF MEMBER ORGANIZATIONS

Scholarship for a spouse, child, stepchild or grandchild of an employee of an InfoComm International member organization or for an employee of an InfoComm International member organization. Must be majoring in audiovisual related fields, such as audio, video, audiovisual, electronics, telecommunications, technical theatre, data networking, software development, and information technology. Minimum of 2.75 GPA required. Must show evidence of AV experience (completed course, job, internship, etc.).

Academic Fields/Career Goals: Communications; Computer Science/Data Processing; Electrical Engineering/Electronics; Filmmaking/Video.

Award: Scholarship for use in freshman, sophomore, junior, senior, or graduate years; not renewable. *Number:* 1–50. *Amount:* $1500.

Eligibility Requirements: Applicant must be enrolled or expecting to enroll full-time at a two-year or four-year or technical institution or university. Applicant must have 3.0 GPA or higher. Available to U.S. and non-U.S. citizens.

Application Requirements: Application form, essay, recommendations or references, transcript. *Deadline:* May 10.

Contact: Ms. Shana Rieger, Membership and Social Media Program Manager
International Communications Industries Foundation
11242 Waples Mill Road, Suite 200
Fairfax, VA 22030
Phone: 703-273-7200 Ext. 3690
Fax: 703-278-8082
E-mail: srieger@infocomm.org

INTERNATIONAL COMMUNICATIONS INDUSTRIES FOUNDATION AV SCHOLARSHIP

Scholarship for students majoring in audiovisual related fields such as audio, video, audiovisual, electronics, telecommunications, technical theatre, data networking, software development, information and technology. Minimum 2.75 GPA required. Must provide evidence of audiovisual knowledge (completed course, job, internship, etc.).

Academic Fields/Career Goals: Communications; Computer Science/Data Processing; Electrical Engineering/Electronics; Filmmaking/Video.

Award: Scholarship for use in freshman, sophomore, junior, senior, or graduate years; not renewable. *Number:* 1–50. *Amount:* $1200.

Eligibility Requirements: Applicant must be enrolled or expecting to enroll full-time at a two-year or four-year or technical institution or university. Applicant must have 3.0 GPA or higher. Available to U.S. and Canadian citizens.

Application Requirements: Application form, essay, recommendations or references, transcript. *Deadline:* May 10.

Contact: Ms. Shana Rieger, Membership and Social Media Program Manager
International Communications Industries Foundation
11242 Waples Mill Road, Suite 200
Fairfax, VA 22030
Phone: 703-273-7200 Ext. 3690
Fax: 703-278-8082
E-mail: srieger@infocomm.org

INTERNATIONAL FOODSERVICE EDITORIAL COUNCIL

http://www.ifeconline.com/

INTERNATIONAL FOODSERVICE EDITORIAL COUNCIL COMMUNICATIONS SCHOLARSHIP

• *See page 96*

JORGE MAS CANOSA FREEDOM FOUNDATION

http://masscholarships.org/

MAS FAMILY SCHOLARSHIP AWARD

• *See page 181*

THE LAGRANT FOUNDATION

http://www.lagrantfoundation.org/

LAGRANT FOUNDATION SCHOLARSHIP FOR GRADUATES

• *See page 97*

LAGRANT FOUNDATION SCHOLARSHIP FOR UNDERGRADUATES

• *See page 97*

NATIONAL ACADEMY OF TELEVISION ARTS & SCIENCES—OHIO VALLEY CHAPTER

http://ohiovalleyemmy.org/

DAVID J. CLARKE MEMORIAL SCHOLARSHIP

One $3000 scholarship offered to a full-time graduate or undergraduate student, majoring in broadcasting (or other designated television major) at an accredited college or university in the designated market area of stations serving the Ohio Valley Chapter of the National Academy of Television Arts and Sciences. The award will be given to a student who has achieved academic excellence; who is involved in co-curricular television activities (through student media, internships, or related employment); who possesses a desire to engage in television as a career; and who has high integrity and personal character. Financial need may also be considered. Must apply online at http://ohiovalleyemmy.org/students/scholarship-application/.

Academic Fields/Career Goals: Communications; Filmmaking/Video; Journalism; TV/Radio Broadcasting.

Award: Scholarship for use in freshman, sophomore, junior, senior, or graduate years; not renewable. *Number:* 1. *Amount:* $3000.

Eligibility Requirements: Applicant must be enrolled or expecting to enroll full-time at a four-year institution or university. Available to U.S. citizens.

Application Requirements: Application form, portfolio. *Deadline:* April 30.

NATIONAL ACADEMY OF TELEVISION ARTS AND SCIENCES

http://www.emmyonline.tv/

DOUGLAS W. MUMMERT SCHOLARSHIP

• See page 142

JIM McKAY MEMORIAL SCHOLARSHIP

The Jim McKay Memorial Scholarship honors sports journalist Jim McKay (1921-2008) and was established in 2009 by the HBO, CBS, NBC, ABC and FOX networks. It is presented at the Sports Emmys each May. It is awarded to a college-bound applicant who demonstrates exceptional talent as a creator of video programming as well as outstanding academic achievement and potential for success in a highly competitive profession.

Academic Fields/Career Goals: Communications; Filmmaking/Video; Journalism; Music; Performing Arts; Photojournalism/Photography; TV/Radio Broadcasting.

Award: Scholarship for use in freshman year; not renewable. *Number:* 1. *Amount:* $10,000.

Eligibility Requirements: Applicant must be high school student and planning to enroll or expecting to enroll full-time at a two-year or four-year institution or university. Available to U.S. citizens.

Application Requirements: Application form, essay, portfolio. *Deadline:* February 26.

Contact: Mr. Adam Sharp, Chair, Scholarship Committee
Phone: 212-586-8424
Fax: 212-246-8129
E-mail: scholarship@emmyonline.tv

MIKE WALLACE MEMORIAL SCHOLARSHIP

The Mike Wallace Memorial Scholarship is funded by a grant from CBS News in honor of longtime correspondent Mike Wallace (1918-2012) and presented each year at the News and Documentary Emmys. It is awarded to a college-bound applicant who demonstrates exceptional talent as a creator of video programming as well as outstanding academic achievement and potential for success in a highly competitive profession.

Academic Fields/Career Goals: Communications; Filmmaking/Video; Journalism; Music; Performing Arts; Photojournalism/Photography; TV/Radio Broadcasting.

Award: Scholarship for use in freshman year; not renewable. *Number:* 1. *Amount:* $10,000.

Eligibility Requirements: Applicant must be high school student and planning to enroll or expecting to enroll full-time at a two-year or four-year institution or university. Available to U.S. citizens.

Application Requirements: Application form, essay, portfolio. *Deadline:* February 26.

Contact: Mr. Adam Sharp, Chair, Scholarship Committee
Phone: 212-586-8424
Fax: 212-246-8129
E-mail: scholarship@emmyonline.tv

NATIONAL ACADEMY OF TELEVISION ARTS AND SCIENCES TRUSTEES SCHOLARSHIP

The Trustees Scholarship was established by the NATAS Board of Trustees to recognize standout graduating high school seniors who intend to pursue degrees in pursuit of a career in any aspect of the television industry.

Academic Fields/Career Goals: Communications; Filmmaking/Video; Journalism; Music; Performing Arts; Photojournalism/Photography; TV/Radio Broadcasting.

Award: Scholarship for use in freshman year; not renewable. *Number:* 1. *Amount:* $10,000.

Eligibility Requirements: Applicant must be high school student and planning to enroll or expecting to enroll full-time at a two-year or four-year institution or university. Available to U.S. citizens.

Application Requirements: Application form, essay, portfolio. *Deadline:* February 26.

Contact: Mr. Adam Sharp, Chair, Scholarship Committee
Phone: 212-586-8424
Fax: 212-246-8129
E-mail: scholarship@emmyonline.tv

RANDY FALCO SCHOLARSHIP

The Falco Scholarship is awarded to a college-bound Hispanic or Latino student who demonstrates exceptional talent as a creator of video programming as well as outstanding academic achievement and potential for success in a highly competitive profession. The $10,000 annual scholarship honors the industry contributions of renowned media executive Randy Falco, currently the President and Chief Executive Officer of Univision Communications Inc. (UCI).

Academic Fields/Career Goals: Communications; Filmmaking/Video; Journalism; Music; Performing Arts; Photojournalism/Photography; TV/Radio Broadcasting.

Award: Scholarship for use in freshman year; not renewable. *Number:* 1. *Amount:* $10,000.

Eligibility Requirements: Applicant must be Hispanic; high school student and planning to enroll or expecting to enroll full-time at a two-year or four-year institution or university. Available to U.S. citizens.

Application Requirements: Application form, essay, portfolio. *Deadline:* February 26.

Contact: Mr. Adam Sharp, Chair, Scholarship Committee
Phone: 212-586-8424
Fax: 212-246-8129
E-mail: scholarship@emmyonline.tv

NATIONAL ACADEMY OF TELEVISION ARTS AND SCIENCES, MICHIGAN CHAPTER

http://natasmichigan.org

DR. LYNNE BOYLE/JOHN SCHIMPF UNDERGRADUATE SCHOLARSHIP

• See page 97

NATIONAL ASSOCIATION OF BLACK JOURNALISTS

http://www.nabj.org/

NABJ SCHOLARSHIP

Scholarship for a student who is currently attending an accredited four-year college or university. Must be enrolled as an undergraduate or graduate student majoring in journalism (print, radio, online, or television). Minimum 2.5 GPA. Must be a member of NABJ. Scholarship value and the number of awards granted varies annually.

Academic Fields/Career Goals: Communications; Journalism; TV/Radio Broadcasting.

Award: Scholarship for use in freshman, sophomore, junior, senior, or graduate years; not renewable.

Eligibility Requirements: Applicant must be enrolled or expecting to enroll full-time at a four-year institution or university. Applicant must have 2.5 GPA or higher. Available to U.S. and non-U.S. citizens.

Application Requirements: Application form, driver's license, essay, interview, recommendations or references, transcript. *Deadline:* March 17.

Contact: Irving Washington, Manager
Phone: 301-445-7100
Fax: 301-445-7101
E-mail: iwashington@nabj.org

NATIONAL ASSOCIATION OF BROADCASTERS

http://www.nab.org/

NATIONAL ASSOCIATION OF BROADCASTERS GRANTS FOR RESEARCH IN BROADCASTING

Award program is intended to fund research on economic, business, social, and policy issues important to station managers and other decision-makers in the United States commercial broadcast industry. Competition is open to all academic personnel. Graduate students and senior undergraduates are invited to submit proposals. For details refer to website http://www.nab.org.

Academic Fields/Career Goals: Communications; Journalism; TV/Radio Broadcasting.

Award: Grant for use in senior, graduate, or postgraduate years; not renewable. *Number:* 2. *Amount:* $5000.

Eligibility Requirements: Applicant must be enrolled or expecting to enroll full-time at a four-year institution or university. Available to U.S. and non-U.S. citizens.

Application Requirements: Application form, recommendations or references, research proposal, budget. *Deadline:* February 1.

Contact: Debbie Milman, Research Director
National Association of Broadcasters
1771 N Street, NW
Washington, DC 20036
Phone: 202-429-5383
Fax: 202-429-4199
E-mail: dmilman@nab.org

NATIONAL ASSOCIATION OF HISPANIC JOURNALISTS (NAHJ)

http://www.nahj.org/

NATIONAL ASSOCIATION OF HISPANIC JOURNALISTS SCHOLARSHIP

One-time award for high school seniors, college undergraduates, and first-year graduate students who are pursuing careers in English- or Spanish-language print, photo, broadcast, or online journalism. Students may major or plan to major in any subject, but must demonstrate a sincere desire to pursue a career in journalism. Must submit resume and work samples. Applications available only on website http://www.nahj.org.

Academic Fields/Career Goals: Communications; Journalism; Photojournalism/Photography; TV/Radio Broadcasting.

Award: Scholarship for use in freshman, sophomore, junior, senior, or graduate years; not renewable. *Amount:* $1000–$2000.

Eligibility Requirements: Applicant must be enrolled or expecting to enroll full-time at a four-year institution or university and must have an interest in photography/photogrammetry/filmmaking or writing. Available to U.S. citizens.

Application Requirements: Application form, essay, financial need analysis, recommendations or references, resume, transcript, work samples. *Deadline:* March 31.

Contact: Virginia Galindo, Program Assistant
Phone: 202-662-7145
E-mail: vgalindo@nahj.org

NATIONAL CATTLEMEN'S FOUNDATION

http://www.nationalcattlemensfoundation.org/

CME BEEF INDUSTRY SCHOLARSHIP
• *See page 102*

NATIONAL DAIRY SHRINE

http://www.dairyshrine.org/

MARSHALL E. MCCULLOUGH-NATIONAL DAIRY SHRINE SCHOLARSHIPS
• *See page 108*

NEBRASKA PRESS ASSOCIATION

http://www.nebpress.com/

NEBRASKA PRESS ASSOCIATION FOUNDATION SCHOLARSHIP
• *See page 97*

NEW JERSEY BROADCASTERS ASSOCIATION

http://www.njba.com/

MICHAEL S. LIBRETTI SCHOLARSHIP

Scholarships for undergraduate students in broadcasting, communication and journalism. Must be a New Jersey resident.

Academic Fields/Career Goals: Communications; Journalism; TV/Radio Broadcasting.

Award: Scholarship for use in freshman, sophomore, junior, or senior years; not renewable. *Number:* 1. *Amount:* up to $5000.

Eligibility Requirements: Applicant must be enrolled or expecting to enroll full-time at a four-year institution or university and resident of New Jersey. Available to U.S. citizens.

Application Requirements: Application form. *Deadline:* varies.

Contact: Mr. Paul Rotella, President and CEO
NJ 08831
Phone: 609-860-0111
Fax: 609-860-0110
E-mail: njba@njba.com

OHIO NEWS MEDIA FOUNDATION

http://www.ohionews.org

HAROLD K. DOUTHIT SCHOLARSHIP
• *See page 98*

OHIO NEWS MEDIA FOUNDATION MINORITY SCHOLARSHIP
• *See page 98*

OHIO NEWS MEDIA FOUNDATION UNIVERSITY JOURNALISM SCHOLARSHIP
• *See page 98*

ONWA ANNUAL SCHOLARSHIP
• *See page 98*

OREGON ASSOCIATION OF BROADCASTERS

http://www.theoab.org/

OAB FOUNDATION SCHOLARSHIP

Award for students to begin or continue their education in broadcast and related studies. Must have a minimum GPA of 3.25. Must be a resident of

Oregon studying in Oregon. For more details, refer to website at http//http://www.TheOAB.org.

Academic Fields/Career Goals: Communications; Journalism; TV/Radio Broadcasting.

Award: Scholarship for use in freshman, sophomore, junior, senior, graduate, or postgraduate years; renewable. *Number:* 4. *Amount:* $2500–$3500.

Eligibility Requirements: Applicant must be enrolled or expecting to enroll full-time at a two-year or four-year institution or university and resident of Oregon. Available to U.S. citizens.

Application Requirements: Application form, essay, financial need analysis, recommendations or references, resume, transcript. *Deadline:* May 3.

Contact: Mr. Bill Johnstone, President and Chief Executive Officer
Oregon Association of Broadcasters
9020 SW Washington Square Road
Suite 140
Portland, OR 97223-4433
Phone: 503-443-2299
Fax: 503-443-2488
E-mail: theoab@theoab.org

OUTDOOR WRITERS ASSOCIATION OF AMERICA

http://www.owaa.org/

OUTDOOR WRITERS ASSOCIATION OF AMERICA - BODIE MCDOWELL SCHOLARSHIP AWARD

One-time award for undergraduate and graduate students who demonstrate outdoor communications talent and intend to make a career in this field. Applicants must include a letter of recommendation from their institution and samples of their outdoor communications work.

Academic Fields/Career Goals: Communications; Environmental Science; Filmmaking/Video; Journalism; Literature/English/Writing; Natural Resources; Photojournalism/Photography; TV/Radio Broadcasting.

Award: Scholarship for use in freshman, sophomore, junior, senior, graduate, or postgraduate years; not renewable. *Number:* 2–6. *Amount:* $1000–$5000.

Eligibility Requirements: Applicant must be enrolled or expecting to enroll full-time at a two-year or four-year or technical institution or university and must have an interest in amateur radio, art, athletics/sports, photography/photogrammetry/filmmaking, or writing. Available to U.S. and non-U.S. citizens.

Application Requirements: Application form, essay. *Deadline:* March 15.

Contact: Ms. Jessica Seitz, Membership and Conference Director
Outdoor Writers Association of America
615 Oak St.
St. 201
Missoula, MT 59801
Phone: 406-728-7434
Fax: 406-728-7445
E-mail: info@owaa.org

POLISH ARTS CLUB OF BUFFALO SCHOLARSHIP FOUNDATION

http://www.pacb.bfn.org/

POLISH ARTS CLUB OF BUFFALO SCHOLARSHIP FOUNDATION TRUST

• See page 144

PRINT AND GRAPHIC SCHOLARSHIP FOUNDATION

http://www.printing.org/

PRINT AND GRAPHICS SCHOLARSHIPS FOUNDATION

Applicant must be interested in a career in graphic communications, printing technology or management, or publishing. Selection is based on academic record, recommendations, biographical information, and extracurricular activities. All applications and letters of recommendation must be submitted online at http://www.pgsf.org. All applications high school and college applicants must be submitted by March 1. Awards are available to applicants outside United States, as long as they are attending a U.S. institution and meet the basic criteria of the Print and Graphics Scholarship Foundation.

Academic Fields/Career Goals: Communications; Graphics/Graphic Arts/Printing.

Award: Scholarship for use in freshman, sophomore, junior, senior, or graduate years; renewable. *Number:* 150–200. *Amount:* $1500–$5000.

Eligibility Requirements: Applicant must be enrolled or expecting to enroll full-time at a two-year or four-year or technical institution or university. Applicant must have 3.0 GPA or higher. Available to U.S. and non-U.S. citizens.

Application Requirements: Application form, essay. *Deadline:* March 1.

Contact: Bernie Eckert, Administrator
Print and Graphic Scholarship Foundation
301 Brush Creek Road
Warrendale, PA 15086
Phone: 412-259-1740
E-mail: pgsf@printing.org

PRINTING INDUSTRY MIDWEST EDUCATION FOUDNATION

http://www.pimw.org/scholarships

PRINTING INDUSTRY MIDWEST EDUCATION FOUNDATION SCHOLARSHIP FUND

The fund offers $1000 renewable scholarships to full-time students enrolled in two- or four-year institutions and technical colleges offering degrees in the print communications discipline. Applicant must be a Minnesota resident and be committed to a career in the print communications industry. Minimum 3.0 GPA required. Priority given to children of PIM member company employees.

Academic Fields/Career Goals: Communications; Flexography; Graphics/Graphic Arts/Printing; Journalism; Marketing; Photojournalism/Photography.

Award: Scholarship for use in freshman, sophomore, junior, or senior years; renewable. *Number:* 5–10. *Amount:* $1000.

Eligibility Requirements: Applicant must be enrolled or expecting to enroll full-time at a two-year or four-year or technical institution or university and resident of Iowa, Minnesota, Nebraska, North Dakota, South Dakota. Applicant must have 3.0 GPA or higher. Available to U.S. citizens.

Application Requirements: Application form, essay. *Deadline:* April 1.

Contact: Kristin Pilling-Davis, Education Director
Printing Industry Midwest Education Foudnation
PIM
1300 Godward St. NE Ste. 2650
Minneapolis, MN 55413
Phone: 612-400-6200
E-mail: kdavis@pimw.org

PUBLIC RELATIONS STUDENT SOCIETY OF AMERICA

http://www.prssa.org/

PUBLIC RELATIONS SOCIETY OF AMERICA MULTICULTURAL AFFAIRS SCHOLARSHIP

• See page 98

RADIO TELEVISION DIGITAL NEWS ASSOCIATION

http://www.rtdna.org

CAROLE SIMPSON SCHOLARSHIP

Carole Simpson is a former member of the RTDNF Board of Trustees. In a career of notable firsts, in 1992 Simpson became the first woman and first African American to moderate a presidential debate. She established the scholarship to encourage and help minority students overcome hurdles along their career path.

Academic Fields/Career Goals: Communications; Journalism; Photojournalism/Photography; TV/Radio Broadcasting.

Award: Scholarship for use in junior or senior years; not renewable. *Number:* 1. *Amount:* $2000.

Eligibility Requirements: Applicant must be American Indian/Alaska Native, Asian/Pacific Islander, Black (non-Hispanic), Hispanic and enrolled or expecting to enroll full-time at a four-year institution or university. Available to U.S. and non-U.S. citizens.

Application Requirements: Application form, essay, portfolio. *Deadline:* January 31.

Contact: Ms. Kate McGarrity, Awards and Programs Manager
Radio Television Digital News Association
529 14th Street, NW
Suite 1240
Washington, DC 20045
Phone: 202-662-7254
E-mail: katem@rtdna.org

ED BRADLEY SCHOLARSHIP

Ed Bradley was the first black White House television correspondent and enjoyed a long career on CBS 60 Minutes. Bradley was recognized by RTDNA in 2000 for his lifetime commitment to excellence in journalism. He created the award in 1994 to recognize top-tier students, particularly minority students, pursuing journalism careers.

Academic Fields/Career Goals: Communications; Journalism; Photojournalism/Photography; TV/Radio Broadcasting.

Award: Scholarship for use in junior or senior years; not renewable. *Number:* 1. *Amount:* $10,000.

Eligibility Requirements: Applicant must be American Indian/Alaska Native, Asian/Pacific Islander, Black (non-Hispanic), Hispanic and enrolled or expecting to enroll full-time at a four-year institution or university. Available to U.S. and non-U.S. citizens.

Application Requirements: Application form, essay, portfolio. *Deadline:* January 31.

Contact: Ms. Kate McGarrity, Awards and Programs Manager
Radio Television Digital News Association
529 14th Street, NW
Suite 1240
Washington, DC 20045
Phone: 202-662-7254
E-mail: katem@rtdna.org

GEORGE FOREMAN TRIBUTE TO LYNDON B. JOHNSON SCHOLARSHIP

George Foreman is a boxing champion, Olympic gold medal winner and celebrated pitchman. As a young man, he was inspired by President Lyndon Johnson and by RTDNF founder Barney Oldfield. The scholarship is a $6,000 award given to a journalism student from the University of Texas at Austin.

Academic Fields/Career Goals: Communications; Journalism; Photojournalism/Photography; TV/Radio Broadcasting.

Award: Scholarship for use in sophomore, junior, or senior years; not renewable. *Number:* 1. *Amount:* $6000.

Eligibility Requirements: Applicant must be enrolled or expecting to enroll full-time at a four-year institution or university and studying in Texas. Available to U.S. and non-U.S. citizens.

Application Requirements: Application form, portfolio. *Deadline:* January 31.

Contact: Ms. Kate McGarrity, Awards and Programs Manager
Radio Television Digital News Association
529 14th Street, NW
Suite 1240
Washington, DC 20045
Phone: 202-662-7254
E-mail: katem@rtdna.org

LEE THORNTON SCHOLARSHIP

Lee Thornton was the first African-American woman to cover the White House for a major news network (CBS) and the first African-American host of All Things Considered on National Public Radio. She served as a faculty member at the Howard University School of Communications, earning a tenured position. Later in her career, she taught at the University of Maryland's Philip Merrill College of Journalism and served a term as the school's interim dean. She held a Master's degree from Michigan State University and a doctorate in mass communications from Northwestern University. Ms. Thornton passed away in 2013 at age 71, and endowed in her estate this scholarship in her name. Students from the University of Maryland and Howard University will be given preference. The recipient of the Lee Thornton Scholarship will receive $2,000 and an invitation to the Excellence in Journalism conference.

Academic Fields/Career Goals: Communications; Journalism.

Award: Scholarship for use in sophomore, junior, or senior years; not renewable. *Number:* 1. *Amount:* $2000.

Eligibility Requirements: Applicant must be enrolled or expecting to enroll full-time at a four-year institution or university and studying in District of Columbia, Maryland. Available to U.S. and non-U.S. citizens.

Application Requirements: Application form, essay, portfolio. *Deadline:* January 31.

Contact: Ms. Kate McGarrity, Awards and Programs Manager
Radio Television Digital News Association
529 14th Street, NW
Suite 1240
Washington, DC 20045
Phone: 202-662-7254
E-mail: katem@rtdna.org

LOU AND CAROLE PRATO SPORTS REPORTING SCHOLARSHIP

In recognition of his service to RTDNA, and his commitment to excellence in journalism, the Lou and Carole Prato Sports Reporting Scholarship was established in 2001. It is awarded to a journalism student who brings Lou's journalism values to covering sports.

Academic Fields/Career Goals: Communications; Journalism; Photojournalism/Photography; Sports-Related/Exercise Science; TV/Radio Broadcasting.

Award: Scholarship for use in sophomore, junior, or senior years; not renewable. *Number:* 1. *Amount:* $1000.

Eligibility Requirements: Applicant must be enrolled or expecting to enroll full-time at a four-year institution or university. Available to U.S. and non-U.S. citizens.

Application Requirements: Application form, essay, portfolio. *Deadline:* January 31.

Contact: Ms. Kate McGarrity, Awards and Programs Manager
Radio Television Digital News Association
529 14th Street, NW
Suite 1240
Washington, DC 20045
Phone: 202-662-7254
E-mail: katem@rtdna.org

MIKE REYNOLDS JOURNALISM SCHOLARSHIP

Mike Reynolds, who died in 1988 at age 45, was managing editor at KCCI-TV in Des Moines, IA. Applicants must have good writing ability, excellent grades, a dedication to the news business, strong interest in pursuing a career in electronic journalism and a demonstrated need for financial assistance.

Academic Fields/Career Goals: Communications; Journalism; Photojournalism/Photography; TV/Radio Broadcasting.

Award: Scholarship for use in sophomore, junior, or senior years; not renewable. *Number:* 1. *Amount:* $1000.

Eligibility Requirements: Applicant must be enrolled or expecting to enroll full-time at a four-year institution or university. Available to U.S. and non-U.S. citizens.

Application Requirements: Application form, essay, portfolio. *Deadline:* January 31.

Contact: Ms. Kate McGarrity, Awards and Programs Manager
Radio Television Digital News Association
529 14th Street, NW
Suite 1240
Washington, DC 20045
Phone: 202-662-7254
E-mail: katem@rtdna.org

RHODE ISLAND FOUNDATION

http://www.rifoundation.org/

J. D. EDSAL SCHOLARSHIP
• See page 99

RDW GROUP INC. MINORITY SCHOLARSHIP FOR COMMUNICATIONS

Award to provide support for minority students who wish to pursue a course of study in communications at the undergraduate or graduate level. Must be a Rhode Island resident and must demonstrate financial need.

Academic Fields/Career Goals: Communications.

Award: Scholarship for use in freshman, sophomore, junior, senior, or graduate years; not renewable. *Amount:* $2000.

Eligibility Requirements: Applicant must be American Indian/Alaska Native, Asian/Pacific Islander, Black (non-Hispanic), Hispanic; enrolled or expecting to enroll full-time at a four-year institution or university and resident of Rhode Island. Available to U.S. citizens.

Application Requirements: Application form, essay, self-addressed stamped envelope with application, transcript. *Deadline:* April 26.

Contact: Libby Monahan, Funds Administrator
  Phone: 401-274-4564 Ext. 3117
  E-mail: libbym@rifoundation.org

ROBERT H. MOLLOHAN FAMILY CHARITABLE FOUNDATION, INC.

http://www.mollohanfoundation.org/

HARRY C. HAMM FAMILY SCHOLARSHIP

The Harry C. Hamm Family Scholarship is awarded to a sophomore, junior, or senior college student who is in serious pursuit of a B.A. in Journalism or Communications at a West Virginia four-year institution. Mr. Hamm was a 50 year veteran reporter/editor with Ogden Newspapers. The applicant must be a graduate of a high school in West Virginia and must have at least a 3.0 GPA.

Academic Fields/Career Goals: Communications; Journalism.

Award: Scholarship for use in sophomore, junior, or senior years; not renewable. *Amount:* $1000.

Eligibility Requirements: Applicant must be high school student; planning to enroll or expecting to enroll full-time at a four-year institution or university; resident of West Virginia and studying in West Virginia. Applicant must have 3.0 GPA or higher. Available to U.S. citizens.

Application Requirements: Application form, essay, recommendations or references, resume, test scores, transcript.

Contact: Aime Shaffer, Program Manager
  Phone: 304-333-6783
  E-mail: ashaffer@wvhtf.org

SOCIETY FOR TECHNICAL COMMUNICATION

http://www.stc.org/

SOCIETY FOR TECHNICAL COMMUNICATION SCHOLARSHIP PROGRAM

Award for study relating to communication of information about technical subjects. Applicants must be full-time graduate students working toward a Master's or Doctoral degree, or undergraduate students working toward a Bachelor's degree. Must have completed at least one year of postsecondary education and have at least one full year of academic work remaining. Two awards available for undergraduate students, two available for graduate students.

Academic Fields/Career Goals: Communications; Science, Technology, and Society.

Award: Scholarship for use in sophomore, junior, senior, or graduate years; not renewable. *Number:* up to 4. *Amount:* up to $1500.

Eligibility Requirements: Applicant must be enrolled or expecting to enroll full-time at a four-year institution or university. Available to U.S. and non-U.S. citizens.

Application Requirements: Application form, essay, recommendations or references, transcript. *Deadline:* February 15.

Contact: Scott DeLoach, Manager, Scholarship Selection Committee
  Society for Technical Communication
  834 C Dekalb Avenue, NE
  Atlanta, GA 30307

SOCIETY FOR TECHNICAL COMMUNICATION–LONE STAR CHAPTER

http://www.stc-dfw.org/

LONE STAR COMMUNITY SCHOLARSHIPS

Scholarship for graduate or undergraduate student working toward a degree or certificate in the technical communication field. We also provide a scholarship for those returning to school to either further their studies in technical communication through approved training courses or career advancement classes. For further information see website http://www.stc-dfw.org.

Academic Fields/Career Goals: Communications.

Award: Scholarship for use in freshman, sophomore, junior, senior, or graduate years; not renewable. *Number:* 1–4.

Eligibility Requirements: Applicant must be Hispanic; enrolled or expecting to enroll full- or part-time at a four-year institution or university and resident of Oklahoma, Texas. Available to U.S. and non-U.S. citizens.

Application Requirements: Application form, recommendations or references, transcript. *Deadline:* March 28.

Contact: Rob Harris, Scholarship Committee Manager
  Phone: 940-391-0167
  E-mail: scholarship@stc-dfw.org

SOCIETY OF MOTION PICTURE AND TELEVISION ENGINEERS

https://www.smpte.org/

LOUIS F. WOLF JR. MEMORIAL SCHOLARSHIP

This scholarship was established to help students further their undergraduate or graduate studies in motion pictures and television, with an emphasis on technology. Open To Currently Enrolled, Full-Time Undergraduate Student Members;, Extra Credit May Be Awarded For Volunteer Work/Leadership.

Academic Fields/Career Goals: Communications; Electrical Engineering/Electronics; Engineering-Related Technologies; Engineering/Technology; Filmmaking/Video; Science, Technology, and Society; TV/Radio Broadcasting.

Award: Scholarship for use in freshman, sophomore, junior, senior, graduate, or postgraduate years; not renewable. *Number:* up to 1. *Amount:* $1000–$5000.

Eligibility Requirements: Applicant must be enrolled or expecting to enroll full-time at a two-year or four-year or technical institution or university. Applicant or parent of applicant must be member of Society of Motion Picture and Television Engineers. Available to U.S. and non-U.S. citizens.

Application Requirements: Application form, essay, financial need analysis, recommendations or references, transcript. *Deadline:* June 1.

Contact: Sally-Ann DAmato, Director of Operations
  Society of Motion Picture and Television Engineers
  SMPTE, 3 Barker Avenue
  White Plains, NY 10601
  Phone: 914-761-1100 Ext. 2375
  E-mail: sdamato@smpte.org

STUDENT PAPER AWARD

Contest for best paper by a current Student Member of SMPTE. Paper must deal with some technical phase of motion pictures, television, photographic instrumentation, or their closely allied arts and sciences. For more information see website http://www.smpte.org.

Academic Fields/Career Goals: Communications; Electrical Engineering/Electronics; Engineering-Related Technologies; Engineering/Technology; Filmmaking/Video; Science, Technology, and Society; TV/Radio Broadcasting.

Award: Prize for use in freshman, sophomore, junior, senior, graduate, or postgraduate years; not renewable. *Number:* 1–2. *Amount:* $1–$1500.

Eligibility Requirements: Applicant must be enrolled or expecting to enroll full- or part-time at a two-year or four-year or technical institution or university. Applicant or parent of applicant must be member of Society of Motion Picture and Television Engineers. Available to U.S. and non-U.S. citizens.

Application Requirements: Application form, entry in a contest, essay, student ID card, transcript. *Deadline:* May 1.

Contact: Sally-Ann DAmato, Director of Operations
Society of Motion Picture and Television Engineers
SMPTE, 3 Barker Avenue
White Plains, NY 10601
Phone: 914-761-1100 Ext. 2375
E-mail: sdamato@smpte.org

SOCIETY OF SATELLITE PROFESSIONALS INTERNATIONAL
http://www.sspi.org/

SSPI INTERNATIONAL SCHOLARSHIPS
• *See page 160*

SPECIALTY EQUIPMENT MARKET ASSOCIATION
http://www.sema.org/

SEMA MEMORIAL SCHOLARSHIP FUND
• *See page 92*

STRAIGHTFORWARD MEDIA
http://www.straightforwardmedia.com/

STRAIGHTFORWARD MEDIA MEDIA & COMMUNICATIONS SCHOLARSHIP
• *See page 99*

SUPPORT CREATIVITY
http://wesupportcreativity.org

SUPPORT CREATIVITY SCHOLARSHIP
• *See page 137*

TAMPA BAY TIMES FUND, INC.
http://www.tampabay.com/fund

CAREER JOURNALISM SCHOLARSHIP
These scholarships target high school seniors in the Times audience area who have a demonstrated interest in pursuing journalism/media as a major in college and as a career. The scholarship is worth up to $2,500 per year and may be renewed annually. Up to 3 winners are selected each year. Students from these Florida counties are eligible to apply: Pinellas, Hillsborough, Pasco, Hernando. Application deadline: January 20. Winners are notified by the end of February. On-line applications only.

Academic Fields/Career Goals: Communications; Journalism; Photojournalism/Photography; TV/Radio Broadcasting.

Award: Scholarship for use in freshman, sophomore, junior, or senior years; not renewable. *Number:* 1–3. *Amount:* $1000–$2500.

Eligibility Requirements: Applicant must be high school student; age 17-19; planning to enroll or expecting to enroll full-time at a four-year institution or university; single and resident of Florida. Applicant must have 3.0 GPA or higher. Available to U.S. citizens.

Application Requirements: Application form, essay, portfolio. *Deadline:* January 20.

Contact: Ms. Nancy Waclawek, Scholarship Administrator
Tampa Bay Times Fund, Inc.
PO Box 1121
St. Petersburg, FL 33731-1121
E-mail: tbtschls@gmail.com

TAMPA BAY TIMES FUND CAREER JOURNALISM SCHOLARSHIPS
• *See page 99*

TEXAS ASSOCIATION OF BROADCASTERS
https://www.tab.org/scholarships/available-scholarships

ANN ARNOLD SCHOLARSHIP
Junior, senior or graduate student enrolled in a broadcast curriculum at a four-year college or university in Texas, demonstrating financial need.

Academic Fields/Career Goals: Communications.

Award: Scholarship for use in junior, senior, graduate, or postgraduate years; not renewable. *Number:* 1. *Amount:* $5000.

Eligibility Requirements: Applicant must be enrolled or expecting to enroll full-time at a four-year institution or university; resident of Texas and studying in Texas. Applicant must have 3.5 GPA or higher. Available to U.S. citizens.

Application Requirements: Application form, essay, financial need analysis. *Deadline:* April 15.

Contact: Mr. Craig Bean, Director, Public Service & EEO
Texas Association of Broadcasters
502 East 11th Street, Suite 200
Austin, TX 78701
Phone: 512-322-9944
Fax: 512-322-0522
E-mail: craig@tab.org

BELO TEXAS BROADCAST EDUCATION FOUNDATION SCHOLARSHIP
Scholarship of $2000 to undergraduate and graduate students enrolled in a fully accredited program of instruction that emphasizes radio or television broadcasting or communications at a four-year college or university in Texas. Student must be a member of the Texas Association of Broadcasters. Must have a GPA of 3.0 minimum.

Academic Fields/Career Goals: Communications; TV/Radio Broadcasting.

Award: Scholarship for use in freshman, sophomore, junior, senior, or graduate years; not renewable. *Number:* 1. *Amount:* $2000.

Eligibility Requirements: Applicant must be enrolled or expecting to enroll full-time at a four-year institution or university and studying in Texas. Applicant or parent of applicant must be member of Texas Association of Broadcasters. Applicant must have 3.0 GPA or higher. Available to U.S. and non-U.S. citizens.

Application Requirements: Application form, essay, financial need analysis, recommendations or references. *Deadline:* May 3.

Contact: Craig Bean, Public Service Manager
Texas Association of Broadcasters
502 East 11th Street, Suite 200
Austin, TX 78701
Phone: 512-322-9944
Fax: 512-322-0522
E-mail: craig@tab.org

BONNER MCLANE TEXAS BROADCAST EDUCATION FOUNDATION SCHOLARSHIP
Scholarship of $2000 to a undergraduate and students enrolled in a fully accredited program of instruction that emphasizes radio or television broadcasting or communications at a four-year college or university in Texas. Student must be a member of the Texas Association of Broadcasters. Must have a GPA of 3.0 minimum.

Academic Fields/Career Goals: Communications; TV/Radio Broadcasting.

Award: Scholarship for use in freshman, sophomore, junior, senior, or graduate years; not renewable. *Number:* 1. *Amount:* $2000.

Eligibility Requirements: Applicant must be enrolled or expecting to enroll full-time at a four-year institution or university and studying in Texas. Applicant or parent of applicant must be member of Texas

Association of Broadcasters. Applicant must have 3.0 GPA or higher. Available to U.S. and non-U.S. citizens.

Application Requirements: Application form, essay, financial need analysis, recommendations or references. *Deadline:* May 3.

Contact: Craig Bean, Public Service Manager
Texas Association of Broadcasters
502 East 11th Street, Suite 200
Austin, TX 78701
Phone: 512-322-9944
Fax: 512-322-0522
E-mail: craig@tab.org

STUDENT TEXAS BROADCAST EDUCATION FOUNDATION SCHOLARSHIP

Scholarship of $2000 to a undergraduate or a graduate student enrolled in a program of instruction that emphasizes radio or television broadcasting or communications at a two-year or technical school in Texas. Student must be a member of the Texas Association of Broadcasters. Must have a GPA of 3.0 minimum.

Academic Fields/Career Goals: Communications; TV/Radio Broadcasting.

Award: Scholarship for use in freshman, sophomore, junior, or senior years; not renewable. *Number:* 1. *Amount:* $2000.

Eligibility Requirements: Applicant must be enrolled or expecting to enroll full-time at a two-year or technical institution and studying in Texas. Applicant or parent of applicant must be member of Texas Association of Broadcasters. Applicant must have 3.0 GPA or higher. Available to U.S. and non-U.S. citizens.

Application Requirements: Application form, essay, financial need analysis, recommendations or references. *Deadline:* May 3.

Contact: Craig Bean, Public Service Manager
Texas Association of Broadcasters
502 East 11th Street, Suite 200
Austin, TX 78701
Phone: 512-322-9944
Fax: 512-322-0522
E-mail: craig@tab.org

TOM REIFF TEXAS BROADCAST EDUCATION FOUNDATION SCHOLARSHIP

Scholarship of $2000 to undergraduate and graduate students enrolled in a fully accredited program of instruction that emphasizes radio or television broadcasting or communications at a four-year college or university in Texas. Student must be a member of the Texas Association of Broadcasters. Must have a GPA of 3.0 minimum.

Academic Fields/Career Goals: Communications; TV/Radio Broadcasting.

Award: Scholarship for use in freshman, sophomore, junior, senior, or graduate years; not renewable. *Number:* 1. *Amount:* $2000.

Eligibility Requirements: Applicant must be enrolled or expecting to enroll full-time at a four-year institution or university and studying in Texas. Applicant or parent of applicant must be member of Texas Association of Broadcasters. Applicant must have 3.0 GPA or higher. Available to U.S. and non-U.S. citizens.

Application Requirements: Application form, essay, financial need analysis, recommendations or references. *Deadline:* May 3.

Contact: Craig Bean, Public Service Manager
Texas Association of Broadcasters
502 East 11th Street, Suite 200
Austin, TX 78701
Phone: 512-322-9944
Fax: 512-322-0522
E-mail: craig@tab.org

UNDERGRADUATE TEXAS BROADCAST EDUCATION FOUNDATION SCHOLARSHIP

Scholarship of $2000 to a undergraduate student enrolled in a fully accredited program of instruction that emphasizes radio or television broadcasting or communications at a four-year college or university in Texas. Student must be a member of the Texas Association of Broadcasters. Must have a GPA of 3.0 minimum.

Academic Fields/Career Goals: Communications; TV/Radio Broadcasting.

Award: Scholarship for use in freshman, sophomore, junior, or senior years; not renewable. *Number:* 1. *Amount:* $2000.

Eligibility Requirements: Applicant must be enrolled or expecting to enroll full-time at a four-year institution or university and studying in Texas. Applicant or parent of applicant must be member of Texas Association of Broadcasters. Applicant must have 3.0 GPA or higher. Available to U.S. and non-U.S. citizens.

Application Requirements: Application form, essay, financial need analysis, recommendations or references. *Deadline:* May 3.

Contact: Craig Bean, Public Service Manager
Texas Association of Broadcasters
502 East 11th Street, Suite 200
Austin, TX 78701
Phone: 512-322-9944
Fax: 512-322-0522
E-mail: craig@tab.org

VANN KENNEDY TEXAS BROADCAST EDUCATION FOUNDATION SCHOLARSHIP

Scholarship of $2000 to a undergraduate or graduate student enrolled in a fully accredited program of instruction that emphasizes radio or television broadcasting or communications at college or university in Texas. Student must be a member of the Texas Association of Broadcasters. Must have a GPA of 3.0 minimum.

Academic Fields/Career Goals: Communications; TV/Radio Broadcasting.

Award: Scholarship for use in freshman, sophomore, junior, or senior years; not renewable. *Number:* 1. *Amount:* $2000.

Eligibility Requirements: Applicant must be enrolled or expecting to enroll full-time at a two-year or four-year institution or university and studying in Texas. Applicant or parent of applicant must be member of Texas Association of Broadcasters. Applicant must have 3.0 GPA or higher. Available to U.S. and non-U.S. citizens.

Application Requirements: Application form, essay, financial need analysis, recommendations or references. *Deadline:* May 3.

Contact: Craig Bean, Public Service Manager
Texas Association of Broadcasters
502 East 11th Street, Suite 200
Austin, TX 78701
Phone: 512-322-9944
Fax: 512-322-0522
E-mail: craig@tab.org

TEXAS GRIDIRON CLUB INC.

http://www.spjfw.org/

TEXAS GRIDIRON CLUB SCHOLARSHIPS

$500 to $4000 scholarships for full-time or part-time college juniors, seniors, or graduate students majoring in newspaper, photojournalism, or broadcast fields. Must be Texas resident or going to school in Texas.

Academic Fields/Career Goals: Communications; Journalism; Photojournalism/Photography; TV/Radio Broadcasting.

Award: Scholarship for use in sophomore, junior, senior, or graduate years; not renewable. *Number:* 10–15. *Amount:* $500–$4000.

Eligibility Requirements: Applicant must be enrolled or expecting to enroll full- or part-time at a four-year institution or university. Applicant must have 2.5 GPA or higher. Available to U.S. citizens.

Application Requirements: Application form, essay, financial need analysis. *Deadline:* December 1.

Contact: Angie Summers, Scholarships Coordinator
Texas Gridiron Club Inc.
709 Houston Street
Arlington, TX 76012
E-mail: asummers@star-telegram.com

TKE EDUCATIONAL FOUNDATION

http://www.tke.org/

GEORGE W. WOOLERY MEMORIAL SCHOLARSHIP

$300 scholarship available to initiated undergraduate members of Tau Kappa Epsilon who are full-time students in good standing with a cumulative GPA of 3.0 or higher. Preference will first be given to a graduate of the TKE Leadership Academy but, if there is no qualified applicant, the scholarship will be open to any other qualified Teke.

Academic Fields/Career Goals: Communications.

Award: Scholarship for use in sophomore, junior, or senior years; not renewable. *Number:* 1. *Amount:* $300.

Eligibility Requirements: Applicant must be enrolled or expecting to enroll full-time at a four-year institution or university; male and must have an interest in leadership. Applicant or parent of applicant must be member of Tau Kappa Epsilon. Applicant must have 3.0 GPA or higher. Available to U.S. and non-U.S. citizens.

Application Requirements: Application form, application form may be submitted online (http://www.tke.org/member_resources/scholarships/apply_online), essay, narrative summary of how TKE membership has benefited applicant, personal photograph, transcript. *Deadline:* March 15.

Contact: Offices of the Grand Chapter
TKE Educational Foundation
7439 Woodland Drive, Suite 100
Indianapolis, IN 46278
E-mail: tkeogc@tke.org

TURF AND ORNAMENTAL COMMUNICATORS ASSOCIATION

http://www.toca.org/

TURF AND ORNAMENTAL COMMUNICATORS ASSOCIATION SCHOLARSHIP PROGRAM
• *See page 111*

UNITED METHODIST COMMUNICATIONS

http://www.umcom.org/

LEONARD M. PERRYMAN COMMUNICATIONS SCHOLARSHIP FOR ETHNIC MINORITY STUDENTS

One-time award to assist United Methodist ethnic minority students who are college students intending to pursue careers in religious communications.

Academic Fields/Career Goals: Communications; Journalism; Photojournalism/Photography; Religion/Theology; TV/Radio Broadcasting.

Award: Scholarship for use in junior or senior years; not renewable. *Number:* 1. *Amount:* $2500.

Eligibility Requirements: Applicant must be Methodist; American Indian/Alaska Native, Asian/Pacific Islander, Black (non-Hispanic), Hispanic and enrolled or expecting to enroll full-time at a two-year or four-year institution or university. Available to U.S. citizens.

Application Requirements: Application form, essay, personal photograph, recommendations or references, transcript. *Deadline:* March 15.

Contact: Michael Neff, Executive Director
Phone: 703-836-4606 Ext. 325
Fax: 703-836-2024
E-mail: mwneff@ashs.org

UNITED NEGRO COLLEGE FUND

http://www.uncf.org/

DIVERSE VOICES IN STORYTELLING SCHOLARSHIP

Need-based program open to full-time, African American students with an interest in a career focused on storytelling in the media/entertainment field. Applicants must attend an accredited HBCU with a declared major in film, creative writing, communications or journalism. Up to $5625.

Academic Fields/Career Goals: Communications; Filmmaking/Video; Journalism; Literature/English/Writing.

Award: Scholarship for use in junior year; renewable.

Eligibility Requirements: Applicant must be Black (non-Hispanic) and enrolled or expecting to enroll full-time at a four-year institution or university. Applicant must have 3.0 GPA or higher. Available to U.S. citizens.

Application Requirements: Application form, essay, financial need analysis. *Deadline:* December 17.

Contact: Mary Williams, Director of Outreach and Recruitment
Phone: 800-331-2244

JACK AND JILL—JACQUELINE MOORE BOWLES SCHOLARSHIP

The Jack and Jill of America Foundation-Jacqueline Moore Bowles scholarship will provide two $2,500 need-based scholarships to returning college students who will be enrolled full-time at an accredited, post secondary institution and who will begin their junior or senior year majoring in Communications.

Academic Fields/Career Goals: Communications.

Award: Scholarship for use in junior or senior years. *Number:* 2. *Amount:* $2500.

Eligibility Requirements: Applicant must be Black (non-Hispanic) and enrolled or expecting to enroll full-time at a four-year institution or university. Applicant must have 3.0 GPA or higher. Available to U.S. citizens.

Application Requirements: Application form, essay, financial need analysis. *Deadline:* October 27.

Contact: Mary Williams, Director of Outreach and Recruitment
Phone: 800-331-2244

JOHN LENNON ENDOWED SCHOLARSHIP PROGRAM

Scholarship up to $5000 based on need, to support deserving students. Must attend one of the 37 UNCF member institutions. Applicants must be majoring in communications, mass communications, mass media arts, music and performing arts.

Academic Fields/Career Goals: Communications; Music; Performing Arts.

Award: Scholarship for use in freshman, sophomore, junior, or senior years.

Eligibility Requirements: Applicant must be Black (non-Hispanic) and enrolled or expecting to enroll at a four-year institution or university. Applicant must have 3.0 GPA or higher. Available to U.S. citizens.

Application Requirements: Application form, financial need analysis. *Deadline:* December 29.

Contact: Mary Williams, Director of Outreach and Recruitment
Phone: 800-331-2244

MICHAEL JACKSON SCHOLARSHIP

One-time scholarships up to $5000 for students majoring in communication arts or social science who are attending UNCF member colleges and universities. Funds may be used for tuition, room and board, books, or to repay federal student loans. Minimum 2.5 GPA required.

Academic Fields/Career Goals: Communications; Social Sciences.

Award: Scholarship for use in freshman, sophomore, junior, senior, or graduate years; not renewable.

Eligibility Requirements: Applicant must be Black (non-Hispanic) and enrolled or expecting to enroll full-time at a four-year institution or university. Applicant must have 2.5 GPA or higher. Available to U.S. citizens.

Application Requirements: Application form, essay. *Deadline:* October 21.

Contact: Mary Williams, Director of Outreach and Recruitment
Phone: 800-331-2244

OSSIE DAVIS ENDOWMENT SCHOLARSHIP PROGRAM
• *See page 146*

SUEZ CORPORATE SCHOLARS PROGRAM
• *See page 94*

UNCF/ALLIANCE DATA SCHOLARSHIP AND INTERNSHIP PROGRAM
• *See page 99*

UNCF/ANTHEM CORPORATE SCHOLARS PROGRAM
• *See page 184*

UNCF/CARNIVAL CORPORATE SCHOLARS PROGRAM
• *See page 184*

VALLEY PRESS CLUB

http://www.valleypressclub.com/

VALLEY PRESS CLUB SCHOLARSHIPS, THE REPUBLICAN SCHOLARSHIP, CHANNEL 22 SCHOLARSHIP

Nonrenewable award for graduating high school seniors from Connecticut and Massachusetts, who are interested in television journalism, photojournalism, broadcast journalism, or print journalism.

Academic Fields/Career Goals: Communications; Journalism; Photojournalism/Photography; TV/Radio Broadcasting.

Award: Scholarship for use in freshman year; not renewable. *Number:* 4–6. *Amount:* $1000.

Eligibility Requirements: Applicant must be high school student; planning to enroll or expecting to enroll full-time at a four-year institution or university; resident of Connecticut, Massachusetts and must have an interest in writing. Available to U.S. citizens.

Application Requirements: Application form, community service, financial need analysis, interview. *Deadline:* April 1.

Contact: Noreen Tassinari, Scholarship Committee Chair
Valley Press Club
PO Box 5475
Springfield, MA 01101
Phone: 413-205-5037
E-mail: ntassinari@thebige.com

VIRGINIA ASSOCIATION OF BROADCASTERS

http://www.vabonline.com/

VIRGINIA ASSOCIATION OF BROADCASTERS SCHOLARSHIP AWARD

Scholarships are available to entering juniors and seniors majoring in mass communications-related courses. Must either be a resident of Virginia or be enrolled at a Virginia college or university. Must be U.S. citizen and enrolled full-time.

Academic Fields/Career Goals: Communications.

Award: Scholarship for use in junior or senior years; renewable. *Number:* 4. *Amount:* $500–$1000.

Eligibility Requirements: Applicant must be enrolled or expecting to enroll full-time at a four-year institution or university; resident of Virginia and studying in Virginia. Available to U.S. and non-U.S. citizens.

Application Requirements: Application form, essay, financial need analysis, transcript. *Deadline:* February 15.

Contact: Ruby Seal, Director of Administration
Phone: 434-977-3716
Fax: 434-979-2439
E-mail: ruby.seal@easterassociates.com

WISCONSIN BROADCASTERS ASSOCIATION FOUNDATION

http://www.wi-broadcasters.org/

WISCONSIN BROADCASTERS ASSOCIATION FOUNDATION SCHOLARSHIP

Four $2000 scholarships offered to assist students enrolled in broadcasting-related educational programs at four-year public or private institutions. Applicants must either have graduated from a Wisconsin high school, or be attending a Wisconsin college or university, must have completed at least 60 credits, and must be planning a career in radio or television broadcasting.

Academic Fields/Career Goals: Communications; TV/Radio Broadcasting.

Award: Scholarship for use in freshman, sophomore, junior, or senior years; not renewable. *Number:* 4. *Amount:* $2000.

Eligibility Requirements: Applicant must be enrolled or expecting to enroll full-time at a four-year institution or university and studying in Wisconsin. Available to U.S. citizens.

Application Requirements: Application form, essay, recommendations or references, transcript. *Deadline:* October 20.

Contact: John Laabs, President
Phone: 608-255-2600
Fax: 608-256-3986
E-mail: jlaabs@aol.com

WOMEN'S BASKETBALL COACHES ASSOCIATION

http://www.wbca.org/

ROBIN ROBERTS/WBCA SPORTS COMMUNICATIONS SCHOLARSHIP AWARD

One-time award for female student athletes who have completed their eligibility and plan to go to graduate school. Must major in communications. Must be nominated by the head coach of women's basketball who is a member of the WBCA.

Academic Fields/Career Goals: Communications; Journalism.

Award: Scholarship for use in senior, graduate, or postgraduate years; not renewable. *Number:* 1. *Amount:* $4000.

Eligibility Requirements: Applicant must be enrolled or expecting to enroll full- or part-time at a four-year institution or university; female and must have an interest in athletics/sports. Available to U.S. and non-U.S. citizens.

Application Requirements: Application form, recommendations or references, statistics. *Deadline:* February 15.

Contact: Betty Jaynes, Consultant
Phone: 770-279-8027 Ext. 102
Fax: 770-279-6290
E-mail: bettyj@wbca.org

WYOMING TRUCKING ASSOCIATION SCHOLARSHIP FUND TRUST

http://www.wytruck.org/

WYOMING TRUCKING ASSOCIATION SCHOLARSHIP TRUST FUND
• See page 95

COMPUTER SCIENCE/ DATA PROCESSING

AIST FOUNDATION

http://www.aistfoundation.org/

ASSOCIATION FOR IRON AND STEEL TECHNOLOGY OHIO VALLEY CHAPTER SCHOLARSHIP
• See page 167

ASSOCIATION FOR IRON AND STEEL TECHNOLOGY WILLY KORF MEMORIAL SCHOLARSHIP
• See page 187

ALICE L. HALTOM EDUCATIONAL FUND

http://www.alhef.org/

ALICE L. HALTOM EDUCATIONAL FUND
• See page 176

AMERICAN FOUNDATION FOR THE BLIND

http://www.afb.org/

PAUL W. RUCKES SCHOLARSHIP

Scholarship of $1000 to an undergraduate or graduate student studying in the field of engineering or in computer, physical, or life sciences. For more information and application requirements, please visit http://www.afb.org/scholarships.asp.

Academic Fields/Career Goals: Computer Science/Data Processing; Electrical Engineering/Electronics; Engineering/Technology; Natural Sciences; Physical Sciences.

Award: Scholarship for use in freshman, sophomore, junior, or senior years; not renewable. *Number:* 1. *Amount:* $1000.

Eligibility Requirements: Applicant must be visually impaired and enrolled or expecting to enroll full-time at a two-year or four-year institution or university. Applicant must be visually impaired. Available to U.S. citizens.

Application Requirements: Application form, essay, proof of post-secondary acceptance and legal blindness, proof of citizenship, FAFSA, recommendations or references, transcript. *Deadline:* April 30.

Contact: Dawn Bodrogi, Information Center
American Foundation for the Blind
11 Penn Plaza, Suite 300
New York, NY 10001
Phone: 212-502-7661
Fax: 212-502-7771
E-mail: afbinfo@afb.net

AMERICAN INDIAN SCIENCE AND ENGINEERING SOCIETY

http://www.aises.org/

A.T. ANDERSON MEMORIAL SCHOLARSHIP PROGRAM
• See page 121

AMERICAN RAILWAY ENGINEERING AND MAINTENANCE OF WAY ASSOCIATION

http://www.aremafoundation.org/

AREMA GRADUATE AND UNDERGRADUATE SCHOLARSHIPS
• See page 204

AMERICAN SOCIETY FOR INFORMATION SCIENCE AND TECHNOLOGY

http://www.asis.org/

JOHN WILEY & SONS BEST JASIST PAPER AWARD

Award of $1500 to recognize the best refereed paper published in the volume year of the JASIT preceding the ASIST annual meeting. John Wiley & Sons Inc., shall contribute $500 towards travel expenses to attend the ASIST annual meeting. No nomination procedure is used for this award. All eligible papers are considered.

Academic Fields/Career Goals: Computer Science/Data Processing; Library and Information Sciences.

Award: Prize for use in freshman, sophomore, junior, senior, graduate, or postgraduate years; not renewable. *Number:* 1. *Amount:* $2000.

Eligibility Requirements: Applicant must be enrolled or expecting to enroll full-time at a four-year institution or university. Available to U.S. and non-U.S. citizens.

Application Requirements: Application form, essay. *Deadline:* varies.

Contact: Awards Coordinator
Phone: 301-495-0900
Fax: 301-495-0810
E-mail: asis@asis.org

ARMED FORCES COMMUNICATIONS AND ELECTRONICS ASSOCIATION, EDUCATIONAL FOUNDATION

http://www.afcea.org/site/?q=foundation/scholarships

AFCEA STEM MAJORS SCHOLARSHIPS FOR UNDERGRADUATE STUDENTS
• See page 122

ARMED FORCES COMMUNICATIONS AND ELECTRONICS ASSOCIATION ROTC SCHOLARSHIP PROGRAM
• See page 151

ARRL FOUNDATION INC.

http://www.arrl.org/

ANDROSCOGGIN AMATEUR RADIO CLUB SCHOLARSHIP

Up to 2 awards to students in the ARRL Maine or New England Division (Maine, New Hampshire, Vermont, Rhode Island, Massachusetts or Connecticut) who have an active technician class amateur radio license or higher. Preference given to students studying computer science, TV/radio electronics, or electrical engineering at a two- or four-year college.

Academic Fields/Career Goals: Computer Science/Data Processing; Electrical Engineering/Electronics; TV/Radio Broadcasting.

Award: Scholarship for use in freshman, sophomore, junior, or senior years; not renewable. *Number:* 1–2. *Amount:* $500–$1000.

Eligibility Requirements: Applicant must be enrolled or expecting to enroll full- or part-time at a two-year or four-year or technical institution; resident of Connecticut, Maine, Massachusetts, New Hampshire, Rhode Island, Vermont and must have an interest in amateur radio. Available to U.S. citizens.

Application Requirements: Application form. *Deadline:* January 31.

Contact: Ms. Mary Hobart, Secretary
Phone: 860-594-0397
E-mail: k1mmh@arrl.org

INDIANAPOLIS AMATEUR RADIO ASSOCIATION SCHOLARSHIP

$1000 award for a student who is a resident of Indiana or the ARRL Central Division (Illinois, Indiana, and Wisconsin). Must be studying electrical or electronics engineering, computer science, or related fields and have an amateur radio license.

Academic Fields/Career Goals: Computer Science/Data Processing; Electrical Engineering/Electronics.

Award: Scholarship for use in freshman, sophomore, junior, or senior years; not renewable. *Number:* 1. *Amount:* $1000.

Eligibility Requirements: Applicant must be enrolled or expecting to enroll full- or part-time at a two-year or four-year or technical institution or university; resident of Illinois, Indiana, Wisconsin and must have an interest in amateur radio. Available to U.S. citizens.

Application Requirements: Application form. *Deadline:* January 31.

Contact: Ms. Mary Hobart, Secretary
Phone: 860-594-0397
E-mail: k1mmh@arrl.org

JAKE MCCLAIN DRIVER, KC5WXA, SCHOLARSHIP

$1000 scholarship for a resident of Tennessee or the ARRL Delta Division (Arkansas, Louisiana, Mississippi, Tennessee). Must have a Technical Class or higher license and provide at least one QLSL card received within the past 12 months. Must be studying electronics, computers, or journalism.

Academic Fields/Career Goals: Computer Science/Data Processing; Electrical Engineering/Electronics; Journalism.

Award: Scholarship for use in freshman, sophomore, junior, or senior years; not renewable. *Number:* 1. *Amount:* $1000.

Eligibility Requirements: Applicant must be enrolled or expecting to enroll full- or part-time at a two-year or four-year or technical institution or university; resident of Arkansas, Louisiana, Mississippi, Tennessee and must have an interest in amateur radio. Available to U.S. citizens.

Application Requirements: Application form. *Deadline:* January 31.

Contact: Ms. Mary Hobart, Secretary
Phone: 860-594-0397
E-mail: k1mmh@arrl.org

MAGNOLIA DX ASSOCIATION SCHOLARSHIP
• See page 217

NORTH FULTON AMATEUR RADIO LEAGUE SCHOLARSHIP

$900 scholarship for an ARRL member who is studying engineering or computer science. Must be a resident in GA and a member of ARRL. If no qualified applicant, preference will be awarded to an applicant from the ARRL Southeastern Division (Alabama, Florida, Georgia, Puerto Rico, and the U.S. Virgin Islands).

Academic Fields/Career Goals: Computer Science/Data Processing; Engineering/Technology.

Award: Scholarship for use in freshman, sophomore, junior, or senior years; not renewable. *Number:* 1. *Amount:* $900.

Eligibility Requirements: Applicant must be enrolled or expecting to enroll full- or part-time at a two-year or four-year or technical institution or university; resident of Alabama, Florida, Georgia, Puerto Rico and must have an interest in amateur radio. Applicant or parent of applicant must be member of American Radio Relay League. Available to U.S. citizens.

Application Requirements: Application form. *Deadline:* January 31.

Contact: Ms. Mary Hobart, Secretary
Phone: 860-594-0397
E-mail: k1mmh@arrl.org

PHD SCHOLARSHIP

One $1000 award for journalism, computer science, or electronic engineering students who are amateur radio operators. Preference given to residents of ARRL Midwest Division (IA, KS, MO, NE). Applicant may be a student who is a child of a deceased amateur radio operator.

Academic Fields/Career Goals: Computer Science/Data Processing; Electrical Engineering/Electronics; Journalism.

Award: Scholarship for use in freshman, sophomore, junior, or senior years; not renewable. *Number:* 1. *Amount:* $1000.

Eligibility Requirements: Applicant must be enrolled or expecting to enroll full-time at a four-year institution or university; resident of Iowa, Kansas, Missouri, Nebraska and must have an interest in amateur radio. Available to U.S. citizens.

Application Requirements: Application form. *Deadline:* January 31.

Contact: Ms. Mary Hobart, Secretary
Phone: 860-594-0397
E-mail: k1mmh@arrl.org

RAY, N0RP, & KATIE, W0KTE, PAUTZ SCHOLARSHIP

One award of up to $1000 is available to a resident of the ARRL Midwest Division (IA, KS, NE, MO) studying electronics or computer science at an accredited four-year college or university. Applicant should possess a general class or higher amateur radio license and be a member of the ARRL.

Academic Fields/Career Goals: Computer Science/Data Processing; Electrical Engineering/Electronics.

Award: Scholarship for use in freshman, sophomore, junior, or senior years; not renewable. *Number:* 1. *Amount:* $500–$1000.

Eligibility Requirements: Applicant must be enrolled or expecting to enroll full- or part-time at a four-year institution or university; resident of Iowa, Kansas, Missouri, Nebraska and must have an interest in amateur radio. Applicant or parent of applicant must be member of American Radio Relay League. Available to U.S. citizens.

Application Requirements: Application form. *Deadline:* January 31.

Contact: Ms. Mary Hobart, Secretary
Phone: 860-594-0397
E-mail: k1mmh@arrl.org

SOUTHEASTERN DX CLUB SCHOLARSHIP

$500 scholarship for an active member of an amateur radio club affiliated with the ARRL. Preference given to students pursuing engineering or computer science. Must be a resident of Georgia. If no qualified applicant, preference will be awarded to an applicant from the ARRL Southeastern Division (Alabama, Florida, Georgia, Puerto Rico and the U.S. Virgin Islands).

Academic Fields/Career Goals: Computer Science/Data Processing; Engineering/Technology.

Award: Scholarship for use in freshman, sophomore, junior, or senior years; not renewable. *Number:* 1. *Amount:* $500.

Eligibility Requirements: Applicant must be enrolled or expecting to enroll full- or part-time at a two-year or four-year or technical institution

or university; resident of Alabama, Florida, Georgia, Puerto Rico and must have an interest in amateur radio. Available to U.S. citizens.

Application Requirements: Application form. *Deadline:* January 31.

Contact: Ms. Mary Hobart, Secretary
Phone: 860-594-0397
E-mail: k1mmh@arrl.org

ASSOCIATION OF FORMER INTELLIGENCE OFFICERS

http://www.afio.com

AFIO UNDERGRADUATE AND GRADUATE SCHOLARSHIPS

• *See page 113*

ASSOCIATION OF STATE DAM SAFETY OFFICIALS (ASDSO)

http://www.DamSafety.org

ASSOCIATION OF STATE DAM SAFETY OFFICIALS (ASDSO) SENIOR UNDERGRADUATE SCHOLARSHIP

• *See page 168*

ASTRONAUT SCHOLARSHIP FOUNDATION

http://www.astronautscholarship.org/

ASTRONAUT SCHOLARSHIP FOUNDATION

• *See page 123*

AUTOMOTIVE WOMEN'S ALLIANCE FOUNDATION

http://awafoundation.org/index.php

AUTOMOTIVE WOMEN'S ALLIANCE FOUNDATION SCHOLARSHIPS

• *See page 81*

BARRY GOLDWATER SCHOLARSHIP AND EXCELLENCE IN EDUCATION FOUNDATION

https://goldwater.scholarsapply.org

BARRY M. GOLDWATER SCHOLARSHIP AND EXCELLENCE IN EDUCATION PROGRAM

• *See page 123*

BHW GROUP

https://thebhwgroup.com/

BHW WOMEN IN STEM SCHOLARSHIP

• *See page 124*

CARDS AGAINST HUMANITY

https://cardsagainsthumanity.com/

SCIENCE AMBASSADOR SCHOLARSHIP

• *See page 124*

CATCHING THE DREAM

http://www.catchingthedream.org/

MATH, ENGINEERING, SCIENCE, BUSINESS, EDUCATION, COMPUTERS SCHOLARSHIPS

• *See page 178*

TRIBAL BUSINESS MANAGEMENT PROGRAM (TBM)
• *See page 82*

DISTIL NETWORKS
http://www.distilnetworks.com

WOMEN FORWARD IN TECHNOLOGY SCHOLARSHIP PROGRAM
• *See page 124*

DIVERSITYCOMM, INC.
http://www.diversitycomm.net/

DIVERSITY IN STEAM MAGAZINE SCHOLARSHIP
• *See page 83*

DOTCOM-MONITOR, INC.
https://www.dotcom-monitor.com/

LOADVIEW WOMEN IN COMPUTING SCHOLARSHIP
Dotcom-Monitor would like to encourage and support female undergraduate students who are pursuing careers in computing by assisting them with the rising cost of higher education. Each year one applicant will be selected to receive the LoadView Women in Computing Scholarship of $1,000 to support their education and pursuit of a career in computing.

Academic Fields/Career Goals: Computer Science/Data Processing; Electrical Engineering/Electronics; Engineering-Related Technologies; Engineering/Technology.

Award: Scholarship for use in freshman, sophomore, junior, or senior years; not renewable. *Number:* 1. *Amount:* $1000.

Eligibility Requirements: Applicant must be enrolled or expecting to enroll full-time at a two-year or four-year or technical institution or university and female. Available to U.S. and non-U.S. citizens.

Application Requirements: Application form, essay. *Deadline:* April 1.

Contact: Jaymi Tripp, Marketing Specialist
MN
E-mail: sales@loadview-testing.com

ELECTRONIC DOCUMENT SYSTEMS FOUNDATION
http://www.edsf.org/

LYNDA BABOYIAN MEMORIAL SCHOLARSHIP
• *See page 178*

FOUNDATION FOR SCIENCE AND DISABILITY
http://stemd.org/

GRANTS FOR DISABLED GRADUATE STUDENTS IN THE SCIENCES
• *See page 106*

GREAT MINDS IN STEM
http://www.greatmindsinstem.org

HENAAC SCHOLARSHIP PROGRAM
• *See page 115*

HAWAIIAN LODGE, F&AM
http://www.hawaiianlodgefreemasons.org

HAWAIIAN LODGE SCHOLARSHIPS
• *See page 86*

INTERNATIONAL COMMUNICATIONS INDUSTRIES FOUNDATION
http://www.infocomm.org/scholarships

ICIF SCHOLARSHIP FOR EMPLOYEES AND DEPENDENTS OF MEMBER ORGANIZATIONS
• *See page 219*

INTERNATIONAL COMMUNICATIONS INDUSTRIES FOUNDATION AV SCHOLARSHIP
• *See page 219*

THE JACKSON LABORATORY
https://www.jax.org

THE JACKSON LABORATORY COLLEGE SCHOLARSHIP PROGRAM
• *See page 126*

LABROOTS INC.
http://www.LabRoots.com

LABROOTS STEM SCHOLARSHIP
• *See page 116*

LOS ANGELES COUNCIL OF BLACK PROFESSIONAL ENGINEERS
http://www.lablackengineers.org/

AL-BEN SCHOLARSHIP FOR ACADEMIC INCENTIVE
• *See page 193*

AL-BEN SCHOLARSHIP FOR PROFESSIONAL MERIT
• *See page 193*

AL-BEN SCHOLARSHIP FOR SCHOLASTIC ACHIEVEMENT
• *See page 193*

MICROSOFT CORPORATION
http://www.microsoft.com/

YOU CAN MAKE A DIFFERENCE SCHOLARSHIP
Scholarship for high school students who want make an impact with technology. All students who submit proposals will receive a free copy of Microsoft Visual Studio NET Academic Edition.

Academic Fields/Career Goals: Computer Science/Data Processing.

Award: Scholarship for use in freshman year; not renewable. *Number:* 10. *Amount:* $5000.

Eligibility Requirements: Applicant must be high school student and planning to enroll or expecting to enroll full- or part-time at a four-year institution or university. Available to U.S. citizens.

Application Requirements: Application form, transcript. *Deadline:* April 30.

Contact: Scholarship Committee
E-mail: scholars@microsoft.com

MORPHISEC
https://www.morphisec.com

WOMEN IN CYBERSECURITY SCHOLARSHIPS
At Morphisec, we believe that diversity drives innovation and we strive to increase the number of women employed in cyber security and related fields. Our current scholarship opportunities are open to female students who are studying for degrees in cyber security, information assurance,

information security, information systems security, an other sub-disciplines of computer science.

Academic Fields/Career Goals: Computer Science/Data Processing.

Award: Scholarship for use in freshman, sophomore, junior, senior, graduate, or postgraduate years; not renewable. *Number:* 3. *Amount:* $1000–$2500.

Eligibility Requirements: Applicant must be enrolled or expecting to enroll full-time at a two-year or four-year institution or university and female. Available to U.S. citizens.

Application Requirements: Application form, essay. *Deadline:* May 15.

Contact: Ursula Ron, Director of Marketing
Morphisec
275 Grove Street Suite 2-400
Newton, MA 02466
Phone: 617-209-2552
E-mail: scholarships@morphisec.com

NASA IDAHO SPACE GRANT CONSORTIUM

http://www.idahospacegrant.org

NASA IDAHO SPACE GRANT CONSORTIUM SCHOLARSHIP PROGRAM
• *See page 126*

NASA/MARYLAND SPACE GRANT CONSORTIUM

http://www.mdspacegrant.org/

NASA MARYLAND SPACE GRANT CONSORTIUM UNDERGRADUATE SCHOLARSHIPS
• *See page 156*

NASA MINNESOTA SPACE GRANT CONSORTIUM

https://www.mnspacegrant.org/

MINNESOTA SPACE GRANT CONSORTIUM SCHOLARSHIP PROGRAM
• *See page 156*

NASA MONTANA SPACE GRANT CONSORTIUM

http://www.spacegrant.montana.edu/

MONTANA SPACE GRANT SCHOLARSHIP PROGRAM
• *See page 156*

NASA'S VIRGINIA SPACE GRANT CONSORTIUM

http://www.vsgc.odu.edu/

COMMUNITY COLLEGE STEM SCHOLARSHIPS
• *See page 126*

UNDERGRADUATE STEM RESEARCH SCHOLARSHIPS
• *See page 127*

NATIONAL SECURITY AGENCY

http://www.nsa.gov/Careers

NATIONAL SECURITY AGENCY STOKES EDUCATIONAL SCHOLARSHIP PROGRAM
Renewable awards for high school students planning to attend a four-year undergraduate institution to study computer science, electrical engineering, or computer engineering. Must be at least 16 to apply. Must be a U.S. citizen. Minimum 3.0 GPA required, and minimum SAT score of 1600. For application visit website http://www.nsa.gov/careers

Academic Fields/Career Goals: Computer Science/Data Processing; Electrical Engineering/Electronics.

Award: Scholarship for use in freshman, sophomore, junior, or senior years; renewable. *Number:* 15–20. *Amount:* $1000–$30,000.

Eligibility Requirements: Applicant must be high school student and planning to enroll or expecting to enroll full-time at a four-year institution or university. Applicant must have 3.0 GPA or higher. Available to U.S. citizens.

Application Requirements: Application form, application form may be submitted online (http://www.nsa.gov/careers), essay, interview, recommendations or references, resume, test scores, transcript. *Deadline:* October 31.

Contact: Anne Clark, Program Manager
National Security Agency
9800 Savage Road, Suite 6779
Fort Meade, MD 20755-6779
Phone: 866-672-4473
Fax: 410-854-3002
E-mail: amclark@nsa.gov

NEVADA NASA SPACE GRANT CONSORTIUM

https://nasa.epscorspo.nevada.edu/

NATIONAL SPACE GRANT CONSORTIUM SCHOLARSHIPS
• *See page 127*

NEXTSTEPU

http://www.nextstepu.com/

$1,500 STEM SCHOLARSHIP
• *See page 120*

NORTH AMERICAN NETWORK OPERATORS GROUP (NANOG)

www/scholarshipamerica.org

NANOG SCHOLARSHIP PROGRAM
The North American Network Operators Group (NANOG), is the professional association for Internet engineering, architecture and operations. Our core focus is on continuous improvement of the data transmission technologies, practices, and facilities that make the Internet function. In an effort to support the next generation of network operators, NANOG has established a scholarship program to assist current undergraduate and graduate level students pursuing a degree in computer engineering, computer science, electrical engineering, network engineering or telecommunications (at the graduate-level only) with $10,000 scholarships. To apply, students must plan to enroll part-time (at least six credits) or full-time in undergraduate or graduate study at an accredited two- or four-year college or university for the entire 2018–2019 academic year. Applicants must have a minimum 3.0 grade point average on a 4.0 scale or its equivalent. Qualified students are encouraged to apply early!

Academic Fields/Career Goals: Computer Science/Data Processing.

Award: Scholarship for use in freshman, sophomore, junior, senior, or graduate years; not renewable. *Number:* 4. *Amount:* $10,000.

Eligibility Requirements: Applicant must be enrolled or expecting to enroll full- or part-time at a two-year or four-year institution. Applicant must have 3.0 GPA or higher. Available to U.S. citizens.

Application Requirements: Application form, essay. *Deadline:* June 2.

Contact: Program Manager
North American Network Operators Group (NANOG)
One Scholarship Way
Saint Peter, MN 56082
Phone: 800-537-4180
E-mail: nanog@scholarshipamerica.org

PACIFIC GAS AND ELECTRIC COMPANY

http://www.scholarshipamerica.org

PG&E BETTER TOGETHER STEM SCHOLARSHIP PROGRAM

PG&E believes in helping students interested in being a part of California's clean energy future, giving them opportunities to learn and succeed in higher education. PG&E is awarding scholarships to help further STEM studies of students in California. Twenty scholarships of $10,000 each and 20 scholarships of $1,000 each are available to high school seniors, current college students, veterans and adults returning to school who are PG&E customers at the time of application and are pursuing a degree in one of the following STEM disciplines: Engineering (electrical, mechanical, computer, industrial or environmental), Computer Science/Information Systems, Cyber Security or Environmental Sciences. Applicants must plan to enroll in full-time undergraduate study for the entire 2018-2019 academic year and be pursuing their first postsecondary degree at a school in California. Scholarships will be awarded based on academic achievement, demonstrated participation and leadership in school and community activities and financial need. Applicable majors include Engineering (electrical, mechanical, computer, industrial or environmental), Computer Science/Information Systems, Cyber Security, and Environmental Sciences.

Academic Fields/Career Goals: Computer Science/Data Processing; Electrical Engineering/Electronics; Environmental Science; Mechanical Engineering.

Award: Scholarship for use in freshman, sophomore, junior, or senior years; not renewable. *Number:* 40. *Amount:* $1000–$10,000.

Eligibility Requirements: Applicant must be enrolled or expecting to enroll full-time at a two-year or four-year or technical institution or university; resident of California and studying in California. Applicant must have 2.5 GPA or higher. Available to U.S. citizens.

Application Requirements: Application form, financial need analysis. *Deadline:* February 5.

Contact: Program Manager
Pacific Gas and Electric Company
Scholarship America
One Scholarship Way
Saint Peter, MN 56082
Phone: 800-537-4180 Ext. 437
E-mail: pge@scholarshipamerica.org

ROBERT H. MOLLOHAN FAMILY CHARITABLE FOUNDATION, INC.

http://www.mollohanfoundation.org/

HIGH TECHNOLOGY SCHOLARS PROGRAM
• *See page 173*

RURAL TECHNOLOGY FUND

http://ruraltechfund.org/

SOCIAL ENTREPRENEURSHIP SCHOLARSHIP

This scholarship is open to students from schools in Kentucky who have a passion for using technology skills to make a positive social change in the world or at home in their communities. Applicants must be an active member of the Student Technology Leadership Program at his or her respective high school.

Academic Fields/Career Goals: Computer Science/Data Processing.

Award: Scholarship for use in freshman year; not renewable. *Number:* 1. *Amount:* $500.

Eligibility Requirements: Applicant must be high school student; planning to enroll or expecting to enroll full- or part-time at a four-year institution and studying in Kentucky. Available to U.S. citizens.

Application Requirements: Application form, essay. *Deadline:* April 15.

SCARLETT FAMILY FOUNDATION SCHOLARSHIP PROGRAM

http://www.scarlettfoundation.org/

SCHOLARSHIP FOR STUDENTS PURSUING A BUSINESS OR STEM DEGREE
• *See page 91*

SEMICONDUCTOR RESEARCH CORPORATION (SRC)

http://www.src.org/

MASTER'S SCHOLARSHIP PROGRAM
• *See page 195*

SIGMA XI, THE SCIENTIFIC RESEARCH SOCIETY

http://www.sigmaxi.org/

SIGMA XI GRANTS-IN-AID OF RESEARCH
• *See page 110*

SILICON VALLEY COMMUNITY FOUNDATION

http://www.siliconvalleycf.org

SAMSUNG@FIRST SCHOLARS

Samsung Semiconductor Inc.'s theme of "Collaborate. Innovate. Grow." has served as the company's mantra to drive technology innovation today and for the next 30 years in Silicon Valley. To help support the valley's continued legacy as the epicenter of innovation and growth in high-tech, the company has made a commitment to the next-generation of innovators by establishing its Samsung@First Scholars program. The scholarship program's goal is to support those outstanding scientists, technologists, engineers, and mathematicians who will lead the world for the next 30 years and beyond. Must be a current undergraduate student entering sophomore, junior or senior year in the upcoming academic school year or an undergraduate senior accepted into a Master's program or a current Master's student. Must be planning to enroll on a full-time basis (as defined by the program of study) in a California, public four-year college/university. Preference given to students enrolling in a school in the greater Bay Area (includes Santa Clara, San Mateo, San Francisco, Marin, Alameda, Contra Costa, Napa, Solano, Sonoma). Declared major in Science, Technology, Engineering or Math (STEM). Preference given to computer science and engineering (CISE) and engineering majors. Minimum grade point average of 3.0 on a 4.0 scale.

Academic Fields/Career Goals: Computer Science/Data Processing; Electrical Engineering/Electronics; Energy and Power Engineering; Engineering-Related Technologies; Engineering/Technology; Marine/Ocean Engineering; Materials Science, Engineering, and Metallurgy; Mathematics; Mechanical Engineering; Science, Technology, and Society; Statistics.

Award: Scholarship for use in sophomore, junior, senior, or graduate years; not renewable. *Number:* 1–3. *Amount:* $1000–$15,000.

Eligibility Requirements: Applicant must be enrolled or expecting to enroll full-time at a four-year institution or university; resident of California and studying in California. Applicant must have 3.0 GPA or higher. Available to U.S. citizens.

Application Requirements: Application form, essay, financial need analysis. *Deadline:* March 21.

Contact: Scholarships Team
Silicon Valley Community Foundation
2440 West El Camino Real
Suite 300
Mountain View, CA 94040
Phone: 650-450-5487
E-mail: scholarships@siliconvalleycf.org

SOCIETY OF WOMEN ENGINEERS

http://societyofwomenengineers.swe.org/

ADMIRAL GRACE MURRAY HOPPER SCHOLARSHIP

Three $1500 scholarships for freshman women pursuing ABET-accredited baccalaureate program in preparation for careers in engineering, engineering technology, and computer science in the United States and Mexico. Preference is given to student in computer-related engineering majors. Minimum 3.5 GPA required.

Academic Fields/Career Goals: Computer Science/Data Processing; Engineering-Related Technologies.

Award: Scholarship for use in freshman year; not renewable. *Number:* 3. *Amount:* $1500.

Eligibility Requirements: Applicant must be enrolled or expecting to enroll full-time at a four-year institution or university and female. Applicant must have 3.5 GPA or higher. Available to U.S. citizens.

Application Requirements: Application form, essay. *Deadline:* May 1.

Contact: Scholarship Committee
    Phone: 800-793-4636
    E-mail: scholarships@swe.org

CUMMINS SCHOLARSHIP
• *See page 197*

HONEYWELL SCHOLARSHIP
• *See page 198*

INVENERGY WOMEN'S NETWORK SCHOLARSHIP
• *See page 212*

LIEBHERR MINING SCHOLARSHIP

Two $1250 scholarships for women pursuing ABET-accredited Baccalaureate programs in preparation for careers in engineering, engineering technology, and computer science in the United States and Mexico. Must be a U.S. citizen and have a minimum 3.0 GPA. One scholarship is renewable for upperclassman. One award is restricted to freshman students and is not renewable.

Academic Fields/Career Goals: Computer Science/Data Processing; Electrical Engineering/Electronics; Engineering/Technology; Mechanical Engineering.

Award: Scholarship for use in freshman, sophomore, junior, or senior years; not renewable. *Number:* 2. *Amount:* $1250.

Eligibility Requirements: Applicant must be enrolled or expecting to enroll full-time at a four-year institution or university and female. Applicant must have 3.0 GPA or higher. Available to U.S. citizens.

Application Requirements: Application form. *Deadline:* February 15.

Contact: Scholarship Committee
    Phone: 800-793-4636
    E-mail: scholarships@swe.org

LILLIAN MOLLER GILBRETH MEMORIAL SCHOLARSHIP
• *See page 198*

LOCKHEED MARTIN CORPORATION SCHOLARSHIP

Eight $2000 scholarships for women pursuing ABET-accredited Baccalaureate programs in preparation for careers in engineering, engineering technology, or computer science in the United States and Mexico. Includes travel grant for the SWE Annual Conference. 3.2 minimum GPA required.

Academic Fields/Career Goals: Computer Science/Data Processing; Electrical Engineering/Electronics; Engineering/Technology.

Award: Scholarship for use in freshman, sophomore, junior, or senior years; not renewable. *Number:* 8. *Amount:* $2000.

Eligibility Requirements: Applicant must be enrolled or expecting to enroll full-time at a four-year institution or university and female. Available to U.S. citizens.

Application Requirements: Application form. *Deadline:* February 15.

Contact: Scholarship Committee
    Phone: 800-793-4636
    E-mail: scholarships@swe.org

ROBERTA BANASZAK GLEITER ENGINEERING ENDEAVOR SCHOLARSHIP
• *See page 199*

SWE REGION E SCHOLARSHIP
• *See page 200*

SWE REGION G JUDY SIMMONS MEMORIAL SCHOLARSHIP
• *See page 200*

SOCIETY OF WOMEN ENGINEERS-DALLAS SECTION

http://www.dallasswe.org/

DALLAS SWE ANNIE COLAÇO COLLEGIATE LEADER SCHOLARSHIP

The scholarship is named in honor of Annie Colaço(1899-1991), the grandmother to SWE lifetime member Nandika D'Souza. Annie Colaço epitomized selfless service and lifelong learning, which is reflected in the SWE mission. $100 award to a student leader and $150 to the SWE student section where the student serves. A maximum of 2 (two) award recipients may be from the same SWE section. The maximum number of awards given annually is 4 (four).

Academic Fields/Career Goals: Computer Science/Data Processing; Engineering/Technology.

Award: Scholarship for use in sophomore, junior, senior, graduate, or postgraduate years; not renewable. *Number:* 1–4. *Amount:* $100–$150.

Eligibility Requirements: Applicant must be enrolled or expecting to enroll full-time at a four-year institution or university; female; resident of Texas and studying in Texas. Applicant must have 3.0 GPA or higher. Available to U.S. citizens.

Application Requirements: Application form, essay, personal photograph. *Deadline:* April 30.

Contact: Shelley Stracener, FY18 President
    E-mail: dallas.swe@gmail.com

SOCIETY OF WOMEN ENGINEERS-ROCKY MOUNTAIN SECTION

http://www.swe-rms.org/

SOCIETY OF WOMEN ENGINEERS-ROCKY MOUNTAIN SECTION SCHOLARSHIP PROGRAM
• *See page 161*

SOCIETY OF WOMEN ENGINEERS-TWIN TIERS SECTION

http://twintiers.swe.org/

SOCIETY OF WOMEN ENGINEERS-TWIN TIERS SECTION SCHOLARSHIP

Scholarship available to female students who reside or attend school in the Twin Tiers SWE section of New York. This is limited to zip codes that begin with 148, 149, 169 and residents of Bradford County, Pennsylvania. Applicant must be accepted or enrolled in an undergraduate degree program in engineering or computer science at an ABET-, CSAB- or SWE-accredited school.

Academic Fields/Career Goals: Computer Science/Data Processing; Engineering-Related Technologies; Engineering/Technology.

Award: Scholarship for use in freshman year; not renewable. *Number:* 5. *Amount:* $2000.

Eligibility Requirements: Applicant must be high school student; planning to enroll or expecting to enroll full-time at a four-year institution or university; female and resident of New York, Pennsylvania. Applicant must have 3.0 GPA or higher. Available to U.S. citizens.

Application Requirements: Application form, autobiography, essay. *Deadline:* March 24.

Contact: Jessica Ortiz
    E-mail: scholarship@swetwintiers.org

SPECIALTY EQUIPMENT MARKET ASSOCIATION

http://www.sema.org/

SEMA MEMORIAL SCHOLARSHIP FUND
• *See page 92*

STRAIGHT NORTH

https://www.straightnorth.com/

STRAIGHT NORTH STEM SCHOLARSHIP
• *See page 92*

TECHNOLOGY FIRST

https://technologyfirst.org/

ROBERT V. MCKENNA SCHOLARSHIPS

Must have at least sophomore standing (30 semester hours) at his/her respective university or college and currently be enrolled as an undergraduate student as defined by the applicant's institution. Must be able to prove that his/her major relates to the information technology field. Approved majors include but are not limited to the following: computer systems, computer science, computer information systems, management information systems, and industrial/computer engineering. Must have a minimum cumulative GPA of 3.0 and a minimum major GPA of 3.25 on a 4.0 scale at the date of submission. Must have a strong interest in pursuing an IT career in Southwest Ohio. Must be a permanent resident of or attend a North Central accredited degree-granting college within the Southwest Ohio region including Adams, Brown, Butler, Champaign, Clark, Clermont, Clinton, Darke, Greene, Hamilton, Logan, Miami, Montgomery, Preble, Shelby and Warren counties. Financial need, character, and personal work ethic will be important selection criteria.

Academic Fields/Career Goals: Computer Science/Data Processing; Engineering-Related Technologies; Engineering/Technology; Health Information Management/Technology; Science, Technology, and Society.

Award: Scholarship for use in sophomore or junior years; not renewable. *Number:* 2–4. *Amount:* $750–$1500.

Eligibility Requirements: Applicant must be enrolled or expecting to enroll full-time at a four-year institution; resident of Ohio and studying in Ohio. Applicant must have 3.0 GPA or higher. Available to U.S. citizens.

Application Requirements: Application form. *Deadline:* March 15.

TEXAS DEPARTMENT OF TRANSPORTATION

http://www.txdot.gov/

CONDITIONAL GRANT PROGRAM
• *See page 212*

TKE EDUCATIONAL FOUNDATION

http://www.tke.org/

ERIC D. DUNNING SCHOLARSHIP

One-time award of $300 given to an undergraduate member of Tau Kappa Epsilon who has demonstrated leadership ability within his chapter, campus, or community. Must be a full-time student in good standing with a GPA of 2.75 or higher. Must be at least a sophomore or higher and be pursuing a degree in engineering, computer science, or any of the pure sciences (chemistry, mathematics, physics, geology, etc.). Preference will be given to Tekes at Missouri University of Science and Technology. If there are no qualified candidates from Beta-Eta Chapter, this scholarship will be open to any Frater who meets the criteria.

Academic Fields/Career Goals: Computer Science/Data Processing; Earth Science; Engineering/Technology; Mathematics; Physical Sciences.

Award: Scholarship for use in sophomore, junior, or senior years; not renewable. *Number:* 1. *Amount:* $300.

Eligibility Requirements: Applicant must be enrolled or expecting to enroll full-time at a four-year institution or university; male and must have an interest in leadership. Applicant or parent of applicant must be member of Tau Kappa Epsilon. Available to U.S. and non-U.S. citizens.

Application Requirements: Application form, application form may be submitted online (http://www.tke.org/member_resources/scholarships/apply_online), essay, personal photograph, transcript. *Deadline:* March 15.

Contact: Offices of the Grand Chapter
TKE Educational Foundation
7439 Woodland Drive, Suite 100
Indianapolis, IN 46278
E-mail: tkeogc@tke.org

UNITED DAUGHTERS OF THE CONFEDERACY

http://www.hqudc.org/

WALTER REED SMITH SCHOLARSHIP
• *See page 184*

UNITED NEGRO COLLEGE FUND

http://www.uncf.org/

BASF/ALFRED CHISHOLM ENDOWED MEMORIAL SCHOLARSHIP
• *See page 93*

DAVIS SCHOLARSHIP FOR WOMEN IN STEM
• *See page 202*

DELL CORPORATE SCHOLARS PROGRAM
• *See page 213*

DISCOVER FINANCIAL SERVICES SCHOLARSHIP
• *See page 93*

GALACTIC UNITE BYTHEWAY SCHOLARSHIP
• *See page 202*

HCN/APRICITY RESOURCES SCHOLARS PROGRAM
• *See page 93*

KIA MOTORS AMERICA STEM/SUSTAINABILITY SCHOLARSHIP
• *See page 175*

MUFG UNION BANK SCHOLARSHIP PROGRAM
• *See page 93*

ORACLE COMMUNITY IMPACT SCHOLARSHIP

Provides scholarship support to African American and Hispanic American students majoring in computer science, computer engineering or mathematics. Applicant must be a matriculating student attending any accredited four-year college or university. Preference is given to students attending a UNCF member institution or other HBCU. Candidates can be either a resident of Northern California or a graduate of a Chicago Public School.

Academic Fields/Career Goals: Computer Science/Data Processing; Mathematics.

Award: Scholarship for use in freshman, sophomore, junior, or senior years.

Eligibility Requirements: Applicant must be Black (non-Hispanic), Hispanic and enrolled or expecting to enroll at a four-year institution or university. Applicant must have 3.0 GPA or higher. Available to U.S. citizens.

Application Requirements: Application form, essay. *Deadline:* December 31.

Contact: Mary Williams, Director of Outreach and Recruitment
Phone: 800-331-2244

ORACLE CORPORATE SCHOLARS PROGRAM
• *See page 184*

PROCTER & GAMBLE GENERAL SCHOLARSHIP
• *See page 94*

PROCTER & GAMBLE STEM SCHOLARSHIP
• *See page 128*

RICOH SCHOLARSHIP PROGRAM
• *See page 94*

SUEZ CORPORATE SCHOLARS PROGRAM
• *See page 94*

UNCF/ALLIANCE DATA SCHOLARSHIP AND INTERNSHIP PROGRAM
• *See page 99*

UNCF/ANTHEM CORPORATE SCHOLARS PROGRAM
• *See page 184*

UNCF/NISSAN SCHOLARSHIP PROGRAM
• *See page 185*

UNCF NORTHROP GRUMMAN SCHOLARSHIP
Scholarship available for a freshman, sophomore, or junior in college who is a U.S. citizen, an African- American, and enrolled full-time as a college undergraduate. Minimum 3.0 GPA required. Must be pursuing a major in computer science, computer engineering, electrical engineering, software engineering, or systems engineering. Must have an unmet financial need.

Academic Fields/Career Goals: Computer Science/Data Processing; Electrical Engineering/Electronics; Engineering/Technology.

Award: Scholarship for use in freshman, sophomore, or junior years; not renewable.

Eligibility Requirements: Applicant must be Black (non-Hispanic) and enrolled or expecting to enroll full-time at a four-year institution or university. Applicant must have 3.0 GPA or higher. Available to U.S. citizens.

Application Requirements: Application form, financial need analysis. *Deadline:* December 29.

Contact: Mary Williams, Director of Outreach and Recruitment
Phone: 800-331-2244

UNCF STEM SCHOLARS PROGRAM
• *See page 175*

WILLIAM WRIGLEY FOUNDATION SCHOLARSHIP
• *See page 95*

UNIVERSITIES SPACE RESEARCH ASSOCIATION
http://www.usra.edu/

UNIVERSITIES SPACE RESEARCH ASSOCIATION SCHOLARSHIP AWARD PROGRAM
• *See page 128*

VERMONT SPACE GRANT CONSORTIUM
http://www.cems.uvm.edu/vsgc

VERMONT SPACE GRANT CONSORTIUM
• *See page 104*

VISIONARY INTEGRATION PROFESSIONALS (VIP)
http://www.trustvip.com/

WOMEN IN TECHNOLOGY SCHOLARSHIP (WITS)
Scholarship for women who are enrolled at, or accepted into, either a two or four-year college or university within the United States. Must be planning a career in computer science, information technology, management information systems, or other related fields. 3.0 GPA or higher required. Selection based upon academic performance, essay, and level of participation in community services and/or extracurricular activities.

Academic Fields/Career Goals: Computer Science/Data Processing; Earth Science; Engineering/Technology.

Award: Scholarship for use in freshman, sophomore, junior, senior, graduate, or postgraduate years; not renewable. *Number:* 1–20. *Amount:* $500–$2500.

Eligibility Requirements: Applicant must be enrolled or expecting to enroll full-time at a two-year or four-year institution or university and female. Applicant must have 3.0 GPA or higher. Available to U.S. citizens.

Application Requirements: Application form, application form may be submitted online (http://www.vipconsulting.com/vip/index.cfm/about-vip/community-support/women-in-technology-scholarship-wits/), community service, essay, explanation of major, transcript. *Deadline:* March 10.

Contact: Dawn Johnson, Marketing Associate
Visionary Integration Professionals (VIP)
80 Iron Point Circle #100
Folsom, CA 95630
Phone: 916-985-9625
E-mail: WITS@vipconsulting.com

WYOMING TRUCKING ASSOCIATION SCHOLARSHIP FUND TRUST
http://www.wytruck.org/

WYOMING TRUCKING ASSOCIATION SCHOLARSHIP TRUST FUND
• *See page 95*

XEROX
http://www.xerox.com//

TECHNICAL MINORITY SCHOLARSHIP
• *See page 203*

CONSTRUCTION ENGINEERING/ MANAGEMENT

AACE INTERNATIONAL
http://www.aacei.org/

AACE INTERNATIONAL COMPETITIVE SCHOLARSHIP
• *See page 130*

AMERICAN COUNCIL OF ENGINEERING COMPANIES OF PENNSYLVANIA (ACEC/PA)

http://www.acecpa.org/

ERIC J. GENNUSO AND LEROY D. (BUD) LOY, JR. SCHOLARSHIP PROGRAM
• *See page 187*

AMERICAN INDIAN SCIENCE AND ENGINEERING SOCIETY

http://www.aises.org/

A.T. ANDERSON MEMORIAL SCHOLARSHIP PROGRAM
• *See page 121*

AMERICAN PUBLIC POWER ASSOCIATION

https://www.publicpower.org/grants-scholarships

DEED EDUCATIONAL SCHOLARSHIP
• *See page 190*

DEED STUDENT INTERNSHIP
• *See page 190*

DEED STUDENT RESEARCH GRANTS
• *See page 204*

DEED TECHNICAL DESIGN PROJECT
• *See page 191*

AMERICAN RAILWAY ENGINEERING AND MAINTENANCE OF WAY ASSOCIATION

http://www.aremafoundation.org/

AREMA GRADUATE AND UNDERGRADUATE SCHOLARSHIPS
• *See page 204*

AMERICAN SOCIETY OF CERTIFIED ENGINEERING TECHNICIANS

http://www.ascet.org/

KURT H. AND DONNA M. SCHULER SMALL GRANT
• *See page 205*

AMERICAN SOCIETY OF HEATING, REFRIGERATING, AND AIR CONDITIONING ENGINEERS, INC.

http://www.ashrae.org/

ASHRAE REGION III BOGGARM SETTY SCHOLARSHIP
• *See page 191*

ARRL FOUNDATION INC.

http://www.arrl.org/

ALFRED E. FRIEND JR., W4CF, MEMORIAL SCHOLARSHIP
• *See page 191*

GARY WAGNER, K3OMI, SCHOLARSHIP
• *See page 191*

ASSOCIATED GENERAL CONTRACTORS EDUCATION AND RESEARCH FOUNDATION

http://www.agcfoundation.org/

AGC EDUCATION AND RESEARCH FOUNDATION UNDERGRADUATE SCHOLARSHIPS
• *See page 207*

JAMES L. ALLHANDS ESSAY COMPETITION
• *See page 207*

WORKFORCE DEVELOPMENT SCHOLARSHIP
Applicant can be anyone who is planning to attend a technical school or approved craft training program in any discipline of construction, including a high school senior, military member, or postsecondary student.

Academic Fields/Career Goals: Construction Engineering/Management; Engineering-Related Technologies; Engineering/Technology; Trade/Technical Specialties.

Award: Scholarship for use in freshman or sophomore years; renewable. *Number:* 10–20. *Amount:* $1000.

Eligibility Requirements: Applicant must be enrolled or expecting to enroll full- or part-time at a two-year or technical institution. Available to U.S. citizens.

Application Requirements: Application form, essay, interview. *Deadline:* June 1.

Contact: Courtney Bishop, Associate Director
Associated General Contractors Education and Research Foundation
2300 Wilson Boulevard
Suite 300
Arlington, VA 22201
Phone: 703-837-5356
Fax: 703-837-5451
E-mail: courtney.bishop@agc.org

ASSOCIATED GENERAL CONTRACTORS OF NEW YORK STATE, LLC

https://www.agcnys.org/programs/scholarship/

ASSOCIATED GENERAL CONTRACTORS NYS SCHOLARSHIP PROGRAM
• *See page 207*

ASSOCIATION OF STATE DAM SAFETY OFFICIALS (ASDSO)

http://www.DamSafety.org

ASSOCIATION OF STATE DAM SAFETY OFFICIALS (ASDSO) SENIOR UNDERGRADUATE SCHOLARSHIP
• *See page 168*

BHW GROUP

https://thebhwgroup.com/

BHW WOMEN IN STEM SCHOLARSHIP
• *See page 124*

BRASKEM ODEBRECHT

http://www.odebrechtaward.com

ODEBRECHT AWARD FOR SUSTAINABLE DEVELOPMENT
• *See page 131*

BROWN AND CALDWELL

http://www.brownandcaldwell.com

ECKENFELDER SCHOLARSHIP
• *See page 169*

MINORITY SCHOLARSHIP PROGRAM
• *See page 169*

COLORADO CONTRACTORS ASSOCIATION INC.

http://www.coloradocontractors.org/

COLORADO CONTRACTORS ASSOCIATION SCHOLARSHIP PROGRAM

Scholarships of $2500 for junior and senior students who are interested in pursuing a career in heavy-highway-municipal-utility construction. Scholarships are only awarded to students who attend the following institutions: Colorado School of Mines, Colorado State University-Fort Collins, Colorado State University-Pueblo.

Academic Fields/Career Goals: Construction Engineering/Management.

Award: Scholarship for use in junior or senior years; not renewable. *Amount:* $2500.

Eligibility Requirements: Applicant must be enrolled or expecting to enroll full- or part-time at a four-year institution or university. Available to U.S. citizens.

Application Requirements: Application form. *Deadline:* varies.

Contact: Scholarship Program Coordinator
Phone: 290-290-6611
Fax: 290-290-9141
E-mail: info@coloradocontractors.org

CONNECTICUT BUILDING CONGRESS SCHOLARSHIP FUND, INC.

http://www.cbc-ct.org

CBC SCHOLARSHIP FUND
• *See page 132*

DIVERSITYCOMM, INC.

http://www.diversitycomm.net/

DIVERSITY IN STEAM MAGAZINE SCHOLARSHIP
• *See page 83*

FLORIDA EDUCATIONAL FACILITIES PLANNERS' ASSOCIATION

http://www.fefpa.org/

FEFPA ASSISTANTSHIP
• *See page 133*

FLORIDA ENGINEERING SOCIETY

http://www.fleng.org/scholarships.cfm

DAVID F. LUDOVICI SCHOLARSHIP
• *See page 192*

FECON SCHOLARSHIP
• *See page 208*

GREATER KANAWHA VALLEY FOUNDATION

http://www.tgkvf.org/

STEVEN ENGINEERING SCHOLARSHIP
• *See page 192*

GREAT MINDS IN STEM

http://www.greatmindsinstem.org

HENAAC SCHOLARSHIP PROGRAM
• *See page 115*

HOUZZ

http://houzz.com

RESIDENTIAL CONSTRUCTION MANAGEMENT SCHOLARSHIP

Houzz is committed to supporting the next generation of construction professionals as they enter the world of residential construction. Open to students studying construction management at the undergraduate or graduate level who want to pursue residential construction management professionally.

Academic Fields/Career Goals: Construction Engineering/Management.

Award: Scholarship for use in freshman, sophomore, junior, senior, or graduate years; not renewable. *Number:* 1. *Amount:* $2500.

Eligibility Requirements: Applicant must be enrolled or expecting to enroll full- or part-time at a two-year or four-year or technical institution or university and studying in Alabama, Alaska, Arizona, Arkansas, California, Colorado, Connecticut, Delaware, District of Columbia, Florida, Georgia, Hawaii, Idaho, Illinois, Indiana, Iowa, Kansas, Kentucky, Louisiana, Maine, Maryland, Massachusetts, Michigan, Minnesota, Mississippi, Missouri, Montana, Nebraska, Nevada, New Hampshire, New Jersey, New Mexico, New York, North Carolina, North Dakota, Ohio, Oklahoma, Oregon, Pennsylvania, Rhode Island, South Carolina, South Dakota, Tennessee, Texas, Utah, Vermont, Virginia, Washington, West Virginia, Wisconsin, Wyoming. Available to U.S. and non-U.S. citizens.

Application Requirements: Application form, essay. *Deadline:* continuous.

Contact: Emily Hurley, Community Manager
E-mail: scholarships@houzz.com

INTERNATIONAL FACILITY MANAGEMENT ASSOCIATION FOUNDATION

http://www.ifmafoundation.org/

IFMA FOUNDATION SCHOLARSHIPS
• *See page 135*

LABROOTS INC.

http://www.LabRoots.com

LABROOTS STEM SCHOLARSHIP
• *See page 116*

MIDWEST ROOFING CONTRACTORS ASSOCIATION

http://www.mrca.org/

MRCA FOUNDATION SCHOLARSHIP PROGRAM
• *See page 135*

NASA'S VIRGINIA SPACE GRANT CONSORTIUM

http://www.vsgc.odu.edu/

COMMUNITY COLLEGE STEM SCHOLARSHIPS
• See page 126

NATIONAL ASPHALT PAVEMENT ASSOCIATION RESEARCH AND EDUCATION FOUNDATION

http://www.asphaltpavement.org

NATIONAL ASPHALT PAVEMENT ASSOCIATION RESEARCH AND EDUCATION FOUNDATION SCHOLARSHIP PROGRAM
• See page 209

NATIONAL CONSTRUCTION EDUCATION FOUNDATION

http://www.abc.org/

TRIMMER EDUCATION FOUNDATION SCHOLARSHIPS FOR CONSTRUCTION MANAGEMENT

Scholarships are available to students in a major related to the construction industry. Applicants must be enrolled at an educational institution with an ABC student chapter, and be current, active members or employed by an ABC member firm. Architecture and most engineering programs are excluded. Applicants must have a minimum overall GPA of 2.85 and 3.0 in the major. If no courses have been taken in the major, a minimum overall GPA of 3.0 is required. Visit website http://www.abc.org.

Academic Fields/Career Goals: Construction Engineering/Management.

Award: Scholarship for use in sophomore, junior, or senior years; not renewable. *Number:* 10–15. *Amount:* up to $5000.

Eligibility Requirements: Applicant must be enrolled or expecting to enroll full-time at a two-year or four-year institution or university. Available to U.S. citizens.

Application Requirements: Application form, essay, financial need analysis, recommendations or references, Student Aid Report (SAR), transcript. *Deadline:* May 22.

Contact: John Strock, Director, Career and Constructions
  Phone: 703-812-2008
  E-mail: strock@abc.org

NEXTSTEPU

http://www.nextstepu.com/

$1,500 STEM SCHOLARSHIP
• See page 120

PLAN NEW HAMPSHIRE

http://www.plannh.org

PLAN NEW HAMPSHIRE SCHOLARSHIP AND FELLOWSHIP PROGRAM
• See page 129

PROFESSIONAL CONSTRUCTION ESTIMATORS ASSOCIATION

http://www.pcea.org/

TED G. WILSON MEMORIAL SCHOLARSHIP FOUNDATION
• See page 211

RCI FOUNDATION

http://www.rcifoundation.org/

LEWIS W. NEWLAN AWARD
• See page 136

ROBERT W. LYONS AWARD
• See page 136

SOCIETY OF WOMEN ENGINEERS

http://societyofwomenengineers.swe.org/

ADA I. PRESSMAN MEMORIAL SCHOLARSHIP
• See page 196

AMERICAN TRANSMISSION CO. SCHOLARSHIP
• See page 196

ANNE MAUREEN WHITNEY BARROW MEMORIAL SCHOLARSHIP
• See page 196

ANNE SHEN SMITH ENDOWED SCHOLARSHIP
• See page 196

BETTY LOU BAILEY SWE REGION F SCHOLARSHIP
• See page 197

B.J. HARROD SCHOLARSHIP
• See page 197

BK KRENZER MEMORIAL REENTRY SCHOLARSHIP
• See page 197

CAROL STEPHENS SWE REGION F SCHOLARSHIP
• See page 197

DR. IVY M. PARKER MEMORIAL SCHOLARSHIP
• See page 197

DOROTHY P. MORRIS SCHOLARSHIP
• See page 198

EXELON SCHOLARSHIP
• See page 198

IBM LINDA SANFORD WOMEN'S TECHNICAL ADVANCEMENT SCHOLARSHIP
• See page 198

LILLIAN MOLLER GILBRETH MEMORIAL SCHOLARSHIP
• See page 198

MARY V. MUNGER MEMORIAL SCHOLARSHIP
• See page 199

OLIVE LYNN SALEMBIER MEMORIAL REENTRY SCHOLARSHIP
• See page 199

ROBERTA BANASZAK GLEITER ENGINEERING ENDEAVOR SCHOLARSHIP
• See page 199

SUSAN MISZKOWICZ SEPTEMBER 11 MEMORIAL SCHOLARSHIP
• See page 199

SWE BALTIMORE-WASHINGTON SECTION SCHOLARSHIP
• See page 199

SWE CENTRAL NEW MEXICO PIONEERS SCHOLARSHIP
• *See page 200*

SWE CENTRAL NEW MEXICO REENTRY SCHOLARSHIP
• *See page 200*

SWE MID-HUDSON SECTION SCHOLARSHIP
• *See page 200*

SWE PHOENIX SECTION SCHOLARSHIP
• *See page 200*

SWE REGION E SCHOLARSHIP
• *See page 200*

SWE REGION G JUDY SIMMONS MEMORIAL SCHOLARSHIP
• *See page 200*

SWE REGION H SCHOLARSHIPS
• *See page 201*

SWE REGION J SCHOLARSHIP
• *See page 201*

TE CONNECTIVITY EXCELLENCE IN ENGINEERING SCHOLARSHIP
• *See page 201*

TURNER CONSTRUCTION SCHOLARSHIP
• *See page 201*

WANDA MUNN SCHOLARSHIP
• *See page 201*

SOCIETY OF WOMEN ENGINEERS-ROCKY MOUNTAIN SECTION

http://www.swe-rms.org/

SOCIETY OF WOMEN ENGINEERS-ROCKY MOUNTAIN SECTION SCHOLARSHIP PROGRAM
• *See page 161*

STRAIGHT NORTH

https://www.straightnorth.com/

STRAIGHT NORTH STEM SCHOLARSHIP
• *See page 92*

TRANSPORTATION ASSOCIATION OF CANADA FOUNDATION

http://www.tac-foundation.ca

TAC FOUNDATION SCHOLARSHIPS
• *See page 213*

TURNER CONSTRUCTION COMPANY

http://www.turnerconstruction.com/

YOUTHFORCE 2020 SCHOLARSHIP PROGRAM
• *See page 137*

UNITED NEGRO COLLEGE FUND

http://www.uncf.org/

UNCF STEM SCHOLARS PROGRAM
• *See page 175*

VECTORWORKS, INC.

http://www.vectorworks.net

VECTORWORKS DESIGN SCHOLARSHIP
• *See page 137*

WIRE REINFORCEMENT INSTITUTE EDUCATION FOUNDATION

http://www.wirereinforcementinstitute.org/

WRI FOUNDATION COLLEGE SCHOLARSHIP PROGRAM
• *See page 214*

COSMETOLOGY

AVACARE MEDICAL

https://avacaremedical.com

AVACARE MEDICAL SCHOLARSHIP
• *See page 115*

JOE FRANCIS HAIRCARE SCHOLARSHIP FOUNDATION

http://www.joefrancis.com

JOE FRANCIS HAIRCARE SCHOLARSHIP FOUNDATION
Cosmetology or Barber School scholarships are awarded for $1200 each, with 26 to 28 scholarships awarded annually. Applicants are evaluated for their potential to successfully complete school, their financial need, and commitment to a long-term career in cosmetology. Window to apply is January 1st to June 1st. Deadline to apply is June 1st. Students who graduate before September of the award year are not eligible to apply. Applications are found on our website (apply online) http://www.joefrancis.com.

Academic Fields/Career Goals: Cosmetology.

Award: Scholarship for use in freshman year; not renewable. *Number:* 26–28. *Amount:* $1200.

Eligibility Requirements: Applicant must be enrolled or expecting to enroll full- or part-time at a technical institution. Available to U.S. citizens.

Application Requirements: Application form, essay, financial need analysis. *Deadline:* June 1.

Contact: Kim Larson, Administrator
Joe Francis Haircare Scholarship Foundation
PO Box 50625
Minneapolis, MN 55405
Phone: 651-769-1757
E-mail: kimlarsonmn@gmail.com

MEDICAL SCRUBS COLLECTION

http://medicalscrubscollection.com

MEDICAL SCRUBS COLLECTION SCHOLARSHIP
• *See page 120*

OREGON STUDENT ASSISTANCE COMMISSION

https://oregonstudentaid.gov/

HUFFSTUTTER FAMILY STYLIST SCHOLARSHIP

Scholarship for students from Oregon or Washington, majoring in cosmetology, beauty, barbering or hairdresser. Must attend an Oregon college offering degrees or certificates in cosmetology or hair design. Based on financial need.

Academic Fields/Career Goals: Cosmetology; Trade/Technical Specialties.

Award: Scholarship for use in freshman or sophomore years; not renewable.

Eligibility Requirements: Applicant must be enrolled or expecting to enroll at a two-year or four-year or technical institution or university; resident of Oregon and studying in Oregon. Available to U.S. citizens.

Application Requirements: Application form. *Deadline:* March 1.

Contact: Melissa Adams, Scholarship Processing Coordinator
    Phone: 541-687-7409
    E-mail: melissa.adams@state.or.us

STRAIGHTFORWARD MEDIA

http://www.straightforwardmedia.com/

STRAIGHTFORWARD MEDIA VOCATIONAL-TECHNICAL SCHOOL SCHOLARSHIP

• *See page 118*

CRIMINAL JUSTICE/ CRIMINOLOGY

AMERICAN CRIMINAL JUSTICE ASSOCIATION-LAMBDA ALPHA EPSILON

http://www.acjalae.org/

AMERICAN CRIMINAL JUSTICE ASSOCIATION-LAMBDA ALPHA EPSILON NATIONAL SCHOLARSHIP

Awarded only to members of the American Criminal Justice Association. One-time award of $100 to $400. Members may reapply each year. Must have minimum 3.0 GPA. Must pursue studies in law/legal services, criminal justice/law, or the social sciences.

Academic Fields/Career Goals: Criminal Justice/Criminology.

Award: Scholarship for use in freshman, sophomore, junior, senior, or graduate years; not renewable. *Number:* 9. *Amount:* $100–$400.

Eligibility Requirements: Applicant must be enrolled or expecting to enroll full- or part-time at a two-year or four-year institution or university. Applicant or parent of applicant must be member of American Criminal Justice Association. Applicant must have 3.0 GPA or higher. Available to U.S. citizens.

Application Requirements: Application form. *Deadline:* December 31.

Contact: Karen Campbell, Executive Secretary
    American Criminal Justice Association-Lambda Alpha Epsilon
    PO Box 601047
    Sacramento, CA 95860-1047
    Phone: 916-484-6553
    E-mail: acjalae@aol.com

AMERICAN SOCIETY OF CRIMINOLOGY

http://www.asc41.com/

AMERICAN SOCIETY OF CRIMINOLOGY GENE CARTE STUDENT PAPER COMPETITION

Award for full-time undergraduate or graduate students. Must submit a conceptual or empirical paper on a subject directly relating to criminology. Papers must be 7500 words or less.

Academic Fields/Career Goals: Criminal Justice/Criminology; Law Enforcement/Police Administration; Law/Legal Services; Social Sciences.

Award: Prize for use in freshman, sophomore, junior, senior, or graduate years; not renewable. *Number:* 3. *Amount:* $200–$500.

Eligibility Requirements: Applicant must be enrolled or expecting to enroll full-time at a four-year institution or university and must have an interest in writing. Available to U.S. and non-U.S. citizens.

Application Requirements: Conceptual or empirical paper on a subject directly relating to criminology, entry in a contest. *Deadline:* April 15.

Contact: Andrew Hochstetlet, Scholarship Committee
    American Society of Criminology
    Iowa State University, 203D East Hall
    Ames, IA 50011-4504
    Phone: 515-294-2841
    E-mail: hochstet@iastate.edu

ASSOCIATION OF CERTIFIED FRAUD EXAMINERS

http://www.acfe.com/

RITCHIE-JENNINGS MEMORIAL SCHOLARSHIP

• *See page 81*

ASSOCIATION OF FORMER INTELLIGENCE OFFICERS

http://www.afio.com

AFIO UNDERGRADUATE AND GRADUATE SCHOLARSHIPS

• *See page 113*

CANTOR CRANE INJURY LAW

https://cantorcrane.com

CANTOR CRANE PERSONAL INJURY LAWYER $1,000 SCHOLARSHIP

In order to help make a college education more affordable opportunity and to help spread awareness about Driving Under the Influence and Distracted Driving, the Arizona law firm of Cantor Crane is offering a $1,000 law student scholarship to help current, or soon-to-be, law students ease the burden of higher education costs. The scholarship funds may be used for law school tuition at a college or university. It is not required that the applicant be enrolled in an educational program at the time of his or her application. The winner will have one year from the date of the award to provide a tuition invoice from the school of their choice. A check for $1,000 will then be sent to the educational institution. Submitting the application is easy. Simply take the pledge to not drive under the influence and to not drive while distracted by things such as texting and fill out the contact information.

Academic Fields/Career Goals: Criminal Justice/Criminology; Law/Legal Services.

Award: Scholarship for use in freshman, sophomore, junior, senior, graduate, or postgraduate years; renewable. *Number:* 1. *Amount:* $1000.

Eligibility Requirements: Applicant must be enrolled or expecting to enroll full- or part-time at a two-year or four-year institution or university. Available to U.S. and non-U.S. citizens.

Application Requirements: Application form. *Deadline:* July 31.

Contact: Tristan Petricca, Media Director
Cantor Crane Injury Law
1 East Washington Street
Suite 1800
Phoenix, AZ 85004
Phone: 602-254-2701
E-mail: t.petricca@dmcantor.com

CONNECTICUT ASSOCIATION OF WOMEN POLICE

http://www.cawp.net/

CONNECTICUT ASSOCIATION OF WOMEN POLICE SCHOLARSHIP

Available to Connecticut residents graduating from an accredited high school, and entering a college or university in Connecticut as a criminal justice major.

Academic Fields/Career Goals: Criminal Justice/Criminology; Law Enforcement/Police Administration.

Award: Scholarship for use in freshman year; not renewable. *Number:* 1–3. *Amount:* $200–$500.

Eligibility Requirements: Applicant must be high school student; planning to enroll or expecting to enroll full-time at a two-year or four-year institution or university; resident of Connecticut and studying in Connecticut. Available to U.S. citizens.

Application Requirements: Application form, essay, financial need analysis, recommendations or references, transcript. *Deadline:* April 30.

Contact: Gail McDonnell, Scholarship Committee
Connecticut Association of Women Police
PO Box 1653
Hartford, CT 06144
Phone: 860-527-7300

CONTINENTAL SOCIETY, DAUGHTERS OF INDIAN WARS

http://www.csdiw.org/

CONTINENTAL SOCIETY, DAUGHTERS OF INDIAN WARS SCHOLARSHIP

Award for a certified Indian tribal member enrolled in an undergraduate degree program in education or social service. Must maintain minimum 3.0 GPA and work with Native Americans in a social service or educational role after graduation. Preference given to those in or entering junior year.

Academic Fields/Career Goals: Criminal Justice/Criminology; Dental Health/Services; Education; Food Science/Nutrition; Health Administration; Health and Medical Sciences; Home Economics; Nursing; Occupational Safety and Health; Oncology; Optometry; Osteopathy; Pharmacy; Public Health; Social Services; Special Education; Therapy/Rehabilitation.

Award: Scholarship for use in sophomore, junior, or senior years; renewable. *Number:* 1. *Amount:* $5000.

Eligibility Requirements: Applicant must be American Indian/Alaska Native and enrolled or expecting to enroll full-time at a two-year or four-year institution or university. Applicant must have 3.0 GPA or higher. Available to U.S. citizens.

Application Requirements: Application form, essay, financial need analysis. *Deadline:* June 15.

Contact: Mrs. J.B. Richards, II, National Scholarship Chairman
Continental Society, Daughters of Indian Wars
PO Box 6695
Chesterfield, MO 63006-6695
Phone: 636-220-2442
E-mail: leslie@khs65.com

INDIANA SHERIFFS' ASSOCIATION

http://www.indianasheriffs.org/

INDIANA SHERIFFS' ASSOCIATION SCHOLARSHIP PROGRAM

Applicant must be an Indiana resident majoring in a criminal justice/law enforcement field at an Indiana college or university. Must be a member or dependent child or grandchild of a member of the association. Must be a full-time student with at least 12 credit hours.

Academic Fields/Career Goals: Criminal Justice/Criminology; Law Enforcement/Police Administration.

Award: Scholarship for use in freshman, sophomore, junior, or senior years; not renewable. *Number:* 40. *Amount:* $500.

Eligibility Requirements: Applicant must be enrolled or expecting to enroll full-time at a two-year or four-year institution or university; resident of Indiana and studying in Indiana. Applicant or parent of applicant must be member of Indiana Sheriffs' Association. Available to U.S. citizens.

Application Requirements: Application form, essay. *Deadline:* April 1.

Contact: Laura Vest, Administrative Director
Indiana Sheriffs' Association
147 East Maryland Street
Indianapolis, IN 46204
Phone: 317-356-3633
E-mail: lvest@indianasheriffs.org

LIVSECURE

https://www.livsecure.com

LIVSECURE STUDENT SCHOLARSHIP

At LivSecure, we are proud to support those who are studying to make our neighborhoods a safer place. If you are currently studying law enforcement, law, criminal justice, or a related field, then you are eligible to submit a security-focused essay for a chance to win a $1,000 scholarship to put toward your college tuition.

Academic Fields/Career Goals: Criminal Justice/Criminology; Law Enforcement/Police Administration; Law/Legal Services.

Award: Scholarship for use in freshman or sophomore years; not renewable. *Number:* 1–3. *Amount:* $500–$1000.

Eligibility Requirements: Applicant must be enrolled or expecting to enroll full- or part-time at a two-year or four-year or technical institution or university.

Application Requirements: Essay. *Deadline:* July 1.

Contact: Megan Nonemacher, Marketing Manager
LivSecure
3803 West Chester Pike
Suite 100
Newtown Square, PA 19073
Phone: 484-420-0314
E-mail: megan.nonemacher@myalarmcenter.com

NAQVI INJURY LAW

http://www.naqvilaw.com/

NAQVI LAW SCHOLARSHIP

This is a primarily needs-based scholarship offered to Nevada high school students and graduates seeking a law-oriented college degree. The application is submitted online, and the successful applicant will receive $2000.

Academic Fields/Career Goals: Criminal Justice/Criminology; Law/Legal Services; Political Science.

Award: Scholarship for use in freshman year; not renewable. *Number:* 1. *Amount:* $2000.

Eligibility Requirements: Applicant must be enrolled or expecting to enroll full-time at a four-year institution or university and resident of Nevada. Applicant must have 3.0 GPA or higher. Available to U.S. citizens.

Application Requirements: Application form, application form may be submitted online (http://naqvilaw.com/scholarship-application/), financial need analysis, transcript. *Deadline:* December 31.

NATIONAL BLACK POLICE ASSOCIATION

http://www.blackpolice.org/

ALPHONSO DEAL SCHOLARSHIP AWARD

$500 scholarship for high school senior and U.S. citizen to attend a two-year college or university. Must study law enforcement or other related criminal justice field. Minimum 2.5 GPA required.

Academic Fields/Career Goals: Criminal Justice/Criminology; Law Enforcement/Police Administration; Law/Legal Services; Social Sciences; Social Services.

Award: Scholarship for use in freshman year; not renewable. *Number:* 4. *Amount:* $500.

Eligibility Requirements: Applicant must be high school student and planning to enroll or expecting to enroll full-time at a two-year or four-year institution or university. Available to U.S. citizens.

Application Requirements: Application form, letter of acceptance, personal photograph, recommendations or references, transcript. *Deadline:* June 1.

Contact: Ronald Hampton, Executive Director
National Black Police Association
30 Kennedy Street, NW, Suite 101
Washington, DC 20011
Phone: 202-986-2070
Fax: 202-986-0410
E-mail: nbpanatofc@worldnet.att.net

NORTH CAROLINA STATE EDUCATION ASSISTANCE AUTHORITY

http://www.ncseaa.edu/

NORTH CAROLINA SHERIFFS' ASSOCIATION UNDERGRADUATE CRIMINAL JUSTICE SCHOLARSHIPS

One-time award for full-time North Carolina resident undergraduate students majoring in criminal justice at a University of North Carolina school. Priority given to child of any North Carolina law enforcement officer. Letter of recommendation from county sheriff required.

Academic Fields/Career Goals: Criminal Justice/Criminology; Law Enforcement/Police Administration.

Award: Scholarship for use in freshman, sophomore, junior, or senior years; not renewable. *Number:* 10. *Amount:* $1000–$2000.

Eligibility Requirements: Applicant must be enrolled or expecting to enroll full-time at a four-year institution or university; resident of North Carolina and studying in North Carolina. Applicant or parent of applicant must have employment or volunteer experience in police/firefighting. Available to U.S. citizens.

Application Requirements: Application form, financial need analysis.

Contact: Michele Goldston, Assistant, Scholarship and Grant Division
North Carolina State Education Assistance Authority
PO Box 13663
Research Triangle Park, NC 27709
Phone: 919-549-8614
E-mail: mgoldston@ncseaa.edu

OREGON ASSOCIATION CHIEFS OF POLICE

http://www.policechief.org/

LAW ENFORCEMENT AND CRIMINAL JUSTICE COLLEGE SCHOLARSHIP PROGRAM

Each year, the Oregon Association Chiefs of Police (OACP) provides $1000 college scholarships to students who plan to enter a law enforcement or other criminal justice career. The OACP is committed to promoting professionalism and we value the presence and contributions of educated men and women in Law Enforcement and Criminal Justice. To further our commitment, the OACP provides competitive college scholarships for qualifying students. The following information will help you determine if you qualify for scholarship consideration and will help you understand the application process. Each year, the Oregon Association Chiefs of Police (OACP) provides $1000 college scholarships to students who plan to enter a law enforcement or other

criminal justice career. The OACP is committed to promoting professionalism and we value the presence and contributions of educated men and women in Law Enforcement and Criminal Justice. To further our commitment, the OACP provides competitive college scholarships for qualifying students. The following information will help you determine if you qualify for scholarship consideration and will help you understand the application process. 1. Have you completed at least 36 college credit hours or 30 semester hours? In lieu of 36 college credit hours have you logged at least 240 hours of service over the last year as a cadet, explorer, or reserve police officer? 2. Have you maintained a grade point average (GPA) of at least 2.5–3. Do you plan to enter a law enforcement or other criminal justice career? Preference will be given to immediate family members of an Oregon Police Officer killed or disabled in the line of duty, as well as dependents of OACP members.

Academic Fields/Career Goals: Criminal Justice/Criminology.

Award: Scholarship for use in freshman, sophomore, junior, senior, graduate, or postgraduate years; not renewable. *Number:* 5. *Amount:* $1000.

Eligibility Requirements: Applicant must be enrolled or expecting to enroll full- or part-time at a two-year or four-year institution or university and resident of Oregon. Applicant must have 2.5 GPA or higher. Available to U.S. citizens.

Application Requirements: Application form, autobiography, personal photograph. *Deadline:* December 31.

Contact: Mrs. Marie Campbell, Association Executive
Oregon Association Chiefs of Police
1191 Capitol Street, NE
Salem, OR 97301
Phone: 503-315-1411
Fax: 503-315-1416
E-mail: marie@victorygrp.com

OREGON STUDENT ASSISTANCE COMMISSION

https://oregonstudentaid.gov/

OREGON ASSOCIATION OF CERTIFIED FRAUD EXAMINERS SCHOLARSHIP

• *See page 90*

SILICON VALLEY COMMUNITY FOUNDATION

http://www.siliconvalleycf.org

HAROLD JOHNSON LAW ENFORCEMENT SCHOLARSHIP

The Harold Johnson Law Enforcement Scholarship was established in memory of Police Chief Harold "Hal" Johnson to provide financial support to students who plan to pursue a career in police work, corrections or other criminal justice fields. This scholarship honors Hal's 29 year law enforcement career, which began in Sacramento, California, in 1955. This scholarship is designed to recognize students who demonstrate a similar passion for public service and who demonstrate academic potential, leadership, and financial need. Must have demonstrated desire and a plan to pursue a career in police work, corrections or other criminal justice fields. Law school students are not eligible. Minimum cumulative grade point average of 2.5 on a 4.0 scale required. Must be a current graduating senior or graduate of a public or private high school in the greater San Francisco Bay Area (includes San Francisco, San Mateo, Marin, Alameda, Contra Costa, Santa Clara, Napa, Solano, Sonoma, Monterey Bay, Santa Cruz, Monterey and San Benito counties); planning to enroll or currently enrolled in a two- or four-year college, university or police academy as a full-time student; and a United States citizen.

Academic Fields/Career Goals: Criminal Justice/Criminology.

Award: Scholarship for use in freshman, sophomore, junior, or senior years; not renewable. *Number:* 1–7. *Amount:* $1000–$5000.

Eligibility Requirements: Applicant must be enrolled or expecting to enroll full-time at a two-year or four-year institution or university and resident of California. Applicant must have 2.5 GPA or higher. Available to U.S. citizens.

Application Requirements: Application form, essay, financial need analysis. *Deadline:* February 21.

Contact: Scholarships Team
Silicon Valley Community Foundation
2440 West El Camino Real
Suite 300
Mountain View, CA 94040
Phone: 650-450-5487
E-mail: scholarships@siliconvalleycf.org

WASHINGTON STATE ASSOCIATION FOR JUSTICE

http://www.washingtonjustice.org/

WASHINGTON STATE ASSOCIATION FOR JUSTICE AMERICAN JUSTICE ESSAY & VIDEO SCHOLARSHIP

As part of the Washington State Association for Justice's (WSAJ) commitment to foster an awareness and understanding of the important role that the civil justice system plays in our society, WSAJ sponsors an annual statewide student essay and video scholarship program. For 2018, WSAJ will award two, $3,750 scholarships, one to an essayist and one to a videographer. The video scholarship winner's piece will be posted on WSAJ's Facebook and Twitter accounts, and may be aired on TV. This scholarship is available to high school seniors who are residents attending high school in Washington state. Students need not attend a Washington college, but must start college within the next two years to receive the funds. If you have questions about the prompt or the practice of law, please contact anita@washingtonjustice.org and we will connect you with an attorney to answer your questions. The prompt for both scholarships is–Forced arbitration clauses in consumer contracts: How do they affect us? Essay option: Write a 700-800 word essay on this subject. Video option: Create a video of no more than 60 seconds in length on this subject in the format of a Public Service Announcement, as well as writing a 300-400 word summary on this subject and the inspiration for the video. The video must be uploaded on YouTube or Vimeo and the link shared with the scholarship committee. WSAJ reserves the right to make the winning video available to the general public. By submitting a video, you grant WSAJ a royalty-free license to copy, distribute, modify, display and perform publicly and otherwise use and authorize others to use your video for any purpose. You also guarantee that no other person, corporation or organization has a copyright interest in your video.

Academic Fields/Career Goals: Criminal Justice/Criminology; Law/Legal Services; Peace and Conflict Studies; Political Science; Public Policy and Administration; Social Sciences.

Award: Scholarship for use in freshman year; not renewable. *Number:* 2. *Amount:* $3750.

Eligibility Requirements: Applicant must be high school student; planning to enroll or expecting to enroll full-time at a four-year institution or university; resident of Washington and studying in Washington. Available to U.S. and non-U.S. citizens.

Application Requirements: Application form, essay. *Deadline:* March 17.

Contact: Anita Yandle, Scholarship Coordinator
Washington State Association for Justice
1809 7th Ave
Suite 1500
Seattle, WA 98101
Phone: 206-464-1011
E-mail: anita@washingtonjustice.org

WIFLE FOUNDATION, INC.

http://www.wifle.org/

WIFLE SCHOLARSHIP

Scholarship to encourage women to pursue a career in federal law enforcement. Applicant must be enrolled in, or be transferring to, a four-year program in criminal justice, social sciences, public administration, chemistry, physics, computer science, or related studies and have a minimum GPA of 3.0. May also be in a graduate program. Must demonstrate commitment to the community through volunteer community service or an internship in a law enforcement agency. Must be a United States citizen.

Academic Fields/Career Goals: Criminal Justice/Criminology; Law Enforcement/Police Administration; Law/Legal Services; Social Sciences.

Award: Scholarship for use in sophomore, junior, senior, graduate, or postgraduate years; not renewable. *Number:* 1–4. *Amount:* $1000–$2500.

Eligibility Requirements: Applicant must be enrolled or expecting to enroll full-time at a four-year institution or university and female. Applicant must have 3.0 GPA or higher. Available to U.S. citizens.

Application Requirements: Application form, community service, essay. *Deadline:* May 1.

Contact: Ms. Catherine Sanz, President
WIFLE Foundation, Inc.
2200 Wilson Boulevard
Suite 102, PMB 204
Arlington, VA 22201
Phone: 301-805-2180
E-mail: wifle@comcast.net

WILLIAMS LAW GROUP

https://familylawyersnewjersey.com/

WILLIAMS LAW GROUP OPPORTUNITY TO GROW SCHOLARSHIP

• *See page 139*

CULINARY ARTS

AMERICAN HOTEL AND LODGING EDUCATIONAL FOUNDATION

http://www.ahlef.org/

AHLEF ANNUAL SCHOLARSHIP GRANT PROGRAM

The program is co-administered with affiliated schools that select the scholarship recipients based upon a set of minimum eligiblity criteria, which includes full-time enrollment status in a U.S. hospitality-related degree granting program, minimum cumulative GPA of 3.0 or higher, U.S. citizenship or permanent U.S. residency. A list of affiliated schools available on https://www.ahlef.org/Scholarships/Academic/AHLEF_School-Nominated_Scholarships/.

Academic Fields/Career Goals: Culinary Arts; Food Service/Hospitality; Hospitality Management; Recreation, Parks, Leisure Studies; Travel/Tourism.

Award: Scholarship for use in junior or senior years; not renewable. *Amount:* $500–$6000.

Eligibility Requirements: Applicant must be enrolled or expecting to enroll full-time at a two-year or four-year institution or university. Applicant must have 3.0 GPA or higher. Available to U.S. citizens.

Application Requirements: Application form, essay, financial need analysis. *Deadline:* February 15.

Contact: Ms. Michelle Poinelli, SVP, Foundation Programs
American Hotel and Lodging Educational Foundation
1250 Eye Street, NW, Suite 1100
Washington, DC 20005
Phone: 202-289-3139
E-mail: scholarships@ahlef.org

AMERICAN HOTEL & LODGING EDUCATIONAL FOUNDATION PEPSI SCHOLARSHIP

Scholarships of $500 to $3000 awarded to graduates of Hospitality High School in Washington, DC. The scholarship recipients are selected by Hospitality High based upon a set of minimum eligibility criteria which includes graduate of Hospitality High, a minimum 2.5 GPA, and at least 250 hours in the hotel/hospitality industry.

Academic Fields/Career Goals: Culinary Arts; Food Service/Hospitality; Hospitality Management; Recreation, Parks, Leisure Studies; Travel/Tourism.

Award: Scholarship for use in freshman, sophomore, junior, or senior years; not renewable. *Amount:* $500–$3000.

Eligibility Requirements: Applicant must be enrolled or expecting to enroll full-time at a two-year or four-year institution or university and resident of District of Columbia. Applicant must have 2.5 GPA or higher. Available to U.S. and non-U.S. citizens.

Application Requirements: Application form, essay, financial need analysis, nomination from Hospitality High School, resume, transcript. *Deadline:* May 1.

Contact: Ms. Kelsey Allagood, Foundation Manager
American Hotel and Lodging Educational Foundation
1201 New York Avenue, NW, Suite 600
Washington, DC 20005
Phone: 202-289-3139
Fax: 202-289-3199
E-mail: scholarships@ahlef.org

ECOLAB SCHOLARSHIP PROGRAM

Award for students enrolled full-time in United States Baccalaureate or associate program leading to degree in hospitality management.

Academic Fields/Career Goals: Culinary Arts; Food Service/Hospitality; Hospitality Management; Recreation, Parks, Leisure Studies; Travel/Tourism.

Award: Scholarship for use in freshman, sophomore, junior, or senior years; not renewable. *Number:* 10–15. *Amount:* $1000–$2000.

Eligibility Requirements: Applicant must be enrolled or expecting to enroll full-time at a two-year or four-year institution or university. Available to U.S. and non-U.S. citizens.

Application Requirements: Application form, essay, financial need analysis, resume, transcript. *Deadline:* May 1.

Contact: Ms. Kelsey Allagood, Foundation Manager
American Hotel and Lodging Educational Foundation
1201 New York Avenue, SW, Suite 600
Washington, DC 20005-3931
Phone: 202-289-3139
Fax: 202-289-3199
E-mail: kallagood@ahlef.org

HYATT HOTELS FUND FOR MINORITY LODGING MANAGEMENT

Scholarship available for African-American, Hispanic, American Indian, Alaskan Native, Asian, or Pacific Islander in a Baccalaureate hospitality management program. Must be at least a junior in a four-year program to receive the scholarship monies.

Academic Fields/Career Goals: Culinary Arts; Food Service/Hospitality; Hospitality Management; Recreation, Parks, Leisure Studies; Travel/Tourism.

Award: Scholarship for use in sophomore, junior, or senior years; not renewable. *Number:* 10–15. *Amount:* $2000.

Eligibility Requirements: Applicant must be American Indian/Alaska Native, Asian/Pacific Islander, Black (non-Hispanic), Hispanic and enrolled or expecting to enroll full-time at a four-year institution or university. Available to U.S. citizens.

Application Requirements: Application form, essay, financial need analysis, recommendations or references, resume, transcript. *Deadline:* May 1.

Contact: Ms. Kelsey Allagood, Foundation Manager
American Hotel and Lodging Educational Foundation
1201 New York Avenue, Suite 600
Washington, DC 20005
Phone: 202-289-3139
Fax: 202-289-3199
E-mail: scholarships@ahlef.org

INCOMING FRESHMAN SCHOLARSHIPS

This program is exclusively for incoming freshman interested in pursuing hospitality-related undergraduate programs. Preference will be given to any applicant who is a graduate of the Educational Institute's Lodging Management Program (LMP, which is a two-year high school program.) Must have a minimum 2.0 GPA.

Academic Fields/Career Goals: Culinary Arts; Food Service/Hospitality; Hospitality Management; Recreation, Parks, Leisure Studies; Travel/Tourism.

Award: Scholarship for use in freshman year; not renewable. *Number:* 5–10. *Amount:* $1000–$2000.

Eligibility Requirements: Applicant must be high school student and planning to enroll or expecting to enroll full-time at a two-year or four-year institution or university. Available to U.S. citizens.

Application Requirements: Application form, essay, financial need analysis, resume, transcript. *Deadline:* May 1.

Contact: Ms. Kelsey Allagood, Foundation Manager
American Hotel and Lodging Educational Foundation
1201 New York Avenue, NW, Suite 600
Washington, DC 20005-3197
Phone: 202-289-3139
Fax: 202-289-3199
E-mail: scholarships@ahlef.org

RAMA SCHOLARSHIP FOR THE AMERICAN DREAM

Schools participating in this program include Bethune-Cookman College, California State Polytechnic University, Cornell University, Florida International University, Georgia State university, Greenville Technical College, Howard University, Johnson & Wales University, New York University, University of Central Florida, University of Houston, University of South Carolina, and Virginia Tech. The participating schools select the student nominees based upon a set of minimum eligibility criteria which include: enrolled in at least 9 credit hours for the fall and spring semesters, majoring in an undergraduate or graduate hospitality management program, minimum GPA of 2.5, U.S. citizenship or permanent resident, and schools must give preference to students of Asian-Indian descent or other minority groups, as well as JHM employees and their dependents.

Academic Fields/Career Goals: Culinary Arts; Food Service/Hospitality; Hospitality Management; Recreation, Parks, Leisure Studies; Travel/Tourism.

Award: Scholarship for use in sophomore, junior, senior, or graduate years; not renewable. *Amount:* $1000–$3000.

Eligibility Requirements: Applicant must be American Indian/Alaska Native, Asian/Pacific Islander, Black (non-Hispanic), Hispanic and enrolled or expecting to enroll full- or part-time at a two-year or four-year institution or university. Applicant must have 2.5 GPA or higher. Available to U.S. citizens.

Application Requirements: Application form, essay, financial need analysis, nomination from school, recommendations or references, transcript. *Deadline:* May 1.

Contact: Ms. Kelsey Allagood, Foundation Manager
American Hotel and Lodging Educational Foundation
1201 New York Avenue, NW, Suite 600
Washington, DC 20005
Phone: 202-289-3139
Fax: 202-289-3199
E-mail: kallagood@ahlef.org

CANFIT

http://www.canfit.org/

CANFIT NUTRITION, PHYSICAL EDUCATION AND CULINARY ARTS SCHOLARSHIP

Awards undergraduate and graduate African-American, American-Indian/Alaska Native, Asian-American, Pacific Islander or Latino/Hispanic students who express financial need and are studying nutrition, physical education, or culinary arts in California. GPA of minimum 2.5 for undergraduates and 3.0 for graduates. See website for essay topic http://www.canfit.org.

Academic Fields/Career Goals: Culinary Arts; Food Science/Nutrition; Food Service/Hospitality; Health and Medical Sciences; Sports-Related/Exercise Science.

Award: Scholarship for use in junior, senior, or graduate years; not renewable. *Number:* 5–10. *Amount:* $500–$1500.

Eligibility Requirements: Applicant must be of African, Chinese, Hispanic, Indian, Japanese heritage; American Indian/Alaska Native, Asian/Pacific Islander, Black (non-Hispanic); enrolled or expecting to enroll full-time at a four-year or technical institution or university; resident of California and studying in California. Applicant must have 2.5 GPA or higher. Available to U.S. citizens.

Application Requirements: Application form, essay, financial need analysis, personal photograph, recommendations or references, transcript. *Deadline:* March 31.

Contact: Ms. Arnell Hinkle, Executive Director
Phone: 510-644-1533 Ext. 12
Fax: 510-644-1535
E-mail: info@canfit.org

CAREERS THROUGH CULINARY ARTS PROGRAM INC.

http://www.ccapinc.org/

CAREERS THROUGH CULINARY ARTS PROGRAM COOKING COMPETITION FOR SCHOLARSHIPS

Applicants must be a senior in a C-CAP designated partner high school in Arizona; Prince George's County, Maryland; Tidewater, Virginia; or the cities of Boston, Chicago, Los Angeles, New York, Philadelphia or Washington, DC. Applicants must be accepted into the cooking competition for scholarships.

Academic Fields/Career Goals: Culinary Arts; Hospitality Management.

Award: Scholarship for use in freshman, sophomore, junior, or senior years; not renewable. *Number:* 50–70. *Amount:* $1000–$90,000.

Eligibility Requirements: Applicant must be high school student; planning to enroll or expecting to enroll full- or part-time at a two-year or four-year or technical institution and resident of Arizona, California, Illinois, Maryland, New York, Pennsylvania, Virginia. Available to U.S. and non-U.S. citizens.

Application Requirements: Application form, entry in a contest, essay, financial need analysis, interview, recommendations or references, test scores, transcript. *Deadline:* varies.

Contact: Check website for local coordinator's contact information.

THE CULINARY TRUST

http://www.theculinarytrust.org/

CULINARY TRUST SCHOLARSHIP PROGRAM FOR CULINARY STUDY AND RESEARCH

Scholarships provides funds to qualified applicants for beginning, continuing, and specialty education courses at accredited culinary schools worldwide, as well as, independent study for research projects. Applicants must have at least, a minimum 3.0 GPA, must write an essay, submit two letters of recommendation. Application fee: $35.

Academic Fields/Career Goals: Culinary Arts; Food Science/Nutrition; Food Service/Hospitality.

Award: Scholarship for use in freshman, sophomore, junior, senior, graduate, or postgraduate years; not renewable. *Number:* 21. *Amount:* $1000–$5000.

Eligibility Requirements: Applicant must be enrolled or expecting to enroll full- or part-time at a two-year or four-year or technical institution or university. Applicant must have 3.0 GPA or higher. Available to U.S. and non-U.S. citizens.

Application Requirements: Application form, application form may be submitted online (http://www.theculinarytrust.org), essay, interview, recommendations or references, resume, transcript. *Fee:* $35. *Deadline:* March 1.

Contact: Heather Johnston, Administrator
The Culinary Trust
PO Box 273
New York, NY 10013
Phone: 888-345-4666
Fax: 888-345-4666
E-mail: heather@theculinarytrust.org

GOLDEN GATE RESTAURANT ASSOCIATION

http://www.ggra.org/

GOLDEN GATE RESTAURANT ASSOCIATION SCHOLARSHIP FOUNDATION

One-time award for any student pursuing a food service degree at a 501(c)(3) institution, or institutions approved by the Board of Trustees. California residency and personal interview in San Francisco is required.

Minimum GPA of 2.75 required. For further information email donnalyn@ggra.org, or visit http://ggra.org/scholarships/.

Academic Fields/Career Goals: Culinary Arts; Hospitality Management.

Award: Scholarship for use in freshman, sophomore, junior, or senior years; renewable. *Number:* 9–15. *Amount:* $1000–$6000.

Eligibility Requirements: Applicant must be enrolled or expecting to enroll full- or part-time at a two-year or four-year or technical institution or university and resident of California. Applicant must have 2.5 GPA or higher. Available to U.S. citizens.

Application Requirements: Application form, essay, financial need analysis, interview. *Deadline:* April 30.

Contact: Donnalyn Murphy, Trustee and Secretary
Golden Gate Restaurant Association
220 Montgomery Street
Suite 990
San Francisco, CA 94104
Phone: 415-781-5350
E-mail: donnalyn@ggra.org

ILLINOIS RESTAURANT ASSOCIATION EDUCATIONAL FOUNDATION

http://www.illinoisrestaurants.org/

ILLINOIS RESTAURANT ASSOCIATION EDUCATIONAL FOUNDATION SCHOLARSHIPS

Scholarship available to Illinois residents enrolled in a food service management, culinary arts, or hospitality management concentration in an accredited program of a two- or four-year college or university. Must be a U.S. citizen.

Academic Fields/Career Goals: Culinary Arts; Food Science/Nutrition; Food Service/Hospitality; Hospitality Management.

Award: Scholarship for use in freshman, sophomore, junior, senior, graduate, or postgraduate years; not renewable. *Number:* 50–70. *Amount:* $1000–$10,000.

Eligibility Requirements: Applicant must be age 17-25; enrolled or expecting to enroll full- or part-time at a two-year or four-year institution or university and resident of Illinois. Applicant or parent of applicant must have employment or volunteer experience in food service, hospitality/hotel administration/operations. Applicant must have 2.5 GPA or higher. Available to U.S. citizens.

Application Requirements: Application form, essay, personal photograph, recommendations or references, transcript. *Deadline:* April 27.

Contact: Jenna Zera, IRA Educational Foundation Scholarship Committee
Illinois Restaurant Association Educational Foundation
33 West Monroe, Suite 250
Chicago, IL 60603
Phone: 312-380-4117
Fax: 312-787-4792

INTERNATIONAL FOODSERVICE EDITORIAL COUNCIL

http://www.ifeconline.com/

INTERNATIONAL FOODSERVICE EDITORIAL COUNCIL COMMUNICATIONS SCHOLARSHIP

• See page 96

JAMES BEARD FOUNDATION INC.

http://www.jamesbeard.org/

ANDREW ZIMMERN "SECOND CHANCES" SCHOLARSHIP

Up to two $10,000 scholarship available to students planning to enroll or currently enrolled at a licensed or accredited culinary school. Student must submit an essay (of 250 words) describing extreme challenges (health, family, military, employment etc.) they have faced, and explain how this scholarship in culinary studies will give them the second chance they deserve in overcoming these hardships.

Academic Fields/Career Goals: Culinary Arts.

Award: Scholarship for use in freshman, sophomore, junior, senior, or graduate years; not renewable. *Number:* 1–2. *Amount:* $10,000.

Eligibility Requirements: Applicant must be enrolled or expecting to enroll full- or part-time at a four-year institution or university. Available to U.S. and non-U.S. citizens.

Application Requirements: Application form, essay. *Deadline:* May 15.

Contact: Scholarship Management Services
James Beard Foundation Inc.
One Scholarship Way
Saint Peter, MN 56082
Phone: 507-931-1682
E-mail: jamesbeard@scholarshipamerica.org

BERN LAXER MEMORIAL SCHOLARSHIP

Scholarship for students seeking careers in food service and hospitality management. Up to one scholarship will be given in one of three programs: culinary, hospitality management, and viticulture/oenology. Program and school must be accredited in accordance with the James Beard Foundation scholarship criteria. Must be resident of Florida and substantiate residency, have a high school diploma or the equivalent, and have a minimum of one-year culinary experience either as a student or employee.

Academic Fields/Career Goals: Culinary Arts; Food Science/Nutrition; Hospitality Management.

Award: Scholarship for use in freshman, sophomore, junior, or senior years; not renewable. *Number:* 1. *Amount:* $11,150.

Eligibility Requirements: Applicant must be enrolled or expecting to enroll full- or part-time at a four-year institution or university and resident of Florida. Available to U.S. and non-U.S. citizens.

Application Requirements: Application form, essay, financial need analysis. *Deadline:* May 15.

Contact: Scholarship Management Services
James Beard Foundation Inc.
One Scholarship Way
Saint Peter, MN 56082
Phone: 507-931-1682
E-mail: jamesbeard@scholarshipamerica.org

CHARLIE TROTTER SCHOLARSHIP

Up to two scholarships of $12,000 for high school seniors or graduates who plan to enroll or students who are already enrolled at least part-time in a course of study at a licensed or accredited culinary school.

Academic Fields/Career Goals: Culinary Arts.

Award: Scholarship for use in freshman, sophomore, junior, or senior years; not renewable. *Number:* 2. *Amount:* $12,000.

Eligibility Requirements: Applicant must be enrolled or expecting to enroll full- or part-time at a four-year institution or university. Available to U.S. citizens.

Application Requirements: Application form, essay, financial need analysis. *Deadline:* May 15.

Contact: Scholarship Management Services
James Beard Foundation Inc.
One Scholarship Way
Saint Peter, MN 56082
E-mail: jamesbeard@scholarshipamerica.org

CHICAGO JBF EATS WEEK SCHOLARSHIP

$11,300 scholarship for residents of the greater Chicago area who are enrolled in an accredited program of hospitality, culinary, baking, or beverage studies. Must be able to verify residency.

Academic Fields/Career Goals: Culinary Arts.

Award: Scholarship for use in freshman, sophomore, junior, or senior years; not renewable. *Number:* 1. *Amount:* $11,300.

Eligibility Requirements: Applicant must be enrolled or expecting to enroll full- or part-time at a four-year institution or university and resident of Illinois. Available to U.S. citizens.

Application Requirements: Application form, essay, financial need analysis. *Deadline:* May 15.

Contact: Scholarship Manager
James Beard Foundation Inc.
One Scholarship Way
Saint Peter, MN 56082
Phone: 507-931-1682
E-mail: jamesbeard@scholarshipamerica.org

CHRISTIAN WOLFFER SCHOLARSHIP

Up to one $5,000 award is available to New York residents planning to enroll or currently enrolled at a licensed or accredited culinary school or wine studies program. Minimum GPA of 3.0 required.

Academic Fields/Career Goals: Culinary Arts.

Award: Scholarship for use in freshman, sophomore, junior, or senior years; not renewable. *Number:* 1. *Amount:* $5000.

Eligibility Requirements: Applicant must be enrolled or expecting to enroll full- or part-time at a two-year or four-year institution or university and resident of New York. Applicant must have 3.0 GPA or higher. Available to U.S. citizens.

Application Requirements: Application form, essay, financial need analysis. *Deadline:* May 15.

Contact: Scholarship Management Services
James Beard Foundation Inc.
One Scholarship Way
Saint Peter, MN 56082
Phone: 507-931-1682
E-mail: jamesbeard@scholarshipamerica.org

CONNECTONE BANK SCHOLARSHIP

Up to one scholarship of $8,500 for high school seniors or graduates who are already enrolled at least part-time in a course of study at a licensed or accredited culinary school. Must reside and/or attend school in New Jersey.

Academic Fields/Career Goals: Culinary Arts.

Award: Scholarship for use in freshman, sophomore, junior, or senior years; not renewable. *Number:* 1. *Amount:* $8500.

Eligibility Requirements: Applicant must be enrolled or expecting to enroll full- or part-time at a two-year or four-year or technical institution or university. Available to U.S. citizens.

Application Requirements: Application form, essay, financial need analysis. *Deadline:* May 15.

Contact: Scholarship Management Services
James Beard Foundation Inc.
One Scholarship Way
Saint Peter, MN 56082
Phone: 507-931-1682
E-mail: jamesbeard@scholarshipamerica.org

HIGH SOUTH BENTONVILLE CULINARY SCHOLARSHIP

Up to one scholarship of $5,150 for high school seniors or graduates who plan to enroll or students who are already enrolled at least part-time in a course of study at a licensed or accredited culinary school. Preference will be given to applicants residing in, or attending school in the state of Arkansas.

Academic Fields/Career Goals: Culinary Arts.

Award: Scholarship for use in freshman, sophomore, junior, or senior years; not renewable. *Number:* 1. *Amount:* $5150.

Eligibility Requirements: Applicant must be enrolled or expecting to enroll full- or part-time at a two-year or four-year or technical institution or university. Available to U.S. citizens.

Application Requirements: Application form, essay, financial need analysis. *Deadline:* May 15.

Contact: Scholarship Management Services
James Beard Foundation Inc.
One Scholarship Way
Saint Peter, MN 56082
Phone: 507-931-1682
E-mail: jamesbeard@scholarshipamerica.org

JAMES BEARD FOUNDATION SCHOLARSHIP PROGRAM

To apply, students must be high school seniors or graduates planning to start or continue a course of study at a licensed or accredited culinary school or food-focused program in the 2018-2019 academic year.

Additional eligibility requirements may apply for some of the James Beard Foundation scholarships. Students complete one application to be considered for all James Beard Foundation scholarships for which one meets the criteria.

Academic Fields/Career Goals: Culinary Arts.

Award: Scholarship for use in freshman, sophomore, junior, or senior years; not renewable. *Number:* 100. *Amount:* $20,000.

Eligibility Requirements: Applicant must be enrolled or expecting to enroll full- or part-time at a four-year institution or university. Available to U.S. citizens.

Application Requirements: Application form, essay, financial need analysis. *Deadline:* May 15.

Contact: Scholarship Manager
James Beard Foundation Inc.
One Scholarship Way
Saint Peter, MN 56082
Phone: 507-931-1682
E-mail: jamesbeard@scholarshipamerica.org

JAMES BEARD LEGACY SCHOLARSHIP

Up to 10 scholarships of $10,000 each for high school seniors or graduates who plan to enroll or students who are already enrolled at least part-time in a course of study at a licensed or accredited program of food or culinary studies. Must be planning to enroll or currently enrolled in a program of study for culinary arts, wine, food history, nutrition, dietetics, continuing education, food writing, food studies, or a related field. Must also demonstrate financial need.

Academic Fields/Career Goals: Culinary Arts.

Award: Scholarship for use in freshman, sophomore, junior, or senior years; not renewable. *Number:* 10. *Amount:* $10,000.

Eligibility Requirements: Applicant must be enrolled or expecting to enroll full-time at a two-year or four-year institution or university.

Application Requirements: Application form, financial need analysis. *Deadline:* May 15.

Contact: Diane Brown, Director of Educational and Community
Programming
Phone: 212-627-1128

MILJENKO "MIKE"GRGICH'S AMERICAN DREAM SCHOLARSHIP

Up to one $5000 award is available to students planning to enroll or currently enrolled at an accredited wine studies program.

Academic Fields/Career Goals: Culinary Arts.

Award: Scholarship for use in freshman, sophomore, junior, senior, or graduate years; not renewable. *Number:* 1. *Amount:* $5000.

Eligibility Requirements: Applicant must be enrolled or expecting to enroll full- or part-time at a four-year institution or university. Available to U.S. and non-U.S. citizens.

Application Requirements: Application form, essay, financial need analysis. *Deadline:* May 15.

Contact: Scholarship Management Services
James Beard Foundation Inc.
One Scholarship Way
Saint Peter, MN 56082
Phone: 507-931-1682
E-mail: jamesbeard@scholarshipamerica.org

PETER KUMP MEMORIAL SCHOLARSHIP

Up to 5 scholarships of $10,000 towards tuition at an accredited or licensed culinary school of student's choice. Candidates must have a minimum of one year of experience in the culinary field, demonstrate financial need, and have at least a 3.0 GPA.

Academic Fields/Career Goals: Culinary Arts.

Award: Scholarship for use in freshman year; not renewable. *Number:* 1–5. *Amount:* $10,000.

Eligibility Requirements: Applicant must be high school student and planning to enroll or expecting to enroll full- or part-time at a four-year institution or university. Applicant must have 3.0 GPA or higher. Available to U.S. and non-U.S. citizens.

Application Requirements: Application form, essay, financial need analysis. *Deadline:* May 15.

Contact: Scholarship Management Services
James Beard Foundation Inc.
One Scholarship Way
Saint Peter, MN 56082
Phone: 507-931-1682
E-mail: jamesbeard@scholarshipamerica.org

ROBERT MONDAVI WINERY MEMORIAL SCHOLARSHIP

Up to one scholarship of $10,000 for a student planning to enroll or currently enrolled in a beverage, wine studies, or hospitality management program or a Master Sommelier program at an accredited culinary school, hospitality institution, college, or university. Must be a U.S. resident, over 21 years of age, and have a high school diploma or GED.

Academic Fields/Career Goals: Culinary Arts.

Award: Scholarship for use in freshman, sophomore, junior, or senior years; not renewable. *Number:* 1. *Amount:* $10,000.

Eligibility Requirements: Applicant must be enrolled or expecting to enroll full- or part-time at a two-year or four-year institution or university.

Application Requirements: Application form. *Deadline:* May 15.

Contact: Diane Brown, Director of Educational and Community
Programming
Phone: 212-627-1128

STEVEN SCHER MEMORIAL SCHOLARSHIP FOR ASPIRING RESTAURANTEURS

One award of $8,000 for a student in a culinary or hospitality management program at an accredited institution. Must detail work experience, submit essay, and include a list of top three favorite restaurants and explain why they have earned that ranking. Special consideration will be given to career changers.

Academic Fields/Career Goals: Culinary Arts.

Award: Scholarship for use in freshman, sophomore, junior, or senior years; not renewable. *Number:* 1. *Amount:* $8000.

Eligibility Requirements: Applicant must be enrolled or expecting to enroll full- or part-time at a two-year or four-year institution or university. Available to U.S. citizens.

Application Requirements: Application form, essay. *Deadline:* May 15.

Contact: Scholarship Management Services
James Beard Foundation Inc.
One Scholarship Way
Saint Peter, MN 56082
Phone: 507-931-1682
E-mail: jamesbeard@scholarshipamerica.org

TASTE AMERICA SCHOLARSHIPS

Up to 10 scholarships of $2,500 each for students residing or attending school in the states that hosted the JBF nationwide celebration of American Taste: Arizona, California (2), Illinois, Louisiana, Massachusetts, Missouri, Pennsylvania, Texas, and Washington.

Academic Fields/Career Goals: Culinary Arts.

Award: Scholarship for use in freshman, sophomore, junior, or senior years; not renewable. *Number:* 1–10. *Amount:* $2500.

Eligibility Requirements: Applicant must be enrolled or expecting to enroll full- or part-time at a two-year or four-year or technical institution or university. Available to U.S. citizens.

Application Requirements: Application form, essay. *Deadline:* May 15.

Contact: Scholarship Management Services
James Beard Foundation Inc.
One Scholarship Way
Saint Peter, MN 56082
Phone: 507-931-1682
E-mail: jamesbeard@scholarshipamerica.org

LES DAMES D'ESCOFFIER INTERNATIONAL, COLORADO CHAPTER

http://www.lesdamescolorado.org

LES DAMES D'ESCOFFIER INTERNATIONAL, COLORADO CHAPTER SCHOLARSHIP

• See page 107

MAINE RESTAURANT ASSOCIATION
http://www.mainerestaurant.com/

MAINE RESTAURANT ASSOCIATION EDUCATION FOUNDATION SCHOLARSHIP FUND
Scholarship available to students (Maine Residents Only) who wish to pursue higher education in culinary arts, restaurant, and hotel or hospitality management. Preference will be given to ProStart students.

Academic Fields/Career Goals: Culinary Arts; Hospitality Management.

Award: Scholarship for use in freshman, sophomore, junior, or senior years; not renewable. *Number:* 1–8. *Amount:* $500–$2000.

Eligibility Requirements: Applicant must be enrolled or expecting to enroll full- or part-time at a two-year or four-year or technical institution or university and resident of Maine. Available to U.S. citizens.

Application Requirements: Application form, essay. *Deadline:* April 28.

Contact: Becky Jacobson, Operations Manager
Maine Restaurant Association
45 Melville St.
Augusta, ME 04330
Phone: 207-623-2178
E-mail: becky@mainerestaurant.com

MARYLAND RESTAURANT ASSOCIATION EDUCATION FOUNDATION
https://www.marylandrestaurants.com/about.html

THE LETITIA B. CARTER SCHOLARSHIP
The Letitia B. Carter Scholarship is presented by the Restaurant Association of Maryland Education Foundation in memory of former CEO of the Restaurant Association of Maryland. This competitive scholarship is awarded to Maryland residents interested in pursuing hospitality-related coursework. It is available to high school students and college students as well as high school, college or corporate instructors and current hospitality industry professionals. ($500 - $2000 scholarship pool)

Academic Fields/Career Goals: Culinary Arts; Food Science/Nutrition; Food Service/Hospitality; Hospitality Management.

Award: Scholarship for use in freshman, sophomore, junior, or senior years; not renewable. *Number:* 1. *Amount:* $500–$2000.

Eligibility Requirements: Applicant must be enrolled or expecting to enroll full- or part-time at a two-year or four-year or technical institution or university and resident of Maryland. Applicant or parent of applicant must have employment or volunteer experience in food service, hospitality/hotel administration/operations. Applicant must have 3.0 GPA or higher. Available to U.S. citizens.

Application Requirements: Application form, essay. *Deadline:* March 16.

Contact: Jessica Waller, Executive Director
Maryland Restaurant Association Education Foundation
6301 Hillside Court
Columbia, MD 21046
Phone: 410-2906800 Ext. 1025
Fax: 410-2906882
E-mail: jwaller@marylandrestaurants.com

MARCIA S. HARRIS LEGACY FUND SCHOLARSHIP
The Marcia S. Harris Legacy Fund Scholarship is presented by the Restaurant Association of Maryland in memory of Marcia S. Harris former CEO of the Restaurant Association of Maryland for more than 20 years. Marcia had a love for life and a love for the foodservice industry that stood out even in the largest crowds. Her passion and dedication to promoting, protecting and improving the foodservice industry is what drove her day in and day out. Applicants should also possess the qualities of passion and dedication and have a strong desire to improve the foodservice industry through the personal pursuit of professionalism. ($500 - $2000 scholarship pool)

Academic Fields/Career Goals: Culinary Arts; Food Science/Nutrition; Food Service/Hospitality; Hospitality Management.

Award: Scholarship for use in freshman, sophomore, junior, or senior years; not renewable. *Number:* 1. *Amount:* $500–$2000.

Eligibility Requirements: Applicant must be enrolled or expecting to enroll full- or part-time at a two-year or four-year or technical institution or university and resident of Maryland. Available to U.S. citizens.

Application Requirements: Application form, essay. *Deadline:* March 16.

Contact: Jessica Waller, Executive Director
Maryland Restaurant Association Education Foundation
6301 Hillside Court
Columbia, MD 21046
Phone: 410-2906800 Ext. 1025
Fax: 410-2906882
E-mail: jwaller@marylandrestaurants.com

NATIONAL RESTAURANT ASSOCIATION EDUCATIONAL FOUNDATION
http://www.chooserestaurants.org

NATIONAL RESTAURANT ASSOCIATION EDUCATIONAL FOUNDATION UNDERGRADUATE SCHOLARSHIPS FOR COLLEGE STUDENTS
• *See page 109*

OREGON STUDENT ASSISTANCE COMMISSION
https://oregonstudentaid.gov/

OREGON WINE BROTHERHOOD SCHOLARSHIP
Award for residents of Oregon or Washington majoring in enology, viticulture, or culinary arts (preference for wine emphasis). Must attend Chemeketa, Central Oregon, Lane, Linn-Benton, Mt. Hood, Southwestern Oregon, Umpqua, Walla Walla Community College, Oregon State University, University of California at Davis, or Washington State University. Apply/compete annually. Financial need may or may not be considered.

Academic Fields/Career Goals: Culinary Arts; Food Science/Nutrition; Hospitality Management.

Award: Scholarship for use in freshman, sophomore, junior, senior, or graduate years; not renewable.

Eligibility Requirements: Applicant must be enrolled or expecting to enroll full-time at a two-year or four-year institution or university; resident of Oregon, Washington and studying in Oregon, Washington. Available to U.S. citizens.

Application Requirements: Application form, financial need analysis. *Deadline:* March 1.

Contact: Melissa Adams, Scholarship Processing Coordinator
Phone: 541-687-7409
E-mail: melissa.adams@state.or.us

TECHNICAL TRAINING FUND SCHOLARSHIP
• *See page 143*

PROFESSIONAL REPS
http://www.professionalreps.com/

HUNGRY TO LEAD SCHOLARSHIP
Those eligible to apply are high school seniors, or college students registered/pre-registered to attend an accredited school in the United States. Applicant must be pursuing a degree in a foodservice/hospitality program, or directly related. The scholarship is merit based on high school records, ACT and/or SAT scores, college transcripts if applicable, and extracurricular activities. Minimum requirements as follows: high school or college cumulative GPA of 2.5, SAT of 1300, or ACT of 18. Applicants will also be judged on their ability to demonstrate leadership capabilities. Top four finalists will be awarded scholarships in the following order: first place, The Amana Leadership Scholarship ($2,500); second place, The Hungry To Lead Scholarship ($1,500); third place, Leadership Recognition Award ($500); fourth place, Leadership Recognition Award ($500)

Academic Fields/Career Goals: Culinary Arts; Food Science/Nutrition; Food Service/Hospitality.

Award: Scholarship for use in freshman, sophomore, junior, or senior years; not renewable. *Number:* 4. *Amount:* $500–$2500.

Eligibility Requirements: Applicant must be enrolled or expecting to enroll full-time at a two-year or four-year or technical institution or university. Applicant must have 2.5 GPA or higher. Available to U.S. and non-U.S. citizens.

Application Requirements: Application form, essay. *Deadline:* July 1.

Contact: Tessa Bucklin
Professional Reps
750 E. Covey Lane #110
Phoenix, AZ 85024
Phone: 877-995-8922
E-mail: scholarships@professionalreps.com

SOUTH CAROLINA RESTAURANT AND LODGING ASSOCIATION

http://www.scrla.org/

SOUTH CAROLINA TOURISM AND HOSPITALITY EDUCATIONAL FOUNDATION SCHOLARSHIPS

The South Carolina Restaurant and Lodging Educational Foundation (SCRLEF) manages scholarships on behalf of a variety of organizations that support hospitality education. These scholarships are designed to assist students who demonstrate an interest in and commitment to the hospitality (restaurant, foodservice, lodging, tourism) industry.

Academic Fields/Career Goals: Culinary Arts; Food Service/Hospitality; Hospitality Management.

Award: Scholarship for use in freshman, sophomore, junior, or senior years; not renewable. *Number:* 5–16. *Amount:* $750–$2500.

Eligibility Requirements: Applicant must be enrolled or expecting to enroll full-time at a two-year or four-year or technical institution or university; resident of South Carolina and studying in South Carolina. Available to U.S. citizens.

Application Requirements: Application form, essay. *Deadline:* May 1.

Contact: Douglas OFlaherty, Vice President
South Carolina Restaurant and Lodging Association
PO Box 7577
Columbia, SC 29202
Phone: 803-765-9000

STRAIGHTFORWARD MEDIA

http://www.straightforwardmedia.com/

STRAIGHTFORWARD MEDIA VOCATIONAL-TECHNICAL SCHOOL SCHOLARSHIP
• See page 118

SUPPORT CREATIVITY

http://wesupportcreativity.org

SUPPORT CREATIVITY SCHOLARSHIP
• See page 137

TEXAS RESTAURANT ASSOCIATION

http://www.restaurantville.com/

W. PRICE, JR. MEMORIAL SCHOLARSHIP

Each year the Texas Restaurant Association awards the W. Price Jr. Memorial Scholarship to students with a growing passion for the foodservice industry. The scholarship is named for W. Price Jr., the first executive director of the Texas Restaurant Association who served from 1953 until 1974. Seven scholarships of $1,000 are awarded to students graduating high school or those currently enrolled in a postsecondary culinary programs.

Academic Fields/Career Goals: Culinary Arts; Food Service/Hospitality.

Award: Scholarship for use in freshman, sophomore, junior, senior, or graduate years; not renewable. *Number:* 5–7. *Amount:* $1000.

Eligibility Requirements: Applicant must be enrolled or expecting to enroll full-time at a two-year or four-year institution or university and resident of Texas. Applicant or parent of applicant must have employment or volunteer experience in food service, hospitality/hotel administration/operations. Available to U.S. citizens.

Application Requirements: Application form, essay. *Deadline:* February 15.

Contact: Jerrica Deloney, Program Manager
Texas Restaurant Association
PO Box 1429
Austin, TX 78767
Phone: 800-395-2872
E-mail: foundation@tramail.org

UNITED NEGRO COLLEGE FUND

http://www.uncf.org/

UNCF/CARNIVAL CORPORATE SCHOLARS PROGRAM
• See page 184

WISCONSIN BAKERS ASSOCIATION (WBA)

http://www.wibakers.com/

ROBERT W. HILLER SCHOLARSHIP FUND

Scholarship of $1000 awarded for students at all levels in a baking/pastry arts-related program that prepares candidates for a retail baking profession. Minimum 2.85 GPA required.

Academic Fields/Career Goals: Culinary Arts; Food Science/Nutrition; Food Service/Hospitality.

Award: Scholarship for use in freshman, sophomore, junior, senior, graduate, or postgraduate years; not renewable. *Amount:* $1000.

Eligibility Requirements: Applicant must be enrolled or expecting to enroll full-time at a two-year or four-year institution or university. Available to U.S. citizens.

Application Requirements: Application form, essay. *Deadline:* December 1.

Contact: Jessica Hoover
Phone: 414-258-5552
Fax: 414-258-5582
E-mail: jessica@wibakers.com

WBA SCHOLARSHIP

The Wisconsin Bakers Association's education committee submitted recommendations to the Board of Governors on Oct. 24, 1983, to implement the WBA Scholarship Program. The first scholarship awards were later presented in 1984. Since then, the WBA has awarded more than $25,000 in WBA Scholarships! Wisconsin residents only can apply for the WBA Scholarship.

Academic Fields/Career Goals: Culinary Arts; Food Science/Nutrition; Food Service/Hospitality.

Award: Scholarship for use in freshman, sophomore, junior, senior, graduate, or postgraduate years; not renewable.

Eligibility Requirements: Applicant must be enrolled or expecting to enroll full- or part-time at a two-year or four-year or technical institution or university and resident of Wisconsin. Available to U.S. citizens.

Application Requirements: Application form, essay, interview. *Deadline:* continuous.

Contact: Jessica Hoover
Phone: 414-258-5552
Fax: 414-258-5582
E-mail: jessica@wibakers.com

WOMEN CHEFS AND RESTAURATEURS

http://www.womenchefs.org/

FRENCH CULINARY INSTITUTE/ITALIAN CULINARY EXPERIENCE SCHOLARSHIP

Scholarship intended for a culinary student wishing to specialize in Italian cuisine. Recipient must be a new enrollment and satisfy all entrance requirements of the FCI. Scholarship award is applied to total program fee.

Academic Fields/Career Goals: Culinary Arts; Food Service/Hospitality.

Award: Scholarship for use in freshman, sophomore, junior, senior, graduate, or postgraduate years; not renewable. *Number:* 1. *Amount:* $5000.

Eligibility Requirements: Applicant must be enrolled or expecting to enroll full-time at a four-year institution or university. Available to U.S. and non-U.S. citizens.

Application Requirements: Application form, essay. *Fee:* $25. *Deadline:* March 31.

Contact: Dori Sacksteder, Director of Programs
　　　　　Phone: 502-581-0300 Ext. 219
　　　　　Fax: 502-589-3602
　　　　　E-mail: dsacksteder@hqtrs.com

DENTAL HEALTH/ SERVICES

101ST AIRBORNE DIVISION ASSOCIATION

http://www.screamingeaglefoundation.org/

AL & WILLIAMARY VISTE SCHOLARSHIP

• *See page 114*

ACLS CERTIFICATION INSTITUTE

https://acls.com

MEDICAL SCHOOL SCHOLARSHIP

It's no secret that medical school is stressful. Between demanding course work and long hours, many students don't have the time of resources to care for their overall well-being. Long periods of stress predisposes students for depression and anxiety. This cycle frequently continues after medical school. Roughly 1 physician commits suicide per day. It is our goal to combat this trend by improving student wellness and removing the stigma around mental health treatment. Award amount of $2,500. Post a video creatively responding to the following prompt: How would you improve student wellness? i.e.: a system you would change, a service/program that would be helpful? Videos should be 30-45 second in length. Upload the video to YouTube and submit the link with your application. Each video should include a brief description with a link to https://acls.com/scholarship and the hashtag #studentwellnessscholarship. Each video must be original. Share the scholarship page on Facebook with the hashtag #studentwellnessscholarship. Complete the application including the student survey. Open to students currently enrolled or accepted to medical school, dental school, or nursing school. Student must be a legal resident of and currently living in the United States. Winner is not based on financial need. Relatives of employees and employees of ACLS Certification Institute and its affiliates are ineligible. Applicant must complete all steps of the application process to be considered.

Academic Fields/Career Goals: Dental Health/Services; Health and Medical Sciences; Nursing; Radiology.

Award: Scholarship for use in freshman, sophomore, junior, senior, or graduate years; not renewable. *Number:* 1. *Amount:* $2500.

Eligibility Requirements: Applicant must be enrolled or expecting to enroll full- or part-time at a two-year or four-year or technical institution or university. Available to U.S. citizens.

Application Requirements: Application form. *Deadline:* November 30.

ALBERTA HERITAGE SCHOLARSHIP FUND

http://www.alis.alberta.ca/

ABORIGINAL HEALTH CAREERS BURSARY

• *See page 167*

JASON LANG SCHOLARSHIP

Award of CAN$1000 to reward the outstanding academic achievement of Alberta postsecondary students who are studying full-time in Alberta.

Must be a Canadian citizen or permanent resident and Alberta resident. Must be enrolled full-time in an undergraduate or professional program, such as law, medicine, pharmacy, or dentistry at an eligible Alberta postsecondary institution. Nominated by Awards Office at institution on the basis of achieving a minimum GPA of 3.2 in the previous academic year. May be awarded up to three times to one student. Contact the Student Awards Office for application deadline. For additional information, see website http://alis.alberta.ca.

Academic Fields/Career Goals: Dental Health/Services; Health and Medical Sciences; Law/Legal Services; Pharmacy.

Award: Scholarship for use in sophomore, junior, or senior years; not renewable.

Eligibility Requirements: Applicant must be Canadian citizen; enrolled or expecting to enroll full-time at a two-year or four-year or technical institution or university; resident of Alberta and studying in Alberta.

Application Requirements: Application form, test scores, transcript. *Deadline:* varies.

Contact: Scholarship Committee
　　　　　Phone: 780-427-8640
　　　　　E-mail: scholarships@gov.ab.ca

NORTHERN ALBERTA DEVELOPMENT COUNCIL BURSARY

Return service bursary awards CAN$6000 per year for up to two years to increase the number of trained professionals in Northern Alberta and to encourage students from Northern Alberta to obtain a postsecondary education. Must be residents of Alberta, and planning to enroll in a full-time postsecondary program in a field in demand in Northern Alberta. Fields in demand include education, health and medical, engineering, technical fields, and social work. Applicants must also be within two years of completion of their postsecondary program. Students must live and work for one year in Northern Alberta for each year of assistance awarded. For additional information, go to website http://alis.alberta.ca.

Academic Fields/Career Goals: Dental Health/Services; Education; Engineering/Technology; Health and Medical Sciences; Social Services.

Award: Scholarship for use in junior or senior years; not renewable.

Eligibility Requirements: Applicant must be Canadian citizen; enrolled or expecting to enroll full-time at a four-year or technical institution or university; resident of Alberta and studying in Alberta.

Application Requirements: Application form, essay, financial need analysis, transcript. *Deadline:* April 30.

Contact: Scholarship Committee
　　　　　Phone: 780-427-8640
　　　　　E-mail: scholarships@gov.ab.ca

AMERICAN ACADEMY OF ORAL AND MAXILLOFACIAL RADIOLOGY

http://www.aaomr.org/

CHARLES R. MORRIS STUDENT RESEARCH AWARD

Award to applicants from accredited programs performing research in oral and maxillofacial radiology. Applicant must be a full-time undergraduate or predoctoral student at the time of research, be nominated by the institution where research was carried out, and submit a manuscript detailing the research project.

Academic Fields/Career Goals: Dental Health/Services.

Award: Grant for use in junior, senior, or graduate years; not renewable. *Number:* 1. *Amount:* $1000.

Eligibility Requirements: Applicant must be enrolled or expecting to enroll full-time at a four-year institution or university. Available to U.S. and non-U.S. citizens.

Application Requirements: Application form, manuscript, recommendations or references. *Deadline:* June 16.

Contact: Dr. Michael Shrout, Executive Director
　　　　　American Academy of Oral and Maxillofacial Radiology
　　　　　Box 1010
　　　　　Evans, GA 30809-1010
　　　　　Phone: 706-271-2881
　　　　　E-mail: mshrout@mcg.edu

AMERICAN DENTAL ASSOCIATION (ADA) FOUNDATION

http://www.adafoundation.org/

AMERICAN DENTAL ASSOCIATION FOUNDATION DENTAL HYGIENE SCHOLARSHIP PROGRAM

Applicant must be enrolled full-time with a minimum of 12 Credit hours as a student in an accredited dental hygiene program accredited by the Commission of Dental Accreditation of the American Dental Association. Must be U.S. citizen, permanent resident is ineligible to apply. Must have a minimum 3.5 GPA on a 4.0 scale. Applicants must be recommended by the dental hygiene program director and may request application materials from that same individual at the school where they are currently enrolled as an entering final year student in a dental hygiene program. Applicants must demonstrate a minimum financial need of $1000.

Academic Fields/Career Goals: Dental Health/Services.

Award: Scholarship for use in senior year; not renewable. *Number:* up to 15. *Amount:* up to $1000.

Eligibility Requirements: Applicant must be enrolled or expecting to enroll full-time at a four-year institution or university. Applicant must have 3.5 GPA or higher. Available to U.S. citizens.

Application Requirements: Application form, essay, financial need analysis, recommendations or references. *Deadline:* April 23.

Contact: Rose Famularo, Coordinator
Phone: 312-440-2763
E-mail: famularor@ada.org

AMERICAN DENTAL ASSOCIATION FOUNDATION DENTAL STUDENT SCHOLARSHIP PROGRAM

One-time award for entering second-year students at a dental school accredited by the American Dental Association Commission on Dental Accreditation. Must have 3.0 GPA, and be enrolled full-time (minimum of 12 hours). Must show financial need and be a U.S. citizen, a permanent resident is ineligible to apply. Applicants may request application materials from associate dean for student affairs at the dental school where they are currently enrolled. An applicant must be recommended to the ADA Foundation by the school official.

Academic Fields/Career Goals: Dental Health/Services.

Award: Scholarship for use in sophomore year; not renewable. *Number:* up to 25. *Amount:* up to $2500.

Eligibility Requirements: Applicant must be enrolled or expecting to enroll full-time at a four-year institution or university. Applicant must have 3.0 GPA or higher. Available to U.S. citizens.

Application Requirements: Application form, essay, financial need analysis, recommendations or references. *Deadline:* October 4.

Contact: Rose Famularo, Coordinator
Phone: 312-440-2763
E-mail: famularor@ada.org

AMERICAN DENTAL EDUCATION ASSOCIATION

http://www.adea.org/

ADEA/SIGMA PHI ALPHA LINDA DEVORE SCHOLARSHIP

The ADEA/Sigma Phi Alpha Linda DeVore Scholarship recognizes the memory and the 30-year dental education career of Linda Rubinstein DeVore. Professor DeVore was active in dental hygiene education, scholarship and public service. She served as President of the American Association of Dental Schools (now ADEA) in 1994, and President of the Supreme Chapter of Sigma Phi Alpha, the national honorary society of the dental hygiene profession, from 1997–98. A $1,000 scholarship is awarded to an individual pursuing allied dental education study at the baccalaureate, master's or doctoral degree levels.

Academic Fields/Career Goals: Dental Health/Services.

Award: Scholarship for use in freshman, sophomore, junior, senior, or graduate years; not renewable. *Number:* 1. *Amount:* $1000.

Eligibility Requirements: Applicant must be enrolled or expecting to enroll full- or part-time at a two-year or four-year or technical institution or university. Available to U.S. and non-U.S. citizens.

Application Requirements: Application form. *Deadline:* November 1.

Contact: Mr. Eric Lund, Professional Development Manager
American Dental Education Association
655 K Street, NW, Suite 800
Washington, DC 20001
Phone: 202-289-7201 Ext. 188
Fax: 202-289-7204
E-mail: lunde@adea.org

AMERICAN DENTAL HYGIENISTS' ASSOCIATION (ADHA) INSTITUTE FOR ORAL HEALTH

http://www.adha.org/institute-for-oral-health

CAROL BAUHS BENSON SCHOLARSHIP

Established in the memory of Carol Bauhs Benson, this scholarship is awarded to students at the Certificate/Associate educational level who have completed (or who will complete by the time of the award) a minimum of one year in a dental hygiene curriculum. This scholarship is restricted to students who reside in the following states: Minnesota, North Dakota, South Dakota or Wisconsin.

Academic Fields/Career Goals: Dental Health/Services.

Award: Scholarship for use in sophomore year; not renewable. *Number:* 1. *Amount:* $1000.

Eligibility Requirements: Applicant must be enrolled or expecting to enroll full-time at a two-year institution or university and resident of Minnesota, North Dakota, South Dakota, Wisconsin. Applicant must have 3.5 GPA or higher. Available to U.S. citizens.

Application Requirements: Application form, essay. *Deadline:* February 1.

Contact: Joan Brazas, Development Manager
American Dental Hygienists' Association (ADHA) Institute
For Oral Health
444 North Michigan Avenue
Suite 400
Chicago, IL 60611
Phone: 312-440-8944
E-mail: institute@adha.net

COLGATE "BRIGHT SMILES, BRIGHT FUTURES" MINORITY SCHOLARSHIP

One time award for members of minority groups currently underrepresented in dental hygiene programs at the certificate educational level. Must be an active student member of ADHA. Applicant must have completed one year of dental hygiene curricula at an accredited dental hygiene program in United States. Applicant must demonstrate GPA of at least 3.0, and financial need of $1500 or more.

Academic Fields/Career Goals: Dental Health/Services.

Award: Scholarship for use in sophomore year; not renewable. *Number:* 1–2. *Amount:* $1250.

Eligibility Requirements: Applicant must be American Indian/Alaska Native, Asian/Pacific Islander, Black (non-Hispanic), Hispanic and enrolled or expecting to enroll full-time at a two-year or technical institution. Applicant or parent of applicant must be member of American Dental Hygienist's Association. Applicant must have 3.0 GPA or higher. Available to U.S. citizens.

Application Requirements: Application form, essay. *Deadline:* February 1.

Contact: Joan Brazas, Development Manager
American Dental Hygienists' Association (ADHA) Institute
For Oral Health
444 North Michigan Avenue
Suite 400
Chicago, IL 60611
Phone: 312-440-8944
E-mail: institute@adha.net

CREST ORAL-B LABORATORIES DENTAL HYGIENE SCHOLARSHIP

Scholarships to baccalaureate degree students who demonstrate intent to encourage professional excellence, promote quality research, and support dental hygiene through public and private education. Must be an active SADHA or ADHA member. Must have completed one year of dental hygiene curricula at an accredited dental hygiene program in United States. Must demonstrate GPA of at least 3.5.

Academic Fields/Career Goals: Dental Health/Services.

Award: Scholarship for use in sophomore, junior, or senior years; not renewable. *Number:* 1–2. *Amount:* $1000.

Eligibility Requirements: Applicant must be enrolled or expecting to enroll full-time at a four-year institution or university. Applicant or parent of applicant must be member of American Dental Hygienist's Association. Applicant must have 3.5 GPA or higher. Available to U.S. citizens.

Application Requirements: Application form, essay. *Deadline:* May 1.

Contact: Joan Brazas, Development Manager
American Dental Hygienists' Association (ADHA) Institute
For Oral Health
444 North Michigan Avenue
Suite 400
Chicago, IL 60611
Phone: 312-440-8944
E-mail: institute@adha.net

HU-FRIEDY/ESTHER WILKINS INSTRUMENT SCHOLARSHIP

These scholarships are awarded to applicants at the certificate/associate or baccalaureate degree level who have completed a minimum of one year in a dental hygiene curriculum. The program awards recipients with the Hu-Friedy dental hygiene instruments of their choice, equivalent to a retail value of $1,000.

Academic Fields/Career Goals: Dental Health/Services.

Award: Scholarship for use in sophomore, junior, or senior years; not renewable. *Amount:* $1000.

Eligibility Requirements: Applicant must be enrolled or expecting to enroll full-time at a two-year or four-year institution or university. Applicant must have 3.0 GPA or higher. Available to U.S. citizens.

Application Requirements: Application form, essay. *Deadline:* February 1.

Contact: Joan Brazas, Development Manager
American Dental Hygienists' Association (ADHA) Institute
For Oral Health
444 North Michigan Avenue
Suite 400
Chicago, IL 60611
Phone: 312-440-8944
E-mail: institute@adha.net

JOHNSON & JOHNSON SCHOLARSHIP

These scholarships are awarded to applicants pursuing a certificate/associate or baccalaureate degree in dental hygiene and have completed a minimum of one year in a dental hygiene curriculum.

Academic Fields/Career Goals: Dental Health/Services.

Award: Scholarship for use in sophomore, junior, or senior years; not renewable. *Number:* 5. *Amount:* $1000.

Eligibility Requirements: Applicant must be enrolled or expecting to enroll full-time at a two-year or four-year institution or university. Applicant must have 3.5 GPA or higher. Available to U.S. citizens.

Application Requirements: Application form, essay. *Deadline:* February 1.

Contact: Joan Brazas, Development Manager
American Dental Hygienists' Association (ADHA) Institute
For Oral Health
444 North Michigan Avenue
Suite 400
Chicago, IL 60611
Phone: 312-440-8944
E-mail: institute@adha.net

KARLA GIRTS MEMORIAL COMMUNITY OUTREACH SCHOLARSHIP

These scholarships are awarded to students enrolled in an associate, baccalaureate or degree completion program and completed a minimum of one year in a dental hygiene curriculum. Applicants will display a commitment to improving oral health within the geriatric population.

Academic Fields/Career Goals: Dental Health/Services.

Award: Scholarship for use in sophomore, junior, or senior years; not renewable. *Number:* 2. *Amount:* $2000.

Eligibility Requirements: Applicant must be enrolled or expecting to enroll full-time at a two-year or four-year institution. Applicant must have 3.0 GPA or higher. Available to U.S. citizens.

Application Requirements: Application form, essay. *Deadline:* February 1.

Contact: Joan Brazas, Development Manager
American Dental Hygienists' Association (ADHA) Institute
For Oral Health
444 North Michigan Avenue
Suite 400
Chicago, IL 60611
Phone: 312-440-8944
E-mail: institute@adha.net

SIGMA PHI ALPHA UNDERGRADUATE SCHOLARSHIP

Awarded to an outstanding Sigma Phi Alpha member pursuing a certificate/associate or baccalaureate degree at a school with an active chapter of the Sigma Phi Alpha Dental Hygiene Honor Society. Applicant must demonstrate GPA of at least 3.5. Must have completed one year of dental hygiene curricula at an accredited dental hygiene program in United States. Must demonstrate a financial need of $1500 or more. Must be an active SADHA or ADHA member.

Academic Fields/Career Goals: Dental Health/Services.

Award: Scholarship for use in sophomore, junior, or senior years; not renewable. *Number:* 1. *Amount:* $1000.

Eligibility Requirements: Applicant must be enrolled or expecting to enroll full-time at a two-year or four-year or technical institution or university. Applicant or parent of applicant must be member of American Dental Hygienist's Association. Applicant must have 3.5 GPA or higher. Available to U.S. citizens.

Application Requirements: Application form, essay. *Deadline:* February 1.

Contact: Joan Brazas, Development Manager
American Dental Hygienists' Association (ADHA) Institute
For Oral Health
444 North Michigan Avenue
Suite 400
Chicago, IL 60611
Phone: 312-440-8944
E-mail: institute@adha.net

WILMA E. MOTLEY SCHOLARSHIP

This scholarship is awarded to applicant(s) pursuing a Baccalaureate degree at an accredited dental hygiene program and will have completed a minimum of one year in a dental hygiene curriculum.

Academic Fields/Career Goals: Dental Health/Services.

Award: Scholarship for use in sophomore, junior, or senior years; not renewable. *Number:* 1. *Amount:* $1000.

Eligibility Requirements: Applicant must be enrolled or expecting to enroll full-time at an institution or university. Applicant must have 3.5 GPA or higher. Available to U.S. citizens.

Application Requirements: Application form, essay. *Deadline:* February 1.

Contact: Joan Brazas, Development Manager
American Dental Hygienists' Association (ADHA) Institute
For Oral Health
444 North Michigan Avenue
Suite 400
Chicago, IL 60611
Phone: 312-440-8944
E-mail: institute@adha.net

AMERICAN INDIAN SCIENCE AND ENGINEERING SOCIETY

http://www.aises.org/

A.T. ANDERSON MEMORIAL SCHOLARSHIP PROGRAM
• See page 121

AMERICAN LEGION AUXILIARY DEPARTMENT OF COLORADO

http://www.alacolorado.com

AMERICAN LEGION AUXILIARY DEPARTMENT OF COLORADO PAST PRESIDENTS' PARLEY HEALTH CARE PROFESSIONAL SCHOLARSHIPNURSES SCHOLARSHIP

• See page 147

AMERICAN LEGION DEPARTMENT OF NORTH DAKOTA

http://www.ndlegion.org/

O. NESHEIM MEMORIAL SCHOLARSHIP

Must be a legal resident of North Dakota and a direct descendent (child, grandchild or great-grandchild) of a U.S. veteran who served honorably. Proof of service and lineage are required. Must have maintained a secondary school GPA of 2.75 or higher. Must be pursuing a degree in some phase of agriculture, human nutrition, or medicine (medical doctor, PA, dentistry, dental hygiene, pharmacy, or chiropractic). Must be a high school senior or a previous Nesheim Scholarship recipient now attending an institution of higher education. The applicant must submit the completed application form. Include and attach an original essay (500 to 750 words, typed, double–spaced, 12 point font with 1" margins) to address the following issues: 1.What are your educational and career goals? 2. How do you plan to accomplish those goals and what part will your education play in attaining those goals? 3. Where do you plan to continue your education and why did you choose that institution? 4. Briefly discuss your secondary education (coursework, extracurricular activities, sports, jobs, volunteerism, etc.) and how you feel they may or may not have helped you prepare for your choice of college, your life, and your career. Provide proof of acceptance into a postsecondary institution in North Dakota that grants Associate or higher degrees. Include a high school transcript. Include 3 letters of reference, all from non-family members, and one of which must be from a U.S. veteran who served honorably. Provide proof of financial need from the educational institution to be attended.

Academic Fields/Career Goals: Dental Health/Services; Food Science/Nutrition; Health Administration; Health and Medical Sciences; Pharmacy.

Award: Scholarship for use in senior year; not renewable.

Eligibility Requirements: Applicant must be high school student; age 17-18; planning to enroll or expecting to enroll full-time at a two-year or four-year or technical institution or university; single; resident of North Dakota and studying in North Dakota. Applicant must have 2.5 GPA or higher. Available to U.S. citizens. Applicant or parent must meet one or more of the following requirements: general military experience; retired from active duty; disabled or killed as a result of military service; prisoner of war; or missing in action.

Application Requirements: Application form, community service, essay, financial need analysis. *Deadline:* April 1.

Contact: Teri Bryant
American Legion Department of North Dakota
405 W. Main Ave. Suite 4A
West Fargo, ND 58078
Phone: 701-293-3120
E-mail: programs@ndlegion.org

ARRL FOUNDATION INC.

http://www.arrl.org/

CAROLE J. STREETER, KB9JBR, SCHOLARSHIP

One $1000 award is available to a student with any class of active Amateur Radio license with preference for basic Morse code capability. Preference for students studying in the health and medical fields. Must demonstrate basic Morse Code proficiency, be a U.S. citizen, and attend an accredited college or university.

Academic Fields/Career Goals: Dental Health/Services; Health and Medical Sciences; Nursing; Oncology; Optometry; Osteopathy; Therapy/Rehabilitation.

Award: Scholarship for use in freshman, sophomore, junior, senior, or graduate years; not renewable. *Number:* 1. *Amount:* $1000.

Eligibility Requirements: Applicant must be enrolled or expecting to enroll full- or part-time at a two-year or four-year institution or university and must have an interest in amateur radio. Available to U.S. citizens.

Application Requirements: Application form. *Deadline:* January 31.

Contact: Ms. Mary Hobart, Secretary
Phone: 860-594-0397
E-mail: k1mmh@arrl.org

MEDICAL AMATEUR RADIO COUNCIL (MARCO) SCHOLARSHIP

• See page 115

ASSOCIATION ON AMERICAN INDIAN AFFAIRS, INC.

http://www.indian-affairs.org/

ELIZABETH AND SHERMAN ASCHE MEMORIAL SCHOLARSHIP FUND

• See page 106

AVACARE MEDICAL

https://avacaremedical.com

AVACARE MEDICAL SCHOLARSHIP

• See page 115

BETHESDA LUTHERAN COMMUNITIES

http://www.bethesdalutherancommunities.org/scholarships

DEVELOPMENTAL DISABILITIES SCHOLASTIC ACHIEVEMENT SCHOLARSHIP FOR COLLEGE STUDENTS WHO ARE LUTHERAN

One-time award for Lutheran students who are currently enrolled in studies related to developmental disabilities. Awards of up to $3000. 3.0 GPA required.

Academic Fields/Career Goals: Dental Health/Services; Education; Health Administration; Health and Medical Sciences; Health Information Management/Technology; Humanities; Religion/Theology; Social Services; Special Education; Therapy/Rehabilitation.

Award: Scholarship for use in freshman, sophomore, junior, or senior years; not renewable. *Number:* 2–3. *Amount:* $500–$3000.

Eligibility Requirements: Applicant must be Lutheran and enrolled or expecting to enroll full-time at a four-year institution or university. Applicant must have 3.0 GPA or higher. Available to U.S. citizens.

Application Requirements: Application form, community service, essay. *Deadline:* May 1.

Contact: Barb Schultz, Program Coordinator
Bethesda Lutheran Communities
600 Hoffmann Drive
Watertown, WI 53094-6294
Phone: 920-206-4427
E-mail: barb.schultz@mailblc.org

BHW GROUP

https://thebhwgroup.com/

BHW WOMEN IN STEM SCHOLARSHIP

• See page 124

CARDS AGAINST HUMANITY

https://cardsagainsthumanity.com/

SCIENCE AMBASSADOR SCHOLARSHIP

• See page 124

CONTINENTAL SOCIETY, DAUGHTERS OF INDIAN WARS

http://www.csdiw.org/

CONTINENTAL SOCIETY, DAUGHTERS OF INDIAN WARS SCHOLARSHIP
• See page 242

DDSRANK

https://www.ddsrank.com

DDSRANK DENTAL SCHOLARSHIP

The DDSRank Dental Scholarship is awarded to one aspiring dental student to help them pay for the cost of tuition or books.

Academic Fields/Career Goals: Dental Health/Services.

Award: Scholarship for use in freshman, sophomore, junior, senior, or graduate years; not renewable. *Number:* 1. *Amount:* $500.

Eligibility Requirements: Applicant must be enrolled or expecting to enroll full-time at a four-year institution or university. Available to U.S. citizens.

Application Requirements: Essay. *Deadline:* September 23.

Contact: Scholarship Administrator
E-mail: scholarships@ddsrank.com

THE EXPERT INSTITUTE

https://www.theexpertinstitute.com

ANNUAL HEALTHCARE AND LIFE SCIENCES SCHOLARSHIP
• See page 170

HAWAIIAN LODGE, F&AM

http://www.hawaiianlodgefreemasons.org

HAWAIIAN LODGE SCHOLARSHIPS
• See page 86

HEALTH PROFESSIONS EDUCATION FOUNDATION

http://www.healthprofessions.ca.gov/

ALLIED HEALTHCARE SCHOLARSHIP PROGRAM
• See page 165

HELLENIC UNIVERSITY CLUB OF PHILADELPHIA

http://www.hucphiladelphia.org/

NICHOLAS S. HETOS, DDS MEMORIAL GRADUATE SCHOLARSHIP

$2000 scholarships for a senior undergraduate or graduate student with financial need pursuing studies leading to a Doctor of Dental Medicine or Doctor of Dental Surgery degree. Must be a U.S. citizen of Greek descent and a resident of particular counties in NJ or PA.

Academic Fields/Career Goals: Dental Health/Services.

Award: Scholarship for use in senior or graduate years; not renewable. *Number:* up to 1. *Amount:* $2000.

Eligibility Requirements: Applicant must be of Greek heritage; enrolled or expecting to enroll full-time at a four-year institution or university and resident of New Jersey, Pennsylvania. Available to U.S. citizens.

Application Requirements: Application form, financial need analysis, transcript. *Deadline:* April 21.

Contact: Anna Hadgis, Scholarship Chairman
Phone: 610-613-4310
E-mail: www.hucphiladelphia.org

HISPANIC DENTAL ASSOCIATION FOUNDATION

http://www.hdassoc.org/

DR. JUAN D. VILLARREAL/HISPANIC DENTAL ASSOCIATION FOUNDATION

Scholarship offered to Hispanic U.S. students who have been accepted into or are currently enrolled in an accredited dental or dental hygiene program in the state of Texas. Scholarship will obligate the grantees to complete the current year of their dental or dental hygiene program. Scholastic achievement, leadership skills, community service and commitment to improving the health of the Hispanic community will all be considered. Must be a current member of the Hispanic Dental Association.

Academic Fields/Career Goals: Dental Health/Services.

Award: Scholarship for use in freshman, sophomore, junior, or senior years; not renewable. *Number:* up to 3. *Amount:* $500–$1000.

Eligibility Requirements: Applicant must be of Hispanic heritage; enrolled or expecting to enroll full-time at a two-year or four-year institution or university; resident of Texas and studying in Texas. Available to U.S. citizens.

Application Requirements: Application form, essay, recommendations or references, transcript. *Deadline:* June 1.

Contact: David Pena, Executive Director
Hispanic Dental Association Foundation
1111 14th Street
Suite 1100
Washington, DC 20005
Phone: 202-629-3726
E-mail: dpena@hdassoc.org

PROCTOR AND GAMBLE ORAL CARE AND HDA FOUNDATION SCHOLARSHIP

Scholarships available to Hispanic students entering into their first year of an accredited dental, dental hygiene, dental assisting, or dental technician program. Scholastic achievement, community service, leadership, and commitment to improving health of the Hispanic community will all be considered. Must be member of the Hispanic Dental Association.

Academic Fields/Career Goals: Dental Health/Services.

Award: Scholarship for use in freshman year; not renewable. *Number:* up to 15. *Amount:* up to $1000.

Eligibility Requirements: Applicant must be high school student and planning to enroll or expecting to enroll full-time at a two-year or four-year or technical institution or university. Available to U.S. citizens.

Application Requirements: Application form, community service, essay, recommendations or references, transcript. *Deadline:* June 1.

Contact: David Pena, Executive Director
Hispanic Dental Association Foundation
1111 14th Street
Suite 1100
Washington, DC 20005
Phone: 202-629-6108
E-mail: dpena@hdassoc.org

INTERMOUNTAIN MEDICAL IMAGING

https://www.aboutimi.com/

INTERMOUNTAIN MEDICAL IMAGING SCHOLARSHIP
• See page 147

INTERNATIONAL ORDER OF THE KING'S DAUGHTERS AND SONS

http://www.iokds.org/

HEALTH CAREERS SCHOLARSHIP

Award for students preparing for careers in medicine, dentistry, pharmacy, physical or occupational therapy, and medical technologies. Must be a U.S. or Canadian citizen, enrolled full-time in a school accredited in the field involved and located in the U.S. or Canada. For all students, except those preparing for an RN degree, application must be for at least the third year of college. RN students must have completed the first year of schooling. Premedicine students are not eligible to apply. For those students seeking degrees of MD or DDS application must be for at least the second year of medical or dental school. Each applicant must supply proof of acceptance in the school involved.

Academic Fields/Career Goals: Dental Health/Services; Health and Medical Sciences; Nursing; Therapy/Rehabilitation.

Award: Scholarship for use in junior, senior, or graduate years; not renewable. *Number:* 20–30. *Amount:* $500–$1000.

Eligibility Requirements: Applicant must be enrolled or expecting to enroll full-time at a four-year institution or university. Available to U.S. and Canadian citizens.

Application Requirements: Application form, essay, itemized budget, recommendations or references, resume, self-addressed stamped envelope with application, transcript. *Deadline:* April 1.

Contact: Director, Health Careers Department
International Order of The King's Daughters and Sons
PO Box 1017
Chautauqua, NY 14722-1017
Phone: 716-357-4951

LABROOTS INC.

http://www.LabRoots.com

LABROOTS STEM SCHOLARSHIP
• See page 116

LAW OFFICES OF PROSPER SHAKED

https://www.prosperlaw.com/

PROSPER SHAKED SCHOLARSHIP FOR FUTURE MEDICAL PROFESSIONALS
• See page 166

MARYLAND STATE HIGHER EDUCATION COMMISSION

http://www.mhec.state.md.us/

GRADUATE AND PROFESSIONAL SCHOLARSHIP PROGRAM-MARYLAND

Graduate and professional scholarships provide need-based financial assistance to students attending a Maryland school of medicine, dentistry, law, pharmacy, social work, or nursing. Funds are provided to specific Maryland colleges and universities. Students must demonstrate financial need and be Maryland residents. Contact institution financial aid office for more information.

Academic Fields/Career Goals: Dental Health/Services; Health and Medical Sciences; Law/Legal Services; Nursing; Social Services.

Award: Scholarship for use in freshman, sophomore, junior, or senior years; renewable. *Number:* up to 584. *Amount:* $1000–$5000.

Eligibility Requirements: Applicant must be enrolled or expecting to enroll full- or part-time at a four-year institution or university; resident of Maryland and studying in Maryland. Available to U.S. citizens.

Application Requirements: Application form, contact institution financial aid office, financial need analysis. *Deadline:* March 1.

Contact: Monica Wheatley, Program Manager
Maryland State Higher Education Commission
839 Bestgate Road, Suite 400
Annapolis, MD 21401
Phone: 410-260-4560
Fax: 410-260-3202
E-mail: mwheatle@mhec.state.md.us

MEDICAL SCRUBS COLLECTION

http://medicalscrubscollection.com

MEDICAL SCRUBS COLLECTION SCHOLARSHIP
• See page 120

MICHAEL MOODY FITNESS

http://www.michaelmoodyfitness.com/

MICHAEL MOODY FITNESS SCHOLARSHIP
• See page 166

NATIONAL DENTAL ASSOCIATION FOUNDATION

http://www.ndaonline.org/

NATIONAL DENTAL ASSOCIATION FOUNDATION COLGATE-PALMOLIVE SCHOLARSHIP PROGRAM (UNDERGRADUATES)

A scholarship of up to $1000 is given to sophomores through juniors in a dental school who are under-represented minority students. Applicants should be a member of NDA. Number of scholarships granted varies.

Academic Fields/Career Goals: Dental Health/Services.

Award: Scholarship for use in sophomore, junior, or senior years; not renewable. *Number:* up to 100. *Amount:* $700–$1000.

Eligibility Requirements: Applicant must be American Indian/Alaska Native, Asian/Pacific Islander, Black (non-Hispanic), Hispanic and enrolled or expecting to enroll full-time at a four-year institution or university. Available to U.S. citizens.

Application Requirements: Application form, financial need analysis, letter of request, recommendations or references, resume, transcript. *Deadline:* May 15.

Contact: Roosevelt Brown, President
Phone: 501-681-6110
Fax: 541-376-4008
E-mail: rbndaf1@comcast.net

OREGON STUDENT ASSISTANCE COMMISSION

https://oregonstudentaid.gov/

CLARK-PHELPS SCHOLARSHIP

Award for high school graduates who are residents of Oregon or Alaska and are studying nursing (undergraduate or graduate), dentistry, or medicine. Must be enrolled in a public institution in Oregon, with preference for Oregon Health and Science University, and working toward a 4-year degree or graduate degree. Must reapply annually for award renewal. Based on financial need.

Academic Fields/Career Goals: Dental Health/Services; Health and Medical Sciences; Nursing.

Award: Scholarship for use in freshman, sophomore, junior, senior, or graduate years; not renewable.

Eligibility Requirements: Applicant must be enrolled or expecting to enroll full-time at a four-year institution or university; resident of Alaska, Oregon and studying in Oregon. Available to U.S. citizens.

Application Requirements: Application form, essay, financial need analysis. *Deadline:* March 1.

Contact: Melissa Adams, Scholarship Processing Coordinator
Phone: 541-687-7409
E-mail: melissa.adams@state.or.us

PLATINUM EDUCATIONAL GROUP

http://www.platinumed.com

PLATINUM EDUCATIONAL GROUP SCHOLARSHIPS PROGRAM FOR EMS, NURSING, AND ALLIED HEALTH
• See page 117

THE RECOVERY VILLAGE

https://www.therecoveryvillage.com/

RECOVERY VILLAGE HEALTHCARE SCHOLARSHIP

A $500 award will be given to a student pursuing a health-related degree program. Areas of study that will be considered include, but are not limited to, counseling, social work, emergency medicine, pre-med, nursing, psychology (with a focus on addiction counseling or a substance-abuse related field). In order to be eligible, students must meet the following criteria: U.S. citizen or permanent U.S. resident; enrolled or accepted in an accredited college or university and plan to continue enrollment; graduating high school seniors who meet the above criteria are encouraged to apply; consent to a talent release, and will provide a digital photograph and quote for display on ARS websites if notified as the winner. Selection will be based upon completed of application, originality (20%), creativity (20%), writing skills (20%), inspiration (20%), and demonstrated interest in addiction treatment and recovery (20%). The winner will be notified following the deadline and the award will be credited to the student's school. Certain information must be provided by the student to The Recovery Village in order for the school to receive the funds.

Academic Fields/Career Goals: Dental Health/Services; Nursing; Occupational Safety and Health; Psychology; Public Health; Public Policy and Administration; Therapy/Rehabilitation.

Award: Scholarship for use in freshman, sophomore, junior, senior, graduate, or postgraduate years; not renewable. *Number:* 1–2. *Amount:* $1–$1000.

Eligibility Requirements: Applicant must be enrolled or expecting to enroll full- or part-time at a two-year or four-year institution or university. Applicant or parent of applicant must have employment or volunteer experience in occupational health and safety. Available to U.S. citizens.

Application Requirements: Application form, essay. *Deadline:* June 30.

Contact: Amy Campbell
E-mail: amy.campbell@laneterralever.com

SCARLETT FAMILY FOUNDATION SCHOLARSHIP PROGRAM

http://www.scarlettfoundation.org/

SCHOLARSHIP FOR STUDENTS PURSUING A BUSINESS OR STEM DEGREE
• *See page 91*

STANLEY DENTISTRY

http://www.stanleysmiles.com

STANLEY DENTISTRY SCHOLARSHIP FUND

Drs. Robert and Bobbi Stanley have created a merit-based scholarship fund for individuals seeking undergraduate or graduate-level education in dentistry or related fields. The scholarship will be in the amount of $500 for the 2019 academic year. The scholarship will be awarded based on academic excellence, the pursuit of further study in dentistry at an accredited college or university in North Carolina, and genuine passion for further study. The scholarship will last for the duration of one year and be paid directly to the winning candidate to use towards tuition and board.

Academic Fields/Career Goals: Dental Health/Services.

Award: Scholarship for use in freshman, sophomore, junior, senior, graduate, or postgraduate years; not renewable. *Number:* 1. *Amount:* $500.

Eligibility Requirements: Applicant must be enrolled or expecting to enroll full-time at a two-year or four-year institution or university and studying in North Carolina. Available to U.S. citizens.

Application Requirements: Application form. *Deadline:* March 15.

Contact: Catherine Shireman, Scholarship Coordinator
Stanley Dentistry
3731 NW Cary Parkway
Suite 201
Cary, NC 27513
Phone: 919-371-4454
E-mail: catherine@stanleysmiles.com

STRAIGHTFORWARD MEDIA

http://www.straightforwardmedia.com/

STRAIGHTFORWARD MEDIA MEDICAL PROFESSIONS SCHOLARSHIP

Scholarship of $500 available to full-time students in any health-related field. Awarded four times per year. Deadlines: March 31, June 30, September 30, and December 31.

Academic Fields/Career Goals: Dental Health/Services; Environmental Health; Health Administration; Health and Medical Sciences; Health Information Management/Technology; Nursing; Occupational Safety and Health; Oncology; Optometry; Osteopathy; Pharmacy; Therapy/Rehabilitation.

Award: Scholarship for use in freshman, sophomore, junior, or senior years; not renewable. *Number:* 4. *Amount:* $500.

Eligibility Requirements: Applicant must be enrolled or expecting to enroll full- or part-time at a two-year or four-year or technical institution or university. Available to U.S. and non-U.S. citizens.

Application Requirements: Essay. *Deadline:* varies.

Contact: Scholarship Committee
Phone: 605-348-3042

STRAIGHTFORWARD MEDIA VOCATIONAL-TECHNICAL SCHOOL SCHOLARSHIP
• *See page 118*

SUPREME GUARDIAN COUNCIL, INTERNATIONAL ORDER OF JOB'S DAUGHTERS

http://www.iojd.org/

GROTTO SCHOLARSHIP

Scholarships of $1500 to aid Job's Daughters students of outstanding ability whom have a sincerity of purpose. High school seniors, or graduates, junior college, technical school, or college students who are in early graduation programs, and pursuing an education in dentistry, preferably with some training in the handicapped field are eligible to apply.

Academic Fields/Career Goals: Dental Health/Services.

Award: Scholarship for use in freshman, sophomore, junior, senior, graduate, or postgraduate years; not renewable. *Number:* 1. *Amount:* $1500.

Eligibility Requirements: Applicant must be age 18-30; enrolled or expecting to enroll full- or part-time at a two-year or four-year or technical institution or university and single female. Applicant or parent of applicant must be member of Jobs Daughters. Available to U.S. and non-U.S. citizens.

Application Requirements: Application form, community service, essay, recommendations or references, transcript. *Deadline:* April 30.

Contact: Christal Bindrich, Scholarship Committee Chairman
Supreme Guardian Council, International Order of Job's Daughters
5351 South Butterfield Way
Greenfield, WI 53221
Phone: 414-423-0016
E-mail: christalbindrich@wi.rr.com

U.S. DEPARTMENT OF HEALTH AND HUMAN SERVICES

http://www.hhs.gov/

U. S. PUBLIC HEALTH SERVICE-HEALTH RESOURCES AND SERVICES ADMINISTRATION, BUREAU OF HEALTH PROFESSIONS SCHOLARSHIPS FOR DISADVANTAGED STUDENTS

One-time award for full-time students from disadvantaged backgrounds enrolled in health professions and nursing programs. Institution must apply for funding and must be eligible to receive SDS funds. Students must contact financial aid office to apply.

Academic Fields/Career Goals: Dental Health/Services; Health and Medical Sciences; Nursing; Therapy/Rehabilitation.

Award: Scholarship for use in freshman, sophomore, junior, senior, or graduate years; not renewable.

Eligibility Requirements: Applicant must be enrolled or expecting to enroll full-time at a two-year or four-year institution or university. Available to U.S. citizens.

Application Requirements: Application form, financial need analysis. *Deadline:* varies.

Contact: Andrea Stampone, Public Health Analyst
U.S. Department of Health and Human Services
Division of Student Loans and Scholarships
Parklawn Building, Suite 9-105
Rockville, MD 20857
Phone: 301-443-4776
Fax: 301-446-0846
E-mail: callcenter@hrsa.gov

DRAFTING

AMERICAN SOCIETY OF CERTIFIED ENGINEERING TECHNICIANS

http://www.ascet.org/

KURT H. AND DONNA M. SCHULER SMALL GRANT
• *See page 205*

MIDWEST ROOFING CONTRACTORS ASSOCIATION

http://www.mrca.org/

MRCA FOUNDATION SCHOLARSHIP PROGRAM
• *See page 135*

NASA'S VIRGINIA SPACE GRANT CONSORTIUM

http://www.vsgc.odu.edu/

COMMUNITY COLLEGE STEM SCHOLARSHIPS
• *See page 126*

NATIONAL ASSOCIATION OF WOMEN IN CONSTRUCTION

http://www.nawic.org/

NAWIC UNDERGRADUATE SCHOLARSHIPS
• *See page 135*

ONLINE LOGO MAKER

http://onlinelogomaker.com

OLM MALALA YOUSAFZAI SCHOLARSHIP
• *See page 143*

PROFESSIONAL CONSTRUCTION ESTIMATORS ASSOCIATION

http://www.pcea.org/

TED G. WILSON MEMORIAL SCHOLARSHIP FOUNDATION
• *See page 211*

SUPPORT CREATIVITY

http://wesupportcreativity.org

SUPPORT CREATIVITY SCHOLARSHIP
• *See page 137*

VECTORWORKS, INC.

http://www.vectorworks.net

VECTORWORKS DESIGN SCHOLARSHIP
• *See page 137*

EARTH SCIENCE

AEG FOUNDATION

http://www.aegfoundation.org/

AEG FOUNDATION MARLIAVE FUND

One-time award to support undergraduate and graduate students studying engineering geology and geological engineering.

Academic Fields/Career Goals: Earth Science; Engineering/Technology; Science, Technology, and Society.

Award: Scholarship for use in senior or graduate years; not renewable. *Number:* 1. *Amount:* $4000.

Eligibility Requirements: Applicant must be enrolled or expecting to enroll full-time at a four-year institution or university. Available to U.S. and Canadian citizens.

Application Requirements: Application form, application form may be submitted online (http://www.aegfoundation.org), essay, recommendations or references, resume, transcript. *Deadline:* February 1.

Contact: Becky Roland, Executive Director
AEG Foundation
PO Box 460518
Denver, CO 80246
Phone: 303-757-2926
Fax: 720-230-4846
E-mail: staff@aegfoundation.org

TILFORD FIELD STUDIES SCHOLARSHIP

Scholarship of $1000 for student members of AEG. Three to four awards are granted annually. For undergraduate students, the scholarship goes toward the cost of a geology field camp course or senior thesis field research. For graduate students, the scholarship would apply to field research.

Academic Fields/Career Goals: Earth Science.

Award: Scholarship for use in freshman, sophomore, junior, senior, graduate, or postgraduate years; not renewable. *Number:* 4–5. *Amount:* $500–$2500.

Eligibility Requirements: Applicant must be enrolled or expecting to enroll full-time at a four-year institution or university. Applicant or parent of applicant must be member of Association of Engineering Geologists. Available to U.S. and non-U.S. citizens.

Application Requirements: Application form, application form may be submitted online (http://www.aegfoundation.org), essay, recommendations or references, resume, transcript. *Deadline:* February 1.

Contact: Becky Roland, AEG Foundation
AEG Foundation
PO Box 460518
Denver, CO 80246
Phone: 303-757-2926
Fax: 720-230-4846
E-mail: staff@aegfoundation.org

ALASKA GEOLOGICAL SOCIETY INC.

http://www.alaskageology.org/

ALASKA GEOLOGICAL SOCIETY SCHOLARSHIP

Scholarship available for a full-time junior or senior undergraduate or graduate student enrolled at any college or university with academic emphasis in earth sciences. Student must have a project based in Alaska or on a topic directly related to Alaskan geology.

Academic Fields/Career Goals: Earth Science.

Award: Scholarship for use in junior, senior, or graduate years; not renewable. *Number:* 3–8. *Amount:* $500–$2500.

Eligibility Requirements: Applicant must be enrolled or expecting to enroll full-time at a four-year institution or university and studying in Alaska. Available to U.S. and non-U.S. citizens.

Application Requirements: Application form, essay. *Deadline:* February 1.

Contact: Susan Karl, Chair of Scholarship Committee
Alaska Geological Society Inc.
Alaska Geological Society
PO Box 101288
Anchorage, AK 99510
Phone: 907-786-7428
E-mail: skarl@usgs.gov

AMERICAN GROUND WATER TRUST

http://www.agwt.org/

AMERICAN GROUND WATER TRUST-AMTROL INC. SCHOLARSHIP

Award for college/university entry-level students intending to pursue a career in ground water-related field. Must either have completed a science/environmental project involving ground water resources or have had vacation work experience related to the environment and natural resources. Must be U.S. citizen or legal resident with minimum 3.0 GPA. Submit two letters of recommendation and transcript.

Academic Fields/Career Goals: Earth Science; Hydrology; Natural Resources.

Award: Scholarship for use in freshman year; not renewable. *Number:* 2. *Amount:* $1500.

Eligibility Requirements: Applicant must be enrolled or expecting to enroll full-time at a four-year institution or university. Applicant must have 3.0 GPA or higher. Available to U.S. citizens.

Application Requirements: Application form, essay. *Deadline:* June 1.

Contact: Andrew Stone, Executive Director
American Ground Water Trust
50 Pleasant Street, Suite 2
Concord, NH 03301-4073
Phone: 603-228-5444
E-mail: trustinfo@agwt.org

AMERICAN GROUND WATER TRUST-BAROID SCHOLARSHIP

Award for entry-level students intending to pursue a career in ground water-related field. Must either have completed a science/environmental project involving ground water resources or have had vacation work experience related to the environment and natural resources. Must be a U.S. citizen or legal resident with minimum 3.0 GPA. Submit two letters of recommendation and transcript.

Academic Fields/Career Goals: Earth Science; Hydrology; Natural Resources.

Award: Scholarship for use in freshman year; not renewable. *Number:* 1. *Amount:* $2000.

Eligibility Requirements: Applicant must be enrolled or expecting to enroll full-time at a four-year institution or university. Applicant must have 3.0 GPA or higher. Available to U.S. citizens.

Application Requirements: Application form, essay. *Deadline:* June 1.

Contact: Andrew Stone, Executive Director
American Ground Water Trust
50 Pleasant Street, Suite 2
Concord, NH 03301-4073
Phone: 603-228-5444
E-mail: trustinfo@agwt.org

AMERICAN GROUND WATER TRUST-THOMAS STETSON SCHOLARSHIP

For students entering their freshman year in a full-time program of study at a four-year accredited university or college located west of the Mississippi River and intending to pursue a career in ground water-related field. Must be U.S. citizen or legal resident with 3.0 GPA or higher. For more information see website http://www.agwt.org.

Academic Fields/Career Goals: Earth Science; Hydrology; Natural Resources.

Award: Scholarship for use in freshman year; not renewable. *Number:* 1. *Amount:* $2000.

Eligibility Requirements: Applicant must be enrolled or expecting to enroll full-time at a four-year institution or university. Applicant must have 3.0 GPA or higher. Available to U.S. citizens.

Application Requirements: Application form, essay. *Deadline:* June 1.

Contact: Andrew Stone, Executive Director
American Ground Water Trust
50 Pleasant Street, Suite 2
Concord, NH 03301-4073
Phone: 603-228-5444
E-mail: trustinfo@agwt.org

AMERICAN INDIAN SCIENCE AND ENGINEERING SOCIETY

http://www.aises.org/

A.T. ANDERSON MEMORIAL SCHOLARSHIP PROGRAM
• See page 121

AMERICAN SOCIETY OF AGRONOMY, CROP SCIENCE SOCIETY OF AMERICA, SOIL SCIENCE SOCIETY OF AMERICA

http://www.agronomy.org

J. FIELDING REED SCHOLARSHIP
• See page 106

ARIZONA HYDROLOGICAL SOCIETY

http://www.azhydrosoc.org/

ARIZONA HYDROLOGICAL SOCIETY SCHOLARSHIP

One-time award to outstanding upper-level undergraduate or graduate students who have demonstrated academic excellence in water resources related fields as a means of encouraging them to continue to develop as water resources professionals. Must be a resident of Arizona and be enrolled in a postsecondary Arizona institution.

Academic Fields/Career Goals: Earth Science; Hydrology; Natural Resources; Nuclear Science; Science, Technology, and Society.

Award: Scholarship for use in junior, senior, or graduate years; not renewable. *Number:* 3. *Amount:* $2000.

Eligibility Requirements: Applicant must be enrolled or expecting to enroll full-time at a two-year or four-year or technical institution or university; resident of Arizona and studying in Arizona. Available to U.S. citizens.

Application Requirements: Application form, essay, financial need analysis, recommendations or references, transcript. *Deadline:* April 30.

Contact: Aregai Tecle, Professor
Phone: 928-523-6642
Fax: 928-556-7112
E-mail: aregai.tecle@nau.edu

ARRL FOUNDATION INC.

http://www.arrl.org/

OLD MAN INTERNATIONAL SIDEBAND SOCIETY (OMISS) SCHOLARSHIP

One $1000 award for a student with an active general class amateur radio license studying science, math, engineering, or a technology-related field at an accredited 4-year college or university. Special consideration given to adult applicants beginning or returning to school. Preference is also given to prior year's recipient if he/she reapplies and continues to meet eligibility requirements. Recipient must provide OMISS members with a brief report of his/her educational studies and amateur radio activities at end of school year.

Academic Fields/Career Goals: Earth Science; Engineering/Technology; Environmental Science; Health and Medical Sciences; Materials Science, Engineering, and Metallurgy; Mathematics; Meteorology/Atmospheric Science; Natural Sciences; Nuclear Science; Physical Sciences.

Award: Scholarship for use in freshman, sophomore, junior, or senior years; not renewable. *Number:* 1. *Amount:* $1000.

Eligibility Requirements: Applicant must be enrolled or expecting to enroll full- or part-time at a four-year institution or university and must have an interest in amateur radio. Available to U.S. citizens.

Application Requirements: Application form. *Deadline:* January 31.

Contact: Ms. Mary Hobart, Secretary
Phone: 860-594-0397
E-mail: k1mmh@arrl.org

ASSOCIATION FOR WOMEN GEOSCIENTISTS (AWG)

http://www.awg.org/

AWG ETHNIC MINORITY SCHOLARSHIP

The Minority Scholarship encourages young women of a minority background, or heritage, to pursue a major and career in the geosciences. The scholarship provides financial support for college expenses and matches the student with a mentor who has a career similar to that desired by the awardee.

Academic Fields/Career Goals: Earth Science; Education; Environmental Science; Gemology; Geography; Hydrology; Meteorology/Atmospheric Science; Museum Studies; Natural Resources; Natural Sciences; Oceanography; Physical Sciences.

Award: Scholarship for use in freshman, sophomore, junior, or senior years; not renewable. *Number:* 1–5. *Amount:* $500–$3000.

Eligibility Requirements: Applicant must be American Indian/Alaska Native, Black (non-Hispanic), Hispanic; enrolled or expecting to enroll full- or part-time at a four-year institution or university and female. Available to U.S. citizens.

Application Requirements: Application form, community service, recommendations or references, statement of academic or career goals, test scores, transcript. *Deadline:* June 30.

Contact: Christina Tapia, Ethnic Minority Scholarship Coordinator

AWG MARIA LUISA CRAWFORD FIELD CAMP SCHOLARSHIP

• *See page 129*

AWG SALT LAKE CHAPTER (SLC) RESEARCH SCHOLARSHIP

• *See page 129*

AWG UNDERGRADUATE EXCELLENCE IN PALEONTOLOGY AWARD

• *See page 123*

JANET CULLEN TANAKA GEOSCIENCES UNDERGRADUATE SCHOLARSHIP

• *See page 129*

LONE STAR RISING CAREER SCHOLARSHIP

The Lone Star Rising Career Scholarship provides professional development funding for women geoscience professionals seeking to resume their geoscience careers after having been out of the work force, or women geoscience students seeking to enter the workforce in a geoscience-related field within the next two years.

Academic Fields/Career Goals: Earth Science; Education; Environmental Science; Gemology; Hydrology; Meteorology/Atmospheric Science; Museum Studies; Natural Resources;
Natural Sciences; Oceanography; Physical Sciences; Science, Technology, and Society.

Award: Scholarship for use in freshman, sophomore, junior, senior, graduate, or postgraduate years; not renewable. *Number:* 1–2. *Amount:* $1–$3000.

Eligibility Requirements: Applicant must be enrolled or expecting to enroll full- or part-time at a two-year or four-year institution or university and single female. Applicant or parent of applicant must have employment or volunteer experience in physical or natural sciences. Available to U.S. citizens.

Application Requirements: Application form, financial need analysis, recommendations or references. *Deadline:* October 31.

Contact: AWG Lone Star Rising Career Scholarship Coordinator
Association for Women Geoscientists (AWG)
AWG Lone Star Chapter
PO Box 542042
Houston, TX 77254
E-mail: awglonestar@gmail.com

OSAGE CHAPTER UNDERGRADUATE SERVICE SCHOLARSHIP

• *See page 129*

SUSAN EKDALE MEMORIAL FIELD CAMP SCHOLARSHIP

The scholarship will be awarded to a female student in the geosciences to help defray field camp expenses. Applicant must be attending a Utah institution of higher learning, or be a Utah resident attending college elsewhere.

Academic Fields/Career Goals: Earth Science; Environmental Science; Hydrology; Meteorology/Atmospheric Science; Museum Studies; Natural Resources; Natural Sciences; Oceanography; Physical Sciences.

Award: Scholarship for use in freshman, sophomore, junior, senior, or graduate years; not renewable. *Amount:* $1000–$2000.

Eligibility Requirements: Applicant must be enrolled or expecting to enroll full- or part-time at a four-year institution or university; female; resident of Utah and studying in Utah. Available to U.S. citizens.

Application Requirements: Application form, essay, letter of eligibility from the department verifying field of study, recommendations or references. *Deadline:* March 12.

Contact: Janae Wallace, Ekdale Scholarship Committee Chair
Association for Women Geoscientists (AWG)
AWG Salt Lake Chapter
PO Box 58691
Salt Lake City, UT 84158-0691
Phone: 801-537-3387
E-mail: janaewallace@utah.gov

ASSOCIATION OF STATE DAM SAFETY OFFICIALS (ASDSO)

http://www.DamSafety.org

ASSOCIATION OF STATE DAM SAFETY OFFICIALS (ASDSO) SENIOR UNDERGRADUATE SCHOLARSHIP

• *See page 168*

ASSOCIATION ON AMERICAN INDIAN AFFAIRS, INC.

http://www.indian-affairs.org/

ELIZABETH AND SHERMAN ASCHE MEMORIAL SCHOLARSHIP FUND

• *See page 106*

ASTRONAUT SCHOLARSHIP FOUNDATION

http://www.astronautscholarship.org/

ASTRONAUT SCHOLARSHIP FOUNDATION

• *See page 123*

BARRY GOLDWATER SCHOLARSHIP AND EXCELLENCE IN EDUCATION FOUNDATION

https://goldwater.scholarsapply.org

BARRY M. GOLDWATER SCHOLARSHIP AND EXCELLENCE IN EDUCATION PROGRAM
• *See page 123*

BHW GROUP

https://thebhwgroup.com/

BHW WOMEN IN STEM SCHOLARSHIP
• *See page 124*

B.O.G. PEST CONTROL

http://www.bogpestcontrol.com/

B.O.G. PEST CONTROL SCHOLARSHIP FUND
• *See page 169*

BROWN AND CALDWELL

http://www.brownandcaldwell.com

ECKENFELDER SCHOLARSHIP
• *See page 169*

MINORITY SCHOLARSHIP PROGRAM
• *See page 169*

CALAVERAS BIG TREES ASSOCIATION

https://bigtrees.org/

EMILY M. HEWITT MEMORIAL SCHOLARSHIP
• *See page 170*

CARDS AGAINST HUMANITY

https://cardsagainsthumanity.com/

SCIENCE AMBASSADOR SCHOLARSHIP
• *See page 124*

DIVERSITYCOMM, INC.

http://www.diversitycomm.net/

DIVERSITY IN STEAM MAGAZINE SCHOLARSHIP
• *See page 83*

GARDEN CLUB OF AMERICA

http://www.gcamerica.org/

ELIZABETH GARDNER NORWEB SUMMER ENVIRONMENTAL STUDIES SCHOLARSHIP
• *See page 107*

GREAT MINDS IN STEM

http://www.greatmindsinstem.org

HENAAC SCHOLARSHIP PROGRAM
• *See page 115*

INDEPENDENT LABORATORIES INSTITUTE SCHOLARSHIP ALLIANCE

http://www.acil.org/

INDEPENDENT LABORATORIES INSTITUTE SCHOLARSHIP ALLIANCE
• *See page 171*

KENTUCKY ENERGY AND ENVIRONMENT CABINET

http://dep.ky.gov

ENVIRONMENTAL PROTECTION SCHOLARSHIP
• *See page 172*

LABROOTS INC.

http://www.LabRoots.com

LABROOTS STEM SCHOLARSHIP
• *See page 116*

THE LAND CONSERVANCY OF NEW JERSEY

http://www.tlc-nj.org/

ROGERS FAMILY SCHOLARSHIP
• *See page 172*

RUSSELL W. MYERS SCHOLARSHIP
• *See page 172*

MEDICAL SCRUBS COLLECTION

http://medicalscrubscollection.com

MEDICAL SCRUBS COLLECTION SCHOLARSHIP
• *See page 120*

MONTANA FEDERATION OF GARDEN CLUBS

http://www.mtfgc.org/

LIFE MEMBER MONTANA FEDERATION OF GARDEN CLUBS SCHOLARSHIP

Applicant must be at least a sophomore, majoring in conservation, horticulture, park or forestry, floriculture, greenhouse management, land management, or related subjects. Must be in need of assistance. Must have a potential for a successful future. Must be ranked in upper half of class or have a minimum 2.7 GPA. Must be a Montana resident and all study must be done in Montana.

Academic Fields/Career Goals: Earth Science; Horticulture/Floriculture; Landscape Architecture; Natural Resources.

Award: Scholarship for use in sophomore, junior, or senior years; not renewable. *Number:* 1. *Amount:* $1000.

Eligibility Requirements: Applicant must be enrolled or expecting to enroll full-time at a four-year institution or university; resident of Montana and studying in Montana. Applicant must have 2.5 GPA or higher. Available to U.S. citizens.

Application Requirements: Driver's license, recommendations or references, transcript. *Deadline:* May 1.

Contact: Joyce Backa, Life Members Scholarship Chairman
Montana Federation of Garden Clubs
513 Skyline Drive
Craig, MT 59404-8712
Phone: 406-235-4229
E-mail: rjback@bresnan.net

NASA FLORIDA SPACE GRANT CONSORTIUM

http://www.floridaspacegrant.org/

FLORIDA SPACE RESEARCH PROGRAM
• *See page 156*

NASA IDAHO SPACE GRANT CONSORTIUM

http://www.idahospacegrant.org

NASA IDAHO SPACE GRANT CONSORTIUM SCHOLARSHIP PROGRAM
• *See page 126*

NASA/MARYLAND SPACE GRANT CONSORTIUM

http://www.mdspacegrant.org/

NASA MARYLAND SPACE GRANT CONSORTIUM UNDERGRADUATE SCHOLARSHIPS
• *See page 156*

NASA MINNESOTA SPACE GRANT CONSORTIUM

https://www.mnspacegrant.org/

MINNESOTA SPACE GRANT CONSORTIUM SCHOLARSHIP PROGRAM
• *See page 156*

NATIONAL ASSOCIATION OF GEOSCIENCE TEACHERS & FAR WESTERN SECTION

http://www.nagt-fws.org

NATIONAL ASSOCIATION OF GEOSCIENCE TEACHERS-FAR WESTERN SECTION SCHOLARSHIP
Academically superior students currently enrolled in school in Hawaii, Nevada, or California are eligible to apply for one of three $500 scholarships to the school of their choice. Must be a high school senior or community college student enrolling full-time (12 quarter units) in a Bachelor's degree program in geology at a four-year institution or an undergraduate geology major enrolling in an upper division field geology course of approximately 30 field mapping days.

Academic Fields/Career Goals: Earth Science.

Award: Scholarship for use in sophomore, junior, or senior years; not renewable. *Number:* 3. *Amount:* $500.

Eligibility Requirements: Applicant must be enrolled or expecting to enroll full- or part-time at a four-year institution or university and studying in California, Hawaii, Nevada. Available to U.S. citizens.

Application Requirements: Application form, endorsement signature of a regular member of NAGT-FWS in the reference letter, recommendations or references, transcript. *Deadline:* April 1.

Contact: Mike Martin, Geology Scholarship Coordinator
Phone: 951-789-5690
E-mail: mmartin@rusd.k12.ca.us

NATIONAL GARDEN CLUBS INC.

http://www.gardenclub.org/

NATIONAL GARDEN CLUBS INC. SCHOLARSHIP PROGRAM
• *See page 109*

NEVADA NASA SPACE GRANT CONSORTIUM

https://nasa.epscorspo.nevada.edu/

NATIONAL SPACE GRANT CONSORTIUM SCHOLARSHIPS
• *See page 127*

NEXTSTEPU

http://www.nextstepu.com/

$1,500 STEM SCHOLARSHIP
• *See page 120*

NGWA FOUNDATION

http://www.ngwa.org/Foundation/Pages/default.aspx

NGWA FOUNDATION'S LEN ASSANTE SCHOLARSHIP
Applicant must be in a field of study that serves, supports, or promotes the groundwater industry. Qualifying majors: geology, hydrology, hydrogeology, environmental sciences, microbiology, and well-drilling two-year associate degree programs. Minimum 2.5 GPA required.

Academic Fields/Career Goals: Earth Science; Environmental Science; Hydrology.

Award: Scholarship for use in freshman, sophomore, junior, senior, graduate, or postgraduate years; not renewable. *Number:* 1–10. *Amount:* $1000–$5000.

Eligibility Requirements: Applicant must be enrolled or expecting to enroll full-time at a two-year or four-year or technical institution or university. Applicant must have 2.5 GPA or higher. Available to U.S. and non-U.S. citizens.

Application Requirements: Application form, essay, personal photograph. *Deadline:* February 15.

Contact: Foundation Administrator
NGWA Foundation
601 Dempsey Road
Westerville, OH 43081
Phone: 614-898-7791 Ext. 1504
E-mail: foundation@ngwa.org

OREGON STUDENT ASSISTANCE COMMISSION

https://oregonstudentaid.gov/

ANDY AITKENHEAD SCHOLARSHIP
• *See page 127*

SEHAR SALEHA AHMAD AND ABRAHIM EKRAMULLAH ZAFAR FOUNDATION SCHOLARSHIP
• *See page 127*

ROCKY MOUNTAIN COAL MINING INSTITUTE

http://www.rmcmi.org/

ROCKY MOUNTAIN COAL MINING INSTITUTE SCHOLARSHIP
• *See page 211*

SCARLETT FAMILY FOUNDATION SCHOLARSHIP PROGRAM

http://www.scarlettfoundation.org/

SCHOLARSHIP FOR STUDENTS PURSUING A BUSINESS OR STEM DEGREE
• *See page 91*

SIGMA XI, THE SCIENTIFIC RESEARCH SOCIETY

http://www.sigmaxi.org/

SIGMA XI GRANTS-IN-AID OF RESEARCH
• *See page 110*

SOIL AND WATER CONSERVATION SOCIETY

http://www.swcs.org

DONALD A. WILLIAMS SCHOLARSHIP SOIL CONSERVATION SCHOLARSHIP
• *See page 103*

SOIL AND WATER CONSERVATION SOCIETY-MISSOURI SHOW-ME CHAPTER

http://www.moswcs.org/

MO SHOW-ME CHAPTER SWCS SCHOLARSHIP
• *See page 111*

SOIL AND WATER CONSERVATION SOCIETY-NEW JERSEY CHAPTER

http://www.geocities.com/njswcs

EDWARD R. HALL SCHOLARSHIP
• *See page 103*

STRAIGHT NORTH

https://www.straightnorth.com/

STRAIGHT NORTH STEM SCHOLARSHIP
• *See page 92*

TKE EDUCATIONAL FOUNDATION

http://www.tke.org/

CARROL C. HALL MEMORIAL SCHOLARSHIP
• *See page 128*

ERIC D. DUNNING SCHOLARSHIP
• *See page 235*

UNICO FOUNDATION INC.

http://www.unico.org/

LOUISE TORRACO MEMORIAL SCHOLARSHIP FOR SCIENCE
• *See page 174*

UNIVERSITIES SPACE RESEARCH ASSOCIATION

http://www.usra.edu/

UNIVERSITIES SPACE RESEARCH ASSOCIATION SCHOLARSHIP AWARD PROGRAM
• *See page 128*

VERMONT SPACE GRANT CONSORTIUM

http://www.cems.uvm.edu/vsgc

VERMONT SPACE GRANT CONSORTIUM
• *See page 104*

VISIONARY INTEGRATION PROFESSIONALS (VIP)

http://www.trustvip.com/

WOMEN IN TECHNOLOGY SCHOLARSHIP (WITS)
• *See page 236*

ECONOMICS

280 GROUP

https://280group.com/contact/280-group-product-management-scholarship/

280 GROUP PRODUCT MANAGEMENT SCHOLARSHIP

The 280 Group is a strategic consulting partner to any business that needs a proven methodology to optimize Product Management and Product Marketing functions in their company. We're excited to be offering three $500 scholarships to students pursuing a Bachelor's or Master's degree in business, economics or a related field. Students who receive the scholarships will also get full access to the Certified Product Manager® Online Course and Exam. This course is valued at $1,495 and will teach students the core skills to be a Product Manager and allow them to earn the prestigious AIPMM (Association of International Product Management and Marketing) Certified Product Manager® credential.

Academic Fields/Career Goals: Economics; Marketing.

Award: Scholarship for use in freshman, sophomore, junior, senior, or graduate years; renewable. *Number:* 3. *Amount:* $500.

Eligibility Requirements: Applicant must be enrolled or expecting to enroll full- or part-time at a four-year institution or university. Applicant must have 2.5 GPA or higher. Available to U.S. and non-U.S. citizens.

Application Requirements: Application form, essay. *Deadline:* November 15.

Contact: Ms. Mira Wooten, Director of Solutions
280 Group
142B Santa Cruz Ave
Los Gatos, CA 95030
Phone: 831-419-3502
E-mail: mira@280group.com

THE ACTUARIAL FOUNDATION

http://www.actuarialfoundation.org

ACTUARY OF TOMORROW—STUART A. ROBERTSON MEMORIAL SCHOLARSHIP
• *See page 175*

CURTIS E. HUNTINGTON MEMORIAL SCHOLARSHIP (FORMERLY THE JOHN CULVER WOODDY SCHOLARSHIP)

The Curtis E. Huntington Memorial Scholarship (formerly the John Culver Wooddy Scholarship) is awarded annually to college seniors who have successfully completed at least one actuarial examination, rank in the top quartile of their class and are nominated by a professor at their school.

Academic Fields/Career Goals: Economics; Finance; Insurance and Actuarial Science; Mathematics; Statistics.

Award: Scholarship for use in senior year; not renewable. *Amount:* $2000.

Eligibility Requirements: Applicant must be enrolled or expecting to enroll full-time at a four-year institution or university. Applicant must have 2.5 GPA or higher. Available to U.S. and non-U.S. citizens.

Application Requirements: Application form, essay. *Deadline:* June 16.

Contact: Curtis E. Huntington Memorial Scholarship
The Actuarial Foundation
475 North Martingale Road, Suite 600
Schaumburg, IL 60173
Phone: 847-706-3535
E-mail: scholarships@actfnd.org

AUTOMOTIVE WOMEN'S ALLIANCE FOUNDATION

http://awafoundation.org/index.php

AUTOMOTIVE WOMEN'S ALLIANCE FOUNDATION SCHOLARSHIPS
• *See page 81*

CATCHING THE DREAM

http://www.catchingthedream.org/

TRIBAL BUSINESS MANAGEMENT PROGRAM (TBM)
• *See page 82*

DISTIL NETWORKS

http://www.distilnetworks.com

WOMEN FORWARD IN TECHNOLOGY SCHOLARSHIP PROGRAM
• *See page 124*

DIVERSITYCOMM, INC.

http://www.diversitycomm.net/

DIVERSITY IN STEAM MAGAZINE SCHOLARSHIP
• *See page 83*

FUKUNAGA SCHOLARSHIP FOUNDATION

http://fukunagascholarship.com

FUKUNAGA SCHOLARSHIP FOUNDATION
• *See page 85*

GOVERNMENT FINANCE OFFICERS ASSOCIATION

http://www.gfoa.org/

MINORITIES IN GOVERNMENT FINANCE SCHOLARSHIP
• *See page 86*

HOUSE OF BLUES MUSIC FORWARD FOUNDATION

https://hobmusicforward.org/

STEVEN J. FINKEL SERVICE EXCELLENCE SCHOLARSHIP
• *See page 180*

TIFFANY GREEN OPERATOR SCHOLARSHIP AWARD
• *See page 96*

INSTITUTE FOR HUMANE STUDIES

http://www.theihs.org/

HUMANE STUDIES FELLOWSHIPS
• *See page 219*

JORGE MAS CANOSA FREEDOM FOUNDATION

http://masscholarships.org/

MAS FAMILY SCHOLARSHIP AWARD
• *See page 181*

NATIONAL ASSOCIATION OF NEGRO BUSINESS AND PROFESSIONAL WOMEN'S CLUBS INC.

http://www.nanbpwc.org/

JULIANNE MALVEAUX SCHOLARSHIP

Scholarship for African-American women who are college sophomores or juniors enrolled in an accredited college or university. Applicants must be majoring in journalism, economics, or a related field. Minimum 3.0 GPA required. Must be a U.S. citizen.

Academic Fields/Career Goals: Economics; Journalism.

Award: Scholarship for use in sophomore or junior years; not renewable. *Number:* 1. *Amount:* $1000.

Eligibility Requirements: Applicant must be Black (non-Hispanic); enrolled or expecting to enroll full-time at a four-year institution or university and female. Applicant must have 3.0 GPA or higher. Available to U.S. citizens.

Application Requirements: Application form, essay, recommendations or references, transcript. *Deadline:* April 30.

Contact: Scholarship Program Director
National Association of Negro Business and Professional
Women's Clubs Inc.
1806 New Hampshire Avenue, NW
Washington, DC 20009-3298
Phone: 202-483-4206
E-mail: info@nanbpwc.org

NATIONAL SECURITY EDUCATION PROGRAM

http://www.iie.org/

NATIONAL SECURITY EDUCATION PROGRAM (NSEP) DAVID L. BOREN UNDERGRADUATE SCHOLARSHIPS
• *See page 139*

NATIONAL SOCIETY DAUGHTERS OF THE AMERICAN REVOLUTION

http://www.dar.org/

NATIONAL SOCIETY DAUGHTERS OF THE AMERICAN REVOLUTION ENID HALL GRISWOLD MEMORIAL SCHOLARSHIP

Scholarship of $1000 awarded to a deserving junior or senior enrolled in an accredited college or university in the United States who is majoring in political science, history, government, or economics.

Academic Fields/Career Goals: Economics; History; Political Science.

Award: Scholarship for use in junior or senior years; not renewable. *Number:* 2. *Amount:* $5000.

Eligibility Requirements: Applicant must be enrolled or expecting to enroll full-time at a four-year institution or university. Available to U.S. citizens.

Application Requirements: Application form, essay, financial need analysis. *Deadline:* February 10.

Contact: Lakeisha Graham, Manager, Office of the Reporter General
Phone: 202-628-1776
Fax: 202-879-3348
E-mail: nsdarscholarships@dar.org

NEW ENGLAND EMPLOYEE BENEFITS COUNCIL

http://www.neebc.org/

NEW ENGLAND EMPLOYEE BENEFITS COUNCIL SCHOLARSHIP PROGRAM
• *See page 89*

OFFICE AND PROFESSIONAL EMPLOYEES INTERNATIONAL UNION

http://www.opeiu.org/

JOHN KELLY LABOR STUDIES SCHOLARSHIP FUND
Scholarship of up to $3000 given to graduate or undergraduate students who have labor studies, social sciences, industrial relation as their major. Ten scholarships are granted. Applicants should be a member or associate member of the union.

Academic Fields/Career Goals: Economics; Social Sciences.

Award: Scholarship for use in freshman, sophomore, junior, senior, or graduate years; not renewable. *Number:* 10. *Amount:* up to $3000.

Eligibility Requirements: Applicant must be enrolled or expecting to enroll full-time at a four-year institution or university. Available to U.S. citizens.

Application Requirements: Application form, essay, transcript. *Deadline:* March 31.

Contact: Mary Mahoney, Secretary-Treasurer
Phone: 202-393-4464
Fax: 202-887-0910
E-mail: mmahoney@opeiudc.org

SCARLETT FAMILY FOUNDATION SCHOLARSHIP PROGRAM

http://www.scarlettfoundation.org/

SCHOLARSHIP FOR STUDENTS PURSUING A BUSINESS OR STEM DEGREE
• *See page 91*

SOCIETY OF AUTOMOTIVE ANALYSTS

http://saaauto.com/

SOCIETY OF AUTOMOTIVE ANALYSTS SCHOLARSHIP
• *See page 91*

STRAIGHTFORWARD MEDIA

http://www.straightforwardmedia.com/

STRAIGHTFORWARD MEDIA BUSINESS SCHOOL SCHOLARSHIP
• *See page 99*

STRAIGHTFORWARD MEDIA LIBERAL ARTS SCHOLARSHIP
• *See page 139*

TRANSPORTATION ASSOCIATION OF CANADA FOUNDATION

http://www.tac-foundation.ca

TAC FOUNDATION SCHOLARSHIPS
• *See page 213*

UNITED NEGRO COLLEGE FUND

http://www.uncf.org/

DISCOVER FINANCIAL SERVICES SCHOLARSHIP
• *See page 93*

MUFG UNION BANK SCHOLARSHIP PROGRAM
• *See page 93*

UBS/PAINEWEBBER SCHOLARSHIP
• *See page 94*

UNCF/KOCH SCHOLARS PROGRAM FOR UNDERGRADUATES
• *See page 94*

WILLIAM WRIGLEY FOUNDATION SCHOLARSHIP
• *See page 95*

EDUCATION

ALBERTA HERITAGE SCHOLARSHIP FUND

http://www.alis.alberta.ca/

ANNA AND JOHN KOLESAR MEMORIAL SCHOLARSHIPS
Award of CAN$1500 to recognize and reward the academic excellence of a high school student entering a Faculty of Education. Must be resident of Alberta and plan to enroll full-time in the first year of an education program. Must be from a family where neither parent obtained a university degree. Selection based on the highest average obtained on three grade 12 subjects. Must be a Canadian citizen or permanent resident. For additional information and application, visit website http://alis.alberta.ca.

Academic Fields/Career Goals: Education; Special Education.

Award: Scholarship for use in freshman year; not renewable. *Number:* 1.

Eligibility Requirements: Applicant must be Canadian citizen; high school student; planning to enroll or expecting to enroll full-time at a two-year or four-year institution or university and resident of Alberta. Applicant must have 3.0 GPA or higher.

Application Requirements: Application form, test scores, transcript. *Deadline:* July 1.

Contact: Scholarship Committee
Phone: 780-427-8640
E-mail: scholarships@gov.ab.ca

LANGUAGES IN TEACHER EDUCATION SCHOLARSHIPS
One-time awards of CAN$2500 to Alberta students enrolled full-time in the final two years of a recognized teacher preparation program in Alberta, taking courses that will allow them to teach languages other than English in Alberta schools. Must be Canadian citizen or permanent resident and a resident of Alberta. Must intend to teach in Alberta after graduation. Nominations by faculty of education. For additional information, visit website http://alis.alberta.ca.

Academic Fields/Career Goals: Education; Foreign Language.

Award: Scholarship for use in junior or senior years; not renewable. *Number:* 16.

Eligibility Requirements: Applicant must be enrolled or expecting to enroll full-time at a four-year institution or university; resident of Alberta and studying in Alberta. Available to Canadian citizens.

Application Requirements: Nomination by institution. *Deadline:* varies.

Contact: Scholarship Committee
Phone: 780-427-8640
E-mail: scholarships@gov.ab.ca

NORTHERN ALBERTA DEVELOPMENT COUNCIL BURSARY

• *See page 251*

AMERICAN FEDERATION OF TEACHERS

http://www.aft.org/

ROBERT G. PORTER SCHOLARS PROGRAM-AFT MEMBERS

Nonrenewable grant provides continuing education for school teachers, paraprofessionals and school-related personnel, higher education faculty and professionals, employees of state and local governments, nurses and other health professionals. Must be member of the American Federation of Teachers for at least one year.

Academic Fields/Career Goals: Education.

Award: Grant for use in freshman, sophomore, junior, or senior years; not renewable. *Number:* up to 10. *Amount:* $1000.

Eligibility Requirements: Applicant must be enrolled or expecting to enroll full- or part-time at a four-year institution or university. Applicant or parent of applicant must have employment or volunteer experience in nursing, teaching/education. Available to U.S. citizens.

Application Requirements: Application form, essay, recommendations or references, statement of need. *Deadline:* March 31.

Contact: Bernadette Bailey, Scholarship Coordinator
American Federation of Teachers
555 New Jersey Avenue, NW
Washington, DC 20001
Phone: 202-879-4481
Fax: 202-879-4406
E-mail: bbailey@aft.org

AMERICAN FOUNDATION FOR THE BLIND

http://www.afb.org/

DELTA GAMMA FOUNDATION FLORENCE MARGARET HARVEY MEMORIAL SCHOLARSHIP

One scholarship of $1000 to an undergraduate or graduate student who has exhibited academic excellence, and is studying in the field of rehabilitation and/or education of persons who are blind or visually impaired. Must submit proof of legal blindness. For additional information and application requirements, refer to website http://www.afb.org/scholarships.asp.

Academic Fields/Career Goals: Education; Therapy/Rehabilitation.

Award: Scholarship for use in freshman, sophomore, junior, or senior years; not renewable. *Number:* 1. *Amount:* $1000.

Eligibility Requirements: Applicant must be visually impaired and enrolled or expecting to enroll full- or part-time at a two-year or four-year institution or university. Applicant must be visually impaired. Available to U.S. citizens.

Application Requirements: Application form, essay, proof of post-secondary acceptance and legal blindness, recommendations or references, transcript. *Deadline:* April 30.

Contact: Dawn Bodrogi, Information Center and Library Coordinator
American Foundation for the Blind
11 Penn Plaza, Suite 300
New York, NY 10001
Phone: 212-502-7661
Fax: 212-502-7771
E-mail: afbinfo@afb.net

RUDOLPH DILLMAN MEMORIAL SCHOLARSHIP

One-time award not open to previous recipients. Four scholarships of $2500 each to undergraduate or graduate students who are studying in the field of rehabilitation and/or education of persons who are blind or visually impaired. One of these grants is specifically for a student who meets all requirements and submits evidence of economic need. Must submit proof of legal blindness. For additional information and application requirements, visit website http://www.afb.org/scholarships.asp.

Academic Fields/Career Goals: Education; Therapy/Rehabilitation.

Award: Scholarship for use in freshman, sophomore, junior, or senior years; not renewable. *Number:* up to 4. *Amount:* $2500.

Eligibility Requirements: Applicant must be visually impaired and enrolled or expecting to enroll full- or part-time at a two-year or four-year institution or university. Applicant must be visually impaired. Available to U.S. citizens.

Application Requirements: Application form, essay, financial need analysis, proof of legal blindness, acceptance letter, recommendations or references, transcript. *Deadline:* April 30.

Contact: Dawn Bodrogi, Information Center and Library Coordinator
American Foundation for the Blind
11 Penn Plaza, Suite 300
New York, NY 10001
Phone: 212-502-7661
Fax: 212-502-7771
E-mail: afbinfo@afb.net

AMERICAN INSTITUTE OF POLISH CULTURE INC.

http://www.ampolinstitute.org/

HARRIET IRSAY SCHOLARSHIP GRANT

• *See page 141*

AMERICAN LEGION AUXILIARY DEPARTMENT OF IOWA

http://www.ialegion.org/ala

AMERICAN LEGION AUXILIARY DEPARTMENT OF IOWA HARRIET HOFFMAN MEMORIAL MERIT AWARD FOR TEACHER TRAINING

One-time award for Iowa residents attending Iowa institutions who are the children, grandchildren, or great-grandchildren of veterans. Preference given to descendants of deceased veterans.

Academic Fields/Career Goals: Education.

Award: Scholarship for use in freshman, sophomore, junior, or senior years; not renewable. *Number:* 1. *Amount:* $400.

Eligibility Requirements: Applicant must be enrolled or expecting to enroll full-time at a four-year institution or university; resident of Iowa and studying in Iowa. Available to U.S. citizens. Applicant or parent must meet one or more of the following requirements: general military experience; retired from active duty; disabled or killed as a result of military service; prisoner of war; or missing in action.

Application Requirements: Application form, essay, financial need analysis, personal photograph, recommendations or references, self-addressed stamped envelope with application, test scores, transcript. *Deadline:* June 1.

Contact: Marlene Valentine, Secretary and Treasurer
American Legion Auxiliary Department of Iowa
720 Lyon Street
Des Moines, IA 50309
Phone: 515-282-7987
Fax: 515-282-7583
E-mail: alasectreas@ialegion.org

AMERICAN LEGION DEPARTMENT OF MISSOURI

http://www.missourilegion.org/

ERMAN W. TAYLOR MEMORIAL SCHOLARSHIP

Two $500 awards are given annually to a student planning on obtaining a degree in education. Applicants must be unmarried Missouri resident below age 21, and must use the scholarship as a full-time student in an accredited college or university. Must be an unmarried descendant of a veteran having served 90 days on active duty in the Army, Air Force, Navy, Marine Corps, or Coast Guard of the United States, and having an honorable discharge.

Academic Fields/Career Goals: Education.

Award: Scholarship for use in freshman year; not renewable. *Number:* 2. *Amount:* $500.

Eligibility Requirements: Applicant must be high school student; planning to enroll or expecting to enroll full-time at a two-year or four-year institution or university; single and resident of Missouri. Available to U.S. citizens. Applicant or parent must meet one or more of the following requirements: general military experience; retired from active duty; disabled or killed as a result of military service; prisoner of war; or missing in action.

Application Requirements: Application form, discharge certificate, essay, test scores. *Deadline:* April 20.

Contact: John Doane, Chairman
Phone: 417-924-8596
Fax: 573-225-1406
E-mail: info@missourilegion.org

AMERICAN MONTESSORI SOCIETY

http://www.amshq.org/

AMERICAN MONTESSORI SOCIETY TEACHER EDUCATION SCHOLARSHIP FUND

One-time award for aspiring Montessori teacher candidates. Requires verification that applicant has been accepted into an AMS Montessori Teacher Education program. Awards are considered on the basis of financial need, a compelling personal statement, and 3 letters of recommendation.

Academic Fields/Career Goals: Education.

Award: Scholarship for use in freshman, sophomore, junior, senior, or graduate years; not renewable. *Number:* 12–20. *Amount:* $1000–$3000.

Eligibility Requirements: Applicant must be enrolled or expecting to enroll full-time at a two-year or four-year or technical institution or university. Available to U.S. and non-U.S. citizens.

Application Requirements: Application form, essay, financial need analysis. *Deadline:* May 1.

Contact: Sophia Merendini, Teacher Education
American Montessori Society
American Montessori Society, 116 East 16th Street, 6th Floor
New York, NY 10003
Phone: 212-358-1250 Ext. 315
E-mail: sophia@amshq.org

AMERICAN PHYSICAL THERAPY ASSOCIATION

http://www.apta.org/honorsawards

MARY MCMILLAN SCHOLARSHIP AWARD

Students may be nominated from physical therapist assistant education programs and physical therapist professional education programs accredited by the Commission on Accreditation in Physical Therapy Education (CAPTE) of the association. Physical therapist assistant education program students must be enrolled in the final year of study. For physical therapist assistant education programs that have a part-time curriculum, all nominees must be in the final year of the curriculum of that institution. Minimum 3.0 GPA required.

Academic Fields/Career Goals: Education; Health and Medical Sciences; Therapy/Rehabilitation.

Award: Scholarship for use in senior, graduate, or postgraduate years; not renewable. *Number:* 1–6. *Amount:* $3000–$5000.

Eligibility Requirements: Applicant must be enrolled or expecting to enroll full-time at a two-year or four-year institution or university. Applicant or parent of applicant must have employment or volunteer experience in physical therapy/rehabilitation. Applicant must have 3.0 GPA or higher. Available to U.S. citizens.

Application Requirements: Application form, community service, essay. *Deadline:* December 1.

Contact: Alissa Patanarut, Senior Honors and Awards Program
Specialist
American Physical Therapy Association
1111 North Fairfax Street
Alexandria, VA 22314
Phone: 800-999-2782 Ext. 3154
E-mail: alissapatanarut@apta.org

AMERICAN SCHOOL OF CLASSICAL STUDIES AT ATHENS

http://www.ascsa.edu.gr/

ASCSA SUMMER SESSION AND SUMMER SEMINARS SCHOLARSHIPS
• *See page 118*

AMERICAN WELDING SOCIETY

http://www.aws.org/

JOHN M. STROPKI STEM SCHOLARSHIP

Awarded to a college undergraduate student. Priority will be given to the sons and daughters of current Lincoln Electric employees in the United States and Canada. Students must have a 3.0 overall GPA, and be attending school full time. One $2,500 scholarship award will be made to any student pursuing a degree as an educator of a STEM subject.

Academic Fields/Career Goals: Education.

Award: Scholarship for use in freshman, sophomore, junior, or senior years; not renewable.

Eligibility Requirements: Applicant must be high school student and planning to enroll or expecting to enroll full-time at a four-year institution. Applicant must have 3.0 GPA or higher. Available to U.S. and Canadian citizens.

Application Requirements: Application form, financial need analysis. *Deadline:* February 15.

Contact: John Douglass, Associate Director, AWS Foundation
Phone: 800-443-9353 Ext. 212
E-mail: jdouglass@aws.org

ARCTIC INSTITUTE OF NORTH AMERICA

http://www.arctic.ucalgary.ca/

JIM BOURQUE SCHOLARSHIP

One-time award of CAN$1000 to Canadian aboriginal student enrolled in postsecondary training in education, environmental studies, traditional knowledge or telecommunications. Must submit, in 500 words or less, a description of their intended program of study and reasons for their choice of program. Must include most recent high school or college/university transcript; a signed letter of recommendation from a community leader, a statement of financial need which indicates funding already received or expected; and proof of enrollment in, or application to, a post secondary institution. Applicants must also provide proof of Canadian Aboriginal descent. Applicants are evaluated based on need, relevance of study, achievements, return of investment and overall presentation of the application.

Academic Fields/Career Goals: Education; Environmental Science; Natural Resources; Natural Sciences.

Award: Scholarship for use in freshman, sophomore, junior, or senior years; not renewable. *Number:* 1.

Eligibility Requirements: Applicant must be of Canadian heritage and Canadian citizen; American Indian/Alaska Native; enrolled or expecting to enroll full-time at a four-year institution or university and resident of Alberta, British Columbia, Manitoba, New Brunswick, Newfoundland, Northwest Territories, Nova Scotia, Ontario, Prince Edward Island, Quebec, Saskatchewan, Yukon.

Application Requirements: Application form, essay, financial need analysis. *Deadline:* July 15.

Contact: Melanie Paulson, Administrative Coordinator
Phone: 403-220-7515
E-mail: arctic@ucalgary.ca

ARIZONA BUSINESS EDUCATION ASSOCIATION

http://www.azbea.org/

ABEA STUDENT TEACHER SCHOLARSHIPS

Scholarships awarded to future business education teachers. Must be member of ABEA. Must be a student in last semester or two of an undergraduate Arizona business education teacher program at an accredited university or four-year college or in a post-Baccalaureate Arizona business education teacher certification program at an accredited university or four-year college.

Academic Fields/Career Goals: Education.

Award: Scholarship for use in junior or senior years; not renewable. *Number:* up to 3. *Amount:* $500.

Eligibility Requirements: Applicant must be enrolled or expecting to enroll full-time at a four-year institution or university and resident of Arizona. Applicant or parent of applicant must be member of Arizona Business Education Association. Available to U.S. citizens.

Application Requirements: Application form, recommendations or references, resume, transcript. *Deadline:* April 1.

Contact: Shirley Eittreim, Scholarships Committee Chair
Arizona Business Education Association
Northland Pioneer College
PO Box 610
Holbrook, AZ 86025
Phone: 928-532-6151
E-mail: sjeittreim@cybertrails.com

ARRL FOUNDATION INC.

http://www.arrl.org/

CTRI/CHRIS SEEBER, KA1GEU, MEMORIAL SCHOLARSHIP

One $500 scholarship for a student with active Amateur Radio license who is studying science, science education, math, math education, engineering, or technology at any accredited 2- or 4-year college or university. Student must reside in ARRL New England Division (Connecticut, Rhode Island, Vermont, Maine, New Hampshire).

Academic Fields/Career Goals: Education; Engineering/Technology; Materials Science, Engineering, and Metallurgy; Mathematics; Natural Sciences; Nuclear Science; Physical Sciences.

Award: Scholarship for use in freshman, sophomore, junior, or senior years; not renewable. *Number:* 1. *Amount:* $500.

Eligibility Requirements: Applicant must be enrolled or expecting to enroll full-time at a two-year or four-year institution or university; resident of Connecticut, Maine, New Hampshire, Rhode Island, Vermont and must have an interest in amateur radio. Available to U.S. citizens.

Application Requirements: Application form. *Deadline:* January 31.

Contact: Ms. Mary Hobart, Secretary
Phone: 860-594-0397
E-mail: k1mmh@arrl.org

ASSOCIATION FOR EDUCATION AND REHABILITATION OF THE BLIND AND VISUALLY IMPAIRED

http://www.aerbvi.org/

WILLIAM AND DOROTHY FERRELL SCHOLARSHIP

Nonrenewable scholarship given in even years for postsecondary education leading to career in services for blind or visually impaired. Applicant must submit proof of legal blindness or visual field impairment of 20 percent or less.

Academic Fields/Career Goals: Education; Health and Medical Sciences; Occupational Safety and Health; Public Policy and Administration; Therapy/Rehabilitation.

Award: Scholarship for use in freshman, sophomore, junior, senior, or graduate years; not renewable. *Number:* 2. *Amount:* $500–$1000.

Eligibility Requirements: Applicant must be visually impaired and enrolled or expecting to enroll full-time at a two-year or four-year institution or university. Applicant must be visually impaired. Available to U.S. and non-U.S. citizens.

Application Requirements: Application form. *Deadline:* March 25.

Contact: Scholarship Coordinator
Association for Education and Rehabilitation of the Blind and Visually Impaired
1703 North Beauregard Street, Suite 440
Alexandria, VA 22311-1744
Phone: 703-671-4500
E-mail: scholarships@aerbvi.org

ASSOCIATION FOR WOMEN GEOSCIENTISTS (AWG)

http://www.awg.org/

AWG ETHNIC MINORITY SCHOLARSHIP
• *See page 260*

AWG MARIA LUISA CRAWFORD FIELD CAMP SCHOLARSHIP
• *See page 129*

AWG SALT LAKE CHAPTER (SLC) RESEARCH SCHOLARSHIP
• *See page 129*

LONE STAR RISING CAREER SCHOLARSHIP
• *See page 260*

ASSOCIATION OF RETIRED TEACHERS OF CONNECTICUT

http://www.artct.org/

ARTC GLEN MOON SCHOLARSHIP

Renewable scholarship to Connecticut high school seniors, who intend to pursue a career in teaching. Must demonstrate a positive financial need.

Academic Fields/Career Goals: Education.

Award: Scholarship for use in freshman year; renewable. *Number:* 2–3. *Amount:* $1500–$2000.

Eligibility Requirements: Applicant must be high school student; planning to enroll or expecting to enroll full- or part-time at a four-year institution or university and resident of Connecticut. Available to U.S. citizens.

Application Requirements: Application form, community service, driver's license, financial need analysis, recommendations or references, test scores, transcript. *Deadline:* March 31.

Contact: Teresa Barton, Scholarship Committee
Phone: 866-343-2782
E-mail: info@ctretiredteachers.org

BETHESDA LUTHERAN COMMUNITIES

http://www.bethesdalutherancommunities.org/scholarships

DEVELOPMENTAL DISABILITIES SCHOLASTIC ACHIEVEMENT SCHOLARSHIP FOR COLLEGE STUDENTS WHO ARE LUTHERAN
• *See page 254*

BULKOFFICESUPPLY.COM

http://www.bulkofficesupply.com

OFFICE SUPPLY SCHOLARSHIP
• *See page 141*

CALIFORNIA STUDENT AID COMMISSION

http://www.csac.ca.gov/

CHILD DEVELOPMENT TEACHER AND SUPERVISOR GRANT PROGRAM
• *See page 203*

CALIFORNIA TEACHERS ASSOCIATION (CTA)

http://www.cta.org/

L. GORDON BITTLE MEMORIAL SCHOLARSHIP

Awards scholarships annually to active SCTA members for study in a teacher preparatory program. Students may reapply each year. Not available to those who are currently working in public schools as members of CTA. Minimum 3.5 GPA.

Academic Fields/Career Goals: Education.

Award: Scholarship for use in freshman, sophomore, junior, senior, or graduate years; not renewable. *Number:* up to 3. *Amount:* $2500.

Eligibility Requirements: Applicant must be enrolled or expecting to enroll full-time at a two-year or four-year institution or university and resident of California. Applicant or parent of applicant must be member of California Teachers Association. Applicant must have 3.5 GPA or higher. Available to U.S. citizens.

Application Requirements: Application form, essay, recommendations or references, transcript. *Deadline:* February 8.

Contact: Janeya Collins, Scholarship Coordinator
California Teachers Association (CTA)
PO Box 921
Burlingame, CA 94011-0921
Phone: 650-552-5468
Fax: 650-552-5001
E-mail: scholarships@cta.org

MARTIN LUTHER KING, JR. MEMORIAL SCHOLARSHIP

Awards for ethnic minority members of the California Teachers Association, their dependent children, and ethnic minority members of Student California Teachers Association who want to pursue degrees or credentials in public education. Minimum 3.5 GPA.

Academic Fields/Career Goals: Education.

Award: Scholarship for use in freshman, sophomore, junior, senior, or graduate years; not renewable. *Amount:* $1000–$2000.

Eligibility Requirements: Applicant must be American Indian/Alaska Native, Asian/Pacific Islander, Black (non-Hispanic), Hispanic; enrolled or expecting to enroll full-time at a two-year or four-year institution or university and resident of California. Applicant or parent of applicant must be member of California Teachers Association. Applicant must have 3.5 GPA or higher. Available to U.S. citizens.

Application Requirements: Application form, essay, financial need analysis, recommendations or references. *Deadline:* March 14.

Contact: Janeya Collins, Scholarship Coordinator
California Teachers Association (CTA)
PO Box 921
Burlingame, CA 94011-0921
Phone: 650-552-5468
Fax: 650-552-5001
E-mail: scholarships@cta.org

CANADIAN INSTITUTE OF UKRAINIAN STUDIES

http://www.cius.ca/

LEO J. KRYSA UNDERGRADUATE SCHOLARSHIP
• *See page 138*

CATCHING THE DREAM

http://www.catchingthedream.org/

MATH, ENGINEERING, SCIENCE, BUSINESS, EDUCATION, COMPUTERS SCHOLARSHIPS
• *See page 178*

NATIVE AMERICAN LEADERSHIP IN EDUCATION (NALE)
• *See page 178*

CONNECTICUT EDUCATION FOUNDATION INC.

http://www.cea.org/cef/

SCHOLARSHIP FOR ETHNIC MINORITY COLLEGE STUDENTS

An award for qualified minority candidates who have been accepted into a teacher preparation program at an accredited Connecticut college or university. Must have a 3.0 GPA.

Academic Fields/Career Goals: Education.

Award: Scholarship for use in freshman, sophomore, junior, or senior years; renewable. *Number:* 1–2. *Amount:* $1000–$2000.

Eligibility Requirements: Applicant must be American Indian/Alaska Native, Asian/Pacific Islander, Black (non-Hispanic), Hispanic; enrolled or expecting to enroll full-time at a two-year or four-year institution or university; resident of Connecticut and studying in Connecticut. Applicant must have 3.0 GPA or higher. Available to U.S. citizens.

Application Requirements: Application form, essay. *Deadline:* May 1.

Contact: Mr. Jeffrey Leake, President
Connecticut Education Foundation Inc.
21 Oak Street, Suite 500
Hartford, CT 06106
Phone: 860-525-5641 Ext. 6308
E-mail: jeffl@cea.org

SCHOLARSHIP FOR MINORITY HIGH SCHOOL STUDENTS

Award for qualified minority candidates who have been accepted into an accredited four-year Connecticut college or university and intend to enter the teaching profession. Must have 3.0 GPA.

Academic Fields/Career Goals: Education.

Award: Scholarship for use in freshman, sophomore, junior, or senior years; renewable. *Number:* 1–2. *Amount:* $1000–$2000.

Eligibility Requirements: Applicant must be American Indian/Alaska Native, Asian/Pacific Islander, Black (non-Hispanic), Hispanic; high school student; planning to enroll or expecting to enroll full-time at a four-year institution or university; resident of Connecticut and studying in Connecticut. Applicant must have 3.0 GPA or higher. Available to U.S. citizens.

Application Requirements: Application form, essay. *Deadline:* May 1.

Contact: Mr. Jeffrey Leake, President
Connecticut Education Foundation Inc.
21 Oak Street, Suite 500
Hartford, CT 06106
Phone: 860-525-5641 Ext. 6308
E-mail: jeffl@cea.org

CONNECTICUT OFFICE OF HIGHER EDUCATION

http://www.ctohe.org

MINORITY TEACHER INCENTIVE GRANT PROGRAM

Program provides up to $5,000 a year for two years of full-time study in a teacher preparation program for the junior or senior year at a Connecticut college or university. Applicant must be African-American, Hispanic/Latino, Asian American or Native American heritage and be nominated by the Education Dean. Program graduates who teach in Connecticut public schools may be eligible for loan reimbursement stipends up to $2,500 per year for up to four years.

Academic Fields/Career Goals: Education.

Award: Grant for use in junior or senior years; renewable. *Number:* 87. *Amount:* $2500–$5000.

Eligibility Requirements: Applicant must be American Indian/Alaska Native, Asian/Pacific Islander, Black (non-Hispanic), Hispanic; enrolled or expecting to enroll full-time at a four-year institution or university; resident of Connecticut and studying in Connecticut. Available to U.S. citizens.

Application Requirements: Application form. *Deadline:* October 15.

Contact: Ms. Lynne Goodwin, Executive Assistant
Connecticut Office of Higher Education
450 Columbus Boulevard
Suite 510
Hartford, CT 06103
Phone: 860-947-1855
E-mail: mtip@ctohe.org

CONTINENTAL SOCIETY, DAUGHTERS OF INDIAN WARS

http://www.csdiw.org/

CONTINENTAL SOCIETY, DAUGHTERS OF INDIAN WARS SCHOLARSHIP
• *See page 242*

CULTURAL SERVICES OF THE FRENCH EMBASSY

http://www.frenchculture.org/

TEACHING ASSISTANT PROGRAM IN FRANCE
• *See page 113*

DECA (DISTRIBUTIVE EDUCATION CLUBS OF AMERICA)

http://www.deca.org/

HARRY A. APPLEGATE SCHOLARSHIP
• *See page 83*

EASTERN STAR-GRAND CHAPTER OF CALIFORNIA

http://www.oescal.org/

SCHOLARSHIPS FOR EDUCATION, BUSINESS AND RELIGION
• *See page 178*

GENERAL BOARD OF HIGHER EDUCATION AND MINISTRY

http://www.gbhem.org

EDITH M. ALLEN SCHOLARSHIP

Scholarship for outstanding African-American graduate or undergraduate students pursuing a degree in education, social work, medicine, and/or other health professions. Must be enrolled at a United Methodist college or university and be an active, full member of the United Methodist Church for at least three years.

Academic Fields/Career Goals: Education; Health and Medical Sciences; Social Services.

Award: Scholarship for use in freshman, sophomore, junior, or senior years; not renewable. *Number:* 2. *Amount:* $1200.

Eligibility Requirements: Applicant must be Methodist; Black (non-Hispanic) and enrolled or expecting to enroll full-time at a four-year institution or university. Available to U.S. citizens.

Application Requirements: Application form, essay. *Deadline:* March 1.

Contact: Ms. Marcie Bigord, Assistant Director of Loans & Scholarships
General Board of Higher Education and Ministry
PO Box 340007
Nashville, TN 37203-0007
Phone: 615-340-7388
Fax: 615-340-7529
E-mail: mbigord@gbhem.org

GENERAL FEDERATION OF WOMEN'S CLUBS OF MASSACHUSETTS

http://www.gfwcma.org/

NEWTONVILLE WOMAN'S CLUB SCHOLARSHIP

Applicant must be a senior in a Massachusetts high school who will enroll in a four-year accredited college or university in a teacher-training program that leads to certification to teach.

Academic Fields/Career Goals: Education.

Award: Scholarship for use in freshman year; not renewable. *Number:* 1. *Amount:* $600.

Eligibility Requirements: Applicant must be high school student; planning to enroll or expecting to enroll full-time at a four-year institution or university and resident of Massachusetts. Available to U.S. citizens.

Application Requirements: Application form, driver's license, essay. *Deadline:* March 1.

Contact: Scholarship Chm
General Federation of Women's Clubs of Massachusetts
P.O. Box 679
Sudbury, MA 01776
E-mail: gfwcma@aol.com

GEORGIA ASSOCIATION OF EDUCATORS

http://www.gae.org/

GAE GFIE SCHOLARSHIP FOR ASPIRING TEACHERS

Scholarships will be awarded to graduating seniors who currently attend a fully accredited public Georgia high school and will attend a fully accredited Georgia college or university within the next twelve months. Must have a 3.0 GPA. Must submit three letters of recommendation. Must have plans to enter the teaching profession.

Academic Fields/Career Goals: Education.

Award: Scholarship for use in freshman year; not renewable. *Number:* up to 20. *Amount:* $1000.

Eligibility Requirements: Applicant must be enrolled or expecting to enroll full-time at a two-year or four-year institution or university; resident of Georgia and studying in Georgia. Applicant must have 3.0 GPA or higher. Available to U.S. citizens.

Application Requirements: Application form, recommendations or references, transcript. *Deadline:* February 1.

Contact: Sharon Henderson, Staff Associate
Phone: 678-837-1114
Fax: 678-837-1150
E-mail: sharon.henderson@gae.org

GOLDEN APPLE FOUNDATION

http://www.goldenapple.org/

GOLDEN APPLE SCHOLARS OF ILLINOIS

Applicants must be between the ages of 16 and 21 and maintain a GPA of 2.5. Eligible applicants must be residents of Illinois studying education in Illinois. Recipients must agree to teach in an Illinois school school-of-need for 5 years.

Academic Fields/Career Goals: Education.

Award: Scholarship for use in freshman, sophomore, junior, or senior years; renewable. *Number:* 200. *Amount:* $23,000.

Eligibility Requirements: Applicant must be age 16-21; enrolled or expecting to enroll full-time at a two-year or four-year institution or university; resident of Illinois and studying in Illinois. Applicant must have 2.5 GPA or higher. Available to U.S. citizens.

Application Requirements: Application form, essay, interview, personal photograph. *Deadline:* February 15.

Contact: Ms. Patricia Kilduff, Director of Recruitment and Placement
Phone: 312-477-7515
E-mail: kilduff@goldenapple.org

GOLDEN KEY INTERNATIONAL HONOUR SOCIETY

http://www.goldenkey.org/

EDUCATION ACHIEVEMENT AWARDS

Awards members who excel in the study of education. Eligible applicants are undergraduate, graduate and postgraduate members who are currently enrolled in classes at a degree-granting program. One winner will receive a $1000 award. The second place winner will receive $750 and the third place winner will receive $500.

Academic Fields/Career Goals: Education.

Award: Prize for use in freshman, sophomore, junior, senior, graduate, or postgraduate years; not renewable. *Number:* 3. *Amount:* $500–$1000.

Eligibility Requirements: Applicant must be enrolled or expecting to enroll full- or part-time at a four-year institution or university. Available to U.S. and non-U.S. citizens.

Application Requirements: Application form, education related paper or report, entry in a contest, essay, recommendations or references, transcript. *Deadline:* March 3.

Contact: Scholarship Program Administrators
Golden Key International Honour Society
PO Box 23737
Nashville, TN 37202-3737
Phone: 800-377-2401
E-mail: scholarships@goldenkey.org

GREATER KANAWHA VALLEY FOUNDATION

http://www.tgkvf.org/

JOSEPH C. BASILE, II MEMORIAL SCHOLARSHIP FUND

Award for residents of West Virginia who are majoring in education. Must be an undergraduate at a college or university in West Virginia. Award based on financial need.

Academic Fields/Career Goals: Education.

Award: Scholarship for use in freshman, sophomore, junior, or senior years; not renewable. *Number:* 1. *Amount:* $1500.

Eligibility Requirements: Applicant must be enrolled or expecting to enroll full-time at a four-year institution or university; resident of West Virginia and studying in West Virginia. Available to U.S. citizens.

Application Requirements: Application form, essay, financial need analysis, recommendations or references, self-addressed stamped envelope with application, test scores, transcript. *Deadline:* January 15.

Contact: Susan Hoover, Scholarship Coordinator
Greater Kanawha Valley Foundation
900 Lee Street East, 16th Floor
Charleston, WV 25301
E-mail: shoover@tgkvf.org

HAWAIIAN LODGE, F&AM

http://www.hawaiianlodgefreemasons.org

HAWAIIAN LODGE SCHOLARSHIPS

• See page 86

HAWAII EDUCATION ASSOCIATION

http://www.heaed.com/

HAWAII EDUCATION ASSOCIATION STUDENT TEACHER SCHOLARSHIP

Scholarship available to student teachers intending to teach in the Hawaii State Department of Education who are enrolled in a State Approved Teacher Education Program as a full-time undergraduate or post baccalaureate candidate in any state-approved or nationally accredited institution of higher learning in the 2018-2019 academic year.

Academic Fields/Career Goals: Education.

Award: Scholarship for use in senior, graduate, or postgraduate years; not renewable. *Number:* 2. *Amount:* $3000.

Eligibility Requirements: Applicant must be enrolled or expecting to enroll full-time at a four-year institution or university. Applicant or parent of applicant must be member of Hawaii Education Association. Available to U.S. citizens.

Application Requirements: Application form, essay, financial need analysis, personal photograph. *Deadline:* June 4.

Contact: Laurie Togami, Scholarship Committee
Hawaii Education Association
1953 South Beretania Street, Suite 5C
Honolulu, HI 96826-1304
Phone: 808-949-6657
E-mail: hea.office@hawaiieducationassociation.org

HIROSHI BARBARA KIM YAMASHITA HEA SCHOLARSHIP

One $2000 scholarship awarded to full-time undergraduate education majors currently attending an accredited institution of higher learning and intending to teach in a Hawaii public school. Minimum 3.2 GPA required.

Academic Fields/Career Goals: Education.

Award: Scholarship for use in freshman, sophomore, junior, or senior years; not renewable. *Number:* 1. *Amount:* $2000.

Eligibility Requirements: Applicant must be enrolled or expecting to enroll full-time at a four-year institution or university. Applicant must have 3.5 GPA or higher. Available to U.S. citizens.

Application Requirements: Application form, essay, financial need analysis, personal photograph. *Deadline:* April 2.

Contact: Laurie Togami, Staff Specialist
Hawaii Education Association
1953 South Beretania Street, Suite 5C
Honolulu, HI 96826
Phone: 808-949-6657
E-mail: hea.office@hawaiieducationassociation.org

ILLINOIS PTA

http://www.illinoispta.org

ILLINOIS PTA SCHOLARSHIP

Scholarship has evolved to encourage Illinois college-bound high school seniors entering the field of education or an education-related field at the college/university of their choice. Minimum 3.0 GPA required.

Academic Fields/Career Goals: Education.

Award: Scholarship for use in freshman year; not renewable. *Number:* 2. *Amount:* $2000–$3000.

Eligibility Requirements: Applicant must be high school student; planning to enroll or expecting to enroll full-time at a four-year institution or university and resident of Illinois. Applicant must have 3.0 GPA or higher. Available to U.S. citizens.

Application Requirements: Application form, application form may be submitted online (http://www.illinoispta.org), community service, essay, personal photograph, resume, test scores, transcript. *Deadline:* February 15.

Contact: Barb Miller, Scholarship Director
Illinois PTA
PO Box 907
Springfield, IL 62705-0907
Phone: 217-528-9617
Fax: 217-528-9490
E-mail: Bmiller@illinoispta.org

ILLINOIS STUDENT ASSISTANCE COMMISSION (ISAC)

http://www.isac.org/

MINORITY TEACHERS OF ILLINOIS SCHOLARSHIP PROGRAM

Award for minority students intending to become school teachers; teaching commitment attached to receipt. Number of scholarships and the individual dollar amounts vary.

Academic Fields/Career Goals: Education.

Award: Scholarship for use in freshman, sophomore, junior, senior, graduate, or postgraduate years; not renewable.

Eligibility Requirements: Applicant must be American Indian/Alaska Native, Asian/Pacific Islander, Black (non-Hispanic), Hispanic; enrolled or expecting to enroll full- or part-time at a two-year or four-year institution or university; resident of Illinois and studying in Illinois. Available to U.S. citizens.

Application Requirements: Application form. *Deadline:* March 1.

Contact: ISAC Call Center Representative
Illinois Student Assistance Commission (ISAC)
1755 Lake Cook Road
Deerfield, IL 60015-5209
Phone: 800-899-4722
E-mail: isac.studentservices@illinois.gov

INDIANA RETIRED TEACHER'S ASSOCIATION (IRTA)

http://www.retiredteachers.org/

INDIANA RETIRED TEACHERS FOUNDATION SCHOLARSHIP

Scholarship available to college sophomores or juniors who are enrolled full-time in an education program at an Indiana college or university for a baccalaureate degree. The applicant must be the child, grandchild, legal dependent or spouse of an active, retired or deceased member of the Indiana State Teachers Retirement Fund and Indiana Retired Teachers Association.

Academic Fields/Career Goals: Education.

Award: Scholarship for use in sophomore or junior years; not renewable. *Number:* 10. *Amount:* $2000.

Eligibility Requirements: Applicant must be enrolled or expecting to enroll full-time at a four-year institution or university; resident of Indiana and studying in Indiana. Applicant or parent of applicant must have employment or volunteer experience in teaching/education. Available to U.S. citizens.

Application Requirements: Application form, community service, essay, financial need analysis. *Deadline:* April 28.

Contact: Executive Director
Indiana Retired Teacher's Association (IRTA)
150 West Market Street, Suite 610
Indianapolis, IN 46204-2812
Phone: 888-454-9333

INTERNATIONAL TECHNOLOGY EDUCATION ASSOCIATION

http://www.iteaconnect.org/

INTERNATIONAL TECHNOLOGY EDUCATION ASSOCIATION UNDERGRADUATE SCHOLARSHIP IN TECHNOLOGY EDUCATION

A scholarship for undergraduate students pursuing a degree in technology education and technological studies. Applicants must be members of the association.

Academic Fields/Career Goals: Education; Engineering/Technology; Science, Technology, and Society.

Award: Scholarship for use in freshman, sophomore, junior, or senior years; not renewable. *Number:* 3. *Amount:* $1000.

Eligibility Requirements: Applicant must be enrolled or expecting to enroll full-time at a four-year institution or university. Applicant or parent of applicant must be member of International Technology Education Association. Applicant must have 2.5 GPA or higher. Available to U.S. and non-U.S. citizens.

Application Requirements: Application form, recommendations or references, resume, transcript. *Deadline:* December 1.

Contact: Scholarship Committee
International Technology Education Association
1914 Association Drive, Suite 201
Reston, VA 20191
Phone: 703-860-2100
Fax: 703-860-0353
E-mail: iteaordr@iris.org

JACK J. ISGUR FOUNDATION

http://www.isgur.org

JACK J. ISGUR FOUNDATION SCHOLARSHIP

Awards scholarships to juniors, seniors, and graduate students with intentions of teaching the humanities in grades kindergarten through 8th grade, preferably in rural Missouri.

Academic Fields/Career Goals: Education; Humanities; Music.

Award: Scholarship for use in junior, senior, graduate, or postgraduate years; not renewable. *Number:* 5–100. *Amount:* $750–$1500.

Eligibility Requirements: Applicant must be enrolled or expecting to enroll full- or part-time at a four-year institution or university. Available to U.S. and non-U.S. citizens.

Application Requirements: Application form, essay, interview. *Deadline:* May 15.

Contact: Mr. Charles Jensen, Administrator, Jack J. Isgur Foundation
Jack J. Isgur Foundation
Stinson Leonard Street Law Firm
1201 Walnut Street, 29th Floor
Kansas City, MO 64106
Phone: 816-691-2760
E-mail: charles.jensen@stinson.com

KANSAS BOARD OF REGENTS

http://www.kansasregents.org/

KANSAS TEACHER SERVICE SCHOLARSHIP

Scholarship to encourage talented students to enter the teaching profession and teach in Kansas in specific curriculum areas or in underserved areas of Kansas. Students must be Kansas residents attending a postsecondary institution in Kansas. For more details, refer to website http://www.kansasregents.org.

Academic Fields/Career Goals: Education.

Award: Scholarship for use in junior, senior, or graduate years; renewable. *Amount:* $2214–$5536.

Eligibility Requirements: Applicant must be enrolled or expecting to enroll full- or part-time at a four-year institution or university; resident of Kansas and studying in Kansas. Applicant must have 3.0 GPA or higher. Available to U.S. citizens.

Application Requirements: Application form, essay, financial need analysis. *Deadline:* May 1.

Contact: Diane Lindeman, Director of Student Financial Assistance
Kansas Board of Regents
1000 SW Jackson, Suite 520
Topeka, KS 66612
Phone: 785-430-4255
Fax: 785-430-4233
E-mail: dlindeman@ksbor.org

MARYLAND STATE HIGHER EDUCATION COMMISSION

http://www.mhec.state.md.us/

JANET L. HOFFMANN LOAN ASSISTANCE REPAYMENT PROGRAM

Provides assistance for repayment of loan debt to Maryland residents working full-time in nonprofit organizations and state or local governments. Must submit Employment Verification Form and Lender Verification Form.

Academic Fields/Career Goals: Education; Law/Legal Services; Nursing; Social Services; Therapy/Rehabilitation.

Award: Grant for use in freshman, sophomore, junior, or senior years; not renewable. *Number:* up to 700. *Amount:* $1500–$10,000.

Eligibility Requirements: Applicant must be enrolled or expecting to enroll full-time at a four-year institution or university; resident of Maryland and studying in Maryland. Applicant or parent of applicant must have employment or volunteer experience in government/politics. Available to U.S. citizens.

Application Requirements: Application form, IRS 1040 form, transcript. *Deadline:* September 30.

Contact: Tamika McKelvin, Office of Student Financial Assistance
Maryland State Higher Education Commission
839 Bestgate Road, Suite 400
Annapolis, MD 21401
Phone: 410-260-4546
Fax: 410-260-3203
E-mail: tmckelvil@mhec.state.md.us

MASSACHUSETTS OFFICE OF STUDENT FINANCIAL ASSISTANCE

http://www.osfa.mass.edu/

EARLY CHILDHOOD EDUCATORS SCHOLARSHIP PROGRAM

• *See page 203*

PARAPROFESSIONAL TEACHER PREPARATION GRANT PROGRAM

Grant providing financial aid assistance to Massachusetts residents, who are currently employed as paraprofessionals in Massachusetts public schools and wish to obtain higher education and become certified as full-time teachers.

Academic Fields/Career Goals: Education.

Award: Grant for use in freshman, sophomore, junior, or senior years; not renewable. *Amount:* $250–$7500.

Eligibility Requirements: Applicant must be enrolled or expecting to enroll full- or part-time at a two-year or four-year institution or university; resident of Massachusetts and studying in Massachusetts. Available to U.S. citizens.

Application Requirements: Application form. *Deadline:* June 1.

Contact: Ms. Jean Szymaniak, Senior Program Assistant
Massachusetts Office of Student Financial Assistance
75 Pleasant Street Third Floor
Malden, MA 02148
Phone: 617-391-6083 Ext. 6083
E-mail: jszymaniak@dhe.mass.edu

MICHAEL MOODY FITNESS

http://www.michaelmoodyfitness.com/

MICHAEL MOODY FITNESS SCHOLARSHIP

• *See page 166*

NASA FLORIDA SPACE GRANT CONSORTIUM

http://www.floridaspacegrant.org/

FLORIDA SPACE RESEARCH PROGRAM

• *See page 156*

NASA RHODE ISLAND SPACE GRANT CONSORTIUM

http://brown/initiatives/ri-space-grant

NASA RISGC SUMMER SCHOLARSHIP FOR UNDERGRADUATE STUDENTS

• *See page 157*

NATIONAL ASSOCIATION FOR CAMPUS ACTIVITIES

http://www.naca.org/

NATIONAL ASSOCIATION FOR CAMPUS ACTIVITIES MID ATLANTIC HIGHER EDUCATION RESEARCH SCHOLARSHIP

• *See page 186*

NATIONAL COUNCIL OF JEWISH WOMEN LOS ANGELES (NCJW L LA)

http://ncjwla.org/

THE SHERMAN AND FRANCES L. TELLER TEACHING CREDENTIAL SCHOLARSHIP

To qualify a candidate must be a K-12 educator pursuing a multiple or single subject TEACHING CREDENTIAL (includes special education and ESL). The applicant must be enrolled at a University of California or California State University campus in the greater Los Angeles area. The applicant may be a man OR woman. The National Council of Jewish Women l Los Angeles (NCJW l LA) provides scholarships, regardless of race, ethnicity, religion, age, gender identity, sexuality or national origin to those who live and attend school in the Greater Los Angeles area, including Los Angeles, Orange, Riverside, and Ventura Counties.

Academic Fields/Career Goals: Education.

Award: Scholarship for use in freshman, sophomore, junior, or senior years; not renewable. *Number:* 2. *Amount:* $2000.

Eligibility Requirements: Applicant must be enrolled or expecting to enroll full- or part-time at an institution or university; resident of California and studying in California. Available to U.S. citizens.

Application Requirements: Application form, essay, financial need analysis. *Deadline:* continuous.

Contact: Stephanie Flax, Scholarship and Program Coordinator
National Council of Jewish Women Los Angeles (NCJW l LA)
543 N. Fairfax Avenue
Los Angeles, CA 90036
Phone: 323-852-8515
E-mail: scholarship@ncjwla.org

NATIONAL COUNCIL OF TEACHERS OF MATHEMATICS

http://www.nctm.org/

PROSPECTIVE SECONDARY TEACHER COURSE WORK SCHOLARSHIPS

Grant provides financial support to college students preparing for teaching secondary school mathematics. Award of $10,000 will be granted in two phases, with $5000 for the recipient's third year of full-time study, and $5000 for fourth year. Must be student members of NCTM and cannot reapply. Must submit proposal, essay, letters of recommendation, and transcripts.

Academic Fields/Career Goals: Education; Mathematics.

Award: Scholarship for use in junior or senior years; not renewable. *Number:* 2. *Amount:* up to $5000.

Eligibility Requirements: Applicant must be enrolled or expecting to enroll full-time at a four-year institution or university. Available to U.S. and non-U.S. citizens.

Application Requirements: Application form, essay, recommendations or references, transcript, written proposal. *Deadline:* May 9.

Contact: Mathematics Education Trust
Phone: 703-620-9840 Ext. 2112
Fax: 703-476-2970
E-mail: exec@nctm.org

NATIONAL INSTITUTE FOR LABOR RELATIONS RESEARCH

http://www.nilrr.org/

APPLEGATE/JACKSON/PARKS FUTURE TEACHER SCHOLARSHIP

Scholarship available to all education majors currently attending institution of higher learning in the United States. High school seniors accepted into a teacher education program may also apply under certain conditions. Award is based on an essay demonstrating knowledge of and interest in the issue of compulsory unionism in education. Specify "Education" or "Future Teacher Scholarship" on any correspondence.

Academic Fields/Career Goals: Education; Special Education.

Award: Scholarship for use in freshman, sophomore, junior, senior, graduate, or postgraduate years; not renewable. *Number:* 1. *Amount:* $1000.

Eligibility Requirements: Applicant must be enrolled or expecting to enroll full- or part-time at a four-year institution or university. Available to U.S. citizens.

Application Requirements: Application form, essay. *Deadline:* December 31.

Contact: Cathy Jones, Scholarship Coordinator
National Institute for Labor Relations Research
5211 Port Royal Road
Springfield, VA 22151
Phone: 703-321-9606 Ext. 2247
E-mail: clj@nrtw.org

NORTH CAROLINA ASSOCIATION OF EDUCATORS

http://www.ncae.org/

MARY MORROW-EDNA RICHARDS SCHOLARSHIP

One-time award for junior year of study in four-year education degree program. Preference given to members of the student branch of the North Carolina Association of Educators. Must be North Carolina resident attending a North Carolina institution. Must agree to teach in North Carolina for two years after graduation. Must be a junior in college when application is filed.

Academic Fields/Career Goals: Education.

Award: Scholarship for use in senior year; not renewable. *Number:* 3–8. *Amount:* up to $1000.

Eligibility Requirements: Applicant must be enrolled or expecting to enroll full-time at a four-year institution or university; resident of North Carolina and studying in North Carolina. Applicant or parent of applicant must be member of Other Student Academic Clubs. Available to U.S. citizens.

Application Requirements: Application form, essay, financial need analysis, recommendations or references, transcript. *Deadline:* January 13.

Contact: Annette Montgomery, Communications Secretary
Phone: 800-662-7924
Fax: 919-839-8229
E-mail: annette.montgomery@ncae.org

OKLAHOMA STATE REGENTS FOR HIGHER EDUCATION

http://www.okhighered.org/

FUTURE TEACHER SCHOLARSHIP-OKLAHOMA

Open to outstanding Oklahoma high school graduates who agree to teach in shortage areas. Must rank in top 15 percent of graduating class or score above 85th percentile on ACT or similar test, or be accepted in an educational program. Students nominated by institution. Reapply to renew. Must attend college/university in Oklahoma.

Academic Fields/Career Goals: Education.

Award: Scholarship for use in freshman, sophomore, junior, senior, or graduate years; not renewable. *Amount:* $500–$1500.

Eligibility Requirements: Applicant must be enrolled or expecting to enroll full- or part-time at a two-year or four-year institution or university; resident of Oklahoma and studying in Oklahoma. Available to U.S. citizens.

Application Requirements: Application form, essay.

Contact: Scholarship Programs Coordinator
Oklahoma State Regents for Higher Education
PO Box 108850
Oklahoma City, OK 73101-8850
Phone: 800-858-1840
E-mail: studentinfo@osrhe.edu

OREGON PTA

http://www.oregonpta.org/

TEACHER EDUCATION SCHOLARSHIP

Nonrenewable scholarships to high school seniors or college students who are Oregon residents who want to teach in Oregon at an elementary or secondary school. The scholarship may be used at any Oregon public college or university that trains teachers or that transfers credits in education.

Academic Fields/Career Goals: Education.

Award: Scholarship for use in freshman, sophomore, junior, or senior years; not renewable. *Number:* 6–13. *Amount:* $500.

Eligibility Requirements: Applicant must be enrolled or expecting to enroll full-time at a two-year or four-year institution or university; resident of Oregon and studying in Oregon. Available to U.S. citizens.

Application Requirements: Application form, essay. *Deadline:* March 21.

Contact: Scholarship Committee
Oregon PTA
4506 Southeast Belmont Street, Suite 108-B
Portland, OR 97215
E-mail: or_office@pta.org

OREGON STUDENT ASSISTANCE COMMISSION

https://oregonstudentaid.gov/

HARRIET A. SIMMONS SCHOLARSHIP

One-time award available to Oregon residents who are enrolled in an elementary or secondary education program in an Oregon public or nonprofit college or university, entering senior or fifth-year, or graduate students in a fifth year for elementary or secondary teaching certificate. Based on financial need.

Academic Fields/Career Goals: Education.

Award: Scholarship for use in senior or graduate years; not renewable.

Eligibility Requirements: Applicant must be enrolled or expecting to enroll full-time at a four-year institution or university and studying in Oregon. Available to U.S. citizens.

Application Requirements: Application form, financial need analysis. *Deadline:* March 1.

Contact: Melissa Adams, Scholarship Processing Coordinator
Phone: 541-687-7409
E-mail: melissa.adams@state.or.us

JAMES CARLSON MEMORIAL SCHOLARSHIP

One-time award for elementary or secondary education majors entering the final year of their program, or graduate students in fifth year for elementary or secondary certificate. Applicants may qualify according to one of the following: (1) Diverse environments (essay required); (2) dependents of Oregon Education Association members (essay recommended); or (3) students committed to teaching autistic children (essay recommended). Based on financial need.

Academic Fields/Career Goals: Education; Special Education.

Award: Scholarship for use in senior or graduate years; not renewable.

Eligibility Requirements: Applicant must be enrolled or expecting to enroll full-time at a four-year institution or university and resident of Oregon. Available to U.S. citizens.

Application Requirements: Application form, essay, financial need analysis. *Deadline:* March 1.

Contact: Melissa Adams, Scholarship Processing Coordinator
Phone: 541-687-7409
E-mail: melissa.adams@state.or.us

OREGON ALPHA DELTA KAPPA SCHOLARSHIP

Award for elementary or secondary education majors entering senior or fifth-year or graduate students in fifth year for elementary or secondary certificate. Oregon four-year public and nonprofit colleges only. Based on financial need.

Academic Fields/Career Goals: Education.

Award: Scholarship for use in freshman, sophomore, junior, senior, or graduate years; not renewable.

Eligibility Requirements: Applicant must be enrolled or expecting to enroll at a four-year institution or university and studying in Oregon. Available to U.S. citizens.

Application Requirements: Application form. *Deadline:* March 1.

Contact: Melissa Adams, Scholarship Processing Coordinator
Phone: 541-687-7409
E-mail: melissa.adams@state.or.us

OREGON COLLEGE SAVINGS PLAN EDUCATION CELEBRATION SCHOLARSHIP

One-time award for education majors studying at least half-time at Oregon public or nonprofit schools. Preference given to college seniors or 5th-year seniors seeking MAT or 2nd-year community college students pursuing AAOT or equivalent. High school seniors must have at least a 3.0 GPA (3.4 preferred) and college students must have a minimum GPA of 3.25. Awardees must be willing to participate in publicity with Oregon 529 College Savings Network. Apply/compete annually. Based on financial need.

Academic Fields/Career Goals: Education.

Award: Scholarship for use in freshman, sophomore, junior, senior, or graduate years; not renewable.

Eligibility Requirements: Applicant must be enrolled or expecting to enroll full- or part-time at a two-year or four-year institution or university and studying in Oregon. Available to U.S. citizens.

Application Requirements: Application form, financial need analysis. *Deadline:* March 1.

Contact: Melissa Adams, Scholarship Processing Coordinator
Phone: 541-687-7409
E-mail: melissa.adams@state.or.us

PADDLE CANADA

http://www.paddlecanada.com

BILL MASON SCHOLARSHIP FUND

The Bill Mason Memorial Scholarship Fund is a tribute to the late Bill Mason, a Canadian recognized both nationally and internationally as an avid canoeist, environmentalist, filmmaker, photographer, artist and public speaker. The scholarship is intended to incorporate some of the characteristics that made Bill Mason unique and to help ensure that the memory, spirit and ideals that he represented are kept fresh in the minds of Canadians. Applicants must demonstrate experience and competency in any or all of the following: canoeing and kayaking skills, wilderness travel experience, wilderness leadership and guiding, environmental issues, communication skills.

Academic Fields/Career Goals: Education; Environmental Science; Natural Resources; Natural Sciences; Recreation, Parks, Leisure Studies; Sports-Related/Exercise Science.

Award: Scholarship for use in sophomore, junior, or senior years; not renewable. *Number:* 1. *Amount:* $943.

Eligibility Requirements: Applicant must be Canadian citizen; enrolled or expecting to enroll full-time at a two-year or four-year institution or university; resident of Alberta, British Columbia, Manitoba, New Brunswick, Newfoundland, Northwest Territories, Nova Scotia, Ontario, Prince Edward Island, Quebec, Saskatchewan, Yukon and studying in Alberta, British Columbia, Manitoba, New Brunswick, Newfoundland, Northwest Territories, Nova Scotia, Ontario, Prince Edward Island, Quebec, Saskatchewan, Yukon. Applicant must have 3.0 GPA or higher.

Application Requirements: Application form, community service, driver's license, financial need analysis. *Deadline:* September 30.

Contact: Mr. Graham Ketcheson, Executive Director
Paddle Canada
PO Box 126 Station Main
Kingston, ON K7L 4V6
CAN
Phone: 888-252-6292 Ext. 11
E-mail: graham@paddlecanada.com

PANCHOLI COSMETIC SURGERY

https://www.drpancholi.com/

PANCHOLI SCHOLARSHIP FOR NEVADA EDUCATORS

Any current Nevada resident who is interested in a career in education and is pursuing a degree is welcome to apply for the $2,000 scholarship—whether you are a high school senior, current education major, or considering returning to school. Eligible candidates must meet the following criteria: 1. Must be a Nevada resident; 2. Must be pursuing a degree or career path in an education-related field at an institution of higher learning the following semester; 3. Must submit one letter of recommendation with valid contact information; 4. Must complete the application form, provide original essay answers, and upload completed application and one letter of reference.

Academic Fields/Career Goals: Education.

Award: Scholarship for use in freshman, sophomore, junior, senior, graduate, or postgraduate years; not renewable. *Number:* 1. *Amount:* $2000.

Eligibility Requirements: Applicant must be enrolled or expecting to enroll full- or part-time at a two-year or four-year institution or university; resident of Nevada and studying in Nevada. Available to U.S. citizens.

Application Requirements: Application form, essay. *Deadline:* June 13.

Contact: Emily Bradley, Marketing Assistant
E-mail: pancholischolarship@gmail.com

PHI DELTA KAPPA INTERNATIONAL

http://www.pdkintl.org/

PHI DELTA KAPPA INTERNATIONAL PROSPECTIVE EDUCATOR SCHOLARSHIPS

High school seniors and current undergraduates who are pursuing careers in teaching are eligible for Prospective Educator Scholarships. Applicants must be connected to the PDK family of associations through membership in Educators Rising, PDK International, and/or Pi Lambda Theta.

Academic Fields/Career Goals: Education.

Award: Scholarship for use in freshman, sophomore, junior, or senior years; not renewable. *Number:* 25–35. *Amount:* $500–$2000.

Eligibility Requirements: Applicant must be enrolled or expecting to enroll full- or part-time at a four-year institution or university. Applicant or parent of applicant must be member of Phi Delta Kappa International. Available to U.S. and non-U.S. citizens.

Application Requirements: Application form, essay. *Deadline:* April 2.

Contact: Katrina Breese, Senior Director of Development & Engagement
Phi Delta Kappa International
PO Box 13090
Arlington, VA 22219
Phone: 812-339-1156
Fax: 812-339-0018
E-mail: scholarships@pdkintl.org

PRESBYTERIAN CHURCH (USA)

http://www.pcusa.org/financialaid

STUDENT OPPORTUNITY SCHOLARSHIP

Designed to assist undergraduate students with their sophomore, junior and senior year of college. Restricted to members of the Presbyterian Church (USA).

Academic Fields/Career Goals: Education; Health and Medical Sciences; Religion/Theology; Social Sciences; Social Services.

Award: Scholarship for use in sophomore, junior, or senior years; renewable. *Number:* 68. *Amount:* up to $3000.

Eligibility Requirements: Applicant must be Presbyterian and enrolled or expecting to enroll full-time at a four-year institution or university. Applicant must have 2.5 GPA or higher. Available to U.S. citizens.

Application Requirements: Application form, essay, financial need analysis, recommendations or references, resume, transcript. *Deadline:* June 1.

Contact: Ms. Laura Bryan, Coordinator, Financial Aid for Studies
Presbyterian Church (USA)
100 Witherspoon Street
Louisville, KY 40202
Phone: 800-728-7228 Ext. 5735
Fax: 502-569-8766
E-mail: finaid@pcusa.org

SARAH KLENKE MEMORIAL TEACHING SCHOLARSHIP

http://www.sarahklenkescholarship.org/

SARAH ELIZABETH KLENKE MEMORIAL TEACHING SCHOLARSHIP

Scholarship for deserving young adults to achieve the goal of becoming teachers. Must have a 2.0 GPA or higher, participate in JROTC or a team sport, and a desire to major in education.

Academic Fields/Career Goals: Education.

Award: Scholarship for use in freshman or senior years; not renewable. *Number:* 1. *Amount:* $1000.

Eligibility Requirements: Applicant must be enrolled or expecting to enroll full-time at a two-year or four-year institution or university. Available to U.S. and non-U.S. citizens.

Application Requirements: Application form, essay, letter from coach or teacher confirming participation in ROTC or team sport, recommendations or references. *Deadline:* April 15.

Contact: William Klenke, Scholarship Committee
Sarah Klenke Memorial Teaching Scholarship
9108 Charred Oak Drive
Bethesda, MD 20817
Phone: 202-412-2812
E-mail: wjk40@yahoo.com

THE SOCIETY FOR THE SCIENTIFIC STUDY OF SEXUALITY

http://www.sexscience.org/

THE SOCIETY FOR THE SCIENTIFIC STUDY OF SEXUALITY STUDENT RESEARCH GRANT

• *See page 120*

SOUTH DAKOTA BOARD OF REGENTS

http://www.sdbor.edu/

SOUTH DAKOTA BOARD OF REGENTS ANNIS I. FOWLER/KADEN SCHOLARSHIP

Scholarship for graduating South Dakota high school seniors to pursue a career in elementary education at a South Dakota public university. University must be one of the following: BHSU, BSU, NSU or USD. Applicants must have a cumulative GPA of 3.0 after three years of high school. One-time award.

Academic Fields/Career Goals: Education.

Award: Scholarship for use in freshman year; not renewable. *Number:* 2. *Amount:* $1000.

Eligibility Requirements: Applicant must be high school student; planning to enroll or expecting to enroll full-time at a four-year institution or university; resident of South Dakota and studying in South Dakota. Applicant must have 3.0 GPA or higher. Available to U.S. citizens.

Application Requirements: Application form, essay. *Deadline:* February 26.

Contact: Kerri Richards, Student Services Coordinator
South Dakota Board of Regents
306 E. Capitol Ave
Ste. 200
Pierre, SD 57501
Phone: 605-773-3455
E-mail: kerri.richards@sdbor.edu

STRAIGHTFORWARD MEDIA

http://www.straightforwardmedia.com/

STRAIGHTFORWARD MEDIA TEACHER SCHOLARSHIP

Scholarship of $500 for students planning to be teachers of any kind and at any level. Must be U.S. citizen. Awarded four times per year. Deadlines are January 14, April 14, July 14, and October 14. For more information, see website at http://www.straightforwardmedia.com/education/form.php.

Academic Fields/Career Goals: Education; Special Education.

Award: Scholarship for use in freshman, sophomore, junior, or senior years; not renewable. *Number:* 4. *Amount:* $500.

Eligibility Requirements: Applicant must be enrolled or expecting to enroll full- or part-time at a two-year or four-year or technical institution or university. Available to U.S. citizens.

Application Requirements: Essay. *Deadline:* varies.

Contact: Scholarship Committee
Phone: 605-348-3042

TEACHER.ORG

http://www.teacher.org

"INSPIRE OUR FUTURE" $2,500 SCHOLARSHIP

Teacher.org offers a $2500 scholarship for college students studying to become teachers or work in the field of education.

Academic Fields/Career Goals: Education.

Award: Scholarship for use in sophomore, junior, senior, graduate, or postgraduate years; not renewable. *Number:* 1. *Amount:* $2500.

Eligibility Requirements: Applicant must be enrolled or expecting to enroll full- or part-time at a two-year or four-year or technical institution or university. Applicant must have 3.5 GPA or higher. Available to U.S. citizens.

Application Requirements: Application form, application form may be submitted online (http://www.teacher.org), essay, transcript. *Deadline:* April 1.

Contact: Salpy Baharian, Co-Founder
Teacher.org
7120 Hayvenhurst Avenue
Van Nuys, CA 91406
Phone: 818-860-8620
E-mail: scholarships@teacher.org

TENNESSEE EDUCATION ASSOCIATION

http://www.teateachers.org/

TEA DON SAHLI-KATHY WOODALL FUTURE TEACHERS OF AMERICA SCHOLARSHIP

Scholarship is available to a high school senior planning to major in education, attending a high school which has an FTA Chapter affiliated with TEA, and planning to enroll in a Tennessee college.

Academic Fields/Career Goals: Education.

Award: Scholarship for use in freshman year; not renewable. *Number:* 1. *Amount:* $1000.

Eligibility Requirements: Applicant must be high school student; planning to enroll or expecting to enroll full-time at a four-year institution or university; resident of Tennessee and studying in Tennessee. Available to U.S. citizens.

Application Requirements: Application form, essay. *Deadline:* March 1.

Contact: Jeanette DeMain
Tennessee Education Association
801 Second Avenue North
Nashville, TN 37201
Phone: 615-242-8392 Ext. 210
E-mail: jdemain@tnea.org

TEA DON SAHLI-KATHY WOODALL MINORITY SCHOLARSHIP

Scholarship is available to a minority high school senior planning to major in education and planning to enroll in a Tennessee college.

Application must be made by an FTA Chapter, or by the student with the recommendation of an active TEA member.

Academic Fields/Career Goals: Education.

Award: Scholarship for use in freshman year; not renewable. *Number:* 1. *Amount:* $1000.

Eligibility Requirements: Applicant must be American Indian/Alaska Native, Asian/Pacific Islander, Black (non-Hispanic), Hispanic; high school student; planning to enroll or expecting to enroll full-time at a four-year institution or university; resident of Tennessee and studying in Tennessee. Available to U.S. citizens.

Application Requirements: Application form, essay. *Deadline:* March 1.

Contact: Jeanette DeMain
Tennessee Education Association
801 Second Avenue North
Nashville, TN 37201
Phone: 615-242-8392 Ext. 210
E-mail: jdemain@tnea.org

TEA DON SAHLI-KATHY WOODALL SONS AND DAUGHTERS SCHOLARSHIP

Scholarship is available to a TEA member's child who is a high school senior, undergraduate or graduate student, and is planning to enroll, or is already enrolled, in a Tennessee college, majoring in education.

Academic Fields/Career Goals: Education.

Award: Scholarship for use in freshman, sophomore, junior, senior, or graduate years; not renewable. *Number:* 1. *Amount:* $1000.

Eligibility Requirements: Applicant must be enrolled or expecting to enroll full-time at a four-year institution or university; resident of Tennessee and studying in Tennessee. Applicant or parent of applicant must be member of Tennessee Education Association. Applicant or parent of applicant must have employment or volunteer experience in teaching/education. Available to U.S. citizens.

Application Requirements: Application form, essay. *Deadline:* March 1.

Contact: Jeanette DeMain
Tennessee Education Association
801 Second North
Nashville, TN 37201
Phone: 615-242-8392 Ext. 210
E-mail: jdemain@tnea.org

TEA DON SAHLI-KATHY WOODALL STEA SCHOLARSHIP

Scholarship is available to undergraduate students who are student TEA members. Application must be made through the local STEA Chapter. Amount varies from $500 to $1000.

Academic Fields/Career Goals: Education.

Award: Scholarship for use in freshman, sophomore, junior, or senior years; not renewable. *Number:* 4. *Amount:* $500–$1000.

Eligibility Requirements: Applicant must be enrolled or expecting to enroll full- or part-time at a four-year institution or university; resident of Tennessee and studying in Tennessee. Available to U.S. citizens.

Application Requirements: Application form, essay. *Deadline:* March 1.

Contact: Jeanette DeMain
Tennessee Education Association
801 Second Avenue North
Nashville, TN 37201
Phone: 615-242-8392 Ext. 210
E-mail: jdemain@tnea.org

TKE EDUCATIONAL FOUNDATION

http://www.tke.org/

CARROL C. HALL MEMORIAL SCHOLARSHIP

• *See page 128*

FRANCIS J. FLYNN MEMORIAL SCHOLARSHIP

Award of $800 for an undergraduate member of TKE who is a full-time student pursuing a degree in mathematics or education. Minimum 2.75

GPA required. Leadership within chapter or campus organizations recognized. Preference will first be given to a member of Theta-Sigma Chapter, but if there is no qualified applicant, the scholarship will be open to any other qualified Teke.

Academic Fields/Career Goals: Education; Mathematics.

Award: Scholarship for use in sophomore, junior, or senior years; not renewable. *Number:* 1. *Amount:* $800.

Eligibility Requirements: Applicant must be enrolled or expecting to enroll full-time at a four-year institution or university; male and must have an interest in leadership. Applicant or parent of applicant must be member of Tau Kappa Epsilon. Available to U.S. and non-U.S. citizens.

Application Requirements: Application form, application form may be submitted online (http://www.tke.org/member_resources/scholarships/apply_online), essay, narrative summary of how TKE membership has benefited applicant, personal photograph, transcript. *Deadline:* March 15.

Contact: Offices of the Grand Chapter
TKE Educational Foundation
7439 Woodland Drive, Suite 100
Indianapolis, IN 46278
E-mail: tkeogc@tke.org

ULMAN CANCER FUND FOR YOUNG ADULTS

http://www.ulmanfund.org/scholarships

JAMES AND PATRICIA SOOD SCHOLARSHIP

The Ulman Cancer Fund for Young Adults is committed to helping young adults continue their education after being affected by cancer through their own diagnosis or the diagnosis of a loved one. Many scholarships offered by UCF share similar applicant criteria. Applicants need only submit one application, which will be considered for any and all scholarships for which the student applies and is eligible.

Academic Fields/Career Goals: Education.

Award: Scholarship for use in freshman, sophomore, junior, senior, or graduate years; not renewable. *Number:* 1. *Amount:* $2500.

Eligibility Requirements: Applicant must be age 15-39 and enrolled or expecting to enroll full- or part-time at a four-year institution or university. Available to U.S. citizens.

Application Requirements: Application form, essay. *Deadline:* March 1.

Contact: Lauriann Parker, Scholarship Coordinator
Ulman Cancer Fund for Young Adults
1215 E. Fort Ave.
Ste. 104
Baltimore, MD 21230
Phone: 410-964-0202 Ext. 105
E-mail: scholarship@ulmanfund.org

UNITED NEGRO COLLEGE FUND

http://www.uncf.org/

PNC FOUNDATION SCHOLARSHIP

Need-based award up to $1650. Candidates must have permanent residency or reside within Central or Northern New Jersey, and majoring in the field of early childhood education or education. The applicants must currently attend a UNCF member institution or an accredited four-year institution in the state of New Jersey.

Academic Fields/Career Goals: Education.

Award: Scholarship for use in freshman, sophomore, junior, or senior years; not renewable.

Eligibility Requirements: Applicant must be Black (non-Hispanic) and enrolled or expecting to enroll at a four-year institution or university. Applicant must have 2.5 GPA or higher. Available to U.S. citizens.

Application Requirements: Application form, essay, financial need analysis. *Deadline:* December 22.

Contact: Mary Williams, Director of Outreach and Recruitment
Phone: 800-331-2244

UNIVERSITY OF WYOMING

http://www.uwyo.edu/scholarships

SUPERIOR STUDENT IN EDUCATION SCHOLARSHIP-WYOMING

Scholarship available each year to sixteen Wyoming high school graduates who plan to teach in Wyoming. The award covers costs of undergraduate tuition at the University of Wyoming or any Wyoming community college.

Academic Fields/Career Goals: Education.

Award: Scholarship for use in freshman, sophomore, junior, or senior years; renewable. *Number:* 16–16. *Amount:* $1000.

Eligibility Requirements: Applicant must be enrolled or expecting to enroll full-time at a two-year or four-year institution or university; resident of Wyoming and studying in Wyoming. Applicant must have 3.0 GPA or higher. Available to U.S. citizens.

Application Requirements: Application form, recommendations or references, test scores, transcript. *Deadline:* October 31.

Contact: Tammy Mack, Assistant Director, Scholarships
University of Wyoming
Department 3335
1000 East University Avenue
Laramie, WY 82071
Phone: 307-766-2412
Fax: 307-766-3800
E-mail: FinAid@uwyo.edu

VERMONT-NEA

http://www.vtnea.org/

VERMONT-NEA/MAIDA F. TOWNSEND SCHOLARSHIP

Scholarship of $1000 to sons and daughters of Vermont-NEA members in their last year of high school, undergraduates, and graduate students. Students majoring in any discipline are eligible to apply, but preference may be given to those majoring in education, or having that intention.

Academic Fields/Career Goals: Education.

Award: Scholarship for use in freshman, sophomore, junior, senior, or graduate years; not renewable. *Number:* 5. *Amount:* $1000.

Eligibility Requirements: Applicant must be enrolled or expecting to enroll full- or part-time at a two-year or four-year or technical institution or university. Applicant or parent of applicant must be member of Vermont-NEA. Applicant or parent of applicant must have employment or volunteer experience in teaching/education. Available to U.S. and non-U.S. citizens.

Application Requirements: Application form, community service, cover letter, essay, recommendations or references, test scores, transcript. *Deadline:* February 1.

Contact: Sandy Perkins, Administrative Assistant
Vermont-NEA
10 Wheelock Street
Montpelier, VT 05602-3737
Phone: 802-223-6375
E-mail: sperkins@vtnea.org

VIRGINIA CONGRESS OF PARENTS AND TEACHERS

http://www.vapta.org/

FRIEDA L. KOONTZ SCHOLARSHIP

Scholarship of $1200 to graduating high school students planning to enter teaching or other youth-serving professions in Virginia. Must be Virginia residents graduating from a Virginia public high school with a Parent-Teacher-Student Association (PTSA) and attending a Virginia college or university. Minimum 2.5 GPA required.

Academic Fields/Career Goals: Education.

Award: Scholarship for use in freshman year; not renewable. *Number:* 1. *Amount:* $1200.

Eligibility Requirements: Applicant must be high school student; planning to enroll or expecting to enroll full-time at a four-year institution or university; resident of Virginia and studying in Virginia.

Applicant or parent of applicant must be member of Parent-Teacher Association/Organization. Applicant must have 2.5 GPA or higher. Available to U.S. citizens.

Application Requirements: Application form, essay, recommendations or references, test scores, transcript. *Deadline:* March 1.

Contact: Daniel Phillips, Scholarship Chair
Phone: 804-264-1234
E-mail: info@vapta.org

GENERAL SCHOLARSHIPS

General scholarships in addition to the Freida L. Koontz and John S. Davis Scholarships. Only graduating students enrolled in a Virginia school that is a PTA or PTSA school may apply. See website for application details.

Academic Fields/Career Goals: Education.

Award: Scholarship for use in freshman year; not renewable. *Number:* 10–20. *Amount:* $1000.

Eligibility Requirements: Applicant must be high school student; planning to enroll or expecting to enroll full-time at a four-year institution or university and resident of Virginia. Applicant or parent of applicant must be member of Parent-Teacher Association/Organization. Applicant must have 2.5 GPA or higher. Available to U.S. citizens.

Application Requirements: Application form, essay, recommendations or references, test scores, transcript. *Deadline:* March 1.

Contact: Daniel Phillips, Scholarship Chair
Phone: 804-264-1234
E-mail: info@vapta.org

S. JOHN DAVIS SCHOLARSHIP

Scholarship of $1200 to Virginia residents graduating from a Virginia public school that has a Parent-Teacher-Student Association (PTSA) or PTA. Must be planning to attend a Virginia college or university and pursuing a career in teaching or qualifying for service with a youth-serving agency in Virginia. Minimum 2.5 GPA required.

Academic Fields/Career Goals: Education.

Award: Scholarship for use in freshman year; not renewable. *Number:* 1. *Amount:* $1200.

Eligibility Requirements: Applicant must be high school student; planning to enroll or expecting to enroll full-time at a four-year institution or university; resident of Virginia and studying in Virginia. Applicant or parent of applicant must be member of Parent-Teacher Association/Organization. Applicant must have 2.5 GPA or higher. Available to U.S. citizens.

Application Requirements: Application form, essay. *Deadline:* March 1.

Contact: Daniel Phillips, Scholarship Chair
Phone: 804-264-1234
E-mail: info@vapta.org

WISCONSIN CONGRESS OF PARENTS AND TEACHERS INC.

http://www.wisconsinpta.org/

BROOKMIRE-HASTINGS SCHOLARSHIPS

One-time award to graduating high school seniors from Wisconsin public schools. Must pursue a degree in education. High school must have an active PTA in good standing of the Wisconsin PTA.

Academic Fields/Career Goals: Education; Special Education.

Award: Scholarship for use in freshman year; not renewable. *Number:* up to 2. *Amount:* $1000.

Eligibility Requirements: Applicant must be high school student; planning to enroll or expecting to enroll full-time at a four-year institution or university and resident of Wisconsin. Available to U.S. citizens.

Application Requirements: Application form, essay, interview, recommendations or references, transcript. *Deadline:* March 1.

Contact: Kim Schwantes, Executive Administrator
Wisconsin Congress of Parents and Teachers Inc.
4797 Hayes Road, Suite 2
Madison, WI 53704-3256
Phone: 608-244-1455

WISCONSIN MATHEMATICS EDUCATION FOUNDATION

http://wmefonline.org/

ARNE ENGEBRETSEN WISCONSIN MATHEMATICS COUNCIL SCHOLARSHIP

Scholarship for Wisconsin high school senior who is planning to study mathematics education and teach mathematics at K-12 level.

Academic Fields/Career Goals: Education; Mathematics.

Award: Scholarship for use in freshman year; not renewable. *Number:* 1. *Amount:* $2000.

Eligibility Requirements: Applicant must be high school student; planning to enroll or expecting to enroll full-time at a four-year institution or university and resident of Wisconsin. Available to U.S. citizens.

Application Requirements: Application form, essay, recommendations or references, resume, transcript. *Deadline:* March 1.

ETHEL A. NEIJAHR WISCONSIN MATHEMATICS COUNCIL SCHOLARSHIP

Scholarship for a Wisconsin resident who is currently enrolled in teacher education programs in a Wisconsin institution studying mathematics education. Minimum GPA of 3.0 required.

Academic Fields/Career Goals: Education; Mathematics.

Award: Scholarship for use in junior or senior years; not renewable. *Number:* 1. *Amount:* $2000.

Eligibility Requirements: Applicant must be enrolled or expecting to enroll full-time at a four-year institution or university; resident of Wisconsin and studying in Wisconsin. Applicant must have 3.0 GPA or higher. Available to U.S. citizens.

Application Requirements: Application form, essay, recommendations or references, resume, transcript. *Deadline:* March 1.

SISTER MARY PETRONIA VAN STRATEN WISCONSIN MATHEMATICS COUNCIL SCHOLARSHIP

Scholarship for a Wisconsin resident who is currently enrolled in teacher education programs in Wisconsin institution studying mathematics education. Minimum GPA of 3.0 required.

Academic Fields/Career Goals: Education; Mathematics.

Award: Scholarship for use in junior or senior years; not renewable. *Number:* 1. *Amount:* $2000.

Eligibility Requirements: Applicant must be enrolled or expecting to enroll full-time at a four-year institution or university; resident of Wisconsin and studying in Wisconsin. Applicant must have 3.0 GPA or higher. Available to U.S. citizens.

Application Requirements: Application form, essay, recommendations or references, resume, transcript. *Deadline:* March 1.

WOMEN BAND DIRECTORS INTERNATIONAL

http://www.womenbanddirectors.org/

CHARLOTTE PLUMMER OWEN MEMORIAL SCHOLARSHIP

One-time award for women instrumental music majors enrolled in a four-year institution. Applicants must be working toward a degree in music education with the intention of becoming a band director. See website for application http://www.womenbanddirectors.org/.

Academic Fields/Career Goals: Education; Music; Performing Arts.

Award: Scholarship for use in freshman, sophomore, junior, or senior years; not renewable. *Number:* 4. *Amount:* $300.

Eligibility Requirements: Applicant must be enrolled or expecting to enroll full-time at a four-year institution or university; female and must have an interest in music/singing. Available to U.S. and non-U.S. citizens.

Application Requirements: Application form, essay, personal photograph, recommendations or references, transcript. *Deadline:* December 1.

Contact: Nicole Aakre-Rubis, Scholarship Chair
Women Band Directors International
16085 Excel Way
Rosemount, MN 55068

MARTHA ANN STARK MEMORIAL SCHOLARSHIP

One-time award for women instrumental music majors enrolled in a four-year institution. Applicants must be working toward a degree in music education with the intention of becoming a band director. Three of the scholarships are designated for college upperclassmen, and one is open to all levels. See website for application http://www.womenbanddirectors.org/.

Academic Fields/Career Goals: Education; Music; Performing Arts.

Award: Scholarship for use in freshman, sophomore, junior, or senior years; not renewable. *Number:* 1. *Amount:* $300.

Eligibility Requirements: Applicant must be enrolled or expecting to enroll full-time at a four-year institution or university; female and must have an interest in music/singing. Available to U.S. and non-U.S. citizens.

Application Requirements: Application form, essay, personal photograph, recommendations or references, transcript. *Deadline:* December 1.

Contact: Nicole Aakre-Rubis, Scholarship Chair
Women Band Directors International
16085 Excel Way
Rosemount, MN 55068

VOLKWEIN MEMORIAL SCHOLARSHIP

One-time award for female instrumental music majors enrolled in a four-year institution. Applicants must be working toward a degree in music education with the intention of becoming a band director. Three of the scholarships are designated for college upperclassmen, and one is open to all levels. See website for application http://www.womenbanddirectors.org/.

Academic Fields/Career Goals: Education; Music; Performing Arts.

Award: Scholarship for use in freshman, sophomore, junior, senior, or graduate years; not renewable. *Number:* 4. *Amount:* $300–$500.

Eligibility Requirements: Applicant must be enrolled or expecting to enroll full-time at a four-year institution or university; female and must have an interest in music/singing. Available to U.S. and non-U.S. citizens.

Application Requirements: Application form, essay, personal photograph, recommendations or references, self-addressed stamped envelope with application, transcript. *Deadline:* December 1.

Contact: Nicole Aakre-Rubis, Scholarship Chair
Women Band Directors International
16085 Excel Way
Rosemount, MN 55068

WOMEN'S SPORTS FOUNDATION

http://www.womenssportsfoundation.org/

DOROTHEA DEITZ ENDOWED MEMORIAL SCHOLARSHIP

The Dorothea Deitz Endowed Memorial Scholarship was established in 2005 by the Dorothea Deitz Memorial Scholarship Fund Board of Trustees to encourage young women in New York to pursue careers in the physical education teaching profession.

Academic Fields/Career Goals: Education.

Award: Scholarship for use in freshman year; not renewable. *Number:* 1–9. *Amount:* $1000.

Eligibility Requirements: Applicant must be high school student; planning to enroll or expecting to enroll full-time at a four-year institution; female and resident of New York. Applicant must have 3.0 GPA or higher. Available to U.S. citizens.

Application Requirements: Application form. *Deadline:* May 31.

Contact: Elizabeth Flores
Phone: 516-307-3915
E-mail: lflores@womenssportsfoundation.org

Y'S MEN INTERNATIONAL

http://www.ysmen.org/

ALEXANDER SCHOLARSHIP LOAN FUND
• *See page 185*

ELECTRICAL ENGINEERING/ ELECTRONICS

AACE INTERNATIONAL

http://www.aacei.org/

AACE INTERNATIONAL COMPETITIVE SCHOLARSHIP
• *See page 130*

AHS INTERNATIONAL—THE VERTICAL FLIGHT TECHNICAL SOCIETY

http://www.vtol.org/

VERTICAL FLIGHT FOUNDATION SCHOLARSHIP
• *See page 148*

AIST FOUNDATION

http://www.aistfoundation.org/

AISI/AIST FOUNDATION PREMIER SCHOLARSHIP

This award is granted to the highest scoring FeMET at StEEL scholarship applicants. $10,000 scholarships are for full-time students of metallurgy, materials science, chemical, electrical, mechanical, environmental, computer science, and industrial engineering. Students must have an interest in a career in the steel industry as demonstrated by an internship or related experience, or who have plans to pursue such experiences during college. Students must commit to a summer internship at a steel producing company (placement assistance is provided) prior to receiving this scholarship. Student may apply during their sophomore and junior years. Applications are accepted from September 1 through December 31 each year.

Academic Fields/Career Goals: Electrical Engineering/Electronics; Materials Science, Engineering, and Metallurgy; Mechanical Engineering.

Award: Scholarship for use in sophomore or junior years; not renewable. *Number:* 1. *Amount:* $10,000.

Eligibility Requirements: Applicant must be enrolled or expecting to enroll full-time at a four-year institution or university. Applicant must have 2.5 GPA or higher. Available to U.S. and non-U.S. citizens.

Application Requirements: Application form, essay, recommendations or references, resume, transcript. *Deadline:* December 31.

Contact: Lori Wharrey, AIST Manager, Board Services
　　　　AIST Foundation
　　　　186 Thorn Hill Road
　　　　Warrendale, PA 15086
　　　　Phone: 724-814-3044
　　　　E-mail: lwharrey@aist.org

AIST WILLIAM E. SCHWABE MEMORIAL SCHOLARSHIP

Scholarship for full-time students of metallurgy, materials science, chemical, mechanical, electrical, environmental, computer science, and industrial engineering. Students must have an interest in a career in the steel industry as demonstrated by an internship or related experience, or who have plans to pursue such experiences during college. Student may apply after first term of freshman year of college. Applications are accepted from 1 Sep through 31 Dec each year. Note: High school students do not qualify but are encouraged to learn about the steel industry and the career opportunities available therein, during their freshman year.

Academic Fields/Career Goals: Electrical Engineering/Electronics; Engineering/Technology; Materials Science, Engineering, and Metallurgy; Mechanical Engineering.

Award: Scholarship for use in sophomore, junior, or senior years; not renewable. *Number:* 1. *Amount:* $3000.

Eligibility Requirements: Applicant must be enrolled or expecting to enroll full-time at a four-year institution or university. Applicant must have 2.5 GPA or higher. Available to U.S. and non-U.S. citizens.

Application Requirements: Application form, essay, recommendations or references, resume, transcript. *Deadline:* December 31.

Contact: Lori Wharrey, AIST Manager, Board Services
　　　　Phone: 724-814-3044
　　　　E-mail: lwharrey@aist.org

ASSOCIATION FOR IRON AND STEEL TECHNOLOGY BENJAMIN F. FAIRLESS SCHOLARSHIP (AIME)
• *See page 186*

ASSOCIATION FOR IRON AND STEEL TECHNOLOGY DAVID H. SAMSON CANADIAN SCHOLARSHIP
• *See page 187*

ASSOCIATION FOR IRON AND STEEL TECHNOLOGY OHIO VALLEY CHAPTER SCHOLARSHIP
• *See page 167*

ASSOCIATION FOR IRON AND STEEL TECHNOLOGY RONALD E. LINCOLN SCHOLARSHIP

Scholarship for full-time students of metallurgy, materials science, chemical, mechanical, electrical, environmental, computer science, and industrial engineering. Students must have an interest in a career in the steel industry as demonstrated by an internship or related experience, or who have plans to pursue such experiences during college. Student may apply after first term of freshman year of college. Applications are accepted from 1 Sep through 31 Dec each year. Note: High school students do not qualify but are encouraged to learn about the steel industry and the career opportunities available therein, during their freshman year.

Academic Fields/Career Goals: Electrical Engineering/Electronics; Materials Science, Engineering, and Metallurgy; Mechanical Engineering.

Award: Scholarship for use in sophomore, junior, or senior years; not renewable. *Number:* 2. *Amount:* $3000.

Eligibility Requirements: Applicant must be enrolled or expecting to enroll full-time at a four-year institution or university. Applicant must have 2.5 GPA or higher. Available to U.S. and non-U.S. citizens.

Application Requirements: Application form, essay, recommendations or references, resume, transcript. *Deadline:* December 31.

Contact: Lori Wharrey, AIST Manager, Board Services
　　　　AIST Foundation
　　　　186 Thorn Hill Road
　　　　Warrendale, PA 15086
　　　　Phone: 724-814-3044
　　　　E-mail: lwharrey@aist.org

ASSOCIATION FOR IRON AND STEEL TECHNOLOGY WILLY KORF MEMORIAL SCHOLARSHIP
• *See page 187*

STEEL ENGINEERING EDUCATION LINK (STEEL) SCHOLARSHIPS

Scholarships are for full-time students of chemical, electrical, mechanical, computer science, environment, and industrial engineering. Students must have an interest in a career in the steel industry as demonstrated by an internship or related experience, or who have plans to pursue such experiences during college. Students must commit to a paid summer internship at a steel producing company (placement assistance is provided) prior to receiving this scholarship. Student may apply during their sophomore and junior years. Applications are accepted from 1 Sep through 31 Dec each year.

Academic Fields/Career Goals: Electrical Engineering/Electronics; Mechanical Engineering.

Award: Scholarship for use in sophomore or junior years; not renewable. *Number:* 1–10. *Amount:* $5000.

Eligibility Requirements: Applicant must be enrolled or expecting to enroll full-time at a four-year institution or university. Applicant must have 2.5 GPA or higher. Available to U.S. and non-U.S. citizens.

Application Requirements: Application form, essay, recommendations or references, resume, transcript. *Deadline:* December 31.

Contact: Lori Wharrey, AIST Manager, Board Services
AIST Foundation
186 Thorn Hill Road
Warrendale, PA 15086
Phone: 724-814-3044
E-mail: lwharrey@aist.org

AMERICAN CHEMICAL SOCIETY, RUBBER DIVISION

http://www.rubber.org/

AMERICAN CHEMICAL SOCIETY, RUBBER DIVISION UNDERGRADUATE SCHOLARSHIP
• *See page 120*

AMERICAN COUNCIL OF ENGINEERING COMPANIES OF PENNSYLVANIA (ACEC/PA)

http://www.acecpa.org/

ERIC J. GENNUSO AND LEROY D. (BUD) LOY, JR. SCHOLARSHIP PROGRAM
• *See page 187*

AMERICAN FOUNDATION FOR THE BLIND

http://www.afb.org/

PAUL W. RUCKES SCHOLARSHIP
• *See page 228*

AMERICAN INDIAN SCIENCE AND ENGINEERING SOCIETY

http://www.aises.org/

A.T. ANDERSON MEMORIAL SCHOLARSHIP PROGRAM
• *See page 121*

AMERICAN INSTITUTE OF AERONAUTICS AND ASTRONAUTICS

http://www.aiaafoundation.org/

AIAA FOUNDATION UNDERGRADUATE SCHOLARSHIPS
• *See page 121*

LEATRICE GREGORY PENDRAY SCHOLARSHIP
• *See page 121*

AMERICAN PUBLIC POWER ASSOCIATION

https://www.publicpower.org/grants-scholarships

DEED EDUCATIONAL SCHOLARSHIP
• *See page 190*

DEED STUDENT INTERNSHIP
• *See page 190*

DEED STUDENT RESEARCH GRANTS
• *See page 204*

DEED TECHNICAL DESIGN PROJECT
• *See page 191*

AMERICAN PUBLIC TRANSPORTATION FOUNDATION

http://www.apta.com/

LOUIS T. KLAUDER SCHOLARSHIP

Scholarships for study towards a career in the rail transit industry as an electrical or mechanical engineer. Must be sponsored by APTA member organization and complete internship with APTA member organization. Minimum GPA of 3.0 required.

Academic Fields/Career Goals: Electrical Engineering/Electronics; Mechanical Engineering.

Award: Scholarship for use in sophomore, junior, senior, or graduate years; renewable. *Number:* 1. *Amount:* $2500.

Eligibility Requirements: Applicant must be enrolled or expecting to enroll full-time at a two-year or four-year institution or university. Applicant must have 3.0 GPA or higher. Available to U.S. and Canadian citizens.

Application Requirements: Application form, essay, financial need analysis, recommendations or references, transcript, verification of enrollment for the current semester, copy of fee schedule from the college/university. *Deadline:* June 16.

Contact: Pamela Boswell, Vice President of Program Management
American Public Transportation Foundation
1666 K Street, NW
Washington, DC 20006-1215
Phone: 202-496-4803
Fax: 202-496-2323
E-mail: pboswell@apta.com

TRANSIT HALL OF FAME SCHOLARSHIP AWARD PROGRAM
• *See page 204*

AMERICAN RAILWAY ENGINEERING AND MAINTENANCE OF WAY ASSOCIATION

http://www.aremafoundation.org/

AREMA GRADUATE AND UNDERGRADUATE SCHOLARSHIPS
• *See page 204*

AMERICAN SOCIETY OF CERTIFIED ENGINEERING TECHNICIANS

http://www.ascet.org/

KURT H. AND DONNA M. SCHULER SMALL GRANT
• *See page 205*

AMERICAN SOCIETY OF HEATING, REFRIGERATING, AND AIR CONDITIONING ENGINEERS, INC.

http://www.ashrae.org/

ALWIN B. NEWTON SCHOLARSHIP

Scholarship available to undergraduate students pursuing a bachelor of science or engineering degree, who are enrolled full-time in a program accredited by the Accreditation Board for Engineering and Technology. Application and additional information on Website http://www.ashrae.org.

Academic Fields/Career Goals: Electrical Engineering/Electronics; Engineering-Related Technologies; Engineering/Technology; Heating,

Air-Conditioning, and Refrigeration Mechanics; Mechanical Engineering; Trade/Technical Specialties.

Award: Scholarship for use in sophomore, junior, or senior years; not renewable. *Number:* 1. *Amount:* $5000.

Eligibility Requirements: Applicant must be enrolled or expecting to enroll full-time at a four-year institution or university. Applicant must have 3.0 GPA or higher. Available to U.S. and non-U.S. citizens.

Application Requirements: Application form, financial need analysis. *Deadline:* December 1.

Contact: Lois Benedict, Scholarship Administrator
Phone: 404-636-8400 Ext. 1120
E-mail: lbenedict@ashrae.org

ASHRAE REGION III BOGGARM SETTY SCHOLARSHIP
• *See page 191*

DUANE HANSON SCHOLARSHIP

One-time, $5000 scholarship available to undergraduate students pursuing a Bachelor of Science or engineering degree, who are enrolled full-time in a program. For study in heating, ventilating, refrigeration, and air conditioning in an ABET-accredited program at an accredited school. See Website for application and additional information, http://www.ashrae.org.

Academic Fields/Career Goals: Electrical Engineering/Electronics; Engineering-Related Technologies; Engineering/Technology; Heating, Air-Conditioning, and Refrigeration Mechanics; Trade/Technical Specialties.

Award: Scholarship for use in freshman, sophomore, junior, or senior years; not renewable. *Number:* 1. *Amount:* $5000.

Eligibility Requirements: Applicant must be enrolled or expecting to enroll full-time at a four-year institution or university. Applicant must have 3.0 GPA or higher. Available to U.S. and non-U.S. citizens.

Application Requirements: Application form, financial need analysis. *Deadline:* December 1.

Contact: Lois Benedict, Scholarship Administrator
Phone: 404-636-8400 Ext. 1120
E-mail: lbenedict@ashrae.org

FRANK M. CODA SCHOLARSHIP

$5000 award to undergraduate students enrolled full-time in an ABET-accredited program leading to Bachelor of Science or engineering degree in a course of study that traditionally has been a preparatory curriculum for the HVAC&R profession. Future service to the HVAC&R profession, character and leadership ability are taken into consideration. For application and additional information see Website, http://www.ashrae.org.

Academic Fields/Career Goals: Electrical Engineering/Electronics; Engineering-Related Technologies; Engineering/Technology; Heating, Air-Conditioning, and Refrigeration Mechanics; Mechanical Engineering; Trade/Technical Specialties.

Award: Scholarship for use in sophomore, junior, or senior years; not renewable. *Number:* 1. *Amount:* $5000.

Eligibility Requirements: Applicant must be enrolled or expecting to enroll full-time at a four-year institution or university and must have an interest in leadership. Applicant must have 3.0 GPA or higher. Available to U.S. and non-U.S. citizens.

Application Requirements: Application form, financial need analysis. *Deadline:* December 1.

Contact: Lois Benedict, Scholarship Administrator
Phone: 404-636-8400 Ext. 1120
E-mail: lbenedict@ashrae.org

GORDON V. R. HOLNESS SCHOLARSHIP

$5000 scholarship available to undergraduate students pursuing a Bachelor of Science or engineering degree, who are enrolled full-time in a program accredited by the Accreditation Board for Engineering and Technology. Application and additional information on Website http://www.ashrae.org.

Academic Fields/Career Goals: Electrical Engineering/Electronics; Engineering/Technology.

Award: Scholarship for use in sophomore, junior, or senior years; not renewable. *Number:* 1. *Amount:* $5000.

Eligibility Requirements: Applicant must be enrolled or expecting to enroll full-time at a four-year institution or university. Applicant must have 3.0 GPA or higher. Available to U.S. citizens.

Application Requirements: Application form, financial need analysis. *Deadline:* December 1.

Contact: Lois Benedict, Scholarship Administrator
Phone: 404-636-8400 Ext. 1120
E-mail: lbenedict@ashrae.org

HENRY ADAMS SCHOLARSHIP

One-time $3000 award for full-time study in heating, ventilating, refrigeration, and air conditioning in an ABET-accredited program at an accredited school. Must be pursuing a Bachelor of Science or engineering degree. See Website for application and additional information, http://www.ashrae.org.

Academic Fields/Career Goals: Electrical Engineering/Electronics; Engineering-Related Technologies; Engineering/Technology; Heating, Air-Conditioning, and Refrigeration Mechanics; Trade/Technical Specialties.

Award: Scholarship for use in freshman, sophomore, junior, or senior years; not renewable. *Number:* 1. *Amount:* $3000.

Eligibility Requirements: Applicant must be enrolled or expecting to enroll full-time at a four-year institution or university and must have an interest in leadership. Applicant must have 3.0 GPA or higher. Available to U.S. and non-U.S. citizens.

Application Requirements: Application form, financial need analysis. *Deadline:* December 1.

Contact: Lois Benedict, Scholarship Administrator
Phone: 404-636-8400 Ext. 1120
E-mail: lbenedict@ashrae.org

LYNN G. BELLENGER SCHOLARSHIP

One-year $5,000 scholarship available to a female undergraduate engineering technology student enrolled full-time in a post-secondary educational institution and pursuing a Bachelor or an Associate degree in a course of study which has traditionally been a preparatory curriculum for the HVAC&R profession.

Academic Fields/Career Goals: Electrical Engineering/Electronics; Engineering-Related Technologies; Engineering/Technology; Heating, Air-Conditioning, and Refrigeration Mechanics; Mechanical Engineering; Trade/Technical Specialties.

Award: Scholarship for use in sophomore, junior, or senior years; not renewable. *Number:* 1. *Amount:* $5000.

Eligibility Requirements: Applicant must be enrolled or expecting to enroll full-time at a two-year or four-year institution or university; female and must have an interest in leadership. Applicant must have 3.0 GPA or higher. Available to U.S. citizens.

Application Requirements: Application form, financial need analysis. *Deadline:* December 1.

Contact: Lois Benedict, Scholarship Administrator
Phone: 404-636-8400 Ext. 1120
E-mail: lbenedict@ashrae.org

REUBEN TRANE SCHOLARSHIP

Undergraduate engineering scholarships awarded in two disbursements of $5000 each at the beginning of the student's junior and senior year. Must be a full-time student enrolled in a Bachelor of Science or engineering degree accredited by the Accreditation Board for Engineering and Technology. See Website for application package and additional information, http://www.ashrae.org.

Academic Fields/Career Goals: Electrical Engineering/Electronics; Energy and Power Engineering; Engineering/Technology; Heating, Air-Conditioning, and Refrigeration Mechanics; Mechanical Engineering; Trade/Technical Specialties.

Award: Scholarship for use in junior or senior years; renewable. *Number:* 4. *Amount:* $10,000.

Eligibility Requirements: Applicant must be enrolled or expecting to enroll full-time at a four-year institution or university and must have an interest in leadership. Applicant must have 3.0 GPA or higher. Available to U.S. and non-U.S. citizens.

Application Requirements: Application form, financial need analysis. *Deadline:* December 1.

Contact: Lois Benedict, Scholarship Administrator
Phone: 404-636-8400 Ext. 1120
E-mail: lbenedict@ashrae.org

WILLIS H. CARRIER SCHOLARSHIPS

Two, one-year scholarships of $10,000 available to undergraduate students enrolled full time in an ABET-accredited program leading to a Bachelor of Science or engineering degree. Minimum 3.0 GPA required. See Website for application and further details, http://www.ashrae.org.

Academic Fields/Career Goals: Electrical Engineering/Electronics; Engineering-Related Technologies; Engineering/Technology; Heating, Air-Conditioning, and Refrigeration Mechanics.

Award: Scholarship for use in sophomore, junior, or senior years; not renewable. *Number:* 2. *Amount:* $10,000.

Eligibility Requirements: Applicant must be enrolled or expecting to enroll full-time at a four-year institution or university. Applicant must have 3.0 GPA or higher. Available to U.S. citizens.

Application Requirements: Application form, financial need analysis. *Deadline:* December 1.

Contact: Lois Benedict, Scholarship Administrator
    Phone: 404-636-8400 Ext. 1120
    E-mail: lbenedict@ashrae.org

AMERICAN SOCIETY OF NAVAL ENGINEERS

http://www.navalengineers.org/

AMERICAN SOCIETY OF NAVAL ENGINEERS SCHOLARSHIP
• *See page 122*

ARMED FORCES COMMUNICATIONS AND ELECTRONICS ASSOCIATION, EDUCATIONAL FOUNDATION

http://www.afcea.org/site/?q=foundation/scholarships

AFCEA STEM MAJORS SCHOLARSHIPS FOR UNDERGRADUATE STUDENTS
• *See page 122*

ARMED FORCES COMMUNICATIONS AND ELECTRONICS ASSOCIATION ROTC SCHOLARSHIP PROGRAM
• *See page 151*

ARRL FOUNDATION INC.

http://www.arrl.org/

ALFRED E. FRIEND JR., W4CF, MEMORIAL SCHOLARSHIP
• *See page 191*

ANDROSCOGGIN AMATEUR RADIO CLUB SCHOLARSHIP
• *See page 229*

BETTY WEATHERFORD, KQ6RE, MEMORIAL SCHOLARSHIP

$1000 award for a student with an Amateur Radio license in any class. Must be studying electrical or communications engineering.

Academic Fields/Career Goals: Electrical Engineering/Electronics; Engineering/Technology.

Award: Scholarship for use in freshman, sophomore, junior, or senior years; not renewable. *Number:* 1. *Amount:* $1000.

Eligibility Requirements: Applicant must be enrolled or expecting to enroll full- or part-time at a two-year or four-year or technical institution or university and must have an interest in amateur radio. Available to U.S. citizens.

Application Requirements: Application form. *Deadline:* January 31.

Contact: Ms. Mary Hobart, Secretary
    Phone: 860-594-0397
    E-mail: k1mmh@arrl.org

CHARLES CLARKE CORDLE MEMORIAL SCHOLARSHIP
• *See page 216*

CHARLES N. FISHER MEMORIAL SCHOLARSHIP
• *See page 122*

DR. JAMES L. LAWSON MEMORIAL SCHOLARSHIP
• *See page 216*

EDMOND A. METZGER SCHOLARSHIP

Scholarship for licensed amateur radio operators, at the novice class or above. Applicants must be undergraduate or graduate electrical engineering students and members of the Amateur Radio Relay League. Preference given to residents of ARRL Central Division (IL, IN, WI) and to students attending school in the Central Division states.

Academic Fields/Career Goals: Electrical Engineering/Electronics.

Award: Scholarship for use in freshman, sophomore, junior, senior, or graduate years; not renewable. *Number:* 1. *Amount:* $500.

Eligibility Requirements: Applicant must be enrolled or expecting to enroll full-time at a four-year institution or university; resident of Illinois, Indiana, Wisconsin; studying in Illinois, Indiana, Wisconsin and must have an interest in amateur radio. Applicant or parent of applicant must be member of American Radio Relay League. Available to U.S. citizens.

Application Requirements: Application form. *Deadline:* January 31.

Contact: Ms. Mary Hobart, Secretary
    Phone: 860-594-0397
    E-mail: k1mmh@arrl.org

FRED R. MCDANIEL MEMORIAL SCHOLARSHIP
• *See page 216*

GARY WAGNER, K3OMI, SCHOLARSHIP
• *See page 191*

INDIANAPOLIS AMATEUR RADIO ASSOCIATION SCHOLARSHIP
• *See page 229*

IRARC MEMORIAL, JOSEPH P. RUBINO, WA4MMD, SCHOLARSHIP

Need-based award available to licensed amateur radio operators. Preference is given to Brevard County, FL residents or to all Florida residents. Must maintain 2.5 GPA and pursue an undergraduate degree or electronic technician certification at an accredited institution.

Academic Fields/Career Goals: Electrical Engineering/Electronics; Engineering/Technology.

Award: Scholarship for use in freshman, sophomore, junior, or senior years; not renewable. *Amount:* $750.

Eligibility Requirements: Applicant must be enrolled or expecting to enroll full-time at a two-year or four-year or technical institution or university; resident of Florida and must have an interest in amateur radio. Applicant must have 2.5 GPA or higher. Available to U.S. citizens.

Application Requirements: Application form, financial need analysis. *Deadline:* January 31.

Contact: Ms. Mary Hobart, Secretary
    Phone: 860-594-0397
    E-mail: k1mmh@arrl.org

IRVING W. COOK, WA0CGS, SCHOLARSHIP
• *See page 216*

JAKE MCCLAIN DRIVER, KC5WXA, SCHOLARSHIP
• *See page 229*

LOIS MANLEY, K7LMZ, AND RANDALL PITCHFORD, WW7ZZ, SCHOLARSHIP
• *See page 206*

L. PHIL AND ALICE J. WICKER SCHOLARSHIP
• *See page 217*

MAGNOLIA DX ASSOCIATION SCHOLARSHIP
• *See page 217*

MISSISSIPPI SCHOLARSHIP
• *See page 122*

ORLANDO HAMCATION SCHOLARSHIP
• *See page 217*

PAUL AND HELEN L. GRAUER SCHOLARSHIP
• *See page 122*

PHD SCHOLARSHIP
• *See page 230*

RAY, N0RP, & KATIE, W0KTE, PAUTZ SCHOLARSHIP
• *See page 230*

WIFDR SCHOLARSHIP
• *See page 122*

ASSOCIATION OF FEDERAL COMMUNICATIONS CONSULTING ENGINEERS

http://www.afcce.org

JULES COHEN SCHOLARSHIP

AFCCE/IEEE-BTS Scholarships provide financial assistance to students who are undertaking a full-time undergraduate or graduate program in engineering or science and demonstrate an interest in careers in telecommunications consulting or broadcast engineering. AFCCE Scholarships generally range between $500 to $2,500 per semester and the IEEE-BTS Jules Cohen Scholarships, administered by the AFCCE, are either $5,000 or $10,000. A single application to the AFCCE will automatically enter the student for consideration for all scholarships for which you are eligible during each semester.

Academic Fields/Career Goals: Electrical Engineering/Electronics; Engineering-Related Technologies; Science, Technology, and Society.

Award: Scholarship for use in junior, senior, or graduate years; not renewable. *Number:* 1–13. *Amount:* $5000–$10,000.

Eligibility Requirements: Applicant must be enrolled or expecting to enroll full-time at a four-year institution or university and studying in Alabama, Alaska, Arizona, Arkansas, California, Colorado, Connecticut, Delaware, District of Columbia, Florida, Georgia, Guam, Hawaii, Idaho, Illinois, Indiana, Iowa, Kansas, Kentucky, Louisiana, Maine, Maryland, Massachusetts, Michigan, Minnesota, Mississippi, Missouri, Montana, Nebraska, Nevada, New Hampshire, New Jersey, New Mexico, New York, North Carolina, North Dakota, Ohio, Oklahoma, Oregon, Pennsylvania, Puerto Rico, Rhode Island, South Carolina, South Dakota, Tennessee, Texas, Utah, Vermont, Virginia, Washington, West Virginia, Wisconsin, Wyoming. Available to U.S. and non-U.S. citizens.

Application Requirements: Application form, essay. *Deadline:* April 30.

Contact: Mr. Marshall Cross, Chair, AFCCE Scholarship Committee
Association of Federal Communications Consulting Engineers
MegaWave Corporation
100 Jackson Road
Devens, MA 01434
Phone: 978-615-7200 Ext. 14
Fax: 978-615-7241
E-mail: mcross@megawave.com

ASSOCIATION OF STATE DAM SAFETY OFFICIALS (ASDSO)

http://www.DamSafety.org

ASSOCIATION OF STATE DAM SAFETY OFFICIALS (ASDSO) SENIOR UNDERGRADUATE SCHOLARSHIP
• *See page 168*

ASTRONAUT SCHOLARSHIP FOUNDATION

http://www.astronautscholarship.org/

ASTRONAUT SCHOLARSHIP FOUNDATION
• *See page 123*

AUTOMOTIVE WOMEN'S ALLIANCE FOUNDATION

http://awafoundation.org/index.php

AUTOMOTIVE WOMEN'S ALLIANCE FOUNDATION SCHOLARSHIPS
• *See page 81*

BARRY GOLDWATER SCHOLARSHIP AND EXCELLENCE IN EDUCATION FOUNDATION

https://goldwater.scholarsapply.org

BARRY M. GOLDWATER SCHOLARSHIP AND EXCELLENCE IN EDUCATION PROGRAM
• *See page 123*

BHW GROUP

https://thebhwgroup.com/

BHW WOMEN IN STEM SCHOLARSHIP
• *See page 124*

BRASKEM ODEBRECHT

http://www.odebrechtaward.com

ODEBRECHT AWARD FOR SUSTAINABLE DEVELOPMENT
• *See page 131*

BROWN AND CALDWELL

http://www.brownandcaldwell.com

ECKENFELDER SCHOLARSHIP
• *See page 169*

MINORITY SCHOLARSHIP PROGRAM
• *See page 169*

CARDS AGAINST HUMANITY

https://cardsagainsthumanity.com/

SCIENCE AMBASSADOR SCHOLARSHIP
• *See page 124*

CATCHING THE DREAM

http://www.catchingthedream.org/

TRIBAL BUSINESS MANAGEMENT PROGRAM (TBM)
• *See page 82*

CENTER FOR ARCHITECTURE

http://www.centerforarchitecture.org

CENTER FOR ARCHITECTURE DESIGN SCHOLARSHIP
• *See page 132*

CLUTCH PREP

http://www.clutchprep.com

CLUTCH PREP STEM SCHOLARSHIP
Clutch Prep is proud to support future STEM professionals. As a company that was founded by STEM scholars to help college students succeed in their studies, we recognize the rigorous academic and financial requirements that come with pursuing the degree. As a result, we are proud to offer a $1,500 scholarship to one student who shows passion & extraordinary commitment to the STEM field.

Academic Fields/Career Goals: Electrical Engineering/Electronics; Engineering-Related Technologies; Engineering/Technology; Mathematics; Science, Technology, and Society.

Award: Scholarship for use in freshman, sophomore, junior, or senior years; not renewable. *Number:* 1. *Amount:* $1500.

Eligibility Requirements: Applicant must be enrolled or expecting to enroll full- or part-time at a two-year or four-year institution or university; resident of Alabama, Alaska, Arizona, Arkansas, California, Colorado, Connecticut, Delaware, District of Columbia, Florida, Georgia, Hawaii, Idaho, Illinois, Indiana, Iowa, Kansas, Kentucky, Louisiana, Maine, Maryland, Massachusetts, Michigan, Minnesota, Mississippi, Missouri, Montana, Nebraska, Nevada, New Hampshire, New Jersey, New Mexico, New York, North Carolina, North Dakota, Ohio, Oklahoma, Oregon, Pennsylvania, Rhode Island, South Carolina, South Dakota, Tennessee, Texas, Utah, Vermont, Virginia, Washington, West Virginia, Wisconsin, Wyoming and studying in Alabama, Alaska, Arizona, Arkansas, California, Colorado, Connecticut, Delaware, District of Columbia, Florida, Georgia, Hawaii, Idaho, Illinois, Indiana, Iowa, Kansas, Kentucky, Louisiana, Maine, Maryland, Massachusetts, Michigan, Minnesota, Mississippi, Missouri, Montana, Nebraska, Nevada, New Hampshire, New Jersey, New Mexico, New York, North Carolina, North Dakota, Ohio, Oklahoma, Oregon, Pennsylvania, Rhode Island, Saskatchewan, South Carolina, South Dakota, Tennessee, Texas, Utah, Vermont, Virginia, Washington, West Virginia, Wisconsin, Wyoming. Available to U.S. citizens.

Application Requirements: Application form. *Deadline:* April 30.

Contact: Christy Lopez, Community Manager
Clutch Prep
2125 Biscayne Blvd
Suite 375
Miami, FL 33137
E-mail: christy@clutchprep.com

DISTIL NETWORKS

http://www.distilnetworks.com

WOMEN FORWARD IN TECHNOLOGY SCHOLARSHIP PROGRAM
• *See page 124*

DIVERSITYCOMM, INC.

http://www.diversitycomm.net/

DIVERSITY IN STEAM MAGAZINE SCHOLARSHIP
• *See page 83*

DOTCOM-MONITOR, INC.

https://www.dotcom-monitor.com/

LOADVIEW WOMEN IN COMPUTING SCHOLARSHIP
• *See page 231*

THE ELECTROCHEMICAL SOCIETY

http://www.electrochem.org/

H.H. DOW MEMORIAL STUDENT ACHIEVEMENT AWARD OF THE INDUSTRIAL ELECTROLYSIS AND

ELECTROCHEMICAL ENGINEERING DIVISION OF THE ELECTROCHEMICAL SOCIETY INC.
• *See page 125*

STUDENT RESEARCH AWARDS OF THE BATTERY DIVISION OF THE ELECTROCHEMICAL SOCIETY INC.
• *See page 125*

FABRICATORS AND MANUFACTURERS ASSOCIATION FOUNDATION

http://www.nutsandboltsfoundation.org/scholarships/

COLLEGE AND TRADE/TECHNICAL SCHOOL SCHOLARSHIPS
• *See page 154*

FLORIDA ENGINEERING SOCIETY

http://www.fleng.org/scholarships.cfm

DAVID F. LUDOVICI SCHOLARSHIP
• *See page 192*

FOUNDATION FOR SCIENCE AND DISABILITY

http://stemd.org/

GRANTS FOR DISABLED GRADUATE STUDENTS IN THE SCIENCES
• *See page 106*

GREATER KANAWHA VALLEY FOUNDATION

http://www.tgkvf.org/

STEVEN ENGINEERING SCHOLARSHIP
• *See page 192*

GREAT MINDS IN STEM

http://www.greatmindsinstem.org

HENAAC SCHOLARSHIP PROGRAM
• *See page 115*

ILLUMINATING ENGINEERING SOCIETY OF NORTH AMERICA– GOLDEN GATE SECTION

http://www.iesgg.org/

ALAN LUCAS MEMORIAL EDUCATIONAL SCHOLARSHIP
• *See page 135*

INDEPENDENT LABORATORIES INSTITUTE SCHOLARSHIP ALLIANCE

http://www.acil.org/

INDEPENDENT LABORATORIES INSTITUTE SCHOLARSHIP ALLIANCE
• *See page 171*

INTERNATIONAL COMMUNICATIONS INDUSTRIES FOUNDATION

http://www.infocomm.org/scholarships

ICIF SCHOLARSHIP FOR EMPLOYEES AND DEPENDENTS OF MEMBER ORGANIZATIONS
• *See page 219*

INTERNATIONAL COMMUNICATIONS INDUSTRIES FOUNDATION AV SCHOLARSHIP
• *See page 219*

INTERNATIONAL SOCIETY FOR OPTICAL ENGINEERING-SPIE

http://www.spie.org/scholarships

SPIE EDUCATIONAL SCHOLARSHIPS IN OPTICAL SCIENCE AND ENGINEERING
• *See page 126*

JORGE MAS CANOSA FREEDOM FOUNDATION

http://masscholarships.org/

MAS FAMILY SCHOLARSHIP AWARD
• *See page 181*

LABROOTS INC.

http://www.LabRoots.com

LABROOTS STEM SCHOLARSHIP
• *See page 116*

LOS ANGELES COUNCIL OF BLACK PROFESSIONAL ENGINEERS

http://www.lablackengineers.org/

AL-BEN SCHOLARSHIP FOR ACADEMIC INCENTIVE
• *See page 193*

AL-BEN SCHOLARSHIP FOR PROFESSIONAL MERIT
• *See page 193*

AL-BEN SCHOLARSHIP FOR SCHOLASTIC ACHIEVEMENT
• *See page 193*

NASA FLORIDA SPACE GRANT CONSORTIUM

http://www.floridaspacegrant.org/

FLORIDA SPACE RESEARCH PROGRAM
• *See page 156*

NASA IDAHO SPACE GRANT CONSORTIUM

http://www.idahospacegrant.org

NASA IDAHO SPACE GRANT CONSORTIUM SCHOLARSHIP PROGRAM
• *See page 126*

NASA MINNESOTA SPACE GRANT CONSORTIUM

https://www.mnspacegrant.org/

MINNESOTA SPACE GRANT CONSORTIUM SCHOLARSHIP PROGRAM
• *See page 156*

NASA MONTANA SPACE GRANT CONSORTIUM

http://www.spacegrant.montana.edu/

MONTANA SPACE GRANT SCHOLARSHIP PROGRAM
• *See page 156*

NASA'S VIRGINIA SPACE GRANT CONSORTIUM

http://www.vsgc.odu.edu/

COMMUNITY COLLEGE STEM SCHOLARSHIPS
• *See page 126*

UNDERGRADUATE STEM RESEARCH SCHOLARSHIPS
• *See page 127*

NATIONAL ASSOCIATION OF WOMEN IN CONSTRUCTION

http://www.nawic.org/

NAWIC UNDERGRADUATE SCHOLARSHIPS
• *See page 135*

NATIONAL BOARD OF BOILER AND PRESSURE VESSEL INSPECTORS

http://www.nationalboard.org/

NATIONAL BOARD TECHNICAL SCHOLARSHIP
• *See page 194*

NATIONAL SECURITY AGENCY

http://www.nsa.gov/Careers

NATIONAL SECURITY AGENCY STOKES EDUCATIONAL SCHOLARSHIP PROGRAM
• *See page 232*

NATIONAL SOCIETY OF PROFESSIONAL ENGINEERS

http://www.nspe.org/

MAUREEN L. AND HOWARD N. BLITMAN, PE SCHOLARSHIP TO PROMOTE DIVERSITY IN ENGINEERING
• *See page 194*

PAUL H. ROBBINS HONORARY SCHOLARSHIP
• *See page 194*

PROFESSIONAL ENGINEERS IN INDUSTRY SCHOLARSHIP
• *See page 194*

NEXTSTEPU

http://www.nextstepu.com/

$1,500 STEM SCHOLARSHIP
• *See page 120*

OREGON STUDENT ASSISTANCE COMMISSION

https://oregonstudentaid.gov/

AMERICAN COUNCIL OF ENGINEERING COMPANIES OF OREGON SCHOLARSHIP
• *See page 210*

HOME BUILDERS FOUNDATION JIM IRVINE STATEWIDE SCHOLARSHIP
• *See page 136*

SOCIETY OF AMERICAN MILITARY ENGINEERS PORTLAND POST SCHOLARSHIP
• *See page 195*

PACIFIC GAS AND ELECTRIC COMPANY

http://www.scholarshipamerica.org

PG&E BETTER TOGETHER STEM SCHOLARSHIP PROGRAM
• *See page 233*

PROFESSIONAL CONSTRUCTION ESTIMATORS ASSOCIATION

http://www.pcea.org/

TED G. WILSON MEMORIAL SCHOLARSHIP FOUNDATION
• *See page 211*

ROBERT H. MOLLOHAN FAMILY CHARITABLE FOUNDATION, INC.

http://www.mollohanfoundation.org/

HIGH TECHNOLOGY SCHOLARS PROGRAM
• *See page 173*

SCARLETT FAMILY FOUNDATION SCHOLARSHIP PROGRAM

http://www.scarlettfoundation.org/

SCHOLARSHIP FOR STUDENTS PURSUING A BUSINESS OR STEM DEGREE
• *See page 91*

SEMICONDUCTOR RESEARCH CORPORATION (SRC)

http://www.src.org/

MASTER'S SCHOLARSHIP PROGRAM
• *See page 195*

SIGMA XI, THE SCIENTIFIC RESEARCH SOCIETY

http://www.sigmaxi.org/

SIGMA XI GRANTS-IN-AID OF RESEARCH
• *See page 110*

SILICON VALLEY COMMUNITY FOUNDATION

http://www.siliconvalleycf.org

SAMSUNG@FIRST SCHOLARS
• *See page 233*

SOCIETY OF AUTOMOTIVE ENGINEERS

https://www.sae.org/participate

BMW/SAE ENGINEERING SCHOLARSHIP
• *See page 160*

EDWARD D. HENDRICKSON/SAE ENGINEERING SCHOLARSHIP
• *See page 160*

TMC/SAE DONALD D. DAWSON TECHNICAL SCHOLARSHIP
• *See page 160*

SOCIETY OF MANUFACTURING ENGINEERS EDUCATION FOUNDATION

http://www.smeef.org/

WILLIAM E. WEISEL SCHOLARSHIP FUND
Scholarship will be given to a full-time undergraduate student enrolled in an engineering or technology degree program in the U.S. or Canada, seeking a career in manufacturing. Consideration will be given to students who intend to apply their knowledge in the sub-specialty of medical robotics. Minimum of 3.0 GPA is required. Scholarships will be limited to United States and Canadian citizens.

Academic Fields/Career Goals: Electrical Engineering/Electronics; Engineering/Technology; Mechanical Engineering; Trade/Technical Specialties.

Award: Scholarship for use in sophomore, junior, or senior years; not renewable. *Number:* 1–10. *Amount:* $1000–$5000.

Eligibility Requirements: Applicant must be enrolled or expecting to enroll full-time at a four-year institution or university. Applicant must have 3.0 GPA or higher. Available to U.S. and Canadian citizens.

Application Requirements: Application form, essay, recommendations or references, resume, transcript. *Deadline:* February 1.

SOCIETY OF MOTION PICTURE AND TELEVISION ENGINEERS

https://www.smpte.org/

LOUIS F. WOLF JR. MEMORIAL SCHOLARSHIP
• *See page 224*

STUDENT PAPER AWARD
• *See page 224*

SOCIETY OF PLASTICS ENGINEERS FOUNDATION (SPE)

http://www.4spe.org/

FLEMING/BLASZCAK SCHOLARSHIP
* See page 195

SOCIETY OF PLASTICS ENGINEERS SCHOLARSHIP PROGRAM
* See page 196

SOCIETY OF WOMEN ENGINEERS

http://societyofwomenengineers.swe.org/

ADA I. PRESSMAN MEMORIAL SCHOLARSHIP
* See page 196

AMERICAN TRANSMISSION CO. SCHOLARSHIP
* See page 196

ANNE MAUREEN WHITNEY BARROW MEMORIAL SCHOLARSHIP
* See page 196

ANNE SHEN SMITH ENDOWED SCHOLARSHIP
* See page 196

BETTY LOU BAILEY SWE REGION F SCHOLARSHIP
* See page 197

B.J. HARROD SCHOLARSHIP
* See page 197

BK KRENZER MEMORIAL REENTRY SCHOLARSHIP
* See page 197

CAROL STEPHENS SWE REGION F SCHOLARSHIP
* See page 197

CUMMINS SCHOLARSHIP
* See page 197

DR. IVY M. PARKER MEMORIAL SCHOLARSHIP
* See page 197

DOROTHY LEMKE HOWARTH MEMORIAL SCHOLARSHIP
* See page 197

DOROTHY P. MORRIS SCHOLARSHIP
* See page 198

EXELON SCHOLARSHIP
* See page 198

GENERAL ELECTRIC WOMEN'S NETWORK SCHOLARSHIP
* See page 212

HONEYWELL SCHOLARSHIP
* See page 198

IBM LINDA SANFORD WOMEN'S TECHNICAL ADVANCEMENT SCHOLARSHIP
* See page 198

INVENERGY WOMEN'S NETWORK SCHOLARSHIP
* See page 212

LIEBHERR MINING SCHOLARSHIP
* See page 234

LILLIAN MOLLER GILBRETH MEMORIAL SCHOLARSHIP
* See page 198

LOCKHEED MARTIN CORPORATION SCHOLARSHIP
* See page 234

MARY V. MUNGER MEMORIAL SCHOLARSHIP
* See page 199

OLIVE LYNN SALEMBIER MEMORIAL REENTRY SCHOLARSHIP
* See page 199

PAULA LORING SIMON SCHOLARSHIP
* See page 199

ROBERTA BANASZAK GLEITER ENGINEERING ENDEAVOR SCHOLARSHIP
* See page 199

SUSAN MISZKOWICZ SEPTEMBER 11 MEMORIAL SCHOLARSHIP
* See page 199

SWE BALTIMORE-WASHINGTON SECTION SCHOLARSHIP
* See page 199

SWE CENTRAL NEW MEXICO PIONEERS SCHOLARSHIP
* See page 200

SWE CENTRAL NEW MEXICO REENTRY SCHOLARSHIP
* See page 200

SWE MID-HUDSON SECTION SCHOLARSHIP
* See page 200

SWE PHOENIX SECTION SCHOLARSHIP
* See page 200

SWE REGION E SCHOLARSHIP
* See page 200

SWE REGION G JUDY SIMMONS MEMORIAL SCHOLARSHIP
* See page 200

SWE REGION H SCHOLARSHIPS
* See page 201

SWE REGION J SCHOLARSHIP
* See page 201

TE CONNECTIVITY EXCELLENCE IN ENGINEERING SCHOLARSHIP
* See page 201

WANDA MUNN SCHOLARSHIP
* See page 201

SOCIETY OF WOMEN ENGINEERS-ROCKY MOUNTAIN SECTION

http://www.swe-rms.org/

SOCIETY OF WOMEN ENGINEERS-ROCKY MOUNTAIN SECTION SCHOLARSHIP PROGRAM
* See page 161

SONS OF NORWAY FOUNDATION

http://www.sonsofnorway.com/foundation

NANCY LORRAINE JENSEN MEMORIAL SCHOLARSHIP
• *See page 202*

SPECIALTY EQUIPMENT MARKET ASSOCIATION

http://www.sema.org/

SEMA MEMORIAL SCHOLARSHIP FUND
• *See page 92*

STRAIGHTFORWARD MEDIA

http://www.straightforwardmedia.com/

STRAIGHTFORWARD MEDIA ENGINEERING SCHOLARSHIP
• *See page 202*

STRAIGHT NORTH

https://www.straightnorth.com/

STRAIGHT NORTH STEM SCHOLARSHIP
• *See page 92*

TAU BETA PI ASSOCIATION

https://www.tbp.org/

TAU BETA PI SCHOLARSHIP PROGRAM
• *See page 202*

TIMOTION

http://www.timotion.com/

TIMOTION ENGINEERING AND EXCELLENCE SCHOLARSHIP
• *See page 213*

TURNER CONSTRUCTION COMPANY

http://www.turnerconstruction.com/

YOUTHFORCE 2020 SCHOLARSHIP PROGRAM
• *See page 137*

UNITED NEGRO COLLEGE FUND

http://www.uncf.org/

BASF/ALFRED CHISHOLM ENDOWED MEMORIAL SCHOLARSHIP
• *See page 93*

DAVIS SCHOLARSHIP FOR WOMEN IN STEM
• *See page 202*

DELL CORPORATE SCHOLARS PROGRAM
• *See page 213*

PROCTER & GAMBLE STEM SCHOLARSHIP
• *See page 128*

SUEZ CORPORATE SCHOLARS PROGRAM
• *See page 94*

UNCF NORTHROP GRUMMAN SCHOLARSHIP
• *See page 236*

UNCF STEM SCHOLARS PROGRAM
• *See page 175*

WILLIAM WRIGLEY FOUNDATION SCHOLARSHIP
• *See page 95*

UNIVERSITIES SPACE RESEARCH ASSOCIATION

http://www.usra.edu/

UNIVERSITIES SPACE RESEARCH ASSOCIATION SCHOLARSHIP AWARD PROGRAM
• *See page 128*

VERMONT SPACE GRANT CONSORTIUM

http://www.cems.uvm.edu/vsgc

VERMONT SPACE GRANT CONSORTIUM
• *See page 104*

WOMEN IN AVIATION, INTERNATIONAL

http://www.wai.org/

DELTA AIR LINES ENGINEERING SCHOLARSHIP
• *See page 163*

XEROX

http://www.xerox.com//

TECHNICAL MINORITY SCHOLARSHIP
• *See page 203*

ENERGY AND POWER ENGINEERING

AMERICAN CHEMICAL SOCIETY, RUBBER DIVISION

http://www.rubber.org/

AMERICAN CHEMICAL SOCIETY, RUBBER DIVISION UNDERGRADUATE SCHOLARSHIP
• *See page 120*

AMERICAN COUNCIL OF ENGINEERING COMPANIES OF PENNSYLVANIA (ACEC/PA)

http://www.acecpa.org/

ERIC J. GENNUSO AND LEROY D. (BUD) LOY, JR. SCHOLARSHIP PROGRAM
• *See page 187*

AMERICAN INDIAN SCIENCE AND ENGINEERING SOCIETY

http://www.aises.org/

A.T. ANDERSON MEMORIAL SCHOLARSHIP PROGRAM
• *See page 121*

AMERICAN NUCLEAR SOCIETY

http://www.ans.org/

DECOMMISSIONING, DECONTAMINATION, AND REUTILIZATION UNDERGRADUATE SCHOLARSHIP

Undergraduate scholarship for students who have completed two or more years in a course of study leading to a degree in nuclear science, nuclear engineering, or a nuclear-related field.

Academic Fields/Career Goals: Energy and Power Engineering; Nuclear Science.

Award: Scholarship for use in junior or senior years; not renewable. *Number:* 1. *Amount:* $2000.

Eligibility Requirements: Applicant must be enrolled or expecting to enroll full-time at a four-year institution or university. Available to U.S. citizens.

Application Requirements: Application form, essay, recommendations or references, transcript. *Deadline:* February 1.

Contact: Scholarship Coordinator
American Nuclear Society
555 North Kensington Avenue
La Grange Park, IL 60526
Phone: 708-352-6611
Fax: 708-352-0499
E-mail: outreach@ans.org

AMERICAN PUBLIC POWER ASSOCIATION

https://www.publicpower.org/grants-scholarships

DEED EDUCATIONAL SCHOLARSHIP
• *See page 190*

DEED STUDENT INTERNSHIP
• *See page 190*

DEED STUDENT RESEARCH GRANTS
• *See page 204*

DEED TECHNICAL DESIGN PROJECT
• *See page 191*

AMERICAN SOCIETY FOR NONDESTRUCTIVE TESTING

http://www.asnt.org

ASNT ENGINEERING UNDERGRADUATE SCHOLARSHIP

The Engineering Undergraduate Scholarship provides incentive to engineering undergraduate students enrolled in colleges and universities in the U.S. to choose nondestructive testing and evaluation as their field of specialization.

Academic Fields/Career Goals: Energy and Power Engineering; Engineering-Related Technologies; Engineering/Technology.

Award: Scholarship for use in freshman, sophomore, junior, or senior years; not renewable. *Number:* 3. *Amount:* $3000.

Eligibility Requirements: Applicant must be enrolled or expecting to enroll full-time at a two-year or four-year institution or university. Applicant or parent of applicant must have employment or volunteer experience in engineering/technology. Available to U.S. citizens.

Application Requirements: Application form, essay. *Deadline:* December 15.

Contact: Jessica Ames, Program Coordinator
American Society for Nondestructive Testing
1711 Arlingate Lane
PO Box 28518
Columbus, OH 43228
E-mail: james@asnt.org

AMERICAN SOCIETY OF CERTIFIED ENGINEERING TECHNICIANS

http://www.ascet.org/

KURT H. AND DONNA M. SCHULER SMALL GRANT
• *See page 205*

AMERICAN SOCIETY OF HEATING, REFRIGERATING, AND AIR CONDITIONING ENGINEERS, INC.

http://www.ashrae.org/

ASHRAE REGION III BOGGARM SETTY SCHOLARSHIP
• *See page 191*

REUBEN TRANE SCHOLARSHIP
• *See page 282*

AMERICAN SOCIETY OF NAVAL ENGINEERS

http://www.navalengineers.org/

AMERICAN SOCIETY OF NAVAL ENGINEERS SCHOLARSHIP
• *See page 122*

ARRL FOUNDATION INC.

http://www.arrl.org/

ALFRED E. FRIEND JR., W4CF, MEMORIAL SCHOLARSHIP
• *See page 191*

GARY WAGNER, K3OMI, SCHOLARSHIP
• *See page 191*

LOIS MANLEY, K7LMZ, AND RANDALL PITCHFORD, WW7ZZ, SCHOLARSHIP
• *See page 206*

WIFDR SCHOLARSHIP
• *See page 122*

ASSOCIATION FOR WOMEN GEOSCIENTISTS (AWG)

http://www.awg.org/

AWG MARIA LUISA CRAWFORD FIELD CAMP SCHOLARSHIP
• *See page 129*

ASSOCIATION OF STATE DAM SAFETY OFFICIALS (ASDSO)

http://www.DamSafety.org

ASSOCIATION OF STATE DAM SAFETY OFFICIALS (ASDSO) SENIOR UNDERGRADUATE SCHOLARSHIP
• *See page 168*

AUTOMOTIVE WOMEN'S ALLIANCE FOUNDATION

http://awafoundation.org/index.php

AUTOMOTIVE WOMEN'S ALLIANCE FOUNDATION SCHOLARSHIPS
• *See page 81*

BARRY GOLDWATER SCHOLARSHIP AND EXCELLENCE IN EDUCATION FOUNDATION

https://goldwater.scholarsapply.org

BARRY M. GOLDWATER SCHOLARSHIP AND EXCELLENCE IN EDUCATION PROGRAM
• *See page 123*

BHW GROUP

https://thebhwgroup.com/

BHW WOMEN IN STEM SCHOLARSHIP
• *See page 124*

BRASKEM ODEBRECHT

http://www.odebrechtaward.com

ODEBRECHT AWARD FOR SUSTAINABLE DEVELOPMENT
• *See page 131*

BROWN AND CALDWELL

http://www.brownandcaldwell.com

ECKENFELDER SCHOLARSHIP
• *See page 169*

MINORITY SCHOLARSHIP PROGRAM
• *See page 169*

CARDS AGAINST HUMANITY

https://cardsagainsthumanity.com/

SCIENCE AMBASSADOR SCHOLARSHIP
• *See page 124*

DISTIL NETWORKS

http://www.distilnetworks.com

WOMEN FORWARD IN TECHNOLOGY SCHOLARSHIP PROGRAM
• *See page 124*

DIVERSITYCOMM, INC.

http://www.diversitycomm.net/

DIVERSITY IN STEAM MAGAZINE SCHOLARSHIP
• *See page 83*

THE ELECTROCHEMICAL SOCIETY

http://www.electrochem.org/

H.H. DOW MEMORIAL STUDENT ACHIEVEMENT AWARD OF THE INDUSTRIAL ELECTROLYSIS AND

ELECTROCHEMICAL ENGINEERING DIVISION OF THE ELECTROCHEMICAL SOCIETY INC.
• *See page 125*

STUDENT RESEARCH AWARDS OF THE BATTERY DIVISION OF THE ELECTROCHEMICAL SOCIETY INC.
• *See page 125*

FLORIDA ENGINEERING SOCIETY

http://www.fleng.org/scholarships.cfm

DAVID F. LUDOVICI SCHOLARSHIP
• *See page 192*

FOUNDATION FOR SCIENCE AND DISABILITY

http://stemd.org/

GRANTS FOR DISABLED GRADUATE STUDENTS IN THE SCIENCES
• *See page 106*

GREATER KANAWHA VALLEY FOUNDATION

http://www.tgkvf.org/

LEOPOLD & ELIZABETH MARMET SCHOLARSHIP
Renewable award to West Virginia residents pursuing full-time postsecondary studies in science, production or conservation of energy, or natural resources. Award may not be used for medical studies. Minimum 2.5 GPA required. Preference given to graduate students.
Academic Fields/Career Goals: Energy and Power Engineering; Natural Resources.
Award: Scholarship for use in freshman, sophomore, junior, senior, or graduate years; renewable. *Amount:* $3000.
Eligibility Requirements: Applicant must be enrolled or expecting to enroll full-time at a four-year institution or university and resident of West Virginia. Applicant must have 2.5 GPA or higher. Available to U.S. citizens.
Application Requirements: Application form, recommendations or references, test scores, transcript. *Deadline:* January 15.
Contact: Susan Hoover, Scholarship Program Officer
　　　Phone: 304-346-3620
　　　E-mail: shoover@tgkvf.org

STEVEN ENGINEERING SCHOLARSHIP
• *See page 192*

GREAT MINDS IN STEM

http://www.greatmindsinstem.org

HENAAC SCHOLARSHIP PROGRAM
• *See page 115*

LABROOTS INC.

http://www.LabRoots.com

LABROOTS STEM SCHOLARSHIP
• *See page 116*

NASA IDAHO SPACE GRANT CONSORTIUM

http://www.idahospacegrant.org

NASA IDAHO SPACE GRANT CONSORTIUM SCHOLARSHIP PROGRAM
• *See page 126*

NEXTSTEPU

http://www.nextstepu.com/

$1,500 STEM SCHOLARSHIP
• *See page 120*

PLAN NEW HAMPSHIRE

http://www.plannh.org

PLAN NEW HAMPSHIRE SCHOLARSHIP AND FELLOWSHIP PROGRAM
• *See page 129*

ROBERT H. MOLLOHAN FAMILY CHARITABLE FOUNDATION, INC.

http://www.mollohanfoundation.org/

HIGH TECHNOLOGY SCHOLARS PROGRAM
• *See page 173*

SCARLETT FAMILY FOUNDATION SCHOLARSHIP PROGRAM

http://www.scarlettfoundation.org/

SCHOLARSHIP FOR STUDENTS PURSUING A BUSINESS OR STEM DEGREE
• *See page 91*

SIGMA XI, THE SCIENTIFIC RESEARCH SOCIETY

http://www.sigmaxi.org/

SIGMA XI GRANTS-IN-AID OF RESEARCH
• *See page 110*

SILICON VALLEY COMMUNITY FOUNDATION

http://www.siliconvalleycf.org

SAMSUNG@FIRST SCHOLARS
• *See page 233*

SOCIETY OF WOMEN ENGINEERS

http://societyofwomenengineers.swe.org/

ADA I. PRESSMAN MEMORIAL SCHOLARSHIP
• *See page 196*

AMERICAN TRANSMISSION CO. SCHOLARSHIP
• *See page 196*

ANNE MAUREEN WHITNEY BARROW MEMORIAL SCHOLARSHIP
• *See page 196*

ANNE SHEN SMITH ENDOWED SCHOLARSHIP
• *See page 196*

BETTY LOU BAILEY SWE REGION F SCHOLARSHIP
• *See page 197*

B.J. HARROD SCHOLARSHIP
• *See page 197*

BK KRENZER MEMORIAL REENTRY SCHOLARSHIP
• *See page 197*

CAROL STEPHENS SWE REGION F SCHOLARSHIP
• *See page 197*

DR. IVY M. PARKER MEMORIAL SCHOLARSHIP
• *See page 197*

DOROTHY LEMKE HOWARTH MEMORIAL SCHOLARSHIP
• *See page 197*

DOROTHY P. MORRIS SCHOLARSHIP
• *See page 198*

EXELON SCHOLARSHIP
• *See page 198*

IBM LINDA SANFORD WOMEN'S TECHNICAL ADVANCEMENT SCHOLARSHIP
• *See page 198*

LILLIAN MOLLER GILBRETH MEMORIAL SCHOLARSHIP
• *See page 198*

MARY V. MUNGER MEMORIAL SCHOLARSHIP
• *See page 199*

OLIVE LYNN SALEMBIER MEMORIAL REENTRY SCHOLARSHIP
• *See page 199*

ROBERTA BANASZAK GLEITER ENGINEERING ENDEAVOR SCHOLARSHIP
• *See page 199*

SUSAN MISZKOWICZ SEPTEMBER 11 MEMORIAL SCHOLARSHIP
• *See page 199*

SWE BALTIMORE-WASHINGTON SECTION SCHOLARSHIP
• *See page 199*

SWE CENTRAL NEW MEXICO PIONEERS SCHOLARSHIP
• *See page 200*

SWE CENTRAL NEW MEXICO REENTRY SCHOLARSHIP
• *See page 200*

SWE MID-HUDSON SECTION SCHOLARSHIP
• *See page 200*

SWE PHOENIX SECTION SCHOLARSHIP
• *See page 200*

SWE REGION E SCHOLARSHIP
• *See page 200*

SWE REGION G JUDY SIMMONS MEMORIAL SCHOLARSHIP
• *See page 200*

SWE REGION H SCHOLARSHIPS
• *See page 201*

SWE REGION J SCHOLARSHIP
• *See page 201*

WANDA MUNN SCHOLARSHIP
• *See page 201*

SOCIETY OF WOMEN ENGINEERS-ROCKY MOUNTAIN SECTION
http://www.swe-rms.org/

SOCIETY OF WOMEN ENGINEERS-ROCKY MOUNTAIN SECTION SCHOLARSHIP PROGRAM
• *See page 161*

STRAIGHTFORWARD MEDIA
http://www.straightforwardmedia.com/

STRAIGHTFORWARD MEDIA ENGINEERING SCHOLARSHIP
• *See page 202*

STRAIGHT NORTH
https://www.straightnorth.com/

STRAIGHT NORTH STEM SCHOLARSHIP
• *See page 92*

TIMOTION
http://www.timotion.com/

TIMOTION ENGINEERING AND EXCELLENCE SCHOLARSHIP
• *See page 213*

UNITED NEGRO COLLEGE FUND
http://www.uncf.org/

DAVIS SCHOLARSHIP FOR WOMEN IN STEM
• *See page 202*

DELL CORPORATE SCHOLARS PROGRAM
• *See page 213*

GALACTIC UNITE BYTHEWAY SCHOLARSHIP
• *See page 202*

UNCF STEM SCHOLARS PROGRAM
• *See page 175*

VERMONT SPACE GRANT CONSORTIUM
http://www.cems.uvm.edu/vsgc

VERMONT SPACE GRANT CONSORTIUM
• *See page 104*

ENGINEERING-RELATED TECHNOLOGIES

AACE INTERNATIONAL
http://www.aacei.org/

AACE INTERNATIONAL COMPETITIVE SCHOLARSHIP
• *See page 130*

AHS INTERNATIONAL—THE VERTICAL FLIGHT TECHNICAL SOCIETY
http://www.vtol.org/

VERTICAL FLIGHT FOUNDATION SCHOLARSHIP
• *See page 148*

AIST FOUNDATION
http://www.aistfoundation.org/

ASSOCIATION FOR IRON AND STEEL TECHNOLOGY BALTIMORE CHAPTER SCHOLARSHIP
Scholarship for child, grandchild, or spouse of a member of the Baltimore Chapter of AIST. Must be high school seniors who are currently enrolled undergraduate students pursuing a career in engineering or metallurgy. Student may reapply each year for the term of their college education.
Academic Fields/Career Goals: Engineering-Related Technologies; Engineering/Technology; Materials Science, Engineering, and Metallurgy.
Award: Scholarship for use in freshman, sophomore, junior, or senior years; not renewable. *Number:* 1. *Amount:* $1500.
Eligibility Requirements: Applicant must be enrolled or expecting to enroll full-time at a four-year institution or university. Applicant or parent of applicant must be member of Association for Iron and Steel Technology. Available to U.S. citizens.
Application Requirements: Application form, essay, test scores, transcript. *Deadline:* April 30.
Contact: Thomas Russo, Program Coordinator
AIST Foundation
1430 Sparrows Point Boulevard
Sparrows Point, MD 21219-1014

ASSOCIATION FOR IRON AND STEEL TECHNOLOGY BENJAMIN F. FAIRLESS SCHOLARSHIP (AIME)
• *See page 186*

ASSOCIATION FOR IRON AND STEEL TECHNOLOGY OHIO VALLEY CHAPTER SCHOLARSHIP
• *See page 167*

AMERICAN CHEMICAL SOCIETY, RUBBER DIVISION
http://www.rubber.org/

AMERICAN CHEMICAL SOCIETY, RUBBER DIVISION UNDERGRADUATE SCHOLARSHIP
• *See page 120*

AMERICAN COUNCIL OF ENGINEERING COMPANIES OF PENNSYLVANIA (ACEC/PA)
http://www.acecpa.org/

ERIC J. GENNUSO AND LEROY D. (BUD) LOY, JR. SCHOLARSHIP PROGRAM
• *See page 187*

AMERICAN INDIAN SCIENCE AND ENGINEERING SOCIETY
http://www.aises.org/

A.T. ANDERSON MEMORIAL SCHOLARSHIP PROGRAM
• *See page 121*

AMERICAN INSTITUTE OF AERONAUTICS AND ASTRONAUTICS

http://www.aiaafoundation.org/

AIAA FOUNDATION UNDERGRADUATE SCHOLARSHIPS
• *See page 121*

LEATRICE GREGORY PENDRAY SCHOLARSHIP
• *See page 121*

AMERICAN PUBLIC POWER ASSOCIATION

https://www.publicpower.org/grants-scholarships

DEED EDUCATIONAL SCHOLARSHIP
• *See page 190*

DEED STUDENT INTERNSHIP
• *See page 190*

DEED STUDENT RESEARCH GRANTS
• *See page 204*

DEED TECHNICAL DESIGN PROJECT
• *See page 191*

AMERICAN PUBLIC TRANSPORTATION FOUNDATION

http://www.apta.com/

TRANSIT HALL OF FAME SCHOLARSHIP AWARD PROGRAM
• *See page 204*

AMERICAN RAILWAY ENGINEERING AND MAINTENANCE OF WAY ASSOCIATION

http://www.aremafoundation.org/

AREMA GRADUATE AND UNDERGRADUATE SCHOLARSHIPS
• *See page 204*

AMERICAN SOCIETY FOR ENGINEERING EDUCATION

http://www.asee.org/

SCIENCE, MATHEMATICS, AND RESEARCH FOR TRANSFORMATION DEFENSE SCHOLARSHIP FOR SERVICE PROGRAM
• *See page 121*

AMERICAN SOCIETY FOR NONDESTRUCTIVE TESTING

http://www.asnt.org

ASNT ENGINEERING UNDERGRADUATE SCHOLARSHIP
• *See page 290*

AMERICAN SOCIETY OF CERTIFIED ENGINEERING TECHNICIANS

http://www.ascet.org/

JOSEPH C. JOHNSON MEMORIAL GRANT

Grant for $750 given to qualified applicants in order to offset the cost of tuition, books and lab fees. Applicant must be a U.S. citizen or a legal resident of the country in which the applicant is currently living, as well as be either a student, certified, regular, registered or associate member of ASCET. Student must be enrolled in an engineering technology program. For further information, visit http://www.ascet.org.

Academic Fields/Career Goals: Engineering-Related Technologies; Engineering/Technology.

Award: Grant for use in freshman, sophomore, junior, or senior years; not renewable. *Number:* 1. *Amount:* $750.

Eligibility Requirements: Applicant must be enrolled or expecting to enroll full- or part-time at a two-year or four-year or technical institution or university. Applicant must have 3.0 GPA or higher. Available to U.S. citizens.

Application Requirements: Application form, financial need analysis, personal photograph. *Deadline:* February 28.

Contact: Mr. Jimmy Lynch, Scholarship Committee Chair
American Society of Certified Engineering Technicians
15621 W. 87th St Pkwy #205
Lenexa, KS 66219
Phone: 773-2427238
E-mail: financialaid@ascet.org

JOSEPH M. PARISH MEMORIAL GRANT

Grant of $500 will be awarded to a student to be used to offset the cost of tuition, books and lab fees. Applicant must be a student member of ASCET and be a U.S. citizen or a legal resident of the country in which the applicant is currently living. The award will be given to full time students enrolled in an engineering technology program; students pursuing a BS degree in engineering are not eligible for this grant. For more information, visit http://www.ascet.org.

Academic Fields/Career Goals: Engineering-Related Technologies; Engineering/Technology.

Award: Grant for use in freshman, sophomore, junior, or senior years; not renewable. *Number:* 1. *Amount:* $500.

Eligibility Requirements: Applicant must be enrolled or expecting to enroll full- or part-time at a two-year or four-year or technical institution or university. Applicant must have 3.0 GPA or higher. Available to U.S. citizens.

Application Requirements: Application form, financial need analysis, personal photograph. *Deadline:* February 28.

Contact: Mr. Jimmy Lynch, Financial Aid Chair
American Society of Certified Engineering Technicians
15621 W. 87th St Pkwy #205
Lenexa, KS 66219
Phone: 733-2427238
E-mail: financialaid@ascet.org

KURT H. AND DONNA M. SCHULER SMALL GRANT
• *See page 205*

AMERICAN SOCIETY OF HEATING, REFRIGERATING, AND AIR CONDITIONING ENGINEERS, INC.

http://www.ashrae.org/

ALWIN B. NEWTON SCHOLARSHIP
• *See page 281*

ASHRAE GENERAL SCHOLARSHIPS

One-time award of $5000 for full-time study in heating, ventilating, refrigeration, and air conditioning in an ABET-accredited program at an accredited school. Must be pursuing a bachelor of science or engineering degree and have a minimum GPA of 3.0. See Website for application and additional information, http://www.ashrae.org.

Academic Fields/Career Goals: Engineering-Related Technologies; Engineering/Technology; Heating, Air-Conditioning, and Refrigeration Mechanics; Trade/Technical Specialties.

Award: Scholarship for use in freshman, sophomore, junior, or senior years; not renewable. *Number:* 2. *Amount:* $5000.

Eligibility Requirements: Applicant must be enrolled or expecting to enroll full-time at a four-year institution or university and must have an interest in leadership. Applicant must have 3.0 GPA or higher. Available to U.S. and non-U.S. citizens.

Application Requirements: Application form, financial need analysis. *Deadline:* December 1.

Contact: Lois Benedict, Scholarship Administrator
    Phone: 404-636-8400 Ext. 1120
    E-mail: lbenedict@ashrae.org

ASHRAE LEGACY SCHOLARSHIP

Scholarship available to undergraduate students pursuing a Bachelor of Science or engineering degree, who are enrolled full-time in a program accredited by the Accreditation Board for Engineering and Technology. Application and additional information on Website http://www.ashrae.org.

Academic Fields/Career Goals: Engineering-Related Technologies; Engineering/Technology; Heating, Air-Conditioning, and Refrigeration Mechanics.

Award: Scholarship for use in sophomore, junior, or senior years. *Number:* 1. *Amount:* $5000.

Eligibility Requirements: Applicant must be enrolled or expecting to enroll full-time at a four-year institution or university. Applicant must have 3.0 GPA or higher. Available to U.S. citizens.

Application Requirements: Application form, financial need analysis. *Deadline:* December 1.

Contact: Lois Benedict, Scholarship Administrator
    Phone: 404-636-8400 Ext. 1120
    E-mail: lbenedict@ashrae.org

ASHRAE REGION III BOGGARM SETTY SCHOLARSHIP
• See page 191

ASHRAE REGION VIII SCHOLARSHIP

One-year scholarship available to undergraduate engineering student enrolled full-time in an ABET-accredited program at a school located within the geographic boundaries of ASHRAE'S Region VIII. This region includes Arkansas, Louisiana, Texas, and Oklahoma as well as Mexico. See Website for application and additional information, http://www.ashrae.org.

Academic Fields/Career Goals: Engineering-Related Technologies; Engineering/Technology.

Award: Scholarship for use in freshman, sophomore, junior, or senior years; not renewable. *Number:* 1. *Amount:* $3000.

Eligibility Requirements: Applicant must be enrolled or expecting to enroll full-time at a four-year institution or university and studying in Arkansas, Louisiana, Oklahoma, Texas. Applicant must have 3.0 GPA or higher. Available to U.S. and non-U.S. citizens.

Application Requirements: Application form, financial need analysis. *Deadline:* December 1.

Contact: Lois Benedict, Scholarship Administrator
    Phone: 404-636-8400 Ext. 1120
    E-mail: lbenedict@ashrae.org

DUANE HANSON SCHOLARSHIP
• See page 282

FRANK M. CODA SCHOLARSHIP
• See page 282

HENRY ADAMS SCHOLARSHIP
• See page 282

LYNN G. BELLENGER SCHOLARSHIP
• See page 282

WILLIS H. CARRIER SCHOLARSHIPS
• See page 283

AMERICAN WELDING SOCIETY
http://www.aws.org/

AIRGAS-JERRY BAKER SCHOLARSHIP

Awarded to full-time undergraduate pursuing a minimum four-year degree in welding engineering or welding engineering technology. Applicant must be a minimum of 18 years of age and have a 3.0 GPA. Priority will be given to those individuals residing or attending school in the states of Alabama, Georgia or Florida.

Academic Fields/Career Goals: Engineering-Related Technologies; Materials Science, Engineering, and Metallurgy.

Award: Scholarship for use in freshman, sophomore, junior, or senior years; not renewable. *Number:* 1. *Amount:* $2500.

Eligibility Requirements: Applicant must be enrolled or expecting to enroll full-time at a four-year institution or university. Applicant must have 3.0 GPA or higher. Available to U.S. and Canadian citizens.

Application Requirements: Application form, essay, financial need analysis. *Deadline:* February 15.

Contact: John Douglass, Associate Director, Scholarships, Foundation
    American Welding Society
    8669 NW 36 Street, Suite 130
    Miami, FL 33166
    Phone: 800-443-9353 Ext. 212
    E-mail: jdouglass@aws.org

AIRGAS-TERRY JARVIS MEMORIAL SCHOLARSHIP

Award for a full-time undergraduate pursuing a minimum four-year degree in welding engineering or welding engineering technology. Must have a minimum 2.8 overall GPA with a 3.0 GPA in engineering courses. Priority given to applicants residing or attending school in Florida, Georgia, or Alabama.

Academic Fields/Career Goals: Engineering-Related Technologies; Engineering/Technology; Materials Science, Engineering, and Metallurgy.

Award: Scholarship for use in freshman, sophomore, junior, or senior years; not renewable. *Number:* 1. *Amount:* $2500.

Eligibility Requirements: Applicant must be enrolled or expecting to enroll full-time at a four-year institution or university. Applicant must have 3.0 GPA or higher. Available to U.S. and Canadian citizens.

Application Requirements: Application form, essay, financial need analysis. *Deadline:* February 15.

Contact: John Douglass, Associate Director Scholarships, Foundation
    American Welding Society
    8669 NW 36 Street, Suite 130
    Miami, FL 33166
    Phone: 800-443-9353 Ext. 212
    E-mail: jdouglass@aws.org

AIR PRODUCTS WOMEN IN GASES AND WELDING SCHOLARSHIP

Awarded to a female pursing higher education in a welding or engineering discipline, who has proven to be an exceptional student and is eager to start her career in the industry. The student must be a U.S. citizen, a full time student with a 2.5 overall GPA, and pursuing a two-year or four-year degree at a U.S. school.

Academic Fields/Career Goals: Engineering-Related Technologies; Engineering/Technology; Materials Science, Engineering, and Metallurgy.

Award: Scholarship for use in freshman, sophomore, junior, or senior years; not renewable. *Number:* 1. *Amount:* $2500.

Eligibility Requirements: Applicant must be enrolled or expecting to enroll full-time at a two-year or four-year institution and female. Applicant must have 3.5 GPA or higher. Available to U.S. citizens.

Application Requirements: Application form, financial need analysis. *Deadline:* February 15.

Contact: Mr. John Douglass, Associate Director
    American Welding Society
    8669 NW 36 Street, Suite 130
    Miami, FL 33166
    Phone: 305-443-9353 Ext. 212
    E-mail: jdouglass@aws.org

AMERICAN WELDING SOCIETY DISTRICT SCHOLARSHIP PROGRAM

Award for students in vocational training, community college, or a degree program in welding or a related field of study. Applicants must be high school graduates or equivalent. Must reside in the United States and attend a U.S. institution. Recipients may reapply. Must include personal statement of career goals.

Academic Fields/Career Goals: Engineering-Related Technologies; Trade/Technical Specialties.

Award: Scholarship for use in freshman, sophomore, junior, or senior years; not renewable. *Number:* 150–200. *Amount:* $100–$2500.

Eligibility Requirements: Applicant must be enrolled or expecting to enroll full- or part-time at a two-year or four-year or technical institution or university. Available to U.S. citizens.

Application Requirements: Application form, financial need analysis. *Deadline:* March 1.

Contact: Mr. John Douglass, Associate Director, Foundation
American Welding Society
8669 NW 36 Street, Suite 130
Miami, FL 33166
Phone: 800-443-9353 Ext. 212
E-mail: jdouglass@aws.org

DONALD F. HASTINGS SCHOLARSHIP

Award for undergraduate pursuing a four-year degree either full-time or part-time in welding engineering or welding engineering technology. Preference given to students residing or attending school in California or Ohio. Submit copy of proposed curriculum. Must rank in upper half of class or have a minimum GPA of 2.5. Must also include acceptance letter.

Academic Fields/Career Goals: Engineering-Related Technologies; Engineering/Technology; Trade/Technical Specialties.

Award: Scholarship for use in freshman, sophomore, junior, or senior years; renewable. *Number:* 1.

Eligibility Requirements: Applicant must be enrolled or expecting to enroll full- or part-time at a four-year institution or university. Applicant must have 3.5 GPA or higher. Available to U.S. citizens.

Application Requirements: Application form, financial need analysis. *Deadline:* February 15.

Contact: Mr. John Douglass, Associate Director, Foundation
American Welding Society
8669 NW 36 Street, Suite 130
Miami, FL 33166
Phone: 800-443-9353 Ext. 212
E-mail: jdouglass@aws.org

EDWARD J. BRADY MEMORIAL SCHOLARSHIP

Award for an undergraduate student pursuing a four-year degree either full- or part-time in welding engineering or welding engineering technology.

Academic Fields/Career Goals: Engineering-Related Technologies; Engineering/Technology; Trade/Technical Specialties.

Award: Scholarship for use in freshman, sophomore, junior, or senior years; not renewable.

Eligibility Requirements: Applicant must be enrolled or expecting to enroll full- or part-time at a four-year institution or university. Available to U.S. citizens.

Application Requirements: Application form, essay, financial need analysis. *Deadline:* February 15.

Contact: Mr. John Douglass, Associate Director, AWS Foundation
American Welding Society
8669 NW 36 Street, Suite 130
Miami, FL 33166
Phone: 305-443-9353 Ext. 212
E-mail: jdouglass@aws.org

HOWARD E. AND WILMA J. ADKINS MEMORIAL SCHOLARSHIP

Award for a full-time junior or senior in welding engineering or welding engineering technology. Preference to welding engineering students and those residing or attending school in Wisconsin or Kentucky. Must have at least 3.2 GPA in engineering, scientific, and technical subjects and a 2.8 GPA overall. No financial need is required to apply. Award may be granted a maximum of two years. Reapply each year. Submit copy of proposed curriculum and an acceptance letter.

Academic Fields/Career Goals: Engineering-Related Technologies; Engineering/Technology; Trade/Technical Specialties.

Award: Scholarship for use in junior or senior years; not renewable.

Eligibility Requirements: Applicant must be enrolled or expecting to enroll full-time at a four-year institution. Available to U.S. citizens.

Application Requirements: Application form, essay, financial need analysis. *Deadline:* February 15.

Contact: Mr. John Douglass, Associate Director, Foundation
American Welding Society
8669 NW 36 Street, Suite 130
Miami, FL 33166
Phone: 800-443-9353 Ext. 212
E-mail: jdouglass@aws.org

JOHN C. LINCOLN MEMORIAL SCHOLARSHIP

Award for an undergraduate pursuing a four-year degree either full time or part time in engineering or welding engineering technology. Priority given to welding engineering students residing or attending school in the states of Ohio or Arizona. Applicant must have a minimum 2.5 overall GPA. Proof of financial need is required to qualify.

Academic Fields/Career Goals: Engineering-Related Technologies; Engineering/Technology; Materials Science, Engineering, and Metallurgy.

Award: Scholarship for use in freshman, sophomore, junior, or senior years; not renewable. *Number:* 1. *Amount:* $3500.

Eligibility Requirements: Applicant must be enrolled or expecting to enroll full- or part-time at a four-year institution. Applicant must have 3.5 GPA or higher. Available to U.S. citizens.

Application Requirements: Application form, financial need analysis. *Deadline:* February 15.

Contact: Mr. John Douglass, Associate Director, Foundation
American Welding Society
8669 NW 36 Street, Suite 130
Miami, FL 33166
Phone: 800-443-9353 Ext. 212
E-mail: jdouglass@aws.org

JOHN M. STROPKI SCHOLARSHIP

Awarded to a college undergraduate student pursuing a minimum four-year Bachelor's degree in welding engineering or a related engineering or science major. Priority will be given to the sons and daughters of current Lincoln Electric employees in the United States and Canada. Students must have a 3.0 overall GPA, and be attending school full time. Three $5,000 scholarship awards will be made to children of current Lincoln Electric employees in the U. S. or Canada pursuing a welding engineering, or related engineering or science Bachelor's degree. One $5,000 scholarship award will be made to any student pursuing a welding engineering, or related engineering or science Bachelor's degree.

Academic Fields/Career Goals: Engineering-Related Technologies; Engineering/Technology.

Award: Scholarship for use in freshman, sophomore, junior, or senior years; not renewable.

Eligibility Requirements: Applicant must be enrolled or expecting to enroll full-time at a four-year institution. Available to U.S. and Canadian citizens.

Application Requirements: Application form, financial need analysis. *Deadline:* February 15.

Contact: Mr. John Douglass, Associate Director, AWS Foundation
American Welding Society
8669 NW 36 Street, #130
Miami, FL 33166
Phone: 305-443-9353 Ext. 212
E-mail: jdouglass@aws.org

MATSUO BRIDGE COMPANY LTD. OF JAPAN SCHOLARSHIP

• *See page 206*

MILLER ELECTRIC INTERNATIONAL WORLD SKILLS COMPETITION SCHOLARSHIP

Applicant must compete in the National Skills USA-VICA Competition for Welding, and advance to the AWS Weld Trials at the AWS International Welding and Fabricating Exposition and Convention, which is held on a bi-annual basis. The winner of the U.S. Weld Trial Competition will receive the scholarship for $10,000 and runner up will

receive $1000. For additional information, see website
http://www.aws.org.

Academic Fields/Career Goals: Engineering-Related Technologies;
Engineering/Technology; Materials Science, Engineering, and
Metallurgy; Trade/Technical Specialties.

Award: Grant for use in freshman, sophomore, junior, or senior years;
renewable.

Eligibility Requirements: Applicant must be enrolled or expecting to
enroll full- or part-time at a four-year institution or university. Available
to U.S. citizens.

Application Requirements: Interview.

Contact: Mr. John Douglass, Associate Director, AWS Foundation
American Welding Society
8669 NW 36 Street, Suite 130
Miami, FL 33166
Phone: 800-443-9353 Ext. 212
E-mail: jdouglass@aws.org

MILLER ELECTRIC MFG. CO. SCHOLARSHIP

Two awards of $3000 each are available for undergraduate students who
will be seniors in a four-year bachelor's degree in welding engineering
technology or welding engineering. Applicant must be U.S. citizen
planning to attend a U.S. institution and have a minimum 3.0 GPA.
Priority given to students attending Ferris State University. Must exhibit a
strong interest in welding equipment and have prior work experience in
the welding equipment field.

Academic Fields/Career Goals: Engineering-Related Technologies;
Engineering/Technology; Materials Science, Engineering, and
Metallurgy; Trade/Technical Specialties.

Award: Scholarship for use in senior year; not renewable.

Eligibility Requirements: Applicant must be enrolled or expecting to
enroll full- or part-time at a four-year institution or university. Applicant
must have 3.0 GPA or higher. Available to U.S. citizens.

Application Requirements: Application form, financial need analysis.
Deadline: February 15.

Contact: Mr. John Douglass, Associate Director, AWS Foundation
American Welding Society
8669 NW 36 Street, Suite 130
Miami, FL 33166
Phone: 800-443-9353 Ext. 212
E-mail: jdouglass@aws.org

PRAXAIR INTERNATIONAL SCHOLARSHIP

Award for a full-time student demonstrating leadership and pursuing a
four-year degree in welding engineering or welding engineering
technology. Priority given to welding engineering students. Must be a
U.S. or Canadian citizen. Financial need is not required. Must have
minimum 2.5 GPA.

Academic Fields/Career Goals: Engineering-Related Technologies;
Engineering/Technology; Materials Science, Engineering, and
Metallurgy.

Award: Scholarship for use in freshman, sophomore, junior, or senior
years; not renewable.

Eligibility Requirements: Applicant must be enrolled or expecting to
enroll full-time at a four-year institution or university. Applicant must
have 3.5 GPA or higher. Available to U.S. and Canadian citizens.

Application Requirements: Application form, financial need analysis.
Deadline: February 15.

Contact: Mr. John Douglass, Associate Director, AWS Foundation
American Welding Society
8669 NW 36 Street, Suite 130
Miami, FL 33166
Phone: 800-443-9353 Ext. 212
E-mail: jdouglass@aws.org

RICHARD J. SEIF TECHNICAL SALES AND MARKETING SCHOLARSHIP

• See page 176

ROBERT G. AND ANNETTE H. PALI SCHOLARSHIP

This scholarship is sponsored by Robert Pali, Past AWS Treasurer, and
his wife, Annette. The student must be a U.S. citizen, with a 3.0 overall
GPA, and be pursuing a Bachelor's degree in engineering, or science
related to math, physics, or chemistry. Preference will be given to
students attending Lafayette College. Preference will be given to women.
Annual award is $3,000. The application deadline is February 15th.

Academic Fields/Career Goals: Engineering-Related Technologies.

Award: Scholarship for use in junior or senior years; renewable.

Eligibility Requirements: Applicant must be enrolled or expecting to
enroll full- or part-time at a four-year institution. Applicant must have 3.0
GPA or higher. Available to U.S. citizens.

Application Requirements: Application form, financial need analysis.
Deadline: February 15.

Contact: Mr. John Douglass, Associate Director, AWS Foundation
American Welding Society
8669 NW 36 Street, #130
Miami, FL 33166
Phone: 305-443-9353 Ext. 212
E-mail: jdouglass@aws.org

VICTOR TECHNOLOGIES AWARD FOR EXCELLENCE IN CUTTING AND WELDING

Awarded to a student who is a senior or in their final year of a 4-year
degree in WET or WE. Minimum 3.0 overall GPA, U.S. citizen.

Academic Fields/Career Goals: Engineering-Related Technologies;
Engineering/Technology.

Award: Scholarship for use in senior year; not renewable.

Eligibility Requirements: Applicant must be enrolled or expecting to
enroll full- or part-time at a four-year institution. Applicant must have 3.0
GPA or higher. Available to U.S. citizens.

Application Requirements: Application form, financial need analysis.
Deadline: February 15.

Contact: Mr. John Douglass, Associate Director, AWS Foundation
American Welding Society
8669 NW 36 Street, Suite 130
Miami, FL 33166
Phone: 305-443-9353 Ext. 212
E-mail: jdouglass@aws.org

VICTOR TECHNOLOGIES CUTTING AND WELDING SCHOLARSHIP

Awarded to an undergraduate pursuing a four-year degree in Welding
Engineering Technology or Welding Engineering.

Academic Fields/Career Goals: Engineering-Related Technologies;
Engineering/Technology; Materials Science, Engineering, and
Metallurgy.

Award: Scholarship for use in freshman, sophomore, or junior years; not
renewable.

Eligibility Requirements: Applicant must be enrolled or expecting to
enroll full- or part-time at a four-year institution. Applicant must have 3.5
GPA or higher. Available to U.S. citizens.

Application Requirements: Application form, financial need analysis.
Deadline: February 15.

Contact: Mr. John Douglass, Associate Director, AWS Foundation
American Welding Society
8669 NW 36 Street, Suite 130
Miami, FL 33166
Phone: 305-443-9353 Ext. 212
E-mail: jdouglass@aws.org

WILLIAM A. AND ANN M. BROTHERS SCHOLARSHIP

Awarded to a full-time undergraduate pursuing a bachelor's degree in
welding or welding-related program at an accredited university.
Applicant must have a minimum 2.5 overall GPA. Proof of financial need
is required.

Academic Fields/Career Goals: Engineering-Related Technologies;
Materials Science, Engineering, and Metallurgy.

Award: Scholarship for use in freshman, sophomore, junior, or senior
years; not renewable.

Eligibility Requirements: Applicant must be enrolled or expecting to
enroll full-time at a four-year institution or university. Applicant must
have 3.5 GPA or higher. Available to U.S. citizens.

Application Requirements: Application form, financial need analysis.
Deadline: February 15.

Contact: Mr. John Douglass, Associate Director, AWS Foundation
American Welding Society
8669 NW 36 Street, Suite 130
Miami, FL 33166
Phone: 800-443-9353 Ext. 212
E-mail: jdouglass@aws.org

WILLIAM A. RICE FAMILY, WOMEN IN WELDING SCHOLARSHIP

Awarded to a female candidate attending one of the following universities: Ferris State University, The Ohio State University, LeTourneau University, Pennsylvania College of Technology, or Montana Tech of the University of Montana. The candidate must be pursuing a Bachelor's degree in welding engineering, welding engineering technology, materials joining engineering, materials joining technology. Applicant must be a citizen of the United States.

Academic Fields/Career Goals: Engineering-Related Technologies; Engineering/Technology; Materials Science, Engineering, and Metallurgy.

Award: Scholarship for use in freshman, sophomore, junior, or senior years; not renewable.

Eligibility Requirements: Applicant must be enrolled or expecting to enroll full- or part-time at a four-year institution and female. Available to U.S. citizens.

Application Requirements: Application form, financial need analysis. *Deadline:* February 15.

Contact: Mr. John Douglass, Associate Director, AWS Foundation
American Welding Society
8669 NW 36 Street, Suite 130
Miami, FL 33166
Phone: 305-443-9353 Ext. 212
E-mail: jdouglass@aws.org

WILLIAM B. HOWELL MEMORIAL SCHOLARSHIP

Awarded to a full-time undergraduate student pursuing a minimum four-year degree in a welding program at an accredited university. Priority will be given to those individuals residing or attending schools in the state of Florida, Michigan, and Ohio. Minimum 2.5 GPA required.

Academic Fields/Career Goals: Engineering-Related Technologies; Engineering/Technology; Materials Science, Engineering, and Metallurgy.

Award: Scholarship for use in freshman, sophomore, junior, or senior years; not renewable.

Eligibility Requirements: Applicant must be enrolled or expecting to enroll full-time at a four-year institution; resident of Florida, Michigan, Ohio and studying in Florida, Michigan, Ohio. Applicant must have 3.5 GPA or higher. Available to U.S. citizens.

Application Requirements: Application form, essay, financial need analysis. *Deadline:* February 15.

Contact: Mr. John Douglass, Associate Director, AWS Foundation
American Welding Society
8669 NW 36 Street, Suite 130
Miami, FL 33166
Phone: 305-443-9353 Ext. 212
E-mail: jdouglass@aws.org

ARMED FORCES COMMUNICATIONS AND ELECTRONICS ASSOCIATION, EDUCATIONAL FOUNDATION

http://www.afcea.org/site/?q=foundation/scholarships

AFCEA STEM MAJORS SCHOLARSHIPS FOR UNDERGRADUATE STUDENTS

• *See page 122*

ARMED FORCES COMMUNICATIONS AND ELECTRONICS ASSOCIATION ROTC SCHOLARSHIP PROGRAM

• *See page 151*

ARRL FOUNDATION INC.

http://www.arrl.org/

DAN HUETTL, WZ7U, MEMORIAL SCHOLARSHIP

$2000 scholarship for a student with active Amateur Radio license who is studying science, technology, engineering, or mathematics at any accredited college or university. Preference will be given to previous recipients if eligibility requirements continue to be met. If no such applicant is identified, preference is given to applicants attending Arizona State University. Minimum 3.0 GPA required. Applicants may receive this scholarship multiple times provided they reapply each year and continue to meet eligibility requirements, up to four years for undergraduate study and up to two years for graduate study.

Academic Fields/Career Goals: Engineering-Related Technologies; Engineering/Technology; Mathematics; Natural Sciences; Nuclear Science; Physical Sciences.

Award: Scholarship for use in freshman, sophomore, junior, senior, or graduate years; not renewable. *Amount:* $2000.

Eligibility Requirements: Applicant must be enrolled or expecting to enroll full-time at a four-year institution or university and must have an interest in amateur radio. Applicant must have 3.0 GPA or higher. Available to U.S. citizens.

Application Requirements: Application form. *Deadline:* January 31.

Contact: Ms. Mary Hobart, Secretary
Phone: 860-594-0397
E-mail: k1mmh@arrl.org

GARY WAGNER, K3OMI, SCHOLARSHIP

• *See page 191*

HENRY BROUGHTON, K2AE, MEMORIAL SCHOLARSHIP

At least one $1000 award is available to students located within 70 miles of Schenectady, NY. Must possess a general class amateur radio license and pursue a Baccalaureate or higher course of study in engineering, sciences, or similar field at an accredited four-year college or university.

Academic Fields/Career Goals: Engineering-Related Technologies; Engineering/Technology.

Award: Scholarship for use in freshman, sophomore, junior, senior, or graduate years; not renewable. *Number:* 1. *Amount:* $1000.

Eligibility Requirements: Applicant must be enrolled or expecting to enroll full- or part-time at a four-year institution or university; resident of New York and must have an interest in amateur radio. Available to U.S. citizens.

Application Requirements: Application form. *Deadline:* January 31.

Contact: Ms. Mary Hobart, Secretary
Phone: 860-594-0397
E-mail: k1mmh@arrl.org

LOIS MANLEY, K7LMZ, AND RANDALL PITCHFORD, WW7ZZ, SCHOLARSHIP

• *See page 206*

WILSE MORGAN, WX7P, MEMORIAL ARRL NORTHWESTERN DIVISION SCHOLARSHIP

• *See page 177*

YASME FOUNDATION SCHOLARSHIP

• *See page 168*

ASSOCIATED GENERAL CONTRACTORS EDUCATION AND RESEARCH FOUNDATION

http://www.agcfoundation.org/

WORKFORCE DEVELOPMENT SCHOLARSHIP

• *See page 237*

ASSOCIATION OF FEDERAL COMMUNICATIONS CONSULTING ENGINEERS

http://www.afcce.org

JULES COHEN SCHOLARSHIP
• *See page 284*

ASSOCIATION OF STATE DAM SAFETY OFFICIALS (ASDSO)

http://www.DamSafety.org

ASSOCIATION OF STATE DAM SAFETY OFFICIALS (ASDSO) SENIOR UNDERGRADUATE SCHOLARSHIP
• *See page 168*

ASTRONAUT SCHOLARSHIP FOUNDATION

http://www.astronautscholarship.org/

ASTRONAUT SCHOLARSHIP FOUNDATION
• *See page 123*

AUTOMOTIVE WOMEN'S ALLIANCE FOUNDATION

http://awafoundation.org/index.php

AUTOMOTIVE WOMEN'S ALLIANCE FOUNDATION SCHOLARSHIPS
• *See page 81*

BARRY GOLDWATER SCHOLARSHIP AND EXCELLENCE IN EDUCATION FOUNDATION

https://goldwater.scholarsapply.org

BARRY M. GOLDWATER SCHOLARSHIP AND EXCELLENCE IN EDUCATION PROGRAM
• *See page 123*

BHW GROUP

https://thebhwgroup.com/

BHW WOMEN IN STEM SCHOLARSHIP
• *See page 124*

BROWN AND CALDWELL

http://www.brownandcaldwell.com

ECKENFELDER SCHOLARSHIP
• *See page 169*

MINORITY SCHOLARSHIP PROGRAM
• *See page 169*

CARDS AGAINST HUMANITY

https://cardsagainsthumanity.com/

SCIENCE AMBASSADOR SCHOLARSHIP
• *See page 124*

CATCHING THE DREAM

http://www.catchingthedream.org/

TRIBAL BUSINESS MANAGEMENT PROGRAM (TBM)
• *See page 82*

THE CLUNKER JUNKER

https://theclunkerjunker.com/

CLUNKER JUNKER CASH FOR CARS AND COLLEGE SCHOLARSHIP

This scholarship is open to all college aged females who are pursuing a degree or certification in an automotive technology field such as engineering, mechanics, design, or auto body at an accredited college or technical school in the Fall of 2018 and/or the Spring of 2019.

Academic Fields/Career Goals: Engineering-Related Technologies; Engineering/Technology; Industrial Design; Transportation.

Award: Scholarship for use in freshman, sophomore, junior, senior, graduate, or postgraduate years; renewable. *Number:* 1. *Amount:* $1000.

Eligibility Requirements: Applicant must be enrolled or expecting to enroll full- or part-time at a two-year or four-year or technical institution or university; female; resident of Alabama, Alaska, Alberta, Arizona, Arkansas, British Columbia, California, Colorado, Connecticut, Delaware, District of Columbia, Florida, Georgia, Guam, Hawaii, Idaho, Illinois, Indiana, Iowa, Kansas, Kentucky, Louisiana, Maine, Manitoba, Maryland, Massachusetts, Michigan, Minnesota, Mississippi, Missouri, Montana, Nebraska, Nevada, New Brunswick, Newfoundland, New Hampshire, New Jersey, New Mexico, New York, North Carolina, North Dakota, Northwest Territories, Nova Scotia, Ohio, Oklahoma, Ontario, Oregon, Pennsylvania, Prince Edward Island, Puerto Rico, Quebec, Rhode Island, Saskatchewan, South Carolina, South Dakota, Tennessee, Texas, Utah, Vermont, Virginia, Washington, West Virginia, Wisconsin, Wyoming, Yukon and studying in Alabama, Alaska, Alberta, Arizona, Arkansas, British Columbia, California, Colorado, Connecticut, Delaware, District of Columbia, Florida, Georgia, Guam, Hawaii, Idaho, Illinois, Indiana, Iowa, Kansas, Kentucky, Louisiana, Maine, Manitoba, Maryland, Massachusetts, Michigan, Minnesota, Mississippi, Missouri, Montana, Nebraska, Nevada, New Brunswick, Newfoundland, New Hampshire, New Jersey, New Mexico, New York, North Carolina, North Dakota, Northwest Territories, Nova Scotia, Ohio, Oklahoma, Ontario, Oregon, Pennsylvania, Prince Edward Island, Puerto Rico, Quebec, Rhode Island, Saskatchewan, South Carolina, South Dakota, Tennessee, Texas, Utah, Vermont, Virginia, West Virginia, Wisconsin, Wyoming, Yukon. Available to U.S. and non-U.S. citizens.

Application Requirements: Essay. *Deadline:* continuous.

Contact: Valerie Mitz, COO
    E-mail: valerie@theclunkerjunker.com

CLUTCH PREP

http://www.clutchprep.com

CLUTCH PREP STEM SCHOLARSHIP
• *See page 285*

CONNECTICUT BUILDING CONGRESS SCHOLARSHIP FUND, INC.

http://www.cbc-ct.org

CBC SCHOLARSHIP FUND
• *See page 132*

DISTIL NETWORKS

http://www.distilnetworks.com

WOMEN FORWARD IN TECHNOLOGY SCHOLARSHIP PROGRAM
• *See page 124*

DIVERSITYCOMM, INC.

http://www.diversitycomm.net/

DIVERSITY IN STEAM MAGAZINE SCHOLARSHIP
• See page 83

DOTCOM-MONITOR, INC.

https://www.dotcom-monitor.com/

LOADVIEW WOMEN IN COMPUTING SCHOLARSHIP
• See page 231

THE ELECTROCHEMICAL SOCIETY

http://www.electrochem.org/

H.H. DOW MEMORIAL STUDENT ACHIEVEMENT AWARD OF THE INDUSTRIAL ELECTROLYSIS AND ELECTROCHEMICAL ENGINEERING DIVISION OF THE ELECTROCHEMICAL SOCIETY INC.
• See page 125

STUDENT RESEARCH AWARDS OF THE BATTERY DIVISION OF THE ELECTROCHEMICAL SOCIETY INC.
• See page 125

ENGINEERS FOUNDATION OF OHIO

http://www.ohioengineer.com/

ENGINEERS FOUNDATION OF OHIO GENERAL FUND SCHOLARSHIP

Applicant must be a college junior or senior at the end of the academic year in which the application is submitted. Must be enrolled full-time at an Ohio college or university in a curriculum leading to a BS degree in engineering or its equivalent. Minimum GPA of 3.0 required. Must be a U.S. citizen and permanent resident of Ohio.

Academic Fields/Career Goals: Engineering-Related Technologies.

Award: Scholarship for use in junior or senior years; not renewable. *Number:* 1. *Amount:* $1000.

Eligibility Requirements: Applicant must be enrolled or expecting to enroll full-time at a four-year institution or university; resident of Ohio and studying in Ohio. Applicant must have 3.0 GPA or higher. Available to U.S. citizens.

Application Requirements: Application form, essay, financial need analysis, recommendations or references, test scores, transcript. *Deadline:* December 15.

Contact: Pam McClure, Manager of Administration
Phone: 614-223-1177
E-mail: efo@ohioengineer.com

LLOYD A. CHACEY, PE-OHIO SOCIETY OF PROFESSIONAL ENGINEERS MEMORIAL SCHOLARSHIP

Scholarship available for a son, daughter, brother, sister, niece, nephew, spouse or grandchild of a current member of the Ohio Society of Professional Engineers, or of a deceased member who was in good standing at the time of his or her death. Must be enrolled full-time at an Ohio college or university in a curriculum leading to a degree in engineering or its equivalent. Must have a minimum of 3.0 GPA. Must be a U.S. citizen and permanent resident of Ohio.

Academic Fields/Career Goals: Engineering-Related Technologies.

Award: Scholarship for use in junior or senior years; renewable. *Number:* up to 2. *Amount:* $2000.

Eligibility Requirements: Applicant must be enrolled or expecting to enroll full-time at a four-year institution or university; resident of Ohio and studying in Ohio. Applicant must have 3.0 GPA or higher. Available to U.S. citizens.

Application Requirements: Application form, essay, financial need analysis, recommendations or references, test scores, transcript. *Deadline:* December 15.

Contact: Pam McClure, Manager of Administration
Phone: 614-223-1177
E-mail: efo@ohioengineer.com

RAYMOND H. FULLER, PE MEMORIAL SCHOLARSHIP

Scholarship of $1000 to graduating high school seniors who will enter their freshman year in college the next fall. Recipients must be accepted for enrollment in an engineering program at an Ohio college or university. Must have a minimum of 3.0 GPA. Must be a U.S. citizen and permanent resident of Ohio. Consideration will be given to the prospective recipient's academic achievement, interest in a career in engineering and financial need as determined by interviews and from references.

Academic Fields/Career Goals: Engineering-Related Technologies.

Award: Scholarship for use in freshman year; not renewable. *Number:* 1. *Amount:* $1000.

Eligibility Requirements: Applicant must be high school student; planning to enroll or expecting to enroll full-time at a four-year institution or university; resident of Ohio and studying in Ohio. Applicant must have 3.0 GPA or higher. Available to U.S. citizens.

Application Requirements: Application form, essay, financial need analysis, interview, recommendations or references, test scores, transcript. *Deadline:* December 15.

Contact: Pam McClure, Manager of Administration
Phone: 614-223-1177
E-mail: efo@ohioengineer.com

FABRICATORS AND MANUFACTURERS ASSOCIATION FOUNDATION

http://www.nutsandboltsfoundation.org/scholarships/

COLLEGE AND TRADE/TECHNICAL SCHOOL SCHOLARSHIPS
• See page 154

FLORIDA ENGINEERING SOCIETY

http://www.fleng.org/scholarships.cfm

DAVID F. LUDOVICI SCHOLARSHIP
• See page 192

FOUNDATION FOR SCIENCE AND DISABILITY

http://stemd.org/

GRANTS FOR DISABLED GRADUATE STUDENTS IN THE SCIENCES
• See page 106

GREAT MINDS IN STEM

http://www.greatmindsinstem.org

HENAAC SCHOLARSHIP PROGRAM
• See page 115

ILLUMINATING ENGINEERING SOCIETY OF NORTH AMERICA

http://www.ies.org/

ROBERT W. THUNEN MEMORIAL SCHOLARSHIPS
• See page 135

INDEPENDENT LABORATORIES INSTITUTE SCHOLARSHIP ALLIANCE

http://www.acil.org/

INDEPENDENT LABORATORIES INSTITUTE SCHOLARSHIP ALLIANCE
• See page 171

INTERNATIONAL FACILITY MANAGEMENT ASSOCIATION FOUNDATION

http://www.ifmafoundation.org/

IFMA FOUNDATION SCHOLARSHIPS
• See page 135

INTERNATIONAL SOCIETY FOR OPTICAL ENGINEERING-SPIE

http://www.spie.org/scholarships

SPIE EDUCATIONAL SCHOLARSHIPS IN OPTICAL SCIENCE AND ENGINEERING
• See page 126

INTERNATIONAL SOCIETY OF AUTOMATION

http://www.isa.org/

ISA EDUCATIONAL FOUNDATION SCHOLARSHIPS

Scholarships to graduate and undergraduate students who demonstrate outstanding potential for long-range contribution to the fields of automation, systems, and control.

Academic Fields/Career Goals: Engineering-Related Technologies.

Award: Scholarship for use in sophomore, junior, or graduate years; not renewable. *Number:* 15–16. *Amount:* $500–$5000.

Eligibility Requirements: Applicant must be enrolled or expecting to enroll full-time at a two-year or four-year or technical institution or university. Applicant must have 2.5 GPA or higher. Available to U.S. and non-U.S. citizens.

Application Requirements: Application form, essay. *Deadline:* February 15.

Contact: Scholarship Committee
International Society of Automation
67 TW Alexander Drive
Research Triangle Park, NC 27709

INTERNATIONAL SOCIETY OF EXPLOSIVES ENGINEERS

http://www.isee.org/

JERRY MCDOWELL FUND

Scholarship of $1500 to $5000 to students whose field of education is related to the commercial explosives industry.

Academic Fields/Career Goals: Engineering-Related Technologies; Engineering/Technology.

Award: Scholarship for use in freshman, sophomore, junior, senior, or graduate years; not renewable. *Number:* 1–3. *Amount:* $1500–$5000.

Eligibility Requirements: Applicant must be enrolled or expecting to enroll full-time at a two-year or four-year institution or university. Available to U.S. and non-U.S. citizens.

Application Requirements: Application form, financial need analysis. *Deadline:* May 1.

Contact: Patrick Lang, Manager, Education Foundation
Phone: 440-349-4400
Fax: 440-349-3788
E-mail: isee@isee.org

JORGE MAS CANOSA FREEDOM FOUNDATION

http://masscholarships.org/

MAS FAMILY SCHOLARSHIP AWARD
• See page 181

LABROOTS INC.

http://www.LabRoots.com

LABROOTS STEM SCHOLARSHIP
• See page 116

LOGISTICS & TRANSPORTATION ASSOCIATION OF NORTH AMERICA

http://www.ltna.org

TRANSPORTATION CLUBS INTERNATIONAL FRED A. HOOPER MEMORIAL SCHOLARSHIP

Merit-based award available to currently enrolled college students majoring in traffic management, transportation, physical distribution, logistics, or a related field. Must have completed at least one year of post-high school education. One-time award of $1500. Must submit three references. Available to citizens of the United States, Canada, and Mexico.

Academic Fields/Career Goals: Engineering-Related Technologies; Transportation.

Award: Scholarship for use in freshman, sophomore, junior, or senior years; not renewable. *Number:* 1. *Amount:* $1500.

Eligibility Requirements: Applicant must be enrolled or expecting to enroll full- or part-time at a two-year or four-year or technical institution or university. Available to U.S. and non-U.S. citizens.

Application Requirements: Application form, essay, personal photograph, recommendations or references, transcript. *Deadline:* April 30.

Contact: Katie deJonge, Executive Director
Phone: 360-898-3344
E-mail: executive.director@ltna.org

LOS ANGELES COUNCIL OF BLACK PROFESSIONAL ENGINEERS

http://www.lablackengineers.org/

AL-BEN SCHOLARSHIP FOR ACADEMIC INCENTIVE
• See page 193

AL-BEN SCHOLARSHIP FOR PROFESSIONAL MERIT
• See page 193

AL-BEN SCHOLARSHIP FOR SCHOLASTIC ACHIEVEMENT
• See page 193

MAINE SOCIETY OF PROFESSIONAL ENGINEERS

http://www.mespe.org/

MAINE SOCIETY OF PROFESSIONAL ENGINEERS VERNON T. SWAINE-ROBERT E. CHUTE SCHOLARSHIP

Nonrenewable scholarship for full-time study for freshmen only. Must be a Maine resident. Application can also be obtained by sending e-mail to rgmglads@twi.net.

Academic Fields/Career Goals: Engineering-Related Technologies; Engineering/Technology.

Award: Scholarship for use in freshman year; not renewable. *Number:* 1–2. *Amount:* $1500.

Eligibility Requirements: Applicant must be high school student; planning to enroll or expecting to enroll full-time at a four-year institution or university; resident of Maine and studying in Maine. Applicant must have 2.5 GPA or higher. Available to U.S. citizens.

Application Requirements: Application form, essay, interview, recommendations or references, self-addressed stamped envelope with application, test scores, transcript. *Deadline:* March 1.

Contact: Robert Martin, Scholarship Committee Chairman
　　　Maine Society of Professional Engineers
　　　1387 Augusta Road
　　　Belgrade, ME 04917
　　　Phone: 207-495-2244
　　　E-mail: rgmglads@twi.net

MANUFACTURERS ASSOCIATION OF MAINE

http://www.mainemfg.com/

MAINE MANUFACTURING CAREER AND TRAINING FOUNDATION SCHOLARSHIP

• *See page 156*

MINERALS, METALS, AND MATERIALS SOCIETY (TMS)

http://www.tms.org/

KAUFMAN CALPHAD SCHOLARSHIP

The applicant must be a student member of Material Advantage. Applicants must be undergraduate sophomores or junior unless otherwise noted. Applicants must be enrolled full time in a metallurgical/materials science engineering program at a qualified college or university. Relatives of members of the funding committee/division are not eligible. Submitted coursework must be relevant to the scholarship for which the student is applying.

Academic Fields/Career Goals: Engineering-Related Technologies; Engineering/Technology; Materials Science, Engineering, and Metallurgy; Mechanical Engineering; Science, Technology, and Society.

Award: Scholarship for use in sophomore or junior years; not renewable. *Number:* 1. *Amount:* $1000.

Eligibility Requirements: Applicant must be enrolled or expecting to enroll full-time at a four-year institution or university. Available to U.S. and non-U.S. citizens.

Application Requirements: Application form, essay. *Deadline:* March 15.

Contact: Ms. Bryn Simpson
　　　E-mail: bsimpson@tms.org

MATERIALS PROCESSING AND MANUFACTURING DIVISION SCHOLARSHIP

The applicant must be a student member of Material Advantage. Applicants must be undergraduate sophomores or junior unless otherwise noted. Applicants must be enrolled full time in a metallurgical/materials science engineering program at a qualified college or university. Relatives of members of the funding committee/division are not eligible. Submitted coursework must be relevant to the scholarship for which the student is applying.

Academic Fields/Career Goals: Engineering-Related Technologies; Engineering/Technology; Materials Science, Engineering, and Metallurgy; Science, Technology, and Society.

Award: Scholarship for use in sophomore or junior years; not renewable. *Number:* 1–2. *Amount:* $2500.

Eligibility Requirements: Applicant must be enrolled or expecting to enroll full-time at a four-year institution or university. Available to U.S. and non-U.S. citizens.

Application Requirements: Application form, essay. *Deadline:* March 15.

Contact: Ms. Bryn Simpson
　　　E-mail: bsimpson@tms.org

TMS/EPD SCHOLARSHIP

The applicant must be a student member of Material Advantage. Applicants must be undergraduate sophomores or junior unless otherwise noted. Applicants must be enrolled full time in a metallurgical/materials science engineering program at a qualified college or university. Relatives of members of the funding committee/division are not eligible. Submitted coursework must be relevant to the scholarship for which the student is applying.

Academic Fields/Career Goals: Engineering-Related Technologies; Engineering/Technology; Materials Science, Engineering, and Metallurgy; Science, Technology, and Society.

Award: Scholarship for use in sophomore or junior years; not renewable. *Number:* 2. *Amount:* $3000.

Eligibility Requirements: Applicant must be enrolled or expecting to enroll full-time at a four-year institution or university. Available to U.S. and non-U.S. citizens.

Application Requirements: Application form, essay. *Deadline:* March 15.

Contact: Ms. Bryn Simpson, TMS Student Awards Program
　　　E-mail: bsimpson@tms.org

TMS/FMD GILBERT CHIN SCHOLARSHIP

The applicant must be a student member of Material Advantage. Applicants must be undergraduate sophomores or junior unless otherwise noted. Applicants must be enrolled full time in a metallurgical/materials science engineering program at a qualified college or university. Relatives of members of the funding committee/division are not eligible. Submitted coursework must be relevant to the scholarship for which the student is applying.

Academic Fields/Career Goals: Engineering-Related Technologies; Engineering/Technology; Materials Science, Engineering, and Metallurgy; Science, Technology, and Society.

Award: Scholarship for use in sophomore or junior years; not renewable. *Number:* 1. *Amount:* $2000.

Eligibility Requirements: Applicant must be enrolled or expecting to enroll full-time at a four-year institution or university. Available to U.S. and non-U.S. citizens.

Application Requirements: Application form, essay. *Deadline:* March 15.

Contact: Ms. Bryn Simpson, TMS Student Awards Program
　　　Phone: 724-776-9000
　　　E-mail: bsimpson@tms.org

TMS/INTERNATIONAL SYMPOSIUM ON SUPERALLOYS SCHOLARSHIP PROGRAM

The applicant must be a student member of Material Advantage. Applicants must be undergraduate sophomores or junior unless otherwise noted. Applicants must be enrolled full time in a metallurgical/materials science engineering program at a qualified college or university. Relatives of members of the funding committee/division are not eligible. Submitted coursework must be relevant to the scholarship for which the student is applying.

Academic Fields/Career Goals: Engineering-Related Technologies; Engineering/Technology; Materials Science, Engineering, and Metallurgy; Science, Technology, and Society.

Award: Scholarship for use in sophomore, junior, senior, or graduate years; not renewable. *Number:* 2. *Amount:* $2000.

Eligibility Requirements: Applicant must be enrolled or expecting to enroll full-time at a four-year institution or university. Available to U.S. and non-U.S. citizens.

Application Requirements: Application form, essay. *Deadline:* March 15.

Contact: Ms. Bryn Simpson
　　　E-mail: bsimpson@tms.org

TMS/LIGHT METALS DIVISION SCHOLARSHIP PROGRAM

The applicant must be a student member of Material Advantage. Applicants must be undergraduate sophomores or junior unless otherwise noted. Applicants must be enrolled full time in a metallurgical/materials science engineering program at a qualified college or university. Relatives of members of the funding committee/division are not eligible. Submitted coursework must be relevant to the scholarship for which the student is applying.

Academic Fields/Career Goals: Engineering-Related Technologies; Engineering/Technology; Materials Science, Engineering, and Metallurgy.

Award: Scholarship for use in sophomore or junior years; not renewable. *Number:* 1. *Amount:* $4000.

Eligibility Requirements: Applicant must be enrolled or expecting to enroll full-time at a four-year institution or university. Available to U.S. and non-U.S. citizens.

Application Requirements: Application form, essay. *Deadline:* March 15.

Contact: Ms. Bryn Simpson
          E-mail: bsimpson@tms.org

TMS OUTSTANDING STUDENT PAPER CONTEST–UNDERGRADUATE

The applicant must be a student member of Material Advantage. Applicants must be an undergraduate student enrolled full-time in a metallurgical/materials science engineering program at a qualified college or university. Papers must be unpublished as of the submission deadline date. Only one paper contest entry per student is accepted. Papers should be of a technical/research nature and may deal with any of the following disciplines: physical and mechanical metallurgy, extractive and process metallurgy, or materials science. The paper should be prepared by one author. It should be the original work of that author as far as possible. If a faculty member is listed as co-author, include a letter from the faculty member confirming that the applicant is the primary author. Papers must be written in English, utilizing good communication skills. The photocopy or digital file submitted must be easily legible. Poor copies of figures and texts are unacceptable. The paper should be neither less than 2,000 nor more than 4,000 words.

Academic Fields/Career Goals: Engineering-Related Technologies; Engineering/Technology; Materials Science, Engineering, and Metallurgy; Science, Technology, and Society.

Award: Prize for use in freshman, sophomore, junior, or senior years; not renewable. *Number:* 2.

Eligibility Requirements: Applicant must be enrolled or expecting to enroll full-time at a four-year institution or university. Available to U.S. and non-U.S. citizens.

Application Requirements: Essay. *Deadline:* May 1.

Contact: Ms. Bryn Simpson
          E-mail: bsimpson@tms.org

TMS/STRUCTURAL MATERIALS DIVISION SCHOLARSHIP

The applicant must be a student member of Material Advantage. Applicants must be undergraduate sophomores or junior unless otherwise noted. Applicants must be enrolled full time in a metallurgical/materials science engineering program at a qualified college or university. Relatives of members of the funding committee/division are not eligible. Submitted coursework must be relevant to the scholarship for which the student is applying.

Academic Fields/Career Goals: Engineering-Related Technologies; Engineering/Technology; Materials Science, Engineering, and Metallurgy; Science, Technology, and Society.

Award: Scholarship for use in sophomore or junior years; not renewable. *Number:* 1. *Amount:* $1000.

Eligibility Requirements: Applicant must be enrolled or expecting to enroll full-time at a four-year institution or university. Available to U.S. and non-U.S. citizens.

Application Requirements: Application form, essay. *Deadline:* March 15.

Contact: Ms. Bryn Simpson
          E-mail: bsimpson@tms.org

NASA IDAHO SPACE GRANT CONSORTIUM

http://www.idahospacegrant.org

NASA IDAHO SPACE GRANT CONSORTIUM SCHOLARSHIP PROGRAM
• *See page 126*

NASA RHODE ISLAND SPACE GRANT CONSORTIUM

http://brown/initiatives/ri-space-grant

NASA RHODE ISLAND SPACE GRANT CONSORTIUM OUTREACH SCHOLARSHIP FOR UNDERGRADUATE STUDENTS

Scholarship for undergraduate students attending a Rhode Island Space Grant Consortium participating institution and studying in any space-related field of science, math, engineering, or other field with applications in space study. Recipients are expected to devote a maximum of 8 hours per week to outreach activities in science education for K-12 children and teachers.

Academic Fields/Career Goals: Engineering-Related Technologies; Mathematics; Science, Technology, and Society.

Award: Scholarship for use in sophomore, junior, or senior years; not renewable. *Number:* up to 2. *Amount:* up to $4000.

Eligibility Requirements: Applicant must be enrolled or expecting to enroll full-time at a four-year institution or university and studying in Rhode Island. Applicant must have 3.0 GPA or higher. Available to U.S. citizens.

Application Requirements: Application form, essay, letter of interest, recommendations or references, resume, transcript. *Deadline:* varies.

Contact: Nancy Ciminelli, Program Manager
          NASA Rhode Island Space Grant Consortium
          Brown University
          Box 1846, Lincoln Field
          Providence, RI 02912
          Phone: 401-863-1151
          Fax: 401-863-3978
          E-mail: nancy_ciminelli@brown.edu

NASA'S VIRGINIA SPACE GRANT CONSORTIUM

http://www.vsgc.odu.edu/

UNDERGRADUATE STEM RESEARCH SCHOLARSHIPS
• *See page 127*

NATIONAL ASSOCIATION FOR THE ADVANCEMENT OF COLORED PEOPLE

http://www.naacp.org/

HUBERTUS W.V. WELLEMS SCHOLARSHIP FOR MALE STUDENTS
• *See page 194*

NATIONAL ASSOCIATION OF WOMEN IN CONSTRUCTION

http://www.nawic.org/

NAWIC UNDERGRADUATE SCHOLARSHIPS
• *See page 135*

NATIONAL SECURITY EDUCATION PROGRAM

http://www.iie.org/

NATIONAL SECURITY EDUCATION PROGRAM (NSEP) DAVID L. BOREN UNDERGRADUATE SCHOLARSHIPS
• *See page 139*

NATIONAL SOCIETY OF BLACK ENGINEERS

https://connect.nsbe.org/Scholarships/ScholarshipList.aspx

NSBE CORPORATE SCHOLARSHIP PROGRAM

The goals of the scholarships are to encourage and reward academic excellence for African-American students, and to promote retention is engineering studies. Scholarships are offered to chemical, mechanical, civil, electrical, environmental, and computer engineering majors who are undergraduate sophomores, juniors, and seniors.

Academic Fields/Career Goals: Engineering-Related Technologies; Engineering/Technology.

Award: Scholarship for use in freshman, sophomore, junior, or senior years; not renewable. *Number:* 3. *Amount:* $2500.

Eligibility Requirements: Applicant must be Black (non-Hispanic) and enrolled or expecting to enroll full- or part-time at a four-year institution or university. Applicant must have 3.0 GPA or higher. Available to U.S. citizens.

Application Requirements: Application form, essay. *Deadline:* June 30.

Contact: Raynashia Goodine, Scholarship Coordinator
National Society of Black Engineers
205 Daingerfield Road
Alexandria VA
E-mail: scholarships@nsbe.org

NATIONAL SOCIETY OF PROFESSIONAL ENGINEERS

http://www.nspe.org/

MAUREEN L. AND HOWARD N. BLITMAN, PE SCHOLARSHIP TO PROMOTE DIVERSITY IN ENGINEERING
• *See page 194*

PAUL H. ROBBINS HONORARY SCHOLARSHIP
• *See page 194*

PROFESSIONAL ENGINEERS IN INDUSTRY SCHOLARSHIP
• *See page 194*

NATIONAL STONE, SAND AND GRAVEL ASSOCIATION (NSSGA)

http://www.nssga.org/

BARRY K. WENDT MEMORIAL SCHOLARSHIP

Scholarship is restricted to a student in an engineering school who plans to pursue a career in the aggregates industry. Eligible students will be enrolled in a mining-related degree program and will have completed at least one year of college coursework.

Academic Fields/Career Goals: Engineering-Related Technologies; Materials Science, Engineering, and Metallurgy.

Award: Scholarship for use in sophomore, junior, or senior years; not renewable. *Number:* 1. *Amount:* up to $2500.

Eligibility Requirements: Applicant must be enrolled or expecting to enroll full-time at a four-year institution or university. Available to U.S. and non-U.S. citizens.

Application Requirements: 300- to 500-word statement of plans for career in the aggregates industry, application form, application form may be submitted online (http://www.nssga.org/education/scholarships/), essay, recommendations or references. *Deadline:* May 29.

Contact: Catherine Whalen, Barry K. Wendt Memorial Scholarship
Committee, c/o NSSGA
National Stone, Sand and Gravel Association (NSSGA)
1605 King Street
Alexandria, VA 22314
Phone: 703-525-8788
Fax: 703-525-7782
E-mail: info@nssga.org

NEXTSTEPU

http://www.nextstepu.com/

$1,500 STEM SCHOLARSHIP
• *See page 120*

OREGON STUDENT ASSISTANCE COMMISSION

https://oregonstudentaid.gov/

FRED FIELDS SCHOLARSHIP
• *See page 182*

PLUMBING-HEATING-COOLING CONTRACTORS EDUCATION FOUNDATION

http://www.phccfoundation.org/scholarships

DELTA FAUCET COMPANY SCHOLARSHIP PROGRAM
• *See page 182*

PHCC EDUCATIONAL FOUNDATION NEED-BASED SCHOLARSHIP
• *See page 182*

PHCC EDUCATIONAL FOUNDATION SCHOLARSHIP PROGRAM
• *See page 182*

ROBERT H. MOLLOHAN FAMILY CHARITABLE FOUNDATION, INC.

http://www.mollohanfoundation.org/

HIGH TECHNOLOGY SCHOLARS PROGRAM
• *See page 173*

ROCKY MOUNTAIN COAL MINING INSTITUTE

http://www.rmcmi.org/

ROCKY MOUNTAIN COAL MINING INSTITUTE SCHOLARSHIP
• *See page 211*

SCARLETT FAMILY FOUNDATION SCHOLARSHIP PROGRAM

http://www.scarlettfoundation.org/

SCHOLARSHIP FOR STUDENTS PURSUING A BUSINESS OR STEM DEGREE
• *See page 91*

SILICON VALLEY COMMUNITY FOUNDATION

http://www.siliconvalleycf.org

SAMSUNG@FIRST SCHOLARS
• *See page 233*

SIMPLEHUMAN

http://www.simplehuman.com/

SIMPLE SOLUTIONS DESIGN COMPETITION

IDSA-endorsed competition to promote creative problem-solving through product design and increase public awareness of industrial design. Applicants must be enrolled in an Industrial Design program or a closely related program at a design school or university and must design a new, innovative product/technology/concept for making household chores easier. Entries evaluated on utility, efficiency, innovation, research, and aesthetics. See website for details http://www.simplehuman.com/design.

Academic Fields/Career Goals: Engineering-Related Technologies; Engineering/Technology; Industrial Design.

Award: Prize for use in freshman, sophomore, junior, or senior years; not renewable. *Number:* 1. *Amount:* $5000.

Eligibility Requirements: Applicant must be enrolled or expecting to enroll full- or part-time at a two-year or four-year or technical institution or university. Available to U.S. and non-U.S. citizens.

Application Requirements: Application form, entry in a contest, one PDF or JPEG of design, specs, materials, explanation. *Deadline:* February 27.

Contact: Sarah Beachler, Marketing and Communications Associate
Phone: 310-436-2278
Fax: 310-538-9196
E-mail: sbeachler@simplehuman.com

SOCIETY FOR IMAGING SCIENCE AND TECHNOLOGY

http://www.imaging.org/

RAYMOND DAVIS SCHOLARSHIP

Award available to an undergraduate junior or senior or graduate student enrolled full-time in an accredited program of photographic, imaging science or engineering. Minimum award is $1000. Applications processed between October 1 and December 15 only.

Academic Fields/Career Goals: Engineering-Related Technologies; Engineering/Technology; Photojournalism/Photography; Science, Technology, and Society.

Award: Scholarship for use in junior, senior, graduate, or postgraduate years; not renewable. *Number:* 1–2. *Amount:* $1000.

Eligibility Requirements: Applicant must be enrolled or expecting to enroll full-time at a four-year institution or university. Available to U.S. and non-U.S. citizens.

Application Requirements: Application form. *Deadline:* October 1.

Contact: Ms. Donna Smith, Executive Assistant
Society for Imaging Science and Technology
7003 Kilworth Lane
Springfield, VA 22151
Phone: 703-642-9090 Ext. 107
E-mail: info@imaging.org

SOCIETY OF AUTOMOTIVE ENGINEERS

https://www.sae.org/participate

BMW/SAE ENGINEERING SCHOLARSHIP
• *See page 160*

EDWARD D. HENDRICKSON/SAE ENGINEERING SCHOLARSHIP
• *See page 160*

RALPH K. HILLQUIST HONORARY SAE SCHOLARSHIP

A $1000 nonrenewable scholarship awarded every other year at the SAE Noise and Vibration Conference. Applicants must be U.S. citizens enrolled full-time as a junior in a U.S. university. A minimum 3.0 GPA with significant academic and leadership achievements is required. The student must also have a declared major in mechanical engineering or an automotive-related engineering discipline, with preference given to those with studies in the areas of expertise related to noise and vibration.

Academic Fields/Career Goals: Engineering-Related Technologies; Engineering/Technology; Mechanical Engineering.

Award: Scholarship for use in junior year; not renewable. *Number:* 1. *Amount:* $1000.

Eligibility Requirements: Applicant must be enrolled or expecting to enroll full-time at a four-year institution or university. Applicant or parent of applicant must be member of Society of Automotive Engineers. Applicant must have 3.0 GPA or higher. Available to U.S. citizens.

Application Requirements: Application form, essay, transcript. *Deadline:* February 1.

Contact: Connie Harnish, SAE Educational Relations
Society of Automotive Engineers
400 Commonwealth Drive
Warrendale, PA 15096-0001
Phone: 724-772-4047
E-mail: connie@sae.org

TMC/SAE DONALD D. DAWSON TECHNICAL SCHOLARSHIP
• *See page 160*

YANMAR/SAE SCHOLARSHIP

Eligible applicants will be citizens of North America (U.S., Canada, Mexico) and will be entering their junior year of undergraduate engineering or enrolled in a postgraduate engineering or related science program. Applicants must be pursuing a course of study or research related to the conservation of energy in transportation, agriculture, construction, and power generation. Emphasis will be placed on research or study related to the internal combustion engine.

Academic Fields/Career Goals: Engineering-Related Technologies; Engineering/Technology; Materials Science, Engineering, and Metallurgy; Mechanical Engineering.

Award: Scholarship for use in junior, senior, or graduate years; renewable. *Number:* 1. *Amount:* $1000.

Eligibility Requirements: Applicant must be enrolled or expecting to enroll full-time at a four-year institution or university. Available to U.S. and non-U.S. citizens.

Application Requirements: Application form, essay, self-addressed stamped envelope with application, test scores, transcript. *Deadline:* April 1.

Contact: Connie Harnish, SAE Educational Relations
Society of Automotive Engineers
400 Commonwealth Drive
Warrendale, PA 15096
Phone: 724-772-4047
E-mail: connie@sae.org

SOCIETY OF MANUFACTURING ENGINEERS EDUCATION FOUNDATION

http://www.smeef.org/

MYRTLE AND EARL WALKER SCHOLARSHIP FUND

Scholarship available to full-time undergraduate students enrolled in a degree program in manufacturing engineering or technology in the United States or Canada. Minimum GPA of 3.0. Scholarship value and number of awards granted varies.

Academic Fields/Career Goals: Engineering-Related Technologies; Engineering/Technology; Mechanical Engineering.

Award: Scholarship for use in freshman, sophomore, junior, or senior years; not renewable. *Number:* 1–25. *Amount:* $1000–$7000.

Eligibility Requirements: Applicant must be enrolled or expecting to enroll full-time at a two-year or four-year or technical institution or university. Applicant must have 3.0 GPA or higher. Available to U.S. and Canadian citizens.

Application Requirements: Application form, essay, recommendations or references, resume, test scores, transcript. *Deadline:* February 1.

Contact: SME Education Foundation
Society of Manufacturing Engineers Education Foundation
One SME Drive, PO Box 930
Dearborn, MI 48121
Phone: 313-425-3300
Fax: 313-425-3411
E-mail: foundation@sme.org

SOCIETY OF MOTION PICTURE AND TELEVISION ENGINEERS

https://www.smpte.org/

LOUIS F. WOLF JR. MEMORIAL SCHOLARSHIP
• *See page 224*

STUDENT PAPER AWARD
• *See page 224*

SOCIETY OF PLASTICS ENGINEERS FOUNDATION (SPE)

http://www.4spe.org/

GULF COAST HURRICANE SCHOLARSHIP
• *See page 196*

SOCIETY OF WOMEN ENGINEERS

http://societyofwomenengineers.swe.org/

ADMIRAL GRACE MURRAY HOPPER SCHOLARSHIP
• *See page 234*

MEREDITH THOMS MEMORIAL SCHOLARSHIP

Five $2700 scholarships for women pursuing ABET-accredited Baccalaureate programs in preparation for careers in engineering and engineering technology in the United States and Mexico. Minimum 3.0 GPA required.

Academic Fields/Career Goals: Engineering-Related Technologies; Engineering/Technology.

Award: Scholarship for use in sophomore, junior, or senior years; not renewable. *Number:* 5. *Amount:* $2700.

Eligibility Requirements: Applicant must be enrolled or expecting to enroll full-time at a four-year institution or university and female. Applicant must have 3.0 GPA or higher. Available to U.S. citizens.

Application Requirements: Application form. *Deadline:* February 15.

Contact: Scholarship Committee
Phone: 800-793-4636
E-mail: scholarships@swe.org

PAST PRESIDENTS SCHOLARSHIP

Two $2000 scholarships for women pursuing ABET-accredited Baccalaureate or graduate programs in preparation for careers in engineering and engineering technology in the United States and Mexico. Must be a U.S. citizen and have a minimum 3.0 GPA.

Academic Fields/Career Goals: Engineering-Related Technologies; Engineering/Technology.

Award: Scholarship for use in sophomore, junior, senior, or graduate years; not renewable. *Number:* 2. *Amount:* $2000.

Eligibility Requirements: Applicant must be enrolled or expecting to enroll full-time at a four-year institution or university and female. Applicant must have 3.0 GPA or higher. Available to U.S. citizens.

Application Requirements: Application form. *Deadline:* February 15.

Contact: Scholarship Committee
Phone: 800-793-4636
E-mail: scholarships@swe.org

ROBERTA BANASZAK GLEITER ENGINEERING ENDEAVOR SCHOLARSHIP
• *See page 199*

ROCHELLE NICOLETTE PERRY MEMORIAL SCHOLARSHIP

One $1000 award for women pursuing ABET-accredited Baccalaureate or graduate programs in preparation for careers in engineering, engineering technology, and computer science in the United States and Mexico. Schools in Region E or H preferred. SWE membership and minimum 3.0 GPA required. Community involvement with planning and participating in events or other organizations preferred. High level of dedication and passion for community, organizations, and engineering in general preferred.

Academic Fields/Career Goals: Engineering-Related Technologies; Engineering/Technology.

Award: Scholarship for use in sophomore, junior, senior, or graduate years; not renewable. *Number:* 1. *Amount:* $1000.

Eligibility Requirements: Applicant must be enrolled or expecting to enroll full-time at a four-year institution or university and female. Applicant or parent of applicant must be member of Society of Women Engineers. Applicant must have 3.0 GPA or higher. Available to U.S. citizens.

Application Requirements: Application form, essay. *Deadline:* February 15.

Contact: Scholarship Committee
Phone: 800-793-4636
E-mail: scholarships@swe.org

SWE CENTRAL INDIANA SECTION SCHOLARSHIP

$2000 scholarship for women pursuing ABET-accredited Baccalaureate programs in preparation for careers in engineering, engineering technology, and computer science in the United States and Mexico. Must be a U.S. citizen, go to school in Indiana or be an Indiana resident, and have a minimum 3.0 GPA.

Academic Fields/Career Goals: Engineering-Related Technologies; Engineering/Technology.

Award: Scholarship for use in sophomore, junior, senior, or graduate years; not renewable. *Number:* 1. *Amount:* $2000.

Eligibility Requirements: Applicant must be enrolled or expecting to enroll full-time at a four-year institution or university and female. Applicant must have 3.0 GPA or higher. Available to U.S. citizens.

Application Requirements: Application form, financial need analysis. *Deadline:* February 15.

Contact: Scholarship Committee
Phone: 800-793-4636
E-mail: scholarships@swe.org

SWE NEW JERSEY SECTION SCHOLARSHIP

Scholarship available for a female New Jersey resident majoring in engineering. Available to incoming freshman. Minimum 3.5 GPA required. Must have attended high school in New Jersey.

Academic Fields/Career Goals: Engineering-Related Technologies; Engineering/Technology.

Award: Scholarship for use in freshman year; not renewable. *Number:* 1. *Amount:* $2000.

Eligibility Requirements: Applicant must be enrolled or expecting to enroll full-time at a four-year institution or university; female and resident of New Jersey. Applicant must have 3.5 GPA or higher. Available to U.S. citizens.

Application Requirements: Application form, essay. *Deadline:* May 1.

Contact: Scholarship Committee
Phone: 800-793-4636
E-mail: scholarships@swe.org

SWE REGION E SCHOLARSHIP
• *See page 200*

SWE REGION G JUDY SIMMONS MEMORIAL SCHOLARSHIP
• *See page 200*

TE CONNECTIVITY EXCELLENCE IN ENGINEERING SCHOLARSHIP
• *See page 201*

SOCIETY OF WOMEN ENGINEERS-ROCKY MOUNTAIN SECTION

http://www.swe-rms.org/

SOCIETY OF WOMEN ENGINEERS-ROCKY MOUNTAIN SECTION SCHOLARSHIP PROGRAM
• *See page 161*

SOCIETY OF WOMEN ENGINEERS-TWIN TIERS SECTION

http://twintiers.swe.org/

SOCIETY OF WOMEN ENGINEERS-TWIN TIERS SECTION SCHOLARSHIP
• *See page 234*

STRAIGHTFORWARD MEDIA

http://www.straightforwardmedia.com/

STRAIGHTFORWARD MEDIA ENGINEERING SCHOLARSHIP
• *See page 202*

STRAIGHT NORTH

https://www.straightnorth.com/

STRAIGHT NORTH STEM SCHOLARSHIP
• *See page 92*

TAG AND LABEL MANUFACTURERS INSTITUTE, INC.

http://www.tlmi.com/

TLMI 4 YEAR COLLEGE DEGREE SCHOLARSHIP PROGRAM

A $5000 scholarship awarded to a sophomore or junior attending a four-year accredited college or university on a full-time basis for their junior or senior year studies. Applicants must demonstrate interest in pursuing a career in the tag and label industry.

Academic Fields/Career Goals: Engineering-Related Technologies; Flexography; Graphics/Graphic Arts/Printing.

Award: Scholarship for use in junior or senior years; not renewable. *Number:* 1–6. *Amount:* $2500–$5000.

Eligibility Requirements: Applicant must be enrolled or expecting to enroll full-time at a four-year institution or university. Applicant must have 3.0 GPA or higher. Available to U.S. and Canadian citizens.

Application Requirements: Application form, interview, portfolio. *Deadline:* March 31.

Contact: Scholarship Committee
Tag and Label Manufacturers Institute, Inc.
One Blackburn Center
Gloucester, MA 01930
Phone: 978-282-1400
E-mail: office@tlmi.com

TAU BETA PI ASSOCIATION

https://www.tbp.org/

TAU BETA PI SCHOLARSHIP PROGRAM
• *See page 202*

TECHNICAL ASSOCIATION OF THE PULP & PAPER INDUSTRY (TAPPI)

http://www.tappi.org/

CORRUGATED PACKAGING DIVISION SCHOLARSHIPS

Award to applicants working full time or part time in the box business and attending day/night school for a graduate or undergraduate degree or to a full-time student in a two- or four-year college, university or technical school. Information can be found at http://www.tappi.org/s_tappi/sec.asp?CID=6101&DID=546695.

Academic Fields/Career Goals: Engineering-Related Technologies; Paper and Pulp Engineering.

Award: Scholarship for use in freshman, sophomore, junior, senior, or graduate years; not renewable. *Number:* 1–4. *Amount:* $1000–$2000.

Eligibility Requirements: Applicant must be enrolled or expecting to enroll full- or part-time at a four-year or technical institution or university. Applicant must have 3.0 GPA or higher. Available to U.S. and non-U.S. citizens.

Application Requirements: Application form. *Deadline:* March 15.

Contact: Mr. Laurence Womack, Director of Standards and Awards
Technical Association of the Pulp & Paper Industry (TAPPI)
15 Technology Parkway South
Peachtree Corners, GA 30092
Phone: 770-209-7276
E-mail: standards@tappi.org

TECHNOLOGY FIRST

https://technologyfirst.org/

ROBERT V. MCKENNA SCHOLARSHIPS
• *See page 235*

TIMOTION

http://www.timotion.com/

TIMOTION ENGINEERING AND EXCELLENCE SCHOLARSHIP
• *See page 213*

TRANSPORTATION ASSOCIATION OF CANADA FOUNDATION

http://www.tac-foundation.ca

TAC FOUNDATION SCHOLARSHIPS
• *See page 213*

TURNER CONSTRUCTION COMPANY

http://www.turnerconstruction.com/

YOUTHFORCE 2020 SCHOLARSHIP PROGRAM
• *See page 137*

UNITED NEGRO COLLEGE FUND

http://www.uncf.org/

DELL CORPORATE SCHOLARS PROGRAM
• *See page 213*

DISCOVER FINANCIAL SERVICES SCHOLARSHIP
• *See page 93*

PROCTER & GAMBLE STEM SCHOLARSHIP
• *See page 128*

UNCF STEM SCHOLARS PROGRAM
• *See page 175*

VECTORWORKS, INC.

http://www.vectorworks.net

VECTORWORKS DESIGN SCHOLARSHIP
• *See page 137*

VERMONT SPACE GRANT CONSORTIUM

http://www.cems.uvm.edu/vsgc

VERMONT SPACE GRANT CONSORTIUM
• *See page 104*

WOMEN IN AEROSPACE FOUNDATION

http://www.womeninaerospace.org/index.html

WIA FOUNDATION SCHOLARSHIP
• *See page 162*

XEROX

http://www.xerox.com//

TECHNICAL MINORITY SCHOLARSHIP
• *See page 203*

ENGINEERING/ TECHNOLOGY

AACE INTERNATIONAL

http://www.aacei.org/

AACE INTERNATIONAL COMPETITIVE SCHOLARSHIP
• *See page 130*

ACI FOUNDATION

http://www.acifoundation.org

ACI FOUNDATION SCHOLARSHIP PROGRAM
• *See page 130*

AEG FOUNDATION

http://www.aegfoundation.org/

AEG FOUNDATION MARLIAVE FUND
• *See page 258*

AHS INTERNATIONAL—THE VERTICAL FLIGHT TECHNICAL SOCIETY

http://www.vtol.org/

VERTICAL FLIGHT FOUNDATION SCHOLARSHIP
• *See page 148*

AIST FOUNDATION

http://www.aistfoundation.org/

AIST ALFRED B. GLOSSBRENNER AND JOHN KLUSCH SCHOLARSHIPS

Scholarship intended to award high school senior who plans on pursuing a degree in metallurgy or engineering. Student must have previous academic excellence in science courses. Applicant must be a dependent of a AIST Northeastern Ohio chapter member.

Academic Fields/Career Goals: Engineering/Technology; Materials Science, Engineering, and Metallurgy.

Award: Scholarship for use in freshman year; not renewable. *Number:* 2. *Amount:* $1000.

Eligibility Requirements: Applicant must be high school student and planning to enroll or expecting to enroll full-time at a four-year institution or university. Applicant or parent of applicant must be member of Association for Iron and Steel Technology. Available to U.S. and non-U.S. citizens.

Application Requirements: Application form, essay, recommendations or references, resume, test scores, transcript. *Deadline:* April 30.

Contact: Richard Kurz, Chapter Secretary
AIST Foundation
22831 East State Street, Route 62
Alliance, OH 44601

AIST WILLIAM E. SCHWABE MEMORIAL SCHOLARSHIP
• *See page 280*

ASSOCIATION FOR IRON AND STEEL TECHNOLOGY BALTIMORE CHAPTER SCHOLARSHIP
• *See page 293*

ASSOCIATION FOR IRON AND STEEL TECHNOLOGY DAVID H. SAMSON CANADIAN SCHOLARSHIP
• *See page 187*

ASSOCIATION FOR IRON AND STEEL TECHNOLOGY MIDWEST CHAPTER BETTY MCKERN SCHOLARSHIP

Scholarship awarded to a graduating female high school senior, or to an undergraduate freshman, sophomore, or junior enrolled in a fully AIST-accredited college or university. Applicant must be in good academic standing. Must be a dependent of an AIST Midwest chapter member.

Academic Fields/Career Goals: Engineering/Technology.

Award: Scholarship for use in freshman, sophomore, junior, or senior years; not renewable. *Number:* 1. *Amount:* $3000.

Eligibility Requirements: Applicant must be enrolled or expecting to enroll full-time at a four-year institution or university and female. Applicant or parent of applicant must be member of Association for Iron and Steel Technology. Available to U.S. and non-U.S. citizens.

Application Requirements: Application form, essay, recommendations or references, resume, test scores, transcript. *Deadline:* March 15.

Contact: AIST Midwest Member Chapter Scholarships Chair
AIST Foundation
c/o Barry Felton
250 West U.S. Highway 12
Burns Harbor, IN 46304

ASSOCIATION FOR IRON AND STEEL TECHNOLOGY MIDWEST CHAPTER DON NELSON SCHOLARSHIP

One scholarship for a graduating high school senior, or undergraduate freshman, sophomore or junior enrolled in a fully AIST-accredited college or university. Applicant must be in good academic standing. Must be a dependent of an AIST Midwest chapter member. May reapply each year for the duration of college education.

Academic Fields/Career Goals: Engineering/Technology.

Award: Scholarship for use in freshman, sophomore, junior, or senior years; not renewable. *Number:* 1. *Amount:* up to $1000.

Eligibility Requirements: Applicant must be enrolled or expecting to enroll full-time at a four-year institution or university. Applicant or parent of applicant must be member of Association for Iron and Steel Technology. Available to U.S. and non-U.S. citizens.

Application Requirements: Application form, essay, recommendations or references, resume, test scores, transcript. *Deadline:* March 15.

Contact: AIST Midwest Member Chapter Scholarships Chair
AIST Foundation
c/o Barry Felton
250 West U.S. Highway 12
Burns Harbor, IN 46304

ASSOCIATION FOR IRON AND STEEL TECHNOLOGY MIDWEST CHAPTER ENGINEERING SCHOLARSHIP

Two four-year scholarships awarded to graduating high school senior or undergraduate freshman, sophomore or junior enrolled in a fully AIST-accredited college or university majoring engineering. Applicant must be in good academic standing. Must be a dependent of an AIST Midwest chapter member. May reapply each year for the duration of college education.

Academic Fields/Career Goals: Engineering/Technology.

Award: Scholarship for use in freshman, sophomore, or junior years; renewable. *Number:* 2. *Amount:* $1500.

Eligibility Requirements: Applicant must be enrolled or expecting to enroll full-time at a four-year institution or university. Applicant or parent of applicant must be member of Association for Iron and Steel Technology. Available to U.S. and non-U.S. citizens.

Application Requirements: Application form, essay, recommendations or references, resume, test scores, transcript. *Deadline:* March 15.

Contact: AIST Midwest Member Chapter Scholarships Chair
AIST Foundation
c/o Barry Felton
250 West U.S. Highway 12
Burns Harbor, IN 46304

ASSOCIATION FOR IRON AND STEEL TECHNOLOGY MIDWEST CHAPTER JACK GILL SCHOLARSHIP

Scholarship for a graduating high school senior, or undergraduate freshman, sophomore, or junior enrolled in a fully AIST-accredited college or university majoring engineering. Applicant must be in good academic standing. Must be a dependent of an AIST Midwest chapter member. May reapply each year for the duration of college education.

Academic Fields/Career Goals: Engineering/Technology.

Award: Scholarship for use in freshman, sophomore, junior, or senior years; not renewable. *Number:* 1. *Amount:* $3000.

Eligibility Requirements: Applicant must be enrolled or expecting to enroll full-time at a four-year institution or university. Applicant or parent of applicant must be member of Association for Iron and Steel Technology. Available to U.S. and non-U.S. citizens.

Application Requirements: Application form, essay, recommendations or references, resume, test scores, transcript. *Deadline:* March 15.

Contact: AIST Midwest Member Chapter Scholarships Chair
AIST Foundation
c/o Barry Felton
250 West U.S. Highway 12
Burns Harbor, IN 46304

ASSOCIATION FOR IRON AND STEEL TECHNOLOGY MIDWEST CHAPTER MEL NICKEL SCHOLARSHIP

Scholarship awarded to a graduating high school senior, or undergraduate freshman, sophomore or junior enrolled in a fully AIST-accredited college or university majoring engineering. Applicant must be in good academic standing. Must be a dependent of an AIST Midwest chapter member. May reapply each year for the term of their college education.

Academic Fields/Career Goals: Engineering/Technology.

Award: Scholarship for use in freshman, sophomore, junior, or senior years; not renewable. *Number:* 1. *Amount:* $3000.

Eligibility Requirements: Applicant must be enrolled or expecting to enroll full-time at a four-year institution or university. Applicant or parent of applicant must be member of Association for Iron and Steel Technology. Available to U.S. and non-U.S. citizens.

Application Requirements: Application form, essay, recommendations or references, resume, test scores, transcript. *Deadline:* March 15.

Contact: AIST Midwest Member Chapter Scholarships Chair
AIST Foundation
c/o Barry Felton
250 West U.S. Highway 12
Burns Harbor, IN 46304

ASSOCIATION FOR IRON AND STEEL TECHNOLOGY MIDWEST CHAPTER NON-ENGINEERING SCHOLARSHIP

Scholarship for graduating high school senior, or undergraduate freshman, sophomore, or junior enrolled in a fully AIST-accredited college or university. Applicant must be in good academic standing and dependent of an AIST Midwest chapter member. Recipients may reapply each year for the term of their college education.

Academic Fields/Career Goals: Engineering/Technology.

Award: Scholarship for use in freshman, sophomore, junior, or senior years; not renewable. *Number:* 3. *Amount:* $1500.

Eligibility Requirements: Applicant must be enrolled or expecting to enroll full-time at a four-year institution or university. Applicant or parent of applicant must be member of Association for Iron and Steel Technology. Available to U.S. and non-U.S. citizens.

Application Requirements: Application form, essay, recommendations or references, resume, test scores, transcript. *Deadline:* March 15.

Contact: AIST Midwest Member Chapter Scholarships Chair
AIST Foundation
c/o Barry Felton
250 West U.S. Highway 12
Burns Harbor, IN 46304

ASSOCIATION FOR IRON AND STEEL TECHNOLOGY MIDWEST CHAPTER WESTERN STATES SCHOLARSHIP

Scholarship of $3000 awarded to a graduating high school senior, or undergraduate freshman, sophomore, junior, or senior enrolled in a fully AIST-accredited college or university. Applicant must be in good academic standing and a dependent of an AIST Midwest chapter member. Recipients may reapply each year for the term of their college education.

Academic Fields/Career Goals: Engineering/Technology.

Award: Scholarship for use in freshman, sophomore, junior, or senior years; not renewable. *Number:* 1. *Amount:* $3000.

Eligibility Requirements: Applicant must be enrolled or expecting to enroll full-time at a four-year institution or university. Applicant or parent of applicant must be member of Association for Iron and Steel Technology. Available to U.S. and non-U.S. citizens.

Application Requirements: Application form, essay, recommendations or references, resume, test scores, transcript. *Deadline:* March 15.

Contact: AIST Midwest Member Chapter Scholarships Chair
AIST Foundation
c/o Barry Felton
250 West U.S. Highway 12
Burns Harbor, IN 46304

ASSOCIATION FOR IRON AND STEEL TECHNOLOGY NORTHWEST MEMBER CHAPTER SCHOLARSHIP

Scholarships of $1000 available to encourage a Pacific Northwest area student to prepare for a career in engineering. Must be the child, grandchild, spouse, or niece/nephew of a member in good standing of the AIST Northwest Chapter. Award based on academic achievements in chemistry, mathematics, and physics.

Academic Fields/Career Goals: Engineering/Technology; Materials Science, Engineering, and Metallurgy.

Award: Scholarship for use in freshman, sophomore, junior, or senior years; not renewable. *Number:* 2. *Amount:* $1000.

Eligibility Requirements: Applicant must be enrolled or expecting to enroll full- or part-time at a four-year institution or university. Applicant or parent of applicant must be member of Association for Iron and Steel Technology. Available to U.S. citizens.

Application Requirements: Application form, essay, recommendations or references, resume, test scores, transcript. *Deadline:* April 30.

Contact: Gerardo Giraldo, AIST Northwest Chapter Secretary
AIST Foundation
2434 Eyres Place West
Seattle, WA 98199
Phone: 206-285-7897
E-mail: acero9938@comcast.net

ASSOCIATION FOR IRON AND STEEL TECHNOLOGY OHIO VALLEY CHAPTER SCHOLARSHIP

• *See page 167*

ASSOCIATION FOR IRON AND STEEL TECHNOLOGY PITTSBURGH CHAPTER SCHOLARSHIP

Scholarships of $2500 for children, stepchildren, grandchildren, or spouse of a member in good standing of the Pittsburgh Chapter. Applicant must be a high school senior or currently enrolled undergraduate preparing for a career in engineering or metallurgy.

Academic Fields/Career Goals: Engineering/Technology; Materials Science, Engineering, and Metallurgy.

Award: Scholarship for use in freshman, sophomore, junior, or senior years; not renewable. *Number:* 2–3. *Amount:* $2500.

Eligibility Requirements: Applicant must be enrolled or expecting to enroll full-time at a four-year institution or university. Applicant or parent of applicant must be member of Association for Iron and Steel Technology. Available to U.S. citizens.

Application Requirements: Application form, essay, recommendations or references, resume, test scores, transcript. *Deadline:* April 30.

Contact: Daniel Kos, Program Coordinator
AIST Foundation
375 Saxonburg Boulevard
Saxonburg, PA 16056
E-mail: dkos@ii-vi.com

ASSOCIATION FOR IRON AND STEEL TECHNOLOGY SOUTHEAST MEMBER CHAPTER SCHOLARSHIP

Scholarship of $3000 for children, stepchildren, grandchildren, or spouse of active Southeast Chapter members who are pursuing a career in engineering, the sciences, or other majors relating to iron and steel production. Students may reapply for the scholarship each year for their term of college.

Academic Fields/Career Goals: Engineering/Technology; Materials Science, Engineering, and Metallurgy.

Award: Scholarship for use in freshman, sophomore, junior, or senior years; renewable. *Number:* 1. *Amount:* $3000.

Eligibility Requirements: Applicant must be enrolled or expecting to enroll full- or part-time at a four-year institution or university. Applicant or parent of applicant must be member of Association for Iron and Steel Technology. Available to U.S. citizens.

Application Requirements: Application form, essay, recommendations or references, resume, test scores, transcript. *Deadline:* April 30.

Contact: Mike Hutson, AIST Southeast Chapter Secretary
AIST Foundation
803 Floyd Street
Kings Mountain, NC 29086
Phone: 704-730-8320
Fax: 704-730-8321
E-mail: mike@johnhutsoncompany.com

ALBERTA HERITAGE SCHOLARSHIP FUND

http://www.alis.alberta.ca/

NORTHERN ALBERTA DEVELOPMENT COUNCIL BURSARY
• *See page 251*

AMERICAN CHEMICAL SOCIETY, RUBBER DIVISION

http://www.rubber.org/

AMERICAN CHEMICAL SOCIETY, RUBBER DIVISION UNDERGRADUATE SCHOLARSHIP
• *See page 120*

AMERICAN COUNCIL OF ENGINEERING COMPANIES OF PENNSYLVANIA (ACEC/PA)

http://www.acecpa.org/

ERIC J. GENNUSO AND LEROY D. (BUD) LOY, JR. SCHOLARSHIP PROGRAM
• *See page 187*

AMERICAN FOUNDATION FOR THE BLIND

http://www.afb.org/

PAUL W. RUCKES SCHOLARSHIP
• *See page 228*

AMERICAN INDIAN SCIENCE AND ENGINEERING SOCIETY

http://www.aises.org/

A.T. ANDERSON MEMORIAL SCHOLARSHIP PROGRAM
• *See page 121*

AMERICAN INSTITUTE OF AERONAUTICS AND ASTRONAUTICS

http://www.aiaafoundation.org/

AIAA FOUNDATION UNDERGRADUATE SCHOLARSHIPS
• *See page 121*

LEATRICE GREGORY PENDRAY SCHOLARSHIP
• *See page 121*

AMERICAN PUBLIC POWER ASSOCIATION

https://www.publicpower.org/grants-scholarships

DEED EDUCATIONAL SCHOLARSHIP
• *See page 190*

DEED STUDENT INTERNSHIP
• *See page 190*

DEED STUDENT RESEARCH GRANTS
• *See page 204*

DEED TECHNICAL DESIGN PROJECT
• *See page 191*

AMERICAN PUBLIC TRANSPORTATION FOUNDATION

http://www.apta.com/

JACK GILSTRAP SCHOLARSHIP

Awarded the APTF scholarship to the applicant with the highest score. Must be in public transportation industry-related fields of study. Must be sponsored by AFTA member organization and complete an internship program with a member organization. Minimum 3.0 GPA required.

Academic Fields/Career Goals: Engineering/Technology; Transportation.

Award: Scholarship for use in sophomore, junior, senior, or graduate years; renewable. *Number:* 1. *Amount:* $2500.

Eligibility Requirements: Applicant must be enrolled or expecting to enroll full-time at a two-year or four-year institution or university. Applicant must have 3.0 GPA or higher. Available to U.S. and Canadian citizens.

Application Requirements: Application form, essay, financial need analysis, recommendations or references, transcript, verification of enrollment for the current semester and copy of fee schedule from the college/university. *Deadline:* June 16.

Contact: Pamela Boswell, Vice President of Program Management
American Public Transportation Foundation
1666 K Street, NW
Washington, DC 20006-1215
Phone: 202-496-4803
Fax: 202-496-2323
E-mail: pboswell@apta.com

TRANSIT HALL OF FAME SCHOLARSHIP AWARD PROGRAM
• *See page 204*

AMERICAN RAILWAY ENGINEERING AND MAINTENANCE OF WAY ASSOCIATION

http://www.aremafoundation.org/

AREMA GRADUATE AND UNDERGRADUATE SCHOLARSHIPS
• See page 204

AMERICAN SOCIETY FOR ENGINEERING EDUCATION

http://www.asee.org/

SCIENCE, MATHEMATICS, AND RESEARCH FOR TRANSFORMATION DEFENSE SCHOLARSHIP FOR SERVICE PROGRAM
• See page 121

AMERICAN SOCIETY FOR NONDESTRUCTIVE TESTING

http://www.asnt.org

ASNT ENGINEERING UNDERGRADUATE SCHOLARSHIP
• See page 290

AMERICAN SOCIETY OF AGRICULTURAL AND BIOLOGICAL ENGINEERS

http://www.asabe.org/

ASABE FOUNDATION SCHOLARSHIP

Award for full-time engineering undergraduate student in the U.S. or Canada. Must be active student member of the American Society of Agricultural Engineers. Must have a minimum of 3.0 GPA. Write for more information and special application procedures. One-time award of $1000. Must have completed one year of school, and must submit paper titled "My Goals in the Engineering Profession".

Academic Fields/Career Goals: Engineering/Technology.

Award: Scholarship for use in sophomore, junior, or senior years; not renewable. *Number:* 1. *Amount:* $1200.

Eligibility Requirements: Applicant must be enrolled or expecting to enroll full-time at a four-year institution or university. Applicant or parent of applicant must be member of Other Student Academic Clubs. Applicant must have 3.0 GPA or higher. Available to U.S. and Canadian citizens.

Application Requirements: Application form, essay, financial need analysis, recommendations or references, resume. *Deadline:* March 15.

Contact: Carol Flautt, Scholarship Program
American Society of Agricultural and Biological Engineers
2950 Niles Road
St. Joseph, MI 49085
Phone: 269-932-7036
Fax: 269-429-3852
E-mail: flautt@asabe.org

AMERICAN SOCIETY OF CERTIFIED ENGINEERING TECHNICIANS

http://www.ascet.org/

JOSEPH C. JOHNSON MEMORIAL GRANT
• See page 294

JOSEPH M. PARISH MEMORIAL GRANT
• See page 294

KURT H. AND DONNA M. SCHULER SMALL GRANT
• See page 205

AMERICAN SOCIETY OF HEATING, REFRIGERATING, AND AIR CONDITIONING ENGINEERS, INC.

http://www.ashrae.org/

ALWIN B. NEWTON SCHOLARSHIP
• See page 281

ASHRAE GENERAL SCHOLARSHIPS
• See page 294

ASHRAE LEGACY SCHOLARSHIP
• See page 295

ASHRAE REGION III BOGGARM SETTY SCHOLARSHIP
• See page 191

ASHRAE REGION IV BENNY BOOTLE SCHOLARSHIP
• See page 130

ASHRAE REGION VIII SCHOLARSHIP
• See page 295

DUANE HANSON SCHOLARSHIP
• See page 282

FRANK M. CODA SCHOLARSHIP
• See page 282

GORDON V. R. HOLNESS SCHOLARSHIP
• See page 282

HENRY ADAMS SCHOLARSHIP
• See page 282

LYNN G. BELLENGER SCHOLARSHIP
• See page 282

REUBEN TRANE SCHOLARSHIP
• See page 282

WILLIS H. CARRIER SCHOLARSHIPS
• See page 283

AMERICAN SOCIETY OF MECHANICAL ENGINEERS AUXILIARY INC.

http://www.asme.org/

ASME AUXILIARY UNDERGRADUATE SCHOLARSHIP CHARLES B. SHARP

Award of $3000 available only to ASME student members to be used in final year of undergraduate study in mechanical engineering. Must be a U.S. citizen.

Academic Fields/Career Goals: Engineering/Technology.

Award: Scholarship for use in junior year; not renewable. *Number:* 1–2. *Amount:* $3000.

Eligibility Requirements: Applicant must be enrolled or expecting to enroll full-time at a four-year institution or university. Applicant or parent of applicant must be member of American Society of Mechanical Engineers. Available to U.S. citizens.

Application Requirements: Application form, financial need analysis. *Deadline:* March 1.

Contact: RuthAnn Bigley, ASME Auxiliary Staff Coordinator
American Society of Mechanical Engineers Auxiliary Inc.
Two Park Avenue
Mailstop RB
New York, NY 10016
Phone: 212-591-7650
E-mail: bigleyr@asme.org

AMERICAN SOCIETY OF NAVAL ENGINEERS

http://www.navalengineers.org/

AMERICAN SOCIETY OF NAVAL ENGINEERS SCHOLARSHIP
• See page 122

AMERICAN SOCIETY OF PLUMBING ENGINEERS

http://www.aspe.org/

ALFRED STEELE ENGINEERING SCHOLARSHIP

Scholarships of $1000 are awarded for the members of American society of plumbing engineers towards education and professional development on plumbing engineering and designing.

Academic Fields/Career Goals: Engineering/Technology; Industrial Design.

Award: Scholarship for use in freshman, sophomore, junior, or senior years; not renewable. *Number:* 5. *Amount:* $1000.

Eligibility Requirements: Applicant must be enrolled or expecting to enroll full-time at a two-year or four-year or technical institution or university. Applicant must have 3.0 GPA or higher. Available to U.S. and non-U.S. citizens.

Application Requirements: Application form, community service, essay, recommendations or references, statement of personal achievement, transcript. *Deadline:* September 1.

Contact: Stacey Kidd, Membership Director
Phone: 773-693-2773
Fax: 773-695-9007
E-mail: skidd@aspe.org

AMERICAN WELDING SOCIETY

http://www.aws.org/

AIRGAS-TERRY JARVIS MEMORIAL SCHOLARSHIP
• See page 295

AIR PRODUCTS WOMEN IN GASES AND WELDING SCHOLARSHIP
• See page 295

DONALD AND SHIRLEY HASTINGS SCHOLARSHIP

Award for U.S. citizen at least 18 years of age pursuing a four-year undergraduate degree in welding engineering or welding engineering technology. Priority given to welding engineering students. Preference is given to students residing or attending school in California or Ohio. Submit copy of proposed curriculum. Minimum GPA of 2.5 required.

Academic Fields/Career Goals: Engineering/Technology; Materials Science, Engineering, and Metallurgy.

Award: Scholarship for use in freshman, sophomore, junior, or senior years; not renewable. *Number:* 1.

Eligibility Requirements: Applicant must be enrolled or expecting to enroll full- or part-time at a four-year institution or university. Available to U.S. citizens.

Application Requirements: Application form, financial need analysis. *Deadline:* February 15.

Contact: Mr. John Douglass, Associate Director, Foundation
American Welding Society
8669 NW 36 Street, Suite 130
Miami, FL 33166
Phone: 800-443-9353 Ext. 212
E-mail: jdouglass@aws.org

DONALD F. HASTINGS SCHOLARSHIP
• See page 296

EDWARD J. BRADY MEMORIAL SCHOLARSHIP
• See page 296

HOWARD E. AND WILMA J. ADKINS MEMORIAL SCHOLARSHIP
• See page 296

JOHN C. LINCOLN MEMORIAL SCHOLARSHIP
• See page 296

JOHN M. STROPKI SCHOLARSHIP
• See page 296

MATSUO BRIDGE COMPANY LTD. OF JAPAN SCHOLARSHIP
• See page 206

MILLER ELECTRIC INTERNATIONAL WORLD SKILLS COMPETITION SCHOLARSHIP
• See page 296

MILLER ELECTRIC MFG. CO. SCHOLARSHIP
• See page 297

PAST PRESIDENTS' SCHOLARSHIP

Scholarship available to students pursuing a bachelor's degree in welding engineering, welding engineering technology, or an engineering program with emphasis on welding. Also open to graduate students pursuing a master's or doctorate in engineering or management.

Academic Fields/Career Goals: Engineering/Technology; Mechanical Engineering.

Award: Scholarship for use in junior or senior years; not renewable.

Eligibility Requirements: Applicant must be enrolled or expecting to enroll full- or part-time at a four-year institution. Available to U.S. citizens.

Application Requirements: Application form, financial need analysis. *Deadline:* February 15.

Contact: Mr. John Douglass, Associate Director, AWS Foundation
American Welding Society
8669 NW 36 Street, Suite 130
Miami, FL 33166
Phone: 305-443-9353 Ext. 212
E-mail: jdouglass@aws.org

PRAXAIR INTERNATIONAL SCHOLARSHIP
• See page 297

RICHARD J. SEIF TECHNICAL SALES AND MARKETING SCHOLARSHIP
• See page 176

ROBERT L. PEASLEE BRAZING SCHOLARSHIP

Award for students pursuing a minimum four-year bachelor's degree in welding engineering or welding engineering technology with an emphasis on brazing applications. Must show brazing coursework. Must be minimum 18 years of age and at least a college junior. 3.0 GPA required.

Academic Fields/Career Goals: Engineering/Technology; Materials Science, Engineering, and Metallurgy.

Award: Scholarship for use in junior or senior years; not renewable.

Eligibility Requirements: Applicant must be enrolled or expecting to enroll full- or part-time at a four-year institution or university. Applicant must have 3.0 GPA or higher. Available to U.S. and Canadian citizens.

Application Requirements: Application form, financial need analysis. *Deadline:* February 15.

Contact: Mr. John Douglass, Associate Director, AWS Foundation
American Welding Society
8669 NW 36 Street, Suite 130
Miami, FL 33166
Phone: 800-443-9353 Ext. 212
E-mail: jdouglass@aws.org

VICTOR TECHNOLOGIES AWARD FOR EXCELLENCE IN CUTTING AND WELDING
• See page 297

VICTOR TECHNOLOGIES CUTTING AND WELDING SCHOLARSHIP
• *See page 297*

WILLIAM A. RICE FAMILY, WOMEN IN WELDING SCHOLARSHIP
• *See page 298*

WILLIAM B. HOWELL MEMORIAL SCHOLARSHIP
• *See page 298*

ANDERSON SOBEL COSMETIC SURGERY
https://www.andersonsobelcosmetic.com/

WISE (WOMEN IN STEM EXCEL) SCHOLARSHIP
The $1,500 WISE Scholarship is open to all Washingtonian women interested in pursuing a career in a STEM field. That includes high school seniors, anyone considering returning to school, and everything in between. We encourage you to apply if you meet the scholarship criteria: 1. Any female student living in Washington State who plans to attend any college or university; 2. Student must be actively pursuing a degree and career path in a STEM-related field at an institution of higher learning; 3. Must be able to provide one letter of recommendation; 4. Complete the application form and provide original essay answers

Academic Fields/Career Goals: Engineering/Technology.

Award: Scholarship for use in freshman, sophomore, junior, senior, graduate, or postgraduate years; not renewable. *Number:* 1. *Amount:* $1500.

Eligibility Requirements: Applicant must be enrolled or expecting to enroll full-time at an institution or university; female; resident of Washington and studying in Washington.

Application Requirements: Application form. *Deadline:* May 5.

Contact: Emily Bradley, Marketing Assistant
Anderson Sobel Cosmetic Surgery
230 Hilliard Ave Suite 2
Asheville, NC 28801
Phone: 828-8283508563
Fax: 28801
E-mail: womeninstemscholarship@gmail.com

ARIZONA PROFESSIONAL CHAPTER OF AISES
http://www.aises.org/scholarships

ARIZONA PROFESSIONAL CHAPTER OF AISES SCHOLARSHIP
Scholarship awarded to American Indian/Alaska Natives attending Arizona schools of higher education pursuing degrees in the sciences, engineering, medicine, natural resources, math, and technology. Student must be a full-time undergraduate student (at least 12 hours per semester) at an accredited two-year or four-year college or university.

Academic Fields/Career Goals: Engineering/Technology; Health and Medical Sciences; Natural Resources; Physical Sciences.

Award: Scholarship for use in freshman, sophomore, junior, or senior years; not renewable.

Eligibility Requirements: Applicant must be American Indian/Alaska Native; enrolled or expecting to enroll full-time at a two-year or four-year institution or university and studying in Arizona. Applicant must have 2.5 GPA or higher. Available to U.S. citizens.

Application Requirements: Application form, essay, portfolio, proof of tribal enrollment, copy of AISES membership card, recommendations or references, resume, transcript. *Deadline:* August 17.

Contact: Jaime Ashike, Scholarship Committee
Arizona Professional Chapter of AISES
PO Box 2528
Phoenix, AZ 85002
Phone: 480-326-0958
E-mail: amazing_butterfly@hotmail.com

ARMED FORCES COMMUNICATIONS AND ELECTRONICS ASSOCIATION, EDUCATIONAL FOUNDATION
http://www.afcea.org/site/?q=foundation/scholarships

AFCEA STEM MAJORS SCHOLARSHIPS FOR UNDERGRADUATE STUDENTS
• *See page 122*

ARMED FORCES COMMUNICATIONS AND ELECTRONICS ASSOCIATION ROTC SCHOLARSHIP PROGRAM
• *See page 151*

ARRL FOUNDATION INC.
http://www.arrl.org/

ALFRED E. FRIEND JR, W4CF, MEMORIAL SCHOLARSHIP
• *See page 191*

ALLEN AND BERTHA WATSON MEMORIAL SCHOLARSHIP
$500 award for the study of science, technology, or engineering. Must be a resident of Oklahoma or attend a 4-year university or college in Oklahoma. If no qualified applicant is identified, an applicant from the ARRL West Gulf Division (Texas and Oklahoma) will be chosen.

Academic Fields/Career Goals: Engineering/Technology; Science, Technology, and Society.

Award: Scholarship for use in freshman, sophomore, junior, or senior years; not renewable. *Number:* 1. *Amount:* $500.

Eligibility Requirements: Applicant must be enrolled or expecting to enroll full- or part-time at a four-year institution or university; resident of Oklahoma and must have an interest in amateur radio. Available to U.S. citizens.

Application Requirements: Application form. *Deadline:* January 31.

Contact: Ms. Mary Hobart, Secretary
Phone: 860-594-0397
E-mail: k1mmh@arrl.org

BETTY WEATHERFORD, KQ6RE, MEMORIAL SCHOLARSHIP
• *See page 283*

CHARLES N. FISHER MEMORIAL SCHOLARSHIP
• *See page 122*

CTRI/CHRIS SEEBER, KA1GEU, MEMORIAL SCHOLARSHIP
• *See page 268*

DAN HUETTL, WZ7U, MEMORIAL SCHOLARSHIP
• *See page 298*

GARY WAGNER, K3OMI, SCHOLARSHIP
• *See page 191*

HENRY BROUGHTON, K2AE, MEMORIAL SCHOLARSHIP
• *See page 298*

IRARC MEMORIAL, JOSEPH P. RUBINO, WA4MMD, SCHOLARSHIP
• *See page 283*

LOIS MANLEY, K7LMZ, AND RANDALL PITCHFORD, WW7ZZ, SCHOLARSHIP
• *See page 206*

MAGNOLIA DX ASSOCIATION SCHOLARSHIP
• *See page 217*

MISSISSIPPI SCHOLARSHIP
• See page 122

NORTH FULTON AMATEUR RADIO LEAGUE SCHOLARSHIP
• See page 230

OLD MAN INTERNATIONAL SIDEBAND SOCIETY (OMISS) SCHOLARSHIP
• See page 259

PAUL AND HELEN L. GRAUER SCHOLARSHIP
• See page 122

SOUTHEASTERN DX CLUB SCHOLARSHIP
• See page 230

WIFDR SCHOLARSHIP
• See page 122

WILSE MORGAN, WX7P, MEMORIAL ARRL NORTHWESTERN DIVISION SCHOLARSHIP
• See page 177

YASME FOUNDATION SCHOLARSHIP
• See page 168

ASM MATERIALS EDUCATION FOUNDATION
http://www.asmfoundation.org/

EDWARD J. DULIS SCHOLARSHIP
Award of $1500 for student members of ASM International studying metallurgy or materials science and engineering. Award is merit based; financial need is not considered.

Academic Fields/Career Goals: Engineering/Technology; Materials Science, Engineering, and Metallurgy.

Award: Scholarship for use in sophomore, junior, or senior years; not renewable. *Number:* 1. *Amount:* $1500.

Eligibility Requirements: Applicant must be enrolled or expecting to enroll full-time at a four-year institution or university. Applicant or parent of applicant must be member of ASM International. Available to U.S. and Canadian citizens.

Application Requirements: Application form, personal photograph. *Deadline:* May 1.

Contact: Jeane Deatherage, Administrator, Foundation Programs
ASM Materials Education Foundation
ASM Materials Education Foundation
9639 Kinsman Rd.
Materials Park, OH 44073-0001
Phone: 440-3385151
E-mail: scholarshipsUG@asminternational.org

GEORGE A. ROBERTS SCHOLARSHIP
Awards for college juniors or seniors studying metallurgy or materials engineering in North America. Applicants must be student members of ASM International. Awards based on need, interest in field, academics, and character.

Academic Fields/Career Goals: Engineering/Technology; Materials Science, Engineering, and Metallurgy.

Award: Scholarship for use in junior or senior years; not renewable. *Number:* 5. *Amount:* $6000.

Eligibility Requirements: Applicant must be enrolled or expecting to enroll full-time at an institution or university. Applicant or parent of applicant must be member of ASM International. Available to U.S. and Canadian citizens.

Application Requirements: Application form, essay, financial need analysis, personal photograph. *Deadline:* May 1.

Contact: Jeane Deatherage, Administrator, Foundation Programs
ASM Materials Education Foundation
9639 Kinsman Road
Materials Park, OH 44073-0002
Phone: 440-338-5151
E-mail: jeane.deatherage@asminternational.org

JOHN M. HANIAK SCHOLARSHIP
Award for student members of ASM International studying metallurgy or materials science and engineering. Must have completed at least one year of college to apply. Award is merit based; financial need is not considered.

Academic Fields/Career Goals: Engineering/Technology; Materials Science, Engineering, and Metallurgy.

Award: Scholarship for use in sophomore, junior, or senior years; not renewable. *Number:* 1. *Amount:* $1500.

Eligibility Requirements: Applicant must be enrolled or expecting to enroll full-time at a four-year institution or university. Applicant or parent of applicant must be member of ASM International. Available to U.S. and Canadian citizens.

Application Requirements: Application form, essay. *Deadline:* May 1.

Contact: Jeane Deatherage, Administrator, Foundation Programs
ASM Materials Education Foundation
9639 Kinsman Road
Materials Park, OH 44073-0002
Phone: 440-338-5151 Ext. 5533
E-mail: scholarshipsUG@asminternational.org

WILLIAM P. WOODSIDE FOUNDER'S SCHOLARSHIP
$10,000 scholarship for college junior or senior studying metallurgy or materials engineering in North America. Must be a student member of ASM International. Award based on need, interest in field, academics, and character.

Academic Fields/Career Goals: Engineering/Technology; Materials Science, Engineering, and Metallurgy.

Award: Scholarship for use in junior or senior years; not renewable. *Number:* 1. *Amount:* $10,000.

Eligibility Requirements: Applicant must be enrolled or expecting to enroll full-time at an institution or university. Applicant or parent of applicant must be member of ASM International. Available to U.S. and Canadian citizens.

Application Requirements: Application form, essay, financial need analysis, personal photograph. *Deadline:* May 1.

Contact: Jeane Deatherage, Administrator, Foundation Programs
ASM Materials Education Foundation
ASM Materials Education Foundation
9639 Kinsman Road
Materials Park, OH 44073
Phone: 440-3385151 Ext. 5533
E-mail: scholarshipsUG@asminternational.org

ASPRS, THE IMAGING AND GEOSPATIAL INFORMATION SOCIETY
http://www.asprs.org/

ABRAHAM ANSON MEMORIAL SCHOLARSHIP
Award to encourage students to pursue education in geospatial science or technology related to photogrammetry, remote sensing, surveying and mapping. Must be enrolled or intending to enroll in a U.S. college or university in geospatial science, surveying and mapping and related fields. Must submit with application a list of all applicable courses taken, a statement of work experience including internships, special projects, technical papers, and courses taught that may support the student's capabilities in this field. For additional information and online application, see website http://www.asprs.org/membership/scholar.html.

Academic Fields/Career Goals: Engineering/Technology; Surveying, Surveying Technology, Cartography, or Geographic Information Science.

Award: Scholarship for use in freshman, sophomore, junior, or senior years; not renewable. *Number:* 1. *Amount:* $2000.

Eligibility Requirements: Applicant must be enrolled or expecting to enroll full-time at a four-year institution or university. Available to U.S. citizens.

Application Requirements: Application form, essay, recommendations or references, resume, transcript. *Deadline:* October 17.

Contact: Scholarship Administrator
Phone: 301-493-0290
E-mail: scholarships@asprs.org

FRANCIS H. MOFFITT MEMORIAL SCHOLARSHIP

Award to encourage upper-division undergraduate and graduate-level students to pursue a course of study in surveying and photogrammetry leading to a career in the mapping profession. Must be enrolled or intending to enroll in a college or university in the U.S. in the field of surveying or photogrammetry. Application must include listing of all courses taken in the field, internships, special projects, courses taught, technical papers that demonstrate applicant's capabilities in the field, two letters of recommendation, and a short statement detailing contributions to the field and future career plans. For additional information, see website http://www.asprs.org.

Academic Fields/Career Goals: Engineering/Technology; Surveying, Surveying Technology, Cartography, or Geographic Information Science.

Award: Scholarship for use in junior or senior years; not renewable. *Number:* 1. *Amount:* $6500.

Eligibility Requirements: Applicant must be enrolled or expecting to enroll full-time at a four-year institution or university. Available to U.S. citizens.

Application Requirements: Application form, essay, recommendations or references, transcript. *Deadline:* October 17.

Contact: Jesse Winch, Scholarship Administrator
Phone: 301-493-0290
E-mail: scholarships@asprs.org

JOHN O. BEHRENS INSTITUTE FOR LAND INFORMATION MEMORIAL SCHOLARSHIP

Award to encourage study in geospatial science or technology or land information systems/records. Must be an undergraduate student enrolled or intending to enroll in a U.S. college or university in the designated field. Application must be submitted electronically and must include a list of completed courses in the field, papers, research reports, or other items produced by the applicant that demonstrate capability in the field, and internships, work experience, special projects or courses taught that support potential excellence in the field. Additional information and application on website http://www.asprs.org/membership/scholar.html.

Academic Fields/Career Goals: Engineering/Technology; Surveying, Surveying Technology, Cartography, or Geographic Information Science.

Award: Scholarship for use in freshman, sophomore, junior, or senior years; not renewable. *Number:* 1. *Amount:* $2000.

Eligibility Requirements: Applicant must be enrolled or expecting to enroll full-time at a four-year institution or university. Available to U.S. citizens.

Application Requirements: Application form, essay, recommendations or references, resume, transcript. *Deadline:* October 17.

Contact: Scholarship Administrator
Phone: 301-493-0290
E-mail: scholarships@asprs.org

KENNETH J. OSBORN MEMORIAL SCHOLARSHIP

Award to encourage students who display the interest and aptitude to enter the profession of surveying, mapping, geospatial information and technology, and photogrammetry. Student must be enrolled or intending to enroll in a college or university in the U.S. in a program of study to prepare for the profession. Application must be submitted electronically. For additional requirements that must accompany electronic application, visit website http://www.asprs.org/membership/scholar.html.

Academic Fields/Career Goals: Engineering/Technology; Surveying, Surveying Technology, Cartography, or Geographic Information Science.

Award: Scholarship for use in freshman, sophomore, junior, or senior years; not renewable. *Number:* 1. *Amount:* $2000.

Eligibility Requirements: Applicant must be enrolled or expecting to enroll full-time at a four-year institution or university. Available to U.S. citizens.

Application Requirements: Application form, essay, recommendations or references, resume, transcript. *Deadline:* October 17.

Contact: Scholarship Administrator
Phone: 301-493-0290
E-mail: scholarships@asprs.org

ROBERT E. ALTENHOFEN MEMORIAL SCHOLARSHIP

One-time award of $2000 available for undergraduate or graduate study in theoretical photogrammetry. Applicant must supply a sample of work in photogrammetry and a statement of plans for future study in the field. Must be a member of ASPRS.

Academic Fields/Career Goals: Engineering/Technology; Surveying, Surveying Technology, Cartography, or Geographic Information Science.

Award: Scholarship for use in junior, senior, or graduate years; not renewable. *Number:* 1. *Amount:* $2000.

Eligibility Requirements: Applicant must be enrolled or expecting to enroll full-time at a four-year institution or university and must have an interest in photography/photogrammetry/filmmaking. Applicant or parent of applicant must be member of American Society for Photogrammetry and Remote Sensing. Available to U.S. and non-U.S. citizens.

Application Requirements: Application form, essay, recommendations or references, transcript, work sample. *Deadline:* October 17.

Contact: Program Manager
ASPRS, The Imaging and Geospatial Information Society
5410 Grosvenor Lane, Suite 210
Bethesda, MD 20814-2160
Phone: 301-493-0290
Fax: 301-493-0208
E-mail: scholarships@asprs.org

ASSOCIATED GENERAL CONTRACTORS EDUCATION AND RESEARCH FOUNDATION

http://www.agcfoundation.org/

WORKFORCE DEVELOPMENT SCHOLARSHIP
• See page 237

ASSOCIATION OF STATE DAM SAFETY OFFICIALS (ASDSO)

http://www.DamSafety.org

ASSOCIATION OF STATE DAM SAFETY OFFICIALS (ASDSO) SENIOR UNDERGRADUATE SCHOLARSHIP
• See page 168

AUTOMOTIVE WOMEN'S ALLIANCE FOUNDATION

http://awafoundation.org/index.php

AUTOMOTIVE WOMEN'S ALLIANCE FOUNDATION SCHOLARSHIPS
• See page 81

BARRY GOLDWATER SCHOLARSHIP AND EXCELLENCE IN EDUCATION FOUNDATION

https://goldwater.scholarsapply.org

BARRY M. GOLDWATER SCHOLARSHIP AND EXCELLENCE IN EDUCATION PROGRAM
• See page 123

BHW GROUP

https://thebhwgroup.com/

BHW WOMEN IN STEM SCHOLARSHIP
• See page 124

BOYS AND GIRLS CLUBS OF GREATER SAN DIEGO

http://www.sdyouth.org/

SPENCE REESE SCHOLARSHIP

Renewable scholarship for graduating high school seniors in the United States for study of law, medicine, engineering, and political science. Awarded based on academic standing, academic ability, financial need, and character.

Academic Fields/Career Goals: Engineering/Technology; Health and Medical Sciences; Law/Legal Services; Political Science.

Award: Scholarship for use in freshman, sophomore, junior, or senior years; not renewable. *Number:* 4. *Amount:* $6000.

Eligibility Requirements: Applicant must be high school student and planning to enroll or expecting to enroll full-time at a four-year institution or university. Applicant must have 3.5 GPA or higher. Available to U.S. citizens.

Application Requirements: Application form, essay, financial need analysis, interview. *Deadline:* March 30.

Contact: Spence Reese Scholarship Administrator
Boys and Girls Clubs of Greater San Diego
4635 Clairemont Mesa Boulevard
San Diego, CA 92117
E-mail: mahazzard@sdyouth.org

BROWN AND CALDWELL

http://www.brownandcaldwell.com

ECKENFELDER SCHOLARSHIP
• *See page 169*

MINORITY SCHOLARSHIP PROGRAM
• *See page 169*

CARDS AGAINST HUMANITY

https://cardsagainsthumanity.com/

SCIENCE AMBASSADOR SCHOLARSHIP
• *See page 124*

CATCHING THE DREAM

http://www.catchingthedream.org/

MATH, ENGINEERING, SCIENCE, BUSINESS, EDUCATION, COMPUTERS SCHOLARSHIPS
• *See page 178*

CENTER FOR ARCHITECTURE

http://www.centerforarchitecture.org

CENTER FOR ARCHITECTURE, DOUGLAS HASKELL AWARD FOR STUDENT JOURNALS
• *See page 132*

THE CLUNKER JUNKER

https://theclunkerjunker.com/

CLUNKER JUNKER CASH FOR CARS AND COLLEGE SCHOLARSHIP
• *See page 299*

CLUTCH PREP

http://www.clutchprep.com

CLUTCH PREP STEM SCHOLARSHIP
• *See page 285*

CONNECTICUT BUILDING CONGRESS SCHOLARSHIP FUND, INC.

http://www.cbc-ct.org

CBC SCHOLARSHIP FUND
• *See page 132*

THE DALLAS FOUNDATION

http://www.dallasfoundation.org/

WHITLEY PLACE SCHOLARSHIP
• *See page 133*

DAVIDSON INSTITUTE FOR TALENT DEVELOPMENT

http://www.davidsongifted.org/

DAVIDSON FELLOWS SCHOLARSHIP PROGRAM
• *See page 124*

DELAWARE HIGHER EDUCATION OFFICE

http://www.doe.k12.de.us

DELAWARE SOLID WASTE AUTHORITY JOHN P. "PAT" HEALY SCHOLARSHIP

Award for legal residents of Delaware who are U.S. citizens or eligible non-citizens. Must be high school seniors or full-time college students in their freshman or sophomore years. Must major in either environmental engineering or environmental sciences at a Delaware college. Selection based on financial need, academic performance, community and school involvement, and leadership ability.

Academic Fields/Career Goals: Engineering/Technology; Environmental Science.

Award: Scholarship for use in freshman or sophomore years; renewable. *Number:* 2. *Amount:* $1500–$2500.

Eligibility Requirements: Applicant must be enrolled or expecting to enroll full-time at a two-year or four-year institution or university; resident of Delaware and must have an interest in leadership. Applicant must have 3.0 GPA or higher. Available to U.S. citizens.

Application Requirements: Application form, financial need analysis. *Deadline:* March 5.

Contact: Ms. Juliet Murawski, Program Administrator
Delaware Higher Education Office
401 Federal Street
Suite 2
Dover, DE 19901
Phone: 302-735-4120
Fax: 302-739-5894
E-mail: dheo@doe.k12.de.us

DISTIL NETWORKS

http://www.distilnetworks.com

WOMEN FORWARD IN TECHNOLOGY SCHOLARSHIP PROGRAM
• *See page 124*

DIVERSITYCOMM, INC.

http://www.diversitycomm.net/

DIVERSITY IN STEAM MAGAZINE SCHOLARSHIP
• *See page 83*

DOTCOM-MONITOR, INC.
https://www.dotcom-monitor.com/

LOADVIEW WOMEN IN COMPUTING SCHOLARSHIP
• *See page 231*

EAA AVIATION FOUNDATION, INC.
http://www.eaa.org/

PAYZER SCHOLARSHIP
• *See page 153*

THE ELECTROCHEMICAL SOCIETY
http://www.electrochem.org/

H.H. DOW MEMORIAL STUDENT ACHIEVEMENT AWARD OF THE INDUSTRIAL ELECTROLYSIS AND ELECTROCHEMICAL ENGINEERING DIVISION OF THE ELECTROCHEMICAL SOCIETY INC.
• *See page 125*

STUDENT RESEARCH AWARDS OF THE BATTERY DIVISION OF THE ELECTROCHEMICAL SOCIETY INC.
• *See page 125*

FABRICATORS AND MANUFACTURERS ASSOCIATION FOUNDATION
http://www.nutsandboltsfoundation.org/scholarships/

COLLEGE AND TRADE/TECHNICAL SCHOOL SCHOLARSHIPS
• *See page 154*

FLORIDA ENGINEERING SOCIETY
http://www.fleng.org/scholarships.cfm

ACEC/FLORIDA SCHOLARSHIP
One-time scholarship of $5000 given to Florida citizen pursuing a bachelor's, master's or doctoral degree in an ABET-approved engineering program or in an accredited land surveying program. Students must be entering their junior, senior, or fifth year of college.

Academic Fields/Career Goals: Engineering/Technology; Surveying, Surveying Technology, Cartography, or Geographic Information Science.

Award: Scholarship for use in junior or senior years; not renewable. *Number:* 1. *Amount:* $5000.

Eligibility Requirements: Applicant must be enrolled or expecting to enroll full-time at a four-year institution or university; resident of Florida and studying in Florida. Available to U.S. citizens.

Application Requirements: Application form, essay. *Deadline:* March 6.

Contact: Chad Faison, Director of Marketing & Communications
Florida Engineering Society
125 South Gadsden Street
Tallahassee, FL 32301
Phone: 850-224-7121
E-mail: cfaison@fleng.org

DAVID F. LUDOVICI SCHOLARSHIP
• *See page 192*

ERIC PRIMAVERA MEMORIAL SCHOLARSHIP
One-time scholarship of $1000 given to students in their junior or senior year in a Florida university engineering program. Minimum 3.0 GPA required.

Academic Fields/Career Goals: Engineering/Technology.

Award: Scholarship for use in junior or senior years; not renewable. *Number:* 1. *Amount:* $1000.

Eligibility Requirements: Applicant must be enrolled or expecting to enroll full-time at an institution or university; resident of Florida and studying in Florida. Applicant must have 3.0 GPA or higher. Available to U.S. citizens.

Application Requirements: Application form. *Deadline:* February 1.

Contact: Amanda Hudson, Director of Information Technology
Florida Engineering Society
125 S Gadsden Street
Tallahassee, FL 32301
Phone: 850-224-7121
E-mail: ahudson@fleng.org

HIGH SCHOOL SCHOLARSHIP
One-time scholarship given to high school seniors who are residents of Florida. Minimum 3.5 GPA required. Applicant must have genuine interest in engineering.

Academic Fields/Career Goals: Engineering/Technology.

Award: Scholarship for use in freshman year; not renewable. *Number:* 6. *Amount:* $1500–$2500.

Eligibility Requirements: Applicant must be high school student; planning to enroll or expecting to enroll full-time at a four-year institution or university and resident of Florida. Applicant or parent of applicant must have employment or volunteer experience in engineering/technology. Applicant must have 3.5 GPA or higher. Available to U.S. citizens.

Application Requirements: Application form, interview. *Deadline:* February 1.

Contact: Amanda Hudson, Director of Information Technology
Florida Engineering Society
125 S Gadsden Street
Tallahassee, FL 32301
Phone: 850-224-7121
E-mail: ahudson@fleng.org

RAYMOND W. MILLER, PE SCHOLARSHIP
One-time scholarship given to students in their junior or senior year in a Florida university engineering program. Minimum 3.0 GPA required.

Academic Fields/Career Goals: Engineering/Technology.

Award: Scholarship for use in junior or senior years; not renewable. *Number:* 1. *Amount:* $1500–$2500.

Eligibility Requirements: Applicant must be enrolled or expecting to enroll full-time at an institution or university; resident of Florida and studying in Florida. Applicant must have 3.0 GPA or higher. Available to U.S. citizens.

Application Requirements: Application form. *Deadline:* February 1.

Contact: Amanda Hudson, Director of Information Technology
Florida Engineering Society
125 S Gadsden Street
Tallahassee, FL 32301
Phone: 850-224-7121
E-mail: ahudson@fleng.org

RICHARD B. GASSETT, PE SCHOLARSHIP
One-time scholarship given to students in their junior or senior year in a Florida university engineering program. Minimum 3.0 GPA required.

Academic Fields/Career Goals: Engineering/Technology.

Award: Scholarship for use in junior or senior years; not renewable. *Number:* 1. *Amount:* $1500–$2500.

Eligibility Requirements: Applicant must be enrolled or expecting to enroll full-time at an institution or university; resident of Florida and studying in Florida. Applicant must have 3.0 GPA or higher. Available to U.S. citizens.

Application Requirements: Application form. *Deadline:* February 1.

Contact: Amanda Hudson, Director of Information Technology
Florida Engineering Society
125 S Gadsden Street
Tallahassee, FL 32301
Phone: 850-224-7121
E-mail: ahudson@fleng.org

FOUNDATION FOR SCIENCE AND DISABILITY

http://stemd.org/

GRANTS FOR DISABLED GRADUATE STUDENTS IN THE SCIENCES

• See page 106

GEORGIA SOCIETY OF PROFESSIONAL ENGINEERS/GEORGIA ENGINEERING FOUNDATION

http://www.gefinc.org/

GEORGIA ENGINEERING FOUNDATION SCHOLARSHIP PROGRAM

Awards scholarships to students who are preparing for a career in engineering or engineering technology. Must be U.S. citizens and legal residents of Georgia. Must be attending or accepted in an ABET-accredited program. Separate applications are available: one for use by high school seniors and new college freshmen and one for use by college upperclassmen.

Academic Fields/Career Goals: Engineering/Technology.

Award: Scholarship for use in freshman, sophomore, junior, or senior years; not renewable. *Number:* 45. *Amount:* $1000–$5000.

Eligibility Requirements: Applicant must be enrolled or expecting to enroll full-time at a four-year institution or university and resident of Georgia. Available to U.S. citizens.

Application Requirements: Application form, personal photograph. *Deadline:* August 31.

Contact: Julie Secrist, Scholarship Committee Chairman
Georgia Society of Professional Engineers/Georgia
Engineering Foundation
233 Peachtree Street, Suite 700, Harris Tower
Atlanta, GA 30303
Phone: 678-449-5522
E-mail: scholarshipchair@gefinc.org

GOLDEN KEY INTERNATIONAL HONOUR SOCIETY

http://www.goldenkey.org/

ENGINEERING/TECHNOLOGY ACHIEVEMENT AWARD

Award to members who excel in the study of engineering or technology. Applicants will be asked to respond to a problem posed by an honorary member within the discipline. One winner will receive a $1000 award. The second place winner will receive $750 and the third place winner will receive $500.

Academic Fields/Career Goals: Engineering/Technology.

Award: Prize for use in freshman, sophomore, junior, senior, graduate, or postgraduate years; not renewable. *Number:* 3. *Amount:* $500–$1000.

Eligibility Requirements: Applicant must be enrolled or expecting to enroll full- or part-time at a four-year institution or university. Available to U.S. and non-U.S. citizens.

Application Requirements: Application form, engineering-related report, cover page from the online registration, entry in a contest, essay, recommendations or references, transcript. *Deadline:* March 3.

Contact: Scholarship Program Administrators
Golden Key International Honour Society
PO Box 23737
Nashville, TN 37202-3737
Phone: 800-377-2401
E-mail: scholarships@goldenkey.org

GREATER KANAWHA VALLEY FOUNDATION

http://www.tgkvf.org/

MATH AND SCIENCE SCHOLARSHIP

• See page 171

STEVEN ENGINEERING SCHOLARSHIP

• See page 192

GREAT MINDS IN STEM

http://www.greatmindsinstem.org

HENAAC SCHOLARSHIP PROGRAM

• See page 115

HELLENIC UNIVERSITY CLUB OF PHILADELPHIA

http://www.hucphiladelphia.org/

DIMITRI J. VERVERELLI MEMORIAL SCHOLARSHIP FOR ARCHITECTURE AND/OR ENGINEERING

• See page 134

IDAHO STATE BROADCASTERS ASSOCIATION

http://www.idahobroadcasters.org/

WAYNE C. CORNILS MEMORIAL SCHOLARSHIP

• See page 180

ILLINOIS SOCIETY OF PROFESSIONAL ENGINEERS

http://www.illinoisengineer.com/

ILLINOIS SOCIETY OF PROFESSIONAL ENGINEERS/MELVIN E. AMSTUTZ MEMORIAL AWARD

Applicant must attend an Illinois university approved by the Accreditation Board of Engineering. Applicant must be at least a junior in university he or she attends, and must prove financial need. Essay must address why applicant wishes to become a professional engineer. Must have a B average.

Academic Fields/Career Goals: Engineering/Technology.

Award: Scholarship for use in junior or senior years; not renewable. *Number:* 1. *Amount:* $1500.

Eligibility Requirements: Applicant must be enrolled or expecting to enroll full-time at a four-year institution and studying in Illinois. Applicant must have 3.0 GPA or higher. Available to U.S. and non-U.S. citizens.

Application Requirements: Application form, application form may be submitted online (http://illinoisengineer.com/scholarships.shtml), essay, financial need analysis, recommendations or references, resume, transcript. *Deadline:* March 31.

Contact: Mrs. Nicole Palmisano, Scholarship Coordinator
Phone: 217-544-7424 Ext. 238
Fax: 217-528-6545
E-mail: NicolePalmisano@illinoisengineer.com

ILLUMINATING ENGINEERING SOCIETY OF NORTH AMERICA

http://www.ies.org/

ROBERT W. THUNEN MEMORIAL SCHOLARSHIPS

• See page 135

INDEPENDENT LABORATORIES INSTITUTE SCHOLARSHIP ALLIANCE

http://www.acil.org/

INDEPENDENT LABORATORIES INSTITUTE SCHOLARSHIP ALLIANCE

• See page 171

INSTITUTE OF INDUSTRIAL ENGINEERS

http://www.iienet.org/

A.O. PUTNAM MEMORIAL SCHOLARSHIP

$700 award for undergraduate students enrolled in any school in the United States and its territories, Canada, and Mexico pursuing a course of study in industrial engineering. The school's industrial engineering program or equivalent must be accredited by an agency or organization recognized by IIE. Priority is given to students who have demonstrated an interest in management consulting. Minimum 3.4 GPA required.

Academic Fields/Career Goals: Engineering/Technology.

Award: Scholarship for use in freshman, sophomore, junior, or senior years; not renewable. *Number:* 1. *Amount:* up to $4000.

Eligibility Requirements: Applicant must be enrolled or expecting to enroll full-time at a four-year institution or university. Applicant or parent of applicant must be member of Institute of Industrial Engineers. Available to U.S. and non-U.S. citizens.

Application Requirements: Application form, nomination, recommendations or references, transcript. *Deadline:* November 15.

Contact: Bonnie Cameron, Operations Administrator
Phone: 770-449-0461 Ext. 105
E-mail: bcameron@iienet.org

C.B. GAMBRELL UNDERGRADUATE SCHOLARSHIP

One-time award for undergraduate industrial engineering students who are U.S. citizens, have graduated from a U.S. high school, and have a class standing above freshman level in an ABET-accredited IE program. Must be a member of Industrial Engineers, have a minimum GPA of 3.4, and be nominated by a department head.

Academic Fields/Career Goals: Engineering/Technology.

Award: Scholarship for use in sophomore, junior, or senior years; not renewable. *Number:* 1. *Amount:* up to $4000.

Eligibility Requirements: Applicant must be enrolled or expecting to enroll full-time at a four-year institution or university. Applicant or parent of applicant must be member of Institute of Industrial Engineers. Available to U.S. citizens.

Application Requirements: Application form, nomination, recommendations or references, transcript. *Deadline:* November 15.

Contact: Bonnie Cameron, Operations Administrator
Phone: 770-449-0461 Ext. 105
E-mail: bcameron@iienet.org

CIE UNDERGRADUATE SCHOLARSHIP

$2000 scholarship will be awarded to an undergraduate industrial engineering student for the best application of corporate social responsibility, resilience, or sustainability principals aligned with classic industrial engineering techniques to a project for an enterprise. Interested candidates must complete an application form, as well as submit a complete description of the project, including provision of a financial analysis using the triple-bottom line definitions of sustainability, showing a positive cash flow or return on investment to the enterprise over the project life. Applicants should have at least a 3.4 GPA.

Academic Fields/Career Goals: Engineering/Technology.

Award: Scholarship for use in freshman, sophomore, junior, or senior years; not renewable. *Number:* 1. *Amount:* $2000.

Eligibility Requirements: Applicant must be enrolled or expecting to enroll full-time at a four-year institution or university. Available to U.S. citizens.

Application Requirements: Application form, project description, recommendations or references, transcript. *Deadline:* February 1.

Contact: Bonnie Cameron, Operations Administrator
Phone: 770-449-0461 Ext. 105
E-mail: bcameron@iienet.org

DWIGHT D. GARDNER SCHOLARSHIP

$3000 scholarship available to undergraduate students enrolled in an industrial engineering program in any school in the United States and its territories, Canada, and Mexico, provided the school's engineering program or equivalent is accredited by an agency recognized by IIE. Must be an IIE member. Minimum 3.4 GPA required. Must be nominated by department head.

Academic Fields/Career Goals: Engineering/Technology.

Award: Scholarship for use in freshman, sophomore, junior, or senior years; not renewable. *Number:* 3. *Amount:* up to $4000.

Eligibility Requirements: Applicant must be enrolled or expecting to enroll full-time at a four-year institution or university. Applicant or parent of applicant must be member of Institute of Industrial Engineers. Available to U.S. and non-U.S. citizens.

Application Requirements: Application form, essay, financial need analysis, nomination, recommendations or references, transcript. *Deadline:* November 15.

Contact: Bonnie Cameron, Operations Administrator
Phone: 770-449-0461 Ext. 105
E-mail: bcameron@iienet.org

HAROLD AND INGE MARCUS SCHOLARSHIP

Available to undergraduate students enrolled in any school in the United States provided the school's engineering program is accredited by an agency recognized by IIE and the student is pursuing a course of study in industrial engineering. This award is intended to recognize academic excellence and noteworthy contribution to the development of the industrial engineering profession. Must have at least a 3.4 GPA.

Academic Fields/Career Goals: Engineering/Technology.

Award: Scholarship for use in freshman, sophomore, junior, or senior years; not renewable. *Amount:* up to $4000.

Eligibility Requirements: Applicant must be enrolled or expecting to enroll full-time at a two-year or four-year institution or university. Available to U.S. citizens.

Application Requirements: Application form, nominations, recommendations or references, transcript. *Deadline:* November 15.

Contact: Bonnie Cameron, Operations Administrator
Phone: 770-449-0461 Ext. 105
E-mail: bcameron@iienet.org

IIE COUNCIL OF FELLOWS UNDERGRADUATE SCHOLARSHIP

Awards to undergraduate students enrolled in any school in the United States and its territories, Canada and Mexico, provided the school's engineering program or equivalent is accredited by an agency recognized by IIE and the student is pursuing a course of study in industrial engineering. Must be IIE member and have minimum 3.4 GPA.

Academic Fields/Career Goals: Engineering/Technology.

Award: Scholarship for use in freshman, sophomore, junior, or senior years; not renewable. *Amount:* up to $4000.

Eligibility Requirements: Applicant must be enrolled or expecting to enroll full-time at a four-year institution or university. Applicant or parent of applicant must be member of Institute of Industrial Engineers. Available to U.S. and non-U.S. citizens.

Application Requirements: Application form, nomination form, recommendations or references, transcript. *Deadline:* November 15.

Contact: Bonnie Cameron, Operations Administrator
Phone: 770-449-0461 Ext. 105
E-mail: bcameron@iienet.org

JOHN L. IMHOFF SCHOLARSHIP

At least one award for a student pursuing an industrial engineering degree who, by academic, employment and/or professional achievements, has made noteworthy contributions to the development of the industrial engineering profession through international understanding. IIE membership is not required. Must have at least a 3.4 GPA.

Academic Fields/Career Goals: Engineering/Technology.

Award: Scholarship for use in freshman, sophomore, junior, or senior years; not renewable. *Number:* 1. *Amount:* $1000.

Eligibility Requirements: Applicant must be enrolled or expecting to enroll full-time at a four-year institution or university. Available to U.S. citizens.

Application Requirements: Application form, essay, nomination, recommendations or references, transcript. *Deadline:* November 15.

Contact: Bonnie Cameron, Operations Administrator
Phone: 770-449-0461 Ext. 105
E-mail: bcameron@iienet.org

LISA ZAKEN AWARD FOR EXCELLENCE

Award for undergraduate and graduate students enrolled in any school, and pursuing a course of study in industrial engineering. Award is intended to recognize excellence in scholarly activities and leadership related to the industrial engineering profession on campus. Must maintain at least a 3.0 GPA.

Academic Fields/Career Goals: Engineering/Technology.

Award: Prize for use in freshman, sophomore, junior, senior, or graduate years; not renewable. *Number:* up to 1. *Amount:* up to $4000.

Eligibility Requirements: Applicant must be enrolled or expecting to enroll full-time at a four-year institution or university. Applicant or parent of applicant must be member of Institute of Industrial Engineers. Applicant must have 3.0 GPA or higher. Available to U.S. and non-U.S. citizens.

Application Requirements: Application form, essay, nomination form, recommendations or references, transcript. *Deadline:* November 15.

Contact: Bonnie Cameron, Operations Administrator
Phone: 770-449-0461 Ext. 105
E-mail: bcameron@iienet.org

MARVIN MUNDEL MEMORIAL SCHOLARSHIP

Scholarship awarded to undergraduate students enrolled in any school in the United States, Canada, or Mexico with an accredited industrial engineering program. Priority given to students who have demonstrated an interest in work measurement and methods engineering. Must be active Institute members with 3.4 GPA or above. Must be nominated by department head or faculty adviser.

Academic Fields/Career Goals: Engineering/Technology.

Award: Scholarship for use in freshman, sophomore, junior, or senior years; not renewable. *Amount:* up to $4000.

Eligibility Requirements: Applicant must be enrolled or expecting to enroll full-time at a four-year institution or university. Applicant or parent of applicant must be member of Institute of Industrial Engineers. Available to U.S. and non-U.S. citizens.

Application Requirements: Application form, nomination, recommendations or references, transcript. *Deadline:* November 15.

Contact: Bonnie Cameron, Operations Administrator
Phone: 770-449-0461 Ext. 105
E-mail: bcameron@iienet.org

PRESIDENTS SCHOLARSHIP

$1000 scholarship available to undergraduate student pursuing a course of study in industrial engineering. This award is intended to recognize excellence in scholarly activities and leadership of the industrial engineering profession. Must be active in a student chapter and must have demonstrated leadership and promoted IIE involvement on campus. Must have at least a 3.4 GPA.

Academic Fields/Career Goals: Engineering/Technology.

Award: Scholarship for use in freshman, sophomore, junior, or senior years; not renewable. *Number:* 1. *Amount:* $1000.

Eligibility Requirements: Applicant must be enrolled or expecting to enroll full-time at a four-year institution or university. Applicant or parent of applicant must be member of Institute of Industrial Engineers. Available to U.S. citizens.

Application Requirements: Application form, nomination, recommendations or references, transcript. *Deadline:* November 15.

Contact: Bonnie Cameron, Operations Administrator
Phone: 770-449-0461 Ext. 105
E-mail: bcameron@iienet.org

SOCIETY FOR HEALTH SYSTEMS SCHOLARSHIP

$1000 award for undergraduate students enrolled full-time in an industrial engineering program in any accredited school in the United States and its territories, Canada and Mexico. Must be pursuing a course of study in industrial engineering and operations research with a definite interest in the area of health care. Must be an active Society for Health Systems student member with a minimum 3.4 GPA. Nomination required.

Academic Fields/Career Goals: Engineering/Technology.

Award: Scholarship for use in freshman, sophomore, junior, or senior years; not renewable. *Amount:* $1000.

Eligibility Requirements: Applicant must be enrolled or expecting to enroll full-time at a four-year institution or university. Available to U.S. citizens.

Application Requirements: Application form, essay, nomination, recommendations or references, resume, transcript. *Deadline:* December 1.

Contact: Bonnie Cameron, Operations Administrator
Phone: 770-449-0461 Ext. 105
E-mail: bcameron@iienet.org

UPS SCHOLARSHIP FOR FEMALE STUDENTS

One-time award for female undergraduate students enrolled at any school in the United States, Canada, or Mexico in an industrial engineering program. Must be a member of Institute of Industrial Engineers, have a minimum GPA of 3.4, and be nominated by a department head.

Academic Fields/Career Goals: Engineering/Technology.

Award: Scholarship for use in freshman, sophomore, junior, or senior years; not renewable. *Number:* 1. *Amount:* up to $4000.

Eligibility Requirements: Applicant must be enrolled or expecting to enroll full-time at a four-year or technical institution or university and female. Applicant or parent of applicant must be member of Institute of Industrial Engineers. Available to U.S. and non-U.S. citizens.

Application Requirements: Application form, nomination, recommendations or references, transcript. *Deadline:* November 15.

Contact: Bonnie Cameron, Operations Administrator
Phone: 770-449-0461 Ext. 105
E-mail: bcameron@iienet.org

UPS SCHOLARSHIP FOR MINORITY STUDENTS

One-time award for minority undergraduate students enrolled at any school in the United States, Canada, or Mexico in an industrial engineering program. Must be a member of Institute of Industrial Engineers. Nominated students by IE department heads will be sent an application package to complete and return before November 15. Minimum GPA of 3.4 required.

Academic Fields/Career Goals: Engineering/Technology.

Award: Scholarship for use in freshman, sophomore, junior, or senior years; not renewable. *Number:* 1. *Amount:* up to $4000.

Eligibility Requirements: Applicant must be American Indian/Alaska Native, Asian/Pacific Islander, Black (non-Hispanic), Hispanic and enrolled or expecting to enroll full-time at a four-year institution or university. Applicant or parent of applicant must be member of Institute of Industrial Engineers. Available to U.S. and non-U.S. citizens.

Application Requirements: Application form, nomination, recommendations or references, transcript. *Deadline:* November 15.

Contact: Bonnie Cameron, Operations Administrator
Phone: 770-449-0461 Ext. 105
E-mail: bcameron@iienet.org

INTERNATIONAL FACILITY MANAGEMENT ASSOCIATION FOUNDATION

http://www.ifmafoundation.org/

IFMA FOUNDATION SCHOLARSHIPS
• See page 135

INTERNATIONAL SOCIETY FOR OPTICAL ENGINEERING-SPIE

http://www.spie.org/scholarships

SPIE EDUCATIONAL SCHOLARSHIPS IN OPTICAL SCIENCE AND ENGINEERING
• See page 126

INTERNATIONAL SOCIETY OF EXPLOSIVES ENGINEERS

http://www.isee.org/

JERRY MCDOWELL FUND
• See page 301

INTERNATIONAL TECHNOLOGY EDUCATION ASSOCIATION

http://www.iteaconnect.org/

INTERNATIONAL TECHNOLOGY EDUCATION ASSOCIATION UNDERGRADUATE SCHOLARSHIP IN TECHNOLOGY EDUCATION
• See page 272

LABROOTS INC.

http://www.LabRoots.com

LABROOTS STEM SCHOLARSHIP
• See page 116

LEAGUE OF UNITED LATIN AMERICAN CITIZENS NATIONAL EDUCATIONAL SERVICE CENTERS INC.

http://www.lnesc.org/

GE/LULAC SCHOLARSHIP
• See page 181

GM/LULAC SCHOLARSHIP

Renewable award for minority students who are pursuing an undergraduate degree in engineering at an accredited college or university. Must maintain a minimum 3.0 GPA. Selection is based in part on the likelihood of pursuing a successful career in engineering.

Academic Fields/Career Goals: Engineering/Technology.

Award: Scholarship for use in freshman, sophomore, junior, or senior years; renewable. *Number:* up to 20. *Amount:* up to $2000.

Eligibility Requirements: Applicant must be American Indian/Alaska Native, Asian/Pacific Islander, Black (non-Hispanic), Hispanic and enrolled or expecting to enroll full-time at a four-year institution or university. Applicant must have 3.0 GPA or higher. Available to U.S. citizens.

Application Requirements: Application form, essay, recommendations or references, transcript. *Deadline:* July 15.

Contact: Scholarship Administrator
League of United Latin American Citizens National
Educational Service Centers Inc.
2000 L Street, NW, Suite 610
Washington, DC 20036
Phone: 202-835-9646 Ext. 10
Fax: 202-835-9685

LOS ANGELES COUNCIL OF BLACK PROFESSIONAL ENGINEERS

http://www.lablackengineers.org/

AL-BEN SCHOLARSHIP FOR ACADEMIC INCENTIVE
• See page 193

AL-BEN SCHOLARSHIP FOR PROFESSIONAL MERIT
• See page 193

AL-BEN SCHOLARSHIP FOR SCHOLASTIC ACHIEVEMENT
• See page 193

MAINE SOCIETY OF PROFESSIONAL ENGINEERS

http://www.mespe.org/

MAINE SOCIETY OF PROFESSIONAL ENGINEERS VERNON T. SWAINE-ROBERT E. CHUTE SCHOLARSHIP
• See page 301

MANUFACTURERS ASSOCIATION OF MAINE

http://www.mainemfg.com/

MAINE MANUFACTURING CAREER AND TRAINING FOUNDATION SCHOLARSHIP
• See page 156

MARINE TECHNOLOGY SOCIETY

http://www.mtsociety.org/

MTS STUDENT SCHOLARSHIP FOR GRADUATING HIGH SCHOOL SENIORS

Scholarship of $2000 available to high school seniors who have been accepted into a full-time undergraduate program and have an interest in marine technology.

Academic Fields/Career Goals: Engineering/Technology; Marine/Ocean Engineering.

Award: Scholarship for use in freshman year; not renewable. *Amount:* $2000.

Eligibility Requirements: Applicant must be high school student and planning to enroll or expecting to enroll full-time at a four-year institution or university. Available to U.S. and non-U.S. citizens.

Application Requirements: Application form, college acceptance letter, essay, recommendations or references, transcript. *Deadline:* April 15.

Contact: Suzanne Voelker, Operations Administrator
Marine Technology Society
5565 Sterrett Place, Suite 108
Columbia, MD 21044
Phone: 410-884-5330
E-mail: suzanne.voelker@mtsociety.org

MASSACHUSETTS ASSOCIATION OF LAND SURVEYORS AND CIVIL ENGINEERS

http://www.malsce.org/

MALSCE SCHOLARSHIPS

A scholarship awarded to a student presently enrolled full time (days) as an undergraduate in an accredited college, university, junior college, technical institute or community college and majoring in land surveying, civil engineering, or environmental engineering. The MALSCE Education Trust may select one or more applicants to receive scholarships per year and currently plans to award one or two scholarships. Typically 2-3 scholarships are awarded each year with varying denominations of $500, $1000 or $2500 each. The MALSCE Education Trust Chair will contact winning applicants. Applicant must be presently enrolled full-time (days) in an accredited college, university, junior college, technical institute, or community college and majoring in land surveying, civil engineering, or environmental engineering; be a Massachusetts resident (based upon parents full-time residence, if still a dependent), however, he/she may attend an out-of-state school; complete and sign the application and give it to a qualified sponsor. A sponsor must be a department head, dean, professor, or instructor who has personal knowledge of the applicant. An applicant's employer may also be a sponsor, if that employer is a MALSCE member in good standing. Friends and relatives of the applicant may not be sponsors. The Trustees will not accept a letter of recommendation from a sponsor other than the types listed above.

Academic Fields/Career Goals: Engineering/Technology; Environmental Science; Surveying, Surveying Technology, Cartography, or Geographic Information Science.

Award: Scholarship for use in sophomore, junior, or senior years; not renewable. *Number:* 1–2. *Amount:* $500–$2000.

Eligibility Requirements: Applicant must be enrolled or expecting to enroll full- or part-time at a two-year or four-year or technical institution or university; resident of Massachusetts and studying in Massachusetts. Available to U.S. citizens.

Application Requirements: Application form, essay. *Deadline:* October 31.

Contact: Mrs. Mary Ann Corcoran, MALSCE Education Trust Chair
Massachusetts Association of Land Surveyors and Civil
Engineers
One Walnut Street
Boston, MA 02108
Phone: 413-841-0355
E-mail: mcorcoran@hillengineers.com

MIDWEST ROOFING CONTRACTORS ASSOCIATION

http://www.mrca.org/

MRCA FOUNDATION SCHOLARSHIP PROGRAM
• *See page 135*

MINERALS, METALS, AND MATERIALS SOCIETY (TMS)

http://www.tms.org/

KAUFMAN CALPHAD SCHOLARSHIP
• *See page 302*

MATERIALS PROCESSING AND MANUFACTURING DIVISION SCHOLARSHIP
• *See page 302*

TMS/EPD SCHOLARSHIP
• *See page 302*

TMS/FMD GILBERT CHIN SCHOLARSHIP
• *See page 302*

TMS/INTERNATIONAL SYMPOSIUM ON SUPERALLOYS SCHOLARSHIP PROGRAM
• *See page 302*

TMS/LIGHT METALS DIVISION SCHOLARSHIP PROGRAM
• *See page 302*

TMS OUTSTANDING STUDENT PAPER CONTEST– UNDERGRADUATE
• *See page 303*

TMS/STRUCTURAL MATERIALS DIVISION SCHOLARSHIP
• *See page 303*

NASA FLORIDA SPACE GRANT CONSORTIUM

http://www.floridaspacegrant.org/

FLORIDA SPACE RESEARCH PROGRAM
• *See page 156*

NASA IDAHO SPACE GRANT CONSORTIUM

http://www.idahospacegrant.org

NASA IDAHO SPACE GRANT CONSORTIUM SCHOLARSHIP PROGRAM
• *See page 126*

NASA/MARYLAND SPACE GRANT CONSORTIUM

http://www.mdspacegrant.org/

NASA MARYLAND SPACE GRANT CONSORTIUM UNDERGRADUATE SCHOLARSHIPS
• *See page 156*

NASA MINNESOTA SPACE GRANT CONSORTIUM

https://www.mnspacegrant.org/

MINNESOTA SPACE GRANT CONSORTIUM SCHOLARSHIP PROGRAM
• *See page 156*

NASA MONTANA SPACE GRANT CONSORTIUM

http://www.spacegrant.montana.edu/

MONTANA SPACE GRANT SCHOLARSHIP PROGRAM
• *See page 156*

NASA RHODE ISLAND SPACE GRANT CONSORTIUM

http://brown/initiatives/ri-space-grant

NASA RHODE ISLAND SPACE GRANT CONSORTIUM UNDERGRADUATE RESEARCH SCHOLARSHIP
• *See page 157*

NASA RISGC SCIENCE EN ESPANOL SCHOLARSHIP FOR UNDERGRADUATE STUDENTS
• *See page 157*

NASA'S VIRGINIA SPACE GRANT CONSORTIUM

http://www.vsgc.odu.edu/

COMMUNITY COLLEGE STEM SCHOLARSHIPS
• *See page 126*

NATIONAL ACTION COUNCIL FOR MINORITIES IN ENGINEERING-NACME INC.

http://www.nacme.org/

NACME SCHOLARS PROGRAM

Renewable award for African-American, American-Indian, or Latino student enrolled in a Baccalaureate engineering program. Award money is given to participating institutions who select applicants and disperse funds. High school seniors must be accepted by a College of Engineering (at the end of the freshman year, NACME assumes a minimum GPA of 2.5 on a scale of 4.0). Two-year community college transfers, i.e., those accepted for their third year of engineering study, must enter with at least a 2.7 cumulative GPA on a scale of a 4.0 and an Associate's Degree in engineering science (or the equivalent program of study). Check website for details, http://www.nacme.org.

Academic Fields/Career Goals: Engineering/Technology.

Award: Scholarship for use in freshman, sophomore, junior, or senior years; renewable.

Eligibility Requirements: Applicant must be American Indian/Alaska Native, Black (non-Hispanic), Hispanic and enrolled or expecting to enroll full-time at a four-year institution or university. Applicant must have 2.5 GPA or higher. Available to U.S. citizens.

Application Requirements: Financial need analysis. *Deadline:* March 15.

Contact: Christopher Smith, Vice President, Scholarships, University
Relations, and Research
National Action Council for Minorities in Engineering-
NACME Inc.
One North Broadway
Suite 601
White Plains, NY 10601-2318
Phone: 914-539-4316
Fax: 914-539-4032
E-mail: scholars@nacme.org

NATIONAL ASSOCIATION FOR THE ADVANCEMENT OF COLORED PEOPLE

http://www.naacp.org/

HUBERTUS W.V. WELLEMS SCHOLARSHIP FOR MALE STUDENTS
• *See page 194*

NATIONAL ASSOCIATION OF WOMEN IN CONSTRUCTION

http://www.nawic.org/

NAWIC UNDERGRADUATE SCHOLARSHIPS
• *See page 135*

NATIONAL SOCIETY OF BLACK ENGINEERS

https://connect.nsbe.org/Scholarships/ScholarshipList.aspx

NSBE CORPORATE SCHOLARSHIP PROGRAM
• *See page 304*

S. D. BECHTEL JR. FOUNDATION ENGINEERING SCHOLARSHIP

The purpose of this scholarship is to provide financial scholarships for students pursuing undergraduate degrees in Engineering and collegiate members of the National Society of Black Engineers (NSBE). Applicants must be NSBE members, majoring in civil engineering or mechanical engineering.

Academic Fields/Career Goals: Engineering/Technology.

Award: Scholarship for use in freshman, sophomore, junior, or senior years; renewable. *Number:* 3. *Amount:* $15,000.

Eligibility Requirements: Applicant must be Black (non-Hispanic) and enrolled or expecting to enroll full- or part-time at a four-year institution or university. Applicant must have 3.0 GPA or higher. Available to U.S. citizens.

Application Requirements: *Deadline:* June 30.

Contact: Raynashia Goodine, Programs Coordinator, Scholarships
National Society of Black Engineers
205 Daingerfield Road
Alexandria, VA 22314
Phone: 703-8372207 Ext. 214
E-mail: scholarships@nsbe.org

NATIONAL SOCIETY OF PROFESSIONAL ENGINEERS

http://www.nspe.org/

MAUREEN L. AND HOWARD N. BLITMAN, PE SCHOLARSHIP TO PROMOTE DIVERSITY IN ENGINEERING
• *See page 194*

PAUL H. ROBBINS HONORARY SCHOLARSHIP
• *See page 194*

PROFESSIONAL ENGINEERS IN INDUSTRY SCHOLARSHIP
• *See page 194*

NEVADA NASA SPACE GRANT CONSORTIUM

https://nasa.epscorspo.nevada.edu/

NATIONAL SPACE GRANT CONSORTIUM SCHOLARSHIPS
• *See page 127*

NEXTSTEPU

http://www.nextstepu.com/

$1,500 STEM SCHOLARSHIP
• *See page 120*

OREGON STUDENT ASSISTANCE COMMISSION

https://oregonstudentaid.gov/

AMERICAN COUNCIL OF ENGINEERING COMPANIES OF OREGON SCHOLARSHIP
• *See page 210*

ANDY AITKENHEAD SCHOLARSHIP
• *See page 127*

HOME BUILDERS FOUNDATION JIM IRVINE STATEWIDE SCHOLARSHIP
• *See page 136*

JEFFREY ALAN SCOGGINS MEMORIAL SCHOLARSHIP

Award for college junior or above for fall term/semester in undergraduate study in engineering at an Oregon four-year nonprofit college or university, Oregon State University is preferred. Membership in the Sigma Chi fraternity is preferred. May reapply for additional year of funding, which may be used towards graduate study. 3.0 GPA is preferred. Based on financial need.

Academic Fields/Career Goals: Engineering/Technology.

Award: Scholarship for use in junior, senior, or graduate years; not renewable.

Eligibility Requirements: Applicant must be enrolled or expecting to enroll full-time at a four-year institution or university; resident of Oregon and studying in Oregon. Available to U.S. citizens.

Application Requirements: Application form, financial need analysis. *Deadline:* March 1.

Contact: Melissa Adams, Scholarship Processing Coordinator
Phone: 541-687-7409
E-mail: melissa.adams@state.or.us

SOCIETY OF AMERICAN MILITARY ENGINEERS PORTLAND POST SCHOLARSHIP
• *See page 195*

PLAN NEW HAMPSHIRE

http://www.plannh.org

PLAN NEW HAMPSHIRE SCHOLARSHIP AND FELLOWSHIP PROGRAM
• *See page 129*

PLUMBING-HEATING-COOLING CONTRACTORS EDUCATION FOUNDATION

http://www.phccfoundation.org/scholarships

DELTA FAUCET COMPANY SCHOLARSHIP PROGRAM
• *See page 182*

PHCC EDUCATIONAL FOUNDATION NEED-BASED SCHOLARSHIP
• *See page 182*

PHCC EDUCATIONAL FOUNDATION SCHOLARSHIP PROGRAM
• *See page 182*

PROFESSIONAL CONSTRUCTION ESTIMATORS ASSOCIATION

http://www.pcea.org/

TED G. WILSON MEMORIAL SCHOLARSHIP FOUNDATION
• *See page 211*

ROBERT H. MOLLOHAN FAMILY CHARITABLE FOUNDATION, INC.

http://www.mollohanfoundation.org/

HIGH TECHNOLOGY SCHOLARS PROGRAM
• *See page 173*

ROCKY MOUNTAIN COAL MINING INSTITUTE

http://www.rmcmi.org/

ROCKY MOUNTAIN COAL MINING INSTITUTE SCHOLARSHIP
• *See page 211*

SALT RIVER PROJECT (SRP)

http://www.srpnet.com/

NAVAJO GENERATING STATION NAVAJO SCHOLARSHIP

Applicants must be enrolled members of the Navajo Nation who will be full-time students at an accredited college or university. Priority will be given to the math, engineering and environmental studies. Awards are made based on the field of study, and academic excellence and achievement. Award amounts are determined by the NGS Scholarship Committee following an evaluation of the Financial Needs Analysis of each applicant.

Academic Fields/Career Goals: Engineering/Technology; Environmental Science; Mathematics.

Award: Scholarship for use in junior year; renewable.

Eligibility Requirements: Applicant must be American Indian/Alaska Native and enrolled or expecting to enroll full-time at a four-year institution or university. Applicant must have 3.0 GPA or higher.

Application Requirements: *Deadline:* April 25.

SCARLETT FAMILY FOUNDATION SCHOLARSHIP PROGRAM

http://www.scarlettfoundation.org/

SCHOLARSHIP FOR STUDENTS PURSUING A BUSINESS OR STEM DEGREE
• *See page 91*

SEMICONDUCTOR RESEARCH CORPORATION (SRC)

http://www.src.org/

MASTER'S SCHOLARSHIP PROGRAM
• *See page 195*

SIGMA XI, THE SCIENTIFIC RESEARCH SOCIETY

http://www.sigmaxi.org/

SIGMA XI GRANTS-IN-AID OF RESEARCH
• *See page 110*

SILICON VALLEY COMMUNITY FOUNDATION

http://www.siliconvalleycf.org

SAMSUNG@FIRST SCHOLARS
• *See page 233*

SIMPLEHUMAN

http://www.simplehuman.com/

SIMPLE SOLUTIONS DESIGN COMPETITION
• *See page 305*

SOCIETY FOR IMAGING SCIENCE AND TECHNOLOGY

http://www.imaging.org/

RAYMOND DAVIS SCHOLARSHIP
• *See page 305*

SOCIETY OF AUTOMOTIVE ENGINEERS

https://www.sae.org/participate

BMW/SAE ENGINEERING SCHOLARSHIP
• *See page 160*

EDWARD D. HENDRICKSON/SAE ENGINEERING SCHOLARSHIP
• *See page 160*

FRED M. YOUNG SR./SAE ENGINEERING SCHOLARSHIP

Scholarship of $4000 awarded at $1000 per year for four years. Applicants must have a 3.75 GPA, rank in the 90th percentile in both math and critical reading on SAT or composite ACT scores, and pursue an engineering degree accredited by ABET. A 3.0 GPA and continued engineering enrollment must be maintained to renew the scholarship.

Academic Fields/Career Goals: Engineering/Technology.

Award: Scholarship for use in freshman year; renewable. *Number:* 1. *Amount:* $1000.

Eligibility Requirements: Applicant must be high school student and planning to enroll or expecting to enroll full-time at a four-year institution or university. Available to U.S. citizens.

Application Requirements: Application form, essay, test scores, transcript. *Deadline:* December 15.

Contact: Connie Harnish, SAE Educational Relations
Society of Automotive Engineers
400 Commonwealth Drive
Warrendale, PA 15096
Phone: 724-772-4047
E-mail: connie@sae.org

RALPH K. HILLQUIST HONORARY SAE SCHOLARSHIP
• *See page 305*

SAE LONG TERM MEMBER SPONSORED SCHOLARSHIP

The scholarship recognizes outstanding SAE student members who actively support SAE and its activities. Applications may be submitted by the student or by the SAE faculty advisor, an SAE Section officer or a community leader. The student must be a junior who will be entering the senior year of undergraduate engineering studies. Number of award varies.

Academic Fields/Career Goals: Engineering/Technology.

Award: Scholarship for use in senior year; not renewable. *Amount:* $1000.

Eligibility Requirements: Applicant must be enrolled or expecting to enroll full-time at a four-year institution or university. Applicant or parent of applicant must be member of Society of Automotive Engineers. Available to U.S. citizens.

Application Requirements: Application form, recommendations or references. *Deadline:* April 1.

Contact: Connie Harnish, SAE Educational Relations
Society of Automotive Engineers
400 Commonwealth Drive
Warrendale, PA 15096
Phone: 724-772-4047
E-mail: connie@sae.org

TAU BETA PI/SAE ENGINEERING SCHOLARSHIP

Six scholarships valued at $1000 each will be awarded for the freshman year only. Applicants must have a 3.75 GPA, rank in the 90th percentile in both math and critical reading for SAT scores or for composite ACT scores, and pursue an engineering program accredited by the engineering accreditation commission of the Accreditation Board for Engineering and Technology.

Academic Fields/Career Goals: Engineering/Technology.

Award: Scholarship for use in freshman year; not renewable. *Number:* 6. *Amount:* $1000.

Eligibility Requirements: Applicant must be high school student and planning to enroll or expecting to enroll full- or part-time at a four-year institution or university. Available to U.S. citizens.

Application Requirements: Application form, essay, test scores, transcript. *Deadline:* December 15.

Contact: Connie Harnish, SAE Educational Relations
Society of Automotive Engineers
400 Commonwealth Drive
Warrendale, PA 15096
Phone: 724-772-4047
E-mail: connie@sae.org

TMC/SAE DONALD D. DAWSON TECHNICAL SCHOLARSHIP
• *See page 160*

YANMAR/SAE SCHOLARSHIP
• *See page 305*

SOCIETY OF MANUFACTURING ENGINEERS EDUCATION FOUNDATION

http://www.smeef.org/

ALBERT E. WISCHMEYER MEMORIAL SCHOLARSHIP AWARD

Applicants must be residents of Western New York State, graduating high school seniors or current undergraduate students enrolled in an accredited degree program in manufacturing engineering, manufacturing engineering technology or mechanical technology in New York. Must have an GPA of 3.0.

Academic Fields/Career Goals: Engineering/Technology.

Award: Scholarship for use in freshman, sophomore, junior, or senior years; not renewable. *Number:* 1–10. *Amount:* $1000–$5000.

Eligibility Requirements: Applicant must be enrolled or expecting to enroll full-time at a four-year institution or university; resident of New York and studying in New York. Applicant must have 3.0 GPA or higher. Available to U.S. citizens.

Application Requirements: Application form, essay, recommendations or references, resume, transcript. *Deadline:* February 1.

ARTHUR AND GLADYS CERVENKA SCHOLARSHIP AWARD

One-time award to full-time students enrolled in a degree program in manufacturing engineering or technology. Preference given to students attending a Florida institution. Minimum 3.0 GPA required.

Academic Fields/Career Goals: Engineering/Technology.

Award: Scholarship for use in freshman, sophomore, junior, or senior years; not renewable. *Number:* 1–10. *Amount:* $1000–$5000.

Eligibility Requirements: Applicant must be enrolled or expecting to enroll full-time at a four-year institution or university. Applicant must have 3.0 GPA or higher. Available to U.S. citizens.

Application Requirements: Application form, essay, recommendations or references, resume, transcript. *Deadline:* February 1.

CATERPILLAR SCHOLARS AWARD FUND

Supports five one-time scholarships for full-time students enrolled in a manufacturing engineering program. Minority applicants may apply as incoming freshmen. Applicants must have an overall minimum GPA of 3.0.

Academic Fields/Career Goals: Engineering/Technology.

Award: Scholarship for use in freshman, sophomore, junior, or senior years; not renewable. *Number:* 1–15. *Amount:* $1000–$5000.

Eligibility Requirements: Applicant must be enrolled or expecting to enroll full-time at a four-year institution or university. Applicant must have 3.0 GPA or higher. Available to U.S. and Canadian citizens.

Application Requirements: Application form, essay, recommendations or references, resume, transcript. *Deadline:* February 1.

CHAPTER 17-ST. LOUIS SCHOLARSHIP

Scholarship will be given to full-time or part-time students enrolled in a manufacturing engineering, industrial technology, or other related program. Must study in Missouri or Illinois. Minimum 2.5 GPA is required.

Academic Fields/Career Goals: Engineering/Technology.

Award: Scholarship for use in freshman, sophomore, junior, or senior years; not renewable.

Eligibility Requirements: Applicant must be enrolled or expecting to enroll full-time at a four-year institution or university and studying in Illinois, Missouri. Applicant must have 2.5 GPA or higher. Available to U.S. and Canadian citizens.

Application Requirements: Application form, essay, recommendations or references, resume, transcript. *Deadline:* February 1.

CHAPTER 198-DOWNRIVER DETROIT SCHOLARSHIP

One-time award for an individual seeking an Associate's degree, Bachelor's degree, or graduate degree in manufacturing, mechanical or industrial engineering, engineering technology, or industrial technology at an accredited public or private college or university in Michigan. Must have a minimum GPA of 2.5. Preference is given to applicants who are a child or grandchild of a current SME Downriver Chapter No. 198 member, a member of its student chapter, or a Michigan resident.

Academic Fields/Career Goals: Engineering/Technology; Industrial Design; Mechanical Engineering; Trade/Technical Specialties.

Award: Scholarship for use in freshman, sophomore, junior, senior, or graduate years; not renewable. *Number:* 1–5. *Amount:* $1000–$5000.

Eligibility Requirements: Applicant must be enrolled or expecting to enroll full-time at a two-year or four-year institution or university and studying in Michigan. Applicant must have 2.5 GPA or higher. Available to U.S. citizens.

Application Requirements: Application form, essay, recommendations or references, resume, student statement letter, test scores, transcript. *Deadline:* February 1.

CHAPTER 23-QUAD CITIES IOWA/ILLINOIS SCHOLARSHIP

Scholarship applicant must be entering freshman or current undergraduate student pursuing a Bachelor's degree in manufacturing engineering or a related field at an accredited college or university in Iowa or Illinois.

Academic Fields/Career Goals: Engineering/Technology.

Award: Scholarship for use in freshman, sophomore, or junior years; not renewable. *Number:* up to 5. *Amount:* $1000–$5000.

Eligibility Requirements: Applicant must be enrolled or expecting to enroll full-time at a four-year institution or university and studying in Illinois, Iowa. Available to U.S. and Canadian citizens.

Application Requirements: Application form, essay, recommendations or references, resume, test scores, transcript. *Deadline:* February 1.

CHAPTER 31-TRI CITY SCHOLARSHIP

Applicants must be seeking a Bachelor's degree in manufacturing, mechanical, or industrial engineering, engineering technology, industrial technology or closely related field of study. Must be enrolled in or plan to attend an accredited college or university in the state of Michigan.

Academic Fields/Career Goals: Engineering/Technology.

Award: Scholarship for use in freshman, sophomore, junior, or senior years; not renewable. *Number:* up to 5. *Amount:* $1000–$5000.

Eligibility Requirements: Applicant must be enrolled or expecting to enroll full-time at a two-year or four-year or technical institution or university and studying in Michigan. Applicant must have 3.0 GPA or higher. Available to U.S. and Canadian citizens.

Application Requirements: Application form, essay, resume, test scores, transcript. *Deadline:* February 1.

CHAPTER 3-PEORIA ENDOWED SCHOLARSHIP

Applicants must be seeking a Bachelor's degree in manufacturing engineering, industrial engineering, manufacturing technology, or a manufacturing-related degree program at either Bradley University (Peoria, Illinois) or Illinois State University (Normal, Illinois).

Academic Fields/Career Goals: Engineering/Technology.

Award: Scholarship for use in freshman, sophomore, or junior years; not renewable. *Number:* up to 5. *Amount:* $1000–$5000.

Eligibility Requirements: Applicant must be enrolled or expecting to enroll full-time at a two-year or four-year or technical institution or university; resident of Illinois and studying in Illinois. Applicant must have 3.0 GPA or higher. Available to U.S. and Canadian citizens.

Application Requirements: Application form, essay, recommendations or references, resume, test scores, transcript. *Deadline:* February 1.

CHAPTER 4-LAWRENCE A. WACKER MEMORIAL SCHOLARSHIP

Awards available to full-time students enrolled in or accepted to a degree program in manufacturing, mechanical or industrial engineering at a college or university in the state of Wisconsin. One scholarship will be granted to a graduating high school senior and the other will be granted to a current undergraduate student. Minimum GPA of 3.0 required.

Academic Fields/Career Goals: Engineering/Technology; Mechanical Engineering.

Award: Scholarship for use in freshman, sophomore, junior, or senior years; not renewable. *Number:* 1–10. *Amount:* $1000–$5000.

Eligibility Requirements: Applicant must be enrolled or expecting to enroll full-time at a four-year institution or university and studying in Wisconsin. Applicant must have 3.0 GPA or higher. Available to U.S. citizens.

Application Requirements: Application form, essay, recommendations or references, resume, transcript. *Deadline:* February 1.

CHAPTER 63-PORTLAND JAMES E. MORROW SCHOLARSHIP

Applicants must be pursuing a career in manufacturing or a related field. Preference will be given to students planning to attend Oregon or southwest Washington schools. Preference will also be given to applicants who reside within the states of Oregon or southwest Washington.

Academic Fields/Career Goals: Engineering/Technology.

Award: Scholarship for use in freshman, sophomore, or junior years; not renewable. *Number:* up to 5. *Amount:* $1000–$5000.

Eligibility Requirements: Applicant must be enrolled or expecting to enroll full-time at a two-year or four-year or technical institution or university; resident of Oregon, Washington and studying in Oregon, Washington. Available to U.S. and Canadian citizens.

Application Requirements: Application form, essay, recommendations or references, resume, transcript. *Deadline:* February 1.

CHAPTER 63-PORTLAND UNCLE BUD SMITH SCHOLARSHIP

Applicants must be pursuing a career in manufacturing or a related field. Preference will be given to students planning to attend Oregon or southwest Washington schools. Preference will also be given to applicants who reside within the states of Oregon or southwest Washington.

Academic Fields/Career Goals: Engineering/Technology.

Award: Scholarship for use in freshman, sophomore, or junior years; not renewable. *Number:* up to 5. *Amount:* $1000–$5000.

Eligibility Requirements: Applicant must be enrolled or expecting to enroll full-time at a two-year or four-year or technical institution or university; resident of Oregon, Washington and studying in Oregon, Washington. Available to U.S. and Canadian citizens.

Application Requirements: Application form, essay, recommendations or references, resume, test scores, transcript. *Deadline:* February 1.

CHAPTER 67-PHOENIX SCHOLARSHIP

Award for a high school senior who plans on enrolling in a manufacturing program technology or manufacturing technology program or an undergraduate student enrolled in a manufacturing engineering technology, manufacturing technology, industrial technology, or closely related program at an accredited college or university in Arizona. Applicants must have an overall GPA of 2.5. Scholarship ranges from $1000 to $5000.

Academic Fields/Career Goals: Engineering/Technology; Industrial Design; Mechanical Engineering; Trade/Technical Specialties.

Award: Scholarship for use in freshman, sophomore, junior, or senior years; not renewable. *Number:* 1–5. *Amount:* $1000–$5000.

Eligibility Requirements: Applicant must be enrolled or expecting to enroll full-time at a two-year or four-year institution or university and studying in Arizona. Applicant must have 2.5 GPA or higher. Available to U.S. citizens.

Application Requirements: Application form, essay, recommendations or references, resume, test scores, transcript. *Deadline:* February 1.

CHAPTER 6-FAIRFIELD COUNTY SCHOLARSHIP

Scholarship applicants must be full-time undergraduate students enrolled in a degree program in manufacturing engineering, technology, or a closely related field in the United States or Canada. Preference is given to residents of, or students studying in, the eastern part of the United States.

Academic Fields/Career Goals: Engineering/Technology.

Award: Scholarship for use in freshman, sophomore, or junior years; not renewable. *Number:* up to 4. *Amount:* $1000–$5000.

Eligibility Requirements: Applicant must be enrolled or expecting to enroll full-time at a two-year or four-year or technical institution. Applicant must have 3.0 GPA or higher. Available to U.S. and Canadian citizens.

Application Requirements: Application form, essay, recommendations or references, resume, test scores, transcript. *Deadline:* February 1.

CHAPTER 93-ALBUQUERQUE SCHOLARSHIP

Scholarship to students entering freshmen or current undergraduate students pursuing a Bachelor's degree in manufacturing engineering or a related field who plan to or are attending an accredited college or university in New Mexico.

Academic Fields/Career Goals: Engineering/Technology.

Award: Scholarship for use in freshman, sophomore, junior, or senior years; not renewable. *Number:* 1–5. *Amount:* $1000–$5000.

Eligibility Requirements: Applicant must be enrolled or expecting to enroll full-time at a four-year institution or university and studying in New Mexico. Available to U.S. citizens.

Application Requirements: Application form, essay, recommendations or references, resume, test scores, transcript. *Deadline:* February 1.

CLARENCE AND JOSEPHINE MYERS SCHOLARSHIP

Applicants must be an undergraduate or graduate student pursuing a degree in engineering or a manufacturing-related field at a college within the state of Indiana.

Academic Fields/Career Goals: Engineering/Technology.

Award: Scholarship for use in freshman, sophomore, junior, or senior years; not renewable. *Number:* up to 5. *Amount:* $1000–$5000.

Eligibility Requirements: Applicant must be enrolled or expecting to enroll full-time at a two-year or four-year or technical institution or university and studying in Indiana. Available to U.S. and Canadian citizens.

Application Requirements: Application form, essay, recommendations or references, test scores, transcript. *Deadline:* February 1.

CLINTON J. HELTON MANUFACTURING SCHOLARSHIP AWARD FUND

One-time award to full-time students enrolled in a degree program in manufacturing engineering or technology at Colorado State University or University of Colorado. Applicants must possess an overall minimum GPA of 3.3.

Academic Fields/Career Goals: Engineering/Technology; Trade/Technical Specialties.

Award: Scholarship for use in freshman, sophomore, junior, or senior years; not renewable. *Number:* 1–5. *Amount:* $1000–$5000.

Eligibility Requirements: Applicant must be enrolled or expecting to enroll full-time at a four-year institution or university and studying in Colorado. Available to U.S. citizens.

Application Requirements: Application form, essay, recommendations or references, test scores, transcript. *Deadline:* February 1.

CONNIE AND ROBERT T. GUNTER SCHOLARSHIP

One-time award will be given for full-time undergraduate students enrolled in a degree program in manufacturing engineering or technology. Minimum 3.5 GPA is required. Must study in Georgia.

Academic Fields/Career Goals: Engineering/Technology.

Award: Scholarship for use in freshman, sophomore, junior, or senior years; not renewable. *Number:* 1–5. *Amount:* $1000–$5000.

Eligibility Requirements: Applicant must be enrolled or expecting to enroll full-time at a four-year institution or university and studying in Georgia. Applicant must have 3.5 GPA or higher. Available to U.S. citizens.

Application Requirements: Application form, essay, recommendations or references, resume, transcript. *Deadline:* February 1.

DETROIT CHAPTER ONE-FOUNDING CHAPTER SCHOLARSHIP

Several awards will be available in each of the following: Associate's degree and equivalent, Baccalaureate degree, and graduate degree programs. Minimum GPA of 3.5 is required. Preference given to undergraduate or graduate student enrolled in a manufacturing engineering or technology program at one of the sponsored institutions.

Academic Fields/Career Goals: Engineering/Technology.

Award: Scholarship for use in freshman, sophomore, junior, senior, or graduate years; not renewable. *Number:* 3. *Amount:* $1000.

Eligibility Requirements: Applicant must be enrolled or expecting to enroll full- or part-time at a two-year or four-year institution or university and studying in Michigan. Applicant must have 3.5 GPA or higher. Available to U.S. citizens.

Application Requirements: Application form, recommendations or references. *Deadline:* February 1.

DIRECTOR'S SCHOLARSHIP AWARD

Scholarship award for full-time undergraduate students enrolled in a manufacturing or related degree program in the United States or Canada. Preference will be given to students who demonstrate leadership skills in a community, academic, or professional environment. Average GPA of 3.5 required.

Academic Fields/Career Goals: Engineering/Technology.

Award: Scholarship for use in freshman, sophomore, junior, or senior years; not renewable. *Number:* 1–5. *Amount:* $1000–$10,000.

Eligibility Requirements: Applicant must be enrolled or expecting to enroll full-time at a four-year institution or university and must have an interest in leadership. Applicant must have 3.5 GPA or higher. Available to U.S. and Canadian citizens.

Application Requirements: Application form, essay, recommendations or references, resume, transcript. *Deadline:* February 1.

EDWARD S. ROTH MANUFACTURING ENGINEERING SCHOLARSHIP

Award to a graduating high school senior, a current full-time undergraduate or graduate student enrolled in an accredited four-year

degree program in manufacturing engineering at a sponsored ABET-accredited school. Minimum GPA of 3.0 and be a U.S. citizen.

Academic Fields/Career Goals: Engineering/Technology.

Award: Scholarship for use in freshman, sophomore, junior, senior, or graduate years; not renewable. *Number:* 1–10. *Amount:* $1000–$5000.

Eligibility Requirements: Applicant must be enrolled or expecting to enroll full-time at a four-year institution or university and studying in California, Florida, Illinois, Massachusetts, Minnesota, Ohio, Texas, Utah. Applicant must have 3.0 GPA or higher. Available to U.S. citizens.

Application Requirements: Application form, interview, recommendations or references, resume, transcript. *Deadline:* February 1.

E. WAYNE KAY COMMUNITY COLLEGE SCHOLARSHIP AWARD

One-time award to full-time students enrolled at an accredited community college or trade school which offers programs in manufacturing or closely related field in the United States or Canada. Minimum GPA of 3.0 required. Scholarship applicants may be entering freshmen or sophomore students with less than 60 college credit hours completed and be seeking a career in manufacturing engineering or technology.

Academic Fields/Career Goals: Engineering/Technology; Trade/Technical Specialties.

Award: Scholarship for use in freshman or sophomore years; not renewable. *Number:* 1–20. *Amount:* $1000–$10,000.

Eligibility Requirements: Applicant must be enrolled or expecting to enroll full-time at a two-year or four-year or technical institution or university. Applicant must have 3.0 GPA or higher. Available to U.S. and Canadian citizens.

Application Requirements: Application form, essay, recommendations or references, resume, transcript. *Deadline:* February 1.

E. WAYNE KAY CO-OP SCHOLARSHIP

Scholarship will be awarded for graduating high school senior or full-time undergraduate student enrolled in a degree program in manufacturing or a closely related field at a two-year community college or trade school in the United States or Canada. Average of 3.0 GPA is required.

Academic Fields/Career Goals: Engineering/Technology.

Award: Scholarship for use in freshman, sophomore, junior, or senior years; not renewable. *Number:* 1–10. *Amount:* $1000–$5000.

Eligibility Requirements: Applicant must be enrolled or expecting to enroll full-time at a two-year or four-year or technical institution or university. Applicant must have 3.0 GPA or higher. Available to U.S. and non-U.S. citizens.

Application Requirements: Application form, essay, recommendations or references, resume, transcript. *Deadline:* February 1.

E. WAYNE KAY HIGH SCHOOL SCHOLARSHIP

Scholarship available for student enrolled full-time in manufacturing engineering or technology program at an accredited college or university. Minimum 3.0 GPA required.

Academic Fields/Career Goals: Engineering/Technology.

Award: Scholarship for use in freshman, sophomore, junior, or senior years; renewable. *Number:* 1–20. *Amount:* $1000–$2500.

Eligibility Requirements: Applicant must be enrolled or expecting to enroll full-time at a four-year institution or university. Applicant must have 3.0 GPA or higher. Available to U.S. and Canadian citizens.

Application Requirements: Application form, essay, recommendations or references, test scores, transcript. *Deadline:* February 1.

E. WAYNE KAY SCHOLARSHIP

Scholarship for full-time undergraduate students enrolled in a degree program in manufacturing engineering, technology, or a closely related field in the United States or Canada. Minimum of 3.0 GPA is required.

Academic Fields/Career Goals: Engineering/Technology; Trade/Technical Specialties.

Award: Scholarship for use in freshman, sophomore, junior, or senior years; not renewable. *Number:* 10–30. *Amount:* $2500–$7500.

Eligibility Requirements: Applicant must be enrolled or expecting to enroll full-time at a four-year institution or university. Applicant must have 3.0 GPA or higher. Available to U.S. and Canadian citizens.

Application Requirements: Application form, essay, recommendations or references, resume, test scores, transcript. *Deadline:* February 1.

FORT WAYNE CHAPTER 56 SCHOLARSHIP

One-time award for an individual seeking an Associate's degree, Bachelor's degree, or graduate degree in manufacturing, mechanical or industrial engineering, engineering technology, or industrial technology at an accredited public or private college or university in Indiana. Must have a minimum GPA of 2.5. Preference given to applicants who are a child or grandchild of a current SME Fort Wayne Chapter No. 56 member, a member of its student chapter, or an Indiana resident.

Academic Fields/Career Goals: Engineering/Technology; Industrial Design; Mechanical Engineering; Trade/Technical Specialties.

Award: Scholarship for use in freshman, sophomore, junior, senior, or graduate years; not renewable. *Number:* 1–10. *Amount:* $1000–$5000.

Eligibility Requirements: Applicant must be enrolled or expecting to enroll full-time at a two-year or four-year institution or university and studying in Indiana. Applicant must have 2.5 GPA or higher. Available to U.S. citizens.

Application Requirements: Application form, essay, recommendations or references, resume, transcript. *Deadline:* February 1.

GUILIANO MAZZETTI SCHOLARSHIP AWARD

One-time award available to full-time students enrolled in a degree program in manufacturing engineering or technology in the United States or Canada. Minimum GPA of 3.0 required.

Academic Fields/Career Goals: Engineering/Technology.

Award: Scholarship for use in freshman, sophomore, junior, or senior years; not renewable. *Number:* 1–10. *Amount:* $1000–$5000.

Eligibility Requirements: Applicant must be enrolled or expecting to enroll full-time at a four-year institution or university. Applicant must have 3.0 GPA or higher. Available to U.S. and Canadian citizens.

Application Requirements: Application form, essay, recommendations or references, resume, transcript. *Deadline:* February 1.

LUCILE B. KAUFMAN WOMEN'S SCHOLARSHIP

Scholarships available for female full-time undergraduate students enrolled in a degree program in manufacturing engineering, technology or a closely related field in the United States or Canada. Minimum of 3.0 GPA is required. Scholarship value and the number of awards granted varies.

Academic Fields/Career Goals: Engineering/Technology.

Award: Scholarship for use in freshman, sophomore, junior, or senior years; not renewable. *Number:* 1–5. *Amount:* $1000–$5000.

Eligibility Requirements: Applicant must be enrolled or expecting to enroll full-time at a four-year institution or university and female. Applicant must have 3.0 GPA or higher. Available to U.S. and Canadian citizens.

Application Requirements: Application form, essay, recommendations or references, resume, transcript. *Deadline:* February 1.

MYRTLE AND EARL WALKER SCHOLARSHIP FUND
• *See page 305*

NORTH CENTRAL REGION 9 SCHOLARSHIP

Award to a full-time student enrolled in a manufacturing, mechanical, or industrial engineering degree program in North Central Region 9 (Iowa, Minnesota, Nebraska, North Dakota, South Dakota, Wisconsin, and the upper peninsula of Michigan). Applicants must have a 3.0 GPA.

Academic Fields/Career Goals: Engineering/Technology; Industrial Design; Mechanical Engineering; Trade/Technical Specialties.

Award: Scholarship for use in freshman, sophomore, junior, or senior years; not renewable. *Number:* 1–10. *Amount:* $1000–$5000.

Eligibility Requirements: Applicant must be enrolled or expecting to enroll full-time at a four-year institution or university and studying in Iowa, Michigan, Minnesota, Nebraska, North Dakota, South Dakota, Wisconsin. Applicant must have 3.0 GPA or higher. Available to U.S. citizens.

Application Requirements: Application form, essay, recommendations or references, resume, transcript. *Deadline:* February 1.

SME FAMILY SCHOLARSHIP

Scholarships awarded to children or grandchildren of Society of Manufacturing Engineers members. Must be graduating high school senior planning to pursue full-time studies for an undergraduate degree in manufacturing engineering, manufacturing engineering technology, or a closely related engineering study at an accredited college or university. Minimum GPA of 3.0 required. Scholarship value and the number of awards granted varies annually.

Academic Fields/Career Goals: Engineering/Technology.

Award: Scholarship for use in freshman, sophomore, junior, or senior years; renewable. *Number:* 1–10. *Amount:* $5000–$80,000.

Eligibility Requirements: Applicant must be enrolled or expecting to enroll full-time at a four-year institution or university. Applicant must have 3.0 GPA or higher. Available to U.S. and non-U.S. citizens.

Application Requirements: Application form, essay, interview, personal photograph, recommendations or references, resume, test scores, transcript. *Deadline:* February 1.

WALT BARTRAM MEMORIAL EDUCATION AWARD

Scholarship available for graduating high school seniors who commit to enroll in, or full-time college or university students pursuing a degree in, manufacturing engineering or a closely related field within the areas of New Mexico, Arizona or Southern California.

Academic Fields/Career Goals: Engineering/Technology.

Award: Scholarship for use in freshman, sophomore, junior, or senior years; not renewable. *Number:* 1. *Amount:* $1500.

Eligibility Requirements: Applicant must be enrolled or expecting to enroll full-time at a four-year institution or university; resident of Arizona, California, New Mexico and studying in Arizona, California, New Mexico. Applicant or parent of applicant must be member of Soil and Water Conservation Society. Available to U.S. and Canadian citizens.

Application Requirements: 2 copies of student statement letter, application form, recommendations or references, resume, transcript. *Deadline:* February 1.

WICHITA CHAPTER 52 SCHOLARSHIP

Award for an individual seeking an Associate's degree, Bachelor's degree, or graduate degree in manufacturing, mechanical or industrial engineering, engineering technology, or industrial technology at an accredited public or private college or university in Kansas, Oklahoma or Missouri. Applicants must have a minimum GPA of 2.5. Preference given to applicants who are a relative of a current SME Wichita Chapter No. 52 member or a Kansas resident.

Academic Fields/Career Goals: Engineering/Technology; Industrial Design; Mechanical Engineering; Trade/Technical Specialties.

Award: Scholarship for use in freshman, sophomore, junior, senior, or graduate years; not renewable. *Number:* 1. *Amount:* up to $1500.

Eligibility Requirements: Applicant must be enrolled or expecting to enroll full-time at a two-year or four-year institution or university and studying in Kansas, Missouri, Oklahoma. Applicant must have 2.5 GPA or higher. Available to U.S. citizens.

Application Requirements: Application form, recommendations or references, resume, student statement letter, transcript. *Deadline:* February 1.

WILLIAM E. WEISEL SCHOLARSHIP FUND
• *See page 287*

SOCIETY OF MOTION PICTURE AND TELEVISION ENGINEERS

https://www.smpte.org/

LOUIS F. WOLF JR. MEMORIAL SCHOLARSHIP
• *See page 224*

STUDENT PAPER AWARD
• *See page 224*

SOCIETY OF PETROLEUM ENGINEERS

http://www.spe.org/

GUS ARCHIE MEMORIAL SCHOLARSHIPS

Renewable award for students who have not attended college or university before and are planning to enroll in a petroleum engineering degree program at a four-year institution. Must have minimum 3.0 GPA.

Academic Fields/Career Goals: Engineering/Technology.

Award: Scholarship for use in freshman, sophomore, junior, or senior years; renewable. *Number:* 1–2. *Amount:* $6000.

Eligibility Requirements: Applicant must be enrolled or expecting to enroll full-time at a four-year institution or university. Applicant must have 3.0 GPA or higher. Available to U.S. and non-U.S. citizens.

Application Requirements: Application form, financial need analysis, personal photograph, recommendations or references, test scores, transcript. *Deadline:* April 30.

Contact: Young Member Program
Society of Petroleum Engineers
PO Box 833836
Richardson, TX 75083
Phone: 972-952-9448
Fax: 972-952-9435
E-mail: studentactivities@spe.org

SOCIETY OF PLASTICS ENGINEERS FOUNDATION (SPE)

http://www.4spe.org/

FLEMING/BLASZCAK SCHOLARSHIP
• *See page 195*

GULF COAST HURRICANE SCHOLARSHIP
• *See page 196*

SOCIETY OF PLASTICS ENGINEERS SCHOLARSHIP PROGRAM
• *See page 196*

SOCIETY OF WOMEN ENGINEERS

http://societyofwomenengineers.swe.org/

ADA I. PRESSMAN MEMORIAL SCHOLARSHIP
• *See page 196*

AMERICAN TRANSMISSION CO. SCHOLARSHIP
• *See page 196*

ANNE MAUREEN WHITNEY BARROW MEMORIAL SCHOLARSHIP
• *See page 196*

ANNE SHEN SMITH ENDOWED SCHOLARSHIP
• *See page 196*

BECHTEL CORPORATION SCHOLARSHIP

Two $1400 scholarships for women pursuing ABET-accredited Baccalaureate programs in preparation for careers in engineering, engineering technology, and computer science in the United States and Mexico. SWE membership and minimum 3.0 GPA required.

Academic Fields/Career Goals: Engineering/Technology.

Award: Scholarship for use in sophomore, junior, or senior years; not renewable. *Number:* 2. *Amount:* $1400.

Eligibility Requirements: Applicant must be enrolled or expecting to enroll full-time at a four-year institution or university and female. Applicant or parent of applicant must be member of Society of Women Engineers. Applicant must have 3.0 GPA or higher. Available to U.S. citizens.

Application Requirements: Application form. *Deadline:* February 15.

Contact: Scholarship Committee
Phone: 800-793-4636
E-mail: scholarships@swe.org

BETTY LOU BAILEY SWE REGION F SCHOLARSHIP
• *See page 197*

BETTY RUTH HOLLANDER SCHOLARSHIP

One $5000 scholarship for women pursuing ABET-accredited baccalaureate programs in preparation for careers in engineering and engineering technology in the United States and Mexico. Must be a U.S. citizen and have a minimum 3.0 GPA.

Academic Fields/Career Goals: Engineering/Technology.

Award: Scholarship for use in senior year; not renewable. *Number:* 1. *Amount:* $5000.

Eligibility Requirements: Applicant must be enrolled or expecting to enroll full-time at a four-year institution or university and female. Applicant must have 3.0 GPA or higher. Available to U.S. citizens.

Application Requirements: Application form. *Deadline:* February 15.

Contact: Scholarship Committee
Phone: 800-793-4636
E-mail: scholarships@swe.org

B.J. HARROD SCHOLARSHIP
• *See page 197*

BK KRENZER MEMORIAL REENTRY SCHOLARSHIP
• *See page 197*

BRILL FAMILY SCHOLARSHIP

$1500 award for a woman pursuing an ABET-accredited Baccalaureate program in preparation for a career in engineering, engineering technology, and computer science in the United States and Mexico. Preference given to a student pursuing study in aeronautical/aerospace engineering or biomedical engineering. Minimum 3.0 GPA required.

Academic Fields/Career Goals: Engineering/Technology.

Award: Scholarship for use in sophomore, junior, or senior years; not renewable. *Number:* 1. *Amount:* $1500.

Eligibility Requirements: Applicant must be enrolled or expecting to enroll full-time at a four-year institution or university and female. Applicant must have 3.0 GPA or higher. Available to U.S. citizens.

Application Requirements: Application form. *Deadline:* February 15.

Contact: Scholarship Committee
Phone: 800-793-4636
E-mail: scholarships@swe.org

CAROL STEPHENS SWE REGION F SCHOLARSHIP
• *See page 197*

CUMMINS SCHOLARSHIP
• *See page 197*

DR. IVY M. PARKER MEMORIAL SCHOLARSHIP
• *See page 197*

DOROTHY LEMKE HOWARTH MEMORIAL SCHOLARSHIP
• *See page 197*

DOROTHY P. MORRIS SCHOLARSHIP
• *See page 198*

DUPONT COMPANY SCHOLARSHIP
• *See page 198*

ELIZABETH MCLEAN MEMORIAL SCHOLARSHIP
• *See page 211*

ELLEN HIPPELI MEMORIAL SCHOLARSHIP

$1000 scholarship for women pursuing ABET-accredited Baccalaureate programs in preparation for careers in engineering, engineering technology, and computer science in the United States and Mexico. U.S. citizenship required. Nuclear engineering major preferred. Minimum 3.5 GPA required.

Academic Fields/Career Goals: Engineering/Technology.

Award: Scholarship for use in freshman year; not renewable. *Number:* 1. *Amount:* $1000.

Eligibility Requirements: Applicant must be high school student; planning to enroll or expecting to enroll full-time at a four-year institution or university and female. Applicant must have 3.5 GPA or higher. Available to U.S. citizens.

Application Requirements: Application form, essay. *Deadline:* May 1.

Contact: Scholarship Committee
Phone: 800-793-4636
E-mail: scholarships@swe.org

EXELON SCHOLARSHIP
• *See page 198*

GENERAL ELECTRIC WOMEN'S NETWORK SCHOLARSHIP
• *See page 212*

HONEYWELL SCHOLARSHIP
• *See page 198*

IBM LINDA SANFORD WOMEN'S TECHNICAL ADVANCEMENT SCHOLARSHIP
• *See page 198*

INVENERGY WOMEN'S NETWORK SCHOLARSHIP
• *See page 212*

JILL S. TIETJEN P.E. SCHOLARSHIP

$1750 award for a woman pursuing an ABET-accredited Baccalaureate program in preparation for a career in engineering and engineering technology in the United States and Mexico. Must be a U.S. citizen and have minimum 3.0 GPA.

Academic Fields/Career Goals: Engineering/Technology.

Award: Scholarship for use in sophomore, junior, or senior years; not renewable. *Number:* 1. *Amount:* $1750.

Eligibility Requirements: Applicant must be enrolled or expecting to enroll full-time at a four-year institution or university and female. Applicant must have 3.0 GPA or higher. Available to U.S. citizens.

Application Requirements: Application form. *Deadline:* February 15.

Contact: Scholarship Committee
Phone: 800-793-4636
E-mail: scholarships@swe.org

JOHN DEERE SWE SCHOLARSHIP

$2000 renewable scholarships for women pursuing ABET-accredited Baccalaureate or graduate programs in preparation for careers in engineering, engineering technology, and computer science in the United States and Mexico. Must be a U.S. citizen and have a minimum 3.0 GPA. Preferred geographic region by state: GA, IL, IN, IA, KS, LA, MI, MN, MO, MT, NE, NC, ND, OH, OK, SD, TN.

Academic Fields/Career Goals: Engineering/Technology.

Award: Scholarship for use in sophomore, junior, senior, or graduate years; not renewable. *Number:* 2. *Amount:* $2000.

Eligibility Requirements: Applicant must be enrolled or expecting to enroll full-time at a four-year institution or university and female. Applicant must have 3.0 GPA or higher. Available to U.S. citizens.

Application Requirements: Application form. *Deadline:* February 15.

Contact: Scholarship Committee
Phone: 800-793-4636
E-mail: scholarships@swe.org

JUDITH RESNICK MEMORIAL SCHOLARSHIP

$3500 scholarship for a women pursuing an ABET-accredited Baccalaureate program in preparation for a career in engineering and engineering technology in the United States and Mexico. Must have a minimum 3.0 GPA, be a member of SWE, and pursue a space-related engineering major.

Academic Fields/Career Goals: Engineering/Technology.

Award: Scholarship for use in sophomore, junior, or senior years; not renewable. *Number:* 1. *Amount:* $3500.

Eligibility Requirements: Applicant must be enrolled or expecting to enroll full-time at a four-year institution or university and female. Applicant or parent of applicant must be member of Society of Women Engineers. Applicant must have 3.0 GPA or higher. Available to U.S. citizens.

Application Requirements: Application form. *Deadline:* February 15.

Contact: Scholarship Committee
Phone: 800-793-4636
E-mail: scholarships@swe.org

LIEBHERR MINING SCHOLARSHIP
• *See page 234*

LILLIAN MOLLER GILBRETH MEMORIAL SCHOLARSHIP
• *See page 198*

LOCKHEED MARTIN CORPORATION SCHOLARSHIP
• *See page 234*

MARY GUNTHER MEMORIAL SCHOLARSHIP

Four $3000 scholarships for women pursuing ABET-accredited Baccalaureate programs in preparation for careers in engineering, engineering technology, and computer science in the United States and Mexico. Preference given to students pursuing studies in architectural and environmental engineering. 3.5 GPA required for freshmen, 3.0 GPA required for all other grades.

Academic Fields/Career Goals: Engineering/Technology.

Award: Scholarship for use in freshman, sophomore, junior, or senior years; not renewable. *Number:* 4. *Amount:* $3000.

Eligibility Requirements: Applicant must be enrolled or expecting to enroll full-time at a four-year institution or university and female. Available to U.S. citizens.

Application Requirements: Application form. *Deadline:* February 15.

Contact: Scholarship Committee
Phone: 800-793-4636
E-mail: scholarships@swe.org

MARY V. MUNGER MEMORIAL SCHOLARSHIP
• *See page 199*

MASWE SCHOLARSHIP

Four $1500 awards for women pursuing ABET-accredited Baccalaureate programs in preparation for careers in engineering and engineering technology in the United States and Mexico. Financial need is taken into consideration. Minimum 3.0 GPA required.

Academic Fields/Career Goals: Engineering/Technology.

Award: Scholarship for use in sophomore, junior, or senior years; not renewable. *Number:* 4. *Amount:* $1500.

Eligibility Requirements: Applicant must be enrolled or expecting to enroll full-time at a four-year institution or university and female. Applicant must have 3.0 GPA or higher. Available to U.S. citizens.

Application Requirements: Application form, financial need analysis. *Deadline:* February 15.

Contact: Scholarship Committee
Phone: 800-793-4636
E-mail: scholarships@swe.org

MEREDITH THOMS MEMORIAL SCHOLARSHIP
• *See page 306*

OLIVE LYNN SALEMBIER MEMORIAL REENTRY SCHOLARSHIP
• *See page 199*

PAST PRESIDENTS SCHOLARSHIP
• *See page 306*

PAULA LORING SIMON SCHOLARSHIP
• *See page 199*

ROBERTA BANASZAK GLEITER ENGINEERING ENDEAVOR SCHOLARSHIP
• *See page 199*

ROCHELLE NICOLETTE PERRY MEMORIAL SCHOLARSHIP
• *See page 306*

SUSAN MISZKOWICZ SEPTEMBER 11 MEMORIAL SCHOLARSHIP
• *See page 199*

SWE BALTIMORE-WASHINGTON SECTION SCHOLARSHIP
• *See page 199*

SWE CENTRAL INDIANA SECTION SCHOLARSHIP
• *See page 306*

SWE CENTRAL NEW MEXICO PIONEERS SCHOLARSHIP
• *See page 200*

SWE CENTRAL NEW MEXICO REENTRY SCHOLARSHIP
• *See page 200*

SWE MID-HUDSON SECTION SCHOLARSHIP
• *See page 200*

SWE NEW JERSEY SECTION SCHOLARSHIP
• *See page 306*

SWE PHOENIX SECTION SCHOLARSHIP
• *See page 200*

SWE REGION E SCHOLARSHIP
• *See page 200*

SWE REGION G JUDY SIMMONS MEMORIAL SCHOLARSHIP
• *See page 200*

SWE REGION H SCHOLARSHIPS
• *See page 201*

SWE REGION J SCHOLARSHIP
• *See page 201*

TE CONNECTIVITY EXCELLENCE IN ENGINEERING SCHOLARSHIP
• *See page 201*

TURNER CONSTRUCTION SCHOLARSHIP
• *See page 201*

WANDA MUNN SCHOLARSHIP
• *See page 201*

SOCIETY OF WOMEN ENGINEERS-DALLAS SECTION

http://www.dallaswe.org/

DALLAS SWE ANNIE COLAÇO COLLEGIATE LEADER SCHOLARSHIP
• *See page 234*

DALLAS SWE HIGH SCHOOL SENIOR SCHOLARSHIP

Scholarship for graduating high school senior women who wish to pursue a degree in engineering. Applicant must be a Texas resident and attend a Texas Region 10 high school. Please refer to website for further details http://www.dallaswe.org/scholarships.

Academic Fields/Career Goals: Engineering/Technology.

Award: Scholarship for use in freshman year; not renewable. *Number:* 2–4. *Amount:* $500–$1000.

Eligibility Requirements: Applicant must be high school student; planning to enroll or expecting to enroll full-time at a four-year institution or university; female and resident of Texas. Applicant must have 3.0 GPA or higher. Available to U.S. citizens.

Application Requirements: Application form, essay, personal photograph. *Deadline:* April 15.

Contact: Shelley Stracener, FY18 President
E-mail: dallas.swe@gmail.com

SOCIETY OF WOMEN ENGINEERS-ROCKY MOUNTAIN SECTION

http://www.swe-rms.org/

SOCIETY OF WOMEN ENGINEERS-ROCKY MOUNTAIN SECTION SCHOLARSHIP PROGRAM
• *See page 161*

SOCIETY OF WOMEN ENGINEERS-TWIN TIERS SECTION

http://twintiers.swe.org/

SOCIETY OF WOMEN ENGINEERS-TWIN TIERS SECTION SCHOLARSHIP
• *See page 234*

SPECIALTY EQUIPMENT MARKET ASSOCIATION

http://www.sema.org/

SEMA MEMORIAL SCHOLARSHIP FUND
• *See page 92*

STRAIGHTFORWARD MEDIA

http://www.straightforwardmedia.com/

STRAIGHTFORWARD MEDIA ENGINEERING SCHOLARSHIP
• *See page 202*

STRAIGHT NORTH

https://www.straightnorth.com/

STRAIGHT NORTH STEM SCHOLARSHIP
• *See page 92*

TAU BETA PI ASSOCIATION

https://www.tbp.org/

TAU BETA PI SCHOLARSHIP PROGRAM
• *See page 202*

TECHNICAL ASSOCIATION OF THE PULP & PAPER INDUSTRY (TAPPI)

http://www.tappi.org/

PAPER AND BOARD DIVISION SCHOLARSHIPS

Award to TAPPI student member or an undergraduate member of a TAPPI Student Chapter enrolled as a college or university undergraduate in an engineering or science program. Must be sophomore, junior, or senior and able to show a significant interest in the paper industry. Information can be found at http://www.tappi.org/s_tappi/sec.asp?CID=6101&DID=546695.

Academic Fields/Career Goals: Engineering/Technology; Paper and Pulp Engineering.

Award: Scholarship for use in sophomore, junior, or senior years; not renewable. *Number:* 1–4. *Amount:* $1000–$1500.

Eligibility Requirements: Applicant must be enrolled or expecting to enroll full-time at a four-year institution or university. Available to U.S. and non-U.S. citizens.

Application Requirements: Application form. *Deadline:* February 15.

Contact: Mr. Laurence Womack, Director of Standards and Awards
Technical Association of the Pulp & Paper Industry (TAPPI)
15 Technology Parkway South
Peachtree Corners, GA 30092
Phone: 770-209-7276
E-mail: standards@tappi.org

TAPPI PROCESS AND PRODUCT QUALITY DIVISION SCHOLARSHIP

The TAPPI Process and Product Quality Scholarship is awarded to TAPPI student members or student chapter members to encourage them to pursue careers in the pulp and paper industry and to develop awareness of quality management.

Academic Fields/Career Goals: Engineering/Technology.

Award: Scholarship for use in sophomore, junior, or senior years; not renewable. *Number:* 1. *Amount:* $1000.

Eligibility Requirements: Applicant must be enrolled or expecting to enroll full-time at a four-year institution or university. Available to U.S. and non-U.S. citizens.

Application Requirements: Application form. *Deadline:* February 15.

Contact: Mr. Charles Bohanan, Director of Standards and Awards
Technical Association of the Pulp & Paper Industry (TAPPI)
15 Technology Parkway South
Peachtree Corners, GA 30092
Phone: 770-209-7276
E-mail: standards@tappi.org

TECHNOLOGY FIRST

https://technologyfirst.org/

ROBERT V. MCKENNA SCHOLARSHIPS
• *See page 235*

TIMOTION

http://www.timotion.com/

TIMOTION ENGINEERING AND EXCELLENCE SCHOLARSHIP
• *See page 213*

TKE EDUCATIONAL FOUNDATION

http://www.tke.org/

ERIC D. DUNNING SCHOLARSHIP
• *See page 235*

TRANSPORTATION ASSOCIATION OF CANADA FOUNDATION

http://www.tac-foundation.ca

TAC FOUNDATION SCHOLARSHIPS
• *See page 213*

TURNER CONSTRUCTION COMPANY

http://www.turnerconstruction.com/

YOUTHFORCE 2020 SCHOLARSHIP PROGRAM
• *See page 137*

UNITED NEGRO COLLEGE FUND

http://www.uncf.org/

BASF/ALFRED CHISHOLM ENDOWED MEMORIAL SCHOLARSHIP
• *See page 93*

DAVIS SCHOLARSHIP FOR WOMEN IN STEM
• *See page 202*

DELL CORPORATE SCHOLARS PROGRAM
• *See page 213*

DISCOVER FINANCIAL SERVICES SCHOLARSHIP
• *See page 93*

GALACTIC UNITE BYTHEWAY SCHOLARSHIP
• *See page 202*

KIA MOTORS AMERICA STEM/SUSTAINABILITY SCHOLARSHIP
• *See page 175*

PROCTER & GAMBLE STEM SCHOLARSHIP
• *See page 128*

RICOH SCHOLARSHIP PROGRAM
• *See page 94*

UNCF/KOCH SCHOLARS PROGRAM FOR UNDERGRADUATES
• *See page 94*

UNCF/NISSAN SCHOLARSHIP PROGRAM
• *See page 185*

UNCF NORTHROP GRUMMAN SCHOLARSHIP
• *See page 236*

UNCF STEM SCHOLARS PROGRAM
• *See page 175*

WILLIAM WRIGLEY FOUNDATION SCHOLARSHIP
• *See page 95*

UNITED STATES SOCIETY ON DAMS

http://www.ussdams.org/

UNITED STATES SOCIETY ON DAMS SCHOLARSHIP AWARD
• *See page 214*

UNIVERSITIES SPACE RESEARCH ASSOCIATION

http://www.usra.edu/

UNIVERSITIES SPACE RESEARCH ASSOCIATION SCHOLARSHIP AWARD PROGRAM
• *See page 128*

VECTORWORKS, INC.

http://www.vectorworks.net

VECTORWORKS DESIGN SCHOLARSHIP
• *See page 137*

VERMONT SPACE GRANT CONSORTIUM

http://www.cems.uvm.edu/vsgc

VERMONT SPACE GRANT CONSORTIUM
• *See page 104*

VISIONARY INTEGRATION PROFESSIONALS (VIP)

http://www.trustvip.com/

WOMEN IN TECHNOLOGY SCHOLARSHIP (WITS)
• See page 236

WISCONSIN SOCIETY OF PROFESSIONAL ENGINEERS

http://www.wspe.org/

WISCONSIN SOCIETY OF PROFESSIONAL ENGINEERS SCHOLARSHIPS

Scholarships are awarded each year to high school seniors having qualifications for success in engineering education. Must be a U.S. citizen and Wisconsin resident, ACT composite score and have a minimum GPA of 3.0.

Academic Fields/Career Goals: Engineering/Technology.

Award: Scholarship for use in freshman year; not renewable. *Number:* 7. *Amount:* $1000–$2000.

Eligibility Requirements: Applicant must be high school student; planning to enroll or expecting to enroll full-time at a four-year institution or university and resident of Wisconsin. Applicant must have 3.0 GPA or higher. Available to U.S. citizens.

Application Requirements: Application form, essay, interview, recommendations or references, self-addressed stamped envelope with application, test scores, transcript. *Deadline:* December 19.

Contact: Al Linder
E-mail: Al.lindner@graef-usa.com

WOMEN IN AEROSPACE FOUNDATION

http://www.womeninaerospace.org/index.html

WIA FOUNDATION SCHOLARSHIP
• See page 162

XEROX

http://www.xerox.com//

TECHNICAL MINORITY SCHOLARSHIP
• See page 203

ENTOMOLOGY

AMERICAN INDIAN SCIENCE AND ENGINEERING SOCIETY

http://www.aises.org/

A.T. ANDERSON MEMORIAL SCHOLARSHIP PROGRAM
• See page 121

AMERICAN SOCIETY OF AGRONOMY, CROP SCIENCE SOCIETY OF AMERICA, SOIL SCIENCE SOCIETY OF AMERICA

http://www.agronomy.org

J. FIELDING REED SCHOLARSHIP
• See page 106

BARRY GOLDWATER SCHOLARSHIP AND EXCELLENCE IN EDUCATION FOUNDATION

https://goldwater.scholarsapply.org

BARRY M. GOLDWATER SCHOLARSHIP AND EXCELLENCE IN EDUCATION PROGRAM
• See page 123

BHW GROUP

https://thebhwgroup.com/

BHW WOMEN IN STEM SCHOLARSHIP
• See page 124

FOUNDATION FOR SCIENCE AND DISABILITY

http://stemd.org/

GRANTS FOR DISABLED GRADUATE STUDENTS IN THE SCIENCES
• See page 106

GREAT MINDS IN STEM

http://www.greatmindsinstem.org

HENAAC SCHOLARSHIP PROGRAM
• See page 115

HORTICULTURAL RESEARCH INSTITUTE

http://www.hriresearch.org/

BRYAN A. CHAMPION MEMORIAL SCHOLARSHIP
• See page 101

CARVILLE M. AKEHURST MEMORIAL SCHOLARSHIP

Scholarship is available to resident of Maryland, Virginia, or West Virginia. Applicant must be enrolled in an accredited undergraduate or graduate landscape/ horticulture program or related discipline at a two- or four-year institution and must have minimum 3.0 GPA. Online application only. http//http://www.HRIresearch.org for complete information.

Academic Fields/Career Goals: Entomology; Horticulture/Floriculture; Landscape Architecture.

Award: Scholarship for use in junior or senior years; not renewable. *Number:* 2. *Amount:* $2000.

Eligibility Requirements: Applicant must be enrolled or expecting to enroll full-time at a two-year or four-year or technical institution or university and resident of Maryland, Virginia, West Virginia. Applicant must have 3.0 GPA or higher. Available to U.S. citizens.

Application Requirements: Application form, essay, financial need analysis, recommendations or references, resume, transcript. *Deadline:* May 31.

Contact: Ms. Teresa Jodon, Executive Director
Horticultural Research Institute
1200 G Street, NW, Suite 800
Washington, DC 20005
Phone: 202-695-2474
Fax: 888-761-7883
E-mail: scholarships@hriresearch.org

TIMOTHY AND PALMER W. BIGELOW JR, SCHOLARSHIP
• See page 101

USREY FAMILY SCHOLARSHIP

Award for students accredited in undergraduate or graduate landscape horticulture program or related discipline at a two- or four-year institution. Preference given to applicants who plan to work within the industry. Must have a minimum 2.5 GPA. For more information, visit website http://www.hriresearch.org.

Academic Fields/Career Goals: Entomology; Horticulture/Floriculture; Landscape Architecture.

Award: Scholarship for use in sophomore, junior, senior, or graduate years; not renewable. *Amount:* $500.

Eligibility Requirements: Applicant must be enrolled or expecting to enroll full-time at a two-year or four-year or technical institution or university and studying in California. Applicant must have 2.5 GPA or higher. Available to U.S. and non-U.S. citizens.

Application Requirements: Application form, application form may be submitted online (http://www.hriresearch.org/index.cfm?page=Content&categoryID=168&ID=5), essay, financial need analysis, recommendations or references, resume, transcript. *Deadline:* May 31.

Contact: Teresa Jodon
Horticultural Research Institute
1200 G Street, NW, Suite 800
Washington, DC 20005
Phone: 202-695-2474
Fax: 888-761-7883
E-mail: scholarships@hriresearch.org

LABROOTS INC.

http://www.LabRoots.com

LABROOTS STEM SCHOLARSHIP
• *See page 116*

MEDICAL SCRUBS COLLECTION

http://medicalscrubscollection.com

MEDICAL SCRUBS COLLECTION SCHOLARSHIP
• *See page 120*

SOIL AND WATER CONSERVATION SOCIETY-MISSOURI SHOW-ME CHAPTER

http://www.moswcs.org/

MO SHOW-ME CHAPTER SWCS SCHOLARSHIP
• *See page 111*

ENVIRONMENTAL HEALTH

AMERICAN INDIAN SCIENCE AND ENGINEERING SOCIETY

http://www.aises.org/

A.T. ANDERSON MEMORIAL SCHOLARSHIP PROGRAM
• *See page 121*

ASSOCIATION OF ENVIRONMENTAL HEALTH ACADEMIC PROGRAMS (AEHAP)

http://www.aehap.org/

STUDENT RESEARCH COMPETITION (SRC)

The purpose of this competition is to provide graduates and undergraduates in their junior or senior year with an opportunity to present their current, recently (within the last 3 months) completed or ongoing individual research on an environmental health related topic to environmental health professionals at the National Environmental Health Association's (NEHA) annual education conference. This is an extraordinary opportunity for students to experience a professional conference, to network with potential employers and to gain experience presenting their work in a formal session and during a poster session. Some students have even landed jobs as a result of winning the competition and meeting their future employer at the conference. Further, the scholarship provides $1,000 in cash and an all-expenses paid trip to NEHA's conference held annually each summer.

Academic Fields/Career Goals: Environmental Health.

Award: Scholarship for use in junior, senior, or graduate years; not renewable. *Amount:* $1000.

Eligibility Requirements: Applicant must be enrolled or expecting to enroll full-time at a four-year institution. Available to U.S. citizens.

Application Requirements: Application form. *Deadline:* February 28.

Contact: Clint Pinion
Association of Environmental Health Academic Programs
(AEHAP)
PO Box 66057
Burien, WA 98166
Phone: 206-522-5272
E-mail: Clint.Pinion@eku.edu

BHW GROUP

https://thebhwgroup.com/

BHW WOMEN IN STEM SCHOLARSHIP
• *See page 124*

BROWN AND CALDWELL

http://www.brownandcaldwell.com

ECKENFELDER SCHOLARSHIP
• *See page 169*

MINORITY SCHOLARSHIP PROGRAM
• *See page 169*

CYNTHIA E. MORGAN SCHOLARSHIP FUND (CEMS)

http://www.cemsfund.com/

CYNTHIA E. MORGAN MEMORIAL SCHOLARSHIP FUND, INC.

Award for a high school junior or senior, or a current college student, who is a Maryland resident and first generation college student. No previous generation (parents or grandparents) may have attended any college/university. Scholarship for use only at a Maryland post-secondary school or medical school. Must be majoring in, or plan to enter, a medical-related field (for example: doctor, nurse, radiologist).

Academic Fields/Career Goals: Environmental Health; Health and Medical Sciences; Health Information Management/Technology; Neurobiology; Nursing; Occupational Safety and Health; Oncology; Osteopathy; Pharmacy; Psychology; Radiology; Therapy/Rehabilitation.

Award: Scholarship for use in freshman, sophomore, junior, senior, graduate, or postgraduate years; not renewable. *Number:* up to 1. *Amount:* $1000.

Eligibility Requirements: Applicant must be enrolled or expecting to enroll full- or part-time at a two-year or four-year or technical institution or university; resident of Maryland and studying in Maryland. Available to U.S. citizens.

Application Requirements: Application form, essay. *Deadline:* February 25.

Contact: Mr. John Kantorski, Founder and President
Cynthia E. Morgan Scholarship Fund (CEMS)
5516 Maudes Way
White Marsh, MD 21162-3417
Phone: 410-458-6312
Fax: 443-927-7321
E-mail: administrator@cemsfund.com

FLORIDA ENVIRONMENTAL HEALTH ASSOCIATION

http://www.feha.org/

FLORIDA ENVIRONMENTAL HEALTH ASSOCIATION EDUCATIONAL SCHOLARSHIP AWARDS

Scholarships offered to students interested in pursuing a career in the field of environmental health, or to enhance an existing career in environmental health. Applicant must be a member of FEHA in good standing.

Academic Fields/Career Goals: Environmental Health; Public Health.

Award: Scholarship for use in junior, senior, graduate, or postgraduate years; not renewable. *Number:* 1–4. *Amount:* $500–$1000.

Eligibility Requirements: Applicant must be enrolled or expecting to enroll full- or part-time at a four-year institution or university. Applicant or parent of applicant must be member of Florida Environmental Health Association. Applicant must have 2.5 GPA or higher. Available to U.S. and non-U.S. citizens.

Application Requirements: Application form, recommendations or references, transcript. *Deadline:* varies.

Contact: Kim Duffek, Scholarship Committee Chair
Florida Environmental Health Association
400 West Robinson Street, Suite S-529
Orlando, FL 32801
Phone: 407-317-7325
E-mail: duffekkj@gmail.com

FOUNDATION FOR SCIENCE AND DISABILITY

http://stemd.org/

GRANTS FOR DISABLED GRADUATE STUDENTS IN THE SCIENCES
• *See page 106*

GREAT MINDS IN STEM

http://www.greatmindsinstem.org

HENAAC SCHOLARSHIP PROGRAM
• *See page 115*

THE JACKSON LABORATORY

https://www.jax.org

THE JACKSON LABORATORY COLLEGE SCHOLARSHIP PROGRAM
• *See page 126*

LABROOTS INC.

http://www.LabRoots.com

LABROOTS STEM SCHOLARSHIP
• *See page 116*

MICHAEL MOODY FITNESS

http://www.michaelmoodyfitness.com/

MICHAEL MOODY FITNESS SCHOLARSHIP
• *See page 166*

NATIONAL ENVIRONMENTAL HEALTH ASSOCIATION/AMERICAN ACADEMY OF SANITARIANS

http://www.neha.org/

NATIONAL ENVIRONMENTAL HEALTH ASSOCIATION/AMERICAN ACADEMY OF SANITARIANS SCHOLARSHIP

One-time award for college juniors, seniors, and graduate students pursuing studies in environmental health sciences or public health. Undergraduates must be enrolled full-time in an approved program that is accredited by the Environmental Health Accreditation Council (EHAC) or a NEHA institutional/educational or sustaining member school.

Academic Fields/Career Goals: Environmental Health; Public Health.

Award: Scholarship for use in junior or senior years; renewable. *Number:* 3–4. *Amount:* $1000–$2000.

Eligibility Requirements: Applicant must be enrolled or expecting to enroll full- or part-time at a four-year institution or university. Available to U.S. citizens.

Application Requirements: Application form, recommendations or references, transcript. *Deadline:* February 1.

Contact: Cindy Dimmitt, Scholarship Coordinator
National Environmental Health Association/American
Academy of Sanitarians
720 South Colorado Boulevard, Suite 1000-N
Denver, CO 80246-1926
Phone: 303-756-9090
Fax: 303-691-9490
E-mail: cdimmitt@neha.org

NATIONAL INSTITUTES OF HEALTH

https://www.training.nih.gov/programs/ugsp

NIH UNDERGRADUATE SCHOLARSHIP PROGRAM FOR STUDENTS FROM DISADVANTAGED BACKGROUNDS
• *See page 116*

NEXTSTEPU

http://www.nextstepu.com/

$1,500 STEM SCHOLARSHIP
• *See page 120*

OREGON STUDENT ASSISTANCE COMMISSION

https://oregonstudentaid.gov/

CHARLES PATRICK SCHOLARSHIP

Scholarship for graduates of Oregon high schools who will enroll as college junior or above for fall term/semester in undergraduate study at an Oregon private nonprofit college. Preference for major in environmental health, environmental students, forestry, natural resources. Preference for career field in environmental sustainability or land management. Based on financial need.

Academic Fields/Career Goals: Environmental Health; Environmental Science; Natural Resources.

Award: Scholarship for use in junior or senior years; renewable.

Eligibility Requirements: Applicant must be enrolled or expecting to enroll at a four-year institution or university; resident of Oregon and studying in Oregon. Applicant must have 3.5 GPA or higher. Available to U.S. citizens.

Application Requirements: Application form. *Deadline:* March 1.

Contact: Melissa Adams, Scholarship Processing Coordinator
Phone: 541-687-7409
E-mail: melissa.adams@state.or.us

WILLIAM E. KEENE MEMORIAL SCHOLARSHIP

Award for residents of Oregon or Washington whose career plans include public health, with strong interest in epidemiology. Preference given to those majoring in public health, epidemiology, environmental health science, health care management, and health education behavioral science. Must be enrolled at least half-time at four-year public and nonprofit colleges or universities. 3.0 GPA preferred. Apply/compete annually. Financial need may or may not be considered.

Academic Fields/Career Goals: Environmental Health; Environmental Science; Health Information Management/Technology; Public Health.

Award: Scholarship for use in freshman, sophomore, junior, or senior years; not renewable.

Eligibility Requirements: Applicant must be enrolled or expecting to enroll full- or part-time at a four-year institution or university and resident of Oregon, Washington. Available to U.S. and non-U.S. citizens.

Application Requirements: Application form. *Deadline:* March 1.

Contact: Melissa Adams, Scholarship Processing Coordinator
Phone: 541-687-7409
E-mail: melissa.adams@state.or.us

SOIL AND WATER CONSERVATION SOCIETY-MISSOURI SHOW-ME CHAPTER

http://www.moswcs.org/

MO SHOW-ME CHAPTER SWCS SCHOLARSHIP
• *See page 111*

STRAIGHTFORWARD MEDIA

http://www.straightforwardmedia.com/

STRAIGHTFORWARD MEDIA MEDICAL PROFESSIONS SCHOLARSHIP
• *See page 257*

STRAIGHT NORTH

https://www.straightnorth.com/

STRAIGHT NORTH STEM SCHOLARSHIP
• *See page 92*

TED ROLLINS AND VALEO GROUPE

http://valeogroupe.us/

TED ROLLINS ECO SCHOLARSHIP
• *See page 183*

WASHINGTON STATE ENVIRONMENTAL HEALTH ASSOCIATION

http://www.wseha.org/

CIND M. TRESER MEMORIAL SCHOLARSHIP PROGRAM
Scholarships are available for undergraduate students pursuing a major in environmental health or related science and intending to practice environmental health. Must be a resident of Washington. For more details see website http://www.wseha.org.

Academic Fields/Career Goals: Environmental Health.

Award: Scholarship for use in junior or senior years; not renewable. *Number:* 1–2. *Amount:* $500–$2000.

Eligibility Requirements: Applicant must be enrolled or expecting to enroll full-time at a four-year institution or university; resident of Washington and studying in Washington. Applicant must have 3.0 GPA or higher. Available to U.S. citizens.

Application Requirements: Application form. *Deadline:* March 15.

Contact: Mr. Charles Treser, Principle Lecturer Emeritus
Washington State Environmental Health Association
Univ. of Washington, SPH, DEOHS
1959 NE Pacific Street, F-226D
Seattle, WA 98195-7234
Phone: 206-616-2097
E-mail: ctreser@uw.edu

WISCONSIN ASSOCIATION FOR FOOD PROTECTION

http://www.wifoodprotection.org

E.H. MARTH FOOD PROTECTION AND FOOD SCIENCES SCHOLARSHIP
Scholarship awarded to promote and sustain interest in the fields of study that may lead to a career in dairy, food, or environmental sanitation. One scholarship is awarded per year and previous applicants and recipients may reapply.

Academic Fields/Career Goals: Environmental Health; Food Science/Nutrition.

Award: Scholarship for use in sophomore, junior, senior, or graduate years; not renewable. *Number:* 1. *Amount:* $1500.

Eligibility Requirements: Applicant must be enrolled or expecting to enroll full-time at a four-year institution or university; resident of Wisconsin and studying in Wisconsin. Available to U.S. citizens.

Application Requirements: Application form, recommendations or references, transcript. *Deadline:* July 1.

Contact: Mr. Jim Wickert, Chairman, Scholarship Committee
Wisconsin Association for Food Protection
3834 Ridgeway Avenue
Madison, WI 53704
Phone: 608-241-2438
E-mail: jwick16060@tds.net

ENVIRONMENTAL SCIENCE

101ST AIRBORNE DIVISION ASSOCIATION

http://www.screamingeaglefoundation.org/

AL & WILLIAMARY VISTE SCHOLARSHIP
• *See page 114*

ABBIE SARGENT MEMORIAL SCHOLARSHIP INC.

http://www.nhfarmbureau.org/

ABBIE SARGENT MEMORIAL SCHOLARSHIP
• *See page 100*

AIR & WASTE MANAGEMENT ASSOCIATION, ALLEGHENY MOUNTAIN SECTION

http://www.ams-awma.org/

ALLEGHENY MOUNTAIN SECTION AIR & WASTE MANAGEMENT ASSOCIATION SCHOLARSHIP
Scholarships for qualified students enrolled in an undergraduate program leading to a career in a field related directly to the environment. Open to current undergraduate students or high school students accepted full-time in a four-year college or university program in Western Pennsylvania or West Virginia. Applicants must have a minimum B average or a 3.0 GPA.

Academic Fields/Career Goals: Environmental Science; Meteorology/Atmospheric Science.

Award: Scholarship for use in freshman, sophomore, junior, or senior years; not renewable. *Number:* 1–5. *Amount:* $500–$2000.

Eligibility Requirements: Applicant must be enrolled or expecting to enroll full-time at a four-year institution or university; resident of Pennsylvania, West Virginia and studying in Pennsylvania, West Virginia. Applicant must have 3.0 GPA or higher. Available to U.S. citizens.

Application Requirements: Application form, community service, essay. *Deadline:* March 31.

Contact: David Testa, Scholarship Chair
Air & Waste Management Association, Allegheny Mountain Section
c/o AECOM
681 Andersen Drive, Foster Plaza 6
Pittsburgh, PA 15220
Phone: 412-503-4560
E-mail: david.testa@aecom.com

AIR & WASTE MANAGEMENT ASSOCIATION–COASTAL PLAINS CHAPTER

http://www.awmacoastalplains.org/

COASTAL PLAINS CHAPTER OF THE AIR AND WASTE MANAGEMENT ASSOCIATION ENVIRONMENTAL STEWARD SCHOLARSHIP

Scholarships awarded to first- or second-year students pursuing a career in environmental science or physical science. Minimum high school and college GPA of 2.5 required. A 500-word paper on personal and professional goals must be submitted.

Academic Fields/Career Goals: Environmental Science; Physical Sciences.

Award: Scholarship for use in freshman or sophomore years; not renewable. *Number:* 5. *Amount:* $800.

Eligibility Requirements: Applicant must be enrolled or expecting to enroll full-time at a two-year or four-year institution or university. Applicant must have 2.5 GPA or higher. Available to U.S. citizens.

Application Requirements: 500-word paper on personal and professional goals, application form, recommendations or references, test scores. *Deadline:* varies.

Contact: Dwain Waters, Treasurer
Air & Waste Management Association–Coastal Plains Chapter
One Energy Place
Pensacola, FL 32520-0328
Phone: 850-444-6527
Fax: 850-444-6217
E-mail: gdwaters@southernco.com

AIST FOUNDATION

http://www.aistfoundation.org/

ASSOCIATION FOR IRON AND STEEL TECHNOLOGY WILLY KORF MEMORIAL SCHOLARSHIP
• *See page 187*

AMERICAN CHEMICAL SOCIETY

http://www.acs.org/

AMERICAN CHEMICAL SOCIETY SCHOLARS PROGRAM
• *See page 187*

AMERICAN COUNCIL OF ENGINEERING COMPANIES OF PENNSYLVANIA (ACEC/PA)

http://www.acecpa.org/

ERIC J. GENNUSO AND LEROY D. (BUD) LOY, JR. SCHOLARSHIP PROGRAM
• *See page 187*

AMERICAN INDIAN SCIENCE AND ENGINEERING SOCIETY

http://www.aises.org/

A.T. ANDERSON MEMORIAL SCHOLARSHIP PROGRAM
• *See page 121*

AMERICAN INSTITUTE OF CHEMICAL ENGINEERS

http://www.aiche.org/

ENVIRONMENTAL DIVISION UNDERGRADUATE STUDENT PAPER AWARD
• *See page 188*

AMERICAN PHYSIOLOGICAL SOCIETY

http://www.the-aps.org

BARBARA A. HORWITZ AND JOHN M. HOROWITZ UNDERGRADUATE RESEARCH AWARDS
• *See page 114*

AMERICAN PUBLIC POWER ASSOCIATION

https://www.publicpower.org/grants-scholarships

DEED EDUCATIONAL SCHOLARSHIP
• *See page 190*

DEED STUDENT INTERNSHIP
• *See page 190*

DEED STUDENT RESEARCH GRANTS
• *See page 204*

DEED TECHNICAL DESIGN PROJECT
• *See page 191*

AMERICAN SOCIETY OF AGRONOMY, CROP SCIENCE SOCIETY OF AMERICA, SOIL SCIENCE SOCIETY OF AMERICA

http://www.agronomy.org

J. FIELDING REED SCHOLARSHIP
• *See page 106*

ARCTIC INSTITUTE OF NORTH AMERICA

http://www.arctic.ucalgary.ca/

JIM BOURQUE SCHOLARSHIP
• *See page 267*

ARRL FOUNDATION INC.

http://www.arrl.org/

OLD MAN INTERNATIONAL SIDEBAND SOCIETY (OMISS) SCHOLARSHIP
• *See page 259*

ROBERT D., W8ST, AND DONNA J., W9DJS, STREETER SCHOLARSHIP

$1000 scholarship for a student with any active amateur radio license class attending college or university. Student should be studying horticulture and/or environmental sciences.

Academic Fields/Career Goals: Environmental Science; Horticulture/Floriculture.

Award: Scholarship for use in freshman, sophomore, junior, or senior years; not renewable. *Number:* 1. *Amount:* $1000.

Eligibility Requirements: Applicant must be enrolled or expecting to enroll full-time at a two-year or four-year or technical institution or university and must have an interest in amateur radio. Available to U.S. citizens.

Application Requirements: Application form. *Deadline:* January 31.

Contact: Ms. Mary Hobart, Secretary
Phone: 860-594-0397
E-mail: k1mmh@arrl.org

W1FDR SCHOLARSHIP
• *See page 122*

ASSOCIATION FOR WOMEN GEOSCIENTISTS (AWG)
http://www.awg.org/

AWG ETHNIC MINORITY SCHOLARSHIP
• *See page 260*

AWG MARIA LUISA CRAWFORD FIELD CAMP SCHOLARSHIP
• *See page 129*

AWG SALT LAKE CHAPTER (SLC) RESEARCH SCHOLARSHIP
• *See page 129*

JANET CULLEN TANAKA GEOSCIENCES UNDERGRADUATE SCHOLARSHIP
• *See page 129*

LONE STAR RISING CAREER SCHOLARSHIP
• *See page 260*

OSAGE CHAPTER UNDERGRADUATE SERVICE SCHOLARSHIP
• *See page 129*

SUSAN EKDALE MEMORIAL FIELD CAMP SCHOLARSHIP
• *See page 260*

ASSOCIATION OF CALIFORNIA WATER AGENCIES
http://www.acwa.com/

ASSOCIATION OF CALIFORNIA WATER AGENCIES SCHOLARSHIPS
• *See page 123*

CLAIR A. HILL SCHOLARSHIP
• *See page 123*

ASSOCIATION OF NEW JERSEY ENVIRONMENTAL COMMISSIONS
http://www.anjec.org/

LECHNER SCHOLARSHIP
Award of $1000 scholarship for a student entering his/her junior or senior year at an accredited New Jersey college or university. Must be a New Jersey resident and have a minimum GPA of 3.0.

Academic Fields/Career Goals: Environmental Science.

Award: Scholarship for use in junior or senior years; not renewable. *Number:* 1. *Amount:* $1000.

Eligibility Requirements: Applicant must be enrolled or expecting to enroll full-time at a four-year institution or university; resident of New Jersey and studying in New Jersey. Applicant must have 3.0 GPA or higher. Available to U.S. citizens.

Application Requirements: Application form, essay, recommendations or references, transcript.

Contact: Jennifer Coffey, Executive Director
Phone: 973-539-7547
Fax: 973-539-7713
E-mail: jcoffey@anjec.org

ASSOCIATION OF STATE DAM SAFETY OFFICIALS (ASDSO)
http://www.DamSafety.org

ASSOCIATION OF STATE DAM SAFETY OFFICIALS (ASDSO) SENIOR UNDERGRADUATE SCHOLARSHIP
• *See page 168*

AUDUBON SOCIETY OF WESTERN PENNSYLVANIA
http://www.aswp.org/

BEULAH FREY ENVIRONMENTAL SCHOLARSHIP
Scholarship available to high school seniors pursuing studies in the environmental and natural sciences. Students who are applying to a two- or four-year college to further their studies in an environmentally-related field are eligible to apply. Scholarship is restricted to the residents of the seven counties around Pittsburgh.

Academic Fields/Career Goals: Environmental Science; Natural Sciences.

Award: Scholarship for use in freshman year; not renewable. *Number:* 1–2. *Amount:* $1000.

Eligibility Requirements: Applicant must be high school student; planning to enroll or expecting to enroll full-time at a two-year or four-year institution or university and resident of Pennsylvania. Available to U.S. citizens.

Application Requirements: Application form, essay, recommendations or references, test scores, transcript. *Deadline:* March 31.

Contact: Patricia O'Neill, Director of Education
Audubon Society of Western Pennsylvania
614 Dorseyville Road
Pittsburgh, PA 15238
Phone: 412-963-6100
Fax: 412-963-6761
E-mail: toneill@aswp.org

AUTOMOTIVE WOMEN'S ALLIANCE FOUNDATION
http://awafoundation.org/index.php

AUTOMOTIVE WOMEN'S ALLIANCE FOUNDATION SCHOLARSHIPS
• *See page 81*

BARRY GOLDWATER SCHOLARSHIP AND EXCELLENCE IN EDUCATION FOUNDATION
https://goldwater.scholarsapply.org

BARRY M. GOLDWATER SCHOLARSHIP AND EXCELLENCE IN EDUCATION PROGRAM
• *See page 123*

BHW GROUP
https://thebhwgroup.com/

BHW WOMEN IN STEM SCHOLARSHIP
• *See page 124*

B.O.G. PEST CONTROL

http://www.bogpestcontrol.com/

B.O.G. PEST CONTROL SCHOLARSHIP FUND
• *See page 169*

BROWN AND CALDWELL

http://www.brownandcaldwell.com

ECKENFELDER SCHOLARSHIP
• *See page 169*

MINORITY SCHOLARSHIP PROGRAM
• *See page 169*

CALAVERAS BIG TREES ASSOCIATION

https://bigtrees.org/

EMILY M. HEWITT MEMORIAL SCHOLARSHIP
• *See page 170*

CARDS AGAINST HUMANITY

https://cardsagainsthumanity.com/

SCIENCE AMBASSADOR SCHOLARSHIP
• *See page 124*

CONSERVATION FEDERATION OF MISSOURI

http://www.confedmo.org/

CHARLES P. BELL CONSERVATION SCHOLARSHIP

Eight scholarships of $250 to $600 for Missouri students and/or teachers whose studies or projects are related to natural science, resource conservation, earth resources, or environmental protection. Must be used for study in Missouri. See application for eligibility details.

Academic Fields/Career Goals: Environmental Science; Natural Resources; Natural Sciences.

Award: Scholarship for use in freshman, sophomore, junior, senior, or graduate years; not renewable. *Number:* 8. *Amount:* $250–$600.

Eligibility Requirements: Applicant must be enrolled or expecting to enroll full- or part-time at a four-year institution or university; resident of Missouri and studying in Missouri. Available to U.S. citizens.

Application Requirements: Application form, community service, financial need analysis. *Deadline:* January 31.

Contact: Laurie Coleman, Membership Director
Conservation Federation of Missouri
728 W Main Street
Jefferson City, MO 65101
Phone: 573-634-2322
Fax: 573-634-8205
E-mail: lcoleman@confedmo.org

COSTA RICAN VACATIONS

http://www.vacationscostarica.com/

COSTA RICAN VACATIONS SCHOLARSHIP

The Costa Rican Vacations scholarship program recognizes and rewards innovation and ideas within the areas of tourism studies and sustainable tourism. Every year Costa Rican Vacations will award two scholarships of $1,000 each to students who are interested in pursuing their studies and their career in tourism, hospitality or sustainable development. Scholarships are not renewable; however, a recipient may re-apply. Additional information can be found on the Costa Rican Vacations website: http://www.vacationscostarica.com/about-us/scholarships/

Academic Fields/Career Goals: Environmental Science; Hospitality Management; Natural Resources; Travel/Tourism.

Award: Scholarship for use in freshman, sophomore, junior, or senior years; not renewable. *Number:* 2. *Amount:* $1000.

Eligibility Requirements: Applicant must be enrolled or expecting to enroll full- or part-time at a four-year institution or university. Applicant must have 3.0 GPA or higher. Available to U.S. and non-U.S. citizens.

Application Requirements: Essay. *Deadline:* February 15.

Contact: Sofía González, Senior Online Content Editor
Phone: 800-606-1860 Ext. 1304
E-mail: scholarships@namutravel.com

DELAWARE HIGHER EDUCATION OFFICE

http://www.doe.k12.de.us

DELAWARE SOLID WASTE AUTHORITY JOHN P. "PAT" HEALY SCHOLARSHIP
• *See page 316*

DISTIL NETWORKS

http://www.distilnetworks.com

WOMEN FORWARD IN TECHNOLOGY SCHOLARSHIP PROGRAM
• *See page 124*

DIVERSITYCOMM, INC.

http://www.diversitycomm.net/

DIVERSITY IN STEAM MAGAZINE SCHOLARSHIP
• *See page 83*

ENVIRONMENTAL PROFESSIONALS' ORGANIZATION OF CONNECTICUT

http://www.epoc.org/

EPOC ENVIRONMENTAL SCHOLARSHIP FUND

Scholarships awarded annually to junior, senior, and graduate level students (full- or part-time) enrolled in accepted programs of study leading the student to become an environmental professional in Connecticut.

Academic Fields/Career Goals: Environmental Science.

Award: Scholarship for use in junior, senior, or graduate years; not renewable. *Number:* 2–3.

Eligibility Requirements: Applicant must be enrolled or expecting to enroll full- or part-time at a four-year institution or university. Available to U.S. citizens.

Application Requirements: Application form, essay, financial need analysis, recommendations or references, transcript. *Deadline:* May 7.

Contact: John Figurelli, Scholarship Fund Coordinator
Environmental Professionals' Organization of Connecticut
PO Box 176
Amston, CT 06231-0176
Phone: 860-513-1473
Fax: 860-228-4902
E-mail: figurelj@wseinc.com

FOUNDATION FOR SCIENCE AND DISABILITY

http://stemd.org/

GRANTS FOR DISABLED GRADUATE STUDENTS IN THE SCIENCES
• *See page 106*

GARDEN CLUB OF AMERICA

http://www.gcamerica.org/

CAROLINE THORN KISSEL SUMMER ENVIRONMENTAL STUDIES SCHOLARSHIP

Scholarship for students to promote environmental studies by students who are either residents of the state of New Jersey or non-residents pursuing study in New Jersey or its surrounding waters. Open to college students, graduate students, Ph.D. candidates, or non-degree-seeking applicants above the high school level. Must be a U.S. citizen.

Academic Fields/Career Goals: Environmental Science.

Award: Scholarship for use in freshman, sophomore, junior, senior, or graduate years; not renewable. *Number:* 1. *Amount:* $3000.

Eligibility Requirements: Applicant must be enrolled or expecting to enroll full- or part-time at a two-year or four-year or technical institution or university; resident of New Jersey and studying in New Jersey. Available to U.S. citizens.

Application Requirements: Application form, essay. *Deadline:* February 5.

Contact: Garden Club of America
Garden Club of America
14 East 60th Street
New York, NY 10022-1006
Phone: 212-753-8287
E-mail: scholarshipapplications@gcamerica.org

CLARA CARTER HIGGINS SUMMER ENVIRONMENTAL STUDIES SCHOLARSHIP

Scholarship to encourage studies and careers in the environmental field, with the opportunity to gain knowledge and experience beyond the regular course of study. Annually funds one Clara Carter Higgins scholar and one or more GCA Summer Environmental Studies scholars at $3,000 per recipient in financial assistance for summer coursework in environmental studies.

Academic Fields/Career Goals: Environmental Science.

Award: Scholarship for use in sophomore, junior, or senior years; not renewable. *Number:* 1. *Amount:* $3000.

Eligibility Requirements: Applicant must be enrolled or expecting to enroll full- or part-time at a four-year institution or university. Available to U.S. citizens.

Application Requirements: Application form, essay. *Deadline:* February 5.

Contact: Garden Club of America
Garden Club of America
14 East 60th Street
New York, NY 10022-1006
Phone: 212-753-8287
E-mail: scholarshipapplications@gcamerica.org

ELIZABETH GARDNER NORWEB SUMMER ENVIRONMENTAL STUDIES SCHOLARSHIP

• See page 107

GCA AWARD IN DESERT STUDIES

One or more awards of $4,000 to promote the study of horticulture, conservation, botany, environmental science, and landscape design relating to the arid landscape. Open to graduate or advanced undergraduate students studying at an accredited U.S. university. Preference given to students wishing to gain practical field experience—specifically, planning and design for sustainability, rainwater harvesting and plant management, etc.—through structured internships at accredited botanical gardens and arboreta.

Academic Fields/Career Goals: Environmental Science; Horticulture/Floriculture; Landscape Architecture.

Award: Prize for use in junior, senior, or graduate years; not renewable. *Number:* 1. *Amount:* $4000.

Eligibility Requirements: Applicant must be enrolled or expecting to enroll full-time at a four-year institution or university. Available to U.S. citizens.

Application Requirements: Application form. *Deadline:* January 15.

Contact: Kenny Zelov, Assistant Director of Horticulture, Desert Botanical Garden
Garden Club of America
1201 North Galvin Parkway
Phoenix, AZ 85008
Phone: 408-481-8162
E-mail: kzelov@dbg.org

GCA AWARDS FOR SUMMER ENVIRONMENTAL STUDIES

$3,000 award to encourage studies and careers in the environmental field, with the opportunity to gain knowledge and experience beyond the regular course of study. Open to college students following their freshman, sophomore, or junior year. Eligibility is open to U.S. citizens and permanent residents who are enrolled in a U.S.–based institution.

Academic Fields/Career Goals: Environmental Science.

Award: Scholarship for use in sophomore, junior, or senior years; not renewable. *Amount:* $3000.

Eligibility Requirements: Applicant must be enrolled or expecting to enroll full-time at a four-year institution or university. Available to U.S. citizens.

Application Requirements: Application form, essay. *Deadline:* February 5.

Contact: Garden Club of America
Garden Club of America
Scholarship Applications
14 East 60th Street
New York, NY 10022-1006
Phone: 212-753-8287
E-mail: scholarshipapplications@gcamerica.org

MARY T. CAROTHERS SUMMER ENVIRONMENTAL STUDIES SCHOLARSHIP

Scholarship to encourage studies and careers in the environmental field, with the opportunity to gain knowledge and experience beyond the regular course of study. Provides financial assistance of $3,000 to one student annually for field work, research, or classroom work. Open to college undergraduates for summer study following the freshman, sophomore, or junior year.

Academic Fields/Career Goals: Environmental Science.

Award: Scholarship for use in sophomore, junior, or senior years; not renewable. *Number:* 1. *Amount:* $3000.

Eligibility Requirements: Applicant must be enrolled or expecting to enroll full-time at a four-year institution or university. Available to U.S. citizens.

Application Requirements: Application form, essay. *Deadline:* February 5.

Contact: Garden Club of America
Garden Club of America
14 East 60th Street
New York, NY 10022-1006
Phone: 212-753-8287
E-mail: scholarshipapplications@gcamerica.org

GREAT MINDS IN STEM

http://www.greatmindsinstem.org

HENAAC SCHOLARSHIP PROGRAM

• See page 115

GREEN CHEMISTRY INSTITUTE-AMERICAN CHEMICAL SOCIETY

http://www.acs.org/greenchemistry

CIBA TRAVEL AWARDS IN GREEN CHEMISTRY

The award sponsors the participation of students (high school, undergraduate, and graduate students) in an American Chemical Society (ACS) technical meeting, conference or training program, having a significant green chemistry or sustainability component, to expand the students' education in green chemistry. The applicant must demonstrate research or educational interest in green chemistry. The award amount is based on estimated travel expenses.

Academic Fields/Career Goals: Environmental Science.

Award: Grant for use in freshman, sophomore, junior, senior, graduate, or postgraduate years; not renewable. *Number:* 3–4. *Amount:* up to $2000.

Eligibility Requirements: Applicant must be enrolled or expecting to enroll full-time at a four-year institution or university. Available to U.S. citizens.

Application Requirements: Application form, application form may be submitted online, essay, recommendations or references, resume, transcript. *Deadline:* October 12.

Contact: Ms. Joyce Kilgore, Program Manager
Green Chemistry Institute-American Chemical Society
1155 16th Street, NW
Washington, DC 20036
Phone: 202-872-6109
E-mail: gci@acs.org

KENNETH G. HANCOCK MEMORIAL AWARD IN GREEN CHEMISTRY

Award of $1000 for the students who have completed their education or research in green chemistry. The scholarship provides national recognition for outstanding student contributions to furthering the goals of green chemistry through research or education.

Academic Fields/Career Goals: Environmental Science.

Award: Prize for use in freshman, sophomore, junior, senior, or graduate years; not renewable. *Number:* 1–2. *Amount:* $1000.

Eligibility Requirements: Applicant must be enrolled or expecting to enroll full-time at a four-year institution or university. Available to U.S. and non-U.S. citizens.

Application Requirements: Application form, application form may be submitted online, essay. *Deadline:* March 1.

Contact: Mrs. Jennifer MacKellar, Program Manager
Green Chemistry Institute-American Chemical Society
1155 16th Street, NW
Washington, DC 20036
Phone: 202-872-6173
E-mail: gci@acs.org

HERB SOCIETY OF AMERICA, WESTERN RESERVE UNIT

http://www.westernreserveherbsociety.org/

HORTICULTURE SCHOLARSHIP FROM FRANCIS SYLVIA ZVERINA
• *See page 101*

HORTICULTURE SCHOLARSHIP OF THE WESTERN RESERVE HERB SOCIETY
• *See page 101*

INDEPENDENT LABORATORIES INSTITUTE SCHOLARSHIP ALLIANCE

http://www.acil.org/

INDEPENDENT LABORATORIES INSTITUTE SCHOLARSHIP ALLIANCE
• *See page 171*

INDIANA WILDLIFE FEDERATION ENDOWMENT

http://www.indianawildlife.org/

CHARLES A. HOLT INDIANA WILDLIFE FEDERATION ENDOWMENT SCHOLARSHIP

A $1000.00 scholarship will be award to one Indiana resident enrolled in a course of study related to resource conservation or environmental education at a sophomore level or above in an accredited college or university. The scholarship recipient will receive priority consideration for an Indiana Wildlife Federation internship position.

Academic Fields/Career Goals: Environmental Science; Natural Resources.

Award: Scholarship for use in sophomore, junior, or senior years; not renewable. *Number:* 1. *Amount:* $1000.

Eligibility Requirements: Applicant must be enrolled or expecting to enroll full-time at a four-year institution or university; resident of Indiana and studying in Indiana. Available to U.S. citizens.

Application Requirements: Application form, essay. *Deadline:* June 1.

Contact: Barbara Simpson, Executive Director
Indiana Wildlife Federation Endowment
708 East Michigan Street
Indianapolis, IN 46202
Phone: 317-875-9453
E-mail: info@indianawildlife.org

INTERTRIBAL TIMBER COUNCIL

http://www.itcnet.org/

TRUMAN D. PICARD SCHOLARSHIP

The program is dedicated to assisting Native American/Native-Alaskan youth seeking careers in natural resources. Graduating senior high school students and those currently attending institutions of higher education are encouraged to apply. A valid tribal/Alaska native corporation's enrollment card is required.

Academic Fields/Career Goals: Environmental Science; Fire Sciences; Natural Resources.

Award: Scholarship for use in freshman, sophomore, junior, senior, or graduate years; not renewable. *Number:* 15–30. *Amount:* $2000–$2500.

Eligibility Requirements: Applicant must be American Indian/Alaska Native and enrolled or expecting to enroll full-time at a two-year or four-year institution or university. Available to U.S. citizens.

Application Requirements: Application form, essay, financial need analysis. *Deadline:* February 7.

Contact: Laura Alvidrez, Education Committee
Intertribal Timber Council
1112 NE 21st Avenue, Suite 4
Portland, OR 97232-2114
Phone: 503-282-4296
E-mail: itc1@teleport.com

KENTUCKY ENERGY AND ENVIRONMENT CABINET

http://dep.ky.gov

ENVIRONMENTAL PROTECTION SCHOLARSHIP
• *See page 172*

LABROOTS INC.

http://www.LabRoots.com

LABROOTS STEM SCHOLARSHIP
• *See page 116*

THE LAND CONSERVANCY OF NEW JERSEY

http://www.tlc-nj.org/

ROGERS FAMILY SCHOLARSHIP
• *See page 172*

RUSSELL W. MYERS SCHOLARSHIP
• *See page 172*

MASSACHUSETTS ASSOCIATION OF LAND SURVEYORS AND CIVIL ENGINEERS

http://www.malsce.org/

MALSCE SCHOLARSHIPS
• *See page 321*

MICHAEL MOODY FITNESS

http://www.michaelmoodyfitness.com/

MICHAEL MOODY FITNESS SCHOLARSHIP
• *See page 166*

NASA IDAHO SPACE GRANT CONSORTIUM

http://www.idahospacegrant.org

NASA IDAHO SPACE GRANT CONSORTIUM SCHOLARSHIP PROGRAM
• *See page 126*

NASA/MARYLAND SPACE GRANT CONSORTIUM

http://www.mdspacegrant.org/

NASA MARYLAND SPACE GRANT CONSORTIUM UNDERGRADUATE SCHOLARSHIPS
• *See page 156*

NASA MINNESOTA SPACE GRANT CONSORTIUM

https://www.mnspacegrant.org/

MINNESOTA SPACE GRANT CONSORTIUM SCHOLARSHIP PROGRAM
• *See page 156*

NASA'S VIRGINIA SPACE GRANT CONSORTIUM

http://www.vsgc.odu.edu/

COMMUNITY COLLEGE STEM SCHOLARSHIPS
• *See page 126*

NATIONAL COUNCIL OF STATE GARDEN CLUBS INC. SCHOLARSHIP

http://www.gardenclub.org/

NATIONAL COUNCIL OF STATE GARDEN CLUBS INC. SCHOLARSHIP
• *See page 108*

NATIONAL GARDEN CLUBS INC.

http://www.gardenclub.org/

NATIONAL GARDEN CLUBS INC. SCHOLARSHIP PROGRAM
• *See page 109*

NATIONAL INSTITUTES OF HEALTH

https://www.training.nih.gov/programs/ugsp

NIH UNDERGRADUATE SCHOLARSHIP PROGRAM FOR STUDENTS FROM DISADVANTAGED BACKGROUNDS
• *See page 116*

NATIONAL SAFETY COUNCIL

http://www.cshema.org/

CAMPUS SAFETY, HEALTH AND ENVIRONMENTAL MANAGEMENT ASSOCIATION SCHOLARSHIP AWARD PROGRAM
One $2000 scholarship available to full-time undergraduate or graduate students in all majors to encourage the study of safety and environmental management. The program is open to all college undergraduate and graduate students in all majors/disciplines enrolled in 12 credit hours per semester, trimester, or quarter.

Academic Fields/Career Goals: Environmental Science; Occupational Safety and Health.

Award: Scholarship for use in freshman, sophomore, junior, senior, or graduate years; not renewable. *Number:* 1. *Amount:* $2000.

Eligibility Requirements: Applicant must be enrolled or expecting to enroll full-time at a four-year institution or university. Available to U.S. and Canadian citizens.

Application Requirements: Application form, essay, transcript. *Deadline:* March 31.

Contact: Scholarship Committee
National Safety Council
120 West 7th Street, Suite 204
Bloomington, IN 47404
Phone: 812-245-8084
Fax: 812-245-0590

NATIONAL SECURITY EDUCATION PROGRAM

http://www.iie.org/

NATIONAL SECURITY EDUCATION PROGRAM (NSEP) DAVID L. BOREN UNDERGRADUATE SCHOLARSHIPS
• *See page 139*

NEW ENGLAND WATER WORKS ASSOCIATION

http://www.newwa.org/

ELSON T. KILLAM MEMORIAL SCHOLARSHIP
• *See page 210*

FRANCIS X. CROWLEY SCHOLARSHIP
• *See page 182*

JOSEPH MURPHY SCHOLARSHIP
• *See page 210*

NEXTSTEPU

http://www.nextstepu.com/

$1,500 STEM SCHOLARSHIP
• *See page 120*

NGWA FOUNDATION

http://www.ngwa.org/Foundation/Pages/default.aspx

NGWA FOUNDATION'S LEN ASSANTE SCHOLARSHIP
• *See page 262*

OHIO ACADEMY OF SCIENCE/OHIO ENVIRONMENTAL EDUCATION FUND

http://www.ohiosci.org/

OHIO ENVIRONMENTAL SCIENCE & ENGINEERING SCHOLARSHIPS

Merit-based, non-renewable, tuition-only scholarships awarded to undergraduate students admitted to Ohio state or private colleges and universities. Must be able to demonstrate knowledge of, and commitment to, careers in environmental sciences or environmental engineering.

Academic Fields/Career Goals: Environmental Science.

Award: Scholarship for use in senior year; not renewable. *Number:* 18. *Amount:* $1250–$2500.

Eligibility Requirements: Applicant must be enrolled or expecting to enroll full- or part-time at a two-year or four-year institution or university and studying in Ohio. Applicant must have 3.0 GPA or higher. Available to U.S. citizens.

Application Requirements: Application form, application form may be submitted online (https://mc04.manuscriptcentral.com/oas), community service, essay, recommendations or references, resume, self-addressed stamped envelope with application, transcript. *Deadline:* April 15.

Contact: Dr. Stephen McConoughey, Chief Executive Officer
Ohio Academy of Science/Ohio Environmental Education Fund
1500 West Third Avenue, Suite 228
Columbus, OH 43212-2817
Phone: 614-488-2228
Fax: 614-488-7629
E-mail: smcconoughey@ohiosci.org

OREGON STUDENT ASSISTANCE COMMISSION

https://oregonstudentaid.gov/

ANDY AITKENHEAD SCHOLARSHIP
• *See page 127*

CHARLES PATRICK SCHOLARSHIP
• *See page 335*

ROBERTS SCHOLARSHIP
• *See page 173*

ROYDEN M. BODLEY SCHOLARSHIP

Award open to Oregon high school graduates who earned their Eagle rank in Boy Scouts of America Cascade Pacific Council. Must be enrolled, or planning to enroll, in an Oregon public or nonprofit college in an undergraduate program in forestry, wildlife conservation, environmental studies, or related fields that continue interest in the outdoors. Must reapply annually to renew award. Must specify the date you were awarded the rank of Eagle Scout and the name of the Council.

Academic Fields/Career Goals: Environmental Science; Natural Resources; Natural Sciences.

Award: Scholarship for use in freshman year; not renewable.

Eligibility Requirements: Applicant must be enrolled or expecting to enroll full-time at a four-year institution or university; male; resident of Oregon and studying in Oregon. Applicant or parent of applicant must be member of Boy Scouts. Available to U.S. citizens.

Application Requirements: Application form, financial need analysis. *Deadline:* March 1.

Contact: Melissa Adams, Scholarship Processing Coordinator
Phone: 541-687-7409
E-mail: melissa.adams@state.or.us

WILLIAM E. KEENE MEMORIAL SCHOLARSHIP
• *See page 335*

OUTDOOR WRITERS ASSOCIATION OF AMERICA

http://www.owaa.org/

OUTDOOR WRITERS ASSOCIATION OF AMERICA - BODIE MCDOWELL SCHOLARSHIP AWARD
• *See page 222*

PACIFIC GAS AND ELECTRIC COMPANY

http://www.scholarshipamerica.org

PG&E BETTER TOGETHER STEM SCHOLARSHIP PROGRAM
• *See page 233*

PADDLE CANADA

http://www.paddlecanada.com

BILL MASON SCHOLARSHIP FUND
• *See page 275*

PLAN NEW HAMPSHIRE

http://www.plannh.org

PLAN NEW HAMPSHIRE SCHOLARSHIP AND FELLOWSHIP PROGRAM
• *See page 129*

SALT RIVER PROJECT (SRP)

http://www.srpnet.com/

NAVAJO GENERATING STATION NAVAJO SCHOLARSHIP
• *See page 324*

SCARLETT FAMILY FOUNDATION SCHOLARSHIP PROGRAM

http://www.scarlettfoundation.org/

SCHOLARSHIP FOR STUDENTS PURSUING A BUSINESS OR STEM DEGREE
• *See page 91*

SHRED NATIONS

https://www.shrednations.com/

SHRED NATIONS SCHOLARSHIP

Shred Nations Scholarship is a one time annual award of up to $5,000 to offset the costs of higher education. The scholarship award may be divided into two separate payments to be paid directly to the applicant's chosen institution of higher education, which must be an accredited university, college or trade school. Applicants must have completed secondary school, or currently be a senior in a secondary school, with a minimum GPA of 3.0 with an interest in business, environmental studies or the shredding and recycling industry. Applicants will be required to submit a nomination from a NAID member. NAID members will be comprised of any employee or owner of a NAID member company. One scholarship will be awarded for the academic year, and past recipients may re-apply to be awarded the scholarship for subsequent years. Shred Nations employees, immediate or extended families are not permitted to be awarded the scholarship. Candidates who plan to make the secure destruction industry a career and whose degree program provides the maximum potential benefit to their respective/perspective employer will be favorably considered. Priority will also be given to family and friends of members of the Shred Nations partner network. All applicants will be evaluated based on the following criteria, and such other considerations as the Selection Committee determines are meritorious to the purposes of the scholarship. The selection committee will analyze the scholar's academic achievement and rigor including high school and college/university transcripts, honors and awards. The scholar's character will be evaluated based upon the recommendation of a NAID member owner/executive. In addition, the scholar's extracurricular activities and merits related to those activities will be examined. The scholar should demonstrate through a 500 and 1,000 word essay how they can use their studies to improve business, environmental responsibility and make future contributions to the community including interest in the secure destruction industry and demonstrate what they value they can provide to a potential company that is hiring them.

Academic Fields/Career Goals: Environmental Science.

Award: Scholarship for use in freshman, sophomore, junior, senior, graduate, or postgraduate years; not renewable. *Number:* 1. *Amount:* $5000.

Eligibility Requirements: Applicant must be enrolled or expecting to enroll full- or part-time at a two-year or four-year or technical institution or university. Applicant must have 3.0 GPA or higher. Available to U.S. citizens.

Application Requirements: Application form, essay. *Deadline:* February 26.

Contact: Mr. Rand LeMarinel, President
Phone: 303-962-5585
E-mail: scholarship@shrednations.com

SIGMA XI, THE SCIENTIFIC RESEARCH SOCIETY

http://www.sigmaxi.org/

SIGMA XI GRANTS-IN-AID OF RESEARCH
• *See page 110*

SOCIETY FOR RANGE MANAGEMENT

http://www.rangelands.org/

MASONIC RANGE SCIENCE SCHOLARSHIP
• *See page 103*

SOIL AND WATER CONSERVATION SOCIETY

http://www.swcs.org

DONALD A. WILLIAMS SCHOLARSHIP SOIL CONSERVATION SCHOLARSHIP
• *See page 103*

SOIL AND WATER CONSERVATION SOCIETY-MISSOURI SHOW-ME CHAPTER

http://www.moswcs.org/

MO SHOW-ME CHAPTER SWCS SCHOLARSHIP
• *See page 111*

SOIL AND WATER CONSERVATION SOCIETY-NEW JERSEY CHAPTER

http://www.geocities.com/njswcs

EDWARD R. HALL SCHOLARSHIP
• *See page 103*

STRAIGHT NORTH

https://www.straightnorth.com/

STRAIGHT NORTH STEM SCHOLARSHIP
• *See page 92*

TAILOR MADE LAWNS

http://www.tailormadelawns.com

TAILOR MADE LAWNS SCHOLARSHIP FUND
• *See page 111*

TECHNICAL ASSOCIATION OF THE PULP & PAPER INDUSTRY (TAPPI)

http://www.tappi.org/

ENVIRONMENTAL WORKING GROUP SCHOLARSHIP

Scholarship for full-time students in a college program or applicants working full-time or part-time in the corrugated industry. Must demonstrate an interest in the corrugated packaging industry.

Academic Fields/Career Goals: Environmental Science; Paper and Pulp Engineering.

Award: Scholarship for use in sophomore, junior, or senior years; not renewable. *Number:* 1. *Amount:* $2500.

Eligibility Requirements: Applicant must be enrolled or expecting to enroll full-time at a four-year institution or university. Applicant must have 3.0 GPA or higher. Available to U.S. and non-U.S. citizens.

Application Requirements: Application form, interview. *Deadline:* February 15.

Contact: Mr. Laurence Womack, Director of Standards and Awards
Technical Association of the Pulp & Paper Industry (TAPPI)
15 Technology Parkway South
Peachtree Corners, GA 30092
Phone: 770-209-7276
E-mail: standards@tappi.org

TED ROLLINS AND VALEO GROUPE

http://valeogroupe.us/

TED ROLLINS ECO SCHOLARSHIP
• *See page 183*

UNICO FOUNDATION INC.

http://www.unico.org/

LOUISE TORRACO MEMORIAL SCHOLARSHIP FOR SCIENCE
• *See page 174*

UNITED NEGRO COLLEGE FUND

http://www.uncf.org/

KIA MOTORS AMERICA STEM/SUSTAINABILITY SCHOLARSHIP
• *See page 175*

SUEZ CORPORATE SCHOLARS PROGRAM
• *See page 94*

UNITED STATES ENVIRONMENTAL PROTECTION AGENCY

http://www.epa.gov/enviroed

NATIONAL NETWORK FOR ENVIRONMENTAL MANAGEMENT STUDIES FELLOWSHIP

Fellowship program designed to provide undergraduate and graduate students with research opportunities at one of EPA's facilities nationwide. EPA awards approximately 40 NNEMS fellowships per year. Selected students receive a stipend for performing their research project. EPA develops an annual catalog of research projects available for student application. Submit a complete application package as described in the annual catalog. Minimum 3.0 GPA required.

Academic Fields/Career Goals: Environmental Science; Natural Resources.

Award: Grant for use in freshman, sophomore, junior, senior, graduate, or postgraduate years; not renewable. *Number:* 20–25.

Eligibility Requirements: Applicant must be enrolled or expecting to enroll full- or part-time at a two-year or four-year institution or university. Applicant must have 3.0 GPA or higher. Available to U.S. citizens.

Application Requirements: Application form, recommendations or references, resume, transcript. *Deadline:* January 22.

Contact: Michael Baker, Acting Director
United States Environmental Protection Agency
Environmental Education Division
1200 Pennsylvania Avenue, NW, MC 1704A
Washington, DC 20460
Phone: 202-564-0446
Fax: 202-564-2754
E-mail: baker.michael@epa.gov

UNITED STATES SOCIETY ON DAMS

http://www.ussdams.org/

UNITED STATES SOCIETY ON DAMS SCHOLARSHIP AWARD
• *See page 214*

EUROPEAN STUDIES

CULTURAL SERVICES OF THE FRENCH EMBASSY

http://www.frenchculture.org/

TEACHING ASSISTANT PROGRAM IN FRANCE
• *See page 113*

FASHION DESIGN

AMERICAN SHEEP INDUSTRY ASSOCIATION

http://www.sheepusa.org/

NATIONAL MAKE IT WITH WOOL COMPETITION

Awards available for entrants ages 13 years & older. Must enter at district and/or state level with home-constructed garment of at least 60 percent wool. Applicant must model garment. National entry fee is $12 for regular contest and $20 for Fashion/Apparel Design students. District and state entry fees may also apply. Complete rules available from State Director, National Coordinator, and online. http://www.NationalMakeItWithWool.com

Academic Fields/Career Goals: Fashion Design.

Award: Prize for use in freshman, sophomore, junior, senior, or graduate years; not renewable. *Number:* 2–26. *Amount:* $25–$1500.

Eligibility Requirements: Applicant must be enrolled or expecting to enroll full- or part-time at a two-year or four-year or technical institution or university; resident of Alberta, California, Colorado, Connecticut, Delaware, Florida, Georgia, Idaho, Illinois, Indiana, Kansas, Kentucky, Maine, Maryland, Massachusetts, Michigan, Minnesota, Missouri, Montana, Nebraska, New Hampshire, New Jersey, New York, North Carolina, North Dakota, Ohio, Oklahoma, Oregon, Pennsylvania, Rhode Island, South Dakota, Tennessee, Texas, Utah, Vermont, Washington, Wisconsin, Wyoming; studying in Alabama, Alaska, Arizona, Arkansas, California, Colorado, Connecticut, Delaware, District of Columbia, Florida, Georgia, Idaho, Illinois, Indiana, Iowa, Kansas, Kentucky, Louisiana, Maine, Maryland, Massachusetts, Michigan, Minnesota, Mississippi, Missouri, Montana, Nebraska, Nevada, New Hampshire, New Jersey, New Mexico, New York, North Carolina, North Dakota, Ohio, Oklahoma, Oregon, Pennsylvania, Rhode Island, South Carolina, South Dakota, Tennessee, Texas, Utah, Vermont, Virginia, Washington, West Virginia, Wisconsin, Wyoming and must have an interest in sewing. Available to U.S. citizens.

Application Requirements: Application form. *Fee:* $12.

Contact: Mary Roediger, National Coordinator
American Sheep Industry Association
PO Box 123
Albany, OH 45710
Phone: 740-591-5149
E-mail: wool@sewtruedesigns.com

CONGRESSIONAL BLACK CAUCUS FOUNDATION, INC.

http://www.cbcfinc.org/

CBC SPOUSES VISUAL ARTS SCHOLARSHIP
• *See page 132*

DECA (DISTRIBUTIVE EDUCATION CLUBS OF AMERICA)

http://www.deca.org/

HARRY A. APPLEGATE SCHOLARSHIP
• *See page 83*

QUALITY BATH

http://www.qualitybath.com

QUALITYBATH.COM SCHOLARSHIP PROGRAM
• *See page 140*

SUPPORT CREATIVITY

http://wesupportcreativity.org

SUPPORT CREATIVITY SCHOLARSHIP
• *See page 137*

FILMMAKING/VIDEO

ACADEMY FOUNDATION OF THE ACADEMY OF MOTION PICTURE ARTS AND SCIENCES

http://www.oscars.org/saa

ACADEMY OF MOTION PICTURE ARTS AND SCIENCES STUDENT ACADEMY AWARDS

Award available to students who have made a narrative, documentary, alternative, foreign or animated film of up to 60 minutes within the curricular structure of an accredited college or university. Initial entry must be on DVD-R. 16mm or larger format print, digital beta-cam tape, HD-Cam or DCP required for further rounds. Prizes awarded in four categories. Each category awards gold ($5000), silver ($3000), and bronze ($2000). Visit website for details and application http://www.oscars.org/saa.

Academic Fields/Career Goals: Filmmaking/Video.

Award: Prize for use in freshman, sophomore, junior, senior, or graduate years; not renewable. *Number:* 3–15. *Amount:* $2000–$5000.

Eligibility Requirements: Applicant must be enrolled or expecting to enroll full-time at a two-year or four-year institution or university. Available to U.S. and non-U.S. citizens.

Application Requirements: 16mm or larger format film print or NTSC digital betacam version of the entry (BetaSP format is not acceptable), DVD, application form, entry in a contest. *Deadline:* April 1.

Contact: Shawn Guthrie, Program Administrator
       Academy Foundation of the Academy of Motion Picture Arts
         and Sciences
       8949 Wilshire Boulevard
       Beverly Hills, CA 90211-1972
       Phone: 310-247-3000 Ext. 3306
       Fax: 310-859-9619
       E-mail: sguthrie@oscars.org

ADC RESEARCH INSTITUTE

http://www.adc.org/

JACK SHAHEEN MASS COMMUNICATIONS SCHOLARSHIP AWARD
• *See page 215*

ASIAN AMERICAN JOURNALISTS ASSOCIATION

http://www.aaja.org/

CIC/ANNA CHENNAULT SCHOLARSHIP
• *See page 217*

ASIAN AMERICAN JOURNALISTS ASSOCIATION, SEATTLE CHAPTER

http://www.aajaseattle.org/

NORTHWEST JOURNALISTS OF COLOR SCHOLARSHIP
• *See page 96*

CHARLES AND LUCILLE KING FAMILY FOUNDATION, INC.

http://www.kingfoundation.org/

CHARLES AND LUCILLE KING FAMILY FOUNDATION SCHOLARSHIPS
• *See page 218*

CONGRESSIONAL BLACK CAUCUS FOUNDATION, INC.

http://www.cbcfinc.org/

CBC SPOUSES VISUAL ARTS SCHOLARSHIP
• *See page 132*

DIVERSITYCOMM, INC.

http://www.diversitycomm.net/

DIVERSITY IN STEAM MAGAZINE SCHOLARSHIP
• *See page 83*

HEMOPHILIA FOUNDATION OF SOUTHERN CALIFORNIA

http://www.hemosocal.org/

EARL JAMES FAHRINGER PERFORMING ARTS SCHOLARSHIP
• *See page 142*

ILLUMINATING ENGINEERING SOCIETY OF NORTH AMERICA– GOLDEN GATE SECTION

http://www.iesgg.org/

ALAN LUCAS MEMORIAL EDUCATIONAL SCHOLARSHIP
• *See page 135*

INTERNATIONAL COMMUNICATIONS INDUSTRIES FOUNDATION

http://www.infocomm.org/scholarships

ICIF SCHOLARSHIP FOR EMPLOYEES AND DEPENDENTS OF MEMBER ORGANIZATIONS
• *See page 219*

INTERNATIONAL COMMUNICATIONS INDUSTRIES FOUNDATION AV SCHOLARSHIP
• *See page 219*

ISLAMIC SCHOLARSHIP FUND

http://islamicscholarshipfund.org/

ISF NATIONAL SCHOLARSHIP
• *See page 119*

NATIONAL ACADEMY OF TELEVISION ARTS & SCIENCES— OHIO VALLEY CHAPTER

http://ohiovalleyemmy.org/

DAVID J. CLARKE MEMORIAL SCHOLARSHIP
• *See page 220*

NATIONAL ACADEMY OF TELEVISION ARTS AND SCIENCES

http://www.emmyonline.tv/

DOUGLAS W. MUMMERT SCHOLARSHIP
• *See page 142*

JIM MCKAY MEMORIAL SCHOLARSHIP
• *See page 220*

MIKE WALLACE MEMORIAL SCHOLARSHIP
• *See page 220*

NATIONAL ACADEMY OF TELEVISION ARTS AND SCIENCES TRUSTEES SCHOLARSHIP
• *See page 220*

RANDY FALCO SCHOLARSHIP
• *See page 220*

NATIONAL ACADEMY OF TELEVISION ARTS AND SCIENCES, MICHIGAN CHAPTER

http://natasmichigan.org

DR. LYNNE BOYLE/JOHN SCHIMPF UNDERGRADUATE SCHOLARSHIP
• *See page 97*

OUTDOOR WRITERS ASSOCIATION OF AMERICA

http://www.owaa.org/

OUTDOOR WRITERS ASSOCIATION OF AMERICA - BODIE MCDOWELL SCHOLARSHIP AWARD
• *See page 222*

POLISH ARTS CLUB OF BUFFALO SCHOLARSHIP FOUNDATION

http://www.pacb.bfn.org/

POLISH ARTS CLUB OF BUFFALO SCHOLARSHIP FOUNDATION TRUST
• *See page 144*

PRINCESS GRACE FOUNDATION-USA

http://www.pgfusa.org/

PRINCESS GRACE AWARDS IN DANCE, THEATER, AND FILM

One-time scholarship for students enrolled full-time in film or video, dance, or theater program. For dance, applicant must have completed at least one year of undergraduate study; for theater, final year of study in either undergraduate or graduate level; and for film, must be in thesis program. The number of scholarships varies from ten to twelve annually.
Academic Fields/Career Goals: Filmmaking/Video; Performing Arts.
Award: Grant for use in sophomore, junior, senior, or graduate years; not renewable. *Number:* 15–25. *Amount:* $5000–$25,000.
Eligibility Requirements: Applicant must be enrolled or expecting to enroll full-time at a four-year institution or university. Available to U.S. citizens.
Application Requirements: Application form, essay, personal photograph, portfolio.
Contact: Ms. Diana Kemppainen, Program Director
Phone: 212-317-1470
E-mail: grants@pgfusa.org

QUALITY BATH

http://www.qualitybath.com

QUALITYBATH.COM SCHOLARSHIP PROGRAM
• *See page 140*

RHODE ISLAND FOUNDATION

http://www.rifoundation.org/

J. D. EDSAL SCHOLARSHIP
• *See page 99*

SOCIETY OF MOTION PICTURE AND TELEVISION ENGINEERS

https://www.smpte.org/

LOUIS F. WOLF JR. MEMORIAL SCHOLARSHIP
• *See page 224*

STUDENT PAPER AWARD
• *See page 224*

SUPPORT CREATIVITY

http://wesupportcreativity.org

SUPPORT CREATIVITY SCHOLARSHIP
• *See page 137*

TELETOON

http://www.teletoon.com/

TELETOON ANIMATION SCHOLARSHIP
• *See page 145*

UNITED NEGRO COLLEGE FUND

http://www.uncf.org/

DIVERSE VOICES IN STORYTELLING SCHOLARSHIP
• *See page 227*

UNIVERSITY FILM AND VIDEO ASSOCIATION

http://www.ufva.org/

UNIVERSITY FILM AND VIDEO ASSOCIATION CAROLE FIELDING STUDENT GRANTS

Up to $4000 is available for production grants in narrative, documentary, experimental, new-media/installation, or animation. Up to $1000 is available for grants in research. Applicant must be sponsored by a faculty person who is an active member of the University Film and Video Association. Fifty percent of award distributed upon completion of project.
Academic Fields/Career Goals: Filmmaking/Video.
Award: Grant for use in freshman, sophomore, junior, senior, or graduate years; not renewable. *Number:* 2–5. *Amount:* $1000–$4000.
Eligibility Requirements: Applicant must be enrolled or expecting to enroll full- or part-time at a two-year or four-year institution or university. Available to U.S. and non-U.S. citizens.
Application Requirements: Application form, essay. *Deadline:* December 15.
Contact: Prof. Laura Vazquez
University Film and Video Association
Northern Illinois University
Department of Communication
DeKalb, IL 60115
Phone: 815-753-7107
E-mail: lvazquez@niu.edu

FINANCE

THE ACTUARIAL FOUNDATION

http://www.actuarialfoundation.org

ACTUARY OF TOMORROW—STUART A. ROBERTSON MEMORIAL SCHOLARSHIP
• *See page 175*

CURTIS E. HUNTINGTON MEMORIAL SCHOLARSHIP (FORMERLY THE JOHN CULVER WOODDY SCHOLARSHIP)
• *See page 263*

AUTOMOTIVE WOMEN'S ALLIANCE FOUNDATION

http://awafoundation.org/index.php

AUTOMOTIVE WOMEN'S ALLIANCE FOUNDATION SCHOLARSHIPS
• *See page 81*

CHECKS SUPERSTORE

http://www.checks-superstore.com/

CHECKS SUPERSTORE SCHOLARSHIP

Checks SuperStore is offering an annual $1,000 scholarship to one college/university student in the United States. The scholarship will be awarded to the student who submits the best overall essay. Essay must be between 500 and 1,000 words long and must fully answer one of the questions. Entry deadline is on August 15th.

Academic Fields/Career Goals: Finance.

Award: Scholarship for use in freshman, sophomore, junior, or senior years; renewable. *Number:* 1. *Amount:* $1000.

Eligibility Requirements: Applicant must be enrolled or expecting to enroll full-time at a four-year institution. Applicant must have 3.0 GPA or higher. Available to U.S. citizens.

Application Requirements: Application form may be submitted online (http://www.checks-superstore.com/scholarship.aspx), essay. *Deadline:* August 15.

Contact: Ryan Skidmore, Scholarship Manager
  E-mail: scholarship@checks-superstore.com

DECA (DISTRIBUTIVE EDUCATION CLUBS OF AMERICA)

http://www.deca.org/

HARRY A. APPLEGATE SCHOLARSHIP
• *See page 83*

DISTIL NETWORKS

http://www.distilnetworks.com

WOMEN FORWARD IN TECHNOLOGY SCHOLARSHIP PROGRAM
• *See page 124*

DIVERSITYCOMM, INC.

http://www.diversitycomm.net/

DIVERSITY IN STEAM MAGAZINE SCHOLARSHIP
• *See page 83*

FUKUNAGA SCHOLARSHIP FOUNDATION

http://fukunagascholarship.com

FUKUNAGA SCHOLARSHIP FOUNDATION
• *See page 85*

GEORGIA GOVERNMENT FINANCE OFFICERS ASSOCIATION

http://www.ggfoa.org/

GGFOA ANNUAL COLLEGE SCHOLARSHIP
• *See page 85*

GOVERNMENT FINANCE OFFICERS ASSOCIATION

http://www.gfoa.org/

FRANK L. GREATHOUSE GOVERNMENT ACCOUNTING SCHOLARSHIP
• *See page 85*

JEFFREY L. ESSER CAREER DEVELOPMENT SCHOLARSHIP
• *See page 85*

OREGON STUDENT ASSISTANCE COMMISSION

https://oregonstudentaid.gov/

OREGON ASSOCIATION OF CERTIFIED FRAUD EXAMINERS SCHOLARSHIP
• *See page 90*

SCARLETT FAMILY FOUNDATION SCHOLARSHIP PROGRAM

http://www.scarlettfoundation.org/

SCHOLARSHIP FOR STUDENTS PURSUING A BUSINESS OR STEM DEGREE
• *See page 91*

SPECIALTY EQUIPMENT MARKET ASSOCIATION

http://www.sema.org/

SEMA MEMORIAL SCHOLARSHIP FUND
• *See page 92*

STRAIGHTFORWARD MEDIA

http://www.straightforwardmedia.com/

STRAIGHTFORWARD MEDIA BUSINESS SCHOOL SCHOLARSHIP
• *See page 99*

STRAIGHT NORTH

https://www.straightnorth.com/

STRAIGHT NORTH STEM SCHOLARSHIP
• *See page 92*

UNITED NEGRO COLLEGE FUND

http://www.uncf.org/

BASF/ALFRED CHISHOLM ENDOWED MEMORIAL SCHOLARSHIP
• *See page 93*

DISCOVER FINANCIAL SERVICES SCHOLARSHIP
• *See page 93*

HCN/APRICITY RESOURCES SCHOLARS PROGRAM
• *See page 93*

MUFG UNION BANK SCHOLARSHIP PROGRAM
• *See page 93*

PROCTER & GAMBLE GENERAL SCHOLARSHIP
• *See page 94*

RICOH SCHOLARSHIP PROGRAM
• *See page 94*

SUEZ CORPORATE SCHOLARS PROGRAM
• *See page 94*

UBS/PAINEWEBBER SCHOLARSHIP
• *See page 94*

UNCF/ANTHEM CORPORATE SCHOLARS PROGRAM
• *See page 184*

UNCF/CARNIVAL CORPORATE SCHOLARS PROGRAM
• *See page 184*

UNCF/NISSAN SCHOLARSHIP PROGRAM
• *See page 185*

VOYA SCHOLARS
• *See page 94*

WILLIAM WRIGLEY FOUNDATION SCHOLARSHIP
• *See page 95*

FIRE SCIENCES

AMERICAN SOCIETY OF CERTIFIED ENGINEERING TECHNICIANS

http://www.ascet.org/

KURT H. AND DONNA M. SCHULER SMALL GRANT
• *See page 205*

CALAVERAS BIG TREES ASSOCIATION

https://bigtrees.org/

EMILY M. HEWITT MEMORIAL SCHOLARSHIP
• *See page 170*

DIVERSITYCOMM, INC.

http://www.diversitycomm.net/

DIVERSITY IN STEAM MAGAZINE SCHOLARSHIP
• *See page 83*

GRAND RAPIDS COMMUNITY FOUNDATION

http://www.grfoundation.org/

HARRY J. MORRIS, JR. EMERGENCY SERVICES SCHOLARSHIP
Scholarship is for students who are residents of Kent, Allegan, Barry, Ionia, Ottawa, Montcalm, Muskegon or Newaygo Counties pursuing an undergraduate certificate or degree at an accredited education program in Michigan in the field of emergency medical technician, paramedic, or firefighter training. Must have a 2.5 cumulative GPA or verified GED Certificate and demonstrate financial need.

Academic Fields/Career Goals: Fire Sciences; Health and Medical Sciences.

Award: Scholarship for use in freshman, sophomore, junior, or senior years; not renewable. *Number:* 1–4. *Amount:* $1000–$1500.

Eligibility Requirements: Applicant must be enrolled or expecting to enroll full- or part-time at a two-year or four-year or technical institution; resident of Michigan and studying in Michigan. Applicant must have 2.5 GPA or higher. Available to U.S. citizens.

Application Requirements: Application form, essay, financial need analysis. *Deadline:* April 1.

Contact: Ms. Ruth Bishop, Education Program Officer
Grand Rapids Community Foundation
185 Oakes SW
Grand Rapids, MI 49503
Phone: 616-454-1751 Ext. 103
E-mail: rbishop@grfoundation.org

INDEPENDENT LABORATORIES INSTITUTE SCHOLARSHIP ALLIANCE

http://www.acil.org/

INDEPENDENT LABORATORIES INSTITUTE SCHOLARSHIP ALLIANCE
• *See page 171*

INTERNATIONAL ASSOCIATION OF FIRE CHIEFS FOUNDATION

http://www.iafcf.org/

INTERNATIONAL ASSOCIATION OF FIRE CHIEFS FOUNDATION SCHOLARSHIP AWARD
One-time award, open to any person who is an active member (volunteer or paid) of an emergency or fire department. Must use the scholarship funds for an accredited, recognized institution of higher education.

Academic Fields/Career Goals: Fire Sciences.

Award: Scholarship for use in freshman, sophomore, junior, senior, or graduate years; not renewable. *Number:* 20–30. *Amount:* $500–$2500.

Eligibility Requirements: Applicant must be enrolled or expecting to enroll full- or part-time at a two-year or four-year or technical institution or university. Applicant must have 2.5 GPA or higher. Available to U.S. and Canadian citizens.

Application Requirements: Application form, essay. *Deadline:* April 29.

Contact: Terry Monroe, Director, Membership and Marketing
Phone: 703-385-1610
Fax: 703-273-9363
E-mail: tmonroe@iafc.org

INTERTRIBAL TIMBER COUNCIL

http://www.itcnet.org/

TRUMAN D. PICARD SCHOLARSHIP
• *See page 341*

LEARNING FOR LIFE

http://www.learning-for-life.org/

INTERNATIONAL ASSOCIATIONS OF FIRE CHIEFS FOUNDATION SCHOLARSHIP
Applicant must be a graduating high school senior in May or June of the year the application is issued and a Fire Service Explorer. The school selected by the applicant must be an accredited public or proprietary institution.

Academic Fields/Career Goals: Fire Sciences.

Award: Scholarship for use in freshman year; not renewable. *Number:* 2. *Amount:* $500.

Eligibility Requirements: Applicant must be high school student and planning to enroll or expecting to enroll full- or part-time at a two-year or four-year institution or university. Applicant or parent of applicant must be member of Explorer Program/Learning for Life. Available to U.S. citizens.

Application Requirements: Application form, essay, personal photograph, recommendations or references, transcript. *Deadline:* July 1.

Contact: William Taylor, Scholarships and Awards Coordinator
E-mail: btaylor@lflmail.org

MARYLAND STATE HIGHER EDUCATION COMMISSION

http://www.mhec.state.md.us/

CHARLES W. RILEY FIRE AND EMERGENCY MEDICAL SERVICES TUITION REIMBURSEMENT PROGRAM
Award intended to reimburse members of rescue organizations serving Maryland communities for tuition costs of course work towards a degree

or certificate in fire service or medical technology. Must attend a two- or four-year school in Maryland. Minimum 2.0 GPA. The scholarship is worth up to $6500.

Academic Fields/Career Goals: Fire Sciences; Health and Medical Sciences; Trade/Technical Specialties.

Award: Scholarship for use in freshman, sophomore, junior, or senior years; not renewable. *Number:* 1–150. *Amount:* $1–$6500.

Eligibility Requirements: Applicant must be enrolled or expecting to enroll full- or part-time at a two-year or four-year institution or university; resident of Maryland and studying in Maryland. Applicant or parent of applicant must have employment or volunteer experience in police/firefighting. Available to U.S. citizens.

Application Requirements: Application form. *Deadline:* June 1.

Contact: Donna Thomas, Office of Student Financial Assistance
 Maryland State Higher Education Commission
 6 North Liberty Street
 Baltimore, MD 21202
 Phone: 410-767-3109
 E-mail: donnae.thomas@maryland.gov

NASA IDAHO SPACE GRANT CONSORTIUM

http://www.idahospacegrant.org

NASA IDAHO SPACE GRANT CONSORTIUM SCHOLARSHIP PROGRAM
• *See page 126*

OREGON STUDENT ASSISTANCE COMMISSION

https://oregonstudentaid.gov/

NWFEDA—NORTHWEST FIRE EQUIPMENT DEALERS ASSOCIATION SCHOLARSHIP

Award for Oregon or Washington residents enrolled at least half-time and studying fire protection/suppression, fire science, fire investigation, or emergency medical services/technology and intending on careers in emergency services. Minimum 3.0 GPA preferred.

Academic Fields/Career Goals: Fire Sciences.

Award: Scholarship for use in freshman, sophomore, junior, senior, or graduate years; not renewable.

Eligibility Requirements: Applicant must be enrolled or expecting to enroll full- or part-time at a two-year or four-year or technical institution or university; resident of Oregon, Washington and studying in Oregon, Washington. Available to U.S. citizens.

Application Requirements: Application form. *Deadline:* March 1.

Contact: Melissa Adams, Scholarship Processing Coordinator
 Phone: 541-687-7409
 E-mail: melissa.adams@state.or.us

STRAIGHTFORWARD MEDIA

http://www.straightforwardmedia.com/

STRAIGHTFORWARD MEDIA VOCATIONAL-TECHNICAL SCHOOL SCHOLARSHIP
• *See page 118*

FLEXOGRAPHY

FOUNDATION OF FLEXOGRAPHIC TECHNICAL ASSOCIATION

http://www.flexography.org/

FOUNDATION OF FLEXOGRAPHIC TECHNICAL ASSOCIATION SCHOLARSHIP COMPETITION

Awards students enrolled in a FFTA Flexo in Education Program with plans to attend a postsecondary institution, or be currently enrolled in a postsecondary institution offering a course of study in flexography. Must demonstrate an interest in a career in flexography, and maintain an overall GPA of at least 3.0. Must reapply.

Academic Fields/Career Goals: Flexography.

Award: Scholarship for use in freshman, sophomore, junior, or senior years; not renewable. *Number:* 6–8. *Amount:* up to $3000.

Eligibility Requirements: Applicant must be enrolled or expecting to enroll full-time at a two-year or four-year or technical institution or university. Applicant must have 3.0 GPA or higher. Available to U.S. and Canadian citizens.

Application Requirements: Application form, application form may be submitted online (http://www.flexography.org), essay, recommendations or references, transcript. *Deadline:* March 15.

Contact: Shelley Rubin, Manager of Educational Programs
 Foundation of Flexographic Technical Association
 3920 Veterans Memorial Highway, Suite 9
 Bohemia, NY 11716
 Phone: 631-737-6020 Ext. 36
 Fax: 631-737-6813

PRINTING INDUSTRY MIDWEST EDUCATION FOUDNATION

http://www.pimw.org/scholarships

PRINTING INDUSTRY MIDWEST EDUCATION FOUNDATION SCHOLARSHIP FUND
• *See page 222*

STRAIGHT NORTH

https://www.straightnorth.com/

STRAIGHT NORTH STEM SCHOLARSHIP
• *See page 92*

TAG AND LABEL MANUFACTURERS INSTITUTE, INC.

http://www.tlmi.com/

TLMI 2 YEAR COLLEGE DEGREE SCHOLARSHIP PROGRAM

Scholarship program for students enrolled at a two-year college or in a degree technical program whose major course work includes courses appropriate for future work in the tag and label manufacturing industry. Must submit statements including personal information, financial circumstances, career and/or educational goals, employment experience, and reasons applicant should be selected for this award.

Academic Fields/Career Goals: Flexography.

Award: Scholarship for use in sophomore year; not renewable. *Number:* 1–4. *Amount:* $500–$1000.

Eligibility Requirements: Applicant must be enrolled or expecting to enroll full-time at a two-year or technical institution. Applicant must have 3.0 GPA or higher. Available to U.S. and Canadian citizens.

Application Requirements: Application form, essay, portfolio. *Deadline:* March 31.

Contact: Scholarship Committee
Tag and Label Manufacturers Institute, Inc.
510 King Street
Suite 410
Alexandria, VA 22314
Phone: 703-645-5086
E-mail: office@tlmi.com

TLMI 4 YEAR COLLEGE DEGREE SCHOLARSHIP PROGRAM
• *See page 307*

FOOD SCIENCE/ NUTRITION

101ST AIRBORNE DIVISION ASSOCIATION

http://www.screamingeaglefoundation.org/

AL & WILLIAMARY VISTE SCHOLARSHIP
• *See page 114*

AACC INTERNATIONAL

http://www.aaccnet.org/

UNDERGRADUATE SCHOLARSHIP AWARD

The purposes of the undergraduate scholarship program are to encourage scholastically outstanding advanced undergraduate students in academic preparation for a career in grain-based food science and technology, and to attract and encourage outstanding students to enter the field of grain-based food science and technology.

Academic Fields/Career Goals: Food Science/Nutrition.

Award: Scholarship for use in freshman, sophomore, junior, or senior years; not renewable. *Number:* 1. *Amount:* $825.

Eligibility Requirements: Applicant must be enrolled or expecting to enroll full-time at an institution or university. Applicant must have 3.0 GPA or higher. Available to U.S. and non-U.S. citizens.

Application Requirements: Application form, essay. *Deadline:* March 3.

Contact: Lauren McGinty, Membership Experience Manager
AACC International
3340 Pilot Knob Road
St. Paul, MN 55121
Phone: 651-454-7250
E-mail: lmcginty@scisoc.org

ACADEMY OF NUTRITION AND DIETETICS

http://www.eatright.org/

ACADEMY OF NUTRITION AND DIETETICS FOUNDATION SCHOLARSHIP PROGRAM

Academy of Nutrition and Dietetics Foundation scholarships are available for undergraduate and graduate students enrolled in programs, including dietetic internships, preparing for entry to dietetics practice as well as dietetics professionals engaged in continuing education at the graduate level. Scholarship funds are provided by many state dietetic associations, dietetic practice groups, past AND leaders and corporate donors. Scholarships require Academy of Nutrition and Dietetics membership. Details available on website: http://eatrightfoundation.org/scholarships-funding/#Scholarships

Academic Fields/Career Goals: Food Science/Nutrition.

Award: Scholarship for use in sophomore, junior, senior, or graduate years; not renewable. *Number:* 200–250. *Amount:* $500–$10,000.

Eligibility Requirements: Applicant must be enrolled or expecting to enroll full- or part-time at a two-year or four-year institution or university. Applicant or parent of applicant must be member of American Dietetic Association. Available to U.S. citizens.

Application Requirements: Application form, essay, financial need analysis. *Deadline:* April 23.

Contact: Laura Nitowski, Foundation Program Coordinator
E-mail: scholarship@eatright.org

AMERICAN INDIAN SCIENCE AND ENGINEERING SOCIETY

http://www.aises.org/

A.T. ANDERSON MEMORIAL SCHOLARSHIP PROGRAM
• *See page 121*

AMERICAN INSTITUTE OF WINE AND FOOD-PACIFIC NORTHWEST CHAPTER

http://www.aiwf.org/

CULINARY, VINIFERA, AND HOSPITALITY SCHOLARSHIP

One-time award available to residents of Washington State. Must be enrolled full-time in an accredited culinary, vinifera, or hospitality program in Washington State. Must have completed two years. Minimum 3.0 GPA required.

Academic Fields/Career Goals: Food Science/Nutrition; Food Service/Hospitality; Hospitality Management.

Award: Scholarship for use in junior or senior years; not renewable. *Number:* 4. *Amount:* $1500.

Eligibility Requirements: Applicant must be enrolled or expecting to enroll full-time at a two-year or four-year or technical institution or university; resident of Washington and studying in Washington. Applicant must have 3.0 GPA or higher. Available to U.S. and non-U.S. citizens.

Application Requirements: Application form, recommendations or references, resume. *Deadline:* continuous.

Contact: Brad Sturman, Scholarship Coordinator
American Institute of Wine and Food-Pacific Northwest Chapter
224 18th Avenue
Kirkland, WA 98033
Phone: 206-679-6228

AMERICAN LEGION DEPARTMENT OF NORTH DAKOTA

http://www.ndlegion.org/

O. NESHEIM MEMORIAL SCHOLARSHIP
• *See page 254*

AMERICAN OIL CHEMISTS' SOCIETY

http://www.aocs.org/

AOCS ANALYTICAL DIVISION STUDENT AWARD
• *See page 190*

AOCS BIOTECHNOLOGY STUDENT EXCELLENCE AWARD
• *See page 105*

AOCS HEALTH AND NUTRITION DIVISION STUDENT EXCELLENCE AWARD

$500 award and certificate to recognize the outstanding merit and performance of a student in the health and nutrition field. Student will present a paper at the Annual Meeting of the Society.

Academic Fields/Career Goals: Food Science/Nutrition.

Award: Prize for use in senior or graduate years; not renewable. *Number:* 1. *Amount:* $500.

Eligibility Requirements: Applicant must be enrolled or expecting to enroll full-time at a four-year institution or university. Available to U.S. and non-U.S. citizens.

Application Requirements: Abstract, application form, essay, recommendations or references. *Deadline:* October 15.

Contact: Barbara Semeraro, Area Manager, Membership
American Oil Chemists' Society
AOCS
PO Box 17190
Urbana, IL 61803
Phone: 217-693-4804
Fax: 217-693-4849
E-mail: awards@aocs.org

AOCS PROCESSING DIVISION AWARDS
• *See page 190*

AMERICAN SOCIETY FOR ENOLOGY AND VITICULTURE
http://www.asev.org/

AMERICAN SOCIETY FOR ENOLOGY AND VITICULTURE SCHOLARSHIPS
• *See page 105*

AVACARE MEDICAL
https://avacaremedical.com

AVACARE MEDICAL SCHOLARSHIP
• *See page 115*

BHW GROUP
https://thebhwgroup.com/

BHW WOMEN IN STEM SCHOLARSHIP
• *See page 124*

CANFIT
http://www.canfit.org/

CANFIT NUTRITION, PHYSICAL EDUCATION AND CULINARY ARTS SCHOLARSHIP
• *See page 245*

CONTINENTAL SOCIETY, DAUGHTERS OF INDIAN WARS
http://www.csdiw.org/

CONTINENTAL SOCIETY, DAUGHTERS OF INDIAN WARS SCHOLARSHIP
• *See page 242*

THE CULINARY TRUST
http://www.theculinarytrust.org/

CULINARY TRUST SCHOLARSHIP PROGRAM FOR CULINARY STUDY AND RESEARCH
• *See page 246*

DIVERSITYCOMM, INC.
http://www.diversitycomm.net/

DIVERSITY IN STEAM MAGAZINE SCHOLARSHIP
• *See page 83*

GREAT MINDS IN STEM
http://www.greatmindsinstem.org

HENAAC SCHOLARSHIP PROGRAM
• *See page 115*

ILLINOIS RESTAURANT ASSOCIATION EDUCATIONAL FOUNDATION
http://www.illinoisrestaurants.org/

ILLINOIS RESTAURANT ASSOCIATION EDUCATIONAL FOUNDATION SCHOLARSHIPS
• *See page 246*

INSTITUTE OF FOOD TECHNOLOGISTS
http://www.ift.org/

ARTHUR SCHRAMM SCHOLARSHIP
One award for an undergraduate student enrolled as a rising sophomore, junior, or senior pursuing an undergraduate degree in food science. Minimum 3.0 GPA required. Applicant must be a student member of IFT at the time of application.

Academic Fields/Career Goals: Food Science/Nutrition.

Award: Scholarship for use in sophomore, junior, or senior years; not renewable. *Number:* 1.

Eligibility Requirements: Applicant must be enrolled or expecting to enroll full-time at a four-year institution or university. Applicant must have 3.0 GPA or higher. Available to U.S. and non-U.S. citizens.

Application Requirements: Application form. *Deadline:* February 15.

Contact: IFT Foundation Coordinator
Institute of Food Technologists
525 West Van Buren, Suite 1000
Chicago, IL 60607
Phone: 312-782-8424
E-mail: info@ift.org

BARBARA B. KEENAN SCHOLARSHIP
One award for an undergraduate student enrolled as a rising sophomore, junior, or senior pursuing an undergraduate degree in food science. Minimum 3.0 GPA required. Applicant must be a student member of IFT at the time of application.

Academic Fields/Career Goals: Food Science/Nutrition.

Award: Scholarship for use in sophomore, junior, or senior years; not renewable. *Number:* 1.

Eligibility Requirements: Applicant must be enrolled or expecting to enroll full-time at a four-year institution or university. Applicant must have 3.0 GPA or higher. Available to U.S. and non-U.S. citizens.

Application Requirements: Application form. *Deadline:* February 15.

Contact: IFT Foundation Coordinator
Institute of Food Technologists
525 West Van Buren, Suite 1000
Chicago, IL 60607
Phone: 312-782-8424
E-mail: info@ift.org

DR. ANN C. HOLLINGSWORTH STUDENT LEADERSHIP SCHOLARSHIP
One award for an undergraduate student enrolled as a rising sophomore, junior, or senior pursuing an undergraduate degree in food science. Minimum 3.0 GPA required. Applicant must be a student member of IFT at the time of application.

Academic Fields/Career Goals: Food Science/Nutrition.

Award: Scholarship for use in sophomore, junior, or senior years; not renewable. *Number:* 1.

Eligibility Requirements: Applicant must be enrolled or expecting to enroll full-time at a four-year institution or university. Applicant must have 3.0 GPA or higher. Available to U.S. and non-U.S. citizens.

Application Requirements: Application form. *Deadline:* February 15.

Contact: IFT Foundation Coordinator
Institute of Food Technologists
525 West Van Buren, Suite 1000
Chicago, IL 60607
Phone: 312-782-8424
E-mail: info@ift.org

EDLONG DAIRY TECHNOLOGIES SCHOLARSHIP

One $2,000 scholarship to a graduate student and one $1,000 scholarship to a junior/senior undergraduate student. The student must be enrolled in a Master's or Ph.D. food science program with a focus in dairy science and/or dairy flavors or pursuing an undergraduate degree in food science with a focus in dairy flavors and/or dairy science at an IFT approved university. Minimum 3.0 GPA required.

Academic Fields/Career Goals: Food Science/Nutrition.

Award: Scholarship for use in junior, senior, graduate, or postgraduate years; not renewable. *Number:* 1. *Amount:* $1000.

Eligibility Requirements: Applicant must be enrolled or expecting to enroll full-time at a four-year institution or university. Applicant must have 3.0 GPA or higher. Available to U.S. and non-U.S. citizens.

Application Requirements: Application form. *Deadline:* February 15.

Contact: IFT Foundation Coordinator
Institute of Food Technologists
525 West Van Buren, Suite 1000
Chicago, IL 60607
Phone: 312-782-8424
E-mail: info@ift.org

EVAN TUREK MEMORIAL SCHOLARSHIP AND INTERNSHIP

• *See page 107*

IFT FOOD ENGINEERING DIVISION SCHOLARSHIP

Available to an undergraduate student who will pursue a research project focusing on any aspect of food process engineering. The research will occur during the academic year or summer. Applicant must be a student member of IFT at the time of application. Will submit a recommendation letter from a research mentor who is a member of the Food Engineering Division of IFT stating that the mentor will supervise the student to do research in their lab.

Academic Fields/Career Goals: Food Science/Nutrition.

Award: Scholarship for use in sophomore, junior, or senior years; not renewable. *Number:* 1. *Amount:* $1000.

Eligibility Requirements: Applicant must be enrolled or expecting to enroll full-time at a four-year institution or university. Applicant must have 3.0 GPA or higher. Available to U.S. and non-U.S. citizens.

Application Requirements: Application form. *Deadline:* February 15.

Contact: IFT Foundation Coordinator
Institute of Food Technologists
525 West Van Buren, Suite 1000
Chicago, IL 60607
Phone: 312-782-8424
E-mail: info@ift.org

IFT FOOD MICROBIOLOGY DIVISION UNDERGRADUATE SCHOLARSHIP

$1000 scholarship available to an undergraduate student studying food microbiology. Minimum 3.0 GPA required. Applicant must be a student member of IFT at the time of application.

Academic Fields/Career Goals: Food Science/Nutrition.

Award: Scholarship for use in sophomore, junior, or senior years; not renewable. *Number:* 1. *Amount:* $1000.

Eligibility Requirements: Applicant must be enrolled or expecting to enroll full-time at a four-year institution or university. Applicant must have 3.0 GPA or higher. Available to U.S. and non-U.S. citizens.

Application Requirements: Application form. *Deadline:* February 15.

Contact: IFT Foundation Coordinator
Institute of Food Technologists
525 West Van Buren, Suite 1000
Chicago, IL 60607
Phone: 312-782-8424
E-mail: info@ift.org

INSTITUTE FOR THERMAL PROCESSING SPECIALISTS IRVING PFLUG MEMORIAL SCHOLARSHIP

One $1500 scholarship for an undergraduate student studying food science, food engineering, or food microbiology as it relates to food preservation. Minimum 3.0 GPA required. Must reapply each year. Applicant must be a student member of IFT at the time of application.

Academic Fields/Career Goals: Food Science/Nutrition.

Award: Scholarship for use in sophomore, junior, or senior years; not renewable. *Number:* 1. *Amount:* $1500.

Eligibility Requirements: Applicant must be enrolled or expecting to enroll full-time at a four-year institution or university. Applicant must have 3.0 GPA or higher. Available to U.S. and non-U.S. citizens.

Application Requirements: Application form. *Deadline:* February 15.

Contact: IFT Foundation Coordinator
Institute of Food Technologists
525 West Van Buren, Suite 1000
Chicago, IL 60607
Phone: 312-782-8424
E-mail: info@ift.org

JOHN POWERS SCHOLARSHIP

One award for an undergraduate student enrolled as a rising sophomore, junior, or senior pursuing an undergraduate degree in food science. Minimum 3.0 GPA required. Applicant must be a student member of IFT at the time of application.

Academic Fields/Career Goals: Food Science/Nutrition.

Award: Scholarship for use in sophomore, junior, or senior years; not renewable. *Number:* 1.

Eligibility Requirements: Applicant must be enrolled or expecting to enroll full-time at a four-year institution or university. Applicant must have 3.0 GPA or higher. Available to U.S. and non-U.S. citizens.

Application Requirements: Application form. *Deadline:* February 15.

Contact: IFT Foundation Coordinator
Institute of Food Technologists
525 West Van Buren, Suite 1000
Chicago, IL 60607
Phone: 312-782-8424
E-mail: info@ift.org

PEPSICO SCHOLARSHIP AND INTERNSHIP

One scholarship and internship at PepsiCo. Applicant must be enrolled in an IFT approved undergraduate or graduate program at the standing of junior or above, majoring in biochemistry, dairy science, food chemistry, food packaging, non-thermal processing or related discipline. Applicant must demonstrate exceptional leadership experience and be an IFT member at the time of application. Must have 3.0 cumulative GPA in food science.

Academic Fields/Career Goals: Food Science/Nutrition; Physical Sciences.

Award: Scholarship for use in junior, senior, or graduate years; not renewable. *Number:* 1. *Amount:* $1000.

Eligibility Requirements: Applicant must be enrolled or expecting to enroll full-time at a four-year institution or university. Applicant must have 3.0 GPA or higher. Available to U.S. citizens.

Application Requirements: Application form, interview. *Deadline:* September 30.

Contact: IFT Foundation Coordinator
Institute of Food Technologists
525 West Van Buren, Suite 1000
Chicago, IL 60607
Phone: 312-782-8424
E-mail: info@ift.org

INTERNATIONAL FOODSERVICE EDITORIAL COUNCIL

http://www.ifeconline.com/

INTERNATIONAL FOODSERVICE EDITORIAL COUNCIL COMMUNICATIONS SCHOLARSHIP

• *See page 96*

JAMES BEARD FOUNDATION INC.

http://www.jamesbeard.org/

BERN LAXER MEMORIAL SCHOLARSHIP
• See page 247

LABROOTS INC.

http://www.LabRoots.com

LABROOTS STEM SCHOLARSHIP
• See page 116

LAW OFFICES OF PROSPER SHAKED

https://www.prosperlaw.com/

PROSPER SHAKED SCHOLARSHIP FOR FUTURE MEDICAL PROFESSIONALS
• See page 166

LES DAMES D'ESCOFFIER INTERNATIONAL, COLORADO CHAPTER

http://www.lesdamescolorado.org

LES DAMES D'ESCOFFIER INTERNATIONAL, COLORADO CHAPTER SCHOLARSHIP
• See page 107

MARYLAND RESTAURANT ASSOCIATION EDUCATION FOUNDATION

https://www.marylandrestaurants.com/about.html

THE LETITIA B. CARTER SCHOLARSHIP
• See page 249

MARCIA S. HARRIS LEGACY FUND SCHOLARSHIP
• See page 249

MEDICAL SCRUBS COLLECTION

http://medicalscrubscollection.com

MEDICAL SCRUBS COLLECTION SCHOLARSHIP
• See page 120

MICHAEL MOODY FITNESS

http://www.michaelmoodyfitness.com/

MICHAEL MOODY FITNESS SCHOLARSHIP
• See page 166

NATIONAL DAIRY SHRINE

http://www.dairyshrine.org/

NATIONAL DAIRY SHRINE/DAIRY MARKETING INC. MILK MARKETING SCHOLARSHIPS
• See page 108

NDS STUDENT RECOGNITION AWARD
• See page 102

NATIONAL POULTRY AND FOOD DISTRIBUTORS ASSOCIATION

http://www.npfda.org/

NATIONAL POULTRY AND FOOD DISTRIBUTORS ASSOCIATION SCHOLARSHIP FOUNDATION
• See page 102

NATIONAL RESTAURANT ASSOCIATION EDUCATIONAL FOUNDATION

http://www.chooserestaurants.org

NATIONAL RESTAURANT ASSOCIATION EDUCATIONAL FOUNDATION UNDERGRADUATE SCHOLARSHIPS FOR COLLEGE STUDENTS
• See page 109

NEXTSTEPU

http://www.nextstepu.com/

$1,500 STEM SCHOLARSHIP
• See page 120

OREGON STUDENT ASSISTANCE COMMISSION

https://oregonstudentaid.gov/

OREGON WINE BROTHERHOOD SCHOLARSHIP
• See page 249

PROFESSIONAL REPS

http://www.professionalreps.com/

HUNGRY TO LEAD SCHOLARSHIP
• See page 249

SCARLETT FAMILY FOUNDATION SCHOLARSHIP PROGRAM

http://www.scarlettfoundation.org/

SCHOLARSHIP FOR STUDENTS PURSUING A BUSINESS OR STEM DEGREE
• See page 91

SCHOOL NUTRITION FOUNDATION

https://schoolnutrition.org/snf/

NANCY CURRY SCHOLARSHIP

Scholarship assists members of the American School Food Service Association and their dependents to pursue educational and career advancement in school food-service or child nutrition.

Academic Fields/Career Goals: Food Science/Nutrition; Food Service/Hospitality.

Award: Scholarship for use in freshman, sophomore, junior, senior, graduate, or postgraduate years; not renewable.

Eligibility Requirements: Applicant must be enrolled or expecting to enroll full- or part-time at a two-year or four-year or technical institution or university. Applicant or parent of applicant must have employment or volunteer experience in food service. Applicant must have 3.0 GPA or higher. Available to U.S. citizens.

Application Requirements: Application form, essay, proof of enrollment, recommendations or references, resume, test scores, transcript. *Deadline:* April 15.

Contact: Ruth O'Brien, Scholarship Manager
School Nutrition Foundation
700 South Washington Street, Suite 300
Alexandria, VA 22314
Phone: 703-739-3900 Ext. 150
E-mail: robrien@asfsa.org

PROFESSIONAL GROWTH SCHOLARSHIP

Scholarships for child nutrition professionals who are pursuing graduate education in a food science management or nutrition-related field of study.

Academic Fields/Career Goals: Food Science/Nutrition; Food Service/Hospitality.

Award: Scholarship for use in freshman, sophomore, junior, senior, graduate, or postgraduate years; not renewable.

Eligibility Requirements: Applicant must be enrolled or expecting to enroll full- or part-time at a two-year or four-year or technical institution or university. Applicant or parent of applicant must have employment or volunteer experience in food service. Applicant must have 3.5 GPA or higher. Available to U.S. citizens.

Application Requirements: Application form, essay, proof of enrollment, official program requirement, recommendations or references, resume, transcript. *Deadline:* April 15.

Contact: Scholarship Manager
School Nutrition Foundation
700 South Washington Street, Suite 300
Alexandria, VA 22314
Phone: 703-739-3900 Ext. 150
Fax: 703-739-3915
E-mail: robrien@asfsa.org

SCHWAN'S FOOD SERVICE SCHOLARSHIP

Program is designed to assist members of the American School Food Service Association and their dependents as they pursue educational advancement in the field of child nutrition.

Academic Fields/Career Goals: Food Science/Nutrition; Food Service/Hospitality.

Award: Scholarship for use in freshman, sophomore, junior, senior, graduate, or postgraduate years; not renewable.

Eligibility Requirements: Applicant must be enrolled or expecting to enroll full- or part-time at a two-year or four-year or technical institution or university. Applicant or parent of applicant must have employment or volunteer experience in food service. Applicant must have 2.5 GPA or higher. Available to U.S. citizens.

Application Requirements: Application form, essay, proof of enrollment, official program requirements, recommendations or references, resume, transcript. *Deadline:* April 15.

Contact: Ruth O'Brien, Scholarship Manager
School Nutrition Foundation
700 South Washington Street, Suite 300
Alexandria, VA 22314
Phone: 703-739-3900 Ext. 150
E-mail: robrien@asfsa.org

SOIL AND WATER CONSERVATION SOCIETY

http://www.swcs.org

DONALD A. WILLIAMS SCHOLARSHIP SOIL CONSERVATION SCHOLARSHIP

• *See page 103*

TOURISM CARES

http://www.tourismcares.org

IATAN RONALD A. SANTANA MEMORIAL SCHOLARSHIP

Scholarship available to a full time or part time student enrolled in the second half of their college career in a travel and tourism or hospitality related program of study at a college or university in the US. Available to citizens or permanent residents from US, Guam or Puerto Rico.

Academic Fields/Career Goals: Food Science/Nutrition; Hospitality Management; Travel/Tourism.

Award: Scholarship for use in sophomore, junior, or senior years; not renewable. *Number:* 6. *Amount:* $2000.

Eligibility Requirements: Applicant must be enrolled or expecting to enroll full- or part-time at a two-year or four-year institution or university. Applicant must have 3.0 GPA or higher. Available to U.S. citizens.

Application Requirements: Application form, essay. *Deadline:* April 1.

Contact: Trish Kelly, Workforce Development Coordinator
Phone: 781-821-5990 Ext. 214
E-mail: scholarships@tourismcares.org

UNITED DAUGHTERS OF THE CONFEDERACY

http://www.hqudc.org/

WALTER REED SMITH SCHOLARSHIP

• *See page 184*

UNITED STATES DEPARTMENT OF AGRICULTURE

http://www.usda.gov/

USDA/1994 TRIBAL SCHOLARS PROGRAM

• *See page 111*

WASHINGTON WINE INDUSTRY FOUNDATION

http://washingtonwinefoundation.org/

WALTER J. CLORE SCHOLARSHIP

• *See page 112*

WHAT DETOX

http://whatdetox.com/meet-the-team/

WHAT DETOX SCHOLARSHIP

The principal aim of this scholarship program is to offer financial support to current undergraduate and graduate students and to encourage serious and deserving students to continue their studies in marketing or nutrition.

Academic Fields/Career Goals: Food Science/Nutrition; Marketing.

Award: Scholarship for use in freshman, sophomore, junior, senior, graduate, or postgraduate years; not renewable. *Number:* 1. *Amount:* $1000.

Eligibility Requirements: Applicant must be enrolled or expecting to enroll full-time at a four-year institution or university. Available to U.S. and non-U.S. citizens.

Application Requirements: Essay. *Deadline:* January 31.

Contact: Christina Johnson, CEO
E-mail: christine@whatdetox.com

WISCONSIN ASSOCIATION FOR FOOD PROTECTION

http://www.wifoodprotection.org

E.H. MARTH FOOD PROTECTION AND FOOD SCIENCES SCHOLARSHIP

• *See page 336*

WISCONSIN BAKERS ASSOCIATION (WBA)

http://www.wibakers.com/

ROBERT W. HILLER SCHOLARSHIP FUND

• *See page 250*

WBA SCHOLARSHIP
• See page 250

FOOD SERVICE/ HOSPITALITY

AMERICAN HOTEL AND LODGING EDUCATIONAL FOUNDATION

http://www.ahlef.org/

AHLEF ANNUAL SCHOLARSHIP GRANT PROGRAM
• See page 244

AMERICAN HOTEL & LODGING EDUCATIONAL FOUNDATION PEPSI SCHOLARSHIP
• See page 244

ECOLAB SCHOLARSHIP PROGRAM
• See page 245

HYATT HOTELS FUND FOR MINORITY LODGING MANAGEMENT
• See page 245

INCOMING FRESHMAN SCHOLARSHIPS
• See page 245

RAMA SCHOLARSHIP FOR THE AMERICAN DREAM
• See page 245

AMERICAN INSTITUTE OF WINE AND FOOD-PACIFIC NORTHWEST CHAPTER

http://www.aiwf.org/

CULINARY, VINIFERA, AND HOSPITALITY SCHOLARSHIP
• See page 351

CALIFORNIA RESTAURANT ASSOCIATION EDUCATIONAL FOUNDATION

http://www.calrest.org/

ACADEMIC SCHOLARSHIP FOR HIGH SCHOOL SENIORS

One-time scholarship awarded to high school seniors to support their education in the restaurant and/or food service industry. Applicants must be citizens of the United States or its territories (American Samoa, Guam, Puerto Rico, and U.S. Virgin Islands).

Academic Fields/Career Goals: Food Service/Hospitality.

Award: Scholarship for use in freshman year; not renewable. *Amount:* up to $2000.

Eligibility Requirements: Applicant must be high school student; planning to enroll or expecting to enroll full-time at a two-year or four-year or technical institution or university and resident of California. Applicant must have 2.5 GPA or higher. Available to U.S. and non-U.S. citizens.

Application Requirements: Application form, essay, interview, recommendations or references, resume, transcript. *Deadline:* April 15.

Contact: Mrs. Kathie Griley, Director, Industry Education
  Phone: 800-765-4842 Ext. 2756
  E-mail: kgriley@calrest.org

ACADEMIC SCHOLARSHIP FOR UNDERGRADUATE STUDENTS

Scholarships awarded to college students to support their education in the restaurant and food service industry. Minimum 2.75 GPA required. Individuals must be citizens of the United States or its territories (American Samoa, Guam, Puerto Rico, and U.S. Virgin Islands).

Academic Fields/Career Goals: Food Service/Hospitality.

Award: Scholarship for use in freshman, sophomore, junior, or senior years; not renewable.

Eligibility Requirements: Applicant must be enrolled or expecting to enroll full-time at a four-year institution or university and resident of California. Applicant must have 2.5 GPA or higher. Available to U.S. and non-U.S. citizens.

Application Requirements: Application form, essay, interview, recommendations or references, transcript. *Deadline:* March 31.

Contact: Mrs. Kathie Griley, Director, Industry Education
  Phone: 800-765-4842 Ext. 2756
  E-mail: kgriley@calrest.org

CANFIT

http://www.canfit.org/

CANFIT NUTRITION, PHYSICAL EDUCATION AND CULINARY ARTS SCHOLARSHIP
• See page 245

COLORADO RESTAURANT ASSOCIATION

http://www.coloradorestaurant.com/

CRA UNDERGRADUATE SCHOLARSHIPS

Scholarship of $1000 to $2000 for applicants intending to pursue education in the undergraduate level in the field of food service or hospitality and have a GPA of at least 2.75.

Academic Fields/Career Goals: Food Service/Hospitality.

Award: Scholarship for use in freshman, sophomore, junior, or senior years; not renewable. *Number:* 15. *Amount:* $1000–$2000.

Eligibility Requirements: Applicant must be enrolled or expecting to enroll full- or part-time at a four-year institution or university. Available to U.S. and non-U.S. citizens.

Application Requirements: Application form, recommendations or references, resume, transcript. *Deadline:* April 6.

Contact: Mary Mino, President
  Phone: 800-522-2972
  Fax: 303-830-2973
  E-mail: info@coloradorestaurant.com

PROSTART SCHOLARSHIPS

Scholarship of $500 to $1000 for applicants currently in high school and intending to pursue education in the field of food service or hospitality and have a GPA of at least 3.0.

Academic Fields/Career Goals: Food Service/Hospitality.

Award: Scholarship for use in freshman year; not renewable. *Number:* 15. *Amount:* $500–$1000.

Eligibility Requirements: Applicant must be high school student and planning to enroll or expecting to enroll full- or part-time at a four-year institution or university. Applicant must have 3.0 GPA or higher. Available to U.S. and non-U.S. citizens.

Application Requirements: Application form, recommendations or references, resume, transcript. *Deadline:* April 6.

Contact: Mary Mino, President
  Phone: 800-522-2972
  Fax: 303-830-2973
  E-mail: info@coloradorestaurant.com

THE CULINARY TRUST

http://www.theculinarytrust.org/

CULINARY TRUST SCHOLARSHIP PROGRAM FOR CULINARY STUDY AND RESEARCH
• See page 246

DECA (DISTRIBUTIVE EDUCATION CLUBS OF AMERICA)

http://www.deca.org/

HARRY A. APPLEGATE SCHOLARSHIP
• *See page 83*

ILLINOIS RESTAURANT ASSOCIATION EDUCATIONAL FOUNDATION

http://www.illinoisrestaurants.org/

ILLINOIS RESTAURANT ASSOCIATION EDUCATIONAL FOUNDATION SCHOLARSHIPS
• *See page 246*

INTERNATIONAL FOODSERVICE EDITORIAL COUNCIL

http://www.ifeconline.com/

INTERNATIONAL FOODSERVICE EDITORIAL COUNCIL COMMUNICATIONS SCHOLARSHIP
• *See page 96*

INTERNATIONAL FOOD SERVICE EXECUTIVES ASSOCIATION

http://www.ifsea.com/

INTERNATIONAL FOOD SERVICE EXECUTIVES ASSOCIATION / WORTHY GOAL SCHOLARSHIP FUND
Scholarships to assist individuals in receiving food service, vocational or hospitality training beyond high school. Applicant must be enrolled or accepted as full-time student in an accredited program at an institution of higher education.

Academic Fields/Career Goals: Food Service/Hospitality.

Award: Scholarship for use in freshman, sophomore, junior, senior, graduate, or postgraduate years; not renewable. *Number:* 1–23,000. *Amount:* $1000–$2000.

Eligibility Requirements: Applicant must be enrolled or expecting to enroll full-time at a two-year or four-year or technical institution or university. Available to U.S. and non-U.S. citizens.

Application Requirements: Application form, essay, financial need analysis, financial statement summary, work experience documentation, recommendations or references, transcript. *Deadline:* March 1.

Contact: David Orosz, Chairman, Board of Trustees, Worthy Goal Foundation
International Food Service Executives Association
4435 Colchester Creek Drive
Cumming, GA 30040
Phone: 952-402-9686
Fax: 317-863-0586
E-mail: dave@orosz.us

LES DAMES D'ESCOFFIER INTERNATIONAL, COLORADO CHAPTER

http://www.lesdamescolorado.org

LES DAMES D'ESCOFFIER INTERNATIONAL, COLORADO CHAPTER SCHOLARSHIP
• *See page 107*

MARYLAND RESTAURANT ASSOCIATION EDUCATION FOUNDATION

https://www.marylandrestaurants.com/about.html

THE LETITIA B. CARTER SCHOLARSHIP
• *See page 249*

MARCIA S. HARRIS LEGACY FUND SCHOLARSHIP
• *See page 249*

MICHAEL MOODY FITNESS

http://www.michaelmoodyfitness.com/

MICHAEL MOODY FITNESS SCHOLARSHIP
• *See page 166*

MISSOURI TRAVEL COUNCIL

http://www.missouritravel.com/

BOB SMITH TOURISM SCHOLARSHIP
One-time award for Missouri resident pursuing hospitality-related major such as hotel/restaurant management or tourism. Applicant must be currently enrolled in an accredited four-year college or university in the state of Missouri. Selection is based on responses to set-forth scholarship criteria.

Academic Fields/Career Goals: Food Service/Hospitality; Hospitality Management; Travel/Tourism.

Award: Scholarship for use in sophomore, junior, or senior years; not renewable. *Number:* 2. *Amount:* $1000.

Eligibility Requirements: Applicant must be enrolled or expecting to enroll full-time at a four-year institution or university; resident of Missouri and studying in Missouri. Applicant must have 3.0 GPA or higher. Available to U.S. citizens.

Application Requirements: Application form, essay. *Deadline:* March 1.

Contact: Mr. Chuck Martin, Executive Director
Missouri Travel Council
1505 East Riverside Drive
Cape Girardeau, MO 63701-2219
Phone: 573-803-3777
E-mail: CMartin@MissouriTravel.com

NATIONAL POULTRY AND FOOD DISTRIBUTORS ASSOCIATION

http://www.npfda.org/

NATIONAL POULTRY AND FOOD DISTRIBUTORS ASSOCIATION SCHOLARSHIP FOUNDATION
• *See page 102*

NATIONAL RESTAURANT ASSOCIATION EDUCATIONAL FOUNDATION

http://www.chooserestaurants.org

NATIONAL RESTAURANT ASSOCIATION EDUCATIONAL FOUNDATION UNDERGRADUATE SCHOLARSHIPS FOR COLLEGE STUDENTS
• *See page 109*

PROFESSIONAL REPS

http://www.professionalreps.com/

HUNGRY TO LEAD SCHOLARSHIP
• *See page 249*

SCHOOL NUTRITION FOUNDATION

https://schoolnutrition.org/snf/

NANCY CURRY SCHOLARSHIP
• See page 354

PROFESSIONAL GROWTH SCHOLARSHIP
• See page 355

SCHWAN'S FOOD SERVICE SCHOLARSHIP
• See page 355

SOUTH CAROLINA RESTAURANT AND LODGING ASSOCIATION

http://www.scrla.org/

SOUTH CAROLINA TOURISM AND HOSPITALITY EDUCATIONAL FOUNDATION SCHOLARSHIPS
• See page 250

TEXAS RESTAURANT ASSOCIATION

http://www.restaurantville.com/

W. PRICE, JR. MEMORIAL SCHOLARSHIP
• See page 250

TOURISM CARES

http://www.tourismcares.org

ASTA PRINCESS CRUISES SCHOLARSHIP

Scholarship available to a full time or part time student enrolled in the second half of their college career in a travel and tourism or hospitality related program of study at a college or university in the US or Canada. Additional two page essay required.

Academic Fields/Career Goals: Food Service/Hospitality; Hospitality Management; Travel/Tourism.

Award: Scholarship for use in sophomore, junior, or senior years; not renewable. *Number:* 1. *Amount:* $2500.

Eligibility Requirements: Applicant must be enrolled or expecting to enroll full- or part-time at a two-year or four-year institution or university. Applicant must have 3.0 GPA or higher. Available to U.S. and Canadian citizens.

Application Requirements: Application form, essay. *Deadline:* April 1.

Contact: Trish Kelly, Workforce Development Coordinator
Phone: 781-821-5990 Ext. 214
E-mail: scholarships@tourismcares.org

NTA LA MACCHIA FAMILY SCHOLARSHIP

Scholarship available to a full time student enrolled in the second half of their college career in a travel and tourism or hospitality related program of study at a college or university in Wisconsin, US or a permanent resident of Wisconsin, US.

Academic Fields/Career Goals: Food Service/Hospitality; Hospitality Management; Travel/Tourism.

Award: Scholarship for use in junior or senior years; not renewable. *Amount:* $2000.

Eligibility Requirements: Applicant must be enrolled or expecting to enroll full-time at a four-year institution or university and resident of Wisconsin. Applicant must have 3.0 GPA or higher. Available to U.S. citizens.

Application Requirements: Application form, essay. *Deadline:* April 1.

Contact: Trish Kelly, Workforce Development Coordinator
Phone: 781-821-5990 Ext. 214
E-mail: scholarships@tourismcares.org

NTA NEW HORIZONS KATHY LETARTE SCHOLARSHIP

One $2000 scholarship awarded to an undergraduate student entering junior or senior year of study. Applicant must be enrolled in a tourism-related program at an accredited four-year college or university. Must have minimum 3.0 GPA. Applicant must be Michigan or Georgia resident. Additional essay required.

Academic Fields/Career Goals: Food Service/Hospitality; Hospitality Management; Travel/Tourism.

Award: Scholarship for use in junior or senior years; not renewable. *Number:* 1. *Amount:* $2000.

Eligibility Requirements: Applicant must be enrolled or expecting to enroll full- or part-time at a four-year institution or university and resident of Georgia, Michigan. Applicant must have 3.0 GPA or higher. Available to U.S. citizens.

Application Requirements: Application form, essay. *Deadline:* April 1.

Contact: Trish Kelly, Workforce Development Coordinator
Tourism Cares
20 Vernon Street
Norwood, MA 02062
Phone: 781-821-5990
Fax: 781-762-6100
E-mail: info@tourismcares.org

NTA OHIO SCHOLARSHIP

Scholarship available to a full time or part time student enrolled in the second half of their college career in a travel and tourism or hospitality related program of study at a college or university in Ohio, US or a permanent resident of Ohio, US.

Academic Fields/Career Goals: Food Service/Hospitality; Hospitality Management; Travel/Tourism.

Award: Scholarship for use in sophomore, junior, or senior years; not renewable.

Eligibility Requirements: Applicant must be enrolled or expecting to enroll full- or part-time at a two-year or four-year institution or university and resident of Ohio. Available to U.S. citizens.

Application Requirements: Application form, essay. *Deadline:* April 1.

Contact: Trish Kelly, Workforce Development Coordinator
Phone: 781-821-5990 Ext. 214
E-mail: scholarships@tourismcares.org

NTA TRAVEL LEADERS SCHOLARSHIP

Scholarship available to a full time student enrolled in the second half of their college career as an undergraduate or a any year of graduate school, in a travel and tourism or hospitality related program of study at a college or university in the US.

Academic Fields/Career Goals: Food Service/Hospitality; Hospitality Management; Travel/Tourism.

Award: Scholarship for use in sophomore, junior, senior, or graduate years; not renewable. *Number:* 7. *Amount:* $2000.

Eligibility Requirements: Applicant must be enrolled or expecting to enroll full-time at a two-year or four-year institution or university. Applicant must have 3.0 GPA or higher. Available to U.S. citizens.

Application Requirements: Application form, essay. *Deadline:* April 1.

Contact: Trish Kelly, Workforce Development Coordinator
Phone: 781-821-5990 Ext. 214
E-mail: scholarships@tourismcares.org

NTA UTAH KEITH GRIFFALL SCHOLARSHIP

Scholarship available to a full time or part time student enrolled in the second half of their college career in a travel and tourism or hospitality related program of study at a college or university in Utah, US or permanent resident of Utah, US.

Academic Fields/Career Goals: Food Service/Hospitality; Hospitality Management; Travel/Tourism.

Award: Scholarship for use in sophomore, junior, or senior years; not renewable. *Number:* 1. *Amount:* $2000.

Eligibility Requirements: Applicant must be enrolled or expecting to enroll full- or part-time at a two-year or four-year institution or university and resident of Utah. Applicant must have 3.0 GPA or higher. Available to U.S. citizens.

Application Requirements: Application form, essay. *Deadline:* April 1.

Contact: Trish Kelly, Workforce Development Coordinator
Phone: 781-821-5990 Ext. 214
E-mail: scholarships@tourismcares.org

UNITED NEGRO COLLEGE FUND

http://www.uncf.org/

NATIONAL BLACK MCDONALD'S OWNERS ASSOCIATION HOSPITALITY SCHOLARS PROGRAM
• See page 94

WISCONSIN BAKERS ASSOCIATION (WBA)

http://www.wibakers.com/

ROBERT W. HILLER SCHOLARSHIP FUND
• See page 250

WBA SCHOLARSHIP
• See page 250

WOMEN CHEFS AND RESTAURATEURS

http://www.womenchefs.org/

FRENCH CULINARY INSTITUTE/ITALIAN CULINARY EXPERIENCE SCHOLARSHIP
• See page 250

WOMEN GROCERS OF AMERICA

http://www.nationalgrocers.org/

MARY MACEY SCHOLARSHIP
• See page 112

FOREIGN LANGUAGE

ACL/NJCL NATIONAL LATIN EXAM

http://www.nle.org/

NATIONAL LATIN EXAM SCHOLARSHIP
• See page 214

ALBERTA HERITAGE SCHOLARSHIP FUND

http://www.alis.alberta.ca/

FELLOWSHIPS FOR FULL-TIME STUDIES IN FRENCH
Awards of between CAN$500 and CAN$1000 per semester to assist Albertans in pursuing postsecondary studies taught in French. Must be Alberta resident, Canadian citizen, or landed immigrant, and plan to register full-time in a postsecondary program in Alberta of at least one semester in length. Must be enrolled in a minimum of three courses per semester which have French as the language of instruction. For additional information and application, see website http://alis.alberta.ca.

Academic Fields/Career Goals: Foreign Language.

Award: Scholarship for use in freshman, sophomore, junior, or senior years; not renewable.

Eligibility Requirements: Applicant must be Canadian citizen; enrolled or expecting to enroll full-time at a two-year or four-year or technical institution or university; resident of Alberta and must have an interest in French language.

Application Requirements: Application form, transcript. *Deadline:* November 15.

Contact: Scholarship Committee
Phone: 780-427-8640
E-mail: scholarships@gov.ab.ca

LANGUAGE BURSARY PROGRAM FOR TEACHING FNMI LANGUAGES
Award of CAN$2500 to assist Alberta teachers, Elders, or instructors who currently provide instruction of an FNMI language and intend to take a summer post-secondary program. Applicants must hold a valid Alberta professional teaching certificate or be working towards Alberta certification, have been teaching in Alberta for a minimum of one year by the end of the current school year, demonstrate a background in FNMI language learning and culture, or have recently initiated the study of an FNMI language. For additional information, see website http://alis.alberta.ca.

Academic Fields/Career Goals: Foreign Language.

Award: Scholarship for use in freshman, sophomore, junior, senior, or graduate years; not renewable. *Number:* up to 2.

Eligibility Requirements: Applicant must be Canadian citizen; enrolled or expecting to enroll full- or part-time at a two-year or four-year institution or university and resident of Alberta. Applicant or parent of applicant must have employment or volunteer experience in teaching/education.

Application Requirements: Application form, recommendations or references. *Deadline:* February 10.

Contact: Scholarship Committee
Phone: 780-427-8640
E-mail: scholarships@gov.ab.ca

LANGUAGES IN TEACHER EDUCATION SCHOLARSHIPS
• See page 265

ALPHA MU GAMMA, THE NATIONAL COLLEGIATE FOREIGN LANGUAGE SOCIETY

http://www.amgnational.org/

NATIONAL ALPHA MU GAMMA SCHOLARSHIPS
One-time award to student members of Alpha Mu Gamma with a minimum 3.5 GPA, who plan to continue study of a foreign language. Must participate in a national scholarship competition. Apply through local chapter advisers. Freshmen are not eligible. Must submit a copy of Alpha Mu Gamma membership certificate. Can study overseas if part of his/her school program.

Academic Fields/Career Goals: Foreign Language.

Award: Scholarship for use in sophomore, junior, or senior years; not renewable. *Number:* 2–3. *Amount:* $500–$1000.

Eligibility Requirements: Applicant must be enrolled or expecting to enroll full- or part-time at a two-year or four-year institution or university. Applicant or parent of applicant must be member of Alpha Mu Gamma. Applicant must have 3.5 GPA or higher. Available to U.S. and non-U.S. citizens.

Application Requirements: Application form, essay. *Deadline:* February 1.

Contact: Ms. Leslie Brazier, Administrative Assistant
Alpha Mu Gamma, The National Collegiate Foreign Language Society
1073 North Benson Rd.
Department of Modern Languages and Literatures-- Fairfield University
Fairfield, CT 06824
Phone: 203-254-4000 Ext. 2676
E-mail: AMGNational@fairfield.edu

AMERICAN CLASSICAL LEAGUE/NATIONAL JUNIOR CLASSICAL LEAGUE

http://www.aclclassics.org/

NATIONAL JUNIOR CLASSICAL LEAGUE SCHOLARSHIP
• See page 214

AMERICAN INSTITUTE OF POLISH CULTURE INC.

http://www.ampolinstitute.org/

HARRIET IRSAY SCHOLARSHIP GRANT
• See page 141

AMERICAN SCHOOL OF CLASSICAL STUDIES AT ATHENS

http://www.ascsa.edu.gr/

ASCSA SUMMER SESSION AND SUMMER SEMINARS SCHOLARSHIPS
• See page 118

ASSOCIATION OF FORMER INTELLIGENCE OFFICERS

http://www.afio.com

AFIO UNDERGRADUATE AND GRADUATE SCHOLARSHIPS
• See page 113

CULTURAL SERVICES OF THE FRENCH EMBASSY

http://www.frenchculture.org/

TEACHING ASSISTANT PROGRAM IN FRANCE
• See page 113

GERMAN ACADEMIC EXCHANGE SERVICE (DAAD)

http://www.daad.org/

DAAD UNIVERSITY SUMMER COURSE GRANT
Scholarships are awarded to full-time degree students of Canadian or U.S. colleges, sophomore/2nd year and higher, for the pursuit of summer courses at universities in Germany. It is open to applicants of any major but there is a prerequisite of at least two years of college-level German (B1) or the equivalent German language fluency. Courses are three to four weeks in duration, take place at many locations in Germany (universities), are taught in German, and topics include German language, literature, current affairs, political science, history, culture, arts, film and media, economics, linguistics, law, translation and interpretation, and test prep for German language proficiency examinations. Accommodations are arranged by the host institution.

Academic Fields/Career Goals: Foreign Language.

Award: Grant for use in sophomore, junior, or senior years; not renewable.

Eligibility Requirements: Applicant must be enrolled or expecting to enroll full-time at a four-year institution or university and must have an interest in German language/culture. Available to U.S. and non-U.S. citizens.

Application Requirements: Application form, essay.

Contact: DAAD New York
          German Academic Exchange Service (DAAD)
          871 UN Plaza
          New York, NY 10017
          Phone: 212-758-3223
          E-mail: daadny@daad.org

KOSCIUSZKO FOUNDATION

http://www.thekf.org

YEAR ABROAD PROGRAM IN POLAND
• See page 138

MINISTRY OF EDUCATION, CULTURE, SPORTS, SCIENCE AND TECHNOLOGY

http://www.mext.go.jp/

JAPAN STUDIES SCHOLARSHIP
This is a one time non-renewable scholarship to engage in the study of the Japanese language or Japanese studies in Japan.

Academic Fields/Career Goals: Foreign Language.

Award: Scholarship for use in sophomore, junior, or senior years; not renewable.

Eligibility Requirements: Applicant must be enrolled or expecting to enroll full-time at a four-year institution; resident of California, Nevada and must have an interest in Asian language. Available to U.S. citizens.

Application Requirements: Application form, interview, personal photograph. *Deadline:* February 9.

Contact: Steven Goldman, Senior Coordinator for Educational Affairs, Consulate General of Japan in San Francisco
          Ministry of Education, Culture, Sports, Science and Technology
          275 Battery St.
          San Francisco, CA 94530
          Phone: 415-780-6086
          E-mail: steven.goldman@sr.mofa.go.jp

NATIONAL ASSOCIATION OF HISPANIC JOURNALISTS (NAHJ)

http://www.nahj.org/

MARIA ELENA SALINAS SCHOLARSHIP
One-time scholarship for high school seniors, college undergraduates, and first-year graduate students who are pursuing careers in Spanish-language broadcast (radio or TV) journalism. Students may major or plan to major in any subject, but must demonstrate a sincere desire to pursue a career in this field. Must submit essays and demo tapes (audio or video) in Spanish. Scholarship includes the opportunity to serve an internship with Univision Spanish-language television news network.

Academic Fields/Career Goals: Foreign Language; Journalism; TV/Radio Broadcasting.

Award: Scholarship for use in freshman, sophomore, junior, senior, or graduate years; not renewable. *Number:* 2. *Amount:* $5000.

Eligibility Requirements: Applicant must be enrolled or expecting to enroll full-time at a four-year institution or university and must have an interest in Spanish language. Available to U.S. citizens.

Application Requirements: Application form, driver's license, essay, financial need analysis, recommendations or references, resume, transcript. *Deadline:* March 31.

Contact: Virginia Galindo, Program Assistant
          Phone: 202-662-7145
          E-mail: vgalindo@nahj.org

NATIONAL SECURITY EDUCATION PROGRAM

http://www.iie.org/

NATIONAL SECURITY EDUCATION PROGRAM (NSEP) DAVID L. BOREN UNDERGRADUATE SCHOLARSHIPS
• See page 139

SOCIETY FOR CLASSICAL STUDIES

http://www.classicalstudies.org/

MINORITY STUDENT SUMMER SCHOLARSHIP
• See page 130

SONS OF ITALY FOUNDATION

http://www.osia.org/sif

ITALIAN LANGUAGE SCHOLARSHIP
• See page 215

SONS OF ITALY NATIONAL LEADERSHIP GRANTS COMPETITION LANGUAGE SCHOLARSHIP

Scholarships for undergraduate students in their junior or senior year of study who are majoring in Italian language studies. Must be a U.S. citizen of Italian descent. For more details see website http://www.osia.org.

Academic Fields/Career Goals: Foreign Language.

Award: Scholarship for use in junior or senior years; not renewable. *Number:* up to 1. *Amount:* $4000–$10,000.

Eligibility Requirements: Applicant must be of Italian heritage and enrolled or expecting to enroll full-time at a four-year institution or university. Available to U.S. citizens.

Application Requirements: Application form, essay, recommendations or references, resume, test scores, transcript. *Fee:* $30. *Deadline:* February 28.

Contact: Ms. Laura Kelly, Scholarship Coordinator
Phone: 202-547-2900
E-mail: scholarships@osia.org

STRAIGHTFORWARD MEDIA

http://www.straightforwardmedia.com/

STRAIGHTFORWARD MEDIA LIBERAL ARTS SCHOLARSHIP
• See page 139

UNITED NATIONS ASSOCIATION OF CONNECTICUT

http://www.unausa.org

UNITED NATIONS ASSOCIATION OF CONNECTICUT SCHOLARSHIP
• See page 147

FUNERAL SERVICES/ MORTUARY SCIENCE

ALABAMA FUNERAL DIRECTORS ASSOCIATION INC.

http://www.alabamafda.org/

ALABAMA FUNERAL DIRECTORS ASSOCIATION SCHOLARSHIP

Two $1000 scholarships available to Alabama residents. Applicant must have been accepted by an accredited mortuary science school and be sponsored by a member of the AFDA. Must maintain a minimum 2.5 GPA. Deadline: no later than 30 days prior to the AFDA mid winter meeting and annual convention.

Academic Fields/Career Goals: Funeral Services/Mortuary Science.

Award: Scholarship for use in freshman, sophomore, junior, or senior years; not renewable. *Number:* 2. *Amount:* $1000.

Eligibility Requirements: Applicant must be enrolled or expecting to enroll full- or part-time at a four-year institution or university and resident of Alabama. Applicant must have 2.5 GPA or higher. Available to U.S. citizens.

Application Requirements: Application form, essay, personal photograph, recommendations or references, transcript, two proofs of residency (such as voter registration, drivers license, or tax returns). *Deadline:* varies.

Contact: Denise Edmisten, Executive Director
Alabama Funeral Directors Association Inc.
7956 Vaughn Road, PO Box 380
Montgomery, AL 36116
Phone: 334-956-8000
Fax: 334-956-8001

AMERICAN BOARD OF FUNERAL SERVICE EDUCATION

http://www.abfse.org/

AMERICAN BOARD OF FUNERAL SERVICE EDUCATION SCHOLARSHIPS

One-time award for students who are enrolled in an accredited funeral science education program and have completed at least one term/semester. Deadlines: March 1 and September 1. For more details see website http//http://www.abfse.org.

Academic Fields/Career Goals: Funeral Services/Mortuary Science.

Award: Scholarship for use in freshman, sophomore, junior, or senior years; not renewable. *Number:* 5–10. *Amount:* $1500–$2500.

Eligibility Requirements: Applicant must be enrolled or expecting to enroll full-time at a two-year or four-year institution or university. Available to U.S. and non-U.S. citizens.

Application Requirements: Application form, autobiography, community service, essay.

Contact: Robert C. Smith III, Executive Director
American Board of Funeral Service Education
992 Mantua Pike
Suite 108
Woodbury Heights, NJ 08097
Phone: 816-233-3747
Fax: 856-579-7354
E-mail: exdir@abfse.org

MISSOURI FUNERAL DIRECTORS & EMBALMERS ASSOCIATION

http://www.mofuneral.org/

MISSOURI FUNERAL DIRECTORS ASSOCIATION SCHOLARSHIPS

Scholarship to Missouri residents pursuing a career in funeral services or mortuary science.

Academic Fields/Career Goals: Funeral Services/Mortuary Science.

Award: Scholarship for use in freshman, sophomore, junior, or senior years; not renewable. *Number:* up to 5. *Amount:* $300–$600.

Eligibility Requirements: Applicant must be enrolled or expecting to enroll full- or part-time at a technical institution and resident of Missouri. Available to U.S. citizens.

Application Requirements: Application form, recommendations or references, resume. *Deadline:* April 15.

Contact: Don Otto, Executive Director
Missouri Funeral Directors & Embalmers Association
1105 Southwest Boulevard, Suite A
Jefferson City, MO 65109
Phone: 573-635-1661
Fax: 573-635-9494
E-mail: info@mofuneral.org

NATIONAL FUNERAL DIRECTORS AND MORTICIANS ASSOCIATION

http://www.nfdma.com/

NATIONAL FUNERAL DIRECTORS AND MORTICIANS ASSOCIATION SCHOLARSHIP

Awards for high school graduates who have preferably worked in or had one year of apprenticeship in the funeral home business.

Academic Fields/Career Goals: Funeral Services/Mortuary Science.

Award: Scholarship for use in freshman year; not renewable. *Number:* 1. *Amount:* $1500.

Eligibility Requirements: Applicant must be high school student and planning to enroll or expecting to enroll full- or part-time at a four-year institution or university. Available to U.S. citizens.

Application Requirements: Application form, recommendations or references, resume, test scores. *Deadline:* April 15.

Contact: Eva Cranford, Scholarship Coordinator
   Phone: 718-625-4656
   E-mail: lladyc23@aol.com

THE ORDER OF THE GOLDEN RULE FOUNDATION

http://www.ogr.org/charitable-foundation

ORDER OF THE GOLDEN RULE FOUNDATION AWARDS OF EXCELLENCE SCHOLARSHIP PROGRAM

One-time scholarship for mortuary science students to prepare for a career in funeral service. Must be enrolled in a mortuary science degree program at an accredited mortuary school, have a minimum 3.0 GPA, commit to working at an independently owned funeral home, and be scheduled to graduate within this calendar year.

Academic Fields/Career Goals: Funeral Services/Mortuary Science.

Award: Scholarship for use in freshman, sophomore, junior, or senior years; not renewable. *Number:* 2. *Amount:* $2000–$3500.

Eligibility Requirements: Applicant must be enrolled or expecting to enroll full- or part-time at a two-year or four-year or technical institution or university. Applicant must have 3.0 GPA or higher. Available to U.S. and non-U.S. citizens.

Application Requirements: Application form, community service, essay. *Deadline:* February 2.

Contact: Jessica Smith, Assistant Executive Director
   The Order of the Golden Rule Foundation
   9101 Burnet Road
   Suite 120
   Austin, TX 78758
   Phone: 800-637-8030
   Fax: 512-334-5514
   E-mail: jsmith@ogr.org

WALLACE S. AND WILMA K. LAUGHLIN FOUNDATION TRUST

http://www.nefda.org/

SWANSON SCHOLARSHIP

Scholarship for a Nebraska student entering the mortuary science program at a Kansas City community college. Must be a US citizen, a high school graduate and have completed Nebraska pre-mortuary science hours. Scholarship value and number of awards varies annually.

Academic Fields/Career Goals: Funeral Services/Mortuary Science.

Award: Scholarship for use in junior or senior years; not renewable. *Number:* 1–10. *Amount:* $1000–$10,000.

Eligibility Requirements: Applicant must be enrolled or expecting to enroll full-time at a two-year institution and resident of Nebraska. Available to U.S. citizens.

Application Requirements: Application form, financial need analysis, interview. *Deadline:* June 30.

Contact: Craig Draucker, Chairman
   Wallace S. and Wilma K. Laughlin Foundation Trust
   PO Box 10
   521 First Street
   Milford, NE 68405
   Phone: 402-761-2217
   E-mail: Staff@nefda.org

GEMOLOGY

AMERICAN INDIAN SCIENCE AND ENGINEERING SOCIETY

http://www.aises.org/

A.T. ANDERSON MEMORIAL SCHOLARSHIP PROGRAM
• *See page 121*

ASSOCIATION FOR WOMEN GEOSCIENTISTS (AWG)

http://www.awg.org/

AWG ETHNIC MINORITY SCHOLARSHIP
• *See page 260*

AWG MARIA LUISA CRAWFORD FIELD CAMP SCHOLARSHIP
• *See page 129*

LONE STAR RISING CAREER SCHOLARSHIP
• *See page 260*

OSAGE CHAPTER UNDERGRADUATE SERVICE SCHOLARSHIP
• *See page 129*

BHW GROUP

https://thebhwgroup.com/

BHW WOMEN IN STEM SCHOLARSHIP
• *See page 124*

STRAIGHT NORTH

https://www.straightnorth.com/

STRAIGHT NORTH STEM SCHOLARSHIP
• *See page 92*

GEOGRAPHY

AMERICAN ASSOCIATION OF GEOGRAPHERS

http://www.aag.org/

DARREL HESS COMMUNITY COLLEGE GEOGRAPHY SCHOLARSHIPS

Two $1,000 scholarships will be awarded to students from community colleges, junior colleges, city colleges, or similar two-year educational institutions who will be transferring as geography majors to four year colleges and universities.

Academic Fields/Career Goals: Geography.

Award: Grant for use in junior year; not renewable. *Number:* 2–4. *Amount:* $1000.

Eligibility Requirements: Applicant must be enrolled or expecting to enroll full-time at a two-year institution. Applicant must have 3.5 GPA or higher. Available to U.S. and non-U.S. citizens.

Application Requirements: Application form, essay. *Deadline:* December 31.

Contact: Ms. Candida Mannozzi, Deputy Director for Operations
American Association of Geographers
Association of American Geographers
1710 16th Street, NW
Washington, DC 20009
Phone: 202-234-1450
E-mail: grantsawards@aag.org

AMERICAN INDIAN SCIENCE AND ENGINEERING SOCIETY

http://www.aises.org/

A.T. ANDERSON MEMORIAL SCHOLARSHIP PROGRAM
• *See page 121*

ASSOCIATION FOR WOMEN GEOSCIENTISTS (AWG)

http://www.awg.org/

AWG ETHNIC MINORITY SCHOLARSHIP
• *See page 260*

AWG SALT LAKE CHAPTER (SLC) RESEARCH SCHOLARSHIP
• *See page 129*

OSAGE CHAPTER UNDERGRADUATE SERVICE SCHOLARSHIP
• *See page 129*

ASSOCIATION OF STATE DAM SAFETY OFFICIALS (ASDSO)

http://www.DamSafety.org

ASSOCIATION OF STATE DAM SAFETY OFFICIALS (ASDSO) SENIOR UNDERGRADUATE SCHOLARSHIP
• *See page 168*

BHW GROUP

https://thebhwgroup.com/

BHW WOMEN IN STEM SCHOLARSHIP
• *See page 124*

BROWN AND CALDWELL

http://www.brownandcaldwell.com

ECKENFELDER SCHOLARSHIP
• *See page 169*

MINORITY SCHOLARSHIP PROGRAM
• *See page 169*

DIVERSITYCOMM, INC.

http://www.diversitycomm.net/

DIVERSITY IN STEAM MAGAZINE SCHOLARSHIP
• *See page 83*

GAMMA THETA UPSILON-INTERNATIONAL GEOGRAPHIC HONOR SOCIETY

http://www.gtuhonors.org/

BUZZARD-MAXFIELD-RICHASON AND RECHLIN SCHOLARSHIP

Award is granted to a student who is a Gamma Theta Upsilon member, majoring in geography, will be a senior undergraduate and who has been accepted into a graduate program in geography.

Academic Fields/Career Goals: Geography.

Award: Scholarship for use in senior or graduate years; not renewable. *Number:* 5. *Amount:* $1000.

Eligibility Requirements: Applicant must be enrolled or expecting to enroll full-time at a four-year institution or university. Applicant or parent of applicant must be member of Gamma Theta Upsilon. Applicant must have 3.0 GPA or higher. Available to U.S. and non-U.S. citizens.

Application Requirements: Application form, recommendations or references, transcript. *Deadline:* May 31.

Contact: Dr. Donald Zeigler, Scholarship Committee
Gamma Theta Upsilon-International Geographic Honor Society
Old Dominion University
1881 University Drive
Virginia Beach, VA 23453
E-mail: dzeigler@odu.edu

THE LAND CONSERVANCY OF NEW JERSEY

http://www.tlc-nj.org/

ROGERS FAMILY SCHOLARSHIP
• *See page 172*

NASA IDAHO SPACE GRANT CONSORTIUM

http://www.idahospacegrant.org

NASA IDAHO SPACE GRANT CONSORTIUM SCHOLARSHIP PROGRAM
• *See page 126*

SCARLETT FAMILY FOUNDATION SCHOLARSHIP PROGRAM

http://www.scarlettfoundation.org/

SCHOLARSHIP FOR STUDENTS PURSUING A BUSINESS OR STEM DEGREE
• *See page 91*

SIGMA XI, THE SCIENTIFIC RESEARCH SOCIETY

http://www.sigmaxi.org/

SIGMA XI GRANTS-IN-AID OF RESEARCH
• *See page 110*

GRAPHICS/GRAPHIC ARTS/ PRINTING

AUTOMOTIVE WOMEN'S ALLIANCE FOUNDATION

http://awafoundation.org/index.php

AUTOMOTIVE WOMEN'S ALLIANCE FOUNDATION SCHOLARSHIPS
• See page 81

CCNMA: LATINO JOURNALISTS OF CALIFORNIA

http://www.ccnma.org/

CCNMA SCHOLARSHIPS
• See page 218

CONGRESSIONAL BLACK CAUCUS FOUNDATION, INC.

http://www.cbcfinc.org/

CBC SPOUSES VISUAL ARTS SCHOLARSHIP
• See page 132

DIVERSITYCOMM, INC.

http://www.diversitycomm.net/

DIVERSITY IN STEAM MAGAZINE SCHOLARSHIP
• See page 83

ELECTRONIC DOCUMENT SYSTEMS FOUNDATION

http://www.edsf.org/

ANDY AND JULIE PLATA HONORARY SCHOLARSHIP
This scholarship is provided to a student in a graphic arts related program who displays an entrepreneurial spirit and is pursuing a career in the graphic communications / printing industry.

Academic Fields/Career Goals: Graphics/Graphic Arts/Printing.

Award: Scholarship for use in freshman, sophomore, junior, senior, or graduate years; not renewable. *Number:* 1. *Amount:* $2000.

Eligibility Requirements: Applicant must be enrolled or expecting to enroll full-time at a two-year or four-year or technical institution or university. Applicant must have 3.0 GPA or higher. Available to U.S. and non-U.S. citizens.

Application Requirements: Application form, community service, essay. *Deadline:* May 1.

Contact: Ms. Brenda Kai, Executive Director
Phone: 817-849-1145
E-mail: brenda.kai@edsf.org

EDSF BOARD OF DIRECTORS SCHOLARSHIPS
Scholarships awarded to full-time students who are committed to pursuing a career in the document management and graphic communications marketplace. The career choices are very broad and include, but are not limited to, computer science and engineering, graphic design, graphic communications, media communications, and business. Preference is given to college-level juniors, seniors and advanced degree students. Minimum 3.0 GPA required.

Academic Fields/Career Goals: Graphics/Graphic Arts/Printing.

Award: Scholarship for use in freshman, sophomore, junior, senior, or graduate years; not renewable. *Number:* 1–40. *Amount:* $1000–$5000.

Eligibility Requirements: Applicant must be enrolled or expecting to enroll full-time at a two-year or four-year institution or university. Applicant must have 3.0 GPA or higher. Available to U.S. and non-U.S. citizens.

Application Requirements: Application form, community service, essay. *Deadline:* May 1.

Contact: Ms. Brenda Kai, Executive Director
Phone: 817-849-1145
E-mail: brenda.kai@edsf.org

HOODS MEMORIAL SCHOLARSHIP
$2000 award for students whose academic focus includes all document management and graphic communications careers with special consideration given to students interested in marketing and public relations. Minimum 3.0 GPA required.

Academic Fields/Career Goals: Graphics/Graphic Arts/Printing.

Award: Scholarship for use in freshman, sophomore, junior, senior, or graduate years; not renewable. *Number:* 1. *Amount:* $2000.

Eligibility Requirements: Applicant must be enrolled or expecting to enroll full-time at a two-year or four-year institution or university. Applicant must have 3.0 GPA or higher. Available to U.S. and non-U.S. citizens.

Application Requirements: Application form, community service, essay. *Deadline:* May 1.

Contact: Ms. Brenda Kai, Executive Director
Phone: 817-849-1145
E-mail: brenda.kai@edsf.org

LYNDA BABOYIAN MEMORIAL SCHOLARSHIP
• See page 178

GOLDEN KEY INTERNATIONAL HONOUR SOCIETY

http://www.goldenkey.org/

VISUAL AND PERFORMING ARTS ACHIEVEMENT AWARDS
• See page 142

INTERNATIONAL FOODSERVICE EDITORIAL COUNCIL

http://www.ifeconline.com/

INTERNATIONAL FOODSERVICE EDITORIAL COUNCIL COMMUNICATIONS SCHOLARSHIP
• See page 96

THE LAGRANT FOUNDATION

http://www.lagrantfoundation.org/

LAGRANT FOUNDATION SCHOLARSHIP FOR GRADUATES
• See page 97

LAGRANT FOUNDATION SCHOLARSHIP FOR UNDERGRADUATES
• See page 97

NATIONAL ASSOCIATION OF HISPANIC JOURNALISTS (NAHJ)

http://www.nahj.org/

NEWHOUSE SCHOLARSHIP PROGRAM
Two-year $5000 annually award for students who are pursuing careers in the newspaper industry as reporters, editors, graphic artists, or photojournalists. Recipient is expected to participate in summer internship at a Newhouse newspaper following their junior year. Students must submit resume and writing samples.

Academic Fields/Career Goals: Graphics/Graphic Arts/Printing; Journalism; Photojournalism/Photography.

Award: Scholarship for use in junior or senior years; not renewable. *Amount:* $5000.

Eligibility Requirements: Applicant must be enrolled or expecting to enroll full-time at a four-year institution or university. Available to U.S. citizens.

Application Requirements: Application form, essay, financial need analysis, recommendations or references, resume, transcript, work samples. *Deadline:* March 31.

Contact: Virginia Galindo, Program Assistant
    Phone: 202-662-7145
    E-mail: vgalindo@nahj.org

NEBRASKA PRESS ASSOCIATION

http://www.nebpress.com/

NEBRASKA PRESS ASSOCIATION FOUNDATION SCHOLARSHIP
• See page 97

NEW ENGLAND PRINTING AND PUBLISHING COUNCIL

http://www.gcsfne.org/

GRAPHIC COMMUNICATIONS SCHOLARSHIP FUND OF NEW ENGLAND

Applicants must be residents of New England who have been admitted to, or are currently attending, an accredited two-year vocational or technical college or a four-year college or university that offers a degree program related to printing or graphic communications. Renewable for up to four years if student maintains 2.5 GPA.

Academic Fields/Career Goals: Graphics/Graphic Arts/Printing.

Award: Scholarship for use in freshman, sophomore, junior, or senior years; renewable. *Number:* 16–35. *Amount:* $1350–$2500.

Eligibility Requirements: Applicant must be enrolled or expecting to enroll full-time at a two-year or four-year or technical institution or university and resident of Connecticut, Maine, Massachusetts, New Hampshire, Rhode Island, Vermont. Applicant must have 2.5 GPA or higher. Available to U.S. citizens.

Application Requirements: Application form, financial need analysis. *Deadline:* June 15.

Contact: Tad Parker, Scholarship Administrator
    New England Printing and Publishing Council
    5 Crystal Pond Road
    Southboro, MA 01772
    E-mail: chair@gcsfne.org

OREGON STUDENT ASSISTANCE COMMISSION

https://oregonstudentaid.gov/

HB DESIGN SCHOLARSHIP

Award for college junior or above studying graphic design or interactive/web design at any U.S. college or university. Semifinalists will be required to e-mail a design sample along with a 200-word description about the concept. Apply/compete annually. Based on financial need.

Academic Fields/Career Goals: Graphics/Graphic Arts/Printing.

Award: Scholarship for use in junior, senior, or graduate years; not renewable.

Eligibility Requirements: Applicant must be enrolled or expecting to enroll full-time at a four-year institution or university and resident of Oregon. Applicant must have 3.0 GPA or higher. Available to U.S. citizens.

Application Requirements: Application form, essay, financial need analysis. *Deadline:* March 1.

Contact: Melissa Adams, Scholarship Processing Coordinator
    Phone: 541-687-7409
    E-mail: melissa.adams@state.or.us

KERDRAGON SCHOLARSHIP
• See page 143

KIRCHHOFF FAMILY FINE ARTS SCHOLARSHIP
• See page 143

PRINT AND GRAPHIC SCHOLARSHIP FOUNDATION

http://www.printing.org/

PRINT AND GRAPHICS SCHOLARSHIPS FOUNDATION
• See page 222

PRINTING INDUSTRY MIDWEST EDUCATION FOUDNATION

http://www.pimw.org/scholarships

PRINTING INDUSTRY MIDWEST EDUCATION FOUNDATION SCHOLARSHIP FUND
• See page 222

QUALITY BATH

http://www.qualitybath.com

QUALITYBATH.COM SCHOLARSHIP PROGRAM
• See page 140

RHODE ISLAND FOUNDATION

http://www.rifoundation.org/

J. D. EDSAL SCHOLARSHIP
• See page 99

ROBERT H. MOLLOHAN FAMILY CHARITABLE FOUNDATION, INC.

http://www.mollohanfoundation.org/

MARY OLIVE EDDY JONES ART SCHOLARSHIP
• See page 140

SUPPORT CREATIVITY

http://wesupportcreativity.org

SUPPORT CREATIVITY SCHOLARSHIP
• See page 137

TAG AND LABEL MANUFACTURERS INSTITUTE, INC.

http://www.tlmi.com/

TLMI 4 YEAR COLLEGE DEGREE SCHOLARSHIP PROGRAM
• See page 307

TECHNICAL ASSOCIATION OF THE PULP & PAPER INDUSTRY (TAPPI)

http://www.tappi.org/

COATING AND GRAPHIC ARTS DIVISION SCHOLARSHIP

Scholarship to encourage talented science and engineering students to pursue careers in the paper industry and to utilize their capabilities in advancing the science and technology of coated paper and paperboard manufacturing and the graphic arts industry. The division may award up to four $1000 awards annually. Information can be found at http://www.tappi.org/s_tappi/sec.asp?CID=6101&DID=546695.

Academic Fields/Career Goals: Graphics/Graphic Arts/Printing; Paper and Pulp Engineering.

Award: Scholarship for use in freshman, sophomore, junior, or senior years; not renewable. *Number:* 1–4. *Amount:* $1000.

Eligibility Requirements: Applicant must be enrolled or expecting to enroll full-time at a four-year institution or university. Applicant must have 3.0 GPA or higher. Available to U.S. and non-U.S. citizens.

Application Requirements: Application form. *Deadline:* March 15.

Contact: Mr. Laurence Womack, Director of Standards and Awards
Technical Association of the Pulp & Paper Industry (TAPPI)
15 Technology Parkway South
Peachtree Corners, GA 30092
Phone: 770-209-7276
E-mail: standards@tappi.org

VECTORWORKS, INC.

http://www.vectorworks.net

VECTORWORKS DESIGN SCHOLARSHIP
• *See page 137*

WORLDSTUDIO FOUNDATION

http://www.aiga.org/

WORLDSTUDIO AIGA SCHOLARSHIPS
• *See page 146*

HEALTH ADMINISTRATION

ALBERTA HERITAGE SCHOLARSHIP FUND

http://www.alis.alberta.ca/

ABORIGINAL HEALTH CAREERS BURSARY
• *See page 167*

ALICE L. HALTOM EDUCATIONAL FUND

http://www.alhef.org/

ALICE L. HALTOM EDUCATIONAL FUND
• *See page 176*

AMERICAN LEGION AUXILIARY DEPARTMENT OF COLORADO

http://www.alacolorado.com

AMERICAN LEGION AUXILIARY DEPARTMENT OF COLORADO PAST PRESIDENTS' PARLEY HEALTH CARE PROFESSIONAL SCHOLARSHIPNURSES SCHOLARSHIP
• *See page 147*

AMERICAN LEGION AUXILIARY DEPARTMENT OF WISCONSIN

http://www.amlegionauxwi.org/

AMERICAN LEGION AUXILIARY DEPARTMENT OF WISCONSIN PAST PRESIDENTS' PARLEY HEALTH CAREER SCHOLARSHIPS

One-time award of $1000. Course of study need not be a four-year program. A hospital, university, or technical school program is also acceptable. Applicant must be a direct descendant, wife, or widow of a veteran. Must submit certification of an American Legion Auxiliary unit president, copy of proof that veteran was in service (i.e. discharge papers), letters of recommendation, transcripts, and essay. Must have minimum 3.5 GPA, show financial need, and be a resident of Wisconsin or member of the Wisconsin American Legion Family. Applications available on website http://www.amlegionauxwi.org.

Academic Fields/Career Goals: Health Administration; Health and Medical Sciences; Nursing.

Award: Scholarship for use in freshman, sophomore, junior, or senior years; not renewable. *Number:* 1–2. *Amount:* $1000.

Eligibility Requirements: Applicant must be enrolled or expecting to enroll full- or part-time at a two-year or four-year or technical institution or university and resident of Wisconsin. Applicant or parent of applicant must be member of American Legion or Auxiliary. Applicant must have 3.5 GPA or higher. Available to U.S. citizens. Applicant or parent must meet one or more of the following requirements: general military experience; retired from active duty; disabled or killed as a result of military service; prisoner of war; or missing in action.

Application Requirements: Application form, essay, financial need analysis. *Deadline:* March 15.

Contact: Bonnie Dorniak, Department Secretary
American Legion Auxiliary Department of Wisconsin
PO Box 140
Portage, WI 53901
Phone: 608-745-0124
Fax: 608-745-1947
E-mail: deptsec@amlegionauxwi.org

AMERICAN LEGION DEPARTMENT OF NORTH DAKOTA

http://www.ndlegion.org/

O. NESHEIM MEMORIAL SCHOLARSHIP
• *See page 254*

THE ARC NEW YORK

https://www.nysarc.org/

JAMES F. REVILLE SCHOLARSHIP

The scholarship, in the amount of $3,000 per recipient, is paid in installments of $1,500 per semester for any year the student is enrolled in college. The scholarship is presented to an individual who intends to pursue a career related to the field of intellectual or other developmental disabilities such as behavioral sciences, social work, nursing, healthcare administration and management or psychology. The funds must be claimed within a four (4) year period from the time the scholarship was awarded. Two (2) scholarships are presented annually. Student must be enrolled full-time in any year of their college education. Student's training must be in a field related to intellectual or other developmental disabilities. Students currently receiving a scholarship through The Arc New York are not eligible to receive simultaneous scholarships. Student must be a New York State resident and/or attending a college or university in New York State. Submit completed application, signed by the Department Chairperson, and one (1) letter of recommendation from a current academic instructor.

Academic Fields/Career Goals: Health Administration; Health and Medical Sciences; Nursing; Social Services; Special Education; Therapy/Rehabilitation.

Award: Scholarship for use in freshman, sophomore, junior, senior, or graduate years; not renewable. *Number:* 2. *Amount:* $3000.

Eligibility Requirements: Applicant must be enrolled or expecting to enroll full-time at a two-year or four-year institution or university; resident of New York and studying in New York.

Application Requirements: Application form. *Deadline:* January 15.

Contact: Maria Simone
The Arc New York
29 British American Boulevard
Latham, NY 12110
Phone: 518-439-8311
Fax: 518-439-1893
E-mail: scholarships@thearcny.org

ASRT FOUNDATION
http://foundation.asrt.org

PROFESSIONAL ADVANCEMENT SCHOLARSHIP
Open to ASRT members only who are certificate, undergraduate or graduate students pursuing any degree or certificate intended to further a career in the radiologic sciences profession. One of the following must also be true: applicant holds an unrestricted state license, is registered by the American Registry of Radiologic Technologists, or registered with an equivalent certifying body.

Academic Fields/Career Goals: Health Administration; Health and Medical Sciences; Oncology; Radiology.

Award: Scholarship for use in freshman, sophomore, junior, senior, graduate, or postgraduate years; not renewable. *Number:* 10–20. *Amount:* up to $2000.

Eligibility Requirements: Applicant must be enrolled or expecting to enroll full- or part-time at a two-year or four-year or technical institution or university. Applicant or parent of applicant must be member of American Society of Radiologic Technologists. Applicant must have 3.0 GPA or higher. Available to U.S. citizens.

Application Requirements: Application form, application form may be submitted online (http://aim.applylists.net), essay, financial need analysis, recommendations or references, resume. *Deadline:* February 1.

AVACARE MEDICAL
https://avacaremedical.com

AVACARE MEDICAL SCHOLARSHIP
• *See page 115*

BETHESDA LUTHERAN COMMUNITIES
http://www.bethesdalutherancommunities.org/scholarships

DEVELOPMENTAL DISABILITIES SCHOLASTIC ACHIEVEMENT SCHOLARSHIP FOR COLLEGE STUDENTS WHO ARE LUTHERAN
• *See page 254*

BHW GROUP
https://thebhwgroup.com/

BHW WOMEN IN STEM SCHOLARSHIP
• *See page 124*

CONTINENTAL SOCIETY, DAUGHTERS OF INDIAN WARS
http://www.csdiw.org/

CONTINENTAL SOCIETY, DAUGHTERS OF INDIAN WARS SCHOLARSHIP
• *See page 242*

FUKUNAGA SCHOLARSHIP FOUNDATION
http://fukunagascholarship.com

FUKUNAGA SCHOLARSHIP FOUNDATION
• *See page 85*

GREATER KANAWHA VALLEY FOUNDATION
http://www.tgkvf.org/

WILLARD H. ERWIN JR. MEMORIAL SCHOLARSHIP FUND
• *See page 179*

HAWAIIAN LODGE, F&AM
http://www.hawaiianlodgefreemasons.org

HAWAIIAN LODGE SCHOLARSHIPS
• *See page 86*

HEALTHCARE INFORMATION AND MANAGEMENT SYSTEMS SOCIETY FOUNDATION
http://www.himss.org/

HIMSS FOUNDATION SCHOLARSHIP PROGRAM
The Foundation Scholarships can be awarded to undergraduate, Master's or Ph.D. students enrolled in a program related to the healthcare information and management systems field. In addition to the $5000 scholarship award, the winner also receives an all-expense paid trip to the Annual HIMSS Conference and Exhibition. Applicants must be member in good standing of HIMS. Primary occupation must be that of student in an accredited program related to the healthcare information or management systems field. The specific degree program is not a critical factor, although it is expected that programs similar to those in industrial engineering, operations research, healthcare informatics, computer science and information systems, mathematics, and quantitative programs in business administration and hospital administration will predominate. Undergraduate applicants must be at least a first-term junior when the scholarship is awarded. Previous Foundation Scholarship winners are ineligible.

Academic Fields/Career Goals: Health Administration; Health and Medical Sciences; Health Information Management/Technology; Science, Technology, and Society.

Award: Scholarship for use in junior, senior, graduate, or postgraduate years; not renewable. *Number:* 4–12. *Amount:* $5000.

Eligibility Requirements: Applicant must be enrolled or expecting to enroll full-time at a four-year institution or university. Applicant or parent of applicant must be member of Healthcare Information and Management Systems Society. Available to U.S. and non-U.S. citizens.

Application Requirements: Application form, community service, essay, recommendations or references, resume, transcript. *Deadline:* October 15.

Contact: Helen Figge, Senior Director, Professional Development, Career Services
Healthcare Information and Management Systems Society Foundation
33 West Monroe Street, Suite 1700
Chicago, IL 60603
Phone: 312-915-9548
E-mail: hfigge@himss.org

HEALTH RESEARCH COUNCIL OF NEW ZEALAND

http://www.hrc.govt.nz/

PACIFIC HEALTH WORKFORCE AWARD

Intended to support students studying towards a health or health-related qualification. The eligible courses of study are: health, health administration, or a recognized qualification aligned with the Pacific Island. Priority given to management training, medical, and nursing students. Applicants should be New Zealand citizens or hold residency in New Zealand at the time of application and be of Pacific Island descent. The value of the awards and dollar value will vary and for one year of study.

Academic Fields/Career Goals: Health Administration; Health and Medical Sciences; Health Information Management/Technology; Nursing.

Award: Scholarship for use in freshman, sophomore, junior, senior, graduate, or postgraduate years; not renewable.

Eligibility Requirements: Applicant must be New Zealander citizen; Asian/Pacific Islander and enrolled or expecting to enroll full-time at a two-year or four-year institution or university. Available to citizens of countries other than the U.S. or Canada.

Application Requirements: Application form, driver's license, essay, financial need analysis, recommendations or references, transcript. *Deadline:* October 10.

Contact: Ngamau Wichman Tou, Manager, Pacific Health Research
Phone: 64 9 3035255
Fax: 64 9 377 9988
E-mail: nwichmantou@hrc.govt.nz

PACIFIC MENTAL HEALTH WORK FORCE AWARD

Intended to provide one year of support for students studying towards a mental health or mental health-related qualification. Eligible courses of study include: nursing, psychology, health, health administration or a recognized qualification aligned with the Pacific Island mental health priority areas. Applicants should be New Zealand citizens or hold residency in New Zealand at the time of application and be of Pacific Island descent.

Academic Fields/Career Goals: Health Administration; Health and Medical Sciences; Health Information Management/Technology; Nursing; Psychology.

Award: Scholarship for use in freshman, sophomore, junior, senior, graduate, or postgraduate years; not renewable.

Eligibility Requirements: Applicant must be New Zealander citizen; Asian/Pacific Islander and enrolled or expecting to enroll full-time at a two-year or four-year institution or university. Available to citizens of countries other than the U.S. or Canada.

Application Requirements: Application form, essay, financial need analysis, recommendations or references, resume, transcript. *Deadline:* October 10.

Contact: Ngamau Wichman Tou, Manager, Pacific Health Research
Phone: 64 9 3035255
Fax: 64 9 377 9988
E-mail: nwichmantou@hrc.govt.nz

INTERMOUNTAIN MEDICAL IMAGING

https://www.aboutimi.com/

INTERMOUNTAIN MEDICAL IMAGING SCHOLARSHIP
• *See page 147*

MEDICAL SCRUBS COLLECTION

http://medicalscrubscollection.com

MEDICAL SCRUBS COLLECTION SCHOLARSHIP
• *See page 120*

MICHAEL MOODY FITNESS

http://www.michaelmoodyfitness.com/

MICHAEL MOODY FITNESS SCHOLARSHIP
• *See page 166*

THE NATIONAL SOCIETY OF THE COLONIAL DAMES OF AMERICA

http://www.nscda.org/

AMERICAN INDIAN NURSE SCHOLARSHIP PROGRAM

Since 1928 The National Society of The Colonial Dames of America has provided a small number of scholarship awards to assist students of American Indian heritage who are pursuing degrees in nursing or in the field of health care and health education. Eligible students receive $1,500 per semester and the money is to be used strictly for tuition, books or fees applicable to the student's approved program. The grant is sent to the school and credited to the student's account. Once a student is accepted, he or she may re-apply for continued funds each semester as long as the student remains in academic good standing.

Academic Fields/Career Goals: Health Administration; Nursing.

Award: Scholarship for use in freshman, sophomore, junior, senior, graduate, or postgraduate years; renewable. *Number:* 2. *Amount:* $500–$1500.

Eligibility Requirements: Applicant must be American Indian/Alaska Native and enrolled or expecting to enroll full-time at a two-year or four-year or technical institution or university. Applicant must have 2.5 GPA or higher. Available to U.S. citizens.

Application Requirements: Application form, autobiography, driver's license, financial need analysis, personal photograph. *Deadline:* June 1.

Contact: NSCDA Membership Manager
Phone: 202-337-2288 Ext. 227
E-mail: dames@dumbartonhouse.org

NEW ENGLAND EMPLOYEE BENEFITS COUNCIL

http://www.neebc.org/

NEW ENGLAND EMPLOYEE BENEFITS COUNCIL SCHOLARSHIP PROGRAM
• *See page 89*

SCARLETT FAMILY FOUNDATION SCHOLARSHIP PROGRAM

http://www.scarlettfoundation.org/

SCHOLARSHIP FOR STUDENTS PURSUING A BUSINESS OR STEM DEGREE
• *See page 91*

STRAIGHTFORWARD MEDIA

http://www.straightforwardmedia.com/

STRAIGHTFORWARD MEDIA MEDICAL PROFESSIONS SCHOLARSHIP
• *See page 257*

UNITED NEGRO COLLEGE FUND

http://www.uncf.org/

HCN/APRICITY RESOURCES SCHOLARS PROGRAM
• *See page 93*

UNCF/ANTHEM CORPORATE SCHOLARS PROGRAM
• *See page 184*

HEALTH AND MEDICAL SCIENCES

ACLS CERTIFICATION INSTITUTE
https://acls.com

MEDICAL SCHOOL SCHOLARSHIP
• *See page 251*

ALBERTA HERITAGE SCHOLARSHIP FUND
http://www.alis.alberta.ca/

ABORIGINAL HEALTH CAREERS BURSARY
• *See page 167*

JASON LANG SCHOLARSHIP
• *See page 251*

NORTHERN ALBERTA DEVELOPMENT COUNCIL BURSARY
• *See page 251*

ALPENA REGIONAL MEDICAL CENTER
http://www.alpenaregionalmedicalcenter.org/

THELMA ORR MEMORIAL SCHOLARSHIP
Two $1500 scholarships for students pursuing a course of study related to human medicine at any state accredited Michigan college or university.
Academic Fields/Career Goals: Health and Medical Sciences.
Award: Scholarship for use in freshman, sophomore, junior, or senior years; not renewable. *Number:* 2. *Amount:* $1500.
Eligibility Requirements: Applicant must be enrolled or expecting to enroll full-time at a four-year institution or university; resident of Michigan and studying in Michigan. Available to U.S. citizens.
Application Requirements: Application form. *Deadline:* April 15.
Contact: Marlene Pear, Director, Voluntary Services
  Phone: 989-356-7351
  E-mail: info@agh.org

AMERICAN INDIAN SCIENCE AND ENGINEERING SOCIETY
http://www.aises.org/

A.T. ANDERSON MEMORIAL SCHOLARSHIP PROGRAM
• *See page 121*

AMERICAN LEGION AUXILIARY DEPARTMENT OF ARIZONA
http://wwwaladeptaz.org

AMERICAN LEGION AUXILIARY DEPARTMENT OF ARIZONA HEALTH CARE OCCUPATION SCHOLARSHIPS
Award for Arizona residents enrolled at an institution in Arizona that awards degrees or certificates in health occupations. Preference given to an immediate family member of a veteran. Must be a U.S. citizen and Arizona resident for at least one year.
Academic Fields/Career Goals: Health and Medical Sciences.
Award: Scholarship for use in freshman, sophomore, junior, senior, graduate, or postgraduate years; not renewable. *Amount:* $500.
Eligibility Requirements: Applicant must be age 17-99; enrolled or expecting to enroll full- or part-time at a two-year or four-year or technical institution or university; resident of Arizona and studying in Arizona. Available to U.S. citizens.

Application Requirements: Application form, essay, financial need analysis, personal photograph. *Deadline:* May 15.
Contact: Mrs. Barbara Matteson, Department Secretary and Treasurer
  American Legion Auxiliary Department of Arizona
  4701 North 19th Avenue, Suite 100
  Phoenix, AZ 85015-3727
  Phone: 602-241-1080
  E-mail: secretary@aladeptaz.org

AMERICAN LEGION AUXILIARY DEPARTMENT OF COLORADO
http://www.alacolorado.com

AMERICAN LEGION AUXILIARY DEPARTMENT OF COLORADO PAST PRESIDENTS' PARLEY HEALTH CARE PROFESSIONAL SCHOLARSHIPNURSES SCHOLARSHIP
• *See page 147*

AMERICAN LEGION AUXILIARY DEPARTMENT OF MAINE
http://www.mainelegion.org/

AMERICAN LEGION AUXILIARY DEPARTMENT OF MAINE PAST PRESIDENTS' PARLEY NURSES SCHOLARSHIP
One-time award for child, grandchild, sister, or brother of veteran. Must be resident of Maine and wishing to continue education at accredited school in medical field. Must submit photo, doctor's statement, and evidence of civic activity. Minimum 3.5 GPA required.
Academic Fields/Career Goals: Health and Medical Sciences; Nursing.
Award: Scholarship for use in freshman, sophomore, junior, or senior years; not renewable. *Number:* 1. *Amount:* $300.
Eligibility Requirements: Applicant must be enrolled or expecting to enroll full-time at a two-year or four-year or technical institution or university and resident of Maine. Applicant or parent of applicant must have employment or volunteer experience in community service. Applicant must have 2.5 GPA or higher. Available to U.S. citizens. Applicant or parent must meet one or more of the following requirements: general military experience; retired from active duty; disabled or killed as a result of military service; prisoner of war; or missing in action.
Application Requirements: Application form, doctor's statement, personal photograph, recommendations or references, transcript. *Deadline:* March 31.
Contact: Mary Wells, Education Chairman
  Phone: 207-532-6007
  E-mail: aladeptsecme@verizon.net

AMERICAN LEGION AUXILIARY DEPARTMENT OF MICHIGAN
http://www.michalaux.org/

AMERICAN LEGION AUXILIARY DEPARTMENT OF MICHIGAN MEDICAL CAREER SCHOLARSHIP
Award for training in Michigan as registered nurse, licensed practical nurse, physical therapist, respiratory therapist, or in any medical career. Must be child, grandchild, great-grandchild, wife, or widow of honorably discharged or deceased veteran who has served during the eligibility dates for American Legion membership. Must be Michigan resident attending a Michigan school.
Academic Fields/Career Goals: Health and Medical Sciences; Nursing; Therapy/Rehabilitation.
Award: Scholarship for use in freshman year; not renewable. *Number:* 10–20. *Amount:* $500.
Eligibility Requirements: Applicant must be enrolled or expecting to enroll full-time at a two-year or four-year or technical institution or university; resident of Michigan and studying in Michigan. Applicant must have 3.5 GPA or higher. Available to U.S. citizens. Applicant must have general military experience.

Application Requirements: Application form, financial need analysis. *Deadline:* March 15.

Contact: Scholarship Coordinator
American Legion Auxiliary Department of Michigan
212 North Verlinden Avenue, Suite B
Lansing, MI 48915
Phone: 517-267-8809 Ext. 21
E-mail: info@michalaux.org

AMERICAN LEGION AUXILIARY DEPARTMENT OF MINNESOTA

http://www.mnala.org

AMERICAN LEGION AUXILIARY DEPARTMENT OF MINNESOTA PAST PRESIDENTS' PARLEY HEALTH CARE SCHOLARSHIP

One-time $1000 award for American Legion Auxiliary Department of Minnesota member for at least three years who is needy and deserving, to begin or continue education in any phase of the health care field. Must be a Minnesota resident, attend a vocational or postsecondary institution and maintain at least a C average in school.

Academic Fields/Career Goals: Health and Medical Sciences.

Award: Scholarship for use in freshman, sophomore, junior, or senior years; not renewable. *Number:* 1–10. *Amount:* $1000.

Eligibility Requirements: Applicant must be enrolled or expecting to enroll full-time at a two-year or four-year or technical institution or university; resident of Minnesota and studying in Minnesota. Applicant or parent of applicant must be member of American Legion or Auxiliary. Available to U.S. citizens.

Application Requirements: Application form, financial need analysis. *Deadline:* March 15.

Contact: Sandie Deutsch, Executive Secretary
American Legion Auxiliary Department of Minnesota
State Veterans Service Building
20 West 12th Street, Room 314
St. Paul, MN 55155
Phone: 651-224-7634

AMERICAN LEGION AUXILIARY DEPARTMENT OF TEXAS

http://www.alatexas.org/

AMERICAN LEGION AUXILIARY DEPARTMENT OF TEXAS PAST PRESIDENTS' PARLEY MEDICAL SCHOLARSHIP

Scholarships available for full-time students pursuing studies in human health care. Must be a resident of Texas. Must be a veteran or child, grandchild, great grandchild of a veteran who served in the Armed Forces during period of eligibility.

Academic Fields/Career Goals: Health and Medical Sciences.

Award: Scholarship for use in freshman, sophomore, junior, or senior years; not renewable. *Number:* 1–10. *Amount:* $1000.

Eligibility Requirements: Applicant must be enrolled or expecting to enroll full-time at a two-year or four-year or technical institution or university and resident of Texas. Available to U.S. citizens. Applicant must have general military experience.

Application Requirements: Application form, community service, financial need analysis, letter stating qualifications and intentions, recommendations or references, transcript. *Deadline:* June 1.

Contact: Paula Raney, State Secretary
Phone: 512-476-7278
Fax: 512-482-8391
E-mail: alatexas@txlegion.org

AMERICAN LEGION AUXILIARY DEPARTMENT OF WISCONSIN

http://www.amlegionauxwi.org/

AMERICAN LEGION AUXILIARY DEPARTMENT OF WISCONSIN PAST PRESIDENTS' PARLEY HEALTH CAREER SCHOLARSHIPS
• See page 366

AMERICAN LEGION DEPARTMENT OF NORTH DAKOTA

http://www.ndlegion.org/

O. NESHEIM MEMORIAL SCHOLARSHIP
• See page 254

AMERICAN OCCUPATIONAL THERAPY FOUNDATION INC.

http://www.aotf.org/

CARLOTTA WELLES SCHOLARSHIP

Award for study leading to an occupational therapy Associate degree at an accredited institution.

Academic Fields/Career Goals: Health and Medical Sciences; Therapy/Rehabilitation.

Award: Scholarship for use in sophomore year; not renewable. *Number:* up to 1. *Amount:* $500–$500.

Eligibility Requirements: Applicant must be enrolled or expecting to enroll full-time at a two-year institution. Applicant or parent of applicant must be member of American Occupational Therapy Association. Available to U.S. citizens.

Application Requirements: Application form, application form may be submitted online (http://www.aotf.org), Curriculum Director's Statement, essay, recommendations or references. *Deadline:* varies.

Contact: Ms. Jeanne Cooper, Scholarship Program Manager
Phone: 240-292-1034
Fax: 240-396-6188
E-mail: JCooper@aotf.org

AMERICAN PHYSICAL THERAPY ASSOCIATION

http://www.apta.org/honorsawards

MARY MCMILLAN SCHOLARSHIP AWARD
• See page 267

AMERICAN PHYSIOLOGICAL SOCIETY

http://www.the-aps.org

BARBARA A. HORWITZ AND JOHN M. HOROWITZ UNDERGRADUATE RESEARCH AWARDS
• See page 114

AMERICAN RESPIRATORY CARE FOUNDATION

http://www.arcfoundation.org/

JIMMY A. YOUNG MEMORIAL EDUCATION RECOGNITION AWARD

Award available to students studying respiratory care at an American Medical Association-approved institution. Preference given to minority students. Must submit letters of recommendation and a paper on a respiratory care topic. Must have a minimum 3.0 GPA.

Academic Fields/Career Goals: Health and Medical Sciences; Therapy/Rehabilitation.

Award: Prize for use in freshman, sophomore, junior, or senior years; not renewable. *Number:* 1. *Amount:* up to $1000.

Eligibility Requirements: Applicant must be enrolled or expecting to enroll full- or part-time at a two-year or four-year institution or university. Applicant must have 3.0 GPA or higher. Available to U.S. citizens.

Application Requirements: Application form, paper on respiratory care topic, recommendations or references, transcript. *Deadline:* June 16.

Contact: Jill Nelson, Administrative Coordinator
American Respiratory Care Foundation
9425 North MacArthur Boulevard, Suite 100
Irving, TX 75063-4706
Phone: 972-243-2272
Fax: 972-484-2720
E-mail: info@arcfoundation.org

MORTON B. DUGGAN, JR. MEMORIAL EDUCATION RECOGNITION AWARD

Awards students with a minimum 3.0 GPA, enrolled in an American Medical Association-approved respiratory care program. Must be U.S. citizen or permanent resident. Need proof of college enrollment. Must submit an original referenced paper on respiratory care. Preference given to Georgia and South Carolina residents. One-time merit-based award of up to $1000, and includes airfare, registration to AARC Congress, and one night's lodging.

Academic Fields/Career Goals: Health and Medical Sciences; Therapy/Rehabilitation.

Award: Scholarship for use in freshman, sophomore, junior, or senior years; not renewable. *Number:* 1. *Amount:* up to $1000.

Eligibility Requirements: Applicant must be enrolled or expecting to enroll full- or part-time at a two-year or four-year institution or university. Applicant must have 3.0 GPA or higher. Available to U.S. citizens.

Application Requirements: Application form, paper on respiratory care, recommendations or references, transcript. *Deadline:* June 16.

Contact: Jill Nelson, Administrative Coordinator
American Respiratory Care Foundation
9425 North MacArthur Boulevard, Suite 100
Irving, TX 75063-4706
Phone: 972-243-2272
Fax: 972-484-2720
E-mail: info@arcfoundation.org

SEPRACOR ACHIEVEMENT AWARD FOR EXCELLENCE IN PULMONARY DISEASE STATE MANAGEMENT

Nominations may be made by anyone by submitting a paper of not more than 1000 words describing why a nominee should be considered for the award. Must be a member of the American Association for Respiratory Care. Must be a respiratory therapist or other healthcare professional, including physician. Nominees must have demonstrated the attainment of positive healthcare outcomes as a direct result of their disease-oriented practice of respiratory care, regardless of care setting.

Academic Fields/Career Goals: Health and Medical Sciences; Therapy/Rehabilitation.

Award: Prize for use in freshman, sophomore, junior, senior, graduate, or postgraduate years; not renewable. *Number:* 1. *Amount:* up to $2500.

Eligibility Requirements: Applicant must be enrolled or expecting to enroll full- or part-time at a four-year institution or university. Applicant or parent of applicant must have employment or volunteer experience in physical therapy/rehabilitation. Available to U.S. and non-U.S. citizens.

Application Requirements: Paper describing why a nominee should be considered for the award, recommendations or references, resume. *Deadline:* June 1.

Contact: Jill Nelson, Administrative Coordinator
American Respiratory Care Foundation
9425 North MacArthur Boulevard, Suite 100
Irving, TX 75063-4706
Phone: 972-243-2272
Fax: 972-484-2720
E-mail: info@arcfoundation.org

THE ARC NEW YORK

https://www.nysarc.org/

JAMES F. REVILLE SCHOLARSHIP
• See page 366

ARIZONA PROFESSIONAL CHAPTER OF AISES

http://www.aises.org/scholarships

ARIZONA PROFESSIONAL CHAPTER OF AISES SCHOLARSHIP
• See page 313

ARRL FOUNDATION INC.

http://www.arrl.org/

CAROLE J. STREETER, KB9JBR, SCHOLARSHIP
• See page 254

MEDICAL AMATEUR RADIO COUNCIL (MARCO) SCHOLARSHIP
• See page 115

OLD MAN INTERNATIONAL SIDEBAND SOCIETY (OMISS) SCHOLARSHIP
• See page 259

W1FDR SCHOLARSHIP
• See page 122

ASRT FOUNDATION

http://foundation.asrt.org

ELEKTA RADIATION THERAPY SCHOLARSHIP

Open to students in the 2nd or 3rd year of an entry-level radiation therapy program. Is a merit-based scholarship awarded on financial need, academic performance, recommendation, and essays.

Academic Fields/Career Goals: Health and Medical Sciences.

Award: Scholarship for use in sophomore, junior, or senior years; not renewable. *Number:* 4. *Amount:* $5000.

Eligibility Requirements: Applicant must be enrolled or expecting to enroll full- or part-time at a two-year or four-year or technical institution or university. Applicant or parent of applicant must be member of American Society of Radiologic Technologists. Applicant must have 3.0 GPA or higher. Available to U.S. citizens.

Application Requirements: Application form, essay, financial need analysis. *Deadline:* February 1.

JERMAN-CAHOON STUDENT SCHOLARSHIP

Merit scholarship for certificate or undergraduate students. Must have completed at least one semester in the radiological sciences to apply (does not include prerequisites). Financial need is a factor. Requirements include 3.0 GPA, recommendation and several short answer essays.

Academic Fields/Career Goals: Health and Medical Sciences; Oncology; Radiology.

Award: Scholarship for use in sophomore or junior years; not renewable. *Number:* 6. *Amount:* up to $2500.

Eligibility Requirements: Applicant must be enrolled or expecting to enroll full- or part-time at a two-year or four-year or technical institution or university. Applicant must have 3.0 GPA or higher. Available to U.S. citizens.

Application Requirements: Application form, application form may be submitted online (http://aim.applyists.net), essay, financial need analysis, recommendations or references, transcript. *Deadline:* February 1.

PROFESSIONAL ADVANCEMENT SCHOLARSHIP
• See page 367

ROYCE OSBORN MINORITY STUDENT SCHOLARSHIP

Minority scholarship for certificate or undergraduate students. Must have completed at least one semester in the radiological sciences to apply (does not include prerequisites). Financial need is a factor. Requirements include 3.0 GPA, recommendation and several short answer essays.

Academic Fields/Career Goals: Health and Medical Sciences; Radiology.

Award: Scholarship for use in sophomore or junior years; not renewable. *Number:* 5. *Amount:* up to $4000.

Eligibility Requirements: Applicant must be American Indian/Alaska Native, Asian/Pacific Islander, Black (non-Hispanic), Hispanic and enrolled or expecting to enroll full- or part-time at a two-year or four-year or technical institution or university. Applicant must have 3.0 GPA or higher. Available to U.S. citizens.

Application Requirements: Application form, application form may be submitted online (http://aim.applyists.net), essay, financial need analysis, recommendations or references, transcript. *Deadline:* February 1.

SIEMENS CLINICAL ADVANCEMENT SCHOLARSHIP

Open to ASRT members only who are medical imaging professionals pursuing a Bachelor's or Master's degree in the radiologic sciences to advance patient care skills or pursuing a certificate in a specialty discipline and seek to enhance their clinical practice skills and provide excellent patient care should apply. One of the following must also be true: applicant holds an unrestricted state license, is registered by the American Registry of Radiologic Technologists, or registered with an equivalent certifying body.

Academic Fields/Career Goals: Health and Medical Sciences; Oncology; Radiology.

Award: Scholarship for use in sophomore, junior, senior, graduate, or postgraduate years; not renewable. *Number:* 4. *Amount:* $5000.

Eligibility Requirements: Applicant must be enrolled or expecting to enroll full- or part-time at a two-year or four-year or technical institution or university. Applicant or parent of applicant must be member of American Society of Radiologic Technologists. Applicant must have 3.0 GPA or higher. Available to U.S. citizens.

Application Requirements: Application form, application form may be submitted online (http://aim.applyists.net), essay, financial need analysis, recommendations or references, resume. *Deadline:* February 1.

VARIAN RADIATION THERAPY ADVANCEMENT SCHOLARSHIP

Merit scholarship for radiation therapists and medical dosimetrists or for current radiologic technologists in an entry-level radiation therapy program. Financial need is a factor. Requirements include recommendation and several short answer essays.

Academic Fields/Career Goals: Health and Medical Sciences; Oncology.

Award: Scholarship for use in sophomore, junior, senior, graduate, or postgraduate years; not renewable. *Number:* 19. *Amount:* $5000.

Eligibility Requirements: Applicant must be enrolled or expecting to enroll full- or part-time at a two-year or four-year or technical institution or university. Applicant must have 3.0 GPA or higher. Available to U.S. citizens.

Application Requirements: Application form, application form may be submitted online (http://aim.applyists.net), essay, financial need analysis, recommendations or references, transcript. *Deadline:* February 1.

ASSOCIATION FOR EDUCATION AND REHABILITATION OF THE BLIND AND VISUALLY IMPAIRED

http://www.aerbvi.org/

WILLIAM AND DOROTHY FERRELL SCHOLARSHIP

• See page 268

ASSOCIATION ON AMERICAN INDIAN AFFAIRS, INC.

http://www.indian-affairs.org/

ELIZABETH AND SHERMAN ASCHE MEMORIAL SCHOLARSHIP FUND

• See page 106

AVACARE MEDICAL

https://avacaremedical.com

AVACARE MEDICAL SCHOLARSHIP

• See page 115

BETHESDA LUTHERAN COMMUNITIES

http://www.bethesdalutherancommunities.org/scholarships

DEVELOPMENTAL DISABILITIES SCHOLASTIC ACHIEVEMENT SCHOLARSHIP FOR COLLEGE STUDENTS WHO ARE LUTHERAN

• See page 254

BHW GROUP

https://thebhwgroup.com/

BHW WOMEN IN STEM SCHOLARSHIP

• See page 124

BIOCOMMUNICATIONS ASSOCIATION

http://www.bca.org

ENDOWMENT FUND FOR EDUCATION GRANT

• See page 218

BOYS AND GIRLS CLUBS OF GREATER SAN DIEGO

http://www.sdyouth.org/

SPENCE REESE SCHOLARSHIP

• See page 316

CANFIT

http://www.canfit.org/

CANFIT NUTRITION, PHYSICAL EDUCATION AND CULINARY ARTS SCHOLARSHIP

• See page 245

CHRISTIANA CARE HEALTH SYSTEMS

http://www.christianacare.org/

RUTH SHAW JUNIOR BOARD SCHOLARSHIP

Offers financial assistance to students currently enrolled in nursing and selected allied health programs. Applicants are selected based on academic achievement and a proven commitment to quality patient care. Students receiving assistance are required to commit to a minimum of one year of employment with Christiana Care.

Academic Fields/Career Goals: Health and Medical Sciences; Nursing.

Award: Scholarship for use in freshman, sophomore, junior, or senior years; not renewable.

Eligibility Requirements: Applicant must be enrolled or expecting to enroll full- or part-time at a four-year institution or university. Applicant or parent of applicant must have employment or volunteer experience in nursing. Available to U.S. citizens.

Application Requirements: Application form, driver's license, recommendations or references, resume, transcript. *Deadline:* April 30.

Contact: Wendy Gable, Scholarship Committee
Christiana Care Health Systems
200 Hygeia Drive, PO Box 6001
Newark, DE 19713
Phone: 302-428-5710
E-mail: wgable@christianacare.org

CONSOLE AND HOLLAWELL

http://www.myinjuryattorney.com/legal-scholarship-2017-2018/

OVERDOSE ATTORNEY SCHOLARSHIP

Overdose Attorney is a website project created by the law firm Console & Hollawell in response to the US opioid epidemic. We started this project in 2017, to help those who lost someone due to an opioid overdose. We're committed to fighting over-prescription, a leader cause of opioid addiction. This includes shutting down pill-pushing doctors and holding drug manufacturers accountable. To raise awareness of this important cause, we're proud to offer our Overdose Lawyer Scholarship. Our hope is that students of the legal or medical professions will help us fight this epidemic. We want qualified applicants to write a brief essay (500 words) to tell us why you deserve this award.

Academic Fields/Career Goals: Health and Medical Sciences; Law/Legal Services.

Award: Scholarship for use in freshman, sophomore, junior, senior, or graduate years; not renewable. *Number:* 1. *Amount:* $1000.

Eligibility Requirements: Applicant must be enrolled or expecting to enroll full-time at a two-year or four-year institution or university. Available to U.S. citizens.

Application Requirements: Essay, personal photograph. *Deadline:* July 15.

Contact: Emily Senski, Digital Marketing Specialist
Console and Hollawell
525 NJ 73, #117
Marlton, NJ 08053

CONTINENTAL SOCIETY, DAUGHTERS OF INDIAN WARS

http://www.csdiw.org/

CONTINENTAL SOCIETY, DAUGHTERS OF INDIAN WARS SCHOLARSHIP
• *See page 242*

CROHN'S & COLITIS FOUNDATION

http://www.ccfa.org/

CROHN'S & COLITIS FOUNDATION OF AMERICA STUDENT RESEARCH FELLOWSHIP AWARDS

Student Research Fellowship Awards will be available for full time research with a mentor investigating a subject relevant to IBD. Mentors may not be a relative of the applicant and may not work in their lab. The mentor must be a faculty member who directs a research project highly relevant to the study of IBD at an accredited institution. Awards will be payable to the institution, not the individual. A complete financial statement and scientific report are due September 1 of the year of the award. All publications arising from work funded by this project must acknowledge support of CCFA. Candidates may be undergraduate, medical or graduate students (not yet engaged in thesis research) in accredited United States institutions. Candidates may not hold similar salary support from other agencies.

Academic Fields/Career Goals: Health and Medical Sciences.

Award: Scholarship for use in freshman, sophomore, junior, senior, or graduate years; not renewable. *Amount:* $2500.

Eligibility Requirements: Applicant must be enrolled or expecting to enroll full-time at a four-year institution or university. Available to U.S. and non-U.S. citizens.

Application Requirements: Application form. *Deadline:* March 15.

Contact: Mr. Moustafa Ibrahim, National Manager of Grants and Contracts
Crohn's & Colitis Foundation
733 Third Avenue
Suite 510
New York, NY 10017
Phone: 646-943-7505
E-mail: grants@ccfa.org

CYNTHIA E. MORGAN SCHOLARSHIP FUND (CEMS)

http://www.cemsfund.com/

CYNTHIA E. MORGAN MEMORIAL SCHOLARSHIP FUND, INC.
• *See page 334*

THE EXPERT INSTITUTE

https://www.theexpertinstitute.com

ANNUAL HEALTHCARE AND LIFE SCIENCES SCHOLARSHIP
• *See page 170*

FOUNDATION FOR SCIENCE AND DISABILITY

http://stemd.org/

GRANTS FOR DISABLED GRADUATE STUDENTS IN THE SCIENCES
• *See page 106*

FOUNDATION FOR SEACOAST HEALTH

http://www.ffsh.org

FOUNDATION FOR SEACOAST HEALTH SCHOLARSHIPS

In keeping with the mission of the organization to invest its resources to improve the health and well being of Seacoast residents, candidates must be pursuing an undergraduate or graduate degree in a health-related field of study. The awards are based primarily on scholastic aptitude and performance, personal achievements, leadership, and community involvement. The applicant's primary residence must be one of the following towns: Portsmouth, Rye, Newcastle, Greenland, Newington, and North Hampton, New Hampshire; Kittery, Elliot and York, Maine.

Academic Fields/Career Goals: Health and Medical Sciences.

Award: Scholarship for use in freshman, sophomore, junior, senior, graduate, or postgraduate years; renewable. *Number:* 2–6. *Amount:* $1000–$5000.

Eligibility Requirements: Applicant must be enrolled or expecting to enroll full- or part-time at a two-year or four-year or technical institution or university and resident of Maine, New Hampshire. Available to U.S. citizens.

Application Requirements: Application form, essay. *Deadline:* April 1.

Contact: Noreen Hodgdon
Foundation for Seacoast Health
100 Campus Drive Suite 1
Portsmouth, NH 03801
Phone: 603-422-8204
Fax: 603-422-8207
E-mail: nhodgdon@communitycampus.org

GENERAL BOARD OF HIGHER EDUCATION AND MINISTRY

http://www.gbhem.org

EDITH M. ALLEN SCHOLARSHIP
• *See page 270*

GENERAL FEDERATION OF WOMEN'S CLUBS OF MASSACHUSETTS

http://www.gfwcma.org/

CATHERINE E. PHILBIN SCHOLARSHIP

One scholarship of up to $500 will be awarded to a graduate or undergraduate student studying public health. Eligible applicants will be residents of Massachusetts. Along with the application, students must send a personal statement of no more than 500 words addressing professional goals and financial need.

Academic Fields/Career Goals: Health and Medical Sciences.

Award: Scholarship for use in freshman, sophomore, junior, senior, or graduate years; not renewable. *Number:* 1. *Amount:* $500.

Eligibility Requirements: Applicant must be enrolled or expecting to enroll full-time at a four-year institution or university and resident of Massachusetts. Available to U.S. citizens.

Application Requirements: Application form, driver's license, essay. *Deadline:* March 1.

Contact: Scholarship Chairman
General Federation of Women's Clubs of Massachusetts
PO Box 679
Sudbury, MA 01776-0679
E-mail: gfwcma@aol.com

GEORGIA BOARD FOR PHYSICIAN WORKFORCE (GBPW)

http://www.gbpw.georgia.gov

PHYSICIANS FOR RURAL AREAS ASSISTANCE PROGRAM

Service repayable medical school scholarship for a maximum of $20,000 per year for four years available to Georgia residents enrolled in U.S. accredited medical school. Repay by practicing medicine for one year in rural Georgia for each year that the scholarship is received. Service payment begins upon completion of residency training.

Academic Fields/Career Goals: Health and Medical Sciences.

Award: Scholarship for use in freshman, sophomore, junior, or senior years; renewable. *Number:* 20–25. *Amount:* up to $20,000.

Eligibility Requirements: Applicant must be enrolled or expecting to enroll full-time at an institution or university and resident of Georgia. Available to U.S. citizens.

Application Requirements: Application form, essay, financial need analysis, interview, personal photograph, proof of GA residency, test scores, transcript. *Deadline:* June 1.

Contact: Ms. Pamela Smith, Administration Manager
Georgia Board for Physician Workforce (GBPW)
2 Peachtree Street, NW
36th Floor
Atlanta, GA 30303
Phone: 404-232-7972
E-mail: psmith@dch.ga.gov

GRAND RAPIDS COMMUNITY FOUNDATION

http://www.grfoundation.org/

HARRY J. MORRIS, JR. EMERGENCY SERVICES SCHOLARSHIP

• *See page 349*

GREATER KANAWHA VALLEY FOUNDATION

http://www.tgkvf.org/

NICHOLAS AND MARY AGNES TRIVILLIAN MEMORIAL SCHOLARSHIP FUND

Renewable award for West Virginia residents pursuing medical or pharmacy programs. Must show financial need and academic merit.

Academic Fields/Career Goals: Health and Medical Sciences; Pharmacy.

Award: Scholarship for use in freshman, sophomore, junior, or senior years; renewable. *Amount:* $1000.

Eligibility Requirements: Applicant must be enrolled or expecting to enroll full-time at a four-year institution or university and resident of West Virginia. Available to U.S. citizens.

Application Requirements: Application form, essay, financial need analysis, recommendations or references, self-addressed stamped envelope with application, test scores, transcript. *Deadline:* January 15.

Contact: Susan Hoover, Scholarship Program Officer
Greater Kanawha Valley Foundation
900 Lee Street East, 16th Floor
Charleston, WV 25301
Phone: 304-346-3620
E-mail: shoover@tgkvf.org

HAWAIIAN LODGE, F&AM

http://www.hawaiianlodgefreemasons.org

HAWAIIAN LODGE SCHOLARSHIPS

• *See page 86*

HEALTHCARE INFORMATION AND MANAGEMENT SYSTEMS SOCIETY FOUNDATION

http://www.himss.org/

HIMSS FOUNDATION SCHOLARSHIP PROGRAM

• *See page 367*

HEALTH PROFESSIONS EDUCATION FOUNDATION

http://www.healthprofessions.ca.gov/

ALLIED HEALTHCARE SCHOLARSHIP PROGRAM

• *See page 165*

HEALTH RESEARCH COUNCIL OF NEW ZEALAND

http://www.hrc.govt.nz/

PACIFIC HEALTH WORKFORCE AWARD

• *See page 368*

PACIFIC MENTAL HEALTH WORK FORCE AWARD

• *See page 368*

HELLENIC UNIVERSITY CLUB OF PHILADELPHIA

http://www.hucphiladelphia.org/

DR. PETER A. THEODOS MEMORIAL GRADUATE SCHOLARSHIP

$2500 scholarship awarded to a senior undergraduate or graduate student with financial need pursuing studies leading to a Doctor of Medicine degree. Must be a U.S. citizen of Greek descent and a resident of particular counties in NJ or PA.

Academic Fields/Career Goals: Health and Medical Sciences.

Award: Scholarship for use in senior or graduate years; not renewable. *Number:* up to 1. *Amount:* up to $1500.

Eligibility Requirements: Applicant must be of Greek heritage; enrolled or expecting to enroll full-time at a four-year institution or university and resident of New Jersey, Pennsylvania. Available to U.S. citizens.

Application Requirements: Application form, financial need analysis, transcript. *Deadline:* April 21.

Contact: Anna Hadgis, Scholarship Chairman
Phone: 610-613-4310
E-mail: www.hucphiladelphia.org

INDIAN HEALTH SERVICES, UNITED STATES DEPARTMENT OF HEALTH AND HUMAN SERVICES
http://www.ihs.gov/scholarship

HEALTH PROFESSIONS PREPARATORY SCHOLARSHIP PROGRAM
• *See page 165*

INDIAN HEALTH SERVICE HEALTH PROFESSIONS PRE-GRADUATE SCHOLARSHIPS
• *See page 125*

INTERMOUNTAIN MEDICAL IMAGING
https://www.aboutimi.com/

INTERMOUNTAIN MEDICAL IMAGING SCHOLARSHIP
• *See page 147*

INTERNATIONAL ORDER OF THE KING'S DAUGHTERS AND SONS
http://www.iokds.org/

HEALTH CAREERS SCHOLARSHIP
• *See page 255*

THE JACKSON LABORATORY
https://www.jax.org

THE JACKSON LABORATORY COLLEGE SCHOLARSHIP PROGRAM
• *See page 126*

KETAMINE CLINICS OF LOS ANGELES
http://www.ketamineclinics.com/

KETAMINE CLINICS OF LOS ANGELES SCHOLARSHIP PROGRAM
• *See page 165*

LABROOTS INC.
http://www.LabRoots.com

LABROOTS STEM SCHOLARSHIP
• *See page 116*

LADIES AUXILIARY TO THE VETERANS OF FOREIGN WARS, DEPARTMENT OF MAINE
http://mainevfw.org/

FRANCES L. BOOTH MEDICAL SCHOLARSHIP SPONSORED BY LAVFW DEPARTMENT OF MAINE
Award for an undergraduate student majoring in the field of medicine who has a parent or grandparent who is a member of the Maine VFW or VFW auxiliary. Applicant must have sponsor from the VFW/Ladies Auxiliary to the Veterans of Foreign Wars.
Academic Fields/Career Goals: Health and Medical Sciences; Humanities; Nursing; Therapy/Rehabilitation.
Award: Scholarship for use in freshman, sophomore, junior, or senior years; renewable. *Number:* 1. *Amount:* $1000.

Eligibility Requirements: Applicant must be enrolled or expecting to enroll full-time at a two-year or four-year institution or university and resident of Maine. Applicant or parent of applicant must be member of Veterans of Foreign Wars or Auxiliary. Applicant must have 3.0 GPA or higher. Available to U.S. citizens.
Application Requirements: Application form, community service, essay, financial need analysis, personal letter, recommendations or references, resume, transcript. *Deadline:* March 31.
Contact: Sheila Webber, Chairman, FBMS
Ladies Auxiliary to the Veterans of Foreign Wars, Department of Maine
PO Box 493
Old Orchard Beach, ME 04064
Phone: 207-934-2405
E-mail: swebber2@maine.rr.com

LAW OFFICES OF PROSPER SHAKED
https://www.prosperlaw.com/

PROSPER SHAKED SCHOLARSHIP FOR FUTURE MEDICAL PROFESSIONALS
• *See page 166*

MAINE OSTEOPATHIC ASSOCIATION
http://www.mainedo.org/

MAINE OSTEOPATHIC ASSOCIATION SCHOLARSHIP
Two awards of $1000 each to students who are residents of Maine and able to present proof of enrollment at an approved osteopathic college.
Academic Fields/Career Goals: Health and Medical Sciences; Osteopathy.
Award: Scholarship for use in freshman, sophomore, junior, senior, graduate, or postgraduate years; not renewable. *Number:* 1–2. *Amount:* $1000.
Eligibility Requirements: Applicant must be enrolled or expecting to enroll full-time at a four-year institution or university and resident of Maine. Available to U.S. citizens.
Application Requirements: Application form. *Deadline:* continuous.
Contact: Amanda Richards, Operations Director
Maine Osteopathic Association
128 State Street, Suite 102
Augusta, ME 04330
Phone: 207-623-1101 Ext. 11
E-mail: arichards@mainedo.org

MARYLAND STATE HIGHER EDUCATION COMMISSION
http://www.mhec.state.md.us/

CHARLES W. RILEY FIRE AND EMERGENCY MEDICAL SERVICES TUITION REIMBURSEMENT PROGRAM
• *See page 349*

GRADUATE AND PROFESSIONAL SCHOLARSHIP PROGRAM-MARYLAND
• *See page 256*

MEDICAL SCRUBS COLLECTION
http://medicalscrubscollection.com

MEDICAL SCRUBS COLLECTION SCHOLARSHIP
• *See page 120*

MICHAEL MOODY FITNESS
http://www.michaelmoodyfitness.com/

MICHAEL MOODY FITNESS SCHOLARSHIP
• *See page 166*

NATIONAL ATHLETIC TRAINERS' ASSOCIATION RESEARCH AND EDUCATION FOUNDATION

http://www.natafoundation.org/

NATIONAL ATHLETIC TRAINERS' ASSOCIATION RESEARCH AND EDUCATION FOUNDATION SCHOLARSHIP PROGRAM

One-time award available to full-time students who are members of NATA. Minimum 3.2 GPA required. Open to undergraduate upperclassmen and graduate/postgraduate students.

Academic Fields/Career Goals: Health and Medical Sciences; Health Information Management/Technology; Sports-Related/Exercise Science; Therapy/Rehabilitation.

Award: Scholarship for use in junior, senior, graduate, or postgraduate years; not renewable. *Number:* 70. *Amount:* $2000.

Eligibility Requirements: Applicant must be enrolled or expecting to enroll full-time at a four-year institution or university. Applicant or parent of applicant must be member of National Athletic Trainers Association. Available to U.S. and non-U.S. citizens.

Application Requirements: Application form, essay, recommendations or references, transcript. *Deadline:* February 10.

Contact: Patsy Brown, Scholarship Coordinator
National Athletic Trainers' Association Research and
    Education Foundation
2952 Stemmons Freeway, Suite 200
Dallas, TX 75247
Phone: 214-637-6282 Ext. 151
Fax: 214-637-2206
E-mail: patsyb@nata.org

NATIONAL INSTITUTES OF HEALTH

https://www.training.nih.gov/programs/ugsp

NIH UNDERGRADUATE SCHOLARSHIP PROGRAM FOR STUDENTS FROM DISADVANTAGED BACKGROUNDS

• See page 116

NEXTSTEPU

http://www.nextstepu.com/

$1,500 STEM SCHOLARSHIP

• See page 120

OREGON COMMUNITY FOUNDATION

http://www.oregoncf.org/

FRANZ STENZEL M.D. AND KATHRYN STENZEL SCHOLARSHIP FUND

Scholarships for Oregon residents, with a focus on three types of students: (a) those pursuing any type of undergraduate degree, (b) those pursuing a nursing education through a two-year, four-year, or graduate program, and (c) medical students.

Academic Fields/Career Goals: Health and Medical Sciences; Nursing.

Award: Scholarship for use in freshman, sophomore, junior, or senior years; renewable. *Number:* up to 70. *Amount:* $2000–$5000.

Eligibility Requirements: Applicant must be enrolled or expecting to enroll full-time at a two-year or four-year institution or university and resident of Oregon. Available to U.S. citizens.

Application Requirements: Application form, recommendations or references. *Deadline:* March 1.

Contact: Dianne Causey, Program Associate for Scholarships and
    Grants
Phone: 503-227-6846 Ext. 1418
E-mail: dcausey@oregoncf.org

OREGON STUDENT ASSISTANCE COMMISSION

https://oregonstudentaid.gov/

ANDY AITKENHEAD SCHOLARSHIP

• See page 127

CHESTER AND HELEN LUTHER SCHOLARSHIP

Award available to graduates of any high school in Oregon or Clark County, Washington. Applicants must also be residents of either Oregon or Clark County, Washington. Must attend a college or university in Oregon or Clark County, Washington, enroll at least half-time, be a first-generation college attendee, and be at least 25 years old as of the March scholarship deadline. Based on financial need.

Academic Fields/Career Goals: Health and Medical Sciences; Nursing.

Award: Scholarship for use in freshman, sophomore, junior, senior, or graduate years; not renewable.

Eligibility Requirements: Applicant must be enrolled or expecting to enroll full- or part-time at a two-year or four-year institution or university; resident of Oregon, Washington and studying in Oregon, Washington. Applicant must have 3.0 GPA or higher. Available to U.S. citizens.

Application Requirements: Application form, financial need analysis. *Deadline:* March 1.

Contact: Melissa Adams, Scholarship Processing Coordinator
Phone: 541-687-7409
E-mail: melissa.adams@state.or.us

CLARK-PHELPS SCHOLARSHIP

• See page 256

FRANZ STENZEL M.D. AND KATHRYN STENZEL SCHOLARSHIP

Open to graduates (including GED recipients and home-schooled graduates) of Oregon high schools. Majoring in medicine (pre-med and graduate-level), nursing, or physician assistant studies. High school seniors must have minimum 2.75 GPA and college students a minimum 2.5 GPA. Must enroll at least half time. Automatically renewable if renewal criteria is met. Based on financial need.

Academic Fields/Career Goals: Health and Medical Sciences; Nursing.

Award: Scholarship for use in freshman, sophomore, junior, senior, or graduate years; renewable.

Eligibility Requirements: Applicant must be enrolled or expecting to enroll full- or part-time at a four-year institution or university and resident of Oregon. Applicant must have 2.5 GPA or higher. Available to U.S. citizens.

Application Requirements: Application form, financial need analysis. *Deadline:* March 1.

Contact: Melissa Adams, Scholarship Processing Coordinator
Phone: 541-687-7409
E-mail: melissa.adams@state.or.us

JOHN MARK TURETZKY SCHOLARSHIP

Scholarship for career in natural medicine or related fields including integrative mental health, oriental medicine, or nutrition. Preference for National College of Natural Medicine, Portland, Oregon. Based on financial need.

Academic Fields/Career Goals: Health and Medical Sciences.

Award: Scholarship for use in freshman, sophomore, junior, or senior years; not renewable.

Eligibility Requirements: Applicant must be enrolled or expecting to enroll at a two-year or four-year institution and resident of Oregon. Available to U.S. citizens.

Application Requirements: Application form. *Deadline:* March 1.

Contact: Melissa Adams, Scholarship Processing Coordinator
Phone: 541-687-7409
E-mail: melissa.adams@state.or.us

MARION A. LINDEMAN SCHOLARSHIP

Award for Willamette View Health Center or Willamette View Terrace employees who have completed one or more years of service. Must be pursuing a degree or certificate in nursing, speech, physical or occupational therapy, or other health-related fields at a public or nonprofit college. Must enroll at least half time in a public or non-profit college and reapply annually for award renewal. Based on financial need.

Academic Fields/Career Goals: Health and Medical Sciences; Nursing; Therapy/Rehabilitation.

Award: Scholarship for use in freshman, sophomore, junior, or senior years; not renewable.

Eligibility Requirements: Applicant must be enrolled or expecting to enroll full- or part-time at a two-year or four-year institution. Applicant or parent of applicant must be affiliated with Willamette View. Available to U.S. citizens.

Application Requirements: Application form, financial need analysis. *Deadline:* March 1.

Contact: Melissa Adams, Scholarship Processing Coordinator
Phone: 541-687-7409
E-mail: melissa.adams@state.or.us

PEARL SCHOLARSHIP

Award for students in Oregon public colleges and universities who are or have been in foster care. College students must have a minimum 3.0 GPA. Must be enrolled at least part-time and studying health sciences. Based on financial need.

Academic Fields/Career Goals: Health and Medical Sciences.

Award: Scholarship for use in freshman, sophomore, junior, or senior years; not renewable.

Eligibility Requirements: Applicant must be enrolled or expecting to enroll full- or part-time at a four-year institution or university and studying in Oregon. Applicant must have 3.0 GPA or higher. Available to U.S. citizens.

Application Requirements: Application form, financial need analysis. *Deadline:* March 1.

Contact: Melissa Adams, Scholarship Processing Coordinator
Phone: 541-687-7409
E-mail: melissa.adams@state.or.us

PACERS FOUNDATION INC.

http://www.pacersfoundation.org/

LINDA CRAIG MEMORIAL SCHOLARSHIP PRESENTED BY ST. VINCENT SPORTS MEDICINE

Scholarship presented by St. Vincent Sports Medicine is for currently-enrolled juniors and seniors with declared majors of medicine, sports medicine, and/or physical therapy. Students must have completed at least 4 semesters and attend a school in Indiana. Minimum 3.0 GPA required.

Academic Fields/Career Goals: Health and Medical Sciences; Sports-Related/Exercise Science; Therapy/Rehabilitation.

Award: Scholarship for use in junior, senior, graduate, or postgraduate years; renewable. *Number:* 1–2. *Amount:* $2000.

Eligibility Requirements: Applicant must be enrolled or expecting to enroll full-time at a two-year or four-year institution or university and studying in Indiana. Applicant must have 3.0 GPA or higher. Available to U.S. citizens.

Application Requirements: Application form, essay, recommendations or references, transcript. *Deadline:* March 1.

Contact: Jami Marsh, Executive Director
Pacers Foundation Inc.
125 South Pennsylvania Street
Indianapolis, IN 46204
Phone: 317-917-2856
E-mail: foundation@pacers.com

PILOT INTERNATIONAL

https://www.pilotinternational.org/

PILOT INTERNATIONAL SCHOLARSHIP

The Pilot International Scholarship was established in 1988 to provide financial Assistance to undergraduate students preparing for a career working with youth leadership and development, helping people with brain safety or fitness, or caring for families during times of need. Scholarships are based on financial need, academic success, and application content.

Academic Fields/Career Goals: Health and Medical Sciences; Nursing; Psychology; Special Education; Therapy/Rehabilitation.

Award: Scholarship for use in freshman, sophomore, or junior years; not renewable. *Number:* 5–10. *Amount:* $500–$1500.

Eligibility Requirements: Applicant must be enrolled or expecting to enroll full- or part-time at a four-year institution or university. Applicant must have 3.0 GPA or higher. Available to U.S. citizens.

Application Requirements: Application form, community service, essay, financial need analysis, personal photograph. *Deadline:* March 15.

Contact: Sierra Martin, Founders Fund Specialist
Pilot International
102 Preston Court
Macon, GA 31210
Phone: 478-477-1208 Ext. 304
Fax: 478-477-6978
E-mail: sierra@pilothq.org

PRESBYTERIAN CHURCH (USA)

http://www.pcusa.org/financialaid

STUDENT OPPORTUNITY SCHOLARSHIP
• *See page 275*

SCARLETT FAMILY FOUNDATION SCHOLARSHIP PROGRAM

http://www.scarlettfoundation.org/

SCHOLARSHIP FOR STUDENTS PURSUING A BUSINESS OR STEM DEGREE
• *See page 91*

SIGMA XI, THE SCIENTIFIC RESEARCH SOCIETY

http://www.sigmaxi.org/

SIGMA XI GRANTS-IN-AID OF RESEARCH
• *See page 110*

THE SOCIETY FOR THE SCIENTIFIC STUDY OF SEXUALITY

http://www.sexscience.org/

THE SOCIETY FOR THE SCIENTIFIC STUDY OF SEXUALITY STUDENT RESEARCH GRANT
• *See page 120*

SOCIETY OF PEDIATRIC NURSES

http://www.pedsnurses.org/

SOCIETY OF PEDIATRIC NURSES EDUCATIONAL SCHOLARSHIP
• *See page 203*

STRAIGHTFORWARD MEDIA

http://www.straightforwardmedia.com/

STRAIGHTFORWARD MEDIA MEDICAL PROFESSIONS SCHOLARSHIP
• *See page 257*

STRAIGHT NORTH

https://www.straightnorth.com/

STRAIGHT NORTH STEM SCHOLARSHIP
• *See page 92*

UNITED NATIONS ASSOCIATION OF CONNECTICUT

http://www.unausa.org

UNITED NATIONS ASSOCIATION OF CONNECTICUT SCHOLARSHIP

• *See page 147*

UNITED NEGRO COLLEGE FUND

http://www.uncf.org/

UNCF STEM SCHOLARS PROGRAM

• *See page 175*

U.S. DEPARTMENT OF HEALTH AND HUMAN SERVICES

http://www.hhs.gov/

U. S. PUBLIC HEALTH SERVICE-HEALTH RESOURCES AND SERVICES ADMINISTRATION, BUREAU OF HEALTH PROFESSIONS SCHOLARSHIPS FOR DISADVANTAGED STUDENTS

• *See page 257*

VESALIUS TRUST FOR VISUAL COMMUNICATION IN THE HEALTH SCIENCES

http://www.vesaliustrust.org/

STUDENT RESEARCH SCHOLARSHIP

Scholarships available to students currently enrolled in an undergraduate or graduate school program of bio-communications (medical illustration) who have completed one full year of the curriculum.

Academic Fields/Career Goals: Health and Medical Sciences.

Award: Scholarship for use in junior, senior, or graduate years; not renewable. *Number:* 10–15. *Amount:* $500.

Eligibility Requirements: Applicant must be enrolled or expecting to enroll full- or part-time at a four-year institution or university and must have an interest in art. Available to U.S. and non-U.S. citizens.

Application Requirements: Application form, portfolio, recommendations or references, resume, transcript. *Deadline:* November 7.

Contact: Wendy Gee, Student Grants and Scholarships
Vesalius Trust for Visual Communication in the Health Sciences
1100 Grundy Lane
San Bruno, CA 94066
Phone: 650-244-4320
E-mail: wendy.hillergee@krames.com

WISCONSIN MEDICAL SOCIETY FOUNDATION

http://www.wisconsinmedicalsocietyfoundation.org

AMY HUNTER-WILSON, MD SCHOLARSHIP

Scholarship assists American Indians with proof of tribal membership who pursue training or advanced education as doctors of medicine, nurses, or in related health careers. Award amounts are determined based on the students field of study and financial need and will vary depending on the number of eligible applicants and funds available.

Academic Fields/Career Goals: Health and Medical Sciences.

Award: Scholarship for use in freshman, sophomore, junior, senior, or graduate years; not renewable.

Eligibility Requirements: Applicant must be American Indian/Alaska Native; enrolled or expecting to enroll full-time at a two-year or four-year or technical institution or university; resident of Wisconsin and studying in Wisconsin. Available to U.S. citizens.

Application Requirements: Application form, essay, financial need analysis. *Deadline:* February 1.

Contact: Ms. Elizabeth Ringle, Scholarship Coordinator
Phone: 866-442-3800
Fax: 608-442-3851

HEALTH INFORMATION MANAGEMENT/ TECHNOLOGY

AHIMA FOUNDATION

http://ahimafoundation.org/

AHIMA FOUNDATION STUDENT MERIT SCHOLARSHIP

Merit scholarships for undergraduate, Master's, and Doctoral health information management students. Must be a member of AHIMA. One standard application for all available scholarships. Applicant must have a minimum cumulative GPA of 3.5 (out of 4.0) or 4.5 (out of 5.0). Applications information is available at: http://ahimafoundation.org/education/MeritScholarships.aspx

Academic Fields/Career Goals: Health Information Management/Technology.

Award: Scholarship for use in sophomore, junior, senior, graduate, or postgraduate years; not renewable. *Number:* 1. *Amount:* $1000–$2500.

Eligibility Requirements: Applicant must be enrolled or expecting to enroll full- or part-time at a two-year or four-year institution or university. Applicant or parent of applicant must be member of American Health Information Management Association. Applicant must have 3.5 GPA or higher. Available to U.S. and non-U.S. citizens.

Application Requirements: Application form, application form may be submitted online (http://ahimafoundation.org/education/MeritScholarships.aspx), community service, essay, program director verification, recommendations or references, transcript. *Deadline:* September 30.

Contact: AHIMA Foundation
AHIMA Foundation
233 North Michigan Avenue, 21st Floor
Chicago, IL 60601-5800
Phone: 312-233-1131
E-mail: fore@ahima.org

ALICE L. HALTOM EDUCATIONAL FUND

http://www.alhef.org/

ALICE L. HALTOM EDUCATIONAL FUND

• *See page 176*

AMERICAN LEGION AUXILIARY DEPARTMENT OF COLORADO

http://www.alacolorado.com

AMERICAN LEGION AUXILIARY DEPARTMENT OF COLORADO PAST PRESIDENTS' PARLEY HEALTH CARE PROFESSIONAL SCHOLARSHIPNURSES SCHOLARSHIP

• *See page 147*

AVACARE MEDICAL

https://avacaremedical.com

AVACARE MEDICAL SCHOLARSHIP

• *See page 115*

BETHESDA LUTHERAN COMMUNITIES

http://www.bethesdalutherancommunities.org/scholarships

DEVELOPMENTAL DISABILITIES SCHOLASTIC ACHIEVEMENT SCHOLARSHIP FOR COLLEGE STUDENTS WHO ARE LUTHERAN
• *See page 254*

BHW GROUP

https://thebhwgroup.com/

BHW WOMEN IN STEM SCHOLARSHIP
• *See page 124*

CYNTHIA E. MORGAN SCHOLARSHIP FUND (CEMS)

http://www.cemsfund.com/

CYNTHIA E. MORGAN MEMORIAL SCHOLARSHIP FUND, INC.
• *See page 334*

FOUNDATION FOR SCIENCE AND DISABILITY

http://stemd.org/

GRANTS FOR DISABLED GRADUATE STUDENTS IN THE SCIENCES
• *See page 106*

HAWAIIAN LODGE, F&AM

http://www.hawaiianlodgefreemasons.org

HAWAIIAN LODGE SCHOLARSHIPS
• *See page 86*

HEALTHCARE INFORMATION AND MANAGEMENT SYSTEMS SOCIETY FOUNDATION

http://www.himss.org/

HIMSS FOUNDATION SCHOLARSHIP PROGRAM
• *See page 367*

HEALTH RESEARCH COUNCIL OF NEW ZEALAND

http://www.hrc.govt.nz/

PACIFIC HEALTH WORKFORCE AWARD
• *See page 368*

PACIFIC MENTAL HEALTH WORK FORCE AWARD
• *See page 368*

INTERMOUNTAIN MEDICAL IMAGING

https://www.aboutimi.com/

INTERMOUNTAIN MEDICAL IMAGING SCHOLARSHIP
• *See page 147*

LABROOTS INC.

http://www.LabRoots.com

LABROOTS STEM SCHOLARSHIP
• *See page 116*

LAW OFFICES OF PROSPER SHAKED

https://www.prosperlaw.com/

PROSPER SHAKED SCHOLARSHIP FOR FUTURE MEDICAL PROFESSIONALS
• *See page 166*

MEDICAL SCRUBS COLLECTION

http://medicalscrubscollection.com

MEDICAL SCRUBS COLLECTION SCHOLARSHIP
• *See page 120*

MICHAEL MOODY FITNESS

http://www.michaelmoodyfitness.com/

MICHAEL MOODY FITNESS SCHOLARSHIP
• *See page 166*

NATIONAL ATHLETIC TRAINERS' ASSOCIATION RESEARCH AND EDUCATION FOUNDATION

http://www.natafoundation.org/

NATIONAL ATHLETIC TRAINERS' ASSOCIATION RESEARCH AND EDUCATION FOUNDATION SCHOLARSHIP PROGRAM
• *See page 376*

NEXTSTEPU

http://www.nextstepu.com/

$1,500 STEM SCHOLARSHIP
• *See page 120*

OREGON STUDENT ASSISTANCE COMMISSION

https://oregonstudentaid.gov/

WILLIAM E. KEENE MEMORIAL SCHOLARSHIP
• *See page 335*

SCARLETT FAMILY FOUNDATION SCHOLARSHIP PROGRAM

http://www.scarlettfoundation.org/

SCHOLARSHIP FOR STUDENTS PURSUING A BUSINESS OR STEM DEGREE
• *See page 91*

STRAIGHTFORWARD MEDIA

http://www.straightforwardmedia.com/

STRAIGHTFORWARD MEDIA MEDICAL PROFESSIONS SCHOLARSHIP
• *See page 257*

STRAIGHT NORTH
https://www.straightnorth.com/

STRAIGHT NORTH STEM SCHOLARSHIP
• *See page 92*

TECHNOLOGY FIRST
https://technologyfirst.org/

ROBERT V. MCKENNA SCHOLARSHIPS
• *See page 235*

ULTRASOUNDTECHNICIANSCHOOLS.COM
http://www.ultrasoundtechnicianschools.com

ULTRASOUNDTECHNICIANSCHOOLS.COM SCHOLARSHIP
We are offering you the chance to win a $1,000 ultrasound technician scholarship. A winner will be selected from the list of all eligible candidates. We will be awarding two different scholarships each year. When one deadline ends, the next scholarship will begin.

Academic Fields/Career Goals: Health Information Management/Technology; Radiology.

Award: Scholarship for use in freshman, sophomore, or junior years; not renewable. *Number:* 2. *Amount:* $1000.

Eligibility Requirements: Applicant must be enrolled or expecting to enroll full-time at a two-year or four-year or technical institution or university. Available to U.S. citizens.

Application Requirements: Application form. *Deadline:* July 15.

Contact: Jennifer Moody, Website Marketing Strategist
UltrasoundTechnicianSchools.com
15500 W 113th St
#200
Lenexa, KS 66219
Phone: 913-254-6000 Ext. 6063
E-mail: jennifer.moody@marketing.keypathedu.com

HEATING, AIR-CONDITIONING, AND REFRIGERATION MECHANICS

AMERICAN INDIAN SCIENCE AND ENGINEERING SOCIETY
http://www.aises.org/

A.T. ANDERSON MEMORIAL SCHOLARSHIP PROGRAM
• *See page 121*

AMERICAN SOCIETY OF HEATING, REFRIGERATING, AND AIR CONDITIONING ENGINEERS, INC.
http://www.ashrae.org/

ALWIN B. NEWTON SCHOLARSHIP
• *See page 281*

ASHRAE GENERAL SCHOLARSHIPS
• *See page 294*

ASHRAE LEGACY SCHOLARSHIP
• *See page 295*

DUANE HANSON SCHOLARSHIP
• *See page 282*

FRANK M. CODA SCHOLARSHIP
• *See page 282*

HENRY ADAMS SCHOLARSHIP
• *See page 282*

LYNN G. BELLENGER SCHOLARSHIP
• *See page 282*

REUBEN TRANE SCHOLARSHIP
• *See page 282*

WILLIS H. CARRIER SCHOLARSHIPS
• *See page 283*

BHW GROUP
https://thebhwgroup.com/

BHW WOMEN IN STEM SCHOLARSHIP
• *See page 124*

PLUMBING-HEATING-COOLING CONTRACTORS EDUCATION FOUNDATION
http://www.phccfoundation.org/scholarships

BRADFORD WHITE CORPORATION SCHOLARSHIP
Scholarship for students enrolled in either an approved four-year PHCC apprenticeship program or at an accredited two-year community college, technical college, or trade school.

Academic Fields/Career Goals: Heating, Air-Conditioning, and Refrigeration Mechanics; Trade/Technical Specialties.

Award: Scholarship for use in freshman, sophomore, junior, or senior years; not renewable. *Number:* 3. *Amount:* $2500.

Eligibility Requirements: Applicant must be enrolled or expecting to enroll full-time at a two-year or technical institution. Applicant must have 2.5 GPA or higher. Available to U.S. and Canadian citizens.

Application Requirements: Application form, essay. *Deadline:* May 1.

Contact: John Zink, Scholarship Coordinator
Phone: 800-533-7694
E-mail: scholarships@naphcc.org

DELTA FAUCET COMPANY SCHOLARSHIP PROGRAM
• *See page 182*

PHCC EDUCATIONAL FOUNDATION NEED-BASED SCHOLARSHIP
• *See page 182*

PHCC EDUCATIONAL FOUNDATION SCHOLARSHIP PROGRAM
• *See page 182*

PROFESSIONAL CONSTRUCTION ESTIMATORS ASSOCIATION
http://www.pcea.org/

TED G. WILSON MEMORIAL SCHOLARSHIP FOUNDATION
• *See page 211*

SOUTH CAROLINA ASSOCIATION OF HEATING AND AIR CONDITIONING CONTRACTORS

http://www.schvac.org/

SOUTH CAROLINA ASSOCIATION OF HEATING AND AIR CONDITIONING CONTRACTORS SCHOLARSHIP

Scholarship of $500 to pursue a career in the heating and air conditioning industry. Participating students must maintain an overall GPA of 2.5 and a GPA of 3.0 in all major topics. Deadline varies.

Academic Fields/Career Goals: Heating, Air-Conditioning, and Refrigeration Mechanics.

Award: Scholarship for use in freshman year; renewable. *Amount:* $500.

Eligibility Requirements: Applicant must be high school student and planning to enroll or expecting to enroll full- or part-time at a technical institution. Applicant must have 2.5 GPA or higher. Available to U.S. and non-U.S. citizens.

Application Requirements: Application form, recommendations or references. *Deadline:* varies.

Contact: Leigh Faircloth, Scholarship Committee
Phone: 800-395-9276
Fax: 803-252-7799
E-mail: staff@schvac.org

STRAIGHTFORWARD MEDIA

http://www.straightforwardmedia.com/

STRAIGHTFORWARD MEDIA VOCATIONAL-TECHNICAL SCHOOL SCHOLARSHIP
• See page 118

STRAIGHT NORTH

https://www.straightnorth.com/

STRAIGHT NORTH STEM SCHOLARSHIP
• See page 92

HISTORIC PRESERVATION AND CONSERVATION

AMERICAN SCHOOL OF CLASSICAL STUDIES AT ATHENS

http://www.ascsa.edu.gr/

ASCSA SUMMER SESSION AND SUMMER SEMINARS SCHOLARSHIPS
• See page 118

COSTUME SOCIETY OF AMERICA

http://www.costumesocietyamerica.com/

ADELE FILENE STUDENT PRESENTER GRANT
• See page 138

STELLA BLUM STUDENT RESEARCH GRANT
• See page 138

THE GEORGIA TRUST FOR HISTORIC PRESERVATION

http://www.georgiatrust.org/

B. PHINIZY SPALDING, HUBERT B. OWENS, AND THE NATIONAL SOCIETY OF THE COLONIAL DAMES OF AMERICA IN THE STATE OF GEORGIA ACADEMIC SCHOLARSHIPS
• See page 113

J. NEEL REID PRIZE
• See page 133

PLAN NEW HAMPSHIRE

http://www.plannh.org

PLAN NEW HAMPSHIRE SCHOLARSHIP AND FELLOWSHIP PROGRAM
• See page 129

HISTORY

AMERICAN FEDERATION OF STATE, COUNTY, AND MUNICIPAL EMPLOYEES

http://www.afscme.org/

AFSCME/UNCF UNION SCHOLARS PROGRAM
• See page 113

AMERICAN SCHOOL OF CLASSICAL STUDIES AT ATHENS

http://www.ascsa.edu.gr/

ASCSA SUMMER SESSION AND SUMMER SEMINARS SCHOLARSHIPS
• See page 118

ASSOCIATION OF FORMER INTELLIGENCE OFFICERS

http://www.afio.com

AFIO UNDERGRADUATE AND GRADUATE SCHOLARSHIPS
• See page 113

CANADIAN INSTITUTE OF UKRAINIAN STUDIES

http://www.cius.ca/

LEO J. KRYSA UNDERGRADUATE SCHOLARSHIP
• See page 138

COSTUME SOCIETY OF AMERICA

http://www.costumesocietyamerica.com/

ADELE FILENE STUDENT PRESENTER GRANT
• See page 138

STELLA BLUM STUDENT RESEARCH GRANT
• See page 138

CULTURAL SERVICES OF THE FRENCH EMBASSY

http://www.frenchculture.org/

TEACHING ASSISTANT PROGRAM IN FRANCE
• *See page 113*

THE GEORGIA TRUST FOR HISTORIC PRESERVATION

http://www.georgiatrust.org/

B. PHINIZY SPALDING, HUBERT B. OWENS, AND THE NATIONAL SOCIETY OF THE COLONIAL DAMES OF AMERICA IN THE STATE OF GEORGIA ACADEMIC SCHOLARSHIPS
• *See page 113*

GREATER SALINA COMMUNITY FOUNDATION

http://www.gscf.org/

KANSAS FEDERATION OF REPUBLICAN WOMEN SCHOLARSHIP

Awards female students currently attending a Kansas college or university with declared major of political science, history, or public administration. Must be entering junior or senior year of undergraduate study, or attending graduate school. Must be Kansas residents and maintain cumulative GPA of 3.0 or better. Applicants must be registered members of the Republican Party. Must be involved in extracurricular activities.

Academic Fields/Career Goals: History; Political Science; Public Policy and Administration.

Award: Scholarship for use in junior, senior, or graduate years; renewable. *Number:* 1. *Amount:* up to $1000.

Eligibility Requirements: Applicant must be enrolled or expecting to enroll full-time at a two-year or four-year institution or university; female; resident of Kansas and studying in Kansas. Applicant must have 3.0 GPA or higher. Available to U.S. citizens.

Application Requirements: Application form, essay. *Deadline:* March 31.

Contact: Michelle Griffin, Scholarship and Affiliate Coordinator
Greater Salina Community Foundation
PO Box 2876
Salina, KS 67402-2876
Phone: 785-823-1800
E-mail: michellegriffin@gscf.org

HAWAIIAN LODGE, F&AM

http://www.hawaiianlodgefreemasons.org

HAWAIIAN LODGE SCHOLARSHIPS
• *See page 86*

INSTITUTE FOR HUMANE STUDIES

http://www.theihs.org/

HUMANE STUDIES FELLOWSHIPS
• *See page 219*

ISLAMIC SCHOLARSHIP FUND

http://islamicscholarshipfund.org/

ISF NATIONAL SCHOLARSHIP
• *See page 119*

LA-PHILOSOPHIE.COM

http://la-philosophie.com

LA-PHILOSOPHIE.COM SCHOLARSHIP
• *See page 119*

THE LYNDON BAINES JOHNSON FOUNDATION

http://www.lbjlibrary.org/page/foundation/

MOODY RESEARCH GRANTS
• *See page 114*

NATIONAL SOCIETY DAUGHTERS OF THE AMERICAN REVOLUTION

http://www.dar.org/

NATIONAL SOCIETY DAUGHTERS OF THE AMERICAN REVOLUTION DR. AURA-LEE A. PITTENGER AND JAMES HOBBS PITTENGER AMERICAN HISTORY SCHOLARSHIP

Scholarship of $2000 each year for up to four consecutive years to a graduating high school senior who will have a concentrated study of a minimum of 24 credit hours in American history or American government while in college. United States citizens residing abroad may apply through a Units Overseas chapter.

Academic Fields/Career Goals: History; Political Science.

Award: Scholarship for use in freshman year; renewable. *Number:* 1. *Amount:* $2000.

Eligibility Requirements: Applicant must be high school student and planning to enroll or expecting to enroll full-time at a four-year institution or university. Available to U.S. citizens.

Application Requirements: Application form, essay. *Deadline:* February 10.

Contact: Lakeisha Graham, Manager, Office of the Reporter General
Phone: 202-628-1776
Fax: 202-879-3348
E-mail: nsdarscholarships@dar.org

NATIONAL SOCIETY DAUGHTERS OF THE AMERICAN REVOLUTION ENID HALL GRISWOLD MEMORIAL SCHOLARSHIP
• *See page 264*

PHI ALPHA THETA HISTORY HONOR SOCIETY, INC.

http://www.phialphatheta.org/

PHI ALPHA THETA PAPER PRIZES

Award for best graduate and undergraduate student papers. Grants $500 prize for best graduate student paper, $500 prize for best undergraduate paper, and four $350 prizes for either graduate or undergraduate papers. All applicants must be members of the association.

Academic Fields/Career Goals: History.

Award: Prize for use in freshman, sophomore, junior, senior, or graduate years; not renewable. *Number:* 6. *Amount:* $350–$500.

Eligibility Requirements: Applicant must be enrolled or expecting to enroll full-time at a four-year institution or university. Applicant or parent of applicant must be member of Phi Alpha Theta. Applicant must have 3.0 GPA or higher. Available to U.S. and non-U.S. citizens.

Application Requirements: Essay, recommendations or references. *Deadline:* June 30.

Contact: Dr. Clayton Drees, Department of History
Phi Alpha Theta History Honor Society, Inc.
Virginia Wesleyan College
1584 Wesleyan Drive
Norfolk, VA 23502-5599
E-mail: cdrees@vwc.edu

PHI ALPHA THETA UNDERGRADUATE STUDENT SCHOLARSHIP

Awards of $1000 available to exceptional juniors entering the senior year and majoring in modern European history (1815 to present). Must be Phi Alpha Theta members. Based on both financial need and merit.

Academic Fields/Career Goals: History.

Award: Scholarship for use in senior year; not renewable. *Number:* 1. *Amount:* $1000.

Eligibility Requirements: Applicant must be enrolled or expecting to enroll full-time at a four-year institution or university. Applicant or parent of applicant must be member of Phi Alpha Theta. Available to U.S. and non-U.S. citizens.

Application Requirements: Application form, recommendations or references, resume, transcript. *Deadline:* March 1.

Contact: Dr. Graydon Tunstall, Executive Director
Phi Alpha Theta History Honor Society, Inc.
University of South Florida
4202 East Fowler Avenue, SOC 107
Tampa, FL 33620-8100
Phone: 800-394-8195
Fax: 813-974-8215
E-mail: info@phialphatheta.org

PHI ALPHA THETA/WESTERN FRONT ASSOCIATION PAPER PRIZE

Essay competition open to full-time undergraduate members of the association. The paper must be from 12 to 15 typed pages and must address the American experience in World War I, must be dealing with virtually any aspect of American involvement during the period from 1912 (second Moroccan crisis) to 1924 (Dawes plan). Primary source material must be used. For further details visit http://www.phialphatheta.org.

Academic Fields/Career Goals: History.

Award: Prize for use in freshman, sophomore, junior, or senior years; not renewable. *Number:* 1. *Amount:* $1000.

Eligibility Requirements: Applicant must be enrolled or expecting to enroll full-time at a four-year institution or university and must have an interest in writing. Applicant or parent of applicant must be member of Phi Alpha Theta. Applicant must have 3.0 GPA or higher. Available to U.S. and non-U.S. citizens.

Application Requirements: 5 copies of the paper, CD-ROM containing a file of the paper and cover letter, application form, essay. *Deadline:* December 1.

Contact: Dr. Graydon Tunstall, Executive Director
Phi Alpha Theta History Honor Society, Inc.
University of South Florida
4202 East Fowler Avenue, SOC 107
Tampa, FL 33620-8100
Phone: 800-394-8195
Fax: 813-974-8215
E-mail: info@phialphatheta.org

PHI ALPHA THETA WORLD HISTORY ASSOCIATION PAPER PRIZE

Awards one undergraduate and one graduate-level prize for papers examining any historical issue with global implications such as: exchange or interchange of cultures, comparison of civilizations or cultures. This is a joint award with the World History Association. Must be a member of the World History Association or Phi Alpha Theta. Paper must have been composed while enrolled at an accredited college or university. Must send in four copies of paper along with professor's letter.

Academic Fields/Career Goals: History; Humanities; International Studies; Social Sciences.

Award: Prize for use in freshman, sophomore, junior, senior, or graduate years; not renewable. *Number:* 2. *Amount:* $500.

Eligibility Requirements: Applicant must be enrolled or expecting to enroll full-time at a four-year institution or university. Applicant or parent of applicant must be member of Other Student Academic Clubs, Phi Alpha Theta. Applicant must have 3.0 GPA or higher. Available to U.S. and non-U.S. citizens.

Application Requirements: 4 copies of paper, abstract, letter from faculty member or professor, recommendations or references. *Deadline:* June 30.

Contact: Prof. Merry Wiesner-Hanks
Phi Alpha Theta History Honor Society, Inc.
Department of History
University of Wisconsin-Madison
Madison, WI 53201
E-mail: merrywh@uwm.edu

SOCIETY FOR CLASSICAL STUDIES

http://www.classicalstudies.org/

MINORITY STUDENT SUMMER SCHOLARSHIP
• See page 130

SOUTHERN BAPTIST HISTORICAL LIBRARY AND ARCHIVES

http://www.sbhla.org/

LYNN E. MAY JR. STUDY GRANT
• See page 114

STRAIGHTFORWARD MEDIA

http://www.straightforwardmedia.com/

STRAIGHTFORWARD MEDIA LIBERAL ARTS SCHOLARSHIP
• See page 139

TOPSFIELD HISTORICAL SOCIETY

http://www.topsfieldhistory.org/

JOHN KIMBALL MEMORIAL TRUST SCHOLARSHIP PROGRAM FOR THE STUDY OF HISTORY

Scholarship grants funds for tuition, books, and other educational and research expenses to undergraduate and graduate students; as well as college, university, and graduate school instructors and professors who have excelled in, and/or have a passion for the study of history and related disciplines; and who reside in, or have a substantial connection to Topsfield, Massachusetts.

Academic Fields/Career Goals: History.

Award: Grant for use in freshman, sophomore, junior, senior, graduate, or postgraduate years; not renewable. *Number:* 10–12. *Amount:* $3000–$5000.

Eligibility Requirements: Applicant must be enrolled or expecting to enroll full- or part-time at a two-year or four-year or technical institution or university; resident of Massachusetts and studying in Massachusetts. Available to U.S. citizens.

Application Requirements: Application form. *Deadline:* April 15.

Contact: Mr. Norman Isler, Trustee, John Kimball Scholarship Program
Topsfield Historical Society
PO Box 323
Topsfield, MA 01983
Phone: 978-887-9724
E-mail: normisler@comcast.net

UNITED DAUGHTERS OF THE CONFEDERACY

http://www.hqudc.org/

HELEN JAMES BREWER SCHOLARSHIP

Award for full-time undergraduate student who is a descendant of a Confederate soldier, sailor or marine. Must be from Alabama, Florida, Georgia, South Carolina, Tennessee or Virginia. Recipient must be enrolled in an accredited college or university and studying history and literature. Must be a member or former member of the Children of the Confederacy. Minimum 3.0 GPA required.

Academic Fields/Career Goals: History; Literature/English/Writing.

Award: Scholarship for use in freshman, sophomore, junior or senior years; renewable. *Number:* 1–2. *Amount:* $800–$1000.

Eligibility Requirements: Applicant must be enrolled or expecting to enroll full-time at a four-year institution or university and resident of Alabama, Florida, Georgia, South Carolina, Tennessee, Virginia. Applicant or parent of applicant must be member of Children of the Confederacy, United Daughters of the Confederacy. Applicant must have 3.0 GPA or higher. Available to U.S. citizens.

Application Requirements: Application form, copy of applicant's birth certificate, copy of confederate ancestor's proof of service, essay, financial need analysis, personal photograph, recommendations or references, self-addressed stamped envelope with application, test scores, transcript. *Deadline:* March 15.

Contact: Ms. Jamie Davis, Second Vice President General
   Phone: 804-355-1636
   E-mail: hqudc@rcn.com

UNITED NEGRO COLLEGE FUND

http://www.uncf.org/

CATHERINE W. PIERCE SCHOLARSHIP
• *See page 140*

UNCF/KOCH SCHOLARS PROGRAM FOR UNDERGRADUATES
• *See page 94*

WILLA CATHER FOUNDATION

http://www.willacather.org/

ANTONETTE WILLA SKUPA TURNER SCHOLARSHIP

The purpose of the Antonette Willa Skupa Turner Scholarship is to provide financial assistance to graduates of Nebraska high schools who plan to enroll as English or history majors in accredited colleges or universities.

Academic Fields/Career Goals: History; Literature/English/Writing.

Award: Scholarship for use in freshman year; not renewable. *Number:* 1. *Amount:* $500.

Eligibility Requirements: Applicant must be high school student; planning to enroll or expecting to enroll full-time at a four-year institution or university and resident of Nebraska. Applicant must have 3.0 GPA or higher. Available to U.S. citizens.

Application Requirements: Application form, essay. *Deadline:* February 28.

Contact: Ashley Olson, Executive Director
   Willa Cather Foundation
   413 North Webster Street
   Red Cloud, NE 68970
   Phone: 402-746-2653
   E-mail: info@willacather.org

HOME ECONOMICS

ABBIE SARGENT MEMORIAL SCHOLARSHIP INC.

http://www.nhfarmbureau.org/

ABBIE SARGENT MEMORIAL SCHOLARSHIP
• *See page 100*

AMERICAN ASSOCIATION OF FAMILY & CONSUMER SERVICES

http://www.aafcs.org/

AMERICAN ASSOCIATION OF FAMILY & CONSUMER SCIENCES NATIONAL UNDERGRADUATE SCHOLARSHIP

The association awards scholarships to individuals who have exhibited the potential to make contributions to the family and consumer sciences profession.

Academic Fields/Career Goals: Home Economics.

Award: Scholarship for use in sophomore, junior, or senior years; not renewable. *Number:* up to 1. *Amount:* up to $5000.

Eligibility Requirements: Applicant must be enrolled or expecting to enroll full-time at a four-year institution or university. Available to U.S. citizens.

Application Requirements: Application form, application form may be submitted online (http://www.aafcs.org), recommendations or references, resume, transcript. *Deadline:* January 15.

CONTINENTAL SOCIETY, DAUGHTERS OF INDIAN WARS

http://www.csdiw.org/

CONTINENTAL SOCIETY, DAUGHTERS OF INDIAN WARS SCHOLARSHIP
• *See page 242*

COSTUME SOCIETY OF AMERICA

http://www.costumesocietyamerica.com/

ADELE FILENE STUDENT PRESENTER GRANT
• *See page 138*

STELLA BLUM STUDENT RESEARCH GRANT
• *See page 138*

FAMILY, CAREER AND COMMUNITY LEADERS OF AMERICA-TEXAS ASSOCIATION

http://www.texasfccla.org/

C.J. DAVIDSON SCHOLARSHIP FOR FCCLA

Renewable award for graduating high school seniors enrolled in full-time program in family and consumer sciences. Must be Texas resident and should study in Texas. Must have minimum GPA of 2.5.

Academic Fields/Career Goals: Home Economics.

Award: Scholarship for use in freshman year; renewable. *Number:* 1–10. *Amount:* up to $18,000.

Eligibility Requirements: Applicant must be high school student; planning to enroll or expecting to enroll full-time at a four-year institution or university; single; resident of Texas and studying in Texas. Applicant or parent of applicant must be member of Family, Career and Community Leaders of America. Applicant must have 2.5 GPA or higher. Available to U.S. citizens.

Application Requirements: Application form, essay, recommendations or references, test scores, transcript. *Deadline:* March 1.

Contact: Staff
   Family, Career and Community Leaders of America-Texas
    Association
   1107 West 45th
   Austin, TX 78756
   Phone: 512-306-0099
   Fax: 512-442-7100
   E-mail: fccla@texasfccla.org

FCCLA REGIONAL SCHOLARSHIPS
• *See page 179*

FCCLA TEXAS FARM BUREAU SCHOLARSHIP
• *See page 179*

INTERNATIONAL FOODSERVICE EDITORIAL COUNCIL
http://www.ifeconline.com/

INTERNATIONAL FOODSERVICE EDITORIAL COUNCIL COMMUNICATIONS SCHOLARSHIP
• *See page 96*

LES DAMES D'ESCOFFIER INTERNATIONAL, COLORADO CHAPTER
http://www.lesdamescolorado.org

LES DAMES D'ESCOFFIER INTERNATIONAL, COLORADO CHAPTER SCHOLARSHIP
• *See page 107*

UNITED DAUGHTERS OF THE CONFEDERACY
http://www.hqudc.org/

WALTER REED SMITH SCHOLARSHIP
• *See page 184*

HORTICULTURE/ FLORICULTURE

ABBIE SARGENT MEMORIAL SCHOLARSHIP INC.
http://www.nhfarmbureau.org/

ABBIE SARGENT MEMORIAL SCHOLARSHIP
• *See page 100*

ALABAMA GOLF COURSE SUPERINTENDENTS ASSOCIATION
http://www.agcsa.org/

ALABAMA GOLF COURSE SUPERINTENDENT'S ASSOCIATION'S DONNIE ARTHUR MEMORIAL SCHOLARSHIP
• *See page 104*

AMERICAN INDIAN SCIENCE AND ENGINEERING SOCIETY
http://www.aises.org/

A.T. ANDERSON MEMORIAL SCHOLARSHIP PROGRAM
• *See page 121*

AMERICAN SOCIETY FOR ENOLOGY AND VITICULTURE
http://www.asev.org/

AMERICAN SOCIETY FOR ENOLOGY AND VITICULTURE SCHOLARSHIPS
• *See page 105*

ARIZONA NURSERY ASSOCIATION
http://www.azna.org/

ARIZONA NURSERY ASSOCIATION FOUNDATION SCHOLARSHIP

Provides research grants and scholarships for the Green Industry. Applicant must be an Arizona resident currently or planning to be enrolled in a horticultural related curriculum at an Arizona university, community college, or continuing education program. See website for further details http://www.azna.org.

Academic Fields/Career Goals: Horticulture/Floriculture.

Award: Scholarship for use in freshman, sophomore, junior, or senior years; renewable. *Number:* 12–16. *Amount:* $500–$3000.

Eligibility Requirements: Applicant must be enrolled or expecting to enroll full- or part-time at a two-year or four-year or technical institution or university. Available to U.S. citizens.

Application Requirements: Application form, recommendations or references, transcript. *Deadline:* April 15.

Contact: Cheryl Goar, Executive Director
   Phone: 480-966-1610
   E-mail: cgoar@azna.org

ARRL FOUNDATION INC.
http://www.arrl.org/

ROBERT D., W8ST, AND DONNA J., W9DJS, STREETER SCHOLARSHIP
• *See page 337*

BHW GROUP
https://thebhwgroup.com/

BHW WOMEN IN STEM SCHOLARSHIP
• *See page 124*

CHS FOUNDATION
http://www.chsfoundation.org/

CHS FOUNDATION HIGH SCHOOL SCHOLARSHIPS
• *See page 100*

CHS FOUNDATION TWO-YEAR COLLEGE SCHOLARSHIPS
• *See page 100*

ENVIRONMENTAL CARE ASSOCIATION OF IDAHO
http://www.eacofidaho.org

ECA SCHOLARSHIP

The scholarship will be given directly to the recipient. Applicants must be a son or daughter of ECA member, OR be employed in the Lawn Care, Pest Control or Grounds Management Industries, OR Applicant must be enrolled as a full-time student in an accredited college level in Pest Control, Lawn Care or related industry. A reference letter and two letters of recommendation are required along with a one-page typed essay stating the benefits of the Lawn Care or Pest Control Industries.

Academic Fields/Career Goals: Horticulture/Floriculture; Trade/Technical Specialties.

Award: Scholarship for use in freshman, sophomore, junior, or senior years; not renewable. *Number:* 1–2. *Amount:* $500.

Eligibility Requirements: Applicant must be enrolled or expecting to enroll full- or part-time at a two-year or four-year or technical institution or university and resident of Idaho.

Application Requirements: Application form, essay. *Deadline:* November 10.

Contact: Ann Bates, Executive Coordinator
Phone: 208-681-4769
E-mail: abates@ecaofidaho.org

FEDERATED GARDEN CLUBS OF CONNECTICUT

http://www.ctgardenclubs.org/

FEDERATED GARDEN CLUBS OF CONNECTICUT INC. SCHOLARSHIPS
• *See page 170*

FEDERATED GARDEN CLUBS OF MARYLAND

http://www.fgcofmd.org/

ROBERT LEWIS BAKER SCHOLARSHIP

Scholarship awards of up to $5000 to encourage the study of ornamental horticulture, and landscape design. Applicants must be high school graduates, current college and/or graduate students, and Maryland residents. Can attend any accredited college/university in the United States.

Academic Fields/Career Goals: Horticulture/Floriculture; Landscape Architecture.

Award: Scholarship for use in freshman, sophomore, junior, senior, or graduate years; not renewable. *Number:* 1. *Amount:* $5000.

Eligibility Requirements: Applicant must be enrolled or expecting to enroll full-time at a four-year institution or university and resident of Maryland. Available to U.S. citizens.

Application Requirements: Application form. *Deadline:* June 30.

Contact: Marjorie Schiebel, Scholarship Chair
Phone: 410-296-6961
E-mail: fgcofmd@aol.com

GARDEN CLUB OF AMERICA

http://www.gcamerica.org/

CORLISS KNAPP ENGLE SCHOLARSHIP IN HORTICULTURE

$3,000 award to support horticultural study at an accredited college, university, or major botanic garden or arboretum. Open to college undergraduates and graduate students, advanced degree candidates, or non-degree-seeking applicants above the high school level. Must be a U.S. citizen or permanent resident enrolled in a U.S. institution.

Academic Fields/Career Goals: Horticulture/Floriculture.

Award: Scholarship for use in freshman, sophomore, junior, senior, or graduate years; not renewable. *Number:* 1. *Amount:* $3000.

Eligibility Requirements: Applicant must be enrolled or expecting to enroll full- or part-time at a four-year institution or university. Available to U.S. citizens.

Application Requirements: Application form, essay. *Deadline:* February 1.

Contact: Garden Club of America
Garden Club of America
14 East 60th Street
New York, NY 10022
Phone: 212-753-8287
E-mail: scholarshipapplications@gcamerica.org

GARDEN CLUB OF AMERICA MONTINE M. FREEMAN SCHOLARSHIP IN NATIVE PLANTS

$3000 scholarship to support study at an accredited college, university, or major botanic garden or arboretum. Projects may include, but are not restricted to, plant propagation, and the acquisition of skills for working with native plant collections, including techniques for incorporating them in managed landscapes. Photographic and written documentation of studies and research projects may be considered. Open to college undergraduates and graduate students, advanced degree candidates, or non-degree-seeking applicants above the high school level.

Academic Fields/Career Goals: Horticulture/Floriculture; Natural Sciences.

Award: Scholarship for use in sophomore, junior, senior, or graduate years; not renewable. *Amount:* $3000.

Eligibility Requirements: Applicant must be enrolled or expecting to enroll full-time at a four-year institution or university. Available to U.S. citizens.

Application Requirements: Application form, essay. *Deadline:* February 1.

Contact: Garden Club of America
Garden Club of America
14 East 60th Street
New York, NY 10022
Phone: 212-753-8287
E-mail: scholarshipapplications@gcamerica.org

GCA AWARD IN DESERT STUDIES
• *See page 340*

GCA SUMMER SCHOLARSHIP IN FIELD BOTANY

Scholarship of $3000 to undergraduate or graduate students up to Master's level wishing to pursue summer field work in botany. All candidates must be U.S. citizens or permanent residents enrolled in a U.S. college or university. Research must be conducted in the Western Hemisphere.

Academic Fields/Career Goals: Horticulture/Floriculture; Natural Sciences.

Award: Scholarship for use in freshman, sophomore, junior, senior, or graduate years; not renewable. *Number:* 1. *Amount:* $3000.

Eligibility Requirements: Applicant must be enrolled or expecting to enroll full-time at a four-year institution or university. Available to U.S. citizens.

Application Requirements: Application form, essay. *Deadline:* February 1.

Contact: Garden Club of America
Garden Club of America
14 East 60th Street
New York, NY 10022-1006
Phone: 212-753-8287
E-mail: scholarshipapplications@gcamerica.org

JOAN K. HUNT AND RACHEL M. HUNT SUMMER SCHOLARSHIP IN FIELD BOTANY

One scholarship of $3,500 towards summer study in field botany to promote the awareness of the importance of botany to horticulture. Open to undergraduates and graduate students up to the Master's degree level with preference given to undergraduate students. Must be a U.S. citizen or permanent resident enrolled in an accredited United States institution.

Academic Fields/Career Goals: Horticulture/Floriculture; Natural Sciences.

Award: Scholarship for use in freshman, sophomore, junior, senior, or graduate years; not renewable. *Number:* 1. *Amount:* $3500.

Eligibility Requirements: Applicant must be enrolled or expecting to enroll full-time at a four-year institution or university. Available to U.S. citizens.

Application Requirements: Application form, essay. *Deadline:* February 1.

Contact: Garden Club of America
Garden Club of America
14 East 60th Street
New York, NY 10022-1006
Phone: 212-753-8287
E-mail: scholarshipapplications@gcamerica.org

KATHARINE M. GROSSCUP SCHOLARSHIPS IN HORTICULTURE

Scholarships of up to $3,500 to encourage the study of horticulture and related fields by providing financial assistance to college sophomores, juniors, seniors, or graduate students who wish to pursue these academic endeavors. Preference is given to students from Ohio, Pennsylvania, West Virginia, Michigan, Indiana, and Kentucky.

Academic Fields/Career Goals: Horticulture/Floriculture; Landscape Architecture.

Award: Scholarship for use in sophomore, junior, senior, or graduate years; not renewable.

Eligibility Requirements: Applicant must be enrolled or expecting to enroll full-time at a four-year institution or university and resident of Indiana, Kentucky, Michigan, Ohio, Pennsylvania, West Virginia. Available to U.S. citizens.

Application Requirements: Application form, essay, interview. *Deadline:* January 8.

Contact: Grosscup Scholarship Committee
Garden Club of America
14 East 60th Street, 3rd Floor
New York, NY 10022-1006
E-mail: grosscupscholarship@gmail.com

LOY MCCANDLESS MARKS SCHOLARSHIP IN TROPICAL HORTICULTURE

Award of $5,000 to graduate or advanced undergraduate student specializing in tropical horticulture, botany, or landscape architecture. Provides an opportunity to study at a leading foreign institution that specializes in the field of tropical plants. Travel must commence within 12 months of the award. Awarded only in even numbered years.

Academic Fields/Career Goals: Horticulture/Floriculture.

Award: Scholarship for use in junior, senior, or graduate years; not renewable. *Number:* 1. *Amount:* $5000.

Eligibility Requirements: Applicant must be enrolled or expecting to enroll full-time at a four-year institution or university. Available to U.S. citizens.

Application Requirements: Application form, essay, interview. *Deadline:* February 1.

Contact: Garden Club of America
Garden Club of America
14 East 60th Street
New York, NY 10022-1006
Phone: 212-753-8287
E-mail: scholarshipapplications@gcamerica.org

SARA SHALLENBERGER BROWN GCA NATIONAL PARKS CONSERVATION SCHOLARSHIP

Scholarship provides training, transportation, and a $250/week stipend for each student as an SCA apprentice crew leader working directly under two experienced leaders on a 3 or 4 week summer trail crew in one of America's national parks. Open to college undergraduates aged 19 to 20, with preference given to those with prior SCA experience.

Academic Fields/Career Goals: Horticulture/Floriculture; Natural Resources.

Award: Scholarship for use in freshman or sophomore years; not renewable.

Eligibility Requirements: Applicant must be age 19-20 and enrolled or expecting to enroll full-time at a four-year institution or university. Available to U.S. citizens.

Application Requirements: Application form. *Deadline:* February 17.

Contact: Marlee Leveille
Garden Club of America
Student Conservation Association
Phone: 603-504-3202
E-mail: mleveille@thesca.org

GOLDEN STATE BONSAI FEDERATION

http://www.gsbf-bonsai.org/

HORTICULTURE SCHOLARSHIPS

Scholarship for study towards a certificate in ornamental horticulture from an accredited school. Applicant must be a current member of a GSBF member club and have a letter of recommendation from club president, or a responsible spokesperson from GSBF. Deadline varies.

Academic Fields/Career Goals: Horticulture/Floriculture.

Award: Scholarship for use in freshman, sophomore, junior, senior, graduate, or postgraduate years; not renewable. *Number:* 1–5. *Amount:* up to $400.

Eligibility Requirements: Applicant must be enrolled or expecting to enroll full-time at a two-year or four-year or technical institution or university. Applicant or parent of applicant must be member of Golden State Bonsai Federation. Available to U.S. citizens.

Application Requirements: Application form, recommendations or references. *Deadline:* varies.

Contact: Abe Far, Grants and Scholarship Committee
Golden State Bonsai Federation
2451 Galahad Road
San Diego, CA 92123
Phone: 619-234-3434
E-mail: abefar@cox.net

GOLF COURSE SUPERINTENDENTS ASSOCIATION OF AMERICA

http://www.eifg.org/

GCSAA SCHOLARS COMPETITION

Competition for outstanding students planning careers in golf course management. Must be full-time college undergraduates currently enrolled in a two-year or more accredited program related to golf course management and have completed one year of program. Must be member of GCSAA.

Academic Fields/Career Goals: Horticulture/Floriculture.

Award: Scholarship for use in sophomore, junior, or senior years; not renewable. *Amount:* $500–$6000.

Eligibility Requirements: Applicant must be enrolled or expecting to enroll full-time at a two-year or four-year institution or university. Applicant or parent of applicant must be member of Golf Course Superintendents Association of America. Available to U.S. and non-U.S. citizens.

Application Requirements: Application form, essay. *Deadline:* June 1.

Contact: Mischia Wright, Associate Director
Golf Course Superintendents Association of America
1421 Research Park Drive
Lawrence, KS 66049
Phone: 800-472-7878 Ext. 4445
Fax: 785-832-4448
E-mail: mwright@gcsaa.org

GREAT MINDS IN STEM

http://www.greatmindsinstem.org

HENAAC SCHOLARSHIP PROGRAM

• See page 115

HERB SOCIETY OF AMERICA, WESTERN RESERVE UNIT

http://www.westernreserveherbsociety.org/

HORTICULTURE SCHOLARSHIP FROM FRANCIS SYLVIA ZVERINA

• See page 101

HORTICULTURE SCHOLARSHIP OF THE WESTERN RESERVE HERB SOCIETY

• See page 101

HORTICULTURAL RESEARCH INSTITUTE

http://www.hriresearch.org/

BRYAN A. CHAMPION MEMORIAL SCHOLARSHIP

• See page 101

CARVILLE M. AKEHURST MEMORIAL SCHOLARSHIP

• See page 333

MUGGETS SCHOLARSHIP

Annual scholarship available to students enrolled in an accredited undergraduate or graduate horticulture, landscape, or related discipline at a two- or four-year institution. Students in vocational agriculture programs will also be considered. High school seniors may apply for this scholarship. Minimum 2.5 GPA required. Online application submission. Visit http//http://www.HRIresearch.org for details.

Academic Fields/Career Goals: Horticulture/Floriculture; Landscape Architecture.

Award: Scholarship for use in sophomore, junior, senior, or graduate years; not renewable. *Number:* 1. *Amount:* $1500.

Eligibility Requirements: Applicant must be enrolled or expecting to enroll full-time at a two-year or four-year or technical institution or university. Applicant must have 2.5 GPA or higher. Available to U.S. and non-U.S. citizens.

Application Requirements: Application form, essay, financial need analysis, recommendations or references, resume, transcript. *Deadline:* May 31.

Contact: Ms. Teresa Jodon, Executive Director
Horticultural Research Institute
1200 G Street, NW, Suite 800
Washington, DC 20005
Phone: 202-695-2474
Fax: 888-761-7883
E-mail: scholarships@hriresearch.org

SPRING MEADOW NURSERY SCHOLARSHIP

Scholarship for the full-time study of horticulture or landscape architecture students in undergraduate or graduate horticulture program or related discipline at a two- or four-year institution. Applicant must have minimum 2.5 GPA. Spring Meadow Nursery's goal is to grant scholarships to students with an interest in woody plant production, woody plant propagation, woody plant breeding, horticultural sales and marketing. Undergraduate: Applicant must have at least a Sophomore standing in a four-year curriculum or Senior standing in a two-year curriculum as of the Fall semester of scholarship application year. Graduate: All applicants in graduate school regardless of year in school may apply. Online application only.

Academic Fields/Career Goals: Horticulture/Floriculture; Landscape Architecture.

Award: Scholarship for use in junior, senior, or graduate years; not renewable. *Number:* 3. *Amount:* $3000.

Eligibility Requirements: Applicant must be enrolled or expecting to enroll full-time at a two-year or four-year or technical institution or university. Applicant must have 2.5 GPA or higher. Available to U.S. and Canadian citizens.

Application Requirements: Application form, essay, financial need analysis, recommendations or references, resume, transcript. *Deadline:* May 31.

Contact: Ms. Teresa Jodon, Executive Director
Horticultural Research Institute
1200 G Street, NW, Suite 800
Washington, DC 20005
Phone: 202-695-2474
Fax: 888-761-7883
E-mail: scholarships@hriresearch.org

TIMOTHY AND PALMER W. BIGELOW JR., SCHOLARSHIP
• See page 101

USREY FAMILY SCHOLARSHIP
• See page 333

IDAHO NURSERY AND LANDSCAPE ASSOCIATION

http://www.inlagrow.org/

IDAHO NURSERY AND LANDSCAPE ASSOCIATION SCHOLARSHIPS

To encourage study of Horticulture, Floriculture, Plant Pathology, Landscape Design, Turfgrass Management, Botany and other allied subjects that pertain to the green industry. Applicant must be an Idaho resident.

Academic Fields/Career Goals: Horticulture/Floriculture.

Award: Scholarship for use in freshman, sophomore, junior, or senior years; not renewable. *Number:* 1–4. *Amount:* $750.

Eligibility Requirements: Applicant must be enrolled or expecting to enroll full- or part-time at a two-year or four-year or technical institution or university; resident of Idaho and studying in Idaho. Available to U.S. citizens.

Application Requirements: Application form, community service, essay. *Deadline:* December 1.

Contact: Ann Bates, Executive Director
Phone: 208-681-4769
Fax: 208-529-0832
E-mail: abates@inlagrow.org

JOSEPH SHINODA MEMORIAL SCHOLARSHIP FOUNDATION

http://www.shinodascholarship.org/

JOSEPH SHINODA MEMORIAL SCHOLARSHIP

One-time award for undergraduates in accredited colleges and universities. Must be furthering their education in the field of floriculture (production, distribution, research, or retail).

Academic Fields/Career Goals: Horticulture/Floriculture.

Award: Scholarship for use in sophomore, junior, or senior years; not renewable. *Number:* 8–15. *Amount:* $1000–$5000.

Eligibility Requirements: Applicant must be enrolled or expecting to enroll full-time at a four-year institution or university. Available to U.S. citizens.

Application Requirements: Application form, essay, financial need analysis, recommendations or references, transcript. *Deadline:* March 30.

Contact: Barbara McCaleb, Executive Secretary
Joseph Shinoda Memorial Scholarship Foundation
234 Via La Paz
San Luis Obispo, CA 93401
Phone: 805-544-0717

LABROOTS INC.

http://www.LabRoots.com

LABROOTS STEM SCHOLARSHIP
• See page 116

THE LAND CONSERVANCY OF NEW JERSEY

http://www.tlc-nj.org/

ROGERS FAMILY SCHOLARSHIP
• See page 172

LANDSCAPE ARCHITECTURE FOUNDATION

http://www.lafoundation.org

RAIN BIRD INTELLIGENT USE OF WATER SCHOLARSHIP

This award recognizes an outstanding landscape architecture, horticulture or irrigation science student. Eligible applicants are in the final two years of undergraduate study with demonstrated commitment to these professions through participation in extracurricular activities and exemplary scholastic achievements.

Academic Fields/Career Goals: Horticulture/Floriculture.

Award: Scholarship for use in junior or senior years; not renewable. *Number:* 1. *Amount:* $2500.

Eligibility Requirements: Applicant must be enrolled or expecting to enroll full- or part-time at a four-year institution or university. Available to U.S. and non-U.S. citizens.

Application Requirements: Application form, essay, personal photograph. *Fee:* $5. *Deadline:* February 1.

Contact: Scholarships Coordinator
Phone: 202-331-7070 Ext. 14
E-mail: scholarships@lafoundation.org

MONTANA FEDERATION OF GARDEN CLUBS

http://www.mtfgc.org/

LIFE MEMBER MONTANA FEDERATION OF GARDEN CLUBS SCHOLARSHIP
• See page 261

NATIONAL GARDEN CLUBS SCHOLARSHIP

Scholarship for a college student majoring in some branch of horticulture. Applicants must have sophomore or higher standing and be a legal resident of Montana.

Academic Fields/Career Goals: Horticulture/Floriculture.

Award: Scholarship for use in sophomore, junior, or senior years; not renewable. *Number:* 1. *Amount:* up to $3500.

Eligibility Requirements: Applicant must be enrolled or expecting to enroll full-time at a four-year institution or university and resident of Montana. Available to U.S. citizens.

Application Requirements: Application form, financial need analysis. *Deadline:* February 28.

Contact: Margaret Yaw, Scholarship Committee, State Chairman
Montana Federation of Garden Clubs
2603 Spring Creek Drive
Bozeman, MT 59715-3621
Phone: 406-587-3621

NATIONAL COUNCIL OF STATE GARDEN CLUBS INC. SCHOLARSHIP

http://www.gardenclub.org/

NATIONAL COUNCIL OF STATE GARDEN CLUBS INC. SCHOLARSHIP
• See page 108

NATIONAL GARDEN CLUBS INC.

http://www.gardenclub.org/

NATIONAL GARDEN CLUBS INC. SCHOLARSHIP PROGRAM
• See page 109

NATIONAL RESTAURANT ASSOCIATION EDUCATIONAL FOUNDATION

http://www.chooserestaurants.org

NATIONAL RESTAURANT ASSOCIATION EDUCATIONAL FOUNDATION UNDERGRADUATE SCHOLARSHIPS FOR COLLEGE STUDENTS
• See page 109

SOIL AND WATER CONSERVATION SOCIETY-NEW JERSEY CHAPTER

http://www.geocities.com/njswcs

EDWARD R. HALL SCHOLARSHIP
• See page 103

SOUTHERN NURSERY ASSOCIATION

http://www.sna.org/

SIDNEY B. MEADOWS SCHOLARSHIP ENDOWMENT FUND

Scholarship of at least $1500 to students enrolled in an accredited undergraduate or graduate ornamental horticulture program or related discipline at a four-year institution. Student must be in a junior or senior or graduate standing at time of application. For undergraduate students minimum grade point average of 2.25 on a scale of 4.0, or 3.0 for graduate students. Students must be a US Citizen and a resident of the following states in the United States: Alabama, Arkansas, Florida, Georgia, Kentucky, Louisiana, Maryland, Mississippi, Missouri, North Carolina, Oklahoma, South Carolina, Tennessee, Texas, Virginia and West Virginia.

Academic Fields/Career Goals: Horticulture/Floriculture.

Award: Scholarship for use in junior, senior, or graduate years; not renewable. *Number:* 10–12. *Amount:* $1500.

Eligibility Requirements: Applicant must be enrolled or expecting to enroll full-time at a four-year institution or university and resident of Alabama, Arkansas, Florida, Georgia, Kentucky, Louisiana, Maryland, Mississippi, Missouri, North Carolina, Oklahoma, South Carolina, Tennessee, Texas, Virginia, West Virginia. Applicant must have 3.0 GPA or higher. Available to U.S. citizens.

Application Requirements: Application form. *Deadline:* May 30.

Contact: Mr. Danny Summers, Executive Vice President
Southern Nursery Association
PO Box 801513
Acworth, GA 30101
Phone: 678-813-1880
E-mail: danny@sbmsef.org

TURF AND ORNAMENTAL COMMUNICATORS ASSOCIATION

http://www.toca.org/

TURF AND ORNAMENTAL COMMUNICATORS ASSOCIATION SCHOLARSHIP PROGRAM
• See page 111

HOSPITALITY MANAGEMENT

AMERICAN HOTEL AND LODGING EDUCATIONAL FOUNDATION

http://www.ahlef.org/

AHLEF ANNUAL SCHOLARSHIP GRANT PROGRAM
• See page 244

AMERICAN EXPRESS SCHOLARSHIP PROGRAM

Award for full- and part-time students in undergraduate program leading to degree in hospitality management. Must be employed at hotel which is a member of AH&LA, and must work a minimum of 20 hours per week. Dependents of hotel employees may also apply.

Academic Fields/Career Goals: Hospitality Management.

Award: Scholarship for use in freshman, sophomore, junior, or senior years; not renewable. *Number:* 5–8. *Amount:* $500–$2000.

Eligibility Requirements: Applicant must be enrolled or expecting to enroll full- or part-time at a two-year or four-year institution or university. Applicant or parent of applicant must have employment or volunteer experience in hospitality/hotel administration/operations. Available to U.S. and non-U.S. citizens.

Application Requirements: Application form, essay, financial need analysis, resume, transcript. *Deadline:* May 1.

Contact: Kelsey Allagood, Foundation Manager
American Hotel and Lodging Educational Foundation
1201 New York Avenue, NW, Suite 600
Washington, DC 20005-3931
Phone: 202-289-3139
Fax: 202-289-3199
E-mail: kallagood@ahlef.org

AMERICAN HOTEL & LODGING EDUCATIONAL FOUNDATION PEPSI SCHOLARSHIP
• *See page 244*

ECOLAB SCHOLARSHIP PROGRAM
• *See page 245*

HYATT HOTELS FUND FOR MINORITY LODGING MANAGEMENT
• *See page 245*

INCOMING FRESHMAN SCHOLARSHIPS
• *See page 245*

RAMA SCHOLARSHIP FOR THE AMERICAN DREAM
• *See page 245*

AMERICAN INSTITUTE OF WINE AND FOOD-PACIFIC NORTHWEST CHAPTER
http://www.aiwf.org/

CULINARY, VINIFERA, AND HOSPITALITY SCHOLARSHIP
• *See page 351*

CAREERS THROUGH CULINARY ARTS PROGRAM INC.
http://www.ccapinc.org/

CAREERS THROUGH CULINARY ARTS PROGRAM COOKING COMPETITION FOR SCHOLARSHIPS
• *See page 246*

CLUB FOUNDATION
http://www.clubfoundation.org/

JOE PERDUE SCHOLARSHIP PROGRAM
Awards for candidates seeking a managerial career in the private club industry and currently attending an accredited four year college or university. Must have completed freshman year and be enrolled full-time. Must have achieved and continue to maintain a GPA of at least 2.5 on a 4.0 scale or a 4.5 on a 6.0 scale.

Academic Fields/Career Goals: Hospitality Management.

Award: Scholarship for use in sophomore, junior, or senior years; not renewable. *Number:* 8. *Amount:* $2500.

Eligibility Requirements: Applicant must be enrolled or expecting to enroll full-time at a four-year institution or university. Applicant must have 2.5 GPA or higher. Available to U.S. citizens.

Application Requirements: Application form, essay. *Deadline:* May 1.

Contact: Carrie Wosicki, Director of Development
E-mail: carrie.wosicki@cmaa.org

COSTA RICAN VACATIONS
http://www.vacationscostarica.com/

COSTA RICAN VACATIONS SCHOLARSHIP
• *See page 339*

DECA (DISTRIBUTIVE EDUCATION CLUBS OF AMERICA)
http://www.deca.org/

HARRY A. APPLEGATE SCHOLARSHIP
• *See page 83*

FUKUNAGA SCHOLARSHIP FOUNDATION
http://fukunagascholarship.com

FUKUNAGA SCHOLARSHIP FOUNDATION
• *See page 85*

GOLDEN GATE RESTAURANT ASSOCIATION
http://www.ggra.org/

GOLDEN GATE RESTAURANT ASSOCIATION SCHOLARSHIP FOUNDATION
• *See page 246*

HAWAII LODGING & TOURISM ASSOCIATION
http://www.hawaiilodging.org

CLEM JUDD, JR. MEMORIAL SCHOLARSHIP
Scholarship for a Hawaii resident who must be able to prove Hawaiian ancestry. Applicant must be enrolled full-time at a U.S. accredited university/college majoring in hotel management. Must have a minimum 3.0 GPA.

Academic Fields/Career Goals: Hospitality Management.

Award: Scholarship for use in junior or senior years; not renewable. *Number:* 2. *Amount:* $1000–$2500.

Eligibility Requirements: Applicant must be Asian/Pacific Islander; enrolled or expecting to enroll full-time at a four-year institution and resident of Hawaii. Applicant must have 3.0 GPA or higher. Available to U.S. citizens.

Application Requirements: Application form, essay, personal photograph, recommendations or references, resume. *Deadline:* July 1.

Contact: Scholarship Committee
Hawaii Lodging & Tourism Association
2270 Kalakaua Avenue, Suite 1506
Honolulu, HI 96815
Phone: 808-923-0407
Fax: 808-924-3843
E-mail: info@hawaiilodging.org

R.W. "BOB" HOLDEN SCHOLARSHIP
One $1000 award for a student attending an accredited university or college in Hawaii, majoring in hotel management. Must be a Hawaii resident and a U.S. citizen. Must have a minimum 3.0 GPA.

Academic Fields/Career Goals: Hospitality Management; Travel/Tourism.

Award: Scholarship for use in junior or senior years; not renewable. *Number:* 1–5. *Amount:* $1000.

Eligibility Requirements: Applicant must be enrolled or expecting to enroll full-time at a four-year institution or university. Applicant must have 3.0 GPA or higher. Available to U.S. citizens.

Application Requirements: Application form, essay, personal photograph, recommendations or references, resume, self-addressed stamped envelope with application, transcript. *Deadline:* July 1.

Contact: Dean Nakasone, Vice President
Hawaii Lodging & Tourism Association
2270 Kalakaua Avenue, Suite 1702
Honolulu, HI 96815
Phone: 808-923-0407
E-mail: info@hawaiilodging.org

HOUSE OF BLUES MUSIC FORWARD FOUNDATION

https://hobmusicforward.org/

STEVEN J. FINKEL SERVICE EXCELLENCE SCHOLARSHIP
• See page 180

TIFFANY GREEN OPERATOR SCHOLARSHIP AWARD
• See page 96

ILLINOIS RESTAURANT ASSOCIATION EDUCATIONAL FOUNDATION

http://www.illinoisrestaurants.org/

ILLINOIS RESTAURANT ASSOCIATION EDUCATIONAL FOUNDATION SCHOLARSHIPS
• See page 246

INTERNATIONAL FOODSERVICE EDITORIAL COUNCIL

http://www.ifeconline.com/

INTERNATIONAL FOODSERVICE EDITORIAL COUNCIL COMMUNICATIONS SCHOLARSHIP
• See page 96

JAMES BEARD FOUNDATION INC.

http://www.jamesbeard.org/

BERN LAXER MEMORIAL SCHOLARSHIP
• See page 247

MAINE RESTAURANT ASSOCIATION

http://www.mainerestaurant.com/

MAINE RESTAURANT ASSOCIATION EDUCATION FOUNDATION SCHOLARSHIP FUND
• See page 249

MARYLAND RESTAURANT ASSOCIATION EDUCATION FOUNDATION

https://www.marylandrestaurants.com/about.html

THE LETITIA B. CARTER SCHOLARSHIP
• See page 249

MARCIA S. HARRIS LEGACY FUND SCHOLARSHIP
• See page 249

MISSOURI TRAVEL COUNCIL

http://www.missouritravel.com/

BOB SMITH TOURISM SCHOLARSHIP
• See page 357

NATIONAL RESTAURANT ASSOCIATION EDUCATIONAL FOUNDATION

http://www.chooserestaurants.org

NATIONAL RESTAURANT ASSOCIATION EDUCATIONAL FOUNDATION UNDERGRADUATE SCHOLARSHIPS FOR COLLEGE STUDENTS
• See page 109

OHIO TRAVEL ASSOCIATION

http://www.ohiotravel.org/

BILL SCHWARTZ MEMORIAL SCHOLARSHIP
Scholarship will be granted to a qualified full-time, Ohio student after the completion of their freshman year. Must be studying hospitality management or travel/tourism with a minimum 2.5 GPA. As part of the scholarship program, the recipient will be invited to various OTA events throughout the year.

Academic Fields/Career Goals: Hospitality Management; Travel/Tourism.

Award: Scholarship for use in sophomore, junior, or senior years; not renewable. *Number:* 1. *Amount:* $1000.

Eligibility Requirements: Applicant must be enrolled or expecting to enroll full-time at a two-year or four-year or technical institution or university; resident of Ohio and studying in Ohio. Applicant or parent of applicant must have employment or volunteer experience in travel and tourism industry. Applicant must have 2.5 GPA or higher. Available to U.S. citizens.

Application Requirements: Application form, financial need analysis, recommendations or references, transcript. *Deadline:* June 15.

Contact: Ms. Betsy Decillis, Membership and Community Manager
Phone: 800-896-4682 Ext. 0#
E-mail: betsy@ohiotravel.org

OREGON STUDENT ASSISTANCE COMMISSION

https://oregonstudentaid.gov/

OREGON WINE BROTHERHOOD SCHOLARSHIP
• See page 249

SCARLETT FAMILY FOUNDATION SCHOLARSHIP PROGRAM

http://www.scarlettfoundation.org/

SCHOLARSHIP FOR STUDENTS PURSUING A BUSINESS OR STEM DEGREE
• See page 91

SILICON VALLEY COMMUNITY FOUNDATION

http://www.siliconvalleycf.org

ANTHONY NARIGI HOSPITALITY SCHOLARSHIP FUND
The Anthony Narigi Hospitality Scholarship Fund was established by the Monterey Plaza Hotel and Spa in loving memory of Anthony Nicholas Narigi, the son of John Narigi, a respected and long-time employee of Monterey Plaza Hotel and Spa. This scholarship will support students who plan to pursue a career in the hospitality industry and who are enrolled or plan to enroll in hospitality trade schools, junior colleges, four-year public or private institutions and graduate programs. Applicant must reside in Monterey County, San Francisco County, Sonoma County, Napa County, Contra Costa County or Santa Clara County. Applicants must be currently employed in the hospitality profession or applying for or enrolled in an educational program pursuing a degree or certificate designed for the hospitality industry, which includes: hotel/motel, spa, restaurant, winery. Applicants must have worked a minimum of 250

hours if currently employed in the hospitality industry or 100 hours if a current student. Applicants must hold a high school diploma. Students must have a minimum GPA of 2.5 on a 4.0 scale.

Academic Fields/Career Goals: Hospitality Management.

Award: Scholarship for use in freshman, sophomore, junior, senior, or graduate years; not renewable. *Number:* 1–5. *Amount:* $1000–$5000.

Eligibility Requirements: Applicant must be enrolled or expecting to enroll full- or part-time at a two-year or four-year or technical institution or university and resident of California. Applicant must have 2.5 GPA or higher. Available to U.S. citizens.

Application Requirements: Application form. *Deadline:* continuous.

Contact: Scholarships Team
Silicon Valley Community Foundation
2440 West El Camino Real
Suite 300
Mountain View, CA 94040
Phone: 650-450-5487
E-mail: scholarships@siliconvalleycf.org

SOUTH CAROLINA RESTAURANT AND LODGING ASSOCIATION

http://www.scrla.org/

SOUTH CAROLINA TOURISM AND HOSPITALITY EDUCATIONAL FOUNDATION SCHOLARSHIPS
• *See page 250*

TOURISM CARES

http://www.tourismcares.org

ASTA PRINCESS CRUISES SCHOLARSHIP
• *See page 358*

IATAN RONALD A. SANTANA MEMORIAL SCHOLARSHIP
• *See page 355*

NTA LA MACCHIA FAMILY SCHOLARSHIP
• *See page 358*

NTA NEW HORIZONS KATHY LETARTE SCHOLARSHIP
• *See page 358*

NTA OHIO SCHOLARSHIP
• *See page 358*

NTA PAT AND JIM HOST SCHOLARSHIP
Scholarship is available for a permanent resident or student in Kentucky

Academic Fields/Career Goals: Hospitality Management; Travel/Tourism.

Award: Scholarship for use in sophomore, junior, senior, or graduate years; not renewable. *Number:* 1. *Amount:* $2000.

Eligibility Requirements: Applicant must be enrolled or expecting to enroll full-time at a two-year or four-year institution or university and resident of Kentucky. Applicant must have 3.0 GPA or higher. Available to U.S. citizens.

Application Requirements: Application form, essay. *Deadline:* April 1.

Contact: Trish Kelly, Workforce Development Coordinator
Tourism Cares
20 Vernon Street
Norwood, MA 02062
Phone: 781-821-5990
Fax: 781-762-6100
E-mail: info@tourismcares.org

NTA TRAVEL LEADERS SCHOLARSHIP
• *See page 358*

NTA UTAH KEITH GRIFFALL SCHOLARSHIP
• *See page 358*

UNITED NEGRO COLLEGE FUND

http://www.uncf.org/

NATIONAL BLACK MCDONALD'S OWNERS ASSOCIATION HOSPITALITY SCHOLARS PROGRAM
• *See page 94*

UNCF/CARNIVAL CORPORATE SCHOLARS PROGRAM
• *See page 184*

HUMANITIES

AMERICAN CLASSICAL LEAGUE/NATIONAL JUNIOR CLASSICAL LEAGUE

http://www.aclclassics.org/

NATIONAL JUNIOR CLASSICAL LEAGUE SCHOLARSHIP
• *See page 214*

AMERICAN SCHOOL OF CLASSICAL STUDIES AT ATHENS

http://www.ascsa.edu.gr/

ASCSA SUMMER SESSION AND SUMMER SEMINARS SCHOLARSHIPS
• *See page 118*

BETHESDA LUTHERAN COMMUNITIES

http://www.bethesdalutherancommunities.org/scholarships

DEVELOPMENTAL DISABILITIES SCHOLASTIC ACHIEVEMENT SCHOLARSHIP FOR COLLEGE STUDENTS WHO ARE LUTHERAN
• *See page 254*

CANADIAN INSTITUTE OF UKRAINIAN STUDIES

http://www.cius.ca/

LEO J. KRYSA UNDERGRADUATE SCHOLARSHIP
• *See page 138*

CATCHING THE DREAM

http://www.catchingthedream.org/

MATH, ENGINEERING, SCIENCE, BUSINESS, EDUCATION, COMPUTERS SCHOLARSHIPS
• *See page 178*

NATIVE AMERICAN LEADERSHIP IN EDUCATION (NALE)
• *See page 178*

CULTURAL SERVICES OF THE FRENCH EMBASSY

http://www.frenchculture.org/

TEACHING ASSISTANT PROGRAM IN FRANCE
• *See page 113*

INSTITUTE FOR HUMANE STUDIES

http://www.theihs.org/

HUMANE STUDIES FELLOWSHIPS
• *See page 219*

JACK J. ISGUR FOUNDATION

http://www.isgur.org

JACK J. ISGUR FOUNDATION SCHOLARSHIP
• *See page 272*

LADIES AUXILIARY TO THE VETERANS OF FOREIGN WARS, DEPARTMENT OF MAINE

http://mainevfw.org/

FRANCES L. BOOTH MEDICAL SCHOLARSHIP SPONSORED BY LAVFW DEPARTMENT OF MAINE
• *See page 375*

LA-PHILOSOPHIE.COM

http://la-philosophie.com

LA-PHILOSOPHIE.COM SCHOLARSHIP
• *See page 119*

MICHAEL MOODY FITNESS

http://www.michaelmoodyfitness.com/

MICHAEL MOODY FITNESS SCHOLARSHIP
• *See page 166*

NOET SCHOLARLY TOOLS

http://www.noet.com

NOET HUMANITIES SCHOLARSHIP
The Noet Humanities Scholarship seeks to award students enrolled in a humanities program at the undergraduate or graduate level. There is one scholarship available at $500. To enter, students must be currently enrolled (or enrolling in the upcoming quarter) in an undergraduate or graduate program in the humanities.

Academic Fields/Career Goals: Humanities.

Award: Scholarship for use in freshman, sophomore, junior, senior, graduate, or postgraduate years; not renewable. *Number:* up to 1. *Amount:* $500–$500.

Eligibility Requirements: Applicant must be enrolled or expecting to enroll full- or part-time at a two-year or four-year institution or university. Available to U.S. and non-U.S. citizens.

Application Requirements: Application form may be submitted online (http://noet.com/scholarships), email address, transcript. *Deadline:* varies.

Contact: Mr. Benjamin Amundgaard, Noet Brand/Product Manager
Noet Scholarly Tools
1313 Commercial Street
Bellingham, WA 98226
Phone: 360-398-5145
E-mail: ben.amundgaard@noet.com

PHI ALPHA THETA HISTORY HONOR SOCIETY, INC.

http://www.phialphatheta.org/

PHI ALPHA THETA WORLD HISTORY ASSOCIATION PAPER PRIZE
• *See page 383*

STRAIGHTFORWARD MEDIA

http://www.straightforwardmedia.com/

STRAIGHTFORWARD MEDIA LIBERAL ARTS SCHOLARSHIP
• *See page 139*

UNITED NEGRO COLLEGE FUND

http://www.uncf.org/

OSSIE DAVIS ENDOWMENT SCHOLARSHIP PROGRAM
• *See page 146*

HUMAN RESOURCES

AUTOMOTIVE WOMEN'S ALLIANCE FOUNDATION

http://awafoundation.org/index.php

AUTOMOTIVE WOMEN'S ALLIANCE FOUNDATION SCHOLARSHIPS
• *See page 81*

FUKUNAGA SCHOLARSHIP FOUNDATION

http://fukunagascholarship.com

FUKUNAGA SCHOLARSHIP FOUNDATION
• *See page 85*

HOUSE OF BLUES MUSIC FORWARD FOUNDATION

https://hobmusicforward.org/

TIFFANY GREEN OPERATOR SCHOLARSHIP AWARD
• *See page 96*

NEW ENGLAND EMPLOYEE BENEFITS COUNCIL

http://www.neebc.org/

NEW ENGLAND EMPLOYEE BENEFITS COUNCIL SCHOLARSHIP PROGRAM
• *See page 89*

SCARLETT FAMILY FOUNDATION SCHOLARSHIP PROGRAM

http://www.scarlettfoundation.org/

SCHOLARSHIP FOR STUDENTS PURSUING A BUSINESS OR STEM DEGREE
• *See page 91*

SHRM FOUNDATION-SOCIETY FOR HUMAN RESOURCE MANAGEMENT

http://www.shrmfoundation.org

SHRM FOUNDATION STUDENT SCHOLARSHIPS

Applicants must be SHRM members and must be pursuing a college degree in HR or a related field. Undergraduates must have a cumulative GPA of at least 3.0 on a 4.0 point scale, and graduate applicants must have at least a 3.5 GPA on a 4.0 scale. Course work in HR management is required. Awards are primarily merit-based.

Academic Fields/Career Goals: Human Resources.

Award: Scholarship for use in junior, senior, or graduate years; not renewable. *Number:* 44. *Amount:* $2500–$10,000.

Eligibility Requirements: Applicant must be enrolled or expecting to enroll full- or part-time at a four-year institution or university. Applicant or parent of applicant must be member of Society for Human Resource Management. Applicant must have 3.0 GPA or higher. Available to U.S. and non-U.S. citizens.

Application Requirements: Application form, community service, essay. *Deadline:* October 10.

Contact: Dorothy Mebane, Manager, Foundation Programs
SHRM Foundation-Society for Human Resource Management
1800 Duke Street
Alexandria, VA 22314
Phone: 703-535-6219
E-mail: dorothy.mebane@shrm.org

UNITED NEGRO COLLEGE FUND

http://www.uncf.org/

ORACLE CORPORATE SCHOLARS PROGRAM
• *See page 184*

PROCTER & GAMBLE GENERAL SCHOLARSHIP
• *See page 94*

SUEZ CORPORATE SCHOLARS PROGRAM
• *See page 94*

UNCF/ALLIANCE DATA SCHOLARSHIP AND INTERNSHIP PROGRAM
• *See page 99*

Y'S MEN INTERNATIONAL

http://www.ysmen.org/

ALEXANDER SCHOLARSHIP LOAN FUND
• *See page 185*

HYDROLOGY

AMERICAN GROUND WATER TRUST

http://www.agwt.org/

AMERICAN GROUND WATER TRUST-AMTROL INC. SCHOLARSHIP
• *See page 259*

AMERICAN GROUND WATER TRUST-BAROID SCHOLARSHIP
• *See page 259*

AMERICAN GROUND WATER TRUST-THOMAS STETSON SCHOLARSHIP
• *See page 259*

AMERICAN INDIAN SCIENCE AND ENGINEERING SOCIETY

http://www.aises.org/

A.T. ANDERSON MEMORIAL SCHOLARSHIP PROGRAM
• *See page 121*

ARIZONA HYDROLOGICAL SOCIETY

http://www.azhydrosoc.org/

ARIZONA HYDROLOGICAL SOCIETY SCHOLARSHIP
• *See page 259*

ASSOCIATION FOR WOMEN GEOSCIENTISTS (AWG)

http://www.awg.org/

AWG ETHNIC MINORITY SCHOLARSHIP
• *See page 260*

AWG MARIA LUISA CRAWFORD FIELD CAMP SCHOLARSHIP
• *See page 129*

AWG SALT LAKE CHAPTER (SLC) RESEARCH SCHOLARSHIP
• *See page 129*

JANET CULLEN TANAKA GEOSCIENCES UNDERGRADUATE SCHOLARSHIP
• *See page 129*

LONE STAR RISING CAREER SCHOLARSHIP
• *See page 260*

OSAGE CHAPTER UNDERGRADUATE SERVICE SCHOLARSHIP
• *See page 129*

SUSAN EKDALE MEMORIAL FIELD CAMP SCHOLARSHIP
• *See page 260*

ASSOCIATION OF CALIFORNIA WATER AGENCIES

http://www.acwa.com/

ASSOCIATION OF CALIFORNIA WATER AGENCIES SCHOLARSHIPS
• *See page 123*

CLAIR A. HILL SCHOLARSHIP
• *See page 123*

BARRY GOLDWATER SCHOLARSHIP AND EXCELLENCE IN EDUCATION FOUNDATION

https://goldwater.scholarsapply.org

BARRY M. GOLDWATER SCHOLARSHIP AND EXCELLENCE IN EDUCATION PROGRAM
• *See page 123*

BHW GROUP

https://thebhwgroup.com/

BHW WOMEN IN STEM SCHOLARSHIP
• *See page 124*

BROWN AND CALDWELL

http://www.brownandcaldwell.com

ECKENFELDER SCHOLARSHIP
• *See page 169*

MINORITY SCHOLARSHIP PROGRAM
• *See page 169*

CALIFORNIA GROUNDWATER ASSOCIATION

http://www.groundh2o.org/

CALIFORNIA GROUNDWATER ASSOCIATION SCHOLARSHIP
Award for California residents who demonstrate an interest in some facet of groundwater technology. One to two $1000 awards. Must use for study in California. Submit letter of recommendation.

Academic Fields/Career Goals: Hydrology; Natural Resources.

Award: Scholarship for use in freshman, sophomore, junior, or senior years; not renewable. *Number:* 1–2. *Amount:* $1000.

Eligibility Requirements: Applicant must be enrolled or expecting to enroll full-time at a two-year or four-year or technical institution or university; resident of California and studying in California. Available to U.S. citizens.

Application Requirements: Application form, essay, recommendations or references, transcript. *Deadline:* April 1.

Contact: Mike Mortensson, Executive Director
California Groundwater Association
PO Box 14369
Santa Rosa, CA 95402
Phone: 707-578-4408
Fax: 707-546-4906
E-mail: wellguy@groundh2o.org

GREAT MINDS IN STEM

http://www.greatmindsinstem.org

HENAAC SCHOLARSHIP PROGRAM
• *See page 115*

KENTUCKY ENERGY AND ENVIRONMENT CABINET

http://dep.ky.gov

ENVIRONMENTAL PROTECTION SCHOLARSHIP
• *See page 172*

THE LAND CONSERVANCY OF NEW JERSEY

http://www.tlc-nj.org/

ROGERS FAMILY SCHOLARSHIP
• *See page 172*

RUSSELL W. MYERS SCHOLARSHIP
• *See page 172*

NGWA FOUNDATION

http://www.ngwa.org/Foundation/Pages/default.aspx

NGWA FOUNDATION'S LEN ASSANTE SCHOLARSHIP
• *See page 262*

SIGMA XI, THE SCIENTIFIC RESEARCH SOCIETY

http://www.sigmaxi.org/

SIGMA XI GRANTS-IN-AID OF RESEARCH
• *See page 110*

SOCIETY OF WOMEN ENGINEERS-ROCKY MOUNTAIN SECTION

http://www.swe-rms.org/

SOCIETY OF WOMEN ENGINEERS-ROCKY MOUNTAIN SECTION SCHOLARSHIP PROGRAM
• *See page 161*

SOIL AND WATER CONSERVATION SOCIETY

http://www.swcs.org

DONALD A. WILLIAMS SCHOLARSHIP SOIL CONSERVATION SCHOLARSHIP
• *See page 103*

SOIL AND WATER CONSERVATION SOCIETY-MISSOURI SHOW-ME CHAPTER

http://www.moswcs.org/

MO SHOW-ME CHAPTER SWCS SCHOLARSHIP
• *See page 111*

STRAIGHT NORTH

https://www.straightnorth.com/

STRAIGHT NORTH STEM SCHOLARSHIP
• *See page 92*

INDUSTRIAL DESIGN

AIST FOUNDATION

http://www.aistfoundation.org/

ASSOCIATION FOR IRON AND STEEL TECHNOLOGY WILLY KORF MEMORIAL SCHOLARSHIP
• *See page 187*

AMERICAN INSTITUTE OF CHEMICAL ENGINEERS

http://www.aiche.org/

SAFETY AND HEALTH NATIONAL STUDENT DESIGN COMPETITION AWARD FOR SAFETY
• *See page 190*

AMERICAN SOCIETY OF PLUMBING ENGINEERS

http://www.aspe.org/

ALFRED STEELE ENGINEERING SCHOLARSHIP
• *See page 312*

AUTOMOTIVE WOMEN'S ALLIANCE FOUNDATION

http://awafoundation.org/index.php

AUTOMOTIVE WOMEN'S ALLIANCE FOUNDATION SCHOLARSHIPS
• *See page 81*

BHW GROUP

https://thebhwgroup.com/

BHW WOMEN IN STEM SCHOLARSHIP
• *See page 124*

CENTER FOR ARCHITECTURE

http://www.centerforarchitecture.org

CENTER FOR ARCHITECTURE DESIGN SCHOLARSHIP
• *See page 132*

THE CLUNKER JUNKER

https://theclunkerjunker.com/

CLUNKER JUNKER CASH FOR CARS AND COLLEGE SCHOLARSHIP
• *See page 299*

FABRICATORS AND MANUFACTURERS ASSOCIATION FOUNDATION

http://www.nutsandboltsfoundation.org/scholarships/

COLLEGE AND TRADE/TECHNICAL SCHOOL SCHOLARSHIPS
• *See page 154*

GREAT MINDS IN STEM

http://www.greatmindsinstem.org

HENAAC SCHOLARSHIP PROGRAM
• *See page 115*

IFDA EDUCATIONAL FOUNDATION

http://www.ifdaef.org/

RUTH CLARK FURNITURE DESIGN SCHOLARSHIP
• *See page 142*

INDUSTRIAL DESIGNERS SOCIETY OF AMERICA

http://www.idsa.org/

INDUSTRIAL DESIGNERS SOCIETY OF AMERICA UNDERGRADUATE SCHOLARSHIP

One-time award to a U.S. citizen or permanent U.S. resident currently enrolled in an industrial design program. Must submit twenty visual examples of work and study full-time.

Academic Fields/Career Goals: Industrial Design.
Award: Scholarship for use in junior year; not renewable. *Number:* 2. *Amount:* $2500.
Eligibility Requirements: Applicant must be enrolled or expecting to enroll full-time at an institution or university. Applicant must have 3.0 GPA or higher. Available to U.S. citizens.
Application Requirements: Application form, recommendations or references, transcript, twenty visual examples of work. *Deadline:* May 18.
Contact: Max Taylor, Executive Assistant
Industrial Designers Society of America
45195 Business Court, Suite 250
Dulles, VA 20166
Phone: 703-707-6000
Fax: 703-787-8501
E-mail: maxt@idsa.org

MANUFACTURERS ASSOCIATION OF MAINE

http://www.mainemfg.com/

MAINE MANUFACTURING CAREER AND TRAINING FOUNDATION SCHOLARSHIP
• *See page 156*

MIDWEST ROOFING CONTRACTORS ASSOCIATION

http://www.mrca.org/

MRCA FOUNDATION SCHOLARSHIP PROGRAM
• *See page 135*

NASA'S VIRGINIA SPACE GRANT CONSORTIUM

http://www.vsgc.odu.edu/

COMMUNITY COLLEGE STEM SCHOLARSHIPS
• *See page 126*

ONLINE LOGO MAKER

http://onlinelogomaker.com

OLM MALALA YOUSAFZAI SCHOLARSHIP
• *See page 143*

RHODE ISLAND FOUNDATION

http://www.rifoundation.org/

JAMES J. BURNS AND C. A. HAYNES SCHOLARSHIP

Award of $1000 for students enrolled in a textile program at an educational institution offering this type of program. Preference given to children of members of National Association of Textile Supervisors. Must demonstrate financial need.

Academic Fields/Career Goals: Industrial Design.
Award: Scholarship for use in freshman, sophomore, junior, or senior years; not renewable. *Amount:* $1000.
Eligibility Requirements: Applicant must be enrolled or expecting to enroll full-time at a two-year or four-year institution or university. Available to U.S. citizens.
Application Requirements: Application form, essay, financial need analysis, recommendations or references, transcript. *Deadline:* June 3.
Contact: Libby Monahan, Funds Administrator
Phone: 401-274-4564 Ext. 3117
E-mail: libbym@rifoundation.org

SIMPLEHUMAN

http://www.simplehuman.com/

SIMPLE SOLUTIONS DESIGN COMPETITION
• See page 305

SOCIETY OF MANUFACTURING ENGINEERS EDUCATION FOUNDATION

http://www.smeef.org/

CHAPTER 198-DOWNRIVER DETROIT SCHOLARSHIP
• See page 325

CHAPTER 67-PHOENIX SCHOLARSHIP
• See page 326

FORT WAYNE CHAPTER 56 SCHOLARSHIP
• See page 328

NORTH CENTRAL REGION 9 SCHOLARSHIP
• See page 328

WICHITA CHAPTER 52 SCHOLARSHIP
• See page 328

SOCIETY OF PLASTICS ENGINEERS FOUNDATION (SPE)

http://www.4spe.org/

FLEMING/BLASZCAK SCHOLARSHIP
• See page 195

GULF COAST HURRICANE SCHOLARSHIP
• See page 196

SOCIETY OF PLASTICS ENGINEERS SCHOLARSHIP PROGRAM
• See page 196

SUPPORT CREATIVITY

http://wesupportcreativity.org

SUPPORT CREATIVITY SCHOLARSHIP
• See page 137

TIMOTION

http://www.timotion.com/

TIMOTION ENGINEERING AND EXCELLENCE SCHOLARSHIP
• See page 213

VECTORWORKS, INC.

http://www.vectorworks.net

VECTORWORKS DESIGN SCHOLARSHIP
• See page 137

INSURANCE AND ACTUARIAL SCIENCE

THE ACTUARIAL FOUNDATION

http://www.actuarialfoundation.org

ACTUARIAL DIVERSITY SCHOLARSHIP
The Actuarial Diversity Scholarship promotes diversity through an annual scholarship program for Black/African American, Hispanic, Native North American and Pacific Islander students. The scholarship award recognizes and encourages the academic achievements of full-time undergraduate students pursuing a degree that may lead to a career in the actuarial profession.

Academic Fields/Career Goals: Insurance and Actuarial Science; Mathematics.

Award: Scholarship for use in freshman, sophomore, junior, or senior years; not renewable. *Amount:* $1000–$4000.

Eligibility Requirements: Applicant must be American Indian/Alaska Native, Asian/Pacific Islander, Black (non-Hispanic), Hispanic and enrolled or expecting to enroll full-time at a two-year or four-year institution or university. Applicant must have 3.0 GPA or higher. Available to U.S. and non-U.S. citizens.

Application Requirements: Application form, essay, personal photograph. *Deadline:* May 1.

Contact: Attn: Actuarial Diversity Scholarship
The Actuarial Foundation
475 North Martingale Road, Suite 600
Schaumburg, IL 60173-2226
Phone: 847-706-3535
E-mail: scholarships@actfnd.org

ACTUARY OF TOMORROW—STUART A. ROBERTSON MEMORIAL SCHOLARSHIP
• See page 175

CURTIS E. HUNTINGTON MEMORIAL SCHOLARSHIP (FORMERLY THE JOHN CULVER WOODDY SCHOLARSHIP)
• See page 263

BHW GROUP

https://thebhwgroup.com/

BHW WOMEN IN STEM SCHOLARSHIP
• See page 124

CARDS AGAINST HUMANITY

https://cardsagainsthumanity.com/

SCIENCE AMBASSADOR SCHOLARSHIP
• See page 124

D.W. SIMPSON & COMPANY

http://www.dwsimpson.com/

D.W. SIMPSON ACTUARIAL SCIENCE SCHOLARSHIP
One-time award for full-time actuarial science students. Must be entering senior year of undergraduate study in actuarial science. GPA of 3.2 or better in actuarial science and an overall GPA of 3.0 or better required. Must have passed at least one actuarial exam and be eligible to work in the U.S. Deadlines: April 30 for fall and October 31 for spring.

Academic Fields/Career Goals: Insurance and Actuarial Science.

Award: Scholarship for use in senior year; not renewable. *Number:* up to 2. *Amount:* up to $1000.

Eligibility Requirements: Applicant must be enrolled or expecting to enroll full-time at a four-year institution or university. Applicant must have 3.0 GPA or higher. Available to U.S. citizens.

Application Requirements: Application form, essay, resume, test scores. *Deadline:* varies.

Contact: Bethany Rave, Partner-Operations
Phone: 312-867-2300
Fax: 312-951-8386
E-mail: scholarship@dwsimpson.com

MISSOURI INSURANCE EDUCATION FOUNDATION

http://www.mief.org

MISSOURI INSURANCE EDUCATION FOUNDATION SCHOLARSHIP

One $2500 scholarship and five $2000 scholarships available to college and university students in their junior or senior year. Must be Missouri resident and attending school in Missouri.

Academic Fields/Career Goals: Insurance and Actuarial Science.

Award: Scholarship for use in junior or senior years; not renewable. *Number:* 6. *Amount:* $2000–$2500.

Eligibility Requirements: Applicant must be enrolled or expecting to enroll full-time at a four-year institution or university; resident of Missouri and studying in Missouri. Applicant must have 2.5 GPA or higher. Available to U.S. citizens.

Application Requirements: Application form, financial need analysis, recommendations or references, transcript. *Deadline:* March 31.

Contact: Amy Hamacher, Assistant
Missouri Insurance Education Foundation
PO Box 1654
Jefferson City, MO 65102
Phone: 573-893-4234
Fax: 573-893-4996
E-mail: miis@midamerica.net

NEW ENGLAND EMPLOYEE BENEFITS COUNCIL

http://www.neebc.org/

NEW ENGLAND EMPLOYEE BENEFITS COUNCIL SCHOLARSHIP PROGRAM
• See page 89

SCARLETT FAMILY FOUNDATION SCHOLARSHIP PROGRAM

http://www.scarlettfoundation.org/

SCHOLARSHIP FOR STUDENTS PURSUING A BUSINESS OR STEM DEGREE
• See page 91

SPENCER EDUCATIONAL FOUNDATION INC.

http://www.spencered.org/

SPENCER EDUCATIONAL FOUNDATION SCHOLARSHIP

Scholarship is available to outstanding applicants who are focused on a career in risk management, insurance, and related disciplines. If student is attending a two year college, he/she must have intentions of transferring to a four year college with proof that he or she is majoring or minoring in Risk Management as it pertains to insurance.

Academic Fields/Career Goals: Insurance and Actuarial Science.

Award: Scholarship for use in junior, senior, graduate, or postgraduate years; renewable. *Number:* 30–40. *Amount:* $5000–$10,000.

Eligibility Requirements: Applicant must be enrolled or expecting to enroll full- or part-time at a two-year or four-year institution or university. Applicant must have 3.0 GPA or higher. Available to U.S. and Canadian citizens.

Application Requirements: Application form, essay. *Deadline:* January 31.

Contact: Ms. Angela Sabatino, Programs Director
Spencer Educational Foundation Inc.
1065 Avenue of the Americas, 13th Floor
New York, NY 10018
Phone: 212-655-6223
E-mail: asabatino@spencered.org

STRAIGHT NORTH

https://www.straightnorth.com/

STRAIGHT NORTH STEM SCHOLARSHIP
• See page 92

UNITED NEGRO COLLEGE FUND

http://www.uncf.org/

UNCF/TRAVELERS INSURANCE SCHOLARSHIP
• See page 185

VOYA SCHOLARS
• See page 94

INTERIOR DESIGN

AMERICAN SOCIETY OF INTERIOR DESIGNERS (ASID) EDUCATION FOUNDATION INC.

http://www.asidfoundation.org

ASID FOUNDATION LEGACY SCHOLARSHIP FOR UNDERGRADUATES

Open to all students in their junior or senior year of undergraduate study enrolled in at least a three-year program of interior design. The award will be given to a creatively outstanding student as demonstrated through their portfolio.

Academic Fields/Career Goals: Interior Design.

Award: Scholarship for use in junior or senior years; not renewable. *Number:* 1. *Amount:* $4000.

Eligibility Requirements: Applicant must be enrolled or expecting to enroll full- or part-time at a four-year institution or university. Available to U.S. citizens.

Application Requirements: Application form, application form may be submitted online (http://www.asidfoundation.org), portfolio, recommendations or references, transcript. *Deadline:* March 12.

Contact: Valerie O'Keefe, Executive Assistant and Foundation Manager
Phone: 202-546-3480
Fax: 202-546-3240
E-mail: foundation@asid.org

ASSOCIATION FOR WOMEN IN ARCHITECTURE FOUNDATION

http://www.awa-la.org/

ASSOCIATION FOR WOMEN IN ARCHITECTURE FOUNDATION SCHOLARSHIP
• See page 131

CENTER FOR ARCHITECTURE

http://www.centerforarchitecture.org

CENTER FOR ARCHITECTURE DESIGN SCHOLARSHIP
• See page 132

HOUZZ

http://houzz.com

RESIDENTIAL DESIGN SCHOLARSHIP
• *See page 134*

SUSTAINABLE RESIDENTIAL DESIGN SCHOLARSHIP
• *See page 134*

IFDA EDUCATIONAL FOUNDATION

http://www.ifdaef.org/

IFDA LEADERS COMMEMORATIVE SCHOLARSHIP

Scholarship available to students who have completed four courses related to the field of interior design. Award is made to a to full-time student. Applicant does not have to be IFDA student member. Applicant must submit 300 to 500 word essay explaining future plans and goals, indicating why they believe that they are deserving of this award. Decision based upon student's academic achievement, awards and accomplishments, future plans and goals, and letter of recommendation. Documents sent along with the application should be sent via email

Academic Fields/Career Goals: Interior Design.

Award: Scholarship for use in sophomore, junior, or senior years; not renewable. *Number:* 1. *Amount:* $1500.

Eligibility Requirements: Applicant must be enrolled or expecting to enroll full-time at a four-year institution or university. Available to U.S. and non-U.S. citizens.

Application Requirements: Application form, essay. *Deadline:* March 31.

Contact: Earline Feldman, Director of Scholarships and Grants
         IFDA Educational Foundation
         112 Hidden Lake
         Canton, GA 30114
         Phone: 770-378-7221
         E-mail: ef.ifda@tapestries.org

IFDA STUDENT MEMBER SCHOLARSHIP

Scholarship available to students who have completed four courses related to the field of interior design. Award of $2000 to full-time student. Applicant must be IFDA student member. Applicant must submit 300 to 500 word essay explaining why they joined IFDA, discuss future plans and goals, and indicate why they are deserving of this award. Decision based upon student's academic achievement, awards and accomplishments, future plans and goals, and letter of recommendation. Documents sent along with the application should be sent individually to the four judges (4 copies).

Academic Fields/Career Goals: Interior Design; Trade/Technical Specialties.

Award: Scholarship for use in sophomore, junior, or senior years; not renewable. *Number:* 1. *Amount:* $2000.

Eligibility Requirements: Applicant must be enrolled or expecting to enroll full-time at a four-year institution or university. Available to U.S. and non-U.S. citizens.

Application Requirements: Application form, essay. *Deadline:* March 31.

Contact: Earline Feldman, Director of Scholarships and Grants
         IFDA Educational Foundation
         112 Hidden Lake Circle
         Canton, GA 30114
         Phone: 770-378-7221
         E-mail: ef.ifda@tapestries.org

PART TIME STUDENT SCHOLARSHIP

$1500 scholarship supported by IFDA Educational Foundation. Applicant must be a part-time student currently enrolled in at least 2 interior design or related field courses in a nationally accredited school in the United States.

Academic Fields/Career Goals: Interior Design.

Award: Scholarship for use in sophomore, junior, or senior years; not renewable. *Number:* 1. *Amount:* $1500.

Eligibility Requirements: Applicant must be enrolled or expecting to enroll part-time at a four-year institution or university. Available to U.S. and non-U.S. citizens.

Application Requirements: Application form, essay. *Deadline:* March 31.

Contact: Earline Feldman, IFDA Director of Scholarships and Grants
         IFDA Educational Foundation
         112 Hidden Lake Circle
         Canton, GA 30114
         Phone: 770-378-7221
         E-mail: ef.ifda@tapestries.org

RUTH CLARK FURNITURE DESIGN SCHOLARSHIP
• *See page 142*

TRICIA LEVANGIE GREEN/SUSTAINABLE SCHOLARSHIP
• *See page 134*

ILLUMINATING ENGINEERING SOCIETY OF NORTH AMERICA

http://www.ies.org/

ROBERT W. THUNEN MEMORIAL SCHOLARSHIPS
• *See page 135*

ILLUMINATING ENGINEERING SOCIETY OF NORTH AMERICA– GOLDEN GATE SECTION

http://www.iesgg.org/

ALAN LUCAS MEMORIAL EDUCATIONAL SCHOLARSHIP
• *See page 135*

INTERNATIONAL FACILITY MANAGEMENT ASSOCIATION FOUNDATION

http://www.ifmafoundation.org/

IFMA FOUNDATION SCHOLARSHIPS
• *See page 135*

NATIONAL ASSOCIATION OF WOMEN IN CONSTRUCTION

http://www.nawic.org/

NAWIC UNDERGRADUATE SCHOLARSHIPS
• *See page 135*

ONLINE LOGO MAKER

http://onlinelogomaker.com

OLM MALALA YOUSAFZAI SCHOLARSHIP
• *See page 143*

OREGON STUDENT ASSISTANCE COMMISSION

https://oregonstudentaid.gov/

HOME BUILDERS FOUNDATION JIM IRVINE STATEWIDE SCHOLARSHIP
• *See page 136*

PLAN NEW HAMPSHIRE

http://www.plannh.org

PLAN NEW HAMPSHIRE SCHOLARSHIP AND FELLOWSHIP PROGRAM
• *See page 129*

QUALITY BATH

http://www.qualitybath.com

QUALITYBATH.COM SCHOLARSHIP PROGRAM
• *See page 140*

SUPPORT CREATIVITY

http://wesupportcreativity.org

SUPPORT CREATIVITY SCHOLARSHIP
• *See page 137*

TURNER CONSTRUCTION COMPANY

http://www.turnerconstruction.com/

YOUTHFORCE 2020 SCHOLARSHIP PROGRAM
• *See page 137*

VECTORWORKS, INC.

http://www.vectorworks.net

VECTORWORKS DESIGN SCHOLARSHIP
• *See page 137*

INTERNATIONAL MIGRATION

UNITED NATIONS ASSOCIATION OF CONNECTICUT

http://www.unausa.org

UNITED NATIONS ASSOCIATION OF CONNECTICUT SCHOLARSHIP
• *See page 147*

INTERNATIONAL STUDIES

ARRL FOUNDATION INC.

http://www.arrl.org/

DON RIEBHOFF MEMORIAL SCHOLARSHIP

One $1000 award available to students with a technician or higher class license for radio operation. Preference given to those pursuing a Baccalaureate or higher degree in international studies at any accredited institution above the high school level. Preference given to ARRL members. Must demonstrate academic merit, financial need, and interest in promoting amateur radio.

Academic Fields/Career Goals: International Studies.

Award: Scholarship for use in freshman, sophomore, junior, senior, or graduate years; not renewable. *Number:* 1. *Amount:* $1000.

Eligibility Requirements: Applicant must be enrolled or expecting to enroll full-time at a four-year institution or university and must have an interest in amateur radio. Applicant or parent of applicant must be member of American Radio Relay League. Available to U.S. citizens.

Application Requirements: Application form, financial need analysis. *Deadline:* January 31.

Contact: Ms. Mary Hobart, Secretary
    Phone: 860-594-0397
    E-mail: k1mmh@arrl.org

ASSOCIATION OF FORMER INTELLIGENCE OFFICERS

http://www.afio.com

AFIO UNDERGRADUATE AND GRADUATE SCHOLARSHIPS
• *See page 113*

AUTOMOTIVE WOMEN'S ALLIANCE FOUNDATION

http://awafoundation.org/index.php

AUTOMOTIVE WOMEN'S ALLIANCE FOUNDATION SCHOLARSHIPS
• *See page 81*

CULTURAL SERVICES OF THE FRENCH EMBASSY

http://www.frenchculture.org/

TEACHING ASSISTANT PROGRAM IN FRANCE
• *See page 113*

ISLAMIC SCHOLARSHIP FUND

http://islamicscholarshipfund.org/

ISF NATIONAL SCHOLARSHIP
• *See page 119*

JORGE MAS CANOSA FREEDOM FOUNDATION

http://masscholarships.org/

MAS FAMILY SCHOLARSHIP AWARD
• *See page 181*

THE LYNDON BAINES JOHNSON FOUNDATION

http://www.lbjlibrary.org/page/foundation/

MOODY RESEARCH GRANTS
• *See page 114*

NATIONAL SECURITY EDUCATION PROGRAM

http://www.iie.org/

NATIONAL SECURITY EDUCATION PROGRAM (NSEP) DAVID L. BOREN UNDERGRADUATE SCHOLARSHIPS
• *See page 139*

PHI ALPHA THETA HISTORY HONOR SOCIETY, INC.

http://www.phialphatheta.org/

PHI ALPHA THETA WORLD HISTORY ASSOCIATION PAPER PRIZE
• *See page 383*

UNITED NATIONS ASSOCIATION OF CONNECTICUT

http://www.unausa.org

UNITED NATIONS ASSOCIATION OF CONNECTICUT SCHOLARSHIP
• *See page 147*

WOMEN IN INTERNATIONAL TRADE (WIIT)

http://www.wiit.org/

WIIT CHARITABLE TRUST SCHOLARSHIP PROGRAM
2 scholarships of $1500 each (one for an undergraduate female student and one for a graduate female student) may be awarded for the summer or fall semester and the spring semester of each year. Applicants must: (1) be currently enrolled or accepted at an undergraduate or graduate program at an accredited U.S. university or college, either full-time or part-time; and (2) demonstrate interest in international development, international relations, international trade, international economics, or international business. A completed application includes a 3–5 page essay, applicant information, and proof of acceptance or current enrollment in an accredited U.S. college or university. All materials should be submitted by email only to info@wiittrust.org using the following subject line-"Submission for WIIT TRUST Essay Writing Contest". Only one submission entry will be accepted from each entrant. Awards are based on the quality of the applicants' essays in response to the assigned topic for that year. Application information is available at https://www.wiit.org/wiit-charitable-trust/; click on "new scholarship program" to download the information for the current year.

Academic Fields/Career Goals: International Studies.

Award: Scholarship for use in freshman, sophomore, junior, senior, graduate, or postgraduate years; not renewable. *Number:* 1–4. *Amount:* $1500.

Eligibility Requirements: Applicant must be enrolled or expecting to enroll full- or part-time at a two-year or four-year institution or university and female. Available to U.S. citizens.

Application Requirements: Application form, essay. *Deadline:* June 15.

Contact: Nancy Travis, Chair, WIIT Charitable Trust
    E-mail: info@wiittrust.org

JOURNALISM

ADC RESEARCH INSTITUTE

http://www.adc.org/

JACK SHAHEEN MASS COMMUNICATIONS SCHOLARSHIP AWARD
• *See page 215*

ALPHA OMEGA COUNCIL OF NEW ENGLAND

http://www.alphaomegacouncil.org/

ALPHA OMEGA SCHOLARSHIP IN MEMORY OF PETER AGRIS
• *See page 215*

AMERICAN INSTITUTE OF POLISH CULTURE INC.

http://www.ampolinstitute.org/

HARRIET IRSAY SCHOLARSHIP GRANT
• *See page 141*

AMERICAN QUARTER HORSE FOUNDATION (AQHF)

http://www.aqha.com/foundation

AQHF JOURNALISM OR COMMUNICATIONS SCHOLARSHIP
• *See page 216*

ARRL FOUNDATION INC.

http://www.arrl.org/

JAKE MCCLAIN DRIVER, KC5WXA, SCHOLARSHIP
• *See page 229*

PHD SCHOLARSHIP
• *See page 230*

ASIAN AMERICAN JOURNALISTS ASSOCIATION

http://www.aaja.org/

CIC/ANNA CHENNAULT SCHOLARSHIP
• *See page 217*

MARY QUON MOY ING MEMORIAL SCHOLARSHIP AWARD
• *See page 217*

VINCENT CHIN MEMORIAL SCHOLARSHIP
• *See page 217*

ASIAN AMERICAN JOURNALISTS ASSOCIATION, SEATTLE CHAPTER

http://www.aajaseattle.org/

NORTHWEST JOURNALISTS OF COLOR SCHOLARSHIP
• *See page 96*

ASSOCIATED PRESS

http://www.aptra.org/

ASSOCIATED PRESS TELEVISION/RADIO ASSOCIATION-CLETE ROBERTS JOURNALISM SCHOLARSHIP AWARDS
Award for college undergraduates and graduate students studying in California, Nevada or Hawaii and pursuing careers in broadcast journalism. Submit application, references, and examples of broadcast-related work.

Academic Fields/Career Goals: Journalism; TV/Radio Broadcasting.
Award: Scholarship for use in freshman, sophomore, junior, or senior years; not renewable. *Number:* 3. *Amount:* $1500.
Eligibility Requirements: Applicant must be enrolled or expecting to enroll full-time at a two-year or four-year institution or university and studying in California, Hawaii, Nevada. Available to U.S. citizens.
Application Requirements: Application form, recommendations or references. *Deadline:* December 14.

Contact: Roberta Gonzales, Scholarship Committee
Associated Press
CBS 5 TV, 855 Battery Street
San Francisco, CA 94111

KATHRYN DETTMAN MEMORIAL JOURNALISM SCHOLARSHIP

One-time award of $1500 for broadcast journalism students, enrolled at a California, Hawaii, or Nevada college or university. Must submit entry form and examples of broadcast-related work.
Academic Fields/Career Goals: Journalism; TV/Radio Broadcasting.
Award: Scholarship for use in freshman, sophomore, junior, or senior years; renewable. *Number:* 1–4. *Amount:* $1500.
Eligibility Requirements: Applicant must be enrolled or expecting to enroll full-time at a two-year or four-year institution or university and studying in California, Hawaii, Nevada. Available to U.S. citizens.
Application Requirements: Application form, examples of broadcast-related work. *Deadline:* December 14.

Contact: Roberta Gonzales, Scholarship Committee
Associated Press
CBS 5 TV, 855 Battery Street
San Francisco, CA 94111

ASSOCIATION FOR WOMEN IN COMMUNICATIONS-SEATTLE PROFESSIONAL CHAPTER

http://www.seattleawc.org/

SEATTLE PROFESSIONAL CHAPTER OF THE ASSOCIATION FOR WOMEN IN COMMUNICATIONS

Scholarship of $3000 for women pursuing journalism in the state of Washington. For more details on eligibility criteria or selection procedure, refer to website at http://www.seattleawc.org/scholarships.html.
Academic Fields/Career Goals: Journalism.
Award: Scholarship for use in sophomore, junior, or senior years; not renewable. *Number:* 2. *Amount:* $3000.
Eligibility Requirements: Applicant must be enrolled or expecting to enroll full-time at a two-year or four-year or technical institution or university; female; resident of Washington and studying in Washington. Available to U.S. citizens.
Application Requirements: Application form, resume, sample of work, cover letter, transcript. *Deadline:* March 16.

Contact: Jaron Snow, Office Administrator
Phone: 425-771-4189
E-mail: awcseattle@verizon.net

BMI FOUNDATION, INC.

http://www.bmifoundation.org/

BMI FOUNDERS AWARD FOR RADIO BROADCASTING
• *See page 218*

CCNMA: LATINO JOURNALISTS OF CALIFORNIA

http://www.ccnma.org/

CCNMA SCHOLARSHIPS
• *See page 218*

COMMUNITY FOUNDATION OF WESTERN MASSACHUSETTS

http://www.communityfoundation.org/

WILLIAM J. (BILL) AND LORETTA M. O'NEIL SCHOLARSHIP

Scholarship available to residents from western MA pursuing English, journalism, or a related field. For details, please see website http://communityfoundation.org/.
Academic Fields/Career Goals: Journalism.
Award: Scholarship for use in freshman, sophomore, junior, senior, or graduate years; not renewable.
Eligibility Requirements: Applicant must be enrolled or expecting to enroll full- or part-time at a two-year or four-year institution or university and resident of Massachusetts. Available to U.S. citizens.
Application Requirements: Application form, essay, financial need analysis, transcript. *Deadline:* March 31.

Contact: Dotty Theriaque, Program Assistant for Scholarships
Community Foundation of Western Massachusetts
1500 Main Street
PO Box 15769
Springfield, MA 01115
Phone: 413-732-2858
Fax: 413-733-8565
E-mail: scholar@communityfoundation.org

CONNECTICUT CHAPTER OF SOCIETY OF PROFESSIONAL JOURNALISTS

http://www.ctspj.org/

CONNECTICUT SPJ BOB EDDY SCHOLARSHIP PROGRAM
• *See page 218*

DOW JONES NEWS FUND

https://dowjonesnewsfund.org/

DOW JONES NEWS FUND HIGH SCHOOL JOURNALISM WORKSHOPS WRITING, PHOTOGRAPHY AND MULTIMEDIA COMPETITION

Participants in DJNF summer workshops are nominated for writing, multimedia and photography awards based on their published work. Scholarships are presented to the best writers, digital producers and photographers to pursue media careers.
Academic Fields/Career Goals: Journalism.
Award: Scholarship for use in freshman year; not renewable. *Number:* 6. *Amount:* $1000.
Eligibility Requirements: Applicant must be high school student and planning to enroll or expecting to enroll full-time at a four-year institution or university. Available to U.S. and non-U.S. citizens.
Application Requirements: Application form, essay, portfolio. *Deadline:* October 1.

Contact: Mrs. Linda Shockley, Managing Director
Dow Jones News Fund
PO Box 300
Princeton, NJ 08543-0300
Phone: 609-452-2820
E-mail: djnf@dowjones.com

FREEDOM FORUM

http://www.newseuminstitute.org

AL NEUHARTH FREE SPIRIT AND JOURNALISM CONFERENCE PROGRAM

One-time award for high school juniors interested in pursuing a career in journalism. Must be actively involved in high school journalism and demonstrate qualities such as being a visionary, an innovative leader, an entrepreneur or a courageous achiever. One student selected from each state and the District of Columbia. Scholars come to Washington D.C. to receive their awards and participate in an all-expense paid journalism conference. See website at http://www.freespirit.org for further information.

Academic Fields/Career Goals: Journalism.

Award: Scholarship for use in freshman year; not renewable. *Number:* 51. *Amount:* $1000.

Eligibility Requirements: Applicant must be high school student; planning to enroll or expecting to enroll full-time at a two-year or four-year institution or university and must have an interest in entrepreneurship, leadership, photography/photogrammetry/filmmaking, or writing. Available to U.S. citizens.

Application Requirements: Application form, essay, personal photograph. *Deadline:* February 1.

Contact: Karen Catone, Director, Al Neuharth Free Spirit Program
Freedom Forum
555 Pennsylvania Avenue, NW
Washington, DC 20001
Phone: 202-292-6271
E-mail: kcatone@freedomforum.org

GEORGIA PRESS EDUCATIONAL FOUNDATION INC.

http://gapress.org/scholarships-internships/

DURWOOD MCALISTER SCHOLARSHIP

Scholarship awarded annually to an outstanding student majoring in print journalism at a Georgia college or university.

Academic Fields/Career Goals: Journalism.

Award: Scholarship for use in freshman, sophomore, junior, senior, or graduate years; not renewable. *Number:* 1. *Amount:* $500–$2000.

Eligibility Requirements: Applicant must be enrolled or expecting to enroll full-time at a two-year or four-year institution or university; resident of Georgia and studying in Georgia. Available to U.S. citizens.

Application Requirements: Application form, essay, financial need analysis, interview, personal photograph. *Deadline:* March 1.

Contact: Sean Ireland, Manager
Phone: 770-454-6776
Fax: 770-454-6778
E-mail: sireland@gapress.org

GEORGIA PRESS EDUCATIONAL FOUNDATION SCHOLARSHIPS

One-time awards to Georgia high school seniors and college undergraduates. Based on prior interest in newspaper journalism. Must be recommended by high school counselor, professor, and/or Georgia Press Educational Foundation member. Must reside and attend school in Georgia.

Academic Fields/Career Goals: Journalism.

Award: Scholarship for use in freshman, sophomore, junior, or senior years; not renewable. *Number:* 1–5. *Amount:* $500–$2000.

Eligibility Requirements: Applicant must be enrolled or expecting to enroll full-time at a two-year or four-year institution or university; resident of Georgia and studying in Georgia. Available to U.S. citizens.

Application Requirements: Application form, essay, financial need analysis, interview, personal photograph. *Deadline:* March 1.

Contact: Sean Ireland, Manager
Georgia Press Educational Foundation Inc.
3066 Mercer University Drive, Suite 200
Atlanta, GA 30341-4137
Phone: 770-454-6776

WILLIAM C. ROGERS SCHOLARSHIP

Scholarship awarded to a junior or senior majoring in the news-editorial sequence. For full-time study only. Must be a resident of Georgia.

Academic Fields/Career Goals: Journalism.

Award: Scholarship for use in junior or senior years; not renewable. *Number:* 1. *Amount:* $500–$2000.

Eligibility Requirements: Applicant must be enrolled or expecting to enroll full-time at a four-year institution or university and resident of Georgia. Available to U.S. citizens.

Application Requirements: Application form, essay, financial need analysis, interview, personal photograph. *Deadline:* March 1.

Contact: Sean Ireland, Manager
Phone: 770-454-6776
Fax: 770-454-6778
E-mail: sireland@gapress.org

IDAHO STATE BROADCASTERS ASSOCIATION

http://www.idahobroadcasters.org/

WAYNE C. CORNILS MEMORIAL SCHOLARSHIP
• *See page 180*

INDIANA BROADCASTERS ASSOCIATION

http://www.indianabroadcasters.org/

INDIANA BROADCASTERS FOUNDATION SCHOLARSHIP

Awards a student majoring in broadcasting, electronic media, or journalism. Must maintain a 3.0 GPA and be a resident of Indiana. One-time award for full-time undergraduate study in Indiana.

Academic Fields/Career Goals: Journalism; TV/Radio Broadcasting.

Award: Scholarship for use in freshman, sophomore, junior, or senior years; not renewable. *Number:* up to 10. *Amount:* $500–$2000.

Eligibility Requirements: Applicant must be enrolled or expecting to enroll full-time at a two-year or four-year or technical institution or university; resident of Indiana and studying in Indiana. Applicant must have 3.0 GPA or higher. Available to U.S. citizens.

Application Requirements: Application form, application form may be submitted online (http://www.indianabroadcasters.org), essay, recommendations or references, transcript. *Deadline:* March 4.

Contact: Gwen Piening, Scholarship Administrator
Indiana Broadcasters Association
3003 East 98th Street, Suite 161
Indianapolis, IN 46280
Phone: 317-573-0119
Fax: 317-573-0895
E-mail: indba@aol.com

INTERNATIONAL FOODSERVICE EDITORIAL COUNCIL

http://www.ifeconline.com/

INTERNATIONAL FOODSERVICE EDITORIAL COUNCIL COMMUNICATIONS SCHOLARSHIP
• *See page 96*

ISLAMIC SCHOLARSHIP FUND

http://islamicscholarshipfund.org/

ISF NATIONAL SCHOLARSHIP
• *See page 119*

JAPANESE AMERICAN CITIZENS LEAGUE (JACL)

http://www.jacl.org/

NATIONAL JACL HEADQUARTERS SCHOLARSHIP
• *See page 107*

JORGE MAS CANOSA FREEDOM FOUNDATION

http://masscholarships.org/

MAS FAMILY SCHOLARSHIP AWARD
• *See page 181*

LA-PHILOSOPHIE.COM

http://la-philosophie.com

LA-PHILOSOPHIE.COM SCHOLARSHIP
• *See page 119*

MAINE COMMUNITY FOUNDATION, INC.

http://www.mainecf.org/

GUY P. GANNETT SCHOLARSHIP FUND

Scholarship for students majoring in journalism or a field reasonably related, including all forms of print, broadcast, or electronic media. Please go to the Maine Community Foundation, Inc. website for application requirements.

Academic Fields/Career Goals: Journalism.

Award: Scholarship for use in freshman year; not renewable.

Eligibility Requirements: Applicant must be high school student; planning to enroll or expecting to enroll full-time at a four-year institution or university and resident of Maine. Available to U.S. citizens.

Application Requirements: Application form, financial need analysis.

Contact: Ms. Amy Pollien, Grants Administration
        Phone: 207-667-9735 Ext. 1109
        E-mail: apollien@mainecf.org

MARYLAND/DELAWARE/DISTRICT OF COLUMBIA PRESS FOUNDATION

http://www.mddcpress.com/

MICHAEL J. POWELL HIGH SCHOOL JOURNALIST OF THE YEAR

Scholarship of $1500 to an outstanding high school student. Applicant must submit five samples of work, mounted on unlined paper, a letter of recommendation from the nominee's advisor, an autobiography geared to the publication activities in which the nominee participated, and the nominee should write a paragraph or two on the most important aspect of scholastic journalism.

Academic Fields/Career Goals: Journalism.

Award: Scholarship for use in freshman year; not renewable. *Number:* 1. *Amount:* $1500.

Eligibility Requirements: Applicant must be high school student; planning to enroll or expecting to enroll full-time at a four-year institution or university; resident of Delaware, District of Columbia, Maryland and must have an interest in writing. Available to U.S. citizens.

Application Requirements: Application form, driver's license, entry in a contest, five sample articles, recommendations or references. *Deadline:* January 31.

Contact: Jennifer Thornberry, Membership Services Coordinator
        Maryland/Delaware/District of Columbia Press Foundation
        60 West Street
        Suite 107
        Annapolis, MD 21401-2479
        Phone: 855-721-6332 Ext. 2
        Fax: 855-721-6332
        E-mail: service@mddcpress.com

MISSISSIPPI ASSOCIATION OF BROADCASTERS

http://www.msbroadcasters.org/

MISSISSIPPI ASSOCIATION OF BROADCASTERS SCHOLARSHIP

Scholarship available to a student enrolled in a fully accredited broadcast curriculum at a Mississippi two- or four-year college.

Academic Fields/Career Goals: Journalism; TV/Radio Broadcasting.

Award: Scholarship for use in freshman, sophomore, junior, or senior years; not renewable. *Number:* up to 8. *Amount:* $2000.

Eligibility Requirements: Applicant must be enrolled or expecting to enroll full-time at a two-year or four-year institution or university; resident of Mississippi and studying in Mississippi. Available to U.S. citizens.

Application Requirements: Application form, extracurricular activities and community involvement also considered, financial need analysis, recommendations or references. *Deadline:* May 1.

Contact: Jackie Lett, Scholarship Coordinator
        Phone: 601-957-9121
        Fax: 601-957-9175
        E-mail: jackie@msbroadcasters.org

MISSISSIPPI PRESS ASSOCIATION EDUCATION FOUNDATION

http://www.mspress.org/displaycommon.cfm?an=1&suba rticlenbr=16

MISSISSIPPI PRESS ASSOCIATION EDUCATION FOUNDATION SCHOLARSHIP

The foundation annually offers $1000 ($500 per semester) scholarships to qualified students enrolled in print journalism, and who are residents of Mississippi. The recipient who maintains a 3.0 GPA. Total value of the scholarship can be as much as $4000 when awarded to an incoming freshman who remains qualified throughout their four years of print journalism education.

Academic Fields/Career Goals: Journalism.

Award: Scholarship for use in freshman, sophomore, junior, or senior years; renewable. *Number:* 1. *Amount:* $1000–$4000.

Eligibility Requirements: Applicant must be enrolled or expecting to enroll full-time at a two-year or four-year institution or university and resident of Mississippi. Applicant must have 3.0 GPA or higher. Available to U.S. citizens.

Application Requirements: Application form, recommendations or references, resume, sample of work. *Deadline:* April 1.

Contact: Beth Boone, Scholarship Coordinator
        Phone: 601-981-3060
        Fax: 601-981-3676
        E-mail: bboone@mspress.org

NATIONAL ACADEMY OF TELEVISION ARTS & SCIENCES— OHIO VALLEY CHAPTER

http://ohiovalleyemmy.org/

DAVID J. CLARKE MEMORIAL SCHOLARSHIP
• *See page 220*

NATIONAL ACADEMY OF TELEVISION ARTS AND SCIENCES

http://www.emmyonline.tv/

DOUGLAS W. MUMMERT SCHOLARSHIP
• *See page 142*

JIM MCKAY MEMORIAL SCHOLARSHIP
• *See page 220*

MIKE WALLACE MEMORIAL SCHOLARSHIP
• *See page 220*

NATIONAL ACADEMY OF TELEVISION ARTS AND SCIENCES TRUSTEES SCHOLARSHIP
• *See page 220*

RANDY FALCO SCHOLARSHIP
• *See page 220*

NATIONAL ACADEMY OF TELEVISION ARTS AND SCIENCES, MICHIGAN CHAPTER

http://natasmichigan.org

DR. LYNNE BOYLE/JOHN SCHIMPF UNDERGRADUATE SCHOLARSHIP

• *See page 97*

NATIONAL ACADEMY OF TELEVISION ARTS AND SCIENCES-NATIONAL CAPITAL/CHESAPEAKE BAY CHAPTER

http://www.natasdc.org/

BETTY ENDICOTT/NTA-NCCB STUDENT SCHOLARSHIP

Scholarship for a full-time sophomore, junior or non-graduating senior student pursuing a career in communication, television or broadcast journalism. Must be enrolled in an accredited four-year college or university in Maryland, Virginia or Washington, D.C. Minimum GPA of 3.0 required. Must demonstrate an aptitude or interest in communication, television or broadcast journalism. Application URL http://capitalemmys.tv/betty_endicott.htm.

Academic Fields/Career Goals: Journalism; TV/Radio Broadcasting.

Award: Scholarship for use in sophomore, junior, or senior years; not renewable. *Number:* 1. *Amount:* $5000.

Eligibility Requirements: Applicant must be enrolled or expecting to enroll full-time at a four-year institution or university and studying in District of Columbia, Maryland, Virginia. Applicant must have 3.0 GPA or higher. Available to U.S. citizens.

Application Requirements: Application form, essay, recommendations or references, resume, transcript, work samples (resume tape in VHS format and radio or television broadcast scripts). *Deadline:* April 22.

Contact: Diane Bruno, Student Affairs Committee
National Academy of Television Arts and Sciences-National
    Capital/Chesapeake Bay Chapter
9405 Russell Road
Silver Spring, MD 20910
Phone: 301-587-3993
E-mail: capitalemmys@aol.com

NATIONAL ASSOCIATION OF BLACK JOURNALISTS

http://www.nabj.org/

ALLISON FISHER SCHOLARSHIP

Scholarship for students currently attending an accredited college or university. Must be majoring in print journalism and maintain a 3.0 GPA. Recipient will attend NABJ convention and participate in the mentor program. Scholarship value and the number of awards granted varies.

Academic Fields/Career Goals: Journalism.

Award: Scholarship for use in freshman, sophomore, junior, senior, or graduate years; not renewable.

Eligibility Requirements: Applicant must be enrolled or expecting to enroll full-time at a four-year institution or university. Applicant must have 3.0 GPA or higher. Available to U.S. and non-U.S. citizens.

Application Requirements: Driver's license, proof of enrollment, recommendations or references. *Deadline:* March 17.

Contact: Irving Washington, Manager
Phone: 301-445-7100
Fax: 301-445-7101
E-mail: iwashington@nabj.org

GERALD BOYD/ROBIN STONE NON-SUSTAINING SCHOLARSHIP

One-time scholarship for students enrolled in an accredited four-year institution. Must be enrolled as an undergraduate or graduate student and maintain a 3.0 GPA. Must major in print journalism. Must be a member of NABJ. Scholarship value and the number of awards granted annually varies.

Academic Fields/Career Goals: Journalism.

Award: Scholarship for use in freshman, sophomore, junior, senior, or graduate years; not renewable.

Eligibility Requirements: Applicant must be enrolled or expecting to enroll full-time at a four-year institution or university. Applicant must have 3.0 GPA or higher. Available to U.S. and non-U.S. citizens.

Application Requirements: 6 samples of work, application form, essay, personal photograph, recommendations or references, transcript. *Deadline:* March 17.

Contact: Irving Washington, Manager
Phone: 301-445-7100
Fax: 301-445-7101
E-mail: iwashington@nabj.org

NABJ SCHOLARSHIP

• *See page 220*

NATIONAL ASSOCIATION OF BLACK JOURNALISTS AND NEWHOUSE FOUNDATION SCHOLARSHIP

Award for high school seniors planning to attend an accredited four-year college or university and major in journalism. Minimum 3.0 GPA required. Must be a member of NABJ. The scholarship value and the number of awards granted varies.

Academic Fields/Career Goals: Journalism.

Award: Scholarship for use in freshman, sophomore, junior, or senior years; not renewable.

Eligibility Requirements: Applicant must be enrolled or expecting to enroll full-time at a four-year institution or university and must have an interest in writing. Applicant must have 3.0 GPA or higher. Available to U.S. and non-U.S. citizens.

Application Requirements: Application form, driver's license, essay, interview, recommendations or references, transcript. *Deadline:* March 17.

Contact: Irving Washington, Manager
Phone: 301-445-7100
Fax: 301-445-7101
E-mail: iwashington@nabj.org

NATIONAL ASSOCIATION OF BLACK JOURNALISTS NON-SUSTAINING SCHOLARSHIP AWARDS

One-time award for college students attending a four-year institution and majoring in journalism. Minimum 2.5 GPA required. Must be a member of NABJ. Scholarship value and the number of awards varies annually.

Academic Fields/Career Goals: Journalism; Photojournalism/Photography; TV/Radio Broadcasting.

Award: Scholarship for use in freshman, sophomore, junior, or senior years; not renewable.

Eligibility Requirements: Applicant must be enrolled or expecting to enroll full-time at a four-year institution or university and must have an interest in writing. Applicant must have 2.5 GPA or higher. Available to U.S. and non-U.S. citizens.

Application Requirements: Application form, driver's license, personal photograph, proof of enrollment, recommendations or references, transcript. *Deadline:* March 17.

Contact: Irving Washington, Manager
Phone: 301-445-7100
Fax: 301-445-7101
E-mail: iwashington@nabj.org

NATIONAL ASSOCIATION OF BROADCASTERS

http://www.nab.org/

NATIONAL ASSOCIATION OF BROADCASTERS GRANTS FOR RESEARCH IN BROADCASTING

• *See page 221*

NATIONAL ASSOCIATION OF HISPANIC JOURNALISTS (NAHJ)

http://www.nahj.org/

GERALDO RIVERA SCHOLARSHIP

Awards available to college undergraduates and graduate students pursuing careers in English- or Spanish-language TV broadcast journalism. Applications available on website, http://www.nahj.org.

Academic Fields/Career Goals: Journalism; TV/Radio Broadcasting.

Award: Scholarship for use in senior or graduate years; not renewable. *Amount:* $1000–$5000.

Eligibility Requirements: Applicant must be enrolled or expecting to enroll full-time at a four-year institution or university. Available to U.S. citizens.

Application Requirements: Application form, financial need analysis, recommendations or references, resume, transcript. *Deadline:* March 31.

Contact: Virginia Galindo, Program Assistant
Phone: 202-662-7145
E-mail: vgalindo@nahj.org

MARIA ELENA SALINAS SCHOLARSHIP
• *See page 360*

NATIONAL ASSOCIATION OF HISPANIC JOURNALISTS SCHOLARSHIP
• *See page 221*

NEWHOUSE SCHOLARSHIP PROGRAM
• *See page 364*

WASHINGTON POST YOUNG JOURNALISTS SCHOLARSHIP

Four-year award of $10,000 for high school seniors in D.C. metropolitan area. Contact educational programs manager for application and information.

Academic Fields/Career Goals: Journalism.

Award: Scholarship for use in freshman year; not renewable. *Amount:* $10,000.

Eligibility Requirements: Applicant must be high school student; planning to enroll or expecting to enroll full-time at a four-year institution or university and resident of District of Columbia, Maryland, Virginia. Available to U.S. citizens.

Application Requirements: Application form, recommendations or references, transcript. *Deadline:* March 31.

Contact: Virginia Galindo, Program Assistant
Phone: 202-662-7145
E-mail: vgalindo@nahj.org

NATIONAL ASSOCIATION OF NEGRO BUSINESS AND PROFESSIONAL WOMEN'S CLUBS INC.

http://www.nanbpwc.org/

JULIANNE MALVEAUX SCHOLARSHIP
• *See page 264*

NATIONAL DAIRY SHRINE

http://www.dairyshrine.org/

MARSHALL E. MCCULLOUGH-NATIONAL DAIRY SHRINE SCHOLARSHIPS
• *See page 108*

NATIONAL PRESS CLUB

http://www.press.org/

NATIONAL PRESS CLUB SCHOLARSHIP FOR JOURNALISM DIVERSITY

Scholarship of $2500 per year awarded to a talented minority student planning to pursue a career in journalism. Applicant must be a high school senior. Must have applied to or been accepted by a college or university for the upcoming year.

Academic Fields/Career Goals: Journalism.

Award: Scholarship for use in freshman year; not renewable. *Number:* 1. *Amount:* $2500.

Eligibility Requirements: Applicant must be American Indian/Alaska Native, Asian/Pacific Islander, Black (non-Hispanic), Hispanic; high school student and planning to enroll or expecting to enroll full-time at a four-year institution or university. Applicant must have 3.0 GPA or higher. Available to U.S. and non-U.S. citizens.

Application Requirements: Application form, essay, financial need analysis, recommendations or references, transcript, work samples demonstrating an ongoing interest in journalism. *Deadline:* March 1.

Contact: Joann Booze, Scholarship Coordinator
Phone: 202-662-7532
Fax: 202-662-7512
E-mail: jbooze@press.org

NATIONAL SCHOLASTIC PRESS ASSOCIATION

http://www.studentpress.org/

NSPA JOURNALISM HONOR ROLL SCHOLARSHIP

Scholarship to student journalists who have achieved a 3.75 or higher GPA and have worked in student media for two or more years.

Academic Fields/Career Goals: Journalism.

Award: Scholarship for use in freshman year; not renewable. *Number:* 1–3. *Amount:* $1000.

Eligibility Requirements: Applicant must be high school student and planning to enroll or expecting to enroll full-time at a four-year institution or university. Applicant or parent of applicant must have employment or volunteer experience in journalism/broadcasting. Available to U.S. and non-U.S. citizens.

Application Requirements: Application form, essay, proof of NSPA membership required, recommendations or references, resume, transcript. *Deadline:* February 15.

Contact: Marisa Dobson, Sponsorship Contest Coordinator
Phone: 612-625-6519
Fax: 612-626-0720
E-mail: marisa@studentpress.org

NATIONAL WRITERS ASSOCIATION FOUNDATION

http://www.nationalwriters.com/

NATIONAL WRITERS ASSOCIATION FOUNDATION SCHOLARSHIPS

Scholarships available to talented young writers with serious interest in any writing field.

Academic Fields/Career Goals: Journalism; Literature/English/Writing.

Award: Scholarship for use in freshman, sophomore, junior, senior, graduate, or postgraduate years; not renewable. *Number:* 1–4. *Amount:* $1000.

Eligibility Requirements: Applicant must be enrolled or expecting to enroll full- or part-time at a two-year or four-year or technical institution or university and must have an interest in writing. Available to U.S. and non-U.S. citizens.

Application Requirements: Application form. *Deadline:* December 31.

Contact: Sandy Whelchel, Executive Director
National Writers Association Foundation
10940 South Parker Road, Suite 508
Parker, CO 80134
Phone: 303-841-0246
Fax: 303-841-2607
E-mail: natlwritersassn@hotmail.com

NATIVE AMERICAN JOURNALISTS ASSOCIATION

http://www.naja.com/

NATIVE AMERICAN JOURNALISTS ASSOCIATION SCHOLARSHIPS
• *See page 97*

NEBRASKA PRESS ASSOCIATION

http://www.nebpress.com/

NEBRASKA PRESS ASSOCIATION FOUNDATION SCHOLARSHIP
• *See page 97*

NEW JERSEY BROADCASTERS ASSOCIATION

http://www.njba.com/

MICHAEL S. LIBRETTI SCHOLARSHIP
• *See page 221*

NEW JERSEY PRESS FOUNDATION

http://www.njpressfoundation.org/

BERNARD KILGORE MEMORIAL SCHOLARSHIP FOR THE NJ HIGH SCHOOL JOURNALIST OF THE YEAR
Program co-sponsored with the Garden State Scholastic Press Association. Winning student is nominated to the Journalism Education Association for the National High School Journalist of the Year Competition. Must be in high school with plans of entering a four-year college or university on a full-time basis. Minimum 3.0 GPA required.

Academic Fields/Career Goals: Journalism.

Award: Scholarship for use in freshman year; not renewable. *Number:* 1. *Amount:* $5000.

Eligibility Requirements: Applicant must be high school student; planning to enroll or expecting to enroll full-time at a four-year institution or university; resident of New Jersey and must have an interest in writing. Applicant must have 3.0 GPA or higher. Available to U.S. citizens.

Application Requirements: Application form, essay, portfolio. *Deadline:* February 28.

Contact: Peggy Arbitell, Business Manager
Phone: 609-406-0600 Ext. 14
E-mail: parbitell@njpa.org

OHIO NEWS MEDIA FOUNDATION

http://www.ohionews.org

HAROLD K. DOUTHIT SCHOLARSHIP
• *See page 98*

OHIO NEWS MEDIA FOUNDATION MINORITY SCHOLARSHIP
• *See page 98*

OHIO NEWS MEDIA FOUNDATION UNIVERSITY JOURNALISM SCHOLARSHIP
• *See page 98*

ONWA ANNUAL SCHOLARSHIP
• *See page 98*

OREGON ASSOCIATION OF BROADCASTERS

http://www.theoab.org/

OAB FOUNDATION SCHOLARSHIP
• *See page 221*

OREGON COMMUNITY FOUNDATION

http://www.oregoncf.org/

JACKSON FOUNDATION JOURNALISM SCHOLARSHIP FUND
Scholarship for students attending an Oregon college or university and majoring in, or with emphasis on, journalism. For both full-time and part-time. Must be a resident of Oregon.

Academic Fields/Career Goals: Journalism.

Award: Scholarship for use in freshman, sophomore, junior, or senior years; renewable. *Number:* 5. *Amount:* $1500–$2000.

Eligibility Requirements: Applicant must be enrolled or expecting to enroll full-time at a four-year institution or university; resident of Oregon and studying in Oregon. Available to U.S. citizens.

Application Requirements: Application form. *Deadline:* March 1.

Contact: Dianne Causey, Program Associate for Scholarships and Grants
Phone: 503-227-6846 Ext. 1418
E-mail: dcausey@oregoncf.org

OREGON STUDENT ASSISTANCE COMMISSION

https://oregonstudentaid.gov/

JACKSON FOUNDATION JOURNALISM SCHOLARSHIP
Renewable award for students at Oregon public and nonprofit colleges who are journalism majors or whose course of study emphasizes journalism. Preference given to students who have taken the SAT and have received good essay scores. Based on financial need.

Academic Fields/Career Goals: Journalism.

Award: Scholarship for use in freshman, sophomore, junior, or senior years; not renewable.

Eligibility Requirements: Applicant must be enrolled or expecting to enroll full-time at a two-year or four-year institution; resident of Oregon and studying in Oregon. Available to U.S. citizens.

Application Requirements: Application form, financial need analysis. *Deadline:* March 1.

Contact: Melissa Adams, Scholarship Processing Coordinator
Phone: 541-687-7409
E-mail: melissa.adams@state.or.us

OUTDOOR WRITERS ASSOCIATION OF AMERICA

http://www.owaa.org/

OUTDOOR WRITERS ASSOCIATION OF AMERICA - BODIE MCDOWELL SCHOLARSHIP AWARD
• *See page 222*

OVERSEAS PRESS CLUB FOUNDATION

http://www.overseaspressclubfoundation.org/

OVERSEAS PRESS CLUB FOUNDATION SCHOLAR AWARDS
Students aspiring to become foreign correspondents can apply. Must write an essay of approximately 500 words concentrating on an area of the world or an international issue that is in keeping with the applicant's

interest. Must be studying at an American college or university or be an American student studying abroad. Winners receive either a $2,000 scholarship or a $3,000 fellowship to be used to fund an experience at an overseas media organization.

Academic Fields/Career Goals: Journalism.

Award: Scholarship for use in freshman, sophomore, junior, senior, or graduate years; not renewable. *Number:* 16. *Amount:* $2000–$3000.

Eligibility Requirements: Applicant must be enrolled or expecting to enroll full-time at a two-year or four-year institution or university and must have an interest in writing. Available to U.S. and non-U.S. citizens.

Application Requirements: Essay. *Deadline:* December 1.

Contact: Jane Reilly, Executive Director
Overseas Press Club Foundation
40 West 45th Street
New York, NY 10036
Phone: 201-493-9087
E-mail: foundation@opcofamerica.org

PALM BEACH ASSOCIATION OF BLACK JOURNALISTS

PALM BEACH ASSOCIATION OF BLACK JOURNALISTS SCHOLARSHIP

Scholarship of $1000 are awarded to African-American graduating high school seniors plan to pursue a degree in journalism-print, television, radio broadcasting or photography industries. Have a GPA of 2.7 or better.

Academic Fields/Career Goals: Journalism; Photojournalism/Photography; TV/Radio Broadcasting.

Award: Scholarship for use in freshman year; not renewable. *Number:* 1. *Amount:* $1000.

Eligibility Requirements: Applicant must be Black (non-Hispanic); high school student and planning to enroll or expecting to enroll full- or part-time at a four-year institution or university. Available to U.S. and non-U.S. citizens.

Application Requirements: Application form, college acceptance proof, driver's license, transcript. *Deadline:* March 30.

Contact: Christopher Smith, Scholarship Chair
Palm Beach Association of Black Journalists
PO Box 19533
West Palm Beach, FL 33416

PHILADELPHIA ASSOCIATION OF BLACK JOURNALISTS

http://www.pabj.org/

PHILADELPHIA ASSOCIATION OF BLACK JOURNALISTS SCHOLARSHIP

One-time award available to deserving high school students in the Delaware Valley who are interested in becoming journalists. Must have a 2.5 GPA. All applicants must state their intention to pursue journalism careers.

Academic Fields/Career Goals: Journalism.

Award: Scholarship for use in freshman, sophomore, junior, or senior years; not renewable. *Number:* 2. *Amount:* up to $1000.

Eligibility Requirements: Applicant must be Black (non-Hispanic); enrolled or expecting to enroll full-time at a four-year institution or university; resident of Pennsylvania and must have an interest in writing. Applicant must have 2.5 GPA or higher. Available to U.S. citizens.

Application Requirements: Application form, driver's license, essay, recommendations or references, transcript. *Deadline:* May 1.

Contact: Manny Smith, Scholarship Committee
Philadelphia Association of Black Journalists
PO Box 8232
Philadelphia, PA 19101
E-mail: manuelsmith@gmail.com

PRINTING INDUSTRY MIDWEST EDUCATION FOUDNATION

http://www.pimw.org/scholarships

PRINTING INDUSTRY MIDWEST EDUCATION FOUNDATION SCHOLARSHIP FUND
• See page 222

QUILL AND SCROLL FOUNDATION

http://www.quillandscroll.org

EDWARD J. NELL MEMORIAL SCHOLARSHIP IN JOURNALISM

Merit-based award for high school seniors planning to major in journalism. Must have won a National Quill and Scroll Writing Award or a Photography or Yearbook Excellence contest. Entry forms available from journalism adviser or Quill and Scroll. Must rank in upper third of class or have a minimum 3.0 GPA.

Academic Fields/Career Goals: Journalism.

Award: Scholarship for use in freshman year; not renewable. *Number:* 1–6. *Amount:* $500–$1500.

Eligibility Requirements: Applicant must be high school student; planning to enroll or expecting to enroll full-time at a four-year institution or university and must have an interest in photography/photogrammetry/filmmaking or writing. Applicant must have 3.0 GPA or higher. Available to U.S. citizens.

Application Requirements: Application form, essay, personal photograph. *Deadline:* May 10.

Contact: JEFFREY BROWNE, Executive Director
Quill and Scroll Foundation
School of Journalism, W111 AJB
Iowa City, IA 52242-1528
Phone: 319-335-3457
E-mail: quill-scroll@uiowa.edu

RADIO TELEVISION DIGITAL NEWS ASSOCIATION

http://www.rtdna.org

CAROLE SIMPSON SCHOLARSHIP
• See page 222

ED BRADLEY SCHOLARSHIP
• See page 223

GEORGE FOREMAN TRIBUTE TO LYNDON B. JOHNSON SCHOLARSHIP
• See page 223

LEE THORNTON SCHOLARSHIP
• See page 223

LOU AND CAROLE PRATO SPORTS REPORTING SCHOLARSHIP
• See page 223

MIKE REYNOLDS JOURNALISM SCHOLARSHIP
• See page 223

ROBERT H. MOLLOHAN FAMILY CHARITABLE FOUNDATION, INC.

http://www.mollohanfoundation.org/

HARRY C. HAMM FAMILY SCHOLARSHIP
• See page 224

SIGMA DELTA CHI FOUNDATION OF WASHINGTON D.C.

http://www.sdxdc.org

SIGMA DELTA CHI SCHOLARSHIPS

One-time award to help pay tuition for full-time students in their junior or senior year demonstrating a clear intention to become journalists. Must demonstrate financial need. Grades and skills are also considered. Must be enrolled in a college or university in the Washington, D.C., metropolitan area. Sponsored by the Society of Professional Journalists.

Academic Fields/Career Goals: Journalism.

Award: Scholarship for use in junior or senior years; not renewable. *Number:* 4–7. *Amount:* $3000–$5000.

Eligibility Requirements: Applicant must be enrolled or expecting to enroll full-time at a four-year institution or university and studying in District of Columbia, Maryland, Virginia. Applicant must have 3.0 GPA or higher. Available to U.S. and non-U.S. citizens.

Application Requirements: Application form, essay, financial need analysis, interview, portfolio. *Deadline:* February 28.

Contact: Maura Judkis
E-mail: scholarship@sdxdc.org

SOCIETY OF PROFESSIONAL JOURNALISTS, LOS ANGELES CHAPTER

http://www.spj.org/losangeles

BILL FARR SCHOLARSHIP

Award available to a student who is either a resident of Los Angeles, Ventura or Orange counties or is enrolled at a university in one of those counties. Must have completed sophomore year and be enrolled in or accepted to a journalism program.

Academic Fields/Career Goals: Journalism.

Award: Scholarship for use in junior, senior, or graduate years; not renewable. *Number:* 1. *Amount:* $500–$1000.

Eligibility Requirements: Applicant must be enrolled or expecting to enroll full-time at a four-year institution or university; resident of California and studying in California. Available to U.S. citizens.

Application Requirements: Application form, essay, financial need analysis, recommendations or references, resume, work samples. *Deadline:* April 15.

Contact: Daniel Garvey, Scholarship Chairman
Society of Professional Journalists, Los Angeles Chapter
1250 Bellflower
Long Beach, CA 90840
Phone: 562-985-5779

CARL GREENBERG SCHOLARSHIP

Award for a student who is either a resident of Los Angeles, Ventura or Orange counties or is enrolled at a university in one of those three California counties. Must have completed sophomore year and be enrolled in or accepted to an investigative or political journalism program.

Academic Fields/Career Goals: Journalism.

Award: Scholarship for use in junior, senior, or graduate years; not renewable. *Number:* 1. *Amount:* $1000.

Eligibility Requirements: Applicant must be enrolled or expecting to enroll full-time at a four-year institution or university; resident of California and studying in California. Available to U.S. citizens.

Application Requirements: Application form, essay, financial need analysis, recommendations or references, resume, work samples. *Deadline:* April 15.

Contact: Daniel Garvey, Scholarship Chairman
Society of Professional Journalists, Los Angeles Chapter
1250 Bellflower
Long Beach, CA 90840
Phone: 562-985-5779

HELEN JOHNSON SCHOLARSHIP

Awards are available to a student who is a resident of Los Angeles, Ventura or Orange counties or is enrolled at a university in one of those three California counties. Must have completed sophomore year and be enrolled in or accepted to a broadcast journalism program.

Academic Fields/Career Goals: Journalism; TV/Radio Broadcasting.

Award: Scholarship for use in junior, senior, or graduate years; not renewable. *Number:* 1. *Amount:* $500–$1000.

Eligibility Requirements: Applicant must be enrolled or expecting to enroll full-time at a four-year institution or university; resident of California and studying in California. Available to U.S. citizens.

Application Requirements: Application form, essay, financial need analysis, recommendations or references, resume, work samples. *Deadline:* April 15.

Contact: Daniel Garvey, Scholarship Chairman
Society of Professional Journalists, Los Angeles Chapter
1250 Bellflower
Long Beach, CA 90840
Phone: 562-985-5779

KEN INOUYE SCHOLARSHIP

Awards are available to a minority student who is either a resident of Los Angeles, Ventura, or Orange counties or is enrolled at a university in one of those three California counties. Must have completed sophomore year and be enrolled in or accepted to a journalism program.

Academic Fields/Career Goals: Journalism.

Award: Scholarship for use in junior, senior, or graduate years; renewable. *Number:* 1. *Amount:* $500–$1000.

Eligibility Requirements: Applicant must be American Indian/Alaska Native, Asian/Pacific Islander, Black (non-Hispanic), Hispanic; enrolled or expecting to enroll full-time at a four-year institution or university; resident of California and studying in California. Available to U.S. citizens.

Application Requirements: Application form, essay, financial need analysis, recommendations or references, resume, work samples. *Deadline:* April 15.

Contact: Daniel Garvey, Scholarship Chairman
Society of Professional Journalists, Los Angeles Chapter
1250 Bellflower
Long Beach, CA 90840
Phone: 562-985-5779

SOCIETY OF PROFESSIONAL JOURNALISTS MARYLAND PRO CHAPTER

http://www.spj.org/mdpro

MARYLAND SPJ PRO CHAPTER COLLEGE SCHOLARSHIP

Scholarships for journalism students whose regular home residence is in Maryland. May attend colleges or universities in Virginia, Washington D.C., or Pennsylvania.

Academic Fields/Career Goals: Journalism.

Award: Scholarship for use in freshman, sophomore, junior, or senior years; not renewable.

Eligibility Requirements: Applicant must be enrolled or expecting to enroll full- or part-time at a four-year institution or university; resident of Maryland and studying in District of Columbia, Maryland, Pennsylvania, Virginia. Available to U.S. citizens.

Application Requirements: Application form, awards or honors received, essay, financial need analysis, recommendations or references, transcript. *Deadline:* May 9.

Contact: Sue Katcef, Scholarship Chair
Society of Professional Journalists Maryland Pro Chapter
402 Fox Hollow Lane
Annapolis, MD 21403
Phone: 301-405-7526
E-mail: susiekk@aol.com

SOUTH ASIAN JOURNALISTS ASSOCIATION (SAJA)

http://www.saja.org/

SAJA JOURNALISM SCHOLARSHIP

Scholarships for students in North America who are of South Asian descent (includes Bangladesh, Bhutan, India, Maldives, Nepal, Pakistan and Sri Lanka, Indo-Caribbean) or those with a demonstrated interest in South Asia or South Asian issues. Must be interested in pursuing journalism. Applicant must be a high school senior, undergraduate student or graduate-level student.

Academic Fields/Career Goals: Journalism.

Award: Scholarship for use in freshman, sophomore, junior, senior, graduate, or postgraduate years; not renewable. *Number:* 1–4. *Amount:* $1000–$2000.

Eligibility Requirements: Applicant must be Asian/Pacific Islander and enrolled or expecting to enroll full-time at a two-year or four-year institution or university. Available to U.S. and non-U.S. citizens.

Application Requirements: Application form, essay, financial need analysis, journalism clips or work samples, portfolio, recommendations or references, resume. *Deadline:* February 15.

Contact: Amita Parashar, Student Committee and Scholarships
    Phone: 202-513-2845
    E-mail: students@saja.org

STRAIGHTFORWARD MEDIA

http://www.straightforwardmedia.com/

STRAIGHTFORWARD MEDIA MEDIA & COMMUNICATIONS SCHOLARSHIP
• *See page 99*

TAMPA BAY TIMES FUND, INC.

http://www.tampabay.com/fund

CAREER JOURNALISM SCHOLARSHIP
• *See page 225*

TAMPA BAY TIMES FUND CAREER JOURNALISM SCHOLARSHIPS
• *See page 99*

TEXAS GRIDIRON CLUB INC.

http://www.spjfw.org/

TEXAS GRIDIRON CLUB SCHOLARSHIPS
• *See page 226*

UNITED METHODIST COMMUNICATIONS

http://www.umcom.org/

LEONARD M. PERRYMAN COMMUNICATIONS SCHOLARSHIP FOR ETHNIC MINORITY STUDENTS
• *See page 227*

UNITED NEGRO COLLEGE FUND

http://www.uncf.org/

DIVERSE VOICES IN STORYTELLING SCHOLARSHIP
• *See page 227*

VALLEY PRESS CLUB

http://www.valleypressclub.com/

VALLEY PRESS CLUB SCHOLARSHIPS, THE REPUBLICAN SCHOLARSHIP, CHANNEL 22 SCHOLARSHIP
• *See page 228*

WOMEN'S BASKETBALL COACHES ASSOCIATION

http://www.wbca.org/

ROBIN ROBERTS/WBCA SPORTS COMMUNICATIONS SCHOLARSHIP AWARD
• *See page 228*

LANDSCAPE ARCHITECTURE

AMERICAN SCHOOL OF CLASSICAL STUDIES AT ATHENS

http://www.ascsa.edu.gr/

ASCSA SUMMER SESSION AND SUMMER SEMINARS SCHOLARSHIPS
• *See page 118*

AMERICAN SOCIETY OF CERTIFIED ENGINEERING TECHNICIANS

http://www.ascet.org/

KURT H. AND DONNA M. SCHULER SMALL GRANT
• *See page 205*

ASSOCIATION FOR WOMEN IN ARCHITECTURE FOUNDATION

http://www.awa-la.org/

ASSOCIATION FOR WOMEN IN ARCHITECTURE FOUNDATION SCHOLARSHIP
• *See page 131*

BHW GROUP

https://thebhwgroup.com/

BHW WOMEN IN STEM SCHOLARSHIP
• *See page 124*

CENTER FOR ARCHITECTURE

http://www.centerforarchitecture.org

CENTER FOR ARCHITECTURE DESIGN SCHOLARSHIP
• *See page 132*

CENTER FOR ARCHITECTURE, DOUGLAS HASKELL AWARD FOR STUDENT JOURNALS
• *See page 132*

CONNECTICUT BUILDING CONGRESS SCHOLARSHIP FUND, INC.

http://www.cbc-ct.org

CBC SCHOLARSHIP FUND
• *See page 132*

THE DALLAS FOUNDATION

http://www.dallasfoundation.org/

WHITLEY PLACE SCHOLARSHIP
• *See page 133*

FEDERATED GARDEN CLUBS OF CONNECTICUT

http://www.ctgardenclubs.org/

FEDERATED GARDEN CLUBS OF CONNECTICUT INC. SCHOLARSHIPS
• *See page 170*

FEDERATED GARDEN CLUBS OF MARYLAND

http://www.fgcofmd.org/

ROBERT LEWIS BAKER SCHOLARSHIP
• *See page 386*

GARDEN CLUB OF AMERICA

http://www.gcamerica.org/

GCA AWARD IN DESERT STUDIES
• *See page 340*

KATHARINE M. GROSSCUP SCHOLARSHIPS IN HORTICULTURE
• *See page 386*

THE GEORGIA TRUST FOR HISTORIC PRESERVATION

http://www.georgiatrust.org/

B. PHINIZY SPALDING, HUBERT B. OWENS, AND THE NATIONAL SOCIETY OF THE COLONIAL DAMES OF AMERICA IN THE STATE OF GEORGIA ACADEMIC SCHOLARSHIPS
• *See page 113*

J. NEEL REID PRIZE
• *See page 133*

HERB SOCIETY OF AMERICA, WESTERN RESERVE UNIT

http://www.westernreserveherbsociety.org/

HORTICULTURE SCHOLARSHIP FROM FRANCIS SYLVIA ZVERINA
• *See page 101*

HORTICULTURE SCHOLARSHIP OF THE WESTERN RESERVE HERB SOCIETY
• *See page 101*

HORTICULTURAL RESEARCH INSTITUTE

http://www.hriresearch.org/

BRYAN A. CHAMPION MEMORIAL SCHOLARSHIP
• *See page 101*

CARVILLE M. AKEHURST MEMORIAL SCHOLARSHIP
• *See page 333*

MUGGETS SCHOLARSHIP
• *See page 388*

SPRING MEADOW NURSERY SCHOLARSHIP
• *See page 388*

TIMOTHY AND PALMER W. BIGELOW JR, SCHOLARSHIP
• *See page 101*

USREY FAMILY SCHOLARSHIP
• *See page 333*

HOUZZ

http://houzz.com

RESIDENTIAL DESIGN SCHOLARSHIP
• *See page 134*

SUSTAINABLE RESIDENTIAL DESIGN SCHOLARSHIP
• *See page 134*

THE LAND CONSERVANCY OF NEW JERSEY

http://www.tlc-nj.org/

RUSSELL W. MYERS SCHOLARSHIP
• *See page 172*

MONTANA FEDERATION OF GARDEN CLUBS

http://www.mtfgc.org/

LIFE MEMBER MONTANA FEDERATION OF GARDEN CLUBS SCHOLARSHIP
• *See page 261*

NATIONAL ASSOCIATION OF WOMEN IN CONSTRUCTION

http://www.nawic.org/

NAWIC UNDERGRADUATE SCHOLARSHIPS
• *See page 135*

NATIONAL GARDEN CLUBS INC.

http://www.gardenclub.org/

NATIONAL GARDEN CLUBS INC. SCHOLARSHIP PROGRAM
• *See page 109*

OREGON STUDENT ASSISTANCE COMMISSION

https://oregonstudentaid.gov/

HOME BUILDERS FOUNDATION JIM IRVINE STATEWIDE SCHOLARSHIP
• *See page 136*

PLAN NEW HAMPSHIRE

http://www.plannh.org

PLAN NEW HAMPSHIRE SCHOLARSHIP AND FELLOWSHIP PROGRAM
• *See page 129*

PROFESSIONAL CONSTRUCTION ESTIMATORS ASSOCIATION

http://www.pcea.org/

TED G. WILSON MEMORIAL SCHOLARSHIP FOUNDATION
• *See page 211*

QUALITY BATH

http://www.qualitybath.com

QUALITYBATH.COM SCHOLARSHIP PROGRAM
• *See page 140*

SUPPORT CREATIVITY

http://wesupportcreativity.org

SUPPORT CREATIVITY SCHOLARSHIP
• *See page 137*

TURNER CONSTRUCTION COMPANY

http://www.turnerconstruction.com/

YOUTHFORCE 2020 SCHOLARSHIP PROGRAM
• *See page 137*

VECTORWORKS, INC.

http://www.vectorworks.net

VECTORWORKS DESIGN SCHOLARSHIP
• *See page 137*

THE WALTER J. TRAVIS SOCIETY

http://www.travissociety.com

THE WALTER J. TRAVIS MEMORIAL SCHOLARSHIP AND THE WALTER J. TRAVIS-RUDY ZOCCHI MEMORIAL SCHOLARSHIP
• *See page 137*

LAW ENFORCEMENT/ POLICE ADMINISTRATION

AMERICAN SOCIETY OF CRIMINOLOGY

http://www.asc41.com/

AMERICAN SOCIETY OF CRIMINOLOGY GENE CARTE STUDENT PAPER COMPETITION
• *See page 241*

ASSOCIATION OF FORMER INTELLIGENCE OFFICERS

http://www.afio.com

AFIO UNDERGRADUATE AND GRADUATE SCHOLARSHIPS
• *See page 113*

CONNECTICUT ASSOCIATION OF WOMEN POLICE

http://www.cawp.net/

CONNECTICUT ASSOCIATION OF WOMEN POLICE SCHOLARSHIP
• *See page 242*

INDIANA SHERIFFS' ASSOCIATION

http://www.indianasheriffs.org/

INDIANA SHERIFFS' ASSOCIATION SCHOLARSHIP PROGRAM
• *See page 242*

ISLAMIC SCHOLARSHIP FUND

http://islamicscholarshipfund.org/

ISF NATIONAL SCHOLARSHIP
• *See page 119*

LEARNING FOR LIFE

http://www.learning-for-life.org/

CAPTAIN JAMES J. REGAN SCHOLARSHIP

Two one-time $500 scholarships are presented annually to Law Enforcement Explorers graduating from high school or from an accredited college program. Evaluation will be based on academic record.

Academic Fields/Career Goals: Law Enforcement/Police Administration.

Award: Scholarship for use in freshman, sophomore, junior, or senior years; not renewable. *Number:* 2. *Amount:* $500.

Eligibility Requirements: Applicant must be enrolled or expecting to enroll full-time at a two-year or four-year or technical institution or university. Applicant or parent of applicant must be member of Explorer Program/Learning for Life. Available to U.S. citizens.

Application Requirements: Application form, essay, personal photograph, recommendations or references, transcript. *Deadline:* March 31.

Contact: William Taylor, Scholarships and Awards Coordinator
Learning for Life
1329 West Walnut Hill Lane, PO Box 152225
Irving, TX 75015-2225
Phone: 972-580-2241
E-mail: btaylor@lflmail.org

SHERYL A. HORAK MEMORIAL SCHOLARSHIP

Award for graduating high school students who are Law Enforcement Explorers joining a program in law enforcement in accredited college or university. Provides a one-time scholarship of $1000.

Academic Fields/Career Goals: Law Enforcement/Police Administration.

Award: Scholarship for use in freshman year; not renewable. *Number:* 1. *Amount:* $1000.

Eligibility Requirements: Applicant must be enrolled or expecting to enroll full-time at a two-year or four-year institution or university. Applicant or parent of applicant must be member of Explorer Program/Learning for Life. Available to U.S. citizens.

Application Requirements: Application form, essay, personal photograph, recommendations or references, transcript. *Deadline:* March 31.

Contact: William Taylor, Scholarships and Awards Coordinator
E-mail: btaylor@lflmail.org

LIVSECURE

https://www.livsecure.com

LIVSECURE STUDENT SCHOLARSHIP
• *See page 242*

NATIONAL BLACK POLICE ASSOCIATION

http://www.blackpolice.org/

ALPHONSO DEAL SCHOLARSHIP AWARD
• *See page 243*

NORTH CAROLINA STATE EDUCATION ASSISTANCE AUTHORITY

http://www.ncseaa.edu/

NORTH CAROLINA SHERIFFS' ASSOCIATION UNDERGRADUATE CRIMINAL JUSTICE SCHOLARSHIPS
• *See page 243*

OREGON STUDENT ASSISTANCE COMMISSION

https://oregonstudentaid.gov/

OREGON ASSOCIATION OF CERTIFIED FRAUD EXAMINERS SCHOLARSHIP
• *See page 90*

WIFLE FOUNDATION, INC.

http://www.wifle.org/

WIFLE SCHOLARSHIP
• *See page 244*

LAW/LEGAL SERVICES

ALBERTA HERITAGE SCHOLARSHIP FUND

http://www.alis.alberta.ca/

JASON LANG SCHOLARSHIP
• *See page 251*

AMERICAN SOCIETY OF CRIMINOLOGY

http://www.asc41.com/

AMERICAN SOCIETY OF CRIMINOLOGY GENE CARTE STUDENT PAPER COMPETITION
• *See page 241*

AUTOMOTIVE WOMEN'S ALLIANCE FOUNDATION

http://awafoundation.org/index.php

AUTOMOTIVE WOMEN'S ALLIANCE FOUNDATION SCHOLARSHIPS
• *See page 81*

BAURKOT & BAURKOT: THE IMMIGRATION LAW GROUP

http://nationalimmigrationlawyers.com/

ATTORNEY RAYMOND LAHOUD SCHOLAR PROGRAM

All scholarship candidates must be enrolled in a 4-year college or university program and about to embark on their sophomore, junior, or senior year; or be accepted, or already enrolled in an ABA-accredited law school and about to embark on their first, second, or third year of law school; wish to pursue, or already be pursuing a career in the legal profession; have maintained a minimum GPA of 3.0 at their current college, university, or law school; and submit an application, resume, unofficial transcripts, and an essay discussing why the candidate wishes to pursue a career in the legal profession. The essay must be no less than 3,000 words. The application deadline is March 1 of each year. Selected candidates will be notified no later than April 1 of the same year. The scholarship may be used by the selected recipient for any education related expense. To learn more, please visit: http://nationalimmigrationlawyers.com/legalscholars/ or e-mail legalscholars@baurkotlaw.com. No phone calls or faxes, please.

Academic Fields/Career Goals: Law/Legal Services.

Award: Scholarship for use in sophomore, junior, senior, graduate, or postgraduate years; not renewable. *Number:* 5. *Amount:* $10,000.

Eligibility Requirements: Applicant must be enrolled or expecting to enroll full-time at a four-year institution or university. Applicant must have 3.0 GPA or higher. Available to U.S. and non-U.S. citizens.

Application Requirements: Application form, essay. *Deadline:* March 1.

Contact: Yenny Bautista, Office Director
Baurkot & Baurkot: The Immigration Law Group
205 South 7th Street
Easton, PA 18042
Phone: 484-544-0022
E-mail: legalscholars@baurkotlaw.com

BENSON & BINGHAM

https://www.bensonbingham.com/

BENSON & BINGHAM ANNUAL SCHOLARSHIP

Entrants for our scholarship must submit a minimum of a 600-word typed essay on one of the following two topics to be judged by partners Joe Benson and Ben Bingham at the conclusion of the deadline: 1. Premises Security: Given the Mandalay Bay Shooting, what steps should hotels take to insure the safety and security of their guests? or 2. Consumer Product Safety: When are the affixed warnings regarding the potential risk of injury obvious enough to warrant not having them? [A product is defective for its failure to be accompanied by suitable and adequate warnings concerning its safe and proper use, if the absence of such warnings renders the product unreasonably dangerous. To be adequate a warning must be: (1) designed to reasonably catch the consumer's attention, (2) that the language be comprehensible and give a fair indication of the specific risks attendant to use of the product, and (3) that warnings be of sufficient intensity justified by the magnitude of the risk.] In order to be eligible for the scholarship award, applicants must adhere to the following scholarship criteria: currently enrolled in or recently accepted to an accredited law school; a United States citizen or permanent resident; have a cumulative GPA of 3.0 or higher. A copy of your college transcript (unofficial) must accompany the application. Proof of law school acceptance or attendance must accompany the application. Applications must be received electronically by August 31, 2018 to the following email address: scholarship@bensonbingham.com. In the subject line, please reference: Benson & Bingham Annual Scholarship Application. One grand prize winner will receive a one-time payment of $2,000 and two one-time runner up awards a payment of $250 to be applied to the law school of their admission/attendance. Essays may be published by Benson & Bingham, so please refrain from submitting anything personal, vulgar or inappropriate for the web. The winner of the award will be announced by October 31st, 2018.

Academic Fields/Career Goals: Law/Legal Services.

Award: Scholarship for use in senior or postgraduate years; not renewable. *Number:* 3–2000. *Amount:* $250.

Eligibility Requirements: Applicant must be enrolled or expecting to enroll full-time at an institution or university; resident of Alabama, Alaska, Alberta, Arizona, Arkansas, British Columbia, California, Colorado, Connecticut, Delaware, District of Columbia, Florida, Georgia, Guam, Hawaii, Idaho, Illinois, Indiana, Iowa, Kansas, Kentucky, Louisiana, Maine, Manitoba, Maryland, Massachusetts, Michigan, Minnesota, Mississippi, Missouri, Montana, Nebraska, Nevada, New Brunswick, Newfoundland, New Hampshire, New Jersey, New Mexico, New York, North Carolina, North Dakota, Northwest Territories, Nova Scotia, Ohio, Oklahoma, Ontario, Oregon, Pennsylvania, Prince Edward Island, Puerto Rico, Quebec, Rhode Island, Saskatchewan, South Carolina, South Dakota, Tennessee, Texas, Utah, Vermont, Virginia, Washington, West Virginia, Wisconsin, Wyoming, Yukon and studying in Alabama, Alaska, Alberta, Arizona, Arkansas, British Columbia, California, Colorado, Connecticut, Delaware, District of Columbia, Florida, Georgia, Guam, Hawaii, Idaho, Illinois, Indiana, Iowa, Kansas, Kentucky, Louisiana, Maine, Manitoba, Maryland, Massachusetts, Michigan, Minnesota, Mississippi, Missouri, Montana, Nebraska, Nevada, New Brunswick, Newfoundland, New Hampshire, New Jersey, New Mexico, New York, North Carolina, North Dakota, Northwest Territories, Nova Scotia, Ohio, Oklahoma, Ontario, Oregon, Pennsylvania, Prince Edward Island, Puerto Rico, Quebec, Rhode Island, Saskatchewan, South Carolina, South Dakota, Tennessee, Texas, Utah, Vermont, Virginia, Washington, West Virginia, Wisconsin, Wyoming, Yukon. Applicant must have 3.0 GPA or higher. Available to U.S. citizens.

Application Requirements: Application form, essay. *Deadline:* August 31.

Contact: Justin Simpson, Scholarship Administrator
Benson & Bingham
11441 Allerton Park Dr. Ste. # 100
Las Vegas, NV 89135
Phone: 702-6846900
E-mail: scholarship@bensonbingham.com

BLACK ENTERTAINMENT AND SPORTS LAWYERS ASSOCIATION INC.

http://www.besla.org/

BESLA SCHOLARSHIP LEGAL WRITING COMPETITION

$1500 award for the best 1000-word, or two-page essay on a compelling legal issue facing the entertainment or sports industry. Essay must be written by law school student who has completed at least one full year at an accredited law school. Minimum GPA of 2.8 required.

Academic Fields/Career Goals: Law/Legal Services.

Award: Scholarship for use in freshman, sophomore, junior, senior, or graduate years; not renewable. *Number:* 2. *Amount:* $1500.

Eligibility Requirements: Applicant must be enrolled or expecting to enroll full-time at a four-year institution or university. Available to U.S. and non-U.S. citizens.

Application Requirements: Application form, essay, resume, transcript. *Deadline:* varies.

Contact: Rev. Phyllicia Hatton, Executive Administrator
Phone: 301-248-1818
Fax: 301-248-0700
E-mail: beslamailbox@aol.com

BOYS AND GIRLS CLUBS OF GREATER SAN DIEGO

http://www.sdyouth.org/

SPENCE REESE SCHOLARSHIP

• See page 316

CANLAS LAW GROUP

https://www.canlaslaw.com/

LEGAL COLLEGE SCHOLARSHIP PROGRAM

Canlas Law Group, APLC, law firm is currently accepting applications for its 2018 college scholarship program. Young people who are interested in this opportunity are challenged to write an essay on a topic of our selection. The winning applicant will be presented with a $500 college scholarship that may be used toward related education expenses.

Academic Fields/Career Goals: Law/Legal Services.

Award: Scholarship for use in freshman, sophomore, junior, or senior years; not renewable. *Number:* 1. *Amount:* $500.

Eligibility Requirements: Applicant must be enrolled or expecting to enroll full-time at a four-year institution or university. Available to U.S. citizens.

Application Requirements: Application form, essay. *Deadline:* June 1.

Contact: Christopher Canlas, Owner
Canlas Law Group
18000 Studebaker Rd
Suite 350
Cerritos, CA 90703
Phone: 323-8884325
E-mail: Canlaslawgroupmarketing@gmail.com

CANTOR CRANE INJURY LAW

https://cantorcrane.com

CANTOR CRANE PERSONAL INJURY LAWYER $1,000 SCHOLARSHIP

• See page 241

CONSOLE AND HOLLAWELL

http://www.myinjuryattorney.com/legal-scholarship-2017-2018/

OVERDOSE ATTORNEY SCHOLARSHIP

• See page 373

DUDLEY DEBOSIER INJURY LAWYERS

http://www.dudleydebosier.com

DUDLEY DEBOSIER LAW SCHOOL SCHOLARSHIP

The Dudley DeBosier Injury Lawyers Law School Scholarship program was organized to enhance the legal educational opportunities available to law students within our community. Dudley DeBosier Injury Lawyers believes a solid legal education foundation is instrumental in a rewarding and fulfilling career. Dudley DeBosier will award two (2) $2,500 scholarships to eligible law school students. To apply and further information, please visit our website.

Academic Fields/Career Goals: Law/Legal Services.

Award: Scholarship for use in senior or graduate years; not renewable. *Number:* 2. *Amount:* $2500.

Eligibility Requirements: Applicant must be enrolled or expecting to enroll full-time at an institution or university. Available to U.S. citizens.

Application Requirements: Application form, essay, personal photograph. *Deadline:* June 2.

Contact: Ms. Elizabeth Demopulos, Director of Marketing
Dudley DeBosier Injury Lawyers
1075 Government Street
Baton Rouge, LA 70802
Phone: 225-379-4902 Ext. 4902
Fax: 225-379-4952
E-mail: EDemopulos@dudleydebosier.com

FALES & FALES, P.A.

https://www.faleslaw.com/

LAW ENFORCEMENT FAMILY MEMBER SCHOLARSHIP

This scholarship will be awarded to a student (undergraduate or graduate) enrolled at either an accredited law school or an accredited university. The student must have a family member (such as a parent, spouse or sibling) who is or was an active duty member of law enforcement, including reserve officers and retired, deceased or disabled officers. To be eligible, a candidate must submit a 1-3 page typed essay describing the impact of the law enforcement member on the candidate's life. Candidates must be full-time students with a current GPA of at least a 3.0. To apply, candidates must submit the following: 1. a completed application (which can be found on our website), 2. A personal essay, and 3. a certified copy of the applicant's current transcript confirming satisfaction of the eligibility requirements listed above.

Academic Fields/Career Goals: Law/Legal Services.

Award: Scholarship for use in freshman, sophomore, junior, senior, graduate, or postgraduate years; not renewable. *Number:* 1. *Amount:* $1000.

Eligibility Requirements: Applicant must be enrolled or expecting to enroll full-time at a four-year institution or university. Applicant or parent of applicant must have employment or volunteer experience in police/firefighting. Applicant must have 3.0 GPA or higher. Available to U.S. citizens.

Application Requirements: Application form, essay. *Deadline:* August 31.

Contact: Anthony Ferguson
Fales & Fales, P.A.
192 Lisbon Street
PO Box 889
Lewiston, ME 04240
Phone: 207-786-0606
Fax: 207-786-2514
E-mail: aferguson@faleslaw.com

FELDMAN LAW FIRM PLLC

http://www.afphoenixcriminalattorney.com/

LAW STUDENT SCHOLARSHIP

The scholarship, in the amount of $1,000, is being offered to assist in the payment of tuition to law school. It is not required that an applicant be enrolled in law school at the time of the submission of his or her application. However, the scholarship funds must be utilized within one year after the date of the announcement of the winner. The $1,000 award will be paid directly to the law school selected by the winner. The scholarship is open to citizens of the United States who are enrolled at, or who intend to enroll at a U.S. law school accredited by the American Bar Association. The application includes the online form; a statement of not more than 100 words telling us why you want to pursue a legal education; and an (optional) essay of not more than 750 words discussing how you will use your law school degree to make a difference in the world.

Academic Fields/Career Goals: Law/Legal Services.

Award: Scholarship for use in freshman, sophomore, junior, senior, or graduate years; not renewable. *Number:* 1. *Amount:* $1000.

Eligibility Requirements: Applicant must be enrolled or expecting to enroll full- or part-time at a four-year institution or university. Available to U.S. citizens.

Application Requirements: Application form, essay. *Deadline:* February 22.

Contact: John Kelly
Feldman Law Firm PLLC
1 E. Washington St., Suite 500
Phoenix, AZ 85004
E-mail: mike@jkphoenixpersonalinjuryattorney.com

LAW SCHOOL SCHOLARSHIP

The scholarship will consist of a direct tuition payment of $1,000 to the law school attended or to be attended by the successful applicant. You need not be attending law school when you submit your application for the scholarship, but the scholarship must be used within a year from the date of the award. This must be for attendance at a law school located in the United States which is accredited by the American Bar Association. U.S. citizens who are currently attending law school (ABA-accredited) or who will be attending law school in the near future are eligible to submit an application for the scholarship. To be considered, an applicant must complete our online application, upload a brief statement (175 words or less) describing how you intend to utilize your law degree, and (optional) upload a statement (1,000 words or less) of how you think your law degree will enable you to make a positive impact on society.

Academic Fields/Career Goals: Law/Legal Services.

Award: Scholarship for use in freshman, sophomore, junior, senior, or graduate years; not renewable. *Number:* 1. *Amount:* $1000.

Eligibility Requirements: Applicant must be enrolled or expecting to enroll full- or part-time at a four-year institution or university. Available to U.S. citizens.

Application Requirements: Application form, essay. *Deadline:* February 22.

Contact: Ryan Tegnelia
Feldman Law Firm PLLC
2820 Camino Del Rio South, Suite 110
San Diego, CA 92108
E-mail: mike@sandiegocriminallawyerrt.com

LAW STUDENT SCHOLARSHIP

The $1,000 scholarship will be applied to defray a portion of the cost of tuition at an ABA-accredited United States law school. It will be a direct tuition payment to that law school. The successful applicant must utilize the scholarship fund within a year after the date of notification that he or she has been selected as the scholarship recipient. We do not require that you be enrolled in law school when you submit your application. United States citizens who are attending, or who plan to attend, a U.S. law school that is accredited by the American Bar Association are eligible to apply for the scholarship. To be considered for the scholarship, you must submit to us a completed online application; a statement (to be uploaded) of 125 words or less indicating why you want to obtain a law degree; and (optional) a statement (to be uploaded) of 900 words or less discussing how your law degree will enable you to make a difference in the world.

Academic Fields/Career Goals: Law/Legal Services.

Award: Scholarship for use in freshman, sophomore, junior, or senior years; not renewable. *Number:* 1. *Amount:* $1000.

Eligibility Requirements: Applicant must be enrolled or expecting to enroll full- or part-time at a four-year institution or university. Available to U.S. citizens.

Application Requirements: Application form, essay. *Deadline:* February 12.

Contact: Adam Feldman
Feldman Law Firm PLLC
1 E. Washington St.
Phoenix, AZ 85004
E-mail: mike@afphoenixcriminalattorney.com

GRAND RAPIDS COMMUNITY FOUNDATION

http://www.grfoundation.org/

WARNER NORCROSS AND JUDD LLP SCHOLARSHIP FOR STUDENTS OF COLOR

Financial assistance to students of color who are residents of Michigan, or attend a college/university/vocational school in Michigan, pursuing a career in law, paralegal, or a legal secretarial program. Law school scholarship ($5000), paralegal scholarship ($2000), legal secretary scholarship ($1000).

Academic Fields/Career Goals: Law/Legal Services.

Award: Scholarship for use in freshman, sophomore, junior, senior, or graduate years; not renewable. *Number:* 1–3. *Amount:* $1000–$5000.

Eligibility Requirements: Applicant must be American Indian/Alaska Native, Asian/Pacific Islander, Black (non-Hispanic), Hispanic; enrolled or expecting to enroll full-time at a two-year or four-year institution or university; resident of Michigan and studying in Michigan. Applicant must have 2.5 GPA or higher. Available to U.S. citizens.

Application Requirements: Application form, essay, financial need analysis. *Deadline:* April 1.

Contact: Ms. Ruth Bishop, Education Program Officer
Grand Rapids Community Foundation
185 Oakes SW
Grand Rapids, MI 49503
Phone: 616-454-1751 Ext. 103
E-mail: rbishop@grfoundation.org

GREATER KANAWHA VALLEY FOUNDATION

http://www.tgkvf.org/

BERNICE PICKINS PARSONS FUND

Renewable award of $1000 open to students pursuing education or training in the fields of library science, nursing, and paraprofessional training in the legal field. Grant based on financial need. Must be a resident of West Virginia; preference given to Jackson county residents.

Academic Fields/Career Goals: Law/Legal Services; Library and Information Sciences; Nursing.

Award: Grant for use in freshman, sophomore, junior, or senior years; renewable. *Amount:* $1000.

Eligibility Requirements: Applicant must be enrolled or expecting to enroll full-time at a two-year or four-year institution or university and resident of West Virginia. Available to U.S. citizens.

Application Requirements: Application form, essay, financial need analysis, recommendations or references, self-addressed stamped envelope with application, test scores, transcript. *Deadline:* January 15.

Contact: Susan Hoover, Scholarship Program Officer
Greater Kanawha Valley Foundation
900 Lee Street East, 16th Floor
Charleston, WV 25301
Phone: 304-346-3620
E-mail: shoover@tgkvf.org

INSTITUTE FOR HUMANE STUDIES

http://www.theihs.org/

HUMANE STUDIES FELLOWSHIPS

• *See page 219*

ISLAMIC SCHOLARSHIP FUND

http://islamicscholarshipfund.org/

ISF NATIONAL SCHOLARSHIP

• *See page 119*

JAPANESE AMERICAN CITIZENS LEAGUE (JACL)

http://www.jacl.org/

NATIONAL JACL HEADQUARTERS SCHOLARSHIP

• *See page 107*

LAW OFFICE OF DAVID P. SHAPIRO

http://www.davidpshapirolaw.com/about-us/

LAW STUDENT SCHOLARSHIP

This is a single scholarship in the amount of $1,000. It will be used by the successful applicant to offset the cost of law school tuition at a United States law school accredited by the American Bar Association. You need not be enrolled in law school at the time of your application, but you must provide us, within one year of being selected as the winner of the award, the name of the ABA-approved law school you will be attending, along with proof of your acceptance at the law school. The scholarship funds will be paid directly to the law school on your behalf. The scholarship is open to applicants who are citizens of the United States who are attending

law school or who plan to do so within the time frame set forth above. To be considered for the award, you must complete the online application form, prepare and upload a brief (100 words or less) statement describing why you are interested in obtaining a law degree, and (ptional) prepare and upload an essay (up to 1,000 words) that describes how obtaining your law school degree will enable you to have a positive impact on the world.

Academic Fields/Career Goals: Law/Legal Services.

Award: Scholarship for use in freshman, sophomore, junior, senior, or graduate years; not renewable. *Number:* 1. *Amount:* $1000.

Eligibility Requirements: Applicant must be enrolled or expecting to enroll full- or part-time at a four-year institution or university. Available to U.S. citizens.

Application Requirements: Application form, essay. *Deadline:* February 2.

Contact: David Shapiro
Law Office of David P. Shapiro
1501 5th Ave #200
San Diego, CA 92101
E-mail: michael@davidpshapirolaw.com

LAW OFFICES OF GOODWIN & SCIESZKA

http://www.1888goodwin.com/

GOODWIN & SCIESZKA INNOVATION SCHOLARSHIP

The Innovation Scholarship will be awarded to three high-achieving students intending to pursue a career in law. Applicants will be judged on their academic performance and their essay addressing one of two law-related questions provided on the application. Applicant must be either a current law student at an accredited law school within the U.S. or at an accredited undergraduate university planning to attend law school.

Academic Fields/Career Goals: Law/Legal Services.

Award: Scholarship for use in freshman, sophomore, junior, senior, or graduate years; not renewable. *Number:* 3. *Amount:* $500–$1000.

Eligibility Requirements: Applicant must be enrolled or expecting to enroll full- or part-time at a two-year or four-year institution or university. Applicant must have 3.0 GPA or higher. Available to U.S. citizens.

Application Requirements: Application form, essay. *Deadline:* June 1.

Contact: Michael Cianfarani
E-mail: mcianfarani@trafficdigitalagency.com

LIVSECURE

https://www.livsecure.com

LIVSECURE STUDENT SCHOLARSHIP

• *See page 242*

LOUTHIAN LAW FIRM, P.A.

http://www.louthianlaw.com/

LOUTHIAN LAW LEGAL SCHOLARSHIP

This scholarship is designed to encourage and award creative authorship. Informing various audiences is part of the legal profession. The ability to clearly and accurately relay a message is crucial, whether it is addressed to a person inquiring about legal services, a client, a judge, or a jury. Scholarship applicants must submit a sample of their writing which has previously been published in a newspaper, magazine, professional blog or academic publication. It is not necessary that the subject matter be related to the law; its primary purpose should be to inform readers.

Academic Fields/Career Goals: Law/Legal Services.

Award: Scholarship for use in freshman year; not renewable. *Amount:* $1000.

Eligibility Requirements: Applicant must be enrolled or expecting to enroll full- or part-time at an institution or university. Available to U.S. citizens.

Application Requirements: Application form, essay. *Deadline:* May 1.

Contact: Nicole Longo
Phone: 919-302-7545
E-mail: nicole@gladiatorlawmarketing.com

MARYLAND STATE HIGHER EDUCATION COMMISSION

http://www.mhec.state.md.us/

GRADUATE AND PROFESSIONAL SCHOLARSHIP PROGRAM-MARYLAND
• *See page 256*

JANET L. HOFFMANN LOAN ASSISTANCE REPAYMENT PROGRAM
• *See page 272*

MORROW & SHEPPARD LLP

https://www.morrowsheppard.com

MORROW & SHEPPARD COLLEGE SCHOLARSHIP

Morrow & Sheppard LLP is a law firm founded by Nick Morrow and John Sheppard. Both partners are Houston lawyers representing clients with cases relating to maritime injuries, truck accidents, oil field accidents, and other types of civil and commercial litigation. It can be very difficult to pay for college, and the expense can be a heavy financial burden. Morrow & Sheppard LLP offers this legal scholarship to students starting their journey into college and to those intending to explore a legal career, as a way to provide financial assistance. The winner of this scholarship will receive $500 towards their education. Any high school senior or current college student who is interested in pursuing law within the U.S. is allowed to apply. For full details see our website: https://www.morrowsheppard.com/college-scholarship/

Academic Fields/Career Goals: Law/Legal Services.

Award: Scholarship for use in freshman, sophomore, junior, or senior years; not renewable. *Number:* 1. *Amount:* $500.

Eligibility Requirements: Applicant must be high school student; planning to enroll or expecting to enroll full- or part-time at a two-year or four-year institution or university and studying in Alabama, Alaska, Arizona, Arkansas, California, Colorado, Connecticut, Delaware, District of Columbia, Florida, Georgia, Hawaii, Idaho, Illinois, Indiana, Iowa, Kansas, Kentucky, Louisiana, Maine, Maryland, Massachusetts, Michigan, Minnesota, Mississippi, Missouri, Montana, Nebraska, Nevada, New Hampshire, New Jersey, New Mexico, New York, North Carolina, North Dakota, Ohio, Oklahoma, Oregon, Pennsylvania, Rhode Island, South Carolina, South Dakota, Tennessee, Texas, Utah, Vermont, Virginia, Washington, West Virginia, Wisconsin, Wyoming. Available to U.S. citizens.

Application Requirements: Application form, essay. *Deadline:* July 10.

Contact: Nick Morrow
Morrow & Sheppard LLP
3701 Kirby Drive, Suite 840
Houston, TX 77098
Phone: 713-489-1206
E-mail: scholarship@morrowsheppard.com

NAQVI INJURY LAW

http://www.naqvilaw.com/

NAQVI LAW SCHOLARSHIP
• *See page 242*

NATIONAL BLACK POLICE ASSOCIATION

http://www.blackpolice.org/

ALPHONSO DEAL SCHOLARSHIP AWARD
• *See page 243*

NATIONAL COURT REPORTERS ASSOCIATION

http://ncra.org

COUNCIL ON APPROVED STUDENT EDUCATION'S SCHOLARSHIP FUND

Applicant must have a writing speed of 140 to 180 words/min; must be in an NCRA certified court reporting program; write a two-page essay on topic chosen for the year; and submit a letter of recommendation.

Academic Fields/Career Goals: Law/Legal Services.

Award: Scholarship for use in sophomore year; not renewable. *Number:* 3. *Amount:* $500–$1500.

Eligibility Requirements: Applicant must be enrolled or expecting to enroll full- or part-time at a two-year or four-year or technical institution. Applicant must have 3.0 GPA or higher. Available to U.S. and Canadian citizens.

Application Requirements: Application form, entry in a contest, essay, recommendations or references, transcript. *Deadline:* April 1.

Contact: Cynthia Andrews, Director, Professional Development Programs
National Court Reporters Association
8224 Old Courthouse Road
Vienna, VA 22182
Phone: 703-584-9058
E-mail: candrews@ncra.org

FRANK SARLI MEMORIAL SCHOLARSHIP

One-time award to a student who is nearing graduation from a trade/technical school or four-year college. Must be enrolled in a court reporting program. Minimum 3.5 GPA required.

Academic Fields/Career Goals: Law/Legal Services.

Award: Scholarship for use in senior year; not renewable. *Number:* 1. *Amount:* $2000.

Eligibility Requirements: Applicant must be enrolled or expecting to enroll full- or part-time at a four-year or technical institution or university. Applicant or parent of applicant must be member of National Federation of Press Women. Applicant must have 3.5 GPA or higher. Available to U.S. and non-U.S. citizens.

Application Requirements: Application form. *Deadline:* February 28.

Contact: B.J. Shorak, Deputy Executive Director
National Court Reporters Association
8224 Old Courthouse Road
Vienna, VA 22182-3808
Phone: 703-556-6272 Ext. 126
Fax: 703-556-6291
E-mail: BJSHORAK@ncra.org

STUDENT MEMBER TUITION GRANT

Four $500 awards for students in good academic standing in a court reporting program. Students are required to write 120 to 200 words/min.

Academic Fields/Career Goals: Law/Legal Services.

Award: Grant for use in freshman, sophomore, junior, or senior years; not renewable. *Number:* 4. *Amount:* $500.

Eligibility Requirements: Applicant must be enrolled or expecting to enroll full- or part-time at a four-year or technical institution or university. Available to U.S. and non-U.S. citizens.

Application Requirements: Application form. *Deadline:* May 31.

Contact: Amy Davidson, Assistant Director of Membership
National Court Reporters Association
8224 Old Courthouse Road
Vienna, VA 22182
Phone: 703-556-6272 Ext. 123
E-mail: adavidson@ncrahq.org

NATIONAL FEDERATION OF PARALEGAL ASSOCIATIONS INC. (NFPA)

http://www.paralegals.org/

NATIONAL FEDERATION OF PARALEGAL ASSOCIATES INC. THOMSON REUTERS SCHOLARSHIP

Applicants must be full- or part-time students enrolled in an accredited paralegal education program or college-level program with emphasis in paralegal studies. Minimum GPA of 3.0 required. NFPA membership is not required. Travel stipend to annual convention, where recipients will receive awards, also provided.

Academic Fields/Career Goals: Law/Legal Services.

Award: Scholarship for use in freshman, sophomore, junior, senior, graduate, or postgraduate years; not renewable. *Number:* 2. *Amount:* $2000–$3000.

Eligibility Requirements: Applicant must be enrolled or expecting to enroll full- or part-time at a two-year or four-year or technical institution or university. Applicant must have 3.0 GPA or higher. Available to U.S. and non-U.S. citizens.

Application Requirements: Application form, essay. *Deadline:* July 1.

Contact: Allison Kastner, Administrative Assistant
National Federation of Paralegal Associations Inc. (NFPA)
9100 Purdue Road
Suite 200
Indianapolis, IN 46268
Phone: 317-454-8312
E-mail: info@paralegals.org

NEW ENGLAND EMPLOYEE BENEFITS COUNCIL

http://www.neebc.org/

NEW ENGLAND EMPLOYEE BENEFITS COUNCIL SCHOLARSHIP PROGRAM
• *See page 89*

OREGON STUDENT ASSISTANCE COMMISSION

https://oregonstudentaid.gov/

OREGON ASSOCIATION OF CERTIFIED FRAUD EXAMINERS SCHOLARSHIP
• *See page 90*

ROBINSON & HENRY, P.C.

https://www.robinsonandhenry.com/

ROBINSON & HENRY FAMILY LAW SCHOLARSHIP

This scholarship is available to high school seniors and current college students nationwide who plan on attending, or are attending, an accredited 4-year college/university or 2-year accredited community college in the Fall of 2018. The Family Law Scholarship is open only to applicants whose parents have gone through a divorce or are planning on pursuing a career in family law.

Academic Fields/Career Goals: Law/Legal Services.

Award: Scholarship for use in freshman, sophomore, junior, or senior years; not renewable. *Number:* 1. *Amount:* $1000.

Eligibility Requirements: Applicant must be enrolled or expecting to enroll full-time at a two-year or four-year institution or university. Applicant must have 3.0 GPA or higher. Available to U.S. citizens.

Application Requirements: Application form, essay. *Deadline:* May 31.

Contact: Amador Cahvez
E-mail: amador@niftymarketing.com

ROBINSON & HENRY INJURY SCHOLARSHIP

This scholarship is available to high school seniors and current college students nationwide who plan on attending, or are attending, an accredited 4-year college/university or 2-year accredited community

college in the Fall of 2018. The applicant or the applicant's family must have been involved in a personal injury accident. Special preferences will be given to members of a family that has recently been injured in a car accident.

Academic Fields/Career Goals: Law/Legal Services.

Award: Scholarship for use in freshman, sophomore, junior, or senior years; not renewable. *Number:* 1. *Amount:* $1500.

Eligibility Requirements: Applicant must be enrolled or expecting to enroll full-time at a two-year or four-year institution or university. Applicant must have 3.0 GPA or higher. Available to U.S. citizens.

Application Requirements: Application form, essay. *Deadline:* May 31.

Contact: Amador Cahvez
E-mail: amador@niftymarketing.com

SOCIETY OF SATELLITE PROFESSIONALS INTERNATIONAL

http://www.sspi.org/

SSPI INTERNATIONAL SCHOLARSHIPS
• *See page 160*

TKE EDUCATIONAL FOUNDATION

http://www.tke.org/

HARRY J. DONNELLY MEMORIAL SCHOLARSHIP
• *See page 93*

UNITARIAN UNIVERSALIST ASSOCIATION

http://www.uua.org/

STANFIELD AND D'ORLANDO ART SCHOLARSHIP
• *See page 146*

UNITED NEGRO COLLEGE FUND

http://www.uncf.org/

SUEZ CORPORATE SCHOLARS PROGRAM
• *See page 94*

VIRGINIA STATE BAR

http://www.vsb.org/

LAW IN SOCIETY AWARD COMPETITION

Participants write an essay in response to a hypothetical situation dealing with legal issues. Awards are based on superior understanding of the value of law in everyday life. The top thirty essays are awarded prizes of a plaque and dictionary/thesaurus set. First place receives $2000 U.S. Savings Bond or $1000 cash; second place, $1,500 bond or $750 cash; third place, $1000 bond or $500 cash; honorable mentions, $200 bond or $100 cash.

Academic Fields/Career Goals: Law/Legal Services.

Award: Prize for use in freshman year; not renewable. *Number:* up to 10. *Amount:* $100–$1000.

Eligibility Requirements: Applicant must be high school student; planning to enroll or expecting to enroll full- or part-time at a four-year institution or university; resident of Virginia and must have an interest in writing. Available to U.S. citizens.

Application Requirements: Application form, entry in a contest, essay. *Deadline:* February 1.

Contact: Sandy Adkins, Public Relations Assistant
Virginia State Bar
707 East Main Street, Suite 1500
Richmond, VA 23219-2800
Phone: 804-775-0594
Fax: 804-775-0582
E-mail: adkins@vsb.org

WASHINGTON STATE ASSOCIATION FOR JUSTICE

http://www.washingtonjustice.org/

WASHINGTON STATE ASSOCIATION FOR JUSTICE AMERICAN JUSTICE ESSAY & VIDEO SCHOLARSHIP
• *See page 244*

WASHINGTON STATE ASSOCIATION FOR JUSTICE PAST PRESIDENTS' SCHOLARSHIP

The Washington State Association for Justice (WSAJ) created the WSAJ Past President's Scholarship Fund in 1991. One $7,500 scholarship will be awarded in 2018. Winners must have 1. Demonstrated academic achievement and planned advancement toward a degree in an institution of higher learning. 2. A documented need for financial assistance. 3. A history of achievement despite having been a victim of injury or overcoming a disability, handicap, or similar challenge. 4. A record of commitment to helping people in need or protecting the rights of injured persons. 5. A plan or commitment to apply your education toward helping people. 6. Residency in Washington State. 7. High school seniors only. Application for this scholarship must be made as follows. Incomplete applications will not be reviewed or considered. 1. Send a letter (written by the student/applicant) to the scholarship committee describing the qualifications of the applicant and explaining the reasons why s/he feels they deserve the scholarship. 2. Include all high school and community college academic transcripts; name, address, and telephone number of two (2) references, at least one of which must be outside of the school environment (please do not submit more than two); brief written financial statement indicating what resources are available to the applicant and why this scholarship is necessary to fund the applicant's college education (copies of FAFSA are acceptable); name, address, telephone number and email (if they have one) of the applicant; any other documentation the applicant wishes to attach in support of their qualifications and; completed Application Checklist form. Applications must be postmarked on or before March 17, 2018.

Academic Fields/Career Goals: Law/Legal Services.

Award: Scholarship for use in freshman year; not renewable. *Number:* 1. *Amount:* $7500.

Eligibility Requirements: Applicant must be high school student; planning to enroll or expecting to enroll full-time at a four-year institution or university and resident of Washington. Applicant or parent of applicant must have employment or volunteer experience in community service. Available to U.S. citizens.

Application Requirements: Application form, driver's license, essay, financial need analysis. *Deadline:* March 17.

Contact: Anita Yandle, Scholarship Coordinator
Washington State Association for Justice
1809 7th Ave
Suite 1500
Seattle, WA 98101
Phone: 206-464-1011
E-mail: anita@washingtonjustice.org

WIFLE FOUNDATION, INC.

http://www.wifle.org/

WIFLE SCHOLARSHIP
• *See page 244*

WILLIAMS LAW GROUP

https://familylawyersnewjersey.com/

WILLIAMS LAW GROUP OPPORTUNITY TO GROW SCHOLARSHIP
• *See page 139*

LIBRARY AND INFORMATION SCIENCES

ALICE L. HALTOM EDUCATIONAL FUND

http://www.alhef.org/

ALICE L. HALTOM EDUCATIONAL FUND
• *See page 176*

AMERICAN SOCIETY FOR INFORMATION SCIENCE AND TECHNOLOGY

http://www.asis.org/

JOHN WILEY & SONS BEST JASIST PAPER AWARD
• *See page 229*

ASSOCIATION OF MOVING IMAGE ARCHIVISTS

https://amianet.org/

AMIA SCHOLARSHIPS PROGRAM

These scholarships, each in the amount of $4,000, are given as financial assistance to students of merit who intend to pursue careers in moving image archiving. The funds are sent directly to the recipients' educational institutions to help cover the costs of tuition or registration fees. Students from any country may apply. Applicants need only submit one application form and one set of supporting documents to be eligible for all three scholarships; however, no applicant will be awarded more than one scholarship.

Academic Fields/Career Goals: Library and Information Sciences.

Award: Scholarship for use in freshman, sophomore, junior, senior, graduate, or postgraduate years; not renewable. *Number:* 4. *Amount:* $4000.

Eligibility Requirements: Applicant must be enrolled or expecting to enroll full-time at a two-year or four-year or technical institution or university. Applicant must have 3.0 GPA or higher. Available to U.S. and non-U.S. citizens.

Application Requirements: Application form, essay. *Deadline:* May 15.

Contact: Kristina Kersels, Events and Operations
Association of Moving Image Archivists
1313 Vine Street
Hollywood, CA 90028
Phone: 323-463-1500
E-mail: kkersels@amianet.org

BIBLIOGRAPHICAL SOCIETY OF AMERICA

http://www.bibsocamer.org/

JUSTIN G. SCHILLER PRIZE FOR BIBLIOGRAPHICAL WORK IN PRE-20TH-CENTURY CHILDREN'S BOOKS

Award for bibliographic work in the field of pre-20th century children's books. Winner will receive a cash award of $2000 and a year's membership in the Society.

Academic Fields/Career Goals: Library and Information Sciences; Literature/English/Writing.

Award: Prize for use in freshman, sophomore, junior, or senior years; not renewable. *Number:* 1. *Amount:* $2000.

Eligibility Requirements: Applicant must be enrolled or expecting to enroll full- or part-time at a four-year institution or university. Available to U.S. and non-U.S. citizens.

Application Requirements: Application form, documentation regarding the approval of a thesis or dissertation or confirming the date of publication, entry in a contest, resume. *Deadline:* September 1.

Contact: Michele Randall, Executive Secretary
Bibliographical Society of America
PO Box 1537, Lenox Hill Station
New York, NY 10021
Phone: 212-452-2710
Fax: 212-452-2710
E-mail: bsa@bibsocamer.org

DIVERSITYCOMM, INC.

http://www.diversitycomm.net/

DIVERSITY IN STEAM MAGAZINE SCHOLARSHIP
• *See page 83*

FLORIDA ASSOCIATION FOR MEDIA IN EDUCATION

http://www.floridamediaed.org/ssyra.html

FAME/SANDY ULM SCHOLARSHIP

Scholarship for students studying to be school library media specialists. The scholarship awards at least $1000 to one or more students each year. Deadlines are September 15 and February 15.

Academic Fields/Career Goals: Library and Information Sciences.

Award: Scholarship for use in freshman year; not renewable. *Amount:* $1000.

Eligibility Requirements: Applicant must be high school student; planning to enroll or expecting to enroll full-time at a two-year or four-year or technical institution or university and studying in Florida. Available to U.S. citizens.

Application Requirements: Application form. *Deadline:* varies.

Contact: Larry Bodkin, Executive Director
Phone: 850-531-8350
Fax: 850-531-8344
E-mail: lbodkin@floridamedia.org

GREATER KANAWHA VALLEY FOUNDATION

http://www.tgkvf.org/

BERNICE PICKINS PARSONS FUND
• *See page 416*

IDAHO LIBRARY ASSOCIATION

http://www.idaholibraries.org/

IDAHO LIBRARY ASSOCIATION GARDNER HANKS SCHOLARSHIP

Scholarship for students who are beginning or continuing formal library education, pursuing a Master's of Library Science degree or Media Generalist certification. Must be an Idaho Library Association member.

Academic Fields/Career Goals: Library and Information Sciences.

Award: Scholarship for use in freshman, sophomore, junior, senior, graduate, or postgraduate years; not renewable. *Number:* 1. *Amount:* $600.

Eligibility Requirements: Applicant must be enrolled or expecting to enroll full-time at a two-year or four-year institution or university and resident of Idaho. Applicant or parent of applicant must be member of Idaho Library Association. Available to U.S. citizens.

Application Requirements: Application form, financial need analysis. *Deadline:* May 31.

Contact: Rami Attebury, Scholarships, Awards, and Recruitment Committee Chair
E-mail: rattebur@uidaho.edu

WISCONSIN LIBRARY ASSOCIATION

http://wla.wisconsinlibraries.org/awards-scholarships/

SCHOLARSHIP FOR THE EDUCATION OF RURAL LIBRARIANS GLORIA HOEGH MEMORIAL FUND

Scholarship awarded to librarians planning to attend a workshop, conference, and/or a continuing education program within or outside Wisconsin. Applicant must be a library employee working in a Wisconsin community with a current population of 5000 or less or who works with library employees in those communities.

Academic Fields/Career Goals: Library and Information Sciences.

Award: Scholarship for use in freshman, sophomore, junior, senior, or graduate years; not renewable. *Number:* 1. *Amount:* $900.

Eligibility Requirements: Applicant must be enrolled or expecting to enroll full- or part-time at a four-year institution or university and resident of Wisconsin. Available to U.S. citizens.

Application Requirements: Application form, essay, financial need analysis. *Deadline:* July 18.

Contact: Ms. Brigitte Rupp Vacha, WLA Conference Liaison
Wisconsin Library Association
4610 S Biltmore Lane
Suite 100
Madison, WI 53718
Phone: 608-245-3640
Fax: 608-245-3646
E-mail: ruppvacha@wisconsinlibraries.org

WLA CONTINUING EDUCATION SCHOLARSHIP

Scholarship awarded to employee who is planning to attend a continuing education program within or outside of Wisconsin. Applicant must be able to communicate the knowledge gained from the continuing education program to fellow librarians and information professionals in Wisconsin, employed in a library and information agency in Wisconsin.

Academic Fields/Career Goals: Library and Information Sciences.

Award: Scholarship for use in freshman, sophomore, junior, senior, graduate, or postgraduate years; not renewable. *Number:* 1.

Eligibility Requirements: Applicant must be enrolled or expecting to enroll full- or part-time at a four-year institution or university and resident of Wisconsin. Available to U.S. citizens.

Application Requirements: Application form. *Deadline:* July 17.

Contact: Ms. Brigitte Rupp Vacha, WLA Conference Liaison
Wisconsin Library Association
4610 S Biltmore Lane
Suite 100
Madison, WI 53718
Phone: 608-245-3640
Fax: 608-245-3646
E-mail: ruppvacha@wisconsinlibraries.org

LITERATURE/ENGLISH/ WRITING

AMERICAN FOUNDATION FOR THE BLIND

http://www.afb.org/

R.L. GILLETTE SCHOLARSHIP

Two scholarships of $1000 each to women who are enrolled in a four-year undergraduate degree program in literature or music. In addition to the general requirements, applicants must submit a performance tape not to exceed 30 minutes, or a creative writing sample. Must submit proof of legal blindness. For additional information and application requirements, refer to website http://www.afb.org/scholarships.asp.

Academic Fields/Career Goals: Literature/English/Writing; Music.

Award: Scholarship for use in freshman, sophomore, junior, or senior years; not renewable. *Number:* up to 2. *Amount:* $1000.

Eligibility Requirements: Applicant must be visually impaired; enrolled or expecting to enroll full-time at a four-year institution or university and female. Applicant must be visually impaired. Available to U.S. citizens.

Application Requirements: Application form, essay, financial need analysis, performance tape (not to exceed 30 minutes) or creative writing sample, proof of legal blindness, acceptance letter, recommendations or references, transcript. *Deadline:* April 30.

Contact: Dawn Bodrogi, Information Center and Library Coordinator
American Foundation for the Blind
11 Penn Plaza, Suite 300
New York, NY 10001
Phone: 212-502-7661
Fax: 212-502-7771
E-mail: afbinfo@afb.net

AMERICAN-SCANDINAVIAN FOUNDATION

http://www.amscan.org/

AMERICAN-SCANDINAVIAN FOUNDATION TRANSLATION PRIZE

Two prizes are awarded for outstanding English translations of poetry, fiction, drama or literary prose originally written in Danish, Finnish, Icelandic, Norwegian or Swedish. The Nadia Christensen Prize includes a $2,500 award, publication of an excerpt in Scandinavian Review, and a commemorative bronze medallion. The Leif and Inger Sjöberg Award, given to an individual whose literature translations have not previously been published, includes a $2,000 award, publication of an excerpt in Scandinavian Review, and a commemorative bronze medallion.

Academic Fields/Career Goals: Literature/English/Writing.

Award: Prize for use in freshman, sophomore, junior, senior, graduate, or postgraduate years; not renewable. *Number:* 2. *Amount:* $2000–$2500.

Eligibility Requirements: Applicant must be enrolled or expecting to enroll full- or part-time at a two-year or four-year or technical institution or university and must have an interest in Scandinavian language. Available to U.S. and non-U.S. citizens.

Application Requirements: Application form. *Deadline:* June 15.

Contact: Carl Fritscher, Fellowships and Grants Officer
Phone: 212-779-3587
E-mail: grants@amscan.org

BIBLIOGRAPHICAL SOCIETY OF AMERICA

http://www.bibsocamer.org/

JUSTIN G. SCHILLER PRIZE FOR BIBLIOGRAPHICAL WORK IN PRE-20TH-CENTURY CHILDREN'S BOOKS

• See page 419

CULTURAL SERVICES OF THE FRENCH EMBASSY

http://www.frenchculture.org/

TEACHING ASSISTANT PROGRAM IN FRANCE

• See page 113

DAVIDSON INSTITUTE FOR TALENT DEVELOPMENT

http://www.davidsongifted.org/

DAVIDSON FELLOWS SCHOLARSHIP PROGRAM

• See page 124

DIVERSITYCOMM, INC.

http://www.diversitycomm.net/

DIVERSITY IN STEAM MAGAZINE SCHOLARSHIP

• See page 83

GOLDEN KEY INTERNATIONAL HONOUR SOCIETY

http://www.goldenkey.org/

LITERARY ACHIEVEMENT AWARDS

Award of $1000 will be given to winners in each of the following four categories: fiction, non-fiction, poetry, and feature writing. Eligible applicants are undergraduate, graduate and postgraduate members who are currently enrolled in classes at a degree-granting program.

Academic Fields/Career Goals: Literature/English/Writing.

Award: Prize for use in freshman, sophomore, junior, senior, graduate, or postgraduate years; not renewable. *Number:* 4. *Amount:* $1000.

Eligibility Requirements: Applicant must be enrolled or expecting to enroll full- or part-time at a four-year institution or university and must have an interest in writing. Available to U.S. and non-U.S. citizens.

Application Requirements: Application form, entry in a contest, essay, original composition. *Deadline:* April 1.

Contact: Scholarship Program Administrators
Golden Key International Honour Society
PO Box 23737
Nashville, TN 37202-3737
Phone: 800-377-2401
E-mail: scholarships@goldenkey.org

INSTITUTE FOR HUMANE STUDIES

http://www.theihs.org/

HUMANE STUDIES FELLOWSHIPS

• See page 219

INTERNATIONAL FOODSERVICE EDITORIAL COUNCIL

http://www.ifeconline.com/

INTERNATIONAL FOODSERVICE EDITORIAL COUNCIL COMMUNICATIONS SCHOLARSHIP

• See page 96

INTERNATIONAL LITERACY ASSOCIATION

https://literacyworldwide.org/home

JEANNE S. CHALL RESEARCH FELLOWSHIP

This fellowship is a US$5,000 grant established to encourage and support reading research by promising scholars. Its special emphasis is to support research efforts in the following areas: beginning reading (theory, research, and practice that improves the effectiveness of learning to read); readability (methods of predicting the difficulty of texts); reading difficulty (diagnosis, treatment, and prevention); stages of reading development; the relation of vocabulary to reading; and diagnosing and teaching adults with limited reading ability. Applicants must be ILA members.

Academic Fields/Career Goals: Literature/English/Writing; Special Education.

Award: Grant for use in senior, graduate, or postgraduate years; not renewable. *Number:* 1. *Amount:* $5000.

Eligibility Requirements: Applicant must be enrolled or expecting to enroll full- or part-time at a four-year institution or university. Available to U.S. and non-U.S. citizens.

Application Requirements: Application form. *Deadline:* January 15.

Contact: Wendy Logan, Executive Programs Manager
E-mail: ILAAwards@reading.org

JAPANESE AMERICAN CITIZENS LEAGUE (JACL)

http://www.jacl.org/

NATIONAL JACL HEADQUARTERS SCHOLARSHIP
• *See page 107*

NATIONAL WRITERS ASSOCIATION FOUNDATION

http://www.nationalwriters.com/

NATIONAL WRITERS ASSOCIATION FOUNDATION SCHOLARSHIPS
• *See page 406*

OUTDOOR WRITERS ASSOCIATION OF AMERICA

http://www.owaa.org/

OUTDOOR WRITERS ASSOCIATION OF AMERICA - BODIE MCDOWELL SCHOLARSHIP AWARD
• *See page 222*

STRAIGHTFORWARD MEDIA

http://www.straightforwardmedia.com/

STRAIGHTFORWARD MEDIA LIBERAL ARTS SCHOLARSHIP
• *See page 139*

UNITED DAUGHTERS OF THE CONFEDERACY

http://www.hqudc.org/

HELEN JAMES BREWER SCHOLARSHIP
• *See page 383*

UNITED NEGRO COLLEGE FUND

http://www.uncf.org/

DIVERSE VOICES IN STORYTELLING SCHOLARSHIP
• *See page 227*

HCN/APRICITY RESOURCES SCHOLARS PROGRAM
• *See page 93*

VIRTUOUS PROM

https://www.virtuousprom.com

KAREN HANSON MEMORIAL SCHOLARSHIP

This scholarship was created in loving memory of Karen Hanson, amazing mother, wife, teacher and friend. Karen was taken from us too soon, but among the many lessons she taught us, it was to face life's challenges with optimism and humor. The Karen Hanson Memorial Scholarship is for anyone planning to or currently pursuing studies in Literature, either at the undergraduate, graduate or post–graduate level. The winner will be awarded $350. In order to apply, applicants must submit a 250+ word essay responding to the following prompt: Life is full of challenges and struggles, and one of the great things literature can do is help us move through and past them with humor. In 250 words or more, describe how an education in Literature can help us move through life with greater joy. Submissions may be written in prose or may be submitted in the form of a short (hopefully humorous!) story. All essays must be submitted to scholarships@virtuousprom.com beginning each year on September 1 and received no later than November 30. Out of the pool of applicants, we will choose three finalists by January 1. Finalists will be chosen based on the coherency and persuasiveness of their essays. We will then notify the finalists and post the three finalists' essays on our blog and on our Facebook page. The winner will be announced January 31 on Facebook.

Academic Fields/Career Goals: Literature/English/Writing.

Award: Scholarship for use in freshman, sophomore, junior, senior, graduate, or postgraduate years; not renewable. *Number:* 1. *Amount:* $350.

Eligibility Requirements: Applicant must be enrolled or expecting to enroll full- or part-time at a two-year or four-year institution or university. Available to U.S. and non-U.S. citizens.

Application Requirements: Essay. *Deadline:* November 30.

Contact: Ms. Megan MacNeal, Creative Director
E-mail: megan@virtuousprom.com

WILLA CATHER FOUNDATION

http://www.willacather.org/

ANTONETTE WILLA SKUPA TURNER SCHOLARSHIP
• *See page 384*

NORMA ROSS WALTER SCHOLARSHIP

Applicants must be female high school seniors who are prospective first year college students and plan to continue their education as English majors in accredited colleges or universities. Selection is based on intellectual promise, creativity, and character of the applicant.

Academic Fields/Career Goals: Literature/English/Writing.

Award: Scholarship for use in freshman year; not renewable. *Number:* 1–3. *Amount:* $1250–$2500.

Eligibility Requirements: Applicant must be high school student; planning to enroll or expecting to enroll full-time at a four-year institution or university; female and resident of Nebraska. Applicant must have 3.0 GPA or higher. Available to U.S. citizens.

Application Requirements: Application form, essay. *Deadline:* January 31.

Contact: Ashley Olson, Executive Director
Willa Cather Foundation
413 North Webster Street
Red Cloud, NE 68970
Phone: 402-746-2653
E-mail: info@willacather.org

MARINE BIOLOGY

AMERICAN INDIAN SCIENCE AND ENGINEERING SOCIETY

http://www.aises.org/

A.T. ANDERSON MEMORIAL SCHOLARSHIP PROGRAM
• *See page 121*

AMERICAN PHYSIOLOGICAL SOCIETY

http://www.the-aps.org

BARBARA A. HORWITZ AND JOHN M. HOROWITZ UNDERGRADUATE RESEARCH AWARDS
• *See page 114*

ASSOCIATION FOR WOMEN GEOSCIENTISTS (AWG)

http://www.awg.org/

AWG UNDERGRADUATE EXCELLENCE IN PALEONTOLOGY AWARD
• *See page 123*

ASSOCIATION ON AMERICAN INDIAN AFFAIRS, INC.

http://www.indian-affairs.org/

ELIZABETH AND SHERMAN ASCHE MEMORIAL SCHOLARSHIP FUND
• *See page 106*

BARRY GOLDWATER SCHOLARSHIP AND EXCELLENCE IN EDUCATION FOUNDATION

https://goldwater.scholarsapply.org

BARRY M. GOLDWATER SCHOLARSHIP AND EXCELLENCE IN EDUCATION PROGRAM
• *See page 123*

CALAVERAS BIG TREES ASSOCIATION

https://bigtrees.org/

EMILY M. HEWITT MEMORIAL SCHOLARSHIP
• *See page 170*

CUSHMAN FOUNDATION FOR FORAMINIFERAL RESEARCH

http://www.cushmanfoundation.org/index.php

LOEBLICH AND TAPPAN STUDENT RESEARCH AWARD
• *See page 170*

DISTIL NETWORKS

http://www.distilnetworks.com

WOMEN FORWARD IN TECHNOLOGY SCHOLARSHIP PROGRAM
• *See page 124*

DIVERSITYCOMM, INC.

http://www.diversitycomm.net/

DIVERSITY IN STEAM MAGAZINE SCHOLARSHIP
• *See page 83*

THE EXPERT INSTITUTE

https://www.theexpertinstitute.com

ANNUAL HEALTHCARE AND LIFE SCIENCES SCHOLARSHIP
• *See page 170*

GREAT MINDS IN STEM

http://www.greatmindsinstem.org

HENAAC SCHOLARSHIP PROGRAM
• *See page 115*

HAWAIIAN LODGE, F&AM

http://www.hawaiianlodgefreemasons.org

HAWAIIAN LODGE SCHOLARSHIPS
• *See page 86*

LABROOTS INC.

http://www.LabRoots.com

LABROOTS STEM SCHOLARSHIP
• *See page 116*

THE LAND CONSERVANCY OF NEW JERSEY

http://www.tlc-nj.org/

ROGERS FAMILY SCHOLARSHIP
• *See page 172*

RUSSELL W. MYERS SCHOLARSHIP
• *See page 172*

LOUISIANA OFFICE OF STUDENT FINANCIAL ASSISTANCE

http://www.osfa.la.gov/

ROCKEFELLER STATE WILDLIFE SCHOLARSHIP
• *See page 172*

MARINE TECHNOLOGY SOCIETY

http://www.mtsociety.org/

CHARLES H. BUSSMAN UNDERGRADUATE SCHOLARSHIP
Scholarship for undergraduate students enrolled full-time in a marine-related field. Must be a member of Marine Technology Society.

Academic Fields/Career Goals: Marine Biology; Marine/Ocean Engineering; Oceanography.

Award: Scholarship for use in freshman, sophomore, junior, or senior years; not renewable. *Amount:* up to $2500.

Eligibility Requirements: Applicant must be enrolled or expecting to enroll full-time at a four-year institution or university. Applicant or parent of applicant must be member of Marine Technology Society. Available to U.S. and non-U.S. citizens.

Application Requirements: Application form, driver's license, proof of acceptance for an undergraduate course, recommendations or references, transcript. *Deadline:* April 15.

Contact: Suzanne Voelker, Operations Administrator
    Phone: 410-884-5330
    Fax: 410-884-9060
    E-mail: suzanne.voelker@mtsociety.org

JOHN C. BAJUS SCHOLARSHIP
Scholarship available to undergraduate and graduate students enrolled full-time in a marine-related field. Must be a MTS student member with demonstrated commitment to community service/volunteer activities.

Academic Fields/Career Goals: Marine Biology; Marine/Ocean Engineering; Oceanography.

Award: Scholarship for use in freshman, sophomore, junior, senior, or graduate years; not renewable. *Amount:* up to $1000.

Eligibility Requirements: Applicant must be enrolled or expecting to enroll full-time at a four-year institution or university. Applicant or parent of applicant must be member of Marine Technology Society. Available to U.S. and non-U.S. citizens.

Application Requirements: Application form, driver's license, recommendations or references, transcript. *Deadline:* April 15.

Contact: Suzanne Voelker, Operations Administrator
    Phone: 410-884-5330
    Fax: 410-884-9060
    E-mail: suzanne.voelker@mtsociety.org

MTS STUDENT SCHOLARSHIP
Scholarships available to both Marine Technology Society members and non-members, undergraduates and graduate students, enrolled full-time in a marine-related field.

Academic Fields/Career Goals: Marine Biology; Marine/Ocean Engineering; Oceanography.

Award: Scholarship for use in freshman, sophomore, junior, senior, or graduate years; not renewable. *Amount:* up to $2000.

Eligibility Requirements: Applicant must be enrolled or expecting to enroll full-time at a four-year institution or university. Available to U.S. and non-U.S. citizens.

Application Requirements: Application form, driver's license, recommendations or references, transcript. *Deadline:* April 15.

Contact: Suzanne Voelker, Operations Administrator
Phone: 410-884-5330
Fax: 410-884-9060
E-mail: suzanne.voelker@mtsociety.org

MTS STUDENT SCHOLARSHIP FOR GRADUATE AND UNDERGRADUATE STUDENTS

Scholarship of $2000 available to undergraduate students who are enrolled full-time in a marine-related field.

Academic Fields/Career Goals: Marine Biology; Marine/Ocean Engineering.

Award: Scholarship for use in freshman, sophomore, junior, senior, or graduate years; not renewable. *Amount:* $2000.

Eligibility Requirements: Applicant must be enrolled or expecting to enroll full-time at a four-year institution or university. Available to U.S. and non-U.S. citizens.

Application Requirements: Application form, essay, recommendations or references, transcript. *Deadline:* April 15.

Contact: Suzanne Voelker, Operations Administrator
Marine Technology Society
5565 Sterrett Place, Suite 108
Columbia, MD 21044
Phone: 410-884-5330
E-mail: suzanne.voelker@mtsociety.org

MTS STUDENT SCHOLARSHIP FOR TWO-YEAR TECHNICAL, ENGINEERING AND COMMUNITY COLLEGE STUDENTS

Scholarship of $2000 available to students enrolled in a two-year technical, engineering, or community college in a marine-related field.

Academic Fields/Career Goals: Marine Biology; Marine/Ocean Engineering.

Award: Scholarship for use in freshman or sophomore years; not renewable. *Amount:* $2000.

Eligibility Requirements: Applicant must be enrolled or expecting to enroll full-time at a two-year institution. Available to U.S. and non-U.S. citizens.

Application Requirements: Application form, essay, recommendations or references, transcript. *Deadline:* April 15.

Contact: Suzanne Voelker, Operations Administrator
Marine Technology Society
5565 Sterrett Place, Suite 108
Columbia, MD 21044
Phone: 410-884-5330
E-mail: suzanne.voelker@mtsociety.org

PAROS-DIGIQUARTZ SCHOLARSHIP

Scholarships available to both MTS members and non-members, undergraduates and graduate students, enrolled full-time in a marine-related field with an interest in marine instrumentation. High school seniors who have been accepted into a full-time undergraduate program in a marine-related field are also eligible to apply.

Academic Fields/Career Goals: Marine Biology; Marine/Ocean Engineering; Oceanography.

Award: Scholarship for use in freshman, sophomore, junior, senior, or graduate years; not renewable. *Amount:* up to $2000.

Eligibility Requirements: Applicant must be enrolled or expecting to enroll full-time at a four-year institution or university. Available to U.S. and non-U.S. citizens.

Application Requirements: Application form, driver's license, recommendations or references, transcript. *Deadline:* April 15.

Contact: Suzanne Voelker, Operations Administrator
Phone: 410-884-5330
Fax: 410-884-9060
E-mail: suzanne.voelker@mtsociety.org

ROV SCHOLARSHIP

Scholarships for undergraduate and graduate students interested in remotely operated vehicles or underwater work that furthers the use of ROVs. Open to MTS student members and non-MTS members.

Academic Fields/Career Goals: Marine Biology; Marine/Ocean Engineering; Oceanography.

Award: Scholarship for use in freshman, sophomore, junior, senior, or graduate years; not renewable. *Amount:* up to $10,000.

Eligibility Requirements: Applicant must be enrolled or expecting to enroll full-time at a four-year institution or university. Available to U.S. and non-U.S. citizens.

Application Requirements: Application form, driver's license, essay, recommendations or references, transcript. *Deadline:* April 15.

Contact: Chuck Richards, Chair, Scholarship Committee
Marine Technology Society
c/o C.A. Richards and Associates Inc.
777 North Eldridge Parkway, Suite 280
Houston, TX 77079

MEDICAL SCRUBS COLLECTION

http://medicalscrubscollection.com

MEDICAL SCRUBS COLLECTION SCHOLARSHIP
• *See page 120*

NEXTSTEPU

http://www.nextstepu.com/

$1,500 STEM SCHOLARSHIP
• *See page 120*

SCARLETT FAMILY FOUNDATION SCHOLARSHIP PROGRAM

http://www.scarlettfoundation.org/

SCHOLARSHIP FOR STUDENTS PURSUING A BUSINESS OR STEM DEGREE
• *See page 91*

SIGMA XI, THE SCIENTIFIC RESEARCH SOCIETY

http://www.sigmaxi.org/

SIGMA XI GRANTS-IN-AID OF RESEARCH
• *See page 110*

SOCIETY FOR INTEGRATIVE AND COMPARATIVE BIOLOGY

http://www.sicb.org/

LIBBIE H. HYMAN MEMORIAL SCHOLARSHIP
• *See page 174*

STRAIGHT NORTH

https://www.straightnorth.com/

STRAIGHT NORTH STEM SCHOLARSHIP
• *See page 92*

UNICO FOUNDATION INC.

http://www.unico.org/

LOUISE TORRACO MEMORIAL SCHOLARSHIP FOR SCIENCE
• *See page 174*

WOMAN'S SEAMEN'S FRIEND SOCIETY OF CONNECTICUT INC.

FINANCIAL SUPPORT FOR MARINE OR MARITIME STUDIES

Applicant must be full-time student. High school students not considered. Award available to U.S. citizens. Must be majoring in marine sciences at any college or university.

Academic Fields/Career Goals: Marine Biology; Oceanography.

Award: Scholarship for use in freshman, sophomore, junior, or senior years; not renewable.

Eligibility Requirements: Applicant must be enrolled or expecting to enroll full-time at a four-year institution or university. Available to U.S. citizens.

Application Requirements: Application form, financial need analysis, recommendations or references, resume, test scores, transcript. *Deadline:* varies.

Contact: Marshall Davidson, Executive Director
Phone: 203-777-2165
Fax: 203-777-5774
E-mail: wsfsofct@earthlink.net

YOUTH MARITIME TRAINING ASSOCIATION

http://ymta.net/

NORM MANLY—YMTA MARITIME EDUCATIONAL SCHOLARSHIPS

The scholarships may be used by students pursuing marine-related and maritime training and education in community colleges, technical and vocational programs, colleges, universities, maritime academies or other educational institutions. Scholarships will be awarded in the amounts of one $5,000, one $3,000, two $2,500, and two $1,000. In addition, Pacific Maritime Magazine will award a $500 scholarship to one of the finalists planning to pursue a seagoing maritime career. Requires 2.5 GPA or submit an additional letter of recommendation from a second teacher.

Academic Fields/Career Goals: Marine Biology; Marine/Ocean Engineering; Oceanography; Trade/Technical Specialties.

Award: Scholarship for use in freshman year; not renewable. *Number:* 6–7. *Amount:* $1000–$5000.

Eligibility Requirements: Applicant must be high school student; planning to enroll or expecting to enroll full- or part-time at a two-year or four-year or technical institution or university and resident of Washington. Applicant must have 2.5 GPA or higher. Available to U.S. citizens.

Application Requirements: Application form, essay. *Deadline:* March 22.

Contact: Alicia Barnes, Director
Youth Maritime Training Association
PO Box 81142
Seattle, WA 98108
Phone: 206-812-5464
E-mail: ymta@pugetmaritime.org

MARINE/OCEAN ENGINEERING

AMERICAN COUNCIL OF ENGINEERING COMPANIES OF PENNSYLVANIA (ACEC/PA)

http://www.acecpa.org/

ERIC J. GENNUSO AND LEROY D. (BUD) LOY, JR. SCHOLARSHIP PROGRAM
• *See page 187*

AMERICAN INDIAN SCIENCE AND ENGINEERING SOCIETY

http://www.aises.org/

A.T. ANDERSON MEMORIAL SCHOLARSHIP PROGRAM
• *See page 121*

AMERICAN SOCIETY OF CERTIFIED ENGINEERING TECHNICIANS

http://www.ascet.org/

KURT H. AND DONNA M. SCHULER SMALL GRANT
• *See page 205*

AMERICAN SOCIETY OF NAVAL ENGINEERS

http://www.navalengineers.org/

AMERICAN SOCIETY OF NAVAL ENGINEERS SCHOLARSHIP
• *See page 122*

ARRL FOUNDATION INC.

http://www.arrl.org/

ALFRED E. FRIEND JR, W4CF, MEMORIAL SCHOLARSHIP
• *See page 191*

LOIS MANLEY, K7LMZ, AND RANDALL PITCHFORD, WW7ZZ, SCHOLARSHIP
• *See page 206*

W I FDR SCHOLARSHIP
• *See page 122*

BARRY GOLDWATER SCHOLARSHIP AND EXCELLENCE IN EDUCATION FOUNDATION

https://goldwater.scholarsapply.org

BARRY M. GOLDWATER SCHOLARSHIP AND EXCELLENCE IN EDUCATION PROGRAM
• *See page 123*

BHW GROUP

https://thebhwgroup.com/

BHW WOMEN IN STEM SCHOLARSHIP
• *See page 124*

BROWN AND CALDWELL

http://www.brownandcaldwell.com

ECKENFELDER SCHOLARSHIP
• *See page 169*

MINORITY SCHOLARSHIP PROGRAM
• *See page 169*

CALAVERAS BIG TREES ASSOCIATION

https://bigtrees.org/

EMILY M. HEWITT MEMORIAL SCHOLARSHIP
• See page 170

DISTIL NETWORKS

http://www.distilnetworks.com

WOMEN FORWARD IN TECHNOLOGY SCHOLARSHIP PROGRAM
• See page 124

DIVERSITYCOMM, INC.

http://www.diversitycomm.net/

DIVERSITY IN STEAM MAGAZINE SCHOLARSHIP
• See page 83

GREATER KANAWHA VALLEY FOUNDATION

http://www.tgkvf.org/

STEVEN ENGINEERING SCHOLARSHIP
• See page 192

GREAT MINDS IN STEM

http://www.greatmindsinstem.org

HENAAC SCHOLARSHIP PROGRAM
• See page 115

HAWAIIAN LODGE, F&AM

http://www.hawaiianlodgefreemasons.org

HAWAIIAN LODGE SCHOLARSHIPS
• See page 86

LABROOTS INC.

http://www.LabRoots.com

LABROOTS STEM SCHOLARSHIP
• See page 116

LOUISIANA OFFICE OF STUDENT FINANCIAL ASSISTANCE

http://www.osfa.la.gov/

ROCKEFELLER STATE WILDLIFE SCHOLARSHIP
• See page 172

MANUFACTURERS ASSOCIATION OF MAINE

http://www.mainemfg.com/

MAINE MANUFACTURING CAREER AND TRAINING FOUNDATION SCHOLARSHIP
• See page 156

MARINE TECHNOLOGY SOCIETY

http://www.mtsociety.org/

CHARLES H. BUSSMAN UNDERGRADUATE SCHOLARSHIP
• See page 423

JOHN C. BAJUS SCHOLARSHIP
• See page 423

MTS STUDENT SCHOLARSHIP
• See page 423

MTS STUDENT SCHOLARSHIP FOR GRADUATE AND UNDERGRADUATE STUDENTS
• See page 424

MTS STUDENT SCHOLARSHIP FOR GRADUATING HIGH SCHOOL SENIORS
• See page 321

MTS STUDENT SCHOLARSHIP FOR TWO-YEAR TECHNICAL, ENGINEERING AND COMMUNITY COLLEGE STUDENTS
• See page 424

PAROS-DIGIQUARTZ SCHOLARSHIP
• See page 424

ROV SCHOLARSHIP
• See page 424

NASA FLORIDA SPACE GRANT CONSORTIUM

http://www.floridaspacegrant.org/

FLORIDA SPACE RESEARCH PROGRAM
• See page 156

NEXTSTEPU

http://www.nextstepu.com/

$1,500 STEM SCHOLARSHIP
• See page 120

SCARLETT FAMILY FOUNDATION SCHOLARSHIP PROGRAM

http://www.scarlettfoundation.org/

SCHOLARSHIP FOR STUDENTS PURSUING A BUSINESS OR STEM DEGREE
• See page 91

SIGMA XI, THE SCIENTIFIC RESEARCH SOCIETY

http://www.sigmaxi.org/

SIGMA XI GRANTS-IN-AID OF RESEARCH
• See page 110

SILICON VALLEY COMMUNITY FOUNDATION

http://www.siliconvalleycf.org

SAMSUNG@FIRST SCHOLARS
• See page 233

SNAME
http://www.sname.org

GENERAL UNDERGRADUATE SCHOLARSHIPS

General Undergraduate Scholarships are part of the SNAME Undergraduate Scholarships Program. It is open to U.S., Canadian and international applicants. SNAME membership required four months prior to the application submission deadline (i.e. February 1). Applicants must study in approved universities with SNAME student sections. Awards are made for one year of study leading to a Bachelor of Science degree in naval architecture, marine engineering, ocean engineering, ship hydrodynamics and wave theory, ship and offshore structures, or in other fields directly related to the marine industry. Applicants must not receive their Bachelor's degree prior to April 15 of the academic year they are applying for their scholarship. Undergraduate scholarships may be awarded to an individual more than once and applicants remain eligible for a graduate scholarship. Applications must be received prior to June 1, with all supporting data by June 15 for Scholarships Committee review. Selection in July based upon Scholarships Committee recommendations and Executive Committee approval. Scholarship funds may be used for student tuition, textbooks, academic fees or other academic related expenses for study and research. Application forms downloaded from the SNAME website are to be submitted electronically to Sofia Iliogrammenou at scholarships@sname.org.

Academic Fields/Career Goals: Marine/Ocean Engineering.

Award: Scholarship for use in freshman, sophomore, junior, or senior years; not renewable. *Amount:* up to $5000.

Eligibility Requirements: Applicant must be enrolled or expecting to enroll full-time at an institution or university. Available to U.S. and non-U.S. citizens.

Application Requirements: Application form, essay. *Deadline:* June 1.

Contact: Sofia Iliogrammenou, Director of Regional Member Services
E-mail: scholarships@sname.org

MANDELL AND LESTER ROSENBLATT UNDERGRADUATE SCHOLARSHIP

First awarded in 2007, the Mandell and Lester Rosenblatt Scholarship provides a maximum of $6,000 to an undergraduate scholar having a passion for naval architecture, marine or ocean engineering, and displaying evidence of professionalism and involvement in SNAME. The Mandell and Lester Rosenblatt Scholarship is part of the SNAME Undergraduate Scholarships Program. It is open to U.S., Canadian and international applicants. SNAME membership required four months prior to the application submission deadline (i.e. February 1). Currently be an actively involved member of a SNAME student section and be committed to future membership. Awards are made for one year of study leading to a Bachelor of Science degree in naval architecture, marine engineering, ocean engineering, ship hydrodynamics and wave theory, ship and offshore structures, or in other fields directly related to the marine industry. Applicants must not receive their Bachelor's degree prior to April 15th of the academic year they are applying for their scholarship. Undergraduate scholarships may be awarded to an individual more than once and applicants remain eligible for a graduate scholarship. Applications must be received prior to June 1, with all supporting data by June 15 for Scholarships Committee review. Selection in July based upon Scholarships Committee recommendations and Executive Committee approval. Scholarship funds may be used for student tuition, textbooks, academic fees or other academic related expenses for study and research. Application forms downloaded from the SNAME website are to be submitted electronically to Sofia Iliogrammenou at scholarships@sname.org.

Academic Fields/Career Goals: Marine/Ocean Engineering.

Award: Scholarship for use in freshman, sophomore, junior, or senior years; not renewable. *Amount:* up to $6000.

Eligibility Requirements: Applicant must be enrolled or expecting to enroll full-time at an institution or university. Available to U.S. and non-U.S. citizens.

Application Requirements: Application form, essay. *Deadline:* June 1.

Contact: Sofia Iliogrammenou, Director of Regional Member Services
E-mail: scholarships@sname.org

ROBERT N. HERBERT UNDERGRADUATE SCHOLARSHIP

First awarded in 2008, the Robert N. Herbert Undergraduate Scholarship provides a maximum award of $6,000 to an undergraduate scholar having a passion for naval architecture, marine or ocean engineering, and displaying evidence of professionalism and involvement in SNAME. The Robert N. Herbert Undergraduate Scholarship is part of the SNAME Undergraduate Scholarships Program. It is open to U.S., Canadian and International applicants. SNAME membership required four months prior to the application submission deadline (i.e. February 1). Currently be an actively involved member of a SNAME student section and be committed to future membership. Awards are made for one year of study leading to a Bachelor of Science degree in naval architecture, marine engineering, ocean engineering, ship hydrodynamics and wave theory, ship and offshore structures, or in other fields directly related to the marine industry. Applicants must not receive their Bachelor's degree prior to April 15th of the academic year they are applying for their scholarship. Undergraduate scholarships may be awarded to an individual more than once and applicants remain eligible for a graduate scholarship. Applications must be received prior to June 1, with all supporting data by June 15 for Scholarships Committee review. Selection in July based upon Scholarships Committee recommendations and Executive Committee approval. Scholarship funds may be used for student tuition, textbooks, academic fees or other academic related expenses for study and research. Application forms downloaded from the SNAME website are to be submitted electronically to Sofia Iliogrammenou at scholarships@sname.org.

Academic Fields/Career Goals: Marine/Ocean Engineering.

Award: Scholarship for use in freshman, sophomore, junior, or senior years; not renewable. *Amount:* up to $6000.

Eligibility Requirements: Applicant must be enrolled or expecting to enroll full-time at an institution or university. Available to U.S. and non-U.S. citizens.

Application Requirements: Application form, essay. *Deadline:* June 1.

Contact: Sofia Iliogrammenou, Director of Regional Member Services
E-mail: scholarships@sname.org

SOCIETY OF WOMEN ENGINEERS
http://societyofwomenengineers.swe.org/

ADA I. PRESSMAN MEMORIAL SCHOLARSHIP

AMERICAN TRANSMISSION CO. SCHOLARSHIP

ANNE MAUREEN WHITNEY BARROW MEMORIAL SCHOLARSHIP

ANNE SHEN SMITH ENDOWED SCHOLARSHIP

BETTY LOU BAILEY SWE REGION F SCHOLARSHIP

B.J. HARROD SCHOLARSHIP

BK KRENZER MEMORIAL REENTRY SCHOLARSHIP

CAROL STEPHENS SWE REGION F SCHOLARSHIP

DR. IVY M. PARKER MEMORIAL SCHOLARSHIP

DOROTHY LEMKE HOWARTH MEMORIAL SCHOLARSHIP

DOROTHY P. MORRIS SCHOLARSHIP

EXELON SCHOLARSHIP

IBM LINDA SANFORD WOMEN'S TECHNICAL ADVANCEMENT SCHOLARSHIP
• See page 198

LILLIAN MOLLER GILBRETH MEMORIAL SCHOLARSHIP
• See page 198

MARY V. MUNGER MEMORIAL SCHOLARSHIP
• See page 199

OLIVE LYNN SALEMBIER MEMORIAL REENTRY SCHOLARSHIP
• See page 199

ROBERTA BANASZAK GLEITER ENGINEERING ENDEAVOR SCHOLARSHIP
• See page 199

SUSAN MISZKOWICZ SEPTEMBER 11 MEMORIAL SCHOLARSHIP
• See page 199

SWE BALTIMORE-WASHINGTON SECTION SCHOLARSHIP
• See page 199

SWE CENTRAL NEW MEXICO PIONEERS SCHOLARSHIP
• See page 200

SWE CENTRAL NEW MEXICO REENTRY SCHOLARSHIP
• See page 200

SWE MID-HUDSON SECTION SCHOLARSHIP
• See page 200

SWE PHOENIX SECTION SCHOLARSHIP
• See page 200

SWE REGION E SCHOLARSHIP
• See page 200

SWE REGION G JUDY SIMMONS MEMORIAL SCHOLARSHIP
• See page 200

SWE REGION H SCHOLARSHIPS
• See page 201

SWE REGION J SCHOLARSHIP
• See page 201

TE CONNECTIVITY EXCELLENCE IN ENGINEERING SCHOLARSHIP
• See page 201

WANDA MUNN SCHOLARSHIP
• See page 201

SOCIETY OF WOMEN ENGINEERS-ROCKY MOUNTAIN SECTION

http://www.swe-rms.org/

SOCIETY OF WOMEN ENGINEERS-ROCKY MOUNTAIN SECTION SCHOLARSHIP PROGRAM
• See page 161

STRAIGHT NORTH

https://www.straightnorth.com/

STRAIGHT NORTH STEM SCHOLARSHIP
• See page 92

YOUTH MARITIME TRAINING ASSOCIATION

http://ymta.net/

NORM MANLY—YMTA MARITIME EDUCATIONAL SCHOLARSHIPS
• See page 425

MARKETING

280 GROUP

https://280group.com/contact/280-group-product-management-scholarship/

280 GROUP PRODUCT MANAGEMENT SCHOLARSHIP
• See page 263

AUTOMOTIVE AFTERMARKET SCHOLARSHIPS

http://www.automotivescholarships.com/

AUTOMOTIVE AFTERMARKET SCHOLARSHIPS
• See page 177

AUTOMOTIVE WOMEN'S ALLIANCE FOUNDATION

http://awafoundation.org/index.php

AUTOMOTIVE WOMEN'S ALLIANCE FOUNDATION SCHOLARSHIPS
• See page 81

BALTIMORE CHAPTER OF THE AMERICAN MARKETING ASSOCIATION

http://www.amabaltimore.org/

UNDERGRADUATE MARKETING EDUCATION MERIT SCHOLARSHIPS
• See page 177

DECA (DISTRIBUTIVE EDUCATION CLUBS OF AMERICA)

http://www.deca.org/

HARRY A. APPLEGATE SCHOLARSHIP
• See page 83

DIGITAL THIRD COAST INTERNET MARKETING

http://www.digitalthirdcoast.net/

DIGITAL MARKETING SCHOLARSHIP
• See page 96

FUKUNAGA SCHOLARSHIP FOUNDATION

http://fukunagascholarship.com

FUKUNAGA SCHOLARSHIP FOUNDATION
• See page 85

HOUSE OF BLUES MUSIC FORWARD FOUNDATION

https://hobmusicforward.org/

TIFFANY GREEN OPERATOR SCHOLARSHIP AWARD
• See page 96

IDAHO STATE BROADCASTERS ASSOCIATION

http://www.idahobroadcasters.org/

WAYNE C. CORNILS MEMORIAL SCHOLARSHIP
• See page 180

INFINITY DENTAL WEB

http://www.infinitydentalweb.com

INTERNET MARKETING SCHOLARSHIP

This year's Infinity Dental Web scholarship seeks to assist students pursuing an education in marketing. With this scholarship, we hope to be able to assist some promising student who will make a contribution to the success of business, and to encourage them to use their skills in promoting quality dental care. Qualifying applicants will answer the essay question provided. The essay should be between 500-750 words. You may upload an essay in Word or PDF format, or you may copy and paste it into the application form. Essays will be judged on both the quality of the writing and the substance of the ideas presented. To be considered, you must submit the application and essay before the deadline. Identify a family dental practice that provides a basic level of dental care to a middle-class clientele. It can be your own dentist or any dentist, as long as the practice has a website. Please identify the practice by giving us the URL of their website. Visualize yourself as a marketing professional who has been hired to help transform this practice to a high-end practice focusing on smile makeovers and catering to a high-income clientele. Describe how you would brand this practice. Give a specific and detailed critique of what you would do to change their website.

Academic Fields/Career Goals: Marketing; Mathematics; Social Sciences; Social Services; Statistics.

Award: Scholarship for use in freshman, sophomore, junior, senior, graduate, or postgraduate years; not renewable. *Number:* 1. *Amount:* $250.

Eligibility Requirements: Applicant must be enrolled or expecting to enroll full- or part-time at a two-year or four-year institution or university. Available to U.S. citizens.

Application Requirements: Essay. *Deadline:* June 30.

Contact: Ms. Amber Mosure, Research Specialist
          Infinity Dental Web
          1839 South Alma School Road
          Suite 200
          Mesa, AZ 85210
          Phone: 480-273-8888
          E-mail: amber@infinitydentalweb.com

INTERNATIONAL FOODSERVICE EDITORIAL COUNCIL

http://www.ifeconline.com/

INTERNATIONAL FOODSERVICE EDITORIAL COUNCIL COMMUNICATIONS SCHOLARSHIP
• See page 96

THE LAGRANT FOUNDATION

http://www.lagrantfoundation.org/

LAGRANT FOUNDATION SCHOLARSHIP FOR GRADUATES
• See page 97

LAGRANT FOUNDATION SCHOLARSHIP FOR UNDERGRADUATES
• See page 97

NATIONAL DAIRY SHRINE

http://www.dairyshrine.org/

NATIONAL DAIRY SHRINE/DAIRY MARKETING INC. MILK MARKETING SCHOLARSHIPS
• See page 108

NATIONAL RESTAURANT ASSOCIATION EDUCATIONAL FOUNDATION

http://www.chooserestaurants.org

NATIONAL RESTAURANT ASSOCIATION EDUCATIONAL FOUNDATION UNDERGRADUATE SCHOLARSHIPS FOR COLLEGE STUDENTS
• See page 109

NEBRASKA PRESS ASSOCIATION

http://www.nebpress.com/

NEBRASKA PRESS ASSOCIATION FOUNDATION SCHOLARSHIP
• See page 97

NEXT STEPS DIGITAL

https://www.nextstepsdigital.com/

NEXT STEPS DIGITAL SCHOLARSHIP

The recipient will receive a one-time $5,000 scholarship to be applied to qualified expenses, including graduate and undergraduate tuition, fees, books, and on-campus room and board for the 2018 Spring Semester. Funds are provided by Next Steps Digital. Payments are issued by Next Steps Digital and made payable to the student's approved college or university and mailed after Dec. 31, 2018 directly to the accredited college or university last designated by the student.

Academic Fields/Career Goals: Marketing.

Award: Scholarship for use in freshman, sophomore, junior, senior, or graduate years; not renewable. *Number:* 1. *Amount:* $5000.

Eligibility Requirements: Applicant must be enrolled or expecting to enroll full-time at a four-year institution or university. Applicant must have 3.5 GPA or higher. Available to U.S. citizens.

Application Requirements: Application form, essay. *Deadline:* December 15.

Contact: Josh Blanton, CMO
          E-mail: josh@nextstepsdigital.com

OHIO NEWS MEDIA FOUNDATION

http://www.ohionews.org

HAROLD K. DOUTHIT SCHOLARSHIP
• See page 98

OHIO NEWS MEDIA FOUNDATION MINORITY SCHOLARSHIP
• See page 98

OHIO NEWS MEDIA FOUNDATION UNIVERSITY JOURNALISM SCHOLARSHIP

ONWA ANNUAL SCHOLARSHIP

PRINTING INDUSTRY MIDWEST EDUCATION FOUDNATION
http://www.pimw.org/scholarships

PRINTING INDUSTRY MIDWEST EDUCATION FOUNDATION SCHOLARSHIP FUND

RHODE ISLAND FOUNDATION
http://www.rifoundation.org/

J. D. EDSAL SCHOLARSHIP

SCARLETT FAMILY FOUNDATION SCHOLARSHIP PROGRAM
http://www.scarlettfoundation.org/

SCHOLARSHIP FOR STUDENTS PURSUING A BUSINESS OR STEM DEGREE

SPECIALTY EQUIPMENT MARKET ASSOCIATION
http://www.sema.org/

SEMA MEMORIAL SCHOLARSHIP FUND

STRAIGHTFORWARD MEDIA
http://www.straightforwardmedia.com/

STRAIGHTFORWARD MEDIA BUSINESS SCHOOL SCHOLARSHIP

STRAIGHTFORWARD MEDIA MEDIA & COMMUNICATIONS SCHOLARSHIP

STRAIGHT NORTH
https://www.straightnorth.com/

STRAIGHT NORTH STEM SCHOLARSHIP

SUPPORT CREATIVITY
http://wesupportcreativity.org

SUPPORT CREATIVITY SCHOLARSHIP

TAMPA BAY TIMES FUND, INC.
http://www.tampabay.com/fund

TAMPA BAY TIMES FUND CAREER JOURNALISM SCHOLARSHIPS

TRIANGLE PEST CONTROL
http://www.trianglepest.com

TRIANGLE PEST CONTROL SCHOLARSHIP

UNITED NEGRO COLLEGE FUND
http://www.uncf.org/

DISCOVER FINANCIAL SERVICES SCHOLARSHIP

HCN/APRICITY RESOURCES SCHOLARS PROGRAM

NATIONAL BLACK MCDONALD'S OWNERS ASSOCIATION HOSPITALITY SCHOLARS PROGRAM

ORACLE CORPORATE SCHOLARS PROGRAM

PROCTER & GAMBLE GENERAL SCHOLARSHIP

RICOH SCHOLARSHIP PROGRAM

SUEZ CORPORATE SCHOLARS PROGRAM

UBS/PAINEWEBBER SCHOLARSHIP

UNCF/ALLIANCE DATA SCHOLARSHIP AND INTERNSHIP PROGRAM

UNCF/ANTHEM CORPORATE SCHOLARS PROGRAM

UNCF/CARNIVAL CORPORATE SCHOLARS PROGRAM

UNCF/NISSAN SCHOLARSHIP PROGRAM

VOYA SCHOLARS

WILLIAM WRIGLEY FOUNDATION SCHOLARSHIP

WHAT DETOX
http://whatdetox.com/meet-the-team/

WHAT DETOX SCHOLARSHIP

WYOMING TRUCKING ASSOCIATION SCHOLARSHIP FUND TRUST

http://www.wytruck.org/

WYOMING TRUCKING ASSOCIATION SCHOLARSHIP TRUST FUND
• See page 95

MATERIALS SCIENCE, ENGINEERING, AND METALLURGY

ACI FOUNDATION

http://www.acifoundation.org

ACI FOUNDATION SCHOLARSHIP PROGRAM
• See page 130

AIST FOUNDATION

http://www.aistfoundation.org/

AISI/AIST FOUNDATION PREMIER SCHOLARSHIP
• See page 280

AIST ALFRED B. GLOSSBRENNER AND JOHN KLUSCH SCHOLARSHIPS
• See page 308

AIST WILLIAM E. SCHWABE MEMORIAL SCHOLARSHIP
• See page 280

ASSOCIATION FOR IRON AND STEEL TECHNOLOGY BALTIMORE CHAPTER SCHOLARSHIP
• See page 293

ASSOCIATION FOR IRON AND STEEL TECHNOLOGY BENJAMIN F. FAIRLESS SCHOLARSHIP (AIME)
• See page 186

ASSOCIATION FOR IRON AND STEEL TECHNOLOGY DAVID H. SAMSON CANADIAN SCHOLARSHIP
• See page 187

ASSOCIATION FOR IRON AND STEEL TECHNOLOGY NORTHWEST MEMBER CHAPTER SCHOLARSHIP
• See page 309

ASSOCIATION FOR IRON AND STEEL TECHNOLOGY OHIO VALLEY CHAPTER SCHOLARSHIP
• See page 167

ASSOCIATION FOR IRON AND STEEL TECHNOLOGY PITTSBURGH CHAPTER SCHOLARSHIP
• See page 309

ASSOCIATION FOR IRON AND STEEL TECHNOLOGY RONALD E. LINCOLN SCHOLARSHIP
• See page 280

ASSOCIATION FOR IRON AND STEEL TECHNOLOGY SOUTHEAST MEMBER CHAPTER SCHOLARSHIP
• See page 310

ASSOCIATION FOR IRON AND STEEL TECHNOLOGY WILLY KORF MEMORIAL SCHOLARSHIP
• See page 187

FERROUS METALLURGY EDUCATION TODAY (FEMET)
Scholarships are for full-time students of metallurgy or materials science engineering. Students must have an interest in a career in the steel industry as demonstrated by an internship or related experience, or who have plans to pursue such experiences during college. Students must commit to a summer internship at a steel producing company (placement assistance is provided) prior to receiving this scholarship. Student may apply during their sophomore and junior years. Applications are accepted from 1 Sep through 31 Dec each year.

Academic Fields/Career Goals: Materials Science, Engineering, and Metallurgy.

Award: Scholarship for use in sophomore or junior years; not renewable. *Number:* 1–10. *Amount:* $5000.

Eligibility Requirements: Applicant must be enrolled or expecting to enroll full-time at a four-year institution or university. Applicant must have 2.5 GPA or higher. Available to U.S. and non-U.S. citizens.

Application Requirements: Application form, essay, recommendations or references, resume, transcript. *Deadline:* December 31.

Contact: Lori Wharrey, AIST Manager, Board Services
AIST Foundation
186 Thorn HIll Road
Warrendale, PA 15086
Phone: 724-814-3044
E-mail: lwharrey@aist.org

AMERICAN CHEMICAL SOCIETY

http://www.acs.org/

AMERICAN CHEMICAL SOCIETY SCHOLARS PROGRAM
• See page 187

AMERICAN CHEMICAL SOCIETY, RUBBER DIVISION

http://www.rubber.org/

AMERICAN CHEMICAL SOCIETY, RUBBER DIVISION UNDERGRADUATE SCHOLARSHIP
• See page 120

AMERICAN COUNCIL OF ENGINEERING COMPANIES OF PENNSYLVANIA (ACEC/PA)

http://www.acecpa.org/

ERIC J. GENNUSO AND LEROY D. (BUD) LOY, JR. SCHOLARSHIP PROGRAM
• See page 187

AMERICAN INDIAN SCIENCE AND ENGINEERING SOCIETY

http://www.aises.org/

A.T. ANDERSON MEMORIAL SCHOLARSHIP PROGRAM
• See page 121

AMERICAN INSTITUTE OF AERONAUTICS AND ASTRONAUTICS

http://www.aiaafoundation.org/

AIAA FOUNDATION UNDERGRADUATE SCHOLARSHIPS
• See page 121

LEATRICE GREGORY PENDRAY SCHOLARSHIP
• See page 121

AMERICAN SOCIETY OF CERTIFIED ENGINEERING TECHNICIANS

http://www.ascet.org/

KURT H. AND DONNA M. SCHULER SMALL GRANT
• See page 205

AMERICAN SOCIETY OF NAVAL ENGINEERS

http://www.navalengineers.org/

AMERICAN SOCIETY OF NAVAL ENGINEERS SCHOLARSHIP
• See page 122

AMERICAN WELDING SOCIETY

http://www.aws.org/

AIRGAS-JERRY BAKER SCHOLARSHIP
• See page 295

AIRGAS-TERRY JARVIS MEMORIAL SCHOLARSHIP
• See page 295

AIR PRODUCTS WOMEN IN GASES AND WELDING SCHOLARSHIP
• See page 295

ARSHAM AMIRIKIAN ENGINEERING SCHOLARSHIP
• See page 206

DONALD AND SHIRLEY HASTINGS SCHOLARSHIP
• See page 312

DONALD J. BENETEAU SCHOLARSHIP

Awarded to an undergraduate student pursuing a full time or part time education in welding or a related program. The applicant must have a minimum overall GPA of 3.0, have proof of financial need, and be a student member of the American Welding Society. The applicant must be a U.S. or Canadian citizen, and plan to attend an academic institution in the U. S. or Canada.

Academic Fields/Career Goals: Materials Science, Engineering, and Metallurgy.

Award: Scholarship for use in freshman, sophomore, junior, or senior years; not renewable.

Eligibility Requirements: Applicant must be enrolled or expecting to enroll full- or part-time at a four-year institution. Applicant must have 3.0 GPA or higher. Available to U.S. and Canadian citizens.

Application Requirements: Application form, financial need analysis. *Deadline:* February 15.

Contact: Mr. John Douglass, Associate Director, Foundation
American Welding Society
8669 NW 36 Street, #130
Miami, FL 33166
Phone: 305-443-9353 Ext. 212
E-mail: jdouglass@aws.org

JOHN C. LINCOLN MEMORIAL SCHOLARSHIP
• See page 296

MATSUO BRIDGE COMPANY LTD. OF JAPAN SCHOLARSHIP
• See page 206

MILLER ELECTRIC INTERNATIONAL WORLD SKILLS COMPETITION SCHOLARSHIP
• See page 296

MILLER ELECTRIC MFG. CO. SCHOLARSHIP
• See page 297

PRAXAIR INTERNATIONAL SCHOLARSHIP
• See page 297

ROBERT L. PEASLEE BRAZING SCHOLARSHIP
• See page 312

ROBERT W. WHITE, SR. SCHOLARSHIP

For a junior or senior college student in a welding program. Preference to students in resistance welding program. Full time, U.S. citizen. Minimum overall GPA 3.2

Academic Fields/Career Goals: Materials Science, Engineering, and Metallurgy.

Award: Scholarship for use in junior or senior years; not renewable.

Eligibility Requirements: Applicant must be enrolled or expecting to enroll full-time at an institution or university. Applicant must have 3.0 GPA or higher. Available to U.S. citizens.

Application Requirements: Application form, financial need analysis. *Deadline:* February 15.

Contact: Mr. John Douglass, Associate Director, AWS Foundation
American Welding Society
8669 NW 36 Street, #130
Miami, FL 33166
Phone: 305-443-9353 Ext. 212
E-mail: jdouglass@aws.org

VICTOR TECHNOLOGIES CUTTING AND WELDING SCHOLARSHIP
• See page 297

WILLIAM A. AND ANN M. BROTHERS SCHOLARSHIP
• See page 297

WILLIAM A. RICE FAMILY, WOMEN IN WELDING SCHOLARSHIP
• See page 298

WILLIAM B. HOWELL MEMORIAL SCHOLARSHIP
• See page 298

ARMED FORCES COMMUNICATIONS AND ELECTRONICS ASSOCIATION, EDUCATIONAL FOUNDATION

http://www.afcea.org/site/?q=foundation/scholarships

AFCEA STEM MAJORS SCHOLARSHIPS FOR UNDERGRADUATE STUDENTS
• See page 122

ARMED FORCES COMMUNICATIONS AND ELECTRONICS ASSOCIATION ROTC SCHOLARSHIP PROGRAM
• See page 151

ARRL FOUNDATION INC.

http://www.arrl.org/

ALFRED E. FRIEND JR, W4CF, MEMORIAL SCHOLARSHIP

CTRI/CHRIS SEEBER, KA1GEU, MEMORIAL SCHOLARSHIP

GARY WAGNER, K3OMI, SCHOLARSHIP

LOIS MANLEY, K7LMZ, AND RANDALL PITCHFORD, WW7ZZ, SCHOLARSHIP

OLD MAN INTERNATIONAL SIDEBAND SOCIETY (OMISS) SCHOLARSHIP

W1FDR SCHOLARSHIP

ASM MATERIALS EDUCATION FOUNDATION

http://www.asmfoundation.org/

EDWARD J. DULIS SCHOLARSHIP

GEORGE A. ROBERTS SCHOLARSHIP

JOHN M. HANIAK SCHOLARSHIP

WILLIAM P. WOODSIDE FOUNDER'S SCHOLARSHIP

ASSOCIATION OF STATE DAM SAFETY OFFICIALS (ASDSO)

http://www.DamSafety.org

ASSOCIATION OF STATE DAM SAFETY OFFICIALS (ASDSO) SENIOR UNDERGRADUATE SCHOLARSHIP

ASTRONAUT SCHOLARSHIP FOUNDATION

http://www.astronautscholarship.org/

ASTRONAUT SCHOLARSHIP FOUNDATION

AUTOMOTIVE WOMEN'S ALLIANCE FOUNDATION

http://awafoundation.org/index.php

AUTOMOTIVE WOMEN'S ALLIANCE FOUNDATION SCHOLARSHIPS

BARRY GOLDWATER SCHOLARSHIP AND EXCELLENCE IN EDUCATION FOUNDATION

https://goldwater.scholarsapply.org

BARRY M. GOLDWATER SCHOLARSHIP AND EXCELLENCE IN EDUCATION PROGRAM

BHW GROUP

https://thebhwgroup.com/

BHW WOMEN IN STEM SCHOLARSHIP

BROWN AND CALDWELL

http://www.brownandcaldwell.com

MINORITY SCHOLARSHIP PROGRAM

DISTIL NETWORKS

http://www.distilnetworks.com

WOMEN FORWARD IN TECHNOLOGY SCHOLARSHIP PROGRAM

DIVERSITYCOMM, INC.

http://www.diversitycomm.net/

DIVERSITY IN STEAM MAGAZINE SCHOLARSHIP

THE ELECTROCHEMICAL SOCIETY

http://www.electrochem.org/

STUDENT RESEARCH AWARDS OF THE BATTERY DIVISION OF THE ELECTROCHEMICAL SOCIETY INC.

FABRICATORS AND MANUFACTURERS ASSOCIATION FOUNDATION

http://www.nutsandboltsfoundation.org/scholarships/

COLLEGE AND TRADE/TECHNICAL SCHOOL SCHOLARSHIPS

GREATER KANAWHA VALLEY FOUNDATION

http://www.tgkvf.org/

STEVEN ENGINEERING SCHOLARSHIP

GREAT MINDS IN STEM

http://www.greatmindsinstem.org

HENAAC SCHOLARSHIP PROGRAM

INDEPENDENT LABORATORIES INSTITUTE SCHOLARSHIP ALLIANCE

http://www.acil.org/

INDEPENDENT LABORATORIES INSTITUTE SCHOLARSHIP ALLIANCE

INTERNATIONAL SOCIETY FOR OPTICAL ENGINEERING-SPIE

http://www.spie.org/scholarships

SPIE EDUCATIONAL SCHOLARSHIPS IN OPTICAL SCIENCE AND ENGINEERING

JORGE MAS CANOSA FREEDOM FOUNDATION

http://masscholarships.org/

MAS FAMILY SCHOLARSHIP AWARD

LABROOTS INC.

http://www.LabRoots.com

LABROOTS STEM SCHOLARSHIP

LOS ANGELES COUNCIL OF BLACK PROFESSIONAL ENGINEERS

http://www.lablackengineers.org/

AL-BEN SCHOLARSHIP FOR ACADEMIC INCENTIVE

AL-BEN SCHOLARSHIP FOR PROFESSIONAL MERIT

AL-BEN SCHOLARSHIP FOR SCHOLASTIC ACHIEVEMENT

MANUFACTURERS ASSOCIATION OF MAINE

http://www.mainemfg.com/

MAINE MANUFACTURING CAREER AND TRAINING FOUNDATION SCHOLARSHIP

MEDICAL SCRUBS COLLECTION

http://medicalscrubscollection.com

MEDICAL SCRUBS COLLECTION SCHOLARSHIP

MIDWEST ROOFING CONTRACTORS ASSOCIATION

http://www.mrca.org/

MRCA FOUNDATION SCHOLARSHIP PROGRAM

MINERALS, METALS, AND MATERIALS SOCIETY (TMS)

http://www.tms.org/

KAUFMAN CALPHAD SCHOLARSHIP

MATERIALS PROCESSING AND MANUFACTURING DIVISION SCHOLARSHIP

TMS/EPD SCHOLARSHIP

TMS/FMD GILBERT CHIN SCHOLARSHIP

TMS/INTERNATIONAL SYMPOSIUM ON SUPERALLOYS SCHOLARSHIP PROGRAM

TMS/LIGHT METALS DIVISION SCHOLARSHIP PROGRAM

TMS OUTSTANDING STUDENT PAPER CONTEST– UNDERGRADUATE

TMS/STRUCTURAL MATERIALS DIVISION SCHOLARSHIP

NASA FLORIDA SPACE GRANT CONSORTIUM

http://www.floridaspacegrant.org/

FLORIDA SPACE RESEARCH PROGRAM

NASA IDAHO SPACE GRANT CONSORTIUM

http://www.idahospacegrant.org

NASA IDAHO SPACE GRANT CONSORTIUM SCHOLARSHIP PROGRAM

NASA/MARYLAND SPACE GRANT CONSORTIUM

http://www.mdspacegrant.org/

NASA MARYLAND SPACE GRANT CONSORTIUM UNDERGRADUATE SCHOLARSHIPS

NASA'S VIRGINIA SPACE GRANT CONSORTIUM

http://www.vsgc.odu.edu/

COMMUNITY COLLEGE STEM SCHOLARSHIPS

UNDERGRADUATE STEM RESEARCH SCHOLARSHIPS

NATIONAL SOCIETY OF PROFESSIONAL ENGINEERS

http://www.nspe.org/

MAUREEN L. AND HOWARD N. BLITMAN, PE SCHOLARSHIP TO PROMOTE DIVERSITY IN ENGINEERING
• *See page 194*

PAUL H. ROBBINS HONORARY SCHOLARSHIP
• *See page 194*

PROFESSIONAL ENGINEERS IN INDUSTRY SCHOLARSHIP
• *See page 194*

NATIONAL STONE, SAND AND GRAVEL ASSOCIATION (NSSGA)

http://www.nssga.org/

BARRY K. WENDT MEMORIAL SCHOLARSHIP
• *See page 304*

NEXTSTEPU

http://www.nextstepu.com/

$1,500 STEM SCHOLARSHIP
• *See page 120*

ROCKY MOUNTAIN COAL MINING INSTITUTE

http://www.rmcmi.org/

ROCKY MOUNTAIN COAL MINING INSTITUTE SCHOLARSHIP
• *See page 211*

SCARLETT FAMILY FOUNDATION SCHOLARSHIP PROGRAM

http://www.scarlettfoundation.org/

SCHOLARSHIP FOR STUDENTS PURSUING A BUSINESS OR STEM DEGREE
• *See page 91*

SEMICONDUCTOR RESEARCH CORPORATION (SRC)

http://www.src.org/

MASTER'S SCHOLARSHIP PROGRAM
• *See page 195*

SIGMA XI, THE SCIENTIFIC RESEARCH SOCIETY

http://www.sigmaxi.org/

SIGMA XI GRANTS-IN-AID OF RESEARCH
• *See page 110*

SILICON VALLEY COMMUNITY FOUNDATION

http://www.siliconvalleycf.org

SAMSUNG@FIRST SCHOLARS
• *See page 233*

SOCIETY OF AUTOMOTIVE ENGINEERS

https://www.sae.org/participate

TMC/SAE DONALD D. DAWSON TECHNICAL SCHOLARSHIP
• *See page 160*

YANMAR/SAE SCHOLARSHIP
• *See page 305*

SOCIETY OF PLASTICS ENGINEERS FOUNDATION (SPE)

http://www.4spe.org/

FLEMING/BLASZCAK SCHOLARSHIP
• *See page 195*

GULF COAST HURRICANE SCHOLARSHIP
• *See page 196*

SOCIETY OF PLASTICS ENGINEERS SCHOLARSHIP PROGRAM
• *See page 196*

SOCIETY OF WOMEN ENGINEERS

http://societyofwomenengineers.swe.org/

AMERICAN TRANSMISSION CO. SCHOLARSHIP
• *See page 196*

ANNE SHEN SMITH ENDOWED SCHOLARSHIP
• *See page 196*

BETTY LOU BAILEY SWE REGION F SCHOLARSHIP
• *See page 197*

B.J. HARROD SCHOLARSHIP
• *See page 197*

BK KRENZER MEMORIAL REENTRY SCHOLARSHIP
• *See page 197*

CAROL STEPHENS SWE REGION F SCHOLARSHIP
• *See page 197*

CUMMINS SCHOLARSHIP
• *See page 197*

DR. IVY M. PARKER MEMORIAL SCHOLARSHIP
• *See page 197*

DOROTHY LEMKE HOWARTH MEMORIAL SCHOLARSHIP
• *See page 197*

DOROTHY P. MORRIS SCHOLARSHIP
• *See page 198*

EXELON SCHOLARSHIP
• *See page 198*

HONEYWELL SCHOLARSHIP
• *See page 198*

IBM LINDA SANFORD WOMEN'S TECHNICAL ADVANCEMENT SCHOLARSHIP
• *See page 198*

LILLIAN MOLLER GILBRETH MEMORIAL SCHOLARSHIP
• *See page 198*

MARY V. MUNGER MEMORIAL SCHOLARSHIP
• *See page 199*

OLIVE LYNN SALEMBIER MEMORIAL REENTRY SCHOLARSHIP
• *See page 199*

ROBERTA BANASZAK GLEITER ENGINEERING ENDEAVOR SCHOLARSHIP
• *See page 199*

SUSAN MISZKOWICZ SEPTEMBER 11 MEMORIAL SCHOLARSHIP
• *See page 199*

SWE BALTIMORE-WASHINGTON SECTION SCHOLARSHIP
• *See page 199*

SWE CENTRAL NEW MEXICO PIONEERS SCHOLARSHIP
• *See page 200*

SWE CENTRAL NEW MEXICO REENTRY SCHOLARSHIP
• *See page 200*

SWE MID-HUDSON SECTION SCHOLARSHIP
• *See page 200*

SWE PHOENIX SECTION SCHOLARSHIP
• *See page 200*

SWE REGION G JUDY SIMMONS MEMORIAL SCHOLARSHIP
• *See page 200*

SWE REGION H SCHOLARSHIPS
• *See page 201*

SWE REGION J SCHOLARSHIP
• *See page 201*

TE CONNECTIVITY EXCELLENCE IN ENGINEERING SCHOLARSHIP
• *See page 201*

WANDA MUNN SCHOLARSHIP
• *See page 201*

SOCIETY OF WOMEN ENGINEERS-ROCKY MOUNTAIN SECTION

http://www.swe-rms.org/

SOCIETY OF WOMEN ENGINEERS-ROCKY MOUNTAIN SECTION SCHOLARSHIP PROGRAM
• *See page 161*

STRAIGHTFORWARD MEDIA

http://www.straightforwardmedia.com/

STRAIGHTFORWARD MEDIA ENGINEERING SCHOLARSHIP
• *See page 202*

STRAIGHT NORTH

https://www.straightnorth.com/

STRAIGHT NORTH STEM SCHOLARSHIP
• *See page 92*

TAU BETA PI ASSOCIATION

https://www.tbp.org/

TAU BETA PI SCHOLARSHIP PROGRAM
• *See page 202*

TURNER CONSTRUCTION COMPANY

http://www.turnerconstruction.com/

YOUTHFORCE 2020 SCHOLARSHIP PROGRAM
• *See page 137*

UNITED NEGRO COLLEGE FUND

http://www.uncf.org/

GALACTIC UNITE BYTHEWAY SCHOLARSHIP
• *See page 202*

PROCTER & GAMBLE STEM SCHOLARSHIP
• *See page 128*

UNCF STEM SCHOLARS PROGRAM
• *See page 175*

VERMONT SPACE GRANT CONSORTIUM

http://www.cems.uvm.edu/vsgc

VERMONT SPACE GRANT CONSORTIUM
• *See page 104*

XEROX

http://www.xerox.com//

TECHNICAL MINORITY SCHOLARSHIP
• *See page 203*

MATHEMATICS

101ST AIRBORNE DIVISION ASSOCIATION

http://www.screamingeaglefoundation.org/

AL & WILLIAMARY VISTE SCHOLARSHIP
• *See page 114*

THE ACTUARIAL FOUNDATION

http://www.actuarialfoundation.org

ACTUARIAL DIVERSITY SCHOLARSHIP
• *See page 397*

ACTUARY OF TOMORROW—STUART A. ROBERTSON MEMORIAL SCHOLARSHIP
• *See page 175*

CURTIS E. HUNTINGTON MEMORIAL SCHOLARSHIP (FORMERLY THE JOHN CULVER WOODDY SCHOLARSHIP)
• *See page 263*

AMERICAN INDIAN SCIENCE AND ENGINEERING SOCIETY

http://www.aises.org/

A.T. ANDERSON MEMORIAL SCHOLARSHIP PROGRAM
• *See page 121*

AMERICAN LEGION DEPARTMENT OF MARYLAND

http://www.mdlegion.org/

AMERICAN LEGION DEPARTMENT OF MARYLAND MATH-SCIENCE SCHOLARSHIP
Scholarship for study in math or the sciences. Must be a Maryland resident and the dependent child of a veteran. Must submit essay, financial need analysis, and transcript with application. Nonrenewable award for freshman. Application available on website http://mdlegion.org.

Academic Fields/Career Goals: Mathematics; Physical Sciences.

Award: Scholarship for use in freshman, sophomore, junior, or senior years; not renewable. *Number:* 1–3. *Amount:* $500–$1500.

Eligibility Requirements: Applicant must be high school student; planning to enroll or expecting to enroll full-time at a two-year or four-year institution or university and resident of Maryland. Applicant or parent of applicant must be member of American Legion or Auxiliary. Available to U.S. citizens.

Application Requirements: Application form, essay, financial need analysis. *Deadline:* April 1.

Contact: Russell Myers, Department Adjutant
American Legion Department of Maryland
101 North Gay, Room E
Baltimore, MD 21202
Phone: 410-752-1405
E-mail: russell@mdlegion.org

AMERICAN MATHEMATICAL ASSOCIATION OF TWO YEAR COLLEGES

http://www.amatyc.org/

CHARLES MILLER SCHOLARSHIP
A grand prize of $3000 for the qualified individual with the highest total score of the student mathematics league exam. Funds to continue education at an accredited four-year institution. In the case of a tie for the grand prize, the scholarship will be evenly divided.

Academic Fields/Career Goals: Mathematics.

Award: Scholarship for use in freshman or sophomore years; not renewable. *Number:* 1. *Amount:* $3000.

Eligibility Requirements: Applicant must be enrolled or expecting to enroll full-time at a two-year institution. Available to U.S. citizens.

Application Requirements: Entry in a contest, test scores. *Deadline:* September 30.

Contact: Dr. Cheryl Cleaves, Interim Executive Director
American Mathematical Association of Two Year Colleges
AMATYC c/o Southwest Tennessee CC
5983 Macon Cove
Memphis, TN 38134
Phone: 901-333-5643
Fax: 901-333-5651
E-mail: amatyc@amatyc.org

AMERICAN SOCIETY FOR ENGINEERING EDUCATION

http://www.asee.org/

SCIENCE, MATHEMATICS, AND RESEARCH FOR TRANSFORMATION DEFENSE SCHOLARSHIP FOR SERVICE PROGRAM
• *See page 121*

ARMED FORCES COMMUNICATIONS AND ELECTRONICS ASSOCIATION, EDUCATIONAL FOUNDATION

http://www.afcea.org/site/?q=foundation/scholarships

AFCEA STEM MAJORS SCHOLARSHIPS FOR UNDERGRADUATE STUDENTS
• *See page 122*

ARMED FORCES COMMUNICATIONS AND ELECTRONICS ASSOCIATION ROTC SCHOLARSHIP PROGRAM
• *See page 151*

ARRL FOUNDATION INC.

http://www.arrl.org/

CTRI/CHRIS SEEBER, KA1GEU, MEMORIAL SCHOLARSHIP
• *See page 268*

DAN HUETTL, WZ7U, MEMORIAL SCHOLARSHIP
• *See page 298*

LOIS MANLEY, K7LMZ, AND RANDALL PITCHFORD, WW7ZZ, SCHOLARSHIP
• *See page 206*

OLD MAN INTERNATIONAL SIDEBAND SOCIETY (OMISS) SCHOLARSHIP
• *See page 259*

W1FDR SCHOLARSHIP
• *See page 122*

ASSOCIATION FOR WOMEN IN MATHEMATICS

http://www.awm-math.org/

ALICE T. SCHAFER MATHEMATICS PRIZE FOR EXCELLENCE IN MATHEMATICS BY AN UNDERGRADUATE WOMAN
One-time merit award for women undergraduates in the math field. Based on quality of performance in math courses and special programs, ability to work independently, interest in math, and performance in competitions. Must be nominated by a professor or an adviser.

Academic Fields/Career Goals: Mathematics.

Award: Prize for use in freshman, sophomore, junior, or senior years; not renewable. *Number:* 1. *Amount:* $250–$1000.

Eligibility Requirements: Applicant must be enrolled or expecting to enroll full-time at a four-year institution or university and female. Available to U.S. citizens.

Application Requirements: Application form. *Deadline:* September 15.

Contact: Steven Ferrucci, Managing Director
Phone: 401-455-4042
E-mail: steven@awm-math.org

AUTOMOTIVE WOMEN'S ALLIANCE FOUNDATION

http://awafoundation.org/index.php

AUTOMOTIVE WOMEN'S ALLIANCE FOUNDATION SCHOLARSHIPS

• See page 81

BARRY GOLDWATER SCHOLARSHIP AND EXCELLENCE IN EDUCATION FOUNDATION

https://goldwater.scholarsapply.org

BARRY M. GOLDWATER SCHOLARSHIP AND EXCELLENCE IN EDUCATION PROGRAM

• See page 123

BHW GROUP

https://thebhwgroup.com/

BHW WOMEN IN STEM SCHOLARSHIP

• See page 124

CALIFORNIA MATHEMATICS COUNCIL-SOUTH

http://www.cmc-math.org/

CALIFORNIA MATHEMATICS COUNCIL-SOUTH SECONDARY EDUCATION SCHOLARSHIPS

Scholarships for students enrolled in accredited Southern California secondary education credential programs with math as a major. Applicants must be members of the California Math Council-South.

Academic Fields/Career Goals: Mathematics.

Award: Scholarship for use in freshman, sophomore, junior, or senior years; renewable. *Number:* 2–5. *Amount:* $100–$2000.

Eligibility Requirements: Applicant must be enrolled or expecting to enroll full- or part-time at a four-year institution or university; resident of California and studying in California. Available to U.S. and non-U.S. citizens.

Application Requirements: Application form, essay, recommendations or references, transcript. *Deadline:* January 31.

Contact: Dr. Sid Kolpas, Professor of Mathematics
Phone: 818-240-1000 Ext. 5378
E-mail: sjkolpas@sprintmail.com

CARDS AGAINST HUMANITY

https://cardsagainsthumanity.com/

SCIENCE AMBASSADOR SCHOLARSHIP

• See page 124

CLUTCH PREP

http://www.clutchprep.com

CLUTCH PREP STEM SCHOLARSHIP

• See page 285

THE DALLAS FOUNDATION

http://www.dallasfoundation.org/

WHITLEY PLACE SCHOLARSHIP

• See page 133

DAVIDSON INSTITUTE FOR TALENT DEVELOPMENT

http://www.davidsongifted.org/

DAVIDSON FELLOWS SCHOLARSHIP PROGRAM

• See page 124

DISTIL NETWORKS

http://www.distilnetworks.com

WOMEN FORWARD IN TECHNOLOGY SCHOLARSHIP PROGRAM

• See page 124

DIVERSITYCOMM, INC.

http://www.diversitycomm.net/

DIVERSITY IN STEAM MAGAZINE SCHOLARSHIP

• See page 83

FOUNDATION FOR SCIENCE AND DISABILITY

http://stemd.org/

GRANTS FOR DISABLED GRADUATE STUDENTS IN THE SCIENCES

• See page 106

GREATER KANAWHA VALLEY FOUNDATION

http://www.tgkvf.org/

MATH AND SCIENCE SCHOLARSHIP

• See page 171

GREAT MINDS IN STEM

http://www.greatmindsinstem.org

HENAAC SCHOLARSHIP PROGRAM

• See page 115

HAWAIIAN LODGE, F&AM

http://www.hawaiianlodgefreemasons.org

HAWAIIAN LODGE SCHOLARSHIPS

• See page 86

INFINITY DENTAL WEB

http://www.infinitydentalweb.com

INTERNET MARKETING SCHOLARSHIP

• See page 429

LABROOTS INC.
http://www.LabRoots.com

LABROOTS STEM SCHOLARSHIP
• *See page 116*

MICHIGAN COUNCIL OF TEACHERS OF MATHEMATICS
http://www.mictm.org/

MIRIAM SCHAEFER SCHOLARSHIP
A scholarship of $2500 is given to a senior or a junior enrolled full-time in undergraduate degree with mathematics specialty. Applicants should be a resident of Michigan but citizenship does not matter.

Academic Fields/Career Goals: Mathematics.

Award: Scholarship for use in junior or senior years; not renewable. *Number:* 3–5. *Amount:* $2500.

Eligibility Requirements: Applicant must be enrolled or expecting to enroll full-time at a four-year institution or university and resident of Michigan. Applicant must have 3.0 GPA or higher. Available to U.S. and non-U.S. citizens.

Application Requirements: Application form, essay. *Deadline:* May 1.

Contact: Mr. Chris Berry, Executive Director
Michigan Council of Teachers of Mathematics
4767 Stadler Road
Monroe, MI 48162
Phone: 734-477-0421
Fax: 734-241-4128
E-mail: info@mictm.org

NASA FLORIDA SPACE GRANT CONSORTIUM
http://www.floridaspacegrant.org/

FLORIDA SPACE RESEARCH PROGRAM
• *See page 156*

NASA IDAHO SPACE GRANT CONSORTIUM
http://www.idahospacegrant.org

NASA IDAHO SPACE GRANT CONSORTIUM SCHOLARSHIP PROGRAM
• *See page 126*

NASA/MARYLAND SPACE GRANT CONSORTIUM
http://www.mdspacegrant.org/

NASA MARYLAND SPACE GRANT CONSORTIUM UNDERGRADUATE SCHOLARSHIPS
• *See page 156*

NASA MINNESOTA SPACE GRANT CONSORTIUM
https://www.mnspacegrant.org/

MINNESOTA SPACE GRANT CONSORTIUM SCHOLARSHIP PROGRAM
• *See page 156*

NASA MONTANA SPACE GRANT CONSORTIUM
http://www.spacegrant.montana.edu/

MONTANA SPACE GRANT SCHOLARSHIP PROGRAM
• *See page 156*

NASA RHODE ISLAND SPACE GRANT CONSORTIUM
http://brown/initiatives/ri-space-grant

NASA RHODE ISLAND SPACE GRANT CONSORTIUM OUTREACH SCHOLARSHIP FOR UNDERGRADUATE STUDENTS
• *See page 303*

NASA RISGC SCIENCE EN ESPANOL SCHOLARSHIP FOR UNDERGRADUATE STUDENTS
• *See page 157*

NASA'S VIRGINIA SPACE GRANT CONSORTIUM
http://www.vsgc.odu.edu/

COMMUNITY COLLEGE STEM SCHOLARSHIPS
• *See page 126*

UNDERGRADUATE STEM RESEARCH SCHOLARSHIPS
• *See page 127*

NATIONAL COUNCIL OF TEACHERS OF MATHEMATICS
http://www.nctm.org/

PROSPECTIVE SECONDARY TEACHER COURSE WORK SCHOLARSHIPS
• *See page 273*

NEVADA NASA SPACE GRANT CONSORTIUM
https://nasa.epscorspo.nevada.edu/

NATIONAL SPACE GRANT CONSORTIUM SCHOLARSHIPS
• *See page 127*

NEXTSTEPU
http://www.nextstepu.com/

$1,500 STEM SCHOLARSHIP
• *See page 120*

OREGON STUDENT ASSISTANCE COMMISSION
https://oregonstudentaid.gov/

ANDY AITKENHEAD SCHOLARSHIP
• *See page 127*

PIRATE'S ALLEY FAULKNER SOCIETY

http://www.wordsandmusic.org/

WILLIAM FAULKNER-WILLIAM WISDOM CREATIVE WRITING COMPETITION

Prizes for unpublished manuscripts written in English. One prize awarded in each category: $7500, novel; $2500, novella; $2000, book-length narrative non-fiction; $1,500, novel-in-progress; $1500, short story; $750, essay; $750, poem; $750 high school short story-student author, $250 sponsoring teacher. Manuscripts must be submitted by e-mail; entry forms and accompanying entry fee ranging from $10 for high school category to $40 for novel must be submitted hard copy by snail mail.

Academic Fields/Career Goals: Mathematics.

Award: Prize for use in freshman, sophomore, junior, senior, graduate, or postgraduate years; not renewable. *Number:* 8. *Amount:* $250–$7500.

Eligibility Requirements: Applicant must be age 15-80; enrolled or expecting to enroll full- or part-time at a two-year or four-year institution or university and must have an interest in English language or writing. Applicant or parent of applicant must have employment or volunteer experience in human services. Available to U.S. and non-U.S. citizens.

Application Requirements: Application form. *Fee:* $25. *Deadline:* May 1.

Contact: Ms. Rosemary James, Director
Pirate's Alley Faulkner Society
624 Pirate's Alley
New Orleans, LA 70116
Phone: 504-586-1609
E-mail: faulkhouse@aol.com

SALT RIVER PROJECT (SRP)

http://www.srpnet.com/

NAVAJO GENERATING STATION NAVAJO SCHOLARSHIP
• *See page 324*

SCARLETT FAMILY FOUNDATION SCHOLARSHIP PROGRAM

http://www.scarlettfoundation.org/

SCHOLARSHIP FOR STUDENTS PURSUING A BUSINESS OR STEM DEGREE
• *See page 91*

SIGMA XI, THE SCIENTIFIC RESEARCH SOCIETY

http://www.sigmaxi.org/

SIGMA XI GRANTS-IN-AID OF RESEARCH
• *See page 110*

SILICON VALLEY COMMUNITY FOUNDATION

http://www.siliconvalleycf.org

SAMSUNG@FIRST SCHOLARS
• *See page 233*

STRAIGHT NORTH

https://www.straightnorth.com/

STRAIGHT NORTH STEM SCHOLARSHIP
• *See page 92*

TKE EDUCATIONAL FOUNDATION

http://www.tke.org/

ERIC D. DUNNING SCHOLARSHIP
• *See page 235*

FRANCIS J. FLYNN MEMORIAL SCHOLARSHIP
• *See page 277*

UNITED NEGRO COLLEGE FUND

http://www.uncf.org/

BASF/ALFRED CHISHOLM ENDOWED MEMORIAL SCHOLARSHIP
• *See page 93*

DAVIS SCHOLARSHIP FOR WOMEN IN STEM
• *See page 202*

GALACTIC UNITE BYTHEWAY SCHOLARSHIP
• *See page 202*

KIA MOTORS AMERICA STEM/SUSTAINABILITY SCHOLARSHIP
• *See page 175*

ORACLE COMMUNITY IMPACT SCHOLARSHIP
• *See page 235*

ORACLE CORPORATE SCHOLARS PROGRAM
• *See page 184*

PROCTER & GAMBLE STEM SCHOLARSHIP
• *See page 128*

UNCF STEM SCHOLARS PROGRAM
• *See page 175*

VOYA SCHOLARS
• *See page 94*

UNIVERSITIES SPACE RESEARCH ASSOCIATION

http://www.usra.edu/

UNIVERSITIES SPACE RESEARCH ASSOCIATION SCHOLARSHIP AWARD PROGRAM
• *See page 128*

VERMONT SPACE GRANT CONSORTIUM

http://www.cems.uvm.edu/vsgc

VERMONT SPACE GRANT CONSORTIUM
• *See page 104*

WISCONSIN MATHEMATICS EDUCATION FOUNDATION

http://wmefonline.org/

ARNE ENGEBRETSEN WISCONSIN MATHEMATICS COUNCIL SCHOLARSHIP
• *See page 279*

ETHEL A. NEIJAHR WISCONSIN MATHEMATICS COUNCIL SCHOLARSHIP
• *See page 279*

SISTER MARY PETRONIA VAN STRATEN WISCONSIN MATHEMATICS COUNCIL SCHOLARSHIP
• *See page 279*

WOMEN IN AEROSPACE FOUNDATION

http://www.womeninaerospace.org/index.html

WIA FOUNDATION SCHOLARSHIP
• *See page 162*

MECHANICAL ENGINEERING

AACE INTERNATIONAL

http://www.aacei.org/

AACE INTERNATIONAL COMPETITIVE SCHOLARSHIP
• *See page 130*

AHS INTERNATIONAL—THE VERTICAL FLIGHT TECHNICAL SOCIETY

http://www.vtol.org/

VERTICAL FLIGHT FOUNDATION SCHOLARSHIP
• *See page 148*

AIST FOUNDATION

http://www.aistfoundation.org/

AISI/AIST FOUNDATION PREMIER SCHOLARSHIP
• *See page 280*

AIST WILLIAM E. SCHWABE MEMORIAL SCHOLARSHIP
• *See page 280*

ASSOCIATION FOR IRON AND STEEL TECHNOLOGY BENJAMIN F. FAIRLESS SCHOLARSHIP (AIME)
• *See page 186*

ASSOCIATION FOR IRON AND STEEL TECHNOLOGY RONALD E. LINCOLN SCHOLARSHIP
• *See page 280*

ASSOCIATION FOR IRON AND STEEL TECHNOLOGY WILLY KORF MEMORIAL SCHOLARSHIP
• *See page 187*

STEEL ENGINEERING EDUCATION LINK (STEEL) SCHOLARSHIPS
• *See page 280*

AMERICAN CHEMICAL SOCIETY, RUBBER DIVISION

http://www.rubber.org/

AMERICAN CHEMICAL SOCIETY, RUBBER DIVISION UNDERGRADUATE SCHOLARSHIP
• *See page 120*

AMERICAN COUNCIL OF ENGINEERING COMPANIES OF PENNSYLVANIA (ACEC/PA)

http://www.acecpa.org/

ERIC J. GENNUSO AND LEROY D. (BUD) LOY, JR. SCHOLARSHIP PROGRAM
• *See page 187*

AMERICAN INDIAN SCIENCE AND ENGINEERING SOCIETY

http://www.aises.org/

A.T. ANDERSON MEMORIAL SCHOLARSHIP PROGRAM
• *See page 121*

AMERICAN INSTITUTE OF AERONAUTICS AND ASTRONAUTICS

http://www.aiaafoundation.org/

AIAA FOUNDATION UNDERGRADUATE SCHOLARSHIPS
• *See page 121*

LEATRICE GREGORY PENDRAY SCHOLARSHIP
• *See page 121*

AMERICAN PUBLIC POWER ASSOCIATION

https://www.publicpower.org/grants-scholarships

DEED EDUCATIONAL SCHOLARSHIP
• *See page 190*

DEED STUDENT INTERNSHIP
• *See page 190*

DEED STUDENT RESEARCH GRANTS
• *See page 204*

DEED TECHNICAL DESIGN PROJECT
• *See page 191*

AMERICAN PUBLIC TRANSPORTATION FOUNDATION

http://www.apta.com/

LOUIS T. KLAUDER SCHOLARSHIP
• *See page 281*

TRANSIT HALL OF FAME SCHOLARSHIP AWARD PROGRAM
• *See page 204*

AMERICAN RAILWAY ENGINEERING AND MAINTENANCE OF WAY ASSOCIATION

http://www.aremafoundation.org/

AREMA GRADUATE AND UNDERGRADUATE SCHOLARSHIPS
• *See page 204*

AMERICAN SOCIETY OF CERTIFIED ENGINEERING TECHNICIANS

http://www.ascet.org/

KURT H. AND DONNA M. SCHULER SMALL GRANT
• *See page 205*

AMERICAN SOCIETY OF HEATING, REFRIGERATING, AND AIR CONDITIONING ENGINEERS, INC.

http://www.ashrae.org/

ALWIN B. NEWTON SCHOLARSHIP
• *See page 281*

ASHRAE REGION III BOGGARM SETTY SCHOLARSHIP
• *See page 191*

FRANK M. CODA SCHOLARSHIP
• *See page 282*

LYNN G. BELLENGER SCHOLARSHIP
• *See page 282*

REUBEN TRANE SCHOLARSHIP
• *See page 282*

AMERICAN SOCIETY OF MECHANICAL ENGINEERS AUXILIARY INC.

http://www.asme.org/

AGNES MALAKATE KEZIOS SCHOLARSHIP
Scholarship to college juniors for use in final year at a four year college. Must be majoring in mechanical engineering, be member of ASME (if available), and exhibit leadership values. Must be U.S. citizen enrolled in a college/university in the United States that has ABET accreditation. Scholarship value is $3000 and the number of awards granted varies.

Academic Fields/Career Goals: Mechanical Engineering.

Award: Scholarship for use in junior or senior years; not renewable. *Number:* 1–2. *Amount:* $3000.

Eligibility Requirements: Applicant must be enrolled or expecting to enroll full-time at a four-year institution or university. Available to U.S. citizens.

Application Requirements: Application form, essay, financial need analysis. *Deadline:* March 1.

Contact: Saraswati Sahay, Undergraduate Scholarships
American Society of Mechanical Engineers Auxiliary Inc.
170 East Opal Drive
Glastonbury, CT 06033
Phone: 860-659-3828
E-mail: uma.sahay@gmail.com

ALLEN J. BALDWIN SCHOLARSHIP
Scholarship available to college juniors for use in final year at a four year college. Must be majoring in mechanical engineering, be member of ASME (if available), and exhibit leadership values. Must be U.S. citizen enrolled in a college/university in the United States that has ABET accreditation. Scholarship value is $2000 and the number of awards granted varies.

Academic Fields/Career Goals: Mechanical Engineering.

Award: Scholarship for use in junior year; not renewable. *Number:* 1–2. *Amount:* $3000.

Eligibility Requirements: Applicant must be enrolled or expecting to enroll full-time at a four-year institution or university. Available to U.S. citizens.

Application Requirements: Application form, driver's license, financial need analysis, recommendations or references, self-addressed stamped envelope with application, transcript. *Deadline:* March 15.

Contact: Saraswati Sahay, Undergraduate Scholarships
American Society of Mechanical Engineers Auxiliary Inc.
170 East Opal Drive
Glastonbury, CT 06033
Phone: 860-659-3828
E-mail: uma.sahay@gmail.com

BERNA LOU CARTWRIGHT SCHOLARSHIP
Scholarship for college juniors for use in final year at a four year college. Must be majoring in mechanical engineering. Must be a U.S. citizen, enrolled in a college/university in the United States that has ABET accreditation. Number of awards varies.

Academic Fields/Career Goals: Mechanical Engineering.

Award: Scholarship for use in junior year; not renewable. *Number:* 1–2. *Amount:* $3000.

Eligibility Requirements: Applicant must be enrolled or expecting to enroll full-time at a four-year institution or university and must have an interest in leadership. Applicant or parent of applicant must be member of Other Student Academic Clubs. Available to U.S. citizens.

Application Requirements: Application form, financial need analysis, recommendations or references, resume, transcript. *Deadline:* March 15.

Contact: Saraswati Sahay, Undergraduate Scholarships
American Society of Mechanical Engineers Auxiliary Inc.
170 East Opal Drive
Glastonbury, CT 06033
Phone: 860-659-3828
E-mail: uma.sahay@gmail.com

SYLVIA W. FARNY SCHOLARSHIP
One-time awards of $2000 to ASME student members for the final year of undergraduate study in mechanical engineering. Must be a U.S. citizen, enrolled in a college/university in the United States that has ABET accreditation. Number of scholarships granted varies.

Academic Fields/Career Goals: Mechanical Engineering.

Award: Scholarship for use in junior year; not renewable. *Number:* 1–2. *Amount:* $3000.

Eligibility Requirements: Applicant must be enrolled or expecting to enroll full-time at a four-year institution or university. Applicant or parent of applicant must be member of Other Student Academic Clubs. Available to U.S. citizens.

Application Requirements: Application form, recommendations or references, transcript. *Deadline:* March 15.

Contact: Saraswati Sahay, Undergraduate Scholarships
American Society of Mechanical Engineers Auxiliary Inc.
170 East Opal Drive
Glastonbury, CT 06033
Phone: 860-659-3828
E-mail: uma.sahay@gmail.com

AMERICAN SOCIETY OF NAVAL ENGINEERS

http://www.navalengineers.org/

AMERICAN SOCIETY OF NAVAL ENGINEERS SCHOLARSHIP
• *See page 122*

AMERICAN WELDING SOCIETY

http://www.aws.org/

PAST PRESIDENTS' SCHOLARSHIP
• *See page 312*

ARRL FOUNDATION INC.

http://www.arrl.org/

ALFRED E. FRIEND JR, W4CF, MEMORIAL SCHOLARSHIP
• *See page 191*

GARY WAGNER, K3OMI, SCHOLARSHIP
• See page 191

W1FDR SCHOLARSHIP
• See page 122

ASSOCIATION OF STATE DAM SAFETY OFFICIALS (ASDSO)

http://www.DamSafety.org

ASSOCIATION OF STATE DAM SAFETY OFFICIALS (ASDSO) SENIOR UNDERGRADUATE SCHOLARSHIP
• See page 168

ASTRONAUT SCHOLARSHIP FOUNDATION

http://www.astronautscholarship.org/

ASTRONAUT SCHOLARSHIP FOUNDATION
• See page 123

AUTOMOTIVE AFTERMARKET SCHOLARSHIPS

http://www.automotivescholarships.com/

AUTOMOTIVE AFTERMARKET SCHOLARSHIPS
• See page 177

AUTOMOTIVE WOMEN'S ALLIANCE FOUNDATION

http://awafoundation.org/index.php

AUTOMOTIVE WOMEN'S ALLIANCE FOUNDATION SCHOLARSHIPS
• See page 81

BARRY GOLDWATER SCHOLARSHIP AND EXCELLENCE IN EDUCATION FOUNDATION

https://goldwater.scholarsapply.org

BARRY M. GOLDWATER SCHOLARSHIP AND EXCELLENCE IN EDUCATION PROGRAM
• See page 123

BHW GROUP

https://thebhwgroup.com/

BHW WOMEN IN STEM SCHOLARSHIP
• See page 124

BRASKEM ODEBRECHT

http://www.odebrechtaward.com

ODEBRECHT AWARD FOR SUSTAINABLE DEVELOPMENT
• See page 131

BROWN AND CALDWELL

http://www.brownandcaldwell.com

ECKENFELDER SCHOLARSHIP
• See page 169

MINORITY SCHOLARSHIP PROGRAM
• See page 169

CARDS AGAINST HUMANITY

https://cardsagainsthumanity.com/

SCIENCE AMBASSADOR SCHOLARSHIP
• See page 124

CENTER FOR ARCHITECTURE

http://www.centerforarchitecture.org

CENTER FOR ARCHITECTURE DESIGN SCHOLARSHIP
• See page 132

CONNECTICUT BUILDING CONGRESS SCHOLARSHIP FUND, INC.

http://www.cbc-ct.org

CBC SCHOLARSHIP FUND
• See page 132

THE DALLAS FOUNDATION

http://www.dallasfoundation.org/

WHITLEY PLACE SCHOLARSHIP
• See page 133

DISTIL NETWORKS

http://www.distilnetworks.com

WOMEN FORWARD IN TECHNOLOGY SCHOLARSHIP PROGRAM
• See page 124

DIVERSITYCOMM, INC.

http://www.diversitycomm.net/

DIVERSITY IN STEAM MAGAZINE SCHOLARSHIP
• See page 83

THE ELECTROCHEMICAL SOCIETY

http://www.electrochem.org/

STUDENT RESEARCH AWARDS OF THE BATTERY DIVISION OF THE ELECTROCHEMICAL SOCIETY INC.
• See page 125

FABRICATORS AND MANUFACTURERS ASSOCIATION FOUNDATION

http://www.nutsandboltsfoundation.org/scholarships/

COLLEGE AND TRADE/TECHNICAL SCHOOL SCHOLARSHIPS
• See page 154

FOUNDATION FOR SCIENCE AND DISABILITY

http://stemd.org/

GRANTS FOR DISABLED GRADUATE STUDENTS IN THE SCIENCES
• *See page 106*

GREATER KANAWHA VALLEY FOUNDATION

http://www.tgkvf.org/

STEVEN ENGINEERING SCHOLARSHIP
• *See page 192*

GREAT MINDS IN STEM

http://www.greatmindsinstem.org

HENAAC SCHOLARSHIP PROGRAM
• *See page 115*

HAWAIIAN LODGE, F&AM

http://www.hawaiianlodgefreemasons.org

HAWAIIAN LODGE SCHOLARSHIPS
• *See page 86*

INDEPENDENT LABORATORIES INSTITUTE SCHOLARSHIP ALLIANCE

http://www.acil.org/

INDEPENDENT LABORATORIES INSTITUTE SCHOLARSHIP ALLIANCE
• *See page 171*

INTERNATIONAL SOCIETY FOR OPTICAL ENGINEERING-SPIE

http://www.spie.org/scholarships

SPIE EDUCATIONAL SCHOLARSHIPS IN OPTICAL SCIENCE AND ENGINEERING
• *See page 126*

JORGE MAS CANOSA FREEDOM FOUNDATION

http://masscholarships.org/

MAS FAMILY SCHOLARSHIP AWARD
• *See page 181*

KENTUCKY ENERGY AND ENVIRONMENT CABINET

http://dep.ky.gov

ENVIRONMENTAL PROTECTION SCHOLARSHIP
• *See page 172*

LABROOTS INC.

http://www.LabRoots.com

LABROOTS STEM SCHOLARSHIP
• *See page 116*

LOS ANGELES COUNCIL OF BLACK PROFESSIONAL ENGINEERS

http://www.lablackengineers.org/

AL-BEN SCHOLARSHIP FOR ACADEMIC INCENTIVE
• *See page 193*

AL-BEN SCHOLARSHIP FOR PROFESSIONAL MERIT
• *See page 193*

AL-BEN SCHOLARSHIP FOR SCHOLASTIC ACHIEVEMENT
• *See page 193*

MANUFACTURERS ASSOCIATION OF MAINE

http://www.mainemfg.com/

MAINE MANUFACTURING CAREER AND TRAINING FOUNDATION SCHOLARSHIP
• *See page 156*

MINERALS, METALS, AND MATERIALS SOCIETY (TMS)

http://www.tms.org/

KAUFMAN CALPHAD SCHOLARSHIP
• *See page 302*

NASA FLORIDA SPACE GRANT CONSORTIUM

http://www.floridaspacegrant.org/

FLORIDA SPACE RESEARCH PROGRAM
• *See page 156*

NASA IDAHO SPACE GRANT CONSORTIUM

http://www.idahospacegrant.org

NASA IDAHO SPACE GRANT CONSORTIUM SCHOLARSHIP PROGRAM
• *See page 126*

NASA MINNESOTA SPACE GRANT CONSORTIUM

https://www.mnspacegrant.org/

MINNESOTA SPACE GRANT CONSORTIUM SCHOLARSHIP PROGRAM
• *See page 156*

NASA MONTANA SPACE GRANT CONSORTIUM

http://www.spacegrant.montana.edu/

MONTANA SPACE GRANT SCHOLARSHIP PROGRAM
• *See page 156*

NASA'S VIRGINIA SPACE GRANT CONSORTIUM

http://www.vsgc.odu.edu/

COMMUNITY COLLEGE STEM SCHOLARSHIPS
• *See page 126*

UNDERGRADUATE STEM RESEARCH SCHOLARSHIPS
• *See page 127*

NATIONAL ASSOCIATION OF WOMEN IN CONSTRUCTION

http://www.nawic.org/

NAWIC UNDERGRADUATE SCHOLARSHIPS
• *See page 135*

NATIONAL BOARD OF BOILER AND PRESSURE VESSEL INSPECTORS

http://www.nationalboard.org/

NATIONAL BOARD TECHNICAL SCHOLARSHIP
• *See page 194*

NATIONAL SOCIETY OF PROFESSIONAL ENGINEERS

http://www.nspe.org/

MAUREEN L. AND HOWARD N. BLITMAN, PE SCHOLARSHIP TO PROMOTE DIVERSITY IN ENGINEERING
• *See page 194*

PAUL H. ROBBINS HONORARY SCHOLARSHIP
• *See page 194*

PROFESSIONAL ENGINEERS IN INDUSTRY SCHOLARSHIP
• *See page 194*

NEVADA NASA SPACE GRANT CONSORTIUM

https://nasa.epscorspo.nevada.edu/

NATIONAL SPACE GRANT CONSORTIUM SCHOLARSHIPS
• *See page 127*

NEXTSTEPU

http://www.nextstepu.com/

$1,500 STEM SCHOLARSHIP
• *See page 120*

OREGON STUDENT ASSISTANCE COMMISSION

https://oregonstudentaid.gov/

AMERICAN COUNCIL OF ENGINEERING COMPANIES OF OREGON SCHOLARSHIP
• *See page 210*

FRED FIELDS SCHOLARSHIP
• *See page 182*

SOCIETY OF AMERICAN MILITARY ENGINEERS PORTLAND POST SCHOLARSHIP
• *See page 195*

PACIFIC GAS AND ELECTRIC COMPANY

http://www.scholarshipamerica.org

PG&E BETTER TOGETHER STEM SCHOLARSHIP PROGRAM
• *See page 233*

PLAN NEW HAMPSHIRE

http://www.plannh.org

PLAN NEW HAMPSHIRE SCHOLARSHIP AND FELLOWSHIP PROGRAM
• *See page 129*

PLUMBING-HEATING-COOLING CONTRACTORS EDUCATION FOUNDATION

http://www.phccfoundation.org/scholarships

DELTA FAUCET COMPANY SCHOLARSHIP PROGRAM
• *See page 182*

PHCC EDUCATIONAL FOUNDATION NEED-BASED SCHOLARSHIP
• *See page 182*

PHCC EDUCATIONAL FOUNDATION SCHOLARSHIP PROGRAM
• *See page 182*

PROFESSIONAL CONSTRUCTION ESTIMATORS ASSOCIATION

http://www.pcea.org/

TED G. WILSON MEMORIAL SCHOLARSHIP FOUNDATION
• *See page 211*

ROBERT H. MOLLOHAN FAMILY CHARITABLE FOUNDATION, INC.

http://www.mollohanfoundation.org/

HIGH TECHNOLOGY SCHOLARS PROGRAM
• *See page 173*

SCARLETT FAMILY FOUNDATION SCHOLARSHIP PROGRAM

http://www.scarlettfoundation.org/

SCHOLARSHIP FOR STUDENTS PURSUING A BUSINESS OR STEM DEGREE
• *See page 91*

SIGMA XI, THE SCIENTIFIC RESEARCH SOCIETY

http://www.sigmaxi.org/

SIGMA XI GRANTS-IN-AID OF RESEARCH
• *See page 110*

SILICON VALLEY COMMUNITY FOUNDATION

http://www.siliconvalleycf.org

SAMSUNG@FIRST SCHOLARS
• See page 233

SOCIETY OF AUTOMOTIVE ENGINEERS

https://www.sae.org/participate

BMW/SAE ENGINEERING SCHOLARSHIP
• See page 160

EDWARD D. HENDRICKSON/SAE ENGINEERING SCHOLARSHIP
• See page 160

RALPH K. HILLQUIST HONORARY SAE SCHOLARSHIP
• See page 305

TMC/SAE DONALD D. DAWSON TECHNICAL SCHOLARSHIP
• See page 160

YANMAR/SAE SCHOLARSHIP
• See page 305

SOCIETY OF MANUFACTURING ENGINEERS EDUCATION FOUNDATION

http://www.smeef.org/

CHAPTER 198-DOWNRIVER DETROIT SCHOLARSHIP
• See page 325

CHAPTER 4-LAWRENCE A. WACKER MEMORIAL SCHOLARSHIP
• See page 326

CHAPTER 67-PHOENIX SCHOLARSHIP
• See page 326

FORT WAYNE CHAPTER 56 SCHOLARSHIP
• See page 328

MYRTLE AND EARL WALKER SCHOLARSHIP FUND
• See page 305

NORTH CENTRAL REGION 9 SCHOLARSHIP
• See page 328

WICHITA CHAPTER 52 SCHOLARSHIP
• See page 328

WILLIAM E. WEISEL SCHOLARSHIP FUND
• See page 287

SOCIETY OF PLASTICS ENGINEERS FOUNDATION (SPE)

http://www.4spe.org/

GULF COAST HURRICANE SCHOLARSHIP
• See page 196

SOCIETY OF WOMEN ENGINEERS

http://societyofwomenengineers.swe.org/

ADA I. PRESSMAN MEMORIAL SCHOLARSHIP
• See page 196

AMERICAN TRANSMISSION CO. SCHOLARSHIP
• See page 196

ANNE MAUREEN WHITNEY BARROW MEMORIAL SCHOLARSHIP
• See page 196

ANNE SHEN SMITH ENDOWED SCHOLARSHIP
• See page 196

BETTY LOU BAILEY SWE REGION F SCHOLARSHIP
• See page 197

B.J. HARROD SCHOLARSHIP
• See page 197

BK KRENZER MEMORIAL REENTRY SCHOLARSHIP
• See page 197

CAROL STEPHENS SWE REGION F SCHOLARSHIP
• See page 197

CUMMINS SCHOLARSHIP
• See page 197

DR. IVY M. PARKER MEMORIAL SCHOLARSHIP
• See page 197

DOROTHY LEMKE HOWARTH MEMORIAL SCHOLARSHIP
• See page 197

DOROTHY P. MORRIS SCHOLARSHIP
• See page 198

DUPONT COMPANY SCHOLARSHIP
• See page 198

EXELON SCHOLARSHIP
• See page 198

GENERAL ELECTRIC WOMEN'S NETWORK SCHOLARSHIP
• See page 212

HONEYWELL SCHOLARSHIP
• See page 198

IBM LINDA SANFORD WOMEN'S TECHNICAL ADVANCEMENT SCHOLARSHIP
• See page 198

INVENERGY WOMEN'S NETWORK SCHOLARSHIP
• See page 212

LIEBHERR MINING SCHOLARSHIP
• See page 234

LILLIAN MOLLER GILBRETH MEMORIAL SCHOLARSHIP
• See page 198

MARY V. MUNGER MEMORIAL SCHOLARSHIP
• See page 199

OLIVE LYNN SALEMBIER MEMORIAL REENTRY SCHOLARSHIP
• See page 199

ROBERTA BANASZAK GLEITER ENGINEERING ENDEAVOR SCHOLARSHIP
• *See page 199*

SUSAN MISZKOWICZ SEPTEMBER 11 MEMORIAL SCHOLARSHIP
• *See page 199*

SWE BALTIMORE-WASHINGTON SECTION SCHOLARSHIP
• *See page 199*

SWE CENTRAL NEW MEXICO PIONEERS SCHOLARSHIP
• *See page 200*

SWE CENTRAL NEW MEXICO REENTRY SCHOLARSHIP
• *See page 200*

SWE MID-HUDSON SECTION SCHOLARSHIP.
• *See page 200*

SWE PHOENIX SECTION SCHOLARSHIP
• *See page 200*

SWE REGION E SCHOLARSHIP
• *See page 200*

SWE REGION H SCHOLARSHIPS
• *See page 201*

SWE REGION J SCHOLARSHIP
• *See page 201*

TE CONNECTIVITY EXCELLENCE IN ENGINEERING SCHOLARSHIP
• *See page 201*

TURNER CONSTRUCTION SCHOLARSHIP
• *See page 201*

VIRGINIA COUNTS/BETTY IRISH SWE FOR LIFE SCHOLARSHIP

$1000 scholarship for women pursuing ABET-accredited Baccalaureate or graduate programs in preparation for careers in mechanical engineering in the United States and Mexico. Must be a U.S. citizen and have a minimum 3.0 GPA. SWE membership required. Preference given to applicants from Arizona or attending an Arizona school.

Academic Fields/Career Goals: Mechanical Engineering.

Award: Scholarship for use in sophomore, junior, senior, or graduate years; not renewable. *Number:* 1. *Amount:* $1000.

Eligibility Requirements: Applicant must be enrolled or expecting to enroll full-time at a four-year institution or university and female. Applicant or parent of applicant must be member of Society of Women Engineers. Applicant must have 3.0 GPA or higher. Available to U.S. citizens.

Application Requirements: Application form. *Deadline:* February 15.

Contact: Scholarship Committee
    Phone: 800-793-4636
    E-mail: scholarships@swe.org

WANDA MUNN SCHOLARSHIP.
• *See page 201*

SOCIETY OF WOMEN ENGINEERS-ROCKY MOUNTAIN SECTION

http://www.swe-rms.org/

SOCIETY OF WOMEN ENGINEERS-ROCKY MOUNTAIN SECTION SCHOLARSHIP PROGRAM
• *See page 161*

SONS OF NORWAY FOUNDATION

http://www.sonsofnorway.com/foundation

NANCY LORRAINE JENSEN MEMORIAL SCHOLARSHIP
• *See page 202*

SPECIALTY EQUIPMENT MARKET ASSOCIATION

http://www.sema.org/

SEMA MEMORIAL SCHOLARSHIP FUND
• *See page 92*

STRAIGHTFORWARD MEDIA

http://www.straightforwardmedia.com/

STRAIGHTFORWARD MEDIA ENGINEERING SCHOLARSHIP
• *See page 202*

STRAIGHT NORTH

https://www.straightnorth.com/

STRAIGHT NORTH STEM SCHOLARSHIP
• *See page 92*

TAU BETA PI ASSOCIATION

https://www.tbp.org/

TAU BETA PI SCHOLARSHIP PROGRAM
• *See page 202*

TIMOTION

http://www.timotion.com/

TIMOTION ENGINEERING AND EXCELLENCE SCHOLARSHIP
• *See page 213*

TURNER CONSTRUCTION COMPANY

http://www.turnerconstruction.com/

YOUTHFORCE 2020 SCHOLARSHIP PROGRAM
• *See page 137*

UNITED NEGRO COLLEGE FUND

http://www.uncf.org/

DAVIS SCHOLARSHIP FOR WOMEN IN STEM
• *See page 202*

GALACTIC UNITE BYTHEWAY SCHOLARSHIP
• *See page 202*

PROCTER & GAMBLE STEM SCHOLARSHIP
• See page 128

SUEZ CORPORATE SCHOLARS PROGRAM
• See page 94

UNCF STEM SCHOLARS PROGRAM
• See page 175

WILLIAM WRIGLEY FOUNDATION SCHOLARSHIP
• See page 95

UNIVERSITIES SPACE RESEARCH ASSOCIATION

http://www.usra.edu/

UNIVERSITIES SPACE RESEARCH ASSOCIATION SCHOLARSHIP AWARD PROGRAM
• See page 128

VERMONT SPACE GRANT CONSORTIUM

http://www.cems.uvm.edu/vsgc

VERMONT SPACE GRANT CONSORTIUM
• See page 104

WOMEN IN AVIATION, INTERNATIONAL

http://www.wai.org/

DELTA AIR LINES ENGINEERING SCHOLARSHIP
• See page 163

XEROX

http://www.xerox.com/

TECHNICAL MINORITY SCHOLARSHIP
• See page 203

METEOROLOGY/ ATMOSPHERIC SCIENCE

AIR & WASTE MANAGEMENT ASSOCIATION, ALLEGHENY MOUNTAIN SECTION

http://www.ams-awma.org/

ALLEGHENY MOUNTAIN SECTION AIR & WASTE MANAGEMENT ASSOCIATION SCHOLARSHIP
• See page 336

AMERICAN INDIAN SCIENCE AND ENGINEERING SOCIETY

http://www.aises.org/

A.T. ANDERSON MEMORIAL SCHOLARSHIP PROGRAM
• See page 121

AMERICAN METEOROLOGICAL SOCIETY

http://www.ametsoc.org/

AMERICAN METEOROLOGICAL SOCIETY MINORITY SCHOLARSHIPS

Two-year scholarship of $3,000 per year for minority students entering their freshman year of college. Must plan to pursue careers in the atmospheric and related oceanic and hydrologic sciences. Must be U.S. citizen or permanent resident to apply.

Academic Fields/Career Goals: Meteorology/Atmospheric Science.

Award: Scholarship for use in freshman year; renewable. *Number:* 3. *Amount:* $3000–$6000.

Eligibility Requirements: Applicant must be of African, Haitian, Hispanic, Indian, Japanese, Korean, Mexican heritage; American Indian/Alaska Native, Asian/Pacific Islander, Black (non-Hispanic); high school student and planning to enroll or expecting to enroll full-time at a two-year or four-year institution or university. Applicant must have 3.0 GPA or higher. Available to U.S. and Canadian citizens.

Application Requirements: Application form, essay. *Deadline:* February 10.

Contact: Donna Fernandez, Development and Student Program Manager
American Meteorological Society
45 Beacon Street
Boston, MA 02108-3693
Phone: 617-227-2426 Ext. 307
E-mail: dfernand@ametsoc.org

AMS FRESHMAN UNDERGRADUATE SCHOLARSHIP

Scholarships will be awarded, based on academic excellence, to high school seniors entering their freshman year of study in the atmospheric, oceanic, or hydrologic sciences. For use in freshman and sophomore years, with second-year funding dependent on successful completion of first year. The scholarship carries a $5,000 stipend.

Academic Fields/Career Goals: Meteorology/Atmospheric Science.

Award: Scholarship for use in freshman year; renewable. *Number:* 14. *Amount:* $2500–$5000.

Eligibility Requirements: Applicant must be high school student and planning to enroll or expecting to enroll full-time at a two-year or four-year or technical institution or university. Applicant must have 3.0 GPA or higher. Available to U.S. and Canadian citizens.

Application Requirements: Application form, essay. *Deadline:* February 10.

Contact: Ms. Donna Fernandez, Development and Student Program Manager
American Meteorological Society
45 Beacon Street
Boston, MA 02108
Phone: 617-227-2426 Ext. 246
E-mail: dfernand@ametsoc.org

FATHER JAMES B. MACELWANE ANNUAL AWARDS

Available to enrolled undergraduates who submit a paper on a phase of atmospheric sciences with a statement from a supervisor on the student's original contribution to the work. Minimum 3.0 GPA required. No more than two students from any one institution may enter papers in one contest. Must submit letter from department head or faculty member confirming applicant's undergraduate status and paper's originality. Must be a U.S. citizen.

Academic Fields/Career Goals: Meteorology/Atmospheric Science.

Award: Prize for use in sophomore, junior, or senior years; not renewable. *Number:* 1. *Amount:* $1000.

Eligibility Requirements: Applicant must be enrolled or expecting to enroll full-time at a two-year or four-year institution or university. Applicant must have 3.0 GPA or higher. Available to U.S. and Canadian citizens.

Application Requirements: *Deadline:* June 10.

Contact: Donna Fernandez, Development and Student Program Manager
E-mail: dfernandez@ametsoc.org

ARRL FOUNDATION INC.

http://www.arrl.org/

OLD MAN INTERNATIONAL SIDEBAND SOCIETY (OMISS) SCHOLARSHIP
• See page 259

ASSOCIATION FOR WOMEN GEOSCIENTISTS (AWG)

http://www.awg.org/

AWG ETHNIC MINORITY SCHOLARSHIP
• See page 260

AWG MARIA LUISA CRAWFORD FIELD CAMP SCHOLARSHIP
• See page 129

AWG SALT LAKE CHAPTER (SLC) RESEARCH SCHOLARSHIP
• See page 129

JANET CULLEN TANAKA GEOSCIENCES UNDERGRADUATE SCHOLARSHIP
• See page 129

LONE STAR RISING CAREER SCHOLARSHIP
• See page 260

OSAGE CHAPTER UNDERGRADUATE SERVICE SCHOLARSHIP
• See page 129

SUSAN EKDALE MEMORIAL FIELD CAMP SCHOLARSHIP
• See page 260

ASTRONAUT SCHOLARSHIP FOUNDATION

http://www.astronautscholarship.org/

ASTRONAUT SCHOLARSHIP FOUNDATION
• See page 123

AUTOMOTIVE WOMEN'S ALLIANCE FOUNDATION

http://awafoundation.org/index.php

AUTOMOTIVE WOMEN'S ALLIANCE FOUNDATION SCHOLARSHIPS
• See page 81

BARRY GOLDWATER SCHOLARSHIP AND EXCELLENCE IN EDUCATION FOUNDATION

https://goldwater.scholarsapply.org

BARRY M. GOLDWATER SCHOLARSHIP AND EXCELLENCE IN EDUCATION PROGRAM
• See page 123

BHW GROUP

https://thebhwgroup.com/

BHW WOMEN IN STEM SCHOLARSHIP
• See page 124

BROWN AND CALDWELL

http://www.brownandcaldwell.com

ECKENFELDER SCHOLARSHIP
• See page 169

MINORITY SCHOLARSHIP PROGRAM
• See page 169

CARDS AGAINST HUMANITY

https://cardsagainsthumanity.com/

SCIENCE AMBASSADOR SCHOLARSHIP
• See page 124

DISTIL NETWORKS

http://www.distilnetworks.com

WOMEN FORWARD IN TECHNOLOGY SCHOLARSHIP PROGRAM
• See page 124

DIVERSITYCOMM, INC.

http://www.diversitycomm.net/

DIVERSITY IN STEAM MAGAZINE SCHOLARSHIP
• See page 83

FOUNDATION FOR SCIENCE AND DISABILITY

http://stemd.org/

GRANTS FOR DISABLED GRADUATE STUDENTS IN THE SCIENCES
• See page 106

GREAT MINDS IN STEM

http://www.greatmindsinstem.org

HENAAC SCHOLARSHIP PROGRAM
• See page 115

LABROOTS INC.

http://www.LabRoots.com

LABROOTS STEM SCHOLARSHIP
• See page 116

THE LAND CONSERVANCY OF NEW JERSEY

http://www.tlc-nj.org/

ROGERS FAMILY SCHOLARSHIP
• See page 172

NASA FLORIDA SPACE GRANT CONSORTIUM

http://www.floridaspacegrant.org/

FLORIDA SPACE RESEARCH PROGRAM
• See page 156

NASA IDAHO SPACE GRANT CONSORTIUM

http://www.idahospacegrant.org

NASA IDAHO SPACE GRANT CONSORTIUM SCHOLARSHIP PROGRAM
• *See page 126*

NASA MINNESOTA SPACE GRANT CONSORTIUM

https://www.mnspacegrant.org/

MINNESOTA SPACE GRANT CONSORTIUM SCHOLARSHIP PROGRAM
• *See page 156*

NASA RHODE ISLAND SPACE GRANT CONSORTIUM

http://brown/initiatives/ri-space-grant

NASA RHODE ISLAND SPACE GRANT CONSORTIUM UNDERGRADUATE RESEARCH SCHOLARSHIP
• *See page 157*

NEXTSTEPU

http://www.nextstepu.com/

$1,500 STEM SCHOLARSHIP
• *See page 120*

SCARLETT FAMILY FOUNDATION SCHOLARSHIP PROGRAM

http://www.scarlettfoundation.org/

SCHOLARSHIP FOR STUDENTS PURSUING A BUSINESS OR STEM DEGREE
• *See page 91*

SIGMA XI, THE SCIENTIFIC RESEARCH SOCIETY

http://www.sigmaxi.org/

SIGMA XI GRANTS-IN-AID OF RESEARCH
• *See page 110*

SOCIETY OF SATELLITE PROFESSIONALS INTERNATIONAL

http://www.sspi.org/

SSPI INTERNATIONAL SCHOLARSHIPS
• *See page 160*

STRAIGHT NORTH

https://www.straightnorth.com/

STRAIGHT NORTH STEM SCHOLARSHIP
• *See page 92*

TKE EDUCATIONAL FOUNDATION

http://www.tke.org/

CARROL C. HALL MEMORIAL SCHOLARSHIP
• *See page 128*

MILITARY AND DEFENSE STUDIES

ARMED FORCES COMMUNICATIONS AND ELECTRONICS ASSOCIATION, EDUCATIONAL FOUNDATION

http://www.afcea.org/site/?q=foundation/scholarships

AFCEA STEM MAJORS SCHOLARSHIPS FOR UNDERGRADUATE STUDENTS
• *See page 122*

ASSOCIATION OF FORMER INTELLIGENCE OFFICERS

http://www.afio.com

AFIO UNDERGRADUATE AND GRADUATE SCHOLARSHIPS
• *See page 113*

BHW GROUP

https://thebhwgroup.com/

BHW WOMEN IN STEM SCHOLARSHIP
• *See page 124*

THE LYNDON BAINES JOHNSON FOUNDATION

http://www.lbjlibrary.org/page/foundation/

MOODY RESEARCH GRANTS
• *See page 114*

NATIONAL MILITARY INTELLIGENCE FOUNDATION

http://www.nmia.org/

NATIONAL MILITARY INTELLIGENCE ASSOCIATION SCHOLARSHIP
Scholarships to support the growth of professional studies in the field of military intelligence and to recognize and reward excellence in the development and transfer of knowledge about military and associated intelligence disciplines.

Academic Fields/Career Goals: Military and Defense Studies.

Award: Scholarship for use in freshman, sophomore, junior, or senior years; not renewable. *Number:* 3. *Amount:* $1000.

Eligibility Requirements: Applicant must be enrolled or expecting to enroll full-time at a four-year institution or university. Applicant or parent of applicant must be member of National Military Intelligence Association. Applicant must have 3.0 GPA or higher. Available to U.S. citizens.

Application Requirements: Application form, test scores. *Deadline:* August 1.

Contact: Dr. Forrest Frank, Secretary-Treasurer
National Military Intelligence Foundation
National Military Intelligence Foundation
PO Box 6844
Arlington, VA 22311
Phone: 434-542-5929
E-mail: ffrank54@comcast.net

SOCIETY OF SATELLITE PROFESSIONALS INTERNATIONAL

http://www.sspi.org/

SSPI INTERNATIONAL SCHOLARSHIPS
• *See page 160*

WOMEN IN DEFENSE (WID), A NATIONAL SECURITY ORGANIZATION

http://wid.ndia.org/

HORIZONS SCHOLARSHIP

Scholarships awarded to provide financial assistance to further educational objectives of women either currently employed in, or planning careers in, defense or national security arenas (not law enforcement or criminal justice). Must be U.S. citizen. Minimum 3.5 GPA required.

Academic Fields/Career Goals: Military and Defense Studies.

Award: Scholarship for use in junior, senior, graduate, or postgraduate years; not renewable. *Number:* 5–6. *Amount:* $500–$10,000.

Eligibility Requirements: Applicant must be enrolled or expecting to enroll full- or part-time at a four-year institution or university and female. Applicant must have 3.5 GPA or higher. Available to U.S. citizens.

Application Requirements: Application form, essay, financial need analysis. *Deadline:* July 1.

Contact: Tameka Brown
Women In Defense (WID), A National Security Organization
2101 Wilson Boulevard, Suite 700
Arlington, VA 22201-3061
Phone: 703-247-2570
E-mail: tbrown@NDIA.ORG

MUSEUM STUDIES

AMERICAN SCHOOL OF CLASSICAL STUDIES AT ATHENS

http://www.ascsa.edu.gr/

ASCSA SUMMER SESSION AND SUMMER SEMINARS SCHOLARSHIPS
• *See page 118*

ASSOCIATION FOR WOMEN GEOSCIENTISTS (AWG)

http://www.awg.org/

AWG ETHNIC MINORITY SCHOLARSHIP
• *See page 260*

AWG SALT LAKE CHAPTER (SLC) RESEARCH SCHOLARSHIP
• *See page 129*

LONE STAR RISING CAREER SCHOLARSHIP
• *See page 260*

OSAGE CHAPTER UNDERGRADUATE SERVICE SCHOLARSHIP
• *See page 129*

SUSAN EKDALE MEMORIAL FIELD CAMP SCHOLARSHIP
• *See page 260*

COSTUME SOCIETY OF AMERICA

http://www.costumesocietyamerica.com/

ADELE FILENE STUDENT PRESENTER GRANT
• *See page 138*

STELLA BLUM STUDENT RESEARCH GRANT
• *See page 138*

THE LYNDON BAINES JOHNSON FOUNDATION

http://www.lbjlibrary.org/page/foundation/

MOODY RESEARCH GRANTS
• *See page 114*

MUSIC

AMERICAN FOUNDATION FOR THE BLIND

http://www.afb.org/

GLADYS C. ANDERSON MEMORIAL SCHOLARSHIP

Non-renewable award available to a legally-blind female undergraduate or graduate student studying religious or classical music. Must submit a letter from a post-secondary institution as proof of enrollment in a program in music. For online application and more information, visit website http://www.afb.org.

Academic Fields/Career Goals: Music.

Award: Scholarship for use in freshman, sophomore, junior, or senior years; not renewable. *Number:* 1. *Amount:* $1000.

Eligibility Requirements: Applicant must be visually impaired; enrolled or expecting to enroll full-time at a four-year institution or university and female. Applicant must be visually impaired. Available to U.S. citizens.

Application Requirements: Application form, essay, proof of enrollment letter from post secondary institution, proof of blindness letter from agency or medical doctor, recommendations or references, transcript. *Deadline:* April 30.

Contact: Dawn Bodrogi, Information Center and Library Coordinator
Phone: 212-502-7661
E-mail: dbodrogi@afb.net

R.L. GILLETTE SCHOLARSHIP
• *See page 420*

AMERICAN LEGION DEPARTMENT OF KANSAS

http://www.ksamlegion.org/

MUSIC COMMITTEE SCHOLARSHIP

One-time award open to a high school senior or college freshman or sophomore. Must be a Kansas resident. Must have distinguished background in the field of music at an approved Kansas junior college, college or university. Award of $1000, with the disbursement as $500 award for each of the two semesters.

Academic Fields/Career Goals: Music; Performing Arts.

Award: Scholarship for use in freshman or sophomore years; not renewable. *Number:* 1. *Amount:* $1000.

Eligibility Requirements: Applicant must be enrolled or expecting to enroll full-time at a two-year or four-year or technical institution or university; resident of Kansas; studying in Kansas and must have an interest in music/singing. Available to U.S. citizens.

Application Requirements: Application form, financial need analysis, personal photograph. *Deadline:* February 15.

Contact: Mike Oppy, Chairman, Scholarship Committee
American Legion Department of Kansas
1314 SW Topeka Boulevard
Topeka, KS 66612
Phone: 785-232-9315

BMI FOUNDATION, INC.

http://www.bmifoundation.org/

BMI STUDENT COMPOSER AWARDS
• *See page 141*

THE CHOPIN FOUNDATION OF THE UNITED STATES

http://www.chopin.org/

SCHOLARSHIP PROGRAM FOR YOUNG AMERICAN PIANISTS

Program is open to qualified American pianists not younger than 14 and not older than 17 years of age on their first year of application. Renewable for up to four years, if eligible. Students will be assisted in preparing music repertoire required for the National Chopin Piano Competition. Must be U.S. citizens or legal residents. For more information, see website http://www.chopin.org.

Academic Fields/Career Goals: Music.

Award: Grant for use in freshman, sophomore, or junior years; renewable. *Number:* 1–10. *Amount:* $1000.

Eligibility Requirements: Applicant must be age 14-17; enrolled or expecting to enroll full- or part-time at a two-year or four-year institution and must have an interest in music. Available to U.S. citizens.

Application Requirements: Application form, personal photograph. *Fee:* $25. *Deadline:* May 15.

Contact: Jadwiga Gewert, Executive Director
The Chopin Foundation of the United States
1440 79th Street Causeway, Suite 117
Miami, FL 33141
Phone: 305-868-0624
E-mail: info@chopin.org

CONGRESSIONAL BLACK CAUCUS FOUNDATION, INC.

http://www.cbcfinc.org/

CBC SPOUSES HEINEKEN USA PERFORMING ARTS SCHOLARSHIP

This program was established in 2000 in honor of the late Curtis Mayfield to ensure that students pursuing a degree in the performing arts receive financial assistance. Performing arts includes theater, drama, comedy, music, dance, opera, marching bands, etc.

Academic Fields/Career Goals: Music; Performing Arts.

Award: Scholarship for use in freshman, sophomore, junior, or senior years; not renewable. *Number:* 10. *Amount:* $3000.

Eligibility Requirements: Applicant must be Black (non-Hispanic); enrolled or expecting to enroll full-time at a two-year or four-year institution or university; studying in Alabama, Alaska, Arizona, Arkansas, California, Colorado, Connecticut, Delaware, District of Columbia, Florida, Georgia, Guam, Hawaii, Idaho, Illinois, Indiana, Iowa, Kansas, Kentucky, Louisiana, Maine, Maryland, Massachusetts, Michigan, Minnesota, Mississippi, Missouri, Montana, Nebraska, Nevada, New Hampshire, New Jersey, New Mexico, New York, North Carolina, North Dakota, Ohio, Oklahoma, Oregon, Pennsylvania, Puerto Rico, Rhode Island, South Carolina, South Dakota, Tennessee, Texas, Utah, Vermont, Virginia, Washington, West Virginia, Wisconsin, Wyoming and must have an interest in music, music/singing, or theater. Applicant must have 2.5 GPA or higher. Available to U.S. citizens.

Application Requirements: Application form, essay, financial need analysis, personal photograph. *Deadline:* April 21.

Contact: Ms. Katrina Finch, Program Administrator, Scholarships
Phone: 202-263-2800
E-mail: scholarships@cbcfinc.org

DAVIDSON INSTITUTE FOR TALENT DEVELOPMENT

http://www.davidsongifted.org/

DAVIDSON FELLOWS SCHOLARSHIP PROGRAM
• *See page 124*

DELTA OMICRON FOUNDATION, INC.

http://www.dofoundation.org

DELTA OMICRON FOUNDATION EDUCATIONAL GRANTS IN MUSIC

Grants are available to use toward tuition awarded to undergraduate and graduate music students at a four-year college or university. Grants primarily available for Delta Omicron Fraternity members but also for non-members depending dependent of available Foundation funding.

Academic Fields/Career Goals: Music.

Award: Grant for use in freshman, sophomore, junior, senior, graduate, or postgraduate years; not renewable. *Number:* 8. *Amount:* $500.

Eligibility Requirements: Applicant must be enrolled or expecting to enroll full- or part-time at a four-year institution or university. Applicant must have 3.5 GPA or higher. Available to U.S. and non-U.S. citizens.

Application Requirements: Application form, community service, personal photograph. *Deadline:* April 30.

Contact: Dr. Jonny Ramsey, President
Delta Omicron Foundation, Inc.
2500 Potomac Parkway
Denton, TX 76210
Phone: 940-566-3170
E-mail: jramsey18@verizon.net

DIVERSITYCOMM, INC.

http://www.diversitycomm.net/

DIVERSITY IN STEAM MAGAZINE SCHOLARSHIP
• *See page 83*

EDMONTON COMMUNITY FOUNDATION

http://www.ecfoundation.org

WINSPEAR FUND

For accomplished Edmonton area students who will study classical music outside Alberta.

Academic Fields/Career Goals: Music.

Award: Scholarship for use in freshman, sophomore, junior, senior, graduate, or postgraduate years; not renewable.

Eligibility Requirements: Applicant must be enrolled or expecting to enroll full- or part-time at a four-year institution or university and resident of Alberta. Available to Canadian citizens.

Application Requirements: Application form. *Deadline:* March 31.

Contact: Anna Opryshko, Student Awards Associate
Phone: 780-426-0015 Ext. 107
Fax: 780-425-0121
E-mail: studentawards@ecfoundation.org

GENERAL FEDERATION OF WOMEN'S CLUBS OF MASSACHUSETTS

http://www.gfwcma.org/

DORCHESTER WOMEN'S CLUB MUSIC SCHOLARSHIP

Scholarship for undergraduate major in voice. Applicant must be a Massachusetts resident and an undergraduate currently enrolled in a four-year accredited college, university or school of music, majoring in voice.

Academic Fields/Career Goals: Music; Performing Arts.

Award: Scholarship for use in sophomore, junior, or senior years; not renewable. *Number:* 1. *Amount:* $500.

Eligibility Requirements: Applicant must be enrolled or expecting to enroll full-time at a four-year institution or university and resident of Massachusetts. Available to U.S. citizens.

Application Requirements: Application form, driver's license, essay, interview. *Deadline:* March 1.

Contact: Scholarship Chairman
General Federation of Women's Clubs of Massachusetts
245 Dutton Road
Sudbury, MA 01776
Phone: 978-443-4569
E-mail: gfwcma@aol.com

GLENN MILLER BIRTHPLACE SOCIETY

http://www.glennmiller.org/

GMBS-3RD PLACE INSTRUMENTAL SCHOLARSHIP

One scholarship for a male or female instrumentalist will be awarded as a competition prize to be used for any education-related expenses. Must submit 10-minute, high-quality audio tape of pieces selected for competition or those of similar style. Applicant is responsible for travel to and lodging during the competition. One-time award for high school seniors and college freshmen.

Academic Fields/Career Goals: Music.

Award: Scholarship for use in freshman year; not renewable. *Number:* 1. *Amount:* up to $1000.

Eligibility Requirements: Applicant must be enrolled or expecting to enroll full-time at a four-year institution or university. Available to U.S. and non-U.S. citizens.

Application Requirements: Application form, essay, performance tape or CD. *Deadline:* March 10.

Contact: Arlene Leonard, Secretary
Glenn Miller Birthplace Society
PO Box 61
Clarinda, IA 51632
Phone: 712-542-2461
Fax: 712-542-2461
E-mail: gmbs@heartland.net

GMBS-BILL BAKER/HANS STARREVELD SCHOLARSHIP

One scholarship for a male or female instrumentalist will be awarded as a competition prize to be used for any education-related expenses. Must submit 10-minute, high-quality audio tape of pieces selected for competition or those of similar style. Applicant is responsible for travel to and lodging during the competition. One-time award for high school seniors and college freshmen.

Academic Fields/Career Goals: Music.

Award: Scholarship for use in freshman year; not renewable. *Number:* 1. *Amount:* up to $2000.

Eligibility Requirements: Applicant must be enrolled or expecting to enroll full-time at a four-year institution or university. Available to U.S. and non-U.S. citizens.

Application Requirements: Application form, essay, performance tape or CD. *Deadline:* March 10.

Contact: Arlene Leonard, Secretary
Glenn Miller Birthplace Society
PO Box 61
Clarinda, IA 51632
Phone: 712-542-2461
Fax: 712-542-2461
E-mail: gmbs@heartland.net

GMBS-RAY EBERLE VOCAL SCHOLARSHIP

One scholarship for a male or female vocalist will be awarded as a competition prize to be used for any education-related expenses. Must submit 10-minute, high-quality audio tape of pieces selected for competition or those of similar style. Applicant is responsible for travel to and lodging during the competition. One-time award for high school seniors and college freshmen.

Academic Fields/Career Goals: Music.

Award: Scholarship for use in freshman year; not renewable. *Number:* 1. *Amount:* up to $4000.

Eligibility Requirements: Applicant must be enrolled or expecting to enroll full-time at a four-year institution. Available to U.S. and non-U.S. citizens.

Application Requirements: Application form, essay, performance tape or CD. *Deadline:* March 10.

Contact: Arlene Leonard, Secretary
Glenn Miller Birthplace Society
PO Box 61
Clarinda, IA 51632
Phone: 712-542-2461
Fax: 712-542-2461
E-mail: gmbs@heartland.net

GRAND RAPIDS COMMUNITY FOUNDATION

http://www.grfoundation.org/

LLEWELLYN L. CAYVAN STRING INSTRUMENT SCHOLARSHIP

Scholarship for undergraduate students studying the violin, the viola, the violoncello, and/or the bass viol. High school students not considered. To apply, submit required application form, transcript, essay, reference.

Academic Fields/Career Goals: Music.

Award: Scholarship for use in freshman, sophomore, junior, senior, or graduate years; not renewable. *Number:* 1–6. *Amount:* $1000–$2000.

Eligibility Requirements: Applicant must be enrolled or expecting to enroll full-time at a four-year institution or university and must have an interest in music. Available to U.S. citizens.

Application Requirements: Application form, essay. *Deadline:* April 1.

Contact: Ms. Ruth Bishop, Education Program Officer
Grand Rapids Community Foundation
185 Oakes SW
Grand Rapids, MI 49503
Phone: 616-454-1751 Ext. 103
E-mail: rbishop@grfoundation.org

GREATER KANAWHA VALLEY FOUNDATION

http://www.tgkvf.org/

HERB SMITH/EUNICE FLEMING SCHOLARSHIP

Renewable award for a West Virginia resident pursuing full-time postsecondary studies in music, theater, musical theatre, and/or dance. Preference given to Fayette, Kanawha, or Wood County residents. Minimum 3.5 GPA required.

Academic Fields/Career Goals: Music; Performing Arts.

Award: Scholarship for use in freshman, sophomore, junior, or senior years; renewable. *Amount:* $500.

Eligibility Requirements: Applicant must be enrolled or expecting to enroll full-time at a four-year institution or university and resident of West Virginia. Applicant must have 3.5 GPA or higher. Available to U.S. citizens.

Application Requirements: Application form, financial need analysis, recommendations or references, test scores, transcript. *Deadline:* January 15.

Contact: Susan Hoover, Scholarship Program Officer
Greater Kanawha Valley Foundation
900 Lee Street East, 16th Floor
Charleston, WV 25301
Phone: 304-346-3620
E-mail: shoover@tgkvf.org

HAPCO MUSIC FOUNDATION INC.

http://www.hapcopromo.org/

TRADITIONAL MARCHING BAND EXTRAVAGANZA SCHOLARSHIP AWARD

Scholarship is offered to deserving students who will continue their participation in any college music program. Minimum 3.0 GPA required. Applicant should have best composite score of 970 SAT or 20 ACT.

Academic Fields/Career Goals: Music.

Award: Scholarship for use in freshman year; not renewable. *Amount:* $250–$1000.

Eligibility Requirements: Applicant must be enrolled or expecting to enroll full-time at a two-year or four-year institution or university and must have an interest in music. Applicant must have 3.0 GPA or higher. Available to U.S. citizens.

Application Requirements: Application form, essay, personal photograph, recommendations or references, test scores, transcript. *Deadline:* varies.

Contact: Joseph McMullen, President
Phone: 407-877-2262
Fax: 407-654-0308
E-mail: hapcopromo@aol.com

HARTFORD JAZZ SOCIETY INC.

http://www.hartfordjazzsociety.com/

HARTFORD JAZZ SOCIETY SCHOLARSHIPS

Scholarship of up to $3000 is awarded to graduating high school senior attending a four-year college or university. Must be a Connecticut resident. Music major with interest in jazz required.

Academic Fields/Career Goals: Music.

Award: Scholarship for use in freshman year; not renewable. *Number:* 2–3. *Amount:* up to $3000.

Eligibility Requirements: Applicant must be high school student; planning to enroll or expecting to enroll full- or part-time at a four-year institution or university; resident of Connecticut and must have an interest in music. Available to U.S. and Canadian citizens.

Application Requirements: Application form, cassette tape or CD, recommendations or references. *Deadline:* May 1.

Contact: Scholarship Committee Chairperson
Hartford Jazz Society Inc.
116 Cottage Grove Road
Bloomfield, CT 06002
Phone: 860-242-6688
Fax: 860-243-8871
E-mail: hartjazzsocinc@aol.com

HEMOPHILIA FOUNDATION OF SOUTHERN CALIFORNIA

http://www.hemosocal.org/

EARL JAMES FAHRINGER PERFORMING ARTS SCHOLARSHIP

• *See page 142*

HOUSE OF BLUES MUSIC FORWARD FOUNDATION

https://hobmusicforward.org/

STEVEN J. FINKEL SERVICE EXCELLENCE SCHOLARSHIP

• *See page 180*

TIFFANY GREEN OPERATOR SCHOLARSHIP AWARD

• *See page 96*

HOUSTON SYMPHONY

http://www.houstonsymphony.org/

HOUSTON SYMPHONY IMA HOGG COMPETITION

Competition for musicians ages 16 to 29 who play standard instruments of the symphony orchestra. Goal is to offer a review by panel of music professionals and further career of an advanced student or a professional

musician. Participants must be U.S. citizens or studying in the United States. Application fee is $30.

Academic Fields/Career Goals: Music.

Award: Prize for use in freshman, sophomore, junior, senior, graduate, or postgraduate years; not renewable. *Number:* 5. *Amount:* $300–$5000.

Eligibility Requirements: Applicant must be age 16-29; enrolled or expecting to enroll full- or part-time at a two-year or four-year or technical institution or university and must have an interest in music. Available to U.S. and non-U.S. citizens.

Application Requirements: Application form, CD with required repertoire, entry in a contest. *Fee:* $30. *Deadline:* February 13.

Contact: Carol Wilson, Manager, Music Matters!
Houston Symphony
615 Louisiana Street, Suite 102
Houston, TX 77002
Phone: 713-238-1447
Fax: 713-224-0453
E-mail: e&o@houstonsymphony.org

HOUSTON SYMPHONY LEAGUE CONCERTO COMPETITION

Competition is open to student musicians 18 years of age or younger who have not yet graduated from high school and who play any standard orchestral instrument or piano. Must live within a 200-mile radius of Houston and submit a screening CD of one movement of their concerto.

Academic Fields/Career Goals: Music.

Award: Prize for use in freshman year; not renewable. *Number:* up to 3. *Amount:* $250–$1000.

Eligibility Requirements: Applicant must be high school student; planning to enroll or expecting to enroll full-time at a two-year or four-year institution; resident of Texas and must have an interest in music. Available to U.S. citizens.

Application Requirements: Application form, CD, entry in a contest. *Fee:* $25. *Deadline:* November 18.

Contact: Carol Wilson, Manager, Music Matters!
Houston Symphony
615 Louisiana Street, Suite 102
Houston, TX 77002
Phone: 713-238-1449
Fax: 713-224-0453
E-mail: e&o@houstonsymphony.org

JACK J. ISGUR FOUNDATION

http://www.isgur.org

JACK J. ISGUR FOUNDATION SCHOLARSHIP

• *See page 272*

NATIONAL ACADEMY OF TELEVISION ARTS AND SCIENCES

http://www.emmyonline.tv/

DOUGLAS W. MUMMERT SCHOLARSHIP

• *See page 142*

JIM MCKAY MEMORIAL SCHOLARSHIP

• *See page 220*

MIKE WALLACE MEMORIAL SCHOLARSHIP

• *See page 220*

NATIONAL ACADEMY OF TELEVISION ARTS AND SCIENCES TRUSTEES SCHOLARSHIP

• *See page 220*

RANDY FALCO SCHOLARSHIP

• *See page 220*

NATIONAL ASSOCIATION OF PASTORAL MUSICIANS

http://www.npm.org/

ELAINE RENDLER-RENE DOSOGNE-GEORGETOWN CHORALE SCHOLARSHIP

Awards NPM members enrolled full-time or part-time in a graduate or undergraduate degree program of studies related to the field of pastoral music. Applicant must intend to work at least two years in the field of pastoral music following graduation or program completion.

Academic Fields/Career Goals: Music; Religion/Theology.

Award: Scholarship for use in freshman, sophomore, junior, senior, or graduate years; not renewable. *Number:* 1. *Amount:* $1000.

Eligibility Requirements: Applicant must be enrolled or expecting to enroll full- or part-time at a two-year or four-year institution or university and must have an interest in music/singing. Applicant or parent of applicant must be member of National Association of Pastoral Musicians. Available to U.S. and non-U.S. citizens.

Application Requirements: Application form, CD of performance, essay, financial need analysis, recommendations or references, resume. *Deadline:* March 5.

Contact: Ms. Kathleen Haley, Director of Membership Services
Phone: 240-247-3000
E-mail: haley@npm.org

FUNK FAMILY MEMORIAL SCHOLARSHIP

Awards NPM members enrolled full-time or part-time in a graduate or undergraduate degree program of studies related to the field of pastoral music. Applicant must intend to work at least two years in the field of pastoral music following graduation or program completion.

Academic Fields/Career Goals: Music; Religion/Theology.

Award: Scholarship for use in freshman, sophomore, junior, senior, or graduate years; not renewable. *Number:* 1. *Amount:* $1000.

Eligibility Requirements: Applicant must be enrolled or expecting to enroll full- or part-time at a two-year or four-year or technical institution or university and must have an interest in music/singing. Applicant or parent of applicant must be member of National Association of Pastoral Musicians. Available to U.S. and non-U.S. citizens.

Application Requirements: Application form, CD of performance, essay, financial need analysis, recommendations or references, resume. *Deadline:* March 5.

Contact: Ms. Kathleen Haley, Director of Membership Services
Phone: 240-247-3000
E-mail: haley@npm.org

GIA PUBLICATION PASTORAL MUSICIAN SCHOLARSHIP

Awards NPM members enrolled full-time or part-time in a graduate or undergraduate degree program of studies related to the field of pastoral music. Applicant must intend to work at least two years in the field of pastoral music following graduation or program completion.

Academic Fields/Career Goals: Music; Religion/Theology.

Award: Scholarship for use in freshman, sophomore, junior, senior, or graduate years; not renewable. *Number:* 1. *Amount:* $2000.

Eligibility Requirements: Applicant must be enrolled or expecting to enroll full- or part-time at a two-year or four-year institution or university and must have an interest in music/singing. Applicant or parent of applicant must be member of National Association of Pastoral Musicians. Available to U.S. and non-U.S. citizens.

Application Requirements: Application form, CD of performance, essay, financial need analysis, recommendations or references, resume. *Deadline:* March 5.

Contact: Ms. Kathleen Haley, Director of Membership Services
Phone: 240-247-3000
E-mail: haley@npm.org

MUSONICS SCHOLARSHIP

Awards NPM members enrolled full-time or part-time in a graduate or undergraduate degree program of studies related to the field of pastoral music. Applicant must intend to work at least two years in the field of pastoral music following graduation or program completion. One award available for graduate study and one award available for undergraduate study.

Academic Fields/Career Goals: Music; Religion/Theology.

Award: Scholarship for use in freshman, sophomore, junior, senior, or graduate years; not renewable. *Number:* 2. *Amount:* $2000.

Eligibility Requirements: Applicant must be enrolled or expecting to enroll full- or part-time at a two-year or four-year institution or university and must have an interest in music/singing. Applicant or parent of applicant must be member of National Association of Pastoral Musicians. Available to U.S. and non-U.S. citizens.

Application Requirements: Application form, CD of performance, essay, financial need analysis, recommendations or references, resume. *Deadline:* March 5.

Contact: Ms. Kathleen Haley, Director of Membership Services
Phone: 240-247-3000
E-mail: haley@npm.org

NATIONAL ASSOCIATION OF PASTORAL MUSICIANS MEMBERS' SCHOLARSHIP

Awards NPM members enrolled full-time or part-time in a graduate or undergraduate degree program of studies related to the field of pastoral music. Applicant must intend to work at least two years in the field of pastoral music following graduation or program completion.

Academic Fields/Career Goals: Music; Religion/Theology.

Award: Scholarship for use in freshman, sophomore, junior, senior, or graduate years; not renewable. *Number:* 1. *Amount:* $3000.

Eligibility Requirements: Applicant must be enrolled or expecting to enroll full- or part-time at a two-year or four-year or technical institution or university and must have an interest in music/singing. Applicant or parent of applicant must be member of National Association of Pastoral Musicians. Available to U.S. and non-U.S. citizens.

Application Requirements: Application form, CD of performance, essay, financial need analysis, recommendations or references, resume. *Deadline:* March 5.

Contact: Ms. Kathleen Haley, Director of Membership Services
Phone: 240-247-3000
E-mail: haley@npm.org

NPM BOARD OF DIRECTORS SCHOLARSHIP

Scholarship for NPM members enrolled full- or part-time in an undergraduate or graduate pastoral music program. Must intend to work at least two years in the field of pastoral music following graduation/program completion.

Academic Fields/Career Goals: Music.

Award: Scholarship for use in freshman, sophomore, junior, senior, or graduate years; not renewable. *Number:* 1. *Amount:* $2000.

Eligibility Requirements: Applicant must be enrolled or expecting to enroll full- or part-time at a two-year or four-year institution or university and must have an interest in music/singing. Applicant or parent of applicant must be member of National Association of Pastoral Musicians. Available to U.S. and non-U.S. citizens.

Application Requirements: Application form, CD of performance, essay, financial need analysis, recommendations or references, resume. *Deadline:* March 5.

Contact: Ms. Kathleen Haley, Director of Membership Services
Phone: 240-247-3000
E-mail: haley@npm.org

NPM KOINONIA/BOARD OF DIRECTORS SCHOLARSHIP

Awards NPM members enrolled full-time or part-time in a graduate or undergraduate degree program of studies related to the field of pastoral music. Applicant must intend to work at least two years in the field of pastoral music following graduation or program completion.

Academic Fields/Career Goals: Music; Religion/Theology.

Award: Scholarship for use in freshman, sophomore, junior, senior, or graduate years; not renewable. *Number:* 1. *Amount:* $2000.

Eligibility Requirements: Applicant must be enrolled or expecting to enroll full- or part-time at a two-year or four-year institution or university and must have an interest in music/singing. Applicant or parent of applicant must be member of National Association of Pastoral Musicians. Available to U.S. and non-U.S. citizens.

Application Requirements: Application form, CD of performance, essay, financial need analysis, recommendations or references, resume. *Deadline:* March 5.

Contact: Ms. Kathleen Haley, Director of Membership Services
  Phone: 240-247-3000
  E-mail: haley@npm.org

NPM PERROT SCHOLARSHIP

Awards NPM members enrolled full-time or part-time in a graduate or undergraduate degree program of studies related to the field of pastoral music. Applicant must intend to work at least two years in the field of pastoral music following graduation or program completion.

Academic Fields/Career Goals: Music.

Award: Scholarship for use in freshman, sophomore, junior, senior, or graduate years; not renewable. *Number:* 1. *Amount:* $3000.

Eligibility Requirements: Applicant must be enrolled or expecting to enroll full- or part-time at a two-year or four-year institution or university. Applicant or parent of applicant must be member of National Association of Pastoral Musicians. Available to U.S. and non-U.S. citizens.

Application Requirements: Application form, CD of performance, essay, financial need analysis, recommendations or references, resume. *Deadline:* March 5.

Contact: Ms. Kathleen Haley, Director of Membership Services
  Phone: 240-247-3000
  E-mail: haley@npm.org

OREGON CATHOLIC PRESS SCHOLARSHIP

Awards NPM members enrolled full-time or part-time in a graduate or undergraduate degree program of studies related to the field of pastoral music. Applicant must intend to work at least two years in the field of pastoral music following graduation or program completion.

Academic Fields/Career Goals: Music; Religion/Theology.

Award: Scholarship for use in freshman, sophomore, junior, senior, or graduate years; not renewable. *Number:* 1. *Amount:* up to $2500.

Eligibility Requirements: Applicant must be enrolled or expecting to enroll full- or part-time at a two-year or four-year institution or university and must have an interest in music/singing. Available to U.S. and non-U.S. citizens.

Application Requirements: Application form, CD of performance, essay, financial need analysis, recommendations or references, resume. *Deadline:* March 5.

Contact: Ms. Kathleen Haley, Director of Membership Services
  Phone: 240-247-3000
  E-mail: haley@npm.org

PALUCH FAMILY FOUNDATION/WORLD LIBRARY PUBLICATIONS SCHOLARSHIP

Awards NPM members enrolled full-time or part-time in a graduate or undergraduate degree program of studies related to the field of pastoral music. Applicant must intend to work at least two years in the field of pastoral music following graduation or program completion.

Academic Fields/Career Goals: Music; Religion/Theology.

Award: Scholarship for use in freshman, sophomore, junior, senior, or graduate years; not renewable. *Number:* 1. *Amount:* up to $2500.

Eligibility Requirements: Applicant must be enrolled or expecting to enroll full- or part-time at a two-year or four-year institution or university and must have an interest in music/singing. Available to U.S. and non-U.S. citizens.

Application Requirements: Application form, CD of performance, essay, financial need analysis, recommendations or references, resume. *Deadline:* March 5.

Contact: Ms. Kathleen Haley, Director of Membership Services
  Phone: 240-247-3000
  E-mail: haley@npm.org

STEVEN C. WARNER SCHOLARSHIP

Scholarship for NPM members enrolled full-or part-time in an undergraduate or graduate pastoral music program. Applicant must intend to work at least two years in the field of pastoral music following graduation/program completion.

Academic Fields/Career Goals: Music.

Award: Scholarship for use in freshman, sophomore, junior, senior, or graduate years; not renewable. *Number:* 1. *Amount:* $1000.

Eligibility Requirements: Applicant must be enrolled or expecting to enroll full- or part-time at a two-year or four-year institution or university and must have an interest in music/singing. Applicant or parent of applicant must be member of National Association of Pastoral Musicians. Available to U.S. and non-U.S. citizens.

Application Requirements: Application form, CD of performance, essay, financial need analysis, recommendations or references, resume. *Deadline:* March 5.

Contact: Ms. Kathleen Haley, Director of Membership Services
  Phone: 240-247-3000
  E-mail: haley@npm.org

OREGON STUDENT ASSISTANCE COMMISSION

https://oregonstudentaid.gov/

FARROLD STEPHENS SCHOLARSHIP

Awards for students that have experience in vocal performance or music education. Must enroll at least half time as college junior or above for fall term working towards a degree as a vocal performer or music educator. Oregon residency is not required. Semifinalists will be invited to submit a non-returnable CD of a musical performance. Financial need may or may not be considered.

Academic Fields/Career Goals: Music.

Award: Scholarship for use in junior, senior, or graduate years; not renewable.

Eligibility Requirements: Applicant must be enrolled or expecting to enroll full- or part-time at a four-year institution or university. Available to U.S. citizens.

Application Requirements: Application form, financial need analysis. *Deadline:* March 1.

Contact: Melissa Adams, Scholarship Processing Coordinator
  Phone: 541-687-7409
  E-mail: melissa.adams@state.or.us

LIMING AND ULMER MUSIC SCHOLARSHIP

Award for undergraduate students who are enrolled at least half-time at any public or non-profit college and majoring in music. Not open to high school seniors. Apply/compete annually. Based on financial need.

Academic Fields/Career Goals: Music.

Award: Scholarship for use in sophomore, junior, or senior years; not renewable.

Eligibility Requirements: Applicant must be enrolled or expecting to enroll full- or part-time at a two-year or four-year institution or university. Available to U.S. citizens.

Application Requirements: Application form, financial need analysis. *Deadline:* March 1.

Contact: Melissa Adams, Scholarship Processing Coordinator
  Phone: 541-687-7409
  E-mail: melissa.adams@state.or.us

TECHNICAL TRAINING FUND SCHOLARSHIP
• *See page 143*

POLISH ARTS CLUB OF BUFFALO SCHOLARSHIP FOUNDATION

http://www.pacb.bfn.org/

POLISH ARTS CLUB OF BUFFALO SCHOLARSHIP FOUNDATION TRUST
• *See page 144*

QUALITY BATH

http://www.qualitybath.com

QUALITYBATH.COM SCHOLARSHIP PROGRAM
• *See page 140*

QUEEN ELISABETH INTERNATIONAL MUSIC COMPETITION OF BELGIUM

http://www.qeimc.be

QUEEN ELISABETH COMPETITION

Competition is open to musicians who have already completed their training and who are ready to launch their international careers. The competition covers the following musical disciplines: piano, voice and violin.

Academic Fields/Career Goals: Music.

Award: Prize for use in freshman, sophomore, junior, senior, graduate, or postgraduate years; not renewable. *Amount:* $1–$33.

Eligibility Requirements: Applicant must be age 18-32; enrolled or expecting to enroll full- or part-time at a two-year or four-year institution or university and must have an interest in music or music/singing. Available to U.S. and non-U.S. citizens.

Application Requirements: Application form, personal photograph. *Fee:* $130. *Deadline:* December 6.

Contact: Nicolas Dernoncourt, Artistic Coordinator
    Phone: 32 2 213 40 50
    E-mail: info@qeimc.be

RHODE ISLAND FOUNDATION

http://www.rifoundation.org/

BACH ORGAN AND KEYBOARD MUSIC SCHOLARSHIP

Scholarship for college music majors who are Rhode Island residents or attending college in Rhode Island. Must demonstrate good grades, financial need, and be an ABO member. Must include music sample.

Academic Fields/Career Goals: Music.

Award: Scholarship for use in freshman, sophomore, junior, or senior years; not renewable. *Amount:* $800–$1000.

Eligibility Requirements: Applicant must be enrolled or expecting to enroll full-time at a two-year or four-year institution or university; resident of Rhode Island and must have an interest in music/singing. Available to U.S. citizens.

Application Requirements: Application form, financial need analysis, recommendations or references, self-addressed stamped envelope with application, transcript. *Deadline:* June 14.

Contact: Libby Monahan, Funds Administrator
    Phone: 401-274-4564 Ext. 3117
    E-mail: libbym@rifoundation.org

UNITED NEGRO COLLEGE FUND

http://www.uncf.org/

JOHN LENNON ENDOWED SCHOLARSHIP PROGRAM

VSA

http://www.kennedy-center.org/education/vsa/

VSA INTERNATIONAL YOUNG SOLOISTS AWARD

Each year outstanding young musicians with disabilities from around the world receive the VSA International Young Soloists Award, $2,000, and the opportunity to perform at the John F. Kennedy Center for the Performing Arts in Washington, D.C., which is live-streamed and archived on the Kennedy Center website. This program is open to soloists and ensembles of any instrument or genre including classical, jazz, hip-hop, rock, and more!

Academic Fields/Career Goals: Music; Performing Arts.

Award: Prize for use in freshman, sophomore, junior, or senior years; not renewable. *Number:* 4. *Amount:* $2000.

Eligibility Requirements: Applicant must be hearing impaired, learning disabled, physically disabled, or visually impaired; age 14-25; enrolled or expecting to enroll full- or part-time at a four-year institution or university and must have an interest in music or music/singing. Applicant must be hearing impaired, learning disabled, physically disabled, or visually impaired. Available to U.S. and non-U.S. citizens.

Application Requirements: Application form. *Deadline:* February 8.

Contact: Megan Bailey, Administrative Assistant
    VSA
    2700 F St NW
    Washington, DC 20566
    Phone: 202-416-8822
    E-mail: vsainfo@kennedy-center.org

WOMEN BAND DIRECTORS INTERNATIONAL

http://www.womenbanddirectors.org/

CHARLOTTE PLUMMER OWEN MEMORIAL SCHOLARSHIP

MARTHA ANN STARK MEMORIAL SCHOLARSHIP

VOLKWEIN MEMORIAL SCHOLARSHIP

NATURAL RESOURCES

AMERICAN GROUND WATER TRUST

http://www.agwt.org/

AMERICAN GROUND WATER TRUST-AMTROL INC. SCHOLARSHIP

AMERICAN GROUND WATER TRUST-BAROID SCHOLARSHIP

AMERICAN GROUND WATER TRUST-THOMAS STETSON SCHOLARSHIP

AMERICAN INDIAN SCIENCE AND ENGINEERING SOCIETY

http://www.aises.org/

A.T. ANDERSON MEMORIAL SCHOLARSHIP PROGRAM

AMERICAN PUBLIC POWER ASSOCIATION

https://www.publicpower.org/grants-scholarships

DEED EDUCATIONAL SCHOLARSHIP

DEED STUDENT INTERNSHIP

DEED STUDENT RESEARCH GRANTS

DEED TECHNICAL DESIGN PROJECT

AMERICAN SOCIETY OF AGRONOMY, CROP SCIENCE SOCIETY OF AMERICA, SOIL SCIENCE SOCIETY OF AMERICA

http://www.agronomy.org

J. FIELDING REED SCHOLARSHIP
• See page 106

AMERICAN WATER RESOURCES ASSOCIATION

http://www.awra.org/

AWRA RICHARD A. HERBERT MEMORIAL SCHOLARSHIP

At least two scholarships are available: one for full-time undergraduate student and one for a full-time graduate student, each working toward a degree in water resources. All applicants must be national AWRA members.

Academic Fields/Career Goals: Natural Resources.

Award: Scholarship for use in freshman, sophomore, junior, senior, or graduate years; not renewable. *Number:* 2–6. *Amount:* $650–$2000.

Eligibility Requirements: Applicant must be enrolled or expecting to enroll full-time at a four-year institution or university. Available to U.S. and non-U.S. citizens.

Application Requirements: Application form, essay. *Deadline:* April 23.

Contact: Jacque Towner, Office Manager
American Water Resources Association
4 West Federal Street, PO Box 1626
Middleburg, VA 20118-1626
Phone: 540-687-8390
E-mail: info@awra.org

ARCTIC INSTITUTE OF NORTH AMERICA

http://www.arctic.ucalgary.ca/

JIM BOURQUE SCHOLARSHIP
• See page 267

ARIZONA HYDROLOGICAL SOCIETY

http://www.azhydrosoc.org/

ARIZONA HYDROLOGICAL SOCIETY SCHOLARSHIP
• See page 259

ARIZONA PROFESSIONAL CHAPTER OF AISES

http://www.aises.org/scholarships

ARIZONA PROFESSIONAL CHAPTER OF AISES SCHOLARSHIP
• See page 313

ASSOCIATION FOR WOMEN GEOSCIENTISTS (AWG)

http://www.awg.org/

AWG ETHNIC MINORITY SCHOLARSHIP
• See page 260

AWG MARIA LUISA CRAWFORD FIELD CAMP SCHOLARSHIP
• See page 129

AWG SALT LAKE CHAPTER (SLC) RESEARCH SCHOLARSHIP
• See page 129

JANET CULLEN TANAKA GEOSCIENCES UNDERGRADUATE SCHOLARSHIP
• See page 129

LONE STAR RISING CAREER SCHOLARSHIP
• See page 260

OSAGE CHAPTER UNDERGRADUATE SERVICE SCHOLARSHIP
• See page 129

SUSAN EKDALE MEMORIAL FIELD CAMP SCHOLARSHIP
• See page 260

ASSOCIATION OF CALIFORNIA WATER AGENCIES

http://www.acwa.com/

ASSOCIATION OF CALIFORNIA WATER AGENCIES SCHOLARSHIPS
• See page 123

CLAIR A. HILL SCHOLARSHIP
• See page 123

ASSOCIATION OF STATE DAM SAFETY OFFICIALS (ASDSO)

http://www.DamSafety.org

ASSOCIATION OF STATE DAM SAFETY OFFICIALS (ASDSO) SENIOR UNDERGRADUATE SCHOLARSHIP
• See page 168

BHW GROUP

https://thebhwgroup.com/

BHW WOMEN IN STEM SCHOLARSHIP
• See page 124

B.O.G. PEST CONTROL

http://www.bogpestcontrol.com/

B.O.G. PEST CONTROL SCHOLARSHIP FUND
• See page 169

BROWN AND CALDWELL

http://www.brownandcaldwell.com

ECKENFELDER SCHOLARSHIP
• See page 169

MINORITY SCHOLARSHIP PROGRAM
• See page 169

CALAVERAS BIG TREES ASSOCIATION

https://bigtrees.org/

EMILY M. HEWITT MEMORIAL SCHOLARSHIP
• See page 170

CALIFORNIA GROUNDWATER ASSOCIATION

http://www.groundh2o.org/

CALIFORNIA GROUNDWATER ASSOCIATION SCHOLARSHIP
• *See page 395*

CONSERVATION FEDERATION OF MISSOURI

http://www.confedmo.org/

CHARLES P. BELL CONSERVATION SCHOLARSHIP
• *See page 339*

COSTA RICAN VACATIONS

http://www.vacationscostarica.com/

COSTA RICAN VACATIONS SCHOLARSHIP
• *See page 339*

DISTIL NETWORKS

http://www.distilnetworks.com

WOMEN FORWARD IN TECHNOLOGY SCHOLARSHIP PROGRAM
• *See page 124*

FOUNDATION FOR SCIENCE AND DISABILITY

http://stemd.org/

GRANTS FOR DISABLED GRADUATE STUDENTS IN THE SCIENCES
• *See page 106*

GARDEN CLUB OF AMERICA

http://www.gcamerica.org/

ELIZABETH GARDNER NORWEB SUMMER ENVIRONMENTAL STUDIES SCHOLARSHIP
• *See page 107*

SARA SHALLENBERGER BROWN GCA NATIONAL PARKS CONSERVATION SCHOLARSHIP
• *See page 387*

GREATER KANAWHA VALLEY FOUNDATION

http://www.tgkvf.org/

LEOPOLD & ELIZABETH MARMET SCHOLARSHIP
• *See page 291*

GREAT MINDS IN STEM

http://www.greatmindsinstem.org

HENAAC SCHOLARSHIP PROGRAM
• *See page 115*

INDIANA WILDLIFE FEDERATION ENDOWMENT

http://www.indianawildlife.org/

CHARLES A. HOLT INDIANA WILDLIFE FEDERATION ENDOWMENT SCHOLARSHIP
• *See page 341*

INTERTRIBAL TIMBER COUNCIL

http://www.itcnet.org/

NATIVE AMERICAN NATURAL RESOURCE RESEARCH SCHOLARSHIP
The Intertribal Timber Council (ITC), in partnership with the USDA Forest Service Southern Research Station is pleased to announce scholarship opportunities for Native American students who are planning or currently conducting tribally relevant research in a natural resource issue. Deadline: January 31, 2018, 5:00 p.m. PST. Award of up to $4,000. The ITC Research Scholarship is designed to support tribally relevant, natural resource based, research being conducted by Native American scholars (graduate or undergraduate). Required Material: The ITC Research Sub-Committee will review and rank only those applications that completely address the following criteria: 1. letter of application. The letter must include your name, permanent mailing address, email address and phone number. Discuss your current educational program and how the proposed research fits into both your degree in natural resources and your future plans; 2. resume; 3. evidence of validated enrollment in a federally recognized tribe or Alaska Native Corporation, as established by the U.S. Government. A photocopy of your enrollment card, front and back, or Certificate of Indian Blood (CIB) is sufficient; 4. mini research proposal. Please keep this concise (4 page maximum not counting budget and justification). Required elements include a) abstract stating research merit and explaining how this research is relevant to tribal natural resource interests b) timeline and methodology c) dissemination plan, including a tribal component d) budget and budget justification; 5. letters of reference/support from an Academic advisor or committee member is required. Additionally, a second letter of support from a tribal resource manager or a tribal representative with tribal approval of the project or the relevancy of the project to the tribe is required. Incomplete applications will not be considered. Applications should be submitted electronically by email (itc1@teleport.com), or (fax: 503-282-1274). Questions regarding the application process can be submitted to ITC (itc1@teleport.com) (phone 503-282-4296) or Adrian Leighton, chair of the ITC Research Sub-Committee (adrian_leighton@skc.edu).

Academic Fields/Career Goals: Natural Resources; Natural Sciences.

Award: Scholarship for use in freshman, sophomore, junior, senior, or graduate years; not renewable. *Amount:* $4000.

Eligibility Requirements: Applicant must be American Indian/Alaska Native and enrolled or expecting to enroll full-time at a four-year institution or university. Available to U.S. citizens.

Application Requirements: Application form, essay. *Deadline:* January 31.

Contact: Education Committee
Intertribal Timber Council
1112 NE 21st Avenue, Suite 4
Portland, OR 97232
Phone: 503-282-4296
Fax: 503-282-1274
E-mail: itc1@teleport.com

TRUMAN D. PICARD SCHOLARSHIP
• *See page 341*

THE LAND CONSERVANCY OF NEW JERSEY

http://www.tlc-nj.org/

ROGERS FAMILY SCHOLARSHIP
• *See page 172*

RUSSELL W. MYERS SCHOLARSHIP
• *See page 172*

LOUISIANA OFFICE OF STUDENT FINANCIAL ASSISTANCE

http://www.osfa.la.gov/

ROCKEFELLER STATE WILDLIFE SCHOLARSHIP
• *See page 172*

MONTANA FEDERATION OF GARDEN CLUBS

http://www.mtfgc.org/

LIFE MEMBER MONTANA FEDERATION OF GARDEN CLUBS SCHOLARSHIP
• *See page 261*

NASA IDAHO SPACE GRANT CONSORTIUM

http://www.idahospacegrant.org

NASA IDAHO SPACE GRANT CONSORTIUM SCHOLARSHIP PROGRAM
• *See page 126*

OHIO FORESTRY ASSOCIATION

http://www.ohioforest.org/

E. B MILLER MEMORIAL SCHOLARSHIP
Minimum of one scholarship will be awarded to provide assistance toward forest resource education to quality college students. Preference given to students attending Ohio colleges and universities.

Academic Fields/Career Goals: Natural Resources.

Award: Scholarship for use in freshman, sophomore, junior, or senior years; not renewable. *Number:* 1–2. *Amount:* $1000–$3000.

Eligibility Requirements: Applicant must be enrolled or expecting to enroll full-time at a two-year or four-year or technical institution or university and resident of Ohio. Available to U.S. citizens.

Application Requirements: Application form, essay. *Deadline:* April 15.

Contact: Gayla Fleming, Association Services
Ohio Forestry Association
507 Main Street
Suite 202
Zanesville, OH 43701
Phone: 888-388-7337
E-mail: gayla@ohioforest.org

OREGON STUDENT ASSISTANCE COMMISSION

https://oregonstudentaid.gov/

CHARLES PATRICK SCHOLARSHIP
• *See page 335*

ROYDEN M. BODLEY SCHOLARSHIP
• *See page 343*

OUTDOOR WRITERS ASSOCIATION OF AMERICA

http://www.owaa.org/

OUTDOOR WRITERS ASSOCIATION OF AMERICA - BODIE MCDOWELL SCHOLARSHIP AWARD
• *See page 222*

PADDLE CANADA

http://www.paddlecanada.com

BILL MASON SCHOLARSHIP FUND
• *See page 275*

PLAN NEW HAMPSHIRE

http://www.plannh.org

PLAN NEW HAMPSHIRE SCHOLARSHIP AND FELLOWSHIP PROGRAM
• *See page 129*

RAILWAY TIE ASSOCIATION

http://www.rta.org/

JOHN MABRY FORESTRY SCHOLARSHIP
One-time award to potential forestry industry leaders. Open to junior and senior undergraduates who will be enrolled in accredited forestry schools. One scholarship is also available to second-year students in a two-year college. Applications reviewed with emphasis on leadership qualities, career objectives, scholastic achievement, and financial need.

Academic Fields/Career Goals: Natural Resources.

Award: Scholarship for use in junior or senior years; not renewable. *Number:* 2. *Amount:* $2000.

Eligibility Requirements: Applicant must be enrolled or expecting to enroll full-time at a two-year or four-year or technical institution or university. Available to U.S. and Canadian citizens.

Application Requirements: Application form, essay, financial need analysis, personal photograph. *Deadline:* June 30.

Contact: Mrs. Barbara Stacey, Website and Committee Coordinator
Railway Tie Association
115 Commerce Drive, Suite C
Fayetteville, GA 30214
Phone: 770-460-5553
E-mail: ties@rta.org

ROCKY MOUNTAIN ELK FOUNDATION

http://www.rmef.org

WILDLIFE LEADERSHIP AWARDS
Program established to recognize, encourage and promote leadership among future wildlife management professionals. Candidates must be an undergraduate in a recognized wildlife program, have at least a junior standing (completed a minimum of 56 semester hours or 108 quarter hours), and have at least one semester or two quarters remaining in their degree program.

Academic Fields/Career Goals: Natural Resources; Natural Sciences.

Award: Scholarship for use in junior or senior years; not renewable. *Number:* 1–5. *Amount:* $3000.

Eligibility Requirements: Applicant must be enrolled or expecting to enroll full-time at a four-year institution or university and must have an interest in wildlife conservation/animal rescue. Available to U.S. and Canadian citizens.

Application Requirements: Application form. *Deadline:* March 1.

Contact: Toni O'Hara, Lands & Conservation Office Administrator
E-mail: tohara@rmef.org

SOCIETY FOR RANGE MANAGEMENT

http://www.rangelands.org/

MASONIC RANGE SCIENCE SCHOLARSHIP
• *See page 103*

SOIL AND WATER CONSERVATION SOCIETY

http://www.swcs.org

DONALD A. WILLIAMS SCHOLARSHIP SOIL CONSERVATION SCHOLARSHIP
• See page 103

SOIL AND WATER CONSERVATION SOCIETY-MISSOURI SHOW-ME CHAPTER

http://www.moswcs.org/

MO SHOW-ME CHAPTER SWCS SCHOLARSHIP
• See page 111

SOIL AND WATER CONSERVATION SOCIETY-NEW JERSEY CHAPTER

http://www.geocities.com/njswcs

EDWARD R. HALL SCHOLARSHIP
• See page 103

SOUTH DAKOTA BOARD OF REGENTS

http://www.sdbor.edu/

SOUTH DAKOTA BOARD OF REGENTS BJUGSTAD SCHOLARSHIP
• See page 104

STRAIGHT NORTH

https://www.straightnorth.com/

STRAIGHT NORTH STEM SCHOLARSHIP
• See page 92

TECHNICAL ASSOCIATION OF THE PULP & PAPER INDUSTRY (TAPPI)

http://www.tappi.org/

WILLIAM L. CULLISON SCHOLARSHIP
Scholarship provides incentive for students to pursue an academic path related to the pulp and paper industry. Eligible students must meet all criteria and will have completed two years of undergraduate school with two years (or three years in a five-year program) remaining. For details, refer to website http://www.tappi.org/s_tappi/doc.asp?CID=6101&DID=561682.
Academic Fields/Career Goals: Natural Resources; Paper and Pulp Engineering.
Award: Scholarship for use in junior or senior years; renewable. *Number:* 1–2. *Amount:* $2000–$4000.
Eligibility Requirements: Applicant must be enrolled or expecting to enroll full-time at a four-year institution or university. Available to U.S. and non-U.S. citizens.
Application Requirements: Application form. *Deadline:* May 1.
Contact: Mr. Laurence Womack, Director of Standards and Awards
Technical Association of the Pulp & Paper Industry (TAPPI)
15 Technology Parkway South
Peachtree Corners, GA 30092
Phone: 770-209-7276
E-mail: standards@tappi.org

UNITED STATES DEPARTMENT OF AGRICULTURE

http://www.usda.gov/

USDA/1994 TRIBAL SCHOLARS PROGRAM
• See page 111

UNITED STATES ENVIRONMENTAL PROTECTION AGENCY

http://www.epa.gov/enviroed

NATIONAL NETWORK FOR ENVIRONMENTAL MANAGEMENT STUDIES FELLOWSHIP
• See page 344

VIRGINIA ASSOCIATION OF SOIL AND WATER CONSERVATION DISTRICTS EDUCATIONAL FOUNDATION INC.

http://www.vaswcd.org/

VASWCD EDUCATIONAL FOUNDATION INC. SCHOLARSHIP AWARDS PROGRAM
Scholarship to provide financial support to Virginia residents majoring in, or showing a strong desire to major in, a course curriculum related to natural resource conservation and/or environmental studies. Applicants must be full-time students who have applied to an undergraduate freshman-level curriculum. Must rank in the top 20 percent of graduating class or have a 3.0 or greater GPA, and demonstrate an active interest in conservation. Recipients may reapply to their individual SWCD for scholarship consideration in ensuing years.
Academic Fields/Career Goals: Natural Resources.
Award: Scholarship for use in freshman year; not renewable. *Number:* 4. *Amount:* $1000.
Eligibility Requirements: Applicant must be high school student; planning to enroll or expecting to enroll full-time at a four-year institution or university and resident of Virginia. Applicant must have 3.0 GPA or higher. Available to U.S. citizens.
Application Requirements: Application form, essay, financial need analysis. *Deadline:* March 1.
Contact: Jennifer Hoysa, District Manager
Phone: 540-316-6984 Ext. 6984
E-mail: jennifer.hoysa@fauquiercounty.gov

WILSON ORNITHOLOGICAL SOCIETY

http://www.wilsonsociety.org/

GEORGE A. HALL/HAROLD F. MAYFIELD AWARD
• See page 118

PAUL A. STEWART AWARDS
• See page 118

NATURAL SCIENCES

AMERICAN CHEMICAL SOCIETY

http://www.acs.org/

AMERICAN CHEMICAL SOCIETY SCHOLARS PROGRAM
• See page 187

AMERICAN FOUNDATION FOR THE BLIND

http://www.afb.org/

PAUL W. RUCKES SCHOLARSHIP
• See page 228

AMERICAN INDIAN SCIENCE AND ENGINEERING SOCIETY

http://www.aises.org/

A.T. ANDERSON MEMORIAL SCHOLARSHIP PROGRAM
• See page 121

AMERICAN PHYSIOLOGICAL SOCIETY

http://www.the-aps.org

BARBARA A. HORWITZ AND JOHN M. HOROWITZ UNDERGRADUATE RESEARCH AWARDS
• See page 114

AMERICAN SOCIETY OF AGRONOMY, CROP SCIENCE SOCIETY OF AMERICA, SOIL SCIENCE SOCIETY OF AMERICA

http://www.agronomy.org

J. FIELDING REED SCHOLARSHIP
• See page 106

ARCTIC INSTITUTE OF NORTH AMERICA

http://www.arctic.ucalgary.ca/

JIM BOURQUE SCHOLARSHIP
• See page 267

ARRL FOUNDATION INC.

http://www.arrl.org/

CTRI/CHRIS SEEBER, KA1GEU, MEMORIAL SCHOLARSHIP
• See page 268

DAN HUETTL, WZ7U, MEMORIAL SCHOLARSHIP
• See page 298

LOIS MANLEY, K7LMZ, AND RANDALL PITCHFORD, WW7ZZ, SCHOLARSHIP
• See page 206

OLD MAN INTERNATIONAL SIDEBAND SOCIETY (OMISS) SCHOLARSHIP
• See page 259

W1FDR SCHOLARSHIP
• See page 122

YASME FOUNDATION SCHOLARSHIP
• See page 168

ASSOCIATION FOR WOMEN GEOSCIENTISTS (AWG)

http://www.awg.org/

AWG ETHNIC MINORITY SCHOLARSHIP
• See page 260

AWG MARIA LUISA CRAWFORD FIELD CAMP SCHOLARSHIP
• See page 129

AWG SALT LAKE CHAPTER (SLC) RESEARCH SCHOLARSHIP
• See page 129

AWG UNDERGRADUATE EXCELLENCE IN PALEONTOLOGY AWARD
• See page 123

JANET CULLEN TANAKA GEOSCIENCES UNDERGRADUATE SCHOLARSHIP
• See page 129

LONE STAR RISING CAREER SCHOLARSHIP
• See page 260

SUSAN EKDALE MEMORIAL FIELD CAMP SCHOLARSHIP
• See page 260

ASSOCIATION OF CALIFORNIA WATER AGENCIES

http://www.acwa.com/

ASSOCIATION OF CALIFORNIA WATER AGENCIES SCHOLARSHIPS
• See page 123

CLAIR A. HILL SCHOLARSHIP
• See page 123

ASSOCIATION OF FORMER INTELLIGENCE OFFICERS

http://www.afio.com

AFIO UNDERGRADUATE AND GRADUATE SCHOLARSHIPS
• See page 113

ASSOCIATION OF STATE DAM SAFETY OFFICIALS (ASDSO)

http://www.DamSafety.org

ASSOCIATION OF STATE DAM SAFETY OFFICIALS (ASDSO) SENIOR UNDERGRADUATE SCHOLARSHIP
• See page 168

ASSOCIATION ON AMERICAN INDIAN AFFAIRS, INC.

http://www.indian-affairs.org/

ELIZABETH AND SHERMAN ASCHE MEMORIAL SCHOLARSHIP FUND
• See page 106

AUDUBON SOCIETY OF WESTERN PENNSYLVANIA

http://www.aswp.org/

BEULAH FREY ENVIRONMENTAL SCHOLARSHIP
• See page 338

BARRY GOLDWATER SCHOLARSHIP AND EXCELLENCE IN EDUCATION FOUNDATION

https://goldwater.scholarsapply.org

BARRY M. GOLDWATER SCHOLARSHIP AND EXCELLENCE IN EDUCATION PROGRAM
• *See page 123*

BHW GROUP

https://thebhwgroup.com/

BHW WOMEN IN STEM SCHOLARSHIP
• *See page 124*

B.O.G. PEST CONTROL

http://www.bogpestcontrol.com/

B.O.G. PEST CONTROL SCHOLARSHIP FUND
• *See page 169*

BROWN AND CALDWELL

http://www.brownandcaldwell.com

ECKENFELDER SCHOLARSHIP
• *See page 169*

MINORITY SCHOLARSHIP PROGRAM
• *See page 169*

CALAVERAS BIG TREES ASSOCIATION

https://bigtrees.org/

EMILY M. HEWITT MEMORIAL SCHOLARSHIP
• *See page 170*

CARDS AGAINST HUMANITY

https://cardsagainsthumanity.com/

SCIENCE AMBASSADOR SCHOLARSHIP
• *See page 124*

CONSERVATION FEDERATION OF MISSOURI

http://www.confedmo.org/

CHARLES P. BELL CONSERVATION SCHOLARSHIP
• *See page 339*

DISTIL NETWORKS

http://www.distilnetworks.com

WOMEN FORWARD IN TECHNOLOGY SCHOLARSHIP PROGRAM
• *See page 124*

DIVERSITYCOMM, INC.

http://www.diversitycomm.net/

DIVERSITY IN STEAM MAGAZINE SCHOLARSHIP
• *See page 83*

THE ELECTROCHEMICAL SOCIETY

http://www.electrochem.org/

STUDENT RESEARCH AWARDS OF THE BATTERY DIVISION OF THE ELECTROCHEMICAL SOCIETY INC.
• *See page 125*

EXPLORERS CLUB

http://www.explorers.org/

YOUTH ACTIVITY FUND
Award given to college students or high school students pursuing a research project in the field of science. Applicants must have two letter of recommendation, one-page description of project, a budget or plan, and proof of student enrollment with dates.

Academic Fields/Career Goals: Natural Sciences; Science, Technology, and Society.

Award: Grant for use in freshman, sophomore, junior, or senior years; not renewable. *Number:* 10–30. *Amount:* $500–$5000.

Eligibility Requirements: Applicant must be enrolled or expecting to enroll full-time at a four-year institution or university. Available to U.S. and non-U.S. citizens.

Application Requirements: Application form, essay, financial need analysis, recommendations or references. *Deadline:* varies.

Contact: Annie Lee, Member Services
Explorers Club
46 East 70th Street
New York, NY 10021
Fax: 212-288-4449
E-mail: alee@explorers.org

FOUNDATION FOR SCIENCE AND DISABILITY

http://stemd.org/

GRANTS FOR DISABLED GRADUATE STUDENTS IN THE SCIENCES
• *See page 106*

GARDEN CLUB OF AMERICA

http://www.gcamerica.org/

FRANCES M. PEACOCK SCHOLARSHIP FOR NATIVE BIRD HABITAT
Up to $4500 award provides financial aid to study areas in the United States that provide seasonal habitat for threatened or endangered native birds and to tend useful information for land-management decisions. Open to college seniors and graduate students only (second-semester juniors may apply for their senior year). In special instances because of two unusually fine candidates or two candidates working on one project, the award may be divided between two candidates.

Academic Fields/Career Goals: Natural Sciences.

Award: Scholarship for use in senior or graduate years; not renewable. *Amount:* $4500.

Eligibility Requirements: Applicant must be enrolled or expecting to enroll full- or part-time at a four-year institution or university. Available to U.S. citizens.

Application Requirements: Application form. *Deadline:* January 15.

Contact: Prof. Irby Lovette, Scholarship Committee
Garden Club of America
Cornell Lab of Ornithology
159 Sapsucker Woods Road
Ithaca, NY 14850-1999
E-mail: ijl2@cornell.edu

GARDEN CLUB OF AMERICA MONTINE M. FREEMAN SCHOLARSHIP IN NATIVE PLANTS
• *See page 386*

GCA SUMMER SCHOLARSHIP IN FIELD BOTANY
• *See page 386*

JOAN K. HUNT AND RACHEL M. HUNT SUMMER SCHOLARSHIP IN FIELD BOTANY
• *See page 386*

GREAT MINDS IN STEM
http://www.greatmindsinstem.org

HENAAC SCHOLARSHIP PROGRAM
• *See page 115*

HERB SOCIETY OF AMERICA, WESTERN RESERVE UNIT
http://www.westernreserveherbsociety.org/

HORTICULTURE SCHOLARSHIP FROM FRANCIS SYLVIA ZVERINA
• *See page 101*

INTERTRIBAL TIMBER COUNCIL
http://www.itcnet.org/

NATIVE AMERICAN NATURAL RESOURCE RESEARCH SCHOLARSHIP
• *See page 459*

KENTUCKY ENERGY AND ENVIRONMENT CABINET
http://dep.ky.gov

ENVIRONMENTAL PROTECTION SCHOLARSHIP
• *See page 172*

LABROOTS INC.
http://www.LabRoots.com

LABROOTS STEM SCHOLARSHIP
• *See page 116*

LAW OFFICES OF PROSPER SHAKED
https://www.prosperlaw.com/

PROSPER SHAKED SCHOLARSHIP FOR FUTURE MEDICAL PROFESSIONALS
• *See page 166*

MEDICAL SCRUBS COLLECTION
http://medicalscrubscollection.com

MEDICAL SCRUBS COLLECTION SCHOLARSHIP
• *See page 120*

NASA IDAHO SPACE GRANT CONSORTIUM
http://www.idahospacegrant.org

NASA IDAHO SPACE GRANT CONSORTIUM SCHOLARSHIP PROGRAM
• *See page 126*

NASA MINNESOTA SPACE GRANT CONSORTIUM
https://www.mnspacegrant.org/

MINNESOTA SPACE GRANT CONSORTIUM SCHOLARSHIP PROGRAM
• *See page 156*

NEVADA NASA SPACE GRANT CONSORTIUM
https://nasa.epscorspo.nevada.edu/

NATIONAL SPACE GRANT CONSORTIUM SCHOLARSHIPS
• *See page 127*

NEXTSTEPU
http://www.nextstepu.com/

$1,500 STEM SCHOLARSHIP
• *See page 120*

OREGON STUDENT ASSISTANCE COMMISSION
https://oregonstudentaid.gov/

ANDY AITKENHEAD SCHOLARSHIP
• *See page 127*

ROBERTS SCHOLARSHIP
• *See page 173*

ROYDEN M. BODLEY SCHOLARSHIP
• *See page 343*

SEHAR SALEHA AHMAD AND ABRAHIM EKRAMULLAH ZAFAR FOUNDATION SCHOLARSHIP
• *See page 127*

PADDLE CANADA
http://www.paddlecanada.com

BILL MASON SCHOLARSHIP FUND
• *See page 275*

ROBERT H. MOLLOHAN FAMILY CHARITABLE FOUNDATION, INC.
http://www.mollohanfoundation.org/

JOHN M. MURPHY SCHOLARSHIP
The John M. Murphy Scholarship is a $500 scholarship that will be awarded to a Pendleton County High School senior who is planning to major in any natural science related field at a West Virginia college or university. Furthermore, the recipient will be eligible for summer internship opportunities within his or her field of study.

Academic Fields/Career Goals: Natural Sciences.

Award: Scholarship for use in senior year; not renewable. *Amount:* $500.

Eligibility Requirements: Applicant must be high school student; planning to enroll or expecting to enroll full- or part-time at a four-year institution or university; resident of West Virginia and studying in West Virginia. Available to U.S. citizens.

Application Requirements: Application form, essay, recommendations or references, resume, test scores, transcript.

Contact: Aime Shaffer, Program Manager
  Phone: 304-333-6783
  E-mail: ashaffer@wvhtf.org

ROCKY MOUNTAIN ELK FOUNDATION

http://www.rmef.org

WILDLIFE LEADERSHIP AWARDS
• *See page 460*

SCARLETT FAMILY FOUNDATION SCHOLARSHIP PROGRAM

http://www.scarlettfoundation.org/

SCHOLARSHIP FOR STUDENTS PURSUING A BUSINESS OR STEM DEGREE
• *See page 91*

SIGMA XI, THE SCIENTIFIC RESEARCH SOCIETY

http://www.sigmaxi.org/

SIGMA XI GRANTS-IN-AID OF RESEARCH
• *See page 110*

SOIL AND WATER CONSERVATION SOCIETY

http://www.swcs.org

DONALD A. WILLIAMS SCHOLARSHIP SOIL CONSERVATION SCHOLARSHIP
• *See page 103*

SOIL AND WATER CONSERVATION SOCIETY-MISSOURI SHOW-ME CHAPTER

http://www.moswcs.org/

MO SHOW-ME CHAPTER SWCS SCHOLARSHIP
• *See page 111*

SOIL AND WATER CONSERVATION SOCIETY-NEW JERSEY CHAPTER

http://www.geocities.com/njswcs

EDWARD R. HALL SCHOLARSHIP
• *See page 103*

STRAIGHT NORTH

https://www.straightnorth.com/

STRAIGHT NORTH STEM SCHOLARSHIP
• *See page 92*

TED ROLLINS AND VALEO GROUPE

http://valeogroupe.us/

TED ROLLINS ECO SCHOLARSHIP
• *See page 183*

UNICO FOUNDATION INC.

http://www.unico.org/

LOUISE TORRACO MEMORIAL SCHOLARSHIP FOR SCIENCE
• *See page 174*

UNITED NATIONS ASSOCIATION OF CONNECTICUT

http://www.unausa.org

UNITED NATIONS ASSOCIATION OF CONNECTICUT SCHOLARSHIP
• *See page 147*

UNITED NEGRO COLLEGE FUND

http://www.uncf.org/

PROCTER & GAMBLE STEM SCHOLARSHIP
• *See page 128*

NEAR AND MIDDLE EAST STUDIES

ASSOCIATION OF FORMER INTELLIGENCE OFFICERS

http://www.afio.com

AFIO UNDERGRADUATE AND GRADUATE SCHOLARSHIPS
• *See page 113*

BHW GROUP

https://thebhwgroup.com/

BHW WOMEN IN STEM SCHOLARSHIP
• *See page 124*

ISLAMIC SCHOLARSHIP FUND

http://islamicscholarshipfund.org/

ISF NATIONAL SCHOLARSHIP
• *See page 119*

UNITED NATIONS ASSOCIATION OF CONNECTICUT

http://www.unausa.org

UNITED NATIONS ASSOCIATION OF CONNECTICUT SCHOLARSHIP
• *See page 147*

NEUROBIOLOGY

101ST AIRBORNE DIVISION ASSOCIATION

http://www.screamingeaglefoundation.org/

AL & WILLIAMARY VISTE SCHOLARSHIP
• *See page 114*

AMERICAN INDIAN SCIENCE AND ENGINEERING SOCIETY

http://www.aises.org/

A.T. ANDERSON MEMORIAL SCHOLARSHIP PROGRAM
• *See page 121*

AMERICAN PHYSIOLOGICAL SOCIETY

http://www.the-aps.org

BARBARA A. HORWITZ AND JOHN M. HOROWITZ UNDERGRADUATE RESEARCH AWARDS
• *See page 114*

AVACARE MEDICAL

https://avacaremedical.com

AVACARE MEDICAL SCHOLARSHIP
• *See page 115*

BARRY GOLDWATER SCHOLARSHIP AND EXCELLENCE IN EDUCATION FOUNDATION

https://goldwater.scholarsapply.org

BARRY M. GOLDWATER SCHOLARSHIP AND EXCELLENCE IN EDUCATION PROGRAM
• *See page 123*

BHW GROUP

https://thebhwgroup.com/

BHW WOMEN IN STEM SCHOLARSHIP
• *See page 124*

CARDS AGAINST HUMANITY

https://cardsagainsthumanity.com/

SCIENCE AMBASSADOR SCHOLARSHIP
• *See page 124*

CYNTHIA E. MORGAN SCHOLARSHIP FUND (CEMS)

http://www.cemsfund.com/

CYNTHIA E. MORGAN MEMORIAL SCHOLARSHIP FUND, INC.
• *See page 334*

DISTIL NETWORKS

http://www.distilnetworks.com

WOMEN FORWARD IN TECHNOLOGY SCHOLARSHIP PROGRAM
• *See page 124*

DIVERSITYCOMM, INC.

http://www.diversitycomm.net/

DIVERSITY IN STEAM MAGAZINE SCHOLARSHIP
• *See page 83*

THE EXPERT INSTITUTE

https://www.theexpertinstitute.com

ANNUAL HEALTHCARE AND LIFE SCIENCES SCHOLARSHIP
• *See page 170*

FOUNDATION FOR SCIENCE AND DISABILITY

http://stemd.org/

GRANTS FOR DISABLED GRADUATE STUDENTS IN THE SCIENCES
• *See page 106*

GREAT MINDS IN STEM

http://www.greatmindsinstem.org

HENAAC SCHOLARSHIP PROGRAM
• *See page 115*

INTERMOUNTAIN MEDICAL IMAGING

https://www.aboutimi.com/

INTERMOUNTAIN MEDICAL IMAGING SCHOLARSHIP
• *See page 147*

KETAMINE CLINICS OF LOS ANGELES

http://www.ketamineclinics.com/

KETAMINE CLINICS OF LOS ANGELES SCHOLARSHIP PROGRAM
• *See page 165*

LABROOTS INC.

http://www.LabRoots.com

LABROOTS STEM SCHOLARSHIP
• *See page 116*

LAW OFFICES OF PROSPER SHAKED

https://www.prosperlaw.com/

PROSPER SHAKED SCHOLARSHIP FOR FUTURE MEDICAL PROFESSIONALS
• *See page 166*

MEDICAL SCRUBS COLLECTION

http://medicalscrubscollection.com

MEDICAL SCRUBS COLLECTION SCHOLARSHIP
• *See page 120*

MICHAEL MOODY FITNESS

http://www.michaelmoodyfitness.com/

MICHAEL MOODY FITNESS SCHOLARSHIP
• *See page 166*

NATIONAL INSTITUTES OF HEALTH

https://www.training.nih.gov/programs/ugsp

NIH UNDERGRADUATE SCHOLARSHIP PROGRAM FOR STUDENTS FROM DISADVANTAGED BACKGROUNDS
• See page 116

NEXTSTEPU

http://www.nextstepu.com/

$1,500 STEM SCHOLARSHIP
• See page 120

SCARLETT FAMILY FOUNDATION SCHOLARSHIP PROGRAM

http://www.scarlettfoundation.org/

SCHOLARSHIP FOR STUDENTS PURSUING A BUSINESS OR STEM DEGREE
• See page 91

STRAIGHT NORTH

https://www.straightnorth.com/

STRAIGHT NORTH STEM SCHOLARSHIP
• See page 92

NUCLEAR SCIENCE

AMERICAN CHEMICAL SOCIETY, RUBBER DIVISION

http://www.rubber.org/

AMERICAN CHEMICAL SOCIETY, RUBBER DIVISION UNDERGRADUATE SCHOLARSHIP
• See page 120

AMERICAN INDIAN SCIENCE AND ENGINEERING SOCIETY

http://www.aises.org/

A.T. ANDERSON MEMORIAL SCHOLARSHIP PROGRAM
• See page 121

AMERICAN NUCLEAR SOCIETY

http://www.ans.org/

AMERICAN NUCLEAR SOCIETY OPERATIONS AND POWER SCHOLARSHIP

Undergraduate scholarship for students who have completed two or more years in a course of study leading to a degree in nuclear science, nuclear engineering, or a nuclear-related field.

Academic Fields/Career Goals: Nuclear Science.

Award: Scholarship for use in junior or senior years; not renewable. *Number:* 1. *Amount:* $2500.

Eligibility Requirements: Applicant must be enrolled or expecting to enroll full- or part-time at a four-year institution or university. Available to U.S. citizens.

Application Requirements: Application form, recommendations or references, transcript. *Deadline:* February 1.

Contact: Scholarship Coordinator
American Nuclear Society
555 North Kensington Avenue
La Grange Park, IL 60526
Phone: 708-352-6611
Fax: 708-352-0499
E-mail: outreach@ans.org

AMERICAN NUCLEAR SOCIETY UNDERGRADUATE SCHOLARSHIPS

Maximum of four scholarships for students who have completed one year in a course of study leading to a degree in nuclear science, nuclear engineering, or a nuclear-related field and who will be sophomores in the upcoming academic year; and a maximum of twenty one scholarships for students who have completed two or more years and will be entering as juniors or seniors. Must be sponsored by ANS member or branch. Must be U.S. citizen or permanent resident.

Academic Fields/Career Goals: Nuclear Science.

Award: Scholarship for use in junior or senior years; not renewable. *Number:* 4–21. *Amount:* $2000.

Eligibility Requirements: Applicant must be enrolled or expecting to enroll full-time at a four-year institution or university. Available to U.S. citizens.

Application Requirements: Application form, recommendations or references, transcript. *Deadline:* February 1.

Contact: Scholarship Coordinator
American Nuclear Society
555 North Kensington Avenue
La Grange Park, IL 60526
Phone: 708-352-6611
Fax: 708-352-0499
E-mail: outreach@ans.org

ANS INCOMING FRESHMAN SCHOLARSHIP

Scholarship for graduating high school seniors who have enrolled or plan to enroll full-time in a nuclear engineering degree program. Scholarships will be awarded based on an applicant's high school academic achievement and course of undergraduate study.

Academic Fields/Career Goals: Nuclear Science.

Award: Scholarship for use in freshman year; not renewable. *Number:* 1–4. *Amount:* $1000.

Eligibility Requirements: Applicant must be high school student and planning to enroll or expecting to enroll full-time at a four-year institution or university. Available to U.S. and non-U.S. citizens.

Application Requirements: Application form, essay, recommendations or references, transcript. *Deadline:* April 1.

Contact: Scholarship Committee
American Nuclear Society
555 North Kensington Avenue
La Grange Park, IL 60526
Phone: 708-352-6611
Fax: 708-352-0499

CHARLES (TOMMY) THOMAS MEMORIAL SCHOLARSHIP DIVISION SCHOLARSHIP

Undergraduate scholarship for students who have completed two or more years in a course of study leading to a degree in nuclear science, nuclear engineering, or a nuclear-related field.

Academic Fields/Career Goals: Nuclear Science.

Award: Scholarship for use in junior or senior years; not renewable. *Number:* 1. *Amount:* $3000.

Eligibility Requirements: Applicant must be enrolled or expecting to enroll full-time at a four-year institution or university. Available to U.S. citizens.

Application Requirements: Application form, recommendations or references, transcript. *Deadline:* February 1.

Contact: Scholarship Coordinator
American Nuclear Society
555 North Kensington Avenue
La Grange Park, IL 60526
Phone: 708-352-6611
Fax: 708-352-0499
E-mail: outreach@ans.org

DECOMMISSIONING, DECONTAMINATION, AND REUTILIZATION UNDERGRADUATE SCHOLARSHIP
• *See page 290*

DELAYED EDUCATION FOR WOMEN SCHOLARSHIPS
One-time award given to enable mature women whose formal studies in nuclear science, nuclear engineering, or related fields have been delayed or interrupted at least one year. Must be U.S. citizen or permanent resident. Minimum GPA of 2.5 required.

Academic Fields/Career Goals: Nuclear Science.

Award: Scholarship for use in freshman, sophomore, junior, or senior years; not renewable. *Number:* 1. *Amount:* $5000.

Eligibility Requirements: Applicant must be enrolled or expecting to enroll full-time at a four-year institution or university and female. Applicant must have 2.5 GPA or higher. Available to U.S. citizens.

Application Requirements: Application form, financial need analysis, recommendations or references, transcript. *Deadline:* February 1.

Contact: Scholarship Coordinator
American Nuclear Society
555 North Kensington Avenue
La Grange Park, IL 60526
Phone: 708-352-6611
Fax: 708-352-0499
E-mail: outreach@ans.org

JOHN AND MURIEL LANDIS SCHOLARSHIP AWARDS
Maximum of eight scholarships are awarded to undergraduate and graduate students who have greater than average financial need. Applicants should be planning a career in nuclear science, nuclear engineering, or a nuclear related field and be enrolled or planning to enroll in a college or university located in the United States, but need not be U.S. citizens.

Academic Fields/Career Goals: Nuclear Science.

Award: Scholarship for use in freshman, sophomore, junior, senior, or graduate years; not renewable. *Number:* 1–8. *Amount:* $5000.

Eligibility Requirements: Applicant must be enrolled or expecting to enroll full-time at a four-year institution or university. Available to U.S. and non-U.S. citizens.

Application Requirements: Application form, financial need analysis, recommendations or references, transcript. *Deadline:* February 1.

Contact: Scholarship Coordinator
American Nuclear Society
555 North Kensington Avenue
La Grange Park, IL 60526
Phone: 708-352-6611
Fax: 708-352-0469
E-mail: outreach@ans.org

JOHN R. LAMARSH SCHOLARSHIP
Undergraduate scholarship for students who have completed two or more years in a course of study leading to a degree in nuclear science, nuclear engineering, or a nuclear-related field.

Academic Fields/Career Goals: Nuclear Science.

Award: Scholarship for use in junior or senior years; not renewable. *Number:* 1. *Amount:* $2000.

Eligibility Requirements: Applicant must be enrolled or expecting to enroll full- or part-time at a four-year institution or university. Available to U.S. citizens.

Application Requirements: Application form, recommendations or references, transcript. *Deadline:* February 1.

Contact: Scholarship Coordinator
American Nuclear Society
555 North Kensington Avenue
La Grange Park, IL 60526
Phone: 708-352-6611
Fax: 708-352-0499
E-mail: outreach@ans.org

JOSEPH R. DIETRICH SCHOLARSHIP
Undergraduate scholarship for students who have completed two or more years in a course of study leading to a degree in nuclear science, nuclear engineering, or a nuclear-related field.

Academic Fields/Career Goals: Nuclear Science.

Award: Scholarship for use in junior or senior years; not renewable. *Number:* 1. *Amount:* $2000.

Eligibility Requirements: Applicant must be enrolled or expecting to enroll full- or part-time at a four-year institution or university. Available to U.S. citizens.

Application Requirements: Application form, recommendations or references, transcript. *Deadline:* February 1.

Contact: Scholarship Coordinator
American Nuclear Society
555 North Kensington Avenue
La Grange Park, IL 60526
Phone: 708-352-6611
Fax: 708-352-0499
E-mail: outreach@ans.org

RAYMOND DISALVO SCHOLARSHIP
Undergraduate scholarship for students who have completed two or more years in a course of study leading to a degree in nuclear science, nuclear engineering, or a nuclear-related field.

Academic Fields/Career Goals: Nuclear Science.

Award: Scholarship for use in junior or senior years; not renewable. *Number:* 1–21. *Amount:* $2000.

Eligibility Requirements: Applicant must be enrolled or expecting to enroll full-time at a four-year institution or university. Available to U.S. and non-U.S. citizens.

Application Requirements: Application form, recommendations or references, sponsorship letter from ANS organization, transcript. *Deadline:* February 1.

Contact: Scholarship Coordinator
Phone: 708-352-6611
Fax: 708-352-0499
E-mail: outreach@ans.org

ROBERT G. LACY SCHOLARSHIP
Undergraduate scholarship for students who have completed two or more years in a course of study leading to a degree in nuclear science, nuclear engineering, or a nuclear-related field.

Academic Fields/Career Goals: Nuclear Science.

Award: Scholarship for use in junior or senior years; not renewable. *Number:* 1. *Amount:* $2000.

Eligibility Requirements: Applicant must be enrolled or expecting to enroll full-time at a four-year institution or university. Available to U.S. and non-U.S. citizens.

Application Requirements: Application form, recommendations or references, sponsorship letter from ANS organization, transcript. *Deadline:* February 1.

Contact: Scholarship Coordinator
Phone: 708-352-6611
Fax: 708-352-0499
E-mail: outreach@ans.org

ROBERT T. "BOB" LINER SCHOLARSHIP
Undergraduate scholarship for students who have completed two or more years in a course of study leading to a degree in nuclear science, nuclear engineering, or a nuclear-related field.

Academic Fields/Career Goals: Nuclear Science.

Award: Scholarship for use in junior or senior years; not renewable. *Number:* 1. *Amount:* $2000.

Eligibility Requirements: Applicant must be enrolled or expecting to enroll full-time at a four-year institution or university. Available to U.S. and non-U.S. citizens.

Application Requirements: Application form, recommendations or references, sponsorship letter from ANS organization, transcript. *Deadline:* February 1.

Contact: Scholarship Coordinator
Phone: 708-352-6611
Fax: 708-352-0499
E-mail: outreach@ans.org

AMERICAN SOCIETY OF NAVAL ENGINEERS

http://www.navalengineers.org/

AMERICAN SOCIETY OF NAVAL ENGINEERS SCHOLARSHIP
• *See page 122*

ARIZONA HYDROLOGICAL SOCIETY

http://www.azhydrosoc.org/

ARIZONA HYDROLOGICAL SOCIETY SCHOLARSHIP
• *See page 259*

ARRL FOUNDATION INC.

http://www.arrl.org/

CTRI/CHRIS SEEBER, KA1GEU, MEMORIAL SCHOLARSHIP
• *See page 268*

DAN HUETTL, WZ7U, MEMORIAL SCHOLARSHIP
• *See page 298*

LOIS MANLEY, K7LMZ, AND RANDALL PITCHFORD, WW7ZZ, SCHOLARSHIP
• *See page 206*

OLD MAN INTERNATIONAL SIDEBAND SOCIETY (OMISS) SCHOLARSHIP
• *See page 259*

W1FDR SCHOLARSHIP
• *See page 122*

BARRY GOLDWATER SCHOLARSHIP AND EXCELLENCE IN EDUCATION FOUNDATION

https://goldwater.scholarsapply.org

BARRY M. GOLDWATER SCHOLARSHIP AND EXCELLENCE IN EDUCATION PROGRAM
• *See page 123*

BHW GROUP

https://thebhwgroup.com/

BHW WOMEN IN STEM SCHOLARSHIP
• *See page 124*

CARDS AGAINST HUMANITY

https://cardsagainsthumanity.com/

SCIENCE AMBASSADOR SCHOLARSHIP
• *See page 124*

DISTIL NETWORKS

http://www.distilnetworks.com

WOMEN FORWARD IN TECHNOLOGY SCHOLARSHIP PROGRAM
• *See page 124*

DIVERSITYCOMM, INC.

http://www.diversitycomm.net/

DIVERSITY IN STEAM MAGAZINE SCHOLARSHIP
• *See page 83*

FOUNDATION FOR SCIENCE AND DISABILITY

http://stemd.org/

GRANTS FOR DISABLED GRADUATE STUDENTS IN THE SCIENCES
• *See page 106*

GREAT MINDS IN STEM

http://www.greatmindsinstem.org

HENAAC SCHOLARSHIP PROGRAM
• *See page 115*

HAWAIIAN LODGE, F&AM

http://www.hawaiianlodgefreemasons.org

HAWAIIAN LODGE SCHOLARSHIPS
• *See page 86*

LABROOTS INC.

http://www.LabRoots.com

LABROOTS STEM SCHOLARSHIP
• *See page 116*

NASA IDAHO SPACE GRANT CONSORTIUM

http://www.idahospacegrant.org

NASA IDAHO SPACE GRANT CONSORTIUM SCHOLARSHIP PROGRAM
• *See page 126*

NASA MINNESOTA SPACE GRANT CONSORTIUM

https://www.mnspacegrant.org/

MINNESOTA SPACE GRANT CONSORTIUM SCHOLARSHIP PROGRAM
• *See page 156*

NATIONAL INSTITUTES OF HEALTH

https://www.training.nih.gov/programs/ugsp

NIH UNDERGRADUATE SCHOLARSHIP PROGRAM FOR STUDENTS FROM DISADVANTAGED BACKGROUNDS
• *See page 116*

NEXTSTEPU

http://www.nextstepu.com/

$1,500 STEM SCHOLARSHIP
• *See page 120*

OREGON STUDENT ASSISTANCE COMMISSION

https://oregonstudentaid.gov/

ANDY AITKENHEAD SCHOLARSHIP
• *See page 127*

SCARLETT FAMILY FOUNDATION SCHOLARSHIP PROGRAM

http://www.scarlettfoundation.org/

SCHOLARSHIP FOR STUDENTS PURSUING A BUSINESS OR STEM DEGREE
• *See page 91*

SIGMA XI, THE SCIENTIFIC RESEARCH SOCIETY

http://www.sigmaxi.org/

SIGMA XI GRANTS-IN-AID OF RESEARCH
• *See page 110*

STRAIGHT NORTH

https://www.straightnorth.com/

STRAIGHT NORTH STEM SCHOLARSHIP
• *See page 92*

TAILOR MADE LAWNS

http://www.tailormadelawns.com

TAILOR MADE LAWNS SCHOLARSHIP FUND
• *See page 111*

UNITED NATIONS ASSOCIATION OF CONNECTICUT

http://www.unausa.org

UNITED NATIONS ASSOCIATION OF CONNECTICUT SCHOLARSHIP
• *See page 147*

UNITED NEGRO COLLEGE FUND

http://www.uncf.org/

PROCTER & GAMBLE STEM SCHOLARSHIP
• *See page 128*

UNIVERSITIES SPACE RESEARCH ASSOCIATION

http://www.usra.edu/

UNIVERSITIES SPACE RESEARCH ASSOCIATION SCHOLARSHIP AWARD PROGRAM
• *See page 128*

NURSING

101ST AIRBORNE DIVISION ASSOCIATION

http://www.screamingeaglefoundation.org/

AL & WILLIAMARY VISTE SCHOLARSHIP
• *See page 114*

ACLS CERTIFICATION INSTITUTE

https://acls.com

MEDICAL SCHOOL SCHOLARSHIP
• *See page 251*

AIR FORCE RESERVE OFFICER TRAINING CORPS

http://www.afrotc.com/

AIR FORCE ROTC FOUR-YEAR NURSING SCHOLARSHIP
Scholarship offers qualified individuals the chance to compete for scholarships of up to $15,000 per academic year. Nursing students can compete for scholarships through the In-College Scholarship Program, or may qualify for a nursing scholarship.

Academic Fields/Career Goals: Nursing.

Award: Scholarship for use in sophomore, junior, or senior years; not renewable. *Amount:* up to $15,000.

Eligibility Requirements: Applicant must be enrolled or expecting to enroll full-time at a four-year institution or university. Available to U.S. citizens.

Application Requirements: Application form. *Deadline:* varies.

Contact: Capt. Elmarko Magee, Chief of Advertising
Air Force Reserve Officer Training Corps
551 East Maxwell Boulevard
Maxwell AFB, AL 36112-6106
Phone: 866-423-7682

ALBERTA HERITAGE SCHOLARSHIP FUND

http://www.alis.alberta.ca/

ABORIGINAL HEALTH CAREERS BURSARY
• *See page 167*

AMARILLO AREA FOUNDATION

http://www.amarilloareafoundation.org/

E. EUGENE WAIDE, MD MEMORIAL SCHOLARSHIP
Scholarship for graduating senior from Ochiltree, Hansford, Lipscomb, Hutchinson, Roberts or Hemphill counties. Applicant must pursue a career as LVN, BSN (junior or senior), or MSN.

Academic Fields/Career Goals: Nursing.

Award: Scholarship for use in freshman, sophomore, junior, senior, or graduate years; not renewable.

Eligibility Requirements: Applicant must be enrolled or expecting to enroll full- or part-time at a two-year or four-year or technical institution or university and resident of Texas. Available to U.S. citizens.

Application Requirements: Application form, personal photograph. *Deadline:* February 1.

Contact: Scholarship Screening Committee
Phone: 806-376-4521
Fax: 806-373-3656

NANCY GERALD MEMORIAL NURSING SCHOLARSHIP
Scholarship of $500 for graduating senior from one of the 26 counties in Texas. Applicant must be majoring in the field of nursing at Amarillo College or West Texas A & M University pursuing AAS, BSN, or MSN degree.

Academic Fields/Career Goals: Nursing.

Award: Scholarship for use in freshman, sophomore, junior, senior, or graduate years; not renewable. *Amount:* $500.

Eligibility Requirements: Applicant must be enrolled or expecting to enroll full- or part-time at a two-year or four-year institution or university; resident of Texas and studying in Texas. Applicant must have 2.5 GPA or higher. Available to U.S. citizens.

Application Requirements: Application form, personal photograph. *Deadline:* February 1.

Contact: Scholarship Screening Committee
Phone: 806-376-4521
Fax: 806-373-3656

AMERICAN ASSOCIATION OF COLLEGES OF NURSING

http://www.aacnnursing.org

AFTERCOLLEGE/AACN NURSING SCHOLARSHIP PROGRAM

The AfterCollege-AACN Scholarship Fund supports students who are seeking a baccalaureate, Master's or doctoral degree in nursing. Special consideration will be given to students in a graduate program with the goal of becoming a nurse educator; students completing an RN-to-BSN or RN-to-MSN program; and those enrolled in an accelerated program. One scholarship in the amount of $2,500 will be awarded each quarter. Nursing scholarship deadlines are March 31, June 30, September 30, and December 31. Please note that all applicants must already be enrolled (not just accepted) at an AACN member institution. To check if your school is a member, see AACN Members. Only finalists are contacted and may be asked to submit letters of recommendation, published articles, awards/honors, etc. to the selection committee. Recipients will be announced within one month of each deadline and contacted to redeem the award. Check out this list of past scholarship recipients. Have questions about this scholarship? You can reach us at scholarships@aftercollege.com, and visit our Official Scholarship Rules for full details!

Academic Fields/Career Goals: Nursing.

Award: Scholarship for use in freshman, sophomore, junior, senior, graduate, or postgraduate years; not renewable. *Number:* 1. *Amount:* $2500.

Eligibility Requirements: Applicant must be enrolled or expecting to enroll full-time at a four-year institution or university. Available to U.S. and non-U.S. citizens.

Application Requirements: Application form. *Deadline:* continuous.

Contact: Catherine Proulx, Communications Assistant
American Association of Colleges of Nursing
655 K Street NW, Suite 750
Washington, DC 20001
Phone: 202-463-6930 Ext. 292
E-mail: cproulx@aacnnursing.org

AMERICAN INDIAN SCIENCE AND ENGINEERING SOCIETY

http://www.aises.org/

A.T. ANDERSON MEMORIAL SCHOLARSHIP PROGRAM
• *See page 121*

AMERICAN LEGION AUXILIARY DEPARTMENT OF ARIZONA

http://wwwaladeptaz.org

AMERICAN LEGION AUXILIARY DEPARTMENT OF ARIZONA NURSES' SCHOLARSHIPS

Award for Arizona residents enrolled in their second year at an institution in Arizona awarding degrees as a registered nurse. Preference given to immediate family member of a veteran. Must be a U.S. citizen and resident of Arizona for one year.

Academic Fields/Career Goals: Nursing.

Award: Scholarship for use in freshman, sophomore, junior, senior, or graduate years; not renewable. *Number:* 4. *Amount:* $600.

Eligibility Requirements: Applicant must be enrolled or expecting to enroll full- or part-time at a two-year or four-year or technical institution or university; resident of Arizona and studying in Arizona. Available to U.S. citizens.

Application Requirements: Application form, essay, financial need analysis, personal photograph. *Deadline:* May 15.

Contact: Mrs. Barbara Matteson, Department Secretary and Treasurer
American Legion Auxiliary Department of Arizona
4701 North 19th Avenue, Suite 100
Phoenix, AZ 85015-3727
Phone: 602-241-1080
E-mail: secretary@aladeptaz.org

AMERICAN LEGION AUXILIARY DEPARTMENT OF CALIFORNIA

http://www.calegionaux.org/

AMERICAN LEGION AUXILIARY DEPARTMENT OF CALIFORNIA PAST PRESIDENTS' PARLEY NURSING SCHOLARSHIPS

Award for student entering into or continuing studies in a nursing program.

Academic Fields/Career Goals: Nursing.

Award: Scholarship for use in freshman, sophomore, junior, or senior years; not renewable. *Number:* 1–2. *Amount:* $4000–$4000.

Eligibility Requirements: Applicant must be enrolled or expecting to enroll full- or part-time at a four-year institution or university and resident of California. Available to U.S. citizens. Applicant must have general military experience.

Application Requirements: Application form, recommendations or references, transcript. *Deadline:* April 4.

Contact: Ruby Kapsalis, Secretary/Treasurer
Phone: 415-862-5092
Fax: 415-861-8365
E-mail: calegionaux@calegionaux.org

AMERICAN LEGION AUXILIARY DEPARTMENT OF COLORADO

http://www.alacolorado.com

AMERICAN LEGION AUXILIARY DEPARTMENT OF COLORADO PAST PRESIDENTS' PARLEY HEALTH CARE PROFESSIONAL SCHOLARSHIPNURSES SCHOLARSHIP
• *See page 147*

AMERICAN LEGION AUXILIARY DEPARTMENT OF IDAHO

http://www.idahoala.org/

AMERICAN LEGION AUXILIARY DEPARTMENT OF IDAHO NURSING SCHOLARSHIP

Scholarship available to veterans or the children of veterans who are majoring in nursing. Applicants must be 17 to 35 years of age and residents of Idaho for five years prior to applying. One-time award of $1000.

Academic Fields/Career Goals: Nursing.

Award: Scholarship for use in freshman, sophomore, junior, or senior years; not renewable. *Number:* 1. *Amount:* $1000.

Eligibility Requirements: Applicant must be age 17-35; enrolled or expecting to enroll full- or part-time at a four-year institution or university and resident of Idaho. Available to U.S. citizens. Applicant or parent must meet one or more of the following requirements: general military experience; retired from active duty; disabled or killed as a result of military service; prisoner of war; or missing in action.

Application Requirements: Application form, financial need analysis, personal photograph, recommendations or references, self-addressed stamped envelope with application, transcript. *Deadline:* May 15.

Contact: Mary Sue Chase, Secretary
American Legion Auxiliary Department of Idaho
905 Warren Street
Boise, ID 83706-3825
Phone: 208-342-7066
Fax: 208-342-7066
E-mail: idalegionaux@msn.com

AMERICAN LEGION AUXILIARY DEPARTMENT OF IOWA

http://www.ialegion.org/ala

AMERICAN LEGION AUXILIARY DEPARTMENT OF IOWA M.V. MCCRAE MEMORIAL NURSES MERIT AWARD

One-time award available to the child of an Iowa American Legion Post member or Iowa American Legion Auxiliary Unit member. Award is for full-time study in an accredited nursing program. Must be U.S. citizen and Iowa resident. Must attend an Iowa institution.

Academic Fields/Career Goals: Nursing.

Award: Scholarship for use in freshman, sophomore, junior, or senior years; not renewable. *Number:* 1. *Amount:* $400.

Eligibility Requirements: Applicant must be enrolled or expecting to enroll full-time at a two-year or four-year or technical institution or university; resident of Iowa and studying in Iowa. Applicant or parent of applicant must be member of American Legion or Auxiliary. Available to U.S. citizens. Applicant or parent must meet one or more of the following requirements: general military experience; retired from active duty; disabled or killed as a result of military service; prisoner of war; or missing in action.

Application Requirements: Application form, essay, financial need analysis, personal photograph, recommendations or references, self-addressed stamped envelope with application, test scores, transcript. *Deadline:* June 1.

Contact: Marlene Valentine, Secretary and Treasurer
American Legion Auxiliary Department of Iowa
720 Lyon Street
Des Moines, IA 50309
Phone: 515-282-7987
Fax: 515-282-7583
E-mail: alasectreas@ialegion.org

AMERICAN LEGION AUXILIARY DEPARTMENT OF MAINE

http://www.mainelegion.org/

AMERICAN LEGION AUXILIARY DEPARTMENT OF MAINE PAST PRESIDENTS' PARLEY NURSES SCHOLARSHIP
• *See page 369*

AMERICAN LEGION AUXILIARY DEPARTMENT OF MASSACHUSETTS

http://www.masslegion-aux.org/

AMERICAN LEGION AUXILIARY DEPARTMENT OF MASSACHUSETTS PAST PRESIDENTS' PARLEY SCHOLARSHIP

One-time awards of $200 to $750 for residents of Massachusetts who are children of living or deceased veterans. Must be between the ages of 16 to 22 years and enrolled full-time at a Massachusetts institution.

Academic Fields/Career Goals: Nursing.

Award: Scholarship for use in freshman, sophomore, junior, or senior years; not renewable. *Number:* 1. *Amount:* $200–$750.

Eligibility Requirements: Applicant must be age 16-22; enrolled or expecting to enroll full-time at a two-year or four-year institution or university and resident of Massachusetts. Available to U.S. citizens. Applicant or parent must meet one or more of the following requirements: general military experience; retired from active duty; disabled or killed as a result of military service; prisoner of war; or missing in action.

Application Requirements: Application form. *Deadline:* April 1.

Contact: Ann Fournier, Secretary and Treasurer
American Legion Auxiliary Department of Massachusetts
State House Room 546-2
Boston, MA 02133
Phone: 617-727-2958
E-mail: masslegion-aux@comcast.net

AMERICAN LEGION AUXILIARY DEPARTMENT OF MICHIGAN

http://www.michalaux.org/

AMERICAN LEGION AUXILIARY DEPARTMENT OF MICHIGAN MEDICAL CAREER SCHOLARSHIP
• *See page 369*

AMERICAN LEGION AUXILIARY DEPARTMENT OF MISSOURI

http://www.missourilegion.org/

AMERICAN LEGION AUXILIARY DEPARTMENT OF MISSOURI PAST PRESIDENTS' PARLEY SCHOLARSHIP

Scholarship of $500 is awarded to high school graduate who has chosen to study nursing. $500 will be awarded upon receipt of verification from the college that student is enrolled. The applicant must be a resident of Missouri and a member of a veteran's family. The applicant must be validated by the sponsoring unit. Check with sponsoring unit for details on required recommendation letters.

Academic Fields/Career Goals: Nursing.

Award: Scholarship for use in freshman year; not renewable. *Number:* 2. *Amount:* $500.

Eligibility Requirements: Applicant must be high school student; planning to enroll or expecting to enroll full-time at a two-year or four-year or technical institution or university and resident of Missouri. Applicant or parent of applicant must be member of American Legion or Auxiliary. Available to U.S. citizens. Applicant or parent must meet one or more of the following requirements: general military experience; retired from active duty; disabled or killed as a result of military service; prisoner of war; or missing in action.

Application Requirements: Application form, personal photograph, resume. *Deadline:* March 1.

Contact: Karen Larson, Department Secretary/Treasurer
American Legion Auxiliary Department of Missouri
600 Ellis Boulevard
Jefferson City, MO 65101
Phone: 573-636-9133
Fax: 573-635-3467
E-mail: dptmoala@embarqmail.com

AMERICAN LEGION AUXILIARY DEPARTMENT OF NORTH DAKOTA

http://www.ndlegion.org/

AMERICAN LEGION AUXILIARY DEPARTMENT OF NORTH DAKOTA PAST PRESIDENTS' PARLEY NURSES SCHOLARSHIP

One-time award for North Dakota resident who is the child, grandchild, or great-grandchild of a member of the American Legion or Auxiliary. Must be a graduate of a North Dakota high school and attending a nursing program in North Dakota. A minimum 2.5 GPA is required.

Academic Fields/Career Goals: Nursing.

Award: Scholarship for use in freshman year; not renewable. *Number:* 5. *Amount:* $500.

Eligibility Requirements: Applicant must be enrolled or expecting to enroll full- or part-time at a four-year institution or university; resident of North Dakota and studying in North Dakota. Applicant or parent of applicant must be member of American Legion or Auxiliary. Applicant must have 2.5 GPA or higher. Available to U.S. citizens. Applicant or parent must meet one or more of the following requirements: general military experience; retired from active duty; disabled or killed as a result of military service; prisoner of war; or missing in action.

Application Requirements: Application form, driver's license, essay, financial need analysis, self-addressed stamped envelope with application, test scores, transcript. *Deadline:* May 15.

Contact: Myrna Ronholm, Department Secretary
American Legion Auxiliary Department of North Dakota
PO Box 1060
Jamestown, ND 58402-1060
Phone: 701-253-5992
E-mail: ala-hq@ndlegion.org

AMERICAN LEGION AUXILIARY DEPARTMENT OF OHIO

http://www.alaohio.org/

AMERICAN LEGION AUXILIARY DEPARTMENT OF OHIO PAST PRESIDENTS' PARLEY NURSES SCHOLARSHIP

One-time award worth $300 to $500 for Ohio residents who are the children or grandchildren of a veteran, living or deceased. Must enroll or be enrolled in a nursing program. Application requests must be received by May 1.

Academic Fields/Career Goals: Nursing.

Award: Scholarship for use in freshman, sophomore, junior, or senior years; not renewable. *Number:* 15–20. *Amount:* $300–$500.

Eligibility Requirements: Applicant must be enrolled or expecting to enroll full-time at a two-year or four-year institution or university and resident of Ohio. Available to U.S. citizens. Applicant or parent must meet one or more of the following requirements: general military experience; retired from active duty; disabled or killed as a result of military service; prisoner of war; or missing in action.

Application Requirements: Application form, recommendations or references. *Deadline:* May 1.

Contact: Katie Tucker, Scholarship Coordinator
Phone: 740-452-8245
Fax: 740-452-2620
E-mail: ala_katie@rrohio.com

AMERICAN LEGION AUXILIARY DEPARTMENT OF OREGON

http://www.alaoregon.org/

AMERICAN LEGION AUXILIARY DEPARTMENT OF OREGON NURSES SCHOLARSHIP

One-time award for Oregon residents who are in their senior year of high school, who are the children of veterans who served during eligibility dates for American Legion membership. Must enroll in a nursing program. Contact local units for application.

Academic Fields/Career Goals: Nursing.

Award: Scholarship for use in freshman year; not renewable. *Number:* 1. *Amount:* $1500.

Eligibility Requirements: Applicant must be high school student; planning to enroll or expecting to enroll full- or part-time at a four-year institution or university and resident of Oregon. Available to U.S. citizens.

Application Requirements: Application form, essay, financial need analysis, interview. *Deadline:* March 20.

Contact: Virginia Biddle, Secretary/Treasurer
American Legion Auxiliary Department of Oregon
PO Box 1730
Wilsonville, OR 97070
Phone: 503-682-3162
E-mail: alaor@pcez.com

AMERICAN LEGION AUXILIARY DEPARTMENT OF PENNSYLVANIA

http://pa-legion.com

AMERICAN LEGION AUXILIARY DEPARTMENT OF PENNSYLVANIA PAST DEPARTMENT PRESIDENTS' MEMORIAL SCHOLARSHIP

Renewable award of $400 given each year to high school seniors. Must be residents of Pennsylvania. Total award $1200

Academic Fields/Career Goals: Nursing.

Award: Scholarship for use in freshman, sophomore, or junior years; renewable. *Number:* 1. *Amount:* $1200.

Eligibility Requirements: Applicant must be high school student; planning to enroll or expecting to enroll full-time at a four-year institution or university; single; resident of Pennsylvania and studying in Pennsylvania. Available to U.S. citizens.

Application Requirements: Application form. *Deadline:* March 15.

Contact: Colleen Watson, Executive Secretary and Treasurer
Phone: 717-763-7545
Fax: 717-763-0617
E-mail: paalad@hotmail.com

AMERICAN LEGION AUXILIARY DEPARTMENT OF WISCONSIN

http://www.amlegionauxwi.org/

AMERICAN LEGION AUXILIARY DEPARTMENT OF WISCONSIN PAST PRESIDENTS' PARLEY HEALTH CAREER SCHOLARSHIPS

• *See page 366*

AMERICAN LEGION AUXILIARY DEPARTMENT OF WISCONSIN PAST PRESIDENTS' PARLEY REGISTERED NURSE SCHOLARSHIP

One-time award of $1000. Applicant must be in nursing school or have positive acceptance to an accredited hospital or university registered nursing program. Applicant must be a direct descendant, wife, or widow of a veteran. Must submit certification of an American Legion Auxiliary unit president, copy of proof that veteran was in service (i.e. discharge papers), letters of recommendation, transcripts, and essay. Must have minimum 3.5 GPA, show financial need, and be a resident of Wisconsin or member of the Wisconsin American Legion Family. Applications available on website http://www.amlegionauxwi.org.

Academic Fields/Career Goals: Nursing.

Award: Scholarship for use in freshman, sophomore, junior, or senior years; not renewable. *Number:* 1–2. *Amount:* $1000.

Eligibility Requirements: Applicant must be enrolled or expecting to enroll full- or part-time at a two-year or four-year or technical institution or university and resident of Wisconsin. Applicant or parent of applicant must be member of American Legion or Auxiliary. Applicant must have 3.5 GPA or higher. Available to U.S. citizens. Applicant or parent must meet one or more of the following requirements: general military experience; retired from active duty; disabled or killed as a result of military service; prisoner of war; or missing in action.

Application Requirements: Application form, essay, financial need analysis. *Deadline:* March 15.

Contact: Bonnie Dorniak, Department Secretary
American Legion Auxiliary Department of Wisconsin
PO Box 140
Portage, WI 53901
Phone: 608-745-0124
Fax: 608-745-1947
E-mail: deptsec@amlegionauxwi.org

AMERICAN LEGION DEPARTMENT OF MISSOURI

http://www.missourilegion.org/

M.D. "JACK" MURPHY MEMORIAL SCHOLARSHIP

One $750 award for two successive semesters will be given to a Missouri resident who is a RN and under the age of 21. Applicant must be unmarried and a descendant of a veteran with at least ninety days active service in the U.S. Army, Navy, Air Force, Marines, or Coast Guard receiving a Honorable Discharge for service. Applicant must have graduated in the top forty percent of their high school class or have a "C" average or equivalent.

Academic Fields/Career Goals: Nursing.

Award: Scholarship for use in freshman year; not renewable. *Number:* 1. *Amount:* $750.

Eligibility Requirements: Applicant must be high school student; planning to enroll or expecting to enroll full-time at a two-year or four-year institution or university; single female and resident of Missouri. Available to U.S. citizens. Applicant or parent must meet one or more of the following requirements: general military experience; retired from active duty; disabled or killed as a result of military service; prisoner of war; or missing in action.

Application Requirements: Application form, copy of the veteran's discharge or separation notice, financial need analysis, test scores. *Deadline:* April 20.

Contact: John Doane, Chairman
American Legion Department of Missouri
PO Box 179
Jefferson City, MO 65102-0179
Phone: 417-924-8186
Fax: 573-893-2980

THE ARC NEW YORK

https://www.nysarc.org/

JAMES F. REVILLE SCHOLARSHIP
• *See page 366*

ARRL FOUNDATION INC.

http://www.arrl.org/

CAROLE J. STREETER, KB9JBR, SCHOLARSHIP
• *See page 254*

MEDICAL AMATEUR RADIO COUNCIL (MARCO) SCHOLARSHIP
• *See page 115*

ASSOCIATION ON AMERICAN INDIAN AFFAIRS, INC.

http://www.indian-affairs.org/

ELIZABETH AND SHERMAN ASCHE MEMORIAL SCHOLARSHIP FUND
• *See page 106*

AVACARE MEDICAL

https://avacaremedical.com

AVACARE MEDICAL SCHOLARSHIP
• *See page 115*

BESTNURSINGDEGREE.COM

https://www.bestnursingdegree.com

BACK TO SCHOOL NURSING SCHOLARSHIP PROGRAM

Are you ready to chase your dream of becoming a nurse, but aren't sure how you'll pay for your education? We want to help you realize your dream of becoming a nurse by offering you the chance to win a $2,500 nursing scholarship. A winner will be randomly selected from the list of all eligible candidates. We award four different scholarships each year. When one deadline ends, the next scholarship will begin. Deadlines are as follows: January 31, April 30, July 30, and October 31. Apply for the scholarship at https://www.bestnursingdegree.com/scholarship/

Academic Fields/Career Goals: Nursing.

Award: Scholarship for use in freshman, sophomore, junior, senior, graduate, or postgraduate years; not renewable. *Number:* 1. *Amount:* $2500.

Eligibility Requirements: Applicant must be enrolled or expecting to enroll full- or part-time at a two-year or four-year or technical institution or university. Available to U.S. citizens.

Application Requirements: Application form. *Deadline:* continuous.

Contact: Joann Do
BestNursingDegree.com
15500 W 113th St Suite 200
Lenexa, KS 66219
Phone: 913-254-6742
E-mail: Joann.Do@marketing.keypathedu.com

BHW GROUP

https://thebhwgroup.com/

BHW WOMEN IN STEM SCHOLARSHIP
• *See page 124*

CANADIAN NURSES FOUNDATION

http://www.cnf-fiic.ca/

CANADIAN NURSES FOUNDATION SCHOLARSHIPS

Study awards are granted annually to Canadian nurses wishing to pursue education and research. Must be a Canadian citizen or permanent resident and provide proof of citizenship. Must be studying in Canada at a Canadian institution. Baccalaureate students must be full-time, masters and doctoral students may be full- or part-time. Additional restrictions vary by specific scholarship.

Academic Fields/Career Goals: Nursing.

Award: Scholarship for use in sophomore, junior, senior, graduate, or postgraduate years; not renewable. *Number:* 50–60. *Amount:* $1500–$9000.

Eligibility Requirements: Applicant must be Canadian citizen and enrolled or expecting to enroll full- or part-time at a four-year institution or university. Applicant or parent of applicant must have employment or volunteer experience in nursing.

Application Requirements: Application form. *Fee:* $30. *Deadline:* February 22.

Contact: Foundation Coordinator
Canadian Nurses Foundation
50 Driveway
Ottawa, ON
CAN
Phone: 613-680-0879 Ext. 221
E-mail: info@cnf-fiic.ca

CHRISTIANA CARE HEALTH SYSTEMS

http://www.christianacare.org/

RUTH SHAW JUNIOR BOARD SCHOLARSHIP
• *See page 372*

CONTINENTAL SOCIETY, DAUGHTERS OF INDIAN WARS

http://www.csdiw.org/

CONTINENTAL SOCIETY, DAUGHTERS OF INDIAN WARS SCHOLARSHIP
• *See page 242*

CYNTHIA E. MORGAN SCHOLARSHIP FUND (CEMS)

http://www.cemsfund.com/

CYNTHIA E. MORGAN MEMORIAL SCHOLARSHIP FUND, INC.
• *See page 334*

DELAWARE COMMUNITY FOUNDATION

https://delcf.org/

MARGARET A. STAFFORD NURSING SCHOLARSHIP
Must be a resident of Delaware to apply planning on Nursing degree

Academic Fields/Career Goals: Nursing.

Award: Scholarship for use in freshman, sophomore, or junior years; not renewable. *Number:* 1–2. *Amount:* $1000–$2000.

Eligibility Requirements: Applicant must be enrolled or expecting to enroll full- or part-time at a two-year or four-year institution or university and resident of Delaware. Applicant must have 3.0 GPA or higher. Available to U.S. citizens.

Application Requirements: Application form, essay, financial need analysis. *Deadline:* March 15.

Contact: Kelly Sheridan, Scholarship Administrator
Delaware Community Foundation
36 The circle
Georgetown, DE 19947
Phone: 302-856-4393
E-mail: ksheridan@delcf.org

DEPARTMENT OF THE ARMY

http://www.goarmy.com/rotc

U.S. ARMY ROTC FOUR-YEAR NURSING SCHOLARSHIP
One-time award for freshman interested in nursing and accepted into an accredited nursing program. Must join ROTC program at the institution, pass physical evaluation, and have minimum GPA of 2.5. Applicant must be a U.S. citizen, have a qualifying SAT or ACT score, and be at least 17 years of age by college enrollment and under 31 years of age at time of graduation. Online application available.

Academic Fields/Career Goals: Nursing.

Award: Scholarship for use in freshman, sophomore, junior, or senior years; renewable. *Number:* 100. *Amount:* $5000–$50,000.

Eligibility Requirements: Applicant must be age 17-26; enrolled or expecting to enroll full-time at a four-year institution or university; resident of Alabama, Alaska, Arizona, Arkansas, California, Colorado, Connecticut, Delaware, District of Columbia, Florida, Georgia, Guam, Hawaii, Idaho, Illinois, Indiana, Iowa, Kansas, Kentucky, Louisiana, Maine, Maryland, Massachusetts, Michigan, Minnesota, Mississippi, Missouri, Montana, Nebraska, Nevada, New Hampshire, New Jersey, New Mexico, New York, North Carolina, North Dakota, Ohio, Oklahoma, Ontario, Oregon, Pennsylvania, Puerto Rico, Rhode Island, South Carolina, South Dakota, Tennessee, Texas, Utah, Vermont, Virginia, Washington, West Virginia, Wisconsin, Wyoming and studying in Alabama, Alaska, Arizona, Arkansas, California, Colorado, Connecticut, Delaware, District of Columbia, Florida, Georgia, Guam, Hawaii, Idaho, Illinois, Indiana, Iowa, Kansas, Kentucky, Louisiana, Maine, Maryland, Massachusetts, Michigan, Minnesota, Mississippi, Missouri, Montana, Nebraska, Nevada, New Hampshire, New Jersey, New Mexico, New York, North Carolina, North Dakota, Ohio, Oklahoma, Ontario, Oregon, Pennsylvania, Puerto Rico, Rhode Island, South Carolina, South Dakota, Tennessee, Texas, Utah, Vermont, Virginia, Washington, West Virginia, Wisconsin, Wyoming. Applicant must have 2.5 GPA or higher. Available to U.S. citizens. Applicant must have national guard experience.

Application Requirements: Application form, essay, interview. *Deadline:* January 10.

Contact: Mr. Timothy Borgerding, Chief of Scholarship Management Branch
Department of the Army
U.S. Army Cadet Command
Building 1002, 204 1st Cavalry Regiment Road
Fort Knox, KY 40121-5123
Phone: 502-624-2309
E-mail: timothy.b.borgerding.civ@mail.mil

DERMATOLOGY NURSES' ASSOCIATION

http://www.dnanurse.org/

CAREER MOBILITY SCHOLARSHIP
Provides financial assistance to members of the Dermatology Nurses' Association (DNA) who are pursuing an undergraduate or graduate degree. The candidate must be a DNA member for two years, and be employed in the specialty of dermatology.

Academic Fields/Career Goals: Nursing.

Award: Scholarship for use in freshman, sophomore, junior, senior, or graduate years; not renewable. *Number:* 2. *Amount:* $2500.

Eligibility Requirements: Applicant must be enrolled or expecting to enroll full- or part-time at a four-year or technical institution or university. Applicant or parent of applicant must be member of Dermatology Nurses' Association. Applicant or parent of applicant must have employment or volunteer experience in nursing. Available to U.S. and non-U.S. citizens.

Application Requirements: Application form, essay, financial need analysis, recommendations or references, transcript. *Deadline:* August 31.

Contact: DNA Recognition Program
Dermatology Nurses' Association
15000 Commerce Parkway
Suite C
Mount Laurel, NJ 08054
Phone: 800-454-4362
Fax: 856-439-0525
E-mail: dna@dnanurse.org

EQUALITY SCHOLARSHIP COLLABORATIVE

http://www.equalityscholarship.org

NURSING SCHOLARSHIP
Applicants must be enrolled or accepted for enrollment by the interview date in an accredited ADN or BSN RN program in California. Master's prepared programs with a BA/BS in a field other than nursing will be considered eligible. Current Kaiser Permanente employees or their dependents, RN reentry programs, or current RN to BSN or MSN programs are not eligible for these scholarships. Diploma programs are not eligible.

Academic Fields/Career Goals: Nursing.

Award: Scholarship for use in freshman, sophomore, junior, senior, or graduate years; not renewable. *Number:* 1–2. *Amount:* $6000.

Eligibility Requirements: Applicant must be enrolled or expecting to enroll full- or part-time at a two-year or four-year institution or university; studying in California and must have an interest in LGBT issues. Applicant or parent of applicant must have employment or volunteer experience in community service. Applicant must have 3.0 GPA or higher. Available to U.S. and non-U.S. citizens.

Application Requirements: Application form, essay, interview. *Deadline:* February 1.

EXCEPTIONALNURSE.COM

http://www.exceptionalnurse.com/

ANNA MAY ROLANDO SCHOLARSHIP AWARD

Scholarship of $500 awarded to a nursing student with a disability. Preference will be given to a graduate student who has demonstrated a commitment to working with people with disabilities.

Academic Fields/Career Goals: Nursing.

Award: Scholarship for use in freshman, sophomore, junior, senior, graduate, or postgraduate years; not renewable. *Number:* 1. *Amount:* $500.

Eligibility Requirements: Applicant must be hearing impaired, learning disabled, physically disabled, or visually impaired and enrolled or expecting to enroll full-time at a four-year institution or university. Applicant must be hearing impaired, learning disabled, physically disabled, or visually impaired. Available to U.S. citizens.

Application Requirements: Application form, essay, medical verification of disability form, recommendations or references, transcript. *Deadline:* June 1.

Contact: Donna Maheady, Founder
E-mail: exceptionalnurse@aol.com

BRUNO ROLANDO SCHOLARSHIP AWARD

Scholarship of $250 awarded to a nursing student with a disability. Preference will be given to a nursing student who is employed at a Veteran's Hospital.

Academic Fields/Career Goals: Nursing.

Award: Scholarship for use in freshman, sophomore, junior, senior, graduate, or postgraduate years; not renewable. *Number:* 1. *Amount:* $250.

Eligibility Requirements: Applicant must be hearing impaired, learning disabled, physically disabled, or visually impaired and enrolled or expecting to enroll full-time at a four-year institution or university. Applicant or parent of applicant must have employment or volunteer experience in nursing. Applicant must be hearing impaired, learning disabled, physically disabled, or visually impaired. Available to U.S. citizens.

Application Requirements: Application form, essay, medical verification of disability form, recommendations or references, transcript. *Deadline:* June 1.

Contact: Donna Maheady, Founder
E-mail: exceptionalnurse@aol.com

CAROLINE SIMPSON MAHEADY SCHOLARSHIP AWARD

Scholarship of $250 awarded to a nursing student with a disability. Preference will be given to an undergraduate student, of Scottish descent, who has demonstrated a commitment to working with people with disabilities.

Academic Fields/Career Goals: Nursing.

Award: Scholarship for use in freshman, sophomore, junior, senior, graduate, or postgraduate years; not renewable. *Number:* 1. *Amount:* $250.

Eligibility Requirements: Applicant must be hearing impaired, learning disabled, physically disabled, or visually impaired and enrolled or expecting to enroll full-time at a four-year institution or university. Applicant must be hearing impaired, learning disabled, physically disabled, or visually impaired. Available to U.S. citizens.

Application Requirements: Application form, essay, medical verification of disability form, recommendations or references, transcript. *Deadline:* June 1.

Contact: Donna Maheady, Founder
E-mail: exceptionalnurse@aol.com

GENEVIEVE SARAN RICHMOND AWARD

Scholarship of $500 awarded to a nursing student with a disability.

Academic Fields/Career Goals: Nursing.

Award: Scholarship for use in freshman, sophomore, junior, senior, graduate, or postgraduate years; not renewable. *Number:* 1. *Amount:* $500.

Eligibility Requirements: Applicant must be hearing impaired, learning disabled, physically disabled, or visually impaired and enrolled or expecting to enroll full-time at a four-year institution or university. Applicant must be hearing impaired, learning disabled, physically disabled, or visually impaired. Available to U.S. citizens.

Application Requirements: Application form, essay, medical verification of disability form, recommendations or references, transcript. *Deadline:* June 1.

Contact: Donna Maheady, Founder
E-mail: exceptionalnurse@aol.com

JILL LAURA CREEDON SCHOLARSHIP AWARD

Scholarship of $500 awarded to a nursing student with a disability or medical challenge.

Academic Fields/Career Goals: Nursing.

Award: Scholarship for use in freshman, sophomore, junior, senior, graduate, or postgraduate years; not renewable. *Number:* 1. *Amount:* $500.

Eligibility Requirements: Applicant must be hearing impaired, learning disabled, physically disabled, or visually impaired and enrolled or expecting to enroll full-time at a four-year institution or university. Applicant must be hearing impaired, learning disabled, physically disabled, or visually impaired. Available to U.S. citizens.

Application Requirements: Application form, essay, medical verification of disability form, recommendations or references, transcript. *Deadline:* June 1.

Contact: Donna Maheady, Founder
E-mail: exceptionalnurse@aol.com

MARY SERRA GILI SCHOLARSHIP AWARD

Scholarship of $250 awarded to a nursing student with a disability.

Academic Fields/Career Goals: Nursing.

Award: Scholarship for use in freshman, sophomore, junior, senior, graduate, or postgraduate years; not renewable. *Number:* 1. *Amount:* $250.

Eligibility Requirements: Applicant must be hearing impaired, learning disabled, physically disabled, or visually impaired and enrolled or expecting to enroll full-time at a four-year institution or university. Applicant must be hearing impaired, learning disabled, physically disabled, or visually impaired. Available to U.S. citizens.

Application Requirements: Application form, essay, medical verification of disability form, recommendations or references, transcript. *Deadline:* June 1.

Contact: Donna Maheady, Founder
E-mail: exceptionalnurse@aol.com

PETER GILI SCHOLARSHIP AWARD

Scholarship of $500 awarded to a nursing student with a disability.

Academic Fields/Career Goals: Nursing.

Award: Scholarship for use in freshman, sophomore, junior, senior, graduate, or postgraduate years; not renewable. *Number:* 1. *Amount:* $500.

Eligibility Requirements: Applicant must be hearing impaired, learning disabled, physically disabled, or visually impaired and enrolled or expecting to enroll full-time at a four-year institution or university. Applicant must be hearing impaired, learning disabled, physically disabled, or visually impaired. Available to U.S. citizens.

Application Requirements: Application form, essay, medical verification of disability form, recommendations or references, transcript. *Deadline:* June 1.

Contact: Donna Maheady, Founder
E-mail: exceptionalnurse@aol.com

THE EXPERT INSTITUTE

https://www.theexpertinstitute.com

ANNUAL HEALTHCARE AND LIFE SCIENCES SCHOLARSHIP

• *See page 170*

FLORIDA NURSES ASSOCIATION

http://www.floridanurse.org/

AGNES NAUGHTON RN-BSN FUND

This fund is established to honor Agnes Naughton who was a lifelong FNA member and the mother of FNA Executive Director Paula Massey. She valued education and this scholarship will assist a RN who is continuing his or her education.

Academic Fields/Career Goals: Nursing.

Award: Scholarship for use in freshman, sophomore, junior, or senior years; not renewable. *Number:* 1. *Amount:* $500.

Eligibility Requirements: Applicant must be enrolled or expecting to enroll full- or part-time at a four-year institution or university; resident of Florida and studying in Florida. Applicant must have 2.5 GPA or higher. Available to U.S. citizens.

Application Requirements: Application form, application form may be submitted online (http://www.floridanurse.org), essay, recommendations or references, transcript, validation of Florida residency.

Contact: Willa Fuller, Executive Director
E-mail: foundation@floridanurse.org

EDNA HICKS FUND SCHOLARSHIP

Applicant should be enrolled in a nationally accredited nursing program. Must be in Associate, Baccalaureate, or Master's degree nursing programs or doctoral programs. Preference given to nurse researchers from South Florida.

Academic Fields/Career Goals: Nursing.

Award: Scholarship for use in freshman, sophomore, junior, senior, graduate, or postgraduate years; not renewable. *Number:* 1. *Amount:* $500.

Eligibility Requirements: Applicant must be enrolled or expecting to enroll full- or part-time at a two-year or four-year institution or university; resident of Florida and studying in Florida. Applicant must have 2.5 GPA or higher. Available to U.S. citizens.

Application Requirements: Application form, driver's license, recommendations or references, transcript. *Deadline:* June 1.

Contact: Willa Fuller, Executive Director
Florida Nurses Association
PO Box 536985
Orlando, FL 32803
E-mail: foundation@floridanurse.org

MARY YORK SCHOLARSHIP FUND

Need criteria for the Mary York Scholarship Fund is not restricted at this time.

Academic Fields/Career Goals: Nursing.

Award: Scholarship for use in freshman, sophomore, junior, senior, graduate, or postgraduate years; not renewable. *Number:* 1. *Amount:* $500.

Eligibility Requirements: Applicant must be enrolled or expecting to enroll full- or part-time at a two-year or four-year or technical institution or university; resident of Florida and studying in Florida. Applicant must have 2.5 GPA or higher. Available to U.S. citizens.

Application Requirements: Application form, essay, financial need analysis, proof of Florida residency, recommendations or references, transcript. *Deadline:* June 1.

Contact: Willa Fuller, Executive Director
Florida Nurses Association
PO Box 536985
Orlando, FL 32803
Phone: 407-896-3261
E-mail: foundation@floridanurse.org

RUTH FINAMORE SCHOLARSHIP FUND

The Ruth Finamore Scholarship Fund is available to all levels of Florida nursing students.

Academic Fields/Career Goals: Nursing.

Award: Scholarship for use in freshman, sophomore, junior, senior, graduate, or postgraduate years; not renewable. *Number:* 1. *Amount:* $500.

Eligibility Requirements: Applicant must be enrolled or expecting to enroll full- or part-time at a two-year or four-year or technical institution

or university; resident of Florida and studying in Florida. Applicant must have 2.5 GPA or higher. Available to U.S. citizens.

Application Requirements: Application form, driver's license, essay, financial need analysis, recommendations or references, transcript, validation of Florida residency. *Deadline:* June 1.

Contact: Willa Fuller, Executive Director
Florida Nurses Association
PO Box 536985
Orlando, FL 32803
E-mail: foundation@floridanurse.org

UNDINE SAMS AND FRIENDS SCHOLARSHIP FUND

The Undine Sams and Friends Scholarship Fund is available statewide to all levels of Nursing students.

Academic Fields/Career Goals: Nursing.

Award: Scholarship for use in freshman, sophomore, junior, senior, or graduate years; not renewable. *Number:* 1. *Amount:* $500.

Eligibility Requirements: Applicant must be enrolled or expecting to enroll full- or part-time at a two-year or four-year or technical institution or university; resident of Florida and studying in Florida. Applicant must have 2.5 GPA or higher. Available to U.S. citizens.

Application Requirements: Application form, application form may be submitted online (http://www.floridanurse.org), financial need analysis, proof of Florida residency, recommendations or references, transcript. *Deadline:* June 1.

Contact: Willa Fuller, Executive Director
Florida Nurses Association
PO Box 536985
Orlando, FL 32803
Phone: 407-896-3261
E-mail: foundation@floridanurse.org

FOUNDATION OF THE NATIONAL STUDENT NURSES' ASSOCIATION

http://www.forevernursing.org

BREAKTHROUGH TO NURSING SCHOLARSHIPS FOR RACIAL/ETHNIC MINORITIES

Available to minority students enrolled in nursing or pre-nursing programs. Awards based on need, scholarship, and health-related activities. Application fee of $10. Send self-addressed stamped envelope with two stamps along with application request. Number of awards varies based on donors.

Academic Fields/Career Goals: Nursing.

Award: Scholarship for use in freshman, sophomore, junior, or senior years; not renewable. *Amount:* $1000–$2500.

Eligibility Requirements: Applicant must be American Indian/Alaska Native, Asian/Pacific Islander, Black (non-Hispanic), Hispanic and enrolled or expecting to enroll full- or part-time at a two-year or four-year institution or university. Available to U.S. citizens.

Application Requirements: Application form, financial need analysis, self-addressed stamped envelope with application, transcript. *Fee:* $10. *Deadline:* January 11.

Contact: Lauren Sperle, FNSNA Staff Specialist
Phone: 718-210-0705 Ext. 111
Fax: 718-797-1186
E-mail: lauren@nsna.org

FOUNDATION OF THE NATIONAL STUDENT NURSES' ASSOCIATION CAREER MOBILITY SCHOLARSHIP

One-time award open to registered nurses enrolled in nursing or licensed practical or vocational nurses enrolled in a program leading to licensure as a registered nurse. The award value is $1000 to $2500 and the number of awards varies. Submit copy of license. Application fee: $10. Send self-addressed stamped envelope.

Academic Fields/Career Goals: Nursing.

Award: Scholarship for use in freshman, sophomore, junior, or senior years; not renewable. *Amount:* $1000–$2500.

Eligibility Requirements: Applicant must be enrolled or expecting to enroll full- or part-time at a two-year or four-year institution or university. Available to U.S. citizens.

Application Requirements: Application form, financial need analysis, self-addressed stamped envelope with application, transcript. *Fee:* $10. *Deadline:* January 11.

Contact: Lauren Sperle, FNSNA Staff Specialist
  Phone: 718-210-0705 Ext. 111
  Fax: 718-797-1186
  E-mail: lauren@nsna.org

FOUNDATION OF THE NATIONAL STUDENT NURSES' ASSOCIATION GENERAL SCHOLARSHIPS

One-time award for National Student Nurses' Association members and nonmembers enrolled in nursing programs. Graduating high school seniors are not eligible. Send self-addressed stamped envelope with two stamps for application.

Academic Fields/Career Goals: Nursing.

Award: Scholarship for use in freshman, sophomore, junior, or senior years; not renewable. *Amount:* $1000–$2500.

Eligibility Requirements: Applicant must be enrolled or expecting to enroll full- or part-time at a two-year or four-year institution or university. Available to U.S. citizens.

Application Requirements: Application form, financial need analysis, self-addressed stamped envelope with application, transcript. *Fee:* $10. *Deadline:* January 11.

Contact: Lauren Sperle, FNSNA Staff Specialist
  Phone: 718-210-0705 Ext. 111
  Fax: 718-797-1186
  E-mail: lauren@nsna.org

FOUNDATION OF THE NATIONAL STUDENT NURSES' ASSOCIATION SPECIALTY SCHOLARSHIP

One-time award available to students currently enrolled in a state-approved school of nursing or prenursing. Must have interest in a specialty area of nursing. The award value is $1000 to $2500 and the number of awards granted varies.

Academic Fields/Career Goals: Nursing.

Award: Scholarship for use in freshman, sophomore, junior, or senior years; not renewable. *Amount:* $1000–$2500.

Eligibility Requirements: Applicant must be enrolled or expecting to enroll full- or part-time at a two-year or four-year institution or university. Available to U.S. citizens.

Application Requirements: Application form, financial need analysis, self-addressed stamped envelope with application, transcript. *Fee:* $10. *Deadline:* January 11.

Contact: Lauren Sperle, FNSNA Staff Specialist
  Phone: 718-210-0705 Ext. 111
  Fax: 718-797-1186
  E-mail: lauren@nsna.org

PROMISE OF NURSING SCHOLARSHIP

Applicants attending nursing school in California, South Florida, Georgia, Illinois, Massachusetts, Michigan, New Jersey, Tennessee, or Dallas/Fort Worth, Texas are eligible. Number of awards granted varies.

Academic Fields/Career Goals: Nursing.

Award: Scholarship for use in freshman, sophomore, junior, or senior years; renewable. *Amount:* $1000–$5000.

Eligibility Requirements: Applicant must be enrolled or expecting to enroll full- or part-time at a two-year or four-year institution or university and studying in California, Florida, Georgia, Illinois, Massachusetts, Michigan, New Jersey, Tennessee, Texas. Available to U.S. citizens.

Application Requirements: Application form, financial need analysis, self-addressed stamped envelope with application, transcript. *Fee:* $10. *Deadline:* January 11.

Contact: Lauren Sperle, FNSNA Staff Specialist
  Phone: 718-210-0705 Ext. 111
  Fax: 718-797-1186
  E-mail: lauren@nsna.org

GENESIS HEALTH SERVICES FOUNDATION

http://www.genesishealth.com/

GALA NURSING SCHOLARSHIPS

Scholarships of $6000 for up to five recipients who are seeking admission to, or have been accepted into, an undergraduate Baccalaureate program in nursing.

Academic Fields/Career Goals: Nursing.

Award: Scholarship for use in freshman, sophomore, junior, or senior years; not renewable. *Number:* up to 5. *Amount:* $6000.

Eligibility Requirements: Applicant must be enrolled or expecting to enroll full-time at a four-year institution or university; resident of Illinois, Iowa and studying in Illinois, Iowa. Available to U.S. citizens.

Application Requirements: Application form, transcript. *Deadline:* March 8.

Contact: Melinda Gowey, Executive Director
  Phone: 563-421-6865
  Fax: 563-421-6869
  E-mail: goweym@genesishealth.com

GOOD SAMARITAN FOUNDATION

http://www.gsftx.org/

GOOD SAMARITAN FOUNDATION SCHOLARSHIP

Scholarship for nursing students in their clinical level of education. Must be a resident of Texas and plan to work in a U.S. health-care system.

Academic Fields/Career Goals: Nursing.

Award: Scholarship for use in freshman, sophomore, junior, senior, graduate, or postgraduate years; renewable. *Amount:* $1000.

Eligibility Requirements: Applicant must be enrolled or expecting to enroll full-time at a four-year institution or university and resident of Texas. Available to U.S. and non-U.S. citizens.

Application Requirements: Application form. *Deadline:* varies.

Contact: Kay Crawford, Scholarship Director
  Phone: 713-529-4646
  Fax: 713-521-1169
  E-mail: kcrawford@gsftx.org

GREATER KANAWHA VALLEY FOUNDATION

http://www.tgkvf.org/

BERNICE PICKINS PARSONS FUND
• *See page 416*

ELEANORA G. WYLIE SCHOLARSHIP

Renewable award for West Virginia residents pursuing postsecondary studies in nursing or gerontology. Minimum 2.5 GPA required. Must show financial need.

Academic Fields/Career Goals: Nursing.

Award: Scholarship for use in freshman, sophomore, junior, senior, or graduate years; renewable. *Amount:* $300.

Eligibility Requirements: Applicant must be enrolled or expecting to enroll full-time at a four-year institution or university and resident of West Virginia. Applicant must have 2.5 GPA or higher. Available to U.S. citizens.

Application Requirements: Application form, financial need analysis, recommendations or references, test scores, transcript. *Deadline:* January 15.

Contact: Susan Hoover, Scholarship Program Officer
  Greater Kanawha Valley Foundation
  900 Lee Street East, 16th Floor
  Charleston, WV 25301
  Phone: 304-346-3620
  E-mail: shoover@tgkvf.org

GUSTAVUS B. CAPITO FUND

Scholarships awarded to students who show financial need and are seeking education in nursing at any accredited college or university with a nursing program in West Virginia. Scholarships are awarded for one or more years. Must be a resident of West Virginia.

Academic Fields/Career Goals: Nursing.

Award: Scholarship for use in freshman, sophomore, junior, or senior years; renewable. *Amount:* $2000.

Eligibility Requirements: Applicant must be enrolled or expecting to enroll full-time at a four-year institution or university; resident of West Virginia and studying in West Virginia. Available to U.S. citizens.

Application Requirements: Application form, essay, financial need analysis, recommendations or references, transcript. *Deadline:* January 15.

Contact: Susan Hoover, Scholarship Program Officer
Greater Kanawha Valley Foundation
900 Lee Street East, 16th Floor
Charleston, WV 25301
Phone: 304-346-3620
E-mail: shoover@tgkvf.org

REBECCA GOLDMAN SCHOLARSHIP

Renewable award for a West Virginia resident pursuing full-time postsecondary studies. Must be studying nursing and have a minimum 3.0 GPA.

Academic Fields/Career Goals: Nursing.

Award: Scholarship for use in freshman, sophomore, junior, or senior years; renewable. *Number:* 1.

Eligibility Requirements: Applicant must be enrolled or expecting to enroll full-time at a four-year institution or university and resident of West Virginia. Applicant must have 3.0 GPA or higher. Available to U.S. citizens.

Application Requirements: Application form, financial need analysis, recommendations or references, test scores, transcript. *Deadline:* January 15.

Contact: Susan Hoover, Scholarship Program Officer
Greater Kanawha Valley Foundation
900 Lee Street East, 16th Floor
Charleston, WV 25301
Phone: 304-346-3620
E-mail: shoover@tgkvf.org

GREAT MINDS IN STEM

http://www.greatmindsinstem.org

HENAAC SCHOLARSHIP PROGRAM
• *See page 115*

GREEN LAW FIRM

https://billgreen.law

GREEN LAW FIRM NURSING HOME & ELDERLY CARE SCHOLARSHIP

Attorney Bill Green and his team at Green Law Firm are committed to improving the quality of care in nursing homes. With over 26 years of experience serving the community and many years fighting against low standards of elderly care, Bill is dedicated to promoting passionate students who are focused on making care homes a 'home' for our senior population. We are pleased to be offering a $1500 nursing scholarship to high-achieving students who are committed to elderly care and pursuing a Baccalaureate degree in nursing. Our hope is to further their professional development and continued competence, allowing them to improve the quality of life for seniors at nursing homes. Applicants will be judged on the content of their application, the essay they provide and on their academic merits. Candidates must be working at a nursing home or in an industry directly related to elderly care and pursuing a Bachelor of Science in Nursing Degree (BSN), including those who already hold a RN certification. Must submit an official copy of their transcript, application and essay. No minimum GPA required.

Academic Fields/Career Goals: Nursing.

Award: Scholarship for use in freshman, sophomore, junior, or senior years; not renewable. *Number:* 1. *Amount:* $1500.

Eligibility Requirements: Applicant must be enrolled or expecting to enroll full- or part-time at a four-year institution or university. Applicant or parent of applicant must have employment or volunteer experience in nursing. Available to U.S. and non-U.S. citizens.

Application Requirements: Application form, essay. *Deadline:* December 31.

Contact: Judi McCabe, Director of Operations
Green Law Firm
3511 Rivers Ave
North Charleston, SC 29405
Phone: 843-747-2455
E-mail: marketing@billgreen.law

HAWAIIAN LODGE, F&AM

http://www.hawaiianlodgefreemasons.org

HAWAIIAN LODGE SCHOLARSHIPS
• *See page 86*

HEALTH PROFESSIONS EDUCATION FOUNDATION

http://www.healthprofessions.ca.gov/

ASSOCIATE DEGREE NURSING SCHOLARSHIP PROGRAM

One-time award to nursing students accepted to or enrolled in associate degree nursing programs. Eligible applicants may receive up to $10,000 per year in financial assistance. Deadlines: Check website http://oshpd.ca.gov/HPEF/. Must be a resident of California. Minimum 2.0 GPA.

Academic Fields/Career Goals: Nursing.

Award: Scholarship for use in freshman, sophomore, junior, or senior years; not renewable. *Number:* 20–40. *Amount:* up to $10,000.

Eligibility Requirements: Applicant must be enrolled or expecting to enroll full- or part-time at a two-year or four-year institution or university; resident of California and studying in California. Available to U.S. citizens.

Application Requirements: Application form, application form may be submitted online (http://calreach.oshpd.ca.gov), community service, essay, financial need analysis, graduation date verification form, verification of language fluency, recommendations or references, transcript. *Deadline:* varies.

Contact: Charlene Almazan, Senior Program Officer
Health Professions Education Foundation
400 R Street
Sacramento, CA 95811
Phone: 800-773-1669
Fax: 916-324-6585
E-mail: HPEF-EMail@oshpd.ca.gov

BACHELOR OF SCIENCE NURSING LOAN REPAYMENT PROGRAM

Repays governmental and commercial loans that were obtained for tuition expenses, books, equipment, and reasonable living expenses associated with attending college. In return for the repayment of educational debt, loan repayment recipients are required to practice full-time in direct patient care in a medically underserved area or county health facility. Deadlines: check website http://oshpd.ca.gov/HPEF. Must be resident of California.

Academic Fields/Career Goals: Nursing.

Award: Grant for use in senior, graduate, or postgraduate years; not renewable. *Number:* 50–70. *Amount:* up to $11,000.

Eligibility Requirements: Applicant must be enrolled or expecting to enroll full- or part-time at a four-year institution or university; resident of California and studying in California. Available to U.S. citizens.

Application Requirements: Application form, application form may be submitted online (http://calreach.oshpd.ca.gov), community service, Employment Verification Form, financial need analysis, recommendations or references, transcript. *Deadline:* varies.

Contact: Charlene Almazan, Senior Program Officer
Health Professions Education Foundation
400 R Street
Sacramento, CA 95811
Phone: 800-773-1669
Fax: 916-324-6585
E-mail: HPEF-EMail@oshpd.ca.gov

BACHELOR OF SCIENCE NURSING SCHOLARSHIP PROGRAM

One-time award to nursing students accepted to or enrolled in baccalaureate degree nursing programs in California. Eligible applicants may receive up to $13,000 per year in financial assistance. Deadlines: check website. Must be resident of California and a U.S. citizen. Minimum 2.0 GPA.

Academic Fields/Career Goals: Nursing.

Award: Scholarship for use in freshman, sophomore, junior, or senior years; not renewable. *Number:* 50–70. *Amount:* up to $13,000.

Eligibility Requirements: Applicant must be age 18-99; enrolled or expecting to enroll full- or part-time at a two-year or four-year institution or university; resident of California and studying in California. Applicant must have 2.5 GPA or higher. Available to U.S. citizens.

Application Requirements: Application form, application form may be submitted online (http://calreach.oshpd.ca.gov/), employment verification form, proof of RN license, verification of language fluency, essay, financial need analysis, recommendations or references, transcript. *Deadline:* varies.

Contact: Charlene Almazan, Senior Program Officer
Health Professions Education Foundation
400 R Street
Sacramento, CA 95811
Phone: 800-773-1669
Fax: 916-324-6585
E-mail: HPEF-EMail@oshpd.ca.gov

VOCATIONAL NURSE & LICENSED VOCATIONAL NURSE TO ASSOCIATE DEGREE NURSING SCHOLARSHIP PROGRAM

Scholarships are available to students who are enrolled or accepted in an accredited Vocational Nurse program. Eligible applicants may receive up to $8,000 per year in financial assistance. Deadlines: Check website http://oshpd.ca.gov/HPEF/. Must be a resident of California. Minimum 2.0 GPA.

Academic Fields/Career Goals: Nursing.

Award: Scholarship for use in freshman or sophomore years; not renewable. *Amount:* $4000–$8000.

Eligibility Requirements: Applicant must be enrolled or expecting to enroll full- or part-time at a two-year or technical institution and resident of California. Available to U.S. citizens.

Application Requirements: Application form, application form may be submitted online (http://calreach.oshpd.ca.gov), community service, essay, financial need analysis, recommendations or references, Student Aid Report (SAR), personal statement, educational debt reporting form, transcript. *Deadline:* varies.

Contact: Meaghan HArrington, Program Officer
Health Professions Education Foundation
400 R Street
Sacramento, CA 95811
Phone: 800-773-1669
Fax: 916-324-6585
E-mail: HPEF-EMail@oshpd.ca.gov

HEALTH RESEARCH COUNCIL OF NEW ZEALAND

http://www.hrc.govt.nz/

PACIFIC HEALTH WORKFORCE AWARD
• See page 368

PACIFIC MENTAL HEALTH WORK FORCE AWARD
• See page 368

ILLINOIS NURSES ASSOCIATION

http://www.illinoisnurses.com/

SONNE SCHOLARSHIP

One-time award of up to $3000 available to nursing students. Funds may be used to cover tuition, fees, or any other cost encountered by students enrolled in Illinois state-approved nursing program. Award limited to U.S. citizens who are residents of Illinois. Recipients will receive a year's free membership in INA upon graduation.

Academic Fields/Career Goals: Nursing.

Award: Scholarship for use in freshman, sophomore, junior, or senior years; not renewable. *Number:* 2–4. *Amount:* $1000–$3000.

Eligibility Requirements: Applicant must be enrolled or expecting to enroll full-time at a four-year institution or university; resident of Illinois and studying in Illinois. Applicant must have 3.5 GPA or higher. Available to U.S. citizens.

Application Requirements: Application form, essay, financial need analysis, recommendations or references, transcript. *Deadline:* March 15.

Contact: Melinda Sweeney, Sonne Scholarship Committee
Illinois Nurses Association
105 West Adams Street, Suite 2101
Chicago, IL 60603
Phone: 312-419-2900 Ext. 222
Fax: 312-419-2920
E-mail: msweeney@illinoisnurses.com

INDEPENDENT COLLEGE FUND OF NEW JERSEY

http://www.njcolleges.org/

C.R. BARD FOUNDATION, INC. NURSING SCHOLARSHIP

Applicant must be entering at least the second semester of their sophomore year or the second semester of the second year of their nursing program and be enrolled full-time at an ICFNJ member college or university. Must maintain a minimum GPA of 3.0.

Academic Fields/Career Goals: Nursing.

Award: Scholarship for use in junior or senior years; not renewable. *Number:* 10. *Amount:* $2500.

Eligibility Requirements: Applicant must be enrolled or expecting to enroll full-time at a four-year institution or university and studying in New Jersey. Applicant must have 3.0 GPA or higher. Available to U.S. citizens.

Application Requirements: Application form, community service, essay, financial need analysis, recommendations or references, resume, transcript. *Deadline:* April 30.

Contact: Ms. Yvette Panella, Scholarship Coordinator
Independent College Fund of New Jersey
797 Springfield Avenue
Summit, NJ 07901
Phone: 908-277-3424
Fax: 908-277-0851
E-mail: scholarships@njcolleges.org

INDIANA HEALTH CARE POLICY INSTITUTE

http://www.ihca.org/

INDIANA HEALTH CARE POLICY INSTITUTE NURSING SCHOLARSHIP

Scholarship is for students pursuing a career in long-term care. One-time award of up to $5000 for Indiana residents studying nursing at an institution in Indiana, Ohio, Kentucky, Illinois or Michigan. Minimum 2.5 GPA required. Total number of awards varies.

Academic Fields/Career Goals: Nursing.

Award: Scholarship for use in freshman, sophomore, junior, or senior years; not renewable. *Number:* 1–5. *Amount:* $750–$5000.

Eligibility Requirements: Applicant must be enrolled or expecting to enroll full- or part-time at a two-year or four-year or technical institution or university; resident of Indiana and studying in Illinois, Indiana,

Kentucky, Michigan, Ohio. Applicant must have 2.5 GPA or higher. Available to U.S. citizens.

Application Requirements: Application form, essay, interview, recommendations or references, transcript. *Deadline:* May 13.

Contact: Dorothy Henry, Executive Director
Indiana Health Care Policy Institute
One North Capitol Avenue, Suite 100
Indianapolis, IN 46204
Phone: 317-616-9028
Fax: 877-298-3749
E-mail: dhenry@ihca.org

INDIAN HEALTH SERVICES, UNITED STATES DEPARTMENT OF HEALTH AND HUMAN SERVICES

http://www.ihs.gov/scholarship

HEALTH PROFESSIONS PREPARATORY SCHOLARSHIP PROGRAM
• *See page 165*

INTERNATIONAL ORDER OF THE KING'S DAUGHTERS AND SONS

http://www.iokds.org/

HEALTH CAREERS SCHOLARSHIP
• *See page 255*

THE JACKSON LABORATORY

https://www.jax.org

THE JACKSON LABORATORY COLLEGE SCHOLARSHIP PROGRAM
• *See page 126*

KETAMINE CLINICS OF LOS ANGELES

http://www.ketamineclinics.com/

KETAMINE CLINICS OF LOS ANGELES SCHOLARSHIP PROGRAM
• *See page 165*

LABROOTS INC.

http://www.LabRoots.com

LABROOTS STEM SCHOLARSHIP
• *See page 116*

LADIES AUXILIARY TO THE VETERANS OF FOREIGN WARS, DEPARTMENT OF MAINE

http://mainevfw.org/

FRANCES L. BOOTH MEDICAL SCHOLARSHIP SPONSORED BY LAVFW DEPARTMENT OF MAINE
• *See page 375*

LAW FIRM OF JACK TOLLIVER, MD & ASSOCIATES, PLLC

http://www.kymedicalmalpractice.com

TOLLIVER ANNUAL NURSING SCHOLARSHIP

Open to current high school seniors living in Kentucky, currently attending a Kentucky high school, and interested in pursuing a nursing degree. Applicants must be applying to a Kentucky college or university

offering an accredited program of study in nursing. Apply through online application only.

Academic Fields/Career Goals: Nursing.

Award: Scholarship for use in freshman year; not renewable. *Number:* 5. *Amount:* $1000.

Eligibility Requirements: Applicant must be high school student; planning to enroll or expecting to enroll full- or part-time at a two-year or four-year institution or university; resident of Kentucky and studying in Kentucky. Available to U.S. citizens.

Application Requirements: Application form, essay. *Deadline:* March 15.

Contact: Nick Gowen
Phone: 502-827-1588
E-mail: nick@kymedicalmalpractice.com

LAW OFFICES OF PROSPER SHAKED

https://www.prosperlaw.com/

PROSPER SHAKED SCHOLARSHIP FOR FUTURE MEDICAL PROFESSIONALS
• *See page 166*

MARION D. AND EVA S. PEEPLES FOUNDATION TRUST SCHOLARSHIP PROGRAM

http://www.jccf.org/apply-for-a-scholarship/

MARION A. AND EVA S. PEEPLES FOUNDATION TRUST SCHOLARSHIP

The Peeples Foundation Trust Fund provides for the awarding of annual scholarships in three fields of study to graduates of Indiana high schools who will attend an Indiana college or university. Eligible students must be pursuing or planning to pursue a major in: Nursing, Dietetics, or Technology Education.

Academic Fields/Career Goals: Nursing.

Award: Scholarship for use in freshman, sophomore, junior, or senior years; renewable. *Number:* 5–20. *Amount:* $1000–$5500.

Eligibility Requirements: Applicant must be enrolled or expecting to enroll full-time at a two-year or four-year or technical institution or university; resident of Indiana and studying in Indiana. Applicant must have 2.5 GPA or higher. Available to U.S. citizens.

Application Requirements: Application form, essay, financial need analysis. *Deadline:* February 21.

Contact: Mrs. Stephanie Fox, Program Officer: Grants and Scholarships
Marion D. and Eva S. Peeples Foundation Trust Scholarship Program
PO Box 217
Franklin, IN 46131
Phone: 317-738-2213
Fax: 317-738-9113
E-mail: stephanief@jccf.org

MARYLAND STATE HIGHER EDUCATION COMMISSION

http://www.mhec.state.md.us/

GRADUATE AND PROFESSIONAL SCHOLARSHIP PROGRAM-MARYLAND
• *See page 256*

JANET L. HOFFMANN LOAN ASSISTANCE REPAYMENT PROGRAM
• *See page 272*

TUITION REDUCTION FOR NON-RESIDENT NURSING STUDENTS

Available to nonresidents of Maryland who attend a two-year or four-year public institution in Maryland. It is renewable provided student maintains academic requirements designated by institution attended. Recipient must agree to serve as a full-time nurse in a hospital or related institution for two to four years.

Academic Fields/Career Goals: Nursing.

Award: Scholarship for use in freshman, sophomore, junior, or senior years; renewable.

Eligibility Requirements: Applicant must be enrolled or expecting to enroll full- or part-time at a two-year or four-year institution and studying in Maryland. Available to U.S. citizens.

Application Requirements: Application form. *Deadline:* varies.

Contact: Robert Parker, Director
Phone: 410-260-4558
E-mail: rparker@mhec.state.md.us

MEDICAL SCRUBS COLLECTION

http://medicalscrubscollection.com

MEDICAL SCRUBS COLLECTION SCHOLARSHIP
• See page 120

MICHAEL MOODY FITNESS

http://www.michaelmoodyfitness.com/

MICHAEL MOODY FITNESS SCHOLARSHIP
• See page 166

MISSISSIPPI NURSES' ASSOCIATION (MNA)

http://www.msnurses.org/

MISSISSIPPI NURSES' ASSOCIATION FOUNDATION SCHOLARSHIP

Scholarship of $1000 to a Mississippi resident. Applicant should major in nursing and be a member of MASN.

Academic Fields/Career Goals: Nursing.

Award: Scholarship for use in freshman, sophomore, junior, or senior years; not renewable. *Number:* 1. *Amount:* $1000.

Eligibility Requirements: Applicant must be enrolled or expecting to enroll full- or part-time at a four-year institution or university and resident of Mississippi. Available to U.S. citizens.

Application Requirements: Application form, essay, recommendations or references, transcript. *Deadline:* October 1.

Contact: Scholarship Committee
Mississippi Nurses' Association (MNA)
31 Woodgreen Place
Madison, MS 39110
Phone: 601-898-0850
E-mail: foundation@msnurses.org

MOUNT SINAI HOSPITAL DEPARTMENT OF NURSING

http://www.mountsinai.org/

BSN STUDENT SCHOLARSHIP/WORK REPAYMENT PROGRAM

$3000 award for senior nursing student or in the last semester/year of the program. Minimum GPA is 3.25.

Academic Fields/Career Goals: Nursing.

Award: Scholarship for use in senior year; not renewable. *Amount:* $3000.

Eligibility Requirements: Applicant must be enrolled or expecting to enroll full-time at a four-year institution or university. Available to U.S. citizens.

Application Requirements: Application form, recommendations or references, resume, transcript. *Deadline:* October 1.

Contact: Maria Vezina, Director, Nursing Education and Recruitment
Mount Sinai Hospital Department of Nursing
One Gustave Levy Place, PO Box 1144
New York, NY 10029

NATIONAL AMERICAN ARAB NURSES ASSOCIATION

http://www.n-aana.org

NATIONAL AMERICAN ARAB NURSES ASSOCIATION SCHOLARSHIPS

The National American Arab Nurses Association (NAANA) annual scholarships, awarded to the most meritorious applicants who are engaged in studying nursing at the Associate degree, Bachelor degree, RN-BSN, or BSN-MSN (Master of Science in Nursing) levels. Annually $500 to $1000 scholarships are awarded, depending on the funds available in a given year. The scholarships should be applied toward tuition and/or books in the academic year they are awarded. Applicants must be enrolled in an accredited nursing program at the time of application, and should be pursuing a nursing program during the year for which the award is made. In order to be eligible, applicants must be of Arab heritage, citizens or permanent residents of the United States, and must reside within the US or its territories; further, applicants must be members of NAANA. Major criteria to be used by the selection committee are 1. academic excellence, exemplified by achievement of a grade point average (GPA) of 3.0 or its equivalent; 2. demonstrated leadership, academic, professional, and/or through student organizations; and 3. evidence of engagement in and contribution to the health care of the Arab American community. Prior recipients of this scholarship are not eligible to apply during the same degree as the first award.

Academic Fields/Career Goals: Nursing.

Award: Scholarship for use in freshman, sophomore, junior, senior, or graduate years; not renewable. *Number:* 1–4. *Amount:* $500–$1000.

Eligibility Requirements: Applicant must be of Arab heritage and Yemeni citizen and enrolled or expecting to enroll full- or part-time at a two-year or four-year institution or university. Applicant must have 3.0 GPA or higher. Available to U.S. citizens.

Application Requirements: Application form, essay. *Deadline:* continuous.

Contact: Mrs. Rose Khalifa, Founder and Past President
National American Arab Nurses Association
18000 West 9 Mile Road
Suite 360
Southfield, MI 48075
Phone: 313-680-5049
E-mail: rosek@metrosolutions.us

NATIONAL ASSOCIATION DIRECTORS OF NURSING ADMINISTRATION

http://www.nadona.org/

NADONA STEPHANIE CARROLL MEMORIAL SCHOLARSHIP

Scholarship is for nursing student enrolled in an accredited nursing program or nursing student in an undergraduate or graduate program. Also for employees in the long term care continuum achieving an LPN/LVN.

Academic Fields/Career Goals: Nursing.

Award: Scholarship for use in freshman, sophomore, junior, senior, graduate, or postgraduate years; not renewable. *Number:* 1–13. *Amount:* $1000–$5000.

Eligibility Requirements: Applicant must be enrolled or expecting to enroll full- or part-time at a two-year or four-year or technical institution or university. Applicant or parent of applicant must have employment or volunteer experience in nursing. Available to U.S. citizens.

Application Requirements: Application form, essay, financial need analysis, personal photograph. *Deadline:* May 1.

Contact: Sherrie Dornberger, Executive Director
National Association Directors of Nursing Administration
1329 E. Kemper Road
Suite 4100A
Springdale, OH 45246
Phone: 800-222-0539
E-mail: info@nadona.org

NATIONAL ASSOCIATION OF HISPANIC NURSES

http://www.nahnnet.org

NAHN SCHOLARSHIPS

Awards are presented to NAHN members only (must be a member for at least 6 months) enrolled in Associate, diploma, Baccalaureate, graduate or practical/vocational nursing programs. Selection based on current academic standing. Scholarship award recipients are a select group of Hispanic students who demonstrate promise of future professional contributions to the nursing profession and who have the potential to act as role models for other aspiring nursing students.

Academic Fields/Career Goals: Nursing.

Award: Scholarship for use in freshman, sophomore, junior, senior, or graduate years; not renewable.

Eligibility Requirements: Applicant must be of Hispanic heritage and enrolled or expecting to enroll full-time at a four-year or technical institution or university. Available to U.S. citizens.

Application Requirements: Application form, essay, recommendations or references, transcript. *Deadline:* varies.

Contact: Celia Besore, Executive Director and CEO
   Phone: 202-387-2477
   Fax: 202-483-7183
   E-mail: info@thehispanicnurses.org

NATIONAL BLACK NURSES ASSOCIATION INC.

http://www.nbna.org/

DR. HILDA RICHARDS SCHOLARSHIP

Scholarship for nurses currently enrolled in a nursing program who are members of NBNA. Applicant must have at least one full year of school remaining.

Academic Fields/Career Goals: Nursing.

Award: Scholarship for use in freshman, sophomore, junior, senior, graduate, or postgraduate years; not renewable. *Number:* 1. *Amount:* $1000–$2000.

Eligibility Requirements: Applicant must be enrolled or expecting to enroll full-time at a two-year or four-year institution or university. Applicant or parent of applicant must be member of National Black Nurses' Association. Applicant or parent of applicant must have employment or volunteer experience in community service. Available to U.S. and non-U.S. citizens.

Application Requirements: Application form, essay, personal photograph, recommendations or references, self-addressed stamped envelope with application, transcript. *Deadline:* April 15.

Contact: Scholarship Committee
   Phone: 301-589-3200
   Fax: 301-589-3223
   E-mail: nbna@erols.com

DR. LAURANNE SAMS SCHOLARSHIP

Award available for NBNA member who is currently enrolled full-time in a nursing program. Applicant must have at least one full year of school remaining. Scholarships will range from $1000 to $2000.

Academic Fields/Career Goals: Nursing.

Award: Scholarship for use in freshman, sophomore, junior, senior, graduate, or postgraduate years; not renewable. *Number:* up to 5. *Amount:* $1000–$2000.

Eligibility Requirements: Applicant must be enrolled or expecting to enroll full-time at a two-year or four-year institution or university. Applicant or parent of applicant must be member of National Black Nurses' Association. Available to U.S. and non-U.S. citizens.

Application Requirements: Application form, essay, recommendations or references, self-addressed stamped envelope with application, transcript. *Deadline:* April 15.

Contact: Scholarship Committee
   Phone: 301-589-3200
   Fax: 301-589-3223
   E-mail: nbna@erols.com

KAISER PERMANENTE SCHOOL OF ANESTHESIA SCHOLARSHIP

Scholarship for nurses currently enrolled in a nursing program who are active members of NBNA. Must have at least one full year of school remaining.

Academic Fields/Career Goals: Nursing.

Award: Scholarship for use in freshman, sophomore, junior, senior, graduate, or postgraduate years; not renewable. *Number:* 1. *Amount:* $1000–$2000.

Eligibility Requirements: Applicant must be enrolled or expecting to enroll full-time at a two-year or four-year institution or university. Applicant or parent of applicant must be member of National Black Nurses' Association. Available to U.S. and non-U.S. citizens.

Application Requirements: Application form, essay, recommendations or references, self-addressed stamped envelope with application, transcript. *Deadline:* April 15.

Contact: Scholarship Committee
   Phone: 301-589-3200
   Fax: 301-589-3223
   E-mail: nbna@erols.com

MARTHA R. DUDLEY LVN/LPN SCHOLARSHIP

Scholarship available for nurses currently enrolled full-time in a nursing program and must be a member of NBNA. Applicant must have at least one full year of school remaining. Scholarships will range from $1000 to $2000.

Academic Fields/Career Goals: Nursing.

Award: Scholarship for use in freshman, sophomore, junior, senior, graduate, or postgraduate years; not renewable. *Number:* 1. *Amount:* $1000–$2000.

Eligibility Requirements: Applicant must be Black (non-Hispanic) and enrolled or expecting to enroll full-time at a two-year or four-year institution or university. Applicant or parent of applicant must be member of National Black Nurses' Association. Applicant or parent of applicant must have employment or volunteer experience in community service. Available to U.S. and non-U.S. citizens.

Application Requirements: Application form, essay, personal photograph, recommendations or references, self-addressed stamped envelope with application, transcript. *Deadline:* April 15.

Contact: Scholarship Committee
   Phone: 301-589-3200
   Fax: 301-589-3223
   E-mail: nbna@erols.com

MAYO FOUNDATIONS SCHOLARSHIP

Scholarship for nurses currently enrolled full-time in a nursing program who are members of NBNA. Applicant must have at least one full year of school remaining.

Academic Fields/Career Goals: Nursing.

Award: Scholarship for use in freshman, sophomore, junior, senior, graduate, or postgraduate years; not renewable. *Number:* 1. *Amount:* $1000–$2000.

Eligibility Requirements: Applicant must be enrolled or expecting to enroll full-time at a two-year or four-year institution or university. Applicant or parent of applicant must be member of National Black Nurses' Association. Available to U.S. and non-U.S. citizens.

Application Requirements: Application form, essay, personal photograph, recommendations or references, self-addressed stamped envelope with application, transcript. *Deadline:* April 15.

Contact: Scholarship Committee
   Phone: 301-589-3200
   Fax: 301-589-3223
   E-mail: nbna@erols.com

NBNA BOARD OF DIRECTORS SCHOLARSHIP

The scholarship enables nurses to grow and better contribute their talents to the health and healthcare of communities. Candidate must be currently enrolled in a nursing program with at least one full year of school remaining and must be a member of NBNA.

Academic Fields/Career Goals: Nursing.

Award: Scholarship for use in freshman, sophomore, junior, senior, graduate, or postgraduate years; not renewable. *Number:* up to 2. *Amount:* $1000–$2000.

Eligibility Requirements: Applicant must be enrolled or expecting to enroll full-time at a two-year or four-year institution or university. Applicant or parent of applicant must be member of National Black Nurses' Association. Applicant or parent of applicant must have employment or volunteer experience in community service. Available to U.S. and non-U.S. citizens.

Application Requirements: Application form, essay, personal photograph, recommendations or references, self-addressed stamped envelope with application, transcript. *Deadline:* April 15.

Contact: Scholarship Committee
Phone: 301-589-3200
Fax: 301-589-3223
E-mail: nbna@erols.com

NURSING SPECTRUM SCHOLARSHIP

Scholarship enables nurses to grow and better contribute their talents to the health and healthcare of communities. Candidate must be currently enrolled in a nursing program and be a member of NBNA. Applicant must have at least one full year of school remaining.

Academic Fields/Career Goals: Nursing.

Award: Scholarship for use in freshman, sophomore, junior, senior, graduate, or postgraduate years; not renewable. *Number:* 1. *Amount:* $1000–$2000.

Eligibility Requirements: Applicant must be enrolled or expecting to enroll full-time at a two-year or four-year institution or university. Applicant or parent of applicant must be member of National Black Nurses' Association. Available to U.S. and non-U.S. citizens.

Application Requirements: Application form, essay, recommendations or references, self-addressed stamped envelope with application, transcript. *Deadline:* April 15.

Contact: Scholarship Committee
Phone: 301-589-3200
Fax: 301-589-3223
E-mail: nbna@erols.com

NATIONAL COUNCIL OF JEWISH WOMEN LOS ANGELES (NCJW L LA)

http://ncjwla.org/

INGER LAWRENCE-M.R. BAUER FOUNDATION NURSING STUDIES SCHOLARSHIP

This award is given to woman or man enrolled in or accepted to a degree program in nursing. Some units toward the degree are preferred, but not required. Applicants to the Inger Lawrence-M.R. Bauer award are also eligible for the June Miller Nursing Education Scholarship. The National Council of Jewish Women l Los Angeles (NCJW l LA) provides scholarships, regardless of race, ethnicity, religion, age, gender identity, sexuality or national origin to those who live and attend school in the Greater Los Angeles area, including Los Angeles, Orange, Riverside, and Ventura Counties.

Academic Fields/Career Goals: Nursing.

Award: Scholarship for use in freshman, sophomore, junior, senior, or graduate years; not renewable. *Number:* 2. *Amount:* $2000.

Eligibility Requirements: Applicant must be enrolled or expecting to enroll full- or part-time at a four-year institution or university; resident of California and studying in California. Available to U.S. citizens.

Application Requirements: Application form, essay, financial need analysis. *Deadline:* continuous.

Contact: Stephanie Flax, Program and Scholarship Coordinator
National Council of Jewish Women Los Angeles (NCJW l LA)
543 North Fairfax Avenue
Los Angeles, CA 90036
Phone: 323-852-8515
E-mail: scholarship@ncjwla.org

THE JUNE MILLER NURSING EDUCATION SCHOLARSHIP

This award is given to woman or man enrolled in or accepted to a degree program in nursing. Some units toward the degree are preferred, but not required. Applicants to the June Miller Nursing Education Scholarship are also eligible for the Inger Lawrence-M.R. Bauer award. The National Council of Jewish Women l Los Angeles (NCJW l LA) provides scholarships, regardless of race, ethnicity, religion, age, gender identity, sexuality or national origin to those who live and attend school in the Greater Los Angeles area, including Los Angeles, Orange, Riverside, and Ventura Counties.

Academic Fields/Career Goals: Nursing.

Award: Scholarship for use in freshman, sophomore, junior, senior, or graduate years; not renewable. *Number:* 4. *Amount:* $2000.

Eligibility Requirements: Applicant must be enrolled or expecting to enroll full- or part-time at a two-year or four-year institution or university; resident of California and studying in California. Available to U.S. citizens.

Application Requirements: Application form, essay, financial need analysis. *Deadline:* continuous.

Contact: Ms. Stephanie Flax, Scholarship and Program Coordinator
National Council of Jewish Women Los Angeles (NCJW l LA)
543 North Fairfax Avenue
Los Angeles, CA 90036
Phone: 323-852-8515
E-mail: scholarship@ncjwla.org

NATIONAL INSTITUTES OF HEALTH

https://www.training.nih.gov/programs/ugsp

NIH UNDERGRADUATE SCHOLARSHIP PROGRAM FOR STUDENTS FROM DISADVANTAGED BACKGROUNDS
• See page 116

NATIONAL SOCIETY DAUGHTERS OF THE AMERICAN REVOLUTION

http://www.dar.org/

NATIONAL SOCIETY DAUGHTERS OF THE AMERICAN REVOLUTION CAROLINE E. HOLT NURSING SCHOLARSHIPS

One-time award for students who are in financial need and have been accepted or are enrolled in an accredited school of nursing. A letter of acceptance into the nursing program or the transcript stating that the applicant is enrolled in the nursing program must be included with the application.

Academic Fields/Career Goals: Nursing.

Award: Scholarship for use in freshman, sophomore, junior, or senior years; not renewable.

Eligibility Requirements: Applicant must be enrolled or expecting to enroll full-time at a two-year or four-year institution or university. Available to U.S. citizens.

Application Requirements: Application form, essay, financial need analysis. *Deadline:* February 10.

Contact: Lakeisha Graham, Manager, Office of the Reporter General
Phone: 202-628-1776
Fax: 202-879-3348
E-mail: nsdarscholarships@dar.org

NATIONAL SOCIETY DAUGHTERS OF THE AMERICAN REVOLUTION MADELINE PICKETT (HALBERT) COGSWELL NURSING SCHOLARSHIP

Scholarship available to students who have been accepted or are currently enrolled in an accredited school of nursing, who are members of NSDAR, descendants of members of NSDAR, or are eligible to be members of NSDAR. A letter of acceptance into the nursing program or transcript showing enrollment in nursing program must be included with the application. DAR member number must be on the application.

Academic Fields/Career Goals: Nursing.

Award: Scholarship for use in freshman, sophomore, junior, or senior years; not renewable. *Amount:* $2500.

Eligibility Requirements: Applicant must be enrolled or expecting to enroll full-time at a two-year or four-year institution or university. Applicant or parent of applicant must be member of Daughters of the American Revolution. Available to U.S. and non-U.S. citizens.

Application Requirements: Application form. *Deadline:* February 15.

Contact: Lakeisha Graham, Manager, Office of the Reporter General
Phone: 202-628-1776
Fax: 202-879-3348
E-mail: nsdarscholarships@dar.org

NATIONAL SOCIETY DAUGHTERS OF THE AMERICAN REVOLUTION MILDRED NUTTING NURSING SCHOLARSHIP

A one-time $1000 scholarship for students who are in financial need and who have been accepted or are currently enrolled in an accredited school of nursing. A letter of acceptance into the nursing program or the transcript stating that the applicant is in the nursing program must be enclosed with the application. Preference will be given to candidates from the Lowell, Massachusetts area.

Academic Fields/Career Goals: Nursing.

Award: Scholarship for use in freshman, sophomore, junior, or senior years; not renewable. *Amount:* $1000.

Eligibility Requirements: Applicant must be enrolled or expecting to enroll full-time at a two-year or four-year institution or university. Available to U.S. citizens.

Application Requirements: Application form, essay, financial need analysis. *Deadline:* February 15.

Contact: Lakeisha Graham, Manager, Office of the Reporter General
Phone: 202-628-1776
Fax: 202-879-3348
E-mail: nsdarscholarships@dar.org

THE NATIONAL SOCIETY OF THE COLONIAL DAMES OF AMERICA

http://www.nscda.org/

AMERICAN INDIAN NURSE SCHOLARSHIP PROGRAM
• *See page 368*

NEW JERSEY STATE NURSES ASSOCIATION

http://www.njsna.org/

INSTITUTE FOR NURSING SCHOLARSHIP

Applicants must be New Jersey residents currently enrolled in a diploma, associate, baccalaureate, master's, or doctoral program in nursing or a related field. The amount awarded in each scholarship will be $1000 per recipient.

Academic Fields/Career Goals: Nursing.

Award: Scholarship for use in freshman, sophomore, junior, senior, graduate, or postgraduate years; not renewable. *Number:* 10. *Amount:* $1000.

Eligibility Requirements: Applicant must be high school student; planning to enroll or expecting to enroll full- or part-time at a two-year or four-year institution or university; resident of New Jersey and studying in New Jersey. Applicant or parent of applicant must have employment or volunteer experience in nursing. Applicant must have 3.0 GPA or higher. Available to U.S. citizens. Applicant must have general military experience.

Application Requirements: Application form, essay, financial need analysis, personal photograph. *Deadline:* February 15.

Contact: Sandy Kerr, Executive Assistant
Phone: 609-883-5335
Fax: 609-883-5343
E-mail: sandy@njsna.org

NEW YORK STATE EMERGENCY NURSES ASSOCIATION (ENA)

http://www.ena.org/

NEW YORK STATE ENA SEPTEMBER 11 SCHOLARSHIP FUND

Scholarships to rescue workers who are going to school to obtain their undergraduate nursing degree. Eligible rescue workers include prehospital care providers, fire fighters, and police officers. The scholarship is not limited geographically. The scholarship winner will also be awarded a complimentary one year ENA membership.

Academic Fields/Career Goals: Nursing.

Award: Scholarship for use in freshman, sophomore, junior, senior, graduate, or postgraduate years; not renewable. *Number:* 1. *Amount:* $2000.

Eligibility Requirements: Applicant must be enrolled or expecting to enroll full- or part-time at a four-year institution or university. Available to U.S. citizens.

Application Requirements: Application form. *Deadline:* varies.

Contact: Educational Services
Phone: 847-460-4123
Fax: 847-460-4005
E-mail: education@ena.org

NEW YORK STATE GRANGE

http://www.nysgrange.org/

JUNE GILL NURSING SCHOLARSHIP

One annual scholarship award to verified NYS Grange member pursuing a career in nursing. Selection based on verification of NYS Grange membership and enrollment in a nursing program, as well as applicant's career statement, academic records, and financial need. Payment made after successful completion of one term.

Academic Fields/Career Goals: Nursing.

Award: Scholarship for use in freshman, sophomore, junior, or senior years; not renewable. *Number:* 1. *Amount:* $1000.

Eligibility Requirements: Applicant must be enrolled or expecting to enroll full-time at a two-year or four-year institution and resident of New York. Applicant or parent of applicant must be member of Grange Association. Available to U.S. citizens.

Application Requirements: Application form, financial need analysis. *Deadline:* April 15.

Contact: Scholarship Committee
New York State Grange
100 Grange Place
Cortland, NY 13045
Phone: 607-756-7553
E-mail: nysgrange@nysgrange.org

NEXTSTEPU

http://www.nextstepu.com/

$1,500 STEM SCHOLARSHIP
• *See page 120*

ODD FELLOWS AND REBEKAHS

http://www.ioofme.org/

ODD FELLOWS AND REBEKAHS ELLEN F. WASHBURN NURSES TRAINING AWARD

Award for high school seniors and college undergraduates to attend an accredited Maine institution and pursue a registered nursing degree. Must have a minimum 2.5 GPA. Can reapply for award for up to four years.

Academic Fields/Career Goals: Nursing.

Award: Scholarship for use in freshman, sophomore, junior, or senior years; renewable. *Number:* up to 30. *Amount:* $150–$400.

Eligibility Requirements: Applicant must be enrolled or expecting to enroll full- or part-time at a two-year or four-year institution or university and studying in Maine. Applicant must have 2.5 GPA or higher. Available to U.S. citizens.

Application Requirements: Application form, financial need analysis, personal photograph, recommendations or references. *Deadline:* April 15.

Contact: Joyce Young, Chairman
Phone: 207-839-4723

ONS FOUNDATION

http://www.onsfoundation.org

ONS FOUNDATION JOSH GOTTHEIL MEMORIAL BONE MARROW TRANSPLANT CAREER DEVELOPMENT AWARDS

Awards available to any professional registered nurse in field of bone marrow transplant nursing for further study in a Bachelor's or Master's program. Submit examples of contributions to BMT nursing.

Academic Fields/Career Goals: Nursing.

Award: Scholarship for use in junior, senior, or graduate years; not renewable. *Number:* 4. *Amount:* $2000.

Eligibility Requirements: Applicant must be enrolled or expecting to enroll full- or part-time at a four-year institution or university. Available to U.S. and non-U.S. citizens.

Application Requirements: Application form, essay, recommendations or references, resume. *Deadline:* December 1.

Contact: Bonny Revo, Executive Assistant
Phone: 412-859-6278
E-mail: brevo@onsfoundation.org

ONS FOUNDATION/ONCOLOGY NURSING CERTIFICATION CORPORATION BACHELOR'S SCHOLARSHIPS

One-time awards to improve oncology nursing by assisting registered nurses in furthering their education. Applicants must hold a current license to practice and be enrolled in an undergraduate nursing degree program at an NLN-accredited school.

Academic Fields/Career Goals: Nursing; Oncology.

Award: Scholarship for use in freshman, sophomore, junior, or senior years; not renewable. *Amount:* $2000.

Eligibility Requirements: Applicant must be enrolled or expecting to enroll full- or part-time at a four-year institution or university. Available to U.S. and non-U.S. citizens.

Application Requirements: Application form, transcript. *Fee:* $5. *Deadline:* February 1.

Contact: Bonny Revo, Executive Assistant
Phone: 412-859-6278
E-mail: brevo@onsfoundation.org

ONS FOUNDATION/PEARL MOORE CAREER DEVELOPMENT AWARDS

Awards to practicing staff nurses who possess or are pursuing a BSN and have two years oncology practice experience.

Academic Fields/Career Goals: Nursing; Oncology.

Award: Prize for use in junior, senior, or graduate years; not renewable. *Number:* 3. *Amount:* $3000.

Eligibility Requirements: Applicant must be enrolled or expecting to enroll full- or part-time at a four-year institution or university. Available to U.S. citizens.

Application Requirements: Application form, recommendations or references. *Deadline:* December 1.

Contact: Bonny Revo, Executive Assistant
Phone: 412-859-6278
E-mail: brevo@onsfoundation.org

OREGON COMMUNITY FOUNDATION

http://www.oregoncf.org/

FRANZ STENZEL M.D. AND KATHRYN STENZEL SCHOLARSHIP FUND
• See page 376

NLN ELLA MCKINNEY SCHOLARSHIP FUND

Award for Oregon high school graduates (or the equivalent) for use in the pursuit of an undergraduate or graduate nursing education. Must attend a nonprofit college or university in Oregon accredited by the NLN Accrediting Commission. For more information, see web http://www.getcollegefunds.org.

Academic Fields/Career Goals: Nursing.

Award: Scholarship for use in freshman, sophomore, junior, or senior years; renewable. *Number:* up to 2. *Amount:* $1000–$2000.

Eligibility Requirements: Applicant must be enrolled or expecting to enroll full-time at a two-year or four-year institution or university; resident of Oregon and studying in Oregon. Available to U.S. citizens.

Application Requirements: Application form, recommendations or references. *Deadline:* March 1.

Contact: Dianne Causey, Program Associate for Scholarships and Grants
Phone: 503-227-6846 Ext. 1418
E-mail: dcausey@oregoncf.org

OREGON STUDENT ASSISTANCE COMMISSION

https://oregonstudentaid.gov/

BERTHA P. SINGER NURSES SCHOLARSHIP

Award for students pursuing a nursing career. Must attend a college or university in Oregon. Minimum GPA of 3.0 required. Proof of enrollment in second year of nursing degree program is required. U.S. Bank employees, their children, or close relatives are not eligible. Based on financial need.

Academic Fields/Career Goals: Nursing.

Award: Scholarship for use in sophomore, junior, senior, or graduate years; not renewable.

Eligibility Requirements: Applicant must be enrolled or expecting to enroll full-time at a four-year institution or university and studying in Oregon. Applicant must have 3.0 GPA or higher. Available to U.S. citizens.

Application Requirements: Application form, financial need analysis. *Deadline:* March 1.

Contact: Melissa Adams, Scholarship Processing Coordinator
Phone: 541-687-7409
E-mail: melissa.adams@state.or.us

CHESTER AND HELEN LUTHER SCHOLARSHIP
• See page 376

CLARK-PHELPS SCHOLARSHIP
• See page 256

FRANZ STENZEL M.D. AND KATHRYN STENZEL SCHOLARSHIP
• See page 376

MARION A. LINDEMAN SCHOLARSHIP
• See page 376

NATIONAL LEAGUE FOR NURSING ELLA MCKINNEY SCHOLARSHIP

Scholarship for students majoring in nursing. Applicants must be graduates (including GED recipients and home-schooled graduates) of Oregon high schools. Preference for applicants enrolling in senior year of undergraduate-level study or final year of graduate-level study. Must enroll in an Oregon college offering nursing programs accredited by the National League for Nursing Accrediting Commission. Based on financial need.

Academic Fields/Career Goals: Nursing.

Award: Scholarship for use in freshman, sophomore, junior, senior, or graduate years; not renewable.

Eligibility Requirements: Applicant must be enrolled or expecting to enroll at a four-year institution or university; resident of Oregon and studying in Oregon. Available to U.S. citizens.

Application Requirements: Application form, financial need analysis. *Deadline:* March 1.

Contact: Melissa Adams, Scholarship Processing Coordinator
Phone: 541-687-7409
E-mail: melissa.adams@state.or.us

WALTER C. AND MARIE C. SCHMIDT SCHOLARSHIP

Scholarship available to Oregon students enrolling in programs to become registered nurses and intending to pursue careers in geriatric health care. Preference given to (1) students attending Lane County Community College, (2) students enrolled in any other two-year college nursing program, (3) students enrolled in a four-year college nursing program. Must enroll at least half time. U.S. Bank employees, their children, or near relatives are not eligible. Based on financial need.

Academic Fields/Career Goals: Nursing.

Award: Scholarship for use in freshman year; not renewable.

Eligibility Requirements: Applicant must be enrolled or expecting to enroll full- or part-time at a two-year or four-year institution or university and resident of Oregon. Available to U.S. citizens.

Application Requirements: Application form, essay, financial need analysis. *Deadline:* March 1.

Contact: Melissa Adams, Scholarship Processing Coordinator
Phone: 541-687-7409
E-mail: melissa.adams@state.or.us

PILOT INTERNATIONAL
https://www.pilotinternational.org/

PILOT INTERNATIONAL SCHOLARSHIP
• *See page 377*

PLATINUM EDUCATIONAL GROUP
http://www.platinumed.com

PLATINUM EDUCATIONAL GROUP SCHOLARSHIPS PROGRAM FOR EMS, NURSING, AND ALLIED HEALTH
• *See page 117*

THE RECOVERY VILLAGE
https://www.therecoveryvillage.com/

RECOVERY VILLAGE HEALTHCARE SCHOLARSHIP
• *See page 256*

RHODE ISLAND FOUNDATION
http://www.rifoundation.org/

ALBERT E. AND FLORENCE W. NEWTON NURSE SCHOLARSHIP

Scholarship for student studying nursing on a full- or part-time basis. Preference will be given to Rhode Island residents committed to practicing in Rhode Island. Must be able to demonstrate financial need. Must be either a licensed RN enrolled in a nursing Baccalaureate degree program; a student enrolled in a Baccalaureate nursing program; a student in a diploma nursing program; or a student in a two-year Associate degree nursing program.

Academic Fields/Career Goals: Nursing.

Award: Scholarship for use in freshman, sophomore, junior, or senior years; renewable. *Amount:* $500–$2000.

Eligibility Requirements: Applicant must be enrolled or expecting to enroll full- or part-time at a two-year or four-year institution or university. Available to U.S. citizens.

Application Requirements: Application form, copy of college acceptance letter, copy of most recent income tax return, essay, financial need analysis, self-addressed stamped envelope with application, transcript. *Deadline:* April 19.

Contact: Libby Monahan, Funds Administrator
Phone: 401-274-4564 Ext. 3117
E-mail: libbym@rifoundation.org

EDWARD J. AND VIRGINIA M. ROUTHIER NURSING SCHOLARSHIP

Renewable scholarship for licensed RNs seeking Baccalaureate or graduate nursing degrees in Rhode Island. Must demonstrate financial need.

Academic Fields/Career Goals: Nursing.

Award: Scholarship for use in freshman, sophomore, junior, senior, or graduate years; renewable. *Amount:* $500–$3000.

Eligibility Requirements: Applicant must be enrolled or expecting to enroll full- or part-time at a four-year institution or university and studying in Rhode Island. Available to U.S. citizens.

Application Requirements: Application form. *Deadline:* April 19.

Contact: Libby Monahan, Funds Administrator
Phone: 401-274-4564 Ext. 3117
E-mail: libbym@rifoundation.org

WILLARD & MARJORIE SCHEIBE NURSING SCHOLARSHIP

Renewable scholarship for Rhode Island residents pursuing LPN, RN, or advanced nursing degrees. Must demonstrate financial need.

Academic Fields/Career Goals: Nursing.

Award: Scholarship for use in freshman, sophomore, junior, senior, or graduate years; renewable.

Eligibility Requirements: Applicant must be enrolled or expecting to enroll full-time at a four-year institution or university and resident of Rhode Island. Available to U.S. citizens.

Application Requirements: Application form, financial need analysis. *Deadline:* April 19.

Contact: Libby Monahan, Funds Administrator
Phone: 401-274-4564 Ext. 3117
E-mail: libbym@rifoundation.org

SCARLETT FAMILY FOUNDATION SCHOLARSHIP PROGRAM
http://www.scarlettfoundation.org/

SCHOLARSHIP FOR STUDENTS PURSUING A BUSINESS OR STEM DEGREE
• *See page 91*

THE SOCIETY FOR THE SCIENTIFIC STUDY OF SEXUALITY
http://www.sexscience.org/

THE SOCIETY FOR THE SCIENTIFIC STUDY OF SEXUALITY STUDENT RESEARCH GRANT
• *See page 120*

SOCIETY OF PEDIATRIC NURSES
http://www.pedsnurses.org/

SOCIETY OF PEDIATRIC NURSES EDUCATIONAL SCHOLARSHIP
• *See page 203*

STRAIGHTFORWARD MEDIA
http://www.straightforwardmedia.com/

STRAIGHTFORWARD MEDIA MEDICAL PROFESSIONS SCHOLARSHIP
• *See page 257*

STRAIGHTFORWARD MEDIA NURSING SCHOOL SCHOLARSHIP

Scholarship of $500 available to students majoring in nursing. Awarded four times per year. Deadlines are April 14, July 14, October 14, and January 14. To apply, go to http://www.straightforwardmedia.com/nursing/form.php.

Academic Fields/Career Goals: Nursing.

Award: Scholarship for use in freshman, sophomore, junior, or senior years; not renewable. *Number:* 4. *Amount:* $500.

Eligibility Requirements: Applicant must be enrolled or expecting to enroll full- or part-time at a two-year or four-year or technical institution or university. Available to U.S. and non-U.S. citizens.

Application Requirements: Essay. *Deadline:* varies.

Contact: Scholarship Committee
Phone: 605-348-3042

STRAIGHT NORTH

https://www.straightnorth.com/

STRAIGHT NORTH STEM SCHOLARSHIP
• See page 92

TAFFORD UNIFORMS

http://www.tafford.com/

TAFFORD UNIFORMS NURSING SCHOLARSHIP PROGRAM

Two scholarships of $1000 each awarded to nursing students enrolled in undergraduate and graduate study. Minimum 2.5 GPA required.

Academic Fields/Career Goals: Nursing.

Award: Scholarship for use in freshman, sophomore, junior, or senior years; not renewable. *Number:* 2. *Amount:* $1000.

Eligibility Requirements: Applicant must be enrolled or expecting to enroll full-time at a two-year or four-year institution or university. Applicant must have 2.5 GPA or higher. Available to U.S. citizens.

Application Requirements: Application form. *Deadline:* continuous.

Contact: Scholarship Coordinator
Phone: 215-643-9666

TOUCHMARK FOUNDATION

http://www.touchmarkfoundation.org/

TOUCHMARK FOUNDATION NURSING SCHOLARSHIP

Students pursuing nursing degrees at any level are encouraged to apply, including nurses interested pursuing advanced degrees in order to teach. Applications reviewed throughout the year. Scholarships are offered to students attending schools in the following states: WI, WA, ID, OR, ND, SD, MN, OK, MT, and AZ.

Academic Fields/Career Goals: Nursing.

Award: Scholarship for use in freshman, sophomore, junior, senior, graduate, or postgraduate years; not renewable. *Number:* 8–16. *Amount:* $1000–$2000.

Eligibility Requirements: Applicant must be enrolled or expecting to enroll full-time at a four-year institution or university and studying in Alberta, Idaho, Minnesota, Montana, North Dakota, Oklahoma, Oregon, South Dakota, Washington, Wisconsin. Available to U.S. citizens.

Application Requirements: Application form, essay, FAFSA, copy of acceptance letter, recommendations or references, transcript. *Deadline:* continuous.

Contact: Bret Cope, Chairman
Touchmark Foundation
5150 SW Griffith Drive
Beaverton, OR 97005
Phone: 503-646-5186
E-mail: bjc@touchmark.com

UNITED DAUGHTERS OF THE CONFEDERACY

http://www.hqudc.org/

PHOEBE PEMBER MEMORIAL SCHOLARSHIP

Award for full-time undergraduate students who are descendants of a Confederate soldier, enrolled in a school of nursing. Must be enrolled in an accredited college or university and have a minimum 3.0 GPA. Submit letter of endorsement from sponsoring Chapter of the United Daughters of the Confederacy.

Academic Fields/Career Goals: Nursing.

Award: Scholarship for use in freshman, sophomore, junior, or senior years; renewable. *Number:* 1–2. *Amount:* $800–$1000.

Eligibility Requirements: Applicant must be enrolled or expecting to enroll full-time at a four-year institution or university. Applicant or parent of applicant must be member of United Daughters of the Confederacy. Applicant must have 3.0 GPA or higher. Available to U.S. citizens.

Application Requirements: Application form, copy of applicant's birth certificate, copy of confederate ancestor's proof of service, essay, financial need analysis, personal photograph, recommendations or

references, self-addressed stamped envelope with application, test scores, transcript. *Deadline:* March 15.

Contact: Ms. Jamie Davis, Second Vice President General
Phone: 804-355-1636
E-mail: hqudc@rcn.com

WALTER REED SMITH SCHOLARSHIP
• See page 184

UNITED NEGRO COLLEGE FUND

http://www.uncf.org/

HCN/APRICITY RESOURCES SCHOLARS PROGRAM
• See page 93

U.S. DEPARTMENT OF HEALTH AND HUMAN SERVICES

http://www.hhs.gov/

U. S. PUBLIC HEALTH SERVICE-HEALTH RESOURCES AND SERVICES ADMINISTRATION, BUREAU OF HEALTH PROFESSIONS SCHOLARSHIPS FOR DISADVANTAGED STUDENTS
• See page 257

VIRGINIA DEPARTMENT OF HEALTH, OFFICE OF MINORITY HEALTH AND HEALTH EQUITY

http://www.vdh.virginia.gov/

MARY MARSHALL PRACTICAL NURSING SCHOLARSHIP (LPN)

Awards for students who are accepted or enrolled as a full-time or part-time student in a practical school of nursing in the state of Virginia. Must be a Virginia resident for at least one year and have submitted a completed application form and a recommendation from the Director regarding scholastic attainment and financial need prior to June 30. Students pursuing a nursing degree not available in Virginia, are not eligible for the scholarship. Scholarship amount varies.

Academic Fields/Career Goals: Nursing.

Award: Scholarship for use in freshman, sophomore, junior, or senior years; not renewable. *Number:* 26–88. *Amount:* $600–$1200.

Eligibility Requirements: Applicant must be enrolled or expecting to enroll full- or part-time at a two-year or four-year or technical institution or university; resident of Virginia and studying in Virginia. Applicant must have 2.5 GPA or higher. Available to U.S. citizens.

Application Requirements: Application form, driver's license, essay, financial need analysis, recommendations or references, transcript. *Deadline:* June 30.

Contact: Miss. Sarahbeth Jones, Communications Specialist
Virginia Department of Health, Office of Minority Health and Health Equity
PO Box 2448, 109 Governor Street, Suite 1016-E
Richmond, VA 23218-2448
Phone: 804-864-7422
Fax: 804-864-7440
E-mail: IncentivePrograms@vdh.virginia.gov

MARY MARSHALL REGISTERED NURSING SCHOLARSHIPS

Scholarship for Virginia residents who have been accepted or is enrollment as a full-time or part-time student in a school of nursing in the state of Virginia. Must demonstrate financial need, verified by the Financial Aid Office/authorized person at the applicant's nursing school. Must also be a resident of Virginia for at least one year and have a minimum 3.0 GPA in required courses. Must have submitted a completed application form and an official grade transcript to The Office of Minority Health and Public Health Policy prior to June 30. If no college courses attempted an official high school transcript or equivalent must be submitted.

Academic Fields/Career Goals: Nursing.

Award: Scholarship for use in freshman, sophomore, junior, or senior years; not renewable. *Number:* 28–95. *Amount:* $600–$2000.

Eligibility Requirements: Applicant must be enrolled or expecting to enroll full- or part-time at a two-year or four-year institution or university; resident of Virginia and studying in Virginia. Applicant must have 2.5 GPA or higher. Available to U.S. citizens.

Application Requirements: Application form, driver's license, essay, financial need analysis, recommendations or references, transcript. *Deadline:* June 30.

Contact: Miss. Sarahbeth Jones, Communications Specialist
Virginia Department of Health, Office of Minority Health and Health Equity
PO Box 2448, 109 Governor Street, Suite 1016-E
Richmond, VA 23218-2448
Phone: 804-864-7422
Fax: 804-864-7440
E-mail: IncentivePrograms@vdh.virginia.gov

WOUND, OSTOMY AND CONTINENCE NURSES SOCIETY

http://www.wocn.org

WOCN ACCREDITED NURSING EDUCATION PROGRAM SCHOLARSHIP

Scholarships are awarded to deserving individuals committed to working within the wound, ostomy and continence nursing specialty. Applicants must agree to support the WOCN Society philosophy and scope of practice. Number of scholarships and the dollar value varies annually. Deadlines: May 1 or November 1.

Academic Fields/Career Goals: Nursing.

Award: Scholarship for use in freshman, sophomore, junior, or senior years; not renewable. *Number:* 20. *Amount:* $2000.

Eligibility Requirements: Applicant must be enrolled or expecting to enroll full-time at a two-year or four-year or technical institution or university. Applicant or parent of applicant must have employment or volunteer experience in nursing. Available to U.S. and non-U.S. citizens.

Application Requirements: Application form. *Deadline:* May 1.

Contact: Heather Martinek, Assistant Executive Director
Wound, Ostomy and Continence Nurses Society
1120 Route 73
Suite 200
Mount Laurel, NJ 08054
Phone: 888-224-9626
Fax: 856-439-0525
E-mail: info@wocn.org

OCCUPATIONAL SAFETY AND HEALTH

AMERICAN INDIAN SCIENCE AND ENGINEERING SOCIETY

http://www.aises.org/

A.T. ANDERSON MEMORIAL SCHOLARSHIP PROGRAM
• *See page 121*

ASSOCIATION FOR EDUCATION AND REHABILITATION OF THE BLIND AND VISUALLY IMPAIRED

http://www.aerbvi.org/

WILLIAM AND DOROTHY FERRELL SCHOLARSHIP
• *See page 268*

BHW GROUP

https://thebhwgroup.com/

BHW WOMEN IN STEM SCHOLARSHIP
• *See page 124*

CONTINENTAL SOCIETY, DAUGHTERS OF INDIAN WARS

http://www.csdiw.org/

CONTINENTAL SOCIETY, DAUGHTERS OF INDIAN WARS SCHOLARSHIP
• *See page 242*

CYNTHIA E. MORGAN SCHOLARSHIP FUND (CEMS)

http://www.cemsfund.com/

CYNTHIA E. MORGAN MEMORIAL SCHOLARSHIP FUND, INC.
• *See page 334*

HAWAIIAN LODGE, F&AM

http://www.hawaiianlodgefreemasons.org

HAWAIIAN LODGE SCHOLARSHIPS
• *See page 86*

INTERMOUNTAIN MEDICAL IMAGING

https://www.aboutimi.com/

INTERMOUNTAIN MEDICAL IMAGING SCHOLARSHIP
• *See page 147*

LAW OFFICES OF PROSPER SHAKED

https://www.prosperlaw.com/

PROSPER SHAKED SCHOLARSHIP FOR FUTURE MEDICAL PROFESSIONALS
• *See page 166*

MICHAEL MOODY FITNESS

http://www.michaelmoodyfitness.com/

MICHAEL MOODY FITNESS SCHOLARSHIP
• *See page 166*

NATIONAL SAFETY COUNCIL

http://www.cshema.org/

CAMPUS SAFETY, HEALTH AND ENVIRONMENTAL MANAGEMENT ASSOCIATION SCHOLARSHIP AWARD PROGRAM
• *See page 342*

THE RECOVERY VILLAGE

https://www.therecoveryvillage.com/

RECOVERY VILLAGE HEALTHCARE SCHOLARSHIP
• *See page 256*

STRAIGHTFORWARD MEDIA

http://www.straightforwardmedia.com/

STRAIGHTFORWARD MEDIA MEDICAL PROFESSIONS SCHOLARSHIP
• *See page 257*

STRAIGHT NORTH

https://www.straightnorth.com/

STRAIGHT NORTH STEM SCHOLARSHIP
• *See page 92*

TEXAS DEPARTMENT OF TRANSPORTATION

http://www.txdot.gov/

CONDITIONAL GRANT PROGRAM
• *See page 212*

OCEANOGRAPHY

AMERICAN INDIAN SCIENCE AND ENGINEERING SOCIETY

http://www.aises.org/

A.T. ANDERSON MEMORIAL SCHOLARSHIP PROGRAM
• *See page 121*

ASSOCIATION FOR WOMEN GEOSCIENTISTS (AWG)

http://www.awg.org/

AWG ETHNIC MINORITY SCHOLARSHIP
• *See page 260*

AWG MARIA LUISA CRAWFORD FIELD CAMP SCHOLARSHIP
• *See page 129*

AWG SALT LAKE CHAPTER (SLC) RESEARCH SCHOLARSHIP
• *See page 129*

JANET CULLEN TANAKA GEOSCIENCES UNDERGRADUATE SCHOLARSHIP
• *See page 129*

LONE STAR RISING CAREER SCHOLARSHIP
• *See page 260*

OSAGE CHAPTER UNDERGRADUATE SERVICE SCHOLARSHIP
• *See page 129*

SUSAN EKDALE MEMORIAL FIELD CAMP SCHOLARSHIP
• *See page 260*

BARRY GOLDWATER SCHOLARSHIP AND EXCELLENCE IN EDUCATION FOUNDATION

https://goldwater.scholarsapply.org

BARRY M. GOLDWATER SCHOLARSHIP AND EXCELLENCE IN EDUCATION PROGRAM
• *See page 123*

BHW GROUP

https://thebhwgroup.com/

BHW WOMEN IN STEM SCHOLARSHIP
• *See page 124*

BROWN AND CALDWELL

http://www.brownandcaldwell.com

ECKENFELDER SCHOLARSHIP
• *See page 169*

MINORITY SCHOLARSHIP PROGRAM
• *See page 169*

CALAVERAS BIG TREES ASSOCIATION

https://bigtrees.org/

EMILY M. HEWITT MEMORIAL SCHOLARSHIP
• *See page 170*

CARDS AGAINST HUMANITY

https://cardsagainsthumanity.com/

SCIENCE AMBASSADOR SCHOLARSHIP
• *See page 124*

DISTIL NETWORKS

http://www.distilnetworks.com

WOMEN FORWARD IN TECHNOLOGY SCHOLARSHIP PROGRAM
• *See page 124*

DIVERSITYCOMM, INC.

http://www.diversitycomm.net/

DIVERSITY IN STEAM MAGAZINE SCHOLARSHIP
• *See page 83*

GREAT MINDS IN STEM

http://www.greatmindsinstem.org

HENAAC SCHOLARSHIP PROGRAM
• *See page 115*

HAWAIIAN LODGE, F&AM

http://www.hawaiianlodgefreemasons.org

HAWAIIAN LODGE SCHOLARSHIPS
• *See page 86*

LABROOTS INC.
http://www.LabRoots.com

LABROOTS STEM SCHOLARSHIP
• *See page 116*

THE LAND CONSERVANCY OF NEW JERSEY
http://www.tlc-nj.org/

ROGERS FAMILY SCHOLARSHIP
• *See page 172*

RUSSELL W. MYERS SCHOLARSHIP
• *See page 172*

LOUISIANA OFFICE OF STUDENT FINANCIAL ASSISTANCE
http://www.osfa.la.gov/

ROCKEFELLER STATE WILDLIFE SCHOLARSHIP
• *See page 172*

MARINE TECHNOLOGY SOCIETY
http://www.mtsociety.org/

CHARLES H. BUSSMAN UNDERGRADUATE SCHOLARSHIP
• *See page 423*

JOHN C. BAJUS SCHOLARSHIP
• *See page 423*

MTS STUDENT SCHOLARSHIP
• *See page 423*

PAROS-DIGIQUARTZ SCHOLARSHIP
• *See page 424*

ROV SCHOLARSHIP
• *See page 424*

NASA MINNESOTA SPACE GRANT CONSORTIUM
https://www.mnspacegrant.org/

MINNESOTA SPACE GRANT CONSORTIUM SCHOLARSHIP PROGRAM
• *See page 156*

NEXTSTEPU
http://www.nextstepu.com/

$1,500 STEM SCHOLARSHIP
• *See page 120*

SCARLETT FAMILY FOUNDATION SCHOLARSHIP PROGRAM
http://www.scarlettfoundation.org/

SCHOLARSHIP FOR STUDENTS PURSUING A BUSINESS OR STEM DEGREE
• *See page 91*

WOMAN'S SEAMEN'S FRIEND SOCIETY OF CONNECTICUT INC.

FINANCIAL SUPPORT FOR MARINE OR MARITIME STUDIES
• *See page 425*

YOUTH MARITIME TRAINING ASSOCIATION
http://ymta.net/

NORM MANLY—YMTA MARITIME EDUCATIONAL SCHOLARSHIPS
• *See page 425*

ONCOLOGY

AMERICAN INDIAN SCIENCE AND ENGINEERING SOCIETY
http://www.aises.org/

A.T. ANDERSON MEMORIAL SCHOLARSHIP PROGRAM
• *See page 121*

AMERICAN LEGION AUXILIARY DEPARTMENT OF COLORADO
http://www.alacolorado.com

AMERICAN LEGION AUXILIARY DEPARTMENT OF COLORADO PAST PRESIDENTS' PARLEY HEALTH CARE PROFESSIONAL SCHOLARSHIPNURSES SCHOLARSHIP
• *See page 147*

ARRL FOUNDATION INC.
http://www.arrl.org/

CAROLE J. STREETER, KB9JBR, SCHOLARSHIP
• *See page 254*

ASRT FOUNDATION
http://foundation.asrt.org

JERMAN-CAHOON STUDENT SCHOLARSHIP
• *See page 371*

PROFESSIONAL ADVANCEMENT SCHOLARSHIP
• *See page 367*

SIEMENS CLINICAL ADVANCEMENT SCHOLARSHIP
• *See page 372*

VARIAN RADIATION THERAPY ADVANCEMENT SCHOLARSHIP
• *See page 372*

AVACARE MEDICAL
https://avacaremedical.com

AVACARE MEDICAL SCHOLARSHIP
• *See page 115*

BHW GROUP

https://thebhwgroup.com/

BHW WOMEN IN STEM SCHOLARSHIP
• *See page 124*

CARDS AGAINST HUMANITY

https://cardsagainsthumanity.com/

SCIENCE AMBASSADOR SCHOLARSHIP
• *See page 124*

CONTINENTAL SOCIETY, DAUGHTERS OF INDIAN WARS

http://www.csdiw.org/

CONTINENTAL SOCIETY, DAUGHTERS OF INDIAN WARS SCHOLARSHIP
• *See page 242*

CYNTHIA E. MORGAN SCHOLARSHIP FUND (CEMS)

http://www.cemsfund.com/

CYNTHIA E. MORGAN MEMORIAL SCHOLARSHIP FUND, INC.
• *See page 334*

THE EXPERT INSTITUTE

https://www.theexpertinstitute.com

ANNUAL HEALTHCARE AND LIFE SCIENCES SCHOLARSHIP
• *See page 170*

GREAT MINDS IN STEM

http://www.greatmindsinstem.org

HENAAC SCHOLARSHIP PROGRAM
• *See page 115*

INTERMOUNTAIN MEDICAL IMAGING

https://www.aboutimi.com/

INTERMOUNTAIN MEDICAL IMAGING SCHOLARSHIP
• *See page 147*

LABROOTS INC.

http://www.LabRoots.com

LABROOTS STEM SCHOLARSHIP
• *See page 116*

LAW OFFICES OF PROSPER SHAKED

https://www.prosperlaw.com/

PROSPER SHAKED SCHOLARSHIP FOR FUTURE MEDICAL PROFESSIONALS
• *See page 166*

MEDICAL SCRUBS COLLECTION

http://medicalscrubscollection.com

MEDICAL SCRUBS COLLECTION SCHOLARSHIP
• *See page 120*

MICHAEL MOODY FITNESS

http://www.michaelmoodyfitness.com/

MICHAEL MOODY FITNESS SCHOLARSHIP
• *See page 166*

NEXTSTEPU

http://www.nextstepu.com/

$1,500 STEM SCHOLARSHIP
• *See page 120*

ONS FOUNDATION

http://www.onsfoundation.org

ONS FOUNDATION/ONCOLOGY NURSING CERTIFICATION CORPORATION BACHELOR'S SCHOLARSHIPS
• *See page 486*

ONS FOUNDATION/PEARL MOORE CAREER DEVELOPMENT AWARDS
• *See page 486*

SCARLETT FAMILY FOUNDATION SCHOLARSHIP PROGRAM

http://www.scarlettfoundation.org/

SCHOLARSHIP FOR STUDENTS PURSUING A BUSINESS OR STEM DEGREE
• *See page 91*

STRAIGHTFORWARD MEDIA

http://www.straightforwardmedia.com/

STRAIGHTFORWARD MEDIA MEDICAL PROFESSIONS SCHOLARSHIP
• *See page 257*

STRAIGHT NORTH

https://www.straightnorth.com/

STRAIGHT NORTH STEM SCHOLARSHIP
• *See page 92*

OPTOMETRY

AMERICAN INDIAN SCIENCE AND ENGINEERING SOCIETY

http://www.aises.org/

A.T. ANDERSON MEMORIAL SCHOLARSHIP PROGRAM
• *See page 121*

AMERICAN LEGION AUXILIARY DEPARTMENT OF COLORADO

http://www.alacolorado.com

AMERICAN LEGION AUXILIARY DEPARTMENT OF COLORADO PAST PRESIDENTS' PARLEY HEALTH CARE PROFESSIONAL SCHOLARSHIPNURSES SCHOLARSHIP
• *See page 147*

AMERICAN OPTOMETRIC FOUNDATION

http://www.aaopt.org/

VISTAKON AWARD OF EXCELLENCE IN CONTACT LENS PATIENT CARE
Open to any fourth-year student attending any school or college of optometry. Must have 3.0 GPA. Student's knowledge of subject matter and skillful, professional clinical contact lens patient care are considered. School makes selection and sends application to AOF.

Academic Fields/Career Goals: Optometry.

Award: Scholarship for use in senior or graduate years; not renewable. *Number:* 19. *Amount:* $1000.

Eligibility Requirements: Applicant must be enrolled or expecting to enroll full-time at a four-year institution or university. Applicant must have 3.0 GPA or higher. Available to U.S. and non-U.S. citizens.

Application Requirements: Application form, recommendations or references. *Deadline:* September 1.

Contact: Alisa Moore, Program Administrator
    Phone: 240-880-3084
    Fax: 301-984-4737
    E-mail: alisam@aaopt.org

ARRL FOUNDATION INC.

http://www.arrl.org/

CAROLE J. STREETER, KB9JBR, SCHOLARSHIP
• *See page 254*

AVACARE MEDICAL

https://avacaremedical.com

AVACARE MEDICAL SCHOLARSHIP
• *See page 115*

BHW GROUP

https://thebhwgroup.com/

BHW WOMEN IN STEM SCHOLARSHIP
• *See page 124*

CARDS AGAINST HUMANITY

https://cardsagainsthumanity.com/

SCIENCE AMBASSADOR SCHOLARSHIP
• *See page 124*

CONTINENTAL SOCIETY, DAUGHTERS OF INDIAN WARS

http://www.csdiw.org/

CONTINENTAL SOCIETY, DAUGHTERS OF INDIAN WARS SCHOLARSHIP
• *See page 242*

THE EXPERT INSTITUTE

https://www.theexpertinstitute.com

ANNUAL HEALTHCARE AND LIFE SCIENCES SCHOLARSHIP
• *See page 170*

GREAT MINDS IN STEM

http://www.greatmindsinstem.org

HENAAC SCHOLARSHIP PROGRAM
• *See page 115*

INDIAN HEALTH SERVICES, UNITED STATES DEPARTMENT OF HEALTH AND HUMAN SERVICES

http://www.ihs.gov/scholarship

HEALTH PROFESSIONS PREPARATORY SCHOLARSHIP PROGRAM
• *See page 165*

INTERMOUNTAIN MEDICAL IMAGING

https://www.aboutimi.com/

INTERMOUNTAIN MEDICAL IMAGING SCHOLARSHIP
• *See page 147*

KETAMINE CLINICS OF LOS ANGELES

http://www.ketamineclinics.com/

KETAMINE CLINICS OF LOS ANGELES SCHOLARSHIP PROGRAM
• *See page 165*

LABROOTS INC.

http://www.LabRoots.com

LABROOTS STEM SCHOLARSHIP
• *See page 116*

LAW OFFICES OF PROSPER SHAKED

https://www.prosperlaw.com/

PROSPER SHAKED SCHOLARSHIP FOR FUTURE MEDICAL PROFESSIONALS
• *See page 166*

MEDICAL SCRUBS COLLECTION

http://medicalscrubscollection.com

MEDICAL SCRUBS COLLECTION SCHOLARSHIP
• *See page 120*

MICHAEL MOODY FITNESS

http://www.michaelmoodyfitness.com/

MICHAEL MOODY FITNESS SCHOLARSHIP
• *See page 166*

NEXTSTEPU

http://www.nextstepu.com/

$1,500 STEM SCHOLARSHIP
• *See page 120*

SCARLETT FAMILY FOUNDATION SCHOLARSHIP PROGRAM

http://www.scarlettfoundation.org/

SCHOLARSHIP FOR STUDENTS PURSUING A BUSINESS OR STEM DEGREE
• *See page 91*

STRAIGHTFORWARD MEDIA

http://www.straightforwardmedia.com/

STRAIGHTFORWARD MEDIA MEDICAL PROFESSIONS SCHOLARSHIP
• *See page 257*

STRAIGHT NORTH

https://www.straightnorth.com/

STRAIGHT NORTH STEM SCHOLARSHIP
• *See page 92*

OSTEOPATHY

AMERICAN INDIAN SCIENCE AND ENGINEERING SOCIETY

http://www.aises.org/

A.T. ANDERSON MEMORIAL SCHOLARSHIP PROGRAM
• *See page 121*

AMERICAN LEGION AUXILIARY DEPARTMENT OF COLORADO

http://www.alacolorado.com

AMERICAN LEGION AUXILIARY DEPARTMENT OF COLORADO PAST PRESIDENTS' PARLEY HEALTH CARE PROFESSIONAL SCHOLARSHIPNURSES SCHOLARSHIP
• *See page 147*

ARRL FOUNDATION INC.

http://www.arrl.org/

CAROLE J. STREETER, KB9JBR, SCHOLARSHIP
• *See page 254*

AVACARE MEDICAL

https://avacaremedical.com

AVACARE MEDICAL SCHOLARSHIP
• *See page 115*

BHW GROUP

https://thebhwgroup.com/

BHW WOMEN IN STEM SCHOLARSHIP
• *See page 124*

CARDS AGAINST HUMANITY

https://cardsagainsthumanity.com/

SCIENCE AMBASSADOR SCHOLARSHIP
• *See page 124*

CONTINENTAL SOCIETY, DAUGHTERS OF INDIAN WARS

http://www.csdiw.org/

CONTINENTAL SOCIETY, DAUGHTERS OF INDIAN WARS SCHOLARSHIP
• *See page 242*

CYNTHIA E. MORGAN SCHOLARSHIP FUND (CEMS)

http://www.cemsfund.com/

CYNTHIA E. MORGAN MEMORIAL SCHOLARSHIP FUND, INC.
• *See page 334*

GREAT MINDS IN STEM

http://www.greatmindsinstem.org

HENAAC SCHOLARSHIP PROGRAM
• *See page 115*

INTERMOUNTAIN MEDICAL IMAGING

https://www.aboutimi.com/

INTERMOUNTAIN MEDICAL IMAGING SCHOLARSHIP
• *See page 147*

LABROOTS INC.

http://www.LabRoots.com

LABROOTS STEM SCHOLARSHIP
• *See page 116*

LAW OFFICES OF PROSPER SHAKED

https://www.prosperlaw.com/

PROSPER SHAKED SCHOLARSHIP FOR FUTURE MEDICAL PROFESSIONALS
• *See page 166*

MAINE OSTEOPATHIC ASSOCIATION

http://www.mainedo.org/

MAINE OSTEOPATHIC ASSOCIATION SCHOLARSHIP
• *See page 375*

MEDICAL SCRUBS COLLECTION

http://medicalscrubscollection.com

MEDICAL SCRUBS COLLECTION SCHOLARSHIP
• *See page 120*

MICHAEL MOODY FITNESS

http://www.michaelmoodyfitness.com/

MICHAEL MOODY FITNESS SCHOLARSHIP
• *See page 166*

NEXTSTEPU

http://www.nextstepu.com/

$1,500 STEM SCHOLARSHIP
• *See page 120*

SCARLETT FAMILY FOUNDATION SCHOLARSHIP PROGRAM

http://www.scarlettfoundation.org/

SCHOLARSHIP FOR STUDENTS PURSUING A BUSINESS OR STEM DEGREE
• *See page 91*

STRAIGHTFORWARD MEDIA

http://www.straightforwardmedia.com/

STRAIGHTFORWARD MEDIA MEDICAL PROFESSIONS SCHOLARSHIP
• *See page 257*

STRAIGHT NORTH

https://www.straightnorth.com/

STRAIGHT NORTH STEM SCHOLARSHIP
• *See page 92*

PAPER AND PULP ENGINEERING

AMERICAN CHEMICAL SOCIETY

http://www.acs.org/

AMERICAN CHEMICAL SOCIETY SCHOLARS PROGRAM
• *See page 187*

AMERICAN INDIAN SCIENCE AND ENGINEERING SOCIETY

http://www.aises.org/

A.T. ANDERSON MEMORIAL SCHOLARSHIP PROGRAM
• *See page 121*

AMERICAN SOCIETY OF HEATING, REFRIGERATING, AND AIR CONDITIONING ENGINEERS, INC.

http://www.ashrae.org/

ASHRAE REGION III BOGGARM SETTY SCHOLARSHIP
• *See page 191*

ARRL FOUNDATION INC.

http://www.arrl.org/

ALFRED E. FRIEND JR., W4CF, MEMORIAL SCHOLARSHIP
• *See page 191*

GARY WAGNER, K3OMI, SCHOLARSHIP
• *See page 191*

W1FDR SCHOLARSHIP
• *See page 122*

BHW GROUP

https://thebhwgroup.com/

BHW WOMEN IN STEM SCHOLARSHIP
• *See page 124*

BROWN AND CALDWELL

http://www.brownandcaldwell.com

ECKENFELDER SCHOLARSHIP
• *See page 169*

MINORITY SCHOLARSHIP PROGRAM
• *See page 169*

CARDS AGAINST HUMANITY

https://cardsagainsthumanity.com/

SCIENCE AMBASSADOR SCHOLARSHIP
• *See page 124*

GREATER KANAWHA VALLEY FOUNDATION

http://www.tgkvf.org/

STEVEN ENGINEERING SCHOLARSHIP
• *See page 192*

GREAT MINDS IN STEM

http://www.greatmindsinstem.org

HENAAC SCHOLARSHIP PROGRAM
• *See page 115*

NEXTSTEPU

http://www.nextstepu.com/

$1,500 STEM SCHOLARSHIP
• *See page 120*

SOCIETY OF WOMEN ENGINEERS

http://societyofwomenengineers.swe.org/

ADA I. PRESSMAN MEMORIAL SCHOLARSHIP
• *See page 196*

AMERICAN TRANSMISSION CO. SCHOLARSHIP
• *See page 196*

ANNE MAUREEN WHITNEY BARROW MEMORIAL SCHOLARSHIP
• *See page 196*

ANNE SHEN SMITH ENDOWED SCHOLARSHIP
• *See page 196*

BETTY LOU BAILEY SWE REGION F SCHOLARSHIP
• *See page 197*

B.J. HARROD SCHOLARSHIP
• *See page 197*

BK KRENZER MEMORIAL REENTRY SCHOLARSHIP
• *See page 197*

CAROL STEPHENS SWE REGION F SCHOLARSHIP
• *See page 197*

DR. IVY M. PARKER MEMORIAL SCHOLARSHIP
• *See page 197*

DOROTHY LEMKE HOWARTH MEMORIAL SCHOLARSHIP
• *See page 197*

DOROTHY P. MORRIS SCHOLARSHIP
• *See page 198*

EXELON SCHOLARSHIP
• *See page 198*

IBM LINDA SANFORD WOMEN'S TECHNICAL ADVANCEMENT SCHOLARSHIP
• *See page 198*

LILLIAN MOLLER GILBRETH MEMORIAL SCHOLARSHIP
• *See page 198*

MARY V. MUNGER MEMORIAL SCHOLARSHIP
• *See page 199*

OLIVE LYNN SALEMBIER MEMORIAL REENTRY SCHOLARSHIP
• *See page 199*

ROBERTA BANASZAK GLEITER ENGINEERING ENDEAVOR SCHOLARSHIP
• *See page 199*

SUSAN MISZKOWICZ SEPTEMBER 11 MEMORIAL SCHOLARSHIP
• *See page 199*

SWE BALTIMORE-WASHINGTON SECTION SCHOLARSHIP
• *See page 199*

SWE CENTRAL NEW MEXICO PIONEERS SCHOLARSHIP
• *See page 200*

SWE CENTRAL NEW MEXICO REENTRY SCHOLARSHIP
• *See page 200*

SWE MID-HUDSON SECTION SCHOLARSHIP
• *See page 200*

SWE PHOENIX SECTION SCHOLARSHIP
• *See page 200*

SWE REGION E SCHOLARSHIP
• *See page 200*

SWE REGION G JUDY SIMMONS MEMORIAL SCHOLARSHIP
• *See page 200*

SWE REGION H SCHOLARSHIPS
• *See page 201*

SWE REGION J SCHOLARSHIP
• *See page 201*

TE CONNECTIVITY EXCELLENCE IN ENGINEERING SCHOLARSHIP
• *See page 201*

TURNER CONSTRUCTION SCHOLARSHIP
• *See page 201*

WANDA MUNN SCHOLARSHIP
• *See page 201*

STRAIGHTFORWARD MEDIA

http://www.straightforwardmedia.com/

STRAIGHTFORWARD MEDIA ENGINEERING SCHOLARSHIP
• *See page 202*

STRAIGHT NORTH

https://www.straightnorth.com/

STRAIGHT NORTH STEM SCHOLARSHIP
• *See page 92*

TECHNICAL ASSOCIATION OF THE PULP & PAPER INDUSTRY (TAPPI)

http://www.tappi.org/

COATING AND GRAPHIC ARTS DIVISION SCHOLARSHIP
• *See page 365*

CORRUGATED PACKAGING DIVISION SCHOLARSHIPS
• *See page 307*

ENGINEERING DIVISION SCHOLARSHIP

Up to two $1500 scholarships offered. One may be awarded to a student who will be in his or her junior year, and the other will be offered to a student who will be in his or her senior year at the beginning of the next academic year. Information can be found at http://www.tappi.org/s_tappi/sec.asp?CID=6101&DID=546695.

Academic Fields/Career Goals: Paper and Pulp Engineering.

Award: Scholarship for use in junior or senior years; not renewable. *Number:* 1–2. *Amount:* $2000.

Eligibility Requirements: Applicant must be enrolled or expecting to enroll full-time at a four-year institution or university. Applicant must have 3.0 GPA or higher. Available to U.S. and non-U.S. citizens.

Application Requirements: Application form. *Deadline:* February 15.

Contact: Mr. Laurence Womack, Director of Standards and Awards
Technical Association of the Pulp & Paper Industry (TAPPI)
15 Technology Parkway South
Peachtree Corners, GA 30092
Phone: 770-209-7276
E-mail: standards@tappi.org

ENVIRONMENTAL WORKING GROUP SCHOLARSHIP
• *See page 344*

PAPER AND BOARD DIVISION SCHOLARSHIPS
• *See page 331*

TAPPI PROCESS CONTROL SCHOLARSHIP
The TAPPI Process Control Scholarship is designed to encourage talented engineering students to pursue careers in the pulp and paper industry and to develop professional skills in process control fields.
Academic Fields/Career Goals: Paper and Pulp Engineering.
Award: Scholarship for use in sophomore, junior, or senior years; not renewable. *Number:* 1. *Amount:* $1000.
Eligibility Requirements: Applicant must be high school student and planning to enroll or expecting to enroll full-time at a two-year or four-year institution or university. Applicant must have 3.0 GPA or higher. Available to U.S. and non-U.S. citizens.
Application Requirements: Application form. *Deadline:* February 15.
Contact: Mr. Laurence Womack, Director of Standards and Awards
Technical Association of the Pulp & Paper Industry (TAPPI)
15 Technology Parkway South
Suite 115
Peachtree Corners, GA 30092
Phone: 770-209-7276
E-mail: standards@tappi.org

WILLIAM L. CULLISON SCHOLARSHIP
• *See page 461*

PEACE AND CONFLICT STUDIES

ASSOCIATION OF FORMER INTELLIGENCE OFFICERS
http://www.afio.com

AFIO UNDERGRADUATE AND GRADUATE SCHOLARSHIPS
• *See page 113*

NATIONAL SECURITY EDUCATION PROGRAM
http://www.iie.org/

NATIONAL SECURITY EDUCATION PROGRAM (NSEP) DAVID L. BOREN UNDERGRADUATE SCHOLARSHIPS
• *See page 139*

UNITED NATIONS ASSOCIATION OF CONNECTICUT
http://www.unausa.org

UNITED NATIONS ASSOCIATION OF CONNECTICUT SCHOLARSHIP
• *See page 147*

VETERANS FOR PEACE-CHAPTER 93
VFP93.org

VETERANS FOR PEACE SCHOLARSHIP
VFP-93 Peace Scholarship is aimed to help Michigan students who are studying peace and conflict resolution, be it a degree program or course. Although originally aimed at veterans this is no longer a requirement. See VFP93.org for further description.
Academic Fields/Career Goals: Peace and Conflict Studies.
Award: Scholarship for use in freshman, sophomore, junior, senior, graduate, or postgraduate years; renewable. *Number:* 1–3. *Amount:* $500–$1000.
Eligibility Requirements: Applicant must be enrolled or expecting to enroll full- or part-time at a four-year institution and resident of Michigan. Available to U.S. citizens.
Application Requirements: Application form. *Deadline:* continuous.
Contact: Bbill Shea, Michigan
Veterans for Peace-Chapter 93
803 john a woods dr
ann arbor, MI 48105
Phone: 734-6620818
E-mail: billshea@umich.edu

WASHINGTON STATE ASSOCIATION FOR JUSTICE
http://www.washingtonjustice.org/

WASHINGTON STATE ASSOCIATION FOR JUSTICE AMERICAN JUSTICE ESSAY & VIDEO SCHOLARSHIP
• *See page 244*

PERFORMING ARTS

AMERICAN LEGION DEPARTMENT OF KANSAS
http://www.ksamlegion.org/

MUSIC COMMITTEE SCHOLARSHIP
• *See page 451*

CONGRESSIONAL BLACK CAUCUS FOUNDATION, INC.
http://www.cbcfinc.org/

CBC SPOUSES HEINEKEN USA PERFORMING ARTS SCHOLARSHIP
• *See page 452*

COSTUME SOCIETY OF AMERICA
http://www.costumesocietyamerica.com/

ADELE FILENE STUDENT PRESENTER GRANT
• *See page 138*

STELLA BLUM STUDENT RESEARCH GRANT
• *See page 138*

GENERAL FEDERATION OF WOMEN'S CLUBS OF MASSACHUSETTS

http://www.gfwcma.org/

DORCHESTER WOMEN'S CLUB MUSIC SCHOLARSHIP
• *See page 452*

GREATER KANAWHA VALLEY FOUNDATION

http://www.tgkvf.org/

HERB SMITH/EUNICE FLEMING SCHOLARSHIP
• *See page 453*

HEMOPHILIA FOUNDATION OF SOUTHERN CALIFORNIA

http://www.hemosocal.org/

EARL JAMES FAHRINGER PERFORMING ARTS SCHOLARSHIP
• *See page 142*

HOSTESS COMMITTEE SCHOLARSHIPS/MISS AMERICA PAGEANT

http://www.missamerica.org/

EUGENIA VELLNER FISCHER AWARD FOR PERFORMING ARTS

Scholarship for Miss America contestants pursuing degree in performing arts. Award available to women who have competed within the Miss America system on the local, state, or national level from 1998 to the present, regardless of whether title was won. One or more scholarships are awarded annually, depending on qualifications of applicants. Late or incomplete applications are not accepted.

Academic Fields/Career Goals: Performing Arts.

Award: Scholarship for use in freshman, sophomore, junior, senior, or graduate years; not renewable.

Eligibility Requirements: Applicant must be enrolled or expecting to enroll full- or part-time at a four-year institution or university; female and must have an interest in beauty pageant. Available to U.S. citizens.

Application Requirements: Application form, essay, financial need analysis, recommendations or references, transcript. *Deadline:* June 30.

Contact: Doreen Lindell Gordon, Controller and Scholarship Administrator
Phone: 609-345-7571 Ext. 27
Fax: 609-347-6079
E-mail: doreen@missamerica.org

ILLUMINATING ENGINEERING SOCIETY OF NORTH AMERICA

http://www.ies.org/

ROBERT W. THUNEN MEMORIAL SCHOLARSHIPS
• *See page 135*

NATIONAL ACADEMY OF TELEVISION ARTS AND SCIENCES

http://www.emmyonline.tv/

DOUGLAS W. MUMMERT SCHOLARSHIP
• *See page 142*

JIM MCKAY MEMORIAL SCHOLARSHIP
• *See page 220*

MIKE WALLACE MEMORIAL SCHOLARSHIP
• *See page 220*

NATIONAL ACADEMY OF TELEVISION ARTS AND SCIENCES TRUSTEES SCHOLARSHIP
• *See page 220*

RANDY FALCO SCHOLARSHIP
• *See page 220*

NATIONAL ACADEMY OF TELEVISION ARTS AND SCIENCES, MICHIGAN CHAPTER

http://natasmichigan.org

DR. LYNNE BOYLE/JOHN SCHIMPF UNDERGRADUATE SCHOLARSHIP
• *See page 97*

NATIONAL OPERA ASSOCIATION

http://www.noa.org/

NOA VOCAL COMPETITION/LEGACY AWARD PROGRAM
• *See page 143*

ONLINE LOGO MAKER

http://onlinelogomaker.com

OLM MALALA YOUSAFZAI SCHOLARSHIP
• *See page 143*

POLISH ARTS CLUB OF BUFFALO SCHOLARSHIP FOUNDATION

http://www.pacb.bfn.org/

POLISH ARTS CLUB OF BUFFALO SCHOLARSHIP FOUNDATION TRUST
• *See page 144*

PRINCESS GRACE FOUNDATION-USA

http://www.pgfusa.org/

PRINCESS GRACE AWARDS IN DANCE, THEATER, AND FILM
• *See page 347*

QUALITY BATH

http://www.qualitybath.com

QUALITYBATH.COM SCHOLARSHIP PROGRAM
• *See page 140*

SERVICE EMPLOYEES INTERNATIONAL UNION (SEIU)

http://www.seiu.org/

SEIU MOE FONER SCHOLARSHIP PROGRAM FOR VISUAL AND PERFORMING ARTS
• *See page 144*

SOUTHEASTERN THEATRE CONFERENCE

http://www.setc.org

POLLY HOLLIDAY SCHOLARSHIP
• *See page 145*

UNITED NEGRO COLLEGE FUND

http://www.uncf.org/

JOHN LENNON ENDOWED SCHOLARSHIP PROGRAM
• *See page 227*

OSSIE DAVIS ENDOWMENT SCHOLARSHIP PROGRAM
• *See page 146*

VSA

http://www.kennedy-center.org/education/vsa/

VSA INTERNATIONAL YOUNG SOLOISTS AWARD
• *See page 457*

WOMEN BAND DIRECTORS INTERNATIONAL

http://www.womenbanddirectors.org/

CHARLOTTE PLUMMER OWEN MEMORIAL SCHOLARSHIP
• *See page 279*

MARTHA ANN STARK MEMORIAL SCHOLARSHIP
• *See page 279*

VOLKWEIN MEMORIAL SCHOLARSHIP
• *See page 279*

PHARMACY

101ST AIRBORNE DIVISION ASSOCIATION

http://www.screamingeaglefoundation.org/

AL & WILLIAMARY VISTE SCHOLARSHIP
• *See page 114*

ALBERTA HERITAGE SCHOLARSHIP FUND

http://www.alis.alberta.ca/

JASON LANG SCHOLARSHIP
• *See page 251*

AMERICAN INDIAN SCIENCE AND ENGINEERING SOCIETY

http://www.aises.org/

A.T. ANDERSON MEMORIAL SCHOLARSHIP PROGRAM
• *See page 121*

AMERICAN LEGION AUXILIARY DEPARTMENT OF COLORADO

http://www.alacolorado.com

AMERICAN LEGION AUXILIARY DEPARTMENT OF COLORADO PAST PRESIDENTS' PARLEY HEALTH CARE PROFESSIONAL SCHOLARSHIPNURSES SCHOLARSHIP
• *See page 147*

AMERICAN LEGION DEPARTMENT OF NORTH DAKOTA

http://www.ndlegion.org/

O. NESHEIM MEMORIAL SCHOLARSHIP
• *See page 254*

ARRL FOUNDATION INC.

http://www.arrl.org/

MEDICAL AMATEUR RADIO COUNCIL (MARCO) SCHOLARSHIP
• *See page 115*

ASSOCIATION FOR FOOD AND DRUG OFFICIALS

http://www.afdo.org/

ASSOCIATION FOR FOOD AND DRUG OFFICIALS SCHOLARSHIP FUND
A $1500 scholarship for students in their third year of college/university who have demonstrated a desire for a career in research, regulatory work, quality control, or teaching in an area related to some aspect of food, drugs, or consumer products safety. Minimum 3.0 GPA required in first two years of undergraduate study. For further information visit website http://www.afdo.org.

Academic Fields/Career Goals: Pharmacy.

Award: Scholarship for use in senior year; not renewable. *Number:* 3. *Amount:* $1500.

Eligibility Requirements: Applicant must be enrolled or expecting to enroll full-time at a four-year institution or university. Applicant must have 3.0 GPA or higher. Available to U.S. and non-U.S. citizens.

Application Requirements: Application form, essay. *Deadline:* March 1.

Contact: Dr. Joanne Brown, Association Manager
Association for Food and Drug Officials
155 W. Market Street, 3rd Floor
York, PA 17401
Phone: 717-757-2888
E-mail: afdo@afdo.org

AVACARE MEDICAL

https://avacaremedical.com

AVACARE MEDICAL SCHOLARSHIP
• *See page 115*

BARRY GOLDWATER SCHOLARSHIP AND EXCELLENCE IN EDUCATION FOUNDATION

https://goldwater.scholarsapply.org

BARRY M. GOLDWATER SCHOLARSHIP AND EXCELLENCE IN EDUCATION PROGRAM
• *See page 123*

BHW GROUP

https://thebhwgroup.com/

BHW WOMEN IN STEM SCHOLARSHIP
• *See page 124*

CONTINENTAL SOCIETY, DAUGHTERS OF INDIAN WARS

http://www.csdiw.org/

CONTINENTAL SOCIETY, DAUGHTERS OF INDIAN WARS SCHOLARSHIP
• *See page 242*

CYNTHIA E. MORGAN SCHOLARSHIP FUND (CEMS)

http://www.cemsfund.com/

CYNTHIA E. MORGAN MEMORIAL SCHOLARSHIP FUND, INC.
• *See page 334*

DISTIL NETWORKS

http://www.distilnetworks.com

WOMEN FORWARD IN TECHNOLOGY SCHOLARSHIP PROGRAM
• *See page 124*

GREATER KANAWHA VALLEY FOUNDATION

http://www.tgkvf.org/

NICHOLAS AND MARY AGNES TRIVILLIAN MEMORIAL SCHOLARSHIP FUND
• *See page 374*

GREAT MINDS IN STEM

http://www.greatmindsinstem.org

HENAAC SCHOLARSHIP PROGRAM
• *See page 115*

HAWAIIAN LODGE, F&AM

http://www.hawaiianlodgefreemasons.org

HAWAIIAN LODGE SCHOLARSHIPS
• *See page 86*

HEALTH PROFESSIONS EDUCATION FOUNDATION

http://www.healthprofessions.ca.gov/

ALLIED HEALTHCARE SCHOLARSHIP PROGRAM
• *See page 165*

INDIAN HEALTH SERVICES, UNITED STATES DEPARTMENT OF HEALTH AND HUMAN SERVICES

http://www.ihs.gov/scholarship

HEALTH PROFESSIONS PREPARATORY SCHOLARSHIP PROGRAM
• *See page 165*

THE JACKSON LABORATORY

https://www.jax.org

THE JACKSON LABORATORY COLLEGE SCHOLARSHIP PROGRAM
• *See page 126*

LAW OFFICES OF PROSPER SHAKED

https://www.prosperlaw.com/

PROSPER SHAKED SCHOLARSHIP FOR FUTURE MEDICAL PROFESSIONALS
• *See page 166*

MEDICAL SCRUBS COLLECTION

http://medicalscrubscollection.com

MEDICAL SCRUBS COLLECTION SCHOLARSHIP
• *See page 120*

NATIONAL COMMUNITY PHARMACIST ASSOCIATION (NCPA) FOUNDATION

http://www.ncpanet.org/

NATIONAL COMMUNITY PHARMACIST ASSOCIATION FOUNDATION PRESIDENTIAL SCHOLARSHIP
One-time award to student members of NCPA. Must be enrolled in an accredited U.S. school or college of pharmacy on a full-time basis. Award based on leadership qualities and accomplishments with a demonstrated interest in independent pharmacy, as well as involvement in extracurricular activities.

Academic Fields/Career Goals: Pharmacy.

Award: Scholarship for use in freshman, sophomore, junior, or senior years; not renewable. *Number:* up to 15. *Amount:* up to $2000.

Eligibility Requirements: Applicant must be enrolled or expecting to enroll full-time at a four-year institution or university and must have an interest in leadership. Applicant must have 2.5 GPA or higher. Available to U.S. citizens.

Application Requirements: Application form, essay, recommendations or references, resume, transcript. *Deadline:* March 15.

Contact: Jackie Lopez, Administrative Assistant
National Community Pharmacist Association (NCPA) Foundation
100 Daingerfield Road
Alexandria, VA 22314
Phone: 703-683-8200
Fax: 703-683-3619
E-mail: jackie.lopez@ncpanet.org

NEXTSTEPU

http://www.nextstepu.com/

$1,500 STEM SCHOLARSHIP
• *See page 120*

PLATINUM EDUCATIONAL GROUP

http://www.platinumed.com

PLATINUM EDUCATIONAL GROUP SCHOLARSHIPS PROGRAM FOR EMS, NURSING, AND ALLIED HEALTH
• *See page 117*

SCARLETT FAMILY FOUNDATION SCHOLARSHIP PROGRAM

http://www.scarlettfoundation.org/

SCHOLARSHIP FOR STUDENTS PURSUING A BUSINESS OR STEM DEGREE
• *See page 91*

STRAIGHTFORWARD MEDIA

http://www.straightforwardmedia.com/

STRAIGHTFORWARD MEDIA MEDICAL PROFESSIONS SCHOLARSHIP
• *See page 257*

STRAIGHTFORWARD MEDIA VOCATIONAL-TECHNICAL SCHOOL SCHOLARSHIP
• *See page 118*

UNITED NEGRO COLLEGE FUND

http://www.uncf.org/

CVS PHARMACY, INC. PHARMACY SCHOLARSHIP
$5000 scholarship for college undergraduate or graduate student pursuing pharmacy studies on a full-time basis. Minimum 3.0 GPA required. Must have demonstrated unmet financial need (as verified by college or university). Open to U.S. citizens, nationals and permanent residents.

Academic Fields/Career Goals: Pharmacy.

Award: Scholarship for use in sophomore, junior, senior, or graduate years; not renewable. *Amount:* $5000.

Eligibility Requirements: Applicant must be Black (non-Hispanic) and enrolled or expecting to enroll full-time at a four-year institution or university. Applicant must have 3.0 GPA or higher. Available to U.S. and non-U.S. citizens.

Application Requirements: Application form, essay, financial need analysis. *Deadline:* April 16.

Contact: Mary Williams, Director of Outreach and Recruitment
Phone: 800-331-2244

PHILOSOPHY

AMERICAN SCHOOL OF CLASSICAL STUDIES AT ATHENS

http://www.ascsa.edu.gr/

ASCSA SUMMER SESSION AND SUMMER SEMINARS SCHOLARSHIPS
• *See page 118*

DAVIDSON INSTITUTE FOR TALENT DEVELOPMENT

http://www.davidsongifted.org/

DAVIDSON FELLOWS SCHOLARSHIP PROGRAM
• *See page 124*

LA-PHILOSOPHIE.COM

http://la-philosophie.com

LA-PHILOSOPHIE.COM SCHOLARSHIP
• *See page 119*

STRAIGHTFORWARD MEDIA

http://www.straightforwardmedia.com/

STRAIGHTFORWARD MEDIA LIBERAL ARTS SCHOLARSHIP
• *See page 139*

UNITED NEGRO COLLEGE FUND

http://www.uncf.org/

UNCF/KOCH SCHOLARS PROGRAM FOR UNDERGRADUATES
• *See page 94*

PHOTOJOURNALISM/ PHOTOGRAPHY

AMERICAN QUARTER HORSE FOUNDATION (AQHF)

http://www.aqha.com/foundation

AQHF JOURNALISM OR COMMUNICATIONS SCHOLARSHIP
• *See page 216*

ASIAN AMERICAN JOURNALISTS ASSOCIATION

http://www.aaja.org/

CIC/ANNA CHENNAULT SCHOLARSHIP
• *See page 217*

MARY QUON MOY ING MEMORIAL SCHOLARSHIP AWARD
• *See page 217*

VINCENT CHIN MEMORIAL SCHOLARSHIP
• *See page 217*

ASIAN AMERICAN JOURNALISTS ASSOCIATION, SEATTLE CHAPTER

http://www.aajaseattle.org/

NORTHWEST JOURNALISTS OF COLOR SCHOLARSHIP
• *See page 96*

CCNMA: LATINO JOURNALISTS OF CALIFORNIA

http://www.ccnma.org/

CCNMA SCHOLARSHIPS
• *See page 218*

COLLEGE PHOTOGRAPHER OF THE YEAR

http://www.cpoy.org/

COLLEGE PHOTOGRAPHER OF THE YEAR COMPETITION

Awards undergraduate and graduate students for juried contest of individual photographs, picture stories and photographic essay and multimedia presentations. Two financial awards in the dollar value of $500 and $1000 are granted, but multiple awards given in the form of Nikon camera equipment and workshop scholarships. Deadline varies.

Academic Fields/Career Goals: Photojournalism/Photography.

Award: Prize for use in freshman, sophomore, junior, senior, or graduate years; not renewable. *Number:* 10. *Amount:* $600–$5000.

Eligibility Requirements: Applicant must be enrolled or expecting to enroll full- or part-time at a four-year institution or university. Available to U.S. and non-U.S. citizens.

Application Requirements: Application form, essay, personal photograph, portfolio. *Deadline:* September 30.

Contact: Jackie Bell, Program Director
College Photographer of the Year
University of Missouri, School of Journalism
109 Lee Hills Hall
Columbia, MO 65211
Phone: 573-882-2198
E-mail: info@cpoy.org

CONNECTICUT CHAPTER OF SOCIETY OF PROFESSIONAL JOURNALISTS

http://www.ctspj.org/

CONNECTICUT SPJ BOB EDDY SCHOLARSHIP PROGRAM
• *See page 218*

INTERNATIONAL FOODSERVICE EDITORIAL COUNCIL

http://www.ifeconline.com/

INTERNATIONAL FOODSERVICE EDITORIAL COUNCIL COMMUNICATIONS SCHOLARSHIP
• *See page 96*

NATIONAL ACADEMY OF TELEVISION ARTS AND SCIENCES

http://www.emmyonline.tv/

DOUGLAS W. MUMMERT SCHOLARSHIP
• *See page 142*

JIM MCKAY MEMORIAL SCHOLARSHIP
• *See page 220*

MIKE WALLACE MEMORIAL SCHOLARSHIP
• *See page 220*

NATIONAL ACADEMY OF TELEVISION ARTS AND SCIENCES TRUSTEES SCHOLARSHIP
• *See page 220*

RANDY FALCO SCHOLARSHIP
• *See page 220*

NATIONAL ASSOCIATION OF BLACK JOURNALISTS

http://www.nabj.org/

NATIONAL ASSOCIATION OF BLACK JOURNALISTS NON-SUSTAINING SCHOLARSHIP AWARDS
• *See page 405*

VISUAL TASK FORCE SCHOLARSHIP

Scholarship for students attending an accredited four-year college or university and majoring in visual journalism. Minimum 3.0 GPA required. Must be a member of NABJ. Scholarship value and the number of scholarships granted varies annually.

Academic Fields/Career Goals: Photojournalism/Photography.

Award: Scholarship for use in freshman, sophomore, junior, senior, or graduate years; not renewable.

Eligibility Requirements: Applicant must be enrolled or expecting to enroll full-time at a four-year institution or university. Applicant must have 3.0 GPA or higher. Available to U.S. and non-U.S. citizens.

Application Requirements: Application form, driver's license, essay, interview, recommendations or references, transcript. *Deadline:* March 17.

Contact: Irving Washington, Manager
Phone: 301-445-7100
Fax: 301-445-7101
E-mail: iwashington@nabj.org

NATIONAL ASSOCIATION OF HISPANIC JOURNALISTS (NAHJ)

http://www.nahj.org/

NATIONAL ASSOCIATION OF HISPANIC JOURNALISTS SCHOLARSHIP
• *See page 221*

NEWHOUSE SCHOLARSHIP PROGRAM
• *See page 364*

NATIVE AMERICAN JOURNALISTS ASSOCIATION

http://www.naja.com/

NATIVE AMERICAN JOURNALISTS ASSOCIATION SCHOLARSHIPS
• *See page 97*

NEBRASKA PRESS ASSOCIATION

http://www.nebpress.com/

NEBRASKA PRESS ASSOCIATION FOUNDATION SCHOLARSHIP
• *See page 97*

OREGON STUDENT ASSISTANCE COMMISSION

https://oregonstudentaid.gov/

KERDRAGON SCHOLARSHIP
• *See page 143*

OUTDOOR WRITERS ASSOCIATION OF AMERICA

http://www.owaa.org/

OUTDOOR WRITERS ASSOCIATION OF AMERICA - BODIE MCDOWELL SCHOLARSHIP AWARD
• *See page 222*

PALM BEACH ASSOCIATION OF BLACK JOURNALISTS

PALM BEACH ASSOCIATION OF BLACK JOURNALISTS SCHOLARSHIP
• *See page 408*

PRINTING INDUSTRY MIDWEST EDUCATION FOUDNATION

http://www.pimw.org/scholarships

PRINTING INDUSTRY MIDWEST EDUCATION FOUNDATION SCHOLARSHIP FUND
• *See page 222*

QUALITY BATH

http://www.qualitybath.com

QUALITYBATH.COM SCHOLARSHIP PROGRAM
• *See page 140*

RADIO TELEVISION DIGITAL NEWS ASSOCIATION

http://www.rtdna.org

CAROLE SIMPSON SCHOLARSHIP
• *See page 222*

ED BRADLEY SCHOLARSHIP
• *See page 223*

GEORGE FOREMAN TRIBUTE TO LYNDON B. JOHNSON SCHOLARSHIP
• *See page 223*

LOU AND CAROLE PRATO SPORTS REPORTING SCHOLARSHIP
• *See page 223*

MIKE REYNOLDS JOURNALISM SCHOLARSHIP
• *See page 223*

SOCIETY FOR IMAGING SCIENCE AND TECHNOLOGY

http://www.imaging.org/

RAYMOND DAVIS SCHOLARSHIP
• *See page 305*

STRAIGHTFORWARD MEDIA

http://www.straightforwardmedia.com/

STRAIGHTFORWARD MEDIA MEDIA & COMMUNICATIONS SCHOLARSHIP
• *See page 99*

SUPPORT CREATIVITY

http://wesupportcreativity.org

SUPPORT CREATIVITY SCHOLARSHIP
• *See page 137*

TAMPA BAY TIMES FUND, INC.

http://www.tampabay.com/fund

CAREER JOURNALISM SCHOLARSHIP
• *See page 225*

TAMPA BAY TIMES FUND CAREER JOURNALISM SCHOLARSHIPS
• *See page 99*

TEXAS GRIDIRON CLUB INC.

http://www.spjfw.org/

TEXAS GRIDIRON CLUB SCHOLARSHIPS
• *See page 226*

UNITARIAN UNIVERSALIST ASSOCIATION

http://www.uua.org/

PAULY D'ORLANDO MEMORIAL ART SCHOLARSHIP
• *See page 146*

UNITED METHODIST COMMUNICATIONS

http://www.umcom.org/

LEONARD M. PERRYMAN COMMUNICATIONS SCHOLARSHIP FOR ETHNIC MINORITY STUDENTS
• *See page 227*

VALLEY PRESS CLUB

http://www.valleypressclub.com/

VALLEY PRESS CLUB SCHOLARSHIPS, THE REPUBLICAN SCHOLARSHIP, CHANNEL 22 SCHOLARSHIP
• *See page 228*

PHYSICAL SCIENCES

101ST AIRBORNE DIVISION ASSOCIATION

http://www.screamingeaglefoundation.org/

AL & WILLIAMARY VISTE SCHOLARSHIP
• *See page 114*

AIR & WASTE MANAGEMENT ASSOCIATION–COASTAL PLAINS CHAPTER

http://www.awmacoastalplains.org/

COASTAL PLAINS CHAPTER OF THE AIR AND WASTE MANAGEMENT ASSOCIATION ENVIRONMENTAL STEWARD SCHOLARSHIP
• *See page 337*

AIST FOUNDATION

http://www.aistfoundation.org/

ASSOCIATION FOR IRON AND STEEL TECHNOLOGY OHIO VALLEY CHAPTER SCHOLARSHIP
• *See page 167*

AMERICAN ASSOCIATION OF PHYSICS TEACHERS

http://aapt.org

BARBARA LOTZE SCHOLARSHIPS FOR FUTURE TEACHERS

Undergraduate students enrolled, or planning to enroll, in physics teacher preparation curricula and high school seniors entering such programs are eligible. Successful applicants receive a stipend of up to $2,000 and a complimentary AAPT Student Membership for one year. The scholarship may be granted to an individual for each of four years. Students who meet the following criteria are eligible to apply for the Barbara Lotze Scholarship for Future Teachers. Applicants must declare their intent to prepare for, and engage in, a career in physics teaching at the high school level and must, at the time the scholarship funds are received by the student, be an undergraduate student enrolled in an accredited two-year college, four-year college or a university; or a high school senior accepted for such enrollment. Must be pursuing, or planning to pursue, a course of study leading toward a career in physics teaching in the high schools. Must be showing promise of success in their studies, and be a citizen of the United States of America. Applications will be accepted at any time and will be considered for recommendation to the Executive Board at each AAPT Winter Meeting. All applications in which all materials, including letters of recommendation, are received by December 1 will be considered for recommendation at the winter meeting of the AAPT Executive Board.

Academic Fields/Career Goals: Physical Sciences.

Award: Scholarship for use in freshman, sophomore, junior, or senior years; not renewable. *Number:* 5–7. *Amount:* $2000.

Eligibility Requirements: Applicant must be enrolled or expecting to enroll full- or part-time at a two-year or four-year institution. Available to U.S. citizens.

Application Requirements: Application form, portfolio. *Deadline:* December 1.

Contact: Mrs. Rachel Sweeney, Executive Assistant
  E-mail: rsweeney@aapt.org

AMERICAN FOUNDATION FOR THE BLIND

http://www.afb.org/

PAUL W. RUCKES SCHOLARSHIP
• *See page 228*

AMERICAN INDIAN SCIENCE AND ENGINEERING SOCIETY

http://www.aises.org/

A.T. ANDERSON MEMORIAL SCHOLARSHIP PROGRAM
• *See page 121*

AMERICAN INSTITUTE OF AERONAUTICS AND ASTRONAUTICS

http://www.aiaafoundation.org/

AIAA FOUNDATION UNDERGRADUATE SCHOLARSHIPS
• *See page 121*

LEATRICE GREGORY PENDRAY SCHOLARSHIP
• *See page 121*

AMERICAN LEGION DEPARTMENT OF MARYLAND

http://www.mdlegion.org/

AMERICAN LEGION DEPARTMENT OF MARYLAND MATH-SCIENCE SCHOLARSHIP
• *See page 437*

AMERICAN SOCIETY FOR ENGINEERING EDUCATION

http://www.asee.org/

SCIENCE, MATHEMATICS, AND RESEARCH FOR TRANSFORMATION DEFENSE SCHOLARSHIP FOR SERVICE PROGRAM
• *See page 121*

AMERICAN SOCIETY OF NAVAL ENGINEERS

http://www.navalengineers.org/

AMERICAN SOCIETY OF NAVAL ENGINEERS SCHOLARSHIP
• *See page 122*

ARIZONA PROFESSIONAL CHAPTER OF AISES

http://www.aises.org/scholarships

ARIZONA PROFESSIONAL CHAPTER OF AISES SCHOLARSHIP
• *See page 313*

ARMED FORCES COMMUNICATIONS AND ELECTRONICS ASSOCIATION, EDUCATIONAL FOUNDATION

http://www.afcea.org/site/?q=foundation/scholarships

AFCEA STEM MAJORS SCHOLARSHIPS FOR UNDERGRADUATE STUDENTS
• *See page 122*

ARMED FORCES COMMUNICATIONS AND ELECTRONICS ASSOCIATION ROTC SCHOLARSHIP PROGRAM
• *See page 151*

ARRL FOUNDATION INC.

http://www.arrl.org/

CTRI/CHRIS SEEBER, KA I GEU, MEMORIAL SCHOLARSHIP
• *See page 268*

DAN HUETTL, WZ7U, MEMORIAL SCHOLARSHIP
• *See page 298*

LOIS MANLEY, K7LMZ, AND RANDALL PITCHFORD, WW7ZZ, SCHOLARSHIP
• *See page 206*

OLD MAN INTERNATIONAL SIDEBAND SOCIETY (OMISS) SCHOLARSHIP
• *See page 259*

WIFDR SCHOLARSHIP
• See page 122

ASSOCIATION FOR WOMEN GEOSCIENTISTS (AWG)

http://www.awg.org/

AWG ETHNIC MINORITY SCHOLARSHIP
• See page 260

AWG MARIA LUISA CRAWFORD FIELD CAMP SCHOLARSHIP
• See page 129

AWG SALT LAKE CHAPTER (SLC) RESEARCH SCHOLARSHIP
• See page 129

JANET CULLEN TANAKA GEOSCIENCES UNDERGRADUATE SCHOLARSHIP
• See page 129

LONE STAR RISING CAREER SCHOLARSHIP
• See page 260

OSAGE CHAPTER UNDERGRADUATE SERVICE SCHOLARSHIP
• See page 129

SUSAN EKDALE MEMORIAL FIELD CAMP SCHOLARSHIP
• See page 260

ASSOCIATION ON AMERICAN INDIAN AFFAIRS, INC.

http://www.indian-affairs.org/

ELIZABETH AND SHERMAN ASCHE MEMORIAL SCHOLARSHIP FUND
• See page 106

BARRY GOLDWATER SCHOLARSHIP AND EXCELLENCE IN EDUCATION FOUNDATION

https://goldwater.scholarsapply.org

BARRY M. GOLDWATER SCHOLARSHIP AND EXCELLENCE IN EDUCATION PROGRAM
• See page 123

BHW GROUP

https://thebhwgroup.com/

BHW WOMEN IN STEM SCHOLARSHIP
• See page 124

CARDS AGAINST HUMANITY

https://cardsagainsthumanity.com/

SCIENCE AMBASSADOR SCHOLARSHIP
• See page 124

CATCHING THE DREAM

http://www.catchingthedream.org/

MATH, ENGINEERING, SCIENCE, BUSINESS, EDUCATION, COMPUTERS SCHOLARSHIPS
• See page 178

NATIVE AMERICAN LEADERSHIP IN EDUCATION (NALE)
• See page 178

THE DALLAS FOUNDATION

http://www.dallasfoundation.org/

WHITLEY PLACE SCHOLARSHIP
• See page 133

DISTIL NETWORKS

http://www.distilnetworks.com

WOMEN FORWARD IN TECHNOLOGY SCHOLARSHIP PROGRAM
• See page 124

DIVERSITYCOMM, INC.

http://www.diversitycomm.net/

DIVERSITY IN STEAM MAGAZINE SCHOLARSHIP
• See page 83

EAA AVIATION FOUNDATION, INC.

http://www.eaa.org/

PAYZER SCHOLARSHIP
• See page 153

THE ELECTROCHEMICAL SOCIETY

http://www.electrochem.org/

H.H. DOW MEMORIAL STUDENT ACHIEVEMENT AWARD OF THE INDUSTRIAL ELECTROLYSIS AND ELECTROCHEMICAL ENGINEERING DIVISION OF THE ELECTROCHEMICAL SOCIETY INC.
• See page 125

STUDENT RESEARCH AWARDS OF THE BATTERY DIVISION OF THE ELECTROCHEMICAL SOCIETY INC.
• See page 125

FOUNDATION FOR SCIENCE AND DISABILITY

http://stemd.org/

GRANTS FOR DISABLED GRADUATE STUDENTS IN THE SCIENCES
• See page 106

GREATER KANAWHA VALLEY FOUNDATION

http://www.tgkvf.org/

MATH AND SCIENCE SCHOLARSHIP
• See page 171

GREAT MINDS IN STEM

http://www.greatmindsinstem.org

HENAAC SCHOLARSHIP PROGRAM
• See page 115

INDEPENDENT LABORATORIES INSTITUTE SCHOLARSHIP ALLIANCE

http://www.acil.org/

INDEPENDENT LABORATORIES INSTITUTE SCHOLARSHIP ALLIANCE
• See page 171

INSTITUTE OF FOOD TECHNOLOGISTS

http://www.ift.org/

PEPSICO SCHOLARSHIP AND INTERNSHIP
• See page 353

LABROOTS INC.

http://www.LabRoots.com

LABROOTS STEM SCHOLARSHIP
• See page 116

THE LAND CONSERVANCY OF NEW JERSEY

http://www.tlc-nj.org/

ROGERS FAMILY SCHOLARSHIP
• See page 172

LOS ANGELES COUNCIL OF BLACK PROFESSIONAL ENGINEERS

http://www.lablackengineers.org/

AL-BEN SCHOLARSHIP FOR ACADEMIC INCENTIVE
• See page 193

AL-BEN SCHOLARSHIP FOR PROFESSIONAL MERIT
• See page 193

AL-BEN SCHOLARSHIP FOR SCHOLASTIC ACHIEVEMENT
• See page 193

MEDICAL SCRUBS COLLECTION

http://medicalscrubscollection.com

MEDICAL SCRUBS COLLECTION SCHOLARSHIP
• See page 120

MICHAEL MOODY FITNESS

http://www.michaelmoodyfitness.com/

MICHAEL MOODY FITNESS SCHOLARSHIP
• See page 166

NASA FLORIDA SPACE GRANT CONSORTIUM

http://www.floridaspacegrant.org/

FLORIDA SPACE RESEARCH PROGRAM
• See page 156

NASA IDAHO SPACE GRANT CONSORTIUM

http://www.idahospacegrant.org

NASA IDAHO SPACE GRANT CONSORTIUM SCHOLARSHIP PROGRAM
• See page 126

NASA/MARYLAND SPACE GRANT CONSORTIUM

http://www.mdspacegrant.org/

NASA MARYLAND SPACE GRANT CONSORTIUM UNDERGRADUATE SCHOLARSHIPS
• See page 156

NASA MINNESOTA SPACE GRANT CONSORTIUM

https://www.mnspacegrant.org/

MINNESOTA SPACE GRANT CONSORTIUM SCHOLARSHIP PROGRAM
• See page 156

NASA'S VIRGINIA SPACE GRANT CONSORTIUM

http://www.vsgc.odu.edu/

UNDERGRADUATE STEM RESEARCH SCHOLARSHIPS
• See page 127

NATIONAL ASSOCIATION FOR THE ADVANCEMENT OF COLORED PEOPLE

http://www.naacp.org/

HUBERTUS W.V. WELLEMS SCHOLARSHIP FOR MALE STUDENTS
• See page 194

NATIONAL INSTITUTES OF HEALTH

https://www.training.nih.gov/programs/ugsp

NIH UNDERGRADUATE SCHOLARSHIP PROGRAM FOR STUDENTS FROM DISADVANTAGED BACKGROUNDS
• See page 116

NATIONAL SOCIETY OF BLACK PHYSICISTS

http://www.nsbp.org/

AMERICAN PHYSICAL SOCIETY CORPORATE-SPONSORED SCHOLARSHIP FOR MINORITY UNDERGRADUATE STUDENTS WHO MAJOR IN PHYSICS

Scholarship available for minority undergraduate students majoring in physics. Award of $2000 per year for new corporate scholars, and $3000 per year for renewal students. In addition, each physics department that hosts one or more APS minority undergraduate scholars and assigns a mentor for their students will receive a $500 award for programs to encourage minority students.

Academic Fields/Career Goals: Physical Sciences.

Award: Scholarship for use in freshman, sophomore, junior, or senior years; not renewable. *Amount:* $2000–$3000.

Eligibility Requirements: Applicant must be American Indian/Alaska Native, Asian/Pacific Islander, Black (non-Hispanic), Hispanic and enrolled or expecting to enroll full- or part-time at a two-year or four-year institution or university. Available to U.S. citizens.

Application Requirements: Application form, recommendations or references, transcript. *Deadline:* December 1.

Contact: Dr. Stephen Roberson, Scholarship Chairman
Phone: 703-536-4207
Fax: 703-536-4203
E-mail: adminofficer@nsbp.org

CHARLES S. BROWN SCHOLARSHIP IN PHYSICS

Scholarship providing and African-American student with financial assistance while enrolled in a physics degree program. Number of awards and dollar value varies.

Academic Fields/Career Goals: Physical Sciences.

Award: Scholarship for use in freshman, sophomore, junior, senior, or graduate years; not renewable.

Eligibility Requirements: Applicant must be Black (non-Hispanic) and enrolled or expecting to enroll full- or part-time at a four-year institution or university. Available to U.S. and non-U.S. citizens.

Application Requirements: Application form, financial need analysis, self-addressed stamped envelope with application. *Deadline:* January 12.

Contact: Scholarship Committee Chair
National Society of Black Physicists
6704G Lee Highway
Arlington, VA 22205
Phone: 703-536-4207
Fax: 703-536-4203
E-mail: scholarship@nsbp.org

ELMER S. IMES SCHOLARSHIP IN PHYSICS

Graduating high school seniors and undergraduate students already enrolled in college as physics majors may apply for the scholarship. U.S citizenship is required.

Academic Fields/Career Goals: Physical Sciences.

Award: Scholarship for use in freshman, sophomore, junior, or senior years; not renewable. *Number:* 1. *Amount:* $1000.

Eligibility Requirements: Applicant must be enrolled or expecting to enroll full-time at a two-year or four-year institution or university. Available to U.S. citizens.

Application Requirements: Application form, driver's license, essay, recommendations or references, resume, transcript. *Deadline:* January 12.

Contact: Scholarship Committee Chair
National Society of Black Physicists
6704G Lee Highway
Arlington, VA 22205
Phone: 703-536-4207
Fax: 703-536-4203
E-mail: scholarship@nsbp.org

HARVEY WASHINGTON BANKS SCHOLARSHIP IN ASTRONOMY

One-time award for an African American student pursuing an undergraduate degree in astronomy/physics.

Academic Fields/Career Goals: Physical Sciences.

Award: Scholarship for use in freshman, sophomore, junior, or senior years; not renewable. *Number:* 1. *Amount:* $1000.

Eligibility Requirements: Applicant must be Black (non-Hispanic) and enrolled or expecting to enroll full-time at a two-year or four-year institution or university. Available to U.S. citizens.

Application Requirements: Application form, essay, recommendations or references, transcript. *Deadline:* January 12.

Contact: Dr. Stephen Roberson, Scholarship Chairman
Phone: 703-536-4207
Fax: 703-536-4203
E-mail: adminofficer@nsbp.org

MICHAEL P. ANDERSON SCHOLARSHIP IN SPACE SCIENCE

One-time award for an African American undergraduate student majoring in space science/physics.

Academic Fields/Career Goals: Physical Sciences.

Award: Scholarship for use in freshman, sophomore, junior, or senior years; not renewable. *Number:* 1. *Amount:* $1000.

Eligibility Requirements: Applicant must be Black (non-Hispanic) and enrolled or expecting to enroll full-time at a two-year or four-year institution or university. Available to U.S. citizens.

Application Requirements: Application form, essay, recommendations or references, transcript. *Deadline:* January 12.

Contact: Dr. Stephen Roberson, Scholarship Chairman
Phone: 703-536-4207
Fax: 703-536-4203
E-mail: adminofficer@nsbp.org

NATIONAL SOCIETY OF BLACK PHYSICISTS AND LAWRENCE LIVERMORE NATIONAL LIBRARY UNDERGRADUATE SCHOLARSHIP

Scholarship for a graduating high school senior or undergraduate student enrolled in a physics major. Scholarship renewable up to four years if student maintains a 3.0 GPA and remains a physics major.

Academic Fields/Career Goals: Physical Sciences.

Award: Scholarship for use in freshman, sophomore, junior, or senior years; renewable. *Number:* 1. *Amount:* $5000.

Eligibility Requirements: Applicant must be Black (non-Hispanic) and enrolled or expecting to enroll full-time at a two-year or four-year institution or university. Applicant must have 3.0 GPA or higher. Available to U.S. citizens.

Application Requirements: Application form, essay, recommendations or references, transcript. *Deadline:* December 1.

Contact: Dr. Stephen Roberson, Scholarship Chairman
Phone: 703-536-4207
Fax: 703-536-4203
E-mail: adminofficer@nsbp.org

RONALD E. MCNAIR SCHOLARSHIP IN SPACE AND OPTICAL PHYSICS

One-time award for African American undergraduate student majoring in physics. Must be U.S. citizen.

Academic Fields/Career Goals: Physical Sciences.

Award: Scholarship for use in freshman, sophomore, junior, or senior years; not renewable. *Number:* 1. *Amount:* $1000.

Eligibility Requirements: Applicant must be Black (non-Hispanic) and enrolled or expecting to enroll full-time at a two-year or four-year institution or university. Available to U.S. citizens.

Application Requirements: Application form, essay, recommendations or references, transcript. *Deadline:* January 12.

Contact: Dr. Stephen Roberson, Scholarship Chairman
Phone: 703-536-4207
Fax: 703-536-4203
E-mail: adminofficer@nsbp.org

WALTER SAMUEL MCAFEE SCHOLARSHIP IN SPACE PHYSICS

One-time scholarship for African American full-time undergraduate student majoring in physics. Must be U.S. citizen.

Academic Fields/Career Goals: Physical Sciences.

Award: Scholarship for use in freshman, sophomore, junior, or senior years; not renewable. *Number:* 1. *Amount:* $1000.

Eligibility Requirements: Applicant must be Black (non-Hispanic) and enrolled or expecting to enroll full-time at a two-year or four-year institution or university. Available to U.S. citizens.

Application Requirements: Application form, essay, recommendations or references, transcript. *Deadline:* January 12.

Contact: Dr. Stephen Roberson, Scholarship Chairman
Phone: 703-536-4207
Fax: 703-536-4203
E-mail: adminofficer@nsbp.org

WILLIE HOBBS MOORE, HARRY L. MORRISON, AND ARTHUR B.C. WALKER PHYSICS SCHOLARSHIPS

Scholarships are intended for African American undergraduate physics majors. Applicants should be either sophomores or juniors. Award for use in junior or senior year of study.

Academic Fields/Career Goals: Physical Sciences.

Award: Scholarship for use in sophomore, junior, or senior years; not renewable. *Number:* 3. *Amount:* $1000.

Eligibility Requirements: Applicant must be Black (non-Hispanic) and enrolled or expecting to enroll full-time at a two-year or four-year institution or university. Available to U.S. citizens.

Application Requirements: Application form, essay, recommendations or references, transcript. *Deadline:* January 12.

Contact: Dr. Stephen Roberson, Scholarship Chairman
Phone: 703-536-4207
Fax: 703-536-4203
E-mail: adminofficer@nsbp.org

NEVADA NASA SPACE GRANT CONSORTIUM

https://nasa.epscorspo.nevada.edu/

NATIONAL SPACE GRANT CONSORTIUM SCHOLARSHIPS
• *See page 127*

NEXTSTEPU

http://www.nextstepu.com/

$1,500 STEM SCHOLARSHIP
• *See page 120*

OREGON STUDENT ASSISTANCE COMMISSION

https://oregonstudentaid.gov/

ANDY AITKENHEAD SCHOLARSHIP
• *See page 127*

SEHAR SALEHA AHMAD AND ABRAHIM EKRAMULLAH ZAFAR FOUNDATION SCHOLARSHIP
• *See page 127*

ROBERT H. MOLLOHAN FAMILY CHARITABLE FOUNDATION, INC.

http://www.mollohanfoundation.org/

HIGH TECHNOLOGY SCHOLARS PROGRAM
• *See page 173*

SCARLETT FAMILY FOUNDATION SCHOLARSHIP PROGRAM

http://www.scarlettfoundation.org/

SCHOLARSHIP FOR STUDENTS PURSUING A BUSINESS OR STEM DEGREE
• *See page 91*

SIGMA XI, THE SCIENTIFIC RESEARCH SOCIETY

http://www.sigmaxi.org/

SIGMA XI GRANTS-IN-AID OF RESEARCH
• *See page 110*

SOCIETY OF PHYSICS STUDENTS

http://www.spsnational.org/

SOCIETY OF PHYSICS STUDENTS LEADERSHIP SCHOLARSHIPS

Scholarships of $2000 to $5000 are awarded to members of Society of Physics Students (SPS) for undergraduate study. The number of awards granted ranges from 17 to 22.

Academic Fields/Career Goals: Physical Sciences.

Award: Scholarship for use in sophomore, junior, or senior years; not renewable. *Number:* 17–22. *Amount:* $2000–$5000.

Eligibility Requirements: Applicant must be enrolled or expecting to enroll full-time at a two-year or four-year institution or university. Applicant or parent of applicant must be member of Society of Physics Students. Available to U.S. and non-U.S. citizens.

Application Requirements: Application form, recommendations or references, transcript. *Deadline:* February 15.

Contact: Scholarship Committee
Society of Physics Students
One Physics Ellipse
College Park, MD 20740
Phone: 301-209-3007
Fax: 301-209-0839
E-mail: sps@aip.org

SOCIETY OF PHYSICS STUDENTS OUTSTANDING STUDENT IN RESEARCH

Available to members of the Society of Physics Students. Winners will receive a $500 honorarium and a $500 award for their SPS Chapter. In addition, expenses for transportation, room, board, and registration for the ICPS will by paid by SPS.

Academic Fields/Career Goals: Physical Sciences.

Award: Prize for use in freshman, sophomore, junior, or senior years; not renewable. *Number:* 1–2. *Amount:* $500–$2500.

Eligibility Requirements: Applicant must be enrolled or expecting to enroll full-time at a two-year or four-year institution or university. Applicant or parent of applicant must be member of Society of Physics Students. Available to U.S. and non-U.S. citizens.

Application Requirements: Abstract, application form, recommendations or references. *Deadline:* April 15.

Contact: Secretary
Society of Physics Students
One Physics Ellipse
College Park, MD 20740
Phone: 301-209-3007
Fax: 301-209-0839
E-mail: sps@aip.org

SOCIETY OF PHYSICS STUDENTS PEGGY DIXON TWO-YEAR COLLEGE SCHOLARSHIP

Scholarship available to Society of Physics Students (SPS) members. Award based on performance both in physics and overall studies, and SPS participation. Must have completed at least one semester or quarter of the introductory physics sequence, and be currently registered in the appropriate subsequent physics courses.

Academic Fields/Career Goals: Physical Sciences.

Award: Scholarship for use in freshman or sophomore years; not renewable. *Number:* 1. *Amount:* $2000.

Eligibility Requirements: Applicant must be enrolled or expecting to enroll full-time at a two-year or four-year institution or university. Applicant or parent of applicant must be member of Society of Physics Students. Available to U.S. and non-U.S. citizens.

Application Requirements: Application form, financial need analysis, letters from at least two faculty members, transcript. *Deadline:* February 15.

Contact: Sacha Purnell, Administrative Assistant
Phone: 301-209-3007
E-mail: sps@aip.org

STRAIGHT NORTH

https://www.straightnorth.com/

STRAIGHT NORTH STEM SCHOLARSHIP
• *See page 92*

TAILOR MADE LAWNS

http://www.tailormadelawns.com

TAILOR MADE LAWNS SCHOLARSHIP FUND
• *See page 111*

TKE EDUCATIONAL FOUNDATION

http://www.tke.org/

CARROL C. HALL MEMORIAL SCHOLARSHIP
• *See page 128*

ERIC D. DUNNING SCHOLARSHIP
• *See page 235*

UNICO FOUNDATION INC.

http://www.unico.org/

LOUISE TORRACO MEMORIAL SCHOLARSHIP FOR SCIENCE
• *See page 174*

UNITED NEGRO COLLEGE FUND

http://www.uncf.org/

BASF/ALFRED CHISHOLM ENDOWED MEMORIAL SCHOLARSHIP
• *See page 93*

KIA MOTORS AMERICA STEM/SUSTAINABILITY SCHOLARSHIP
• *See page 175*

UNCF STEM SCHOLARS PROGRAM
• *See page 175*

UNIVERSITIES SPACE RESEARCH ASSOCIATION

http://www.usra.edu/

UNIVERSITIES SPACE RESEARCH ASSOCIATION SCHOLARSHIP AWARD PROGRAM
• *See page 128*

VERMONT SPACE GRANT CONSORTIUM

http://www.cems.uvm.edu/vsgc

VERMONT SPACE GRANT CONSORTIUM
• *See page 104*

XEROX

http://www.xerox.com//

TECHNICAL MINORITY SCHOLARSHIP
• *See page 203*

POLITICAL SCIENCE

AMERICAN FEDERATION OF STATE, COUNTY, AND MUNICIPAL EMPLOYEES

http://www.afscme.org/

AFSCME/UNCF UNION SCHOLARS PROGRAM
• *See page 113*

JERRY CLARK MEMORIAL SCHOLARSHIP
Renewable award for a student majoring in political science for his or her junior and senior years of study. Must be a child of an AFSCME member. Minimum 2.5 GPA required. Once awarded, the scholarship will be renewed for the senior year provided the student remains enrolled full-time as a political science major.

Academic Fields/Career Goals: Political Science.

Award: Scholarship for use in junior or senior years; renewable. *Number:* 2. *Amount:* $5000.

Eligibility Requirements: Applicant must be enrolled or expecting to enroll full-time at a four-year institution or university. Applicant or parent of applicant must be member of American Federation of State, County, and Municipal Employees. Applicant must have 2.5 GPA or higher. Available to U.S. citizens.

Application Requirements: Application form, proof of parent, transcript. *Deadline:* July 1.

Contact: Philip Allen, Scholarship Coordinator
Phone: 202-429-1250
Fax: 202-429-1293
E-mail: pallen@asscme.org

ARAB AMERICAN SCHOLARSHIP FOUNDATION

http://www.lahc.org/

LEBANESE AMERICAN HERITAGE CLUB'S SCHOLARSHIP FUND
• *See page 216*

ASSOCIATION OF FORMER INTELLIGENCE OFFICERS

http://www.afio.com

AFIO UNDERGRADUATE AND GRADUATE SCHOLARSHIPS
• *See page 113*

BOYS AND GIRLS CLUBS OF GREATER SAN DIEGO

http://www.sdyouth.org/

SPENCE REESE SCHOLARSHIP
• *See page 316*

CULTURAL SERVICES OF THE FRENCH EMBASSY

http://www.frenchculture.org/

TEACHING ASSISTANT PROGRAM IN FRANCE
• *See page 113*

GOVERNMENT FINANCE OFFICERS ASSOCIATION

http://www.gfoa.org/

MINORITIES IN GOVERNMENT FINANCE SCHOLARSHIP
• See page 86

GREATER SALINA COMMUNITY FOUNDATION

http://www.gscf.org/

KANSAS FEDERATION OF REPUBLICAN WOMEN SCHOLARSHIP
• See page 382

HARRY S. TRUMAN SCHOLARSHIP FOUNDATION

http://www.truman.gov/

HARRY S. TRUMAN SCHOLARSHIP
Scholarships for U.S. citizens or U.S. nationals who are college or university students with junior-level academic standing and who wish to attend professional or graduate school to prepare for careers in government or the nonprofit and advocacy sectors. Candidates must be nominated by their institution. Public service and leadership record considered. Visit website http://www.truman.gov for further information and application.

Academic Fields/Career Goals: Political Science; Public Policy and Administration.

Award: Scholarship for use in junior year; renewable. *Number:* 65. *Amount:* $30,000.

Eligibility Requirements: Applicant must be enrolled or expecting to enroll full-time at a four-year institution or university and must have an interest in leadership. Available to U.S. citizens.

Application Requirements: Application form, interview, policy proposal, recommendations or references. *Deadline:* February 5.

Contact: Tonji Wade, Program Officer
Harry S. Truman Scholarship Foundation
712 Jackson Place, NW
Washington, DC 20006
Phone: 202-395-4831
Fax: 202-395-6995
E-mail: office@truman.gov

INSTITUTE FOR HUMANE STUDIES

http://www.theihs.org/

HUMANE STUDIES FELLOWSHIPS
• See page 219

LA-PHILOSOPHIE.COM

http://la-philosophie.com

LA-PHILOSOPHIE.COM SCHOLARSHIP
• See page 119

THE LYNDON BAINES JOHNSON FOUNDATION

http://www.lbjlibrary.org/page/foundation/

MOODY RESEARCH GRANTS
• See page 114

NAQVI INJURY LAW

http://www.naqvilaw.com/

NAQVI LAW SCHOLARSHIP
• See page 242

NATIONAL SOCIETY DAUGHTERS OF THE AMERICAN REVOLUTION

http://www.dar.org/

NATIONAL SOCIETY DAUGHTERS OF THE AMERICAN REVOLUTION DR. AURA-LEE A. PITTENGER AND JAMES HOBBS PITTENGER AMERICAN HISTORY SCHOLARSHIP
• See page 382

NATIONAL SOCIETY DAUGHTERS OF THE AMERICAN REVOLUTION ENID HALL GRISWOLD MEMORIAL SCHOLARSHIP
• See page 264

STRAIGHTFORWARD MEDIA

http://www.straightforwardmedia.com/

STRAIGHTFORWARD MEDIA LIBERAL ARTS SCHOLARSHIP
• See page 139

TKE EDUCATIONAL FOUNDATION

http://www.tke.org/

BRUCE B. MELCHERT SCHOLARSHIP
One-time award of $300 given to an undergraduate member of Tau Kappa Epsilon with sophomore, junior, or senior standing. Must be pursuing a degree in political science or government and have a record of leadership within his fraternity and other campus organizations. Should have as a goal to serve in a political or government position. Recent head and shoulders photograph must be submitted with application. Minimum 3.0 GPA required. Preference will first be given to a member of Beta-Theta Chapter but, if there is no qualified applicant, the scholarship will be open to any other qualified Teke.

Academic Fields/Career Goals: Political Science.

Award: Scholarship for use in sophomore, junior, or senior years; not renewable. *Number:* 1. *Amount:* $300.

Eligibility Requirements: Applicant must be enrolled or expecting to enroll full-time at a four-year institution or university; male and must have an interest in leadership. Applicant or parent of applicant must be member of Tau Kappa Epsilon. Applicant must have 3.0 GPA or higher. Available to U.S. and non-U.S. citizens.

Application Requirements: Application form, application form may be submitted online (http://www.tke.org/member_resources/scholarships/apply_online), essay, narrative summary of how TKE membership has benefited applicant, personal photograph, transcript. *Deadline:* March 15.

Contact: Offices of the Grand Chapter
TKE Educational Foundation
7439 Woodland Drive, Suite 100
Indianapolis, IN 46278
E-mail: tkeogc@tke.org

UNITED NATIONS ASSOCIATION OF CONNECTICUT

http://www.unausa.org

UNITED NATIONS ASSOCIATION OF CONNECTICUT SCHOLARSHIP
• See page 147

UNITED NEGRO COLLEGE FUND

http://www.uncf.org/

OSSIE DAVIS ENDOWMENT SCHOLARSHIP PROGRAM
• *See page 146*

SUEZ CORPORATE SCHOLARS PROGRAM
• *See page 94*

UNCF/KOCH SCHOLARS PROGRAM FOR UNDERGRADUATES
• *See page 94*

WASHINGTON CROSSING FOUNDATION

http://www.gwcf.org/

WASHINGTON CROSSING FOUNDATION SCHOLARSHIP

Merit-based awards available to high school seniors who are planning a career in government service. Must write an essay stating reason for deciding on a career in public service. Minimum 3.0 GPA required.

Academic Fields/Career Goals: Political Science; Public Policy and Administration.

Award: Scholarship for use in freshman year; not renewable. *Amount:* $500–$5000.

Eligibility Requirements: Applicant must be high school student and planning to enroll or expecting to enroll full-time at a four-year institution or university. Applicant must have 3.0 GPA or higher. Available to U.S. citizens.

Application Requirements: Application form, essay, interview, personal photograph. *Deadline:* January 15.

Contact: Washington Crossing Foundation
Washington Crossing Foundation
PO Box 503
Levittown, PA 19058-0503
Phone: 215-949-8841
E-mail: info@gwcf.org

WASHINGTON STATE ASSOCIATION FOR JUSTICE

http://www.washingtonjustice.org/

WASHINGTON STATE ASSOCIATION FOR JUSTICE AMERICAN JUSTICE ESSAY & VIDEO SCHOLARSHIP
• *See page 244*

WILLIAMS LAW GROUP

https://familylawyersnewjersey.com/

WILLIAMS LAW GROUP OPPORTUNITY TO GROW SCHOLARSHIP
• *See page 139*

PSYCHOLOGY

AMERICAN FEDERATION OF STATE, COUNTY, AND MUNICIPAL EMPLOYEES

http://www.afscme.org/

AFSCME/UNCF UNION SCHOLARS PROGRAM
• *See page 113*

AVACARE MEDICAL

https://avacaremedical.com

AVACARE MEDICAL SCHOLARSHIP
• *See page 115*

BHW GROUP

https://thebhwgroup.com/

BHW WOMEN IN STEM SCHOLARSHIP
• *See page 124*

CYNTHIA E. MORGAN SCHOLARSHIP FUND (CEMS)

http://www.cemsfund.com/

CYNTHIA E. MORGAN MEMORIAL SCHOLARSHIP FUND, INC.
• *See page 334*

HEALTH PROFESSIONS EDUCATION FOUNDATION

http://www.healthprofessions.ca.gov/

ALLIED HEALTHCARE SCHOLARSHIP PROGRAM
• *See page 165*

HEALTH RESEARCH COUNCIL OF NEW ZEALAND

http://www.hrc.govt.nz/

PACIFIC MENTAL HEALTH WORK FORCE AWARD
• *See page 368*

INDIAN HEALTH SERVICES, UNITED STATES DEPARTMENT OF HEALTH AND HUMAN SERVICES

http://www.ihs.gov/scholarship

HEALTH PROFESSIONS PREPARATORY SCHOLARSHIP PROGRAM
• *See page 165*

INTERMOUNTAIN MEDICAL IMAGING

https://www.aboutimi.com/

INTERMOUNTAIN MEDICAL IMAGING SCHOLARSHIP
• *See page 147*

KETAMINE CLINICS OF LOS ANGELES

http://www.ketamineclinics.com/

KETAMINE CLINICS OF LOS ANGELES SCHOLARSHIP PROGRAM
• *See page 165*

LABROOTS INC.

http://www.LabRoots.com

LABROOTS STEM SCHOLARSHIP
• *See page 116*

LA-PHILOSOPHIE.COM

http://la-philosophie.com

LA-PHILOSOPHIE.COM SCHOLARSHIP
• *See page 119*

MEDICAL SCRUBS COLLECTION

http://medicalscrubscollection.com

MEDICAL SCRUBS COLLECTION SCHOLARSHIP
• *See page 120*

MICHAEL MOODY FITNESS

http://www.michaelmoodyfitness.com/

MICHAEL MOODY FITNESS SCHOLARSHIP
• *See page 166*

PILOT INTERNATIONAL

https://www.pilotinternational.org/

PILOT INTERNATIONAL SCHOLARSHIP
• *See page 377*

THE RECOVERY VILLAGE

https://www.therecoveryvillage.com/

RECOVERY VILLAGE HEALTHCARE SCHOLARSHIP
• *See page 256*

SIGMA XI, THE SCIENTIFIC RESEARCH SOCIETY

http://www.sigmaxi.org/

SIGMA XI GRANTS-IN-AID OF RESEARCH
• *See page 110*

THE SOCIETY FOR THE SCIENTIFIC STUDY OF SEXUALITY

http://www.sexscience.org/

THE SOCIETY FOR THE SCIENTIFIC STUDY OF SEXUALITY STUDENT RESEARCH GRANT
• *See page 120*

STRAIGHTFORWARD MEDIA

http://www.straightforwardmedia.com/

STRAIGHTFORWARD MEDIA LIBERAL ARTS SCHOLARSHIP
• *See page 139*

UNITED NEGRO COLLEGE FUND

http://www.uncf.org/

HCN/APRICITY RESOURCES SCHOLARS PROGRAM
• *See page 93*

VIRTUOUS PROM

https://www.virtuousprom.com

VIRTUOUS PROM PEACE SCHOLARSHIP
This scholarship is for women studying in the areas of psychology, anthropology, sociology and theology at both the undergraduate and graduate level.
Academic Fields/Career Goals: Psychology.
Award: Scholarship for use in freshman, sophomore, junior, senior, graduate, or postgraduate years; not renewable. *Number:* 1. *Amount:* $250.
Eligibility Requirements: Applicant must be enrolled or expecting to enroll full- or part-time at a two-year or four-year institution or university and female. Available to U.S. and non-U.S. citizens.
Application Requirements: Essay. *Deadline:* January 31.
Contact: Ms. Megan MacNeal, Creative Director
E-mail: megan@virtuousprom.com

WILLIAMS LAW GROUP

https://familylawyersnewjersey.com/

WILLIAMS LAW GROUP OPPORTUNITY TO GROW SCHOLARSHIP
• *See page 139*

PUBLIC HEALTH

ASSOCIATION ON AMERICAN INDIAN AFFAIRS, INC.

http://www.indian-affairs.org/

ELIZABETH AND SHERMAN ASCHE MEMORIAL SCHOLARSHIP FUND
• *See page 106*

AVACARE MEDICAL

https://avacaremedical.com

AVACARE MEDICAL SCHOLARSHIP
• *See page 115*

CONTINENTAL SOCIETY, DAUGHTERS OF INDIAN WARS

http://www.csdiw.org/

CONTINENTAL SOCIETY, DAUGHTERS OF INDIAN WARS SCHOLARSHIP
• *See page 242*

THE EXPERT INSTITUTE

https://www.theexpertinstitute.com

ANNUAL HEALTHCARE AND LIFE SCIENCES SCHOLARSHIP
• *See page 170*

FLORIDA ENVIRONMENTAL HEALTH ASSOCIATION

http://www.feha.org/

FLORIDA ENVIRONMENTAL HEALTH ASSOCIATION EDUCATIONAL SCHOLARSHIP AWARDS
• *See page 335*

HAWAIIAN LODGE, F&AM

http://www.hawaiianlodgefreemasons.org

HAWAIIAN LODGE SCHOLARSHIPS
• *See page 86*

INTERMOUNTAIN MEDICAL IMAGING

https://www.aboutimi.com/

INTERMOUNTAIN MEDICAL IMAGING SCHOLARSHIP
• *See page 147*

THE JACKSON LABORATORY

https://www.jax.org

THE JACKSON LABORATORY COLLEGE SCHOLARSHIP PROGRAM
• *See page 126*

LABROOTS INC.

http://www.LabRoots.com

LABROOTS STEM SCHOLARSHIP
• *See page 116*

LAW OFFICES OF PROSPER SHAKED

https://www.prosperlaw.com/

PROSPER SHAKED SCHOLARSHIP FOR FUTURE MEDICAL PROFESSIONALS
• *See page 166*

MEDICAL SCRUBS COLLECTION

http://medicalscrubscollection.com

MEDICAL SCRUBS COLLECTION SCHOLARSHIP
• *See page 120*

MICHAEL MOODY FITNESS

http://www.michaelmoodyfitness.com/

MICHAEL MOODY FITNESS SCHOLARSHIP
• *See page 166*

NATIONAL ENVIRONMENTAL HEALTH ASSOCIATION/AMERICAN ACADEMY OF SANITARIANS

http://www.neha.org/

NATIONAL ENVIRONMENTAL HEALTH ASSOCIATION/AMERICAN ACADEMY OF SANITARIANS SCHOLARSHIP
• *See page 335*

NATIONAL INSTITUTES OF HEALTH

https://www.training.nih.gov/programs/ugsp

NIH UNDERGRADUATE SCHOLARSHIP PROGRAM FOR STUDENTS FROM DISADVANTAGED BACKGROUNDS
• *See page 116*

NEW ENGLAND EMPLOYEE BENEFITS COUNCIL

http://www.neebc.org/

NEW ENGLAND EMPLOYEE BENEFITS COUNCIL SCHOLARSHIP PROGRAM
• *See page 89*

OREGON STUDENT ASSISTANCE COMMISSION

https://oregonstudentaid.gov/

LAURENCE R. FOSTER MEMORIAL SCHOLARSHIP
One-time award to students enrolled or planning to enroll in a public health degree program. First preference given to those working in the public health field and those pursuing a graduate degree in public health. Second preference given to undergraduates entering junior or senior year health programs may apply if seeking a public health career, and not private practice. Applicants from diverse environments preferred. Based on financial need.

Academic Fields/Career Goals: Public Health.

Award: Scholarship for use in junior, senior, or graduate years; not renewable.

Eligibility Requirements: Applicant must be enrolled or expecting to enroll full- or part-time at a four-year institution or university. Available to U.S. citizens.

Application Requirements: Application form, essay, financial need analysis. *Deadline:* March 1.

Contact: Melissa Adams, Scholarship Processing Coordinator
    Phone: 541-687-7409
    E-mail: melissa.adams@state.or.us

WILLIAM E. KEENE MEMORIAL SCHOLARSHIP
• *See page 335*

PLATINUM EDUCATIONAL GROUP

http://www.platinumed.com

PLATINUM EDUCATIONAL GROUP SCHOLARSHIPS PROGRAM FOR EMS, NURSING, AND ALLIED HEALTH
• *See page 117*

THE RECOVERY VILLAGE

https://www.therecoveryvillage.com/

RECOVERY VILLAGE HEALTHCARE SCHOLARSHIP
• *See page 256*

THE SOCIETY FOR THE SCIENTIFIC STUDY OF SEXUALITY

http://www.sexscience.org/

THE SOCIETY FOR THE SCIENTIFIC STUDY OF SEXUALITY STUDENT RESEARCH GRANT
• *See page 120*

SOUTH CAROLINA PUBLIC HEALTH ASSOCIATION

http://www.scpha.com/

SOUTH CAROLINA PUBLIC HEALTH ASSOCIATION PUBLIC HEALTH SCHOLARSHIPS

Current member of the SCPHA with more than 6 hours remaining and enrolled in a accredited higher education program for public health or related field. Dantzler- exhibit significant commitment to the public health profession through volunteer and/or professional activity as indicated on the application. Public Health Scholarship- exhibit significant commitment to the public health profession through volunteer and/or professional activity as indicated on the application.

Academic Fields/Career Goals: Public Health.

Award: Scholarship for use in freshman, sophomore, junior, senior, graduate, or postgraduate years; not renewable. *Number:* 2. *Amount:* $500–$750.

Eligibility Requirements: Applicant must be enrolled or expecting to enroll full- or part-time at a four-year institution or university. Applicant must have 3.5 GPA or higher. Available to U.S. citizens.

Application Requirements: Application form, proof of number of hours remaining, transcript. *Deadline:* March 31.

Contact: Mr. Larry White, Scholarship Committee Chair
South Carolina Public Health Association
PO Box 3051
Conway, SC 29528
Phone: 843-488-1329 Ext. 225
Fax: 843-488-1330
E-mail: larry@smokefreehorry.org

PUBLIC POLICY AND ADMINISTRATION

AMERICAN INSTITUTE OF POLISH CULTURE INC.

http://www.ampolinstitute.org/

HARRIET IRSAY SCHOLARSHIP GRANT
• *See page 141*

AMERICAN LEGION AUXILIARY DEPARTMENT OF ARIZONA

http:/wwwaladeptaz.org

AMERICAN LEGION AUXILIARY DEPARTMENT OF ARIZONA WILMA HOYAL-MAXINE CHILTON MEMORIAL SCHOLARSHIP
• *See page 215*

ASSOCIATION FOR EDUCATION AND REHABILITATION OF THE BLIND AND VISUALLY IMPAIRED

http://www.aerbvi.org/

WILLIAM AND DOROTHY FERRELL SCHOLARSHIP
• *See page 268*

ASSOCIATION OF FORMER INTELLIGENCE OFFICERS

http://www.afio.com

AFIO UNDERGRADUATE AND GRADUATE SCHOLARSHIPS
• *See page 113*

THE DALLAS FOUNDATION

http://www.dallasfoundation.org/

WHITLEY PLACE SCHOLARSHIP
• *See page 133*

GEORGIA GOVERNMENT FINANCE OFFICERS ASSOCIATION

http://www.ggfoa.org/

GGFOA ANNUAL COLLEGE SCHOLARSHIP
• *See page 85*

GOVERNMENT FINANCE OFFICERS ASSOCIATION

http://www.gfoa.org/

JEFFREY L. ESSER CAREER DEVELOPMENT SCHOLARSHIP
• *See page 85*

MINORITIES IN GOVERNMENT FINANCE SCHOLARSHIP
• *See page 86*

GREATER SALINA COMMUNITY FOUNDATION

http://www.gscf.org/

KANSAS FEDERATION OF REPUBLICAN WOMEN SCHOLARSHIP
• *See page 382*

HARRY S. TRUMAN SCHOLARSHIP FOUNDATION

http://www.truman.gov/

HARRY S. TRUMAN SCHOLARSHIP
• *See page 510*

JAPANESE AMERICAN CITIZENS LEAGUE (JACL)

http://www.jacl.org/

NATIONAL JACL HEADQUARTERS SCHOLARSHIP
• *See page 107*

MICHAEL MOODY FITNESS

http://www.michaelmoodyfitness.com/

MICHAEL MOODY FITNESS SCHOLARSHIP
• *See page 166*

NATIONAL ACADEMY OF TELEVISION ARTS AND SCIENCES

http://www.emmyonline.tv/

DOUGLAS W. MUMMERT SCHOLARSHIP
• *See page 142*

NEW ENGLAND EMPLOYEE BENEFITS COUNCIL

http://www.neebc.org/

NEW ENGLAND EMPLOYEE BENEFITS COUNCIL SCHOLARSHIP PROGRAM
• *See page 89*

THE RECOVERY VILLAGE

https://www.therecoveryvillage.com/

RECOVERY VILLAGE HEALTHCARE SCHOLARSHIP
• *See page 256*

WASHINGTON CROSSING FOUNDATION

http://www.gwcf.org/

WASHINGTON CROSSING FOUNDATION SCHOLARSHIP
• *See page 511*

WASHINGTON STATE ASSOCIATION FOR JUSTICE

http://www.washingtonjustice.org/

WASHINGTON STATE ASSOCIATION FOR JUSTICE AMERICAN JUSTICE ESSAY & VIDEO SCHOLARSHIP
• *See page 244*

RADIOLOGY

101ST AIRBORNE DIVISION ASSOCIATION

http://www.screamingeaglefoundation.org/

AL & WILLIAMARY VISTE SCHOLARSHIP
• *See page 114*

ACLS CERTIFICATION INSTITUTE

https://acls.com

MEDICAL SCHOOL SCHOLARSHIP
• *See page 251*

AMERICAN INDIAN SCIENCE AND ENGINEERING SOCIETY

http://www.aises.org/

A.T. ANDERSON MEMORIAL SCHOLARSHIP PROGRAM
• *See page 121*

ASRT FOUNDATION

http://foundation.asrt.org

JERMAN-CAHOON STUDENT SCHOLARSHIP
• *See page 371*

PROFESSIONAL ADVANCEMENT SCHOLARSHIP
• *See page 367*

ROYCE OSBORN MINORITY STUDENT SCHOLARSHIP
• *See page 372*

SIEMENS CLINICAL ADVANCEMENT SCHOLARSHIP
• *See page 372*

CYNTHIA E. MORGAN SCHOLARSHIP FUND (CEMS)

http://www.cemsfund.com/

CYNTHIA E. MORGAN MEMORIAL SCHOLARSHIP FUND, INC.
• *See page 334*

HEALTH PROFESSIONS EDUCATION FOUNDATION

http://www.healthprofessions.ca.gov/

ALLIED HEALTHCARE SCHOLARSHIP PROGRAM
• *See page 165*

LABROOTS INC.

http://www.LabRoots.com

LABROOTS STEM SCHOLARSHIP
• *See page 116*

MEDICAL SCRUBS COLLECTION

http://medicalscrubscollection.com

MEDICAL SCRUBS COLLECTION SCHOLARSHIP
• *See page 120*

NEXTSTEPU

http://www.nextstepu.com/

$1,500 STEM SCHOLARSHIP
• *See page 120*

PLATINUM EDUCATIONAL GROUP

http://www.platinumed.com

PLATINUM EDUCATIONAL GROUP SCHOLARSHIPS PROGRAM FOR EMS, NURSING, AND ALLIED HEALTH
• *See page 117*

ULTRASOUNDTECHNICIANSCHOOLS.COM

http://www.ultrasoundtechnicianschools.com

ULTRASOUNDTECHNICIANSCHOOLS.COM SCHOLARSHIP
• *See page 380*

REAL ESTATE

APPRAISAL INSTITUTE EDUCATION TRUST

http://www.aiedtrust.org/

AIET MINORITIES AND WOMEN EDUCATIONAL SCHOLARSHIP

Awarded to minorities and women undergraduate students pursuing academic degrees in real estate appraisal or related fields.

Academic Fields/Career Goals: Real Estate.

Award: Scholarship for use in freshman, sophomore, junior, senior, graduate, or postgraduate years; not renewable. *Amount:* $1000.

Eligibility Requirements: Applicant must be hearing impaired, learning disabled, physically disabled, or visually impaired; American Indian/Alaska Native, Asian/Pacific Islander, Black (non-Hispanic), Hispanic; enrolled or expecting to enroll full- or part-time at a four-year institution or university and female. Applicant must be hearing impaired, learning disabled, physically disabled, or visually impaired. Applicant must have 2.5 GPA or higher. Available to U.S. citizens.

Application Requirements: Application form, essay, financial need analysis, personal photograph, recommendations or references, resume, transcript. *Deadline:* April 15.

Contact: Sarah Walsh
Appraisal Institute Education Trust
200 West Madison
Suite 1500
Chicago, IL 60607
Phone: 312-335-4133
Fax: 312-335-4134
E-mail: educationtrust@appraisalinstitute.org

APPRAISAL INSTITUTE EDUCATION TRUST EDUCATION SCHOLARSHIPS

Awarded on the basis of academic excellence, this scholarship helps finance the educational endeavors of undergraduate and graduate students concentrating in real estate appraisal, land economics, real estate or allied fields.

Academic Fields/Career Goals: Real Estate.

Award: Scholarship for use in sophomore, junior, senior, or graduate years; not renewable. *Amount:* $1000–$2000.

Eligibility Requirements: Applicant must be enrolled or expecting to enroll full-time at a four-year institution or university. Available to U.S. citizens.

Application Requirements: Application form, essay, recommendations or references, resume, transcript. *Deadline:* February 15.

Contact: Sarah Walsh, Coordinator
Appraisal Institute Education Trust
200 West Madison
Suite 1500
Chicago, IL 60606
Phone: 312-335-4133
Fax: 312-335-4134
E-mail: educationtrust@appraisalinstitute.org

C.A.R. SCHOLARSHIP FOUNDATION

http://www.car.org/

C.A.R. SCHOLARSHIP FOUNDATION AWARD

Scholarships to students enrolled at a California College or University for professions which are centered on, or support a career in real estate transactional activity. Must have maintained a cumulative GPA of 2.6 or higher.

Academic Fields/Career Goals: Real Estate.

Award: Scholarship for use in sophomore, junior, senior, graduate, or postgraduate years; not renewable. *Number:* 10–25. *Amount:* $2000–$4000.

Eligibility Requirements: Applicant must be enrolled or expecting to enroll full- or part-time at a two-year or four-year institution or university; resident of California and studying in California. Applicant must have 2.5 GPA or higher. Available to U.S. citizens.

Application Requirements: Application form, driver's license, essay, interview. *Deadline:* April 6.

Contact: Lindsey Moss, Scholarship Coordinator
C.A.R. Scholarship Foundation
525 South Virgil Avenue
Los Angeles, CA 90020
Phone: 213-739-8217
Fax: 213-739-7278
E-mail: scholarship@car.org

ILLINOIS REAL ESTATE EDUCATIONAL FOUNDATION

http://www.ilreef.org/

ILLINOIS REAL ESTATE EDUCATIONAL FOUNDATION ACADEMIC SCHOLARSHIPS

Awards for Illinois residents attending an accredited two-or four-year junior college, college or university in Illinois. Must have completed 30 college credit hours and be pursuing a degree with an emphasis in real estate. Must be a U.S. citizen.

Academic Fields/Career Goals: Real Estate.

Award: Scholarship for use in freshman, sophomore, junior, or senior years; not renewable. *Amount:* $1000.

Eligibility Requirements: Applicant must be enrolled or expecting to enroll full-time at a two-year or four-year institution or university; resident of Illinois and studying in Illinois. Available to U.S. citizens.

Application Requirements: Application form, essay, recommendations or references, resume, transcript. *Deadline:* April 1.

Contact: Laurie Clayton, Foundation Manager
Illinois Real Estate Educational Foundation
522 South 5th Street, PO Box 2607
Springfield, IL 62708
Phone: 866-854-7333
Fax: 217-529-5893
E-mail: lclayton@iar.org

THOMAS F. SEAY SCHOLARSHIP

Award of $2000 to students pursuing a degree with an emphasis in real estate. Must be a U.S. citizen and attending any accredited U.S. college or university full-time. Must have completed at least 30 college credit hours. Minimum 3.5 GPA required.

Academic Fields/Career Goals: Real Estate.

Award: Scholarship for use in junior or senior years; not renewable. *Amount:* $2000.

Eligibility Requirements: Applicant must be enrolled or expecting to enroll full-time at a four-year institution or university; resident of Illinois and studying in Illinois. Applicant must have 3.5 GPA or higher. Available to U.S. citizens.

Application Requirements: Application form, community service, essay, recommendations or references, resume, transcript. *Deadline:* April 1.

Contact: Laurie Clayton, Foundation Manager
Illinois Real Estate Educational Foundation
522 South 5th Street, PO Box 2607
Springfield, IL 62708
Phone: 866-854-7333
Fax: 217-529-5893
E-mail: lclayton@iar.org

NEW JERSEY ASSOCIATION OF REALTORS

http://www.njar.com/

NEW JERSEY ASSOCIATION OF REALTORS EDUCATIONAL FOUNDATION SCHOLARSHIP PROGRAM

One-time awards for New Jersey residents who are high school seniors pursuing studies in real estate or allied fields. Preference to students considering a career in real estate. Must be member of NJAR or relative of a member. Selected candidates are interviewed in June. Must be a U.S. citizen.

Academic Fields/Career Goals: Real Estate.

Award: Scholarship for use in freshman year; not renewable. *Number:* 20–32. *Amount:* $1000–$2500.

Eligibility Requirements: Applicant must be high school student; planning to enroll or expecting to enroll full-time at a four-year institution or university and resident of New Jersey. Applicant or parent of applicant must be member of New Jersey Association of Realtors. Available to U.S. citizens.

Application Requirements: Application form, essay, financial need analysis, interview, letter of verification of realtor/realtor associate/association staff, transcript. *Deadline:* April 9.

Contact: Diane Hatley, Educational Foundation
New Jersey Association of Realtors
PO Box 2098
Edison, NJ 08818
Phone: 732-494-5616
Fax: 732-494-4723

STRAIGHTFORWARD MEDIA

http://www.straightforwardmedia.com/

STRAIGHTFORWARD MEDIA VOCATIONAL-TECHNICAL SCHOOL SCHOLARSHIP
• *See page 118*

RECREATION, PARKS, LEISURE STUDIES

AMERICAN HOTEL AND LODGING EDUCATIONAL FOUNDATION

http://www.ahlef.org/

AHLEF ANNUAL SCHOLARSHIP GRANT PROGRAM
• *See page 244*

AMERICAN HOTEL & LODGING EDUCATIONAL FOUNDATION PEPSI SCHOLARSHIP
• *See page 244*

ECOLAB SCHOLARSHIP PROGRAM
• *See page 245*

HYATT HOTELS FUND FOR MINORITY LODGING MANAGEMENT
• *See page 245*

INCOMING FRESHMAN SCHOLARSHIPS
• *See page 245*

RAMA SCHOLARSHIP FOR THE AMERICAN DREAM
• *See page 245*

CALAVERAS BIG TREES ASSOCIATION

https://bigtrees.org/

EMILY M. HEWITT MEMORIAL SCHOLARSHIP
• *See page 170*

THE LAND CONSERVANCY OF NEW JERSEY

http://www.tlc-nj.org/

ROGERS FAMILY SCHOLARSHIP
• *See page 172*

RUSSELL W. MYERS SCHOLARSHIP
• *See page 172*

MICHAEL MOODY FITNESS

http://www.michaelmoodyfitness.com/

MICHAEL MOODY FITNESS SCHOLARSHIP
• *See page 166*

NATIONAL RECREATION AND PARK ASSOCIATION

http://www.nrpa.org/

AFRS STUDENT SCHOLARSHIP
Applicant must be currently enrolled in a NRPA accredited recreation/parks curriculum or related field. Number of awards varies.

Academic Fields/Career Goals: Recreation, Parks, Leisure Studies.

Award: Scholarship for use in freshman or sophomore years; not renewable. *Amount:* $500.

Eligibility Requirements: Applicant must be enrolled or expecting to enroll full- or part-time at a four-year institution or university. Applicant must have 3.0 GPA or higher. Available to U.S. citizens.

Application Requirements: Application form, essay, recommendations or references, test scores, transcript. *Deadline:* June 1.

Contact: Jessica Lytle, Senior Manager
Phone: 703-858-2150
Fax: 703-858-0974
E-mail: jlytle@nrpa.org

PADDLE CANADA

http://www.paddlecanada.com

BILL MASON SCHOLARSHIP FUND
• *See page 275*

SHAPE AMERICA

http://www.shapeamerica.org/

RUTH ABERNATHY PRESIDENTIAL SCHOLARSHIP
Three award for undergraduate students and two for graduate students in January of each year. Must be majoring in the field of health, physical education, recreation or dance. Undergraduate awards are in the amount of $1,250 each and graduate awards are in the amount of $1,750 each. Recipients also receive a complimentary three-year SHAPE America membership. Applicant must be current member of SHAPE America

Academic Fields/Career Goals: Recreation, Parks, Leisure Studies; Sports-Related/Exercise Science.

Award: Scholarship for use in junior, senior, or graduate years; not renewable. *Number:* 5. *Amount:* $1250–$1750.

Eligibility Requirements: Applicant must be enrolled or expecting to enroll full-time at a four-year institution or university and must have an interest in leadership. Applicant must have 3.5 GPA or higher. Available to U.S. and non-U.S. citizens.

Application Requirements: Application form. *Deadline:* October 15.

Contact: Patti Hartle, Executive Administrator
SHAPE America
1900 Association Drive
Reston, VA 20191
Phone: 703-476-3405
E-mail: phartle@shapeamerica.org

SOIL AND WATER CONSERVATION SOCIETY-MISSOURI SHOW-ME CHAPTER

http://www.moswcs.org/

MO SHOW-ME CHAPTER SWCS SCHOLARSHIP
• *See page 111*

THE WALTER J. TRAVIS SOCIETY

http://www.travissociety.com

THE WALTER J. TRAVIS MEMORIAL SCHOLARSHIP AND THE WALTER J. TRAVIS-RUDY ZOCCHI MEMORIAL SCHOLARSHIP
• *See page 137*

RELIGION/THEOLOGY

AMERICAN SCHOOL OF CLASSICAL STUDIES AT ATHENS

http://www.ascsa.edu.gr/

ASCSA SUMMER SESSION AND SUMMER SEMINARS SCHOLARSHIPS
• *See page 118*

BETHESDA LUTHERAN COMMUNITIES

http://www.bethesdalutherancommunities.org/scholarships

DEVELOPMENTAL DISABILITIES SCHOLASTIC ACHIEVEMENT SCHOLARSHIP FOR COLLEGE STUDENTS WHO ARE LUTHERAN
• *See page 254*

EASTERN STAR-GRAND CHAPTER OF CALIFORNIA

http://www.oescal.org/

SCHOLARSHIPS FOR EDUCATION, BUSINESS AND RELIGION
• *See page 178*

ED E. AND GLADYS HURLEY FOUNDATION

ED E. AND GLADYS HURLEY FOUNDATION SCHOLARSHIP

Provides scholarships up to $1000 per year per student. Applicant must be Protestant enrolled or expecting to enroll full or part-time at a two-year or four-year institution or university and studying in Texas. Available to U.S. citizens.

Academic Fields/Career Goals: Religion/Theology.

Award: Scholarship for use in freshman, sophomore, junior, senior, graduate, or postgraduate years; not renewable. *Number:* 100–150. *Amount:* up to $1000.

Eligibility Requirements: Applicant must be Protestant; enrolled or expecting to enroll full- or part-time at a two-year or four-year institution or university; resident of Arkansas, Louisiana, Texas and studying in Texas. Available to U.S. citizens.

Application Requirements: Application form, financial need analysis, recommendations or references. *Deadline:* April 30.

Contact: Rose Davis, Financial Aid Coordinator
Ed E. and Gladys Hurley Foundation
Houston Graduate School-Theology
2501 Central Parkway, Suite A19
Houston, TX 77092
Phone: 713-942-9505
E-mail: rdavis@hgst.edu

LA-PHILOSOPHIE.COM

http://la-philosophie.com

LA-PHILOSOPHIE.COM SCHOLARSHIP
• *See page 119*

NATIONAL ASSOCIATION OF PASTORAL MUSICIANS

http://www.npm.org/

ELAINE RENDLER-RENE DOSOGNE-GEORGETOWN CHORALE SCHOLARSHIP
• *See page 455*

FUNK FAMILY MEMORIAL SCHOLARSHIP
• *See page 455*

GIA PUBLICATION PASTORAL MUSICIAN SCHOLARSHIP
• *See page 455*

MUSONICS SCHOLARSHIP
• *See page 455*

NATIONAL ASSOCIATION OF PASTORAL MUSICIANS MEMBERS' SCHOLARSHIP
• *See page 455*

NPM KOINONIA/BOARD OF DIRECTORS SCHOLARSHIP
• *See page 455*

OREGON CATHOLIC PRESS SCHOLARSHIP
• *See page 456*

PALUCH FAMILY FOUNDATION/WORLD LIBRARY PUBLICATIONS SCHOLARSHIP
• *See page 456*

OREGON STUDENT ASSISTANCE COMMISSION

https://oregonstudentaid.gov/

BEN SELLING SCHOLARSHIP

Award for Oregon residents enrolling as undergraduate sophomores, juniors, or seniors. Minimum college GPA of 3.5 required. Recipients must attend any Oregon or U.S. Rabbinical public and nonprofit college. Apply/compete annually.

Academic Fields/Career Goals: Religion/Theology.

Award: Scholarship for use in sophomore, junior, or senior years; not renewable.

Eligibility Requirements: Applicant must be Jewish and enrolled or expecting to enroll full-time at a two-year or four-year institution. Applicant must have 3.5 GPA or higher. Available to U.S. citizens.

Application Requirements: Application form, financial need analysis. *Deadline:* March 1.

Contact: Melissa Adams, Scholarship Processing Coordinator
Phone: 541-687-7409
E-mail: melissa.adams@state.or.us

PRESBYTERIAN CHURCH (USA)

http://www.pcusa.org/financialaid

STUDENT OPPORTUNITY SCHOLARSHIP
• *See page 275*

THE SOCIETY FOR THE SCIENTIFIC STUDY OF SEXUALITY

http://www.sexscience.org/

THE SOCIETY FOR THE SCIENTIFIC STUDY OF SEXUALITY STUDENT RESEARCH GRANT
• *See page 120*

SOUTHERN BAPTIST HISTORICAL LIBRARY AND ARCHIVES

http://www.sbhla.org/

LYNN E. MAY JR. STUDY GRANT
• *See page 114*

UNITARIAN UNIVERSALIST ASSOCIATION

http://www.uua.org/

ROY H. POLLACK SCHOLARSHIP
Scholarship given to a junior or senior student with academic excellence and good character, studying for ordained ministry who actively participates in extracurricular activities at their theological school. Applicant must be pursuing in Divinity degree.

Academic Fields/Career Goals: Religion/Theology.

Award: Scholarship for use in junior or senior years; not renewable.

Eligibility Requirements: Applicant must be Unitarian Universalist and enrolled or expecting to enroll full- or part-time at a four-year institution or university. Available to U.S. citizens.

Application Requirements: Application form, financial need analysis. *Deadline:* April 15.

Contact: Ms. Hillary Goodridge, Program Director
Phone: 617-971-9600
Fax: 617-971-0029
E-mail: uufp@aol.com

UNITED METHODIST COMMUNICATIONS

http://www.umcom.org/

LEONARD M. PERRYMAN COMMUNICATIONS SCHOLARSHIP FOR ETHNIC MINORITY STUDENTS
• *See page 227*

SCIENCE, TECHNOLOGY, AND SOCIETY

ADELANTE! U.S. EDUCATION LEADERSHIP FUND

http://www.adelantefund.org/

ADELANTE FUND SCHOLARSHIPS
• *See page 175*

AEG FOUNDATION

http://www.aegfoundation.org/

AEG FOUNDATION MARLIAVE FUND
• *See page 258*

AMERICAN INDIAN SCIENCE AND ENGINEERING SOCIETY

http://www.aises.org/

A.T. ANDERSON MEMORIAL SCHOLARSHIP PROGRAM
• *See page 121*

AMERICAN INSTITUTE OF AERONAUTICS AND ASTRONAUTICS

http://www.aiaafoundation.org/

AIAA FOUNDATION UNDERGRADUATE SCHOLARSHIPS
• *See page 121*

LEATRICE GREGORY PENDRAY SCHOLARSHIP
• *See page 121*

AMERICAN LEGION DEPARTMENT OF TENNESSEE

http://www.tennesseelegion.org/

JROTC SCHOLARSHIP
One scholarship of $3000 available to a Tennessee JROTC cadet who has been awarded either The American Legion General Military Excellence, or The American Legion Scholastic Award Medal and The American Legion Certificate. JROTC Senior Instructor must provide the recommendation for the award. Information and recommendation forms are provided each JROTC Unit in Tennessee. Must be U.S. citizen.

Academic Fields/Career Goals: Science, Technology, and Society.

Award: Scholarship for use in freshman, sophomore, junior, or senior years; not renewable. *Number:* 1. *Amount:* $3000.

Eligibility Requirements: Applicant must be high school student; planning to enroll or expecting to enroll full- or part-time at a four-year institution or university; resident of Tennessee and studying in Tennessee. Applicant or parent of applicant must have employment or volunteer experience in journalism/broadcasting. Available to U.S. citizens.

Application Requirements: Application form. *Deadline:* April 15.

Contact: Dean Tuttle, Department Adjutant
American Legion Department of Tennessee
318 Donelson Pike
Nashville, TN 37214
Phone: 615-391-5088
E-mail: Adjutant@TNLegion.org

AMERICAN SCHOOL OF CLASSICAL STUDIES AT ATHENS

http://www.ascsa.edu.gr/

ASCSA SUMMER SESSION AND SUMMER SEMINARS SCHOLARSHIPS
• *See page 118*

ARIZONA HYDROLOGICAL SOCIETY

http://www.azhydrosoc.org/

ARIZONA HYDROLOGICAL SOCIETY SCHOLARSHIP
• *See page 259*

ARRL FOUNDATION INC.

http://www.arrl.org/

ALLEN AND BERTHA WATSON MEMORIAL SCHOLARSHIP
• *See page 313*

WILSE MORGAN, WX7P, MEMORIAL ARRL NORTHWESTERN DIVISION SCHOLARSHIP
• See page 177

YASME FOUNDATION SCHOLARSHIP
• See page 168

ASSOCIATION FOR WOMEN GEOSCIENTISTS (AWG)

http://www.awg.org/

LONE STAR RISING CAREER SCHOLARSHIP
• See page 260

ASSOCIATION OF FEDERAL COMMUNICATIONS CONSULTING ENGINEERS

http://www.afcce.org

JULES COHEN SCHOLARSHIP
• See page 284

ASSOCIATION OF STATE DAM SAFETY OFFICIALS (ASDSO)

http://www.DamSafety.org

ASSOCIATION OF STATE DAM SAFETY OFFICIALS (ASDSO) SENIOR UNDERGRADUATE SCHOLARSHIP
• See page 168

AUTOMOTIVE WOMEN'S ALLIANCE FOUNDATION

http://awafoundation.org/index.php

AUTOMOTIVE WOMEN'S ALLIANCE FOUNDATION SCHOLARSHIPS
• See page 81

BHW GROUP

https://thebhwgroup.com/

BHW WOMEN IN STEM SCHOLARSHIP
• See page 124

BROWN AND CALDWELL

http://www.brownandcaldwell.com

ECKENFELDER SCHOLARSHIP
• See page 169

CATCHING THE DREAM

http://www.catchingthedream.org/

MATH, ENGINEERING, SCIENCE, BUSINESS, EDUCATION, COMPUTERS SCHOLARSHIPS
• See page 178

NATIVE AMERICAN LEADERSHIP IN EDUCATION (NALE)
• See page 178

CLUTCH PREP

http://www.clutchprep.com

CLUTCH PREP STEM SCHOLARSHIP
• See page 285

DAVIDSON INSTITUTE FOR TALENT DEVELOPMENT

http://www.davidsongifted.org/

DAVIDSON FELLOWS SCHOLARSHIP PROGRAM
• See page 124

DISTIL NETWORKS

http://www.distilnetworks.com

WOMEN FORWARD IN TECHNOLOGY SCHOLARSHIP PROGRAM
• See page 124

DIVERSITYCOMM, INC.

http://www.diversitycomm.net/

DIVERSITY IN STEAM MAGAZINE SCHOLARSHIP
• See page 83

EXPLORERS CLUB

http://www.explorers.org/

YOUTH ACTIVITY FUND
• See page 463

FOUNDATION FOR SCIENCE AND DISABILITY

http://stemd.org/

GRANTS FOR DISABLED GRADUATE STUDENTS IN THE SCIENCES
• See page 106

HAWAIIAN LODGE, F&AM

http://www.hawaiianlodgefreemasons.org

HAWAIIAN LODGE SCHOLARSHIPS
• See page 86

HEALTHCARE INFORMATION AND MANAGEMENT SYSTEMS SOCIETY FOUNDATION

http://www.himss.org/

HIMSS FOUNDATION SCHOLARSHIP PROGRAM
• See page 367

INTERNATIONAL TECHNOLOGY EDUCATION ASSOCIATION

http://www.iteaconnect.org/

INTERNATIONAL TECHNOLOGY EDUCATION ASSOCIATION UNDERGRADUATE SCHOLARSHIP IN TECHNOLOGY EDUCATION
• See page 272

THE JACKSON LABORATORY

https://www.jax.org

THE JACKSON LABORATORY COLLEGE SCHOLARSHIP PROGRAM
• *See page 126*

LABROOTS INC.

http://www.LabRoots.com

LABROOTS STEM SCHOLARSHIP
• *See page 116*

MICHAEL MOODY FITNESS

http://www.michaelmoodyfitness.com/

MICHAEL MOODY FITNESS SCHOLARSHIP
• *See page 166*

MINERALS, METALS, AND MATERIALS SOCIETY (TMS)

http://www.tms.org/

KAUFMAN CALPHAD SCHOLARSHIP
• *See page 302*

MATERIALS PROCESSING AND MANUFACTURING DIVISION SCHOLARSHIP
• *See page 302*

TMS/EPD SCHOLARSHIP
• *See page 302*

TMS/FMD GILBERT CHIN SCHOLARSHIP
• *See page 302*

TMS/INTERNATIONAL SYMPOSIUM ON SUPERALLOYS SCHOLARSHIP PROGRAM
• *See page 302*

TMS OUTSTANDING STUDENT PAPER CONTEST–UNDERGRADUATE
• *See page 303*

TMS/STRUCTURAL MATERIALS DIVISION SCHOLARSHIP
• *See page 303*

NASA IDAHO SPACE GRANT CONSORTIUM

http://www.idahospacegrant.org

NASA IDAHO SPACE GRANT CONSORTIUM SCHOLARSHIP PROGRAM
• *See page 126*

NASA RHODE ISLAND SPACE GRANT CONSORTIUM

http://brown/initiatives/ri-space-grant

NASA RHODE ISLAND SPACE GRANT CONSORTIUM OUTREACH SCHOLARSHIP FOR UNDERGRADUATE STUDENTS
• *See page 303*

NASA'S VIRGINIA SPACE GRANT CONSORTIUM

http://www.vsgc.odu.edu/

UNDERGRADUATE STEM RESEARCH SCHOLARSHIPS
• *See page 127*

NEXTSTEPU

http://www.nextstepu.com/

$1,500 STEM SCHOLARSHIP
• *See page 120*

R & D SYSTEMS INC.

https://www.rndsystems.com/

R&D SYSTEMS SCHOLARSHIP PROGRAM
Scholarship available to students with majors in a science-related field as well as high school students planning on majoring in a science field. High school students must submit a written statement addressing the following topics: Make a top ten list of your favorite emerging technologies.
Academic Fields/Career Goals: Science, Technology, and Society.
Award: Scholarship for use in freshman, sophomore, junior, senior, graduate, or postgraduate years; not renewable. *Number:* 1. *Amount:* $1500.
Eligibility Requirements: Applicant must be enrolled or expecting to enroll full- or part-time at a two-year or four-year institution or university. Available to U.S. and non-U.S. citizens.
Application Requirements: Application form, essay. *Deadline:* July 8.
Contact: Lisa Ikariyama
      E-mail: Lisa.Ikariyama@bio-techne.com

SIGMA XI, THE SCIENTIFIC RESEARCH SOCIETY

http://www.sigmaxi.org/

SIGMA XI GRANTS-IN-AID OF RESEARCH
• *See page 110*

SILICON VALLEY COMMUNITY FOUNDATION

http://www.siliconvalleycf.org

SAMSUNG@FIRST SCHOLARS
• *See page 233*

SOCIETY FOR IMAGING SCIENCE AND TECHNOLOGY

http://www.imaging.org/

RAYMOND DAVIS SCHOLARSHIP
• *See page 305*

SOCIETY FOR TECHNICAL COMMUNICATION

http://www.stc.org/

SOCIETY FOR TECHNICAL COMMUNICATION SCHOLARSHIP PROGRAM
• *See page 224*

SOCIETY OF MOTION PICTURE AND TELEVISION ENGINEERS

https://www.smpte.org/

LOUIS F. WOLF JR. MEMORIAL SCHOLARSHIP
• *See page 224*

STUDENT PAPER AWARD
• *See page 224*

SOCIETY OF PLASTICS ENGINEERS FOUNDATION (SPE)

http://www.4spe.org/

GULF COAST HURRICANE SCHOLARSHIP
• *See page 196*

SOIL AND WATER CONSERVATION SOCIETY

http://www.swcs.org

DONALD A. WILLIAMS SCHOLARSHIP SOIL CONSERVATION SCHOLARSHIP
• *See page 103*

SOIL AND WATER CONSERVATION SOCIETY-MISSOURI SHOW-ME CHAPTER

http://www.moswcs.org/

MO SHOW-ME CHAPTER SWCS SCHOLARSHIP
• *See page 111*

STRAIGHT NORTH

https://www.straightnorth.com/

STRAIGHT NORTH STEM SCHOLARSHIP
• *See page 92*

TECHNOLOGY FIRST

https://technologyfirst.org/

ROBERT V. MCKENNA SCHOLARSHIPS
• *See page 235*

THERMO FISHER SCIENTIFIC

https://www.thermofisher.com/antibodyscholarship

THERMO FISHER SCIENTIFIC ANTIBODY SCHOLARSHIP PROGRAM

The Thermo Fisher Scientific Antibody Scholarship program, awarded annually, is open to graduate and undergraduate students studying biology, chemistry, biochemistry or a related life science field. Applicants are required to demonstrate a strong academic background along with a true passion for science. A total of six scholarships are available for the 2018-2019 academic year; two $10,000 awards and four $5,000 awards will be awarded on August 8, 2018. Complete rules and the application form can be found on our website at http://www.thermofisher.com/antibodyscholarship

Academic Fields/Career Goals: Science, Technology, and Society.

Award: Scholarship for use in freshman, sophomore, junior, senior, graduate, or postgraduate years; not renewable. *Number:* 6. *Amount:* $5000–$10,000.

Eligibility Requirements: Applicant must be enrolled or expecting to enroll full- or part-time at a two-year or four-year institution or university. Applicant must have 3.0 GPA or higher. Available to U.S. and non-U.S. citizens.

Application Requirements: Application form, essay. *Deadline:* May 31.

Contact: Mrs. Sue Boggs, Scholarship Coordinator
Thermo Fisher Scientific
3747 N Meridian Rd
Rockford, IL 61101
Phone: 815-6684973
E-mail: antibodyscholarship@thermofisher.com

UNITED NEGRO COLLEGE FUND

http://www.uncf.org/

PROCTER & GAMBLE STEM SCHOLARSHIP
• *See page 128*

UNIVERSITIES SPACE RESEARCH ASSOCIATION

http://www.usra.edu/

UNIVERSITIES SPACE RESEARCH ASSOCIATION SCHOLARSHIP AWARD PROGRAM
• *See page 128*

VERMONT SPACE GRANT CONSORTIUM

http://www.cems.uvm.edu/vsgc

VERMONT SPACE GRANT CONSORTIUM
• *See page 104*

WOMEN IN AEROSPACE FOUNDATION

http://www.womeninaerospace.org/index.html

WIA FOUNDATION SCHOLARSHIP
• *See page 162*

SOCIAL SCIENCES

AMERICAN FEDERATION OF STATE, COUNTY, AND MUNICIPAL EMPLOYEES

http://www.afscme.org/

AFSCME/UNCF UNION SCHOLARS PROGRAM
• *See page 113*

AMERICAN INDIAN SCIENCE AND ENGINEERING SOCIETY

http://www.aises.org/

A.T. ANDERSON MEMORIAL SCHOLARSHIP PROGRAM
• *See page 121*

AMERICAN SOCIETY OF CRIMINOLOGY

http://www.asc41.com/

AMERICAN SOCIETY OF CRIMINOLOGY GENE CARTE STUDENT PAPER COMPETITION
• *See page 241*

BHW GROUP

https://thebhwgroup.com/

BHW WOMEN IN STEM SCHOLARSHIP
• *See page 124*

CANADIAN INSTITUTE OF UKRAINIAN STUDIES

http://www.cius.ca/

LEO J. KRYSA UNDERGRADUATE SCHOLARSHIP
• *See page 138*

CATCHING THE DREAM

http://www.catchingthedream.org/

MATH, ENGINEERING, SCIENCE, BUSINESS, EDUCATION, COMPUTERS SCHOLARSHIPS
• *See page 178*

CULTURAL SERVICES OF THE FRENCH EMBASSY

http://www.frenchculture.org/

TEACHING ASSISTANT PROGRAM IN FRANCE
• *See page 113*

INDIAN HEALTH SERVICES, UNITED STATES DEPARTMENT OF HEALTH AND HUMAN SERVICES

http://www.ihs.gov/scholarship

HEALTH PROFESSIONS PREPARATORY SCHOLARSHIP PROGRAM
• *See page 165*

INFINITY DENTAL WEB

http://www.infinitydentalweb.com

INTERNET MARKETING SCHOLARSHIP
• *See page 429*

INSTITUTE FOR HUMANE STUDIES

http://www.theihs.org/

HUMANE STUDIES FELLOWSHIPS
• *See page 219*

LA-PHILOSOPHIE.COM

http://la-philosophie.com

LA-PHILOSOPHIE.COM SCHOLARSHIP
• *See page 119*

MICHAEL MOODY FITNESS

http://www.michaelmoodyfitness.com/

MICHAEL MOODY FITNESS SCHOLARSHIP
• *See page 166*

NATIONAL BLACK POLICE ASSOCIATION

http://www.blackpolice.org/

ALPHONSO DEAL SCHOLARSHIP AWARD
• *See page 243*

NATIONAL SECURITY EDUCATION PROGRAM

http://www.iie.org/

NATIONAL SECURITY EDUCATION PROGRAM (NSEP) DAVID L. BOREN UNDERGRADUATE SCHOLARSHIPS
• *See page 139*

OFFICE AND PROFESSIONAL EMPLOYEES INTERNATIONAL UNION

http://www.opeiu.org/

JOHN KELLY LABOR STUDIES SCHOLARSHIP FUND
• *See page 265*

PARAPSYCHOLOGY FOUNDATION

http://www.parapsychology.org/

CHARLES T. AND JUDITH A. TART STUDENT INCENTIVE
An annual incentive is awarded to promote the research of an undergraduate or graduate student, who shows dedication to work within parapsychology. For more details see website http://www.parapsychology.org.

Academic Fields/Career Goals: Social Sciences.

Award: Scholarship for use in freshman, sophomore, junior, senior, graduate, or postgraduate years; not renewable. *Number:* 1. *Amount:* $500.

Eligibility Requirements: Applicant must be enrolled or expecting to enroll full-time at a two-year or four-year institution or university. Available to U.S. citizens.

Application Requirements: Application form, essay, recommendations or references, transcript. *Deadline:* October 15.

Contact: Lisette Coly, Vice President
Phone: 212-628-1550
Fax: 212-628-1559
E-mail: office@parapsychology.org

EILEEN J. GARRETT SCHOLARSHIP FOR PARAPSYCHOLOGICAL RESEARCH
Scholarship requires applicants to demonstrate academic interest in the science of parapsychology through completed research, term papers, and courses for which credit was received. Those with only a general interest will not be considered. Visit website for additional information.

Academic Fields/Career Goals: Social Sciences.

Award: Scholarship for use in freshman, sophomore, junior, senior, graduate, or postgraduate years; not renewable. *Number:* 1. *Amount:* $3000.

Eligibility Requirements: Applicant must be enrolled or expecting to enroll full-time at a two-year or four-year institution or university. Available to U.S. citizens.

Application Requirements: Application form, essay, recommendations or references, transcript. *Deadline:* July 15.

Contact: Lisette Coly, Vice President
Parapsychology Foundation
PO Box 1562
New York, NY 10021-0043
Phone: 212-628-1550
Fax: 212-628-1559
E-mail: office@parapsychology.org

PHI ALPHA THETA HISTORY HONOR SOCIETY, INC.

http://www.phialphatheta.org/

PHI ALPHA THETA WORLD HISTORY ASSOCIATION PAPER PRIZE
• *See page 383*

PRESBYTERIAN CHURCH (USA)

http://www.pcusa.org/financialaid

STUDENT OPPORTUNITY SCHOLARSHIP
• *See page 275*

SIGMA XI, THE SCIENTIFIC RESEARCH SOCIETY

http://www.sigmaxi.org/

SIGMA XI GRANTS-IN-AID OF RESEARCH
• *See page 110*

THE SOCIETY FOR THE SCIENTIFIC STUDY OF SEXUALITY

http://www.sexscience.org/

THE SOCIETY FOR THE SCIENTIFIC STUDY OF SEXUALITY STUDENT RESEARCH GRANT
• *See page 120*

STRAIGHTFORWARD MEDIA

http://www.straightforwardmedia.com/

STRAIGHTFORWARD MEDIA LIBERAL ARTS SCHOLARSHIP
• *See page 139*

UNITED NEGRO COLLEGE FUND

http://www.uncf.org/

HCN/APRICITY RESOURCES SCHOLARS PROGRAM
• *See page 93*

MICHAEL JACKSON SCHOLARSHIP
• *See page 227*

OSSIE DAVIS ENDOWMENT SCHOLARSHIP PROGRAM
• *See page 146*

SUEZ CORPORATE SCHOLARS PROGRAM
• *See page 94*

WASHINGTON STATE ASSOCIATION FOR JUSTICE

http://www.washingtonjustice.org/

WASHINGTON STATE ASSOCIATION FOR JUSTICE AMERICAN JUSTICE ESSAY & VIDEO SCHOLARSHIP
• *See page 244*

WIFLE FOUNDATION, INC.

http://www.wifle.org/

WIFLE SCHOLARSHIP
• *See page 244*

WILLIAMS LAW GROUP

https://familylawyersnewjersey.com/

WILLIAMS LAW GROUP OPPORTUNITY TO GROW SCHOLARSHIP
• *See page 139*

Y'S MEN INTERNATIONAL

http://www.ysmen.org/

ALEXANDER SCHOLARSHIP LOAN FUND
• *See page 185*

SOCIAL SERVICES

ALBERTA HERITAGE SCHOLARSHIP FUND

http://www.alis.alberta.ca/

NORTHERN ALBERTA DEVELOPMENT COUNCIL BURSARY
• *See page 251*

AMERICAN FEDERATION OF STATE, COUNTY, AND MUNICIPAL EMPLOYEES

http://www.afscme.org/

AFSCME/UNCF UNION SCHOLARS PROGRAM
• *See page 113*

AMERICAN LEGION AUXILIARY DEPARTMENT OF ARIZONA

http:/wwwaladeptaz.org

AMERICAN LEGION AUXILIARY DEPARTMENT OF ARIZONA WILMA HOYAL-MAXINE CHILTON MEMORIAL SCHOLARSHIP
• *See page 215*

THE ARC NEW YORK

https://www.nysarc.org/

JAMES F. REVILLE SCHOLARSHIP
• *See page 366*

BETHESDA LUTHERAN COMMUNITIES

http://www.bethesdalutherancommunities.org/scholarships

DEVELOPMENTAL DISABILITIES SCHOLASTIC ACHIEVEMENT SCHOLARSHIP FOR COLLEGE STUDENTS WHO ARE LUTHERAN
• *See page 254*

COMMUNITY FOUNDATION OF WESTERN MASSACHUSETTS

http://www.communityfoundation.org/

HELEN HAMILTON SCHOLARSHIP FUND
Scholarship for students pursuing degrees in social services, housing studies, urban design, and other related fields with a preference for students who have demonstrated a commitment to community service.

For more information, please see website
http://communityfoundation.org/.

Academic Fields/Career Goals: Social Services; Urban and Regional Planning.

Award: Scholarship for use in freshman, sophomore, junior, senior, or graduate years; not renewable.

Eligibility Requirements: Applicant must be enrolled or expecting to enroll full- or part-time at a two-year or four-year institution or university and resident of Massachusetts. Applicant or parent of applicant must have employment or volunteer experience in community service. Available to U.S. citizens.

Application Requirements: Application form, essay, financial need analysis, transcript. *Deadline:* March 31.

Contact: Dotty Theriaque, Program Assistant for Scholarships
Community Foundation of Western Massachusetts
1500 Main Street
PO Box 15769
Springfield, MA 01115
Phone: 413-732-2858
Fax: 413-733-8565
E-mail: scholar@communityfoundation.org

CONTINENTAL SOCIETY, DAUGHTERS OF INDIAN WARS

http://www.csdiw.org/

CONTINENTAL SOCIETY, DAUGHTERS OF INDIAN WARS SCHOLARSHIP
• *See page 242*

GENERAL BOARD OF HIGHER EDUCATION AND MINISTRY

http://www.gbhem.org

EDITH M. ALLEN SCHOLARSHIP
• *See page 270*

HEALTH PROFESSIONS EDUCATION FOUNDATION

http://www.healthprofessions.ca.gov/

ALLIED HEALTHCARE SCHOLARSHIP PROGRAM
• *See page 165*

INFINITY DENTAL WEB

http://www.infinitydentalweb.com

INTERNET MARKETING SCHOLARSHIP
• *See page 429*

MARYLAND STATE HIGHER EDUCATION COMMISSION

http://www.mhec.state.md.us/

GRADUATE AND PROFESSIONAL SCHOLARSHIP PROGRAM-MARYLAND
• *See page 256*

JANET L. HOFFMANN LOAN ASSISTANCE REPAYMENT PROGRAM
• *See page 272*

MICHAEL MOODY FITNESS

http://www.michaelmoodyfitness.com/

MICHAEL MOODY FITNESS SCHOLARSHIP
• *See page 166*

NATIONAL BLACK POLICE ASSOCIATION

http://www.blackpolice.org/

ALPHONSO DEAL SCHOLARSHIP AWARD
• *See page 243*

PRESBYTERIAN CHURCH (USA)

http://www.pcusa.org/financialaid

STUDENT OPPORTUNITY SCHOLARSHIP
• *See page 275*

UNITED COMMUNITY SERVICES FOR WORKING FAMILIES

http://www.ucswf.org

TED BRICKER SCHOLARSHIP

One-time award available to child of a union member who is a parent or guardian. Must be a member of a union affiliated with the Berks County United Labor Council, AFL-CIO. Must submit essay that is clear, concise, persuasive, and shows a commitment to the community.

Academic Fields/Career Goals: Social Services.

Award: Scholarship for use in freshman year; not renewable. *Number:* 1. *Amount:* up to $250.

Eligibility Requirements: Applicant must be high school student; planning to enroll or expecting to enroll full-time at a four-year institution or university and resident of Pennsylvania. Applicant or parent of applicant must be member of AFL-CIO. Available to U.S. citizens.

Application Requirements: Application form, essay, financial need analysis, transcript. *Deadline:* July 31.

Contact: Victoria Henshaw, Executive Director
United Community Services for Working Families
1251 North Front Street
Reading, PA 19601
Phone: 610-374-3319 Ext. 104
E-mail: vhenshaw@ucswf.org

UNITED NEGRO COLLEGE FUND

http://www.uncf.org/

HCN/APRICITY RESOURCES SCHOLARS PROGRAM
• *See page 93*

WILLIAMS LAW GROUP

https://familylawyersnewjersey.com/

WILLIAMS LAW GROUP OPPORTUNITY TO GROW SCHOLARSHIP
• *See page 139*

Y'S MEN INTERNATIONAL

http://www.ysmen.org/

ALEXANDER SCHOLARSHIP LOAN FUND
• *See page 185*

SPECIAL EDUCATION

ALBERTA HERITAGE SCHOLARSHIP FUND

http://www.alis.alberta.ca/

ANNA AND JOHN KOLESAR MEMORIAL SCHOLARSHIPS
• *See page 265*

AMERICAN LEGION AUXILIARY DEPARTMENT OF ARIZONA

http:/wwwaladeptaz.org

AMERICAN LEGION AUXILIARY DEPARTMENT OF ARIZONA WILMA HOYAL-MAXINE CHILTON MEMORIAL SCHOLARSHIP
• *See page 215*

THE ARC NEW YORK

https://www.nysarc.org/

JAMES F. REVILLE SCHOLARSHIP
• *See page 366*

JOSEPH T. WEINGOLD SCHOLARSHIP
Two (2) scholarships are presented annually. The scholarship, in the amount of $3,000 per recipient, is paid in installments of $1,500 for two (2) semesters. The funds must be claimed within a four (4) year period from the time the scholarship was awarded. Applications will be distributed to interested students by the University's Department of Special Education. Students will send applications directly to The Arc New York State Office. Students must be enrolled in a New York State degree program, leading to a special education certification. Students currently receiving a scholarship through The Arc New York are not eligible to receive simultaneous scholarships. Upon selection, student must send confirmation of enrollment and course schedule. Submit completed application, signed by Department Chairperson, and one (1) letter of recommendation from a current academic instructor.

Academic Fields/Career Goals: Special Education.

Award: Scholarship for use in freshman, sophomore, junior, senior, or graduate years; not renewable. *Number:* 2. *Amount:* $3000.

Eligibility Requirements: Applicant must be enrolled or expecting to enroll full- or part-time at a two-year or four-year institution or university; resident of New York and studying in New York.

Application Requirements: Application form. *Deadline:* January 15.

Contact: Maria Simone
The Arc New York
29 British American Boulevard
Latham, NY 12110
Phone: 518-439-8311
Fax: 518-439-1893
E-mail: scholarships@thearcny.org

BETHESDA LUTHERAN COMMUNITIES

http://www.bethesdalutherancommunities.org/scholarships

DEVELOPMENTAL DISABILITIES SCHOLASTIC ACHIEVEMENT SCHOLARSHIP FOR COLLEGE STUDENTS WHO ARE LUTHERAN
• *See page 254*

CONTINENTAL SOCIETY, DAUGHTERS OF INDIAN WARS

http://www.csdiw.org/

CONTINENTAL SOCIETY, DAUGHTERS OF INDIAN WARS SCHOLARSHIP
• *See page 242*

ILLINOIS STUDENT ASSISTANCE COMMISSION (ISAC)

http://www.isac.org/

ILLINOIS SPECIAL EDUCATION TEACHER TUITION WAIVER
Teachers or students who are pursuing a career in special education as public, private or parochial preschool, elementary or secondary school teachers in Illinois may be eligible for this program. This program will exempt such individuals from paying tuition and mandatory fees at an eligible institution, for up to four years. The individual dollar amount awarded are subject to sufficient annual appropriations by the Illinois General Assembly.

Academic Fields/Career Goals: Special Education.

Award: Scholarship for use in freshman, sophomore, junior, senior, or graduate years; renewable.

Eligibility Requirements: Applicant must be enrolled or expecting to enroll full- or part-time at a four-year institution or university; resident of Illinois and studying in Illinois. Applicant must have 2.5 GPA or higher. Available to U.S. citizens.

Application Requirements: Application form. *Deadline:* March 1.

Contact: ISAC Call Center Representative
Illinois Student Assistance Commission (ISAC)
1755 Lake Cook Road
Deerfield, IL 60015-5209
Phone: 800-899-4722
E-mail: isac.studentservices@illinois.gov

INTERNATIONAL LITERACY ASSOCIATION

https://literacyworldwide.org/home

JEANNE S. CHALL RESEARCH FELLOWSHIP
• *See page 421*

MICHAEL MOODY FITNESS

http://www.michaelmoodyfitness.com/

MICHAEL MOODY FITNESS SCHOLARSHIP
• *See page 166*

NATIONAL INSTITUTE FOR LABOR RELATIONS RESEARCH

http://www.nilrr.org/

APPLEGATE/JACKSON/PARKS FUTURE TEACHER SCHOLARSHIP
• *See page 273*

OREGON STUDENT ASSISTANCE COMMISSION

https://oregonstudentaid.gov/

JAMES CARLSON MEMORIAL SCHOLARSHIP
• *See page 274*

MARY ELIZABETH GUEST SCHOLARSHIP
Renewable award for graduates of Oregon high schools (not open to graduating high school seniors) who are attending 4-year private or

nonprofit colleges and universities. For those studying special education, with a preference for teaching students with severe behavioral disorders. Based on financial need and must meet Expected Family Contribution (EFC) limitations

Academic Fields/Career Goals: Special Education.

Award: Scholarship for use in sophomore, junior, or senior years; renewable.

Eligibility Requirements: Applicant must be enrolled or expecting to enroll full-time at a four-year institution or university and resident of Oregon. Available to U.S. citizens.

Application Requirements: Application form, financial need analysis. *Deadline:* March 1.

Contact: Melissa Adams, Scholarship Processing Coordinator
Phone: 541-687-7409
E-mail: melissa.adams@state.or.us

PILOT INTERNATIONAL

https://www.pilotinternational.org/

PILOT INTERNATIONAL SCHOLARSHIP
• *See page 377*

STRAIGHTFORWARD MEDIA

http://www.straightforwardmedia.com/

STRAIGHTFORWARD MEDIA TEACHER SCHOLARSHIP
• *See page 276*

WISCONSIN CONGRESS OF PARENTS AND TEACHERS INC.

http://www.wisconsinpta.org/

BROOKMIRE-HASTINGS SCHOLARSHIPS
• *See page 278*

SPORTS-RELATED/ EXERCISE SCIENCE

101ST AIRBORNE DIVISION ASSOCIATION

http://www.screamingeaglefoundation.org/

AL & WILLIAMARY VISTE SCHOLARSHIP
• *See page 114*

AMERICAN INDIAN SCIENCE AND ENGINEERING SOCIETY

http://www.aises.org/

A.T. ANDERSON MEMORIAL SCHOLARSHIP PROGRAM
• *See page 121*

AMERICAN PHYSIOLOGICAL SOCIETY

http://www.the-aps.org

BARBARA A. HORWITZ AND JOHN M. HOROWITZ UNDERGRADUATE RESEARCH AWARDS
• *See page 114*

BAT AND BALL GAME

https://batandballgame.com/

BAT AND BALL GAME WOMEN'S SPORTS SCHOLARSHIP

Women in Sports: It's a theme that has been gaining popularity and momentum for decades now. While more and more female athletes are emerging, the realm of professional sports remains male-dominated. At Bat and Ball Game, we'd like to take do our part to promote greater awareness while empowering women through sports–and we're proud to announce our women's sports scholarship, which includes one award to a deserving young athlete. Write an original essay on one of the following topics: Are there women in sports today that you see as role models? Who and why?; Why is baseball important to the sporting world in general?; Where will the sport of baseball be 10 years from now?; In your perspective, how has sport changed in the last two decades? Applicants' essays will be judged on thoughtfulness, creativity, and a demonstrated knowledge of sport. All scholarship essays must be submitted in English and should be 400 to 600 words in length. Submissions will be accepted from 12/01/2018 to 05/30/2019. Submit your essay and personal details via email to scholarship@batandballgame.com. Note that in accordance with the terms and conditions of this scholarship, your bio and essay may be published on Bat and Ball Game's website, blog, and social media platforms including Twitter, and Facebook. The scholarship winner must provide the following: proof of identity and confirmation of their current enrollment at an accredited institution. Qualifying universities and colleges include accredited institutions listed on the U.S. Department of Education website. Any school transfers are subject to the same accreditation guidelines. The board of judges will make its decision by 06/15/2018 date, after which the scholarship winner will be notified. Funds are provided by Bat and Ball Game, and will be deposited directly to the winners' bank accounts or made payable to their universities' Financial Aid departments. There is no application fee for participation in this women's sports scholarship opportunity.

Academic Fields/Career Goals: Sports-Related/Exercise Science.

Award: Scholarship for use in freshman, sophomore, junior, or senior years; not renewable. *Number:* 1. *Amount:* $1000.

Eligibility Requirements: Applicant must be physically disabled; enrolled or expecting to enroll full- or part-time at a two-year or four-year institution and female. Applicant must be physically disabled. Available to U.S. and non-U.S. citizens.

Application Requirements: Essay. *Deadline:* May 30.

Contact: Andrew Shields
Bat and Ball Game
8345 NW 66th Street, #C7592
Miami, FL 33166-7896
Phone: 844-873-2875
E-mail: scholarship@batandballgame.com

CANFIT

http://www.canfit.org/

CANFIT NUTRITION, PHYSICAL EDUCATION AND CULINARY ARTS SCHOLARSHIP
• *See page 245*

MICHAEL MOODY FITNESS

http://www.michaelmoodyfitness.com/

MICHAEL MOODY FITNESS SCHOLARSHIP
• *See page 166*

NATIONAL ATHLETIC TRAINERS' ASSOCIATION RESEARCH AND EDUCATION FOUNDATION

http://www.natafoundation.org/

NATIONAL ATHLETIC TRAINERS' ASSOCIATION RESEARCH AND EDUCATION FOUNDATION SCHOLARSHIP PROGRAM

NEXTSTEPU

http://www.nextstepu.com/

$1,500 STEM SCHOLARSHIP

PACERS FOUNDATION INC.

http://www.pacersfoundation.org/

LINDA CRAIG MEMORIAL SCHOLARSHIP PRESENTED BY ST. VINCENT SPORTS MEDICINE

PADDLE CANADA

http://www.paddlecanada.com

BILL MASON SCHOLARSHIP FUND

RADIO TELEVISION DIGITAL NEWS ASSOCIATION

http://www.rtdna.org

LOU AND CAROLE PRATO SPORTS REPORTING SCHOLARSHIP

SCARLETT FAMILY FOUNDATION SCHOLARSHIP PROGRAM

http://www.scarlettfoundation.org/

SCHOLARSHIP FOR STUDENTS PURSUING A BUSINESS OR STEM DEGREE

SHAPE AMERICA

http://www.shapeamerica.org/

RUTH ABERNATHY PRESIDENTIAL SCHOLARSHIP

STRAIGHTFORWARD MEDIA

http://www.straightforwardmedia.com/

STRAIGHTFORWARD MEDIA VOCATIONAL-TECHNICAL SCHOOL SCHOLARSHIP

THE WALTER J. TRAVIS SOCIETY

http://www.travissociety.com

THE WALTER J. TRAVIS MEMORIAL SCHOLARSHIP AND THE WALTER J. TRAVIS-RUDY ZOCCHI MEMORIAL SCHOLARSHIP

Y'S MEN INTERNATIONAL

http://www.ysmen.org/

ALEXANDER SCHOLARSHIP LOAN FUND

STATISTICS

THE ACTUARIAL FOUNDATION

http://www.actuarialfoundation.org

ACTUARY OF TOMORROW—STUART A. ROBERTSON MEMORIAL SCHOLARSHIP

CURTIS E. HUNTINGTON MEMORIAL SCHOLARSHIP (FORMERLY THE JOHN CULVER WOODDY SCHOLARSHIP)

AMERICAN INDIAN SCIENCE AND ENGINEERING SOCIETY

http://www.aises.org/

A.T. ANDERSON MEMORIAL SCHOLARSHIP PROGRAM

ARMED FORCES COMMUNICATIONS AND ELECTRONICS ASSOCIATION, EDUCATIONAL FOUNDATION

http://www.afcea.org/site/?q=foundation/scholarships

AFCEA STEM MAJORS SCHOLARSHIPS FOR UNDERGRADUATE STUDENTS

AUTOMOTIVE WOMEN'S ALLIANCE FOUNDATION

http://awafoundation.org/index.php

AUTOMOTIVE WOMEN'S ALLIANCE FOUNDATION SCHOLARSHIPS

DIVERSITYCOMM, INC.

http://www.diversitycomm.net/

DIVERSITY IN STEAM MAGAZINE SCHOLARSHIP

GREAT MINDS IN STEM

http://www.greatmindsinstem.org

HENAAC SCHOLARSHIP PROGRAM
• *See page 115*

INFINITY DENTAL WEB

http://www.infinitydentalweb.com

INTERNET MARKETING SCHOLARSHIP
• *See page 429*

LABROOTS INC.

http://www.LabRoots.com

LABROOTS STEM SCHOLARSHIP
• *See page 116*

NEXTSTEPU

http://www.nextstepu.com/

$1,500 STEM SCHOLARSHIP
• *See page 120*

SILICON VALLEY COMMUNITY FOUNDATION

http://www.siliconvalleycf.org

SAMSUNG@FIRST SCHOLARS
• *See page 233*

UNITED NEGRO COLLEGE FUND

http://www.uncf.org/

KIA MOTORS AMERICA STEM/SUSTAINABILITY SCHOLARSHIP
• *See page 175*

VOYA SCHOLARS
• *See page 94*

SURVEYING, SURVEYING TECHNOLOGY, CARTOGRAPHY, OR GEOGRAPHIC INFORMATION SCIENCE

AMERICAN CONGRESS ON SURVEYING AND MAPPING

http://landsurveyorsunited.com/acsm

ACSM FELLOWS SCHOLARSHIP

One-time award available to a student with a junior or higher standing in any ACSM discipline (surveying, mapping, geographic information systems, and geodetic science). Must be ACSM member.

Academic Fields/Career Goals: Surveying, Surveying Technology, Cartography, or Geographic Information Science.

Award: Scholarship for use in freshman, sophomore, junior, or senior years; not renewable. *Number:* 1. *Amount:* $2000.

Eligibility Requirements: Applicant must be enrolled or expecting to enroll full- or part-time at a four-year institution or university. Applicant or parent of applicant must be member of American Congress on Surveying and Mapping. Available to U.S. citizens.

Application Requirements: Application form, essay, membership proof, recommendations or references, transcript. *Deadline:* October 1.

Contact: Ilse Genovese, Communications Director
American Congress on Surveying and Mapping
6 Montgomery Village Avenue, Suite 403
Gaithersburg, MD 20879
Phone: 240-632-9716 Ext. 113
Fax: 240-632-1321
E-mail: ilse.genovese@acsm.net

ACSM LOWELL H. AND DOROTHY LOVING UNDERGRADUATE SCHOLARSHIP

Scholarship available for a junior or senior in a college or university in the U.S. studying surveying. Program of study must include courses in two of the following areas: land surveying, geometric geodesy, photogrammetry/remote sensing, or analysis and design of spatial measurement systems.

Academic Fields/Career Goals: Surveying, Surveying Technology, Cartography, or Geographic Information Science.

Award: Scholarship for use in freshman, sophomore, junior, or senior years; not renewable. *Number:* 1. *Amount:* $2500.

Eligibility Requirements: Applicant must be enrolled or expecting to enroll full- or part-time at a four-year institution or university. Applicant or parent of applicant must be member of American Congress on Surveying and Mapping. Available to U.S. citizens.

Application Requirements: Application form, essay, membership proof, recommendations or references, transcript. *Deadline:* October 1.

Contact: Ilse Genovese, Communications Director
American Congress on Surveying and Mapping
6 Montgomery Village Avenue, Suite 403
Gaithersbutg, MD 20879
Phone: 240-632-9716
Fax: 240-632-1321
E-mail: ilse.genovese@acsm.net

AMERICAN ASSOCIATION FOR GEODETIC SURVEYING JOSEPH F. DRACUP SCHOLARSHIP AWARD

Award for students enrolled in a four-year degree program in surveying (or in closely-related degree programs such as geomatics or surveying engineering). Preference given to applicants from programs with significant focus on geodetic surveying. Must be ACSM member.

Academic Fields/Career Goals: Surveying, Surveying Technology, Cartography, or Geographic Information Science.

Award: Scholarship for use in freshman, sophomore, junior, or senior years; not renewable. *Number:* 1. *Amount:* $2000.

Eligibility Requirements: Applicant must be enrolled or expecting to enroll full- or part-time at a four-year institution or university. Applicant or parent of applicant must be member of American Congress on Surveying and Mapping. Available to U.S. and non-Canadian citizens.

Application Requirements: Application form, essay, recommendations or references, transcript. *Deadline:* October 1.

Contact: Ilse Genovese, ACSM Communications Director
American Congress on Surveying and Mapping
6 Montgomery Village Avenue, Suite 403
Gaithersburg, MD 20879
Phone: 240-632-9716 Ext. 113
Fax: 240-632-1321
E-mail: ilse.genovese@acsm.net

BERNTSEN INTERNATIONAL SCHOLARSHIP IN SURVEYING

Award of $1500 for full-time students enrolled in a four-year degree program in surveying or in a closely-related degree program, such as geomatics or surveying engineering. Must be ACSM member.

Academic Fields/Career Goals: Surveying, Surveying Technology, Cartography, or Geographic Information Science.

Award: Scholarship for use in freshman, sophomore, junior, or senior years; not renewable. *Number:* 1. *Amount:* $1500.

Eligibility Requirements: Applicant must be enrolled or expecting to enroll full-time at a four-year institution or university. Applicant or parent of applicant must be member of American Congress on Surveying and Mapping. Available to U.S. citizens.

Application Requirements: Application form, essay, recommendations or references, transcript. *Deadline:* October 1.

Contact: Ilse Genovese, ACSM Communications Director
American Congress on Surveying and Mapping
6 Montgomery Village Avenue, Suite 403
Gaithersburg, MD 20879
Phone: 240-632-9716 Ext. 113
Fax: 240-632-1321
E-mail: ilse.genovese@acsm.net

BERNTSEN INTERNATIONAL SCHOLARSHIP IN SURVEYING TECHNOLOGY

Award for full-time undergraduate students enrolled in a two-year degree program in surveying technology. For U.S. study only. Must be a member of the American Congress on Surveying and Mapping. See website for application and more details http://www.acsm.net/scholar.html.

Academic Fields/Career Goals: Surveying, Surveying Technology, Cartography, or Geographic Information Science.

Award: Scholarship for use in freshman or sophomore years; not renewable. *Number:* 1. *Amount:* $500.

Eligibility Requirements: Applicant must be enrolled or expecting to enroll full-time at a two-year or four-year institution. Applicant or parent of applicant must be member of American Congress on Surveying and Mapping. Available to U.S. and non-Canadian citizens.

Application Requirements: Application form, essay, proof of membership in ACSM, recommendations or references, transcript. *Deadline:* varies.

Contact: Ilse Genovese, ACSM Communications Director
American Congress on Surveying and Mapping
6 Montgomery Village Avenue, Suite 403
Gaithersburg, MD 20879
Phone: 240-632-9716 Ext. 113
Fax: 240-632-1321
E-mail: ilse.genovese@acsm.net

CADY MCDONNELL MEMORIAL SCHOLARSHIP

Award of $1000 for female surveying student. Must be a resident of one of the following western states: Alaska, Arizona, California, Colorado, Hawaii, Idaho, Montana, Nevada, New Mexico, Oregon, Utah, Washington, and Wyoming. Must provide proof of legal home residence and be a member of the American Congress on Surveying and Mapping.

Academic Fields/Career Goals: Surveying, Surveying Technology, Cartography, or Geographic Information Science.

Award: Scholarship for use in freshman, sophomore, junior, or senior years; not renewable. *Number:* 1. *Amount:* $1000.

Eligibility Requirements: Applicant must be enrolled or expecting to enroll full- or part-time at a two-year or four-year institution or university; female and resident of Alaska, Arizona, California, Colorado, Hawaii, Idaho, Montana, Nevada, New Mexico, Oregon, Utah, Washington, Wyoming. Applicant or parent of applicant must be member of American Congress on Surveying and Mapping. Available to U.S. citizens.

Application Requirements: Application form, essay, financial need analysis, proof of residence, membership proof, personal statement, recommendations or references, transcript. *Deadline:* October 1.

Contact: Ilse Genovese, ACSM Communications Director
American Congress on Surveying and Mapping
6 Montgomery Village Avenue, Suite 403
Gaithersburg, MD 20879
Phone: 240-632-9716 Ext. 113
Fax: 240-632-1321
E-mail: ilse.genovese@acsm.net

NETTIE DRACUP MEMORIAL SCHOLARSHIP

Award for undergraduate student enrolled in a four-year geodetic surveying program at an accredited college or university. Must be U.S. citizen. Must be ACSM member.

Academic Fields/Career Goals: Surveying, Surveying Technology, Cartography, or Geographic Information Science.

Award: Scholarship for use in freshman, sophomore, junior, or senior years; not renewable. *Number:* 2. *Amount:* $2000.

Eligibility Requirements: Applicant must be enrolled or expecting to enroll full-time at a four-year institution or university. Applicant or parent of applicant must be member of American Congress on Surveying and Mapping. Available to U.S. citizens.

Application Requirements: ACSM membership proof, application form, essay, financial need analysis, recommendations or references, transcript. *Deadline:* October 1.

Contact: Ilse Genovese, Communications Director
American Congress on Surveying and Mapping
6 Montgomery Village Avenue, Suite 403
Gaithersburg, MD 20879
Phone: 240-632-9716 Ext. 113
Fax: 240-632-1321
E-mail: ilse.genovese@acsm.net

SCHONSTEDT SCHOLARSHIP IN SURVEYING

Award preference given to applicants with junior or senior standing in a four-year program in surveying. Schonstedt donates magnetic locator to surveying program at each recipient's school. Must be ACSM member.

Academic Fields/Career Goals: Surveying, Surveying Technology, Cartography, or Geographic Information Science.

Award: Scholarship for use in junior or senior years; not renewable. *Number:* 2. *Amount:* $1500.

Eligibility Requirements: Applicant must be enrolled or expecting to enroll full-time at a four-year institution or university. Applicant or parent of applicant must be member of American Congress on Surveying and Mapping. Available to U.S. citizens.

Application Requirements: ACSM membership proof, application form, essay, recommendations or references, transcript. *Deadline:* October 1.

Contact: Ilse Genovese, Communications Director
American Congress on Surveying and Mapping
6 Montgomery Village Avenue, Suite 403
Gaithersburg, MD 20879
Phone: 240-632-9716 Ext. 113
Fax: 240-632-1321
E-mail: ilse.genovese@acsm.net

TRI-STATE SURVEYING AND PHOTOGRAMMETRY KRIS M. KUNZE MEMORIAL SCHOLARSHIP
• *See page 176*

AMERICAN COUNCIL OF ENGINEERING COMPANIES OF PENNSYLVANIA (ACEC/PA)

http://www.acecpa.org/

ERIC J. GENNUSO AND LEROY D. (BUD) LOY, JR. SCHOLARSHIP PROGRAM
• *See page 187*

AMERICAN INDIAN SCIENCE AND ENGINEERING SOCIETY

http://www.aises.org/

A.T. ANDERSON MEMORIAL SCHOLARSHIP PROGRAM
• *See page 121*

AMERICAN SOCIETY OF CERTIFIED ENGINEERING TECHNICIANS

http://www.ascet.org/

KURT H. AND DONNA M. SCHULER SMALL GRANT
• *See page 205*

ASPRS, THE IMAGING AND GEOSPATIAL INFORMATION SOCIETY

http://www.asprs.org/

ABRAHAM ANSON MEMORIAL SCHOLARSHIP
• *See page 314*

FRANCIS H. MOFFITT MEMORIAL SCHOLARSHIP
• *See page 315*

JOHN O. BEHRENS INSTITUTE FOR LAND INFORMATION MEMORIAL SCHOLARSHIP
• *See page 315*

KENNETH J. OSBORN MEMORIAL SCHOLARSHIP
• *See page 315*

ROBERT E. ALTENHOFEN MEMORIAL SCHOLARSHIP
• *See page 315*

ASSOCIATED GENERAL CONTRACTORS OF NEW YORK STATE, LLC

https://www.agcnys.org/programs/scholarship/

ASSOCIATED GENERAL CONTRACTORS NYS SCHOLARSHIP PROGRAM
• *See page 207*

ASSOCIATION OF CALIFORNIA WATER AGENCIES

http://www.acwa.com/

ASSOCIATION OF CALIFORNIA WATER AGENCIES SCHOLARSHIPS
• *See page 123*

CLAIR A. HILL SCHOLARSHIP
• *See page 123*

ASSOCIATION OF STATE DAM SAFETY OFFICIALS (ASDSO)

http://www.DamSafety.org

ASSOCIATION OF STATE DAM SAFETY OFFICIALS (ASDSO) SENIOR UNDERGRADUATE SCHOLARSHIP
• *See page 168*

BROWN AND CALDWELL

http://www.brownandcaldwell.com

ECKENFELDER SCHOLARSHIP
• *See page 169*

MINORITY SCHOLARSHIP PROGRAM
• *See page 169*

FLORIDA ENGINEERING SOCIETY

http://www.fleng.org/scholarships.cfm

ACEC/FLORIDA SCHOLARSHIP
• *See page 317*

LABROOTS INC.

http://www.LabRoots.com

LABROOTS STEM SCHOLARSHIP
• *See page 116*

THE LAND CONSERVANCY OF NEW JERSEY

http://www.tlc-nj.org/

ROGERS FAMILY SCHOLARSHIP
• *See page 172*

RUSSELL W. MYERS SCHOLARSHIP
• *See page 172*

MASSACHUSETTS ASSOCIATION OF LAND SURVEYORS AND CIVIL ENGINEERS

http://www.malsce.org/

MALSCE SCHOLARSHIPS
• *See page 321*

NEXTSTEPU

http://www.nextstepu.com/

$1,500 STEM SCHOLARSHIP
• *See page 120*

OREGON STUDENT ASSISTANCE COMMISSION

https://oregonstudentaid.gov/

PROFESSIONAL LAND SURVEYORS OF OREGON SCHOLARSHIP
Award for students enrolled in Oregon public and nonprofit colleges and engaged in a course of study leading to land-surveying career. Must intend to take Fundamentals of Land Surveying exam. Additional essay stating education/career goals and their relation to land surveying is required. Based on financial need.

Academic Fields/Career Goals: Surveying, Surveying Technology, Cartography, or Geographic Information Science.

Award: Scholarship for use in freshman, sophomore, junior, or senior years; not renewable.

Eligibility Requirements: Applicant must be enrolled or expecting to enroll full-time at a two-year or four-year institution or university and studying in Oregon. Available to U.S. citizens.

Application Requirements: Application form, essay, financial need analysis. *Deadline:* March 1.

Contact: Melissa Adams, Scholarship Processing Coordinator
Phone: 541-687-7409
E-mail: melissa.adams@state.or.us

PROFESSIONAL CONSTRUCTION ESTIMATORS ASSOCIATION

http://www.pcea.org/

TED G. WILSON MEMORIAL SCHOLARSHIP FOUNDATION
• *See page 211*

RHODE ISLAND SOCIETY OF PROFESSIONAL LAND SURVEYORS

http://www.rispls.org/

PIERRE H. GUILLEMETTE SCHOLARSHIP

Scholarship available to any Rhode Island resident enrolled in a certificate or degree program in land surveying at a qualified institution of higher learning.

Academic Fields/Career Goals: Surveying, Surveying Technology, Cartography, or Geographic Information Science.

Award: Scholarship for use in freshman, sophomore, junior, or senior years; not renewable.

Eligibility Requirements: Applicant must be enrolled or expecting to enroll full- or part-time at a four-year institution or university and resident of Rhode Island. Available to U.S. citizens.

Application Requirements: Application form, resume, transcript.
Deadline: October 30.

Contact: Scholarship Coordinator
Rhode Island Society of Professional Land Surveyors
PO Box 544
East Greenwich, RI 02818
Phone: 401-294-1262
E-mail: info@rispls.org

SOIL AND WATER CONSERVATION SOCIETY-MISSOURI SHOW-ME CHAPTER

http://www.moswcs.org/

MO SHOW-ME CHAPTER SWCS SCHOLARSHIP
• *See page 111*

THERAPY/ REHABILITATION

101ST AIRBORNE DIVISION ASSOCIATION

http://www.screamingeaglefoundation.org/

AL & WILLIAMARY VISTE SCHOLARSHIP
• *See page 114*

ALBERTA HERITAGE SCHOLARSHIP FUND

http://www.alis.alberta.ca/

ABORIGINAL HEALTH CAREERS BURSARY
• *See page 167*

AMERICAN FOUNDATION FOR THE BLIND

http://www.afb.org/

DELTA GAMMA FOUNDATION FLORENCE MARGARET HARVEY MEMORIAL SCHOLARSHIP
• *See page 266*

RUDOLPH DILLMAN MEMORIAL SCHOLARSHIP
• *See page 266*

AMERICAN INDIAN SCIENCE AND ENGINEERING SOCIETY

http://www.aises.org/

A.T. ANDERSON MEMORIAL SCHOLARSHIP PROGRAM
• *See page 121*

AMERICAN LEGION AUXILIARY DEPARTMENT OF COLORADO

http://www.alacolorado.com

AMERICAN LEGION AUXILIARY DEPARTMENT OF COLORADO PAST PRESIDENTS' PARLEY HEALTH CARE PROFESSIONAL SCHOLARSHIPNURSES SCHOLARSHIP
• *See page 147*

AMERICAN LEGION AUXILIARY DEPARTMENT OF MICHIGAN

http://www.michalaux.org/

AMERICAN LEGION AUXILIARY DEPARTMENT OF MICHIGAN MEDICAL CAREER SCHOLARSHIP
• *See page 369*

AMERICAN OCCUPATIONAL THERAPY FOUNDATION INC.

http://www.aotf.org/

CARLOTTA WELLES SCHOLARSHIP
• *See page 370*

AMERICAN PHYSICAL THERAPY ASSOCIATION

http://www.apta.org/honorsawards

MARY MCMILLAN SCHOLARSHIP AWARD
• *See page 267*

AMERICAN RESPIRATORY CARE FOUNDATION

http://www.arcfoundation.org/

JIMMY A. YOUNG MEMORIAL EDUCATION RECOGNITION AWARD
• *See page 370*

MORTON B. DUGGAN, JR. MEMORIAL EDUCATION RECOGNITION AWARD
• *See page 371*

SEPRACOR ACHIEVEMENT AWARD FOR EXCELLENCE IN PULMONARY DISEASE STATE MANAGEMENT
• *See page 371*

THE ARC NEW YORK

https://www.nysarc.org/

JAMES F. REVILLE SCHOLARSHIP
• *See page 366*

ARRL FOUNDATION INC.

http://www.arrl.org/

CAROLE J. STREETER, KB9JBR, SCHOLARSHIP
• *See page 254*

ASSOCIATION FOR EDUCATION AND REHABILITATION OF THE BLIND AND VISUALLY IMPAIRED

http://www.aerbvi.org/

WILLIAM AND DOROTHY FERRELL SCHOLARSHIP
• *See page 268*

AVACARE MEDICAL

https://avacaremedical.com

AVACARE MEDICAL SCHOLARSHIP
• *See page 115*

BETHESDA LUTHERAN COMMUNITIES

http://www.bethesdalutherancommunities.org/scholarships

DEVELOPMENTAL DISABILITIES SCHOLASTIC ACHIEVEMENT SCHOLARSHIP FOR COLLEGE STUDENTS WHO ARE LUTHERAN
• *See page 254*

CONTINENTAL SOCIETY, DAUGHTERS OF INDIAN WARS

http://www.csdiw.org/

CONTINENTAL SOCIETY, DAUGHTERS OF INDIAN WARS SCHOLARSHIP
• *See page 242*

CYNTHIA E. MORGAN SCHOLARSHIP FUND (CEMS)

http://www.cemsfund.com/

CYNTHIA E. MORGAN MEMORIAL SCHOLARSHIP FUND, INC.
• *See page 334*

THE EXPERT INSTITUTE

https://www.theexpertinstitute.com

ANNUAL HEALTHCARE AND LIFE SCIENCES SCHOLARSHIP
• *See page 170*

HEALTH PROFESSIONS EDUCATION FOUNDATION

http://www.healthprofessions.ca.gov/

ALLIED HEALTHCARE SCHOLARSHIP PROGRAM
• *See page 165*

INTERMOUNTAIN MEDICAL IMAGING

https://www.aboutimi.com/

INTERMOUNTAIN MEDICAL IMAGING SCHOLARSHIP
• *See page 147*

INTERNATIONAL ORDER OF THE KING'S DAUGHTERS AND SONS

http://www.iokds.org/

HEALTH CAREERS SCHOLARSHIP
• *See page 255*

KETAMINE CLINICS OF LOS ANGELES

http://www.ketamineclinics.com/

KETAMINE CLINICS OF LOS ANGELES SCHOLARSHIP PROGRAM
• *See page 165*

LADIES AUXILIARY TO THE VETERANS OF FOREIGN WARS, DEPARTMENT OF MAINE

http://mainevfw.org/

FRANCES L. BOOTH MEDICAL SCHOLARSHIP SPONSORED BY LAVFW DEPARTMENT OF MAINE
• *See page 375*

LAW OFFICES OF PROSPER SHAKED

https://www.prosperlaw.com/

PROSPER SHAKED SCHOLARSHIP FOR FUTURE MEDICAL PROFESSIONALS
• *See page 166*

MARYLAND STATE HIGHER EDUCATION COMMISSION

http://www.mhec.state.md.us/

JANET L. HOFFMANN LOAN ASSISTANCE REPAYMENT PROGRAM
• *See page 272*

MEDICAL SCRUBS COLLECTION

http://medicalscrubscollection.com

MEDICAL SCRUBS COLLECTION SCHOLARSHIP
• *See page 120*

MICHAEL MOODY FITNESS

http://www.michaelmoodyfitness.com/

MICHAEL MOODY FITNESS SCHOLARSHIP
• *See page 166*

NATIONAL AMBUCS INC.

http://www.ambucs.org/

AMBUCS SCHOLARS-SCHOLARSHIPS FOR THERAPISTS
• *See page 148*

NATIONAL ATHLETIC TRAINERS' ASSOCIATION RESEARCH AND EDUCATION FOUNDATION

http://www.natafoundation.org/

NATIONAL ATHLETIC TRAINERS' ASSOCIATION RESEARCH AND EDUCATION FOUNDATION SCHOLARSHIP PROGRAM
• See page 376

NATIONAL SOCIETY DAUGHTERS OF THE AMERICAN REVOLUTION

http://www.dar.org/

NATIONAL SOCIETY DAUGHTERS OF THE AMERICAN REVOLUTION OCCUPATIONAL THERAPY SCHOLARSHIP

Scholarship of $1000 for students who are in financial need and have been accepted or are attending an accredited school of occupational therapy including art, music or physical therapy. A letter of acceptance into the occupational therapy program or the transcript stating the applicant is in the occupational therapy program must be included with the application.

Academic Fields/Career Goals: Therapy/Rehabilitation.

Award: Scholarship for use in freshman, sophomore, junior, senior, or graduate years; not renewable. *Amount:* $1000.

Eligibility Requirements: Applicant must be enrolled or expecting to enroll full- or part-time at a two-year or four-year institution or university. Available to U.S. citizens.

Application Requirements: Application form, essay, financial need analysis. *Deadline:* February 15.

Contact: Lakeisha Graham, Manager, Office of the Reporter General
   Phone: 202-628-1776
   Fax: 202-879-3348
   E-mail: nsdarscholarships@dar.org

OREGON STUDENT ASSISTANCE COMMISSION

https://oregonstudentaid.gov/

MARION A. LINDEMAN SCHOLARSHIP
• See page 376

PACERS FOUNDATION INC.

http://www.pacersfoundation.org/

LINDA CRAIG MEMORIAL SCHOLARSHIP PRESENTED BY ST. VINCENT SPORTS MEDICINE
• See page 377

PILOT INTERNATIONAL

https://www.pilotinternational.org/

PILOT INTERNATIONAL SCHOLARSHIP
• See page 377

THE RECOVERY VILLAGE

https://www.therecoveryvillage.com/

RECOVERY VILLAGE HEALTHCARE SCHOLARSHIP
• See page 256

SCARLETT FAMILY FOUNDATION SCHOLARSHIP PROGRAM

http://www.scarlettfoundation.org/

SCHOLARSHIP FOR STUDENTS PURSUING A BUSINESS OR STEM DEGREE
• See page 91

STRAIGHTFORWARD MEDIA

http://www.straightforwardmedia.com/

STRAIGHTFORWARD MEDIA MEDICAL PROFESSIONS SCHOLARSHIP
• See page 257

UNITED NEGRO COLLEGE FUND

http://www.uncf.org/

HCN/APRICITY RESOURCES SCHOLARS PROGRAM
• See page 93

U.S. DEPARTMENT OF HEALTH AND HUMAN SERVICES

http://www.hhs.gov/

U. S. PUBLIC HEALTH SERVICE-HEALTH RESOURCES AND SERVICES ADMINISTRATION, BUREAU OF HEALTH PROFESSIONS SCHOLARSHIPS FOR DISADVANTAGED STUDENTS
• See page 257

TRADE/TECHNICAL SPECIALTIES

AIRCRAFT ELECTRONICS ASSOCIATION EDUCATIONAL FOUNDATION

http://www.aea.net/

DUTCH AND GINGER ARVER SCHOLARSHIP
• See page 149

GARMIN-JERRY SMITH MEMORIAL SCHOLARSHIP
• See page 149

GARMIN SCHOLARSHIP
• See page 149

LEE TARBOX MEMORIAL SCHOLARSHIP
• See page 149

LOWELL GAYLOR MEMORIAL SCHOLARSHIP
• See page 149

MID-CONTINENT INSTRUMENT SCHOLARSHIP
• See page 150

ALBERTA HERITAGE SCHOLARSHIP FUND

http://www.alis.alberta.ca/

REGISTERED APPRENTICESHIP PROGRAM/CAREER AND TECHNOLOGIES STUDIES (RAPS/CTS) SCHOLARSHIPS

Scholarships of CAN$1000 available for high school graduates who are registered as apprentices in a trade while in high school to encourage recipients to continue their apprenticeship or occupational training programs after graduation. Must be a Canadian citizen or landed immigrant and Alberta resident. For more details see website http://alis.alberta.ca.

Academic Fields/Career Goals: Trade/Technical Specialties.

Award: Scholarship for use in freshman year; not renewable. *Number:* 500.

Eligibility Requirements: Applicant must be enrolled or expecting to enroll full-time at a technical institution and resident of Alberta. Available to Canadian citizens.

Application Requirements: Application form, essay, recommendations or references. *Deadline:* June 30.

Contact: Scholarship Committee
Phone: 780-427-8640
E-mail: scholarships@gov.ab.ca

AMERICAN CHEMICAL SOCIETY

http://www.acs.org/

AMERICAN CHEMICAL SOCIETY SCHOLARS PROGRAM
• *See page 187*

AMERICAN LEGION DEPARTMENT OF PENNSYLVANIA

http://www.pa-legion.com/

ROBERT W. VALIMONT ENDOWMENT FUND SCHOLARSHIP (PART II)

Scholarships for any Pennsylvania high school senior seeking admission to a two-year college, post-high school trade/technical school, or training program. Must attend school in Pennsylvania. Continuation of award is based on grades. Renewable award of $600. Number of awards varies from year to year. Membership in an American Legion post in Pennsylvania is not required, but it must be documented if it does apply.

Academic Fields/Career Goals: Trade/Technical Specialties.

Award: Scholarship for use in freshman year; renewable. *Amount:* $600.

Eligibility Requirements: Applicant must be high school student; planning to enroll or expecting to enroll full-time at a two-year or technical institution; resident of Pennsylvania and studying in Pennsylvania. Applicant must have 2.5 GPA or higher. Available to U.S. citizens.

Application Requirements: Application form, financial need analysis, test scores, transcript. *Deadline:* May 30.

Contact: Debbie Watson, Emblem Sales Supervisor
American Legion Department of Pennsylvania
PO Box 2324
Harrisburg, PA 17105-2324
Phone: 717-730-9100
Fax: 717-975-2836
E-mail: hq@pa-legion.com

AMERICAN SOCIETY OF CERTIFIED ENGINEERING TECHNICIANS

http://www.ascet.org/

KURT H. AND DONNA M. SCHULER SMALL GRANT
• *See page 205*

AMERICAN SOCIETY OF HEATING, REFRIGERATING, AND AIR CONDITIONING ENGINEERS, INC.

http://www.ashrae.org/

ALWIN B. NEWTON SCHOLARSHIP
• *See page 281*

ASHRAE GENERAL SCHOLARSHIPS
• *See page 294*

DUANE HANSON SCHOLARSHIP
• *See page 282*

FRANK M. CODA SCHOLARSHIP
• *See page 282*

HENRY ADAMS SCHOLARSHIP
• *See page 282*

LYNN G. BELLENGER SCHOLARSHIP
• *See page 282*

REUBEN TRANE SCHOLARSHIP
• *See page 282*

AMERICAN WELDING SOCIETY

http://www.aws.org/

AMERICAN WELDING SOCIETY DISTRICT SCHOLARSHIP PROGRAM
• *See page 296*

ARSHAM AMIRIKIAN ENGINEERING SCHOLARSHIP
• *See page 206*

DONALD F. HASTINGS SCHOLARSHIP
• *See page 296*

EDWARD J. BRADY MEMORIAL SCHOLARSHIP
• *See page 296*

HOWARD E. AND WILMA J. ADKINS MEMORIAL SCHOLARSHIP
• *See page 296*

MILLER ELECTRIC INTERNATIONAL WORLD SKILLS COMPETITION SCHOLARSHIP
• *See page 296*

MILLER ELECTRIC MFG. CO. SCHOLARSHIP
• *See page 297*

ASSOCIATED GENERAL CONTRACTORS EDUCATION AND RESEARCH FOUNDATION

http://www.agcfoundation.org/

WORKFORCE DEVELOPMENT SCHOLARSHIP
• *See page 237*

AUTOMOTIVE AFTERMARKET SCHOLARSHIPS

http://www.automotivescholarships.com/

AUTOMOTIVE AFTERMARKET SCHOLARSHIPS
• *See page 177*

ENVIRONMENTAL CARE ASSOCIATION OF IDAHO

http://www.eacofidaho.org

ECA SCHOLARSHIP
• *See page 385*

FABRICATORS AND MANUFACTURERS ASSOCIATION FOUNDATION

http://www.nutsandboltsfoundation.org/scholarships/

COLLEGE AND TRADE/TECHNICAL SCHOOL SCHOLARSHIPS
• *See page 154*

GRAND RAPIDS COMMUNITY FOUNDATION

http://www.grfoundation.org/

DAROOGE FAMILY SCHOLARSHIP FOR CONSTRUCTION TRADES
• *See page 133*

IFDA EDUCATIONAL FOUNDATION

http://www.ifdaef.org/

IFDA STUDENT MEMBER SCHOLARSHIP
• *See page 399*

MANUFACTURERS ASSOCIATION OF MAINE

http://www.mainemfg.com/

MAINE MANUFACTURING CAREER AND TRAINING FOUNDATION SCHOLARSHIP
• *See page 156*

MARYLAND STATE HIGHER EDUCATION COMMISSION

http://www.mhec.state.md.us/

CHARLES W. RILEY FIRE AND EMERGENCY MEDICAL SERVICES TUITION REIMBURSEMENT PROGRAM
• *See page 349*

MIDWEST ROOFING CONTRACTORS ASSOCIATION

http://www.mrca.org/

MRCA FOUNDATION SCHOLARSHIP PROGRAM
• *See page 135*

NATIONAL ASSOCIATION OF WOMEN IN CONSTRUCTION

http://www.nawic.org/

NAWIC CONSTRUCTION TRADES SCHOLARSHIP
Scholarship for women pursuing a trade apprenticeship program. Only for students attending school in the United States or Canada.

Academic Fields/Career Goals: Trade/Technical Specialties.

Award: Scholarship for use in sophomore or junior years; not renewable. *Number:* 1. *Amount:* $1000–$2000.

Eligibility Requirements: Applicant must be enrolled or expecting to enroll full-time at a technical institution. Available to U.S. and Canadian citizens.

Application Requirements: Application form, essay, transcript. *Deadline:* March 15.

Contact: Scholarship Committee
National Association of Women in Construction
327 South Adams Street
Fort Worth, TX 76104
Phone: 817-877-5551
Fax: 817-877-0324

NAWIC UNDERGRADUATE SCHOLARSHIPS
• *See page 135*

NEXTSTEPU

http://www.nextstepu.com/

$1,500 STEM SCHOLARSHIP
• *See page 120*

NORTH CAROLINA COMMUNITY COLLEGE SYSTEM-STUDENT DEVELOPMENT SERVICES

http://www.nccommunitycolleges.edu/student-services

WACHOVIA TECHNICAL SCHOLARSHIP PROGRAM
One scholarship per college valued at $500 each. These scholarships are distributed among the 58 colleges in the community college system, which may be distributed in two payments: fall semester, $250; and spring semester, $250. To qualify as a candidate for these scholarships, a person must meet the following criteria: 1. Is a full-time student enrolled in the second year of a two-year educational/technical program. 2. Demonstrate financial need. 3. Demonstrate scholastic promise. 4. Use the scholarship to pay for tuition, books, and transportation. The recipients of the scholarships will be selected each year from applicants meeting the above criteria at local colleges.

Academic Fields/Career Goals: Trade/Technical Specialties.

Award: Scholarship for use in freshman or sophomore years; not renewable. *Amount:* $500.

Eligibility Requirements: Applicant must be enrolled or expecting to enroll full-time at a two-year or technical institution; resident of North Carolina and studying in North Carolina. Available to U.S. citizens.

Application Requirements: Application form, essay. *Deadline:* continuous.

Contact: Charletta Sims Evans, Associate Director of Student
Development Services
Phone: 919-807-7106
E-mail: simsc@nccommunitycolleges.edu

OIL & ENERGY SERVICE PROFESSIONALS

http://www.thinkoesp.org

DAVE NELSEN SCHOLARSHIPS
OESP is always eager to honor members who are propelling the industry, as well as supporting future energy professionals, who will one day become the backbone of our industry. Focusing on the future, The Dave Nelsen Scholarship, established in 1999, has given out more than $300,000 to students interested in pursuing careers in the energy service industry. Through our generous sponsors, OESP awards between three and six $5,000 scholarships each year. The Association seeks sponsors willing to donate $2,500 to our worthy recipients, with OESP pleased to continually provide matching funds. To be considered, scholarship candidates are asked to write a 500–word essay, highlighting how their educational background has prepared them for career success. Applicants are also asked to share their career goals for the next 5–10 years.

Academic Fields/Career Goals: Trade/Technical Specialties.

Award: Scholarship for use in freshman, sophomore, junior, or senior years; not renewable. *Number:* 3–6. *Amount:* $5000.

Eligibility Requirements: Applicant must be enrolled or expecting to enroll full- or part-time at a two-year or four-year or technical institution. Available to U.S. citizens.

Application Requirements: Application form, essay. *Deadline:* April 2.

OREGON SHEEP GROWERS ASSOCIATION

http://www.sheeporegon.com

OREGON SHEEP GROWERS ASSOCIATION MEMORIAL SCHOLARSHIP
• *See page 110*

OREGON STUDENT ASSISTANCE COMMISSION

https://oregonstudentaid.gov/

DAVID L. MASSEE EDUCATION SCHOLARSHIP

Award for students who are enrolled at least half time in trade or vocational programs in private or two-year public colleges in the U.S. Automatically renewable if renewal criteria is met.

Academic Fields/Career Goals: Trade/Technical Specialties.

Award: Scholarship for use in freshman, sophomore, junior, or senior years; not renewable.

Eligibility Requirements: Applicant must be enrolled or expecting to enroll full- or part-time at a two-year institution. Available to U.S. citizens.

Application Requirements: Application form. *Deadline:* March 1.

Contact: Melissa Adams, Scholarship Processing Coordinator
Phone: 541-687-7409
E-mail: melissa.adams@state.or.us

HUFFSTUTTER FAMILY STYLIST SCHOLARSHIP
• *See page 241*

JIM AND DIANNA MURPHY SCHOLARSHIP

Scholarship for graduates of Oregon high schools (including GED recipients and home-schooled graduates) who are majoring in programs to become diesel mechanic/technician, driver/operator of commercial vehicle/bus/truck, and related areas leading to a career in the commercial trucking industry or in diesel technologies. Must enroll at least half-time at a Oregon two-year community college or for-profit school. Financial need may or may not be considered.

Academic Fields/Career Goals: Trade/Technical Specialties.

Award: Scholarship for use in freshman or sophomore years; not renewable.

Eligibility Requirements: Applicant must be enrolled or expecting to enroll full- or part-time at a two-year or technical institution; resident of Oregon and studying in Oregon. Available to U.S. citizens.

Application Requirements: Application form. *Deadline:* March 1.

Contact: Melissa Adams, Scholarship Processing Coordinator
Phone: 541-687-7409
E-mail: melissa.adams@state.or.us

TECHNICAL TRAINING FUND SCHOLARSHIP
• *See page 143*

PLUMBING-HEATING-COOLING CONTRACTORS EDUCATION FOUNDATION

http://www.phccfoundation.org/scholarships

BRADFORD WHITE CORPORATION SCHOLARSHIP
• *See page 380*

DELTA FAUCET COMPANY SCHOLARSHIP PROGRAM
• *See page 182*

PHCC EDUCATIONAL FOUNDATION NEED-BASED SCHOLARSHIP
• *See page 182*

PHCC EDUCATIONAL FOUNDATION SCHOLARSHIP PROGRAM
• *See page 182*

PROFESSIONAL CONSTRUCTION ESTIMATORS ASSOCIATION

http://www.pcea.org/

TED G. WILSON MEMORIAL SCHOLARSHIP FOUNDATION
• *See page 211*

ROCKY MOUNTAIN COAL MINING INSTITUTE

http://www.rmcmi.org/

ROCKY MOUNTAIN COAL MINING INSTITUTE TECHNICAL SCHOLARSHIP

Scholarship for a first or second year student at a two-year technical/trade school in good standing at the time of selection. The student must be in a discipline related to potential use in the coal mining industry. Must be U.S. citizen and a legal resident of one of the Rocky Mountain Coal Mining Institute member states.

Academic Fields/Career Goals: Trade/Technical Specialties.

Award: Scholarship for use in freshman or sophomore years; not renewable. *Number:* 8. *Amount:* $1000.

Eligibility Requirements: Applicant must be enrolled or expecting to enroll full-time at a technical institution and resident of Arizona, Colorado, Montana, New Mexico, North Dakota, Texas, Utah, Wyoming. Available to U.S. citizens.

Application Requirements: Application form, essay, interview. *Deadline:* February 1.

Contact: Shahreen Salam, Executive Assistant
Rocky Mountain Coal Mining Institute
8057 South Yukon Way
Littleton, CO 80128-5510
Phone: 303-948-3300
Fax: 303-948-1132
E-mail: mail@rmcmi.org

SOCIETY OF MANUFACTURING ENGINEERS EDUCATION FOUNDATION

http://www.smeef.org/

CHAPTER 198-DOWNRIVER DETROIT SCHOLARSHIP
• *See page 325*

CHAPTER 67-PHOENIX SCHOLARSHIP
• *See page 326*

CLINTON J. HELTON MANUFACTURING SCHOLARSHIP AWARD FUND
• *See page 327*

E. WAYNE KAY COMMUNITY COLLEGE SCHOLARSHIP AWARD
• *See page 327*

E. WAYNE KAY SCHOLARSHIP
• *See page 327*

FORT WAYNE CHAPTER 56 SCHOLARSHIP
• *See page 328*

NORTH CENTRAL REGION 9 SCHOLARSHIP
• See page 328

WICHITA CHAPTER 52 SCHOLARSHIP
• See page 328

WILLIAM E. WEISEL SCHOLARSHIP FUND
• See page 287

SOCIETY OF PLASTICS ENGINEERS FOUNDATION (SPE)

http://www.4spe.org/

FLEMING/BLASZCAK SCHOLARSHIP
• See page 195

GULF COAST HURRICANE SCHOLARSHIP
• See page 196

SOCIETY OF PLASTICS ENGINEERS SCHOLARSHIP PROGRAM
• See page 196

SPECIALTY EQUIPMENT MARKET ASSOCIATION

http://www.sema.org/

SEMA MEMORIAL SCHOLARSHIP FUND
• See page 92

STRAIGHTFORWARD MEDIA

http://www.straightforwardmedia.com/

STRAIGHTFORWARD MEDIA VOCATIONAL-TECHNICAL SCHOOL SCHOLARSHIP
• See page 118

TRUCKER TO TRUCKER, LLC

http://www.truckertotrucker.com/

TRUCKER TO TRUCKER SCHOLARSHIP

$500 Scholarship to attend a commercial driver's training program in the US. Applicants will need to fill out a short online application and upload a 300-500 word essay.

Academic Fields/Career Goals: Trade/Technical Specialties.

Award: Scholarship for use in freshman, sophomore, junior, or senior years; not renewable. *Number:* 2. *Amount:* $500.

Eligibility Requirements: Applicant must be age 18-99 and enrolled or expecting to enroll full-time at a technical institution. Available to U.S. citizens.

Application Requirements: Application form, essay. *Deadline:* November 15.

Contact: Scholarship Coordinator
E-mail: scholarship@truckertotrucker.com

UNITED COMMUNITY SERVICES FOR WORKING FAMILIES

http://www.ucswf.org

RONALD LORAH MEMORIAL SCHOLARSHIP

One-time award available to a union member, spouse of a union member, or child of a union member. Must be a resident of Pennsylvania. Must submit essay that is clear, concise, persuasive and show an understanding of unions.

Academic Fields/Career Goals: Trade/Technical Specialties.

Award: Scholarship for use in freshman, sophomore, junior, or senior years; not renewable. *Number:* 2. *Amount:* $500–$750.

Eligibility Requirements: Applicant must be enrolled or expecting to enroll full-time at a two-year or four-year or technical institution or university and resident of Pennsylvania. Applicant or parent of applicant must be member of AFL-CIO. Available to U.S. citizens.

Application Requirements: Application form, essay, financial need analysis, transcript. *Deadline:* July 31.

Contact: Victoria Henshaw, Executive Director
United Community Services for Working Families
1251 North Front Street
Reading, PA 19601
E-mail: vhenshaw@ucswf.org

VERMONT SPACE GRANT CONSORTIUM

http://www.cems.uvm.edu/vsgc

VERMONT SPACE GRANT CONSORTIUM
• See page 104

WOMEN IN LOGISTICS, NORTHERN CALIFORNIA

http://www.womeninlogistics.org/

WOMEN IN LOGISTICS SCHOLARSHIP
• See page 185

WOMEN'S JEWELRY ASSOCIATION

http://www.womensjewelryassociation.com

WOMEN'S JEWELRY ASSOCIATION STUDENT SCHOLARSHIP
• See page 146

WYOMING TRUCKING ASSOCIATION SCHOLARSHIP FUND TRUST

http://www.wytruck.org/

WYOMING TRUCKING ASSOCIATION SCHOLARSHIP TRUST FUND
• See page 95

YOUTH MARITIME TRAINING ASSOCIATION

http://ymta.net/

NORM MANLY—YMTA MARITIME EDUCATIONAL SCHOLARSHIPS
• See page 425

TRANSPORTATION

AMERICAN BUS ASSOCIATION

https://www.buses.org/

ABA ACADEMIC MERIT SCHOLARSHIPS

Academic Merit Scholarships are open to both ABA and non-ABA Members. The applicant must be a freshman, sophomore; junior, senior, or graduate student at an accredited University (4-year university/college or junior college) and must have a declared major or course of study relevant to the transportation, travel and tourism industry and must possess a cumulative GPA of 3.4 or higher. Two scholarships are awarded, in the amount $5,000 each. Apply online between December 7th and April 6th. Create an account to submit applications, as well as check the status of your applications and make any necessary changes before the program deadline.

Academic Fields/Career Goals: Transportation; Travel/Tourism.

Award: Scholarship for use in freshman, sophomore, junior, senior, graduate, or postgraduate years; not renewable. *Number:* 2. *Amount:* $5000.

Eligibility Requirements: Applicant must be enrolled or expecting to enroll full-time at a four-year institution. Applicant must have 3.5 GPA or higher. Available to U.S. and Canadian citizens.

Application Requirements: Application form, essay. *Deadline:* April 6.

Contact: Zoe Deloglos, Special Projects Coordinator
American Bus Association
111 K Street NE
9th Floor
Washington, DC 20002
Phone: 202-202-218-7222
Fax: 202-202-842-0850
E-mail: zdeloglos@buses.org

ABA DIVERSITY SCHOLARSHIPS

The Diversity Scholarship focuses on broadening the number of traditionally underrepresented groups in the management and operation ranks of the transportation, travel, and tourism industry. Eligible candidates must have completed, at a minimum, their first year of college at an accredited university; must have a declared major or course of study relevant to the transportation, travel, and tourism industry; and must have a cumulative 3.0 GPA. Applicants are required to submit a 500-word essay discussing the role they hope to play in advancing the future of the transportation, motorcoach, travel, and tourism/hospitality industry.

Academic Fields/Career Goals: Transportation; Travel/Tourism.

Award: Scholarship for use in sophomore, junior, or senior years; not renewable. *Number:* 1. *Amount:* $5000.

Eligibility Requirements: Applicant must be enrolled or expecting to enroll full- or part-time at an institution or university. Applicant must have 3.0 GPA or higher. Available to U.S. and Canadian citizens.

Application Requirements: Application form, essay. *Deadline:* April 6.

Contact: Zoe Deloglos, Special Projects Coordinator
American Bus Association
111 K Street NE
9th Floor
Washington, DC 20002
Phone: 202-202-218-7222
Fax: 202-202-842-0850
E-mail: zdeloglos@buses.org

AMERICAN COUNCIL OF ENGINEERING COMPANIES OF PENNSYLVANIA (ACEC/PA)

http://www.acecpa.org/

ERIC J. GENNUSO AND LEROY D. (BUD) LOY, JR. SCHOLARSHIP PROGRAM
• *See page 187*

AMERICAN INDIAN SCIENCE AND ENGINEERING SOCIETY

http://www.aises.org/

A.T. ANDERSON MEMORIAL SCHOLARSHIP PROGRAM
• *See page 121*

AMERICAN PUBLIC TRANSPORTATION FOUNDATION

http://www.apta.com/

DAN REICHARD JR. SCHOLARSHIP
• *See page 176*

DR. GEORGE M. SMERK SCHOLARSHIP

Scholarship for study towards a career in career in public transit management. Must be sponsored by APTA member organization.

Minimum GPA of 3.0 required. College sophomores (30 hours or more satisfactorily completed), juniors, seniors, or those seeking advanced degrees may apply.

Academic Fields/Career Goals: Transportation.

Award: Scholarship for use in sophomore, junior, senior, or graduate years; not renewable. *Number:* 1. *Amount:* $2500.

Eligibility Requirements: Applicant must be enrolled or expecting to enroll full-time at a two-year or four-year institution or university. Applicant must have 3.0 GPA or higher. Available to U.S. citizens.

Application Requirements: Application form, essay, financial need analysis, recommendations or references, test scores, transcript, verification of enrollment for the fall semester, copy of fee schedule from the college/university. *Deadline:* June 16.

Contact: Pamela Boswell, Vice President of Program Management
American Public Transportation Foundation
1666 K Street, NW
Washington, DC 20006-1215
Phone: 202-496-4803
Fax: 202-496-2323
E-mail: pboswell@apta.com

DONALD C. HYDE ESSAY PROGRAM

Award of $500 for the best response to the required essay component of the program.

Academic Fields/Career Goals: Transportation.

Award: Prize for use in sophomore, junior, senior, or graduate years; not renewable. *Number:* 1. *Amount:* $500.

Eligibility Requirements: Applicant must be enrolled or expecting to enroll full-time at a two-year or four-year institution or university. Applicant must have 3.0 GPA or higher. Available to U.S. and Canadian citizens.

Application Requirements: Application form, entry in a contest, essay, financial need analysis, recommendations or references, transcript. *Deadline:* June 16.

Contact: Pamela Boswell, Vice President of Program Management
American Public Transportation Foundation
1666 K Street, NW
Washington, DC 20006-1215
Phone: 202-496-4803
Fax: 202-496-2323
E-mail: pboswell@apta.com

JACK GILSTRAP SCHOLARSHIP
• *See page 310*

PARSONS BRINCKERHOFF-JIM LAMMIE SCHOLARSHIP

Scholarship for study in public transportation engineering field. Must be sponsored by APTA member organization and complete internship with APTA member organization. Minimum GPA of 3.0 required.

Academic Fields/Career Goals: Transportation.

Award: Scholarship for use in sophomore, junior, senior, or graduate years; renewable. *Number:* 1. *Amount:* $2500.

Eligibility Requirements: Applicant must be enrolled or expecting to enroll full-time at a two-year or four-year institution or university. Applicant must have 3.0 GPA or higher. Available to U.S. and Canadian citizens.

Application Requirements: Application form, essay, financial need analysis, recommendations or references, transcript, verification of enrollment for the current year and copy of fee schedule from the college/university. *Deadline:* June 16.

Contact: Pamela Boswell, Vice President of Program Management
American Public Transportation Foundation
1666 K Street, NW
Washington, DC 20006-1215
Phone: 202-496-4803
Fax: 202-496-2323
E-mail: pboswell@apta.com

TRANSIT HALL OF FAME SCHOLARSHIP AWARD PROGRAM
• *See page 204*

AMERICAN SOCIETY OF CERTIFIED ENGINEERING TECHNICIANS

http://www.ascet.org/

KURT H. AND DONNA M. SCHULER SMALL GRANT
• *See page 205*

ASSOCIATED GENERAL CONTRACTORS OF NEW YORK STATE, LLC

https://www.agcnys.org/programs/scholarship/

ASSOCIATED GENERAL CONTRACTORS NYS SCHOLARSHIP PROGRAM
• *See page 207*

AUTOMOTIVE WOMEN'S ALLIANCE FOUNDATION

http://awafoundation.org/index.php

AUTOMOTIVE WOMEN'S ALLIANCE FOUNDATION SCHOLARSHIPS
• *See page 81*

THE CLUNKER JUNKER

https://theclunkerjunker.com/

CLUNKER JUNKER CASH FOR CARS AND COLLEGE SCHOLARSHIP
• *See page 299*

LOGISTICS & TRANSPORTATION ASSOCIATION OF NORTH AMERICA

http://www.ltna.org

ALICE GLAISYER WARFIELD MEMORIAL SCHOLARSHIP

Award is available to currently enrolled students majoring in transportation, logistics, traffic management, or related fields. Available to citizens of the United States, Canada, and Mexico. See website for application, http://www.transportationclubinternational.com/.

Academic Fields/Career Goals: Transportation.

Award: Scholarship for use in freshman, sophomore, junior, or senior years; not renewable. *Number:* 1. *Amount:* $1500.

Eligibility Requirements: Applicant must be enrolled or expecting to enroll full- or part-time at a two-year or four-year or technical institution or university. Applicant or parent of applicant must be member of Transportation Club International. Available to U.S. and non-U.S. citizens.

Application Requirements: Application form, essay, personal photograph, recommendations or references, transcript. *Deadline:* April 30.

Contact: Katie deJonge, Executive Director
Phone: 360-898-3344
E-mail: executive.director@ltna.org

DENNY LYDIC SCHOLARSHIP

Award is available to currently enrolled college students majoring in transportation, logistics, traffic management, or related fields. Available to citizens of the United States, Canada, and Mexico. See website for application, http://www.transportationclubinternational.com/.

Academic Fields/Career Goals: Transportation.

Award: Scholarship for use in freshman, sophomore, junior, or senior years; not renewable. *Number:* 1. *Amount:* $1000.

Eligibility Requirements: Applicant must be enrolled or expecting to enroll full- or part-time at a two-year or four-year or technical institution or university. Applicant or parent of applicant must be member of Transportation Club International. Available to U.S. and non-U.S. citizens.

Application Requirements: Application form, essay, personal photograph, recommendations or references, transcript. *Deadline:* April 30.

Contact: Katie deJonge, Executive Director
Phone: 360-898-3344
E-mail: executive.director@ltna.org

TEXAS TRANSPORTATION SCHOLARSHIP

Merit-based award for a student who is at least a sophomore studying transportation, traffic management, and related fields. Must have been enrolled in a school in Texas during some phase of education (elementary, secondary, high school). Must include photo and submit three references. One-time scholarship of $1000. See website for application http://www.transportationclubinternational.com/.

Academic Fields/Career Goals: Transportation.

Award: Scholarship for use in sophomore, junior, or senior years; not renewable. *Number:* 1. *Amount:* $1000.

Eligibility Requirements: Applicant must be enrolled or expecting to enroll full- or part-time at a two-year or four-year or technical institution or university. Applicant or parent of applicant must be member of Transportation Club International. Available to U.S. citizens.

Application Requirements: Application form, essay, personal photograph, recommendations or references, transcript. *Deadline:* April 30.

Contact: Katie deJonge, Executive Director
Phone: 360-898-3344
E-mail: executive.director@ltna.org

TRANSPORTATION CLUBS INTERNATIONAL CHARLOTTE WOODS SCHOLARSHIP

Award available to an enrolled college student majoring in transportation or traffic management. Must be a member or a dependent of a member of Transportation Clubs International. Must have completed at least one year of post-high school education. One-time award of $1000. See website for application http://www.transportationclubsinternational.com/.

Academic Fields/Career Goals: Transportation.

Award: Scholarship for use in freshman, sophomore, junior, or senior years; not renewable. *Number:* 1. *Amount:* $1000.

Eligibility Requirements: Applicant must be enrolled or expecting to enroll full- or part-time at a two-year or four-year or technical institution or university. Applicant or parent of applicant must be member of Transportation Club International. Available to U.S. and non-U.S. citizens.

Application Requirements: Application form, essay, personal photograph, recommendations or references, transcript. *Deadline:* April 30.

Contact: Crystal Hunter, Program Manager
Phone: 800-377-2401
E-mail: awards@goldenkey.org

TRANSPORTATION CLUBS INTERNATIONAL FRED A. HOOPER MEMORIAL SCHOLARSHIP
• *See page 301*

TRANSPORTATION CLUBS INTERNATIONAL GINGER AND FRED DEINES CANADA SCHOLARSHIP

One-time award for a student of Canadian heritage, who is attending college or university in Canada or the United States and majoring in transportation, traffic management, logistics, or a related field. Academic merit is considered. See website for application http://www.transportationclubsinternational.com/.

Academic Fields/Career Goals: Transportation.

Award: Scholarship for use in freshman, sophomore, junior, or senior years; not renewable. *Number:* 1. *Amount:* $1500.

Eligibility Requirements: Applicant must be of Canadian heritage and Canadian citizen and enrolled or expecting to enroll full- or part-time at a two-year or four-year or technical institution or university. Applicant or parent of applicant must be member of Transportation Club International.

Application Requirements: Application form, essay, personal photograph, recommendations or references, transcript. *Deadline:* April 30.

Contact: Katie deJonge, Executive Director
Phone: 360-898-3344
E-mail: executive.director@ltna.org

TRANSPORTATION CLUBS INTERNATIONAL GINGER AND FRED DEINES MEXICO SCHOLARSHIP

Scholarship of $2000 for a Mexican student who is enrolled in an accredited institution of higher learning in a vocational or degree program in the fields of transportation, logistics or traffic management, or related fields. May be enrolled in a U.S. or Canadian institution. See website for application http://www.transportationclubinternational.com/.

Academic Fields/Career Goals: Transportation.

Award: Scholarship for use in freshman, sophomore, junior, or senior years; not renewable. *Number:* 1. *Amount:* $2000.

Eligibility Requirements: Applicant must be Mexican citizen and enrolled or expecting to enroll full- or part-time at a two-year or four-year or technical institution or university. Applicant or parent of applicant must be member of Transportation Club International. Available to Canadian and non-U.S. citizens.

Application Requirements: Application form, essay, personal photograph, recommendations or references, transcript. *Deadline:* April 30.

Contact: Katie deJonge, Executive Director
    Phone: 360-898-3344
    E-mail: executive.director@ltna.org

NATIONAL CUSTOMS BROKERS AND FORWARDERS ASSOCIATION OF AMERICA

http://www.ncbfaa.org/

NATIONAL CUSTOMS BROKERS AND FORWARDERS ASSOCIATION OF AMERICA SCHOLARSHIP AWARD

One-time award for employees of National Customs Broker & Forwarders Association of America, Inc. (NCBFAA) regular member organizations and their children. Must be studying transportation logistics or international trade full time. Require minimum 2.0 GPA.

Academic Fields/Career Goals: Transportation.

Award: Scholarship for use in freshman, sophomore, junior, or senior years; not renewable. *Number:* 1. *Amount:* $5000.

Eligibility Requirements: Applicant must be enrolled or expecting to enroll full-time at a four-year institution or university. Available to U.S. citizens.

Application Requirements: Essay. *Deadline:* January 8.

Contact: Mr. Tom Mathers, Director, Communications
    National Customs Brokers and Forwarders Association of America
    1200 18th Street, NW, Suite 901
    Washington, DC 20036
    Phone: 202-466-0222
    E-mail: tom@ncbfaa.org

OREGON STUDENT ASSISTANCE COMMISSION

https://oregonstudentaid.gov/

WESTERN ASSOCIATION OF STATE HIGHWAY AND TRANSPORTATION OFFICIALS SCHOLARSHIP

Award for students planning to enroll at least part-time as college juniors or above for fall term/semester at any four-year college or university. Career interest preference for transportation or a transportation-related field. Apply/compete annually. Based on financial need.

Academic Fields/Career Goals: Transportation.

Award: Scholarship for use in junior or senior years; not renewable.

Eligibility Requirements: Applicant must be enrolled or expecting to enroll full- or part-time at a four-year institution or university and resident of Oregon. Applicant must have 3.0 GPA or higher. Available to U.S. citizens.

Application Requirements: Application form, essay, financial need analysis. *Deadline:* March 1.

Contact: Melissa Adams, Scholarship Processing Coordinator
    Phone: 541-687-7409
    E-mail: melissa.adams@state.or.us

PLAN NEW HAMPSHIRE

http://www.plannh.org

PLAN NEW HAMPSHIRE SCHOLARSHIP AND FELLOWSHIP PROGRAM
• See page 129

SPECIALTY EQUIPMENT MARKET ASSOCIATION

http://www.sema.org/

SEMA MEMORIAL SCHOLARSHIP FUND
• See page 92

WOMEN IN LOGISTICS, NORTHERN CALIFORNIA

http://www.womeninlogistics.org/

WOMEN IN LOGISTICS SCHOLARSHIP
• See page 185

WYOMING TRUCKING ASSOCIATION SCHOLARSHIP FUND TRUST

http://www.wytruck.org/

WYOMING TRUCKING ASSOCIATION SCHOLARSHIP TRUST FUND
• See page 95

TRAVEL/TOURISM

AMERICAN BUS ASSOCIATION

https://www.buses.org/

ABA ACADEMIC MERIT SCHOLARSHIPS
• See page 538

ABA DIVERSITY SCHOLARSHIPS
• See page 539

AMERICAN HOTEL AND LODGING EDUCATIONAL FOUNDATION

http://www.ahlef.org/

AHLEF ANNUAL SCHOLARSHIP GRANT PROGRAM
• See page 244

AMERICAN HOTEL & LODGING EDUCATIONAL FOUNDATION PEPSI SCHOLARSHIP
• See page 244

ECOLAB SCHOLARSHIP PROGRAM
• See page 245

HYATT HOTELS FUND FOR MINORITY LODGING MANAGEMENT
• See page 245

INCOMING FRESHMAN SCHOLARSHIPS
• See page 245

RAMA SCHOLARSHIP FOR THE AMERICAN DREAM

COSTA RICAN VACATIONS
http://www.vacationscostarica.com/

COSTA RICAN VACATIONS SCHOLARSHIP

FUKUNAGA SCHOLARSHIP FOUNDATION
http://fukunagascholarship.com

FUKUNAGA SCHOLARSHIP FOUNDATION

HAWAII LODGING & TOURISM ASSOCIATION
http://www.hawaiilodging.org

R.W. "BOB" HOLDEN SCHOLARSHIP

MISSOURI TRAVEL COUNCIL
http://www.missouritravel.com/

BOB SMITH TOURISM SCHOLARSHIP

OHIO TRAVEL ASSOCIATION
http://www.ohiotravel.org/

BILL SCHWARTZ MEMORIAL SCHOLARSHIP

TOURISM CARES
http://www.tourismcares.org

ASTA HOLLAND AMERICA LINE UNDERGRADUATE SCHOLARSHIP
Scholarship available to a full time or part time student enrolled in the second half of their college career in a travel and tourism or hospitality related program of study at a college or university in the US or Canada.
Academic Fields/Career Goals: Travel/Tourism.
Award: Scholarship for use in sophomore, junior, or senior years; not renewable. *Number:* 1. *Amount:* $2500.
Eligibility Requirements: Applicant must be enrolled or expecting to enroll full- or part-time at a two-year or four-year institution or university. Applicant must have 3.0 GPA or higher. Available to U.S. and Canadian citizens.
Application Requirements: Application form, financial need analysis. *Deadline:* April 1.
Contact: Trish Kelly, Workforce Development Coordinator
  Phone: 781-821-5990 Ext. 214
  E-mail: scholarships@tourismcares.org

ASTA PRINCESS CRUISES SCHOLARSHIP

IATAN RONALD A. SANTANA MEMORIAL SCHOLARSHIP

NTA LA MACCHIA FAMILY SCHOLARSHIP

NTA NEW HORIZONS KATHY LETARTE SCHOLARSHIP

NTA OHIO SCHOLARSHIP

NTA PAT AND JIM HOST SCHOLARSHIP

NTA TRAVEL LEADERS SCHOLARSHIP

NTA UTAH KEITH GRIFFALL SCHOLARSHIP

UNITED NEGRO COLLEGE FUND
http://www.uncf.org/

UNCF/CARNIVAL CORPORATE SCHOLARS PROGRAM

TV/RADIO BROADCASTING

ADC RESEARCH INSTITUTE
http://www.adc.org/

JACK SHAHEEN MASS COMMUNICATIONS SCHOLARSHIP AWARD

ALABAMA BROADCASTERS ASSOCIATION
http://www.al-ba.com/

ALABAMA BROADCASTERS ASSOCIATION SCHOLARSHIP
Scholarship available to Alabama residents studying broadcasting at any accredited Alabama technical school, 2- or 4-year college, or university.
Academic Fields/Career Goals: TV/Radio Broadcasting.
Award: Scholarship for use in junior or senior years; not renewable. *Number:* up to 4. *Amount:* up to $2500.
Eligibility Requirements: Applicant must be enrolled or expecting to enroll full-time at a two-year or four-year or technical institution or university; resident of Alabama and studying in Alabama. Available to U.S. citizens.
Application Requirements: Application form, recommendations or references. *Deadline:* April 30.
Contact: Sharon Tinsley, President
  Phone: 205-982-5001
  Fax: 205-982-0015
  E-mail: stinsley@al-ba.com

ALBERTA HERITAGE SCHOLARSHIP FUND
http://www.alis.alberta.ca/

TIESSEN FOUNDATION BROADCAST SCHOLARSHIP
CAN$750 to recognize an outstanding Alberta high school student and to encourage and assist them with their post-secondary studies at any recognized post-secondary institution in Canada that offers degree or diploma programs in broadcasting. For additional information, see website http://alis.alberta.ca.
Academic Fields/Career Goals: TV/Radio Broadcasting.
Award: Scholarship for use in freshman year; not renewable.
Eligibility Requirements: Applicant must be Canadian citizen; high school student; planning to enroll or expecting to enroll full-time at a two-year or four-year or technical institution or university and resident of Alberta.

Application Requirements: Application form, essay, recommendations or references. *Deadline:* June 1.

Contact: Scholarship Committee
Phone: 780-427-8640
E-mail: scholarships@gov.ab.ca

ARRL FOUNDATION INC.

http://www.arrl.org/

ANDROSCOGGIN AMATEUR RADIO CLUB SCHOLARSHIP
• *See page 229*

ASIAN AMERICAN JOURNALISTS ASSOCIATION

http://www.aaja.org/

CIC/ANNA CHENNAULT SCHOLARSHIP
• *See page 217*

MARY QUON MOY ING MEMORIAL SCHOLARSHIP AWARD
• *See page 217*

VINCENT CHIN MEMORIAL SCHOLARSHIP
• *See page 217*

ASIAN AMERICAN JOURNALISTS ASSOCIATION, SEATTLE CHAPTER.

http://www.aajaseattle.org/

NORTHWEST JOURNALISTS OF COLOR SCHOLARSHIP
• *See page 96*

ASSOCIATED PRESS

http://www.aptra.org/

ASSOCIATED PRESS TELEVISION/RADIO ASSOCIATION-CLETE ROBERTS JOURNALISM SCHOLARSHIP AWARDS
• *See page 401*

KATHRYN DETTMAN MEMORIAL JOURNALISM SCHOLARSHIP
• *See page 402*

CALIFORNIA BROADCASTERS FOUNDATION

http://www.cabroadcasters.org/

CALIFORNIA BROADCASTERS FOUNDATION INTERN SCHOLARSHIP

Two $500 scholarships awarded to radio interns and two $500 scholarships awarded to television interns each semester. Any enrolled college student working as an intern at any California Broadcasters Foundation or Association member radio or television station is eligible. No minimum number of hours per week required. Immediate family of current Foundation Board Members are not eligible. Deadlines: June 18 for fall and December 10 for spring.

Academic Fields/Career Goals: TV/Radio Broadcasting.

Award: Scholarship for use in freshman, sophomore, junior, senior, graduate, or postgraduate years; not renewable. *Number:* up to 4. *Amount:* $500.

Eligibility Requirements: Applicant must be enrolled or expecting to enroll full- or part-time at a two-year or four-year or technical institution or university and resident of California. Available to U.S. citizens.

Application Requirements: Application form, essay, recommendations or references. *Deadline:* varies.

Contact: Mark Powers, Government Affairs
California Broadcasters Foundation
915 L Street, Suite 1150
Sacramento, CA 95814
Phone: 916-444-2237
E-mail: cbapowers@cabroadcasters.org

CCNMA: LATINO JOURNALISTS OF CALIFORNIA

http://www.ccnma.org/

CCNMA SCHOLARSHIPS
• *See page 218*

CHARLES AND LUCILLE KING FAMILY FOUNDATION, INC.

http://www.kingfoundation.org/

CHARLES AND LUCILLE KING FAMILY FOUNDATION SCHOLARSHIPS
• *See page 218*

HAWAII ASSOCIATION OF BROADCASTERS INC.

http://www.hawaiibroadcasters.com/

HAWAII ASSOCIATION OF BROADCASTERS SCHOLARSHIP

Renewable scholarship for full-time college students with the career goal of working in the broadcast industry in Hawaii upon graduation. Minimum GPA of 2.75 required. Number of awards granted ranges between twenty and thirty. For more information, visit website http://www.hawaiibroadcasters.com.

Academic Fields/Career Goals: TV/Radio Broadcasting.

Award: Scholarship for use in freshman, sophomore, junior, or senior years; renewable. *Number:* 20–30. *Amount:* $500–$4500.

Eligibility Requirements: Applicant must be enrolled or expecting to enroll full-time at a two-year or four-year institution or university. Applicant must have 2.5 GPA or higher. Available to U.S. and non-U.S. citizens.

Application Requirements: Application form, recommendations or references, transcript. *Deadline:* April 30.

Contact: Scholarship Committee
Hawaii Association of Broadcasters Inc.
PO Box 61562
Honolulu, HI 96839
Phone: 808-599-1455
Fax: 808-599-7784

IDAHO STATE BROADCASTERS ASSOCIATION

http://www.idahobroadcasters.org/

WAYNE C. CORNILS MEMORIAL SCHOLARSHIP
• *See page 180*

ILLUMINATING ENGINEERING SOCIETY OF NORTH AMERICA

http://www.ies.org/

ROBERT W. THUNEN MEMORIAL SCHOLARSHIPS
• *See page 135*

INDIANA BROADCASTERS ASSOCIATION

http://www.indianabroadcasters.org/

**INDIANA BROADCASTERS FOUNDATION
SCHOLARSHIP**
• See page 403

ISLAMIC SCHOLARSHIP FUND

http://islamicscholarshipfund.org/

ISF NATIONAL SCHOLARSHIP
• See page 119

LOUISIANA ASSOCIATION OF BROADCASTERS

http://www.broadcasters.org/

BROADCAST SCHOLARSHIP PROGRAM

Scholarship to students enrolled and attending classes, full-time, in a fully accredited broadcast curriculum at a Louisiana four-year college. Must be a Louisiana resident and maintain a minimum 2.5 GPA. Previous LAB Scholarship Award winners are eligible.

Academic Fields/Career Goals: TV/Radio Broadcasting.

Award: Scholarship for use in junior or senior years; not renewable. *Number:* 2. *Amount:* $2000.

Eligibility Requirements: Applicant must be enrolled or expecting to enroll full-time at a four-year institution or university; resident of Louisiana and studying in Louisiana. Applicant must have 2.5 GPA or higher. Available to U.S. citizens.

Application Requirements: Application form, essay. *Deadline:* February 1.

Contact: Polly Johnson, Louisiana
Louisiana Association of Broadcasters
660 Florida Street
Baton Rouge, LA 70801
Phone: 225-267-4522
E-mail: pollyjohnson@broadcasters.org

MICHIGAN ASSOCIATION OF BROADCASTERS FOUNDATION

http://www.michmab.com/

WXYZ-TV BROADCASTING SCHOLARSHIP

One-time $1000 scholarship to assist students who are actively pursuing a career in a broadcast-related field. No limit on the number of awards within the program. Interested applicants should send a cover letter, resume, letters of recommendation, and an essay (200 to 300 words). The scholarship is open to Michigan residents currently attending college in Michigan.

Academic Fields/Career Goals: TV/Radio Broadcasting.

Award: Scholarship for use in freshman year; not renewable. *Number:* 1. *Amount:* $1000.

Eligibility Requirements: Applicant must be high school student; planning to enroll or expecting to enroll full-time at a two-year or four-year institution or university; resident of Michigan and studying in Michigan. Available to U.S. citizens.

Application Requirements: Application form, driver's license, essay, recommendations or references. *Deadline:* January 15.

Contact: Julie Sochay, Executive Vice President
Michigan Association of Broadcasters Foundation
819 North Washington Avenue
Lansing, MI 48906
Phone: 517-484-7444
Fax: 517-484-5810
E-mail: mabf@michmab.com

MISSISSIPPI ASSOCIATION OF BROADCASTERS

http://www.msbroadcasters.org/

**MISSISSIPPI ASSOCIATION OF BROADCASTERS
SCHOLARSHIP**
• See page 404

MISSOURI BROADCASTERS ASSOCIATION SCHOLARSHIP PROGRAM

http://www.mbaweb.org/

**MISSOURI BROADCASTERS ASSOCIATION
SCHOLARSHIP PROGRAM**

Scholarship for a Missouri resident enrolled or planning to enroll in a broadcast or related curriculum which provides training and expertise applicable to a broadcast operation. Must maintain a GPA of at least 3.0 or equivalent. Multiple awards may be assigned each year and the amount of the scholarship will vary.

Academic Fields/Career Goals: TV/Radio Broadcasting.

Award: Scholarship for use in freshman, sophomore, junior, or senior years; not renewable. *Number:* 3–5. *Amount:* $1000–$2500.

Eligibility Requirements: Applicant must be enrolled or expecting to enroll full-time at a two-year or four-year institution or university; resident of Missouri and studying in Missouri. Applicant must have 3.0 GPA or higher. Available to U.S. citizens.

Application Requirements: Application form, essay, financial need analysis. *Deadline:* March 31.

Contact: Ms. Terry Harper, Director of Member Services
Phone: 573-636-6692
Fax: 573-634-8258
E-mail: tharper@mbaweb.org

MONTANA BROADCASTERS ASSOCIATION

http://www.mtbroadcasters.org/

**GREAT FALLS BROADCASTERS ASSOCIATION
SCHOLARSHIP**

Scholarship available to a student who has graduated from a north-central Montana high school (Cascade, Meagher, Judith Basin, Fergus, Choteau, Teton, Pondera, Glacier, Toole, Liberty, Hill, Blaine, Phillips, and Valley counties) and is enrolled as at least a second year student in radio-TV at any public or private Montana college or university.

Academic Fields/Career Goals: TV/Radio Broadcasting.

Award: Scholarship for use in sophomore year; not renewable. *Number:* 1. *Amount:* $2000–$5000.

Eligibility Requirements: Applicant must be enrolled or expecting to enroll full-time at a two-year or four-year institution or university; resident of Montana and studying in Montana. Available to U.S. citizens.

Application Requirements: Application form, essay, recommendations or references, transcript. *Deadline:* March 15.

Contact: Gregory McDonald, Scholarship Coordinator
Montana Broadcasters Association
HC 70 PO Box 98
Bonner, MT 59823
Phone: 406-244-4622
Fax: 406-244-5518
E-mail: mba@mtbroadcasters.org

NATIONAL ACADEMY OF TELEVISION ARTS & SCIENCES— OHIO VALLEY CHAPTER

http://ohiovalleyemmy.org/

DAVID J. CLARKE MEMORIAL SCHOLARSHIP
• See page 220

NATIONAL ACADEMY OF TELEVISION ARTS AND SCIENCES

http://www.emmyonline.tv/

DOUGLAS W. MUMMERT SCHOLARSHIP
• See page 142

JIM MCKAY MEMORIAL SCHOLARSHIP
• See page 220

MIKE WALLACE MEMORIAL SCHOLARSHIP
• See page 220

NATIONAL ACADEMY OF TELEVISION ARTS AND SCIENCES TRUSTEES SCHOLARSHIP
• See page 220

RANDY FALCO SCHOLARSHIP
• See page 220

NATIONAL ACADEMY OF TELEVISION ARTS AND SCIENCES, MICHIGAN CHAPTER

http://natasmichigan.org

DR. LYNNE BOYLE/JOHN SCHIMPF UNDERGRADUATE SCHOLARSHIP
• See page 97

NATIONAL ACADEMY OF TELEVISION ARTS AND SCIENCES-NATIONAL CAPITAL/CHESAPEAKE BAY CHAPTER

http://www.natasdc.org/

BETTY ENDICOTT/NTA-NCCB STUDENT SCHOLARSHIP
• See page 405

NATIONAL ASSOCIATION OF BLACK JOURNALISTS

http://www.nabj.org/

NABJ SCHOLARSHIP
• See page 220

NATIONAL ASSOCIATION OF BLACK JOURNALISTS NON-SUSTAINING SCHOLARSHIP AWARDS
• See page 405

NATIONAL ASSOCIATION OF BROADCASTERS

http://www.nab.org/

NATIONAL ASSOCIATION OF BROADCASTERS GRANTS FOR RESEARCH IN BROADCASTING
• See page 221

NATIONAL ASSOCIATION OF HISPANIC JOURNALISTS (NAHJ)

http://www.nahj.org/

GERALDO RIVERA SCHOLARSHIP
• See page 406

MARIA ELENA SALINAS SCHOLARSHIP
• See page 360

NATIONAL ASSOCIATION OF HISPANIC JOURNALISTS SCHOLARSHIP
• See page 221

NATIONAL DAIRY SHRINE

http://www.dairyshrine.org/

MARSHALL E. MCCULLOUGH-NATIONAL DAIRY SHRINE SCHOLARSHIPS
• See page 108

NEW JERSEY BROADCASTERS ASSOCIATION

http://www.njba.com/

MICHAEL S. LIBRETTI SCHOLARSHIP
• See page 221

NORTH CAROLINA ASSOCIATION OF BROADCASTERS

http://www.ncbroadcast.com/

NCAB SCHOLARSHIP
One-time scholarship for high school seniors enrolled as full-time students in a North Carolina college or university with an interest in broadcasting. Must be between ages 17 and 20.

Academic Fields/Career Goals: TV/Radio Broadcasting.

Award: Scholarship for use in freshman year; not renewable. *Number:* 2. *Amount:* $10,000.

Eligibility Requirements: Applicant must be high school student; age 17-20; planning to enroll or expecting to enroll full-time at a two-year or four-year institution or university and studying in North Carolina. Available to U.S. citizens.

Application Requirements: Application form, essay, recommendations or references, transcript. *Deadline:* April 15.

Contact: Lisa Reynolds, Executive Manager
North Carolina Association of Broadcasters
PO Box 627
Raleigh, NC 27602
Phone: 919-821-7300
Fax: 919-839-0304

OREGON ASSOCIATION OF BROADCASTERS

http://www.theoab.org/

OAB FOUNDATION SCHOLARSHIP
• See page 221

OUTDOOR WRITERS ASSOCIATION OF AMERICA

http://www.owaa.org/

OUTDOOR WRITERS ASSOCIATION OF AMERICA - BODIE MCDOWELL SCHOLARSHIP AWARD
• See page 222

PALM BEACH ASSOCIATION OF BLACK JOURNALISTS

PALM BEACH ASSOCIATION OF BLACK JOURNALISTS SCHOLARSHIP
• *See page 408*

POLISH ARTS CLUB OF BUFFALO SCHOLARSHIP FOUNDATION

http://www.pacb.bfn.org/

POLISH ARTS CLUB OF BUFFALO SCHOLARSHIP FOUNDATION TRUST
• *See page 144*

RADIO TELEVISION DIGITAL NEWS ASSOCIATION

http://www.rtdna.org

CAROLE SIMPSON SCHOLARSHIP
• *See page 222*

ED BRADLEY SCHOLARSHIP
• *See page 223*

GEORGE FOREMAN TRIBUTE TO LYNDON B. JOHNSON SCHOLARSHIP
• *See page 223*

LOU AND CAROLE PRATO SPORTS REPORTING SCHOLARSHIP
• *See page 223*

MIKE REYNOLDS JOURNALISM SCHOLARSHIP
• *See page 223*

RHODE ISLAND FOUNDATION

http://www.rifoundation.org/

J. D. EDSAL SCHOLARSHIP
• *See page 99*

SOCIETY OF MOTION PICTURE AND TELEVISION ENGINEERS

https://www.smpte.org/

LOUIS F. WOLF JR. MEMORIAL SCHOLARSHIP
• *See page 224*

STUDENT PAPER AWARD
• *See page 224*

SOCIETY OF PROFESSIONAL JOURNALISTS, LOS ANGELES CHAPTER

http://www.spj.org/losangeles

HELEN JOHNSON SCHOLARSHIP
• *See page 409*

STRAIGHTFORWARD MEDIA

http://www.straightforwardmedia.com/

STRAIGHTFORWARD MEDIA MEDIA & COMMUNICATIONS SCHOLARSHIP
• *See page 99*

TAMPA BAY TIMES FUND, INC.

http://www.tampabay.com/fund

CAREER JOURNALISM SCHOLARSHIP
• *See page 225*

TAMPA BAY TIMES FUND CAREER JOURNALISM SCHOLARSHIPS
• *See page 99*

TEXAS ASSOCIATION OF BROADCASTERS

https://www.tab.org/scholarships/available-scholarships

BELO TEXAS BROADCAST EDUCATION FOUNDATION SCHOLARSHIP
• *See page 225*

BONNER MCLANE TEXAS BROADCAST EDUCATION FOUNDATION SCHOLARSHIP
• *See page 225*

STUDENT TEXAS BROADCAST EDUCATION FOUNDATION SCHOLARSHIP
• *See page 226*

TOM REIFF TEXAS BROADCAST EDUCATION FOUNDATION SCHOLARSHIP
• *See page 226*

UNDERGRADUATE TEXAS BROADCAST EDUCATION FOUNDATION SCHOLARSHIP
• *See page 226*

VANN KENNEDY TEXAS BROADCAST EDUCATION FOUNDATION SCHOLARSHIP
• *See page 226*

TEXAS GRIDIRON CLUB INC.

http://www.spjfw.org/

TEXAS GRIDIRON CLUB SCHOLARSHIPS
• *See page 226*

UNITED METHODIST COMMUNICATIONS

http://www.umcom.org/

LEONARD M. PERRYMAN COMMUNICATIONS SCHOLARSHIP FOR ETHNIC MINORITY STUDENTS
• *See page 227*

VALLEY PRESS CLUB

http://www.valleypressclub.com/

VALLEY PRESS CLUB SCHOLARSHIPS, THE REPUBLICAN SCHOLARSHIP, CHANNEL 22 SCHOLARSHIP
• *See page 228*

WISCONSIN BROADCASTERS ASSOCIATION FOUNDATION

http://www.wi-broadcasters.org/

WISCONSIN BROADCASTERS ASSOCIATION FOUNDATION SCHOLARSHIP
• *See page 228*

WOWT-TV OMAHA, NEBRASKA

http://www.wowt.com/

WOWT-TV BROADCASTING SCHOLARSHIP PROGRAM

Two annual scholarships of $1000 for high school graduates in the Channel 6 viewing area of Nebraska. Must be pursuing a full-time career in broadcasting and have a minimum GPA of 3.0.

Academic Fields/Career Goals: TV/Radio Broadcasting.

Award: Scholarship for use in freshman year; not renewable. *Number:* 2. *Amount:* $1000.

Eligibility Requirements: Applicant must be high school student; planning to enroll or expecting to enroll full-time at a two-year or four-year institution or university and resident of Nebraska. Applicant must have 3.0 GPA or higher. Available to U.S. citizens.

Application Requirements: Application form, community service, essay, interview. *Deadline:* March 15.

Contact: Brandy Gerry, Programming and Community Affairs Manager
WOWT-TV Omaha, Nebraska
3501 Farnam Street
Omaha, NE 68131
Phone: 402-346-6666
E-mail: scholarship@wowt.com

URBAN AND REGIONAL PLANNING

AMERICAN PLANNING ASSOCIATION

http://www.planning.org/

JUDITH MCMANUS PRICE SCHOLARSHIP

Women and minority (African American, Hispanic American, or Native American) students enrolled in an approved Planning Accreditation Board (PAB) planning program who are citizens of the United States, intend to pursue careers as practicing planners in the public sector, and are able to demonstrate a genuine financial need are eligible to apply for this scholarship. For further information visit https://www.planning.org/scholarships/apa/

Academic Fields/Career Goals: Urban and Regional Planning.

Award: Scholarship for use in freshman, sophomore, junior, senior, or graduate years; not renewable. *Amount:* $2000–$5000.

Eligibility Requirements: Applicant must be American Indian/Alaska Native, Black (non-Hispanic), Hispanic and enrolled or expecting to enroll full-time at a four-year institution or university. Available to U.S. citizens.

Application Requirements: Application form, essay, financial need analysis. *Deadline:* April 30.

Contact: Christine Ott, Senior Development Officer
American Planning Association
205 N. Michigan Avenue
Suite 1200
Chicago, IL 60601
Phone: 312-786-6345
E-mail: cott@planning.org

AMERICAN SCHOOL OF CLASSICAL STUDIES AT ATHENS

http://www.ascsa.edu.gr/

ASCSA SUMMER SESSION AND SUMMER SEMINARS SCHOLARSHIPS

• *See page 118*

ASSOCIATION OF STATE DAM SAFETY OFFICIALS (ASDSO)

http://www.DamSafety.org

ASSOCIATION OF STATE DAM SAFETY OFFICIALS (ASDSO) SENIOR UNDERGRADUATE SCHOLARSHIP

• *See page 168*

CENTER FOR ARCHITECTURE

http://www.centerforarchitecture.org

CENTER FOR ARCHITECTURE, DOUGLAS HASKELL AWARD FOR STUDENT JOURNALS

• *See page 132*

COMMUNITY FOUNDATION OF WESTERN MASSACHUSETTS

http://www.communityfoundation.org/

HELEN HAMILTON SCHOLARSHIP FUND

• *See page 524*

CONNECTICUT CHAPTER OF THE AMERICAN PLANNING ASSOCIATION

http://www.ccapa.org/

DIANA DONALD SCHOLARSHIP

One-time award of $2500 for full-time students enrolled in a graduate or undergraduate program in city planning or a closely related field. Must be resident of Connecticut and study in Connecticut. Deadline varies.

Academic Fields/Career Goals: Urban and Regional Planning.

Award: Scholarship for use in freshman, sophomore, junior, senior, or graduate years; not renewable. *Number:* up to 1. *Amount:* up to $2500.

Eligibility Requirements: Applicant must be enrolled or expecting to enroll full-time at a four-year institution or university; resident of Connecticut and studying in Connecticut. Available to U.S. and non-U.S. citizens.

Application Requirements: Application form, essay, financial need analysis, recommendations or references, transcript. *Deadline:* varies.

Contact: Mary Savage-Dunham, Town Planner
Connecticut Chapter of the American Planning Association
75 Main Street
Southington, CT 06489
Phone: 860-276-6248
E-mail: savagem@southington.org

INTERNATIONAL FACILITY MANAGEMENT ASSOCIATION FOUNDATION

http://www.ifmafoundation.org/

IFMA FOUNDATION SCHOLARSHIPS

• *See page 135*

THE LAND CONSERVANCY OF NEW JERSEY

http://www.tlc-nj.org/

ROGERS FAMILY SCHOLARSHIP

• *See page 172*

RUSSELL W. MYERS SCHOLARSHIP

• *See page 172*

PLAN NEW HAMPSHIRE

http://www.plannh.org

PLAN NEW HAMPSHIRE SCHOLARSHIP AND FELLOWSHIP PROGRAM
• *See page 129*

TRANSPORTATION ASSOCIATION OF CANADA FOUNDATION

http://www.tac-foundation.ca

TAC FOUNDATION SCHOLARSHIPS
• *See page 213*

VECTORWORKS, INC.

http://www.vectorworks.net

VECTORWORKS DESIGN SCHOLARSHIP
• *See page 137*

WOMEN'S STUDIES

AMERICAN FEDERATION OF STATE, COUNTY, AND MUNICIPAL EMPLOYEES

http://www.afscme.org/

AFSCME/UNCF UNION SCHOLARS PROGRAM
• *See page 113*

NATIONAL ASSOCIATION OF WATER COMPANIES-NEW JERSEY CHAPTER

http://www.nawc.org

NATIONAL ASSOCIATION OF WATER COMPANIES-NEW JERSEY CHAPTER SCHOLARSHIP

For college students interested in a career in the water utility industry or any related field. Must be U.S. citizen, five-year resident of New Jersey, high school senior or college student attending or enrolled in a New Jersey college or university. Must maintain a 3.0 GPA.

Academic Fields/Career Goals: Women's Studies.

Award: Scholarship for use in freshman, sophomore, junior, senior, or graduate years; not renewable. *Number:* 2. *Amount:* $2500.

Eligibility Requirements: Applicant must be enrolled or expecting to enroll full- or part-time at a two-year or four-year institution or university; resident of New Jersey and studying in New Jersey. Applicant must have 3.0 GPA or higher. Available to U.S. citizens.

Application Requirements: Application form, essay. *Deadline:* April 1.

Contact: Gail Brady, Scholarship Committee Chairperson
National Association of Water Companies-New Jersey Chapter
Middlesex Water Co
1500 Ronson Rd.
Iselin, NJ 08830
Phone: 973-669-5807
E-mail: gbradygbconsult@verizon.net

NATIONAL INSTITUTES OF HEALTH

https://www.training.nih.gov/programs/ugsp

NIH UNDERGRADUATE SCHOLARSHIP PROGRAM FOR STUDENTS FROM DISADVANTAGED BACKGROUNDS
• *See page 116*

THE SOCIETY FOR THE SCIENTIFIC STUDY OF SEXUALITY

http://www.sexscience.org/

THE SOCIETY FOR THE SCIENTIFIC STUDY OF SEXUALITY STUDENT RESEARCH GRANT
• *See page 120*

UNITED NATIONS ASSOCIATION OF CONNECTICUT

http://www.unausa.org

UNITED NATIONS ASSOCIATION OF CONNECTICUT SCHOLARSHIP
• *See page 147*

WILLIAMS LAW GROUP

https://familylawyersnewjersey.com/

WILLIAMS LAW GROUP OPPORTUNITY TO GROW SCHOLARSHIP

• *See page 139*

Nonacademic/Noncareer Criteria

CIVIC, PROFESSIONAL, SOCIAL, OR UNION AFFILIATION

AIR LINE PILOTS ASSOCIATION, INTERNATIONAL

http://www.alpa.org/

AIRLINE PILOTS ASSOCIATION SCHOLARSHIP PROGRAM

Scholarship for children of medically retired, long-term disabled, or deceased pilot members of the Air Line Pilots Association. The total monetary value is $12,000 with $3000 disbursed annually to the recipient for four consecutive years, provided that a GPA of 3.0 is maintained. An additional $2000 per year is available which may be awarded to one or two additional applicants as a one-year special award, which is not renewable.

Award: Scholarship for use in freshman, sophomore, junior, or senior years; renewable. *Number:* 1–3. *Amount:* $1000–$12,000.

Eligibility Requirements: Applicant must be enrolled or expecting to enroll full-time at a four-year institution or university. Applicant or parent of applicant must be member of Airline Pilots Association. Applicant must have 3.0 GPA or higher. Available to U.S. and Canadian citizens.

Application Requirements: Application form, financial need analysis. *Deadline:* April 1.

Contact: Yvonne Willits, Coordinator
Phone: 703-689-4107
Fax: 703-481-5575
E-mail: Yvonne.Willits@alpa.org

ALBERTA AGRICULTURE FOOD AND RURAL DEVELOPMENT 4-H BRANCH

http://www.4h.ab.ca/

ALBERTA AGRICULTURE FOOD AND RURAL DEVELOPMENT 4-H SCHOLARSHIP PROGRAM

Awards will be given to current and incoming students attending any institute of higher learning. Must have been a member of the Alberta 4-H Program and be a Canadian citizen. Must be a resident of Alberta.

Award: Scholarship for use in freshman, sophomore, junior, senior, or graduate years; not renewable. *Number:* 115–120. *Amount:* $200–$1500.

Eligibility Requirements: Applicant must be enrolled or expecting to enroll full-time at a two-year or four-year or technical institution or university and resident of Alberta. Applicant or parent of applicant must be member of National 4-H. Available to Canadian citizens.

Application Requirements: Application form, essay, recommendations or references, transcript. *Deadline:* May 5.

Contact: Susann Stone, Scholarship Coordinator
Phone: 780-682-2153
Fax: 780-682-3784
E-mail: foundation@4hab.com

AMERICAN DENTAL ASSISTANTS ASSOCIATION

http://www.adaausa.org

JULIETTE A. SOUTHARD SCHOLARSHIP

Leadership-based award available to ADAA members enrolled in a dental assisting program.

Award: Scholarship for use in freshman, sophomore, junior, senior, graduate, or postgraduate years; not renewable. *Number:* 1–10. *Amount:* $1–$750.

Eligibility Requirements: Applicant must be enrolled or expecting to enroll full- or part-time at a two-year or four-year or technical institution or university. Applicant or parent of applicant must be member of American Dental Assistants Association. Available to U.S. citizens.

Application Requirements: Application form, essay, financial need analysis. *Deadline:* March 15.

Contact: Mr. Jay Kasper, Associate Executive Director
American Dental Assistants Association
140 N Bloomingdale Rd
Bloomingdale, IL 60108
Phone: 630-9944247
Fax: 630-3518490
E-mail: jaykasper@adaausa.org

AMERICAN FEDERATION OF STATE, COUNTY, AND MUNICIPAL EMPLOYEES

http://www.afscme.org/

AMERICAN FEDERATION OF STATE, COUNTY, AND MUNICIPAL EMPLOYEES SCHOLARSHIP PROGRAM

Scholarship for family dependents of American Federation of State, County, and Municipal Employees members. Must be a graduating high school senior planning to pursue postsecondary education at a four-year institution. Submit proof of parent's membership. Renewable award of $2000.

Award: Scholarship for use in freshman, sophomore, junior, or senior years; renewable. *Number:* 13. *Amount:* $2000.

Eligibility Requirements: Applicant must be high school student and planning to enroll or expecting to enroll full-time at a four-year institution or university. Applicant or parent of applicant must be member of American Federation of State, County, and Municipal Employees. Available to U.S. citizens.

Application Requirements: Application form, essay, recommendations or references, test scores, transcript. *Deadline:* December 31.

Contact: Philip Allen, Scholarship Coordinator
Phone: 202-429-1250
Fax: 202-429-1293
E-mail: pallen@asscme.org

UNION PLUS CREDIT CARD SCHOLARSHIP PROGRAM

One-time award for AFSCME members, their spouses and dependent children. Graduate students and grandchildren are not eligible.

Award: Scholarship for use in freshman, sophomore, junior, or senior years; not renewable. *Amount:* $500–$4000.

Eligibility Requirements: Applicant must be enrolled or expecting to enroll full-time at a two-year or four-year or technical institution or university. Applicant or parent of applicant must be member of American Federation of State, County, and Municipal Employees. Available to U.S. citizens.

Application Requirements: Application form, driver's license, essay, recommendations or references, transcript. *Deadline:* January 31.

Contact: Philip Allen, Scholarship Coordinator
Phone: 202-429-1250
Fax: 202-429-1293
E-mail: pallen@asscme.org

AMERICAN FEDERATION OF TEACHERS

http://www.aft.org/

ROBERT G. PORTER SCHOLARS PROGRAM-AMERICAN FEDERATION OF TEACHERS DEPENDENTS

Scholarship of up to $8000 for high school seniors who are dependents of AFT members. Must submit transcript, test scores, essay, and recommendations with application. Must be U.S. citizen.

Award: Scholarship for use in freshman year; renewable. *Number:* 4. *Amount:* $8000.

Eligibility Requirements: Applicant must be high school student and planning to enroll or expecting to enroll full-time at a four-year institution or university. Applicant or parent of applicant must be member of American Federation of Teachers. Applicant or parent of applicant must have employment or volunteer experience in nursing, teaching/education. Available to U.S. citizens.

Application Requirements: Application form, community service, essay, recommendations or references, test scores, transcript. *Deadline:* March 31.

Contact: Ms. Nina Newkirk, Scholarship Coordinator
Phone: 202-393-5696
E-mail: nnewkirk@aft.org

AMERICAN LEGION AUXILIARY DEPARTMENT OF CONNECTICUT

http://www.ct.legion.org/

AMERICAN LEGION AUXILIARY DEPARTMENT OF CONNECTICUT MEMORIAL EDUCATIONAL GRANT

Half the number of available grants are awarded to children of veterans who are also residents of CT. Remaining grants awarded to child or grandchild of a member (or member at time of death) of the CT Departments of the American Legion/American Legion Auxiliary, regardless of residency; or are members of the CT Departments of the American Legion Auxiliary/Sons of the American Legion, regardless of residency. Contact local unit President. Must include list of community service activities.

Award: Grant for use in freshman, sophomore, junior, or senior years; not renewable. *Number:* 4. *Amount:* $500.

Eligibility Requirements: Applicant must be age 16-23; enrolled or expecting to enroll full-time at a two-year or four-year or technical institution or university; resident of Connecticut and studying in Mississippi. Applicant or parent of applicant must be member of American Legion or Auxiliary. Available to U.S. citizens. Applicant must have general military experience.

Application Requirements: Application form, community service, essay, financial need analysis. *Deadline:* March 10.

Contact: Nancy Hansen, State Secretary
American Legion Auxiliary Department of Connecticut
PO Box 266
Rocky Hill, CT 06067-0266
Phone: 860-616-2343
Fax: 860-616-2342
E-mail: ctaladept@gmail.com

AMERICAN LEGION AUXILIARY DEPARTMENT OF CONNECTICUT PAST PRESIDENTS' PARLEY MEMORIAL EDUCATION GRANT

The program gives preference a child or grandchild of an ex-service woman, who was or is a member of the CT departments of the American Legion/American Legion Auxiliary. In the event of a deficiency of preferred applicants, award may be granted to child or grandchild of a member of the CT Departments of the American Legion/American Legion Auxiliary or Sons of the American Legion. Minimum three-year membership required, or three years prior to death. Contact local unit President. Must include list of community service activities.

Award: Grant for use in freshman, sophomore, junior, or senior years; not renewable. *Number:* 4. *Amount:* $500.

Eligibility Requirements: Applicant must be age 16-23; enrolled or expecting to enroll full-time at a two-year or four-year or technical institution or university and resident of Connecticut. Applicant or parent of applicant must be member of American Legion or Auxiliary. Available to U.S. citizens. Applicant must have general military experience.

Application Requirements: Application form, community service, financial need analysis. *Deadline:* March 10.

Contact: Nancy Hansen, State Secretary
American Legion Auxiliary Department of Connecticut
PO Box 266
Rocky Hill, CT 06067-0266
Phone: 860-616-2343
Fax: 860-616-2342
E-mail: ctaladept@gmail.com

AMERICAN LEGION AUXILIARY DEPARTMENT OF MISSOURI

http://www.missourilegion.org/

AMERICAN LEGION AUXILIARY DEPARTMENT OF MISSOURI LELA MURPHY SCHOLARSHIP

Scholarship of $500 for high school graduate. $250 will be awarded each semester. Applicant must be Missouri resident and the granddaughter or great-granddaughter of a living or deceased Auxiliary member. Sponsoring unit and department must validate application.

Award: Scholarship for use in freshman year; not renewable. *Number:* 1. *Amount:* $500.

Eligibility Requirements: Applicant must be high school student; planning to enroll or expecting to enroll full-time at a two-year or four-year or technical institution or university; female and resident of Missouri. Applicant or parent of applicant must be member of American Legion or Auxiliary. Available to U.S. citizens. Applicant or parent must meet one or more of the following requirements: general military experience; retired from active duty; disabled or killed as a result of military service; prisoner of war; or missing in action.

Application Requirements: Application form. *Deadline:* March 1.

Contact: Karen Larson, Department Secretary/Treasurer
American Legion Auxiliary Department of Missouri
600 Ellis Boulevard
Jefferson City, MO 65101
Phone: 573-636-9133
Fax: 573-635-3467
E-mail: dptmoala@embarqmail.com

AMERICAN LEGION AUXILIARY DEPARTMENT OF MISSOURI NATIONAL PRESIDENT'S SCHOLARSHIP

State-level award. Offers one $500 scholarship. Applicant must complete 50 hours of community service during their high school years. Sponsoring unit and department must validate application. Applicant must be a Missouri resident.

Award: Scholarship for use in freshman year; not renewable. *Number:* 1. *Amount:* $500.

Eligibility Requirements: Applicant must be high school student; planning to enroll or expecting to enroll full-time at a two-year or four-year or technical institution or university and resident of Missouri. Applicant or parent of applicant must be member of American Legion or Auxiliary. Available to U.S. citizens. Applicant or parent must meet one or more of the following requirements: general military experience; retired from active duty; disabled or killed as a result of military service; prisoner of war; or missing in action.

Application Requirements: Application form, community service, resume. *Deadline:* March 1.

Contact: Karen Larson, Department Secretary/Treasurer
American Legion Auxiliary Department of Missouri
600 Ellis Boulevard
Jefferson City, MO 65101
Phone: 573-636-9133
Fax: 573-635-3467
E-mail: dptmoala@embarqmail.com

AMERICAN LEGION AUXILIARY DEPARTMENT OF NEBRASKA

http://www.nebraskalegionaux.net/

AMERICAN LEGION AUXILIARY DEPARTMENT OF NEBRASKA RUBY PAUL CAMPAIGN FUND SCHOLARSHIP

One-time award for Nebraska residents who are children, grandchildren, or great-grandchildren of an American Legion Auxiliary member, or who have been members of the American Legion, American Legion Auxiliary, or Sons of the American Legion or Auxiliary for two years prior to issuing the application. Must rank in upper third of class or have minimum 3.0 GPA.

Award: Scholarship for use in freshman year; not renewable. *Number:* 1–3. *Amount:* $100–$300.

Eligibility Requirements: Applicant must be high school student; planning to enroll or expecting to enroll full-time at a four-year institution or university and resident of Nebraska. Applicant or parent of applicant must be member of American Legion or Auxiliary. Applicant must have 3.0 GPA or higher. Available to U.S. citizens. Applicant or parent must meet one or more of the following requirements: general military experience; retired from active duty; disabled or killed as a result of military service; prisoner of war; or missing in action.

Application Requirements: Application form, essay, financial need analysis, letter of acceptance, proof of enrollment, recommendations or references, test scores, transcript. *Deadline:* March 15.

Contact: Jacki O'Neill, Department Secretary
Phone: 402-466-1808
E-mail: neaux@alltel.net

AMERICAN LEGION AUXILIARY DEPARTMENT OF OREGON

http://www.alaoregon.org/

AMERICAN LEGION AUXILIARY DEPARTMENT OF OREGON SPIRIT OF YOUTH SCHOLARSHIP

One-time award available to Oregon high school seniors. Must be a current female junior member of the American Legion Auxiliary with a three-year membership history. Apply through local units.

Award: Scholarship for use in freshman year; not renewable. *Number:* 1. *Amount:* $1000.

Eligibility Requirements: Applicant must be high school student; planning to enroll or expecting to enroll full- or part-time at a four-year institution or university; female and resident of Oregon. Applicant or parent of applicant must be member of American Legion or Auxiliary. Available to U.S. citizens.

Application Requirements: Application form, essay, financial need analysis, interview. *Deadline:* February 1.

Contact: Virginia Biddle, Secretary/Treasurer
American Legion Auxiliary Department of Oregon
PO Box 1730
Wilsonville, OR 97070
Phone: 503-682-3162
E-mail: alaor@pcez.com

AMERICAN LEGION AUXILIARY DEPARTMENT OF SOUTH DAKOTA

http://www.sdlegion-aux.org/

AMERICAN LEGION AUXILIARY DEPARTMENT OF SOUTH DAKOTA COLLEGE SCHOLARSHIPS

One-time award of $500 to assist veterans children or auxiliary members' children from South Dakota ages 16 to 22 to secure an education at a four-year school. Write for more information.

Award: Scholarship for use in freshman, sophomore, junior, or senior years; not renewable. *Number:* 2. *Amount:* $500.

Eligibility Requirements: Applicant must be age 16-22; enrolled or expecting to enroll full-time at a four-year institution or university and resident of South Dakota. Applicant or parent of applicant must be member of American Legion or Auxiliary. Available to U.S. and non-U.S. citizens. Applicant or parent must meet one or more of the following requirements: general military experience; retired from active duty; disabled or killed as a result of military service; prisoner of war; or missing in action.

Application Requirements: Application form, entry in a contest, essay, financial need analysis, recommendations or references. *Deadline:* March 1.

Contact: Dianne Hudson, Executive Secretary
American Legion Auxiliary Department of South Dakota
PO Box 1819
Sioux Falls, SD 57101
Phone: 605-338-9774
Fax: 605-332-3032
E-mail: legionauxiliary.sd@gmail.com

AMERICAN LEGION AUXILIARY DEPARTMENT OF SOUTH DAKOTA SENIOR SCHOLARSHIP

Award of $400 for current senior member of South Dakota American Legion Auxiliary who has been a member for three years. Based on financial need.

Award: Scholarship for use in freshman year; not renewable. *Number:* 1. *Amount:* $400.

Eligibility Requirements: Applicant must be high school student; planning to enroll or expecting to enroll full-time at a two-year or four-year or technical institution; female and resident of South Dakota. Applicant or parent of applicant must be member of American Legion or Auxiliary. Available to U.S. and non-U.S. citizens. Applicant or parent must meet one or more of the following requirements: general military experience; retired from active duty; disabled or killed as a result of military service; prisoner of war; or missing in action.

Application Requirements: Application form, essay, financial need analysis, recommendations or references, transcript. *Deadline:* March 1.

Contact: Dianne Hudson, Executive Secretary
American Legion Auxiliary Department of South Dakota
PO Box 1819
Sioux Falls, SD 57101
Phone: 605-338-9774
Fax: 605-332-3032
E-mail: legionauxiliary.sd@gmail.com

AMERICAN LEGION AUXILIARY DEPARTMENT OF SOUTH DAKOTA THELMA FOSTER SCHOLARSHIP FOR SENIOR AUXILIARY MEMBERS

One-time award of $300 must be used within twelve months for a current senior member of the South Dakota American Legion Auxiliary who has been a member for three years. Applicant may be a high school senior or older and must be female.

Award: Scholarship for use in freshman year; not renewable. *Number:* 1. *Amount:* $300.

Eligibility Requirements: Applicant must be enrolled or expecting to enroll full-time at a four-year institution or university and female. Applicant or parent of applicant must be member of American Legion or Auxiliary. Available to U.S. and non-U.S. citizens. Applicant or parent must meet one or more of the following requirements: general military experience; retired from active duty; disabled or killed as a result of military service; prisoner of war; or missing in action.

Application Requirements: Application form, essay, financial need analysis, recommendations or references. *Deadline:* March 1.

Contact: Dianne Hudson, Executive Secretary
American Legion Auxiliary Department of South Dakota
PO Box 1819
Sioux Falls, SD 57101
Phone: 605-338-9774
Fax: 605-332-3032
E-mail: legionauxiliary.sd@gmail.com

AMERICAN LEGION AUXILIARY DEPARTMENT OF UTAH

http://www.legion-aux.org/

AMERICAN LEGION AUXILIARY DEPARTMENT OF UTAH NATIONAL PRESIDENT'S SCHOLARSHIP

Scholarships available for graduating high school seniors. Must be a resident of Utah, a U.S. citizen, and the direct descendant of a veteran.

Award: Scholarship for use in freshman year; not renewable. *Number:* 15. *Amount:* $1000–$2500.

Eligibility Requirements: Applicant must be high school student; planning to enroll or expecting to enroll full-time at a two-year or four-year or technical institution or university; single and resident of Utah. Applicant or parent of applicant must be member of American Legion or Auxiliary. Available to U.S. citizens. Applicant or parent must meet one or more of the following requirements: general military experience; retired from active duty; disabled or killed as a result of military service; prisoner of war; or missing in action.

Application Requirements: Application form, essay, recommendations or references, statement of parent's military service, test scores, transcript. *Deadline:* March 1.

Contact: Lucia Anderson, Public Relations Manager and Associate Editor
Phone: 801-539-1015
Fax: 801-521-9191
E-mail: landerson@legion-aux.org

AMERICAN LEGION AUXILIARY DEPARTMENT OF WISCONSIN

http://www.amlegionauxwi.org/

AMERICAN LEGION AUXILIARY DEPARTMENT OF WISCONSIN DELLA VAN DEUREN MEMORIAL SCHOLARSHIP

One-time award of $1000 for Wisconsin residents. Applicant or mother of applicant must be a member of an American Legion Auxiliary unit. Must submit certification of an American Legion Auxiliary unit president, copy of proof that veteran was in service (i.e. discharge papers), letters of recommendation, transcripts, and essay. Minimum 3.5 GPA required. Must demonstrate financial need. Applications available on website http://www.amlegionauxwi.org.

Award: Scholarship for use in freshman, sophomore, junior, or senior years; not renewable. *Number:* 2. *Amount:* $1000.

Eligibility Requirements: Applicant must be enrolled or expecting to enroll full- or part-time at a two-year or four-year or technical institution or university; female and resident of Wisconsin. Applicant or parent of applicant must be member of American Legion or Auxiliary. Applicant must have 3.5 GPA or higher. Available to U.S. citizens. Applicant or parent must meet one or more of the following requirements: general military experience; retired from active duty; disabled or killed as a result of military service; prisoner of war; or missing in action.

Application Requirements: Application form, essay, financial need analysis. *Deadline:* March 15.

Contact: Bonnie Dorniak, Department Secretary
American Legion Auxiliary Department of Wisconsin
PO Box 140
Portage, WI 53901
Phone: 608-745-0124
Fax: 608-745-1947
E-mail: deptsec@amlegionauxwi.org

AMERICAN LEGION AUXILIARY DEPARTMENT OF WISCONSIN H.S. AND ANGELINE LEWIS SCHOLARSHIPS

One-time award of $1000. Applicant must be a direct descendant, wife, or widow of a veteran. Must submit certification of an American Legion Auxiliary unit president, copy of proof that veteran was in service (i.e. discharge papers), letters of recommendation, transcripts, and essay. Must submit minimum 3.5 GPA, show financial need, and be a resident of Wisconsin or member of the Wisconsin American Legion Family. Applications available on website http://www.amlegionauxwi.org.

Award: Scholarship for use in freshman, sophomore, junior, senior, graduate, or postgraduate years; not renewable. *Number:* 5–6. *Amount:* $1000.

Eligibility Requirements: Applicant must be enrolled or expecting to enroll full- or part-time at a two-year or four-year or technical institution or university and resident of Wisconsin. Applicant or parent of applicant must be member of American Legion or Auxiliary. Applicant must have 3.5 GPA or higher. Available to U.S. citizens. Applicant or parent must meet one or more of the following requirements: general military experience; retired from active duty; disabled or killed as a result of military service; prisoner of war; or missing in action.

Application Requirements: Application form, essay, financial need analysis. *Deadline:* March 15.

Contact: Bonnie Dorniak, Department Secretary
American Legion Auxiliary Department of Wisconsin
PO Box 140
Portage, WI 53901
Phone: 608-745-0124
Fax: 608-745-1947
E-mail: deptsec@amlegionauxwi.org

AMERICAN LEGION AUXILIARY DEPARTMENT OF WISCONSIN MERIT AND MEMORIAL SCHOLARSHIPS

One-time award of $1000. Applicant must be a direct descendant, wife, or widow of a veteran. Must submit certification of an American Legion Auxiliary unit president, copy of proof that veteran was in service (i.e. discharge papers), letters of recommendation, transcripts, and essay. Must have minimum 3.5 GPA, show financial need, and be a resident of Wisconsin or member of the Wisconsin American Legion Family. Applications available on website http://www.amlegionauxwi.org.

Award: Scholarship for use in freshman, sophomore, junior, or senior years; not renewable. *Number:* 7. *Amount:* $1000.

Eligibility Requirements: Applicant must be enrolled or expecting to enroll full- or part-time at a two-year or four-year or technical institution or university and resident of Wisconsin. Applicant or parent of applicant must be member of American Legion or Auxiliary. Applicant must have 3.5 GPA or higher. Available to U.S. citizens. Applicant or parent must meet one or more of the following requirements: general military experience; retired from active duty; disabled or killed as a result of military service; prisoner of war; or missing in action.

Application Requirements: Application form, essay, financial need analysis. *Deadline:* March 15.

Contact: Bonnie Dorniak, Department Secretary
American Legion Auxiliary Department of Wisconsin
PO Box 140
Portage, WI 53901
Phone: 608-745-0124
Fax: 608-745-1947
E-mail: deptsec@amlegionauxwi.org

AMERICAN LEGION AUXILIARY DEPARTMENT OF WISCONSIN PRESIDENT'S SCHOLARSHIPS

One-time award of $1000. The mother of the applicant or the applicant must be a member of the Wisconsin American Legion Auxiliary. Must submit certification of an American Legion Auxiliary unit president, copy of proof that veteran was in service (i.e. discharge papers), letters of recommendation, transcripts, and essay. Must have minimum 3.5 GPA, show financial need, and be a resident of Wisconsin. Applications available on website http://www.legion-aux.org.

Award: Scholarship for use in freshman, sophomore, junior, or senior years; not renewable. *Number:* 3. *Amount:* $1000.

Eligibility Requirements: Applicant must be enrolled or expecting to enroll full- or part-time at a four-year institution or university and resident of Wisconsin. Applicant or parent of applicant must be member of American Legion or Auxiliary. Applicant must have 3.5 GPA or higher. Available to U.S. citizens. Applicant or parent must meet one or more of the following requirements: general military experience; retired from active duty; disabled or killed as a result of military service; prisoner of war; or missing in action.

Application Requirements: Application form, essay, financial need analysis. *Deadline:* March 15.

Contact: Bonnie Dorniak, Department Secretary
American Legion Auxiliary Department of Wisconsin
PO Box 140
Portage, WI 53901
Phone: 608-745-0124
Fax: 608-745-1947
E-mail: deptsec@amlegionauxwi.org

AMERICAN LEGION AUXILIARY NATIONAL HEADQUARTERS

http://www.ALAforVeterans.org

AMERICAN LEGION AUXILIARY NON-TRADITIONAL STUDENTS SCHOLARSHIPS

One-time award for students returning to the classroom after some period of time in which his/her formal schooling was interrupted or a student who has had at least one year of college and is in need of financial assistance to pursue an undergraduate degree. Must be a member of the American Legion, American Legion Auxiliary or Sons of the American Legion.

Award: Scholarship for use in freshman, sophomore, junior, senior, graduate, or postgraduate years; not renewable. *Number:* 5. *Amount:* $2000.

Eligibility Requirements: Applicant must be enrolled or expecting to enroll full- or part-time at a two-year or four-year or technical institution or university. Applicant or parent of applicant must be member of American Legion or Auxiliary. Available to U.S. citizens.

Application Requirements: Application form, essay, financial need analysis. *Deadline:* March 1.

Contact: Kristin Hinshaw, Program Coordinator
American Legion Auxiliary National Headquarters
8945 North Meridian Street
Suite 200
Indianapolis, IN 46260
Phone: 317-569-4500 Ext. 4556
E-mail: Education@ALAforVeterans.org

AMERICAN LEGION AUXILIARY SPIRIT OF YOUTH SCHOLARSHIPS FOR JUNIOR MEMBERS

Renewable scholarship for graduating high school seniors. Must be a woman and a current junior member of the American Legion Auxiliary, with a three-year membership history.

Award: Scholarship for use in freshman, sophomore, junior, or senior years; not renewable. *Number:* 5. *Amount:* $5000.

Eligibility Requirements: Applicant must be high school student; planning to enroll or expecting to enroll full-time at a two-year or four-year or technical institution or university and female. Applicant or parent of applicant must be member of American Legion or Auxiliary. Applicant must have 3.0 GPA or higher. Available to U.S. citizens.

Application Requirements: Application form, essay. *Deadline:* March 1.

Contact: Kristin Hinshaw, Program Coordinator
American Legion Auxiliary National Headquarters
8945 North Meridian Street
Suite 200
Indianapolis, IN 46260
Phone: 317-569-4500 Ext. 4556
E-mail: Education@ALAforVeterans.org

AMERICAN LEGION DEPARTMENT OF IDAHO

http://www.idaholegion.com/

AMERICAN LEGION DEPARTMENT OF IDAHO SCHOLARSHIP

One-time award of $500 to $750 for residents of Idaho studying at an Idaho institution. Must be related to a Idaho American Member.

Award: Scholarship for use in freshman year; not renewable. *Number:* 1–3. *Amount:* $500–$750.

Eligibility Requirements: Applicant must be high school student; planning to enroll or expecting to enroll full-time at a two-year or four-year institution or university; resident of Idaho and studying in Idaho. Applicant or parent of applicant must be member of American Legion or Auxiliary. Available to U.S. citizens. Applicant or parent must meet one or more of the following requirements: general military experience; retired from active duty; disabled or killed as a result of military service; prisoner of war; or missing in action.

Application Requirements: Application form, community service, essay, financial need analysis. *Deadline:* June 1.

Contact: Abe Abrahamson, Adjutant
American Legion Department of Idaho
901 West Warren Street
Boise, ID 83706-3825
Phone: 208-342-7061
E-mail: idlegion@mindspring.com

AMERICAN LEGION DEPARTMENT OF ILLINOIS

http://www.illegion.org/

AMERICANISM ESSAY CONTEST SCHOLARSHIP

Scholarship for students in 7th to 12th grades of any accredited Illinois high school. Must write a 500-word essay on selected topic.

Award: Prize for use in freshman year; not renewable. *Number:* 1–60. *Amount:* $100–$1200.

Eligibility Requirements: Applicant must be high school student; planning to enroll or expecting to enroll full- or part-time at a two-year or four-year institution or university; resident of Illinois and must have an interest in writing. Applicant or parent of applicant must be member of American Legion or Auxiliary. Available to U.S. citizens.

Application Requirements: Application form, essay. *Deadline:* February 1.

Contact: Christy Rich, Executive Administrative Assistant
American Legion Department of Illinois
2720 East Lincoln Street
Bloomington, IL 61704
Phone: 309-663-0361
E-mail: hdqs@illegion.org

AMERICAN LEGION DEPARTMENT OF ILLINOIS BOY SCOUT/EXPLORER SCHOLARSHIP

Scholarship for a graduating high school senior who is a qualified Boy Scout or Explorer and a resident of Illinois. Must write a 500-word essay on Legion's Americanism and Boy Scout programs.

Award: Scholarship for use in freshman year; not renewable. *Number:* 1–5. *Amount:* $200–$1000.

Eligibility Requirements: Applicant must be high school student; planning to enroll or expecting to enroll full- or part-time at a four-year institution or university and resident of Illinois. Applicant or parent of applicant must be member of Boy Scouts. Available to U.S. citizens.

Application Requirements: Application form, essay. *Deadline:* April 30.

Contact: Christy Rich, Executive Administrative Assistant
American Legion Department of Illinois
2720 East Lincoln Street
Bloomington, IL 61704
Phone: 309-663-0361
E-mail: hdqs@illegion.org

AMERICAN LEGION DEPARTMENT OF INDIANA

http://www.indianalegion.org

AMERICAN LEGION FAMILY SCHOLARSHIP

Scholarship open to children and grandchildren of current members of The American Legion, American Legion Auxiliary, and The Sons of the American Legion. Also open to the children and grandchildren of deceased members who were current paid members of the above organizations at the time of their death. Applicants must be attending or planning to attend an Indiana institution of higher education.

Award: Scholarship for use in freshman, sophomore, junior, or senior years; not renewable.

Eligibility Requirements: Applicant must be enrolled or expecting to enroll full- or part-time at a two-year or four-year or technical institution or university; resident of Indiana and studying in Indiana. Applicant or parent of applicant must be member of American Legion or Auxiliary. Applicant must have 3.5 GPA or higher. Available to U.S. citizens.

Application Requirements: Application form, essay. *Deadline:* April 2.

Contact: Butch Miller, Program Director
American Legion Department of Indiana
5440 Herbert Lord Rd
Indianapolis, IN 46216
Phone: 317-6301300
Fax: 317-237-9891
E-mail: bmiller@indianalegion.org

AMERICAN LEGION DEPARTMENT OF IOWA

http://www.ialegion.org/

AMERICAN LEGION DEPARTMENT OF IOWA EAGLE SCOUT OF THE YEAR SCHOLARSHIP

Three one-time award for Eagle Scouts who are residents of Iowa. For full-time study only.

Award: Scholarship for use in freshman year; not renewable. *Number:* up to 3. *Amount:* $250–$1000.

Eligibility Requirements: Applicant must be high school student; planning to enroll or expecting to enroll full-time at a two-year or four-year institution or university; male and resident of Iowa. Applicant or parent of applicant must be member of Boy Scouts. Available to U.S. citizens.

Application Requirements: Application form, entry in a contest, recommendations or references. *Deadline:* March 1.

Contact: Program Director
American Legion Department of Iowa
720 Lyon Street
Des Moines, IA 50309
Phone: 515-282-5068

AMERICAN LEGION DEPARTMENT OF KANSAS

http://www.ksamlegion.org/

ALBERT M. LAPPIN SCHOLARSHIP

Scholarship for children of the members of Kansas American Legion or its auxiliary. Membership must have been active for the past three years. The children of deceased members are also eligible if parents' dues were paid at the time of death. Applicant must be a son/daughter of a veteran. Must be high school senior or college freshman or sophomore. Must use award at a Kansas college, university, or trade school.

Award: Scholarship for use in freshman or sophomore years; not renewable. *Number:* 1. *Amount:* $1000.

Eligibility Requirements: Applicant must be enrolled or expecting to enroll full-time at a two-year or four-year or technical institution or university; resident of Kansas and studying in Kansas. Applicant or parent of applicant must be member of American Legion or Auxiliary. Available to U.S. citizens.

Application Requirements: Application form, essay, financial need analysis, personal photograph. *Deadline:* February 15.

Contact: Mike Oppy, Chairman, Scholarship Committee
American Legion Department of Kansas
1314 SW Topeka Boulevard
Topeka, KS 66612
Phone: 785-232-9513

CHARLES W. AND ANNETTE HILL SCHOLARSHIP

Scholarship of $1000 to the descendants of veterans who are American Legion members or American Legion Auxiliary members holding membership for the past three consecutive years. Descendants of deceased members can also apply. Must be high school seniors or college

freshmen or sophomores in a Kansas institution. Scholarship for use at an approved college, university, or trade school in Kansas. Must maintain a 3.0 GPA. Disbursement: $500 at beginning each semester for one year.

Award: Scholarship for use in freshman or sophomore years; not renewable. *Number:* 1. *Amount:* $1000.

Eligibility Requirements: Applicant must be enrolled or expecting to enroll full-time at a two-year or four-year or technical institution or university; resident of Kansas and studying in Kansas. Applicant or parent of applicant must be member of American Legion or Auxiliary. Applicant must have 3.0 GPA or higher. Available to U.S. citizens.

Application Requirements: Application form, essay, financial need analysis, personal photograph. *Deadline:* February 15.

Contact: Mike Oppy, Chairman, Scholarship Committee
American Legion Department of Kansas
1314 SW Topeka Boulevard
Topeka, KS 66612
Phone: 785-232-9315

HUGH A. SMITH SCHOLARSHIP FUND

One-year scholarship of $500 to the children of American Legion/Auxiliary members holding membership for the past three consecutive years. Children of a deceased member can also apply. Parent of the applicant must be a veteran. Must be high school seniors or college freshmen or sophomores in a Kansas institution. Scholarship for use at an approved college, university, or trade school in Kansas. Must maintain a C average in college.

Award: Scholarship for use in freshman or sophomore years; not renewable. *Number:* 1. *Amount:* $500.

Eligibility Requirements: Applicant must be enrolled or expecting to enroll full-time at a two-year or four-year or technical institution or university; resident of Kansas and studying in Kansas. Applicant or parent of applicant must be member of American Legion or Auxiliary. Available to U.S. citizens.

Application Requirements: Application form, essay, financial need analysis, personal photograph. *Deadline:* February 15.

Contact: Mike Oppy, Chairman, Scholarship Committee
American Legion Department of Kansas
1314 SW Topeka Boulevard
Topeka, KS 66612
Phone: 785-232-9315

ROSEDALE POST 346 SCHOLARSHIP

Two scholarships of $1500 each awarded to the children of American Legion members or of American Legion Auxiliary members holding membership for the past three consecutive years. Children of a deceased member can also apply. Parent of the applicant must be a veteran. Must be high school seniors or college freshmen or sophomores in a Kansas institution. Scholarship for use at an approved college, university, or trade school in Kansas. Must maintain a C average in college.

Award: Scholarship for use in freshman or sophomore years; not renewable. *Number:* 2. *Amount:* $1500.

Eligibility Requirements: Applicant must be enrolled or expecting to enroll full-time at a two-year or four-year or technical institution or university; resident of Kansas and studying in Kansas. Applicant or parent of applicant must be member of American Legion or Auxiliary. Available to U.S. citizens.

Application Requirements: Application form, essay, financial need analysis, personal photograph. *Deadline:* February 15.

Contact: Mike Oppy, Chairman, Scholarship Committee
American Legion Department of Kansas
1314 SW Topeka Boulevard
Topeka, KS 66612
Phone: 785-232-9315

TED AND NORA ANDERSON SCHOLARSHIPS

Scholarship of $1000 for each semester (one year only) given to the descendant of American Legion members who are holding membership for the past three consecutive years. Children of a deceased member can also apply. Must be high school seniors or college freshmen or sophomores in a Kansas institution. Scholarship for use at an approved college, university, or trade school in Kansas. Must maintain a C average in college.

Award: Scholarship for use in freshman or sophomore years; not renewable. *Number:* 1. *Amount:* $1000.

Eligibility Requirements: Applicant must be enrolled or expecting to enroll full-time at a two-year or four-year or technical institution or

university; resident of Kansas and studying in Kansas. Applicant or parent of applicant must be member of American Legion or Auxiliary. Available to U.S. citizens.

Application Requirements: Application form, essay, financial need analysis, personal photograph. *Deadline:* February 15.

Contact: Mike Oppy, Chairman, Scholarship Committee
American Legion Department of Kansas
1314 SW Topeka Boulevard
Topeka, KS 66612
Phone: 785-232-9315

AMERICAN LEGION DEPARTMENT OF MAINE

http://www.mainelegion.org/

JAMES V. DAY SCHOLARSHIP

One-time $500 award for a Maine resident whose parent is a member of the American Legion or Auxiliary in Maine, or is a member of Sons of the American Legion in Maine. Must be a U.S. citizen. Based on character and financial need.

Award: Scholarship for use in freshman, sophomore, junior, or senior years; not renewable. *Number:* 1–2. *Amount:* up to $500.

Eligibility Requirements: Applicant must be enrolled or expecting to enroll full-time at a two-year or four-year or technical institution or university and resident of Maine. Applicant or parent of applicant must be member of American Legion or Auxiliary. Available to U.S. citizens. Applicant or parent must meet one or more of the following requirements: general military experience; retired from active duty; disabled or killed as a result of military service; prisoner of war; or missing in action.

Application Requirements: Application form, recommendations or references, transcript. *Deadline:* May 1.

Contact: Mr. Paul L'Heureux, Department Adjutant
American Legion Department of Maine
PO Box 900
Waterville, ME 04903
Phone: 207-873-3229
Fax: 207-872-0501
E-mail: legionme@mainelegion.org

AMERICAN LEGION DEPARTMENT OF MARYLAND

http://www.mdlegion.org/

AMERICAN LEGION DEPARTMENT OF MARYLAND GENERAL SCHOLARSHIP FUND

Nonrenewable scholarship for veterans or children of veterans who served in the Armed Forces during dates of eligibility for American Legion membership. Merit-based award. Application available on website http://mdlegion.org.

Award: Scholarship for use in freshman, sophomore, junior, or senior years; not renewable. *Number:* 1–10. *Amount:* $500–$1000.

Eligibility Requirements: Applicant must be high school student; planning to enroll or expecting to enroll full-time at a two-year or four-year institution or university and resident of Maryland. Applicant or parent of applicant must be member of American Legion or Auxiliary. Available to U.S. citizens.

Application Requirements: Application form, essay, financial need analysis. *Deadline:* April 1.

Contact: Russell Myers, Department Adjutant
American Legion Department of Maryland
101 North Gay, Room E
Baltimore, MD 21202
Phone: 410-752-1405
E-mail: russell@mdlegion.org

THE AMERICAN LEGION, DEPARTMENT OF MINNESOTA

http://www.mnlegion.org/

AMERICAN LEGION DEPARTMENT OF MINNESOTA MEMORIAL SCHOLARSHIP

Scholarship available to Minnesota residents who are dependents of members of the Minnesota American Legion or Auxiliary. One-time award of $500 for study at a Minnesota institution or neighboring state with reciprocating agreement. See website for application information http://www.mnlegion.org.

Award: Scholarship for use in freshman, sophomore, junior, or senior years; not renewable. *Number:* 6. *Amount:* $500.

Eligibility Requirements: Applicant must be enrolled or expecting to enroll full- or part-time at a two-year or four-year or technical institution or university; resident of Minnesota and studying in Iowa, Minnesota, North Dakota, South Dakota, Wisconsin. Applicant or parent of applicant must be member of American Legion or Auxiliary. Available to U.S. citizens. Applicant or parent must meet one or more of the following requirements: general military experience; retired from active duty; disabled or killed as a result of military service; prisoner of war; or missing in action.

Application Requirements: Application form, essay, financial need analysis. *Deadline:* April 1.

Contact: Jennifer Kelley, Program Coordinator
The American Legion, Department of Minnesota
20 West 12th Street, Room 300-A
St. Paul, MN 55155
Phone: 651-291-1800
E-mail: department@mnlegion.org

MINNESOTA LEGIONNAIRES INSURANCE TRUST SCHOLARSHIP

Scholarship for Minnesota residents who are veterans or dependents of veterans. One-time award of $500 for study at a Minnesota institution or neighboring state with reciprocating agreement. All applications must be approved and recommended by a post of the American Legion. See website for application information http://www.mnlegion.org.

Award: Scholarship for use in freshman, sophomore, junior, or senior years; not renewable. *Number:* 3. *Amount:* $500.

Eligibility Requirements: Applicant must be enrolled or expecting to enroll full- or part-time at a two-year or four-year or technical institution or university; resident of Minnesota and studying in Iowa, Minnesota, North Dakota, South Dakota, Wisconsin. Applicant or parent of applicant must be member of American Legion or Auxiliary. Available to U.S. citizens. Applicant or parent must meet one or more of the following requirements: general military experience; retired from active duty; disabled or killed as a result of military service; prisoner of war; or missing in action.

Application Requirements: Application form, essay, financial need analysis. *Deadline:* April 1.

Contact: Jennifer Kelley, Program Coordinator
The American Legion, Department of Minnesota
20 West 12th Street, Room 300-A
St. Paul, MN 55155
Phone: 651-291-1800
E-mail: department@mnlegion.org

AMERICAN LEGION DEPARTMENT OF MISSOURI

http://www.missourilegion.org/

CHARLES L. BACON MEMORIAL SCHOLARSHIP

Two awards of $500 are given to members of The American Legion, the American Legion Auxiliary, or the Sons of The American Legion, or a descendant of a member of any thereof. Applicants must be unmarried Missouri resident below age 21, and must use the scholarship as a full-time student in an accredited college or university in Missouri. Must submit proof of American Legion membership.

Award: Scholarship for use in freshman year; not renewable. *Number:* 2. *Amount:* $500.

Eligibility Requirements: Applicant must be high school student; planning to enroll or expecting to enroll full-time at a two-year or four-year institution or university; single and resident of Missouri. Applicant or parent of applicant must be member of American Legion or Auxiliary. Available to U.S. citizens. Applicant or parent must meet one or more of the following requirements: general military experience; retired from active duty; disabled or killed as a result of military service; prisoner of war; or missing in action.

Application Requirements: Application form, discharge certificate, financial need analysis, test scores. *Deadline:* April 20.

Contact: John Doane, Chairman
Phone: 417-924-8596
Fax: 573-225-1406
E-mail: info@missourilegion.org

AMERICAN LEGION DEPARTMENT OF NEBRASKA

http://www.nebraskalegion.net/

MAYNARD JENSEN AMERICAN LEGION MEMORIAL SCHOLARSHIP

Scholarship for dependents or grandchildren of members, prisoner-of-war, missing-in-action veterans, killed-in-action veterans, or any deceased veterans of the American Legion. One-time award is based on academic achievement and financial need for Nebraska residents attending Nebraska institutions. Several scholarships of $500 each. Must have minimum 2.5 GPA and must submit school certification of GPA.

Award: Scholarship for use in freshman, sophomore, junior, or senior years; not renewable. *Number:* 1–10. *Amount:* $500.

Eligibility Requirements: Applicant must be enrolled or expecting to enroll full-time at a two-year or four-year or technical institution or university; resident of Nebraska and studying in Nebraska. Applicant or parent of applicant must be member of American Legion or Auxiliary. Applicant must have 3.5 GPA or higher. Available to U.S. citizens.

Application Requirements: Application form, financial need analysis. *Deadline:* March 1.

Contact: Brent Hagel-Pitt, Administrator
American Legion Department of Nebraska
P.O. Box 5205
Lincoln, NE 68505
Phone: 402-464-6338
E-mail: actdirlegion@windstream.net

AMERICAN LEGION DEPARTMENT OF OHIO

http://www.ohiolegion.com/

OHIO AMERICAN LEGION SCHOLARSHIPS

One-time award for full-time students attending an accredited institution. Open to students of any postsecondary academic year. Must have minimum 3.0 GPA. Must be a member of the American Legion, a direct descendent of a Legionnaire (living or deceased), or surviving spouse or child of a deceased U.S. military person who died on active duty or of injuries received on active duty.

Award: Scholarship for use in freshman, sophomore, junior, or senior years; not renewable. *Number:* 15–18. *Amount:* $2000–$3000.

Eligibility Requirements: Applicant must be enrolled or expecting to enroll full-time at a two-year or four-year or technical institution or university. Applicant or parent of applicant must be member of American Legion or Auxiliary. Applicant must have 3.0 GPA or higher. Available to U.S. and non-U.S. citizens. Applicant or parent must meet one or more of the following requirements: general military experience; retired from active duty; disabled or killed as a result of military service; prisoner of war; or missing in action.

Application Requirements: Application form, resume, transcript. *Deadline:* April 15.

Contact: Donald Lanthorn, Service Director
American Legion Department of Ohio
60 Big Run Road, PO Box 8007
Delaware, OH 43015
Phone: 740-362-7478
Fax: 740-362-1429
E-mail: dlanthorn@iwaynet.net

AMERICAN LEGION DEPARTMENT OF PENNSYLVANIA

http://www.pa-legion.com/

JOSEPH P. GAVENONIS COLLEGE SCHOLARSHIP (PLAN I)

Scholarships for Pennsylvania residents seeking a four-year degree from a Pennsylvania college or university. Must be the child of a member of a Pennsylvania American Legion post. Must be a graduating high school senior. Award amount and number of awards determined annually. Renewable award. Must maintain 2.5 GPA in college. Total number of awards varies.

Award: Scholarship for use in freshman year; renewable. *Amount:* $500–$1000.

Eligibility Requirements: Applicant must be high school student; planning to enroll or expecting to enroll full-time at a four-year institution or university; resident of Pennsylvania and studying in Pennsylvania. Applicant or parent of applicant must be member of American Legion or Auxiliary. Applicant must have 2.5 GPA or higher. Available to U.S. citizens.

Application Requirements: Application form, financial need analysis, test scores, transcript. *Deadline:* May 30.

Contact: Debbie Watson, Emblem Sales Supervisor
American Legion Department of Pennsylvania
PO Box 2324
Harrisburg, PA 17105-2324
Phone: 717-730-9100
Fax: 717-975-2836
E-mail: hq@pa-legion.com

AMERICAN LEGION DEPARTMENT OF TENNESSEE

http://www.tennesseelegion.org/

AMERICAN LEGION DEPARTMENT OF TENNESSEE EAGLE SCOUT OF THE YEAR

$3000 scholarship for graduating high school seniors who are Eagle Scouts, enrolled either part-time or full-time for study in accredited colleges or universities. Deadline varies.

Award: Scholarship for use in freshman, sophomore, junior, or senior years; not renewable. *Number:* 1. *Amount:* $3000.

Eligibility Requirements: Applicant must be high school student; age 15–18; planning to enroll or expecting to enroll full- or part-time at a four-year institution or university; male; resident of Tennessee and studying in Tennessee. Applicant or parent of applicant must be member of Boy Scouts. Available to U.S. citizens.

Application Requirements: Application form, community service, personal photograph, portfolio. *Deadline:* March 1.

Contact: Dean Tuttle, Department Adjutant
American Legion Department of Tennessee
318 Donelson Pike
Nashville, TN 37214
Phone: 615-391-5088
E-mail: Adjutant@TNLegion.org

AMERICAN LEGION DEPARTMENT OF VERMONT

http://www.vtlegion.org

AMERICAN LEGION EAGLE SCOUT OF THE YEAR

Awarded to the Boy Scout chosen for outstanding service to his religious institution, school, and community. Must receive the award and reside in Vermont.

Award: Scholarship for use in freshman year; not renewable. *Number:* 1. *Amount:* $1000.

Eligibility Requirements: Applicant must be high school student; planning to enroll or expecting to enroll full-time at a two-year or four-year or technical institution or university and resident of Vermont. Applicant or parent of applicant must be member of Boy Scouts. Applicant or parent of applicant must have employment or volunteer experience in community service. Available to U.S. citizens.

Application Requirements: Application form, community service, essay, personal photograph. *Deadline:* March 1.

Contact: Ronald LaRose, Chairman
American Legion Department of Vermont
PO Box 396
Montpelier, VT 05601-0396
Phone: 802-223-7131
E-mail: alvthq@myfairpoint.net

AMERICAN LEGION DEPARTMENT OF WASHINGTON

http://www.walegion.org/

AMERICAN LEGION DEPARTMENT OF WASHINGTON CHILDREN AND YOUTH SCHOLARSHIPS

One-time award for the son or daughter of a Washington American Legion or Auxiliary member, living or deceased. Must be high school senior and Washington resident planning to attend an accredited institution of higher education in Washington. Award based on need.

Award: Scholarship for use in freshman year; not renewable. *Number:* 2. *Amount:* $1500–$2500.

Eligibility Requirements: Applicant must be high school student; planning to enroll or expecting to enroll full- or part-time at a four-year institution or university and resident of Washington. Applicant or parent of applicant must be member of American Legion or Auxiliary. Available to U.S. citizens.

Application Requirements: Application form, financial need analysis. *Deadline:* April 1.

Contact: Department Adjutant
American Legion Department of Washington
PO Box 3917
Lacey, WA 98509
Phone: 360-491-4373
E-mail: americanlegion@walegion.org

AMERICAN LEGION DEPARTMENT OF WEST VIRGINIA

http://www.wvlegion.org/

SONS OF THE AMERICAN LEGION WILLIAM F. "BILL" JOHNSON MEMORIAL SCHOLARSHIP

Applicant is required to write an essay based on a different question each year. Award is given during the second semester of college provided the winner has passing grades in the first semester. Must submit a copy of passing GPA of their first semester of college. Must be a resident of West Virginia and the child or grandchild of a member of The American Legion. Deadline each year is May 15th.

Award: Scholarship for use in freshman year; not renewable.

Eligibility Requirements: Applicant must be high school student; planning to enroll or expecting to enroll full-time at a two-year or four-year institution or university; resident of West Virginia and studying in West Virginia. Applicant or parent of applicant must be member of American Legion or Auxiliary. Available to U.S. citizens. Applicant or parent must meet one or more of the following requirements: general military experience; retired from active duty; disabled or killed as a result of military service; prisoner of war; or missing in action.

Application Requirements: Application form, essay. *Deadline:* May 15.

Contact: Mr. Miles Epling, Department Adjutant
American Legion Department of West Virginia
2016 Kanawha Boulevard East, P.O. Box 3191
Charleston, WV 25332
Phone: 304-343-7591
E-mail: wvlegion@suddenlinkmail.com

AMERICAN POSTAL WORKERS UNION

http://www.apwu.org/

E.C. HALLBECK SCHOLARSHIP FUND

Scholarship for children of American Postal Workers Union members. Applicant must be a child, grandchild, stepchild, or legally adopted child of an active member, Retirees Department member, or deceased member of American Postal Workers Union. Must be a senior attending high school or other corresponding secondary school. Must be 18 years or older. Recipient must attend accredited community college or university as a full-time student. Scholarship will be $1000 for each year of four consecutive years of college. Scholarship will provide five area winners. For additional information and to download applications go to website http://www.apwu.org.

Award: Scholarship for use in freshman year; renewable. *Number:* 5. *Amount:* $1000.

Eligibility Requirements: Applicant must be high school student and planning to enroll or expecting to enroll full-time at a two-year or four-year or technical institution or university. Applicant or parent of applicant must be member of American Postal Workers Union. Applicant or parent of applicant must have employment or volunteer experience in federal/postal service. Available to U.S. citizens.

Application Requirements: Application form, essay, recommendations or references, test scores, transcript. *Deadline:* March 15.

Contact: Terry Stapleton, Secretary and Treasurer
American Postal Workers Union
1300 L Street, NW
Washington, DC 20005
Phone: 202-842-4215
Fax: 202-842-8530

VOCATIONAL SCHOLARSHIP PROGRAM

A scholarship for a child, grandchild, stepchild, or legally adopted child of an active member, Retiree's Department member, or deceased member of the American Postal Workers Union. Applicant must be a senior attending high school who plans on attending an accredited vocational school or community college vocational program as a full-time student. The award is $1000 per year consecutively or until completion of the course. For additional information see website http://www.apwu.org.

Award: Scholarship for use in freshman year; renewable. *Number:* 5. *Amount:* $1000.

Eligibility Requirements: Applicant must be high school student and planning to enroll or expecting to enroll full-time at a four-year institution or university. Applicant or parent of applicant must be member of American Postal Workers Union. Applicant or parent of applicant must have employment or volunteer experience in federal/postal service. Available to U.S. citizens.

Application Requirements: Application form, essay, recommendations or references, test scores, transcript. *Deadline:* March 15.

Contact: Terry Stapleton, Secretary and Treasurer
American Postal Workers Union
1300 L Street, NW
Washington, DC 20005
Phone: 202-842-4215
Fax: 202-842-8530

AMERICAN QUARTER HORSE FOUNDATION (AQHF)

http://www.aqha.com/foundation

AQHF GENERAL SCHOLARSHIP

Ideal candidates are current AQHA or AQHYA members.

Award: Scholarship for use in sophomore, junior, senior, graduate, or postgraduate years; renewable. *Number:* 1–15. *Amount:* $4000.

Eligibility Requirements: Applicant must be enrolled or expecting to enroll full-time at a two-year or four-year or technical institution or university. Applicant or parent of applicant must be member of American Quarter Horse Association. Applicant must have 2.5 GPA or higher. Available to U.S. and non-U.S. citizens.

Application Requirements: Application form, financial need analysis. *Deadline:* December 1.

Contact: Scholarship Office
American Quarter Horse Foundation (AQHF)
2601 East Interstate 40
Amarillo, TX 79104
Phone: 806-378-5029
E-mail: foundation@aqha.org

AQHF RACING SCHOLARSHIPS

Scholarships for applicants who have experience within the racing industry or are seeking a career in the industry. Applicants seeking a career in the racing industry may specialize in veterinary medicine, racetrack management or other related fields.

Award: Scholarship for use in freshman, sophomore, junior, senior, graduate, or postgraduate years; renewable. *Number:* 1–5. *Amount:* $4000–$8000.

Eligibility Requirements: Applicant must be enrolled or expecting to enroll full-time at a two-year or four-year or technical institution or university. Applicant or parent of applicant must be member of American Quarter Horse Association. Applicant or parent of applicant must have employment or volunteer experience in designated career field, harness racing. Applicant must have 2.5 GPA or higher. Available to U.S. and non-U.S. citizens.

Application Requirements: Application form, financial need analysis. *Deadline:* December 1.

Contact: Scholarship Office
American Quarter Horse Foundation (AQHF)
2601 East Interstate 40
Amarillo, TX 79104
Phone: 806-378-5029
E-mail: foundation@aqha.org

AQHF YOUTH SCHOLARSHIPS

Ideal candidates are members of AQHA or AQHYA who have completed a minimum of three years cumulative membership; exhibit an affinity for the American Quarter Horse, and demonstrate leadership potential.

Award: Scholarship for use in freshman, sophomore, junior, senior, or graduate years; renewable. *Number:* 1–15. *Amount:* $8000.

Eligibility Requirements: Applicant must be high school student and planning to enroll or expecting to enroll full-time at a two-year or four-year or technical institution or university. Applicant or parent of applicant must be member of American Quarter Horse Association. Applicant must have 3.5 GPA or higher. Available to U.S. and non-U.S. citizens.

Application Requirements: Application form, financial need analysis. *Deadline:* December 1.

Contact: Scholarship Office
American Quarter Horse Foundation (AQHF)
2601 East Interstate 40
Amarillo, TX 79104
Phone: 806-378-5029
E-mail: foundation@aqha.org

ARIZONA QUARTER HORSE YOUTH SCHOLARSHIP

Ideal candidate is an AQHA or AQHYA member from Arizona who is a current or previous member of the Arizona Quarter Horse Youth Association, and must be actively involved with AzQHA.

Award: Scholarship for use in freshman, sophomore, junior, senior, or graduate years; renewable. *Number:* 1. *Amount:* $5000.

Eligibility Requirements: Applicant must be enrolled or expecting to enroll full-time at a two-year or four-year or technical institution or university and resident of Arizona. Applicant or parent of applicant must be member of American Quarter Horse Association. Applicant must have 2.5 GPA or higher. Available to U.S. citizens.

Application Requirements: Application form, financial need analysis. *Deadline:* December 1.

Contact: Scholarship Office
American Quarter Horse Foundation (AQHF)
2601 East Interstate 40
Amarillo, TX 79104
Phone: 806-378-5029
E-mail: foundation@aqha.org

ARIZONA QUARTER RACING SCHOLARSHIP

Ideal candidate is an AQHA or AQHYA member from Arizona who has experience within, or is seeking a career in the racing industry. Recipient may specialize in veterinary medicine, racetrack management or other related field.

Award: Scholarship for use in freshman, sophomore, junior, senior, graduate, or postgraduate years; not renewable. *Number:* 1. *Amount:* $500.

Eligibility Requirements: Applicant must be enrolled or expecting to enroll full-time at a two-year or four-year or technical institution or university; resident of Arizona and must have an interest in animal/agricultural competition. Applicant or parent of applicant must be member of American Quarter Horse Association. Applicant or parent of applicant must have employment or volunteer experience in designated career field, harness racing. Applicant must have 2.5 GPA or higher. Available to U.S. citizens.

Application Requirements: Application form, financial need analysis. *Deadline:* December 1.

Contact: Scholarship Office
American Quarter Horse Foundation (AQHF)
2601 East Interstate 40
Amarillo, TX 79104
Phone: 806-378-5029
E-mail: foundation@aqha.org

BOON SAN KITTY SCHOLARSHIP

Ideal candidate is a current AQHA or AQHYA member.

Award: Scholarship for use in freshman, sophomore, junior, or senior years; renewable. *Number:* 1. *Amount:* $7500.

Eligibility Requirements: Applicant must be high school student and planning to enroll or expecting to enroll full-time at a two-year or four-year institution or university. Applicant or parent of applicant must be member of American Quarter Horse Association. Applicant must have 3.0 GPA or higher. Available to U.S. and non-U.S. citizens.

Application Requirements: Application form, financial need analysis. *Deadline:* December 1.

Contact: Scholarship Office
American Quarter Horse Foundation (AQHF)
2601 East Interstate 40
Amarillo, TX 79104
Phone: 806-378-5029
E-mail: foundation@aqha.org

CHRISTOPHER LAWRENCE JUNKER NEBRASKA SCHOLARSHIP

Ideal candidate is an AQHA or AQHYA member from Nebraska.

Award: Scholarship for use in freshman, sophomore, junior, or senior years; not renewable. *Number:* 1. *Amount:* $500.

Eligibility Requirements: Applicant must be enrolled or expecting to enroll full-time at a two-year or four-year or technical institution or university and resident of Nebraska. Applicant or parent of applicant must be member of American Quarter Horse Association. Applicant must have 2.5 GPA or higher. Available to U.S. citizens.

Application Requirements: Application form, financial need analysis. *Deadline:* December 1.

Contact: Scholarship Office
American Quarter Horse Foundation (AQHF)
2601 East Interstate 40
Amarillo, TX 79104
Phone: 806-378-5029
E-mail: foundation@aqha.org

DR. GERALD O'CONNOR MICHIGAN QHY SCHOLARSHIP

Ideal candidate is an AQHA or AQHYA member from Michigan. Scholarship is available once every four years.

Award: Scholarship for use in freshman, sophomore, junior, senior, or graduate years; renewable. *Number:* 1. *Amount:* $2000.

Eligibility Requirements: Applicant must be enrolled or expecting to enroll full-time at a two-year or four-year or technical institution or university; resident of Michigan and must have an interest in animal/agricultural competition. Applicant or parent of applicant must be member of American Quarter Horse Association. Applicant must have 2.5 GPA or higher. Available to U.S. citizens.

Application Requirements: Application form, financial need analysis. *Deadline:* December 1.

Contact: Scholarship Office
American Quarter Horse Foundation (AQHF)
2601 East Interstate 40
Amarillo, TX 79104
Phone: 806-378-5029
E-mail: foundation@aqha.org

DOGWOOD SCHOLARSHIP

Ideal candidate is a current AQHA or AQHYA member.

Award: Scholarship for use in freshman, sophomore, junior, or senior years; renewable. *Number:* 1. *Amount:* $5000.

Eligibility Requirements: Applicant must be enrolled or expecting to enroll full-time at a two-year or four-year or technical institution or university. Applicant or parent of applicant must be member of American Quarter Horse Association. Applicant must have 3.0 GPA or higher. Available to U.S. and non-U.S. citizens.

Application Requirements: Application form, financial need analysis. *Deadline:* December 1.

Contact: Scholarship Office
American Quarter Horse Foundation (AQHF)
2601 East Interstate 40
Amarillo, TX 79104
Phone: 806-378-5029
E-mail: foundation@aqha.org

EXCELLENCE IN EQUINE & AGRICULTURAL INVOLVEMENT SCHOLARSHIP

Ideal candidate is an AQHA or AQHYA member who exemplifies the characteristics of leadership and excellence acquired through participation in equine and or agriculture activities. Applicant should not compete in AQHA-approved shows.

Award: Scholarship for use in freshman, sophomore, junior, senior, or graduate years; renewable. *Number:* 1. *Amount:* $25,000.

Eligibility Requirements: Applicant must be enrolled or expecting to enroll full-time at a two-year or four-year institution or university. Applicant or parent of applicant must be member of American Quarter Horse Association. Applicant or parent of applicant must have employment or volunteer experience in agriculture. Applicant must have 3.5 GPA or higher. Available to U.S. and non-U.S. citizens.

Application Requirements: Application form, financial need analysis. *Deadline:* December 1.

Contact: Scholarship Office
American Quarter Horse Foundation (AQHF)
2601 East Interstate 40
Amarillo, TX 79104
Phone: 806-378-5029
E-mail: foundation@aqha.org

FARM AND RANCH HERITAGE SCHOLARSHIP

Ideal candidates are AQHA or AQHYA members from farming and or ranching backgrounds who represent the outstanding education, expertise and life skills gained through participation in agricultural activities. Applicants may not compete in AQHA-approved shows.

Award: Scholarship for use in freshman, sophomore, junior, senior, or graduate years; renewable. *Number:* 1–4. *Amount:* $12,500.

Eligibility Requirements: Applicant must be enrolled or expecting to enroll full-time at a two-year or four-year institution or university. Applicant or parent of applicant must be member of American Quarter Horse Association. Applicant or parent of applicant must have employment or volunteer experience in agriculture, farming. Applicant must have 3.0 GPA or higher. Available to U.S. and non-U.S. citizens.

Application Requirements: Application form, financial need analysis. *Deadline:* December 1.

Contact: Scholarship Office
American Quarter Horse Foundation (AQHF)
2601 East Interstate 40
Amarillo, TX 79104
Phone: 806-378-5029
E-mail: foundation@aqha.org

GUY STOOPS PROFESSIONAL HORSEMEN'S FAMILY SCHOLARSHIP

Ideal candidates are AQHA or AQHYA members whose parent(s) are a current member of the AQHA Professional Horsemen's Association, with membership in good standing for three or more years.

Award: Scholarship for use in freshman, sophomore, junior, or senior years; renewable. *Number:* 1. *Amount:* $3000.

Eligibility Requirements: Applicant must be enrolled or expecting to enroll full-time at a two-year or four-year or technical institution or university. Applicant or parent of applicant must be member of American Quarter Horse Association, Professional Horsemen Association. Applicant must have 2.5 GPA or higher. Available to U.S. and non-U.S. citizens.

Application Requirements: Application form, financial need analysis. *Deadline:* December 1.

Contact: Scholarship Office
American Quarter Horse Foundation (AQHF)
2601 East Interstate 40
Amarillo, TX 79104
Phone: 806-378-5029
E-mail: foundation@aqha.org

INDIANA QUARTER HORSE YOUTH SCHOLARSHIP

Ideal candidate is an AQHA or AQHYA member from Indiana who is a current member of the Indiana Quarter Horse Association, and has maintained two or more years membership with that association.

Award: Scholarship for use in freshman, sophomore, junior, or senior years; not renewable. *Number:* 1. *Amount:* $1500.

Eligibility Requirements: Applicant must be enrolled or expecting to enroll full-time at a two-year or four-year or technical institution or university and resident of Indiana. Applicant or parent of applicant must be member of American Quarter Horse Association. Applicant must have 2.5 GPA or higher. Available to U.S. citizens.

Application Requirements: Application form, financial need analysis. *Deadline:* December 1.

Contact: Scholarship Office
American Quarter Horse Foundation (AQHF)
2601 East Interstate 40
Amarillo, TX 79104
Phone: 806-378-5029
E-mail: foundation@aqha.org

JAMES F. AND DORIS M. BARTON SCHOLARSHIP

Ideal candidate is an AQHA or AQHYA member from New York who is a current member of the Empire State Youth Quarter Horse Association.

Award: Scholarship for use in freshman, sophomore, junior, or senior years; renewable. *Number:* 1. *Amount:* $5000.

Eligibility Requirements: Applicant must be enrolled or expecting to enroll full-time at a two-year or four-year institution or university and resident of New York. Applicant or parent of applicant must be member of American Quarter Horse Association. Applicant must have 3.0 GPA or higher. Available to U.S. citizens.

Application Requirements: Application form, financial need analysis. *Deadline:* December 1.

Contact: Scholarship Office
American Quarter Horse Foundation (AQHF)
2601 East Interstate 40
Amarillo, TX 79104
Phone: 806-378-5029
E-mail: foundation@aqha.org

JOAN CAIN FLORIDA QUARTER HORSE YOUTH SCHOLARSHIP

Ideal candidate is an AQHA or AQHYA member from Florida who is a current member of the Florida Quarter Horse Youth Association, and has maintained two or more years of membership.

Award: Scholarship for use in freshman, sophomore, junior, or senior years; not renewable. *Number:* 1. *Amount:* $1000.

Eligibility Requirements: Applicant must be enrolled or expecting to enroll full-time at a two-year or four-year or technical institution or university and resident of Florida. Applicant or parent of applicant must be member of American Quarter Horse Association. Applicant must have 2.5 GPA or higher. Available to U.S. citizens.

Application Requirements: Application form, financial need analysis. *Deadline:* December 1.

Contact: Scholarship Office
American Quarter Horse Foundation (AQHF)
2601 East Interstate 40
Amarillo, TX 79104
Phone: 806-378-5029
E-mail: foundation@aqha.org

JOYCE WYATT PENNSYLVANIA QUARTER HORSE YOUTH SCHOLARSHIP

Ideal candidate is an AQHA or AQHYA member from Pennsylvania. Scholarship is available once every four years.

Award: Scholarship for use in freshman, sophomore, junior, senior, or graduate years; renewable. *Number:* 1. *Amount:* $2000.

Eligibility Requirements: Applicant must be enrolled or expecting to enroll full-time at a two-year or four-year or technical institution or university and resident of Pennsylvania. Applicant or parent of applicant must be member of American Quarter Horse Association. Applicant must have 3.0 GPA or higher. Available to U.S. citizens.

Application Requirements: Application form, financial need analysis. *Deadline:* December 1.

Contact: Scholarship Office
American Quarter Horse Foundation (AQHF)
2601 East Interstate 40
Amarillo, TX 79104
Phone: 806-378-5029
E-mail: foundation@aqha.org

NEBRASKA QUARTER HORSE YOUTH SCHOLARSHIP

Ideal candidate is an AQHA or AQHYA member from Nebraska.

Award: Scholarship for use in freshman, sophomore, junior, or senior years; renewable. *Number:* 1. *Amount:* $2000.

Eligibility Requirements: Applicant must be enrolled or expecting to enroll full-time at a two-year or four-year or technical institution or university and resident of Nebraska. Applicant or parent of applicant must be member of American Quarter Horse Association. Applicant must have 2.5 GPA or higher. Available to U.S. citizens.

Application Requirements: Application form, financial need analysis. *Deadline:* December 1.

Contact: Scholarship Office
American Quarter Horse Foundation (AQHF)
2601 East Interstate 40
Amarillo, TX 79104
Phone: 806-378-5029
E-mail: foundation@aqha.org

SCOOP VESSELS SCHOLARSHIP

Ideal candidate is a member of AQHA who demonstrates a strong work ethic and financial need.

Award: Scholarship for use in junior or senior years; renewable. *Number:* 1. *Amount:* $5000.

Eligibility Requirements: Applicant must be enrolled or expecting to enroll full-time at a four-year institution or university. Applicant or parent of applicant must be member of American Quarter Horse Association. Applicant must have 2.5 GPA or higher. Available to U.S. and non-U.S. citizens.

Application Requirements: Application form, financial need analysis. *Deadline:* December 1.

Contact: Scholarship Office
American Quarter Horse Foundation (AQHF)
2601 East Interstate 40
Amarillo, TX 79104
Phone: 806-378-5029
E-mail: foundation@aqha.org

SWAYZE WOODRUFF MEMORIAL MID-SOUTH SCHOLARSHIP

Ideal candidate is an AQHA or AQHYA member from Alabama, Arkansas, Louisiana, Mississippi or Tennessee who competes in AQHA-approved shows.

Award: Scholarship for use in freshman, sophomore, junior, or senior years; renewable. *Number:* 1. *Amount:* $9000.

Eligibility Requirements: Applicant must be enrolled or expecting to enroll full-time at a two-year or four-year institution or university; resident of Alabama, Arkansas, Louisiana, Mississippi, Tennessee and must have an interest in animal/agricultural competition. Applicant or parent of applicant must be member of American Quarter Horse Association. Applicant must have 2.5 GPA or higher. Available to U.S. citizens.

Application Requirements: Application form. *Deadline:* December 1.

Contact: Scholarship Office
American Quarter Horse Foundation (AQHF)
2601 East Interstate 40
Amarillo, TX 79104
Phone: 806-378-5029
E-mail: foundation@aqha.org

AMERICAN WATER SKI EDUCATIONAL FOUNDATION

http://www.waterskihalloffame.com/

AMERICAN WATER SKI EDUCATIONAL FOUNDATION SCHOLARSHIP

Awards for incoming college sophomores through incoming seniors who are members of USA Water Ski. Awards are based upon academics, leadership, extracurricular activities, recommendations, essay and financial need.

Award: Scholarship for use in sophomore, junior, or senior years; renewable. *Number:* 5. *Amount:* $1500–$3000.

Eligibility Requirements: Applicant must be enrolled or expecting to enroll full-time at a two-year or four-year institution or university. Applicant or parent of applicant must be member of USA Water Ski. Available to U.S. citizens.

Application Requirements: Application form, essay, financial need analysis, recommendations or references, self-addressed stamped envelope with application, transcript. *Deadline:* March 1.

Contact: Carole Lowe, Scholarship Director
Phone: 863-324-2472 Ext. 127
Fax: 863-324-3996
E-mail: awsefhalloffame@cs.com

AMVETS AUXILIARY

http://amvetsaux.org/

AMVETS NATIONAL LADIES AUXILIARY SCHOLARSHIP

One-time award of up to $1000 for a member of AMVETS or the Auxiliary. Applicant may also be the family member of a member. Award for full-time study at any accredited U.S. institution. Minimum 2.5 GPA required.

Award: Scholarship for use in sophomore, junior, or senior years; not renewable. *Number:* up to 7. *Amount:* $750–$1000.

Eligibility Requirements: Applicant must be enrolled or expecting to enroll full-time at a two-year or four-year or technical institution. Applicant or parent of applicant must be member of AMVETS Auxiliary. Applicant must have 2.5 GPA or higher. Available to U.S. citizens. Applicant or parent must meet one or more of the following requirements: general military experience; retired from active duty; disabled or killed as a result of military service; prisoner of war; or missing in action.

Application Requirements: Application form, essay, recommendations or references, transcript. *Deadline:* June 1.

Contact: Kellie Haggerty, Executive Administrator
AMVETS Auxiliary
4647 Forbes Boulevard
Lanham, MD 20706-4380
Phone: 301-459-6255
Fax: 301-459-5403
E-mail: auxhdqs@amvets.org

APPALOOSA HORSE CLUB-APPALOOSA YOUTH PROGRAM

http://www.appaloosayouth.com/

APPALOOSA YOUTH EDUCATIONAL SCHOLARSHIPS

Scholarship of up to $1000 available for members or dependents of members of the Appaloosa Youth Association or Appaloosa Horse Club. Based on academics, leadership, sportsmanship, and horsemanship. Printable application is available at website, http://www.appaloosayouth.com.

Award: Scholarship for use in freshman, sophomore, junior, or senior years; not renewable. *Number:* 6–8. *Amount:* $100–$1000.

Eligibility Requirements: Applicant must be enrolled or expecting to enroll full-time at a two-year or four-year institution or university and must have an interest in animal/agricultural competition or leadership. Applicant or parent of applicant must be member of Appaloosa Horse Club/Appaloosa Youth Association. Applicant must have 3.5 GPA or higher. Available to U.S. citizens.

Application Requirements: Application form, entry in a contest, essay, personal photograph, recommendations or references, test scores, transcript. *Deadline:* June 1.

Contact: Anna Brown, AYF Coordinator
Appaloosa Horse Club-Appaloosa Youth Program
2720 West Pullman Road
Moscow, ID 83843
Phone: 208-882-5578 Ext. 264
Fax: 208-882-8150
E-mail: youth@appaloosa.com

ARRL FOUNDATION INC.

http://www.arrl.org/

YOU'VE GOT A FRIEND IN PENNSYLVANIA SCHOLARSHIP

One-time award available to licensed general class or extra class amateur radio operators. Must be a member of American Radio Relay League and have an A or equivalent grade point average including graded courses in mathematics, science, and languages and excluding grades in sports or physical education. Must also be a resident of the Commonwealth of Pennsylvania.

Award: Scholarship for use in freshman, sophomore, junior, senior, graduate, or postgraduate years; not renewable. *Number:* 2. *Amount:* $2000.

Eligibility Requirements: Applicant must be enrolled or expecting to enroll full-time at a two-year or four-year or technical institution or university; resident of Pennsylvania and must have an interest in amateur radio. Applicant or parent of applicant must be member of American Radio Relay League. Applicant must have 3.5 GPA or higher. Available to U.S. citizens.

Application Requirements: Application form. *Deadline:* January 31.

Contact: Ms. Mary Hobart, Secretary
Phone: 860-594-0397
E-mail: k1mmh@arrl.org

AUTOMOTIVE RECYCLERS ASSOCIATION SCHOLARSHIP FOUNDATION

http://www.a-r-a.org/

AUTOMOTIVE RECYCLERS ASSOCIATION SCHOLARSHIP FOUNDATION SCHOLARSHIP

Scholarships are available for the post-high school educational pursuits of the children of employees of direct ARA member companies.

Award: Scholarship for use in freshman, sophomore, junior, or senior years; not renewable.

Eligibility Requirements: Applicant must be enrolled or expecting to enroll full-time at a two-year or four-year institution or university. Applicant or parent of applicant must be member of Automotive Recyclers Association. Applicant must have 3.0 GPA or higher. Available to U.S. and non-U.S. citizens.

Application Requirements: Application form, letter verifying parents' employment, personal photograph, transcript. *Deadline:* March 15.

Contact: Kelly Badillo, Director, Member Services
Automotive Recyclers Association Scholarship Foundation
3975 Fair Ridge Drive, Suite 20-North
Fairfax, VA 22033
Phone: 703-385-1001 Ext. 26
Fax: 703-385-1494
E-mail: kelly@a-r-a.org

CALIFORNIA GRANGE FOUNDATION

http://www.csgfoundation.org/

CALIFORNIA GRANGE FOUNDATION SCHOLARSHIP

Scholarship program available for Grange members residing in California who wish to attend a higher institution of learning of their choice.

Award: Scholarship for use in freshman, sophomore, junior, or senior years; renewable. *Number:* 5–8. *Amount:* $250–$1000.

Eligibility Requirements: Applicant must be enrolled or expecting to enroll full- or part-time at a two-year or four-year or technical institution or university and resident of California. Applicant or parent of applicant must be member of Grange Association. Available to U.S. citizens.

Application Requirements: Application form, community service, essay, financial need analysis, recommendations or references, transcript. *Deadline:* April 1.

Contact: Mrs. Leslie Parker, Executive Assistant
California Grange Foundation
3830 U Street
Sacramento, CA 95817
Phone: 916-454-5805 Ext. 21
Fax: 916-739-8189
E-mail: info@californiagrange.org

CALIFORNIA STATE PARENT-TEACHER ASSOCIATION

http://www.capta.org/

CONTINUING EDUCATION-PTA VOLUNTEERS SCHOLARSHIP

Scholarships are available annually from the California State PTA to be used for continuing education at accredited colleges, universities, trade or technical schools. These scholarships recognize volunteer service in PTA and enable PTA volunteers to continue their education.

Award: Scholarship for use in freshman, sophomore, junior, senior, or graduate years; not renewable. *Amount:* $500.

Eligibility Requirements: Applicant must be enrolled or expecting to enroll full- or part-time at a two-year or four-year or technical institution or university and resident of California. Applicant or parent of applicant must be member of Parent-Teacher Association/Organization. Applicant or parent of applicant must have employment or volunteer experience in community service. Available to U.S. citizens.

Application Requirements: Application form, copy of membership card, essay, recommendations or references, transcript. *Deadline:* November 15.

Contact: Becky Reece, Scholarship and Award Chairman
California State Parent-Teacher Association
930 Georgia Street
Los Angeles, CA 90015-1322
Phone: 213-620-1100
Fax: 213-620-1141

CALIFORNIA TEACHERS ASSOCIATION (CTA)

http://www.cta.org/

CALIFORNIA TEACHERS ASSOCIATION SCHOLARSHIP FOR DEPENDENT CHILDREN

Awards scholarships annually for dependent children of active, retired, or deceased members of California Teachers Association. Minimum 3.5 GPA required.

Award: Scholarship for use in freshman, sophomore, junior, senior, or graduate years; not renewable. *Number:* up to 25. *Amount:* $2500.

Eligibility Requirements: Applicant must be enrolled or expecting to enroll full-time at a two-year or four-year or technical institution or university. Applicant or parent of applicant must be member of California Teachers Association. Applicant must have 3.5 GPA or higher. Available to U.S. citizens.

Application Requirements: Application form, essay, recommendations or references, transcript. *Deadline:* February 8.

Contact: Janeya Collins, Scholarship Coordinator
California Teachers Association (CTA)
PO Box 921
Burlingame, CA 94011-0921
Phone: 650-552-5468
Fax: 650-552-5001
E-mail: scholarships@cta.org

CALIFORNIA TEACHERS ASSOCIATION SCHOLARSHIP FOR MEMBERS

Must be an active member of California Teachers Association (including members working on an emergency credential). Available for study in a degree, credential, or graduate program.

Award: Scholarship for use in freshman, sophomore, junior, senior, or graduate years; not renewable. *Number:* 5. *Amount:* $2500.

Eligibility Requirements: Applicant must be enrolled or expecting to enroll full-time at a two-year or four-year institution or university and resident of California. Applicant or parent of applicant must be member of California Teachers Association. Applicant or parent of applicant must have employment or volunteer experience in teaching/education. Applicant must have 3.0 GPA or higher. Available to U.S. citizens.

Application Requirements: Application form, essay, recommendations or references, transcript. *Deadline:* February 8.

Contact: Janeya Collins, Scholarship Coordinator
California Teachers Association (CTA)
PO Box 921
Burlingame, CA 94011-0921
Phone: 650-552-5468
E-mail: scholarships@cta.org

CIVIL AIR PATROL, USAF AUXILIARY

http://www.gocivilairpatrol.com/

CIVIL AIR PATROL ACADEMIC SCHOLARSHIPS

One-time award for active members of the Civil Air Patrol to pursue undergraduate, graduate, or trade or technical education. Must be a current CAP member. Significant restrictions apply. Not open to the general public.

Award: Scholarship for use in freshman, sophomore, junior, senior, or graduate years; not renewable. *Number:* up to 40. *Amount:* $1000–$7500.

Eligibility Requirements: Applicant must be enrolled or expecting to enroll full-time at a two-year or four-year or technical institution or university. Applicant or parent of applicant must be member of Civil Air Patrol. Available to U.S. citizens.

Application Requirements: Application form, essay, personal photograph, recommendations or references, resume, test scores, transcript. *Deadline:* January 31.

Contact: Kelly Easterly, Assistant Program Manager
Civil Air Patrol, USAF Auxiliary
105 South Hansell Street, Building 714
Maxwell Air Force Base, AL 36112-6332
Phone: 334-953-8640
Fax: 334-953-6699
E-mail: cpr@capnhq.gov

COMMUNITY BANKERS ASSOCIATION OF ILLINOIS

http://www.cbai.com/

COMMUNITY BANKERS ASSOC OF IL CHILD OF A BANKER SCHOLARSHIP

Must be a child or grandchild of an eligible CBAI member banker or be a part-time employee of an eligible CBAI member bank.

Award: Prize for use in freshman year; renewable. *Number:* 3. *Amount:* $4000.

Eligibility Requirements: Applicant must be high school student; planning to enroll or expecting to enroll full-time at a two-year or four-year or technical institution or university and resident of Illinois. Applicant or parent of applicant must be member of Community Banker Association of Illinois. Available to U.S. citizens.

Application Requirements: Application form. *Deadline:* August 15.

Contact: Ms. Bobbi Watson, Administrative Assistant
Community Bankers Association of Illinois
CBAI
901 Community Drive
Springfield, IL 62715
Phone: 800-736-2224
E-mail: bobbiw@cbai.com

COMMUNITY FOUNDATION OF WESTERN MASSACHUSETTS

http://www.communityfoundation.org/

HORACE HILL SCHOLARSHIP

Scholarships are given to children or grandchildren of a member of the Springfield Newspapers 25-Year Club. For more information or application, visit http://www.communityfoundation.org.

Award: Scholarship for use in freshman, sophomore, junior, senior, or graduate years; not renewable. *Amount:* up to $1000.

Eligibility Requirements: Applicant must be enrolled or expecting to enroll full- or part-time at a two-year or four-year institution or university and resident of Massachusetts. Applicant or parent of applicant must be member of Springfield Newspaper 25-Year Club. Available to U.S. citizens.

Application Requirements: Application form, Student Aid Report (SAR), transcript. *Deadline:* March 31.

Contact: Dotty Theriaque, Program Assistant for Scholarships
Community Foundation of Western Massachusetts
1500 Main Street
PO Box 15769
Springfield, MA 01115
Phone: 413-732-2858
Fax: 413-733-8565
E-mail: scholar@communityfoundation.org

EASTERN ORTHODOX COMMITTEE ON SCOUTING

http://www.eocs.org/

EASTERN ORTHODOX COMMITTEE ON SCOUTING SCHOLARSHIPS

One-time award for high school seniors planning to attend a four-year institution. Must be a registered member of a Boy or Girl Scout unit, an Eagle Scout or Gold Award recipient, active member of an Eastern Orthodox Church, and recipient of the Alpha Omega religious award.

Award: Scholarship for use in freshman year; not renewable. *Number:* 2. *Amount:* $500–$1000.

Eligibility Requirements: Applicant must be Eastern Orthodox; high school student; planning to enroll or expecting to enroll full-time at a four-year institution or university and single. Applicant or parent of applicant must be member of Boy Scouts, Girl Scouts. Available to U.S. citizens.

Application Requirements: Application form, community service, recommendations or references, self-addressed stamped envelope with application, test scores, transcript. *Deadline:* May 1.

Contact: George Boulukos, Scholarship Chairman
Eastern Orthodox Committee on Scouting
862 Guy Lombardo Avenue
Freeport, NY 11520
Phone: 516-868-4050
E-mail: geobou03@aol.com

EASTERN SURFING ASSOCIATION (ESA)

http://www.surfesa.org/

ESA MARSH SCHOLARSHIP PROGRAM

Grants are awarded to ESA current members in good standing on the basis of academics and U.S. citizenship rather than athletic ability.

Award: Scholarship for use in freshman, sophomore, junior, or senior years; not renewable. *Number:* 2. *Amount:* up to $8000.

Eligibility Requirements: Applicant must be enrolled or expecting to enroll full-time at a four-year institution or university. Applicant or parent of applicant must be member of Eastern Surfing Association. Available to U.S. citizens.

Application Requirements: Application form, essay, recommendations or references, transcript. *Deadline:* May 15.

Contact: Debbie Hodges, Scholarship Committee
Phone: 757-233-1790
E-mail: centralhq@surfesa.org

ELKS NATIONAL FOUNDATION

http://www.elks.org/enf

ELKS EMERGENCY EDUCATIONAL GRANTS

Grant available to children of Elks members who are deceased or totally disabled. Disability must be proven by recent doctors note. Parent must have been a member for at least a year before the date of death or onset of disability. Applicants for the one-year renewable awards must be unmarried, under the age of 23, be a full-time undergraduate student, and demonstrate financial need. They must also maintain a minimum 2.0 GPA.

Award: Scholarship for use in freshman, sophomore, junior, or senior years; not renewable. *Amount:* $1000–$4000.

Eligibility Requirements: Applicant must be enrolled or expecting to enroll full-time at a two-year or four-year institution or university and single. Applicant or parent of applicant must be member of Elks Club. Available to U.S. citizens.

Application Requirements: Application form, community service, essay, financial need analysis. *Deadline:* October 31.

Contact: Elks National Foundation Scholarship Office
Elks National Foundation
2750 North Lakeview Avenue
Chicago, IL 60614-2256
Phone: 773-755-4732
E-mail: scholarship@elks.org

ELKS NATIONAL FOUNDATION LEGACY AWARDS

$4,000 four-year scholarships available for children and grandchildren of Elks in good standing. Parent or grandparent must have been an Elk for two years and continue to be a member in good standing. Must be high school senior and apply through the related member's Elks Lodge. Applications available after September 1 online only, enf.elks.org/leg. Must be submitted online through the website.

Award: Scholarship for use in freshman, sophomore, junior, or senior years; renewable. *Number:* 250. *Amount:* $4000.

Eligibility Requirements: Applicant must be high school student and planning to enroll or expecting to enroll full-time at a four-year institution or university. Applicant or parent of applicant must be member of Elks Club. Available to U.S. citizens.

Application Requirements: Application form, community service, essay. *Deadline:* January 26.

Contact: Elks National Foundation Scholarship Office
Elks National Foundation
2750 North Lakeview Avenue
Chicago, IL 60614-2256
Phone: 773-755-4732
E-mail: scholarship@elks.org

FEDERATION OF AMERICAN CONSUMERS AND TRAVELERS

http://www.usafact.org

FEDERATION OF AMERICAN CONSUMERS AND TRAVELERS EDUCATIONAL GRANT PROGRAM

Approximately $75,000 will be awarded this year to members and their immediate families, with the hope of increasing accessibility to advanced education. Some of the highlights of this new program include a single application can be submitted for all types of education, from trade schools to graduate programs, no deadlines! Applications will be accepted year round and will be reviewed quarterly, awards will occur four times annually, and for the first time, graduate students may apply. The program will begin accepting applications on January 1, 2018.

Award: Grant for use in freshman, sophomore, junior, senior, graduate, or postgraduate years; not renewable. *Number:* 4–10. *Amount:* $250–$10,000.

Eligibility Requirements: Applicant must be enrolled or expecting to enroll full-time at a two-year or four-year or technical institution or university. Applicant or parent of applicant must be member of Federation of American Consumers and Travelers. Available to U.S. citizens.

Application Requirements: Application form, community service, essay. *Deadline:* continuous.

Contact: Vicki Rolens, Managing Director
Federation of American Consumers and Travelers
PO Box 104
Edwardsville, IL 62025
Phone: 800-872-3228 Ext. 10
E-mail: vrolens@usafact.org

FIRST CATHOLIC SLOVAK LADIES ASSOCIATION

http://www.fcsla.org/

FIRST CATHOLIC SLOVAK LADIES ASSOCIATION HIGH SCHOOL SCHOLARSHIPS

Scholarship for high school students. A written report of approximately 250 words on "What This High School Scholarship Will Do for Me" must be submitted with application. Candidate must have been a beneficial member of the Association for at least three years prior to date of application.

Award: Scholarship for use in freshman year; renewable. *Number:* up to 32. *Amount:* $1000.

Eligibility Requirements: Applicant must be high school student and planning to enroll or expecting to enroll full-time at a four-year institution or university. Applicant or parent of applicant must be member of First Catholic Slovak Ladies Association. Available to U.S. and Canadian citizens.

Application Requirements: Application form, community service, essay, personal photograph, transcript. *Deadline:* March 1.

Contact: Director of Fraternal Scholarships
First Catholic Slovak Ladies Association
24950 Chagrin Boulevard
Beachwood, OH 44122
Phone: 800-464-4642
E-mail: info@fcsla.com

FLEET RESERVE ASSOCIATION EDUCATION FOUNDATION

http://www.fra.org/foundation

COLONEL HAZEL ELIZABETH BENN U.S.M.C. SCHOLARSHIP

Scholarship only for U.S. citizens who are unmarried, dependent children of a member in good standing of the FRA, currently or at time of death, who served or is now serving in the U.S. Navy as an enlisted medical rating assigned to and serving with the U.S. Marine Corps. Must be enrolled as a freshman or sophomore undergraduate at a state or regionally accredited institution of post-secondary education located in the United States.

Award: Scholarship for use in freshman or sophomore years; not renewable. *Number:* 1–5. *Amount:* $1000–$2000.

Eligibility Requirements: Applicant must be enrolled or expecting to enroll full-time at a two-year or four-year institution and single. Applicant or parent of applicant must be member of Fleet Reserve Association/Auxiliary. Available to U.S. citizens.

Application Requirements: Application form, community service, essay, financial need analysis. *Deadline:* April 15.

Contact: Mrs. Alicia Landis, Program Administrator
Phone: 703-683-1400 Ext. 107
E-mail: scholars@fra.org

DORAN/BLAIR SCHOLARSHIPS

Applicant or sponsor has to be a member in good standing of the FRA, currently or at time of death. Applicant must be an FRA member; spouse; dependent biological, step, or adoptive child; or biological, step, or adoptive grandchild; or biological, step, or adoptive great grandchild of the FRA member. Applicant must be a U.S. citizen, registered as a full time student in an accredited college located in the United States of America.

Award: Scholarship for use in freshman, sophomore, junior, senior, graduate, or postgraduate years; not renewable. *Number:* 1–20. *Amount:* $1000–$5000.

Eligibility Requirements: Applicant must be enrolled or expecting to enroll full-time at a two-year or four-year institution or university.

Applicant or parent of applicant must be member of Fleet Reserve Association/Auxiliary. Available to U.S. citizens. Applicant must have served in the Coast Guard.

Application Requirements: Application form, community service, essay, financial need analysis. *Deadline:* April 15.

Contact: Mrs. Alicia Landis, Program Administrator
> *Phone:* 703-683-1400 Ext. 107
> *E-mail:* scholars@fra.org

GIRL SCOUTS OF CONNECTICUT

http://www.gsofct.org/

EMILY CHAISON GOLD AWARD SCHOLARSHIP

An annual scholarship of $750 is awarded each year to one Gold Award recipient from the state of Connecticut during her senior year.

Award: Scholarship for use in freshman year; not renewable. *Number:* 1. *Amount:* $750.

Eligibility Requirements: Applicant must be high school student; planning to enroll or expecting to enroll full-time at a four-year institution or university; female and resident of Connecticut. Applicant or parent of applicant must be member of Girl Scouts. Available to U.S. citizens.

Application Requirements: Application form, community service, essay, recommendations or references. *Deadline:* April 1.

Contact: Nancy Bussman, Scholarship Committee
> Girl Scouts of Connecticut
> 340 Washington Street
> Hartford, CT 06106
> *Phone:* 203-239-2922
> *E-mail:* nbussman@gsofct.org

GLASS, MOLDERS, POTTERY, PLASTICS AND ALLIED WORKERS INTERNATIONAL UNION

http://www.gmpiu.org/

GMP MEMORIAL SCHOLARSHIP PROGRAM

Six college scholarships of $4000 per year available to the sons and daughters of members of the union. Renewable each year for a full four-year college program if adequate academic standards are maintained. Four vocational/technical/two-year Associate degree scholarships of $2000 also available (not to exceed the cost of the program).

Award: Scholarship for use in freshman year; renewable. *Number:* 10. *Amount:* $2000–$4000.

Eligibility Requirements: Applicant must be high school student and planning to enroll or expecting to enroll full-time at a two-year or four-year or technical institution or university. Applicant or parent of applicant must be member of Glass, Molders, Pottery, Plastics and Allied Workers International Union. Available to U.S. and Canadian citizens.

Application Requirements: Application form, test scores. *Deadline:* November 1.

Contact: Bruce Smith, International Secretary and Treasurer
> Glass, Molders, Pottery, Plastics and Allied Workers
> International Union
> 608 East Baltimore Pike, PO Box 607
> Media, PA 19063
> *Phone:* 610-565-5051 Ext. 220
> *Fax:* 610-565-0983

GOLDEN KEY INTERNATIONAL HONOUR SOCIETY

http://www.goldenkey.org/

GEICO LIFE SCHOLARSHIP

Ten $1000 awards will be given to outstanding students while balancing additional responsibilities. Must have completed at least 12 undergraduate credit hours in the previous year. Must be enrolled at the time of application and must be working toward a Baccalaureate degree.

Award: Scholarship for use in freshman, sophomore, junior, or senior years; not renewable. *Number:* 10. *Amount:* $1000.

Eligibility Requirements: Applicant must be enrolled or expecting to enroll full- or part-time at a four-year institution or university. Applicant or parent of applicant must be member of Golden Key National Honor Society. Available to U.S. and non-U.S. citizens.

Application Requirements: Application form, essay, recommendations or references, transcript. *Deadline:* April 1.

Contact: Scholarship Program Administrators
> Golden Key International Honour Society
> PO Box 23737
> Nashville, TN 37202
> *Phone:* 800-377-2401

GOLDEN KEY STUDY ABROAD SCHOLARSHIPS

Ten $1000 scholarships will be awarded each year to assist students in the pursuit of a study abroad program. Eligible members are undergraduate members who are currently enrolled in a study abroad program or will be enrolled in the academic year immediately following the granting of the award. Deadlines: April 15 and October 20.

Award: Scholarship for use in freshman, sophomore, junior, or senior years; not renewable. *Number:* 10. *Amount:* $1000.

Eligibility Requirements: Applicant must be enrolled or expecting to enroll full-time at a four-year institution or university. Applicant or parent of applicant must be member of Golden Key National Honor Society. Available to U.S. and non-U.S. citizens.

Application Requirements: Application form, description of the planned academic program, essay, transcript. *Deadline:* varies.

Contact: Scholarship Program Administrators
> Golden Key International Honour Society
> PO Box 23737
> Nashville, TN 37202-3737
> *Phone:* 800-377-2401
> *E-mail:* scholarships@goldenkey.org

GOLF COURSE SUPERINTENDENTS ASSOCIATION OF AMERICA

http://www.eifg.org/

GOLF COURSE SUPERINTENDENTS ASSOCIATION OF AMERICA LEGACY AWARD

Awards of $1500 for the children or grandchildren of Golf Course Superintendents Association of America members. Applicants must be enrolled full-time at an accredited institution of higher learning, or for high school seniors, they must have been accepted at such an institution for the next academic year.

Award: Scholarship for use in freshman, sophomore, junior, or senior years; not renewable. *Number:* 20. *Amount:* $1500.

Eligibility Requirements: Applicant must be enrolled or expecting to enroll full-time at a two-year or four-year or technical institution or university. Applicant or parent of applicant must be member of Golf Course Superintendents Association of America. Available to U.S. and non-U.S. citizens.

Application Requirements: Application form, essay. *Deadline:* April 15.

Contact: Mischia Wright, Associate Director
> Golf Course Superintendents Association of America
> 1421 Research Park Drive
> Lawrence, KS 66049
> *Phone:* 800-472-7878 Ext. 4445
> *Fax:* 785-832-4448
> *E-mail:* mwright@gcsaa.org

JOSEPH S. GARSKE COLLEGIATE GRANT PROGRAM

Award available to children/step children of GCSAA members who have been active members for five or more consecutive years for use at an accredited college or trade school. Applicant must be a graduating high school senior and be accepted at an institution of higher learning for the upcoming year.

Award: Scholarship for use in freshman year; not renewable. *Number:* 1–5. *Amount:* $500–$2500.

Eligibility Requirements: Applicant must be high school student and planning to enroll or expecting to enroll full-time at a two-year or four-year or technical institution or university. Applicant or parent of applicant must be member of Golf Course Superintendents Association of America. Available to U.S. and non-U.S. citizens.

Application Requirements: Application form, essay. *Deadline:* March 15.

Contact: Mischia Wright, Associate Director
Golf Course Superintendents Association of America
1421 Research Park Drive
Lawrence, KS 66049
Phone: 800-472-7878 Ext. 4445
Fax: 785-832-4448
E-mail: mwright@gcsaa.org

HAWAII EDUCATION ASSOCIATION

http://www.heaed.com/

HAWAII EDUCATION ASSOCIATION CONTINUING COLLEGE STUDENT SCHOLARSHIP

Scholarships will be awarded to continuing, full-time college students pursuing a career in education (preference will be given to those in preK-12 teaching) in any two- or four-year state or nationally accredited institution of higher learning in the 2018–2019 academic year.

Award: Scholarship for use in freshman, sophomore, junior, or senior years; not renewable. *Number:* 2. *Amount:* $2000.

Eligibility Requirements: Applicant must be enrolled or expecting to enroll full-time at a two-year or four-year institution or university. Applicant or parent of applicant must be member of Hawaii Education Association. Available to U.S. citizens.

Application Requirements: Application form, essay, financial need analysis, personal photograph. *Deadline:* April 2.

Contact: Laurie Togami, Staff Specialist
Phone: 808-949-6657
Fax: 808-944-2032
E-mail: hea.office@heaed.com

HAWAII EDUCATION ASSOCIATION HIGH SCHOOL STUDENT SCHOLARSHIP

Scholarship available to high school seniors planning on attending four-year college/university. Must be HEA members, children of HEA members, or grandchildren or legally adopted grandchildren of HEA members. Members must be in good standing and shall have been members for at least one year.

Award: Scholarship for use in freshman year; not renewable. *Number:* 2. *Amount:* $2000.

Eligibility Requirements: Applicant must be high school student; planning to enroll or expecting to enroll full-time at a four-year institution or university and resident of Hawaii. Applicant or parent of applicant must be member of Hawaii Education Association. Available to U.S. citizens.

Application Requirements: Application form, essay, financial need analysis, personal photograph. *Deadline:* April 2.

Contact: Laurie Togami, Scholarship Committee
Hawaii Education Association
1953 South Beretania Street, Suite 5C
Honolulu, HI 96826-1304
Phone: 808-949-6657
E-mail: hea.office@hawaiieducationassociation.org

HELLENIC UNIVERSITY CLUB OF PHILADELPHIA

http://www.hucphiladelphia.org/

PAIDEIA SCHOLARSHIP

$3000 merit scholarship awarded to the child of a Hellenic University Club of Philadelphia member. Must be a U.S. citizen of Greek descent and a resident of particular counties in NJ or PA.

Award: Scholarship for use in freshman, sophomore, junior, or senior years; not renewable. *Number:* 1. *Amount:* up to $3000.

Eligibility Requirements: Applicant must be of Greek heritage; enrolled or expecting to enroll full-time at a four-year institution or university and resident of New Jersey, Pennsylvania. Applicant or parent of applicant must be member of Hellenic University Club of Pennsylvania. Available to U.S. citizens.

Application Requirements: Application form, financial need analysis, transcript. *Deadline:* April 3.

Contact: Anna Hadgis, Scholarship Chairman
Phone: 610-613-4310
E-mail: www.hucphiladelphia.org

HONOR SOCIETY OF PHI KAPPA PHI

http://www.PhiKappaPhi.org/

LITERACY GRANT COMPETITION

Grants up to $2500 are awarded to Phi Kappa Phi members for projects relating to a broad definition of literacy (math, science, music, art, reading, health, etc.). These projects should fulfill the spirit of volunteerism and community. Eligible applicants must be Active members of Phi Kappa Phi.

Award: Grant for use in freshman, sophomore, junior, senior, graduate, or postgraduate years; not renewable. *Number:* up to 18. *Amount:* $300–$2500.

Eligibility Requirements: Applicant must be enrolled or expecting to enroll full- or part-time at a two-year or four-year or technical institution or university. Applicant or parent of applicant must be member of Phi Kappa Phi. Available to U.S. and non-U.S. citizens.

Application Requirements: Application form, itemized budget. *Deadline:* April 1.

Contact: Mrs. Kelli Partin, Programs Coordinator
Honor Society of Phi Kappa Phi
7576 Goodwood Boulevard
Baton Rouge, LA 70806
Phone: 225-388-4917 Ext. 35
Fax: 225-388-4900
E-mail: kpartin@phikappaphi.org

INDEPENDENT OFFICE PRODUCTS AND FURNITURE DEALERS ASSOCIATION

http://www.iopfda.org/

NOPA AND OFDA SCHOLARSHIP AWARD

Candidates must have graduated from high school or its equivalent before July 1 of the year in which they would use the scholarship. Must have an academic record sufficient to be accepted by an accredited college, junior college, or technical institute. Must be a relative of a member of NOPA or OFDA.

Award: Scholarship for use in freshman, sophomore, junior, or senior years; not renewable. *Number:* up to 25. *Amount:* $2000.

Eligibility Requirements: Applicant must be enrolled or expecting to enroll full- or part-time at a two-year or four-year or technical institution or university. Applicant or parent of applicant must be member of Independent Office Products and Furniture Dealers Association. Available to U.S. and non-U.S. citizens.

Application Requirements: Application form, recommendations or references, transcript. *Deadline:* March 16.

Contact: Billie Zidek, Scholarship Administrator
Phone: 703-549-9040 Ext. 121
E-mail: bzidek@iopfda.org

INTERNATIONAL BROTHERHOOD OF TEAMSTERS SCHOLARSHIP FUND

http://www.teamster.org/

JAMES R. HOFFA MEMORIAL SCHOLARSHIP FUND

Scholarships available to children of members of the International Brotherhood of Teamsters (in good standing). The $10,000 awards are renewed on an annual basis. Also awarded are a one-time $1000 awards (non-renewable). The recipient must plan to attend a four-year institution and must maintain 3.0 GPA.

Award: Scholarship for use in freshman, sophomore, junior, or senior years; renewable. *Number:* 1–100. *Amount:* $1000–$10,000.

Eligibility Requirements: Applicant must be high school student and planning to enroll or expecting to enroll full-time at a four-year institution or university. Applicant or parent of applicant must be member of International Brotherhood of Teamsters. Applicant must have 3.0 GPA or higher. Available to U.S. and Canadian citizens.

Application Requirements: Application form, entry in a contest, list of activities, recommendations or references, test scores, transcript. *Deadline:* March 31.

Contact: Mrs. Traci Jacobs, Administrative Manager
International Brotherhood of Teamsters Scholarship Fund
25 Louisiana Avenue, NW
Washington, DC 20001
Phone: 202-624-8735
Fax: 202-624-7457
E-mail: tjacobs@teamster.org

INTERNATIONAL CHEMICAL WORKERS UNION

http://www.icwuc.org/

WALTER L. MITCHELL MEMORIAL AWARDS

Award available to children of International Chemical Workers Union members. Applicants must be starting their freshman year of college.

Award: Scholarship for use in freshman year; not renewable. *Number:* 12. *Amount:* $1500.

Eligibility Requirements: Applicant must be high school student and planning to enroll or expecting to enroll full-time at a two-year or four-year or technical institution or university. Applicant or parent of applicant must be member of International Chemical Workers Union. Available to U.S. citizens.

Application Requirements: Application form, biographical questionnaire, test scores, transcript. *Deadline:* April 23.

Contact: Sue Everhart, Secretary for Research and Education
International Chemical Workers Union
1799 Akron-Peninsula Road
Akron, OH 44313
Phone: 330-926-1444 Ext. 134
Fax: 330-926-0816
E-mail: severhart@icwuc.org

INTERNATIONAL UNION OF BRICKLAYERS AND ALLIED CRAFTWORKERS

http://www.bacweb.org/

CANADIAN BATES SCHOLARSHIP PROGRAM

BAC's Canadian Bates Scholarship program is administered by Universities Canada, located in Ottawa, Ontario. Three students are selected annually to receive a stipend of either $1500 CDN or $1200 CDN per year for up to four consecutive years providing the student maintains satisfactory academic progress. To apply, the student must be the son or daughter of a Canadian BAC member in good standing of a Canadian BAC Local, and a graduating high school senior who plans to attend college in the fall.

Award: Scholarship for use in freshman, sophomore, junior, or senior years; renewable. *Number:* 3. *Amount:* $1200–$1500.

Eligibility Requirements: Applicant must be Canadian citizen; high school student; planning to enroll or expecting to enroll full-time at a four-year institution or university and resident of British Columbia, Manitoba, New Brunswick, Newfoundland, Northwest Territories, Nova Scotia, Prince Edward Island, Quebec, Saskatchewan, Yukon. Applicant or parent of applicant must be member of International Union of Bricklayers and Allied Craftworkers.

Application Requirements: Application form. *Deadline:* May 15.

Contact: Kimberly Ward
International Union of Bricklayers and Allied Craftworkers
620 F Street, NW
Washington, DC 20004
Phone: 202-383-3887
E-mail: askbac@bacweb.org

U.S. BATES SCHOLARSHIP PROGRAM

The U.S. Bates Scholarship awards a stipend of $2500 per year for up to four years to three students annually. The program is open to sons and daughters of U.S. BAC members (in good standing) of U.S. BAC Locals who are in their junior year of high school, and who either have taken or plan to take the standardized PSAT exam.

Award: Scholarship for use in freshman, sophomore, junior, or senior years; renewable. *Number:* 3. *Amount:* $2500.

Eligibility Requirements: Applicant must be high school student; planning to enroll or expecting to enroll full-time at a four-year institution or university and resident of Alabama, Alaska, American Samoa, Arizona, Arkansas, California, Colorado, Connecticut, Delaware, District of Columbia, Florida, Georgia, Guam, Hawaii, Idaho, Illinois, Indiana, Iowa, Kansas, Kentucky, Louisiana, Maine, Maryland, Massachusetts, Michigan, Minnesota, Mississippi, Missouri, Montana, Nebraska, Nevada, New Hampshire, New Jersey, New Mexico, New York, North Carolina, North Dakota, Northern Mariana Islands, Ohio, Oklahoma, Oregon, Pennsylvania, Puerto Rico, Rhode Island, South Carolina, South Dakota, Tennessee, Texas, Utah, Vermont, Virginia, Washington, West Virginia, Wisconsin, Wyoming. Applicant or parent of applicant must be member of International Union of Bricklayers and Allied Craftworkers. Available to U.S. citizens.

Application Requirements: Application form. *Deadline:* March 31.

Contact: Kimberly Ward
International Union of Bricklayers and Allied Craftworkers
620 F Street, NW
Washington, DC 20004
Phone: 202-383-3887
E-mail: askbac@bacweb.org

ITALIAN CATHOLIC FEDERATION

http://www.icf.org/

ITALIAN CATHOLIC FEDERATION FIRST YEAR SCHOLARSHIP

Scholarship for undergraduate students of the Catholic faith and of Italian heritage (or children or grand children of non-Italian ICF members). Must have minimum 3.2 GPA. Must live in AZ, CA, IL and NV.

Award: Scholarship for use in freshman year; not renewable. *Number:* 180–200. *Amount:* $400.

Eligibility Requirements: Applicant must be Roman Catholic; high school student; planning to enroll or expecting to enroll full-time at a two-year or four-year or technical institution or university and resident of Arizona, California, Illinois, Nevada. Applicant or parent of applicant must be member of Italian Catholic Federation. Available to U.S. citizens.

Application Requirements: Application form, essay, financial need analysis, recommendations or references, test scores, transcript. *Deadline:* March 15.

Contact: Scholarship Committee
Italian Catholic Federation
ICF Central Council Office
8393 Capwell Drive, Suite 110
Oakland, CA 94621
Phone: 510-633-9058
Fax: 510-633-9758

JUNIOR ACHIEVEMENT

http://www.ja.org/

JOE FRANCOMANO SCHOLARSHIP

Renewable award to high school seniors who have demonstrated academic achievement, leadership skills, and financial need. May be used at any accredited post secondary educational institution for any field of study resulting in a Baccalaureate degree. Must have completed JA Company Program or JA Economics.

Award: Scholarship for use in freshman year; renewable. *Number:* 1. *Amount:* $5000.

Eligibility Requirements: Applicant must be high school student; planning to enroll or expecting to enroll full-time at a four-year institution or university and must have an interest in leadership. Applicant or parent of applicant must be member of Junior Achievement. Applicant must have 3.0 GPA or higher. Available to U.S. citizens.

Application Requirements: Application form, essay, financial need analysis, recommendations or references, transcript. *Deadline:* February 1.

Contact: Gwen Rose, Scholarship Coordinator
Phone: 719-540-6134
E-mail: dterry@ja.org

KAPPA ALPHA THETA FOUNDATION

http://www.kappaalphathetafoundation.org/

KAPPA ALPHA THETA FOUNDATION NON-DEGREE EDUCATIONAL GRANT PROGRAM

Kappa Alpha Theta Foundation grants provide funds for collegian and alumnae members of Kappa Alpha Theta Fraternity for leadership training and non-degree educational and service-learning opportunities. Individual collegian and alumnae members of the Fraternity and college and alumnae chapters are eligible to apply.

Award: Grant for use in freshman, sophomore, junior, senior, graduate, or postgraduate years; not renewable. *Number:* 1. *Amount:* $100–$5000.

Eligibility Requirements: Applicant must be enrolled or expecting to enroll full- or part-time at an institution or university and female. Applicant or parent of applicant must be member of Greek Organization. Available to U.S. and non-U.S. citizens.

Application Requirements: Application form. *Deadline:* continuous.

Contact: Mary Kate Kronzer, Programs Manager
Phone: 317-876-8593 Ext. 113
E-mail: mkronzer@kappaalphatheta.org

KAPPA ALPHA THETA FOUNDATION SCHOLARSHIP PROGRAM

Kappa Alpha Theta Foundation awards scholarships to graduate and undergraduate members of Kappa Alpha Theta Fraternity. Scholarships are awarded based upon academic performance, fraternity activities, campus and/or community activities, financial need (for need-based awards), and references.

Award: Scholarship for use in sophomore, junior, senior, graduate, or postgraduate years; not renewable. *Amount:* $1000–$12,000.

Eligibility Requirements: Applicant must be enrolled or expecting to enroll full- or part-time at a two-year or four-year institution or university and female. Applicant or parent of applicant must be member of Greek Organization. Available to U.S. and non-U.S. citizens.

Application Requirements: Application form, community service, essay, financial need analysis. *Deadline:* March 7.

Contact: Mary Kate Kronzer, Programs Manager
Phone: 317-876-8593 Ext. 113
E-mail: mkronzer@kappaalphatheta.edu

KNIGHTS OF COLUMBUS

http://www.kofc.org/

FOURTH DEGREE PRO DEO AND PRO PATRIA (CANADA)

Renewable scholarships for members of Canadian Knights of Columbus councils and their children who are entering first year of study for Baccalaureate degree. Based on academic excellence. Award not limited to Fourth Degree members.

Award: Scholarship for use in freshman year; renewable. *Amount:* $1500.

Eligibility Requirements: Applicant must be Roman Catholic; Canadian citizen and enrolled or expecting to enroll full-time at a four-year institution or university. Applicant or parent of applicant must be member of Knights of Columbus. Applicant must have 3.0 GPA or higher.

Application Requirements: Application form, recommendations or references, test scores, transcript. *Deadline:* May 1.

FOURTH DEGREE PRO DEO AND PRO PATRIA SCHOLARSHIPS

Award available to students entering freshman year at a Catholic university or college in United States. Applicant must be a member or child of a member of Knights of Columbus or Columbian Squires. Scholarships are awarded on the basis of academic excellence. Minimum 3.0 GPA required. See website for additional information http://www.kofc.org.

Award: Scholarship for use in freshman, sophomore, junior, or senior years; renewable. *Amount:* $1500.

Eligibility Requirements: Applicant must be Roman Catholic and enrolled or expecting to enroll full-time at a four-year institution or university. Applicant or parent of applicant must be member of Columbian Squires, Knights of Columbus. Applicant must have 3.0 GPA or higher. Available to U.S. citizens.

Application Requirements: Application form, essay, recommendations or references, test scores, transcript. *Deadline:* March 1.

Contact: Rev. Donald Barry, Scholarship Coordinator
Knights of Columbus
Department of Scholarships, PO Box 1670
New Haven, CT 06507-0901
Phone: 202-336-6800
Fax: 202-408-8102
E-mail: info@kofc.org

FRANCIS P. MATTHEWS AND JOHN E. SWIFT EDUCATIONAL TRUST SCHOLARSHIPS

Available to dependent children of Knights of Columbus who died or became permanently disabled while in military service during a time of conflict, from a cause connected with military service, or who died as the result of criminal violence while in the performance of their duties as full-time law enforcement officers or firemen. The scholarship is awarded at a Catholic college in the amount not covered by other financial aid for tuition up to $25,000 annually.

Award: Scholarship for use in freshman, sophomore, junior, or senior years; renewable. *Amount:* up to $25,000.

Eligibility Requirements: Applicant must be Roman Catholic and enrolled or expecting to enroll full-time at a four-year institution or university. Applicant or parent of applicant must be member of Knights of Columbus. Available to U.S. citizens. Applicant or parent must meet one or more of the following requirements: general military experience; retired from active duty; disabled or killed as a result of military service; prisoner of war; or missing in action.

Application Requirements: Application form, proof of parent's military service or employment in law enforcement services. *Deadline:* March 1.

JOHN W. MCDEVITT (FOURTH DEGREE) SCHOLARSHIPS

Scholarship for students entering freshman year at a Catholic college or university in United States. Applicant must submit Pro Deo and Pro Patria Scholarship application. Must be a member or wife, son, or daughter of a member of the Knights of Columbus. Minimum 3.0 GPA required. See website for additional information http://www.fofc.org.

Award: Scholarship for use in freshman year; renewable. *Amount:* $1500.

Eligibility Requirements: Applicant must be Roman Catholic and enrolled or expecting to enroll full-time at a four-year institution or university. Applicant or parent of applicant must be member of Knights of Columbus. Applicant must have 3.0 GPA or higher. Available to U.S. citizens.

Application Requirements: Application form, recommendations or references, test scores, transcript. *Deadline:* March 1.

PERCY J. JOHNSON ENDOWED SCHOLARSHIPS

Renewable scholarship for young men entering freshman year at a Catholic college or university. Applicants must submit Pro Deo and Pro Patria Scholarship application and a copy of Student Aid Report (SAR). Must be a member or a son of a member of the Knights of Columbus. Must also rank in upper third of class or have 3.0 GPA. See website for additional information http://www.kofc.org.

Award: Scholarship for use in freshman year; renewable. *Amount:* $1500.

Eligibility Requirements: Applicant must be Roman Catholic; enrolled or expecting to enroll full-time at a four-year institution or university and male. Applicant or parent of applicant must be member of Knights of Columbus. Applicant must have 3.0 GPA or higher. Available to U.S. citizens.

Application Requirements: Application form, financial need analysis, recommendations or references, test scores, transcript. *Deadline:* March 1.

LADIES AUXILIARY OF THE FLEET RESERVE ASSOCIATION

http://www.fra.org/

LADIES AUXILIARY OF THE FLEET RESERVE ASSOCIATION SCHOLARSHIP

Scholarship for members; spouses; dependent biological, step or adoptive child; or biological, step or adoptive grandchild of LA FRA or FRA member in good standing, currently or at time of death. Applicant must be a U.S. citizen, registered as a full-time student in an accredited college located in the United States.

Award: Scholarship for use in freshman, sophomore, junior, or senior years; not renewable. *Amount:* $1500.

Eligibility Requirements: Applicant must be enrolled or expecting to enroll full-time at a four-year institution or university and female. Applicant or parent of applicant must be member of Fleet Reserve Association/Auxiliary. Available to U.S. citizens. Applicant or parent must meet one or more of the following requirements: Coast Guard, Marine Corps, or Navy experience; retired from active duty; disabled or killed as a result of military service; prisoner of war; or missing in action.

Application Requirements: Application form, essay, recommendations or references, transcript. *Deadline:* April 15.

Contact: National Scholarship Chair
Ladies Auxiliary of the Fleet Reserve Association
PO Box 3459
Pahrump, NV 89041-3459
Phone: 775-751-3309

SAM ROSE MEMORIAL SCHOLARSHIP

Scholarship for members; spouses; dependent biological, step or adoptive child; or biological, step or adoptive grandchild of LA FRA or FRA member in good standing, currently or at time of death. Applicant must be a U.S. citizen, registered as a full-time student in an accredited college located in the United States.

Award: Scholarship for use in freshman, sophomore, junior, or senior years; not renewable. *Amount:* $1500.

Eligibility Requirements: Applicant must be enrolled or expecting to enroll full-time at a four-year institution or university. Applicant or parent of applicant must be member of Fleet Reserve Association/Auxiliary. Available to U.S. citizens. Applicant or parent must meet one or more of the following requirements: Coast Guard, Marine Corps, or Navy experience; retired from active duty; disabled or killed as a result of military service; prisoner of war; or missing in action.

Application Requirements: Application form, essay, recommendations or references, transcript. *Deadline:* April 15.

Contact: National Scholarship Chair
Ladies Auxiliary of the Fleet Reserve Association
PO Box 3459
Pahrump, NV 89041-3459
Phone: 775-751-3309

LEARNING ALLY

http://www.learningally.org

MARION HUBER LEARNING THROUGH LISTENING AWARDS

Awards presented to Learning Ally members who are high school seniors with learning disabilities, in recognition of extraordinary leadership, scholarship, enterprise and service to others. Must have minimum 3.0 GPA.

Award: Prize for use in freshman year; not renewable. *Number:* 6. *Amount:* $2000–$6000.

Eligibility Requirements: Applicant must be learning disabled; high school student and planning to enroll or expecting to enroll full-time at a two-year or four-year institution. Applicant or parent of applicant must be member of Learning Ally. Applicant must be learning disabled. Applicant must have 3.0 GPA or higher. Available to U.S. citizens.

Application Requirements: Application form, community service, essay. *Deadline:* May 31.

Contact: Jessica Kooper, Director of Engagement Marketing
Learning Ally
20 Roszel Road
Princeton, NJ 08540
Phone: 609-243-3089
E-mail: naa@learningally.org

MARY P. OENSLAGER SCHOLASTIC ACHIEVEMENT AWARDS

Award presented to Learning Ally members who are college seniors and blind or visually impaired, in recognition of extraordinary leadership, scholarship, enterprise, and service to others.

Award: Prize for use in senior or graduate years; not renewable. *Number:* 3–9. *Amount:* $1000–$6000.

Eligibility Requirements: Applicant must be visually impaired and enrolled or expecting to enroll full-time at a four-year institution or university. Applicant or parent of applicant must be member of Learning Ally. Applicant must be visually impaired. Applicant must have 3.0 GPA or higher. Available to U.S. citizens.

Application Requirements: Application form, community service, essay. *Deadline:* May 31.

Contact: Jessica Kooper, Director of Engagement Marketing
Learning Ally
20 Roszel Road
Princeton, NJ 08540
Phone: 609-243-7082
E-mail: naa@learningally.org

MINNESOTA AFL-CIO

http://www.mnaflcio.org/

MARTIN DUFFY ADULT LEARNER SCHOLARSHIP AWARD

Scholarship available for union members affiliated with the Minnesota AFL-CIO or the Minnesota Joint Council 32. May be used at any postsecondary institution in Minnesota. Information available on website at http://www.mnaflcio.org.

Award: Scholarship for use in freshman, sophomore, junior, or senior years; not renewable. *Number:* 4. *Amount:* $500.

Eligibility Requirements: Applicant must be enrolled or expecting to enroll full-time at a four-year institution or university; resident of Minnesota and studying in Minnesota. Applicant or parent of applicant must be member of AFL-CIO. Available to U.S. citizens.

Application Requirements: Application form. *Deadline:* April 30.

Contact: Computer Information Specialist
Minnesota AFL-CIO
175 Aurora Avenue
St. Paul, MN 55103
Phone: 651-227-7647
Fax: 651-227-3801

MINNESOTA AFL-CIO SCHOLARSHIPS

Applicant must be attending a college or university located in Minnesota. Must have a parent or legal guardian, who has held a one year membership in a local union which is an affiliate of the Minnesota AFL-CIO. Winners are selected by lot. Academic eligibility based on a straight "B" average or better. See website http://www.mnaflcio.org for information and application.

Award: Scholarship for use in freshman year; not renewable. *Number:* up to 5. *Amount:* $1000.

Eligibility Requirements: Applicant must be high school student; planning to enroll or expecting to enroll full-time at a two-year or four-year or technical institution or university and studying in Minnesota. Applicant or parent of applicant must be member of AFL-CIO. Applicant must have 3.0 GPA or higher. Available to U.S. citizens.

Application Requirements: Application form, transcript. *Deadline:* April 30.

Contact: Computer Information Specialist
Minnesota AFL-CIO
175 Aurora Avenue
St. Paul, MN 55103
Phone: 651-227-7647
Fax: 651-227-3801

NATIONAL ALLIANCE OF POSTAL AND FEDERAL EMPLOYEES (NAPFE)

http://www.napfe.com/

ASHBY B. CARTER MEMORIAL SCHOLARSHIP FUND FOUNDERS AWARD

Scholarships available to high school seniors. Must be a U.S. citizen. Applicant must be a dependent of NAPFE Labor Union member with a minimum three year membership. Applicant must take the SAT on or before March 1 of the year they apply for award.

Award: Scholarship for use in freshman year; not renewable. *Number:* 3. *Amount:* $2000–$5000.

Eligibility Requirements: Applicant must be high school student and planning to enroll or expecting to enroll full-time at a four-year institution or university. Applicant or parent of applicant must be member of National Alliance of Postal and Federal Employees. Available to U.S. citizens.

Application Requirements: Application form, community service, personal photograph, recommendations or references, self-addressed stamped envelope with application, test scores, transcript. *Deadline:* April 1.

Contact: Melissa Jeffries-Stewart, Director
Phone: 202-939-6325 Ext. 239
Fax: 202-939-6389
E-mail: headquarters@napfe.org

NATIONAL ASSOCIATION FOR THE ADVANCEMENT OF COLORED PEOPLE

http://www.naacp.org/

AGNES JONES JACKSON SCHOLARSHIP

Scholarship for undergraduate and graduate students who have been members of the NAACP for at least one year, or fully paid life members. Undergraduates must have 2.5 GPA and graduate students must have 3.0 GPA.

Award: Scholarship for use in freshman, sophomore, junior, senior, or graduate years; not renewable. *Number:* 1. *Amount:* $1500–$2500.

Eligibility Requirements: Applicant must be American Indian/Alaska Native, Asian/Pacific Islander, Black (non-Hispanic), Hispanic and enrolled or expecting to enroll full- or part-time at a two-year or four-year institution or university. Applicant or parent of applicant must be member of National Association for the Advancement of Colored People. Available to U.S. citizens.

Application Requirements: Application form, evidence of NAACP membership, financial need analysis, recommendations or references, transcript. *Deadline:* March 7.

Contact: Victor Goode, Attorney
Phone: 410-580-5760
E-mail: info@naacp.org

NATIONAL ASSOCIATION FOR THE SELF-EMPLOYED

http://www.NASE.org/

NASE SCHOLARSHIPS

Scholarship of $4000 for high school students or college undergraduates enrolled in full-time program of study. Total number of available awards varies. Applicants must be children or dependents of NASE Members and between the ages of 16 and 24.

Award: Scholarship for use in freshman, sophomore, junior, or senior years; not renewable. *Amount:* $4000.

Eligibility Requirements: Applicant must be age 16-24; enrolled or expecting to enroll full-time at a four-year institution or university and must have an interest in leadership. Applicant or parent of applicant must be member of National Association for the Self-Employed. Available to U.S. citizens.

Application Requirements: Application form, application form may be submitted online (http://www.nase.org/Membership/MembersBenefits/BenefitDetails.aspx ?BenefitId=71), essay, financial need analysis, recommendations or references, resume, transcript. *Deadline:* April 1.

Contact: Molly Nelson, Member Communications Manager
Phone: 202-466-2100
Fax: 202-466-2123
E-mail: mnelson@NASEadmin.org

NATIONAL ASSOCIATION OF ENERGY SERVICE COMPANIES

http://www.aesc.net/

ASSOCIATION OF ENERGY SERVICE COMPANIES SCHOLARSHIP PROGRAM

Applicant must be the legal dependent of an employee of an AESC member company, or an employee. Dependents of company officers are not eligible. Must submit application to local AESC chapter chairman. Application must include ACT or SAT test scores.

Award: Scholarship for use in freshman, sophomore, junior, senior, or graduate years; renewable. *Number:* 150–200. *Amount:* $1000.

Eligibility Requirements: Applicant must be enrolled or expecting to enroll full-time at a two-year or four-year or technical institution or university. Applicant or parent of applicant must be member of Association of Energy Service Companies. Available to U.S. and non-U.S. citizens.

Application Requirements: Application form, essay. *Deadline:* March 14.

Contact: Susan Dudley, Administrative Assistant
Phone: 800-692-0771
Fax: 713-781-7542
E-mail: sdudley@aesc.net

NATIONAL ASSOCIATION OF LETTER CARRIERS

http://www.nalc.org/

COSTAS G. LEMONOPOULOS SCHOLARSHIP

Scholarships to children of NALC members attending public, four-year colleges or universities supported by the state of Florida or St. Petersburg Junior College. Scholarships are renewable one time.

Award: Scholarship for use in freshman, sophomore, junior, or senior years; renewable. *Number:* 1–20.

Eligibility Requirements: Applicant must be enrolled or expecting to enroll full-time at a two-year or four-year institution or university and studying in Florida. Applicant or parent of applicant must be member of National Association of Letter Carriers. Available to U.S. citizens.

Application Requirements: Application form, recommendations or references, transcript. *Deadline:* June 1.

Contact: Ann Porch, Membership Committee
Phone: 202-393-4695
E-mail: nalcinf@nalc.org

JOHN T. DONELON SCHOLARSHIP

Scholarship for sons and daughters of NALC members who are high school seniors when making application. The $1000 scholarship will be renewable for four years.

Award: Scholarship for use in freshman year; renewable. *Number:* 5. *Amount:* $1000.

Eligibility Requirements: Applicant must be high school student and planning to enroll or expecting to enroll full-time at a four-year institution or university. Applicant or parent of applicant must be member of National Association of Letter Carriers. Available to U.S. citizens.

Application Requirements: Application form, recommendations or references, transcript. *Deadline:* December 31.

Contact: Ann Porch, Membership Committee
Phone: 202-393-4695
E-mail: nalcinf@nalc.org

UNION PLUS SCHOLARSHIP PROGRAM

One-time cash award available for undergraduate and graduate study programs. Scholarship ranges from $500 to $4000. Three awards are granted. Must be children of members of NALC.

Award: Scholarship for use in freshman year; not renewable. *Number:* 3. *Amount:* $500–$4000.

Eligibility Requirements: Applicant must be high school student and planning to enroll or expecting to enroll full-time at a four-year institution or university. Applicant or parent of applicant must be member of National Association of Letter Carriers. Available to U.S. citizens.

Application Requirements: Application form, recommendations or references, transcript. *Deadline:* January 31.

Contact: Ann Porch, Membership Committee
  Phone: 202-393-4695
  E-mail: nalcinf@nalc.org

WILLIAM C. DOHERTY SCHOLARSHIP FUND

Five scholarships of $4000 each are awarded to children of members in NALC. Renewable for three consecutive years thereafter providing the winner maintains satisfactory grades. Applicant must be a high school senior when making application.

Award: Scholarship for use in freshman year; renewable. *Number:* 5. *Amount:* $4000.

Eligibility Requirements: Applicant must be high school student and planning to enroll or expecting to enroll full-time at a four-year institution or university. Applicant or parent of applicant must be member of National Association of Letter Carriers. Available to U.S. citizens.

Application Requirements: Application form, test scores, transcript. *Deadline:* December 31.

Contact: Ann Porch, Membership Committee
  Phone: 202-393-4695
  E-mail: nalcinf@nalc.org

NATIONAL ASSOCIATION OF SECONDARY SCHOOL PRINCIPALS

http://www.nhs.us/

NATIONAL HONOR SOCIETY SCHOLARSHIP PROGRAM

One-time award to senior National Honor Society members who are in good standing with their active chapter. Application process opens in the fall, and members receive application instructions from their NHS adviser. Program information is available on the NHS website at https://www.nhs.us/students/the-nhs-scholarship.

Award: Scholarship for use in freshman year; not renewable. *Number:* 600.

Eligibility Requirements: Applicant must be high school student and planning to enroll or expecting to enroll full-time at a two-year or four-year institution or university. Applicant or parent of applicant must be member of National Honor Society. Available to U.S. and non-U.S. citizens.

Application Requirements: Application form, essay. *Deadline:* January 30.

Contact: Ms. Elancia Felder, Program Manager
  E-mail: scholarship@nhs.us

NATIONAL BETA CLUB

http://www.betaclub.org/

NATIONAL BETA CLUB SCHOLARSHIP

Applicant must be in twelfth grade and a member of the National Beta Club. Must be nominated by school chapter of the National Beta Club, therefore, applications will not be sent to the individual students. Renewable and nonrenewable awards available. Contact school Beta Club sponsor for more information.

Award: Scholarship for use in freshman year; renewable. *Number:* 221. *Amount:* $1000–$15,000.

Eligibility Requirements: Applicant must be high school student and planning to enroll or expecting to enroll full-time at a two-year or four-year institution or university. Applicant or parent of applicant must be member of National Beta Club. Available to U.S. citizens.

Application Requirements: Application form, application form may be submitted online, essay, recommendations or references, test scores, transcript. *Fee:* $10. *Deadline:* December 10.

Contact: Mrs. Joan Burnett, Scholarship Coordinator
  Phone: 864-583-4553
  Fax: 864-542-9300
  E-mail: jburnett@betaclub.org

NATIONAL FFA ORGANIZATION

http://www.ffa.org

NATIONAL FFA COLLEGIATE SCHOLARSHIP PROGRAM

Scholarships to high school seniors planning to enroll in a full-time course of study at an accredited vocational/technical school, college or university. A smaller number of awards are available to currently enrolled undergraduates. Most awards require the applicant be an FFA member. Some awards are available to non-members.

Award: Scholarship for use in freshman, sophomore, junior, or senior years; not renewable. *Number:* 1700–1800. *Amount:* $500–$29,000.

Eligibility Requirements: Applicant must be age 17-23 and enrolled or expecting to enroll full-time at a two-year or four-year or technical institution or university. Applicant or parent of applicant must be member of Future Farmers of America. Available to U.S. citizens.

Application Requirements: Application form. *Deadline:* February 1.

Contact: Scholarship Program Manager
  National FFA Organization
  PO Box 68960
  Indianapolis, IN 46268
  Phone: 317-802-6099
  E-mail: scholarships@ffa.org

NATIONAL FOSTER PARENT ASSOCIATION

http://www.nfpaonline.org/

NATIONAL FOSTER PARENT ASSOCIATION YOUTH SCHOLARSHIP

Award for high school senior who will be entering first year of college, comparable education, or training program. Six $1000 awards, three for foster children currently in foster care with an NFPA member family, and one each for birth and adopted children of foster parents. NFPA family membership required ($35 membership fee).

Award: Scholarship for use in freshman year; not renewable. *Number:* 6. *Amount:* $1000.

Eligibility Requirements: Applicant must be high school student and planning to enroll or expecting to enroll full- or part-time at a two-year or four-year or technical institution or university. Applicant or parent of applicant must be member of National Foster Parent Association. Available to U.S. citizens.

Application Requirements: Application form, driver's license, essay, recommendations or references, test scores, transcript. *Deadline:* March 31.

Contact: Karen Jorgenson, Executive Director
  National Foster Parent Association
  7512 Stanich Avenue, Suite 6
  Gig Harbor, WA 98335
  Phone: 253-853-4000
  Fax: 253-853-4001
  E-mail: info@nfpaonline.org

NATIONAL JUNIOR ANGUS ASSOCIATION

http://www.angus.org/njaa/

ANGUS FOUNDATION SCHOLARSHIPS

Applicants must have at one time been a National Junior Angus Association member and currently be a junior, regular or life member of the association. Must have applied to undergraduate studies in any field. Applicants must have a minimum 2.0 GPA. See website for further information and to download application.

Award: Scholarship for use in freshman, sophomore, junior, senior, or graduate years; not renewable. *Number:* 75–90. *Amount:* $250–$5000.

Eligibility Requirements: Applicant must be enrolled or expecting to enroll full-time at a two-year or four-year or technical institution or university. Applicant or parent of applicant must be member of American Angus Association. Available to U.S. and Canadian citizens.

Application Requirements: Application form, recommendations or references, transcript. *Deadline:* May 1.

Contact: Mr. Milford Jenkins, Angus Foundation President
National Junior Angus Association
3201 Frederick Avenue
St. Joseph, MO 64506
Phone: 816-383-5100 Ext. 163
Fax: 816-383-5146
E-mail: mjenkins@angusfoundation.org

NATIONAL SOCIETY DAUGHTERS OF THE AMERICAN REVOLUTION

http://www.dar.org/

NATIONAL SOCIETY DAUGHTERS OF THE AMERICAN REVOLUTION LILLIAN AND ARTHUR DUNN SCHOLARSHIP

A $2500 scholarship awarded for up to four years to well-qualified, deserving sons and daughters of members of the NSDAR. Outstanding recipients will be considered for an additional period of up to four years of study. Must include DAR member number.

Award: Scholarship for use in freshman, sophomore, junior, or senior years; renewable. *Amount:* $2500.

Eligibility Requirements: Applicant must be enrolled or expecting to enroll full-time at a four-year institution or university. Applicant or parent of applicant must be member of Daughters of the American Revolution. Available to U.S. citizens.

Application Requirements: Application form, financial need analysis. *Deadline:* February 15.

Contact: Lakeisha Graham, Manager, Office of the Reporter General
Phone: 202-628-1776
Fax: 202-879-3348
E-mail: nsdarscholarships@dar.org

NATIONAL SOCIETY OF COLLEGIATE SCHOLARS (NSCS)

http://www.nscs.org/

NSCS EXEMPLARY SCHOLAR AWARD

Scholarship of $1000 available to outstanding undergraduates among the NSCS members for their high academic achievement as well as additional scholarly pursuits outside of the classroom. They should exemplify the NSCS mission: "Honoring and inspiring academic excellence and engaged citizenship for a lifetime" and show integrity in everything they do. Must have a completed profile and resume in NSCS database. Apply on website http://www.nscs.org/exemplary_scholar_award.

Award: Scholarship for use in freshman, sophomore, junior, or senior years; not renewable. *Number:* 3. *Amount:* $1000.

Eligibility Requirements: Applicant must be enrolled or expecting to enroll full- or part-time at a four-year institution or university and must have an interest in leadership. Applicant or parent of applicant must be member of National Society of Collegiate Scholars. Available to U.S. and non-U.S. citizens.

Application Requirements: Application form. *Deadline:* April 30.

Contact: Stephen Loflin, Executive Director
Phone: 202-965-9000
E-mail: nscs@nscs.org

NSCS MERIT AWARD

Fifty merit awards to outstanding new NSCS members around the country. Student is chosen based upon how they exemplify the mission of NSCS. Must have a resume in the NSCS database and be a member who has joined between August of the previous year and July of the present year. Must have a minimum GPA of 3.4 and be enrolled in an accredited institution. For additional information, see website http://www.nscs.org.

Award: Scholarship for use in freshman, sophomore, junior, or senior years; not renewable. *Number:* 50. *Amount:* $1000.

Eligibility Requirements: Applicant must be enrolled or expecting to enroll full- or part-time at a two-year or four-year or technical institution or university. Applicant or parent of applicant must be member of

National Society of Collegiate Scholars. Available to U.S. and non-U.S. citizens.

Application Requirements: Application form, recommendations or references, resume, transcript. *Deadline:* July 31.

Contact: Stephen Loflin, Executive Director
Phone: 202-965-9000
E-mail: nscs@nscs.org

NSCS SCHOLAR ABROAD SCHOLARSHIP

Scholarship for an active NSCS member who has been accepted to and enrolled in an accredited study abroad program. One $5000 scholarship is awarded each fall and spring semester and one $2500 scholarship is awarded for the summer term. Must have profile and resume in NSCS database and have a minimum 3.4 GPA. Apply at website http://www.nscs.org/scholar-abroad-scholarship.

Award: Scholarship for use in freshman, sophomore, junior, or senior years; not renewable. *Number:* 3. *Amount:* $2500–$5000.

Eligibility Requirements: Applicant must be enrolled or expecting to enroll full-time at a two-year or four-year institution or university. Applicant or parent of applicant must be member of National Society of Collegiate Scholars. Available to U.S. and non-U.S. citizens.

Application Requirements: Application form, resume. *Deadline:* April 15.

Contact: Stephen Loflin, Executive Director
Phone: 202-965-9000
E-mail: nscs@nscs.org

NATIONAL SOCIETY OF HIGH SCHOOL SCHOLARS

http://www.nshss.org

CLAES NOBEL ACADEMIC SCHOLARSHIPS

Scholarships for high school students planning to attend four-year colleges or universities who are members of NSHSS. Minimum 3.5 GPA required.

Award: Scholarship for use in freshman year; not renewable. *Number:* 10. *Amount:* $5000.

Eligibility Requirements: Applicant must be high school student; planning to enroll or expecting to enroll full-time at a four-year institution or university and must have an interest in leadership. Applicant or parent of applicant must be member of National Society of High School Scholars. Applicant must have 3.5 GPA or higher. Available to U.S. and non-U.S. citizens.

Application Requirements: Application form, essay, personal photograph. *Deadline:* March 10.

Contact: Dr. Susan Thurman, Scholarship Director
National Society of High School Scholars
1936 North Druid Hills Road
Atlanta, GA 30319
Phone: 404-235-5500
E-mail: scholarships@nshss.org

NATIONAL SCHOLAR AWARDS FOR NSHSS MEMBERS

Scholarship of $1000 for undergraduate study. Applicant must be a member of NSHSS.

Award: Scholarship for use in freshman year; not renewable. *Number:* 85. *Amount:* $1000.

Eligibility Requirements: Applicant must be high school student; planning to enroll or expecting to enroll full-time at a two-year or four-year or technical institution or university and must have an interest in leadership. Applicant or parent of applicant must be member of National Society of High School Scholars. Applicant must have 3.5 GPA or higher. Available to U.S. and non-U.S. citizens.

Application Requirements: Application form, essay, personal photograph. *Deadline:* March 10.

Contact: Dr. Susan Thurman, Scholarship Director
National Society of High School Scholars
1936 North Druid Hills road
Atlanta, GA 30319
Phone: 404-235-5500
E-mail: scholarships@nshss.org

ROBERT P. SHEPPARD LEADERSHIP AWARD FOR NSHSS MEMBERS

Scholarship of $1000 awarded to an NSHSS member demonstrating outstanding dedication to community service and initiative in volunteer activities.

Award: Scholarship for use in freshman year; not renewable. *Number:* 5. *Amount:* $1000–$2500.

Eligibility Requirements: Applicant must be high school student; planning to enroll or expecting to enroll full-time at a four-year institution or university and must have an interest in leadership. Applicant or parent of applicant must be member of National Society of High School Scholars. Applicant must have 3.5 GPA or higher. Available to U.S. and non-U.S. citizens.

Application Requirements: Application form, essay, personal photograph. *Deadline:* March 15.

Contact: Dr. Susan Thurman, Scholarship Director
National Society of High School Scholars
1936 North Druid Hills Road
Atlanta, GA 30319
Phone: 404-235-5500
E-mail: scholarships@nshss.org

NEW YORK STATE GRANGE

http://www.nysgrange.org/

SUSAN W. FREESTONE EDUCATION AWARD

Grants for members of Junior Grange and Subordinate Grange in New York State. Students must enroll in an approved two or four-year college in New York State. Second grants available with reapplication.

Award: Scholarship for use in freshman or sophomore years; not renewable. *Number:* 1–4. *Amount:* $1000.

Eligibility Requirements: Applicant must be high school student; planning to enroll or expecting to enroll full-time at a two-year or four-year institution; resident of New York and studying in New York. Applicant or parent of applicant must be member of Grange Association. Applicant must have 2.5 GPA or higher. Available to U.S. citizens.

Application Requirements: Application form, financial need analysis. *Deadline:* April 15.

Contact: Scholarship Committee
New York State Grange
100 Grange Place
Cortland, NY 13045
Phone: 607-756-7553
E-mail: nysgrange@nysgrange.org

NORTHEASTERN LOGGERS' ASSOCIATION INC.

http://www.northernlogger.com/

NORTHEASTERN LOGGERS' ASSOCIATION SCHOLARSHIPS

Scholarships available to those whose family is a member of the Northeastern Loggers' Association or whose family member is an employee of an Industrial or Associate Members of the Northeastern Loggers' Association. Must submit paper on topic of "What it means to grow up in the forest industry."

Award: Scholarship for use in freshman, sophomore, junior, or senior years; not renewable. *Number:* 6–10. *Amount:* $500–$1000.

Eligibility Requirements: Applicant must be enrolled or expecting to enroll full-time at a two-year or four-year or technical institution or university. Applicant or parent of applicant must be member of Northeastern Loggers Association. Available to U.S. and Canadian citizens.

Application Requirements: Application form, essay. *Deadline:* March 31.

Contact: Mona Lincoln, Director, Training and Safety
Phone: 315-369-3078
Fax: 315-369-3736
E-mail: mona@northernlogger.com

NORTH EAST ROOFING EDUCATIONAL FOUNDATION

http://www.nerca.org/

NORTH EAST ROOFING EDUCATIONAL FOUNDATION SCHOLARSHIP

Applicants must be a member of NERCA, their employees, or their respective immediate family. Immediate family is defined as self, spouse, or child. The child may be natural, legally adopted, or a stepchild. Also must be a high school senior or graduate who plans to enroll in a full-time undergraduate course of study at an accredited two-year or four-year college, university, or vocational-technical school.

Award: Scholarship for use in freshman, sophomore, junior, or senior years; not renewable. *Number:* 11. *Amount:* up to $2000.

Eligibility Requirements: Applicant must be enrolled or expecting to enroll full-time at a two-year or four-year or technical institution or university. Applicant or parent of applicant must be member of North East Roofing Contractors Association. Available to U.S. and Canadian citizens.

Application Requirements: Application form, recommendations or references, self-addressed stamped envelope with application, transcript. *Deadline:* May 1.

Contact: Patsy Sweeney, Clerk
North East Roofing Educational Foundation
150 Grossman Drive Street, Suite 313
Braintree, MA 02184
Phone: 781-849-0555
Fax: 781-849-3223
E-mail: info@nerca.org

OFFICE AND PROFESSIONAL EMPLOYEES INTERNATIONAL UNION

http://www.opeiu.org/

OFFICE AND PROFESSIONAL EMPLOYEES INTERNATIONAL UNION HOWARD COUGHLIN MEMORIAL SCHOLARSHIP FUND

Scholarship of twelve full-time awards of $6000 and six part-time awards of $2400 is given to undergraduate students. Applicants should be a member or associate member of the Union.

Award: Scholarship for use in freshman, sophomore, junior, or senior years; not renewable. *Number:* 18. *Amount:* $2400–$6000.

Eligibility Requirements: Applicant must be enrolled or expecting to enroll full- or part-time at a two-year or four-year or technical institution or university. Applicant or parent of applicant must be member of Office and Professional Employees International Union. Available to U.S. citizens.

Application Requirements: Application form, SAT/CAT scores, transcript. *Deadline:* March 31.

Contact: Mary Mahoney, Secretary-Treasurer
Phone: 202-393-4464
Fax: 202-887-0910
E-mail: mmahoney@opeiudc.org

OKLAHOMA ALUMNI & ASSOCIATES OF FHA, HERO AND FCCLA INC.

http://www.okalumni.org

OKLAHOMA ALUMNI & ASSOCIATES OF FHA, HERO, AND FCCLA INC. SCHOLARSHIP

One-time award for FCCLA members who will be pursuing a postsecondary education. Must be a resident of Oklahoma. Scholarship value is $1500. Two scholarships are granted.

Award: Scholarship for use in freshman year; not renewable. *Number:* 2. *Amount:* $1500.

Eligibility Requirements: Applicant must be high school student; planning to enroll or expecting to enroll full-time at a two-year or four-year or technical institution or university and resident of Oklahoma. Applicant or parent of applicant must be member of Family, Career and Community Leaders of America. Applicant must have 3.0 GPA or higher. Available to U.S. citizens.

Application Requirements: Application form, essay. *Deadline:* February 1.

Contact: Denise Morris, State FCCLA Adviser
Oklahoma Alumni & Associates of FHA, HERO and FCCLA Inc.
1500 West Seventh Avenue
Stillwater, OK 74074
Phone: 405-743-5467
E-mail: denise.morris@careertech.ok.gov

OREGON STUDENT ASSISTANCE COMMISSION

https://oregonstudentaid.gov/

AFSCME: AMERICAN FEDERATION OF STATE, COUNTY, AND MUNICIPAL EMPLOYEES LOCAL 2067 SCHOLARSHIP

Award for active members in good standing or spouses, children, or grandchildren of active members in good standing of Oregon AFSCME Local 2067. Qualifying members must have been active in AFSCME Local 2067 one+ year as of the March scholarship deadline. Oregon residency is not required. Minimum 2.5 GPA.

Award: Scholarship for use in freshman, sophomore, junior, or senior years; not renewable.

Eligibility Requirements: Applicant must be enrolled or expecting to enroll full- or part-time at a four-year institution or university. Applicant or parent of applicant must be member of American Federation of State, County, and Municipal Employees. Applicant must have 2.5 GPA or higher. Available to U.S. citizens.

Application Requirements: Application form, essay, financial need analysis.

Contact: Melissa Adams, Scholarship Processing Coordinator
Phone: 541-687-7409
E-mail: melissa.adams@state.or.us

AMERICAN FEDERATION OF STATE, COUNTY, AND MUNICIPAL EMPLOYEES OREGON COUNCIL #75—WILLIAM LUCY SCHOLARSHIP

Eligible members of Oregon AFSCME Council #75 and their dependents, grandchildren, and spouses. Qualifying members must have been active in the Oregon Council one+ year as of the March scholarship deadline or have been a member one+ year preceding the date of layoff, death, disability, or retirement. Preference to majors in labor studies or political science. Part-time enrollment (minimum six credit hours) or graduate program enrollment will be considered only for active members, spouses, domestic partners, or laid-off members. Based on financial need.

Award: Scholarship for use in freshman, sophomore, junior, senior, or graduate years; not renewable.

Eligibility Requirements: Applicant must be enrolled or expecting to enroll full- or part-time at a four-year institution or university. Applicant or parent of applicant must be member of Teamsters. Applicant must have 3.0 GPA or higher. Available to U.S. citizens.

Application Requirements: Application form, essay. *Deadline:* March 1.

Contact: Melissa Adams, Scholarship Processing Coordinator
Phone: 541-687-7409
E-mail: melissa.adams@state.or.us

AMERICAN FEDERATION OF STATE, COUNTY, AND MUNICIPAL EMPLOYEES OREGON COUNCIL # 75 SCHOLARSHIP

Renewable award for active, laid-off, retired, or disabled members in good standing or spouses (including life partners and their children), natural children, or grandchildren of active, laid-off, retired, disabled, or deceased members of AFSCME Council #75 in good standing. Qualifying members must have been active in AFSCME Council # 75 one year or more as of the March 1 scholarship deadline or have been a member one year or more preceding the date of layoff, death, disability, or retirement. Enrollment of at least half-time is required. Financial need may or may not be considered.

Award: Scholarship for use in freshman, sophomore, junior, senior, or graduate years; renewable.

Eligibility Requirements: Applicant must be enrolled or expecting to enroll full- or part-time at a two-year or four-year institution or university and resident of Yukon. Applicant or parent of applicant must be member of American Federation of State, County, and Municipal Employees. Available to U.S. citizens.

Application Requirements: Application form, essay, financial need analysis.

Contact: Melissa Adams, Scholarship Processing Coordinator
Phone: 541-687-7409
E-mail: melissa.adams@state.or.us

CLYDE C. CROSBY/JOSEPH M. EDGAR AND THOMAS J. MALLOY MEMORIAL SCHOLARSHIP

Renewable scholarship available for a graduating high school senior with a minimum 3.0 cumulative GPA who is a child, or dependent stepchild of an active, retired, disabled, or deceased member of local union affiliated with Teamsters 37. Member must have been active for at least one year. Scholarship is automatically renewable if renewal criteria met. Based on financial need

Award: Scholarship for use in freshman, sophomore, junior, or senior years; renewable.

Eligibility Requirements: Applicant must be high school student and planning to enroll or expecting to enroll full-time at a four-year institution or university. Applicant or parent of applicant must be member of Teamsters. Applicant must have 3.0 GPA or higher. Available to U.S. citizens.

Application Requirements: Application form, financial need analysis. *Deadline:* March 1.

Contact: Melissa Adams, Scholarship Processing Coordinator
Phone: 541-687-7409
E-mail: melissa.adams@state.or.us

INTERNATIONAL BROTHERHOOD OF ELECTRICAL WORKERS LOCAL 280 SCHOLARSHIP

One-time award available for children or grandchildren of active or retired members of IBEW Local 280. Must be graduating high school seniors enrolling as first-time freshman in any college or university in the U.S.

Award: Scholarship for use in freshman year; not renewable.

Eligibility Requirements: Applicant must be enrolled or expecting to enroll full- or part-time at a four-year institution or university. Applicant or parent of applicant must be member of International Brotherhood of Electrical Workers. Available to U.S. citizens.

Application Requirements: Application form. *Deadline:* March 1.

Contact: Melissa Adams, Scholarship Processing Coordinator
Phone: 541-687-7409
E-mail: melissa.adams@state.or.us

INTERNATIONAL UNION OF OPERATING ENGINEERS LOCAL 701 SCHOLARSHIP

One-time award available for graduating high school seniors who are children of International Union of Operating Engineers Local 701 members.

Award: Scholarship for use in freshman year; not renewable.

Eligibility Requirements: Applicant must be high school student and planning to enroll or expecting to enroll full- or part-time at a four-year institution or university. Applicant or parent of applicant must be member of International Union of Operating Engineers. Available to U.S. citizens.

Application Requirements: Application form. *Deadline:* March 1.

Contact: Melissa Adams, Scholarship Processing Coordinator
Phone: 541-687-7409
E-mail: melissa.adams@state.or.us

JOSH HIETER MEMORIAL/TEAMSTERS LOCAL 223 SCHOLARSHIP

One-time award for active members or dependent children or stepchildren of active, retired, disabled, or deceased members of Local 223 of the Joint Council of Teamsters #37. Member must have been active 1+ year as of the March scholarship deadline or have been a member 1+ year preceding the date of retirement, disability, or death. For use at an Oregon public or non-profit college. Minimum 3.0 GPA is preferred.

Award: Scholarship for use in freshman, sophomore, junior, or senior years; not renewable.

Eligibility Requirements: Applicant must be enrolled or expecting to enroll full-time at a two-year or four-year or technical institution or university and studying in Oregon. Applicant or parent of applicant must be member of Teamsters. Available to U.S. citizens.

Application Requirements: Application form, essay. *Deadline:* March 1.

Contact: Melissa Adams, Scholarship Processing Coordinator
Phone: 541-687-7409
E-mail: melissa.adams@state.or.us

NORTHWEST AUTOMATIC VENDING ASSOCIATION SCHOLARSHIP

One-time award to recent high school graduates who are first-time freshmen and are dependents or grandchildren of members or employees of Northwest Automatic Vending Association. Oregon residency not required. For use at public or nonprofit universities only.

Award: Scholarship for use in freshman year; not renewable.

Eligibility Requirements: Applicant must be high school student and planning to enroll or expecting to enroll full-time at a four-year institution or university. Applicant or parent of applicant must be member of Northwest Automatic Vending Association. Available to U.S. citizens.

Application Requirements: Application form. *Deadline:* March 1.

Contact: Melissa Adams, Scholarship Processing Coordinator
Phone: 541-687-7409
E-mail: melissa.adams@state.or.us

OREGON STATE FISCAL ASSOCIATION SCHOLARSHIP

One-time award for OSFA members or their dependents. Members must enroll in an Oregon public or nonprofit institution at least half-time and must study public administration, finance, economics, or related fields. Children of members must enroll full-time in an Oregon institution and may enter any program of study. Must reapply annually. Based on financial need.

Award: Scholarship for use in freshman, sophomore, junior, senior, or graduate years; not renewable.

Eligibility Requirements: Applicant must be enrolled or expecting to enroll full- or part-time at a two-year or four-year institution or university; resident of Oregon and studying in Oregon. Applicant or parent of applicant must be member of Oregon State Fiscal Association. Available to U.S. citizens.

Application Requirements: Application form, financial need analysis. *Deadline:* March 1.

Contact: Melissa Adams, Scholarship Processing Coordinator
Phone: 541-687-7409
E-mail: melissa.adams@state.or.us

TEAMSTERS COUNCIL 37 FEDERAL CREDIT UNION SCHOLARSHIP

One-time award for members (or dependents of members) of Council 37 Federal Credit Union who are active for one year as of the March deadline, in a local that is affiliated with the Joint Council of Teamsters 37. GPA preference between 2.0 and 3.0. Must enroll at least half-time. Financial need may or may not be considered.

Award: Scholarship for use in freshman, sophomore, junior, or senior years; not renewable.

Eligibility Requirements: Applicant must be enrolled or expecting to enroll full- or part-time at a two-year or four-year institution or university. Applicant or parent of applicant must be member of Teamsters. Available to U.S. citizens.

Application Requirements: Application form. *Deadline:* March 1.

Contact: Melissa Adams, Scholarship Processing Coordinator
Phone: 541-687-7409
E-mail: melissa.adams@state.or.us

TEAMSTERS LOCAL 305 SCHOLARSHIP

Renewable award for graduating Oregon high school seniors who are dependents of eligible members of Local 305 of the Joint Council of Teamsters #37. Members must have been active at least one year as of the March deadline. Scholarship is automatically renewable if renewal criteria is met.

Award: Scholarship for use in freshman year; renewable.

Eligibility Requirements: Applicant must be high school student and planning to enroll or expecting to enroll full-time at a four-year institution or university. Applicant or parent of applicant must be member of Teamsters. Available to U.S. citizens.

Application Requirements: Application form. *Deadline:* March 1.

Contact: Melissa Adams, Scholarship Processing Coordinator
Phone: 541-687-7409
E-mail: melissa.adams@state.or.us

PENNSYLVANIA FEDERATION OF DEMOCRATIC WOMEN INC.

http://www.pafedofdemwomen.org

PENNSYLVANIA FEDERATION OF DEMOCRATIC WOMEN INC. ANNUAL SCHOLARSHIP AWARDS

Award of up to $1000 for any female resident of Pennsylvania who is a sophomore or junior at an accredited college or university and is a registered Democrat. Award is for their Junior or senior year. Applicants must possess a Democratic Party family background and be an active participant in activities of the Democratic Party.

Award: Scholarship for use in junior or senior years; not renewable. *Number:* 1–5. *Amount:* $250–$1000.

Eligibility Requirements: Applicant must be enrolled or expecting to enroll full-time at a four-year institution or university; female and resident of Pennsylvania. Applicant or parent of applicant must be member of Democratic Party. Available to U.S. citizens.

Application Requirements: Application form, essay. *Deadline:* April 1.

Contact: Michelle Price, Scholarship Chair
Pennsylvania Federation of Democratic Women Inc.
462 W Grant Street
Easton, PA 18042
Phone: 610-235-9599
E-mail: mbernsonprice@gmail.com

PENNSYLVANIA MASONIC YOUTH FOUNDATION

http://www.pmyf.org/

PENNSYLVANIA MASONIC YOUTH FOUNDATION EDUCATIONAL ENDOWMENT FUND SCHOLARSHIPS

Grants for members, children, stepchildren, grandchildren, siblings, or dependents of members in good standing of a Pennsylvania Masonic Lodge, or members in good standing of a PA Masonic-sponsored youth group. Applicants must be high school graduates or high school seniors pursuing a college education. Minimum GPA 3.0. Proof of relationship to a member of a Lodge under the jurisdiction of the Right Worshipful Grand Lodge of Free and Accepted Masons of PA is required, or proof of membership in one of the youth groups it sponsors.

Award: Grant for use in freshman, sophomore, junior, or senior years; not renewable. *Number:* 25–75. *Amount:* $1000–$3000.

Eligibility Requirements: Applicant must be enrolled or expecting to enroll full-time at a two-year or four-year or technical institution or university. Applicant or parent of applicant must be member of Freemasons. Applicant must have 3.0 GPA or higher. Available to U.S. and non-U.S. citizens.

Application Requirements: Application form, essay, financial need analysis. *Deadline:* March 15.

Contact: Amy Nace, Executive Assistant
Pennsylvania Masonic Youth Foundation
1244 Bainbridge Road
Elizabethtown, PA 17022
Phone: 717-367-1536 Ext. 2
Fax: 717-367-0616
E-mail: pmyf@pagrandlodge.org

PHILIPINO-AMERICAN ASSOCIATION OF NEW ENGLAND

http://www.pamas.org/

PAMAS RESTRICTED SCHOLARSHIP AWARD

Award of $500 for any sons or daughters of PAMAS members who are currently active in PAMAS projects and activities. Must be of Filipino descent, a resident of New England, a high school senior at the time of award, and have college acceptance letter from accredited institution.

Application Requirements: Application form. *Deadline:* March 1.

Contact: Melissa Adams, Scholarship Processing Coordinator
Phone: 541-687-7409
E-mail: melissa.adams@state.or.us

Minimum of 3.3 GPA required. For application details visit http://www.pamas.org.

Award: Scholarship for use in freshman year; not renewable. *Number:* 1. *Amount:* $500.

Eligibility Requirements: Applicant must be Asian/Pacific Islander; high school student; planning to enroll or expecting to enroll full-time at a four-year institution or university and resident of Connecticut, Maine, Massachusetts, New Hampshire, Rhode Island, Vermont. Applicant or parent of applicant must be member of Philipino-American Association. Available to U.S. citizens.

Application Requirements: Application form, college acceptance letter, essay, recommendations or references, transcript. *Deadline:* May 31.

Contact: Amanda Kalb, First Vice President
Phone: 617-471-3513
E-mail: balic2ss@comcast.net

PHI SIGMA KAPPA INTERNATIONAL HEADQUARTERS
http://www.phisigmakappa.org/

WENDEROTH UNDERGRADUATE SCHOLARSHIP
Available to sophomores and juniors on the basis of academic criteria. Must submit an essay and letter of recommendation along with the application.

Award: Scholarship for use in sophomore or junior years; not renewable. *Number:* 1–4. *Amount:* $1750–$4000.

Eligibility Requirements: Applicant must be enrolled or expecting to enroll full-time at a four-year institution or university. Applicant or parent of applicant must be member of Phi Sigma Kappa. Available to U.S. and non-U.S. citizens.

Application Requirements: Application form, essay, personal photograph, recommendations or references, resume, transcript. *Deadline:* January 31.

Contact: Michael Carey, Executive Director
Phone: 317-573-5420
Fax: 317-573-5430
E-mail: michael@phisigmakappa.org

ZETA SCHOLARSHIP
Scholarships are available following a generous gift to the Phi Sigma Kappa Foundation from the Zeta Alumni Association. Phi Sig or a child of a Phi Sig having minimum 3.0 GPA are eligible to apply.

Award: Scholarship for use in freshman, sophomore, junior, senior, or graduate years; not renewable. *Number:* 2. *Amount:* $2500.

Eligibility Requirements: Applicant must be enrolled or expecting to enroll full-time at a four-year institution or university. Applicant or parent of applicant must be member of Phi Sigma Kappa. Applicant must have 3.0 GPA or higher. Available to U.S. citizens.

Application Requirements: Application form, community service, personal photograph, recommendations or references, resume, test scores, transcript. *Deadline:* January 31.

Contact: Scholarship Program Coordinator
Phi Sigma Kappa International Headquarters
2925 East 96th Street
Indianapolis, IN 46240
Phone: 317-573-5420
Fax: 317-573-5430

PHI SIGMA PI NATIONAL HONOR FRATERNITY
http://www.phisigmapi.org/

RICHARD CECIL TODD AND CLAUDA PENNOCK TODD TRIPOD SCHOLARSHIP
Scholarship to promote the future academic opportunity of brothers (members) of the fraternity, who have excelled in embodying the ideals of scholarship, leadership, and fellowship. One-time award for full-time student, sophomore level or higher, with minimum 3.0 GPA.

Award: Scholarship for use in sophomore, junior, or senior years; not renewable. *Number:* 1. *Amount:* up to $1500.

Eligibility Requirements: Applicant must be enrolled or expecting to enroll full-time at a two-year or four-year institution or university and must have an interest in leadership. Applicant or parent of applicant must be member of Greek Organization. Applicant must have 3.0 GPA or higher. Available to U.S. and non-U.S. citizens.

Application Requirements: Application form, driver's license, essay, recommendations or references, transcript. *Deadline:* April 15.

Contact: Suzanne Schaffer, Executive Director
Phone: 717-299-4710
Fax: 717-390-3054
E-mail: schaffer@phisigmapi.org

PONY OF THE AMERICAS CLUB INC.
http://www.poac.org/

POAC NATIONAL SCHOLARSHIP
Two to four renewable awards that may be used for any year or any institution but must be for full-time undergraduate study. Application and transcript required. Award restricted to those who have interest in animal or agricultural competition and active involvement in Pony Of the Americas organization.

Award: Scholarship for use in freshman, sophomore, junior, or senior years; not renewable. *Number:* 2–4. *Amount:* $500–$1000.

Eligibility Requirements: Applicant must be enrolled or expecting to enroll full- or part-time at a two-year or four-year or technical institution or university and must have an interest in animal/agricultural competition. Applicant or parent of applicant must be member of Pony of the Americas Club. Available to U.S. and non-U.S. citizens.

Application Requirements: Application form, driver's license, entry in a contest, essay, recommendations or references, transcript. *Deadline:* March 1.

Contact: Joyse Banister, Scholarship Administrator/CEO
Pony Of the Americas Club Inc.
3828 South Emerson Avenue
Indianapolis, IN 46203
Phone: 317-788-0107
Fax: 317-788-8974
E-mail: officemanager@poac.org

PROFESSIONAL HORSEMEN'S SCHOLARSHIP FUND INC.
http://www.nationalpha.com/

PROFESSIONAL HORSEMEN'S SCHOLARSHIP FUND
Scholarship provides financial assistance from a fund established for children of professional members of the Professional Horseman's Association who have been professional members for more than two years and who are enrolled in an approved school for the advancement of their education beyond the secondary level.

Award: Scholarship for use in freshman, sophomore, junior, senior, graduate, or postgraduate years; not renewable. *Number:* 10–20. *Amount:* $500–$1000.

Eligibility Requirements: Applicant must be enrolled or expecting to enroll full-time at a two-year or four-year or technical institution or university. Applicant or parent of applicant must be member of Professional Horsemen Association. Available to U.S. and non-U.S. citizens.

Application Requirements: Application form, autobiography, essay, financial need analysis, interview. *Deadline:* May 1.

Contact: Mrs. Ann Grenci, Chairman, Scholarship Committee
Phone: 561-707-9094
E-mail: foxhill33@aol.com

PROJECT BEST SCHOLARSHIP FUND
http://www.projectbest.com/

PROJECT BEST SCHOLARSHIP
One-time award of $1000 to $2000 for employees or children or spouses of employees working for a company or labor union in the construction industry that is affiliated with Project BEST. Must be residents of West

Virginia, Pennsylvania, or Ohio and attend a West Virginia or Ohio postsecondary institution. Must be U.S. citizens.

Award: Scholarship for use in freshman, sophomore, junior, senior, or graduate years; renewable. *Number:* 11–22. *Amount:* $1000–$2000.

Eligibility Requirements: Applicant must be enrolled or expecting to enroll full-time at a two-year or four-year institution or university; resident of Ohio, Pennsylvania, West Virginia and studying in Ohio, West Virginia. Applicant or parent of applicant must be member of AFL-CIO. Applicant or parent of applicant must have employment or volunteer experience in construction. Available to U.S. citizens.

Application Requirements: Application form. *Deadline:* continuous.

Contact: Ginny Favede, Director
Project BEST Scholarship Fund
21 Armory Drive
Wheeling, WV 26003
Phone: 304-242-0520
E-mail: projectbest@projectbest.com

PUEBLO OF ISLETA, DEPARTMENT OF EDUCATION

http://www.isletapueblo.com/

HIGHER EDUCATION SUPPLEMENTAL SCHOLARSHIP ISLETA PUEBLO HIGHER EDUCATION DEPARTMENT

Applicants must be students seeking a postsecondary degree. The degree granting institution must be a nationally accredited vocational or postsecondary institution offering a certificate, Associate, Bachelor's, Master's, or Doctoral degree. Enrolled tribal members of the Isleta Pueblo may apply for this scholarship if they also apply for additional scholarships from different sources. Deadlines: April 1 for summer, November 1 for spring and July 1 for fall.

Award: Scholarship for use in freshman, sophomore, junior, senior, graduate, or postgraduate years; renewable.

Eligibility Requirements: Applicant must be American Indian/Alaska Native and enrolled or expecting to enroll full- or part-time at a two-year or four-year or technical institution or university. Applicant or parent of applicant must be member of Ice Skating Institute. Available to U.S. citizens.

Application Requirements: Application form, certificate of Indian blood, class schedule, financial need analysis, transcript. *Deadline:* varies.

Contact: Higher Education Director
Pueblo of Isleta, Department of Education
PO Box 1270
Isleta, NM 87022
Phone: 505-869-2680
Fax: 505-869-7690
E-mail: isletahighered@yahoo.com

RED ANGUS ASSOCIATION OF AMERICA

http://www.redangus.org/

4 RAAA/JUNIOR RED ANGUS SCHOLARSHIP

Scholarship of $500 given to active members of the National Junior Red Angus Association. Must be high school seniors or college underclassmen.

Award: Scholarship for use in freshman or sophomore years; not renewable. *Number:* 2. *Amount:* $500.

Eligibility Requirements: Applicant must be enrolled or expecting to enroll full-time at a two-year or four-year institution or university. Applicant or parent of applicant must be member of National Junior Red Angus Association. Available to U.S. citizens.

Application Requirements: Application form, personal photograph, recommendations or references, transcript. *Deadline:* March 31.

Contact: Betty Grimshaw, Association Administrative Director
Phone: 940-387-3502
Fax: 940-383-4036
E-mail: betty@redangus.org

DEE SONSTEGARD MEMORIAL SCHOLARSHIP

Scholarship of $500 given to active members of the National Junior Red Angus Association. Must be high school seniors or college underclassmen.

Award: Scholarship for use in freshman or sophomore years; not renewable. *Number:* 2. *Amount:* $500.

Eligibility Requirements: Applicant must be enrolled or expecting to enroll full-time at a two-year or four-year institution or university. Applicant or parent of applicant must be member of National Junior Red Angus Association. Available to U.S. citizens.

Application Requirements: Application form, personal photograph, recommendations or references, transcript. *Deadline:* March 31.

Contact: Betty Grimshaw, Association Administrative Director
Phone: 940-387-3502
Fax: 940-383-4036
E-mail: betty@redangus.org

FARM AND RANCH CONNECTION SCHOLARSHIP

Scholarship of $500 given to active members of the National Junior Red Angus Association. Must be high school seniors or college underclassmen.

Award: Scholarship for use in freshman or sophomore years; not renewable. *Number:* 1. *Amount:* $500.

Eligibility Requirements: Applicant must be enrolled or expecting to enroll full-time at a two-year or four-year institution or university. Applicant or parent of applicant must be member of National Junior Red Angus Association. Available to U.S. citizens.

Application Requirements: Application form, personal photograph, recommendations or references, transcript. *Deadline:* March 31.

Contact: Betty Grimshaw, Association Administrative Director
Phone: 940-387-3502
Fax: 940-383-4036
E-mail: betty@redangus.org

LEONARD A. LORENZEN MEMORIAL SCHOLARSHIP

Scholarship of $500 given to active members of the National Junior Red Angus Association. Must be high school seniors or college underclassmen.

Award: Scholarship for use in freshman or sophomore years; not renewable. *Number:* 2. *Amount:* $500.

Eligibility Requirements: Applicant must be enrolled or expecting to enroll full-time at a two-year or four-year institution or university. Applicant or parent of applicant must be member of National Junior Red Angus Association. Available to U.S. citizens.

Application Requirements: Application form, personal photograph, recommendations or references, transcript. *Deadline:* March 31.

Contact: Betty Grimshaw, Association Administrative Director
Phone: 940-387-3502
Fax: 940-383-4036
E-mail: betty@redangus.org

THE RESERVE OFFICERS ASSOCIATION

http://www.roa.org/

HENRY J. REILLY MEMORIAL SCHOLARSHIP-HIGH SCHOOL SENIORS AND FIRST YEAR FRESHMEN

One-time award for high school seniors or college freshmen who are U.S. citizens and children or grandchildren of active members of the Reserve Officers Association. Must demonstrate leadership, have minimum 3.0 GPA and 1250 on the SAT. Must submit sponsor verification. College freshmen must submit college transcript.

Award: Scholarship for use in freshman year; not renewable. *Number:* 25–30. *Amount:* $1000.

Eligibility Requirements: Applicant must be enrolled or expecting to enroll full-time at a four-year institution or university and must have an interest in leadership. Applicant or parent of applicant must be member of Reserve Officers Association. Applicant must have 3.0 GPA or higher. Available to U.S. citizens. Applicant or parent must meet one or more of the following requirements: general military experience; retired from active duty; disabled or killed as a result of military service; prisoner of war; or missing in action.

Application Requirements: Application form, essay, test scores, transcript. *Deadline:* May 15.

Contact: Rebecca Riedler, Executive Administrator
Phone: 202-646-7706
E-mail: scholarship@roa.org

HENRY J. REILLY MEMORIAL UNDERGRADUATE SCHOLARSHIP PROGRAM FOR COLLEGE ATTENDEES

One-time award of $1000 for members and children or grandchildren of members of the Reserve Officers Association or its Auxiliary. Must be a U.S. citizen, 26 years old or younger, and enrolled at an accredited four-year institution. Must submit sponsor verification. Minimum 3.0 GPA required. Submit SAT or ACT scores; contact for score requirements.

Award: Scholarship for use in freshman, sophomore, junior, or senior years; not renewable. *Number:* 25–30. *Amount:* $1000.

Eligibility Requirements: Applicant must be enrolled or expecting to enroll full-time at a two-year or four-year institution or university. Applicant or parent of applicant must be member of Reserve Officers Association. Applicant must have 3.0 GPA or higher. Available to U.S. citizens. Applicant or parent must meet one or more of the following requirements: general military experience; retired from active duty; disabled or killed as a result of military service; prisoner of war; or missing in action.

Application Requirements: Application form, essay, sponsor verification, test scores, transcript. *Deadline:* May 15.

Contact: Rebecca Riedler, Executive Administrator
Phone: 202-646-7706
E-mail: scholarship@roa.org

RETAIL, WHOLESALE AND DEPARTMENT STORE UNION

http://www.rwdsu.org/

ALVIN E. HEAPS MEMORIAL SCHOLARSHIP

Scholarship for RWDSU members or members of an RWDSU family. Applicant must submit 500-word essay on the benefits of union membership. See website for application, http://www.rwdsu.info/heapsscholar.htm.

Award: Scholarship for use in freshman, sophomore, junior, or senior years; not renewable.

Eligibility Requirements: Applicant must be enrolled or expecting to enroll full- or part-time at a two-year or four-year institution or university. Applicant or parent of applicant must be member of Retail, Wholesale and Department Store Union. Available to U.S. citizens.

Application Requirements: Application form, essay, transcript. *Deadline:* varies.

Contact: Scholarship Committee
Phone: 212-684-5300
Fax: 212-779-2809

RHODE ISLAND FOUNDATION

http://www.rifoundation.org/

EDWARD LEON DUHAMEL FREEMASONS SCHOLARSHIP

Renewable scholarship for descendants of members of Franklin Lodge in Westerly Rhode Island. Must be accepted into an accredited postsecondary institution. Must demonstrate scholastic achievement, financial need, and good citizenship.

Award: Scholarship for use in freshman, sophomore, junior, or senior years; renewable. *Amount:* $500–$1000.

Eligibility Requirements: Applicant must be enrolled or expecting to enroll full-time at a four-year institution or university. Applicant or parent of applicant must be member of Freemasons. Available to U.S. citizens.

Application Requirements: Application form, essay, financial need analysis, self-addressed stamped envelope with application, transcript. *Deadline:* varies.

Contact: Libby Monahan, Funds Administrator
Phone: 401-274-4564 Ext. 3117
E-mail: libbym@rifoundation.org

SERVICE EMPLOYEES INTERNATIONAL UNION (SEIU)

http://www.seiu.org/

SEIU JESSE JACKSON SCHOLARSHIP PROGRAM

Renewable scholarship of $5000 given to a student whose work and aspirations for economic and social justice reflect the values and accomplishments of the Rev. Jackson.

Award: Scholarship for use in freshman, sophomore, junior, or senior years; renewable. *Number:* 1. *Amount:* $5000.

Eligibility Requirements: Applicant must be enrolled or expecting to enroll full-time at a four-year institution or university. Applicant or parent of applicant must be member of Service Employees International Union. Available to U.S. citizens.

Application Requirements: Application form, essay. *Deadline:* March 1.

Contact: c/o Scholarship Program Administrators, Inc.
Phone: 615-320-3149
Fax: 615-320-3151
E-mail: info@spaprog.com

SEIU JOHN GEAGAN SCHOLARSHIP

Scholarship to SEIU members or their children or SEIU local union staff. Priority will be given to those applicants who are not served by traditional education institutions-typically adults who have been in the workforce and have decided to go, or return to, college.

Award: Scholarship for use in freshman, sophomore, junior, or senior years; not renewable. *Number:* 1. *Amount:* $2500.

Eligibility Requirements: Applicant must be enrolled or expecting to enroll full-time at a two-year or four-year or technical institution or university. Applicant or parent of applicant must be member of Service Employees International Union. Available to U.S. citizens.

Application Requirements: Application form, essay. *Deadline:* March 1.

Contact: c/o Scholarship Program Administrators, Inc.
Phone: 615-320-3149
Fax: 615-320-3151
E-mail: info@spaprog.com

SEIU NORA PIORE SCHOLARSHIP PROGRAM

Renewable award of $4375 to SEIU members enrolled full-time in an undergraduate study. Applicant's financial need will be considered during the selection process.

Award: Scholarship for use in freshman, sophomore, junior, or senior years; renewable. *Number:* 1. *Amount:* $4375.

Eligibility Requirements: Applicant must be enrolled or expecting to enroll full-time at a four-year institution or university. Applicant or parent of applicant must be member of Service Employees International Union. Available to U.S. citizens.

Application Requirements: Application form. *Deadline:* March 1.

Contact: c/o Scholarship Program Administrators, Inc.
Phone: 615-320-3149
Fax: 615-320-3151
E-mail: info@spaprog.com

SEIU SCHOLARSHIP PROGRAM

Fifteen $1000 scholarships available in annual installments for up to four years. Applicants must graduate from a high school or GED program by August. Must be enrolled as a full-time college freshman by the fall semester at an accredited, four-year college or university.

Award: Scholarship for use in freshman year; renewable. *Number:* 15. *Amount:* $1000.

Eligibility Requirements: Applicant must be high school student and planning to enroll or expecting to enroll full-time at a four-year institution or university. Applicant or parent of applicant must be member of Service Employees International Union. Available to U.S. citizens.

Application Requirements: Application form. *Deadline:* March 1.

Contact: c/o Scholarship Program Administrators, Inc.
Phone: 615-320-3149
Fax: 615-320-3151
E-mail: info@spaprog.com

SIGMA ALPHA MU

http://www.sam-fdn.org

UNDERGRADUATE ACHIEVEMENT AWARDS

Scholarship for seniors or juniors of undergraduate students enrolled full-time study. Must be member of Sigma Alpha Mu Foundation. Scholarship value varies.

Award: Scholarship for use in junior or senior years; not renewable. *Number:* 2.

Eligibility Requirements: Applicant must be enrolled or expecting to enroll full-time at a four-year institution or university. Applicant or parent of applicant must be member of Sigma Alpha Mu Foundation. Available to U.S. citizens.

Application Requirements: Application form. *Deadline:* February 1.

Contact: Maria Mandel, Director of Scholarships and Donor Relations
Phone: 317-789-8339
Fax: 317-824-1505
E-mail: mariam@sam-fdn.org

YOUNG SCHOLARS PROGRAM

Scholarship for candidates achieving a 3.75 GPA (or equivalent) for courses taken in the academic term of the undergraduate study. Must be member of Sigma Alpha Mu Foundation. Deadline varies.

Award: Scholarship for use in freshman, sophomore, junior, or senior years; not renewable. *Amount:* $500.

Eligibility Requirements: Applicant must be enrolled or expecting to enroll full-time at a four-year institution or university. Applicant or parent of applicant must be member of Sigma Alpha Mu Foundation. Applicant must have 2.5 GPA or higher. Available to U.S. citizens.

Application Requirements: Application form.

Contact: Maria Mandel, Director of Scholarships and Donor Relations
Phone: 317-789-8339
Fax: 317-824-1505
E-mail: mariam@sam-fdn.org

SIGMA CHI FOUNDATION

http://foundation.sigmachi.org

GENERAL SCHOLARSHIP GRANTS

Applicants must have completed three semesters (or four quarters) of undergraduate study to be considered for current year awards. Funds are available for tuition/fees payments only.

Award: Scholarship for use in sophomore, junior, or senior years; not renewable.

Eligibility Requirements: Applicant must be enrolled or expecting to enroll full-time at a four-year institution or university and male. Applicant or parent of applicant must be member of Sigma Chi Fraternity. Available to U.S. and non-U.S. citizens.

Application Requirements: Application form, financial need analysis, recommendations or references, transcript. *Deadline:* April 13.

Contact: Heidi Holley, Scholarship Administrator
Phone: 847-869-3655 Ext. 270
Fax: 847-869-4906
E-mail: heidi.holley@sigmachi.org

SLOVAK GYMNASTIC UNION SOKOL, USA

http://www.sokolusa.org/

SOKOL, USA/MILAN GETTING SCHOLARSHIP

Available to members of SOKOL, U.S.A who have been in good standing for at least three years. Must have plans to attend college. Renewable for a maximum of four years, based upon academic achievement. Minimum GPA 2.5 required.

Award: Grant for use in freshman, sophomore, junior, or senior years; renewable. *Number:* 4–8. *Amount:* $500.

Eligibility Requirements: Applicant must be enrolled or expecting to enroll full-time at a four-year institution or university. Applicant or parent of applicant must be member of SOKOL, USA. Applicant must have 2.5 GPA or higher. Available to U.S. citizens.

Application Requirements: Application form. *Deadline:* April 1.

Contact: Milan Kovac, Fraternal Secretary
Slovak Gymnastic Union SOKOL, USA
301 Pine Street
P.O. Box 677
Boonton, NJ 07005-0677
Phone: 973-676-0281
E-mail: sokolusahqs@aol.com

SLOVENIAN WOMEN'S UNION SCHOLARSHIP FOUNDATION

http://www.swusf.org

SLOVENIAN WOMEN'S UNION OF AMERICA SCHOLARSHIP FOUNDATION

one time award for full-time study only. Essay, transcripts, letters of recommendation from principal/teacher, financial need form, photo, civic and church activities information required. Open to high school seniors. One graduate school scholarship of $2,000 available to student majoring in education. Membership in Slovenian Women's Union not required. Applicant must be of Slovenian ancestry. One Graduate school scholarship of $2,000 available to student majoring in science, mathematics, or engineering. Membership in Slovenian Women's Union not required. Applicant must be of Slovenian ancestry.

Award: Scholarship for use in freshman, sophomore, junior, senior, or graduate years; not renewable. *Number:* 6–12. *Amount:* $1000–$2000.

Eligibility Requirements: Applicant must be enrolled or expecting to enroll full- or part-time at a two-year or four-year or technical institution or university. Applicant or parent of applicant must be member of Slovenian Women's Union of America. Available to U.S. citizens.

Application Requirements: Application form, autobiography, community service, essay, financial need analysis, personal photograph. *Deadline:* March 1.

Contact: Mary Turvey, Director
Slovenian Women's Union Scholarship Foundation
4 Lawrence Drive
Marquette, MI 49855
Phone: 906-249-4288
E-mail: mturvey@aol.com

SOIL AND WATER CONSERVATION SOCIETY

http://www.swcs.org

MELVILLE H. COHEE STUDENT LEADER CONSERVATION SCHOLARSHIP

The scholarship honors SWCS members who succeed as leaders in their studies, volunteerism, and work. Members who are in their junior or senior year of full-time undergraduate study or pursuing graduate level studies with a natural resource conservation orientation at a properly accredited college or university are eligible.

Award: Scholarship for use in junior, senior, graduate, or postgraduate years; not renewable. *Number:* 1. *Amount:* up to $500.

Eligibility Requirements: Applicant must be enrolled or expecting to enroll full-time at a four-year institution or university. Applicant or parent of applicant must be member of Soil and Water Conservation Society. Available to U.S. and non-U.S. citizens.

Application Requirements: Application form, essay, recommendations or references, transcript. *Deadline:* February 13.

Contact: SWCS Scholarships Program Coordinator
Soil and Water Conservation Society
945 SW Ankeny Road
Ankeny, IA 50023-9723
Phone: 515-289-2331 Ext. 114
E-mail: scholarships@swcs.org

SONS OF NORWAY FOUNDATION

http://www.sonsofnorway.com/foundation

ASTRID G. CATES AND MYRTLE BEINHAUER SCHOLARSHIP FUNDS

Merit award available to students ages 17 to 22 who are current members, children, or grandchildren of members of the Sons of Norway. School transcript required. Academic potential and clarity of study plan is key criterion for award. Minimum 3.0 GPA required.

Award: Scholarship for use in freshman, sophomore, junior, or senior years; not renewable. *Number:* 2–7. *Amount:* $1000–$3000.

Eligibility Requirements: Applicant must be age 17-22 and enrolled or expecting to enroll full-time at a two-year or four-year or technical institution or university. Applicant or parent of applicant must be member of Mutual Benefit Society. Applicant must have 3.0 GPA or higher. Available to U.S. citizens.

Application Requirements: Application form, application form may be submitted online (http://www.sonsofnorway.com/foundation), community service, essay, personal photograph, recommendations or references, test scores, transcript. *Deadline:* March 1.

Contact: Scholarship Coordinator
Sons of Norway Foundation
1455 West Lake Street
Minneapolis, MN 55408-2666
Phone: 612-827-3611
E-mail: foundation@sofn.com

SOUTH CAROLINA STATE EMPLOYEES ASSOCIATION

http://www.scsea.com/

RICHLAND/LEXINGTON SCSEA SCHOLARSHIP

Scholarships available to SCSEA members or their relatives, with priority given to Richland-Lexington Chapter members, spouses and/or children of Chapter members. The awardees must be currently enrolled at a recognized and accredited college, university, trade school or other institution of higher learning and must have completed at least one academic semester/quarter.

Award: Scholarship for use in sophomore, junior, senior, graduate, or postgraduate years; not renewable. *Number:* 3. *Amount:* $750.

Eligibility Requirements: Applicant must be enrolled or expecting to enroll full-time at a two-year or four-year institution or university and resident of South Carolina. Applicant or parent of applicant must be member of Society of Architectural Historians. Available to U.S. citizens.

Application Requirements: Application form, essay, transcript. *Deadline:* March 12.

Contact: Broadus Jamerson, Executive Director
Phone: 803-765-0680
Fax: 803-779-6558
E-mail: scsea@scsea.com

SUPREME GUARDIAN COUNCIL, INTERNATIONAL ORDER OF JOB'S DAUGHTERS

http://www.iojd.org/

SUPREME GUARDIAN COUNCIL SCHOLARSHIP

Scholarships of $750 to aid Job's Daughters students of outstanding ability whom have a sincerity of purpose. High school seniors, or graduates, junior college, technical school, or college students who are in early graduation programs, are eligible to apply.

Award: Scholarship for use in freshman, sophomore, junior, senior, graduate, or postgraduate years; not renewable. *Number:* 5–10. *Amount:* $750.

Eligibility Requirements: Applicant must be age 18-30; enrolled or expecting to enroll full- or part-time at a two-year or four-year or technical institution or university and single female. Applicant or parent of applicant must be member of Jobs Daughters. Available to U.S. and non-U.S. citizens.

Application Requirements: Application form, community service, essay, financial need analysis, recommendation from Executive Bethel Guardian Council, achievements outside of Job's Daughters, recommendations or references. *Deadline:* April 30.

Contact: Christal Bindrich, Scholarship Committee Chairman
Supreme Guardian Council, International Order of Job's Daughters
5351 South Butterfield Way
Greenfield, WI 53221
Phone: 414-423-0016
E-mail: christalbindrich@wi.rr.com

SUSIE HOLMES MEMORIAL SCHOLARSHIP

Scholarships of $1000 awarded to Job's Daughters high school students with a minimum of 2.5 GPA.

Award: Scholarship for use in freshman, sophomore, junior, senior, graduate, or postgraduate years; not renewable. *Number:* 1. *Amount:* $1000.

Eligibility Requirements: Applicant must be age 18-30; enrolled or expecting to enroll full-time at a two-year or four-year or technical institution or university and single female. Applicant or parent of applicant must be member of Jobs Daughters. Applicant must have 2.5 GPA or higher. Available to U.S. and non-U.S. citizens.

Application Requirements: Application form, community service, essay, recommendations or references, test scores, transcript. *Deadline:* April 30.

Contact: Christal Bindrich, Scholarship Committee Chairman
Supreme Guardian Council, International Order of Job's Daughters
5351 South Butterfield Way
Greenfield, WI 53221
Phone: 414-423-0016
E-mail: christalbindrich@wi.rr.com

TEXAS AFL-CIO

http://www.texasaflcio.org/

TEXAS AFL-CIO SCHOLARSHIP PROGRAM

Award for sons or daughters of members of unions affiliated with the Texas AFL-CIO and the appropriate Central Labor Council. Selection by interview/testing process. One-time awards of $1000. Applicant must be a graduating high school senior and Texas resident. Previous winners may apply for a limited number of continuing scholarships.

Award: Scholarship for use in freshman, sophomore, junior, or senior years; not renewable. *Number:* 20–35. *Amount:* $1000.

Eligibility Requirements: Applicant must be high school student; planning to enroll or expecting to enroll full-time at a two-year or four-year or technical institution or university and resident of Texas. Applicant or parent of applicant must be member of AFL-CIO. Available to U.S. citizens.

Application Requirements: Application form, essay, financial need analysis, interview, personal photograph. *Deadline:* January 31.

Contact: Mr. Edward Sills, Director of Communications
Texas AFL-CIO
PO Box 12727
Austin, TX 78701
Phone: 512-477-6195
Fax: 512-477-2962
E-mail: ed@texasaflcio.org

TKE EDUCATIONAL FOUNDATION

http://www.tke.org/

CHARLES J. TRABOLD SCHOLARSHIP

One-time award of $1200 given to an undergraduate member of Tau Kappa Epsilon who has demonstrated leadership ability within his chapter, campus, or community. Must be a full-time student in good standing with a GPA of 3.0 or higher. Preference will first be given to a member of Kappa-Kappa Chapter (Monmouth) but, if there is no qualified applicant, the scholarship will be open to any other qualified Teke.

Award: Scholarship for use in sophomore, junior, or senior years; not renewable. *Number:* 1. *Amount:* $1200.

Eligibility Requirements: Applicant must be enrolled or expecting to enroll full-time at a four-year institution or university; male and must have an interest in leadership. Applicant or parent of applicant must be member of Tau Kappa Epsilon. Applicant must have 3.0 GPA or higher. Available to U.S. and non-U.S. citizens.

Application Requirements: Application form, application form may be submitted online (http://www.tke.org/member_resources/scholarships/apply_online), essay, personal photograph, transcript. *Deadline:* March 15.

Contact: Offices of the Grand Chapter
TKE Educational Foundation
7439 Woodland Drive, Suite 100
Indianapolis, IN 46278
E-mail: tkeogc@tke.org

CHARLES R. WALGREEN, JR. LEADERSHIP AWARD

This $1400 leadership award is given in recognition of academic achievement with a GPA of at least 3.0 or higher and recognizes outstanding leadership, as demonstrated by activities and accomplishments within the chapter, on campus and in the community.

Award: Scholarship for use in sophomore, junior, or senior years; not renewable. *Number:* 1. *Amount:* $1400.

Eligibility Requirements: Applicant must be enrolled or expecting to enroll full-time at a four-year institution or university; male and must have an interest in leadership. Applicant or parent of applicant must be member of Tau Kappa Epsilon. Applicant must have 3.0 GPA or higher. Available to U.S. and non-U.S. citizens.

Application Requirements: Application form, application form may be submitted online (http://www.tke.org/member_resources/scholarships/apply_online), essay, personal photograph, transcript. *Deadline:* March 15.

Contact: Offices of the Grand Chapter
TKE Educational Foundation
7439 Woodland Drive, Suite 100
Indianapolis, IN 46278
E-mail: tkeogc@tke.org

CHARLES R. WALGREEN, JR. SCHOLARSHIP AWARD

Award given in recognition of outstanding leadership, as demonstrated by the activities and accomplishments of an individual within the chapter, on campus and in the community, while maintaining a good academic record. All initiated undergraduate members of TKE, in good standing with a cumulative GPA of 2.5 or higher, are eligible to apply.

Award: Scholarship for use in sophomore, junior, or senior years; not renewable. *Number:* 1. *Amount:* $1400.

Eligibility Requirements: Applicant must be enrolled or expecting to enroll full-time at a four-year institution or university; male and must have an interest in leadership. Applicant or parent of applicant must be member of Tau Kappa Epsilon. Applicant must have 2.5 GPA or higher. Available to U.S. and non-U.S. citizens.

Application Requirements: Application form, application form may be submitted online (http://www.tke.org/member_resources/scholarships/apply_online), essay, narrative summary of how TKE membership has benefited applicant, personal photograph, transcript. *Deadline:* March 15.

Contact: Offices of the Grand Chapter
TKE Educational Foundation
7439 Woodland Drive, Suite 100
Indianapolis, IN 46278
E-mail: tkeogc@tke.org

CHRISTOPHER GRASSO SCHOLARSHIP

One-time award of $200 given to an undergraduate member of Tau Kappa Epsilon who has demonstrated leadership ability within his chapter, campus, or community. Must be a full-time student in good standing with a GPA of 2.5 or higher. Preference should be given to any member of Alpha-Tau Chapter who applies but is not restricted to members of Alpha-Tau.

Award: Scholarship for use in sophomore, junior, or senior years; not renewable. *Number:* 1. *Amount:* $200.

Eligibility Requirements: Applicant must be enrolled or expecting to enroll full-time at a four-year institution or university; male and must have an interest in leadership. Applicant or parent of applicant must be member of Tau Kappa Epsilon. Applicant must have 2.5 GPA or higher. Available to U.S. and non-U.S. citizens.

Application Requirements: Application form, application form may be submitted online (http://www.tke.org/member_resources/scholarships/apply_online), essay, personal photograph, transcript. *Deadline:* March 15.

Contact: Offices of the Grand Chapter
TKE Educational Foundation
7439 Woodland Drive, Suite 100
Indianapolis, IN 46278
E-mail: tkeogc@tke.org

DONALD A. AND JOHN R. FISHER MEMORIAL SCHOLARSHIP

One-time award of $800 given to an undergraduate member of Tau Kappa Epsilon, who has demonstrated leadership ability within his chapter, campus, or community. Must be a full-time student in good standing with a GPA of 3.0 or higher.

Award: Scholarship for use in sophomore, junior, or senior years; not renewable. *Number:* 1. *Amount:* $800.

Eligibility Requirements: Applicant must be enrolled or expecting to enroll full-time at a four-year institution or university; male and must have an interest in leadership. Applicant or parent of applicant must be member of Tau Kappa Epsilon. Applicant must have 3.0 GPA or higher. Available to U.S. and non-U.S. citizens.

Application Requirements: Application form, application form may be submitted online (http://www.tke.org/member_resources/scholarships/apply_online), essay, personal photograph, transcript. *Deadline:* March 15.

Contact: Offices of the Grand Chapter
TKE Educational Foundation
7439 Woodland Drive, Suite 100
Indianapolis, IN 46278
E-mail: tkeogc@tke.org

DORIS AND ELMER H. SCHMITZ, SR. MEMORIAL SCHOLARSHIP

One-time award of $300 given to an undergraduate member of Tau Kappa Epsilon from Wisconsin who has demonstrated leadership ability within his chapter, campus, or community. Must be a full-time student in good standing with a GPA of 2.5 or higher. Preference will first be given to a member from the state of Wisconsin but, if there is no qualified applicant, the scholarship will be open to any other qualified Teke.

Award: Scholarship for use in sophomore, junior, or senior years; not renewable. *Number:* 1. *Amount:* $300.

Eligibility Requirements: Applicant must be enrolled or expecting to enroll full-time at a four-year institution or university; male; resident of Wisconsin and must have an interest in leadership. Applicant or parent of applicant must be member of Tau Kappa Epsilon. Applicant must have 2.5 GPA or higher. Available to U.S. and non-U.S. citizens.

Application Requirements: Application form, application form may be submitted online (http://www.tke.org/member_resources/scholarships/apply_online), essay, narrative summary of how TKE membership has benefited applicant, personal photograph, transcript. *Deadline:* March 15.

Contact: Offices of the Grand Chapter
TKE Educational Foundation
7439 Woodland Drive, Suite 100
Indianapolis, IN 46278
E-mail: tkeogc@tke.org

DWAYNE R. WOERPEL MEMORIAL LEADERSHIP SCHOLARSHIP

$500 award available to an undergraduate Tau Kappa Epsilon member who is a full-time student and graduate of the TKE Leadership Academy. Applicants should have demonstrated leadership qualities in service to the Fraternity and to the civic and religious community while maintaining a 3.0 GPA or higher. Preference will first be given to a graduate of the TKE Leadership Academy but, if there is no qualified applicant, the scholarship will be open to any other qualified Teke.

Award: Scholarship for use in sophomore, junior, or senior years; not renewable. *Number:* 1. *Amount:* $500.

Eligibility Requirements: Applicant must be enrolled or expecting to enroll full-time at a four-year institution or university; male and must have an interest in leadership. Applicant or parent of applicant must be member of Tau Kappa Epsilon. Applicant must have 3.0 GPA or higher. Available to U.S. and non-U.S. citizens.

Application Requirements: Application form, application form may be submitted online (http://www.tke.org/member_resources/scholarships/apply_online), essay, personal photograph, transcript. *Deadline:* March 15.

Contact: Offices of the Grand Chapter
TKE Educational Foundation
7439 Woodland Drive, Suite 100
Indianapolis, IN 46278
E-mail: tkeogc@tke.org

EUGENE C. BEACH MEMORIAL SCHOLARSHIP

One-time award of $300 given to an undergraduate member of Tau Kappa Epsilon who has demonstrated leadership ability within chapter, campus, or community. Must be a full-time student in good standing with a GPA of 3.0 or higher.

Award: Scholarship for use in freshman, sophomore, junior, or senior years; not renewable. *Number:* 1. *Amount:* $300.

Eligibility Requirements: Applicant must be enrolled or expecting to enroll full-time at a four-year institution or university; male and must have an interest in leadership. Applicant or parent of applicant must be member of Tau Kappa Epsilon. Applicant must have 3.0 GPA or higher. Available to U.S. and non-U.S. citizens.

Application Requirements: Application form, application form may be submitted online (http://www.tke.org/member_resources/scholarships/apply_online), essay, narrative summary of how TKE membership has benefited applicant, personal photograph, transcript. *Deadline:* March 15.

Contact: Offices of the Grand Chapter
TKE Educational Foundation
7439 Woodland Drive, Suite 100
Indianapolis, IN 46278
E-mail: tkeogc@tke.org

FATHER TIMOTHY VAKOC MEMORIAL SCHOLARSHIP

This scholarship is available to any undergraduate member of Tau Kappa Epsilon who is a full-time student. Preference will first be given to members of Theta-Rho Chapter but if no qualified individual applies, the award will be open to any member of TKE.

Award: Scholarship for use in sophomore, junior, or senior years; not renewable. *Number:* 1. *Amount:* $400.

Eligibility Requirements: Applicant must be enrolled or expecting to enroll full-time at a four-year institution or university; male and must have an interest in leadership. Applicant or parent of applicant must be member of Tau Kappa Epsilon. Available to U.S. and non-U.S. citizens.

Application Requirements: Application form, application form may be submitted online (http://www.tke.org/member_resources/scholarships/apply_online), essay, personal photograph, transcript. *Deadline:* March 15.

Contact: Offices of the Grand Chapter
TKE Educational Foundation
7439 Woodland Drive, Suite 100
Indianapolis, IN 46278
E-mail: tkeogc@tke.org

GABE ANAYA SCHOLARSHIP

One-time award of $300 given to an undergraduate member of Tau Kappa Epsilon who has demonstrated leadership ability within his chapter, campus, or community. Must be a full-time student in good standing with a GPA of 2.75 or higher. Preference will be given to members from Alpha-Omicron chapter.

Award: Scholarship for use in sophomore, junior, or senior years; not renewable. *Number:* 1. *Amount:* $300.

Eligibility Requirements: Applicant must be enrolled or expecting to enroll full-time at a four-year institution or university; male and must have an interest in leadership. Applicant or parent of applicant must be member of Tau Kappa Epsilon. Available to U.S. and non-U.S. citizens.

Application Requirements: Application form, application form may be submitted online (http://www.tke.org/member_resources/scholarships/apply_online), essay, personal photograph, transcript. *Deadline:* March 15.

Contact: Offices of the Grand Chapter
TKE Educational Foundation
7439 Woodland Drive, Suite 100
Indianapolis, IN 46278
E-mail: tkeogc@tke.org

J.D. WILLIAMS SCHOLARSHIP

One-time award of $500 given to an undergraduate member of Tau Kappa Epsilon who has demonstrated leadership ability within his

chapter, campus, or community. Must be a full-time student in good standing.

Award: Scholarship for use in sophomore, junior, or senior years; not renewable. *Number:* 1. *Amount:* $500.

Eligibility Requirements: Applicant must be enrolled or expecting to enroll full-time at a four-year institution or university; male and must have an interest in leadership. Applicant or parent of applicant must be member of Tau Kappa Epsilon. Available to U.S. and non-U.S. citizens.

Application Requirements: Application form, application form may be submitted online (http://www.tke.org/member_resources/scholarships/apply_online), essay, personal photograph, transcript. *Deadline:* March 15.

Contact: Offices of the Grand Chapter
TKE Educational Foundation
7439 Woodland Drive, Suite 100
Indianapolis, IN 46278
E-mail: tkeogc@tke.org

JOHN A. COURSON SCHOLARSHIP

This $2200 distinguished scholastic award is the highest academic honor awarded to a member of Tau Kappa Epsilon. Award is given in recognition of academic achievement with a GPA of at least 3.0 or higher and recognizes outstanding leadership, as demonstrated by activities and accomplishments within the chapter, on campus and in the community.

Award: Scholarship for use in sophomore, junior, or senior years; not renewable. *Number:* 1. *Amount:* $2200.

Eligibility Requirements: Applicant must be enrolled or expecting to enroll full-time at a four-year institution or university; male and must have an interest in leadership. Applicant or parent of applicant must be member of Tau Kappa Epsilon. Applicant must have 3.0 GPA or higher. Available to U.S. and non-U.S. citizens.

Application Requirements: Application form, application form may be submitted online (http://www.tke.org/member_resources/scholarships/apply_online), essay, personal photograph, transcript. *Deadline:* March 15.

Contact: Offices of the Grand Chapter
TKE Educational Foundation
7439 Woodland Drive, Suite 100
Indianapolis, IN 46278
E-mail: tkeogc@tke.org

J. RUSSEL SALSBURY MEMORIAL SCHOLARSHIP

One-time award of $200 given to an undergraduate member of Tau Kappa Epsilon who has demonstrated leadership ability within his chapter, campus, or community. Must be a full-time student in good standing with a GPA of 3.0 or higher.

Award: Scholarship for use in sophomore, junior, or senior years; not renewable. *Number:* 1. *Amount:* $200.

Eligibility Requirements: Applicant must be enrolled or expecting to enroll full-time at a four-year institution or university; male and must have an interest in leadership. Applicant or parent of applicant must be member of Tau Kappa Epsilon. Applicant must have 3.0 GPA or higher. Available to U.S. and non-U.S. citizens.

Application Requirements: Application form, application form may be submitted online (http://www.tke.org/member_resources/scholarships/apply_online), essay, personal photograph, transcript. *Deadline:* March 15.

Contact: Offices of the Grand Chapter
TKE Educational Foundation
7439 Woodland Drive, Suite 100
Indianapolis, IN 46278
E-mail: tkeogc@tke.org

KENNETH L. DUKE, SR. MEMORIAL SCHOLARSHIP

One-time award of $200 given to an undergraduate member of Tau Kappa Epsilon who has demonstrated leadership ability within his chapter, campus, or community. Must be a full-time student in good standing with a GPA of 2.5 or higher.

Award: Scholarship for use in sophomore, junior, or senior years; not renewable. *Number:* 1. *Amount:* $200.

Eligibility Requirements: Applicant must be enrolled or expecting to enroll full-time at a four-year institution or university; male and must have an interest in leadership. Applicant or parent of applicant must be member of Tau Kappa Epsilon. Applicant must have 2.5 GPA or higher. Available to U.S. and non-U.S. citizens.

Application Requirements: Application form, application form may be submitted online (http://www.tke.org/member_resources/scholarships/apply_online), essay, personal photograph, transcript. *Deadline:* March 15.

Contact: Offices of the Grand Chapter
TKE Educational Foundation
7439 Woodland Drive, Suite 100
Indianapolis, IN 46278
E-mail: tkeogc@tke.org

LENWOOD S. COCHRAN SCHOLARSHIP

One-time award of $1000 given to an undergraduate member of Tau Kappa Epsilon who has demonstrated leadership ability within his chapter, campus, or community. Must be a full-time student in good standing with a GPA of 3.0 or higher. Preference will first be given to a member of Sigma-Psi and Gamma-Mu, but if there is no qualified applicant, the scholarship will be open to any other qualified Teke.

Award: Scholarship for use in sophomore, junior, or senior years; not renewable. *Number:* 1. *Amount:* $1000.

Eligibility Requirements: Applicant must be enrolled or expecting to enroll full-time at a four-year institution or university; male and must have an interest in leadership. Applicant or parent of applicant must be member of Tau Kappa Epsilon. Applicant must have 3.0 GPA or higher. Available to U.S. and non-U.S. citizens.

Application Requirements: Application form, application form may be submitted online (http://www.tke.org/member_resources/scholarships/apply_online), essay, personal photograph, transcript. *Deadline:* March 15.

Contact: Offices of the Grand Chapter
TKE Educational Foundation
7439 Woodland Drive, Suite 100
Indianapolis, IN 46278
E-mail: tkeogc@tke.org

LON G. JUSTICE SCHOLARSHIP

One-time award of $1000 given to an undergraduate member of Tau Kappa Epsilon. Must be a full-time student in good standing with a GPA of 3.0 or higher and with exceptional academic achievement. Must demonstrate exceptional leadership abilities in campus, community, and Fraternity activities and have a demonstrated record of personal achievement (e.g. awards, citations, Fraternity, campus or community recognitions).

Award: Scholarship for use in sophomore, junior, or senior years; not renewable. *Number:* 1. *Amount:* $1000.

Eligibility Requirements: Applicant must be enrolled or expecting to enroll full-time at a four-year institution or university; male and must have an interest in leadership. Applicant or parent of applicant must be member of Tau Kappa Epsilon. Applicant must have 3.0 GPA or higher. Available to U.S. and non-U.S. citizens.

Application Requirements: Application form, application form may be submitted online (http://www.tke.org/member_resources/scholarships/apply_online), essay, personal photograph, transcript. *Deadline:* March 15.

Contact: Offices of the Grand Chapter
TKE Educational Foundation
7439 Woodland Drive, Suite 100
Indianapolis, IN 46278
E-mail: tkeogc@tke.org

MICHAEL CERUSSI LEADERSHIP SCHOLARSHIP

One-time award of $200 given to an undergraduate member of Tau Kappa Epsilon who has demonstrated leadership ability within his chapter, campus, or community. Awarded to a past or present jeweled officer with a minimum 3.0 GPA. Members from Nu Chapter are preferred, but if there is no qualified applicant, the scholarship will be open to any other eligible Teke.

Award: Scholarship for use in sophomore, junior, or senior years; not renewable. *Number:* 1. *Amount:* $200.

Eligibility Requirements: Applicant must be enrolled or expecting to enroll full-time at a four-year institution or university; male and must have an interest in leadership. Applicant or parent of applicant must be member of Tau Kappa Epsilon. Applicant must have 3.0 GPA or higher. Available to U.S. and non-U.S. citizens.

Application Requirements: Application form, application form may be submitted online

(http://www.tke.org/member_resources/scholarships/apply_online), essay, personal photograph, transcript. *Deadline:* March 15.

Contact: Offices of the Grand Chapter
TKE Educational Foundation
7439 Woodland Drive, Suite 100
Indianapolis, IN 46278
E-mail: tkeogc@tke.org

MICHAEL J. MORIN MEMORIAL SCHOLARSHIP

One-time award of $300 for any undergraduate member of Tau Kappa Epsilon who has demonstrated leadership capacity within his chapter, on campus or the community. Must have a cumulative GPA of 3.0 or higher and be a full-time student in good standing.

Award: Scholarship for use in sophomore, junior, or senior years; not renewable. *Number:* 1. *Amount:* $300.

Eligibility Requirements: Applicant must be enrolled or expecting to enroll full-time at a four-year institution or university; male and must have an interest in leadership. Applicant or parent of applicant must be member of Tau Kappa Epsilon. Applicant must have 3.0 GPA or higher. Available to U.S. and non-U.S. citizens.

Application Requirements: Application form, application form may be submitted online (http://www.tke.org/member_resources/scholarships/apply_online), essay, narrative summary of how TKE membership has benefited applicant, personal photograph, transcript. *Deadline:* March 15.

Contact: Offices of the Grand Chapter
TKE Educational Foundation
7439 Woodland Drive, Suite 100
Indianapolis, IN 46278
E-mail: tkeogc@tke.org

MILES GRAY MEMORIAL SCHOLARSHIP

One-time award of $300 given to an undergraduate member of Tau Kappa Epsilon who has demonstrated leadership ability within his chapter, campus, or community. Must be a full-time student in good standing with a GPA of 3.0 or higher.

Award: Scholarship for use in sophomore, junior, or senior years; not renewable. *Number:* 1. *Amount:* $300.

Eligibility Requirements: Applicant must be enrolled or expecting to enroll full-time at a four-year institution or university; male and must have an interest in leadership. Applicant or parent of applicant must be member of Tau Kappa Epsilon. Applicant must have 3.0 GPA or higher. Available to U.S. and non-U.S. citizens.

Application Requirements: Application form, application form may be submitted online (http://www.tke.org/member_resources/scholarships/apply_online), essay, personal photograph, transcript. *Deadline:* March 15.

Contact: Offices of the Grand Chapter
TKE Educational Foundation
7439 Woodland Drive, Suite 100
Indianapolis, IN 46278
E-mail: tkeogc@tke.org

ROBERT D. PLANCK SCHOLARSHIP

One-time award of $300 given to an undergraduate member of Tau Kappa Epsilon. Must be a full-time student in good standing and demonstrate financial need. Preference will first be given to a member in the state of Texas but, if there is no qualified applicant, the scholarship will be open to any other qualified Teke.

Award: Scholarship for use in sophomore, junior, or senior years; not renewable. *Number:* 1. *Amount:* $300.

Eligibility Requirements: Applicant must be enrolled or expecting to enroll full-time at a four-year institution or university and male. Applicant or parent of applicant must be member of Tau Kappa Epsilon. Available to U.S. and non-U.S. citizens.

Application Requirements: Application form, application form may be submitted online (http://www.tke.org/member_resources/scholarships/apply_online), essay, financial need analysis, personal photograph, transcript. *Deadline:* March 15.

Contact: Offices of the Grand Chapter
TKE Educational Foundation
7439 Woodland Drive, Suite 100
Indianapolis, IN 46278
E-mail: tkeogc@tke.org

RONALD REAGAN LEADERSHIP AWARD

One-time award of $1100 for initiated undergraduate member of Tau Kappa Epsilon, given in recognition of outstanding leadership, as demonstrated by activities and accomplishments within chapter, on campus, and in community. Minimum 3.0 GPA required.

Award: Scholarship for use in sophomore, junior, or senior years; not renewable. *Number:* 1. *Amount:* $1100.

Eligibility Requirements: Applicant must be enrolled or expecting to enroll full-time at a four-year institution or university; male and must have an interest in leadership. Applicant or parent of applicant must be member of Tau Kappa Epsilon. Applicant must have 3.0 GPA or higher. Available to U.S. and non-U.S. citizens.

Application Requirements: Application form, application form may be submitted online (http://www.tke.org/member_resources/scholarships/apply_online), essay, narrative summary of how TKE membership has benefited applicant, personal photograph, transcript. *Deadline:* March 15.

Contact: Offices of the Grand Chapter
TKE Educational Foundation
7439 Woodland Drive, Suite 100
Indianapolis, IN 46278
E-mail: tkeogc@tke.org

T.J. SCHMITZ SCHOLARSHIP

$500 award for an initiated undergraduate member of TKE. Must be a full-time student in good standing with a minimum cumulative GPA of 3.0. Must have demonstrated leadership capability within chapter, campus, or community.

Award: Scholarship for use in sophomore, junior, or senior years; not renewable. *Number:* 1. *Amount:* $500.

Eligibility Requirements: Applicant must be enrolled or expecting to enroll full-time at a four-year institution or university; male and must have an interest in leadership. Applicant or parent of applicant must be member of Tau Kappa Epsilon. Applicant must have 3.0 GPA or higher. Available to U.S. and non-U.S. citizens.

Application Requirements: Application form, application form may be submitted online (http://www.tke.org/member_resources/scholarships/apply_online), essay, narrative summary of how TKE membership has benefited applicant, personal photograph, transcript. *Deadline:* March 15.

Contact: Offices of the Grand Chapter
TKE Educational Foundation
7439 Woodland Drive, Suite 100
Indianapolis, IN 46278
E-mail: tkeogc@tke.org

TKE SERVANT LEADERSHIP SCHOLARSHIP

$800 award open to all initiated undergraduate and graduate studies members of Tau Kappa Epsilon who are currently enrolled students in good standing with a cumulative GPA of 3.0 or higher. Applicants must have a demonstrated record of leadership in service to others. Applicants may apply themselves or may be nominated by any alumnus, his chapter, the chapter's alumni association, school administration official, or faculty member. Awards will be made annually, with the recipients for each biennium prior to the International Conclave of TKE acknowledged and recognized as servant leaders before the Grand Chapter at Conclave.

Award: Scholarship for use in freshman, sophomore, junior, senior, or graduate years; not renewable. *Number:* 1. *Amount:* $800.

Eligibility Requirements: Applicant must be enrolled or expecting to enroll full-time at a four-year institution or university; male and must have an interest in leadership. Applicant or parent of applicant must be member of Tau Kappa Epsilon. Applicant must have 3.0 GPA or higher. Available to U.S. and non-U.S. citizens.

Application Requirements: Application form, application form may be submitted online (http://www.tke.org/member_resources/scholarships/apply_online), essay, personal photograph, transcript. *Deadline:* March 15.

Contact: Offices of the Grand Chapter
TKE Educational Foundation
7439 Woodland Drive, Suite 100
Indianapolis, IN 46278
E-mail: tkeogc@tke.org

WALLACE MCCAULEY MEMORIAL SCHOLARSHIP

One-time $300 award to undergraduate member of Tau Kappa Epsilon with junior or senior standing. Must have demonstrated understanding of the importance of good alumni relations. Must have excelled in the development, promotion, and execution of programs which increase alumni contact, awareness, and participation in fraternity activities. Minimum 3.0 GPA required.

Award: Scholarship for use in junior or senior years; not renewable. *Number:* 1. *Amount:* $300.

Eligibility Requirements: Applicant must be enrolled or expecting to enroll full-time at a four-year institution or university; male and must have an interest in leadership. Applicant or parent of applicant must be member of Tau Kappa Epsilon. Applicant must have 3.0 GPA or higher. Available to U.S. and non-U.S. citizens.

Application Requirements: Application form, application form may be submitted online (http://www.tke.org/member_resources/scholarships/apply_online), essay, narrative summary of how TKE membership has benefited applicant, personal photograph, transcript. *Deadline:* March 15.

Contact: Offices of the Grand Chapter
TKE Educational Foundation
7439 Woodland Drive, Suite 100
Indianapolis, IN 46278
E-mail: tkeogc@tke.org

WILLIAM V. MUSE SCHOLARSHIP

Award of $400 given to an undergraduate member of Tau Kappa Epsilon who has completed at least 30 semester hours of course work. Applicant should demonstrate leadership within chapter and maintain 3.0 GPA. Preference will first be given to a member of Epsilon-Upsilon Chapter but, if there is no qualified applicant, the scholarship will be open to any other qualified Teke.

Award: Scholarship for use in sophomore, junior, or senior years; not renewable. *Number:* 1. *Amount:* $400.

Eligibility Requirements: Applicant must be enrolled or expecting to enroll full-time at a four-year institution or university; male and must have an interest in leadership. Applicant or parent of applicant must be member of Tau Kappa Epsilon. Applicant must have 3.0 GPA or higher. Available to U.S. and non-U.S. citizens.

Application Requirements: Application form, application form may be submitted online (http://www.tke.org/member_resources/scholarships/apply_online), essay, narrative summary of how TKE membership has benefited applicant, personal photograph, transcript. *Deadline:* March 15.

Contact: Offices of the Grand Chapter
TKE Educational Foundation
7439 Woodland Drive, Suite 100
Indianapolis, IN 46278
E-mail: tkeogc@tke.org

WILLIAM WILSON MEMORIAL SCHOLARSHIP

One-time award given to undergraduate member of Tau Kappa Epsilon with junior or senior standing. Must have demonstrated understanding of the importance of good alumni relations. Must have excelled in the development, promotion, and execution of programs which increase alumni contact, awareness, and participation in fraternity activities. If there are no applicants who meet the alumni relations criteria, the scholarship will be open to any other qualified Teke, in recognition of academic achievement with a Grade Point Average of at least 2.5 or higher and recognized outstanding leadership within the chapter and on campus.

Award: Scholarship for use in junior or senior years; not renewable. *Number:* 1. *Amount:* $300.

Eligibility Requirements: Applicant must be enrolled or expecting to enroll full-time at a four-year institution or university; male and must have an interest in leadership. Applicant or parent of applicant must be member of Tau Kappa Epsilon. Applicant must have 3.0 GPA or higher. Available to U.S. and non-U.S. citizens.

Application Requirements: Application form, application form may be submitted online (http://www.tke.org/member_resources/scholarships/apply_online), essay, narrative summary of how TKE membership has benefited applicant, personal photograph, transcript. *Deadline:* March 15.

Contact: Offices of the Grand Chapter
TKE Educational Foundation
7439 Woodland Drive, Suite 100
Indianapolis, IN 46278
E-mail: tkeogc@tke.org

UNION PLUS SCHOLARSHIP PROGRAM

http://www.unionplus.org/

UNION PLUS EDUCATION FOUNDATION SCHOLARSHIP PROGRAM

One-time cash award for current or retired union members in good standing, in unions affiliated with the AFL-CIO, their spouses, and dependent children. Based upon academic achievement, character, leadership, career goals, social awareness of the labor movement and financial need. Must be from Canada or U.S., including Puerto Rico and the Virgin Islands. Members must apply online at our website: https://www.unionplus.org/benefits/money/union-plus-scholarships.

Award: Scholarship for use in freshman, sophomore, junior, senior, or graduate years; not renewable. *Number:* 100–120. *Amount:* $500–$4000.

Eligibility Requirements: Applicant must be enrolled or expecting to enroll full- or part-time at a two-year or four-year or technical institution or university and studying in Alabama, Alaska, Arizona, Arkansas, California, Colorado, Connecticut, Delaware, District of Columbia, Florida, Georgia, Hawaii, Idaho, Illinois, Indiana, Iowa, Kansas, Kentucky, Louisiana, Maine, Maryland, Massachusetts, Michigan, Minnesota, Mississippi, Missouri, Montana, Nebraska, Nevada, New Hampshire, New Jersey, New Mexico, New York, North Carolina, North Dakota, Ohio, Oklahoma, Oregon, Pennsylvania, Rhode Island, South Carolina, South Dakota, Tennessee, Texas, Utah, Vermont, Virginia, Washington, West Virginia, Wisconsin, Wyoming. Applicant or parent of applicant must be member of AFL-CIO. Applicant must have 2.5 GPA or higher. Available to U.S. and non-U.S. citizens.

Application Requirements: Application form, essay. *Deadline:* January 31.

Contact: Shana Higgins, Program Assistant
Union Plus Scholarship Program
Union Privilege, 1100 First Street, NE
Suite 850
Washington, DC 20002
Phone: 202-778-9836
E-mail: shiggins@unionprivilege.org

UNITED DAUGHTERS OF THE CONFEDERACY

http://www.hqudc.org/

BARBARA JACKSON SICHEL MEMORIAL SCHOLARSHIP

Renewable award for undergraduate students who are descendant of a Confederate soldier, sailor or marine. Must be enrolled in an accredited college or university. Minimum of 3.0 GPA required. Submit a letter of endorsement from sponsoring Chapter of the United Daughters of the Confederacy.

Award: Scholarship for use in freshman, sophomore, junior, or senior years; renewable. *Number:* 1–2. *Amount:* $800–$1000.

Eligibility Requirements: Applicant must be enrolled or expecting to enroll full-time at a four-year institution or university. Applicant or parent of applicant must be member of United Daughters of the Confederacy. Applicant must have 3.0 GPA or higher. Available to U.S. citizens.

Application Requirements: Application form, essay, financial need analysis, personal photograph, proof of confederate ancestor's service, copy of applicant's birth certificate, recommendations or references, self-addressed stamped envelope with application, test scores, transcript. *Deadline:* March 15.

Contact: Ms. Jamie Davis, Second Vice President General
Phone: 804-355-1636
E-mail: hqudc@rcn.com

CHARLOTTE M. F. BENTLEY/NEW YORK CHAPTER 103 SCHOLARSHIP

Renewable award for undergraduate students who are descendant of a Confederate soldier, sailor or marine. Must be enrolled in an accredited college or university. Minimum of 3.0 GPA required. Must be members of United Daughters of the Confederacy and Children of the Confederacy from New York.

Award: Scholarship for use in freshman, sophomore, junior, or senior years; renewable. *Number:* 1–2. *Amount:* $800–$1000.

Eligibility Requirements: Applicant must be enrolled or expecting to enroll full-time at a four-year institution or university and resident of New York. Applicant or parent of applicant must be member of Children of the Confederacy, United Daughters of the Confederacy. Applicant must have 3.0 GPA or higher. Available to U.S. citizens.

Application Requirements: Application form, essay, financial need analysis, personal photograph, proof of confederate ancestor's service, copy of applicant's birth certificate, recommendations or references, self-addressed stamped envelope with application, test scores, transcript. *Deadline:* March 15.

Contact: Ms. Jamie Davis, Second Vice President General
Phone: 804-355-1636
E-mail: hqudc@rcn.com

ELIZABETH AND WALLACE KINGSBURY SCHOLARSHIP

Award for full-time undergraduate students who are descendants of a Confederate soldier, studying at an accredited college or university. Must have been a member of the Children of the Confederacy for a minimum of three years. Minimum 3.0 GPA required.

Award: Scholarship for use in freshman, sophomore, junior, or senior years; renewable. *Number:* 1–2. *Amount:* $800–$1000.

Eligibility Requirements: Applicant must be enrolled or expecting to enroll full-time at a four-year institution or university. Applicant or parent of applicant must be member of Children of the Confederacy. Applicant must have 3.0 GPA or higher. Available to U.S. citizens.

Application Requirements: Application form, copy of applicant's birth certificate, copy of confederate ancestor's proof of service, essay, financial need analysis, personal photograph, recommendations or references, self-addressed stamped envelope with application, test scores, transcript. *Deadline:* March 15.

Contact: Ms. Jamie Davis, Second Vice President General
Phone: 804-355-1636
E-mail: hqudc@rcn.com

GERTRUDE BOTTS-SAUCIER SCHOLARSHIP

Award for full-time undergraduate students who are descendants of a Confederate soldier, sailor or marine. Must be from Texas, Mississippi or Louisiana. Must be enrolled in an accredited college or university and have a minimum 3.0 GPA. Submit application and letter of endorsement from sponsoring chapter of the United Daughters of the Confederacy.

Award: Scholarship for use in freshman, sophomore, junior, or senior years; renewable. *Number:* 1–2. *Amount:* $800–$1000.

Eligibility Requirements: Applicant must be enrolled or expecting to enroll full-time at a four-year institution or university and resident of Louisiana, Mississippi, Texas. Applicant or parent of applicant must be member of United Daughters of the Confederacy. Applicant must have 3.0 GPA or higher. Available to U.S. citizens.

Application Requirements: Application form, copy of applicant's birth certificate, copy of confederate ancestor's proof of service, essay, financial need analysis, personal photograph, recommendations or references, self-addressed stamped envelope with application, test scores, transcript. *Deadline:* March 15.

Contact: Ms. Jamie Davis, Second Vice President General
Phone: 804-355-1636
E-mail: hqudc@rcn.com

LOLA B. CURRY SCHOLARSHIP

Award for full-time undergraduate students from Alabama who are descendants of a Confederate soldier. Must be enrolled in an accredited college or university in Alabama. Minimum 3.0 GPA required. Submit letter of endorsement from sponsoring chapter of the United Daughters of the Confederacy.

Award: Scholarship for use in freshman, sophomore, junior, or senior years; renewable. *Number:* 1–2. *Amount:* $800–$1000.

Eligibility Requirements: Applicant must be enrolled or expecting to enroll full-time at a four-year institution or university; resident of Alabama and studying in Alabama. Applicant or parent of applicant must be member of United Daughters of the Confederacy. Applicant must have 3.0 GPA or higher. Available to U.S. citizens.

Application Requirements: Application form, copy of applicant's birth certificate, copy of confederate ancestor's proof of service, essay, financial need analysis, personal photograph, recommendations or references, self-addressed stamped envelope with application, test scores, transcript. *Deadline:* March 15.

Contact: Ms. Jamie Davis, Second Vice President General
Phone: 804-355-1636
E-mail: hqudc@rcn.com

UNITED DAUGHTERS OF THE CONFEDERACY UNDERGRADUATE SCHOLARSHIPS

Renewable award for undergraduate students who are descendants of an eligible Confederate soldier. Must be enrolled in an accredited college or university. Minimum 3.0 GPA required. Applicants must be endorsed by the President and the Second Vice President/Education Chairman of Chapter and Division, and by the Second Vice President General. Applications are submitted through local chapters.

Award: Scholarship for use in freshman, sophomore, junior, or senior years; renewable. *Number:* 18–30. *Amount:* $800–$1000.

Eligibility Requirements: Applicant must be enrolled or expecting to enroll full-time at a two-year or four-year institution or university. Applicant or parent of applicant must be member of United Daughters of the Confederacy. Applicant must have 3.0 GPA or higher. Available to U.S. citizens.

Application Requirements: Application form, copy of applicant's birth certificate, copy of confederate ancestor's proof of service, essay, financial need analysis, personal photograph, recommendations or references, self-addressed stamped envelope with application, test scores, transcript. *Deadline:* March 15.

Contact: Ms. Jamie Davis, Second Vice President General
Phone: 804-355-1636
E-mail: hqudc@rcn.com

WINNIE DAVIS-CHILDREN OF THE CONFEDERACY SCHOLARSHIP

Award for full-time undergraduate students who are descendants of a Confederate soldier, enrolled in an accredited college or university. Recipient must be, or have been until age of 18, a participating member of the Children of the Confederacy and approved by the Third Vice President General. Minimum 3.0 GPA required.

Award: Scholarship for use in freshman, sophomore, junior, or senior years; renewable. *Number:* 1–2. *Amount:* $800–$1000.

Eligibility Requirements: Applicant must be enrolled or expecting to enroll full-time at a four-year institution or university. Applicant or parent of applicant must be member of Children of the Confederacy. Applicant must have 3.0 GPA or higher. Available to U.S. citizens.

Application Requirements: Application form, copy of applicant's birth certificate, copy of confederate ancestor's proof of service, essay, financial need analysis, personal photograph, recommendations or references, self-addressed stamped envelope with application, test scores, transcript. *Deadline:* March 15.

Contact: Ms. Jamie Davis, Second Vice President General
Phone: 804-355-1636
E-mail: hqudc@rcn.com

UNITED FOOD AND COMMERCIAL WORKERS INTERNATIONAL UNION

http://www.ufcw.org/

JAMES A. SUFFRIDGE UNITED FOOD AND COMMERCIAL WORKERS SCHOLARSHIP PROGRAM

Scholarships available to graduating high school seniors and college students during the specific program year. Must be an active member of UFCW or unmarried dependent under age 20 of a UFCW member. Scholarship is disbursed over a four-year period.

Award: Scholarship for use in freshman, sophomore, junior, or senior years; renewable. *Number:* 14–20. *Amount:* up to $8000.

Eligibility Requirements: Applicant must be enrolled or expecting to enroll full- or part-time at a two-year or four-year or technical institution or university. Applicant or parent of applicant must be member of United Food and Commercial Workers. Available to U.S. and Canadian citizens.

Application Requirements: Application form, community service, essay, transcript. *Deadline:* April 15.

Contact: Field Assistant
United Food and Commercial Workers International Union
1775 K Street, NW
Washington, DC 20006
Phone: 202-223-3111
Fax: 202-721-8008
E-mail: scholarship@ufcw.org

UNITED STATES BOWLING CONGRESS

http://www.bowl.com/

GIFT FOR LIFE SCHOLARSHIP

The Gift for Life Scholarships are available to any USBC Youth member currently in high school and holding a GPA of 2.5 or better who can demonstrate financial need.

Award: Scholarship for use in freshman year; not renewable. *Number:* 12. *Amount:* $1000.

Eligibility Requirements: Applicant must be high school student; planning to enroll or expecting to enroll full- or part-time at a two-year or four-year or technical institution or university and must have an interest in bowling. Applicant or parent of applicant must be member of Young American Bowling Alliance. Available to U.S. citizens.

Application Requirements: Application form, essay. *Deadline:* December 1.

Contact: Roger Noordhoek, Senior Director of Youth Marketing
United States Bowling Congress
621 Six Flags Drive
Arlington, TX 76011
Phone: 800-514-2695 Ext. 8308
E-mail: contactus@ibcyouth.com

USBC ALBERTA E. CROWE STAR OF TOMORROW AWARD

Award annually recognizes star qualities in a female USBC Youth member who competes in the sport of bowling. Star qualities include distinguished certified bowling performances on the local, state and national level, academic achievement and extra-curricular activities.

Award: Scholarship for use in freshman, sophomore, junior, or senior years; not renewable. *Number:* 1. *Amount:* $6000.

Eligibility Requirements: Applicant must be enrolled or expecting to enroll full-time at a two-year or four-year or technical institution or university; female and must have an interest in bowling. Applicant or parent of applicant must be member of Young American Bowling Alliance. Applicant must have 3.0 GPA or higher. Available to U.S. citizens.

Application Requirements: Application form, essay. *Deadline:* December 1.

Contact: Roger Noordhoek, Senior Director of Youth Marketing
United States Bowling Congress
621 Six Flags Drive
Arlington, TX 76011
Phone: 800-514-BOWL Ext. 8308
E-mail: contactus@ibcyouth.com

USBC ANNUAL ZEB SCHOLARSHIP

Scholarship is awarded to a USBC Youth member who achieves academic success and gives back to his/her community through service. Candidates must have a current GPA of 3.0 or better.

Award: Scholarship for use in freshman, sophomore, junior, or senior years; not renewable. *Number:* 1. *Amount:* $2500.

Eligibility Requirements: Applicant must be high school student; planning to enroll or expecting to enroll full- or part-time at a two-year or four-year or technical institution or university and must have an interest in bowling. Applicant or parent of applicant must be member of Young American Bowling Alliance. Applicant or parent of applicant must have employment or volunteer experience in community service. Applicant must have 3.0 GPA or higher. Available to U.S. citizens.

Application Requirements: Application form, essay. *Deadline:* December 1.

Contact: Roger Noordhoek, Senior Director of Youth Marketing
United States Bowling Congress
621 Six Flags Drive
Arlington, TX 76011
Phone: 800-514-BOWL Ext. 8308
E-mail: contactus@ibcyouth.com

USBC CHUCK HALL STAR OF TOMORROW SCHOLARSHIP

Scholarship annually recognizes star qualities in a male USBC Youth member who competes in the sport of bowling. Award is given to a male high school senior or college student and must be a current USBC Youth or USBC member in good standing.

Award: Scholarship for use in freshman, sophomore, junior, or senior years; renewable. *Number:* 1. *Amount:* $6000.

Eligibility Requirements: Applicant must be enrolled or expecting to enroll full-time at a two-year or four-year or technical institution or university; male and must have an interest in bowling. Applicant or parent of applicant must be member of Young American Bowling Alliance. Applicant must have 3.0 GPA or higher. Available to U.S. citizens.

Application Requirements: Application form, essay. *Deadline:* December 1.

Contact: Roger Noordhoek, Senior Director of Youth Marketing
United States Bowling Congress
621 Six Flags Drive
Arlington, TX 76011
Phone: 800-514-BOWL Ext. 8308
E-mail: contactus@ibcyouth.com

USBC EARL ANTHONY MEMORIAL SCHOLARSHIP

Annually recognizes five USBC Youth bowlers for their community involvement and academic achievements.

Award: Scholarship for use in freshman, sophomore, junior, or senior years; not renewable. *Number:* 5. *Amount:* $5000.

Eligibility Requirements: Applicant must be high school student; planning to enroll or expecting to enroll full- or part-time at a two-year or four-year or technical institution or university and must have an interest in bowling. Applicant or parent of applicant must be member of Young American Bowling Alliance. Applicant must have 3.0 GPA or higher. Available to U.S. citizens.

Application Requirements: Application form, community service, essay. *Deadline:* December 1.

Contact: Roger Noordhoek, Senior Director of Youth Marketing
United States Bowling Congress
621 Six Flags Drive
Arlington, TX 76011
Phone: 800-514-BOWL Ext. 8308
E-mail: contactus@ibcyouth.com

USBC YOUTH AMBASSADOR OF THE YEAR (M/F)

Annually recognizes one male and one female USBC Youth bowler for his/her exemplary contributions to the sport of bowling, academic accomplishments and community involvement.

Award: Scholarship for use in freshman year; not renewable. *Number:* 2. *Amount:* $1500.

Eligibility Requirements: Applicant must be high school student; planning to enroll or expecting to enroll full- or part-time at a two-year or four-year or technical institution or university and must have an interest in bowling. Applicant or parent of applicant must be member of Young American Bowling Alliance. Available to U.S. citizens.

Application Requirements: Application form, essay. *Deadline:* December 1.

Contact: Roger Noordhoek, Senior Director of Youth Marketing
United States Bowling Congress
621 Six Flags Drive
Arlington, TX 76011
Phone: 800-514-BOWL Ext. 8308
E-mail: contactus@ibcyouth.com

UNITED STATES MARINE CORPS SCHOLARSHIP FOUNDATION, INC.

http://www.mcsf.org/

MARINE CORPS SCHOLARSHIP FOUNDATION

Available to the sons and daughters of active duty, veteran, and deceased Marines, and to the children of qualifying Navy Corpsmen, whose family income does not exceed $96,000. Must submit proof of parent's service. Apply online at mcsf.org and or email Scholarship@mcsf.org for further information.

Award: Scholarship for use in freshman, sophomore, junior, or senior years; not renewable. *Number:* 2000–2300. *Amount:* $1500–$10,000.

Eligibility Requirements: Applicant must be enrolled or expecting to enroll full- or part-time at a two-year or four-year or technical institution or university. Applicant or parent of applicant must be member of American Legion or Auxiliary. Available to U.S. citizens.

Application Requirements: Application form, essay, financial need analysis. *Deadline:* March 1.

Contact: Jeanna Adams, Assistant Director, Scholarship Programs
Phone: 866-496-5462
E-mail: scholarship@mcsf.org

UNITED STATES SUBMARINE VETERANS

https://www.ussvi.org/Documents.asp?Type=Scholarship|Application

UNITED STATES SUBMARINE VETERANS INC. NATIONAL SCHOLARSHIP PROGRAM

Program requires the sponsor to be a qualified Base Member or Member-at-Large in good standing. Must demonstrate financial need, have a minimum 2.5 GPA, and submit an essay. Open to children, stepchildren, and grandchildren of qualified members. Applicants must be between the ages of 17 to 23 and must be unmarried.

Award: Scholarship for use in freshman, sophomore, junior, or senior years; not renewable. *Number:* 2–18. *Amount:* $950–$1500.

Eligibility Requirements: Applicant must be age 17-23; enrolled or expecting to enroll full-time at a two-year or four-year or technical institution or university and single. Applicant or parent of applicant must be member of Veterans of Foreign Wars or Auxiliary. Applicant or parent of applicant must have employment or volunteer experience in seafaring/fishing industry. Applicant must have 3.0 GPA or higher. Available to U.S. citizens. Applicant or parent must meet one or more of the following requirements: Navy experience; retired from active duty; disabled or killed as a result of military service; prisoner of war; or missing in action.

Application Requirements: Application form, essay, financial need analysis, recommendations or references, transcript. *Deadline:* April 15.

Contact: Paul Orstad, National Scholarship Chairman
United States Submarine Veterans
30 Surrey Lane
Norwich, CT 06369-6541
Phone: 860-334-6457
E-mail: hogan343@aol.com

USA BMX

http://usabmx.com

BOB WARNICKE MEMORIAL SCHOLARSHIP PROGRAM

Scholarship assists students and their families in meeting the costs of undergraduate or trade school education. Applicant must be a high school senior, graduate or attending a postsecondary school at the time of application, or accepted and plan to attend an accredited postsecondary school as a full-time or part-time student for the complete award year. Must be an active member or official of USA BMX.

Award: Scholarship for use in freshman, sophomore, junior, senior, graduate, or postgraduate years; not renewable.

Eligibility Requirements: Applicant must be enrolled or expecting to enroll full- or part-time at a two-year or four-year or technical institution or university. Applicant or parent of applicant must be member of National Bicycle League. Available to U.S. and non-U.S. citizens.

Application Requirements: Application form, essay, personal photograph. *Deadline:* March 6.

Contact: Scholarship Committee
Phone: 480-961-1903

UTILITY WORKERS UNION OF AMERICA

http://www.uwua.net/

UTILITY WORKERS UNION OF AMERICA SCHOLARSHIP AWARDS PROGRAM

Renewable award for high school juniors who are children of active members of the Utility Workers Union of America. Must take the PSAT National Merit Scholarship Qualifying Test in junior year and plan to enter college in the fall after high school graduation.

Award: Scholarship for use in freshman, sophomore, junior, or senior years; renewable. *Number:* 2. *Amount:* $500–$2000.

Eligibility Requirements: Applicant must be high school student and planning to enroll or expecting to enroll full-time at a four-year institution or university. Applicant or parent of applicant must be member of Utility Workers Union of America. Available to U.S. citizens.

Application Requirements: Application form. *Deadline:* May 31.

Contact: Ms. Stacy Paulo, Executive Assistant to the National Secretary-Treasurer
Utility Workers Union of America
1300 L St. NW
Suite 1200
Washington, DC 20002
Phone: 202-899-2851
Fax: 202-899-2852
E-mail: spaulo@uwua.net

WESTERN FRATERNAL LIFE ASSOCIATION

http://www.wflains.org

WESTERN FRATERNAL LIFE NATIONAL SCHOLARSHIP

Western Fraternal Life Association is pleased to announce 25 national scholarships for its eligible members. The 25 national scholarships include the following: 1. one four-year academic scholarship, $1,000 per year for a total of $4,000; 2. two $1,000 scholarships to either community college or vocational/trade school; 3. one $1,000 community involvement scholarship; 4. one $1,000 non-traditional student scholarship. Traditional and non-traditional students are eligible. Must be a Western Fraternal Life Association member in good standing for two years prior to the application deadline. A member is an individual who has life insurance or an annuity with Western. High school seniors may apply. Members who are qualified for the National Scholarship may also qualify for state and local lodge scholarships. You are eligible to win this scholarship four times.

Award: Scholarship for use in freshman, sophomore, junior, senior, graduate, or postgraduate years; renewable. *Number:* 25. *Amount:* $1000.

Eligibility Requirements: Applicant must be enrolled or expecting to enroll full-time at a two-year or four-year or technical institution or university and resident of Colorado, Illinois, Iowa, Kansas, Louisiana, Michigan, Minnesota, Missouri, Nebraska, North Dakota, Oklahoma, Oregon, Pennsylvania, South Dakota, Texas, Washington, Wisconsin. Applicant or parent of applicant must be member of Western Fraternal Life Association. Available to U.S. citizens.

Application Requirements: Application form, essay. *Deadline:* March 1.

Contact: Darcy Hilton, Member Programs Coordinator
Western Fraternal Life Association
1900 First Avenue NE
Cedar Rapids, IA 52402
Phone: 877-935-2467 Ext. 131
Fax: 319-363-8806
E-mail: dhilton@wflains.org

WISCONSIN ASSOCIATION FOR FOOD PROTECTION

http://www.wifoodprotection.org

WAFP MEMORIAL SCHOLARSHIP

Scholarship for a child or dependent of a current or deceased WAFP member, or the applicant may be a WAFP student member. Must have been accepted into an accredited degree program in a university, college, or technical institute.

Award: Scholarship for use in sophomore, junior, senior, or graduate years; not renewable. *Number:* 1. *Amount:* $1000.

Eligibility Requirements: Applicant must be enrolled or expecting to enroll full-time at a two-year or four-year or technical institution or university. Applicant or parent of applicant must be member of Wisconsin Association for Food Protection. Available to U.S. and non-U.S. citizens.

Application Requirements: Application form. *Deadline:* July 1.

Contact: Mr. Jim Wickert, Scholarship Committee Chairman
Wisconsin Association for Food Protection
3834 Ridgeway Avenue
Madison, WI 53704
Phone: 608-241-2438
E-mail: jwick16060@tds.net

WYOMING FARM BUREAU FEDERATION

http://www.wyfb.org/

LIVINGSTON FAMILY - H.J. KING MEMORIAL SCHOLARSHIP

One-time award given to graduates of Wyoming high schools. Must attend a Wyoming junior college or the University of Wyoming. Minimum 2.5 GPA required. If Applicant is under 18 years of age, the applicant must have an immediate family member or guardian that is a current member of the Wyoming Farm Bureau Federation at the time of applying.

Award: Scholarship for use in freshman, sophomore, junior, senior, or graduate years; not renewable. *Number:* 1. *Amount:* $1500.

Eligibility Requirements: Applicant must be enrolled or expecting to enroll full-time at a two-year or four-year institution or university; resident of Wyoming and studying in Wyoming. Applicant or parent of applicant must be member of Wyoming Farm Bureau. Applicant must have 2.5 GPA or higher. Available to U.S. and non-U.S. citizens.

Application Requirements: Application form, financial need analysis, personal photograph. *Deadline:* March 1.

Contact: McKenzi Digby, Administrative Assistant
Wyoming Farm Bureau Federation
PO Box 1348
Laramie, WY 82073
Phone: 307-721-7719
E-mail: mdigby@wyfb.org

WYOMING FARM BUREAU CONTINUING EDUCATION SCHOLARSHIPS

Award to students attending a two-year college in Wyoming or the University of Wyoming. Must be a resident of Wyoming and if 18 years or older, must be a current member of the Wyoming Farm Bureau Federation. If under 18, applicant must have an immediate family member or guardian that is a current member of the Wyoming Farm Bureau Federation at the time of applying. Must submit at least two semesters of college grade transcripts. Freshmen must submit first semester grades and proof of enrollment in second semester. Minimum 2.5 GPA.

Award: Scholarship for use in freshman, sophomore, junior, or graduate years; not renewable. *Number:* 3. *Amount:* $500.

Eligibility Requirements: Applicant must be enrolled or expecting to enroll full-time at a two-year or four-year institution or university; resident of Wyoming and studying in Wyoming. Applicant or parent of applicant must be member of Wyoming Farm Bureau. Applicant must have 2.5 GPA or higher. Available to U.S. and non-U.S. citizens.

Application Requirements: Application form, financial need analysis, personal photograph. *Deadline:* March 1.

Contact: McKenzi Digby, Administrative Assistant
Wyoming Farm Bureau Federation
PO Box 1348
Laramie, WY 82073
Phone: 307-721-7719
E-mail: mdigby@wyfb.org

WYOMING FARM BUREAU FEDERATION SCHOLARSHIPS

Five $500 scholarships will be given to graduates of Wyoming high schools. Eligible candidates must be enrolled in a two-year college in Wyoming or the University of Wyoming and must have a minimum 2.5 GPA. If 18 years or older, applicant must be a current paid member of the Wyoming Farm Bureau Federation at the time of applying. If under 18, applicant must have an immediate family member or guardian that is a current member of the Wyoming Farm Bureau Federation.

Award: Scholarship for use in freshman, sophomore, junior, senior, or graduate years; not renewable. *Number:* 5. *Amount:* $500.

Eligibility Requirements: Applicant must be enrolled or expecting to enroll full-time at a two-year or four-year institution or university; resident of Wyoming and studying in Wyoming. Applicant or parent of applicant must be member of Wyoming Farm Bureau. Applicant must have 2.5 GPA or higher. Available to U.S. and non-U.S. citizens.

Application Requirements: Application form, financial need analysis, personal photograph. *Deadline:* March 1.

Contact: McKenzi Digby, Administrative Assistant
Wyoming Farm Bureau Federation
PO Box 1348
Laramie, WY 82073
Phone: 307-721-7719
E-mail: mdigby@wyfb.org

CORPORATE AFFILIATION

AMERICAN LEGION DEPARTMENT OF WEST VIRGINIA

http://www.wvlegion.org/

AMERICAN LEGION DEPARTMENT OF WEST VIRGINIA BOARD OF REGENTS SCHOLARSHIP

One-time prize awarded annually to the winner of the West Virginia American Legion State Oratorical Scholarship Program Contest. Must be in ninth to twelfth grade of an accredited West Virginia high school to compete. For use at a West Virginia institution only.

Award: Scholarship for use in freshman year; not renewable. *Number:* 1. *Amount:* up to $2000.

Eligibility Requirements: Applicant must be high school student; planning to enroll or expecting to enroll full-time at a four-year institution or university; resident of West Virginia; studying in West Virginia and must have an interest in public speaking. Applicant or parent of applicant must be affiliated with A.T. Cross. Available to U.S. citizens.

Application Requirements: Application form. *Deadline:* December 29.

Contact: Mr. Miles Epling, State Adjutant
American Legion Department of West Virginia
2016 Kanawha Boulevard East, PO Box 3191
Charleston, WV 25311
Phone: 304-343-7591
E-mail: wvlegion@suddenlinkmail.com

DEMOLAY FOUNDATION INCORPORATED

http://www.demolay.org/

FRANK S. LAND SCHOLARSHIP

Scholarship awarded to members of DeMolay International only, who have not yet reached the age of 21, to assist in financing their education. Must be U.S. resident.

Award: Scholarship for use in freshman, sophomore, junior, or senior years; not renewable. *Number:* 10–15. *Amount:* $1000.

Eligibility Requirements: Applicant must be enrolled or expecting to enroll full-time at a two-year or four-year institution or university; male; resident of Alabama, Alaska, Arizona, Arkansas, California, Colorado, Connecticut, Delaware, District of Columbia, Florida, Georgia, Hawaii, Idaho, Illinois, Indiana, Iowa, Kansas, Kentucky, Louisiana, Maine, Maryland, Massachusetts, Michigan, Minnesota, Mississippi, Missouri, Montana, Nebraska, Nevada, New Hampshire, New Jersey, New Mexico, New York, North Carolina, North Dakota, Ohio, Oklahoma, Oregon, Pennsylvania, Rhode Island, South Carolina, South Dakota, Tennessee, Texas, Utah, Vermont, Virginia, Washington, West Virginia, Wisconsin, Wyoming and studying in Alabama, Alaska, Arizona, Arkansas, California, Colorado, Connecticut, Delaware, District of Columbia, Florida, Georgia, Hawaii, Idaho, Illinois, Indiana, Iowa, Kansas, Kentucky, Louisiana, Maine, Maryland, Massachusetts, Michigan, Minnesota, Mississippi, Missouri, Montana, Nebraska, Nevada, New Hampshire, New Jersey, New Mexico, New York, North Carolina, North Dakota, Ohio, Oklahoma, Oregon, Pennsylvania, Rhode Island, South Carolina, South Dakota, Tennessee, Texas, Utah, Vermont, Virginia, Washington, West Virginia, Wisconsin, Wyoming. Applicant or parent of applicant must be affiliated with DeMolay. Available to U.S. citizens.

Application Requirements: Application form, financial need analysis. *Deadline:* April 1.

Contact: Mr. Frank Kell, Scholarship Committee Chairman
DeMolay Foundation Incorporated
10200 Northwest Ambassador Drive
Kansas City, MO 64153
Phone: 800-336-6529
E-mail: scholarships@demolay.org

DONALDSON COMPANY

http://www.donaldson.com/

THE DONALDSON COMPANY, INC. SCHOLARSHIP PROGRAM

Scholarships for children of U.S. employees of Donaldson Company Inc. Any form of accredited postsecondary education is eligible. The amount of the award can range from $2000 to $3000 for each year of full-time study and may be renewed for up to a total of three years. The number of scholarships awarded is limited to a maximum of 25 percent of the number of applicants.

Award: Scholarship for use in freshman, sophomore, junior, or senior years; renewable. *Amount:* $2000–$3000.

Eligibility Requirements: Applicant must be enrolled or expecting to enroll full-time at a two-year or four-year or technical institution or university. Applicant or parent of applicant must be affiliated with Donaldson Company. Available to U.S. citizens.

Application Requirements: Application form, essay, financial need analysis. *Deadline:* March 15.

Contact: Norm Linnell, Vice President, General Counsel and Secretary
Phone: 952-887-3631
Fax: 952-887-3005
E-mail: norm.linnell@donaldson.com

THE FORD FAMILY FOUNDATION

http://www.tfff.org

SCHOLARSHIP PROGRAM FOR SONS AND DAUGHTERS OF EMPLOYEES OF ROSEBURG FOREST PRODUCTS CO.

Kenneth W. Ford and The Ford Family Foundation established the Ford Sons & Daughters Program to provide scholarships to sons and daughters of Roseburg Forest Products Co. employees as they pursue education beyond high school. Each year, up to 10% of all eligible applicants are selected to receive the Ford Sons & Daughters Scholarship. An applicant must be a dependent child or stepchild (age 21 or younger) of an employee of Roseburg Forest Products Co. The employee must be full-time and have been employed by Roseburg Forest Products Co. for a minimum of 18 months as of March 1 of the application year.

Award: Scholarship for use in freshman, sophomore, junior, or senior years; renewable. *Number:* 30–47. *Amount:* $3000–$5000.

Eligibility Requirements: Applicant must be enrolled or expecting to enroll full-time at a two-year or four-year or technical institution or university. Applicant or parent of applicant must be affiliated with Roseburg Forest Products.

Application Requirements: Application form, essay, interview. *Deadline:* March 1.

Contact: Tricia Tate, Scholarship Programs Manager
The Ford Family Foundation
44 Club Road, Suite 100
Eugene, OR 97401
Phone: 541-485-6211
Fax: 541-485-6223
E-mail: fordscholarships@tfff.org

GANNETT FOUNDATION

http://www.gannettfoundation.org/

GANNETT FOUNDATION/MADELYN P. JENNINGS SCHOLARSHIP AWARD

One-time awards for high school students whose parents are current full-time Gannett Company employees. Must be planning to attend a 4-year college or university for full-time study in the fall after graduation. Students must meet all requirements for participation in the National Merit Scholarship Program and take the PSAT/NMSQT in their junior year of high school. For more information, email the Gannett Benefits Team at Gannett Co., Inc., gannettbenefits@gannett.com.

Award: Scholarship for use in freshman year; not renewable. *Number:* 6. *Amount:* $3000.

Eligibility Requirements: Applicant must be high school student and planning to enroll or expecting to enroll full-time at a four-year institution or university. Applicant or parent of applicant must be affiliated with Gannett Company, Inc.. Available to U.S. citizens.

Application Requirements: Application form. *Deadline:* March 26.

Contact: Tiffany Sanford, Senior Benefits Analyst
Gannett Foundation
7950 Jones Branch Drive
McLean, VA 22107
Phone: 703-854-6446
E-mail: tsanford@gannett.com

GATEWAY PRESS INC. OF LOUISVILLE

http://www.gatewaypressinc.com/

GATEWAY PRESS SCHOLARSHIP

Scholarship for graduating high school seniors whose parents have been employees of Gateway Press Inc. for a minimum of 5 years. Applicant must be accepted at a college or university and maintain a minimum GPA of 2.25.

Award: Scholarship for use in freshman year; renewable. *Amount:* up to $3000.

Eligibility Requirements: Applicant must be high school student and planning to enroll or expecting to enroll full-time at a four-year institution or university. Applicant or parent of applicant must be affiliated with Gateway Press Inc.. Available to U.S. citizens.

Application Requirements: Application form, recommendations or references, transcript. *Deadline:* January 1.

Contact: Chris Georgehead, Human Resources Manager
Phone: 502-454-0431
Fax: 502-459-7930
E-mail: kit@gatewaypressinc.com

HERMAN O. WEST FOUNDATION

http://www.westpharma.com/

HERMAN O. WEST FOUNDATION SCHOLARSHIP PROGRAM

Awards up to fourteen scholarships per year to high school seniors who will be attending college in the fall after graduation. The scholarship may only be applied toward tuition cost up to $3000 per year for up to four years. Available only to children of active employees of West Pharmaceutical Services, Inc.

Award: Scholarship for use in freshman, sophomore, junior, or senior years; renewable. *Number:* 1–14. *Amount:* $3000–$12,000.

Eligibility Requirements: Applicant must be high school student and planning to enroll or expecting to enroll full-time at a two-year or four-year institution or university. Applicant or parent of applicant must be affiliated with West Pharmaceuticals. Available to U.S. citizens.

Application Requirements: Application form, essay. *Deadline:* January 31.

Contact: Laura Pit, Manager, Community Affairs
Herman O. West Foundation
530 Herman O West Drive
Exton, PA 19341
Phone: 610-594-3046
E-mail: laura.pitt@westpharma.com

JOHNSON CONTROLS INC.

http://www.johnsoncontrols.com/

JOHNSON CONTROLS FOUNDATION SCHOLARSHIP PROGRAM

Available to high school seniors who are children of Johnson Controls, Inc. U.S. employees only. 20 one-time awards of $2000 and 40 renewable scholarships of $2000 a year for up to four years.

Award: Scholarship for use in freshman year; renewable. *Number:* up to 60. *Amount:* $2000.

Eligibility Requirements: Applicant must be high school student and planning to enroll or expecting to enroll full-time at a four-year institution or university. Applicant or parent of applicant must be affiliated with Johnson Controls, Inc.. Applicant must have 3.5 GPA or higher. Available to U.S. citizens.

Application Requirements: Application form, application form may be submitted online, community service, essay, recommendations or references, test scores, transcript. *Deadline:* March 13.

Contact: Marlene Griffith, Human Resources Administration Coordinator
Phone: 414-524-2425
Fax: 414-524-2299
E-mail: marlene.f.griffith@jci.com

OREGON STUDENT ASSISTANCE COMMISSION

https://oregonstudentaid.gov/

ALBINA FUEL COMPANY SCHOLARSHIP

Scholarship available to a dependent child of a current Albina Fuel Company employee. The employee must have been employed for at least one full year as of October 1 prior to the scholarship deadline. Must reapply annually. Oregon residency not required.

Award: Scholarship for use in freshman, sophomore, junior, or senior years; not renewable.

Eligibility Requirements: Applicant must be enrolled or expecting to enroll full-time at a four-year institution. Applicant or parent of applicant must be affiliated with Albina Fuel Company. Available to U.S. citizens.

Application Requirements: Application form, essay. *Deadline:* March 1.

Contact: Melissa Adams, Scholarship Processing Coordinator
Phone: 541-687-7409
E-mail: melissa.adams@state.or.us

A. VICTOR ROSENFELD SCHOLARSHIP

Award for dependents of employees of Calbag Metals who have worked for that company for three or more years prior to the March 1 scholarship deadline. Applicants must be enrolled at any public or nonprofit U.S. college or university. Must reapply annually for award renewal. FAFSA required, based on financial need.

Award: Scholarship for use in freshman, sophomore, junior, or senior years; not renewable.

Eligibility Requirements: Applicant must be enrolled or expecting to enroll full-time at a four-year institution or university and resident of Oregon, Washington. Applicant or parent of applicant must be affiliated with Calbag Metals. Available to U.S. citizens.

Application Requirements: Application form, essay, financial need analysis. *Deadline:* March 1.

Contact: Melissa Adams, Scholarship Processing Coordinator
Phone: 541-687-7409
E-mail: melissa.adams@state.or.us

ESSEX GENERAL CONSTRUCTION SCHOLARSHIP

Award for an employee, or dependent of a current employee of Essex General Construction. Employee must have been continuously employed at Essex for one year or more at no fewer than 20 hours per week as of the application deadline. Oregon residency is not required. Must be a high school graduate enrolling as an undergraduate in a college or university in the U.S. Must reapply each year to renew award for up to four years.

Award: Scholarship for use in freshman, sophomore, junior, or senior years; not renewable.

Eligibility Requirements: Applicant must be enrolled or expecting to enroll full- or part-time at a four-year institution or university. Applicant or parent of applicant must be affiliated with Essex General Construction. Available to U.S. citizens.

Application Requirements: Application form. *Deadline:* March 1.

Contact: Melissa Adams, Scholarship Processing Coordinator
Phone: 541-687-7409
E-mail: melissa.adams@state.or.us

GLENN JACKSON SCHOLARS SCHOLARSHIPS

Renewable award for Oregon graduating high school seniors who are dependents of employees or retirees of Oregon Department of Transportation or Parks and Recreation Department. Employees must have worked in their department at least three years as of the scholarship deadline. Must enroll in a public or non-profit college. Scholarship is automatically renewable if renewal criteria met. Financial need may or may not be considered.

Award: Scholarship for use in freshman, sophomore, junior, or senior years; renewable.

Eligibility Requirements: Applicant must be high school student; planning to enroll or expecting to enroll full- or part-time at a two-year or four-year institution or university and resident of Oregon. Applicant or parent of applicant must be affiliated with Oregon Department of Transportation Parks and Recreation. Available to U.S. citizens.

Application Requirements: Application form, financial need analysis. *Deadline:* March 1.

Contact: Melissa Adams, Scholarship Processing Coordinator
Phone: 541-687-7409
E-mail: melissa.adams@state.or.us

OREGON TRUCKING ASSOCIATION SAFETY MANAGEMENT COUNCIL SCHOLARSHIP

One-time award available to a child of an Oregon Trucking Association member, or child of an employee of OTA member. Applicants must be graduating high school seniors planning to attend a public or nonprofit college or university. Oregon residency is not required.

Award: Scholarship for use in freshman year; not renewable.

Eligibility Requirements: Applicant must be high school student and planning to enroll or expecting to enroll full-time at a four-year institution. Applicant or parent of applicant must be affiliated with Oregon Trucking Association. Available to U.S. citizens.

Application Requirements: Application form. *Deadline:* March 1.

Contact: Melissa Adams, Scholarship Processing Coordinator
Phone: 541-687-7409
E-mail: melissa.adams@state.or.us

RICHARD F. BRENTANO MEMORIAL SCHOLARSHIP

Award for legal dependents of eligible employees of Waste Control Systems Inc., and subsidiaries. Employees must be employed at least one year as of the March 1 scholarship deadline. Must reapply annually to renew award.

Award: Scholarship for use in freshman, sophomore, junior, or senior years; not renewable.

Eligibility Requirements: Applicant must be enrolled or expecting to enroll full-time at a four-year institution or university. Applicant or parent of applicant must be affiliated with Waste Control Systems, Inc.. Applicant must have 3.0 GPA or higher. Available to U.S. citizens.

Application Requirements: Application form. *Deadline:* March 1.

Contact: Melissa Adams, Scholarship Processing Coordinator
Phone: 541-687-7409
E-mail: melissa.adams@state.or.us

ROBERT D. FORSTER SCHOLARSHIP

Dependents of eligible employees of Walsh Construction Co. Eligible employees must have been employed by Walsh Construction 3+ years (1000+ hours each year) as of the March scholarship deadline. Based on financial need. May be used at any four-year college or university in the U.S.

Award: Scholarship for use in freshman, sophomore, junior, or senior years; renewable.

Eligibility Requirements: Applicant must be enrolled or expecting to enroll full-time at a four-year institution or university. Applicant or parent of applicant must be affiliated with Walsh Construction Company. Available to U.S. citizens.

Application Requirements: Application form, financial need analysis. *Deadline:* March 1.

Contact: Melissa Adams, Scholarship Processing Coordinator
Phone: 541-687-7409
E-mail: melissa.adams@state.or.us

ROGER W. EMMONS MEMORIAL SCHOLARSHIP

Scholarship available to children and grandchildren of owners or employees (for at least three years) of regular members of the Oregon Refuse and Recycling Association. Award may be used at any accredited U.S. public or nonprofit college or university. Scholarship is automatically renewable if renewal criteria met.

Award: Scholarship for use in freshman year; renewable.

Eligibility Requirements: Applicant must be high school student and planning to enroll or expecting to enroll full-time at a four-year institution or university. Applicant or parent of applicant must be affiliated with Oregon Refuse and Recycling Association. Available to U.S. citizens.

Application Requirements: Application form. *Deadline:* March 1.

Contact: Melissa Adams, Scholarship Processing Coordinator
Phone: 541-687-7409
E-mail: melissa.adams@state.or.us

STIMSON LUMBER COMPANY SCHOLARSHIP

Renewable award for dependents of Stimson Lumber Company employees who are graduating seniors.

Award: Scholarship for use in freshman year; renewable.

Eligibility Requirements: Applicant must be high school student and planning to enroll or expecting to enroll full-time at a two-year or four-year institution. Applicant or parent of applicant must be affiliated with Stimson Lumber Company. Applicant must have 3.0 GPA or higher. Available to U.S. citizens.

Application Requirements: Application form. *Deadline:* March 1.

Contact: Melissa Adams, Scholarship Processing Coordinator
Phone: 541-687-7409
E-mail: melissa.adams@state.or.us

TAYLOR MADE LABELS SCHOLARSHIP

Award available to dependents of eligible employees of Taylor Made Label Company. Employee must have been employed by Taylor Made for a minimum of one year as of the March scholarship deadline. Applicant must reapply annually for award renewal. Financial need may or may not be considered.

Award: Scholarship for use in freshman, sophomore, junior, or senior years; not renewable.

Eligibility Requirements: Applicant must be enrolled or expecting to enroll full- or part-time at a four-year institution or university. Applicant or parent of applicant must be affiliated with Taylor Made Label Company. Available to U.S. citizens.

Application Requirements: Application form. *Deadline:* March 1.

Contact: Melissa Adams, Scholarship Processing Coordinator
Phone: 541-687-7409
E-mail: melissa.adams@state.or.us

WALTER DAVIES SCHOLARSHIP

Award for eligible employees or dependents of eligible employees of U.S. Bank. Must be an Oregon high school graduate. Oregon residency is not required; must re-apply annually. Based on financial need.

Award: Scholarship for use in freshman, sophomore, junior, or senior years; not renewable.

Eligibility Requirements: Applicant must be enrolled or expecting to enroll full- or part-time at a four-year institution or university. Applicant or parent of applicant must be affiliated with U.S. Bancorp. Available to U.S. citizens.

Application Requirements: Application form, financial need analysis. *Deadline:* March 1.

Contact: Melissa Adams, Scholarship Processing Coordinator
Phone: 541-687-7409
E-mail: melissa.adams@state.or.us

WILLETT AND MARGUERITE LAKE SCHOLARSHIP

Scholarships for dependents and grandchildren of eligible employees of Bonita Pioneer Packaging Company who have been employed by the company for two years. May be used at public and non-profit colleges only. Reapply annually. Financial need may or may not be considered.

Award: Scholarship for use in freshman, sophomore, junior, or senior years; not renewable.

Eligibility Requirements: Applicant must be enrolled or expecting to enroll full-time at a four-year institution or university. Applicant or parent of applicant must be affiliated with Bonita Pioneer Packaging Company. Available to U.S. citizens.

Application Requirements: Application form. *Deadline:* March 1.

Contact: Melissa Adams, Scholarship Processing Coordinator
Phone: 541-687-7409
E-mail: melissa.adams@state.or.us

WOODARD FAMILY SCHOLARSHIP

Scholarships are available to employees and dependents of eligible employees of Kimwood Corporation. Awards may be used at Oregon public and nonprofit colleges only. May reapply annually for award. Financial need may or may not be considered.

Award: Scholarship for use in freshman, sophomore, junior, or senior years; not renewable.

Eligibility Requirements: Applicant must be enrolled or expecting to enroll full-time at a two-year or four-year institution and studying in Oregon. Applicant or parent of applicant must be affiliated with Kimwood Corporation or Middlefield Village. Available to U.S. citizens.

Application Requirements: Application form, financial need analysis. *Deadline:* March 1.

Contact: Melissa Adams, Scholarship Processing Coordinator
Phone: 541-687-7409
E-mail: melissa.adams@state.or.us

RHODE ISLAND FOUNDATION

http://www.rifoundation.org/

A.T. CROSS SCHOLARSHIP

Renewable scholarships ranging from $1000 to $3000 for new applicants and from $300 to $2000 for renewals are available to children of full-time employees of A.T. Cross Company. Must be Rhode Island residents.

Award: Scholarship for use in freshman, sophomore, junior, or senior years; renewable. *Amount:* $1000–$3000.

Eligibility Requirements: Applicant must be enrolled or expecting to enroll full-time at a four-year institution or university and resident of Rhode Island. Applicant or parent of applicant must be affiliated with A.T. Cross. Available to U.S. citizens.

Application Requirements: Application form, essay, financial need analysis, recommendations or references, self-addressed stamped envelope with application, transcript. *Deadline:* May 15.

Contact: Libby Monahan, Funds Administrator
Phone: 401-274-4564 Ext. 3117
E-mail: libbym@rifoundation.org

THEODORE R. AND VIVIAN M. JOHNSON SCHOLARSHIP FOUNDATION INC.

http://www.jsf.bz/

THEODORE R. AND VIVIAN M. JOHNSON SCHOLARSHIP PROGRAM FOR CHILDREN OF UPS EMPLOYEES OR UPS RETIREES

The children of United Parcel Service employees or retirees who live in Florida are eligible for scholarship funds to attend college or vocational school in Florida. Awards are for undergraduate study only and ranges from $1000 to $10,000. Community college students and vocational school students may receive a maximum of $10,000 per year.

Award: Scholarship for use in freshman, sophomore, junior, or senior years; renewable. *Number:* 1–205. *Amount:* $1000–$10,000.

Eligibility Requirements: Applicant must be enrolled or expecting to enroll full- or part-time at a two-year or four-year or technical institution or university; resident of Florida and studying in Florida. Applicant or parent of applicant must be affiliated with Universal American Financial Corporation. Available to U.S. citizens.

Application Requirements: Application form, financial need analysis. *Deadline:* April 15.

Contact: Alexa Thelen, Program Manager
Theodore R. and Vivian M. Johnson Scholarship Foundation Inc.
Scholarship Management Services
One Scholarship Way
Saint Peter, MN 56082
Phone: 507-931-1682
E-mail: athelen@scholarshipamerica.org

TRIANGLE COMMUNITY FOUNDATION

http://www.trianglecf.org

GEORGE AND MARY NEWTON SCHOLARSHIP

Anyone between 16-25, who has received or is expecting a high school degree or equivalent and whose parent or legal guardian is an employee of Newton Instrument Company, Inc., may apply. Applicant must have applied to the institution he or she plans to attend, and must intend to enroll within one year of the application deadline. Recipients will be selected on the basis of academic achievement, financial need, school and community activities, and work experience and educational goals.

Award: Scholarship for use in freshman, sophomore, junior, or senior years; renewable. *Number:* 1. *Amount:* $1000.

Eligibility Requirements: Applicant must be age 16-25; enrolled or expecting to enroll full-time at a two-year or four-year or technical institution or university and resident of North Carolina. Applicant or parent of applicant must be affiliated with Newton Instrument Company. Available to U.S. citizens.

Application Requirements: Application form. *Deadline:* March 15.

Contact: Mrs. Sarah Battersby, Scholarships and Donor Services Officer
Phone: 919-474-8370 Ext. 4015
E-mail: Scholarships@trianglecf.org

WALMART FOUNDATION

http://foundation.walmart.com/

WALMART ASSOCIATE SCHOLARSHIP

The Walmart Foundation offers scholarship programs that benefit qualified Walmart associates. Applicants must be employed with any division of Walmart for at least six consecutive months prior to the application due date for the award period in which the associate is applying. Applicants must have graduated high school/home school or obtained a GED or be a graduating high school senior who intends to enroll in a college or university upon graduation.
http://foundation.walmart.com/our-focus/associate-scholarships

Award: Scholarship for use in freshman, sophomore, junior, senior, or graduate years; renewable. *Amount:* up to $16,000.

Eligibility Requirements: Applicant must be enrolled or expecting to enroll full- or part-time at a two-year or four-year or technical institution or university. Applicant or parent of applicant must be affiliated with Wal-Mart Foundation. Available to U.S. citizens.

Application Requirements: Application form, application form may be submitted online (http://foundation.walmart.com/our-focus/associate-scholarships), community service, entry in a contest, financial need analysis. *Deadline:* varies.

Contact: Walmart Foundation Scholarship Administrator
Walmart Foundation
702 SW 8th Street
Bentonville, AR 72716-0150
Fax: 479-273-6850
E-mail: W.Mschol@wal-mart.com

WALMART DEPENDENT SCHOLARSHIP

The Walmart Foundation offers scholarship programs that benefit qualified Walmart associates and their high school senior dependents. Applicants must be the dependent of an actively employed Walmart associate (employee) within any division of Walmart for at least six consecutive months as of April 1 and must be a high school or home school senior graduating or earning a GED between August 1 and July 31. Applicants must have a cumulative high school grade point average (GPA) of at least 2.0 on a 4-point scale. See website for details, https://walmart.scholarsapply.org/dependent/

Award: Scholarship for use in freshman, sophomore, junior, or senior years; renewable. *Amount:* up to $13,000.

Eligibility Requirements: Applicant must be high school student and planning to enroll or expecting to enroll full-time at a two-year or four-year or technical institution or university. Applicant or parent of applicant must be affiliated with Wal-Mart Foundation. Available to U.S. citizens.

Application Requirements: Application form, application form may be submitted online (http://foundation.walmart.com/our-focus/associate-scholarships), entry in a contest, financial need analysis, transcript. *Deadline:* April 1.

Contact: Walmart Foundation Scholarship Administrator
Walmart Foundation
702 SW 8th Street
Bentonville, AR 72716-0150
Fax: 479-273-6850
E-mail: W.Mschol@wal-mart.com

EMPLOYMENT/ VOLUNTEER EXPERIENCE

1-800-HANSONS

http://www.hansons.com

1-800-HANSONS SCHOLARSHIP PROGRAM

To be eligible, applicant must have a minimum of a 3.3 cumulative GPA and submit a 1000–1500-word essay. There are no other requirements for this scholarship, just the desire and drive to be successful in life. Please answer one of the following essay questions: What do you consider to be the single most important societal problem? Why? What do you think your chosen industry will be like in the next 10 years? What is the purpose of life? If you won the lottery for a million dollars, what would you do with it? Mail your official transcript and essay to 1-800-HANSONS, ATTN: Hansons Scholarship Program, c/o Brian Elias, 977 E 14 Mile Road, Troy, MI 48083. Be sure to include your name, address, phone number, and email address so we can contact you if you win!

Award: Scholarship for use in freshman, sophomore, junior, senior, graduate, or postgraduate years; not renewable. *Number:* 8. *Amount:* $500–$5000.

Eligibility Requirements: Applicant must be enrolled or expecting to enroll full- or part-time at a two-year or four-year institution or university. Available to U.S. and non-U.S. citizens.

Application Requirements: Essay. *Deadline:* October 15.

Contact: Theresa Baughman
1-800-HANSONS
977 E 14 Mile Rd
Troy, MI 48083
Phone: 248-5813030 Ext. 1011
E-mail: tbaughman@hansons.com

1DENTAL.COM

https://www.1dental.com/

1DENTAL SCHOLARSHIP

1Dental is offering a $500 college scholarship to eligible high school seniors and college students who apply. You can apply by visiting 1Dental's scholarship page (https://www.1dental.com/scholarship/) and filling out our scholarship. We offer this scholarship every year. Deadline is December 21, 2018.

Award: Scholarship for use in freshman, sophomore, junior, senior, or graduate years; not renewable. *Number:* 1. *Amount:* $500.

Eligibility Requirements: Applicant must be enrolled or expecting to enroll full-time at a two-year or four-year or technical institution or university. Available to U.S. citizens.

Application Requirements: Application form. *Deadline:* December 21.

Contact: Natasha G, 1Dental Scholarship Coordinator
E-mail: scholarships@1dental.com

1ST CAVALRY DIVISION ASSOCIATION

https://www.1CDA.org

1ST CAVALRY DIVISION ASSOCIATION SCHOLARSHIP FOUNDATION

Scholarship opportunities for members of the 1st Cavalry Division Association and their children.

Award: Grant for use in freshman, sophomore, junior, or senior years; renewable. *Amount:* $1200.

Eligibility Requirements: Applicant must be enrolled or expecting to enroll full- or part-time at a two-year or four-year or technical institution. Available to U.S. and non-U.S. citizens. Applicant or parent must meet one or more of the following requirements: Army experience; retired from active duty; disabled or killed as a result of military service; prisoner of war; or missing in action.

Application Requirements: Application form. *Deadline:* August 1.

Contact: Ms. Dara Wydler, Executive Director
Phone: 254-547-6537
E-mail: firstcav@1cda.org

4MYCASH.COM, LLC

https://www.4mycash.com

4MYCASH ST. LOUIS HARD MONEY SCHOLARSHIP

The 4MyCash St. Louis Hard Money Scholarship was created to help students interested in higher education reach their goal of attending college or university. Each year students who have lived in St. Louis, MO, at some point in their lives, will have the chance to provide a short essay. Applicants are asked to explain how their experience living in St. Louis has shaped them as individuals. St. Louis is a dynamic and historic city faced with many challenges, but it is also one of opportunity and growth. We encourage applicants to consider some of those challenges and opportunities in their essay. A committee will select a winner by the end of November. One winner will be selected and receive $1000 towards higher education.

Award: Scholarship for use in freshman, sophomore, junior, senior, graduate, or postgraduate years; renewable. *Number:* 1. *Amount:* $1000.

Eligibility Requirements: Applicant must be enrolled or expecting to enroll full- or part-time at a two-year or four-year or technical institution or university. Available to U.S. citizens.

Application Requirements: Application form, essay. *Deadline:* November 30.

Contact: Mr. Andrew Polsky, Manager
4MyCash.com, LLC
7750 Maryland Avenue
#50004
St. Louis, MO 63105
Phone: 310-764-7656
E-mail: andrew@4mycash.com

A-1 AUTO TRANSPORT, INC.

https://www.a1autotransport.com/a-1-auto-transport-scholarship/

A-1 AUTO TRANSPORT SCHOLARSHIP

The scholarship will be sent directly to the school/university/college financial aid office. 3 awards of $1000, $500 and $250.

Award: Scholarship for use in freshman, sophomore, junior, senior, graduate, or postgraduate years; renewable. *Number:* 3. *Amount:* $250–$1000.

Eligibility Requirements: Applicant must be enrolled or expecting to enroll full- or part-time at a two-year or four-year or technical institution or university. Applicant must have 3.0 GPA or higher. Available to U.S. and non-U.S. citizens.

Application Requirements: Essay. *Deadline:* March 10.

Contact: Joe Webster
       Phone: 831-778-4529
       E-mail: scholarships@a1autotransport.com

ACADGILD

https://acadgild.com

ACADGILD MERIT-BASED SCHOLARSHIPS

AcadGild believes that accessing affordable and convenient eLearning options for upskilling is the smartest way to beat the high costs associated with traditional learning resulting in eventual massive college dropout rates. To make things easier for meritorious students and their families, AcadGild has decided to award $10,000 annually in scholarships to students signing up for its courses in Technology, Analytics, Design, and Digital Marketing. The majority of the scholarships are partial-course fee awards. A limited number of full-course fee awards to are also given to highly motivated students.

Award: Scholarship for use in freshman, sophomore, junior, senior, or graduate years; renewable. *Number:* 200–1000. *Amount:* $200–$1000.

Eligibility Requirements: Applicant must be hearing impaired, learning disabled, physically disabled, or visually impaired; American Indian/Alaska Native, Asian/Pacific Islander, Black (non-Hispanic), Hispanic; age 13-65 and enrolled or expecting to enroll full- or part-time at a technical institution or university. Applicant must be hearing impaired, learning disabled, physically disabled, or visually impaired. Available to U.S. and non-U.S. citizens. Applicant or parent must meet one or more of the following requirements: general military experience; retired from active duty; disabled or killed as a result of military service; prisoner of war; or missing in action.

Application Requirements: Essay. *Deadline:* December 31.

Contact: Kuldeeplore Sharma
       AcadGild
       340 S Lemon Ave #9212
       Walnut 91789
       Phone: 888-884-8355
       E-mail: kuldeep@acadgild.com

ACES: THE SOCIETY FOR EDITING

https://aceseditors.org/

BILL WALSH SCHOLARSHIP

The Walsh Scholarship will make its first award in early 2018 (and annually after that) to an applicant who demonstrates the talent and passion for language that Bill Walsh devoted his life to and who aspires to pursue the craft of editing the news.

Award: Scholarship for use in junior, senior, or graduate years; not renewable. *Number:* 1. *Amount:* $3000.

Eligibility Requirements: Applicant must be enrolled or expecting to enroll full-time at a four-year institution or university. Available to U.S. and non-U.S. citizens.

Application Requirements: Application form, essay. *Deadline:* November 15.

Contact: Mr. Alex Cruden
       E-mail: alex@aceseditors.org

AIR TRAFFIC CONTROL ASSOCIATION INC.

http://www.atca.org/

AIR TRAFFIC CONTROL ASSOCIATION SCHOLARSHIP

Scholarships for students in programs leading to a bachelor's degree or higher in aviation-related courses of study, and for full-time employees engaged in advanced study to improve their skills in air traffic control or aviation. Visit website for additional information http://www.atca.org.

Award: Scholarship for use in freshman, sophomore, junior, senior, graduate, or postgraduate years; not renewable. *Number:* 7–12. *Amount:* $2000–$10,000.

Eligibility Requirements: Applicant must be enrolled or expecting to enroll full- or part-time at a two-year or four-year institution or university and must have an interest in aviation. Applicant or parent of applicant must have employment or volunteer experience in air traffic control. Available to U.S. and non-U.S. citizens.

Application Requirements: Application form, essay, financial need analysis. *Deadline:* May 1.

Contact: Tim Wagner, Membership Manager
       Air Traffic Control Association Inc.
       1101 King Street, Suite 300
       Alexandria, VA 22314
       Phone: 703-299-2430
       E-mail: info@atca.org

BUCKINGHAM MEMORIAL SCHOLARSHIP

Scholarships granted to children of air traffic control specialists pursuing a bachelor's degree or higher in any course of study. Must be the child, natural or by adoption, of a person serving, or having served as an air traffic control specialist, be it with the U.S. government, U.S. military, or in a private facility in the United States.

Award: Scholarship for use in freshman, sophomore, junior, senior, or graduate years; not renewable. *Number:* 1–4. *Amount:* $2000–$10,000.

Eligibility Requirements: Applicant must be enrolled or expecting to enroll full- or part-time at a four-year institution or university. Applicant or parent of applicant must have employment or volunteer experience in air traffic control. Available to U.S. citizens.

Application Requirements: Application form, community service, essay, financial need analysis, personal photograph. *Deadline:* May 1.

Contact: Tim Wagner, Membership Manager
       Air Traffic Control Association Inc.
       1101 King Street
       Suite 300
       Alexandria, VA 22314
       Phone: 703-299-2430 Ext. 314
       E-mail: info@atca.org

ALABAMA SOCIETY OF CERTIFIED PUBLIC ACCOUNTANTS

http://www.ascpa.org/

ASCPA EDUCATIONAL FOUNDATION SCHOLARSHIP

Scholarships available for students with a declared major in accounting. Must have completed intermediate accounting courses (I and II) with a 3.0 average in all accounting courses, and a 3.0 average overall. Available for fourth or fifth year of study. Must be U.S. citizen or hold permanent resident status. Must have one full year of study remaining. 300 word essay.

Award: Scholarship for use in senior or graduate years; not renewable. *Number:* 34–38. *Amount:* $1500–$2500.

Eligibility Requirements: Applicant must be enrolled or expecting to enroll full-time at a four-year institution or university; resident of Alabama and studying in Alabama. Applicant must have 3.0 GPA or higher. Available to U.S. citizens.

Application Requirements: Application form, essay. *Deadline:* March 16.

Contact: Ms. Diane Christy, Vice President of Communications
       Alabama Society of Certified Public Accountants
       1041 Longfield Court
       Montgomery, AL 36117
       Phone: 334-386-5752
       E-mail: dchristy@ascpa.org

ALERTONE SERVICES, LLC

https://www.alert-1.com/

ALERT1 STUDENT FOR SENIORS SCHOLARSHIP

Plan to help seniors in the future? You could be grandma's caregiver or the next great innovator for seniors. Whether you're pursuing technology or the arts, you're committed to improve senior care. To reward your hard work, Alert1 wants to give you a helping hand. As America's #1 medical alert, we're all about helping future leaders in senior care. Alert1 is offering a $250 scholarship to a student attending an accredited U.S. college or university who wants to help seniors. To apply for this scholarship, follow the instructions below. Submit the online application form and answer the following three questions (under 300 words each):

What is your experience with seniors? What is the most important lesson you've learned from seniors? How will you help seniors in your chosen career?

Award: Scholarship for use in freshman, sophomore, junior, senior, or graduate years; not renewable. *Number:* 1. *Amount:* $250.

Eligibility Requirements: Applicant must be enrolled or expecting to enroll full-time at a two-year or four-year institution or university. Available to U.S. citizens.

Application Requirements: Application form, essay, personal photograph. *Deadline:* January 5.

Contact: Marketing Associate
AlertOne Services, LLC
1000 Commerce Park Drive
Williamsport, PA 17701
Phone: 800-693-5433 Ext. 6129
E-mail: abigial.delker@alert1.com

ALEXANDER GRAHAM BELL ASSOCIATION FOR THE DEAF AND HARD OF HEARING

http://www.agbell.org/

AG BELL COLLEGE SCHOLARSHIP PROGRAM

Available to students with pre-lingual bilateral hearing loss in the moderate-severe to profound range who attend a mainstream and accredited college or university on a full-time basis. Specific eligibility criteria, submission guidelines, deadline and application available on AG Bell website at http://www.agbell.org.

Award: Scholarship for use in freshman, sophomore, junior, senior, graduate, or postgraduate years; not renewable. *Number:* 20–40. *Amount:* $1500–$5000.

Eligibility Requirements: Applicant must be hearing impaired; enrolled or expecting to enroll full-time at a four-year institution or university; resident of Alabama, Alaska, Alberta, American Samoa, Arizona, Arkansas, British Columbia, California, Colorado, Connecticut, Delaware, District of Columbia, Florida, Georgia, Guam, Hawaii, Idaho, Illinois, Indiana, Iowa, Kansas, Kentucky, Louisiana, Maine, Manitoba, Maryland, Massachusetts, Michigan, Minnesota, Mississippi, Missouri, Montana, Nebraska, Nevada, New Brunswick, Newfoundland, New Hampshire, New Jersey, New Mexico, New York, North Carolina, North Dakota, Northern Mariana Islands, Northwest Territories, Nova Scotia, Ohio, Oklahoma, Ontario, Oregon, Pennsylvania, Prince Edward Island, Puerto Rico, Quebec, Rhode Island, Saskatchewan, South Carolina, South Dakota, Tennessee, Texas, Utah, Vermont, Virginia, Washington, West Virginia, Wisconsin, Wyoming, Yukon and studying in Alabama, Alaska, Alberta, American Samoa, Arizona, Arkansas, British Columbia, California, Colorado, Connecticut, Delaware, District of Columbia, Florida, Georgia, Guam, Hawaii, Idaho, Illinois, Indiana, Iowa, Kansas, Kentucky, Louisiana, Maine, Manitoba, Maryland, Massachusetts, Michigan, Minnesota, Mississippi, Missouri, Montana, Nebraska, Nevada, New Brunswick, Newfoundland, New Hampshire, New Jersey, New Mexico, New York, North Carolina, North Dakota, Northern Mariana Islands, Northwest Territories, Nova Scotia, Ohio, Oklahoma, Ontario, Oregon, Pennsylvania, Prince Edward Island, Puerto Rico, Quebec, Rhode Island, Saskatchewan, South Carolina, South Dakota, Tennessee, Texas, Utah, Vermont, Virginia, Washington, West Virginia, Wisconsin, Wyoming, Yukon. Applicant must be hearing impaired. Applicant must have 3.5 GPA or higher. Available to U.S. and non-U.S. citizens.

Application Requirements: Application form, essay. *Deadline:* March 8.

Contact: Ms. Lisa Chutjian, Chief Development Officer
Phone: 202-337-5220
E-mail: scholarships@agbell.org

ALGAECAL INC.

https://www.algaecal.com/

ALGAECAL SCHOLARSHIP

The AlgaeCal Scholarship originated from the desire to financially assist students in pursuit of higher education as they face the challenge of significantly rising costs of obtaining a college degree. Also, it stemmed from the need for greater focus on the critical issue of health and well-being. With two-thirds of the U.S. reported to be overweight, and one-third obese, more dialogue and solutions are obviously still in need to manage and correct this huge rising health crisis. Applicants will download and fill out an AlgaeCal Health Scholarships Application Form and write an essay up to 750 words, describing "If you could, what, if any, changes to programs, policies, and education etc. would you implement for the general health/ well being of the average modern person?"

Award: Scholarship for use in freshman, sophomore, junior, senior, graduate, or postgraduate years; not renewable. *Number:* 1. *Amount:* $1000.

Eligibility Requirements: Applicant must be age 18-99 and enrolled or expecting to enroll full- or part-time at a two-year or four-year or technical institution or university. Applicant must have 3.0 GPA or higher. Available to U.S. and non-U.S. citizens.

Application Requirements: Essay. *Deadline:* June 30.

Contact: Mr. Philip Wong
Phone: 877-9165901
E-mail: philip@algaecal.com

ALLIANCE FOR YOUNG ARTISTS AND WRITERS INC.

http://www.artandwriting.org/

SCHOLASTIC ART AND WRITING AWARDS

Public, private, or home-school students in the U.S., Canada, or American schools abroad enrolled in grades 7–12 are eligible to participate in the Scholastic Awards in 29 categories of art and wiring. The Scholastic Awards are adjudicated without knowledge of the artists/writers identity using three criteria: originality, technical skill, and emergence of personal voice or vision.

Award: Scholarship for use in freshman year; not renewable. *Number:* 89. *Amount:* $500–$10,000.

Eligibility Requirements: Applicant must be high school student and planning to enroll or expecting to enroll full- or part-time at a two-year or four-year or technical institution or university. Available to U.S. and non-U.S. citizens.

Application Requirements: Application form, essay, personal photograph, portfolio. *Fee:* $5. *Deadline:* continuous.

Contact: General Information
Alliance for Young Artists and Writers Inc.
557 Broadway
New York, NY 10012
Phone: 212-343-7700
E-mail: info@artandwriting.org

ALLTHEROOMS

http://alltherooms.com

ROOM TO TRAVEL - STUDY ABROAD SCHOLARSHIP

University students enrolled in or enrolling in a study abroad program with their university must submit a 600-800 worded essay on what inspires them to travel and the benefits they stand to gain from their study abroad experience. Winning submission receives $1,000 to be used on study abroad costs. Submissions must be received no later than August 1st, 2018 and winner will be announced prior to the 2018 Fall semester. Eligible students have U.S. citizenship or residency and is enrolled in or enrolling in a study abroad program at an accredited university.

Award: Prize for use in freshman, sophomore, junior, or senior years; renewable. *Number:* 1. *Amount:* $1000.

Eligibility Requirements: Applicant must be enrolled or expecting to enroll full-time at a four-year institution or university. Available to U.S. citizens.

Application Requirements: Essay. *Deadline:* August 1.

Contact: Victor Bosselaar
AllTheRooms
712 5th Avenue, 14th FL
New York, NY 10019
Phone: 203-561-9767
E-mail: victor.bosselaar@gmail.com

ALZHEIMER'S FOUNDATION OF AMERICA

https://alzfdn.org/

AFA TEENS FOR ALZHEIMER'S AWARENESS COLLEGE SCHOLARSHIP

Alzheimer's disease doesn't just affect the people who have been diagnosed with it; it also affects their loved ones, caregivers and people of all ages, including children. Each year, AFA holds a scholarship essay contest which asks students to describe how Alzheimer's disease changed or impacted their lives. Whether they've had a loved one with the disease, volunteered or worked as a caretaker or are just passionate about the cause, the next generation of leaders in the fight against Alzheimer's have a story tell. We want to hear it! All high school seniors who are U.S. citizens or permanent residents and plan to enter a four year college/university in 2018 are invited to take part in the 2018 contest. In 2017, AFA awarded $25,000 in college scholarships to students across the country through the program. In addition to the scholarships, the grand prize winner and runners up had their essays featured in AFA's Care Quarterly magazine, which has a national readership of approximately 250,000 people.

Award: Scholarship for use in freshman year; not renewable. *Number:* 25–5000. *Amount:* $500.

Eligibility Requirements: Applicant must be high school student and planning to enroll or expecting to enroll full-time at a four-year institution or university. Available to U.S. citizens.

Application Requirements: Application form. *Deadline:* February 15.

Contact: Sherry Cheng

AMERICAN ALPINE CLUB

https://americanalpineclub.org/

AMERICAN ALPINE CLUB RESEARCH GRANTS

AAC Research Grants support scientific endeavors in mountains and crags around the world. We fund projects that contribute vital knowledge of our climbing environment, enrich our understanding of global climber impacts and support and improve the health and sustainability of mountain environments and habitats. AAC Research Grants are powered by the Alliance for Sustainable Energy and supported by the following endowments: Lara-Karena Bitenieks Kellogg Memorial Fund, Scott Fischer Memorial Fund, Arthur K. Gilkey Memorial Fund and the Bedayn Research Fund. In addition to their relevance, applications are considered in terms of their scientific or technical quality and merit: qualifications of the applicant, strength of the research framework, dissemination plans, merit of the investigation, financial contribution the AAC grant would make to the total research budget. Application Period: November 15 to January 15 each year. Each grant recipient becomes an AAC Researcher, sharing their experiences, lessons learned, and findings with fellow climbers and the research community.

Award: Grant for use in sophomore, junior, senior, graduate, or postgraduate years; not renewable. *Number:* 8–15. *Amount:* $1500.

Eligibility Requirements: Applicant must be enrolled or expecting to enroll full- or part-time at a four-year institution or university. Available to U.S. and non-U.S. citizens.

Application Requirements: Application form. *Deadline:* January 15.

Contact: Anna Kramer, Grants Manager
Phone: 3033840110
E-mail: grants@americanalpineclub.org

AMERICAN ASSOCIATION OF TEACHERS OF JAPANESE BRIDGING CLEARINGHOUSE FOR STUDY ABROAD IN JAPAN

http://www.aatj.org

BRIDGING SCHOLARSHIP FOR STUDY ABROAD IN JAPAN

Scholarships for U.S. students studying abroad in Japan on semester or year-long programs. Deadlines: April 10 and October 10.

Award: Scholarship for use in sophomore, junior, or senior years; not renewable. *Number:* 70–120. *Amount:* $2500–$4000.

Eligibility Requirements: Applicant must be enrolled or expecting to enroll full-time at a two-year or four-year institution or university. Available to U.S. citizens.

Application Requirements: Application form, essay. *Deadline:* April 10.

Contact: Susan Schmidt
E-mail: susan.schmidt@colorado.edu

AMERICAN COUNCIL OF THE BLIND

http://www.acb.org/

AMERICAN COUNCIL OF THE BLIND SCHOLARSHIPS

Merit-based award available to undergraduate students who are legally blind in both eyes. Submit certificate of legal blindness and proof of acceptance at an accredited postsecondary institution, as well as scholarship application, high school or college transcripts and other supporting documents (see directions on http://www.acb.org). Deadline: February 15.

Award: Scholarship for use in freshman, sophomore, junior, senior, graduate, or postgraduate years; not renewable. *Number:* 16–20. *Amount:* $1000–$4500.

Eligibility Requirements: Applicant must be visually impaired and enrolled or expecting to enroll full- or part-time at a two-year or four-year or technical institution or university. Applicant must be visually impaired. Applicant must have 3.0 GPA or higher. Available to U.S. citizens.

Application Requirements: Application form, community service, interview. *Deadline:* February 15.

Contact: Dee Theien, Scholarship Coordinator
American Council of the Blind
6300 Shingle Creek Pkwy
Suite 195
Brooklyn Center, MN 55430
Phone: 612-332-3242
E-mail: info@acb.org

AMERICAN DENTAL ASSISTANTS ASSOCIATION

http://www.adaausa.org

JULIETTE A. SOUTHARD SCHOLARSHIP
• *See page 549*

AMERICAN FEDERATION OF TEACHERS

http://www.aft.org/

ROBERT G. PORTER SCHOLARS PROGRAM-AMERICAN FEDERATION OF TEACHERS DEPENDENTS
• *See page 550*

AMERICAN LEGION AUXILIARY DEPARTMENT OF MASSACHUSETTS

http://www.masslegion-aux.org/

AMERICAN LEGION AUXILIARY DEPARTMENT OF MASSACHUSETTS DEPARTMENT PRESIDENT'S SCHOLARSHIP

Awarded to children of veterans who served in the armed forces during the eligibility dates specified by the legion. The applicant must complete 50 hours of community service during high school years to be eligible for this scholarship.

Award: Scholarship for use in freshman, sophomore, junior, or senior years; not renewable. *Number:* 12. *Amount:* $200–$750.

Eligibility Requirements: Applicant must be age 16-22; enrolled or expecting to enroll full-time at a two-year or four-year institution or university and resident of Massachusetts. Available to U.S. citizens. Applicant or parent must meet one or more of the following requirements: general military experience; retired from active duty;

disabled or killed as a result of military service; prisoner of war; or missing in action.

Application Requirements: Application form. *Deadline:* April 1.

Contact: Ann Fournier, Secretary and Treasurer
American Legion Auxiliary Department of Massachusetts
State House Room 546-2
Boston, MA 02133
Phone: 617-727-2958
E-mail: masslegion-aux@comcast.net

AMERICAN LEGION AUXILIARY DEPARTMENT OF NORTH DAKOTA

http://www.ndlegion.org/

AMERICAN LEGION AUXILIARY DEPARTMENT OF NORTH DAKOTA NATIONAL PRESIDENT'S SCHOLARSHIP

Three division scholarships for children of veterans who served in the Armed Forces during eligible dates for American Legion membership. Must be U.S. citizen and a high school senior with a minimum 2.5 GPA. Must be entered by local American Legion Auxiliary Unit.

Award: Scholarship for use in freshman year; not renewable. *Number:* 3. *Amount:* $1000–$2500.

Eligibility Requirements: Applicant must be high school student; planning to enroll or expecting to enroll full-time at a four-year institution or university; resident of North Dakota and studying in North Dakota. Applicant or parent of applicant must have employment or volunteer experience in community service. Applicant must have 2.5 GPA or higher. Available to U.S. citizens. Applicant or parent must meet one or more of the following requirements: general military experience; retired from active duty; disabled or killed as a result of military service; prisoner of war; or missing in action.

Application Requirements: Application form, essay, financial need analysis, proof of 50 hours voluntary service, recommendations or references, test scores, transcript. *Deadline:* March 1.

Contact: Myrna Runholm, Department Secretary
Phone: 701-253-5992
Fax: 701-952-5993
E-mail: ala-hq@ndlegion.org

AMERICAN LEGION AUXILIARY DEPARTMENT OF PENNSYLVANIA

http://pa-legion.com

AMERICAN LEGION AUXILIARY DEPARTMENT OF PENNSYLVANIA SCHOLARSHIP FOR DEPENDENTS OF LIVING VETERANS

Renewable award of $600 for high school seniors who are residents of Pennsylvania. Applicants must enroll in a program of full-time study. Total $2,400 award.

Award: Scholarship for use in freshman, sophomore, junior, or senior years; renewable. *Number:* 1. *Amount:* $600.

Eligibility Requirements: Applicant must be high school student; planning to enroll or expecting to enroll full-time at a four-year institution or university; single; resident of Pennsylvania and studying in Pennsylvania. Available to U.S. citizens.

Application Requirements: Application form. *Deadline:* March 15.

Contact: Colleen Watson, Executive Secretary and Treasurer
Phone: 717-763-7545
Fax: 717-763-0617
E-mail: paalad@hotmail.com

AMERICAN LEGION AUXILIARY DEPARTMENT OF WISCONSIN

http://www.amlegionauxwi.org/

AMERICAN LEGION AUXILIARY DEPARTMENT OF WISCONSIN DELLA VAN DEUREN MEMORIAL SCHOLARSHIP

• *See page 552*

AMERICAN LEGION AUXILIARY DEPARTMENT OF WISCONSIN H.S. AND ANGELINE LEWIS SCHOLARSHIPS

• *See page 552*

AMERICAN LEGION AUXILIARY DEPARTMENT OF WISCONSIN MERIT AND MEMORIAL SCHOLARSHIPS

• *See page 552*

AMERICAN LEGION AUXILIARY DEPARTMENT OF WISCONSIN PRESIDENT'S SCHOLARSHIPS

• *See page 552*

AMERICAN LEGION AUXILIARY NATIONAL HEADQUARTERS

http://www.ALAforVeterans.org

AMERICAN LEGION AUXILIARY CHILDREN OF WARRIORS NATIONAL PRESIDENTS' SCHOLARSHIP

One-time scholarship for high school children of veterans who served in the Armed Forces during the eligibility dates for The American Legion. The applicant must complete 50 hours of community service during his/her high school years to be eligible for one of these scholarships.

Award: Scholarship for use in freshman year; not renewable. *Number:* 15. *Amount:* $5000.

Eligibility Requirements: Applicant must be high school student and planning to enroll or expecting to enroll full-time at a four-year institution or university. Available to U.S. citizens. Applicant or parent must meet one or more of the following requirements: general military experience; retired from active duty; disabled or killed as a result of military service; prisoner of war; or missing in action.

Application Requirements: Application form, community service, essay. *Deadline:* March 1.

Contact: Kristin Hinshaw, Program Coordinator
American Legion Auxiliary National Headquarters
8945 North Meridian Street
Suite 200
Indianapolis, IN 46260
Phone: 317-569-4500 Ext. 4556
E-mail: Education@ALAforVeterans.org

AMERICAN LEGION DEPARTMENT OF MARYLAND

http://www.mdlegion.org/

AMERICAN LEGION DEPARTMENT OF MARYLAND GENERAL SCHOLARSHIP FUND

• *See page 555*

AMERICAN LEGION, DEPARTMENT OF MARYLAND, HIGH SCHOOL ORATORICAL SCHOLARSHIP CONTEST

Scholarship awarded to winner of the Department of MD High School Oratorical Contest. Applicants must apply at their local Posts and compete in and win their Post, County, and District level competitions for eligibility. The winner of this contest goes on to compete at Nationals for a chance at $18,000 first prize scholarship. For details http://www.legion.org/oratorical

Award: Scholarship for use in freshman, sophomore, junior, or senior years; not renewable. *Number:* 1–7. *Amount:* $500–$2000.

Eligibility Requirements: Applicant must be high school student; planning to enroll or expecting to enroll full-time at a two-year or four-year institution or university and resident of Maryland. Available to U.S. citizens.

Application Requirements: *Deadline:* January 10.

Contact: Russell Myers, Department Adjutant
American Legion Department of Maryland
101 North Gay Street
Room E
Baltimore, MD 21202
Phone: 410-752-1405
E-mail: russell@mdlegion.org

MARYLAND BOYS STATE SCHOLARSHIP

Scholarship awarded from applicants that have graduated from Maryland Boys State program. Applications must be received by May 1st of the Boys State graduate's SR year in High School. Application available at http://www.mdlegion.org/Forms/bsschol.pdf

Award: Scholarship for use in freshman, sophomore, junior, or senior years; not renewable. *Number:* 1–10. *Amount:* $500.

Eligibility Requirements: Applicant must be high school student; planning to enroll or expecting to enroll full-time at a two-year or four-year institution or university; male and resident of Maryland. Available to U.S. citizens.

Application Requirements: Application form. *Deadline:* May 1.

Contact: Russell Myers, Department Adjutant
American Legion Department of Maryland
101 North Gay Street
Room E
Baltimore, MD 21202
Phone: 410-752-1405
E-mail: russell@mdlegion.org

AMERICAN LEGION DEPARTMENT OF VERMONT

http://www.vtlegion.org

AMERICAN LEGION EAGLE SCOUT OF THE YEAR
• *See page 556*

AMERICAN POSTAL WORKERS UNION

http://www.apwu.org/

E.C. HALLBECK SCHOLARSHIP FUND
• *See page 557*

VOCATIONAL SCHOLARSHIP PROGRAM
• *See page 557*

AMERICAN QUARTER HORSE FOUNDATION (AQHF)

http://www.aqha.com/foundation

AQHF RACING SCHOLARSHIPS
• *See page 558*

ARIZONA QUARTER RACING SCHOLARSHIP
• *See page 558*

EXCELLENCE IN EQUINE & AGRICULTURAL INVOLVEMENT SCHOLARSHIP
• *See page 559*

FARM AND RANCH HERITAGE SCHOLARSHIP
• *See page 559*

AMERICAN SAVINGS FOUNDATION

http://www.asfdn.org/

ROBERT T. KENNEY SCHOLARSHIP PROGRAM AT THE AMERICAN SAVINGS FOUNDATION

Scholarship awards range from $1,000 to $3,000 for students entering any year of a two- or four-year undergraduate program or technical/vocational program at an accredited institution. Applicant must be a resident of one of the 64 Connecticut towns within our service area. Minimum 2.5 GPA required.

Award: Scholarship for use in freshman, sophomore, junior, or senior years; renewable. *Number:* 400. *Amount:* $1000–$2500.

Eligibility Requirements: Applicant must be enrolled or expecting to enroll full-time at a two-year or four-year or technical institution or university and resident of Connecticut. Applicant must have 2.5 GPA or higher.

Application Requirements: Application form, essay, financial need analysis. *Deadline:* March 31.

Contact: Heather Hokunson, Associate Program Officer - Scholarships
Phone: 860-827-2572
Fax: 860-832-4582
E-mail: hhokunson@asfdn.org

AMERICAN SCHOOL OF CLASSICAL STUDIES AT ATHENS

http://www.ascsa.edu.gr/

CHARLES M. EDWARDS SCHOLARSHIP

Edwards scholarship is for participation in the ASCSA Summer Session program only. It is not for funding at the student's home institution.

Award: Scholarship for use in junior or senior years; not renewable. *Number:* 1. *Amount:* $500.

Eligibility Requirements: Applicant must be enrolled or expecting to enroll part-time at a four-year institution or university. Available to U.S. and non-U.S. citizens.

Application Requirements: Application form. *Fee:* $25. *Deadline:* January 15.

Contact: ASCSA Committee on the Summer Sessions
American School of Classical Studies at Athens
6-8 Charlton Street
Princeton, NJ 08540
E-mail: ssapplication@ascsa.org

AMERICAN SOCIETY OF SAFETY ENGINEERS (ASSE) FOUNDATION

http://foundation.asse.org

FAMILY SCHOLARSHIP FUND

The Family Scholarship Fund is available to children and spouses of individuals who lost their lives in a workplace incident. Applicants will need to provide incident background and documentation for verification. Applications are accepted on a rolling basis and must be completed online. The ASSE Foundation is grateful for the exceptional service of the men and women who serve in the US military. The Family Scholarship Fund criteria do not include military personnel lost in the line of duty.

Award: Scholarship for use in freshman, sophomore, junior, senior, graduate, or postgraduate years; not renewable. *Number:* 1–2. *Amount:* $5000–$10,000.

Eligibility Requirements: Applicant must be enrolled or expecting to enroll full- or part-time at a two-year or four-year or technical institution or university. Available to U.S. citizens.

Application Requirements: Application form, essay, interview, personal photograph. *Deadline:* continuous.

Contact: Family Scholarship Fund Coordinator
E-mail: assefoundation@asse.org

AMERICAN TRAFFIC SAFETY SERVICES FOUNDATION

http://www.atssa.com/TheFoundation

ROADWAY WORKER MEMORIAL SCHOLARSHIP PROGRAM

Scholarship provides financial assistance for post-high school education to the dependents of roadway workers killed or permanently disabled in work zone construction or maintenance activities within the work zone, including mobile operations and the installation of roadside safety features. Spouses of fallen workers and parents with custody or legal guardianship of surviving children are also eligible.

Award: Scholarship for use in freshman, sophomore, junior, senior, graduate, or postgraduate years; not renewable. *Number:* 2–5. *Amount:* $5000–$10,000.

Eligibility Requirements: Applicant must be enrolled or expecting to enroll full- or part-time at a two-year or four-year or technical institution or university. Applicant or parent of applicant must have employment or volunteer experience in construction, roadway work, transportation industry. Available to U.S. citizens.

Application Requirements: Application form, community service, essay, financial need analysis, interview. *Deadline:* February 15.

Contact: Neil Mullanaphy, Foundation Director
American Traffic Safety Services Foundation
15 Riverside Parkway, Suite 100
Fredericksburg, VA 22406-1077
Phone: 540-368-1701 Ext. 3885
E-mail: neil.mullanaphy@atssa.com

ANCHOR SCHOLARSHIP FOUNDATION

http://www.anchorscholarship.com

ANCHOR SCHOLARSHIP FOUNDATION

Must be dependent child or spouse of U.S. Navy service member (active, retired, or honorably discharged) and meet eligibility criteria which is posted on our website. Dependent child must be pursuing their first Bachelor's degree full-time at a 4-year college or university. Spouse applicants may attend either full or part-time at either a 2-year or 4-year college or university in pursuit of their first Associate's or Bachelor's degree. We use a two part on-line application (eligibility and scholarship). Once your eligibility has been confirmed, you will be given access to the scholarship application. Be prepared to submit sponsor's full name, rank/rate, list of duty stations, home-ports, ship hull numbers, dates served aboard and supporting documentation. Selection based on academics, extracurricular activities, character, and financial need.

Award: Scholarship for use in freshman, sophomore, junior, or senior years; not renewable. *Number:* 35–43. *Amount:* $2000–$5000.

Eligibility Requirements: Applicant must be enrolled or expecting to enroll full- or part-time at a two-year or four-year institution or university. Available to U.S. citizens. Applicant or parent must meet one or more of the following requirements: Navy experience; retired from active duty; disabled or killed as a result of military service; prisoner of war; or missing in action.

Application Requirements: Application form, essay, financial need analysis. *Deadline:* March 1.

Contact: Mrs. Ingrid Turner, Director of Operations
Anchor Scholarship Foundation
138 South Rosemont Road
Suite 206
Virginia Beach, VA 23452
Phone: 757-777-4724
E-mail: scholarshipadmin@anchorscholarship.com

ANKIN LAW

http://ankinlaw.com

ANKIN LAW OFFICE ANNUAL COLLEGE SCHOLARSHIP

Ankin Law understands the financial challenges college students face. Every year we offer a $1,500 scholarship to an undergraduate or law school student who submits the best essay addressing the topic below. The submission deadline is July 15, 2018. Qualified applicants will 1. submit a fully completed application no later than July 15, 2018; be enrolled as a full-time student in an accredited community college, college or university, or an accredited law school or graduate school starting in the fall of 2018; 3. submit their own original work; 4. provide proof of enrollment should his/her submission be selected. 2018 Essay Prompt: Write an essay of 1,500 words or less on the following topic: How can businesses lessen the risk of personal injury to either employees or customers? The Ankin Law College Scholarship for 2018 requires that you submit a completed application no later than July 15, 2018. Applications received after July 15, 2018 will not be considered. Applications may only be submitted through the website. http://ankinlaw.com/aaaa_scholarship/ A submission via any other channel will not be considered. Ankin Law, in its sole discretion will pick the scholarship winner. The winner will be selected from all eligible applications and will be announced on AnkinLaw.com by September 1, 2018. The winning applicant will be notified by email. The funds will be distributed after the winner has been announced and proof of post-high school enrollment has been verified. The winner's essay submission may be published on AnkinLaw.com. The Ankin Law Office College

Scholarship and AnkinLaw.com reserve the right to publish submissions received. Ankin Law has the sole right to resolve any disputes which may arise in the selection of the award winner. There will only be one award allotted.

Award: Scholarship for use in freshman, sophomore, junior, senior, or graduate years; not renewable. *Number:* 1. *Amount:* $1500.

Eligibility Requirements: Applicant must be enrolled or expecting to enroll full-time at a two-year or four-year institution or university. Available to U.S. and non-U.S. citizens.

Application Requirements: Application form, essay. *Deadline:* July 15.

Contact: Mr. Howard Ankin, Partner
Ankin Law
10 North Dearborn, Suite 500
Chicago, IL 60602
Phone: 844-600-0000
E-mail: ankinlaw123@gmail.com

ANTHONY MUNOZ FOUNDATION

http://www.munozfoundation.org

ANTHONY MUNOZ SCHOLARSHIPS

The Anthony Muñoz Scholarship Fund was created by Anthony Muñoz and his family to support greater Cincinnati high school youth in achieving their dreams of attending a local college or university. Applications for the scholarship fund will be accepted starting January 1st, 2018 through May 1st, 2018. Recipients of The Anthony Muñoz Scholarship Fund must meet several requirements to apply for this scholarship. This includes, but is not limited to attending a high school in our greater Cincinnati Impact Area; being enrolled in or entering an eligible greater Cincinnati/Tri-State college or university; and displaying a desire to overcome adversity and demonstrate a financial need. The scholarship fund application and eligibility requirements can be found at http://www.munozfoundation.org.

Award: Scholarship for use in freshman, sophomore, junior, or senior years; renewable. *Number:* 7. *Amount:* $20,000.

Eligibility Requirements: Applicant must be high school student; planning to enroll or expecting to enroll full-time at a four-year institution; resident of Indiana, Kentucky, Ohio and studying in Indiana, Kentucky, Ohio. Applicant must have 2.5 GPA or higher. Available to U.S. citizens.

Application Requirements: Application form, essay, financial need analysis, interview. *Deadline:* May 1.

Contact: Mrs. Victoria Knepp, Director of Marketing and Events
Anthony Munoz Foundation
8919 Rossash Road
Cincinnati, OH 45236
Phone: 513-772-4900
Fax: 513-772-4911
E-mail: vknepp@munozfoundation.org

ARCHITECTURAL PRECAST ASSOCIATION

http://www.archprecast.org

TOM CORY MEMORIAL SCHOLARSHIP

One $2000 scholarship available to college upperclassmen, Master's, and doctoral students. Must be studying architecture and have a minimum 3.0 GPA.

Award: Scholarship for use in junior, senior, graduate, or postgraduate years; not renewable. *Number:* 1. *Amount:* $2000.

Eligibility Requirements: Applicant must be enrolled or expecting to enroll full-time at a four-year institution or university. Applicant must have 3.0 GPA or higher. Available to U.S. and Canadian citizens.

Application Requirements: Application form. *Deadline:* March 31.

Contact: Mrs. Lisa Collier, Meeting Planner/Program Manager
Architectural Precast Association
325 John Knox Road
Suite L103
Tallahassee, FL 32303
Phone: 850-224-0711
E-mail: info@archprecast.org

THE ARC NEW YORK

https://www.nysarc.org/

ARTHUR W. PENSE SCHOLARSHIP

About the Scholarship: One (1) scholarship is presented annually. The scholarship, in the amount of $3,000, is paid in installments of $1,500 per semester. The funds must be claimed within a four (4) year period from the time the scholarship was awarded. Applications will be distributed to interested students by the University's Department of Physical or Occupational Therapy. Students will complete and submit applications directly to The Arc New York. Students must be enrolled in a degree program in physical or occupational therapy and may include a 2-3 month fieldwork program as part of their degree. Individuals currently receiving a scholarship through The Arc New York are not eligible to receive simultaneous scholarships. Student must be a New York State resident and/or attending a college or university in New York State. Submit completed application, signed by the Department Chairperson, and one (1) letter of recommendation from a current academic instructor.

Award: Scholarship for use in freshman, sophomore, junior, senior, or graduate years; not renewable. *Number:* 1. *Amount:* $3000.

Eligibility Requirements: Applicant must be enrolled or expecting to enroll full- or part-time at a four-year institution or university; resident of New York and studying in New York. Available to U.S. and non-U.S. citizens.

Application Requirements: Application form. *Deadline:* January 15.

Contact: Maria Simone
The Arc New York
29 British American Boulevard
Latham, NY 12110
Phone: 518-439-8311
Fax: 518-439-1893
E-mail: scholarships@thearcny.org

ARC OF WASHINGTON TRUST FUND

http://www.arctrustfund.org/

ARC OF WASHINGTON TRUST FUND STIPEND PROGRAM

Stipends of up to $5000 will be awarded to upper division or graduate students at institutions in the State of Washington. Applicants must have a previous history of involvement and future interest in the field of intellectual and/or developmental disabilities. The application can be downloaded from the website http://www.arctrustfund.org/Student-Stipends

Award: Scholarship for use in junior, senior, graduate, or postgraduate years; not renewable. *Number:* 4–5. *Amount:* $4000–$5000.

Eligibility Requirements: Applicant must be enrolled or expecting to enroll full-time at a four-year institution or university; resident of Washington and studying in Washington. Applicant or parent of applicant must have employment or volunteer experience in community service, designated career field, helping people with disabilities, human services, medicine (physician/surgeon), nursing, physical therapy/rehabilitation, teaching/education. Available to U.S. citizens.

Application Requirements: Application form, essay. *Deadline:* March 31.

Contact: Diana Stadden, Administrative Assistant
ARC of Washington Trust Fund
2638 State Avenue NE
Olympia, WA 98506
Phone: 360-357-5596 Ext. 6
E-mail: info@arctrustfund.org

ARKANSAS SINGLE PARENT SCHOLARSHIP FUND

http://www.aspsf.org/

ARKANSAS SINGLE PARENT SCHOLARSHIP FUND

Visit our website for full eligibility and program information: http://www.aspsf.org/scholarships/how-to-apply/

Award: Scholarship for use in freshman, sophomore, junior, or senior years; not renewable. *Number:* 1–2400. *Amount:* $1–$2000.

Eligibility Requirements: Applicant must be enrolled or expecting to enroll full- or part-time at a two-year or four-year or technical institution or university and resident of Arkansas. Available to U.S. and non-U.S. citizens.

Application Requirements: Application form, essay, financial need analysis, interview. *Deadline:* continuous.

ARMENIAN RELIEF SOCIETY OF EASTERN USA INC.-REGIONAL OFFICE

http://www.arseastusa.org/

ARMENIAN RELIEF SOCIETY UNDERGRADUATE SCHOLARSHIP

Applicant must be an undergraduate student of Armenian heritage attending an accredited four-year college or university in the United States. Award for full-time students only. Must be U.S. or Canadian citizen. High school students may not apply.

Award: Scholarship for use in freshman, sophomore, or junior years; not renewable. *Number:* 10–25. *Amount:* $1000–$1500.

Eligibility Requirements: Applicant must be Armenian citizen and enrolled or expecting to enroll full-time at a four-year institution or university. Applicant must have 3.0 GPA or higher. Available to U.S. and Canadian citizens.

Application Requirements: Application form, essay, financial need analysis. *Deadline:* April 1.

Contact: Mrs. Vartouhie Chiloyan, Scholarship Committee
Armenian Relief Society of Eastern USA Inc.-Regional Office
80 Bigelow Avenue, Suite 200
Watertown, MA 02472
Phone: 617-926-3801
E-mail: arseastus@gmail.com

ARRL FOUNDATION INC.

http://www.arrl.org/

TED, W4VHF, AND ITICE, K4LVV, GOLDTHORPE SCHOLARSHIP

One $500 scholarship to a student attending a four-year college or university and possessing an active amateur radio license. Financial need and active volunteer service in the community will be taken into consideration.

Award: Scholarship for use in freshman, sophomore, junior, or senior years; not renewable. *Number:* 1. *Amount:* $500.

Eligibility Requirements: Applicant must be enrolled or expecting to enroll full- or part-time at a four-year institution or university and must have an interest in amateur radio. Applicant or parent of applicant must have employment or volunteer experience in community service. Available to U.S. citizens.

Application Requirements: Application form, community service, financial need analysis. *Deadline:* January 31.

Contact: Ms. Mary Hobart, Secretary
Phone: 860-594-0397
E-mail: k1mmh@arrl.org

ARTBA

http://www.artba.org/

ARTBA-TDF LANFORD FAMILY HIGHWAY WORKERS MEMORIAL SCHOLARSHIP PROGRAM

The ARTBA-TDF Highway Worker Memorial Scholarship Program provides financial assistance to help the sons, daughters or legally adopted children of highway workers killed or permanently disabled in the line of duty pursue post-high school education. Minimum 2.5 GPA required.

Award: Scholarship for use in freshman, sophomore, junior, senior, graduate, or postgraduate years; not renewable. *Amount:* $1000–$5000.

Eligibility Requirements: Applicant must be enrolled or expecting to enroll full- or part-time at a two-year or four-year or technical institution or university. Applicant or parent of applicant must have employment or volunteer experience in construction, roadway work, transportation industry. Applicant must have 2.5 GPA or higher. Available to U.S. citizens.

Application Requirements: Application form, essay, financial need analysis, personal photograph. *Deadline:* April 6.

Contact: Eileen Houlihan, District of Columbia
ARTBA
250 E Street SW
Suite 900
Washington, DC 20024
Phone: 202-683-1019
E-mail: ehoulihan@artba.org

ASIAN PACIFIC COMMUNITY FUND

http://www.apcf.org/

ROYAL BUSINESS BANK SCHOLARSHIP PROGRAM

Royal Business Bank is committed to supporting economically-challenged youth residing in its business service territories to fulfill their dreams of obtaining a higher education.

Award: Scholarship for use in freshman year; not renewable. *Number:* 20. *Amount:* $1000.

Eligibility Requirements: Applicant must be high school student; planning to enroll or expecting to enroll full-time at a two-year or four-year institution or university and resident of California, Nevada. Applicant must have 3.0 GPA or higher. Available to U.S. citizens.

Application Requirements: Application form, community service. *Deadline:* March 28.

Contact: Ms. Karen Fan, Marketing Manager
Asian Pacific Community Fund
1145 Wilshire Boulevard
Suite 105
Los Angeles, CA 90017
Phone: 213-624-6400 Ext. 6
Fax: 213-624-6406
E-mail: scholarships@apcf.org

TAIWANESE AMERICAN SCHOLARSHIP FUND

The Taiwanese American Scholarship Fund is focused on helping economically-challenged Taiwanese American youth fulfill their dreams of obtaining higher education. To be eligible, a student must be 1. a U.S. citizen or U.S. permanent resident (holders of a Permanent Resident Card) and a direct blood descendant of a Taiwanese citizen; 2. a high school senior or first year college student residing in the United States; 3. plan to attend a university or college as a full-time first or second year student in the fall of 2018 in the United States (if selected, high school seniors must submit college acceptance letter for verification); 4. have a minimum cumulative unweighted high school/college GPA of 3.0; 5. have a household income at or below the Federal/State/County Low Income Level (must be able to show 2017 or 2018 tax return should applicant be selected for award). The scholarship is open to all majors. Previous award recipients are eligible to apply as long as they meet the eligibility requirements.

Award: Scholarship for use in freshman or sophomore years; renewable. *Number:* 10. *Amount:* $5000.

Eligibility Requirements: Applicant must be of Chinese heritage; Asian/Pacific Islander and enrolled or expecting to enroll full-time at a four-year institution or university. Applicant must have 3.0 GPA or higher. Available to U.S. citizens.

Application Requirements: Application form. *Deadline:* March 28.

Contact: Ms. Karen Fan, Marketing Manager
Asian Pacific Community Fund
1145 Wilshire Boulevard
Suite 105
Los Angeles, CA 90017
Phone: 213-624-6400 Ext. 6
Fax: 213-624-6406
E-mail: scholarships@apcf.org

ASIAN REPORTER

http://www.arfoundation.net/

ASIAN REPORTER SCHOLARSHIP

Scholarship available to graduating high school student or currently enrolled college student of Asian descent. Must be a resident of

Washington or Oregon and attend school full-time in either state. Minimum 3.25 GPA required. Must demonstrate financial need, and involvement in community or school-related activities.

Award: Scholarship for use in freshman, sophomore, junior, senior, graduate, or postgraduate years; not renewable. *Number:* 2–9. *Amount:* $1000–$2000.

Eligibility Requirements: Applicant must be Asian/Pacific Islander; age 17-40; enrolled or expecting to enroll full- or part-time at a two-year or four-year or technical institution or university; resident of Oregon, Washington and studying in Oregon, Washington. Applicant must have 3.0 GPA or higher. Available to U.S. citizens.

Application Requirements: Application form, community service, essay, financial need analysis, personal photograph. *Deadline:* March 1.

Contact: Jason Lim, Program Director
Phone: 503-283-0595
Fax: 503-283-4445
E-mail: arfoundation@asianreporter.com

ASSURED LIFE ASSOCIATION

http://assuredlife.org

ASSURED LIFE ASSOCIATION ENDOWMENT SCHOLARSHIP PROGRAM

Award for full-time study at a trade/technical school, two-year college, four-year college or university. Applicant must be a benefit member, or a child or grandchild of a benefit member, of Assured Life Association of Colorado. Applicant may reapply each year he/she is a full-time student.

Award: Scholarship for use in freshman, sophomore, junior, senior, or graduate years; not renewable. *Number:* 65–75. *Amount:* $500–$2500.

Eligibility Requirements: Applicant must be enrolled or expecting to enroll full-time at a two-year or four-year or technical institution or university. Applicant must have 2.5 GPA or higher. Available to U.S. and Canadian citizens.

Application Requirements: Application form, community service, essay, personal photograph. *Deadline:* March 15.

Contact: Mr. Jerome Christensen, Vice President
Assured Life Association
PO Box 3169
Englewood, CO 80155
Phone: 303-468-3820
E-mail: jlc@assuredlife.org

AYN RAND INSTITUTE

https://www.aynrand.org

ATLAS SHRUGGED ESSAY CONTEST

Annual Essay Contest on Ayn Rand's novel, Atlas Shrugged, for college/university and 12th grade students. Essays will be judged on whether the student is able to argue for and justify his or her view–not on whether the Institute agrees with the view the student expresses. Judges will look for writing that is clear, articulate and logically organized. Winning essays must demonstrate an outstanding grasp of the philosophic meaning of Atlas Shrugged. For complete rules and guidelines, visit https://www.aynrand.org/students/essay-contests#atlasshrugged-1

Award: Prize for use in freshman, sophomore, junior, senior, graduate, or postgraduate years; not renewable. *Number:* 236. *Amount:* $50–$10,000.

Eligibility Requirements: Applicant must be enrolled or expecting to enroll full- or part-time at a two-year or four-year or technical institution or university. Available to U.S. and non-U.S. citizens.

Application Requirements: Essay. *Deadline:* May 15.

Contact: Anthony Loy, Student Outreach Coordinator
Ayn Rand Institute
2121 Alton Parkway, Suite 250
Irvine, CA 92606
Phone: 949-222-6550 Ext. 269
Fax: 949-222-6558
E-mail: essays@aynrand.org

BARONE DEFENSE FIRM

http://baronedefensefirm.com/

BARONE DEFENSE FIRM WIN BACK YOUR LIFE SCHOLARSHIP

The Win Back Your Life scholarship is open to apply to for any student who is currently enrolled in an accredited community college, undergraduate, or graduate program in the United States. Students who are currently incoming first-year college students and have graduated high school or possesses a GED may also apply. For complete information, please visit http://baronedefensefirm.com/#scholarship

Award: Scholarship for use in freshman, sophomore, junior, senior, graduate, or postgraduate years; not renewable. *Number:* 1. *Amount:* $1000.

Eligibility Requirements: Applicant must be enrolled or expecting to enroll full- or part-time at a two-year or four-year or technical institution or university. Applicant must have 3.0 GPA or higher. Available to U.S. and non-U.S. citizens.

Application Requirements: Application form, essay. *Deadline:* July 31.

Contact: Patrick Barone
    E-mail: info@baronedefensefirm.com

BILLINGS & BARRETT

https://billingsandbarrett.com/

BILLINGS & BARRETT FIRST IN FAMILY SCHOLARSHIP

Being blessed enough to graduate from college, as well as law school, Billings and Barrett recognize that while many people may have the talent and fortitude to go onto higher education, many lack the opportunity to do so simply due to their family situation. And yet, a select number of Americans are able to overcome those obstacles and become the first member of their family to go off to college. But, while they were able to walk the difficult road to get there, there is still a difficult road ahead. With that in mind, to help them on that road, Billings and Barrett are excited to introduce their First in Family Scholarship, designed to support individuals who want to further their education and are the first members of their families to attend college. For more information, please visit: https://billingsandbarrett.com/#scholarship

Award: Scholarship for use in freshman, sophomore, junior, senior, graduate, or postgraduate years; not renewable. *Number:* 1. *Amount:* $1000.

Eligibility Requirements: Applicant must be enrolled or expecting to enroll full- or part-time at a two-year or four-year or technical institution or university. Applicant must have 3.0 GPA or higher. Available to U.S. and non-U.S. citizens.

Application Requirements: Application form, essay. *Deadline:* September 30.

Contact: Peter Billings
    E-mail: info@billingsandbarrett.com

BOUNCE ENERGY

http://www.bounceenergy.com

BE MORE SCHOLARSHIP

Bounce Energy is excited to announce its fourth annual "BE More" Scholarship! The scholarship is open to all high school senior and college students who live or attend school in the state of Texas. The $2,500 scholarship will be awarded to three qualifying students. In order to be eligible for the scholarship, students must meet the requirements below, submit an online application, and write a short essay of no more than 500 words.

Award: Scholarship for use in freshman, sophomore, junior, senior, graduate, or postgraduate years; not renewable. *Number:* 3. *Amount:* $2500.

Eligibility Requirements: Applicant must be age 13-24; enrolled or expecting to enroll full- or part-time at a two-year or four-year or technical institution or university; resident of Texas and studying in Texas. Applicant must have 3.0 GPA or higher. Available to U.S. and non-U.S. citizens.

Application Requirements: Application form, essay. *Deadline:* June 30.

Contact: Scholarship Coordinator
    Bounce Energy
    12 Greenway Plaza
    Suite 250
    Houston, TX 77046
    Phone: 855-4526862
    E-mail: BEscholarship@directenergy.com

BRYAN CAMERON EDUCATION FOUNDATION

http://www.bryancameroneducationfoundation.org/index.php

CAMERON IMPACT SCHOLARSHIP

The Bryan Cameron Education Foundation awards four-year, full-tuition, merit-based undergraduate scholarships to exceptional high school students who have demonstrated excellence in academics, extracurricular activities, leadership, and community service. The Cameron Impact Scholar is unique among their high-achieving peers in their desire to make an impact on their communities and in the world at large. Our Scholar aspires to contribute to positive forces for change and plans to tailor their education to that end.

Award: Scholarship for use in freshman, sophomore, junior, or senior years; renewable. *Number:* 10–15. *Amount:* $20,000–$50,000.

Eligibility Requirements: Applicant must be high school student and planning to enroll or expecting to enroll full-time at a four-year institution or university. Applicant must have 3.5 GPA or higher. Available to U.S. citizens.

Application Requirements: Application form. *Deadline:* September 14.

Contact: Mrs. Amie Lucas, Executive Director
    Bryan Cameron Education Foundation
    8939 S. Sepulveda Boulevard
    Suite 110, #772
    Los Angeles, CA 90045
    Phone: 917-7567798
    E-mail: amie@bryancameronef.org

BUY-RITE BEAUTY

https://www.buyritebeauty.com/

BUY-RITES ANNUAL BEAUTY SCHOOL SCHOLARSHIP

Buy-Rite Beauty will be awarding a $1,000 scholarship to a hairstylist or cosmetology student who best exemplifies our core beliefs. We want to hear about their most meaningful achievement and how it relates to your future as a hairstylist. The contest is open to U.S. residents. No purchase necessary. All participants must have applied to or be enrolled in as full-time beautician/cosmetology students. To apply, students will submit an essay detailing their most meaningful achievement and how it relates to their future as a hairstylist. The essay should be between 500-1000 words. Send a Word doc attachment to scholarship@buyritebeauty.com with your essay submission. The file name should be your full name, state, and date of birth. For example, Chipper-Jones-GA-4-24-1972. All submission emails must contain the student's full name, date of birth, email address, postal address, school they are currently enrolled in and/or applied to, and a phone number to contact. Buy-Rite Beauty will select the winner based on the best essay as determined by our internal panel of judges. Selection criteria will include, but is not limited to: Compelling and engaging description of essay topic; Thematic consistency throughout the submission around the central thesis; Proper spelling and grammar usage throughout the submission. Buy-Rite Beauty will select the winner during the month of December and will announce the winner on the website pending notification of the student and his or her family.

Award: Scholarship for use in freshman, sophomore, junior, or senior years; not renewable. *Number:* 1. *Amount:* $1000.

Eligibility Requirements: Applicant must be enrolled or expecting to enroll full-time at a two-year or four-year or technical institution or university. Available to U.S. citizens.

Application Requirements: Essay. *Deadline:* December 1.

Contact: Scholarships
    E-mail: scholarship@buyritebeauty.com

BY KIDS FOR KIDS, CO.

http://bkfkeducation.com

SALLIE MAE® MAKE COLLEGE HAPPEN CHALLENGE

Students are challenged to creatively answer the question, "How do you plan to pay for college?" Entries can be in the form of a video, photo, essay, song, or poem (be creative!).To enter, answer a few questions then either share a link to your creative entry or upload it. Registration is currently open. The contest launches November 1, 2016 at noon (12:00 p.m.) ET and ends December 31, 2016 at 5:00 p.m. (ET). See website for details, http://www.makecollegehappenchallenge.com

Award: Prize for use in freshman, sophomore, junior, or senior years; not renewable. *Number:* 10. *Amount:* $1000–$15,000.

Eligibility Requirements: Applicant must be age 14-18 and enrolled or expecting to enroll full- or part-time at a two-year or four-year or technical institution or university. Available to U.S. citizens.

Application Requirements: Application form. *Deadline:* December 31.

Contact: Operations & Events Manager
    Phone: 203-321-1226
    E-mail: info@bkfk.com

CALIFORNIA COMMUNITY COLLEGES

http://www.cccco.edu/

EOPS (EXTENDED OPPORTUNITY PROGRAMS AND SERVICES)/CARE (COOPERATIVE AGENCIES RESOURCES FOR EDUCATION)

Renewable award available to California residents and individuals who are exempt from paying nonresident tuition. Individuals must be enrolled as a full-time student at a two-year publicly-funded California community college. EOPS students must fulfill program-specific income and educational disadvantage eligibility requirements. CARE students must be in EOPS, currently receive CalWORKs/TANF, have at least one child under fourteen years of age at time of acceptance into CARE program, be a single head of household, and age 18 or older. EOPS students may also qualify for CARE if their dependent child(ren) receive CalWORKs/TANF cash aid even if the student (i.e., parent) is not a cash aid recipient. Contact local college EOPS/CARE office for an application and more information about supportive services and grants. To locate nearest community college campus, see http://www.cccco.edu/

Award: Grant for use in freshman or sophomore years; renewable. *Number:* 10,000–85,000. *Amount:* $100–$1000.

Eligibility Requirements: Applicant must be enrolled or expecting to enroll full-time at a two-year institution; single; resident of California and studying in California. Available to U.S. citizens.

Application Requirements: Application form, financial need analysis. *Deadline:* continuous.

Contact: Contact local community college EOPS/CARE program.

CALIFORNIA COUNCIL OF THE BLIND

http://www.ccbnet.org/

CALIFORNIA COUNCIL OF THE BLIND SCHOLARSHIPS

Scholarships available to blind student applicants who are California residents entering or continuing studies at an accredited college, university, or vocational training school. Must be a full-time student registered for at least twelve under-graduate units for the entire academic year. Applications must be typed and all blanks must be filled to be considered for scholarship. Applications available at website http://www.ccbnet.org.

Award: Scholarship for use in freshman, sophomore, junior, senior, graduate, or postgraduate years; not renewable. *Number:* 6–20. *Amount:* $1000–$3500.

Eligibility Requirements: Applicant must be visually impaired; enrolled or expecting to enroll full-time at a two-year or four-year or technical institution or university; resident of California and studying in California. Applicant must be visually impaired. Available to U.S. and non-U.S. citizens.

Application Requirements: Application form, essay, interview. *Deadline:* May 15.

Contact: Scholarship Chair, CA Council of the Blind
    California Council of the Blind
    1303 J Street, Suite 400
    Sacramento, CA 95814-2900
    Phone: 916-441-2100
    E-mail: ccotb@ccbnet.org

CALIFORNIA STATE PARENT-TEACHER ASSOCIATION

http://www.capta.org/

CONTINUING EDUCATION-PTA VOLUNTEERS SCHOLARSHIP

• See page 561

GRADUATING HIGH SCHOOL SENIOR SCHOLARSHIP

Available to high school seniors graduating between January 1 and June 30 of the current academic year from high schools in California with a PTA/PTSA unit in good standing. Must be a California resident. Must have volunteered in the school and community volunteer service.

Award: Scholarship for use in freshman year; renewable. *Amount:* $500.

Eligibility Requirements: Applicant must be high school student; planning to enroll or expecting to enroll full-time at a two-year or four-year or technical institution or university and resident of California. Applicant or parent of applicant must have employment or volunteer experience in community service. Available to U.S. citizens.

Application Requirements: Application form, community service, copy of current PTA/PTSA membership card, essay, recommendations or references, transcript. *Deadline:* February 1.

Contact: Becky Reece, Scholarship and Award Chairman
    California State Parent-Teacher Association
    930 Georgia Street
    Los Angeles, CA 90015-1322
    Phone: 213-620-1100
    Fax: 213-620-1411
    E-mail: info@capta.org

CALIFORNIA STUDENT AID COMMISSION

http://www.csac.ca.gov/

LAW ENFORCEMENT PERSONNEL DEPENDENTS SCHOLARSHIP

Provides college grants to needy dependents of California law enforcement officers, officers and employees of the Department of Corrections and Department of Youth Authority, and firefighters killed or disabled in the line of duty.

Award: Grant for use in freshman, sophomore, junior, or senior years; renewable. *Amount:* $100–$13,665.

Eligibility Requirements: Applicant must be enrolled or expecting to enroll full- or part-time at a two-year or four-year institution or university; resident of California and studying in California. Applicant or parent of applicant must have employment or volunteer experience in police/firefighting. Available to U.S. citizens.

Application Requirements: Application form, birth certificate, death certificate of parents or spouse, police report, financial need analysis, transcript. *Deadline:* continuous.

Contact: Catalina Mistler, Chief, Program Administration and Services
    Division
    California Student Aid Commission
    PO Box 419026
    Rancho Cordova, CA 95741-9026
    Phone: 916-464-7268
    Fax: 916-526-8004
    E-mail: studentsupport@csac.ca.gov

CALIFORNIA TABLE GRAPE COMMISSION

http://www.freshcaliforniagrapes.com/

CALIFORNIA TABLE GRAPE FARM WORKERS SCHOLARSHIP PROGRAM

Applicants must be high school graduates who plan to attend any college or university in California. The applicant, a parent, or a legal guardian must have worked in the California table grape harvest during the last season. School activities, personal references, and financial need are considered. Must be a U.S. citizen.

Award: Scholarship for use in freshman year; not renewable. *Number:* 3. *Amount:* $16,000.

Eligibility Requirements: Applicant must be enrolled or expecting to enroll full-time at a four-year institution or university and studying in California. Applicant or parent of applicant must have employment or volunteer experience in agriculture. Available to U.S. citizens.

Application Requirements: Application form, essay, recommendations or references, test scores, transcript. *Deadline:* March 19.

Contact: Scholarship Coordinator
California Table Grape Commission
392 West Fallbrook, Suite 101
Fresno, CA 93711-6150
Phone: 559-447-8350
Fax: 559-447-9184

CALIFORNIA TEACHERS ASSOCIATION (CTA)

http://www.cta.org/

CALIFORNIA TEACHERS ASSOCIATION SCHOLARSHIP FOR MEMBERS
• *See page 562*

CAMP NETWORK

https://www.campnetwork.com/

CAMP COUNSELOR APPRECIATION SCHOLARSHIP

All applicants must be U.S. citizens and current high school seniors attending school in the United States; anticipating completion of high school diploma at time of application; carrying a minimum 3.0 GPA currently. Please create a short, exciting video (3-5 minutes max) that explains your experience as a camp counselor, how you exhibit the 5 qualities above, and how you intend to use your college degree. Upload your video to DropBox.com, YouTube, Vimeo, or another reputable file sharing service (make sure the visibility is set to public). To submit your application send an email to scholarships@campnetwork.com. Please include your full name, school year, name of the college you plan to or are already attending, and a link to your video. By submitting this form you agree to allow Camp Network to use your video for promotional purposes.

Award: Scholarship for use in freshman year; not renewable. *Number:* 1–2. *Amount:* $1000.

Eligibility Requirements: Applicant must be high school student and planning to enroll or expecting to enroll full-time at an institution or university. Applicant must have 3.0 GPA or higher. Available to U.S. citizens.

Application Requirements: Application form. *Deadline:* November 1.

Contact: Andrew Downing
Camp Network
1033 Demonbreun St
Suite 300
Nashville, TN 37203
E-mail: scholarships@campnetwork.com

CARDSDIRECT INC.

https://www.cardsdirect.com/

FUTURE DESIGNER SCHOLARSHIP

At CardsDirect our job is to capture a moment that resonates with our customers and present it through our greeting cards. We want your help designing our next top-selling holiday card and are proud to offer our first-ever scholarship program. Two winners of our Future Designer Scholarship will receive a $2,500 scholarship to a secondary institution of their choice and will have their designs featured as products on our site. Applicants must be at least 17 years old and already accepted or enrolled in this educational organization. One entry per person. Please see the all information about the scholarship here: https://www.cardsdirect.com/scholarship.aspx. Original artwork, photographs, or computer graphics can be submitted online as a JPEG (.jpg), via email. Artwork is open to any 2-dimensional medium, including oil, acrylic, pastel, watercolor, pencil, mixed media, digital illustration and more. Original artwork can be sent by taking a digital photograph or by scanning the image. Artwork must be at least 300 dpi and a maximum file size of 5 MB. You can incorporate text into your card design, but it is not a requirement. We do not need text for the interior of the card. We are looking to expand our holiday card selection with designs geared toward December holidays and seasonal greetings. Here are some ideas to help get you started: winter or mountain landscapes, Christmas themed still life such as ornaments, animals or wildlife in the snow, and Santa portraits. Use your imagination to create a unique holiday card. This giveaway is open to U.S. residents who are 17 years of age and older (proof of age and identity must be furnished upon request). Must be either a full-time student enrolled in a post-secondary education institution (this includes junior colleges and vocational schools) or one that has been formally accepted into such post-secondary educational institution and will begin school within the next calendar year. This giveaway is not open to employees, agents, independent dealers and affiliates of CardsDirect and its agents, as well as affiliates and immediate family members of all such persons.

Award: Scholarship for use in freshman, sophomore, junior, senior, graduate, or postgraduate years; not renewable. *Number:* 2. *Amount:* $2500.

Eligibility Requirements: Applicant must be enrolled or expecting to enroll full- or part-time at a two-year or four-year or technical institution or university. Available to U.S. citizens.

Application Requirements: *Deadline:* November 1.

Contact: Leah Sanchez, Brand Manager
CardsDirect Inc.
12750 Merit Drive
Suite 900
Dallas, TX 75251
Phone: 866-700 Ext. 5030
E-mail: scholarship@cardsdirect.com

CARING.COM

http://caring.com

CARING.COM STUDENT-CAREGIVER BI-ANNUAL SCHOLARSHIP

There are two deadlines for this scholarship every calendar year, one in December and one over the summer. The application can always be found at caring.com/scholarship. Additionally, previous winners' submissions can be found at caring.com/scholars. We encourage applicants to view previous winners' submissions when completing their own applications.

Award: Scholarship for use in freshman, sophomore, junior, senior, graduate, or postgraduate years; not renewable. *Number:* 2. *Amount:* $1500.

Eligibility Requirements: Applicant must be enrolled or expecting to enroll full- or part-time at a two-year or four-year or technical institution or university. Available to U.S. and non-U.S. citizens.

Application Requirements: Application form. *Deadline:* continuous.

Contact: Daniel Tachna-Fram, Product Management Intern
E-mail: tfram@caring.com

CEDAR EDUCATION LENDING, LLC

http://www.cedaredlending.com

$500 BECAUSE COLLEGE IS EXPENSIVE SCHOLARSHIP

The $500 Because College is Expensive Scholarship is open to all students and those planning on enrolling within 12 months. The winner will be determined by random drawing and then contacted directly and announced on the Scholarship page. Apply online only at cedaredlending.com

Award: Scholarship for use in freshman, sophomore, junior, senior, graduate, or postgraduate years; not renewable. *Number:* 2. *Amount:* $500.

Eligibility Requirements: Applicant must be enrolled or expecting to enroll full- or part-time at a two-year or four-year institution or university. Available to U.S. citizens.

Application Requirements: Application form. *Deadline:* continuous.

Contact: John Kara
Cedar Education Lending, LLC
82 Donnybrook Dr
Demarest, NJ 07627
E-mail: john@cedaredlending.com

CENTER FOR REINTEGRATION

http://www.reintegration.com

BAER REINTEGRATION SCHOLARSHIP

The goal of the Baer Reintegration Scholarship is to help people with schizophrenia, schizoaffective disorder or bipolar disorder acquire the educational and vocational skills necessary to reintegrate into society, secure jobs, and regain their lives

Award: Scholarship for use in freshman, sophomore, junior, senior, graduate, or postgraduate years; renewable. *Number:* 20–30. *Amount:* $1000–$30,000.

Eligibility Requirements: Applicant must be enrolled or expecting to enroll full- or part-time at a two-year or four-year or technical institution or university. Available to U.S. citizens.

Application Requirements: Application form, essay, financial need analysis. *Deadline:* January 31.

Contact: Baer Reintegration Scholarship
Center for Reintegration
PO Box 35218
Phildelphia, PA 19128
E-mail: baerscholarships@reintegration.com

CENTRAL SCHOLARSHIP

http://www.central-scholarship.org

LESSANS FAMILY SCHOLARSHIP

Scholarship available for Jewish students from Maryland who attend undergraduate colleges, universities or vocational schools full-time. Students can attend any accredited U.S. college or university. Awards are based on need and merit. The scholarship committee determines award amounts. For more information, visit website http://www.centralsb.org.

Award: Scholarship for use in freshman year; renewable. *Number:* 2. *Amount:* $2000.

Eligibility Requirements: Applicant must be Jewish; of Jewish heritage; high school student; planning to enroll or expecting to enroll full-time at a two-year or four-year institution or university and resident of Maryland. Applicant must have 3.0 GPA or higher. Available to U.S. citizens.

Application Requirements: Application form, essay, financial need analysis, interview. *Deadline:* April 1.

Contact: Angela Harrison, Program Manager
Phone: 410-415-5558
Fax: 410-415-5501
E-mail: aharrison@central-scholarship.org

STRAUS SCHOLARSHIP PROGRAM FOR UNDERGRADUATE EDUCATION

Scholarship provides assistance to Maryland residents who are full-time undergraduate students in their sophomore, junior, or senior years at an accredited college or university. Renewable grants of up to $5000 each per year will be awarded. If the recipient graduates within four years with a cumulative GPA of 3.0 or higher, an additional $5000 grant will be awarded to apply toward student loan debt.

Award: Scholarship for use in sophomore, junior, or senior years; renewable. *Number:* 5–8. *Amount:* $2500–$5000.

Eligibility Requirements: Applicant must be enrolled or expecting to enroll full-time at a four-year institution or university and resident of Maryland. Applicant must have 3.0 GPA or higher. Available to U.S. citizens.

Application Requirements: Application form, essay, financial need analysis, interview. *Deadline:* April 1.

Contact: Angela Harrison, Program Manager
Phone: 410-415-5558
Fax: 410-415-5501
E-mail: aharrison@central-scholarship.org

CGTRADER

https://www.cgtrader.com/

ANNUAL CGTRADER SCHOLARSHIP

Each semester CGTrader challenges students to dig into the field of technology writing an essay on how innovative technologies are transforming our lives. Enter the CGTrader Scholarship challenge to win $3,000 for your education bills. The best submission will be awarded $2,000 while the two runners-up will receive $500 each. How to enter? Write and submit an original essay on the topic "The future of technology in education." Visit our scholarship website at https://www.cgtrader.com/scholarships

Award: Scholarship for use in freshman, sophomore, junior, senior, graduate, or postgraduate years; renewable. *Number:* 3. *Amount:* $500–$2000.

Eligibility Requirements: Applicant must be high school student; age 18-99; planning to enroll or expecting to enroll full- or part-time at a two-year or four-year or technical institution or university; resident of Alabama, Alaska, Alberta, Arizona, Arkansas, British Columbia, California, Colorado, Connecticut, Delaware, District of Columbia, Florida, Georgia, Guam, Hawaii, Idaho, Illinois, Indiana, Iowa, Kansas, Kentucky, Louisiana, Maine, Manitoba, Maryland, Massachusetts, Michigan, Minnesota, Mississippi, Missouri, Montana, Nebraska, Nevada, New Brunswick, Newfoundland, New Hampshire, New Jersey, New Mexico, New York, North Carolina, North Dakota, Northwest Territories, Nova Scotia, Ohio, Oklahoma, Ontario, Oregon, Pennsylvania, Prince Edward Island, Puerto Rico, Quebec, Rhode Island, Saskatchewan, South Carolina, South Dakota, Tennessee, Texas, Utah, Vermont, Virginia, Washington, West Virginia, Wisconsin, Wyoming, Yukon and studying in Alabama, Alaska, Alberta, Arizona, Arkansas, British Columbia, California, Colorado, Connecticut, Delaware, District of Columbia, Florida, Georgia, Guam, Hawaii, Idaho, Illinois, Indiana, Iowa, Kansas, Kentucky, Louisiana, Maine, Manitoba, Maryland, Massachusetts, Michigan, Minnesota, Mississippi, Missouri, Montana, Nebraska, Nevada, New Brunswick, Newfoundland, New Hampshire, New Jersey, New Mexico, New York, North Carolina, North Dakota, Northwest Territories, Nova Scotia, Ohio, Oklahoma, Ontario, Oregon, Pennsylvania, Prince Edward Island, Puerto Rico, Quebec, Rhode Island, Saskatchewan, South Carolina, South Dakota, Tennessee, Texas, Utah, Vermont, Virginia, Washington, West Virginia, Wisconsin, Wyoming, Yukon. Applicant must have 2.5 GPA or higher. Available to U.S. and non-U.S. citizens.

Application Requirements: Essay. *Deadline:* June 1.

Contact: Laura Paskauskaite, Scholarship Administrator
CGTrader
Antakalnio st. 17
Vilnius 10312
E-mail: laura@cgtrader.com

CHARLES E. BOYK LAW OFFICES, LLC

https://www.charlesboyk-law.com/

BOYK LAW VETERAN SCHOLARSHIP

As part of our Military Messages campaign, the Ohio car accident lawyers of Charles E. Boyk Law Offices, LLC are pleased to announce its first annual 2015 US Veteran Scholarship for college students. The personal injury law firm located in Toledo, Ohio represents victims of car accidents, motorcycle accidents, defective drug and medical device cases, nursing home neglect cases, dog bite injuries, and all other personal injury accident matters throughout the entire state. The scholarship has been created as part of Boyk Law's continued commitment to the service men and women of the United States Armed Forces and their continuing education. The Veteran Scholarship is $2,000.00 and will be awarded to a student who is currently attending an accredited college or university, who has either served in the Armed Forces or is the child of a US Veteran. For more information, please visit: https://www.charlesboyk-law.com/#scholarship

Award: Scholarship for use in freshman, sophomore, junior, senior, graduate, or postgraduate years; not renewable. *Number:* 1. *Amount:* $2000.

Eligibility Requirements: Applicant must be enrolled or expecting to enroll full- or part-time at a two-year or four-year or technical institution or university. Applicant must have 3.0 GPA or higher. Available to U.S. citizens. Applicant must have general military experience.

Application Requirements: Application form, essay. *Deadline:* May 15.

Contact: Charles Boyk
E-mail: SEO@charlesboyk-law.com

CHRISTIAN COMMUNITY CREDIT UNION

https://www.mycccu.com/

SCHOLARSHIPS FOR SUCCESS

Christian Community Credit Union's 2018 Scholarships for Success Program is awarding $60,000 in scholarships. Awardees will receive multi-year scholarships of $1,000 per year! The scholarship program is open to members of Christian Community Credit Union with a Checking Account (newly-opened or existing). The scholarship application deadline is March 31, 2018 and scholarships will be awarded by mid-May. For a scholarship application and/or Credit Union membership information, please call 800.347.CCCU (2228) or visit http://www.myCCCU.com/scholarship.

Award: Scholarship for use in freshman, sophomore, junior, senior, graduate, or postgraduate years; renewable. *Number:* 60. *Amount:* $1000.

Eligibility Requirements: Applicant must be Christian and enrolled or expecting to enroll full-time at a two-year or four-year or technical institution or university. Available to U.S. citizens.

Application Requirements: Application form, community service, driver's license, essay. *Deadline:* March 31.

Contact: Marketing
Phone: 800-347-2228
E-mail: info@mycccu.com

CHRISTIAN RECORD SERVICES INC.

http://www.christianrecord.org

ANNE LOWE SCHOLARSHIPS

One-time award for legally blind or blind college undergraduates. Submit application, essay-autobiography, photo, references, and financial information by April 1.

Award: Scholarship for use in freshman, sophomore, junior, or senior years; not renewable. *Number:* 1–5. *Amount:* $1000.

Eligibility Requirements: Applicant must be visually impaired and enrolled or expecting to enroll full-time at a four-year institution or university. Applicant must be visually impaired. Available to U.S. citizens.

Application Requirements: Application form, autobiography, driver's license, essay, financial need analysis, personal photograph. *Deadline:* April 1.

Contact: Mrs. Taumi Baker, Asst. to the President
Christian Record Services Inc.
PO Box 6097
Lincoln, NE 68506
Phone: 402-488-0981 Ext. 240
E-mail: taumi.baker@christianrecord.org

CHURCH HILL CLASSICS

http://www.diplomaframe.com/

FRAME MY FUTURE SCHOLARSHIP CONTEST

Submit an original creation that communicates: This is how I want to Frame My Future. Some examples of creative entry pieces are: photos, collages, drawings, poem, painting, graphic design piece, short typed essay, or anything you can create in an image.

Award: Scholarship for use in freshman, sophomore, junior, senior, graduate, or postgraduate years; not renewable. *Number:* 1–3. *Amount:* $500–$5000.

Eligibility Requirements: Applicant must be enrolled or expecting to enroll full-time at a two-year or four-year or technical institution or university. Available to U.S. citizens.

Application Requirements: Application form. *Deadline:* March 1.

Contact: Chris Angelone, Digital Marketing Associate
Church Hill Classics
594 Pepper Street
Monroe, CT 06468
Phone: 203-268-1598 Ext. 186
E-mail: christopher@diplomaframe.com

CLARA LIONEL FOUNDATION

http://claralionelfoundation.org

CLARA LIONEL FOUNDATION GLOBAL SCHOLARSHIP PROGRAM

Applicants to the Clara Lionel Foundation Global Scholarship Program must be a citizen or native of Brazil, Barbados, Cuba, Haiti, Grenada, Guyana, or Jamaica. Applicants must have been born in one of these countries as part of the application you will need to provide a copy of your birth certificate. Eligible to study in the United States and been accepted to an accredited four-year college or university located in the United States. As part of your application, you will need to upload a copy of your acceptance letter. A first time college student (with fewer than 12 college credits unless those credits were earned in high school) planning to enroll in full-time undergraduate study at an accredited four-year college or university in the United States.

Award: Scholarship for use in freshman year; renewable. *Number:* 5–10. *Amount:* $5000–$50,000.

Eligibility Requirements: Applicant must be Hispanic, Latin American/Caribbean citizen and enrolled or expecting to enroll full-time at a four-year institution or university. Available to U.S. and non-Canadian citizens.

Application Requirements: Application form, essay. *Deadline:* August 1.

CLOTHINGRIC.COM

http://www.clothingric.com

CLOTHINGRIC.COM ANNUAL STUDENT SCHOLARSHIP

A strong and prosperous community ClothingRIC is all set to take initiative and showed many levels of involvement in the betterment of society. And to do so, we've initiated a student reward program for students who show exceptional interest in education and have limited resources to carry it with zeal and zest. With the purpose of encouraging this highly praiseworthy value, we are pleased to announce that the winning contestant will be eligible to receive $1000 scholarship for tuition fee. The sole purpose of this scholarship program is to lend a helping hand to students who are going through financial hardships. This scholarship will surely help them to overcome their financial obstacles to a great extent

Award: Scholarship for use in freshman, sophomore, junior, senior, graduate, or postgraduate years; not renewable. *Number:* 1. *Amount:* $1000.

Eligibility Requirements: Applicant must be American Indian/Alaska Native, Asian/Pacific Islander, Black (non-Hispanic), Hispanic; age 18-35 and enrolled or expecting to enroll full-time at a two-year or four-year or technical institution or university. Available to U.S. citizens.

Application Requirements: Application form. *Deadline:* October 31.

Contact: Mr. John Spears
Phone: 004-00441582965165
E-mail: johnlspears@clothingric.com

CODA INTERNATIONAL

http://www.coda-international.org

MILLIE BROTHER SCHOLARSHIP FOR CHILDREN OF DEAF ADULTS

Scholarship awarded to any higher education student who is the hearing child of deaf parents. One-time award based on transcripts, letters of reference, and an essay.

Award: Scholarship for use in freshman, sophomore, junior, senior, or graduate years; not renewable. *Number:* 2–5. *Amount:* $1000–$3000.

Eligibility Requirements: Applicant must be enrolled or expecting to enroll full- or part-time at a two-year or four-year or technical institution or university. Available to U.S. and non-U.S. citizens.

Application Requirements: Application form, essay. *Deadline:* April 1.

Contact: Dr. Jennie Pyers, Chair, CODA Scholarship Committee
CODA International
Wellesley College, 106 Central Street
Wellesley, MA 02481
Phone: 413-650-2632
E-mail: scholarships@coda-international.org

COGBURN LAW OFFICES

http://cogburnlaw.com/

COGBURN LAW OFFICES ANNUAL SCHOLARSHIP

Cogburn Law Offices offers a broad range of services, with an emphasis on personal injury and consumer law. We understand the increasing costs of college tuition is making it more difficult to obtain a college degree for many outstanding students across the nation. Therefore, every year we offer a $5,000 scholarship to a student who submits the strongest essay focusing on a given topic.

Award: Scholarship for use in freshman, sophomore, junior, or senior years; not renewable. *Number:* 1. *Amount:* $5000.

Eligibility Requirements: Applicant must be enrolled or expecting to enroll full-time at a two-year or four-year institution or university. Available to U.S. citizens.

Application Requirements: Application form, essay. *Deadline:* July 15.

Contact: Pat McCune, Scholarship Coordinator
Cogburn Law Offices
PO Box 1596
620B Academy Drive
Northbrook, IL 60065
Phone: 847-940-4000
E-mail: pat@marketjd.com

COLLEGE NOW GREATER CLEVELAND, INC.

http://www.collegenowgc.org/

COLLEGE NOW GREATER CLEVELAND ADULT LEARNER PROGRAM SCHOLARSHIP

Scholarship for students pursuing first associate or bachelor's degree in an eligible two- or four-year program. Individuals already having a bachelor's degree are not eligible. Students must be 19 years old or older and must have interrupted the education for at least one year. Applicants must be a resident of Ashtabula, Cuyahoga, Geauga, Lake, Lorain, Mahoning, Medina, Portage, Stark, Summit or Trumbull County. Student must meet income guidelines and maintain a 2.5 GPA. Student must be attending a public or private not for profit institution.

Award: Scholarship for use in freshman, sophomore, junior, or senior years; renewable. *Number:* 100–200. *Amount:* $1000–$4000.

Eligibility Requirements: Applicant must be enrolled or expecting to enroll full- or part-time at a two-year or four-year or technical institution or university and resident of Ohio. Applicant must have 2.5 GPA or higher. Available to U.S. citizens.

Application Requirements: Application form, essay, financial need analysis. *Deadline:* April 15.

Contact: Mr. Robert Durham, Director of Scholarship Services and Financial Aid
College Now Greater Cleveland, Inc.
50 Public Square, Suite 1800
Cleveland, OH 44113
Phone: 216-635-0450
E-mail: rdurham@collegenowgc.org

COLORADO MASONS BENEVOLENT FUND ASSOCIATION

http://www.cmbfa.org/scholarship

COLORADO MASONS BENEVOLENT FUND SCHOLARSHIPS

Applicants must be graduating seniors from a Colorado public high school accepted at a Colorado postsecondary institution. The maximum grant is $7000 renewable over four years. Obtain scholarship materials and specific requirements from high school counselor, or our website (http://www.cmbfa.org/scholarships). One-year vocational grants are also available, usually $1000.

Award: Scholarship for use in freshman, sophomore, junior, or senior years; renewable. *Number:* 6–8. *Amount:* $1000–$7000.

Eligibility Requirements: Applicant must be high school student; planning to enroll or expecting to enroll full-time at a two-year or four-year or technical institution or university; resident of Colorado and studying in Colorado. Available to U.S. citizens.

Application Requirements: Application form, essay, financial need analysis, interview. *Deadline:* March 15.

Contact: Grover Sardeson, Scholarship Administrator
Colorado Masons Benevolent Fund Association
P.O. Box 703
Westminster, CO 80036-0703
Phone: 719-623-5349
E-mail: education@cmbfa.org

COLUMBUS CITIZENS FOUNDATION

http://www.columbuscitizensfd.org/scholarships/scholarships.html

COLUMBUS CITIZENS FOUNDATION COLLEGE SCHOLARSHIP PROGRAM

CCF recipients receive a four-year scholarship that helps underwrite the cost of their college tuition. CCF scholarships, while generous, provide assistance towards tuition but will not cover payment for all school costs. Applications and all support documents must be submitted to FACTS Grant and Aid Assessment in February each year for entering the freshman year of college in fall 2018. Visit the CCF website (columbuscitizensfd.org) for all eligibility information and application instructions.

Award: Scholarship for use in freshman, sophomore, junior, or senior years; renewable.

Eligibility Requirements: Applicant must be of Italian heritage; high school student and planning to enroll or expecting to enroll full-time at a four-year institution or university. Applicant must have 3.0 GPA or higher. Available to U.S. citizens.

Application Requirements: Application form, essay, financial need analysis, interview. *Deadline:* February 17.

Contact: Antonella Recchia, Director, Scholarships/Opportunities Office
Columbus Citizens Foundation
8 E. 69th Street
New York, NY 10021
Phone: 212-249-9923
Fax: 212-517-7619
E-mail: arecchia@columbuscitizens.org

COMCAST LEADERS AND ACHIEVERS SCHOLARSHIP PROGRAM

http://corporate.comcast.com/our-values/community-investment/youth-education-leadership#accordion-2

COMCAST LEADERS AND ACHIEVERS SCHOLARSHIP

Nominees must be full-time high school seniors, must demonstrate a strong commitment to community service and display leadership abilities. Minimum 2.8 GPA required. Must be nominated by their high school principal. Employees of Comcast, its subsidiaries and affiliates, and their families, are not eligible. E-mail for nomination form: comcast@spaprog.com.

Award: Scholarship for use in freshman year; not renewable. *Amount:* $1000.

Eligibility Requirements: Applicant must be high school student and planning to enroll or expecting to enroll full-time at a two-year or four-year institution or university. Applicant or parent of applicant must have employment or volunteer experience in community service. Applicant must have 3.0 GPA or higher. Available to U.S. and non-U.S. citizens.

Application Requirements: Community service. *Deadline:* January 29.

Contact: Executive Director
Comcast Leaders and Achievers Scholarship Program
1500 Market Street, East Tower, 33rd Floor
Philadelphia, PA 19102
Phone: 866-851-4274
E-mail: comcast@spaprog.com

COMMUNITY BANKERS ASSOCIATION OF ILLINOIS

http://www.cbai.com/

COMMUNITY BANKERS ASSOC. OF IL ESSAY CONTEST

Open to Illinois high school seniors who are sponsored by a CBAI member bank. Student bank employees, immediate families of bank employees, board members, stockholders, CBAI employees, and judges are ineligible. Twelve awards are available at $1,000/year for up to four years of higher education; 12 additional one-time $500 awards are also available. For more details see website http://www.cbai.com.

Award: Prize for use in freshman year; renewable. *Number:* 12–24. *Amount:* $500–$4000.

Eligibility Requirements: Applicant must be high school student; planning to enroll or expecting to enroll full-time at a two-year or four-year or technical institution or university and resident of Illinois. Available to U.S. citizens.

Application Requirements: Application form, essay. *Deadline:* February 7.

Contact: Ms. Bobbi Watson, Administrative Ast.
Community Bankers Association of Illinois
CBAI
901 Community Drive
Springfield, IL 62703-5184
Phone: 800-7362224
E-mail: bobbiw@cbai.com

CONNECTICUT OFFICE OF HIGHER EDUCATION

http://www.ctohe.org

GOVERNOR'S SCHOLARSHIP PROGRAM—NEED/MERIT SCHOLARSHIP

This program provides scholarships to eligible Connecticut residents attending eligible institutions of higher education in Connecticut. Eligibility is based on a minimum SAT score of 1800, or a minimum ACT score of 27 and/or top 20% ranking in the students junior year high school class. Applications must be filed through the students high school counseling office. In addition, all students must file a Free Application for Federal Student Aid (FAFSA) and, as a result, have an Expected Family Contribution (EFC) equal to or less than the annual allowable maximum EFC. Both the application and FAFSA must be processed by February 15th.

Award: Scholarship for use in sophomore, junior, or senior years; renewable. *Number:* 1967. *Amount:* $2275–$5250.

Eligibility Requirements: Applicant must be enrolled or expecting to enroll full- or part-time at a two-year or four-year institution or university; resident of Connecticut and studying in Connecticut. Applicant must have 3.5 GPA or higher. Available to U.S. citizens.

Application Requirements: Application form, financial need analysis. *Deadline:* February 15.

Contact: Ms. Lynne Goodwin, Student Financial Aid Consultant
Connecticut Office of Higher Education
450 Columbus Boulevard
Suite 510
Hartford, CT 06103
Phone: 860-947-1855
E-mail: sfa@ctohe.org

ROBERTA B. WILLIS SCHOLARSHIP PROGRAM—NEED-BASED GRANT

This program provides need-based grants to eligible Connecticut residents attending eligible institutions of higher education in Connecticut. Students must file a Free Application for Federal Student Aid (FAFSA) by their college's deadline, if applicable. Students, as a result of filing the FAFSA, must have an Expected Family Contribution (EFC) equal to or less than the allowable annual EFC. There is no application to fill out.

Award: Grant for use in freshman, sophomore, junior, or senior years; renewable. *Amount:* $1–$4500.

Eligibility Requirements: Applicant must be enrolled or expecting to enroll full- or part-time at a two-year or four-year institution or university; resident of Connecticut and studying in Connecticut. Available to U.S. citizens.

Application Requirements: Financial need analysis. *Deadline:* continuous.

Contact: Ms. Lynne Goodwin, Financial Aid Consultant
Connecticut Office of Higher Education
450 Columbus Boulevard
Suite 510
Hartford, CT 06103
Phone: 860-947-1855
E-mail: sfa@ctohe.org

COUNCIL OF CITIZENS WITH LOW VISION INTERNATIONAL C/O AMERICAN COUNCIL OF THE BLIND

http://www.cclvi.org/

FRED SCHEIGERT SCHOLARSHIP

The Council of Citizens with Low Vision International (CCLVI) annually awards three scholarships in the amount of $3,000 each to one full-time entering freshman, undergraduate and graduate college student who are low vision, maintain a strong GPA and are involved in their school and local community. The application process annually opens January 1 at 12:01am eastern and the materials must annually be received by March 1 at 11:59pm eastern. Please see website for details. Scholarship funds will be awarded for the upcoming academic year. To read the scholarship guidelines and complete an online application, please visit https://www.cclvi.org.

Award: Scholarship for use in freshman, graduate, or postgraduate years; not renewable. *Number:* 3. *Amount:* $3000.

Eligibility Requirements: Applicant must be visually impaired and enrolled or expecting to enroll full-time at a four-year or technical institution or university. Applicant must be visually impaired. Applicant must have 3.5 GPA or higher. Available to U.S. and non-U.S. citizens.

Application Requirements: Application form, interview. *Deadline:* March 15.

Contact: Lindsey Tilden, Chair
Phone: 844-460-0625
E-mail: scholarship@cclvi.org

COUPONSURF.COM

http://couponsurf.com/

COUPONSURF ENTREPRENEURS SCHOLARSHIP

CouponSurf understands the importance of entrepreneurship towards building a better future. To that end, we are proud to announce a $1,000 scholarship to be awarded to a student who shows exceptional entrepreneurial skills and passion. The money can go towards financing the student's entrepreneurial idea, tuition for the 2018 fall semester, or towards attending a special entrepreneurial conference or boot camp. This scholarship is open to high school seniors and university students in accredited school programs and is for the 2018-2019 spring semester. Please review the eligibility requirements and application process below and remember, there will only be one winner. All applicants must include your full name, email, phone number, mailing address, 500 to 1,000 word essay; and a recommendation letter from a mentor, teacher or a professor. This scholarship is available to all applicants who meet the following criteria: 1. Must not have a college degree from a 4-year institution; 2. Must be enrolled in a 4-year institution or have a high school diploma. Please submit a 500 to 1,000-word essay in PDF or Word Doc format to the attached submission form along with your full name, address and contact details. We also require an unofficial copy of your high school transcript or college transcript. The essay topic is as follows: We want to hear about your entrepreneurial passion and idea. Therefore, we request you write an essay explaining what the entrepreneurial venture is and what the return on investment could be. In the essay, explain why you would be the best candidate for this scholarship Why do you want to obtain a college degree? And how will this scholarship help you achieve your goals? Alternatively, you can send a video (less than 5 minutes) talking about the venture. Please submit through the CouponSurf.com Scholarship Application Form.

Award: Scholarship for use in freshman, sophomore, junior, or senior years; not renewable. *Number:* 1. *Amount:* $1000.

Eligibility Requirements: Applicant must be enrolled or expecting to enroll full- or part-time at a two-year or four-year or technical institution or university. Available to U.S. and non-U.S. citizens.

Application Requirements: Essay. *Deadline:* December 31.

Contact: Scott Smith, Digital Product Manager
CouponSurf.com
402 Main Street, Suite 100-224
Metuchen, NJ 08840

COURAGE KENNY REHABILITATION INSTITUTE, VOCATIONAL SERVICES DEPARTMENT

http://www.allinahealth.org/couragekenny

SCHOLARSHIP FOR PEOPLE WITH DISABILITIES

Award provides financial assistance to students with sensory or physical disabilities. May reapply each year. Applicant must be pursuing educational goals or technical expertise beyond high school. Must be U.S. citizen and resident of Minnesota, or participate in Courage Kenny Rehabilitation Services. A Statement of Intention essay must be submitted along with application form - http://www.allinahealth.org/Courage-Kenny-Rehabilitation-Institute/Programs-and-services/Scholarship-for-people-with-disabilities/

Award: Scholarship for use in freshman, sophomore, junior, or senior years; not renewable. *Number:* 15–19. *Amount:* $500–$1000.

Eligibility Requirements: Applicant must be hearing impaired, physically disabled, or visually impaired; enrolled or expecting to enroll full-time at a two-year or four-year or technical institution or university and resident of Minnesota. Applicant must be hearing impaired, physically disabled, or visually impaired. Available to U.S. citizens.

Application Requirements: Application form, essay, financial need analysis, interview. *Deadline:* May 31.

Contact: Ms. Leanne Jackson, Vocational Evaluator
Courage Kenny Rehabilitation Institute, Vocational Services Department
Courage Kenny Rehabilitation Institute
MR #78404
Minneapolis, MN 55422
Phone: 612-775-2564
E-mail: leanne.jackson-butala@allina.com

CROSLEY LAW FIRM

https://crosleylaw.com

CROSLEY LAW FIRM DISTRACTED DRIVING SCHOLARSHIP

We understand how challenging it can be to finance a college education, especially while juggling classes, work, extra-curricular activities, and more. To help students get some relief and focus on their education, Crosley Law Firm is proud to offer a $500 scholarship twice a year to a currently enrolled college student or high school senior. The focus of the scholarship is distracted driving. Every single day, distracted driving kills 8 and injures 1,161 people nationwide, according to the Centers for Disease Control and Prevention. These staggering and eye-opening statistics are why we advocate for safe driving habits and why we are offering this scholarship. Applicants must have a 3.0 or higher GPA to apply. In order to apply, scholarship applicants must submit the following materials at the time of submission: confirmation of enrollment at a community college or 4-year institution, and an essay that is between 750 and 2,000 words in length and discusses how distracted driving has impacted your life. The scholarship is offered twice per year, and applications are accepted year-round. The two deadlines each year are: December 31 at 11:59 p.m. and June 30 at 11:59 p.m. https://crosleylaw.com/500-scholarship-college-student-high-school-senior-national/

Award: Scholarship for use in freshman, sophomore, junior, senior, graduate, or postgraduate years; renewable. *Number:* 2. *Amount:* $500.

Eligibility Requirements: Applicant must be enrolled or expecting to enroll full- or part-time at a two-year or four-year institution or university. Applicant must have 3.0 GPA or higher. Available to U.S. citizens.

Application Requirements: Application form, essay. *Deadline:* continuous.

Contact: Chip LaFleur, Marketing Manager
Crosley Law Firm
2632 Broadway St
Suite 101 South
San Antonio, TX 78215
Phone: 210-529 Ext. 3000
Fax: 210-444 Ext. 1561
E-mail: info@crosleylawscholarship.com

CSA MEDICAL SUPPLY

https://csamedicalsupply.com

CSA MEDICAL SUPPLY COLLEGE SCHOLARSHIP

CSA Medical Supply.com is excited to offer our inaugural college scholarship designed to aid college students with mobility disabilities in their academic endeavors. One student will be awarded a $500 scholarship. In order to qualify for this scholarship you must submit an essay, poem, or short story about the chosen topic "Personnel Challenge". This scholarship is open to all students with mobility disabilities enrolled at an accredited 4-year institution.

Award: Scholarship for use in freshman, sophomore, junior, or senior years; renewable. *Number:* 1. *Amount:* $500.

Eligibility Requirements: Applicant must be physically disabled and enrolled or expecting to enroll full-time at a four-year institution or university. Applicant must be physically disabled. Applicant must have 3.0 GPA or higher. Available to U.S. citizens.

Application Requirements: Essay. *Deadline:* May 30.

Contact: Aaron Kish, Director of Marking
CSA Medical Supply
725 N HWY A1A
STE A106
Jupiter, FL 33477
Phone: 561-203-2191 Ext. 7018
Fax: 561-203-7932
E-mail: scholarships@csamedicalsupply.com

DANIELS FUND

http://www.danielsfund.org

BOUNDLESS OPPORTUNITY SCHOLARSHIP

The Boundless Opportunity Scholarship (BOS) is designed to benefit highly-motivated non-traditional students who recognize the power of education to create a better life for themselves and their families. The scholarship is available at select two- and four-year colleges and universities in Colorado, New Mexico, Utah, and Wyoming. The Daniels Fund, the legacy of cable television pioneer Bill Daniels, awards grants to partnering colleges and universities who then provide need-based scholarships to successful student applicants. The BOS program serves seven non-traditional student populations, and is intended to help students able to demonstrate the need for financial assistance as they invest in themselves through continued education. Partnering schools choose to offer the BOS program to one or more of these defined student populations: adults entering or returning to college, GED recipients, former foster care youth, former juvenile justice youth, returning military, individuals pursuing EMT/paramedic training, individuals pursuing Early Childhood Education (ECE) certification. Not all schools will offer Boundless Opportunity Scholarships to all student populations; please check with your school.

Award: Scholarship for use in freshman, sophomore, junior, or senior years; renewable.

Eligibility Requirements: Applicant must be enrolled or expecting to enroll full- or part-time at a two-year or four-year institution or university; resident of Colorado, New Mexico, Utah, Wyoming and studying in Colorado, New Mexico, Utah, Wyoming. Available to U.S. citizens.

Application Requirements: Application form, essay, interview. *Deadline:* continuous.

Contact: Laura Steffen, Vice President, Scholar Recruitment &
Selection
Daniels Fund
101 Monroe Street
Denver, CO 80206
Phone: 720-941-4455
E-mail: lsteffen@danielsfund.org

DANIELS SCHOLARSHIP PROGRAM

The Daniels Scholarship Program provides a four-year, annually-renewable college scholarship for graduating high school seniors in Colorado, New Mexico, Utah, and Wyoming who demonstrate exceptional character, leadership, and a commitment to serving their communities. It is a "last dollar" scholarship that pays toward tuition and fees, room and board, books and supplies, and miscellaneous educational expenses. Scholars may attend any nonprofit accredited school in the United States. For more information, visit http://www.DanielsFund.org/Scholarships.

Award: Scholarship for use in freshman, sophomore, junior, or senior years; renewable. *Number:* 230.

Eligibility Requirements: Applicant must be high school student; planning to enroll or expecting to enroll full-time at a two-year or four-year institution or university and resident of Colorado, New Mexico, Utah, Wyoming. Available to U.S. citizens.

Application Requirements: Application form, community service, essay, financial need analysis, interview, personal photograph. *Deadline:* November 30.

Contact: Laura Steffen, Vice President, Scholar Recruitment &
Selection
Daniels Fund
101 Monroe Street
Denver, CO 80206
Phone: 720-941-4455
E-mail: lsteffen@danielsfund.org

DANLEY'S GARAGE BUILDERS

https://www.danleysgarageworld.com/

DANLEY'S GARAGE BUILDERS SCHOLARSHIP

Tell us about a teacher that has inspired you in your life and how that has affected you. Give us an introduction to who you are and how this teacher inspired you to be who you are today and who you will be moving forward. Acceptable essays will be between 700 and 1,000 words long that answer the question, "What Teacher Has Inspired You?". All entries should be sent to scholarship@danleys.com. Each scholarship entry must include a photo of yourself, your phone number, your home address and proof of enrollment/acceptance to a college or university.

Award: Scholarship for use in freshman, sophomore, junior, or senior years; not renewable. *Number:* 1. *Amount:* $1000.

Eligibility Requirements: Applicant must be enrolled or expecting to enroll full- or part-time at a two-year or four-year institution or university. Available to U.S. citizens.

Application Requirements: Essay, personal photograph. *Deadline:* November 15.

Contact: Carl K
Phone: 7084374100 ext. 4029
E-mail: scholarship@danleys.com

DAVID S. WYMAN INSTITUTE OF HOLOCAUST STUDIES

http://www.wymaninstitute.org

JOSIAH E. DUBOIS, JR. COLLEGE SCHOLARSHIP ESSAY CONTEST

This college scholarship essay contest is open to either seniors enrolled in a US accredited high school program, including home schooled students. They may win an award to able applied to their freshman year of college expenses. Students are required to write an essay that describes how you have applied, or would apply, the lessons of the DuBois story to your own life, focusing on core values such as decency, honor, and respect for our common humanity. One entry per student. Essays should be between

500-1,000 words in length. Complete details can be found at: http://new.wymaninstitute.org/resources/josiah-e-dubois-jr-college-scholarship-essay-contest/

Award: Scholarship for use in freshman year; not renewable. *Number:* 1–3. *Amount:* $1000–$2500.

Eligibility Requirements: Applicant must be high school student and planning to enroll or expecting to enroll full- or part-time at a two-year or four-year institution or university. Available to U.S. citizens.

Application Requirements: *Deadline:* June 15.

Contact: Ms. Joanna Goodwin
E-mail: info@mepdn.org

DELAWARE HIGHER EDUCATION OFFICE

http://www.doe.k12.de.us

EDUCATIONAL BENEFITS FOR CHILDREN OF DECEASED VETERANS

Applicant must have been a resident of the state of Delaware for three or more consecutive years prior to the date of application. If the applicant's parent is a member of the armed forces, the parent must have been a resident of Delaware at the time of death or declaration of missing in action or prisoner of war status. Applicant must be a U.S. citizen or eligible non-citizen. Applicant must be between the ages of 16 and 24. Applicant must be the child of one of the following: member of the armed forces whose cause of death was service-related; member of the armed forces who is being held or was held as a prisoner of war; member of the armed forces who is officially declared missing in action; state police officer whose cause of death was service-related; or state employee of the Department of Transportation routinely employed in job-related activities upon the state highway system whose cause of death was job-related.

Award: Grant for use in freshman, sophomore, junior, or senior years; renewable. *Amount:* $10,000–$12,000.

Eligibility Requirements: Applicant must be age 16-24; enrolled or expecting to enroll full-time at a two-year or four-year institution or university and resident of Delaware. Applicant or parent of applicant must have employment or volunteer experience in police/firefighting. Available to U.S. citizens. Applicant or parent must meet one or more of the following requirements: general military experience; retired from active duty; disabled or killed as a result of military service; prisoner of war; or missing in action.

Application Requirements: Application form. *Deadline:* June 4.

Contact: Ms. Juliet Murawski, Program Administrator
Delaware Higher Education Office
401 Federal Street
Suite 2
Dover, DE 19901
Phone: 302-735-4120
Fax: 302-739-5894
E-mail: dheo@doe.k12.de.us

DEMAS LAW GROUP, P.C.

http://www.injury-attorneys.com/

DEMAS LAW GROUP SCHOLARSHIP

Demas Law Group will be awarding $1,000 to a qualifying student who has demonstrated a meaningful commitment to improving their local community. The legal team at Demas Law Group values education, and we're thrilled to offer this scholarship to a deserving student who's not only helping build a better community today, but positively shaping the future of that community for a better tomorrow.

Award: Scholarship for use in freshman, sophomore, junior, or senior years; not renewable. *Number:* 1. *Amount:* $1000.

Eligibility Requirements: Applicant must be enrolled or expecting to enroll full-time at a four-year institution or university. Applicant must have 3.0 GPA or higher. Available to U.S. citizens.

Application Requirements: Application form, driver's license, essay. *Deadline:* May 2.

Contact: Sylvia Zawadzka
E-mail: sylvia@injury-attorneys.com

DEMOLAY FOUNDATION INCORPORATED
http://www.demolay.org/

FRANK S. LAND SCHOLARSHIP
• *See page 588*

DEPARTMENT OF THE ARMY
http://www.goarmy.com/rotc

ARMY ROTC GREEN TO GOLD SCHOLARSHIP PROGRAM FOR TWO-YEAR, THREE-YEAR AND FOUR-YEAR SCHOLARSHIPS, ACTIVE DUTY ENLISTED PERSONNEL

Award for junior year for use at a four-year institution for Army enlisted personnel. Merit considered. Must also be member of the school's ROTC program. Must pass physical and have completed two years of active duty. Applicant must be at least seventeen years of age by college enrollment and under thirty-one years of age in the year of graduation. Submit recommendations from Commanding Officer and Field Grade Commander. Include DODMERB Physical Forms and DA Form 2A.

Award: Scholarship for use in junior or graduate years; renewable. *Number:* 200–400.

Eligibility Requirements: Applicant must be age 17-30; enrolled or expecting to enroll full-time at a four-year institution or university; resident of Alabama, Alaska, Arizona, Arkansas, California, Colorado, Connecticut, Delaware, District of Columbia, Florida, Georgia, Guam, Hawaii, Idaho, Illinois, Indiana, Iowa, Kansas, Kentucky, Louisiana, Maine, Maryland, Massachusetts, Michigan, Minnesota, Mississippi, Missouri, Montana, Nebraska, Nevada, New Hampshire, New Jersey, New Mexico, New York, North Carolina, North Dakota, Ohio, Oklahoma, Ontario, Oregon, Pennsylvania, Puerto Rico, Rhode Island, South Carolina, South Dakota, Tennessee, Texas, Utah, Vermont, Virginia, Washington, West Virginia, Wisconsin, Wyoming and studying in Alabama, Alaska, Arizona, Arkansas, California, Colorado, Connecticut, Delaware, District of Columbia, Florida, Georgia, Guam, Hawaii, Idaho, Illinois, Indiana, Iowa, Kansas, Kentucky, Louisiana, Maine, Maryland, Massachusetts, Michigan, Minnesota, Mississippi, Missouri, Montana, Nebraska, Nevada, New Hampshire, New Jersey, New Mexico, New York, North Carolina, North Dakota, Ohio, Oklahoma, Ontario, Oregon, Pennsylvania, Puerto Rico, Rhode Island, South Carolina, South Dakota, Tennessee, Texas, Utah, Vermont, Virginia, Washington, West Virginia, Wisconsin, Wyoming. Applicant must have 2.5 GPA or higher. Available to U.S. citizens. Applicant must have served in the Army.

Application Requirements: Application form, essay, personal photograph. *Deadline:* December 1.

Contact: Mr. Timothy Borgerding, Scholarship Management Branch
Department of the Army
Building 1002, 204 1st Cavalry Regiment Road
Fort Knox, KY 40121-5123
Phone: 502-624-2309
E-mail: timothy.b.borgerding.civ@mail.mil

ARMY (ROTC) RESERVE OFFICERS TRAINING CORPS TWO-, THREE-, FOUR-YEAR CAMPUS-BASED SCHOLARSHIPS

One-time award for college freshmen, sophomores, or juniors or students with BA who need two years to obtain graduate degree. Must be a member of school's ROTC program. Must pass physical. Minimum 2.5 GPA required. Professor of Military Science must submit application. Applicant must be at least 17 when enrolled in college and under thirty-one years of age in the year of graduation. Must be U.S. citizen/national at time of award. Open year-round.

Award: Scholarship for use in freshman, sophomore, junior, senior, or graduate years; renewable. *Number:* 2000–3500. *Amount:* $10,000–$120,000.

Eligibility Requirements: Applicant must be age 17-30; enrolled or expecting to enroll full-time at a four-year institution or university; resident of Alabama, Alaska, Arizona, Arkansas, California, Colorado, Connecticut, Delaware, District of Columbia, Florida, Georgia, Guam, Hawaii, Idaho, Illinois, Indiana, Iowa, Kansas, Kentucky, Louisiana, Maine, Maryland, Massachusetts, Michigan, Minnesota, Mississippi, Missouri, Montana, Nebraska, Nevada, New Hampshire, New Jersey, New Mexico, New York, North Carolina, North Dakota, Ohio, Oklahoma, Ontario, Oregon, Pennsylvania, Puerto Rico, Rhode Island, South Carolina, South Dakota, Tennessee, Texas, Utah, Vermont, Virginia, Washington, West Virginia, Wisconsin, Wyoming and studying in Alabama, Alaska, Arizona, Arkansas, California, Colorado, Connecticut, Delaware, District of Columbia, Florida, Georgia, Guam, Hawaii, Idaho, Illinois, Indiana, Iowa, Kansas, Kentucky, Louisiana, Maine, Maryland, Massachusetts, Michigan, Minnesota, Mississippi, Missouri, Montana, Nebraska, Nevada, New Hampshire, New Jersey, New Mexico, New York, North Carolina, North Dakota, Ohio, Oklahoma, Oregon, Pennsylvania, Puerto Rico, Rhode Island, South Carolina, South Dakota, Tennessee, Texas, Utah, Vermont, Virginia, Washington, West Virginia, Wisconsin, Wyoming and studying in Alabama, Alaska, Arizona, Arkansas, California, Colorado, Connecticut, Delaware, District of Columbia, Florida, Georgia, Guam, Hawaii, Idaho, Illinois, Indiana, Iowa, Kansas, Kentucky, Louisiana, Maine, Maryland, Massachusetts, Michigan, Minnesota, Mississippi, Missouri, Montana, Nebraska, Nevada, New Hampshire, New Jersey, New Mexico, New York, North Carolina, North Dakota, Ohio, Oklahoma, Oregon, Pennsylvania, Puerto Rico, Rhode Island, South Carolina, South Dakota, Tennessee, Texas, Utah, Vermont, Virginia, Washington, West Virginia, Wisconsin, Wyoming. Applicant must have 2.5 GPA or higher. Available to U.S. citizens. Applicant must have served in the Army.

Application Requirements: Application form, interview. *Deadline:* continuous.

Contact: Mr. Timothy Borgerding, Incentives Division Chief
Department of the Army
U.S. Army Cadet Command
Building 1002, 204 1st Cavalry Regiment Road
Fort Knox, KY 40121-5123
Phone: 502-624-2309
E-mail: timothy.b.borgerding.civ@mail.mil

U.S. ARMY ROTC FOUR-YEAR COLLEGE SCHOLARSHIP

One-time award for students entering college for the first time, or freshmen in a documented five-year degree program. Must join school's ROTC program, pass physical, and submit teacher evaluations. Must be a U.S. citizen and have a qualifying SAT or ACT score. Applicant must be at least seventeen years of age by college enrollment and under thirty-one years of age in the year of graduation. Online application available.

Award: Scholarship for use in freshman year; renewable. *Number:* 1000–2500. *Amount:* $9000–$150,000.

Eligibility Requirements: Applicant must be high school student; age 17-26; planning to enroll or expecting to enroll full-time at a four-year institution or university; resident of Alabama, Alaska, Arizona, Arkansas, California, Colorado, Connecticut, Delaware, District of Columbia, Florida, Georgia, Guam, Hawaii, Idaho, Illinois, Indiana, Iowa, Kansas, Kentucky, Louisiana, Maine, Maryland, Massachusetts, Michigan, Minnesota, Mississippi, Missouri, Montana, Nebraska, Nevada, New Hampshire, New Jersey, New Mexico, New York, North Carolina, North Dakota, Ohio, Oklahoma, Oregon, Pennsylvania, Puerto Rico, Rhode Island, South Carolina, South Dakota, Tennessee, Texas, Utah, Vermont, Virginia, Washington, West Virginia, Wisconsin, Wyoming and studying in Alabama, Alaska, Arizona, Arkansas, California, Colorado, Connecticut, Delaware, District of Columbia, Florida, Georgia, Guam, Hawaii, Idaho, Illinois, Indiana, Iowa, Kansas, Kentucky, Louisiana, Maine, Maryland, Massachusetts, Michigan, Minnesota, Mississippi, Missouri, Montana, Nebraska, Nevada, New Hampshire, New Jersey, New Mexico, New York, North Carolina, North Dakota, Ohio, Oklahoma, Ontario, Oregon, Pennsylvania, Puerto Rico, Rhode Island, South Carolina, South Dakota, Tennessee, Texas, Utah, Vermont, Virginia, Washington, West Virginia, Wisconsin, Wyoming. Applicant must have 2.5 GPA or higher. Available to U.S. citizens. Applicant must have national guard experience.

Application Requirements: Application form, essay, interview. *Deadline:* January 10.

Contact: Ms. Kathleen Barnes, Supervisor, Human Resources Specialist
Department of the Army
U.S. Army Cadet Command
Building 1002, 204 1st Cavalry Regiment Road
Fort Knox, KY 40121-5123
Phone: 502-624-7371
E-mail: kathleen.m.barnes19.civ@mail.mil

U.S. ARMY ROTC FOUR-YEAR HISTORICALLY BLACK COLLEGE/UNIVERSITY SCHOLARSHIP

One-time award for students attending college for the first time Must attend a historically black college or university and must join school's ROTC program. Must pass physical. Must have a qualifying SAT or ACT score and minimum GPA of 2.5. Applicant must be at least 17 by college enrollment and under thirty-one years of age in the year of graduation. Must be a U.S. citizen/national at time of award. Application available online.

Award: Scholarship for use in freshman, sophomore, junior, senior, or graduate years; renewable. *Number:* 20–200. *Amount:* $9000–$40,000.

Eligibility Requirements: Applicant must be age 17-26; enrolled or expecting to enroll full-time at a four-year institution or university;

resident of Alabama, Alaska, Arizona, Arkansas, California, Colorado, Connecticut, Delaware, District of Columbia, Florida, Georgia, Guam, Hawaii, Idaho, Illinois, Indiana, Iowa, Kansas, Kentucky, Louisiana, Maine, Maryland, Massachusetts, Michigan, Minnesota, Mississippi, Missouri, Montana, Nebraska, Nevada, New Hampshire, New Jersey, New Mexico, New York, North Carolina, North Dakota, Ohio, Oklahoma, Ontario, Oregon, Pennsylvania, Puerto Rico, Rhode Island, South Carolina, South Dakota, Tennessee, Texas, Utah, Vermont, Virginia, Washington, West Virginia, Wisconsin, Wyoming and studying in Alabama, Alaska, Arizona, Arkansas, California, Colorado, Connecticut, Delaware, District of Columbia, Florida, Georgia, Guam, Hawaii, Idaho, Illinois, Indiana, Iowa, Kansas, Kentucky, Louisiana, Maine, Maryland, Massachusetts, Michigan, Minnesota, Mississippi, Missouri, Montana, Nebraska, Nevada, New Hampshire, New Jersey, New Mexico, New York, North Carolina, North Dakota, Ohio, Oklahoma, Ontario, Oregon, Pennsylvania, Puerto Rico, Rhode Island, South Carolina, South Dakota, Tennessee, Texas, Utah, Vermont, Virginia, Washington, West Virginia, Wisconsin, Wyoming. Applicant must have 2.5 GPA or higher. Available to U.S. citizens. Applicant must have national guard experience.

Application Requirements: Application form, essay, interview. *Deadline:* January 10.

Contact: Ms. Kathleen Barnes, Supervisor, Human Resources Specialist
Department of the Army
U.S. Army Cadet Command
Building 1002, 204 1st Cavalry Regiment Road
Fort Knox, KY 40121-5123
Phone: 502-624-7371
E-mail: kathleen.m.barnes19.civ@mail.mil

U.S. ARMY ROTC GUARANTEED RESERVE FORCES DUTY (GRFD), (ARNG/USAR) AND DEDICATED ARNG SCHOLARSHIPS

One-time award for college freshmen, sophomores, and juniors, or two-year graduate degree students. Must be a member of school's ROTC program. Must pass physical. Minimum 2.5 GPA required. Applicant must be at least seventeen years of age when enrolled in college and under thirty-one years of age in the year of graduation. Must be a U.S. citizen/national at the time of award.

Award: Scholarship for use in freshman, sophomore, junior, senior, or graduate years; renewable. *Number:* 1000–3000. *Amount:* $10,000–$120,000.

Eligibility Requirements: Applicant must be age 17-30; enrolled or expecting to enroll full-time at a four-year institution or university; resident of Alabama, Alaska, Arizona, Arkansas, California, Colorado, Connecticut, Delaware, District of Columbia, Florida, Georgia, Guam, Hawaii, Idaho, Illinois, Indiana, Iowa, Kansas, Kentucky, Louisiana, Maine, Maryland, Massachusetts, Michigan, Minnesota, Mississippi, Missouri, Montana, Nebraska, Nevada, New Hampshire, New Jersey, New Mexico, New York, North Carolina, North Dakota, Ohio, Oklahoma, Oregon, Pennsylvania, Puerto Rico, Rhode Island, South Carolina, South Dakota, Tennessee, Texas, Utah, Vermont, Virginia, Washington, West Virginia, Wisconsin, Wyoming and studying in Alabama, Alaska, Arizona, Arkansas, California, Colorado, Connecticut, Delaware, District of Columbia, Florida, Georgia, Guam, Hawaii, Idaho, Illinois, Indiana, Iowa, Kansas, Kentucky, Louisiana, Maine, Maryland, Massachusetts, Michigan, Minnesota, Mississippi, Missouri, Montana, Nebraska, Nevada, New Hampshire, New Jersey, New Mexico, New York, North Carolina, North Dakota, Ohio, Oklahoma, Oregon, Pennsylvania, Puerto Rico, Rhode Island, Saskatchewan, South Carolina, South Dakota, Tennessee, Texas, Utah, Vermont, Virginia, Washington, West Virginia, Wisconsin, Wyoming. Applicant must have 2.5 GPA or higher. Available to U.S. citizens. Applicant must have national guard experience.

Application Requirements: Application form, interview. *Deadline:* continuous.

Contact: Mr. Kenneth Suratt, Program Manager
Department of the Army
U.S. Army Cadet Command
Building 1002, 204 1st Cavalry Regiment Road
Fort Knox, KY 40121-5123
Phone: 502-624-1257
E-mail: kenneth.s.suratt.ctr@mail.mil

U.S. ARMY ROTC MILITARY JUNIOR COLLEGE (MJC) SCHOLARSHIP

One-time award for high school graduates who wish to attend a two-year military junior college. Must serve simultaneously in the Army National Guard or Reserve and qualify for the ROTC Advanced Course. Must have a minimum GPA of 2.5. Must be a U.S. citizen/national at time of award. Must also be eighteen years of age by October 1 and under twenty-seven years of age on June 30 in the year of graduation. On-line application available. Must be used at one of five military junior colleges. See Professor of Military Science at college for application.

Award: Scholarship for use in freshman or sophomore years; renewable. *Number:* 110–150. *Amount:* $5600–$52,000.

Eligibility Requirements: Applicant must be age 18-26; enrolled or expecting to enroll full-time at a two-year institution; resident of Alabama, Alaska, Arizona, Arkansas, California, Colorado, Connecticut, Delaware, District of Columbia, Florida, Georgia, Guam, Hawaii, Idaho, Illinois, Indiana, Iowa, Kansas, Kentucky, Louisiana, Maine, Maryland, Massachusetts, Michigan, Minnesota, Mississippi, Missouri, Montana, Nebraska, Nevada, New Hampshire, New Jersey, New Mexico, New York, North Carolina, North Dakota, Ohio, Oklahoma, Oregon, Pennsylvania, Puerto Rico, Rhode Island, South Carolina, South Dakota, Tennessee, Texas, Utah, Vermont, Virginia, Washington, West Virginia, Wisconsin, Wyoming and studying in Alabama, Alaska, Arizona, Arkansas, California, Colorado, Connecticut, Delaware, District of Columbia, Florida, Georgia, Guam, Hawaii, Idaho, Illinois, Indiana, Iowa, Kansas, Kentucky, Louisiana, Maine, Maryland, Massachusetts, Michigan, Minnesota, Mississippi, Missouri, Montana, Nebraska, Nevada, New Hampshire, New Jersey, New Mexico, New York, North Carolina, North Dakota, Ohio, Oklahoma, Oregon, Pennsylvania, Puerto Rico, Rhode Island, South Carolina, South Dakota, Tennessee, Texas, Utah, Vermont, Virginia, Washington, West Virginia, Wisconsin, Wyoming. Applicant must have 2.5 GPA or higher. Available to U.S. citizens. Applicant must have national guard experience.

Application Requirements: Application form, essay, interview. *Deadline:* July 25.

Contact: Mr. Larry Waller, Program Manager
Department of the Army
U.S. Army Cadet Command
Building 1002, 204 1st Cavalry Regiment Road
Fort Knox, KY 40121-5123
Phone: 502-624-7023
E-mail: larry.j.waller.civ@mail.mil

DESERVE MODERN

http://www.DeserveModern.com

DESERVE MODERN SCHOLARSHIP

Deserve Modern Scholarship is open to high school juniors & seniors, all college, and graduate level students. There are no other exclusionary criteria. Applications are rolling (you can apply any time) and finalists will be announced the week of May 1st annually with the winner announced later in May. Apply online at http://www.DeserveModern.com

Award: Scholarship for use in freshman, sophomore, junior, senior, graduate, or postgraduate years; not renewable. *Number:* 1. *Amount:* $250.

Eligibility Requirements: Applicant must be age 16-99 and enrolled or expecting to enroll full- or part-time at a two-year or four-year or technical institution or university. Available to U.S. and non-U.S. citizens.

Application Requirements: Application form. *Deadline:* continuous.

Contact: Craig Brooker
E-mail: deservemodern@gmail.com

DESIGN MY COSTUME

http://designmycostume.com/

DESIGN MY COSTUME SCHOLARSHIP

Design My Costume are offering a $2,000 scholarship fund for U.S. high school students intending to pursue further study in fashion or similar subjects and trades. We understand how the ever rising costs of education are weighing heavily on students, and how taking on part or full time jobs to make ends meet can interfere with the pursuit of your chosen career.

With this scholarship fund we hope to reduce some of this burden and free you up to focus exclusively on your studies. The scholarship fund will be divided up as follows: The winner will receive $1,000, the runner-up will receive $500, the second and third runners-up will receive $250 each. The amount awarded will be paid out as an education related expenditure in the form of either bank transfer or check. We are looking for students to submit essays on subjects related to clothing and sewing, preferably with a focus on embroidery machines, sewing machines, embroidery and sewing combo machines or the latest sewing and embroidery machines reviews. The scholarship prizes will be awarded based on the quality, resourcefulness, and unique content of the essay. More details and reference links are available on the scholarship page of our website. If you are a current high school student intending to study fashion or a similar trade through an accredited university, college or fashion school in the U.S. in 2018, then you're eligible to apply for the Design My Costume Scholarship. If you would like to submit an application for this scholarship, then go to our website, where you will find the application form available for download on our scholarship page. You will need to fill out your name and mailing details, and the essay should be a minimum of 400 words. You will need to attach a copy of your school or undergraduate transcript along with the application. To be considered for this year's scholarship, your application must be submitted by the 30th December 2018. The winners will be made public on the 15th January 2019. The process for accepting applications for the 2018 scholarship will open on the 1st January 2018. By applying for the Design My Costume Scholarship, you will be agreeing to have your name, photograph and essay published on our website, in our monthly newsletter, and on our social media pages, should you be awarded one of the prizes.

Award: Scholarship for use in freshman, junior, or senior years; renewable. *Number:* 1. *Amount:* $2000.

Eligibility Requirements: Applicant must be enrolled or expecting to enroll full- or part-time at a two-year or four-year or technical institution or university. Available to U.S. and non-U.S. citizens.

Application Requirements: Application form, essay, personal photograph. *Deadline:* December 30.

Contact: Denis Lubojanski, Design My Costume Scholarship
Design My Costume
Flat C, 7 Gloucester Street
London SW1V 2DB
Phone: 11-7554447547
E-mail: denislubojanski@gmail.com

DIAMANTE, INC.

http://www.diamanteinc.org/

LATINO DIAMANTE SCHOLARSHIP FUND

Awards for Hispanic high school seniors recognizing their contributions to the community and their leadership qualities. Graduating high school seniors in North Carolina who plan to enroll at North Carolina institutions of higher education, and first-year undergraduates can apply for this scholarship. Must maintain a GPA of at least 2.5.

Award: Scholarship for use in freshman year; not renewable. *Number:* 2. *Amount:* $500.

Eligibility Requirements: Applicant must be Hispanic; enrolled or expecting to enroll full- or part-time at a two-year or four-year institution or university; resident of North Carolina; studying in North Carolina and must have an interest in leadership. Applicant or parent of applicant must have employment or volunteer experience in community service. Applicant must have 2.5 GPA or higher. Available to U.S. citizens.

Application Requirements: Application form, community service, essay, recommendations or references, transcript.

DIBELLA LAW OFFICES, P.C.

https://www.dibellalawoffice.com/

2018 DIBELLA LAW OFFICES, P.C. SCHOLARSHIP

This scholarship is open to graduating high school seniors and current undergraduate college students with a 3.0 or higher GPA who are committed to leaving a mark on the world. The application includes an essay section to tell us about your academic goals and how those goals will help you give back to the community; the introduction is to be 100-200 words, and the essay is to be 500-1000 words. The winner will be announced June 19th, 2018.

Award: Scholarship for use in freshman, sophomore, junior, or senior years; not renewable. *Number:* 1. *Amount:* $500.

Eligibility Requirements: Applicant must be enrolled or expecting to enroll full- or part-time at a two-year or four-year institution or university. Applicant must have 3.0 GPA or higher. Available to U.S. citizens.

Application Requirements: Application form, essay. *Deadline:* May 16.

Contact: Sam Greer
E-mail: sgreer@slsconsulting.com

DISABLED AMERICAN VETERANS

http://www.dav.org/

JESSE BROWN MEMORIAL YOUTH SCHOLARSHIP PROGRAM

The Jesse Brown Memorial Youth Scholarship Program honors former National Service Officer and Secretary of Veterans Affairs Jesse Brown. It is given in memory of a DAV leader dedicated to veterans, through the recognition of those who carry on his legacy of service. This scholarship is awarded to youth volunteers who are committed to serving veterans. Each year, one outstanding applicant receives the top scholarship in the amount of $20,000 to help fund their higher education. In addition, the top winner and parent/guardian receive round-trip airfare (lowest non-refundable fare), hotel accommodations, and per diem for three days to attend the DAV National Convention. The winner will be presented the award and be recognized for their dedication and commitment to veterans. Additional scholarships are awarded annually in the following amounts: second prize of $15,000, third prize of $10,000, fourth prize of $7,500 (two awarded annually), fifth prize of $5,000 (three awarded annually).

Award: Scholarship for use in freshman, sophomore, junior, senior, graduate, or postgraduate years; renewable. *Number:* 8. *Amount:* $5000–$20,000.

Eligibility Requirements: Applicant must be enrolled or expecting to enroll full- or part-time at a two-year or four-year or technical institution or university. Applicant or parent of applicant must have employment or volunteer experience in community service, helping people with disabilities. Available to U.S. citizens.

Application Requirements: Application form, community service, essay. *Deadline:* February 10.

Contact: Ms. Kati Geoppinger, Supervisor of Voluntary Services
Disabled American Veterans
3725 Alexandria Pike
Cold Spring, KY 41076
Phone: 859-442-1012
E-mail: kgeoppinger@dav.org

DISABLEDPERSON INC. COLLEGE SCHOLARSHIP

http://www.disabledperson.com/

DISABLEDPERSON INC. NATIONAL COLLEGE SCHOLARSHIP AWARD FOR COLLEGE STUDENTS WITH DISABILITIES

Essay contest for college students with disabilities who are enrolled as full-time students in a two- or four-year accredited college or university. Length of the essay must not exceed 1000 words. We offer two scholarships per school year.

Award: Scholarship for use in freshman, sophomore, junior, senior, graduate, or postgraduate years; not renewable. *Number:* 1. *Amount:* $2000.

Eligibility Requirements: Applicant must be hearing impaired, learning disabled, physically disabled, or visually impaired and enrolled or expecting to enroll full- or part-time at a two-year or four-year or technical institution or university. Applicant must be hearing impaired, learning disabled, physically disabled, or visually impaired. Available to U.S. citizens.

Application Requirements: Application form, essay. *Deadline:* March 31.

Contact: Michael Corso, Programs Manager
disABLEDperson Inc. College Scholarship
PO Box 230636
Encinitas, CA 92023
E-mail: scholarships@disabledperson.com

DOLLARS 4 TIC SCHOLARS

http://www.dollars4ticscholars.org/

DOLLARS 4 TIC SCHOLARS TOURETTE SYNDROME SCHOLARSHIP

A minimum GPA of 2.5 and a letter of diagnosis of Tourette Syndrome are required. No fee is required to apply. Required components include application, essay, video, FAFSA SAR and financial information, transcripts, letter of acceptance, letter of diagnosis, and three letters of recommendation. Students have the option to apply online and mail in supporting documents (transcript, FAFSA and diagnosis) or complete the entire application process via mailing. Students can find the complete scholarship information by going to our website at http://www.dollars4ticscholars.org/application.

Award: Scholarship for use in freshman, sophomore, junior, or senior years; not renewable. *Number:* 5. *Amount:* $1000.

Eligibility Requirements: Applicant must be enrolled or expecting to enroll full-time at a two-year or four-year institution or university. Applicant must have 2.5 GPA or higher. Available to U.S. citizens.

Application Requirements: Application form, essay, financial need analysis. *Deadline:* April 15.

Contact: Diane Diamantis, President
Dollars 4 Tic Scholars
21801 Little Bear Lane
Boca Raton, FL 33428
Phone: 561-4879526
Fax: 561-4879526
E-mail: info@dollars4ticscholars.org

DOLPHIN SCHOLARSHIP FOUNDATION

http://www.dolphinscholarship.org/

DOLPHIN SCHOLARSHIPS

Renewable award for undergraduate and vocational study. Applicant's sponsor must meet one of the following requirements: be current/former member of the U.S. Navy who qualified in submarines and served in the Submarine Force for at least eight years; current or former member of the Navy who served in submarine support activities for at least ten years; Medically discharged or; died while on active duty in the Submarine Force. Must be single, under age 24.

Award: Scholarship for use in freshman, sophomore, junior, or senior years; renewable. *Number:* 25–30. *Amount:* $2000–$3400.

Eligibility Requirements: Applicant must be enrolled or expecting to enroll full-time at a two-year or four-year or technical institution or university and married. Available to U.S. citizens.

Application Requirements: Application form, community service, essay, financial need analysis, personal photograph. *Deadline:* March 15.

Contact: Mr. Andrew Clark, Executive Director
Dolphin Scholarship Foundation
4966 Euclid Road
Suite 109
Virginia Beach, VA 23462
Phone: 757-671-3200 Ext. 4
E-mail: scholars@dolphinscholarship.org

DOMNICK CUNNINGHAM AND WHALEN

https://www.dcwlaw.com/

DOMNICK CUNNINGHAM & WHALEN ELDER ABUSE PREVENTION

As part of our dedication to achieving a more equitable system of caring for those who have suffered serious harm or who are significantly impacted by nursing home abuse and neglect, we are proud to announce the creation of the Domnick Cunningham & Whalen Elder Abuse Prevention Scholarship. This annual award of $1,000 shall be given to a higher education student who demonstrates an interest in developing legislative solutions to problems of elder abuse and access to care. Identify a current problem facing seniors in nursing homes or assisted living facilities and propose legislation that can help address the issue and provide protections for the elderly. For more information, please visit: https://www.dcwlaw.com/west-palm-beach-personal-injury-lawyer/#scholarship

Award: Scholarship for use in freshman, sophomore, junior, senior, graduate, or postgraduate years; not renewable. *Number:* 1. *Amount:* $1000.

Eligibility Requirements: Applicant must be enrolled or expecting to enroll full- or part-time at a two-year or four-year or technical institution or university. Applicant must have 3.0 GPA or higher. Available to U.S. and non-U.S. citizens.

Application Requirements: Application form, essay. *Deadline:* July 31.

Contact: Sean Domnick
E-mail: info@dcwlaw.com

DONALDSON COMPANY

http://www.donaldson.com/

THE DONALDSON COMPANY, INC. SCHOLARSHIP PROGRAM

• *See page 588*

DONTPAYFULL.COM

https://www.dontpayfull.com/

$500 ANNUAL STUDENT SCHOLARSHIP

We want to invest in students who need financial help. This is why we are glad to announce the opening of "DontPayFull Student Scholarship", sponsored exclusively by DontPayFull.com. We offer $500 every year (not renewable) to one eligible student across each institution type (High School, College or University) in the United States.

Award: Scholarship for use in freshman, junior, graduate, or postgraduate years; not renewable. *Number:* 1. *Amount:* $500.

Eligibility Requirements: Applicant must be enrolled or expecting to enroll full- or part-time at a two-year or four-year or technical institution or university. Available to U.S. and non-Canadian citizens.

Application Requirements: Application form, essay. *Deadline:* October 31.

Contact: Irina Vasilescu, 500$ Annual Student Scholarship
DontPayFull.com
str. Zece Mese no 9, Bucharest, Romania
Bucharest
E-mail: irinav@dontpayfull.com

DRONE PILOT GROUND SCHOOL

https://www.dronepilotgroundschool.com

DRONE TECHNOLOGY COLLEGE SCHOLARSHIP

The Drone Technology College Scholarship will be awarded to current U.S. undergraduates who have an interest in pushing the drone industry forward, as demonstrated in an essay of 750-1,000 words. Successful applicants will write thorough, thoughtful essays that dive deeply into the topic, and will have a strong letter of support. Visit the scholarship webpage to learn more, and to apply.

Award: Prize for use in freshman, sophomore, junior, or senior years; not renewable. *Number:* 2. *Amount:* $1000.

Eligibility Requirements: Applicant must be enrolled or expecting to enroll full- or part-time at a two-year or four-year institution or university. Available to U.S. and non-U.S. citizens.

Application Requirements: Application form, autobiography, essay. *Deadline:* May 1.

Contact: Mr. Alan Perlman
Drone Pilot Ground School
746 Harpeth Knoll Road
Nashville, TN 37221
Phone: 888-3828053
E-mail: support@dronepilotgroundschool.com

EDGAR ALLEN POE LITERARY SOCIETY

http://www.ravens.org/

DISTINGUISHED RAVEN FAC MEMORIAL SCHOLARSHIP

Scholarship provides educational assistance to the descendants of those Lao/Hmong who served alongside the Ravens in defense of their country.

Award: Scholarship for use in freshman, sophomore, junior, or senior years; not renewable. *Number:* 10. *Amount:* $1000–$2500.

Eligibility Requirements: Applicant must be of Lao/Hmong heritage; Asian/Pacific Islander and enrolled or expecting to enroll full-time at a two-year or four-year or technical institution or university. Available to U.S. and non-U.S. citizens.

Application Requirements: Application form, essay. *Deadline:* February 29.

Contact: Col. Jerry Milam, Scholarship Chairman
Edgar Allen Poe Literary Society
4320 Saddle Ridge Trail
Flower Mound, TX 75028
Phone: 972-691-2569
E-mail: spikemilam@verizon.net

EDUCATOR, INC.

https://www.educator.com/

ANNUAL $2,400 STUDENT SCHOLARSHIP

Both current college students and rising freshmen are eligible for this scholarship. The scholarships will be awarded to two students ($1000 for 1st and $500 for 2nd), and the money will be transferred to their University to go towards the tuition fee. 3rd/4th/5th place winners will be emailed a login for their Annual Educator.com subscription. The students will be chosen based on their academic achievements and essay. The choice will be made by a scholarship committee of two Educator Co-Founders, and two Educator.com Instructors. To apply, applicants need to submit a scan of their most recent transcript (High School is ok for rising freshmen) plus one 500-1000 word essay on "What is the greatest problem in education today and how would you change it?" Educator.com will only consider the work for this scholarship, and will not use it for any other purposes. Application Deadline: August 31st, 2018. Application Results Announcement: October 1st, 2018. Scholarship Amount: 1st place: $1000, 2nd place: $500, 3rd/4th/5th: 1 Annual Subscription to Educator.com ($300 value each). Requirements: Most recent transcript (High School is ok for rising freshmen) plus 500–1000 word essay on "What is the greatest problem in education today and how would you change it?"

Award: Scholarship for use in freshman, sophomore, or junior years; renewable. *Number:* 5. *Amount:* $300–$1000.

Eligibility Requirements: Applicant must be enrolled or expecting to enroll full- or part-time at a two-year or four-year or technical institution or university. Available to U.S. and non-U.S. citizens.

Application Requirements: Application form, essay. *Deadline:* August 31.

Contact: Sarah Woods
E-mail: sarah@educator.com

ELEARNERS.COM

http://www.elearners.com

ELEARNERS ONLINE STUDENT SCHOLARSHIP

Entering to win our free scholarship for college is fast and easy. All you have to do is complete a short form to tell us a little about yourself and answer one essay question in 250 words or less. What is the essay question you ask? We want you to tell us: How has choosing an online college enabled you to finish your education?

Award: Scholarship for use in freshman, sophomore, junior, senior, graduate, or postgraduate years; not renewable. *Number:* 1–2. *Amount:* $1000.

Eligibility Requirements: Applicant must be enrolled or expecting to enroll full- or part-time at a two-year or four-year or technical institution or university. Available to U.S. citizens.

Application Requirements: Application form, driver's license, essay. *Deadline:* February 28.

Contact: Scholarship Organizer
E-mail: militaryscholarships@elearners.com

ELECTRONIC SECURITY ASSOCIATION (ESA)

http://www.esaweb.org

ESA YOUTH SCHOLARSHIP PROGRAM

One-time award for high school seniors entering postsecondary education, who are deserving sons or daughters of police and fire officials. The number of awards granted varies annually.

Award: Scholarship for use in freshman year; not renewable. *Amount:* $500–$10,000.

Eligibility Requirements: Applicant must be high school student; age 15-20 and planning to enroll or expecting to enroll full-time at a four-year institution or university. Applicant or parent of applicant must have employment or volunteer experience in police/firefighting. Available to U.S. citizens.

Application Requirements: Application form, essay, proof of acceptance to college or university, proof of parent/guardian occupation, recommendations or references, resume, test scores, transcript. *Deadline:* March 28.

Contact: Laurie Knox, Vice President of Communications and Public Relations
Electronic Security Association (ESA)
6333 North State Highway 161
Suite 350
Irving, TX 75038
Phone: 888-447-1689 Ext. 6825
E-mail: laurie.knox@esaweb.org

ELIZABETH GREENSHIELDS FOUNDATION

http://www.elizabethgreenshieldsfoundation.org

THE ELIZABETH GREENSHIELDS FOUNDATION GRANT

The Elizabeth Greenshields Foundation provides financial grants to art students and artists in the early or developmental stage of their career. The Foundation focuses solely on those who work in a representational style of painting, drawing, sculpture or printmaking and who are committed to making the practice of their art a lifetime career. Candidates must be at least 18 years of age at the time of submitting their application. Grants are made directly to the beneficiaries, not through other organizations. First grants are in the amount of CDN$15,000; second and third grants, in the amount of CDN$18,000. Important: The Foundation does not accept applications from commercial artists, graphic designers and illustrators; photographers; cartoonists; animation artists; video artists, filmmakers and digital artists; craft-makers; artists who work in the decorative arts; or any artist whose work falls primarily into these categories. The Foundation does not provide funding for the pursuit of abstract or non-objective art. Applications may only be accessed through the Foundation's website. The Foundation does not mail or provide application forms to applicants.

Award: Grant for use in freshman, sophomore, junior, senior, graduate, or postgraduate years; not renewable. *Number:* 40–70. *Amount:* $10,500–$13,000.

Eligibility Requirements: Applicant must be enrolled or expecting to enroll full- or part-time at a two-year or four-year institution or university. Available to U.S. and non-U.S. citizens.

Application Requirements: Application form, personal photograph, portfolio. *Deadline:* continuous.

Contact: Ms. Emily Bergsma, Applications Coordinator
Phone: 514-937-9225
E-mail: info@greenshieldsfoundation.ca

ENVIRONMENTAL LITIGATION GROUP P.C.

https://www.elglaw.com/

ENVIRONMENTAL LITIGATION GROUP, P.C. ASBESTOS SCHOLARSHIP

The eligibility requirements for our 2018 Scholarship Program are the following: must be 18 years old and a U.S. citizen; must be enrolled full-time in a U.S. based accredited two-year or four-year university, community college, junior college, or a graduate degree program; must have a minimum Grade Point Average of 3.0 or higher; must be a student who witnessed a parent, sibling, immediate family member or close friend fighting cancer; must apply to the contest via online form available on our website at https://www.elglaw.com/scholarship/. Must provide the written essay by the deadline of July 31, 2018. The three winners will be chosen by the end of August 2018 and notified by email.

Award: Scholarship for use in freshman, sophomore, junior, senior, or graduate years; not renewable. *Number:* 3. *Amount:* $2000–$5000.

Eligibility Requirements: Applicant must be enrolled or expecting to enroll full-time at a two-year or four-year institution or university. Applicant must have 3.0 GPA or higher. Available to U.S. citizens.

Application Requirements: Essay, personal photograph. *Deadline:* July 31.

Contact: Ciprian Oltean
Environmental Litigation Group P.C.
2160 Highland Avenue
Suite 200
Birmingham, AL 35205
Phone: (760) 696-7959
E-mail: ciprian@elglaw.com

EOD WARRIOR FOUNDATION

http://www.eodwarriorfoundation.org

EXPLOSIVE ORDNANCE DISPOSAL MEMORIAL SCHOLARSHIP

Award based on academic merit, community involvement, and financial need for the children, grandchildren, and spouses of military Explosive Ordnance Disposal technicians. This scholarship is for students enrolled or planning to enroll full-time as an undergraduate in a U.S. accredited two year, four year college. Applications are only available on the website at http://www.eodwarriorfoundation.org.

Award: Scholarship for use in freshman, sophomore, junior, or senior years; not renewable. *Number:* 25–75. *Amount:* $1000–$5000.

Eligibility Requirements: Applicant must be enrolled or expecting to enroll full-time at a two-year or four-year institution or university. Applicant or parent of applicant must have employment or volunteer experience in explosive ordnance disposal. Available to U.S. citizens. Applicant or parent must meet one or more of the following requirements: general military experience; retired from active duty; disabled or killed as a result of military service; prisoner of war; or missing in action.

Application Requirements: Application form, application form may be submitted online (http://www.eodmemorial.org/scholarship), community service, essay, recommendations or references, transcript. *Deadline:* March 15.

Contact: Nicole Motsek, Executive Director
EOD Warrior Foundation
33735 Snickersville Turnpike
PO Box 309
Bluemont, VA 20135
Phone: 540-554-4550
E-mail: nicole.motsek@eodmemorial.org

EQUALITY SCHOLARSHIP COLLABORATIVE

http://www.equalityscholarship.org

EQUALITY SCHOLARSHIPS FOR COMMUNITY COLLEGE TRANSFER STUDENTS

eQuality scholarships for community college transfer students recognize northern and central California community college students for their service to the lesbian/gay/bisexual/transgender community. Applicants must plan to attend or have begun attending an accredited 4-year college or university for the first time in the award year.

Award: Scholarship for use in junior or senior years; not renewable. *Number:* 1–2. *Amount:* $6000.

Eligibility Requirements: Applicant must be enrolled or expecting to enroll full- or part-time at a four-year institution or university; resident of California and must have an interest in LGBT issues. Applicant or parent of applicant must have employment or volunteer experience in community service. Available to U.S. and non-U.S. citizens.

Application Requirements: Application form, essay, interview. *Deadline:* February 1.

SCHOLARSHIPS FOR HIGH SCHOOL GRADUATES

eQuality Scholarships for high school graduates recognize graduating high school seniors and recent graduates in northern and central California students for their service to the lesbian/gay/bisexual/transgender community. Applicants must plan to attend or have begun attending an accredited post-secondary institution for the first time in the award year.

Award: Scholarship for use in freshman, sophomore, junior, or senior years; not renewable. *Number:* 11–12. *Amount:* $6000.

Eligibility Requirements: Applicant must be enrolled or expecting to enroll full- or part-time at a two-year or four-year or technical institution or university; resident of California and must have an interest in LGBT issues. Applicant or parent of applicant must have employment or volunteer experience in community service. Available to U.S. and non-U.S. citizens.

Application Requirements: Application form, community service, essay, interview. *Deadline:* February 1.

ESSAYHUB

https://essayhub.com/

ESSAY WRITING CONTEST BY ESSAYHUB

Any individual choosing to participate in this contest must be undergoing high school or higher level education (university, college). Every submission must meet the minimum word count requirement of 500 words to 1000 words max. All work for this essay contest must be written in English. We understand that the world is multilingual and we would enjoy reading such interesting works in their original language, however it would make conducting such an event nearly impossible. Fill our application form located on this page to take part in the contest. Or send your works in Word or Doc type files as to allow easy access to them to the email address support@essayhub.com with subject line Essay Writing Contest. The email submission requirements need you to place your name in the work itself and in the text of the email letter itself. Example: Essay Writing Contest–Joseph Smith. Avoid continuously looking to debate whether you should be the winner or trying to convince the judges why you think you deserved to win. All judging is done anonymously and based solely on the quality of the essay writer's work. This allows for only the best essays to win. We do not accept the submission of any kind of scholarship essay. Plagiarism is a no go. All those found guilty will be disqualified without being notified. No excuses, no exceptions. There are many referencing guides available on our website for you to use in case you get stuck. In the case of a resubmission from a previous contest it will not be taken into account and regarded as plagiarism. Make sure to include your correct contact information so we may get a hold of you if you have won.

Award: Scholarship for use in freshman, sophomore, junior, senior, graduate, or postgraduate years; not renewable. *Number:* 3. *Amount:* $500.

Eligibility Requirements: Applicant must be hearing impaired, learning disabled, physically disabled, or visually impaired; American Indian/Alaska Native, Asian/Pacific Islander, Black (non-Hispanic),

Hispanic; enrolled or expecting to enroll full- or part-time at a two-year or four-year institution or university and must have an interest in writing. Applicant must be hearing impaired, learning disabled, physically disabled, or visually impaired. Available to U.S. and non-U.S. citizens.

Application Requirements: Essay. *Deadline:* April 30.

Contact: Miss. Tia Moreen
Gardena
E-mail: tia.moreen@gmail.com

EVANS SCHOLARS FOUNDATION

http://www.wgaesf.org

CHICK EVANS SCHOLARSHIP FOR CADDIES

Full tuition and housing scholarship renewable up to four years for high school seniors who have worked at least two years as a caddie at a Western Golf Association member club. Must demonstrate financial need, excellent academics and outstanding character. Visit http://www.wgaesf.org for more information.

Award: Scholarship for use in freshman, sophomore, junior, or senior years; renewable. *Number:* 270. *Amount:* $100,000.

Eligibility Requirements: Applicant must be high school student; age 17-19; planning to enroll or expecting to enroll full-time at a four-year institution or university; single and studying in Colorado, Illinois, Indiana, Kansas, Michigan, Minnesota, Missouri, Ohio, Oregon, Pennsylvania, Washington, Wisconsin. Available to U.S. and non-U.S. citizens.

Application Requirements: Application form, essay, financial need analysis, interview, personal photograph. *Deadline:* September 30.

Contact: Scholarship Committee
Phone: 847-724-4600
E-mail: applications@wgaesf.org

EVERIPEDIA INC.

https://www.everipedia.com

EVERIPEDIA TECH TITANS DIVERSITY SCHOLARSHIP

All too often, underrepresented minorities (including members of the LGBT community) have to work extra hard to gain the same respect/status as a non-minority individual in a similar position. To this end, we at Everipedia have created a list of individuals that we believe deserve recognition for their work. The Everipedia Tech Titans Diversity Scholarship aims to bring awareness and recognition to these men and women working tirelessly across the globe in search of the truth in science and technology. The Everipedia Tech Titans Diversity Scholarship was established by Everipedia, Inc. in 2017. It aims to increase awareness of minorities in STEM areas, along with the challenges they face around the world. Applicants, instead of writing an essay, will create a Wikipedia-style biography page for a person of their choice. A sample list of individuals will be provided, but applicants are free to chose their own. Our scholarship offers an award of $1000 and is open to all incoming and current college students. Must be a sophomore, junior, or senior in high school, or currently enrolled in a college/university. Must be fluent in English. Submissions with poor grammar will not be considered.

Award: Scholarship for use in freshman, sophomore, junior, senior, graduate, or postgraduate years; not renewable. *Number:* 1. *Amount:* $1000.

Eligibility Requirements: Applicant must be enrolled or expecting to enroll full- or part-time at a two-year or four-year or technical institution or university. Available to U.S. and non-U.S. citizens.

Application Requirements: *Deadline:* December 1.

Contact: Mr. Travis Moore, CTO
Everipedia Inc.
972 Hilgard Ave
PH2
Los Angeles, CA 90024
Phone: 702-723-6417
E-mail: scholarships@everipedia.com

EXPRESSVPN

https://www.expressvpn.com

EXPRESSVPN FUTURE OF PRIVACY SCHOLARSHIP

Enter by submitting a short essay exploring the following prompt: If you had the combined powers of all the world's leaders, what would be your 10-year plan to ensure the next generation has the right to privacy? Essay should be 300-400 words in length. Please submit your entry to scholarship@expressvpn.com by August 31, 2018, no later than 11:59 PM, Pacific Standard Time. Essays must be written in English. Applicants must be currently enrolled in either a high school, undergraduate school, or graduate school located in the United States or United Kingdom. There is no age or citizenship requirement. Essays must be sent via email only. One entry per student. Multiple entries per student will be disregarded. Essays must be submitted online by August 31, 2018, no later than 11:59 PM, Pacific Standard Time. The winner will be announced before or on Saturday, October 13, 2018. The prize will be awarded by international wire transfer. The winner will be required to provide his/her bank information in order to complete the bank transfer. The winner must submit a valid ID and proof of enrollment in a high school, undergraduate school, or graduate school located in the United States or United Kingdom.

Award: Scholarship for use in freshman, sophomore, junior, senior, graduate, or postgraduate years; renewable. *Number:* 1. *Amount:* $5000.

Eligibility Requirements: Applicant must be enrolled or expecting to enroll full- or part-time at a two-year or four-year or technical institution or university. Available to U.S. and non-Canadian citizens.

Application Requirements: Essay. *Deadline:* August 31.

Contact: Scholarship Manager
ExpressVPN
Road Town
Tortola
British Virgin Islands
E-mail: scholarship@expressvpn.com

FEDERAL RESOURCES

http://www.federalresources.com

WARRIOR'S LEGACY SCHOLARSHIP FUND

This scholarship is designed to recognize and financially assist college-bound high school seniors or currently enrolled college students at an accredited institution whose parent/guardian is an active, retired, or volunteer service member of Law Enforcement, the Armed Forces, or First Responders. Students must show proof of service, proof of GPA (3.0), and proof of attendance at the accredited institution. Applicant must be a US Citizen or Permanent Resident. Visit http://www.federalresources.com/scholarship/ to apply.

Award: Scholarship for use in freshman, sophomore, junior, or senior years; not renewable. *Number:* 1. *Amount:* $5000.

Eligibility Requirements: Applicant must be enrolled or expecting to enroll full-time at a two-year or four-year or technical institution or university. Applicant or parent of applicant must have employment or volunteer experience in police/firefighting. Applicant must have 3.0 GPA or higher. Available to U.S. citizens.

Application Requirements: Application form. *Deadline:* May 31.

Contact: Scholarship Committee
Federal Resources
235G Log Canoe Circle
Stevensville, MD 21666
Phone: 800-8921099
E-mail: scholarships@federalresources.com

FELDCO WINDOWS, SIDING AND DOORS

http://www.4feldco.com

FELDCO WINDOWS, SIDING AND DOORS SCHOLARSHIP

Acceptable essays will be between 700-1,000 words long that answer the question: How has your family contributed to who you are today? All entries should be sent to scholarship@4feldco.com. Send your entry to us as an email attachment and include your full name, a headshot of yourself (.png or.jpg format), mobile phone number and address in the email. The scholarship will be awarded to the applicant that best demonstrates in their own words, how their family has contributed to who they are today. Please use the full word limit (700-1,000 words) to best describe how your family has shaped your life. Deadlines to submit are January 15th and July 15th of each year indefinitely. Applications received after the deadline will be considered for the following deadline. Proof of enrollment must be provided with your email submission. This can include a digital scan of your unofficial transcript, letter from admissions or acceptance letter on a school letterhead.

Award: Scholarship for use in freshman, sophomore, junior, or senior years; renewable. *Number:* 1. *Amount:* $1000.

Eligibility Requirements: Applicant must be enrolled or expecting to enroll full-time at a four-year institution or university. Available to U.S. citizens.

Application Requirements: Essay, personal photograph. *Deadline:* continuous.

Contact: Carl Krzeczkowski
E-mail: carlk@4feldco.com

FELDMAN & ROYLE, ATTORNEYS AT LAW

http://www.feldmanroyle.com/

AUTISM SCHOLARSHIPS

Feldman & Royle, Attorneys at Law is pleased to announce two annual scholarships for individuals diagnosed with Autism Spectrum Disorder (ASD or Autism). The scholarships are designed to assist applicants in furthering their education. Each of the $1,000 scholarships will be for tuition at an educational institution chosen by the applicant. All those who have ASD (DSM-5) are eligible for the scholarships, which will be used to assist you in furthering your educational goals. We may request proof of your ASD diagnosis. Feldman & Royle is offering two annual scholarships. Both of them are for $1,000, and will be used to defray the cost of tuition for a secondary school, community college, trade school or college. You are eligible for a scholarship whether or not you currently attend school. After being awarded the scholarship, you will have one year within which to provide us with a tuition invoice from the educational institution you have chosen to attend. A check for $1,000 will then be issued to the institution.

Award: Scholarship for use in freshman, sophomore, junior, senior, graduate, or postgraduate years; not renewable. *Number:* 2. *Amount:* $1,000.

Eligibility Requirements: Applicant must be learning disabled and enrolled or expecting to enroll full- or part-time at a two-year or four-year or technical institution or university. Applicant must be learning disabled. Available to U.S. citizens.

Application Requirements: Application form, essay. *Deadline:* November 7.

Contact: Adam Feldman
E-mail: michael@feldmanroyle.com

FELDMAN LAW FIRM PLLC

http://www.afphoenixcriminalattorney.com/

AUTISM SCHOLARSHIP

The scholarship is in the amount of $1,000, and is being offered as an incentive to those persons diagnosed with ASD to continue their education. The scholarship fund will be applied to defray a portion of the tuition cost for attendance at a university or college, junior college, or vocational school. Applicants do not have to be enrolled in school at the time of submission of their application, but the scholarship fund must be used within one year from the date of the award. The scholarship being offered by The Feldman Law Firm is open to anyone who has been diagnosed with ASD (DSM-V) who would like to continue their education at a vocational school, college or university. In order to fulfill the requirements for the application process, you must fill out the online application; prepare and upload a statement (up to 100 words in length) telling us your educational goals; and (optional) prepare and upload an essay (up to 850 words in length) discussing how ASD has affected your education.

Award: Scholarship for use in freshman, sophomore, junior, or senior years; not renewable. *Number:* 1. *Amount:* $1000.

Eligibility Requirements: Applicant must be learning disabled and enrolled or expecting to enroll full- or part-time at a two-year or four-year or technical institution or university. Applicant must be learning disabled. Available to U.S. citizens.

Application Requirements: Application form, essay. *Deadline:* February 15.

Contact: Adam Feldman
Feldman Law Firm PLLC
1 E. Washington St.
Phoenix, AZ 85004
E-mail: mike@afphoenixcriminalattorney.com

DISABLED VETERANS SCHOLARSHIP

The Feldman Law Firm will be awarding an educational scholarship for the benefit of disabled veterans. The scholarship will be for $1,000, and it will provide tuition assistance for the successful applicant. It is being offered to encourage disabled veterans to continue their education, and provide financial assistance toward that goal. The $1,000 disabled veteran scholarship is offered to eligible applicants who wish to attend a trade or vocational school, or a college or junior college. Applicants do not have to be enrolled in a school at the time they submit their application. We do require, however, that the scholarship funds be used within a year after the date on which it is awarded. The winning applicant will provide us with a tuition invoice from the educational institution he or she has chosen, and we will pay $1,000 directly to the school. In order to apply for the scholarship, you must be a veteran of any branch of the Armed Forces of the United States. You must also have a disability rating of 30% or higher. Applicants must fill out and complete the online application form and provide us with (upload) a statement of 125 words or less discussing your educational goals. (Optional) Provide us with (upload) an essay of not more than 850 words discussing how your military service has made an impact on your life. In addition, we may request proof of your veteran status, and proof of your disability. The application, together with any upload(s), must be submitted by February 5, 2018. The winning applicant will be notified on or before March 5, 2018. The winner will be selected by Adam Feldman, founder of The Feldman Law Firm, in his sole discretion.

Award: Scholarship for use in freshman, sophomore, junior, senior, graduate, or postgraduate years; not renewable. *Number:* 1. *Amount:* $1000.

Eligibility Requirements: Applicant must be physically disabled and enrolled or expecting to enroll full- or part-time at a two-year or four-year or technical institution or university. Applicant must be physically disabled. Available to U.S. citizens. Applicant or parent must meet one or more of the following requirements: general military experience; retired from active duty; disabled or killed as a result of military service; prisoner of war; or missing in action.

Application Requirements: Application form, essay. *Deadline:* February 5.

Contact: Adam Feldman
Phone: 602-540-7887
E-mail: mike@afphoenixcriminalattorney.com

FIG TECH INC.

http://www.figloans.com

$1,000 SCHOLARSHIP FOR SOCIAL IMPACT

Everyone at Fig is driven by their passion for helping communities become financially healthy, so we have created the Fig Loans Scholarship to help students who aspire to be a positive force for change in their communities. Since decision-making at the local level is becoming an important part of civic life, being a good citizen is more important than ever, and Fig is committed to supporting that growth in our home, Houston. The Fig Loans scholarship is one of the many ways we hope to empower the leaders of tomorrow. If you have the desire to make a difference with your career, we would love to hear your story! Must be a full-time student enrolled in a two year, four year, or graduate program attending school or have a permanent address in the greater Texas area (if your parents live in Texas and you grew up here, you are eligible). All majors are welcome; positive impact on communities comes in all different forms and we celebrate that. Must be a permanent residents or U.S. citizen. Please submit a current college transcript, resume, 400 to 800 word essay on the following topic: At Fig, we are committed to taking down the predatory lending system, you can learn more about our story at http://www.figloans.com/about. What is an issue in your community that you are passionate about? How did you become passionate about this issue, have you been involved with solving that issue, and how do you plan to use your education to affect long lasting change. The deadline for submission is October 15, 2018. Please send your resume, current college transcript and essay to scholarship@figloans.com. Please also include your name in the title of your email. After the submission deadline, our team will review all applications and select a winner.

Award: Scholarship for use in freshman, sophomore, junior, senior, graduate, or postgraduate years; not renewable. *Number:* 1. *Amount:* $1000.

Eligibility Requirements: Applicant must be age 18-65; enrolled or expecting to enroll full- or part-time at a two-year or four-year or technical institution or university and studying in Texas. Available to U.S. citizens.

Application Requirements: Essay. *Deadline:* October 15.

Contact: Zara Mohidin, Scholarship Chair
Phone: 832-80200344
E-mail: scholarship@figloans.com

FINALLY SOLD

http://www.finallysold.com

FINALLY SOLD IMPACT MAKER SCHOLARSHIP

The Finally Sold Impact Maker Scholarships are merit based scholarships designed for those who really feel that they can make a lasting impact in their chosen career. We are looking for passionate candidates who can articulate why going to their chosen school will allow them to ultimately make a difference in their field. Don't worry about your grades or SAT scores, because we won't look at those. Rather, we are looking for people who can demonstrate that they possess such traits and characteristics as: creativity, ambition, passion, resourcefulness, entrepreneurship, influence and persuasion. All you need to do is submit a short video and write a short essay pitching why you think we should pick you. We even award bonus points and extra credit for applicants such as our Influencer and Recruitment BONUS that rewards those who cross promote their video and our program. We also have bonuses for those who submit their application early or pass a short quiz about our company. Please see our site for more details.

Award: Scholarship for use in freshman, sophomore, junior, senior, graduate, or postgraduate years; renewable. *Number:* 6. *Amount:* $500.

Eligibility Requirements: Applicant must be age 16-99; enrolled or expecting to enroll full- or part-time at a two-year or four-year or technical institution or university; resident of Alabama, Alaska, Arizona, Arkansas, California, Colorado, Connecticut, Delaware, District of Columbia, Florida, Georgia, Hawaii, Idaho, Illinois, Indiana, Iowa, Kansas, Kentucky, Louisiana, Maine, Maryland, Massachusetts, Michigan, Minnesota, Mississippi, Missouri, Montana, Nebraska, Nevada, New Hampshire, New Jersey, New Mexico, New York, North Carolina, North Dakota, Ohio, Oklahoma, Oregon, Pennsylvania, Rhode Island, South Carolina, South Dakota, Tennessee, Texas, Utah, Vermont, Virginia, Washington, West Virginia, Wisconsin, Wyoming and studying in Arizona, Arkansas, California, Colorado, Connecticut, Delaware, District of Columbia, Florida, Georgia, Hawaii, Idaho, Illinois, Indiana, Iowa, Kansas, Kentucky, Louisiana, Maine, Maryland, Massachusetts, Michigan, Minnesota, Mississippi, Missouri, Montana, Nebraska, Nevada, New Hampshire, New Jersey, New Mexico, New York, North Carolina, North Dakota, Ohio, Oklahoma, Oregon, Pennsylvania, Rhode Island, South Carolina, South Dakota, Tennessee, Texas, Utah, Vermont, Virginia, Washington, West Virginia, Wisconsin, Wyoming. Available to U.S. citizens.

Application Requirements: Application form, essay. *Deadline:* continuous.

Contact: Douglas Schwartz, Scholarship Manager
Finally Sold
11225 N 28 Dr.,
Suite C218
Phoenix, AZ 85029
Phone: 480-469-5814
E-mail: Scholarships@FinallySold.com

FINANCE AUTHORITY OF MAINE

http://www.famemaine.com/

TUITION WAIVER PROGRAMS

Provides tuition waivers for children and spouses of EMS personnel, firefighters, and law enforcement officers who have been killed in the line of duty and for students who were foster children under the custody of the Department of Human Services when they graduated from high school. Waivers valid at the University of Maine System, the Maine Technical College System, and Maine Maritime Academy. Applicant must reside and study in Maine.

Award: Grant for use in freshman, sophomore, junior, or senior years; renewable. *Number:* 30.

Eligibility Requirements: Applicant must be enrolled or expecting to enroll full- or part-time at a two-year or four-year institution or university; resident of Maine and studying in Maine. Applicant or parent of applicant must have employment or volunteer experience in police/firefighting. Available to U.S. citizens.

Application Requirements: Application form. *Deadline:* continuous.

Contact: Jennifer Lanphear, Education Programs Officer
Finance Authority of Maine
5 Community Drive
Augusta, ME 04332
Phone: 207-620-3548
E-mail: education@famemaine.com

FINANCIAL SERVICE CENTERS OF NEW YORK

http://www.fscny.org

FSCNY YOUNG LEADERS SCHOLARSHIP

Applicants will be considered based on the following criteria: academic achievement; demonstrated leadership in their school; and demonstrated involvement in their community, contributing at least 50 valuable hours of volunteer service each year of high school. Applicants must be seniors attending public high schools in New York City's five boroughs or surrounding New York counties. After an initial review of all applications, the finalists will be selected for interviews with the Selection Committee. Interviews will be scheduled in late March for selected candidates. Students will be notified if they have been selected to receive an award by April 13, 2018. Award recipients may be invited to receive their awards at FSCNY's 26th Annual Conference Scholarship Luncheon, to be held at the Brooklyn Marriott Hotel April 26, 2018. Additional details will be made available to scholarship winners at a later date. Several scholarships will be issued to selected recipients consisting of a one-time cash award to be applied towards the cost of their freshman year of study at an accredited two- or four-year college or university. The cash award for each of the selected winners will range between $2,000 and $7,500 based on the recommendations of the Selection Committee.

Award: Scholarship for use in freshman year; not renewable. *Number:* 1–10. *Amount:* $2000–$7500.

Eligibility Requirements: Applicant must be high school student; planning to enroll or expecting to enroll full- or part-time at a two-year or four-year institution or university; resident of New York and must have an interest in leadership. Available to U.S. citizens.

Application Requirements: Application form, community service, essay, interview. *Deadline:* March 9.

Contact: LeeAnn Thomson
E-mail: lthompson@fisca.org

FIT SMALL BUSINESS

http://www.fitsmallbusiness.com

BUSINESS PLAN SCHOLARSHIP FOR STUDENTS WITH DISABILITIES

The Business Plan Scholarship is awarded twice a year, once during the fall semester and once during the spring semester. The winner is judged primarily on the merit of their 500-1000 word response to the essay prompt 'What I learned from writing a business plan'

Award: Scholarship for use in freshman, sophomore, junior, senior, graduate, or postgraduate years; not renewable. *Number:* 1. *Amount:* $1000.

Eligibility Requirements: Applicant must be hearing impaired, learning disabled, physically disabled, or visually impaired and enrolled or expecting to enroll full- or part-time at a two-year or four-year or technical institution or university. Applicant must be hearing impaired, learning disabled, physically disabled, or visually impaired. Available to U.S. and non-U.S. citizens.

Application Requirements: Essay. *Deadline:* November 1.

Contact: Mr. Marc Prosser, Publisher
E-mail: mprosser@fitsmallbusiness.com

FLORIDA PTA/PTSA

http://www.floridapta.org/

FLORIDA PTA/PTSA ANNUAL SCHOLARSHIP

Non-Renewable scholarship of $2000 awarded to students enrolled full-time in their undergraduate study.

Award: Scholarship for use in freshman year; not renewable. *Number:* 2. *Amount:* $2000.

Eligibility Requirements: Applicant must be high school student; planning to enroll or expecting to enroll full-time at a two-year or four-year or technical institution or university and resident of Florida. Applicant must have 2.5 GPA or higher.

Application Requirements: Application form, community service, essay, financial need analysis. *Deadline:* February 1.

Contact: Scholarship Chair, Scholarship Chair
Florida PTA/PTSA
1747 Orlando Central Parkway
Orlando, FL 32809
Phone: 407-855-7604
Fax: 407-240-9577
E-mail: scholarship@floridapta.org

FOUNDATION FOR SIGHT AND SOUND

http://fssny.org

HELP AMERICA HEAR SCHOLARSHIP

The scholarship is open nationally to high school seniors who have a hearing loss, which requires the use of hearing aid(s) in their daily life. The purpose of this scholarship is to help students with hearing challenges reach their full potential by giving them the gift of sound. This will further allow the students to build confidence and self-esteem as they prepare to begin their college or vocational school education. The recipient of this scholarship will be selected by an independent group of judges to be determined by the Foundation For Sight & Sound, a 501c3 Not for Profit Corporation. The scholarship will award one student per school year, currently wearing hearing aid(s). Cochlear users may enter this and will only receive the financial award. The scholarship recipient will receive two state-of-the-art ReSound Hearing Aids which best fit his/her hearing loss, along with a $1000 scholarship to the student's college or vocational school of choice.

Award: Scholarship for use in freshman year; not renewable. *Number:* 1. *Amount:* $1000.

Eligibility Requirements: Applicant must be hearing impaired; high school student and planning to enroll or expecting to enroll full- or part-time at a two-year or four-year or technical institution or university. Applicant must be hearing impaired. Available to U.S. citizens.

Application Requirements: Application form, essay, personal photograph. *Deadline:* March 25.

Contact: Ms. Marissa Marinucci, Office Assistant
Foundation for Sight and Sound
Foundation For Sight and Sound
PO Box 1245
Smithtown, NY 11787
Phone: 631-366-3461
E-mail: info@fssny.org

FOUNDATION OF THE 1ST CAVALRY DIVISION ASSOCIATION

https://www.1cda.org/

FOUNDATION OF THE 1ST CAVALRY DIVISION ASSOCIATION (IA DRANG) SCHOLARSHIP

Award for children and grandchildren of soldiers of 1st Cavalry Division, U.S. Air Force Forward Air Controllers and A1E pilots, and war correspondents who served in designated qualifying units which were involved in battles of the Ia Drang Valley during the period of November 3-19, 1965. Include self-addressed stamped envelope. More information on http://www.1cda.org.

Award: Grant for use in freshman, sophomore, junior, or senior years; not renewable. *Number:* 2–8. *Amount:* $600–$1200.

Eligibility Requirements: Applicant must be enrolled or expecting to enroll full- or part-time at a two-year or four-year or technical institution or university. Available to U.S. citizens. Applicant or parent must meet one or more of the following requirements: Air Force or Army experience; retired from active duty; disabled or killed as a result of military service; prisoner of war; or missing in action.

Application Requirements: Application form. *Deadline:* continuous.

Contact: Ms. Dara Wydler, Executive Director
Foundation of the 1st Cavalry Division Association
302 North Main Street
Copperas Cove, TX 76522-1703
Phone: 254-547-6537
E-mail: firstcav@1cda.org

FOUNDATION OF THE 1ST CAVALRY DIVISION ASSOCIATION SCHOLARSHIP

Scholarships for children of soldiers of the 1st Cavalry Division who died or have been declared permanently and totally (100%) disabled from combat with the 1st Cavalry Division or Soldiers currently assigned to the Division (includes spouse and children). Show proof of service with the division, relationship to parent, death or disability of parent, and acceptance at higher education institution. Include self-addressed stamped envelope.

Award: Grant for use in freshman, sophomore, junior, or senior years; not renewable. *Number:* 1–8. *Amount:* $600–$1200.

Eligibility Requirements: Applicant must be enrolled or expecting to enroll full- or part-time at a two-year or four-year or technical institution or university. Available to U.S. citizens. Applicant or parent must meet one or more of the following requirements: national guard experience; retired from active duty; disabled or killed as a result of military service; prisoner of war; or missing in action.

Application Requirements: Application form. *Deadline:* August 1.

Contact: Ms. Dara Wydler, Executive Director
Foundation of the 1st Cavalry Division Association
302 North Main Street
Copperas Cove, TX 76522-1703
Phone: 254-547-6537
E-mail: firstcav@1cda.org

FRATERNAL ORDER OF POLICE ASSOCIATES OF OHIO INC.

http://www.fopaohio.org/

FRATERNAL ORDER OF POLICE ASSOCIATES, STATE LODGE OF OHIO INC., SCHOLARSHIP FUND

Scholarship available to a graduating high school senior whose parent or guardian is a member in good standing of the Fraternal Order of Police, State Lodge of Ohio Inc. The amount of each scholarship will be up to $4000 payable over a four-year period. A one-time award of $500 will be given to the first runner-up. Scholarships will be awarded on the basis of scholastic merit, economic need and goals in life.

Award: Scholarship for use in freshman year; renewable. *Number:* 1–4. *Amount:* $500–$1000.

Eligibility Requirements: Applicant must be high school student; planning to enroll or expecting to enroll full-time at a four-year institution or university and resident of Ohio. Applicant or parent of applicant must have employment or volunteer experience in police/firefighting. Available to U.S. citizens.

Application Requirements: Application form, community service, essay, financial need analysis, personal photograph, proof of guardianship, recommendations or references, test scores, transcript. *Deadline:* May 1.

Contact: Mr. Michael Esposito, FOPA Scholarship Assistance Program
Fraternal Order of Police Associates of Ohio Inc.
PO Box 14564
Cincinnati, OH 45250-0564
Phone: 513-684-4755
E-mail: mje@fopaohio.org

FREEDOM ALLIANCE

https://freedomalliance.org

FREEDOM ALLIANCE SCHOLARSHIP FUND

Freedom Alliance Scholarship Fund applicants must be one of the following: the dependent son or daughter of a U.S. soldier, sailor, airman, guardsman or Marine who has become 100% permanently disabled as a result of an combat mission or training accident; the dependent son or daughter of a U.S. soldier, sailor, airman, guardsman or Marine who has been killed in action; the dependent son or daughter of a U.S. soldier, sailor, airman, guardsman or Marine who has been classified as a Prisoner of War (POW) or Missing in Action (MIA). All applicants must also meet the following eligibility requirements in order to qualify for a Freedom Alliance scholarship: currently in their senior year of high school, a high school graduate or a currently enrolled full time undergraduate student; under the age of 26 at the time of application; have a GPA of 2.0 or higher. Eligible students can visit our website, http://www.fascholarship.com, and complete the application to start the process.

Award: Scholarship for use in freshman, sophomore, junior, or senior years; renewable. *Number:* 250–326. *Amount:* $500–$3500.

Eligibility Requirements: Applicant must be age 17-25 and enrolled or expecting to enroll full-time at a two-year or four-year or technical institution or university. Applicant must have 2.5 GPA or higher. Available to U.S. citizens.

Application Requirements: Application form, essay, personal photograph. *Deadline:* continuous.

Contact: Wanda Cruz, Programs Assistant
Freedom Alliance
22570 Markey Court
Suite 240
Dulles, VA 20166
Phone: 800-475-6620
E-mail: info@fascholarship.com

FRIENDS OF THE MINNESOTA ORCHESTRA (FORMERLY WAMSO)

https://friendsofminnesotaorchestra.org/

YOUNG ARTIST COMPETITION

Awards of $500 to $5000 and/or performnce awards for graduates, undergraduates, and early career artists through age 25 as of 1/20/2019. Applicant must reside or study in U.S. or Canada.

Award: Prize for use in freshman, sophomore, junior, senior, graduate, or postgraduate years; not renewable. *Number:* 8. *Amount:* $500–$5000.

Eligibility Requirements: Applicant must be age 15-25; enrolled or expecting to enroll full- or part-time at a two-year or four-year or technical institution or university and must have an interest in music. Available to U.S. and non-U.S. citizens.

Application Requirements: Application form. *Fee:* $75. *Deadline:* September 30.

Contact: James Waldo, Young Artist Competition Co-Chair
E-mail: yac@mnorch.org

FUNNEWJERSEY.COM INC.

http://www.funnewjersey.com

FUNNEWJERSEY.COM SCHOLARSHIP

FunNewJersey.com is awarding scholarships to New Jersey residents who plan on attending an institution of higher learning at one of the many distinguished colleges and/or universities in state. Applicants must submit an essay about New Jersey. Themes may include the following: What is so special about New Jersey? What should tourists, visitors and non-residents know about NJ that they might not know? Do you have any memories of New Jersey that are special? What is your favorite local attraction or place? What makes your town, city, neighborhood or community unique? These are merely suggestions: please feel free to come up with your own creative responses. Applicants must also submit a resume.

Award: Scholarship for use in freshman year; not renewable. *Number:* 1–3. *Amount:* $100–$1000.

Eligibility Requirements: Applicant must be high school student; planning to enroll or expecting to enroll full-time at a two-year or four-year or technical institution or university; resident of New Jersey and studying in New Jersey. Available to U.S. citizens.

Application Requirements: Essay. *Deadline:* April 15.

Contact: Ms. Ray Gallagher, Managing Content Editor
FunNewJersey.com Inc.
241 Forsgate Drive
Suite 113
Jamesburg, NJ 08831
Phone: 732-298-0615 Ext. 551
E-mail: ray@funnewjersey.com

GENERAL FEDERATION OF WOMEN'S CLUBS OF MASSACHUSETTS

http://www.gfwcma.org/

GENERAL FEDERATION OF WOMEN'S CLUBS OF MASSACHUSETTS NICKEL FOR NOTES MUSIC SCHOLARSHIP

Scholarship for high school seniors majoring in piano, instrument, music education, music therapy or voice. Applicant must be a senior in a Massachusetts High School.

Award: Scholarship for use in freshman year; not renewable. *Number:* 1. *Amount:* $500.

Eligibility Requirements: Applicant must be high school student; planning to enroll or expecting to enroll full-time at a four-year institution or university and resident of Massachusetts. Available to U.S. citizens.

Application Requirements: Application form, essay. *Deadline:* March 1.

Contact: Scholarship Chm
General Federation of Women's Clubs of Massachusetts
P.O. Box 679
Sudbury, MA 01776
Phone: 978-443-4569
E-mail: gfwcma@aol.com

GENERAL FEDERATION OF WOMEN'S CLUBS OF MASSACHUSETTS PENNIES FOR ART SCHOLARSHIP

Scholarship for graduating high school senior who is resident of Massachusetts majoring in art. Must submit three (3) pieces of original artwork in three (3) different mediums (no sculpture). Matting is required except for oil on stretched canvas.

Award: Scholarship for use in freshman year; not renewable. *Number:* 1. *Amount:* $500.

Eligibility Requirements: Applicant must be high school student; planning to enroll or expecting to enroll full-time at a four-year institution or university and resident of Massachusetts. Available to U.S. citizens.

Application Requirements: Application form, driver's license, essay, portfolio. *Deadline:* March 1.

Contact: Scholarship Chm
General Federation of Women's Clubs of Massachusetts
P.O. Box 679
Sudbury, MA 01776
E-mail: gfwcma@aol.com

GEORGIA PRESS EDUCATIONAL FOUNDATION INC.

http://gapress.org/scholarships-internships/

KIRK SUTLIVE SCHOLARSHIP

Scholarship awarded annually to a student majoring in either the news-editorial or public relations sequence.

Award: Scholarship for use in freshman, sophomore, junior, or senior years; not renewable. *Number:* 1. *Amount:* $500–$2000.

Eligibility Requirements: Applicant must be enrolled or expecting to enroll full-time at a four-year institution or university; resident of Georgia and studying in Georgia. Available to U.S. citizens.

Application Requirements: Application form, essay, financial need analysis, interview, personal photograph. *Deadline:* March 1.

Contact: Sean Ireland, Manager
Phone: 770-454-6776
Fax: 770-454-6778
E-mail: sireland@gapress.org

MORRIS NEWSPAPER CORPORATION SCHOLARSHIP

Scholarship awarded annually to an outstanding print journalism student. Applications are submitted through newspapers in the Morris Newspaper Corporation chain and recipients are named by the Foundation.

Award: Scholarship for use in freshman, sophomore, junior, or senior years; not renewable. *Number:* 1. *Amount:* $500–$2000.

Eligibility Requirements: Applicant must be enrolled or expecting to enroll full-time at a two-year or four-year institution or university; resident of Georgia and studying in Georgia. Available to U.S. citizens.

Application Requirements: Application form, essay, financial need analysis, interview, personal photograph. *Deadline:* March 1.

Contact: Sean Ireland, Manager
Phone: 770-454-6776
Fax: 770-454-6778
E-mail: sireland@gapress.org

GEORGIA STUDENT FINANCE COMMISSION

http://www.GAfutures.org

GEORGIA HERO SCHOLARSHIP

Provides assistance with cost of attendance to members of the Georgia National Guard and U.S. Military Reservists who were deployed overseas on active duty service, on or after February 1, 2003, to a location designated as a combat zone, and the children and spouses of such members of the Georgia National Guard and U.S. Military Reserves. Students must be attending an eligible college or university in Georgia.

Award: Scholarship for use in freshman, sophomore, junior, or senior years; not renewable. *Number:* 200–350. *Amount:* $2000.

Eligibility Requirements: Applicant must be enrolled or expecting to enroll full- or part-time at a two-year or four-year or technical institution or university; resident of Georgia and studying in Georgia. Available to U.S. citizens.

Application Requirements: Application form.

Contact: Ms. Pennie Strong, Vice President, Student Aid Services
Georgia Student Finance Commission
2082 East Exchange Place
Tucker, GA 30084
Phone: 770-724-9014
Fax: 770-724-9249
E-mail: pennies@gsfc.org

GEORGIA PUBLIC SAFETY MEMORIAL GRANT

Public Safety Memorial Grant provides assistance to the dependent children of Georgia public safety officers who were permanently disabled or killed in the line of duty. Funds may be used toward the cost of attendance at eligible colleges or universities in Georgia.

Award: Grant for use in freshman, sophomore, junior, or senior years; not renewable. *Number:* 20–40. *Amount:* $2000–$18,000.

Eligibility Requirements: Applicant must be enrolled or expecting to enroll full-time at a two-year or four-year or technical institution or university; resident of Georgia and studying in Georgia. Applicant or parent of applicant must have employment or volunteer experience in police/firefighting. Available to U.S. citizens.

Application Requirements: Application form. *Deadline:* continuous.

Contact: Ms. Pennie Strong, Vice President, Student Aid Services
Georgia Student Finance Commission
2082 East Exchange Place
Tucker, GA 30084
Phone: 770-724-9014
Fax: 770-724-9249
E-mail: pennies@gsfc.org

GEORGIA TUITION EQUALIZATION GRANT (GTEG)

The Georgia Tuition Equalization Grant (GTEG) provides grant assistance toward educational costs to Georgia residents enrolled at an eligible private college or university. Students must be enrolled full-time in an undergraduate program of study leading to an undergraduate

Award: Grant for use in freshman, sophomore, junior, or senior years; renewable. *Number:* 46,000. *Amount:* $317–$475.

Eligibility Requirements: Applicant must be enrolled or expecting to enroll full-time at a two-year or four-year institution or university; resident of Georgia and studying in Georgia. Available to U.S. citizens.

Application Requirements: Application form.

Contact: Ms. Pennie Strong, Vice President, Student Aid Services
Georgia Student Finance Commission
2082 East Exchange Place
Tucker, GA 30084
Phone: 770-724-9014
Fax: 770-724-9249
E-mail: pennies@gsfc.org

ZELL MILLER SCHOLARSHIP PROGRAM

Zell Miller Scholarship is a merit-based award available to Georgia residents, similar to the HOPE Scholarship, but with more stringent academic requirements and a higher level of tuition assistance. A Zell Miller Scholarship recipient must graduate from high school with a minimum 3.7 HOPE Calculated (approved core courses) grade point average combined and earned 4 credits of academic rigor, with a minimum SAT score of 1,200 on the math and reading portions or a minimum composite ACT score of 26 in single national test administration. Students must maintain a minimum 3.3 cumulative postsecondary grade point average to remain eligible. Students are provided full-tuition assistance while pursuing an undergraduate degree and they must attend an eligible college or university in Georgia. A seven-year limit exists for students first receiving the Zell Miller Scholarship during the 2011-2012 academic year (FY12) or later.

Award: Scholarship for use in freshman, sophomore, junior, or senior years; renewable. *Number:* 200,000. *Amount:* $534–$5004.

Eligibility Requirements: Applicant must be enrolled or expecting to enroll full- or part-time at a two-year or four-year or technical institution or university; resident of Georgia and studying in Georgia. Applicant must have 3.5 GPA or higher. Available to U.S. citizens.

Application Requirements: Application form.

Contact: Ms. Pennie Strong, Vice President, Student Aid Services
Georgia Student Finance Commission
2082 East Exchange Place
Tucker, GA 30084
Phone: 770-724-9014
Fax: 770-724-9249
E-mail: pennies@gsfc.org

GERSOWITZ LIBO & KOREK, P.C.

https://www.lawyertime.com

GARDINER FOUNDATION SCHOLARSHIP

For a young person, losing a family member can be a devastating experience. However, losing multiple family members all at once is almost unthinkable. That's what happened to Dexter Gardiner, who on July 9, 2006 lost six family members in a tragic car accident on the Bronx River Parkway. Yet despite the loss, Dexter chose to use the tragedy as a way to help others who have experienced similar situations in losing beloved family members unexpectedly. Needless to say, for those left behind, especially children whose college education may suddenly be in doubt due to financial concerns, the world can suddenly seem very uncertain.

Award: Scholarship for use in sophomore or senior years; renewable. *Number:* 4–5. *Amount:* $1500.

Eligibility Requirements: Applicant must be enrolled or expecting to enroll full-time at an institution or university. Available to U.S. citizens.

Application Requirements: Application form, essay. *Deadline:* July 15.

Contact: Mr. Bryan Powell
E-mail: scholarship@lawyertime.com

GIFT BASKETS PLUS

http://www.giftbasketsplus.com

HIGH SCHOOL GRADUATE SCHOLARSHIP CONTEST

We are announcing the Gift Baskets Plus college scholarship contest for $500. The rules are simple. Seniors in high school will submit an essay of at least 600 words, entitled "The perfect high school graduation gift." Each essay must be submitted by email to scholarship@giftbasketsplus.com. To qualify, each submission must contain a PDF of the essay; student's full name; destination college (or colleges if not yet selected); email address; mailing address; date of birth. Qualifying essays will be published on GiftBasketsPlus.com. Essays must be submitted by May 1st, to be considered. The winner will be announced on June 1. Once qualified, one essay will be selected for a $500 scholarship based on the number of social shares that essay gets. Winners will be notified by email and scholarships will be mailed by check. Good luck, students!

Award: Prize for use in freshman, sophomore, junior, senior, or graduate years; not renewable. *Number:* 1. *Amount:* $500.

Eligibility Requirements: Applicant must be enrolled or expecting to enroll full-time at a two-year or four-year or technical institution or university. Available to U.S. citizens.

Application Requirements: Essay. *Deadline:* May 1.

Contact: Tamara Watson, Marketing Manager
Phone: 800-520-6657

GOENNOUNCE, LLC

http://GoEnnounce.com/about

GOENNOUNCE YOURSELF $500 MONTHLY SCHOLARSHIP

Our $500 monthly scholarship is a monthly scholarship open to all high school students and college freshmen, sophomores, and juniors. Once you apply, you're considered every month based on the updates you're posting. Not essay or GPA–based. Who are you as a student? An athlete, a history ace, a star on the drums, class treasurer, a student volunteer, or something completely different? We want to reward you for being you and for e–announcing your school progress and accomplishments each month.

Award: Prize for use in freshman, sophomore, or junior years; renewable. *Number:* 12. *Amount:* $500.

Eligibility Requirements: Applicant must be enrolled or expecting to enroll full-time at a two-year or four-year institution or university. Available to U.S. citizens.

Application Requirements: *Deadline:* continuous.

GOLDSTEIN AND BASHNER

https://www.eglaw.com/

COMBATING CAMPUS ISSUES SCHOLARSHIP

Each year, a $1,000 award will be presented to an especially promising higher education student who shares our determination and articulates a clear vision about how he or she will work to advance advocacy initiatives and solutions for on-campus problems. For more information, please visit: http://www.eglaw.com/nassau-county-injury/#scholarship

Award: Scholarship for use in freshman, sophomore, junior, senior, graduate, or postgraduate years; not renewable. *Number:* 1. *Amount:* $1000.

Eligibility Requirements: Applicant must be enrolled or expecting to enroll full- or part-time at a two-year or four-year or technical institution or university. Applicant must have 3.0 GPA or higher. Available to U.S. and non-U.S. citizens.

Application Requirements: Application form, essay. *Deadline:* May 15.

Contact: Neal Goldstein
E-mail: help.eglaw@gmail.com

GOLF COURSE SUPERINTENDENTS ASSOCIATION OF AMERICA

http://www.eifg.org/

GOLF COURSE SUPERINTENDENTS ASSOCIATION OF AMERICA LEGACY AWARD
• *See page 564*

JOSEPH S. GARSKE COLLEGIATE GRANT PROGRAM
• *See page 564*

GORDON LAW GROUP

https://www.gordonlawltd.com

GORDON LAW GROUP ANNUAL SCHOLARSHIP

Gordon Law Group is offering one $1,000 scholarship to an undergraduate or law school student who submits the best essay addressing the following topic: Should internet advertisers be subject to the same advertising requirements as those who advertise offline?

Award: Scholarship for use in freshman, sophomore, junior, or senior years; not renewable. *Number:* 1. *Amount:* $1000.

Eligibility Requirements: Applicant must be enrolled or expecting to enroll full-time at a two-year or four-year institution or university. Available to U.S. citizens.

Application Requirements: Essay. *Deadline:* July 15.

Contact: Pat McCune
E-mail: pat@marketjd.com

GREATER GOOD SCIENCE CENTER

https://ggsc.berkeley.edu/

THE PURPOSE CHALLENGE

The Purpose Challenge is a campaign to help high school seniors find their purpose in life, write better essays for their college applications, and apply for $25,000 in scholarship money. An innovative and inspiring new online tool, The Purpose Challenge, draws on decades of research into the roots and benefits of purpose. The toolkit incorporates video content, reading materials, and brief written exercises such as imagining your ideal life at age 40, to help high school seniors reflect on and refine their sense of purpose. Additionally, it contains step-by-step guidance on how to write a meaningful college essay, along with providing sample essays for review. Teens can then inject their newly fleshed out sense of purpose in their college application essay and win up to $25,000 for college! Learn more at http://www.purposechallenge.org. Why Purpose? We believe purpose is critically important: Research has shown that a strong sense of purpose, a commitment to something that is both personally rewarding and beneficial to others, is linked to improved health, well-being, and success. A stronger sense of purpose can make a significant difference in a young person's life path, setting them on a course for a more successful, meaningful life.

Award: Prize for use in freshman year; not renewable. *Number:* 6. *Amount:* $5000–$25,000.

Eligibility Requirements: Applicant must be high school student and planning to enroll or expecting to enroll full-time at a four-year institution or university. Available to U.S. citizens.

Application Requirements: Essay. *Deadline:* February 1.

Contact: Administrator
Phone: 310-826-0123
E-mail: opportunities@purposechallenge.org

GREATER WASHINGTON URBAN LEAGUE

http://www.gwul.org/

SAFEWAY/GREATER WASHINGTON URBAN LEAGUE SCHOLARSHIP

Award to graduating high school students who reside in the service area of the League. Applicants must complete an essay on a subject selected by the sponsors and must have completed 90 percent of their school district's community service requirement. Minimum GPA of 2.7 required.

Award: Scholarship for use in freshman year; not renewable. *Number:* 6. *Amount:* $3000.

Eligibility Requirements: Applicant must be high school student; planning to enroll or expecting to enroll full-time at a four-year institution or university and resident of District of Columbia. Applicant or parent of applicant must have employment or volunteer experience in community service. Available to U.S. citizens.

Application Requirements: Application form, community service, entry in a contest, essay, test scores. *Deadline:* February 12.

Contact: Audrey Epperson, Director of Education
Phone: 202-265-8200
Fax: 202-387-7019
E-mail: aepperson@gwul.org

GRUNGO COLARULO

https://gcinjurylaw.com/

GRUNGO COLARULO GIVING BACK TO THE COMMUNITY SCHOLARSHIP

The Giving Back to the Community scholarship is open to apply to for any student who is currently enrolled in an accredited community college, undergraduate, or graduate program in the United States. Students who are currently incoming first-year college students and have graduated high school or possesses a GED may also apply. For complete information on this scholarship, please visit https://gcinjurylaw.com/#scholarship

Award: Scholarship for use in freshman, sophomore, junior, senior, graduate, or postgraduate years; not renewable. *Number:* 1. *Amount:* $500.

Eligibility Requirements: Applicant must be enrolled or expecting to enroll full- or part-time at a two-year or four-year or technical institution or university. Applicant must have 3.0 GPA or higher. Available to U.S. and non-U.S. citizens.

Application Requirements: Application form, community service, essay. *Deadline:* October 31.

Contact: Richard Grungo
E-mail: rgrungo@gcinjurylaw.com

HAGAN SCHOLARSHIP FOUNDATION

https://haganscholarships.org/

HAGAN SCHOLARSHIP

The Purpose of the Hagan Scholarship is to provide each recipient with the opportunity to obtain a four-year college education and graduate college debt free; and to provide a practical understanding of important life skills not typically taught as a part of the school curriculum. These life skills are taught via Workshops, Schwab Scholar Accounts, and Study Abroad.

Award: Scholarship for use in freshman, sophomore, junior, senior, or graduate years; renewable. *Number:* 300. *Amount:* $40,000.

Eligibility Requirements: Applicant must be high school student; planning to enroll or expecting to enroll full-time at a four-year institution or university; resident of Alabama, Alaska, Arizona, Arkansas, California, Colorado, Florida, Georgia, Idaho, Illinois, Indiana, Iowa, Kansas, Kentucky, Louisiana, Maine, Maryland, Massachusetts, Michigan, Minnesota, Mississippi, Missouri, Montana, Nebraska, Nevada, New Hampshire, New Mexico, New York, North Carolina, North Dakota, Ohio, Oklahoma, Oregon, Pennsylvania, South Carolina, South Dakota, Tennessee, Texas, Utah, Vermont, Virginia, Washington, West Virginia, Wisconsin, Wyoming and studying in Alabama, Alaska, Arizona, Arkansas, California, Colorado, Connecticut, Delaware, Florida, Georgia, Hawaii, Idaho, Illinois, Indiana, Iowa, Kansas, Kentucky, Louisiana, Maine, Maryland, Massachusetts, Michigan, Minnesota, Mississippi, Missouri, Montana, Nebraska, Nevada, New Hampshire, New Jersey, New Mexico, New York, North Carolina, North Dakota, Ohio, Oklahoma, Oregon, Pennsylvania, South Carolina, South Dakota, Tennessee, Texas, Utah, Vermont, Virginia, Washington, West Virginia, Wisconsin, Wyoming. Applicant must have 3.5 GPA or higher. Available to U.S. citizens.

Application Requirements: Application form, driver's license, essay, financial need analysis, personal photograph. *Deadline:* November 15.

Contact: Mr. Dan Hagan, Trustee
Hagan Scholarship Foundation
PO Box 1225
Columbia, MO 65205
E-mail: scholarships@hsfmo.org

HANSCOM FEDERAL CREDIT UNION

https://www.hfcu.org/

JOHN F. CONDON MEMORIAL SCHOLARSHIP

To qualify, you must be a member at the time of application and you must be planning to enroll in an accredited program of higher education. Other considerations include academic performance, extracurricular activities, community service and financial need.

Award: Prize for use in freshman year; not renewable. *Number:* 5. *Amount:* $1500.

Eligibility Requirements: Applicant must be high school student and planning to enroll or expecting to enroll full- or part-time at a two-year or four-year institution or university. Available to U.S. citizens.

Application Requirements: Application form, essay. *Deadline:* March 11.

Contact: Cara Powers, Scholarship Administrator
Hanscom Federal Credit Union
1610 Eglin St
Hanscom AFB, MA 01731
Phone: 781-698-2203
E-mail: cpowers@hfcu.org

HARDWICK & PENDERGAST, P.S.

http://www.hardwickpendergast.com/

HARDWICK & PENDERGAST, P.S. SCHOLARSHIP

At Hardwick & Pendergast, P.S. we understand the importance of a good education. That is why we are thrilled to be able to help one deserving student with their post-secondary education expenses. This scholarship is open to graduating high-school seniors and currently-enrolled college students who have earned a 3.0 or higher GPA. Applications and additional information can be found on our website!

Award: Scholarship for use in freshman, sophomore, junior, or senior years; not renewable. *Number:* 1. *Amount:* $500.

Eligibility Requirements: Applicant must be enrolled or expecting to enroll full- or part-time at a two-year or four-year institution or university. Applicant must have 3.0 GPA or higher. Available to U.S. citizens.

Application Requirements: Application form, essay. *Deadline:* July 12.

Contact: Mr. Ronnie Gee, Scholarship Manager
Phone: 323-254-1510
E-mail: info@hardwickpendergast.com

HARNESS HORSE YOUTH FOUNDATION

http://www.hhyf.org/

CURT GREENE MEMORIAL SCHOLARSHIP

One-time award with preference given to those under age 24 who have a passion for harness racing. Based on need, merit, need, and passion for harness racing. Available for study in any field. May reapply.

Award: Scholarship for use in freshman, sophomore, junior, or senior years; not renewable. *Number:* 1–2. *Amount:* $2500.

Eligibility Requirements: Applicant must be age 18-24; enrolled or expecting to enroll full-time at a two-year or four-year or technical institution or university and must have an interest in animal/agricultural competition. Applicant or parent of applicant must have employment or volunteer experience in harness racing. Applicant must have 2.5 GPA or higher. Available to U.S. and Canadian citizens.

Application Requirements: Application form, community service, essay, financial need analysis, personal photograph. *Deadline:* April 30.

Contact: Ellen Taylor, Executive Director
Phone: 317-9080029
E-mail: ellen@hhyf.org

HARNESS TRACKS OF AMERICA

http://www.harnesstracks.com/

HTA/HAROLD SNYDER MEMORIAL SCHOLARSHIPS

One-time, merit-based award of $5000 for students actively involved in harness racing or the children of licensed drivers, trainers, breeders, or caretakers, living or deceased. Based on financial need, academic merit, and active harness racing involvement by applicant or family member. High school seniors may apply for the following school year award.

Award: Scholarship for use in freshman, sophomore, junior, senior, or graduate years; not renewable. *Number:* 3. *Amount:* $5000.

Eligibility Requirements: Applicant must be enrolled or expecting to enroll full-time at a two-year or four-year or technical institution or university. Applicant or parent of applicant must have employment or volunteer experience in harness racing. Available to U.S. and Canadian citizens.

Application Requirements: Application form, essay, financial need analysis. *Deadline:* June 26.

Contact: Ms. Heather McColloch, Executive Assistant
Harness Tracks of America
10705 Northfield Rd.
Northfield, OH 44067
Phone: 330-467-4101 Ext. 2204
E-mail: hmccolloch@northfieldpark.com

HARRINGTON FAMILY FOUNDATION

http://harringtonfamilyfoundation.org

OREGON COMMUNITY QUARTERBACK SCHOLARSHIP

The Oregon Community Quarterback Scholarship is a renewable four-year collegiate scholarship program for Oregon high school seniors who are emerging leaders, and plan to attend an Oregon university, college or trade school. This need-based scholarship focuses on an individual's involvement in his or her community, rather than academic or athletic performance. Four scholarships will be awarded for the 2018/19 academic year. Each scholarship is worth $2,500 per year, for a total of $10,000 per student. The scholarship is valid only at an Oregon accredited college, university or trade school. Interviews with the Harrington Family Foundation Scholarship Committee may be conducted for scholarship finalists. To learn more visit harringtonfamilyfoundation.org.

Award: Scholarship for use in freshman, sophomore, junior, or senior years; renewable. *Number:* 4. *Amount:* $10,000.

Eligibility Requirements: Applicant must be age 17-99; enrolled or expecting to enroll full-time at a two-year or four-year or technical institution or university; resident of Oregon and studying in Oregon. Available to U.S. and non-U.S. citizens.

Application Requirements: Application form, essay, financial need analysis. *Deadline:* April 2.

Contact: Mrs. Madeline Guzzo, Scholarship Manager
Harrington Family Foundation
1816 NW Overton Street
Portland, OR 97209
Phone: 855-868-3549
E-mail: madeline@harringtonfamilyfoundation.org

HAWAII EDUCATION ASSOCIATION

http://www.heaed.com/

HAWAII EDUCATION ASSOCIATION CONTINUING COLLEGE STUDENT SCHOLARSHIP

• See page 565

HAWAII EDUCATION ASSOCIATION HIGH SCHOOL STUDENT SCHOLARSHIP

• See page 565

HAWAII SCHOOLS FEDERAL CREDIT UNION

http://www.hawaiischoolsfcu.org/

EDWIN KUNIYUKI MEMORIAL SCHOLARSHIP

Annual scholarship for an incoming college freshman in recognition of academic excellence. Applicant must be Hawaii Schools Federal Credit Union member at the time the application is submitted.

Award: Scholarship for use in freshman year; not renewable. *Number:* 1. *Amount:* $1000.

Eligibility Requirements: Applicant must be high school student; planning to enroll or expecting to enroll full-time at a two-year or four-year or technical institution or university and resident of Hawaii. Applicant must have 2.5 GPA or higher. Available to U.S. citizens.

Application Requirements: Application form, essay. *Deadline:* February 16.

Contact: Mr. Stuart Asahina, Vice President
Hawaii Schools Federal Credit Union
233 Vineyard Street
Honolulu, HI 96813
Phone: 808-521-0302 Ext. 6236
Fax: 808-538-3231
E-mail: sasahina@hawaiischoolsfcu.org

HBCUCONNECT.COM

http://www.hbcuconnect.com/

HBCUCONNECT.COM MINORITY SCHOLARSHIP PROGRAM

Scholarship to minorities attending a historically Black college or university. Must attend or be enrolled into an HBCU. Selection based on quality of content in the online registration, and/or an essay, and financial need.

Award: Scholarship for use in freshman, sophomore, junior, senior, graduate, or postgraduate years; not renewable. *Number:* 1. *Amount:* $1000–$2500.

Eligibility Requirements: Applicant must be American Indian/Alaska Native, Asian/Pacific Islander, Black (non-Hispanic), Hispanic and enrolled or expecting to enroll full- or part-time at a two-year or four-year institution or university. Available to U.S. citizens.

Application Requirements: Application form, essay. *Deadline:* continuous.

Contact: Mr. William Moss, CEO
Phone: 614-416-5515
Fax: 614-864-8901
E-mail: wrmoss@hbcuconnect.com

HELEN DILLER FAMILY FOUNDATION

http://www.dillerteenawards.org

DILLER TEEN TIKKUN OLAM AWARDS

The Diller Teen Tikkun Olam Awards celebrate tikkun olam, or repairing the world. The Diller Family Foundation knows that supporting Jewish teen leadership today means creating and inspiring future generations of strong Jewish leaders in the global community. The Awards provide $36,000 for each recipient so that they may use it to further their project or education. If the funds will be used towards education, they will be sent directly to the college or university. Some recipients choose to divide the award between their education and philanthropic work. Applicants must demonstrate leadership via a specific community service project that is already underway. Applications presenting a project that has not yet been initiated will not be considered. Examples of past recipients' work can be found on our website, http://www.dillerteenawards.org.

Award: Prize for use in freshman, sophomore, junior, senior, graduate, or postgraduate years; not renewable. *Number:* 15. *Amount:* $36,000.

Eligibility Requirements: Applicant must be Jewish; of Jewish heritage; age 13-19 and enrolled or expecting to enroll full- or part-time at a two-year or four-year or technical institution or university. Available to U.S. citizens.

Application Requirements: Application form, community service. *Deadline:* January 8.

Contact: Ms. Lindsay Merbaum, Marketing and Outreach Coordinator
Helen Diller Family Foundation
121 Steuart Street
San Francisco, CA 94105
Phone: 415-512-6438
E-mail: lindsaym@sfjcf.org

HEMOPHILIA FOUNDATION OF SOUTHERN CALIFORNIA

http://www.hemosocal.org/

CHRISTOPHER MARK PITKIN MEMORIAL SCHOLARSHIP

Scholarship open to all members of the hemophilia community, including spouses and siblings. Applicants must be pursuing a college or technical/trade school education. Applicants must be part of the HFSC Service Area - Counties of Los Angeles, Orange, Santa Barbara, San Luis Obispo, Riverside, San Bernardino, Ventura, Inyo, and Kern.

Award: Scholarship for use in freshman, sophomore, junior, senior, graduate, or postgraduate years; not renewable. *Number:* 5–11. *Amount:* $250–$1000.

Eligibility Requirements: Applicant must be physically disabled; enrolled or expecting to enroll full- or part-time at a two-year or four-year or technical institution or university and resident of California. Applicant must be physically disabled. Available to U.S. citizens.

Application Requirements: Application form, essay. *Deadline:* June 29.

Contact: Laura Desai, Operations Manager
Hemophilia Foundation of Southern California
959 E Walnut St Suite 114
Pasadena, CA 91106
Phone: 626-765-6656
Fax: 626-765-6657
E-mail: info@hemosocal.org

HENKEL CONSUMER ADHESIVES INC.

http://www.ducktapeclub.com/

DUCK BRAND DUCT TAPE "STUCK AT PROM" SCHOLARSHIP CONTEST

Contest is open to residents of the United States and Canada. Must be 14 years or older. The Grand Prize winners will each receive a $10000 scholarship, the second place students will each receive $5000, and third place winners will each receive $3000. The remaining seven "runner-up" couples will each receive a $1000 prize. Additionally, the Singles Category winner will receive a $1000 prize.

Award: Prize for use in freshman, sophomore, junior, or senior years; not renewable. *Number:* 1–11. *Amount:* $1000–$10,000.

Eligibility Requirements: Applicant must be high school student; planning to enroll or expecting to enroll full- or part-time at a two-year or four-year or technical institution or university and resident of Alabama, Alaska, Alberta, Arizona, Arkansas, British Columbia, California, Connecticut, Delaware, District of Columbia, Florida, Georgia, Guam, Hawaii, Idaho, Illinois, Indiana, Iowa, Kansas, Kentucky, Louisiana, Maine, Manitoba, Massachusetts, Michigan, Minnesota, Mississippi, Missouri, Montana, Nebraska, Nevada, New Brunswick, Newfoundland, New Hampshire, New Jersey, New Mexico, New York, North Carolina, North Dakota, Northwest Territories, Nova Scotia, Ohio, Oklahoma, Ontario, Oregon, Pennsylvania, Prince Edward Island, Puerto Rico, Rhode Island, Saskatchewan, South Carolina, South Dakota, Tennessee, Texas, Utah, Virginia, Washington, West Virginia, Wisconsin, Wyoming, Yukon. Available to U.S. and Canadian citizens.

Application Requirements: Application form, personal photograph. *Deadline:* May 31.

Contact: Consumer Relations, ShurTech Brands Consumer Relations Department
Henkel Consumer Adhesives Inc.
32150 Just Imagine Drive
Avon, OH 44011-1355
Phone: 800-321-1733

HERB KOHL EDUCATIONAL FOUNDATION INC.

http://www.kohleducation.org/

HERB KOHL EXCELLENCE SCHOLARSHIP PROGRAM

Scholarships of $10,000 to Wisconsin high school graduates awarded annually in a competitive selection process. Applicants must be Wisconsin residents. Recipients are chosen for their demonstrated academic potential, outstanding leadership, citizenship, community service, integrity and other special talents.

Award: Scholarship for use in freshman, sophomore, junior, or senior years; not renewable. *Number:* 100. *Amount:* $10,000.

Eligibility Requirements: Applicant must be high school student; planning to enroll or expecting to enroll full- or part-time at a two-year or four-year or technical institution or university and resident of Wisconsin. Available to U.S. and non-U.S. citizens.

Application Requirements: Application form, community service, essay. *Deadline:* November 4.

Contact: Ms. Kim Marggraf, Director
Phone: 920-457-1727
E-mail: marggraf@excel.net

THE HIGGINS FIRM

https://www.thehigginsfirm.com

JUDGE BILL HIGGINS PUBLIC SERVICE SCHOLARSHIP

The applicant must be currently enrolled in an accredited community college, undergraduate, or graduate program. This also includes incoming first- year college students who are high school graduates or possess a GED. For more information visit: https://www.thehigginsfirm.com/medical-malpractice.html#scholarship.

Award: Scholarship for use in freshman, sophomore, junior, senior, graduate, or postgraduate years; not renewable. *Number:* 1. *Amount:* $500.

Eligibility Requirements: Applicant must be enrolled or expecting to enroll full- or part-time at a two-year or four-year or technical institution or university. Applicant must have 3.0 GPA or higher. Available to U.S. and non-U.S. citizens.

Application Requirements: Application form, community service, essay. *Deadline:* July 21.

Contact: Jim Higgins
E-mail: info@higginsfirm.com

HIGH INCOME PARENTS.COM

http://www.highincomeparents.com

MELISSA READ MEMORIAL SCHOLARSHIP

Here at High Income Parents, we value education, and we especially value education at a reduced cost. The value of the scholarship is currently at $2000. Students at technical, community and four-year colleges are welcome to apply. Your enrollment and good standing will be verified if you are selected as a finalist. There will be five finalists selected by me and then judged by a select group of teachers. This year's topic question is: What is the worst financial decision you have made and what did you learn from it? Send the essay with other information in a.doc file (written in Microsoft Word) as an email attachment to tom@highincomeparents.com with the subject line Melissa Read Memorial Scholarship. You can start to submit the applications May 1st.

Award: Scholarship for use in freshman, sophomore, junior, or senior years; not renewable. *Number:* 1. *Amount:* $2000.

Eligibility Requirements: Applicant must be enrolled or expecting to enroll full-time at a two-year or four-year or technical institution or university. Available to U.S. citizens.

Application Requirements: Essay. *Deadline:* July 1.

Contact: Dr. Tom Rairdon
E-mail: Tom@highincomeparents.com

HISPANIC ANNUAL SALUTE

http://www.hispanicannualsalute.org/

HISPANIC ANNUAL SALUTE SCHOLARSHIP

Scholarships of $2000 are awarded to graduating high school seniors. Program is intended to help foster a strong Hispanic presence within colleges and universities that will ultimately lead to active community leadership and volunteerism. Applicant must maintain a minimum GPA of 2.5.

Award: Scholarship for use in freshman year; not renewable. *Number:* 10. *Amount:* $2000.

Eligibility Requirements: Applicant must be Hispanic; high school student and planning to enroll or expecting to enroll full-time at a four-year institution or university. Applicant or parent of applicant must have employment or volunteer experience in community service. Applicant must have 2.5 GPA or higher. Available to U.S. citizens.

Application Requirements: Application form, essay, recommendations or references, test scores. *Deadline:* December 4.

Contact: Dan Sandos, President
Phone: 303-699-0715
Fax: 303-627-4205
E-mail: dcsandos@aol.com

HISPANIC METROPOLITAN CHAMBER SCHOLARSHIPS

http://www.hmccoregon.com/

HISPANIC METROPOLITAN CHAMBER SCHOLARSHIPS

Scholarships to encourage Hispanics to pursue higher education. Applicant must have a minimum 3.00 GPA. The award is available only to Hispanic students from Oregon and Southwest Washington.

Award: Scholarship for use in freshman, sophomore, junior, senior, graduate, or postgraduate years; not renewable. *Number:* 45–50. *Amount:* $2000–$8000.

Eligibility Requirements: Applicant must be of Hispanic heritage; enrolled or expecting to enroll full- or part-time at a two-year or four-year institution or university and resident of Oregon. Applicant must have 3.0 GPA or higher. Available to U.S. and non-Canadian citizens.

Application Requirements: Application form, community service, essay. *Deadline:* January 29.

Contact: MaryAnn Potter, Scholarship Director
Hispanic Metropolitan Chamber Scholarships
P.O. Box 1837
Portland, OR 97207
Phone: 503-222-0280
E-mail: scholarship@hmccoregon.com

THE HIV LEAGUE

http://www.hivleague.org

THE HIV LEAGUE SCHOLARSHIP

The HIV League seeks to identify and award scholarships to the most promising students living with HIV as evidenced by their educational accomplishments, leadership, and service. If you choose to not have your name publicized, this will not hurt your chances in being awarded an HIV League Scholarship. If you do, however, choose to have your name publicized, we will always ask permission from you first. Also, if you choose to have your name publicized, this will give you the opportunity to have your voice heard as a student living with HIV amongst different publications and media outlets. If you have any further questions about this portion of the scholarship application, please do not hesitate to email our Executive Director, Daniel Szymczyk, at daniel@hivleague.org.

Award: Scholarship for use in freshman, sophomore, junior, senior, graduate, or postgraduate years; not renewable. *Number:* 4. *Amount:* $7000.

Eligibility Requirements: Applicant must be enrolled or expecting to enroll full-time at a two-year or four-year or technical institution or university. Applicant must have 2.5 GPA or higher. Available to U.S. citizens.

Application Requirements: Application form, essay, interview. *Deadline:* January 31.

Contact: Mr. Daniel Szymczyk, Founder / Executive Director
The HIV League
PO Box 7033
New York, NY 10008-7033
Phone: 828-467-4025
E-mail: daniel@hivleague.org

HOFOSS DEVALL

https://www.hdinjurylaw.com/

HOFFOSS DEVALL LOUISIANA SAFE DRIVER SCHOLARSHIP

The Hoffoss Devall Louisiana Safe Driver Scholarship is a $2,000 scholarship for a Louisiana high school senior who is enrolled in a two-year to five-year institution in Louisiana in 2018. To apply for this scholarship, create a short (30-120 second video) or submit an essay (must be at least 1,000 words) telling us about one of the following things: 1. Explain why you do not support or promote distracted driving (i.e. driving while texting or drinking); 2. Explain how you prevent distracted driving and promote safe driving practices for yourself, friends, or family by providing specific examples. If you're submitting a video application, upload your video to YouTube. Fill out the application with supporting essay, and include a link to your video on YouTube. If you're submitting an essay application, fill out the application and include your full essay (must be at least 1,000 words) in the appropriate submission box. Applications are due April 30, 2018.

Award: Scholarship for use in freshman year; not renewable. *Number:* 1. *Amount:* $2000.

Eligibility Requirements: Applicant must be high school student; planning to enroll or expecting to enroll full- or part-time at a two-year or four-year or technical institution or university; resident of Louisiana and studying in Louisiana. Available to U.S. citizens.

Application Requirements: Application form, essay. *Deadline:* April 30.

Contact: Scholarship Coordinator
E-mail: coordinator@ourscholarship.io

HOFFOSS DEVALL PROBLEM SOLVING SCHOLARSHIP

The Hoffoss Devall Problem Solving Scholarship is a $2,000 scholarship for a college or first-year law student who is enrolled in a two-year to five-year institution, graduate school or law school in 2018. To apply for this scholarship, create a short (2-4 minute video) OR submit an essay (must be at least 1,000 words) answering this prompt: If you had $1 million, what problem would you try to solve? And how would you do it? Who would you work with? Why would you try to solve that particular problem? If you're submitting a video application, upload your video to YouTube. Fill out the application with supporting essay, and include a link to your video on YouTube. If you're submitting an essay application, fill out the application and include your full essay (must be at least 1,000 words) in the appropriate submission box. Applications are due April 30, 2018.

Award: Scholarship for use in freshman, sophomore, junior, senior, or graduate years; not renewable. *Number:* 1. *Amount:* $2000.

Eligibility Requirements: Applicant must be enrolled or expecting to enroll full- or part-time at a two-year or four-year or technical institution or university. Available to U.S. citizens.

Application Requirements: Application form, essay. *Deadline:* April 30.

Contact: Scholarship Coordinator
E-mail: coordinator@ourscholarship.io

HOME IMPROVEMENT SOLUTIONS

http://www.myhomeimprovementsolutions.com

HOME IMPROVEMENT SCHOLARSHIP BY HOME IMPROVEMENT SOLUTIONS

Under this scholarship program, an applicant needs to write 1000-1500 words on the given topics that you can check out from our site and submit your content on our site. Then our experts will analyze the quality of the content and announce the name of the winner. Winner will win $500 as a reward

Award: Scholarship for use in freshman, sophomore, junior, senior, graduate, or postgraduate years; not renewable.

Eligibility Requirements: Applicant must be American Indian/Alaska Native, Asian/Pacific Islander, Black (non-Hispanic), Hispanic and enrolled or expecting to enroll full- or part-time at a two-year or four-year or technical institution or university.

Application Requirements: Application form. *Deadline:* December 15.

Contact: Chris Diaz, Home Improvement Solutions Scholarship
Home Improvement Solutions
2389 joes road
Millerton, NY 12546
Phone: 518-663-0295
E-mail: info@myhomeimprovementsolutions.com

HOMUS

https://homus.org

HOMUS SCHOLARSHIP PROGRAM

Since its conception in 1991, electronic commerce, or e-commerce, has made revolutionary changes in the way people do business transactions. Prior to e-commerce, consumers had to purchase items directly from a physical store. Now almost every transaction can be done online, thanks to the emergence of e-commerce. And our magazine is helping consumers to make a right decision before while shopping online. College is a big step forward in achieving student's goals and we would like to be a part of the educational life of students. That's why we are providing $3000 E-Commerce Research Scholarship program for all students currently enrolled in a college or university! Homus.org offers the opportunity for all who want to apply for the scholarship by researching and covering the following topic "E-Commerce Trends. How E-Commerce Will Change Retail Business in Next 10 Years."

Award: Scholarship for use in freshman, sophomore, junior, senior, graduate, or postgraduate years; renewable. *Number:* 1. *Amount:* $3000.

Eligibility Requirements: Applicant must be hearing impaired, learning disabled, physically disabled, or visually impaired; American Indian/Alaska Native, Asian/Pacific Islander, Black (non-Hispanic), Hispanic; high school student and planning to enroll or expecting to enroll full- or part-time at a two-year or four-year or technical institution or university. Applicant must be hearing impaired, learning disabled, physically disabled, or visually impaired. Available to U.S. and non-U.S. citizens.

Application Requirements: Application form, essay. *Deadline:* September 15.

Contact: Mr. David Croll, Senior Manager
Homus
4318 Oakwood Avenue
New York, NY 10021
Phone: 1-2126395961
E-mail: hello@homus.org

HOOVER PRESIDENTIAL FOUNDATION

http://www.hooverpresidentialfoundation.org/travel-grant.php

HERBERT HOOVER UNCOMMON STUDENT AWARD

Award for juniors attending an Iowa high school or home school program only. Grades and test scores are not evaluated. Applicants are chosen on the basis of submitted project proposals. Those chosen will complete their proposed project and make a presentation to receive $1500. Three are chosen for $5000 scholarships.

Award: Scholarship for use in freshman or sophomore years; not renewable. *Number:* 15. *Amount:* $1500–$5000.

Eligibility Requirements: Applicant must be high school student; planning to enroll or expecting to enroll full-time at a two-year or four-year or technical institution or university and resident of Iowa. Available to U.S. citizens.

Application Requirements: Application form. *Deadline:* March 15.

Contact: Ms. Delene McConnaha, Membership and Academic Programs Manager
Hoover Presidential Foundation
PO Box 696
302 Parkside Drive
West Branch, IA 52358-0696
Phone: 319-643-5327
E-mail: DMcConnaha@HooverPF.org

HOSPITAL CENTRAL SERVICES INC.

http://www.giveapint.org/

HOSPITAL CENTRAL SERVICES STUDENT VOLUNTEER SCHOLARSHIP

Award to a graduating high school senior. Must have completed a minimum of 135 hours of volunteer service to the Blood Center in no less than a two calendar year period. Minimum 2.5 GPA required. Children of employees of Hospital Central Services or its affiliates are not eligible.

Award: Scholarship for use in freshman year; not renewable. *Number:* up to 2. *Amount:* $1000.

Eligibility Requirements: Applicant must be high school student and planning to enroll or expecting to enroll full- or part-time at a two-year or four-year institution or university. Applicant or parent of applicant must have employment or volunteer experience in community service. Applicant must have 2.5 GPA or higher. Available to U.S. citizens.

Application Requirements: Application form, recommendations or references, test scores, transcript. *Deadline:* March 31.

Contact: Sandra Thomas, Director of Development and Customer Service
Hospital Central Services Inc.
1465 Valley Center Parkway
Bethlehem, PA 18017
Phone: 610-691-5850 Ext. 292

HOSTESS COMMITTEE SCHOLARSHIPS/MISS AMERICA PAGEANT

http://www.missamerica.org/

MISS AMERICA COMMUNITY SERVICE SCHOLARSHIPS

Award to assist in the expansion of scholarship provision throughout the state and local programs. Each eligible state will receive a $1000 scholarship for a contestant demonstrating exemplary community service initiatives. Only opened to those contestants competing at the state level.

Award: Scholarship for use in freshman, sophomore, junior, senior, or graduate years; not renewable. *Amount:* $1000.

Eligibility Requirements: Applicant must be enrolled or expecting to enroll full- or part-time at a four-year institution or university; female and must have an interest in beauty pageant. Applicant or parent of applicant must have employment or volunteer experience in community service. Available to U.S. citizens.

Application Requirements: Application form. *Deadline:* varies.

Contact: Doreen Lindell Gordon, Controller and Scholarship Administrator
Phone: 609-345-7571 Ext. 27
Fax: 609-347-6079
E-mail: doreen@missamerica.org

HOSTGATOR

https://www.hostgator.com/

HOSTGATOR WEBSITE SCHOLARSHIP

Three $1,500 scholarships are available to students of all majors currently enrolled in 2- or 4-year university programs who answer the essay question, "How has the internet impacted your education?" Please see website for more details, https://www.hostgator.com/blog/hostgator-website-scholarship/

Award: Scholarship for use in freshman, sophomore, junior, senior, or graduate years; not renewable. *Number:* 3. *Amount:* $1500.

Eligibility Requirements: Applicant must be enrolled or expecting to enroll full- or part-time at a two-year or four-year institution or university. Available to U.S. citizens.

Application Requirements: Essay. *Deadline:* November 30.

HOUSE OF BLUES MUSIC FORWARD FOUNDATION

https://hobmusicforward.org/

LIVE NATION—US CONCERTS SCHOLARSHIP AWARD

This $10,000 scholarship is open to students interested in the five core areas of the Live Nation business: concert promotion and venue operation, sponsorship and advertising, ticketing, e-commerce and artist management. Finalists for this scholarship will also be considered for an internship opportunity with Live Nation Entertainment.

Award: Scholarship for use in junior or senior years; not renewable. *Number:* 1. *Amount:* $10,000.

Eligibility Requirements: Applicant must be enrolled or expecting to enroll full-time at a four-year institution or university and must have an interest in music or music/singing. Applicant must have 3.0 GPA or higher.

Application Requirements: Application form, essay. *Deadline:* March 31.

Contact: Ms. Nazanin Fatemian, House of Blues Music Forward Foundation
House of Blues Music Forward Foundation
7060 Hollywood Boulevard, Floor 2
Los Angeles, CA 90028
Phone: 323-821-3946
E-mail: nfatemian@hobmusicforward.org

HOUSTON COMMUNITY SERVICES

AZTECA SCHOLARSHIP

Scholarships are awarded annually to a male and a female high school senior planning to attend a university or a college as first-time, first-year students. Must be a Houston Area resident.

Award: Scholarship for use in freshman year; not renewable. *Number:* 2. *Amount:* $500.

Eligibility Requirements: Applicant must be of Hispanic heritage; high school student; planning to enroll or expecting to enroll full-time at a two-year or four-year institution or university and resident of Texas. Available to U.S. citizens.

Application Requirements: Application form, essay, personal photograph. *Deadline:* April 28.

Contact: Edward Castillo, Coordinator
Houston Community Services
5115 Harrisburg Boulevard
Houston, TX 77011
Phone: 713-926-8771
Fax: 713-926-8771
E-mail: hcsaztlan@sbcglobal.net

HOW TO WIN COLLEGE SCHOLARSHIPS

https://how2winscholarships.com

SAVOR SUMMER COLLEGE SCHOLARSHIP

This is a $500 scholarship award open to high school sophomores, juniors, and seniors in the 2018-2019 school year. There is no income limit for this scholarship opportunity. To read the full list of requirements and to download the application, please visit https://how2winscholarships.com.

Award: Scholarship for use in freshman year; not renewable. *Number:* 1. *Amount:* $500.

Eligibility Requirements: Applicant must be high school student and planning to enroll or expecting to enroll full-time at a two-year or four-year institution or university. Applicant must have 3.0 GPA or higher. Available to U.S. citizens.

Application Requirements: Application form, essay. *Deadline:* July 1.

Contact: Monica Matthews, Author, Site/Business Owner
How to Win College Scholarships
PO Box 94
Jeddo, MI 48032
Phone: 810-434-4390
E-mail: info@how2winscholarships.com

HUBSHOUT

http://hubshout.com/

HUBSHOUT INTERNET MARKETING SCHOLARSHIP

The HubShout Internet Marketing Scholarship is designed to help students who are on the path to any type of technical, business, or marketing career that will involve online marketing. Students who have completed at least one year of post-secondary education and have at least a 3.0 GPA are encouraged to apply. Graduate students are also welcome to apply. This is an ongoing scholarship and applications are reviewed twice per year.

Award: Scholarship for use in sophomore, junior, senior, graduate, or postgraduate years; not renewable. *Number:* 1. *Amount:* $1000.

Eligibility Requirements: Applicant must be enrolled or expecting to enroll full-time at a two-year or four-year or technical institution or university. Applicant must have 3.0 GPA or higher. Available to U.S. citizens.

Application Requirements: Application form. *Deadline:* continuous.

Contact: Chad Hill
HubShout
200 Little Falls Street
Suite 207
Falls Church, VA 22046
Phone: 888-266-6432
E-mail: chad@hubshout.com

HUMANA FOUNDATION

http://www.humanafoundation.org/

HUMANA FOUNDATION SCHOLARSHIP PROGRAM

Applicants must be under 25 years of age and a United States citizen. Must be a dependent of a Humana Inc. employee. For more information, visit website http://www.humanafoundation.org.

Award: Scholarship for use in freshman, sophomore, junior, or senior years; renewable. *Number:* 74–75. *Amount:* $1500–$3000.

Eligibility Requirements: Applicant must be enrolled or expecting to enroll full-time at a two-year or four-year institution or university. Available to U.S. citizens.

Application Requirements: Application form, financial need analysis. *Deadline:* April 17.

Contact: Charles Jackson, Consultant
Humana Foundation
500 West Main Street, Room 208
Louisville, KY 40202
Phone: 502-580-1245
E-mail: cjackson@humana.com

IDAHO STATE BOARD OF EDUCATION

http://www.boardofed.idaho.gov/

IDAHO GOVERNOR'S CUP SCHOLARSHIP

Idaho Governor's Cup is a renewable scholarship available to Idaho residents enrolled full-time in an undergraduate academic or vocational-technical program at an eligible Idaho public or private college or university. A minimum GPA of 2.8 is required. Applicants must demonstrate commitment to public service and be able to document service. Applicants must be a high school seniors and U.S. citizens.

Award: Scholarship for use in freshman year; renewable. *Number:* 20–40. *Amount:* $3000.

Eligibility Requirements: Applicant must be high school student; planning to enroll or expecting to enroll full-time at a two-year or four-year institution or university; resident of Idaho and studying in Idaho. Applicant or parent of applicant must have employment or volunteer experience in community service. Applicant must have 2.5 GPA or higher. Available to U.S. citizens.

Application Requirements: Application form, community service, essay, portfolio. *Deadline:* February 15.

Contact: Sarah Bettweiser
E-mail: sarah@idahogovernorscup.org

INDIANA LIBRARY FEDERATION

http://www.ilfonline.org/

SUE MARSH WELLER SCHOLARSHIP FUND

Scholarships are provided for undergraduate or graduate students entering or currently enrolled in a program to receive educational certification in the field of school library media services. For more details, visit http//http://www.ilfonline.org.

Award: Scholarship for use in freshman, sophomore, junior, senior, or graduate years; not renewable.

Eligibility Requirements: Applicant must be enrolled or expecting to enroll full-time at a four-year institution or university; resident of Indiana and studying in Indiana. Available to U.S. citizens.

Application Requirements: Application form, essay. *Deadline:* June 30.

Contact: Tisa Davis, Communications Manager
Indiana Library Federation
941 E. 86th St.
Suite 260
Indianapolis, IN 46240
Phone: 317-257-2040 Ext. 104
Fax: 317-257-1389
E-mail: tdavis@ilfonline.org

INTERNATIONAL ASSOCIATION OF FIRE FIGHTERS

http://www.iaff.org/

W. H. "HOWIE" MCCLENNAN SCHOLARSHIP

Sons, daughters, or legally adopted children of IAFF members killed in the line of duty who are planning to attend an institution of higher learning can apply. Award of $2500 for each year. Renewable up to four years. Applicant must have a GPA of 2.0.

Award: Scholarship for use in freshman year; renewable. *Number:* 20–25. *Amount:* $2500.

Eligibility Requirements: Applicant must be enrolled or expecting to enroll full- or part-time at a two-year or four-year or technical institution. Applicant or parent of applicant must have employment or volunteer experience in police/firefighting. Available to U.S. citizens.

Application Requirements: Application form, essay, financial need analysis, recommendations or references, transcript. *Deadline:* February 1.

Contact: L. Harrington, International Association of Fire Fighters
International Association of Fire Fighters
1750 New York Avenue, NW
Education Department, 3rd Floor
Washington, DC 20006-5395
Phone: 202-737-8484
Fax: 202-737-8418

INTERNATIONAL COLLEGE COUNSELORS

http://www.internationalcollegecounselors.com

INTERNATIONAL COLLEGE COUNSELORS SCHOLARSHIP

International College Counselors is giving away two (2) $250 scholarships. High school freshmen, sophomores or juniors must write an essay that addresses the following topic: Brag about your high school or homeschool experience. What do you like best about it? Essays must not exceed 500 words. Two winning essays will be selected: one (1) from a student in Miami Dade County, Broward County, or Palm Beach County; and one (1) at large winner from anywhere in the world, domestic or international, including home schooled students. Each winner will receive a $250 check. The goal of the International College Counselors Scholarship is to increase awareness of the value of higher education among students.

Award: Scholarship for use in freshman year; not renewable. *Number:* 2. *Amount:* $250.

Eligibility Requirements: Applicant must be high school student and planning to enroll or expecting to enroll full-time at a two-year or four-year or technical institution or university. Available to U.S. and non-U.S. citizens.

Application Requirements: Application form, essay. *Deadline:* March 30.

Contact: Cheree Liebowitz, Director of Marketing
International College Counselors
3107 Stirling Road
Suite 208
Ft. Lauderdale, FL 33312
E-mail: info@internationalcollegecounselors.com

INTERNATIONAL DAIRY DELI BAKERY ASSOCIATION

http://www.iddba.org

INTERNATIONAL DAIRY DELI BAKERY ASSOCIATION'S SCHOLARSHIP FOR GROWING THE FUTURE

Applicants must work for a member of IDDBA at least 13 hours per week while attending classes. Applicants are eligible for two awards per year.

Award: Scholarship for use in freshman, sophomore, junior, senior, or graduate years; not renewable. *Number:* 200–300. *Amount:* $500–$2000.

Eligibility Requirements: Applicant must be enrolled or expecting to enroll full- or part-time at a two-year or four-year or technical institution or university. Applicant or parent of applicant must have employment or volunteer experience in food service. Applicant must have 2.5 GPA or higher. Available to U.S. and non-U.S. citizens.

Application Requirements: Application form. *Deadline:* continuous.

Contact: Mr. Jonathan Whalley, Education Coordinator
International Dairy Deli Bakery Association
636 Science Dr.
Madison, WI 53711
Phone: 608-310-5000
E-mail: scholarships@iddba.org

INTERNATIONAL FLIGHT SERVICES ASSOCIATION

http://www.ifsanet.com

AMI SCHOLARSHIP AWARD

Individuals are selected based on scholastic merit and dedication to an advanced education. Priority is given to those with an onboard hospitality focus, or relationship with member company.

Award: Scholarship for use in freshman, sophomore, junior, senior, graduate, or postgraduate years; not renewable. *Number:* 1. *Amount:* $4500.

Eligibility Requirements: Applicant must be enrolled or expecting to enroll full- or part-time at an institution or university. Applicant must have 3.0 GPA or higher. Available to U.S. and non-U.S. citizens.

Application Requirements: Application form, essay, financial need analysis. *Deadline:* April 30.

Contact: Ms. Kelly McLendon, Programs Manager
International Flight Services Association
1100 Johnson Ferry Road
Suite 300
Atlanta, GA 30342
Phone: 678-303-3042
E-mail: kmclendon@kellencompany.com

DHL AIRLINE BUSINESS SOLUTIONS SCHOLARSHIP AWARD

Individuals are selected to receive the award based on scholastic merit and dedication to an advanced education. Must be an employee of a current IFSA member company in good standing, or a relative of an employee of a current IFSA member company. Please address financial need within essay.

Award: Scholarship for use in freshman, sophomore, junior, or senior years; not renewable. *Number:* 1. *Amount:* $2250.

Eligibility Requirements: Applicant must be enrolled or expecting to enroll full- or part-time at an institution or university. Applicant or parent of applicant must have employment or volunteer experience in hospitality/hotel administration/operations. Applicant must have 3.0 GPA or higher. Available to U.S. and non-U.S. citizens.

Application Requirements: Application form, essay, recommendations or references, transcript. *Deadline:* May 14.

Contact: Ms. Kelly McLendon, Programs Manager
International Flight Services Association
1100 Johnson Ferry Road, NE
Suite 300
Atlanta, GA 30342
Phone: 678-303-3042
E-mail: kmclendon@kellencompany.com

FLYING FOOD GROUP SCHOLARSHIP AWARD

Individuals are selected to receive the award based on scholastic merit and dedication to an advanced education. Must be an employee of a current IFSA member company in good standing, or a relative of an employee of a current IFSA member company.

Award: Scholarship for use in freshman, sophomore, junior, or senior years; not renewable. *Number:* 1. *Amount:* $2250.

Eligibility Requirements: Applicant must be enrolled or expecting to enroll full- or part-time at an institution or university. Applicant or parent of applicant must have employment or volunteer experience in hospitality/hotel administration/operations. Applicant must have 3.0 GPA or higher. Available to U.S. and non-U.S. citizens.

Application Requirements: Application form, essay, recommendations or references, transcript. *Deadline:* May 14.

Contact: Ms. Kelly McLendon, Programs Manager
International Flight Services Association
1100 Johnson Ferry Road, NE
Suite 300
Atlanta, GA 30342
Phone: 678-303-3042
E-mail: kmclendon@kellencompany.com

IFSA MEMBER FAMILY SCHOLARSHIP AWARD

Individuals are selected based upon scholastic merit and dedication to pursuing an advanced degree. Must be an employee of a current IFSA member company in good standing, or a relative of an employee of a current IFSA member company.

Award: Scholarship for use in freshman, sophomore, junior, or senior years; not renewable. *Number:* 2. *Amount:* $2250.

Eligibility Requirements: Applicant must be enrolled or expecting to enroll full- or part-time at an institution or university. Applicant or parent of applicant must have employment or volunteer experience in hospitality/hotel administration/operations. Applicant must have 3.0 GPA or higher. Available to U.S. and non-U.S. citizens.

Application Requirements: Application form, essay, recommendations or references, transcript. *Deadline:* May 14.

Contact: Ms. Kelly McLendon, Programs Manager
International Flight Services Association
1100 Johnson Ferry Road, NE
Suite 300
Atlanta, GA 30342
Phone: 678-303-3042
E-mail: kmclendon@kellencompany.com

JOHN & GINNIE LONG SCHOLARSHIP AWARD

Individuals are selected to receive the award based on scholastic merit and dedication to an advanced education. Must be an employee of a current IFSA member company in good standing, or a relative of an employee of a current IFSA member company.

Award: Scholarship for use in freshman, sophomore, junior, or senior years; not renewable. *Number:* 1. *Amount:* $2250.

Eligibility Requirements: Applicant must be enrolled or expecting to enroll full- or part-time at an institution or university. Applicant or parent of applicant must have employment or volunteer experience in hospitality/hotel administration/operations. Applicant must have 3.0 GPA or higher. Available to U.S. and non-U.S. citizens.

Application Requirements: Application form, essay, recommendations or references, transcript. *Deadline:* May 14.

Contact: Ms. Kelly McLendon, Programs Manager
International Flight Services Association
1100 Johnson Ferry Road, NE
Suite 300
Atlanta, GA 30342
Phone: 678-303-3042
E-mail: kmclendon@kellencompany.com

JOHN LOUIS FOUNDATION SCHOLARSHIP AWARD

Individuals are selected to receive the award based on scholastic merit and dedication to an advanced education. Must be an employee of a current IFSA member company in good standing, or a relative of an employee of a current IFSA member company. Please address financial need within essay.

Award: Scholarship for use in freshman, sophomore, junior, or senior years; not renewable. *Number:* 1. *Amount:* $5000.

Eligibility Requirements: Applicant must be enrolled or expecting to enroll full- or part-time at an institution or university. Applicant or parent of applicant must have employment or volunteer experience in hospitality/hotel administration/operations. Applicant must have 3.0 GPA or higher. Available to U.S. and non-U.S. citizens.

Application Requirements: Application form, essay, recommendations or references, transcript. *Deadline:* May 14.

Contact: Ms. Kelly McLendon, Programs Manager
International Flight Services Association
1100 Johnson Ferry Road, NE
Suite 300
Atlanta, GA 30342
Phone: 678-303-3042
E-mail: kmclendon@kellencompany.com

KING NUT COMPANIES SCHOLARSHIP AWARD

Individuals are selected to receive the award based on scholastic merit and dedication to an advanced education. Must be an employee of a current IFSA member company in good standing, or a relative of an employee of a current IFSA member company. Please address financial need within essay.

Award: Scholarship for use in freshman, sophomore, junior, or senior years; not renewable. *Number:* 1. *Amount:* $2250.

Eligibility Requirements: Applicant must be enrolled or expecting to enroll full- or part-time at an institution or university. Applicant or parent of applicant must have employment or volunteer experience in hospitality/hotel administration/operations. Applicant must have 3.0 GPA or higher. Available to U.S. and non-U.S. citizens.

Application Requirements: Application form, essay, recommendations or references, transcript. *Deadline:* May 14.

Contact: Ms. Kelly McLendon, Programs Manager
International Flight Services Association
1100 Johnson Ferry Road, NE
Suite 300
Atlanta, GA 30342
Phone: 678-303-3042
E-mail: kmclendon@kellencompany.com

OAKFIELD FARMS SOLUTIONS SCHOLARSHIP AWARD

Individuals are selected to receive the award based on scholastic merit and dedication to pursuing a career in onboard services operations. Must be an employee of a current IFSA member company in good standing, or a relative of an employee of a current IFSA member company.

Award: Scholarship for use in freshman, sophomore, junior, or senior years; not renewable. *Number:* 1. *Amount:* $5000.

Eligibility Requirements: Applicant must be enrolled or expecting to enroll full- or part-time at an institution or university. Applicant or parent of applicant must have employment or volunteer experience in hospitality/hotel administration/operations. Applicant must have 3.0 GPA or higher. Available to U.S. and non-U.S. citizens.

Application Requirements: Application form, essay, recommendations or references, transcript. *Deadline:* May 14.

Contact: Ms. Kelly McLendon, Programs Manager
International Flight Services Association
1100 Johnson Ferry Road, NE
Suite 300
Atlanta, GA 30342
Phone: 678-303-3042
E-mail: kmclendon@kellencompany.com

WESSCO INTERNATIONAL SCHOLARSHIP AWARD

Individuals are selected to receive the award based on scholastic merit and dedication to an advanced education. Must be an employee of a current IFSA member company in good standing, or a relative of an employee of a current IFSA member company. Please address financial need within essay.

Award: Scholarship for use in freshman, sophomore, junior, or senior years; not renewable. *Number:* 1. *Amount:* $5000.

Eligibility Requirements: Applicant must be enrolled or expecting to enroll full- or part-time at an institution or university. Applicant or parent of applicant must have employment or volunteer experience in hospitality/hotel administration/operations. Applicant must have 3.0 GPA or higher. Available to U.S. and non-U.S. citizens.

Application Requirements: Application form, essay, recommendations or references, transcript. *Deadline:* May 14.

Contact: Ms. Kelly McLendon, Programs Manager
International Flight Services Association
1100 Johnson Ferry Road, NE
Suite 300
Atlanta, GA 30342
Phone: 678-303-3042
E-mail: kmclendon@kellencompany.com

IOVATE HEALTH SCIENCES INTERNATIONAL INC.

http://www.iovate.com/

SIX STAR PRO NUTRITION SCHOLARSHIP AWARD

Through the Six Star Greatness is Earned Scholarship Award initiative, Six Star is making a difference in the lives of American high school and post-secondary students by awarding one male and one female who showcase an active lifestyle a $15,000 bursary (for a total of $30,000) to put towards their college or university education. To qualify applicants must submit either a 1000 word essay or a 3-minute video telling us how you excel in all three aspects of your life, including athletics, academics and community involvement. Our ideal candidate should be currently attending post-secondary education institution or a high school senior student planning to attend (18 to 22 years of age); have a minimum of 3.0 GPA; be a leader on campus and excels as the overall student; have demonstrated a strong work ethic in the community, in the classroom and on the field. Submit written essays no longer than 1,000 words, or a video submissions up to 3 minutes in length. Creative entries highly recommended. Tell us how you excel in all three aspects of your life, including athletics, academics and community involvement. Entries encouraged to have a sports/fitness focus. Send a written submission with a photo of your choice (minimum requirement). Creative submission recommended including highlight reels, video essays, video testimonials, etc. See website, http://www.sixstarpro.com/scholarship/.

Award: Scholarship for use in freshman, sophomore, junior, senior, or graduate years; not renewable. *Number:* 2. *Amount:* $15,000.

Eligibility Requirements: Applicant must be age 18-22 and enrolled or expecting to enroll full- or part-time at a two-year or four-year or technical institution or university. Applicant must have 3.0 GPA or higher. Available to U.S. citizens.

Application Requirements: Essay, personal photograph. *Deadline:* April 30.

Contact: Daniel Smith, Scholarship Program
Iovate Health Sciences International Inc.
3880 Jeffrey Boulevard
Blasdell, NY 14219
E-mail: daniel.smith@iovate.com

IOWA STUDENT LOAN

http://www.IowaStudentLoan.org/

COME 2 IOWA (C2IA) SENIOR SCHOLARSHIP

To participate in the C2IA Senior Scholarship, eligible students may register at http://www.IowaStudentLoan.org/Come2Iowa

Award: Scholarship for use in freshman year; not renewable. *Number:* 5. *Amount:* $1000.

Eligibility Requirements: Applicant must be high school student; age 13-99; planning to enroll or expecting to enroll full- or part-time at a two-year or four-year or technical institution or university; resident of Illinois, Minnesota, Missouri, Nebraska, South Dakota, Wisconsin and studying in Iowa. Available to U.S. citizens.

Application Requirements: Application form. *Deadline:* May 31.

Contact: Ryan Baker, Lender Liaison and Communication Specialist
Iowa Student Loan
6775 Vista Drive
West Des Moines, IA 50266
Phone: 515-273-7225
E-mail: scholarship@studentloan.org

IOWA FINANCIAL KNOW-HOW CHALLENGE: SENIOR SCHOLARSHIP

Thirty $2,000 scholarships for Iowa high school seniors who plan to attend college in fall 2018. To qualify, students must register by February 16, 2018, complete two online financial literacy tutorials and complete a related financial literacy assessment test. Go to http://www.IowaStudentLoan.org/SeniorScholarship to register and see details.

Award: Scholarship for use in freshman year; not renewable. *Number:* 30. *Amount:* $2000.

Eligibility Requirements: Applicant must be high school student; planning to enroll or expecting to enroll full- or part-time at a two-year or four-year or technical institution or university and resident of Iowa. Available to U.S. citizens.

Application Requirements: Application form. *Deadline:* February 16.

Contact: Julie Cahalan, Communications Specialist
Iowa Student Loan
Iowa Student Loan
6775 Vista Drive
West Des Moines, IA 50266
Phone: 800-243-7552 Ext. 7226
E-mail: scholarship@studentloan.org

JACKIE ROBINSON FOUNDATION

http://www.jackierobinson.org/

JACKIE ROBINSON SCHOLARSHIP

Scholarship for graduating high school seniors accepted to accredited four-year colleges or universities. Must be a minority student, United States citizen, involved in community service and demonstrate leadership potential and financial need. See website for additional details.

Award: Scholarship for use in freshman, sophomore, junior, or senior years; renewable. *Number:* 40-60. *Amount:* $6000-$6000.

Eligibility Requirements: Applicant must be American Indian/Alaska Native, Asian/Pacific Islander, Black (non-Hispanic), Hispanic; high school student; age 18-22; planning to enroll or expecting to enroll full-time at a four-year institution or university and must have an interest in leadership. Applicant or parent of applicant must have employment or volunteer experience in community service. Applicant must have 3.0 GPA or higher. Available to U.S. citizens.

Application Requirements: Application form, application form may be submitted online (http://jackierobinson.org), community service, essay, financial need analysis, recommendations or references, test scores, transcript. *Deadline:* February 15.

Contact: Mr. John Shaw, Scholarship Application
Jackie Robinson Foundation
75 Varick Street, 2nd Floor
New York, NY 10013
Phone: 212-290-8600
Fax: 212-290-8081
E-mail: scholarships@jackierobinson.org

JAMES F. BYRNES FOUNDATION

http://www.byrnesscholars.org/

JAMES F. BYRNES SCHOLARSHIP

Renewable award for residents of South Carolina ages in their Senior year High School, with one or both parents deceased. Must show financial need; a satisfactory scholastic record; and qualities of character, ability, and enterprise. Award is for undergraduate study. Results of SAT must be provided. Information available on website http://www.byrnesscholars.org.

Award: Scholarship for use in freshman year; renewable. *Number:* 6-10. *Amount:* $14,000.

Eligibility Requirements: Applicant must be high school student; age 17-19; planning to enroll or expecting to enroll full-time at a four-year institution and resident of South Carolina. Available to U.S. citizens.

Application Requirements: Application form, autobiography, essay, financial need analysis, interview, personal photograph. *Deadline:* February 1.

Contact: Kenya White, Executive Secretary
James F. Byrnes Foundation
PO Box 6781
Columbia, SC 29260-6781
Phone: 803-254-9325
E-mail: info@byrnesscholars.org

JEANNETTE RANKIN WOMEN'S SCHOLARSHIP FUND

http://www.rankinfoundation.org/

JEANNETTE RANKIN WOMEN'S SCHOLARSHIP FUND

Applicants must be low-income women, age 35 or older, who are U.S. citizens or permanent residents of the U.S. pursuing a technical/vocational education, an associate degree, or a first bachelor's degree at a regionally or ACICS accredited college. Applications are available on our website http://www.rankinfoundation.org/students/application/ from November through March.

Award: Scholarship for use in freshman, sophomore, junior, or senior years; renewable. *Number:* 25–50. *Amount:* $2000.

Eligibility Requirements: Applicant must be enrolled or expecting to enroll full- or part-time at a two-year or four-year or technical institution or university and female. Available to U.S. citizens.

Application Requirements: Application form, essay, financial need analysis. *Deadline:* March 1.

Contact: LaTrena Stokes, Program Scholarship Manager
Jeannette Rankin Women's Scholarship Fund
1 Huntington Road, #701
Athens, GA 30606
Phone: 706-208-1211
E-mail: info@rankinfoundation.org

JOHN B. FABRIELE, III, LLC

https://www.fabrielelaw.com/

FABRIELE DISABILITY AWARENESS SCHOLARSHIP

Applicants must have a minimum cumulative GPA of 3.3 or higher. Applicants must be enrolled in an institution of higher education in the fall semester of 2018. If the applicant is still awaiting admission or deciding on a school when submitting the application, that is fine. However, before granting the scholarship we will need to ensure that the applicant is enrolled for the fall of 2018. Applicants must submit a 500-word statement in response to the following the prompt. Mail your application to 214 Route 18 #2A, East Brunswick, NJ 08816. Address your letter to The Fabriele Disability Awareness Scholarship. Please visit https://www.fabrielelaw.com/#scholarship for complete information.

Award: Scholarship for use in freshman, sophomore, junior, senior, graduate, or postgraduate years; not renewable. *Number:* 1. *Amount:* $1000.

Eligibility Requirements: Applicant must be enrolled or expecting to enroll full- or part-time at a two-year or four-year or technical institution or university. Applicant must have 3.0 GPA or higher. Available to U.S. and non-U.S. citizens.

Application Requirements: Application form, essay. *Deadline:* May 31.

Contact: John Fabriele
John B. Fabriele, III, LLC
214 Route 18, Suite 2A
East Brunswick, NJ 08816

JOHN F. KENNEDY LIBRARY FOUNDATION

http://www.jfklibrary.org/

PROFILE IN COURAGE ESSAY CONTEST

Essay contest open to all high school students, grades nine to twelve. Students in U.S. territories and U.S. citizens attending schools overseas may also apply. All essays will be judged on the overall originality of topic and the clear communication of ideas through language. Winner and their nominating teacher are invited to Kennedy Library to accept award. Winner receives $3000, nomination teacher receives grant of $500; second place receives $1000 and five finalists receive $500.

Award: Prize for use in freshman year; not renewable. *Number:* 7. *Amount:* $500–$10,000.

Eligibility Requirements: Applicant must be high school student and planning to enroll or expecting to enroll full-time at a four-year institution. Available to U.S. citizens.

Application Requirements: Application form, essay. *Deadline:* continuous.

Contact: Esther Kohn, Essay Contest Coordinator
John F. Kennedy Library Foundation
Columbia Point
Boston, MA 02125
Phone: 617-514-1649
E-mail: profiles@nara.gov

JOHNSON ATTORNEYS GROUP

https://californiainjuryaccidentlawyer.com/

NEVER DRINK AND DRIVE SCHOLARSHIP

Our hope is that this scholarship helps to raise awareness among young people about the dangers of drinking and driving. It's our mission to eliminate drunk driving and ensure the safety of all.

Award: Scholarship for use in freshman, sophomore, junior, senior, graduate, or postgraduate years; renewable. *Number:* 1. *Amount:* $1000.

Eligibility Requirements: Applicant must be enrolled or expecting to enroll full-time at a two-year or four-year institution or university. Available to U.S. citizens.

Application Requirements: Essay, personal photograph. *Deadline:* March 11.

Contact: Ms. Susan Schaben, Marketing
Johnson Attorneys Group
4440 Von Karman ave
Newport Beach 92660
Phone: 800-2356801
E-mail: Susan@jaglegal.com

JUNK A CAR

https://www.junkacar.com/

JUNK A CAR 2018 SCHOLARSHIP

Junk A Car recognizes the importance of a secondary education. As a part of our ongoing commitment to community service, we are offering a $1,000 scholarship. Junk A Car uses the profits from our Cash for Junk Cars business to finance this scholarship opportunity. Incoming freshman must be enrolled full-time in a U.S. high school or in a home school program. High school graduates planning to become a full time student at an accredited college or university are also eligible. Existing college students must be full-time students enrolled in an accredited U.S. college or university. Send us an email to scholarships@junkacarworldwide.com and include the following information: your full name, address, phone number and email address; a 350 to 500 word essay explaining why you feel you deserve a scholarship from Junk A Car. If your education has been interrupted and you are not currently enrolled in high school or college, please include an explanation in your essay; the name of the high school or college in which you are currently enrolled. If you are currently not in high school or college, please include an explanation in your application essay; if you are an incoming freshman, restarting your education or not currently enrolled in a high school or college, please include the name of the college you plan to attend. If you are an incoming freshman you must be planning to be a full-time student. We will reply to all applications within 24 hours to confirm receipt of your application. We may require additional information after your application has been received. All payments will be made directly to your college or university. If you are selected, you may be asked to allow us to feature your story on our website. Participation is not required and you will not be asked to participate in a feature article until after the scholarship has been awarded. All applications are confidential. You will find the complete scholarship information by going to our website: https://www.junkacar.com/scholarships

Award: Scholarship for use in freshman, sophomore, junior, or senior years; not renewable. *Number:* 1. *Amount:* $1000.

Eligibility Requirements: Applicant must be enrolled or expecting to enroll full-time at a four-year institution or university. Available to U.S. citizens.

Application Requirements: Application form, essay. *Deadline:* June 1.

Contact: Peter Greenblum
Junk A Car
483 Kings Highway
3rd Floor
Brooklyn, NY 11223
Phone: 888-323-7128
E-mail: scholarships@junkacarworldwide.com

J. WALTER THOMPSON

https://www.jwt.com/en/

HELEN LANSDOWNE RESOR SCHOLARSHIP

The Helen Lansdowne Resor Scholarship is an international opportunity that awards up to $10,000 for five creative women. Winners also get an internship at J. Walter Thompson, one-on-one mentorship and first-look placement upon graduation. So, who is Helen? A game changer, that's who. It started in 1908, when Helen Lansdowne was hired by J. Walter Thompson Cincinnati as the industry's first female copywriter. She soon moved to the New York office, where she rose through the ranks as a creative powerhouse. She hired and mentored dozens of creative women, ensuring that the female voice was represented in J. Walter Thompson's work. Who's eligible? Female students registered at an undergraduate, graduate, and/or portfolio school with at least 12 months of school left as of May 14, 2018. To throw your headband into the ring, apply! Visit http://www.jwt.com/ https://www.jwt.com/hlrscholarship/

Award: Scholarship for use in freshman, sophomore, junior, senior, graduate, or postgraduate years; not renewable. *Number:* 5. *Amount:* $10,000.

Eligibility Requirements: Applicant must be enrolled or expecting to enroll full- or part-time at a two-year or four-year or technical institution or university and female. Applicant must have 2.5 GPA or higher. Available to U.S. and non-U.S. citizens.

Application Requirements: Application form, essay, portfolio. *Deadline:* May 14.

Contact: Jessica Watson, HR Project Manager
J. Walter Thompson
466 Lexington Avenue
2nd Floor, J. Walter Thompson
New York, NY 10017
Phone: 212-210-6072
E-mail: hlrscholarship@jwt.com

KAUFMAN & STIGGER, PLLC

http://www.getthetiger.com/

THE ALBERTA C. KAUFMAN SCHOLARSHIP

In order to honor his late mother, Attorney Marshall Kaufman of Kentucky's Kaufman & Stigger, PLLC wished to offer a scholarship to graduating high school seniors and current college students. Alberta C. Kaufman encouraged her son to further his education and to eventually attend law school. It is in that spirit of support that we are sponsoring The Alberta C. Kaufman Scholarship.

Award: Scholarship for use in freshman, sophomore, junior, or senior years; not renewable. *Number:* 1. *Amount:* $500.

Eligibility Requirements: Applicant must be enrolled or expecting to enroll full- or part-time at a two-year or four-year institution or university and resident of Kentucky. Applicant must have 3.0 GPA or higher. Available to U.S. citizens.

Application Requirements: Application form, essay. *Deadline:* May 9.

Contact: Linda Brumleve
Kaufman & Stigger, PLLC
7513 New La Grange Road
Louisville, KY 40222
Phone: 502-458-5555
Fax: 502-458-9101
E-mail: lbrumleve@kstrial.com

KELLER LAW OFFICES

http://www.kellerlawoffices.com/

KELLER LAW OFFICES SCHOLARSHIP FOR HIGHER EDUCATION

The goal of this scholarship is to provide financial assistance to a worthy student. We understand that there are a lot of outstanding young people who, without financial assistance would not be able to go to college. Medical, social or financial obstacles can make higher education a mere dream to some students. Every year, to help open the door to the world of higher education, Keller Law Offices will offer a $1,000 scholarship to a student who submits the strongest essay focusing on the given topic.

Award: Scholarship for use in freshman, sophomore, junior, senior, or graduate years; not renewable. *Number:* 1. *Amount:* $1000.

Eligibility Requirements: Applicant must be enrolled or expecting to enroll full-time at a two-year or four-year institution or university. Available to U.S. citizens.

Application Requirements: Application form, essay. *Deadline:* July 15.

Contact: Pat McCune
E-mail: pat@marketjd.com

KELLEY & CANTERBURY, LLC

http://kelleyandcanterbury.com/

KELLEY & CANTERBURY, LLC ALASKA CURIOSITY SCHOLARSHIP

The team at Kelley & Canterbury, LLC has called Alaska home for decades. We devote our lives to helping people throughout Anchorage when they are wrongfully injured. But we did not get here alone. We have teachers and mentors to support us, clients to teach us, family members to inspire us, and a community believing in us. To do the same for an Alaska student, to be the community that supports them; that would be the greatest honor. We sincerely want to pay it forward and help a student achieve his or her own dreams. That is why we are providing a scholarship to one student so that he or she has the financial support needed to take this world by storm, one goal at a time. If you are an Alaska high school senior or college student who will be enrolled in a two-year to five-year institution (college, graduate school, law school, etc.) in Alaska in 2018, apply for the Kelley & Canterbury, LLC Alaska Curiosity Scholarship of $1000. A minimum GPA is not required.

Award: Scholarship for use in freshman, sophomore, junior, senior, or graduate years; not renewable. *Number:* 1. *Amount:* $1500.

Eligibility Requirements: Applicant must be enrolled or expecting to enroll full- or part-time at a two-year or four-year or technical institution or university and studying in Alabama, Alaska, Arizona, Arkansas, California, Colorado, Connecticut, Delaware, District of Columbia, Florida, Georgia, Hawaii, Idaho, Illinois, Indiana, Iowa, Kansas, Kentucky, Louisiana, Maine, Maryland, Massachusetts, Michigan, Minnesota, Mississippi, Missouri, Montana, Nebraska, Nevada, New Hampshire, New Jersey, New Mexico, New York, North Carolina, North Dakota, Ohio, Oklahoma, Oregon, Pennsylvania, Rhode Island, South Carolina, South Dakota, Tennessee, Texas, Utah, Vermont, Virginia, Washington, West Virginia, Wisconsin, Wyoming. Available to U.S. citizens.

Application Requirements: Essay. *Deadline:* May 30.

Contact: Scholarship Coordinator
Kelley & Canterbury, LLC
821 N Street, # 205
Anchorage, AK 99501
Phone: 513-444-2016
E-mail: coordinator@ourscholarship.io

KELLY LAW TEAM

http://www.jkphoenixpersonalinjuryattorney.com/

AUTISM/ASD SCHOLARSHIP

The Kelly Law Team (KLT) is pleased to announce that it will be offering a scholarship in the amount of $1,000 for individuals with autism. The scholarship will be used to assist in the pursuit secondary or post-secondary educational opportunities. The $1,000 scholarship will be in the form of a tuition payment for the attendance at a university, college, junior college, or trade or vocational school. It is not required that the individual be enrolled in an educational program at the time of the submission of his or her application, but must be used within a year after the award. The funds will be provided directly to the educational institution chosen by the winner. Applicants must be United States citizens who have been diagnosed with ASD. The completed application must be submitted to us no later than February 8, 2018. The application will consist of (a) the online application, (b) a statement of 100 words or less explaining how the scholarship will assist in achieving your educational goals, and (c) an optional essay (1,000 words or less) on how autism has affected your education. We may also ask you to provide us with evidence of your diagnosis. The winner will be chosen on or before March 8, 2018. The winner will be selected at the discretion of John Kelly, whose decision will be final.

Award: Scholarship for use in freshman, sophomore, junior, senior, graduate, or postgraduate years; not renewable. *Number:* 1. *Amount:* $1000.

Eligibility Requirements: Applicant must be learning disabled and enrolled or expecting to enroll full- or part-time at a two-year or four-year or technical institution or university. Applicant must be learning disabled. Available to U.S. citizens.

Application Requirements: Application form, essay. *Deadline:* February 8.

Contact: John Kelly
Phone: 602-283-4122
E-mail: michael@jkphoenixpersonalinjuryattorney.com

DISABLED VETERAN SCHOLARSHIP

This is a $1,000 scholarship being offered to disabled veterans. The winning applicant may use the award to defray the tuition cost at a secondary school, trade or vocational school, junior college, college or university. It is not required that an applicant be attending school at the time of the submission of his or her application. The successful applicant will have one year from the date of the announcement of the award to provide KLT with evidence of acceptance at a school. The funds will be paid directly to the education institution chosen by the applicant, to be applied to tuition. Eligibility for the scholarship is for veterans of any branch of the United States Armed Forces who have a disability rating of 30% or higher. We may request proof of your disability and/or your veteran status. To apply for the scholarship, the following actions are required: 1. complete the online application. You must also indicate your agreement with the terms and conditions of the scholarship program; 2. upload a statement of up to 100 words setting forth your educational goals; and 3. (optional) upload an essay (1,000 words or less) discussing the effect your military service has had on your life.

Award: Scholarship for use in freshman, sophomore, junior, or senior years; not renewable. *Number:* 1. *Amount:* $1000.

Eligibility Requirements: Applicant must be physically disabled and enrolled or expecting to enroll full- or part-time at a two-year or four-year or technical institution or university. Applicant must be physically disabled. Available to U.S. citizens. Applicant or parent must meet one or more of the following requirements: general military experience; retired from active duty; disabled or killed as a result of military service; prisoner of war; or missing in action.

Application Requirements: Application form, essay. *Deadline:* February 9.

Contact: John Kelly
Kelly Law Team
1 E. Washington St., Suite 500
Phoenix, AZ 85004
E-mail: mike@jkphoenixpersonalinjuryattorney.com

DISABLED VETERAN SCHOLARSHIP

Our firm and its founder, Ryan J. Tegnelia, believe that one way we can show our thanks to disabled veterans is by helping them fulfill their educational goals. We are doing this by providing a scholarship which we hope will encourage disabled veterans to continue their education, whether at a trade or vocational school, or at the university, junior college or college level. It is a $1,000 tuition scholarship, which will be paid directly to the school that the winning applicant chooses to attend. There is no requirement that applicants be enrolled at school when they submit their application. However, the funds must be used within a year after the successful applicant is notified that he or she has won the scholarship. An applicant must be a disabled veteran of the Armed Forces of the United States (any branch). Your disability rating must be at least 30%. Our application process is simple and straightforward. To be considered for the scholarship, you should complete the online application, upload a short statement setting forth your educational goals, and (optional)

upload an essay consisting of 1,000 words or less discussing how your military service has affected your life.

Award: Scholarship for use in freshman, sophomore, junior, or senior years; not renewable. *Number:* 1. *Amount:* $1000.

Eligibility Requirements: Applicant must be physically disabled and enrolled or expecting to enroll full- or part-time at a two-year or four-year or technical institution or university. Applicant must be physically disabled. Available to U.S. citizens. Applicant or parent must meet one or more of the following requirements: general military experience; retired from active duty; disabled or killed as a result of military service; prisoner of war; or missing in action.

Application Requirements: Application form, essay. *Deadline:* February 13.

Contact: Ryan Tegnelia
Kelly Law Team
2820 Camino Del Rio South, Suite 110
San Diego, CA 92108
E-mail: mike@sandiegocriminallawyerrt.com

KEVIN'S REVIEW

http://www.kevinsreview.com

KEVIN'S REVIEW NCLEX ASSISTANCE SCHOLARSHIP

In order to stay true to our student-centered intent and mission, KevinsReview.com is introducing a new and very unique scholarship. Platinum Tests and Feuer Nursing Review has also joined us in this mission. Both have graciously contributed for each award recipient! The scholarship is awarded on a quarterly basis, meaning there will be 4 award recipients each year. Each recipient of the scholarship will receive 1. an award of $250, enough to cover half or more of the cost of an NCLEX Review Course or an NCLEX Application; 2. lifetime access to Platinum Tests, a Computerized Adaptive Testing simulator that can predict your NCLEX readiness ($80 value); 3. three months of access to Feuer Nursing Review's Comprehensive NCLEX Review ($375 value). Drawings will take place February 1st, May 1st, August 1st, and November 1st of each year. This money is meant to help pay for remedial classes, if necessary, or to help allay the costs of re-registration and re-application. Students must upload proof that they have unsuccessfully attempted the NCLEX. This can be in the form of NCLEX "Quick Results" (a screenshot from the Pearson Vue website), or a photo or photocopy of your NCLEX notification letter in the mail. Students must upload proof that they are either attempting the NCLEX again or are undergoing a paid NCLEX Review or remedial course. This can be in the form of a receipt or confirmation email from Pearson Vue, your State Board of Nursing, or an NCLEX Review company. Apply and upload your documents here! http://www.kevinsreview.com/nclex/nclex-assistance.php

Award: Prize for use in sophomore or senior years; renewable. *Number:* 4. *Amount:* $715.

Eligibility Requirements: Applicant must be enrolled or expecting to enroll full- or part-time at a two-year or four-year or technical institution or university. Available to U.S. and non-U.S. citizens.

Application Requirements: Application form. *Deadline:* continuous.

Contact: Kevin Pan
Phone: 630-776-5801
E-mail: kevin@kevinsreview.com

KIDGUARD

http://www.kidguard.com/

KIDGUARD FOR EDUCATION ESSAY SCHOLARSHIP

Do you think parents should monitor their children's phones and online activities? We want to hear your honest opinion. The personal opinion expressed in your essay will in no way affect whether or not you are awarded the scholarship. We respect that everyone has their own opinions on the topic and want to hear what you have to say. We want to stress that word count is not a deciding factor in this contest. However, this is a writing contest and you are expected to express your well-thought-out ideas clearly, supported with research and evidence.

Award: Scholarship for use in freshman, sophomore, junior, senior, graduate, or postgraduate years; not renewable. *Number:* 1–2. *Amount:* $500–$1500.

Eligibility Requirements: Applicant must be enrolled or expecting to enroll full-time at a two-year or four-year or technical institution or university. Available to U.S. and non-U.S. citizens.

Application Requirements: Essay. *Deadline:* March 31.

Contact: Jessica Chang
KidGuard
117 W. 9th Street, Suite 1009
Los Angeles, CA 90015
E-mail: jessica@kidguard.com

KIDGUARD FOR EDUCATION ESSAY SCHOLARSHIP FOR HIGH SCHOOL

Statistics show that 42% of teenagers with tech access have been cyberbullied over the past year and that 1 in 4 have been bullied more than once. We believe that you as high school students can give us invaluable feedback. We want to hear your honest opinion. The personal opinion expressed in your essay will in no way affect whether or not you are awarded the scholarship. We respect that everyone has their own opinions on the topic and want to hear what you have to say. There are two parts in the application: essay contest and survey questions (optional.) Please visit our site for more information.

Award: Scholarship for use in freshman, sophomore, junior, or senior years; not renewable. *Number:* 1–3. *Amount:* $500–$1000.

Eligibility Requirements: Applicant must be high school student and planning to enroll or expecting to enroll full-time at a two-year or four-year institution or university. Available to U.S. and non-U.S. citizens.

Application Requirements: Essay. *Deadline:* March 31.

Contact: Jessica Chang
KidGuard
117 West 9th Street, Suite 1009
Los Angeles, CA 90015
E-mail: jessica@kidguard.com

KITCHEN GUIDES

http://www.kitchensguides.com/

SMART KITCHEN IMPROVEMENT SCHOLARSHIP BY KITCHEN GUIDES

Under this scholarship, applicants have to write 1000 words article on the cooking related niche. Topics will provide by us, so you just need to pick one from them and start writing on it and submit it on our website

Award: Scholarship for use in freshman, sophomore, junior, senior, graduate, or postgraduate years; not renewable. *Number:* 1. *Amount:* $500.

Eligibility Requirements: Applicant must be hearing impaired, learning disabled, physically disabled, or visually impaired; American Indian/Alaska Native, Asian/Pacific Islander, Black (non-Hispanic), Hispanic; high school student; age 15-40 and planning to enroll or expecting to enroll full- or part-time at a two-year or four-year or technical institution or university. Applicant must be hearing impaired, learning disabled, physically disabled, or visually impaired. Available to U.S. and non-U.S. citizens. Applicant must have general military experience.

Application Requirements: Application form. *Deadline:* October 15.

Contact: Kitchen Guides. Steven Burton, Kitchen Guides
Kitchen Guides
3548 Wyatt Street
Boca Raton, FL 33432
Phone: 651-3938087
E-mail: info@kitchensguides.com

KOGAN AND DISALVO, P.A.

https://www.kogan-disalvo.com/

KOGAN & DISALVO PERSONAL INJURY LAW AUTONOMOUS VEHICLES SCHOLARSHIP

Kogan & DiSalvo Personal Injury Law is honored to offer the Kogan & DiSalvo Law Firm Autonomous Vehicles Scholarship to a worthy and enthusiastic student. Eligibility for this $1,000 scholarship requires the applicant to meet each of the following criteria: applicant must be accepted to/enrolled in an accredited undergraduate college, university or graduate school, and pursuing an education in the legal field; applicant must demonstrate strong academic standing with a minimum GPA of 3.0;

applicant has demonstrated an academic career inclusive of outstanding service to the community, strong initiative to pursue higher education and superlative leadership. For more information, please visit: https://masseyattorneys.com/#scholarship

Award: Scholarship for use in freshman, sophomore, junior, senior, graduate, or postgraduate years; not renewable. *Number:* 1. *Amount:* $1000.

Eligibility Requirements: Applicant must be enrolled or expecting to enroll full- or part-time at a two-year or four-year or technical institution or university. Applicant must have 3.0 GPA or higher. Available to U.S. and non-U.S. citizens.

Application Requirements: Application form, essay. *Deadline:* July 31.

Contact: Darryl Kogan
E-mail: scholarship@koganinjurylaw.com

KOPFLER AND HERMANN, ATTORNEYS AT LAW

https://kopflerhermann.com/

KOPFLER & HERMANN OVERCOMING ADVERSITY SCHOLARSHIP

Kopfler & Hermann, personal injury attorneys based in Houma, Louisiana, is pleased to announce our annual scholarship in the amount of $1,000 to a student who has overcome adversity in their life and has emerged stronger. With decades of legal experience, injury lawyer Joe Kopfler has been serving the Gulf Coast since 1992 and is committed to seeing that justice is served for those injured workers and accident victims. The time immediately following a serious accident can be one of the most difficult for those involved and their families, which is why our firm seeks to help those impacted fight for full compensation for their injuries and any other damages. Similarly, we admire those who are able to overcome adversity and in this vein have established the Overcoming Adversity Scholarship. For more information, please visit: https://kopflerhermann.com/#scholarship

Award: Scholarship for use in freshman, sophomore, junior, senior, graduate, or postgraduate years; not renewable. *Number:* 1. *Amount:* $1000.

Eligibility Requirements: Applicant must be enrolled or expecting to enroll full- or part-time at a two-year or four-year or technical institution or university. Applicant must have 3.0 GPA or higher. Available to U.S. and non-U.S. citizens.

Application Requirements: Application form, essay. *Deadline:* July 31.

Contact: Joseph Kopfler
E-mail: info@kopflerhermann.com

LANDSCAPE ARCHITECTURE FOUNDATION

http://www.lafoundation.org

ASLA COUNCIL OF FELLOWS SCHOLARSHIP

This scholarship was established to: 1) aid outstanding students with unmet financial need; 2) increase participation of economically disadvantaged and under-represented populations; and 3) enrich the profession of landscape architecture through a more diverse population. Eligible applicants must be Student ASLA members and third, fourth, or fifth-year undergraduates in Landscape Architecture Accreditation Board (LAAB) accredited programs.

Award: Scholarship for use in junior or senior years; not renewable. *Number:* 1–3. *Amount:* $5000.

Eligibility Requirements: Applicant must be enrolled or expecting to enroll full- or part-time at a four-year institution or university. Available to U.S. citizens.

Application Requirements: Application form, essay, financial need analysis, personal photograph. *Fee:* $5. *Deadline:* February 1.

Contact: Scholarships Coordinator
Phone: 202-331-7070 Ext. 14
E-mail: scholarships@lafoundation.org

COURTLAND PAUL SCHOLARSHIP

This scholarship honors the memory of Courtland P. Paul, FASLA (1927-2003) and his lifelong commitment to the landscape architecture profession. A native Californian, he became one of the state's first licensed landscape architects in 1954. Mr. Paul and Peridian International, the landscape architecture firm he founded over fifty years ago, were well known for community design and master planning, and for the golf courses, hotels, and theme parks they created in Southern California and throughout the world.

Award: Scholarship for use in junior or senior years; not renewable. *Number:* 1. *Amount:* $5000.

Eligibility Requirements: Applicant must be enrolled or expecting to enroll full- or part-time at a four-year institution or university. Available to U.S. citizens.

Application Requirements: Application form, essay, financial need analysis, personal photograph. *Fee:* $5. *Deadline:* February 1.

Contact: Scholarships Coordinator
　　　Phone: 202-331-7070 Ext. 14
　　　E-mail: scholarships@lafoundation.org

EDSA MINORITY SCHOLARSHIP

Scholarship established to help African American, Hispanic, Native American and minority students of other cultural and ethnic backgrounds to continue their landscape architecture education as they pursue a graduate degree or enter into their final two years of undergraduate study.

Award: Scholarship for use in junior, senior, or graduate years; not renewable. *Number:* 1. *Amount:* $5000.

Eligibility Requirements: Applicant must be American Indian/Alaska Native, Asian/Pacific Islander, Black (non-Hispanic), Hispanic and enrolled or expecting to enroll full- or part-time at a four-year institution or university. Available to U.S. and non-U.S. citizens.

Application Requirements: Application form, essay, personal photograph. *Fee:* $5. *Deadline:* February 1.

Contact: Scholarships Coordinator
　　　Phone: 202-331-7070 Ext. 14
　　　E-mail: scholarships@lafoundation.org

HAWAII CHAPTER/DAVID T. WOOLSEY SCHOLARSHIP

The award provides funds for educational or professional development purposes for a third-, fourth-, or fifth-year undergraduate or graduate student of landscape architecture in a Landscape Architecture Accreditation Board (LAAB) accredited program. Student must be a permanent resident of Hawaii.

Award: Scholarship for use in junior, senior, or graduate years; not renewable. *Number:* 1–2000.

Eligibility Requirements: Applicant must be enrolled or expecting to enroll full- or part-time at a four-year institution or university and resident of Hawaii. Available to U.S. and non-U.S. citizens.

Application Requirements: Application form, essay, personal photograph. *Fee:* $5. *Deadline:* February 1.

Contact: Scholarships Coordinator
　　　Phone: 202-331-7070 Ext. 14
　　　E-mail: scholarships@lafoundation.org

LANDSCAPE FORMS DESIGN FOR PEOPLE SCHOLARSHIP

This $3,000 scholarship honors landscape architecture students with a proven contribution to the design of public spaces that integrate landscape design and the use of amenities to promote social interaction.

Award: Scholarship for use in senior year; not renewable. *Number:* 1. *Amount:* $3000.

Eligibility Requirements: Applicant must be enrolled or expecting to enroll full-time at a four-year institution or university. Available to U.S. and non-U.S. citizens.

Application Requirements: Application form, essay, personal photograph. *Fee:* $5. *Deadline:* February 1.

Contact: Scholarships Coordinator
　　　Phone: 202-331-7070 Ext. 14
　　　E-mail: scholarships@lafoundation.org

STEVEN G. KING PLAY ENVIRONMENTS SCHOLARSHIP

This $5,000 scholarship, created by Steven G. King, FASLA, founder and Chairman of Landscape Structures Inc., recognizes a student who has high potential in the design of play environments. This student must show an interest in the value of integrating playgrounds into parks, schools and other play environments and understand the significant social and educational value of play. Key qualities in the student receiving the Scholarship are creativity, openness to innovation, and a demonstrated interest in park and playground planning.

Award: Scholarship for use in junior, senior, or graduate years; not renewable. *Number:* 1. *Amount:* $5000.

Eligibility Requirements: Applicant must be enrolled or expecting to enroll full- or part-time at a four-year institution or university. Available to U.S. and non-U.S. citizens.

Application Requirements: Application form, essay, personal photograph. *Fee:* $5. *Deadline:* February 1.

Contact: Scholarships Coordinator
　　　Phone: 202-331-7070 Ext. 14
　　　E-mail: scholarships@lafoundation.org

LARSON JEWELERS

http://www.larsonjewelers.com

BAND WITH SUCCESS SCHOLARSHIP

Larson Jewelers created the Band With Success Scholarship to band together with both men and women who want to further their education and strive for a successful future. We are proud to offer scholarships to any students, age 16 and older, attending high school or enrolled in undergraduate, graduate and vocational programs in the US. Larson Jewelers understands the financial difficulties of higher education and would like to help. The application consists of three short essay questions involving career goals and extra-curricular activities and the winner will be announced on our website.

Award: Scholarship for use in freshman, sophomore, junior, senior, or graduate years; not renewable. *Number:* 1–2. *Amount:* $1000.

Eligibility Requirements: Applicant must be enrolled or expecting to enroll full-time at a two-year or four-year or technical institution or university. Available to U.S. citizens.

Application Requirements: Application form, essay. *Deadline:* April 15.

Contact: Scholarship Coordinator
　　　E-mail: service@larsonjewelers.com

LATIN AMERICAN EDUCATIONAL FOUNDATION

http://www.laef.org/

LATIN AMERICAN EDUCATIONAL FOUNDATION SCHOLARSHIPS

Scholarship for Colorado residents of Hispanic heritage. Applicant should be accepted in an accredited college, university or vocational school. Must maintain a minimum GPA of 3.0.

Award: Scholarship for use in freshman, sophomore, junior, senior, or graduate years; renewable. *Number:* 100–120. *Amount:* $500–$2000.

Eligibility Requirements: Applicant must be of Hispanic heritage; enrolled or expecting to enroll full- or part-time at a two-year or four-year institution or university and resident of Colorado. Applicant must have 3.0 GPA or higher. Available to U.S. citizens.

Application Requirements: Application form, community service, essay, financial need analysis, interview, personal photograph. *Deadline:* February 15.

Contact: Karley Arguello, Scholarship Selection Committee
　　　Latin American Educational Foundation
　　　561 Santa Fe Drive
　　　Denver, CO 80204
　　　Phone: 303-446-0541 Ext. 10
　　　E-mail: karguello@laef.org

LA UNIDAD LATINA FOUNDATION

http://www.lulf.org/

LA UNIDAD LATINA FOUNDATION DREAM SCHOLARSHIP

From the beginning our scholarship has welcomed and awarded undocumented scholars. Due to the changing political climate and increased need in the community, we launched the DREAM fund in 2015 whose focus would be on DREAMERS, DACA-mented, and undocumented scholars. Since 2015 we have awarded over $15,000 in scholarships from this fund alone.

Award: Scholarship for use in sophomore, junior, senior, graduate, or postgraduate years; not renewable. *Number:* 8–12. *Amount:* $1000.

Eligibility Requirements: Applicant must be of Hispanic, Latin American/Caribbean, Mexican, Nicaraguan heritage and enrolled or expecting to enroll full- or part-time at a two-year or four-year or technical institution or university. Applicant must have 3.0 GPA or higher.

Application Requirements: Application form, community service. *Deadline:* October 1.

Contact: Julio Casado, President
    E-mail: lulf@lulfoundation.org

LA UNIDAD LATINA FOUNDATION NATIONAL SCHOLARSHIP

Since our founding in 1999, our flagship scholarship has awarded over $200,000 in scholarships to scholars with financial needs who have demonstrated academic excellence, exceptional leadership and a commitment to impacting the Latino community. Scholarships are available on a competitive basis to undergraduate four-year college, and graduate students who meet the following criteria and abide by the following requirements: 1. must have minimum cumulative GPA above 2.80 out of a 4.0 GPA scale; 2. cumulative GPAs below 2.80 do not qualify for a scholarship; 3. must be currently enrolled in an eligible Bachelor's or Master's degree program at an accredited four-year college or university; 4. must have completed at least one full-time year of study for undergraduate applicants; 5. must reside in the United States. Required Documentation: 1. unofficial copy of University transcript. If selected as a finalist, you will be required to submit an official University-issued transcript; 2. letter of recommendation from university administrator/faculty or community leader demonstrating student leadership and commitment to civic service. (200-350 words). Only when requested by LULF: Official university-issued academic transcript(s) required and included in application. Graduate students are required to submit graduate and undergraduate transcripts. Applications are only accepted during the application period. Letters of recommendation are to be sent electronically. Mailed letters of recommendation must be postmarked by the deadline. Do not send letters of recommendation by registered mail or another delivery service that requires a signature, as we are sometimes unavailable to sign for deliveries. You will be notified when to submit an official transcript. We accept unofficial copies of transcripts both electronically and by mail. Send electronic transcripts to LULF@lulfoundation.org. Send paper transcripts to our mailing address above listed above. Applications that do not fit all of the criteria or do not meet the above mentioned requirements will be rejected.

Award: Scholarship for use in sophomore, junior, senior, graduate, or postgraduate years; not renewable. *Number:* 10–20. *Amount:* $500–$1000.

Eligibility Requirements: Applicant must be of Hispanic, Latin American/Caribbean, Mexican, Nicaraguan heritage and enrolled or expecting to enroll full- or part-time at a two-year or four-year or technical institution or university. Applicant must have 3.0 GPA or higher. Available to U.S. and non-U.S. citizens.

Application Requirements: Application form, community service. *Deadline:* October 1.

Contact: Julio Casado, President
    E-mail: lulf@lulfoundation.org

LAW OFFICE OF DAVID D. WHITE, PLLC

http://www.wm-attorneys.com/

ANNUAL TRAUMATIC BRAIN INJURY SCHOLARSHIPS

The Law Office of David D. White takes pleasure in announcing the establishment of an annual scholarship program for the benefit of persons who have suffered traumatic brain injury (TBI). The scholarship program consists of two scholarships, offered annually,* both in the amount of $1,000. The scholarships will take the form of tuition payments for attendance at a school of the applicant's choosing. This may be a university, a college (or a community college), a secondary school, or a trade school. And you do not have to be enrolled as a student currently in order to apply. In order to be eligible to apply for a scholarship, you must have been diagnosed with TBI. We may ask you to provide us with proof of the diagnosis. The winners will have a year in which to provide an invoice for tuition from their school, and we will then pay $1,000 to the school toward the cost reflected in the invoice.

Award: Scholarship for use in freshman, sophomore, junior, senior, graduate, or postgraduate years; not renewable. *Number:* 2. *Amount:* $1000.

Eligibility Requirements: Applicant must be learning disabled and enrolled or expecting to enroll full- or part-time at a two-year or four-year or technical institution or university. Applicant must be learning disabled. Available to U.S. citizens.

Application Requirements: Application form, essay. *Deadline:* November 3.

Contact: David White
    E-mail: michael@wm-attorneys.com

LAW OFFICE OF DAVID P. SHAPIRO

http://www.davidpshapirolaw.com/about-us/

AUTISM SCHOLARSHIP

This is a one-time scholarship in the amount of $1,000. It will be applied to offset the cost of tuition at a college, university, junior college, trade or vocational school, or community college. You do not have to be currently enrolled in the educational institution in order to apply for the scholarship. The winner will have one year from the date of the award in which to provide us with the name of the school you will be attending. The check for $1,000 will be issued directly to that school on the winner's behalf. Anyone who has been diagnosed with ASD (DSM-V) and is interested in furthering their educational goals is invited to apply for the scholarship. We reserve the right to request proof of the diagnosis. The application process requires the one complete the online application form, upload a brief statement (100 words or less) telling us how the money will be used for your educational plans if you are awarded the scholarship, and (optional) upload an essay (1,000 words or less) on the impact ASD has had on your education.

Award: Scholarship for use in freshman, sophomore, junior, or senior years; not renewable. *Number:* 1. *Amount:* $1000.

Eligibility Requirements: Applicant must be learning disabled and enrolled or expecting to enroll full- or part-time at a two-year or four-year or technical institution or university. Applicant must be learning disabled. Available to U.S. citizens.

Application Requirements: Application form, essay. *Deadline:* February 12.

Contact: David Shapiro
    Law Office of David P. Shapiro
    1501 5th Ave #200
    San Diego, CA 92101
    E-mail: michael@davidpshapirolaw.com

LAW OFFICE OF HENRY QUEENER

https://queenerlaw.com/

LAW OFFICE OF HENRY QUEENER ANNUAL SCHOLARSHIP

Benjamin Franklin once said: "An investment in knowledge pays the best interest". The Law Office of Henry Queener is proud to announce our investment in knowledge. Every year we offer a $1,500 scholarship to an exceptional student who submits the strongest essay focusing on the given topic.

Award: Scholarship for use in freshman, sophomore, junior, or senior years; not renewable. *Number:* 1. *Amount:* $1500.

Eligibility Requirements: Applicant must be high school student and planning to enroll or expecting to enroll full-time at a two-year or four-year institution or university. Available to U.S. citizens.

Application Requirements: Application form, essay. *Deadline:* July 15.

Contact: Pat McCune, Scholarship Coordinator
    Law Office of Henry Queener
    PO Box 1596
    Northbrook, IL 60065
    Phone: 847-940-4000
    E-mail: pat@marketjd.com

LAW OFFICE OF MATTHEW L. SHARP

https://mattsharplaw.com/

LAW OFFICE OF MATTHEW L. SHARP ANNUAL SCHOLARSHIP

At The Law Office of Matthew L Sharp we understand the increasing costs of college tuition makes it more difficult to graduate college for many outstanding students across the nation. Therefore, every year we offer a $1,000 scholarship to a student who submits the strongest essay focusing on the given topic.

Award: Scholarship for use in freshman, sophomore, junior, or senior years; not renewable. *Number:* 1. *Amount:* $1000.

Eligibility Requirements: Applicant must be enrolled or expecting to enroll full-time at a two-year or four-year institution or university. Available to U.S. citizens.

Application Requirements: Application form, essay. *Deadline:* July 15.

Contact: Pat McCune
    E-mail: pat@marketjd.com

LAW OFFICE OF MATTHEW SHRUM

http://www.shrumlawoffice.com/

ANNUAL SINGLE MOTHERS SCHOLARSHIP

The Law Office of Matthew Shrum is delighted to announce the offering of two annual scholarships of $1,000 each for the benefit of single mothers who wish to continue their education. The scholarship is open to single mothers who wish to continue their education on the secondary or post-secondary level. The scholarships will be paid to defray tuition costs at their chosen school. There are two scholarships being offered annually by the Law Office of Matthew Shrum. Each is in the amount of $1,000. The winners will receive the award for payment of tuition in connection with their enrollment/attendance at a college (including community college), trade school or secondary school. Each winner will have a period of one year from the award date in order to provide to us a tuition invoice from the school of her choice. We will then issue a check payable to the order of the school in the sum of $1,000.

Award: Scholarship for use in freshman, sophomore, junior, senior, graduate, or postgraduate years; not renewable. *Number:* 2. *Amount:* $1000.

Eligibility Requirements: Applicant must be enrolled or expecting to enroll full- or part-time at a two-year or four-year or technical institution or university and single female. Available to U.S. citizens.

Application Requirements: Application form, essay. *Deadline:* November 9.

Contact: Matthew Shrum
    E-mail: michael@shrumlawoffice.com

LAW OFFICES OF DAVID A. BLACK

http://www.dbphoenixcriminallawyer.com

SCHOLARSHIP FOR DISABLED VETERANS

The Law Offices of David A. Black has announced the establishment of a scholarship for disabled veterans. This is a scholarship that will assist in the payment of tuition to the educational institution chosen by the successful applicant. The scholarship is in the form of tuition assistance at a college or university, junior college, trade school or vocational school. Applicants need not be enrolled at an educational institution at the time they submit their application, but the scholarship must be utilized within one year from the date of the award. The scholarship funds will be paid directly to the school to defray a portion of the tuition cost. In order to be considered for the scholarship, you must be a veteran of the United States Armed Forces and have a 30% or higher disability rating. Your completed online application, together with all uploads, is due no later than January 15, 2018. To apply for the disabled veteran scholarship, you must 1. complete and submit the online application; 2. upload a short statement (not more than 100 words) telling us your educational goals. (Optional) Upload an essay of not more than 800 words on the topic of how your military service has affected your life. The winner will be selected at the sole discretion of David A. Black, founder of the Law Offices of David A. Black. Mr. Black's decision will be made, and the winner will be notified, on or before March 15, 2018.

Award: Scholarship for use in freshman, sophomore, junior, senior, graduate, or postgraduate years; not renewable. *Number:* 1. *Amount:* $1000.

Eligibility Requirements: Applicant must be physically disabled and enrolled or expecting to enroll full- or part-time at a two-year or four-year or technical institution or university. Applicant must be physically disabled. Available to U.S. citizens. Applicant or parent must meet one or more of the following requirements: general military experience; retired from active duty; disabled or killed as a result of military service; prisoner of war; or missing in action.

Application Requirements: Application form, essay. *Deadline:* January 15.

Contact: David Black
    Law Offices of David A. Black
    40 North Central Avenue, Suite 1400
    Phoenix, AZ 85004
    Phone: 480-280-8028
    E-mail: michael@dbphoenixcriminallawyer.com

LAW OFFICES OF DIANNE SAWAYA LLC

https://dlslawfirm.com/

LAW OFFICES OF DIANNE SAWAYA DENVER SAFE DRIVER SCHOLARSHIP

If you are a high school senior in Colorado or college student enrolled in a two to five-year institution in the United States, apply today for the $1,000 Law Offices of Dianne Sawaya Denver Safe Driver Scholarship. A minimum GPA is not required. Read the Instructions and Terms and Conditions for more eligibility information. To apply for this scholarship, create a short (30-120 second video) orsubmit an essay (must be at least 1,000 words) telling us about one of the following things: 1. Explain why you do not support or promote distracted driving (Ex: driving while texting or drinking); 2. Explain how you prevent distracted driving and promote safe driving practices for yourself, friends, or family by providing specific examples. If you're submitting a video application, upload your video to YouTube. Fill out the application with supporting essay, and include a link to your video on YouTube. If you're submitting an essay application, fill out the application and include your full essay (must be at least 1,000 words) in the appropriate submission box.

Award: Scholarship for use in freshman, sophomore, junior, or senior years; not renewable. *Number:* 1. *Amount:* $1000.

Eligibility Requirements: Applicant must be enrolled or expecting to enroll full- or part-time at a two-year or four-year or technical institution or university. Available to U.S. citizens.

Application Requirements: Application form, essay. *Deadline:* May 31.

Contact: Scholarship Coordinator
    E-mail: coordinator@ourscholarship.io

LAW OFFICES OF JUDD S. NEMIRO, PLLC

http://www.jnphoenixfamilylawyer.com/

ANNUAL DYSLEXIA SCHOLARSHIP

The Law Offices of Judd S. Nemiro, PLLC takes pleasure in announcing its annual dyslexia scholarship program. The program consists of two awards annually, each for $1,000, for tuition assistance at an educational institution. We offer these scholarships in order to help those with Dyslexia in continuing their education. You must be diagnosed with Dyslexia. We may ask for proof of the diagnosis. Two scholarships are being offered annually, and each is in the sum of $1,000. Each scholarship will take the form of a tuition payment for enrollment at a university, college, community college, trade school, or secondary school. You need not be currently enrolled at an educational institution at the time you submit your application. The winners, within a year from the award date, will provide us with a tuition invoice from the school they will be attending. A $1,000 check will then be forwarded to the school.

Award: Scholarship for use in freshman, sophomore, junior, senior, graduate, or postgraduate years; not renewable. *Number:* 2. *Amount:* $1000.

Eligibility Requirements: Applicant must be learning disabled and enrolled or expecting to enroll full- or part-time at a two-year or four-year or technical institution or university. Applicant must be learning disabled. Available to U.S. citizens.

Application Requirements: Application form, essay. *Deadline:* November 4.

Contact: Judd Nemiro
E-mail: michael@jnphoenixfamilylawyer.com

LAW OFFICES OF MARK SHERMAN, LLC

markshermanlaw.com

MARK SHERMAN LAW JUVENILE JUSTICE SCHOLARSHIP

The Law Offices of Mark Sherman, based in Stamford, Connecticut, is pleased to announce that we are offering a scholarship in the amount of $1,000 to one student who has an interest in working with young people who have already been convicted of a crime and been sent to jail. We want to support them in seizing new opportunities and giving them the means to be a success in their community. This student may have also experienced and overcome adversity in their life and can relate to these juveniles who are rebuilding their lives once out of jail. For more information, please visit:
https://www.markshermanlaw.com/#scholarship

Award: Scholarship for use in freshman, sophomore, junior, senior, graduate, or postgraduate years; not renewable. *Number:* 1. *Amount:* $1000.

Eligibility Requirements: Applicant must be enrolled or expecting to enroll full- or part-time at a two-year or four-year or technical institution or university. Applicant must have 3.0 GPA or higher. Available to U.S. and non-U.S. citizens.

Application Requirements: Application form, essay. *Deadline:* July 31.

Contact: Mark Sherman
E-mail: info@markshermanlaw.com

LAW OFFICES OF SEAN M. CLEARY

https://www.seanclearypa.com/

LAW OFFICES OF SEAN M. CLEARY SCHOLARSHIP

The Offices of Sean M. Cleary is not interested just in helping people recover compensation after suffering an accident, but we are also happy to provide financial help for students who pursue higher education. Approximately 3 out of 100,000 people were killed during 2015 in DUI accidents in the United States, with one of those three people being under the age of 21; the numbers being even higher if we are talking about the state of Florida. With this in mind, in 2018 we are offering a $1,000 scholarship for the student who will help bring more attention over the dangerous consequences of teens driving under the influence of alcohol. To submit your essay or if you are searching for more information on the subject, go to https://www.seanclearypa.com/scholarship/

Award: Scholarship for use in freshman, sophomore, junior, or senior years; renewable. *Number:* 1. *Amount:* $1000.

Eligibility Requirements: Applicant must be enrolled or expecting to enroll full-time at a four-year institution or university. Applicant must have 3.0 GPA or higher. Available to U.S. citizens.

Application Requirements: Essay, personal photograph. *Deadline:* August 31.

Contact: Mr. Sean Cleary, Atty.
Law Offices of Sean M. Cleary
19 W Flagler St #618
Miami, FL 33130
Phone: 1-305-416-9805
E-mail: sean@seanclearypa.com

LAW OFFICES OF SHERYL R. RENTZ, P.C.

http://www.srrentzlaw.com/

LAW OFFICES OF SHERYL R. RENTZ 2018 SCHOLARSHIP

The Law Offices of Sheryl R. Rentz 2018 Scholarship is our way of thanking those students who have gone above and beyond in order to give back to their local communities. Students who have earned at least a 3.0 GPA in the classroom while pursuing the betterment of the world outside of the classroom are welcome to apply to this scholarship. Applicants should be graduating high school seniors or current undergraduate students. U.S. Citizenship or Permanent Residency is required. Please visit our website for additional information and to submit an application today: http://www.srrentzlaw.com/scholarship/

Award: Scholarship for use in freshman, sophomore, junior, or senior years; not renewable. *Number:* 1. *Amount:* $500.

Eligibility Requirements: Applicant must be enrolled or expecting to enroll full- or part-time at a two-year or four-year institution or university. Applicant must have 3.0 GPA or higher. Available to U.S. citizens.

Application Requirements: Application form, essay. *Deadline:* May 2.

Contact: Mr. Sam Greer, Scholarship Manager
Law Offices of Sheryl R. Rentz, P.C.
65 N. Raymond Avenue, Suite 230
Pasadena, CA 91103
Phone: 323-254-1510 Ext. 119
E-mail: sgreer@slsconsulting.com

LAW OFFICES OF TRAGOS, SARTES AND TRAGOS

https://tragoslaw.com/

TRAGOS WRITE YOUR OWN LAW SCHOLARSHIP

This scholarship is offered to any student currently enrolled in an accredited community college, undergraduate, or graduate program in the United States. This includes incoming first-year college students who are high school graduates or possess a GED. All eligible candidates must be in good academic standing, with a minimum cumulative GPA of 3.0 or above. For more complete information, visit https://tragoslaw.com/#scholarship.

Award: Scholarship for use in freshman, sophomore, junior, senior, graduate, or postgraduate years; not renewable. *Number:* 1. *Amount:* $500.

Eligibility Requirements: Applicant must be enrolled or expecting to enroll full- or part-time at a two-year or four-year or technical institution or university. Applicant must have 3.0 GPA or higher. Available to U.S. and non-U.S. citizens.

Application Requirements: Application form, essay. *Deadline:* May 31.

Contact: George Tragos
E-mail: info@tragoslaw.com

LEAGUE FOUNDATION

http://www.leaguefoundation.org/

LEAGUE FOUNDATION ACADEMIC SCHOLARSHIP

The LEAGUE Foundation provides financial resources for U.S. Citizens that are self- identified as Gay, Lesbian, Bisexual, and Transgender high school seniors entering their first year of institutions of higher learning. The scholarship application opens annually in January and closes in April with awards distributed in the summer of each year. For scholarship criteria: http://www.leaguefoundation.org.

Award: Scholarship for use in freshman year; not renewable. *Number:* 4–8. *Amount:* $1500–$2500.

Eligibility Requirements: Applicant must be high school student; planning to enroll or expecting to enroll full-time at a two-year or four-year or technical institution or university and must have an interest in LGBT issues. Applicant must have 3.0 GPA or higher. Available to U.S. citizens.

Application Requirements: Application form, community service, essay, personal photograph. *Deadline:* April 30.

Contact: Mr. Mark Patterson, Executive Director
LEAGUE Foundation
208 South Akard Street
Room 20th Floor
Dallas, TX 75202
Phone: 469-571-2279
E-mail: info@leaguefoundation.org

LEMBERG LAW

http://www.lemberglaw.com

LEMBERG LAW AMERICAN DREAM $1,250 UNDERGRADUATE SCHOLARSHIP

Open to students who are immigrants to the U.S. and who are U.S. citizens, (Class of 2018) who plan to enroll full-time in an accredited two-year or four-year college or university in the U.S. during the 2018-2019 school year; or undergraduate students who will be enrolled full-time in an accredited two-year or four-year college or university in the U.S. during the 2018-2019 school year. Please submit an essay (maximum of 2,000 characters, or about 400 words) about interesting differences between the U.S. legal system and that of your country of origin or another country.

Award: Scholarship for use in freshman, sophomore, junior, or senior years; not renewable. *Number:* 1. *Amount:* $1250.

Eligibility Requirements: Applicant must be of African, Albanian, Arab, Armenian, Arumanian/Ulacedo-Romanian, Australian, Belgian, Bulgarian, Canadian, Central European, Chinese, Croatian/Serbian, Cypriot, Danish, Dutch, Eastern European, English, European Union, Finnish, former Soviet Union, French, German, Greek, Haitian, Hispanic, Hungarian, Icelandic, Indian, Irish, Israeli, Italian, Japanese, Jewish, Korean, Lao/Hmong, Latin American/Caribbean, Latvian, Lebanese, Lithuanian, Mexican, Mongolian, New Zealander, Nicaraguan, Norwegian, Polish, Portuguese, Rumanian, Russian, Scandinavian, Scottish, Slavic/Czech, Spanish, Sub-Saharan African, Swedish, Swiss, Syrian, Turkish, Ukrainian, Vietnamese, Welsh, Yemeni heritage and enrolled or expecting to enroll full-time at a two-year or four-year institution or university. Available to U.S. and non-U.S. citizens.

Application Requirements: Application form, essay. *Deadline:* March 31.

Contact: Ceasar DiMauro, Scholarship Manager
E-mail: scholarship2018@lemberglaw.org

LEPENDORF & SILVERSTEIN, P.C.

http://www.lependorf.com/

2018 LEPENDORF & SILVERSTEIN, P.C. SCHOLARSHIP

This scholarship is open to graduating high school seniors and current undergraduate college students with a 3.0 or higher GPA who have demonstrated a commitment to bettering their community. The application includes an essay section to tell us about your academic goals and how those goals will help you give back to the community; the introduction is to be 100-200 words, and the essay is to be 500-1000 words. The winner will be announced Monday, June 13th 2018. Additional information and applications can be found on our website.

Award: Scholarship for use in freshman, sophomore, junior, or senior years; not renewable. *Number:* 1. *Amount:* $500.

Eligibility Requirements: Applicant must be enrolled or expecting to enroll full- or part-time at a two-year or four-year institution or university. Applicant must have 3.0 GPA or higher. Available to U.S. citizens.

Application Requirements: Application form, essay. *Deadline:* May 9.

Contact: Sam Greer
Phone: 323-254-1510 Ext. 119
E-mail: lependorf@gmail.com

LEP FOUNDATION FOR YOUTH EDUCATION

http://www.lepfoundation.org/applications

CURE—CANCER SUPPORT SCHOLARSHIP

The Lep Foundation for Youth Education was formed in 2009 with the specific mission of providing financial assistance to support disabled students who demonstrate academic success and the motivation to move forward despite their disabilities. In addition, the Foundation was proud to have introduced the Cure Cancer Support Scholarship in 2016 to assist students diagnosed with childhood and adolescent cancers. The Lep Foundation is a non-profit charity with 501c3 tax exempt status (E.I.N. #27-0817346).

Award: Scholarship for use in freshman, sophomore, junior, senior, graduate, or postgraduate years; not renewable. *Number:* 1. *Amount:* $5000.

Eligibility Requirements: Applicant must be enrolled or expecting to enroll full- or part-time at a two-year or four-year or technical institution or university. Available to U.S. citizens.

Application Requirements: Application form, essay, financial need analysis. *Deadline:* June 1.

Contact: Scholarship Committee
Lep Foundation for Youth Education
9 Whispering Spring Dr.
Millstone Twp., NJ 08510
E-mail: lepfoundation@aol.com

JOHN LEPPING MEMORIAL SCHOLARSHIP

The Lep Foundation for Youth Education was formed in 2009 with the specific mission of providing financial assistance to support disabled students who demonstrate academic success and the motivation to move forward despite their disabilities. In addition, the Foundation was proud to have introduced the Cure Cancer Support Scholarship in 2016 to assist students diagnosed with childhood and adolescent cancers. The Lep Foundation is a non-profit charity with 501c3 tax exempt status (E.I.N. #27-0817346).

Award: Scholarship for use in freshman, sophomore, junior, senior, graduate, or postgraduate years; not renewable. *Number:* 1–5. *Amount:* $5000.

Eligibility Requirements: Applicant must be enrolled or expecting to enroll full- or part-time at a two-year or four-year or technical institution or university and resident of New Jersey, New York, Pennsylvania. Available to U.S. citizens.

Application Requirements: Application form, essay, financial need analysis. *Deadline:* May 1.

Contact: Scholarship Committee
Lep Foundation for Youth Education
9 Whispering Spring Dr.
Millstone Twp., NJ 08510
E-mail: lepfoundation@aol.com

LEVY LAW OFFICES

https://levylawoffices.com/

LEVY LAW OFFICES CINCINNATI SAFE DRIVER SCHOLARSHIP

If you are a high school senior in Ohio or Kentucky or college student enrolled in a two to five-year institution in Ohio or Kentucky in 2018 apply today for the $2500 Levy Law Offices Cincinnati Safe Driver Scholarship. A minimum GPA is not required. Read the Instructions and Terms and Conditions for more eligibility information. To apply for this scholarship, create a short (2-3 minute video) telling us about one of the following things: 1. Explain why you do not support or promote distracted driving (i.e. driving while texting or drinking); 2. Explain how you prevent distracted driving and promote safe driving practices for yourself, friends, or family by providing specific examples. As you're submitting a video application, upload your video to YouTube. Fill out the application with supporting essay, and include a link to your video on YouTube. Applications are due March 30, 2018.

Award: Scholarship for use in freshman, sophomore, junior, senior, or graduate years; not renewable. *Number:* 1. *Amount:* $2500.

Eligibility Requirements: Applicant must be enrolled or expecting to enroll full- or part-time at a two-year or four-year or technical institution or university; resident of Kentucky, Ohio and studying in Kentucky, Ohio. Available to U.S. citizens.

Application Requirements: Application form. *Deadline:* March 30.

Contact: Scholarship Coordinator
E-mail: coordinator@ourscholarship.io

LIFESAVER ESSAYS

https://lifesaveressays.com

LIFE SAVER ESSAYS ESSAY WRITING CONTEST

Lifesaver Essays, an academic help platform, announces its third Essay Writing Contest. We welcome entries from passionate writers. So feel free to pick up your laptop, activate your caudate nucleus and get the juices flowing! Anyone, from any country, is free to apply. Apply online via https://lifesaveressays.com. There is no entry fee. The essay should be at least 900 words and not over 1300 words. Our team of writers have come out with a list of topics that are interesting, engaging and fun to write on. Choose one topic. All essays must be absolutely original and in your own words. Images are allowed. You are free to use images but they must be copyright-free or appropriately cited. Submissions are accepted only in Microsoft Word documents (doc or docx). The cover page of your essay must contain your complete details such as your full name, phone number, and email. The essay must be written in English. Multiple entries are allowed. The Essay Writing Contest is open from August 9 to 11:59 PM to November 30, PDT. The top three winners will be announced on December 15. One winner will be chosen every week as a Surprise Winner and they will get a consolation prize. You can send as many entries as you like.

Award: Prize for use in freshman, sophomore, junior, senior, graduate, or postgraduate years; not renewable. *Number:* 5–11. *Amount:* $10–$200.

Eligibility Requirements: Applicant must be enrolled or expecting to enroll full- or part-time at a two-year or four-year or technical institution or university. Available to U.S. and non-U.S. citizens.

Application Requirements: Essay. *Deadline:* November 30.

Contact: Mr. John Paulson, Co-founder, Lifesaver Essays
Lifesaver Essays
505, Oakland City Center,
14th Street, Suite 900
Oakland, CA 94612
Phone: 510-775-1061
E-mail: help@lifesaveressays.com

LIVE POETS SOCIETY AND JUST POETRY!!! MAGAZINE

http://www.highschoolpoetrycontest.com/

NATIONAL HIGH SCHOOL POETRY CONTEST

Award to encourage the youth of America in the pursuit of literary exploration and excellence, and to help provide a venue in which American High School students may share their poetic works. All U.S. high school students are eligible to enter this contest by submitting an original poem of 20 lines or less according to the Official Rules and Entry Procedures on our website, http://www.highschoolpoetrycontest.com, under the 'To Enter' tab.

Award: Scholarship for use in freshman year; not renewable. *Number:* 1–9. *Amount:* $100–$1000.

Eligibility Requirements: Applicant must be high school student and planning to enroll or expecting to enroll full-time at a two-year or four-year institution or university. Available to U.S. citizens.

Application Requirements: *Deadline:* continuous.

Contact: Mr. D Edwards, Editor
Live Poets Society and JUST POETRY!!! magazine
PO Box 8841
Turnersville, NJ 08012
E-mail: info@highschoolpoetrtycontest.com

MAGIC JOHNSON FOUNDATION INC.

http://www.magicjohnson.org/

TAYLOR MICHAELS SCHOLARSHIP FUND

Scholarship to provide support for deserving minority high school students who exemplify a strong potential for academic achievement but face social-economic conditions that hinder them from reaching their full potential. Must have strong community service involvement.

Award: Scholarship for use in freshman year; renewable. *Amount:* $1000–$5000.

Eligibility Requirements: Applicant must be American Indian/Alaska Native, Asian/Pacific Islander, Black (non-Hispanic), Hispanic; high school student and planning to enroll or expecting to enroll full-time at a four-year institution or university. Applicant or parent of applicant must have employment or volunteer experience in community service. Applicant must have 2.5 GPA or higher. Available to U.S. and non-U.S. citizens.

Application Requirements: Application form, community service, essay, recommendations or references, transcript. *Deadline:* February 5.

Contact: Scholarship Coordinator
Magic Johnson Foundation Inc.
9100 Wilshire Boulevard, Suite 700, East Tower
Beverly Hills, CA 90212
Phone: 310-246-4400

MAINE STATE SOCIETY FOUNDATION OF WASHINGTON, DC INC.

http://mainestatesociety.org/foundation/

MAINE STATE SOCIETY FOUNDATION SCHOLARSHIP

Scholarship(s) awarded to full-time students enrolled in undergraduate courses at a four-year degree-granting, nonprofit institution in Maine. Must be Maine resident. All inquiries must be accompanied by a self-addressed stamped envelope. Applicant must be 25 or younger.

Award: Scholarship for use in sophomore or junior years; not renewable. *Number:* 5–10. *Amount:* $1000–$2500.

Eligibility Requirements: Applicant must be enrolled or expecting to enroll full-time at a four-year institution or university; resident of Maine and studying in Maine. Applicant must have 3.0 GPA or higher. Available to U.S. citizens.

Application Requirements: Application form, essay. *Deadline:* March 15.

Contact: Jessica Stewart
E-mail: mssfscholarship@gmail.com

MAINOR WORTH INJURY LAWYERS

https://mainorwirth.com/

MAINOR WIRTH INJURY LAWYERS SCHOLARSHIP

Mainor Wirth Injury Lawyers, located in Las Vegas, Nevada, is dedicated to helping members of our community become successful and achieve their goals. Medical, social or financial obstacles can make higher education a mere dream to some students. Therefore, every year we offer a $1,000 scholarship to the student who submits the strongest essay focusing on the given topic.

Award: Scholarship for use in freshman, sophomore, junior, or senior years; not renewable. *Number:* 1. *Amount:* $1000.

Eligibility Requirements: Applicant must be enrolled or expecting to enroll full-time at a two-year or four-year institution or university. Available to U.S. citizens.

Application Requirements: Application form, essay. *Deadline:* July 15.

Contact: Bradly Mainor, Senior Partner
Mainor Worth Injury Lawyers
6018 South Fort Apache Road
Suite 150
Las Vegas, NV 89148
Phone: 702-464-5000

MANA DE SAN DIEGO

http://www.manasd.org/

MANA DE SAN DIEGO SYLVIA CHAVEZ MEMORIAL SCHOLARSHIP

Scholarship for Latinas with permanent residence in San Diego County who are enrolled or about to enroll in a two-year, four-year, or graduate program. Must have a minimum 2.75 GPA and demonstrate financial need. For an application and additional information visit http://www.sdmana.org.

Award: Scholarship for use in freshman, sophomore, junior, or senior years; not renewable. *Amount:* $500–$2000.

Eligibility Requirements: Applicant must be Hispanic; enrolled or expecting to enroll full- or part-time at a two-year or four-year institution or university; female; resident of California and must have an interest in leadership. Applicant or parent of applicant must have employment or volunteer experience in community service. Available to U.S. citizens.

Application Requirements: Application form, essay, recommendations or references, transcript. *Deadline:* February 13.

Contact: Lucy Hernandez, Scholarship Director
MANA de San Diego
PO Box 81364
San Diego, CA 92138-1364
Phone: 619-225-9594
Fax: 619-225-0500
E-mail: scholarships@sdmana.org

MARYLAND ASSOCIATION OF PRIVATE COLLEGES AND CAREER SCHOOLS

http://www.mapccs.org/

MARYLAND ASSOCIATION OF PRIVATE COLLEGES AND CAREER SCHOOLS SCHOLARSHIP

Awards for study at Maryland private colleges and career schools only. Must enroll in private college or career school same year high school is completed.

Award: Scholarship for use in freshman year; not renewable. *Number:* 50–75. *Amount:* $500–$2000.

Eligibility Requirements: Applicant must be high school student; planning to enroll or expecting to enroll full- or part-time at a technical institution and studying in Maryland. Available to U.S. and non-U.S. citizens.

Application Requirements: Application form, essay. *Deadline:* continuous.

Contact: Frank Russell, Administrative Manager
Maryland Association of Private Colleges and Career Schools
5305 Village Center Drive
Suite 295
Columbia, MD 21044
Phone: 410-282-4012
E-mail: info@mapccs.org

MARYLAND STATE HIGHER EDUCATION COMMISSION

http://www.mhec.state.md.us/

EDWARD T. CONROY MEMORIAL SCHOLARSHIP PROGRAM

Scholarship for dependents of deceased or 100 percent disabled U.S. Armed Forces personnel; the son, daughter, or surviving spouse of a victim of the September 11, 2001 terrorist attacks who died as a result of the attacks on the World Trade Center in New York City, the attack on the Pentagon in Virginia, or the crash of United Airlines Flight 93 in Pennsylvania; a POW/MIA of the Vietnam Conflict or his/her son or daughter; the son, daughter or surviving spouse (who has not remarried) of a state or local public safety employee or volunteer who died in the line of duty; or a state or local public safety employee or volunteer who was 100 percent disabled in the line of duty. Must be Maryland resident at time of disability. Submit applicable VA certification. Must be at least 16 years of age and attend Maryland institution.

Award: Scholarship for use in freshman, sophomore, junior, or senior years; renewable. *Number:* up to 121. *Amount:* $7200–$9000.

Eligibility Requirements: Applicant must be age 16-24; enrolled or expecting to enroll full- or part-time at a two-year or four-year institution or university; resident of Maryland and studying in Maryland. Applicant or parent of applicant must have employment or volunteer experience in police/firefighting. Available to U.S. citizens. Applicant or parent must meet one or more of the following requirements: general military experience; retired from active duty; disabled or killed as a result of military service; prisoner of war; or missing in action.

Application Requirements: Application form, birth and death certificate, disability papers. *Deadline:* July 15.

Contact: Linda Asplin, Office of Student Financial Assistance
Maryland State Higher Education Commission
839 Bestgate Road, Suite 400
Annapolis, MD 21401-3013
Phone: 410-260-4563
Fax: 410-260-3203
E-mail: lasplin@mhec.state.md.us

MASSACHUSETTS OFFICE OF STUDENT FINANCIAL ASSISTANCE

http://www.osfa.mass.edu/

AGNES M. LINDSAY SCHOLARSHIP

Scholarships for students with demonstrated financial need who are from rural areas of Massachusetts and attend public institutions of higher education in Massachusetts. Deadline varies.

Award: Scholarship for use in freshman, sophomore, junior, or senior years; not renewable. *Number:* 20–35. *Amount:* $250–$1100.

Eligibility Requirements: Applicant must be enrolled or expecting to enroll full-time at a two-year or four-year institution or university; resident of Massachusetts and studying in Massachusetts. Available to U.S. citizens.

Application Requirements: Application form, financial need analysis. *Deadline:* continuous.

Contact: Robert Brun, Director of Scholarships and Grants
Phone: 617-727-9420
Fax: 617-727-0667
E-mail: osfa@osfa.mass.edu

CHRISTIAN A. HERTER MEMORIAL SCHOLARSHIP

Renewable award for Massachusetts residents who are in the tenth and eleventh grades, and whose socio-economic backgrounds and environment may inhibit their ability to attain educational goals. Must exhibit severe personal or family-related difficulties, medical problems, or have overcome a personal obstacle. Provides up to 50 percent of the student's calculated need, as determined by federal methodology, at the college of their choice within the continental United States.

Award: Scholarship for use in freshman, sophomore, junior, or senior years; renewable. *Number:* 25–100. *Amount:* $500–$20,000.

Eligibility Requirements: Applicant must be high school student; planning to enroll or expecting to enroll full-time at a two-year or four-year or technical institution or university; resident of Massachusetts and studying in Illinois, Indiana, Iowa, Kansas, Kentucky, Louisiana, Maine, Manitoba, Maryland, Massachusetts. Applicant must have 2.5 GPA or higher. Available to U.S. citizens.

Application Requirements: Application form, community service, financial need analysis, interview. *Deadline:* February 1.

Contact: Robert Brun, Director of Scholarships and Grants
Phone: 617-727-9420
Fax: 617-727-0667
E-mail: osfa@osfa.mass.edu

DSS ADOPTED CHILDREN TUITION WAIVER

Need-based tuition waiver for Massachusetts residents who are full-time undergraduate students. Must attend a Massachusetts public institution of higher education and be under 24 years of age. File the FAFSA after January 1. Contact school financial aid office for more information.

Award: Scholarship for use in freshman, sophomore, junior, or senior years; renewable.

Eligibility Requirements: Applicant must be enrolled or expecting to enroll full-time at a two-year or four-year institution; resident of Massachusetts and studying in District of Columbia, Massachusetts, Pennsylvania, Vermont. Available to U.S. and non-Canadian citizens.

Application Requirements: Application form.

Contact: Robert Brun, Director of Scholarships and Grants
Phone: 617-727-9420
Fax: 617-727-0667
E-mail: osfa@osfa.mass.edu

JOHN AND ABIGAIL ADAMS SCHOLARSHIP

Scholarship to reward and inspire student achievement, attract more high-performing students to Massachusetts public higher education, and provide families of college-bound students with financial assistance. Must be a U.S. citizen or an eligible non-citizen. There is no application process for the scholarship. Students who are eligible will be notified in the fall of their senior year in high school.

Award: Scholarship for use in freshman, sophomore, junior, or senior years; renewable. *Amount:* $125–$1742.

Eligibility Requirements: Applicant must be high school student; planning to enroll or expecting to enroll full-time at a two-year or four-year institution or university; resident of Massachusetts and studying in

Massachusetts. Applicant must have 3.0 GPA or higher. Available to U.S. citizens.

Application Requirements: *Deadline:* continuous.

Contact: Clantha McCurdy, Senior Deputy Commissioner
Massachusetts Office of Student Financial Assistance
75 Pleasant Street, 3rd Floor
Malden, MA 02148
Phone: 617-391-6098

MASSACHUSETTS ASSISTANCE FOR STUDENT SUCCESS PROGRAM

Provides need-based financial assistance to Massachusetts residents to attend undergraduate postsecondary institutions in Massachusetts, Pennsylvania, Vermont, and District of Columbia. High school seniors may apply. Expected Family Contribution (EFC) should be $3850. Timely filing of FAFSA required.

Award: Grant for use in freshman, sophomore, junior, or senior years; not renewable. *Number:* 47,000–50,000. *Amount:* $400–$1600.

Eligibility Requirements: Applicant must be enrolled or expecting to enroll full-time at a two-year or four-year or technical institution or university; resident of Massachusetts and studying in District of Columbia, Massachusetts, Pennsylvania, Vermont. Available to U.S. citizens.

Application Requirements: Financial need analysis. *Deadline:* May 1.

Contact: Robert Brun, Director of Scholarships and Grants
Phone: 617-727-9420
Fax: 617-727-0667
E-mail: osfa@osfa.mass.edu

MASSACHUSETTS CASH GRANT PROGRAM

A need-based grant to assist with mandatory fees and non-state supported tuition. This supplemental award is available to Massachusetts residents, who are undergraduates at public two-year, four-year colleges and universities in Massachusetts. Must file FAFSA before May 1. Contact college financial aid office for information.

Award: Grant for use in freshman, sophomore, junior, or senior years; renewable. *Amount:* $200–$2500.

Eligibility Requirements: Applicant must be enrolled or expecting to enroll full- or part-time at a two-year or four-year institution or university; resident of Massachusetts and studying in Massachusetts. Available to U.S. citizens.

Application Requirements: Financial need analysis. *Deadline:* continuous.

Contact: Robert Brun, Director of Scholarships and Grants
Phone: 617-727-9420
Fax: 617-727-0667
E-mail: osfa@osfa.mass.edu

MASSACHUSETTS GILBERT MATCHING STUDENT GRANT PROGRAM

Grants for permanent Massachusetts residents attending an independent, regionally accredited Massachusetts school or school of nursing full time. Must be U.S. citizen and permanent legal resident of Massachusetts. File the Free Application for Federal Student Aid after January 1. Contact college financial aid office for complete details and deadlines.

Award: Grant for use in freshman, sophomore, junior, or senior years; not renewable. *Number:* 8000–9500. *Amount:* $200–$2500.

Eligibility Requirements: Applicant must be enrolled or expecting to enroll full-time at a four-year institution or university; resident of Massachusetts and studying in Massachusetts. Available to U.S. citizens.

Application Requirements: Financial need analysis.

Contact: Robert Brun, Senior Associate Commissioner
Massachusetts Office of Student Financial Assistance
75 Pleasant Street, 3rd Floor
Malden, MA 02148
Phone: 617-391-6099
E-mail: rbrub@dhe.mass.edu

MASSACHUSETTS PART-TIME GRANT PROGRAM

Award for permanent Massachusetts residents who have enrolled part-time for at least one year in a state-approved postsecondary school. The recipient must not have a bachelor's degree. FAFSA must be filed before May 1. Contact college financial aid office for further information.

Award: Grant for use in freshman, sophomore, junior, or senior years; not renewable. *Amount:* $200–$1700.

Eligibility Requirements: Applicant must be enrolled or expecting to enroll part-time at a two-year or four-year or technical institution or university; resident of Massachusetts and studying in Massachusetts. Available to U.S. citizens.

Application Requirements: Financial need analysis. *Deadline:* May 1.

Contact: Robert Brun, Director of Scholarships and Grants
Phone: 617-727-9420
Fax: 617-727-0667
E-mail: osfa@osfa.mass.edu

MASSACHUSETTS PUBLIC SERVICE GRANT PROGRAM

Scholarships for children and/or spouses of deceased members of fire, police, and corrections departments, who were killed in the line of duty. Awards Massachusetts residents attending Massachusetts institutions. Applicant should have not received a prior bachelor's degree or its equivalent.

Award: Grant for use in freshman, sophomore, junior, or senior years; not renewable. *Amount:* $6360–$15,411.

Eligibility Requirements: Applicant must be enrolled or expecting to enroll full-time at a two-year or four-year institution or university; resident of Massachusetts and studying in Massachusetts. Applicant or parent of applicant must have employment or volunteer experience in police/firefighting. Available to U.S. citizens.

Application Requirements: Application form, financial need analysis. *Deadline:* May 1.

Contact: Alison Connolly
Massachusetts Office of Student Financial Assistance
75 Pleasant Street Third Floor
Malden, MA 02148
Phone: 617-391-6073
E-mail: osfa@osfa.mass.edu

PAUL TSONGAS SCHOLARSHIP PROGRAM

Scholarship to recognize achievement and reward Massachusetts students, who have graduated from high school within three years with a GPA of 3.75 and a SAT score of at least 1200, and who also meet the one year residency requirement for tuition classification at the state colleges. This scholarship is awarded directly by the state university, as part of the admissions process. Interested applicants should contact the college directly, however, there is not a specific application for the Tsongas Scholarship. Students are selected and offered the scholarship by the appropriate college staff.

Award: Scholarship for use in freshman, sophomore, junior, or senior years; renewable. *Number:* 20–45. *Amount:* $11,500–$14,850.

Eligibility Requirements: Applicant must be high school student; planning to enroll or expecting to enroll full-time at a two-year or four-year institution; resident of Massachusetts and studying in Massachusetts. Applicant must have 3.5 GPA or higher. Available to U.S. citizens.

Application Requirements: Application form. *Deadline:* continuous.

Contact: Robert Brun, Director of Scholarships and Grants
Phone: 617-727-9420
Fax: 617-727-0667
E-mail: osfa@osfa.mass.edu

MASSEY AND ASSOCIATES, PC

https://www.masseyattorneys.com/

MASSEY & ASSOCIATES: JUSTICE FOR ALL SCHOLARSHIP

Massey & Associates, personal injury attorneys based in Chattanooga, Tennessee, is pleased to announce that we are offering a scholarship in the amount of $1,000 to one student who has experienced and overcome adversity in their life and justice was served - we would like to hear about the positive effects this justice had on yourself and your community. For more information, please visit: https://masseyattorneys.com/#scholarship

Award: Scholarship for use in freshman, sophomore, junior, senior, graduate, or postgraduate years; not renewable. *Number:* 1. *Amount:* $1000.

Eligibility Requirements: Applicant must be enrolled or expecting to enroll full- or part-time at a two-year or four-year or technical institution or university. Applicant must have 3.0 GPA or higher. Available to U.S. and non-U.S. citizens.

Application Requirements: Application form, essay. *Deadline:* July 31.

Contact: Gary Massey
E-mail: info@masseyattorneys.com

MATRIX HEALTH GROUP

https://matrixhealthgroup.com

JOE HOLIBAUGH MEMORIAL SCHOLARSHIP

$1500 scholarship for men and women with hemophilia and an inhibitor. Joe Holibaugh (1971- 2006) Living with severe hemophilia and an inhibitor, Joe met many challenges, but he faced these difficulties as opportunities to grow, embracing life fully with his entire being. Joe worked hard to impart this approach to others, bringing many together with his unique style of wit and humor. Joe's work lives on in the hearts of his many friends and family who love him dearly. He will always be remembered for his strength, love and resolve to make a difference for the bleeding disorders community.

Award: Scholarship for use in freshman, sophomore, junior, senior, graduate, or postgraduate years; not renewable. *Number:* 1. *Amount:* $1500.

Eligibility Requirements: Applicant must be physically disabled and enrolled or expecting to enroll full-time at a two-year or four-year or technical institution or university. Applicant must be physically disabled. Applicant must have 2.5 GPA or higher. Available to U.S. citizens.

Application Requirements: Application form, essay. *Deadline:* August 1.

Contact: Athenna Harrison, HFA Office Manager
Matrix Health Group
820 First Street NE, Suite 720
Washington, DC 20002
Phone: 202-675-6984
E-mail: a.harrison@hemophiliafed.org

MARK COATS MEMORIAL SCHOLARSHIP

$1500 scholarship for men and women with Hemophilia. Mark Coats (1956-1963) was just a young child when he passed from hemophilia-related issues. Mark was born in an entirely different era of bleeding disorders treatment and was not able to live a near normal life as most people with hemophilia do today. With his smiling eyes and sweet grin, we are reminded that every child deserves a chance to lead a full and happy life. We look to Mark as a reminder of what living with a bleeding disorder was like not that long ago and how blessed we are to have the treatments and medical advances we have today.

Award: Scholarship for use in freshman, sophomore, junior, senior, graduate, or postgraduate years; not renewable. *Number:* 1. *Amount:* $1500.

Eligibility Requirements: Applicant must be physically disabled and enrolled or expecting to enroll full-time at a two-year or four-year or technical institution or university. Applicant must be physically disabled. Applicant must have 2.5 GPA or higher. Available to U.S. citizens.

Application Requirements: Application form, essay. *Deadline:* August 1.

Contact: Athenna Harrison, HFA Office Manager
Matrix Health Group
820 First Street NE, Suite 720
Washington, DC 20002
Phone: 202-675-6984
E-mail: a.harrison@hemophiliafed.org

MIKE HYLTON MEMORIAL SCHOLARSHIP

$1500 scholarship for MEN with hemophilia or von Willebrand Disease and their immediate family members. Mike Hylton (1945-1998) A man of great character and steadiness, Mike faced some of the most physically daunting and mortal challenges that people with severe hemophilia could encounter. During the blood crisis of the 1980s, Mike met the challenges with class and a concern for others not only in the bleeding disorder community, but also those affected with HIV. He was a thoughtful, analytical and spiritual individual - patient and tolerant of others, but certainly willing and capable to express his opinions and beliefs. While some felt it was more important to speak, he knew that it was more effective to listen. Mike found great comfort in his faith and family.

Award: Scholarship for use in freshman, sophomore, junior, senior, graduate, or postgraduate years; not renewable. *Number:* 1. *Amount:* $1500.

Eligibility Requirements: Applicant must be physically disabled; enrolled or expecting to enroll full-time at a two-year or four-year or technical institution or university and male. Applicant must be physically disabled. Applicant must have 2.5 GPA or higher. Available to U.S. citizens.

Application Requirements: Application form, essay. *Deadline:* August 1.

Contact: Athenna Harrison, HFA Office Manager
Matrix Health Group
820 First St NE Ste 720
Washington DC, DC 20002
Phone: 202-675-6984
E-mail: a.harrison@hemophiliafed.org

MILLIE GONZALEZ MEMORIAL SCHOLARSHIP

$1500 scholarship for women with hemophilia or von Willebrand Disease. Millie Gonzalez (1953-2001) was a devoted wife and mother as well as a pioneer dedicated to advocacy. Millie promoted awareness of the unique struggles faced by women with a bleeding disorder and those caring for an individual affected by a bleeding disorder. She was married to Papo Gonzalez, a person with hemophilia and well known advocate in his own right, who passed prior to Millie. She was a tireless advocate not only for women, but also for people of Hispanic heritage affected with bleeding disorders. Although loving, compassionate and gentle, Millie had the heart of a tiger and fought each day for her own survival while inspiring others to achieve and succeed.

Award: Scholarship for use in freshman, sophomore, junior, senior, graduate, or postgraduate years; not renewable. *Number:* 1. *Amount:* $1500.

Eligibility Requirements: Applicant must be physically disabled; enrolled or expecting to enroll full-time at a two-year or four-year or technical institution or university and female. Applicant must be physically disabled. Applicant must have 2.5 GPA or higher. Available to U.S. citizens.

Application Requirements: Application form, essay. *Deadline:* August 1.

Contact: Athenna Harrison
Matrix Health Group
820 First Street NE, Suite 720
Washington, DC 20002
Phone: 202-675-6984
E-mail: a.harrison@hemophiliafed.org

RON NIEDERMAN MEMORIAL SCHOLARSHIP

$1500 scholarship for men with hemophilia or von Willebrand Disease and their immediate family members. Born with severe hemophilia when treatment for people with bleeding disorders was nonexistent predisposed Ron, as with many of his generation, to a lifetime of pain, struggle for better care, and the fight against stigma and prejudice. Ron endured challenges and faced each with grace and an air of, "I can handle that, no problem." He exemplified the meaning of compassion towards others and practiced more than preached what it meant to be an advocate. He was a great friend and a trusted source of advice and wisdom. Ron's commitment to the bleeding disorder community was surpassed only by his love for his family.

Award: Scholarship for use in freshman, sophomore, junior, senior, graduate, or postgraduate years; not renewable. *Number:* 1. *Amount:* $1500.

Eligibility Requirements: Applicant must be physically disabled; enrolled or expecting to enroll full-time at a two-year or four-year or technical institution or university and male. Applicant must be physically disabled. Applicant must have 2.5 GPA or higher. Available to U.S. citizens.

Application Requirements: Application form, essay. *Deadline:* August 1.

Contact: Athenna Harrison, HFA Office Manager
Matrix Health Group
820 First Street NE, Suite 720
Washington, DC 20002
Phone: 202-675-6984
E-mail: a.harrison@hemophiliafed.org

TIM KENNEDY MEMORIAL SCHOLARSHIP

$1500 scholarship for MEN with hemophilia. Tim Kennedy (1962- 2011) Those who knew Tim remember his ability to make most anyone smile and share a hearty laugh. Though life had dealt him a rough hand, Tim kept an air about him that was truly inspiring. As a father and husband, the love he showed his two children and wife knew no bounds. As a friend, he was always ready to listen, share and comfort - most often with his signature sense of humor. As a member of the bleeding disorders community, Tim was devoted to helping his peers look past their health conditions and enjoy every moment of life for all it's worth.

Award: Scholarship for use in freshman, sophomore, junior, senior, graduate, or postgraduate years; not renewable. *Number:* 1. *Amount:* $1500.

Eligibility Requirements: Applicant must be physically disabled; enrolled or expecting to enroll full-time at a two-year or four-year or technical institution or university and male. Applicant must be physically disabled. Applicant must have 2.5 GPA or higher. Available to U.S. citizens.

Application Requirements: Application form, essay. *Deadline:* August 1.

Contact: Athenna Harrison, HFA Office Manager
Matrix Health Group
820 First Street, NE, Suite 720
Washington, DC 20002
Phone: 202-675-6984
E-mail: a.harrison@hemophiliafed.org

MEDIGO GMBH

https://www.medigo.com/en

MEDIGO SCHOLARSHIP PROGRAM

MEDIGO strives to remove barriers to healthcare for our patients. We firmly believe that education should be equally as accessible for students. We are proud to offer a scholarship of $2,000, with the aim of supporting one promising student through their college or university degree. We are looking to reward a student who best aligns with our values of diversity and inclusion. Applicants are asked to write an essay on diversity in the workplace.

Award: Scholarship for use in freshman, sophomore, junior, or senior years; renewable. *Number:* 1. *Amount:* $2000.

Eligibility Requirements: Applicant must be enrolled or expecting to enroll full- or part-time at a four-year institution or university. Available to U.S. and non-U.S. citizens.

Application Requirements: Essay. *Deadline:* September 1.

Contact: Mr. Samuel Rucker, MEDIGO
Medigo GMBH
Rosenthaler Str. 13
Berlin 10119
Phone: 49-1632212215
E-mail: scholarship@medigo.com

MENSA FOUNDATION

mensafoundation.org

U.S. SCHOLARSHIP PROGRAM

The scholarship program is an essay based program open to students of all ages. Mensa membership is not required.

Award: Scholarship for use in freshman, sophomore, junior, senior, graduate, or postgraduate years; not renewable. *Number:* 100–150. *Amount:* $600–$2500.

Eligibility Requirements: Applicant must be enrolled or expecting to enroll full- or part-time at a two-year or four-year institution or university. Available to U.S. citizens.

Application Requirements: Application form, essay. *Deadline:* January 15.

Contact: Jill Beckham, Foundation Director
Mensa Foundation
1229 Corporate Dr W
Arlington, TX 76006
Phone: 817-607-5577
Fax: 817-649-5232
E-mail: director@mensafoundation.org

MES FOUNDATION

http://www.mesfoundation.org

RICHARD H. PIERCE MEMORIAL SCHOLARSHIP

A $5,000 scholarship per student per year will be awarded. Scholarships will be renewable for up to 4 years (depending on the grade level of the student). A total of 10 scholarships will be awarded to eligible students in 2018. Application period runs from January 1st–April 1st. Recipients must be a Maine resident entering first year of post-secondary education; intend to enroll/be enrolled in a 2 or 4 year degree-granting college or university accredited by the Association of Schools and Colleges; and show a strong desire to complete degree program.

Award: Scholarship for use in freshman, sophomore, junior, or senior years; renewable. *Number:* 10. *Amount:* $5000.

Eligibility Requirements: Applicant must be enrolled or expecting to enroll full-time at a two-year or four-year institution or university and resident of Maine. Available to U.S. citizens.

Application Requirements: Application form, community service, essay, financial need analysis. *Deadline:* April 1.

Contact: Kristie Hurlburt, Program Director
MES Foundation
PO Box 1296
Alfred, ME 04002
Phone: 207-791-3600
E-mail: khurlburt@mesfoundation.org

MINDSUMO

http://www.mindsumo.com

MINDSUMO 15-MINUTE SCHOLARSHIP

This is the first year we are launching this scholarship program to run in conjunction with our standard MindSumo platform. In terms of total payouts we have provided to college students for merit-based performance on solving business and engineering challenges, we have paid out $600,000 over the last 4 years. Now we want to convert a portion of our prize pool to be dedicated to scholarships. Our reward structure is unique in that the number of winners and the award amount depends on the number of submissions. Our objective is to reward a larger proportion of applicants to encourage them through the tough scholarship application process rather than limit winners to a small select few. Please see website for details, http://www.mindsumo.com/scholarships.

Award: Scholarship for use in freshman, sophomore, junior, senior, graduate, or postgraduate years; not renewable. *Number:* 250–500. *Amount:* $40–$200.

Eligibility Requirements: Applicant must be enrolled or expecting to enroll full- or part-time at a two-year or four-year or technical institution or university. Available to U.S. and non-U.S. citizens.

Application Requirements: *Deadline:* continuous.

Contact: Mr. John Huang, Manager
MindSumo
33 New Montgomery
Suite 220
San Francisco, CA 94105
Phone: 843-453-5176
E-mail: john@mindsumo.com

MINNESOTA MASONIC CHARITIES

http://www.mnmasoniccharities.org

MINNESOTA MASONIC CHARITIES SIGNATURE SCHOLARSHIP

Signature Scholarships are provided each year to students attending a Minnesota high school with a GPA of 3.9 or higher. Applicants must plan to enroll in a four-year college program.

Award: Scholarship for use in freshman, sophomore, junior, or senior years; renewable. *Number:* 5. *Amount:* $5000.

Eligibility Requirements: Applicant must be high school student; planning to enroll or expecting to enroll full-time at a four-year institution or university and resident of Minnesota. Applicant must have 3.5 GPA or higher. Available to U.S. citizens.

Application Requirements: Application form, essay. *Deadline:* February 15.

Contact: Ms. Deb Cutsinger, Scholarships Manager
Minnesota Masonic Charities
11501 Masonic Home Drive
Bloomington, MN 55437
Phone: 952-948-6206
E-mail: deb.cutsinger@mnmasonic.org

MINNESOTA MASONIC CHARITIES UNDERGRADUATE SCHOLARSHIP

Undergraduate Scholarships are provided each year to current college freshman, sophomores or juniors who graduated from a Minnesota high school and have a GPA of 3.0 or above. Applicants must be enrolled in a four-year college program.

Award: Scholarship for use in sophomore, junior, or senior years; renewable. *Number:* 20. *Amount:* $2000.

Eligibility Requirements: Applicant must be enrolled or expecting to enroll full-time at a four-year institution or university and resident of Minnesota. Applicant must have 3.0 GPA or higher. Available to U.S. citizens.

Application Requirements: Application form, essay. *Deadline:* February 15.

Contact: Ms. Deb Cutsinger, Scholarships Manager
Minnesota Masonic Charities
11501 Masonic Home Drive
Bloomington, MN 55437
Phone: 952-948-6206
E-mail: deb.cutsinger@mnmasonic.org

MINNESOTA OFFICE OF HIGHER EDUCATION

http://www.ohe.state.mn.us

SAFETY OFFICERS' SURVIVOR GRANT PROGRAM

Grant for eligible survivors of Minnesota public safety officers killed in the line of duty. Safety officers who have been permanently or totally disabled in the line of duty are also eligible. Must be used at a Minnesota institution participating in State Grant Program. Write for details. Must submit proof of death or disability and Public Safety Officers Benefit Fund Certificate. Must apply for renewal each year. Five-year limit on awards.

Award: Grant for use in freshman, sophomore, junior, senior, or graduate years; not renewable. *Number:* 1–10. *Amount:* $1–$13,840.

Eligibility Requirements: Applicant must be enrolled or expecting to enroll full- or part-time at a two-year or four-year or technical institution or university; resident of Minnesota and studying in Minnesota. Applicant or parent of applicant must have employment or volunteer experience in police/firefighting. Available to U.S. citizens.

Application Requirements: Application form. *Deadline:* continuous.

Contact: Brenda Larter, Program Administrator
Phone: 651-355-0612
E-mail: brenda.larter@state.mn.us

MISSISSIPPI OFFICE OF STUDENT FINANCIAL AID

http://www.mississippi.edu/financialaid

LAW ENFORCEMENT OFFICERS/FIREMEN SCHOLARSHIP

Financial assistance to dependent children and spouses of any Mississippi law enforcement officer, full-time fire fighter or volunteer fire fighter who has suffered fatal injuries or wounds or become permanently and totally disabled as a result of injuries or wounds which occurred in the performance of the official and appointed duties of his or her office. This financial assistance is offered as an eight semester tuition and room scholarship at any state-supported college or university in Mississippi.

Award: Scholarship for use in freshman, sophomore, junior, or senior years; renewable. *Number:* 18–30. *Amount:* $2010–$12,854.

Eligibility Requirements: Applicant must be enrolled or expecting to enroll full-time at a two-year or four-year institution or university; resident of Mississippi and studying in Mississippi. Applicant or parent of applicant must have employment or volunteer experience in police/firefighting. Applicant must have 2.5 GPA or higher. Available to U.S. citizens.

Application Requirements: Application form. *Deadline:* continuous.

Contact: Program Administrator
Mississippi Office of Student Financial Aid
3825 Ridgewood Road
Jackson, MS 39211
Phone: 601-432-6997
Fax: 601-432 Ext. 6527
E-mail: sfa@mississippi.edu

MITCHELL INSTITUTE

http://www.mitchellinstitute.org/

SENATOR GEORGE J. MITCHELL SCHOLARSHIP RESEARCH INSTITUTE

The Mitchell Institute awards scholarships to graduating students from every public high school in Maine each year. The 2018 scholarship award is in the amount of $9500, and Mitchell Scholars have up to six years to use the funds. An award check in the amount of $2375 will be disbursed to each Scholar annually for up to four years.

Award: Scholarship for use in freshman, sophomore, junior, or senior years; renewable. *Number:* 135. *Amount:* $9500.

Eligibility Requirements: Applicant must be high school student; planning to enroll or expecting to enroll full- or part-time at a two-year or four-year or technical institution or university and resident of Maine. Available to U.S. and non-U.S. citizens.

Application Requirements: Application form, community service, essay, financial need analysis. *Deadline:* April 1.

Contact: Kim Gustafson, Scholarship Director
Mitchell Institute
75 Washington Avenue
Suite 2E
Portland, ME 04101
Phone: 207-773-7700
E-mail: kgustafson@mitchellinstitute.org

MLD WEALTH MANAGEMENT GROUP

http://mywealthmanagement.ca/

ANNUAL MLD SCHOLASTIC SCHOLARSHIP

MLD Wealth Management is offering an annual scholarship to all the students from that meet our qualifications. This scholarship is based on merit, financial need, and community participation. The winning applicant will receive $3000 towards their education costs. Scholarship details: http://mywealthmanagement.ca/scholarsip2018/

Award: Scholarship for use in freshman, sophomore, junior, senior, graduate, or postgraduate years; not renewable. *Number:* 1. *Amount:* $3000.

Eligibility Requirements: Applicant must be enrolled or expecting to enroll full-time at a two-year or four-year institution or university. Applicant must have 3.0 GPA or higher. Available to U.S. and Canadian citizens.

Application Requirements: Application form, essay, interview, personal photograph. *Deadline:* May 10.

Contact: Mr. Chris Hilliard, PR Manager
MLD Wealth Management Group
239 8th Avenue SW
Suite 200
Calgary T2P 1B9
Phone: 604-360-5161
Fax: 403-410-9668
E-mail: pr@mywealthmanagement.ca

MUCHGAMES.COM

http://www.muchgames.com

MUCHGAMES.COM STUDENT RESEARCH GRANT OF $1500

This research grant is for students that are interested in researching the social and psychological effects of video game addiction.

Award: Grant for use in senior, graduate, or postgraduate years; renewable. *Number:* 1. *Amount:* $1500.

Eligibility Requirements: Applicant must be enrolled or expecting to enroll full- or part-time at a four-year institution or university. Applicant must have 3.0 GPA or higher. Available to U.S. citizens.

Application Requirements: Essay. *Deadline:* April 30.

Contact: miss. Tara Veino, Support Coordinator
Muchgames.com
701 E. Bridger Ave
Las Vegas, NV 89101
Phone: 646-703-1630
E-mail: learn@muchgames.com

THE MULLER FIRM, LTD

https://chicagodivorceattys.com/

THE MULLER FIRM, LTD ANNUAL SCHOLARSHIP

The Muller Firm, LTD. is committed to the idea that higher education plays an important role in helping young people begin a fulfilling career and in developing responsible citizens. Every year we offer a $1,000 scholarship to help high school students who wish to pursue higher education as well as students currently enrolled in an undergraduate or law school program. Our scholarship recipient is chosen from the essay submissions addressing the given topic.

Award: Scholarship for use in freshman, sophomore, junior, or senior years; not renewable. *Number:* 1. *Amount:* $1000.

Eligibility Requirements: Applicant must be enrolled or expecting to enroll full-time at a two-year or four-year institution or university. Available to U.S. citizens.

Application Requirements: Application form, essay. *Deadline:* July 15.

Contact: Pat McCune, Scholarship Coordinator
The Muller Firm, LTD
PO Box 1596
Northbrook, IL 60065
Phone: 847-940-4000
Fax: 847-940-4000
E-mail: pat@marketjd.com

NATIONAL AIDS MEMORIAL

http://www.aidsmemorial.org

PEDRO ZAMORA YOUNG LEADERS SCHOLARSHIP

The Pedro Zamora Young Leaders Scholarship is open to all current high school seniors, and college freshman, sophomores and juniors (ages 27 and younger) who demonstrate an active commitment to fighting HIV/AIDS and taking on roles of public service and leadership. Examples include (but are not limited to): serving in peer-education and prevention programs; working in the reproductive-health and sexual health field; pursuing a medical degree to work with HIV-positive individuals; international service providing AIDS-related care and/or HIV-prevention education; research in established and emerging technologies designed to mitigate the epidemic; or activism and social change efforts that address issues contributing to the epidemic, like education and drug sentencing reform, employment and economic justice issues, housing and homelessness. All applicants must describe their current leadership efforts/experience, its significance to the HIV/AIDS epidemic, as well as their how their future career plans or public service will be an extension of their current efforts. Applicants must provide at least one letter of recommendation from a teacher, program coordinator, supervisor/ally/community leader who is directly involved in their HIV/AIDS-related service, leadership, or field of study. A panel of community leaders will judge the applications. Submissions must include the following five items: 1. A complete application; 2. A brief personal statement (not to exceed 500 words) describing some of the ways that you provide service and/or leadership in the fight against HIV/AIDS and how your studies, career plans, or public service will contribute to the fight against HIV/AIDS; 3. A written essay, not to exceed 1,500 words, in which you reflect on the ways in which your life has been impacted by HIV/AIDS; explore and describe the ways in which you are providing public service or leadership that makes a difference in the lives of people with HIV/AIDS, or people at risk; and detail how the scholarship will help you in your career path and how that career will allow you to continue to fight HIV/AIDS in a way that makes a difference; 4. At least one written letter of recommendation from a teacher, program coordinator, supervisor/ally/community leader or other adult who is directly involved in your HIV/AIDS-related service, leadership, or field of study; 5. A transcript from current high school or college that demonstrates a minimum 2.5 GPA overall, or in the immediate past two semesters or three trimesters.

Award: Scholarship for use in freshman, sophomore, junior, or senior years; not renewable. *Number:* 8–10. *Amount:* $5000.

Eligibility Requirements: Applicant must be enrolled or expecting to enroll full- or part-time at a two-year or four-year institution or university and studying in Alabama, Alaska, Arizona, Arkansas, California, Colorado, Connecticut, Delaware, District of Columbia, Florida, Georgia, Hawaii, Idaho, Illinois, Indiana, Iowa, Kansas, Kentucky, Louisiana, Maine, Maryland, Massachusetts, Michigan, Minnesota, Mississippi, Missouri, Montana, Nebraska, Nevada, New Hampshire, New Jersey, New Mexico, New York, North Carolina, North Dakota, Ohio, Oklahoma, Oregon, Pennsylvania, Puerto Rico, Rhode Island, South Carolina, South Dakota, Tennessee, Texas, Utah, Vermont, Virginia, Washington, West Virginia, Wisconsin, Wyoming. Applicant must have 2.5 GPA or higher. Available to U.S. citizens.

Application Requirements: Application form, essay. *Deadline:* May 31.

Contact: Matt Kennedy, Operations Associate
National AIDS Memorial
National AIDS Memorial
870 Market Street, Suite 965
San Francisco, CA 94102
Phone: 415-765-0446
E-mail: mkennedy@aidsmemorial.org

NATIONAL ASSOCIATION FOR CAMPUS ACTIVITIES

http://www.naca.org/

ALAN DAVIS SCHOLARSHIP

The Alan Davis Scholarship recipient possesses an inspired spirit and creative spark. This individual is innovative and forward thinking in regards to the events and opportunities available to the student body. Must be active in at minimum two on-campus student organizations or activities as well as hold a significant leadership position in one of the organizations. Must have demonstrated significant contributions to their campus communities and demonstrated creative efforts on and off campus. The awarded scholar embodies the core qualities of both NACA and Riddle & Bloom: creativity, originality, pride for his/her school and unparalleled ambition and vision.

Award: Scholarship for use in sophomore, junior, or senior years; not renewable. *Number:* 1. *Amount:* $5000.

Eligibility Requirements: Applicant must be enrolled or expecting to enroll full-time at a two-year or four-year institution or university and must have an interest in leadership. Applicant must have 3.0 GPA or higher. Available to U.S. citizens.

Application Requirements: Application form, essay. *Deadline:* June 30.

Contact: Executive Assistant
E-mail: scholarships@naca.org

JOHN ZAGUNIS STUDENT LEADER SCHOLARSHIP

Scholarships will be awarded to undergraduate or graduate students maintaining a cumulative GPA of 3.0 or better at the time of the application and during the academic term in which the scholarship is awarded. Applicants should demonstrate leadership skills and abilities while holding a significant leadership position on campus. Applicants must submit two letters of recommendation and a description of the applicant's leadership activities, skills, abilities and accomplishments. Must be enrolled in a college/university in the NACA Mid Atlantic & Mid America.

Award: Scholarship for use in freshman, sophomore, junior, senior, or graduate years; not renewable. *Number:* 1. *Amount:* $300.

Eligibility Requirements: Applicant must be enrolled or expecting to enroll full-time at a two-year or four-year institution or university; studying in Delaware, District of Columbia, Illinois, Indiana, Kentucky, Maryland, Michigan, New Jersey, New York, Ohio, Ontario, Pennsylvania, West Virginia and must have an interest in leadership. Applicant must have 3.0 GPA or higher. Available to U.S. citizens.

Application Requirements: Application form, essay. *Deadline:* December 31.

Contact: Executive Assistant
E-mail: scholarships@naca.org

LORI RHETT MEMORIAL SCHOLARSHIP

Scholarships will be given to undergraduate or graduate students in the NACA West Region with a cumulative GPA of 2.5 or better at the time of the application and during the academic term in which the scholarship is awarded. Must demonstrate significant leadership skill and ability while holding a significant leadership position on campus. Applicants must have made contributions via volunteer involvement, either on or off campus.

Award: Scholarship for use in freshman, sophomore, junior, senior, or graduate years; not renewable. *Number:* 1. *Amount:* $300.

Eligibility Requirements: Applicant must be enrolled or expecting to enroll full-time at a two-year or four-year institution or university; studying in Alaska, Arizona, British Columbia, California, Colorado, Idaho, Nevada, New Mexico, Oregon, Utah, Washington and must have an interest in leadership. Applicant or parent of applicant must have employment or volunteer experience in community service. Applicant must have 2.5 GPA or higher. Available to U.S. citizens.

Application Requirements: Application form, essay. *Deadline:* September 30.

Contact: Executive Assistant
   E-mail: scholarships@naca.org

NATIONAL ASSOCIATION FOR CAMPUS ACTIVITIES MID ATLANTIC UNDERGRADUATE SCHOLARSHIP FOR STUDENT LEADERS

Scholarship for undergraduate students who are in good standing at the time of the application and during the academic term in which the scholarship is awarded. Applicants must maintain a 2.5 GPA, demonstrate leadership skills and abilities while holding a significant leadership position on campus or in community, and have made significant contributions via volunteer involvement. Eligible students must be attending a college or university within the NACA Mid Atlantic Region.

Award: Scholarship for use in freshman, sophomore, junior, or senior years; not renewable. *Number:* 1–2. *Amount:* $300.

Eligibility Requirements: Applicant must be enrolled or expecting to enroll full- or part-time at a two-year or four-year institution or university; studying in Delaware, District of Columbia, Maryland, New Jersey, New York, Ontario, Pennsylvania and must have an interest in leadership. Applicant or parent of applicant must have employment or volunteer experience in community service. Applicant must have 2.5 GPA or higher. Available to U.S. citizens.

Application Requirements: Application form, essay. *Deadline:* September 30.

Contact: Executive Assistant
   E-mail: scholarships@naca.org

NATIONAL ASSOCIATION FOR CAMPUS ACTIVITIES SOUTH REGION STUDENT LEADER SCHOLARSHIP

Scholarships will be given to full-time undergraduate students in good standing at the time of the application and during the academic term in which the scholarship is awarded. Must demonstrate significant leadership skill and ability while holding a significant leadership position on campus. Applicants must have made contributions via volunteer involvement, either on or off campus. Must be enrolled in a college/university in the NACA South Region, including the US Virgin Islands.

Award: Scholarship for use in freshman, sophomore, junior, or senior years; not renewable. *Number:* 1–4. *Amount:* $300.

Eligibility Requirements: Applicant must be enrolled or expecting to enroll full-time at a two-year or four-year institution or university; studying in Alabama, Florida, Georgia, Mississippi, North Carolina, South Carolina, Tennessee, Virginia and must have an interest in leadership. Applicant or parent of applicant must have employment or volunteer experience in community service. Available to U.S. citizens.

Application Requirements: Application form, essay. *Deadline:* March 31.

Contact: Executive Assistant
   E-mail: scholarships@naca.org

TESE CALDARELLI MEMORIAL SCHOLARSHIP

Scholarship available to undergraduate or graduate students with a minimum 3.0 GPA. Must demonstrate significant leadership skills and hold a significant position on campus. Must have made significant contributions via volunteer involvement on or off campus. Must attend school in the NACA Mid Atlantic or Mid America Regions.

Award: Scholarship for use in freshman, sophomore, junior, senior, or graduate years; not renewable. *Number:* 1. *Amount:* $300.

Eligibility Requirements: Applicant must be enrolled or expecting to enroll full-time at a two-year or four-year institution or university; studying in Delaware, District of Columbia, Illinois, Indiana, Kentucky, Maryland, Michigan, New Jersey, New York, Ohio, Ontario, Pennsylvania, West Virginia and must have an interest in leadership. Applicant or parent of applicant must have employment or volunteer experience in community service. Applicant must have 3.0 GPA or higher. Available to U.S. citizens.

Application Requirements: Application form, essay. *Deadline:* December 31.

Contact: Executive Assistant
   E-mail: scholarships@naca.org

NATIONAL COUNCIL OF JEWISH WOMEN LOS ANGELES (NCJW L LA)

http://ncjwla.org/

THE DODELL WOMEN'S EMPOWERMENT SCHOLARSHIP

To qualify, an applicant must be re-entering or continuing school in order to learn a marketable skill which will lead to economic self-sufficiency. The applicant must be a woman 25 years of age or older for whom the opportunity to return to school will lead to economic independence. The applicant can be either married or single, with or without children. The National Council of Jewish Women l Los Angeles (NCJW l LA) provides scholarships, regardless of race, ethnicity, religion, age, gender identity, sexuality or national origin to those who live and attend school in the Greater Los Angeles area, including Los Angeles, Orange, Riverside, and Ventura Counties.

Award: Scholarship for use in freshman, sophomore, junior, senior, or graduate years; not renewable. *Number:* 2. *Amount:* $1000.

Eligibility Requirements: Applicant must be enrolled or expecting to enroll full- or part-time at a two-year or four-year or technical institution or university; female; resident of California and studying in California. Available to U.S. citizens.

Application Requirements: Application form, essay, financial need analysis. *Deadline:* continuous.

Contact: Ms. Stephanie Flax, Scholarship and Program Coordinator
   National Council of Jewish Women Los Angeles (NCJW l LA)
   543 North Fairfax Avenue
   Los Angeles, CA 90036
   Phone: 323-852-8515
   E-mail: Scholarship@ncjwla.org

SOPHIE GREENSTADT SCHOLARSHIP FOR MID-LIFE WOMEN

To qualify, an applicant must be re-entering or continuing school in order to learn a marketable skill which will lead to economic self-sufficiency. The applicant must be a woman 35 years of age or older for whom the opportunity to return to school will lead to economic independence. The applicant can be either married or single, with or without children. The National Council of Jewish Women l Los Angeles (NCJW l LA) provides scholarships, regardless of race, ethnicity, religion, age, gender identity, sexuality or national origin to those who live and attend school in the Greater Los Angeles area, including Los Angeles, Orange, Riverside, and Ventura Counties.

Award: Scholarship for use in freshman, sophomore, junior, senior, or graduate years; not renewable. *Number:* 1. *Amount:* $1000.

Eligibility Requirements: Applicant must be enrolled or expecting to enroll full- or part-time at a two-year or four-year or technical institution or university; female; resident of California and studying in California. Available to U.S. citizens.

Application Requirements: Application form, essay, financial need analysis. *Deadline:* continuous.

Contact: Stephanie Flax, Scholarship and Program Coordinator
National Council of Jewish Women Los Angeles (NCJW l LA)
543 North Fairfax Avenue
Los Angeles, CA 90036
Phone: 323-852-8515
E-mail: scholarship@ncjala.org

STEPHEN L. TELLER & RICHARD HOTSON TV, CINEMA, AND THEATER SCHOLARSHIP

To qualify, an applicant must be a full-time student enrolled in a Community College Film/ Television/ Cinema/Theater program, and preparing for a career in film, television, or theater production (not acting). Applicant must have completed 12 units of classes in their school's Film/TV/Cinema/Theater program. The National Council of Jewish Women l Los Angeles (NCJW l LA) provides scholarships, regardless of race, ethnicity, religion, age, gender identity, sexuality or national origin to those who live and attend school in the Greater Los Angeles area, including Los Angeles, Orange, Riverside, and Ventura Counties.

Award: Scholarship for use in freshman, sophomore, junior, or senior years; not renewable. *Number:* 2. *Amount:* $1000.

Eligibility Requirements: Applicant must be enrolled or expecting to enroll full-time at a two-year institution; resident of California and studying in California. Available to U.S. citizens.

Application Requirements: Application form, essay, financial need analysis. *Deadline:* continuous.

Contact: Stephanie Flax, Scholarship and Program Coordinator
National Council of Jewish Women Los Angeles (NCJW l LA)
543 North Fairfax Avenue
Los Angeles, CA 90036
Phone: 323-852-8515
E-mail: scholarship@ncjwla.org

SUSAN SCHULMAN BEGLEY MEMORIAL SCHOLARSHIP

This award is given to a woman who is establishing herself as a head of household and a single parent, and - due to extreme circumstances following the dissolution of an abusive or emotionally traumatic relationship - has no other adequate financial means, and requires funds to meet immediate needs for herself and her children, including rent & food. The National Council of Jewish Women l Los Angeles (NCJW l LA) provides scholarships, regardless of race, ethnicity, religion, age, gender identity, sexuality or national origin to those who live and attend school in the Greater Los Angeles area, including Los Angeles, Orange, Riverside, and Ventura Counties.

Award: Scholarship for use in freshman, sophomore, junior, senior, graduate, or postgraduate years; not renewable. *Number:* 1. *Amount:* $1000.

Eligibility Requirements: Applicant must be enrolled or expecting to enroll full- or part-time at a two-year or four-year or technical institution or university; single female; resident of California and studying in California. Available to U.S. citizens.

Application Requirements: Application form, essay, financial need analysis. *Deadline:* continuous.

Contact: Stephanie Flax, Scholarship and Program Coordinator
National Council of Jewish Women Los Angeles (NCJW l LA)
543 North Fairfax Avenue
Los Angeles, CA 90036
Phone: 323-852-8515
E-mail: scholarship@ncjwla.org

NATIONAL FEDERATION OF STATE POETRY SOCIETIES (NFSPS)

http://www.nfsps.com/

NATIONAL FEDERATION OF STATE POETRY SOCIETIES' COLLEGE UNDERGRADUATE POETRY (CUP) COMPETITION

Open to students enrolled in a degree program at an accredited U.S. college or university. Awards $500 plus publication and 75

complimentary chapbooks marketed on Amazon.com. Winners get invitation, travel stipend of $300, and convention perks to read their work at NFSPS Annual Convention. Online submission of titled manuscript containing exactly ten original poems. For more information, visit NFSPS website, http://www.nfsps.com, Poetry Contests tab.

Award: Prize for use in freshman, sophomore, junior, or senior years; not renewable. *Number:* 2. *Amount:* $500.

Eligibility Requirements: Applicant must be enrolled or expecting to enroll full-time at a two-year or four-year institution or university and must have an interest in writing. Available to U.S. and non-U.S. citizens.

Application Requirements: Application form. *Fee:* $10. *Deadline:* January 31.

Contact: Shirley Blackwell, Chairman
National Federation of State Poetry Societies (NFSPS)
PO Box 1352
Los Lunas, NM 87031
E-mail: sonneteer@earthlink.net

NATIONAL FEDERATION OF THE BLIND (NFB)

http://www.nfb.org/scholarships

AAF KENNETH JERNIGAN SCHOLARSHIP FOR $12,000

The American Action Fund for Blind Children & Adults $12,000 award to honor the top blind college student residing in and attending an accredited institution in the US or Puerto Rico. Winner receives financial assistance to attend NFB convention to receive scholarship.

Award: Scholarship for use in freshman, sophomore, junior, senior, graduate, or postgraduate years; not renewable. *Number:* 1. *Amount:* $12,000.

Eligibility Requirements: Applicant must be visually impaired and enrolled or expecting to enroll full- or part-time at a two-year or four-year institution or university. Applicant must be visually impaired. Available to U.S. citizens.

Application Requirements: Application form, essay, interview. *Deadline:* March 31.

Contact: Patti Chang, Chairperson
National Federation of the Blind (NFB)
NFB Scholarship Committee
200 East Wells Street
Baltimore, MD 21230
Phone: 410-659-9314 Ext. 2415
E-mail: scholarships@nfb.org

CHARLES AND MELVA T. OWEN SCHOLARSHIP FOR $10,000

Merit-based scholarship requires academic excellence and leadership, permanently resides in United States/Puerto Rico, and accredited institution's degree program (in US/PR) directed toward financial independence (excludes degrees in religious studies or solely for cultural education). Winner assisted to attend NFB annual convention to receive this award. Membership not required. USA Citizenship is not a requirement, but if the student's home is not in the US/PR, then the student is not eligible.

Award: Scholarship for use in freshman, sophomore, junior, senior, graduate, or postgraduate years; not renewable. *Number:* 1. *Amount:* $10,000.

Eligibility Requirements: Applicant must be visually impaired and enrolled or expecting to enroll full- or part-time at a two-year or four-year institution or university. Applicant must be visually impaired. Available to U.S. and non-U.S. citizens.

Application Requirements: Application form, essay, interview. *Deadline:* March 31.

Contact: Ms. Patti Chang, Chairperson, NFB Scholarship Committee
National Federation of the Blind (NFB)
200 East Wells Street
Baltimore, MD 21230
Phone: 410-659-9314 Ext. 2415
E-mail: scholarships@nfb.org

NATIONAL FFA ORGANIZATION

http://www.ffa.org

NATIONAL FFA COLLEGIATE SCHOLARSHIP PROGRAM
• *See page 570*

NATIONAL INSTITUTE FOR LABOR RELATIONS RESEARCH

http://www.nilrr.org/

NATIONAL INSTITUTE FOR LABOR RELATIONS RESEARCH WILLIAM B. RUGGLES JOURNALISM SCHOLARSHIP

One-time award for undergraduate or graduate study in journalism, mass communications or related major. Submit 500-word essay demonstrating an understanding of the right-to-work principle. High school seniors accepted into certified journalism school may apply. Specify "Journalism" or "Ruggles" scholarship on any correspondence.

Award: Scholarship for use in freshman, sophomore, junior, senior, graduate, or postgraduate years; not renewable. *Number:* 1. *Amount:* $2000.

Eligibility Requirements: Applicant must be enrolled or expecting to enroll full- or part-time at a four-year institution or university; resident of Alabama, Alaska, Arizona, Arkansas, California, Colorado, Connecticut, Delaware, District of Columbia, Florida, Georgia, Guam, Hawaii, Idaho, Illinois, Indiana, Iowa, Kansas, Kentucky, Louisiana, Maine, Maryland, Massachusetts, Michigan, Minnesota, Mississippi, Missouri, Montana, Nebraska, Nevada, New Hampshire, New Jersey, New Mexico, New York, North Carolina, North Dakota, Ohio, Oklahoma, Oregon, Pennsylvania, Puerto Rico, Rhode Island, South Carolina, South Dakota, Tennessee, Texas, Utah, Vermont, Virginia, Washington, West Virginia, Wisconsin, Wyoming; studying in Alabama, Alaska, Arizona, Arkansas, California, Colorado, Connecticut, Delaware, District of Columbia, Florida, Georgia, Guam, Hawaii, Idaho, Illinois, Indiana, Iowa, Kansas, Kentucky, Louisiana, Maine, Maryland, Massachusetts, Michigan, Minnesota, Mississippi, Missouri, Montana, Nebraska, Nevada, New Hampshire, New Jersey, New Mexico, New York, North Carolina, North Dakota, Ohio, Oklahoma, Oregon, Pennsylvania, Puerto Rico, Rhode Island, South Carolina, South Dakota, Tennessee, Texas, Utah, Vermont, Virginia, Washington, West Virginia, Wisconsin, Wyoming and must have an interest in writing. Available to U.S. citizens.

Application Requirements: Application form, essay. *Deadline:* December 31.

Contact: Cathy Jones, Scholarship Coordinator
National Institute for Labor Relations Research
5211 Port Royal Road, Suite 510
Springfield, VA 22151
Phone: 703-321-9606 Ext. 2247
E-mail: clj@nrtw.org

NATIONAL MILITARY FAMILY ASSOCIATION

http://www.MilitaryFamily.org

NATIONAL MILITARY FAMILY ASSOCIATION'S MILITARY SPOUSE SCHOLARSHIPS

Scholarships ranging from $500 to $1000 are awarded to spouses of Uniformed Services members (active duty, National Guard and Reserve, retirees, and survivors) for professional funding such as licensure and certification or any level of degree. Award number and amount varies. You must be a military spouse with a valid ID card to apply.

Award: Scholarship for use in freshman, sophomore, junior, senior, graduate, or postgraduate years; not renewable. *Number:* 400–600. *Amount:* $500–$1000.

Eligibility Requirements: Applicant must be enrolled or expecting to enroll full- or part-time at a two-year or four-year or technical institution or university and married. Available to U.S. and non-U.S. citizens. Applicant or parent must meet one or more of the following requirements: general military experience; retired from active duty; disabled or killed as a result of military service; prisoner of war; or missing in action.

Application Requirements: Application form, essay. *Deadline:* continuous.

Contact: Spouse Education + Employment Program Manager
National Military Family Association
3601 Eisenhower Avenue
Suite 425
Alexandria, VA 22304
Phone: 703-931-6632
E-mail: scholarships@militaryfamily.org

NATIONAL MULTIPLE SCLEROSIS SOCIETY

http://www.nmss.org/

NATIONAL MULTIPLE SCLEROSIS SOCIETY SCHOLARSHIP PROGRAM

Scholarships available to high school seniors and graduates (or GED) with MS, or who are children of people with MS. Must be attending a postsecondary school for the first time. All applicants must meet the basic eligibility criteria, fully complete the online application and mail supporting documents by deadline. The program is competitive in nature, and not all applicants will be selected for an award. Scholarship finalists will be selected on the basis of demonstrated financial need, academic record, leadership and participation in school or community activities, work experience, an outside appraisal, goals and aspirations, special circumstances, and an essay (written by the applicant) regarding the impact of MS on their life. More information can be found at http://www.nationalmssociety.org

Award: Scholarship for use in freshman year; not renewable. *Number:* 400. *Amount:* $1500.

Eligibility Requirements: Applicant must be physically disabled and enrolled or expecting to enroll full- or part-time at a two-year or four-year institution or university. Applicant must be physically disabled. Available to U.S. citizens.

Application Requirements: Application form, driver's license, essay, financial need analysis, personal photograph. *Deadline:* January 15.

Contact: Scholarship Management Services
Phone: 507-931-1682
E-mail: mssociety@scholarshipamerica.org

NATIONAL PRESS FOUNDATION

http://www.nationalpress.org/

EVERT CLARK/SETH PAYNE AWARD

Award to recognize outstanding reporting and writing in any field of science. Limited to non-technical, print journalism only. Articles published in newspapers (including college newspapers), magazines, and newsletters are eligible. Both freelancers and staff writers are eligible. THIS IS FOR WRITERS 30 YEARS OF AGE OR YOUNGER.,

Award: Prize for use in freshman, sophomore, junior, senior, graduate, or postgraduate years; not renewable. *Number:* 1000.

Eligibility Requirements: Applicant must be enrolled or expecting to enroll full- or part-time at a two-year or four-year or technical institution or university. Available to U.S. and Canadian citizens.

Application Requirements: Application form, portfolio. *Deadline:* June 30.

Contact: Dianeq McGurgan, Administrator
National Press Foundation
P.O. Box 910
Hedgesville, WV 25427
Phone: 304-754-6786
E-mail: diane@casw.org

NATIONAL SOCIETY FOR HISTOTECHNOLOGY

http://nsh.org/

IRWIN S. LERNER STUDENT SCHOLARSHIPS

Student scholarships support the educational endeavors of aspiring histotechnologists.

Award: Scholarship for use in freshman, sophomore, junior, or senior years; not renewable. *Number:* 5. *Amount:* $500.

Eligibility Requirements: Applicant must be enrolled or expecting to enroll full- or part-time at a two-year or four-year institution or university. Available to U.S. and non-U.S. citizens.

Application Requirements: Application form. *Deadline:* March 1.

Contact: Natalie Paskoski
Phone: 4435354060
E-mail: natalie@nsh.org

NATSO FOUNDATION

http://www.natso.com/

BILL MOON SCHOLARSHIP

Available to employees or dependents of NATSO-affiliated truck stops/travel plazas. Visit website at http://www.natsofoundation.org for additional information.

Award: Scholarship for use in freshman, sophomore, junior, senior, or graduate years; not renewable. *Number:* 13. *Amount:* $2500.

Eligibility Requirements: Applicant must be enrolled or expecting to enroll full- or part-time at a two-year or four-year institution or university. Applicant or parent of applicant must have employment or volunteer experience in transportation industry. Available to U.S. and non-U.S. citizens.

Application Requirements: Application form, essay, financial need analysis, recommendations or references, signature from employer, transcript. *Deadline:* April 14.

Contact: Sharon Corigliano, Executive Director
Phone: 703-549-2100 Ext. 8561
Fax: 703-684-9667
E-mail: scorigliano@natso.com

NEBRASKA'S COORDINATING COMMISSION FOR POSTSECONDARY EDUCATION

https://ccpe.nebraska.gov/

NEBRASKA OPPORTUNITY GRANT

Available to undergraduates attending a participating postsecondary institution in Nebraska. Must demonstrate financial need. Nebraska residency required. Awards determined by each participating institution. Student must complete the Free Application for Federal Student Aid (FAFSA) to apply. Contact financial aid office at institution for additional information.

Award: Grant for use in freshman, sophomore, junior, or senior years; not renewable. *Amount:* $100–$4139.

Eligibility Requirements: Applicant must be enrolled or expecting to enroll full- or part-time at a two-year or four-year or technical institution or university; resident of Nebraska and studying in Nebraska. Available to U.S. citizens.

Application Requirements: Application form, financial need analysis. *Deadline:* continuous.

Contact: Mr. J. Ritchie Morrow, Financial Aid Officer
Nebraska's Coordinating Commission for Postsecondary Education
140 North 8th Street, Suite 300
PO Box 95005
Lincoln, NE 68509-5005
Phone: 402-471-2847
E-mail: Ritchie.Morrow@nebraska.gov

NEED

http://www.needld.org/

UNMET NEED GRANT PROGRAM

The program provides "last dollar" funding to lower-income students that still have a need for aid after all federal, state, local and private scholarships and grants have been secured. Must be a U.S. citizen, high school graduate, resident of one of nine participating counties in Southwestern Pennsylvania (Allegheny, Armstrong, Beaver, Butler, Fayette, Greene, Lawrence, Washington or Westmoreland county), and have a minimum 2.0 GPA.

Award: Grant for use in freshman, sophomore, junior, or senior years; not renewable. *Number:* 10–500. *Amount:* $1000–$3500.

Eligibility Requirements: Applicant must be Black (non-Hispanic); enrolled or expecting to enroll full-time at a two-year or four-year or technical institution or university and resident of Pennsylvania. Available to U.S. citizens.

Application Requirements: Application form, essay, financial need analysis, personal photograph. *Deadline:* May 31.

Contact: Mrs. Rhonda Brooks, Director of Student Services
NEED
The Law and Finance Building
429 Fourth Avenue, 20th Floor
Pittsburgh, PA 15219
Phone: 412-566-2760
Fax: 412-471-6643
E-mail: rbrooks@needld.org

NERDIFY

https://gonerdify.com/

NERDY BOT SCHOLARSHIP

High school and university students from all over the world are eligible to participate. To participate send your essay to scholarship@nerdy-bot.com. The essay should be written in English and contain no more than 500 words. Number of entries is limited. One person can send only one essay. Submitted essays should not contain any form of plagiarism. In case of the plagiarism detections the entry will be disqualified without any prior notice. We will evaluate your content, grammar and writing skills. Therefore, before, submitting the application, you should take your time to edit and review your essay thoroughly. Your essay should be authentic; polished up in terms of structure, style and grammar; demonstrate depth of your ideas. Three essays with the highest score based on the criteria above will win the Nerdy Bot essay contest. The results will be published on the website and on our official Facebook page. Only the scholarship winners will be contacted by Nerdify team members via email.

Award: Scholarship for use in freshman, sophomore, junior, senior, graduate, or postgraduate years; renewable. *Number:* 3. *Amount:* $1000.

Eligibility Requirements: Applicant must be enrolled or expecting to enroll full- or part-time at a four-year institution or university. Available to U.S. and non-U.S. citizens.

Application Requirements: Essay. *Deadline:* February 28.

Contact: Nerdify Scholarship Committee
Nerdify
995 Market St, San Francisco, California 94103
San Francisco 94103
Phone: +1224-444-6373
E-mail: scholarship@nerdy-bot.com

NEW JERSEY HIGHER EDUCATION STUDENT ASSISTANCE AUTHORITY

http://www.hesaa.org/

LAW ENFORCEMENT OFFICER MEMORIAL SCHOLARSHIP

Scholarships for full-time undergraduate study at approved New Jersey institutions for the dependent children of New Jersey law enforcement officers killed in the line of duty. Value of scholarship will be established annually. Deadline varies.

Award: Scholarship for use in freshman, sophomore, or junior years; not renewable.

Eligibility Requirements: Applicant must be enrolled or expecting to enroll full-time at a two-year or four-year institution or university; resident of New Jersey and studying in New Jersey. Applicant or parent of applicant must have employment or volunteer experience in police/firefighting. Available to U.S. citizens.

Application Requirements: Application form.

Contact: Jean Hathoway, Assistant Director of Special Grants and
Scholarships
New Jersey Higher Education Student Assistance Authority
PO Box 540
Trenton, NJ 08625
Phone: 609-588-3266

SURVIVOR TUITION BENEFITS PROGRAM

The scholarship provides tuition fees for spouses and dependents of law
enforcement officers, fire, or emergency services personnel killed in the
line of duty. Eligible recipients may attend any independent institution in
the state; however, the annual value of the grant cannot exceed the
highest tuition charged at a New Jersey public institution.

Award: Scholarship for use in freshman, sophomore, junior, or senior
years; renewable.

Eligibility Requirements: Applicant must be enrolled or expecting to
enroll full- or part-time at a two-year or four-year institution or
university; resident of New Jersey and studying in New Jersey. Applicant
or parent of applicant must have employment or volunteer experience in
police/firefighting. Available to U.S. citizens.

Application Requirements: Application form.

Contact: Jean Hathoway, Assistant Director of Special Grants and
Scholarships
New Jersey Higher Education Student Assistance Authority
PO Box 540
Trenton, NJ 08625
Phone: 609-588-3266
E-mail: jhathaway@hesaa.org

NEW JERSEY STATE GOLF ASSOCIATION

NJSGA.org

NEW JERSEY STATE GOLF ASSOCIATION CADDIE SCHOLARSHIP

Caddie Scholarship Foundation, which has provided over $10 million in
college tuition grants to over 2,700 deserving caddie scholars from our
member clubs, since its inception in 1947.

Award: Scholarship for use in freshman, sophomore, junior, or senior
years; not renewable. *Number:* 145. *Amount:* $3500–$6000.

Eligibility Requirements: Applicant must be enrolled or expecting to
enroll full-time at a two-year or four-year or technical institution or
university and resident of New Jersey. Applicant or parent of applicant
must have employment or volunteer experience in private club/caddying.
Applicant must have 2.5 GPA or higher. Available to U.S. citizens.

Application Requirements: Application form, financial need analysis.
Deadline: March 1.

Contact: Ms. Sheila Menendez, Education Director
New Jersey State Golf Association
PO Box 6947
Freehold, NJ 07728
Phone: 848-8636481
E-mail: Menendeznjsga@optonline.net

NEW YORK WOMEN IN COMMUNICATIONS

https://nywici.org/

NEW YORK WOMEN IN COMMUNICATIONS SCHOLARSHIPS

New York Women in Communications, Inc, cultivates leaders in our field
by providing financial support, opportunities for professional
development and mentoring, and entrée to a diverse community of
communications professionals. We are the largest foundation for
women's communications scholarships in the U.S.

Award: Scholarship for use in freshman, sophomore, junior, senior, or
graduate years; not renewable. *Number:* 18–22. *Amount:* $2500–$10,000.

Eligibility Requirements: Applicant must be enrolled or expecting to
enroll full-time at a four-year institution or university; resident of
Connecticut, New Jersey, New York, Pennsylvania and studying in New
York. Applicant must have 3.0 GPA or higher. Available to U.S. and non-
U.S. citizens.

Application Requirements: Application form, essay. *Deadline:*
January 26.

Contact: Anna McManus, Membership Director
New York Women in Communications
355 Lexington Ave
Floor 15
New York, NY 10017
Phone: 212-2972133
E-mail: info@nywici.org

NICODEMUS WILDERNESS PROJECT

http://www.wildernessproject.org/

APPRENTICE ECOLOGIST SCHOLARSHIP

The Apprentice Ecologist Scholarship is open to students interested in
protecting wildlife and the environment. This program elevates young
people into leadership roles by engaging them in environmental
stewardship and conservation projects that benefit native ecosystems and
local communities. Applicants should demonstrate personal initiative,
leadership, and dedication in their projects.

Award: Scholarship for use in freshman, sophomore, junior, or senior
years; not renewable. *Number:* 3. *Amount:* $250–$1000.

Eligibility Requirements: Applicant must be age 13-21 and enrolled or
expecting to enroll full- or part-time at a two-year or four-year or
technical institution or university. Available to U.S. and non-U.S.
citizens.

Application Requirements: Essay. *Deadline:* December 31.

Contact: Dr. Robert Dudley, Director
Nicodemus Wilderness Project
115 Cornell Dr. SE, #40712
Albuquerque, NM 87196-0712
E-mail: mail@wildernessproject.org

NIKKO COSMETIC SURGERY CENTER

http://www.drnikko.com/

BREAST CANCER SURVIVOR SCHOLARSHIPS

Nikko Cosmetic Surgery Center has announced that it will offer two
$1,000 scholarships annually for breast cancer survivors. The
scholarships are aimed at assisting breast cancer survivors in the pursuit
of their educational goals. Nikko Cosmetic Surgery Center is offering
two annual scholarships of $1,000 each. The funds will be paid in the
form of tuition for attendance at an educational institution. The tuition
can be for secondary or for post-secondary education, including college,
trade school, and community college. You do not have to be attending
school at this time to be eligible for a scholarship. Within a year after the
award date, the winner must provide to Nikko Cosmetic Surgery Center a
tuition invoice for the chosen school. A check will then be issued to the
institution for $1,000. To be eligible, you must be a U.S. citizen who has
been diagnosed with breast cancer.

Award: Scholarship for use in freshman, sophomore, junior, senior,
graduate, or postgraduate years; not renewable. *Number:* 2. *Amount:*
$1000.

Eligibility Requirements: Applicant must be physically disabled and
enrolled or expecting to enroll full- or part-time at a two-year or four-year
or technical institution or university. Applicant must be physically
disabled. Available to U.S. citizens.

Application Requirements: Application form, essay. *Deadline:*
September 30.

Contact: Dr. Anthony Nikko
E-mail: michael@drnikko.com

NISEI STUDENT RELOCATION COMMEMORATIVE FUND

http://www.nsrcfund.org/

NISEI STUDENT RELOCATION COMMEMORATIVE FUND

Eligibility: only high school seniors of Southeast Asian (Vietnam,
Cambodia, Laos) ancestry living in the U.S. Deadline to apply varies.
Scholarships awarded in a different city/region each year. Check the
website (http://www.nsrcfund.org) for current information or email:
jeanhibino@aol.com.

Award: Scholarship for use in freshman year; not renewable. *Number:* 30–50. *Amount:* $250–$2000.

Eligibility Requirements: Applicant must be Lao/Hmong, Vietnamese heritage; Asian/Pacific Islander; high school student and planning to enroll or expecting to enroll full- or part-time at a two-year or four-year or technical institution or university. Available to U.S. citizens.

Application Requirements: Application form, community service, essay, financial need analysis.

Contact: Ms. Jean Hibino, Executive Secretary
Nisei Student Relocation Commemorative Fund
19 Scenic Drive
Portland, CT 06480
E-mail: jeanhibino@aol.com

NO BULL SPORTS

http://nobullsports.org/

NO BULL SPORTS SCHOLARSHIP

No Bull Sports is a non-profit organization dedicated to uniting, educating, and empowering young women. When we set out to build a community of female athletes from all walks of life, a cornerstone of our mission was to offer scholarships to deserving high school students. No Bull Sports provides smart, trailblazing, talented young women the financial resources they need to achieve their academic and athletic goals. No Bull Sports is excited to award our quarterly scholarships of $5,000 in March, June, and December to a deserving female high school sophomore, junior or senior to pursue her dreams on and off the field. We will award $15,000 worth of scholarships over the course of a calendar year; awarded 3xs/year, each scholarship is worth $5,000.

Award: Scholarship for use in freshman year; not renewable.

Eligibility Requirements: Applicant must be high school student and planning to enroll or expecting to enroll full- or part-time at a two-year or four-year or technical institution or university. Available to U.S. citizens.

Application Requirements: Application form, essay. *Deadline:* continuous.

Contact: Bridget W.
No Bull Sports
653 W Fallbrook Ave. #101
Fresno, CA 93711
Phone: 877-307-1451
E-mail: hello@nobullsports.org

NOPLAG PLAGIARISM CHECKER

http://noplag.com/

NOPLAG SCHOLARSHIP ESSAY CONTEST

We are happy to announce the start of the Noplag Scholarship Essay contest. In comparison with other writing contests our goal is to help you become successful and nowadays proper education is a key component. We hope that our aid in the amount of $3500 will help the winner in his education in full or partially. Plus, you will have a good chance to test your writing skills and maybe pump them up by participating in this contest.

Award: Scholarship for use in freshman, sophomore, junior, or senior years; not renewable. *Number:* 3. *Amount:* $300–$2500.

Eligibility Requirements: Applicant must be enrolled or expecting to enroll full- or part-time at a two-year or four-year or technical institution or university. Available to U.S. and non-U.S. citizens.

Application Requirements: Application form, essay. *Deadline:* June 25.

Contact: CEO
E-mail: aleks@noplag.com

NORTH CAROLINA ASSOCIATION OF EDUCATORS

http://www.ncae.org/

NORTH CAROLINA ASSOCIATION OF EDUCATORS MARTIN LUTHER KING JR. SCHOLARSHIP

One-time award for high school seniors who are North Carolina residents to attend a postsecondary institution. Must be a U.S. citizen. Based upon financial need, GPA, and essay. Must have a GPA of at least 3.5 on a 5.0 scale or a 2.5 on a 4.0 scale.

Award: Scholarship for use in freshman year; not renewable. *Number:* 2–4. *Amount:* $500–$1000.

Eligibility Requirements: Applicant must be high school student; age 16-18; planning to enroll or expecting to enroll full-time at a two-year or four-year institution or university and resident of North Carolina. Applicant must have 2.5 GPA or higher. Available to U.S. citizens.

Application Requirements: Application form, community service, essay, financial need analysis. *Deadline:* February 5.

Contact: Derevana Leach, Scholarship Coordinator
North Carolina Association of Educators
700 S Salisbury St
Raleigh, NC 27601
Phone: 919-832-3000 Ext. 203
E-mail: derevana.leach@ncae.org

NORTH CAROLINA DIVISION OF VOCATIONAL REHABILITATION SERVICES

http://www.dhhs.state.nc.us/

TRAINING SUPPORT FOR YOUTH WITH DISABILITIES

Public service program that helps persons with disabilities obtain competitive employment. To qualify: student must have a mental, physical or learning disability that is an impediment to employment. A Rehabilitation Counselor along with the eligible student individually develops a rehabilitation program to achieve an employment outcome which requires post secondary training. Financial assistance is based on NC Division of Vocational Rehabilitation demonstrated financial need and type of program in which the student enrolls.

Award: Grant for use in freshman, sophomore, junior, senior, or graduate years; renewable.

Eligibility Requirements: Applicant must be hearing impaired, learning disabled, physically disabled, or visually impaired; enrolled or expecting to enroll full- or part-year at a two-year or four-year or technical institution or university and resident of North Carolina. Applicant must be hearing impaired, learning disabled, physically disabled, or visually impaired. Available to U.S. citizens.

Application Requirements: Application form, financial need analysis, interview. *Deadline:* continuous.

Contact: Stephanie Hanes, Program Specialist for Transition
North Carolina Division of Vocational Rehabilitation Services
2801 Mail Service Center
Raleigh, NC 27699-2801
Phone: 919-855-3576
E-mail: stephanie.hanes@dhhs.nc.gov

NORTH CAROLINA VIETNAM VETERANS, INC.

http://www.ncvvi.org

NC VIETNAM VETERANS, INC., SCHOLARSHIP PROGRAM

Scholarship is awarded to Vietnam Veterans, their spouses or their offspring including adopted. Students who successfully attend a Lessons of Vietnam class prior to or during the year of submission are eligible. A 600-900 word essay on a different topic each year relating to the Vietnam War era is required.

Award: Scholarship for use in freshman, sophomore, junior, or senior years; not renewable. *Number:* 1–6. *Amount:* $500–$1500.

Eligibility Requirements: Applicant must be enrolled or expecting to enroll full-time at a two-year or four-year or technical institution or university and resident of North Carolina. Available to U.S. and non-U.S. citizens.

Application Requirements: Application form, essay. *Deadline:* February 28.

NORTH DAKOTA UNIVERSITY SYSTEM

http://www.ndus.edu/

NORTH DAKOTA ACADEMIC SCHOLARSHIP

This scholarship rewards ND resident high school students for taking rigorous coursework, and meeting minimum grade and testing requirements in high school. To qualify for payment, students must be enrolled full time, meet the minimum cumulative GPA requirement of 2.75 and be maintaining degree progress. Awards are $750/sem or $500/qtr up to a total of $6,000 lifetime. Students have up to 6 years following high school to utilize the scholarship.

Award: Scholarship for use in freshman, sophomore, junior, senior, or graduate years; renewable. *Number:* 1–3000. *Amount:* $500–$2250.

Eligibility Requirements: Applicant must be high school student; planning to enroll or expecting to enroll full-time at a two-year or four-year institution or university; resident of North Dakota and studying in North Dakota. Applicant must have 3.0 GPA or higher. Available to U.S. citizens.

Application Requirements: Application form.

Contact: Brenda Zastoupil, Director of Financial Aid
North Dakota University System
600 E Blvd Ave, Dept. 21
Bismarck, ND 58505-0602
Phone: 701-328-2906
Fax: 701-328-2979
E-mail: brenda.zastoupil@ndus.edu

NORTH DAKOTA CAREER AND TECHNICAL EDUCATION SCHOLARSHIP

This scholarship rewards ND resident high school students for taking rigorous coursework, and meeting minimum grade and testing requirements in high school. To qualify for payment, students must be enrolled full time, meet the minimum cumulative GPA requirements of 2.75 and be maintaining degree progress. Awards are $750/sem. or $500/qtr. up to a total of $6,000 lifetime. Students have up to 6 years following high school to utilize the scholarship.

Award: Scholarship for use in freshman, sophomore, junior, senior, or graduate years; renewable. *Number:* 1–3000. *Amount:* $500–$2250.

Eligibility Requirements: Applicant must be high school student; planning to enroll or expecting to enroll full-time at a two-year or four-year institution or university; resident of North Dakota and studying in North Dakota. Applicant must have 3.0 GPA or higher. Available to U.S. citizens.

Application Requirements: Application form.

Contact: Brenda Zastoupil, Director of Financial Aid
North Dakota University System
600 E Blvd Ave, Dept. 21
Bismarck, ND 58505-0602
Phone: 701-328-2906
Fax: 701-328-2979
E-mail: brenda.zastoupil@ndus.edu

NORTH DAKOTA INDIAN SCHOLARSHIP PROGRAM

The North Dakota Indian Scholarship program was established to provide scholarship awards to Native American Students attending qualifying colleges or universities within North Dakota. Students must be ND residents as defined by the college, enrolled full time, and maintain a GPA of at least 2.0. Awards are available to both undergraduate and graduate students. Students who maintain a 3.50 cumulative GPA qualify for the scholarship based on merit. Students who have a GPA lower than 3.50 must show unmet need. The priority application date is July 15. Not all eligible applicants are awarded due to limited appropriations.

Award: Scholarship for use in freshman, sophomore, junior, senior, or graduate years; not renewable. *Number:* 1–270. *Amount:* $1–$2000.

Eligibility Requirements: Applicant must be American Indian/Alaska Native; enrolled or expecting to enroll full-time at a two-year or four-year or technical institution or university; resident of North Dakota and studying in North Dakota. Available to U.S. citizens.

Application Requirements: Application form, financial need analysis. *Deadline:* July 15.

Contact: Brenda Zastoupil, Director of Financial Aid
North Dakota University System
600 E Blvd Ave, Dept. 21
Bismarck, ND 58505-0602
Phone: 701-328-2906
Fax: 701-328-2979
E-mail: brenda.zastoupil@ndus.edu

NORTH DAKOTA SCHOLARS PROGRAM

The purpose of the ND Scholars Scholarship is to retain within ND, the brightest and best students who are pursuing post-secondary education. The scholarship amount equates to the tuition charged at the Scholar's eligible institution, not to exceed the highest regular resident undergraduate tuition rate in the NDUS system. This program provides merit-based, full-tuition scholarships to ND high school graduates who attend a qualifying college within ND. High school juniors who score in the top 95th percentile of all ND ACT test-takers prior to July 1 of the year preceding their freshman year of college will be considered as a candidate for this award. Not all eligible students will qualify due to limited appropriations. This scholarship is renewable for up to three years. Recipients must be enrolled at qualifying institutions in ND at full-time status (12 cr. minimum per semester) and must maintain a cumulative GPA of 3.50.

Award: Scholarship for use in freshman, sophomore, junior, or senior years; renewable. *Number:* 1–140. *Amount:* $3462–$11,666.

Eligibility Requirements: Applicant must be high school student; planning to enroll or expecting to enroll full-time at a two-year or four-year institution or university; resident of North Dakota and studying in North Dakota. Available to U.S. citizens.

Application Requirements: *Deadline:* June 30.

Contact: Brenda Zastoupil, Director of Financial Aid
North Dakota University System
600 E Blvd Ave, Dept. 21
Bismarck, ND 58505-0602
Phone: 701-328-2906
Fax: 701-328-2979
E-mail: brenda.zastoupil@ndus.edu

NORTH DAKOTA STATE STUDENT INCENTIVE GRANT PROGRAM

The North Dakota State Grant is the premier need-based state grant in North Dakota. Maximum award of $975 per semester or $650 per quarter. The North Dakota State Grant supports ND residents attending an eligible college or university within North Dakota in a program of study that is at least one year in length. The FAFSA is required annually. Awards are available for up to 8 full-time equivalent semesters or 12 full-time equivalent quarters of undergraduate study. Students must meet the SAP guidelines of their institution and meet all title IV eligibility criteria, including having verification complete, if required.

Award: Grant for use in freshman, sophomore, junior, or senior years; not renewable. *Number:* 1–7000. *Amount:* $1–$2925.

Eligibility Requirements: Applicant must be enrolled or expecting to enroll full- or part-time at a two-year or four-year institution or university; resident of North Dakota and studying in North Dakota. Available to U.S. citizens.

Application Requirements: *Deadline:* continuous.

Contact: Brenda Zastoupil, Director of Financial Aid
North Dakota University System
600 E Blvd Ave, Dept. 21
Bismarck, ND 58505-0602
Phone: 701-328-2906
Fax: 701-328-2979
E-mail: brenda.zastoupil@ndus.edu

NORTHWESTERN MUTUAL FOUNDATION

http://www.scholarshipamerica.org

NORTHWESTERN MUTUAL CHILDHOOD CANCER SURVIVOR SCHOLARSHIP

Ten $5,000 scholarship renewable up to one year or until a Bachelor's degree is earned, whichever occurs first, on the basis of maintaining full-time enrollment and a cumulative GPA of 2.5 on a 4.0 scale (or equivalent). The Northwestern Mutual Childhood Cancer Sibling Scholarship program assists siblings of individuals affected by childhood cancer, and who plan to continue their education in college or vocational school programs. The scholarship program will award up to 10 renewable $5,000 scholarships. To apply, students must be U.S. citizens and siblings of individuals who are in current treatment, have survived or passed away from pediatric childhood cancer. Applicants must be age 25 or under and planning to enroll in full-time undergraduate study at an accredited two- or four-year college, university or vocational-technical school for the entire upcoming academic year. Applicants must have a minimum grade point average of 2.5 on a 4.0 scale (or the equivalent) and demonstrate financial need.

Award: Scholarship for use in freshman, sophomore, junior, or senior years; renewable. *Number:* 10. *Amount:* $5000.

Eligibility Requirements: Applicant must be enrolled or expecting to enroll full-time at a two-year or four-year or technical institution or university. Applicant must have 2.5 GPA or higher. Available to U.S. citizens.

Application Requirements: Application form. *Deadline:* March 30.

Contact: Program Manager
Northwestern Mutual Foundation
One Scholarship Way
Saint Peter, MN 56082
Phone: 800-537-4180
E-mail: jsowder@scholarshipamerica.org

NURSERECRUITER.COM

https://www.nurserecruiter.com

NURSERECRUITER.COM SCHOLARSHIP

For over 18 years, NurseRecruiter.com has connected hundreds of thousands of nurses with jobs nationwide. We're all aware of the nursing shortage and its impact on healthcare in America and we want to help. As part of our commitment to attract the best and the brightest to the nursing profession we are proud to announce that we are founding the NurseRecruiter.com Scholarship with an initial $10,000 in nursing scholarships to people who want to further their education and make the world a better place at the same time. Do you know someone who wants to become a nurse? If you know someone interested in pursuing a career in nursing please let them know about our scholarship, we would be happy to help them along their path to becoming a nurse. It is the policy and practice of the NurseRecruiter.com scholarship program to treat all scholarship applicants with dignity and respect and to provide equal opportunity to all persons without regard to color, race, religion, sex, national origin, citizenship, age, disability, marital status, pregnancy, sexual orientation, military status or any other category protected by law.

Award: Scholarship for use in freshman, sophomore, junior, senior, graduate, or postgraduate years; not renewable. *Number:* 1–10. *Amount:* $1000–$5000.

Eligibility Requirements: Applicant must be enrolled or expecting to enroll full- or part-time at a two-year or four-year institution or university. Available to U.S. and non-U.S. citizens.

Application Requirements: Application form, essay. *Deadline:* continuous.

Contact: Peter Frouman, Scholarship Coordinator
NurseRecruiter.com
c/o Nurse Recruiter
113 Cherry Street, #26760
Seattle, WA 98104
Phone: 800-243-3407
Fax: 866-608-1781
E-mail: support@nurserecruiter.com

OHIO DEPARTMENT OF HIGHER EDUCATION

http://www.ohiohighered.org

CHOOSE OHIO FIRST SCHOLARSHIP

Choose Ohio First awards competitive scholarship funding to Ohio's colleges and universities to support undergraduate and qualifying graduate students in innovative STEMM academic programs. Designated Choose Ohio First programs are integrated with regional economies, meeting statewide educational needs, facilitating the completion of baccalaureate degrees in cost effective manners, and recruiting underrepresented STEMM student groups including women and students of color.

Award: Scholarship for use in freshman, sophomore, junior, or senior years; renewable. *Number:* 2643. *Amount:* $1500–$7368.

Eligibility Requirements: Applicant must be enrolled or expecting to enroll full- or part-time at a two-year or four-year institution or university; resident of Ohio and studying in Ohio. Available to U.S. and non-U.S. citizens.

Application Requirements: *Deadline:* continuous.

Contact: Ms. Mandie Maxwell, Assistant Director
Ohio Department of Higher Education
Ohio Department of Higher Education
25 South Front Street
Columbus, OH 43215
Phone: 614-644-9602
E-mail: amaxwell@highered.ohio.gov

OHIO COLLEGE OPPORTUNITY GRANT

OCOG provides grant money to Ohio residents who demonstrate the highest levels of financial need (as determined by the results of the FAFSA) who are enrolled at Ohio public colleges or universities; Ohio private, non-profit colleges or universities; Ohio private, for-profit institutions; or eligible Pennsylvania institutions.

Award: Grant for use in freshman, sophomore, junior, or senior years; not renewable. *Amount:* $1056–$2832.

Eligibility Requirements: Applicant must be enrolled or expecting to enroll full- or part-time at a two-year or four-year institution or university; resident of Ohio and studying in Ohio, Pennsylvania.

Application Requirements: *Deadline:* October 1.

Contact: Tamika Braswell, Director
Ohio Department of Higher Education
25 South Front Street
Columbus, OH 43215
Phone: 614-728-8862
E-mail: ocog_admin@highered.ohio.gov

OHIO SAFETY OFFICERS COLLEGE MEMORIAL FUND

Renewable award covering up to full tuition is available to children and surviving spouses of peace officers, other safety officers and fire fighters killed in the line of duty in any state. Children must be under 26 years of age. Dollar value of each award varies. Must be an Ohio resident and enroll full-time or part-time at an Ohio college or university. Any spouse/child of a member of the armed services of the U.S., who has been killed in the line duty during Operation Enduring Freedom, Operation Iraqi Freedom or a combat zone designated by the President of the United States. Dollar value of each award varies.

Award: Scholarship for use in freshman, sophomore, junior, or senior years; renewable. *Amount:* $8115.

Eligibility Requirements: Applicant must be enrolled or expecting to enroll full- or part-time at a two-year or four-year institution or university; resident of Ohio and studying in Ohio. Available to U.S. citizens.

Application Requirements: *Deadline:* continuous.

Contact: Ramah Church, Program Manager
Ohio Department of Higher Education
25 South Front Street
Columbus, OH 43215
Phone: 614-752-9528
E-mail: osom_admin@highered.ohio.gov

OHIO WAR ORPHANS SCHOLARSHIP

Aids Ohio residents attending an eligible college in Ohio. Must be between the ages of 16 and 25, the child of a disabled or deceased veteran, and enrolled full-time. Must maintain a minimum GPA of 2.0. Renewable up to five years. Amount of award varies. Must include Form DD214.

Award: Scholarship for use in freshman, sophomore, junior, or senior years; renewable.

Eligibility Requirements: Applicant must be age 16-25; enrolled or expecting to enroll full-time at a two-year or four-year institution or university; resident of Ohio and studying in Ohio. Available to U.S. citizens. Applicant must have general military experience.

Application Requirements: Application form. *Deadline:* May 15.

Contact: Ramah Church, Program Manager
Ohio Department of Higher Education
25 South Front Street
Columbus, OH 43215
Phone: 614-752-9528
E-mail: rchurch@highered.ohio.gov

ONE LOVE FOUNDATION

http://www.joinonelove.org

ONE LOVE FOUNDATION PETS VS. PARTNERS SCHOLARSHIP

Pets can and will take advantage of our love. And we forgive them because they're cute and fluffy and don't know any better. But people should know better. Help us highlight the gray areas between love and control by creating your own #OKforpetsnotpartners meme the educates others about unhealthy relationship behaviors. Yep,.. it's that fun and easy! http://www.petsvspartners.com

Award: Scholarship for use in freshman, sophomore, junior, senior, graduate, or postgraduate years; not renewable. *Number:* 3. *Amount:* $500.

Eligibility Requirements: Applicant must be age 18-26 and enrolled or expecting to enroll full- or part-time at a two-year or four-year or technical institution or university. Available to U.S. and non-U.S. citizens.

Application Requirements: *Deadline:* December 31.

Contact: April Wright
One Love Foundation
119 Pondfield Rd
PO Box 368
Bronxville, NY 10708
E-mail: thatsnotlove@joinonelove.org

ONLINEPSYCHOLOGYDEGREES.COM

http://www.onlinepsychologydegrees.com/

ONLINEPSYCHOLOGYDEGREES.COM EDUCATION SCHOLARSHIPS

If you're ready to begin your career of helping change lives, get started by applying for the OnlinePsychologyDegrees.com $1,000 scholarship. Apply now, and then find the psychology programs that fit your career path.

Award: Scholarship for use in freshman, sophomore, junior, senior, graduate, or postgraduate years; renewable. *Number:* 2. *Amount:* $1000.

Eligibility Requirements: Applicant must be enrolled or expecting to enroll full- or part-time at a two-year or four-year or technical institution or university and resident of Alabama, Alaska, Arizona, Arkansas, California, Colorado, Connecticut, Delaware, District of Columbia, Georgia, Hawaii, Idaho, Illinois, Indiana, Iowa, Kansas, Kentucky, Louisiana, Maine, Manitoba, Maryland, Massachusetts, Michigan, Minnesota, Mississippi, Missouri, Montana, Nebraska, Nevada, New Hampshire, New Jersey, New Mexico, North Carolina, North Dakota, Northwest Territories, Ohio, Oklahoma, Ontario, Oregon, Pennsylvania, South Carolina, South Dakota, Tennessee, Texas, Utah, Vermont, Virginia, Washington, West Virginia, Wisconsin, Wyoming. Available to U.S. citizens.

Application Requirements: Application form, essay. *Deadline:* January 15.

Contact: Jennifer Moody, Site Manager
OnlinePsychologyDegrees.com
15500 W 113th St
#200
Lenexa, KS 66219
Phone: 913-2546000
E-mail: jennifer.moody@marketing.keypathedu.com

OREGON STUDENT ASSISTANCE COMMISSION

https://oregonstudentaid.gov/

FRIENDS OF BILL RUTHERFORD EDUCATION SCHOLARSHIP

Award for children of individuals serving in the Oregon State Legislature or holding statewide elected office (Governor, Treasurer, Attorney General, Secretary of State, Commissioner of Labor, or Superintendent of Public Instruction); this does not include judicial positions. For use at public and nonprofit colleges in the U.S. Financial need may or may not be considered.

Award: Scholarship for use in freshman, sophomore, junior, or senior years; not renewable.

Eligibility Requirements: Applicant must be enrolled or expecting to enroll full-time at a four-year institution or university. Applicant or parent of applicant must have employment or volunteer experience in government/politics. Available to U.S. citizens.

Application Requirements: Application form, financial need analysis. *Deadline:* March 1.

Contact: Melissa Adams, Scholarship Processing Coordinator
Phone: 541-687-7409
E-mail: melissa.adams@state.or.us

ORGANIZATION FOR AUTISM RESEARCH

http://www.researchautism.org

LISA HIGGINS HUSSMAN SCHOLARSHIP

The Lisa Higgins Hussman Scholarship supports students with autism attending two or four year universities, life skills or postsecondary programs, or vocational, technical, or trade schools. Hussman applicants typically make up the pool of talented students who face daily challenges related to autism and attend programs that assist in skill-building, job-readiness, and other transition-related skills.

Award: Scholarship for use in freshman, sophomore, junior, or senior years; not renewable. *Number:* 20. *Amount:* $3000.

Eligibility Requirements: Applicant must be enrolled or expecting to enroll full-time at a two-year or four-year or technical institution or university. Available to U.S. citizens.

Application Requirements: Application form, essay. *Deadline:* May 7.

Contact: Executive Director
Phone: 703-243-3466
E-mail: scholarship@researchautism.org

SCHWALLIE FAMILY SCHOLARSHIP

The Schwallie Family Scholarship supports students with autism attending two or four year universities. Schwallie applicants typically pursue degrees at four year universities and have a diagnosis of Asperger Syndrome.

Award: Scholarship for use in freshman, sophomore, junior, or senior years; not renewable. *Number:* 20. *Amount:* $3000.

Eligibility Requirements: Applicant must be enrolled or expecting to enroll full-time at a two-year or four-year institution or university. Available to U.S. citizens.

Application Requirements: Application form, essay. *Deadline:* May 7.

Contact: Executive Director
Phone: 703-243-3466
E-mail: scholarship@researchautism.org

ORGONE BIOPHYSICAL RESEARCH LABORATORY

http://www.orgonelab.org/hochberg.htm

LOU HOCHBERG-UNIVERSITY/COLLEGE ESSAY AWARDS

An award of up to $500 will be given for the best university/college-level student research paper, addressing Wilhelm Reich's sociological discoveries.

Award: Prize for use in freshman, sophomore, junior, senior, graduate, or postgraduate years; not renewable. *Number:* 1. *Amount:* $100–$500.

Eligibility Requirements: Applicant must be enrolled or expecting to enroll full- or part-time at a two-year or four-year or technical institution or university. Available to U.S. and Canadian citizens.

Application Requirements: Essay. *Deadline:* continuous.

Contact: James DeMeo, Director
   E-mail: demeo@orgonelab.org

OSAGE NATION EDUCATION DEPARTMENT

https://www.osagenation-nsn.gov/what-we-do/education-department

OSAGE NATION HIGHER EDUCATION SCHOLARSHIP

The Osage Nation provides scholarships to legally enrolled members of the Osage Nation who are attending colleges and universities throughout the United States and abroad. The annual qualifying application opens on May 15th and closes on June 15th of each year.

Award: Scholarship for use in freshman, sophomore, junior, senior, graduate, or postgraduate years; renewable. *Number:* 1–1200. *Amount:* $150–$5000.

Eligibility Requirements: Applicant must be American Indian/Alaska Native and enrolled or expecting to enroll full- or part-time at a two-year or four-year institution or university. Available to U.S. citizens.

Application Requirements: Application form. *Deadline:* June 15.

Contact: Katie May, Program Manager
   Osage Nation Education Department
   Scholarship Management Services
   One Scholarship Way
   Saint Peter, MN 56082
   Phone: 855-758-8609
   E-mail: OsageNation@scholarshipamerica.org

OUTRIGGER DUKE KAHANAMOKU FOUNDATION

http://www.dukefoundation.org

ODKF GENERAL SCHOLARSHIP AWARD

The Outrigger Duke Kahanamoku Foundation ("ODKF") is an organization created to support the development and growth of individual athletes and teams that compete in local, national and international athletic competitions. As a tribute to Olympic swimmer and gold medal winner Duke Kahanamoku, our scholarships are awarded to competitors in water sports and volleyball. General scholarships are open to student athletes who are Hawaii residents currently competing in water sports or volleyball, who intended to compete in sports in college, have a 3.0 G.P.A. or higher and involved in community service.

Award: Scholarship for use in freshman, sophomore, junior, or senior years; not renewable. *Number:* 30–50. *Amount:* $1450–$15,000.

Eligibility Requirements: Applicant must be enrolled or expecting to enroll full-time at a four-year institution or university; resident of Hawaii and must have an interest in athletics/sports. Applicant must have 3.0 GPA or higher. Available to U.S. citizens.

Application Requirements: Application form, community service, essay, financial need analysis, personal photograph. *Deadline:* March 1.

Contact: Ms. Kathryn Currier, Administrator
   Outrigger Duke Kahanamoku Foundation
   PO Box 160924
   Honolulu, HI 96816
   Phone: 808-545-4880
   E-mail: info@dukefoundation.org

PACERS FOUNDATION INC.

http://www.pacersfoundation.org/

PACERS TEAMUP SCHOLARSHIP

Scholarship is awarded to Indiana high school seniors for their first year of undergraduate study at any accredited four-year college or university or two-year college or junior college. Primary selection criteria is student involvement in community service.

Award: Scholarship for use in freshman year; not renewable. *Number:* 5. *Amount:* $2000.

Eligibility Requirements: Applicant must be enrolled or expecting to enroll full-time at a two-year or four-year institution or university and resident of Indiana. Applicant or parent of applicant must have employment or volunteer experience in community service. Available to U.S. citizens.

Application Requirements: Application form, community service, essay, recommendations or references, transcript. *Deadline:* March 1.

Contact: Jami Marsh, Executive Director
   Pacers Foundation Inc.
   125 South Pennsylvania Street
   Indianapolis, IN 46204
   Phone: 317-917-2856
   E-mail: foundation@pacers.com

PANHELLENIC SCHOLARSHIP FOUNDATION

https://www.panhellenicsf.org/

PANHELLENIC SCHOLARSHIP AWARDS

The PanHellenic Scholarship Awards are offered to recognize and reward students who have demonstrated exceptional academic performance as well as provide meaningful support to those with the greatest financial need. The application can be downloaded directly from our website, http://www.panhellenicsf.org. $250,000 in scholarships will be awarded to exceptional undergraduates of Hellenic descent from across the United States. The awards are offered at two levels: twenty (20) Awards of $10,000 based on academic achievement and financial need; and twenty (20) Awards of $2,500 based solely on academic achievement. To be eligible to apply for a scholarship, applicants must: be U.S. citizens or U.S. permanent residents; be of Hellenic descent; be a full-time undergraduate student at an accredited 4-year university in Fall 2016; and have a minimum 3.5 cumulative GPA. Award recipients are selected by an Academic Committee appointed by the Foundation's Board of Directors. This Committee works independently and makes its decisions based on established criteria set forth in the scholarship application. All award recipients are required to attend the Awards Ceremony & Gala, where they will receive their scholarship.

Award: Scholarship for use in freshman, sophomore, junior, or senior years; not renewable. *Number:* 40. *Amount:* $2500–$10,000.

Eligibility Requirements: Applicant must be of Cypriot, Greek heritage and enrolled or expecting to enroll full-time at a four-year institution or university. Applicant must have 3.5 GPA or higher. Available to U.S. citizens.

Application Requirements: Application form, autobiography, essay, financial need analysis, personal photograph, portfolio. *Deadline:* January 31.

Contact: Mr. Peter Korbakes, Director of Scholarships
   PanHellenic Scholarship Foundation
   17 North Wabash
   Suite 600
   Chicago, IL 60602
   Phone: 312-357-6432
   E-mail: pkorbakes@panhellenicsf.org

PAPERCHECK

https://www.papercheck.com/

PAPERCHECK, LLC—CHARLES SHAFAE' SCHOLARSHIP FUND

Awards one $1,000 scholarships each year to winners of the Papercheck essay contest. Must be enrolled at an accredited four-year college or university. Must maintain a cumulative GPA of at least 3.2. Scholarship guidelines available at https://www.papercheck.com/papercheck-scholarship/.

Award: Scholarship for use in freshman, sophomore, junior, or senior years; not renewable. *Number:* 1. *Amount:* $1000.

Eligibility Requirements: Applicant must be enrolled or expecting to enroll full-time at a four-year institution or university. Applicant must have 3.0 GPA or higher. Available to U.S. citizens.

Application Requirements: Application form, essay. *Deadline:* January 31.

Contact: Mr. Darren Shafae, Scholarship Coordinator
Papercheck
3905 State Street
Suite 7-516
Santa Barbara, CA 93105
Phone: 866-693-3348
E-mail: scholarships@papercheck.com

PARIAN LAW FIRM, LLC

https://westgalawyer.com/

THE EDUCATIONAL JUSTICE SCHOLARSHIP

We are offering $1,000.00 to a student currently enrolled in a community college, junior college, undergraduate, or graduate program. The Education Equality Scholarship rewards hard-working individuals seeking future education, security, and financial stability. The Education Equality Scholarship is available regardless of a student's major selection and current educational year. For more information, please visit: https://westgalawyer.com/#scholarship

Award: Scholarship for use in freshman, sophomore, junior, senior, graduate, or postgraduate years; not renewable. *Number:* 1. *Amount:* $1000.

Eligibility Requirements: Applicant must be enrolled or expecting to enroll full- or part-time at a two-year or four-year or technical institution or university. Applicant must have 3.0 GPA or higher. Available to U.S. and non-U.S. citizens.

Application Requirements: Application form, essay. *Deadline:* May 15.

Contact: Cade Parian
E-mail: marketing@westgalawyer.com

PEACOCK PRODUCTIONS, INC.

http://amefund.com

AUDRIA M. EDWARDS SCHOLARSHIP FUND

Peacock Productions, Inc. administers the Audria M. Edwards Scholarship Fund, and is funded by donations, variety show proceeds, and community fundraisers. Individuals are eligible for scholarships if they 1. will be pursuing post-secondary, under-graduate education in an accredited institution or program during the coming school year; 2. are lesbian, gay, bisexual, or transgender or have a LGBT parent; 3. have resided for at least one year in the state of Oregon or in Clark, Cowlitz, Skamania, or Wahkiakum counties in Washington. To apply, complete the application form, compile a one-page essay, and submit two letters of recommendation and a transcript. Read and sign the affidavit at the end of the application form and mail the form and enclosures on or before May 1st to: The Audria M. Edwards Scholarship Fund, P.O. Box 16337, Portland, OR 97292. A committee appointed by Peacock Productions, Inc. will review materials from all applicants and select finalists on the basis of the following qualifications: clarity of career and educational goals; potential to succeed in an educational program; experience as a volunteer or service-oriented leader; commitment to the LGBTQ community; capacity for overcoming difficult circumstances and making the most of personal assets. All finalists will be interviewed before the Review Committee who determines who will receive scholarships and how much funding each will receive. Checks will be mailed to students's schools and credited to their student accounts before the beginning of the school year. Funds can be used for tuition, fees, and on-campus room and board charges, but cannot be applied toward off-campus housing, transportation, dependent care, or other personal expenses. Awards are presented annually at Peacock in the Park in Portland, Oregon. For more information visit http://www.amefund.org.

Award: Scholarship for use in freshman, sophomore, junior, or senior years; not renewable. *Number:* 8–15. *Amount:* $1000–$5000.

Eligibility Requirements: Applicant must be enrolled or expecting to enroll full- or part-time at a two-year or four-year or technical institution or university and resident of Oregon, Washington. Available to U.S. citizens.

Application Requirements: Application form, community service, essay, financial need analysis, interview. *Deadline:* May 1.

Contact: Kimberlee Van Patten, Co-Founder
Peacock Productions, Inc.
PO Box 16337
Portland, OR 97292
E-mail: info@peacockinthepark.org

PENNSYLVANIA BURGLAR AND FIRE ALARM ASSOCIATION

http://www.pbfaa.com/

PENNSYLVANIA BURGLAR AND FIRE ALARM ASSOCIATION YOUTH SCHOLARSHIP PROGRAM

Non-renewable scholarships available to sons and daughters of active Pennsylvania police and fire personnel, and volunteer fire department personnel for full-time study at a two- or four-year college, or university. Must be a senior attending a Pennsylvania high school. Scholarship amount in the range of $500 to $6500.

Award: Scholarship for use in freshman year; not renewable. *Number:* 6–8. *Amount:* $500–$6500.

Eligibility Requirements: Applicant must be high school student; planning to enroll or expecting to enroll full-time at a two-year or four-year institution or university and resident of Pennsylvania. Applicant or parent of applicant must have employment or volunteer experience in police/firefighting. Available to U.S. citizens.

Application Requirements: Application form, essay, resume, test scores, transcript. *Deadline:* March 1.

Contact: Dale Eller, Executive Director
Phone: 814-838-3093
Fax: 814-838-5127
E-mail: info@pbfaa.com

PENNSYLVANIA FEDERATION OF DEMOCRATIC WOMEN INC.

http://www.pafedofdemwomen.org

PENNSYLVANIA FEDERATION OF DEMOCRATIC WOMEN INC. ANNUAL SCHOLARSHIP AWARDS

• See page 574

PENNSYLVANIA HIGHER EDUCATION ASSISTANCE AGENCY

http://www.pheaa.org/

BLIND OR DEAF BENEFICIARY GRANT PROGRAM

This state-funded program provides financial aid to blind or deaf students attending a postsecondary institution. This program awards funds on a first-come, first-served basis.

Award: Grant for use in freshman, sophomore, junior, or senior years; not renewable. *Amount:* $500.

Eligibility Requirements: Applicant must be hearing impaired or visually impaired; enrolled or expecting to enroll full- or part-time at a two-year or four-year or technical institution or university and resident of Pennsylvania. Applicant must be hearing impaired or visually impaired.

Application Requirements: Application form. *Deadline:* March 31.

Contact: Keith New, Director of Public Relations
Phone: 717-720-2509
E-mail: knew@pheaa.org

PENNSYLVANIA STATE GRANT PROGRAM

Award for Pennsylvania residents attending an approved postsecondary institution as undergraduates in a program of at least two years duration. Renewable for up to eight semesters if applicants show continued need and academic progress. Must submit FAFSA. Number of awards granted varies annually. Scholarship value is $200 to $4340. Deadlines: May 1 and August 1.

Award: Grant for use in freshman, sophomore, junior, or senior years; renewable. *Amount:* $200–$4340.

Eligibility Requirements: Applicant must be enrolled or expecting to enroll full- or part-time at a two-year or four-year or technical institution or university and resident of Pennsylvania. Available to U.S. citizens.

Application Requirements: Application form, financial need analysis.

Contact: Keith New, Director of Public Relations
Pennsylvania Higher Education Assistance Agency
1200 North Seventh Street
Harrisburg, PA 17102-1444
Phone: 717-720-2509

PET LIFESTYLE AND YOU (P.L.A.Y.)

https://www.petplay.com/

SCHOLARS HELPING COLLARS SCHOLARSHIP

Students from across the U.S. are invited to apply for P.L.A.Y.'s annual Scholars Helping Collars Scholarship. This $1,000 scholarship rewards one student who can tell the best story, describing the impact he or she made in the life of a rescue animal or animal welfare cause in general. The contest is open to U.S. residents. No purchase necessary. All participants must be enrolled as a full-time high school senior. Entries are limited to one submission per person. Immediate family members of P.L.A.Y. employees are excluded from this contest. All essay submissions must be received by 11:59pm PT on Wednesday, February 28, 2018. To apply, students will submit an essay with 2-3 photos of their volunteer efforts to help animals in need and how that involvement has changed their lives or shaped their perceptions on the importance of animal welfare by February 28, 2018. The essay should be between 500-1000 words. Send a Word doc attachment to SCHOLARSHIP@ PETPLAY.COM with your essay submission. The file name should be your full name, state, and date of birth. For example, Chipper-Jones-GA-4-24-1992. 2-3 photos of your volunteer efforts to help animals in need. In the body of your email, include student's full name, date of birth, email address, postal address, high school they are currently enrolled in, and a phone number to contact. P.L.A.Y. will select the winner based on the best essay as determined by our internal panel of judges. Selection criteria will include, but is not limited to: compelling and engaging description of volunteer efforts and their impact on the personal life of the student; thematic consistency throughout the submission around the central thesis; proper spelling and grammar usage throughout the submission. Following the February 28th deadline, P.L.A.Y. will select the winner during the month of March and will announce the winner in April 2018 on the website pending notification of the student and his or her family. Please note that winner must provide proof of acceptance to college/university of choice prior to receiving the grand prize.

Award: Scholarship for use in freshman year; not renewable. *Number:* 1. *Amount:* $1000.

Eligibility Requirements: Applicant must be high school student; planning to enroll or expecting to enroll full-time at a four-year institution or university and must have an interest in wildlife conservation/animal rescue. Available to U.S. citizens.

Application Requirements: Essay. *Deadline:* February 28.

Contact: Scholarships
  E-mail: scholarship@petplay.com

PHOENIX PRIDE

https://phoenixpride.org/

PHOENIX PRIDE SCHOLARSHIP PROGRAM

The $5000 Pride Scholarship Fund was established to provide scholarships for students who identify as Lesbian, Gay, Bisexual, Transgendered, or Queer or are the dependent of a self identified LGBTQ parent. The fund was created by Phoenix Pride to support LGBTQ students in furthering their educational goals. Must be a student currently attending an accredited school in Arizona; or a May graduate from a high school in Maricopa County, accepted at an Arizona college for the following school year. Must intend to enroll as a full-time student while receiving the scholarship (minimum 12 credits for undergraduate, 9 credits for graduate per semester); and self-identify as a member of the LGBTQ community with a record of involvement in the LGBTQ community or be a dependent of self identified LGBTQ parent. One additional award available at $1,000 for a student involved in high school sports at the junior varsity or varsity level. Financial need as determined by the Free Application for Federal Student Aid (http://www.fafsa.ed.gov/). Minimum 2.5 cumulative GPA in high school or college courses. A previously awarded student may apply and be considered for subsequent awards along with new applicants, but the scholarship is not automatically renewed. A student will not be awarded for more than a total of four years on the scholarship.

Award: Scholarship for use in freshman, sophomore, junior, senior, graduate, or postgraduate years; not renewable. *Number:* 9. *Amount:* $1000–$5000.

Eligibility Requirements: Applicant must be enrolled or expecting to enroll full-time at a two-year or four-year institution or university; resident of Arizona and studying in Arizona. Applicant must have 2.5 GPA or higher. Available to U.S. citizens.

Application Requirements: Application form, community service. *Deadline:* April 27.

Contact: Mr. Ryan Starzyk, Director at Large, Chairman, Education & Outreach Committee
  Phoenix Pride
  1430 N 5th St
  Phoenix, AZ 85004
  Phone: 480-5161922
  E-mail: ryans@phoenixpride.org

PILOT INTERNATIONAL

https://www.pilotinternational.org/

BECKY BURROWS MEMORIAL SCHOLARSHIP

The Becky Burrows Memorial Scholarships are for graduate or undergraduate students who are re-entering the job market, beginning "second careers", or seeking to improve their professional skills for their current occupation by continuing their education in that field. Students must pursue courses of study that further Pilot International's mission to transform communities through education and service in the area of preparing youth for service, encouraging brain safety and health, and supporting those who care for others.

Award: Scholarship for use in freshman, sophomore, junior, senior, graduate, or postgraduate years; not renewable. *Number:* 1–5. *Amount:* $500–$1000.

Eligibility Requirements: Applicant must be enrolled or expecting to enroll full-time at a four-year institution or university. Applicant must have 3.5 GPA or higher. Available to U.S. citizens.

Application Requirements: Application form, community service, essay, financial need analysis, personal photograph. *Deadline:* March 15.

Contact: Sierra Martin
  Phone: 478-477-1208 Ext. 304
  E-mail: sierra@pilothq.org

KC INTERNATIONAL SCHOLARSHIP

Scholarship for International Students ONLY

Award: Scholarship for use in freshman, sophomore, junior, senior, graduate, or postgraduate years; not renewable. *Amount:* $2500.

Eligibility Requirements: Applicant must be enrolled or expecting to enroll full-time at a four-year institution. Applicant must have 3.5 GPA or higher.

Application Requirements: Application form, community service, essay, financial need analysis, personal photograph, portfolio. *Deadline:* March 15.

Contact: Sierra Martin, Founders Fund Specialist
  Pilot International
  102 Preston Court
  Macon, GA 31210
  Phone: 478-477-1208 Ext. 304
  Fax: 478-477-6978
  E-mail: sierra@pilothq.org

RUBY NEWHALL MEMORIAL SCHOLARSHIP

An applicant for the Ruby Newhall Memorial Scholarship must be from a foreign country, pursuing a degree in the United States or Canada. The field of study must be of a nature that it improves the quality of life for the community in their home country. The applicant must have spent at least one semester in a college in the United States or Canada by the application submission date and have a cumulative grade point average of 3.0 on a 4.0 scale. The applicant must be a full time student and remain a full time student for the duration of the scholarship. The student must have a documented Visa at the time the application is completed, submitted, graded and the scholarship is awarded. Failure to have a valid Visa at any time during this process could disqualify the student.

Award: Scholarship for use in freshman, sophomore, junior, senior, or graduate years; not renewable. *Number:* 5–10. *Amount:* $1500.

Eligibility Requirements: Applicant must be enrolled or expecting to enroll full- or part-time at a four-year institution or university. Applicant must have 3.0 GPA or higher. Available to Canadian and non-U.S. citizens.

Application Requirements: Application form, community service, essay, financial need analysis, personal photograph. *Deadline:* March 15.

Contact: Sierra Martin, Founders Fund Specialist
Pilot International
102 Preston Court
Macon, GA 31210
Phone: 478-477-1208 Ext. 304
Fax: 478-477-6978
E-mail: sierra@pilothq.org

PINE CONE FOUNDATION (PCF)

http://pineconefoundation.org/

PINE CONE FOUNDATION SCHOLARSHIP

The Pine Cone Foundation (PCF) is a 501c3 organization that awards multi-year scholarships to financially-disadvantaged students with documented learning disabilities across the state of California who aspire to attend community college. PCF is a private family foundation aiming to positively impact LD students' lives in California by making college more accessible and financially feasible. Once awarded a scholarship, it's a year-round support program that can total up to $5,500 over a 3 year period. Please visit our website to learn more about our 501c3 organization: pineconefoundation.org. The PCF scholarship program assists eligible students based in California with documented learning disabilities who demonstrate academic promise and are approved for the Board of Governors Fee Waiver (BOGFW). Because the BOGFW waives enrollment fees, we support students with covering book and prescription glasses costs, as well as health service, student center, parking permit and Universal Transit Pass fees. Students seeking associate, bachelor, technical and vocational degrees at one of 113 California-based community colleges can apply if they meet these criteria: 1. must have a documented specific learning disability (SLD); 2.,ust be a graduating high school senior; 3. must plan to enroll at a CA community college; 4. must demonstrate financial need via BOGFW approval; 5. must have a GPA of 2.5 or higher; and 5. must be a U.S. citizen and CA resident.

Award: Scholarship for use in freshman, sophomore, or junior years; renewable. *Number:* 1–5. *Amount:* $500–$5500.

Eligibility Requirements: Applicant must be learning disabled; American Indian/Alaska Native, Asian/Pacific Islander, Black (non-Hispanic), Hispanic; high school student; age 16-19; planning to enroll or expecting to enroll full- or part-time at a two-year or four-year institution; resident of California and studying in California. Applicant must be learning disabled. Applicant must have 2.5 GPA or higher. Available to U.S. citizens.

Application Requirements: Application form, essay, financial need analysis, personal photograph. *Deadline:* April 14.

Contact: PCF Admin Team
Pine Cone Foundation (PCF)
5758 Geary Blvd. #164
San Francisco, CA 94121
E-mail: admin@pineconefoundation.com

PLAINTIFF RELIEF

http://plaintiffrelief.com/

PLAINTIFF RELIEF SCHOLARSHIP

We are excited to offer one $1,000 scholarship to a high school senior who demonstrates academic achievement, exhibits leadership ability, participates in community service activities, and demonstrates financial need. Applicants must be U.S. citizens or permanent residents and current high school seniors at the time of their application. Current college students are not eligible to apply.

Award: Scholarship for use in senior year; not renewable. *Number:* 1. *Amount:* $1000.

Eligibility Requirements: Applicant must be high school student and planning to enroll or expecting to enroll full-time at a four-year institution or university. Available to U.S. citizens.

Application Requirements: Application form. *Deadline:* November 1.

Contact: Alex Miller
Plaintiff Relief
3379 Peachtree Road NE, Suite 555
Atlanta, GA 30326
Phone: 866-301-0084
E-mail: alex@plaintiffrelief.com

POLSON AND POLSON, P.C.

https://www.polsonlawfirm.com/

POLSON & POLSON, P.C. CONQUERING ADVERSITY SCHOLARSHIP

The Polson & Polson, P.C. Conquering Adversity Scholarship is available to individuals currently enrolled in a course of study at any duly accredited community or junior college, undergraduate or graduate degree program anywhere in the United States. Also eligible are high school graduates or GED holders who are about to embark on college-level studies. For full details, please visit https://www.polsonlawfirm.com/#scholarship.

Award: Scholarship for use in freshman, sophomore, junior, senior, graduate, or postgraduate years; not renewable. *Number:* 1. *Amount:* $500.

Eligibility Requirements: Applicant must be enrolled or expecting to enroll full- or part-time at a two-year or four-year or technical institution or university. Applicant must have 3.0 GPA or higher. Available to U.S. and non-U.S. citizens.

Application Requirements: Application form, essay. *Deadline:* October 31.

Contact: Mark Polson
E-mail: info@alabamaduidefense.com

PORTUGUESE AMERICAN LEADERSHIP COUNCIL OF THE UNITED STATES

http://www.palcus.org

PALCUS NATIONAL SCHOLARSHIP PROGRAM

PALCUS has established a merit-based scholarship program to support outstanding undergraduate and graduate college students of Portuguese ancestry toward fulfilling their higher education goals. Visit http://www.palcus.org/scholarship for details.

Award: Scholarship for use in sophomore, junior, senior, or graduate years; not renewable. *Number:* 4. *Amount:* $1000.

Eligibility Requirements: Applicant must be of Portuguese heritage and enrolled or expecting to enroll full-time at a four-year institution or university. Applicant must have 3.0 GPA or higher. Available to U.S. citizens.

Application Requirements: Application form, community service, essay. *Deadline:* July 31.

Contact: Mrs. Gracielle Camilo, Executive Assistant
Portuguese American Leadership Council of the United States
9255 Center St., Ste. 404
Manassas, VA 20110
Phone: 202-466-4664
E-mail: palcus@palcus.org

PORTUGUESE FOUNDATION INC.

https://www.facebook.com/pfict/

PORTUGUESE FOUNDATION SCHOLARSHIP PROGRAM

Eligibility: Student must be of Portuguese ancestry, resident of Connecticut, U.S. citizen or a permanent resident, applying for, or currently in college, full-time student in an undergraduate degree conferring program or a part-time student in a master's or doctorate program.

Award: Scholarship for use in freshman, sophomore, junior, senior, graduate, or postgraduate years; not renewable. *Number:* 1–4. *Amount:* $4000.

Eligibility Requirements: Applicant must be high school student; planning to enroll or expecting to enroll full- or part-time at a two-year or four-year or technical institution or university and resident of Connecticut. Applicant must have 2.5 GPA or higher. Available to U.S. citizens.

Application Requirements: Application form, community service, essay, personal photograph. *Deadline:* April 15.

Contact: Gabe Serrano
Portuguese Foundation Inc.
PO Box 331441
West Hartford, CT 06133-1441
Phone: 860-236-9350
E-mail: pfict90@gmail.com

POTENTIAL MAGAZINE

http://potentialmagazine.com/

COUNTDOWN TO COLLEGE SCHOLARSHIP

This scholarship is for college-bound teens in grades 9th-12th. The scholarship does not require specific test scores, GPA, or class ranking. Parents can also register but will need to designate a student to receive the award. In order to be awarded the scholarship, you must be a current C2C eNews subscriber at the time of the drawing. Winner will be notified via e-mail! You will also be receiving Potential Magazine's free weekly "Countdown to College" (C2C) eNewsletter with additional scholarship opportunities, ACT/SAT prep tips, college prep info, and more.

Award: Scholarship for use in freshman year; not renewable. *Number:* 1. *Amount:* $500.

Eligibility Requirements: Applicant must be high school student and planning to enroll or expecting to enroll full- or part-time at a two-year or four-year institution or university. Available to U.S. citizens.

Application Requirements: Application form. *Deadline:* May 4.

Contact: Editor
Potential Magazine
61 Market Place E
Montgomery, AL 36117
Phone: 334-578-7810
E-mail: editor@potentialmagazine.com

"DON'T WAIT TO REACH YOUR POTENTIAL" SCHOLARSHIP

This scholarship is for college-bound teens in grades 9th-12th residing in the state of Alabama. The scholarship does not require specific test scores, GPA, or class ranking. Parents can also register but will need to designate a student to receive the award. In order to be awarded the scholarship, you must be a current C2C eNews subscriber at the time of the drawing. Winner will be notified via e-mail! You will also be receiving Potential Magazine's free weekly "Countdown to College" (C2C) eNewsletter with additional scholarship opportunities, ACT/SAT prep tips, college prep info, and more.

Award: Scholarship for use in freshman year; not renewable. *Number:* 1. *Amount:* $500.

Eligibility Requirements: Applicant must be high school student; planning to enroll or expecting to enroll full- or part-time at a two-year or four-year institution or university and resident of Alabama. Available to U.S. citizens.

Application Requirements: Application form. *Deadline:* May 4.

Contact: Editor
Potential Magazine
61 Market Place E
Montgomery, AL 36117
Phone: 334-578-7810
E-mail: editor@potentialmagazine.com

PRICE BENOWITZ LLP

http://pricebenowitz.com/

AMATO SANITA BRIGHTER FUTURE SCHOLARSHIP

For more information please visit
https://criminallawpennsylvania.com/2017-amato-sanita-brighter-future-scholarship/

Award: Scholarship for use in freshman, sophomore, junior, senior, or graduate years; not renewable. *Number:* 1. *Amount:* $500.

Eligibility Requirements: Applicant must be enrolled or expecting to enroll full- or part-time at a two-year or four-year or technical institution or university. Applicant must have 3.0 GPA or higher. Available to U.S. citizens.

Application Requirements: Essay. *Deadline:* March 31.

Contact: Amato Sanita
E-mail: info@criminallawpennsylvania.com

ANGIE DIPIETRO WOMEN IN BUSINESS SCHOLARSHIP

This scholarship is available to any female student who is pursuing post-secondary education (community college, undergraduate college, graduate school, business school, or law school) at an accredited U.S. institution. Please visit http://marylandcriminallaws.com/#scholarship for more information on this opportunity.

Award: Scholarship for use in freshman, sophomore, junior, senior, or graduate years; not renewable. *Number:* 1. *Amount:* $500.

Eligibility Requirements: Applicant must be enrolled or expecting to enroll full- or part-time at a two-year or four-year institution or university and female. Applicant must have 3.0 GPA or higher. Available to U.S. citizens.

Application Requirements: Essay. *Deadline:* March 31.

Contact: Angie DiPietro
E-mail: info@marylandcriminallaws.com

KAREN RILEY PORTER GOOD WORKS SCHOLARSHIP

Karin Riley Porter believes strongly in advancing the cause of the criminal justice system and criminal defense services by ensuring that everyone within the Commonwealth of Virginia receives fair representation and that those who are dedicated to that calling can realize their full academic potential. For more information, please visit https://www.virginia-criminallawyer.com/#scholarship

Award: Scholarship for use in freshman, sophomore, junior, senior, graduate, or postgraduate years; not renewable. *Number:* 1. *Amount:* $500.

Eligibility Requirements: Applicant must be enrolled or expecting to enroll full-time at a four-year institution or university. Applicant must have 3.0 GPA or higher. Available to U.S. citizens.

Application Requirements: Essay. *Deadline:* December 15.

Contact: Karin Riley Porter
E-mail: info@virginia-criminallawyer.com

KERRI CASTELLINI WOMEN'S LEADERSHIP SCHOLARSHIP

This scholarship is open to any female student enrolled full-time in a community college, private or public undergraduate college or university, graduate program, business school, or law school in the United States. All candidates who apply for this scholarship must be in good academic standing and possess a minimum cumulative GPA of 3.0 or higher. For more information, please visit:
https://trustandestateslawyers.com/#scholarship

Award: Scholarship for use in freshman, sophomore, junior, senior, graduate, or postgraduate years; not renewable. *Number:* 1. *Amount:* $500.

Eligibility Requirements: Applicant must be enrolled or expecting to enroll full-time at a two-year or four-year institution or university and female. Applicant must have 3.0 GPA or higher. Available to U.S. and non-U.S. citizens.

Application Requirements: Essay. *Deadline:* December 15.

Contact: Kerri Castellini
E-mail: info@trustandestateslawyers.com

KUSH ARORA FEDERAL CRIMINAL JUSTICE REFORM SCHOLARSHIP

Mr. Arora understands that the success of the criminal justice system depends on the success of the bright young women and men who are pursuing their academic and professional dreams today. To help them achieve their goals, and to further bolster the system that he so proudly serves, Mr. Arora has established the Kush Arora Criminal Justice Reform Scholarship. For more information, please visit https://maryland-criminallawyer.com/#scholarship.

Award: Scholarship for use in freshman, sophomore, junior, senior, graduate, or postgraduate years; not renewable. *Number:* 1. *Amount:* $500.

Eligibility Requirements: Applicant must be enrolled or expecting to enroll full-time at a two-year or four-year institution or university. Applicant must have 3.0 GPA or higher. Available to U.S. and non-U.S. citizens.

Application Requirements: Essay. *Deadline:* December 15.

Contact: Kush Arora
E-mail: info@maryland-criminallawyer.com

NATALIA SEGERMEISTER DREAM ACT SCHOLARSHIP

The April Cockerham DREAM Act scholarship is designed to support individuals who are interested in making a difference in the lives of immigrants and other non-native individuals living in the United States. For more information, please visit http://thevisafirm.com/#scholarship.

Award: Scholarship for use in freshman, sophomore, junior, senior, or graduate years; not renewable. *Number:* 1. *Amount:* $500.

Eligibility Requirements: Applicant must be enrolled or expecting to enroll full- or part-time at a two-year or four-year or technical institution or university. Applicant must have 3.0 GPA or higher. Available to U.S. citizens.

Application Requirements: Essay. *Deadline:* March 31.

Contact: Natalia Segermeister
E-mail: info@thevisafirm.com

PRICE BENOWITZ MAKE A DIFFERENCE SCHOLARSHIP

Applicants must submit an approximate 750-word essay responding to the following prompt: 1) How will your dreams make a meaningful impact on the world? 2) How will you take the practical steps to achieve these dreams? This scholarship is offered to any student currently enrolled in an accredited community college, undergraduate, or graduate program. This includes incoming first-year college students who are high school graduates or possess a GED. Candidates must have an interest in social justice, as demonstrated by past and present volunteer, professional, and educational experiences. Eligible candidates must be in good academic standing with a minimum cumulative GPA of 3.0 or higher. For more complete information, please visit our scholarship page at: http://criminallawyerwashingtondc.com/#scholarship

Award: Scholarship for use in freshman, sophomore, junior, senior, graduate, or postgraduate years; not renewable. *Number:* 1. *Amount:* $500.

Eligibility Requirements: Applicant must be enrolled or expecting to enroll full- or part-time at a two-year or four-year or technical institution or university. Applicant must have 3.0 GPA or higher. Available to U.S. and non-U.S. citizens.

Application Requirements: Application form, essay. *Deadline:* May 31.

Contact: Glenn Ivey
E-mail: scholarship@criminallawyerwashingtondc.com

PRICE BENOWITZ SOCIAL JUSTICE SCHOLARSHIP

To further this vision of making the world a better and more equitable place, our firm offers a scholarship to individuals who have demonstrated an outstanding commitment to social justice and community outreach. For more information, please visit https://pricebenowitz.com/#scholarship.

Award: Scholarship for use in freshman, sophomore, junior, senior, graduate, or postgraduate years; not renewable. *Number:* 1. *Amount:* $500.

Eligibility Requirements: Applicant must be enrolled or expecting to enroll full- or part-time at a two-year or four-year institution or university. Applicant must have 3.0 GPA or higher. Available to U.S. and non-U.S. citizens.

Application Requirements: Essay. *Deadline:* April 30.

Contact: David Benowitz
E-mail: info@pricebenowitz.com

SETH OKIN GOOD DEEDS SCHOLARSHIP

Mr. Okin is proud to contribute to the national discussion on community service and helping to enable those in pursuit of educational goals with the ultimate purpose of creating a meaningful life of service to others. For more information, please visit https://criminallawyermaryland.net/#scholarship.

Award: Scholarship for use in freshman, sophomore, junior, senior, or graduate years; not renewable. *Number:* 1. *Amount:* $500.

Eligibility Requirements: Applicant must be enrolled or expecting to enroll full- or part-time at a two-year or four-year institution or university. Applicant must have 3.0 GPA or higher. Available to U.S. citizens.

Application Requirements: Essay. *Deadline:* September 30.

Contact: Seth Okin
E-mail: info@criminallawyermaryland.net

THOMAS SOLDAN HEALTHY COMMUNITIES SCHOLARSHIP

To further champion the cause of developing healthy communities, Mr. Soldan is investing in the future and has offered a scholarship of $500 to any student in a post-secondary education seeking means to encourage sustainable and local health-initiatives in his or her own community. For more information, visit http://virginialawfirm.net/#scholarship.

Award: Scholarship for use in freshman, sophomore, junior, senior, or graduate years; not renewable. *Number:* 1. *Amount:* $500.

Eligibility Requirements: Applicant must be enrolled or expecting to enroll full- or part-time at a two-year or four-year institution or university. Applicant must have 3.0 GPA or higher. Available to U.S. citizens.

Application Requirements: Essay. *Deadline:* September 30.

Contact: Thomas Soldan
E-mail: info@virginialawfirm.net

PRIDE FOUNDATION

http://www.PrideFoundation.org/

PRIDE FOUNDATION SCHOLARSHIP PROGRAM

Pride Foundation provides scholarships to current and future lesbian, gay, bisexual, transgender, and straight-ally student leaders from Alaska, Idaho, Montana, Oregon, and Washington. Our scholarships cover most accredited post-secondary schools, including community colleges; 4-year public or private colleges and universities; trade or certificate programs; and graduate, medical, or law school.

Award: Scholarship for use in freshman, sophomore, junior, senior, graduate, or postgraduate years; not renewable. *Number:* 85–125. *Amount:* $1000–$24,000.

Eligibility Requirements: Applicant must be enrolled or expecting to enroll full- or part-time at a two-year or four-year or technical institution or university; resident of Alaska, Idaho, Montana, Oregon, Washington and must have an interest in LGBT issues. Available to U.S. and non-U.S. citizens.

Application Requirements: Application form, essay. *Deadline:* January 15.

Contact: Craig Williams, Office Manager
Pride Foundation
2014 E. Madison St
Suite 300
Seattle, WA 98122
Phone: 206-323-3318
Fax: 206-323-1017
E-mail: scholarships@pridefoundation.org

PROJECT BEST SCHOLARSHIP FUND

http://www.projectbest.com/

PROJECT BEST SCHOLARSHIP

• See page 575

PROMOCODESFORYOU.COM

https://www.promocodesforyou.com

PROMOCODESFORYOU.COM STUDENT SAVINGS SCHOLARSHIP

At PromoCodesForYou.com, our goal is to provide a resource to help you save money. We know that the financial burden of college can be overwhelming, so we are here with a scholarship to help you reach your career goals. In 750 words or less, tell us what you wish to achieve once you have earned your college degree and why you believe that you will succeed in accomplishing that goal.

Award: Scholarship for use in freshman, sophomore, or junior years; not renewable. *Number:* 1. *Amount:* $1000.

Eligibility Requirements: Applicant must be age 16-22 and enrolled or expecting to enroll full-time at a two-year or four-year or technical institution or university. Available to U.S. and Canadian citizens.

Application Requirements: Application form, essay. *Deadline:* December 10.

Contact: Manager of Scholarship
E-mail: scholarship@promocodesforyou.com

PROMPT

http://prompt.com

PROMPT'S $20,000 SCHOLARSHIP

Apply for Prompt's $20,000 Scholarship, The Easiest Scholarship Application in History. All you have to do is upload your favorite essay you are using for your college applications. Your GPA, test scores, family income, race, activities, and random adult coloring book you did while bored in class do not matter! The only thing that matters is telling us something compelling about yourself. If you don't have an essay yet, you can start your application now and upload the essay later. If your colleges do not require essays, then submit anything you feel is compelling. Make sure you get started today as we're giving away $2,000 the 15th of every month before our big $10,000 Grand Prize deadline on January 15th. If your essay doesn't win this month, you can always upload a new one for next month. Best of luck!

Award: Scholarship for use in freshman year; not renewable. *Number:* 14. *Amount:* $2000–$10,000.

Eligibility Requirements: Applicant must be high school student and planning to enroll or expecting to enroll full-time at a two-year or four-year institution or university. Available to U.S. and non-U.S. citizens.

Application Requirements: Essay, interview. *Deadline:* continuous.

Contact: Jordan Haines, Co-Founder
Prompt
110 E 25th St.
New York, NY 07070
Phone: 844-577-6678
E-mail: scholarship@prompt.com

PUEBLO OF SAN JUAN, DEPARTMENT OF EDUCATION

OHKAY OWINGEH TRIBAL SCHOLARSHIP OF THE PUEBLO OF SAN JUAN

Scholarship for residents of New Mexico enrolled either full-time or part-time in accredited colleges or universities. Minimum GPA of 2.0 required. Must complete required number of hours of community service in the San Juan Pueblo. Up to thirty scholarships are granted and the value of the award ranges from $300 to $600. Deadline varies.

Award: Scholarship for use in freshman, sophomore, junior, or senior years; renewable. *Number:* 1–30. *Amount:* $300–$600.

Eligibility Requirements: Applicant must be American Indian/Alaska Native; enrolled or expecting to enroll full- or part-time at a two-year or four-year or technical institution or university and resident of New Mexico. Applicant or parent of applicant must have employment or volunteer experience in community service. Available to U.S. citizens.

Application Requirements: Application form, letter of acceptance, transcript. *Deadline:* varies.

Contact: Adam Garcia, Education Coordinator
Phone: 505-852-3477
Fax: 505-852-3030
E-mail: wevog68@valornet.com

POP'AY SCHOLARSHIP

Scholarship for members of Pueblo of San Juan tribe pursuing their first Associate or Baccalaureate degree. Must complete a minimum of 20 hours of community service within the San Juan Pueblo. Scholarship value is $2500. Seventeen awards are granted. Deadlines: December 30 for spring, April 30 for summer, and June 30 for fall.

Award: Scholarship for use in freshman, sophomore, junior, or senior years; renewable. *Number:* up to 17. *Amount:* $2500.

Eligibility Requirements: Applicant must be American Indian/Alaska Native; enrolled or expecting to enroll full-time at a two-year or four-year institution or university and resident of New Mexico. Applicant or parent of applicant must have employment or volunteer experience in community service. Available to U.S. citizens.

Application Requirements: Application form, letter of acceptance, transcript. *Deadline:* varies.

Contact: Adam Garcia, Education Coordinator
Phone: 505-852-3477
Fax: 505-852-3030
E-mail: wevog68@valornet.com

QUALITY FORMATIONS LTD.

https://www.qualitycompanyformations.co.uk/

QUALITY COMPANY FORMATIONS SCHOLARSHIP

Our scholarship is open to all students studying at an officially recognised or listed UK and US higher learning or further education institution, and it is specifically designed to supplement each student's annual income, to enable them to spend more time pursuing and developing a new business idea. Whether you would like to attend a trade show, invest in new materials for a prototype, or you simply need some financial help to set up your first company, our scholarship seeks to provide you with all the support you need to succeed.

Award: Scholarship for use in freshman, sophomore, junior, senior, graduate, or postgraduate years; renewable. *Number:* 6. *Amount:* $1250.

Eligibility Requirements: Applicant must be enrolled or expecting to enroll full- or part-time at an institution or university. Available to U.S. and non-U.S. citizens.

Application Requirements: Application form, essay. *Deadline:* July 27.

Contact: Mr. Chris Wilson, Scholarship Manager
Quality Formations Ltd.
71-75 Shelton Street
Covent Garden
London WC2H 9JQ
Phone: 20-39080044
E-mail: c.woodley@qualityformations.co.uk

RAILROAD PASSENGERS ASSOCIATION

https://www.narprail.org/

RAILROAD PASSENGERS ASSOCIATION SCHOLARSHIP

The Rail Passengers' Association (RPA) works to ensure that people have access to quality rail and transit options across the country. Rail transit is vital to providing students with seamless and safe transportation to school. RPA wants to support students in their education and is offering you (or a student you nominate) the chance to win a scholarship prize to help you pay for your higher education during the 2018-2019 school year. Every $20 is an entry to win.

Award: Scholarship for use in freshman, sophomore, junior, senior, graduate, or postgraduate years; not renewable. *Number:* 1. *Amount:* $10,000.

Eligibility Requirements: Applicant must be enrolled or expecting to enroll full- or part-time at a two-year or four-year or technical institution or university. Available to U.S. citizens.

Application Requirements: *Fee:* $20. *Deadline:* April 26.

Contact: Paige Zupan, WCPG
Railroad Passengers Association
207 Front Street
3rd Floor
New York, NY 10038
Phone: 212-233-1670
E-mail: paige@weinsteincarnegie.com

REACH HIGHER MONTANA

http://www.ReachHigherMontana.org

REACH HIGHER MONTANA SCHOLARSHIPS

To qualify, applicants must be: Montana high school seniors, Montana residents who graduated from a Montana high school and are currently attending a Montana college or university, planning on attending school at least half time, maintaining a 2.5 grade point average (GPA). To apply: Scholarship applications are available Dec. 1 - Jan. 15. Watch our website for here for more details and the application: http://www.ReachHigherMontana.org.

Award: Scholarship for use in freshman, sophomore, junior, or senior years; not renewable. *Number:* 75. *Amount:* $1000.

Eligibility Requirements: Applicant must be enrolled or expecting to enroll full- or part-time at a two-year or four-year or technical institution or university; resident of Montana and studying in Montana. Applicant must have 2.5 GPA or higher. Available to U.S. citizens.

Application Requirements: Application form, personal photograph. *Deadline:* January 31.

Contact: Melissa Huntington, Special Projects Manager
Reach Higher Montana
40 W 6th Ave
Helena, MT 59601
Phone: 406-422-1275 Ext. 801
E-mail: MHuntington@ReachHigherMontana.org

REHABCENTER.NET

http://www.rehabcenter.net/

REHABCENTER.NET

RehabCenter.net is proud to award $10,000 in scholarships this year to three students, who share their vision on the dangers of drug and alcohol abuse. The scholarship award monies may only be used toward tuition, or expenses related to your education. There is no cost to enter the contest. Scholarship winners will be notified via email, and we'll make a public announcement of each winner within 30 days of the announcement. Three awards will be given to qualifying students who write the winning essays for first, second, and third places. We're looking for essays that describe the views of those passionate about drug and alcohol addiction and the effects it has on people, their health, society, and more. Maybe you have a loved one who has struggled with drug or alcohol abuse, or maybe you have struggled in the past, maybe you're currently struggling and trying to find the help you need. We welcome and encourage you to enter the contest, share your story, and profess your dedication to addiction awareness efforts. It's not necessary that you have a history with drug and alcohol addiction to enter the contest. The only thing necessary is your commitment to expressing your views for: 1. The ways in which addiction affects society today. 2. What can we do to reduce these effects, help people, and lessen the burden of addiction on society? Essay submissions should be no longer than 1,200 words. Applicants will be awarded based on the quality of the content, degree of originality, and personal style. Contest judges will be in search of essays that are not only structured and organized well, but with strong, logical arguments.

Award: Scholarship for use in freshman, sophomore, junior, senior, graduate, or postgraduate years; renewable. *Number:* 1–3. *Amount:* $3000–$6000.

Eligibility Requirements: Applicant must be enrolled or expecting to enroll full-time at a two-year or four-year or technical institution or university and resident of Alabama, Alaska, Alberta, Arizona, Arkansas, California, Colorado, Connecticut, Delaware, District of Columbia, Florida, Georgia, Hawaii, Idaho, Illinois, Indiana, Iowa, Kansas, Kentucky, Louisiana, Maine, Manitoba, Maryland, Massachusetts, Michigan, Minnesota, Mississippi, Missouri, Montana, Nebraska, Nevada, New Brunswick, Newfoundland, New Hampshire, New Jersey, New Mexico, New York, North Carolina, North Dakota, Ohio, Oklahoma, Oregon, Pennsylvania, Prince Edward Island, Puerto Rico, Rhode Island, South Carolina, South Dakota, Tennessee, Texas, Utah, Vermont, Virginia, Washington, West Virginia, Wisconsin, Wyoming. Available to U.S. citizens.

Application Requirements: Essay. *Deadline:* continuous.

Contact: Joe Belfry, Outreach Coordinator
RehabCenter.net
483 Mandalay Avenue
Clearwater, FL 33767
Phone: 231-360-2055
E-mail: joe@rehabcenter.net

RHINE LAW FIRM, P.C.

https://www.carolinaaccidentattorneys.com/

STRIVE FOR EXCELLENCE SCHOLARSHIP 2018

This scholarship is open to graduating high school seniors and current undergraduate college students with a 3.0 or higher GPA who are bettering themselves through education. The application includes an essay section to tell us about your academic goals and how those goals will help you leave your mark on the world; the introduction is to be 100-200 words, and the essay is to be 500-1000 words. The winner will be announced September 26th, 2018, and the application must be submitted no later than 11:59 on August 29th, 2018. Additional information and applications can be found on our website.

Award: Scholarship for use in freshman, sophomore, junior, or senior years; not renewable. *Number:* 1. *Amount:* $500.

Eligibility Requirements: Applicant must be enrolled or expecting to enroll full- or part-time at a two-year or four-year institution or university. Applicant must have 3.0 GPA or higher. Available to U.S. citizens.

Application Requirements: Application form, essay. *Deadline:* August 29.

Contact: Joel Rhine, Lead Attorney
Rhine Law Firm, P.C.
1612 Military Cutoff Road, Suite 300
Wilmington, NC 28403
Phone: 910-772-9960
E-mail: attorneys@rhinelawfirm.com

RISK MANAGEMENT ASSOCIATION FOUNDATION

http://www.scholarshipamerica.org

THE RISK MANAGEMENT ASSOCIATION FOUNDATION SCHOLARSHIP PROGRAM

The Risk Management Association (RMA) Foundation scholarship program is awarding over $200,000 in renewable scholarships, ranging from $2,000 to $5,000 each, to current undergraduates interested in pursuing a career in the banking industry. To be eligible, student must be a citizen or permanent resident of the United States or Canada and have completed a minimum of two years of college. All applicants must be currently enrolled full-time at an accredited four-year college or university in the United States or Canada and have a minimum grade point average (GPA) of 3.0 on a 4.0 scale overall. Applicants do not have to be a current RMA member, but they must join (free) and remain a member to receive and renew their scholarship. Website: https://www.scholarsapply.org/rma/.

Award: Scholarship for use in junior or senior years; renewable. *Number:* 40. *Amount:* $2000–$5000.

Eligibility Requirements: Applicant must be enrolled or expecting to enroll full-time at a four-year institution. Applicant must have 3.0 GPA or higher. Available to U.S. and Canadian citizens.

Application Requirements: Application form. *Deadline:* October 22.

Contact: Program Manager
Risk Management Association Foundation
One Scholarship Way
Scholarship America
Saint Peter, MN 56082
Phone: 800-537-4180
E-mail: rma@scholarshipamerica.org

RJT CRIMINAL DEFENSE

http://www.sandiegocriminallawyerrt.com/

AUTISM SCHOLARSHIP

RJT Criminal Defense is pleased to be offering a $1,000 educational scholarship for people who have been diagnosed with autism (now known as Autism Spectrum Disorder (ASD)). The scholarship will be used to offset a portion of the tuition at an educational institution chosen by the successful applicant. The aim of the program is to encourage those with autism to continue their education. This is a $1,000 scholarship consisting of tuition assistance at a trade or vocational school, or a college, junior college or university. The scholarship funds will be paid directly to the educational institution selected by the successful applicant. The scholarship money must be used within 1 year after the date of the award. It is not required that an applicant be enrolled in school at the time the application is submitted. The application is open to any United States citizen who has been diagnosed with ASD who wishes to continue his or her education at a trade school, vocational school, or on the college or junior college level. Complete the online application and upload a short statement (125 words or less) setting forth your educational goals. (Optional) Upload an essay (800 words or less) discussing the impact autism has had on your education. We may also require that you provide us with proof of your diagnosis. All application materials must be completed and submitted to us no later than February 5, 2018. The winner will be selected by Ryan J. Tegnelia of RJT Criminal Defense, in his sole discretion. Mr. Tegnelia will announce the winner of the scholarship on or before March 5, 2018.

Award: Scholarship for use in freshman, sophomore, junior, senior, graduate, or postgraduate years; not renewable. *Number:* 1. *Amount:* $1000.

Eligibility Requirements: Applicant must be learning disabled and enrolled or expecting to enroll full- or part-time at a two-year or four-year or technical institution or university. Applicant must be learning disabled. Available to U.S. citizens.

Application Requirements: Application form, essay. *Deadline:* February 5.

Contact: Ryan Tegnelia
RJT Criminal Defense
2820 Camino Del Rio South, Suite 110
San Diego, CA 92108
E-mail: mike@sandiegocriminallawyerrt.com

RON BROWN SCHOLAR FUND

http://www.ronbrown.org/

RON BROWN SCHOLAR PROGRAM

The program seeks to identify African-American high school seniors who will make significant contributions to the society. Applicants must excel academically, show exceptional leadership potential, participate in community service activities, and demonstrate financial need. Must be a U.S. citizen or hold permanent resident visa. Must plan to attend a four-year college or university. Deadlines: November 1 and January 9.

Award: Scholarship for use in freshman, sophomore, junior, or senior years; renewable. *Number:* 10–20. *Amount:* $10,000–$40,000.

Eligibility Requirements: Applicant must be Black (non-Hispanic); high school student and planning to enroll or expecting to enroll full-time at a four-year institution or university. Available to U.S. citizens.

Application Requirements: Application form, community service, essay, financial need analysis, interview, personal photograph. *Deadline:* January 9.

Contact: Ms. Vanessa Evans-Grevious, Vice President
Ron Brown Scholar Fund
485 Hillsdale Drive
Suite 206
CHARLOTTESVILLE, VA 22901
Phone: 434-964-1588
E-mail: info@ronbrown.org

ROVER.COM

https://www.rover.com/

ROVER SITTER SCHOLARSHIP CONTEST

At Rover, we are passionate about helping people achieve their educational goals. Whether you are living off of insta-coffee or insta-noodles, we get it–and we would like to help fund your brain fuel for the coming school year. Just write a 400–500 word essay for your chance to win $500! If you're not already, become a sitter on Rover.com to gain eligibility for the scholarship!

Award: Scholarship for use in freshman, sophomore, junior, senior, or graduate years; not renewable. *Number:* 2. *Amount:* $500.

Eligibility Requirements: Applicant must be enrolled or expecting to enroll full- or part-time at a two-year or four-year institution or university. Applicant must have 2.5 GPA or higher. Available to U.S. citizens.

Application Requirements: Application form, essay. *Deadline:* August 31.

Contact: Rover.com
Rover.com
2101 4th Avenue
#400
Seattle, WA 98121
Phone: 888-453-7889

ST. ANDREW'S SOCIETY OF WASHINGTON, DC

http://www.saintandrewsociety.org/

ST. ANDREW'S SOCIETY OF WASHINGTON DC FOUNDERS' SCHOLARSHIP

In honor of the 250th Anniversary of our St. Andrew's Society's 18th c. founding, the Society has established The St. Andrew's Society Founders' Prize. Made possible by generous donations in the name of James & Mary Dawson and Donald Malcolm MacArthur, this Scholarship is an annual award in the amount of $7,500 made to an outstanding Scottish or Scottish-American scholar. It is available for US students of Scottish descent or UK students born in Scotland to study in the UK or in the United States. Special attention will be given to applicants whose work would demonstrably contribute to enhanced knowledge of Scottish history or culture. Must be a college junior, senior, or graduate student to apply. Need for financial assistance and academic record considered. Visit website for details and application.

Award: Scholarship for use in junior, senior, or graduate years; not renewable. *Number:* 1. *Amount:* $7500.

Eligibility Requirements: Applicant must be of Scottish heritage; enrolled or expecting to enroll full-time at a four-year institution or university and resident of Delaware, District of Columbia, Maryland, New Jersey, North Carolina, Pennsylvania, Virginia, West Virginia. Available to U.S. and non-Canadian citizens.

Application Requirements: Application form, essay, financial need analysis, interview. *Deadline:* April 30.

Contact: T.J. Holland, Chairman, Scholarships Committee
E-mail: scholarships@saintandrewsociety.org

ST. ANDREW'S SOCIETY OF WASHINGTON DC SCHOLARSHIPS

The St. Andrew's Society of Washington DC Scholarships Program awards are available for US students of Scottish descent or UK students born in Scotland to study in the UK or in the United States. Special attention will be given to applicants whose work would demonstrably contribute to enhanced knowledge of Scottish history or culture. Must be a college junior, senior, or graduate student to apply. Need for financial assistance and academic record considered. Visit website for details and application.

Award: Scholarship for use in junior, senior, or graduate years; not renewable. *Number:* 1–8. *Amount:* $500–$15,000.

Eligibility Requirements: Applicant must be of Scottish heritage; enrolled or expecting to enroll full-time at a four-year institution or university and resident of Delaware, District of Columbia, Maryland, New Jersey, North Carolina, Pennsylvania, Virginia, West Virginia. Available to U.S. and non-Canadian citizens.

Application Requirements: Application form, essay, financial need analysis, interview. *Deadline:* April 30.

Contact: Mr. T.J. Holland, Chairman, Scholarships Committee
E-mail: scholarships@saintandrewsociety.org

ST. CLAIRE REGIONAL MEDICAL CENTER

http://www.st-claire.org/

SR. MARY JEANNETTE WESS, S.N.D. SCHOLARSHIP

Scholarships available for undergraduates in their junior or senior year of study, or graduate students. Must have graduated from an eastern Kentucky high school in one of the following counties: Bath, Carter, Elliott, Fleming, Lewis, Magoffin, Menifee, Montgomery, Morgan, Rowan, or Wolfe. Must demonstrate academic achievement, leadership, service, and financial need.

Award: Scholarship for use in junior, senior, or graduate years; renewable. *Number:* 2. *Amount:* $750.

Eligibility Requirements: Applicant must be enrolled or expecting to enroll full-time at a four-year institution or university; resident of Kentucky and must have an interest in leadership. Applicant or parent of applicant must have employment or volunteer experience in community service. Available to U.S. and non-U.S. citizens.

Application Requirements: Application form, financial need analysis, recommendations or references, self-addressed stamped envelope with application, transcript. *Deadline:* varies.

Contact: Tom Lewis, Director of Development
Phone: 606-783-6511
Fax: 606-783-6795
E-mail: telewis@st-claire.org

SALUTE TO EDUCATION, INC.

http://www.stescholarships.org/

SALUTE TO EDUCATION SCHOLARSHIP

Through a unique partnership with the community in South Florida, the Miami-Dade and Broward County Ford and Lincoln Dealers and Ford Motor Company have awarded over $3.7 million in scholarships to more than 4,300 deserving public and private high school seniors in both counties. Salute to Education, Inc., established in 1994, is a non-profit organization funded through dealership contributions, corporate support from Ford Motor Company and other fundraising events & efforts. Salute to Education is one of South Florida's largest private scholarship foundations. In June 2018, Salute to Education will be granting $168,000 in scholarships and brand new laptops to 112 graduating high school seniors in Miami-Dade and Broward County (South Florida). For more information about the scholarship and the application criteria, please visit the website at http://www.stescholarships.org/

Award: Scholarship for use in freshman year; not renewable. *Number:* 112. *Amount:* $1500.

Eligibility Requirements: Applicant must be high school student; age 16-19; planning to enroll or expecting to enroll full-time at a four-year institution or university and resident of Florida. Applicant must have 3.0 GPA or higher. Available to U.S. citizens.

Application Requirements: Application form, community service, essay, financial need analysis. *Deadline:* February 9.

Contact: Rebecca Klein, Program Coodinator
Salute to Education, Inc.
PO Box 833425
Miami, FL 33173
Phone: 305-799-6726
E-mail: steinfo@stescholarships.org

SCHOLAR SERVE

https://www.scholarserve.org

SCHOLAR SERVE AWARDS

Scholar Serve recognizes and supports college and graduate students who apply their knowledge to serving others in their communities. In addition to the recognition, the organization matches recipients to mentors who assist with their service initiatives and provide career guidance. Any full-time undergraduate or graduate student in the United States is eligible to apply. Scholar Serve recipients may receive up to $3,000. Scholar Serve reserves the right to review applications and select recipients at its discretion. The number and amount of awards may vary over time. We do not give preference to graduate students over undergraduates. We look for students who have done well in their academic studies. This does not mean you have to have a 4.0. All of our previous recipients have had a cumulative GPA of 3.0 or better, but we do not have a minimum GPA requirement. When reviewing applications we are looking for students who are volunteering and leading in ways that will enable them to engage in service and advance their career goals beyond the time when they are in school. Most recipients have used the funding they receive for their service efforts and volunteer projects. However, this is not required and is at the discretion of the recipient. U.S. citizenship is not required. All recipients for the 2018 Scholar Serve awards will be notified by March 15, 2018. We make every effort to contact each applicant to provide notification that their application has been received. We thoroughly review every application that is submitted. Late submission will not be considered.

Award: Scholarship for use in freshman, sophomore, junior, senior, graduate, or postgraduate years; not renewable. *Number:* 5–10. *Amount:* $500–$3000.

Eligibility Requirements: Applicant must be enrolled or expecting to enroll full-time at a four-year institution or university. Applicant must have 3.0 GPA or higher. Available to U.S. and non-U.S. citizens.

Application Requirements: Application form, community service. *Deadline:* February 15.

Contact: Angela Courtney, President
E-mail: contact@scholarserve.org

SCHOLARSHIP AMERICA

https://www.abbvieImmunologyScholarship.com/

ABBVIE IMMUNOLOGY SCHOLARSHIP

The AbbVie Immunology Scholarship is designed to provide financial support for exceptional students living with chronic inflammatory diseases. Scholarships of up to $15,000 each will be awarded, dependent upon type of degree pursued. Applicants must be legal residents of the U.S. and diagnosed by a healthcare professional with one of the following: ankylosing spondylitis (AS), Crohn's disease (CD), hidradenitis suppurativa (HS), juvenile idiopathic arthritis (JIA), psoriasis (Ps), psoriatic arthritis (PsA), rheumatoid arthritis (RA), ulcerative colitis (UC), or uveitis (UV). Qualified applicants must plan to enroll in undergraduate (associate's, bachelor's) or graduate (master's, MD, JD, doctorate) study at an accredited two- or four-year college, university or vocational-technical school in the U.S. for the 2018-19 academic year. Scholarships will be awarded based on academic excellence, community involvement, and ability to serve as a positive role model in the immunology community.

Award: Scholarship for use in freshman, sophomore, junior, senior, or graduate years; not renewable. *Amount:* $15,000.

Eligibility Requirements: Applicant must be physically disabled; enrolled or expecting to enroll full- or part-time at a two-year or four-year or technical institution or university and studying in Alabama, Alaska, Arizona, Arkansas, California, Colorado, Connecticut, Delaware, District of Columbia, Florida, Georgia, Hawaii, Idaho, Illinois, Indiana, Iowa, Kansas, Kentucky, Louisiana, Maine, Maryland, Massachusetts, Michigan, Minnesota, Mississippi, Missouri, Montana, Nebraska, Nevada, New Hampshire, New Jersey, New Mexico, New York, North Carolina, North Dakota, Ohio, Oklahoma, Oregon, Pennsylvania, Rhode Island, South Carolina, South Dakota, Tennessee, Texas, Utah, Vermont, Virginia, Washington, West Virginia, Wisconsin, Wyoming. Applicant must be physically disabled. Available to U.S. citizens.

Application Requirements: Application form. *Deadline:* January 9.

Contact: Program Manager
Scholarship America
Scholarship America
One Scholarship Way
Saint Peter, MN 56082
Phone: 507-931-0651
E-mail: AbbVieImmunology@scholarshipamerica.org

SELECTBLINDS.COM

http://www.selectblinds.com

SELECTBLINDS.COM $1000 COLLEGE SCHOLARSHIP

We love and value innovation, education, and passion, and we have created a scholarship based around that. We want to see your innovative spirit and learn what you are passionate about. It could earn you $1,000 to use toward your college expenses! Here is what you need to know: Applicants must submit an idea on one of these two items (video, photos or images, infographic, etc. Creativity is encouraged.): 1) What is the most creative thing you can do with window coverings? or 2)Come up with new technology for window coverings. Applicants must also submit a 250 to750 word essay that answers one of the following questions: 1) What do you want to do to make the world a better place? 2) What is the importance of your major/area of study in today's society? 3) What are your most meaningful achievements, and how do they relate to your field of study? 4) Why did you choose your field of study, and where do you see yourself in 10 years? 5) Why are you a good candidate to receive this scholarship? Applicants must submit a transcript. An unofficial transcript is acceptable. Applicants may email their submissions or links to their submissions to scholarship@selectshops.com.

Award: Scholarship for use in freshman, sophomore, junior, senior, graduate, or postgraduate years; not renewable. *Number:* 1. *Amount:* $1000.

Eligibility Requirements: Applicant must be enrolled or expecting to enroll full- or part-time at a two-year or four-year or technical institution or university. Applicant must have 2.5 GPA or higher. Available to U.S. citizens.

Application Requirements: Essay, personal photograph. *Deadline:* June 15.

Contact: Nate Kennedy, Vice President, Operations
SelectBlinds.com
1910 S Stapley Dr
Ste 137
Mesa, AZ 85204
Phone: 480-302-5163
E-mail: scholarship@selectshops.com

SEXNER & ASSOCIATES LLC

http://www.sexner.com/personal-injury/

MITCHELL S. SEXNER & ASSOCIATES LLC SCHOLARSHIP

This scholarship opportunity is available to graduating high school students or currently enrolled undergraduate college students who have maintained a 3.0 or higher GPA and are current U.S. Citizens or current U.S. Permanent Residents. Students must complete the application and a short essay demonstrating their commitment to their education and improving their community; both items, as well as additional information are available on our website: http://www.sexner.com/personal-injury/scholarship/

Award: Scholarship for use in freshman, sophomore, junior, or senior years; not renewable. *Number:* 1. *Amount:* $500.

Eligibility Requirements: Applicant must be enrolled or expecting to enroll full-time at a two-year or four-year institution. Applicant must have 3.0 GPA or higher. Available to U.S. citizens.

Application Requirements: Application form, essay. *Deadline:* May 15.

Contact: Mitch Sexner
Sexner & Associates LLC
2126 W Van Buren St.
Chicago, IL 60612
E-mail: mitch@sexner.com

SHAWN SUKUMAR ATTORNEY AT LAW

https://www.washingtondccriminallawyer.net/

SHAWN SUKUMAR CRIMINAL JUSTICE REFORM SCHOLARSHIP

This scholarship is offered to any student currently enrolled in an accredited community college, undergraduate, or graduate program in the United States. This includes incoming first-year college students who are high school graduates or possess a GED. The scholarship candidate must possess an interest in social justice, as demonstrated by past and present volunteer, professional, and educational experiences. For more information, please visit http://www.washingtondccriminallawyer.net/#scholarship

Award: Scholarship for use in freshman, sophomore, junior, senior, graduate, or postgraduate years; not renewable. *Number:* 1. *Amount:* $500.

Eligibility Requirements: Applicant must be enrolled or expecting to enroll full- or part-time at a two-year or four-year or technical institution or university. Applicant must have 3.0 GPA or higher. Available to U.S. and non-U.S. citizens.

Application Requirements: Application form, essay. *Deadline:* May 31.

Contact: Shawn Sukumar
E-mail: scholarships@washingtondccriminallawyer.net

SHELVING.COM

http://www.shelving.com/

SHELVING.COM BUSINESS SCHOLARSHIP

This scholarship offers three prizes ranging from $500–$1500 to any currently-enrolled student taking a business-related line of study, ranging from MBAs to retail/warehouse management and any other relevant fields.

Award: Prize for use in freshman, sophomore, junior, or senior years; not renewable. *Number:* 3. *Amount:* $500–$1500.

Eligibility Requirements: Applicant must be enrolled or expecting to enroll full-time at a four-year institution or university. Applicant must have 2.5 GPA or higher. Available to U.S. citizens.

Application Requirements: Application form, essay. *Deadline:* June 30.

Contact: Mr. Timothy Allen, SEO Analyst
Shelving.com
340 E. Big Beaver Rd
Troy, MI 48084
Phone: 248-234-1221
E-mail: tallen@trafficdigitalagency.com

SILICON VALLEY COMMUNITY FOUNDATION

http://www.siliconvalleycf.org

ABBY SOBRATO SCHOLARSHIP

The Abby Sobrato Scholarship was established by John Matthew Sobrato in memory of his mother. A teacher herself, she inspired him to go into teaching and always pushed for equal opportunity for everyone. This scholarship seeks to honor those values and provide expanded opportunities for students attending Latino College Prep Academy (LCPA), Luis Valdez Leadership Academy (LVLA) and B. Roberto Cruz Leadership Academy (RCLA) in San José, Calif., through significant scholarship support that will facilitate college access and success. The selection committee looks for students who demonstrate academic potential, involvement in community or school activities and contributed to their campus in a meaningful way. Renewable scholarship recipients must be willing to actively participate in mentoring activities, college and career success trainings, and summer internship opportunities.

Award: Scholarship for use in freshman or sophomore years; renewable. *Number:* 70. *Amount:* $12,000.

Eligibility Requirements: Applicant must be enrolled or expecting to enroll full- or part-time at a two-year or four-year institution or university and resident of California. Applicant must have 2.5 GPA or higher. Available to U.S. and non-Canadian citizens.

Application Requirements: Application form, essay, financial need analysis. *Deadline:* February 21.

Contact: Scholarships Team
Silicon Valley Community Foundation
2440 West El Camino Real
Suite 300
Mountain View, CA 94040
Phone: 650-450-5487
E-mail: scholarships@siliconvalleycf.org

BOBETTE BIBO GUGLIOTTA MEMORIAL SCHOLARSHIP FOR CREATIVE WRITING

For students majoring in the creative writing field and who have demonstrated creative writing ability. This scholarship was created in 1995 to honor the late Bobette Bibo Gugliotta, author of several books, including Katzimo: Mysterious Mesa; Pigboat 39, about a World War II submarine; and Women of Mexico: The Consecrated and the Commoners, 1519-1900. Her family and friends remember her as wife, mother, hostess and one who was "never bored, never tired, always curious."

Award: Scholarship for use in freshman year; not renewable. *Number:* 2. *Amount:* $1000.

Eligibility Requirements: Applicant must be enrolled or expecting to enroll full-time at a four-year institution; resident of California and must have an interest in writing. Available to U.S. and non-Canadian citizens.

Application Requirements: Application form, essay, financial need analysis. *Deadline:* February 21.

Contact: Scholarships Team
Silicon Valley Community Foundation
2440 West El Camino Real
Suite 300
Mountain View, CA 94040
Phone: 650-450-5487
E-mail: scholarships@siliconvalleycf.org

CURRY AWARD FOR GIRLS AND YOUNG WOMEN

This fund was established by Eleanor Williams Curry, an active civic leader on the Peninsula. Scholarships are awarded to young women who are self-motivated, need financial support and attempt to achieve despite tremendous obstacles. Young women who have dropped out of school for reasons beyond their control, or have undergone unusual hardships to remain in school are encouraged to apply. The selection committee also considers circumstances related to possible ethnic or racial discrimination, physical disability or the choice of a nontraditional area of study. Open to young woman aged 18 to 26; maximum cumulative grade point average of 3.3 on a 4.0 scale. Must have demonstrated financial hardship and be a current resident of San Mateo County, preference given to residents of East Palo Alto, East Menlo Park, Redwood City and San Mateo. Must be a current graduating high school senior, graduate or G.E.D. certificate holder; preference given to students who attend(ed) East Palo Alto Academy, East Side College Prep, Menlo Atherton, Sequoia, Carlmont and San Mateo high schools. Must also be planning to enroll or currently enrolled in a two- or four-year college or university as a full-time student and a United States citizen or eligible non-citizen (eligible non-citizens include United States legal residents and A.B. 540 students).

Award: Scholarship for use in freshman, sophomore, or junior years; not renewable. *Number:* 10. *Amount:* $1000.

Eligibility Requirements: Applicant must be age 18-26; enrolled or expecting to enroll full-time at a two-year or four-year institution or university; female and resident of California. Applicant must have 2.5 GPA or higher. Available to U.S. and non-Canadian citizens.

Application Requirements: Application form, essay, financial need analysis. *Deadline:* February 21.

Contact: Scholarships Team
Silicon Valley Community Foundation
2440 West El Camino Real
Suite 300
Mountain View, CA 94040
Phone: 650-450-5487
E-mail: scholarships@siliconvalleycf.org

HAZEL REED BAUMEISTER SCHOLARSHIP PROGRAM

This program was established in 2001 through the Trust of Mrs. Hazel Reed Baumeister, a longtime resident of Burlingame. The purpose of the scholarship, established in her memory, is to support high school graduates of high academic achievement who would be unable to pursue higher education without financial assistance. The selection committee looks for academic promise, documented perseverance in activities outside the classroom, the quality of the personal statement and personal characteristics such as honesty, good judgment and commitment to serving the community. Students may apply to both the Crain Educational Grant Program and the Hazel Reed Baumeister Scholarship Program, but may receive only one of these scholarships. Must have demonstrated community involvement over a period of several years; have a minimum cumulative grade point average of 3.5 on a 4.0 scale; have demonstrated financial hardship; be a graduating high school senior or graduate of a public or private high school in San Mateo County or Santa Clara County; planning to enroll or currently enrolled in a four-year college or university as a full-time student; and be a United States citizen.

Award: Scholarship for use in freshman, sophomore, junior, or senior years; not renewable. *Number:* 1–15. *Amount:* $1000–$5000.

Eligibility Requirements: Applicant must be enrolled or expecting to enroll full-time at a four-year institution or university and resident of California. Applicant must have 3.5 GPA or higher. Available to U.S. citizens.

Application Requirements: Application form, essay, financial need analysis. *Deadline:* February 21.

Contact: Scholarships Team
Silicon Valley Community Foundation
2440 West El Camino Real
Suite 300
Mountain View, CA 94040
Phone: 650-450-5487
E-mail: scholarships@siliconvalleycf.org

HUANG LEADERSHIP DEVELOPMENT SCHOLARSHIP

The Huang Leadership Development Scholarship was established by Bob and Lily Huang in recognition of the loyalty and dedication of SYNNEX employees worldwide. Bob, founder, past CEO and past chairman of the board of SYNNEX Corporation, and his wife Lily wish to recognize those who worked and contributed to the success of SYNNEX by providing scholarship opportunities to support those employees, past employees and dependents that choose to further their personal leadership development through higher education for the future prosperity of the globalized world. Bob and Lily wish to continue this rich legacy by improving the lives of those seeking to better themselves through higher education and become leaders and mentors in their own right. Scholarship recipients will be selected based on academic achievement excellence and leadership qualities as evidenced by their

personal statement, letters of reference, school and community activities. Open to current employee or past employee, or a legal dependent or grandchild of a current or past employee of SYNNEX Corporation, or its subsidiaries who left the company in good standing; current employee or past employee, or a legal dependent or grandchild of a current or past employee that worked for SYNNEX Corporation or its subsidiaries for a minimum of three years at the time of the application deadline. Must have demonstrated academic excellence and leadership qualities through activities in school, community or social service activities. Must be accepted into and confirmed intent to enroll or be enrolled on a full-time basis in an undergraduate program in a four-year college or university ranked as a top college or university according to the current year's U.S. News and World Report's college/university rankings or comparable source. Award recipients must be willing to share their experience with their peers and future applicants.

Award: Scholarship for use in freshman, sophomore, junior, or senior years; renewable. *Number:* 1–10. *Amount:* $1000–$34,000.

Eligibility Requirements: Applicant must be enrolled or expecting to enroll full-time at a four-year institution or university. Available to U.S. and non-U.S. citizens.

Application Requirements: Application form, essay. *Deadline:* May 9.

Contact: Scholarships Team
Silicon Valley Community Foundation
2440 West El Camino Real
Suite 300
Mountain View, CA 94040
Phone: 650-450-5487
E-mail: scholarships@siliconvalleycf.org

SIMMONS AND FLETCHER, P.C.

https://www.simmonsandfletcher.com/

SIMMONS AND FLETCHER, P.C., LAW MARKETING SCHOLARSHIP

In order to be considered for the Law Marketing Scholarship, applicants must submit an essay. The aim of the essay is to propose and discuss a marketing strategy for personal injury law. The essay should focus on how personal injury law is helping people recover from tragic events. Essays should propose a marketing ad or idea that presents personal injury attorneys in a positive light. The essay should also include a description as to the medium (video, audio, print) that the ad would be presented in and where it would be marketed. The essay should be as long as is necessary to fully explain marketing proposal. All essays should be typed in a legible, 12-point size font.

Award: Scholarship for use in freshman year; not renewable. *Number:* 2. *Amount:* $500–$1000.

Eligibility Requirements: Applicant must be enrolled or expecting to enroll full-time at a two-year or four-year or technical institution or university; resident of Alberta, British Columbia, Guam, Manitoba, New Brunswick, Newfoundland, Northwest Territories, Nova Scotia, Ontario, Prince Edward Island, Puerto Rico, Quebec, Saskatchewan, Yukon and studying in Alberta, British Columbia, Guam, Manitoba, New Brunswick, Newfoundland, Northwest Territories, Nova Scotia, Ontario, Prince Edward Island, Puerto Rico, Quebec, Saskatchewan, Yukon. Applicant must have 2.5 GPA or higher. Available to U.S. citizens.

Application Requirements: Essay. *Deadline:* July 1.

Contact: Paul Cannon, Trial Attorney
Phone: 713-932-0777

SOCIETY FOR APPLIED ANTHROPOLOGY

http://www.sfaa.net/

ANNUAL SFAA STUDENT ENDOWED AWARD

The Student Endowed Award consists of a $500 travel stipend to cover costs of attending the annual meeting, plus a one-year SfAA membership, (which includes a one year subscription to the journals Human Organization and Practicing Anthropology).

Award: Prize for use in freshman, sophomore, junior, senior, graduate, or postgraduate years; not renewable. *Number:* 1. *Amount:* $500.

Eligibility Requirements: Applicant must be enrolled or expecting to enroll full- or part-time at a two-year or four-year institution or university. Available to U.S. and non-U.S. citizens.

Application Requirements: Application form, essay. *Deadline:* December 20.

Contact: Trish Colvin, Office Manager
Society for Applied Anthropology
PO Box 2436
Oklahoma City, OK 73101
Phone: 405-843-5113
Fax: 405-843-8553
E-mail: info@sfaa.net

SOCIETY OF DAUGHTERS OF THE UNITED STATES ARMY

SOCIETY OF DAUGHTERS OF THE UNITED STATES ARMY SCHOLARSHIPS

Scholarship for daughters or granddaughters of career warrant or commissioned officer in the U.S. Army who is on active duty; retired from active duty after 20 years of service; medically retired before 20 years of active service; died while on active duty or died after retiring from active duty. Send the following information to request an application: applicant's name, name of officer, rank, component (active, reserve, retired), dates of active duty service, and relationship to the applicant. Send information only, no documentation at this time. Send to Mary P. Maroney, DUSA Scholarship Chairman, 11804 Grey Birch Place, Reston, VA 20191. Application available November 1 - March 1.

Award: Scholarship for use in freshman, sophomore, junior, or senior years; not renewable. *Number:* 8–12. *Amount:* $1000.

Eligibility Requirements: Applicant must be enrolled or expecting to enroll full-time at a two-year or four-year or technical institution or university and female. Applicant must have 3.0 GPA or higher. Available to U.S. citizens. Applicant or parent must meet one or more of the following requirements: national guard experience; retired from active duty; disabled or killed as a result of military service; prisoner of war; or missing in action.

Application Requirements: Application form, essay. *Deadline:* March 1.

Contact: Mary Maroney, Chairperson, Memorial and Scholarship Funds
Society of Daughters of the United States Army
11804 Grey Birch Place
Reston, VA 20191

SONS OF ITALY FOUNDATION

http://www.osia.org/sif

GENERAL STUDY SCHOLARSHIPS

Through the Sons of Italy Foundation (SIF), and hundreds of thousands of family members located in all fifty states and the District of Columbia, the Order Sons and Daughters of Italy in America (OSDIA) has awarded nearly $61 million in scholarships to date. In past years, the SIF has offered 10 to 12 merit-based scholarships (National Leadership Grants), ranging from $4,000 to $25,000, in a nationwide competition. These figures and the number of scholarships may vary according to funding each year. A number of General Study Scholarships are available. Only one application is required to be eligible for all General Study Scholarships.

Award: Scholarship for use in freshman, sophomore, junior, senior, graduate, or postgraduate years; not renewable. *Number:* 6–12. *Amount:* $4000–$25,000.

Eligibility Requirements: Applicant must be of Italian heritage and enrolled or expecting to enroll full-time at a four-year institution or university. Available to U.S. citizens.

Application Requirements: Application form, essay. *Fee:* $35. *Deadline:* February 28.

Contact: Carly Jerome, Director of Programming
Sons of Italy Foundation
219 E Street NE
Washington, DC 20002
Phone: 202-547-2900
E-mail: scholarships@osia.org

HENRY SALVATORI SCHOLARSHIP FOR GENERAL STUDY

Through the Sons of Italy Foundation (SIF), and hundreds of thousands of family members located in all fifty states and the District of Columbia, the Order Sons and Daughters of Italy in America (OSDIA) has awarded nearly $61 million in scholarships to date. In past years, the SIF has offered 10 to 12 merit-based scholarships (National Leadership Grants), ranging from $4,000 to $25,000, in a nationwide competition. These figures and the number of scholarships may vary according to funding each year. Established by the late philanthropist and businessman for whom it is named, the Henry Salvatori Scholarship for General Study is a grant awarded to a college-bound high school senior who demonstrates exceptional leadership, distinguished scholarship, and a deep understanding and respect for the principles upon which our nation was founded: liberty, freedom, and equality.

Award: Scholarship for use in freshman year; not renewable. *Number:* 1. *Amount:* $4000–$25,000.

Eligibility Requirements: Applicant must be of Italian heritage; high school student and planning to enroll or expecting to enroll full-time at a four-year institution. Available to U.S. citizens.

Application Requirements: Application form, essay. *Fee:* $35. *Deadline:* February 28.

Contact: Carly Jerome, Director of Programming
Sons of Italy Foundation
219 E Street NE
Washington, DC 20002
Phone: 202-547-2900
E-mail: scholarships@osia.org

SOUND MONEY DEFENSE LEAGUE

http://soundmoneydefense.org

MONEY METALS EXCHANGE SCHOLARSHIP PROGRAM

Money Metals Exchange, a national precious dealer recently ranked Best in the USA, has teamed up with the Sound Money Defense League to help qualified students pay for the ever-rising costs of higher education. These groups have just introduced the first gold-backed scholarship of the modern era, setting aside 100 oz. of physical gold for scholarships to outstanding undergraduate and graduate students who display deep understanding of economics and monetary policy. Money Metals Exchange and the Sound Money Defense League will be awarding this scholarship to two incoming or current undergraduate students and two graduate students each year. Judged Scholarship Award: Undergraduate Student First Place: $2,000, Undergraduate Student Runner Up: $1,000, Graduate Student First Place: $2,000, Graduate Student Runner Up: $1,000; People's Choice Award, First Place: $500. Application, resume, and essay must be submitted by September 30. For more information, visit moneymetals.com/scholarship

Award: Scholarship for use in freshman, sophomore, junior, senior, or graduate years; not renewable. *Number:* 5. *Amount:* $500–$2000.

Eligibility Requirements: Applicant must be enrolled or expecting to enroll full-time at a two-year or four-year or technical institution or university. Available to U.S. and non-U.S. citizens.

Application Requirements: Application form, essay. *Deadline:* September 30.

Contact: Mr. Jp Cortez, Assistant Director
Sound Money Defense League
15720 Brixham Hill Avenue
Charlotte, NC 28277
E-mail: jp.cortez@soundmoneydefense.org

SOUTH CAROLINA TUITION GRANTS COMMISSION

http://www.sctuitiongrants.org/

SOUTH CAROLINA TUITION GRANTS PROGRAM

Need-based grant set aside for students attending eligible independent colleges in South Carolina. Student must be a South Carolina resident. Must apply annually by submitting the Free Application for Federal Student Aid (FAFSA). Freshmen must graduate in top 75% of high school class OR score 900 on SAT/19 on ACT OR graduate with at least 2.0 on SC Uniform Grading Scale. Upperclassmen must pass a minimum of 24 credit hours annually.

Award: Grant for use in freshman, sophomore, junior, or senior years; renewable. *Amount:* $100–$3200.

Eligibility Requirements: Applicant must be enrolled or expecting to enroll full-time at a two-year or four-year institution or university;

resident of South Carolina and studying in South Carolina. Available to U.S. citizens.

Application Requirements: Financial need analysis. *Deadline:* June 30.

Contact: Zachary Christian, Financial Aid Counselor
South Carolina Tuition Grants Commission
115 Atrium Way, Suite 102
Columbia, SC 29223
Phone: 803-896-1120
E-mail: zachary@sctuitiongrants.org

SPINE SURGEON DR. VICTOR HAYES

https://tampabaybackpaindoctor.com/

TAMPA BAY SPINE CENTER ROAD TO RECOVERY SCHOLARSHIP

Submit a 750-word essay that thoughtfully describes a time in your life in which you suffered a physical or emotional setback in which you recovered and what that recovery has meant to you. Current official transcript from the applicant's school (first-year college students may submit an official transcript from their most recent school, as well as an unofficial transcript from their current post-secondary institution). For more complete information, please visit: http://tampabaybackpaindoctor.com/#scholarship

Award: Scholarship for use in freshman, sophomore, junior, senior, graduate, or postgraduate years; not renewable. *Number:* 1. *Amount:* $500.

Eligibility Requirements: Applicant must be enrolled or expecting to enroll full- or part-time at a two-year or four-year or technical institution or university. Applicant must have 3.0 GPA or higher. Available to U.S. and non-U.S. citizens.

Application Requirements: Application form, essay. *Deadline:* July 1.

Contact: Dr. Victor Hayes
E-mail: info@tampabaybackpaindoctor.com

STEALTHY AND WEALTHY

http://stealthyandwealthy.com

STEALTHY AND WEALTHY STUDENT ENTREPRENEUR GRANT

Whether you have an idea for an app, a blog or a vlog, a talent for creating products that you want to sell online, a savvy method for investing, or a technological innovation that you want to get off the ground, we want to help. This grant is for anyone interested in building their own business or side hustle to help them get ahead while they are in school. The money can be used for marketing your business, purchasing materials, setting up at a trade show, launching an online store, or whatever your business or idea needs to help you succeed. To give back to the next generation of entrepreneurs and brilliant minds, we have created a grant that will go directly to the student who will be working to build their future. There is one grant that will be awarded each fall to a college student in the United States. This grant will be a $250 one-time gift given to the student who is selected. The money is intended to be used as an investment or to help build a personal side business for the future entrepreneur.

Award: Grant for use in freshman, sophomore, junior, senior, graduate, or postgraduate years; not renewable. *Number:* 1–2. *Amount:* $250–$1000.

Eligibility Requirements: Applicant must be enrolled or expecting to enroll full- or part-time at a two-year or four-year or technical institution or university. Available to U.S. and non-U.S. citizens.

Application Requirements: Application form, essay. *Deadline:* August 21.

Contact: Scott Patten, Editor in Chief
E-mail: scott@stealthyandwealthy.com

STEINBERG, GOODMAN AND KALISH

https://www.sgklawyers.com/

STEINBERG, GOODMAN AND KALISH SCHOLARSHIP

Steinberg, Goodman & Kalish is pleased to announce that every year we will offer a $1,000 scholarship to the student who submits the strongest essay focusing on the given topic. The current topic is "Should pharmaceutical companies be allowed to promote drugs for uses that were not FDA approved?" The application must be completed online and the deadline is July 15, 2018.

Award: Scholarship for use in freshman, sophomore, junior, or senior years; not renewable. *Number:* 1. *Amount:* $1000.

Eligibility Requirements: Applicant must be enrolled or expecting to enroll full-time at a two-year or four-year institution or university. Available to U.S. citizens.

Application Requirements: Application form, essay. *Deadline:* July 15.

Contact: Pat McCune, Scholarship Coordinator
Steinberg, Goodman and Kalish
PO Box 1596
Northbrook, IL 60065
Phone: 847-940-4000
Fax: 847-940-4000
E-mail: pat@marketjd.com

STONEWALL COMMUNITY FOUNDATION

http://www.stonewallfoundation.org/

HARRY BARTEL MEMORIAL SCHOLARSHIP

LGBT students in New York City who are 23 years or younger with a record of community service can apply for this scholarship. Deadline varies. Applications available through Youth Program at The LGBT Center in Manhattan.

Award: Scholarship for use in freshman, sophomore, junior, senior, graduate, or postgraduate years; not renewable. *Number:* 1–2. *Amount:* $500.

Eligibility Requirements: Applicant must be enrolled or expecting to enroll full-time at a two-year or four-year or technical institution or university and must have an interest in LGBT issues. Applicant or parent of applicant must have employment or volunteer experience in community service. Available to U.S. citizens.

Application Requirements: Application form.

Contact: Natasha Jones, Director of Youth Leadership and Engagement
Stonewall Community Foundation
c/o The Lesbian, Gay, Bisexual, and Transgender Community Center
208 West 13th Street
New York, NY 10011
Phone: 212-620-7310
E-mail: youth@gaycenter.org

TRAUB-DICKER RAINBOW SCHOLARSHIP

Non-renewable scholarships available to women-identified lesbians who are involved in LGBTQ activism. Must be graduating high school seniors planning to attend a recognized college, or already matriculated college students in any year of study, including graduate school.

Award: Scholarship for use in freshman, sophomore, junior, senior, graduate, or postgraduate years; not renewable. *Number:* 3–4. *Amount:* $1000–$3000.

Eligibility Requirements: Applicant must be enrolled or expecting to enroll full- or part-time at a four-year institution or university and female. Available to U.S. citizens.

Application Requirements: Application form, essay.

Contact: Carlie Steen, Program Manager
Stonewall Community Foundation
Stonewall Community Foundation
1270 Broadway, Suite 501
New York, NY 10001
Phone: 212-457.1349
E-mail: grants@stonewallfoundation.org

STROLLER DEPOT

https://www.strollerdepot.com/

$1,000 STROLLER DEPOT SCHOLARSHIP

Stroller Depot is offering one $1,000 scholarship to a student who is currently enrolled or accepted to a higher education program; is a young parent (age 18-30), with 1 or more children; and has a GPA of at least 3.5. The scholarship submissions must be received by December 15.

Award: Scholarship for use in freshman, sophomore, junior, senior, graduate, or postgraduate years; not renewable. *Number:* 1. *Amount:* $1000.

Eligibility Requirements: Applicant must be age 18-30 and enrolled or expecting to enroll full- or part-time at a two-year or four-year institution or university. Applicant must have 3.0 GPA or higher. Available to U.S. and non-U.S. citizens.

Application Requirements: Essay. *Deadline:* December 15.

STROM & ASSOCIATES
https://stromlawyers.com

STROM & ASSOCIATES ANNUAL SCHOLARSHIP

Strom & Associates understands the increasing costs of college tuition makes it more difficult to graduate college for many outstanding students across the nation. Therefore, we are offering one $1,500 scholarship. The scholarship committee will select the student who submits the best essay focusing on the given topic.

Award: Scholarship for use in freshman, sophomore, junior, or senior years; not renewable. *Number:* 1. *Amount:* $1500.

Eligibility Requirements: Applicant must be enrolled or expecting to enroll full-time at a two-year or four-year institution or university. Available to U.S. citizens.

Application Requirements: Application form, essay. *Deadline:* July 15.

Contact: Neal Strom, Partner
Strom & Associates
180 N. LaSalle Suite #2510
Chicago, IL 60601
Phone: 312-609-0400

STUDY.COM
study.com

ARMY ROTC STUDY.COM SCHOLARSHIP

A $500 academic award will be given to a student enrolled in Army ROTC at their college or university. Study.com wants to recognize students who have the dedication and strength of character necessary to be successful in the competitive ROTC program. For more information, please visit https://study.com/pages/Army_ROTC_Scholarship.html

Award: Scholarship for use in freshman, sophomore, or junior years; renewable. *Number:* 1. *Amount:* $500.

Eligibility Requirements: Applicant must be enrolled or expecting to enroll full- or part-time at a two-year or four-year institution or university. Available to U.S. citizens. Applicant must have national guard experience.

Application Requirements: Application form, personal photograph. *Deadline:* April 1.

Contact: Koby Wong, Study.com Scholarship Manager
Phone: 650-9621200
E-mail: koby@email.study.com

STUDY.COM CLEP SCHOLARSHIP

Study.com will be supporting three students pursuing CLEP credit. CLEP exams are a proven and efficient way for both traditional and non-traditional students from all walks of life to gain college credit. For more information, please visit https://study.com/academy/popular/studycom-clep-scholarship-application-form-information.html

Award: Scholarship for use in freshman, sophomore, or junior years; renewable. *Number:* 1–3. *Amount:* $250–$500.

Eligibility Requirements: Applicant must be enrolled or expecting to enroll full- or part-time at a two-year or four-year institution or university. Available to U.S. citizens.

Application Requirements: Application form, personal photograph. *Deadline:* April 1.

Contact: Koby Wong, Study.com Scholarship Manager
Phone: 650-9621200
E-mail: koby@email.study.com

STUDY.COM SCHOLARSHIP FOR FLORIDA STUDENTS

The Study.com Scholarship for Florida Students provides a $500 academic award to a student pursuing their undergraduate college degree from a college or university in Florida. At Study.com, we believe every student has a right to an affordable, high-quality education, and with this scholarship we hope to ease the heavy burden of college tuition. Please visit the following link for more info: https://study.com/pages/Scholarship_for_Florida_Students.html

Award: Scholarship for use in freshman, sophomore, or junior years; renewable. *Number:* 1. *Amount:* $500.

Eligibility Requirements: Applicant must be enrolled or expecting to enroll full- or part-time at a two-year or four-year institution or university and studying in Florida. Available to U.S. citizens.

Application Requirements: Application form, personal photograph. *Deadline:* April 1.

Contact: Koby Wong, Study.com Scholarship Manager
Phone: 650-9621200
E-mail: koby@email.study.com

STUDY.COM SCHOLARSHIP FOR TEXAS STUDENTS

The Study.com Scholarship for Texas Students provides a $500 academic award to a student pursuing their undergraduate college degree from any college or university in Texas. At Study.com, we believe every student has a right to an affordable, high-quality education, and with this scholarship we hope to ease the heavy burden of college tuition. For more info, please visit https://study.com/pages/Scholarship_for_Texas_Students.html.

Award: Scholarship for use in freshman, sophomore, or junior years; renewable. *Number:* 1–500.

Eligibility Requirements: Applicant must be enrolled or expecting to enroll full- or part-time at a two-year or four-year institution or university and studying in Texas. Available to U.S. citizens.

Application Requirements: Application form, personal photograph. *Deadline:* April 1.

Contact: Koby Wong, Study.com Scholarship Manager
Phone: 650-9621200
E-mail: koby@email.study.com

TECHNOSOFT INNOVATIONS, INC.
https://www.technosoftinv.com/

TECHNOSOFT INNOVATIONS SCHOLARSHIP PROGRAM

Technosoft Innovations is glad to inform you that we are offering a scholarship of $500 to the students of your university for the academic year 2018-2019. Please send the scholarship application before May 31, 2018 on innovations@technosofteng.com with the subject line "Application for Scholarship Program 2018-2019." Visit https://www.technosoftinv.com/electronic-products.html#scholarship for detailed information. To apply for the scholarship you need to submit a 1000 words essay on either one of these topics: 1. Recent Developments in the Medical Industry; or 2. Recent Developments in the Electronics Industry. We will accept only 100% original essay. Any plagiarism will instantly lead to disqualification. Each applicant can make only one submission. Applicants under the age of 18 years will be disqualified. Winner of the scholarship will be declared on June 15, 2018.

Award: Scholarship for use in freshman, sophomore, junior, senior, graduate, or postgraduate years; renewable. *Number:* 1. *Amount:* $500.

Eligibility Requirements: Applicant must be high school student and planning to enroll or expecting to enroll full- or part-time at a two-year or four-year or technical institution or university. Available to U.S. and Canadian citizens.

Application Requirements: Essay, personal photograph. *Deadline:* May 31.

Contact: Rayburn Rozario, Marketing Head
Technosoft Innovations, Inc.
900 Perimeter Park Drive
Suite C
Morrisville, NC 27590
Phone: 313-265-2622
E-mail: innovations@technosofteng.coml

TELEVISION ACADEMY FOUNDATION
http://www.televisionacademy.com/foundation

TELEVISION ACADEMY FOUNDATION

A competition for excellence in college student video, digital, and film productions. Rules and guidelines are updated annually in the fall at televisionacademyfoundation.org. Awards of up to $10,000. Open to those students who have produced their video while enrolled in a community college, college, or university in the United States.

Award: Prize for use in freshman, sophomore, junior, senior, graduate, or postgraduate years; not renewable. *Number:* 16. *Amount:* $2000–$10,000.

Eligibility Requirements: Applicant must be enrolled or expecting to enroll full- or part-time at a two-year or four-year or technical institution or university. Available to U.S. citizens.

Application Requirements: Application form, personal photograph. *Deadline:* continuous.

Contact: Liz Korda, Director, Awards Dept
Television Academy Foundation
5220 Lankershim Boulevard
North Hollywood, CA 91601
Phone: 818-754-2800
E-mail: ctasupport@televisionacademy.com

TENNESSEE STUDENT ASSISTANCE CORPORATION

http://www.tn.gov/collegepays

DEPENDENT CHILDREN SCHOLARSHIP PROGRAM

Scholarship for Tennessee residents who are dependent children of a Tennessee law enforcement officer, fireman, or an emergency medical service technician who have been killed or totally and permanently disabled while performing duties within the scope of such employment. The scholarship is awarded to full-time undergraduate students for a maximum of four academic years or the period required for the completion of the program of study.

Award: Scholarship for use in freshman, sophomore, junior, or senior years; renewable.

Eligibility Requirements: Applicant must be enrolled or expecting to enroll full-time at a two-year or four-year institution or university; resident of Tennessee and studying in Tennessee. Available to U.S. citizens.

Application Requirements: Application form. *Deadline:* July 15.

Contact: Ms. Kathy Stripling, Grant and Scholarship Analyst
Tennessee Student Assistance Corporation
Parkway Towers
404 James Robertson Parkway, Suite 1510
Nashville, TN 37243-0820
Phone: 615-253-7480
E-mail: kathy.stripling@tn.gov

HELPING HEROES GRANT

Provides assistance to Tennessee veterans who have been awarded the Iraq Campaign Medal, Afghanistan Campaign Medal, or Global War on Terrorism Expeditionary Medal (on or after 9/11/01) and who meet eligibility requirements for the program. Award is $1,000 per semester for 12 or more semester hours or $500 for 6-11 semester hours. For more information, visit http://www.TN.gov/collegepays.

Award: Grant for use in freshman, sophomore, junior, or senior years; renewable. *Amount:* $1000–$2000.

Eligibility Requirements: Applicant must be enrolled or expecting to enroll full- or part-time at a two-year or four-year institution or university; resident of Tennessee and studying in Tennessee. Available to U.S. citizens. Applicant must have general military experience.

Application Requirements: Application form. *Deadline:* September 1.

Contact: Mr. Robert Biggers, Assistant Executive Director of Grant & Scholarship Programs
Tennessee Student Assistance Corporation
Parkway Towers
404 James Robertson Parkway, Suite 1510
Nashville, TN 37243
Phone: 615-253-7453
E-mail: robert.biggers@tn.gov

HOPE ASPIRE AWARD

$750 supplement per semester for four-year institutions, $250 per semester for two-year instititutions. Must meet Tennessee HOPE

Scholarship requirements and Adjusted Gross Income (AGI) attributable to the parents or to the independent student must be $36,000 or less.

Award: Scholarship for use in freshman, sophomore, junior, or senior years; renewable. *Amount:* $500–$1500.

Eligibility Requirements: Applicant must be enrolled or expecting to enroll full- or part-time at a two-year or four-year institution or university; resident of Tennessee and studying in Tennessee. Applicant must have 3.0 GPA or higher. Available to U.S. citizens.

Contact: Mr. Robert Biggers, Assistant Executive Director of Grant & Scholarships Programs
Tennessee Student Assistance Corporation
Parkway Towers
404 James Robertson Parkway, Suite 1510
Nashville, TN 37243-0820
Phone: 615-253-7453
E-mail: robert.biggers@tn.gov

NED MCWHERTER SCHOLARS PROGRAM

Award for Tennessee high school seniors with high academic ability. Must have minimum high school GPA of 3.5 and a score of 29 on the ACT or SAT equivalent. Must attend a college or university in Tennessee. Must be a Tennessee resident and U.S. citizen or permanent resident. For more information, visit website http://tn.gov/collegepays.

Award: Scholarship for use in freshman, sophomore, junior, or senior years; renewable. *Amount:* $6000.

Eligibility Requirements: Applicant must be enrolled or expecting to enroll full-time at a two-year or four-year or technical institution or university; resident of Tennessee and studying in Tennessee. Applicant must have 3.5 GPA or higher. Available to U.S. citizens.

Application Requirements: Application form. *Deadline:* February 15.

Contact: Ms. Kathy Stripling, Grants and Scholarship Analyst
Tennessee Student Assistance Corporation
404 James Robertson Parkway, Suite 1510
Parkway Towers
Nashville, TN 37243-0820
Phone: 615-253-7480
E-mail: kathy.stripling@tn.gov

TELS -HOPE WITH GENERAL ASSEMBLY MERIT SCHOLARSHIP (GAMS)

Students who qualify for the HOPE Scholarship can receive GAMS by earning a minimum 3.75 GPA and a 29 or above on the ACT (or SAT equivalent). The supplemental award is $500 per semester. Must be a Tennessee resident. For more information, visit http://www.tn.gov/collegepays.

Award: Scholarship for use in freshman, sophomore, junior, or senior years; renewable.

Eligibility Requirements: Applicant must be enrolled or expecting to enroll full- or part-time at a two-year or four-year institution or university; resident of Tennessee and studying in Tennessee. Applicant must have 3.5 GPA or higher. Available to U.S. citizens.

Contact: Mr. Robert Biggers, Assistant Executive Director of Grant & Scholarship Programs
Tennessee Student Assistance Corporation
Parkway Towers
404 James Robertson Parkway, Suite 1510
Nashville, TN 37243-0820
Phone: 615-253-7453
E-mail: robert.biggers@tn.gov

TENNESSEE DUAL ENROLLMENT GRANT

Grant for study at an eligible Tennessee postsecondary institution awarded to juniors and seniors in a Tennessee high school who have been admitted to undergraduate study while still pursuing a high school diploma. For more information, visit website http://www.tn.gov/collegepays.

Award: Grant for use in freshman year; renewable.

Eligibility Requirements: Applicant must be high school student; planning to enroll or expecting to enroll part-time at a two-year or four-year or technical institution or university; resident of Tennessee and studying in Tennessee. Available to U.S. citizens.

Application Requirements: Application form. *Deadline:* continuous.

Contact: Mr. Robert Biggers, Assistant Executive Director of Grant &
Scholarship Programs
Tennessee Student Assistance Corporation
Parkway Towers
404 James Robertson Parkway, Suite 1510
Nashville, TN 37243-0820
Phone: 615-253-7453
E-mail: robert.biggers@tn.gov

TENNESSEE HOPE ACCESS GRANT

Non-renewable award of $2,750 for students at four-year colleges or $1,750 for students at two-year colleges. Entering freshmen must have a minimum GPA of 2.75, ACT score of 18-20 (or SAT equivalent), and adjusted gross income attributable to the student must be $36,000 or less. Recipients will become eligible for Tennessee HOPE Scholarship by meeting HOPE Scholarship renewal criteria. TN residents may graduate from high schools located in states other than Tennessee in certain exceptions.

Award: Grant for use in freshman, sophomore, junior, or senior years; not renewable. *Amount:* $1750–$2750.

Eligibility Requirements: Applicant must be enrolled or expecting to enroll full- or part-time at a two-year or four-year institution or university; resident of Tennessee and studying in Tennessee. Applicant must have 3.0 GPA or higher. Available to U.S. citizens.

Application Requirements: Application form, financial need analysis. *Deadline:* September 1.

Contact: Mr. Robert Biggers, Assistant Executive Director of Grant &
Scholarship Programs
Tennessee Student Assistance Corporation
Parkway Towers
404 James Robertson Parkway, Suite 1510
Nashville, TN 37243-0820
Phone: 615-253-7453
E-mail: robert.biggers@tn.gov

TENNESSEE HOPE FOSTER CHILD TUITION GRANT

Renewable tuition award available for recipients of the HOPE Scholarship or HOPE Access Grant. Student must have been in Tennessee state custody as a foster child for at least one year after reaching age 14. Award amount varies and shall not exceed the tuition and mandatory fees at an eligible Tennessee public postsecondary institution. For additional information, visit website http://www.tn.gov/collegepays.

Award: Scholarship for use in freshman, sophomore, junior, or senior years; renewable.

Eligibility Requirements: Applicant must be enrolled or expecting to enroll full- or part-time at a two-year or four-year institution or university; resident of Tennessee and studying in Tennessee. Applicant must have 3.0 GPA or higher. Available to U.S. citizens.

Application Requirements: Application form.

Contact: Mr. Robert Biggers, Assistant Executive Director of Grant &
Scholarship Programs
Tennessee Student Assistance Corporation
Parkway Towers
404 James Robertson Parkway, Suite 1510
Nashville, TN 37243-0820
Phone: 615-253-7453
E-mail: robert.biggers@tn.gov

TENNESSEE HOPE SCHOLARSHIP

Students must achieve a minimum 3.0 GPA or 21 or above on the ACT to qualify for the scholarship. Award amount is $1,750 for per semester at four-year institutions and $1,500 per semester at two-year institutions for entering freshmen who first received HOPE in fall 2015 and thereafter. Award amount is $2,000 per semester at four-year institutions and $1,000 per semester at two-year institutions for students who first received HOPE between fall 2009 and summer 2015. Must be a Tennessee resident attending an eligible postsecondary institution in Tennessee. For more information, visit http://www.TN.gov/CollegePays.

Award: Scholarship for use in freshman, sophomore, junior, or senior years; renewable. *Amount:* $2000–$4500.

Eligibility Requirements: Applicant must be enrolled or expecting to enroll full-time at a two-year or four-year institution or university; resident of Tennessee and studying in Tennessee. Applicant must have 3.0 GPA or higher. Available to U.S. citizens.

Application Requirements: *Deadline:* September 1.
Contact: Mr. Robert Biggers, Assistant Executive Director of Grant &
Scholarship Programs
Tennessee Student Assistance Corporation
Parkway Towers
404 James Robertson Parkway, Suite 1510
Nashville, TN 37243-0820
Phone: 615-253-7453
E-mail: robert.biggers@tn.gov

TENNESSEE STUDENT ASSISTANCE AWARD

Award to assist financially-needy Tennessee residents attending an approved college or university within the state. Applicants must have a valid Expected Family Contribution (EFC) of $2100 or less. Students are encourage to complete the FAFSA as soon as possible after October 1 for priority consideration. To apply, go to http://www.fafsa.gov. For more information, go to http://www.tn.gov/collegepays

Award: Grant for use in freshman, sophomore, junior, or senior years; renewable. *Amount:* $1000–$4000.

Eligibility Requirements: Applicant must be enrolled or expecting to enroll full- or part-time at a two-year or four-year or technical institution or university; resident of Tennessee and studying in Tennessee. Available to U.S. citizens.

Application Requirements: Financial need analysis.

Contact: Mrs. Leah Louallen, Director of Grants and Scholarship
Programs
Tennessee Student Assistance Corporation
Parkway Towers
404 James Robertson Parkway, Suite 1510
Nashville, TN 37243-0820
Phone: 615-253-7478
E-mail: leah.louallen@tn.gov

TERRY FOX HUMANITARIAN AWARD
http://terryfoxawards.ca/

TERRY FOX HUMANITARIAN AWARD

The Terry Fox Humanitarian Award is granted to Canadian students working towards their first post-secondary degree or diploma. Criteria includes commitment to voluntary humanitarian work, courage in overcoming obstacles, excellence in academics, fitness and amateur sports. Maximum value of award is CAN$28,000 for a maximum of four years ($7000 annually, subject to renewal).

Award: Scholarship for use in freshman, sophomore, junior, or senior years; renewable. *Number:* 20. *Amount:* $21,931.

Eligibility Requirements: Applicant must be Canadian citizen; enrolled or expecting to enroll full-time at a two-year or four-year institution or university; resident of Alberta, British Columbia, Manitoba, New Brunswick, Newfoundland, Northwest Territories, Nova Scotia, Ontario, Prince Edward Island, Quebec, Saskatchewan, Yukon and studying in Alberta, British Columbia, Manitoba, New Brunswick, Newfoundland, Northwest Territories, Nova Scotia, Ontario, Prince Edward Island, Quebec, Saskatchewan, Yukon. Applicant or parent of applicant must have employment or volunteer experience in community service.

Application Requirements: Application form, essay, interview. *Deadline:* February 1.

Contact: Mr. Ayden Thow, Awards Coordinator
Terry Fox Humanitarian Award
AQ 5003, 8888 University Drive
Burnaby, BC V5A 1S6
CAN
Phone: 778-782-3057
Fax: 778-782-3311
E-mail: info@terryfoxawards.ca

TETHERBOX
http://www.tetherbox.com/

$1,000 CREATIVE VIDEO CHALLENGE COLLEGE SCHOLARSHIP

Make a creative funny, heartwarming, or informational video for the opportunity to win a $1,000 college scholarship. The assignment for the TetherBox Creative Video Challenge College Scholarship is to make a commercial about TetherBox College Care Packages or a video related to care packages, being away from home, etc. Video length should be at least 1 minute but no longer than 4 minutes. You have full creative control on how you storyboard and shoot your video, but here is a few thoughts to help add context: Situation: Think of unique situations, locations, occurrences, etc. or think of common situations, occurrences and locations that you can put a creative, humorous or heartwarming twist on; Dialogue/Narrative: Develop hilarious or touching dialogue and/or narratives; Perspective: Find creative and unique angles and shots; Effects: Try and make use of different video styles and effects to get the video just the way you want it; Think Creatively: Think back on your favorite commercials and the most popular viral commercials on the web and see what unique ideas you can come up with. Go to http://www.tetherbox.com/scholarship and complete the brief application. When your commercial is ready, upload your video to a file sharing site like Dropbox or Google Drive and send the link to info@tetherbox.com, along with a short bio including your name, year in school, and expected graduation date and a brief overview explaining your video concept. Submission deadline: March 31. Your personal safety is paramount so please be safe. Entry is subject to the official rules and conditions. By submitting your video to TetherBox for scholarship consideration you agree to assign all rights and ownership of the video to TetherBox and you grant TetherBox full permission to re-publish, edit and otherwise freely use your video in any manner without notice or compensation.

Award: Scholarship for use in freshman, sophomore, junior, or senior years; not renewable. *Number:* 1. *Amount:* $1000.

Eligibility Requirements: Applicant must be enrolled or expecting to enroll full-time at a four-year or technical institution or university. Available to U.S. citizens.

Application Requirements: Application form. *Deadline:* March 31.

Contact: Lynn Holdsworth, Co-Founder
TetherBox
5 Walter E. Foran Blvd.
Suite 2002
Flemington, NJ 08822
Phone: 908-246-3934
Fax: 866-302-2255
E-mail: lynn.holdsworth@tetherbox.com

TEXAS AFL-CIO

http://www.texasaflcio.org/

TEXAS AFL-CIO SCHOLARSHIP PROGRAM
• *See page 579*

TEXAS ASSOCIATION OF DEVELOPING COLLEGES

http://www.txadc.org

THE URBAN SCHOLARSHIPS FUND

Eligibility - United States citizen or eligible non-citizen (permanent resident card I-551 front and back copy) Texas resident, graduate of high school from 29 urban cities: Abilene, Amarillo, Arlington, Austin, Beaumont, Brownsville, Carrollton, Corpus Christi, Dallas, Denton, El Paso, Fort Worth, Frisco, Garland, Grand Prairie, Houston, Irving, Killeen, Laredo, Lubbock, McAllen, McKinney, Mesquite, Midland, Pasadena, Plano, San Antonio, Waco and Wichita Falls

Award: Scholarship for use in freshman, sophomore, junior, or senior years; not renewable. *Number:* 450–500. *Amount:* $700–$1000.

Eligibility Requirements: Applicant must be age 16-65; enrolled or expecting to enroll full-time at a two-year or four-year or technical institution or university and resident of Texas. Available to U.S. citizens.

Application Requirements: Financial need analysis. *Deadline:* July 10.

Contact: Ms. Janice Jackson, Office Programs Administrator
Texas Association of Developing Colleges
1140 Empire Central Drive 550
Dallas, TX 75247
Phone: 214-630-2511
E-mail: janice.jackson@txadc.org

TEXAS MUTUAL INSURANCE COMPANY

http://www.texasmutual.com/

TEXAS MUTUAL INSURANCE COMPANY SCHOLARSHIP PROGRAM

A scholarship program open to qualified family members of policyholder employees who died from on-the-job injuries or accidents, policyholder employees who qualify for lifetime income benefits pursuant to the Texas Workers Compensation Act, and family members of injured employees who qualify for lifetime income benefits.

Award: Scholarship for use in freshman, sophomore, junior, or senior years; not renewable. *Number:* 1–25. *Amount:* $600–$6000.

Eligibility Requirements: Applicant must be enrolled or expecting to enroll full-time at a two-year or four-year or technical institution or university. Applicant must have 2.5 GPA or higher. Available to U.S. and non-U.S. citizens.

Application Requirements: Application form, financial need analysis. *Deadline:* continuous.

Contact: Temetria McVea, Executive Assistant to the President
Texas Mutual Insurance Company
6210 East Highway 290
Austin, TX 78723
Phone: 512-224-3907
E-mail: tmcvea@texasmutual.com

THRIVENT STUDENT RESOURCES

https://www.thriventstudentresources.com/

THRIVENT STUDENT RESOURCES SCHOLARSHIP

Thrivent Student Resources is giving away eight $5,000 scholarships to help current undergraduate students plan and pay for college. There will be two drawings of four winners each. The first drawing is April 2, 2018. The second drawing is July 2, 2018. If you are a winner, you'll be contacted by Thrivent Student Resources shortly after that date.

Award: Scholarship for use in freshman, sophomore, junior, senior, graduate, or postgraduate years; not renewable. *Number:* 8. *Amount:* $5000.

Eligibility Requirements: Applicant must be enrolled or expecting to enroll full- or part-time at a two-year or four-year or technical institution or university and resident of Alabama, Alaska, Arizona, Arkansas, California, Colorado, Connecticut, Delaware, District of Columbia, Georgia, Hawaii, Idaho, Illinois, Indiana, Iowa, Kansas, Kentucky, Louisiana, Maine, Maryland, Massachusetts, Michigan, Minnesota, Mississippi, Missouri, Montana, Nebraska, Nevada, New Hampshire, New Jersey, New Mexico, North Carolina, North Dakota, Ohio, Oklahoma, Oregon, Pennsylvania, South Carolina, South Dakota, Tennessee, Texas, Utah, Vermont, Virginia, Washington, West Virginia, Wisconsin, Wyoming. Available to U.S. citizens.

Application Requirements: Application form, financial need analysis. *Deadline:* June 30.

Contact: Julie Heltunen, Marketing agent for Thrivent Student Resources
E-mail: julie@peytonave.com

TONALAW

https://www.tonalaw.com/

TONALAW VETERAN'S SCHOLARSHIP

The TonaLaw Veteran's Scholarship is only open to students attending school in the United States. Students must have served in the U.S. Military and provide proof of service. Applicant must be a student at an accredited school, or be accepted to begin school at an accredited school within 6 months of application. All funds will be dispersed to scholarship recipient within 30 days of being announced as the winner.

Award: Scholarship for use in freshman, sophomore, junior, senior, graduate, or postgraduate years; not renewable. *Number:* 1–2. *Amount:* $1000–$2000.

Eligibility Requirements: Applicant must be enrolled or expecting to enroll full- or part-time at a two-year or four-year or technical institution or university. Available to U.S. citizens. Applicant must have general military experience.

Application Requirements: Application form, essay. *Deadline:* July 31.

Contact: Mackenzie Fox, Marketing Director
TonaLaw
870 Middle Country Road
St James, NY 11780
Phone: 631-780-5355 Ext. 22
Fax: 631-780-5685
E-mail: mac@tonalaw.com

TOPPRODUCTS.COM

http://topproducts.com/

TOPPRODUCTS SINGLE MOTHER SCHOLARSHIP

At TopProducts, we firmly believe in the power of education and giving back to the local community, especially single parent families. We understand the financial strain going to college can place on any family, let alone mothers who not only want to go further their education, but also must raise their children and run the household every day on their own. As strong advocates of both higher education and family values, we are pleased to help single moms who have shown strong scholastic ability throughout their high school or college years get the financial help they need to create a secure future for their children. Please review the eligibility requirements and application process below and remember, there will only be one winner. All applicants must include your full name, mail, phone number, mailing address, and 1,200 to 1,500 word essay. Application Deadline: Dec 31. This scholarship is available to all single mothers who meet the following criteria: 1. Must be a single parent and have custodial care of one or more children under 18, 2. Must not have a college degree from a 4-year institution, 3. Must be enrolled in a 4-year institution or have a high school diploma. Please submit a 1,200 to 1,500 word essay in PDF or Word Doc format to the attached submission form along with your full name, address, and contact details. We also require an unofficial copy of your high school transcript or college transcript. The essay topic is as follows: We want to hear your story. Therefore, we request you write a personal narrative describing yourself, your family and what education means to you. Why do you want to obtain a college degree? And how will this scholarship help you achieve your goals? Please submit through the TopProducts.com Scholarship Application Form.

Award: Scholarship for use in freshman, sophomore, junior, or senior years; not renewable. *Number:* 1. *Amount:* $1000.

Eligibility Requirements: Applicant must be enrolled or expecting to enroll full- or part-time at a two-year or four-year or technical institution or university and single female. Available to U.S. and non-U.S. citizens.

Application Requirements: Essay. *Deadline:* December 31.

TORHOERMAN LAW LLC

http://torhoermanlaw.com

TORHOERMAN LAW DISTRACTED DRIVING ESSAY SCHOLARSHIP

In accordance with our End Distracted Driving campaign, student contestants will be asked to discuss the dangers of distracted driving and what steps our society can take to put an end to this issue. The student with the best overall response will receive $1,000 to go towards their education costs. Contestants can choose to submit either a written essay or a video response to our essay topic prompt.

Award: Scholarship for use in freshman, sophomore, junior, or senior years; not renewable. *Number:* 1. *Amount:* $1000.

Eligibility Requirements: Applicant must be enrolled or expecting to enroll full-time at a two-year or four-year institution or university. Available to U.S. citizens.

Application Requirements: Autobiography, essay. *Deadline:* April 1.

Contact: Mr. Jordan Terry, Marketing Team
Phone: 618-656-4400
E-mail: JTerry@THLawyer.com

TPA SCHOLARSHIP TRUST FOR THE HEARING IMPAIRED

https://www.tpahq.org/scholarshiptrust/

TPA SCHOLARSHIP TRUST FOR THE HEARING IMPAIRED

Scholarships are awarded to deaf or hearing-impaired persons of any age, race, or religion for specialized education, mechanical devices, or medical or specialized treatment. Based on financial need.

Award: Scholarship for use in freshman, sophomore, junior, senior, graduate, or postgraduate years; not renewable. *Amount:* $100–$1000.

Eligibility Requirements: Applicant must be hearing impaired and enrolled or expecting to enroll full- or part-time at a two-year or four-year or technical institution or university. Applicant must be hearing impaired. Available to U.S. citizens.

Application Requirements: Application form, financial need analysis, personal photograph. *Deadline:* continuous.

Contact: Venita Sedodo, Trust Secretary
TPA Scholarship Trust for the Hearing Impaired
2041 Exchange Drive
Saint Charles, MO 63303
Phone: 636-724-2227
E-mail: vsedodo@tpahq.org

TRANSFER TIMES

http://www.transfertimes.com

TRANSFER TIMES $6,000 SCHOLARSHIP

Transfer Times awards two $6000 scholarships per academic year to a two-year student who is transferring to a four-year school that advertises with Transfer Times (or $2,000 if the student chooses another four-year school to attend). Ten finalists are chosen at random and then given the opportunity to submit answers to essay questions. See online entry form for complete contest rules: https://www.transfertimes.com/scholarship.html. Deadlines: Fall Contest, December 1; Spring Contest, May 1.

Award: Scholarship for use in junior or senior years; not renewable. *Number:* 2. *Amount:* $6000.

Eligibility Requirements: Applicant must be enrolled or expecting to enroll full-time at a four-year institution. Available to U.S. citizens.

Application Requirements: Application form. *Deadline:* May 1.

Contact: Rachel Schaar, Account Manager
Transfer Times
2360 N. 124th St., Suite 202
Wauwatosa, WI 53226
Phone: 414-831-0184 Ext. 205
Fax: 414-727-5600
E-mail: rachel@transfertimes.com

TRANSTUTORS

http://www.transtutors.com/scholarship

TRANSTUTORS SCHOLARSHIP

Transtutors scholarship program wants to help students get aids for their studies. We really value good education for all. We have a very simple criteria of writing an essay on your college experience, how do you see it changing and what can be done so that you get best experience. Check more information at: http://www.transtutors.com/scholarship/

Award: Scholarship for use in freshman, sophomore, junior, senior, graduate, or postgraduate years; renewable. *Number:* 3. *Amount:* $1000.

Eligibility Requirements: Applicant must be American Indian/Alaska Native, Asian/Pacific Islander, Black (non-Hispanic), Hispanic and enrolled or expecting to enroll full- or part-time at a two-year or four-year institution or university. Available to U.S. and non-U.S. citizens.

Application Requirements: Essay, personal photograph. *Deadline:* November 30.

Contact: Aditya Singhal, Co-Founder
Transtutors
500startups
6th Floor Del Norte, 814 Mission Street
San Francisco, CA 94103
Phone: 415-619-1033
E-mail: aditya.singhal@transtutors.com

TRAVELNURSESOURCE.COM

https://www.travelnursesource.com/

FUTURE U.S. NURSE SCHOLARSHIP

Travel Nurse Source is awarding a $2,000 scholarship to a nursing student who composes a winning essay to our scholarship essay contest. We would like you to author your personal narrative including a brief introduction about yourself, your interests, and anything else you feel explains your story and reason for wanting this scholarship. Then in a 750-1000 word essay, please tell us about (1) your desire to become a registered nurse and how you plan to contribute to society as an RN, and (2) the significance that receiving this scholarship would have on you.

Award: Scholarship for use in freshman, sophomore, junior, or senior years; not renewable. *Number:* 1. *Amount:* $2000.

Eligibility Requirements: Applicant must be enrolled or expecting to enroll full- or part-time at a two-year or four-year or technical institution or university. Applicant must have 2.5 GPA or higher. Available to U.S. citizens.

Application Requirements: Essay. *Deadline:* October 13.

Contact: Troy Diffenderfer
E-mail: troy@track5media.com

TROPHYCENTRAL INC.

https://www.trophycentral.com

TROPHYCENTRAL SPORTSMANSHIP AND COMPASSION SCHOLARSHIP AWARD

TrophyCentral is thrilled to be able to offer a qualifying high school senior a $1,000 scholarship award to be applied to their first year's tuition to a college or university. The ideal candidate will attend a registered public or private high school in the U.S.; have a minimum high school GPA of 3.25 (out of 4.0) or equivalent through the first semester of their junior year; have demonstrated a unique or special form of sportsmanship, kindness or compassion; and will be attending college beginning in academic year 2019. Although not required, special attention will be given to applicants who are the first in their generation to attend college and entering a branch of the military (ex. ROTC).

Award: Scholarship for use in freshman year; not renewable. *Number:* 1. *Amount:* $1000.

Eligibility Requirements: Applicant must be high school student and planning to enroll or expecting to enroll full- or part-time at a two-year or four-year institution or university. Applicant must have 3.0 GPA or higher. Available to U.S. citizens.

Application Requirements: Application form, essay. *Deadline:* September 30.

Contact: Mr. Neil Rader, Founder and President
TrophyCentral Inc.
PO Box 155
Katonah, NY 10536
E-mail: scholarship@trophycentral.com

TRUCKER TO TRUCKER, LLC

http://www.truckertotrucker.com/

TRUCKERTOTRUCKER.COM COLLEGE SCHOLARSHIP

$500 college scholarship for individuals and their family members who are part of the transportation industry.

Award: Scholarship for use in freshman, sophomore, junior, senior, graduate, or postgraduate years; not renewable. *Number:* 2. *Amount:* $500.

Eligibility Requirements: Applicant must be age 17-99 and enrolled or expecting to enroll full-time at a two-year or four-year institution or university. Applicant or parent of applicant must have employment or volunteer experience in transportation industry. Available to U.S. citizens.

Application Requirements: Application form, essay. *Deadline:* June 1.

Contact: Scholarship Coordinator
E-mail: scholarship@truckertotrucker.com

TUITION EXCHANGE INC.

http://www.tuitionexchange.org/

TUITION EXCHANGE SCHOLARSHIPS

The Tuition Exchange is an association of over 670 colleges and universities awarding over 7200 full or substantial scholarships each year for children and other family members of faculty and staff employed at participating institutions. Students must maintain satisfactory academic progress and a cumulative GPA as established by each institution. Application procedures and deadlines vary by school. Contact Tuition Exchange Liaison Officer at home institution for details.

Award: Scholarship for use in freshman, sophomore, junior, senior, graduate, or postgraduate years; renewable. *Number:* 7000–9000. *Amount:* $4190–$52,140.

Eligibility Requirements: Applicant must be enrolled or expecting to enroll full- or part-time at a two-year or four-year institution or university. Applicant or parent of applicant must have employment or volunteer experience in teaching/education. Available to U.S. and non-U.S. citizens.

Application Requirements: Application form. *Deadline:* continuous.

Contact: Mr. Robert Shorb, Executive Director/CEO
Tuition Exchange Inc.
3 Bethesda Metro Center
Suite 700
Bethesda, MD 20814
Phone: 301-941-1827
E-mail: info@tuitionexchange.org

TURBOSQUID

https://www.turbosquid.com/

TURBOSQUID SPRING SCHOLARSHIP

TurboSquid has established a scholarship program to help identify and nurture future talent in the 3D industry. The topic for our initial scholarship is The Importance of Diversity for the 3D Industry. We want to hear from the future artists (or fans) of our industry. Let us know why you think it's important for 3D companies to diversify their workforce, or tell us what the 3D industry can do to better meet the needs of diverse consumers for whom they produce content or both. Research and write an essay on the following topic, The Importance of Diversity for the 3D Industry. Essay length should be 500-1000 words. You must be an active and graduating high school senior, or currently and actively enrolled as a full-time undergraduate or graduate college student with a minimum 3.0 minimum GPA.

Award: Scholarship for use in freshman, sophomore, junior, senior, or graduate years; not renewable. *Number:* 1. *Amount:* $5000.

Eligibility Requirements: Applicant must be enrolled or expecting to enroll full-time at a two-year or four-year or technical institution or university. Applicant must have 3.0 GPA or higher. Available to U.S. and non-U.S. citizens.

Application Requirements: Essay. *Deadline:* July 31.

Contact: DeLonna Day, Content Marketing Associate
E-mail: scholarships@turbosquid.com

TWO TEN FOOTWEAR FOUNDATION

http://www.twoten.org/

TWO TEN FOOTWEAR FOUNDATION SCHOLARSHIP

Renewable, merit and need-based award available to students who have 500 hours work experience in footwear, leather, or allied industries during year of application, or have a parent employed in one of these fields for at least two years. Must have proof of employment and maintain 2.5 GPA.

Award: Scholarship for use in freshman, sophomore, junior, or senior years; renewable. *Number:* 300–350. *Amount:* $2500–$5000.

Eligibility Requirements: Applicant must be enrolled or expecting to enroll full- or part-time at a two-year or four-year institution or university; resident of Alabama, Alaska, Arizona, Arkansas, California, Colorado, Connecticut, Delaware, Florida, Georgia, Hawaii, Idaho, Illinois, Indiana, Iowa, Kansas, Kentucky, Louisiana, Maine, Maryland, Massachusetts, Michigan, Minnesota, Mississippi, Missouri, Montana, Nebraska, Nevada, New Hampshire, New Jersey, New Mexico, New York, North Carolina, North Dakota, Ohio, Oklahoma, Ontario, Oregon, Pennsylvania, Puerto Rico, Rhode Island, South Carolina, South Dakota, Tennessee, Texas, Utah, Vermont, Virginia, Washington, West Virginia, Wisconsin, Wyoming and studying in Alabama, Alaska, Arizona, Arkansas, California, Colorado, Connecticut, Delaware, Florida, Georgia, Hawaii, Idaho, Illinois, Indiana, Iowa, Kansas, Kentucky, Louisiana, Maine, Maryland, Massachusetts, Michigan, Minnesota, Mississippi, Missouri, Montana, Nebraska, Nevada, New Hampshire, New Jersey, New Mexico, New York, North Carolina, North Dakota, Ohio, Oklahoma, Oregon, Pennsylvania, Puerto Rico, Rhode Island, South Carolina, South Dakota, Tennessee, Texas, Utah, Vermont, Virginia, Washington, West Virginia, Wisconsin, Wyoming. Applicant or parent of applicant must have employment or volunteer experience in leather/footwear industry. Applicant must have 2.5 GPA or higher. Available to U.S. citizens.

Application Requirements: Application form, essay, financial need analysis. *Deadline:* April 5.

Contact: Liz Watson, Scholarship Program Manager
Phone: 781-736-1500
E-mail: scholarship@twoten.org

UCB, INC.

http://www.ucb.com/

UCB FAMILY EPILEPSY SCHOLARSHIP

In 2018, UCB, Inc. will award 32 one-time scholarships to people living with epilepsy, their family members and caregivers who are pursuing higher educations. Thirty scholarships of up to $5,000 each will be awarded to outstanding applicants who demonstrate academic and personal achievement. In addition, 2 Epilepsy Leader Scholarships of $10,000 each will be awarded to outstanding applicants who demonstrate academic and personal achievement as well as a passion for advocacy, serving the epilepsy community and a persevering spirit. Students of all ages are welcome to apply and the scholarship can be used for a two-year, four-year, trade or specialty school.

Award: Scholarship for use in freshman, sophomore, junior, senior, or graduate years; not renewable. *Number:* 32. *Amount:* $5000–$10,000.

Eligibility Requirements: Applicant must be physically disabled and enrolled or expecting to enroll full- or part-time at a two-year or four-year or technical institution or university. Applicant must be physically disabled. Available to U.S. citizens.

Application Requirements: Application form, community service, essay, personal photograph. *Deadline:* March 5.

Contact: Mrs. Amy Bryant, UCB Family Epilepsy Scholarship Program
UCB, Inc.
c/o Summit Medical Communications
1421 East Broad Street, Suite 340
Fuquay-Varina, NC 27526
Phone: 866-825-1920
E-mail: ucbepilepsyscholarship@summitmedcomm.com

ULMAN CANCER FUND FOR YOUNG ADULTS

http://www.ulmanfund.org/scholarships

JACQUELINE SHEARER MEMORIAL SCHOLARSHIP

The Ulman Cancer Fund for Young Adults is committed to helping young adults continue their education after being affected by cancer through their own diagnosis or the diagnosis of a loved one. Many scholarships offered by UCF share similar applicant criteria. Applicants need only submit one application, which will be considered for any and all scholarships for which the student applies and is eligible.

Award: Scholarship for use in freshman, sophomore, junior, or senior years; not renewable. *Number:* 2. *Amount:* $2500.

Eligibility Requirements: Applicant must be age 15-39; enrolled or expecting to enroll full- or part-time at a four-year institution or university and resident of District of Columbia, Maryland, Virginia. Available to U.S. citizens.

Application Requirements: Application form, essay. *Deadline:* March 1.

Contact: Lauriann Parker, Scholarship Coordinator
Ulman Cancer Fund for Young Adults
1215 E. Fort Ave.
Ste. 104
Baltimore, MD 21230
Phone: 410-964-0202 Ext. 105
E-mail: scholarship@ulmanfund.org

JAMIE L. ROBERTS MEMORIAL SCHOLARSHIP AWARD

The Ulman Cancer Fund for Young Adults is committed to helping young adults continue their education after being affected by cancer through their own diagnosis or the diagnosis of a loved one. Many scholarships offered by UCF share similar applicant criteria. Applicants need only submit one application, which will be considered for any and all scholarships for which the student applies and is eligible.

Award: Scholarship for use in freshman, sophomore, junior, senior, or graduate years; not renewable. *Number:* 6. *Amount:* $2500.

Eligibility Requirements: Applicant must be age 15-39 and enrolled or expecting to enroll full- or part-time at a four-year institution or university. Available to U.S. citizens.

Application Requirements: Application form, essay. *Deadline:* March 1.

Contact: Lauriann Parker, Scholarship Coordinator
Ulman Cancer Fund for Young Adults
1215 E. Fort Ave.
Ste. 104
Baltimore, MD 21230
Phone: 410-964-0202 Ext. 105
E-mail: scholarship@ulmanfund.org

JEFFREY P. MEYER MEMORIAL SCHOLARSHIP

The Ulman Cancer Fund for Young Adults is committed to helping young adults continue their education after being affected by cancer through their own diagnosis or the diagnosis of a loved one. Many scholarships offered by UCF share similar applicant criteria. Applicants need only submit one application, which will be considered for any and all scholarships for which the student applies and is eligible.

Award: Scholarship for use in freshman, sophomore, junior, senior, or graduate years; not renewable. *Number:* 1. *Amount:* $2500.

Eligibility Requirements: Applicant must be age 15-39 and enrolled or expecting to enroll full- or part-time at a four-year institution or university. Applicant or parent of applicant must have employment or volunteer experience in community service. Available to U.S. citizens.

Application Requirements: Application form, essay. *Deadline:* March 1.

Contact: Lauriann Parker, Scholarship Coordinator
Ulman Cancer Fund for Young Adults
1215 E. Fort Ave.
Ste. 104
Baltimore, MD 21230
Phone: 410-964-0202 Ext. 105
E-mail: scholarship@ulmanfund.org

JILL WEAVER STARKMAN SCHOLARSHIP

The Ulman Cancer Fund for Young Adults is committed to helping young adults continue their education after being affected by cancer through their own diagnosis or the diagnosis of a loved one. Many scholarships offered by UCF share similar applicant criteria. Applicants need only submit one application, which will be considered for any and all scholarships for which the student applies and is eligible.

Award: Scholarship for use in freshman, sophomore, junior, senior, or graduate years; not renewable. *Number:* 1. *Amount:* $2500.

Eligibility Requirements: Applicant must be age 15-39 and enrolled or expecting to enroll full- or part-time at a four-year institution or university. Applicant or parent of applicant must have employment or volunteer experience in community service. Available to U.S. citizens.

Application Requirements: Application form, community service, essay. *Deadline:* March 1.

Contact: Lauriann Parker, Scholarship Coordinator
Ulman Cancer Fund for Young Adults
1215 E. Fort Ave.
Ste. 104
Baltimore, MD 21230
Phone: 410-964-0202 Ext. 105
E-mail: scholarship@ulmanfund.org

JOHN HANLEY MEMORIAL SCHOLARSHIP

The Ulman Cancer Fund for Young Adults is committed to helping young adults continue their education after being affected by cancer through their own diagnosis or the diagnosis of a loved one. Many scholarships offered by UCF share similar applicant criteria. Applicants need only submit one application, which will be considered for any and all scholarships for which the student applies and is eligible.

Award: Scholarship for use in freshman, sophomore, junior, or senior years; not renewable. *Number:* 6. *Amount:* $2500.

Eligibility Requirements: Applicant must be age 15-25 and enrolled or expecting to enroll full- or part-time at a four-year institution or university. Available to U.S. citizens.

Application Requirements: Application form, essay. *Deadline:* March 1.

Contact: Lauriann Parker, Scholarship Coordinator
Ulman Cancer Fund for Young Adults
1215 E. Fort Ave.
Ste. 104
Baltimore, MD 21230
Phone: 410-964-0202 Ext. 105
E-mail: scholarship@ulmanfund.org

LISA HIGGINS-HUSSMAN FOUNDATION SCHOLARSHIP

The Ulman Cancer Fund for Young Adults is committed to helping young adults continue their education after being affected by cancer through their own diagnosis or the diagnosis of a loved one. Many scholarships offered by UCF share similar applicant criteria. Applicants need only submit one application, which will be considered for any and all scholarships for which the student applies and is eligible.

Award: Scholarship for use in freshman, sophomore, junior, senior, or graduate years; not renewable. *Number:* 1. *Amount:* $2500.

Eligibility Requirements: Applicant must be age 15-39; enrolled or expecting to enroll full- or part-time at a four-year institution or university and resident of District of Columbia, Maryland, Virginia. Available to U.S. citizens.

Application Requirements: Application form, essay. *Deadline:* March 1.

Contact: Lauriann Parker, Scholarship Coordinator
Ulman Cancer Fund for Young Adults
1215 E. Fort Ave.
Ste. 104
Baltimore, MD 21230
Phone: 410-964-0202 Ext. 105
E-mail: scholarship@ulmanfund.org

MARILYN YETSO MEMORIAL SCHOLARSHIP

Provides support for the financial needs of college students who have a parent with cancer or who have lost a parent to cancer. Currently attending, or accepted to, a two- or four-year college, university or vocational program (including graduate and professional schools). Must be a resident of, or attending or planning to attend an educational institution in: Maryland, Virginia, or Washington, D.C.

Award: Scholarship for use in freshman, sophomore, junior, or senior years; not renewable. *Number:* 1–2. *Amount:* $1000.

Eligibility Requirements: Applicant must be age 15-39; enrolled or expecting to enroll full- or part-time at a two-year or four-year or technical institution or university and resident of District of Columbia, Maryland, Virginia. Available to U.S. citizens.

Application Requirements: Application form, essay, financial need analysis. *Deadline:* March 1.

Contact: Lauriann Parker, Scholarship Coordinator
Ulman Cancer Fund for Young Adults
1215 E. Fort Ave.
Ste. 104
Baltimore, MD 21230
Phone: 410-964-0202 Ext. 105
E-mail: scholarship@ulmanfund.org

OLIVIA M. MARQUART SCHOLARSHIP

The Olivia M. Marquart Scholarship was established in honor of a friend, sister, and daughter who continues to demonstrate strength and courage throughout her battle with Synovial Sarcomas in her lungs. The scholarship is awarded annually to a young adult who is either a cancer survivor or currently undergoing treatment. The recipient must demonstrate financial need and be a US citizen attending a college or university in the US. The applicant must reside in Pennsylvania.

Award: Scholarship for use in freshman, sophomore, junior, or senior years; not renewable. *Number:* 1. *Amount:* $2500.

Eligibility Requirements: Applicant must be age 15-39; enrolled or expecting to enroll full- or part-time at a four-year institution or university and resident of Pennsylvania. Available to U.S. citizens.

Application Requirements: Application form, essay. *Deadline:* March 1.

Contact: Lauriann Parker, Scholarship Coordinator
Ulman Cancer Fund for Young Adults
1215 E. Fort Ave.
Ste. 104
Baltimore, MD 21230
Phone: 410-964-0202 Ext. 105
E-mail: scholarship@ulmanfund.org

PERLITA LIWANAG MEMORIAL SCHOLARSHIP

The Perlita Liwanag Memorial Scholarship was established in memory of Perlita Liwanag who lost her life to pancreatic cancer. The purpose of this scholarship is to support the financial needs of a deserving young adult in the Washington, DC metro area (Maryland, Northern Virginia and DC) seeking higher education within the U.S.

Award: Scholarship for use in freshman, sophomore, junior, or senior years; not renewable. *Number:* 1. *Amount:* $2500.

Eligibility Requirements: Applicant must be age 15-39; enrolled or expecting to enroll full- or part-time at a four-year institution or university and resident of District of Columbia, Maryland, Virginia. Available to U.S. citizens.

Application Requirements: Application form, essay. *Deadline:* March 1.

Contact: Lauriann Parker, Scholarship Coordinator
Ulman Cancer Fund for Young Adults
1215 E. Fort Ave.
Ste. 104
Baltimore, MD 21230
Phone: 410-964-0202 Ext. 105
E-mail: scholarship@ulmanfund.org

SATOLA FAMILY SCHOLARSHIP

The Satola Family Scholarship Award was established in 2009 to support the financial needs of young adults who have been affected by cancer, and are seeking higher education. The Satola family wishes to recognize students who have battled cancer or have shown selflessness in supporting a loved one through their cancer experience. This award seeks to honor the applicant who best demonstrates courage, spirit, and determination. The Satola Family Scholarship Award is available to applicants who are young adult cancer survivors diagnosed between the ages of 15-39 OR young adults who have lost a parent/guardian/sibling to cancer OR have a parent/guardian/sibling that has been diagnosed or undergoing treatment for cancer while they were a young adult. Candidates must be degree-seeking and United States citizens.

Award: Scholarship for use in freshman, sophomore, junior, or senior years; not renewable. *Number:* 1. *Amount:* $2500.

Eligibility Requirements: Applicant must be age 15-39 and enrolled or expecting to enroll full- or part-time at a four-year institution or university. Available to U.S. citizens.

Application Requirements: Application form, essay. *Deadline:* March 1.

Contact: Lauriann Parker, Scholarship Coordinator
Ulman Cancer Fund for Young Adults
1215 E. Fort Ave.
Ste. 104
Baltimore, MD 21230
Phone: 410-964-0202 Ext. 105
E-mail: scholarship@ulmanfund.org

SEAN SILVER MEMORIAL SCHOLARSHIP AWARD

Sean Silver was a graduate of Columbia College in Chicago, managing to obtain his degree while in extensive treatment for a rare from of Sarcoma named Chordoma. Sean studies focused on music journalism, combining his passions of music and writing into what he hoped would be a fruitful career as a rock journalist. While undergoing multiple surgeries, radiation and chemotherapy courses, he persevered to obtain his degree from Columbia at the age of 31. Less than a year after graduating from Columbia, Sean lost his battle on May 13, 2007. The Sean Silver Memorial Scholarship Award is available to applicants who are degree seeking United States citizens, age 15-30 at the time of application. Applicants must be currently undergoing active treatment for cancer.

Award: Scholarship for use in freshman, sophomore, junior, or senior years; not renewable. *Number:* 2. *Amount:* $5000.

Eligibility Requirements: Applicant must be age 17-30 and enrolled or expecting to enroll full- or part-time at a four-year institution. Available to U.S. citizens.

Application Requirements: Application form, community service, essay. *Deadline:* March 1.

Contact: Ulman Cancer Fund Scholarship Program Coordinator
Ulman Cancer Fund for Young Adults
1215 East Fort Avenue
Suite 104
Baltimore, MD 21230
Phone: 410-964-0202 Ext. 105
E-mail: scholarship@ulmanfund.org

VERA YIP MEMORIAL SCHOLARSHIP

The Vera Yip Memorial Scholarship Award was established to support the financial needs of young adults who are impacted by cancer and seeking higher education. Vera was committed to promoting a love of learning and helped to inspire and empower others to pursue their personal, educational and professional dreams in the face of adversity. This award seeks to honor the applicant who best demonstrates the courage, determination, motivation and dedication that Vera displayed during her lifetime.

Award: Scholarship for use in freshman, sophomore, junior, or senior years; not renewable. *Number:* 1. *Amount:* $2500.

Eligibility Requirements: Applicant must be age 17-35; enrolled or expecting to enroll full- or part-time at a four-year institution or university; resident of District of Columbia, Maryland, Virginia and studying in District of Columbia, Maryland, Virginia. Available to U.S. citizens.

Application Requirements: Application form, community service, essay. *Deadline:* March 1.

Contact: Lauriann Parker, Scholarship Coordinator
Ulman Cancer Fund for Young Adults
1215 E. Fort Ave.
Ste. 104
Baltimore, MD 21230
Phone: 410-964-0202 Ext. 105
E-mail: scholarship@ulmanfund.org

VITTORIA DIANNA RICARDO MEMORIAL SCHOLARSHIP

The Vittoria Dianna Ricardo Memorial Scholarship is in honor of a worldly woman who preferred to stay out of the limelight and remain quite and reserved. An immigrant from Italy, she worked hard to raise a family and care for her husband who was sick with kidney disease. She lost her battle with lung cancer in 2008. The degree-seeking applicant must be either a cancer survivor or has supported a family member through their cancer experience. Candidates must demonstrate financial need, and be enrolled in any accredited four-year college or university. Applicants must have a 3.0 GPA or better. Freshman may apply but must have a cumulative high school GPA of 3.0 or better.

Award: Scholarship for use in sophomore, junior, senior, or graduate years; not renewable. *Number:* 1. *Amount:* $2500.

Eligibility Requirements: Applicant must be age 17-39 and enrolled or expecting to enroll full- or part-time at a four-year institution or university. Applicant must have 3.0 GPA or higher. Available to U.S. citizens.

Application Requirements: Application form, essay. *Deadline:* March 1.

Contact: Lauriann Parker, Scholarship Coordinator
Ulman Cancer Fund for Young Adults
1215 E. Fort Ave.
Ste. 104
Baltimore, MD 21230
Phone: 410-964-0202 Ext. 105
E-mail: scholarship@ulmanfund.org

UNICO FOUNDATION INC.

http://www.unico.org/

ALPHONSE A. MIELE SCHOLARSHIP

Candidates must be of Italian heritage and reside in the home state of an active UNICO Chapter. Applications must be submitted online. Scholarship is available to a graduating high school senior. This scholarship is valued at $6,000; paid out at $1,500 per year, over four years. Candidates are to go to the UNICO National website (http://www.unico.org), and click on the Scholarship tab. They will find complete information and submission instructions.

Award: Scholarship for use in freshman, sophomore, junior, or senior years; renewable. *Number:* 1. *Amount:* $1500.

Eligibility Requirements: Applicant must be of Italian heritage; high school student; planning to enroll or expecting to enroll full-time at a four-year institution or university and resident of California, Connecticut, Delaware, Florida, Illinois, Massachusetts, Minnesota, Missouri, New Jersey, New York, Pennsylvania, Tennessee, Wisconsin. Applicant must have 3.0 GPA or higher. Available to U.S. citizens.

Application Requirements: Application form, essay, financial need analysis. *Deadline:* April 15.

Contact: Joan Tidona, Scholarship Director
Phone: 973-808-0035
Fax: 973-808-0043
E-mail: uniconational@unico.org

BERNARD AND CAROLYN TORRACO MEMORIAL NURSING SCHOLARSHIP PROGRAM

$2,500 award for students currently enrolled in an accredited nursing degree program in the United States, completing core nursing courses at either an associate degree School of Nursing, a collegiate School of Nursing, or a diploma School of Nursing. Proof of enrollment must be provided. Preference will be given to applicants demonstrating financial need. A current FAFSA Student Aid Report (SAR) or previous year tax return is required. A candidate must hold U.S. citizenship and reside in the home state of an active UNICO chapter. Applications must be submitted online. Candidates are to go to the UNICO National website (http://www.unico.org), and click on the Scholarship tab. There they will find complete information and submission instructions.

Award: Scholarship for use in freshman, sophomore, junior, or senior years; not renewable. *Number:* 10. *Amount:* $2500.

Eligibility Requirements: Applicant must be enrolled or expecting to enroll full- or part-time at a two-year or four-year institution or university and resident of California, Connecticut, Delaware, Florida, Illinois, Maryland, Massachusetts, Minnesota, Missouri, New Jersey, New York, Pennsylvania, Tennessee, Virginia, Wisconsin. Applicant must have 3.0 GPA or higher. Available to U.S. citizens.

Application Requirements: Application form, financial need analysis. *Deadline:* April 15.

Contact: Joan Tidona, Scholarship Director
Phone: 973-808-0035
Fax: 973-808-0043
E-mail: uniconational@unico.org

DIMATTIO CELLI FAMILY STUDY ABROAD SCHOLARSHIP

This award is for study in Italy. Candidates must be currently enrolled, full-time, in an accredited college/university in the United States. The study abroad program must be eligible for credit by the student's college/university. Candidates must be of Italian heritage and reside in the home state of an active UNICO Chapter. Applications must be submitted online. Candidates are to go to the UNICO National website (http://www.unico.org), and click on the Scholarship tab. There they will find complete information and submission instructions.

Award: Scholarship for use in freshman, sophomore, junior, or senior years; not renewable. *Number:* 2. *Amount:* $1250.

Contact: Lauriann Parker, Scholarship Coordinator
Ulman Cancer Fund for Young Adults
1215 E. Fort Ave.
Ste. 104
Baltimore, MD 21230
Phone: 410-964-0202 Ext. 105
E-mail: scholarship@ulmanfund.org

Eligibility Requirements: Applicant must be of Italian heritage; enrolled or expecting to enroll full-time at a four-year institution or university and resident of California, Connecticut, Florida, Illinois, Maryland, Massachusetts, Minnesota, New Jersey, New York, Pennsylvania, Tennessee, Virginia, Wisconsin. Applicant must have 3.0 GPA or higher. Available to U.S. citizens.

Application Requirements: Application form. *Deadline:* March 1.

Contact: Joan Tidona, Scholarship Director
     Phone: 973-808-0035
     Fax: 973-808-0043
     E-mail: uniconational@unico.org

ELLA T. GRASSO LITERARY SCHOLARSHIP

Application is open to matriculated college students. The candidate is required to submit a short story or essay celebrating their Italian heritage. Participants must reside in the home state of an active UNICO Chapter. Applications must be submitted online. Candidates are to go to the UNICO National website (http://www.unico.org), and click on the Scholarship tab. There they will find complete information and submission instructions.

Award: Scholarship for use in sophomore, junior, senior, graduate, or postgraduate years; not renewable. *Number:* 2. *Amount:* $1000.

Eligibility Requirements: Applicant must be of Italian heritage; enrolled or expecting to enroll full-time at a four-year institution or university and resident of California, Connecticut, Delaware, Florida, Illinois, Maryland, Massachusetts, Minnesota, Missouri, New Jersey, New York, Pennsylvania, Tennessee, Virginia, Wisconsin. Applicant must have 3.0 GPA or higher. Available to U.S. citizens.

Application Requirements: Application form, essay. *Deadline:* April 15.

Contact: Joan Tidona, Scholarship Director
     Phone: 973-808-0035
     Fax: 973-808-0043
     E-mail: uniconational@unico.org

GUGLIELMO MARCONI ENGINEERING SCHOLARSHIP

An applicant must be a United States citizen of Italian heritage, currently enrolled full time in an accredited campus based college/university, pursuing an Engineering Degree. A candidate must reside in the home state of an active UNICO Chapter. Applications must be submitted online. Candidates are to go to the UNICO National website (http://www.unico.org), and click on the Scholarship tab. There they will find complete information and submission instructions. Preference is given to candidates demonstrating financial need.

Award: Scholarship for use in sophomore, junior, senior, or graduate years; not renewable. *Number:* 1. *Amount:* $1250.

Eligibility Requirements: Applicant must be of Italian heritage; enrolled or expecting to enroll full-time at a four-year institution or university and resident of California, Connecticut, Delaware, Florida, Illinois, Maryland, Massachusetts, Minnesota, Missouri, New Jersey, New York, Pennsylvania, Tennessee, Virginia, Wisconsin. Applicant must have 3.0 GPA or higher. Available to U.S. citizens.

Application Requirements: Application form, essay, financial need analysis. *Deadline:* April 15.

Contact: Joan Tidona, Scholarship Director
     Phone: 973-808-0035
     Fax: 973-808-0043
     E-mail: uniconational@unico.org

INSERRA SCHOLARSHIPS

The UNICO Foundation will grant two scholarships valued at $2,500 to students currently attending, fulltime, an accredited campus based college/university in the United States pursuing a degree. Candidates must be of Italian heritage and reside in the home state of an active UNICO Chapter. Applications must be submitted online. Candidates are to go to the UNICO National website (http://www.unico.org), and click on the Scholarship tab. They will find complete information and submission instructions.

Award: Scholarship for use in sophomore, junior, senior, or graduate years; not renewable. *Number:* 2. *Amount:* $2500.

Eligibility Requirements: Applicant must be of Italian heritage; enrolled or expecting to enroll full-time at a four-year institution or university and resident of California, Connecticut, Delaware, Florida, Illinois, Maryland, Massachusetts, Missouri, New Jersey, New York, Pennsylvania, Tennessee, Virginia, Wisconsin. Applicant must have 3.0 GPA or higher. Available to U.S. citizens.

Application Requirements: Application form, essay, financial need analysis. *Deadline:* April 15.

Contact: Joan Tidona, Scholarship Director
     Phone: 973-808-0035
     Fax: 973-808-0043
     E-mail: uniconational@unico.org

MAJOR DON S. GENTILE SCHOLARSHIP

Candidates must be of Italian heritage and reside in the home state of an active UNICO Chapter. Applications must be submitted online. Scholarship is available to a graduating high school senior. This scholarship is valued at $6,000; paid out at $1,500 per year, over four years. Candidates are to go to the UNICO National website (http://www.unico.org), and click on the Scholarship tab. They will find complete information and submission instructions.

Award: Scholarship for use in freshman, sophomore, junior, or senior years; renewable. *Number:* 1. *Amount:* $1500.

Eligibility Requirements: Applicant must be of Italian heritage; high school student; planning to enroll or expecting to enroll full-time at a four-year institution or university and resident of California, Connecticut, Delaware, Florida, Illinois, Massachusetts, New Jersey, New York, Pennsylvania, Tennessee, Wisconsin. Applicant must have 3.0 GPA or higher. Available to U.S. citizens.

Application Requirements: Application form, essay, financial need analysis. *Deadline:* April 15.

Contact: Joan Tidona, Scholarship Director
     Phone: 973-808-0035
     Fax: 973-808-0043
     E-mail: uniconational@unico.org

MARIA AND PAOLO ALESSIO SOUTHERN ITALY SCHOLARSHIP

The UNICO Foundation will provide a scholarship, valued at $2,500 to a student enrolled full-time, in an accredited college/university program in the United States pursuing a degree. An applicant must be a United States citizen of Southern Italian heritage, specifically the regions of: Abruzzo, Basilicata, Campania, Calabria, Latium, Molise, Puglia, Sardinia, Sicilia. Applications must be submitted online. Candidates are to go to the UNICO National website (http://www.unico.org), and click on the Scholarship tab. There they will find complete information and submission instructions. Financial need is a consideration.

Award: Scholarship for use in sophomore, junior, or senior years; not renewable. *Number:* 1. *Amount:* $2500.

Eligibility Requirements: Applicant must be of Italian heritage and enrolled or expecting to enroll full-time at a four-year institution or university. Applicant must have 3.0 GPA or higher. Available to U.S. citizens.

Application Requirements: Application form, financial need analysis. *Deadline:* April 15.

Contact: Joan Tidona, Scholarship Director
     Phone: 973-808-0035
     Fax: 973-808-0043
     E-mail: uniconational@unico.org

RALPH J. TORRACO SCHOLARSHIP

The UNICO Foundation will grant two scholarships valued at $2,500 each, to students enrolled full-time, in an accredited college/university program in the United States pursuing a degree. A nominee must hold United States citizenship. This program is open to applicants of all ethnicities. Candidates must reside in the home state of an active UNICO Chapter. Applications must be submitted online. Candidates are to go to the UNICO National website (http://www.unico.org), and click on the Scholarship tab. There they will find complete information and submission instructions. Preference is given to candidates demonstrating financial need.

Award: Scholarship for use in sophomore, junior, senior, or graduate years; not renewable. *Number:* 2. *Amount:* $2500.

Eligibility Requirements: Applicant must be enrolled or expecting to enroll full-time at a four-year institution or university and resident of California, Connecticut, Delaware, Florida, Illinois, Maryland, Massachusetts, Minnesota, Missouri, New Jersey, New York, Pennsylvania, Tennessee, Virginia, Wisconsin. Applicant must have 3.0 GPA or higher. Available to U.S. citizens.

Application Requirements: Application form, essay, financial need analysis. *Deadline:* April 15.

Contact: Joan Tidona, Scholarship Director
  Phone: 973-808-0035
  Fax: 973-808-0043
  E-mail: uniconational@unico.org

THEODORE MAZZA SCHOLARSHIP

Candidates must be of Italian heritage and reside in the home state of an active UNICO Chapter. Applications must be submitted online. This scholarship, available to a graduating high school senior, is valued at $6,000; paid out at $1,500 per year, over four years. Candidates are to go to the UNICO National website (http://www.unico.org), and click on the Scholarship tab. They will find complete information and submission instructions.

Award: Scholarship for use in freshman, sophomore, junior, or senior years; renewable. *Number:* 1. *Amount:* $1500.

Eligibility Requirements: Applicant must be high school student; planning to enroll or expecting to enroll full-time at a four-year institution or university and resident of California, Connecticut, Delaware, Florida, Illinois, Maryland, Massachusetts, Minnesota, Missouri, New Jersey, New York, Pennsylvania, Tennessee, Virginia, Wisconsin. Applicant must have 3.0 GPA or higher. Available to U.S. citizens.

Application Requirements: Application form, essay, financial need analysis. *Deadline:* April 15.

Contact: Joan Tidona, Scholarship Director
  Phone: 973-808-0035
  Fax: 973-808-0043
  E-mail: uniconational@unico.org

WILLIAM C. DAVINI SCHOLARSHIP

Candidates must be of Italian heritage and reside in the home state of an active UNICO Chapter. Applications must be submitted online. This scholarship, available to a graduating high school senior, is valued at $6,000; paid out at $1,500 per year, over four years. Candidates are to go to the UNICO National website (http://www.unico.org), and click on the Scholarship tab. They will find complete information and submission instructions.

Award: Scholarship for use in freshman, sophomore, junior, or senior years; renewable. *Number:* 1. *Amount:* $1500.

Eligibility Requirements: Applicant must be high school student; planning to enroll or expecting to enroll full-time at a four-year institution or university and resident of California, Connecticut, Delaware, Florida, Illinois, Maryland, Massachusetts, Minnesota, Missouri, New Jersey, New York, Pennsylvania, Tennessee, Virginia, Wisconsin. Applicant must have 3.0 GPA or higher. Available to U.S. citizens.

Application Requirements: Application form, essay, financial need analysis. *Deadline:* April 15.

Contact: Joan Tidona, Scholarship Director
  Phone: 973-808-0035
  Fax: 973-808-0043
  E-mail: uniconational@unico.org

UNION PLUS SCHOLARSHIP PROGRAM

http://www.unionplus.org/

UNION PLUS EDUCATION FOUNDATION SCHOLARSHIP PROGRAM
• *See page 584*

UNITED STATES BOWLING CONGRESS

http://www.bowl.com/

USBC ANNUAL ZEB SCHOLARSHIP
• *See page 585*

UNITED STATES SUBMARINE VETERANS

https://www.ussvi.org/Documents.asp?Type=Scholarship|Application

UNITED STATES SUBMARINE VETERANS INC. NATIONAL SCHOLARSHIP PROGRAM
• *See page 586*

UNITED TRANSPORTATION UNION INSURANCE ASSOCIATION

http://www.utuia.org/

UTUIA SCHOLARSHIP

Scholarships of $2000 awarded to undergraduate students. Requirements of a UTUIA scholarship applicant are that he or she be a U.S. citizen, at least a high school senior or equivalent, and age 25 or under. Applicants must be associated with the UTUIA by either owning a UTUIA insurance policy, or by being the child or grandchild of a current UTUIA policyholder. Scholarship applicants must also be associated with the SMART Transportation Division by belonging to the union, or by being the child or grandchild of an active or lifetime SMART Transportation Division member. Applicants also must be accepted for admittance, or already enrolled, for at least 12 credit hours per quarter or semester at a recognized institution of higher learning (university, college or junior college, nursing or technical school offering college credit).

Award: Scholarship for use in freshman, sophomore, junior, or senior years; renewable. *Number:* 50. *Amount:* $2000.

Eligibility Requirements: Applicant must be enrolled or expecting to enroll full-time at a two-year or four-year or technical institution or university. Available to U.S. citizens.

Application Requirements: Application form. *Deadline:* March 31.

Contact: Beth Thomas, Compensation Specialist
  Phone: 216-227-5254

UNIVERSITY CONSORTIUM FOR LIBERIA

http://ucliberia.com/

JOSEPH N. BOAKAI SR. HIGHER EDUCATION SCHOLARSHIP

The University Consortium for Liberia (UCL) Scholarship Program was established in 2015 by the UCL Board of Directors. A special scholarship was established on behalf of Joseph N. Boakai, Sr., the Vice President of the Republic of Liberia, in dedication of his support to educate our youth. The UCL Scholarship program is open to Liberian students and/or students of Liberian decent pursuing a post-secondary education at a U.S. College or University. Priority will be given to students applying to a UCL college/university noted below who are considered Institutional Partners.

Award: Scholarship for use in freshman, sophomore, junior, senior, graduate, or postgraduate years; not renewable. *Number:* 5–10. *Amount:* $500–$1000.

Eligibility Requirements: Applicant must be Black (non-Hispanic) and enrolled or expecting to enroll full- or part-time at a two-year or four-year or technical institution or university. Applicant must have 3.0 GPA or higher. Available to U.S. and non-U.S. citizens.

Application Requirements: Application form. *Deadline:* May 15.

Contact: HON. Cynthia Blandford, University Consortium for Liberia Scholarship Committee
  E-mail: uclscholarship@gmail.com

U.S. COAST GUARD

http://www.gocoastguard/cspi

COLLEGE STUDENT PRE-COMMISSIONING INITIATIVE (CSPI)

See scholarship information at the following website, http://www.gocoastguard/cspi

Award: Scholarship for use in junior or senior years; renewable. *Number:* 70. *Amount:* $12,850.

Eligibility Requirements: Applicant must be physically disabled or visually impaired; American Indian/Alaska Native, Asian/Pacific Islander, Black (non-Hispanic), Hispanic; age 19-28 and enrolled or expecting to enroll full-time at a four-year institution or university. Applicant must be physically disabled or visually impaired. Applicant must have 2.5 GPA or higher. Available to U.S. citizens. Applicant must have served in the Coast Guard.

Application Requirements: Application form, financial need analysis, interview. *Deadline:* continuous.

Contact: Lt. Patrick Bennett
U.S. Coast Guard
2703 Martin Luther King JR Ave SE
Washington, DC 20593
Phone: 202-795-6855
E-mail: patrick.g.bennett@uscg.mil

VALUEPENGUIN

http://www.valuepenguin.com

VALUEPENGUIN SCHOLARSHIP

The cost of education in the U.S. is on the rise. In addition, the National Center for Education Statistics reports that only 12.8% of undergraduate students receive private grants. These facts illustrate how difficult it is for many students across the nation to afford basic necessities, such as textbooks and transportation. let alone tuition. In our coverage of personal finance, we've discovered how these issues have far reaching effects on an individual's financial well being. Oftentimes; they continue to be a burden well after graduation. That's why ValuePenguin is offering a $2,000 scholarship to eligible undergraduate students in the U.S. To be considered for the scholarship, submit a 500 to 750 word response (for a total word count of 1,000 to 1,500) to each of the following two questions: 1) What is a non-essential item or activity you splurge on regularly in college? How much do you think you have spent on it since starting college and do you think it's worthwhile? 2) If you had to teach a personal finance class to college students, what are the top three topics you would cover and why?

Award: Scholarship for use in freshman, sophomore, junior, or senior years; not renewable. *Number:* 1. *Amount:* $2000.

Eligibility Requirements: Applicant must be enrolled or expecting to enroll full- or part-time at a two-year or four-year institution or university and studying in Alabama, Alaska, Arizona, Arkansas, California, Colorado, Connecticut, Delaware, District of Columbia, Florida, Georgia, Guam, Hawaii, Idaho, Illinois, Indiana, Iowa, Kansas, Kentucky, Louisiana, Maine, Maryland, Massachusetts, Michigan, Minnesota, Mississippi, Missouri, Montana, Nebraska, Nevada, New Hampshire, New Jersey, New Mexico, New York, North Carolina, North Dakota, Ohio, Oklahoma, Oregon, Pennsylvania, Puerto Rico, Rhode Island, South Carolina, South Dakota, Tennessee, Texas, Utah, Vermont, Virginia, Washington, West Virginia, Wisconsin, Wyoming. Available to U.S. and non-U.S. citizens.

Application Requirements: Application form, essay. *Deadline:* December 15.

Contact: Rebecca Wessell, Scholarship Manager
ValuePenguin
597 5th Avenue
Floor 5
New York, NY 10017
Phone: 646-248-5684
E-mail: scholarships@valuepenguin.com

VANILLA PILGRIM FOUNDATION

https://www.vanillapilgrim.com/

2018 OPEN ESSAY COMPETITION

There are plenty of scholarships for the athletic, the intelligent, minorities, the handicapped, the needy. We think it is time to have a scholarship for the "Everyday Joe" or "Plain Jane." We think you are just as special. In 400-500 words, tell us what makes you the most vanilla/boring person in the world. Each month we establish a winner and announce the name as well as post the essay to serve as a model for others. Every May we will judge the 12 winners to see who wins the $700 dollar scholarship.

Award: Scholarship for use in freshman, sophomore, junior, senior, graduate, or postgraduate years; not renewable. *Number:* 1. *Amount:* $700.

Eligibility Requirements: Applicant must be enrolled or expecting to enroll full- or part-time at a two-year or four-year or technical institution or university and resident of Alabama, Alaska, Arizona, Arkansas, California, Colorado, Connecticut, Delaware, District of Columbia, Florida, Georgia, Hawaii, Idaho, Illinois, Indiana, Iowa, Kansas, Kentucky, Louisiana, Maine, Maryland, Massachusetts, Michigan, Minnesota, Mississippi, Missouri, Montana, Nebraska, Nevada, New Hampshire, New Jersey, New Mexico, New York, North Carolina, North Dakota, Ohio, Oklahoma, Oregon, Pennsylvania, Rhode Island, South Carolina, South Dakota, Tennessee, Texas, Utah, Vermont, Virginia, Washington, West Virginia, Wisconsin, Wyoming. Available to U.S. citizens.

Application Requirements: Essay. *Fee:* $4. *Deadline:* May 1.

Contact: Mr. John Allred
E-mail: vanillapilgrimfoundation@gmail.com

VETERANAID.ORG

https://www.veteranaid.org

VETERAN BENEFITS SCHOLARSHIP

VeteranAid.org Veterans Benefits Scholarship: Three $2,000 scholarships available to students enrolled in an Associate's degree, Bachelor's degree, or graduate level program at an accredited 2-year college or 4-year university. Each eligible student will submit a 500-750 word essay on the following essay topic: give an example of one veterans benefit and explain how it helps senior veterans, then propose your own benefit to help senior veterans.

Award: Scholarship for use in freshman, sophomore, junior, senior, graduate, or postgraduate years; not renewable. *Number:* 3. *Amount:* $2000.

Eligibility Requirements: Applicant must be enrolled or expecting to enroll full-time at a two-year or four-year institution or university. Available to U.S. citizens.

Application Requirements: Essay. *Deadline:* December 31.

Contact: Sarah Johnson
Phone: 888-907-3272
E-mail: scholarship@veteranaid.org

VETERANS UNITED FOUNDATION

http://www.enhancelives.com

VETERANS UNITED FOUNDATION SCHOLARSHIP

This scholarship is for a surviving spouse or a surviving child of a deceased service member or a deceased veteran, or a veteran with 100% service connected disability currently pursuing post-secondary education. The program's primary goal is to assist veterans and their families by awarding up to ten $50,000 scholarships per semester to help pay for tuition, fees, room and board, books, and supplies pertinent to degree. For more information visit http://www.enhancelives.com/scholarships

Award: Scholarship for use in freshman, sophomore, junior, senior, graduate, or postgraduate years; not renewable. *Number:* 1–10. *Amount:* $1–$50,000.

Eligibility Requirements: Applicant must be enrolled or expecting to enroll full-time at a two-year or four-year or technical institution or university. Available to U.S. citizens. Applicant or parent must meet one or more of the following requirements: general military experience; retired from active duty; disabled or killed as a result of military service; prisoner of war; or missing in action.

Application Requirements: Application form, driver's license, essay, financial need analysis, personal photograph. *Deadline:* March 30.

Contact: Jessica Mueller, Foundation Outreach Coordinator
E-mail: foundation@veteransunited.com

WARD LAW GROUP, PL

http://thecoveragelawyer.com/

WARD LAW GROUP BETTER FUTURE SCHOLARSHIP

This scholarship is offered to any student currently enrolled in an accredited community college, undergraduate, or graduate program in the United States. This includes incoming first-year college students who are high school graduates or possess a GED. For more information please visit following webpage: http://thecoveragelawyer.com/#scholarship

Award: Scholarship for use in freshman, sophomore, junior, senior, graduate, or postgraduate years; not renewable. *Number:* 1. *Amount:* $500.

Eligibility Requirements: Applicant must be enrolled or expecting to enroll full- or part-time at a two-year or four-year or technical institution or university. Applicant must have 3.0 GPA or higher. Available to U.S. and non-U.S. citizens.

Application Requirements: Application form, essay. *Deadline:* January 31.

Contact: Gregory Ward
E-mail: info@thecoveragelawyer.com

WESTERN INTERSTATE COMMISSION FOR HIGHER EDUCATION

http://www.wiche.edu/

WICHE'S WESTERN UNDERGRADUATE EXCHANGE (WUE)

Students from designated states can enroll in two- and four-year undergraduate programs at some 160 public institutions in participating Western states and pay 150 percent of resident tuition, or less. Applicants apply directly to the admissions office at participating institution. Applicants must indicate that they want to be considered for the WUE tuition discount. Participating institutions and the majors available at the WUE rate are listed at http://wiche.edu/wue.

Award: Scholarship for use in freshman, sophomore, junior, or senior years; renewable.

Eligibility Requirements: Applicant must be enrolled or expecting to enroll full-time at a two-year or four-year institution or university; resident of Alaska, Arizona, California, Colorado, Guam, Hawaii, Idaho, Montana, Nevada, New Mexico, North Dakota, Oregon, South Dakota, Utah, Washington, Wyoming and studying in Alaska, Arizona, California, Colorado, Hawaii, Idaho, Montana, Nevada, New Mexico, North Dakota, Oregon, South Dakota, Utah, Washington, Wyoming. Available to U.S. citizens.

Application Requirements: Application form, driver's license. *Deadline:* continuous.

Contact: Ms. Kim Nawrocki, Administrative Assistant, Student Exchange
Western Interstate Commission for Higher Education
3035 Center Green Drive
Boulder, CO 80301
Phone: 303-541-0270
E-mail: knawrocki@wiche.edu

WHITLEY LAW FIRM

https://whitleylawfirm.com/

WHITLEY LAW FIRM OPIOID CRISIS SCHOLARSHIP

In 2016 it is believed that 64,000 Americans died from drug overdoses, 21 percent more than the rate in 2015, according to the Centers for Disease Control and Prevention. Driving overdose deaths are opioids such as prescription painkillers, heroin, and fentanyl. Whitley would like to announce they have established the Whitley Law Firm Opioid Crisis Scholarship in the amount of $1,500 to support up and coming lawyers and raise the awareness of this ongoing epidemic. For more information, please visit: https://whitleylawfirm.com/#scholarship

Award: Scholarship for use in freshman, sophomore, junior, senior, graduate, or postgraduate years; not renewable. *Number:* 1. *Amount:* $1500.

Eligibility Requirements: Applicant must be enrolled or expecting to enroll full- or part-time at a two-year or four-year or technical institution or university. Applicant must have 3.0 GPA or higher.

Application Requirements: Application form, essay. *Deadline:* July 31.

Contact: Robert Whitley
E-mail: info@whitleylawfirm.com

WOLTERMAN LAW OFFICE, LPA

https://www.woltermanlaw.com/

WOLTERMAN LAW OFFICE LPA HOPE FOR THE FUTURE SCHOLARSHIP

Are you an Ohio student who will be enrolled in an Ohio two-year to five-year institution next year? Do you need help paying for schooling or supplies? You are not alone. College is not cheap, but we don't want that to stop you from pursuing this irreplaceable experience. At Wolterman Law Office LPA, we have experienced first-hand the benefits of higher education. That is why we are offering a $1500 scholarship to help one Ohio student go to college, law school, or other institute of higher education. To apply, create a short (30–120 second) video and accompanying essay or submit an essay (must be at least 1,000 words), telling us the following things: 1. What does community leadership mean to you?; 2. How have you made your Ohio community a better place? Please provide specific examples showing your commitment to community service and leadership. Applications are due May 6th, 2018.

Award: Scholarship for use in freshman, sophomore, junior, senior, or graduate years; not renewable. *Number:* 1. *Amount:* $1500.

Eligibility Requirements: Applicant must be enrolled or expecting to enroll full- or part-time at a two-year or four-year or technical institution or university; resident of Ohio and studying in Ohio. Available to U.S. citizens.

Application Requirements: Application form, essay. *Deadline:* May 6.

Contact: Scholarship Coordinator
E-mail: coordinator@ourscholarship.io

WOMEN MARINES ASSOCIATION

http://www.womenmarines.org

ETHYL AND ARMIN WIEBKE MEMORIAL SCHOLARSHIPS

One scholarship awarded each year to a qualified applicant.

Award: Scholarship for use in freshman, sophomore, junior, senior, graduate, or postgraduate years; not renewable. *Number:* 1. *Amount:* $1500.

Eligibility Requirements: Applicant must be enrolled or expecting to enroll full-time at a two-year or four-year institution or university. Applicant must have 3.0 GPA or higher. Available to U.S. citizens.

Application Requirements: Application form, community service, essay, personal photograph. *Deadline:* February 28.

Contact: Col. Dorothy Stover-Kendrick, Scholarship Chair
Women Marines Association
PO Box 134
Stilwell, KS 66085
Phone: 888-525-1943 Ext. 101
E-mail: scholarship@womenmarines.org

THE LILY H. GRIDLEY MEMORIAL SCHOLARSHIP

see http://www.womenmarines.org

Award: Scholarship for use in freshman, sophomore, junior, senior, graduate, or postgraduate years; not renewable. *Amount:* $1500.

Eligibility Requirements: Applicant must be enrolled or expecting to enroll full-time at a two-year or four-year or technical institution or university. Applicant must have 3.0 GPA or higher. Available to U.S. citizens.

Application Requirements: Application form, community service, essay, personal photograph. *Deadline:* February 28.

Contact: Col. Dorothy Stover-Kendrick, Scholarship Chair
Women Marines Association
PO Box 134
Stilwell, KS 66085
Phone: 888-525-1943 Ext. 101
E-mail: scholarship@womenmarines.org

WMA MEMORIAL SCHOLARSHIPS

To be eligible for a WMA scholarships applicants must meet one of the following qualifications: 1. Have served, or be serving in the United States Marine Corps or Reserve; 2. Be a direct descendant by blood, legal adoption or stepchild of a Marine on active duty, or who has served honorably in the United States Marine Corps, Regular or Reserve; 3. Be a sibling or a descendant of a sibling by blood, legal adoption, or step-child of a Marine on active duty, or who has served honorably in the United States Marine Corps, Regular or Reserve; 4. Be a spouse of a Marine; or 5. Have completed two (2) years in the Marine Corps JROTC program.

Award: Scholarship for use in freshman, sophomore, junior, senior, graduate, or postgraduate years; not renewable. *Amount:* $1500–$3000.

Eligibility Requirements: Applicant must be high school student and planning to enroll or expecting to enroll full-time at a two-year or four-year or technical institution or university. Applicant must have 3.0 GPA or higher. Available to U.S. citizens.

Application Requirements: Application form, community service, essay, personal photograph. *Deadline:* February 28.

Contact: Col. Dorothy Stover-Kendrick, Scholarship Chair
Women Marines Association
PO Box 134
Stilwell, KS 66085
Phone: 888-525-1943 Ext. 101
E-mail: scholarship@womenmarines.org

WOMEN'S JEWELRY ASSOCIATION

http://www.womensjewelryassociation.com

MEMBER GRANTS

This grant is available to WJA Members only and is valid towards any type of professional growth.

Award: Grant for use in freshman, sophomore, junior, senior, graduate, or postgraduate years; renewable. *Number:* 12–25. *Amount:* $500–$1000.

Eligibility Requirements: Applicant must be enrolled or expecting to enroll full- or part-time at a two-year or four-year or technical institution or university and female. Available to U.S. and non-U.S. citizens.

Application Requirements: Application form, essay. *Deadline:* January 31.

Contact: Sue Elliott
E-mail: Selliott@gia.edu

WOMEN'S JEWELRY ASSOCIATIONS VETERANS GRANT

This award is given to a woman veteran of the US armed forces who wants to pursue a Jewelry career. It is a grant and does not have to be used for school, but could be used as a start-up grant for their business. It is essay based and is sponsored by Jewelers Mutual.

Award: Grant for use in freshman, sophomore, junior, senior, graduate, or postgraduate years; renewable. *Number:* 1. *Amount:* $5000.

Eligibility Requirements: Applicant must be enrolled or expecting to enroll full- or part-time at a two-year or four-year or technical institution or university and female. Available to U.S. citizens. Applicant or parent must meet one or more of the following requirements: general military experience; retired from active duty; disabled or killed as a result of military service; prisoner of war; or missing in action.

Application Requirements: Application form, essay. *Deadline:* April 15.

Contact: Isabel Cajulis
E-mail: icajulis@reedexpo.com

WONDERSHARE PDFELEMENT

https://pdf.wondershare.com

2018 PDFELEMENT $1000 SCHOLARSHIP

PDFelement is a PDF editing software that provides business solutions for universities, non-profit organizations, government entities, and small to mid-sized businesses. Our goal is provide simple PDF software that lets you work smarter with office documents. With that in mind, we want to invite you to apply for a "PDFs and I" story contest. The winning student will be awarded with $1,000, and the 10 runners-up will receive PDFelement 6 (Valued at $59.95) for free!

Award: Scholarship for use in freshman, sophomore, junior, senior, graduate, or postgraduate years; renewable. *Number:* 1–11. *Amount:* $500–$1000.

Eligibility Requirements: Applicant must be learning disabled; American Indian/Alaska Native; age 18-35 and enrolled or expecting to enroll full-time at a four-year institution or university. Applicant must be learning disabled. Available to U.S. and non-U.S. citizens. Applicant or parent must meet one or more of the following requirements: general military experience; retired from active duty; disabled or killed as a result of military service; prisoner of war; or missing in action.

Application Requirements: Essay, portfolio. *Deadline:* June 15.

Contact: Maggie Chou
Alberta
E-mail: scholarship@wondershare.com

YORKVILLE GOODS LLC

http://yorkvilleblankets.com/

YORKVILLE BLANKETS ASD SCHOLARSHIP

Yorkville Blanket Company's mission to provide comfort to everybody who needs it does not end with making blankets. In order to continue pursuing our mission, we have created the Yorkville Blankets ASD Scholarship for prospective or current college students who are living with ASD as well as students who are parents, siblings, and children of somebody on the autism spectrum to earn an award of $1000 toward continuing their education. The scholarship was created to help provide a means to pursue a post-secondary education for those whose lives have been impacted by Autism Spectrum Disorder (ASD).

Award: Scholarship for use in freshman, sophomore, junior, or senior years; not renewable. *Number:* 1. *Amount:* $1000.

Eligibility Requirements: Applicant must be learning disabled and enrolled or expecting to enroll full- or part-time at a two-year or four-year or technical institution or university. Applicant must be learning disabled. Available to U.S. citizens.

Application Requirements: Essay. *Deadline:* June 1.

Contact: Mr. Thomas Nolan, Owner
Yorkville Goods LLC
65 Linden Dr
Berlin, CT 06037
Phone: 860-335-2447
E-mail: yorkvilleblankets@gmail.com

YOUTH FOUNDATION INC.

http://fdnweb.org/youthfdn

ALEXANDER AND MAUDE HADDEN SCHOLARSHIP

Youth Foundation offers exceptional students with financial need an award of $2500 to $4000 per year which is renewable for four years at the foundation's discretion. Minimum GPA of 3.5 required, community service and extra curricular activities expected. Must write Foundation for information and application request form.

Award: Scholarship for use in freshman, sophomore, junior, or senior years; renewable. *Number:* 96–108. *Amount:* $2500–$4000.

Eligibility Requirements: Applicant must be enrolled or expecting to enroll full-time at a four-year institution or university and resident of Yukon. Applicant or parent of applicant must have employment or volunteer experience in community service. Applicant must have 3.5 GPA or higher. Available to U.S. citizens.

Application Requirements: Application form, community service, essay, financial need analysis, personal photograph. *Deadline:* February 28.

Contact: Ms. Johanna Lee, Executive Administrator
Phone: 212-840-6291
Fax: 212-840-6747
E-mail: YouthFdn@aol.com

ZELUS RECOVERY

http://zelusrecovery.com/

ZELUS RECOVERY $1000 COLLEGE SCHOLARSHIP

Zelus Recovery specializes in treating adolescents and young adults with substance abuse problems. Our goal is to help young people find their way back to health and happiness so they can become contributing members of society. We have created the Zelus Recovery Scholarship for undergraduate and postgraduates students to further that message.

Award: Scholarship for use in freshman, sophomore, junior, senior, graduate, or postgraduate years; not renewable. *Number:* 1. *Amount:* $1000.

Eligibility Requirements: Applicant must be enrolled or expecting to enroll full- or part-time at a two-year or four-year or technical institution or university. Available to U.S. citizens.

Application Requirements: Essay. *Deadline:* August 1.

Contact: Jason Zelus, Executive Director
Zelus Recovery
1965 S. Eagle Road Suite 140
Meridian, ID 83642
Phone: 208-957-6514
Fax: 208-957-6506
E-mail: info@zelusrecovery.com

ZIPRECRUITER
https://www.ziprecruiter.com/

ZIPRECRUITER $3,000 SCHOLARSHIP
ZipRecruiter is offering $3,000 to the college or university student with the most creative entry about their home or college town. The Grand Prize Winner will receive the $3,000 scholarship. The best entries within each city will have their entries posted on our website, and will receive recognition as a ZipRecruiter Scholar Finalist. More information may be found at https://www.ziprecruiter.com/scholarship.

Award: Prize for use in freshman, sophomore, junior, senior, graduate, or postgraduate years; renewable. *Number:* 1. *Amount:* $3000.

Eligibility Requirements: Applicant must be enrolled or expecting to enroll full- or part-time at a two-year or four-year or technical institution or university. Applicant must have 2.5 GPA or higher. Available to U.S. citizens.

Application Requirements: Application form, essay. *Deadline:* September 30.

Contact: Richard Fendler, Marketing Associate
E-mail: richard@ziprecruiter.com

IMPAIRMENT

ACADGILD
https://acadgild.com

ACADGILD MERIT-BASED SCHOLARSHIPS
• *See page 593*

ALEXANDER GRAHAM BELL ASSOCIATION FOR THE DEAF AND HARD OF HEARING
http://www.agbell.org/

AG BELL COLLEGE SCHOLARSHIP PROGRAM
• *See page 594*

AMERICAN COUNCIL OF THE BLIND
http://www.acb.org/

AMERICAN COUNCIL OF THE BLIND SCHOLARSHIPS
• *See page 595*

ARRL FOUNDATION INC.
http://www.arrl.org/

CHALLENGE MET SCHOLARSHIP
Multiple $500 awards are available to students with any active amateur radio license who are studying at an accredited two- or four-year college,
university, or technical school. Preference to applicants with documented learning disabilities (by physician or school) and indications that applicant is putting forth substantial effort regardless of resulting academic grades.

Award: Scholarship for use in freshman, sophomore, junior, or senior years; not renewable. *Amount:* $500.

Eligibility Requirements: Applicant must be hearing impaired, learning disabled, physically disabled, or visually impaired; enrolled or expecting to enroll full- or part-time at a two-year or four-year or technical institution or university and must have an interest in amateur radio. Applicant must be hearing impaired, learning disabled, physically disabled, or visually impaired. Available to U.S. citizens.

Application Requirements: Application form. *Deadline:* January 31.

Contact: Ms. Mary Hobart, Secretary
Phone: 860-594-0397
E-mail: k1mmh@arrl.org

BIOMARIN PHARMACEUTICAL INC.
http://www.biomarin.com/

RARE SCHOLARS
BioMarin Pharmaceutical Inc. has established a scholarship program to assist high school seniors, graduates, current postsecondary undergraduates, or graduate level students who have been diagnosed by a physician as having any form of mucopolysaccharidoses (MPS) disease, phenylketonuria (PKU), or Batten disease, regardless of treatment status. This program is administered by Scholarship America, the nation's largest designer and manager of scholarships, tuition assistance and other education support programs for corporations, foundations, associations, and individuals. Awards are granted without regard to race, color, creed, religion, sexual orientation, age, gender, disability, or national origin.

Award: Scholarship for use in freshman, sophomore, junior, or senior years; not renewable. *Number:* 1–5. *Amount:* $2500–$20,000.

Eligibility Requirements: Applicant must be learning disabled or physically disabled and enrolled or expecting to enroll full-time at a two-year or four-year or technical institution or university. Applicant must be learning disabled or physically disabled. Applicant must have 3.0 GPA or higher. Available to U.S. citizens.

Application Requirements: Application form. *Deadline:* March 30.

Contact: Allison Carleton, Senior Associate, Corporate Communications
Phone: 415-455-7588
E-mail: allison.carleton@bmrn.com

MATRIX HEALTH GROUP BLEEDING DISORDERS
https://matrixhealthgroup.com

JOE HOLIBAUGH MEMORIAL SCHOLARSHIP
• *See page 644*

MARK COATS MEMORIAL SCHOLARSHIP
• *See page 644*

MIKE HYLTON MEMORIAL SCHOLARSHIP
• *See page 644*

MILLIE GONZALEZ MEMORIAL SCHOLARSHIP
• *See page 644*

RON NIEDERMAN MEMORIAL SCHOLARSHIP
• *See page 644*

TIM KENNEDY MEMORIAL SCHOLARSHIP
• *See page 645*

BRIDGES FOR THE DEAF AND HARD OF HEARING

http://www.bridgesfordeafandhh.org/

LINDA COWDEN MEMORIAL SCHOLARSHIP

The Linda Cowden Memorial Scholarship is awarded to Deaf or hard of hearing students or hearing students preparing to work in a profession serving the Deaf and/or hard of hearing communities. Applicants must live in the agency's 16 county service area in middle Tennessee.

Award: Scholarship for use in freshman, sophomore, junior, senior, graduate, or postgraduate years; not renewable. *Number:* 1. *Amount:* $1000.

Eligibility Requirements: Applicant must be hearing impaired; enrolled or expecting to enroll full- or part-time at a two-year or four-year or technical institution or university and resident of Tennessee. Applicant must be hearing impaired. Available to U.S. citizens.

Application Requirements: Application form, essay, interview. *Deadline:* April 1.

Contact: Rebecca Nofi
Bridges for the Deaf and Hard of Hearing
935 Edgehill Avenue
Nashville, TN 37203
Phone: 615-248-8828
E-mail: rn@bridgesfordeafandhh.org

CALIFORNIA COUNCIL OF THE BLIND

http://www.ccbnet.org/

CALIFORNIA COUNCIL OF THE BLIND SCHOLARSHIPS
• *See page 602*

RHONDA KING MEMORIAL SCHOLARSHIP

The individual must be either a resident of, or attending an accredited college or university in Sacramento, Yolo, Placer, or El Dorado Counties. It is not required that a resident of Sacramento, Yolo, Placer or El Dorado Counties be attending an institution in California to submit an application.

Award: Scholarship for use in junior, senior, graduate, or postgraduate years; not renewable. *Number:* 1. *Amount:* $500.

Eligibility Requirements: Applicant must be visually impaired and enrolled or expecting to enroll full-time at a four-year institution or university. Applicant must be visually impaired. Applicant must have 2.5 GPA or higher. Available to U.S. and non-U.S. citizens.

Application Requirements: Application form, application form may be submitted online (http://www.ccbnet.org), essay, interview, recommendations or references, transcript. *Deadline:* July 17.

Contact: Leslie Thom, Scholarship Committee Chair
California Council of the Blind
ACB Capitol Chapter, California Council of the Blind
E-mail: lathom@comcast.net

CHRISTIAN RECORD SERVICES INC.

http://www.christianrecord.org

ANNE LOWE SCHOLARSHIPS
• *See page 605*

COLLEGE WOMEN'S ASSOCIATION OF JAPAN

http://www.cwaj.org/

SCHOLARSHIP FOR THE VISUALLY IMPAIRED TO STUDY ABROAD

Scholarship for visually impaired Japanese nationals or permanent residents of Japan who have been accepted into an undergraduate or graduate degree program at an accredited English-speaking university or research institution. Former recipients of CWAJ awards and members of CWAJ are ineligible. Award value is JPY3 million. Deadline on or between November 1 and November 30.

Award: Scholarship for use in junior or senior years; not renewable. *Number:* 1.

Eligibility Requirements: Applicant must be visually impaired; of Japanese heritage and Japanese citizen and enrolled or expecting to enroll full-time at a four-year institution or university. Applicant must be visually impaired. Available to citizens of countries other than the U.S. or Canada.

Application Requirements: Application form, certificate of disability, essay, recommendations or references, test scores, transcript. *Fee:* $10. *Deadline:* varies.

Contact: Scholarship Committee
E-mail: scholarship@cwaj.org

SCHOLARSHIP FOR THE VISUALLY IMPAIRED TO STUDY IN JAPAN

Scholarship for visually impaired Japanese or permanent resident students for graduate or undergraduate study in Japan. Former recipients of CWAJ awards and members of CWAJ are ineligible. Award Value is JPY2.0 million. Deadline on or between November 1 and November 30.

Award: Scholarship for use in junior or senior years; not renewable. *Number:* 1–2.

Eligibility Requirements: Applicant must be visually impaired; of Japanese heritage and Japanese citizen and enrolled or expecting to enroll full-time at a four-year institution or university. Applicant must be visually impaired. Available to citizens of countries other than the U.S. or Canada.

Application Requirements: Application form, certificate of disability, essay, recommendations or references, self-addressed stamped envelope with application, transcript. *Fee:* $10. *Deadline:* varies.

Contact: Scholarship Committee
E-mail: scholarship@cwaj.org

COUNCIL OF CITIZENS WITH LOW VISION INTERNATIONAL C/O AMERICAN COUNCIL OF THE BLIND

http://www.cclvi.org/

FRED SCHEIGERT SCHOLARSHIP
• *See page 607*

COURAGE KENNY REHABILITATION INSTITUTE, VOCATIONAL SERVICES DEPARTMENT

http://www.allinahealth.org/couragekenny

SCHOLARSHIP FOR PEOPLE WITH DISABILITIES
• *See page 608*

CSA MEDICAL SUPPLY

https://csamedicalsupply.com

CSA MEDICAL SUPPLY COLLEGE SCHOLARSHIP
• *See page 608*

CYSTIC FIBROSIS SCHOLARSHIP FOUNDATION

http://www.cfscholarship.org/

CYSTIC FIBROSIS SCHOLARSHIP

One-time $1000 to $10,000 scholarships for young adults with cystic fibrosis to be used to further their education after high school. Awards may be used for tuition, books, and fees. Students may reapply in subsequent years.

Award: Scholarship for use in freshman, sophomore, junior, or senior years; not renewable. *Number:* 40–50. *Amount:* $1000–$10,000.

Eligibility Requirements: Applicant must be physically disabled and enrolled or expecting to enroll full-time at a two-year or four-year or technical institution or university. Applicant must be physically disabled. Available to U.S. citizens.

Application Requirements: Application form, essay, financial need analysis, recommendations or references, test scores, transcript. *Deadline:* March 21.

Contact: Mary Bottorff, President
Cystic Fibrosis Scholarship Foundation
2814 Grant Street
Evanston, IL 60201
Phone: 847-328-0127
Fax: 847-328-0127
E-mail: mkbcfsf@aol.com

DISABLEDPERSON INC. COLLEGE SCHOLARSHIP

http://www.disabledperson.com/

DISABLEDPERSON INC. NATIONAL COLLEGE SCHOLARSHIP AWARD FOR COLLEGE STUDENTS WITH DISABILITIES
• *See page 612*

EASTERN AMPUTEE GOLF ASSOCIATION

http://www.eagagolf.org/

EASTERN AMPUTEE GOLF ASSOCIATION SCHOLARSHIP FUND

Three (3) $1000 college scholarships are available to any EAGA amputee member and/or a member of his or her family. Amputee is define as one who has had the loss of a limb at a major joint (i.e. Ankle, Wrist etc.) due to trauma or congenital birth defect. Award recipients do not need to be in attendance. Award covers each of the four school years depending on when applications are accepted. Award recipient must maintain a 2.0 GPA.

Award: Scholarship for use in freshman, sophomore, junior, or senior years; renewable. *Number:* 1–6. *Amount:* $1000.

Eligibility Requirements: Applicant must be physically disabled and enrolled or expecting to enroll full-time at a two-year or four-year institution or university. Applicant must be physically disabled. Available to U.S. citizens.

Application Requirements: Application form, community service, essay, financial need analysis, personal photograph. *Fee:* $15. *Deadline:* July 1.

Contact: Mr. Robert Buck, Executive Director
Eastern Amputee Golf Association
20 15 Amherst Drive
Bethlehem, PA 18015-5606
Phone: 610-867-9295
Fax: 610-867-9295
E-mail: rbuck18015@verizon.net

EDMONTON COMMUNITY FOUNDATION

http://www.ecfoundation.org

CHARMAINE LETOURNEAU SCHOLARSHIP

For Deaf or hard of hearing students who are residents of Alberta.

Award: Scholarship for use in freshman, sophomore, junior, or senior years; not renewable.

Eligibility Requirements: Applicant must be hearing impaired; enrolled or expecting to enroll full- or part-time at a two-year or four-year or technical institution or university and resident of Alberta. Applicant must be hearing impaired. Available to Canadian citizens.

Application Requirements: Application form. *Deadline:* August 31.

Contact: Anna Opryshko, Student Awards Associate
Phone: 780-426-0015 Ext. 107
Fax: 780-425-0121
E-mail: studentawards@ecfoundation.org

ELAINE CHAPIN MEMORIAL SCHOLARSHIP FUND

https://sites.google.com/site/theelainechapinfund/

ELAINE CHAPIN MEMORIAL SCHOLARSHIP FUND

Scholarship program that benefits students whose lives are impacted by multiple sclerosis.

Award: Scholarship for use in freshman, sophomore, junior, or senior years; not renewable. *Number:* 8. *Amount:* $500–$1000.

Eligibility Requirements: Applicant must be physically disabled; age 17-99 and enrolled or expecting to enroll full-time at a two-year or four-year or technical institution or university. Applicant must be physically disabled. Available to U.S. citizens.

Application Requirements: Application form, essay. *Deadline:* April 30.

Contact: Joseph Chapin
Elaine Chapin Memorial Scholarship Fund
33 Kassebaum Lane
Suite 103
St. Louis, MO 63129
E-mail: elainechapinfund@gmail.com

ESSAYHUB

https://essayhub.com/

ESSAY WRITING CONTEST BY ESSAYHUB
• *See page 615*

FELDMAN & ROYLE, ATTORNEYS AT LAW

http://www.feldmanroyle.com/

AUTISM SCHOLARSHIPS
• *See page 617*

FELDMAN LAW FIRM PLLC

http://www.afphoenixcriminalattorney.com/

AUTISM SCHOLARSHIP
• *See page 617*

DISABLED VETERANS SCHOLARSHIP
• *See page 617*

FIT SMALL BUSINESS

http://www.fitsmallbusiness.com

BUSINESS PLAN SCHOLARSHIP FOR STUDENTS WITH DISABILITIES
• *See page 618*

FOUNDATION FOR SIGHT AND SOUND

http://fssny.org

HELP AMERICA HEAR SCHOLARSHIP
• *See page 619*

GREAT LAKES HEMOPHILIA FOUNDATION

http://www.glhf.org/

GLHF INDIVIDUAL CLASS SCHOLARSHIP

Scholarship available to members of the Wisconsin bleeding disorder community, individuals with a bleeding disorder and their immediate families. Provides funding assistance for tuition and enrollment fees relevant to continuing education in a non-traditional or non-degree format.

Award: Scholarship for use in freshman, sophomore, junior, or senior years; not renewable. *Number:* 1. *Amount:* up to $500.

Eligibility Requirements: Applicant must be physically disabled; enrolled or expecting to enroll full- or part-time at a two-year or four-year or technical institution or university and resident of Wisconsin. Applicant must be physically disabled. Available to U.S. citizens.

Application Requirements: Application form, essay, recommendations or references, transcript. *Deadline:* varies.

Contact: Karin Koppen, Program Services Coordinator
Great Lakes Hemophilia Foundation
638 North 18 Street, Suite 108
Milwaukee, WI 53233
Phone: 414-257-0200
Fax: 414-257-1225
E-mail: kkoppen@glhf.org

GREAT LAKES HEMOPHILIA FOUNDATION EDUCATION SCHOLARSHIP

This scholarship not only targets the traditional college and vocational students, but also looks at retraining adults with bleeding disorders who are finding it difficult to function in their chosen field because of health complications. It also targets parents of children with bleeding disorders who through career advancement can better meet the financial needs of caring for their child.

Award: Scholarship for use in freshman, sophomore, junior, senior, graduate, or postgraduate years; not renewable. *Number:* 5–6. *Amount:* $500–$2000.

Eligibility Requirements: Applicant must be physically disabled; enrolled or expecting to enroll full- or part-time at a two-year or four-year or technical institution or university and resident of Wisconsin. Applicant must be physically disabled. Available to U.S. citizens.

Application Requirements: Application form, essay, recommendations or references, transcript. *Deadline:* May 1.

Contact: Karin Koppen, Program Services Coordinator
Great Lakes Hemophilia Foundation
638 North 18 Street, Suite 108
Milwaukee, WI 53233
Phone: 414-257-0200
Fax: 414-257-1225
E-mail: kkoppen@glhf.org

HEMOPHILIA FEDERATION OF AMERICA

http://www.hemophiliafed.org/

HFA EDUCATIONAL SCHOLARSHIPS

This scholarship is for students with a bleeding disorder who are attending/planning to attend a postsecondary school.

Award: Scholarship for use in freshman, sophomore, junior, senior, graduate, or postgraduate years; not renewable. *Number:* 2. *Amount:* $2000.

Eligibility Requirements: Applicant must be physically disabled and enrolled or expecting to enroll full- or part-time at a two-year or four-year or technical institution or university. Applicant must be physically disabled. Applicant must have 3.0 GPA or higher. Available to U.S. citizens.

Application Requirements: Application form, essay, financial need analysis. *Deadline:* May 15.

Contact: Athenna Harrison, Educational Scholarship Committee
Hemophilia Federation of America
820 First Street NE
Suite 720
Washington, DC 20002
Phone: 202-675-6984
Fax: 972-616-6211
E-mail: scholarships@hemophiliafed.org

HFA PARENT/SIBLING/CHILD EDUCATIONAL SCHOLARSHIP

Each year, HFA awards scholarships to promising students in the bleeding disorders community. This scholarship is geared towards those who are immediately related to someone with a bleeding disorder.

Award: Scholarship for use in freshman, sophomore, junior, senior, graduate, or postgraduate years; not renewable. *Number:* 1. *Amount:* $2000.

Eligibility Requirements: Applicant must be physically disabled and enrolled or expecting to enroll full- or part-time at a two-year or four-year or technical institution or university. Applicant must be physically disabled. Applicant must have 3.0 GPA or higher. Available to U.S. citizens.

Application Requirements: Application form, essay, financial need analysis. *Deadline:* May 15.

Contact: Athenna Harrison, Educational Scholarship Committee
Hemophilia Federation of America
820 First Street NE
Suite 720
Washington, DC 20002
Phone: 202-675-6984
Fax: 972-616-6211
E-mail: scholarships@hemophiliafed.org

HEMOPHILIA FOUNDATION OF SOUTHERN CALIFORNIA

http://www.hemosocal.org/

CHRISTOPHER MARK PITKIN MEMORIAL SCHOLARSHIP

• *See page 625*

HOMUS

https://homus.org

HOMUS SCHOLARSHIP PROGRAM

• *See page 627*

ILLINOIS COUNCIL OF THE BLIND

http://www.icbonline.org/

FLOYD R. CARGILL SCHOLARSHIP

Award for a visually impaired Illinois resident attending or planning to attend an Illinois college. One-time award of $1000.

Award: Scholarship for use in freshman, sophomore, junior, or senior years; not renewable. *Number:* 1. *Amount:* $1000.

Eligibility Requirements: Applicant must be visually impaired; enrolled or expecting to enroll full-time at a two-year or four-year or technical institution or university; resident of Illinois and studying in Illinois. Applicant must be visually impaired. Applicant must have 3.5 GPA or higher. Available to U.S. citizens.

Application Requirements: Application form, recommendations or references, test scores, transcript. *Deadline:* July 15.

Contact: Maggie Ulrich, Office Manager
Phone: 217-523-4967
E-mail: icb@icbonline.org

KELLY LAW TEAM

http://www.jkphoenixpersonalinjuryattorney.com/

AUTISM/ASD SCHOLARSHIP

• *See page 633*

DISABLED VETERAN SCHOLARSHIP

• *See page 634*

DISABLED VETERAN SCHOLARSHIP

• *See page 634*

KITCHEN GUIDES

http://www.kitchensguides.com/

SMART KITCHEN IMPROVEMENT SCHOLARSHIP BY KITCHEN GUIDES

• *See page 635*

LAW OFFICE OF DAVID D. WHITE, PLLC

http://www.wm-attorneys.com/

ANNUAL TRAUMATIC BRAIN INJURY SCHOLARSHIPS
• *See page 637*

LAW OFFICE OF DAVID P. SHAPIRO

http://www.davidpshapirolaw.com/about-us/

AUTISM SCHOLARSHIP
• *See page 637*

LAW OFFICES OF DAVID A. BLACK

http://www.dbphoenixcriminallawyer.com

SCHOLARSHIP FOR DISABLED VETERANS
• *See page 638*

LAW OFFICES OF JUDD S. NEMIRO, PLLC

http://www.jnphoenixfamilylawyer.com/

ANNUAL DYSLEXIA SCHOLARSHIP
• *See page 638*

LEAD FOUNDATION OF COLORADO

https://www.leadcolorado.org

THE LEAD FOUNDATION SCHOLARSHIP
https://www.leadcolorado.org

Award: Scholarship for use in freshman, sophomore, junior, or senior years; not renewable. *Number:* 2. *Amount:* $1000.

Eligibility Requirements: Applicant must be learning disabled and enrolled or expecting to enroll full-time at a two-year or four-year or technical institution or university. Applicant must be learning disabled. Available to U.S. citizens.

Application Requirements: Application form, essay. *Deadline:* continuous.

Contact: Ms. Kathryn Carruth, Executive Director
LEAD Foundation of Colorado
POB 2516
Colorado Springs, CO 80901
Phone: 806-7892369
E-mail: director@leadcolorado.org

LEARNING ALLY

http://www.learningally.org

MARION HUBER LEARNING THROUGH LISTENING AWARDS
• *See page 568*

MARY P. OENSLAGER SCHOLASTIC ACHIEVEMENT AWARDS
• *See page 568*

LIGHTHOUSE GUILD

http://www.lighthouseguild.org

LIGHTHOUSE GUILD SCHOLARSHIP PROGRAM
Annual merit based scholarship program for college-bound high school and graduate school students who are legally blind. The submission deadline is March 31st. Ten - fifteen scholarships will be awarded to college bound high school seniors and one - two for graduate students.

Award: Scholarship for use in freshman, graduate, or postgraduate years; not renewable. *Number:* 15. *Amount:* $10,000.

Eligibility Requirements: Applicant must be visually impaired and enrolled or expecting to enroll full-time at a four-year institution or university. Applicant must be visually impaired. Applicant must have 3.0 GPA or higher. Available to U.S. citizens.

Application Requirements: Application form, community service, essay. *Deadline:* March 31.

Contact: Mr. Gordon Rovins, Director of Special Programs
Lighthouse Guild
250 West 64th Street
New York, NY 10023
Phone: 212-769-7801
E-mail: scholars@lighthouseguild.org

NATIONAL CENTER FOR LEARNING DISABILITIES, INC.

http://ncld.org

ANNE FORD AND ALLEGRA FORD THOMAS SCHOLARSHIP
The Allegra Ford Thomas Scholarship is a one-time $2,500 scholarship awarded to a graduating high school senior with a documented learning disability (LD) and/or ADHD who will be enrolled in a two-year community college, a vocational or technical training program, or a specialized program for students with LD and/or ADHD in the fall. The Anne Ford Scholarship is a $10,000 scholarship ($2,500/year over four years) granted to a graduating high school senior with a documented learning disability (LD) and/or ADHD who will be enrolled in a full-time Bachelor's degree program in the fall.

Award: Scholarship for use in freshman, sophomore, junior, or senior years; not renewable. *Number:* 2. *Amount:* $2500–$10,000.

Eligibility Requirements: Applicant must be learning disabled; high school student and planning to enroll or expecting to enroll full-time at a two-year or four-year or technical institution or university. Applicant must be learning disabled. Applicant must have 3.0 GPA or higher. Available to U.S. citizens.

Application Requirements: Application form, essay, financial need analysis. *Deadline:* November 1.

Contact: Natalie Tamburello, Manager
Phone: 212-545-7510
E-mail: afscholarship@ncld.org

NATIONAL COUNCIL OF JEWISH WOMEN NEW YORK SECTION

http://www.ncjwny.org/

JACKSON-STRICKS SCHOLARSHIP
Scholarship provides financial aid to a person with significant physical challenges for academic study or vocational training that leads to independent living.

Award: Scholarship for use in sophomore, junior, senior, graduate, or postgraduate years; not renewable. *Number:* 1–2. *Amount:* $1500–$2500.

Eligibility Requirements: Applicant must be physically disabled; enrolled or expecting to enroll full- or part-time at a two-year or four-year institution or university and studying in New York. Applicant must be physically disabled. Available to U.S. and non-U.S. citizens.

Application Requirements: Application form, essay. *Deadline:* March 31.

Contact: Naomi Skop Richter, Jackson-Stricks Scholarship Committee
National Council of Jewish Women New York Section
241 West 72 Street
New York, NY 10023
Phone: 212-687-5030 Ext. 461
E-mail: jss@ncjwny.org

NATIONAL FEDERATION OF THE BLIND (NFB)

http://www.nfb.org/scholarships

AAF KENNETH JERNIGAN SCHOLARSHIP FOR $12,000
• *See page 649*

CHARLES AND MELVA T. OWEN MEMORIAL SCHOLARSHIP FOR $5,000

Merit-based scholarship requires academic excellence and leadership, permanent residency in United States/Puerto Rico, and accredited institution's degree program (in U.S./PR) directed toward financial independence (excludes degrees in religious studies or solely for cultural education). Winner assisted to attend NFB annual convention to receive this award. Membership not required.

Award: Scholarship for use in freshman, sophomore, junior, senior, graduate, or postgraduate years; not renewable. *Number:* 2. *Amount:* $5000.

Eligibility Requirements: Applicant must be visually impaired and enrolled or expecting to enroll full- or part-time at a two-year or four-year institution or university. Applicant must be visually impaired. Available to U.S. and non-U.S. citizens.

Application Requirements: Application form, application form may be submitted online (https://nfb.org//scholarships), essay, interview, proof of legal blindness in both eyes, recommendations or references, test scores, transcript. *Deadline:* March 31.

Contact: Ms. Patti Chang, Chairperson, NFB Scholarship Committee
National Federation of the Blind (NFB)
200 East Wells Street
Baltimore, MD 21230
Phone: 410-659-9314 Ext. 2415
E-mail: scholarships@nfb.org

CHARLES AND MELVA T. OWEN SCHOLARSHIP FOR $10,000

• See page 649

LARRY STREETER MEMORIAL SCHOLARSHIP FOR $3,000

$3000 scholarship for legally blind, permanent residents of the U.S. or Puerto Rico, pursuing a postsecondary degree at an accredited institution in U.S. or PR. Created to assist blind students to elevate their quality of life, equipping them to be active, productive participants in their family, community, and the workplace.

Award: Scholarship for use in freshman, sophomore, junior, or senior years; not renewable. *Number:* 1. *Amount:* $3000.

Eligibility Requirements: Applicant must be visually impaired and enrolled or expecting to enroll full- or part-time at a four-year institution or university. Applicant must be visually impaired. Available to U.S. citizens.

Application Requirements: Application form, essay, financial need analysis, proof of blindness in both eyes, transcript. *Deadline:* March 31.

Contact: Ms. Patti Chang, Chairperson, NFB Scholarship Program
National Federation of the Blind (NFB)
200 East Wells Street
Baltimore, MD 21230
Phone: 410-659-9314 Ext. 2415
E-mail: scholarships@nfb.org

NATIONAL FEDERATION OF THE BLIND SCHOLARSHIP FOR $3,000

$3000 scholarship for legally blind, permanent residents of the U.S. or Puerto Rico, pursuing a postsecondary degree at an accredited institution in U.S. or PR. Selection is merit-based on academic excellence and leadership. With NFB assistance, winner attends NFB annual convention to receive award. Membership in NFB is not required.

Award: Scholarship for use in freshman, sophomore, junior, senior, graduate, or postgraduate years; not renewable. *Number:* 20. *Amount:* $3000.

Eligibility Requirements: Applicant must be visually impaired and enrolled or expecting to enroll full- or part-time at a two-year or four-year institution or university. Applicant must be visually impaired. Available to U.S. and non-U.S. citizens.

Application Requirements: Application form, application form may be submitted online (https://nfb.org//scholarships), essay, interview, proof of legal blindness in both eyes, recommendations or references, test scores, transcript. *Deadline:* March 31.

Contact: Ms. Patti Chang, Chairperson, Scholarship Committee
National Federation of the Blind (NFB)
200 East Wells Street
Baltimore, MD 21230
Phone: 410-659-9314 Ext. 2415
E-mail: scholarships@nfb.org

NATIONAL FEDERATION OF THE BLIND SCHOLARSHIP FOR $7,000

$7000 scholarship for legally blind, permanent residents of the U.S. or Puerto Rico, pursuing a postsecondary degree at an accredited institution in U.S. or PR. Selection is merit-based on academic excellence and leadership. With NFB assistance, winner attends NFB annual convention to receive award. Membership in NFB is not required.

Award: Scholarship for use in freshman, sophomore, junior, senior, graduate, or postgraduate years; not renewable. *Number:* 2. *Amount:* $7000.

Eligibility Requirements: Applicant must be visually impaired and enrolled or expecting to enroll full- or part-time at a two-year or four-year institution or university. Applicant must be visually impaired. Available to U.S. and non-U.S. citizens.

Application Requirements: Application form, application form may be submitted online (http://www.nfb.org//scholarships), entry in a contest, essay, interview, proof of legal blindness in both eyes, recommendations or references, test scores, transcript. *Deadline:* March 31.

Contact: Ms. Patti Chang, Chairperson, NFB Scholarship Committee
National Federation of the Blind (NFB)
200 East Wells Street
Baltimore, MD 21230
Phone: 410-659-9314 Ext. 2415
E-mail: scholarships@nfb.org

NFB SCHOLARSHIP FOR $5,000

$5000 scholarships for legally blind, permanent residents of the U.S. or Puerto Rico, pursuing a postsecondary degree at an accredited institution in U.S. or PR. Selection is merit-based on academic excellence and leadership. With NFB assistance, winner attends NFB annual convention to receive award. Membership in NFB is not required.

Award: Scholarship for use in freshman, sophomore, junior, senior, graduate, or postgraduate years; not renewable. *Number:* 4. *Amount:* $5000.

Eligibility Requirements: Applicant must be visually impaired and enrolled or expecting to enroll full- or part-time at a two-year or four-year institution or university. Applicant must be visually impaired. Available to U.S. and non-U.S. citizens.

Application Requirements: Application form, application form may be submitted online (http://www.nfb.org//scholarships), entry in a contest, essay, interview, proof of legal blindness in both eyes, recommendations or references, test scores, transcript. *Deadline:* March 31.

Contact: Ms. Patti Chang, Chairperson, NFB Scholarship Program
National Federation of the Blind (NFB)
200 East Wells Street
Baltimore, MD 21230
Phone: 410-659-9314 Ext. 2415
E-mail: scholarships@nfb.org

NATIONAL FEDERATION OF THE BLIND OF CALIFORNIA

http://www.nfbcal.org/

GERALD DRAKE MEMORIAL SCHOLARSHIP

One-time award for legally blind students pursuing an undergraduate or graduate degree. Must be a California resident and full-time student.

Award: Scholarship for use in freshman, sophomore, junior, senior, or graduate years; not renewable. *Number:* up to 5. *Amount:* $1500.

Eligibility Requirements: Applicant must be visually impaired; enrolled or expecting to enroll full-time at a four-year institution or university and resident of California. Applicant must be visually impaired. Available to U.S. and non-U.S. citizens.

Application Requirements: Application form. *Deadline:* March 31.

Contact: Robert Stigile, President
Phone: 818-342-6524
Fax: 818-344-7930
E-mail: nfbcal@yahoo.com

JULIE LANDUCCI SCHOLARSHIP

Award for legally blind students pursuing an undergraduate or graduate degree. Must be a California resident and full-time student. Award available to U.S. citizens.

Award: Scholarship for use in freshman, sophomore, junior, senior, or graduate years; renewable. *Number:* 1. *Amount:* up to $2000.

Eligibility Requirements: Applicant must be visually impaired; enrolled or expecting to enroll full-time at a four-year institution or university and resident of California. Applicant must be visually impaired. Available to U.S. citizens.

Application Requirements: Application form. *Deadline:* March 31.

Contact: Robert Stigile, President
　　　　Phone: 818-342-6524
　　　　Fax: 818-344-7930
　　　　E-mail: nfbcal@yahoo.com

LA VYRL "PINKY" JOHNSON MEMORIAL SCHOLARSHIP

One-time award up to $2000 for legally blind students pursuing an undergraduate or graduate degree. Must be a California resident and full-time student.

Award: Scholarship for use in freshman, sophomore, junior, senior, or graduate years; renewable. *Number:* 1. *Amount:* $2000.

Eligibility Requirements: Applicant must be visually impaired; enrolled or expecting to enroll full-time at a four-year institution or university and resident of California. Applicant must be visually impaired. Available to U.S. citizens.

Application Requirements: Application form. *Deadline:* March 31.

Contact: Robert Stigile, President
　　　　Phone: 818-342-6524
　　　　Fax: 818-344-7930
　　　　E-mail: nfbcal@yahoo.com

LAWRENCE "MUZZY" MARCELINO MEMORIAL SCHOLARSHIP

Scholarship provides financial assistance for graduate or undergraduate education to blind students in California. Any legally blind student may apply for a scholarship but must attend the convention of the National Federation of the Blind of California. Selection is based first on academic merit and second on financial need.

Award: Scholarship for use in freshman, sophomore, junior, senior, or graduate years; renewable. *Number:* up to 4. *Amount:* $1500.

Eligibility Requirements: Applicant must be visually impaired; enrolled or expecting to enroll full-time at a four-year institution or university and resident of California. Applicant must be visually impaired. Available to U.S. citizens.

Application Requirements: Application form. *Deadline:* March 15.

Contact: Robert Stigile, President
　　　　Phone: 818-342-6524
　　　　Fax: 818-344-7930
　　　　E-mail: nfbcal@yahoo.com

NATIONAL FEDERATION OF THE BLIND OF CALIFORNIA MERIT SCHOLARSHIPS

Scholarships to qualified blind students pursuing undergraduate or graduate studies in order to achieve an academic degree. This opportunity is also available to high school seniors preparing to enter undergraduate programs.

Award: Scholarship for use in freshman, sophomore, junior, senior, or graduate years; renewable. *Number:* up to 5. *Amount:* $1000.

Eligibility Requirements: Applicant must be visually impaired; enrolled or expecting to enroll full-time at a four-year institution or university and resident of California. Applicant must be visually impaired. Available to U.S. citizens.

Application Requirements: Application form. *Deadline:* March 15.

Contact: Robert Stigile, President
　　　　Phone: 818-342-6524
　　　　Fax: 818-344-7930
　　　　E-mail: nfbcal@yahoo.com

NATIONAL FEDERATION OF THE BLIND OF MISSOURI

http://www.nfbmo.org/

NATIONAL FEDERATION OF THE BLIND OF MISSOURI SCHOLARSHIP PROGRAM FOR LEGALLY BLIND STUDENTS

Awards are based on achievement and commitment to community. Recipients must be legally blind, live in Missouri, and maintain a GPA greater than 2.5.Amount of money each year available for program will vary.

Award: Scholarship for use in sophomore or senior years; not renewable. *Number:* 1–3. *Amount:* $500–$2500.

Eligibility Requirements: Applicant must be visually impaired; enrolled or expecting to enroll full- or part-time at a two-year or four-year or technical institution or university; resident of Missouri and studying in Missouri. Applicant must be visually impaired. Applicant must have 2.5 GPA or higher. Available to U.S. citizens.

Application Requirements: Application form, essay, interview. *Deadline:* February 1.

Contact: Shelia Wright, President
　　　　National Federation of the Blind of Missouri
　　　　7928 NW Milrey Drive
　　　　Kansas City, MO 64152
　　　　Phone: 816-741-6402
　　　　E-mail: scholarship@nfbmo.org

NATIONAL KIDNEY FOUNDATION OF INDIANA INC.

http://www.kidneyindiana.org/

NATIONAL KIDNEY FOUNDATION OF INDIANA SCHOLARSHIP

Scholarship provides financial assistance for kidney dialysis and transplant patients to pursue post-secondary education. Applicant must be resident of Indiana over the age of 18. Must have a high school diploma or its equivalent. Applications are reviewed by committee to choose awardees.

Award: Scholarship for use in freshman, sophomore, junior, or senior years; not renewable. *Number:* 2–8. *Amount:* $250–$1500.

Eligibility Requirements: Applicant must be physically disabled; enrolled or expecting to enroll full- or part-time at a two-year or four-year or technical institution or university and resident of Indiana. Applicant must be physically disabled. Available to U.S. citizens.

Application Requirements: Application form, essay. *Deadline:* March 30.

Contact: Nicki Howard, Public Health Coordinator
　　　　National Kidney Foundation of Indiana Inc.
　　　　National Kidney Foundation of Indiana
　　　　911 E. 86th St, Suite 100
　　　　Indianapolis, IN 46240
　　　　Phone: 317-722-5640
　　　　E-mail: nhoward@kidneyindiana.org

NATIONAL MULTIPLE SCLEROSIS SOCIETY

http://www.nmss.org/

NATIONAL MULTIPLE SCLEROSIS SOCIETY SCHOLARSHIP PROGRAM

• See page 650

NATIONAL PKU NEWS

http://www.pkunews.org/

ROBERT GUTHRIE PKU SCHOLARSHIP AND AWARDS

Scholarship for persons with phenylketonuria (PKU) who are on a special diet for PKU treatment. Award is for full-time or part-time study at any accredited U.S. institution. Up to 8 scholarships of between $500 and $3500 are granted.

Award: Scholarship for use in freshman, sophomore, junior, or senior years; not renewable. *Number:* 4–8. *Amount:* $500–$3500.

Eligibility Requirements: Applicant must be physically disabled and enrolled or expecting to enroll full- or part-time at a two-year or four-year or technical institution or university. Applicant must be physically disabled. Available to U.S. and non-U.S. citizens.

Application Requirements: Application form, essay, personal photograph, recommendations or references, resume, test scores, transcript. *Deadline:* October 15.

Contact: Virginia Schuett, Director
  Phone: 206-525-8140
  E-mail: schuett@pkunews.org

NIKKO COSMETIC SURGERY CENTER
http://www.drnikko.com/

BREAST CANCER SURVIVOR SCHOLARSHIPS
• *See page 652*

NORTH CAROLINA DIVISION OF VOCATIONAL REHABILITATION SERVICES
http://www.dhhs.state.nc.us/

TRAINING SUPPORT FOR YOUTH WITH DISABILITIES
• *See page 653*

OPTIMIST INTERNATIONAL FOUNDATION
http://www.optimist.org/

COMMUNICATION CONTEST FOR THE DEAF AND HARD OF HEARING
College scholarship (district level) for young people through grade twelve in the U.S. and Canada, to CEGEP in Quebec and grade thirteen in the Caribbean. Students interested in participating must submit the results of an audiogram conducted no longer than twenty four months prior to the date of the contest from a qualified audiologist. Students must be certified to have a hearing loss of forty decibels or more and supported by the audiogram to be eligible to compete. Students attending either public school or schools providing special services are eligible to enter if criteria are met.

Award: Scholarship for use in freshman, sophomore, junior, or senior years; not renewable. *Number:* 1–30. *Amount:* up to $2500.

Eligibility Requirements: Applicant must be hearing impaired and enrolled or expecting to enroll full- or part-time at a two-year or four-year or technical institution or university. Applicant must be hearing impaired. Available to U.S. and Canadian citizens.

Application Requirements: Application form, entry in a contest, self-addressed stamped envelope with application, speech/presentation, audiogram. *Deadline:* varies.

Contact: Dana Thomas, Director of International Programs
  Optimist International Foundation
  4494 Lindell Boulevard
  St. Louis, MO 63108
  Phone: 800-500-8130
  Fax: 314-371-6006
  E-mail: programs@optimist.org

OREGON COMMUNITY FOUNDATION
http://www.oregoncf.org/

HARRY LUDWIG SCHOLARSHIP FUND
Scholarship for visually impaired students for use in the pursuit of a postsecondary education at a college or university. For full-time students only.

Award: Scholarship for use in freshman, sophomore, junior, or senior years; renewable. *Number:* 1–3. *Amount:* $500–$5000.

Eligibility Requirements: Applicant must be visually impaired and enrolled or expecting to enroll full-time at a four-year institution or university. Applicant must be visually impaired. Available to U.S. citizens.

Application Requirements: Application form, recommendations or references. *Deadline:* March 1.

Contact: Dianne Causey, Program Associate for Scholarships and Grants
  Phone: 503-227-6846 Ext. 1418
  E-mail: dcausey@oregoncf.org

OREGON STUDENT ASSISTANCE COMMISSION
https://oregonstudentaid.gov/

HARRY LUDWIG MEMORIAL SCHOLARSHIP
Award for visually-impaired Oregon residents planning to enroll full-time in undergraduate or graduate studies at an Oregon college or university. Must document visual impairment with a letter from a physician. Must reapply for award annually. Based on financial need.

Award: Scholarship for use in freshman, sophomore, junior, senior, or graduate years; not renewable.

Eligibility Requirements: Applicant must be visually impaired; enrolled or expecting to enroll full-time at a two-year or four-year institution or university; resident of Oregon and studying in Oregon. Applicant must be visually impaired. Available to U.S. citizens.

Application Requirements: Application form, financial need analysis. *Deadline:* March 1.

Contact: Melissa Adams, Scholarship Processing Coordinator
  Phone: 541-687-7409
  E-mail: melissa.adams@state.or.us

SALEM FOUNDATION ANSEL & MARIE SOLIE SCHOLARSHIP
Award is available to visually impaired Oregon residents planning to enroll in full-time undergraduate studies. Award may be used only at a four-year public or nonprofit Oregon college or university. Apply/compete annually. Financial need may or may not be considered.

Award: Scholarship for use in freshman, sophomore, junior, or senior years; not renewable.

Eligibility Requirements: Applicant must be visually impaired; enrolled or expecting to enroll full-time at a four-year institution or university; resident of Oregon and studying in Oregon. Applicant must be visually impaired. Available to U.S. citizens.

Application Requirements: Application form. *Deadline:* March 1.

Contact: Melissa Adams, Scholarship Processing Coordinator
  Phone: 541-687-7409
  E-mail: melissa.adams@state.or.us

PENNSYLVANIA HIGHER EDUCATION ASSISTANCE AGENCY
http://www.pheaa.org/

BLIND OR DEAF BENEFICIARY GRANT PROGRAM
• *See page 658*

PETAZI
https://petazi.com/

NURTURE FOR NATURE SCHOLARSHIP
One $1200 scholarship created to help raise everyone's awareness about protecting animals and the environment. All students located and currently studying in the United States or Canada are eligible to apply for this scholarship. Valid statements of current academic status as evidence that candidates are currently attending college. Students can apply by writing an inspirational short story about animals/ pets. Upon sharing it with us, we will then share it online via Petazi websites. The winner of the $1200 prize will be the one whose entry/story receives the most likes after we post all the entries on our Petazi Facebook page. See website for details, https://petazi.com/scholarship

Award: Scholarship for use in freshman, sophomore, junior, senior, graduate, or postgraduate years; renewable. *Number:* 1. *Amount:* $1200.

Eligibility Requirements: Applicant must be hearing impaired, learning disabled, physically disabled, or visually impaired; American Indian/Alaska Native, Asian/Pacific Islander, Black (non-Hispanic), Hispanic and enrolled or expecting to enroll full- or part-time at a two-year or four-year institution or university. Applicant must be hearing impaired, learning disabled, physically disabled, or visually impaired. Available to U.S. and non-U.S. citizens. Applicant or parent must meet one or more of the following requirements: general military experience; retired from active duty; disabled or killed as a result of military service; prisoner of war; or missing in action.

Application Requirements: Application form, personal photograph. *Deadline:* June 30.

Contact: Ms. Rose Larson
Petazi
Petazi Scholarship Office
316A Cecil Street
Chicago, IL 60605
Phone: 331-207-4154
E-mail: scholarship@petazi.com

PINE CONE FOUNDATION (PCF)

http://pineconefoundation.org/

PINE CONE FOUNDATION SCHOLARSHIP
• *See page 660*

RJT CRIMINAL DEFENSE

http://www.sandiegocriminallawyerrt.com/

AUTISM SCHOLARSHIP
• *See page 664*

RYU FAMILY FOUNDATION, INC.

SEOL BONG SCHOLARSHIP

One-time award to support and advance education and research. Must be Korean residing in DE, PA, NJ, NY, CT, VT, RI, NH, MA, or ME. Minimum 3.5 GPA required.

Award: Scholarship for use in freshman, sophomore, junior, senior, or graduate years; not renewable. *Number:* 21. *Amount:* $2000–$3000.

Eligibility Requirements: Applicant must be learning disabled; of Korean heritage; Asian/Pacific Islander; enrolled or expecting to enroll full-time at a four-year institution or university; resident of Connecticut, Delaware, Maine, Massachusetts, New Hampshire, New Jersey, New York, Pennsylvania, Rhode Island, Vermont and studying in Connecticut, Delaware, Maine, Massachusetts, New Hampshire, New Jersey, New York, Pennsylvania, Rhode Island, Vermont. Applicant must be learning disabled. Applicant must have 3.5 GPA or higher. Available to U.S. and non-Canadian citizens.

Application Requirements: Application form, essay, financial need analysis, personal photograph, portfolio, recommendations or references, resume, test scores, transcript. *Deadline:* November 15.

Contact: Jenny Kang, Scholarship Secretary
Phone: 973-692-9696 Ext. 20
E-mail: jennyk@toplineus.com

SCHOLARSHIP AMERICA

https://www.abbvieImmunologyScholarship.com/

ABBVIE IMMUNOLOGY SCHOLARSHIP
• *See page 666*

WELLS FARGO SCHOLARSHIP PROGRAM FOR PEOPLE WITH DISABILITIES

The Wells Fargo Scholarship Program for People with Disabilities is designed to help people with disabilities obtain the education or training necessary to succeed in the career path of their choice. To apply, you must have an identified disability (defined as someone who has, or considers themselves to have, a long-term or recurring issue that impacts one or more major life activity). Applicants must be high school seniors or graduates planning to enroll or who are already enrolled in full- or half-time undergraduate study at an accredited two- or four-year college or university in the United States for the 2018-2019 academic year. The program will award up to $2,500 renewable scholarships for full-time students and up to $1,250 renewable scholarships for half-time students. Visit https://scholarsapply.org/pwdscholarship for more information and to apply.

Award: Scholarship for use in freshman, sophomore, junior, or senior years; renewable. *Number:* 25. *Amount:* $2500.

Eligibility Requirements: Applicant must be hearing impaired, learning disabled, physically disabled, or visually impaired and enrolled or expecting to enroll full- or part-time at a two-year or four-year institution or university. Applicant must be hearing impaired, learning disabled, physically disabled, or visually impaired. Applicant must have 2.5 GPA or higher. Available to U.S. citizens.

Application Requirements: Application form. *Deadline:* November 28.

Contact: Program Manager
Scholarship America
Scholarship America
One Scholarship Way
Saint Peter, MN 56082
Phone: 844-402-0357
E-mail: pwdscholarship@scholarshipamerica.org

SERTOMA, INC.

http://www.sertoma.org/

SERTOMA SCHOLARSHIP FOR STUDENTS WHO ARE HARD OF HEARING OR DEAF

Applicants must have a minimum of 40dB bilateral hearing loss, as evidenced on audiogram by an SRT. Must have a minimum cumulative 3.2 GPA on a 4.0 unweighted scale.

Award: Scholarship for use in freshman, sophomore, junior, or senior years; not renewable. *Number:* 45–50. *Amount:* $1000.

Eligibility Requirements: Applicant must be hearing impaired and enrolled or expecting to enroll full-time at a four-year institution or university. Applicant must be hearing impaired. Applicant must have 3.0 GPA or higher. Available to U.S. citizens.

Application Requirements: Application form, Audiogram (Proof of Hearing Loss), recommendations or references, transcript. *Deadline:* May 1.

Contact: Mrs. Bridget Almond, Mission Development Officer, Internal Marketing
Phone: 816-333-8300
E-mail: Balmond@sertomahq.org

SISTER KENNY REHABILITATION INSTITUTE

http://www.allina.com/ahs/ski.nsf

INTERNATIONAL ART SHOW FOR ARTISTS WITH DISABILITIES

One-time award for artwork submitted by artists of any age with visual, hearing, physical, or learning impairment. Contact Sister Kenny Rehabilitation Institute for show information. This is a one-time prize, not an academic scholarship.

Award: Prize for use in freshman, sophomore, junior, senior, or graduate years; not renewable. *Number:* 25–70. *Amount:* $25–$500.

Eligibility Requirements: Applicant must be hearing impaired, learning disabled, physically disabled, or visually impaired; enrolled or expecting to enroll full- or part-time at a four-year institution or university and must have an interest in art. Applicant must be hearing impaired, learning disabled, physically disabled, or visually impaired. Available to U.S. and non-U.S. citizens.

Application Requirements: Application form, entry in a contest. *Deadline:* March 17.

Contact: Laura Swift, Administrative Assistant
Sister Kenny Rehabilitation Institute
800 East 28th Street
Minneapolis, MN 55407-3799
Phone: 612-863-4466
Fax: 612-863-8942
E-mail: laura.swift@allina.com

STICKLER INVOLVED PEOPLE

https://stickler.org/

DR. GUNNAR B. STICKLER SCHOLARSHIP

Applicant must have a diagnosis of Stickler syndrome and submit letter from physician with application. Scholarship is renewable yearly with 3.0 GPA goals letter provided from school.

Award: Scholarship for use in freshman, sophomore, junior, or senior years; renewable. *Number:* 1. *Amount:* $500.

Eligibility Requirements: Applicant must be hearing impaired, physically disabled, or visually impaired; high school student and planning to enroll or expecting to enroll full-time at a four-year institution. Applicant must be hearing impaired, physically disabled, or visually impaired. Applicant must have 3.0 GPA or higher. Available to U.S. citizens.

Application Requirements: Application form. *Deadline:* June 15.

Contact: James Brown, Scholarship Committee Chair
Stickler Involved People
Gunnar B. Stickler Scholarship Award
PO Box 775
Cologne, NJ 08213

TPA SCHOLARSHIP TRUST FOR THE HEARING IMPAIRED

https://www.tpahq.org/scholarshiptrust/

TPA SCHOLARSHIP TRUST FOR THE HEARING IMPAIRED
• See page 675

UCB, INC.

http://www.ucb.com/

UCB FAMILY EPILEPSY SCHOLARSHIP
• See page 677

UNITED STATES ASSOCIATION FOR BLIND ATHLETES

http://www.usaba.org/

ARTHUR E. AND HELEN COPELAND SCHOLARSHIPS

Scholarship for a full-time college student who is blind or visually impaired. All applicants must be current members of USABA.

Award: Scholarship for use in freshman, sophomore, junior, or senior years; not renewable. *Number:* 1–2. *Amount:* $500.

Eligibility Requirements: Applicant must be visually impaired and enrolled or expecting to enroll full-time at a four-year institution or university. Applicant must be visually impaired. Available to U.S. citizens.

Application Requirements: Application form, driver's license, proof of acceptance, recommendations or references, transcript. *Deadline:* October 1.

Contact: Mark Lucas, Executive Director
United States Association for Blind Athletes
33 North Institute Street
Colorado Springs, CO 80903
Phone: 719-630-0422 Ext. 13
Fax: 719-630-0616
E-mail: mlucas@usaba.org

U.S. COAST GUARD

http://www.gocoastguard/cspi

COLLEGE STUDENT PRE-COMMISSIONING INITIATIVE (CSPI)
• See page 681

WISCONSIN DEPARTMENT OF VETERANS AFFAIRS (WDVA)

http://www.dva.state.wi.us/

VETERANS EDUCATION (VETED) REIMBURSEMENT GRANT

The grant is for eligible Wisconsin veterans enrolled at approved schools who have not yet earned a BS/BA. Reimburses up to 120 credits or eight semesters at the UW Madison rate for the same number of credits taken in one semester or term. The number of credits or semesters is based on length of time serving on active duty in the armed forces (active duty for training does not apply). Application is due no later than 60 days after the course start date. The student must earn a 2.0 or better for the semester. An eligible veteran will have entered active duty as a Wisconsin resident or lived in state for twelve consecutive months since entering active duty.

Award: Grant for use in freshman, sophomore, junior, or senior years; renewable. *Amount:* $1340–$4000.

Eligibility Requirements: Applicant must be hearing impaired, learning disabled, physically disabled, or visually impaired; age 18-75; enrolled or expecting to enroll full- or part-time at a two-year or four-year or technical institution or university; resident of Wisconsin and studying in Minnesota, Wisconsin. Applicant must be hearing impaired, learning disabled, physically disabled, or visually impaired. Applicant must have 3.5 GPA or higher. Available to U.S. citizens. Applicant must have general military experience.

Application Requirements: Application form. *Deadline:* July 15.

Contact: Miss. Leslie Busby-Amegashie, Agency Liaison and Regional Coordinator
Wisconsin Department of Veterans Affairs (WDVA)
201 West Washington Street
PO Box 7843
Madison, WI 53707-7843
Phone: 800-947-8387 Ext. 63575
Fax: 608-267-0403 Ext. 3575
E-mail: leslie.busby-amegashie@dva.wisconsin.gov

WISCONSIN HIGHER EDUCATIONAL AID BOARD

http://www.heab.wi.gov/

HANDICAPPED STUDENT GRANT-WISCONSIN

One-time award available to residents of Wisconsin who have severe or profound hearing or visual impairment. Must be enrolled at least half-time at a nonprofit institution. If the handicap prevents the student from attending a Wisconsin school, the award may be used out-of-state in a specialized college. Refer to website for further details http://www.heab.state.wi.us.

Award: Grant for use in freshman, sophomore, junior, or senior years; not renewable. *Amount:* $250–$1800.

Eligibility Requirements: Applicant must be hearing impaired or visually impaired; enrolled or expecting to enroll full- or part-time at a four-year institution or university and resident of Wisconsin. Applicant must be hearing impaired or visually impaired. Available to U.S. citizens.

Application Requirements: Application form, financial need analysis. *Deadline:* continuous.

Contact: Sandy Thomas, Program Coordinator
Wisconsin Higher Educational Aid Board
PO Box 7885
Madison, WI 53707-7885
Phone: 608-266-0888
Fax: 608-267-2808
E-mail: sandy.thomas@wi.gov

WONDERSHARE PDFELEMENT

https://pdf.wondershare.com

2018 PDFELEMENT $1000 SCHOLARSHIP
• *See page 684*

YORKVILLE GOODS LLC

http://yorkvilleblankets.com/

YORKVILLE BLANKETS ASD SCHOLARSHIP
• *See page 684*

MILITARY SERVICE: AIR FORCE

AIR FORCE AID SOCIETY

http://www.afas.org/

GENERAL HENRY H. ARNOLD EDUCATION GRANT PROGRAM

Need- based grants awarded to dependent sons and daughters of active duty, Title 10 AGR/Reserve, Title 32 AGR performing full-time active duty, retired, retired reserve and deceased Air Force members; spouses of active members and Title 10 AGR/Reservist; and surviving spouses of deceased personnel for their undergraduate studies. Dependent children must be unmarried and under the age of 23. High school seniors may apply. Minimum 2.0 GPA is required. Students must reapply and compete each year. Full-time enrollment status required.

Award: Grant for use in freshman, sophomore, junior, or senior years; not renewable. *Number:* 3000. *Amount:* $500–$4000.

Eligibility Requirements: Applicant must be enrolled or expecting to enroll full-time at a two-year or four-year or technical institution or university. Available to U.S. citizens. Applicant or parent must meet one or more of the following requirements: national guard experience; retired from active duty; disabled or killed as a result of military service; prisoner of war; or missing in action.

Application Requirements: Application form, financial need analysis. *Deadline:* April 30.

Contact: Education Programs
Air Force Aid Society
241 18th Street South, Suite 202
Arlington, VA 22202
Phone: 703-972-2647
Fax: 866-896-5637
E-mail: ED@afas-hq.org

AIR FORCE RESERVE OFFICER TRAINING CORPS

http://www.afrotc.com/

AFROTC HBCU SCHOLARSHIP PROGRAM

Up to $15,000 awarded to student studying at a historically black college or university (HBCU). Please refer to website for more information http://www.afrotc.com/scholarships/incolschol/minority/hbcu.php.

Award: Scholarship for use in freshman, sophomore, junior, or senior years; not renewable. *Number:* up to 15. *Amount:* up to $15,000.

Eligibility Requirements: Applicant must be Black (non-Hispanic) and enrolled or expecting to enroll full-time at a four-year institution or university. Available to U.S. citizens. Applicant must have national guard experience.

Application Requirements: Application form. *Deadline:* varies.

Contact: Elmarko Magee, Chief of Advertising
Air Force Reserve Officer Training Corps
551 East Maxwell Boulevard
Maxwell AFB, AL 36112
Phone: 866-423-7682

AFROTC HSI SCHOLARSHIP PROGRAM

$15,000 scholarships to students at colleges and universities defined as Hispanic Serving Institutions by the United States Department of Education. Student must already be enrolled in school to receive award.

Award: Scholarship for use in freshman, sophomore, junior, or senior years; not renewable. *Number:* up to 15. *Amount:* $15,000.

Eligibility Requirements: Applicant must be enrolled or expecting to enroll full-time at a four-year institution or university. Available to U.S. citizens. Applicant must have national guard experience.

Application Requirements: Application form. *Deadline:* varies.

Contact: Capt. Elmarko Magee, Chief of Advertising
Phone: 334-953-2278
E-mail: elmarko.magee@maxwell.af.mil

AIR FORCE ROTC COLLEGE SCHOLARSHIP

Scholarship program provides three- and four-year scholarships in three different types to high school seniors. All scholarship cadets receive a nontaxable monthly allowance (stipend) during the academic year. For more details refer to website http://www.afrotc.com/scholarships/hsschol/types.php.

Award: Scholarship for use in freshman, sophomore, junior, or senior years; renewable. *Number:* 2000–4000. *Amount:* $9000–$15,000.

Eligibility Requirements: Applicant must be age 17-30 and enrolled or expecting to enroll full-time at a two-year or four-year institution or university. Applicant must have 3.0 GPA or higher. Available to U.S. citizens. Applicant or parent must meet one or more of the following requirements: Air Force experience; retired from active duty; disabled or killed as a result of military service; prisoner of war; or missing in action.

Application Requirements: Application form, interview, test scores, transcript. *Deadline:* December 1.

Contact: Ty Christian, Chief Air Force ROTC Advertising Manager
Air Force Reserve Officer Training Corps
551 East Maxwell Boulevard
Maxwell Air Force Base, AL 36112-6106
Phone: 334-953-2278
Fax: 334-953-4384
E-mail: ty.christian@maxwell.af.mil

AIRMEN MEMORIAL FOUNDATION/AIR FORCE SERGEANTS ASSOCIATION

http://www.hqafsa.org/

AIRMEN MEMORIAL FOUNDATION SCHOLARSHIP

Scholarship for full-time undergraduate studies of dependent children of Air Force, Air Force Reserve Command and Air National Guard members in active duty, retired or veteran status. Must be under age of 23, have minimum combined score of 1650 on SAT or 24 on ACT, and a minimum GPA of 3.5.

Award: Scholarship for use in freshman, sophomore, junior, or senior years; not renewable. *Number:* 20. *Amount:* $500–$2000.

Eligibility Requirements: Applicant must be enrolled or expecting to enroll full-time at a four-year institution or university. Applicant must have 3.5 GPA or higher. Available to U.S. and non-U.S. citizens. Applicant or parent must meet one or more of the following requirements: national guard experience; retired from active duty; disabled or killed as a result of military service; prisoner of war; or missing in action.

Application Requirements: Application form, essay, recommendations or references, transcript. *Deadline:* March 31.

Contact: Melanie Shirley, Scholarship Coordinator
Phone: 301-899-3500
Fax: 301-899-8136
E-mail: staff@afsahq.org

CHIEF MASTER SERGEANTS OF THE AIR FORCE SCHOLARSHIP PROGRAM

Scholarship to financially assist the full-time undergraduate studies of dependent children of Air Force, Air Force Reserve Command and Air National Guard enlisted members in active duty, retired or veteran status. Must be under age twenty-three and participate in the Airmen Memorial Foundation Scholarship Program. Must have minimum combined score of 1650 on SAT or 24 on ACT, and a minimum GPA of 3.5.

Award: Scholarship for use in freshman, sophomore, junior, or senior years; not renewable. *Number:* up to 30. *Amount:* $500–$3000.

Eligibility Requirements: Applicant must be enrolled or expecting to enroll full-time at a four-year institution or university. Applicant must have 3.5 GPA or higher. Available to U.S. and non-U.S. citizens. Applicant or parent must meet one or more of the following requirements: national guard experience; retired from active duty; disabled or killed as a result of military service; prisoner of war; or missing in action.

Application Requirements: Application form, essay, recommendations or references, transcript. *Deadline:* March 31.

Contact: Melanie Shirley, Scholarship Coordinator
Phone: 301-899-3500
Fax: 301-899-8136
E-mail: staff@afsahq.org

DEPARTMENT OF VETERANS AFFAIRS (VA)

http://www.gibill.va.gov/

MONTGOMERY GI BILL (SELECTED RESERVE)

Educational assistance program for members of the selected reserve of the Army, Navy, Air Force, Marine Corps and Coast Guard, as well as the Army and Air National Guard. Available to all reservists and National Guard personnel who commit to a six-year obligation, and remain in the Reserve or Guard during the six years. Award is renewable. Monthly benefit is $309 for up to thirty-six months for full-time.

Award: Scholarship for use in freshman, sophomore, junior, senior, or postgraduate years; renewable.

Eligibility Requirements: Applicant must be enrolled or expecting to enroll full- or part-time at a two-year or four-year or technical institution or university. Available to U.S. citizens. Applicant or parent must meet one or more of the following requirements: general military experience; retired from active duty; disabled or killed as a result of military service; prisoner of war; or missing in action.

Application Requirements: Application form. *Deadline:* continuous.

Contact: Keith Wilson, Director, Education Service
Phone: 888-442-4551

DIVERSITYCOMM, INC.

http://www.diversitycomm.net/

US VETERANS MAGAZINE SCHOLARSHIP

We would like you to tell your story in a brief narrative, starting with an introduction about who you are, your interests, and anything else you feel we should know about you. Then, please provide your entry in a 300-500 word essay about your college experience so far, and your future career plans. Graphic or creative presentations are welcome as well.

Award: Scholarship for use in freshman, sophomore, junior, or senior years; renewable. *Number:* 1. *Amount:* $500.

Eligibility Requirements: Applicant must be enrolled or expecting to enroll full- or part-time at a two-year or four-year institution or university. Available to U.S. citizens. Applicant must have general military experience.

Application Requirements: Essay. *Deadline:* August 15.

ELEARNERS.COM

http://www.elearners.com

ELEARNERS MILITARY SCHOLARSHIP

To help ease the burden, eLearners and EducationDynamics is awarding a new $1,000 scholarship to two lucky students who are veterans, active duty service members or spouses of service members or veterans.

Winners can use this one-time payment for whatever they choose. The draw will be held on or about September 2nd and recipients will be notified by mail or phone.

Award: Scholarship for use in freshman, sophomore, junior, senior, graduate, or postgraduate years; not renewable. *Number:* 1–2. *Amount:* $1000.

Eligibility Requirements: Applicant must be age 18-99 and enrolled or expecting to enroll full- or part-time at a two-year or four-year or technical institution or university. Available to U.S. citizens. Applicant must have general military experience.

Application Requirements: Driver's license, essay. *Deadline:* February 28.

Contact: Scholarship Organizer
E-mail: militaryscholarships@elearners.com

FOUNDATION OF THE 1ST CAVALRY DIVISION ASSOCIATION

https://www.1cda.org/

FOUNDATION OF THE 1ST CAVALRY DIVISION ASSOCIATION (IA DRANG) SCHOLARSHIP

• See page 619

FOUNDATION OF THE 1ST CAVALRY DIVISION ASSOCIATION SCHOLARSHIP

• See page 619

IMAGINE AMERICA FOUNDATION

http://www.imagine-america.org

MILITARY AWARD PROGRAM (MAP)

The Military Award Program offers scholarships for veterans and other military students who decide to pursue career college training. This $1,000 career education award is available to any qualified active duty, reservist, honorably discharged or retired veteran of a U.S. military service branch for attendance at a participating career college.

Award: Scholarship for use in freshman, sophomore, junior, or senior years; not renewable. *Number:* 1500. *Amount:* $1000.

Eligibility Requirements: Applicant must be enrolled or expecting to enroll full- or part-time at a two-year or four-year or technical institution. Available to U.S. citizens. Applicant must have general military experience.

Application Requirements: Application form. *Deadline:* continuous.

Contact: Lee Doubleday, Student Services Representative
Imagine America Foundation
12001 Sunrise Valley Drive, Suite 203
Reston, VA 20191
Phone: 571-267-3015
E-mail: leroyd@imagine-america.org

INDIANA DEPARTMENT OF VETERANS AFFAIRS

http://www.in.gov/dva

RESIDENT TUITION FOR ACTIVE DUTY MILITARY PERSONNEL

Applicant must be a nonresident of Indiana serving on active duty and stationed in Indiana and attending any state-supported college or university. Dependents remain eligible for the duration of their enrollment, even if the active duty person is no longer in Indiana. Entitlement is to the resident tuition rate.

Award: Grant for use in freshman, sophomore, junior, senior, graduate, or postgraduate years; renewable.

Eligibility Requirements: Applicant must be enrolled or expecting to enroll full- or part-time at a two-year or four-year or technical institution or university and studying in Indiana. Available to U.S. citizens. Applicant or parent must meet one or more of the following requirements: Air Force or Army experience; retired from active duty; disabled or killed as a result of military service; prisoner of war; or missing in action.

Application Requirements: Application form. *Deadline:* continuous.

Contact: Michael Hamm, State Service Officer
Phone: 317-232-3910
Fax: 317-232-7721
E-mail: mhamm@dva.in.gov

KITCHEN GUIDES

http://www.kitchensguides.com/

SMART KITCHEN IMPROVEMENT SCHOLARSHIP BY KITCHEN GUIDES
• See page 635

PETAZI

https://petazi.com/

NURTURE FOR NATURE SCHOLARSHIP
• See page 692

WISCONSIN DEPARTMENT OF VETERANS AFFAIRS (WDVA)

http://www.dva.state.wi.us/

VETERANS EDUCATION (VETED) REIMBURSEMENT GRANT
• See page 694

MILITARY SERVICE: AIR FORCE NATIONAL GUARD

AIR FORCE AID SOCIETY

http://www.afas.org/

GENERAL HENRY H. ARNOLD EDUCATION GRANT PROGRAM
• See page 695

AIR FORCE RESERVE OFFICER TRAINING CORPS

http://www.afrotc.com/

AFROTC HBCU SCHOLARSHIP PROGRAM
• See page 695

AFROTC HSI SCHOLARSHIP PROGRAM
• See page 695

AIRMEN MEMORIAL FOUNDATION/AIR FORCE SERGEANTS ASSOCIATION

http://www.hqafsa.org/

AIRMEN MEMORIAL FOUNDATION SCHOLARSHIP
• See page 695

CHIEF MASTER SERGEANTS OF THE AIR FORCE SCHOLARSHIP PROGRAM
• See page 696

ALABAMA COMMISSION ON HIGHER EDUCATION

http://www.ache.alabama.gov/

ALABAMA NATIONAL GUARD EDUCATIONAL ASSISTANCE PROGRAM
Renewable award aids Alabama residents who are members of the Alabama National Guard and are enrolled in a nationally recognized accredited college in Alabama. Forms must be signed by a representative of the Alabama Military Department and financial aid officer. Recipient must be in a degree-seeking program.

Award: Scholarship for use in freshman, sophomore, junior, senior, or graduate years; not renewable. *Number:* 400–800. *Amount:* $100–$2000.

Eligibility Requirements: Applicant must be enrolled or expecting to enroll full- or part-time at a two-year or four-year or technical institution or university; resident of Alabama and studying in Alabama. Available to U.S. citizens. Applicant must have national guard experience.

Application Requirements: Application form, financial need analysis. *Deadline:* continuous.

Contact: Cheryl Newton, Grants Coordinator
Phone: 334-242-2273
Fax: 334-242-2269
E-mail: cheryl.newton@ache.alabama.gov

DELAWARE ARMY NATIONAL GUARD

http://www.delawarenationalguard.com/

STATE TUITION ASSISTANCE
You must enlist in the Delaware Air or Army National Guard to be eligible for this scholarship award. Award providing tuition assistance for any member of the Air or Army National Guard attending a Delaware two-year or four-year college. Awards are renewable. Applicant's minimum GPA must be 2.0.

Award: Scholarship for use in freshman, sophomore, junior, or senior years; renewable. *Number:* 1–200. *Amount:* $1–$10,000.

Eligibility Requirements: Applicant must be enrolled or expecting to enroll full- or part-time at a two-year or four-year institution or university and studying in Delaware. Available to U.S. citizens. Applicant or parent must meet one or more of the following requirements: national guard experience; retired from active duty; disabled or killed as a result of military service; prisoner of war; or missing in action.

Application Requirements: Application form. *Deadline:* continuous.

Contact: Robert Csizmadia, State Tuition Assistance Manager
Delaware Army National Guard
1 Vavala Way
New Castle, DE 19720
Phone: 302-326-7012
E-mail: robert.l.csizmadianfg@mail.mil

DEPARTMENT OF VETERANS AFFAIRS (VA)

http://www.gibill.va.gov/

MONTGOMERY GI BILL (SELECTED RESERVE)
• See page 696

RESERVE EDUCATION ASSISTANCE PROGRAM
The program provides educational assistance to members of National Guard and reserve components. Selected Reserve and Individual Ready Reserve (IRR) who are called or ordered to active duty service in response to a war or national emergency as declared by the president or Congress are eligible. For further information see website http://www.GIBILL.va.gov.

Award: Scholarship for use in freshman, sophomore, junior, senior, graduate, or postgraduate years; renewable.

Eligibility Requirements: Applicant must be enrolled or expecting to enroll full- or part-time at a two-year or four-year or technical institution or university. Available to U.S. citizens. Applicant or parent must meet one or more of the following requirements: general military experience; retired from active duty; disabled or killed as a result of military service; prisoner of war; or missing in action.

Application Requirements: Application form. *Deadline:* continuous.

Contact: Keith Wilson, Director, Education Service
   Phone: 888-442-4551

DIVERSITYCOMM, INC.

http://www.diversitycomm.net/

US VETERANS MAGAZINE SCHOLARSHIP

• *See page 696*

ELEARNERS.COM

http://www.elearners.com

ELEARNERS MILITARY SCHOLARSHIP

• *See page 696*

ENLISTED ASSOCIATION OF THE NATIONAL GUARD OF NEW JERSEY

http://www.eang-nj.org/

CSM VINCENT BALDASSARI MEMORIAL SCHOLARSHIP PROGRAM

Scholarships open to the legal children of New Jersey National Guard Members who are also members of the Enlisted Association. Also open to any drilling guardsperson who is a member of the Enlisted Association. Along with application, submit proof of parent's membership and a letter stating the reason for applying and future intents.

Award: Scholarship for use in freshman, sophomore, junior, senior, graduate, or postgraduate years; not renewable. *Number:* 5. *Amount:* $1000.

Eligibility Requirements: Applicant must be enrolled or expecting to enroll full- or part-time at a two-year or four-year or technical institution or university and resident of New Jersey. Available to U.S. and non-U.S. citizens. Applicant or parent must meet one or more of the following requirements: national guard experience; retired from active duty; disabled or killed as a result of military service; prisoner of war; or missing in action.

Application Requirements: Application form, essay, personal photograph, recommendations or references, transcript. *Deadline:* May 15.

Contact: Michael Amoroso, Scholarship Committee Chairman
   Phone: 609-562-0754
   Fax: 609-562-0731
   E-mail: michael.c@us.army.mil

USAA SCHOLARSHIP

Scholarship of $1000 open to any drilling guardsperson (need not be a member of the EANGNJ).

Award: Scholarship for use in freshman, sophomore, junior, senior, graduate, or postgraduate years; not renewable. *Number:* 1. *Amount:* $1000.

Eligibility Requirements: Applicant must be enrolled or expecting to enroll full- or part-time at a two-year or four-year or technical institution or university. Available to U.S. and non-U.S. citizens. Applicant or parent must meet one or more of the following requirements: national guard experience; retired from active duty; disabled or killed as a result of military service; prisoner of war; or missing in action.

Application Requirements: Application form, essay, personal photograph, transcript. *Deadline:* May 15.

Contact: Michael Amoroso, Scholarship Committee Chairman
   Phone: 609-562-0754
   Fax: 609-562-0731
   E-mail: michael.c@us.army.mil

ILLINOIS STUDENT ASSISTANCE COMMISSION (ISAC)

http://www.isac.org/

ILLINOIS NATIONAL GUARD GRANT PROGRAM

Active duty members of the Illinois National Guard, or who are within 12 months of discharge, and who have completed one full year of service are eligible. May be used for study at Illinois two- or four-year public colleges for a maximum of the equivalent of four academic years of full-time enrollment. Deadlines: October 1 of the academic year for full year, March 1 for second/third term, or June 15 for the summer term.

Award: Grant for use in freshman, sophomore, junior, senior, or graduate years; not renewable.

Eligibility Requirements: Applicant must be enrolled or expecting to enroll full- or part-time at a two-year or four-year institution or university; resident of Illinois and studying in Illinois. Available to U.S. citizens. Applicant or parent must meet one or more of the following requirements: national guard experience; retired from active duty; disabled or killed as a result of military service; prisoner of war; or missing in action.

Application Requirements: Application form. *Deadline:* October 1.

Contact: ISAC Call Center Representative
   Illinois Student Assistance Commission (ISAC)
   1755 Lake Cook Road
   Deerfield, IL 60015-5209
   Phone: 800-899-4722
   E-mail: isac.studentservices@illinois.gov

IMAGINE AMERICA FOUNDATION

http://www.imagine-america.org

MILITARY AWARD PROGRAM (MAP)

• *See page 696*

INDIANA COMMISSION FOR HIGHER EDUCATION

http://www.in.gov/che

INDIANA NATIONAL GUARD SUPPLEMENTAL GRANT

The award is a supplement to the Indiana Higher Education Grant program. Applicants must be members of the Indiana National Guard. All Guard paperwork must be completed prior to the start of each semester. The FAFSA must be received by March 10. Award covers certain tuition and fees at select public colleges.

Award: Grant for use in freshman, sophomore, junior, or senior years; not renewable. *Number:* 503–925. *Amount:* $20–$7110.

Eligibility Requirements: Applicant must be enrolled or expecting to enroll full- or part-time at a two-year or four-year institution or university; resident of Indiana and studying in Indiana. Available to U.S. citizens. Applicant or parent must meet one or more of the following requirements: national guard experience; retired from active duty; disabled or killed as a result of military service; prisoner of war; or missing in action.

Application Requirements: Application form. *Deadline:* March 10.

Contact: Kathryn Moore, Grants Counselor
   Indiana Commission for Higher Education
   150 West Market Street, Suite 500
   Indianapolis, IN 46204-2805
   Phone: 317-232-2350
   Fax: 317-232-2360
   E-mail: kmoore@ssaci.in.gov

INDIANA DEPARTMENT OF VETERANS AFFAIRS

http://www.in.gov/dva

NATIONAL GUARD SCHOLARSHIP EXTENSION PROGRAM

A scholarship extension applicant is eligible for a tuition scholarship under Indiana Code 21-13-5-4 for a period not to exceed the period of scholarship extension the applicant served on active duty as a member of the National Guard (mobilized and deployed). Must apply not later than one (1) year after the applicant ceases to be a member of the Indiana National Guard. Applicant should apply through the education officer of their last unit of assignment.

Award: Grant for use in freshman, sophomore, junior, or senior years; renewable.

Eligibility Requirements: Applicant must be enrolled or expecting to enroll full- or part-time at a two-year or four-year or technical institution or university; resident of Indiana and studying in Indiana. Available to U.S. citizens. Applicant must have national guard experience.

Application Requirements: Application form. *Deadline:* continuous.

Contact: Pamela Moody, National Guard Education Officer
Indiana Department of Veterans Affairs
302 West Washington Street, Room E-120
Indianapolis, IN 46204
Phone: 317-964-7017
E-mail: pamela.moody@in.ngb.army.mil

NATIONAL GUARD TUITION SUPPLEMENT PROGRAM

Applicant must be a member of the Indiana National Guard, in active drilling status, who has not been AWOL during the last 12 months, does not possess a bachelor's degree, possesses the requisite academic qualifications, meets the requirements of the state-supported college or university, and meets all National Guard requirements.

Award: Grant for use in freshman, sophomore, junior, or senior years; renewable.

Eligibility Requirements: Applicant must be enrolled or expecting to enroll full- or part-time at a two-year or four-year or technical institution or university; resident of Indiana and studying in Indiana. Available to U.S. citizens. Applicant must have national guard experience.

Application Requirements: Application form. *Deadline:* continuous.

Contact: Michael Hamm, State Service Officer
Phone: 317-232-3910
Fax: 317-232-7721
E-mail: mhamm@dva.in.gov

TUITION AND FEE REMISSION FOR CHILDREN AND SPOUSES OF NATIONAL GUARD MEMBERS

Award to an individual whose father, mother or spouse was a member of the Indiana National Guard and suffered a service-connected death while serving on state active duty (which includes mobilized and deployed for federal active duty). The student must be eligible to pay the resident tuition rate at the state-supported college or university and must possess the requisite academic qualifications.

Award: Grant for use in freshman, sophomore, junior, or senior years; renewable.

Eligibility Requirements: Applicant must be enrolled or expecting to enroll full- or part-time at a two-year or four-year or technical institution or university and studying in Indiana. Available to U.S. citizens. Applicant or parent must meet one or more of the following requirements: national guard experience; retired from active duty; disabled or killed as a result of military service; prisoner of war; or missing in action.

Application Requirements: Application form. *Deadline:* continuous.

Contact: Courtney Carr, Adjutant General
Indiana Department of Veterans Affairs
2002 South Holt Road
Indianapolis, IN 46241
Phone: 317-247-3559
E-mail: c.carr@in.ngb.army.mil

IOWA COLLEGE STUDENT AID COMMISSION

http://www.iowacollegeaid.gov/

IOWA NATIONAL GUARD EDUCATION ASSISTANCE PROGRAM

Program provides postsecondary grant assistance to members of Iowa National Guard Units. Must study at a postsecondary institution in Iowa.

Award: Grant for use in freshman, sophomore, junior, or senior years; not renewable.

Eligibility Requirements: Applicant must be enrolled or expecting to enroll full- or part-time at a two-year or four-year or technical institution or university; resident of Iowa and studying in Iowa. Available to U.S. citizens. Applicant must have national guard experience.

Application Requirements: Application form. *Deadline:* July 1.

Contact: Tracy Davis, Executive Officer 1
Iowa College Student Aid Commission
430 E Grand Avenue, FL 3
Des Moines, IA 50309-1920
Phone: 877-272-4456

KENTUCKY HIGHER EDUCATION ASSISTANCE AUTHORITY (KHEAA)

http://www.kheaa.com/

KENTUCKY NATIONAL GUARD TUITION AWARD

Provides tuition assistance for active members of the Kentucky National Guard to attend a Kentucky college or university. Guard members may apply through their unit.

Award: Grant for use in freshman, sophomore, junior, or senior years; renewable. *Number:* 1000–1500. *Amount:* $100–$11,500.

Eligibility Requirements: Applicant must be enrolled or expecting to enroll full- or part-time at a two-year or four-year or technical institution or university; resident of Kentucky and studying in Kentucky. Available to U.S. citizens. Applicant must have national guard experience.

Application Requirements: Application form. *Deadline:* continuous.

Contact: Charles Newton
Kentucky Higher Education Assistance Authority (KHEAA)
Boone National Guard
Frankfort, KY 40601
Phone: 502-607-1039
E-mail: charles.d.newton@nfg.mail.mil

KITCHEN GUIDES

http://www.kitchensguides.com/

SMART KITCHEN IMPROVEMENT SCHOLARSHIP BY KITCHEN GUIDES

• *See page 635*

LOUISIANA NATIONAL GUARD, JOINT TASK FORCE LA

http://geauxguard.com/organization/joint-force-headquarters-jfhq-la/

LOUISIANA NATIONAL GUARD STATE TUITION EXEMPTION PROGRAM

Renewable award for college undergraduates to receive tuition exemption upon satisfactory performance in the Louisiana National Guard. Applicant must attend a state-funded institution in Louisiana, be a resident and registered voter in Louisiana, meet the academic and residency requirements of the university attended, and provide documentation of Louisiana National Guard enlistment. The exemption can be used for up to 15 semesters. Minimum 2.5 GPA required.

Award: Scholarship for use in freshman, sophomore, junior, or senior years; renewable.

Eligibility Requirements: Applicant must be enrolled or expecting to enroll full- or part-time at a two-year or four-year or technical institution or university; resident of Louisiana and studying in Louisiana. Applicant must have 2.5 GPA or higher. Available to U.S. citizens. Applicant or parent must meet one or more of the following requirements: national guard experience; retired from active duty; disabled or killed as a result of military service; prisoner of war; or missing in action.

Application Requirements: Application form, test scores, transcript. *Deadline:* continuous.

Contact: Jona Hughes, Education Services Officer
Louisiana National Guard, Joint Task Force LA
Building 35, Jackson Barracks, JI-PD
New Orleans, LA 70146-0330
Phone: 504-278-8531 Ext. 8304
Fax: 504-278-8025
E-mail: hughesj@la-arng.ngb.army.mil

NORTH CAROLINA NATIONAL GUARD

http://nc.ng.mil/Pages/default.aspx

NORTH CAROLINA NATIONAL GUARD TUITION ASSISTANCE PROGRAM

Scholarship for members of the North Carolina Air and Army National Guard who will remain in the service for two years following the period for which assistance is provided. Must reapply for each academic period. For use at approved North Carolina institutions.

Award: Grant for use in freshman, sophomore, junior, senior, or graduate years; not renewable. *Amount:* $100–$3440.

Eligibility Requirements: Applicant must be enrolled or expecting to enroll full- or part-time at a two-year or four-year or technical institution or university; resident of North Carolina and studying in North Carolina. Available to U.S. citizens. Applicant or parent must meet one or more of the following requirements: national guard experience; retired from active duty; disabled or killed as a result of military service; prisoner of war; or missing in action.

Application Requirements: Application form. *Deadline:* continuous.

Contact: Ms. Stacy Steinmetz, NCTAP Manager
North Carolina National Guard
1636 Gold Star Drive
Raleigh, NC 27607
Phone: 919-664-6272
E-mail: stacy.m.steinmetz.nfg@mail.mil

OHIO NATIONAL GUARD

http://www.ong.ohio.gov/

OHIO NATIONAL GUARD SCHOLARSHIP PROGRAM

Scholarships are for undergraduate studies at an approved Ohio post-secondary institution. Applicants must enlist for six or three years of Selective Service Reserve Duty in the Ohio National Guard. Scholarship pays 100% instructional and general fees for public institutions and an average of cost of public universities is available for private schools. May reapply up to four years of studies (12 quarters or 8 semesters) for six year enlistment and two years of studies (6 quarters or 4 semesters) for three year enlistment. Deadlines: July 1 (fall), November 1 (winter quarter/spring semester), February 1 (spring quarter), April 1 (summer).

Award: Scholarship for use in freshman, sophomore, junior, or senior years; not renewable. *Number:* up to 3500. *Amount:* up to $4006.

Eligibility Requirements: Applicant must be enrolled or expecting to enroll full- or part-time at a two-year or four-year or technical institution or university; resident of Ohio and studying in Ohio. Available to U.S. citizens. Applicant must have national guard experience.

Application Requirements: Application form. *Deadline:* varies.

Contact: Mrs. Toni Davis, Grants Administrator
Ohio National Guard
2825 West Dublin Granville Road, ONGSP
Columbus, OH 43235-2789
Phone: 614-336-7143
Fax: 614-336-7318
E-mail: toni.davis7@us.army.mil

PENNSYLVANIA HIGHER EDUCATION ASSISTANCE AGENCY

http://www.pheaa.org/

POSTSECONDARY EDUCATION GRATUITY PROGRAM

The program offers waiver of tuition and fees for children of Pennsylvania police officers, firefighters, rescue or ambulance squad members, corrections facility employees, or National Guard members who died in line of duty after January 1, 1976.

Award: Grant for use in freshman, sophomore, junior, or senior years; renewable.

Eligibility Requirements: Applicant must be enrolled or expecting to enroll full-time at a two-year or four-year institution or university; resident of Pennsylvania and studying in Pennsylvania. Available to U.S. citizens. Applicant or parent must meet one or more of the following requirements: national guard experience; retired from active duty; disabled or killed as a result of military service; prisoner of war; or missing in action.

Application Requirements: Application form. *Deadline:* July 1.

Contact: Keith New, Director of Public Relations
Phone: 717-720-2509
E-mail: knew@pheaa.org

PETAZI

https://petazi.com/

NURTURE FOR NATURE SCHOLARSHIP
• See page 692

WISCONSIN DEPARTMENT OF VETERANS AFFAIRS (WDVA)

http://www.dva.state.wi.us/

VETERANS EDUCATION (VETED) REIMBURSEMENT GRANT
• See page 694

MILITARY SERVICE: ARMY

1ST CAVALRY DIVISION ASSOCIATION

https://www.1CDA.org

1ST CAVALRY DIVISION ASSOCIATION SCHOLARSHIP FOUNDATION
• See page 592

AMERICAN LEGION AUXILIARY DEPARTMENT OF KENTUCKY

http://www.kylegion.org/

AMERICAN LEGION AUXILIARY DEPARTMENT OF KENTUCKY LAURA BLACKBURN MEMORIAL SCHOLARSHIP

Scholarship to the child, grandchild, or great grandchild of a veteran who served in the Armed Forces. Applicant must be a Kentucky resident.

Award: Scholarship for use in freshman year; not renewable. *Number:* 1. *Amount:* $1000.

Eligibility Requirements: Applicant must be high school student; planning to enroll or expecting to enroll full-time at a four-year institution or university and resident of Kentucky. Available to U.S. citizens. Applicant or parent must meet one or more of the following requirements: Army experience; retired from active duty; disabled or killed as a result of military service; prisoner of war; or missing in action.

Application Requirements: Application form, financial need analysis, transcript. *Deadline:* March 31.

Contact: Betty Cook, Secretary and Treasurer
Phone: 270-932-7533
Fax: 270-932-7672
E-mail: secretarykyala@aol.com

ARMY OFFICERS' WIVES CLUB OF GREATER WASHINGTON AREA

http://www.aowcgwa.org/

ARMY OFFICERS WIVES CLUB OF THE GREATER WASHINGTON AREA SCHOLARSHIP

Scholarship for high school seniors, college students or children or spouses of U.S. Army personnel. Scholarship awards are based on scholastic merit and community involvement.

Award: Scholarship for use in freshman, sophomore, junior, or senior years; not renewable. *Number:* 1–3. *Amount:* $100–$500.

Eligibility Requirements: Applicant must be enrolled or expecting to enroll full-time at a four-year institution or university. Available to U.S. citizens. Applicant or parent must meet one or more of the following requirements: Army experience; retired from active duty; disabled or killed as a result of military service; prisoner of war; or missing in action.

Application Requirements: Application form, essay, military dependent ID card, recommendations or references, self-addressed stamped envelope with application, transcript. *Deadline:* March 31.

Contact: Janis Waller, Scholarship Committee Chair
Army Officers' Wives Club of Greater Washington Area
12025 William and Mary Circle
Woodbridge, VA 22192-1634

DEPARTMENT OF THE ARMY

http://www.goarmy.com/rotc

ARMY ROTC GREEN TO GOLD SCHOLARSHIP PROGRAM FOR TWO-YEAR, THREE-YEAR AND FOUR-YEAR SCHOLARSHIPS, ACTIVE DUTY ENLISTED PERSONNEL

• *See page 610*

ARMY (ROTC) RESERVE OFFICERS TRAINING CORPS TWO-, THREE-, FOUR-YEAR CAMPUS-BASED SCHOLARSHIPS

• *See page 610*

U.S. ARMY ROTC FOUR-YEAR COLLEGE SCHOLARSHIP

• *See page 610*

U.S. ARMY ROTC FOUR-YEAR HISTORICALLY BLACK COLLEGE/UNIVERSITY SCHOLARSHIP

• *See page 610*

U.S. ARMY ROTC MILITARY JUNIOR COLLEGE (MJC) SCHOLARSHIP

• *See page 611*

DEPARTMENT OF VETERANS AFFAIRS (VA)

http://www.gibill.va.gov/

MONTGOMERY GI BILL (SELECTED RESERVE)

• *See page 696*

DIVERSITYCOMM, INC.

http://www.diversitycomm.net/

US VETERANS MAGAZINE SCHOLARSHIP

• *See page 696*

ELEARNERS.COM

http://www.elearners.com

ELEARNERS MILITARY SCHOLARSHIP

• *See page 696*

FOUNDATION OF THE 1ST CAVALRY DIVISION ASSOCIATION

https://www.1cda.org/

FOUNDATION OF THE 1ST CAVALRY DIVISION ASSOCIATION (IA DRANG) SCHOLARSHIP

• *See page 619*

FOUNDATION OF THE 1ST CAVALRY DIVISION ASSOCIATION SCHOLARSHIP

• *See page 619*

IMAGINE AMERICA FOUNDATION

http://www.imagine-america.org

MILITARY AWARD PROGRAM (MAP)

• *See page 696*

INDIANA DEPARTMENT OF VETERANS AFFAIRS

http://www.in.gov/dva

RESIDENT TUITION FOR ACTIVE DUTY MILITARY PERSONNEL

• *See page 696*

KITCHEN GUIDES

http://www.kitchensguides.com/

SMART KITCHEN IMPROVEMENT SCHOLARSHIP BY KITCHEN GUIDES

• *See page 635*

PETAZI

https://petazi.com/

NURTURE FOR NATURE SCHOLARSHIP

• *See page 692*

SOCIETY OF DAUGHTERS OF THE UNITED STATES ARMY

SOCIETY OF DAUGHTERS OF THE UNITED STATES ARMY SCHOLARSHIPS

• *See page 669*

STUDY.COM

study.com

ARMY ROTC STUDY.COM SCHOLARSHIP

• *See page 671*

WISCONSIN DEPARTMENT OF VETERANS AFFAIRS (WDVA)

http://www.dva.state.wi.us/

VETERANS EDUCATION (VETED) REIMBURSEMENT GRANT

• *See page 694*

WOMEN'S ARMY CORPS VETERANS' ASSOCIATION

http://www.armywomen.org/

WOMEN'S ARMY CORPS VETERANS' ASSOCIATION SCHOLARSHIP

Scholarship to graduating high school senior showing academic promise. Must be a child, grandchild, niece or nephew of an Army servicewoman. Minimum cumulative GPA of 3.5 required. Applicants must plan to enroll in a degree program as a full-time student at an accredited college or university in the United States.

Award: Scholarship for use in freshman year; not renewable. *Number:* 1. *Amount:* $1500.

Eligibility Requirements: Applicant must be high school student and planning to enroll or expecting to enroll full-time at a four-year institution or university. Applicant must have 2.5 GPA or higher. Available to U.S. citizens. Applicant or parent must meet one or more of the following requirements: Army experience; retired from active duty; disabled or killed as a result of military service; prisoner of war; or missing in action.

Application Requirements: Application form. *Deadline:* April 1.

Contact: Eldora Engebretson, Scholarship Committee
    Phone: 623-566-9299
    E-mail: info@armywomen.org

MILITARY SERVICE: ARMY NATIONAL GUARD

ALABAMA COMMISSION ON HIGHER EDUCATION

http://www.ache.alabama.gov/

ALABAMA NATIONAL GUARD EDUCATIONAL ASSISTANCE PROGRAM

• *See page 697*

CONNECTICUT ARMY NATIONAL GUARD

http://ct.ng.mil/Pages/default.aspx

CONNECTICUT ARMY NATIONAL GUARD 100% TUITION WAIVER

Program is for any active member of the Connecticut Army National Guard in good standing. Must be a resident of Connecticut attending any Connecticut state (public) university, community-technical college or regional vocational-technical school. The total number of available awards is unlimited.

Award: Scholarship for use in freshman, sophomore, junior, or senior years; not renewable. *Amount:* $16,000.

Eligibility Requirements: Applicant must be age 17-65; enrolled or expecting to enroll full- or part-time at a two-year or four-year or technical institution or university; resident of Connecticut and studying in Connecticut. Available to U.S. and non-U.S. citizens. Applicant or parent must meet one or more of the following requirements: national guard experience; retired from active duty; disabled or killed as a result of military service; prisoner of war; or missing in action.

Application Requirements: Application form. *Deadline:* July 1.

Contact: Capt. Jeremy Lingenfelser, Education Services Officer
    Connecticut Army National Guard
    360 Broad Street
    Hartford, CT 06105-3795
    Phone: 860-524-4816
    Fax: 860-524-4904
    E-mail: education@ct.ngb.army.mil

DELAWARE ARMY NATIONAL GUARD

http://www.delawarenationalguard.com/

STATE TUITION ASSISTANCE

• *See page 697*

DEPARTMENT OF THE ARMY

http://www.goarmy.com/rotc

U.S. ARMY ROTC FOUR-YEAR COLLEGE SCHOLARSHIP

• *See page 610*

U.S. ARMY ROTC FOUR-YEAR HISTORICALLY BLACK COLLEGE/UNIVERSITY SCHOLARSHIP

• *See page 610*

U.S. ARMY ROTC GUARANTEED RESERVE FORCES DUTY (GRFD), (ARNG/USAR) AND DEDICATED ARNG SCHOLARSHIPS

• *See page 611*

U.S. ARMY ROTC MILITARY JUNIOR COLLEGE (MJC) SCHOLARSHIP

• *See page 611*

DEPARTMENT OF VETERANS AFFAIRS (VA)

http://www.gibill.va.gov/

MONTGOMERY GI BILL (SELECTED RESERVE)

• *See page 696*

RESERVE EDUCATION ASSISTANCE PROGRAM

• *See page 697*

DIVERSITYCOMM, INC.

http://www.diversitycomm.net/

US VETERANS MAGAZINE SCHOLARSHIP

• *See page 696*

ELEARNERS.COM

http://www.elearners.com

ELEARNERS MILITARY SCHOLARSHIP

• *See page 696*

ENLISTED ASSOCIATION OF THE NATIONAL GUARD OF NEW JERSEY

http://www.eang-nj.org/

CSM VINCENT BALDASSARI MEMORIAL SCHOLARSHIP PROGRAM

• *See page 698*

USAA SCHOLARSHIP

• *See page 698*

FLEET RESERVE ASSOCIATION EDUCATION FOUNDATION

http://www.fra.org/foundation

TREADWELL/PRINGLE SCHOLARSHIPS

Scholarship for members; spouses; dependent biological, step or adoptive children; or biological, step or adoptive grandchildren of a FRA member in good standing, currently or at time of death. Applicant must be a U.S.

citizen, registered as a full-time student in an accredited college located in the United States.

Award: Scholarship for use in freshman, sophomore, junior, senior, graduate, or postgraduate years; not renewable.

Eligibility Requirements: Applicant must be enrolled or expecting to enroll full-time at a two-year or four-year institution or university. Available to U.S. citizens. Applicant must have national guard experience.

Application Requirements: Application form, community service, essay, financial need analysis. *Deadline:* April 15.

Contact: Alicia Landis, Program Administrator
    Phone: 703-683-1400
    E-mail: scholars@fra.org

FOUNDATION OF THE 1ST CAVALRY DIVISION ASSOCIATION

https://www.1cda.org/

FOUNDATION OF THE 1ST CAVALRY DIVISION ASSOCIATION SCHOLARSHIP
• *See page 619*

ILLINOIS STUDENT ASSISTANCE COMMISSION (ISAC)

http://www.isac.org/

ILLINOIS NATIONAL GUARD GRANT PROGRAM
• *See page 698*

IMAGINE AMERICA FOUNDATION

http://www.imagine-america.org

MILITARY AWARD PROGRAM (MAP)
• *See page 696*

INDIANA COMMISSION FOR HIGHER EDUCATION

http://www.in.gov/che

INDIANA NATIONAL GUARD SUPPLEMENTAL GRANT
• *See page 698*

INDIANA DEPARTMENT OF VETERANS AFFAIRS

http://www.in.gov/dva

NATIONAL GUARD SCHOLARSHIP EXTENSION PROGRAM
• *See page 698*

NATIONAL GUARD TUITION SUPPLEMENT PROGRAM
• *See page 699*

TUITION AND FEE REMISSION FOR CHILDREN AND SPOUSES OF NATIONAL GUARD MEMBERS
• *See page 699*

IOWA COLLEGE STUDENT AID COMMISSION

http://www.iowacollegeaid.gov/

IOWA NATIONAL GUARD EDUCATION ASSISTANCE PROGRAM
• *See page 699*

KENTUCKY HIGHER EDUCATION ASSISTANCE AUTHORITY (KHEAA)

http://www.kheaa.com/

KENTUCKY NATIONAL GUARD TUITION AWARD
• *See page 699*

KITCHEN GUIDES

http://www.kitchensguides.com/

SMART KITCHEN IMPROVEMENT SCHOLARSHIP BY KITCHEN GUIDES
• *See page 635*

LOUISIANA NATIONAL GUARD, JOINT TASK FORCE LA

http://geauxguard.com/organization/joint-force-headquarters-jfhq-la/

LOUISIANA NATIONAL GUARD STATE TUITION EXEMPTION PROGRAM
• *See page 699*

NORTH CAROLINA NATIONAL GUARD

http://nc.ng.mil/Pages/default.aspx

NORTH CAROLINA NATIONAL GUARD TUITION ASSISTANCE PROGRAM
• *See page 700*

OHIO NATIONAL GUARD

http://www.ong.ohio.gov/

OHIO NATIONAL GUARD SCHOLARSHIP PROGRAM
• *See page 700*

PENNSYLVANIA HIGHER EDUCATION ASSISTANCE AGENCY

http://www.pheaa.org/

POSTSECONDARY EDUCATION GRATUITY PROGRAM
• *See page 700*

PETAZI

https://petazi.com/

NURTURE FOR NATURE SCHOLARSHIP
• *See page 692*

SOCIETY OF DAUGHTERS OF THE UNITED STATES ARMY

SOCIETY OF DAUGHTERS OF THE UNITED STATES ARMY SCHOLARSHIPS
• *See page 669*

STUDY.COM

study.com

ARMY ROTC STUDY.COM SCHOLARSHIP
• *See page 671*

WISCONSIN DEPARTMENT OF VETERANS AFFAIRS (WDVA)

http://www.dva.state.wi.us/

VETERANS EDUCATION (VETED) REIMBURSEMENT GRANT
• *See page 694*

MILITARY SERVICE: COAST GUARD

DEPARTMENT OF VETERANS AFFAIRS (VA)

http://www.gibill.va.gov/

MONTGOMERY GI BILL (SELECTED RESERVE)
• *See page 696*

DIVERSITYCOMM, INC.

http://www.diversitycomm.net/

US VETERANS MAGAZINE SCHOLARSHIP
• *See page 696*

ELEARNERS.COM

http://www.elearners.com

ELEARNERS MILITARY SCHOLARSHIP
• *See page 696*

FLEET RESERVE ASSOCIATION EDUCATION FOUNDATION

http://www.fra.org/foundation

DORAN/BLAIR SCHOLARSHIPS
• *See page 563*

FLEET RESERVE ASSOCIATION EDUCATION FOUNDATION SCHOLARSHIPS

Applicant or sponsor has to be an FRA non-member, living, on active duty, reserve, retired, or honorably discharged veteran of the Navy, Marine Corps or Coast Guard. The applicant must be an FRA non-member; spouse; dependent biological, step, or adoptive child; or biological, step, or adoptive grandchild; or biological, step, or adoptive great grandchild of the FRA non-member. Applicant must be a U.S. citizen, registered as a full-time student in an accredited college located in the United States of America.

Award: Scholarship for use in freshman, sophomore, junior, senior, graduate, or postgraduate years; not renewable. *Number:* 1–10. *Amount:* $1000–$5000.

Eligibility Requirements: Applicant must be enrolled or expecting to enroll full-time at a two-year or four-year institution or university. Available to U.S. citizens. Applicant must have served in the Coast Guard.

Application Requirements: Application form, community service, essay, financial need analysis. *Deadline:* April 15.

Contact: Alicia Landis, Program Administrator
　　　　　Phone: 703-683-1400 Ext. 107
　　　　　E-mail: scholars@fra.org

TREADWELL/PRINGLE SCHOLARSHIPS
• *See page 702*

IMAGINE AMERICA FOUNDATION

http://www.imagine-america.org

MILITARY AWARD PROGRAM (MAP)
• *See page 696*

KITCHEN GUIDES

http://www.kitchensguides.com/

SMART KITCHEN IMPROVEMENT SCHOLARSHIP BY KITCHEN GUIDES
• *See page 635*

LADIES AUXILIARY OF THE FLEET RESERVE ASSOCIATION

http://www.fra.org/

LADIES AUXILIARY OF THE FLEET RESERVE ASSOCIATION SCHOLARSHIP
• *See page 567*

SAM ROSE MEMORIAL SCHOLARSHIP
• *See page 568*

PETAZI

https://petazi.com/

NURTURE FOR NATURE SCHOLARSHIP
• *See page 692*

TAILHOOK EDUCATIONAL FOUNDATION

http://www.tailhook.org/

TAILHOOK EDUCATIONAL FOUNDATION SCHOLARSHIP

Applicant must be a high school graduate and the natural, step or adopted son or daughter of a current or former Naval Aviator, Naval Flight Officer or Naval Air-crewman. Individuals or children of individuals serving or having served on board a U.S. Navy Aircraft Carrier in ship's company or the Air Wing also eligible.

Award: Scholarship for use in freshman, sophomore, junior, or senior years; not renewable. *Number:* 100. *Amount:* $2500–$15,000.

Eligibility Requirements: Applicant must be enrolled or expecting to enroll full-time at a two-year or four-year institution or university. Applicant must have 3.0 GPA or higher. Available to U.S. citizens. Applicant or parent must meet one or more of the following requirements: Coast Guard experience; retired from active duty; disabled or killed as a result of military service; prisoner of war; or missing in action.

Application Requirements: Application form, essay. *Deadline:* March 1.

Contact: Rodger Welch, Executive Director
　　　　　Tailhook Educational Foundation
　　　　　9696 Businesspark Avenue
　　　　　San Diego, CA 92131
　　　　　Phone: 800-269-8267
　　　　　Fax: 858-578-8839
　　　　　E-mail: rlw@tailhook.net

U.S. COAST GUARD

http://www.gocoastguard/cspi

COLLEGE STUDENT PRE-COMMISSIONING INITIATIVE (CSPI)
• *See page 681*

WISCONSIN DEPARTMENT OF VETERANS AFFAIRS (WDVA)

http://www.dva.state.wi.us/

VETERANS EDUCATION (VETED) REIMBURSEMENT GRANT
• *See page 694*

MILITARY SERVICE: GENERAL

ACADGILD

https://acadgild.com

ACADGILD MERIT-BASED SCHOLARSHIPS
• *See page 593*

AMERICAN LEGION AUXILIARY DEPARTMENT OF ALABAMA

http://www.legional.org/

AMERICAN LEGION AUXILIARY DEPARTMENT OF ALABAMA SCHOLARSHIP PROGRAM

Merit-based scholarships for Alabama residents, preferably ages 17 to 25, who are children or grandchildren of veterans of World War I, World War II, Korea, Vietnam, Operation Desert Storm, Beirut, Grenada, or Panama. Submit proof of relationship and service record. Renewable awards of $850 each. Must send self-addressed stamped envelope for application.

Award: Scholarship for use in freshman, sophomore, junior, or senior years; renewable. *Number:* up to 40. *Amount:* $850.

Eligibility Requirements: Applicant must be age 17-25; enrolled or expecting to enroll full-time at a four-year institution or university and resident of Alabama. Applicant must have 3.5 GPA or higher. Available to U.S. citizens. Applicant or parent must meet one or more of the following requirements: general military experience; retired from active duty; disabled or killed as a result of military service; prisoner of war; or missing in action.

Application Requirements: Application form, birth certificate, service record, financial need analysis, personal photograph, recommendations or references, self-addressed stamped envelope with application, test scores, transcript. *Deadline:* April 1.

Contact: Education and Scholarship Chairperson
American Legion Auxiliary Department of Alabama
120 North Jackson Street
Montgomery, AL 36104-3811
Phone: 334-262-1176
Fax: 334-262-1176
E-mail: americanlegionaux1@juno.com

AMERICAN LEGION AUXILIARY DEPARTMENT OF CALIFORNIA

http://www.calegionaux.org/

AMERICAN LEGION AUXILIARY DEPARTMENT OF CALIFORNIA GENERAL SCHOLARSHIP

Award ranges from $500 to $1000 for high school senior or graduate of an accredited high school who has not been able to begin college due to circumstances of illness or finance. Student must attend a California college or university. Deadline March 16.

Award: Scholarship for use in freshman, sophomore, junior, or senior years; not renewable. *Amount:* $500–$1000.

Eligibility Requirements: Applicant must be high school student; planning to enroll or expecting to enroll full- or part-time at a two-year or four-year institution or university; resident of California and studying in California. Available to U.S. citizens. Applicant must have general military experience.

Application Requirements: Application form. *Deadline:* March 16.

Contact: Ruby Kapsalis, Secretary/Treasurer
Phone: 415-862-5092
Fax: 415-861-8365
E-mail: calegionaux@calegionaux.org

AMERICAN LEGION AUXILIARY DEPARTMENT OF CONNECTICUT

http://www.ct.legion.org/

AMERICAN LEGION AUXILIARY DEPARTMENT OF CONNECTICUT MEMORIAL EDUCATIONAL GRANT
• *See page 550*

AMERICAN LEGION AUXILIARY DEPARTMENT OF CONNECTICUT PAST PRESIDENTS' PARLEY MEMORIAL EDUCATION GRANT
• *See page 550*

AMERICAN LEGION AUXILIARY DEPARTMENT OF IOWA

http://www.ialegion.org/ala

AMERICAN LEGION AUXILIARY DEPARTMENT OF IOWA CHILDREN OF VETERANS MERIT AWARD

One-time award available to a high school senior, child of a veteran who served in the armed forces during eligibility dates for American Legion membership. Must be U.S. citizen and Iowa resident enrolled at an Iowa institution.

Award: Scholarship for use in freshman year; not renewable. *Number:* 10. *Amount:* $400.

Eligibility Requirements: Applicant must be high school student; planning to enroll or expecting to enroll full- or part-time at a two-year or four-year or technical institution or university; resident of Iowa and studying in Iowa. Available to U.S. citizens. Applicant or parent must meet one or more of the following requirements: general military experience; retired from active duty; disabled or killed as a result of military service; prisoner of war; or missing in action.

Application Requirements: Application form, essay, financial need analysis, personal photograph. *Deadline:* June 1.

Contact: Marlene Valentine, Executive Director
American Legion Auxiliary Department of Iowa
720 Lyon Street
Des Moines, IA 50309
Phone: 515-282-7987
E-mail: alasectreas@ialegion.org

AMERICAN LEGION AUXILIARY DEPARTMENT OF KENTUCKY

http://www.kylegion.org/

AMERICAN LEGION AUXILIARY DEPARTMENT OF KENTUCKY MARY BARRETT MARSHALL SCHOLARSHIP

Scholarship to the daughter or grand daughter of a veteran in The American Legion. Applicant must attend a Kentucky college, and demonstrate financial need.

Award: Scholarship for use in freshman year; not renewable. *Number:* 1. *Amount:* $1000.

Eligibility Requirements: Applicant must be high school student; planning to enroll or expecting to enroll full-time at a four-year institution or university; female and studying in Kentucky. Available to U.S. citizens. Applicant or parent must meet one or more of the following requirements: general military experience; retired from active duty; disabled or killed as a result of military service; prisoner of war; or missing in action.

Application Requirements: Application form, financial need analysis, transcript. *Deadline:* April 1.

Contact: Betty Cook, Secretary and Treasurer
Phone: 270-932-7533
Fax: 270-932-7672
E-mail: secretarykyala@aol.com

AMERICAN LEGION AUXILIARY DEPARTMENT OF MAINE

http://www.mainelegion.org/

AMERICAN LEGION AUXILIARY DEPARTMENT OF MAINE DANIEL E. LAMBERT MEMORIAL SCHOLARSHIP

Scholarships to assist young men and women in continuing their education beyond high school. Must demonstrate financial need, must be a resident of the State of Maine, U.S. citizen, and parent must be a veteran.

Award: Scholarship for use in freshman year; not renewable. Number: up to 2. Amount: $1000.

Eligibility Requirements: Applicant must be high school student; planning to enroll or expecting to enroll full-time at a four-year institution or university and resident of Maine. Available to U.S. citizens. Applicant or parent must meet one or more of the following requirements: general military experience; retired from active duty; disabled or killed as a result of military service; prisoner of war; or missing in action.

Application Requirements: Application form, financial need analysis. Deadline: May 1.

Contact: Mary Wells, Education Chairman
Phone: 207-532-6007
E-mail: aladeptsecme@verizon.net

AMERICAN LEGION AUXILIARY DEPARTMENT OF MASSACHUSETTS

http://www.masslegion-aux.org/

AMERICAN LEGION AUXILIARY DEPARTMENT OF MASSACHUSETTS DEPARTMENT PRESIDENT'S SCHOLARSHIP

• See page 595

AMERICAN LEGION AUXILIARY DEPARTMENT OF MICHIGAN

http://www.michalaux.org/

AMERICAN LEGION AUXILIARY DEPARTMENT OF MICHIGAN MEMORIAL SCHOLARSHIP

Scholarship for daughter, granddaughter, and great-granddaughter of any honorably discharged or deceased veteran of U.S. wars or conflicts. Must be Michigan resident for minimum of one year, female between 16 and 21 years, and attend college in Michigan. Must include copy of military discharge and copy of parent or guardian's IRS 1040 form.

Award: Scholarship for use in freshman or sophomore years; not renewable. Number: 10–20. Amount: $500.

Eligibility Requirements: Applicant must be age 16-21; enrolled or expecting to enroll full-time at a two-year or four-year or technical institution or university; female; resident of Michigan and studying in Michigan. Applicant must have 3.5 GPA or higher. Available to U.S. citizens. Applicant must have general military experience.

Application Requirements: Application form, financial need analysis. Deadline: March 15.

Contact: Scholarship Coordinator
American Legion Auxiliary Department of Michigan
212 North Verlinden Avenue, Suite B
Lansing, MI 48915
Phone: 517-267-8809 Ext. 21
E-mail: info@michalaux.org

AMERICAN LEGION AUXILIARY DEPARTMENT OF MICHIGAN SCHOLARSHIP FOR NON-TRADITIONAL STUDENT

Applicant must be a dependent of a veteran. Must be one of the following: nontraditional student returning to classroom after some period of time in which their education was interrupted, student over the age of 22 attending college for the first time to pursue a degree, or student over the age of 22 attending a trade or vocational school. Applicants must be Michigan residents only and attend Michigan institution. Judging based on need, character/leadership, scholastic standing, and initiative/goal.

Award: Scholarship for use in freshman, sophomore, junior, or senior years; renewable. Number: 1. Amount: $500.

Eligibility Requirements: Applicant must be age 22-99; enrolled or expecting to enroll full- or part-time at a two-year or four-year or technical institution or university; resident of Michigan and studying in Michigan. Available to U.S. citizens. Applicant must have general military experience.

Application Requirements: Application form, financial need analysis. Deadline: March 15.

Contact: Scholarship Coordinator
American Legion Auxiliary Department of Michigan
212 North Verlinden Avenue, Suite B
Lansing, MI 48915
Phone: 517-267-8809 Ext. 21
E-mail: info@michalaux.org

AMERICAN LEGION AUXILIARY NATIONAL PRESIDENT'S SCHOLARSHIP

One-time scholarship for son or daughter of veterans, who were in armed forces during the eligibility dates for American Legion membership. Must be high school senior. Only one candidate per Auxiliary Unit. Applicant must complete 50 hours of volunteer service in the community. Must submit essay of no more than 1000 words on a specified topic.

Award: Scholarship for use in freshman year; not renewable. Number: 15. Amount: $2500–$3500.

Eligibility Requirements: Applicant must be high school student and planning to enroll or expecting to enroll full-time at a two-year or four-year institution or university. Available to U.S. citizens. Applicant must have general military experience.

Application Requirements: Application form, community service, essay, financial need analysis. Deadline: March 1.

Contact: Scholarship Coordinator
American Legion Auxiliary Department of Michigan
212 North Verlinden Avenue, Suite B
Lansing, MI 48915
Phone: 517-267-8809 Ext. 21
E-mail: info@michalaux.org

AMERICAN LEGION AUXILIARY SPIRIT OF YOUTH SCHOLARSHIP

Scholarship valued at $5000 is available to one Junior American Legion Auxiliary member in each division. The applicant must have held membership in the American Legion Auxiliary for the past three years, must hold a current membership card, and must continue to maintain their membership throughout the four-year scholarship period.

Award: Scholarship for use in freshman, sophomore, junior, or senior years; renewable. Number: 5. Amount: $5000.

Eligibility Requirements: Applicant must be high school student; planning to enroll or expecting to enroll full-time at a two-year or four-year or technical institution or university and female. Applicant must have 3.0 GPA or higher. Available to U.S. citizens. Applicant must have general military experience.

Application Requirements: Application form, essay, financial need analysis. Deadline: March 1.

Contact: Scholarship Coordinator
American Legion Auxiliary Department of Michigan
212 North Verlinden Avenue, Suite B
Lansing, MI 48915
Phone: 517-267-8809 Ext. 21
E-mail: info@michalaux.org

AMERICAN LEGION AUXILIARY DEPARTMENT OF MINNESOTA

http://www.mnala.org

AMERICAN LEGION AUXILIARY DEPARTMENT OF MINNESOTA SCHOLARSHIPS

Seven $1000 awards for the sons, daughters, grandsons, or granddaughters of veterans who served in the Armed Forces during specific eligibility dates. Must be a Minnesota resident, a high school senior or graduate, in need of financial assistance, of good character, having a good scholastic record and at least a C average. Must be planning to attend a Minnesota post secondary institution.

Award: Scholarship for use in freshman, sophomore, junior, or senior years; not renewable. *Number:* 1–7. *Amount:* $1000.

Eligibility Requirements: Applicant must be enrolled or expecting to enroll full-time at a two-year or four-year or technical institution or university; resident of Minnesota and studying in Minnesota. Available to U.S. citizens. Applicant or parent must meet one or more of the following requirements: general military experience; retired from active duty; disabled or killed as a result of military service; prisoner of war; or missing in action.

Application Requirements: Application form, essay, financial need analysis. *Deadline:* March 15.

Contact: Sandie Deutsch, Executive Secretary
American Legion Auxiliary Department of Minnesota
State Veterans Service Building
20 West 12th Street, Room 314
St. Paul, MN 55155
Phone: 651-224-7634
E-mail: sandie@mnala.org

AMERICAN LEGION AUXILIARY DEPARTMENT OF MISSOURI

http://www.missourilegion.org/

AMERICAN LEGION AUXILIARY DEPARTMENT OF MISSOURI LELA MURPHY SCHOLARSHIP
• *See page 550*

AMERICAN LEGION AUXILIARY DEPARTMENT OF MISSOURI NATIONAL PRESIDENT'S SCHOLARSHIP
• *See page 550*

AMERICAN LEGION AUXILIARY DEPARTMENT OF NEBRASKA

http://www.nebraskalegionaux.net/

AMERICAN LEGION AUXILIARY DEPARTMENT OF NEBRASKA RUBY PAUL CAMPAIGN FUND SCHOLARSHIP
• *See page 551*

AMERICAN LEGION AUXILIARY DEPARTMENT OF NORTH DAKOTA

http://www.ndlegion.org/

AMERICAN LEGION AUXILIARY DEPARTMENT OF NORTH DAKOTA NATIONAL PRESIDENT'S SCHOLARSHIP
• *See page 596*

AMERICAN LEGION AUXILIARY DEPARTMENT OF OHIO

http://www.alaohio.org/

AMERICAN LEGION AUXILIARY DEPARTMENT OF OHIO CONTINUING EDUCATION FUND

One-time award for Ohio residents who are the children or grandchildren of veterans, living or deceased, honorably discharged during eligibility dates for American Legion membership. Awards are for undergraduate use, based on need. Freshmen not eligible. Application must be signed by a unit representative.

Award: Scholarship for use in sophomore, junior, or senior years; not renewable. *Number:* 15. *Amount:* $200.

Eligibility Requirements: Applicant must be enrolled or expecting to enroll full-time at a two-year or four-year institution or university and resident of Ohio. Available to U.S. citizens. Applicant or parent must meet one or more of the following requirements: general military experience; retired from active duty; disabled or killed as a result of military service; prisoner of war; or missing in action.

Application Requirements: Application form, financial need analysis, transcript. *Deadline:* November 1.

Contact: Katie Tucker, Scholarship Coordinator
Phone: 740-452-8245
Fax: 740-452-2620
E-mail: ala_katie@rrohio.com

AMERICAN LEGION AUXILIARY DEPARTMENT OF OHIO DEPARTMENT PRESIDENT'S SCHOLARSHIP

Scholarship for children or grandchildren of veterans who served in Armed Forces during eligibility dates for American Legion membership. Must be high school senior, ages 16 to 18, Ohio resident, and U.S. citizen. Award for full-time undergraduate study. One-time award of $1000 to $1500.

Award: Scholarship for use in freshman year; not renewable. *Number:* 2. *Amount:* $1000–$1500.

Eligibility Requirements: Applicant must be high school student; age 16-18; planning to enroll or expecting to enroll full-time at a two-year or four-year institution or university and resident of Ohio. Available to U.S. citizens. Applicant or parent must meet one or more of the following requirements: general military experience; retired from active duty; disabled or killed as a result of military service; prisoner of war; or missing in action.

Application Requirements: Application form, essay, financial need analysis, recommendations or references, transcript. *Deadline:* March 1.

Contact: Department Scholarship Coordinator
American Legion Auxiliary Department of Ohio
PO Box 2760
Zanesville, OH 43702-2760
Phone: 740-452-8245
Fax: 740-452-2620

AMERICAN LEGION AUXILIARY DEPARTMENT OF SOUTH DAKOTA

http://www.sdlegion-aux.org/

AMERICAN LEGION AUXILIARY DEPARTMENT OF SOUTH DAKOTA COLLEGE SCHOLARSHIPS
• *See page 551*

AMERICAN LEGION AUXILIARY DEPARTMENT OF SOUTH DAKOTA SENIOR SCHOLARSHIP
• *See page 551*

AMERICAN LEGION AUXILIARY DEPARTMENT OF SOUTH DAKOTA THELMA FOSTER SCHOLARSHIP FOR SENIOR AUXILIARY MEMBERS
• *See page 551*

AMERICAN LEGION AUXILIARY DEPARTMENT OF TEXAS

http://www.alatexas.org/

AMERICAN LEGION AUXILIARY DEPARTMENT OF TEXAS GENERAL EDUCATION SCHOLARSHIP

Scholarships available for Texas residents. Must be a child of a veteran who served in the Armed Forces during eligibility dates. Some additional criteria used for selection are recommendations, academics, and finances.

Award: Scholarship for use in freshman, sophomore, junior, or senior years; not renewable. *Number:* 1–10. *Amount:* $500.

Eligibility Requirements: Applicant must be enrolled or expecting to enroll full-time at a two-year or four-year or technical institution or university and resident of Texas. Available to U.S. citizens. Applicant must have general military experience.

Application Requirements: Application form, community service, financial need analysis, letter stating qualifications and intentions, recommendations or references, resume, transcript. *Deadline:* June 1.

Contact: Paula Raney, State Secretary
American Legion Auxiliary Department of Texas
PO Box 140407
Austin, TX 78714
Phone: 512-476-7278
Fax: 512-482-8391
E-mail: alatexas@txlegion.org

AMERICAN LEGION AUXILIARY DEPARTMENT OF UTAH

http://www.legion-aux.org/

AMERICAN LEGION AUXILIARY DEPARTMENT OF UTAH NATIONAL PRESIDENT'S SCHOLARSHIP
• *See page 552*

AMERICAN LEGION AUXILIARY DEPARTMENT OF WISCONSIN

http://www.amlegionauxwi.org/

AMERICAN LEGION AUXILIARY DEPARTMENT OF WISCONSIN DELLA VAN DEUREN MEMORIAL SCHOLARSHIP
• *See page 552*

AMERICAN LEGION AUXILIARY DEPARTMENT OF WISCONSIN H.S. AND ANGELINE LEWIS SCHOLARSHIPS
• *See page 552*

AMERICAN LEGION AUXILIARY DEPARTMENT OF WISCONSIN MERIT AND MEMORIAL SCHOLARSHIPS
• *See page 552*

AMERICAN LEGION AUXILIARY DEPARTMENT OF WISCONSIN PRESIDENT'S SCHOLARSHIPS
• *See page 552*

AMERICAN LEGION AUXILIARY NATIONAL HEADQUARTERS

http://www.ALAforVeterans.org

AMERICAN LEGION AUXILIARY CHILDREN OF WARRIORS NATIONAL PRESIDENTS' SCHOLARSHIP
• *See page 596*

AMERICAN LEGION DEPARTMENT OF IDAHO

http://www.idaholegion.com/

AMERICAN LEGION DEPARTMENT OF IDAHO SCHOLARSHIP
• *See page 553*

AMERICAN LEGION DEPARTMENT OF MAINE

http://www.mainelegion.org/

AMERICAN LEGION DEPARTMENT OF MAINE CHILDREN AND YOUTH SCHOLARSHIP

Scholarships available to high school seniors, college students, and veterans who are residents of Maine. Must be in upper half of high school class. One-time award of $500.

Award: Scholarship for use in freshman, sophomore, junior, or senior years; not renewable. *Number:* 7. *Amount:* $500.

Eligibility Requirements: Applicant must be enrolled or expecting to enroll full-time at a two-year or four-year or technical institution or university and resident of Maine. Available to U.S. citizens. Applicant or parent must meet one or more of the following requirements: general military experience; retired from active duty; disabled or killed as a result of military service; prisoner of war; or missing in action.

Application Requirements: Application form, essay, financial need analysis, recommendations or references, transcript. *Deadline:* May 1.

Contact: Mr. Paul L'Heureux, Department Adjutant
American Legion Department of Maine
PO Box 900
Waterville, ME 04903
Phone: 207-873-3229
Fax: 207-872-0501
E-mail: legionme@mainelegion.org

DANIEL E. LAMBERT MEMORIAL SCHOLARSHIP

One-time award for undergraduate and graduate student whose parents are veterans. Award is based on financial need and good character. Must be U.S. citizen. Applicant must show evidence of being enrolled, or attending accredited college or vocational technical school. Scholarship value is from $500 to $1000.

Award: Scholarship for use in freshman, sophomore, junior, or senior years; not renewable. *Number:* 1–2. *Amount:* $500–$1000.

Eligibility Requirements: Applicant must be enrolled or expecting to enroll full-time at a two-year or four-year or technical institution or university and resident of Maine. Available to U.S. citizens. Applicant or parent must meet one or more of the following requirements: general military experience; retired from active duty; disabled or killed as a result of military service; prisoner of war; or missing in action.

Application Requirements: Application form, recommendations or references. *Deadline:* May 1.

Contact: Mr. Paul L'Heureux, Department Adjutant
American Legion Department of Maine
PO Box 900
Waterville, ME 04903
Phone: 207-873-3229
Fax: 207-872-0501
E-mail: legionme@mainelegion.org

JAMES V. DAY SCHOLARSHIP
• *See page 555*

AMERICAN LEGION DEPARTMENT OF MICHIGAN

http://www.michiganlegion.org/

GUY M. WILSON SCHOLARSHIPS

Scholarship for undergraduate use at a Michigan college. Must be resident of Michigan and the son, daughter, grandchild, or great grandchild of a veteran, living or deceased. Must submit copy of veteran's honorable discharge. Must have minimum 2.5 GPA. Total number of awards given vary each year depending upon the number of applications received. Applicants have to refer the website for the deadline.

Award: Scholarship for use in freshman year; not renewable. *Number:* 9. *Amount:* $500.

Eligibility Requirements: Applicant must be high school student; planning to enroll or expecting to enroll full- or part-time at a two-year or four-year institution or university; resident of Michigan and studying in Michigan. Applicant must have 2.5 GPA or higher. Available to U.S. citizens. Applicant or parent must meet one or more of the following requirements: general military experience; retired from active duty; disabled or killed as a result of military service; prisoner of war; or missing in action.

Application Requirements: Application form, essay, financial need analysis. *Deadline:* January 8.

Contact: Programs Coordinator
American Legion Department of Michigan
212 North Verlinden Avenue, Suite A
Lansing, MI 48915
Phone: 517-371-4720 Ext. 23
E-mail: legion@michiganlegion.org

WILLIAM D. AND JEWELL W. BREWER SCHOLARSHIP TRUSTS

One-time award for residents of Michigan who are the son, daughter, grandchild, or great grandchild of veterans, living or deceased. Must submit copy of veteran's honorable discharge. Several scholarships of $500 each. Must have minimum 2.5 GPA. Scholarship can be applied to any college or university within the United States.

Award: Scholarship for use in freshman, sophomore, junior, or senior years; not renewable. *Number:* 4. *Amount:* $500.

Eligibility Requirements: Applicant must be enrolled or expecting to enroll full- or part-time at a two-year or four-year institution or university and resident of Michigan. Applicant must have 2.5 GPA or higher. Available to U.S. citizens. Applicant or parent must meet one or more of the following requirements: general military experience; retired from active duty; disabled or killed as a result of military service; prisoner of war; or missing in action.

Application Requirements: Application form, essay, financial need analysis. *Deadline:* January 8.

Contact: Programs Coordinator
American Legion Department of Michigan
212 North Verlinden Avenue, Suite A
Lansing, MI 48915
Phone: 517-371-4720 Ext. 23
E-mail: legion@michiganlegion.org

THE AMERICAN LEGION, DEPARTMENT OF MINNESOTA

http://www.mnlegion.org/

AMERICAN LEGION DEPARTMENT OF MINNESOTA MEMORIAL SCHOLARSHIP
• *See page 555*

MINNESOTA LEGIONNAIRES INSURANCE TRUST SCHOLARSHIP
• *See page 555*

AMERICAN LEGION DEPARTMENT OF MISSOURI

http://www.missourilegion.org/

CHARLES L. BACON MEMORIAL SCHOLARSHIP
• *See page 555*

LILLIE LOIS FORD SCHOLARSHIP FUND

Two awards of $1000 each are given each year to one boy and one girl. Applicant must have attended a full session of Missouri Boys/Girls State or Missouri Cadet Patrol Academy. Must be a Missouri resident below

age 21, attending an accredited college/university as a full-time student. Must be an unmarried descendant of a veteran having served at least 90 days on active duty in the Army, Air Force, Navy, Marine Corps, or Coast Guard of the United States.

Award: Scholarship for use in freshman year; not renewable. *Number:* 2. *Amount:* $1000.

Eligibility Requirements: Applicant must be high school student; planning to enroll or expecting to enroll full-time at a two-year or four-year institution or university; single and resident of Missouri. Available to U.S. citizens. Applicant or parent must meet one or more of the following requirements: general military experience; retired from active duty; disabled or killed as a result of military service; prisoner of war; or missing in action.

Application Requirements: Application form, copy of the veteran's discharge certificate, financial need analysis, test scores. *Deadline:* April 20.

Contact: John Doane, Chairman, Education and Scholarship Committee
American Legion Department of Missouri
PO Box 179
Jefferson City, MO 65102-0179
Phone: 417-924-8186

AMERICAN LEGION DEPARTMENT OF OHIO

http://www.ohiolegion.com/

OHIO AMERICAN LEGION SCHOLARSHIPS
• *See page 556*

AMERICAN LEGION DEPARTMENT OF WEST VIRGINIA

http://www.wvlegion.org/

SONS OF THE AMERICAN LEGION WILLIAM F. "BILL" JOHNSON MEMORIAL SCHOLARSHIP
• *See page 557*

AMVETS AUXILIARY

http://amvetsaux.org/

AMVETS NATIONAL LADIES AUXILIARY SCHOLARSHIP
• *See page 560*

ARKANSAS DEPARTMENT OF HIGHER EDUCATION

http://www.adhe.edu/

MILITARY DEPENDENT'S SCHOLARSHIP PROGRAM

Renewable waiver of tuition, fees, room and board undergraduate students seeking a bachelor's degree or certificate of completion at any public college, university or technical school in Arkansas who qualify as a spouse or dependent child of an Arkansas resident who has been declared to be missing in action, killed in action, a POW, or killed on ordnance delivery, or a veteran who has been declared to be 100 percent totally and permanently disabled during, or as a result of, active military service.

Award: Scholarship for use in freshman, sophomore, junior, or senior years; renewable.

Eligibility Requirements: Applicant must be enrolled or expecting to enroll full-time at a two-year or four-year or technical institution or university; resident of Arkansas and studying in Arkansas. Available to U.S. citizens. Applicant or parent must meet one or more of the following requirements: general military experience; retired from active duty; disabled or killed as a result of military service; prisoner of war; or missing in action.

Application Requirements: Application form. *Deadline:* June 1.

Contact: Lisa Smith, Director of Financial Aid
Arkansas Department of Higher Education
423 Main Street Suite 400
Little Rock, AR 72201-3818
Phone: 501-371-2000
E-mail: lisa.smith@adhe.edu

CHARLES E. BOYK LAW OFFICES, LLC

https://www.charlesboyk-law.com/

BOYK LAW VETERAN SCHOLARSHIP

• *See page 604*

DEFENSE COMMISSARY AGENCY

http://www.militaryscholar.org/

SCHOLARSHIPS FOR MILITARY CHILDREN

One-time award to unmarried dependents of military personnel for full-time undergraduate study at a four-year institution. Minimum 3.0 GPA required. Further information and applications available at website http://www.militaryscholar.org.

Award: Scholarship for use in freshman, sophomore, or junior years; not renewable. *Number:* 700. *Amount:* $2000.

Eligibility Requirements: Applicant must be enrolled or expecting to enroll full-time at a four-year institution or university and single. Applicant must have 3.0 GPA or higher. Available to U.S. citizens. Applicant or parent must meet one or more of the following requirements: general military experience; retired from active duty; disabled or killed as a result of military service; prisoner of war; or missing in action.

Application Requirements: Application form, essay. *Deadline:* February 16.

Contact: Mr. Bernard Cote
Phone: 856-573-9400
E-mail: militaryscholar@scholarshipmanagers.com

DELAWARE HIGHER EDUCATION OFFICE

http://www.doe.k12.de.us

EDUCATIONAL BENEFITS FOR CHILDREN OF DECEASED VETERANS

• *See page 609*

DEPARTMENT OF VETERANS AFFAIRS (VA)

http://www.gibill.va.gov/

MONTGOMERY GI BILL (ACTIVE DUTY) CHAPTER 30

Award provides up to thirty-six months of education benefits to eligible veterans for college, business school, technical courses, vocational courses, correspondence courses, apprenticeships/job training, or flight training. Must be an eligible veteran with an Honorable Discharge and have high school diploma or GED before applying for benefits.

Award: Scholarship for use in freshman, sophomore, junior, senior, or graduate years; renewable.

Eligibility Requirements: Applicant must be enrolled or expecting to enroll full- or part-time at a two-year or four-year or technical institution or university. Available to U.S. citizens. Applicant or parent must meet one or more of the following requirements: general military experience; retired from active duty; disabled or killed as a result of military service; prisoner of war; or missing in action.

Application Requirements: Application form. *Deadline:* continuous.

Contact: Keith Wilson, Director, Education Service
Phone: 888-442-4551

MONTGOMERY GI BILL (SELECTED RESERVE)

• *See page 696*

RESERVE EDUCATION ASSISTANCE PROGRAM

• *See page 697*

SURVIVORS AND DEPENDENTS EDUCATIONAL ASSISTANCE (CHAPTER 35)-VA

Monthly $860 benefits for up to 45 months. Must be spouses or children under age 26 of current veterans missing in action or of deceased or totally and permanently disabled (service-related) service persons. For more information visit the following website http://www.gibill.va.gov.

Award: Scholarship for use in freshman, sophomore, junior, or senior years; renewable.

Eligibility Requirements: Applicant must be enrolled or expecting to enroll full- or part-time at a two-year or four-year or technical institution or university. Available to U.S. and non-U.S. citizens. Applicant or parent must meet one or more of the following requirements: general military experience; retired from active duty; disabled or killed as a result of military service; prisoner of war; or missing in action.

Application Requirements: Application form. *Deadline:* continuous.

Contact: Keith Wilson, Director, Education Service
Phone: 888-442-4551

DIVERSITYCOMM, INC.

http://www.diversitycomm.net/

US VETERANS MAGAZINE SCHOLARSHIP

• *See page 696*

ELEARNERS.COM

http://www.elearners.com

ELEARNERS MILITARY SCHOLARSHIP

• *See page 696*

EOD WARRIOR FOUNDATION

http://www.eodwarriorfoundation.org

EXPLOSIVE ORDNANCE DISPOSAL MEMORIAL SCHOLARSHIP

• *See page 615*

FELDMAN LAW FIRM PLLC

http://www.afphoenixcriminalattorney.com/

DISABLED VETERANS SCHOLARSHIP

• *See page 617*

FLORIDA STATE DEPARTMENT OF EDUCATION

http://www.floridastudentfinancialaid.org/

SCHOLARSHIPS FOR CHILDREN & SPOUSES OF DECEASED OR DISABLED VETERANS

Renewable scholarships for children and spouses of deceased or disabled veterans. Children must be between the ages of 16 and 22, and attend an eligible Florida postsecondary institution and enrolled at least part-time. Must ensure that the Florida Department of Veterans Affairs certifies the applicant's eligibility. Must maintain GPA of 2.0. For more details, visit the website at http://www.FloridaStudentFinancialAid.org/SSFAD/home/uamain.htm.

Award: Scholarship for use in freshman, sophomore, junior, or senior years; renewable.

Eligibility Requirements: Applicant must be age 16-22; enrolled or expecting to enroll full- or part-time at a two-year or four-year or technical institution or university; resident of Florida and studying in Florida. Available to U.S. citizens. Applicant or parent must meet one or more of the following requirements: general military experience; retired from active duty; disabled or killed as a result of military service; prisoner of war; or missing in action.

Application Requirements: Application form. *Deadline:* April 1.

Contact: Florida Department of Education, Office of Student Financial
Assistance, Customer Service
Florida State Department of Education
325 West Gaines Street
Tallahassee, FL 32399
Phone: 888-827-2004
E-mail: osfa@fldoe.org

ILLINOIS AMVETS

http://www.ilamvets.org/

ILLINOIS AMVETS LADIES AUXILIARY WORCHID SCHOLARSHIPS

Applicant must be an Illinois high school senior and be the child of an
honorably discharged, deceased veteran who served after September 15,
1940. Amount varies yearly.

Award: Scholarship for use in freshman year; not renewable.

Eligibility Requirements: Applicant must be high school student;
planning to enroll or expecting to enroll full-time at a two-year or four-
year or technical institution or university and resident of Illinois.
Available to U.S. citizens. Applicant or parent must meet one or more of
the following requirements: general military experience; retired from
active duty; disabled or killed as a result of military service; prisoner of
war; or missing in action.

Application Requirements: Application form, financial need analysis.
Deadline: March 1.

Contact: Ashley Murphy, Communications Director
Illinois AMVETS
PO Box 372
Groveland, IL 61535
Phone: 800-638-8387
E-mail: ashley@ilamvets.org

ILLINOIS STUDENT ASSISTANCE COMMISSION (ISAC)

http://www.isac.org/

ILLINOIS VETERAN GRANT PROGRAM-IVG

Awards qualified veterans and pays eligible tuition and fees for study in
Illinois public universities or community colleges. Program eligibility
units are based on the enrolled hours for a particular term, not the dollar
amount of the benefits paid. Applications are available at college
financial aid office and can be submitted any time during the academic
year for which assistance is being requested.

Award: Grant for use in freshman, sophomore, junior, senior, or graduate
years; renewable.

Eligibility Requirements: Applicant must be enrolled or expecting to
enroll full- or part-time at a two-year or four-year institution or
university; resident of Illinois and studying in Illinois. Available to U.S.
citizens. Applicant or parent must meet one or more of the following
requirements: general military experience; retired from active duty;
disabled or killed as a result of military service; prisoner of war; or
missing in action.

Application Requirements: Application form. *Deadline:* continuous.

Contact: ISAC Call Center Representative
Illinois Student Assistance Commission (ISAC)
1755 Lake Cook Road
Deerfield, IL 60015-5209
Phone: 800-899-4722
E-mail: isac.studentservices@illinois.gov

IMAGINE AMERICA FOUNDATION

http://www.imagine-america.org

MILITARY AWARD PROGRAM (MAP)

• *See page 696*

INDIANA DEPARTMENT OF VETERANS AFFAIRS

http://www.in.gov/dva

CHILD OF DISABLED VETERAN GRANT OR PURPLE HEART RECIPIENT GRANT

Free tuition at Indiana state-supported colleges or universities for
children of disabled veterans or Purple Heart recipients. Must submit
form DD214 or service record. Covers tuition and mandatory fees.

Award: Grant for use in freshman, sophomore, junior, senior, graduate, or
postgraduate years; renewable.

Eligibility Requirements: Applicant must be enrolled or expecting to
enroll full- or part-time at a two-year or four-year institution or
university; resident of Indiana and studying in Indiana. Available to U.S.
citizens. Applicant must have general military experience.

Application Requirements: Application form. *Deadline:* continuous.

Contact: Michael Hamm, State Service Officer
Phone: 317-232-3910
Fax: 317-232-7721
E-mail: mhamm@dva.in.gov

DEPARTMENT OF VETERANS AFFAIRS FREE TUITION FOR CHILDREN OF POW/MIA'S IN VIETNAM

Renewable award for residents of Indiana who are the children of
veterans declared missing in action or prisoner-of-war after January 1,
1960. Provides tuition at Indiana state-supported institutions for
undergraduate study.

Award: Grant for use in freshman, sophomore, junior, senior, graduate, or
postgraduate years; renewable.

Eligibility Requirements: Applicant must be enrolled or expecting to
enroll full- or part-time at a two-year or four-year institution or
university; resident of Indiana and studying in Indiana. Available to U.S.
citizens. Applicant must have general military experience.

Application Requirements: Application form. *Deadline:* continuous.

Contact: Michael Hamm, State Service Officer
Phone: 317-232-3910
Fax: 317-232-7721
E-mail: mhamm@dva.in.gov

KANSAS COMMISSION ON VETERANS AFFAIRS

http://www.kcva.org/

KANSAS EDUCATIONAL BENEFITS FOR CHILDREN OF MIA, POW, AND DECEASED VETERANS OF THE VIETNAM WAR

Scholarship awarded to students who are children of veterans. Must show
proof of parent's status as missing in action, prisoner-of-war, or killed in
action in the Vietnam War. Kansas residence required of veteran at time
of entry to service. Must attend a state-supported postsecondary school.

Award: Scholarship for use in freshman, sophomore, junior, or senior
years; not renewable. *Number:* 1.

Eligibility Requirements: Applicant must be enrolled or expecting to
enroll full-time at a two-year or four-year or technical institution or
university and studying in Kansas. Available to U.S. citizens. Applicant
or parent must meet one or more of the following requirements: general
military experience; retired from active duty; disabled or killed as a result
of military service; prisoner of war; or missing in action.

Application Requirements: Application form, birth certificate, school
acceptance letter, military discharge of veteran. *Deadline:* varies.

Contact: Wayne Bollig, Program Director
Phone: 785-296-3976
Fax: 785-296-1462
E-mail: wbollig@kcva.org

KELLY LAW TEAM

http://www.jkphoenixpersonalinjuryattorney.com/

DISABLED VETERAN SCHOLARSHIP

• *See page 634*

DISABLED VETERAN SCHOLARSHIP

• *See page 634*

KITCHEN GUIDES

http://www.kitchensguides.com/

SMART KITCHEN IMPROVEMENT SCHOLARSHIP BY KITCHEN GUIDES

• *See page 635*

KNIGHTS OF COLUMBUS

http://www.kofc.org/

FRANCIS P. MATTHEWS AND JOHN E. SWIFT EDUCATIONAL TRUST SCHOLARSHIPS

• *See page 567*

LAW OFFICES OF DAVID A. BLACK

http://www.dbphoenixcriminallawyer.com

SCHOLARSHIP FOR DISABLED VETERANS

• *See page 638*

LOUISIANA DEPARTMENT OF VETERAN AFFAIRS

http://www.vetaffairs.la.gov

LOUISIANA DEPARTMENT OF VETERANS AFFAIRS STATE EDUCATIONAL AID PROGRAM

Waiver of tuition and school-imposed fees at any state supported college, university, or technical institute in Louisiana for dependent children, aged 16-25, of service connected disabled veterans, service connected deceased veterans, or veterans rated 100% service connected due to individual unemployability. Tuition waiver also available for an non-remarried surviving spouse of a service connected deceased veteran. Residency restricted to Louisiana.

Award: Scholarship for use in freshman, sophomore, junior, or senior years; not renewable.

Eligibility Requirements: Applicant must be age 16-25; enrolled or expecting to enroll full-time at a two-year or four-year or technical institution or university; resident of Louisiana and studying in Louisiana. Available to U.S. citizens. Applicant or parent must meet one or more of the following requirements: general military experience; retired from active duty; disabled or killed as a result of military service; prisoner of war; or missing in action.

Application Requirements: Application form. *Deadline:* continuous.

Contact: Mr. Barry Robinson, Regional Manager/Training Officer
Louisiana Department of Veteran Affairs
PO Box 94095 Capitol Station
Baton Rouge, LA 70804-9095
Phone: 225-219-5017
Fax: 225-219-5590
E-mail: barry.robinson@vetaffairs.la.gov

MAINE VETERANS SERVICES

http://www.maine.gov/dvem/bvs

VETERANS DEPENDENTS EDUCATIONAL BENEFITS-MAINE

Tuition waiver award for dependent children who have not reached their 22nd birthday or spouses of veterans permanently and totally disabled resulting from service-connected disability; died from a service-connected disability; at time of death was totally and permanently disabled due to service-connected disability, but whose death was not related to the service-connected disability; or member of the Armed Forces on active duty who has been listed for more than 90 days as missing in action, captured or forcibly detained or interned in the line of duty. Benefits apply only to the University of Maine System, Maine community colleges and Maine Maritime Academy. Must be high school

graduate. Must submit with application proof of veteran's VA disability along with dependent verification paperwork such as birth, marriage, or adoption certificate and proof of enrollment in degree program.

Award: Scholarship for use in freshman, sophomore, junior, or senior years; not renewable.

Eligibility Requirements: Applicant must be enrolled or expecting to enroll full- or part-time at a two-year or four-year institution or university; resident of Maine and studying in Maine. Available to U.S. citizens. Applicant or parent must meet one or more of the following requirements: general military experience; retired from active duty; disabled or killed as a result of military service; prisoner of war; or missing in action.

Application Requirements: Application form, see application.

Contact: Mrs. Paula Gagnon, Office Associate II
Maine Veterans Services
State House Station 117
Augusta, ME 04333-0117
Phone: 207-430-6035
Fax: 207-626-4471
E-mail: mainebvs@maine.gov

MARYLAND STATE HIGHER EDUCATION COMMISSION

http://www.mhec.state.md.us/

EDWARD T. CONROY MEMORIAL SCHOLARSHIP PROGRAM

• *See page 642*

VETERANS OF THE AFGHANISTAN AND IRAQ CONFLICTS SCHOLARSHIP PROGRAM

Provides financial assistance to Maryland resident U.S. Armed Forces personnel who served in Afghanistan or Iraq conflicts and their children or spouses who are attending Maryland institutions.

Award: Scholarship for use in freshman, sophomore, junior, or senior years; renewable. *Number:* 123. *Amount:* $8850.

Eligibility Requirements: Applicant must be enrolled or expecting to enroll full- or part-time at a two-year or four-year institution or university; resident of Maryland and studying in Maryland. Available to U.S. citizens. Applicant or parent must meet one or more of the following requirements: general military experience; retired from active duty; disabled or killed as a result of military service; prisoner of war; or missing in action.

Application Requirements: Application form, birth certificate/marriage certificate, documentation of military order, financial need analysis. *Deadline:* March 1.

Contact: Linda Asplin, Program Administrator
Maryland State Higher Education Commission
839 Bestgate Road, Suite 400
Annapolis, MD 21401-3013
Phone: 410-260-4563
Fax: 410-260-3203
E-mail: lasplin@mhec.state.md.us

MILITARY ORDER OF THE PURPLE HEART

http://www.purpleheart.org/

MILITARY ORDER OF THE PURPLE HEART SCHOLARSHIP

Scholarship for Military Order of the Purple Heart (MOPH) Members/spouses or children, stepchildren, adopted children or grandchildren, veterans killed-in-action or veterans who died of wounds and did not have the opportunity to join the MOPH. Must submit $15 application fee, essay, high school/college transcript, two letters of recommendation and list of extracurricular and volunteer activities. Must be U.S. citizen and high school graduate with minimum GPA of 2.75 and accepted or enrolled as a full-time student at a U.S. college, university or trade school at the time the scholarship is awarded.

Award: Scholarship for use in freshman, sophomore, junior, or senior years; not renewable. *Number:* 84–87. *Amount:* $2500–$7500.

Eligibility Requirements: Applicant must be enrolled or expecting to enroll full-time at a two-year or four-year or technical institution or

university. Applicant must have 3.0 GPA or higher. Available to U.S. citizens. Applicant or parent must meet one or more of the following requirements: general military experience; retired from active duty; disabled or killed as a result of military service; prisoner of war; or missing in action.

Application Requirements: Application form, community service, essay. *Fee:* $15. *Deadline:* January 26.

Contact: Stewart Mckeown, Scholarship Coordinator
Phone: 703-642-5360
E-mail: scholarship@purpleheart.org

NATIONAL MILITARY FAMILY ASSOCIATION

http://www.MilitaryFamily.org

NATIONAL MILITARY FAMILY ASSOCIATION'S MILITARY SPOUSE SCHOLARSHIPS

• *See page 650*

NEW JERSEY DEPARTMENT OF MILITARY AND VETERANS AFFAIRS

http://www.state.nj.us/military

NEW JERSEY WAR ORPHANS TUITION ASSISTANCE

$500 scholarship to children of those service personnel who died while in the military or due to service-connected disabilities, or who are officially listed as missing in action by the U.S. Department of Defense. Must be a resident of New Jersey for at least one year immediately preceding the filing of the application and be between the ages of 16 and 21 at the time of application.

Award: Scholarship for use in freshman, sophomore, junior, or senior years; renewable. *Amount:* $500.

Eligibility Requirements: Applicant must be age 16-21; enrolled or expecting to enroll full-time at a four-year institution or university and resident of New Jersey. Available to U.S. citizens. Applicant or parent must meet one or more of the following requirements: general military experience; retired from active duty; disabled or killed as a result of military service; prisoner of war; or missing in action.

Application Requirements: Application form, transcript. *Deadline:* varies.

Contact: Patricia Richter, Grants Manager
New Jersey Department of Military and Veterans Affairs
PO Box 340
Trenton, NJ 08625-0340
Phone: 609-530-6854
Fax: 609-530-6970
E-mail: patricia.richter@njdmava.state.nj.us

POW-MIA TUITION BENEFIT PROGRAM

Free undergraduate college tuition provided to any child born or adopted before or during the period of time his or her parent was officially declared a prisoner of war or person missing in action after January 1, 1960. The POW-MIA must have been a New Jersey resident at the time he or she entered the service. Child of veteran must attend either a public or private institution in New Jersey. A copy of DD 1300 must be furnished with the application. Minimum 2.5 GPA required.

Award: Scholarship for use in freshman, sophomore, junior, or senior years; renewable.

Eligibility Requirements: Applicant must be enrolled or expecting to enroll full-time at a two-year or four-year or technical institution or university; resident of New Jersey and studying in New Jersey. Applicant must have 2.5 GPA or higher. Available to U.S. citizens. Applicant or parent must meet one or more of the following requirements: general military experience; retired from active duty; disabled or killed as a result of military service; prisoner of war; or missing in action.

Application Requirements: Application form, copy of DD 1300, transcript. *Deadline:* varies.

Contact: Patricia Richter, Grants Manager
New Jersey Department of Military and Veterans Affairs
PO Box 340
Trenton, NJ 08625-0340
Phone: 609-530-6854
Fax: 609-530-6970
E-mail: patricia.richter@njdmava.state.nj.us

VETERANS TUITION CREDIT PROGRAM-NEW JERSEY

Award for New Jersey resident veterans who served in the armed forces between December 31, 1960, and May 7, 1975. Must have been a New Jersey resident at time of induction or discharge or for two years immediately prior to application.

Award: Scholarship for use in freshman, sophomore, junior, or senior years; renewable. *Amount:* $200–$400.

Eligibility Requirements: Applicant must be enrolled or expecting to enroll full- or part-time at a two-year or four-year or technical institution or university and resident of New Jersey. Available to U.S. citizens. Applicant or parent must meet one or more of the following requirements: general military experience; retired from active duty; disabled or killed as a result of military service; prisoner of war; or missing in action.

Application Requirements: Application form. *Deadline:* varies.

Contact: Patricia Richter, Grants Manager
New Jersey Department of Military and Veterans Affairs
PO Box 340
Trenton, NJ 08625-0340
Phone: 609-530-6854
Fax: 609-530-6970
E-mail: patricia.richter@njdmava.state.nj.us

NEW MEXICO COMMISSION ON HIGHER EDUCATION

http://www.hed.state.nm.us/

VIETNAM VETERANS' SCHOLARSHIP PROGRAM

Renewable scholarship program created to provide aid for Vietnam veterans who are undergraduate and graduate students attending public postsecondary institutions or select private colleges in New Mexico. Private colleges include: College of Santa Fe, St. John's College and College of the Southwest.

Award: Scholarship for use in freshman, sophomore, junior, or senior years; renewable. *Number:* 1.

Eligibility Requirements: Applicant must be enrolled or expecting to enroll full-time at a two-year or four-year institution; resident of New Mexico and studying in New Mexico. Available to U.S. citizens. Applicant or parent must meet one or more of the following requirements: general military experience; retired from active duty; disabled or killed as a result of military service; prisoner of war; or missing in action.

Application Requirements: Application form, certification by the NM Veteran's commission. *Deadline:* varies.

Contact: Tashina Moore, Director of Financial Aid
New Mexico Commission on Higher Education
1068 Cerrillos Road
Santa Fe, NM 87505-1650
Phone: 505-476-6549
Fax: 505-476-6511
E-mail: tashina.banks-moore@state.nm.us

NEW MEXICO DEPARTMENT OF VETERANS' SERVICES

http://www.nmdvs.org

NEW MEXICO WARTIME VETERANS SCHOLARSHIP

Award for Wartime Veterans who have been a New Mexico resident for a minimum of ten years and are attending state-funded postsecondary schools. Must have been awarded a campaign medal such as the Southwest Asia Service Medal, Global War on Terrorism Expeditionary Medal, Iraq Campaign Medal, Afghanistan Campaign Medal or any other medal issued for service in the Armed Forces of the United States in support of any U.S. Military Campaign or armed conflict as defined by congress or presidential order or service after August 1, 1990.

Award: Scholarship for use in freshman, sophomore, junior, senior, or graduate years; renewable. *Number:* 100. *Amount:* $3500–$4000.

Eligibility Requirements: Applicant must be enrolled or expecting to enroll full- or part-time at a two-year or four-year or technical institution or university; resident of New Mexico and studying in New Mexico. Available to U.S. citizens. Applicant must have general military experience.

Application Requirements: Application form.

Contact: Mr. Dale Movius, Director, State Benefits
New Mexico Department of Veterans' Services
407 Galiesteo St, Room 134
Santa Fe, NM 87501
Phone: 505-827-6374
E-mail: dalej.movius@state.nm.us

NEW YORK STATE HIGHER EDUCATION SERVICES CORPORATION

http://www.hesc.ny.gov

NEW YORK VIETNAM/PERSIAN GULF/AFGHANISTAN VETERANS TUITION AWARDS

Scholarship for veterans who served in Vietnam, the Persian Gulf, or Afghanistan. Must be a New York resident attending a New York institution. Must establish eligibility by September 1.

Award: Scholarship for use in freshman, sophomore, junior, or senior years; renewable.

Eligibility Requirements: Applicant must be enrolled or expecting to enroll full- or part-time at a two-year or four-year or technical institution or university; resident of New York and studying in New York. Available to U.S. citizens. Applicant or parent must meet one or more of the following requirements: general military experience; retired from active duty; disabled or killed as a result of military service; prisoner of war; or missing in action.

Application Requirements: Application form, financial need analysis. *Deadline:* May 1.

REGENTS AWARD FOR CHILD OF VETERAN

Award for students whose parent, as a result of service in U.S. Armed Forces during war or national emergency, died; suffered a 40 percent or more disability; or is classified as missing in action or a prisoner of war. Veteran must be current New York State resident or have been so at time of death. Student must be a New York resident, attending, or planning to attend, college in New York State. Must establish eligibility before applying for payment.

Award: Scholarship for use in freshman, sophomore, junior, or senior years; not renewable. *Amount:* up to $450.

Eligibility Requirements: Applicant must be enrolled or expecting to enroll full-time at a two-year or four-year institution or university; resident of New York and studying in New York. Available to U.S. citizens. Applicant or parent must meet one or more of the following requirements: general military experience; retired from active duty; disabled or killed as a result of military service; prisoner of war; or missing in action.

Application Requirements: Application form, proof of eligibility. *Deadline:* May 1.

Contact: Rita McGivern, Student Information
New York State Higher Education Services Corporation
99 Washington Avenue, Room 1320
Albany, NY 12255
E-mail: rmcgivern@hesc.com

N.H. DEPARTMENT OF EDUCATION, DIVISION OF HIGHER EDUCATION - HIGHER EDUCATION COMMISSION

http://www.education.nh.gov/highered

SCHOLARSHIPS FOR ORPHANS OF VETERANS

Scholarship to provide financial assistance (room, board, books and supplies) to children of parents who served in World War II, Korean Conflict, Vietnam (Southeast Asian Conflict) or the Gulf Wars, or any other operation for which the armed forces expeditionary medal or theater of operations service medal was awarded to the veteran. Must be

between the ages of 16 and 25 to qualify and be residents of New Hampshire studying at public New Hampshire colleges and universities.

Award: Scholarship for use in freshman, sophomore, junior, senior, graduate, or postgraduate years; renewable. *Number:* 1. *Amount:* $1000–$2500.

Eligibility Requirements: Applicant must be age 16-25; enrolled or expecting to enroll full-time at a two-year or four-year institution or university; resident of New Hampshire and studying in New Hampshire. Available to U.S. citizens. Applicant or parent must meet one or more of the following requirements: general military experience; retired from active duty; disabled or killed as a result of military service; prisoner of war; or missing in action.

Application Requirements: Application form. *Deadline:* September 1.

Contact: Mrs. Pat Moquin, Program Assistant II
N.H. Department of Education, Division of Higher Education - Higher Education Commission
101 Pleasant Street
Concord, NH 03301
Phone: 603-271-0289
E-mail: patricia.moquin@doe.nh.gov

NORTH CAROLINA DIVISION OF VETERANS AFFAIRS

http://www.milvets.nc.gov/

NORTH CAROLINA VETERANS SCHOLARSHIPS CLASS I-A

Scholarships for children of certain deceased, disabled or POW/MIA veterans. Award value is $4500 per nine-month academic year in private colleges and junior colleges. No limit on number awarded each year.

Award: Scholarship for use in freshman, sophomore, junior, or senior years; renewable. *Amount:* $4500.

Eligibility Requirements: Applicant must be enrolled or expecting to enroll full-time at a two-year or four-year or technical institution or university; resident of North Carolina and studying in North Carolina. Available to U.S. citizens. Applicant or parent must meet one or more of the following requirements: general military experience; retired from active duty; disabled or killed as a result of military service; prisoner of war; or missing in action.

Application Requirements: Application form, financial need analysis, interview, transcript. *Deadline:* continuous.

Contact: Charles Smith, Assistant Secretary
Phone: 919-733-3851
Fax: 919-733-2834
E-mail: charlie.smith@ncmail.net

NORTH CAROLINA VETERANS SCHOLARSHIPS CLASS I-B

Awards for children of veterans rated by USDVA as 100 percent disabled due to wartime service as defined in the law, and currently or at time of death drawing compensation for such disability. Parent must have been a North Carolina resident at time of entry into service. Duration of the scholarship is four academic years (8 semesters) if used within 8 years. No limit on number awarded each year.

Award: Scholarship for use in freshman, sophomore, junior, or senior years; renewable. *Amount:* $1500.

Eligibility Requirements: Applicant must be enrolled or expecting to enroll full- or part-time at a two-year or four-year or technical institution or university; resident of North Carolina and studying in North Carolina. Available to U.S. citizens. Applicant or parent must meet one or more of the following requirements: general military experience; retired from active duty; disabled or killed as a result of military service; prisoner of war; or missing in action.

Application Requirements: Application form, financial need analysis, interview, transcript. *Deadline:* continuous.

Contact: Charles Smith, Assistant Secretary
Phone: 919-733-3851
Fax: 919-733-2834
E-mail: charlie.smith@ncmail.net

NORTH CAROLINA VETERANS SCHOLARSHIPS CLASS II

Awards for children of veterans rated by USDVA as much as 20 percent but less than 100 percent disabled due to wartime service as defined in the law, or awarded Purple Heart Medal for wounds received. Parent must have been a North Carolina resident at time of entry into service. Duration of the scholarship is four academic years (8 semesters) if used within 8 years. Free tuition and exemption from certain mandatory fees as set forth in the law in Public, Community and Technical Colleges.

Award: Scholarship for use in freshman, sophomore, junior, or senior years; renewable. *Number:* up to 100. *Amount:* $4500.

Eligibility Requirements: Applicant must be enrolled or expecting to enroll full- or part-time at a two-year or four-year or technical institution or university; resident of North Carolina and studying in North Carolina. Available to U.S. citizens. Applicant or parent must meet one or more of the following requirements: general military experience; retired from active duty; disabled or killed as a result of military service; prisoner of war; or missing in action.

Application Requirements: Application form, financial need analysis, interview, transcript. *Deadline:* March 1.

Contact: Charles Smith, Assistant Secretary
  Phone: 919-733-3851
  Fax: 919-733-2834
  E-mail: charlie.smith@ncmail.net

NORTH CAROLINA VETERANS SCHOLARSHIPS CLASS III

Awards for children of a deceased war veteran, who was honorably discharged and who does not qualify under any other provision within this synopsis or veteran who served in a combat zone or waters adjacent to a combat zone and received a campaign badge or medal and who does not qualify under any other provision within this synopsis. Duration of the scholarship is four academic years (8 semesters) if used within 8 years.

Award: Scholarship for use in freshman, sophomore, junior, or senior years; renewable. *Number:* up to 100. *Amount:* $4500.

Eligibility Requirements: Applicant must be enrolled or expecting to enroll full- or part-time at a two-year or four-year or technical institution or university; resident of North Carolina and studying in North Carolina. Available to U.S. citizens. Applicant or parent must meet one or more of the following requirements: general military experience; retired from active duty; disabled or killed as a result of military service; prisoner of war; or missing in action.

Application Requirements: Application form, financial need analysis, interview, transcript. *Deadline:* March 1.

Contact: Charles Smith, Assistant Secretary
  Phone: 919-733-3851
  Fax: 919-733-2834
  E-mail: charlie.smith@ncmail.net

NORTH CAROLINA VETERANS SCHOLARSHIPS CLASS IV

Awards for children of veterans, who were prisoner of war or missing in action. Duration of the scholarship is four academic years (8 semesters) if used within 8 years. No limit on number awarded each year. Award value is $4500 per nine-month academic year in private colleges and junior colleges.

Award: Scholarship for use in freshman, sophomore, junior, or senior years; renewable. *Amount:* $4500.

Eligibility Requirements: Applicant must be enrolled or expecting to enroll full- or part-time at a two-year or four-year or technical institution or university; resident of North Carolina and studying in North Carolina. Available to U.S. citizens. Applicant or parent must meet one or more of the following requirements: general military experience; retired from active duty; disabled or killed as a result of military service; prisoner of war; or missing in action.

Application Requirements: Application form, financial need analysis, interview, transcript. *Deadline:* continuous.

Contact: Charles Smith, Assistant Secretary
  Phone: 919-733-3851
  Fax: 919-733-2834
  E-mail: charlie.smith@ncmail.net

OHIO DEPARTMENT OF HIGHER EDUCATION

http://www.ohiohighered.org

OHIO WAR ORPHANS SCHOLARSHIP
• *See page 655*

PETAZI

https://petazi.com/

NURTURE FOR NATURE SCHOLARSHIP
• *See page 692*

THE RESERVE OFFICERS ASSOCIATION

http://www.roa.org/

HENRY J. REILLY MEMORIAL SCHOLARSHIP-HIGH SCHOOL SENIORS AND FIRST YEAR FRESHMEN
• *See page 576*

HENRY J. REILLY MEMORIAL UNDERGRADUATE SCHOLARSHIP PROGRAM FOR COLLEGE ATTENDEES
• *See page 577*

RETIRED ENLISTED ASSOCIATION

http://www.trea.org/

RETIRED ENLISTED ASSOCIATION SCHOLARSHIP

One-time award for dependent children or grandchildren of a TREA member or TREA auxiliary member in good standing.

Award: Scholarship for use in freshman, sophomore, junior, senior, graduate, or postgraduate years; not renewable. *Amount:* $1000–$1500.

Eligibility Requirements: Applicant must be enrolled or expecting to enroll full-time at a two-year or four-year or technical institution or university. Available to U.S. citizens. Applicant or parent must meet one or more of the following requirements: general military experience; retired from active duty; disabled or killed as a result of military service; prisoner of war; or missing in action.

Application Requirements: Application form, copy of IRS tax forms, essay, financial need analysis, personal photograph, recommendations or references, test scores, transcript. *Deadline:* April 30.

Contact: Donnell Minnis, Executive Assistant
  Phone: 303-752-0660
  Fax: 303-752-0835
  E-mail: execasst@trea.org

SCHOLARSHIP AMERICA

http://www.scholarshipamerica.org

WELLS FARGO VETERANS SCHOLARSHIP PROGRAM

The Wells Fargo Veterans Scholarship Program is designed to help meet the needs of veterans after military benefits and other grants and scholarships have been utilized. The scholarship program will award renewable scholarships for up to $7,000 per year to honorably-discharged veterans or spouses of disabled veterans who are high school or GED graduates and who have served in the United States military. Qualified applicants must have a minimum grade point average of 2.5 on a 4.0 scale or its equivalent and plan to enroll in full-time undergraduate or graduate (first Masters degree) study at an accredited two- or four-year college, university, or vocational-technical school. Each award renewal will increase by $1,000 over the previous year to encourage program completion. Visit http://www.scholarsapply.org/wellsfargoveterans for more information and to apply.

Award: Scholarship for use in freshman, sophomore, junior, senior, or graduate years; renewable.

Eligibility Requirements: Applicant must be enrolled or expecting to enroll part-time at a two-year or four-year or technical institution or university. Applicant must have 2.5 GPA or higher. Available to U.S. citizens. Applicant must have general military experience.

Application Requirements: Application form. *Deadline:* February 28.

Contact: Program Manager Scholarship America
Scholarship America
One Scholarship Way
St. Peter, MN 56082
Phone: 800-537-4180
E-mail: wellsfargoveterans@scholarshipamerica.org

SOUTH CAROLINA DIVISION OF VETERANS AFFAIRS

http://www.govoepp.state.sc.us/vetaff.htm

TUITION ASSISTANCE FOR CERTAIN WAR VETERANS' CHILDREN

Free tuition for South Carolina residents whose parent is a resident, wartime veteran, and meets one of these criteria; awarded Purple Heart or Congressional Medal of Honor; permanently and totally disabled by VA or killed as a result of military service; prisoner of war; or missing in action. Must be age 18–26 and enrolled or expecting to enroll full or part-time at a state supported two-year or four-year technical institution or university in South Carolina. Complete information and qualifications for this award are on website http://www.govoepp.state.sc.us.

Award: Scholarship for use in freshman, sophomore, junior, or senior years; not renewable.

Eligibility Requirements: Applicant must be age 18-26; enrolled or expecting to enroll full- or part-time at a two-year or four-year or technical institution or university; resident of South Carolina and studying in South Carolina. Available to U.S. citizens. Applicant or parent must meet one or more of the following requirements: general military experience; retired from active duty; disabled or killed as a result of military service; prisoner of war; or missing in action.

Application Requirements: Application form. *Deadline:* continuous.

Contact: Adm. Dorian Sease-Phillips, Free Tuition Coordinator
South Carolina Division of Veterans Affairs
6437 Garners Ferry Rd
Columbia, SC 29209
Phone: 803-647-2434
Fax: 803-647 Ext. 2312
E-mail: dorian.sease-phillips@va.gov

TENNESSEE STUDENT ASSISTANCE CORPORATION

http://www.tn.gov/collegepays

HELPING HEROES GRANT
• *See page 672*

TONALAW

https://www.tonalaw.com/

TONALAW VETERAN'S SCHOLARSHIP
• *See page 674*

UNIVERSITY OF WYOMING

http://www.uwyo.edu/scholarships

VIETNAM VETERANS AWARD-WYOMING

Scholarship available to Wyoming residents who served in the armed forces between August 5, 1964 and May 7, 1975, and received a Vietnam service medal.

Award: Scholarship for use in freshman, sophomore, junior, or senior years; renewable.

Eligibility Requirements: Applicant must be enrolled or expecting to enroll full- or part-time at a two-year or four-year institution or university and resident of Wyoming. Available to U.S. citizens. Applicant or parent must meet one or more of the following requirements: general military experience; retired from active duty; disabled or killed as a result of military service; prisoner of war; or missing in action.

Application Requirements: Application form. *Deadline:* continuous.

Contact: Tammy Mack, Assistant Director, Scholarships
University of Wyoming
Department 3335
1000 East University Avenue
Laramie, WY 82071
Phone: 307-766-2412
Fax: 307-766-3800
E-mail: FinAid@uwyo.edu

VETERANS UNITED FOUNDATION

http://www.enhancelives.com

VETERANS UNITED FOUNDATION SCHOLARSHIP
• *See page 682*

VIRGINIA DEPARTMENT OF VETERANS SERVICES

http://www.dvs.virginia.gov/

VIRGINIA MILITARY SURVIVORS AND DEPENDENTS EDUCATION PROGRAM

Scholarships for post-secondary students between ages 16 and 29 to attend Virginia state-supported institutions. Must be child or surviving spouse of veteran who has either been permanently or totally disabled due to war or other armed conflict; died as a result of war or other armed conflict; or been listed as a POW or MIA. Parent must also meet Virginia residency requirements.

Award: Scholarship for use in freshman, sophomore, junior, senior, or graduate years; renewable.

Eligibility Requirements: Applicant must be age 16-29; enrolled or expecting to enroll full-time at a two-year or four-year or technical institution or university; resident of Virginia and studying in Virginia. Available to U.S. citizens. Applicant or parent must meet one or more of the following requirements: general military experience; retired from active duty; disabled or killed as a result of military service; prisoner of war; or missing in action.

Application Requirements: Application form, DD214 of service member, birth certificate of applicant, marriage certificate, acceptance letter from institution. *Deadline:* varies.

Contact: Mrs. Doris Sullivan, Coordinator
Virginia Department of Veterans Services
1351 Hershberger Road, Suite 220
Roanoke, VA 24012
Phone: 540-561-6625
Fax: 540-857-7573

WISCONSIN DEPARTMENT OF VETERANS AFFAIRS (WDVA)

http://www.dva.state.wi.us/

VETERANS EDUCATION (VETED) REIMBURSEMENT GRANT
• *See page 694*

WOMEN'S JEWELRY ASSOCIATION

http://www.womensjewelryassociation.com

WOMEN'S JEWELRY ASSOCIATIONS VETERANS GRANT
• *See page 684*

WONDERSHARE PDFELEMENT

https://pdf.wondershare.com

2018 PDFELEMENT $1000 SCHOLARSHIP
• *See page 684*

MILITARY SERVICE: MARINES

DIVERSITYCOMM, INC.

http://www.diversitycomm.net/

US VETERANS MAGAZINE SCHOLARSHIP
• *See page 696*

ELEARNERS.COM

http://www.elearners.com

ELEARNERS MILITARY SCHOLARSHIP
• *See page 696*

IMAGINE AMERICA FOUNDATION

http://www.imagine-america.org

MILITARY AWARD PROGRAM (MAP)
• *See page 696*

LADIES AUXILIARY OF THE FLEET RESERVE ASSOCIATION

http://www.fra.org/

LADIES AUXILIARY OF THE FLEET RESERVE ASSOCIATION SCHOLARSHIP
• *See page 567*

SAM ROSE MEMORIAL SCHOLARSHIP
• *See page 568*

MARINE CORPS TANKERS ASSOCIATION INC.

http://www.USMarinetankers.org/

MARINE CORPS TANKERS ASSOCIATION, JOHN CORNELIUS/MAX ENGLISH SCHOLARSHIP

Award for Marine tankers or former Marine tankers, or dependents of Marines who served in a tank unit and are on active duty, retired, reserve or have been honorably discharged. Applicant must be a high school graduate or planning to graduate in June. May be enrolled in college, undergraduate or graduate or have previously attended college. Must be a member of MCTA or intends to join in the future.

Award: Scholarship for use in freshman, sophomore, junior, senior, or graduate years; not renewable. *Number:* 10. *Amount:* up to $2000.

Eligibility Requirements: Applicant must be enrolled or expecting to enroll full-time at a two-year or four-year or technical institution or university. Available to U.S. citizens. Applicant or parent must meet one or more of the following requirements: Marine Corps experience; retired from active duty; disabled or killed as a result of military service; prisoner of war; or missing in action.

Application Requirements: Application form, essay, personal photograph, recommendations or references, test scores, transcript. *Deadline:* March 15.

Contact: Phil Morell, Scholarship Chair
Marine Corps Tankers Association Inc.
1112 Alpine Heights Road
Alpine, CA 91901-2814
Phone: 619-445-8423
Fax: 619-445-8423
E-mail: mpmorell@cox.net

PETAZI

https://petazi.com/

NURTURE FOR NATURE SCHOLARSHIP
• *See page 692*

MILITARY SERVICE: NAVY

ANCHOR SCHOLARSHIP FOUNDATION

http://www.anchorscholarship.com

ANCHOR SCHOLARSHIP FOUNDATION
• *See page 598*

DIVERSITYCOMM, INC.

http://www.diversitycomm.net/

US VETERANS MAGAZINE SCHOLARSHIP
• *See page 696*

ELEARNERS.COM

http://www.elearners.com

ELEARNERS MILITARY SCHOLARSHIP
• *See page 696*

GAMEWARDENS OF VIETNAM ASSOCIATION INC.

http://www.tf116.org/

GAMEWARDENS OF VIETNAM SCHOLARSHIP

Scholarship for entering freshman who is a descendant of a U.S. Navy man or woman who worked with TF-116 in Vietnam. One-time award, but applicant may reapply.

Award: Scholarship for use in freshman year; not renewable. *Number:* 1–3. *Amount:* $500.

Eligibility Requirements: Applicant must be high school student; age 16-21 and planning to enroll or expecting to enroll full-time at a two-year or four-year or technical institution or university. Applicant must have 2.5 GPA or higher. Available to U.S. and non-U.S. citizens. Applicant or parent must meet one or more of the following requirements: Navy experience; retired from active duty; disabled or killed as a result of military service; prisoner of war; or missing in action.

Application Requirements: Application form, recommendations or references, resume, test scores, transcript. *Deadline:* April 1.

Contact: David Ajax, Scholarship Coordinator
Gamewardens of Vietnam Association Inc.
6630 Perry Court
Arvada, CO 80003
Phone: 303-426-6385
Fax: 303-426-6186
E-mail: dpajax@comcast.net

IMAGINE AMERICA FOUNDATION

http://www.imagine-america.org

MILITARY AWARD PROGRAM (MAP)
• *See page 696*

LADIES AUXILIARY OF THE FLEET RESERVE ASSOCIATION

http://www.fra.org/

LADIES AUXILIARY OF THE FLEET RESERVE ASSOCIATION SCHOLARSHIP
• *See page 567*

SAM ROSE MEMORIAL SCHOLARSHIP
• *See page 568*

PETAZI

https://petazi.com/

NURTURE FOR NATURE SCHOLARSHIP
• *See page 692*

UDT-SEAL ASSOCIATION

http://www.nswfoundation.org/

HAD RICHARDS UDT-SEAL MEMORIAL SCHOLARSHIP
One-time award for dependent children of UDT-SEAL association members. Freshmen given priority. Applicant may not be older than 22 and not married. Must be U.S. citizen.

Award: Scholarship for use in freshman, sophomore, junior, or senior years; not renewable. *Number:* 1–2.

Eligibility Requirements: Applicant must be enrolled or expecting to enroll full-time at a two-year or four-year institution or university and single. Available to U.S. citizens. Applicant or parent must meet one or more of the following requirements: Navy experience; retired from active duty; disabled or killed as a result of military service; prisoner of war; or missing in action.

Application Requirements: Application form, essay, personal photograph, proof of active duty or parent/spouse's active duty, test scores, transcript. *Deadline:* varies.

Contact: Robert Rieve, President and CEO
Phone: 757-363-7490
E-mail: info@nswfoundation.org

NAVAL SPECIAL WARFARE SCHOLARSHIP
Awards given to active duty SEAL's, SWCC's, and other active duty military serving in a Naval Special Warfare command or their spouses and dependents.

Award: Scholarship for use in freshman, sophomore, junior, or senior years; not renewable. *Number:* 80–100.

Eligibility Requirements: Applicant must be enrolled or expecting to enroll full- or part-time at a two-year or four-year institution or university. Available to U.S. citizens. Applicant or parent must meet one or more of the following requirements: Navy experience; retired from active duty; disabled or killed as a result of military service; prisoner of war; or missing in action.

Application Requirements: Application form, essay, personal photograph, proof of active duty or parent/spouse's active duty, transcript.

Contact: Robert Rieve, President and CEO
Phone: 757-363-7490
E-mail: info@nswfoundation.org

UDT-SEAL SCHOLARSHIP
Award for dependent children of UDT-SEAL association members. Freshmen given priority. Applicant may not be older than 22 and not married. Must be U.S. citizen.

Award: Scholarship for use in freshman, sophomore, junior, or senior years; not renewable. *Number:* 10–20.

Eligibility Requirements: Applicant must be enrolled or expecting to enroll full-time at a two-year or four-year or technical institution or university and single. Available to U.S. citizens. Applicant or parent must meet one or more of the following requirements: Navy experience; retired from active duty; disabled or killed as a result of military service; prisoner of war; or missing in action.

Application Requirements: Application form, essay, personal photograph, proof of active duty or parent/spouse's active duty, test scores, transcript. *Deadline:* varies.

Contact: Robert Rieve, President and CEO
Phone: 757-363-7490
E-mail: info@nswfoundation.org

UNITED STATES SUBMARINE VETERANS

https://www.ussvi.org/Documents.asp?Type=Scholarship|Application

UNITED STATES SUBMARINE VETERANS INC. NATIONAL SCHOLARSHIP PROGRAM
• *See page 586*

WINGS OVER AMERICA SCHOLARSHIP FOUNDATION

http://www.wingsoveramerica.us/

WINGS OVER AMERICA SCHOLARSHIP FOUNDATION
Applicant must be graduates of an accredited high school or the equivalent home school or institution and must plan to attend an accredited academic institution. Scholarship awardees must be enrolled full-time in order to receive their award. Awards may be used for tuition and tuition-related fees only.

Award: Scholarship for use in freshman, sophomore, or junior years; not renewable. *Number:* 50. *Amount:* $3000.

Eligibility Requirements: Applicant must be enrolled or expecting to enroll full-time at a two-year or four-year or technical institution or university. Available to U.S. citizens. Applicant must have served in the Navy.

Application Requirements: Application form, community service, essay. *Deadline:* February 1.

Contact: Melissa Garrison, Scholarship Administrator
Wings Over America Scholarship Foundation
4966 Euclid Drive
Suite 109
Virginia Beach, VA 23452
Phone: 757-671-3200 Ext. 2
E-mail: scholarship@wingsoveramerica.us

NATIONALITY OR ETHNIC HERITAGE

1-800-HANSONS

http://www.hansons.com

1-800-HANSONS SCHOLARSHIP PROGRAM
• *See page 592*

1DENTAL.COM

https://www.1dental.com/

1DENTAL SCHOLARSHIP
• *See page 592*

1ST CAVALRY DIVISION ASSOCIATION

https://www.1CDA.org

1ST CAVALRY DIVISION ASSOCIATION SCHOLARSHIP FOUNDATION
• *See page 592*

365 PET INSURANCE

https://365petinsurance.com/

MINORITY STUDENTS IN VETERINARY MEDICINE SCHOLARSHIP

The Minority Students in Veterinary Medicine Scholarship is for students currently enrolled in or accepted to a veterinary school in the USA. This scholarship serves to meet the economic needs of minority students to encourage enrollment in veterinary medicine programs to help diversify the population of veterinarians entering the workforce.

Award: Scholarship for use in sophomore, junior, senior, graduate, or postgraduate years; not renewable. *Number:* 1. *Amount:* $500.

Eligibility Requirements: Applicant must be of Mexican heritage; American Indian/Alaska Native, Asian/Pacific Islander, Black (non-Hispanic), Hispanic; enrolled or expecting to enroll full-time at a four-year institution or university; resident of Alabama, Alaska, Arizona, Arkansas, California, Colorado, Connecticut, Delaware, District of Columbia, Florida, Georgia, Guam, Hawaii, Idaho, Illinois, Indiana, Iowa, Kansas, Kentucky, Louisiana, Maine, Maryland, Massachusetts, Michigan, Minnesota, Mississippi, Missouri, Montana, Nebraska, Nevada, New Hampshire, New Jersey, New Mexico, New York, North Carolina, North Dakota, Ohio, Oklahoma, Oregon, Pennsylvania, Puerto Rico, Rhode Island, South Carolina, South Dakota, Tennessee, Texas, Utah, Vermont, Virginia, Washington, West Virginia, Wisconsin, Wyoming and studying in Alabama, Alaska, Arizona, Arkansas, California, Colorado, Connecticut, Delaware, District of Columbia, Florida, Georgia, Hawaii, Idaho, Illinois, Indiana, Iowa, Kansas, Kentucky, Louisiana, Maine, Maryland, Massachusetts, Michigan, Minnesota, Mississippi, Missouri, Montana, Nebraska, Nevada, New Hampshire, New Jersey, New Mexico, New York, North Carolina, North Dakota, Ohio, Oklahoma, Oregon, Pennsylvania, Rhode Island, South Carolina, South Dakota, Tennessee, Texas, Utah, Vermont, Virginia, Washington, West Virginia, Wisconsin, Wyoming. Available to U.S. citizens.

Application Requirements: Application form, essay. *Deadline:* December 31.

Contact: Mr. Jason Lee, 10400 NE 4th St
Bellevue, WA 98004
E-mail: jason@365petinsurance.com

4MYCASH.COM, LLC

https://www.4mycash.com

4MYCASH ST. LOUIS HARD MONEY SCHOLARSHIP
• *See page 592*

THE 5 STRONG SCHOLARSHIP FOUNDATION, INC.

http://5strongscholars.org

5 STRONG SCHOLARS SCHOLARSHIP

The applicants must reside in the Metropolitan Atlanta area (Cobb, Fulton, Clayton, Fayette, Douglas, Gwinett, DeKalb, etc.). If chosen, applicants must be able to attend bi-monthly college prep sessions. Minimum requirements: GPA: 2.5 and ACT: 21, SAT: 1010

Award: Scholarship for use in freshman, sophomore, junior, or senior years; renewable. *Number:* 25. *Amount:* $10,000–$16,000.

Eligibility Requirements: Applicant must be American Indian/Alaska Native, Asian/Pacific Islander, Black (non-Hispanic), Hispanic; high school student; age 17-19; planning to enroll or expecting to enroll full-time at a four-year institution or university; resident of Georgia and studying in Georgia. Applicant must have 3.0 GPA or higher. Available to U.S. citizens.

Application Requirements: Application form, interview. *Deadline:* December 31.

Contact: Drew Ragland
The 5 Strong Scholarship Foundation, Inc.
103 Pinegate Rd
Peachtree City 30269
E-mail: 5strongscholars@gmail.com

A-1 AUTO TRANSPORT, INC.

https://www.a1autotransport.com/a-1-auto-transport-scholarship/

A-1 AUTO TRANSPORT SCHOLARSHIP
• *See page 592*

ACADGILD

https://acadgild.com

ACADGILD MERIT-BASED SCHOLARSHIPS
• *See page 593*

ACES: THE SOCIETY FOR EDITING

https://aceseditors.org/

BILL WALSH SCHOLARSHIP
• *See page 593*

AIR FORCE AID SOCIETY

http://www.afas.org/

GENERAL HENRY H. ARNOLD EDUCATION GRANT PROGRAM
• *See page 695*

AIR FORCE RESERVE OFFICER TRAINING CORPS

http://www.afrotc.com/

AFROTC HBCU SCHOLARSHIP PROGRAM
• *See page 695*

AIR TRAFFIC CONTROL ASSOCIATION INC.

http://www.atca.org/

AIR TRAFFIC CONTROL ASSOCIATION SCHOLARSHIP
• *See page 593*

BUCKINGHAM MEMORIAL SCHOLARSHIP
• *See page 593*

ALABAMA SOCIETY OF CERTIFIED PUBLIC ACCOUNTANTS

http://www.ascpa.org/

ASCPA EDUCATIONAL FOUNDATION SCHOLARSHIP
• *See page 593*

ALBERTA HERITAGE SCHOLARSHIP FUND

http://www.alis.alberta.ca/

ADULT HIGH SCHOOL EQUIVALENCY SCHOLARSHIPS

Awards of CAN$500 to recognize and reward the academic achievement of mature students in the attainment of high school equivalency and provide an incentive for students to continue their education at the postsecondary level. Applicants must be residents of Alberta, have been out of high school for a minimum of three years prior to commencing a high school equivalency program, and be enrolled full-time in a high school equivalency program. Must be nominated by high school. See website for additional information and application http://alis.alberta.ca.

Award: Scholarship for use in freshman year; not renewable. *Number:* up to 200.

Eligibility Requirements: Applicant must be Canadian citizen; enrolled or expecting to enroll full-time at a two-year or four-year or technical institution or university and resident of Alberta. Applicant must have 3.0 GPA or higher.

Application Requirements: Application form, nomination. *Deadline:* September 1.

Contact: Scholarship Committee
Alberta Heritage Scholarship Fund
9940 106th Street, Fourth Floor
PO Box 28000, Station Main
Edmonton, AB T5J 4R4
CAN
Phone: 780-427-8640
Fax: 780-422-4516
E-mail: scholarships@gov.ab.ca

ALBERTA CENTENNIAL SCHOLARSHIPS-ALBERTA

25 awards of CAN$2005 have been established to commemorate the province of Alberta's centennial. Must be Canadian citizens or permanent residents of Canada and Alberta residents. Awards students entering any level of postsecondary study at any university, college, technical institute, or apprenticeship program in Canada. Each high school in Alberta nominates a recipient and all are considered for the 25 awards. For additional information and application form, visit website http://alis.alberta.ca.

Award: Scholarship for use in freshman, sophomore, junior, or senior years; not renewable. *Number:* 25.

Eligibility Requirements: Applicant must be Canadian citizen; high school student; planning to enroll or expecting to enroll full-time at a two-year or four-year or technical institution or university and resident of Alberta.

Application Requirements: Nomination from high school counselors. *Deadline:* June 1.

Contact: Scholarship Committee
Phone: 780-427-8640
E-mail: scholarships@gov.ab.ca

ALEXANDER RUTHERFORD SCHOLARSHIPS FOR HIGH SCHOOL ACHIEVEMENT

Award of up to CAN$2500 available to high school students who are residents of Alberta and plan to enroll or are enrolled in a full-time postsecondary program of at least one semester. Awarded on the basis of achieving an 75 percent average on five designated subjects in grades 10, 11, and 12. Application deadlines are May 1 for September start date and December 1 for January start date. For additional information, see website http://alis.alberta.ca.

Award: Scholarship for use in freshman year; not renewable.

Eligibility Requirements: Applicant must be Canadian citizen; high school student; planning to enroll or expecting to enroll full-time at a two-year or four-year or technical institution or university and resident of Alberta.

Application Requirements: Application form, transcript. *Deadline:* varies.

Contact: Scholarship Committee
Phone: 780-427-8640
E-mail: scholarships@gov.ab.ca

CHARLES S. NOBLE JUNIOR FOOTBALL SCHOLARSHIPS

Scholarships of up to CAN$1000 available to reward the athletic and academic excellence of junior football players at universities, colleges, and technical institutes in Alberta. Must be Alberta residents and enrolled full-time in an undergraduate, professional, or graduate program at a university, college, or technical institute in Alberta. Must be a playing member on an Alberta junior football team and maintain 2.0 average in the previous semester. Students entering their first semester of post-secondary study do not have to meet this requirement. Interested applicants should contact their team coach or manager as nominations must come from the football team. For additional information, visit website http://alis.alberta.ca.

Award: Scholarship for use in freshman, sophomore, junior, senior, or graduate years; not renewable. *Number:* 30.

Eligibility Requirements: Applicant must be Canadian citizen; enrolled or expecting to enroll full-time at a two-year or four-year or technical institution or university; resident of Alberta; studying in Alberta and must have an interest in athletics/sports.

Application Requirements: Nomination from junior football team. *Deadline:* October 1.

Contact: Scholarship Committee
Phone: 780-427-8640
E-mail: scholarships@gov.ab.ca

CHARLES S. NOBLE JUNIOR HOCKEY SCHOLARSHIPS

Awards of CAN$2000 to reward the athletic and academic excellence of junior hockey league players and to provide an incentive and means for these players to continue their postsecondary education. Must be Alberta residents and enrolled full-time at a postsecondary institution in Alberta. Interested applicants should contact their team coach or manager, as nominations must come from the participant's hockey team. Applicants must have maintained a minimum average of 2.0 on a 4.0 scale in their previous semester. Students entering their first semester of post-secondary study do not have to meet this requirement. For additional information, see website http://alis.alberta.ca.

Award: Scholarship for use in freshman, sophomore, junior, or senior years; not renewable. *Number:* 10.

Eligibility Requirements: Applicant must be Canadian citizen; enrolled or expecting to enroll full-time at a two-year or four-year or technical institution or university; resident of Alberta; studying in Alberta and must have an interest in athletics/sports.

Application Requirements: Application form, essay, transcript. *Deadline:* December 1.

Contact: Scholarship Committee
Phone: 780-427-8640
E-mail: scholarships@gov.ab.ca

INTERNATIONAL EDUCATION AWARDS-UKRAINE

Awards of CAN$5000 to enable Alberta post-secondary students, post-graduates, professionals, and scholars to undertake career-related training, research, or study in Ukraine, and Ukrainian post-secondary students, post-graduates, professionals and scholars to undertake career-related training, research, or study in Alberta. Selection will be based on academic merit, past accomplishments, the purpose or validity of the proposal, reference letter, and institutional support and benefit to the recipient's institution. For additional information and application, see website http://alis.alberta.ca.

Award: Scholarship for use in freshman, sophomore, junior, or senior years; not renewable. *Number:* 5.

Eligibility Requirements: Applicant must be Canadian, Ukrainian citizen; enrolled or expecting to enroll full-time at a two-year or four-year or technical institution or university and studying in Alberta. Available to Canadian and non-U.S. citizens.

Application Requirements: Application form, recommendations or references. *Deadline:* February 1.

Contact: Scholarship Committee
Phone: 780-427-8640
E-mail: scholarships@gov.ab.ca

JIMMIE CONDON ATHLETIC SCHOLARSHIPS

Award of CAN$1800 available to Alberta residents enrolled full-time in an undergraduate, professional, or graduate program at a university, college, or technical institute in Alberta. Must be a member of a designated sports team or a Provincial Disabled Athletic Team recognized by the Alberta Athlete Development Program, and must be nominated by coach. For additional information, go to website http://alis.alberta.ca.

Award: Scholarship for use in freshman, sophomore, junior, or senior years; not renewable.

Eligibility Requirements: Applicant must be Canadian citizen; enrolled or expecting to enroll full-time at a two-year or four-year or technical institution or university; resident of Alberta; studying in Alberta and must have an interest in athletics/sports.

Application Requirements: Application form, nomination by athletic coach. *Deadline:* continuous.

Contact: Scholarship Committee
Phone: 780-427-8640
E-mail: scholarships@gov.ab.ca

JO-ANNE KOCH-ABC SOCIETY SCHOLARSHIP

Up to two scholarships of CAN$500 supporting gifted learners in their post-secondary studies. Applicants must have completed Grade 12 requirements at a publicly funded high school in Alberta and plan to pursue post-secondary studies. Applicants must meet the criteria for Giftedness as determined by their school jurisdiction. Preference will be given to applicants who have received extra support for their learning needs. For additional information, see website http://alis.alberta.ca.

Award: Scholarship for use in freshman year; not renewable. *Number:* up to 2.

Eligibility Requirements: Applicant must be Canadian citizen; high school student; planning to enroll or expecting to enroll full-time at a two-year or four-year institution or university and resident of Alberta.

Application Requirements: Application form, essay, recommendations or references. *Deadline:* April 1.

Contact: Scholarship Committee
Phone: 780-427-8640
E-mail: scholarships@gov.ab.ca

KEYERA ENERGY-PETER J. RENTON MEMORIAL SCHOLARSHIP

The scholarship is intended to assist and encourage Alberta students to pursue full-time studies in a post-secondary program in a field related to the oil and gas industry. CAN$3,000 for first year of study and CAN$3,000 renewable in second year providing recipient remains in good standing and continues into the second year. Family of Keyera Energy employees are eligible to apply. Relatives of the selection committee members are not eligible. For additional information, see website http://alis.alberta.ca.

Award: Scholarship for use in freshman or sophomore years; renewable.

Eligibility Requirements: Applicant must be Canadian citizen; high school student; planning to enroll or expecting to enroll full-time at a two-year or four-year or technical institution or university; resident of Alberta and studying in Alberta.

Application Requirements: Application form, essay, recommendations or references. *Deadline:* May 1.

Contact: Scholarship Committee
Phone: 780-427-8640
E-mail: scholarships@gov.ab.ca

LAURENCE DECORE AWARDS FOR STUDENT LEADERSHIP

Awards of CAN$1,000 for postsecondary students who have demonstrated outstanding dedication and leadership to fellow students and to their community. Must be Alberta residents who are currently enrolled in a minimum of three full courses at a designated Alberta postsecondary institution. Selected on the basis of involvement in either student government or student societies, clubs, or organizations. For additional information, visit website http://alis.alberta.ca.

Award: Scholarship for use in freshman, sophomore, junior, or senior years; not renewable. *Number:* 100.

Eligibility Requirements: Applicant must be Canadian citizen; enrolled or expecting to enroll full- or part-time at a two-year or four-year or technical institution or university; resident of Alberta; studying in Alberta and must have an interest in leadership.

Application Requirements: Application form, nomination from school. *Deadline:* March 1.

Contact: Scholarship Committee
Phone: 780-427-8640
E-mail: scholarships@gov.ab.ca

LOUISE MCKINNEY POST-SECONDARY SCHOLARSHIPS

Student awards of up to CAN$2500 to residents of Alberta who are enrolled at a university, college, or technical institute in the second or subsequent year of full-time study. Alberta students studying out-of-province because their program of study is not offered in Alberta will be considered for a scholarship if their class standing is in the top two percent of their program. Deadlines vary. For additional information, go to website http://alis.alberta.ca.

Award: Scholarship for use in sophomore, junior, or senior years; not renewable.

Eligibility Requirements: Applicant must be Canadian citizen; enrolled or expecting to enroll full-time at a two-year or four-year or technical institution or university and resident of Alberta.

Application Requirements: Application form, test scores, transcript. *Deadline:* varies.

Contact: Scholarship Committee
Phone: 780-427-8640
E-mail: scholarships@gov.ab.ca

PERSONS CASE SCHOLARSHIPS

Awards of up to CAN$5000 to assist female students whose studies will ultimately contribute to the advancement of women, or who are studying in a field that is non-traditional for women. Applicants must be residents of Alberta and enrolled full-time at a postsecondary institution in Alberta. Students studying out-of-province may be considered for this award if their program of study is not available in Alberta. Selection is based on chosen program of study, financial need, and academic achievement. For additional information and application, visit website http://alis.alberta.ca.

Award: Scholarship for use in freshman, sophomore, junior, senior, or graduate years; not renewable.

Eligibility Requirements: Applicant must be Canadian citizen; enrolled or expecting to enroll full-time at a four-year institution or university; female; resident of Alberta and studying in Alberta. Applicant must have 3.0 GPA or higher.

Application Requirements: Application form, essay, financial need analysis, resume, transcript. *Deadline:* September 30.

Contact: Scholarship Committee
Phone: 780-427-8640
E-mail: scholarships@gov.ab.ca

QUEEN ELIZABETH II GOLDEN JUBILEE CITIZENSHIP MEDAL

Award of CAN$5000, a medal and a letter of commendation from the Lieutenant Governor to recognize the eight most outstanding students among the recipients of a Premier's Citizenship Award in recognition of the Queen's Golden Jubilee. Applicant must be a Canadian citizen or permanent resident and be nominated for this award. For additional information, see website http://alis.alberta.ca.

Award: Prize for use in freshman year; not renewable. *Number:* 8.

Eligibility Requirements: Applicant must be Canadian citizen; high school student; planning to enroll or expecting to enroll full-time at a four-year institution or university and resident of Alberta.

Application Requirements: Nomination. *Deadline:* June 1.

Contact: Scholarship Committee
Phone: 780-427-8640
E-mail: scholarships@gov.ab.ca

RUTHERFORD SCHOLARS

Award of CAN $2500 for Alberta residents based of results obtained on Diploma Examinations in English 30, or Francais 30, Social Studies 30, and three other subjects. Averages normally are in the 98.0 to 98.8 percent range. Only the first writing of the diploma exam will be considered. No application is required. Recipients are selected from all Alexander Rutherford Scholarship applications received before August 1.

Award: Scholarship for use in freshman year; not renewable. *Number:* 10.

Eligibility Requirements: Applicant must be Canadian citizen; high school student; planning to enroll or expecting to enroll full-time at a four-year institution or university and resident of Alberta.

Application Requirements: Test scores, transcript. *Deadline:* August 1.

Contact: Scholarship Committee
Phone: 780-427-8640
E-mail: scholarships@gov.ab.ca

ALERTONE SERVICES, LLC

https://www.alert-1.com/

ALERT1 STUDENT FOR SENIORS SCHOLARSHIP
• See page 593

ALEXANDER GRAHAM BELL ASSOCIATION FOR THE DEAF AND HARD OF HEARING

http://www.agbell.org/

AG BELL COLLEGE SCHOLARSHIP PROGRAM
• *See page 594*

ALGAECAL INC.

https://www.algaecal.com/

ALGAECAL SCHOLARSHIP
• *See page 594*

ALLIANCE FOR YOUNG ARTISTS AND WRITERS INC.

http://www.artandwriting.org/

SCHOLASTIC ART AND WRITING AWARDS
• *See page 594*

ALLTHEROOMS

http://alltherooms.com

ROOM TO TRAVEL - STUDY ABROAD SCHOLARSHIP
• *See page 594*

ALZHEIMER'S FOUNDATION OF AMERICA

https://alzfdn.org/

AFA TEENS FOR ALZHEIMER'S AWARENESS COLLEGE SCHOLARSHIP
• *See page 595*

AMERICAN ALPINE CLUB

https://americanalpineclub.org/

AMERICAN ALPINE CLUB RESEARCH GRANTS
• *See page 595*

AMERICAN ASSOCIATION OF TEACHERS OF JAPANESE BRIDGING CLEARINGHOUSE FOR STUDY ABROAD IN JAPAN

http://www.aatj.org

BRIDGING SCHOLARSHIP FOR STUDY ABROAD IN JAPAN
• *See page 595*

AMERICAN COUNCIL OF THE BLIND

http://www.acb.org/

AMERICAN COUNCIL OF THE BLIND SCHOLARSHIPS
• *See page 595*

AMERICAN DENTAL ASSISTANTS ASSOCIATION

http://www.adaausa.org

JULIETTE A. SOUTHARD SCHOLARSHIP
• *See page 549*

AMERICAN INDIAN EDUCATION FUND

http://www.aiefprogram.org/

AMERICAN INDIAN EDUCATION FUND SCHOLARSHIP
AIEF provides scholarships to Native American, Alaska Native, and Native Hawaiian students studying undergraduate and graduate studies. Please check out our website at http://www.aiefprogram.org for more information!

Award: Scholarship for use in freshman, sophomore, junior, senior, or graduate years; not renewable. *Number:* 200. *Amount:* $2000.

Eligibility Requirements: Applicant must be American Indian/Alaska Native and enrolled or expecting to enroll full- or part-time at a two-year or four-year or technical institution or university. Available to U.S. citizens.

Application Requirements: Application form, community service, essay, personal photograph. *Deadline:* April 4.

Contact: RaeAnne Schad, AIEF Program Specialist
American Indian Education Fund
2401 Eglin Street
Rapid City, SD 57703
Phone: 866-866-8642
E-mail: rschad@nativepartnership.org

AMERICAN INDIAN GRADUATE CENTER

http://www.aigcs.org/

ACCENTURE AMERICAN INDIAN SCHOLARSHIP
Scholarships awarded to American Indian and Alaska Natives from U.S. federally recognized tribes. This program is for first year college freshmen (undergraduate) students. Must have a cumulative GPA of a 3.25 on a 4.0 scale and demonstrate financial need. Areas of study: engineering, computer science, operations management, finance, marketing and business.

Award: Scholarship for use in freshman year; renewable. *Number:* 10. *Amount:* $10,000.

Eligibility Requirements: Applicant must be American Indian/Alaska Native; high school student and planning to enroll or expecting to enroll full-time at a four-year institution or university. Available to U.S. citizens.

Application Requirements: Application form, community service, essay, financial need analysis, personal photograph. *Deadline:* May 1.

Contact: Marveline Vallo Gabbard, Program Associate
American Indian Graduate Center
3701 San Mateo Boulevard, NE, Suite 200
Albuquerque, NM 87110
Phone: 505-881-4584
E-mail: fellowships@aigcs.org

WELLS FARGO SCHOLARSHIP AMERICAN INDIAN SCHOLARSHIP
Must be an enrolled member of a U.S. federally recognized American Indian or Alaska Native tribe. Be pursuing a degree in the banking, resort management, gaming operations, management and administration, including accounting, finance, information technology and human resources. Must have a cumulative GPA of a 3.0 on a 4.0 scale and demonstrate financial need.

Award: Scholarship for use in junior, senior, or graduate years; renewable. *Number:* 2. *Amount:* $5000.

Eligibility Requirements: Applicant must be American Indian/Alaska Native and enrolled or expecting to enroll full-time at a four-year institution or university. Applicant must have 3.0 GPA or higher. Available to U.S. citizens.

Application Requirements: Application form, community service, essay, financial need analysis, personal photograph. *Deadline:* May 1.

Contact: Marveline Vallo Gabbard, Program Associate
American Indian Graduate Center
3701 San Mateo Boulevard, NE, Suite 200
Albuquerque, NM 87110
Phone: 505-881-4584
E-mail: fellowships@aigcs.org

AMERICAN INSTITUTE FOR FOREIGN STUDY

http://www.aifsabroad.com/

AIFS DIVERSITYABROAD.COM SCHOLARSHIP

Scholarships are available for students studying abroad on any program offered by a DiversityAbroad.com member organization. African-American, Asian-American, Hispanic/Latino and Native-American students are strongly encouraged to apply. Visit http://www.aifsabroad.com/scholarships.asp for more information.

Award: Scholarship for use in freshman, sophomore, junior, or senior years; not renewable. *Number:* up to 20. *Amount:* up to $1000.

Eligibility Requirements: Applicant must be American Indian/Alaska Native, Asian/Pacific Islander, Black (non-Hispanic), Hispanic; enrolled or expecting to enroll full-time at a two-year or four-year institution or university and must have an interest in international exchange. Applicant must have 3.5 GPA or higher. Available to U.S. citizens.

Application Requirements: Application form, essay, personal photograph, recommendations or references, resume, transcript. *Fee:* $95. *Deadline:* varies.

Contact: David Mauro, Admissions Counselor
American Institute for Foreign Study
River Plaza, 9 West Broad Street
Stamford, CT 06902-3788
Phone: 800-727-2437 Ext. 5163
Fax: 203-399-5463
E-mail: dmauro@aifs.com

AIFS-HACU SCHOLARSHIPS

Scholarships to outstanding Hispanic students to study abroad with AIFS. Available to students attending HACU member schools. Students will receive scholarships of up to 50 percent of the full program fee. Students must meet all standard AIFS eligibility requirements. Deadlines: April 15 for fall, October 1 for spring, and March 15 for summer.

Award: Scholarship for use in freshman, sophomore, junior, or senior years; not renewable. *Number:* up to 1. *Amount:* $6000–$8000.

Eligibility Requirements: Applicant must be Hispanic; enrolled or expecting to enroll full-time at a two-year or four-year institution or university and must have an interest in international exchange. Applicant must have 3.0 GPA or higher. Available to U.S. and non-U.S. citizens.

Application Requirements: Application form, essay, personal photograph, recommendations or references, transcript. *Fee:* $95. *Deadline:* varies.

Contact: David Mauro, Admissions Counselor
American Institute for Foreign Study
1 High Ridge Park
Stamford, CT 06905
Phone: 800-727-2437 Ext. 5163
Fax: 203-399-5463
E-mail: dmauro@aifs.com

AMERICAN LEGION AUXILIARY DEPARTMENT OF MASSACHUSETTS

http://www.masslegion-aux.org/

AMERICAN LEGION AUXILIARY DEPARTMENT OF MASSACHUSETTS DEPARTMENT PRESIDENT'S SCHOLARSHIP
• See page 595

AMERICAN LEGION AUXILIARY DEPARTMENT OF WISCONSIN

http://www.amlegionauxwi.org/

AMERICAN LEGION AUXILIARY DEPARTMENT OF WISCONSIN DELLA VAN DEUREN MEMORIAL SCHOLARSHIP
• See page 552

AMERICAN LEGION AUXILIARY DEPARTMENT OF WISCONSIN H.S. AND ANGELINE LEWIS SCHOLARSHIPS
• See page 552

AMERICAN LEGION AUXILIARY DEPARTMENT OF WISCONSIN MERIT AND MEMORIAL SCHOLARSHIPS
• See page 552

AMERICAN LEGION AUXILIARY DEPARTMENT OF WISCONSIN PRESIDENT'S SCHOLARSHIPS
• See page 552

AMERICAN LEGION AUXILIARY NATIONAL HEADQUARTERS

http://www.ALAforVeterans.org

AMERICAN LEGION AUXILIARY CHILDREN OF WARRIORS NATIONAL PRESIDENTS' SCHOLARSHIP
• See page 596

AMERICAN LEGION DEPARTMENT OF MARYLAND

http://www.mdlegion.org/

AMERICAN LEGION DEPARTMENT OF MARYLAND GENERAL SCHOLARSHIP FUND
• See page 555

AMERICAN LEGION, DEPARTMENT OF MARYLAND, HIGH SCHOOL ORATORICAL SCHOLARSHIP CONTEST
• See page 596

MARYLAND BOYS STATE SCHOLARSHIP
• See page 597

AMERICAN LEGION DEPARTMENT OF WASHINGTON

http://www.walegion.org/

AMERICAN LEGION DEPARTMENT OF WASHINGTON CHILDREN AND YOUTH SCHOLARSHIPS
• See page 557

AMERICAN LEGION DEPARTMENT OF WEST VIRGINIA

http://www.wvlegion.org/

AMERICAN LEGION DEPARTMENT OF WEST VIRGINIA BOARD OF REGENTS SCHOLARSHIP
• See page 588

AMERICAN SAVINGS FOUNDATION

http://www.asfdn.org/

ROBERT T. KENNEY SCHOLARSHIP PROGRAM AT THE AMERICAN SAVINGS FOUNDATION
• See page 597

AMERICAN SCHOOL OF CLASSICAL STUDIES AT ATHENS

http://www.ascsa.edu.gr/

CHARLES M. EDWARDS SCHOLARSHIP
• See page 597

AMERICAN SOCIETY OF SAFETY ENGINEERS (ASSE) FOUNDATION

http://foundation.asse.org

FAMILY SCHOLARSHIP FUND
• See page 597

ANCHOR SCHOLARSHIP FOUNDATION

http://www.anchorscholarship.com

ANCHOR SCHOLARSHIP FOUNDATION
• See page 598

ANKIN LAW

http://ankinlaw.com

ANKIN LAW OFFICE ANNUAL COLLEGE SCHOLARSHIP
• See page 598

ANTHONY MUNOZ FOUNDATION

http://www.munozfoundation.org

ANTHONY MUNOZ SCHOLARSHIPS
• See page 598

ARCHITECTURAL PRECAST ASSOCIATION

http://www.archprecast.org

TOM CORY MEMORIAL SCHOLARSHIP
• See page 598

THE ARC NEW YORK

https://www.nysarc.org/

ARTHUR W. PENSE SCHOLARSHIP
• See page 599

ARC OF WASHINGTON TRUST FUND

http://www.arctrustfund.org/

ARC OF WASHINGTON TRUST FUND STIPEND PROGRAM
• See page 599

ARKANSAS SINGLE PARENT SCHOLARSHIP FUND

http://www.aspsf.org/

ARKANSAS SINGLE PARENT SCHOLARSHIP FUND
• See page 599

ARMENIAN RELIEF SOCIETY OF EASTERN USA INC.-REGIONAL OFFICE

http://www.arseastusa.org/

ARMENIAN RELIEF SOCIETY UNDERGRADUATE SCHOLARSHIP
• See page 599

ARMENIAN STUDENTS ASSOCIATION OF AMERICA INC.

http://www.asainc.org/

ARMENIAN STUDENTS ASSOCIATION OF AMERICA INC. SCHOLARSHIPS

One-time award for students of Armenian descent. Must be an undergraduate in sophomore, junior, or senior years, or graduate student, attending an accredited U.S. institution. Award based on need, merit, and character. Application fee: $15.

Award: Scholarship for use in sophomore, junior, senior, or graduate years; not renewable. *Number:* 35. *Amount:* $3300–$6700.

Eligibility Requirements: Applicant must be of Armenian heritage and enrolled or expecting to enroll full-time at a four-year institution or university. Available to U.S. citizens.

Application Requirements: Application form, essay, financial need analysis. *Fee:* $15. *Deadline:* March 15.

Contact: Nathalie Yaghoobian, ASA Scholarship Committee
  Phone: 401-461-6114
  Fax: 401-461-6112
  E-mail: asa@asainc.org

ARTBA

http://www.artba.org/

ARTBA-TDF LANFORD FAMILY HIGHWAY WORKERS MEMORIAL SCHOLARSHIP PROGRAM
• See page 599

ASIAN PACIFIC COMMUNITY FUND

http://www.apcf.org/

ROYAL BUSINESS BANK SCHOLARSHIP PROGRAM
• See page 600

TAIWANESE AMERICAN SCHOLARSHIP FUND
• See page 600

ASIAN PROFESSIONAL EXTENSION INC.

http://www.apex-ny.org/

APEX SCHOLARSHIP

Scholarship to students based on academic excellence, personal essays, letters of recommendation, extracurricular activities/volunteer service, and financial need. Two winners will receive scholarships of $500 and $1000. Deadline varies.

Award: Scholarship for use in freshman, sophomore, junior, senior, or graduate years; not renewable. *Number:* 2. *Amount:* $500–$1000.

Eligibility Requirements: Applicant must be American Indian/Alaska Native or Asian/Pacific Islander and enrolled or expecting to enroll full- or part-time at a four-year institution or university. Available to U.S. citizens.

Application Requirements: Application form, entry in a contest, essay, financial need analysis, recommendations or references, transcript. *Deadline:* varies.

Contact: Trang Le-Chan, Deputy Director of Programs
  Phone: 212-748-1225 Ext. 101
  Fax: 212-748-1250
  E-mail: trang.le-chan@apex-ny.org

ASIAN REPORTER

http://www.arfoundation.net/

ASIAN REPORTER SCHOLARSHIP
• *See page 600*

ASSOCIATION ON AMERICAN INDIAN AFFAIRS, INC.

http://www.indian-affairs.org/

ADOLPH VAN PELT SPECIAL FUND FOR INDIAN SCHOLARSHIPS

Scholarship is open to undergraduate students pursuing a Bachelor's degree in any curriculum. Must be an American Indian/Alaska Native. See http://www.indian-affairs.org for specific details. Must be seeking an Associate's degree or higher at an accredited school.

Award: Scholarship for use in freshman, sophomore, junior, or senior years; not renewable. *Number:* 5–15. *Amount:* up to $1500.

Eligibility Requirements: Applicant must be American Indian/Alaska Native and enrolled or expecting to enroll full-time at a two-year or four-year or technical institution or university. Available to U.S. citizens.

Application Requirements: Application form, essay, Tribal Enrollment. *Deadline:* June 1.

Contact: Lisa Wyzlic, Director of Scholarship Programs
Association on American Indian Affairs, Inc.
966 Hungerford Drive, Suite 12-B
Rockville, MD 20850
Phone: 240-314-7155
Fax: 240-314-7155
E-mail: lw.aaia@indian-affairs.org

ALLOGAN SLAGLE MEMORIAL SCHOLARSHIP

Scholarship available for American Indian/Alaska Native undergraduate and graduate students who are members of tribes that are not yet recognized by the federal government. Students must apply each year. See http://www.indian-affairs.org for specific details. Must be seeking an Associate's degree or higher at an accredited school.

Award: Scholarship for use in freshman, sophomore, junior, senior, or graduate years; not renewable. *Number:* 4–8. *Amount:* $1500.

Eligibility Requirements: Applicant must be American Indian/Alaska Native and enrolled or expecting to enroll full-time at a two-year or four-year or technical institution or university. Available to U.S. citizens.

Application Requirements: Application form, essay, Tribal Enrollment. *Deadline:* June 1.

Contact: Lisa Wyzlic, Director of Scholarship Programs
Association on American Indian Affairs, Inc.
966 Hungerford Drive, Suite 12-B
Rockville, MD 20850
Phone: 240-314-7155
Fax: 240-314-7159
E-mail: lw.aaia@indian-affairs.org

DAVID RISLING EMERGENCY AID SCHOLARSHIP

This scholarship is very limited in the amount available as well as the situation covered (eviction, utility disconnection, child removed from daycare for non-payment, some very limited car expenses for commuting students). Scholarship is for acute, temporary, unexpected emergencies that would keep students from attending school. Tuition, books, computers and other expected expenses are NOT considered emergencies. Must be Native American/Alaska Native. See our website at http://www.indian-affairs.org for details AND call the Rockville office prior to submission to see if funding is available and if your situation qualifies as an emergency. We do not fund summer session or expenses incurred over the summer.

Award: Scholarship for use in freshman, sophomore, junior, senior, or graduate years; not renewable. *Amount:* $100–$400.

Eligibility Requirements: Applicant must be American Indian/Alaska Native and enrolled or expecting to enroll full-time at a two-year or four-year institution or university. Available to U.S. citizens.

Application Requirements: Application form, essay, financial need analysis, recommendations or references, transcript, Tribal Enrollment,

financial aid award letter, full time class schedule, explanation of need, proof of need. *Deadline:* continuous.

Contact: Lisa Wyzlic, Director of Scholarship Programs
Association on American Indian Affairs, Inc.
966 Hungerford Drive, Suite 12-B
Rockville, MD 20850
Phone: 240-314-7155
Fax: 240-314-7159
E-mail: lw.aaia@indian-affairs.org

DISPLACED HOMEMAKER SCHOLARSHIP

This undergraduate scholarship is for men and women 30+ who would not otherwise be able to complete their educational goals due to family responsibilities. Must be an American Indian/Alaska Native. See our website http://www.indian-affairs.org for complete details. Must be an Associate's degree or higher. Must be an accredited institution.

Award: Scholarship for use in freshman, sophomore, junior, or senior years; not renewable. *Number:* 2–10. *Amount:* $1500.

Eligibility Requirements: Applicant must be American Indian/Alaska Native and enrolled or expecting to enroll full-time at a two-year or four-year or technical institution or university. Available to U.S. citizens.

Application Requirements: Application form, essay, Tribal Enrollment. *Deadline:* June 3.

Contact: Lisa Wyzlic, Director of Scholarship Programs
Association on American Indian Affairs, Inc.
966 Hungerford Drive, Suite 12-B
Rockville, MD 20850
Phone: 240-314-7155
Fax: 240-314-7159
E-mail: lw.aaia@indian-affairs.org

OWANAH ANDERSON SCHOLARSHIP

This scholarship is for Native American and Alaska Native undergraduate women who are entering their Junior year of college. Students must be enrolled in a federally recognized tribe. Students must be seeking a Bachelors Degree and may be enrolled in any curriculum. This scholarship renews each semester through the student's Senior year pending satisfactory progress. Each award is $1,500 per school year. $750 is disbursed in late September and $750 is disbursed in late January. This scholarship is for two years only. See our website at http://www.indian-affairs.org for complete details.

Award: Scholarship for use in junior year; renewable. *Number:* 1–5. *Amount:* $1500.

Eligibility Requirements: Applicant must be American Indian/Alaska Native; enrolled or expecting to enroll full-time at a four-year institution or university and female. Available to U.S. citizens.

Application Requirements: Application form, copy of Tribal Enrollment, essay. *Deadline:* June 1.

Contact: Lisa Wyzlic, Director of Scholarship Program
Association on American Indian Affairs, Inc.
966 Hungerford Drive, Suite 12-B
Rockville, DC 20850
Phone: 240-314-7155
Fax: 240-314-7159
E-mail: lw.aaia@indian-affairs.org

ASSURED LIFE ASSOCIATION

http://assuredlife.org

ASSURED LIFE ASSOCIATION ENDOWMENT SCHOLARSHIP PROGRAM
• *See page 600*

AWEBER COMMUNICATIONS

http://www.aweber.com/

AWEBER DEVELOPING FUTURES SCHOLARSHIP

The AWeber Developing Futures Scholarship, which grants a $2,500 scholarship to one college student each year, is awarded to undergraduate students studying in the Business/Marketing/Communications fields, as they pursue their educational and professional goals. It is AWeber's mission to help entrepreneurs and small business owners be successful as they connect with and grow their communities. As part of that mission, we know that drive is something that is nurtured over time–and it all begins with investing in the young individuals who will be the entrepreneurs, business owners and hard-working professionals of the future. See more at http://www.aweber.com/email-marketing-scholarship.htm#sthash.SVlP9Kh4.dpuf

Award: Scholarship for use in freshman, sophomore, junior, or senior years; not renewable. *Number:* 1. *Amount:* $2500.

Eligibility Requirements: Applicant must be enrolled or expecting to enroll full- or part-time at a four-year institution or university. Available to U.S. and non-U.S. citizens.

Application Requirements: Essay. *Deadline:* May 31.

Contact: Ms. Rebecca Pollard
    E-mail: rebeccap@aweber.com

AYN RAND INSTITUTE

https://www.aynrand.org

ATLAS SHRUGGED ESSAY CONTEST
• *See page 600*

BARONE DEFENSE FIRM

http://baronedefensefirm.com/

BARONE DEFENSE FIRM WIN BACK YOUR LIFE SCHOLARSHIP
• *See page 601*

BILLINGS & BARRETT

https://billingsandbarrett.com/

BILLINGS & BARRETT FIRST IN FAMILY SCHOLARSHIP
• *See page 601*

MATRIX HEALTH GROUP BLEEDING DISORDERS

https://matrixhealthgroup.com

JOE HOLIBAUGH MEMORIAL SCHOLARSHIP
• *See page 644*

MARK COATS MEMORIAL SCHOLARSHIP
• *See page 644*

MIKE HYLTON MEMORIAL SCHOLARSHIP
• *See page 644*

MILLIE GONZALEZ MEMORIAL SCHOLARSHIP
• *See page 644*

RON NIEDERMAN MEMORIAL SCHOLARSHIP
• *See page 644*

TIM KENNEDY MEMORIAL SCHOLARSHIP
• *See page 645*

BLACKFEET NATION HIGHER EDUCATION PROGRAM

http://www.blackfeetnation.com/

BLACKFEET NATION HIGHER EDUCATION GRANT

Grants of $2800-$3000 will be awarded to students who are enrolled members of the Blackfeet Tribe and actively pursuing an undergraduate degree. Must submit a certification of Blackfeet blood.

Award: Grant for use in freshman, sophomore, junior, or senior years; not renewable. *Number:* 180. *Amount:* $2800–$3000.

Eligibility Requirements: Applicant must be American Indian/Alaska Native and enrolled or expecting to enroll full-time at a two-year or four-year or technical institution or university. Available to U.S. citizens.

Application Requirements: Application form, certification of Blackfeet blood, essay, financial need analysis, transcript. *Deadline:* March 1.

Contact: Conrad LaFromboise, Director
    Blackfeet Nation Higher Education Program
    PO Box 850
    Browning, MT 59417
    Phone: 406-338-7539
    Fax: 406-338-7529
    E-mail: bhep@3rivers.net

BOUNCE ENERGY

http://www.bounceenergy.com

BE MORE SCHOLARSHIP
• *See page 601*

BRYAN CAMERON EDUCATION FOUNDATION

http://www.bryancameroneducationfoundation.org/index.php

CAMERON IMPACT SCHOLARSHIP
• *See page 601*

BUREAU OF INDIAN AFFAIRS OFFICE OF INDIAN EDUCATION PROGRAMS

http://www.bie.edu/

BUREAU OF INDIAN EDUCATION GRANT PROGRAM

Grants are provided to supplement financial assistance to eligible American Indian/Alaska Native students entering college seeking a Baccalaureate degree. A student must be a member of, or at least one-quarter degree Indian blood descendent of a member of an American Indian tribe who are eligible for the special programs and services provided by the United States through the Bureau of Indian Affairs to Indians because of their status as Indians.

Award: Grant for use in freshman year; not renewable.

Eligibility Requirements: Applicant must be American Indian/Alaska Native; high school student and planning to enroll or expecting to enroll full-time at a two-year or four-year institution or university. Available to U.S. citizens.

Application Requirements: Application form, recommendations or references, test scores, transcript. *Deadline:* varies.

Contact: Paulina Bell, Office Automation Assistant
    Phone: 202-208-6123
    Fax: 202-208-3312

BUY-RITE BEAUTY

https://www.buyritebeauty.com/

BUY-RITES ANNUAL BEAUTY SCHOOL SCHOLARSHIP
• *See page 601*

BY KIDS FOR KIDS, CO.

http://bkfkeducation.com

SALLIE MAE® MAKE COLLEGE HAPPEN CHALLENGE
• *See page 602*

CABRILLO CIVIC CLUBS OF CALIFORNIA INC.

http://www.cabrillocivicclubs.org/scholarship.asp

CABRILLO CIVIC CLUBS OF CALIFORNIA SCHOLARSHIP

Applicants must be graduating California high school seniors of Portuguese heritage and American citizenship, with an overall 3.5 GPA.

Award: Scholarship for use in freshman year; not renewable. *Number:* 75–100. *Amount:* $500.

Eligibility Requirements: Applicant must be of Portuguese heritage; high school student; planning to enroll or expecting to enroll full-time at a technical institution and resident of California. Applicant must have 3.5 GPA or higher. Available to U.S. citizens.

Application Requirements: Application form, driver's license, personal photograph, recommendations or references, resume, self-addressed stamped envelope with application, transcript. *Deadline:* March 15.

Contact: Breck Austin, Scholarship Chairperson
Cabrillo Civic Clubs of California Inc.
2174 South Coast Highway
Oceanside, CA 92054
E-mail: shampoobla@sbcglobal.net

CAFÉ BUSTELO

http://cafebustelo.com

CAFE BUSTELO EL CAFE DEL FUTURO SCHOLARSHIP ESSAY CONTEST

Café Bustelo and the Hispanic Association of Colleges and Universities (HACU) have teamed up to present El Café del Futuro Scholarship Essay Contest. Eligible students can enter for a chance to win one of nine $5,000 college scholarships. Permanent legal residents of the 50 United States and D.C., age 18 or older and of Latino decent, that are currently enrolled full-time in a college of university, are eligible to apply for the scholarship. To enter/apply, complete the online application on the HACU website: http://www.hacu.net; and respond to and upload your original essay on the following topic: Describe how your Latino heritage, family, and the community in which you grew up have impacted your desire and motivation to obtain a college degree. Additionally, describe what you intend to accomplish with your degree and how you will give back to your community. Attach the required supporting documents to the application.

Award: Scholarship for use in freshman, sophomore, junior, or senior years; not renewable. *Number:* 9. *Amount:* $5000.

Eligibility Requirements: Applicant must be of Hispanic heritage and enrolled or expecting to enroll full-time at a four-year institution or university. Available to U.S. citizens.

Application Requirements: Application form, essay. *Deadline:* May 26.

Contact: Hispanic Association of Colleges & Universities
Café Bustelo
8415 Datapoint Drive, Suite 400
San Antonio, TX 78229
Phone: 210-692-3805
Fax: 210-692-0823
E-mail: hacu@hacu.net

CALIFORNIA COMMUNITY COLLEGES

http://www.cccco.edu/

EOPS (EXTENDED OPPORTUNITY PROGRAMS AND SERVICES)/CARE (COOPERATIVE AGENCIES RESOURCES FOR EDUCATION)
• *See page 602*

CALIFORNIA COUNCIL OF THE BLIND

http://www.ccbnet.org/

CALIFORNIA COUNCIL OF THE BLIND SCHOLARSHIPS
• *See page 602*

CAMP NETWORK

https://www.campnetwork.com/

CAMP COUNSELOR APPRECIATION SCHOLARSHIP
• *See page 603*

CARDSDIRECT INC.

https://www.cardsdirect.com/

FUTURE DESIGNER SCHOLARSHIP
• *See page 603*

CARING.COM

http://caring.com

CARING.COM STUDENT-CAREGIVER BI-ANNUAL SCHOLARSHIP
• *See page 603*

CEDAR EDUCATION LENDING, LLC

http://www.cedaredlending.com

$500 BECAUSE COLLEGE IS EXPENSIVE SCHOLARSHIP
• *See page 603*

CENTER FOR REINTEGRATION

http://www.reintegration.com

BAER REINTEGRATION SCHOLARSHIP
• *See page 604*

CENTRAL COUNCIL, TLINGIT AND HAIDA INDIAN TRIBES OF ALASKA

http://www.hied.org/

ALUMNI STUDENT ASSISTANCE PROGRAM

The program provides annual scholarship awards to all enrolled Tlingit or Haida tribal members regardless of service area, community affiliation, origination, residence, tribal compact, or signatory status.

Award: Scholarship for use in freshman, sophomore, junior, senior, graduate, or postgraduate years; not renewable. *Number:* 1–100. *Amount:* $300–$500.

Eligibility Requirements: Applicant must be American Indian/Alaska Native and enrolled or expecting to enroll full-time at a two-year or four-year institution or university. Applicant must have 2.5 GPA or higher. Available to U.S. citizens.

Application Requirements: Application form, community service, essay, financial need analysis, recommendations or references, transcript, tribal enrollment certification form, letter of admission. *Deadline:* September 15.

Contact: Miss. Leslie Rae Isturis, Education Specialist
Central Council, Tlingit and Haida Indian Tribes of Alaska
3239 Hospital Drive
Juneau, AK 99801
Phone: 907-463-7375
Fax: 907-463-7173
E-mail: listuris@ccthita.org

COLLEGE STUDENT ASSISTANCE PROGRAM

A federally funded program which authorizes a program of assistance, by educational grants, to Indians seeking higher education. Awards available only to enrolled T&H members. Minimum 2.0 GPA required.

Award: Scholarship for use in freshman, sophomore, junior, senior, graduate, or postgraduate years; renewable. *Number:* 1–200. *Amount:* up to $2000.

Eligibility Requirements: Applicant must be American Indian/Alaska Native and enrolled or expecting to enroll full-time at a two-year or four-year institution or university. Available to U.S. citizens.

Application Requirements: Application form, letter of admission, test scores, transcript. *Deadline:* May 15.

Contact: Miss. Leslie Rae Isturis, Education Specialist
Central Council, Tlingit and Haida Indian Tribes of Alaska
3239 Hospital Drive
Juneau, AK 99801
Phone: 907-463-7375
Fax: 907-463-7173
E-mail: listuris@ccthita.org

CENTRAL SCHOLARSHIP

http://www.central-scholarship.org

LESSANS FAMILY SCHOLARSHIP
• *See page 604*

STRAUS SCHOLARSHIP PROGRAM FOR UNDERGRADUATE EDUCATION
• *See page 604*

CGTRADER

https://www.cgtrader.com/

ANNUAL CGTRADER SCHOLARSHIP
• *See page 604*

CHARLES E. BOYK LAW OFFICES, LLC

https://www.charlesboyk-law.com/

BOYK LAW VETERAN SCHOLARSHIP
• *See page 604*

CHEROKEE NATION OF OKLAHOMA

http://www.cherokee.org/

CHEROKEE NATION HIGHER EDUCATION SCHOLARSHIP

A supplementary program that provides financial assistance to Cherokee Nation Members only. It is a need-based program which provides assistance in seeking a Bachelor's degree.

Award: Scholarship for use in freshman, sophomore, junior, or senior years; renewable. *Number:* up to 2800. *Amount:* $100–$1000.

Eligibility Requirements: Applicant must be American Indian/Alaska Native and enrolled or expecting to enroll full-time at a four-year institution or university. Applicant must have 2.5 GPA or higher. Available to U.S. citizens.

Application Requirements: Test scores, transcript, written request for application. *Deadline:* June 13.

Contact: Nita Wilson, Higher Education Specialist
Cherokee Nation of Oklahoma
PO Box 948
Tahlequah, OK 74465
Phone: 918-458-6195
E-mail: nwilson@cherokee.org

CHICANA/LATINA FOUNDATION

http://www.chicanalatina.org/

SCHOLARSHIPS FOR LATINA STUDENTS ENROLLED IN COLLEGES/UNIVERSITIES IN NORTHERN CALIFORNIA

Scholarships are awarded to female Latina students enrolled in two-year, four-year or graduate levels. Applicants must be from and/or attending colleges in the nine counties of Northern California listed on the application.

Award: Scholarship for use in freshman, sophomore, junior, or senior years; not renewable. *Number:* 25–30. *Amount:* $1500.

Eligibility Requirements: Applicant must be of Hispanic heritage; enrolled or expecting to enroll full-time at a two-year or four-year institution or university; female and resident of California. Available to U.S. citizens.

Application Requirements: Application form, essay, interview. *Deadline:* March 31.

Contact: Stephanie Segovia, Program Director
Chicana/Latina Foundation
1419 Burlingame Avenue, Suite W2
Burlingame, CA 94010
Phone: 650-548-1049
E-mail: stephanie@chicanalatina.org

CHINESE AMERICAN ASSOCIATION OF MINNESOTA

http://www.caam.org/

CHINESE AMERICAN ASSOCIATION OF MINNESOTA (CAAM) SCHOLARSHIPS

Merit and need scholarships of $1000 each are available for college and graduate students of Chinese descent and a resident of Minnesota. Applicants will be evaluated on their academic records, leadership qualities, and community service.

Award: Scholarship for use in freshman, sophomore, junior, senior, or graduate years; not renewable. *Amount:* $1000.

Eligibility Requirements: Applicant must be of Chinese heritage; Asian/Pacific Islander; enrolled or expecting to enroll full-time at a two-year or four-year or technical institution or university and resident of Minnesota. Available to U.S. citizens.

Application Requirements: Application form, financial need analysis, recommendations or references, SAT score. *Deadline:* November 15.

Contact: Scholarship Committee
Chinese American Association of Minnesota
PO Box 582584
Minneapolis, MN 55458-2584

CHRISTIAN COMMUNITY CREDIT UNION

https://www.mycccu.com/

SCHOLARSHIPS FOR SUCCESS
• *See page 605*

CHRISTIAN RECORD SERVICES INC.

http://www.christianrecord.org

ANNE LOWE SCHOLARSHIPS
• *See page 605*

CHURCH HILL CLASSICS

http://www.diplomaframe.com/

FRAME MY FUTURE SCHOLARSHIP CONTEST
• *See page 605*

CITIZEN POTAWATOMI NATION

http://www.potawatomi.org/

CITIZEN POTAWATOMI NATION TRIBAL SCHOLARSHIP

Provides financial assistance for payment of tuition for members of the Citizen Potawatomi Nation. Minimum 2.0 GPA required. Deadlines are December 1 for spring, August 1 for fall, and June 1 for summer. Award amount varies from $750 to $1500.

Award: Scholarship for use in freshman, sophomore, junior, senior, or graduate years; renewable. *Amount:* $750–$1500.

Eligibility Requirements: Applicant must be American Indian/Alaska Native and enrolled or expecting to enroll full- or part-time at a two-year or four-year or technical institution or university. Available to U.S. citizens.

Application Requirements: Application form, financial need analysis, test scores, transcript. *Deadline:* varies.

Contact: Charles Clark, Director, Tribal Rolls
Phone: 800-880-9880
Fax: 405-275-0198
E-mail: cclark@potawatomi.org

CLARA LIONEL FOUNDATION

http://claralionelfoundation.org

CLARA LIONEL FOUNDATION GLOBAL SCHOLARSHIP PROGRAM
• *See page 605*

CLOTHINGRIC.COM

http://www.clothingric.com

CLOTHINGRIC.COM ANNUAL STUDENT SCHOLARSHIP
• *See page 605*

CODA INTERNATIONAL

http://www.coda-international.org

MILLIE BROTHER SCHOLARSHIP FOR CHILDREN OF DEAF ADULTS
• *See page 605*

COGBURN LAW OFFICES

http://cogburnlaw.com/

COGBURN LAW OFFICES ANNUAL SCHOLARSHIP
• *See page 606*

COLLEGEBOUND FOUNDATION

http://www.collegeboundfoundation.org/

LORENZO FELDER SCHOLARSHIP

You must: be an African-American male; be a graduate of a Baltimore City public school; have a cumulative GPA of 3.0 or better; have demonstrated financial need; have verifiable community service or extracurricular activity; write an essay of 500-1,000 words describing the environment you live in and the most meaningful contribution you have made as a volunteer in your community.

Award: Scholarship for use in freshman year; not renewable. *Number:* 1–3. *Amount:* $1000–$1500.

Eligibility Requirements: Applicant must be Black (non-Hispanic); high school student; planning to enroll or expecting to enroll full-time at a two-year or four-year institution; male and resident of Maryland. Applicant must have 3.0 GPA or higher. Available to U.S. citizens.

Application Requirements: Application form, community service, essay. *Deadline:* March 1.

Contact: Jennifer Covahey, Associate Program Director, Scholarship
Programs
CollegeBound Foundation
300 Water Street, Suite 300
Baltimore, MD 21202
Phone: 410-783-2905 Ext. 207
E-mail: jcovahey@collegeboundfoundation.org

COLLEGE NOW GREATER CLEVELAND, INC.

http://www.collegenowgc.org/

COLLEGE NOW GREATER CLEVELAND ADULT LEARNER PROGRAM SCHOLARSHIP
• *See page 606*

COLLEGE WOMEN'S ASSOCIATION OF JAPAN

http://www.cwaj.org/

SCHOLARSHIP FOR THE VISUALLY IMPAIRED TO STUDY ABROAD
• *See page 686*

SCHOLARSHIP FOR THE VISUALLY IMPAIRED TO STUDY IN JAPAN
• *See page 686*

COLORADO MASONS BENEVOLENT FUND ASSOCIATION

http://www.cmbfa.org/scholarship

COLORADO MASONS BENEVOLENT FUND SCHOLARSHIPS
• *See page 606*

COLUMBUS CITIZENS FOUNDATION

http://www.columbuscitizensfd.org/scholarships/scholarships.html

COLUMBUS CITIZENS FOUNDATION COLLEGE SCHOLARSHIP PROGRAM
• *See page 606*

COMMUNITY BANKERS ASSOCIATION OF ILLINOIS

http://www.cbai.com/

COMMUNITY BANKERS ASSOC OF IL CHILD OF A BANKER SCHOLARSHIP
• *See page 562*

COMMUNITY BANKERS ASSOC. OF IL ESSAY CONTEST
• *See page 607*

COMMUNITY FOUNDATION OF WESTERN MASSACHUSETTS

http://www.communityfoundation.org/

HELLESPONT SOCIETY SCHOLARSHIP FUND

Scholarship available to high school graduates who attend a two or four year college, who are persons of Greek descent, with a preference given to descendants of past Hellespont Society Members. For more information, please see website http://communityfoundation.org/.

Award: Scholarship for use in freshman year; not renewable.

Eligibility Requirements: Applicant must be of Greek heritage; high school student; planning to enroll or expecting to enroll full- or part-time at a two-year or four-year institution and resident of Massachusetts. Available to U.S. citizens.

Application Requirements: Application form, essay, financial need analysis, transcript. *Deadline:* March 31.

Contact: Dotty Theriaque, Program Assistant for Scholarships
Community Foundation of Western Massachusetts
1500 Main Street
PO Box 15769
Springfield, MA 01115
Phone: 413-732-2858
Fax: 413-733-8565
E-mail: scholar@communityfoundation.org

CONGRESSIONAL BLACK CAUCUS FOUNDATION, INC.

http://www.cbcfinc.org/

CBC SPOUSES EDUCATION SCHOLARSHIP

The CBC Spouses Education Scholarship was established in 1988 by the spouses of Congressional Black Caucus members in response to federal cuts in spending for education programs and scholarships, which disproportionately affect people of color. This scholarship awards scholarships to academically talented and highly motivated students of all majors who intend to pursue full-time undergraduate, graduate, or doctoral degrees.

Award: Scholarship for use in freshman, sophomore, junior, senior, or graduate years; not renewable. *Number:* 250–350. *Amount:* $500–$8200.

Eligibility Requirements: Applicant must be Black (non-Hispanic); enrolled or expecting to enroll full-time at a two-year or four-year institution or university and studying in Alabama, Alaska, Arizona, Arkansas, California, Colorado, Connecticut, Delaware, District of Columbia, Florida, Georgia, Guam, Hawaii, Idaho, Illinois, Indiana, Iowa, Kansas, Kentucky, Louisiana, Maine, Maryland, Massachusetts, Michigan, Minnesota, Mississippi, Missouri, Montana, Nebraska, Nevada, New Hampshire, New Jersey, New Mexico, New York, North Carolina, North Dakota, Ohio, Oklahoma, Oregon, Pennsylvania, Puerto Rico, Rhode Island, South Carolina, South Dakota, Tennessee, Texas, Utah, Vermont, Virginia, Washington, West Virginia, Wisconsin, Wyoming. Applicant must have 2.5 GPA or higher. Available to U.S. citizens.

Application Requirements: Application form, essay, financial need analysis, personal photograph. *Deadline:* May 19.

Contact: Ms. Katrina Finch, Program Administrator, Scholarships
Phone: 202-263-2800
E-mail: scholarships@cbcfinc.org

CONNECTICUT ASSOCIATION OF LATINOS IN HIGHER EDUCATION (CALAHE)

http://www.calahe.org/

CONNECTICUT ASSOCIATION OF LATINOS IN HIGHER EDUCATION SCHOLARSHIPS

Must demonstrate involvement with, and commitment to, activities that promote Latinos in pursuit of education. Must have a 2.75 GPA, be a U.S. citizen or permanent resident, be a resident of Connecticut.

Award: Scholarship for use in freshman, sophomore, junior, or senior years; not renewable. *Number:* 20. *Amount:* $1000.

Eligibility Requirements: Applicant must be of Hispanic heritage; enrolled or expecting to enroll full-time at a two-year or four-year institution or university and resident of Connecticut. Applicant must have 2.5 GPA or higher. Available to U.S. citizens.

Application Requirements: Application form, essay, financial need analysis. *Deadline:* May 4.

Contact: Dr. Wilson Luna, Gateway Community-Technical College
Connecticut Association of Latinos in Higher Education
(CALAHE)
20 Church Street
New Haven, CT 06510
Phone: 203-285-2210
E-mail: wluna@gatewayct.edu

CONNECTICUT OFFICE OF HIGHER EDUCATION

http://www.ctohe.org

GOVERNOR'S SCHOLARSHIP PROGRAM—NEED/MERIT SCHOLARSHIP
• *See page 607*

ROBERTA B. WILLIS SCHOLARSHIP PROGRAM—NEED-BASED GRANT
• *See page 607*

COUNCIL OF CITIZENS WITH LOW VISION INTERNATIONAL C/O AMERICAN COUNCIL OF THE BLIND

http://www.cclvi.org/

FRED SCHEIGERT SCHOLARSHIP
• *See page 607*

COUPONSURF.COM

http://couponsurf.com/

COUPONSURF ENTREPRENEURS SCHOLARSHIP
• *See page 607*

COURAGE KENNY REHABILITATION INSTITUTE, VOCATIONAL SERVICES DEPARTMENT

http://www.allinahealth.org/couragekenny

SCHOLARSHIP FOR PEOPLE WITH DISABILITIES
• *See page 608*

COZZY.ORG

https://cozzy.org

COZZY.ORG CUSTOMER SUPPORT SCHOLARSHIP

The Cozzy team is excited to offer a $2,500 scholarship to one winner. The scholarship is available to any undergraduate and postgraduate college student. The $2,500 scholarship grant can be used toward course materials, books, and other educational resources. To participate in our scholarship program, you need to research and cover the following topic The future of the commerce. How the internet will change the consumption in 10 years? The essay should include title, 1000-1500 words, at least 3 research materials used. You must be a student pursuing any degree or majors in any degree. You must be above 18 years. We reserve all rights to verify your date of college enrollment or high school/college graduation. Essay must be unique, demonstrate deep understanding of the topic and research skills. We would like to see your expertise supported by data and statistics.

Award: Scholarship for use in freshman, junior, senior, graduate, or postgraduate years; renewable. *Number:* 1. *Amount:* $2500.

Eligibility Requirements: Applicant must be age 18-99 and enrolled or expecting to enroll full- or part-time at a four-year institution or university. Available to U.S. and non-U.S. citizens.

Application Requirements: Essay. *Deadline:* October 30.

Contact: Mr. Brian Landarson
E-mail: finance@cozzy.org

CROATIAN SCHOLARSHIP FUND

http://www.croatianscholarship.org/

CROATIAN SCHOLARSHIP FUND

Scholarship for students of Croatian heritage. Award based on academic achievement and financial need. Must demonstrate appropriate degree selection. Scholarships are awarded depending on availability of funds and number of applicants.

Award: Scholarship for use in freshman, sophomore, junior, or senior years; renewable. *Amount:* $1500.

Eligibility Requirements: Applicant must be of Croatian/Serbian heritage; age 18-25 and enrolled or expecting to enroll full-time at a four-year institution or university. Applicant must have 2.5 GPA or higher. Available to U.S. and non-U.S. citizens.

Application Requirements: Application form, application form may be submitted online, autobiography, financial need analysis, personal photograph, recommendations or references, test scores, transcript. *Deadline:* May 15.

Contact: Vesna Brekalo, Scholarship Liaison
Croatian Scholarship Fund
31 Mesa Vista Court
PO Box 290
San Ramon, CA 94583
Phone: 925-556-6263
Fax: 925-556-6263
E-mail: vbrekalo@msn.com

CROSLEY LAW FIRM

https://crosleylaw.com

CROSLEY LAW FIRM DISTRACTED DRIVING SCHOLARSHIP
• *See page 608*

CSA MEDICAL SUPPLY

https://csamedicalsupply.com

CSA MEDICAL SUPPLY COLLEGE SCHOLARSHIP
• *See page 608*

THE DALLAS FOUNDATION

http://www.dallasfoundation.org/

DR. DAN J. AND PATRICIA S. PICKARD SCHOLARSHIP
The Dr. Dan J. and Patricia S. Pickard Scholarship Fund was established at the Dallas Foundation in 2004 to assist African-American male students in Dallas County. Dr. Pickard was an optometrist and founder of the Pickard eye clinic. He believed that if you did something nice for someone and they do something nice for someone else, you can affect the lives of many people. The Scholarship Fund is his way of "passing it on".

Award: Scholarship for use in freshman year; renewable. *Number:* 1–2. *Amount:* $1000–$2000.

Eligibility Requirements: Applicant must be Black (non-Hispanic); high school student; planning to enroll or expecting to enroll full-time at a two-year or four-year institution; male; resident of Texas and studying in Texas. Applicant must have 2.5 GPA or higher. Available to U.S. citizens.

Application Requirements: Application form, community service, essay, financial need analysis, recommendations or references, transcript. *Deadline:* April 1.

Contact: Ms. Rachel Lasseter, Program Associate
The Dallas Foundation
900 Jackson Street, Suite 705
Dallas, TX 75202
Phone: 214-741-9898
Fax: 214-741-9848
E-mail: scholarships@dallasfoundation.org

DANIELS FUND

http://www.danielsfund.org

BOUNDLESS OPPORTUNITY SCHOLARSHIP
• *See page 608*

DANIELS SCHOLARSHIP PROGRAM
• *See page 609*

DANLEY'S GARAGE BUILDERS

https://www.danleysgarageworld.com/

DANLEY'S GARAGE BUILDERS SCHOLARSHIP
• *See page 609*

DAVID S. WYMAN INSTITUTE OF HOLOCAUST STUDIES

http://www.wymaninstitute.org

JOSIAH E. DUBOIS, JR. COLLEGE SCHOLARSHIP ESSAY CONTEST
• *See page 609*

DEMAS LAW GROUP, P.C.

http://www.injury-attorneys.com/

DEMAS LAW GROUP SCHOLARSHIP
• *See page 609*

DEMOLAY FOUNDATION INCORPORATED

http://www.demolay.org/

FRANK S. LAND SCHOLARSHIP
• *See page 588*

DEPARTMENT OF THE ARMY

http://www.goarmy.com/rotc

ARMY ROTC GREEN TO GOLD SCHOLARSHIP PROGRAM FOR TWO-YEAR, THREE-YEAR AND FOUR-YEAR SCHOLARSHIPS, ACTIVE DUTY ENLISTED PERSONNEL
• *See page 610*

ARMY (ROTC) RESERVE OFFICERS TRAINING CORPS TWO-, THREE-, FOUR-YEAR CAMPUS-BASED SCHOLARSHIPS
• *See page 610*

U.S. ARMY ROTC FOUR-YEAR COLLEGE SCHOLARSHIP
• *See page 610*

U.S. ARMY ROTC FOUR-YEAR HISTORICALLY BLACK COLLEGE/UNIVERSITY SCHOLARSHIP
• *See page 610*

U.S. ARMY ROTC GUARANTEED RESERVE FORCES DUTY (GRFD), (ARNG/USAR) AND DEDICATED ARNG SCHOLARSHIPS
• *See page 611*

U.S. ARMY ROTC MILITARY JUNIOR COLLEGE (MJC) SCHOLARSHIP
• *See page 611*

DESERVE MODERN

http://www.DeserveModern.com

DESERVE MODERN SCHOLARSHIP
• *See page 611*

DESIGN MY COSTUME

http://designmycostume.com/

DESIGN MY COSTUME SCHOLARSHIP
• *See page 611*

DIAMANTE, INC.

http://www.diamanteinc.org/

LATINO DIAMANTE SCHOLARSHIP FUND
• *See page 612*

DIBELLA LAW OFFICES, P.C.

https://www.dibellalawoffice.com/

2018 DIBELLA LAW OFFICES, P.C. SCHOLARSHIP
• *See page 612*

DISABLED AMERICAN VETERANS

http://www.dav.org/

JESSE BROWN MEMORIAL YOUTH SCHOLARSHIP PROGRAM
• *See page 612*

DISABLEDPERSON INC. COLLEGE SCHOLARSHIP

http://www.disabledperson.com/

DISABLEDPERSON INC. NATIONAL COLLEGE SCHOLARSHIP AWARD FOR COLLEGE STUDENTS WITH DISABILITIES
• *See page 612*

DISCIPLESHIP MINISTRIES

http://umcyoungpeople.org

RICHARD S. SMITH SCHOLARSHIP
Open to racial/ethnic minority youth only. Must be a United Methodist Youth who has been active in local church for at least one year prior to application. Must be a graduating senior in high school (who maintained at least a "C" average) entering the first year of undergraduate study and be pursuing a "church-related" career.

Award: Scholarship for use in freshman year; not renewable. *Number:* 1–5. *Amount:* $100–$1300.

Eligibility Requirements: Applicant must be Methodist; American Indian/Alaska Native, Asian/Pacific Islander, Black (non-Hispanic), Hispanic; high school student and planning to enroll or expecting to enroll full-time at a two-year or four-year or technical institution or university. Applicant must have 2.5 GPA or higher. Available to U.S. citizens.

Application Requirements: Application form, essay, financial need analysis. *Deadline:* March 1.

Contact: Kelsey Tinker Hannum, Grant and Scholarships Administrator
Phone: 615-340-7184
E-mail: youngpeople@umcdiscipleship.org

DIVERSITYCOMM, INC.

http://www.diversitycomm.net/

BLACK EOE JOURNAL SCHOLARSHIP
For the 2018 fall semester, Black EOE Journal will be offering a $500 scholarship that is available to African–American undergraduate students. As one of the strongest growing African American publications in our nation, the Black EOE Journal informs, educates, and provides equal opportunity in corporate America. We provide the latest and most important diversity news spanning every industry, business and profession. This includes up-to-date statistics on workforce diversity, B2B trends, noteworthy conferences, business opportunities and role model spotlights. The Black EOE Journal is the ultimate African American Career & Business connection! We would like you to tell your story in a brief narrative, starting with an introduction about who you are, your interests, and anything else you feel we should know about you. Then, please provide your entry in a 300-500 word essay about your

college experience so far, and your future career plans. Graphic or creative presentations are welcome as well. The scholarship will be awarded to the applicant who best demonstrates a genuine desire and goal of using the scholarship to advance in their field, and an overall passion for knowledge.

Award: Scholarship for use in freshman, sophomore, junior, or senior years. *Number:* 1. *Amount:* $500.

Eligibility Requirements: Applicant must be of African heritage; Black (non-Hispanic) and enrolled or expecting to enroll full- or part-time at a four-year institution or university. Available to U.S. citizens.

Application Requirements: Application form, essay. *Deadline:* August 15.

HISPANIC NETWORK MAGAZINE SCHOLARSHIP
For the 2018 Fall Semester, Hispanic Network Magazine will be offering a $500 scholarship that is available to Hispanic undergraduate students. The Hispanic Network Magazine is a valuable source to assist with your Multicultural Hiring and Supplier needs. Our goal is to create an environment of teamwork in which Latin Americans and other minorities have access to all applicable business and career opportunities. We are an information source designed to bring promising, talented people together with potential employers and customers throughout the business community. Requirements: We would like you to tell your story in a brief narrative, starting with an introduction about who you are, your interests, and anything else you feel we should know about you. Then, please provide your entry in a 300-500 word essay about your college experience so far, and your future career plans. Graphic or creative presentations are welcome as well.

Award: Scholarship for use in freshman, sophomore, junior, or senior years; renewable. *Number:* 1. *Amount:* $500.

Eligibility Requirements: Applicant must be Hispanic and enrolled or expecting to enroll full- or part-time at a four-year institution or university. Available to U.S. citizens.

Application Requirements: Application form, essay. *Deadline:* August 15.

DOLLARS 4 TIC SCHOLARS

http://www.dollars4ticscholars.org/

DOLLARS 4 TIC SCHOLARS TOURETTE SYNDROME SCHOLARSHIP
• *See page 613*

DOLPHIN SCHOLARSHIP FOUNDATION

http://www.dolphinscholarship.org/

DOLPHIN SCHOLARSHIPS
• *See page 613*

DOMNICK CUNNINGHAM AND WHALEN

https://www.dcwlaw.com/

DOMNICK CUNNINGHAM & WHALEN ELDER ABUSE PREVENTION
• *See page 613*

DONALDSON COMPANY

http://www.donaldson.com/

THE DONALDSON COMPANY, INC. SCHOLARSHIP PROGRAM
• *See page 588*

DONTPAYFULL.COM

https://www.dontpayfull.com/

$500 ANNUAL STUDENT SCHOLARSHIP
• *See page 613*

DRONE PILOT GROUND SCHOOL

https://www.dronepilotgroundschool.com

DRONE TECHNOLOGY COLLEGE SCHOLARSHIP
• *See page 613*

EDGAR ALLEN POE LITERARY SOCIETY

http://www.ravens.org/

DISTINGUISHED RAVEN FAC MEMORIAL SCHOLARSHIP
• *See page 614*

EDMONTON COMMUNITY FOUNDATION

http://www.ecfoundation.org

BELCOURT BROSSEAU METIS AWARDS
The Fund provides awards so that Métis Albertans demonstrating financial need, commitment, and a desire to be gainfully employed can realize self-sufficient through the advancement of their post-secondary education and skills development.

Award: Scholarship for use in freshman, sophomore, junior, senior, or graduate years; not renewable.

Eligibility Requirements: Applicant must be Canadian citizen; enrolled or expecting to enroll full- or part-time at a two-year or four-year or technical institution or university; resident of Alberta and studying in Alberta, British Columbia, Manitoba, New Brunswick, Newfoundland, Northwest Territories, Nova Scotia, Ontario, Prince Edward Island, Quebec, Saskatchewan, Yukon.

Application Requirements: Application form. *Deadline:* March 31.

Contact: Anna Opryshko, Student Awards Associate
Phone: 780-426-0015 Ext. 107
Fax: 780-425-0121
E-mail: studentawards@ecfoundation.org

EDUCATOR, INC.

https://www.educator.com/

ANNUAL $2,400 STUDENT SCHOLARSHIP
• *See page 614*

ELEARNERS.COM

http://www.elearners.com

ELEARNERS ONLINE STUDENT SCHOLARSHIP
• *See page 614*

ELIZABETH GREENSHIELDS FOUNDATION

http://www.elizabethgreenshieldsfoundation.org

THE ELIZABETH GREENSHIELDS FOUNDATION GRANT
• *See page 614*

ENVIRONMENTAL LITIGATION GROUP P.C.

https://www.elglaw.com/

ENVIRONMENTAL LITIGATION GROUP, P.C. ASBESTOS SCHOLARSHIP
• *See page 615*

EPSILON SIGMA ALPHA

http://www.epsilonsigmaalpha.org/scholarships

EPSILON SIGMA ALPHA FOUNDATION SCHOLARSHIPS
Awards for various fields of study. Required GPA vary with scholarship. Applications must be sent to the Epsilon Sigma Alpha designated state counselor. See website at http://www.esaintl.com/esaf for further information, application forms, and a list of state counselors.

Award: Scholarship for use in freshman, sophomore, junior, senior, graduate, or postgraduate years; not renewable. *Number:* 125–175. *Amount:* $350–$7500.

Eligibility Requirements: Applicant must be American Indian/Alaska Native, Asian/Pacific Islander, Black (non-Hispanic), Hispanic and enrolled or expecting to enroll full- or part-time at a two-year or four-year or technical institution or university. Applicant must have 3.0 GPA or higher. Available to U.S. and non-U.S. citizens.

Application Requirements: Application form, essay, recommendations or references, test scores, transcript. *Fee:* $5. *Deadline:* February 1.

Contact: Kathy Loyd, Scholarship Chairman
Epsilon Sigma Alpha
1222 NW 651
Blairstown, MO 64726
Phone: 660-678-2611
Fax: 660-747-0807
E-mail: kloyd@knoxy.net

EQUALITY SCHOLARSHIP COLLABORATIVE

http://www.equalityscholarship.org

EQUALITY SCHOLARSHIPS FOR COMMUNITY COLLEGE TRANSFER STUDENTS
• *See page 615*

SCHOLARSHIPS FOR HIGH SCHOOL GRADUATES
• *See page 615*

ESSAYHUB

https://essayhub.com/

ESSAY WRITING CONTEST BY ESSAYHUB
• *See page 615*

EVANS SCHOLARS FOUNDATION

http://www.wgaesf.org

CHICK EVANS SCHOLARSHIP FOR CADDIES
• *See page 616*

EVERIPEDIA INC.

https://www.everipedia.com

EVERIPEDIA TECH TITANS DIVERSITY SCHOLARSHIP
• *See page 616*

EXPRESSVPN

https://www.expressvpn.com

EXPRESSVPN FUTURE OF PRIVACY SCHOLARSHIP
• *See page 616*

FEDERAL RESOURCES

http://www.federalresources.com

WARRIOR'S LEGACY SCHOLARSHIP FUND
• *See page 616*

FELDCO WINDOWS, SIDING AND DOORS

http://www.4feldco.com

FELDCO WINDOWS, SIDING AND DOORS SCHOLARSHIP
• *See page 616*

FELDMAN & ROYLE, ATTORNEYS AT LAW

http://www.feldmanroyle.com/

AUTISM SCHOLARSHIPS
• *See page 617*

FELDMAN LAW FIRM PLLC

http://www.afphoenixcriminalattorney.com/

AUTISM SCHOLARSHIP
• *See page 617*

DISABLED VETERANS SCHOLARSHIP
• *See page 617*

FIG TECH INC.

http://www.figloans.com

$1,000 SCHOLARSHIP FOR SOCIAL IMPACT
• *See page 617*

FINALLY SOLD

http://www.finallysold.com

FINALLY SOLD IMPACT MAKER SCHOLARSHIP
• *See page 618*

FINANCIAL SERVICE CENTERS OF NEW YORK

http://www.fscny.org

FSCNY YOUNG LEADERS SCHOLARSHIP
• *See page 618*

FIRST CATHOLIC SLOVAK LADIES ASSOCIATION

http://www.fcsla.org/

FIRST CATHOLIC SLOVAK LADIES ASSOCIATION FRATERNAL SCHOLARSHIP AWARD

Must be FCSLA member in good standing for at least three years. Must attend accredited college in the United States or Canada in undergraduate or graduate degree program. Must submit certified copy of college acceptance. Award value is $1250 for undergraduate and $1750 for graduate students.

Award: Scholarship for use in freshman, sophomore, junior, senior, or graduate years; not renewable. *Number:* 133. *Amount:* $1250–$1750.

Eligibility Requirements: Applicant must be of Slavic/Czech heritage and enrolled or expecting to enroll full-time at a two-year or four-year institution or university. Available to U.S. and Canadian citizens.

Application Requirements: Application form, driver's license, essay, personal photograph, recommendations or references, test scores, transcript. *Deadline:* March 1.

Contact: Dorothy Szumski, Director of Fraternal Scholarships
First Catholic Slovak Ladies Association
24950 Chagrin Boulevard
Beachwood, OH 44122
Phone: 216-464-8015 Ext. 134
Fax: 216-464-9260
E-mail: info@fcsla.com

FIT SMALL BUSINESS

http://www.fitsmallbusiness.com

BUSINESS PLAN SCHOLARSHIP FOR STUDENTS WITH DISABILITIES
• *See page 618*

FLORIDA PTA/PTSA

http://www.floridapta.org/

FLORIDA PTA/PTSA ANNUAL SCHOLARSHIP
• *See page 619*

FLORIDA STATE DEPARTMENT OF EDUCATION

http://www.floridastudentfinancialaid.org/

JOSE MARTI SCHOLARSHIP CHALLENGE GRANT FUND

Award available to Hispanic-American students who were born in, or whose parent was born in a Hispanic country. Must be a Florida resident, be enrolled full-time in Florida at an eligible school, and have a GPA of 3.0 or above. Must be U.S. citizen or eligible non-citizen. FAFSA must be processed by May 15. For more details, visit the website at http://www.FloridaStudentFinancialAid.org/SSFAD/home/uamain.htm.

Award: Scholarship for use in freshman, sophomore, junior, or senior years; renewable. *Amount:* $2000.

Eligibility Requirements: Applicant must be of Hispanic heritage; high school student; planning to enroll or expecting to enroll full-time at a two-year or four-year institution or university; resident of Florida and studying in Florida. Applicant must have 3.0 GPA or higher. Available to U.S. citizens.

Application Requirements: Application form, financial need analysis. *Deadline:* April 1.

Contact: Florida Department of Education, Office of Student Financial Assistance, Customer Service
Florida State Department of Education
325 West Gaines Street
Tallahassee, FL 32399
Phone: 888-827-2004
E-mail: osfa@fldoe.org

FOUNDATION FOR SIGHT AND SOUND

http://fssny.org

HELP AMERICA HEAR SCHOLARSHIP
• *See page 619*

FOUNDATION OF THE 1ST CAVALRY DIVISION ASSOCIATION

https://www.1cda.org/

FOUNDATION OF THE 1ST CAVALRY DIVISION ASSOCIATION (IA DRANG) SCHOLARSHIP
• *See page 619*

FOUNDATION OF THE 1ST CAVALRY DIVISION ASSOCIATION SCHOLARSHIP

• See page 619

FREEDOM ALLIANCE

https://freedomalliance.org

FREEDOM ALLIANCE SCHOLARSHIP FUND

• See page 620

THE FREEMAN FOUNDATION/INSTITUTE OF INTERNATIONAL EDUCATION

https://www.iie.org/

FREEMAN AWARDS FOR STUDY IN ASIA

The Freeman-ASIA program is designed to support U.S.-based undergraduates with demonstrated financial need who are planning to study abroad in East or Southeast Asia. The program's goal is to increase the number of U.S. citizens and permanent residents with first-hand exposure to and understanding of Asia and its peoples and cultures. Award recipients are required to share their experiences with their home campuses or communities to encourage study abroad by others and fulfill the program's goal of increasing understanding of Asia in the United States. Award amounts vary from $3,000 to $7,000 depending on the study abroad program length and financial need. More information can be found on the program's website: https://www.iie.org/Programs/Freeman-ASIA/

Award: Scholarship for use in freshman, sophomore, junior, or senior years; not renewable. *Amount:* $3000.

Eligibility Requirements: Applicant must be enrolled or expecting to enroll full- or part-time at a two-year or four-year institution or university. Applicant must have 2.5 GPA or higher. Available to U.S. citizens.

Application Requirements: Application form, essay, financial need analysis. *Deadline:* continuous.

FRIENDS OF COAL LADIES AUXILIARY

friendsofcoalladies.com

FRIENDS OF COAL SCHOLARSHIPS

We serve as many individuals as we can each year depending on our funding each year.

Award: Scholarship for use in freshman year; not renewable. *Number:* 20,000. *Amount:* $2000.

Eligibility Requirements: Applicant must be enrolled or expecting to enroll full- or part-time at a two-year or four-year or technical institution or university. Applicant must have 3.0 GPA or higher. Available to U.S. citizens.

Application Requirements: Application form, community service. *Deadline:* continuous.

Contact: Regina Fairchild, Chair
Friends of Coal Ladies Auxiliary
Post Office Box 1109
Beckley, WV 25802
Phone: 304-255-1457 Ext. 20
E-mail: rf961@suddenlink.net

FRIENDS OF THE MINNESOTA ORCHESTRA (FORMERLY WAMSO)

https://friendsofminnesotaorchestra.org/

YOUNG ARTIST COMPETITION

• See page 620

FUNNEWJERSEY.COM INC.

http://www.funnewjersey.com

FUNNEWJERSEY.COM SCHOLARSHIP

• See page 620

GENERAL BOARD OF HIGHER EDUCATION AND MINISTRY

http://www.gbhem.org

BISHOP JOSEPH B. BETHEA SCHOLARSHIP

Undergraduate scholarship for full-time African American students. Must be a member of the Southeastern Jurisdiction Black Methodists for Church Renewal (SEJBMCR) and an active, full member of a United Methodist Church for at least one year prior to applying. Must be U.S. citizen or permanent resident, maintain a GPA of 2.8, and demonstrate financial need.

Award: Scholarship for use in freshman, sophomore, junior, or senior years; not renewable.

Eligibility Requirements: Applicant must be Methodist; Black (non-Hispanic) and enrolled or expecting to enroll full-time at a four-year institution or university. Available to U.S. citizens.

Application Requirements: Application form, essay. *Deadline:* March 1.

Contact: Ms. Marcie Bigord, Assistant Director of Loans & Scholarships
General Board of Higher Education and Ministry
PO Box 340007
Nashville, TN 37203-0007
Phone: 615-340-7388
Fax: 615-340-7529
E-mail: mbigord@gbhem.org

GENERAL FEDERATION OF WOMEN'S CLUBS OF MASSACHUSETTS

http://www.gfwcma.org/

GENERAL FEDERATION OF WOMEN'S CLUBS OF MASSACHUSETTS NICKEL FOR NOTES MUSIC SCHOLARSHIP

• See page 620

GENERAL FEDERATION OF WOMEN'S CLUBS OF MASSACHUSETTS PENNIES FOR ART SCHOLARSHIP

• See page 620

GEORGIA PRESS EDUCATIONAL FOUNDATION INC.

http://gapress.org/scholarships-internships/

KIRK SUTLIVE SCHOLARSHIP

• See page 621

MORRIS NEWSPAPER CORPORATION SCHOLARSHIP

• See page 621

GEORGIA STUDENT FINANCE COMMISSION

http://www.GAfutures.org

GEORGIA HERO SCHOLARSHIP

• See page 621

GEORGIA PUBLIC SAFETY MEMORIAL GRANT

• See page 621

GEORGIA TUITION EQUALIZATION GRANT (GTEG)
• *See page 621*

ZELL MILLER SCHOLARSHIP PROGRAM
• *See page 621*

GERSOWITZ LIBO & KOREK, P.C.
https://www.lawyertime.com

GARDINER FOUNDATION SCHOLARSHIP
• *See page 621*

GIFT BASKETS PLUS
http://www.giftbasketsplus.com

HIGH SCHOOL GRADUATE SCHOLARSHIP CONTEST
• *See page 622*

GOENNOUNCE, LLC
http://GoEnnounce.com/about

GOENNOUNCE YOURSELF $500 MONTHLY SCHOLARSHIP
• *See page 622*

GOLDSTEIN AND BASHNER
https://www.eglaw.com/

COMBATING CAMPUS ISSUES SCHOLARSHIP
• *See page 622*

GOLF COURSE SUPERINTENDENTS ASSOCIATION OF AMERICA
http://www.eifg.org/

GOLF COURSE SUPERINTENDENTS ASSOCIATION OF AMERICA LEGACY AWARD
• *See page 564*

JOSEPH S. GARSKE COLLEGIATE GRANT PROGRAM
• *See page 564*

GORDON LAW GROUP
https://www.gordonlawltd.com

GORDON LAW GROUP ANNUAL SCHOLARSHIP
• *See page 622*

GREATER GOOD SCIENCE CENTER
https://ggsc.berkeley.edu/

THE PURPOSE CHALLENGE
• *See page 622*

GREENHOUSE SCHOLARS
https://greenhousescholars.org/

GREENHOUSE SCHOLARS
Greenhouse Scholars' vision is to create a community of leaders who will evolve the communities of the world. We are not a typical scholarship: we support each Scholar through a special community and with a unique program that provides critical personal and professional support, plus financial subsidies. Our Whole Person approach, consisting of 8 program components, is designed to connect our Scholars to opportunities and experiences, while also cultivating skill sets and meaningful relationships. We look for high-performing high school seniors who come from low-income communities and have demonstrated true leadership and positive community contributions. Applicants must be/have: 1) a graduating high school senior who is planning to attend a 4-year, accredited institution, 2) a resident of selected states, 3) a minimum un-weighted, cumulative GPA of 3.5, and 4) an annual household income no greater than $70,000 for a family of four. For application information, please visit: https://greenhousescholars.org/our-scholars/become-a-scholar/.

Award: Scholarship for use in freshman, sophomore, junior, or senior years; renewable. *Number:* 15–25. *Amount:* $1000–$5000.

Eligibility Requirements: Applicant must be high school student; planning to enroll or expecting to enroll full-time at a four-year institution or university; resident of Colorado, Georgia, Illinois, North Carolina and studying in Alabama, Alaska, Arizona, Arkansas, California, Colorado, Connecticut, Delaware, District of Columbia, Florida, Georgia, Hawaii, Idaho, Illinois, Indiana, Iowa, Kansas, Kentucky, Louisiana, Maine, Maryland, Michigan, Mississippi, Missouri, Montana, Nebraska, Nevada, New Hampshire, New Jersey, New Mexico, New York, North Carolina, North Dakota, Ohio, Oklahoma, Oregon, Pennsylvania, Rhode Island, South Carolina, South Dakota, Tennessee, Texas, Utah, Vermont, Virginia, Washington, West Virginia, Wisconsin, Wyoming. Applicant must have 3.5 GPA or higher. Available to U.S. citizens.

Application Requirements: Application form, community service, essay, financial need analysis, interview, personal photograph. *Deadline:* December 1.

Contact: Lindsey Price, Senior Associate - Program
Greenhouse Scholars
1881 9th Street, Suite 200
Boulder, CO 80302
Phone: 720-449-7444
E-mail: scholars@greenhousescholars.org

GRUNGO COLARULO
https://gcinjurylaw.com/

GRUNGO COLARULO GIVING BACK TO THE COMMUNITY SCHOLARSHIP
• *See page 623*

HAGAN SCHOLARSHIP FOUNDATION
https://haganscholarships.org/

HAGAN SCHOLARSHIP
• *See page 623*

HANSCOM FEDERAL CREDIT UNION
https://www.hfcu.org/

JOHN F. CONDON MEMORIAL SCHOLARSHIP
• *See page 623*

HARDWICK & PENDERGAST, P.S.
http://www.hardwickpendergast.com/

HARDWICK & PENDERGAST, P.S. SCHOLARSHIP
• *See page 623*

HARRINGTON FAMILY FOUNDATION
http://harringtonfamilyfoundation.org

OREGON COMMUNITY QUARTERBACK SCHOLARSHIP
• *See page 624*

HAWAII EDUCATION ASSOCIATION

http://www.heaed.com/

HAWAII EDUCATION ASSOCIATION CONTINUING COLLEGE STUDENT SCHOLARSHIP
• *See page 565*

HAWAII EDUCATION ASSOCIATION HIGH SCHOOL STUDENT SCHOLARSHIP
• *See page 565*

HAWAII SCHOOLS FEDERAL CREDIT UNION

http://www.hawaiischoolsfcu.org/

EDWIN KUNIYUKI MEMORIAL SCHOLARSHIP
• *See page 624*

HBCUCONNECT.COM

http://www.hbcuconnect.com/

HBCUCONNECT.COM MINORITY SCHOLARSHIP PROGRAM
• *See page 624*

HEALTH PRODUCTS FOR YOU

https://www.healthproductsforyou.com/

HPFY DISABILITY SCHOLARSHIP
This scholarship of $500 will be awarded to a deserving high school senior who plans to attend a vocational or academic college. Applicant can also be a student currently enrolled in college. Must be a current high school senior or a college student living with a documented disability. If the applicant is a high school student, then he or she should be planning to attend an undergraduate program in a 2 or 4 -year University/College or Technical College in the fall of the academic year following high-school graduation. Schools must be in the USA. Enrollment status in school or college must be full time or half time. To apply for the HPFY Disability Scholarship, email the following to scholarship@ healthproductsforyou.comby August 15th: personal information, including full name, date of birth, mailing address and phone number; proof of enrollment which can be a enrollment certificate or transcript of your most recent GPA (does not affect the selection); medical documents to prove the disability; an essay of minimum 500 words that speaks about your personal trials and triumphs in life related to your illness or disability and how that has defined the person you are today; any supporting documents or letters of recommendations from teachers, mentors or advisers that you would like the selection committee to consider. If all the eligibility requirements are met, the recipient will be selected on the basis of their essay and the supporting documents. The selected recipient of the $500 scholarship will be notified by email and featured on the Giving Day page on our website by the second week of September.

Award: Scholarship for use in freshman, sophomore, junior, senior, graduate, or postgraduate years; not renewable. *Number:* 1. *Amount:* $500.

Eligibility Requirements: Applicant must be enrolled or expecting to enroll full- or part-time at a two-year or four-year or technical institution or university. Available to U.S. and non-U.S. citizens.

Application Requirements: Essay. *Deadline:* August 15.

Contact: Mrs. Gazala Bohra
    E-mail: gazala@hpfy.com

HELEN DILLER FAMILY FOUNDATION

http://www.dillerteenawards.org

DILLER TEEN TIKKUN OLAM AWARDS
• *See page 624*

HELLENIC TIMES SCHOLARSHIP FUND

http://www.htsf.org/

HELLENIC TIMES SCHOLARSHIP FUND
One-time award to students of Greek/Hellenic descent. Must be between the ages of 17 and 25. For use in any year of undergraduate education. Employees of the Hellenic Times and their families are not eligible.

Award: Scholarship for use in freshman, sophomore, junior, or senior years; not renewable. *Number:* 30–40. *Amount:* $500–$10,000.

Eligibility Requirements: Applicant must be of Greek heritage; age 17-25 and enrolled or expecting to enroll full-time at a two-year or four-year or technical institution or university. Available to U.S. and non-U.S. citizens.

Application Requirements: Application form, financial need analysis, recommendations or references, resume, transcript. *Deadline:* February 19.

Contact: Nick Katsoris, President of Scholarship Fund
    Hellenic Times Scholarship Fund
    823 11th Avenue, Fifth Floor
    New York, NY 10019-3535
    Phone: 212-986-6881
    Fax: 212-977-3662
    E-mail: htsfund@aol.com

HELLENIC UNIVERSITY CLUB OF NEW YORK

http://www.hucny.com

HELLENIC UNIVERSITY CLUB UNDERGRADUATE SCHOLARSHIP AWARDS PROGRAM
The Hellenic University Club Undergraduate Scholarship Awards are offered in recognition and honor of Greek American students who have exemplified high scholastic achievement. The Hellenic University Club of New York will offer a total of four (4) awards of $1,500 each based on academic achievement and financial need. All applicants must meet the eligibility requirements and submit a complete Hellenic University Club Undergraduate Scholarship Application to the organization. Must be a high school student that will graduate in spring 2018 from a state certified high school, or equivalent, and will enroll at an accredited university/college in the U.S. in fall 2018 as a full-time student pursuing a Bachelor's degree; must be U.S. citizens or U.S. permanent residents and living in the tri-state New York area (New York, New Jersey and Connecticut); must be of Hellenic descent, at least one great grandparent with Hellenic roots; must have a cumulative average of at least 90% (or 3.5 GPA) or be in the top 10% of their class; must have a minimum SAT score of 1800/2400 (old SAT) or 1300/1600 (new SAT) and/or minimum ACT score of 27/36; must be able to demonstrate financial need. For more information, visit our website: http://www.hucny.com

Award: Grant for use in freshman year; not renewable. *Number:* 4. *Amount:* $1500.

Eligibility Requirements: Applicant must be of Cypriot, Greek heritage; high school student; planning to enroll or expecting to enroll full-time at a four-year institution or university and resident of Connecticut, New Jersey, New York. Applicant must have 3.5 GPA or higher. Available to U.S. citizens.

Application Requirements: Application form, essay. *Deadline:* April 1.

HELLENIC UNIVERSITY CLUB OF PHILADELPHIA

http://www.hucphiladelphia.org/

CHRISTOPHER DEMETRIS SCHOLARSHIP
$1500 scholarship for a full-time student enrolled in a degree program at an accredited four-year college or university. High school seniors accepted for enrollment in such a degree program may also apply. Must be a U.S. citizen of Greek descent and a resident of particular counties in NJ or PA.

Award: Scholarship for use in freshman, sophomore, junior, or senior years; not renewable. *Amount:* up to $1500.

Eligibility Requirements: Applicant must be of Greek heritage; enrolled or expecting to enroll full-time at a four-year institution or university and resident of New Jersey, Pennsylvania. Available to U.S. citizens.

Application Requirements: Application form, financial need analysis, transcript. *Deadline:* April 3.

Contact: Anna Hadgis, Scholarship Chairman
         Phone: 610-613-4310
         E-mail: www.hucphiladelphia.org

DR. NICHOLAS PADIS MEMORIAL GRADUATE SCHOLARSHIP

$5000 scholarship for a qualifying senior undergraduate or graduate student pursuing a full-time degree at an accredited university or professional school. Must be a U.S. citizen of Greek descent and a resident of particular counties in NJ or PA. Academic excellence is the primary consideration for this scholarship.

Award: Scholarship for use in senior or graduate years; not renewable. *Number:* up to 1. *Amount:* up to $5000.

Eligibility Requirements: Applicant must be of Greek heritage; enrolled or expecting to enroll full-time at a four-year institution or university and resident of New Jersey, Pennsylvania. Available to U.S. citizens.

Application Requirements: Application form, financial need analysis, transcript. *Deadline:* April 3.

Contact: Anna Hadgis, Scholarship Chairman
         Phone: 610-613-4310
         E-mail: www.hucphiladelphia.org

DORIZAS MEMORIAL SCHOLARSHIP

$3000 award for a full-time student enrolled in a degree program at an accredited four-year college or university. Must be a U.S. citizen of Greek descent and a resident of particular counties in NJ or PA.

Award: Scholarship for use in freshman, sophomore, junior, or senior years; not renewable. *Amount:* up to $3000.

Eligibility Requirements: Applicant must be of Greek heritage; enrolled or expecting to enroll full-time at a four-year institution or university and resident of New Jersey, Pennsylvania. Available to U.S. citizens.

Application Requirements: Application form, financial need analysis, transcript. *Deadline:* April 3.

Contact: Anna Hadgis, Scholarship Chairman
         Phone: 610-613-4310
         E-mail: www.hucphiladelphia.org

FOUNDERS SCHOLARSHIP

$3000 award for a full-time student enrolled in a degree program at an accredited four-year college or university. Must be a U.S. citizen of Greek descent and a resident of particular counties in NJ or PA.

Award: Scholarship for use in freshman, sophomore, junior, or senior years; not renewable. *Amount:* up to $3000.

Eligibility Requirements: Applicant must be of Greek heritage; enrolled or expecting to enroll full-time at a four-year institution or university and resident of New Jersey, Pennsylvania. Available to U.S. citizens.

Application Requirements: Application form, financial need analysis, transcript. *Deadline:* April 3.

Contact: Anna Hadgis, Scholarship Chairman
         Phone: 610-613-4310
         E-mail: www.hucphiladelphia.org

PAIDEIA SCHOLARSHIP
• See page 565

HEMOPHILIA FOUNDATION OF SOUTHERN CALIFORNIA

http://www.hemosocal.org/

CHRISTOPHER MARK PITKIN MEMORIAL SCHOLARSHIP
• See page 625

HENKEL CONSUMER ADHESIVES INC.

http://www.ducktapeclub.com/

DUCK BRAND DUCT TAPE "STUCK AT PROM" SCHOLARSHIP CONTEST
• See page 625

HERB KOHL EDUCATIONAL FOUNDATION INC.

http://www.kohleducation.org/

HERB KOHL EXCELLENCE SCHOLARSHIP PROGRAM
• See page 625

THE HIGGINS FIRM

https://www.thehigginsfirm.com

JUDGE BILL HIGGINS PUBLIC SERVICE SCHOLARSHIP
• See page 625

HIGH INCOME PARENTS.COM

http://www.highincomeparents.com

MELISSA READ MEMORIAL SCHOLARSHIP
• See page 625

HISPANIC ANNUAL SALUTE

http://www.hispanicannualsalute.org/

HISPANIC ANNUAL SALUTE SCHOLARSHIP
• See page 626

HISPANIC HERITAGE FOUNDATION

http://hispanicheritage.org/

HISPANIC HERITAGE FOUNDATION YOUTH AWARDS

The Hispanic Heritage Foundation's Youth Awards honors Latino high school seniors who excel in the classroom and community and for their focus in various categories including: Business & Entrepreneurship, Community Service, Education, Healthcare & Science, Media & Entertainment, Science, Technology, and Engineering, & Mathematics (STEM). Three awards for each student category are given in each of the different regions across the country. In addition, one Regional Award winning student from each category will be selected as the National Youth Award recipient in his or her respective category. Youth Awards begin with a high-profile, national search through a celebrity-based multimedia campaign that includes partnerships with more than 5,000 high schools and hundreds of colleges, media, elected officials, businesses and organizations. Approximately 10,000 applications are collected from qualified juniors who are honored as seniors in the fall. Students have an average GPA of 3.5 or higher, and are promoted as role models to inspire others and shatter negative stereotypes. Youth Awardees can receive grants for education or community projects to encourage social innovation and entrepreneurship. Eligibility: Must be graduating from an accredited high school in the Spring of 2019; Must have an un-weighted 3.0 GPA on a 4.0 scale; Must be of Hispanic Heritage including (includes Spain, Brazil, Philippines); Planning to enroll full-time in a bachelor's degree program at an accredited higher education institution in the fall directly after your graduation from high school. If selected, attendance to the regional ceremony is mandatory. Travel to the ceremony will be at the recipient's expense. Completed online application including a letter of recommendation, transcript and essay questions. Applicant must be a Permanent Resident, DACA, U.S. Citizen or Eligible Non-Citizen. For more information please see http://www.HispanicHeritage.org.

Award: Grant for use in freshman year; not renewable. *Number:* 190–200. *Amount:* $1000–$3500.

Eligibility Requirements: Applicant must be Hispanic; high school student and planning to enroll or expecting to enroll full-time at a two-year or four-year institution or university. Applicant must have 3.0 GPA or higher. Available to U.S. citizens.

Application Requirements: Application form, essay.

Contact: Brenda Camarillo, Youth Awards Program Manager
Hispanic Heritage Foundation
333 S Grand Ave.
Los Angeles, CA 90071
Phone: 323-7437339
E-mail: brenda@hispanicheritage.org

HISPANIC METROPOLITAN CHAMBER SCHOLARSHIPS

http://www.hmccoregon.com/

HISPANIC METROPOLITAN CHAMBER SCHOLARSHIPS
• *See page 626*

HISPANIC SCHOLARSHIP FUND

http://HSF.net

HSF/GENERAL COLLEGE SCHOLARSHIP PROGRAM

Merit-based award for U.S. citizens, permanent residents, eligible non-citizens or DACA of Hispanic heritage with plans to enroll full time in an accredited U.S. 4 year university in the upcoming academic year. Applicants must have a minimum 3.0 GPA. Must complete FAFSA or state based financial aid (if available). Must include official transcript. Award ranges from $500-$5,000 depending on need. For additional information please go to HSF.net

Award: Scholarship for use in freshman, sophomore, junior, senior, graduate, or postgraduate years; not renewable. *Number:* 2200–5000. *Amount:* $500–$5000.

Eligibility Requirements: Applicant must be of Hispanic heritage and enrolled or expecting to enroll full-time at a four-year institution or university. Applicant must have 3.0 GPA or higher. Available to U.S. citizens.

Application Requirements: Application form, community service, essay, financial need analysis, personal photograph. *Deadline:* March 30.

Contact: Ms. Ricardo Deleon, COO
Hispanic Scholarship Fund
1411 West 190th Street
Suite 700
Gardena, CA 90248
Phone: 310-975-3700
E-mail: scholar1@hsf.net

THE HIV LEAGUE

http://www.hivleague.org

THE HIV LEAGUE SCHOLARSHIP
• *See page 626*

HOFOSS DEVALL

https://www.hdinjurylaw.com/

HOFFOSS DEVALL LOUISIANA SAFE DRIVER SCHOLARSHIP
• *See page 626*

HOFFOSS DEVALL PROBLEM SOLVING SCHOLARSHIP
• *See page 626*

HOME IMPROVEMENT SOLUTIONS

http://www.myhomeimprovementsolutions.com

HOME IMPROVEMENT SCHOLARSHIP BY HOME IMPROVEMENT SOLUTIONS
• *See page 626*

HOMUS

https://homus.org

HOMUS SCHOLARSHIP PROGRAM
• *See page 627*

HOOVER PRESIDENTIAL FOUNDATION

http://www.hooverpresidentialfoundation.org/travel-grant.php

HERBERT HOOVER UNCOMMON STUDENT AWARD
• *See page 627*

HOPI TRIBE

http://www.hopi-nsn.gov/

BIA HIGHER EDUCATION GRANT

Grant provides financial support for eligible Hopi individuals pursuing postsecondary education. Minimum 2.5 CGPA required. Deadlines are July 1 for fall, and December 1 for spring.

Award: Grant for use in freshman, sophomore, junior, or senior years; not renewable. *Number:* 1–150. *Amount:* $50–$2500.

Eligibility Requirements: Applicant must be American Indian/Alaska Native and enrolled or expecting to enroll full-time at a two-year or four-year institution or university. Applicant must have 2.5 GPA or higher. Available to U.S. citizens.

Application Requirements: Application form, financial need analysis, test scores, transcript, verification of Hopi Indian blood. *Deadline:* varies.

Contact: Theresa Lomakema, Financial Aid Processor/Monitor
Phone: 928-734-3533
E-mail: info@hopi.nsn.us

HOPI EDUCATION AWARD

Grant provides financial support for eligible Hopi individuals pursuing postsecondary education. Minimum 2.5 CGPA required. Deadlines are April 1 for summer, July 1 for fall, and December 1 for spring.

Award: Scholarship for use in freshman, sophomore, junior, or senior years; not renewable. *Number:* 1–400. *Amount:* $50–$2500.

Eligibility Requirements: Applicant must be American Indian/Alaska Native and enrolled or expecting to enroll full- or part-time at a two-year or four-year institution or university. Applicant must have 2.5 GPA or higher. Available to U.S. citizens.

Application Requirements: Application form, financial need analysis, test scores, transcript, verification of Hopi Indian blood. *Deadline:* varies.

Contact: Theresa Lomakema, Financial Aid Processor/Monitor
Phone: 928-734-3533
E-mail: info@hopi.nsn.us

TRIBAL PRIORITY AWARD

Scholarship provides financial support for eligible Hopi individuals pursuing postsecondary education. Minimum 3.0 GPA required.

Award: Scholarship for use in junior or senior years; not renewable. *Number:* 1–5. *Amount:* $2500–$15,000.

Eligibility Requirements: Applicant must be American Indian/Alaska Native and enrolled or expecting to enroll full-time at a two-year or four-year institution or university. Applicant must have 3.0 GPA or higher. Available to U.S. citizens.

Application Requirements: Application form, financial need analysis, interview, recommendations or references, test scores, transcript, verification of Hopi Indian blood. *Deadline:* July 1.

Contact: Theresa Lomakema, Financial Aid Processor/Monitor
Phone: 928-734-3533
E-mail: info@hopi.nsn.us

HOSTGATOR

https://www.hostgator.com/

HOSTGATOR WEBSITE SCHOLARSHIP
• *See page 627*

HOUSE OF BLUES MUSIC FORWARD FOUNDATION

https://hobmusicforward.org/

LIVE NATION—US CONCERTS SCHOLARSHIP AWARD
• *See page 628*

HOUSTON COMMUNITY SERVICES

AZTECA SCHOLARSHIP
• *See page 628*

HOW TO WIN COLLEGE SCHOLARSHIPS

https://how2winscholarships.com

SAVOR SUMMER COLLEGE SCHOLARSHIP
• *See page 628*

HUBSHOUT

http://hubshout.com/

HUBSHOUT INTERNET MARKETING SCHOLARSHIP
• *See page 628*

HUMANA FOUNDATION

http://www.humanafoundation.org/

HUMANA FOUNDATION SCHOLARSHIP PROGRAM
• *See page 628*

INDIANA LIBRARY FEDERATION

http://www.ilfonline.org/

SUE MARSH WELLER SCHOLARSHIP FUND
• *See page 629*

INDIAN AMERICAN CULTURAL ASSOCIATION

http://www.iasf.org/

INDIAN AMERICAN SCHOLARSHIP FUND

Scholarships for descendants of families who are from modern-day India and are graduating from public or private high schools in Georgia. They must be enrolled in four-year colleges or universities. There are both academic and need-based awards available through this program.

Award: Scholarship for use in freshman year; renewable. *Number:* 3. *Amount:* $500–$5000.

Eligibility Requirements: Applicant must be of Indian heritage; Asian/Pacific Islander; high school student; planning to enroll or expecting to enroll full-time at a four-year institution or university and resident of Georgia. Applicant must have 3.0 GPA or higher. Available to U.S. citizens.

Application Requirements: Application form, essay, financial need analysis, IRS 1040 form, resume, test scores, transcript. *Deadline:* varies.

Contact: Rajesh Kurup, Scholarship Coordinator
    E-mail: rajnina@mindspring.com

INTERNATIONAL ASSOCIATION OF BLACK ACTUARIES

http://www.blackactuaries.org

IABA SCHOLARSHIP

The International Association of Black Actuaries scholarship program advances its mission by providing scholarships at the undergraduate and graduate level to qualified black students who are interested in pursuing an actuarial career. IABA's mission is to contribute to an increase in the number of black actuaries and to influence the successful career development, civic growth and achievement of black actuaries.

Award: Scholarship for use in freshman, sophomore, junior, senior, or graduate years; not renewable. *Number:* 25–35. *Amount:* $3000–$5000.

Eligibility Requirements: Applicant must be Black (non-Hispanic) and enrolled or expecting to enroll full-time at a two-year or four-year institution or university. Applicant must have 3.0 GPA or higher. Available to U.S. and non-U.S. citizens.

Application Requirements: Application form, essay. *Deadline:* March 31.

Contact: Kate Weaver, Executive Director
    E-mail: iaba@blackactuaries.org

INTERNATIONAL COLLEGE COUNSELORS

http://www.internationalcollegecounselors.com

INTERNATIONAL COLLEGE COUNSELORS SCHOLARSHIP
• *See page 629*

INTERNATIONAL DAIRY DELI BAKERY ASSOCIATION

http://www.iddba.org

INTERNATIONAL DAIRY DELI BAKERY ASSOCIATION'S SCHOLARSHIP FOR GROWING THE FUTURE
• *See page 629*

INTERNATIONAL FLIGHT SERVICES ASSOCIATION

http://www.ifsanet.com

AMI SCHOLARSHIP AWARD
• *See page 629*

INTERNATIONAL ORDER OF THE KING'S DAUGHTERS AND SONS

http://www.iokds.org/

INTERNATIONAL ORDER OF THE KING'S DAUGHTERS AND SONS NORTH AMERICAN INDIAN SCHOLARSHIP

Scholarships available for Native American students. Proof of reservation registration, college acceptance letter, and financial aid office address required. Merit-based award. Send self-addressed stamped envelope. Must maintain minimum 2.5 GPA.

Award: Scholarship for use in freshman, sophomore, junior, or senior years; renewable. *Number:* 45–60. *Amount:* $500–$650.

Eligibility Requirements: Applicant must be American Indian/Alaska Native and enrolled or expecting to enroll full-time at a two-year or four-year or technical institution or university. Applicant must have 2.5 GPA or higher. Available to U.S. and Canadian citizens.

Application Requirements: Application form, essay, financial need analysis, recommendations or references, self-addressed stamped envelope with application, transcript, written documentation of reservation registration. *Deadline:* varies.

Contact: Scholarship Committee
    Phone: 312-799-8015
    E-mail: lillyfellowship@poetryfoundation.org

INTERNATIONAL UNION OF BRICKLAYERS AND ALLIED CRAFTWORKERS

http://www.bacweb.org/

CANADIAN BATES SCHOLARSHIP PROGRAM
• *See page 566*

IOVATE HEALTH SCIENCES INTERNATIONAL INC.

http://www.iovate.com/

SIX STAR PRO NUTRITION SCHOLARSHIP AWARD
• *See page 631*

IOWA STUDENT LOAN

http://www.IowaStudentLoan.org/

COME 2 IOWA (C2IA) SENIOR SCHOLARSHIP
• *See page 631*

IOWA FINANCIAL KNOW-HOW CHALLENGE: SENIOR SCHOLARSHIP
• *See page 631*

ITALIAN-AMERICAN CHAMBER OF COMMERCE OF CHICAGO

http://www.iacc-chicago.com/

ITALIAN-AMERICAN CHAMBER OF COMMERCE OF CHICAGO SCHOLARSHIP

One-time awards for Illinois residents of Italian descent. Available to high school seniors and college students for use at a four-year institution. Applicants must have a 3.5 GPA. Must reside in Cook, Du Page, Kane, Lake, McHenry, or Will counties of Illinois. Must submit a letter including a biographical account of themselves and two letters of recommendation, one from a teacher and one from their counselor.

Award: Scholarship for use in freshman, sophomore, junior, or senior years; not renewable. *Number:* 1. *Amount:* up to $1000.

Eligibility Requirements: Applicant must be of Italian heritage; enrolled or expecting to enroll full-time at a four-year institution and resident of Illinois. Applicant must have 2.5 GPA or higher. Available to U.S. and non-U.S. citizens.

Application Requirements: Application form, essay, personal photograph, recommendations or references, self-addressed stamped envelope with application, transcript. *Deadline:* May 31.

Contact: Frank Pugno, Scholarship Chairman
Italian-American Chamber of Commerce of Chicago
30 South Michigan Avenue, Suite 504
Chicago, IL 60603
Phone: 312-553-9137 Ext. 13
Fax: 312-553-9142
E-mail: info.chicago@italchambers.net

JACKIE ROBINSON FOUNDATION

http://www.jackierobinson.org/

JACKIE ROBINSON SCHOLARSHIP
• *See page 631*

JA LIVING LEGACY

http://www.jalivinglegacy.org/

TERI AND ART IWASAKI SCHOLARSHIP

The scholarship is to support the rising costs of education. Applicant must be a descendent of a Japanese-American World War II veteran that served in the United States military units. Descendants include grandchild, great grandchild, grand niece/nephew as well as extended family.

Award: Scholarship for use in freshman year; not renewable. *Number:* 1. *Amount:* $2000.

Eligibility Requirements: Applicant must be of Japanese heritage; Asian/Pacific Islander; high school student and planning to enroll or expecting to enroll full- or part-time at an institution or university. Available to U.S. citizens.

Application Requirements: *Deadline:* continuous.

JAMES F. BYRNES FOUNDATION

http://www.byrnesscholars.org/

JAMES F. BYRNES SCHOLARSHIP
• *See page 631*

JEANNETTE RANKIN WOMEN'S SCHOLARSHIP FUND

http://www.rankinfoundation.org/

JEANNETTE RANKIN WOMEN'S SCHOLARSHIP FUND
• *See page 632*

JEWISH VOCATIONAL SERVICE LOS ANGELES

http://www.jvsla.org/

JVS SCHOLARSHIP PROGRAM

Need-based scholarships to support Jewish students from Los Angeles County in their pursuit of college, graduate, and vocational education. Applicants must be Jewish, permanent residents of Los Angeles, maintain a minimum 2.7 GPA for undergraduates and 3.0 GPA for graduates, and demonstrate verifiable financial need.

Award: Scholarship for use in freshman, sophomore, junior, senior, or graduate years; not renewable. *Number:* 150–200. *Amount:* $750–$5000.

Eligibility Requirements: Applicant must be Jewish; of Jewish heritage; enrolled or expecting to enroll full-time at a two-year or four-year or technical institution or university and resident of California. Applicant must have 3.0 GPA or higher. Available to U.S. citizens.

Application Requirements: Application form, community service, essay, financial need analysis, interview. *Deadline:* March 31.

Contact: Patricia Sills, Scholarship Program Manager
Jewish Vocational Service Los Angeles
6505 Wilshire Boulevard, Suite 200
Los Angeles, CA 90048
Phone: 323-761-8888 Ext. 8868
E-mail: scholarship@jvsla.org

JEWISH WAR VETERANS OF THE UNITED STATES OF AMERICA

http://www.jwv.org/

BERNARD ROTBERG MEMORIAL SCHOLARSHIPS

This is a grant for high school seniors (at the time of application) to help them pay the costs of their tuition. Applicants must have been accepted by an accredited college, university, community college, or hospital school of nursing as a member of the freshman class entering in the fall of the year the student graduates. Applicants must be a direct descendant (children, grand-children, great-grand-children, etc.) of Jewish War Veterans members in good standing. All members, including posthumous members, must have joined before 2013.

Award: Grant for use in freshman year; not renewable. *Number:* 1. *Amount:* $1000.

Eligibility Requirements: Applicant must be high school student and planning to enroll or expecting to enroll full-time at a two-year or four-year institution or university. Available to U.S. citizens.

Application Requirements: Application form. *Deadline:* May 27.

JOHN B. FABRIELE, III, LLC

https://www.fabrielelaw.com/

FABRIELE DISABILITY AWARENESS SCHOLARSHIP
• *See page 632*

JOHN F. KENNEDY LIBRARY FOUNDATION

http://www.jfklibrary.org/

PROFILE IN COURAGE ESSAY CONTEST
• *See page 632*

JOHN M. AZARIAN MEMORIAL ARMENIAN YOUTH SCHOLARSHIP FUND

http://azariangroup.com/scholarship.html

JOHN M. AZARIAN MEMORIAL ARMENIAN YOUTH SCHOLARSHIP FUND

Grants awarded to undergraduate students of Armenian descent, attending a full-time four-year college or university within the United States. Compelling financial need is the main criteria. Minimum 2.5 GPA required. Activity / involvement in the Armenian church / community a plus.

Award: Grant for use in freshman, sophomore, junior, or senior years; not renewable. *Number:* 1–5. *Amount:* $500–$5000.

Eligibility Requirements: Applicant must be of Armenian heritage and enrolled or expecting to enroll full-time at a four-year institution or university. Applicant must have 2.5 GPA or higher. Available to U.S. citizens.

Application Requirements: Application form, autobiography, essay, financial need analysis, personal photograph. *Deadline:* May 30.

Contact: Mr. John Azarian, CEO
John M. Azarian Memorial Armenian Youth Scholarship Fund
The Azarian Group, LLC, The Azarian Building
6 Prospect Street, Suite 2A
Midland Park, NJ 07432
Phone: 201-444-7111 Ext. 101
E-mail: jazarian@azariangroup.com

JOHNSON ATTORNEYS GROUP

https://californiainjuryaccidentlawyer.com/

NEVER DRINK AND DRIVE SCHOLARSHIP
• *See page 632*

JUNK A CAR

https://www.junkacar.com/

JUNK A CAR 2018 SCHOLARSHIP
• *See page 632*

JVS CHICAGO

http://jvschicago.org/

JEWISH FEDERATION OF METROPOLITAN CHICAGO ACADEMIC SCHOLARSHIP PROGRAM

Educational scholarship funds from grants administered by the Jewish Federation of Metropolitan Chicago are available for Jewish college and graduate students. Approximately $500,000 is available each year for full-time students, predominantly those legally domiciled in the metropolitan Chicago area, with career promise in their chosen fields. Assistance is available primarily for those with FINANCIAL NEED who are pursuing careers in the helping professions.

Award: Scholarship for use in junior, senior, graduate, or postgraduate years; not renewable. *Number:* 100–125. *Amount:* $1000–$8000.

Eligibility Requirements: Applicant must be Jewish; of Jewish heritage and enrolled or expecting to enroll full-time at a four-year institution or university. Available to U.S. citizens.

Application Requirements: Application form, financial need analysis. *Deadline:* February 1.

Contact: Sally Yarberry, Scholarship Administrator
JVS Chicago
216 W. Jackson Blvd.
Suite 700
Chicago, IL 60606
Phone: 312-673-3444
E-mail: jvsscholarship@jvschicago.org

J. WALTER THOMPSON

https://www.jwt.com/en/

HELEN LANSDOWNE RESOR SCHOLARSHIP
• *See page 633*

KANSAS BOARD OF REGENTS

http://www.kansasregents.org/

KANSAS ETHNIC MINORITY SCHOLARSHIP

Scholarship program designed to assist financially needy, academically competitive students who are identified as members of any of the following ethnic/racial groups: African-American, American Indian or Alaskan Native, Asian or Pacific Islander, or Hispanic. Priority is given to applicants who are freshmen. Students must be Kansas residents attending postsecondary institutions in Kansas. For more details refer to website http://www.kansasregents.org/students/student_financial_aid/scholarships_and_grants.

Award: Scholarship for use in freshman, sophomore, junior, or senior years; renewable. *Number:* 100–250. *Amount:* $50–$1850.

Eligibility Requirements: Applicant must be American Indian/Alaska Native, Asian/Pacific Islander, Black (non-Hispanic), Hispanic; enrolled or expecting to enroll full-time at a two-year or four-year institution or university; resident of Kansas and studying in Kansas. Applicant must have 3.0 GPA or higher. Available to U.S. citizens.

Application Requirements: Application form, financial need analysis. *Deadline:* May 1.

Contact: Diane Lindeman, Director of Student Financial Assistance
Kansas Board of Regents
1000 SW Jackson, Suite 520
Topeka, KS 66612
Phone: 785-430-4255
Fax: 785-430-4233
E-mail: dlindeman@ksbor.org

KAUFMAN & STIGGER, PLLC

http://www.getthetiger.com/

THE ALBERTA C. KAUFMAN SCHOLARSHIP
• *See page 633*

KELLER LAW OFFICES

http://www.kellerlawoffices.com/

KELLER LAW OFFICES SCHOLARSHIP FOR HIGHER EDUCATION
• *See page 633*

KELLEY & CANTERBURY, LLC

http://kelleyandcanterbury.com/

KELLEY & CANTERBURY, LLC ALASKA CURIOSITY SCHOLARSHIP
• *See page 633*

KELLY LAW TEAM
http://www.jkphoenixpersonalinjuryattorney.com/

AUTISM/ASD SCHOLARSHIP
• *See page 633*

DISABLED VETERAN SCHOLARSHIP
• *See page 634*

DISABLED VETERAN SCHOLARSHIP
• *See page 634*

KENTUCKY HIGHER EDUCATION ASSISTANCE AUTHORITY (KHEAA)
http://www.kheaa.com/

COLLEGE ACCESS PROGRAM (CAP) GRANT
Award for U.S. citizens and Kentucky residents seeking their first undergraduate degree. Applicants enrolled in sectarian institutions are not eligible. Must submit Free Application for Federal Student Aid to demonstrate financial need. Funding is limited. Awards are made on a first-come, first-serve basis.

Award: Grant for use in freshman, sophomore, junior, or senior years; not renewable. *Number:* 45,500–47,000. *Amount:* $475–$1900.

Eligibility Requirements: Applicant must be enrolled or expecting to enroll full- or part-time at a two-year or four-year or technical institution or university; resident of Kentucky and studying in Kentucky. Available to U.S. citizens.

Application Requirements: Application form. *Deadline:* continuous.

Contact: Sheila Roe, Program Coordinator
Kentucky Higher Education Assistance Authority (KHEAA)
PO Box 798
Frankfort, KY 40602-0798
Phone: 800-928-8926 Ext. 67393
E-mail: sroe@kheaa.com

KEVIN'S REVIEW
http://www.kevinsreview.com

KEVIN'S REVIEW NCLEX ASSISTANCE SCHOLARSHIP
• *See page 634*

KIDGUARD
http://www.kidguard.com/

KIDGUARD FOR EDUCATION ESSAY SCHOLARSHIP
• *See page 634*

KIDGUARD FOR EDUCATION ESSAY SCHOLARSHIP FOR HIGH SCHOOL
• *See page 635*

KIMBO FOUNDATION
http://www.kimbofoundation.org/

KIMBO FOUNDATION SCHOLARSHIP
Scholarship available to Korean-American students only. Full time study only. Application deadline varies every year.

Award: Scholarship for use in freshman, sophomore, junior, senior, graduate, or postgraduate years; not renewable. *Number:* 30–50. *Amount:* $1500.

Eligibility Requirements: Applicant must be of Korean heritage; Asian/Pacific Islander and enrolled or expecting to enroll full-time at a two-year or four-year or technical institution or university. Available to citizens of countries other than the U.S. or Canada.

Application Requirements: Application form, copy of household income tax return, essay, recommendations or references, transcript. *Deadline:* varies.

Contact: Jennifer Chung, Program Coordinator
Kimbo Foundation
430 Shotwell Street
San Francisco, CA 94110
Phone: 415-285-4100
Fax: 415-285-4103
E-mail: info@kimbofoundation.org

KITCHEN GUIDES
http://www.kitchensguides.com/

SMART KITCHEN IMPROVEMENT SCHOLARSHIP BY KITCHEN GUIDES
• *See page 635*

KNIGHTS OF COLUMBUS
http://www.kofc.org/

FOURTH DEGREE PRO DEO AND PRO PATRIA (CANADA)
• *See page 567*

KOGAN AND DISALVO, P.A.
https://www.kogan-disalvo.com/

KOGAN & DISALVO PERSONAL INJURY LAW AUTONOMOUS VEHICLES SCHOLARSHIP
• *See page 635*

KOPFLER AND HERMANN, ATTORNEYS AT LAW
https://kopflerhermann.com/

KOPFLER & HERMANN OVERCOMING ADVERSITY SCHOLARSHIP
• *See page 635*

KOREAN AMERICAN SCHOLARSHIP FOUNDATION
http://www.kasf.org/

KOREAN-AMERICAN SCHOLARSHIP FOUNDATION EASTERN REGION SCHOLARSHIPS
Scholarships available to Korean-American and Korean students enrolled in a full-time undergraduate or graduate program in the United States. Selection based on financial need, academic achievement, school activities, and community services. Each applicant must submit an application to the respective KASF region. For more details and an application see website http://www.kasf.org.

Award: Scholarship for use in freshman, sophomore, junior, senior, or graduate years; not renewable. *Amount:* $1000.

Eligibility Requirements: Applicant must be of Korean heritage; Asian/Pacific Islander; enrolled or expecting to enroll full-time at a four-year institution or university and studying in Delaware, District of Columbia, Kentucky, Maryland, North Carolina, Pennsylvania, Virginia, West Virginia. Available to U.S. and non-U.S. citizens.

Application Requirements: Application form, essay, financial need analysis, personal photograph, recommendations or references, self-addressed stamped envelope with application, transcript. *Deadline:* May 31.

Contact: Dr. Brandon Yi, Scholarship Committee
Korean American Scholarship Foundation
803 Russell Avenue, Suite 2C
Reston, VA 20879
E-mail: eastern@kasf.org

KOREAN-AMERICAN SCHOLARSHIP FOUNDATION NORTHEASTERN REGION SCHOLARSHIPS

Scholarships available to Korean-American and Korean students enrolled in a full-time undergraduate or graduate program in the United States. Selection based on financial need, academic achievement, school activities, and community services. Each applicant must submit an application to the respective KASF region. For more details and an application see website http://www.kasf.org.

Award: Scholarship for use in freshman, sophomore, junior, senior, graduate, or postgraduate years; not renewable. *Number:* 60. *Amount:* $1000–$2500.

Eligibility Requirements: Applicant must be of Korean heritage; Asian/Pacific Islander; enrolled or expecting to enroll full-time at a four-year institution or university and studying in Connecticut, Maine, Massachusetts, New Hampshire, New Jersey, New York, Rhode Island, Vermont. Available to U.S. citizens.

Application Requirements: Application form, essay, financial need analysis, personal photograph, recommendations or references, transcript. *Deadline:* June 23.

Contact: Mr. William Kim, Scholarship Committee Chairman
Korean American Scholarship Foundation
51 West Overlook
Port Washington, NY 11050
Phone: 516-883-1142
Fax: 516-883-1964
E-mail: kim.william@gmail.com

KOREAN-AMERICAN SCHOLARSHIP FOUNDATION SOUTHERN REGION SCHOLARSHIPS

Scholarships available to Korean-American and Korean students enrolled in a full-time undergraduate or graduate program in the United States. Selection based on financial need, academic achievement, school activities, and community services. Each applicant must submit an application to the respective KASF region. For more details and an application see website http://www.kasf.org.

Award: Scholarship for use in freshman, sophomore, junior, senior, or graduate years; not renewable. *Number:* up to 45. *Amount:* $1000.

Eligibility Requirements: Applicant must be of Korean heritage; Asian/Pacific Islander; enrolled or expecting to enroll full-time at a four-year institution or university and studying in Alabama, Arkansas, Florida, Georgia, Louisiana, Mississippi, North Carolina, Oklahoma, South Carolina, Tennessee, Texas. Available to U.S. citizens.

Application Requirements: Application form, essay, financial need analysis, personal photograph, recommendations or references, transcript. *Deadline:* June 10.

Contact: Dr. Sam Sook Chung, Scholarship Committee
Korean American Scholarship Foundation
2989 Preston Drive
Rex, GA 30273
Phone: 770-968-6768
E-mail: samsookchung@hotmail.com

KOREAN-AMERICAN SCHOLARSHIP FOUNDATION WESTERN REGION SCHOLARSHIPS

Scholarships available to Korean-American and Korean students enrolled in a full-time undergraduate or graduate program in the United States. Selection based on financial need, academic achievement, school activities, and community services. Each applicant must submit an application to the respective KASF region. For more details and an application see website http://www.kasf.org.

Award: Scholarship for use in freshman, sophomore, junior, senior, or graduate years; not renewable. *Amount:* $2000.

Eligibility Requirements: Applicant must be of Korean heritage; Asian/Pacific Islander; enrolled or expecting to enroll full-time at a four-year institution or university and studying in Alaska, Arizona, California, Colorado, Hawaii, Idaho, Montana, Nevada, New Mexico, Oregon, Utah, Washington, Wyoming. Applicant must have 3.0 GPA or higher. Available to U.S. citizens.

Application Requirements: Application form, essay, financial need analysis, personal photograph, recommendations or references, transcript. *Deadline:* May 31.

Contact: KASF Western Regional Chapter
Korean American Scholarship Foundation
3435 Wilshire Boulevard, Suite 2450B
Los Angeles, CA 90010
Phone: 213-380-5273
Fax: 213-380-5273
E-mail: western@kasf.org

KOSCIUSZKO FOUNDATION

http://www.thekf.org

MASSACHUSETTS FEDERATION OF POLISH WOMEN'S CLUBS SCHOLARSHIPS

Nonrenewable award to American students of Polish descent for sophomore, junior, and senior year who are attending an accredited four-year college or university. The scholarship is awarded to residents of Massachusetts. If no residents of Massachusetts apply, the award(s) may be offered to residents of New England. Applicants must submit proof of Polish ancestry. Minimum 3.0 GPA required.

Award: Scholarship for use in sophomore, junior, or senior years; not renewable. *Number:* 1–3. *Amount:* $1250.

Eligibility Requirements: Applicant must be of Polish heritage; enrolled or expecting to enroll full-time at a four-year institution or university and resident of Connecticut, Maine, Massachusetts, New Hampshire, Rhode Island, Vermont. Applicant must have 3.0 GPA or higher. Available to U.S. citizens.

Application Requirements: Application form, application form may be submitted online (http://www.thekf.org/kf/scholarships/tuition/mfpw/), essay, financial need analysis, personal photograph, proof of Polish ancestry, recommendations or references, transcript. *Fee:* $35. *Deadline:* January 16.

Contact: Ms. Addy Tymczyszyn, Scholarship and Grant Officer for Americans
Kosciuszko Foundation
15 East 65th Street
New York, NY 10065
Phone: 212-734-2130 Ext. 210
E-mail: Addy@thekf.org

POLISH AMERICAN CLUB OF NORTH JERSEY SCHOLARSHIPS

Scholarships of $1000 to $1700 awarded to qualified students for full-time undergraduate and graduate studies at accredited colleges and universities in the United States. The scholarship is renewable. U.S. citizens of Polish descent and Polish citizens with permanent residency status in the United States with minimum GPA of 3.0 are eligible. Applicants must be members of the Polish American Club of North Jersey.

Award: Scholarship for use in freshman, sophomore, junior, senior, or graduate years; not renewable. *Number:* 1–5. *Amount:* $1000–$1700.

Eligibility Requirements: Applicant must be of Polish heritage; enrolled or expecting to enroll full-time at a four-year institution or university and resident of New Jersey. Applicant must have 3.0 GPA or higher. Available to U.S. citizens.

Application Requirements: Application form, essay, personal photograph, proof of Polish ancestry, recommendations or references, transcript. *Fee:* $35. *Deadline:* January 15.

Contact: Ms. Addy Tymczyszyn, Scholarship and Grant Officer for Americans
Kosciuszko Foundation
15 East 65th Street
New York, NY 10065
Phone: 212-734-2130 Ext. 210
E-mail: addy@thekf.org

POLISH NATIONAL ALLIANCE OF BROOKLYN USA INC. SCHOLARSHIPS

Scholarships of $2000 available to qualified undergraduate students for full-time studies at accredited colleges and universities in the United States. U.S. citizens of Polish descent and Polish citizens with permanent residency status in the United States with minimum GPA of 3.0 are eligible. Applicants must be members in good standing of the Polish National Alliance of Brooklyn Lodge#1903.

Award: Scholarship for use in freshman, sophomore, junior, or senior years; not renewable. *Number:* 1–2. *Amount:* $2000.

Eligibility Requirements: Applicant must be of Polish heritage; enrolled or expecting to enroll full-time at a four-year institution or university and resident of New York. Applicant must have 3.0 GPA or higher. Available to U.S. and non-Canadian citizens.

Application Requirements: Application form, essay, personal photograph, proof of Polish ancestry, recommendations or references, transcript. *Fee:* $35. *Deadline:* January 5.

Contact: Ms. Addy Tymczyszyn, Scholarship and Grant Officer for
        Americans
        Kosciuszko Foundation
        15 East 65th Street
        New York, NY 10065
        Phone: 212-734-2130 Ext. 210
        E-mail: Addy@thekf.org

TOMASZKIEWICZ-FLORIO SCHOLARSHIP

The Tomaszkiewicz-Florio Scholarship supports Kosciuszko Foundation's Summer language and culture program at the Jagiellonian University in Krakow, Poland. The scholarship covers program fees (tuition, 3 meals a day, sightseeing on weekends and a shared room) for a 3 week intensive language program. Some funding may be awarded towards airfare. High school seniors who expect to be 18 and have a high school diploma by the first day of the program may apply. Credit is available. Students who receive scholarship funding are responsible for $95 non-refundable registration fees, airfare and spending money. Group flights are available.

Award: Scholarship for use in freshman, sophomore, junior, or senior years; not renewable. *Number:* up to 13. *Amount:* $1985.

Eligibility Requirements: Applicant must be of Polish heritage and enrolled or expecting to enroll full-time at a four-year institution or university. Applicant must have 3.0 GPA or higher. Available to U.S. citizens.

Application Requirements: Application fee, application form, essay, financial need analysis, personal photograph, recommendations or references, transcript. *Fee:* $35. *Deadline:* April 15.

Contact: Addy Tymczyszyn, Summer Study Abroad Coordinator
        Kosciuszko Foundation
        15 East 65th Street
        New York, NY 10065
        Phone: 212-734-2130 Ext. 210

LANDSCAPE ARCHITECTURE FOUNDATION

http://www.lafoundation.org

ASLA COUNCIL OF FELLOWS SCHOLARSHIP
• See page 635

COURTLAND PAUL SCHOLARSHIP
• See page 635

EDSA MINORITY SCHOLARSHIP
• See page 636

HAWAII CHAPTER/DAVID T. WOOLSEY SCHOLARSHIP
• See page 636

LANDSCAPE FORMS DESIGN FOR PEOPLE SCHOLARSHIP
• See page 636

STEVEN G. KING PLAY ENVIRONMENTS SCHOLARSHIP
• See page 636

LARSON JEWELERS

http://www.larsonjewelers.com

BAND WITH SUCCESS SCHOLARSHIP
• See page 636

LATIN AMERICAN EDUCATIONAL FOUNDATION

http://www.laef.org/

LATIN AMERICAN EDUCATIONAL FOUNDATION SCHOLARSHIPS
• See page 636

LA UNIDAD LATINA FOUNDATION

http://www.lulf.org/

LA UNIDAD LATINA FOUNDATION DREAM SCHOLARSHIP
• See page 636

LA UNIDAD LATINA FOUNDATION NATIONAL SCHOLARSHIP
• See page 637

LAW OFFICE OF DAVID D. WHITE, PLLC

http://www.wm-attorneys.com/

ANNUAL TRAUMATIC BRAIN INJURY SCHOLARSHIPS
• See page 637

LAW OFFICE OF DAVID P. SHAPIRO

http://www.davidpshapirolaw.com/about-us/

AUTISM SCHOLARSHIP
• See page 637

LAW OFFICE OF HENRY QUEENER

https://queenerlaw.com/

LAW OFFICE OF HENRY QUEENER ANNUAL SCHOLARSHIP
• See page 637

LAW OFFICE OF MATTHEW L. SHARP

https://mattsharplaw.com/

LAW OFFICE OF MATTHEW L. SHARP ANNUAL SCHOLARSHIP
• See page 638

LAW OFFICE OF MATTHEW SHRUM

http://www.shrumlawoffice.com/

ANNUAL SINGLE MOTHERS SCHOLARSHIP
• See page 638

LAW OFFICES OF DAVID A. BLACK

http://www.dbphoenixcriminallawyer.com

SCHOLARSHIP FOR DISABLED VETERANS
• See page 638

LAW OFFICES OF DIANNE SAWAYA LLC

https://dlslawfirm.com/

LAW OFFICES OF DIANNE SAWAYA DENVER SAFE DRIVER SCHOLARSHIP
• See page 638

LAW OFFICES OF JUDD S. NEMIRO, PLLC

http://www.jnphoenixfamilylawyer.com/

ANNUAL DYSLEXIA SCHOLARSHIP
• *See page 638*

LAW OFFICES OF MARK SHERMAN, LLC

markshermanlaw.com

MARK SHERMAN LAW JUVENILE JUSTICE SCHOLARSHIP
• *See page 639*

LAW OFFICES OF SEAN M. CLEARY

https://www.seanclearypa.com/

LAW OFFICES OF SEAN M. CLEARY SCHOLARSHIP
• *See page 639*

LAW OFFICES OF SHERYL R. RENTZ, P.C.

http://www.srrentzlaw.com/

LAW OFFICES OF SHERYL R. RENTZ 2018 SCHOLARSHIP
• *See page 639*

LAW OFFICES OF TRAGOS, SARTES AND TRAGOS

https://tragoslaw.com/

TRAGOS WRITE YOUR OWN LAW SCHOLARSHIP
• *See page 639*

LEAGUE FOUNDATION

http://www.leaguefoundation.org/

LEAGUE FOUNDATION ACADEMIC SCHOLARSHIP
• *See page 639*

LEAGUE OF UNITED LATIN AMERICAN CITIZENS NATIONAL EDUCATIONAL SERVICE CENTERS INC.

http://www.lnesc.org/

LULAC NATIONAL SCHOLARSHIP FUND
Awards scholarships to Hispanic students who are enrolled or planning to enroll in accredited colleges or universities in the United States. Applicants must be U.S. citizens or legal residents. Scholarships may be used for the payment of tuition, academic fees, room, board and the purchase of required educational materials. For additional information visit website http://www.lnesc.org to see a list of participating councils or send a self-addressed stamped envelope.

Award: Scholarship for use in freshman, sophomore, junior, or senior years; not renewable. *Number:* 1000. *Amount:* $250–$2000.

Eligibility Requirements: Applicant must be Hispanic and enrolled or expecting to enroll full-time at a two-year or four-year institution or university. Available to U.S. citizens.

Application Requirements: Application form, driver's license, essay, financial need analysis, interview, recommendations or references, self-addressed stamped envelope with application, test scores, transcript. *Deadline:* March 31.

Contact: Scholarship Coordinator
League of United Latin American Citizens National
   Educational Service Centers Inc.
2000 L Street, NW, Suite 610
Washington, DC 20036
Phone: 202-835-9646
Fax: 202-835-9685

LEMBERG LAW

http://www.lemberglaw.com

LEMBERG LAW AMERICAN DREAM $1,250 UNDERGRADUATE SCHOLARSHIP
• *See page 640*

LEPENDORF & SILVERSTEIN, P.C.

http://www.lependorf.com/

2018 LEPENDORF & SILVERSTEIN, P.C. SCHOLARSHIP
• *See page 640*

LEP FOUNDATION FOR YOUTH EDUCATION

http://www.lepfoundation.org/applications

CURE—CANCER SUPPORT SCHOLARSHIP
• *See page 640*

JOHN LEPPING MEMORIAL SCHOLARSHIP
• *See page 640*

LEVY LAW OFFICES

https://levylawoffices.com/

LEVY LAW OFFICES CINCINNATI SAFE DRIVER SCHOLARSHIP
• *See page 640*

LIFESAVER ESSAYS

https://lifesaveressays.com

LIFE SAVER ESSAYS ESSAY WRITING CONTEST
• *See page 640*

LIGHTHOUSE GUILD

http://www.lighthouseguild.org

LIGHTHOUSE GUILD SCHOLARSHIP PROGRAM
• *See page 689*

LIVE POETS SOCIETY AND JUST POETRY!!! MAGAZINE

http://www.highschoolpoetrycontest.com/

NATIONAL HIGH SCHOOL POETRY CONTEST
• *See page 641*

MAGIC JOHNSON FOUNDATION INC.

http://www.magicjohnson.org/

TAYLOR MICHAELS SCHOLARSHIP FUND
• *See page 641*

MAINE STATE SOCIETY FOUNDATION OF WASHINGTON, DC INC.

http://mainestatesociety.org/foundation/

MAINE STATE SOCIETY FOUNDATION SCHOLARSHIP
• *See page 641*

MAINOR WORTH INJURY LAWYERS

https://mainorwirth.com/

MAINOR WIRTH INJURY LAWYERS SCHOLARSHIP
• *See page 641*

MANA DE SAN DIEGO

http://www.manasd.org/

MANA DE SAN DIEGO SYLVIA CHAVEZ MEMORIAL SCHOLARSHIP
• *See page 641*

MARYLAND ASSOCIATION OF PRIVATE COLLEGES AND CAREER SCHOOLS

http://www.mapccs.org/

MARYLAND ASSOCIATION OF PRIVATE COLLEGES AND CAREER SCHOOLS SCHOLARSHIP
• *See page 642*

MASSACHUSETTS OFFICE OF STUDENT FINANCIAL ASSISTANCE

http://www.osfa.mass.edu/

AGNES M. LINDSAY SCHOLARSHIP
• *See page 642*

CHRISTIAN A. HERTER MEMORIAL SCHOLARSHIP
• *See page 642*

DSS ADOPTED CHILDREN TUITION WAIVER
• *See page 642*

JOHN AND ABIGAIL ADAMS SCHOLARSHIP
• *See page 642*

MASSACHUSETTS ASSISTANCE FOR STUDENT SUCCESS PROGRAM
• *See page 643*

MASSACHUSETTS CASH GRANT PROGRAM
• *See page 643*

MASSACHUSETTS GILBERT MATCHING STUDENT GRANT PROGRAM
• *See page 643*

MASSACHUSETTS PART-TIME GRANT PROGRAM
• *See page 643*

MASSACHUSETTS PUBLIC SERVICE GRANT PROGRAM
• *See page 643*

PAUL TSONGAS SCHOLARSHIP PROGRAM
• *See page 643*

MASSEY AND ASSOCIATES, PC

https://www.masseyattorneys.com/

MASSEY & ASSOCIATES: JUSTICE FOR ALL SCHOLARSHIP
• *See page 643*

MEDIGO GMBH

https://www.medigo.com/en

MEDIGO SCHOLARSHIP PROGRAM
• *See page 645*

MENOMINEE INDIAN TRIBE OF WISCONSIN

http://www.menominee-nsn.gov/

MENOMINEE INDIAN TRIBE ADULT VOCATIONAL TRAINING PROGRAM
Renewable award for enrolled Menominee tribal members to use at vocational or technical schools. Must be at least 1/4 Menominee and show proof of Indian blood. Must complete financial aid form.

Award: Grant for use in freshman or sophomore years; renewable. *Number:* 50–70. *Amount:* $100–$2200.

Eligibility Requirements: Applicant must be American Indian/Alaska Native and enrolled or expecting to enroll full- or part-time at a two-year or technical institution. Available to U.S. citizens.

Application Requirements: Application form, financial need analysis, proof of Indian blood. *Deadline:* varies.

Contact: Virginia Nuske, Education Director
Menominee Indian Tribe of Wisconsin
PO Box 910
Keshena, WI 54135
Phone: 715-799-5110
Fax: 715-799-5102
E-mail: vnuske@mitw.org

MENOMINEE INDIAN TRIBE OF WISCONSIN HIGHER EDUCATION GRANTS
Renewable award for only enrolled Menominee tribal members to use at a two- or four-year college or university. Must be at least 1/4 Menominee and show proof of Indian blood. Must complete the Free Application for Federal Student Aid (FAFSA)financial aid form and demonstrate financial need.

Award: Grant for use in freshman, sophomore, junior, or senior years; renewable. *Number:* 136. *Amount:* $100–$2200.

Eligibility Requirements: Applicant must be American Indian/Alaska Native and enrolled or expecting to enroll full- or part-time at a two-year or four-year institution or university. Available to U.S. citizens.

Application Requirements: Application form, financial need analysis, proof of Indian blood. *Deadline:* continuous.

Contact: Virginia Nuske, Education Director
Menominee Indian Tribe of Wisconsin
PO Box 910
Keshena, WI 54135
Phone: 715-799-5110
Fax: 715-799-5102
E-mail: vnuske@mitw.org

MENSA FOUNDATION

mensafoundation.org

U.S. SCHOLARSHIP PROGRAM
• *See page 645*

MES FOUNDATION

http://www.mesfoundation.org

RICHARD H. PIERCE MEMORIAL SCHOLARSHIP
• See page 645

THE MIAMI FOUNDATION

http://www.miamifoundation.org

RODNEY THAXTON/MARTIN E. SEGAL SCHOLARSHIP

Award available to a graduating high school senior who is African American and a Miami-Dade county area resident. Must demonstrate a commitment to social justice and have financial need. For additional information and application, visit website at http://www.dadecommunityfoundation.org.

Award: Scholarship for use in freshman year; not renewable. *Number:* 11. *Amount:* $1000.

Eligibility Requirements: Applicant must be Black (non-Hispanic); high school student; planning to enroll or expecting to enroll full-time at a four-year institution or university and resident of Florida. Available to U.S. citizens.

Application Requirements: Application form, resume, transcript. *Deadline:* April 17.

Contact: Lauren Mayfield, Programs Assistant
The Miami Foundation
40 NW 3rd Street
Miami, FL 33128
Phone: 305-371-2711
E-mail: lmayfield@miamifoundation.org

SIDNEY M. ARONOVITZ SCHOLARSHIP

Award available for minority students who are seniors at a Miami-Dade county public school or GED recipient from Miami-Dade area. Must be enrolled or planning to enroll in a college or university and plan to live and work in South Florida. Must have a minimum of 3.0 GPA. Additional information and application on website http://www.dadecommunityfoundation.org.

Award: Scholarship for use in freshman year; not renewable. *Number:* 1. *Amount:* $500.

Eligibility Requirements: Applicant must be American Indian/Alaska Native, Black (non-Hispanic), Hispanic; high school student; planning to enroll or expecting to enroll full-time at a four-year institution or university and resident of Florida. Applicant must have 3.0 GPA or higher. Available to U.S. citizens.

Application Requirements: Application form, financial need analysis, transcript. *Deadline:* March 20.

Contact: Lauren Mayfield, Programs Assistant
The Miami Foundation
40 NW 3rd Street
Miami, FL 33128
Phone: 305-371-2711
E-mail: lmayfield@miamifoundation.org

MINDSUMO

http://www.mindsumo.com

MINDSUMO 15-MINUTE SCHOLARSHIP
• See page 645

MINNESOTA MASONIC CHARITIES

http://www.mnmasoniccharities.org

MINNESOTA MASONIC CHARITIES SIGNATURE SCHOLARSHIP
• See page 645

MINNESOTA MASONIC CHARITIES UNDERGRADUATE SCHOLARSHIP
• See page 646

MINNESOTA OFFICE OF HIGHER EDUCATION

http://www.ohe.state.mn.us

MINNESOTA INDIAN SCHOLARSHIP

The Minnesota Indian Scholarship Program provides postsecondary financial assistance to eligible Minnesota resident students who are of one-fourth or more American Indian ancestry and demonstrate financial need for an award. Scholarships are available to eligible American Indian undergraduate students enrolled at least ¾ time and graduate students enrolled at least half time. The award amount is based on need up to $4,000 per year for undergraduate students and up to $6,000 for graduate students.

Award: Scholarship for use in freshman, sophomore, junior, senior, graduate, or postgraduate years; not renewable.

Eligibility Requirements: Applicant must be of Arumanian/Ulacedo-Romanian heritage; American Indian/Alaska Native; high school student; planning to enroll or expecting to enroll full- or part-time at a two-year or four-year or technical institution or university; resident of Minnesota and studying in Minnesota. Available to U.S. and Canadian citizens.

Application Requirements: Application form, financial need analysis. *Deadline:* continuous.

Contact: Meghan Flores, State Grant Manager
Phone: 651-355-0610
E-mail: meghan.flores@state.mn.us

MITCHELL INSTITUTE

http://www.mitchellinstitute.org/

SENATOR GEORGE J. MITCHELL SCHOLARSHIP RESEARCH INSTITUTE
• See page 646

MLD WEALTH MANAGEMENT GROUP

http://mywealthmanagement.ca/

ANNUAL MLD SCHOLASTIC SCHOLARSHIP
• See page 646

MUCHGAMES.COM

http://www.muchgames.com

MUCHGAMES.COM STUDENT RESEARCH GRANT OF $1500
• See page 646

THE MULLER FIRM, LTD

https://chicagodivorceattys.com/

THE MULLER FIRM, LTD ANNUAL SCHOLARSHIP
• See page 647

MYSTERY WEEKLY MAGAZINE

https://www.mysteryweekly.com

2018 EMERGING MYSTERY WRITER SCHOLARSHIP

Selection of the Mystery Weekly Magazine scholarship recipient will be based entirely on the creative writing requirement. Your story submission must be a previously unpublished 1000-6000 word mystery. Any mystery fiction sub-genre is acceptable. The final decision will be made by independent judges respected in the crime writing community.

Award: Scholarship for use in freshman, sophomore, junior, senior, graduate, or postgraduate years; not renewable. *Number:* 1. *Amount:* $250.

Eligibility Requirements: Applicant must be enrolled or expecting to enroll full- or part-time at a two-year or four-year or technical institution or university. Available to U.S. and Canadian citizens.

Application Requirements: Application form. *Deadline:* May 30.

Contact: Kerry Carter, Editor
Mystery Weekly Magazine
3-35 Stone Church Road
Suite 213
Ancaster, ON L9K 1S5
CAN
E-mail: info@mysteryweekly.com

NAACP LEGAL DEFENSE AND EDUCATIONAL FUND INC.

http://www.naacpldf.org/

HERBERT LEHMAN SCHOLARSHIP PROGRAM

Renewable award for successful African-American high school seniors and freshmen to attend a four-year college on a full-time basis. Candidates are required to be U.S. citizens and must have outstanding potential as evidenced by their high school academic records, test scores, and personal essays.

Award: Scholarship for use in freshman, sophomore, junior, or senior years; renewable. *Number:* 25–30. *Amount:* $2000.

Eligibility Requirements: Applicant must be Black (non-Hispanic) and enrolled or expecting to enroll full-time at a four-year institution or university. Applicant must have 2.5 GPA or higher. Available to U.S. citizens.

Application Requirements: Application form, community service, essay, personal photograph, recommendations or references, resume, test scores, transcript. *Deadline:* March 31.

Contact: Program Director
NAACP Legal Defense and Educational Fund Inc.
99 Hudson Street
Suite 1600
New York, NY 10013
Phone: 212-965-2225
Fax: 212-219-1595
E-mail: scholarships@naacpldf.org

NANA (NORTHWEST ALASKA NATIVE ASSOCIATION) REGIONAL CORPORATION

http://www.nana.com/

ROBERT AQQALUK NEWLIN SR. MEMORIAL TRUST SCHOLARSHIP

Scholarship for NANA shareholders, descendants of NANA shareholders, or dependents of NANA shareholders or their descendants. Applicant must be enrolled or accepted for admittance at a postsecondary educational institution or vocational school.

Award: Scholarship for use in freshman, sophomore, junior, or senior years; not renewable. *Number:* 250–400. *Amount:* $1000–$2000.

Eligibility Requirements: Applicant must be American Indian/Alaska Native and enrolled or expecting to enroll full- or part-time at a two-year or four-year or technical institution or university. Available to U.S. citizens.

Application Requirements: Application form, college acceptance letter, enrollment proof, financial need analysis, recommendations or references, transcript. *Deadline:* varies.

Contact: Erica Nelson, Education Director
NANA (Northwest Alaska Native Association) Regional Corporation
PO Box 509
Kotzebue, AK 99752
Phone: 907-442-1607
Fax: 907-442-2289
E-mail: erica.nelson@nana.org

NATIONAL AIDS MEMORIAL

http://www.aidsmemorial.org

PEDRO ZAMORA YOUNG LEADERS SCHOLARSHIP
• *See page 647*

NATIONAL ASSOCIATION FOR CAMPUS ACTIVITIES

http://www.naca.org/

ALAN DAVIS SCHOLARSHIP
• *See page 647*

JOHN ZAGUNIS STUDENT LEADER SCHOLARSHIP
• *See page 647*

LORI RHETT MEMORIAL SCHOLARSHIP
• *See page 648*

NATIONAL ASSOCIATION FOR CAMPUS ACTIVITIES MID ATLANTIC UNDERGRADUATE SCHOLARSHIP FOR STUDENT LEADERS
• *See page 648*

NATIONAL ASSOCIATION FOR CAMPUS ACTIVITIES SOUTH REGION STUDENT LEADER SCHOLARSHIP
• *See page 648*

TESE CALDARELLI MEMORIAL SCHOLARSHIP
• *See page 648*

NATIONAL ASSOCIATION FOR THE ADVANCEMENT OF COLORED PEOPLE

http://www.naacp.org/

AGNES JONES JACKSON SCHOLARSHIP
• *See page 569*

NATIONAL ASSOCIATION OF COLORED WOMEN'S CLUBS

http://www.nacwc.org/

HALLIE Q. BROWN SCHOLARSHIP

One-time $1000-$2000 scholarship for high school graduates who have completed at least one semester in a postsecondary accredited institution with a minimum "C" average.

Award: Scholarship for use in freshman year; not renewable. *Number:* 4–6. *Amount:* $1000–$2000.

Eligibility Requirements: Applicant must be Black (non-Hispanic); high school student and planning to enroll or expecting to enroll full-time at a two-year or four-year institution or university. Available to U.S. citizens.

Application Requirements: Application form, recommendations or references, transcript. *Deadline:* March 30.

Contact: Dr. Gerldine Jenkins, Program Coordinator
National Association of Colored Women's Clubs
Program Coordinator
Washington, DC 20009
Phone: 202-667-4080
Fax: 202-667-2574

NATIONAL ASSOCIATION OF NEGRO BUSINESS AND PROFESSIONAL WOMEN'S CLUBS INC.

http://www.nanbpwc.org/

NATIONAL SCHOLARSHIP

Scholarship for African-American graduating high school seniors with a minimum 3.0 GPA. Must submit 300-word essay on the topic "Why Education is Important to Me."

Award: Scholarship for use in freshman year; not renewable. *Number:* 6–8. *Amount:* $500–$1000.

Eligibility Requirements: Applicant must be Black (non-Hispanic); high school student and planning to enroll or expecting to enroll full-time at a four-year institution or university. Applicant must have 3.0 GPA or higher. Available to U.S. citizens.

Application Requirements: Application form, community service, essay, recommendations or references, test scores, transcript. *Deadline:* March 1.

Contact: Twyla Whitby, National Director of Education Scholarship Program
National Association of Negro Business and Professional Women's Clubs Inc.
1806 New Hampshire Avenue, NW
Washington, DC 20009-3298
Phone: 202-483-4206
E-mail: info@nanbpwc.org

NATIONAL COLLEGIATE CANCER FOUNDATION

http://collegiatecancer.org/

NATIONAL COLLEGIATE CANCER FOUNDATION SCHOLARSHIPS

The National Collegiate Cancer Foundation was established to provide services and support to young adults whose lives have been impacted by cancer and who have continued with their education throughout treatment or after their treatment. The NCCF Survivor Scholarship Program$1,000 competitive awards will be judged based on the criteria listed below. Applicants must meet all of the requirements listed: 1. Must be a cancer survivor or current patient; 2. Must be between the ages of 18-35. An exception will be made if you are 17 and entering college in the fall following application; 3. U.S. citizen or permanent resident; 4. Attending or planning to attend an accredited college, university or vocational institution in pursuit of an Associate, Bachelor, Master's, doctorate or certificate. Applicants will be evaluated based on six criteria: displaying a "Will Win" attitude with respect to his or her cancer experience; quality of essays; financial need; overall story of cancer survivorship; commitment to education; quality of recommendations. The National Collegiate Cancer Foundation is proud to provide financial assistance to young adults pursuing their education who have lost a parent or guardian to cancer. The Legacy Scholarship Program $1,000 competitive awards will be judged based on the criteria listed below. Applicants must meet all of the requirements listed below: 1. Must have lost a parent or guardian to cancer; 2. Must be between the ages of 18-35. An exception will be made if you are 17 and entering college; 3. U.S. citizen or permanent resident; 4. Attending or planning to attend an accredited college, university, or vocational institution in pursuit of an Associate, Bachelor, Master's, doctorate or certificate. Applicants will be evaluated based on the following criteria: journey, encouragement, financial need, notable accomplishments, quality of recommendations.

Award: Scholarship for use in freshman, sophomore, junior, senior, graduate, or postgraduate years; not renewable. *Number:* 50. *Amount:* $1000.

Eligibility Requirements: Applicant must be age 17-35 and enrolled or expecting to enroll full- or part-time at a two-year or four-year or technical institution or university. Available to U.S. citizens.

Application Requirements: Application form, essay, financial need analysis. *Deadline:* May 15.

Contact: Meghan Rodgers
National Collegiate Cancer Foundation
8334 N. Brook Lane
Bethesda, MD 20814
Phone: 240-5156262
E-mail: info@collegiatecancer.org

NATIONAL COUNCIL OF JEWISH WOMEN LOS ANGELES (NCJW L LA)

http://ncjwla.org/

THE DODELL WOMEN'S EMPOWERMENT SCHOLARSHIP
• *See page 648*

THE SINGERMAN/NOSSECK MEMORIAL SCHOLARSHIP

To qualify a candidate must be enrolling or enrolled in a trade school (online course ok) that leads to certification (i.e. massage therapy, dental assistant, CNA), in order to learn a marketable skill which will lead to

economic self-sufficiency. The scholarship is intended to ease the burden of the applicant starting or continuing their education, and is not limited to a particular field of study. The National Council of Jewish Women l Los Angeles (NCJW l LA) provides scholarships, regardless of race, ethnicity, religion, age, gender identity, sexuality or national origin to those who live and attend school in the Greater Los Angeles area, including Los Angeles, Orange, Riverside, and Ventura Counties.

Award: Scholarship for use in freshman, sophomore, junior, or senior years; not renewable. *Number:* 1. *Amount:* $1000.

Eligibility Requirements: Applicant must be enrolled or expecting to enroll full- or part-time at a technical institution; resident of California and studying in California. Available to U.S. citizens.

Application Requirements: Application form, essay, financial need analysis. *Deadline:* continuous.

Contact: Stephanie Flax, Scholarship and Program Coordinator
National Council of Jewish Women Los Angeles (NCJW l LA)
543 North Fairfax Avenue
Los Angeles, CA 90036
Phone: 323-852-8515
E-mail: scholarship@ncjwla.org

SOPHIE GREENSTADT SCHOLARSHIP FOR MID-LIFE WOMEN
• *See page 648*

STEPHEN L. TELLER & RICHARD HOTSON TV, CINEMA, AND THEATER SCHOLARSHIP
• *See page 649*

SUSAN SCHULMAN BEGLEY MEMORIAL SCHOLARSHIP
• *See page 649*

NATIONAL FEDERATION OF STATE POETRY SOCIETIES (NFSPS)

http://www.nfsps.com/

NATIONAL FEDERATION OF STATE POETRY SOCIETIES' COLLEGE UNDERGRADUATE POETRY (CUP) COMPETITION
• *See page 649*

NATIONAL FEDERATION OF THE BLIND (NFB)

http://www.nfb.org/scholarships

AAF KENNETH JERNIGAN SCHOLARSHIP FOR $12,000
• *See page 649*

CHARLES AND MELVA T. OWEN SCHOLARSHIP FOR $10,000
• *See page 649*

NATIONAL FFA ORGANIZATION

http://www.ffa.org

NATIONAL FFA COLLEGIATE SCHOLARSHIP PROGRAM
• *See page 570*

NATIONAL INSTITUTE FOR LABOR RELATIONS RESEARCH

http://www.nilrr.org/

NATIONAL INSTITUTE FOR LABOR RELATIONS RESEARCH WILLIAM B. RUGGLES JOURNALISM SCHOLARSHIP
• *See page 650*

NATIONAL ITALIAN AMERICAN FOUNDATION

http://www.niaf.org/

NATIONAL ITALIAN AMERICAN FOUNDATION CATEGORY I SCHOLARSHIP

Award available to Italian-American students who have outstanding potential and high academic achievements. Minimum 3.5 GPA required. Must be a U.S. citizen and be enrolled in an accredited institution of higher education. Application can only be submitted online. For further information, deadlines, and online application visit website http://www.niaf.org/scholarships/index.asp.

Award: Scholarship for use in freshman, sophomore, junior, senior, graduate, or postgraduate years; not renewable. *Number:* 40–45. *Amount:* $2500–$10,000.

Eligibility Requirements: Applicant must be of Italian heritage and enrolled or expecting to enroll full-time at a two-year or four-year institution or university. Applicant must have 3.5 GPA or higher. Available to U.S. citizens.

Application Requirements: Application form, essay, recommendations or references, transcript. *Deadline:* March 2.

Contact: NIAF Education and Culture Department
National Italian American Foundation
1860 19th Street, NW
Washington, DC 20009
Phone: 202-387-0600
E-mail: scholarships@niaf.org

NATIONAL MILITARY FAMILY ASSOCIATION

http://www.MilitaryFamily.org

NATIONAL MILITARY FAMILY ASSOCIATION'S MILITARY SPOUSE SCHOLARSHIPS
• *See page 650*

NATIONAL MULTIPLE SCLEROSIS SOCIETY

http://www.nmss.org/

NATIONAL MULTIPLE SCLEROSIS SOCIETY SCHOLARSHIP PROGRAM
• *See page 650*

NATIONAL PRESS FOUNDATION

http://www.nationalpress.org/

EVERT CLARK/SETH PAYNE AWARD
• *See page 650*

NATIONAL SOCIETY DAUGHTERS OF THE AMERICAN REVOLUTION

http://www.dar.org/

NATIONAL SOCIETY DAUGHTERS OF THE AMERICAN REVOLUTION AMERICAN INDIAN SCHOLARSHIP

One-time scholarship available to Native Americans. All awards are judged based on financial need and academic achievement. Undergraduate students are given preference. GPA of 2.75 or higher is required. Deadline is February 15th each calendar year

Award: Scholarship for use in freshman, sophomore, junior, senior, or graduate years; not renewable. *Amount:* $4000.

Eligibility Requirements: Applicant must be American Indian/Alaska Native and enrolled or expecting to enroll full-time at a two-year or four-year or technical institution or university. Available to U.S. citizens.

Application Requirements: Application form, essay. *Deadline:* February 15.

Contact: Lakeisha Graham, Manager, Office of the Reporter General
Phone: 202-628-1776
Fax: 202-879-3348
E-mail: nsdarscholarships@dar.org

NATIONAL SOCIETY DAUGHTERS OF THE AMERICAN REVOLUTION FRANCES CRAWFORD MARVIN AMERICAN INDIAN SCHOLARSHIP

Nonrenewable award available for a Native American to attend any two- or four-year college or university. Must demonstrate financial need, academic achievement, and have a 3.0 GPA or higher. Must submit a self-addressed stamped envelope to be considered.

Award: Scholarship for use in freshman, sophomore, junior, or senior years; not renewable. *Number:* 1.

Eligibility Requirements: Applicant must be American Indian/Alaska Native and enrolled or expecting to enroll full-time at a two-year or four-year institution or university. Applicant must have 3.0 GPA or higher. Available to U.S. citizens.

Application Requirements: Application form, financial need analysis. *Deadline:* February 15.

Contact: Lakeisha Graham, Manager, Office of the Reporter General
Phone: 202-628-1776
Fax: 202-879-3348
E-mail: nsdarscholarships@dar.org

NATIONAL SOCIETY FOR HISTOTECHNOLOGY

http://nsh.org/

IRWIN S. LERNER STUDENT SCHOLARSHIPS
• *See page 650*

NATIVE VISION SCHOLARSHIP

http://www.nativevision.org/

NATIVEVISION

Scholarship available to any Native American high school senior who has been accepted to college.

Award: Scholarship for use in freshman year; not renewable. *Number:* 2. *Amount:* $5000.

Eligibility Requirements: Applicant must be American Indian/Alaska Native; high school student and planning to enroll or expecting to enroll full-time at a four-year institution or university. Applicant must have 3.0 GPA or higher. Available to U.S. and non-U.S. citizens.

Application Requirements: Application form, community service, essay, financial need analysis. *Deadline:* May 12.

Contact: Marlena Hammen, Scholarship Coordinator
Native Vision Scholarship
415 North Washington Street
4th Floor
Baltimore, MD 21231
Phone: 443-287-5167
Fax: 410-955-2010
E-mail: mhammen@jhu.edu

NEBRASKA'S COORDINATING COMMISSION FOR POSTSECONDARY EDUCATION

https://ccpe.nebraska.gov/

NEBRASKA OPPORTUNITY GRANT
• *See page 651*

NEED

http://www.needld.org/

UNMET NEED GRANT PROGRAM
• *See page 651*

NERDIFY

https://gonerdify.com/

NERDY BOT SCHOLARSHIP
• *See page 651*

NEW JERSEY STATE GOLF ASSOCIATION

NJSGA.org

NEW JERSEY STATE GOLF ASSOCIATION CADDIE SCHOLARSHIP
• *See page 652*

NEW YORK STATE HIGHER EDUCATION SERVICES CORPORATION

http://www.hesc.ny.gov

NEW YORK STATE AID TO NATIVE AMERICANS
Award for enrolled members of a New York State tribe and their children who are attending or planning to attend a New York State college and who are New York State residents. Deadlines: July 15 for the fall semester, December 31 for the spring semester, and May 20 for summer session.

Award: Scholarship for use in freshman, sophomore, junior, or senior years; renewable. *Amount:* $85–$2000.

Eligibility Requirements: Applicant must be American Indian/Alaska Native; enrolled or expecting to enroll full- or part-time at a two-year or four-year or technical institution or university; resident of New York and studying in New York. Available to U.S. citizens.

Application Requirements: Application form, financial need analysis, recommendations or references, transcript. *Deadline:* varies.

Contact: Native American Education Unit
New York State Higher Education Services Corporation
EBA Room 475
Albany, NY 12234
Phone: 518-474-0537

NEW YORK WOMEN IN COMMUNICATIONS

https://nywici.org/

NEW YORK WOMEN IN COMMUNICATIONS SCHOLARSHIPS
• *See page 652*

N.H. DEPARTMENT OF EDUCATION, DIVISION OF HIGHER EDUCATION - HIGHER EDUCATION COMMISSION

http://www.education.nh.gov/highered

SCHOLARSHIPS FOR ORPHANS OF VETERANS
• *See page 714*

NICODEMUS WILDERNESS PROJECT

http://www.wildernessproject.org/

APPRENTICE ECOLOGIST SCHOLARSHIP
• *See page 652*

NIKKO COSMETIC SURGERY CENTER

http://www.drnikko.com/

BREAST CANCER SURVIVOR SCHOLARSHIPS
• *See page 652*

NISEI STUDENT RELOCATION COMMEMORATIVE FUND

http://www.nsrcfund.org/

NISEI STUDENT RELOCATION COMMEMORATIVE FUND
• *See page 652*

NO BULL SPORTS

http://nobullsports.org/

NO BULL SPORTS SCHOLARSHIP
• *See page 653*

NOPLAG PLAGIARISM CHECKER

http://noplag.com/

NOPLAG SCHOLARSHIP ESSAY CONTEST
• *See page 653*

NORTH CAROLINA ASSOCIATION OF EDUCATORS

http://www.ncae.org/

NORTH CAROLINA ASSOCIATION OF EDUCATORS MARTIN LUTHER KING JR. SCHOLARSHIP
• *See page 653*

NORTH CAROLINA DIVISION OF VOCATIONAL REHABILITATION SERVICES

http://www.dhhs.state.nc.us/

TRAINING SUPPORT FOR YOUTH WITH DISABILITIES
• *See page 653*

NORTH CAROLINA SOCIETY OF HISPANIC PROFESSIONALS

http://www.thencshp.org/

NORTH CAROLINA HISPANIC COLLEGE FUND SCHOLARSHIP
Four-year renewable scholarship for Hispanic students. Must have graduated from a North Carolina high school within the past two years, have a four-year cumulative GPA of 2.5, and be accepted into a two- or four-year college or university. Preference is given to full-time students but part-time students may apply. Preference will be given to foreign-born applicants or native-born children of foreign-born parents. Applications are available online at http://www.thencshp.org/.

Award: Scholarship for use in freshman, sophomore, junior, or senior years; renewable. *Amount:* $500–$2500.

Eligibility Requirements: Applicant must be Hispanic; enrolled or expecting to enroll full- or part-time at a two-year or four-year institution or university and resident of North Carolina. Applicant must have 2.5 GPA or higher. Available to U.S. and non-U.S. citizens.

Application Requirements: Application form, application form may be submitted online (http://www.thencshp.org), transcript. *Deadline:* continuous.

Contact: Marco Zarate, President
North Carolina Society of Hispanic Professionals
8450 Chapel Hill Road, Suite 209
Cary, NC 27513
Phone: 919-467-8424
Fax: 919-469-1785
E-mail: mailbox@thencshp.org

NORTH CAROLINA VIETNAM VETERANS, INC.

http://www.ncvvi.org

NC VIETNAM VETERANS, INC., SCHOLARSHIP PROGRAM
• *See page 653*

NORTH DAKOTA UNIVERSITY SYSTEM

http://www.ndus.edu/

NORTH DAKOTA ACADEMIC SCHOLARSHIP
• *See page 654*

NORTH DAKOTA CAREER AND TECHNICAL EDUCATION SCHOLARSHIP
• *See page 654*

NORTH DAKOTA INDIAN SCHOLARSHIP PROGRAM
• *See page 654*

NORTH DAKOTA SCHOLARS PROGRAM
• *See page 654*

NORTH DAKOTA STATE STUDENT INCENTIVE GRANT PROGRAM
• *See page 654*

NORTHERN CHEYENNE TRIBAL EDUCATION DEPARTMENT

http://www.cheyennenation.com

NORTHERN CHEYENNE TRIBAL EDUCATION DEPARTMENT
Scholarships are provided to enrolled Northern Cheyenne members only.

Award: Scholarship for use in freshman, sophomore, junior, senior, or graduate years; renewable. *Number:* 90. *Amount:* $100–$7000.

Eligibility Requirements: Applicant must be American Indian/Alaska Native and enrolled or expecting to enroll full- or part-time at a two-year or four-year institution or university. Available to U.S. citizens.

Application Requirements: Application form, essay, financial need analysis. *Deadline:* December 1.

Contact: Norma Bixby, Director
Northern Cheyenne Tribal Education Department
Box 307
Lame Deer, MT 59043
Phone: 406-477-6602
Fax: 406-477-8150
E-mail: norma.bixby@cheyennenation.com

NORTHWEST DANISH ASSOCIATION

http://www.northwestdanish.org

NORTHWEST DANISH ASSOCIATION SCHOLARSHIP
The scholarship program is designated for people with some kind of Danish connection, living in WA or Oregon states, but study may be at any other location in the United States.

Award: Scholarship for use in freshman, sophomore, junior, senior, or graduate years; not renewable. *Number:* 1–5. *Amount:* $500–$1000.

Eligibility Requirements: Applicant must be of Danish heritage; enrolled or expecting to enroll full-time at a two-year or four-year institution or university and resident of Oregon, Washington. Available to U.S. citizens.

Application Requirements: Application form, essay, financial need analysis. *Deadline:* April 30.

Contact: Dr. Edith Christensen, Scholarship Awards
Northwest Danish Association
1833 N. 105th St.
Suite 101
Seattle, WA 98133
Phone: 206-523-3263
E-mail: seattle@nwdanish.org

NORTHWESTERN MUTUAL FOUNDATION

http://www.scholarshipamerica.org

NORTHWESTERN MUTUAL CHILDHOOD CANCER SURVIVOR SCHOLARSHIP
• *See page 654*

NOVUS BIOLOGICALS, LLC

https://www.novusbio.com

NOVUS BIOLOGICALS SCHOLARSHIP PROGRAM
Applicants must have a major declared in a science related field and must be enrolled or accepted for enrollment (Baccalaureate, graduate, associate degree, or diploma) with a declared major in a science related field. Fill out the scholarship application form and submit a transcript of all college/post-secondary coursework (if high school student submit high school transcript). This may be an official or unofficial copy. Submit a written statement addressing the following topics: Submit a 140 character statement/tweet on your favorite scientist. Write a personal statement of 500 words or less on how you plan to use your degree to further advance science in your field of interest.

Award: Scholarship for use in freshman, sophomore, junior, senior, graduate, or postgraduate years; not renewable. *Number:* 1. *Amount:* $1500.

Eligibility Requirements: Applicant must be enrolled or expecting to enroll full- or part-time at a two-year or four-year institution or university. Available to U.S. and non-U.S. citizens.

Application Requirements: Application form, essay. *Deadline:* July 20.

Contact: Lisa Ikariyama
Novus Biologicals, LLC
8100 Southpark Way
Unit A-8
Littleton, CO 80120
Phone: 303-7301950
E-mail: lisa@novusbio.com

NURSERECRUITER.COM

https://www.nurserecruiter.com

NURSERECRUITER.COM SCHOLARSHIP
• *See page 655*

OCA

http://www.ocanational.org/

OCA-UPS FOUNDATION GOLD MOUNTAIN SCHOLARSHIP
Scholarships for Asian Pacific Americans who are the first person in their immediate family to attend college. Must be entering first year of college in the upcoming fall. Please check out http//http://www.ocanational.org for more information.

Award: Scholarship for use in freshman, sophomore, junior, or senior years; not renewable. *Number:* 15. *Amount:* $2000.

Eligibility Requirements: Applicant must be Asian/Pacific Islander; high school student and planning to enroll or expecting to enroll full-time at a two-year or four-year institution or university. Applicant must have 3.0 GPA or higher. Available to U.S. citizens.

Application Requirements: Application form, essay, financial need analysis. *Deadline:* continuous.

Contact: Andrew Lo, Programs Associate
OCA
1322 18th Street, NW
Washington, DC 20036
Phone: 202-223-5500
E-mail: oca@ocanational.org

OFFICE OF NAVAJO NATION SCHOLARSHIP AND FINANCIAL ASSISTANCE

http://www.onnsfa.org/

CHIEF MANUELITO SCHOLARSHIP PROGRAM

Award programs established to recognize and award undergraduate students with high test scores and GPA of 3.0. Priorities to Navajo Nation applicants. Must be enrolled as a full-time undergraduate and pursue a degree program leading to a Baccalaureate. For further details visit website http://www.onnsfa.org/docs/polproc.pdf.

Award: Scholarship for use in freshman, sophomore, junior, or senior years; not renewable. *Number:* 1. *Amount:* $7000.

Eligibility Requirements: Applicant must be American Indian/Alaska Native and enrolled or expecting to enroll full-time at a two-year or four-year institution or university. Applicant must have 3.0 GPA or higher. Available to U.S. citizens.

Application Requirements: Application form, financial need analysis, test scores, transcript. *Deadline:* April 1.

Contact: Maxine Damon, Financial Aid Counselor
Phone: 800-243-2956
Fax: 928-871-6561
E-mail: maxinedamon@navajo.org

OHIO DEPARTMENT OF HIGHER EDUCATION

http://www.ohiohighered.org

CHOOSE OHIO FIRST SCHOLARSHIP
• *See page 655*

OHIO COLLEGE OPPORTUNITY GRANT
• *See page 655*

OHIO SAFETY OFFICERS COLLEGE MEMORIAL FUND
• *See page 655*

OHIO WAR ORPHANS SCHOLARSHIP
• *See page 655*

ONEIDA TRIBE OF INDIANS OF WISCONSIN

http://www.oneida-nsn.gov

ONEIDA HIGHER EDUCATION SCHOLARSHIP PROGRAM

Renewable award available to enrolled members of the Oneida Tribe of Indians of Wisconsin, who are accepted into an accredited postsecondary institution within the United States. Must have a high school diploma, HSED or GED. Maximum funding varies based on the post-secondary costs and level of degree seeking. Please see website for more details.

Award: Grant for use in freshman, sophomore, junior, senior, graduate, or postgraduate years; renewable.

Eligibility Requirements: Applicant must be American Indian/Alaska Native and enrolled or expecting to enroll full- or part-time at a two-year or four-year or technical institution or university. Available to U.S. citizens.

Application Requirements: Application form, financial need analysis. *Deadline:* continuous.

Contact: Higher Education Advisor
Oneida Tribe of Indians of Wisconsin
PO Box 365
Oneida, WI 54155
Phone: 920-869-4033
E-mail: highered@oneidanation.org

ONE LOVE FOUNDATION

http://www.joinonelove.org

ONE LOVE FOUNDATION PETS VS. PARTNERS SCHOLARSHIP
• *See page 656*

ONLINEPSYCHOLOGYDEGREES.COM

http://www.onlinepsychologydegrees.com/

ONLINEPSYCHOLOGYDEGREES.COM EDUCATION SCHOLARSHIPS
• *See page 656*

OREGON NATIVE AMERICAN CHAMBER OF COMMERCE SCHOLARSHIP

http://www.onacc.org/

OREGON NATIVE AMERICAN CHAMBER OF COMMERCE SCHOLARSHIP

Scholarships available to Native American students studying in Oregon. Must verify Native American status and be actively involved in the Native American community.

Award: Scholarship for use in freshman, sophomore, junior, or senior years; not renewable. *Number:* 1. *Amount:* $1000.

Eligibility Requirements: Applicant must be American Indian/Alaska Native; enrolled or expecting to enroll full- or part-time at a four-year institution or university and studying in Oregon. Available to U.S. and Canadian citizens.

Application Requirements: Application form, proof of Native American descent, transcript. *Deadline:* varies.

Contact: James Parker, Director of Operations
Phone: 503-894-4525
E-mail: support@onacc.org

ORGANIZATION FOR AUTISM RESEARCH

http://www.researchautism.org

LISA HIGGINS HUSSMAN SCHOLARSHIP
• *See page 656*

SCHWALLIE FAMILY SCHOLARSHIP
• *See page 656*

ORGONE BIOPHYSICAL RESEARCH LABORATORY

http://www.orgonelab.org/hochberg.htm

LOU HOCHBERG-UNIVERSITY/COLLEGE ESSAY AWARDS
• *See page 656*

ORTHODOX UNION

http://ou.org

SARA AND MAX GOLDSAMMLER SCHOLARSHIP FUND

This award is open to any Jewish student. Applicants should write a short essay describing in 500 to 1000 words how they have demonstrated leadership ability both in and outside of school.

Award: Scholarship for use in freshman, sophomore, junior, or senior years; not renewable. *Number:* 3. *Amount:* $300–$1000.

Eligibility Requirements: Applicant must be Jewish; of Jewish heritage and enrolled or expecting to enroll full- or part-time at a two-year or four-year or technical institution or university. Available to U.S. citizens.

Application Requirements: Application form, essay. *Deadline:* August 10.

Contact: Mrs. Rachel Shammah, Alumni Assistant
Orthodox Union
11 Broadway
New York, NY 10004
Phone: 212-613-8155
E-mail: shammahr@ncsy.org

OSAGE NATION EDUCATION DEPARTMENT

https://www.osagenation-nsn.gov/what-we-do/education-department

OSAGE NATION HIGHER EDUCATION SCHOLARSHIP
• *See page 657*

OUR WORLD UNDERWATER SCHOLARSHIP SOCIETY

http://www.owuscholarship.org/

OUR WORLD UNDERWATER SCHOLARSHIP SOCIETY

Annual award for individual planning to pursue a career in a water-related discipline through practical exposure to various fields and leaders of underwater endeavors. Scuba experience required. Must be at least 21 but not yet 26. Scholarship value is $25,000 for the North American Rolex Scholar, open to North American citizens only. The European Rolex Scholarship is open to European citizens and the Australasian Rolex Scholarship is open to citizens of the Australasian region.

Award: Scholarship for use in junior or senior years; not renewable. *Number:* 3. *Amount:* $70,000.

Eligibility Requirements: Applicant must be Australian, Canadian, Dutch, European Union, Finnish, French, German, Irish, Mexican, New Zealander, Scottish, Spanish, Swedish, Swiss citizen; age 21-26; enrolled or expecting to enroll full- or part-time at a two-year or four-year or technical institution or university and must have an interest in athletics/sports. Available to U.S. and non-U.S. citizens.

Application Requirements: Application form, autobiography, community service, driver's license, essay, interview. *Fee:* $50. *Deadline:* November 30.

Contact: Roberta Flanders, Scholarship Application Coordinator
Our World Underwater Scholarship Society
PO Box 6157
Woodridge, IL 60517
Phone: 630-969-6690
E-mail: execadmin@owuscholarship.org

OUTRIGGER DUKE KAHANAMOKU FOUNDATION

http://www.dukefoundation.org

ODKF GENERAL SCHOLARSHIP AWARD
• *See page 657*

PANHELLENIC SCHOLARSHIP FOUNDATION

https://www.panhellenicsf.org/

PANHELLENIC SCHOLARSHIP AWARDS
• *See page 657*

PAPERCHECK

https://www.papercheck.com/

PAPERCHECK, LLC—CHARLES SHAFAE' SCHOLARSHIP FUND
• *See page 657*

PARIAN LAW FIRM, LLC

https://westgalawyer.com/

THE EDUCATIONAL JUSTICE SCHOLARSHIP
• *See page 658*

PEACOCK PRODUCTIONS, INC.

http://amefund.com

AUDRIA M. EDWARDS SCHOLARSHIP FUND
• *See page 658*

PENNSYLVANIA FEDERATION OF DEMOCRATIC WOMEN INC.

http://www.pafedofdemwomen.org

PENNSYLVANIA FEDERATION OF DEMOCRATIC WOMEN INC. ANNUAL SCHOLARSHIP AWARDS
• *See page 574*

PENNSYLVANIA HIGHER EDUCATION ASSISTANCE AGENCY

http://www.pheaa.org/

BLIND OR DEAF BENEFICIARY GRANT PROGRAM
• *See page 658*

PENNSYLVANIA STATE GRANT PROGRAM
• *See page 658*

PETAZI

https://petazi.com/

NURTURE FOR NATURE SCHOLARSHIP
• *See page 692*

PETER AND ALICE KOOMRUIAN FUND

PETER AND ALICE KOOMRUIAN ARMENIAN EDUCATION FUND

Award for students of Armenian descent to pursue postsecondary studies in any field at any accredited college or university in the U.S. Submit student identification and letter of enrollment. Must rank in upper third of class or have minimum GPA of 3.0.

Award: Scholarship for use in freshman, sophomore, junior, senior, or graduate years; not renewable. *Number:* 4–10. *Amount:* $1000–$5000.

Eligibility Requirements: Applicant must be Armenian citizen and enrolled or expecting to enroll full-time at a two-year or four-year institution or university. Applicant must have 3.0 GPA or higher. Available to U.S. and non-U.S. citizens.

Application Requirements: Application form, personal photograph. *Deadline:* April 30.

Contact: Mr. Terenik Koujakian, Awards Committee Member
Peter and Alice Koomruian Fund
16654 1/2 Calneva Drive
Encino, CA 91436
Phone: 818-990-7454
E-mail: terenikkoujakian@hotmail.com

PETER DOCTOR MEMORIAL INDIAN SCHOLARSHIP FOUNDATION INC.

PETER DOCTOR MEMORIAL INDIAN SCHOLARSHIP FOUNDATION INC.

One-time award available to enrolled New York State Iroquois Indian students. Must be a full-time student at the Freshman level and above.

Award: Scholarship for use in freshman, sophomore, junior, senior, or graduate years; not renewable. *Number:* 2. *Amount:* $700–$1500.

Eligibility Requirements: Applicant must be American Indian/Alaska Native; enrolled or expecting to enroll full-time at a two-year or four-year or technical institution or university and resident of New York. Available to U.S. citizens.

Application Requirements: Application form, driver's license, financial need analysis, recommendations or references, tribal certification. *Deadline:* May 31.

Contact: Clara Hill, Treasurer
Peter Doctor Memorial Indian Scholarship Foundation Inc.
PO Box 431
Basom, NY 14013
Phone: 716-542-2025
E-mail: ceh3936@hughes.net

PET LIFESTYLE AND YOU (P.L.A.Y.)

https://www.petplay.com/

SCHOLARS HELPING COLLARS SCHOLARSHIP

• *See page 659*

PHILIPINO-AMERICAN ASSOCIATION OF NEW ENGLAND

http://www.pamas.org/

BLESSED LEON OF OUR LADY OF THE ROSARY AWARD

Award for any Filipino-American high school student. Must be of Filipino descent, and have a minimum GPA of 3.3. Application details are available at http://www.pamas.org.

Award: Scholarship for use in freshman year; not renewable. *Number:* 1. *Amount:* $250.

Eligibility Requirements: Applicant must be Asian/Pacific Islander; high school student; planning to enroll or expecting to enroll full-time at a two-year or four-year or technical institution or university and resident of Connecticut, Maine, Massachusetts, New Hampshire, Rhode Island, Vermont. Available to U.S. citizens.

Application Requirements: Application form, college acceptance letter, essay, recommendations or references, transcript. *Deadline:* May 31.

Contact: Amanda Kalb, First Vice President
Phone: 617-471-3513
E-mail: balic2ss@comcast.net

PAMAS RESTRICTED SCHOLARSHIP AWARD

• *See page 574*

RAVENSCROFT FAMILY AWARD

Award for any Filipino-American high school student, who is active in the Filipino community. Must be of Filipino descent, a resident of New England, and have a minimum GPA of 3.3. Application details are available at http://www.pamas.org.

Award: Scholarship for use in freshman year; not renewable. *Number:* 1. *Amount:* $250.

Eligibility Requirements: Applicant must be Asian/Pacific Islander; high school student; planning to enroll or expecting to enroll full-time at a four-year institution or university and resident of Connecticut, Maine, Massachusetts, New Hampshire, Rhode Island, Vermont. Available to U.S. citizens.

Application Requirements: Application form, college acceptance letter, essay, recommendations or references, transcript. *Deadline:* May 31.

Contact: Amanda Kalb, First Vice President
Phone: 617-471-3513
E-mail: balic2ss@comcast.net

PHOENIX PRIDE

https://phoenixpride.org/

PHOENIX PRIDE SCHOLARSHIP PROGRAM

• *See page 659*

PILOT INTERNATIONAL

https://www.pilotinternational.org/

BECKY BURROWS MEMORIAL SCHOLARSHIP

• *See page 659*

KC INTERNATIONAL SCHOLARSHIP

• *See page 659*

RUBY NEWHALL MEMORIAL SCHOLARSHIP

• *See page 659*

PINE CONE FOUNDATION (PCF)

http://pineconefoundation.org/

PINE CONE FOUNDATION SCHOLARSHIP

• *See page 660*

PLAINTIFF RELIEF

http://plaintiffrelief.com/

PLAINTIFF RELIEF SCHOLARSHIP

• *See page 660*

POLISH HERITAGE ASSOCIATION OF MARYLAND

http://www.pha-md.org/

POLISH HERITAGE SCHOLARSHIP

$2500 scholarships given to individuals of Polish descent (at least two Polish grandparents) who demonstrates academic excellence, financial need, and promotes their Polish Heritage. Must be a legal Maryland resident.

Award: Scholarship for use in freshman, sophomore, junior, or senior years; not renewable. *Number:* 1–9. *Amount:* $1500–$2500.

Eligibility Requirements: Applicant must be of Polish heritage; enrolled or expecting to enroll full-time at a two-year or four-year institution or university and resident of Maryland. Available to U.S. citizens.

Application Requirements: Application form, essay, financial need analysis, interview, recommendations or references, transcript. *Deadline:* March 15.

Contact: Thomas Hollowak, Scholarship Chair
Phone: 410-837-4268
E-mail: thollowalk@ubmail.ubalt.edu

POLISH WOMEN'S ALLIANCE

http://www.pwaa.org/

POLISH WOMEN'S ALLIANCE ACADEMIC COLLEGE UNDERGRADUATE SCHOLARSHIPS

Scholarships are given to members of the Polish Women's Alliance of America who have been in good standing for five years. Awards are given for the sophomore, junior, and senior year level of undergraduate study. For details visit website http://www.pwaa.org.

Award: Scholarship for use in sophomore, junior, or senior years; renewable. *Number:* 5. *Amount:* $1000.

Eligibility Requirements: Applicant must be of Polish heritage and enrolled or expecting to enroll full-time at a four-year institution or university. Available to U.S. citizens.

Application Requirements: Application form, essay, personal photograph, transcript. *Deadline:* May 15.

Contact: Sharon Zago, Vice President and Scholarship Chairman
Phone: 847-384-1208
E-mail: vpres@pwaa.org

POLSON AND POLSON, P.C.

https://www.polsonlawfirm.com/

POLSON & POLSON, P.C. CONQUERING ADVERSITY SCHOLARSHIP

* *See page 660*

PORTUGUESE AMERICAN LEADERSHIP COUNCIL OF THE UNITED STATES

http://www.palcus.org

PALCUS NATIONAL SCHOLARSHIP PROGRAM

* *See page 660*

POTENTIAL MAGAZINE

http://potentialmagazine.com/

COUNTDOWN TO COLLEGE SCHOLARSHIP

* *See page 661*

"DON'T WAIT TO REACH YOUR POTENTIAL" SCHOLARSHIP

* *See page 661*

PRESBYTERIAN CHURCH (USA)

http://www.pcusa.org/financialaid

NATIVE AMERICAN SUPPLEMENTAL GRANT

Award for Undergrad students who are registered Members of a Native American Tribe. Students must be members of a PC(USA) church.

Award: Grant for use in freshman, sophomore, junior, or senior years; not renewable.

Eligibility Requirements: Applicant must be Presbyterian; American Indian/Alaska Native and enrolled or expecting to enroll full-time at a four-year institution or university. Available to U.S. citizens.

Application Requirements: Application form. *Deadline:* June 1.

Contact: Ms. Laura Bryan, Coordinator, Financial Aid for Studies
Presbyterian Church (USA)
100 Witherspoon Street
Louisville, KY 40202
Phone: 800-728-7228 Ext. 5735
Fax: 502-569-8766
E-mail: finaid@pcusa.org

PRICE BENOWITZ LLP

http://pricebenowitz.com/

AMATO SANITA BRIGHTER FUTURE SCHOLARSHIP

* *See page 661*

ANGIE DIPIETRO WOMEN IN BUSINESS SCHOLARSHIP

* *See page 661*

KAREN RILEY PORTER GOOD WORKS SCHOLARSHIP

* *See page 661*

KERRI CASTELLINI WOMEN'S LEADERSHIP SCHOLARSHIP

* *See page 661*

KUSH ARORA FEDERAL CRIMINAL JUSTICE REFORM SCHOLARSHIP

* *See page 661*

NATALIA SEGERMEISTER DREAM ACT SCHOLARSHIP

* *See page 662*

PRICE BENOWITZ MAKE A DIFFERENCE SCHOLARSHIP

* *See page 662*

PRICE BENOWITZ SOCIAL JUSTICE SCHOLARSHIP

* *See page 662*

SETH OKIN GOOD DEEDS SCHOLARSHIP

* *See page 662*

STEVE DUCKETT CONSERVATION SCHOLARSHIP

As a dedicated local attorney and an active member of Ducks Unlimited, Steve Duckett is an outspoken proponent of conservation initiatives throughout the country. He believes that it is our responsibility as American citizens to be active stewards of the land that we inherited from our forefathers. To learn more, visit https://www.virginiacriminallaws.com/#scholarship.

Award: Scholarship for use in freshman, sophomore, junior, senior, or graduate years; not renewable. *Number:* 1. *Amount:* $500.

Eligibility Requirements: Applicant must be enrolled or expecting to enroll full- or part-time at a two-year or four-year or technical institution or university. Applicant must have 3.0 GPA or higher. Available to U.S. citizens.

Application Requirements: Essay. *Deadline:* September 30.

Contact: Steve Duckett
E-mail: info@virginiacriminallaws.com

THOMAS SOLDAN HEALTHY COMMUNITIES SCHOLARSHIP

* *See page 662*

PRIDE FOUNDATION

http://www.PrideFoundation.org/

PRIDE FOUNDATION SCHOLARSHIP PROGRAM

* *See page 662*

PROMOCODESFORYOU.COM

https://www.promocodesforyou.com

PROMOCODESFORYOU.COM STUDENT SAVINGS SCHOLARSHIP

* *See page 662*

PROMPT

http://prompt.com

PROMPT'S $20,000 SCHOLARSHIP

* *See page 663*

PUEBLO OF ISLETA, DEPARTMENT OF EDUCATION

http://www.isletapueblo.com/

HIGHER EDUCATION SUPPLEMENTAL SCHOLARSHIP ISLETA PUEBLO HIGHER EDUCATION DEPARTMENT

* *See page 576*

PUEBLO OF SAN JUAN, DEPARTMENT OF EDUCATION

OHKAY OWINGEH TRIBAL SCHOLARSHIP OF THE PUEBLO OF SAN JUAN

* *See page 663*

POP'AY SCHOLARSHIP
• *See page 663*

QUALITY FORMATIONS LTD.
https://www.qualitycompanyformations.co.uk/

QUALITY COMPANY FORMATIONS SCHOLARSHIP
• *See page 663*

RAILROAD PASSENGERS ASSOCIATION
https://www.narprail.org/

RAILROAD PASSENGERS ASSOCIATION SCHOLARSHIP
• *See page 663*

REACH HIGHER MONTANA
http://www.ReachHigherMontana.org

REACH HIGHER MONTANA SCHOLARSHIPS
• *See page 663*

REHABCENTER.NET
http://www.rehabcenter.net/

REHABCENTER.NET
• *See page 664*

RHINE LAW FIRM, P.C.
https://www.carolinaaccidentattorneys.com/

STRIVE FOR EXCELLENCE SCHOLARSHIP 2018
• *See page 664*

RISK MANAGEMENT ASSOCIATION FOUNDATION
http://www.scholarshipamerica.org

THE RISK MANAGEMENT ASSOCIATION FOUNDATION SCHOLARSHIP PROGRAM
• *See page 664*

RJT CRIMINAL DEFENSE
http://www.sandiegocriminallawyerrt.com/

AUTISM SCHOLARSHIP
• *See page 664*

ROMAN CATHOLIC DIOCESE OF TULSA
http://www.dioceseoftulsa.org

MAE LASSLEY OSAGE SCHOLARSHIP
This scholarship fund gives the Catholic Church an opportunity to continue it's educational work with the Osage Tribe.

Award: Scholarship for use in freshman, sophomore, junior, senior, or graduate years; renewable. *Amount:* $500–$1000.

Eligibility Requirements: Applicant must be Roman Catholic; American Indian/Alaska Native and enrolled or expecting to enroll full-time at a two-year or four-year institution or university. Applicant must have 2.5 GPA or higher. Available to U.S. citizens.

Application Requirements: Application form, financial need analysis. *Deadline:* April 15.

Contact: Mrs. Sarah Jameson, Director, Youth, Young Adult and
   Campus Ministry
   Roman Catholic Diocese of Tulsa
   Roman Catholic Diocese of Tulsa
   PO Box 690240
   Tulsa, OK 74169-0240
   Phone: 918-307-4939
   E-mail: sarah.jameson@dioceseoftulsa.org

RON BROWN SCHOLAR FUND
http://www.ronbrown.org/

RON BROWN SCHOLAR PROGRAM
• *See page 665*

ROVER.COM
https://www.rover.com/

ROVER SITTER SCHOLARSHIP CONTEST
• *See page 665*

RYU FAMILY FOUNDATION, INC.

SEOL BONG SCHOLARSHIP
• *See page 693*

SACHS FOUNDATION
http://www.sachsfoundation.org/

SACHS FOUNDATION SCHOLARSHIPS
Award to undergraduate students based on performance, financial need, and applicant's area of study and life goals. Must be African-American and a resident of Colorado for five or more years. Minimum 3.0 GPA required to apply.

Award: Scholarship for use in freshman year; renewable. *Number:* 50. *Amount:* $6000.

Eligibility Requirements: Applicant must be Black (non-Hispanic); high school student; planning to enroll or expecting to enroll full-time at a two-year or four-year institution or university and resident of Colorado. Applicant must have 3.0 GPA or higher. Available to U.S. citizens.

Application Requirements: Application form, autobiography, essay, financial need analysis, interview, personal photograph. *Deadline:* March 15.

Contact: Lisa Harris, Secretary and Treasurer
   Phone: 719-633-2353
   E-mail: lisa@sachsfoundation.org

SAINT ANDREW'S SOCIETY OF THE STATE OF NEW YORK
http://www.standrewsny.org/

ST. ANDREWS SCHOLARSHIP
Scholarship for senior undergraduate students who will obtain a Bachelor's degree from an accredited college or university in the spring and can demonstrate the significance of studying in Scotland. Proof of application to their selected school will be required for finalists. Applicant must be of Scottish descent.

Award: Scholarship for use in senior year; not renewable. *Number:* 2. *Amount:* $20,000–$30,000.

Eligibility Requirements: Applicant must be of Scottish heritage and enrolled or expecting to enroll full-time at a four-year institution or university. Applicant must have 2.5 GPA or higher. Available to U.S. citizens.

Application Requirements: Application form. *Deadline:* December 15.

Contact: Brigid Tucker, Director of Operations
   Phone: 212-223-4248
   Fax: 212-223-0748
   E-mail: office@standrewsny.org

ST. ANDREW'S SOCIETY OF WASHINGTON, DC

http://www.saintandrewsociety.org/

ST. ANDREW'S SOCIETY OF WASHINGTON DC FOUNDERS' SCHOLARSHIP
• *See page 665*

ST. ANDREW'S SOCIETY OF WASHINGTON DC SCHOLARSHIPS
• *See page 665*

SALUTE TO EDUCATION, INC.

http://www.stescholarships.org/

SALUTE TO EDUCATION SCHOLARSHIP
• *See page 666*

SALVADORAN AMERICAN LEADERSHIP AND EDUCATIONAL FUND

http://www.salef.org/

FULFILLING OUR DREAMS SCHOLARSHIP FUND
Up to 60 scholarships ranging from $500 to $2500 will be awarded to students who come from a Latino heritage. Must have a 2.5 GPA. See website for more details, http://www.salef.org.

Award: Scholarship for use in freshman, sophomore, junior, senior, graduate, or postgraduate years; not renewable. *Number:* 50–60. *Amount:* $500–$2500.

Eligibility Requirements: Applicant must be of Hispanic, Latin American/Caribbean heritage; enrolled or expecting to enroll full- or part-time at a two-year or four-year institution or university; resident of California and studying in California. Applicant must have 2.5 GPA or higher. Available to U.S. and non-U.S. citizens.

Application Requirements: Application form, community service, essay, financial need analysis, interview, personal photograph, recommendations or references, resume, self-addressed stamped envelope with application, test scores, transcript. *Deadline:* June 30.

Contact: Mayra Soriano, Educational and Youth Programs Manager
Salvadoran American Leadership and Educational Fund
1625 West Olympic Boulevard, Suite 718
Los Angeles, CA 90015
Phone: 213-480-1052
Fax: 213-487-2530
E-mail: msoriano@salef.org

SANTO DOMINGO SCHOLARSHIP PROGRAM

SANTO DOMINGO SCHOLARSHIP
An organization instituted for the welfare of the Santo Domingo Pueblo enrolled members. Santo Domingo Tribe—Education Office offers scholarships in Higher Education and Adult Education. To be considered an applicant, you must fill out an application. Deadlines: Fall semester—March 1 and Spring semester—October 1.

Award: Scholarship for use in freshman, sophomore, junior, or senior years; renewable. *Amount:* $200–$1000.

Eligibility Requirements: Applicant must be American Indian/Alaska Native and enrolled or expecting to enroll full- or part-time at a two-year or four-year or technical institution or university. Applicant must have 2.5 GPA or higher. Available to U.S. citizens.

Application Requirements: Application form, certificate of Indian blood, financial need analysis, recommendations or references, transcript. *Deadline:* varies.

Contact: Rita Lujan, Education Director
Santo Domingo Scholarship Program
PO Box 160
Santo Domingo Pueblo, NM 87052
Phone: 505-465-2214 Ext. 2211
Fax: 505-465-2542
E-mail: rlujan@kewa-nsn.us

SCHOLAR SERVE

https://www.scholarserve.org

SCHOLAR SERVE AWARDS
• *See page 666*

SCHOLARSHIP AMERICA

https://www.abbvieImmunologyScholarship.com/

ABBVIE IMMUNOLOGY SCHOLARSHIP
• *See page 666*

SELECTBLINDS.COM

http://www.selectblinds.com

SELECTBLINDS.COM $1000 COLLEGE SCHOLARSHIP
• *See page 666*

SEXNER & ASSOCIATES LLC

http://www.sexner.com/personal-injury/

MITCHELL S. SEXNER & ASSOCIATES LLC SCHOLARSHIP
• *See page 667*

SHAWN SUKUMAR ATTORNEY AT LAW

https://www.washingtondccriminallawyer.net/

SHAWN SUKUMAR CRIMINAL JUSTICE REFORM SCHOLARSHIP
• *See page 667*

SHELVING.COM

http://www.shelving.com/

SHELVING.COM BUSINESS SCHOLARSHIP
• *See page 667*

SILICON VALLEY COMMUNITY FOUNDATION

http://www.siliconvalleycf.org

ABBY SOBRATO SCHOLARSHIP
• *See page 667*

BOBETTE BIBO GUGLIOTTA MEMORIAL SCHOLARSHIP FOR CREATIVE WRITING
• *See page 667*

CURRY AWARD FOR GIRLS AND YOUNG WOMEN
• *See page 667*

CYNTHIA H. KUO SCHOLARSHIP
The Cynthia H. Kuo scholarship fund was established in loving memory of Cynthia by her husband, Dale Chen and best friend, Elisa Yu. Cynthia was always passionate about caring for people. She especially liked being part of a big Christian family, and helping people in need from time to time. Before her passing, she organized a Christian fellowship program to

support young overseas Chinese students studying in the Bay Area seeking to worship God in the local Christian community. In order to honor Cynthia and fulfill her wishes, her friends and family established this scholarship for Chinese students actively involved in the Christian faith and/or Christian youth groups in June 2012. Must be a Chinese student who is either first-generation in the U.S. or born overseas, planning to attend a four-year college in the U.S. on a full-time basis; actively involved in the Christian faith or Christian youth group for the last two years; graduating high school senior or current college student with a minimum grade point average of 3.0 on a 4.0 scale; and have demonstrated financial need.

Award: Scholarship for use in freshman, sophomore, junior, or senior years; not renewable. *Number:* 1–5. *Amount:* $1000–$5000.

Eligibility Requirements: Applicant must be Christian; of Chinese heritage; Asian/Pacific Islander and enrolled or expecting to enroll full-time at a four-year institution or university. Applicant must have 3.0 GPA or higher. Available to U.S. and non-U.S. citizens.

Application Requirements: Application form. *Deadline:* March 17.

Contact: Scholarships Team
Silicon Valley Community Foundation
2440 West El Camino Real
Suite 300
Mountain View, CA 94040
Phone: 650-450-5487
E-mail: scholarships@siliconvalleycf.org

HAZEL REED BAUMEISTER SCHOLARSHIP PROGRAM
• *See page 668*

HUANG LEADERSHIP DEVELOPMENT SCHOLARSHIP
• *See page 668*

LATINOS IN TECHNOLOGY SCHOLARSHIP

The Latinos in Technology Scholarship was established by the Hispanic Foundation of Silicon Valley, a public foundation dedicated to inspiring community philanthropy and engaging people to invest in the educational achievement and leadership development of a thriving Hispanic community in Silicon Valley. This program will give up to 100 Latino students the support they need to graduate from college; an educational opportunity they would not have access to otherwise. Additionally, scholarship recipients will be considered for summer internships with sponsoring corporate investors. By implementing this program in Silicon Valley, HFSV will be able to directly address the local education gap among Latinos as well as begin to close the high tech employment diversity gap. Must be of Latino or Hispanic origin (as defined by U.S. Census Bureau) and have a declared major in and been accepted into a STEM program. Must be a current college student entering their junior or senior year in the 2018 academic school year and planning to enroll on a full-time or part-time basis. Preference will be given to full-time and rising junior students. Must be a graduate of a high school in the following Northern California counties: Alameda County, Contra Costa County, Marin County, Napa County, San Francisco County, San Mateo County, Santa Clara County, Santa Cruz County, Solano County, Sonoma County and Yolo County; or a graduate of a high school not in the above counties, but enrolled at a college/university within the 11 listed counties. Minimum cumulative college grade point average of 2.5. Must have demonstrated financial need and be a United States citizen or eligible non-citizen (eligible non-citizens include United States legal residents and students who have obtained Deferred Action for Childhood Arrivals).

Award: Scholarship for use in junior or senior years; renewable. *Number:* 60–100. *Amount:* $1000–$30,000.

Eligibility Requirements: Applicant must be of Hispanic, Mexican heritage; enrolled or expecting to enroll full- or part-time at a four-year institution or university and resident of California. Applicant must have 2.5 GPA or higher. Available to U.S. and non-Canadian citizens.

Application Requirements: Application form, essay, financial need analysis. *Deadline:* September 20.

Contact: Scholarships Team
Silicon Valley Community Foundation
2440 West El Camino Real
Suite 300
Mountain View, CA 94040
Phone: 650-450-5487
E-mail: scholarships@siliconvalleycf.org

TANG SCHOLARSHIP

Mr. Edward C. Tang established this award in 2007 to provide financial assistance to gay, lesbian, bisexual and transgender (g/l/b/t) Asian and Pacific Islanders (API) for post-secondary education. This scholarship is to help GLBT youth proudly achieve educational pursuits and dreams without shame. This scholarship awards up to four outstanding students annually, a scholarship of up to $15,000. These scholarships are renewable for a maximum of three additional years (for a total of four years), provided each student annually meets the renewal requirements. Must be self-identified as Asian/Pacific Islander (at least 25 percent Asian/Pacific Islander ancestry), lesbian, gay, bisexual or transgender and involved in the LGBT community; a graduate of a high school in one of the nine Bay Area counties: Alameda, Contra Costa, Marin, San Francisco, San Mateo, Santa Clara, Napa, Sonoma or Solano; a full-time (minimum 12 units for all semesters/quarters) enrollment in an accredited two- or four-year college, community college, university, graduate school or vocational school; a minimum GPA of 3.0 on a scale of 4.0; a demonstrated academic promise; a demonstrated financial hardship; and a United States citizen or legal resident between the ages of 17 and 25 on or before April 30, 2018.

Award: Scholarship for use in freshman, sophomore, junior, senior, or graduate years; renewable. *Number:* 1–4. *Amount:* $1000–$60,000.

Eligibility Requirements: Applicant must be Asian/Pacific Islander; age 17-25; enrolled or expecting to enroll full-time at a two-year or four-year or technical institution or university; resident of California and must have an interest in LGBT issues. Applicant must have 3.0 GPA or higher. Available to U.S. and non-U.S. citizens.

Application Requirements: Application form, essay, financial need analysis, interview. *Deadline:* April 30.

Contact: Scholarships Team
Silicon Valley Community Foundation
2440 West El Camino Real
Suite 300
Mountain View, CA 94040
Phone: 650-450-5487
E-mail: scholarships@siliconvalleycf.org

SIMMONS AND FLETCHER, P.C.

https://www.simmonsandfletcher.com/

SIMMONS AND FLETCHER, P.C., LAW MARKETING SCHOLARSHIP
• *See page 668*

SNOW, CARPIO & WEEKLEY, PLC

http://workinjuryaz.com

SCW DREAMERS SCHOLARSHIP

Must be a DREAMer with a GPA of 3.0 or higher. This is a video submission scholarship. For all requirements and more info please visit our website http://workinjuryaz.com/tucson-social-security-disability-attorneys/#dreamers. Only submissions on our website will be considered.

Award: Scholarship for use in freshman or sophomore years; not renewable. *Number:* 2. *Amount:* $2500.

Eligibility Requirements: Applicant must be of Hispanic heritage; age 16-25 and enrolled or expecting to enroll full- or part-time at a two-year or four-year institution or university. Applicant must have 3.0 GPA or higher. Available to U.S. and non-U.S. citizens.

Application Requirements: Application form. *Deadline:* May 31.

Contact: April Snow
E-mail: snowcarpioaz@gmail.com

SOCIETY FOR APPLIED ANTHROPOLOGY

http://www.sfaa.net/

ANNUAL SFAA STUDENT ENDOWED AWARD
• *See page 668*

BEATRICE MEDICINE AWARDS

The Society for Applied Anthropology honors the memory of Dr. Beatrice Medicine with an annual student travel scholarship for Native

Americans/First Nations. The scholarship provides financial support for two students (graduate or undergraduate) to attend the annual meeting of the Society. Two awards ($500 each) will be made to attend the Annual Meeting of the SfAA.

Award: Prize for use in freshman, sophomore, junior, senior, or graduate years; not renewable. *Number:* 2. *Amount:* $500.

Eligibility Requirements: Applicant must be American Indian/Alaska Native and enrolled or expecting to enroll full- or part-time at a two-year or four-year institution or university. Available to U.S. and non-U.S. citizens.

Application Requirements: Application form, essay. *Deadline:* December 20.

Contact: Trish Colvin, Office Manager
Society for Applied Anthropology
PO Box 2436
Oklahoma City, OK 73101
Phone: 405-843-5113
Fax: 405-843-8553
E-mail: info@sfaa.net

SOCIETY OF DAUGHTERS OF THE UNITED STATES ARMY

SOCIETY OF DAUGHTERS OF THE UNITED STATES ARMY SCHOLARSHIPS
• *See page 669*

SONS OF ITALY FOUNDATION
http://www.osia.org/sif

GENERAL STUDY SCHOLARSHIPS
• *See page 669*

HENRY SALVATORI SCHOLARSHIP FOR GENERAL STUDY
• *See page 669*

SONS OF ITALY FOUNDATION'S NATIONAL LEADERSHIP GRANT COMPETITION
Scholarships for undergraduate or graduate students who are U.S. citizens of Italian descent. Must demonstrate academic excellence. For more details see Website, http://www.osia.org.

Award: Scholarship for use in freshman, sophomore, junior, senior, or graduate years; not renewable. *Number:* 9–10. *Amount:* $4000–$10,000.

Eligibility Requirements: Applicant must be of Italian heritage and enrolled or expecting to enroll full-time at a four-year institution or university. Available to U.S. citizens.

Application Requirements: Application form, community service, essay, recommendations or references, resume, test scores, transcript. *Fee:* $30. *Deadline:* February 28.

Contact: Ms. Laura Kelly
Phone: 202-547-2900
Fax: 202-546-8168
E-mail: scholarships@osia.org

SONS OF ITALY NATIONAL LEADERSHIP GRANTS COMPETITION/ HENRY SALVATORI SCHOLARSHIP
Scholarships for college-bound high school seniors who demonstrate exceptional leadership, distinguished scholarship, and a deep understanding and respect for the principles upon which our nation was founded: liberty, freedom, and equality. Must be a U.S. citizen of Italian descent. For more details see website http://www.osia.org.

Award: Scholarship for use in freshman year; not renewable. *Number:* up to 1. *Amount:* up to $5000.

Eligibility Requirements: Applicant must be of Italian heritage; high school student and planning to enroll or expecting to enroll full-time at a four-year institution or university. Available to U.S. citizens.

Application Requirements: Application form, community service, essay, recommendations or references, resume, test scores, transcript. *Fee:* $30. *Deadline:* February 27.

Contact: Ms. Laura Kelly
Phone: 202-547-2900
Fax: 202-546-8168
E-mail: scholarships@osia.org

SOUND MONEY DEFENSE LEAGUE
http://soundmoneydefense.org

MONEY METALS EXCHANGE SCHOLARSHIP PROGRAM
• *See page 669*

SOURCE SUPPLY COMPANY
http://sourcesupplycompany.com/

SOURCE SUPPLY SCHOLARSHIP
To apply for the 2014-2015 Source Supply Scholarship, respond to the following essay prompt in 1,000 words: Please discuss the importance of keeping the environment clean. How does recycling make an impact on the environment? And how can the systems we, as a nation, have in place be improved? To be eligible, please email your essay to info@sourcesupplycompany.com by May 31, 2015. Please be sure to reference Source Supply College Scholarship Essay Content in the subject line of your email.

Award: Scholarship for use in freshman, sophomore, or junior years; not renewable. *Number:* up to 1. *Amount:* $1000–$1000.

Eligibility Requirements: Applicant must be American Indian/Alaska Native, Asian/Pacific Islander, Black (non-Hispanic), Hispanic and enrolled or expecting to enroll full-time at a two-year or four-year or technical institution or university. Available to U.S. citizens.

Application Requirements: Entry in a contest, essay. *Deadline:* May 31.

Contact: Dave Brown, Owner
Source Supply Company
6 Bellecor Drive
Suite 104
New Castle, PA 19720
Phone: 302-328-5110
E-mail: Info@SourceSupplyCompany.com

SOUTH CAROLINA TUITION GRANTS COMMISSION
http://www.sctuitiongrants.org/

SOUTH CAROLINA TUITION GRANTS PROGRAM
• *See page 669*

SPINE SURGEON DR. VICTOR HAYES
https://tampabaybackpaindoctor.com/

TAMPA BAY SPINE CENTER ROAD TO RECOVERY SCHOLARSHIP
• *See page 670*

STATE EMPLOYEES ASSOCIATION OF NORTH CAROLINA (SEANC)
http://www.seanc.org/

STATE EMPLOYEES ASSOCIATION OF NORTH CAROLINA (SEANC) SCHOLARSHIPS
Scholarships available to SEANC members, their spouses and dependents seeking postsecondary education. Awarded in three categories: based on academic merit, financial need, and awards for SEANC members only. For application and more information visit http://www.seanc.org/.

Award: Scholarship for use in freshman, sophomore, junior, or senior years; not renewable. *Number:* 47. *Amount:* $500–$1000.

Eligibility Requirements: Applicant must be enrolled or expecting to enroll full-time at a two-year or four-year or technical institution or

university and resident of North Carolina. Applicant must have 3.5 GPA or higher. Available to U.S. citizens.

Application Requirements: Application form, financial need analysis. *Deadline:* April 15.

Contact: Renee Vaughan
Phone: 919-833-6436

STEALTHY AND WEALTHY

http://stealthyandwealthy.com

STEALTHY AND WEALTHY STUDENT ENTREPRENEUR GRANT
• *See page 670*

STEINBERG, GOODMAN AND KALISH

https://www.sgklawyers.com/

STEINBERG, GOODMAN AND KALISH SCHOLARSHIP
• *See page 670*

STONEWALL COMMUNITY FOUNDATION

http://www.stonewallfoundation.org/

TRAUB-DICKER RAINBOW SCHOLARSHIP
• *See page 670*

STRAIGHTFORWARD MEDIA

http://www.straightforwardmedia.com/

STRAIGHTFORWARD MEDIA MINORITY SCHOLARSHIP

Four scholarships a year offered to students who are members of racial or ethnic minority groups and who are currently enrolled in or planning to enroll in postsecondary education. For more information, see website at http://www.straightforwardmedia.com/minority/form.php.

Award: Scholarship for use in freshman, sophomore, junior, or senior years; not renewable. *Number:* 4. *Amount:* $500.

Eligibility Requirements: Applicant must be American Indian/Alaska Native, Asian/Pacific Islander, Black (non-Hispanic), Hispanic and enrolled or expecting to enroll full- or part-time at a two-year or four-year or technical institution or university. Available to U.S. and non-U.S. citizens.

Application Requirements: Essay. *Deadline:* varies.

Contact: Scholarship Committee
Phone: 605-348-3042

STROLLER DEPOT

https://www.strollerdepot.com/

$1,000 STROLLER DEPOT SCHOLARSHIP
• *See page 670*

STROM & ASSOCIATES

https://stromlawyers.com

STROM & ASSOCIATES ANNUAL SCHOLARSHIP
• *See page 671*

STUDY.COM

study.com

ARMY ROTC STUDY.COM SCHOLARSHIP
• *See page 671*

STUDY.COM CLEP SCHOLARSHIP
• *See page 671*

STUDY.COM SCHOLARSHIP FOR FLORIDA STUDENTS
• *See page 671*

STUDY.COM SCHOLARSHIP FOR TEXAS STUDENTS
• *See page 671*

SWISS BENEVOLENT SOCIETY

http://www.sbssf.com/

SWISS BENEVOLENT SOCIETY OF SAN FRANCISCO SCHOLARSHIPS

The Swiss Benevolent Society helps qualified applicants obtain a higher education in any field of endeavor at any accredited university or college in the United States. The scholarships are limited to students who are residents of Northern California. Students may apply every year while enrolled. Applicants must be of Swiss descent by demonstrating that applicant or at least one parent is a Swiss national; must be registered with the Swiss Consulate General of San Francisco (or carry a valid Swiss passport); must have resided in Northern California for a minimum of three years preceding the date of initial application; must have applied for admission to any accredited institution of higher learning in the United States offering a Baccalaureate or graduate degree. (In exceptional cases, students attending a community college or an accredited vocational school in California may be considered); and must be a full time student, 12 undergraduate or 9 graduate units per term. Additional requirements regarding scholastic merit and financial need, as well as the application form and guidelines, are available on the SBSSF website. Only complete applications, including all supporting documents, postmarked no later than April 30th, can be considered.

Award: Scholarship for use in freshman, sophomore, junior, senior, graduate, or postgraduate years; renewable.

Eligibility Requirements: Applicant must be of Swiss heritage; enrolled or expecting to enroll full-time at a two-year or four-year or technical institution or university and resident of California. Applicant must have 2.5 GPA or higher.

Application Requirements: Application form, essay, financial need analysis. *Deadline:* April 30.

Contact: John Andrew, Scholarship Committee Chair
Swiss Benevolent Society
Pier 17, Suite 600
San Francisco, CA 94111
E-mail: scholarships@sbssf.com

SWISS BENEVOLENT SOCIETY OF CHICAGO

http://www.sbschicago.org/

SWISS BENEVOLENT SOCIETY OF CHICAGO SCHOLARSHIPS

Scholarship for undergraduate college students of Swiss descent, having permanent residence in Illinois or Southern Wisconsin. Must have 3.3 GPA. High school students need a 26 on ACT or 1050 on SAT.

Award: Scholarship for use in freshman, sophomore, or junior years; not renewable. *Number:* 30. *Amount:* $500–$2500.

Eligibility Requirements: Applicant must be of Swiss heritage; enrolled or expecting to enroll full-time at a four-year institution or university and resident of Illinois, Wisconsin. Available to U.S. citizens.

Application Requirements: Application form, essay. *Deadline:* April 15.

Contact: John Paluch, Chair
Swiss Benevolent Society of Chicago
PO Box 2137
Chicago, IL 60690-2137
Phone: 847-491-8081
E-mail: education@sbschicago.org

SWISS BENEVOLENT SOCIETY OF NEW YORK

http://www.sbsny.org/

MEDICUS STUDENT EXCHANGE

One-time award to students of Swiss nationality or parentage. Open to U.S. residents for study in Switzerland and to Swiss residents for study in the U.S. Must be proficient in foreign language of instruction.

Award: Grant for use in junior, senior, or graduate years; not renewable. *Number:* 1–10. *Amount:* $2000–$10,000.

Eligibility Requirements: Applicant must be of Swiss heritage; enrolled or expecting to enroll full-time at a four-year institution or university and must have an interest in foreign language. Applicant must have 2.5 GPA or higher. Available to U.S. and non-Canadian citizens.

Application Requirements: Application form. *Fee:* $75. *Deadline:* March 31.

Contact: Scholarship Committee
Swiss Benevolent Society of New York
500 Fifth Avenue, Suite 1800
New York, NY 10110
Phone: 212-246-0655

PELLEGRINI SCHOLARSHIP GRANTS

Award to students who have a minimum 3.0 GPA and show financial need. Must submit proof of Swiss nationality or descent. Must be a permanent resident of Connecticut, Delaware, New Jersey, New York, or Pennsylvania.

Award: Scholarship for use in freshman, sophomore, junior, senior, or graduate years; not renewable. *Number:* 50. *Amount:* $500–$5000.

Eligibility Requirements: Applicant must be of Swiss heritage; enrolled or expecting to enroll full-time at a two-year or four-year or technical institution or university and resident of Connecticut, Delaware, New Jersey, New York, Pennsylvania. Applicant must have 3.0 GPA or higher. Available to U.S. citizens.

Application Requirements: Application form, financial need analysis. *Fee:* $75. *Deadline:* March 31.

Contact: Scholarship Committee
Swiss Benevolent Society of New York
500 Fifth Avenue, Room 1800
New York, NY 10110
Phone: 212-246-0655

TECHNOSOFT INNOVATIONS, INC.

https://www.technosoftinv.com/

TECHNOSOFT INNOVATIONS SCHOLARSHIP PROGRAM

• See page 671

TELEVISION ACADEMY FOUNDATION

http://www.televisionacademy.com/foundation

TELEVISION ACADEMY FOUNDATION

• See page 671

TELIOS LAW PLLC

http://telioslaw.com

TELIOS LAW EXCELSIOR SCHOLARSHIP

The Telios Law Excelsior Scholarship application is open to any high school student or recent high school graduate who is a Colorado resident and will be enrolled full-time for the 2018-2019 school year as a freshman or sophomore at a college or university that has an emphasis on spiritual formation in the Christian faith. For complete information, please visit http://telioslaw.com/scholarships. Excelsior is a Latin word meaning "ever higher". It evokes the pursuit of excellence (think of the inspiring passages of Philippians 3:1-16 and 4:8) and is particularly fitting given the mountain regions of Colorado. Whether it be climbing a Fourteener, studying a 500-page treatise, writing a novel, creating a work of art, performing at a recital, or leading a team to victory, the desire to climb higher, think deeper, run faster, write better, or improve any other laudable skill is summed up in the phrase "ever higher". Telios Law believes that this desire to excel can be used as a gift to benefit and love those around us. Telios Law also believes that striving to excel simply and only for one's own sake is vanity. We seek to excel in the work we do while also encouraging and supporting that attitude in others with the Telios Law Excelsior Scholarship.

Award: Scholarship for use in freshman, sophomore, junior, or senior years; renewable. *Number:* 1. *Amount:* $1000.

Eligibility Requirements: Applicant must be enrolled or expecting to enroll full-time at a two-year or four-year institution or university and resident of Colorado.

Application Requirements: Application form, essay. *Deadline:* January 15.

Contact: Mr. Joshua Romero, Outreach Coordinator
Telios Law PLLC
P.O. Box 3488
Monument, CO 80132
Phone: 855-748-4201
E-mail: tell@telioslaw.com

TELIOS LAW SOJOURNER SCHOLARSHIP

The Telios Law Sojourner Scholarship application is open to any high school student or recent high school graduate who has spent three or more years of his or her life as a third-culture missionary kid and will be enrolled full-time for the 2018-2019 school year as a freshman or sophomore at a college or university that has an emphasis on spiritual formation in the Christian faith. For complete information, please visit http://telioslaw.com/scholarships. A sojourner lives between cultures, and this is often the experience of a third-culture missionary kid. For MKs, a key to transitioning back "home" is figuring out how to flourish in a new culture. Behind this struggle is the desire put into pop culture terms by singer and songwriter Adele, who wrote, "But I want to live / And not just survive." We all have a longing for what ancient Greek philosophers called eudaimonia, which roughly translates to "happiness, welfare, or human flourishing." Telios Law believes that we as humans were made to flourish, and we want to contribute to that flourishing, not only through doing our legal work well, but by helping MKs in particular pursue their flourishing as they transition back.

Award: Scholarship for use in freshman, sophomore, junior, or senior years; renewable. *Number:* 1. *Amount:* $1000.

Eligibility Requirements: Applicant must be enrolled or expecting to enroll full-time at a two-year or four-year institution or university.

Application Requirements: Application form, essay. *Deadline:* January 15.

Contact: Mr. Joshua Romero, Outreach Coordinator
Telios Law PLLC
P.O. Box 3488
Monument, CO 80132
Phone: 855-748-4201
E-mail: tell@telioslaw.com

TENNESSEE STUDENT ASSISTANCE CORPORATION

http://www.tn.gov/collegepays

DEPENDENT CHILDREN SCHOLARSHIP PROGRAM

• See page 672

HELPING HEROES GRANT

• See page 672

HOPE ASPIRE AWARD

• See page 672

NED MCWHERTER SCHOLARS PROGRAM

• See page 672

TELS -HOPE WITH GENERAL ASSEMBLY MERIT SCHOLARSHIP (GAMS)

• See page 672

TENNESSEE DUAL ENROLLMENT GRANT
• *See page 672*

TENNESSEE HOPE ACCESS GRANT
• *See page 673*

TENNESSEE HOPE FOSTER CHILD TUITION GRANT
• *See page 673*

TENNESSEE HOPE SCHOLARSHIP
• *See page 673*

TENNESSEE STUDENT ASSISTANCE AWARD
• *See page 673*

TERRY FOX HUMANITARIAN AWARD
http://terryfoxawards.ca/

TERRY FOX HUMANITARIAN AWARD
• *See page 673*

TETHERBOX
http://www.tetherbox.com/

$1,000 CREATIVE VIDEO CHALLENGE COLLEGE SCHOLARSHIP
• *See page 673*

TEXAS ASSOCIATION OF DEVELOPING COLLEGES
http://www.txadc.org

THE URBAN SCHOLARSHIPS FUND
• *See page 674*

TEXAS BLACK BAPTIST SCHOLARSHIP COMMITTEE
http://www.bgct.org/

TEXAS BLACK BAPTIST SCHOLARSHIP
Renewable award for Texas residents attending a Baptist educational institution in Texas. Must be of African-American descent with a minimum 2.0 GPA. Must be a member in good standing of a Baptist church.

Award: Scholarship for use in freshman, sophomore, junior, or senior years; renewable. *Amount:* $1600.

Eligibility Requirements: Applicant must be Baptist; Black (non-Hispanic); enrolled or expecting to enroll full- or part-time at a two-year or four-year institution or university; resident of Texas and studying in Texas. Available to U.S. citizens.

Application Requirements: Application form, driver's license, financial need analysis, interview, personal photograph, portfolio, recommendations or references, resume, test scores, transcript. *Deadline:* continuous.

Contact: Charlie Singleton, Director
　　　　Phone: 214-828-5130
　　　　Fax: 214-828-5284
　　　　E-mail: charlie.singleton@bgct.org

TEXAS MUTUAL INSURANCE COMPANY
http://www.texasmutual.com/

TEXAS MUTUAL INSURANCE COMPANY SCHOLARSHIP PROGRAM
• *See page 674*

THRIVENT STUDENT RESOURCES
https://www.thriventstudentresources.com/

THRIVENT STUDENT RESOURCES SCHOLARSHIP
• *See page 674*

TONALAW
https://www.tonalaw.com/

TONALAW VETERAN'S SCHOLARSHIP
• *See page 674*

TOPPRODUCTS.COM
http://topproducts.com/

TOPPRODUCTS SINGLE MOTHER SCHOLARSHIP
• *See page 675*

TORHOERMAN LAW LLC
http://torhoermanlaw.com

TORHOERMAN LAW DISTRACTED DRIVING ESSAY SCHOLARSHIP
• *See page 675*

TPA SCHOLARSHIP TRUST FOR THE HEARING IMPAIRED
https://www.tpahq.org/scholarshiptrust/

TPA SCHOLARSHIP TRUST FOR THE HEARING IMPAIRED
• *See page 675*

TRANSFER TIMES
http://www.transfertimes.com

TRANSFER TIMES $6,000 SCHOLARSHIP
• *See page 675*

TRANSTUTORS
http://www.transtutors.com/scholarship

TRANSTUTORS SCHOLARSHIP
• *See page 675*

TRAVELNURSESOURCE.COM
https://www.travelnursesource.com/

FUTURE U.S. NURSE SCHOLARSHIP
• *See page 676*

TROPHYCENTRAL INC.
https://www.trophycentral.com

TROPHYCENTRAL SPORTSMANSHIP AND COMPASSION SCHOLARSHIP AWARD
• *See page 676*

TURBOSQUID
https://www.turbosquid.com/

TURBOSQUID SPRING SCHOLARSHIP
• *See page 676*

UCB, INC.

http://www.ucb.com/

UCB FAMILY EPILEPSY SCHOLARSHIP
• *See page 677*

ULMAN CANCER FUND FOR YOUNG ADULTS

http://www.ulmanfund.org/scholarships

JACQUELINE SHEARER MEMORIAL SCHOLARSHIP
• *See page 677*

JAMIE L. ROBERTS MEMORIAL SCHOLARSHIP AWARD
• *See page 677*

JEFFREY P. MEYER MEMORIAL SCHOLARSHIP
• *See page 677*

JILL WEAVER STARKMAN SCHOLARSHIP
• *See page 677*

JOHN HANLEY MEMORIAL SCHOLARSHIP
• *See page 678*

LISA HIGGINS-HUSSMAN FOUNDATION SCHOLARSHIP
• *See page 678*

MARILYN YETSO MEMORIAL SCHOLARSHIP
• *See page 678*

OLIVIA M. MARQUART SCHOLARSHIP
• *See page 678*

PERLITA LIWANAG MEMORIAL SCHOLARSHIP
• *See page 678*

SATOLA FAMILY SCHOLARSHIP
• *See page 678*

SEAN SILVER MEMORIAL SCHOLARSHIP AWARD
• *See page 678*

VERA YIP MEMORIAL SCHOLARSHIP
• *See page 679*

VITTORIA DIANNA RICARDO MEMORIAL SCHOLARSHIP
• *See page 679*

UNICO FOUNDATION INC.

http://www.unico.org/

ALPHONSE A. MIELE SCHOLARSHIP
• *See page 679*

BERNARD AND CAROLYN TORRACO MEMORIAL NURSING SCHOLARSHIP PROGRAM
• *See page 679*

DIMATTIO CELLI FAMILY STUDY ABROAD SCHOLARSHIP
• *See page 679*

ELLA T. GRASSO LITERARY SCHOLARSHIP
• *See page 680*

GUGLIELMO MARCONI ENGINEERING SCHOLARSHIP
• *See page 680*

INSERRA SCHOLARSHIPS
• *See page 680*

MAJOR DON S. GENTILE SCHOLARSHIP
• *See page 680*

MARIA AND PAOLO ALESSIO SOUTHERN ITALY SCHOLARSHIP
• *See page 680*

RALPH J. TORRACO SCHOLARSHIP
• *See page 680*

THEODORE MAZZA SCHOLARSHIP
• *See page 681*

WILLIAM C. DAVINI SCHOLARSHIP
• *See page 681*

UNION PLUS SCHOLARSHIP PROGRAM

http://www.unionplus.org/

UNION PLUS EDUCATION FOUNDATION SCHOLARSHIP PROGRAM
• *See page 584*

UNITED NEGRO COLLEGE FUND

http://www.uncf.org/

ABCNJ LEADERSHIP IMPACT SCHOLARSHIP

This scholarship program has been created to provide two merit-based scholarships (one male and one female) in the amount of $2,250 to entering college freshmen who are active members of a congregation which is in covenant with the American Baptist Churches of New Jersey (ABCNJ) member churches and who will attend any accredited four year college or university.

Award: Scholarship for use in freshman year; not renewable. *Number:* 2. *Amount:* $2250.

Eligibility Requirements: Applicant must be Baptist; Black (non-Hispanic); enrolled or expecting to enroll full-time at a four-year institution or university and resident of Florida, New Jersey, New York. Applicant must have 3.0 GPA or higher. Available to U.S. citizens.

Application Requirements: Application form, essay. *Deadline:* July 9.

Contact: Mary Williams, Director of Outreach and Recruitment
　　　Phone: 800-331-2244

BEVERLY J. GILLIAM SCHOLARSHIP FOR FOREIGN STUDY

The Beverly J. Gilliam Scholarship for Foreign Study offers financial assistance up to $6,500 to students who are accepted into recognized summer study abroad programs. The scholarship's goals are to help students obtain international experiences that will allow them to become better world citizens and successfully compete in the global job market. This program will allow UNCF students to experience diverse cultures and participate within challenging overseas' academic environments. The applicants must be enrolled at one of the UNCF's member institutions as a sophomore or junior and have a minimum 2.7 GPA.

Award: Scholarship for use in sophomore or junior years; not renewable.

Eligibility Requirements: Applicant must be Black (non-Hispanic) and enrolled or expecting to enroll at a four-year institution or university. Applicant must have 2.5 GPA or higher. Available to U.S. citizens.

Application Requirements: Application form, essay. *Deadline:* May 22.

Contact: Mary Williams, Director of Outreach and Recruitment
　　　Phone: 800-331-2244

BLANCHE FORD ENDOWMENT SCHOLARSHIP FUND

The Blanche Ford Endowment Scholarship Fund was established in memory of Blanche Elizabeth Ford as a tribute to the love, grace, and compassion that she exemplified. The Fund provides up to $10,000 need-based scholarship awards renewable through university graduation. Applicant must be a sophomore at one of the 37 UNCF member institutions, have unmet financial need and evidence of community service commitment/involvement.

Award: Scholarship for use in junior year; renewable.

Eligibility Requirements: Applicant must be Black (non-Hispanic) and enrolled or expecting to enroll full-time at a four-year institution or university. Applicant must have 3.0 GPA or higher. Available to U.S. citizens.

Application Requirements: Application form, essay, financial need analysis. *Deadline:* May 29.

Contact: Mary Williams, Director of Outreach and Recruitment
Phone: 800-331-2244

CHARLESTON FAMILY TRUST SCHOLARSHIP

3 awards of up to $3,000 based upon a students unmet financial need.

Award: Scholarship for use in freshman, sophomore, junior, or senior years. *Number:* 3.

Eligibility Requirements: Applicant must be Black (non-Hispanic) and enrolled or expecting to enroll full-time at a four-year institution or university. Applicant must have 2.5 GPA or higher. Available to U.S. citizens.

Application Requirements: Application form, essay, financial need analysis. *Deadline:* January 19.

Contact: Mary Williams, Director of Outreach and Recruitment
Phone: 800-331-2244

CITY OF CHICAGO SCHOLARSHIP

Scholarship directed to students who are dependents of current or retired employees (parent, legal guardian, or foster parent) of the City of Chicago and their sister agencies. Applicants must attend HBCU or UNCF-affiliated colleges and have a financial.

Award: Scholarship for use in freshman, sophomore, junior, or senior years.

Eligibility Requirements: Applicant must be Black (non-Hispanic) and enrolled or expecting to enroll at a four-year institution or university. Applicant must have 2.5 GPA or higher. Available to U.S. citizens.

Application Requirements: Application form. *Deadline:* December 8.

Contact: Mary Williams, Director of Outreach and Recruitment
Phone: 800-331-2244

CYNTHIA DENISE ROBINSON HORTON SCHOLARSHIP

The Cynthia D. Horton Scholarship is open to any African American student, with a 2.5 GPA, attending an HBCU with preference given to a UNCF school, with unmet financial need.

Award: Scholarship for use in freshman, sophomore, junior, or senior years.

Eligibility Requirements: Applicant must be Black (non-Hispanic) and enrolled or expecting to enroll at a two-year or four-year institution or university. Applicant must have 2.5 GPA or higher. Available to U.S. citizens.

Application Requirements: Application form, essay, financial need analysis. *Deadline:* March 31.

Contact: Mary Williams, Director of Outreach and Recruitment
Phone: 800-331-2244

DEBORAH L. VINCENT/FAHRO EDUCATION SCHOLARSHIP

Up to $1500 award for residents of federally assisted housing or a recipient of assistance through the Community Development Block Grant program in Florida. Must be a high school senior and meet income requirements as defined by HUD for public/assisted housing and Community Development Block Grant targeted area recipients. Must have a sponsor that is an active member of FAHRO as a housing authority/agency or community development agency that is willing to support travel expenses to attend Annual Convention awards banquet to receive scholarship if selected. Minimum 2.5 GPA required.

Award: Scholarship for use in freshman year; renewable.

Eligibility Requirements: Applicant must be Black (non-Hispanic); high school student; planning to enroll or expecting to enroll full-time at a two-year or four-year institution and resident of Florida. Applicant must have 2.5 GPA or higher. Available to U.S. citizens.

Application Requirements: Application form, financial need analysis. *Deadline:* July 10.

Contact: Mary Williams, Director of Outreach and Recruitment
Phone: 800-331-2244

DELTA AIR LINES NEW YORK SCHOLARSHIPS

The Delta Air Lines Foundation in partnership with UNCF has established a scholarship program of up to $5000 for students who reside in or are permanent residents of the State of New York. The scholarship is open to freshmen through 5th year seniors, with unmet financial need. Applicant can be currently enrolled as a full-time student at any U.S located, accredited 4-year college or university. Graduating high school seniors select "freshman" as your classification.

Award: Scholarship for use in freshman, sophomore, junior, or senior years; not renewable.

Eligibility Requirements: Applicant must be Black (non-Hispanic); enrolled or expecting to enroll full-time at a four-year institution or university and resident of New York. Applicant must have 2.5 GPA or higher. Available to U.S. citizens.

Application Requirements: Application form, financial need analysis. *Deadline:* August 18.

Contact: Mary Williams, Director of Outreach and Recruitment
Phone: 800-331-2244

DR. PEPPER SNAPPLE GROUP SCHOLARSHIP

The Dr Pepper Snapple Group Scholarship is open to full-time students who are currently enrolled at an HBCU (Historically Black College or University). Candidates must possess a minimum of a 3.0 GPA on a 4.0 scale and submit a 500 word essay defining their academic achievements, accomplishments and their future career aspirations.

Award: Scholarship for use in freshman, sophomore, or junior years. *Number:* 2. *Amount:* $2500.

Eligibility Requirements: Applicant must be Black (non-Hispanic) and enrolled or expecting to enroll full-time at a four-year institution or university. Applicant must have 3.0 GPA or higher. Available to U.S. citizens.

Application Requirements: Application form, essay. *Deadline:* May 1.

Contact: Mary Williams, Director of Outreach and Recruitment
Phone: 800-331-2244

EDNA BLUM SCHOLARSHIP FOR NYC RESIDENTS

he Edna M. Blum Endowed Scholarship for NYC Residents is open students with an unmet financial need attending colleges/universities throughout the United States. The scholarship will provide an award up to $5,000 depending on the financial need of the student as verified by the attending University or College. Candidates must be from one of the 5 boroughs, be a full time student at an accredited 4 year college or university, be a US citizen or permanent resident.

Award: Scholarship for use in freshman, sophomore, junior, senior, or graduate years; not renewable.

Eligibility Requirements: Applicant must be Black (non-Hispanic); enrolled or expecting to enroll full-time at a four-year institution or university and resident of New York. Applicant must have 2.5 GPA or higher. Available to U.S. citizens.

Application Requirements: Application form, financial need analysis. *Deadline:* October 13.

Contact: Mary Williams, Director of Outreach and Recruitment
Phone: 800-331-2244

ELAINE B. HANCOCK ENDOWED SCHOLARSHIP

The Elaine B. Hancock Endowed Scholarship is open to African-American students at UNCF member institutions and/or Howard University. Applicants must be full-time juniors or seniors with 3.0 GPA. Up to $5,000 depending on the financial need of the student.

Award: Scholarship for use in junior or senior years; renewable.

Eligibility Requirements: Applicant must be Black (non-Hispanic) and enrolled or expecting to enroll full-time at a four-year institution or university. Applicant must have 3.0 GPA or higher. Available to U.S. citizens.

Application Requirements: Application form, financial need analysis. *Deadline:* November 3.

Contact: Mary Williams, Director of Outreach and Recruitment
Phone: 800-331-2244

EUNICE WALKER JOHNSON SCHOLARSHIP

UNCF will be awarding scholarships up to $5,000 to students attending one of the 37 UNCF member HBCUs or Selma University in Alabama. Applicants must have minimum GPA of 3.0 and unmet financial need.

Award: Scholarship for use in freshman, sophomore, junior, or senior years.

Eligibility Requirements: Applicant must be Black (non-Hispanic) and enrolled or expecting to enroll full-time at a four-year institution or university. Applicant must have 3.0 GPA or higher. Available to U.S. citizens.

Application Requirements: Application form, financial need analysis. *Deadline:* September 29.

Contact: Mary Williams, Director of Outreach and Recruitment
Phone: 800-331-2244

FOOT LOCKER FOUNDATION, INC.-UNCF SCHOLARSHIP

Scholarship of up to $5000 for African American high school seniors or students attending or planning to attend a UNCF member college or university. Minimum GPA of 2.5 required. Officers and directors of the Foundation and of Foot Locker, Inc. and its affiliates and family members of these officers and directors are not eligible to apply.

Award: Scholarship for use in freshman, sophomore, junior, or senior years; not renewable.

Eligibility Requirements: Applicant must be Black (non-Hispanic) and enrolled or expecting to enroll full-time at a four-year institution or university. Applicant must have 2.5 GPA or higher. Available to U.S. citizens.

Application Requirements: Application form, essay, financial need analysis. *Deadline:* May 12.

Contact: Mary Williams, Director of Outreach and Recruitment
Phone: 800-331-2244

FORT WAYNE INDIANA SCHOLARSHIP PROGRAM

Up to $3000 need based scholarship for students who are permanent residents of Indiana. Applicants must be current freshman, sophomore or juniors enrolled full time at any accredited four-year institution at the time of application. Applicants may pursue a major in any field, however, preference will be given to students majoring in the natural sciences, accounting, finance, marketing, informational systems or business management related studies.

Award: Scholarship for use in freshman, sophomore, or junior years.

Eligibility Requirements: Applicant must be Black (non-Hispanic); enrolled or expecting to enroll full-time at a four-year institution or university and resident of Indiana. Applicant must have 2.5 GPA or higher. Available to U.S. citizens.

Application Requirements: Application form, essay, financial need analysis. *Deadline:* October 31.

Contact: Mary Williams, Director of Outreach and Recruitment
Phone: 800-331-2244

JACK AND JILL OF AMERICA FOUNDATION SCHOLARSHIP

Up to $2500 scholarship available to any African-American high school senior who will be a full time college student next year. Dependents of members of Jack and Jill of America are not eligible to apply. Minimum 3.0 GPA required. Must be a citizen or permanent resident of the United States. Preference shall be given to applicants who participated in the Jack and Jill of America Leadership Module, however, students who have not participated are eligible to apply.

Award: Scholarship for use in freshman year; not renewable.

Eligibility Requirements: Applicant must be Black (non-Hispanic); high school student and planning to enroll or expecting to enroll full-time at an institution or university. Applicant must have 3.0 GPA or higher. Available to U.S. citizens.

Application Requirements: Application form, essay, financial need analysis. *Deadline:* July 14.

Contact: Mary Williams, Director of Outreach and Recruitment
Phone: 800-331-2244

JAY CHARLES LEVINE SCHOLARSHIP

The Jay Charles Levine Scholarship will provide a $3,000 tuition scholarship for graduating high school seniors from the state of Michigan. Applicants must be residents of Michigan with at least a 2.75 GPA on a 4.0 scale, and must be enrolling at a UNCF member school as a full-time student.

Award: Scholarship for use in freshman year. *Amount:* $3000.

Eligibility Requirements: Applicant must be Black (non-Hispanic); high school student; planning to enroll or expecting to enroll at a four-year institution or university and resident of Michigan. Applicant must have 2.5 GPA or higher. Available to U.S. citizens.

Application Requirements: Application form, essay. *Deadline:* August 1.

Contact: Mary Williams, Director of Outreach and Recruitment
Phone: 800-331-2244

JOSEPH A. TOWLES AFRICAN STUDY ABROAD SCHOLARSHIP

Up to $10,000 scholarship enabling black Americans, conscious of their African descent, to have an opportunity to experience the richness of African cultures. Available to UNCF students who have been accepted into a study abroad program in Africa and have a minimum 3.0 GPA.

Award: Scholarship for use in sophomore, junior, or graduate years; not renewable.

Eligibility Requirements: Applicant must be Black (non-Hispanic) and enrolled or expecting to enroll full-time at a four-year institution or university. Applicant must have 3.0 GPA or higher. Available to U.S. citizens.

Application Requirements: Application form, essay. *Deadline:* December 1.

Contact: Mary Williams, Director of Outreach and Recruitment
Phone: 800-331-2244

JUNE AND WYLIE SELDEN MEMORIAL ENDOWMENT

In memory of June and Wylie Selden, students will receive a need-based scholarship to assist in furthering their college education. The scholarship is available to current undergraduate students who are enrolled at a UNCF member institution.

Award: Scholarship for use in freshman, sophomore, junior, or senior years; not renewable.

Eligibility Requirements: Applicant must be Black (non-Hispanic) and enrolled or expecting to enroll at a four-year institution or university. Applicant must have 2.5 GPA or higher. Available to U.S. citizens.

Application Requirements: Application form, essay, financial need analysis. *Deadline:* September 22.

Contact: Mary Williams, Director of Outreach and Recruitment
Phone: 800-331-2244

KROGER MICHIGAN SCHOLARSHIP

One-time scholarship of up to $4500 available to graduating high school seniors that reside in the Michigan area. Minimum 2.5 GPA required.

Award: Scholarship for use in freshman year; not renewable. *Number:* 1. *Amount:* $4500.

Eligibility Requirements: Applicant must be Black (non-Hispanic); high school student; planning to enroll or expecting to enroll full-time at a four-year institution or university and resident of Michigan. Applicant must have 2.5 GPA or higher. Available to U.S. citizens.

Application Requirements: Application form. *Deadline:* June 2.

Contact: Mary Williams, Director of Outreach and Recruitment
Phone: 800-331-2244

LIBERTY MUTUAL INSURANCE LEADA@LIBERTY SCHOLARSHIP

The plan commits Massachusetts public colleges and universities to providing a series of financial incentives to students who begin their studies at one of 15 community colleges, earn an associate degree within two and a half years, and then transfer to a state university or University of Massachusetts campus to earn a baccalaureate degree. The student must be a current freshman or sophomore enrolled full-time at a Community College in Massachusetts and planning to transfer to a State University or to the University of Massachusetts. Students must be enrolled in the Commonwealth Commitment program before earning their first 15 credits at a Community College. Up to $2500 scholarship and save an average 40% off the cost of a traditional bachelor's degree

Award: Scholarship for use in freshman or sophomore years; not renewable.

Eligibility Requirements: Applicant must be Black (non-Hispanic); enrolled or expecting to enroll full-time at a two-year or four-year institution or university and studying in Massachusetts. Applicant must have 3.0 GPA or higher. Available to U.S. citizens.

Application Requirements: Application form, essay, financial need analysis. *Deadline:* December 15.

Contact: Mary Williams, Director of Outreach and Recruitment
 Phone: 800-331-2244

MALCOLM X SCHOLARSHIP FOR EXCEPTIONAL COURAGE

The Malcolm X Scholarship for "Exceptional Courage" is directed towards undergraduate students, who are enrolled at one of the UNCF Institutions. The scholarship was developed by Spike Lee to increase the awareness about the life and contributions of Malcolm X within society. The program will provide up to $4000 scholarship support for students, who have overcome difficult circumstances or challenges in pursuit of their college education.

Award: Grant for use in freshman, sophomore, junior, or senior years.

Eligibility Requirements: Applicant must be Black (non-Hispanic) and enrolled or expecting to enroll at a four-year institution or university. Applicant must have 2.5 GPA or higher. Available to U.S. citizens.

Application Requirements: Application form, essay. *Deadline:* September 29.

Contact: Mary Williams, Director of Outreach and Recruitment
 Phone: 800-331-2244

MAYS FAMILY SCHOLARSHIP FUND

The Mays Family Scholarship Fund has decided to provide 3 scholarships to students who reside in or are permanent residents of Arkansas, Illinois, Indiana or Michigan. Applicants must attend Howard University, other HBCU's, or one of the following institutions: University of Chicago, Michigan State University, Western Michigan University, Indiana State University, University of Arkansas, Indiana University, or the University of Illinois. Must have unmet financial need and have minimum GPA of 2.8.

Award: Scholarship for use in freshman, sophomore, or junior years; not renewable. *Number:* 3. *Amount:* $1500.

Eligibility Requirements: Applicant must be Black (non-Hispanic); enrolled or expecting to enroll at a four-year institution or university and resident of Arkansas, Illinois, Indiana, Michigan. Applicant must have 2.5 GPA or higher. Available to U.S. citizens.

Application Requirements: Application form, essay, financial need analysis. *Deadline:* June 16.

Contact: Mary Williams, Director of Outreach and Recruitment
 Phone: 800-331-2244

PENNSYLVANIA STATE EMPLOYEES COMBINED CAMPAIGN SCHOLARSHIP (SECA)

Up to $4000 scholarship program for qualified students entering or enrolled in a UNCF member college/university. Applicant must be Pell Grant eligible and have a demonstrated financial need.

Award: Scholarship for use in freshman, sophomore, junior, senior, or graduate years.

Eligibility Requirements: Applicant must be Black (non-Hispanic); enrolled or expecting to enroll full-time at a two-year or four-year institution or university and resident of Pennsylvania. Applicant must have 2.5 GPA or higher. Available to U.S. citizens.

Application Requirements: Application form, financial need analysis. *Deadline:* August 4.

Contact: Mary Williams, Director of Outreach and Recruitment
 Phone: 800-331-2244

RAY CHARLES ENDOWED SCHOLARSHIP

3 scholarship awards of up to $4,500 will help African-American students with high academic promise to defray their significant financial need. Applicants must be African-American college juniors enrolled full-time at a UNCF member institution. Must have minimum cumulative GPA of 3.0 and have unmet financial need.

Award: Scholarship for use in junior year; renewable. *Number:* 3.

Eligibility Requirements: Applicant must be Black (non-Hispanic) and enrolled or expecting to enroll full-time at a four-year institution or university. Applicant must have 3.0 GPA or higher. Available to U.S. citizens.

Application Requirements: Application form, financial need analysis. *Deadline:* January 26.

Contact: Mary Williams, Director of Outreach and Recruitment
 Phone: 800-331-2244

UNCF GENERAL SCHOLARSHIP PROGRAM

Up to $5000 scholarships for students enrolled full-time and attending UNCF Institutes. Must have a demonstrated financial need. Minimum 2.5 GPA required. This application information will be used to match students to specific programs administered by UNCF. For more information see website, http://www.uncf.org.

Award: Scholarship for use in freshman, sophomore, junior, senior, or graduate years; not renewable.

Eligibility Requirements: Applicant must be Black (non-Hispanic) and enrolled or expecting to enroll full-time at a four-year institution or university. Applicant must have 2.5 GPA or higher. Available to U.S. citizens.

Application Requirements: Application form, financial need analysis. *Deadline:* March 16.

Contact: Mary Williams, Director of Outreach and Recruitment
 Phone: 800-331-2244

UNCF HONDA SCHOLARSHIP

The UNCF Honda Manufacturing of Indiana Scholarship Program is a scholarship for high school students who are permanent residents of the state of Indiana. Applicants must be current high school senior/entering college freshman, must be enrolled in a Student Development and/or Student Leadership program or current college freshmen/rising sophomore in college AND enrolled FULL TIME at a U.S. located, accredited post-secondary educational institution. Priority will be given to students who are majoring in one of the field(s) related to Science, Technology, Engineering or Math (STEM).

Award: Scholarship for use in freshman year. *Amount:* $2500.

Eligibility Requirements: Applicant must be Black (non-Hispanic); high school student; planning to enroll or expecting to enroll full-time at a two-year or four-year institution or university and resident of Indiana. Applicant must have 2.5 GPA or higher. Available to U.S. citizens.

Application Requirements: Application form, essay. *Deadline:* June 16.

Contact: Mary Williams, Director of Outreach and Recruitment
 Phone: 800-331-2244

USA FUNDS SCHOLARSHIP

Scholarships of up to $5,000 to assist students and their families in gaining access to postsecondary education at UNCF or other HBCU colleges/universities in Indiana. Students must be resident of Indiana and be a U.S. citizen or permanent resident. Minimum 2.5 GPA required.

Award: Scholarship for use in freshman, sophomore, junior, or senior years; not renewable.

Eligibility Requirements: Applicant must be Black (non-Hispanic); enrolled or expecting to enroll full-time at a four-year institution or university; resident of Indiana and studying in Indiana. Applicant must have 2.5 GPA or higher. Available to U.S. citizens.

Application Requirements: Application form, essay. *Deadline:* August 31.

Contact: Mary Williams, Director of Outreach and Recruitment
 Phone: 800-331-2244

VERTUS HARDIMAN ENDOWED SCHOLARSHIP

The Vertus Hardiman Endowed Scholarship is open to students at HBCUs. Candidates must have a minimum GPA of 3.0 on a 4.0 scale. Current college freshman should use their final GPA from high school. The scholarship will provide an award up to $5,000 depending on the financial need of the student as verified by the attending University or College.

Award: Grant for use in freshman, sophomore, junior, or senior years; not renewable.

Eligibility Requirements: Applicant must be Black (non-Hispanic) and enrolled or expecting to enroll at a four-year institution or university. Applicant must have 3.0 GPA or higher. Available to U.S. citizens.

Application Requirements: Application form, essay, financial need analysis. *Deadline:* October 11.

Contact: Mary Williams, Director of Outreach and Recruitment
 Phone: 800-331-2244

VOYA UNCF MALE INITIATIVE

Scholarship for male, African-American colleges sophomores attending UNCF affiliated colleges or universities on a full-time basis. Must have a demonstrated unmet, financial need as verified by college or university. Minimum 2.5 GPA required.

Award: Scholarship for use in sophomore year; not renewable.

Eligibility Requirements: Applicant must be Black (non-Hispanic); enrolled or expecting to enroll full-time at a four-year institution or university and male. Applicant must have 2.5 GPA or higher. Available to U.S. citizens.

Application Requirements: Application form, essay, financial need analysis. *Deadline:* November 17.

Contact: Mary Williams, Director of Outreach and Recruitment
Phone: 800-331-2244

UNITED SOUTH AND EASTERN TRIBES INC.

http://www.usetinc.org/

UNITED SOUTH AND EASTERN TRIBES SCHOLARSHIP FUND

One-time scholarship for Native American students who are members of United South and Eastern Tribes, enrolled or accepted in a postsecondary educational institution.

Award: Scholarship for use in freshman, sophomore, junior, or senior years; not renewable. *Number:* 4–8. *Amount:* $500.

Eligibility Requirements: Applicant must be Indian citizen; American Indian/Alaska Native and enrolled or expecting to enroll full- or part-time at a four-year institution or university.

Application Requirements: Application form, essay, financial need analysis, proof of tribal enrollment, transcript. *Deadline:* April 30.

Contact: Theresa Embry, Executive Assistant to Director
United South and Eastern Tribes Inc.
711 Stewarts Ferry Pike, Suite 100
Nashville, TN 37214-2634
Phone: 615-872-7900
Fax: 615-872-7417

UNITED STATES HISPANIC LEADERSHIP INSTITUTE

http://www.ushli.org/

DR. JUAN ANDRADE, JR. SCHOLARSHIP

Scholarship for young Hispanic leaders. Applicants must be enrolled or accepted for enrollment as a full-time student in a four-year institution in the United States or U.S. territories, and demonstrate a verifiable need for financial support. At least one parent must be of Hispanic ancestry.

Award: Scholarship for use in freshman, sophomore, junior, or senior years; not renewable. *Number:* 30. *Amount:* $500–$1000.

Eligibility Requirements: Applicant must be Hispanic and enrolled or expecting to enroll full-time at a two-year or four-year institution or university. Available to U.S. citizens.

Application Requirements: Application form, driver's license, essay, personal photograph, recommendations or references, resume, transcript. *Deadline:* January 11.

Contact: Isabel Reyes, Scholarship Coordinator
Phone: 312-427-8683
Fax: 312-427-5183
E-mail: ireyes@ushli.org

UNITED TRANSPORTATION UNION INSURANCE ASSOCIATION

http://www.utuia.org/

UTUIA SCHOLARSHIP
• *See page 681*

UNIVERSITY CONSORTIUM FOR LIBERIA

http://ucliberia.com/

JOSEPH N. BOAKAI SR. HIGHER EDUCATION SCHOLARSHIP
• *See page 681*

U.S. COAST GUARD

http://www.gocoastguard/cspi

COLLEGE STUDENT PRE-COMMISSIONING INITIATIVE (CSPI)
• *See page 681*

US PAN ASIAN AMERICAN CHAMBER OF COMMERCE EDUCATION FOUNDATION

http://www.uspaacc.com/

AMPCUS HALLMARK SCHOLARSHIP

The applicant should demonstrate academic achievement of 3.3 GPA or higher, leadership in extracurricular activities, involvement in community service, and financial need. The amount of the scholarship depends on the sponsors' contributions and varies between $2000 and $5000.

Award: Scholarship for use in freshman year; renewable. *Amount:* $2000–$5000.

Eligibility Requirements: Applicant must be Asian/Pacific Islander; high school student and planning to enroll or expecting to enroll full-time at a four-year institution or university. Applicant must have 3.0 GPA or higher. Available to U.S. citizens.

Application Requirements: Application form. *Deadline:* March 17.

Contact: Diana Yee, Program Associate
US Pan Asian American Chamber of Commerce Education
Foundation
1329 18th Street N.W.
Washington D.C. 20036
Phone: 202-378-1121
E-mail: diana@uspaacc.com

INGERSOLL RAND SCHOLARSHIP

The applicant should demonstrate academic achievement of 3.3 GPA or higher, leadership in extracurricular activities, involvement in community service, and financial need. The amount of the scholarship depends on the sponsors' contributions and varies between $2000 and $5000.

Award: Scholarship for use in freshman year; not renewable. *Amount:* $2000–$5000.

Eligibility Requirements: Applicant must be Asian/Pacific Islander; high school student and planning to enroll or expecting to enroll full-time at a four-year institution or university. Available to U.S. citizens.

Application Requirements: Application form. *Deadline:* March 17.

Contact: Diana Yee, Program Associate
US Pan Asian American Chamber of Commerce Education
Foundation
1329 18th Street N.W.
Washington D.C. 20036
Phone: 202-378-1121
E-mail: Diana@uspaacc.com

PEPSICO HALLMARK SCHOLARSHIPS

The applicant should demonstrate academic achievement of 3.3 GPA or higher, leadership in extracurricular activities, involvement in community service, and financial need. The amount of the scholarship depends on the sponsors' contributions and varies between $2000 and $5000.

Award: Scholarship for use in freshman year; not renewable. *Number:* 1. *Amount:* $2000–$5000.

Eligibility Requirements: Applicant must be Asian/Pacific Islander; high school student and planning to enroll or expecting to enroll full-time at an institution or university. Available to U.S. citizens.

Application Requirements: Application form. *Deadline:* March 17.

Contact: Diana Yee
US Pan Asian American Chamber of Commerce Education
Foundation
1329 18th Street N.W.
Washington D.C. 20036
Phone: 202-378-1121
E-mail: diana@uspaacc.com

UPS HALLMARK SCHOLARSHIPS

The applicant should demonstrate academic achievement of 3.3 GPA or higher, leadership in extracurricular activities, involvement in community service, and financial need. The amount of the scholarship depends on the sponsors' contributions and varies between $2000 and $5000.

Award: Scholarship for use in freshman year; not renewable. *Amount:* $2000–$5000.

Eligibility Requirements: Applicant must be Asian/Pacific Islander; high school student and planning to enroll or expecting to enroll full-time at an institution or university. Available to U.S. citizens.

Application Requirements: Application form. *Deadline:* March 17.

Contact: Diana Yee
US Pan Asian American Chamber of Commerce Education
Foundation
1329 18th Street N.W.
Washington D.C. 20036
Phone: 202-378-1121

WINWIN PRODUCTS, INC. SCHOLARSHIP

The applicant should demonstrate academic achievement of 3.3 GPA or higher, leadership in extracurricular activities, involvement in community service, and financial need. The amount of the scholarship depends on the sponsors' contributions and varies between $2000 and $5000.

Award: Scholarship for use in freshman year; not renewable. *Amount:* $2000–$5000.

Eligibility Requirements: Applicant must be Asian/Pacific Islander; high school student and planning to enroll or expecting to enroll full-time at a four-year institution or university. Available to U.S. citizens.

Application Requirements: Application form. *Deadline:* March 13.

Contact: Diana Yee, Program Associate
US Pan Asian American Chamber of Commerce Education
Foundation
1329 18th Street N.W.
Washington, D.C. 20036
Phone: 202-378-1121
Fax: 202-296-5221
E-mail: diana@uspaacc.com

VALUEPENGUIN

http://www.valuepenguin.com

VALUEPENGUIN SCHOLARSHIP

• *See page 682*

VANILLA PILGRIM FOUNDATION

https://www.vanillapilgrim.com/

2018 OPEN ESSAY COMPETITION

• *See page 682*

VETERANAID.ORG

https://www.veteranaid.org

VETERAN BENEFITS SCHOLARSHIP

• *See page 682*

VETERANS UNITED FOUNDATION

http://www.enhancelives.com

VETERANS UNITED FOUNDATION SCHOLARSHIP

• *See page 682*

WARD LAW GROUP, PL

http://thecoveragelawyer.com/

WARD LAW GROUP BETTER FUTURE SCHOLARSHIP

• *See page 682*

WESTERN INTERSTATE COMMISSION FOR HIGHER EDUCATION

http://www.wiche.edu/

WICHE'S WESTERN UNDERGRADUATE EXCHANGE (WUE)

• *See page 683*

WHITE EARTH TRIBAL COUNCIL

http://www.whiteearth.com/

WHITE EARTH SCHOLARSHIP PROGRAM

Renewable scholarship for students who are enrolled in postsecondary institutions. Must have a GPA of 2.5. Must be U.S. citizen.

Award: Scholarship for use in freshman, sophomore, junior, senior, graduate, or postgraduate years; renewable. *Number:* 200. *Amount:* $3000.

Eligibility Requirements: Applicant must be American Indian/Alaska Native and enrolled or expecting to enroll full- or part-time at a two-year or four-year or technical institution or university. Applicant must have 2.5 GPA or higher. Available to U.S. citizens.

Application Requirements: Application form, financial need analysis, transcript. *Deadline:* May 31.

Contact: Leslie Nessman, Scholarship Manager
Phone: 218-983-3285
Fax: 218-983-4299

WHITLEY LAW FIRM

https://whitleylawfirm.com/

WHITLEY LAW FIRM OPIOID CRISIS SCHOLARSHIP

• *See page 683*

WILLIAM E. DOCTER EDUCATIONAL FUND/ST. MARY ARMENIAN CHURCH

http://www.wedfund.org/

WILLIAM ERVANT DOCTER EDUCATIONAL FUND

Grant up to $2000 available to worthy students regardless of age, gender, or level of education or training. Funds given to American citizens of Armenian ancestry to pursue studies and training in the United States or Canada.

Award: Grant for use in freshman, sophomore, junior, senior, graduate, or postgraduate years; not renewable. *Number:* 20. *Amount:* $1000–$2000.

Eligibility Requirements: Applicant must be of Armenian heritage and enrolled or expecting to enroll full- or part-time at a two-year or four-year or technical institution or university. Available to U.S. citizens.

Application Requirements: Application form, essay, financial need analysis, proof of U.S. citizenship, test scores, transcript. *Deadline:* June 30.

Contact: Edward Alexander, Scholarship Committee Chairman
Fax: 202-364-1441
E-mail: wedfund@aol.com

WISCONSIN HIGHER EDUCATIONAL AID BOARD

http://www.heab.wi.gov/

MINORITY UNDERGRADUATE RETENTION GRANT-WISCONSIN

The grant provides financial assistance to African-American, Native-American, Hispanic, and former citizens of Laos, Vietnam, and Cambodia, for study in Wisconsin. Must be Wisconsin resident, enrolled at least half-time in Wisconsin Technical College System schools, non-profit independent colleges and universities, and tribal colleges. Refer to website for further details http://www.heab.state.wi.us.

Award: Grant for use in sophomore, junior, or senior years; not renewable. *Amount:* $250–$2500.

Eligibility Requirements: Applicant must be American Indian/Alaska Native, Asian/Pacific Islander, Black (non-Hispanic), Hispanic; enrolled or expecting to enroll full- or part-time at a two-year or four-year or technical institution or university; resident of Wisconsin and studying in Wisconsin. Available to U.S. and non-U.S. citizens.

Application Requirements: Application form, financial need analysis. *Deadline:* continuous.

Contact: Mary Lou Kuzdas, Program Coordinator
Wisconsin Higher Educational Aid Board
PO Box 7885
Madison, WI 53707-7885
Phone: 608-267-2212
Fax: 608-267-2808
E-mail: mary.kuzdas@wi.gov

WISCONSIN NATIVE AMERICAN/INDIAN STUDENT ASSISTANCE GRANT

Grants for Wisconsin residents who are at least one-quarter American Indian. Must be attending a college or university within the state. Refer to website for further details, http://www.heab.state.wi.us.

Award: Grant for use in freshman, sophomore, junior, or senior years; not renewable. *Amount:* $250–$1100.

Eligibility Requirements: Applicant must be American Indian/Alaska Native; enrolled or expecting to enroll full- or part-time at a two-year or four-year or technical institution or university; resident of Wisconsin and studying in Wisconsin. Available to U.S. citizens.

Application Requirements: Application form, financial need analysis. *Deadline:* continuous.

Contact: Sandra Thomas, Program Coordinator
Wisconsin Higher Educational Aid Board
PO Box 7885
Madison, WI 53707-7885
Phone: 608-266-0888
Fax: 608-267-2808
E-mail: sandy.thomas@wi.gov

WOLTERMAN LAW OFFICE, LPA

https://www.woltermanlaw.com/

WOLTERMAN LAW OFFICE LPA HOPE FOR THE FUTURE SCHOLARSHIP
• *See page 683*

WOMEN MARINES ASSOCIATION

http://www.womenmarines.org

ETHYL AND ARMIN WIEBKE MEMORIAL SCHOLARSHIPS
• *See page 683*

THE LILY H. GRIDLEY MEMORIAL SCHOLARSHIP
• *See page 683*

WMA MEMORIAL SCHOLARSHIPS
• *See page 683*

WOMEN OF THE EVANGELICAL LUTHERAN CHURCH IN AMERICA

http://www.womenoftheelca.org/

AMELIA KEMP SCHOLARSHIP

Scholarship for ELCA women who are of an ethnic minority in undergraduate, graduate, professional, or vocational courses of study. Must be at least 21 years old and hold membership in the ELCA. Must have experienced an interruption of two or more years in education since the completion of high school.

Award: Scholarship for use in freshman, sophomore, junior, senior, or graduate years; not renewable. *Number:* 1. *Amount:* up to $1000.

Eligibility Requirements: Applicant must be Lutheran; American Indian/Alaska Native, Asian/Pacific Islander, Black (non-Hispanic), Hispanic; enrolled or expecting to enroll full- or part-time at a two-year or four-year or technical institution or university and female. Available to U.S. citizens.

Application Requirements: Application form, recommendations or references, resume, transcript. *Deadline:* February 15.

Contact: Emily Hansen, Scholarship Committee
Phone: 800-638-3522 Ext. 2736
Fax: 773-380-2419
E-mail: womenelca@elca.org

WOMEN'S JEWELRY ASSOCIATION

http://www.womensjewelryassociation.com

MEMBER GRANTS
• *See page 684*

WOMEN'S JEWELRY ASSOCIATIONS VETERANS GRANT
• *See page 684*

WONDERSHARE PDFELEMENT

https://pdf.wondershare.com

2018 PDFELEMENT $1000 SCHOLARSHIP
• *See page 684*

YORKVILLE GOODS LLC

http://yorkvilleblankets.com/

YORKVILLE BLANKETS ASD SCHOLARSHIP
• *See page 684*

ZAMI NOBLA

http://www.zaminobla.org

AUDRE LORDE SCHOLARSHIP FUND

Must be an out black lesbian or lesbian of color who is 40 years old or older attending any technical, undergraduate or graduate school located in the United States. Must be accepted or registered at a post-secondary educational institution for full or part-time attendance as defined by the institution. Must also have a cumulative high school/college/or technical school grade point average of 3.0 or higher. Please do not submit an application if you do not meet the eligibility requirements as your application will not be reviewed. No exceptions to the eligibility requirements are considered. The Fund does not offer scholarships for weekend programs, summer sessions, research, special projects, or for study out of the country.

Award: Scholarship for use in freshman, sophomore, junior, senior, graduate, or postgraduate years; renewable. *Number:* 1–6. *Amount:* $1000.

Eligibility Requirements: Applicant must be American Indian/Alaska Native, Asian/Pacific Islander, Black (non-Hispanic), Hispanic; enrolled or expecting to enroll full- or part-time at a two-year or four-year or technical institution or university and female. Applicant must have 3.0 GPA or higher. Available to U.S. citizens.

Application Requirements: Application form, essay, interview, personal photograph.

Contact: Ms. Mary Anne Adams, Founding Director
ZAMI NOBLA
PO Box 90986
Atlanta, GA 30364
Phone: 404-647-4754
E-mail: zaminobla@zaminobla.org

ZELUS RECOVERY

http://zelusrecovery.com/

ZELUS RECOVERY $1000 COLLEGE SCHOLARSHIP
• *See page 684*

ZIPRECRUITER

https://www.ziprecruiter.com/

ZIPRECRUITER $3,000 SCHOLARSHIP
• *See page 685*

RELIGIOUS AFFILIATION

1-800-HANSONS

http://www.hansons.com

1-800-HANSONS SCHOLARSHIP PROGRAM
• *See page 592*

1DENTAL.COM

https://www.1dental.com/

1DENTAL SCHOLARSHIP
• *See page 592*

1ST CAVALRY DIVISION ASSOCIATION

https://www.1CDA.org

1ST CAVALRY DIVISION ASSOCIATION SCHOLARSHIP FOUNDATION
• *See page 592*

365 PET INSURANCE

https://365petinsurance.com/

MINORITY STUDENTS IN VETERINARY MEDICINE SCHOLARSHIP
• *See page 719*

4MYCASH.COM, LLC

https://www.4mycash.com

4MYCASH ST. LOUIS HARD MONEY SCHOLARSHIP
• *See page 592*

A-1 AUTO TRANSPORT, INC.

https://www.a1autotransport.com/a-1-auto-transport-scholarship/

A-1 AUTO TRANSPORT SCHOLARSHIP
• *See page 592*

ACADGILD

https://acadgild.com

ACADGILD MERIT-BASED SCHOLARSHIPS
• *See page 593*

ACES: THE SOCIETY FOR EDITING

https://aceseditors.org/

BILL WALSH SCHOLARSHIP
• *See page 593*

AIR FORCE AID SOCIETY

http://www.afas.org/

GENERAL HENRY H. ARNOLD EDUCATION GRANT PROGRAM
• *See page 695*

AIR TRAFFIC CONTROL ASSOCIATION INC.

http://www.atca.org/

AIR TRAFFIC CONTROL ASSOCIATION SCHOLARSHIP
• *See page 593*

BUCKINGHAM MEMORIAL SCHOLARSHIP
• *See page 593*

ALABAMA SOCIETY OF CERTIFIED PUBLIC ACCOUNTANTS

http://www.ascpa.org/

ASCPA EDUCATIONAL FOUNDATION SCHOLARSHIP
• *See page 593*

ALERTONE SERVICES, LLC

https://www.alert-1.com/

ALERT1 STUDENT FOR SENIORS SCHOLARSHIP
• *See page 593*

ALEXANDER GRAHAM BELL ASSOCIATION FOR THE DEAF AND HARD OF HEARING

http://www.agbell.org/

AG BELL COLLEGE SCHOLARSHIP PROGRAM
• *See page 594*

ALGAECAL INC.

https://www.algaecal.com/

ALGAECAL SCHOLARSHIP
• *See page 594*

ALLIANCE FOR YOUNG ARTISTS AND WRITERS INC.

http://www.artandwriting.org/

SCHOLASTIC ART AND WRITING AWARDS
• *See page 594*

ALLTHEROOMS
http://alltherooms.com

ROOM TO TRAVEL - STUDY ABROAD SCHOLARSHIP
• *See page 594*

ALZHEIMER'S FOUNDATION OF AMERICA
https://alzfdn.org/

AFA TEENS FOR ALZHEIMER'S AWARENESS COLLEGE SCHOLARSHIP
• *See page 595*

AMERICAN ALPINE CLUB
https://americanalpineclub.org/

AMERICAN ALPINE CLUB RESEARCH GRANTS
• *See page 595*

AMERICAN ASSOCIATION OF TEACHERS OF JAPANESE BRIDGING CLEARINGHOUSE FOR STUDY ABROAD IN JAPAN
http://www.aatj.org

BRIDGING SCHOLARSHIP FOR STUDY ABROAD IN JAPAN
• *See page 595*

AMERICAN BAPTIST FINANCIAL AID PROGRAM
http://www.abhms.org/

AMERICAN BAPTIST HOME MISSION SOCIETIES FINANCIAL AID PROGRAM

The American Baptist Financial Aid Program supports American Baptist college students, graduate students, and seminarians. Applicants must hold an active membership in an American Baptist church, maintain a GPA of 2.75 or higher, and be enrolled at an accredited institution in the United States or Puerto Rico.

Award: Scholarship for use in freshman, sophomore, junior, senior, or graduate years; not renewable. *Number:* 1–250. *Amount:* $500–$1000.

Eligibility Requirements: Applicant must be Baptist and enrolled or expecting to enroll full-time at a four-year institution or university. Applicant must have 3.0 GPA or higher. Available to U.S. citizens.

Application Requirements: Application form, essay, financial need analysis. *Deadline:* April 30.

Contact: Rev. Sarah Strosahl-Kagi, Director of Emerging Leaders and Scholarships Program
American Baptist Financial Aid Program
PO Box 851
Valley Forge, PA 19482-0851
Phone: 800-222-3872 Ext. 2462
Fax: 610-768-2470
E-mail: sarah.strosahl-kagi@abhms.org

AMERICAN COUNCIL OF THE BLIND
http://www.acb.org/

AMERICAN COUNCIL OF THE BLIND SCHOLARSHIPS
• *See page 595*

AMERICAN DENTAL ASSISTANTS ASSOCIATION
http://www.adaausa.org

JULIETTE A. SOUTHARD SCHOLARSHIP
• *See page 549*

AMERICAN LEGION AUXILIARY DEPARTMENT OF MASSACHUSETTS
http://www.masslegion-aux.org/

AMERICAN LEGION AUXILIARY DEPARTMENT OF MASSACHUSETTS DEPARTMENT PRESIDENT'S SCHOLARSHIP
• *See page 595*

AMERICAN LEGION AUXILIARY DEPARTMENT OF WISCONSIN
http://www.amlegionauxwi.org/

AMERICAN LEGION AUXILIARY DEPARTMENT OF WISCONSIN DELLA VAN DEUREN MEMORIAL SCHOLARSHIP
• *See page 552*

AMERICAN LEGION AUXILIARY DEPARTMENT OF WISCONSIN H.S. AND ANGELINE LEWIS SCHOLARSHIPS
• *See page 552*

AMERICAN LEGION AUXILIARY DEPARTMENT OF WISCONSIN MERIT AND MEMORIAL SCHOLARSHIPS
• *See page 552*

AMERICAN LEGION AUXILIARY DEPARTMENT OF WISCONSIN PRESIDENT'S SCHOLARSHIPS
• *See page 552*

AMERICAN LEGION AUXILIARY NATIONAL HEADQUARTERS
http://www.ALAforVeterans.org

AMERICAN LEGION AUXILIARY CHILDREN OF WARRIORS NATIONAL PRESIDENTS' SCHOLARSHIP
• *See page 596*

AMERICAN LEGION DEPARTMENT OF MARYLAND
http://www.mdlegion.org/

AMERICAN LEGION DEPARTMENT OF MARYLAND GENERAL SCHOLARSHIP FUND
• *See page 555*

AMERICAN LEGION, DEPARTMENT OF MARYLAND, HIGH SCHOOL ORATORICAL SCHOLARSHIP CONTEST
• *See page 596*

MARYLAND BOYS STATE SCHOLARSHIP
• *See page 597*

AMERICAN LEGION DEPARTMENT OF WASHINGTON

http://www.walegion.org/

AMERICAN LEGION DEPARTMENT OF WASHINGTON CHILDREN AND YOUTH SCHOLARSHIPS
• *See page 557*

AMERICAN SAVINGS FOUNDATION

http://www.asfdn.org/

ROBERT T. KENNEY SCHOLARSHIP PROGRAM AT THE AMERICAN SAVINGS FOUNDATION
• *See page 597*

AMERICAN SCHOOL OF CLASSICAL STUDIES AT ATHENS

http://www.ascsa.edu.gr/

CHARLES M. EDWARDS SCHOLARSHIP
• *See page 597*

AMERICAN SEPHARDI FOUNDATION

http://www.americansephardifederation.org/

BROOME AND ALLEN BOYS CAMP AND SCHOLARSHIP FUND
The Broome and Allen Scholarship is awarded to students of Sephardic origin or those working in Sephardic studies. Both graduate and undergraduate degree candidates as well as those doing research projects will be considered. It is awarded for one year and must be renewed for successive years. Enclose copy of tax returns with application.

Award: Scholarship for use in freshman, sophomore, junior, senior, graduate, or postgraduate years; not renewable. *Number:* 20–60. *Amount:* $500–$2000.

Eligibility Requirements: Applicant must be Jewish and enrolled or expecting to enroll full- or part-time at a two-year or four-year or technical institution or university. Available to U.S. and non-U.S. citizens.

Application Requirements: Application form, copy of tax returns, essay, financial need analysis, recommendations or references, transcript. *Deadline:* May 15.

Contact: Ms. Ellen Cohen, Membership and Outreach Coordinator
American Sephardi Foundation
15 West 16th Street
New York, NY 10011
Phone: 212-294-8350 Ext. 4
Fax: 212-294-8348
E-mail: ecohen@asf.cjh.org

AMERICAN SOCIETY OF SAFETY ENGINEERS (ASSE) FOUNDATION

http://foundation.asse.org

FAMILY SCHOLARSHIP FUND
• *See page 597*

ANCHOR SCHOLARSHIP FOUNDATION

http://www.anchorscholarship.com

ANCHOR SCHOLARSHIP FOUNDATION
• *See page 598*

ANKIN LAW

http://ankinlaw.com

ANKIN LAW OFFICE ANNUAL COLLEGE SCHOLARSHIP
• *See page 598*

ANTHONY MUNOZ FOUNDATION

http://www.munozfoundation.org

ANTHONY MUNOZ SCHOLARSHIPS
• *See page 598*

ARCHITECTURAL PRECAST ASSOCIATION

http://www.archprecast.org

TOM CORY MEMORIAL SCHOLARSHIP
• *See page 598*

THE ARC NEW YORK

https://www.nysarc.org/

ARTHUR W. PENSE SCHOLARSHIP
• *See page 599*

ARC OF WASHINGTON TRUST FUND

http://www.arctrustfund.org/

ARC OF WASHINGTON TRUST FUND STIPEND PROGRAM
• *See page 599*

ARKANSAS SINGLE PARENT SCHOLARSHIP FUND

http://www.aspsf.org/

ARKANSAS SINGLE PARENT SCHOLARSHIP FUND
• *See page 599*

ARMENIAN RELIEF SOCIETY OF EASTERN USA INC.-REGIONAL OFFICE

http://www.arseastusa.org/

ARMENIAN RELIEF SOCIETY UNDERGRADUATE SCHOLARSHIP
• *See page 599*

ARTBA

http://www.artba.org/

ARTBA-TDF LANFORD FAMILY HIGHWAY WORKERS MEMORIAL SCHOLARSHIP PROGRAM
• *See page 599*

ASIAN PACIFIC COMMUNITY FUND

http://www.apcf.org/

ROYAL BUSINESS BANK SCHOLARSHIP PROGRAM
• *See page 600*

ASIAN REPORTER

http://www.arfoundation.net/

ASIAN REPORTER SCHOLARSHIP
• *See page 600*

ASSOCIATION OF ENVIRONMENTAL HEALTH ACADEMIC PROGRAMS (AEHAP)

http://www.aehap.org/

NSF INTERNATIONAL SCHOLAR PROGRAM
Award available for college junior or senior in an AEHAP Environmental Health Academic Program. Student will spend summer on an independent research project in conjunction with their home university and NSF International and the AEHAP Office. Must have consent and commitment from advisor to help develop and oversee research project. Stipend will be paid in two sums, and advisor will receive $500 stipend.
Award: Scholarship for use in junior or senior years; not renewable. *Number:* 1. *Amount:* $3500.

Eligibility Requirements: Applicant must be enrolled or expecting to enroll full-time at a four-year institution or university. Available to U.S. citizens.

Application Requirements: Application form, essay. *Deadline:* December 31.

Contact: Clint Pinion, AEHAP - NSF Scholarship Committee
Association of Environmental Health Academic Programs (AEHAP)
P.O. Box 66057
Burien, WA 98166
Phone: 206-5225272
E-mail: Clint.Pinion@eku.edu

ASSURED LIFE ASSOCIATION

http://assuredlife.org

ASSURED LIFE ASSOCIATION ENDOWMENT SCHOLARSHIP PROGRAM
• *See page 600*

AWEBER COMMUNICATIONS

http://www.aweber.com/

AWEBER DEVELOPING FUTURES SCHOLARSHIP
• *See page 725*

AYN RAND INSTITUTE

https://www.aynrand.org

ATLAS SHRUGGED ESSAY CONTEST
• *See page 600*

BARONE DEFENSE FIRM

http://baronedefensefirm.com/

BARONE DEFENSE FIRM WIN BACK YOUR LIFE SCHOLARSHIP
• *See page 601*

BILLINGS & BARRETT

https://billingsandbarrett.com/

BILLINGS & BARRETT FIRST IN FAMILY SCHOLARSHIP
• *See page 601*

MATRIX HEALTH GROUP SPRX BLEEDING DISORDERS

https://matrixhealthgroup.com

JOE HOLIBAUGH MEMORIAL SCHOLARSHIP
• *See page 644*

MARK COATS MEMORIAL SCHOLARSHIP
• *See page 644*

MIKE HYLTON MEMORIAL SCHOLARSHIP
• *See page 644*

MILLIE GONZALEZ MEMORIAL SCHOLARSHIP
• *See page 644*

RON NIEDERMAN MEMORIAL SCHOLARSHIP
• *See page 644*

TIM KENNEDY MEMORIAL SCHOLARSHIP
• *See page 645*

BOUNCE ENERGY

http://www.bounceenergy.com

BE MORE SCHOLARSHIP
• *See page 601*

BRYAN CAMERON EDUCATION FOUNDATION

http://www.bryancameroneducationfoundation.org/index.php

CAMERON IMPACT SCHOLARSHIP
• *See page 601*

BUY-RITE BEAUTY

https://www.buyritebeauty.com/

BUY-RITES ANNUAL BEAUTY SCHOOL SCHOLARSHIP
• *See page 601*

BY KIDS FOR KIDS, CO.

http://bkfkeducation.com

SALLIE MAE® MAKE COLLEGE HAPPEN CHALLENGE
• *See page 602*

CALIFORNIA COUNCIL OF THE BLIND

http://www.ccbnet.org/

CALIFORNIA COUNCIL OF THE BLIND SCHOLARSHIPS
• *See page 602*

CAMP NETWORK

https://www.campnetwork.com/

CAMP COUNSELOR APPRECIATION SCHOLARSHIP
• *See page 603*

CARDSDIRECT INC.

https://www.cardsdirect.com/

FUTURE DESIGNER SCHOLARSHIP
• *See page 603*

CARING.COM

http://caring.com

CARING.COM STUDENT-CAREGIVER BI-ANNUAL SCHOLARSHIP
• *See page 603*

CATHOLIC UNITED FINANCIAL

http://www.catholicunitedfinancial.org

POST HIGH SCHOOL TUITION SCHOLARSHIPS
Catholic United Financial membership requirement of 2 years by application deadline.

Award: Scholarship for use in freshman, sophomore, junior, or senior years; not renewable. *Number:* 600. *Amount:* $300–$500.

Eligibility Requirements: Applicant must be Roman Catholic and enrolled or expecting to enroll full- or part-time at a two-year or four-year or technical institution or university. Available to U.S. citizens.

Application Requirements: Application form, personal photograph. *Deadline:* April 30.

Contact: Member Engagement Department
Phone: 18005686670
E-mail: engage@catholicunited.org

CEDAR EDUCATION LENDING, LLC

http://www.cedaredlending.com

$500 BECAUSE COLLEGE IS EXPENSIVE SCHOLARSHIP
• *See page 603*

CENTER FOR REINTEGRATION

http://www.reintegration.com

BAER REINTEGRATION SCHOLARSHIP
• *See page 604*

CENTRAL SCHOLARSHIP

http://www.central-scholarship.org

LESSANS FAMILY SCHOLARSHIP
• *See page 604*

STRAUS SCHOLARSHIP PROGRAM FOR UNDERGRADUATE EDUCATION
• *See page 604*

CGTRADER

https://www.cgtrader.com/

ANNUAL CGTRADER SCHOLARSHIP
• *See page 604*

CHARLES E. BOYK LAW OFFICES, LLC

https://www.charlesboyk-law.com/

BOYK LAW VETERAN SCHOLARSHIP
• *See page 604*

CHRISTIAN COMMUNITY CREDIT UNION

https://www.mycccu.com/

SCHOLARSHIPS FOR SUCCESS
• *See page 605*

CHRISTIAN RECORD SERVICES INC.

http://www.christianrecord.org

ANNE LOWE SCHOLARSHIPS
• *See page 605*

CHURCH HILL CLASSICS

http://www.diplomaframe.com/

FRAME MY FUTURE SCHOLARSHIP CONTEST
• *See page 605*

CLARA LIONEL FOUNDATION

http://claralionelfoundation.org

CLARA LIONEL FOUNDATION GLOBAL SCHOLARSHIP PROGRAM
• *See page 605*

CLOTHINGRIC.COM

http://www.clothingric.com

CLOTHINGRIC.COM ANNUAL STUDENT SCHOLARSHIP
• *See page 605*

CODA INTERNATIONAL

http://www.coda-international.org

MILLIE BROTHER SCHOLARSHIP FOR CHILDREN OF DEAF ADULTS
• *See page 605*

COGBURN LAW OFFICES

http://cogburnlaw.com/

COGBURN LAW OFFICES ANNUAL SCHOLARSHIP
• *See page 606*

COLLEGE NOW GREATER CLEVELAND, INC.

http://www.collegenowgc.org/

COLLEGE NOW GREATER CLEVELAND ADULT LEARNER PROGRAM SCHOLARSHIP
• *See page 606*

COLORADO MASONS BENEVOLENT FUND ASSOCIATION

http://www.cmbfa.org/scholarship

COLORADO MASONS BENEVOLENT FUND SCHOLARSHIPS
• *See page 606*

COLUMBUS CITIZENS FOUNDATION

http://www.columbuscitizensfd.org/scholarships/scholarships.html

COLUMBUS CITIZENS FOUNDATION COLLEGE SCHOLARSHIP PROGRAM
• *See page 606*

COMMUNITY BANKERS ASSOCIATION OF ILLINOIS

http://www.cbai.com/

COMMUNITY BANKERS ASSOC OF IL CHILD OF A BANKER SCHOLARSHIP
• *See page 562*

COMMUNITY BANKERS ASSOC. OF IL ESSAY CONTEST
• *See page 607*

CONNECTICUT OFFICE OF HIGHER EDUCATION

http://www.ctohe.org

GOVERNOR'S SCHOLARSHIP PROGRAM—NEED/MERIT SCHOLARSHIP
• *See page 607*

ROBERTA B. WILLIS SCHOLARSHIP PROGRAM—NEED-BASED GRANT
• *See page 607*

COUNCIL OF CITIZENS WITH LOW VISION INTERNATIONAL C/O AMERICAN COUNCIL OF THE BLIND

http://www.cclvi.org/

FRED SCHEIGERT SCHOLARSHIP
• *See page 607*

COUPONSURF.COM

http://couponsurf.com/

COUPONSURF ENTREPRENEURS SCHOLARSHIP
• *See page 607*

COURAGE KENNY REHABILITATION INSTITUTE, VOCATIONAL SERVICES DEPARTMENT

http://www.allinahealth.org/couragekenny

SCHOLARSHIP FOR PEOPLE WITH DISABILITIES
• *See page 608*

CROSLEY LAW FIRM

https://crosleylaw.com

CROSLEY LAW FIRM DISTRACTED DRIVING SCHOLARSHIP
• *See page 608*

CSA MEDICAL SUPPLY

https://csamedicalsupply.com

CSA MEDICAL SUPPLY COLLEGE SCHOLARSHIP
• *See page 608*

DANIEL P. BUTTAFUOCO & ASSOCIATES

http://www.1800nowhurt.com

YOUNG CHRISTIAN LEADERS SCHOLARSHIP

Two awards of $1000 given each month to students under the age of 24 who are either high school seniors entering college or are currently full-time undergraduates. Must be a full-time resident of either New York, New Jersey, Connecticut, or Pennsylvania. Applications submitted by the 15th of the month will be considered in the following month's selection process. (e.g., apply by April 15th for a May award). Each applicant may receive a maximum total of three awards per 12-month period. Must be an attending, active members of a local church and have a minimum 3.0 GPA.

Award: Scholarship for use in freshman, sophomore, junior, or senior years; not renewable. *Amount:* $1000.

Eligibility Requirements: Applicant must be Christian; age 18-24; enrolled or expecting to enroll full-time at a four-year institution or university and resident of Connecticut, New Jersey, New York, Pennsylvania. Applicant must have 3.0 GPA or higher. Available to U.S. citizens.

Application Requirements: Application form, essay, personal photograph.

Contact: Ms. Maciel Almonte, Scholarship Administrator
Daniel P. Buttafuoco & Associates
9 Broadman Parkway
Jersey City, NJ 07305
Phone: 201-432-7300
E-mail: info@yclscholarship.org

DANIELS FUND

http://www.danielsfund.org

BOUNDLESS OPPORTUNITY SCHOLARSHIP
• *See page 608*

DANIELS SCHOLARSHIP PROGRAM
• *See page 609*

DANLEY'S GARAGE BUILDERS

https://www.danleysgarageworld.com/

DANLEY'S GARAGE BUILDERS SCHOLARSHIP
• *See page 609*

DAVID S. WYMAN INSTITUTE OF HOLOCAUST STUDIES

http://www.wymaninstitute.org

JOSIAH E. DUBOIS, JR. COLLEGE SCHOLARSHIP ESSAY CONTEST
• *See page 609*

DEMAS LAW GROUP, P.C.

http://www.injury-attorneys.com/

DEMAS LAW GROUP SCHOLARSHIP
• *See page 609*

DEMOLAY FOUNDATION INCORPORATED

http://www.demolay.org/

FRANK S. LAND SCHOLARSHIP
• See page 588

DEPARTMENT OF THE ARMY

http://www.goarmy.com/rotc

ARMY ROTC GREEN TO GOLD SCHOLARSHIP PROGRAM FOR TWO-YEAR, THREE-YEAR AND FOUR-YEAR SCHOLARSHIPS, ACTIVE DUTY ENLISTED PERSONNEL
• See page 610

ARMY (ROTC) RESERVE OFFICERS TRAINING CORPS TWO-, THREE-, FOUR-YEAR CAMPUS-BASED SCHOLARSHIPS
• See page 610

U.S. ARMY ROTC FOUR-YEAR COLLEGE SCHOLARSHIP
• See page 610

U.S. ARMY ROTC FOUR-YEAR HISTORICALLY BLACK COLLEGE/UNIVERSITY SCHOLARSHIP
• See page 610

U.S. ARMY ROTC GUARANTEED RESERVE FORCES DUTY (GRFD), (ARNG/USAR) AND DEDICATED ARNG SCHOLARSHIPS
• See page 611

U.S. ARMY ROTC MILITARY JUNIOR COLLEGE (MJC) SCHOLARSHIP
• See page 611

DESERVE MODERN

http://www.DeserveModern.com

DESERVE MODERN SCHOLARSHIP
• See page 611

DESIGN MY COSTUME

http://designmycostume.com/

DESIGN MY COSTUME SCHOLARSHIP
• See page 611

DIBELLA LAW OFFICES, P.C.

https://www.dibellalawoffice.com/

2018 DIBELLA LAW OFFICES, P.C. SCHOLARSHIP
• See page 612

DISABLED AMERICAN VETERANS

http://www.dav.org/

JESSE BROWN MEMORIAL YOUTH SCHOLARSHIP PROGRAM
• See page 612

DISABLEDPERSON INC. COLLEGE SCHOLARSHIP

http://www.disabledperson.com/

DISABLEDPERSON INC. NATIONAL COLLEGE SCHOLARSHIP AWARD FOR COLLEGE STUDENTS WITH DISABILITIES
• See page 612

DISCIPLESHIP MINISTRIES

http://umcyoungpeople.org

DAVID W. SELF SCHOLARSHIP
Must be a United Methodist Youth who has been active in local church for at least one year prior to application. Must be a graduating senior in high school entering the first year of undergraduate study. Must be pursuing a "church-related" career and should have maintained at least a "C" average throughout high school.

Award: Scholarship for use in freshman year; not renewable. *Number:* 1–5. *Amount:* $100–$1000.

Eligibility Requirements: Applicant must be Methodist; high school student and planning to enroll or expecting to enroll full-time at a two-year or four-year institution or university. Applicant must have 2.5 GPA or higher. Available to U.S. citizens.

Application Requirements: Application form, essay, financial need analysis. *Deadline:* March 1.

Contact: Kelsey Tinker Hannum, Grant and Scholarships Administrator
Phone: 615-340-7184
E-mail: youngpeople@umcdiscipleship.org

RICHARD S. SMITH SCHOLARSHIP
• See page 732

DOLLARS 4 TIC SCHOLARS

http://www.dollars4ticscholars.org/

DOLLARS 4 TIC SCHOLARS TOURETTE SYNDROME SCHOLARSHIP
• See page 613

DOLPHIN SCHOLARSHIP FOUNDATION

http://www.dolphinscholarship.org/

DOLPHIN SCHOLARSHIPS
• See page 613

DOMNICK CUNNINGHAM AND WHALEN

https://www.dcwlaw.com/

DOMNICK CUNNINGHAM & WHALEN ELDER ABUSE PREVENTION
• See page 613

DONALDSON COMPANY

http://www.donaldson.com/

THE DONALDSON COMPANY, INC. SCHOLARSHIP PROGRAM
• See page 588

DONTPAYFULL.COM

https://www.dontpayfull.com/

$500 ANNUAL STUDENT SCHOLARSHIP
• See page 613

DRONE PILOT GROUND SCHOOL
https://www.dronepilotgroundschool.com

DRONE TECHNOLOGY COLLEGE SCHOLARSHIP
• *See page 613*

EASTERN ORTHODOX COMMITTEE ON SCOUTING
http://www.eocs.org/

EASTERN ORTHODOX COMMITTEE ON SCOUTING SCHOLARSHIPS
• *See page 562*

EDGAR ALLEN POE LITERARY SOCIETY
http://www.ravens.org/

DISTINGUISHED RAVEN FAC MEMORIAL SCHOLARSHIP
• *See page 614*

EDUCATOR, INC.
https://www.educator.com/

ANNUAL $2,400 STUDENT SCHOLARSHIP
• *See page 614*

ELEARNERS.COM
http://www.elearners.com

ELEARNERS ONLINE STUDENT SCHOLARSHIP
• *See page 614*

ELIZABETH GREENSHIELDS FOUNDATION
http://www.elizabethgreenshieldsfoundation.org

THE ELIZABETH GREENSHIELDS FOUNDATION GRANT
• *See page 614*

ENVIRONMENTAL LITIGATION GROUP P.C.
https://www.elglaw.com/

ENVIRONMENTAL LITIGATION GROUP, P.C. ASBESTOS SCHOLARSHIP
• *See page 615*

EQUALITY SCHOLARSHIP COLLABORATIVE
http://www.equalityscholarship.org

EQUALITY SCHOLARSHIPS FOR COMMUNITY COLLEGE TRANSFER STUDENTS
• *See page 615*

SCHOLARSHIPS FOR HIGH SCHOOL GRADUATES
• *See page 615*

ESSAYHUB
https://essayhub.com/

ESSAY WRITING CONTEST BY ESSAYHUB
• *See page 615*

EVANS SCHOLARS FOUNDATION
http://www.wgaesf.org

CHICK EVANS SCHOLARSHIP FOR CADDIES
• *See page 616*

EVERIPEDIA INC.
https://www.everipedia.com

EVERIPEDIA TECH TITANS DIVERSITY SCHOLARSHIP
• *See page 616*

EXPRESSVPN
https://www.expressvpn.com

EXPRESSVPN FUTURE OF PRIVACY SCHOLARSHIP
• *See page 616*

FADEL EDUCATIONAL FOUNDATION, INC.
http://www.fadelfoundation.org/

ANNUAL AWARD PROGRAM
Grants of $800 to $3500 awarded on the basis of merit and financial need.

Award: Grant for use in freshman, sophomore, junior, senior, or graduate years; renewable. *Number:* 6–8. *Amount:* $800–$3500.

Eligibility Requirements: Applicant must be Muslim faith and enrolled or expecting to enroll full- or part-time at a two-year or four-year or technical institution or university. Available to U.S. citizens.

Application Requirements: Application form, essay, financial need analysis. *Deadline:* May 28.

Contact: Mr. Ayman Fadel, Secretary
      E-mail: secretary@fadelfoundation.org

FEDERAL RESOURCES
http://www.federalresources.com

WARRIOR'S LEGACY SCHOLARSHIP FUND
• *See page 616*

FELDCO WINDOWS, SIDING AND DOORS
http://www.4feldco.com

FELDCO WINDOWS, SIDING AND DOORS SCHOLARSHIP
• *See page 616*

FELDMAN & ROYLE, ATTORNEYS AT LAW
http://www.feldmanroyle.com/

AUTISM SCHOLARSHIPS
• *See page 617*

FELDMAN LAW FIRM PLLC

http://www.afphoenixcriminalattorney.com/

AUTISM SCHOLARSHIP
• *See page 617*

DISABLED VETERANS SCHOLARSHIP
• *See page 617*

FIG TECH INC.

http://www.figloans.com

$1,000 SCHOLARSHIP FOR SOCIAL IMPACT
• *See page 617*

FINALLY SOLD

http://www.finallysold.com

FINALLY SOLD IMPACT MAKER SCHOLARSHIP
• *See page 618*

FINANCE AUTHORITY OF MAINE

http://www.famemaine.com/

TUITION WAIVER PROGRAMS
• *See page 618*

FINANCIAL SERVICE CENTERS OF NEW YORK

http://www.fscny.org

FSCNY YOUNG LEADERS SCHOLARSHIP
• *See page 618*

FIT SMALL BUSINESS

http://www.fitsmallbusiness.com

BUSINESS PLAN SCHOLARSHIP FOR STUDENTS WITH DISABILITIES
• *See page 618*

FLORIDA PTA/PTSA

http://www.floridapta.org/

FLORIDA PTA/PTSA ANNUAL SCHOLARSHIP
• *See page 619*

FOUNDATION FOR CHRISTIAN COLLEGE LEADERS

http://www.collegechristianleader.com/

FOUNDATION FOR COLLEGE CHRISTIAN LEADERS SCHOLARSHIP

Applicant must be accepted to or currently enrolled in an undergraduate degree program. Candidate must demonstrate Christian leadership. Combined income of parents and student must be less than $60,000. Minimum 3.0 GPA required.

Award: Scholarship for use in freshman, sophomore, junior, senior, or graduate years; not renewable.

Eligibility Requirements: Applicant must be Christian; enrolled or expecting to enroll full- or part-time at a four-year institution or university and must have an interest in leadership. Applicant must have 3.0 GPA or higher. Available to U.S. citizens.

Application Requirements: Application form, financial need analysis, interview, leadership assessment form, cover sheet, recommendations or references. *Deadline:* May 7.

Contact: Scholarship Committee
Phone: 858-481-0848
Fax: 858-481-0848
E-mail: lmhays@aol.com

FOUNDATION FOR SIGHT AND SOUND

http://fssny.org

HELP AMERICA HEAR SCHOLARSHIP
• *See page 619*

FOUNDATION OF THE 1ST CAVALRY DIVISION ASSOCIATION

https://www.1cda.org/

FOUNDATION OF THE 1ST CAVALRY DIVISION ASSOCIATION (IA DRANG) SCHOLARSHIP
• *See page 619*

FOUNDATION OF THE 1ST CAVALRY DIVISION ASSOCIATION SCHOLARSHIP
• *See page 619*

FREEDOM ALLIANCE

https://freedomalliance.org

FREEDOM ALLIANCE SCHOLARSHIP FUND
• *See page 620*

FREEDOM FROM RELIGION FOUNDATION

http://www.ffrf.org/

FREEDOM FROM RELIGION FOUNDATION MICHAEL HAKEEM MEMORIAL ONGOING COLLEGE ESSAY COMPETITION

Any currently enrolled college student may submit essay. Any college-bound high school seniors enter our high school contest. "My morals do not come from God, they come from.." is the open-ended topic offered to ongoing college students in the Michael Hakeem Memorial Contest. College students are asked to write essays of 450-650 words due by July 1, with winners announced in August. All the rules and online application are here: https://www.surveymonkey.com/r/B8F3235

Award: Scholarship for use in freshman, sophomore, junior, or senior years; not renewable. *Number:* 6–20. *Amount:* $200–$3000.

Eligibility Requirements: Applicant must be age 16-24; enrolled or expecting to enroll full- or part-time at a two-year or four-year or technical institution or university and must have an interest in writing. Available to U.S. and Canadian citizens.

Application Requirements: Application form, essay. *Deadline:* July 1.

Contact: FFRF College Essay Contest
Freedom From Religion Foundation
PO Box 750
Madison, WI 53701

FREEDOM FROM RELIGION FOUNDATION WILLIAM J. SCHULZ MEMORIAL COLLEGE-BOUND HIGH SCHOOL SENIOR ESSAY COMPETITION

College-bound high school seniors write on the topic: "If there was one thing I could tell my family or a believer about why I'm a nonbeliever, this would be it." June 1 deadline. Word limits of 350 words, with winners announced in July. See all rules at: https://www.surveymonkey.com/r/QBHT9XG

Award: Scholarship for use in freshman year; not renewable. *Number:* 6–20. *Amount:* $200–$3000.

Eligibility Requirements: Applicant must be high school student; age 15-20; planning to enroll or expecting to enroll full- or part-time at a two-year or four-year or technical institution or university and must have an interest in writing. Available to U.S. and Canadian citizens.

Application Requirements: Application form, essay. *Deadline:* June 1.

Contact: High School Essay Competition
Freedom From Religion Foundation
PO Box 750
Madison, WI 53701

FRIENDS OF COAL LADIES AUXILIARY

friendsofcoalladies.com

FRIENDS OF COAL SCHOLARSHIPS
• *See page 735*

FRIENDS OF THE MINNESOTA ORCHESTRA (FORMERLY WAMSO)

https://friendsofminnesotaorchestra.org/

YOUNG ARTIST COMPETITION
• *See page 620*

FUNNEWJERSEY.COM INC.

http://www.funnewjersey.com

FUNNEWJERSEY.COM SCHOLARSHIP
• *See page 620*

GENERAL BOARD OF HIGHER EDUCATION AND MINISTRY

http://www.gbhem.org

BISHOP JOSEPH B. BETHEA SCHOLARSHIP
• *See page 735*

E. CRAIG BRANDENBURG GRADUATE AWARD

Scholarship for students 35 years of age or older, desiring to continue their education or to go into a second career. Must be enrolled full time at an accredited institution, and be active, full-time members of the United Methodist Church for at least one year.

Award: Scholarship for use in freshman, sophomore, junior, senior, or graduate years; not renewable.

Eligibility Requirements: Applicant must be Methodist and enrolled or expecting to enroll full-time at a four-year institution or university. Available to U.S. citizens.

Application Requirements: Application form, essay. *Deadline:* March 1.

Contact: Ms. Marcie Bigord, Assistant Director of Loans & Scholarships
General Board of Higher Education and Ministry
PO Box 340007
Nashville, TN 37203-0007
Phone: 615-340-7388
Fax: 615-340-7529
E-mail: mbigord@gbhem.org

HELEN AND ALLEN BROWN SCHOLARSHIP

Scholarship for outstanding high school graduates and undergraduate college students who are members of the Nashville District of the Tennessee Annual Conference of UMC or members of the New Orleans District of the Louisiana Annual Conference of UMC. Must have been full and active members of The United Methodist Church for at least three years and maintain a GPA of 3.0.

Award: Scholarship for use in freshman, sophomore, junior, or senior years; not renewable.

Eligibility Requirements: Applicant must be Methodist and enrolled or expecting to enroll full-time at a four-year institution or university. Applicant must have 3.0 GPA or higher. Available to U.S. citizens.

Application Requirements: Application form, essay. *Deadline:* March 1.

Contact: Ms. Marcie Bigord, Assistant Director of Loans & Scholarships
General Board of Higher Education and Ministry
PO Box 340007
Nashville, TN 37203-0007
Phone: 615-340-7388
Fax: 615-340-7529
E-mail: mbigord@gbhem.org

THE REV. DR. KAREN LAYMAN GIFT OF HOPE

$1000 scholarship to United Methodist undergraduate students who are full-time, active members of UMC for at least three years prior to applying. Must demonstrate leadership in the United Methodist Church and be enrolled in a full-time degree program at a regionally accredited U.S. institution. Cumulative GPA of 3.0 or higher required.

Award: Scholarship for use in freshman, sophomore, junior, or senior years; not renewable. *Amount:* $1000.

Eligibility Requirements: Applicant must be Methodist; enrolled or expecting to enroll full-time at a two-year or four-year institution or university and must have an interest in leadership. Applicant must have 3.0 GPA or higher. Available to U.S. and non-Canadian citizens.

Application Requirements: Application form, essay. *Deadline:* March 1.

Contact: Ms. Marcie Bigord, Assistant Director of Loans & Scholarships
General Board of Higher Education and Ministry
PO Box 340007
Nashville, TN 37203-0007
Phone: 615-340-7388
Fax: 615-340-7529
E-mail: mbigord@gbhem.org

GENERAL FEDERATION OF WOMEN'S CLUBS OF MASSACHUSETTS

http://www.gfwcma.org/

GENERAL FEDERATION OF WOMEN'S CLUBS OF MASSACHUSETTS NICKEL FOR NOTES MUSIC SCHOLARSHIP
• *See page 620*

GENERAL FEDERATION OF WOMEN'S CLUBS OF MASSACHUSETTS PENNIES FOR ART SCHOLARSHIP
• *See page 620*

GEORGIA PRESS EDUCATIONAL FOUNDATION INC.

http://gapress.org/scholarships-internships/

KIRK SUTLIVE SCHOLARSHIP
• *See page 621*

MORRIS NEWSPAPER CORPORATION SCHOLARSHIP
• *See page 621*

GEORGIA STUDENT FINANCE COMMISSION

http://www.GAfutures.org

GEORGIA HERO SCHOLARSHIP
• *See page 621*

GEORGIA PUBLIC SAFETY MEMORIAL GRANT
• *See page 621*

GEORGIA TUITION EQUALIZATION GRANT (GTEG)
• *See page 621*

ZELL MILLER SCHOLARSHIP PROGRAM
• *See page 621*

GERSOWITZ LIBO & KOREK, P.C.

https://www.lawyertime.com

GARDINER FOUNDATION SCHOLARSHIP

• *See page 621*

GIFT BASKETS PLUS

http://www.giftbasketsplus.com

HIGH SCHOOL GRADUATE SCHOLARSHIP CONTEST

• *See page 622*

GOENNOUNCE, LLC

http://GoEnnounce.com/about

GOENNOUNCE YOURSELF $500 MONTHLY SCHOLARSHIP

• *See page 622*

GOLDSTEIN AND BASHNER

https://www.eglaw.com/

COMBATING CAMPUS ISSUES SCHOLARSHIP

• *See page 622*

GOLF COURSE SUPERINTENDENTS ASSOCIATION OF AMERICA

http://www.eifg.org/

GOLF COURSE SUPERINTENDENTS ASSOCIATION OF AMERICA LEGACY AWARD

• *See page 564*

JOSEPH S. GARSKE COLLEGIATE GRANT PROGRAM

• *See page 564*

GORDON LAW GROUP

https://www.gordonlawltd.com

GORDON LAW GROUP ANNUAL SCHOLARSHIP

• *See page 622*

GREATER GOOD SCIENCE CENTER

https://ggsc.berkeley.edu/

THE PURPOSE CHALLENGE

• *See page 622*

GREATER KANAWHA VALLEY FOUNDATION

http://www.tgkvf.org/

STUART & LUCILLE ARMSTRONG SCHOLARSHIP

Renewable scholarship for an Episcopalian in the Diocese of West Virginia. Must maintain a 3.0 GPA and continue to pursue the same major or degree program. Seminarians are not eligible. Preference given to applicants from St. Christopher in Charleston.

Award: Scholarship for use in freshman, sophomore, junior, or senior years; renewable. *Amount:* $1000.

Eligibility Requirements: Applicant must be Episcopalian; enrolled or expecting to enroll full-time at a four-year institution or university and resident of West Virginia. Applicant must have 3.0 GPA or higher. Available to U.S. citizens.

Application Requirements: Application form, essay, financial need analysis, name and location of home parish along with Rectors name and contact information, recommendations or references, test scores, transcript. *Deadline:* January 15.

Contact: Susan Hoover, Scholarship Program Officer
Greater Kanawha Valley Foundation
900 Lee Street East, 16th Floor
Charleston, WV 25301
Phone: 304-346-3620
E-mail: shoover@tgkvf.org

GREENHOUSE SCHOLARS

https://greenhousescholars.org/

GREENHOUSE SCHOLARS

• *See page 736*

GRUNGO COLARULO

https://gcinjurylaw.com/

GRUNGO COLARULO GIVING BACK TO THE COMMUNITY SCHOLARSHIP

• *See page 623*

HANSCOM FEDERAL CREDIT UNION

https://www.hfcu.org/

JOHN F. CONDON MEMORIAL SCHOLARSHIP

• *See page 623*

HARDWICK & PENDERGAST, P.S.

http://www.hardwickpendergast.com/

HARDWICK & PENDERGAST, P.S. SCHOLARSHIP

• *See page 623*

HARRINGTON FAMILY FOUNDATION

http://harringtonfamilyfoundation.org

OREGON COMMUNITY QUARTERBACK SCHOLARSHIP

• *See page 624*

HAWAII EDUCATION ASSOCIATION

http://www.heaed.com/

HAWAII EDUCATION ASSOCIATION CONTINUING COLLEGE STUDENT SCHOLARSHIP

• *See page 565*

HAWAII EDUCATION ASSOCIATION HIGH SCHOOL STUDENT SCHOLARSHIP

• *See page 565*

HAWAII SCHOOLS FEDERAL CREDIT UNION

http://www.hawaiischoolsfcu.org/

EDWIN KUNIYUKI MEMORIAL SCHOLARSHIP

• *See page 624*

HBCUCONNECT.COM

http://www.hbcuconnect.com/

HBCUCONNECT.COM MINORITY SCHOLARSHIP PROGRAM
• *See page 624*

HEALTH PRODUCTS FOR YOU

https://www.healthproductsforyou.com/

HPFY DISABILITY SCHOLARSHIP
• *See page 737*

HELEN DILLER FAMILY FOUNDATION

http://www.dillerteenawards.org

DILLER TEEN TIKKUN OLAM AWARDS
• *See page 624*

HEMOPHILIA FOUNDATION OF SOUTHERN CALIFORNIA

http://www.hemosocal.org/

CHRISTOPHER MARK PITKIN MEMORIAL SCHOLARSHIP
• *See page 625*

HENKEL CONSUMER ADHESIVES INC.

http://www.ducktapeclub.com/

DUCK BRAND DUCT TAPE "STUCK AT PROM" SCHOLARSHIP CONTEST
• *See page 625*

HERB KOHL EDUCATIONAL FOUNDATION INC.

http://www.kohleducation.org/

HERB KOHL EXCELLENCE SCHOLARSHIP PROGRAM
• *See page 625*

THE HIGGINS FIRM

https://www.thehigginsfirm.com

JUDGE BILL HIGGINS PUBLIC SERVICE SCHOLARSHIP
• *See page 625*

HIGH INCOME PARENTS.COM

http://www.highincomeparents.com

MELISSA READ MEMORIAL SCHOLARSHIP
• *See page 625*

HISPANIC METROPOLITAN CHAMBER SCHOLARSHIPS

http://www.hmccoregon.com/

HISPANIC METROPOLITAN CHAMBER SCHOLARSHIPS
• *See page 626*

THE HIV LEAGUE

http://www.hivleague.org

THE HIV LEAGUE SCHOLARSHIP
• *See page 626*

HOFOSS DEVALL

https://www.hdinjurylaw.com/

HOFFOSS DEVALL LOUISIANA SAFE DRIVER SCHOLARSHIP
• *See page 626*

HOFFOSS DEVALL PROBLEM SOLVING SCHOLARSHIP
• *See page 626*

HOME IMPROVEMENT SOLUTIONS

http://www.myhomeimprovementsolutions.com

HOME IMPROVEMENT SCHOLARSHIP BY HOME IMPROVEMENT SOLUTIONS
• *See page 626*

HOMUS

https://homus.org

HOMUS SCHOLARSHIP PROGRAM
• *See page 627*

HOOVER PRESIDENTIAL FOUNDATION

http://www.hooverpresidentialfoundation.org/travel-grant.php

HERBERT HOOVER UNCOMMON STUDENT AWARD
• *See page 627*

HOSTGATOR

https://www.hostgator.com/

HOSTGATOR WEBSITE SCHOLARSHIP
• *See page 627*

HOUSE OF BLUES MUSIC FORWARD FOUNDATION

https://hobmusicforward.org/

LIVE NATION—US CONCERTS SCHOLARSHIP AWARD
• *See page 628*

HOUSTON COMMUNITY SERVICES

AZTECA SCHOLARSHIP
• *See page 628*

HOW TO WIN COLLEGE SCHOLARSHIPS

https://how2winscholarships.com

SAVOR SUMMER COLLEGE SCHOLARSHIP
• *See page 628*

HUBSHOUT

http://hubshout.com/

HUBSHOUT INTERNET MARKETING SCHOLARSHIP
• *See page 628*

HUMANA FOUNDATION

http://www.humanafoundation.org/

HUMANA FOUNDATION SCHOLARSHIP PROGRAM
• *See page 628*

INDIANA LIBRARY FEDERATION

http://www.ilfonline.org/

SUE MARSH WELLER SCHOLARSHIP FUND
• *See page 629*

INTERNATIONAL COLLEGE COUNSELORS

http://www.internationalcollegecounselors.com

INTERNATIONAL COLLEGE COUNSELORS SCHOLARSHIP
• *See page 629*

INTERNATIONAL DAIRY DELI BAKERY ASSOCIATION

http://www.iddba.org

INTERNATIONAL DAIRY DELI BAKERY ASSOCIATION'S SCHOLARSHIP FOR GROWING THE FUTURE
• *See page 629*

INTERNATIONAL FLIGHT SERVICES ASSOCIATION

http://www.ifsanet.com

AMI SCHOLARSHIP AWARD
• *See page 629*

IOVATE HEALTH SCIENCES INTERNATIONAL INC.

http://www.iovate.com/

SIX STAR PRO NUTRITION SCHOLARSHIP AWARD
• *See page 631*

IOWA STUDENT LOAN

http://www.IowaStudentLoan.org/

COME 2 IOWA (C2IA) SENIOR SCHOLARSHIP
• *See page 631*

IOWA FINANCIAL KNOW-HOW CHALLENGE: SENIOR SCHOLARSHIP
• *See page 631*

ITALIAN CATHOLIC FEDERATION

http://www.icf.org/

ITALIAN CATHOLIC FEDERATION FIRST YEAR SCHOLARSHIP
• *See page 566*

JAMES F. BYRNES FOUNDATION

http://www.byrnesscholars.org/

JAMES F. BYRNES SCHOLARSHIP
• *See page 631*

JEANNETTE RANKIN WOMEN'S SCHOLARSHIP FUND

http://www.rankinfoundation.org/

JEANNETTE RANKIN WOMEN'S SCHOLARSHIP FUND
• *See page 632*

JEWISH VOCATIONAL SERVICE LOS ANGELES

http://www.jvsla.org/

JVS SCHOLARSHIP PROGRAM
• *See page 741*

JOHN B. FABRIELE, III, LLC

https://www.fabrielelaw.com/

FABRIELE DISABILITY AWARENESS SCHOLARSHIP
• *See page 632*

JOHN F. KENNEDY LIBRARY FOUNDATION

http://www.jfklibrary.org/

PROFILE IN COURAGE ESSAY CONTEST
• *See page 632*

JOHNSON ATTORNEYS GROUP

https://californiainjuryaccidentlawyer.com/

NEVER DRINK AND DRIVE SCHOLARSHIP
• *See page 632*

JUNK A CAR

https://www.junkacar.com/

JUNK A CAR 2018 SCHOLARSHIP
• *See page 632*

JVS CHICAGO

http://jvschicago.org/

JEWISH FEDERATION OF METROPOLITAN CHICAGO ACADEMIC SCHOLARSHIP PROGRAM
• *See page 742*

J. WALTER THOMPSON

https://www.jwt.com/en/

HELEN LANSDOWNE RESOR SCHOLARSHIP
• *See page 633*

KAUFMAN & STIGGER, PLLC

http://www.getthetiger.com/

THE ALBERTA C. KAUFMAN SCHOLARSHIP
• *See page 633*

KELLER LAW OFFICES

http://www.kellerlawoffices.com/

KELLER LAW OFFICES SCHOLARSHIP FOR HIGHER EDUCATION
• *See page 633*

KELLEY & CANTERBURY, LLC

http://kelleyandcanterbury.com/

KELLEY & CANTERBURY, LLC ALASKA CURIOSITY SCHOLARSHIP
• *See page 633*

KELLY LAW TEAM

http://www.jkphoenixpersonalinjuryattorney.com/

AUTISM/ASD SCHOLARSHIP
• *See page 633*

DISABLED VETERAN SCHOLARSHIP
• *See page 634*

DISABLED VETERAN SCHOLARSHIP
• *See page 634*

KEVIN'S REVIEW

http://www.kevinsreview.com

KEVIN'S REVIEW NCLEX ASSISTANCE SCHOLARSHIP
• *See page 634*

KIDGUARD

http://www.kidguard.com/

KIDGUARD FOR EDUCATION ESSAY SCHOLARSHIP
• *See page 634*

KIDGUARD FOR EDUCATION ESSAY SCHOLARSHIP FOR HIGH SCHOOL
• *See page 635*

KITCHEN GUIDES

http://www.kitchensguides.com/

SMART KITCHEN IMPROVEMENT SCHOLARSHIP BY KITCHEN GUIDES
• *See page 635*

KNIGHTS OF COLUMBUS

http://www.kofc.org/

FOURTH DEGREE PRO DEO AND PRO PATRIA (CANADA)
• *See page 567*

FOURTH DEGREE PRO DEO AND PRO PATRIA SCHOLARSHIPS
• *See page 567*

FRANCIS P. MATTHEWS AND JOHN E. SWIFT EDUCATIONAL TRUST SCHOLARSHIPS
• *See page 567*

JOHN W. MCDEVITT (FOURTH DEGREE) SCHOLARSHIPS
• *See page 567*

PERCY J. JOHNSON ENDOWED SCHOLARSHIPS
• *See page 567*

KOGAN AND DISALVO, P.A.

https://www.kogan-disalvo.com/

KOGAN & DISALVO PERSONAL INJURY LAW AUTONOMOUS VEHICLES SCHOLARSHIP
• *See page 635*

KOPFLER AND HERMANN, ATTORNEYS AT LAW

https://kopflerhermann.com/

KOPFLER & HERMANN OVERCOMING ADVERSITY SCHOLARSHIP
• *See page 635*

LANDSCAPE ARCHITECTURE FOUNDATION

http://www.lafoundation.org

ASLA COUNCIL OF FELLOWS SCHOLARSHIP
• *See page 635*

COURTLAND PAUL SCHOLARSHIP
• *See page 635*

EDSA MINORITY SCHOLARSHIP
• *See page 636*

HAWAII CHAPTER/DAVID T. WOOLSEY SCHOLARSHIP
• *See page 636*

LANDSCAPE FORMS DESIGN FOR PEOPLE SCHOLARSHIP
• *See page 636*

STEVEN G. KING PLAY ENVIRONMENTS SCHOLARSHIP
• *See page 636*

LARSON JEWELERS

http://www.larsonjewelers.com

BAND WITH SUCCESS SCHOLARSHIP
• *See page 636*

LATIN AMERICAN EDUCATIONAL FOUNDATION

http://www.laef.org/

LATIN AMERICAN EDUCATIONAL FOUNDATION SCHOLARSHIPS
• *See page 636*

LA UNIDAD LATINA FOUNDATION

http://www.lulf.org/

LA UNIDAD LATINA FOUNDATION DREAM SCHOLARSHIP
• *See page 636*

LA UNIDAD LATINA FOUNDATION NATIONAL SCHOLARSHIP
• *See page 637*

LAW OFFICE OF DAVID D. WHITE, PLLC

http://www.wm-attorneys.com/

ANNUAL TRAUMATIC BRAIN INJURY SCHOLARSHIPS
• *See page 637*

LAW OFFICE OF DAVID P. SHAPIRO

http://www.davidpshapirolaw.com/about-us/

AUTISM SCHOLARSHIP
• *See page 637*

LAW OFFICE OF HENRY QUEENER

https://queenerlaw.com/

LAW OFFICE OF HENRY QUEENER ANNUAL SCHOLARSHIP
• *See page 637*

LAW OFFICE OF MATTHEW L. SHARP

https://mattsharplaw.com/

LAW OFFICE OF MATTHEW L. SHARP ANNUAL SCHOLARSHIP
• *See page 638*

LAW OFFICE OF MATTHEW SHRUM

http://www.shrumlawoffice.com/

ANNUAL SINGLE MOTHERS SCHOLARSHIP
• *See page 638*

LAW OFFICES OF DAVID A. BLACK

http://www.dbphoenixcriminallawyer.com

SCHOLARSHIP FOR DISABLED VETERANS
• *See page 638*

LAW OFFICES OF DIANNE SAWAYA LLC

https://dlslawfirm.com/

LAW OFFICES OF DIANNE SAWAYA DENVER SAFE DRIVER SCHOLARSHIP
• *See page 638*

LAW OFFICES OF JUDD S. NEMIRO, PLLC

http://www.jnphoenixfamilylawyer.com/

ANNUAL DYSLEXIA SCHOLARSHIP
• *See page 638*

LAW OFFICES OF MARK SHERMAN, LLC

markshermanlaw.com

MARK SHERMAN LAW JUVENILE JUSTICE SCHOLARSHIP
• *See page 639*

LAW OFFICES OF SEAN M. CLEARY

https://www.seanclearypa.com/

LAW OFFICES OF SEAN M. CLEARY SCHOLARSHIP
• *See page 639*

LAW OFFICES OF SHERYL R. RENTZ, P.C.

http://www.srrentzlaw.com/

LAW OFFICES OF SHERYL R. RENTZ 2018 SCHOLARSHIP
• *See page 639*

LAW OFFICES OF TRAGOS, SARTES AND TRAGOS

https://tragoslaw.com/

TRAGOS WRITE YOUR OWN LAW SCHOLARSHIP
• *See page 639*

LEAGUE FOUNDATION

http://www.leaguefoundation.org/

LEAGUE FOUNDATION ACADEMIC SCHOLARSHIP
• *See page 639*

LEMBERG LAW

http://www.lemberglaw.com

LEMBERG LAW AMERICAN DREAM $1,250 UNDERGRADUATE SCHOLARSHIP
• *See page 640*

LEPENDORF & SILVERSTEIN, P.C.

http://www.lependorf.com/

2018 LEPENDORF & SILVERSTEIN, P.C. SCHOLARSHIP
• *See page 640*

LEP FOUNDATION FOR YOUTH EDUCATION

http://www.lepfoundation.org/applications

CURE—CANCER SUPPORT SCHOLARSHIP
• *See page 640*

JOHN LEPPING MEMORIAL SCHOLARSHIP
• *See page 640*

LEVY LAW OFFICES

https://levylawoffices.com/

LEVY LAW OFFICES CINCINNATI SAFE DRIVER SCHOLARSHIP
• *See page 640*

LIFESAVER ESSAYS

https://lifesaveressays.com

LIFE SAVER ESSAYS ESSAY WRITING CONTEST
• *See page 640*

LIGHTHOUSE GUILD

http://www.lighthouseguild.org

LIGHTHOUSE GUILD SCHOLARSHIP PROGRAM
• *See page 689*

LIVE POETS SOCIETY AND JUST POETRY!!! MAGAZINE

http://www.highschoolpoetrycontest.com/

NATIONAL HIGH SCHOOL POETRY CONTEST
• *See page 641*

MAINE STATE SOCIETY FOUNDATION OF WASHINGTON, DC INC.

http://mainestatesociety.org/foundation/

MAINE STATE SOCIETY FOUNDATION SCHOLARSHIP
• *See page 641*

MAINOR WORTH INJURY LAWYERS

https://mainorwirth.com/

MAINOR WIRTH INJURY LAWYERS SCHOLARSHIP
• *See page 641*

MARYLAND ASSOCIATION OF PRIVATE COLLEGES AND CAREER SCHOOLS

http://www.mapccs.org/

MARYLAND ASSOCIATION OF PRIVATE COLLEGES AND CAREER SCHOOLS SCHOLARSHIP
• *See page 642*

MASSACHUSETTS OFFICE OF STUDENT FINANCIAL ASSISTANCE

http://www.osfa.mass.edu/

AGNES M. LINDSAY SCHOLARSHIP
• *See page 642*

CHRISTIAN A. HERTER MEMORIAL SCHOLARSHIP
• *See page 642*

DSS ADOPTED CHILDREN TUITION WAIVER
• *See page 642*

JOHN AND ABIGAIL ADAMS SCHOLARSHIP
• *See page 642*

MASSACHUSETTS ASSISTANCE FOR STUDENT SUCCESS PROGRAM
• *See page 643*

MASSACHUSETTS CASH GRANT PROGRAM
• *See page 643*

MASSACHUSETTS GILBERT MATCHING STUDENT GRANT PROGRAM
• *See page 643*

MASSACHUSETTS PART-TIME GRANT PROGRAM
• *See page 643*

MASSACHUSETTS PUBLIC SERVICE GRANT PROGRAM
• *See page 643*

PAUL TSONGAS SCHOLARSHIP PROGRAM
• *See page 643*

MASSEY AND ASSOCIATES, PC

https://www.masseyattorneys.com/

MASSEY & ASSOCIATES: JUSTICE FOR ALL SCHOLARSHIP
• *See page 643*

MEDIGO GMBH

https://www.medigo.com/en

MEDIGO SCHOLARSHIP PROGRAM
• *See page 645*

MENSA FOUNDATION

mensafoundation.org

U.S. SCHOLARSHIP PROGRAM
• *See page 645*

MES FOUNDATION

http://www.mesfoundation.org

RICHARD H. PIERCE MEMORIAL SCHOLARSHIP
• *See page 645*

MINDSUMO

http://www.mindsumo.com

MINDSUMO 15-MINUTE SCHOLARSHIP
• *See page 645*

MINNESOTA MASONIC CHARITIES

http://www.mnmasoniccharities.org

MINNESOTA MASONIC CHARITIES SIGNATURE SCHOLARSHIP
• *See page 645*

MINNESOTA MASONIC CHARITIES UNDERGRADUATE SCHOLARSHIP
• *See page 646*

MITCHELL INSTITUTE

http://www.mitchellinstitute.org/

SENATOR GEORGE J. MITCHELL SCHOLARSHIP RESEARCH INSTITUTE
• *See page 646*

MLD WEALTH MANAGEMENT GROUP

http://mywealthmanagement.ca/

ANNUAL MLD SCHOLASTIC SCHOLARSHIP
• *See page 646*

MUCHGAMES.COM

http://www.muchgames.com

MUCHGAMES.COM STUDENT RESEARCH GRANT OF $1500
• *See page 646*

THE MULLER FIRM, LTD

https://chicagodivorceattys.com/

THE MULLER FIRM, LTD ANNUAL SCHOLARSHIP
• *See page 647*

NATIONAL AIDS MEMORIAL

http://www.aidsmemorial.org

PEDRO ZAMORA YOUNG LEADERS SCHOLARSHIP
• *See page 647*

NATIONAL ASSOCIATION FOR CAMPUS ACTIVITIES

http://www.naca.org/

ALAN DAVIS SCHOLARSHIP
• *See page 647*

JOHN ZAGUNIS STUDENT LEADER SCHOLARSHIP
• *See page 647*

LORI RHETT MEMORIAL SCHOLARSHIP
• *See page 648*

NATIONAL ASSOCIATION FOR CAMPUS ACTIVITIES MID ATLANTIC UNDERGRADUATE SCHOLARSHIP FOR STUDENT LEADERS
• *See page 648*

NATIONAL ASSOCIATION FOR CAMPUS ACTIVITIES SOUTH REGION STUDENT LEADER SCHOLARSHIP
• *See page 648*

TESE CALDARELLI MEMORIAL SCHOLARSHIP
• *See page 648*

NATIONAL COLLEGIATE CANCER FOUNDATION

http://collegiatecancer.org/

NATIONAL COLLEGIATE CANCER FOUNDATION SCHOLARSHIPS
• *See page 750*

NATIONAL COUNCIL OF JEWISH WOMEN LOS ANGELES (NCJW L LA)

http://ncjwla.org/

THE DODELL WOMEN'S EMPOWERMENT SCHOLARSHIP
• *See page 648*

THE SINGERMAN/NOSSECK MEMORIAL SCHOLARSHIP
• *See page 750*

SOPHIE GREENSTADT SCHOLARSHIP FOR MID-LIFE WOMEN
• *See page 648*

STEPHEN L. TELLER & RICHARD HOTSON TV, CINEMA, AND THEATER SCHOLARSHIP
• *See page 649*

SUSAN SCHULMAN BEGLEY MEMORIAL SCHOLARSHIP
• *See page 649*

NATIONAL FEDERATION OF STATE POETRY SOCIETIES (NFSPS)

http://www.nfsps.com/

NATIONAL FEDERATION OF STATE POETRY SOCIETIES' COLLEGE UNDERGRADUATE POETRY (CUP) COMPETITION
• *See page 649*

NATIONAL FEDERATION OF THE BLIND (NFB)

http://www.nfb.org/scholarships

AAF KENNETH JERNIGAN SCHOLARSHIP FOR $12,000
• *See page 649*

CHARLES AND MELVA T. OWEN SCHOLARSHIP FOR $10,000
• *See page 649*

NATIONAL FFA ORGANIZATION

http://www.ffa.org

NATIONAL FFA COLLEGIATE SCHOLARSHIP PROGRAM
• *See page 570*

NATIONAL INSTITUTE FOR LABOR RELATIONS RESEARCH

http://www.nilrr.org/

NATIONAL INSTITUTE FOR LABOR RELATIONS RESEARCH WILLIAM B. RUGGLES JOURNALISM SCHOLARSHIP
• *See page 650*

NATIONAL MILITARY FAMILY ASSOCIATION

http://www.MilitaryFamily.org

NATIONAL MILITARY FAMILY ASSOCIATION'S MILITARY SPOUSE SCHOLARSHIPS
• *See page 650*

NATIONAL MULTIPLE SCLEROSIS SOCIETY

http://www.nmss.org/

NATIONAL MULTIPLE SCLEROSIS SOCIETY SCHOLARSHIP PROGRAM
• *See page 650*

NATIONAL PRESS FOUNDATION

http://www.nationalpress.org/

EVERT CLARK/SETH PAYNE AWARD
• *See page 650*

NATIONAL SOCIETY FOR HISTOTECHNOLOGY

http://nsh.org/

IRWIN S. LERNER STUDENT SCHOLARSHIPS
• *See page 650*

NEBRASKA'S COORDINATING COMMISSION FOR POSTSECONDARY EDUCATION

https://ccpe.nebraska.gov/

NEBRASKA OPPORTUNITY GRANT
• *See page 651*

NEED

http://www.needld.org/

UNMET NEED GRANT PROGRAM
• *See page 651*

NERDIFY

https://gonerdify.com/

NERDY BOT SCHOLARSHIP
• *See page 651*

NEW JERSEY STATE GOLF ASSOCIATION

NJSGA.org

NEW JERSEY STATE GOLF ASSOCIATION CADDIE SCHOLARSHIP
• *See page 652*

NEW YORK WOMEN IN COMMUNICATIONS

https://nywici.org/

NEW YORK WOMEN IN COMMUNICATIONS SCHOLARSHIPS
• *See page 652*

N.H. DEPARTMENT OF EDUCATION, DIVISION OF HIGHER EDUCATION - HIGHER EDUCATION COMMISSION

http://www.education.nh.gov/highered

SCHOLARSHIPS FOR ORPHANS OF VETERANS
• *See page 714*

NICODEMUS WILDERNESS PROJECT

http://www.wildernessproject.org/

APPRENTICE ECOLOGIST SCHOLARSHIP
• *See page 652*

NIKKO COSMETIC SURGERY CENTER

http://www.drnikko.com/

BREAST CANCER SURVIVOR SCHOLARSHIPS
• *See page 652*

NO BULL SPORTS

http://nobullsports.org/

NO BULL SPORTS SCHOLARSHIP
• *See page 653*

NOPLAG PLAGIARISM CHECKER

http://noplag.com/

NOPLAG SCHOLARSHIP ESSAY CONTEST
• *See page 653*

NORTH CAROLINA ASSOCIATION OF EDUCATORS

http://www.ncae.org/

NORTH CAROLINA ASSOCIATION OF EDUCATORS MARTIN LUTHER KING JR. SCHOLARSHIP
• *See page 653*

NORTH CAROLINA DIVISION OF VOCATIONAL REHABILITATION SERVICES

http://www.dhhs.state.nc.us/

TRAINING SUPPORT FOR YOUTH WITH DISABILITIES
• *See page 653*

NORTH CAROLINA VIETNAM VETERANS, INC.

http://www.ncvvi.org

NC VIETNAM VETERANS, INC., SCHOLARSHIP PROGRAM
• *See page 653*

NORTH DAKOTA UNIVERSITY SYSTEM

http://www.ndus.edu/

NORTH DAKOTA ACADEMIC SCHOLARSHIP
• *See page 654*

NORTH DAKOTA CAREER AND TECHNICAL EDUCATION SCHOLARSHIP
• *See page 654*

NORTH DAKOTA INDIAN SCHOLARSHIP PROGRAM
• *See page 654*

NORTH DAKOTA SCHOLARS PROGRAM
• *See page 654*

NORTH DAKOTA STATE STUDENT INCENTIVE GRANT PROGRAM
• *See page 654*

NORTHWESTERN MUTUAL FOUNDATION
http://www.scholarshipamerica.org

NORTHWESTERN MUTUAL CHILDHOOD CANCER SURVIVOR SCHOLARSHIP
• *See page 654*

NOVUS BIOLOGICALS, LLC
https://www.novusbio.com

NOVUS BIOLOGICALS SCHOLARSHIP PROGRAM
• *See page 753*

NURSERECRUITER.COM
https://www.nurserecruiter.com

NURSERECRUITER.COM SCHOLARSHIP
• *See page 655*

OHIO DEPARTMENT OF HIGHER EDUCATION
http://www.ohiohighered.org

CHOOSE OHIO FIRST SCHOLARSHIP
• *See page 655*

OHIO COLLEGE OPPORTUNITY GRANT
• *See page 655*

OHIO SAFETY OFFICERS COLLEGE MEMORIAL FUND
• *See page 655*

OHIO WAR ORPHANS SCHOLARSHIP
• *See page 655*

ONE LOVE FOUNDATION
http://www.joinonelove.org

ONE LOVE FOUNDATION PETS VS. PARTNERS SCHOLARSHIP
• *See page 656*

ONLINEPSYCHOLOGYDEGREES.COM
http://www.onlinepsychologydegrees.com/

ONLINEPSYCHOLOGYDEGREES.COM EDUCATION SCHOLARSHIPS
• *See page 656*

ORGANIZATION FOR AUTISM RESEARCH
http://www.researchautism.org

LISA HIGGINS HUSSMAN SCHOLARSHIP
• *See page 656*

SCHWALLIE FAMILY SCHOLARSHIP
• *See page 656*

ORGONE BIOPHYSICAL RESEARCH LABORATORY
http://www.orgonelab.org/hochberg.htm

LOU HOCHBERG-UNIVERSITY/COLLEGE ESSAY AWARDS
• *See page 656*

ORTHODOX UNION
http://ou.org

SARA AND MAX GOLDSAMMLER SCHOLARSHIP FUND
• *See page 754*

OUR WORLD UNDERWATER SCHOLARSHIP SOCIETY
http://www.owuscholarship.org/

OUR WORLD UNDERWATER SCHOLARSHIP SOCIETY
• *See page 755*

OUTRIGGER DUKE KAHANAMOKU FOUNDATION
http://www.dukefoundation.org

ODKF GENERAL SCHOLARSHIP AWARD
• *See page 657*

PANHELLENIC SCHOLARSHIP FOUNDATION
https://www.panhellenicsf.org/

PANHELLENIC SCHOLARSHIP AWARDS
• *See page 657*

PAPERCHECK
https://www.papercheck.com/

PAPERCHECK, LLC—CHARLES SHAFAE' SCHOLARSHIP FUND
• *See page 657*

PARIAN LAW FIRM, LLC
https://westgalawyer.com/

THE EDUCATIONAL JUSTICE SCHOLARSHIP
• *See page 658*

PEACOCK PRODUCTIONS, INC.
http://amefund.com

AUDRIA M. EDWARDS SCHOLARSHIP FUND
• *See page 658*

PENNSYLVANIA FEDERATION OF DEMOCRATIC WOMEN INC.

http://www.pafedofdemwomen.org

PENNSYLVANIA FEDERATION OF DEMOCRATIC WOMEN INC. ANNUAL SCHOLARSHIP AWARDS
• *See page 574*

PENNSYLVANIA HIGHER EDUCATION ASSISTANCE AGENCY

http://www.pheaa.org/

BLIND OR DEAF BENEFICIARY GRANT PROGRAM
• *See page 658*

PET LIFESTYLE AND YOU (P.L.A.Y.)

https://www.petplay.com/

SCHOLARS HELPING COLLARS SCHOLARSHIP
• *See page 659*

PHOENIX PRIDE

https://phoenixpride.org/

PHOENIX PRIDE SCHOLARSHIP PROGRAM
• *See page 659*

PILOT INTERNATIONAL

https://www.pilotinternational.org/

BECKY BURROWS MEMORIAL SCHOLARSHIP
• *See page 659*

KC INTERNATIONAL SCHOLARSHIP
• *See page 659*

RUBY NEWHALL MEMORIAL SCHOLARSHIP
• *See page 659*

PINE CONE FOUNDATION (PCF)

http://pineconefoundation.org/

PINE CONE FOUNDATION SCHOLARSHIP
• *See page 660*

PLAINTIFF RELIEF

http://plaintiffrelief.com/

PLAINTIFF RELIEF SCHOLARSHIP
• *See page 660*

POLSON AND POLSON, P.C.

https://www.polsonlawfirm.com/

POLSON & POLSON, P.C. CONQUERING ADVERSITY SCHOLARSHIP
• *See page 660*

PORTUGUESE AMERICAN LEADERSHIP COUNCIL OF THE UNITED STATES

http://www.palcus.org

PALCUS NATIONAL SCHOLARSHIP PROGRAM
• *See page 660*

POTENTIAL MAGAZINE

http://potentialmagazine.com/

COUNTDOWN TO COLLEGE SCHOLARSHIP
• *See page 661*

"DON'T WAIT TO REACH YOUR POTENTIAL" SCHOLARSHIP
• *See page 661*

PRESBYTERIAN CHURCH (USA)

http://www.pcusa.org/financialaid

NATIONAL PRESBYTERIAN COLLEGE SCHOLARSHIP
Scholarships between $1000 and $2500 available to incoming undergraduate enrolled in full-time programs in colleges associated with the Presbyterian Church (U.S.A.). Applicants must have a minimum GPA of 2.5 and demonstrate financial need. Students are required to participate in campus ministry or a worshiping community proximate to the college they attend and respond to an annual essay question exploring aspects of vocation.

Award: Scholarship for use in freshman, sophomore, junior, or senior years; not renewable. *Number:* 25–100. *Amount:* $1000–$2500.

Eligibility Requirements: Applicant must be Presbyterian and enrolled or expecting to enroll full-time at a four-year institution or university. Applicant must have 2.5 GPA or higher. Available to U.S. and non-U.S. citizens.

Application Requirements: Application form, essay, financial need analysis. *Deadline:* March 1.

Contact: Ms. Laura Bryan, Coordinator, Financial Aid for Studies
Presbyterian Church (USA)
100 Witherspoon Street
Louisville, KY 40202-1396
Phone: 800-728-7228 Ext. 5735
E-mail: finaid@pcusa.org

NATIVE AMERICAN SUPPLEMENTAL GRANT
• *See page 757*

SAMUEL ROBINSON AWARD
Prize granted to full-time junior and senior students attending a Presbyterian related college or university who successfully recite answers to the Westminster Shorter Catechism and write an essay on an assigned topic.

Award: Prize for use in junior or senior years; not renewable. *Number:* 16. *Amount:* $250–$5000.

Eligibility Requirements: Applicant must be Presbyterian and enrolled or expecting to enroll full-time at a four-year institution or university. Available to U.S. citizens.

Application Requirements: Application form, entry in a contest, essay. *Deadline:* April 1.

Contact: Ms. Laura Bryan, Coordinator, Financial Aid for Studies
Presbyterian Church (USA)
100 Witherspoon Street
Louisville, KY 40202
Phone: 800-728-7228 Ext. 5735
Fax: 502-569-8766
E-mail: finaid@pcusa.org

PRICE BENOWITZ LLP

http://pricebenowitz.com/

AMATO SANITA BRIGHTER FUTURE SCHOLARSHIP
• *See page 661*

ANGIE DIPIETRO WOMEN IN BUSINESS SCHOLARSHIP
• *See page 661*

KAREN RILEY PORTER GOOD WORKS SCHOLARSHIP
• *See page 661*

KERRI CASTELLINI WOMEN'S LEADERSHIP SCHOLARSHIP
• *See page 661*

KUSH ARORA FEDERAL CRIMINAL JUSTICE REFORM SCHOLARSHIP
• *See page 661*

NATALIA SEGERMEISTER DREAM ACT SCHOLARSHIP
• *See page 662*

PRICE BENOWITZ MAKE A DIFFERENCE SCHOLARSHIP
• *See page 662*

PRICE BENOWITZ SOCIAL JUSTICE SCHOLARSHIP
• *See page 662*

SETH OKIN GOOD DEEDS SCHOLARSHIP
• *See page 662*

STEVE DUCKETT CONSERVATION SCHOLARSHIP
• *See page 757*

THOMAS SOLDAN HEALTHY COMMUNITIES SCHOLARSHIP
• *See page 662*

PRIDE FOUNDATION

http://www.PrideFoundation.org/

PRIDE FOUNDATION SCHOLARSHIP PROGRAM
• *See page 662*

PROMOCODESFORYOU.COM

https://www.promocodesforyou.com

PROMOCODESFORYOU.COM STUDENT SAVINGS SCHOLARSHIP
• *See page 662*

PROMPT

http://prompt.com

PROMPT'S $20,000 SCHOLARSHIP
• *See page 663*

RAILROAD PASSENGERS ASSOCIATION

https://www.narprail.org/

RAILROAD PASSENGERS ASSOCIATION SCHOLARSHIP
• *See page 663*

REACH HIGHER MONTANA

http://www.ReachHigherMontana.org

REACH HIGHER MONTANA SCHOLARSHIPS
• *See page 663*

REHABCENTER.NET

http://www.rehabcenter.net/

REHABCENTER.NET
• *See page 664*

RHINE LAW FIRM, P.C.

https://www.carolinaaccidentattorneys.com/

STRIVE FOR EXCELLENCE SCHOLARSHIP 2018
• *See page 664*

RISK MANAGEMENT ASSOCIATION FOUNDATION

http://www.scholarshipamerica.org

THE RISK MANAGEMENT ASSOCIATION FOUNDATION SCHOLARSHIP PROGRAM
• *See page 664*

RJT CRIMINAL DEFENSE

http://www.sandiegocriminallawyerrt.com/

AUTISM SCHOLARSHIP
• *See page 664*

ROMAN CATHOLIC DIOCESE OF TULSA

http://www.dioceseoftulsa.org

MAE LASSLEY OSAGE SCHOLARSHIP
• *See page 758*

RON BROWN SCHOLAR FUND

http://www.ronbrown.org/

RON BROWN SCHOLAR PROGRAM
• *See page 665*

ROVER.COM

https://www.rover.com/

ROVER SITTER SCHOLARSHIP CONTEST
• *See page 665*

ST. ANDREW'S SOCIETY OF WASHINGTON, DC

http://www.saintandrewsociety.org/

ST. ANDREW'S SOCIETY OF WASHINGTON DC FOUNDERS' SCHOLARSHIP
• *See page 665*

ST. ANDREW'S SOCIETY OF WASHINGTON DC SCHOLARSHIPS
• *See page 665*

SALUTE TO EDUCATION, INC.
http://www.stescholarships.org/

SALUTE TO EDUCATION SCHOLARSHIP
• *See page 666*

SCHOLAR SERVE
https://www.scholarserve.org

SCHOLAR SERVE AWARDS
• *See page 666*

SCHOLARSHIP AMERICA
https://www.abbvieImmunologyScholarship.com/

ABBVIE IMMUNOLOGY SCHOLARSHIP
• *See page 666*

SELECTBLINDS.COM
http://www.selectblinds.com

SELECTBLINDS.COM $1000 COLLEGE SCHOLARSHIP
• *See page 666*

SEXNER & ASSOCIATES LLC
http://www.sexner.com/personal-injury/

MITCHELL S. SEXNER & ASSOCIATES LLC SCHOLARSHIP
• *See page 667*

SHAWN SUKUMAR ATTORNEY AT LAW
https://www.washingtondccriminallawyer.net/

SHAWN SUKUMAR CRIMINAL JUSTICE REFORM SCHOLARSHIP
• *See page 667*

SHELVING.COM
http://www.shelving.com/

SHELVING.COM BUSINESS SCHOLARSHIP
• *See page 667*

SILICON VALLEY COMMUNITY FOUNDATION
http://www.siliconvalleycf.org

ABBY SOBRATO SCHOLARSHIP
• *See page 667*

BOBETTE BIBO GUGLIOTTA MEMORIAL SCHOLARSHIP FOR CREATIVE WRITING
• *See page 667*

CURRY AWARD FOR GIRLS AND YOUNG WOMEN
• *See page 667*

CYNTHIA H. KUO SCHOLARSHIP
• *See page 759*

HAZEL REED BAUMEISTER SCHOLARSHIP PROGRAM
• *See page 668*

HUANG LEADERSHIP DEVELOPMENT SCHOLARSHIP
• *See page 668*

SIMMONS AND FLETCHER, P.C.
https://www.simmonsandfletcher.com/

SIMMONS AND FLETCHER, P.C., LAW MARKETING SCHOLARSHIP
• *See page 668*

SOCIETY FOR APPLIED ANTHROPOLOGY
http://www.sfaa.net/

ANNUAL SFAA STUDENT ENDOWED AWARD
• *See page 668*

SOCIETY OF DAUGHTERS OF THE UNITED STATES ARMY
SOCIETY OF DAUGHTERS OF THE UNITED STATES ARMY SCHOLARSHIPS
• *See page 669*

SONS OF ITALY FOUNDATION
http://www.osia.org/sif

GENERAL STUDY SCHOLARSHIPS
• *See page 669*

HENRY SALVATORI SCHOLARSHIP FOR GENERAL STUDY
• *See page 669*

SOUND MONEY DEFENSE LEAGUE
http://soundmoneydefense.org

MONEY METALS EXCHANGE SCHOLARSHIP PROGRAM
• *See page 669*

SOUTH CAROLINA TUITION GRANTS COMMISSION
http://www.sctuitiongrants.org/

SOUTH CAROLINA TUITION GRANTS PROGRAM
• *See page 669*

SPINE SURGEON DR. VICTOR HAYES
https://tampabaybackpaindoctor.com/

TAMPA BAY SPINE CENTER ROAD TO RECOVERY SCHOLARSHIP
• *See page 670*

STATE EMPLOYEES ASSOCIATION OF NORTH CAROLINA (SEANC)
http://www.seanc.org/

STATE EMPLOYEES ASSOCIATION OF NORTH CAROLINA (SEANC) SCHOLARSHIPS
• *See page 761*

STEALTHY AND WEALTHY

http://stealthyandwealthy.com

STEALTHY AND WEALTHY STUDENT ENTREPRENEUR GRANT
• *See page 670*

STEINBERG, GOODMAN AND KALISH

https://www.sgklawyers.com/

STEINBERG, GOODMAN AND KALISH SCHOLARSHIP
• *See page 670*

STONEWALL COMMUNITY FOUNDATION

http://www.stonewallfoundation.org/

TRAUB-DICKER RAINBOW SCHOLARSHIP
• *See page 670*

STROLLER DEPOT

https://www.strollerdepot.com/

$1,000 STROLLER DEPOT SCHOLARSHIP
• *See page 670*

STROM & ASSOCIATES

https://stromlawyers.com

STROM & ASSOCIATES ANNUAL SCHOLARSHIP
• *See page 671*

STUDY.COM

study.com

ARMY ROTC STUDY.COM SCHOLARSHIP
• *See page 671*

STUDY.COM CLEP SCHOLARSHIP
• *See page 671*

STUDY.COM SCHOLARSHIP FOR FLORIDA STUDENTS
• *See page 671*

STUDY.COM SCHOLARSHIP FOR TEXAS STUDENTS
• *See page 671*

TECHNOSOFT INNOVATIONS, INC.

https://www.technosoftinv.com/

TECHNOSOFT INNOVATIONS SCHOLARSHIP PROGRAM
• *See page 671*

TELEVISION ACADEMY FOUNDATION

http://www.televisionacademy.com/foundation

TELEVISION ACADEMY FOUNDATION
• *See page 671*

TENNESSEE STUDENT ASSISTANCE CORPORATION

http://www.tn.gov/collegepays

HELPING HEROES GRANT
• *See page 672*

HOPE ASPIRE AWARD
• *See page 672*

NED MCWHERTER SCHOLARS PROGRAM
• *See page 672*

TELS -HOPE WITH GENERAL ASSEMBLY MERIT SCHOLARSHIP (GAMS)
• *See page 672*

TENNESSEE DUAL ENROLLMENT GRANT
• *See page 672*

TENNESSEE HOPE ACCESS GRANT
• *See page 673*

TENNESSEE HOPE FOSTER CHILD TUITION GRANT
• *See page 673*

TENNESSEE HOPE SCHOLARSHIP
• *See page 673*

TENNESSEE STUDENT ASSISTANCE AWARD
• *See page 673*

TETHERBOX

http://www.tetherbox.com/

$1,000 CREATIVE VIDEO CHALLENGE COLLEGE SCHOLARSHIP
• *See page 673*

TEXAS ASSOCIATION OF DEVELOPING COLLEGES

http://www.txadc.org

THE URBAN SCHOLARSHIPS FUND
• *See page 674*

TEXAS BLACK BAPTIST SCHOLARSHIP COMMITTEE

http://www.bgct.org/

TEXAS BLACK BAPTIST SCHOLARSHIP
• *See page 764*

TEXAS MUTUAL INSURANCE COMPANY

http://www.texasmutual.com/

TEXAS MUTUAL INSURANCE COMPANY SCHOLARSHIP PROGRAM
• *See page 674*

THRIVENT STUDENT RESOURCES

https://www.thriventstudentresources.com/

THRIVENT STUDENT RESOURCES SCHOLARSHIP
• *See page 674*

TONALAW
https://www.tonalaw.com/

TONALAW VETERAN'S SCHOLARSHIP
• *See page 674*

TOPPRODUCTS.COM
http://topproducts.com/

TOPPRODUCTS SINGLE MOTHER SCHOLARSHIP
• *See page 675*

TORHOERMAN LAW LLC
http://torhoermanlaw.com

TORHOERMAN LAW DISTRACTED DRIVING ESSAY SCHOLARSHIP
• *See page 675*

TPA SCHOLARSHIP TRUST FOR THE HEARING IMPAIRED
https://www.tpahq.org/scholarshiptrust/

TPA SCHOLARSHIP TRUST FOR THE HEARING IMPAIRED
• *See page 675*

TRANSFER TIMES
http://www.transfertimes.com

TRANSFER TIMES $6,000 SCHOLARSHIP
• *See page 675*

TRANSTUTORS
http://www.transtutors.com/scholarship

TRANSTUTORS SCHOLARSHIP
• *See page 675*

TRAVELNURSESOURCE.COM
https://www.travelnursesource.com/

FUTURE U.S. NURSE SCHOLARSHIP
• *See page 676*

TROPHYCENTRAL INC.
https://www.trophycentral.com

TROPHYCENTRAL SPORTSMANSHIP AND COMPASSION SCHOLARSHIP AWARD
• *See page 676*

TURBOSQUID
https://www.turbosquid.com/

TURBOSQUID SPRING SCHOLARSHIP
• *See page 676*

UCB, INC.
http://www.ucb.com/

UCB FAMILY EPILEPSY SCHOLARSHIP
• *See page 677*

ULMAN CANCER FUND FOR YOUNG ADULTS
http://www.ulmanfund.org/scholarships

JACQUELINE SHEARER MEMORIAL SCHOLARSHIP
• *See page 677*

JAMIE L. ROBERTS MEMORIAL SCHOLARSHIP AWARD
• *See page 677*

JEFFREY P. MEYER MEMORIAL SCHOLARSHIP
• *See page 677*

JILL WEAVER STARKMAN SCHOLARSHIP
• *See page 677*

JOHN HANLEY MEMORIAL SCHOLARSHIP
• *See page 678*

LISA HIGGINS-HUSSMAN FOUNDATION SCHOLARSHIP
• *See page 678*

MARILYN YETSO MEMORIAL SCHOLARSHIP
• *See page 678*

OLIVIA M. MARQUART SCHOLARSHIP
• *See page 678*

PERLITA LIWANAG MEMORIAL SCHOLARSHIP
• *See page 678*

SATOLA FAMILY SCHOLARSHIP
• *See page 678*

SEAN SILVER MEMORIAL SCHOLARSHIP AWARD
• *See page 678*

VERA YIP MEMORIAL SCHOLARSHIP
• *See page 679*

VITTORIA DIANNA RICARDO MEMORIAL SCHOLARSHIP
• *See page 679*

UNICO FOUNDATION INC.
http://www.unico.org/

ALPHONSE A. MIELE SCHOLARSHIP
• *See page 679*

BERNARD AND CAROLYN TORRACO MEMORIAL NURSING SCHOLARSHIP PROGRAM
• *See page 679*

DIMATTIO CELLI FAMILY STUDY ABROAD SCHOLARSHIP
• *See page 679*

ELLA T. GRASSO LITERARY SCHOLARSHIP
• *See page 680*

GUGLIELMO MARCONI ENGINEERING SCHOLARSHIP
• *See page 680*

INSERRA SCHOLARSHIPS
• *See page 680*

MAJOR DON S. GENTILE SCHOLARSHIP
• *See page 680*

MARIA AND PAOLO ALESSIO SOUTHERN ITALY SCHOLARSHIP
• *See page 680*

RALPH J. TORRACO SCHOLARSHIP
• *See page 680*

THEODORE MAZZA SCHOLARSHIP
• *See page 681*

WILLIAM C. DAVINI SCHOLARSHIP
• *See page 681*

UNION PLUS SCHOLARSHIP PROGRAM

http://www.unionplus.org/

UNION PLUS EDUCATION FOUNDATION SCHOLARSHIP PROGRAM
• *See page 584*

UNITARIAN UNIVERSALIST ASSOCIATION

http://www.uua.org/

CHILDREN OF UNITARIAN UNIVERSALIST MINISTERS
Non-renewable scholarship available to children of Unitarian Universalist Ministers to defray undergraduate college expenses. Dollar value and number of awards varies. Priority is given to applicants whose family income does not exceed $50,000.

Award: Scholarship for use in freshman, sophomore, junior, or senior years; not renewable.

Eligibility Requirements: Applicant must be Unitarian Universalist and enrolled or expecting to enroll full- or part-time at a four-year institution or university. Available to U.S. citizens.

Application Requirements: Application form. *Deadline:* July 31.

Contact: Ms. Hillary Goodridge, Program Director
　　　Phone: 617-971-9600
　　　Fax: 617-971-0029
　　　E-mail: uufp@aol.com

JOSEPH SUMNER SMITH SCHOLARSHIP
Funds are available for Unitarian Universalist (UU) students attending Antioch (including satellite and nonresidential campuses) and Harvard. While there is no restriction on the course of studies the student may elect to pursue, nor any restrictions on choice of career, student interested in pursuing the ministry after graduation are especially urged to apply.

Award: Scholarship for use in freshman, sophomore, junior, senior, or graduate years; not renewable. *Amount:* $500–$1000.

Eligibility Requirements: Applicant must be Unitarian Universalist and enrolled or expecting to enroll full- or part-time at a two-year or four-year or technical institution or university. Available to U.S. citizens.

Application Requirements: Application form. *Deadline:* April 30.

Contact: Ms. Hillary Goodridge, Program Director
　　　Phone: 617-971-9600
　　　Fax: 617-971-0029
　　　E-mail: uufp@aol.com

UNITED NEGRO COLLEGE FUND

http://www.uncf.org/

ABCNJ LEADERSHIP IMPACT SCHOLARSHIP
• *See page 765*

UNITED TRANSPORTATION UNION INSURANCE ASSOCIATION

http://www.utuia.org/

UTUIA SCHOLARSHIP
• *See page 681*

UNIVERSITY CONSORTIUM FOR LIBERIA

http://ucliberia.com/

JOSEPH N. BOAKAI SR. HIGHER EDUCATION SCHOLARSHIP
• *See page 681*

U.S. COAST GUARD

http://www.gocoastguard/cspi

COLLEGE STUDENT PRE-COMMISSIONING INITIATIVE (CSPI)
• *See page 681*

VALUEPENGUIN

http://www.valuepenguin.com

VALUEPENGUIN SCHOLARSHIP
• *See page 682*

VANILLA PILGRIM FOUNDATION

https://www.vanillapilgrim.com/

2018 OPEN ESSAY COMPETITION
• *See page 682*

VETERANAID.ORG

https://www.veteranaid.org

VETERAN BENEFITS SCHOLARSHIP
• *See page 682*

VETERANS UNITED FOUNDATION

http://www.enhancelives.com

VETERANS UNITED FOUNDATION SCHOLARSHIP
• *See page 682*

WARD LAW GROUP, PL

http://thecoveragelawyer.com/

WARD LAW GROUP BETTER FUTURE SCHOLARSHIP
• *See page 682*

WESTERN INTERSTATE COMMISSION FOR HIGHER EDUCATION

http://www.wiche.edu/

WICHE'S WESTERN UNDERGRADUATE EXCHANGE (WUE)
• *See page 683*

WHITLEY LAW FIRM

https://whitleylawfirm.com/

WHITLEY LAW FIRM OPIOID CRISIS SCHOLARSHIP
* See page 683

WOLTERMAN LAW OFFICE, LPA

https://www.woltermanlaw.com/

WOLTERMAN LAW OFFICE LPA HOPE FOR THE FUTURE SCHOLARSHIP
* See page 683

WOMEN MARINES ASSOCIATION

http://www.womenmarines.org

ETHYL AND ARMIN WIEBKE MEMORIAL SCHOLARSHIPS
* See page 683

THE LILY H. GRIDLEY MEMORIAL SCHOLARSHIP
* See page 683

WMA MEMORIAL SCHOLARSHIPS
* See page 683

WOMEN OF THE EVANGELICAL LUTHERAN CHURCH IN AMERICA

http://www.womenoftheelca.org/

AMELIA KEMP SCHOLARSHIP
* See page 771

BELMER/FLORA PRINCE SCHOLARSHIP
Scholarship for women who have experienced an interruption of two or more years in education since the completion of high school. Must be member of ELCA and be at least 21 years old.

Award: Scholarship for use in freshman, sophomore, junior, senior, or graduate years; not renewable. *Number:* 2. *Amount:* up to $1000.

Eligibility Requirements: Applicant must be Lutheran; enrolled or expecting to enroll full- or part-time at a two-year or four-year or technical institution or university and female. Available to U.S. citizens.

Application Requirements: Application form, recommendations or references, resume, transcript. *Deadline:* February 15.

Contact: Emily Hansen, Scholarship Committee
Phone: 800-638-3522 Ext. 2736
Fax: 773-380-2419
E-mail: womenelca@elca.org

WOMEN'S JEWELRY ASSOCIATION

http://www.womensjewelryassociation.com

MEMBER GRANTS
* See page 684

WOMEN'S JEWELRY ASSOCIATIONS VETERANS GRANT
* See page 684

YORKVILLE GOODS LLC

http://yorkvilleblankets.com/

YORKVILLE BLANKETS ASD SCHOLARSHIP
* See page 684

ZELUS RECOVERY

http://zelusrecovery.com/

ZELUS RECOVERY $1000 COLLEGE SCHOLARSHIP
* See page 684

ZIPRECRUITER

https://www.ziprecruiter.com/

ZIPRECRUITER $3,000 SCHOLARSHIP
* See page 685

RESIDENCE

180 MEDICAL, INC.

http://www.180medical.com

180 MEDICAL COLLEGE SCHOLARSHIP PROGRAM
Seven $1,000 scholarships will be awarded to students attending a two-year, four-year, or graduate school program full time in the fall are eligible to apply. Applicants must be under a physician's care for a spinal cord injury, spina bifida, transverse myelitis, neurogenic bladder, or ostomy (ileostomy, colostomy, or urostomy). Must be a legal resident in the United States. Deadline is June 1st.

Award: Scholarship for use in freshman, sophomore, junior, senior, graduate, or postgraduate years; not renewable. *Number:* 7. *Amount:* $1000.

Eligibility Requirements: Applicant must be enrolled or expecting to enroll full-time at a two-year or four-year or technical institution or university and resident of Alabama, Alaska, Alberta, Arizona, Arkansas, California, Colorado, Connecticut, Delaware, District of Columbia, Florida, Georgia, Guam, Hawaii, Idaho, Illinois, Indiana, Iowa, Kansas, Kentucky, Louisiana, Maine, Manitoba, Maryland, Massachusetts, Michigan, Minnesota, Mississippi, Missouri, Montana, Nebraska, Nevada, New Hampshire, New Jersey, New Mexico, New York, North Carolina, North Dakota, Ohio, Oklahoma, Oregon, Pennsylvania, Puerto Rico, Rhode Island, Saskatchewan, South Carolina, South Dakota, Tennessee, Texas, Utah, Vermont, Virginia, Washington, West Virginia, Wisconsin, Wyoming. Available to U.S. citizens.

Application Requirements: Application form, essay. *Deadline:* June 1.

365 PET INSURANCE

https://365petinsurance.com/

MINORITY STUDENTS IN VETERINARY MEDICINE SCHOLARSHIP
* See page 719

THE 5 STRONG SCHOLARSHIP FOUNDATION, INC.

http://5strongscholars.org

5 STRONG SCHOLARS SCHOLARSHIP
* See page 719

ALABAMA COMMISSION ON HIGHER EDUCATION

http://www.ache.alabama.gov/

ALABAMA NATIONAL GUARD EDUCATIONAL ASSISTANCE PROGRAM
* See page 697

ALABAMA STUDENT ASSISTANCE PROGRAM

Scholarship award of $300 to $5000 per academic year given to undergraduate students residing in the state of Alabama and attending a college or university in Alabama.

Award: Grant for use in freshman, sophomore, junior, or senior years; not renewable. *Number:* 3500–4500. *Amount:* $300–$5000.

Eligibility Requirements: Applicant must be enrolled or expecting to enroll full- or part-time at a two-year or four-year or technical institution or university; resident of Alabama and studying in Alabama. Available to U.S. citizens.

Application Requirements: Application form, financial need analysis. *Deadline:* continuous.

Contact: Cheryl Newton, Grants Coordinator
Phone: 334-242-2273
Fax: 334-242-2269
E-mail: cheryl.newton@ache.alabama.gov

ALABAMA STUDENT ASSISTANCE PROGRAM

Grant award of $300 to $5000 per academic year given to undergraduate students residing in the state of Alabama and attending a college or university in Alabama.

Award: Grant for use in freshman, sophomore, junior, or senior years; not renewable. *Number:* 3500–4500. *Amount:* $300–$5000.

Eligibility Requirements: Applicant must be enrolled or expecting to enroll full- or part-time at a two-year or four-year or technical institution or university; resident of Alabama and studying in Alabama. Available to U.S. citizens.

Application Requirements: *Deadline:* continuous.

Contact: Cheryl Newton, Grants Coordinator
Phone: 334-242-2273
Fax: 334-242-2269
E-mail: cheryl.newton@ache.alabama.gov

ALABAMA STUDENT GRANT PROGRAM

Nonrenewable awards available to Alabama residents for undergraduate study at certain independent colleges within the state. Both full and half-time students are eligible. Deadlines: September 15, January 15, and February 15.

Award: Grant for use in freshman, sophomore, junior, or senior years; not renewable. *Number:* 3500–5500. *Amount:* $200–$1200.

Eligibility Requirements: Applicant must be enrolled or expecting to enroll full- or part-time at a four-year institution or university; resident of Alabama and studying in Alabama. Available to U.S. citizens.

Application Requirements: Application form. *Deadline:* continuous.

Contact: Cheryl Newton, Grants Coordinator
Phone: 334-242-2273
Fax: 334-242-2269
E-mail: cheryl.newton@ache.alabama.gov

POLICE OFFICERS AND FIREFIGHTERS SURVIVORS EDUCATION ASSISTANCE PROGRAM-ALABAMA

Provides tuition, fees, books, and supplies to dependents of full-time police officers and firefighters killed or totally disabled in the line of duty. Must attend an Alabama public college as an undergraduate. Must be Alabama resident.

Award: Scholarship for use in freshman, sophomore, junior, or senior years; renewable. *Number:* 15–30. *Amount:* $1600–$12,000.

Eligibility Requirements: Applicant must be enrolled or expecting to enroll full- or part-time at a two-year or technical institution or university; resident of Alabama and studying in Alabama. Available to U.S. citizens.

Application Requirements: Application form. *Deadline:* continuous.

Contact: Cheryl Newton, Grants Coordinator
Phone: 334-242-2273
Fax: 334-242-2269
E-mail: cheryl.newton@ache.alabama.gov

ALABAMA DEPARTMENT OF VETERANS AFFAIRS

http://www.va.alabama.gov/

ALABAMA G.I. DEPENDENTS SCHOLARSHIP PROGRAM

The scholarship is for dependents of eligible disabled Alabama veterans. This scholarship will be the payer of last resort after all other grants and scholarships have been utilized for required education expenses. The scholarship pays up to the DoD Tuition Assistance Cap (currently $250 per credit hour) and up to $1,000 for the combination of required textbooks and laboratory fees per semester. Child or stepchild must initiate training before 26th birthday; age 30 deadline may apply in certain situations. No age deadline for spouses or widows. The veteran and the step child's parent must have been married prior the child's 19th birthday.

Award: Scholarship for use in freshman, sophomore, junior, or senior years; renewable.

Eligibility Requirements: Applicant must be enrolled or expecting to enroll full- or part-time at a two-year or four-year or technical institution or university; resident of Alabama and studying in Alabama. Available to U.S. citizens.

Application Requirements: Application form.

Contact: Kayla Kyle, Department Operations Manager
Alabama Department of Veterans Affairs
PO Box 1509
Montgomery, AL 36102-1509
Phone: 334-242-5077

ALABAMA SOCIETY OF CERTIFIED PUBLIC ACCOUNTANTS

http://www.ascpa.org/

ASCPA EDUCATIONAL FOUNDATION SCHOLARSHIP

• *See page 593*

ALASKA COMMISSION ON POSTSECONDARY EDUCATION

http://www.acpe.alaska.gov

ALASKA PERFORMANCE SCHOLARSHIP

To qualify, students must take a specific, rigorous high school curriculum; earn a minimum 2.5 GPA; and do well on college or career readiness exam. Students apply by completing the FAFSA by the annual deadline. Awards can be used at any regionally accredited college or university in Alaska, or for approved career and technical education programs in the state. Students must use scholarship within 6 years of high school graduation. Students cannot receive award for more than 8 semesters.

Award: Scholarship for use in freshman, sophomore, junior, senior, graduate, or postgraduate years; not renewable. *Amount:* $500–$4755.

Eligibility Requirements: Applicant must be enrolled or expecting to enroll full- or part-time at a two-year or four-year or technical institution or university; resident of Alaska and studying in Alaska. Applicant must have 2.5 GPA or higher. Available to U.S. and non-U.S. citizens.

Application Requirements: *Deadline:* continuous.

Contact: Adam Weed, Special Programs Coordinator
Alaska Commission on Postsecondary Education
3030 Vintage Blvd
Juneau, AK 99801
Phone: 907-465-6685
E-mail: customer_service@acpe.state.ak.us

ALASK EDUCATION GRANT

The Alaska legislature created the Alask Education Grant Program (AEG) to provide need-based financial assistance to eligible Alaska students attending qualifying postsecondary educational institutions in Alaska. Students apply by completing the FAFSA annually.

Award: Grant for use in freshman, sophomore, junior, or senior years; not renewable. *Amount:* $500–$4000.

Eligibility Requirements: Applicant must be enrolled or expecting to enroll full- or part-time at a two-year or four-year institution or university; resident of Alaska and studying in Alaska. Available to U.S. and non-U.S. citizens.

Application Requirements: *Deadline:* continuous.

Contact: Adam Weed, Special Programs Coordinator
        Alaska Commission on Postsecondary Education
        3030 Vintage Blvd
        Juneau, AK 99801
        Phone: 907-465-6685
        E-mail: customer_service@acpe.state.ak.us

ALBERTA AGRICULTURE FOOD AND RURAL DEVELOPMENT 4-H BRANCH

http://www.4h.ab.ca/

ALBERTA AGRICULTURE FOOD AND RURAL DEVELOPMENT 4-H SCHOLARSHIP PROGRAM
• *See page 549*

ALBERTA HERITAGE SCHOLARSHIP FUND

http://www.alis.alberta.ca/

ADULT HIGH SCHOOL EQUIVALENCY SCHOLARSHIPS
• *See page 719*

ALBERTA APPRENTICESHIP AND INDUSTRY TRAINING SCHOLARSHIPS
Awards of CAN$1000 to recognize the accomplishments of Alberta high school students taking the registered apprenticeship program and to encourage recipients to continue their apprenticeship training after completing high school. Must be a Canadian citizen or landed immigrant and a resident of Alberta, must have completed the requirements for high school graduation between August 1 and July 31 of the current year and must be registered as an Alberta apprentice in a trade while still attending high school. For additional information, please visit website http://alis.alberta.ca.

Award: Scholarship for use in freshman year; not renewable.

Eligibility Requirements: Applicant must be enrolled or expecting to enroll full-time at a two-year or four-year or technical institution or university and resident of Alberta. Available to Canadian citizens.

Application Requirements: Application form, employer recommendation, essay, recommendations or references. *Deadline:* June 30.

Contact: Scholarship Committee
        Phone: 780-427-8640
        E-mail: scholarships@gov.ab.ca

ALBERTA CENTENNIAL SCHOLARSHIPS-ALBERTA
• *See page 720*

ALBERTA PRE-APPRENTICESHIP SCHOLARSHIPS
CAN$1000 to encourage those completing pre-apprenticeship programs to continue in the trades and complete their training. Programs must include at least four weeks of trades-related instruction, not including work experience. Applicants must be registered apprentices and demonstrate financial need. For additional information, see website http://alis.alberta.ca.

Award: Scholarship for use in freshman or sophomore years; not renewable. *Number:* 11.

Eligibility Requirements: Applicant must be enrolled or expecting to enroll full-time at a technical institution; resident of Alberta and studying in Alberta. Available to Canadian citizens.

Application Requirements: Application form, essay, recommendations or references, transcript. *Deadline:* June 30.

Contact: Scholarship Committee
        Phone: 780-427-8640
        E-mail: scholarships@gov.ab.ca

ALEXANDER RUTHERFORD SCHOLARSHIPS FOR HIGH SCHOOL ACHIEVEMENT
• *See page 720*

CHARLES S. NOBLE JUNIOR FOOTBALL SCHOLARSHIPS
• *See page 720*

CHARLES S. NOBLE JUNIOR HOCKEY SCHOLARSHIPS
• *See page 720*

CHINA-ALBERTA AWARD FOR EXCELLENCE IN CHINESE
Award of CAN$500 for Canadian citizens or permanent residents who are Alberta residents currently enrolled in Grade 12. Must have taken high school Chinese Language and Culture Program 10 and 20 and currently be enrolled or have completed level 30; and have obtained an average of 80% in all courses, and a minimum average of 90% in Chinese Language and Culture 10 and 20. Applicant's parents or a parent must reside in Alberta. For more information, see website http://alis.alberta.ca/.

Award: Grant for use in freshman year; not renewable.

Eligibility Requirements: Applicant must be high school student; planning to enroll or expecting to enroll full-time at a four-year institution or university and resident of Alberta.

Application Requirements: Application form, essay, recommendations or references, transcript. *Deadline:* April 30.

Contact: Scholarship Committee
        Phone: 780-427-8640
        E-mail: scholarships@gov.ab.ca

DUKE AND DUTCHESS OF CAMBRIDGE SCHOLARSHIP
Awards of CAN$2500 available to students who have been in government care and have overcome significant challenges in their lives while pursing their postsecondary studies. Eligible students must be Advancing Futures Bursary recipients and be returning to full-time postsecondary studies. Awarded on the basis of academic achievement; the highest GPA (grade point average) while working toward a degree, diploma, or certificate. Advancing Futures Bursary recipients who are taking postsecondary upgrading courses or attending a specialized high school are also eligible. For more information, see website http://alis.alberta.ca/.

Award: Scholarship for use in freshman, sophomore, junior, or senior years; not renewable. *Number:* 25.

Eligibility Requirements: Applicant must be enrolled or expecting to enroll full-time at a four-year institution or university and resident of Alberta.

Application Requirements: Application form, transcript. *Deadline:* August 1.

Contact: Scholarship Committee
        Phone: 780-427-8640
        E-mail: scholarships@gov.ab.ca

JIMMIE CONDON ATHLETIC SCHOLARSHIPS
• *See page 720*

JO-ANNE KOCH-ABC SOCIETY SCHOLARSHIP
• *See page 721*

KEYERA ENERGY-PETER J. RENTON MEMORIAL SCHOLARSHIP
• *See page 721*

LAURENCE DECORE AWARDS FOR STUDENT LEADERSHIP
• *See page 721*

LOUISE MCKINNEY POST-SECONDARY SCHOLARSHIPS
• *See page 721*

PERSONS CASE SCHOLARSHIPS
• *See page 721*

PRAIRIE BASEBALL ACADEMY SCHOLARSHIPS

Scholarships of between CAN$500 and CAN$2500 reward athletic and academic excellence of Alberta baseball players, and provides an incentive and means for these players to continue with their postsecondary education. Must be Alberta residents and enrolled full-time at a postsecondary institution in Alberta. Applicants must be a participant in the Prairie Baseball Academy and must have achieved a minimum GPA of 2.0 in their previous semester. For additional information, visit website http://alis.alberta.ca.

Award: Scholarship for use in freshman, sophomore, junior, or senior years; not renewable.

Eligibility Requirements: Applicant must be enrolled or expecting to enroll full-time at a two-year or four-year or technical institution or university; resident of Alberta; studying in Alberta and must have an interest in athletics/sports. Available to Canadian citizens.

Application Requirements: Application form, community service, recommendations or references. *Deadline:* October 15.

Contact: Scholarship Committee
Phone: 780-427-8640
E-mail: scholarships@gov.ab.ca

QUEEN ELIZABETH II GOLDEN JUBILEE CITIZENSHIP MEDAL

• *See page 721*

RUTHERFORD SCHOLARS

• *See page 721*

ALBUQUERQUE COMMUNITY FOUNDATION

http://www.albuquerquefoundation.org/

NEW MEXICO MANUFACTURED HOUSING SCHOLARSHIP PROGRAM

The scholarship is to be used for study in a four-year college or university. The total number of available awards and the dollar value of each award varies. Deadline varies. Refer to website for details and application http://www.albuquerquefoundation.org.

Award: Scholarship for use in freshman year; not renewable. *Number:* 1–2. *Amount:* $740–$1000.

Eligibility Requirements: Applicant must be high school student; planning to enroll or expecting to enroll full-time at a four-year institution or university; resident of New Mexico and studying in New Mexico. Applicant must have 3.0 GPA or higher. Available to U.S. citizens.

Application Requirements: Application form, recommendations or references, resume, test scores, transcript.

Contact: Ms. Nancy Johnson, Grant Director
Albuquerque Community Foundation
PO Box 25266
Albuquerque, NM 87125
Phone: 505-883-6240
E-mail: njohnson@albuquerquefoundation.org

SUSSMAN-MILLER EDUCATIONAL ASSISTANCE FUND

The program provides financial aid to enable students to continue with an undergraduate program. This is a gap program based on financial need. Must be resident of New Mexico. Minimum 3.0 GPA required. Deadline varies. The fund requests not to write or call for information. Please visit website http://www.albuquerquefoundation.org for complete information.

Award: Scholarship for use in freshman, sophomore, junior, or senior years; not renewable. *Number:* 25–30. *Amount:* $500–$2500.

Eligibility Requirements: Applicant must be enrolled or expecting to enroll full-time at a two-year or four-year institution or university and resident of New Mexico. Applicant must have 3.0 GPA or higher. Available to U.S. citizens.

Application Requirements: Application form, essay, financial need analysis, recommendations or references, resume, test scores, transcript.

Contact: Ms. Nancy Johnson, Grant Director
Albuquerque Community Foundation
PO Box 25266
Albuquerque, NM 87125
Phone: 505-883-6240
E-mail: njohnson@albuquerquefoundation.org

YOUTH IN FOSTER CARE SCHOLARSHIP PROGRAM

This award is designed to support youth who have been in the New Mexico foster care system.

Award: Scholarship for use in freshman, sophomore, junior, or senior years; not renewable. *Number:* 1–4. *Amount:* $500–$1000.

Eligibility Requirements: Applicant must be age 17-21; enrolled or expecting to enroll full- or part-time at a two-year or four-year or technical institution or university and resident of New Mexico. Available to U.S. citizens.

Application Requirements: Application form, essay, resume, transcript. *Deadline:* March 18.

Contact: Ms. Nancy Johnson, Grant Director
Albuquerque Community Foundation
PO Box 25266
Albuquerque, NM 87125
Phone: 505-883-6240
E-mail: njohnson@albuquerquefoundation.org

ALERT SCHOLARSHIP

http://www.alertmagazine.org/

ALERT SCHOLARSHIP

$500 scholarship for the best essay on drug / alcohol abuse from each state. Applicant must be current high school senior in Alaska, Nebraska, Oregon, Washington, Idaho, Montana, Minnesota, Wyoming, Colorado, North Dakota, or South Dakota. Minimum 2.5 GPA required. For more information visit: http://www.alertmagazine.org/scholarship.php.

Award: Scholarship for use in freshman year; not renewable. *Amount:* $500.

Eligibility Requirements: Applicant must be high school student; planning to enroll or expecting to enroll full- or part-time at a four-year institution or university; resident of Alaska, Colorado, Idaho, Minnesota, Montana, Nebraska, North Dakota, Oregon, South Dakota, Washington, Wyoming and must have an interest in writing. Applicant must have 2.5 GPA or higher. Available to U.S. citizens.

Application Requirements: Essay, personal photograph. *Deadline:* continuous.

Contact: Alert Magazine
Phone: 208-375-7911
Fax: 208-376-0770
E-mail: alertmagazine@aol.com

THE ALEXANDER FOUNDATION

http://www.thealexanderfoundation.org/

THE ALEXANDER FOUNDATION SCHOLARSHIP PROGRAM

Alexander scholarships provide financial assistance to undergraduate or graduate students accepted or enrolled in Colorado institutions of higher education. Applicants must be gay, lesbian, bisexual, or transgendered and reside in Colorado, must demonstrate financial need, and should be active/supporting/contributing members of the community.

Award: Scholarship for use in freshman, sophomore, junior, senior, graduate, or postgraduate years; not renewable. *Number:* 6–35. *Amount:* $300–$3000.

Eligibility Requirements: Applicant must be enrolled or expecting to enroll full- or part-time at a two-year or four-year or technical institution or university; resident of Colorado; studying in Colorado and must have an interest in LGBT issues. Available to U.S. citizens.

Application Requirements: Application form, essay, financial need analysis, recommendations or references, transcript. *Deadline:* April 15.

Contact: Scholarship Committee
The Alexander Foundation
PO Box 1995
Denver, CO 80201-1995
Phone: 303-331-7733
Fax: 303-331-1953
E-mail: infoalexander@thealexanderfoundation.org

ALEXANDER GRAHAM BELL ASSOCIATION FOR THE DEAF AND HARD OF HEARING

http://www.agbell.org/

AG BELL COLLEGE SCHOLARSHIP PROGRAM
• *See page 594*

ALS ASSOCIATION

http://webdc.alsa.org/site/PageServer?pagename=DC_homepage

PAULA KOVARICK SEGALMAN FAMILY SCHOLARSHIP FUND

The Paula Kovarick Segalman Family Scholarship Fund for ALS was established by the Segalman Family to provide educational funding to students affected by ALS, also known as Lou Gehrig's disease. ALS is a fatal disease affecting families physically, emotionally and financially. The cost of care for someone with ALS can exceed $200,000 a year. The fund looks to alleviate some of the additional financial burdens that families will face when paying for college. Applicant must have a parent or legal guardian currently battling ALS or who has passed away from the disease. Annual household income must be less than $50,000. See the URL link for more about the scholarship, eligibility requirements, and the application process http://webdc.alsa.org/site/PageNavigator/DC_Chapter/DC_6_Paula_Segalman_Scholarship.html

Award: Scholarship for use in freshman, sophomore, junior, or senior years; not renewable. *Amount:* up to $25,000.

Eligibility Requirements: Applicant must be age 17-25; enrolled or expecting to enroll full-time at a two-year or four-year or technical institution or university and resident of District of Columbia, Maryland, Virginia. Applicant must have 2.5 GPA or higher. Available to U.S. citizens.

Application Requirements: Essay. *Deadline:* May 1.

Contact: Judy Taylor
ALS Association
7507 Standish Place
Rockville, MD 20855
Phone: 240-672-3742 Ext. 213
E-mail: info@ALSinfo.org

AMERICAN LEGION AUXILIARY DEPARTMENT OF ALABAMA

http://www.legional.org/

AMERICAN LEGION AUXILIARY DEPARTMENT OF ALABAMA SCHOLARSHIP PROGRAM
• *See page 705*

AMERICAN LEGION AUXILIARY DEPARTMENT OF CALIFORNIA

http://www.calegionaux.org/

AMERICAN LEGION AUXILIARY DEPARTMENT OF CALIFORNIA GENERAL SCHOLARSHIP
• *See page 705*

AMERICAN LEGION AUXILIARY DEPARTMENT OF CONNECTICUT

http://www.ct.legion.org/

AMERICAN LEGION AUXILIARY DEPARTMENT OF CONNECTICUT MEMORIAL EDUCATIONAL GRANT
• *See page 550*

AMERICAN LEGION AUXILIARY DEPARTMENT OF CONNECTICUT PAST PRESIDENTS' PARLEY MEMORIAL EDUCATION GRANT
• *See page 550*

AMERICAN LEGION AUXILIARY DEPARTMENT OF IOWA

http://www.ialegion.org/ala

AMERICAN LEGION AUXILIARY DEPARTMENT OF IOWA CHILDREN OF VETERANS MERIT AWARD
• *See page 705*

AMERICAN LEGION AUXILIARY DEPARTMENT OF KENTUCKY

http://www.kylegion.org/

AMERICAN LEGION AUXILIARY DEPARTMENT OF KENTUCKY LAURA BLACKBURN MEMORIAL SCHOLARSHIP
• *See page 700*

AMERICAN LEGION AUXILIARY DEPARTMENT OF MAINE

http://www.mainelegion.org/

AMERICAN LEGION AUXILIARY DEPARTMENT OF MAINE DANIEL E. LAMBERT MEMORIAL SCHOLARSHIP
• *See page 706*

AMERICAN LEGION AUXILIARY DEPARTMENT OF MASSACHUSETTS

http://www.masslegion-aux.org/

AMERICAN LEGION AUXILIARY DEPARTMENT OF MASSACHUSETTS DEPARTMENT PRESIDENT'S SCHOLARSHIP
• *See page 595*

AMERICAN LEGION AUXILIARY DEPARTMENT OF MICHIGAN

http://www.michalaux.org/

AMERICAN LEGION AUXILIARY DEPARTMENT OF MICHIGAN MEMORIAL SCHOLARSHIP
• *See page 706*

AMERICAN LEGION AUXILIARY DEPARTMENT OF MICHIGAN SCHOLARSHIP FOR NON-TRADITIONAL STUDENT
• *See page 706*

AMERICAN LEGION AUXILIARY DEPARTMENT OF MINNESOTA

http://www.mnala.org

AMERICAN LEGION AUXILIARY DEPARTMENT OF MINNESOTA SCHOLARSHIPS

• *See page 707*

AMERICAN LEGION AUXILIARY DEPARTMENT OF MISSOURI

http://www.missourilegion.org/

AMERICAN LEGION AUXILIARY DEPARTMENT OF MISSOURI LELA MURPHY SCHOLARSHIP

• *See page 550*

AMERICAN LEGION AUXILIARY DEPARTMENT OF MISSOURI NATIONAL PRESIDENT'S SCHOLARSHIP

• *See page 550*

AMERICAN LEGION AUXILIARY DEPARTMENT OF NEBRASKA

http://www.nebraskalegionaux.net/

AMERICAN LEGION AUXILIARY DEPARTMENT OF NEBRASKA RUBY PAUL CAMPAIGN FUND SCHOLARSHIP

• *See page 551*

AMERICAN LEGION AUXILIARY DEPARTMENT OF NORTH DAKOTA

http://www.ndlegion.org/

AMERICAN LEGION AUXILIARY DEPARTMENT OF NORTH DAKOTA NATIONAL PRESIDENT'S SCHOLARSHIP

• *See page 596*

AMERICAN LEGION AUXILIARY DEPARTMENT OF NORTH DAKOTA SCHOLARSHIPS

One-time award for North Dakota residents who are already attending a North Dakota institution of higher learning. Contact local or nearest American Legion Auxiliary Unit for more information. Must be a U.S. citizen.

Award: Scholarship for use in sophomore, junior, senior, or graduate years; not renewable. *Number:* 3. *Amount:* $400.

Eligibility Requirements: Applicant must be enrolled or expecting to enroll full-time at a two-year or four-year or technical institution or university; resident of North Dakota and studying in North Dakota. Available to U.S. citizens.

Application Requirements: Application form, driver's license, essay, financial need analysis, recommendations or references, self-addressed stamped envelope with application, test scores, transcript. *Deadline:* January 15.

Contact: Myrna Runholm, Department Secretary
American Legion Auxiliary Department of North Dakota
PO Box 1060
Jamestown, ND 58402-1060
Phone: 701-253-5992
E-mail: ala-hq@ndlegion.org

AMERICAN LEGION AUXILIARY DEPARTMENT OF OHIO

http://www.alaohio.org/

AMERICAN LEGION AUXILIARY DEPARTMENT OF OHIO CONTINUING EDUCATION FUND

• *See page 707*

AMERICAN LEGION AUXILIARY DEPARTMENT OF OHIO DEPARTMENT PRESIDENT'S SCHOLARSHIP

• *See page 707*

AMERICAN LEGION AUXILIARY DEPARTMENT OF OREGON

http://www.alaoregon.org/

AMERICAN LEGION AUXILIARY DEPARTMENT OF OREGON DEPARTMENT GRANTS

One-time award for educational use in the state of Oregon. Must be a resident of Oregon who is the child or widow of a veteran or the wife of a disabled veteran.

Award: Scholarship for use in freshman year; not renewable. *Number:* 2. *Amount:* $1000.

Eligibility Requirements: Applicant must be enrolled or expecting to enroll full- or part-time at a two-year or four-year or technical institution or university and resident of Oregon. Available to U.S. citizens.

Application Requirements: Application form, essay, financial need analysis, interview. *Deadline:* February 10.

Contact: Virginia Biddle, Secretary/Treasurer
American Legion Auxiliary Department of Oregon
PO Box 1730
Wilsonville, OR 97070
Phone: 503-682-3162
E-mail: alaor@pcez.com

AMERICAN LEGION AUXILIARY DEPARTMENT OF OREGON NATIONAL PRESIDENT'S SCHOLARSHIP

One-time award for children of veterans who served in the Armed Forces during eligibility dates for American Legion membership. Must be high school senior and Oregon resident. Must be entered by a local American Legion auxiliary unit. Three scholarships of varying amounts.

Award: Scholarship for use in freshman year; not renewable. *Number:* 3. *Amount:* $1000–$2500.

Eligibility Requirements: Applicant must be high school student; planning to enroll or expecting to enroll full-time at a four-year institution or university and resident of Oregon. Available to U.S. citizens.

Application Requirements: Application form, essay, financial need analysis, interview. *Deadline:* February 1.

Contact: Virginia Biddle, Secretary/Treasurer
American Legion Auxiliary Department of Oregon
PO Box 1730
Wilsonville, OR 97070
Phone: 503-682-3162
E-mail: alaor@pcez.com

AMERICAN LEGION AUXILIARY DEPARTMENT OF OREGON SPIRIT OF YOUTH SCHOLARSHIP

• *See page 551*

AMERICAN LEGION AUXILIARY DEPARTMENT OF PENNSYLVANIA

http://pa-legion.com

AMERICAN LEGION AUXILIARY DEPARTMENT OF PENNSYLVANIA SCHOLARSHIP FOR DEPENDENTS OF DISABLED OR DECEASED VETERANS

Renewable award of $600 to high school seniors who are residents of Pennsylvania. Applicants must enroll in full-time studies.

Award: Scholarship for use in freshman year; renewable. *Number:* 1. *Amount:* $600.

Eligibility Requirements: Applicant must be high school student; planning to enroll or expecting to enroll full-time at a four-year institution or university and resident of Pennsylvania. Available to U.S. citizens.

Application Requirements: Application form. *Deadline:* March 15.

Contact: Colleen Watson, Executive Secretary and Treasurer
Phone: 717-763-7545
Fax: 717-763-0617
E-mail: paalad@hotmail.com

AMERICAN LEGION AUXILIARY DEPARTMENT OF PENNSYLVANIA SCHOLARSHIP FOR DEPENDENTS OF LIVING VETERANS
• *See page 596*

AMERICAN LEGION AUXILIARY DEPARTMENT OF SOUTH DAKOTA

http://www.sdlegion-aux.org/

AMERICAN LEGION AUXILIARY DEPARTMENT OF SOUTH DAKOTA COLLEGE SCHOLARSHIPS
• *See page 551*

AMERICAN LEGION AUXILIARY DEPARTMENT OF SOUTH DAKOTA SENIOR SCHOLARSHIP
• *See page 551*

AMERICAN LEGION AUXILIARY DEPARTMENT OF TEXAS

http://www.alatexas.org/

AMERICAN LEGION AUXILIARY DEPARTMENT OF TEXAS GENERAL EDUCATION SCHOLARSHIP
• *See page 708*

AMERICAN LEGION AUXILIARY DEPARTMENT OF UTAH

http://www.legion-aux.org/

AMERICAN LEGION AUXILIARY DEPARTMENT OF UTAH NATIONAL PRESIDENT'S SCHOLARSHIP
• *See page 552*

AMERICAN LEGION AUXILIARY DEPARTMENT OF WISCONSIN

http://www.amlegionauxwi.org/

AMERICAN LEGION AUXILIARY DEPARTMENT OF WISCONSIN DELLA VAN DEUREN MEMORIAL SCHOLARSHIP
• *See page 552*

AMERICAN LEGION AUXILIARY DEPARTMENT OF WISCONSIN H.S. AND ANGELINE LEWIS SCHOLARSHIPS
• *See page 552*

AMERICAN LEGION AUXILIARY DEPARTMENT OF WISCONSIN MERIT AND MEMORIAL SCHOLARSHIPS
• *See page 552*

AMERICAN LEGION AUXILIARY DEPARTMENT OF WISCONSIN PRESIDENT'S SCHOLARSHIPS
• *See page 552*

AMERICAN LEGION DEPARTMENT OF ARIZONA

http://www.azlegion.org/programs

AMERICAN LEGION DEPARTMENT OF ARIZONA HIGH SCHOOL ORATORICAL CONTEST

Each student must present an 8 to 10 minute prepared oration on any part of the U.S. Constitution without any notes, podiums, or coaching. The student will then be asked to do a 3 to 5 minute oration on one of four possible topics. Which one of the four topics will not be known in advance, so students must be prepared to respond to any of the four. Open to students in grades 9 to 12.

Award: Scholarship for use in freshman year; not renewable. *Number:* 10–20. *Amount:* $50–$1500.

Eligibility Requirements: Applicant must be high school student; planning to enroll or expecting to enroll full-time at a two-year or four-year institution or university; resident of Arizona and must have an interest in public speaking. Available to U.S. citizens.

Application Requirements: Application form. *Deadline:* January 1.

Contact: Roger Munchbach, Department Oratorical Chairman
American Legion Department of Arizona
4701 North 19th Avenue, Suite 200
Phoenix, AZ 85015-3799
Phone: 602-264-7706
E-mail: legionoratoricalcontest@msn.com

AMERICAN LEGION DEPARTMENT OF ARKANSAS

http://www.arklegion.homestead.com/

AMERICAN LEGION DEPARTMENT OF ARKANSAS HIGH SCHOOL ORATORICAL CONTEST

Oratorical contest open to students in ninth to twelfth grades of any accredited Arkansas high school. Begins with finalists at the post level and proceeds through area and district levels to national contest.

Award: Prize for use in freshman year; not renewable. *Number:* 4. *Amount:* $1250–$3500.

Eligibility Requirements: Applicant must be high school student; planning to enroll or expecting to enroll full-time at a four-year institution or university; resident of Arkansas and must have an interest in public speaking. Applicant must have 2.5 GPA or higher. Available to U.S. citizens.

Application Requirements: Application form, entry in a contest, personal photograph, recommendations or references. *Deadline:* December 15.

Contact: William Winchell, Department Adjutant
American Legion Department of Arkansas
PO Box 3280
Little Rock, AR 72203-3280
Phone: 501-375-1104
Fax: 501-375-4236
E-mail: alegion@swbell.net

AMERICAN LEGION DEPARTMENT OF HAWAII

http://www.legion.org/

AMERICAN LEGION DEPARTMENT OF HAWAII HIGH SCHOOL ORATORICAL CONTEST

Oratorical contest open to students in ninth to twelfth grades of any accredited Hawaii high school. Must be under 20 years of age. Speech contests begin in January at post level and continue on to the national competition. Contact local American Legion Post or department for deadlines and application details.

Award: Prize for use in freshman year; not renewable. *Number:* 1–3. *Amount:* $50–$1500.

Eligibility Requirements: Applicant must be high school student; age 14-20; planning to enroll or expecting to enroll full-time at a four-year institution or university and resident of Hawaii. Available to U.S. citizens.

Application Requirements: Application form. *Deadline:* January 1.

Contact: Adm. Bernard Lee, Department Adjutant
American Legion Department of Hawaii
612 McCully Street
Honolulu, HI 96826-3935
Phone: 808-946-6383
E-mail: aldepthi@hawaii.rr.com

AMERICAN LEGION DEPARTMENT OF IDAHO

http://www.idaholegion.com/

AMERICAN LEGION DEPARTMENT OF IDAHO SCHOLARSHIP
• *See page 553*

AMERICAN LEGION DEPARTMENT OF ILLINOIS

http://www.illegion.org/

AMERICANISM ESSAY CONTEST SCHOLARSHIP
• *See page 553*

AMERICAN LEGION DEPARTMENT OF ILLINOIS BOY SCOUT/EXPLORER SCHOLARSHIP
• *See page 553*

AMERICAN LEGION DEPARTMENT OF ILLINOIS HIGH SCHOOL ORATORICAL CONTEST

Single oratorical contest with winners advancing to the next level. Open to students in 9th to 12th grades of any accredited Illinois high school. Seniors must be in attendance as of January 1. Must contact local American Legion post or department headquarters for complete information and applications, which will be available in the fall.

Award: Scholarship for use in freshman year; not renewable. *Number:* 1–30. *Amount:* $100–$2000.

Eligibility Requirements: Applicant must be high school student; planning to enroll or expecting to enroll full- or part-time at a four-year institution or university; resident of Illinois and must have an interest in English language or public speaking. Available to U.S. citizens.

Application Requirements: Application form. *Fee:* $125.

Contact: Christy Rich, Executive Administrative Assistant
American Legion Department of Illinois
2720 East Lincoln Street
Bloomington, IL 61704
Phone: 309-663-0361
Fax: 309-663-5783
E-mail: hdqs@illegion.org

AMERICAN LEGION DEPARTMENT OF INDIANA

http://www.indianalegion.org

AMERICAN LEGION DEPARTMENT OF INDIANA, AMERICANISM AND GOVERNMENT TEST

Study guides are provided to high schools. Students take a test and write an essay. One male and one female student from each grade (10 to 12) are selected as state winners. Tests must be ordered by September 29.

Award: Scholarship for use in freshman, sophomore, junior, or senior years; not renewable. *Number:* 6. *Amount:* $1000.

Eligibility Requirements: Applicant must be high school student; planning to enroll or expecting to enroll full- or part-time at a two-year or four-year or technical institution or university and resident of Indiana. Available to U.S. citizens.

Application Requirements: Application form. *Deadline:* December 1.

Contact: Butch Miller, Program Director
American Legion Department of Indiana
5440 Herbert Lord Rd
Indianapolis, IN 46216
Phone: 317-6301300
Fax: 317-237-9891
E-mail: bmiller@indianalegion.org

AMERICAN LEGION DEPARTMENT OF INDIANA HIGH SCHOOL ORATORICAL CONTEST

Oratorical contest open to students in grades nine to twelve of any accredited Indiana high school or home schooled students in an equivalent grade. All contestants must be a citizen of or lawful permanent resident of the United States. Students may only enter one district/zone/state competition. The student must compete in the district in which his/her sponsoring post is located. Speech contests begin in November at post level and continue on to national competition. Contact local American Legion post for application details or visit our website at http//http://www.indianalegion.org.

Award: Scholarship for use in freshman, sophomore, junior, or senior years; not renewable. *Amount:* $200–$3400.

Eligibility Requirements: Applicant must be high school student; planning to enroll or expecting to enroll full- or part-time at a two-year or four-year or technical institution or university; resident of Indiana and must have an interest in public speaking. Available to U.S. citizens.

Application Requirements: Application form. *Deadline:* December 15.

Contact: Butch Miller, Program Director
American Legion Department of Indiana
5440 Herbert Lord Rd
Indianapolis, IN 46216
Phone: 317-6301300
Fax: 317-237-9891
E-mail: bmiller@indianalegion.org

AMERICAN LEGION FAMILY SCHOLARSHIP
• *See page 553*

FRANK W. MCHALE MEMORIAL SCHOLARSHIPS

One-time award for Indiana high school junior boys who participated in The American Legion Hoosier Boys State Program. Must be nominated by Boys State official while in attendance at Hoosier Boys State. Write for more information and deadline.

Award: Scholarship for use in freshman, sophomore, junior, or senior years; not renewable. *Number:* 3. *Amount:* $800.

Eligibility Requirements: Applicant must be high school student; planning to enroll or expecting to enroll full- or part-time at a two-year or four-year or technical institution or university; male; resident of Indiana and must have an interest in leadership. Available to U.S. citizens.

Application Requirements: Application form, essay.

Contact: Butch Miller, Program Director
American Legion Department of Indiana
5440 Herbert Lord Rd
Indianapolis, IN 46216
Phone: 317-6301300
Fax: 317-237-9891
E-mail: bmiller@indianalegion.org

AMERICAN LEGION DEPARTMENT OF IOWA

http://www.ialegion.org/

AMERICAN LEGION DEPARTMENT OF IOWA EAGLE SCOUT OF THE YEAR SCHOLARSHIP
• *See page 554*

AMERICAN LEGION DEPARTMENT OF IOWA HIGH SCHOOL ORATORICAL CONTEST

All contestants in the department of Iowa American Legion High School Oratorical Contest shall be citizens or lawful permanent residents of the United States. The department of Iowa American Legion High School Oratorical Contest shall consist of one contestant from each of the three area contests. The area contest shall consist of one contestant from each district in the designated Area.

Award: Prize for use in freshman year; not renewable. *Number:* up to 3. *Amount:* $1000–$2000.

Eligibility Requirements: Applicant must be high school student; planning to enroll or expecting to enroll full-time at a two-year or four-year institution or university; resident of Iowa and must have an interest in public speaking. Available to U.S. citizens.

Application Requirements: Application form, entry in a contest. *Deadline:* varies.

Contact: Programs Director
Phone: 515-282-5068
Fax: 515-282-7583
E-mail: programs@ialegion.org

AMERICAN LEGION DEPARTMENT OF IOWA OUTSTANDING SENIOR BASEBALL PLAYER

One-time award for Iowa residents who participated in the American Legion Senior Baseball Program and display outstanding sportsmanship, athletic ability, and proven academic achievements. Must be recommended by Baseball Committee.

Award: Scholarship for use in freshman year; not renewable. *Number:* 1. *Amount:* $750–$1500.

Eligibility Requirements: Applicant must be high school student; age 15-18; planning to enroll or expecting to enroll full-time at a two-year or four-year institution or university; resident of Iowa and must have an interest in athletics/sports. Available to U.S. citizens.

Application Requirements: Application form, entry in a contest, recommendations or references. *Deadline:* July 15.

Contact: Programs Director
Phone: 515-282-5068
Fax: 515-282-7583
E-mail: programs@ialegion.org

AMERICAN LEGION DEPARTMENT OF KANSAS

http://www.ksamlegion.org/

ALBERT M. LAPPIN SCHOLARSHIP
• *See page 554*

AMERICAN LEGION DEPARTMENT OF KANSAS HIGH SCHOOL ORATORICAL CONTEST

Awards a total of $2400 ($1500, $500, $250, and $150) in scholarships to the top four winners in each state. The state winner's school receives $500. The top three contestants in the nation are awarded scholarships totaling $48,000 ($18,000, $16,000, and $14,000).

Award: Prize for use in freshman year; not renewable. *Number:* 4. *Amount:* $150–$18,000.

Eligibility Requirements: Applicant must be high school student; planning to enroll or expecting to enroll full-time at a four-year institution or university; resident of Kansas and must have an interest in public speaking. Available to U.S. citizens.

Application Requirements: Application form. *Deadline:* January 15.

Contact: Jeff Bond, Oratorical Contest Committee
American Legion Department of Kansas
1314 SW Topeka Boulevard
Topeka, KS 66612
Phone: 785-232-9315

CHARLES W. AND ANNETTE HILL SCHOLARSHIP
• *See page 554*

DR. CLICK COWGER BASEBALL SCHOLARSHIP

Scholarship available to a high school senior or college freshman or sophomore enrolled in a Kansas institution. Applicant may intend to enroll in a junior college, university or trade school in Kansas only. Must be a male and should play or has played Kansas American Legion baseball. Must be an average or a better student scholastically.

Award: Scholarship for use in freshman or sophomore years; not renewable. *Number:* 1. *Amount:* $500.

Eligibility Requirements: Applicant must be enrolled or expecting to enroll full-time at a two-year or four-year or technical institution or university; male; resident of Kansas; studying in Kansas and must have an interest in athletics/sports. Available to U.S. citizens.

Application Requirements: Application form, essay, financial need analysis, personal photograph. *Deadline:* July 15.

Contact: Mike Oppy, Chairman, Scholarship Committee
American Legion Department of Kansas
1314 SW Topeka Boulevard
Topeka, KS 66612
Phone: 785-232-9315

HUGH A. SMITH SCHOLARSHIP FUND
• *See page 554*

PAUL FLAHERTY ATHLETIC SCHOLARSHIP

Scholarship available to high school seniors, college level freshmen or sophomores enrolled or intending to enroll in an approved junior college, college, university, or trade school. Must have participated in any form of high school athletics. Must be an average or a better student scholastically.

Award: Scholarship for use in freshman or sophomore years; not renewable. *Number:* 1. *Amount:* $250.

Eligibility Requirements: Applicant must be enrolled or expecting to enroll full-time at a two-year or four-year or technical institution or university; resident of Kansas; studying in Kansas and must have an interest in athletics/sports. Available to U.S. citizens.

Application Requirements: Application form, essay, financial need analysis, personal photograph. *Deadline:* July 15.

Contact: Mike Oppy, Chairman, Scholarship Committee
American Legion Department of Kansas
1314 SW Topeka Boulevard
Topeka, KS 66612
Phone: 785-232-9513

ROSEDALE POST 346 SCHOLARSHIP
• *See page 554*

TED AND NORA ANDERSON SCHOLARSHIPS
• *See page 554*

AMERICAN LEGION DEPARTMENT OF MAINE

http://www.mainelegion.org/

AMERICAN LEGION DEPARTMENT OF MAINE CHILDREN AND YOUTH SCHOLARSHIP
• *See page 708*

DANIEL E. LAMBERT MEMORIAL SCHOLARSHIP
• *See page 708*

JAMES V. DAY SCHOLARSHIP
• *See page 555*

AMERICAN LEGION DEPARTMENT OF MARYLAND

http://www.mdlegion.org/

AMERICAN LEGION DEPARTMENT OF MARYLAND GENERAL SCHOLARSHIP FUND
• *See page 555*

AMERICAN LEGION, DEPARTMENT OF MARYLAND, HIGH SCHOOL ORATORICAL SCHOLARSHIP CONTEST
• *See page 596*

MARYLAND BOYS STATE SCHOLARSHIP
• *See page 597*

AMERICAN LEGION DEPARTMENT OF MICHIGAN

http://www.michiganlegion.org/

AMERICAN LEGION DEPARTMENT OF MICHIGAN ORATORICAL SCHOLARSHIP PROGRAM

Oratorical contest open to students in ninth to twelfth grades of any accredited Michigan high school or state accredited home school. Five one-time awards of varying amounts. State winner advances to National Competition for scholarship money ranging from $14,000 to $18,000. Application Due in November

Award: Scholarship for use in freshman year; not renewable. *Number:* 5. *Amount:* $800–$1500.

Eligibility Requirements: Applicant must be high school student; planning to enroll or expecting to enroll full- or part-time at a two-year or four-year institution or university; resident of Michigan and must have an interest in public speaking. Available to U.S. citizens.

Application Requirements: Application form, essay. *Deadline:* November 18.

Contact: Programs Coordinator
American Legion Department of Michigan
212 North Verlinden Avenue
Lansing, MI 48915
Phone: 517-371-4720 Ext. 23
E-mail: legion@michiganlegion.org

GUY M. WILSON SCHOLARSHIPS
• *See page 708*

WILLIAM D. AND JEWELL W. BREWER SCHOLARSHIP TRUSTS
• *See page 709*

THE AMERICAN LEGION, DEPARTMENT OF MINNESOTA

http://www.mnlegion.org/

AMERICAN LEGION DEPARTMENT OF MINNESOTA HIGH SCHOOL ORATORICAL CONTEST

Oratorical contest open to students in ninth to twelfth grades of any accredited Minnesota high school or home-schooled students. Must be Minnesota resident. Speech must be student's original work on the general subject of the Constitution. Speech contests begin in December at local Legion post level and continue on to the national competition. See website for specific topic and application details http://www.mnlegion.org.

Award: Scholarship for use in freshman year; not renewable. *Number:* 4. *Amount:* $500–$1500.

Eligibility Requirements: Applicant must be high school student; planning to enroll or expecting to enroll full- or part-time at a two-year or four-year or technical institution or university; resident of Minnesota and must have an interest in public speaking. Available to U.S. citizens.

Application Requirements: *Deadline:* November 30.

Contact: Jennifer Kelley, Program Coordinator
The American Legion, Department of Minnesota
20 West 12th Street, Room 300-A
St. Paul, MN 55155
Phone: 651-291-1800
E-mail: department@mnlegion.org

AMERICAN LEGION DEPARTMENT OF MINNESOTA MEMORIAL SCHOLARSHIP
• *See page 555*

MINNESOTA LEGIONNAIRES INSURANCE TRUST SCHOLARSHIP
• *See page 555*

AMERICAN LEGION DEPARTMENT OF MISSOURI

http://www.missourilegion.org/

CHARLES L. BACON MEMORIAL SCHOLARSHIP
• *See page 555*

LILLIE LOIS FORD SCHOLARSHIP FUND
• *See page 709*

AMERICAN LEGION DEPARTMENT OF MONTANA

http://www.mtlegion.org/

AMERICAN LEGION DEPARTMENT OF MONTANA HIGH SCHOOL ORATORICAL CONTEST

Applicants participate in a statewide memorized oratorical contest on the U.S. Constitution. Four places are awarded. Must be a Montana high school student. Contact state adjutant American Legion Department of Montana for further details. Each state winner who competes in the first round of the national contest will receive a $1000 scholarship. Participants in the second round who do not advance to the national final round will receive an additional $1000 scholarship.

Award: Scholarship for use in freshman year; not renewable. *Number:* 1–4. *Amount:* $450–$2000.

Eligibility Requirements: Applicant must be high school student; planning to enroll or expecting to enroll full-time at a two-year or four-year or technical institution or university; resident of Montana and must have an interest in public speaking. Available to U.S. citizens.

Application Requirements: *Deadline:* February 26.

Contact: Gary White, Department Adjutant
American Legion Department of Montana
PO Box 6075
Helena, MT 59602
Phone: 406-324-3989
E-mail: amlegmt29@mtlegion29.org

AMERICAN LEGION DEPARTMENT OF NEBRASKA

http://www.nebraskalegion.net/

AMERICAN LEGION DEPARTMENT OF NEBRASKA HIGH SCHOOL ORATORICAL CONTEST

Local high school winners advance to District. Fifteen District Winners advance to Area contest. Area contestants awarded $100. Four Area winners advance to State contest. State prizes range from $200 to $1000. State winner advances to National contest. National prizes range from $14,000 to $18,000.

Award: Prize for use in freshman year; not renewable. *Number:* 4–19. *Amount:* $100–$1000.

Eligibility Requirements: Applicant must be high school student; planning to enroll or expecting to enroll full- or part-time at a two-year or four-year or technical institution or university; resident of Nebraska and must have an interest in public speaking. Available to U.S. citizens.

Application Requirements: *Deadline:* October 1.

Contact: Brent Hagel-Pitt, Administrator
American Legion Department of Nebraska
P.O. Box 5205
Lincoln, NE 68505
Phone: 402-464-6338
E-mail: actdirlegion@windstream.net

AMERICAN LEGION DEPARTMENT OF NEBRASKA JIM HURLBERT MEMORIAL BASEBALL SCHOLARSHIP

Award to a Nebraska American Legion Baseball player in last year of eligibility and/or graduating senior. One applicant nominated by each Senior American Legion Baseball team. Student must attend a postsecondary educational institution within the state of Nebraska, and must have maintained a GPA in the upper half of his/her graduating class.

Award: Scholarship for use in freshman year; not renewable. *Number:* 1–4. *Amount:* $500.

Eligibility Requirements: Applicant must be high school student; planning to enroll or expecting to enroll full-time at a two-year or four-year or technical institution or university; resident of Nebraska; studying in Nebraska and must have an interest in athletics/sports. Applicant must have 3.5 GPA or higher. Available to U.S. citizens.

Application Requirements: Application form, community service, financial need analysis. *Deadline:* June 15.

Contact: Brent Hagel-Pitt, Administrator
American Legion Department of Nebraska
P.O. Box 5205
Lincoln, NE 68505
Phone: 402-464-6338
E-mail: actdirlegion@windstream.net

MAYNARD JENSEN AMERICAN LEGION MEMORIAL SCHOLARSHIP

• *See page 556*

AMERICAN LEGION DEPARTMENT OF NEW YORK

http://www.ny.legion.org/

AMERICAN LEGION DEPARTMENT OF NEW YORK HIGH SCHOOL ORATORICAL CONTEST

Oratorical contest open to students under 20 years in 9th-12th grades of any accredited New York high school. Speech contests begin in November at post levels and continue to national competition. Must be U.S. citizen or permanent resident. Payments are made directly to college and are awarded over a four-year period. Deadline varies.

Award: Scholarship for use in freshman year; not renewable. *Amount:* $2000–$6000.

Eligibility Requirements: Applicant must be high school student; planning to enroll or expecting to enroll full-time at a four-year institution or university; resident of New York and must have an interest in public speaking. Available to U.S. citizens.

Application Requirements: Application form, entry in a contest. *Deadline:* varies.

Contact: Richard Pedro, Department Adjutant
American Legion Department of New York
112 State Street, Suite 400
Albany, NY 12207
Phone: 518-463-2215
Fax: 518-427-8443
E-mail: newyork@legion.org

AMERICAN LEGION DEPARTMENT OF NORTH CAROLINA

http://www.nclegion.org/

AMERICAN LEGION DEPARTMENT OF NORTH CAROLINA HIGH SCHOOL ORATORICAL CONTEST

This is a speaking contest. The objective of the contest is to develop a deeper knowledge and appreciation of the U.S. Constitution, develop leadership qualities, the ability to think and speak clearly and intelligently, and prepare for acceptance of duties, responsibilities, rights, and privileges of American citizenship. Open to North Carolina high school students. Must be U.S. citizen or lawful permanent resident. The contestant must have a prepared eight to ten minute oration on some aspect of the Constitution of the United States, as well as 4 three to five minute discourses on specific assigned topics to test the speaker's knowledge of the subject.

Award: Scholarship for use in freshman year; not renewable. *Number:* 5. *Amount:* $1000–$2500.

Eligibility Requirements: Applicant must be high school student; planning to enroll or expecting to enroll full-time at a two-year or four-year or technical institution or university; resident of North Carolina and must have an interest in public speaking. Available to U.S. citizens.

Application Requirements: *Deadline:* December 22.

Contact: Deborah Rose, Department Executive Secretary
American Legion Department of North Carolina
4 North Blount Street, PO Box 26657
Raleigh, NC 27611-6657
Phone: 919-832-7506
E-mail: drose-nclegion@nc.rr.com

AMERICAN LEGION DEPARTMENT OF NORTH DAKOTA

http://www.ndlegion.org/

AMERICAN LEGION DEPARTMENT OF NORTH DAKOTA NATIONAL HIGH SCHOOL ORATORICAL CONTEST

Oratorical contest for high school students in grades nine to twelve. Contestants must prepare to speak on the topic of the U.S. Constitution. Must graduate from an accredited North Dakota high school. Contest begins at the local level and continues to the national level. Several one-time awards of $100 to $2000.

Award: Prize for use in freshman, sophomore, junior, or senior years; not renewable. *Number:* 38. *Amount:* $100–$2000.

Eligibility Requirements: Applicant must be high school student; age 14-18; planning to enroll or expecting to enroll full-time at a four-year institution or university; resident of Alberta, North Dakota; studying in North Dakota and must have an interest in public speaking. Available to U.S. citizens.

Application Requirements: Application form. *Deadline:* October 30.

Contact: Teri Bryant
American Legion Department of North Dakota
405 West Main Avenue, Suite 4A
West Fargo, ND 58078
Phone: 701-293-3120
E-mail: programs@ndlegion.org

HATTIE TEDROW MEMORIAL FUND SCHOLARSHIP

Applicants must be legal residents of North Dakota, high school seniors, and direct descendants of a veteran with honorable service in the U.S. military. The student will have two years from the date of graduation from high school to use his/her award.

Award: Scholarship for use in freshman, sophomore, junior, or senior years; not renewable. *Amount:* $200–$500.

Eligibility Requirements: Applicant must be high school student; age 17-18; planning to enroll or expecting to enroll full-time at a two-year or four-year or technical institution or university; resident of North Dakota and studying in North Dakota. Available to U.S. citizens.

Application Requirements: Application form, essay. *Deadline:* March 15.

Contact: Teri Bryant
American Legion Department of North Dakota
405 West Main Avenue, Suite 4A
West Fargo, ND 58078
Phone: 701-293-3120
E-mail: programs@ndlegion.org

AMERICAN LEGION DEPARTMENT OF OREGON

http://www.orlegion.org/

AMERICAN LEGION DEPARTMENT OF OREGON HIGH SCHOOL ORATORICAL CONTEST

Students give two orations, one prepared and one extemporaneous on an assigned topic pertaining to the Constitution of the United States of America. Awards are given at Post, District, and State level with the state winner advancing to the National level contest. Open to students enrolled in high schools within the state of Oregon.

Award: Scholarship for use in freshman year; not renewable. *Number:* up to 4. *Amount:* $200–$500.

Eligibility Requirements: Applicant must be high school student; planning to enroll or expecting to enroll full-time at a four-year institution or university; resident of Oregon and must have an interest in public speaking. Available to U.S. citizens.

Application Requirements: Application form, entry in a contest. *Deadline:* December 1.

Contact: Barry Snyder, Adjutant
Phone: 503-685-5006
Fax: 503-968-5432
E-mail: orlegion@aol.com

AMERICAN LEGION DEPARTMENT OF PENNSYLVANIA

http://www.pa-legion.com/

AMERICAN LEGION DEPARTMENT OF PENNSYLVANIA HIGH SCHOOL ORATORICAL CONTEST

Oratorical contest open to students in 9th-12th grades of any accredited Pennsylvania high school. Speech contests begin in January at post level and continue on to national competition. Contact local American Legion post for deadlines and application details. Three one-time awards ranging from $7500 for first place, second place $5000, and third place $4000.

Award: Prize for use in freshman year; not renewable. *Number:* 3. *Amount:* $4000–$7500.

Eligibility Requirements: Applicant must be high school student; planning to enroll or expecting to enroll full-time at a two-year or four-year or technical institution or university; resident of Pennsylvania and must have an interest in public speaking. Available to U.S. citizens.

Application Requirements: Application form, entry in a contest. *Deadline:* varies.

Contact: Colleen Washinger, Executive Secretary
American Legion Department of Pennsylvania
PO Box 2324
Harrisburg, PA 17105-2324
Phone: 717-730-9100
Fax: 717-975-2836
E-mail: hq@pa-legion.com

JOSEPH P. GAVENONIS COLLEGE SCHOLARSHIP (PLAN I)
• *See page 556*

AMERICAN LEGION DEPARTMENT OF SOUTH DAKOTA

http://www.sdlegion.org/

AMERICAN LEGION DEPARTMENT OF SOUTH DAKOTA HIGH SCHOOL ORATORICAL CONTEST

Provide an 8 to 10 minute oration on some phase of the U.S. Constitution. Be prepared to speak extemporaneously for 3 to 5 minutes on specified articles or amendments. Compete at Local, District, and State levels. State winner goes on to National Contest and opportunity to win $18,000 in scholarships. Contact local American Legion post for contest dates.

Award: Prize for use in freshman, sophomore, junior, or senior years; not renewable. *Number:* 1–4. *Amount:* $200–$1000.

Eligibility Requirements: Applicant must be enrolled or expecting to enroll full-time at a two-year or four-year or technical institution or university; resident of South Dakota and must have an interest in public speaking. Available to U.S. citizens.

Application Requirements: Entry in a contest, oration. *Deadline:* varies.

Contact: Dennis Brendan, Department Adjutant
American Legion Department of South Dakota
PO Box 67
Watertown, SD 57201-0067
Phone: 605-886-3604
Fax: 605-886-2870
E-mail: sdlegion@dailypost.com

AMERICAN LEGION DEPARTMENT OF TENNESSEE

http://www.tennesseelegion.org/

AMERICAN LEGION DEPARTMENT OF TENNESSEE EAGLE SCOUT OF THE YEAR
• *See page 556*

AMERICAN LEGION DEPARTMENT OF TENNESSEE HIGH SCHOOL ORATORICAL CONTEST

Scholarship for graduating Tennessee high school seniors enrolled either part-time or full-time in accredited colleges or universities.

Award: Scholarship for use in freshman, sophomore, junior, or senior years; not renewable. *Number:* 1–3. *Amount:* $1000–$3000.

Eligibility Requirements: Applicant must be high school student; planning to enroll or expecting to enroll full- or part-time at a two-year or four-year institution or university; resident of Tennessee and must have an interest in public speaking. Available to U.S. citizens.

Application Requirements: Application form, essay.

Contact: Dean Tuttle, Department Adjutant
American Legion Department of Tennessee
318 Donelson Pike
Nashville, TN 37214
Phone: 615-391-5088
E-mail: Adjutant@TNLegion.org

AMERICAN LEGION DEPARTMENT OF TEXAS

http://www.txlegion.org/

AMERICAN LEGION DEPARTMENT OF TEXAS HIGH SCHOOL ORATORICAL CONTEST

Scholarships will be given to the winners of oratorical contests. Contestants must be in high school with plans to further their education in a postsecondary institution. The winner of first place will be certified to national headquarters as the Texas representative in the quarter finals and the department will award a $2000 scholarship to the college of the applicant's choice. The department champion will receive additional scholarships each time he/she advances to the next level.

Award: Prize for use in freshman year; not renewable. *Number:* up to 20. *Amount:* $500–$2000.

Eligibility Requirements: Applicant must be high school student; planning to enroll or expecting to enroll full-time at a two-year or four-year or technical institution or university; resident of Texas and must have an interest in public speaking. Available to U.S. citizens.

Application Requirements: Application form, copy of prepared oration, entry in a contest, essay, interview. *Deadline:* varies.

Contact: Robert Squyres, Director of Internal Affairs
American Legion Department of Texas
3401 Ed Bluestein Boulevard
Austin, TX 78721-2902
Phone: 512-472-4138
Fax: 512-472-0603
E-mail: programs@txlegion.org

AMERICAN LEGION DEPARTMENT OF VERMONT

http://www.vtlegion.org

AMERICAN LEGION DEPARTMENT OF VERMONT DEPARTMENT SCHOLARSHIPS

Awards for high school seniors who attend a Vermont high school or similar school in an adjoining state whose parents are legal residents of Vermont, or reside in an adjoining state and attend a Vermont secondary school.

Award: Scholarship for use in freshman year; not renewable. *Number:* 1–12. *Amount:* $500–$1500.

Eligibility Requirements: Applicant must be high school student; planning to enroll or expecting to enroll full- or part-time at a two-year or four-year or technical institution or university and resident of New Hampshire, New York, Vermont. Available to U.S. citizens.

Application Requirements: Application form, essay, financial need analysis. *Deadline:* April 1.

Contact: Huzon "Jerry" Stewart, Chairman
American Legion Department of Vermont
PO Box 396
Montpelier, VT 05601-0396
Phone: 802-223-7131
E-mail: alvthq@myfairpoint.net

AMERICAN LEGION DEPARTMENT OF VERMONT HIGH SCHOOL ORATORICAL CONTEST

Students in grades 9 to 12 are eligible to compete. Must attend an accredited Vermont high school. Must be a U.S. citizen. Selection based on oration.

Award: Prize for use in freshman year; not renewable. *Number:* 1–2. *Amount:* $200–$1500.

Eligibility Requirements: Applicant must be high school student; planning to enroll or expecting to enroll full- or part-time at a two-year or four-year or technical institution or university; resident of Vermont and must have an interest in public speaking. Available to U.S. citizens.

Application Requirements: Application form. *Deadline:* January 1.

Contact: Karlene DeVine, Chairman
American Legion Department of Vermont
126 State Street
Montpelier, VT 05601
Phone: 802-223-7131
E-mail: alvthq@myfairpoint.net

AMERICAN LEGION EAGLE SCOUT OF THE YEAR
• *See page 556*

AMERICAN LEGION DEPARTMENT OF VIRGINIA

http://www.valegion.org/

AMERICAN LEGION DEPARTMENT OF VIRGINIA HIGH SCHOOL ORATORICAL CONTEST

Three one-time awards of up to $1100. Oratorical contest open to applicants who are winners of the Virginia department oratorical contest and who attend high school in Virginia. Competitors must demonstrate their knowledge of the U.S. Constitution. Must be students in ninth to twelfth grades at accredited Virginia high schools.

Award: Prize for use in freshman year; not renewable. *Number:* 3. *Amount:* $600–$1100.

Eligibility Requirements: Applicant must be high school student; planning to enroll or expecting to enroll full-time at a four-year institution or university and resident of Virginia. Available to U.S. citizens.

Application Requirements: Application form, entry in a contest. *Deadline:* December 1.

Contact: Dale Chapman, Adjutant
American Legion Department of Virginia
1708 Commonwealth Avenue
Richmond, VA 23230
Phone: 804-353-6606
Fax: 804-358-1940
E-mail: eeccleston@valegion.org

AMERICAN LEGION DEPARTMENT OF WASHINGTON

http://www.walegion.org/

AMERICAN LEGION DEPARTMENT OF WASHINGTON CHILDREN AND YOUTH SCHOLARSHIPS
• *See page 557*

AMERICAN LEGION DEPARTMENT OF WEST VIRGINIA

http://www.wvlegion.org/

AMERICAN LEGION DEPARTMENT OF WEST VIRGINIA BOARD OF REGENTS SCHOLARSHIP
• *See page 588*

AMERICAN LEGION DEPARTMENT OF WEST VIRGINIA HIGH SCHOOL ORATORICAL CONTEST

Oratorical Scholarship Program Contest open to students in ninth to twelfth grades of any accredited West Virginia high school. Speech contests begin in January at post level and continue on to national competition. Contact local American Legion Post for deadlines and application details, or American Legion State Headquarters 304-343-7591.

Award: Scholarship for use in freshman year; not renewable. *Number:* 25–39. *Amount:* $200.

Eligibility Requirements: Applicant must be high school student; planning to enroll or expecting to enroll full-time at a four-year institution or university; resident of West Virginia; studying in West Virginia and must have an interest in public speaking. Available to U.S. citizens.

Application Requirements: Application form. *Deadline:* December 29.

Contact: Mr. Miles Epling, Department Adjutant
American Legion Department of West Virginia
2016 Kanawha Boulevard East, PO Box 3191
Charleston, WV 25311
Phone: 304-343-7591
E-mail: wvlegion@suddenlinkmail.com

SONS OF THE AMERICAN LEGION WILLIAM F. "BILL" JOHNSON MEMORIAL SCHOLARSHIP
• *See page 557*

AMERICAN QUARTER HORSE FOUNDATION (AQHF)

http://www.aqha.com/foundation

ARIZONA QUARTER HORSE YOUTH SCHOLARSHIP
• *See page 558*

ARIZONA QUARTER RACING SCHOLARSHIP
• *See page 558*

CHRISTOPHER LAWRENCE JUNKER NEBRASKA SCHOLARSHIP
• *See page 558*

DR. GERALD O'CONNOR MICHIGAN QHY SCHOLARSHIP
• *See page 558*

INDIANA QUARTER HORSE YOUTH SCHOLARSHIP
• *See page 559*

JAMES F. AND DORIS M. BARTON SCHOLARSHIP
• *See page 559*

JOAN CAIN FLORIDA QUARTER HORSE YOUTH SCHOLARSHIP
• *See page 559*

JOYCE WYATT PENNSYLVANIA QUARTER HORSE YOUTH SCHOLARSHIP
• *See page 559*

NEBRASKA QUARTER HORSE YOUTH SCHOLARSHIP
• *See page 560*

SWAYZE WOODRUFF MEMORIAL MID-SOUTH SCHOLARSHIP
• *See page 560*

AMERICAN SAVINGS FOUNDATION

http://www.asfdn.org/

ROBERT T. KENNEY SCHOLARSHIP PROGRAM AT THE AMERICAN SAVINGS FOUNDATION
• *See page 597*

ANTHONY MUNOZ FOUNDATION

http://www.munozfoundation.org

ANTHONY MUNOZ SCHOLARSHIPS
• *See page 598*

THE ARC NEW YORK

https://www.nysarc.org/

ARTHUR W. PENSE SCHOLARSHIP
• *See page 599*

ARC OF WASHINGTON TRUST FUND

http://www.arctrustfund.org/

ARC OF WASHINGTON TRUST FUND STIPEND PROGRAM
• *See page 599*

ARIZONA COMMISSION FOR POSTSECONDARY EDUCATION

https://highered.az.gov/

LEVERAGING EDUCATIONAL ASSISTANCE PARTNERSHIP

Grants to financially needy students, who enroll in and attend postsecondary education or training in Arizona schools. Program was formerly known as the State Student Incentive Grant or SSIG Program.

Award: Grant for use in freshman, sophomore, junior, senior, or graduate years; not renewable. *Amount:* $100–$2500.

Eligibility Requirements: Applicant must be enrolled or expecting to enroll full- or part-time at a two-year or four-year or technical institution or university; resident of Arizona and studying in Arizona. Available to U.S. citizens.

Application Requirements: Application form, financial need analysis, transcript. *Deadline:* April 30.

Contact: Mila Zaporteza, Business Manager and LEAP Financial Aid Manager
Arizona Commission for Postsecondary Education
2020 North Central Avenue, Suite 650
Phoenix, AZ 85004-4503
Phone: 602-258-2435 Ext. 102
Fax: 602-258-2483
E-mail: mila@azhighered.gov

ARIZONA PRIVATE SCHOOL ASSOCIATION

http://www.arizonapsa.org/

ARIZONA PRIVATE SCHOOL ASSOCIATION SCHOLARSHIP

Scholarships are for graduating students from Arizona and the high school determines the recipients of the awards. Each spring the Arizona Private School Association awards two $1000 scholarships to every private high school in Arizona.

Award: Scholarship for use in freshman year; not renewable. *Number:* 600. *Amount:* $1000.

Eligibility Requirements: Applicant must be high school student; planning to enroll or expecting to enroll full-time at a four-year institution or university and resident of Arizona. Available to U.S. citizens.

Application Requirements: Application form, essay. *Deadline:* April 30.

Contact: Fred Lockhart, Executive Director
Arizona Private School Association
202 East McDowell Road, Suite 273
Phoenix, AZ 85004
Phone: 602-254-5199
Fax: 602-254-5073
E-mail: apsa@eschelon.com

ARKANSAS DEPARTMENT OF HIGHER EDUCATION

http://www.adhe.edu/

ARKANSAS ACADEMIC CHALLENGE SCHOLARSHIP PROGRAM

Awards for Arkansas residents who are graduating high school seniors, currently enrolled college students and nontraditional students to study at an approved Arkansas institution. Must have at least a 19 ACT composite score (or the equivalent). Renewable up to three additional years.

Award: Scholarship for use in freshman, sophomore, junior, senior, or graduate years; renewable. *Number:* 30,000–35,000. *Amount:* $1000–$5000.

Eligibility Requirements: Applicant must be enrolled or expecting to enroll full- or part-time at a two-year or four-year institution or university; resident of Arkansas and studying in Arkansas. Available to U.S. citizens.

Application Requirements: Application form, financial need analysis. *Deadline:* June 1.

Contact: Jonathan Coleman, Financial Aid Manager
Phone: 501-371-2000
E-mail: jonathan.coleman@adhe.edu

ARKANSAS GOVERNOR'S SCHOLARS PROGRAM

Awards for outstanding Arkansas high school seniors. Applicants who attain 32 or above on ACT, 1410 or above on SAT and have an academic 3.5 GPA, or are selected as National Merit or National Achievement finalists may receive an award equal to tuition, mandatory fees, room, and board up to $10,000 per year at any Arkansas institution. If any of the seventy-five (75) counties is not represented, the Department of Higher Education shall select a student from each non-represented county with the highest qualifications who was not initially qualified. Students from these counties will be awarded $5000 per year at any Arkansas institution.

Award: Scholarship for use in freshman, sophomore, junior, senior, or graduate years; renewable. *Number:* 75–375. *Amount:* $4000–$10,000.

Eligibility Requirements: Applicant must be high school student; planning to enroll or expecting to enroll full-time at a two-year or four-year institution or university; resident of Arkansas and studying in Arkansas. Applicant must have 3.5 GPA or higher. Available to U.S. citizens.

Application Requirements: Application form, community service. *Deadline:* February 1.

Contact: Jonathan Coleman, Financial Aid Manager
Phone: 501-371-2000
E-mail: jonathan.coleman@adhe.edu

LAW ENFORCEMENT OFFICERS' DEPENDENTS SCHOLARSHIP–ARKANSAS

Scholarship for dependents, under 23 years old, of Arkansas law-enforcement officers killed or permanently disabled in the line of duty. Renewable award is a waiver of tuition, fees, and room at two- or four-year Arkansas institution. Submit birth certificate, death certificate, and claims commission report of findings of fact. Proof of disability from State Claims Commission may also be submitted.

Award: Scholarship for use in freshman, sophomore, junior, or senior years; renewable.

Eligibility Requirements: Applicant must be enrolled or expecting to enroll full- or part-time at a two-year or four-year or technical institution or university; resident of Arkansas and studying in Arkansas. Available to U.S. citizens.

Application Requirements: Application form. *Deadline:* June 1.

Contact: Lisa Smith, Program Specialist
Arkansas Department of Higher Education
423 Main Street Suite 400
Little Rock, AR 72201-3818
Phone: 501-371-2000
E-mail: lisa.smith@adhe.edu

MILITARY DEPENDENT'S SCHOLARSHIP PROGRAM
• *See page 709*

ARKANSAS SINGLE PARENT SCHOLARSHIP FUND

http://www.aspsf.org/

ARKANSAS SINGLE PARENT SCHOLARSHIP FUND
• *See page 599*

ARKANSAS STUDENT LOAN AUTHORITY

http://www.asla.info/

R. PRESTON WOODRUFF JR. SCHOLARSHIP

Up to twenty $1,000 scholarships awarded annually. Online entries only and only one entry per applicant. Eligible entries will be drawn at random to select the scholarship winners. Winners must submit a 500-word essay in order to receive a $1,000 scholarship. One renewable scholarship (up to 4 years) will be awarded to the student with the most outstanding essay.

Award: Scholarship for use in freshman, sophomore, junior, senior, or graduate years; renewable. *Number:* 20. *Amount:* $1000.

Eligibility Requirements: Applicant must be enrolled or expecting to enroll full- or part-time at a two-year or four-year or technical institution or university and resident of Arkansas. Available to U.S. citizens.

Application Requirements: Application form. *Deadline:* April 1.

Contact: Amy Neathery, Higher Education Programs Manager
Arkansas Student Loan Authority
3801 Woodland Heights
Suite 200
Little Rock, AR 72212
Phone: 800-443-6030 Ext. 4130
E-mail: aneathery@asla.info

ARRL FOUNDATION INC.

http://www.arrl.org/

ALBERT H. HIX, W8AH, MEMORIAL SCHOLARSHIP

One-time $500 award available to general class or higher class amateur radio operators. Preference is given to the residents of the West Virginia section who are attending postsecondary school in the West Virginia section. Minimum GPA of 3.0 or higher required.

Award: Scholarship for use in freshman, sophomore, junior, or senior years; not renewable. *Number:* 1. *Amount:* $500.

Eligibility Requirements: Applicant must be enrolled or expecting to enroll full-time at a two-year or four-year or technical institution or university; resident of West Virginia; studying in West Virginia and must have an interest in amateur radio. Applicant must have 3.0 GPA or higher. Available to U.S. citizens.

Application Requirements: Application form. *Deadline:* January 31.

Contact: Ms. Mary Hobart, Secretary
Phone: 860-594-0397
E-mail: k1mmh@arrl.org

ARRL ROCKY MOUNTAIN DIVISION SCHOLARSHIP

One $500 award to a student with an active amateur radio license attending an accredited two- or four-year college or university. Preference given to residents of the ARRL Rocky Mountain Division (Colorado, New Mexico, Utah or Wyoming). Must be a U.S. citizen, and a graduating high school senior or undergraduate student. Must submit a letter of recommendation from a sitting officer of an ARRL-affiliated club attesting to regular activity on the amateur radio spectrum and within the Amateur Radio community.

Award: Scholarship for use in freshman, sophomore, junior, or senior years; not renewable. *Number:* 1. *Amount:* $500.

Eligibility Requirements: Applicant must be enrolled or expecting to enroll full- or part-time at a two-year or four-year institution or university; resident of Colorado, New Mexico, Utah, Wyoming and must have an interest in amateur radio. Available to U.S. citizens.

Application Requirements: Application form. *Deadline:* January 31.

Contact: Ms. Mary Hobart, Secretary
Phone: 860-594-0397
E-mail: k1mmh@arrl.org

ATLANTA RADIO CLUB SCHOLARSHIP

One $500 scholarship for a Georgia resident who is a student with an active Amateur Radio license studying at an accredited 4-year college or university. Must be between the ages of 17 and 25 at the time of the award. Preference is given to students performing at a high academic level.

Award: Scholarship for use in freshman, sophomore, junior, senior, or graduate years; not renewable. *Number:* 1. *Amount:* $500.

Eligibility Requirements: Applicant must be age 17-25; enrolled or expecting to enroll full- or part-time at a four-year institution or university; resident of Georgia and must have an interest in amateur radio. Available to U.S. citizens.

Application Requirements: Application form. *Deadline:* January 31.

Contact: Ms. Mary Hobart, Secretary
Phone: 860-594-0397
E-mail: k1mmh@arrl.org

BYRON BLANCHARD, N1EKV, MEMORIAL SCHOLARSHIP

One $500 scholarship for a student in residence in ARRL New England Division (Massachusetts, New Hampshire, Connecticut, Rhode Island, Vermont and Maine). Must have an active Amateur Radio License Class license.

Award: Scholarship for use in freshman, sophomore, junior, or senior years; not renewable. *Number:* 1. *Amount:* $500.

Eligibility Requirements: Applicant must be enrolled or expecting to enroll full- or part-time at a two-year or four-year or technical institution or university; resident of Connecticut, Maine, Massachusetts, New Hampshire, Rhode Island, Vermont and must have an interest in amateur radio. Available to U.S. citizens.

Application Requirements: Application form. *Deadline:* January 31.

Contact: Ms. Mary Hobart, Secretary
Phone: 860-594-0397
E-mail: k1mmh@arrl.org

CENTRAL ARIZONA DX ASSOCIATION SCHOLARSHIP

One $1000 award is a available to a student who is an Arizona resident and who possesses a Technician class or higher radio license. Must have a cumulative GPA of 3.2 or above. Graduating high school students will be considered before current college students.

Award: Scholarship for use in freshman, sophomore, junior, or senior years; not renewable. *Number:* 1. *Amount:* $1000.

Eligibility Requirements: Applicant must be enrolled or expecting to enroll full- or part-time at a two-year or four-year institution or university; resident of Arizona and must have an interest in amateur radio. Available to U.S. citizens.

Application Requirements: Application form. *Deadline:* January 31.

Contact: Ms. Mary Hobart, Secretary
Phone: 860-594-0397
E-mail: k1mmh@arrl.org

CHICAGO FM CLUB SCHOLARSHIP FUND

Multiple awards available to amateur radio operators with technician license who are U.S. citizens or within 3 months of citizenship. Preference given to residents of FCC Ninth Call District (Indiana, Illinois, Wisconsin) pursuing post-secondary course of study at accredited 2- or 4-year college or trade school.

Award: Scholarship for use in freshman, sophomore, junior, or senior years; not renewable. *Amount:* $500.

Eligibility Requirements: Applicant must be enrolled or expecting to enroll full-time at a two-year or four-year or technical institution or university; resident of Illinois, Indiana, Wisconsin and must have an interest in amateur radio. Available to U.S. citizens.

Application Requirements: Application form. *Deadline:* January 31.

Contact: Ms. Mary Hobart, Secretary
Phone: 860-594-0397
E-mail: k1mmh@arrl.org

DAVID KNAUS MEMORIAL SCHOLARSHIP

One $1500 award for a student with an active amateur radio license pursuing a Bachelor's degree or a 2-year Associate's degree. Preference given to a resident of Wisconsin or, if no qualified applicant from Wisconsin, to applicant from the ARRL Central Division (Illinois, Indiana, Wisconsin).

Award: Scholarship for use in freshman, sophomore, junior, or senior years; not renewable. *Number:* 1. *Amount:* $1500.

Eligibility Requirements: Applicant must be enrolled or expecting to enroll full- or part-time at a two-year or four-year institution; resident of Illinois, Indiana, Wisconsin and must have an interest in amateur radio. Available to U.S. citizens.

Application Requirements: Application form. *Deadline:* January 31.

Contact: Ms. Mary Hobart, Secretary
　　　Phone: 860-594-0397
　　　E-mail: k1mmh@arrl.org

GWINNETT AMATEUR RADIO SOCIETY SCHOLARSHIP

One $1000 award available to a Georgia resident possessing an active amateur radio license. Preference is given to students from Gwinnett County, GA or from the state of Georgia studying at four-year colleges or universities.

Award: Scholarship for use in freshman, sophomore, junior, or senior years; not renewable. *Number:* 1. *Amount:* $1000.

Eligibility Requirements: Applicant must be enrolled or expecting to enroll full- or part-time at a four-year institution or university; resident of Georgia and must have an interest in amateur radio. Available to U.S. citizens.

Application Requirements: Application form. *Deadline:* January 31.

Contact: Ms. Mary Hobart, Secretary
　　　Phone: 860-594-0397
　　　E-mail: k1mmh@arrl.org

HARRY A. HODGES, W6YOO, SCHOLARSHIP

$1000 scholarship award for a student with a Technician class amateur radio license. Preference will be given to applicants from San Diego County, California. If no qualified applicant is identified, preference will be given to an applicant from California. Applicant must demonstrate activity and interest in radio service or some technical proficiency by participarting in some form of radio related activities such as emergency communications, equipment construction, community radio services, scouting, etc. Must be performing at a high academic level or an at-risk youth with at least two counselor or teacher recommendationsas to how and why they have turned their lives around.

Award: Scholarship for use in freshman, sophomore, junior, or senior years; not renewable. *Number:* 1. *Amount:* $1000.

Eligibility Requirements: Applicant must be enrolled or expecting to enroll full- or part-time at a two-year or four-year or technical institution or university; resident of California and must have an interest in amateur radio. Available to U.S. citizens.

Application Requirements: Application form. *Deadline:* January 31.

Contact: Ms. Mary Hobart, Secretary
　　　Phone: 860-594-0397
　　　E-mail: k1mmh@arrl.org

JACKSON COUNTY ARA SCHOLARSHIP

One $1000 award for a student with an active Technician class or higher amateur radio license. Must be a student from Louisiana or attending school in Louisiana. Must be attending a 4-year college or university and have a minimum 3.0 GPA.

Award: Scholarship for use in freshman, sophomore, junior, or senior years; not renewable. *Number:* 1. *Amount:* $1000.

Eligibility Requirements: Applicant must be enrolled or expecting to enroll full- or part-time at a four-year institution or university; resident of Louisiana; studying in Louisiana and must have an interest in amateur radio. Applicant must have 3.0 GPA or higher. Available to U.S. citizens.

Application Requirements: Application form. *Deadline:* January 31.

Contact: Ms. Mary Hobart, Secretary
　　　Phone: 860-594-0397
　　　E-mail: k1mmh@arrl.org

JAMES COTHRAN, KD3NI, SCHOLARSHIP

$2000 scholarship for a student with any active Amateur Radio License Class who is a resident of the Atlantic Division (DE, MD, PA, Southern NJ, Western NY), the Roanoke Division (NC, SC, VA, WV), the Southeastern Division (AL, FL, GA) or Washington, D.C.

Award: Scholarship for use in freshman, sophomore, junior, or senior years; not renewable. *Number:* 1. *Amount:* $2000.

Eligibility Requirements: Applicant must be enrolled or expecting to enroll full-time at a two-year or four-year or technical institution or university; resident of Alabama, Delaware, District of Columbia, Florida, Georgia, Maryland, New Jersey, New York, North Carolina, Pennsylvania, South Carolina, Virginia, West Virginia and must have an interest in amateur radio. Available to U.S. citizens.

Application Requirements: Application form. *Deadline:* January 31.

Contact: Ms. Mary Hobart, Secretary
　　　Phone: 860-594-0397
　　　E-mail: k1mmh@arrl.org

MARY LOU BROWN SCHOLARSHIP

Multiple awards available to amateur radio operators with a general class license. Preference given to residents of Alaska, Idaho, Montana, Oregon, and Washington pursuing Baccalaureate or higher course of study. GPA of 3.0 or higher required. Must demonstrate interest in promoting Amateur Radio Service.

Award: Scholarship for use in freshman, sophomore, junior, senior, or graduate years; not renewable. *Amount:* $2500.

Eligibility Requirements: Applicant must be enrolled or expecting to enroll full-time at a four-year institution or university; resident of Alaska, Idaho, Montana, Oregon, Washington and must have an interest in amateur radio. Applicant must have 3.0 GPA or higher. Available to U.S. citizens.

Application Requirements: Application form. *Deadline:* January 31.

Contact: Ms. Mary Hobart, Secretary
　　　Phone: 860-594-0397
　　　E-mail: k1mmh@arrl.org

NEW ENGLAND AMATEUR RADIO FESTIVAL (NEAR–FEST) MEMORIAL SCHOLARSHIP

One $1500 award for a student with an Amateur Radio license in any class located in the ARRL New England Division (Maine, New Hampshire, Vermont, Rhode Island, Connecticut, Massachusetts). First preference given to Extra Class, second preference given to General Class, third preference given to Technician Class. Applicants must have held an amateur radio license for a minimum of one year prior to date of application. May be used to obtain any undergraduate degree or a two-year technical school in radio communications.

Award: Scholarship for use in freshman, sophomore, junior, or senior years; not renewable. *Number:* 1. *Amount:* $1500.

Eligibility Requirements: Applicant must be enrolled or expecting to enroll full- or part-time at a four-year or technical institution or university; resident of Connecticut, Maine, Massachusetts, New Hampshire, Rhode Island, Vermont and must have an interest in amateur radio. Available to U.S. citizens.

Application Requirements: Application form. *Deadline:* January 31.

Contact: Ms. Mary Hobart, Secretary
　　　Phone: 860-594-0397
　　　E-mail: k1mmh@arrl.org

NEW ENGLAND FEMARA SCHOLARSHIP

One-time award of $2000 available to students licensed as amateur radio operator technicians. Multiple awards per year. Preference is given to the residents of Vermont, Maine, New Hampshire, Rhode Island, Massachusetts, or Connecticut.

Award: Scholarship for use in freshman, sophomore, junior, or senior years; not renewable. *Amount:* $2000.

Eligibility Requirements: Applicant must be enrolled or expecting to enroll full-time at a four-year institution or university; resident of Connecticut, Maine, Massachusetts, New Hampshire, Rhode Island, Vermont and must have an interest in amateur radio. Available to U.S. citizens.

Application Requirements: Application form. *Deadline:* January 31.

Contact: Ms. Mary Hobart, Secretary
　　　Phone: 860-594-0397
　　　E-mail: k1mmh@arrl.org

NORMAN E. STROHMEIER, W2VRS, MEMORIAL SCHOLARSHIP

One $500 award is available to students who are residents of western New York and who possess technician class or higher amateur radio licenses. Preference is given to graduating high school seniors with a 3.2 GPA. Must provide documentation of amateur radio activities and achievements and any honor from community service.

Award: Scholarship for use in freshman, sophomore, junior, or senior years; not renewable. *Number:* 1. *Amount:* $500.

Eligibility Requirements: Applicant must be enrolled or expecting to enroll full- or part-time at a two-year or four-year or technical institution or university; resident of New York and must have an interest in amateur radio. Available to U.S. citizens.

Application Requirements: Application form, community service. *Deadline:* January 31.

Contact: Ms. Mary Hobart, Secretary
   Phone: 860-594-0397
   E-mail: k1mmh@arrl.org

OZAUKEE RADIO CLUB, W9CQO, SCHOLARSHIP

One $2000 scholarship for a Wisconsin student with an active general class amateur radio license. Must be under 26 years of age and pursuing full-time studies at a four-year undergraduate degree-granting institution.

Award: Scholarship for use in freshman, sophomore, junior, or senior years; not renewable. *Number:* 1. *Amount:* $2000.

Eligibility Requirements: Applicant must be enrolled or expecting to enroll full-time at a four-year institution or university; resident of Wisconsin and must have an interest in amateur radio. Available to U.S. citizens.

Application Requirements: Application form. *Deadline:* January 31.

Contact: Ms. Mary Hobart, Secretary
   Phone: 860-594-0397
   E-mail: k1mmh@arrl.org

PEORIA AREA AMATEUR RADIO CLUB SCHOLARSHIP

One $500 award is available to residents of the Central Illinois counties of Peoria, Tazewell, Woodford, Knox, McLean, Fulton, Logan, Marshall, and Stark. Applicants must possess a technician class or higher amateur radio license and attend an accredited two- or four-year college or university.

Award: Scholarship for use in freshman, sophomore, junior, or senior years; not renewable. *Number:* 1. *Amount:* $500.

Eligibility Requirements: Applicant must be enrolled or expecting to enroll full- or part-time at a two-year or four-year institution or university; resident of Illinois and must have an interest in amateur radio. Available to U.S. citizens.

Application Requirements: Application form. *Deadline:* January 31.

Contact: Ms. Mary Hobart, Secretary
   Phone: 860-594-0397
   E-mail: k1mmh@arrl.org

SIX METER CLUB OF CHICAGO SCHOLARSHIP

One-time $500 award for licensed amateur radio operators. Preference given to students with grade point average of 2.5 or better and in good academic standing. Must be a resident of Illinois, or resident of ARRL Central Division (Indiana, Wisconsin) attending school at a regionally accredited technical school, community college, college, or university and pursuing an undergraduate degree.

Award: Scholarship for use in freshman, sophomore, junior, or senior years; not renewable. *Number:* 1. *Amount:* $500.

Eligibility Requirements: Applicant must be enrolled or expecting to enroll full- or part-time at a two-year or four-year or technical institution or university; resident of Illinois, Indiana, Wisconsin and must have an interest in amateur radio. Applicant must have 2.5 GPA or higher. Available to U.S. citizens.

Application Requirements: Application form. *Deadline:* January 31.

Contact: Ms. Mary Hobart, Secretary
   Phone: 860-594-0397
   E-mail: k1mmh@arrl.org

THOMAS W. PORTER, W8KYZ, SCHOLARSHIP HONORING MICHAEL DAUGHERTY, W8LSE

One $1000 award available to a student with a technician class or higher amateur radio license. Preference given to students from Ohio or West Virginia at accredited 2- or 4-year colleges/universities or technical schools.

Award: Scholarship for use in freshman, sophomore, junior, or senior years; not renewable. *Number:* 1. *Amount:* $1000.

Eligibility Requirements: Applicant must be enrolled or expecting to enroll full- or part-time at a two-year or four-year or technical institution or university; resident of Ohio, West Virginia and must have an interest in amateur radio. Available to U.S. citizens.

Application Requirements: Application form. *Deadline:* January 31.

Contact: Ms. Mary Hobart, Secretary
   Phone: 860-594-0397
   E-mail: k1mmh@arrl.org

TOM AND JUDITH COMSTOCK SCHOLARSHIP

One-time award of $2000 for high school seniors. Preference given to residents of Texas and Oklahoma. Must be licensed amateur radio operator and be accepted at a two- or four-year institution.

Award: Scholarship for use in freshman year; not renewable. *Number:* 1. *Amount:* $2000.

Eligibility Requirements: Applicant must be high school student; planning to enroll or expecting to enroll full-time at a two-year or four-year institution or university; resident of Oklahoma, Texas and must have an interest in amateur radio. Available to U.S. citizens.

Application Requirements: Application form. *Deadline:* January 31.

Contact: Ms. Mary Hobart, Secretary
   Phone: 860-594-0397
   E-mail: k1mmh@arrl.org

WAYNE NELSON, KB4UT, MEMORIAL SCHOLARSHIP

One $1000 award for a U.S. citizen and Florida resident studying in a technical field at any four-year college or university. May have any class of active Amateur Radio license. Preference given to resident of Central FL (Orange, Seminole, Osceola, Lake, Volusia, Brevard and Polk counties). If none identified, residence in FL. Minimum GPA of 3.0 or better on a 4.0 scale in high school or for the previous undergraduate year.

Award: Scholarship for use in freshman, sophomore, junior, or senior years; not renewable. *Number:* 1. *Amount:* $1000.

Eligibility Requirements: Applicant must be enrolled or expecting to enroll full-time at a four-year institution or university; resident of Florida and must have an interest in amateur radio. Applicant must have 3.0 GPA or higher. Available to U.S. citizens.

Application Requirements: Application form. *Deadline:* January 31.

Contact: Ms. Mary Hobart, Secretary
   Phone: 860-594-0397
   E-mail: k1mmh@arrl.org

WILLIAM BENNETT, W7PHO, MEMORIAL SCHOLARSHIP

One $500 award is available to residents of ARRL's Northwest, Pacific, and Southwest divisions. Must have a general class or higher amateur radio license, attend a four-year college or university, and have a minimum 3.0 GPA.

Award: Scholarship for use in freshman, sophomore, junior, or senior years; not renewable. *Number:* 1. *Amount:* $500.

Eligibility Requirements: Applicant must be enrolled or expecting to enroll full- or part-time at a four-year institution or university; resident of Arizona, California, Colorado, Idaho, Montana, Nevada, New Mexico, Oregon, Utah, Washington, Wyoming and must have an interest in amateur radio. Applicant must have 3.0 GPA or higher. Available to U.S. citizens.

Application Requirements: Application form. *Deadline:* January 31.

Contact: Ms. Mary Hobart, Secretary
   Phone: 860-594-0397
   E-mail: k1mmh@arrl.org

YANKEE CLIPPER CONTEST CLUB YOUTH SCHOLARSHIP

One-time award available to active general class or higher licensed amateur radio operators. Must reside and attend an accredited college or university within a175-mile radius of YCCC Center in Erving, MA. Recipient must be 22 years or younger as of June 1 of the year of the grant.

Award: Scholarship for use in freshman, sophomore, junior, or senior years; not renewable. *Number:* 1. *Amount:* $1200.

Eligibility Requirements: Applicant must be enrolled or expecting to enroll full-time at a two-year or four-year institution or university; resident of Connecticut, Maine, Massachusetts, New Hampshire, New Jersey, New York, Pennsylvania, Rhode Island, Vermont and must have an interest in amateur radio. Available to U.S. citizens.

Application Requirements: Application form. *Deadline:* January 31.

Contact: Ms. Mary Hobart, Secretary
Phone: 860-594-0397
E-mail: k1mmh@arrl.org

YOU'VE GOT A FRIEND IN PENNSYLVANIA SCHOLARSHIP
• *See page 561*

ZACHARY TAYLOR STEVENS SCHOLARSHIP

One $750 award is available to students who possess a technician class or higher amateur radio license. Preference will be given to residents of Michigan, Ohio, and West Virginia. Must attend an accredited 2-year or 4-year college, university, or technical school.

Award: Scholarship for use in freshman, sophomore, junior, or senior years; not renewable. *Number:* 1. *Amount:* $750.

Eligibility Requirements: Applicant must be enrolled or expecting to enroll full- or part-time at a two-year or four-year or technical institution or university; resident of Michigan, Ohio, West Virginia and must have an interest in amateur radio. Available to U.S. citizens.

Application Requirements: Application form. *Deadline:* January 31.

Contact: Ms. Mary Hobart, Secretary
Phone: 860-594-0397
E-mail: k1mmh@arrl.org

ASIAN PACIFIC COMMUNITY FUND
http://www.apcf.org/

ROYAL BUSINESS BANK SCHOLARSHIP PROGRAM
• *See page 600*

ASIAN REPORTER
http://www.arfoundation.net/

ASIAN REPORTER SCHOLARSHIP
• *See page 600*

BARSKI LAW FIRM
http://www.barskilaw.com

BARSKI LAW FIRM SCHOLARSHIP

Scholarship for student(s) to attend an Arizona institution of higher education based upon merit, need and community service.

Award: Scholarship for use in freshman, sophomore, junior, or senior years; not renewable. *Number:* 2500.

Eligibility Requirements: Applicant must be enrolled or expecting to enroll full-time at a two-year or four-year or technical institution or university; resident of Arizona and studying in Arizona. Applicant must have 3.0 GPA or higher. Available to U.S. and non-U.S. citizens.

Application Requirements: Application form, financial need analysis. *Deadline:* June 1.

Contact: Chris Barski
Barski Law Firm
8700 E. Via de Ventura, Suite 140
Scottsdale, AZ 85258
Phone: (602) 441-4700
E-mail: cbarski@barskilaw.com

BLUE GRASS ENERGY
http://www.bgenergy.com/

BLUE GRASS ENERGY ACADEMIC SCHOLARSHIP

Scholarships for Kentucky high school seniors living with parents or guardians who are members of Blue Grass Energy. Must have minimum GPA of 3.0 and have demonstrated academic achievement, extracurricular involvement and financial need. For application and information, visit website http://www.bgenergy.com/forStudents.aspx.

Award: Scholarship for use in freshman year; not renewable. *Number:* 10. *Amount:* $1000.

Eligibility Requirements: Applicant must be high school student; planning to enroll or expecting to enroll full-time at a two-year or four-year or technical institution or university and resident of Kentucky. Applicant must have 3.0 GPA or higher. Available to U.S. citizens.

Application Requirements: Application form, essay, explanation of how scholarship is necessary to further education, financial need analysis, resume, test scores, transcript. *Deadline:* April 1.

Contact: Ms. Magen Howard, Communications Adviser
Phone: 859-885-2104
E-mail: magenh@bgenergy.com

BOETTCHER FOUNDATION
http://www.boettcherfoundation.org/

BOETTCHER FOUNDATION SCHOLARSHIP

Merit-based scholarship available to graduating seniors in the state of Colorado. Selection based on academic achievement, leadership, service and character. Renewable for four years and can be used at any Colorado university or college. Includes full tuition and fees, living stipend of $2800 per year, and a stipend for books.

Award: Scholarship for use in freshman, sophomore, junior, or senior years; renewable. *Number:* 42. *Amount:* $13,000–$40,000.

Eligibility Requirements: Applicant must be high school student; planning to enroll or expecting to enroll full-time at a four-year institution or university; resident of Colorado; studying in Colorado and must have an interest in leadership. Available to U.S. citizens.

Application Requirements: Application form, essay, interview. *Deadline:* November 1.

Contact: Ms. Stephanie Panion, Scholarship Program Coordinator
Boettcher Foundation
600 17th Street, Suite 2210 S
Denver, CO 80202-5422
Phone: 303-285-6207
E-mail: scholarships@boettcherfoundation.org

BOUNCE ENERGY
http://www.bounceenergy.com

BE MORE SCHOLARSHIP
• *See page 601*

BREYER LAW OFFICES, P.C.
https://www.breyerlaw.com/

ARRIVE ALIVE, DON'T DRINK & DRIVE! 2018 SCHOLARSHIP CONTEST

This contest is open to all Arizona high school and college students. We are asking students to create a message to their friends, peers, and the community that will leave a lasting impression on the dangers of driving under the influence of drugs and alcohol in any of the five categories: 1. Essays, 250 words or less; 2. Videos, 2 minutes or less; 3. Graphic Designs; 4. Poems; 5. Illustrations. Submit your entry on Facebook at: https://www.facebook.com/HusbandAndWifeLawTeam

Award: Scholarship for use in freshman, sophomore, junior, or senior years; not renewable. *Number:* 5. *Amount:* $1000.

Eligibility Requirements: Applicant must be enrolled or expecting to enroll full- or part-time at a two-year or four-year institution or university and resident of Arizona. Applicant must have 3.0 GPA or higher. Available to U.S. citizens.

Application Requirements: Application form, essay. *Deadline:* April 2.

Contact: Olivia Eldridge, Scholarship Manager
Breyer Law Offices, P.C.
3840 East Ray Road
Phoenix, AZ 85044
Phone: 480-588-8508
E-mail: olivia@breyerlaw.com

BRIDGES FOR THE DEAF AND HARD OF HEARING

http://www.bridgesfordeafandhh.org/

LINDA COWDEN MEMORIAL SCHOLARSHIP
• See page 686

CABRILLO CIVIC CLUBS OF CALIFORNIA INC.

http://www.cabrillocivicclubs.org/scholarship.asp

CABRILLO CIVIC CLUBS OF CALIFORNIA SCHOLARSHIP
• See page 726

CALIFORNIA ASSOCIATION OF WINE GRAPE GROWERS FOUNDATION

http://www.cawgfoundation.org/

CALIFORNIA WINE GRAPE GROWERS FOUNDATION SCHOLARSHIP

Scholarship for high school seniors whose parents or legal guardians are vineyard employees of wine grape growers. Recipients may study the subject of their choice at any campus of the University of California system, the California State University system, or the California Community College system.

Award: Scholarship for use in freshman year; renewable. *Number:* 6–7. *Amount:* $2000–$8000.

Eligibility Requirements: Applicant must be high school student; planning to enroll or expecting to enroll full-time at a two-year or four-year institution or university; resident of California and studying in California. Available to U.S. citizens.

Application Requirements: Application form, community service, essay, financial need analysis. *Deadline:* March 24.

Contact: Carolee Williams, Assistant Executive Director
California Association of Wine Grape Growers Foundation
1121 L Street, #304
Sacramento, CA 95814
Phone: 916-379-8995
E-mail: carolee@cawg.org

CALIFORNIA COMMUNITY COLLEGES

http://www.ccccco.edu/

EOPS (EXTENDED OPPORTUNITY PROGRAMS AND SERVICES)/CARE (COOPERATIVE AGENCIES RESOURCES FOR EDUCATION)
• See page 602

CALIFORNIA COUNCIL OF THE BLIND

http://www.ccbnet.org/

CALIFORNIA COUNCIL OF THE BLIND SCHOLARSHIPS
• See page 602

CALIFORNIA GRANGE FOUNDATION

http://www.csgfoundation.org/

CALIFORNIA GRANGE FOUNDATION SCHOLARSHIP
• See page 561

CALIFORNIA INTERSCHOLASTIC FEDERATION

http://www.cifstate.org/

CIF SCHOLAR-ATHLETE OF THE YEAR

Honors one male and one female statewide and is based on excellence in athletics, academics and character.

Award: Scholarship for use in freshman year; not renewable. *Number:* 2. *Amount:* $5000.

Eligibility Requirements: Applicant must be high school student; planning to enroll or expecting to enroll full-time at a four-year institution or university; resident of California and must have an interest in athletics/sports. Applicant must have 3.5 GPA or higher. Available to U.S. citizens.

Application Requirements: Application form, community service, essay. *Deadline:* February 11.

Contact: Jade Chin, Assistant to the Executive Director
California Interscholastic Federation
4658 Duckhorn Dr
Sacramento, CA 95624
Phone: 916-239-4477
E-mail: jchin@cifstate.org

CIF SPIRIT OF SPORT AWARD

This award seeks to recognize student-athletes who display good sportsmanship and school leadership, regardless of athletic ability.

Award: Scholarship for use in freshman year; not renewable. *Number:* 6. *Amount:* $500.

Eligibility Requirements: Applicant must be high school student; planning to enroll or expecting to enroll full-time at a four-year institution or university; resident of California and must have an interest in athletics/sports. Available to U.S. citizens.

Application Requirements: Application form, community service, essay. *Deadline:* continuous.

Contact: Jade Chin, Assistant to the Executive Director
California Interscholastic Federation
4658 Duckhorn Dr.
Sacramento, CA 95624
Phone: 916-239-4477
E-mail: jchin@cifstate.org

CALIFORNIA JUNIOR MISS SCHOLARSHIP PROGRAM

http://www.ajm.org/

CALIFORNIA JUNIOR MISS SCHOLARSHIP PROGRAM

Scholarship program to recognize and reward outstanding high school junior females in the areas of academics, leadership, athletics, public speaking, and the performing arts. Must be single, U.S. citizen, and resident of California. Minimum 3.0 GPA required.

Award: Scholarship for use in freshman year; not renewable. *Number:* 25. *Amount:* $500–$10,000.

Eligibility Requirements: Applicant must be high school student; age 15-17; planning to enroll or expecting to enroll full-time at a four-year institution or university; single female; resident of California and must have an interest in beauty pageant, leadership, or public speaking. Applicant must have 3.0 GPA or higher. Available to U.S. citizens.

Application Requirements: Application form, essay, interview, test scores, transcript. *Deadline:* varies.

Contact: Joan McDonald, Chairman
California Junior Miss Scholarship Program
385 Via Montanosa
Encinitas, CA 92024
Phone: 760-420-4177
E-mail: jmcdonald@bellmicro.com

CALIFORNIA SCHOOL LIBRARY ASSOCIATION

http://www.csla.net/

CSLA NORTHERN REGION PARAPROFESSIONAL SCHOLARSHIP

This scholarship is intended to assist a school library paraprofessional who is enrolled in a 2-year paraprofessional program working towards the goal of becoming a school library media technician, or enrolled in a class to support the library program through job-related skills.

Award: Scholarship for use in freshman or sophomore years; not renewable. *Number:* 1–2. *Amount:* $500–$500.

Eligibility Requirements: Applicant must be enrolled or expecting to enroll full- or part-time at a two-year institution and resident of California. Available to U.S. citizens.

Application Requirements: Application form, essay, recommendations or references, transcript. *Deadline:* September 30.

Contact: Jessica Lee, CSLA Northern Region Scholarship Committee
California School Library Association
California School Library Association
6444 E. Spring Street #237
Long Beach, CA 90815-1553
Phone: 888-655-8480
E-mail: info@csla.net

CALIFORNIA STATE PARENT-TEACHER ASSOCIATION

http://www.capta.org/

CONTINUING EDUCATION-PTA VOLUNTEERS SCHOLARSHIP
• *See page 561*

GRADUATING HIGH SCHOOL SENIOR SCHOLARSHIP
• *See page 602*

CALIFORNIA STUDENT AID COMMISSION

http://www.csac.ca.gov/

CAL GRANT C

Award for California residents who are enrolled in a short-term vocational training program. Program must lead to a recognized degree or certificate. Course length must be a minimum of 4 months and no longer than 24 months. Students must be attending an approved California institution and show financial need.

Award: Grant for use in freshman or sophomore years; renewable. *Number:* up to 7761. *Amount:* $576–$3168.

Eligibility Requirements: Applicant must be enrolled or expecting to enroll full- or part-time at a two-year or technical institution; resident of California and studying in California. Available to U.S. citizens.

Application Requirements: Application form, financial need analysis, GPA verification. *Deadline:* March 2.

Contact: Catalina Mistler, Chief, Program Administration and Services Division
California Student Aid Commission
PO Box 419026
Rancho Cordova, CA 95741-9026
Phone: 916-464-7268
Fax: 916-526-8004
E-mail: studentsupport@csac.ca.gov

COMPETITIVE CAL GRANT A

Award for California residents who are not recent high school graduates attending an approved college or university within the state. Must show financial need and meet minimum 3.00 GPA requirement.

Award: Grant for use in freshman, sophomore, junior, or senior years; renewable. *Number:* 1000–2000. *Amount:* $5472–$12,192.

Eligibility Requirements: Applicant must be enrolled or expecting to enroll full- or part-time at a two-year or four-year institution or university; resident of California and studying in California. Applicant must have 3.0 GPA or higher. Available to U.S. citizens.

Application Requirements: Application form, financial need analysis, GPA verification. *Deadline:* March 2.

Contact: Catalina Mistler, Chief, Program Administration and Services Division
California Student Aid Commission
PO Box 419026
Rancho Cordova, CA 95741-9026
Phone: 916-464-7268
Fax: 916-526-8004
E-mail: studentsupport@csac.ca.gov

ENTITLEMENT CAL GRANT B

Provide grant funds for access costs for low-income students in an amount not to exceed $1648 and tuition/fee expenses of up to $12,192. Must be California residents and enroll in an undergraduate academic program of not less than one academic year at a qualifying postsecondary institution. Must show financial need and meet the minimum 2.00 GPA requirement.

Award: Grant for use in freshman, sophomore, junior, or senior years; renewable. *Number:* 61,340. *Amount:* $700–$13,665.

Eligibility Requirements: Applicant must be enrolled or expecting to enroll full- or part-time at a two-year or four-year or technical institution or university; resident of California and studying in California. Available to U.S. citizens.

Application Requirements: Application form, financial need analysis. *Deadline:* March 2.

Contact: Catalina Mistler, Chief, Program Administration and Services Division
California Student Aid Commission
PO Box 419026
Rancho Cordova, CA 95741-9026
Phone: 916-464-7268
Fax: 916-526-8004
E-mail: studentsupport@csac.ca.gov

LAW ENFORCEMENT PERSONNEL DEPENDENTS SCHOLARSHIP
• *See page 602*

CALIFORNIA TEACHERS ASSOCIATION (CTA)

http://www.cta.org/

CALIFORNIA TEACHERS ASSOCIATION SCHOLARSHIP FOR MEMBERS
• *See page 562*

CAREER COLLEGES AND SCHOOLS OF TEXAS

http://www.ccst.org/

CAREER COLLEGES AND SCHOOLS OF TEXAS SCHOLARSHIP PROGRAM

One-time award available to graduating high school seniors who plan to attend a Texas trade or technical institution. Must be a Texas resident. Criteria selection, which is determined independently by each school's guidance counselors, may be based on academic excellence, financial need, or student leadership. Must be U.S. citizen. Deadline: continuous.

Award: Scholarship for use in freshman year; not renewable. *Number:* up to 27,770. *Amount:* $1000.

Eligibility Requirements: Applicant must be high school student; planning to enroll or expecting to enroll full- or part-time at a technical institution; resident of Texas and studying in Texas. Available to U.S. citizens.

Application Requirements: Application form, recommendations or references. *Deadline:* continuous.

Contact: Jennifer George, Association Manager
Career Colleges and Schools of Texas
823 Congress Avenue, Suite 230
Austin, TX 78701
Phone: 512-479-0425 Ext. 17
Fax: 512-495-9031
E-mail: jgeorge@eami.com

CENTRAL SCHOLARSHIP
http://www.central-scholarship.org

LESSANS FAMILY SCHOLARSHIP
• See page 604

STRAUS SCHOLARSHIP PROGRAM FOR UNDERGRADUATE EDUCATION
• See page 604

CGTRADER
https://www.cgtrader.com/

ANNUAL CGTRADER SCHOLARSHIP
• See page 604

CHICAGO AREA BUSINESS AVIATION ASSOCIATION
http://www.cabaa.com

CABAA/FLIGHTSAFETY CORPORATE SCHEDULER AND DISPATCHER TRAINING AWARD
The CABAA Education Foundation, along with FlightSafety, will award a 2018 applicant a FlightSafety Corporate Scheduler/Dispatcher Initial. This approved course addresses the unique needs of individuals serving, or planning to serve as corporate aircraft schedulers/dispatchers. The course is designed to provide individuals with practical information, which will enable them to function as integral members of the corporate travel team. All subject matter is approached from a scheduler/dispatcher's perspective, using real-world examples and scenarios. CABAA and FlightSafety have teamed up to offer this award to promote professional development for a career in business aviation. The winner will be notified by phone and presented the award at the annual CABAA Golf Classic held on August 7th, 2018. The recipients presence is required at the time of award presentation. For more information about the course visit resources.flightsafety.com

Award: Scholarship for use in senior year; not renewable. *Number:* 1. *Amount:* $4000.

Eligibility Requirements: Applicant must be enrolled or expecting to enroll full- or part-time at a two-year or four-year or technical institution or university or resident of Illinois, Indiana, Iowa, Michigan, Missouri, Wisconsin. Applicant must have 3.0 GPA or higher. Available to U.S. citizens.

Application Requirements: Application form, essay. *Deadline:* May 1.

Contact: Brian Zankowski
Lake Villa, IL 60046
Phone: 224-931-8064
E-mail: scholarships@cabaa.com

CABAA/FLIGHTSAFETY MAINTENANCE PROFESSIONAL TRAINING AWARD
One recipient will be awarded the Citation Sovereign Maintenance Initial course. This course is designed to meet the training requirements of aviation maintenance professionals maintaining Citation Sovereign aircraft. The retail value of this award is approximately $18,000. The recipient of the award must be a college student who graduated with a degree in Aircraft Maintenance and holds a current A&P license. The winners will be notified by phone and presented the award at the annual CABAA Golf Classic held on August 7th, 2018. The recipients presence is required at the time of award presentation at the award presentations. CABAA and FlightSafety have teamed up to offer these awards to promote continuing professional development during a business aviation career. These awards are established to encourage all to reach the highest level of achievement in their aviation studies and career. For more information on the course, visit resources.flightsafety.com

Award: Scholarship for use in senior year; not renewable. *Number:* 1. *Amount:* $18,000.

Eligibility Requirements: Applicant must be enrolled or expecting to enroll full- or part-time at a two-year or four-year or technical institution or university and resident of Illinois, Indiana, Iowa, Michigan, Missouri, Wisconsin. Applicant must have 2.5 GPA or higher. Available to U.S. citizens.

Application Requirements: Application form, essay. *Deadline:* May 1.

Contact: Brian Zankowski
Lake Villa, IL 60046
Phone: 224-931-8064
E-mail: scholarships@cabaa.com

CHICANA/LATINA FOUNDATION
http://www.chicanalatina.org/

SCHOLARSHIPS FOR LATINA STUDENTS ENROLLED IN COLLEGES/UNIVERSITIES IN NORTHERN CALIFORNIA
• See page 728

CHINESE AMERICAN ASSOCIATION OF MINNESOTA
http://www.caam.org/

CHINESE AMERICAN ASSOCIATION OF MINNESOTA (CAAM) SCHOLARSHIPS
• See page 728

COLLEGEBOUND FOUNDATION
http://www.collegeboundfoundation.org/

BALTIMORE RAVENS SCHOLARSHIP PROGRAM
The Baltimore Ravens established this scholarship program to enable local youth to continue their education on a collegiate level. The team has a long-standing history of service to local communities, and this fund will support those who do the same. In addition, this renewable scholarship will be based on financial need and academic achievement. You must: have a cumulative 3.0 GPA or better; demonstrate financial need (include a SAR if available); be accepted to and attend a 4-year college or university; have verifiable community service; submit one (1) reference from an individual who can attest to your commitment to helping others; submit one (1) reference from a teacher, school counselor or administrator; and submit a 1-2 page essay describing the environment in which you live, and the most meaningful contribution you have made as a volunteer to the betterment of your community.

Award: Scholarship for use in freshman, sophomore, junior, or senior years; renewable. *Number:* 1–5. *Amount:* $1–$5000.

Eligibility Requirements: Applicant must be high school student; planning to enroll or expecting to enroll full-time at a four-year institution or university and resident of Maryland. Applicant must have 3.0 GPA or higher. Available to U.S. citizens.

Application Requirements: Application form, community service, essay, interview. *Deadline:* March 1.

Contact: Jennifer Covahey, Associate Program Director, Scholarship Programs
CollegeBound Foundation
300 Water Street, Suite 300
Baltimore, MD 21202
E-mail: jcovahey@collegeboundfoundation.org

COLLEGEBOUND FOUNDATION LAST DOLLAR GRANT
The Last Dollar Grant is a need-based award for Baltimore City public high school graduates whose expected family contribution and financial aid package total less than the cost to attend college. Students who are awarded a CollegeBound Foundation Last Dollar Grant are eligible to receive a grant of up to $3,000 per year, renewable for up to six (6) years of college. Students must be a graduating senior from a Baltimore City public high school. Applicants must demonstrate financial need and be eligible to receive a Pell Grant. Family income must not exceed $75,000 annually.

Award: Grant for use in freshman, sophomore, junior, or senior years; renewable. *Number:* 60–70. *Amount:* $500–$3000.

Eligibility Requirements: Applicant must be high school student; planning to enroll or expecting to enroll full-time at a four-year institution or university and resident of Maryland. Available to U.S. citizens.

Application Requirements: Application form, financial need analysis. *Deadline:* June 1.

Contact: Jennifer Covahey, Associate Program Director, Scholarship Programs
CollegeBound Foundation
300 Water Street
Suite 300
Baltimore, MD 21202
Phone: 410-783-2905 Ext. 207
Fax: 410-727-5786
E-mail: jcovahey@collegeboundfoundation.org

DUNBAR CLASS OF 1958 SCHOLARSHIP

The Dunbar Class of 1958 established this scholarship with the intention to give back to the community in which they were raised and went to school. The Class of 1958 views Dunbar as the source of their many successes, and hopes to provide financial assistance so that current graduates have the same opportunities to succeed. You must: be a senior at Paul Laurence Dunbar High School; have a cumulative high school GPA between a 2.0 and a 3.0; and demonstrate financial need.

Award: Scholarship for use in freshman, sophomore, junior, or senior years; not renewable. *Number:* 1–3. *Amount:* $1–$1000.

Eligibility Requirements: Applicant must be high school student; planning to enroll or expecting to enroll full-time at a two-year or four-year institution or university and resident of Maryland. Applicant must have 2.5 GPA or higher. Available to U.S. citizens.

Application Requirements: Application form, essay. *Deadline:* March 1.

Contact: Ms. Jennifer Covahey, Associate Program Director of Scholarships
CollegeBound Foundation
300 Water Street
Baltimore, MD 21202
Phone: 410-783-2905 Ext. 207
E-mail: jcovahey@collegeboundfoundation.org

HY ZOLET STUDENT ATHLETE SCHOLARSHIP

You must be a Baltimore City public high school student-athlete; have a cumulative 2.5 GPA or better; submit at least two (2) letters verifying your participation in high school athletics and evidence you possess the qualities Hy Zolet exemplified, including a good work ethic, fairness and courage, in addition to outstanding leadership and athletic skills; and submit an essay describing your academic and professional goals, why you have chosen them and what you have done to prepare yourself thus far (500-1,000 words; 2-4 pages).

Award: Scholarship for use in freshman, sophomore, junior, or senior years; renewable. *Number:* 4. *Amount:* $1000.

Eligibility Requirements: Applicant must be high school student; planning to enroll or expecting to enroll full-time at a four-year institution or university; resident of Maryland and must have an interest in athletics/sports. Applicant must have 2.5 GPA or higher. Available to U.S. citizens.

Application Requirements: Application form, essay. *Deadline:* March 1.

Contact: Jennifer Covahey, Associate Program Director, Scholarship Programs
CollegeBound Foundation
300 Water Street
Suite 300
Baltimore, MD 21202
Phone: 410-783-2905 Ext. 207
E-mail: jcovahey@collegeboundfoundation.org

KHIA "DJ K-SWIFT" MEMORIAL SCHOLARSHIP

You must: have a cumulative 2.5 GPA or better; submit SAT (CR+M) scores; demonstrate financial need; and submit an essay (500 words) describing the importance of a college education and why you should receive this award.

Award: Scholarship for use in freshman year; not renewable. *Number:* 1–2. *Amount:* $1–$1000.

Eligibility Requirements: Applicant must be high school student; planning to enroll or expecting to enroll full-time at a two-year or four-year institution and resident of Maryland. Applicant must have 2.5 GPA or higher. Available to U.S. citizens.

Application Requirements: Application form. *Deadline:* March 1.

Contact: Ms. Jennifer Covahey, Associate Program Director of Scholarships
CollegeBound Foundation
300 Water Street
Suite 300
Baltimore, MD 21202
Phone: 410-783-2905 Ext. 207
E-mail: jcovahey@collegeboundfoundation.org

LORENZO FELDER SCHOLARSHIP
• *See page 729*

MANAGERIAL AND PROFESSIONAL SOCIETY (MAPS) OF BALTIMORE MERIT SCHOLARSHIP

You must: have a cumulative 3.0 GPA or better; an SAT (CR+M) score of at least 950; verifiable community service; and submit an essay (500-1,000 words) describing the importance of a college education and community service you have been involved in. Only dues-paying MAPS members and their immediate family members are eligible to apply. Winners must attend a MAPS quarterly meeting held in September.

Award: Scholarship for use in freshman year; not renewable. *Number:* 1–3. *Amount:* $500–$1000.

Eligibility Requirements: Applicant must be high school student; planning to enroll or expecting to enroll full-time at a two-year or four-year institution and resident of Maryland. Applicant must have 3.0 GPA or higher. Available to U.S. citizens.

Application Requirements: Application form, essay. *Deadline:* March 1.

Contact: Ms. Jennifer Covahey, Associate Program Director of Scholarships
CollegeBound Foundation
300 Water Street
Baltimore, MD 21202
E-mail: jcovahey@collegeboundfoundation.org

COLLEGE NOW GREATER CLEVELAND, INC.

http://www.collegenowgc.org/

COLLEGE NOW GREATER CLEVELAND ADULT LEARNER PROGRAM SCHOLARSHIP
• *See page 606*

COLLEGE SUCCESS FOUNDATION

http://www.collegesuccessfoundation.org/

GOVERNORS' SCHOLARSHIP FOR FOSTER YOUTH PROGRAM

The Washington State Governor's Scholarship for Foster Youth is a scholarship program that helps young men and women from foster care continue their education and earn a college degree from Washington state. Eligible students must meet specific criteria. The program has been supported by the current and former governors in Proceeds from the Governor's Cup, an annual golf tournament, provide funding for approximately 30-50 new scholars each year. Scholarship award amounts range from $2000 to $4000 depending on the college of attendance. The scholarship can be accessed for up to five years to complete an undergraduate study. Students much be enrolled full-time and maintain satisfactory academic progress in order to renew the scholarship each year.

Award: Scholarship for use in freshman, sophomore, junior, or senior years; renewable. *Number:* 30–50. *Amount:* $2000–$4000.

Eligibility Requirements: Applicant must be high school student; planning to enroll or expecting to enroll full- or part-time at a two-year or four-year institution or university; resident of Washington and studying in Washington. Available to U.S. citizens.

Application Requirements: Application form, application form may be submitted online (http://www.collegesuccessfoundation.org/wa/students/governors-eligibility), essay, recommendations or references, transcript. *Deadline:* March 9.

Contact: Erica Meier, Director, Scholarship Services
        Phone: 425-416-2000
        Fax: 425-416-2001
        E-mail: info@collegesuccessfoundation.org

COLORADO COMMISSION ON HIGHER EDUCATION

http://highered.colorado.gov/cche/mission.html

COLORADO STUDENT GRANT

Grants for Colorado residents attending eligible public, private, or vocational institutions within the state. Students must complete a Free Application for Federal Student Aid (FAFSA) and demonstrate need. Application deadlines vary by institution. Renewable award for undergraduates. Contact the financial aid office at the college/institution for application and more information.

Award: Grant for use in freshman, sophomore, junior, or senior years; not renewable. *Amount:* $300–$5000.

Eligibility Requirements: Applicant must be enrolled or expecting to enroll full- or part-time at a two-year or four-year or technical institution; resident of Colorado and studying in Colorado. Available to U.S. citizens.

Application Requirements: Application form, financial need analysis. *Deadline:* continuous.

Contact: Celina Duran, Financial Aid Administrator
        Colorado Commission on Higher Education
        1560 Broadway
        Suite 1600
        Denver, CO 80202
        Phone: 303-866-2723
        E-mail: celina.duran@dhe.state.co.us

COLORADO EDUCATIONAL SERVICES AND DEVELOPMENT ASSOCIATION

http://www.cesda.org

CESDA DIVERSITY SCHOLARSHIPS

Award for underrepresented, economically, and disadvantaged high school seniors planning to pursue undergraduate studies at a Colorado college or university. Must be Colorado resident. Applicant must be a first generation student, or member of an underrepresented ethnic or racial minority, and/or show financial need. Minimum 2.8 GPA required.

Award: Scholarship for use in freshman year; not renewable. *Number:* 6. *Amount:* $1000.

Eligibility Requirements: Applicant must be high school student; planning to enroll or expecting to enroll full- or part-time at a two-year or four-year or technical institution or university; resident of Colorado and studying in Colorado. Applicant must have 3.0 GPA or higher. Available to U.S. and non-Canadian citizens.

Application Requirements: Application form, essay, financial need analysis. *Deadline:* April 1.

Contact: Maria Castro Barajas, CESDA Chair
        Colorado Educational Services and Development Association
        Center for Community, Suite 485
        108 UCB
        Boulder, CO 80309
        Phone: 303-492-2178
        E-mail: maria.barajas@colorado.edu

COLORADO MASONS BENEVOLENT FUND ASSOCIATION

http://www.cmbfa.org/scholarship

COLORADO MASONS BENEVOLENT FUND SCHOLARSHIPS

• *See page 606*

COMMUNITY BANKERS ASSOCIATION OF GEORGIA

http://www.cbaofga.com/

JULIAN AND JAN HESTER MEMORIAL SCHOLARSHIP

Scholarship available to Georgia high school seniors who will be entering a Georgia two- or four-year college or university, or a program at a technical institution. Recipients will be named on the basis of merit, and family financial need is not considered. Application must be sponsored by a local community bank, and must include an essay on community banking and what it represents.

Award: Scholarship for use in freshman year; not renewable. *Number:* 4. *Amount:* $1000.

Eligibility Requirements: Applicant must be high school student; planning to enroll or expecting to enroll full-time at a two-year or four-year or technical institution or university; resident of Georgia and studying in Georgia. Available to U.S. citizens.

Application Requirements: Application form, community service, recommendations or references, test scores, transcript. *Deadline:* March 30.

Contact: Lauren Dismuke, Public Relations and Marketing Coordinator
        Phone: 770-541-4490
        Fax: 770-541-4496
        E-mail: lauren@cbaofga.com

COMMUNITY BANKERS ASSOCIATION OF ILLINOIS

http://www.cbai.com/

COMMUNITY BANKERS ASSOC OF IL CHILD OF A BANKER SCHOLARSHIP

• *See page 562*

COMMUNITY BANKERS ASSOC. OF IL ESSAY CONTEST

• *See page 607*

COMMUNITY FOUNDATION OF WESTERN MASSACHUSETTS

http://www.communityfoundation.org/

CALEB L. BUTLER SCHOLARSHIP

Scholarship for graduating high school seniors from western MA who are in the custody of the Department of Children and Families (DCF), formerly the Department of Social Services (DSS). Preference given to former or current residents of Hillcrest Educational Centers. For more information, please see website http://communityfoundation.org/.

Award: Scholarship for use in freshman year; not renewable.

Eligibility Requirements: Applicant must be high school student; planning to enroll or expecting to enroll full- or part-time at a two-year or four-year institution or university and resident of Massachusetts. Available to U.S. citizens.

Application Requirements: Application form, essay, financial need analysis, transcript. *Deadline:* March 31.

Contact: Dotty Theriaque, Program Assistant for Scholarships
        Community Foundation of Western Massachusetts
        1500 Main Street
        PO Box 15769
        Springfield, MA 01115
        Phone: 413-732-2858
        Fax: 413-733-8565
        E-mail: scholar@communityfoundation.org

CHRISTINE MITUS ROSE MEMORIAL SCHOLARSHIP

Scholarship for students who have had a parent die; preference to those who have had a parent die from cancer. Must be from western Massachusetts. For more information, see website http://communityfoundation.org/.

Award: Scholarship for use in freshman, sophomore, junior, senior, or graduate years; not renewable.

Eligibility Requirements: Applicant must be enrolled or expecting to enroll full- or part-time at a two-year or four-year institution or university and resident of Massachusetts. Available to U.S. citizens.

Application Requirements: Application form, essay, financial need analysis, transcript. *Deadline:* March 31.

Contact: Dotty Theriaque, Program Assistant for Scholarships
Community Foundation of Western Massachusetts
1500 Main Street
PO Box 15769
Springfield, MA 01115
Phone: 413-732-2858
Fax: 413-733-8565
E-mail: scholar@communityfoundation.org

DIANA & LEON FEFFER SCHOLARSHIP

Scholarship available to residents of western Massachusetts. For more information, please see website http://communityfoundation.org/.

Award: Scholarship for use in freshman, sophomore, junior, senior, or graduate years; not renewable.

Eligibility Requirements: Applicant must be enrolled or expecting to enroll full- or part-time at a two-year or four-year institution or university and resident of Massachusetts. Available to U.S. citizens.

Application Requirements: Application form, essay, financial need analysis, transcript. *Deadline:* March 31.

Contact: Dotty Theriaque, Program Assistant for Scholarships
Community Foundation of Western Massachusetts
1500 Main Street
PO Box 15769
Springfield, MA 01115
Phone: 413-732-2858
Fax: 413-733-8565
E-mail: scholar@communityfoundation.org

FRED K. LANE SCHOLARSHIP

Scholarship for graduating high school seniors who are past or current members (individual or family) or employees of the Orchards Golf Course in South Hadley. For more information, see website http://communityfoundation.org/.

Award: Scholarship for use in freshman year; not renewable.

Eligibility Requirements: Applicant must be high school student; planning to enroll or expecting to enroll full- or part-time at a two-year or four-year institution or university and resident of Massachusetts. Available to U.S. citizens.

Application Requirements: Application form, essay, financial need analysis, transcript. *Deadline:* March 31.

Contact: Dotty Theriaque, Program Assistant for Scholarships
Community Foundation of Western Massachusetts
1500 Main Street
PO Box 15769
Springfield, MA 01115
Phone: 413-732-2858
Fax: 413-733-8565
E-mail: scholar@communityfoundation.org

HELLESPONT SOCIETY SCHOLARSHIP FUND

• See page 729

HORACE HILL SCHOLARSHIP

• See page 562

JAMES L. SHRIVER SCHOLARSHIP

Scholarships available to students from western MA pursuing technical careers. For additional information, see website communityfoundation.org/.

Award: Scholarship for use in freshman, sophomore, junior, senior, or graduate years; not renewable.

Eligibility Requirements: Applicant must be enrolled or expecting to enroll full- or part-time at a four-year institution or university and resident of Massachusetts. Available to U.S. citizens.

Application Requirements: Application form, essay, financial need analysis. *Deadline:* March 31.

Contact: Dotty Theriaque, Program Assistant for Scholarships
Community Foundation of Western Massachusetts
1500 Main Street
PO Box 15769
Springfield, MA 01115
Phone: 413-732-2858
Fax: 413-733-8565
E-mail: scholar@communityfoundation.org

KIMBER RICHTER FAMILY SCHOLARSHIP

Scholarship available to graduating high school seniors of the Baha'i faith from western Massachusetts. For more information, see website http://communityfoundation.org/.

Award: Scholarship for use in freshman year; not renewable.

Eligibility Requirements: Applicant must be high school student; planning to enroll or expecting to enroll full- or part-time at a two-year or four-year institution or university and resident of Massachusetts. Available to U.S. citizens.

Application Requirements: Application form, essay, financial need analysis, transcript. *Deadline:* March 31.

Contact: Dotty Theriaque, Program Assistant for Scholarships
Community Foundation of Western Massachusetts
1500 Main Street
PO Box 15769
Springfield, MA 01115
Phone: 413-732-2858
Fax: 413-733-8565
E-mail: scholar@communityfoundation.org

VIRGINILLO-FALVO SCHOLARSHIP FUND

Scholarship for needy youth of western Massachusetts to attend college. For more information, please see website http://communityfoundation.org/.

Award: Scholarship for use in freshman, sophomore, junior, senior, or graduate years; not renewable.

Eligibility Requirements: Applicant must be enrolled or expecting to enroll full- or part-time at a two-year or four-year institution or university and resident of Massachusetts. Available to U.S. citizens.

Application Requirements: Application form, essay, financial need analysis, transcript. *Deadline:* March 31.

Contact: Dotty Theriaque, Program Assistant for Scholarships
Community Foundation of Western Massachusetts
1500 Main Street
PO Box 15769
Springfield, MA 01115
Phone: 413-732-2858
Fax: 413-733-8565
E-mail: scholar@communityfoundation.org

WILLIAM A. AND VINNIE E. DEXTER SCHOLARSHIP

Scholarship for graduating high school seniors in western Massachusetts. For more information, please see website http://communityfoundation.org/.

Award: Scholarship for use in freshman year; not renewable.

Eligibility Requirements: Applicant must be high school student; planning to enroll or expecting to enroll full- or part-time at a two-year or four-year institution or university and resident of Massachusetts. Available to U.S. citizens.

Application Requirements: Application form, essay, financial need analysis, transcript. *Deadline:* March 31.

Contact: Dotty Theriaque, Program Assistant for Scholarships
Community Foundation of Western Massachusetts
1500 Main Street
PO Box 15769
Springfield, MA 01115
Phone: 413-732-2858
Fax: 413-733-8565
E-mail: scholar@communityfoundation.org

CONNECTICUT ARMY NATIONAL GUARD

http://ct.ng.mil/Pages/default.aspx

CONNECTICUT ARMY NATIONAL GUARD 100% TUITION WAIVER
• See page 702

CONNECTICUT ASSOCIATION OF LATINOS IN HIGHER EDUCATION (CALAHE)

http://www.calahe.org/

CONNECTICUT ASSOCIATION OF LATINOS IN HIGHER EDUCATION SCHOLARSHIPS
• See page 730

CONNECTICUT COMMUNITY FOUNDATION

http://www.conncf.org/

REGIONAL AND RESTRICTED SCHOLARSHIP AWARD PROGRAM

Supports accredited college or university study for residents of the Connecticut community twenty-one town service area. In addition, a variety of restricted award programs are based on specific fund criteria (residency, school, course of study, etc.). Scholarships are awarded on a competitive basis with consideration given to academic record, extracurricular activities, work experience, financial need, reference letter, and an essay.

Award: Scholarship for use in freshman, sophomore, junior, or senior years; renewable. *Number:* 200–300. *Amount:* $2000–$5000.

Eligibility Requirements: Applicant must be enrolled or expecting to enroll full-time at a two-year or four-year institution or university and resident of Connecticut. Applicant must have 3.0 GPA or higher. Available to U.S. citizens.

Application Requirements: Application form, community service, essay, financial need analysis. *Deadline:* March 15.

Contact: Ms. Tallitha Richardson, Program and Scholarship Associate
Connecticut Community Foundation
43 Field Street
Waterbury, CT 06702
Phone: 203-753-1315 Ext. 126
E-mail: scholarships@conncf.org

CONNECTICUT OFFICE OF HIGHER EDUCATION

http://www.ctohe.org

GOVERNOR'S SCHOLARSHIP PROGRAM—NEED/MERIT SCHOLARSHIP
• See page 607

ROBERTA B. WILLIS SCHOLARSHIP PROGRAM—NEED-BASED GRANT
• See page 607

CONNECTICUT WOMEN'S HALL OF FAME

http://www.cwhf.org

EILEEN KRAUS SCHOLARSHIP

The Eileen Kraus Scholarship honors Connecticut Women's Hall of Fame 2002 Inductee Eileen Kraus and recognizes an outstanding young Connecticut woman embarking on her first year of college or university. Applicants should be a female residing in Connecticut in their final year of high school or a recent high school graduate. She must be intending to enroll in her first year of college or university in the fall of the year the scholarship is awarded to obtain an Associate or Bachelor degree. Applicants should visit the scholarship website for an application form and instructions. A two-page essay is required answering the question, "Among the 118 Inductees of the Hall, who do you find the most inspiring, and how do you see the legacy of this woman reflected in your own goals?" Deadline for submission is February 15, 2018. Award winner will be announced by March 31, 2018. Award recipient is asked to attend the CWHF 25th Annual Induction Ceremony in November 2018, in Hartford, CT.

Award: Scholarship for use in freshman year; not renewable. *Number:* 1. *Amount:* $5000.

Eligibility Requirements: Applicant must be high school student; planning to enroll or expecting to enroll full- or part-time at a two-year or four-year institution or university; female and resident of Connecticut. Applicant must have 3.0 GPA or higher. Available to U.S. citizens.

Application Requirements: Application form, essay. *Deadline:* February 15.

Contact: Ms. Tina Carlson, Programs Coordinator
Connecticut Women's Hall of Fame
Connecticut Women's Hall of Fame
320 Fitch Street
New Haven, CT 06515
Phone: 203-392-9008
E-mail: scholarships@cwhf.org

CORPORATION FOR OHIO APPALACHIAN DEVELOPMENT (COAD)

http://www.coadinc.org/

DAVID V. STIVISON APPALACHIAN COMMUNITY ACTION SCHOLARSHIP FUND

Provides financial assistance to students who are residents in the Corporation for Ohio Appalachian Development's service area and want to attend college but lack the required resources. Individual income must not exceed 200 percent of Federal Poverty Level. See website for application information - http://www.coadinc.org/scholarships

Award: Scholarship for use in freshman, sophomore, junior, or senior years; not renewable. *Number:* 1–30. *Amount:* $500–$1500.

Eligibility Requirements: Applicant must be enrolled or expecting to enroll full-time at a two-year or four-year institution or university and resident of Ohio. Available to U.S. citizens.

Application Requirements: Application form, financial need analysis, personal photograph. *Deadline:* April 1.

Contact: Allyssa Mefford, Operations Director
Phone: 740-594-8499 Ext. 213
E-mail: amefford@coadinc.org

COURAGE KENNY REHABILITATION INSTITUTE, VOCATIONAL SERVICES DEPARTMENT

http://www.allinahealth.org/couragekenny

SCHOLARSHIP FOR PEOPLE WITH DISABILITIES
• See page 608

THE DALLAS FOUNDATION

http://www.dallasfoundation.org/

THE AKIN AYODELE SCHOLARSHIP IN MEMORY OF MICHAEL TILMON

Michael Tilmon was a best friend and teammate of Dallas Cowboy Akin Ayodele while at MacArthur High School. Sadly, he passed away in a car accident in March of 1997. This scholarship program is intended to honor those who demonstrate the type of character and integrity that Michael possessed.

Award: Scholarship for use in freshman year; not renewable. *Amount:* $10,000.

Eligibility Requirements: Applicant must be high school student; planning to enroll or expecting to enroll full-time at a two-year or four-year institution or university and resident of Texas.

Application Requirements: Application form, transcript. *Deadline:* April 15.

Contact: Rachel Lasseter, Program Associate
Phone: 214-741-9898
E-mail: scholarships@dallasfoundation.org

DR. DAN J. AND PATRICIA S. PICKARD SCHOLARSHIP
• See page 731

DR. DON AND ROSE MARIE BENTON SCHOLARSHIP

Award is available to students, parents of students and volunteers who have been affiliated with Trinity River Mission in Dallas, Texas. Must be enrolled in a graduate or undergraduate program in a regionally accredited college or university. Scholarship is renewable for two years if the student maintains a specified grade point average and fulfills all reporting requirements as determined by the Scholarship Committee.

Award: Scholarship for use in freshman, sophomore, junior, senior, graduate, or postgraduate years; renewable. Number: 1–3. Amount: $1500.

Eligibility Requirements: Applicant must be enrolled or expecting to enroll full-time at a two-year or four-year institution or university and resident of Texas.

Application Requirements: Application form, transcript. Deadline: April 1.

Contact: Ms. Dolores Sosa Green, Trinity River Mission
The Dallas Foundation
2060 Singleton Boulevard, Suite 104
Dallas, TX 75212
Phone: 214-744-5648

THE LANDON RUSNAK SCHOLARSHIP

The Landon Rusnak Scholarship Fund was established at The Dallas Foundation in 2007. This scholarship is established by the employees of LEAM Drilling Systems, Inc. and Conroe Machine, LLC in memory of Landon Rusnak, son of David and Janet Rusnak and brother of Cady Rusnak. Landon's sister Cady is an active member of the Mexia High School Black Cat Band.

Award: Scholarship for use in freshman year; not renewable. Number: 1. Amount: $3000.

Eligibility Requirements: Applicant must be high school student; planning to enroll or expecting to enroll full-time at a two-year or four-year institution or university; resident of Texas and must have an interest in music.

Application Requirements: Application form, financial need analysis, transcript. Deadline: February 28.

Contact: Rachel Lasseter, Program Associate
Phone: 214-741-9898
E-mail: scholarships@dallasfoundation.org

THE MAYOR'S CHESAPEAKE ENERGY SCHOLARSHIP

The Mayor's Chesapeake Energy Scholarship was established at The Dallas Foundation by Chesapeake Energy Corporation. The goal of the Fund is to make a college degree or vocational certification possible for minority and socially disadvantaged youth. Graduating students in the Dallas ISD are eligible to apply. Applicants should be female or a member of a minority group. Applicants must have participated in the Education is Freedom program.

Award: Scholarship for use in freshman, sophomore, junior, or senior years; renewable. Amount: $20,000.

Eligibility Requirements: Applicant must be high school student; planning to enroll or expecting to enroll full-time at a two-year or four-year or technical institution or university and resident of Texas. Applicant must have 3.0 GPA or higher. Available to U.S. citizens.

Application Requirements: Application form, financial need analysis, test scores, transcript. Deadline: April 15.

Contact: Rachel Lasseter, Program Associate
Phone: 214-741-9898
E-mail: scholarships@dallasfoundation.org

TOMMY TRANCHIN AWARD

Established at The Dallas Foundation to support students with physical, emotional or intellectual disabilities who have excelled or shown promise in a chosen field of interest. Tommy's family wants to recognize his creativity and his refusal to allow his disability to limit his personal growth by helping others to develop their own talents. Applicants should be residents of North Texas.

Award: Scholarship for use in freshman year; not renewable. Amount: $1500.

Eligibility Requirements: Applicant must be high school student; planning to enroll or expecting to enroll full-time at a two-year or four-year or technical institution or university and resident of Texas.

Application Requirements: Application form, physical, proof of physical, emotional or intellectual disability. Deadline: March 5.

Contact: Rachel Lasseter, Program Associate
Phone: 214-741-9898
E-mail: scholarships@dallasfoundation.org

DANIEL P. BUTTAFUOCO & ASSOCIATES

http://www.1800nowhurt.com

YOUNG CHRISTIAN LEADERS SCHOLARSHIP
• See page 777

DANIELS FUND

http://www.danielsfund.org

BOUNDLESS OPPORTUNITY SCHOLARSHIP
• See page 608

DANIELS SCHOLARSHIP PROGRAM
• See page 609

DAVID J. CROUSE & ASSOCIATES

https://crouselawgroup.com/

DAVID J. CROUSE & ASSOCIATES PUBLIC SERVICE SCHOLARSHIP FOR COLLEGE STUDENTS

If you are a college student (Washington State resident) who is planning to pursue a career in public service and are enrolled in a 2-5 year U.S. institution in 2018-2019, apply today for the $2,000 David J. Crouse & Associates Public Service Scholarship. This scholarship will be awarded annually to one college student (which can be any college in the United States) who is a Washington State resident. This scholarship is designed for the student who desires to serve their community through joining the military, police, fire, or any other form of public service (medical, humanitarian, charitable, ministry, etc.). There is no preference to the form of public service intended. We look forward to helping one college student each year to continue his or her education. David J. Crouse previously served in the United States Air Force, Washington Air National Guard and as a city police officer. He and the rest of the team here at David J. Crouse & Associates are excited to help someone else pursue their public service dream. To apply, create a short (30-120 second) video telling us how you plan to better your community through service in the military, police, or another form of public service. Also, please tell us how continuing your education will help you achieve your goals. Upload your video to YouTube. Fill out the application and include a link to your video on YouTube. Applications are due June 1, 2018 for the 2018-2019 college year. For all future years, applications are due by May 1 for the following school year.

Award: Scholarship for use in sophomore, junior, senior, or graduate years; not renewable. Number: 1. Amount: $2000.

Eligibility Requirements: Applicant must be enrolled or expecting to enroll full- or part-time at a two-year or four-year or technical institution or university and resident of Washington. Applicant must have 2.5 GPA or higher. Available to U.S. citizens.

Application Requirements: Application form. Deadline: June 1.

Contact: Scholarship Coordinator
Phone: 513-444-2016
E-mail: coordinator@ourscholarship.io

DAVID J. CROUSE & ASSOCIATES PUBLIC SERVICE SCHOLARSHIP FOR HIGH SCHOOL STUDENTS

If you are a graduating Washington State high school student planning to enroll in a 2-5-year institution to pursue a career in public service, apply today for the $2,000 David J. Crouse & Associates Public Service Scholarship. This scholarship will be awarded annually to a graduating student of any Washington high school. This scholarship is designed for the student who desires to serve their community through joining the military, police, fire, or any other form of public service (medical, humanitarian, charitable, ministry, etc.). There is no preference to the form of public service intended. We look forward to helping one high school student each year to continue his or her education. David J. Crouse previously served in the United States Air Force, Washington Air National Guard and as a city police officer. He and the rest of the team here at David J. Crouse & Associates are excited to help someone else pursue their public service dream. To apply, create a short (30-120 second) video telling us how you plan to better your community through service in the military, police, or another form of public service. Also, please tell us how continuing your education will help you achieve your goals! Upload your video to YouTube. Fill out the application and include a link to your video on YouTube. Applications are due June 1, 2018 for the 2018-2019 college year. For all future years, applications are due by May 1 for the following school year.

Award: Scholarship for use in freshman year; not renewable. *Number:* 1. *Amount:* $2000.

Eligibility Requirements: Applicant must be high school student; planning to enroll or expecting to enroll full- or part-time at a two-year or four-year or technical institution or university and resident of Washington. Applicant must have 2.5 GPA or higher. Available to U.S. citizens.

Application Requirements: Application form. *Deadline:* June 1.

Contact: Scholarship Coordinator
Phone: 513-444-2016
E-mail: coordinator@ourscholarship.io

DELAWARE HIGHER EDUCATION OFFICE

http://www.doe.k12.de.us

B. BRADFORD BARNES MEMORIAL SCHOLARSHIP

Must be a legal resident of Delaware; a high school senior who ranks in upper quarter of class and has a combined score of 1290 on the SAT; and enrolled full-time at the University of Delaware. File the Free Application for Federal Student Aid (FAFSA) prior to the application deadline.

Award: Scholarship for use in freshman, sophomore, junior, or senior years; renewable. *Number:* 1. *Amount:* $15,000–$20,000.

Eligibility Requirements: Applicant must be high school student; planning to enroll or expecting to enroll full-time at an institution or university; resident of Delaware and studying in Delaware. Applicant must have 3.5 GPA or higher. Available to U.S. citizens.

Application Requirements: Application form, essay, financial need analysis. *Deadline:* March 5.

Contact: Ms. Juliet Murawski, Program Administrator
Delaware Higher Education Office
401 Federal Street
Suite 2
Dover, DE 19901
Phone: 302-735-4120
Fax: 302-739-5894
E-mail: dheo@doe.k12.de.us

CHARLES L. HEBNER MEMORIAL SCHOLARSHIP

Must be a legal resident of Delaware; a U.S. citizen or eligible non-citizen; a high school senior who ranks in upper half of class and has a combined score of 1000 on the SAT; enrolled full-time at the University of Delaware or Delaware State University; and majoring in the humanities or social sciences. Preference will be given to political science majors. Must file the Free Application for Federal Student Aid (FAFSA) prior to the application deadline.

Award: Scholarship for use in freshman, sophomore, junior, or senior years; renewable. *Number:* 2. *Amount:* $15,000–$20,000.

Eligibility Requirements: Applicant must be high school student; planning to enroll or expecting to enroll full-time at an institution or university; resident of Delaware and studying in Delaware. Applicant must have 2.5 GPA or higher. Available to U.S. citizens.

Application Requirements: Application form, essay, financial need analysis. *Deadline:* March 5.

Contact: Ms. Juliet Murawski, Program Administrator
Delaware Higher Education Office
401 Federal Street
Suite 2
Dover, DE 19901
Phone: 302-735-4120
Fax: 302-739-5894
E-mail: dheo@doe.k12.de.us

DIAMOND STATE SCHOLARSHIP

Award for legal residents of Delaware who are U.S. citizens or eligible non-citizens. Must be enrolled as a full-time student in a degree program at a nonprofit, regionally accredited institution. Minimum 3.0 GPA required. High school seniors should rank in upper quarter of class and have a combined score of at least 1290 on the SAT.

Award: Scholarship for use in freshman year; renewable. *Number:* 30–50. *Amount:* $1250.

Eligibility Requirements: Applicant must be high school student; planning to enroll or expecting to enroll full-time at a four-year institution or university and resident of Delaware. Applicant must have 3.0 GPA or higher. Available to U.S. citizens.

Application Requirements: Application form, essay. *Deadline:* March 5.

Contact: Ms. Juliet Murawski, Program Administrator
Delaware Higher Education Office
401 Federal Street
Suite 2
Dover, DE 19901
Phone: 302-735-4120
Fax: 302-739-5894
E-mail: dheo@doe.k12.de.us

EDUCATIONAL BENEFITS FOR CHILDREN OF DECEASED VETERANS
• *See page 609*

FIRST STATE MANUFACTURED HOUSING ASSOCIATION SCHOLARSHIP

Award for legal residents of Delaware who are high school seniors or former graduates seeking to further their education. Must have been a resident of a manufactured home for at least one year prior to the application. Evaluated on scholastic record, financial need, essay, and recommendations. Award for any type of accredited two- or four-year degree program, or for any accredited training, licensing, or certification program.

Award: Scholarship for use in freshman, sophomore, junior, or senior years; not renewable. *Number:* 1. *Amount:* $1000.

Eligibility Requirements: Applicant must be enrolled or expecting to enroll full- or part-time at a two-year or four-year or technical institution or university and resident of Delaware. Available to U.S. citizens.

Application Requirements: Application form, essay, financial need analysis. *Deadline:* March 5.

Contact: Ms. Juliet Murawski, Program Administrator
Delaware Higher Education Office
401 Federal Street
Suite 2
Dover, DE 19901
Phone: 302-735-4120
Fax: 302-739-5894
E-mail: dheo@doe.k12.de.us

HERMAN M. HOLLOWAY, SR. MEMORIAL SCHOLARSHIP

Must be a legal resident of Delaware; a U.S. citizen or eligible non-citizen; a high school senior who is ranked in upper half of class and has a combined score of at least 1000 on the SAT; and enrolled full-time at Delaware State University. Must file the Free Application for Federal Student Aid (FAFSA) prior to the application deadline.

Award: Scholarship for use in freshman, sophomore, junior, or senior years; renewable. *Number:* 1. *Amount:* $15,000–$20,000.

Eligibility Requirements: Applicant must be high school student; planning to enroll or expecting to enroll full-time at an institution or university; resident of Delaware and studying in Delaware. Applicant must have 2.5 GPA or higher. Available to U.S. citizens.

Application Requirements: Application form, essay, financial need analysis. *Deadline:* March 5.

Contact: Ms. Juliet Murawski, Program Administrator
Delaware Higher Education Office
401 Federal Street
Suite 2
Dover, DE 19901
Phone: 302-735-4120
Fax: 302-739-5894
E-mail: dheo@doe.k12.de.us

SCHOLARSHIP INCENTIVE PROGRAM (SCIP)

Award for legal residents of Delaware who are U.S. citizens or eligible non-citizens. The application process for ScIP requires three steps: 1. Complete the Free Application for Federal Student Aid (FAFSA) by April 15, 2018, 2. Provide your academic records to the Delaware Higher Education Office by July 2, 2018 to dheo@doe.k12.de.us, 3. Log onto your student account at http://www.de.gov/scholarships to provide your anticipated college enrollment information for 2018-2019 by July 2, 2018. Applicants must demonstrate substantial financial need, as determined using the Free Application for Federal Student Aid (FAFSA); have a minimum cumulative, unweighted grade point average of 2.5 on a 4.0 scale, (grades submitted on a weighted scale will be recalculated to unweighted); enroll full-time in an undergraduate degree program at a nonprofit, regionally accredited institution in Delaware; or enroll full-time in an out-of-state, nonprofit, regionally accredited college in an undergraduate or graduate degree program that is not offered at the University of Delaware, Delaware State University of Delaware Technical Community College.

Award: Grant for use in freshman, sophomore, junior, senior, or graduate years; not renewable. *Number:* 700–1000. *Amount:* $1000.

Eligibility Requirements: Applicant must be enrolled or expecting to enroll full-time at a two-year or four-year institution or university; resident of Delaware and studying in Delaware. Applicant must have 2.5 GPA or higher. Available to U.S. citizens.

Application Requirements: Application form, financial need analysis. *Deadline:* April 15.

Contact: Ms. Juliet Murawski, Program Administrator
Delaware Higher Education Office
401 Federal Street
Suite 2
Dover, DE 19901
Phone: 302-735-4120
Fax: 302-739-5894
E-mail: dheo@doe.k12.dc.us

DEMOLAY FOUNDATION INCORPORATED

http://www.demolay.org/

FRANK S. LAND SCHOLARSHIP

• *See page 588*

DENVER FOUNDATION

http://www.denverfoundation.org/

REISHER FAMILY SCHOLARSHIP FUND

Scholarships awarded to Colorado residents who attend Metropolitan State College, the University of Northern Colorado, and the University of Colorado at Denver. Sophomores or transferring juniors who do not have sufficient funding to otherwise complete their degrees are eligible to apply. Must have at least a 3.0 GPA.

Award: Scholarship for use in sophomore or junior years; not renewable.

Eligibility Requirements: Applicant must be enrolled or expecting to enroll full-time at a four-year institution or university; resident of Colorado and studying in Colorado. Applicant must have 3.0 GPA or higher. Available to U.S. citizens.

Application Requirements: Application form. *Deadline:* varies.

Contact: Karla Bieniulis, Scholarship Committee
Phone: 303-300-1790 Ext. 103
Fax: 303-300-6547
E-mail: info@denverfoundation.org

DEPARTMENT OF THE ARMY

http://www.goarmy.com/rotc

ARMY ROTC GREEN TO GOLD SCHOLARSHIP PROGRAM FOR TWO-YEAR, THREE-YEAR AND FOUR-YEAR SCHOLARSHIPS, ACTIVE DUTY ENLISTED PERSONNEL

• *See page 610*

ARMY (ROTC) RESERVE OFFICERS TRAINING CORPS TWO-, THREE-, FOUR-YEAR CAMPUS-BASED SCHOLARSHIPS

• *See page 610*

U.S. ARMY ROTC FOUR-YEAR COLLEGE SCHOLARSHIP

• *See page 610*

U.S. ARMY ROTC FOUR-YEAR HISTORICALLY BLACK COLLEGE/UNIVERSITY SCHOLARSHIP

• *See page 610*

U.S. ARMY ROTC GUARANTEED RESERVE FORCES DUTY (GRFD), (ARNG/USAR) AND DEDICATED ARNG SCHOLARSHIPS

• *See page 611*

U.S. ARMY ROTC MILITARY JUNIOR COLLEGE (MJC) SCHOLARSHIP

• *See page 611*

DIAMANTE, INC.

http://www.diamanteinc.org/

LATINO DIAMANTE SCHOLARSHIP FUND

• *See page 612*

DISTRICT OF COLUMBIA OFFICE OF THE STATE SUPERINTENDENT OF EDUCATION

http://www.osse.dc.gov/

DC TUITION ASSISTANCE GRANT PROGRAM (DCTAG)

Grant pays the difference between in-state and out-of-state tuition and fees at any public college or university in the United States, Guam, Puerto Rico or U.S. Virgin Islands, up to $10,000 per year. It also pays up to $2500 per year of tuition and fees at private colleges and universities in the Washington metropolitan area and at historically black colleges and universities throughout the United States. Students must be enrolled in a degree-granting program at an eligible institution, and be domiciled in the District of Columbia.

Award: Grant for use in freshman, sophomore, junior, or senior years; not renewable. *Number:* 5999–6000. *Amount:* $2500–$10,000.

Eligibility Requirements: Applicant must be enrolled or expecting to enroll full- or part-time at a two-year or four-year institution or university and resident of District of Columbia. Available to U.S. citizens.

Application Requirements: Application form, financial need analysis. *Deadline:* June 30.

Contact: Dr. Antoinette Mitchell, Assistant Superintendent,
Postsecondary and Career Education
District of Columbia Office of the State Superintendent of Education
810 First Street, NE, 3rd Floor
Washington, DC 20002
Phone: 202-727-2824
E-mail: antoinette.mitchell@dc.gov

DIXIE BOYS BASEBALL

http://www.dixie.org/boys

DIXIE BOYS BASEBALL BERNIE VARNADORE SCHOLARSHIP PROGRAM

Eleven scholarships presented annually to deserving high school seniors who have participated in the Dixie Boys Baseball Program. Citizenship, scholarship, residency in a state with Dixie Baseball Programs and financial need are considered in determining the awards.

Award: Scholarship for use in freshman year; not renewable. *Number:* 11. *Amount:* $1250.

Eligibility Requirements: Applicant must be high school student; planning to enroll or expecting to enroll full-time at a two-year or four-year institution or university; resident of Alabama, Arkansas, Florida, Georgia, Louisiana, Mississippi, North Carolina, South Carolina, Tennessee, Texas, Virginia and must have an interest in athletics/sports. Available to U.S. citizens.

Application Requirements: Application form, financial need analysis, personal photograph. *Deadline:* April 1.

Contact: Mr. James Jones, Commissioner/CEO
Dixie Boys Baseball
PO Box 8263
Dothan, AL 36304
Phone: 334-793-3331
E-mail: jjones29@sw.rr.com

DIXIE YOUTH SCHOLARSHIP PROGRAM

Scholarships are presented annually to deserving high school seniors who participated in the Dixie Youth Baseball program while age 12 and under. Financial need is considered. Scholarship value is $2000.

Award: Scholarship for use in freshman year; not renewable. *Number:* 70. *Amount:* $2000.

Eligibility Requirements: Applicant must be high school student; planning to enroll or expecting to enroll full-time at a two-year or four-year or technical institution or university; resident of Alabama, Arkansas, Florida, Georgia, Louisiana, Mississippi, North Carolina, South Carolina, Tennessee, Texas, Virginia and must have an interest in athletics/sports. Available to U.S. citizens.

Application Requirements: Application form, essay, financial need analysis, personal photograph. *Deadline:* March 15.

Contact: Scholarship Chairman
Dixie Boys Baseball
PO Box 877
Marshall, TX 75671-0877
E-mail: dyb@dixie.org

DON'T MESS WITH TEXAS

http://www.dontmesswithtexas.org/

DON'T MESS WITH TEXAS SCHOLARSHIP PROGRAM

Scholarship for Texas graduating high school seniors who plan to attend accredited two- or four-year colleges or public or private universities in Texas.

Award: Scholarship for use in freshman year; not renewable. *Number:* 2–3. *Amount:* $2000–$6000.

Eligibility Requirements: Applicant must be high school student; planning to enroll or expecting to enroll full- or part-time at a two-year or four-year institution or university; resident of Texas and studying in Texas. Available to U.S. and non-U.S. citizens.

Application Requirements: Application form, essay. *Deadline:* March 26.

Contact: Brenda Flores-Dollar, Programs Manager
Don't Mess With Texas
Texas Department of Transportation
Don't mess with Texas, 150 E. Riverside Dr.
Austin, TX 78704
Phone: 512-486-5904
E-mail: scholarship@dontmesswithtexas.org

DUDLEY DEBOSIER INJURY LAWYERS

http://www.dudleydebosier.com

DUDLEY DEBOSIER SCHOLARSHIP PROGRAM

The Dudley DeBosier Scholarship Program is designed to help students in our community who are interested in attending college upon graduation from high school. That is because our law firm is committed to giving back to our community and the education system. At Dudley DeBosier, we believe education is an important foundation for creating gratifying and advantageous careers. We are proud to support the youth in our community by providing this opportunity, and we look forward to helping students achieve their goals to attend college!

Award: Scholarship for use in freshman year; not renewable. *Number:* 9. *Amount:* $1000–$2000.

Eligibility Requirements: Applicant must be high school student; planning to enroll or expecting to enroll full-time at a two-year or four-year or technical institution or university and resident of Louisiana. Available to U.S. citizens.

Application Requirements: Application form, essay, personal photograph. *Deadline:* March 17.

Contact: Ms. Elizabeth Demopulos, Director of Marketing
Dudley DeBosier Injury Lawyers
1075 Government Street
Baton Rouge, LA 70802
Phone: 225-379-4902 Ext. 4902
Fax: 225-379-4952
E-mail: EDemopulos@dudleydebosier.com

EAST BAY COLLEGE FUND

http://www.eastbaycollegefund.org/

GREAT EXPECTATIONS AWARD

Program provides renewable scholarships, mentoring, college counseling, and life skills training. Must have at least 3.0 cumulative GPA. Restricted to graduating seniors of Oakland, California public high schools.

Award: Scholarship for use in freshman, sophomore, junior, or senior years; renewable. *Number:* 50. *Amount:* $16,000.

Eligibility Requirements: Applicant must be high school student; planning to enroll or expecting to enroll full-time at a four-year institution or university and resident of California. Applicant must have 3.0 GPA or higher. Available to U.S. citizens.

Application Requirements: Application form, application form may be submitted online (https://www.scholarselect.com/scholarships/13454-2014-east-bay-college-fund-great-expectations-scholarship-program), essay, financial need analysis, interview, recommendations or references, transcript. *Deadline:* February 13.

Contact: Yancie Davis, College Access and Success Manager
East Bay College Fund
2201 Broadway, Suite 208
Oakland, CA 94612
Phone: 510-836-8900
Fax: 510-550-7876
E-mail: yancie@eastbaycollegefund.org

EAST LOS ANGELES COMMUNITY UNION (TELACU) SCHOLARSHIP PROGRAM

http://www.telacu.com/

TELACU EDUCATION FOUNDATION

Applicant must be a first-generation college student from a low-income family and have a minimum GPA of 2.5. Must attend partnering colleges and universities and be enrolled full-time for the entire academic year. California applicants: Must be permanent resident of unincorporated East Los Angeles, Bell Gardens, Commerce, Huntington Park, City of Los Angeles, Montebello, Monterey Park, Pico Rivera, Pomona and the Inland Empire, Santa Ana, South Gate, or other communities selected by foundation. Texas applicants: Must be permanent resident of San Antonio or Austin. Illinois Applicants: Must be permanent resident of Greater Chicagoland Area. New York applicants: Must be permanent resident of the state of New York.

Award: Scholarship for use in freshman, sophomore, junior, or senior years; not renewable. *Number:* 350–600. *Amount:* $500–$7500.

Eligibility Requirements: Applicant must be enrolled or expecting to enroll full-time at a two-year or four-year institution or university and resident of California, Illinois, New York, Texas. Applicant must have 2.5 GPA or higher. Available to U.S. citizens.

Application Requirements: Application form, essay, financial need analysis, interview, recommendations or references, resume, test scores, transcript. *Deadline:* March 14.

Contact: Mr. Daniel Garcia, Associate Director
East Los Angeles Community Union (TELACU) Scholarship Program
5400 East Olympic Boulevard
Los Angeles, CA 90022
Phone: 323-721-1655 Ext. 486
E-mail: dgarcia@TELACU.com

EDMONTON COMMUNITY FOUNDATION

http://www.ecfoundation.org

BELCOURT BROSSEAU METIS AWARDS
• *See page 733*

CHARMAINE LETOURNEAU SCHOLARSHIP
• *See page 687*

EDMUND F. MAXWELL FOUNDATION

http://www.maxwell.org/

EDMUND F. MAXWELL FOUNDATION SCHOLARSHIP

Scholarships awarded to residents of western Washington to attend accredited independent colleges or universities. Awards up to $5000 per year based on need, merit, citizenship, and activities. Renewable for up to four years if academic progress is suitable and financial need is unchanged.

Award: Scholarship for use in freshman year; renewable. *Number:* 95.

Eligibility Requirements: Applicant must be enrolled or expecting to enroll full-time at a four-year institution or university and resident of Washington. Available to U.S. citizens.

Application Requirements: Application form, essay, financial need analysis. *Deadline:* April 30.

Contact: Shannon Valderas, Administrator
Edmund F. Maxwell Foundation
PO Box 55548
Seattle, WA 98155
E-mail: admin@maxwell.org

EDWARDS SCHOLARSHIP FUND

http://www.edwardsfund.org

EDWARDS SCHOLARSHIP

The Edwards Scholarship is for legal, permanent residents of the City of Boston, MA only. Applicants must be residents of Boston from the beginning of their junior year in high school to the present. Recipients must maintain a 2.0 GPA on a 4-point scale or a comparable GPA on another scale. Students must apply on-line.

Award: Scholarship for use in freshman, sophomore, junior, or senior years; renewable. *Number:* 136. *Amount:* $2500–$3000.

Eligibility Requirements: Applicant must be enrolled or expecting to enroll full-time at a two-year or four-year institution or university and resident of Massachusetts. Available to U.S. citizens.

Application Requirements: Application form, essay, financial need analysis. *Deadline:* March 15.

Contact: Kathryn Osmond, Director
Edwards Scholarship Fund
89 South Street
Suite 603
Boston, MA 02111
Phone: 617-737-3400
E-mail: info@edwardsfund.org

ELEVATE PEST CONTROL

https://elevatepestcontrol.com/

COLORADO ROFL SCHOLARSHIP

Make us laugh the hardest and you could be awarded a $500 scholarship. Take a minute from your serious academic life and make us laugh. Submit a joke, a story, a quick video (3 minutes or less), anything. All submissions need to be homemade by you. Do not copy funny jokes, stories, or videos from the internet. We want to see your personal creativity. This is the main submission for the scholarship and also what we will weigh the most heavily when choosing our recipient.

Award: Scholarship for use in freshman year; not renewable. *Number:* 1. *Amount:* $500.

Eligibility Requirements: Applicant must be enrolled or expecting to enroll full-time at a two-year or four-year or technical institution or university and resident of Colorado. Available to U.S. citizens.

Application Requirements: Application form. *Deadline:* April 30.

UTAH ROFL SCHOLARSHIP

Make us laugh the hardest and you could be awarded a $500 scholarship. Take a minute from your serious academic life and make us laugh. Submit a joke, a story, a quick video (3 minutes or less), anything. All submissions need to be homemade by you. Do not copy funny jokes, stories, or videos from the internet. We want to see your personal creativity. This is the main submission for the scholarship and also what we will weigh the most heavily when choosing our recipient.

Award: Scholarship for use in freshman year; not renewable. *Number:* 1. *Amount:* $500.

Eligibility Requirements: Applicant must be enrolled or expecting to enroll full-time at a two-year or four-year or technical institution or university and resident of Utah. Available to U.S. citizens.

Application Requirements: Application form. *Deadline:* April 30.

ENLISTED ASSOCIATION OF THE NATIONAL GUARD OF NEW JERSEY

http://www.eang-nj.org/

CSM VINCENT BALDASSARI MEMORIAL SCHOLARSHIP PROGRAM
• *See page 698*

EQUALITY SCHOLARSHIP COLLABORATIVE

http://www.equalityscholarship.org

EQUALITY SCHOLARSHIPS FOR COMMUNITY COLLEGE TRANSFER STUDENTS
• *See page 615*

SCHOLARSHIPS FOR HIGH SCHOOL GRADUATES
• *See page 615*

ESSAYJOLT.COM

http://www.essayjolt.com/

ESSAYJOLT SCHOLARSHIP

Essay contest open to high school juniors and seniors who may be citizens of any country, but must live in New Jersey. Essays are judged on originality, insight, and quality of writing by an independent panel of writers and editors. Only one winner is selected. See website for current essay question and guidelines http://www.essayjolt.com.

Award: Prize for use in freshman year; not renewable. *Number:* 1. *Amount:* $500.

Eligibility Requirements: Applicant must be high school student; planning to enroll or expecting to enroll full- or part-time at a two-year or four-year or technical institution or university; resident of New Jersey and must have an interest in writing. Available to U.S. and non-U.S. citizens.

Application Requirements: Entry in a contest, essay. *Deadline:* varies.

Contact: Meg Hartmann, Director
Phone: 917-575-3165
E-mail: scholarship@essayjolt.com

FINALLY SOLD

http://www.finallysold.com

FINALLY SOLD IMPACT MAKER SCHOLARSHIP
• *See page 618*

FINANCE AUTHORITY OF MAINE

http://www.famemaine.com/

STATE OF MAINE GRANT PROGRAM

Scholarship for residents of Maine, attending an eligible school in Maine,Connecticut, Massachusetts, New Hampshire, Rhode Island, or Vermont. Award based on need. Students attending out-of-state institutions must be participating in the New England Regional Tuition Break Program to be eligible. Students must apply annually. Complete free application for Federal Student Aid to apply. One-time award for undergraduate study. For further information see website http://www.famemaine.com.

Award: Grant for use in freshman, sophomore, junior, or senior years; not renewable. *Number:* 14,096. *Amount:* $1700.

Eligibility Requirements: Applicant must be enrolled or expecting to enroll full- or part-time at a two-year or four-year or technical institution or university; resident of Maine and studying in Connecticut, Maine, Massachusetts, New Hampshire, Rhode Island, Vermont. Available to U.S. citizens.

Application Requirements: Financial need analysis. *Deadline:* May 1.

Contact: Jennifer Lanphear, Education Programs Officer
Finance Authority of Maine
5 Community Drive
Augusta, ME 04332
Phone: 207-620-3548
E-mail: education@famemaine.com

TUITION WAIVER PROGRAMS
• *See page 618*

FINANCIAL SERVICE CENTERS OF NEW YORK

http://www.fscny.org

FSCNY YOUNG LEADERS SCHOLARSHIP
• *See page 618*

FLORIDA ASSOCIATION FOR MEDIA IN EDUCATION

http://www.floridamediaed.org/ssyra.html

INTELLECTUAL FREEDOM STUDENT SCHOLARSHIP

Scholarship in the amount of $1000 is awarded annually to a graduating senior from a high school in Florida. Only students whose library media specialists are members of FAME are eligible. Essays written by senior students will be submitted to the FAME Intellectual Freedom Committee.

Award: Scholarship for use in freshman year; not renewable. *Number:* 1. *Amount:* $1000.

Eligibility Requirements: Applicant must be high school student; planning to enroll or expecting to enroll full-time at a two-year or four-year or technical institution or university and resident of Florida. Available to U.S. citizens.

Application Requirements: Application form, essay. *Deadline:* March 15.

Contact: Larry Bodkin, Executive Director
Phone: 850-531-8350
Fax: 850-531-8344
E-mail: lbodkin@floridamedia.org

FLORIDA PTA/PTSA

http://www.floridapta.org/

FLORIDA PTA/PTSA ANNUAL SCHOLARSHIP
• *See page 619*

FLORIDA PTA/PTSA COMMUNITY/JUNIOR COLLEGE SCHOLARSHIP

One time award of $1000 to high school students who enrolled in a community or junior college. Must be a resident of Florida for at least 2 years. Must be a U.S. citizen and have at least a two-year attendance in a Florida PTA/PTSA high school. Minimum 2.5 GPA or higher.

Award: Scholarship for use in freshman year; not renewable. *Number:* 1–2. *Amount:* $1000.

Eligibility Requirements: Applicant must be enrolled or expecting to enroll full-time at a two-year institution and resident of Florida. Applicant must have 2.5 GPA or higher. Available to U.S. citizens.

Application Requirements: Application form, essay, proof of enrollment, recommendations or references. *Deadline:* March 1.

Contact: Scholarship Chair, Scholarship Chair
Florida PTA/PTSA
1747 Orlando Central Parkway
Orlando, FL 32809
Phone: 407-855-7604
Fax: 407-240-9577
E-mail: scholarship@floridapta.org

FLORIDA PTA/PTSA VOCATIONAL/TECHNICAL SCHOLARSHIP

Scholarship of $1000 is awarded to graduating senior enrolled full-time in a vocational/technical institution within the state of Florida. Must have at least a two-year attendance in a Florida PTA/PTSA high school. Minimum GPA is 2.0.

Award: Scholarship for use in freshman year; not renewable. *Number:* 3. *Amount:* $1000.

Eligibility Requirements: Applicant must be high school student; planning to enroll or expecting to enroll full-time at a two-year or technical institution; resident of Florida and studying in Florida. Available to U.S. citizens.

Application Requirements: Application form, essay, proof of enrollment, recommendations or references. *Deadline:* March 1.

Contact: Scholarship Chair, Scholarship Chair
Florida PTA/PTSA
1747 Orlando Central Parkway
Orlando, FL 32809
Phone: 407-855-7604
Fax: 407-240-9577
E-mail: scholarship@floridapta.org

FLORIDA STATE DEPARTMENT OF EDUCATION

http://www.floridastudentfinancialaid.org/

ACCESS TO BETTER LEARNING AND EDUCATION GRANT

Grant program provides tuition assistance to Florida undergraduate students enrolled in degree programs at eligible private Florida colleges or universities. Must be a U.S. citizen or eligible non-citizen and must meet Florida residency requirements. The participating institution determines application procedures, deadlines, and student eligibility. An eligible student must complete and submit the FAFSA in order to receive program funding. For more details, visit the website at http://www.FloridaStudentFinancialAid.org/SSFAD/home/uamain.htm.

Award: Grant for use in freshman, sophomore, junior, or senior years; renewable. *Amount:* up to $1500.

Eligibility Requirements: Applicant must be enrolled or expecting to enroll full-time at a four-year institution or university; resident of Florida and studying in Florida. Available to U.S. citizens.

Application Requirements: Application form.

Contact: Florida Department of Education, Office of Student Financial
Assistance, Customer Service
Florida State Department of Education
325 West Gaines Street
Tallahassee, FL 32399
Phone: 888-827-2007
E-mail: osfa@fldoe.org

FIRST GENERATION MATCHING GRANT PROGRAM

Need-based grants to Florida resident undergraduate students who are
enrolled in state universities and community colleges in Florida and
whose parents have not earned baccalaureate degrees. Available state
funds are contingent upon matching contributions from private sources
on a dollar-for-dollar basis. Institutions determine application procedures,
deadlines, and student eligibility. For more details, visit the website at
http://www.FloridaStudentFinancialAid.org/SSFAD/home/uamain.htm.

Award: Grant for use in freshman, sophomore, junior, or senior years;
renewable.

Eligibility Requirements: Applicant must be enrolled or expecting to
enroll full- or part-time at a two-year or four-year institution or
university; resident of Florida and studying in Florida. Available to U.S.
citizens.

Application Requirements: Application form, financial need analysis.

Contact: Florida Department of Education, Office of Student Financial
Assistance, Customer Service
Florida State Department of Education
325 West Gaines Street
Tallahassee, FL 32399
Phone: 888-827-2004
E-mail: osfa@fldoe.org

FLORIDA BRIGHT FUTURES SCHOLARSHIP PROGRAM

Three lottery-funded scholarships reward Florida high school graduates
for high academic achievement. Program is comprised of the following
three awards: Florida Academic Scholars Award, Florida Medallion
Scholars Award and Florida Gold Seal Vocational Scholars Award. An
eligible student must complete and submit the FAFSA in order to receive
program funding. For more details, visit the website at
http://www.FloridaStudentFinancialAid.org/SSFAD/home/uamain.htm.

Award: Scholarship for use in freshman, sophomore, junior, or senior
years; renewable.

Eligibility Requirements: Applicant must be high school student;
planning to enroll or expecting to enroll full- or part-time at a two-year or
four-year or technical institution or university; resident of Florida and
studying in Florida. Applicant must have 3.0 GPA or higher. Available to
U.S. citizens.

Application Requirements: Application form, application form may be
submitted online, community service, test scores, transcript.

Contact: Florida Department of Education, Office of Student Financial
Assistance, Customer Service
Florida State Department of Education
325 West Gaines Street
Tallahassee, FL 32399
Phone: 888-827-2004
E-mail: osfa@fldoe.org

FLORIDA POSTSECONDARY STUDENT ASSISTANCE GRANT

Scholarships to degree-seeking, resident, undergraduate students who
demonstrate substantial financial need and are enrolled in eligible degree-
granting private colleges and universities not eligible under the Florida
Private Student Assistance Grant. FSAG is a decentralized program, and
each participating institution determines application procedures,
deadlines and student eligibility. Number of awards varies. For more
details, visit the website at
http://www.FloridaStudentFinancialAid.org/SSFAD/home/uamain.htm.

Award: Grant for use in freshman, sophomore, junior, or senior years;
renewable. *Amount:* $200–$2610.

Eligibility Requirements: Applicant must be enrolled or expecting to
enroll full-time at a two-year or four-year institution or university;
resident of Florida and studying in Florida. Available to U.S. citizens.

Application Requirements: Financial need analysis.

Contact: Florida Department of Education, Office of Student Financial
Assistance, Customer Service
Florida State Department of Education
325 West Gaines Street
Tallahassee, FL 32399
Phone: 888-827-2004
E-mail: osfa@fldoe.org

FLORIDA PRIVATE STUDENT ASSISTANCE GRANT

Grants for Florida residents who are U.S. citizens or eligible non-citizens
attending eligible private, nonprofit, four-year colleges and universities
in Florida. Must be a full-time student and demonstrate substantial
financial need. For renewal, must have earned a minimum cumulative
GPA of 2.0 at the last institution attended. For more details, visit the
website at
http://www.FloridaStudentFinancialAid.org/SSFAD/home/uamain.htm.

Award: Grant for use in freshman, sophomore, junior, or senior years;
renewable. *Amount:* $200–$2610.

Eligibility Requirements: Applicant must be enrolled or expecting to
enroll full-time at a four-year institution or university; resident of Florida
and studying in Florida. Available to U.S. citizens.

Application Requirements: Application form, financial need analysis.

Contact: Florida Department of Education, Office of Student Financial
Assistance, Customer Service
Florida State Department of Education
325 West Gaines Street
Tallahassee, FL 32399
Phone: 888-827-2004
E-mail: osfa@fldoe.org

FLORIDA PUBLIC STUDENT ASSISTANCE GRANT

Grants for Florida residents, U.S. citizens or eligible non-citizens who
attend state universities and public community colleges and demonstrate
substantial financial need. For renewal, must have earned a minimum
cumulative GPA of 2.0 at the last institution attended. For more details,
visit the website at
http://www.FloridaStudentFinancialAid.org/SSFAD/home/uamain.htm.

Award: Grant for use in freshman, sophomore, junior, or senior years;
renewable. *Amount:* $200–$2610.

Eligibility Requirements: Applicant must be enrolled or expecting to
enroll full- or part-time at a two-year or four-year institution or
university; resident of Florida and studying in Florida. Available to U.S.
citizens.

Application Requirements: Application form, financial need analysis.

Contact: Florida Department of Education, Office of Student Financial
Assistance, Customer Service
Florida State Department of Education
325 West Gaines Street
Tallahassee, FL 32399
Phone: 888-827-2004
E-mail: osfa@fldoe.org

FLORIDA STUDENT ASSISTANCE GRANT-CAREER EDUCATION

Need-based grant program available to Florida residents enrolled in
certificate programs of 450 or more clock hours at participating
community colleges or career centers operated by district school boards.
FSAG-CE is a decentralized state of Florida program, which means that
each participating institution determines application procedures,
deadlines, student eligibility, and award amounts. For more details, visit
the website at
http://www.FloridaStudentFinancialAid.org/SSFAD/home/uamain.htm.

Award: Grant for use in freshman, sophomore, junior, or senior years;
renewable. *Amount:* $200–$2610.

Eligibility Requirements: Applicant must be enrolled or expecting to
enroll full- or part-time at a two-year or technical institution; resident of
Florida and studying in Florida. Available to U.S. citizens.

Application Requirements: Application form may be submitted online,
financial need analysis.

Contact: Florida Department of Education, Office of Student Financial
Assistance, Customer Service
Florida State Department of Education
325 West Gaines Street
Tallahassee, FL 32399
Phone: 888-827-2004
E-mail: osfa@fldoe.org

FLORIDA WORK EXPERIENCE PROGRAM

Need-based program providing eligible Florida residents work experiences that will complement and reinforce their educational and career goals. Must maintain GPA of 2.0. Postsecondary institution will determine applicant's eligibility, number of hours to be worked per week, and the award amount. For more details, visit the website at http://www.FloridaStudentFinancialAid.org/SSFAD/home/uamain.htm.

Award: Grant for use in freshman, sophomore, junior, or senior years; renewable.

Eligibility Requirements: Applicant must be enrolled or expecting to enroll full- or part-time at a two-year or four-year institution or university; resident of Florida and studying in Florida. Available to U.S. citizens.

Application Requirements: Financial need analysis.

Contact: Florida Department of Education, Office of Student Financial Assistance, Customer Service
Florida State Department of Education
325 West Gaines Street
Tallahassee, FL 32399
Phone: 888-827-2004
E-mail: osfa@fldoe.com

JOSE MARTI SCHOLARSHIP CHALLENGE GRANT FUND

• *See page 734*

MARY MCLEOD BETHUNE SCHOLARSHIP

Renewable award to Florida residents with a GPA of 3.0 or above, who will attend Bethune-Cookman University, Edward Waters College, Florida A&M University, or Florida Memorial University. Must not have previously received a baccalaureate degree. Must demonstrate financial need as specified by the institution. For more details, visit the website at http://www.FloridaStudentFinancialAid.org/SSFAD/home/uamain.htm.

Award: Scholarship for use in freshman, sophomore, junior, or senior years; renewable. *Amount:* $3000.

Eligibility Requirements: Applicant must be enrolled or expecting to enroll full-time at a four-year institution or university; resident of Florida and studying in Florida. Applicant must have 3.0 GPA or higher. Available to U.S. citizens.

Application Requirements: Financial need analysis.

Contact: Florida Department of Education, Office of Student Financial Assistance, Customer Service
Florida State Department of Education
325 West Gaines Street
Tallahassee, FL 32399
Phone: 888-827-2004
E-mail: osfa@fldoe.org

SCHOLARSHIPS FOR CHILDREN & SPOUSES OF DECEASED OR DISABLED VETERANS

• *See page 710*

WILLIAM L. BOYD IV FLORIDA RESIDENT ACCESS GRANT

Renewable awards to Florida undergraduate residents attending an eligible private, nonprofit Florida college or university. Postsecondary institution will determine applicant's eligibility. Renewal applicant must have earned a minimum institutional GPA of 2.0. An eligible student must complete and submit the FAFSA in order to receive program funding. For more details, visit the website at http://www.FloridaStudentFinancialAid.org/SSFAD/home/uamain.htm.

Award: Grant for use in freshman, sophomore, junior, or senior years; renewable. *Amount:* up to $3000.

Eligibility Requirements: Applicant must be enrolled or expecting to enroll full-time at a four-year institution or university; resident of Florida and studying in Florida. Available to U.S. citizens.

Application Requirements: Application form.

Contact: Florida Department of Education, Office of Student Financial Assistance, Customer Service
Florida State Department of Education
325 West Gaines Street
Tallahassee, FL 32399
Phone: 888-827-2004
E-mail: osfa@fldoe.org

FLORIDA WOMEN'S STATE GOLF ASSOCIATION

CLUB EMPLOYEES AND DEPENDENTS SCHOLARSHIP

Scholarship was designed to employees, and dependents of employees, of FSGA Member Clubs that utilize the GHIN Handicap System.

Award: Scholarship for use in freshman, sophomore, junior, or senior years; renewable. *Number:* 1. *Amount:* $500–$2000.

Eligibility Requirements: Applicant must be enrolled or expecting to enroll full-time at a two-year or four-year or technical institution or university; resident of Florida and must have an interest in golf. Applicant must have 3.0 GPA or higher. Available to U.S. citizens.

Application Requirements: Application form, application form may be submitted online (http://www.fsga.org/sections/Foundation/College-Scholarships/38), community service, essay, financial need analysis, personal photograph, recommendations or references, test scores, transcript. *Deadline:* June 1.

Contact: Kyle Walkiewicz, Director of Junior Golf
Florida Women's State Golf Association
12630 Telecom Drive
Tampa, FL 33637
Phone: 813-632-3742
Fax: 813-910-2125
E-mail: kyle@fsga.org

FSGA SCHOLARS

FSGA Scholars is a scholarship program made possible by the Florida State Golf Association and our Future of Golf Foundation. In the Spring each year, the FSGA selects a minimum of five golfers from the FJT's graduating class to be awarded a renewable four-year scholarship. A total of $10,000 in college scholarships will be awarded each year, resulting in $40,000 granted to each graduating class.

Award: Scholarship for use in freshman, sophomore, junior, or senior years; renewable. *Number:* 1–8. *Amount:* $500–$2000.

Eligibility Requirements: Applicant must be high school student; planning to enroll or expecting to enroll full-time at a two-year or four-year or technical institution or university; resident of Florida and must have an interest in golf. Applicant must have 3.0 GPA or higher. Available to U.S. citizens.

Application Requirements: Application form, application form may be submitted online (http://www.fsga.org/sections/Foundation/College-Scholarships/38), community service, essay, financial need analysis, personal photograph, recommendations or references, test scores, transcript. *Deadline:* July 1.

Contact: Kyle Walkiewica, Director of Junior Golf
Florida Women's State Golf Association
12630 Telecom Drive
Tampa, FL 33637
Phone: 813-632-3742
Fax: 813-910-2125
E-mail: kyle@fsga.org

SARAH E. HUNEYCUTT SCHOLARSHIP

This four-year scholarship of $5000 per academic year ($20,000 total) is awarded annually to a deserving high school senior woman who is a Florida resident, will be attending an accredited Florida college or university, has demonstrated an interest in golf but is not eligible for a golf athletic scholarship, shows financial need, and maintains a grade point average of 3.0 or higher.

Award: Scholarship for use in freshman, sophomore, junior, or senior years; renewable. *Number:* 1–5. *Amount:* $5000.

Eligibility Requirements: Applicant must be high school student; planning to enroll or expecting to enroll full-time at a two-year or four-year or technical institution or university; female; resident of Florida; studying in Florida and must have an interest in golf. Applicant must have 3.0 GPA or higher. Available to U.S. citizens.

Application Requirements: Application form, application form may be submitted online (http://www.jggsf.org/), community service, essay, financial need analysis, personal photograph, test scores, transcript. *Deadline:* June 1.

Contact: Jan Demarco, President
E-mail: jan@jggsf.org

THE FORD FAMILY FOUNDATION

http://www.tfff.org

FORD OPPORTUNITY PROGRAM

Hallie E. Ford and The Ford Family Foundation established the Ford Opportunity Scholarship Program to provide scholarships to college students who are single parents with custody of dependent children (18 years of age or younger) and be the head of household as defined by IRS regulations. Recipients must have at least one year remaining in their undergraduate program and attend college in their home start of Oregon or California and plan to pursue an associate or bachelor's degree. Minimum 3.0 GPA required.

Award: Scholarship for use in freshman, sophomore, junior, senior, graduate, or postgraduate years; renewable. *Number:* 30–50. *Amount:* $1000–$25,000.

Eligibility Requirements: Applicant must be enrolled or expecting to enroll full-time at a two-year or four-year institution or university; single; resident of California, Oregon and studying in California, Oregon. Applicant must have 3.0 GPA or higher. Available to U.S. citizens.

Application Requirements: Application form, essay, financial need analysis, interview. *Deadline:* March 1.

Contact: Tricia Tate, Scholarship Programs Manager
The Ford Family Foundation
44 Club Road, Suite 100
Eugene, OR 97401
Phone: 541-485-6211
Fax: 541-485-6223
E-mail: fordscholarships@tfff.org

FORD RESTART PROGRAM

The Ford Family Foundation established the Ford ReStart Scholarship Program to encourage adults, age 25 or older, to begin or return to full-time, post-secondary education. Each year, up to 46 applicants are selected from Oregon and Siskiyou County, California to receive a Ford ReStart scholarship. An applicant must be at least 25 years old by March 1 of the application year, be no more than halfway through their degree program, and seek an associate's degree or a bachelor's degree at an eligible institution in CA or OR (and not previously have earned a bachelor's degree).

Award: Scholarship for use in freshman, sophomore, junior, senior, graduate, or postgraduate years; renewable. *Number:* 46. *Amount:* $1000–$25,000.

Eligibility Requirements: Applicant must be enrolled or expecting to enroll full-time at a two-year or four-year institution or university; resident of California, Oregon and studying in California, Oregon. Applicant must have 3.0 GPA or higher. Available to U.S. citizens.

Application Requirements: Application form, essay, financial need analysis, interview. *Deadline:* March 1.

Contact: Tricia Tate, Scholarship Programs Manager
The Ford Family Foundation
44 Club Road, Suite 100
Eugene, OR 97401
Phone: 541-485-6211
Fax: 541-485-6223
E-mail: fordscholarships@tfff.org

FORD SCHOLARS PROGRAM

The Ford Scholars Program is need-based and open to 1) graduating high school seniors and, 2) entering college freshmen and (3) continuing community college students ready to transfer to a four-year college, who are seeking a bachelor's degree in Oregon or California. This program is available to residents of Oregon and Siskiyou County, California. The Ford Scholars Program was created by Kenneth W. Ford (1908-1997), a founder of The Ford Family Foundation, to assist students who otherwise would find it impossible, or at least very difficult, to obtain a college degree without financial assistance.

Award: Scholarship for use in freshman, sophomore, junior, senior, graduate, or postgraduate years; renewable. *Number:* 100–120. *Amount:* $1000–$25,000.

Eligibility Requirements: Applicant must be enrolled or expecting to enroll full-time at a two-year or four-year institution or university; resident of California, Oregon and studying in California, Oregon. Applicant must have 3.0 GPA or higher. Available to U.S. citizens.

Application Requirements: Application form, essay, financial need analysis, interview. *Deadline:* March 1.

Contact: Tricia Tate, Scholarship Programs Manager
The Ford Family Foundation
44 Club Road, Suite 100
Eugene, OR 97401
Phone: 541-485-6211
Fax: 541-485-6223
E-mail: fordscholarships@tfff.org

FRANCIS OUIMET SCHOLARSHIP FUND

http://www.ouimet.org

FRANCIS OUIMET SCHOLARSHIP

Since 1949, The Francis Ouimet Scholarship Fund has awarded nearly $34 Million in need-based college tuition assistance to students who have given at least two years of service to golf as caddies, pro shop work, or course superintendent operations at a Massachusetts golf course. The Ouimet Scholarship is unique in that it is renewable for up to four years. Ouimet awards range from $1,000 to $15,000 per year, depending on financial need and ranking in our competitive evaluation process. The value of the award over four years can be $10,000 to $40,000, or more. Nearly 5,700 young people have received Ouimet Scholarships, and many have gone on to prestigious positions of leadership in business and professional careers.

Award: Scholarship for use in freshman, sophomore, junior, or senior years; not renewable. *Amount:* $1000–$15,000.

Eligibility Requirements: Applicant must be enrolled or expecting to enroll full-time at a two-year or four-year institution or university; resident of Massachusetts and must have an interest in golf. Available to U.S. citizens.

Application Requirements: Application form, community service, essay, financial need analysis, interview, personal photograph. *Deadline:* December 1.

Contact: Mrs. Michelle Edwards, Director of Scholarships
Francis Ouimet Scholarship Fund
300 Arnold Palmer Boulevard
Norton, MA 02766
Phone: 774-4309090
Fax: 774-4307474
E-mail: MichelleE@ouimet.org

FRATERNAL ORDER OF POLICE ASSOCIATES OF OHIO INC.

http://www.fopaohio.org/

FRATERNAL ORDER OF POLICE ASSOCIATES, STATE LODGE OF OHIO INC., SCHOLARSHIP FUND

• *See page 619*

FRESH START SCHOLARSHIP FOUNDATION

http://www.freshstartscholarship.org

FRESH START SCHOLARSHIP

Must be entering an undergraduate program at a college or university in Delaware. Scholarship offering a fresh start to women who are returning to school after a hiatus of at least two years to better their life and opportunities. Applicants must be Delaware residents or employed in Delaware for at least 12 months. U.S. Citizenship or Permanent Resident status required.

Award: Scholarship for use in freshman, sophomore, junior, or senior years; not renewable. *Number:* 25–30. *Amount:* $1000–$4000.

Eligibility Requirements: Applicant must be enrolled or expecting to enroll full- or part-time at a two-year or four-year institution or university; female; resident of Delaware and studying in Delaware. Applicant must have 2.5 GPA or higher. Available to U.S. citizens.

Application Requirements: Application form, essay, financial need analysis. *Deadline:* May 15.

Contact: Scholarship Chair
Fresh Start Scholarship Foundation
Fresh Start Scholarship Foundation
PO Box 7784
Wilmington, DE 19803
Phone: 302-397-3440
E-mail: fsscholar@comcast.net

FRIENDS OF 440 SCHOLARSHIP FUND INC.

http://www.440scholarship.org/

FRIENDS OF 440 SCHOLARSHIP FUND, INC.

Scholarships to students who are dependents of workers who were injured or killed in the course and scope of their employment and who are eligible to receive benefits under the Florida Workers' Compensation system, or are dependents of those primarily engaged in the administration of the Florida Workers' Compensation Law.

Award: Scholarship for use in freshman, sophomore, junior, or senior years; renewable. *Number:* 1–60. *Amount:* $500–$6000.

Eligibility Requirements: Applicant must be enrolled or expecting to enroll full-time at a two-year or four-year or technical institution or university and resident of Florida. Available to U.S. and non-U.S. citizens.

Application Requirements: Application form, copy of tax return, transcript. *Deadline:* February 28.

Contact: Ms. Lori Gerson, Managing Director
Phone: 305-423-8710
Fax: 305-670-0716
E-mail: info@440scholarship.org

FULFILLMENT FUND

http://www.fulfillment.org/

FULFILLMENT FUND SCHOLARSHIPS

Award is for undergraduates. Serving students in seven partner high schools, Fremont, Hamilton, Locke, Los Angeles, Manual Arts, Crenshaw and Wilson. Only students who participated in the Fulfillment Fund High School Program for at least two years are eligible to apply for the scholarship.

Award: Scholarship for use in freshman, sophomore, junior, or senior years; not renewable. *Amount:* $1000–$1500.

Eligibility Requirements: Applicant must be enrolled or expecting to enroll full- or part-time at a four-year institution or university and resident of California. Available to U.S. citizens.

Application Requirements: Application form. *Deadline:* varies.

Contact: Darcine Thomas, Community Outreach Manager
Phone: 323-900-8753
Fax: 323-525-3095

FUNNEWJERSEY.COM INC.

http://www.funnewjersey.com

FUNNEWJERSEY.COM SCHOLARSHIP

• *See page 620*

GATTI, KELTNER, BIENVENU & MONTESI

https://www.gkbm.com/

MONTESI SCHOLARSHIP

$2500 scholarship for a student who submits an original essay on how Driving and Texting has affected their life or an experience of how it has impacted someone they know. Winner must show proof of acceptance or active enrollment in undergrad school.

Award: Scholarship for use in freshman, sophomore, junior, or senior years; not renewable. *Number:* 1. *Amount:* $2500.

Eligibility Requirements: Applicant must be enrolled or expecting to enroll full-time at a two-year or four-year or technical institution or university and resident of Arkansas, Mississippi, Tennessee. Available to U.S. citizens.

Application Requirements: Essay. *Deadline:* May 30.

Contact: Chloe Zollinger
E-mail: gkbmlaw@gmail.com

GENERAL FEDERATION OF WOMEN'S CLUBS OF MASSACHUSETTS

http://www.gfwcma.org/

GENERAL FEDERATION OF WOMEN'S CLUBS OF MASSACHUSETTS NICKEL FOR NOTES MUSIC SCHOLARSHIP

• *See page 620*

GENERAL FEDERATION OF WOMEN'S CLUBS OF MASSACHUSETTS PENNIES FOR ART SCHOLARSHIP

• *See page 620*

GENERAL FEDERATION OF WOMEN'S CLUBS OF VERMONT

BARBARA JEAN BARKER MEMORIAL SCHOLARSHIP

Applicants must be Vermont residents who need addition education to advance their position in the workplace.

Award: Grant for use in freshman, sophomore, junior, senior, or graduate years; renewable. *Number:* 2. *Amount:* $1000.

Eligibility Requirements: Applicant must be enrolled or expecting to enroll full- or part-time at a two-year or four-year or technical institution or university; female and resident of Vermont. Available to U.S. citizens.

Application Requirements: Application form, driver's license, financial need analysis, interview. *Deadline:* March 15.

Contact: Mrs. Betty Haggerty
General Federation of Women's Clubs of Vermont
16 Taylor St
Bellows Falls, VT 05101
Phone: 802-463-4159
E-mail: hubett@hotmail.com

GEORGIA PRESS EDUCATIONAL FOUNDATION INC.

http://gapress.org/scholarships-internships/

KIRK SUTLIVE SCHOLARSHIP

• *See page 621*

MORRIS NEWSPAPER CORPORATION SCHOLARSHIP

• *See page 621*

GEORGIA STUDENT FINANCE COMMISSION

http://www.GAfutures.org

GEORGIA HERO SCHOLARSHIP

• *See page 621*

GEORGIA PUBLIC SAFETY MEMORIAL GRANT

• *See page 621*

GEORGIA TUITION EQUALIZATION GRANT (GTEG)

• *See page 621*

ZELL MILLER SCHOLARSHIP PROGRAM

• *See page 621*

GIRL SCOUTS OF CONNECTICUT

http://www.gsofct.org/

EMILY CHAISON GOLD AWARD SCHOLARSHIP

• *See page 564*

GOLDBERG & OSBORNE
https://1800theeagle.com

ARIZONA DON'T TEXT AND DRIVE SCHOLARSHIP

We invite anyone who lives in the United States and knows someone who lives in Arizona currently attending college or trade school, or getting ready to attend one, to make the pledge not to text and drive. That means you can pledge not to text and drive and enter the scholarship drawing either on your behalf or on behalf of someone else. We award one (1) $1,000 scholarship every month. New scholarships begin on the first day of each month and close on the last day of each month. Applications do not carry forward from month to month so please return and take the don't text and drive pledge again to apply for a new month. Winners are announced on our Facebook and Twitter feeds.

Award: Scholarship for use in freshman, sophomore, junior, senior, graduate, or postgraduate years; not renewable. *Number:* 1. *Amount:* $1000.

Eligibility Requirements: Applicant must be enrolled or expecting to enroll full- or part-time at a two-year or four-year or technical institution or university; resident of Arizona and studying in Arizona. Available to U.S. citizens.

Application Requirements: Application form. *Deadline:* continuous.

Contact: Mr. Dan Bradley, Marketing Director
Goldberg & Osborne
2815 S Alma School Rd
Mesa, AZ 85210
Phone: 602-808-6600
E-mail: scholarships@1800theeagle.com

NATIONAL DON'T TEXT AND DRIVE SCHOLARSHIP

Applicants for the Second Quarter 2018 National Goldberg & Osborne Don't Text and Drive College Scholarship must either be attending college or trade school currently or planning to attend college or trade school this semester or the fall 2018 semester. You can pledge not to text and drive and enter the scholarship drawing either on your behalf or on behalf of someone else. We award one (1) $1,000 scholarship every over month (bimonthly) for a total of six scholarships per year. New scholarships begin on the first day of every other month and close on the last day of every other month. Applications do not carry forward from one bimonthly period to the next so please return and take the don't text and drive pledge again to apply for a new period. Winners are announced on our Facebook and Twitter feeds.

Award: Scholarship for use in freshman, sophomore, junior, senior, graduate, or postgraduate years; not renewable. *Number:* 1. *Amount:* $1000.

Eligibility Requirements: Applicant must be enrolled or expecting to enroll full- or part-time at a two-year or four-year or technical institution or university and resident of Alabama, Alaska, Arizona, Arkansas, California, Colorado, Connecticut, Delaware, District of Columbia, Florida, Georgia, Hawaii, Idaho, Illinois, Indiana, Iowa, Kansas, Kentucky, Louisiana, Maine, Maryland, Massachusetts, Michigan, Minnesota, Mississippi, Missouri, Montana, Nebraska, Nevada, New Hampshire, New Jersey, New Mexico, New York, North Carolina, North Dakota, Ohio, Oklahoma, Oregon, Pennsylvania, Rhode Island, South Carolina, South Dakota, Tennessee, Texas, Utah, Vermont, Virginia, Washington, West Virginia, Wisconsin, Wyoming. Available to U.S. citizens.

Application Requirements: Application form. *Deadline:* continuous.

Contact: Mr. Dan Bradley, Marketing Director
Goldberg & Osborne
2815 S Alma School Rd
Mesa, AZ 85210
Phone: 602-808-6600
E-mail: scholarships@1800theeagle.com

GREATER KANAWHA VALLEY FOUNDATION
http://www.tgkvf.org/

C. RAYMOND & DELSIA R. COLLINS SCHOLARSHIP

Renewable award for a full-time student who is a resident of West Virginia pursing postsecondary studies. Must demonstrate academic excellence.

Award: Scholarship for use in freshman, sophomore, junior, or senior years; renewable. *Amount:* $1000.

Eligibility Requirements: Applicant must be enrolled or expecting to enroll full-time at a four-year institution or university and resident of West Virginia. Available to U.S. citizens.

Application Requirements: Application form, financial need analysis, recommendations or references, test scores, transcript. *Deadline:* January 15.

Contact: Susan Hoover, Scholarship Program Officer
Greater Kanawha Valley Foundation
900 Lee Street East, 16th Floor
Charleston, WV 25301
Phone: 304-346-3620
E-mail: shoover@tgkvf.org

DRS. CHARLENE & CHARLES BYRD SCHOLARSHIP

Renewable award for a West Virginia resident pursuing full-time postsecondary studies. Minimum 2.5 GPA required.

Award: Scholarship for use in freshman, sophomore, junior, or senior years; renewable. *Amount:* $1000.

Eligibility Requirements: Applicant must be enrolled or expecting to enroll full-time at a four-year institution or university and resident of West Virginia. Applicant must have 2.5 GPA or higher. Available to U.S. citizens.

Application Requirements: Application form, recommendations or references, transcript. *Deadline:* January 15.

Contact: Susan Hoover, Scholarship Program Officer
Greater Kanawha Valley Foundation
900 Lee Street East, 16th Floor
Charleston, WV 25301
Phone: 304-346-3620
E-mail: shoover@tgkvf.org

EVANS MEMORIAL SCHOLARSHIP

Renewable award available to West Virginia resident who is enrolling or has enrolled in a two-year or four-year college/university in West Virginia. Must demonstrate financial need.

Award: Scholarship for use in freshman, sophomore, junior, or senior years; renewable. *Amount:* $1000.

Eligibility Requirements: Applicant must be enrolled or expecting to enroll full-time at a two-year or four-year institution or university; resident of West Virginia and studying in West Virginia. Available to U.S. citizens.

Application Requirements: Application form, financial need analysis, test scores, transcript. *Deadline:* January 15.

Contact: Susan Hoover, Scholarship Program Officer
Greater Kanawha Valley Foundation
900 Lee Street East, 16th Floor
Charleston, WV 25301
Phone: 304-346-3620
E-mail: shoover@tgkvf.org

HENRY E. KING SCHOLARSHIP FUND

Award available for immediate family members of owners, or employees, of companies that are current members of, and have been members of, the Home Builders Association of Greater Charleston, West Virginia. Award to be used for full-time study in a two- or four-year college/university. Must be a resident of West Virginia and demonstrate financial need. Renewable only for current members.

Award: Scholarship for use in freshman, sophomore, junior, or senior years; not renewable. *Amount:* $1000.

Eligibility Requirements: Applicant must be enrolled or expecting to enroll full-time at a two-year or four-year institution or university and resident of West Virginia. Available to U.S. citizens.

Application Requirements: Application form, financial need analysis, transcript. *Deadline:* January 15.

Contact: Susan Hoover, Scholarship Program Officer
Greater Kanawha Valley Foundation
900 Lee Street East, 16th Floor
Charleston, WV 25301
Phone: 304-346-3620
E-mail: shoover@tgkvf.org

JAMES & MARIANNE LANE SCHOLARSHIP

Renewable award for a West Virginia resident pursuing postsecondary studies. Minimum 2.5 GPA required. Preference given to students attending Washington & Jefferson College.

Award: Scholarship for use in freshman, sophomore, junior, or senior years; renewable.

Eligibility Requirements: Applicant must be enrolled or expecting to enroll full-time at a four-year institution or university and resident of West Virginia. Applicant must have 2.5 GPA or higher. Available to U.S. citizens.

Application Requirements: Application form, recommendations or references, test scores, transcript. *Deadline:* January 15.

Contact: Susan Hoover, Scholarship Program Officer
Greater Kanawha Valley Foundation
900 Lee Street East, 16th Floor
Charleston, WV 25301
Phone: 304-346-3620
E-mail: shoover@tgkvf.org

KID'S CHANCE OF WEST VIRGINIA SCHOLARSHIP

Award for children (between the ages of 16 and 25) of a parent injured in a WV work-related accident. Preference shall be given to students with financial need, academic performance, leadership abilities, demonstrated and potential contributions to school and community who are pursuing any field of study in any accredited trade, vocational school, college, or university. Must attach a copy of the order or letter from the worker's compensation carrier granting a permanent total disability award or dependent's benefits.

Award: Scholarship for use in freshman, sophomore, junior, or senior years; renewable. *Amount:* $2000.

Eligibility Requirements: Applicant must be age 16-25; enrolled or expecting to enroll full-time at a two-year or four-year or technical institution or university; resident of West Virginia and must have an interest in leadership. Available to U.S. citizens.

Application Requirements: Application form, essay, financial need analysis, recommendations or references, transcript, worker's compensation order/letter. *Deadline:* January 15.

Contact: Susan Hoover, Scholarship Program Officer
Greater Kanawha Valley Foundation
900 Lee Street East, 16th Floor
Charleston, WV 25301
Phone: 304-346-3620
E-mail: shoover@tgkvf.org

LAWRENCE C. YEARDLEY SCHOLARSHIP

Renewable award for resident of West Virginia pursuing postsecondary studies. Must demonstrate academic excellence, financial need, and have a minimum 2.5 GPA.

Award: Scholarship for use in freshman, sophomore, junior, or senior years; renewable. *Amount:* $1000.

Eligibility Requirements: Applicant must be enrolled or expecting to enroll full-time at a four-year institution or university and resident of West Virginia. Applicant must have 2.5 GPA or higher. Available to U.S. citizens.

Application Requirements: Application form, financial need analysis, recommendations or references, test scores, transcript. *Deadline:* January 15.

Contact: Susan Hoover, Scholarship Program Officer
Greater Kanawha Valley Foundation
900 Lee Street East, 16th Floor
Charleston, WV 25301
Phone: 304-346-3620
E-mail: shoover@tgkvf.org

LEFF MOORE SCHOLARSHIP

Renewable award for a West Virginia resident pursuing full-time postsecondary studies. Must be affiliated with the Democratic Party and demonstrate financial need. Minimum 2.5 GPA required.

Award: Scholarship for use in freshman, sophomore, junior, or senior years; renewable.

Eligibility Requirements: Applicant must be enrolled or expecting to enroll full-time at a four-year institution or university and resident of West Virginia. Applicant must have 2.5 GPA or higher. Available to U.S. citizens.

Application Requirements: Application form, financial need analysis, recommendations or references, transcript. *Deadline:* January 15.

Contact: Susan Hoover, Scholarship Program Officer
Greater Kanawha Valley Foundation
900 Lee Street East, 16th Floor
Charleston, WV 25301
Phone: 304-346-3620
E-mail: shoover@tgkvf.org

MABEL W. WALKER SCHOLARSHIP

Renewable award for West Virginia residents pursuing full-time postsecondary studies. Minimum 2.5 GPA required. Preference given to residents of Campbell Creek and then Upper Kanawha.

Award: Scholarship for use in freshman, sophomore, junior, or senior years; renewable. *Amount:* $1000.

Eligibility Requirements: Applicant must be enrolled or expecting to enroll full-time at a four-year institution or university and resident of West Virginia. Applicant must have 2.5 GPA or higher. Available to U.S. citizens.

Application Requirements: Application form, financial need analysis, recommendations or references, test scores, transcript. *Deadline:* January 15.

Contact: Susan Hoover, Scholarship Program Officer
Greater Kanawha Valley Foundation
900 Lee Street East, 16th Floor
Charleston, WV 25301
Phone: 304-346-3620
E-mail: shoover@tgkvf.org

MILLIE SNYDER SCHOLARSHIP

Renewable award for a West Virginia resident pursuing full-time postsecondary studies. Must be a member of Weight Watchers. Minimum 2.5 GPA required.

Award: Scholarship for use in freshman, sophomore, junior, or senior years; renewable. *Amount:* $1000.

Eligibility Requirements: Applicant must be enrolled or expecting to enroll full-time at a four-year institution or university and resident of West Virginia. Applicant must have 2.5 GPA or higher. Available to U.S. citizens.

Application Requirements: Application form, financial need analysis, recommendations or references, transcript. *Deadline:* January 15.

Contact: Susan Hoover, Scholarship Program Officer
Greater Kanawha Valley Foundation
900 Lee Street East, 16th Floor
Charleston, WV 25301
Phone: 304-346-3620
E-mail: shoover@tgkvf.org

NORMAN S. AND BETTY M. FITZHUGH FUND

Award available to West Virginia residents who demonstrate academic excellence and financial need to attend any accredited college or university. Scholarships are awarded for full-time study for one or more years.

Award: Scholarship for use in freshman, sophomore, junior, or senior years; renewable. *Number:* 1. *Amount:* $750.

Eligibility Requirements: Applicant must be enrolled or expecting to enroll full-time at a two-year or four-year or technical institution or university and resident of West Virginia. Available to U.S. citizens.

Application Requirements: Application form, essay, financial need analysis, recommendations or references, transcript. *Deadline:* January 15.

Contact: Susan Hoover, Scholarship Program Officer
Greater Kanawha Valley Foundation
900 Lee Street East, 16th Floor
Charleston, WV 25301
Phone: 304-346-3620
E-mail: shoover@tgkvf.org

O'HAIR SCHOLARSHIP

Renewable award for West Virginia residents pursuing full-time postsecondary studies. Must demonstrate academic ability. Minimum 2.5 GPA required.

Award: Scholarship for use in freshman, sophomore, junior, or senior years; renewable. *Amount:* $1000.

Eligibility Requirements: Applicant must be enrolled or expecting to enroll full-time at a four-year institution or university and resident of West Virginia. Applicant must have 2.5 GPA or higher. Available to U.S. citizens.

Application Requirements: Application form, financial need analysis, recommendations or references, test scores, transcript. *Deadline:* January 15.

Contact: Susan Hoover, Scholarship Program Officer
Greater Kanawha Valley Foundation
900 Lee Street East, 16th Floor
Charleston, WV 25301
Phone: 304-346-3620
E-mail: shoover@tgkvf.org

RHUDY SCHOLARSHIP

Renewable award for a West Virginia resident pursuing full-time postsecondary studies. Minimum 2.5 GPA required. Must demonstrate academic ability and financial need.

Award: Scholarship for use in freshman, sophomore, junior, or senior years; renewable. *Amount:* $500.

Eligibility Requirements: Applicant must be enrolled or expecting to enroll full-time at a four-year institution or university and resident of West Virginia. Applicant must have 2.5 GPA or higher. Available to U.S. citizens.

Application Requirements: Application form, financial need analysis, recommendations or references, test scores, transcript. *Deadline:* January 15.

Contact: Susan Hoover, Scholarship Program Officer
Greater Kanawha Valley Foundation
900 Lee Street East, 16th Floor
Charleston, WV 25301
Phone: 304-346-3620
E-mail: shoover@tgkvf.org

R. RAY SINGLETON FUND

Renewable award available for undergraduate or graduate study in a West Virginia college/university. Applicant must be resident of Kanawha, Boone, Clay, Putnam, Lincoln, or Fayette counties, and demonstrate financial need and academic excellence.

Award: Scholarship for use in freshman, sophomore, junior, senior, or graduate years; renewable. *Amount:* $1000.

Eligibility Requirements: Applicant must be enrolled or expecting to enroll full-time at a four-year institution or university; resident of West Virginia and studying in West Virginia. Available to U.S. citizens.

Application Requirements: Application form, financial need analysis, transcript. *Deadline:* January 15.

Contact: Susan Hoover, Scholarship Program Officer
Greater Kanawha Valley Foundation
900 Lee Street East, 16th Floor
Charleston, WV 25301
Phone: 304-346-3620
E-mail: shoover@tgkvf.org

RUTH ANN JOHNSON SCHOLARSHIP

Renewable award for a full-time postsecondary student who is a resident of West Virginia. Must demonstrate academic excellence. Minimum 2.5 GPA required.

Award: Scholarship for use in freshman, sophomore, junior, or senior years; renewable. *Amount:* $1000.

Eligibility Requirements: Applicant must be enrolled or expecting to enroll full-time at a four-year institution or university and resident of West Virginia. Applicant must have 2.5 GPA or higher. Available to U.S. citizens.

Application Requirements: Application form, financial need analysis, recommendations or references, test scores, transcript. *Deadline:* January 15.

Contact: Susan Hoover, Scholarship Program Officer
Greater Kanawha Valley Foundation
900 Lee Street East, 16th Floor
Charleston, WV 25301
Phone: 304-346-3620
E-mail: shoover@tgkvf.org

STUART & LUCILLE ARMSTRONG SCHOLARSHIP

• *See page 782*

THALHEIMER FAMILY SUPPLEMENTAL SCHOLARSHIP

Award available to West Virginia students who are current scholarship winners to provide supplemental funds for goods and services necessary for the student to attend college. Must be a resident of Kanawha, Putnam, Boone, Clay, Fayette, or Lincoln counties and submit a written request for additional aid, listing all financial aid that has been awarded and reason for request.

Award: Scholarship for use in freshman, sophomore, junior, or senior years; not renewable. *Amount:* $1000.

Eligibility Requirements: Applicant must be enrolled or expecting to enroll full-time at a two-year or four-year institution or university and resident of West Virginia. Available to U.S. citizens.

Application Requirements: Application form, financial need analysis, letter requesting aid, transcript. *Deadline:* January 15.

Contact: Susan Hoover, Scholarship Program Officer
Greater Kanawha Valley Foundation
900 Lee Street East, 16th Floor
Charleston, WV 25301
Phone: 304-346-3620
E-mail: shoover@tgkvf.org

WEST VIRGINIA GOLF ASSOCIATION FUND

Award of $1000 available to students at any accredited West Virginia college or university. This fund is open to individuals who (1) have played golf in WV as an amateur for recreation or competition, or (2) have been or are presently employed in WV as a caddie, groundskeeper, bag boy, etc. Must also include a reference by a coach, golf professional, or employer and an essay explaining how the game of golf has made an impact in applicant's life.

Award: Scholarship for use in freshman, sophomore, junior, or senior years; not renewable. *Number:* 2. *Amount:* $1000.

Eligibility Requirements: Applicant must be enrolled or expecting to enroll full-time at a two-year or four-year or technical institution or university; resident of West Virginia; studying in West Virginia and must have an interest in golf. Available to U.S. citizens.

Application Requirements: Application form, essay, recommendations or references, transcript. *Deadline:* January 15.

Contact: Susan Hoover, Scholarship Program Officer
Greater Kanawha Valley Foundation
900 Lee Street East, 16th Floor
Charleston, WV 25301
Phone: 304-346-3620
E-mail: shoover@tgkvf.org

W. P. BLACK SCHOLARSHIP FUND

Renewable award for West Virginia residents who demonstrate academic excellence and financial need and who are enrolled in an undergraduate program in any accredited college or university.

Award: Scholarship for use in freshman, sophomore, junior, or senior years; renewable. *Amount:* $1000.

Eligibility Requirements: Applicant must be enrolled or expecting to enroll full-time at a four-year institution or university and resident of West Virginia. Available to U.S. citizens.

Application Requirements: Application form, essay, financial need analysis, recommendations or references, self-addressed stamped envelope with application, test scores, transcript. *Deadline:* January 15.

Contact: Susan Hoover, Scholarship Coordinator
Greater Kanawha Valley Foundation
900 Lee Street East, 16th Floor
Charleston, WV 25301
Phone: 304-346-3620
E-mail: shoover@tgkvf.org

GREATER SEATTLE BUSINESS ASSOCIATION

http://thegsba.org/

GSBA SCHOLARSHIP FUND

GSBA awards educational scholarships to LGBTQ and allied students who are committed to making a difference in the world. Our scholarships range up to $13,000 annually and are meant to provide significant support as you pursue your educational goals.

Award: Scholarship for use in freshman, sophomore, junior, or senior years; renewable. *Number:* 40–45. *Amount:* $2000–$13,000.

Eligibility Requirements: Applicant must be enrolled or expecting to enroll full- or part-time at a two-year or four-year or technical institution or university; resident of Washington and must have an interest in LGBT issues. Available to U.S. and non-U.S. citizens.

Application Requirements: Application form, community service, essay, financial need analysis, interview. *Deadline:* January 12.

Contact: Travis Mears, Director of Development and Scholarship
Programs
Greater Seattle Business Association
400 East Pine Street
Suite 322
Seattle, WA 98122
Phone: 206-363-9188
E-mail: travis@thegsba.org

GREATER WASHINGTON URBAN LEAGUE

http://www.gwul.org/

SAFEWAY/GREATER WASHINGTON URBAN LEAGUE SCHOLARSHIP
• *See page 622*

GREAT LAKES HEMOPHILIA FOUNDATION

http://www.glhf.org/

GLHF INDIVIDUAL CLASS SCHOLARSHIP
• *See page 687*

GREAT LAKES HEMOPHILIA FOUNDATION EDUCATION SCHOLARSHIP
• *See page 688*

GREENHOUSE SCHOLARS

https://greenhousescholars.org/

GREENHOUSE SCHOLARS
• *See page 736*

HAGAN SCHOLARSHIP FOUNDATION

https://haganscholarships.org/

HAGAN SCHOLARSHIP
• *See page 623*

HARRINGTON FAMILY FOUNDATION

http://harringtonfamilyfoundation.org

OREGON COMMUNITY QUARTERBACK SCHOLARSHIP
• *See page 624*

HAWAII EDUCATION ASSOCIATION

http://www.heaed.com/

HAWAII EDUCATION ASSOCIATION HIGH SCHOOL STUDENT SCHOLARSHIP
• *See page 565*

HAWAII SCHOOLS FEDERAL CREDIT UNION

http://www.hawaiischoolsfcu.org/

EDWIN KUNIYUKI MEMORIAL SCHOLARSHIP
• *See page 624*

HAWAII STATE POSTSECONDARY EDUCATION COMMISSION

HAWAII STATE STUDENT INCENTIVE GRANT

Grants are given to residents of Hawaii who are enrolled in a participating Hawaiian state school. Funds are for undergraduate tuition only. Applicants must submit a financial need analysis.

Award: Grant for use in freshman, sophomore, junior, or senior years; renewable. *Number:* 470. *Amount:* $200–$2000.

Eligibility Requirements: Applicant must be enrolled or expecting to enroll full- or part-time at a two-year or four-year or technical institution or university; resident of Hawaii and studying in Hawaii. Available to U.S. citizens.

Application Requirements: Application form, financial need analysis. *Deadline:* continuous.

Contact: Janine Oyama, Financial Aid Specialist
Hawaii State Postsecondary Education Commission
University of Hawaii
Honolulu, HI 96822
Phone: 808-956-6066

HELLENIC UNIVERSITY CLUB OF NEW YORK

http://www.hucny.com

HELLENIC UNIVERSITY CLUB UNDERGRADUATE SCHOLARSHIP AWARDS PROGRAM
• *See page 737*

HELLENIC UNIVERSITY CLUB OF PHILADELPHIA

http://www.hucphiladelphia.org/

CHRISTOPHER DEMETRIS SCHOLARSHIP
• *See page 737*

DR. NICHOLAS PADIS MEMORIAL GRADUATE SCHOLARSHIP
• *See page 738*

DORIZAS MEMORIAL SCHOLARSHIP
• *See page 738*

FOUNDERS SCHOLARSHIP
• *See page 738*

PAIDEIA SCHOLARSHIP
• *See page 565*

HEMOPHILIA FOUNDATION OF SOUTHERN CALIFORNIA

http://www.hemosocal.org/

CHRISTOPHER MARK PITKIN MEMORIAL SCHOLARSHIP
• *See page 625*

HENKEL CONSUMER ADHESIVES INC.

http://www.ducktapeclub.com/

DUCK BRAND DUCT TAPE "STUCK AT PROM" SCHOLARSHIP CONTEST
• *See page 625*

HERB KOHL EDUCATIONAL FOUNDATION INC.

http://www.kohleducation.org/

HERB KOHL EXCELLENCE SCHOLARSHIP PROGRAM
• *See page 625*

HISPANIC METROPOLITAN CHAMBER SCHOLARSHIPS

http://www.hmccoregon.com/

HISPANIC METROPOLITAN CHAMBER SCHOLARSHIPS
• *See page 626*

HOFOSS DEVALL

https://www.hdinjurylaw.com/

HOFFOSS DEVALL LOUISIANA SAFE DRIVER SCHOLARSHIP
• *See page 626*

HOOVER PRESIDENTIAL FOUNDATION

http://www.hooverpresidentialfoundation.org/travel-grant.php

HERBERT HOOVER UNCOMMON STUDENT AWARD
• *See page 627*

HOUSTON COMMUNITY SERVICES

AZTECA SCHOLARSHIP
• *See page 628*

HUMANE SOCIETY OF THE UNITED STATES

http://www.hsus.org/

SHAW-WORTH MEMORIAL SCHOLARSHIP

Scholarship for a New England high school senior, who has made a meaningful contribution to animal protection over a significant amount of time. Passive liking of animals or the desire to enter an animal care field does not justify the award.

Award: Scholarship for use in freshman year; not renewable. *Number:* 1. *Amount:* $2000.

Eligibility Requirements: Applicant must be high school student; planning to enroll or expecting to enroll full-time at a four-year institution or university and resident of Connecticut, Maine, Massachusetts, New Hampshire, Rhode Island, Vermont. Available to U.S. citizens.

Application Requirements: Essay, recommendations or references. *Deadline:* March 17.

Contact: Administrator
Humane Society of the United States
PO Box 619
Jacksonville, VT 05342-0619
Phone: 802-368-2790
Fax: 802-368-2756

IDAHO STATE BOARD OF EDUCATION

http://www.boardofed.idaho.gov/

IDAHO GOVERNOR'S CUP SCHOLARSHIP
• *See page 628*

IDAHO OPPORTUNITY SCHOLARSHIP

The Idaho Opportunity Scholarship is an award open to Idaho citizens who have graduated from Idaho high schools. The application is open to any high school or college students who attended an Idaho high school, are Idaho residents, and are attending or who are planning on attending an eligible Idaho college or university. Students must be earning their first undergraduate degree. The required GPA is a 3.0 and applicants must show need by completing the FAFSA by March 1 each year. The award is renewable for a total of 4 years.

Award: Scholarship for use in freshman, sophomore, junior, or senior years; renewable. *Number:* 700–2000. *Amount:* $1–$3500.

Eligibility Requirements: Applicant must be enrolled or expecting to enroll full-time at a two-year or four-year or technical institution or university; resident of Idaho and studying in Idaho. Applicant must have 3.0 GPA or higher. Available to U.S. citizens.

Application Requirements: Application form, financial need analysis. *Deadline:* March 1.

Contact: Joy Miller, Scholarships Program Manager
Idaho State Board of Education
650 W. State St., #307
Boise, ID 83720
Phone: 208-332 Ext. 1595
E-mail: joy.miller@osbe.idaho.gov

ILLINOIS AMVETS

http://www.ilamvets.org/

ILLINOIS AMVETS JUNIOR ROTC SCHOLARSHIPS

One year, $1000 scholarship (non-renewal) for high school seniors who have taken the ACT or SAT tests and are children or grandchildren of veterans or active-duty. Student must be enrolled in JROTC program.

Award: Scholarship for use in freshman year; not renewable. *Amount:* $1000.

Eligibility Requirements: Applicant must be high school student; planning to enroll or expecting to enroll full-time at a two-year or four-year or technical institution or university and resident of Illinois. Available to U.S. citizens.

Application Requirements: Application form, essay, financial need analysis. *Deadline:* March 1.

Contact: Ashley Murphy, Communications Director
Illinois AMVETS
PO Box 372
Groveland, IL 61535
Phone: 800-638-8387
E-mail: ashley@ilamvets.org

ILLINOIS AMVETS LADIES AUXILIARY MEMORIAL SCHOLARSHIP

Applicant must be an Illinois student and a child of a veteran who served after September 15, 1940 and was honorably discharged or is presently serving in the military. Must submit SAT or ACT scores, high school rank and grades.

Award: Scholarship for use in freshman year; not renewable.

Eligibility Requirements: Applicant must be high school student; planning to enroll or expecting to enroll full-time at a two-year or four-year or technical institution or university and resident of Illinois. Available to U.S. citizens.

Application Requirements: Application form, financial need analysis. *Deadline:* March 1.

Contact: Ashley Murphy, Communications Director
Illinois AMVETS
PO Box 372
Groveland, IL 61535
Phone: 800-638-8387
E-mail: ashley@ilamvets.org

ILLINOIS AMVETS LADIES AUXILIARY WORCHID SCHOLARSHIPS
• *See page 711*

ILLINOIS AMVETS SERVICE FOUNDATION SCHOLARSHIP

Applicant must be an Illinois high school senior and be the child or grandchild of veteran or active duty.

Award: Scholarship for use in freshman year; not renewable. *Amount:* $1000.

Eligibility Requirements: Applicant must be high school student; planning to enroll or expecting to enroll full-time at a two-year or four-year or technical institution or university; resident of Illinois and studying in Illinois. Available to U.S. citizens.

Application Requirements: Application form, community service, essay, financial need analysis. *Deadline:* March 1.

Contact: Ashley Murphy, Communications Director
Illinois AMVETS
PO Box 372
Groveland, IL 61535
Phone: 800-638-8387
E-mail: ashley@ilamvets.org

ILLINOIS AMVETS TRADE SCHOOL SCHOLARSHIP

Applicant must be an Illinois high school senior who has been accepted in a pre-approved trade school program. Must be a child or grandchild of a veteran or active-duty.

Award: Scholarship for use in freshman year; not renewable. *Amount:* $1000.

Eligibility Requirements: Applicant must be high school student; planning to enroll or expecting to enroll full-time at a technical institution and resident of Illinois. Available to U.S. citizens.

Application Requirements: Application form, essay. *Deadline:* March 1.

Contact: Ashley Murphy, Communications Director
Illinois AMVETS
PO Box 372
Groveland, IL 61535
Phone: 800-638-8387
E-mail: ashley@ilamvets.org

ILLINOIS COUNCIL OF THE BLIND

http://www.icbonline.org/

FLOYD R. CARGILL SCHOLARSHIP
• *See page 688*

ILLINOIS COUNTIES ASSOCIATION

http://www.illinoiscountiesassociation.org/

ILLINOIS COUNTIES ASSOCIATION SCHOLARSHIP

Preferential treatment will be given to: 1) individuals demonstrating a dedicated pursuit toward a career in government, public service or public administration as evidenced by involvement in a course of study, work and volunteer service or internships in public, government, community and/or legislative environments; and, 2) students with immediate family members employed by a county participating in the Nationwide Retirement Solutions 457 program.

Award: Scholarship for use in freshman year; not renewable. *Number:* 15. *Amount:* $3000.

Eligibility Requirements: Applicant must be high school student; planning to enroll or expecting to enroll full-time at a four-year institution or university and resident of Illinois. Applicant must have 3.0 GPA or higher. Available to U.S. citizens.

Application Requirements: Application form, essay, financial need analysis. *Deadline:* April 28.

Contact: Ariana Antonacci, Scholarship Coordinator
Illinois Counties Association
100 East Washington
Springfield, IL 62701
Phone: 217-528-3434
E-mail: ariana@frontlineco.com

ILLINOIS STUDENT ASSISTANCE COMMISSION (ISAC)

http://www.isac.org/

GRANT PROGRAM FOR DEPENDENTS OF POLICE, FIRE, OR CORRECTIONAL OFFICERS

Awards available to Illinois residents who are dependents of police, fire, and correctional officers killed or disabled in line of duty. Provides for tuition and fees at approved Illinois institutions. Number of grants and individual dollar amount awarded vary.

Award: Grant for use in freshman, sophomore, junior, senior, graduate, or postgraduate years; renewable.

Eligibility Requirements: Applicant must be enrolled or expecting to enroll full- or part-time at a two-year or four-year or technical institution or university; resident of Illinois and studying in Illinois. Available to U.S. citizens.

Application Requirements: Application form. *Deadline:* October 1.

Contact: ISAC Call Center Representative
Illinois Student Assistance Commission (ISAC)
1755 Lake Cook Road
Deerfield, IL 60015-5209
Phone: 800-899-4722
E-mail: isac.studentservices@illinois.gov

HIGHER EDUCATION LICENSE PLATE PROGRAM-HELP

Grants for students who attend Illinois colleges for which the special collegiate license plates are available. The Illinois Secretary of State issues the license plates, and part of the proceeds are used for grants for undergraduate students attending these colleges, to pay tuition and mandatory fees.

Award: Grant for use in freshman, sophomore, junior, or senior years; not renewable.

Eligibility Requirements: Applicant must be enrolled or expecting to enroll full- or part-time at a two-year or four-year institution or university; resident of Illinois and studying in Illinois. Available to U.S. citizens.

Application Requirements: Application form, financial need analysis. *Deadline:* continuous.

Contact: ISAC Call Center Representative
Illinois Student Assistance Commission (ISAC)
1755 Lake Cook Road
Deerfield, IL 60015-5209
Phone: 800-899-4722
E-mail: isac.studentservices@illinois.gov

ILLINOIS MONETARY AWARD PROGRAM

Awards to Illinois residents enrolled in a minimum of 3 hours per term in a degree program at an approved Illinois institution. See website for complete list of participating schools. Must demonstrate financial need, based on the information provided on the Free Application for Federal Student Aid. Number of grants and the individual dollar amount awarded vary. Deadline: As soon as possible after October 1 of the year before the student will enter college.

Award: Grant for use in freshman, sophomore, junior, or senior years; renewable. *Amount:* $2850.

Eligibility Requirements: Applicant must be enrolled or expecting to enroll full- or part-time at a two-year or four-year or technical institution or university; resident of Illinois and studying in Illinois. Available to U.S. citizens.

Application Requirements: Application form, financial need analysis. *Deadline:* June 30.

Contact: ISAC Call Center Representative
Illinois Student Assistance Commission (ISAC)
1755 Lake Cook Road
Deerfield, IL 60015-5209
Phone: 800-899-4722
E-mail: isac.studentservices@illinois.gov

ILLINOIS NATIONAL GUARD GRANT PROGRAM
• *See page 698*

ILLINOIS VETERAN GRANT PROGRAM-IVG
• *See page 711*

INDIANA COMMISSION FOR HIGHER EDUCATION

http://www.in.gov/che

FRANK O'BANNON GRANT PROGRAM

A need-based, tuition-restricted program for students attending Indiana public, private, or proprietary institutions seeking a first undergraduate degree. Students (and parents of dependent students) who are U.S. citizens and Indiana residents must file the FAFSA yearly by the March 10 deadline.

Award: Grant for use in freshman, sophomore, junior, or senior years; not renewable. *Number:* 48,408–70,239. *Amount:* $200–$10,992.

Eligibility Requirements: Applicant must be enrolled or expecting to enroll full-time at a two-year or four-year or technical institution or university; resident of Indiana and studying in Indiana. Available to U.S. citizens.

Application Requirements: Application form, FAFSA, financial need analysis. *Deadline:* March 10.

Contact: Grants Counselor
Indiana Commission for Higher Education
150 West Market Street, Suite 500
Indianapolis, IN 46204-2805
Phone: 317-232-2350
Fax: 317-232-3260
E-mail: grants@ssaci.state.in.us

INDIANA NATIONAL GUARD SUPPLEMENTAL GRANT
• *See page 698*

PART-TIME GRANT PROGRAM

Program is designed to encourage part-time undergraduates to start and complete their Associate or Baccalaureate degrees or certificates by subsidizing part-time tuition costs. It is a term-based award that is based on need. State residency requirements must be met and a FAFSA must be filed. Eligibility is determined at the institutional level subject to approval by SSACI.

Award: Grant for use in freshman, sophomore, junior, or senior years; not renewable. *Number:* 4680–6700. *Amount:* $20–$4000.

Eligibility Requirements: Applicant must be enrolled or expecting to enroll part-time at a two-year or four-year or technical institution or university; resident of Indiana and studying in Indiana. Available to U.S. citizens.

Application Requirements: Application form, financial need analysis. *Deadline:* continuous.

Contact: Grants Counselor
Indiana Commission for Higher Education
150 West Market Street, Suite 500
Indianapolis, IN 46204-2805
Phone: 317-232-2350
Fax: 317-232-3260
E-mail: grants@ssaci.state.in.us

INDIANA DEPARTMENT OF VETERANS AFFAIRS

http://www.in.gov/dva

CHILD OF DISABLED VETERAN GRANT OR PURPLE HEART RECIPIENT GRANT
• *See page 711*

DEPARTMENT OF VETERANS AFFAIRS FREE TUITION FOR CHILDREN OF POW/MIA'S IN VIETNAM
• *See page 711*

NATIONAL GUARD SCHOLARSHIP EXTENSION PROGRAM
• *See page 698*

NATIONAL GUARD TUITION SUPPLEMENT PROGRAM
• *See page 699*

INDIANA LIBRARY FEDERATION

http://www.ilfonline.org/

SUE MARSH WELLER SCHOLARSHIP FUND
• *See page 629*

INDIAN AMERICAN CULTURAL ASSOCIATION

http://www.iasf.org/

INDIAN AMERICAN SCHOLARSHIP FUND
• *See page 740*

INTELLECTUAL PROPERTY OWNERS EDUCATION FOUNDATION

https://www.ipoef.org/

IP VIDEO CONTEST

Create a 60 second video about the importance of IP. There are cash prizes and scholarships up to $7,500 awarded to three age categories: 13-15 years old, 16-18 years old, 19+ years old. In addition, there is a category to enter for charity. The winner will receive a $5,000 cash donation for the charity of his/her choice. All finalists qualify for a cash prize for the most likes on Facebook.

Award: Prize for use in freshman, sophomore, junior, senior, graduate, or postgraduate years; not renewable. *Number:* 5. *Amount:* $2000–$7500.

Eligibility Requirements: Applicant must be enrolled or expecting to enroll full- or part-time at a two-year or four-year or technical institution or university and resident of Alabama, Alaska, Arizona, Arkansas, California, Colorado, Connecticut, Delaware, District of Columbia, Florida, Georgia, Hawaii, Idaho, Illinois, Indiana, Iowa, Kansas, Kentucky, Louisiana, Maine, Maryland, Massachusetts, Michigan, Minnesota, Mississippi, Missouri, Montana, Nebraska, Nevada, New Hampshire, New Jersey, New Mexico, New York, North Carolina, North Dakota, Ohio, Oklahoma, Oregon, Pennsylvania, Rhode Island, South Carolina, South Dakota, Tennessee, Texas, Utah, Vermont, Virginia, Washington, West Virginia, Wisconsin, Wyoming. Available to U.S. citizens.

Application Requirements: Application form, personal photograph. *Deadline:* July 1.

Contact: Kristen Garrett, Office and Project Manager
Intellectual Property Owners Education Foundation
1501 M Street, NW
Washington, DC 20005
Phone: 202-507-4500
E-mail: Foundation@ipo.org

INTER-COUNTY ENERGY

http://www.intercountyenergy.net/

INTER-COUNTY ENERGY SCHOLARSHIP

One $1,000 scholarship given to a high school senior in each of Inter-County Energy's six directorial districts: Boyle, Lincoln, Mercer, Garrard, Casey and Marion. Applicant's parent or legal guardian must be a member of Inter-County Energy with the primary residence being on the cooperative lines.

Award: Scholarship for use in freshman year; not renewable. *Number:* 6. *Amount:* $1000.

Eligibility Requirements: Applicant must be high school student; planning to enroll or expecting to enroll full-time at a four-year institution or university and resident of Kentucky. Available to U.S. citizens.

Application Requirements: Application form, autobiography, community service, financial need analysis. *Deadline:* March 20.

Contact: April Burgess, Member Services Advisor
Inter-County Energy
PO Box 87
Danville, KY 40423
Phone: 859-936-7822
Fax: 859-236-5012
E-mail: april@intercountyenergy.net

INTERNATIONAL UNION OF BRICKLAYERS AND ALLIED CRAFTWORKERS

http://www.bacweb.org/

CANADIAN BATES SCHOLARSHIP PROGRAM
• *See page 566*

U.S. BATES SCHOLARSHIP PROGRAM
• *See page 566*

IOWA COLLEGE STUDENT AID COMMISSION

http://www.iowacollegeaid.gov/

IOWA NATIONAL GUARD EDUCATION ASSISTANCE PROGRAM
• *See page 699*

IOWA TUITION GRANT PROGRAM

Program assists students who attend independent postsecondary institutions in Iowa. Iowa residents currently enrolled, or planning to enroll, for at least 3 semester hours at one of the eligible Iowa postsecondary institutions may apply. Awards currently range from $100 to $5650. Grants may not exceed the difference between independent college and university tuition fees and the average tuition fees at the three public Regent universities.

Award: Grant for use in freshman, sophomore, junior, or senior years; not renewable. *Number:* 16,500–19,000. *Amount:* $100–$5650.

Eligibility Requirements: Applicant must be enrolled or expecting to enroll full- or part-time at a two-year or four-year institution or university; resident of Iowa and studying in Iowa. Available to U.S. citizens.

Application Requirements: Financial need analysis. *Deadline:* July 1.

Contact: Tristan Lynn, Executive Officer 1
Iowa College Student Aid Commission
430 E Grand Avenue, FL 3
Des Moines, IA 50309-1920
Phone: 515-725-3409
E-mail: tristan.lynn@iowa.gov

IOWA VOCATIONAL-TECHNICAL TUITION GRANT PROGRAM

Program provides need-based financial assistance to Iowa residents enrolled in career education (vocational-technical), and career option programs at Iowa area community colleges. Grants range from $150 to $1200, depending on the length of the program, financial need, and available funds.

Award: Grant for use in freshman or sophomore years; not renewable. *Number:* 2500–3500. *Amount:* $150–$1200.

Eligibility Requirements: Applicant must be enrolled or expecting to enroll full- or part-time at a two-year or technical institution; resident of Iowa and studying in Iowa. Available to U.S. citizens.

Application Requirements: Financial need analysis. *Deadline:* July 1.

Contact: Tristan Lynn, Executive Officer 1
Iowa College Student Aid Commission
430 E Grand Avenue, FL 3
Des Moines, IA 50309-1920
Phone: 515-725-3409
E-mail: tristan.lynn@iowa.gov

IOWA STUDENT LOAN

http://www.IowaStudentLoan.org/

COME 2 IOWA (C2IA) SENIOR SCHOLARSHIP
• *See page 631*

IOWA FINANCIAL KNOW-HOW CHALLENGE: SENIOR SCHOLARSHIP
• *See page 631*

ITALIAN-AMERICAN CHAMBER OF COMMERCE OF CHICAGO

http://www.iacc-chicago.com/

ITALIAN-AMERICAN CHAMBER OF COMMERCE OF CHICAGO SCHOLARSHIP
• *See page 741*

ITALIAN CATHOLIC FEDERATION

http://www.icf.org/

ITALIAN CATHOLIC FEDERATION FIRST YEAR SCHOLARSHIP
• *See page 566*

JACKSON ENERGY COOPERATIVE

http://www.jacksonenergy.com/

JACKSON ENERGY SCHOLARSHIP ESSAY CONTEST

Applicant must be a high school senior. Scholarships are awarded to winners in an essay contest. Applicants, their parents, or legal guardians must be members of Jackson Energy Cooperative; may not be a spouse or an employee or director of Jackson Energy. Scholarships are paid directly to winner's college, university, or institution of higher education.

Award: Scholarship for use in freshman, sophomore, junior, or senior years; not renewable. *Number:* 8. *Amount:* $2000.

Eligibility Requirements: Applicant must be high school student; planning to enroll or expecting to enroll full-time at a two-year or four-year or technical institution or university and resident of Kentucky. Available to U.S. citizens.

Application Requirements: Application form, essay. *Deadline:* November 25.

Contact: Karen Combs, Kentucky
Jackson Energy Cooperative
115 Jackson Energy Lane
McKee, KY 40447
Phone: 606-364-9223
E-mail: karencombs@jacksonenergy.com

JAMES F. BYRNES FOUNDATION

http://www.byrnesscholars.org/

JAMES F. BYRNES SCHOLARSHIP
• *See page 631*

J. CRAIG AND PAGE T. SMITH SCHOLARSHIP FOUNDATION

http://www.jcraigsmithfoundation.org/

FIRST IN FAMILY SCHOLARSHIP

Scholarships are available for graduating Alabama high school seniors. Must be planning to enroll in an Alabama institution in fall and pursue a four-year degree. Students who apply must want to give back to their community by volunteer and civic work. Special consideration will be given to applicants who would be the first in either their mother's or father's family (or both) to attend college.

Award: Scholarship for use in freshman year; renewable. *Number:* 10. *Amount:* $12,500–$15,000.

Eligibility Requirements: Applicant must be high school student; planning to enroll or expecting to enroll full-time at a four-year institution or university; resident of Alabama and studying in Alabama. Applicant must have 2.5 GPA or higher. Available to U.S. citizens.

Application Requirements: Application form, community service, essay, financial need analysis, recommendations or references, test scores, transcript. *Deadline:* January 15.

Contact: Ahrian Tyler, Administrator/Chairman of the Board
 Phone: 205-250-6669
 Fax: 205-328-7234
 E-mail: ahrian@jcraigsmithfoundation.org

JEWISH VOCATIONAL SERVICE LOS ANGELES

http://www.jvsla.org/

JVS SCHOLARSHIP PROGRAM
• *See page 741*

J. WOOD PLATT CADDIE SCHOLARSHIP TRUST

http://www.plattcaddiescholarship.org/

J. WOOD PLATT CADDIE SCHOLARSHIP TRUST
The Platt Caddie Scholarship is available to individuals who caddie at Golf Association of Philadelphia Member Clubs and is solely based on financial need, as a result of submitting the FAFSA application and other financial documents. This is not an athletic or golf scholarship.

Award: Scholarship for use in freshman, sophomore, junior, senior, or graduate years; renewable. *Amount:* $1000–$10,000.

Eligibility Requirements: Applicant must be enrolled or expecting to enroll full-time at a two-year or four-year or technical institution or university and resident of Delaware, New Jersey, Pennsylvania. Available to U.S. and non-U.S. citizens.

Application Requirements: Application form, essay, financial need analysis, interview. *Deadline:* November 30.

Contact: Mr. Bradley Kane, Director, Platt Caddie Scholarship
 J. Wood Platt Caddie Scholarship Trust
 1974 Sproul Road
 Suite 400
 Broomall, PA 19008
 Phone: 610-687-2340 Ext. 21
 Fax: 610-687-2082
 E-mail: bkane@gapgolf.org

KANSAS BOARD OF REGENTS

http://www.kansasregents.org/

KANSAS ETHNIC MINORITY SCHOLARSHIP
• *See page 742*

KAUFMAN & STIGGER, PLLC

http://www.getthetiger.com/

THE ALBERTA C. KAUFMAN SCHOLARSHIP
• *See page 633*

KENTUCKY ASSOCIATION OF ELECTRIC COOPERATIVES, INC.

http://www.kaec.com/

WOMEN IN RURAL ELECTRIFICATION (WIRE) SCHOLARSHIPS
Scholarship available to Kentucky students who are juniors or seniors in a Kentucky college or university and have 60 credit hours by the fall semester. Immediate family of student must be served by one of the state's 24 rural electric distribution cooperatives. Awards based on academic achievement, extracurricular activities, career goals, recommendations.

Award: Scholarship for use in junior, senior, graduate, or postgraduate years; not renewable. *Number:* 3. *Amount:* $1000.

Eligibility Requirements: Applicant must be enrolled or expecting to enroll full-time at a two-year or four-year or technical institution or university; resident of Kentucky and studying in Kentucky. Available to U.S. citizens.

Application Requirements: Application form. *Deadline:* June 8.

Contact: Mary Beth Dennis, Director of Events & Youth Programs
 Kentucky Association of Electric Cooperatives, Inc.
 PO Box 32170
 Louisville, KY 40232
 Phone: 502-815-6302
 E-mail: mbdennis@kaec.org

KENTUCKY DEPARTMENT OF VETERANS AFFAIRS

http://www.veterans.ky.gov/

DEPARTMENT OF VETERANS AFFAIRS TUITION WAIVER-KY KRS 164-507
Scholarship available to college students who are residents of Kentucky under the age of 26.

Award: Scholarship for use in freshman, sophomore, junior, or senior years; not renewable. *Number:* 400.

Eligibility Requirements: Applicant must be enrolled or expecting to enroll full- or part-time at a two-year or four-year institution or university and resident of Kentucky. Available to U.S. citizens.

Application Requirements: Application form. *Deadline:* varies.

Contact: Barbara Sipek, Tuition Waiver Coordinator
 Phone: 502-595-4447
 E-mail: barbaraa.sipek@ky.gov

KENTUCKY HIGHER EDUCATION ASSISTANCE AUTHORITY (KHEAA)

http://www.kheaa.com/

COLLEGE ACCESS PROGRAM (CAP) GRANT
• *See page 743*

EARLY CHILDHOOD DEVELOPMENT SCHOLARSHIP
Awards scholarship with conditional service commitment for part-time students currently employed by participating ECD facility or providing training in ECD for an approved organization. For more information, visit website http://www.kheaa.com.

Award: Scholarship for use in freshman, sophomore, junior, or senior years; not renewable. *Number:* 500–1100. *Amount:* $100–$1800.

Eligibility Requirements: Applicant must be enrolled or expecting to enroll part-time at a two-year or four-year institution or university; resident of Kentucky and studying in Kentucky. Available to U.S. citizens.

Application Requirements: Application form. *Deadline:* continuous.

Contact: Danny Prather, Program Coordinator
 Kentucky Higher Education Assistance Authority (KHEAA)
 PO Box 798
 Frankfort, KY 40602-0798
 Phone: 800-928-8926 Ext. 67399
 E-mail: danprather@kheaa.com

KENTUCKY EDUCATIONAL EXCELLENCE SCHOLARSHIP (KEES)
Annual award based on yearly high school GPA and highest ACT or SAT score received by high school graduation. Awards are renewable, if required cumulative GPA is maintained at a Kentucky postsecondary school. Must be a Kentucky resident, and a graduate of a Kentucky high school. Low-income students who qualify for the free/reduced lunch program at least one year of high school may receive supplemental awards for passing scores on Advanced Placement (AP) or International Baccalaureate (IB) exams.

Award: Scholarship for use in freshman, sophomore, junior, or senior years; renewable. *Number:* 70,500. *Amount:* $125–$2500.

Eligibility Requirements: Applicant must be enrolled or expecting to enroll full- or part-time at a two-year or four-year or technical institution or university; resident of Kentucky and studying in British Columbia. Available to U.S. citizens.

Application Requirements: *Deadline:* continuous.

Contact: Becky Gilpatrick, Director of Student Aid Services
Kentucky Higher Education Assistance Authority (KHEAA)
PO Box 798
Frankfort, KY 40602
Phone: 800-928-8926 Ext. 67394
E-mail: rgilpatrick@kheaa.com

KENTUCKY NATIONAL GUARD TUITION AWARD
• *See page 699*

KENTUCKY TUITION GRANT (KTG)
Grants available to Kentucky residents who are full-time undergraduates at an independent college within the state. Based on financial need. Must submit FAFSA.

Award: Grant for use in freshman, sophomore, junior, or senior years; not renewable. *Number:* 10,000–12,500. *Amount:* $200–$2920.

Eligibility Requirements: Applicant must be enrolled or expecting to enroll full-time at a two-year or four-year institution or university; resident of Kentucky and studying in Kentucky. Available to U.S. citizens.

Application Requirements: Application form. *Deadline:* continuous.

Contact: Sheila Roe, Grant Program Coordinator
Kentucky Higher Education Assistance Authority (KHEAA)
PO Box 798
Frankfort, KY 40602-0798
Phone: 800-928-8926 Ext. 67393
E-mail: sroe@kheaa.com

KOSCIUSZKO FOUNDATION
http://www.thekf.org

MASSACHUSETTS FEDERATION OF POLISH WOMEN'S CLUBS SCHOLARSHIPS
• *See page 744*

POLISH AMERICAN CLUB OF NORTH JERSEY SCHOLARSHIPS
• *See page 744*

POLISH NATIONAL ALLIANCE OF BROOKLYN USA INC. SCHOLARSHIPS
• *See page 744*

LANDSCAPE ARCHITECTURE FOUNDATION
http://www.lafoundation.org

HAWAII CHAPTER/DAVID T. WOOLSEY SCHOLARSHIP
• *See page 636*

LATIN AMERICAN EDUCATIONAL FOUNDATION
http://www.laef.org/

LATIN AMERICAN EDUCATIONAL FOUNDATION SCHOLARSHIPS
• *See page 636*

LEE-JACKSON EDUCATIONAL FOUNDATION
http://www.lee-jackson.org/

LEE-JACKSON EDUCATIONAL FOUNDATION SCHOLARSHIP COMPETITION
Essay contest for junior and senior Virginia high school students. Must demonstrate appreciation for the exemplary character and soldierly virtues of Generals Robert E. Lee and Thomas J. "Stonewall" Jackson. Three one-time awards of $1000 in each of Virginia's eight regions. A bonus scholarship of $1000 will be awarded to the author of the best essay in each of the eight regions. An additional award of $8000 will go to the essay judged the best in the state.

Award: Scholarship for use in freshman, sophomore, junior, or senior years; not renewable. *Number:* 27. *Amount:* $1000–$10,000.

Eligibility Requirements: Applicant must be high school student; planning to enroll or expecting to enroll full-time at a four-year institution or university; resident of Virginia and must have an interest in writing. Available to U.S. citizens.

Application Requirements: Application form, entry in a contest, essay, transcript. *Deadline:* December 21.

Contact: Stephanie Leech, Administrator
Lee-Jackson Educational Foundation
PO Box 8121
Charlottesville, VA 22906
Phone: 434-977-1861
E-mail: salp_leech@yahoo.com

LEP FOUNDATION FOR YOUTH EDUCATION
http://www.lepfoundation.org/applications

JOHN LEPPING MEMORIAL SCHOLARSHIP
• *See page 640*

LEVY LAW OFFICES
https://levylawoffices.com/

LEVY LAW OFFICES CINCINNATI SAFE DRIVER SCHOLARSHIP
• *See page 640*

LIBERTY GRAPHICS INC.
http://www.lgtees.com

ANNUAL LIBERTY GRAPHICS ART CONTEST
One-time scholarship to the successful student who submits the winning artwork depicting appreciation of the natural environment of Maine. Applicants must be residents of Maine and be a high school seniors. Original works in traditional flat media are the required format. Photography, sculpture and computer-generated work cannot be considered. Multiple submissions are allowed.

Award: Prize for use in freshman year; not renewable. *Number:* 1. *Amount:* $1000.

Eligibility Requirements: Applicant must be high school student; planning to enroll or expecting to enroll full- or part-time at a two-year or four-year or technical institution or university; resident of Maine and must have an interest in art. Available to U.S. citizens.

Application Requirements: Application form. *Deadline:* March 12.

Contact: Mr. Jay Sproul, Scholarship Coordinator
Liberty Graphics Inc.
PO Box 5
44 Main Street
Liberty, ME 04949
Phone: 207-589-4596
E-mail: jay@lgtees.com

LOGAN TELEPHONE CO-OP

LOGAN TELEPHONE COOPERATIVE SCHOLARSHIP
Students will receive half of the money their first semester and must maintain a 2.5 GPA in order to receive the second half of their money.

Award: Scholarship for use in freshman year; not renewable. *Number:* 3. *Amount:* $2000.

Eligibility Requirements: Applicant must be high school student; planning to enroll or expecting to enroll full-time at a two-year or four-year or technical institution or university and resident of Kentucky. Available to U.S. citizens.

Application Requirements: Application form, personal photograph. *Deadline:* April 20.

Contact: Kristen Herndon, Marketing/PR Manager
    Phone: 270-5424121 Ext. 229
    E-mail: kherndon@loganphone.com

LOS ALAMOS NATIONAL LABORATORY FOUNDATION

http://www.lanlfoundation.org/

LOS ALAMOS EMPLOYEES' SCHOLARSHIP

Scholarship supports students in Northern New Mexico who are pursuing undergraduate degrees in fields that will serve the region. Financial need, diversity, and regional representation are integral components of the selections process. Applicant should be a permanent resident of Northern New Mexico with at least a 3.25 cumulative GPA and 19 ACT or 930 SAT score.

Award: Scholarship for use in freshman, sophomore, junior, or senior years; renewable. *Number:* 100. *Amount:* $1000–$20,000.

Eligibility Requirements: Applicant must be enrolled or expecting to enroll full- or part-time at a two-year or four-year institution or university and resident of New Mexico. Available to U.S. and non-U.S. citizens.

Application Requirements: Application form, essay, personal photograph. *Deadline:* January 15.

Contact: John McDermon, Scholarship Program Manager
    Phone: 505-753-8890 Ext. 15
    Fax: 505-753-8915
    E-mail: scholarships@lanlfoundation.org

LOUISIANA DEPARTMENT OF VETERAN AFFAIRS

http://www.vetaffairs.la.gov

LOUISIANA DEPARTMENT OF VETERANS AFFAIRS STATE EDUCATIONAL AID PROGRAM

• *See page 712*

LOUISIANA NATIONAL GUARD, JOINT TASK FORCE LA

http://geauxguard.com/organization/joint-force-headquarters-jfhq-la/

LOUISIANA NATIONAL GUARD STATE TUITION EXEMPTION PROGRAM

• *See page 699*

LOUISIANA OFFICE OF STUDENT FINANCIAL ASSISTANCE

http://www.osfa.la.gov/

TAYLOR OPPORTUNITY PROGRAM FOR STUDENTS HONORS LEVEL

Program awards 8 semesters or 12 terms of tuition to any Louisiana State postsecondary institution plus $400 stipend per semester. Program awards 8 semesters or 12 terms of an amount equal to the weighted average public tuition to students attending a LAICU (Louisiana Association of Independent Colleges and Universities) institution plus $400 stipend per semester. Program awards 8 semesters or 12 terms of an amount equal to the weighted average public tuition to two out-of-state Institutions for Hearing Impaired Students: Gallaudet University and Rochester Institute of Technology plus $400 stipend per semester. Program awards $1744 per year to Approved Proprietary and Cosmetology schools plus a stipend of $800 per year. When you submit the FAFSA, you have automatically applied for all four levels of TOPS, for Federal Pell Grants and Go Grants and for Federal Student Loans. Please do not send separate letters of application to the TOPS office.

Award: Scholarship for use in freshman, sophomore, junior, or senior years; renewable. *Number:* 9661. *Amount:* $836–$6736.

Eligibility Requirements: Applicant must be enrolled or expecting to enroll full-time at a two-year or four-year or technical institution or university; resident of Louisiana and studying in Louisiana. Applicant must have 3.0 GPA or higher. Available to U.S. citizens.

Application Requirements: Application form, application form may be submitted online (http://www.osfa.la.gov), FAFSA, test scores, transcript. *Deadline:* July 1.

Contact: Public Information
    Louisiana Office of Student Financial Assistance
    PO Box 91202
    Baton Rouge, LA 70821-9202
    Phone: 800-259-5626 Ext. 1012
    Fax: 225-208-1496
    E-mail: custserv@osfa.la.gov

TAYLOR OPPORTUNITY PROGRAM FOR STUDENTS OPPORTUNITY LEVEL

Program awards 8 semesters or 12 terms of tuition to any Louisiana State postsecondary institution. Program awards 8 semesters or 12 terms of an amount equal to the weighted average public tuition to students attending a LAICU (Louisiana Association of Independent Colleges and Universities) institution. Program awards 8 semesters or 12 terms of an amount equal to the weighted average public tuition to two out-of-state Institutions for Hearing Impaired Students: Gallaudet University and Rochester Institute of Technology. Program awards $1744 per year to Approved Proprietary and Cosmetology schools. When you submit the FAFSA, you have automatically applied for all four levels of TOPS, and for Federal Pell Grants and Go Grants. Please do not send separate letters of application to the TOPS office.

Award: Scholarship for use in freshman, sophomore, junior, or senior years; renewable. *Number:* 24,633. *Amount:* $436–$5936.

Eligibility Requirements: Applicant must be enrolled or expecting to enroll full-time at a two-year or four-year or technical institution or university; resident of Louisiana and studying in Louisiana. Applicant must have 2.5 GPA or higher. Available to U.S. citizens.

Application Requirements: Application form, application form may be submitted online (http://www.osfa.la.gov), FAFSA, test scores, transcript. *Deadline:* July 1.

Contact: Public Information
    Louisiana Office of Student Financial Assistance
    PO Box 91202
    Baton Rouge, LA 70821-9202
    Phone: 800-259-5626 Ext. 1012
    Fax: 225-208-1496
    E-mail: custserv@osfa.la.gov

TAYLOR OPPORTUNITY PROGRAM FOR STUDENTS PERFORMANCE LEVEL

Program awards 8 semesters or 12 terms of tuition to any Louisiana State postsecondary institution plus $200 stipend per semester. Program awards 8 semesters or 12 terms of an amount equal to the weighted average public tuition to students attending a LAICU (Louisiana Association of Independent Colleges and Universities) institution plus $200 stipend per semester. Program awards 8 semesters or 12 terms of an amount equal to the weighted average public tuition to two out-of-state Institutions for Hearing Impaired Students: Gallaudet University and Rochester Institute of Technology plus $200 stipend per semester. Program awards $1744 plus $400 per year to Approved Proprietary and Cosmetology schools. When you submit the FAFSA, you have automatically applied for all four levels of TOPS, for Federal Pell Grants and Go Grants and for Federal Student Loans. Please do not send separate letters of application to the TOPS office.

Award: Scholarship for use in freshman, sophomore, junior, or senior years; renewable. *Number:* 11,928. *Amount:* $636–$6336.

Eligibility Requirements: Applicant must be enrolled or expecting to enroll full-time at a two-year or four-year or technical institution or university; resident of Louisiana and studying in Louisiana. Applicant must have 3.0 GPA or higher. Available to U.S. citizens.

Application Requirements: Application form, application form may be submitted online (http://www.osfa.la.gov), FAFSA, test scores, transcript. *Deadline:* July 1.

Contact: Public Information
    Louisiana Office of Student Financial Assistance
    PO Box 91202
    Baton Rouge, LA 70821-9202
    Phone: 800-259-5626 Ext. 1012
    Fax: 225-208-1496
    E-mail: custserv@osfa.la.gov

TAYLOR OPPORTUNITY PROGRAM FOR STUDENTS TECH LEVEL

Program awards an amount equal to tuition for up to 4 semesters and two summers of technical training at a Louisiana postsecondary institution that offers a vocational or technical education certificate or diploma program, or a non-academic degree program; or up to $1744 to an approved Proprietary or Cosmetology school. Must have completed the TOPS Opportunity core curriculum or the TOPS Tech core curriculum, must have achieved a 2.50 grade point average over the core curriculum only, and must have achieved an ACT score of 17 or an SAT score of 810. Program awards an amount equal to the weighted average public tuition for technical programs to students attending a LAICU private institution for technical training. When you submit the FAFSA, you have automatically applied for all four levels of TOPS, for Federal Pell Grants and Go Grants and Federal Student Loans. Please do not send separate letters of application to the TOPS office.

Award: Scholarship for use in freshman or sophomore years; renewable. *Number:* 1671. *Amount:* $436–$3985.

Eligibility Requirements: Applicant must be enrolled or expecting to enroll full-time at a technical institution; resident of Louisiana and studying in Louisiana. Applicant must have 2.5 GPA or higher. Available to U.S. citizens.

Application Requirements: Application form, application form may be submitted online (http://www.osfa.la.gov), FAFSA, test scores, transcript. *Deadline:* July 1.

Contact: Public Information
Louisiana Office of Student Financial Assistance
PO Box 91202
Baton Rouge, LA 70821-9202
Phone: 800-259-5626 Ext. 1012
Fax: 225-208-1496
E-mail: custserv@osfa.la.gov

MAINE COMMUNITY COLLEGE SYSTEM

http://www.mccs.me.edu/

EMBARK-SUPPORT FOR THE COLLEGE JOURNEY

Scholarship for high school students who in their junior year have not made plans for college but are academically capable of success in college. Recipients are selected by their school principal or Guidance Director. Students must be entering a Maine Community College. Refer to website http://www.mccs.me.edu/our-programs/programs-for-high-school-students/early-college/

Award: Scholarship for use in freshman or sophomore years; renewable. *Number:* 400–500. *Amount:* $2000.

Eligibility Requirements: Applicant must be high school student; planning to enroll or expecting to enroll full-time at a two-year institution; resident of Maine and studying in Maine. Available to U.S. citizens.

Application Requirements: Application form, financial need analysis. *Deadline:* April 15.

Contact: Mercedes Pour, Director of College Access
Maine Community College System
54 Lighthouse Circle
South Portland, ME 04106
Phone: 207-699-4897
E-mail: mpour@mccs.me.edu

MAINE COMMUNITY FOUNDATION, INC.

http://www.mainecf.org/

JOSEPH W. MAYO ALS SCHOLARSHIP FUND

Please go to the Maine Community Foundation, Inc. website for application requirements

Award: Scholarship for use in freshman, sophomore, junior, or senior years; not renewable.

Eligibility Requirements: Applicant must be enrolled or expecting to enroll full-time at a two-year or four-year institution or university and resident of Maine. Available to U.S. citizens.

Application Requirements: Application form.

Contact: Ms. Amy Pollien, Grants Administration
Phone: 207-667-9735 Ext. 1109
E-mail: apollien@mainecf.org

MAINE STATE SOCIETY FOUNDATION OF WASHINGTON, DC INC.

http://mainestatesociety.org/foundation/

MAINE STATE SOCIETY FOUNDATION SCHOLARSHIP

• *See page 641*

MAINE VETERANS SERVICES

http://www.maine.gov/dvem/bvs

VETERANS DEPENDENTS EDUCATIONAL BENEFITS-MAINE

• *See page 712*

MAKING THE TURN AGAINST PARKINSON'S

http://www.makingtheturngolf.com/3/scholarship-award.htm

MAKING THE TURN AGAINST PARKINSON'S SCHOLARSHIP

Making the Turn Against Parkinson's will award a $5,000 scholarship to the student demonstrating the most effort and creativity in achieving the Scholarship Committee's objectives of raising awareness and developing a greater understanding of what it means to live with Parkinson's disease. Additional honorable mention scholarships may be awarded at the discretion of the committee.

Award: Scholarship for use in freshman, sophomore, junior, senior, graduate, or postgraduate years; not renewable. *Number:* 1–4. *Amount:* $500–$5000.

Eligibility Requirements: Applicant must be enrolled or expecting to enroll full-time at a two-year or four-year institution or university and resident of Michigan. Available to U.S. citizens.

Application Requirements: Application form, driver's license. *Deadline:* March 1.

Contact: Mr. Todd Gardner, President
Williamston, MI 48895
E-mail: scholarship@makingtheturngolf.com

MANA DE SAN DIEGO

http://www.manasd.org/

MANA DE SAN DIEGO SYLVIA CHAVEZ MEMORIAL SCHOLARSHIP

• *See page 641*

MARYLAND STATE HIGHER EDUCATION COMMISSION

http://www.mhec.state.md.us/

DELEGATE SCHOLARSHIP PROGRAM-MARYLAND

Delegate scholarships help Maryland residents attending Maryland degree-granting institutions, certain career schools, or nursing diploma schools. May attend out-of-state institution if Maryland Higher Education Commission deems major to be unique and not offered at a Maryland institution. Free Application for Federal Student Aid may be required. Students interested in this program should apply by contacting their legislative district delegate.

Award: Scholarship for use in freshman, sophomore, junior, or senior years; not renewable. *Number:* up to 3500. *Amount:* $200–$8650.

Eligibility Requirements: Applicant must be enrolled or expecting to enroll full- or part-time at a two-year or four-year or technical institution or university; resident of Maryland and studying in Maryland. Available to U.S. citizens.

Application Requirements: Application form, FAFSA. *Deadline:* continuous.

Contact: Monica Wheatley, Office of Student Financial Assistance
Maryland State Higher Education Commission
839 Bestgate Road, Suite 400
Annapolis, MD 21401-3013
Phone: 800-974-1024
Fax: 410-260-3200
E-mail: osfamail@mhec.state.md.us

EDWARD T. CONROY MEMORIAL SCHOLARSHIP PROGRAM

• *See page 642*

HOWARD P. RAWLINGS EDUCATIONAL EXCELLENCE AWARDS EDUCATIONAL ASSISTANCE GRANT

Award for Maryland residents accepted or enrolled in a full-time undergraduate degree or certificate program at a Maryland institution or hospital nursing school. Must submit financial aid form by March 1. Must earn 2.0 GPA in college to maintain award.

Award: Grant for use in freshman, sophomore, junior, or senior years; renewable. *Number:* 15,000–30,000. *Amount:* $400–$2700.

Eligibility Requirements: Applicant must be enrolled or expecting to enroll full-time at a two-year or four-year institution or university; resident of Maryland and studying in Maryland. Available to U.S. citizens.

Application Requirements: Application form, financial need analysis. *Deadline:* March 1.

Contact: Office of Student Financial Assistance
Maryland State Higher Education Commission
839 Bestgate Road, Suite 400
Annapolis, MD 21401-3013
Phone: 800-974-1024
Fax: 410-260-3200
E-mail: osfamail@mhec.state.md.us

HOWARD P. RAWLINGS EDUCATIONAL EXCELLENCE AWARDS GUARANTEED ACCESS GRANT

Award for Maryland resident enrolling full-time in an undergraduate program at a Maryland institution. Must be under 21 at time of first award and begin college within one year of completing high school in Maryland with a minimum 2.5 GPA. Must have an annual family income less than 130 percent of the federal poverty level guideline.

Award: Grant for use in freshman, sophomore, junior, or senior years; renewable. *Number:* up to 1000. *Amount:* $400–$14,800.

Eligibility Requirements: Applicant must be enrolled or expecting to enroll full-time at a two-year or four-year institution or university; resident of Maryland and studying in Maryland. Applicant must have 3.5 GPA or higher. Available to U.S. citizens.

Application Requirements: Application form, financial need analysis, transcript. *Deadline:* March 1.

Contact: Theresa Lowe, Office of Student Financial Assistance
Maryland State Higher Education Commission
839 Bestgate Road, Suite 400
Annapolis, MD 21401-3013
Phone: 410-260-4555
Fax: 410-260-3200
E-mail: osfamail@mhec.state.md.us

J.F. TOLBERT MEMORIAL STUDENT GRANT PROGRAM

Awards of $500 granted to Maryland residents attending a private career school in Maryland. The scholarship deadline continues.

Award: Grant for use in freshman or sophomore years; not renewable. *Number:* 522. *Amount:* $500.

Eligibility Requirements: Applicant must be enrolled or expecting to enroll full-time at a technical institution; resident of Maryland and studying in Maryland. Available to U.S. citizens.

Application Requirements: Application form, financial need analysis. *Deadline:* continuous.

Contact: Glenda Hamlet, Office of Student Financial Assistance
Maryland State Higher Education Commission
839 Bestgate Road, Suite 400
Annapolis, MD 21401-3013
Phone: 800-974-1024
Fax: 410-260-3200
E-mail: osfamail@mhec.state.md.us

PART-TIME GRANT PROGRAM-MARYLAND

Funds provided to Maryland colleges and universities. Eligible students must be enrolled on a part-time basis (6 to 11 credits) in an undergraduate degree program. Must demonstrate financial need and also be Maryland resident. Contact financial aid office at institution for more information.

Award: Grant for use in freshman, sophomore, junior, or senior years; renewable. *Number:* 1800–9000. *Amount:* $200–$1500.

Eligibility Requirements: Applicant must be enrolled or expecting to enroll part-time at a two-year or four-year institution or university; resident of Maryland and studying in Maryland. Available to U.S. citizens.

Application Requirements: Application form, financial need analysis. *Deadline:* March 1.

Contact: Monica Wheatley, Program Manager
Maryland State Higher Education Commission
839 Bestgate Road, Suite 400
Annapolis, MD 21401
Phone: 410-260-4560
Fax: 410-260-3202
E-mail: mwheatle@mhec.state.md.us

SENATORIAL SCHOLARSHIPS-MARYLAND

Renewable award for Maryland residents attending a Maryland degree-granting institution, nursing diploma school, or certain private career schools. May be used out-of-state only if Maryland Higher Education Commission deems major to be unique and not offered at Maryland institution. The scholarship value is $400 to $7000.

Award: Scholarship for use in freshman, sophomore, junior, or senior years; renewable. *Number:* up to 7000. *Amount:* $400–$7000.

Eligibility Requirements: Applicant must be enrolled or expecting to enroll full- or part-time at a two-year or four-year or technical institution or university; resident of Maryland and studying in Maryland. Available to U.S. citizens.

Application Requirements: Application form, financial need analysis, test scores. *Deadline:* March 1.

Contact: Monica Wheatley, Office of Student Financial Assistance
Maryland State Higher Education Commission
839 Bestgate Road, Suite 400
Annapolis, MD 21401-3013
Phone: 800-974-1024
Fax: 410-260-3200
E-mail: osfamail@mhec.state.md.us

TUITION WAIVER FOR FOSTER CARE RECIPIENTS

Applicant must be a high school graduate or GED recipient and under the age of 21. Must either have resided in a foster care home in Maryland at the time of high school graduation or GED reception, or until 14th birthday, and been adopted after 14th birthday. Applicant, if status approved, will be exempt from paying tuition and mandatory fees at a public college in Maryland.

Award: Grant for use in freshman, sophomore, junior, senior, or graduate years; renewable.

Eligibility Requirements: Applicant must be enrolled or expecting to enroll full- or part-time at a two-year or four-year institution or university; resident of Maryland and studying in Maryland. Available to U.S. citizens.

Application Requirements: Application form, financial need analysis, must inquire at financial aid office of schools. *Deadline:* March 1.

Contact: Robert Parker, Director
Phone: 410-260-4558
E-mail: rparker@mhec.state.md.us

VETERANS OF THE AFGHANISTAN AND IRAQ CONFLICTS SCHOLARSHIP PROGRAM

• *See page 712*

WORKFORCE SHORTAGE STUDENT ASSISTANCE GRANT PROGRAM

Scholarship of $4000 available to students who will be required to major in specific areas and will be obligated to serve in the state of Maryland after completion of degree.

Award: Scholarship for use in freshman, sophomore, junior, or senior years; renewable. *Number:* 1300. *Amount:* $4000.

Eligibility Requirements: Applicant must be enrolled or expecting to enroll full- or part-time at a two-year or four-year institution or university; resident of Maryland and studying in Maryland. Available to U.S. citizens.

Application Requirements: Application form, certain majors require additional documentation, essay, financial need analysis, recommendations or references, resume, transcript. *Deadline:* July 1.

Contact: Maura Sappington, Program Manager
Maryland State Higher Education Commission
839 Bestgate Road, Suite 400
Annapolis, MD 21401-3013
Phone: 410-260-4569
Fax: 410-260-3203
E-mail: msapping@mhec.state.md.us

MASSACHUSETTS OFFICE OF STUDENT FINANCIAL ASSISTANCE

http://www.osfa.mass.edu/

AGNES M. LINDSAY SCHOLARSHIP
• *See page 642*

CHRISTIAN A. HERTER MEMORIAL SCHOLARSHIP
• *See page 642*

DSS ADOPTED CHILDREN TUITION WAIVER
• *See page 642*

JOHN AND ABIGAIL ADAMS SCHOLARSHIP
• *See page 642*

MASSACHUSETTS ASSISTANCE FOR STUDENT SUCCESS PROGRAM
• *See page 643*

MASSACHUSETTS CASH GRANT PROGRAM
• *See page 643*

MASSACHUSETTS GILBERT MATCHING STUDENT GRANT PROGRAM
• *See page 643*

MASSACHUSETTS PART-TIME GRANT PROGRAM
• *See page 643*

MASSACHUSETTS PUBLIC SERVICE GRANT PROGRAM
• *See page 643*

PAUL TSONGAS SCHOLARSHIP PROGRAM
• *See page 643*

MCCURRY FOUNDATION INC.

http://www.mccurryfoundation.org/

MCCURRY FOUNDATION SCHOLARSHIP
Scholarship open to all public high school seniors, with preference given to applicants from Clay, Duval, Nassau, and St. Johns Counties, Florida and from Glynn County, Georgia. Scholarship emphasizes leadership, work ethic, and academic excellence. A minimum GPA of 3.0 is required and family income cannot exceed a maximum of $75,000 (AGI).

Award: Scholarship for use in freshman, sophomore, junior, or senior years; renewable. *Number:* 1–10. *Amount:* $1000–$1500.

Eligibility Requirements: Applicant must be high school student; planning to enroll or expecting to enroll full-time at a two-year or four-year or technical institution or university; single; resident of Florida, Georgia and must have an interest in leadership. Applicant must have 3.0 GPA or higher. Available to U.S. citizens.

Application Requirements: Application form, essay, financial need analysis, interview. *Deadline:* February 15.

Contact: Leslie Fine, Scholarship Selection Committee
Phone: 904-910-4414
E-mail: info@mccurryfoundation.org

MES FOUNDATION

http://www.mesfoundation.org

RICHARD H. PIERCE MEMORIAL SCHOLARSHIP
• *See page 645*

THE MIAMI FOUNDATION

http://www.miamifoundation.org

ALAN R. EPSTEIN SCHOLARSHIP
Award available for a high school senior who is a Dade county resident. Must have a 3.0 GPA and attach a copy of acceptance letter to two- or four-year college or university. For additional information and application, visit website at http://www.dadecommunityfoundation.org.

Award: Scholarship for use in freshman year; not renewable.

Eligibility Requirements: Applicant must be high school student; planning to enroll or expecting to enroll full-time at a two-year or four-year institution or university and resident of Florida. Applicant must have 3.0 GPA or higher. Available to U.S. citizens.

Application Requirements: Acceptance letter, personal statement, application form, financial need analysis, recommendations or references, transcript. *Deadline:* April 10.

Contact: Lauren Mayfield, Programs Assistant
The Miami Foundation
40 NW 3rd Street
Miami, FL 33128
Phone: 305-371-2711
E-mail: lmayfield@miamifoundation.org

RODNEY THAXTON/MARTIN E. SEGAL SCHOLARSHIP
• *See page 748*

SIDNEY M. ARONOVITZ SCHOLARSHIP
• *See page 748*

MICHIGAN DEPARTMENT OF TREASURY - STUDENT FINANCIAL SERVICES BUREAU

http://www.michigan.gov/mistudentaid

CHILDREN OF VETERANS TUITION GRANT
The program is designed to provide undergraduate tuition assistance to certain children older than 16 and less than 26 years of age who have been Michigan residents for the 12 months prior to application. To be eligible, a student must be the natural or adopted child of a Michigan veteran. Stepchildren of the veteran are not eligible. The veteran must have been a legal resident of Michigan immediately before entering military service and must not have later resided outside of Michigan for more than two years; or the veteran must have established legal residency in Michigan after entering military service.

Award: Grant for use in freshman, sophomore, junior, or senior years; renewable.

Eligibility Requirements: Applicant must be age 16-26; enrolled or expecting to enroll full- or part-time at a four-year institution or university; resident of Michigan and studying in Michigan. Available to U.S. citizens.

Application Requirements: Application form.

Contact: Student Scholarships and Grants
Michigan Department of Treasury - Student Financial Services
Bureau
PO Box 30462
Lansing, MI 48909
Phone: 888-447-2687
E-mail: mistudentaid@michigan.gov

MICHIGAN COMPETITIVE SCHOLARSHIP

Renewable awards for Michigan resident to pursue undergraduate study at a Michigan institution. Awards limited to tuition. Must attain SAT score of at least 1200. Must maintain at least a 2.0 grade point average and meet the college's academic progress requirements. Must file Free Application for Federal Student Aid.

Award: Scholarship for use in freshman, sophomore, junior, or senior years; renewable.

Eligibility Requirements: Applicant must be enrolled or expecting to enroll full- or part-time at a two-year or four-year institution or university; resident of Michigan and studying in Michigan. Available to U.S. citizens.

Application Requirements: Application form, financial need analysis.

Contact: Student Scholarships and Grants
Michigan Department of Treasury - Student Financial Services
Bureau
PO Box 30462
Lansing, MI 48909
Phone: 888-447-2687
E-mail: mistudentaid@michigan.gov

MICHIGAN TUITION GRANT

Need-based program. Students must be Michigan residents and attend a Michigan private, nonprofit, degree-granting college. Must file the Free Application for Federal Student Aid and meet the college's academic progress requirements.

Award: Grant for use in freshman, sophomore, junior, or senior years; renewable.

Eligibility Requirements: Applicant must be enrolled or expecting to enroll full- or part-time at a four-year institution or university; resident of Michigan and studying in Michigan. Available to U.S. citizens.

Application Requirements: Application form, financial need analysis. *Deadline:* June 30.

Contact: Student Scholarships and Grants
Michigan Department of Treasury - Student Financial Services
Bureau
PO Box 30462
Lansing, MI 48909
Phone: 888-447-2687
E-mail: mistudentaid@michigan.gov

TUITION INCENTIVE PROGRAM

The Tuition Incentive Program (TIP) was established in 1987 under the Annual Higher Education Appropriations Act as an incentive program that encourages eligible students to complete high school by providing tuition assistance for the first two years of college and beyond. Students must be enrolled in courses leading to an associate degree or certificate. Certificate courses are defined as at least a one-year training program that leads to a certificate (or other recognized educational credential), which prepares students for gainful employment in a recognized occupation. Students must meet a Medicaid eligibility history requirement. Eligible students must apply prior to high school graduation (high school diploma or its recognized equivalent). The program targets students with financial need so students are encouraged to also complete the FAFSA. Funds are appropriated annually in the Higher Education Appropriations Act. This program is administered by the Student Scholarships and Grants Division. http://www.michigan.gov/mistudentaid/0,4636,7-128-60969_61016-274565—,00.html

Award: Grant for use in freshman, sophomore, junior, or senior years; renewable.

Eligibility Requirements: Applicant must be enrolled or expecting to enroll full- or part-time at a two-year or four-year institution or university; resident of Michigan and studying in Michigan. Available to U.S. citizens.

Application Requirements: Application form. *Deadline:* continuous.

Contact: Student Scholarships and Grants
Michigan Department of Treasury - Student Financial Services
Bureau
PO Box 30462
Lansing, MI 48909
Phone: 888-447-2687
E-mail: mistudentaid@michigan.gov

MINNESOTA AFL-CIO

http://www.mnaflcio.org/

MARTIN DUFFY ADULT LEARNER SCHOLARSHIP AWARD

• See page 568

MINNESOTA MASONIC CHARITIES

http://www.mnmasoniccharities.org

MINNESOTA MASONIC CHARITIES LEGACY SCHOLARSHIP

Legacy Scholarships are provided each year to students graduating from a Minnesota high school with a GPA of 3.6 to 3.89. Applicants must plan to enroll in a four-year college program.

Award: Scholarship for use in freshman, sophomore, junior, or senior years; renewable. *Number:* 10. *Amount:* $4000.

Eligibility Requirements: Applicant must be high school student; planning to enroll or expecting to enroll full-time at a four-year institution and resident of Minnesota. Applicant must have 3.5 GPA or higher. Available to U.S. citizens.

Application Requirements: Application form, essay. *Deadline:* February 15.

Contact: Ms. Deb Cutsinger, Scholarships Manager
Minnesota Masonic Charities
11501 Masonic Home Drive
Bloomington, MN 55437
Phone: 952-948-6206
E-mail: deb.cutsinger@mnmasonic.org

MINNESOTA MASONIC CHARITIES SIGNATURE SCHOLARSHIP

• See page 645

MINNESOTA MASONIC CHARITIES UNDERGRADUATE SCHOLARSHIP

• See page 646

MINNESOTA OFFICE OF HIGHER EDUCATION

http://www.ohe.state.mn.us

MINNESOTA GI BILL PROGRAM

The Minnesota GI Bill program provides postsecondary financial assistance to eligible Minnesota veterans and service members as well as eligible spouses and children of deceased or severely disabled eligible Minnesota veterans. Full-time undergraduate or graduate students may be eligible to receive up to $1,000 per semester or term and part-time students may be eligible to receive up to $500 per semester or term. Eligible students may receive up to $3,000 per award year and up to the lifetime maximum of $10,000.

Award: Grant for use in freshman, sophomore, junior, senior, graduate, or postgraduate years; not renewable. *Amount:* $50–$3000.

Eligibility Requirements: Applicant must be enrolled or expecting to enroll full- or part-time at a two-year or four-year or technical institution or university; resident of Minnesota and studying in Minnesota. Available to U.S. citizens.

Application Requirements: Application form. *Deadline:* continuous.

Contact: Meghan Flores, State Grant Manager
Phone: 651-355-0610
E-mail: meghan.flores@state.mn.us

MINNESOTA INDIAN SCHOLARSHIP
• *See page 748*

MINNESOTA STATE GRANT PROGRAM

Need-based grant program available for Minnesota residents attending Minnesota colleges. Student covers 50% of cost with remainder covered by Pell Grant, parent contribution and state grant. Students apply with FAFSA and colleges administer the program on campus.

Award: Grant for use in freshman, sophomore, junior, or senior years; not renewable. *Number:* 71,000–120,000. *Amount:* $100–$11,334.

Eligibility Requirements: Applicant must be enrolled or expecting to enroll full- or part-time at a two-year or four-year or technical institution or university; resident of Minnesota and studying in Minnesota. Available to U.S. citizens.

Application Requirements: Application form, financial need analysis. *Deadline:* continuous.

Contact: Grant Staff
Minnesota Office of Higher Education
1450 Energy Park Drive, Suite 350
St. Paul, MN 55108
Phone: 651-642-0567 Ext. 2

MINNESOTA STATE VETERANS' DEPENDENTS ASSISTANCE PROGRAM

Tuition assistance to dependents of persons considered to be prisoner-of-war or missing in action after August 1, 1958. Must be Minnesota resident attending Minnesota two- or four-year school.

Award: Scholarship for use in freshman, sophomore, junior, or senior years; renewable. *Number:* 100–200. *Amount:* $249–$250.

Eligibility Requirements: Applicant must be enrolled or expecting to enroll full- or part-time at a two-year or four-year institution; resident of Minnesota and studying in Minnesota. Available to U.S. citizens.

Application Requirements: Application form. *Deadline:* continuous.

Contact: Meghan Flores, State Grant Manager
Phone: 651-355-0610
E-mail: meghan.flores@state.mn.us

POSTSECONDARY CHILD CARE GRANT PROGRAM-MINNESOTA

Grant available for students who are not receiving MFIP (TANF) and have children in day care. Based on financial need. Cannot exceed actual child care costs or maximum award chart (based on income). Must be Minnesota resident. For use at Minnesota two- or four-year school, including public technical colleges. Available until student has attended college for the equivalent of four full-time academic years.

Award: Grant for use in freshman, sophomore, junior, or senior years; not renewable. *Number:* 1–3500. *Amount:* $100–$2800.

Eligibility Requirements: Applicant must be enrolled or expecting to enroll full- or part-time at a two-year or four-year or technical institution or university; resident of Minnesota and studying in Minnesota. Available to U.S. citizens.

Application Requirements: Application form, financial need analysis. *Deadline:* continuous.

Contact: Brenda Larter, Program Administrator
Minnesota Office of Higher Education
1450 Energy Park Drive, Suite 350
St. Paul, MN 55108-5227
Phone: 651-355-0612
E-mail: brenda.larter@state.mn.us

SAFETY OFFICERS' SURVIVOR GRANT PROGRAM
• *See page 646*

MISSISSIPPI OFFICE OF STUDENT FINANCIAL AID

http://www.mississippi.edu/financialaid

HIGHER EDUCATION LEGISLATIVE PLAN (HELP)

Eligible applicant must be resident of Mississippi and apply for the first time as a freshman and/or sophomore student who graduated from high school within the immediate past two years. Must demonstrate need as determined by the results of the FAFSA, documenting an average family adjusted gross income of $36,500 or less over the prior two years. Must be enrolled full-time at a Mississippi college or university, have a GPA of 2.5, have completed a specific high school core curriculum, and have scored 20 on the ACT.

Award: Grant for use in freshman, sophomore, junior, or senior years; renewable. *Number:* 2912. *Amount:* $340–$7344.

Eligibility Requirements: Applicant must be enrolled or expecting to enroll full-time at a two-year or four-year institution or university; resident of Mississippi and studying in Mississippi. Applicant must have 3.0 GPA or higher. Available to U.S. citizens.

Application Requirements: Application form, financial need analysis. *Deadline:* March 31.

Contact: Program Administrator
Mississippi Office of Student Financial Aid
3825 Ridgewood Road
Jackson, MS 39211
Phone: 601-432-6997
Fax: 601-432 Ext. 6527
E-mail: sfa@mississippi.edu

LAW ENFORCEMENT OFFICERS/FIREMEN SCHOLARSHIP
• *See page 646*

MISSISSIPPI EMINENT SCHOLARS GRANT

Award for an entering freshmen or as a renewal for sophomore, junior or senior, who are residents of Mississippi. Applicants must achieve a GPA of 3.5 and must have scored 29 on the ACT. Must enroll full-time at an eligible Mississippi college or university.

Award: Grant for use in freshman, sophomore, junior, or senior years; not renewable. *Number:* 2726. *Amount:* $1157–$2500.

Eligibility Requirements: Applicant must be enrolled or expecting to enroll full-time at a two-year or four-year institution or university; resident of Mississippi and studying in Mississippi. Applicant must have 3.5 GPA or higher. Available to U.S. citizens.

Application Requirements: Application form. *Deadline:* September 15.

Contact: Program Administrator
Mississippi Office of Student Financial Aid
3825 Ridgewood Road
Jackson, MS 39211
Phone: 601-432-6997
Fax: 601-432 Ext. 6527
E-mail: sfa@mississippi.edu

MISSISSIPPI RESIDENT TUITION ASSISTANCE GRANT

Must be a resident of Mississippi enrolled full-time at an eligible Mississippi college or university. Must maintain a minimum 2.5 GPA each semester. MTAG awards may be up to $500 per academic year for freshman and sophomores and $1000 per academic year for juniors and seniors.

Award: Grant for use in freshman, sophomore, junior, or senior years; not renewable. *Amount:* $17–$1000.

Eligibility Requirements: Applicant must be enrolled or expecting to enroll full-time at a two-year or four-year institution or university; resident of Mississippi and studying in Mississippi. Applicant must have 2.5 GPA or higher. Available to U.S. citizens.

Application Requirements: Application form. *Deadline:* September 15.

Contact: Program Administrator
Mississippi Office of Student Financial Aid
3825 Ridgewood Road
Jackson, MS 39211
Phone: 601-432-6997
Fax: 601-432 Ext. 6527
E-mail: sfa@mississippi.edu

NISSAN SCHOLARSHIP

Renewable award for Mississippi residents attending a Mississippi institution. Must be graduating from a Mississippi high school in the current year. The scholarship will pay full tuition and a book allowance. Minimum GPA of 2.5 as well as an ACT composite of at least 20 or combined SAT scores of 940 or better. Must demonstrate financial need and leadership abilities.

Award: Scholarship for use in freshman, sophomore, junior, or senior years; renewable. *Number:* 1. *Amount:* $8280.

Eligibility Requirements: Applicant must be high school student; planning to enroll or expecting to enroll full-time at a two-year or four-year institution or university; resident of Mississippi and studying in Mississippi. Applicant must have 2.5 GPA or higher. Available to U.S. citizens.

Application Requirements: Application form, essay, financial need analysis. *Deadline:* March 1.

Contact: Program Administrator
Mississippi Office of Student Financial Aid
3825 Ridgewood Road
Jackson, MS 39211
Phone: 601-432-6997
Fax: 601-432 Ext. 6527
E-mail: sfa@mississippi.edu

MISSOURI CONSERVATION AGENTS ASSOCIATION SCHOLARSHIP

http://www.moagent.com/

MISSOURI CONSERVATION AGENTS ASSOCIATION SCHOLARSHIP

Scholarship of up to $500 per student per year for full-time undergraduate students who reside in the state of Missouri. The applicant must be a U.S. citizen.

Award: Scholarship for use in freshman, sophomore, junior, or senior years; not renewable. *Amount:* up to $500.

Eligibility Requirements: Applicant must be enrolled or expecting to enroll full-time at a four-year or technical institution or university and resident of Missouri. Applicant must have 2.5 GPA or higher. Available to U.S. citizens.

Application Requirements: Essay, transcript. *Deadline:* February 1.

Contact: Brian Ham, Scholarship Committee
Phone: 573-896-8628

MISSOURI DEPARTMENT OF HIGHER EDUCATION

http://www.dhe.mo.gov/

ACCESS MISSOURI FINANCIAL ASSISTANCE PROGRAM

Need-based program that provides awards to students who are enrolled full-time and have an expected family contribution (EFC) of $12,000 or less based on their Free Application for Federal Student Aid (FAFSA). Awards vary depending on EFC and the type of postsecondary school.

Award: Grant for use in freshman, sophomore, junior, or senior years; not renewable.

Eligibility Requirements: Applicant must be enrolled or expecting to enroll full-time at a two-year or technical institution or university; resident of Missouri and studying in Missouri. Applicant must have 2.5 GPA or higher. Available to U.S. citizens.

Application Requirements: FAFSA on file by April 1.

Contact: Information Center
Phone: 800-473-6757 Ext. 4
Fax: 573-751-6635
E-mail: info@dhe.mo.gov

MARGUERITE ROSS BARNETT MEMORIAL SCHOLARSHIP

Scholarship was established for students who are employed while attending school part-time. Must be enrolled at least half-time but less than full-time at a participating Missouri postsecondary school, be employed and compensated for at least 20 hours per week, be 18 years of age, be a Missouri resident and a U.S. citizen or a permanent resident.

Award: Scholarship for use in freshman, sophomore, junior, or senior years; renewable.

Eligibility Requirements: Applicant must be enrolled or expecting to enroll part-time at a two-year or four-year or technical institution or university; resident of Missouri and studying in Missouri. Applicant must have 2.5 GPA or higher. Available to U.S. citizens.

Application Requirements: FAFSA on file by August 1. *Deadline:* August 1.

Contact: Information Center
Phone: 800-473-6757 Ext. 4
Fax: 573-751-6635
E-mail: info@dhe.mo.gov

MISSOURI HIGHER EDUCATION ACADEMIC SCHOLARSHIP (BRIGHT FLIGHT)

Program encourages top-ranked high school seniors to attend approved Missouri postsecondary schools. Must be a Missouri resident and a U.S. citizen or permanent resident. Must have a composite score on the ACT or SAT in the top 5 percent of all Missouri students taking those tests. Students with scores in the top 3 percent are eligible for an annual award of up to $3000 (up to $1500 each semester). Students with scores in the top 4% and 5% are eligible for an annual award of up to $1000 (up to $500 each semester). Award amounts, and the availability of the award for students in the 4% and 5%, are subject to change based on the amount of funding allocated for the program in the legislative session.

Award: Scholarship for use in freshman, sophomore, junior, or senior years; renewable. *Amount:* $1000–$3000.

Eligibility Requirements: Applicant must be enrolled or expecting to enroll full-time at a two-year or four-year or technical institution or university; resident of Missouri and studying in Missouri. Applicant must have 2.5 GPA or higher. Available to U.S. citizens.

Application Requirements: Test scores.

Contact: Information Center
Phone: 800-473-6757 Ext. 4
Fax: 573-751-6635
E-mail: info@dhe.mo.gov

MITCHELL INSTITUTE

http://www.mitchellinstitute.org/

SENATOR GEORGE J. MITCHELL SCHOLARSHIP RESEARCH INSTITUTE

• See page 646

MODERN LAW

https://mymodernlaw.com

DIVORCE PREVENTION SCHOLARSHIP

https://mymodernlaw.com/scholarship/

Award: Scholarship for use in freshman year; not renewable. *Number:* 1. *Amount:* $500.

Eligibility Requirements: Applicant must be enrolled or expecting to enroll full- or part-time at a two-year or four-year or technical institution or university and resident of Arizona. Available to U.S. citizens.

Application Requirements: Application form, essay. *Deadline:* March 1.

MONTANA UNIVERSITY SYSTEM, OFFICE OF COMMISSIONER OF HIGHER EDUCATION

http://www.mus.edu

MONTANA UNIVERSITY SYSTEM HONOR SCHOLARSHIP

Scholarship will be awarded annually to high school seniors graduating from accredited Montana high schools. The MUS Honor Scholarship is a four year renewable scholarship that waives tuition at one of the Montana University System campuses or one of the three community colleges (Flathead Valley in Kalispell, Miles in Miles City or Dawson in Glendive). The scholarship must be used within 9 months after high school graduation. Applicant must have a minimum GPA of 3.4.

Award: Scholarship for use in freshman, sophomore, junior, or senior years; renewable. *Number:* 200. *Amount:* $16,000–$24,000.

Eligibility Requirements: Applicant must be high school student; planning to enroll or expecting to enroll full-time at a two-year or four-year institution or university; resident of Montana and studying in Montana. Applicant must have 3.5 GPA or higher. Available to U.S. citizens.

Application Requirements: Application form. *Deadline:* March 15.

Contact: Sheila Newlun, Grants and Scholarship Coordinator
Phone: 406-449-9168
Fax: 406-444-1869
E-mail: snewlun@montana.edu

MOUNT VERNON URBAN RENEWAL AGENCY

http://www.ci.mount-vernon.ny.us/

MAYORS EDUCATIONAL ASSISTANCE PROGRAM

Awards offered only to the low and moderate income residents of the city of Mount Vernon for the purpose of pursuing higher education at a vocational/technical school or college.

Award: Grant for use in freshman, sophomore, junior, or senior years; renewable.

Eligibility Requirements: Applicant must be enrolled or expecting to enroll full-time at a two-year or four-year or technical institution or university and resident of New York. Applicant must have 3.5 GPA or higher. Available to U.S. citizens.

Application Requirements: Application form, essay, financial need analysis. *Deadline:* July 1.

Contact: Mary Fleming, Director, Scholarship Programs
Mount Vernon Urban Renewal Agency
Department of Planning, One Roosevelt Square, City Hall
Mount Vernon, NY 10550
Phone: 914-699-7230
E-mail: mfleming@ci.mount-vernon.ny.us

NATIONAL COUNCIL OF JEWISH WOMEN LOS ANGELES (NCJW L LA)

http://ncjwla.org/

THE DODELL WOMEN'S EMPOWERMENT SCHOLARSHIP
• *See page 648*

THE SINGERMAN/NOSSECK MEMORIAL SCHOLARSHIP
• *See page 750*

SOPHIE GREENSTADT SCHOLARSHIP FOR MID-LIFE WOMEN
• *See page 648*

STEPHEN L. TELLER & RICHARD HOTSON TV, CINEMA, AND THEATER SCHOLARSHIP
• *See page 649*

SUSAN SCHULMAN BEGLEY MEMORIAL SCHOLARSHIP
• *See page 649*

SYLVIA AND SAMUEL SCHULMAN MEMORIAL SCHOLARSHIP

To qualify, an applicant must be a single mother entering or continuing school in an accredited institution in order to learn a marketable skill, which will lead to economic independence. The award is made in two payments of $500.00. The second payment will be received after written confirmation of status and current school transcripts from the recipient. The National Council of Jewish Women l Los Angeles (NCJW l LA) provides scholarships, regardless of race, ethnicity, religion, age, gender identity, sexuality or national origin to those who live and attend school in the Greater Los Angeles area, including Los Angeles, Orange, Riverside, and Ventura Counties.

Award: Scholarship for use in freshman, sophomore, junior, or senior years; not renewable. *Number:* 1. *Amount:* $1000.

Eligibility Requirements: Applicant must be enrolled or expecting to enroll full- or part-time at a two-year or four-year or technical institution or university; single female; resident of California and studying in California. Available to U.S. citizens.

Application Requirements: Application form, essay, financial need analysis. *Deadline:* continuous.

Contact: Stephanie Flax, Scholarship and Program Coordinator
National Council of Jewish Women Los Angeles (NCJW l LA)
543 N Fairfax Avenue
Los Angeles, CA 90036
Phone: 323-852-8515
E-mail: scholarship@ncjwla.org

NATIONAL DEFENSE TRANSPORTATION ASSOCIATION-SCOTT ST. LOUIS CHAPTER

http://www.ndtascottstlouis.org/

NATIONAL DEFENSE TRANSPORTATION ASSOCIATION, SCOTT AIR FORCE BASE-ST. LOUIS AREA CHAPTER SCHOLARSHIP

The Scott/St. Louis Chapter of the NDTA intends to award a minimum of two (2) scholarships of $3500 each and four (4) scholarships of $2000 each. Additional awards may be granted pending availability of funds. Scholarships are open to any high school student that meets the eligibility criteria. High school students must be reside and go to school in Illinois or Missouri. College applicants must be a full-time student in the following states: CO, IA, IL, IN, KS, MI, MN, MO, MT, ND, NE, SD, WI, or WY.

Award: Scholarship for use in freshman, sophomore, junior, or senior years; not renewable. *Number:* 6. *Amount:* $2000–$3500.

Eligibility Requirements: Applicant must be enrolled or expecting to enroll full-time at a two-year or four-year institution or university; resident of Illinois, Missouri and studying in Colorado, Illinois, Indiana, Iowa, Kansas, Michigan, Minnesota, Missouri, Montana, Nebraska, North Dakota, South Dakota, Wisconsin, Wyoming. Applicant must have 3.0 GPA or higher. Available to U.S. citizens.

Application Requirements: Application form, community service, essay, recommendations or references, test scores, transcript. *Deadline:* March 1.

Contact: Mr. Michael Carnes, Chairman, Professional Development Committee
National Defense Transportation Association-Scott St. Louis Chapter
PO Box 25486
Scott AFB, IL 62225
Phone: 618-229-4756
E-mail: michael.carnes.ctr@ustranscom.mil

NATIONAL EXPRESS AUTO TRANSPORT

https://nxautotransport.com

NATIONAL EXPRESS AUTO TRANSPORT SCHOLARSHIP

Those wishing to apply must submit 1000 words or more regarding auto transport. Examples of this type of writing would include but not be limited to topics such as open carrier transport, enclosed auto transport, door-to-door car shipping, classic cars, exotic cars, green auto transport solutions, to name a few that are related to the industry. Applicants are encouraged to dig deep when making these essays. You can provide interviews, links to authoritative sources, etc. Each submission will be placed on this page with attribution to the author. The work must be completely original and not submitted or be found anywhere else. Any plagiarized / copied articles will be rejected. Applicants are also encouraged to share their article link as much as possible through social media or through other venues that will help the article gain traction and be seen by others. Winners will have their submission converted to a blog post with them as a guest author on our site using that same url and it will remain on our site the the main blog. The submissions for those that did not win but are well written will remain on our scholarship page as well. https://nxautotransport.com/scholarship

Award: Scholarship for use in freshman, sophomore, junior, senior, graduate, or postgraduate years; not renewable. *Number:* 2. *Amount:* $400–$1100.

Eligibility Requirements: Applicant must be age 18-99; enrolled or expecting to enroll full- or part-time at a two-year or four-year or technical institution or university; resident of American Samoa, Northern Mariana Islands, Yukon and studying in American Samoa, Northern Mariana Islands, Yukon. Applicant must have 3.0 GPA or higher. Available to U.S. citizens.

Application Requirements: Essay. *Deadline:* February 4.

Contact: Mr. Carl Rodriguez, General Manager
National Express Auto Transport
7950 NW 53RD ST
#337
MiamI, FL 33173
Phone: 800-2847177 Ext. 404
Fax: 305-4593305
E-mail: admin@neatransport.com

NATIONAL FEDERATION OF THE BLIND OF CALIFORNIA

http://www.nfbcal.org/

GERALD DRAKE MEMORIAL SCHOLARSHIP
• *See page 690*

JULIE LANDUCCI SCHOLARSHIP
• *See page 691*

LA VYRL "PINKY" JOHNSON MEMORIAL SCHOLARSHIP
• *See page 691*

LAWRENCE "MUZZY" MARCELINO MEMORIAL SCHOLARSHIP
• *See page 691*

NATIONAL FEDERATION OF THE BLIND OF CALIFORNIA MERIT SCHOLARSHIPS
• *See page 691*

NATIONAL FEDERATION OF THE BLIND OF MISSOURI

http://www.nfbmo.org/

NATIONAL FEDERATION OF THE BLIND OF MISSOURI SCHOLARSHIP PROGRAM FOR LEGALLY BLIND STUDENTS
• *See page 691*

NATIONAL INSTITUTE FOR LABOR RELATIONS RESEARCH

http://www.nilrr.org/

NATIONAL INSTITUTE FOR LABOR RELATIONS RESEARCH WILLIAM B. RUGGLES JOURNALISM SCHOLARSHIP
• *See page 650*

NATIONAL KIDNEY FOUNDATION OF INDIANA INC.

http://www.kidneyindiana.org/

NATIONAL KIDNEY FOUNDATION OF INDIANA SCHOLARSHIP
• *See page 691*

NEBRASKA'S COORDINATING COMMISSION FOR POSTSECONDARY EDUCATION

https://ccpe.nebraska.gov/

NEBRASKA OPPORTUNITY GRANT
• *See page 651*

NEED

http://www.needld.org/

UNMET NEED GRANT PROGRAM
• *See page 651*

NEVADA OFFICE OF THE STATE TREASURER

http://www.nevadatreasurer.gov/

GOVERNOR GUINN MILLENNIUM SCHOLARSHIP

Scholarship for Nevada residents. Student must graduate from a public or private high school within Nevada with a minimum GPA of 3.25. Must complete core curriculum. Maximum award is $10,000. Student must acknowledge award and use it within 6 years of high school graduation.

Award: Scholarship for use in freshman, sophomore, junior, or senior years; renewable. *Number:* 1. *Amount:* up to $10,000.

Eligibility Requirements: Applicant must be enrolled or expecting to enroll full-time at a two-year or four-year institution or university; resident of Nevada and studying in Nevada. Available to U.S. citizens.

Application Requirements: Application form may be submitted online (http://nevadatreasurer.gov), high schools determine eligibility; student must accept award. *Deadline:* varies.

Contact: Linda English, Executive Director
Phone: 702-486-3889
Fax: 702-486-3246
E-mail: info@nevadatreasurer.gov

NEW ENGLAND BOARD OF HIGHER EDUCATION

http://www.nebhe.org/tuitionbreak

NEW ENGLAND REGIONAL STUDENT PROGRAM-TUITION BREAK

Tuition discount for residents of six New England states (Connecticut, Maine, Massachusetts, New Hampshire, Rhode Island, Vermont). Students pay reduced out-of-state tuition at public colleges or universities in other New England states when enrolling in certain majors not offered at public institutions in home state. Details are available at http://www.nebhe.org/tuitionbreak.

Award: Scholarship for use in freshman, sophomore, junior, senior, or graduate years; renewable.

Eligibility Requirements: Applicant must be enrolled or expecting to enroll full- or part-time at a two-year or four-year institution or university; resident of Connecticut, Maine, Massachusetts, New Hampshire, Rhode Island, Vermont and studying in Connecticut, Maine, Massachusetts, New Hampshire, Rhode Island, Vermont. Available to U.S. citizens.

Application Requirements: Application form. *Deadline:* continuous.

Contact: Wendy Lindsay, Senior Director of Regional Student Program
New England Board of Higher Education
45 Temple Place
Boston, MA 02111
Phone: 617-533-9511
E-mail: tuitionbreak@nebhe.org

NEW JERSEY DEPARTMENT OF MILITARY AND VETERANS AFFAIRS

http://www.state.nj.us/military

NEW JERSEY WAR ORPHANS TUITION ASSISTANCE
• *See page 713*

POW-MIA TUITION BENEFIT PROGRAM
• *See page 713*

VETERANS TUITION CREDIT PROGRAM-NEW JERSEY
• *See page 713*

NEW JERSEY HALL OF FAME

http://njhalloffame.org/

NJHOF ARÊTE SCHOLARSHIP AWARD

The New Jersey Hall of Fame is proud to announce the renewal of the Arete Scholarship Fund. The Arête Scholarships will be awarded to a deserving male and female student graduating in 2018 from a New Jersey high school. Each recipient will receive a $5,000 scholarship from the New Jersey Hall of Fame (NJHOF). Arête is a concept that Plato referred to more than 3,000 years ago that refers to the act of actualizing one's highest sense of self. The term Arête essentially means that the individual should strive to pursue their passions in life, and realize their dreams regardless of their circumstances or the adversities that they are likely to face on the path to greatness. The successful applicants will embody the meaning of Arête, and will distinguish themselves as New Jerseyans who are on their way to realizing their dreams. The NJHOF Arête Scholarship Award will be one of the highest honors that the NJHOF and the state of NJ. can bestow upon a student, and each student will be recognized at the NJHOF's annual Induction Ceremony! The recipients of the Arête scholarship are young people who demonstrate that sense of Jersey pride and that willingness to go above and beyond the call of duty. The successful applicants must demonstrate the qualities such as academic engagement, moral character, and a commitment to their community. These recipients do not necessarily have to be at the very top of their school class from an academic standpoint, but should demonstrate a focus in school and life, and have a well thought out plan on how they intend to realize their highest sense of self: their Arête.

Award: Scholarship for use in freshman year; not renewable. *Number:* 2. *Amount:* $5000.

Eligibility Requirements: Applicant must be high school student; planning to enroll or expecting to enroll full- or part-time at a two-year or four-year institution or university and resident of New Jersey. Available to U.S. citizens.

Application Requirements: Application form. *Deadline:* March 17.

Contact: Ms. Emaleigh Kaithern
E-mail: emaleigh@princetonscgroup.com

NEW JERSEY HIGHER EDUCATION STUDENT ASSISTANCE AUTHORITY

http://www.hesaa.org/

LAW ENFORCEMENT OFFICER MEMORIAL SCHOLARSHIP
• *See page 651*

NEW JERSEY STUDENT TUITION ASSISTANCE REWARD SCHOLARSHIP II

Earn an associate degree from the home New Jersey county college as an NJ STARS recipient and graduate with a cumulative GPA of 3.25 or higher. Family income (taxable and untaxed income) must be less than $250,000 as derived from the FAFSA. NJ STARS II students may receive up to $1,250 per semester, paid completely by the State, after all other sources of federal and State grants and scholarships are applied to tuition charges.

Award: Scholarship for use in junior or senior years; renewable.

Eligibility Requirements: Applicant must be enrolled or expecting to enroll full-time at a four-year institution or university; resident of New Jersey and studying in New Jersey. Applicant must have 3.0 GPA or higher. Available to U.S. citizens.

Application Requirements: Application form. *Deadline:* continuous.

Contact: Jossette Greene, Program Officer
Phone: 609-584-4480
E-mail: jgreene@hesaa.org

NEW JERSEY WORLD TRADE CENTER SCHOLARSHIP

Scholarship was established by the legislature to aid the dependent children and surviving spouses of New Jersey residents who were killed in the terrorist attacks, or who are missing and officially presumed dead as a direct result of the attacks; applies to instate and out-of-state institutions for students seeking undergraduate degrees.

Award: Scholarship for use in freshman, sophomore, junior, or senior years; not renewable. *Amount:* $1–$6500.

Eligibility Requirements: Applicant must be enrolled or expecting to enroll full-time at a two-year or four-year institution or university and resident of New Jersey. Available to U.S. citizens.

Application Requirements: Application form.

Contact: Jean Hathaway, Assistant Director of Special Grants and Scholarships
New Jersey Higher Education Student Assistance Authority
PO Box 540
Trenton, NJ 08625
Phone: 609-588-3266
E-mail: jhathaway@hesaa.org

NJ STUDENT TUITION ASSISTANCE REWARD SCHOLARSHIP

Students must enroll in a full time course of study at their home county colleges. The award covers tuition charges for up to 18 credit hours per term.

Award: Scholarship for use in freshman or sophomore years; renewable. *Amount:* $500–$2600.

Eligibility Requirements: Applicant must be enrolled or expecting to enroll full-time at a two-year institution; resident of New Jersey and studying in New Jersey. Applicant must have 3.0 GPA or higher. Available to U.S. citizens.

Application Requirements: Application form.

Contact: Ms. Jossette Greene, Program Officer
New Jersey Higher Education Student Assistance Authority
PO Box 540
Trenton, NJ 08625
Phone: 609-584-4480
E-mail: jgreene@hessa.org

PART-TIME TUITION AID GRANT FOR COUNTY COLLEGES

Provides financial aid to eligible part-time undergraduate students enrolled for 9 to 11 credits at New Jersey community colleges.

Award: Grant for use in freshman or sophomore years; not renewable. *Amount:* $500–$1900.

Eligibility Requirements: Applicant must be enrolled or expecting to enroll part-time at a two-year institution; resident of New Jersey and studying in New Jersey. Available to U.S. citizens.

Application Requirements: Application form, financial need analysis.

Contact: Jean Hathoway, AS of Grants and Scholarships
New Jersey Higher Education Student Assistance Authority
PO Box 540
Trenton, NJ 08625
Phone: 609-584-4480
E-mail: jhathaway@hesaa.org

SURVIVOR TUITION BENEFITS PROGRAM
• *See page 652*

TUITION AID GRANT

The program provides grants to eligible undergraduate students attending participating in-state institutions.

Award: Grant for use in freshman, sophomore, junior, or senior years; not renewable. *Amount:* $1012–$12,190.

Eligibility Requirements: Applicant must be enrolled or expecting to enroll full-time at a two-year or four-year institution or university; resident of New Jersey and studying in New Jersey. Available to U.S. citizens.

Application Requirements: Application form, financial need analysis.

Contact: Kathyrn Safran, Director of Grants and Scholarships
New Jersey Higher Education Student Assistance Authority
PO Box 540
Trenton, NJ 08625
Phone: 609-584-4480
E-mail: ksafran@hesaa.org

NEW JERSEY STATE GOLF ASSOCIATION

NJSGA.org

NEW JERSEY STATE GOLF ASSOCIATION CADDIE SCHOLARSHIP

• See page 652

NEW JERSEY VIETNAM VETERANS' MEMORIAL FOUNDATION

http://www.njvvmf.org/college-scholarships

NEW JERSEY VIETNAM VETERANS' MEMORIAL FOUNDATION SCHOLARSHIP

Applicant must be a New Jersey resident, be a graduating high school senior, and visited the New Jersey Vietnam Veteran's Memorial (on their own /class trip/ scholarship tour).

Award: Scholarship for use in freshman year; not renewable. *Number:* 2. *Amount:* $2500.

Eligibility Requirements: Applicant must be high school student; planning to enroll or expecting to enroll full-time at a two-year or four-year or technical institution or university and resident of New Jersey. Available to U.S. citizens.

Application Requirements: Application form, essay. *Deadline:* April 14.

NEW MEXICO COMMISSION ON HIGHER EDUCATION

http://www.hed.state.nm.us/

COLLEGE AFFORDABILITY GRANT

Grant available to New Mexico students with financial need who do not qualify for other state grants and scholarships to attend and complete educational programs at a New Mexico public college or university. Student must have unmet need after all other financial aid has been awarded. Student may not be receiving any other state grants or scholarships. Renewable upon satisfactory academic progress.

Award: Grant for use in freshman, sophomore, junior, or senior years; renewable. *Number:* 1. *Amount:* up to $1000.

Eligibility Requirements: Applicant must be enrolled or expecting to enroll full- or part-time at a two-year or four-year institution or university; resident of New Mexico and studying in New Mexico. Available to U.S. citizens.

Application Requirements: Application form, FAFSA, financial need analysis. *Deadline:* continuous.

Contact: Tashina Acker, Director of Financial Aid
New Mexico Commission on Higher Education
1068 Cerrillos Road
Santa Fe, NM 87505-1650
Phone: 505-476-6549
Fax: 505-476-6511
E-mail: tashina.banks-moore@state.nm.us

LEGISLATIVE ENDOWMENT SCHOLARSHIPS

Renewable scholarships to provide aid for undergraduate students with substantial financial need who are attending public postsecondary institutions in New Mexico. Four-year schools may award up to $2500 per academic year, two-year schools may award up to $1000 per academic year. Deadlines varies.

Award: Scholarship for use in freshman, sophomore, junior, or senior years; renewable. *Number:* 1. *Amount:* $1000–$2500.

Eligibility Requirements: Applicant must be enrolled or expecting to enroll full- or part-time at a two-year or four-year institution or university; resident of New Mexico and studying in New Mexico. Available to U.S. citizens.

Application Requirements: Application form, FAFSA, financial need analysis. *Deadline:* varies.

Contact: Tashina Moore, Director of Financial Aid
New Mexico Commission on Higher Education
1068 Cerrillos Road
Santa Fe, NM 87505-1650
Phone: 505-475-6549
Fax: 505-476-6511
E-mail: tashina.banks-moore@state.nm.us

LEGISLATIVE LOTTERY SCHOLARSHIP

Renewable Scholarship for New Mexico high school graduates or GED recipients who plan to attend an eligible New Mexico public college or university. Must be enrolled full-time and maintain 2.5 GPA.

Award: Scholarship for use in freshman year; renewable. *Number:* 1.

Eligibility Requirements: Applicant must be high school student; planning to enroll or expecting to enroll full-time at a four-year institution or university; resident of New Mexico and studying in New Mexico. Applicant must have 3.5 GPA or higher. Available to U.S. citizens.

Application Requirements: Application form, FAFSA. *Deadline:* varies.

Contact: Tashina Moore, Director of Financial Aid
New Mexico Commission on Higher Education
1068 Cerrillos Road
Santa Fe, NM 87505
Phone: 505-476-6549
Fax: 505-476-6511
E-mail: tashina.banks-moore@state.nm.us

NEW MEXICO SCHOLARS' PROGRAM

Renewable award program created to encourage New Mexico high school students to attend public postsecondary institutions or the following private colleges in New Mexico: College of Santa Fe, St. John's College, College of the Southwest. For details visit http://fin.hed.state.nm.us.

Award: Scholarship for use in freshman year; renewable. *Number:* 1.

Eligibility Requirements: Applicant must be high school student; planning to enroll or expecting to enroll full-time at a two-year or four-year institution; resident of New Mexico and studying in New Mexico. Available to U.S. citizens.

Application Requirements: Application form, FAFSA, financial need analysis, test scores. *Deadline:* varies.

Contact: Tashina Moore, Director of Financial Aid
New Mexico Commission on Higher Education
1068 Cerrillos Road
Santa Fe, NM 87505-1650
Phone: 505-476-6549
Fax: 505-476-6511
E-mail: tashina.banks-moore@state.nm.us

NEW MEXICO STUDENT INCENTIVE GRANT

Grant created to provide aid for undergraduate students with substantial financial need who are attending public colleges or universities or the following eligible colleges in New Mexico: College of Santa Fe, St. John's College, College of the Southwest, Institute of American Indian Art, Crownpoint Institute of Technology, Dine College and Southwestern Indian Polytechnic Institute. Part-time students are eligible for pro-rated awards.

Award: Grant for use in freshman, sophomore, junior, or senior years; not renewable. *Number:* 1. *Amount:* $200–$2500.

Eligibility Requirements: Applicant must be enrolled or expecting to enroll full- or part-time at a two-year or four-year or technical institution or university; resident of New Mexico and studying in New Mexico. Available to U.S. citizens.

Application Requirements: Application form, FAFSA, financial need analysis. *Deadline:* varies.

Contact: Tashina Moore, Director of Financial Aid
New Mexico Commission on Higher Education
1068 Cerrillos Road
Santa Fe, NM 87505-1650
Phone: 505-476-6549
Fax: 505-476-6511
E-mail: tashina.banks-moore@state.nm.us

VIETNAM VETERANS' SCHOLARSHIP PROGRAM

• See page 713

NEW MEXICO DEPARTMENT OF VETERANS' SERVICES

http://www.nmdvs.org

CHILDREN OF DECEASED VETERANS SCHOLARSHIP-NEW MEXICO

Award for New Mexico residents who are children of veterans killed as a result of service, prisoner of war, or veterans missing in action. Must be between ages 16 and 26. For use at New Mexico schools for undergraduate study. Must submit parent's death certificate and DD form 214.

Award: Scholarship for use in freshman, sophomore, junior, or senior years; not renewable. *Number:* 49–50. *Amount:* $300.

Eligibility Requirements: Applicant must be age 16-26; enrolled or expecting to enroll full- or part-time at a two-year or four-year or technical institution or university; resident of New Mexico and studying in New Mexico. Available to U.S. citizens.

Application Requirements: Application form.

Contact: Mr. Dale Movius, Director, State Benefits
New Mexico Department of Veterans' Services
407 Galisteo St, Room 134
Santa Fe, NM 87501
Phone: 505-827-6300
E-mail: dalej.movius@state.nm.us

NEW MEXICO VIETNAM VETERAN SCHOLARSHIP

Award for Vietnam veterans who have been New Mexico residents for a minimum of ten years and are attending state-funded postsecondary schools. Must have been awarded the Vietnam Campaign medal. Must submit DD 214 and discharge papers.

Award: Scholarship for use in freshman, sophomore, junior, or senior years; renewable. *Number:* 100. *Amount:* $3500–$4000.

Eligibility Requirements: Applicant must be enrolled or expecting to enroll full- or part-time at a two-year or four-year or technical institution or university; resident of New Mexico and studying in New Mexico. Available to U.S. citizens.

Application Requirements: Application form.

Contact: Mr. Dale Movius, Director, State Benefits
New Mexico Department of Veterans' Services
407 Galisteo St, Room 134
Santa Fe, NM 87501
Phone: 505-827-6300
E-mail: Dalej.movius@state.nm.us

NEW MEXICO WARTIME VETERANS SCHOLARSHIP

• See page 713

NEW YORK STATE EDUCATION DEPARTMENT

http://www.highered.nysed.gov/

SCHOLARSHIP FOR ACADEMIC EXCELLENCE

Renewable award for New York residents. Scholarship winners must attend a college or university in New York. 2000 scholarships are for $1500 and 6000 are for $500. The selection criteria used are based on Regents test scores or rank in class or local exam. Must be U.S. citizen or permanent resident.

Award: Scholarship for use in freshman year; renewable. *Number:* up to 8000. *Amount:* $500–$1500.

Eligibility Requirements: Applicant must be high school student; planning to enroll or expecting to enroll full-time at a two-year or four-year institution or university; resident of New York and studying in New York. Available to U.S. citizens.

Application Requirements: Application form. *Deadline:* December 19.

Contact: Lewis Hall, Supervisor
Phone: 518-486-1319
Fax: 518-486-5346
E-mail: scholar@mail.nysed.gov

NEW YORK STATE GRANGE

http://www.nysgrange.org/

SUSAN W. FREESTONE EDUCATION AWARD

• See page 572

NEW YORK STATE HIGHER EDUCATION SERVICES CORPORATION

http://www.hesc.ny.gov

NEW YORK AID FOR PART-TIME STUDY (APTS)

Renewable scholarship provides tuition assistance to part-time undergraduate students who are New York residents, meet income eligibility requirements and are attending New York accredited institutions. Deadline varies. Must be U.S. citizen.

Award: Grant for use in freshman, sophomore, junior, or senior years; renewable. *Amount:* up to $2000.

Eligibility Requirements: Applicant must be enrolled or expecting to enroll part-time at a two-year or four-year institution or university; resident of New York and studying in New York. Available to U.S. citizens.

Application Requirements: Application form, financial need analysis. *Deadline:* varies.

Contact: Student Information
New York State Higher Education Services Corporation
99 Washington Avenue, Room 1320
Albany, NY 12255
Phone: 518-473-3887
Fax: 518-474-2839

NEW YORK MEMORIAL SCHOLARSHIPS FOR FAMILIES OF DECEASED POLICE OFFICERS, FIRE FIGHTERS, AND PEACE OFFICERS

Renewable scholarship for children, spouses and financial dependents of deceased fire fighters, volunteer firefighters, police officers, peace officers and emergency medical service workers who died in the line of duty. Provides up to the cost of SUNY educational expenses.

Award: Scholarship for use in freshman, sophomore, junior, or senior years; renewable.

Eligibility Requirements: Applicant must be enrolled or expecting to enroll full-time at a four-year institution or university; resident of New York and studying in New York. Available to U.S. citizens.

Application Requirements: Application form, financial need analysis, transcript. *Deadline:* May 1.

Contact: Scholarships
Phone: 888-697-4372

NEW YORK STATE AID TO NATIVE AMERICANS

• See page 752

NEW YORK STATE TUITION ASSISTANCE PROGRAM

Award for New York state residents attending a New York postsecondary institution. Must be full-time student in approved program with tuition over $200 per year. Must show financial need and not be in default in any other state program. Renewable award of $500 to $5000 dependent on family income and tuition charged.

Award: Grant for use in freshman, sophomore, junior, or senior years; renewable. *Number:* 350,000–360,000. *Amount:* $500–$5000.

Eligibility Requirements: Applicant must be enrolled or expecting to enroll full-time at a two-year or four-year institution or university; resident of New York and studying in New York. Available to U.S. citizens.

Application Requirements: Application form, financial need analysis. *Deadline:* May 1.

Contact: Student Information
New York State Higher Education Services Corporation
99 Washington Avenue, Room 1400
Albany, NY 12255
Phone: 888-697-4372

NEW YORK VIETNAM/PERSIAN GULF/AFGHANISTAN VETERANS TUITION AWARDS
• *See page 714*

REGENTS AWARD FOR CHILD OF VETERAN
• *See page 714*

SCHOLARSHIPS FOR ACADEMIC EXCELLENCE
Renewable awards of up to $1500 for academically outstanding New York State high school graduates planning to attend an approved postsecondary institution in New York State. For full-time study only. Contact high school guidance counselor to apply.

Award: Scholarship for use in freshman, sophomore, junior, or senior years; renewable. *Number:* up to 8000. *Amount:* $500–$1500.

Eligibility Requirements: Applicant must be high school student; planning to enroll or expecting to enroll full-time at a four-year institution or university; resident of New York and studying in New York. Available to U.S. citizens.

Application Requirements: Application form. *Deadline:* varies.

Contact: Rita McGivern, Student Information
New York State Higher Education Services Corporation
99 Washington Avenue, Room 1320
Albany, NY 12255
E-mail: scholarship@hesc.com

NEW YORK WOMEN IN COMMUNICATIONS
https://nywici.org/

NEW YORK WOMEN IN COMMUNICATIONS SCHOLARSHIPS
• *See page 652*

N.H. DEPARTMENT OF EDUCATION, DIVISION OF HIGHER EDUCATION - HIGHER EDUCATION COMMISSION
http://www.education.nh.gov/highered

SCHOLARSHIPS FOR ORPHANS OF VETERANS
• *See page 714*

NORTH CAROLINA ASSOCIATION OF EDUCATORS
http://www.ncae.org/

NORTH CAROLINA ASSOCIATION OF EDUCATORS MARTIN LUTHER KING JR. SCHOLARSHIP
• *See page 653*

NORTH CAROLINA BAR FOUNDATION
http://www.ncbar.org/

NORTH CAROLINA BAR ASSOCIATION YOUNG LAWYERS DIVISION SCHOLARSHIP
Renewable award for children or step-children of North Carolina Law Enforcement Officers killed or permanently disabled in the line of duty, studying full-time in accredited colleges or universities. Must be resident of North Carolina and under 26 years of age for first time application. The number of awards and the dollar value of the award varies annually.

Award: Scholarship for use in freshman, sophomore, junior, senior, graduate, or postgraduate years; renewable.

Eligibility Requirements: Applicant must be enrolled or expecting to enroll full-time at a two-year or four-year or technical institution or university and resident of North Carolina. Available to U.S. citizens.

Application Requirements: Application form, essay, financial need analysis, personal photograph. *Deadline:* June 1.

Contact: Ms. Jacquelyn Terrell, Director of Divisions Activities, YLD Staff Liaison
North Carolina Bar Foundation
PO Box 3688
Cary, NC 27519
Phone: 919-657-0561
E-mail: jterrell@ncbar.org

NORTH CAROLINA DIVISION OF VETERANS AFFAIRS
http://www.milvets.nc.gov/

NORTH CAROLINA VETERANS SCHOLARSHIPS CLASS I-A
• *See page 714*

NORTH CAROLINA VETERANS SCHOLARSHIPS CLASS I-B
• *See page 714*

NORTH CAROLINA VETERANS SCHOLARSHIPS CLASS II
• *See page 714*

NORTH CAROLINA VETERANS SCHOLARSHIPS CLASS III
• *See page 715*

NORTH CAROLINA VETERANS SCHOLARSHIPS CLASS IV
• *See page 715*

NORTH CAROLINA DIVISION OF VOCATIONAL REHABILITATION SERVICES
http://www.dhhs.state.nc.us/

TRAINING SUPPORT FOR YOUTH WITH DISABILITIES
• *See page 653*

NORTH CAROLINA NATIONAL GUARD
http://nc.ng.mil/Pages/default.aspx

NORTH CAROLINA NATIONAL GUARD TUITION ASSISTANCE PROGRAM
• *See page 700*

NORTH CAROLINA SOCIETY OF HISPANIC PROFESSIONALS
http://www.thencshp.org/

NORTH CAROLINA HISPANIC COLLEGE FUND SCHOLARSHIP
• *See page 752*

NORTH CAROLINA STATE EDUCATION ASSISTANCE AUTHORITY
http://www.ncseaa.edu/

AUBREY LEE BROOKS SCHOLARSHIPS
A renewable scholarship for graduating high school seniors who are residents of designated North Carolina counties: Alamance, Bertie, Caswell, Durham. Forsyth, Granville, Guilford, Orange, Person, Rockingham, Stokes, Surry, Swain and Warren counties. The scholarship may be used at North Carolina State University, the University of North Carolina at Chapel Hill or the University of North Carolina at Greensboro. Scholarship is renewable, provided the recipient has continued financial need, remains enrolled full-time at an eligible

institution and maintains specified academic standards. Additional details and application at http://www.CFNC.org/Brooks

Award: Scholarship for use in freshman, sophomore, junior, or senior years; renewable. *Number:* 17. *Amount:* $12,000.

Eligibility Requirements: Applicant must be high school student; planning to enroll or expecting to enroll full-time at a four-year institution or university; resident of North Carolina and studying in North Carolina. Available to U.S. citizens.

Application Requirements: Application form, essay, financial need analysis, interview. *Deadline:* continuous.

Contact: Ms. Rashonn Albritton, Scholarship and Grant Manager
North Carolina State Education Assistance Authority
PO Box 13663
Research Triangle Park, NC 27709-3663
Phone: 919-248-4681
E-mail: ralbritton@ncseaa.edu

JAGANNATHAN SCHOLARSHIP

Available to graduating high school seniors who plan to enroll as college freshmen in a full-time degree program at one of the constituent institutions of The University of North Carolina. Applicant must be resident of North Carolina. Applicant must document financial need.

Award: Scholarship for use in freshman year; renewable.

Eligibility Requirements: Applicant must be enrolled or expecting to enroll full-time at a four-year institution or university; resident of North Carolina and studying in North Carolina. Applicant must have 3.0 GPA or higher. Available to U.S. citizens.

Application Requirements: Application form, financial need analysis. *Deadline:* January 15.

Contact: Edna Williams, Manager, Award and Loan Origination Services
North Carolina State Education Assistance Authority
PO Box 13663
Research Triangle Park, NC 27709
Phone: 919-549-8614
E-mail: ewilliams@ncseaa.edu

NORTH CAROLINA COMMUNITY COLLEGE GRANT PROGRAM

Grants are available to North Carolina residents who demonstrate financial need and are enrolled at NC community colleges. The applicant must be a NC resident for tuition purposes; enroll for at least six credit hours per semester in a curriculum program; meet the Satisfactory Academic Progress requirements of the institution. Eligibility is determined based on the same criteria as the Federal Pell Grant; students not eligible for the Federal Pell Grant may be considered for the grant based on the expected family contribution (EFC). Student who have earned a Bachelor's (four-year) degree already are ineligible. Applicants must complete the Free Application for Federal Student Aid (FAFSA). Consideration is automatic once the FAFSA is filed. Please contact the financial aid office at the local community college for more specific information regarding institutional processes.

Award: Grant for use in freshman or sophomore years; not renewable.

Eligibility Requirements: Applicant must be enrolled or expecting to enroll full- or part-time at a two-year or technical institution; resident of North Carolina and studying in North Carolina. Available to U.S. citizens.

Application Requirements: Financial need analysis. *Deadline:* continuous.

Contact: Edna Williams, Manager, Award & Loan Origination Services
North Carolina State Education Assistance Authority
PO Box 13663
Research Triangle Park, NC 27709-3663
Phone: 919-549-8614
Fax: 919-248-4687
E-mail: ewilliams@ncseaa.edu

UNIVERSITY OF NORTH CAROLINA NEED-BASED GRANT

Applicants must be enrolled in at least 6 credit hours at one of sixteen UNC system universities. Eligibility based on need; award varies, consideration for grant automatic when FAFSA is filed. Late applications may be denied due to insufficient funds.

Award: Grant for use in freshman, sophomore, junior, or senior years; renewable.

Eligibility Requirements: Applicant must be enrolled or expecting to enroll full- or part-time at an institution or university; resident of North Carolina and studying in North Carolina. Available to U.S. citizens.

Application Requirements: Application form, financial need analysis.

Contact: Edna Williams, Manager, Award and Loan Origination Services
North Carolina State Education Assistance Authority
PO Box 13663
Research Triangle Park, NC 27709
Phone: 919-549-8614
E-mail: ewilliams@ncseaa.edu

NORTH CAROLINA VIETNAM VETERANS, INC.

http://www.ncvvi.org

NC VIETNAM VETERANS, INC., SCHOLARSHIP PROGRAM
• *See page 653*

NORTH DAKOTA FARMERS UNION

http://www.ndfu.org

STANLEY MOORE FUI FOUNDATION REGIONAL SCHOLARSHIP

Written essay or oral presentation outlining personal and professional goals and involvement with Farmers Union. Priority given to ag-related study.

Award: Scholarship for use in freshman, sophomore, junior, or senior years; not renewable. *Number:* 1–3. *Amount:* $1500.

Eligibility Requirements: Applicant must be enrolled or expecting to enroll full-time at a two-year or four-year or technical institution or university and resident of Minnesota, Montana, North Dakota, South Dakota, Wisconsin. Available to U.S. citizens.

Application Requirements: Application form, community service, essay, interview. *Deadline:* April 22.

Contact: David Velde
North Dakota Farmers Union
1118 Broadway
Alexandria, MN 56308
Phone: 320-763-6561

NORTH DAKOTA UNIVERSITY SYSTEM

http://www.ndus.edu/

NORTH DAKOTA ACADEMIC SCHOLARSHIP
• *See page 654*

NORTH DAKOTA CAREER AND TECHNICAL EDUCATION SCHOLARSHIP
• *See page 654*

NORTH DAKOTA INDIAN SCHOLARSHIP PROGRAM
• *See page 654*

NORTH DAKOTA SCHOLARS PROGRAM
• *See page 654*

NORTH DAKOTA STATE STUDENT INCENTIVE GRANT PROGRAM
• *See page 654*

NORTHWEST DANISH ASSOCIATION

http://www.northwestdanish.org

NORTHWEST DANISH ASSOCIATION SCHOLARSHIP
• *See page 753*

OHIO DEPARTMENT OF HIGHER EDUCATION

http://www.ohiohighered.org

CHOOSE OHIO FIRST SCHOLARSHIP
• *See page 655*

OHIO COLLEGE OPPORTUNITY GRANT
• *See page 655*

OHIO SAFETY OFFICERS COLLEGE MEMORIAL FUND
• *See page 655*

OHIO WAR ORPHANS SCHOLARSHIP
• *See page 655*

OHIO-MICHIGAN ASSOCIATION OF CAREER COLLEGES AND SCHOOLS

http://www.omaccs.org/

LEADS! SCHOLARSHIP
One-time scholarship for graduating high school seniors enrolling in a career college or school that is a participating member of OMACCS. The applicant must be an Ohio or Michigan high school student with a 2.0 GPA or better and does not have to demonstrate a financial need. The scholarship amount and the number of scholarships granted varies.

Award: Scholarship for use in freshman, sophomore, junior, or senior years; not renewable. *Number:* 200–250. *Amount:* $1500–$40,000.

Eligibility Requirements: Applicant must be high school student; planning to enroll or expecting to enroll full- or part-time at a two-year or four-year or technical institution; resident of Michigan, Ohio and studying in Michigan, Ohio. Available to U.S. and non-U.S. citizens.

Application Requirements: Application form, essay. *Deadline:* April 6.

Contact: Denise Putigano, Admin Asst
Ohio-Michigan Association of Career Colleges and Schools
2109 Stella Ct
Ste 125
Columbus, OH 43215
Phone: 614-487-8180
E-mail: admin@omaccs.org

OHIO NATIONAL GUARD

http://www.ong.ohio.gov/

OHIO NATIONAL GUARD SCHOLARSHIP PROGRAM
• *See page 700*

OKLAHOMA ALUMNI & ASSOCIATES OF FHA, HERO AND FCCLA INC.

http://www.okalumni.org

OKLAHOMA ALUMNI & ASSOCIATES OF FHA, HERO, AND FCCLA INC. SCHOLARSHIP
• *See page 572*

OKLAHOMA STATE REGENTS FOR HIGHER EDUCATION

http://www.okhighered.org/

OKLAHOMA TUITION AID GRANT
Award for Oklahoma residents enrolled at an Oklahoma institution at least part time each semester in a degree program. May be enrolled in two- or four-year or approved vocational-technical institution. Award for students attending public institutions or private colleges. Application is made through FAFSA.

Award: Grant for use in freshman, sophomore, junior, or senior years; not renewable. *Amount:* $1000–$1300.

Eligibility Requirements: Applicant must be enrolled or expecting to enroll full- or part-time at a two-year or four-year or technical institution or university; resident of Oklahoma and studying in Oklahoma. Available to U.S. citizens.

Application Requirements: Application form, financial need analysis.

Contact: Mrs. Linette McMurtrey, Scholarship Programs Coordinator
Oklahoma State Regents for Higher Education
655 Research Parkway, Suite 200
Oklahoma City, OK 73104
Phone: 405-225-9131
E-mail: lmcmurtrey@osrhe.edu

REGIONAL UNIVERSITY BACCALAUREATE SCHOLARSHIP
Renewable award for Oklahoma residents attending one of 11 participating Oklahoma public universities. Must have an ACT composite score of at least 30 or be a National Merit semifinalist or commended student. In addition to the award amount, each recipient will receive a resident tuition waiver from the institution. Must maintain a 3.25 GPA. Deadlines vary depending upon the institution attended.

Award: Scholarship for use in freshman, sophomore, junior, or senior years; renewable. *Amount:* $3000.

Eligibility Requirements: Applicant must be enrolled or expecting to enroll full-time at an institution or university; resident of Oklahoma and studying in Oklahoma. Available to U.S. citizens.

Application Requirements: Application form.

Contact: Scholarship Programs Coordinator
Oklahoma State Regents for Higher Education
PO Box 108850
Oklahoma City, OK 73101-8850
Phone: 405-858-1840
E-mail: studentinfo@osrhe.edu

WILLIAM P. WILLIS SCHOLARSHIP
Renewable award for low-income Oklahoma residents attending an Oklahoma institution. Must be a full-time undergraduate. Deadline varies.

Award: Scholarship for use in freshman, sophomore, junior, or senior years; renewable. *Amount:* $2000–$3000.

Eligibility Requirements: Applicant must be enrolled or expecting to enroll full-time at a two-year or four-year institution or university; resident of Oklahoma and studying in Oklahoma. Available to U.S. citizens.

Application Requirements: Application form.

Contact: Scholarship Programs Coordinator
Oklahoma State Regents for Higher Education
PO Box 108850
Oklahoma City, OK 73101-8850
Phone: 405-858-1840
E-mail: studentinfo@osrhe.edu

ONE MILLION DEGREES

http://www.onemilliondegrees.org

ONE MILLION DEGREES SCHOLARSHIP SUPPORT PROGRAM
The One Million Degrees Scholarship Program offers groundbreaking, whole-student programming to low-income, highly motivated community college students. OMD provides scholars with financial, academic, personal and professional supports to ensure students are on track to graduate and prepared for their next step. One Million Degrees currently partners with all seven City Colleges of Chicago, Harper College, Prairie State College and South Suburban College.

Award: Scholarship for use in freshman, sophomore, junior, or senior years; renewable. *Number:* 400–500. *Amount:* $1000.

Eligibility Requirements: Applicant must be enrolled or expecting to enroll full-time at a two-year institution; resident of Illinois and studying in Illinois. Available to U.S. and non-Canadian citizens.

Application Requirements: Application form, essay, financial need analysis. *Deadline:* May 16.

Contact: Magali Perez, Scholar Recruitment Manager
E-mail: apply@onemilliondegrees.org

ONLINEPSYCHOLOGYDEGREES.COM

http://www.onlinepsychologydegrees.com/

ONLINEPSYCHOLOGYDEGREES.COM EDUCATION SCHOLARSHIPS
• *See page 656*

OREGON COMMUNITY FOUNDATION

http://www.oregoncf.org/

ERNEST ALAN AND BARBARA PARK MEYER SCHOLARSHIP FUND

Scholarship for Oregon high school graduates for use in the pursuit of a postsecondary education (undergraduate or graduate) at a nonprofit two- or four-year college or university.

Award: Scholarship for use in freshman, sophomore, junior, or senior years; renewable. *Number:* up to 5. *Amount:* $1000–$4500.

Eligibility Requirements: Applicant must be enrolled or expecting to enroll full-time at a two-year or four-year or technical institution or university and resident of Oregon. Available to U.S. citizens.

Application Requirements: Application form, recommendations or references. *Deadline:* March 1.

Contact: Dianne Causey, Program Associate for Scholarships and Grants
Phone: 503-227-6846 Ext. 1418
E-mail: dcausey@oregoncf.org

FRIENDS OF BILL RUTHERFORD EDUCATION FUND

Scholarship for Oregon high school graduates or GED recipients who are dependent children of individuals holding statewide elected office or currently serving in the Oregon State Legislature. Students must be enrolled full-time in a two- or four-year college or university. For more information, see web http://www.getcollegefunds.org.

Award: Scholarship for use in freshman, sophomore, junior, or senior years; renewable. *Number:* 1–2. *Amount:* $1000–$2500.

Eligibility Requirements: Applicant must be enrolled or expecting to enroll full-time at a two-year or four-year institution or university and resident of Oregon. Available to U.S. citizens.

Application Requirements: Application form, recommendations or references. *Deadline:* March 1.

Contact: Dianne Causey, Program Associate for Scholarships and Grants
Phone: 503-227-6846 Ext. 1418
E-mail: dcausey@oregoncf.org

MARY E. HORSTKOTTE SCHOLARSHIP FUND

Award available for academically talented and financially needy students for use in the pursuit of a postsecondary education. Must be an Oregon resident. For full-time study only.

Award: Scholarship for use in freshman, sophomore, junior, or senior years; not renewable. *Number:* 1–10. *Amount:* $2000.

Eligibility Requirements: Applicant must be enrolled or expecting to enroll full-time at a two-year or four-year or technical institution or university and resident of Oregon. Available to U.S. citizens.

Application Requirements: Application form, recommendations or references. *Deadline:* March 1.

Contact: Dianne Causey, Program Associate for Scholarships and Grants
Phone: 503-227-6846 Ext. 1418
E-mail: dcausey@oregoncf.org

RUBE AND MINAH LESLIE EDUCATIONAL FUND

Scholarship for Oregon residents for the pursuit of a postsecondary education. Selection is based on financial need.

Award: Scholarship for use in freshman, sophomore, junior, or senior years; renewable. *Number:* up to 50. *Amount:* $2000.

Eligibility Requirements: Applicant must be enrolled or expecting to enroll full-time at a two-year or four-year institution or university and resident of Oregon. Available to U.S. citizens.

Application Requirements: Application form, financial need analysis. *Deadline:* March 1.

Contact: Dianne Causey, Program Associate for Scholarships and Grants
Phone: 503-227-6846 Ext. 1418
E-mail: dcausey@oregoncf.org

OREGON STUDENT ASSISTANCE COMMISSION

https://oregonstudentaid.gov/

AMERICAN FEDERATION OF STATE, COUNTY, AND MUNICIPAL EMPLOYEES OREGON COUNCIL # 75 SCHOLARSHIP
• *See page 573*

ANDEO SCHOLARSHIP

One-time award for graduating seniors (including GED recipients and home-schooled seniors) of Oregon or Washington high schools. Must have hosted an international student through ANDEO International Homestays during the current academic year or the year immediately prior to the current year and taken 3+ years of a foreign language by the end of the current academic year. Minimum 3.5 GPA preferred. financial need may or may not be considered. Must enroll at least half time at any public or non-profit U.S. college or university.

Award: Scholarship for use in freshman year; not renewable.

Eligibility Requirements: Applicant must be high school student; planning to enroll or expecting to enroll full- or part-time at a four-year institution or university and resident of Oregon, Washington. Applicant must have 3.5 GPA or higher. Available to U.S. citizens.

Application Requirements: Application form, financial need analysis. *Deadline:* March 1.

Contact: Melissa Adams, Scholarship Processing Coordinator
Phone: 541-687-7409
E-mail: melissa.adams@state.or.us

A. VICTOR ROSENFELD SCHOLARSHIP
• *See page 589*

BANK OF THE CASCADES SCHOLARSHIP

Award for residents of Oregon or Washington who are dependents of eligible employees of Bank of the Cascades. Eligible employee must have been employed by Bank of the Cascades one+ year as of the March scholarship deadline. Must be attending a public or nonprofit college with a preferred GPA of at least 2.5.

Award: Scholarship for use in freshman, sophomore, junior, or senior years; not renewable.

Eligibility Requirements: Applicant must be enrolled or expecting to enroll full-time at a four-year institution or university and resident of Idaho, Oregon, Washington. Applicant must have 2.5 GPA or higher. Available to U.S. citizens.

Application Requirements: Application form, essay. *Deadline:* March 1.

Contact: Melissa Adams, Scholarship Processing Coordinator
Phone: 541-687-7409
E-mail: melissa.adams@state.or.us

BENJAMIN FRANKLIN/EDITH GREEN SCHOLARSHIP

Scholarship for graduating seniors of Oregon high schools, enrolling in an Oregon public college. Based on financial need.

Award: Scholarship for use in freshman year; not renewable.

Eligibility Requirements: Applicant must be high school student; planning to enroll or expecting to enroll at a four-year institution or university; resident of Oregon and studying in Oregon. Available to U.S. citizens.

Application Requirements: Application form. *Deadline:* March 1.

Contact: Melissa Adams, Scholarship Processing Coordinator
Phone: 541-687-7409
E-mail: melissa.adams@state.or.us

BLUE WOLFE SCHOLARSHIP

Scholarship for graduates (including GED recipients) of Oregon high schools, preference to graduates of Portland high schools. Preference to Portland residents. Applicants must enroll in Oregon public and for-profit colleges only. GPA 2.5-3.0 for high school seniors, minimum GPA 3.0 for college students. Enrollment must be at least half time. Financial need may or may not be considered.

Award: Scholarship for use in freshman, sophomore, junior, or senior years; not renewable.

Eligibility Requirements: Applicant must be enrolled or expecting to enroll full- or part-time at a four-year institution or university; resident of Oregon and studying in Oregon. Applicant must have 2.5 GPA or higher. Available to U.S. citizens.

Application Requirements: Application form. *Deadline:* March 1.

Contact: Melissa Adams, Scholarship Processing Coordinator
    Phone: 541-687-7409
    E-mail: melissa.adams@state.or.us

DOROTHY CAMPBELL MEMORIAL SCHOLARSHIP

Renewable award for female Oregon high school graduates with a minimum 2.75 GPA. Must submit essay describing strong, continuing interest in golf and the contribution that sport has made to applicant's development. Preference for participation in high school golf team (including intramural), if available, and planning to enroll at a four-year Oregon public or nonprofit college. Based on financial need.

Award: Scholarship for use in freshman year; renewable.

Eligibility Requirements: Applicant must be enrolled or expecting to enroll full-time at a four-year institution or university; female; resident of Oregon; studying in Oregon and must have an interest in golf. Applicant must have 2.5 GPA or higher. Available to U.S. citizens.

Application Requirements: Application form, essay, financial need analysis. *Deadline:* March 1.

Contact: Melissa Adams, Scholarship Processing Coordinator
    Phone: 541-687-7409
    E-mail: melissa.adams@state.or.us

FORD OPPORTUNITY PROGRAM

Renewable award for Oregon or Siskiyou County residents who are single heads of household with custody of a dependent child or children and without the support of a domestic partner. Must be planning to earn a Bachelor's degree and study full-time at an Oregon or California college or university. Minimum cumulative GPA of 3.0 or 700+ GED score. If minimum requirements are not met, special recommendation form required (see high school counselor or contact OSAC). FAFSA required. Based on financial need and must meet Expected Family Contribution (EFC) limitations.

Award: Scholarship for use in freshman, sophomore, junior, or senior years; renewable.

Eligibility Requirements: Applicant must be enrolled or expecting to enroll full-time at a four-year institution or university; single; resident of California, Oregon and studying in California, Oregon. Applicant must have 3.0 GPA or higher. Available to U.S. citizens.

Application Requirements: Application form, essay, financial need analysis, interview. *Deadline:* March 1.

Contact: Ford Family Foundation Scholarship Office
    Oregon Student Assistance Commission
    44 Club Road, Suite 100
    Eugene, OR 97401
    Phone: 877-864-2872
    E-mail: fordscholarships@tfff.org

FORD RESTART PROGRAM

Award to support nontraditional, full-time adult students who wish to begin or continue education at the postsecondary level in Oregon or California, at a public or non-profit college. Must be an Oregon or Siskiyou County resident and at least 25 years of age by the application deadline. Must have a high school diploma or GED certificate and must not have previously earned a Bachelor's degree. A Restart Reference Form is required and must be submitted with the application. Strong preference given to applicants with little or no recent college experience. Based on financial need and must meet Expected Family Contribution (EFC) limitations.

Award: Scholarship for use in freshman, sophomore, junior, or senior years; renewable.

Eligibility Requirements: Applicant must be enrolled or expecting to enroll full-time at a four-year institution or university; resident of California, Oregon and studying in California, Oregon. Applicant must have 3.0 GPA or higher. Available to U.S. citizens.

Application Requirements: Application form, financial need analysis, interview. *Deadline:* March 1.

Contact: Melissa Adams, Scholarship Processing Coordinator
    Phone: 541-687-7409
    E-mail: melissa.adams@state.or.us

FORD SCHOLARS PROGRAM

Renewable award for Oregon or Siskiyou County residents who are graduating high school seniors, GED recipients or students at the point of transferring from a community college to a four-year college in Oregon or California. Must have minimum cumulative GPA of 3.0 or 700+ GED score, be planning to earn a Bachelor's degree, and be enrolled as a full-time student at a public or non-profit college. If minimum requirements are not met, special recommendation form required (see high school counselor or contact OSAC). Based on financial need and must meet Expected Family Contribution (EFC) limitations.

Award: Scholarship for use in freshman, sophomore, junior, or senior years; renewable.

Eligibility Requirements: Applicant must be enrolled or expecting to enroll full-time at a four-year institution or university; resident of California, Oregon and studying in California, Oregon. Applicant must have 3.0 GPA or higher. Available to U.S. citizens.

Application Requirements: Application form, financial need analysis, interview. *Deadline:* March 1.

Contact: Melissa Adams, Scholarship Processing Coordinator
    Phone: 541-687-7409
    E-mail: melissa.adams@state.or.us

FRANZ STENZEL M.D. AND KATHRYN STENZEL II SCHOLARSHIP

Preference: Nontraditional students, first-generation college students, and students approaching the final year of their programs. Minimum GPA for high school students (first-time freshman), 2.75; college students, 2.50. Not open to medicine, nursing, or physician assistant. Must enroll at least half time. Based on financial need.

Award: Scholarship for use in freshman, sophomore, junior, or senior years; renewable.

Eligibility Requirements: Applicant must be enrolled or expecting to enroll full- or part-time at a four-year institution or university and resident of Oregon. Applicant must have 2.5 GPA or higher. Available to U.S. citizens.

Application Requirements: Application form. *Deadline:* March 1.

Contact: Melissa Adams, Scholarship Processing Coordinator
    Phone: 541-687-7409
    E-mail: melissa.adams@state.or.us

GLENN JACKSON SCHOLARS SCHOLARSHIPS

• *See page 590*

HARRY LUDWIG MEMORIAL SCHOLARSHIP

• *See page 692*

IDA M. CRAWFORD SCHOLARSHIP

Scholarship available to graduates of accredited Oregon high schools. Not available to applicants majoring in law, medicine, theology, teaching, or music. U.S. Bank employees, their children or near relatives, are not eligible. Reapply annually for award renewal. Based on financial need.

Award: Scholarship for use in freshman year; not renewable.

Eligibility Requirements: Applicant must be enrolled or expecting to enroll full-time at a four-year institution and resident of Oregon. Applicant must have 3.5 GPA or higher. Available to U.S. citizens.

Application Requirements: Application form, financial need analysis. *Deadline:* March 1.

Contact: Melissa Adams, Scholarship Processing Coordinator
    Phone: 541-687-7409
    E-mail: melissa.adams@state.or.us

LYNDA PILGER MEMORIAL SCHOLARSHIP

One-time award available to graduating seniors (including home-schooled seniors) of Oregon high schools. Minimum GPA of 2.75. Award must be used at a four-year public college or university in the United States. Must submit an essay describing work in the area of animal rights or animal welfare and how a college education will enhance efforts in these areas. Financial need may or may not be considered.

Award: Scholarship for use in freshman year; not renewable.

Eligibility Requirements: Applicant must be high school student; planning to enroll or expecting to enroll full-time at a four-year institution or university and resident of Oregon. Available to U.S. citizens.

Application Requirements: Application form, essay. *Deadline:* March 1.

Contact: Melissa Adams, Scholarship Processing Coordinator
Phone: 541-687-7409
E-mail: melissa.adams@state.or.us

MARIA C. JACKSON/GENERAL GEORGE A. WHITE SCHOLARSHIP

Available to Oregon residents who served or whose parents serve or have served in the U.S. Armed Forces and resided in Oregon at time of enlistment. Must have at least 3.75 GPA and submit documentation of service. (No GPA requirement for graduate-level students and students attending a technical school). U.S. Bank employees, their children, and near relatives are not eligible. Based on financial need.

Award: Scholarship for use in freshman, sophomore, junior, senior, or graduate years; not renewable.

Eligibility Requirements: Applicant must be enrolled or expecting to enroll full-time at a two-year or four-year or technical institution or university; resident of Oregon and studying in Oregon. Available to U.S. citizens.

Application Requirements: Application form, financial need analysis. *Deadline:* March 1.

Contact: Melissa Adams, Scholarship Processing Coordinator
Phone: 541-687-7409
E-mail: melissa.adams@state.or.us

MARY DUBY HONDERICH SCHOLARSHIP

Scholarship for Oregon residents, preference for Marion County. Major in nursing at an Oregon public or nonprofit college. Must enroll at least half time. Minimum GPA 3.80. Financial need may or may not be considered.

Award: Scholarship for use in freshman, sophomore, junior, or senior years; not renewable.

Eligibility Requirements: Applicant must be enrolled or expecting to enroll full- or part-time at a four-year institution or university; resident of Oregon and studying in Oregon. Applicant must have 3.5 GPA or higher. Available to U.S. citizens.

Application Requirements: Application form. *Deadline:* March 1.

Contact: Melissa Adams, Scholarship Processing Coordinator
Phone: 541-687-7409
E-mail: melissa.adams@state.or.us

OREGON ALBACORE COMMISSION SCHOLARSHIP

One-time award for first-time freshmen or undergraduates enrolled at least half-time at any college or university in the U.S. Open to Oregon commercially licensed albacore tuna landing permit holders, their captains, and their children and dependents who have paid assessments to the Oregon Albacore Commission within the past year; and processors, employees and their children and dependents where the business has purchased Oregon albacore tuna and paid assessments to the Oregon Albacore Commission within the past year. Financial need may or may not be considered. Apply/compete for additional year of funding.

Award: Scholarship for use in freshman, sophomore, junior, or senior years; not renewable.

Eligibility Requirements: Applicant must be enrolled or expecting to enroll full- or part-time at a two-year or four-year institution or university and resident of Oregon. Available to U.S. citizens.

Application Requirements: Application form. *Deadline:* March 1.

Contact: Melissa Adams, Scholarship Processing Coordinator
Phone: 541-687-7409
E-mail: melissa.adams@state.or.us

OREGON HEAD START ASSOCIATION—FRANK ROBERTS SCHOLARSHIP

Scholarship for graduating high school seniors (including GED recipients and home-schooled seniors) who participated in a Head Start program. Preference for first-generation college attendee. Must attend an Oregon public or nonprofit college. Preference for minimum SAT 1090 combined scores or ACT composite of 21. Must enroll at least half time. Based on financial need.

Award: Scholarship for use in freshman year; not renewable.

Eligibility Requirements: Applicant must be high school student; planning to enroll or expecting to enroll full- or part-time at a two-year or four-year institution or university; resident of Oregon and studying in Oregon. Applicant must have 3.5 GPA or higher. Available to U.S. citizens.

Application Requirements: Application form. *Deadline:* March 1.

Contact: Melissa Adams, Scholarship Processing Coordinator
Phone: 541-687-7409
E-mail: melissa.adams@state.or.us

OREGON STATE FISCAL ASSOCIATION SCHOLARSHIP
• *See page 574*

OREGON STUDENT ACCESS COMMISSION EMPLOYEE AND DEPENDENTS SCHOLARSHIP

Award for eligible employees of the Office of Student Access and Completion and their dependents. Children and dependents must enroll full-time and be 23 or under as of the March scholarship deadline. Employees must enroll at least half time. Apply/compete annually.

Award: Scholarship for use in freshman, sophomore, junior, or senior years; not renewable.

Eligibility Requirements: Applicant must be enrolled or expecting to enroll full- or part-time at a four-year institution or university and resident of Oregon. Available to U.S. citizens.

Application Requirements: Application form. *Deadline:* March 1.

Contact: Melissa Adams, Scholarship Processing Coordinator
Phone: 541-687-7409
E-mail: melissa.adams@state.or.us

PACIFIC NW FEDERAL CREDIT UNION SCHOLARSHIP

Scholarship available to members of Pacific North West Federal Credit Union. Must submit an essay on 'Why My Credit Union is an Important Consumer Choice.' Immediate family members of Pacific NW Federal Credit Union employees and credit union elected or appointed officials are not eligible.

Award: Scholarship for use in freshman, sophomore, junior, or senior years; not renewable.

Eligibility Requirements: Applicant must be enrolled or expecting to enroll full-time at a four-year institution or university and resident of Oregon, Washington. Available to U.S. citizens.

Application Requirements: Application form, essay. *Deadline:* March 1.

Contact: Melissa Adams, Scholarship Processing Coordinator
Phone: 541-687-7409
E-mail: melissa.adams@state.or.us

PETER CROSSLEY MEMORIAL SCHOLARSHIP

Renewable award for graduating seniors of Oregon public alternative high schools. Must be highly motivated to succeed despite overcoming a severe personal obstacle or challenge during high school career. Must plan to enroll at least half-time in an Oregon college or university. Preferred GPA is between 2.0 and 3.5. Based on financial need.

Award: Scholarship for use in freshman year; not renewable.

Eligibility Requirements: Applicant must be high school student; planning to enroll or expecting to enroll full- or part-time at a four-year institution or university; resident of Oregon and studying in Oregon. Available to U.S. citizens.

Application Requirements: Application form, essay, financial need analysis. *Deadline:* March 1.

Contact: Melissa Adams, Scholarship Processing Coordinator
Phone: 541-687-7409
E-mail: melissa.adams@state.or.us

SALEM ELECTRIC COOPERATIVE SCHOLARSHIP

Award for high school graduates (including GED recipients and home-schooled graduates) who is or whose parents/legal guardians are receiving service from Salem Electric at their primary residence. Salem Electric staff, board members, and immediate family are not eligible. Apply/compete annually.

Award: Scholarship for use in freshman, sophomore, junior, or senior years; not renewable.

Eligibility Requirements: Applicant must be enrolled or expecting to enroll full-time at a four-year institution or university and resident of Oregon. Available to U.S. citizens.

Application Requirements: Application form. *Deadline:* March 1.

Contact: Melissa Adams, Scholarship Processing Coordinator
Phone: 541-687-7409
E-mail: melissa.adams@state.or.us

SALEM FOUNDATION ANSEL & MARIE SOLIE SCHOLARSHIP

• *See page 692*

SEIU LOCAL 503/OPEU STUDENT FINANCIAL AID SCHOLARSHIP

Award for students who are SEIU Local 503/OPEU active members; laid-off members; children, grandchildren, spouses, or domestic partners of active or retired members in good standing; or dependents of deceased members who were active members at time of death. Qualifying members must have been active (full membership dues payer) 1+ year as of the March scholarship deadline. Children, grandchildren, or dependents of qualifying members must be 24 or younger as of the March scholarship deadline, must enroll full time, and will be considered only for undergraduate programs. Part-time enrollment (minimum six credit hours) or graduate program enrollment will be considered only for active members, spouses, domestic partners, or laid-off members. Based on financial need.

Award: Scholarship for use in freshman, sophomore, junior, senior, or graduate years; not renewable.

Eligibility Requirements: Applicant must be enrolled or expecting to enroll full- or part-time at a four-year institution or university and resident of Oregon. Available to U.S. citizens.

Application Requirements: Application form, financial need analysis. *Deadline:* March 1.

Contact: Melissa Adams, Scholarship Processing Coordinator
Phone: 541-687-7409
E-mail: melissa.adams@state.or.us

W.C. AND PEARL CAMPBELL SCHOLARSHIP

One-time award for graduating seniors of Oregon high schools. 1220+ combined math and critical reading SAT scores or ACT composite of 27+ required. Minimum GPA of 3.85 required. Based on financial need.

Award: Scholarship for use in freshman year; not renewable.

Eligibility Requirements: Applicant must be high school student; planning to enroll or expecting to enroll full-time at a four-year institution or university; resident of Oregon and studying in Oregon. Applicant must have 3.5 GPA or higher. Available to U.S. citizens.

Application Requirements: Application form, financial need analysis. *Deadline:* March 1.

Contact: Melissa Adams, Scholarship Processing Coordinator
Phone: 541-687-7409
E-mail: melissa.adams@state.or.us

OUTRIGGER DUKE KAHANAMOKU FOUNDATION

http://www.dukefoundation.org

ODKF GENERAL SCHOLARSHIP AWARD

• *See page 657*

PACERS FOUNDATION INC.

http://www.pacersfoundation.org/

PACERS TEAMUP SCHOLARSHIP

• *See page 657*

PACIFIC AND ASIAN AFFAIRS COUNCIL

http://www.paachawaii.org/

PAAC ACADEMIC SCHOLARSHIPS

PAAC's academic scholarships are available to college-bound seniors and underclassmen attending Hawaii public or private high school. Applicants must be active in PAAC's high school program (PAAC clubs or PAAC After-School Classes).

Award: Scholarship for use in freshman year; not renewable. *Number:* 5. *Amount:* $300–$1000.

Eligibility Requirements: Applicant must be high school student; planning to enroll or expecting to enroll full-time at a two-year or four-year or technical institution or university and resident of Hawaii. Available to U.S. and non-U.S. citizens.

Application Requirements: Application form, essay. *Deadline:* April 2.

Contact: Jason Shon, High School Program Director
Pacific and Asian Affairs Council
1601 East-West Road, 4th Floor
Honolulu, HI 96848
Phone: 808-944-7759
E-mail: hs@paachawaii.org

PEACOCK PRODUCTIONS, INC.

http://amefund.com

AUDRIA M. EDWARDS SCHOLARSHIP FUND

• *See page 658*

PENNSYLVANIA BURGLAR AND FIRE ALARM ASSOCIATION

http://www.pbfaa.com/

PENNSYLVANIA BURGLAR AND FIRE ALARM ASSOCIATION YOUTH SCHOLARSHIP PROGRAM

• *See page 658*

PENNSYLVANIA FEDERATION OF DEMOCRATIC WOMEN INC.

http://www.pafedofdemwomen.org

PENNSYLVANIA FEDERATION OF DEMOCRATIC WOMEN INC. ANNUAL SCHOLARSHIP AWARDS

• *See page 574*

PENNSYLVANIA HIGHER EDUCATION ASSISTANCE AGENCY

http://www.pheaa.org/

BLIND OR DEAF BENEFICIARY GRANT PROGRAM

• *See page 658*

PENNSYLVANIA STATE GRANT PROGRAM

• *See page 658*

POSTSECONDARY EDUCATION GRATUITY PROGRAM

• *See page 700*

READY TO SUCCEED SCHOLARSHIP PROGRAM

RTSS provides scholarships to high academic achievers that, in combination with the Pennsylvania State Grant Program, offer a total award up to $2,000 for full-time and $1,000 for part-time students. The minimum award is $500. Awards can be used to cover tuition, books, fees, supplies, and living expenses. Students must be nominated by their post-secondary institution for participation in the program. Funding is limited for the program and awards are made on a first-come, first-served basis. The program, which is funded by the Pennsylvania General Assembly, provides awards to high-achieving students whose annual family income does not exceed $110,000.

Award: Scholarship for use in sophomore, junior, or senior years; not renewable. *Amount:* $500–$2000.

Eligibility Requirements: Applicant must be enrolled or expecting to enroll full- or part-time at a two-year or four-year or technical institution or university; resident of Pennsylvania and studying in Pennsylvania. Applicant must have 3.5 GPA or higher.

Application Requirements: Application form, financial need analysis.

Contact: Keith New, Director of Public Relations
    Phone: 717-720-2509
    E-mail: knew@pheaa.org

PETER DOCTOR MEMORIAL INDIAN SCHOLARSHIP FOUNDATION INC.

PETER DOCTOR MEMORIAL INDIAN SCHOLARSHIP FOUNDATION INC.
• *See page 756*

PFUND FOUNDATION

http://www.pfundfoundation.org

PFUND FOUNDATION SCHOLARSHIP PROGRAM

The PFund Foundation Scholarship Program annually awards $60,000 in scholarships to Lesbian, Gay, Bisexual, Transgender, Queer and allied students in recognition of their courageous leadership, community service and academic achievement. Powered by a diverse panel of community leaders who select scholars each year and numerous donors who establish the scholarship awards, the PFund Scholarship Program is developing every generation of LGBTQ leadership. Scholarship awards range from $1,000 to $10,000. To learn more about how to apply, visit http://www.PFundFoundation.org for the Scholarship Guidelines & Application Form or contact (612) 870-1806 or email: scholarships@pfundfoundation.org

Award: Scholarship for use in freshman, sophomore, junior, senior, graduate, or postgraduate years; not renewable. *Number:* 15–30. *Amount:* $2000–$10,000.

Eligibility Requirements: Applicant must be enrolled or expecting to enroll full- or part-time at a two-year or four-year or technical institution or university; resident of Iowa, Minnesota, North Dakota, South Dakota, Wisconsin and studying in Iowa, Minnesota, North Dakota, South Dakota, Wisconsin. Available to U.S. and non-U.S. citizens.

Application Requirements: Application form, community service, essay. *Deadline:* January 15.

Contact: Trina Olson, Executive Director
    PFund Foundation
    2801 21st Ave. S
    Suite 132B
    Minneapolis, MN 55407
    Phone: 612-870-1806
    E-mail: scholarships@pfundfoundation.org

PHILIPINO-AMERICAN ASSOCIATION OF NEW ENGLAND

http://www.pamas.org/

BLESSED LEON OF OUR LADY OF THE ROSARY AWARD
• *See page 756*

PAMAS RESTRICTED SCHOLARSHIP AWARD
• *See page 574*

RAVENSCROFT FAMILY AWARD
• *See page 756*

PHOENIX PRIDE

https://phoenixpride.org/

PHOENIX PRIDE SCHOLARSHIP PROGRAM
• *See page 659*

PINE CONE FOUNDATION (PCF)

http://pineconefoundation.org/

PINE CONE FOUNDATION SCHOLARSHIP
• *See page 660*

PINE TREE STATE 4-H CLUB FOUNDATION/4-H POSTSECONDARY SCHOLARSHIP

http://www.umaine.edu/

PARKER-LOVEJOY SCHOLARSHIP

One-time scholarship of $1000 is available to a graduating high school senior. Applicants must be residents of Maine.

Award: Scholarship for use in freshman year; not renewable. *Number:* 1. *Amount:* $1000.

Eligibility Requirements: Applicant must be high school student; planning to enroll or expecting to enroll full-time at a two-year or four-year institution or university and resident of Maine. Available to U.S. citizens.

Application Requirements: Application form. *Deadline:* March 14.

Contact: Angela Martin, Administrative Assistant
    Phone: 207-581-3739
    Fax: 207-581-1387
    E-mail: angela.martin@maine.edu

WAYNE S. RICH SCHOLARSHIP

Scholarship for an outstanding Maine or New Hampshire 4-H member for postsecondary study. Awarded to a Maine student in odd numbered years and a New Hampshire student in even numbered years.

Award: Scholarship for use in freshman year; not renewable. *Number:* 1. *Amount:* up to $1000.

Eligibility Requirements: Applicant must be high school student; planning to enroll or expecting to enroll full-time at a two-year or four-year institution or university and resident of Maine, New Hampshire. Available to U.S. citizens.

Application Requirements: Application form. *Deadline:* March 14.

Contact: Angela Martin, Administrative Assistant
    Phone: 207-581-3739
    Fax: 207-581-1387
    E-mail: angela.martin@maine.edu

POINTE PEST CONTROL

http://pointepestcontrol.net

GREEN PEST SERVICES SCHOLARSHIP

$750 scholarship available to graduating high school seniors and college freshman who are residents of D.C. and Maryland. Minimum 3.0 GPA required.

Award: Scholarship for use in freshman year; not renewable. *Number:* 4. *Amount:* $750.

Eligibility Requirements: Applicant must be enrolled or expecting to enroll full- or part-time at a two-year or four-year or technical institution or university; resident of Maryland and studying in District of Columbia. Applicant must have 3.0 GPA or higher. Available to U.S. citizens.

Application Requirements: Application form, financial need analysis. *Deadline:* April 14.

Contact: Jodelle Maglaya, Communications Manager
    E-mail: pr@pointepestcontrol.net

ILLINOIS SCHOLARSHIP

$750 scholarship available to graduating high school seniors and college freshman who are residents of Illinois. Minimum 3.0 GPA required.

Award: Scholarship for use in freshman year; not renewable. *Number:* 4. *Amount:* $750.

Eligibility Requirements: Applicant must be enrolled or expecting to enroll full- or part-time at a two-year or four-year or technical institution or university and resident of Illinois. Applicant must have 3.0 GPA or higher. Available to U.S. citizens.

Application Requirements: Application form, financial need analysis. *Deadline:* April 14.

Contact: Jodelle Maglaya, Communications Manager
E-mail: pr@pointepestcontrol.net

VIRGINIA GREEN PEST SERVICES

$750 scholarship available to graduating high school seniors and college freshman who are residents of Virginia. Minimum 3.0 GPA required.

Award: Scholarship for use in freshman year; not renewable. *Number:* 4. *Amount:* $750.

Eligibility Requirements: Applicant must be enrolled or expecting to enroll full- or part-time at a two-year or four-year or technical institution or university and resident of Virginia. Applicant must have 3.0 GPA or higher. Available to U.S. citizens.

Application Requirements: Application form, financial need analysis. *Deadline:* April 14.

Contact: Jodelle Maglaya, Communications Manager
E-mail: pr@pointepestcontrol.net

POLISH HERITAGE ASSOCIATION OF MARYLAND

http://www.pha-md.org/

POLISH HERITAGE SCHOLARSHIP
• *See page 756*

PORTUGUESE FOUNDATION INC.

https://www.facebook.com/pfict/

PORTUGUESE FOUNDATION SCHOLARSHIP PROGRAM
• *See page 660*

POTENTIAL MAGAZINE

http://potentialmagazine.com/

"DON'T WAIT TO REACH YOUR POTENTIAL" SCHOLARSHIP
• *See page 661*

PRESCOTT AUDUBON SOCIETY

prescottaudubon.org

ENVIRONMENTAL SCHOLARSHIP

A $1000 scholarship awarded to a degree-seeking, continuing college student who is passionate about the environment and/or conservation. Must be from Mohave or Yavapai County (home residence), and/or enrolled at a college operating in Yavapai or Mohave County, Arizona.

Award: Scholarship for use in freshman, sophomore, junior, or senior years; not renewable. *Number:* 1. *Amount:* $1000.

Eligibility Requirements: Applicant must be enrolled or expecting to enroll full- or part-time at a two-year or four-year institution or university and resident of Arizona. Available to U.S. citizens.

Application Requirements: Application form, essay. *Deadline:* December 8.

Contact: Scholarship Committee
E-mail: scholarship@prescottaudubon.org

PRIDE FOUNDATION

http://www.PrideFoundation.org/

PRIDE FOUNDATION SCHOLARSHIP PROGRAM
• *See page 662*

PROJECT BEST SCHOLARSHIP FUND

http://www.projectbest.com/

PROJECT BEST SCHOLARSHIP
• *See page 575*

PUEBLO OF SAN JUAN, DEPARTMENT OF EDUCATION

OHKAY OWINGEH TRIBAL SCHOLARSHIP OF THE PUEBLO OF SAN JUAN
• *See page 663*

POP'AY SCHOLARSHIP
• *See page 663*

REACH HIGHER MONTANA

http://www.ReachHigherMontana.org

REACH HIGHER MONTANA SCHOLARSHIPS
• *See page 663*

REHABCENTER.NET

http://www.rehabcenter.net/

REHABCENTER.NET
• *See page 664*

RENEE B. FISHER FOUNDATION

http://www.rbffoundation.org/

MILTON FISHER SCHOLARSHIP FOR INNOVATION AND CREATIVITY

Renewable scholarship for exceptionally innovative and creative high school juniors, seniors, and college freshmen who are graduating or have graduated from a Connecticut or New York City metro area high school (and plan to attend or are attending college anywhere in the U.S.) or are graduating or have graduated from any high school in the U.S. who plan to attend (or are attending) college in CT or NYC. You must graduate from a high school in the U.S. and complete an exceptionally innovative and creative project: solved artistic, scientific, or technical problems in new or unusual ways, come up with a distinctive solution to problems faced by your school, community or family or created a new group, organization, or institution that serves an important need. For more information, please contact http://www.rbffoundation.org

Award: Scholarship for use in freshman, sophomore, junior, or senior years; renewable. *Number:* 1–8. *Amount:* $250–$20,000.

Eligibility Requirements: Applicant must be enrolled or expecting to enroll full-time at a four-year or technical institution or university; resident of Alabama, Alaska, Arizona, Arkansas, California, Colorado, Connecticut, Delaware, District of Columbia, Florida, Georgia, Hawaii, Idaho, Illinois, Indiana, Iowa, Kansas, Kentucky, Louisiana, Maine, Maryland, Massachusetts, Michigan, Minnesota, Mississippi, Missouri, Montana, Nebraska, Nevada, New Hampshire, New Jersey, New Mexico, New York, North Carolina, North Dakota, Ohio, Oklahoma, Oregon, Pennsylvania, Rhode Island, South Carolina, South Dakota, Tennessee, Texas, Utah, Vermont, Virginia, Washington, West Virginia, Wisconsin, Wyoming and studying in Alabama, Alaska, Arizona, Arkansas, California, Colorado, Connecticut, Delaware, District of Columbia, Florida, Georgia, Hawaii, Idaho, Illinois, Indiana, Iowa, Kansas, Kentucky, Louisiana, Maine, Maryland, Massachusetts, Michigan, Minnesota, Mississippi, Missouri, Montana, Nebraska, Nevada, New Hampshire, New Jersey, New Mexico, New York, North Carolina, North Dakota, Ohio, Oklahoma, Oregon, Pennsylvania, Rhode Island, South Carolina, South Dakota, Tennessee, Texas, Utah, Vermont, Virginia, Washington, West Virginia, Wisconsin, Wyoming. Available to U.S. and non-U.S. citizens.

Application Requirements: Application form, essay. *Deadline:* April 30.

Contact: Milton Fisher Scholarship Liaison
Renee B. Fisher Foundation
70 Audubon Street
New Haven, CT 06510
Phone: 203-777-2386
E-mail: mfscholarship@gmail.com

RHODE ISLAND FOUNDATION

http://www.rifoundation.org/

ALDO FREDA LEGISLATIVE PAGES SCHOLARSHIP

Awarded to support Rhode Island Legislative Pages enrolled in a college or university. Must show scholastic achievement and good citizenship. Must be accepted into a full-time accredited postsecondary institution or graduate program. Must be a Rhode Island resident and a citizen of the United States.

Award: Scholarship for use in freshman, sophomore, junior, senior, or graduate years; not renewable. *Number:* 2–3. *Amount:* $1000–$1500.

Eligibility Requirements: Applicant must be enrolled or expecting to enroll full- or part-time at a two-year or four-year institution or university and resident of Rhode Island. Available to U.S. citizens.

Application Requirements: Application form, essay, financial need analysis, recommendations or references, transcript. *Deadline:* June 3.

Contact: Libby Monahan, Funds Administrator
Phone: 401-274-4564 Ext. 3117
E-mail: libbym@rifoundation.org

ANDREW BELL SCHOLARSHIP

Scholarships to high school graduates pursuing a post-secondary education. Must demonstrate financial need.

Award: Scholarship for use in freshman, sophomore, junior, or senior years; not renewable.

Eligibility Requirements: Applicant must be enrolled or expecting to enroll full-time at a two-year or four-year or technical institution or university and resident of Rhode Island. Available to U.S. citizens.

Application Requirements: Application form, financial need analysis. *Deadline:* continuous.

Contact: Urban League of Rhode Island
Phone: 401-351-5000

A.T. CROSS SCHOLARSHIP

• *See page 591*

BRUCE AND MARJORIE SUNDLUN SCHOLARSHIP

Scholarships for low-income single parents seeking to upgrade their career skills. Preference given to single parents previously receiving state support, and also for those previously incarcerated. Must be a Rhode Island resident and must attend school in the state.

Award: Scholarship for use in freshman, sophomore, junior, or senior years; not renewable. *Amount:* up to $1500.

Eligibility Requirements: Applicant must be enrolled or expecting to enroll full- or part-time at a two-year or four-year or technical institution or university; single; resident of Rhode Island and studying in Rhode Island. Available to U.S. and non-U.S. citizens.

Application Requirements: Application form, essay, financial need analysis, recommendations or references, self-addressed stamped envelope with application, transcript. *Deadline:* June 14.

Contact: Libby Monahan, Funds Administrator
Phone: 401-274-4564 Ext. 3117
E-mail: libbym@rifoundation.org

LILY AND CATELLO SORRENTINO MEMORIAL SCHOLARSHIP

Scholarships for Rhode Island residents. Applicant must be 25 years or older wishing to attend college or university in Rhode Island (only students attending non-parochial schools). Must demonstrate financial need. Preference given to first-time applicants. Financial need must be demonstrated.

Award: Scholarship for use in freshman, sophomore, junior, or senior years; not renewable. *Amount:* $500–$1000.

Eligibility Requirements: Applicant must be enrolled or expecting to enroll full- or part-time at a four-year institution or university; resident of Rhode Island and studying in Rhode Island. Available to U.S. citizens.

Application Requirements: Application form, financial need analysis, self-addressed stamped envelope with application, transcript. *Deadline:* May 1.

Contact: Libby Monahan, Funds Administrator
Phone: 401-274-4564 Ext. 3117
E-mail: libbym@rifoundation.org

NONDRAS HURST VOLL SCHOLARSHIP

Scholarship for single mothers transitioning off public assistance who are enrolled or planning to enroll in college certificate or degree program. Must be a Rhode Island resident and demonstrate financial need.

Award: Scholarship for use in freshman, sophomore, junior, or senior years; not renewable.

Eligibility Requirements: Applicant must be enrolled or expecting to enroll full- or part-time at a two-year or four-year institution or university; single female and resident of Rhode Island. Available to U.S. citizens.

Application Requirements: Application form, copy of U.S. income tax return, list of dependent children, copy of financial aid award letter if applicable, essay, financial need analysis, transcript. *Deadline:* April 19.

Contact: Fund for Community Progress, Nondas Hurst Voll Scholarship Committee
Rhode Island Foundation
90 Jefferson Boulevard
Suite B
Warwick, RI 02888
Phone: 401-941-7100

PATTY & MELVIN ALPERIN FIRST GENERATION SCHOLARSHIP

Renewable scholarship for Rhode Island high school seniors whose parents did not graduate from college. Must be accepted or enrolled in an accredited two- or four-year college and demonstrate financial need.

Award: Scholarship for use in freshman year; renewable. *Amount:* $1000.

Eligibility Requirements: Applicant must be high school student; planning to enroll or expecting to enroll full- or part-time at a two-year or four-year institution or university and resident of Rhode Island. Available to U.S. citizens.

Application Requirements: Application form, financial need analysis, transcript. *Deadline:* May 1.

Contact: Libby Monahan, Funds Administrator
Phone: 401-274-4564 Ext. 3117
E-mail: libbym@rifoundation.org

RHODE ISLAND ASSOCIATION OF FORMER LEGISLATORS SCHOLARSHIP

One-time award of $1500 for graduating high school seniors who are Rhode Island residents. Must have a history of substantial voluntary involvement in community service. Must be accepted into an accredited post-secondary institution and should be able to demonstrate financial need.

Award: Scholarship for use in freshman year; not renewable. *Number:* 4–5. *Amount:* $1500.

Eligibility Requirements: Applicant must be high school student; planning to enroll or expecting to enroll full-time at a four-year institution or university and resident of Rhode Island. Available to U.S. citizens.

Application Requirements: Application form, essay, financial need analysis, recommendations or references, self-addressed stamped envelope with application, test scores, transcript. *Deadline:* May 1.

Contact: Libby Monahan, Funds Administrator
Phone: 401-274-4564 Ext. 3117
E-mail: libbym@rifoundation.org

RHODE ISLAND COMMISSION ON WOMEN/FREDA GOLDMAN EDUCATION AWARD

Scholarship to assist women with transportation, child-care, tutoring, educational materials, and/or other support services. Must be pursuing education or job training beyond high school. Preference given to highly motivated, self-supporting, low-income women completing a first undergraduate degree or certificate program.

Award: Scholarship for use in freshman, sophomore, junior, or senior years; not renewable. *Amount:* $500–$1000.

Eligibility Requirements: Applicant must be enrolled or expecting to enroll full- or part-time at a four-year institution or university; female and resident of Rhode Island. Available to U.S. citizens.

Application Requirements: Application form, essay, recommendations or references, self-addressed stamped envelope with application, transcript. *Deadline:* June 14.

Contact: Libby Monahan, Funds Administrator
Phone: 401-274-4564 Ext. 3117
E-mail: libbym@rifoundation.org

UNITED ITALIAN AMERICAN INC. SCHOLARSHIP

For Rhode Island residents with financial need who wish to attend a two- or four-year college or university. Scholarship is based on merit as evidenced by superior achievement and leadership in school and/or community.

Award: Scholarship for use in freshman, sophomore, junior, or senior years; not renewable.

Eligibility Requirements: Applicant must be enrolled or expecting to enroll full-time at a two-year or four-year institution or university; resident of Rhode Island and must have an interest in leadership. Available to U.S. citizens.

Application Requirements: Application form, community service, financial need analysis, transcript. *Deadline:* June 3.

Contact: Libby Monahan, Funds Administrator
Phone: 401-274-4564 Ext. 3117
E-mail: libbym@rifoundation.org

ROBERT H. MOLLOHAN FAMILY CHARITABLE FOUNDATION, INC.

http://www.mollohanfoundation.org/

CARL R. MORRIS MEMORIAL SCHOLARSHIP

The Carl. R. Morris Memorial Scholarship is a $1000 scholarship that will be awarded to a resident of Calhoun County that best emulates Mr. Morris' commitment to community and education. The student must be enrolled, or planning to enroll, at Alderson-Broaddus College, Glenville State College, or West Virginia University, must have at least a 3.0 GPA, and must have demonstrated financial need.

Award: Scholarship for use in freshman, sophomore, junior, or senior years; not renewable. *Number:* 1–60. *Amount:* $1000.

Eligibility Requirements: Applicant must be enrolled or expecting to enroll full-time at a four-year institution or university; resident of West Virginia and studying in West Virginia. Applicant must have 3.0 GPA or higher. Available to U.S. citizens.

Application Requirements: Application form, essay, recommendations or references, resume, test scores, transcript.

Contact: Aime Shaffer, Program Manager
Phone: 304-333-6783
E-mail: ashaffer@wvhtf.org

DR. ROBERTO F. CUNANAN MEMORIAL SCHOLARSHIP

The Dr. Roberto F. Cunanan Memorial Scholarship was created to honor Dr. Cunanan's energetic spirit and loving heart. This $1000 scholarship is awarded to a Bridgeport High School student who is enrolled or planning to enroll at a West Virginia college or university, and who is an active participant in both academics and athletics.

Award: Scholarship for use in freshman, sophomore, junior, or senior years; not renewable. *Number:* 1–60. *Amount:* $1000.

Eligibility Requirements: Applicant must be high school student; planning to enroll or expecting to enroll full-time at a four-year institution or university; resident of West Virginia and must have an interest in athletics/sports. Available to U.S. citizens.

Application Requirements: Application form, essay, recommendations or references, resume, test scores, transcript.

Contact: Aime Shaffer, Program Manager
Phone: 304-333-6783
E-mail: ashaffer@wvhtf.org

HELEN HOLT MOLLOHAN SCHOLARSHIP

The Helen Holt Mollohan Scholarship is a $1000 scholarship that is awarded to a West Virginia female who is enrolled, or planning to enroll, at Glenville State College. This young woman should exhibit strong character, integrity, service to community, concern for others, and high standards of scholarship, like the late Mrs. Mollohan herself.

Award: Scholarship for use in freshman, sophomore, junior, or senior years; renewable. *Amount:* $1000.

Eligibility Requirements: Applicant must be high school student; planning to enroll or expecting to enroll full-time at a four-year institution or university; female; resident of West Virginia and studying in West Virginia. Available to U.S. citizens.

Application Requirements: Application form, essay, recommendations or references, resume, transcript.

Contact: Aime Shaffer, Program Manager
Phone: 304-333-6783
E-mail: ashaffer@wvhtf.org

ROOTHBERT FUND INC.

http://www.roothbertfund.org/

ROOTHBERT FUND INC. SCHOLARSHIP

Scholarships are open to all in the United States regardless of sex, age, color, nationality or religious background. The award must be used in the following states: CT, DC, DE, MA, MD, ME, NC, NH, NJ, NY, OH, PA, RI, VA, VT, or WV. Preference will be given to those who can satisfy high scholastic requirements and are considering careers in education. The Fund seeks candidates who are motivated by spiritual values, and works to foster fellowship among them.

Award: Scholarship for use in freshman, sophomore, junior, senior, or graduate years; renewable. *Number:* 50–60. *Amount:* $2000–$3000.

Eligibility Requirements: Applicant must be enrolled or expecting to enroll full-time at a two-year or four-year or technical institution or university; resident of Connecticut, Delaware, District of Columbia, Maine, Maryland, Massachusetts, New Hampshire, New Jersey, New York, North Carolina, Ohio, Pennsylvania, Rhode Island, Virginia, West Virginia and studying in Connecticut, Delaware, District of Columbia, Maryland, Massachusetts, New Hampshire, New Jersey, New York, Ohio, Pennsylvania, Rhode Island, Vermont, Virginia, West Virginia. Available to U.S. and non-U.S. citizens.

Application Requirements: Application form, essay, financial need analysis, interview, personal photograph. *Deadline:* February 1.

Contact: Percy Preston, Office Manager
Roothbert Fund Inc.
475 Riverside Drive, Room 1622
New York, NY 10115
Phone: 212-870-3116
E-mail: office@roothbertfund.org

RYU FAMILY FOUNDATION, INC.

SEOL BONG SCHOLARSHIP

• *See page 693*

SACHS FOUNDATION

http://www.sachsfoundation.org/

SACHS FOUNDATION SCHOLARSHIPS

• *See page 758*

ST. ANDREW'S SOCIETY OF WASHINGTON, DC

http://www.saintandrewsociety.org/

ST. ANDREW'S SOCIETY OF WASHINGTON DC FOUNDERS' SCHOLARSHIP

• *See page 665*

ST. ANDREW'S SOCIETY OF WASHINGTON DC SCHOLARSHIPS

• *See page 665*

ST. CLAIRE REGIONAL MEDICAL CENTER
http://www.st-claire.org/

SR. MARY JEANNETTE WESS, S.N.D. SCHOLARSHIP
• See page 665

SALT RIVER ELECTRIC COOPERATIVE CORPORATION
http://www.srelectric.com/

SALT RIVER ELECTRIC SCHOLARSHIP PROGRAM
Scholarships available to Kentucky high school seniors who reside in Salt River Electric Service area or the primary residence of their parents/guardian is in the service area. Must be enrolled or plan to enroll in a postsecondary institution. Minimum GPA of 2.5 required. Must demonstrate financial need. Must submit a 500-word essay on a topic chosen from the list on the website. Application and additional information available on website http://www.srelectric.com.

Award: Scholarship for use in freshman year; not renewable. *Number:* 4. *Amount:* $1000.

Eligibility Requirements: Applicant must be high school student; planning to enroll or expecting to enroll full- or part-time at a two-year or four-year or technical institution or university and resident of Kentucky. Applicant must have 2.5 GPA or higher. Available to U.S. citizens.

Application Requirements: Application form, community service, essay, financial need analysis, personal photograph, transcript. *Deadline:* April 4.

Contact: Nicky Rapier, Scholarship Coordinator
Phone: 502-348-3931
Fax: 502-348-1993
E-mail: nickyr@srelectric.com

SALUTE TO EDUCATION, INC.
http://www.stescholarships.org/

SALUTE TO EDUCATION SCHOLARSHIP
• See page 666

SALVADORAN AMERICAN LEADERSHIP AND EDUCATIONAL FUND
http://www.salef.org/

FULFILLING OUR DREAMS SCHOLARSHIP FUND
• See page 759

THE SAN DIEGO FOUNDATION
http://www.sdfoundation.org/

COMMON SCHOLARSHIP APPLICATION
The Common Scholarship Application uses one online form to access more than 100 scholarships. Scholarships are available for graduating high school seniors, undergraduates, graduate students and adult re-entry students who are attending 2-year colleges, 4-year universities, trade/vocational schools, graduate, medical and professional schools and teaching credential programs. Scholarships range from $500 to more than $5,000 and, depending on the scholarship, can pay for tuition, room and board, books, fees and other related expenses. Note that almost all of our scholarships require San Diego County residency.

Award: Scholarship for use in freshman, sophomore, junior, senior, or graduate years; renewable. *Number:* 95–110. *Amount:* $500–$5000.

Eligibility Requirements: Applicant must be enrolled or expecting to enroll full- or part-time at a two-year or four-year or technical institution or university and resident of California. Applicant must have 2.5 GPA or higher. Available to U.S. citizens.

Application Requirements: Application form, essay. *Deadline:* February 1.

Contact: Daniel Stigall, Scholarships Coordinator
E-mail: scholarships@sdfoundation.org

SCHOLARSHIPOWL.COM
http://www.scholarshipowl.com

YOU DESERVE IT! SCHOLARSHIP
Everyone 16 years of age or older is eligible to apply who is enrolled or plans to be enrolled next semester to college. The scholarship renews every month and expires on the 29th of each month. See website for details. For an application, please go to https://scholarshipowl.com/awards/you-deserve-it-scholarship.

Award: Scholarship for use in freshman, sophomore, junior, senior, graduate, or postgraduate years; not renewable. *Number:* 10. *Amount:* $1000.

Eligibility Requirements: Applicant must be enrolled or expecting to enroll full- or part-time at a two-year or four-year or technical institution or university; resident of Alabama, Alaska, Alberta, Arizona, Arkansas, British Columbia, California, Colorado, Connecticut, Delaware, District of Columbia, Florida, Georgia, Guam, Hawaii, Idaho, Illinois, Indiana, Iowa, Kansas, Kentucky, Louisiana, Maine, Manitoba, Maryland, Massachusetts, Michigan, Minnesota, Mississippi, Missouri, Montana, Nebraska, Nevada, New Brunswick, Newfoundland, New Hampshire, New Jersey, New Mexico, New York, North Carolina, North Dakota, Northwest Territories, Nova Scotia, Ohio, Oklahoma, Ontario, Oregon, Pennsylvania, Prince Edward Island, Puerto Rico, Quebec, Saskatchewan, South Carolina, South Dakota, Tennessee, Texas, Utah, Vermont, Virginia, Washington, West Virginia, Wisconsin, Wyoming, Yukon and studying in Alabama, Alaska, Alberta, Arizona, Arkansas, British Columbia, California, Colorado, Connecticut, Delaware, District of Columbia, Florida, Georgia, Guam, Hawaii, Idaho, Illinois, Indiana, Iowa, Kansas, Kentucky, Louisiana, Maine, Manitoba, Maryland, Massachusetts, Michigan, Minnesota, Mississippi, Missouri, Montana, Nebraska, Nevada, New Brunswick, Newfoundland, New Hampshire, New Jersey, New Mexico, New York, North Carolina, North Dakota, Northwest Territories, Nova Scotia, Ohio, Oklahoma, Ontario, Oregon, Pennsylvania, Prince Edward Island, Puerto Rico, Quebec, Saskatchewan, South Carolina, South Dakota, Tennessee, Texas, Utah, Vermont, Virginia, Washington, West Virginia, Wisconsin, Wyoming, Yukon. Available to U.S. citizens.

Application Requirements: Application form. *Deadline:* continuous.

Contact: Mr. Mark Galea
ScholarshipOwl.com
210/2, Manwel Dimech Street
Slimena slm1050
MLT
E-mail: contact@scholarshipowl.com

SHELBY ENERGY COOPERATIVE
http://www.shelbyenergy.com/

SHELBY ENERGY COOPERATIVE SCHOLARSHIPS
Scholarships for high school seniors in Kentucky, whose parents or guardians are Shelby Energy members. Award based on financial need, academic excellence, community and school involvement, and essay.

Award: Scholarship for use in freshman year; not renewable. *Number:* 6. *Amount:* $1000.

Eligibility Requirements: Applicant must be high school student; planning to enroll or expecting to enroll full-time at a four-year institution or university and resident of Kentucky. Available to U.S. citizens.

Application Requirements: Application form, community service, financial need analysis. *Deadline:* March 10.

Contact: Ms. Candi Waford, Manager, Member Services
Shelby Energy Cooperative
620 Old Finchville Road
Shelbyville, KY 40065
Phone: 502-633-4420
Fax: 502-633-2387
E-mail: candi@shelbyenergy.com

SHERBENZ-RYAN EDUCATION FOUNDATION

http://www.scholarshipamerica.org

STERBENZ-RYAN SCHOLARSHIP

The Sterbenz-Ryan Scholarship is to assist students residing in Minnesota and Wisconsin who plan to enroll full-time in undergraduate study at an accredited two- or four- year college, university, or vocational-technical school in the United States for the entire upcoming academic year. Qualified applicants must be high school seniors, high school graduates or current postsecondary undergraduates residing in Minnesota or Wisconsin with a grade point average of 2.5 to 3.5 on a 4.0 scale, or its equivalent. Scholarships up to $15,000 are available for students attending four-year schools and up to $5,000 for students attending two-year schools. Awards are renewable on the basis of satisfactory academic performance. Qualified students are encouraged to apply early!

Award: Scholarship for use in freshman, sophomore, or junior years; renewable. *Number:* 44. *Amount:* $5000–$15,000.

Eligibility Requirements: Applicant must be enrolled or expecting to enroll full-time at a two-year or four-year or technical institution or university and resident of Minnesota, Wisconsin. Applicant must have 2.5 GPA or higher. Available to U.S. citizens.

Application Requirements: Application form. *Deadline:* June 15.

Contact: Program Manager
Sherbenz-Ryan Education Foundation
Scholarship America
One Scholarship Way
St. Peter, MN 56082
Phone: 507-931-1682
E-mail: sterbenz-ryan@scholarshipamerica.org

SILICON VALLEY COMMUNITY FOUNDATION

http://www.siliconvalleycf.org

ABBY SOBRATO SCHOLARSHIP
• See page 667

BAC LOCAL 3 SULLIVAN KRAW SCHOLARSHIP

The BAC Local 3 Sullivan Kraw Scholarship is for employees and/or family members of current employees of the Bricklayers and Allied Craftworkers Local 3 CA who plan to attend an accredited college or university. Must be a qualifying member in good standing of BAC 3 CA for at least five years immediately preceding the date of application; a current graduating high school senior, high school graduate or undergraduate planning to attend a college or university in California on a full-time basis; have a minimum cumulative grade point average of 3.0 on a 4.0 scale; and be a United States citizen.

Award: Scholarship for use in freshman, sophomore, junior, or senior years; not renewable. *Number:* 1–19. *Amount:* $1000–$2500.

Eligibility Requirements: Applicant must be enrolled or expecting to enroll full-time at a four-year institution or university and resident of California. Applicant must have 3.0 GPA or higher. Available to U.S. citizens.

Application Requirements: Application form. *Deadline:* continuous.

Contact: Scholarships Team
Silicon Valley Community Foundation
2440 West El Camino Real
Suite 300
Mountain View, CA 94040
Phone: 650-450-5487
E-mail: scholarships@siliconvalleycf.org

BOBETTE BIBO GUGLIOTTA MEMORIAL SCHOLARSHIP FOR CREATIVE WRITING
• See page 667

CRAIN EDUCATIONAL GRANTS PROGRAM

This program was established in 1987 in memory of Dr. R. Carter Crain and Mildred E. Crain, through Mrs. Crain's will. The purpose of the scholarship is to enable high school graduates to pursue courses of study that they would otherwise be unable to follow due to limited financial means. The selection committee looks for academic promise,

documented perseverance in activities outside the classroom, the quality of the personal statement and personal characteristics such as honesty, good judgment and commitment to serving the community. Students may apply to both the Crain Educational Grant Program and the Hazel Reed Baumeister Scholarship Program, but may receive only one of these scholarships. Must have demonstrated community involvement over a period of several years; have a minimum cumulative grade point average of 3.5 on a 4.0 scale; have demonstrated financial hardship; must be a graduating high school senior or graduate of a public or private high school in San Mateo County or Santa Clara County; planning to enroll or enrolled in a four-year college or university as a full-time student; and a United States citizen.

Award: Scholarship for use in freshman year; not renewable. *Number:* 10. *Amount:* $1000–$5000.

Eligibility Requirements: Applicant must be enrolled or expecting to enroll full-time at a four-year institution or university and resident of California. Applicant must have 3.5 GPA or higher. Available to U.S. citizens.

Application Requirements: Application form, community service, essay, financial need analysis. *Deadline:* February 21.

Contact: Scholarships Team
Silicon Valley Community Foundation
2440 West El Camino Real
Suite 300
Mountain View, CA 94040
Phone: 650-450-5487
E-mail: scholarships@siliconvalleycf.org

CURRY AWARD FOR GIRLS AND YOUNG WOMEN
• See page 667

HAZEL REED BAUMEISTER SCHOLARSHIP PROGRAM
• See page 668

KRISHNAN-SHAH FAMILY SCHOLARSHIP

The Krishnan-Shah Family Scholarship was established by Ajay Shah, Lata Krishnan and their family. This scholarship program seeks to support financially needy students with academic potential and demonstrated community involvement, and provide meaningful and ongoing financial support to ensure that students complete their undergraduate degree. Open to a graduating high school senior residing in the greater Silicon Valley Region (includes Santa Clara County, San Mateo County, San Francisco County, Alameda County and Santa Cruz County), or current community college student who graduated from a high school within the five listed counties. Must be a first generation college student (neither parent earned a four-year college degree), pursuing first undergraduate degree and planning to enroll in a four-year college or university on a full-time basis in the upcoming fall session. Maximum cumulative grade point average of 3.75 on a 4.0 scale. Must have demonstrated involvement in activities (extracurricular, volunteer, paid, etc.) and demonstrated financial need or hardship.

Award: Scholarship for use in freshman, sophomore, junior, or senior years; not renewable. *Number:* 1–5. *Amount:* $1000–$40,000.

Eligibility Requirements: Applicant must be enrolled or expecting to enroll full-time at a four-year institution or university and resident of California. Applicant must have 3.5 GPA or higher.

Application Requirements: Application form, essay, financial need analysis. *Deadline:* February 21.

Contact: Scholarships Team
Silicon Valley Community Foundation
2440 West El Camino Real
Suite 300
Mountain View, CA 94040
Phone: 650-450-5487
E-mail: scholarships@siliconvalleycf.org

LATINOS IN TECHNOLOGY SCHOLARSHIP
• See page 760

MARIE A. CALDERILLA SCHOLARSHIP

This program was established in 2007 through a generous gift from Marie A. Calderilla, pictured, who believed deeply in the importance of education. The purpose of this scholarship is to enable women to pursue courses of study that they would otherwise be unable to follow due to limited financial means. The selection committee looks for academic promise, women who have demonstrated a commitment to completing a degree or certificate program or to increasing their work skills, and personal characteristics such as honesty, good judgment and perseverance. Recipients are eligible for up to three years of funding; however, students must meet renewal requirements to continue to receive the award. Students enrolled in a four-year degree program at a San Mateo County Community College District college are eligible for up to four years of funding. Open to a female student, pursuing first undergraduate degree or certificate program. Must be a graduating high school senior or re-entry student planning to attend a college in the San Mateo County Community College District (Cañada College, College of San Mateo and Skyline Community College). Must have demonstrated financial hardship, be serious about improving her life through education, and a United States citizen or eligible non-citizen (eligible non-citizens include United States legal residents and A.B. 540 students).

Award: Scholarship for use in freshman, sophomore, junior, or senior years; renewable. *Number:* 1–30. *Amount:* $1000–$20,000.

Eligibility Requirements: Applicant must be enrolled or expecting to enroll full- or part-time at a two-year or four-year or technical institution or university; female; resident of California and studying in California. Available to U.S. and non-U.S. citizens.

Application Requirements: Application form, essay, financial need analysis. *Deadline:* April 18.

Contact: Scholarships Team
Silicon Valley Community Foundation
2440 West El Camino Real
Suite 300
Mountain View, CA 94040
Phone: 650-450-5487
E-mail: scholarships@siliconvalleycf.org

PENINSULA REGENT CHARITABLE FOUNDATION EDUCATIONAL GRANT PROGRAM

This program is made possible through the generous contributions of the residents of The Peninsula Regent. Educational grants between $1,000 and $10,000 each will be awarded annually. The program has been created to help employees and/or their dependents with the costs of higher education or the costs of attending courses, including those offered at community colleges and vocational schools. Open to current employee of TPR for at least 90 days as of the application deadline, or dependents of an employee who has worked at the TPR for at least 90 days as of the application deadline, or past TPR scholarship recipient and employee of the TPR who was employed for at least 90 days. Preference will be given to applicants with strong educational motivation, perseverance and involvement outside the classroom, and personal characteristics such as honesty and good judgment. The selection committee will also strongly consider applicants who have dropped out of school for reasons beyond their control or have undergone unusual hardships to remain in school. Must have demonstrated financial hardship and be a United States citizen or legal resident.

Award: Scholarship for use in freshman, sophomore, junior, or senior years; not renewable. *Number:* 1–30. *Amount:* $1000–$10,000.

Eligibility Requirements: Applicant must be enrolled or expecting to enroll full- or part-time at a two-year or four-year or technical institution or university and resident of California. Available to U.S. and non-U.S. citizens.

Application Requirements: Application form, essay, financial need analysis. *Deadline:* March 21.

Contact: Scholarships Team
Silicon Valley Community Foundation
2440 West El Camino Real
Suite 300
Mountain View, CA 94040
Phone: 650-450-5487
E-mail: scholarships@siliconvalleycf.org

RALPH HALE AND MARTHA L. RUPPERT EDUCATIONAL SCHOLARSHIP

The Ruppert Educational Grant Program was established through a trust and bequest agreement by Ralph Hale Ruppert and Lenore Martha Ruppert in memory of their mothers, Nellie Hale Ruppert and Amanda Miller Edwards. The program is designed to assist young people who have financial need and are willing to help themselves. Scholarships are awarded to "late bloomers"–those students who show academic promise and improvement during the last years of high school or in the first few years of college, but are unlikely to receive other scholarships because of their low GPAs. Applicant must be a "late bloomer" who demonstrates

academic promise and continuous grade point average improvement during high school or college. Must demonstrate community involvement. Maximum cumulative grade point average of 3.3 on a 4.0 scale. Must demonstrate financial hardship. Must be a graduating high school senior or graduate of a public or private high school in San Mateo County, San Francisco County, or Santa Clara County and planning to enroll or be enrolled in a two- or four-year college, university or vocational school as a full-time student. Must be a United States citizen or eligible non-citizen (eligible non-citizens include United States legal residents and A.B. 540 students).

Award: Scholarship for use in freshman, sophomore, junior, or senior years; not renewable. *Number:* 1–30. *Amount:* $1000–$10,000.

Eligibility Requirements: Applicant must be enrolled or expecting to enroll full-time at a two-year or four-year or technical institution or university and resident of California. Applicant must have 2.5 GPA or higher. Available to U.S. and non-U.S. citizens.

Application Requirements: Application form, essay, financial need analysis. *Deadline:* February 21.

Contact: Scholarships Team
Silicon Valley Community Foundation
2440 West El Camino Real
Suite 300
Mountain View, CA 94040
Phone: 650-450-5487
E-mail: scholarships@siliconvalleycf.org

ROSHAN RAHBARI SCHOLARSHIP FUND

This scholarship was established in loving memory of Roshan Rahbari, a former student of West Valley Community College and a graduate of Leland High School in San Jose, California. In his 18 years of life Roshan touched the lives of many. He believed in harmony among people of different backgrounds and had a rainbow of friends. He was sensitive to the plight of people in need of help and saw everyone as an individual worthy of respect. His dream was to become a psychologist for young people, and it is in his kind spirit that his parents established this scholarship fund to help young people realize their dreams. The Roshan Rahbari Scholarship Fund seeks to support outstanding community college students with financial need to transfer to and complete their bachelor's degrees at four-year colleges and universities. Must be current resident of California; current community college student transferring to a four-year college or university on a part-time or full-time basis; have a minimum cumulative grade point average of 3.0; have demonstrated service to community or school; have demonstrated financial need; and have character qualities such as integrity, compassion and generosity.

Award: Scholarship for use in sophomore, junior, or senior years; renewable. *Number:* 1–4. *Amount:* $1000–$5000.

Eligibility Requirements: Applicant must be enrolled or expecting to enroll full- or part-time at a four-year institution or university and resident of California. Applicant must have 3.0 GPA or higher. Available to U.S. citizens.

Application Requirements: Application form, essay, financial need analysis. *Deadline:* June 1.

Contact: Scholarships Team
Silicon Valley Community Foundation
2440 West El Camino Real
Suite 300
Mountain View, CA 94040
Phone: 650-450-5487
E-mail: scholarships@siliconvalleycf.org

TANG SCHOLARSHIP

• See page 760

WINE GROUP SCHOLARSHIPS

The Wine Group Scholarship Fund was established in 2009 by a group of owners of The Wine Group LLC (TWG). Its mission is to provide the children, grandchildren or legal dependents of TWG's employees with financial assistance to pursue or continue postsecondary education in any area of study. Must be a child, legal dependent or grandchild of a full-time employee of TWG. Employee must have at least one year of continuous, full-time service with TWG as of Feb. 28 of the year in which the scholarship will be awarded. Employee must be employed with TWG at the time scholarship award selections are made. Children, legal dependents and grandchildren of current and former owners of TWG are not eligible. Scholarship winners of TWG Merit Scholarship will demonstrate a desirable mix of a high level of academic performance, strong communication and leadership skills, and participation in extra-curricular activities. Current graduating high school senior planning to attend a two- or four-year college/university program on a full-time (12 or more units/credits per quarter/semester) or part-time (a minimum of 6 to a maximum of 11 units/credits per quarter/semester) basis or current full-time or part-time college student. Minimum cumulative grade point average of 3.0 on a 4.0 scale. Scholarship winners of TWG Opportunity Scholarship will demonstrate a desirable mix of educational motivation, perseverance and demonstrated financial need or hardship. Applicant must be planning to enroll or currently enrolled in a two- or four-year college or vocational school on a part-time or full-time basis (as defined by the school of attendance). Must have demonstrated financial need or hardship with a maximum family income of $150,000.

Award: Scholarship for use in freshman, sophomore, junior, or senior years; not renewable. *Number:* 1–10. *Amount:* $1000–$10,000.

Eligibility Requirements: Applicant must be enrolled or expecting to enroll full- or part-time at a two-year or four-year or technical institution or university and resident of California. Applicant must have 3.0 GPA or higher. Available to U.S. citizens.

Application Requirements: Application form, essay, financial need analysis. *Deadline:* February 21.

Contact: Scholarships Team
Silicon Valley Community Foundation
2440 West El Camino Real
Suite 300
Mountain View, CA 94040
Phone: 650-450-5487
E-mail: scholarships@siliconvalleycf.org

SIMMONS AND FLETCHER, P.C.

https://www.simmonsandfletcher.com/

SIMMONS AND FLETCHER, P.C., LAW MARKETING SCHOLARSHIP
• *See page 668*

SIMON FOUNDATION FOR EDUCATION AND HOUSING

http://www.sfeh.org/

SIMON SCHOLARS PROGRAM
Scholarships are given to high school seniors at qualified high schools in Atlanta, GA, Santa Fe and Albuquerque, NM, and Anaheim, Santa Ana, Oceanside, or Garden Grove, CA. Deadlines vary for each region. For more details visit website http://www.simonscholars.org.

Award: Scholarship for use in freshman year; not renewable. *Number:* 100. *Amount:* $16,000.

Eligibility Requirements: Applicant must be high school student; planning to enroll or expecting to enroll full-time at a two-year or four-year institution or university and resident of California, Georgia, New Mexico. Applicant must have 3.0 GPA or higher. Available to U.S. citizens.

Application Requirements: Application form, community service, essay, financial need analysis, interview, recommendations or references, test scores, transcript. *Deadline:* varies.

Contact: Dr. Heather Huntley, Director of Partnerships and
Development
Phone: 949-270-3622
Fax: 949-729-8072
E-mail: heatherh@simonscholars.org

SOUTH CAROLINA COMMISSION ON HIGHER EDUCATION

http://www.che.sc.gov/

PALMETTO FELLOWS SCHOLARSHIP PROGRAM
Renewable award for qualified high school seniors in South Carolina to attend a four-year South Carolina institution. The scholarship must be applied directly towards the cost of attendance, less any other gift aid received.

Award: Scholarship for use in freshman year; renewable. *Number:* 4846. *Amount:* $6700–$7500.

Eligibility Requirements: Applicant must be high school student; planning to enroll or expecting to enroll full-time at a four-year institution or university; resident of South Carolina and studying in South Carolina. Applicant must have 3.5 GPA or higher. Available to U.S. citizens.

Application Requirements: Application form, test scores, transcript. *Deadline:* December 15.

Contact: Dr. Karen Woodfaulk, Director of Student Services
South Carolina Commission on Higher Education
1333 Main Street, Suite 200
Columbia, SC 29201
Phone: 803-737-2244
Fax: 803-737-3610
E-mail: kwoodfaulk@che.sc.gov

SOUTH CAROLINA HOPE SCHOLARSHIP
A merit-based scholarship for eligible first-time entering freshman attending a four-year South Carolina institution. Minimum GPA of 3.0 required. Must be a resident of South Carolina.

Award: Scholarship for use in freshman year; not renewable. *Number:* 2605. *Amount:* $2800.

Eligibility Requirements: Applicant must be high school student; planning to enroll or expecting to enroll full-time at a four-year institution or university; resident of South Carolina and studying in South Carolina. Applicant must have 3.0 GPA or higher. Available to U.S. citizens.

Application Requirements: Transcript. *Deadline:* continuous.

Contact: Gerrick Hampton, Scholarship Coordinator
South Carolina Commission on Higher Education
1333 Main Street, Suite 200
Columbia, SC 29201
Phone: 803-737-4544
Fax: 803-737-3610
E-mail: ghampton@che.sc.gov

SOUTH CAROLINA NEED-BASED GRANTS PROGRAM
Award based on FAFSA. A student may receive up to $2500 annually for full-time and up to $1250 annually for part-time study. The grant must be applied directly towards the cost of college attendance for a maximum of eight full-time equivalent terms.

Award: Grant for use in freshman, sophomore, junior, senior, or graduate years; renewable. *Number:* 1–26,730. *Amount:* $1250–$2500.

Eligibility Requirements: Applicant must be enrolled or expecting to enroll full- or part-time at a two-year or four-year or technical institution or university; resident of South Carolina and studying in South Carolina. Available to U.S. citizens.

Application Requirements: Application form, financial need analysis. *Deadline:* continuous.

Contact: Dr. Karen Woodfaulk, Director of Student Service
South Carolina Commission on Higher Education
1333 Main Street, Suite 200
Columbia, SC 29201
Phone: 803-737-2244
Fax: 803-737-2297
E-mail: kwoodfaulk@che.sc.gov

SOUTH CAROLINA DIVISION OF VETERANS AFFAIRS

http://www.govoepp.state.sc.us/vetaff.htm

TUITION ASSISTANCE FOR CERTAIN WAR VETERANS' CHILDREN
• *See page 716*

SOUTH CAROLINA STATE EMPLOYEES ASSOCIATION

http://www.scsea.com/

RICHLAND/LEXINGTON SCSEA SCHOLARSHIP
• *See page 579*

SOUTH CAROLINA TUITION GRANTS COMMISSION

http://www.sctuitiongrants.org/

SOUTH CAROLINA TUITION GRANTS PROGRAM
• *See page 669*

SOUTH DAKOTA BOARD OF REGENTS

http://www.sdbor.edu/

SOUTH DAKOTA OPPORTUNITY SCHOLARSHIP

Renewable scholarship may be worth up to $6200 over four years to students who take a rigorous college-prep curriculum while in high school and stay in the state for their postsecondary education.

Award: Scholarship for use in freshman, sophomore, junior, or senior years; renewable. *Number:* 1000–4100. *Amount:* $1300–$2300.

Eligibility Requirements: Applicant must be high school student; planning to enroll or expecting to enroll full-time at a two-year or four-year or technical institution or university; resident of South Dakota and studying in South Dakota. Applicant must have 3.0 GPA or higher. Available to U.S. citizens.

Application Requirements: Application form. *Deadline:* September 1.

Contact: Kerri Richards, Student Services Coordinator
South Dakota Board of Regents
306 East Capitol, Suite 200
Pierre, SD 57501
Phone: 605-773-3455
E-mail: info@sdbor.edu

SOUTH FLORIDA FAIR AND PALM BEACH COUNTY EXPOSITIONS INC.

http://www.southfloridafair.com/

SOUTH FLORIDA FAIR COLLEGE SCHOLARSHIP

Renewable award of up to $4000 for students who might not otherwise have an opportunity to pursue a college education. Must be a permanent resident of Florida.

Award: Scholarship for use in freshman, sophomore, junior, or senior years; renewable. *Number:* 10. *Amount:* $1000–$4000.

Eligibility Requirements: Applicant must be enrolled or expecting to enroll full- or part-time at a four-year institution or university and resident of Florida. Available to U.S. and non-U.S. citizens.

Application Requirements: Application form, community service, essay, recommendations or references, self-addressed stamped envelope with application, test scores, transcript. *Deadline:* October 15.

Contact: Scholarship Committee
South Florida Fair and Palm Beach County Expositions Inc.
PO Box 210367
West Palm Beach, FL 33421-0367
Phone: 561-790-5245

STATE EMPLOYEES ASSOCIATION OF NORTH CAROLINA (SEANC)

http://www.seanc.org/

STATE EMPLOYEES ASSOCIATION OF NORTH CAROLINA (SEANC) SCHOLARSHIPS
• *See page 761*

STEPHEN PHILLIPS MEMORIAL SCHOLARSHIP FUND, INC.

http://www.phillips-scholarship.org/

STEPHEN PHILLIPS MEMORIAL SCHOLARSHIP FUND, INC.

A renewable award open to full-time undergraduate students with financial need who display academic achievement, a commitment to serving others (in school, in the community or at home,) a strong work ethic, and leadership qualities. A U.S. citizen or noncitizen who has a current lawful presence in the United States and has a work permit, and is a permanent resident of a New England state. Qualifying students may attend college anywhere in the U.S. For more details see website http://www.phillips-scholarship.org.

Award: Scholarship for use in freshman, sophomore, junior, or senior years; renewable. *Number:* 125–135. *Amount:* $3000–$18,000.

Eligibility Requirements: Applicant must be enrolled or expecting to enroll full-time at a four-year institution or university and resident of Connecticut, Maine, Massachusetts, New Hampshire, Rhode Island, Vermont. Applicant must have 3.0 GPA or higher. Available to U.S. citizens.

Application Requirements: Application form, community service, essay, financial need analysis. *Deadline:* May 1.

Contact: Ms. Barbara Iler, Executive Director
Stephen Phillips Memorial Scholarship Fund, Inc.
PO Box 870
Salem, MA 01970
Phone: 978-744-2111
E-mail: staff@spscholars.org

STEPHEN T. MARCHELLO SCHOLARSHIP FOUNDATION

http://www.stmfoundation.org/

A LEGACY OF HOPE SCHOLARSHIPS FOR SURVIVORS OF CHILDHOOD CANCER

Scholarship of up to $2,000 of a one time grant for postsecondary undergraduate education. Applicant must be a survivor of childhood cancer. Must submit a letter from doctor, clinic, or hospital where cancer treatment was received. Residents of CO and MT are eligible. Must be U.S. citizen. Minimum 2.5 GPA required.

Award: Scholarship for use in freshman year; not renewable. *Number:* 1–10. *Amount:* $200–$1500.

Eligibility Requirements: Applicant must be high school student; age 17–20; planning to enroll or expecting to enroll full- or part-time at a two-year or four-year or technical institution or university and resident of Colorado, Montana. Applicant must have 3.5 GPA or higher. Available to U.S. citizens.

Application Requirements: Application form, essay. *Deadline:* March 15.

Contact: Mr. Mario Marchello, Secretary
Stephen T. Marchello Scholarship Foundation
1170 East Long Place
Centennial, CO 80122
Phone: 303-886-5018
E-mail: stmfoundation@hotmail.com

SWISS BENEVOLENT SOCIETY

http://www.sbssf.com/

SWISS BENEVOLENT SOCIETY OF SAN FRANCISCO SCHOLARSHIPS
• *See page 762*

SWISS BENEVOLENT SOCIETY OF CHICAGO

http://www.sbschicago.org/

SWISS BENEVOLENT SOCIETY OF CHICAGO SCHOLARSHIPS
• *See page 762*

SWISS BENEVOLENT SOCIETY OF NEW YORK

http://www.sbsny.org/

PELLEGRINI SCHOLARSHIP GRANTS
• *See page 763*

TAMPA BAY TIMES FUND, INC.

http://www.tampabay.com/fund

BARNES SCHOLARSHIP

The Barnes Scholarships were established in 1999 to help college-bound teens who are high academic achievers, who have overcome significant obstacles in their lives and who have financial need. Each of the four winners is eligible to receive up to $15,000 per year for four years to attend any nationally accredited non-profit college or university. The scholarship may be used to pay for expenses related to the cost of college attendance. The students must be enrolled full-time and remain in good academic standing to continue to receive the scholarship. High school seniors from these Florida counties are eligible to apply: Hernando, Pasco, Pinellas, Hillsborough. Application period: August 1 to October 21. On-line applications only.

Award: Scholarship for use in freshman, sophomore, junior, or senior years; renewable. *Number:* 1–4. *Amount:* $1000–$15,000.

Eligibility Requirements: Applicant must be high school student; age 17-19; planning to enroll or expecting to enroll full-time at a four-year institution or university; single and resident of Florida. Applicant must have 3.0 GPA or higher. Available to U.S. citizens.

Application Requirements: Application form, community service, essay, interview. *Deadline:* October 21.

Contact: Ms. Nancy Waclawek, Scholarship Administrator
Tampa Bay Times Fund, Inc.
PO Box 1121
St. Petersburg, FL 33731-1121
E-mail: tbtschls@gmail.com

TAMPA BAY TIMES FUND BARNES SCHOLARSHIP

Four high school seniors from the Tampa Bay Times' audience area are selected each year and each are awarded up to $15,000 annually for four years to attend any nationally accredited college or university. Criteria for the scholarship include high academic achievement, financial need, evidence of having overcome significant obstacles in life, and community service.

Award: Scholarship for use in freshman, sophomore, junior, or senior years; renewable. *Number:* 4. *Amount:* $15,000.

Eligibility Requirements: Applicant must be high school student; age 18-22; planning to enroll or expecting to enroll full-time at a four-year institution or university; single and resident of Florida. Applicant must have 3.0 GPA or higher. Available to U.S. citizens.

Application Requirements: Application form, community service, essay, financial need analysis, interview. *Deadline:* October 15.

Contact: Nancy Waclawek, Scholarship Administrator
Phone: 813-340-4125
E-mail: tbtschls@gmail.com

TELIOS LAW PLLC

http://telioslaw.com

TELIOS LAW EXCELSIOR SCHOLARSHIP
• *See page 763*

TENNESSEE STUDENT ASSISTANCE CORPORATION

http://www.tn.gov/collegepays

DEPENDENT CHILDREN SCHOLARSHIP PROGRAM
• *See page 672*

HELPING HEROES GRANT
• *See page 672*

HOPE ASPIRE AWARD
• *See page 672*

NED MCWHERTER SCHOLARS PROGRAM
• *See page 672*

REDUCTION IN FORCE TUITION ASSISTANCE BENEFIT

Tuition assistance of up to $11,600 ($5,800 per year) at the schools, institutions, and entities governed by the Tennessee Board of Regents and the University of Tennessee Board of Trustees, as well as state certified apprenticeship programs. Tuition assistance benefits are available for a two-year period beginning when an employee is separated due to a reduction in force. GED classes are also available through the Tennessee Department of Labor and Workforce Development's Career Centers, and testing fees will be covered under the tuition assistance benefit. This program is NOT offered to the general public, but only as one of the benefits provided to State employees who are impacted by the Reduction in Force.

Award: Scholarship for use in freshman, sophomore, junior, or senior years; not renewable.

Eligibility Requirements: Applicant must be enrolled or expecting to enroll full- or part-time at a two-year or four-year or technical institution or university; resident of Tennessee and studying in Tennessee. Available to U.S. citizens.

Application Requirements: Application form.

Contact: Mr. Tim Phelps, Associate Executive Director, Grants and Scholarships
Tennessee Student Assistance Corporation
404 James Robertson Parkway
Nashville, TN 37243
Phone: 615-253-7441
Fax: 615-741-6101
E-mail: tim.phelps@tn.gov

TELS -HOPE WITH GENERAL ASSEMBLY MERIT SCHOLARSHIP (GAMS)
• *See page 672*

TENNESSEE DUAL ENROLLMENT GRANT
• *See page 672*

TENNESSEE HOPE ACCESS GRANT
• *See page 673*

TENNESSEE HOPE FOSTER CHILD TUITION GRANT
• *See page 673*

TENNESSEE HOPE SCHOLARSHIP
• *See page 673*

TENNESSEE HOPE SCHOLARSHIP FOR NONTRADITIONAL STUDENTS

Nontraditional students must be age 25 or older and be an entering freshman in an eligible post-secondary institution or have not been enrolled for at least two (2) years after last attending any post-secondary institution and is now enrolled at an eligible post-secondary institution. Student's and spouse's adjusted gross income must be $36,000 or less on IRS tax form. Students at four-year institutions and two-year institutions with on-campus housing: up to $1750 per full-time semester as a freshmen and sophomore; then up to $2,250 per full-time enrollment semester as a junior and senior. Students at two-year Institutions: up to $1,500 per full-time enrollment semester as a freshman and sophomore.

Award: Scholarship for use in freshman, sophomore, junior, or senior years; renewable.

Eligibility Requirements: Applicant must be enrolled or expecting to enroll full-time at a two-year or four-year institution or university; resident of Tennessee and studying in Tennessee. Applicant must have 2.5 GPA or higher. Available to U.S. citizens.

Application Requirements: Application form. *Deadline:* continuous.

Contact: Mr. Tim Phelps, Associate Executive Director, Grants and
Scholarships
Tennessee Student Assistance Corporation
404 James Robertson Parkway
Nashville, TN 37243
Phone: 615-253-7441
Fax: 615-741-6101
E-mail: tim.phelps@tn.gov

TENNESSEE RECONNECT GRANT

Applicants must be enrolled in a federal Title IV eligible curriculum of
courses leading to a certificate or associate degree. Must not have
previously earned an Associate degree or Baccalaureate degree and enroll
in and attend at least six (6) hours at an eligible institution. Must maintain
a minimum 2.0 cumulative GPA at the end of the academic year as
determined by the institution and participate in a college success
program, as determined by the Tennessee Higher Education Commission.

Award: Scholarship for use in freshman, sophomore, junior, or senior
years; renewable.

Eligibility Requirements: Applicant must be enrolled or expecting to
enroll at an institution or university; resident of Tennessee and studying
in Tennessee. Available to U.S. citizens.

Application Requirements: Application form. *Deadline:* continuous.

Contact: Mr. Tim Phelps, Associate Executive Director, Grants and
Scholarships
Tennessee Student Assistance Corporation
404 James Robertson Parkway
Nashville, TN 37243
Phone: 615-253-7441
Fax: 615-741-6101
E-mail: tim.phelps@tn.gov

TENNESSEE STUDENT ASSISTANCE AWARD
• *See page 673*

TERRY FOUNDATION
http://www.terryfoundation.org/

TERRY FOUNDATION SCHOLARSHIP

Scholarships to Texas high school seniors who have been admitted to:
University of Texas at Austin; Texas A&M University at College Station;
University of Houston; Texas State University; University of Texas at
San Antonio; University of Texas at Dallas; University of North Texas;
Texas Tech University; Texas Woman's University; Texas A&M at
Galveston; Sam Houston State University; University of Texas at El
Paso; or University of Texas at Arlington. Scholarship is based upon
leadership potential and character; scholastic record and ability; and
financial need.

Award: Scholarship for use in freshman, sophomore, junior, or senior
years; renewable. *Number:* 253.

Eligibility Requirements: Applicant must be high school student;
planning to enroll or expecting to enroll full-time at a four-year
institution or university; resident of Texas; studying in Texas and must
have an interest in leadership. Applicant must have 3.0 GPA or higher.
Available to U.S. citizens.

Application Requirements: Application form, essay, financial need
analysis, interview.

Contact: Jodie Koszegi, Scholarship Program Director
Terry Foundation
3104 Edloe, Suite 205
Houston, TX 77027
Phone: 713-552-0002
Fax: 713-622-6352
E-mail: jkoszegi@terryfoundation.org

TERRY FOUNDATION TRANSFER SCHOLARSHIP

Scholarships to Texas high school seniors who have been admitted to:
University of Texas at Austin; Texas A&M University at College Station;
University of Houston; Texas State University; University of Texas at
San Antonio; University of Texas at Dallas; University of North Texas;
Texas Tech University; Texas Woman's University; Texas A&M
University at Galveston; Sam Houston State University; University of
Texas at El Paso; University of Texas at Arlington. Scholarship is based
upon leadership potential and character; scholastic record and ability; and
financial need.

Award: Scholarship for use in sophomore, junior, or senior years;
renewable. *Number:* 120. *Amount:* $13,500.

Eligibility Requirements: Applicant must be enrolled or expecting to
enroll full-time at a four-year institution or university; resident of Texas;
studying in Texas and must have an interest in leadership. Applicant must
have 2.5 GPA or higher. Available to U.S. citizens.

Application Requirements: Application form, essay, financial need
analysis, interview.

Contact: Jodie Koszegi, Scholarship Program Director
Terry Foundation
3104 Edloe, Suite 205
Houston, TX 77027
Phone: 713-552-0002
Fax: 713-622-6352
E-mail: jkoszegi@terryfoundation.org

TERRY FOX HUMANITARIAN AWARD
http://terryfoxawards.ca/

TERRY FOX HUMANITARIAN AWARD
• *See page 673*

TEXAS 4-H YOUTH DEVELOPMENT FOUNDATION
http://texas4hfoundation.org/

TEXAS 4-H OPPORTUNITY SCHOLARSHIP

Renewable award for Texas 4-H members to attend a Texas college or
university. Minimum GPA of 2.5 required. Must attend full-time.

Award: Scholarship for use in freshman, sophomore, junior, or senior
years; renewable. *Number:* 225. *Amount:* $1500–$15,000.

Eligibility Requirements: Applicant must be enrolled or expecting to
enroll full-time at a two-year or four-year or technical institution; resident
of Texas; studying in Texas and must have an interest in
animal/agricultural competition. Applicant must have 2.5 GPA or higher.
Available to U.S. citizens.

Application Requirements: Application form, essay, financial need
analysis, interview, recommendations or references, test scores,
transcript. *Deadline:* varies.

Contact: Jim Reeves, Executive Director
Phone: 979-845-1213
Fax: 979-845-6495
E-mail: jereeves@ag.tamu.edu

TEXAS AFL-CIO
http://www.texasaflcio.org/

TEXAS AFL-CIO SCHOLARSHIP PROGRAM
• *See page 579*

TEXAS ASSOCIATION OF DEVELOPING COLLEGES
http://www.txadc.org

THE URBAN SCHOLARSHIPS FUND
• *See page 674*

TEXAS BLACK BAPTIST SCHOLARSHIP COMMITTEE
http://www.bgct.org/

TEXAS BLACK BAPTIST SCHOLARSHIP
• *See page 764*

TEXAS HIGHER EDUCATION COORDINATING BOARD

http://www.collegeforalltexans.com/

TEXAS EDUCATIONAL OPPORTUNITY GRANT (TEOG)

Provides grant aid to students with financial need attending public two-year colleges. For initial award, student must be enrolled at least half-time and awarded in the first 30 hours (or its equivalent) of an associate's degree or certificate program (excluding credits for dual enrollment or by examination). For renewal award, student must also maintain a minimum overall GPA of 2.50 and successfully complete a minimum of 75% of classes attempted during the school year.

Award: Grant for use in freshman, sophomore, junior, or senior years; renewable. *Amount:* $1–$8000.

Eligibility Requirements: Applicant must be enrolled or expecting to enroll full- or part-time at a two-year institution; resident of Texas and studying in Texas. Available to U.S. citizens.

Application Requirements: Financial need analysis.

Contact: Student Financial Aid Programs
    Phone: 888-311-8881

TOP 10% SCHOLARSHIP PROGRAM

Funding for Initial Awards is not available for the 2018-19 academic year and only renewal award students are eligible for this program. Renewal students must demonstrate financial need and complete the FAFSA by the state priority deadline of March 15. Renewal students must maintain a minimum overall GPA of 3.25, successfully complete at least 30 SCH each year, and successfully complete at least 75% of the hours attempted each year.

Award: Scholarship for use in junior or senior years; renewable. *Amount:* up to $2000.

Eligibility Requirements: Applicant must be enrolled or expecting to enroll full-time at a two-year or four-year institution or university; resident of Texas and studying in Texas. Applicant must have 3.0 GPA or higher. Available to U.S. citizens.

Application Requirements: Financial need analysis.

Contact: Student Financial Aid Programs
    Phone: 888-311-8881

TOWARD EXCELLENCE, ACCESS, AND SUCCESS (TEXAS) GRANT

Renewable aid for students enrolled at least three-quarter time in a public four-year college or university in Texas within sixteen months of graduation from high school. Must demonstrate financial need and have completed the Foundation, Recommended, or DAP Curriculum in high school. For renewal awards, must also maintain a minimum GPA of 2.5 and complete a minimum of 24 SCH's each year. Amount of award is determined by the financial aid office of each school. Priority FAFSA completion deadline is March 15. Contact the college/university financial aid office for additional eligibility information.

Award: Grant for use in freshman, sophomore, junior, or senior years; renewable. *Amount:* $1–$8000.

Eligibility Requirements: Applicant must be enrolled or expecting to enroll full- or part-time at a four-year institution or university; resident of Texas and studying in Texas. Available to U.S. citizens.

Application Requirements: Financial need analysis. *Deadline:* March 15.

Contact: Student Financial Aid Programs
    Phone: 888-311-8881

TEXAS OUTDOOR WRITERS ASSOCIATION

http://www.towa.org/

TEXAS OUTDOOR WRITERS ASSOCIATION SCHOLARSHIP

Annual merit award available to students attending an accredited Texas college or university preparing for a career which would incorporate communications skills about the outdoors, environmental conservation, or resource management. Minimum 2.5 GPA required. Submit writing/photo samples.

Award: Scholarship for use in freshman, sophomore, junior, senior, or graduate years; not renewable. *Number:* 1–2. *Amount:* $2000.

Eligibility Requirements: Applicant must be enrolled or expecting to enroll full- or part-time at a two-year or four-year institution or university; resident of Texas; studying in Texas and must have an interest in writing. Applicant must have 2.5 GPA or higher. Available to U.S. citizens.

Application Requirements: Application form. *Deadline:* February 1.

Contact: Judy Mills, Scholarship Co-Chair
    Texas Outdoor Writers Association
    14871 Estrellita
    Houston, TX 77060
    Phone: 281-448-5811
    E-mail: offtheroad.mills@earthlink.net

TEXAS SOCIETY, MILITARY ORDER OF THE STARS AND BARS

http://www.texasmosb.com/

TEXAS SOCIETY, MILITARY ORDER OF THE STARS AND BARS SCHOLARSHIP

The award is given on the basis of scholastics, extracurricular activities, recommendations, and financial need. Applicants must prove genealogical descent or blood relationship to a Confederate Officer, or government official of the Confederacy. Application and complete rules may be found on the Texas Society, Military Order of the Stars and Bars website.

Award: Scholarship for use in freshman, sophomore, junior, or senior years; not renewable. *Number:* 1. *Amount:* $500–$500.

Eligibility Requirements: Applicant must be enrolled or expecting to enroll full- or part-time at a two-year or four-year or technical institution or university and resident of Texas. Available to U.S. citizens.

Application Requirements: Application form, community service, essay, financial need analysis, genealogical proof, recommendations or references, transcript. *Deadline:* March 1.

Contact: Mr. James Templin, Texas Society Scholarship Chairman
    Texas Society, Military Order of the Stars and Bars
    2500 Woodlawn Drive
    Ennis, TX 75119-7644
    Phone: 972-878-2752
    E-mail: hjtemp@sbcglobal.net

TEXAS TENNIS FOUNDATION

http://www.texastennisfoundation.com/

TEXAS TENNIS FOUNDATION SCHOLARSHIPS AND ENDOWMENTS

College scholarships for highly recommended students residing in Texas, with an interest in tennis. Financial need is considered. Must be between the ages of 17 and 19. Refer to website for details http://www.texastennisfoundation.com/web90/scholarships/tenniscampsscholarships.asp.

Award: Scholarship for use in freshman, sophomore, junior, or senior years; not renewable. *Number:* 10. *Amount:* $1000.

Eligibility Requirements: Applicant must be age 17-19; enrolled or expecting to enroll full-time at a two-year or four-year or technical institution or university; resident of Texas and must have an interest in athletics/sports. Available to U.S. citizens.

Application Requirements: Application form, copy of parent or guardian's federal tax return, essay, financial need analysis, personal photograph, recommendations or references, test scores, transcript. *Deadline:* April 15.

Contact: Van Barry, Executive Director
    Phone: 512-443-1334 Ext. 201
    Fax: 512-443-4748
    E-mail: vbarry@texas.usta.com

THEODORE R. AND VIVIAN M. JOHNSON SCHOLARSHIP FOUNDATION INC.

http://www.jsf.bz/

THEODORE R. AND VIVIAN M. JOHNSON SCHOLARSHIP PROGRAM FOR CHILDREN OF UPS EMPLOYEES OR UPS RETIREES
• *See page 591*

THRIVENT STUDENT RESOURCES

https://www.thriventstudentresources.com/

THRIVENT STUDENT RESOURCES SCHOLARSHIP
• *See page 674*

TIDEWATER SCHOLARSHIP FOUNDATION

http://www.accesscollege.org/

ACCESS SCHOLARSHIP/LAST DOLLAR AWARD
A renewable scholarship of $500 to $1000 for the undergraduates participating in Norfolk, Portsmouth, and Virginia Beach, Virginia secure scholarships and financial aid for college.

Award: Scholarship for use in freshman year; renewable. *Amount:* $500–$1000.

Eligibility Requirements: Applicant must be high school student; planning to enroll or expecting to enroll full-time at a two-year or four-year institution or university and resident of Virginia. Applicant must have 2.5 GPA or higher. Available to U.S. citizens.

Application Requirements: Application form, financial need analysis. *Deadline:* May 1.

Contact: Bonnie Sutton, President and Chief Executive Officer
Phone: 757-962-6113
Fax: 757-962-7314
E-mail: bsutton@accesscollege.org

TIGER WOODS FOUNDATION

http://www.tigerwoodsfoundation.org/

ALFRED "TUP" HOLMES MEMORIAL SCHOLARSHIP
Given yearly to one worthy Atlanta metropolitan area graduating high school senior who has displayed high moral character while demonstrating leadership potential and academic excellence. Must be U.S. citizen. Minimum 3.0 GPA required.

Award: Scholarship for use in freshman year; not renewable. *Number:* 1. *Amount:* $2500.

Eligibility Requirements: Applicant must be high school student; planning to enroll or expecting to enroll full-time at a two-year or four-year institution or university and resident of Georgia. Applicant must have 3.0 GPA or higher. Available to U.S. citizens.

Application Requirements: Application form, community service, essay, recommendations or references, test scores, transcript. *Deadline:* April 1.

Contact: Michelle Kim, Scholarship and Grant Coordinator
Phone: 949-725-3003
Fax: 949-725-3002
E-mail: grants@tigerwoodsfoundation.org

TKE EDUCATIONAL FOUNDATION

http://www.tke.org/

DORIS AND ELMER H. SCHMITZ, SR. MEMORIAL SCHOLARSHIP
• *See page 580*

TORTOISE CAPITAL ADVISORS, LLC

http://www.tortoiseadvisors.com

TORTOISE YOUNG ENTREPRENEURS SCHOLARSHIP
The program is designed to give deserving students a leg up in their academic endeavors. In turn, we hope their educational experience will help them mold an entrepreneurial mindset that helps them conceive or support firms that create innovative products, processes and solutions. To be eligible, applicants must: be a permanent resident of Kansas or Missouri who is enrolled or plans to enroll in a full-time undergraduate course of study towards a Bachelor's degree, or; be a non-resident of either state who is enrolled or plans to enroll as a full-time student in a four-year Bachelor's program at a Kansas or Missouri accredited university or college, and; have a minimum 3.3 grade-point average (on a 4.0 scale or equivalent) and a minimum ACT score of 24 or minimum SAT score of 1680 (includes writing section).

Award: Scholarship for use in freshman, sophomore, junior, or senior years; not renewable. *Number:* 3. *Amount:* $1000–$3000.

Eligibility Requirements: Applicant must be enrolled or expecting to enroll full-time at a four-year institution or university; resident of Kansas, Missouri and studying in Kansas, Missouri. Applicant must have 3.0 GPA or higher. Available to U.S. citizens.

Application Requirements: Application form, application form may be submitted online (http://www.tortoiseadvisors.com/scholarship), community service, essay, recommendations or references, test scores, transcript. *Deadline:* February 28.

Contact: Ben Fraser, Scholarship Coordinator
E-mail: scholarship@tortoiseadvisors.com

TOWNSHIP OFFICIALS OF ILLINOIS

http://www.toi.org/

TOWNSHIP OFFICIALS OF ILLINOIS SCHOLARSHIP PROGRAM
The scholarships are awarded to graduating Illinois high school seniors who have a B average or above, have demonstrated an active interest in school activities, who have submitted an essay on "The Importance of Township Government", high school transcript, and letters of recommendation. Students must attend Illinois institutions, either four-year or junior colleges. Must be full-time student. Must complete an interview with a current township official.

Award: Scholarship for use in freshman year; not renewable. *Number:* 7. *Amount:* $1500.

Eligibility Requirements: Applicant must be high school student; planning to enroll or expecting to enroll full-time at a two-year or four-year institution or university; resident of Illinois and studying in Illinois. Applicant must have 3.0 GPA or higher. Available to U.S. citizens.

Application Requirements: Application form, essay, interview. *Deadline:* March 1.

Contact: Amy Rourke, Associate Editor
Township Officials of Illinois
3217 Northfield Dr
Springfield, IL 62701-1804
Phone: 217-744-2212
E-mail: amy@toi.org

TRIANGLE COMMUNITY FOUNDATION

http://www.trianglecf.org

GEORGE AND MARY NEWTON SCHOLARSHIP
• *See page 591*

TRONFELD WEST & DURRETT

https://twdinjurylaw.com/

TRONFELD WEST & DURRETT STEP BY STEP SCHOLARSHIP
If you are a high school or college student in Virginia and will be enrolled in a two-year to five-year institute for the impending school year, apply today for the Tronfeld West & Durrett Step by Step Scholarship. Five (5) hard-working, creative, dreamers will be awarded $1,500 scholarships to

take their first big steps towards their goals. There is no minimum GPA. To apply, create a short 3-5 minute video or submit a written essay telling us what your dreams are. What goals are you setting for yourself over the next 5, 10, or 20 years? What steps are you going to take to get where you're going? What do you want to do in college? What challenges do you expect along the way? How will you overcome them? Finally, tell us how Tronfeld West & Durrett Step-by-Step Scholarship will help you in your first big step. Remember no goals are too lofty and no dreams are too big–shoot for the moon! Most importantly, be creative. To get started on your application, go to our scholarship page and be sure to include a link to your video on YouTube or your written essay. Applications are due May 1, 2018.

Award: Scholarship for use in freshman, sophomore, junior, senior, or graduate years; not renewable. *Number:* 5. *Amount:* $1500.

Eligibility Requirements: Applicant must be enrolled or expecting to enroll full- or part-time at a two-year or four-year institution or university; resident of Virginia and studying in Virginia. Available to U.S. citizens.

Application Requirements: Application form, essay. *Deadline:* May 1.

Contact: Scholarship Coordinator
    Phone: 513-444-2016
    E-mail: coordinator@ourscholarship.io

TWO TEN FOOTWEAR FOUNDATION

http://www.twoten.org/

CLASSIC SCHOLARSHIPS

Two Ten offers footwear employees and their families higher education scholarships to two or four year undergraduate programs based on financial need, academic ability and personal promise.

Award: Scholarship for use in freshman, sophomore, junior, or senior years; renewable. *Number:* 300–350. *Amount:* $2500–$5000.

Eligibility Requirements: Applicant must be enrolled or expecting to enroll full- or part-time at a two-year or four-year or technical institution or university; resident of Alabama, Alaska, Arizona, Arkansas, California, Colorado, Connecticut, Delaware, Florida, Georgia, Hawaii, Idaho, Illinois, Indiana, Iowa, Kansas, Kentucky, Louisiana, Maine, Maryland, Massachusetts, Michigan, Minnesota, Mississippi, Missouri, Montana, Nebraska, Nevada, New Hampshire, New Jersey, New Mexico, New York, North Carolina, North Dakota, Ohio, Oklahoma, Oregon, Pennsylvania, Puerto Rico, Rhode Island, South Carolina, South Dakota, Tennessee, Texas, Utah, Vermont, Virginia, Washington, West Virginia, Wisconsin, Wyoming and studying in Alabama, Alaska, Arizona, Arkansas, California, Colorado, Connecticut, Delaware, Florida, Georgia, Hawaii, Idaho, Illinois, Indiana, Iowa, Kansas, Kentucky, Louisiana, Maine, Maryland, Massachusetts, Michigan, Minnesota, Mississippi, Missouri, Montana, Nebraska, Nevada, New Hampshire, New Jersey, New Mexico, New York, North Carolina, North Dakota, Ohio, Oklahoma, Oregon, Pennsylvania, Puerto Rico, Rhode Island, South Carolina, South Dakota, Tennessee, Texas, Utah, Vermont, Virginia, Washington, West Virginia, Wisconsin, Wyoming. Applicant must have 2.5 GPA or higher. Available to U.S. citizens.

Application Requirements: Application form, community service, essay, financial need analysis. *Deadline:* April 5.

Contact: Liz Watson, Scholarship Program Manager
    Phone: 781-736-1500
    E-mail: scholarship@twoten.org

TWO TEN FOOTWEAR FOUNDATION SCHOLARSHIP

• *See page 676*

TWO TEN FOUNDATION FOOTWEAR DESIGN SCHOLARSHIP

Unlike our traditional college scholarships, the Footwear Design Scholarship is available to any student who is studying design with a focus on footwear. This program was created in 2003 to assist students with a demonstrated interest and skill in pursuing a career in footwear design. Applicants are evaluated by design potential and financial need. Awards of up to $3,000 annually are renewable for up to four years of undergraduate study.

Award: Scholarship for use in freshman, sophomore, junior, or senior years; renewable. *Number:* 5. *Amount:* $3000.

Eligibility Requirements: Applicant must be enrolled or expecting to enroll full- or part-time at a two-year or four-year or technical institution or university; resident of Alabama, Alaska, Arizona, Arkansas,
California, Colorado, Connecticut, Delaware, Florida, Georgia, Hawaii, Idaho, Illinois, Indiana, Iowa, Kansas, Kentucky, Louisiana, Maine, Maryland, Massachusetts, Michigan, Minnesota, Mississippi, Missouri, Montana, Nebraska, Nevada, New Hampshire, New Jersey, New Mexico, New York, North Carolina, North Dakota, Ohio, Oklahoma, Oregon, Pennsylvania, Puerto Rico, Rhode Island, South Carolina, South Dakota, Tennessee, Texas, Utah, Vermont, Virginia, Washington, West Virginia, Wisconsin, Wyoming and studying in Alabama, Alaska, Arizona, Arkansas, California, Colorado, Connecticut, Delaware, Florida, Georgia, Hawaii, Idaho, Illinois, Indiana, Iowa, Kansas, Kentucky, Louisiana, Maine, Maryland, Massachusetts, Michigan, Minnesota, Mississippi, Missouri, Montana, Nebraska, Nevada, New Hampshire, New Jersey, New Mexico, New York, North Carolina, North Dakota, Nova Scotia, Ohio, Oklahoma, Oregon, Pennsylvania, Puerto Rico, Rhode Island, South Carolina, South Dakota, Tennessee, Texas, Utah, Vermont, Virginia, Washington, West Virginia, Wisconsin, Wyoming. Applicant must have 2.5 GPA or higher. Available to U.S. citizens.

Application Requirements: Application form, essay, financial need analysis, portfolio. *Deadline:* April 5.

Contact: Liz Watson, Scholarship Program Manager
    Phone: 781-736-1500
    E-mail: scholarship@twoten.org

ULMAN CANCER FUND FOR YOUNG ADULTS

http://www.ulmanfund.org/scholarships

JACQUELINE SHEARER MEMORIAL SCHOLARSHIP
• *See page 677*

LISA HIGGINS-HUSSMAN FOUNDATION SCHOLARSHIP
• *See page 678*

MARILYN YETSO MEMORIAL SCHOLARSHIP
• *See page 678*

OLIVIA M. MARQUART SCHOLARSHIP
• *See page 678*

PERLITA LIWANAG MEMORIAL SCHOLARSHIP
• *See page 678*

VERA YIP MEMORIAL SCHOLARSHIP
• *See page 679*

UNICO FOUNDATION INC.

http://www.unico.org/

ALPHONSE A. MIELE SCHOLARSHIP
• *See page 679*

BERNARD AND CAROLYN TORRACO MEMORIAL NURSING SCHOLARSHIP PROGRAM
• *See page 679*

DIMATTIO CELLI FAMILY STUDY ABROAD SCHOLARSHIP
• *See page 679*

ELLA T. GRASSO LITERARY SCHOLARSHIP
• *See page 680*

GUGLIELMO MARCONI ENGINEERING SCHOLARSHIP
• *See page 680*

INSERRA SCHOLARSHIPS
• *See page 680*

MAJOR DON S. GENTILE SCHOLARSHIP
• *See page 680*

RALPH J. TORRACO SCHOLARSHIP
• *See page 680*

THEODORE MAZZA SCHOLARSHIP
• *See page 681*

WILLIAM C. DAVINI SCHOLARSHIP
• *See page 681*

UNITED DAUGHTERS OF THE CONFEDERACY
http://www.hqudc.org/

CHARLOTTE M. F. BENTLEY/NEW YORK CHAPTER 103 SCHOLARSHIP
• *See page 584*

GERTRUDE BOTTS-SAUCIER SCHOLARSHIP
• *See page 584*

LOLA B. CURRY SCHOLARSHIP
• *See page 584*

UNITED NEGRO COLLEGE FUND
http://www.uncf.org/

ABCNJ LEADERSHIP IMPACT SCHOLARSHIP
• *See page 765*

DEBORAH L. VINCENT/FAHRO EDUCATION SCHOLARSHIP
• *See page 766*

DELTA AIR LINES NEW YORK SCHOLARSHIPS
• *See page 766*

EDNA BLUM SCHOLARSHIP FOR NYC RESIDENTS
• *See page 766*

FORT WAYNE INDIANA SCHOLARSHIP PROGRAM
• *See page 767*

JAY CHARLES LEVINE SCHOLARSHIP
• *See page 767*

KROGER MICHIGAN SCHOLARSHIP
• *See page 767*

MAYS FAMILY SCHOLARSHIP FUND
• *See page 768*

PENNSYLVANIA STATE EMPLOYEES COMBINED CAMPAIGN SCHOLARSHIP (SECA)
• *See page 768*

UNCF HONDA SCHOLARSHIP
• *See page 768*

USA FUNDS SCHOLARSHIP
• *See page 768*

UNIVERSITY OF WYOMING
http://www.uwyo.edu/scholarships

VIETNAM VETERANS AWARD-WYOMING
• *See page 716*

UTAH HIGHER EDUCATION ASSISTANCE AUTHORITY
http://www.uheaa.org/

HIGHER EDUCATION SUCCESS STIPEND PROGRAM
Award available to students with substantial financial need for use at any of the participating Utah institutions. The student must be a Utah resident. Contact the financial aid office of the participating institution for requirements and deadlines.

Award: Grant for use in freshman, sophomore, junior, or senior years; not renewable. *Number:* 1000–5000. *Amount:* $300–$4000.

Eligibility Requirements: Applicant must be enrolled or expecting to enroll full- or part-time at a two-year or four-year or technical institution or university; resident of Utah and studying in Utah. Available to U.S. citizens.

Application Requirements: Financial need analysis. *Deadline:* continuous.

Contact: Financial Office
Utah Higher Education Assistance Authority
Participating college or university

VANILLA PILGRIM FOUNDATION
https://www.vanillapilgrim.com/

2018 OPEN ESSAY COMPETITION
• *See page 682*

VERMONT STUDENT ASSISTANCE CORPORATION
http://www.vsac.org/

VERMONT INCENTIVE GRANTS
Grants for Vermont residents based on financial need. Must meet needs test. Must be college undergraduate enrolled full-time at an approved post secondary institution. Only available to Vermont residents.

Award: Grant for use in freshman, sophomore, junior, or senior years; not renewable. *Amount:* $850–$12,050.

Eligibility Requirements: Applicant must be enrolled or expecting to enroll full-time at a two-year or four-year or technical institution or university and resident of Vermont. Available to U.S. citizens.

Application Requirements: Application form, financial need analysis. *Deadline:* continuous.

Contact: Grant Program
Vermont Student Assistance Corporation
PO Box 2000
Winooski, VT 05404-2000
Phone: 800-882-4166

VERMONT PART-TIME STUDENT GRANTS
For undergraduates carrying less than twelve credits per semester who have not received a bachelor's degree. Must be Vermont resident. Based on financial need. Complete Vermont Financial Aid Packet to apply. May be used at any approved post-secondary institution.

Award: Grant for use in freshman, sophomore, junior, or senior years; not renewable. *Amount:* $425–$9040.

Eligibility Requirements: Applicant must be enrolled or expecting to enroll part-time at a two-year or four-year or technical institution or university and resident of Vermont. Available to U.S. citizens.

Application Requirements: Application form, financial need analysis. *Deadline:* continuous.

Contact: Grant Program
Vermont Student Assistance Corporation
PO Box 2000
Winooski, VT 05404-2000
Phone: 888-882-4166

VIRGINIA DEPARTMENT OF EDUCATION

http://www.doe.virginia.gov

GRANVILLE P. MEADE SCHOLARSHIP

The Granville P. Meade Scholarship provides financial assistance to students who have achieved academically, but who are financially unable to attend college. High school seniors only are eligible to apply for scholarship. Students are selected based upon GPA, standardized test scores, letters of recommendations, extra curricular activities, and financial need. Interested students are asked to submit scholarship applications to their high school principals by March 16.

Award: Scholarship for use in freshman year; renewable. *Amount:* $2000.

Eligibility Requirements: Applicant must be high school student; planning to enroll or expecting to enroll full-time at a two-year or four-year institution or university and resident of Virginia. Applicant must have 2.5 GPA or higher. Available to U.S. citizens.

Application Requirements: Application form, financial need analysis. *Deadline:* March 16.

Contact: Mr. Joseph Wharff, School Counseling Connections Specialist
Virginia Department of Education
101 N. 14th Street
Richmond, VA 23218
Phone: 804-225-3370
E-mail: joseph.wharff@doe.virginia.gov

VIRGINIA DEPARTMENT OF VETERANS SERVICES

http://www.dvs.virginia.gov/

VIRGINIA MILITARY SURVIVORS AND DEPENDENTS EDUCATION PROGRAM

• *See page 716*

VIRGINIA STATE COUNCIL OF HIGHER EDUCATION

http://www.schev.edu/

VIRGINIA COMMONWEALTH AWARD

Need-based award for undergraduate or graduate study at a Virginia public two- or four-year college, or university. Undergraduates must be Virginia residents. The application and awards process are administered by the financial aid office at the Virginia public institution where the student is enrolled. Dollar value of each award varies. Contact college financial aid office for application and deadlines.

Award: Grant for use in freshman, sophomore, junior, or senior years; not renewable.

Eligibility Requirements: Applicant must be enrolled or expecting to enroll full- or part-time at a two-year or four-year institution or university; resident of Virginia and studying in Virginia. Available to U.S. citizens.

Application Requirements: Financial need analysis.

Contact: Contact the financial aid office of participating Virginia public college.

VIRGINIA GUARANTEED ASSISTANCE PROGRAM

Awards to undergraduate students proportional to their need, up to full tuition, fees and book allowance. Must be a graduate of a Virginia high school. High school GPA of 2.5 required. Must be enrolled full-time in a public Virginia two- or four-year institution and demonstrate financial need. Must maintain minimum college GPA of 2.0 for renewal awards.

Award: Grant for use in freshman, sophomore, junior, or senior years; not renewable.

Eligibility Requirements: Applicant must be enrolled or expecting to enroll full-time at a two-year or four-year institution or university; resident of Virginia and studying in Virginia. Available to U.S. citizens.

Application Requirements: Financial need analysis.

Contact: Contact the financial aid office of participating Virginia public college.

VIRGINIA TUITION ASSISTANCE GRANT PROGRAM (PRIVATE INSTITUTIONS)

Awards for undergraduate students. Also available to graduate and first professional degree students pursuing a health-related degree program. Not to be used for religious study. Must be U.S. citizen or eligible non-citizen, Virginia domiciled, and enrolled full-time at an approved private, nonprofit college within Virginia. Information and application available from participating Virginia colleges financial aid office. Visit http://www.schev.edu and click on Financial Aid.

Award: Grant for use in freshman, sophomore, junior, senior, or graduate years; renewable. *Amount:* $800–$3200.

Eligibility Requirements: Applicant must be enrolled or expecting to enroll full-time at a four-year institution or university; resident of Virginia and studying in Virginia. Available to U.S. citizens.

Application Requirements: Application form. *Deadline:* July 31.

Contact: Contact the financial aid office of the participating private nonprofit Virginia college or university.

WASHINGTON HOSPITAL HEALTHCARE SYSTEM

http://www.whhs.com/

WASHINGTON HOSPITAL EMPLOYEE ASSOCIATION SCHOLARSHIP

Scholarship for a dependent of a Washington Hospital Employee. Must be a graduating senior, community college student, transferring community college student, or a student attending a four-year institution.

Award: Scholarship for use in freshman, sophomore, junior, or senior years; not renewable. *Number:* 1. *Amount:* $2000.

Eligibility Requirements: Applicant must be enrolled or expecting to enroll full- or part-time at a two-year or four-year or technical institution or university and resident of California. Available to U.S. citizens.

Application Requirements: Application form, driver's license, essay, recommendations or references, test scores, transcript. *Deadline:* March 5.

Contact: Scholarship Chair, c/o Personnel Department
Washington Hospital Healthcare System
2500 Mowry Avenue
Fremont, CA 94538
Phone: 510-818-6220

WASHINGTON STATE PARENT TEACHER ASSOCIATION SCHOLARSHIP PROGRAM

http://www.wastatepta.org/

WASHINGTON STATE PARENT TEACHER ASSOCIATION SCHOLARSHIPS FOUNDATION

One-time scholarships for students who have graduated from a public high school in the state of Washington, and who greatly need financial help to begin full-time postsecondary education.

Award: Scholarship for use in freshman year; not renewable. *Number:* 60–80. *Amount:* $1000–$2000.

Eligibility Requirements: Applicant must be high school student; planning to enroll or expecting to enroll full-time at a four-year institution or university and resident of Washington. Available to U.S. citizens.

Application Requirements: Application form, community service, essay, financial need analysis, recommendations or references, transcript. *Deadline:* March 31.

Contact: Mr. Bill Williams, Executive Director
Phone: 253-565-2153
Fax: 253-565-7753
E-mail: jcarpenter@wastatepta.org

WASHINGTON STUDENT ACHIEVEMENT COUNCIL

COLLEGE BOUND SCHOLARSHIP

This program provides financial assistance to low-income students who want to achieve the dream of a college education. The application is a two-step process. Eligible students should complete an application during their 7th or 8th grade year via http://www.collegebound.wa.gov. The second step requires students to submit a financial aid application their senior year of high school and every year of college for income verification. Additional scholarship pledge requirements can be found at http://www.collegebound.wa.gov.

Award: Scholarship for use in freshman, sophomore, junior, or senior years; renewable.

Eligibility Requirements: Applicant must be enrolled or expecting to enroll full- or part-time at a two-year or four-year or technical institution or university; resident of Washington and studying in Washington.

Application Requirements: Application form. *Deadline:* June 30.

Contact: Sarah Weiss, Associate Director
Washington Student Achievement Council
917 Lakeridge Way SW
Olympia, WA 98502
Phone: 888-535-0747
E-mail: collegebound@wsac.wa.gov

WATSON-BROWN FOUNDATION INC.

http://www.watson-brown.org/

WATSON-BROWN FOUNDATION SCHOLARSHIP

Scholarships are awarded based on academic merit and financial need. Students must be from designated counties in Georgia or South Carolina and may attend any four- year, accredited, non-profit U.S. college or university. Renewable scholarships are awarded on two levels: $3000 and $5000.

Award: Scholarship for use in freshman, sophomore, junior, or senior years; renewable. *Number:* 200. *Amount:* $3000–$5000.

Eligibility Requirements: Applicant must be enrolled or expecting to enroll full-time at a four-year institution or university and resident of Georgia, South Carolina. Applicant must have 3.0 GPA or higher. Available to U.S. citizens.

Application Requirements: Application form, essay, financial need analysis, IRS Form 1040, recommendations or references, test scores, transcript. *Deadline:* February 15.

Contact: Sarah Drury, Director, Scholarships and Alumni Relations
Watson-Brown Foundation Inc.
310 Tom Watson Way
Thomson, GA 30824
Phone: 706-595-8886
E-mail: skdrury@watson-brown.org

WESTERN FRATERNAL LIFE ASSOCIATION

http://www.wflains.org

WESTERN FRATERNAL LIFE NATIONAL SCHOLARSHIP

• *See page 587*

WESTERN INTERSTATE COMMISSION FOR HIGHER EDUCATION

http://www.wiche.edu/

WICHE'S WESTERN UNDERGRADUATE EXCHANGE (WUE)

• *See page 683*

WEST VIRGINIA HIGHER EDUCATION POLICY COMMISSION-STUDENT SERVICES

http://www.wvhepc.edu

WEST VIRGINIA HIGHER EDUCATION GRANT PROGRAM

Award available for West Virginia resident for one year immediately preceding the date of application, high school graduate or the equivalent,

demonstrate financial need, and enroll as a full-time undergraduate at an approved university or college located in West Virginia or Pennsylvania.

Award: Grant for use in freshman, sophomore, junior, or senior years; not renewable. *Number:* 18,000–21,000. *Amount:* $300–$2700.

Eligibility Requirements: Applicant must be enrolled or expecting to enroll full-time at a two-year or four-year institution or university; resident of West Virginia and studying in Pennsylvania, West Virginia. Available to U.S. citizens.

Application Requirements: Financial need analysis. *Deadline:* April 15.

Contact: Judy Smith, Senior Project Coordinator
West Virginia Higher Education Policy Commission-Student Services
1018 Kanawha Boulevard East, Suite 700
Charleston, WV 25301-2827
Phone: 304-558-4618
E-mail: judy.kee@wvhepc.edu

WILLIAM D. SQUIRES EDUCATIONAL FOUNDATION INC.

http://www.wmdsquiresfoundation.org/

WILLIAM D. SQUIRES SCHOLARSHIP

$4000 Scholarship award. Renewable up to $16,000. For graduating high school seniors from Ohio planning to pursue a four year program. The William D. Squires Scholarship is primarily financial need based but students must also have a clear career goal and be highly motivated. Minimum 3.2 GPA is required. Free to apply: http://www.wmdsquiresfoundation.org

Award: Scholarship for use in freshman, sophomore, junior, or senior years; renewable. *Number:* 15. *Amount:* $4000.

Eligibility Requirements: Applicant must be high school student; planning to enroll or expecting to enroll full-time at a four-year institution or university and resident of Ohio. Available to U.S. citizens.

Application Requirements: Application form, essay, financial need analysis. *Deadline:* April 5.

Contact: Scholarship Director
William D. Squires Educational Foundation Inc.
PO Box 2940
Jupiter, FL 33468
Phone: 561-741-7751
E-mail: info@wmdsquiresfoundation.org

WILLIAM F. COOPER SCHOLARSHIP TRUST

WILLIAM F. COOPER SCHOLARSHIP

Scholarship to provide financial assistance to women living within the state of Georgia for undergraduate studies. Cannot be used for law, theology or medicine fields of study. Nursing is an approved area of study. For more details visit website http://www.wachoviascholars.com.

Award: Scholarship for use in freshman, sophomore, junior, or senior years; renewable. *Amount:* $1000.

Eligibility Requirements: Applicant must be enrolled or expecting to enroll full- or part-time at a four-year institution or university; female and resident of Georgia. Available to U.S. citizens.

Application Requirements: Application form, federal tax form 1040, W-2 forms, financial need analysis, recommendations or references, test scores, transcript. *Deadline:* April 1.

Contact: Sally King, Program Coordinator
Phone: 800-576-5135
Fax: 864-268-7160
E-mail: sallyking@bellsouth.net

WILLIAM G. AND MARIE SELBY FOUNDATION

http://www.selbyfdn.org/

SELBY SCHOLAR PROGRAM

Must be a resident of Sarasota, Manatee, Charlotte, or Desoto counties in Florida. Scholarships awarded up to $7,000 annually, not to exceed 1/3 of individual's financial need. Renewable for four years if student is full-time undergraduate at accredited college or university and maintains 3.0 GPA. Must demonstrate financial need and values of leadership and service to the community. STUDENTS WHO ARE ALREADY ATTENDING A 4-YEAR COLLEGE ARE NOT ELIGIBLE TO APPLY.

Award: Scholarship for use in freshman, sophomore, junior, or senior years; renewable. *Number:* 40. *Amount:* $1000–$7000.

Eligibility Requirements: Applicant must be enrolled or expecting to enroll full-time at a four-year institution or university; resident of Florida and must have an interest in leadership. Applicant must have 3.0 GPA or higher. Available to U.S. citizens.

Application Requirements: Application form, essay, financial need analysis, interview. *Deadline:* April 1.

Contact: Evan Jones, Grants and Scholarships Manager
William G. and Marie Selby Foundation
1800 Second Street, Suite 954
Sarasota, FL 34236
Phone: 941-957-0442
E-mail: ejones@selbyfdn.org

WISCONSIN DEPARTMENT OF VETERANS AFFAIRS (WDVA)

http://www.dva.state.wi.us/

VETERANS EDUCATION (VETED) REIMBURSEMENT GRANT
• *See page 694*

WISCONSIN HIGHER EDUCATIONAL AID BOARD

http://www.heab.wi.gov/

HANDICAPPED STUDENT GRANT-WISCONSIN
• *See page 694*

MINORITY UNDERGRADUATE RETENTION GRANT-WISCONSIN
• *See page 771*

TALENT INCENTIVE PROGRAM GRANT

Grant assists residents of Wisconsin who are attending a nonprofit institution in Wisconsin, and who have substantial financial need. Must meet income criteria, be considered economically and educationally disadvantaged, and be enrolled at least half-time. Refer to website for further details http://www.heab.state.wi.us.

Award: Grant for use in freshman, sophomore, junior, or senior years; renewable. *Amount:* $250–$1800.

Eligibility Requirements: Applicant must be enrolled or expecting to enroll full- or part-time at a two-year or four-year or technical institution or university; resident of Wisconsin and studying in Wisconsin. Available to U.S. citizens.

Application Requirements: Application form, financial need analysis, nomination by financial aid office. *Deadline:* continuous.

Contact: Colette Brown, Program Coordinator
Wisconsin Higher Educational Aid Board
PO Box 7885
Madison, WI 53707-7885
Phone: 608-266-1665
Fax: 608-267-2808
E-mail: colette.brown@wi.gov

WISCONSIN ACADEMIC EXCELLENCE SCHOLARSHIP

Renewable award for high school seniors with the highest GPA in graduating class. Must be a Wisconsin resident attending a nonprofit Wisconsin institution full-time. Scholarship value is $2250 toward tuition each year for up to four years. Must maintain 3.0 GPA for renewal. Refer to your high school counselor for more details.

Award: Scholarship for use in freshman year; renewable. *Amount:* up to $2250.

Eligibility Requirements: Applicant must be high school student; planning to enroll or expecting to enroll full-time at a two-year or four-year or technical institution or university; resident of Wisconsin and studying in Wisconsin. Applicant must have 3.0 GPA or higher. Available to U.S. citizens.

Application Requirements: Application form, test scores, transcript. *Deadline:* continuous.

Contact: Nancy Wilkison, Program Coordinator
Wisconsin Higher Educational Aid Board
PO Box 7885
Madison, WI 53707-7885
Phone: 608-267-2213
Fax: 608-267-2808
E-mail: nancy.wilkison@wi.gov

WISCONSIN HIGHER EDUCATION GRANTS (WHEG)

Grants for residents of Wisconsin enrolled at least half-time in degree or certificate programs at a University of Wisconsin Institution, Wisconsin Technical College or an approved Tribal College. Must show financial need. Refer to website for further details http://www.heab.wi.gov.

Award: Grant for use in freshman, sophomore, junior, or senior years; not renewable. *Amount:* $250–$3000.

Eligibility Requirements: Applicant must be enrolled or expecting to enroll full- or part-time at a two-year or four-year or technical institution or university; resident of Wisconsin and studying in Wisconsin. Available to U.S. citizens.

Application Requirements: Application form, financial need analysis. *Deadline:* continuous.

Contact: Sandra Thomas, Program Coordinator
Wisconsin Higher Educational Aid Board
PO Box 7885
Madison, WI 53707-7885
Phone: 608-266-0888
Fax: 608-267-2808
E-mail: sandy.thomas@heab.state.wi.us

WISCONSIN NATIVE AMERICAN/INDIAN STUDENT ASSISTANCE GRANT
• *See page 771*

WISCONSIN SCHOOL COUNSELOR ASSOCIATION

http://www.wscaweb.org/

WISCONSIN SCHOOL COUNSELOR ASSOCIATION HIGH SCHOOL SCHOLARSHIP

Scholarship is available to high school seniors in Wisconsin who plan to attend a two-year or four-year postsecondary institution in the fall. Students are asked to submit an essay that describes how a school counselor or school counseling program has impacted their life.

Award: Scholarship for use in freshman year; not renewable. *Number:* 2–4. *Amount:* $1000.

Eligibility Requirements: Applicant must be high school student; planning to enroll or expecting to enroll full-time at a two-year or four-year institution or university and resident of Wisconsin. Available to U.S. citizens.

Application Requirements: Application form, essay. *Deadline:* November 1.

Contact: Katie Nechodom, WSCA Professional Recognition and Scholarship Coordinator
E-mail: nechodomk@gmail.com

WOLTERMAN LAW OFFICE, LPA

https://www.woltermanlaw.com/

WOLTERMAN LAW OFFICE LPA HOPE FOR THE FUTURE SCHOLARSHIP
• *See page 683*

WOMEN IN DEFENSE MICHIGAN

http://wid-mi.org/

WOMEN IN DEFENSE HORIZONS-MICHIGAN SCHOLARSHIP

The program focuses on the following preferred fields of study: security studies, military history, government relations, engineering, computer science, physics, mathematics, business (as it relates to national security or defense), law (as it relates to national security or defense), international relations, political science, economics. Others will be considered if the applicant can successfully demonstrate relevance to a career in the areas of national security or defense. Awards are based on academic achievement, participation in defense and national security activities, field of study, work experience, statements of objectives, recommendations, and financial need. Awards are made without regard to race, creed, color, or religion. HORIZONS-Michigan reserves the right to revise, suspend or discontinue this program without notice.

Award: Scholarship for use in junior, senior, graduate, or postgraduate years; not renewable. *Number:* 1–4. *Amount:* $1500–$5000.

Eligibility Requirements: Applicant must be enrolled or expecting to enroll full- or part-time at a two-year or four-year or technical institution or university; female; resident of Michigan and studying in Michigan. Applicant must have 3.0 GPA or higher. Available to U.S. citizens.

Application Requirements: Application form, driver's license, essay, financial need analysis. *Deadline:* May 12.

Contact: Melanie Stager, Director of Scholarships
E-mail: scholarships@wid-mi.org

WYOMING DEPARTMENT OF EDUCATION

http://edu.wyoming.gov/

DOUVAS MEMORIAL SCHOLARSHIP

Available to Wyoming residents who are first-generation Americans. Must be between 18 and 22 years old. Must be used at any Wyoming public institution of higher education for study in freshman year.

Award: Scholarship for use in freshman year; not renewable. *Number:* 1. *Amount:* $500.

Eligibility Requirements: Applicant must be age 18-22; enrolled or expecting to enroll full- or part-time at a two-year or four-year institution or university; resident of Wyoming and studying in Wyoming. Available to U.S. citizens.

Application Requirements: Application form. *Deadline:* April 30.

Contact: Bruce Hayes, Education Consultant
Wyoming Department of Education
2300 Capitol Avenue
Hathaway Building, 2nd Floor
Cheyenne, WY 82002
Phone: 307-777-6198
E-mail: bruce.hayes@wyo.gov

HATHAWAY SCHOLARSHIP

Scholarship for Wyoming students to pursue postsecondary education within the state. Award ranges from $840 to $1680 per semester. Deadline varies.

Award: Scholarship for use in freshman, sophomore, junior, senior, or graduate years; renewable. *Amount:* $840–$1680.

Eligibility Requirements: Applicant must be enrolled or expecting to enroll full- or part-time at a two-year or four-year institution or university; resident of Wyoming and studying in Wyoming. Applicant must have 2.5 GPA or higher. Available to U.S. citizens.

Application Requirements: Application form. *Deadline:* continuous.

Contact: Mr. Bradley Barker III, Hathaway Scholarship Consultant
Wyoming Department of Education
2300 Capitol Avenue
Hathaway Building
Cheyenne, WY 82002
Phone: 307-777-6226
E-mail: hathawayscholarship@wyo.gov

WYOMING FARM BUREAU FEDERATION

http://www.wyfb.org/

LIVINGSTON FAMILY - H.J. KING MEMORIAL SCHOLARSHIP
• *See page 587*

WYOMING FARM BUREAU CONTINUING EDUCATION SCHOLARSHIPS
• *See page 587*

WYOMING FARM BUREAU FEDERATION SCHOLARSHIPS
• *See page 588*

YOUTH FOUNDATION INC.

http://fdnweb.org/youthfdn

ALEXANDER AND MAUDE HADDEN SCHOLARSHIP
• *See page 684*

TALENT/INTEREST AREA

1-800-HANSONS

http://www.hansons.com

1-800-HANSONS SCHOLARSHIP PROGRAM
• *See page 592*

1DENTAL.COM

https://www.1dental.com/

1DENTAL SCHOLARSHIP
• *See page 592*

1ST CAVALRY DIVISION ASSOCIATION

https://www.1CDA.org

1ST CAVALRY DIVISION ASSOCIATION SCHOLARSHIP FOUNDATION
• *See page 592*

365 PET INSURANCE

https://365petinsurance.com/

MINORITY STUDENTS IN VETERINARY MEDICINE SCHOLARSHIP
• *See page 719*

A-1 AUTO TRANSPORT, INC.

https://www.a1autotransport.com/a-1-auto-transport-scholarship/

A-1 AUTO TRANSPORT SCHOLARSHIP
• *See page 592*

ACADGILD

https://acadgild.com

ACADGILD MERIT-BASED SCHOLARSHIPS
• *See page 593*

ACES: THE SOCIETY FOR EDITING

https://aceseditors.org/

BILL WALSH SCHOLARSHIP
• *See page 593*

AIR FORCE AID SOCIETY

http://www.afas.org/

GENERAL HENRY H. ARNOLD EDUCATION GRANT PROGRAM
• *See page 695*

AIR TRAFFIC CONTROL ASSOCIATION INC.

http://www.atca.org/

AIR TRAFFIC CONTROL ASSOCIATION SCHOLARSHIP
• *See page 593*

BUCKINGHAM MEMORIAL SCHOLARSHIP
• *See page 593*

ALABAMA SOCIETY OF CERTIFIED PUBLIC ACCOUNTANTS

http://www.ascpa.org/

ASCPA EDUCATIONAL FOUNDATION SCHOLARSHIP
• *See page 593*

ALBERTA HERITAGE SCHOLARSHIP FUND

http://www.alis.alberta.ca/

CHARLES S. NOBLE JUNIOR FOOTBALL SCHOLARSHIPS
• *See page 720*

CHARLES S. NOBLE JUNIOR HOCKEY SCHOLARSHIPS
• *See page 720*

JIMMIE CONDON ATHLETIC SCHOLARSHIPS
• *See page 720*

LAURENCE DECORE AWARDS FOR STUDENT LEADERSHIP
• *See page 721*

PRAIRIE BASEBALL ACADEMY SCHOLARSHIPS
• *See page 800*

ALERTONE SERVICES, LLC

https://www.alert-1.com/

ALERT1 STUDENT FOR SENIORS SCHOLARSHIP
• *See page 593*

ALERT SCHOLARSHIP

http://www.alertmagazine.org/

ALERT SCHOLARSHIP
• *See page 800*

THE ALEXANDER FOUNDATION

http://www.thealexanderfoundation.org/

THE ALEXANDER FOUNDATION SCHOLARSHIP PROGRAM
• *See page 800*

ALEXANDER GRAHAM BELL ASSOCIATION FOR THE DEAF AND HARD OF HEARING

http://www.agbell.org/

AG BELL COLLEGE SCHOLARSHIP PROGRAM
• *See page 594*

ALGAECAL INC.

https://www.algaecal.com/

ALGAECAL SCHOLARSHIP
• *See page 594*

ALLIANCE FOR YOUNG ARTISTS AND WRITERS INC.

http://www.artandwriting.org/

SCHOLASTIC ART AND WRITING AWARDS
• *See page 594*

ALLTHEROOMS

http://alltherooms.com

ROOM TO TRAVEL - STUDY ABROAD SCHOLARSHIP
• *See page 594*

ALZHEIMER'S FOUNDATION OF AMERICA

https://alzfdn.org/

AFA TEENS FOR ALZHEIMER'S AWARENESS COLLEGE SCHOLARSHIP
• *See page 595*

AMERICAN ALPINE CLUB

https://americanalpineclub.org/

AMERICAN ALPINE CLUB RESEARCH GRANTS
• *See page 595*

AMERICAN ASSOCIATION OF TEACHERS OF JAPANESE BRIDGING CLEARINGHOUSE FOR STUDY ABROAD IN JAPAN

http://www.aatj.org

BRIDGING SCHOLARSHIP FOR STUDY ABROAD IN JAPAN
• *See page 595*

AMERICAN COUNCIL OF THE BLIND

http://www.acb.org/

AMERICAN COUNCIL OF THE BLIND SCHOLARSHIPS
• *See page 595*

AMERICAN INSTITUTE FOR FOREIGN STUDY

http://www.aifsabroad.com/

AIFS AFFILIATE SCHOLARSHIPS

Students from colleges and universities that participate in the AIFS Affiliates program are eligible. Application fee: $95. For more details, visit http://www.aifsabroad.com/scholarships.asp.

Award: Scholarship for use in freshman, sophomore, junior, or senior years; not renewable.

Eligibility Requirements: Applicant must be enrolled or expecting to enroll full-time at a two-year or four-year institution or university and must have an interest in international exchange. Available to U.S. and non-U.S. citizens.

Application Requirements: Application form, essay, personal photograph, recommendations or references, transcript. *Fee:* $95. *Deadline:* varies.

Contact: David Mauro, Admissions Counselor
American Institute for Foreign Study
River Plaza, 9 West Broad Street
Stamford, CT 06902-3788
Phone: 800-727-2437 Ext. 5163
Fax: 203-399-5463
E-mail: dmauro@aifs.com

AIFS DIVERSITYABROAD.COM SCHOLARSHIP
• See page 723

AIFS GENERATION STUDY ABROAD SCHOLARSHIPS

Awards available to undergraduates on an AIFS study abroad program. Applicants must demonstrate leadership potential, have a minimum 3.0 cumulative GPA, and meet program requirements. The program application fee is $95. Deadlines: April 15 for fall, October 1 for spring, and March 1 for summer.

Award: Scholarship for use in freshman, sophomore, junior, or senior years; not renewable. *Number:* up to 130. *Amount:* $500–$1000.

Eligibility Requirements: Applicant must be enrolled or expecting to enroll full-time at a two-year or four-year institution or university and must have an interest in international exchange or leadership. Applicant must have 3.0 GPA or higher. Available to U.S. and non-U.S. citizens.

Application Requirements: Application form, essay, personal photograph, recommendations or references, transcript. *Fee:* $95. *Deadline:* varies.

Contact: David Mauro, Admissions Counselor
American Institute for Foreign Study
1 High Ridge Park
Stamford, CT 06905
Phone: 800-727-2437 Ext. 5163
Fax: 203-399-5463
E-mail: dmauro@aifs.com

AIFS GILMAN SCHOLARSHIP BONUS-$500 SCHOLARSHIPS

Award of $500 available to each undergraduate recipient for use toward an AIFS program. More information is available at http://www.iie.org/gilman.

Award: Scholarship for use in freshman, sophomore, junior, or senior years; not renewable. *Amount:* $500.

Eligibility Requirements: Applicant must be enrolled or expecting to enroll full-time at a four-year institution or university and must have an interest in international exchange. Available to U.S. and non-U.S. citizens.

Application Requirements: Application form, essay, personal photograph, recommendations or references, transcript. *Fee:* $95. *Deadline:* varies.

Contact: David Mauro, Admissions Counselor
American Institute for Foreign Study
1 High Ridge Park
Stamford, CT 06905
Phone: 800-727-2437 Ext. 5163
Fax: 203-399-5463
E-mail: dmauro@aifs.com

AIFS-HACU SCHOLARSHIPS
• See page 723

AIFS STUDY AGAIN SCHOLARSHIPS

Students who studied abroad on an AIFS summer program will receive a $1000 scholarship to study abroad on an AIFS semester or academic year catalog program or a $500 scholarship toward a summer catalog program. Students who studied abroad on an AIFS semester or academic year program will receive a $500 scholarship toward a summer catalog program or a $1000 scholarship toward a semester program in a different academic year. Deadlines: April 15 for fall, October 15 for spring, and March 1 for summer.

Award: Scholarship for use in freshman, sophomore, junior, or senior years; not renewable. *Amount:* $500–$1000.

Eligibility Requirements: Applicant must be enrolled or expecting to enroll full-time at a two-year or four-year institution or university and must have an interest in international exchange. Applicant must have 2.5 GPA or higher. Available to U.S. and non-U.S. citizens.

Application Requirements: Application form, essay, personal photograph, recommendations or references, transcript. *Fee:* $95. *Deadline:* varies.

Contact: David Mauro, Admissions Counselor
American Institute for Foreign Study
1 High Ridge Park
Stamford, CT 06905
Phone: 800-727-2437 Ext. 5163
Fax: 203-399-5463
E-mail: dmauro@aifs.com

AMERICAN JEWISH LEAGUE FOR ISRAEL

http://www.americanjewishleague.org/

AMERICAN JEWISH LEAGUE FOR ISRAEL SCHOLARSHIP PROGRAM

Scholarship provides support with tuition for a full year of study (September to May) at one of seven Israeli universities, Bar Ilan, Ben Gurion, Haifa, Hebrew, Tel Aviv, Technion, and Weizmann, Interdisciplinary Center at Herzliya. Additional information is available on website http://www.americanjewishleague.org/ScholarshipInformation.html.

Award: Scholarship for use in freshman, sophomore, junior, or senior years; not renewable. *Number:* 3–15. *Amount:* $2000.

Eligibility Requirements: Applicant must be enrolled or expecting to enroll full-time at a four-year institution or university and must have an interest in Jewish culture. Available to U.S. citizens.

Application Requirements: Application form, essay, personal and academic aspirations, recommendations or references, transcript. *Deadline:* May 1.

Contact: Mr. Karl Zukerman, University Scholarship Fund
American Jewish League for Israel
4485 Hazleton Lane
Wellington, FL 33449
Fax: 561-963-2923
E-mail: kdzwork@aol.com

AMERICAN LEGION AUXILIARY DEPARTMENT OF MASSACHUSETTS

http://www.masslegion-aux.org/

AMERICAN LEGION AUXILIARY DEPARTMENT OF MASSACHUSETTS DEPARTMENT PRESIDENT'S SCHOLARSHIP
• See page 595

AMERICAN LEGION AUXILIARY DEPARTMENT OF WISCONSIN

http://www.amlegionauxwi.org/

AMERICAN LEGION AUXILIARY DEPARTMENT OF WISCONSIN DELLA VAN DEUREN MEMORIAL SCHOLARSHIP
• *See page 552*

AMERICAN LEGION AUXILIARY DEPARTMENT OF WISCONSIN H.S. AND ANGELINE LEWIS SCHOLARSHIPS
• *See page 552*

AMERICAN LEGION AUXILIARY DEPARTMENT OF WISCONSIN MERIT AND MEMORIAL SCHOLARSHIPS
• *See page 552*

AMERICAN LEGION AUXILIARY DEPARTMENT OF WISCONSIN PRESIDENT'S SCHOLARSHIPS
• *See page 552*

AMERICAN LEGION AUXILIARY NATIONAL HEADQUARTERS

http://www.ALAforVeterans.org

AMERICAN LEGION AUXILIARY CHILDREN OF WARRIORS NATIONAL PRESIDENTS' SCHOLARSHIP
• *See page 596*

AMERICAN LEGION BASEBALL

http://www.legion.org/baseball

AMERICAN LEGION BASEBALL SCHOLARSHIP
Awarded to graduated seniors who were nominated by American Legion Baseball coach who demonstrate outstanding academics, citizenship, community spirit, leadership and financial need.

Award: Scholarship for use in freshman, sophomore, junior, senior, graduate, or postgraduate years; not renewable. *Number:* 1–51. *Amount:* $500–$2500.

Eligibility Requirements: Applicant must be high school student; planning to enroll or expecting to enroll full-time at a two-year or four-year or technical institution or university and must have an interest in athletics/sports. Applicant must have 2.5 GPA or higher. Available to U.S. and non-Canadian citizens.

Application Requirements: Application form, personal photograph. *Deadline:* July 15.

Contact: Mr. Steve Cloud, Assistant National Program Coordinator
American Legion Baseball
PO Box 1055
Indianapolis, IN 46206
Phone: 317-630-1213
E-mail: baseball@legion.org

AMERICAN LEGION DEPARTMENT OF ARIZONA

http://www.azlegion.org/programs

AMERICAN LEGION DEPARTMENT OF ARIZONA HIGH SCHOOL ORATORICAL CONTEST
• *See page 803*

AMERICAN LEGION DEPARTMENT OF ARKANSAS

http://www.arklegion.homestead.com/

AMERICAN LEGION DEPARTMENT OF ARKANSAS HIGH SCHOOL ORATORICAL CONTEST
• *See page 803*

AMERICAN LEGION DEPARTMENT OF ILLINOIS

http://www.illegion.org/

AMERICANISM ESSAY CONTEST SCHOLARSHIP
• *See page 553*

AMERICAN LEGION DEPARTMENT OF ILLINOIS HIGH SCHOOL ORATORICAL CONTEST
• *See page 804*

AMERICAN LEGION DEPARTMENT OF INDIANA

http://www.indianalegion.org

AMERICAN LEGION DEPARTMENT OF INDIANA HIGH SCHOOL ORATORICAL CONTEST
• *See page 804*

FRANK W. MCHALE MEMORIAL SCHOLARSHIPS
• *See page 804*

AMERICAN LEGION DEPARTMENT OF IOWA

http://www.ialegion.org/

AMERICAN LEGION DEPARTMENT OF IOWA HIGH SCHOOL ORATORICAL CONTEST
• *See page 804*

AMERICAN LEGION DEPARTMENT OF IOWA OUTSTANDING SENIOR BASEBALL PLAYER
• *See page 805*

AMERICAN LEGION DEPARTMENT OF KANSAS

http://www.ksamlegion.org/

AMERICAN LEGION DEPARTMENT OF KANSAS HIGH SCHOOL ORATORICAL CONTEST
• *See page 805*

DR. CLICK COWGER BASEBALL SCHOLARSHIP
• *See page 805*

PAUL FLAHERTY ATHLETIC SCHOLARSHIP
• *See page 805*

AMERICAN LEGION DEPARTMENT OF MARYLAND

http://www.mdlegion.org/

AMERICAN LEGION DEPARTMENT OF MARYLAND GENERAL SCHOLARSHIP FUND
• *See page 555*

AMERICAN LEGION, DEPARTMENT OF MARYLAND, HIGH SCHOOL ORATORICAL SCHOLARSHIP CONTEST
• *See page 596*

MARYLAND BOYS STATE SCHOLARSHIP
• *See page 597*

AMERICAN LEGION DEPARTMENT OF MICHIGAN

http://www.michiganlegion.org/

AMERICAN LEGION DEPARTMENT OF MICHIGAN ORATORICAL SCHOLARSHIP PROGRAM
• *See page 805*

THE AMERICAN LEGION, DEPARTMENT OF MINNESOTA

http://www.mnlegion.org/

AMERICAN LEGION DEPARTMENT OF MINNESOTA HIGH SCHOOL ORATORICAL CONTEST
• *See page 806*

AMERICAN LEGION DEPARTMENT OF MONTANA

http://www.mtlegion.org/

AMERICAN LEGION DEPARTMENT OF MONTANA HIGH SCHOOL ORATORICAL CONTEST
• *See page 806*

AMERICAN LEGION DEPARTMENT OF NEBRASKA

http://www.nebraskalegion.net/

AMERICAN LEGION DEPARTMENT OF NEBRASKA HIGH SCHOOL ORATORICAL CONTEST
• *See page 806*

AMERICAN LEGION DEPARTMENT OF NEBRASKA JIM HURLBERT MEMORIAL BASEBALL SCHOLARSHIP
• *See page 806*

AMERICAN LEGION DEPARTMENT OF NEW YORK

http://www.ny.legion.org/

AMERICAN LEGION DEPARTMENT OF NEW YORK HIGH SCHOOL ORATORICAL CONTEST
• *See page 807*

AMERICAN LEGION DEPARTMENT OF NORTH CAROLINA

http://www.nclegion.org/

AMERICAN LEGION DEPARTMENT OF NORTH CAROLINA HIGH SCHOOL ORATORICAL CONTEST
• *See page 807*

AMERICAN LEGION DEPARTMENT OF NORTH DAKOTA

http://www.ndlegion.org/

AMERICAN LEGION DEPARTMENT OF NORTH DAKOTA NATIONAL HIGH SCHOOL ORATORICAL CONTEST
• *See page 807*

AMERICAN LEGION DEPARTMENT OF OREGON

http://www.orlegion.org/

AMERICAN LEGION DEPARTMENT OF OREGON HIGH SCHOOL ORATORICAL CONTEST
• *See page 807*

AMERICAN LEGION DEPARTMENT OF PENNSYLVANIA

http://www.pa-legion.com/

AMERICAN LEGION DEPARTMENT OF PENNSYLVANIA HIGH SCHOOL ORATORICAL CONTEST
• *See page 808*

AMERICAN LEGION DEPARTMENT OF SOUTH DAKOTA

http://www.sdlegion.org/

AMERICAN LEGION DEPARTMENT OF SOUTH DAKOTA HIGH SCHOOL ORATORICAL CONTEST
• *See page 808*

AMERICAN LEGION DEPARTMENT OF TENNESSEE

http://www.tennesseelegion.org/

AMERICAN LEGION DEPARTMENT OF TENNESSEE HIGH SCHOOL ORATORICAL CONTEST
• *See page 808*

AMERICAN LEGION DEPARTMENT OF TEXAS

http://www.txlegion.org/

AMERICAN LEGION DEPARTMENT OF TEXAS HIGH SCHOOL ORATORICAL CONTEST
• *See page 808*

AMERICAN LEGION DEPARTMENT OF VERMONT

http://www.vtlegion.org

AMERICAN LEGION DEPARTMENT OF VERMONT HIGH SCHOOL ORATORICAL CONTEST
• *See page 808*

AMERICAN LEGION DEPARTMENT OF WASHINGTON

http://www.walegion.org/

AMERICAN LEGION DEPARTMENT OF WASHINGTON CHILDREN AND YOUTH SCHOLARSHIPS
• *See page 557*

AMERICAN LEGION DEPARTMENT OF WEST VIRGINIA

http://www.wvlegion.org/

AMERICAN LEGION DEPARTMENT OF WEST VIRGINIA BOARD OF REGENTS SCHOLARSHIP
• *See page 588*

AMERICAN LEGION DEPARTMENT OF WEST VIRGINIA HIGH SCHOOL ORATORICAL CONTEST
• *See page 809*

AMERICAN MUSEUM OF NATURAL HISTORY

https://www.amnh.org/our-research/richard-gilder-graduate-school

YOUNG NATURALIST AWARDS
Essay contest open to students in grades 7-12 who are currently enrolled in a public, private, parochial, or home school in the United States, Canada, the U.S. territories, or a U.S.-sponsored school abroad. Essays must be based on an original scientific investigation conducted by the student. See website for guidelines http://www.amnh.org/nationalcenter/youngnaturalistawards/read.html.

Award: Prize for use in freshman year; not renewable. *Number:* 1.

Eligibility Requirements: Applicant must be high school student; planning to enroll or expecting to enroll part-time at a four-year institution or university and must have an interest in writing. Available to Canadian citizens.

Application Requirements: Application form, essay, personal photograph. *Deadline:* March 1.

Contact: Maria Rios, Assistant Director, Fellowships and Student Affairs
American Museum of Natural History
79th st @ Cental Park West
NY, NY 10024
Phone: 212-769-5017
E-mail: fellowships-rggs@amnh.org

AMERICAN QUARTER HORSE FOUNDATION (AQHF)

http://www.aqha.com/foundation

ARIZONA QUARTER RACING SCHOLARSHIP
• *See page 558*

DR. GERALD O'CONNOR MICHIGAN QHY SCHOLARSHIP
• *See page 558*

SWAYZE WOODRUFF MEMORIAL MID-SOUTH SCHOLARSHIP
• *See page 560*

AMERICAN SAVINGS FOUNDATION

http://www.asfdn.org/

ROBERT T. KENNEY SCHOLARSHIP PROGRAM AT THE AMERICAN SAVINGS FOUNDATION
• *See page 597*

AMERICAN SCHOOL OF CLASSICAL STUDIES AT ATHENS

http://www.ascsa.edu.gr/

CHARLES M. EDWARDS SCHOLARSHIP
• *See page 597*

AMERICAN SOCIETY OF SAFETY ENGINEERS (ASSE) FOUNDATION

http://foundation.asse.org

FAMILY SCHOLARSHIP FUND
• *See page 597*

AMERICAN STRING TEACHERS ASSOCIATION

http://www.astaweb.com/

NATIONAL SOLO COMPETITION
Twenty-six individual awards. Instrument categories are violin, viola, cello, double bass, classical guitar, and harp. Applicants competing in Junior Division must be under age 19. Senior Division competitors must be ages 19 to 25. Application fee is $75. Visit website for application forms. Applicant must be a member of ASTA.

Award: Prize for use in freshman, sophomore, junior, senior, or graduate years; not renewable. *Number:* 26.

Eligibility Requirements: Applicant must be age 19-25; enrolled or expecting to enroll full- or part-time at a two-year or four-year or technical institution or university and must have an interest in music. Available to U.S. and Canadian citizens.

Application Requirements: Application form, entry in a contest, proof of age, proof of membership. *Fee:* $75. *Deadline:* varies.

Contact: Laura Kobayashi, Committee Chair
American String Teachers Association
4153 Chain Bridge Road
Fairfax, VA 22030
Phone: 703-279-2113
Fax: 703-279-2114
E-mail: lkobayas@myway.com

ANCHOR SCHOLARSHIP FOUNDATION

http://www.anchorscholarship.com

ANCHOR SCHOLARSHIP FOUNDATION
• *See page 598*

ANKIN LAW

http://ankinlaw.com

ANKIN LAW OFFICE ANNUAL COLLEGE SCHOLARSHIP
• *See page 598*

ANTHONY MUNOZ FOUNDATION

http://www.munozfoundation.org

ANTHONY MUNOZ SCHOLARSHIPS
• *See page 598*

APPALOOSA HORSE CLUB-APPALOOSA YOUTH PROGRAM

http://www.appaloosayouth.com/

APPALOOSA YOUTH EDUCATIONAL SCHOLARSHIPS
• *See page 560*

ARCHITECTURAL PRECAST ASSOCIATION

http://www.archprecast.org

TOM CORY MEMORIAL SCHOLARSHIP
• *See page 598*

THE ARC NEW YORK

https://www.nysarc.org/

ARTHUR W. PENSE SCHOLARSHIP
• *See page 599*

ARKANSAS SINGLE PARENT SCHOLARSHIP FUND

http://www.aspsf.org/

ARKANSAS SINGLE PARENT SCHOLARSHIP FUND
• *See page 599*

ARMENIAN RELIEF SOCIETY OF EASTERN USA INC.-REGIONAL OFFICE

http://www.arseastusa.org/

ARMENIAN RELIEF SOCIETY UNDERGRADUATE SCHOLARSHIP
• *See page 599*

ARRL FOUNDATION INC.

http://www.arrl.org/

ALAN G. THORPE, K1TMW, MEMORIAL SCHOLARSHIP FUND

One $1000 scholarship for a student with active Amateur Radio license who is studying at any accredited 4-year college or university.

Award: Scholarship for use in freshman, sophomore, junior, or senior years; not renewable. *Number:* 1. *Amount:* $1000.

Eligibility Requirements: Applicant must be enrolled or expecting to enroll full- or part-time at a two-year or four-year or technical institution or university and must have an interest in amateur radio. Available to U.S. citizens.

Application Requirements: Application form. *Deadline:* January 31.

Contact: Ms. Mary Hobart, Secretary
Phone: 860-594-0397
E-mail: k1mmh@arrl.org

ALBERT H. HIX, W8AH, MEMORIAL SCHOLARSHIP
• *See page 811*

ARRL ROCKY MOUNTAIN DIVISION SCHOLARSHIP
• *See page 811*

ATLANTA RADIO CLUB SCHOLARSHIP
• *See page 811*

BILL, W2ONV, AND ANN SALERNO MEMORIAL SCHOLARSHIP

Two, one-time $1000 awards are available to students who possess any amateur radio license. Must have a 3.7 GPA or higher. Aggregate annual income of the family household should not exceed $100,000. Must attend an accredited four year college or university.

Award: Scholarship for use in freshman, sophomore, junior, senior, or graduate years; not renewable. *Number:* 2. *Amount:* $1000.

Eligibility Requirements: Applicant must be enrolled or expecting to enroll full-time at a four-year institution or university and must have an interest in amateur radio. Available to U.S. citizens.

Application Requirements: Application form, financial need analysis. *Deadline:* January 31.

Contact: Ms. Mary Hobart, Secretary
Phone: 860-594-0397
E-mail: k1mmh@arrl.org

BYRON BLANCHARD, N1EKV, MEMORIAL SCHOLARSHIP
• *See page 811*

CENTRAL ARIZONA DX ASSOCIATION SCHOLARSHIP
• *See page 811*

CHALLENGE MET SCHOLARSHIP
• *See page 685*

CHICAGO FM CLUB SCHOLARSHIP FUND
• *See page 811*

DAVID KNAUS MEMORIAL SCHOLARSHIP
• *See page 811*

DAYTON AMATEUR RADIO ASSOCIATION SCHOLARSHIPS

Four $1000 awards are available to students with any active amateur radio license. Must attend an accredited four-year college or university.

Award: Scholarship for use in freshman, sophomore, junior, or senior years; not renewable. *Number:* 4. *Amount:* $1000.

Eligibility Requirements: Applicant must be enrolled or expecting to enroll full- or part-time at a four-year institution or university and must have an interest in amateur radio. Available to U.S. citizens.

Application Requirements: Application form. *Deadline:* January 31.

Contact: Ms. Mary Hobart, Secretary
Phone: 860-594-0397
E-mail: k1mmh@arrl.org

ERNEST L. BAULCH, W2TX, AND MARCIA E. BAULCH, WA2AKJ, SCHOLARSHIP

$3500 scholarship for a student with any active Amateur Radio License Class license who is studying at a four-year college or university.

Award: Scholarship for use in freshman, sophomore, junior, or senior years; not renewable. *Number:* 1. *Amount:* $3500.

Eligibility Requirements: Applicant must be enrolled or expecting to enroll full-time at a four-year institution or university and must have an interest in amateur radio. Available to U.S. citizens.

Application Requirements: Application form. *Deadline:* January 31.

Contact: Ms. Mary Hobart, Secretary
Phone: 860-594-0397
E-mail: k1mmh@arrl.org

GENERAL FUND SCHOLARSHIP

Available to students who are amateur radio operators. Students can be licensed in any class of operators. Nonrenewable award for use in undergraduate years. Multiple awards per year.

Award: Scholarship for use in freshman, sophomore, junior, or senior years; not renewable. *Amount:* $2000.

Eligibility Requirements: Applicant must be enrolled or expecting to enroll full-time at a four-year institution or university and must have an interest in amateur radio. Available to U.S. citizens.

Application Requirements: Application form. *Deadline:* January 31.

Contact: Ms. Mary Hobart, Secretary
Phone: 860-594-0397
E-mail: k1mmh@arrl.org

GWINNETT AMATEUR RADIO SOCIETY SCHOLARSHIP
• *See page 812*

HARRY A. HODGES, W6YOO, SCHOLARSHIP
• *See page 812*

HELEN LAUGHLIN AM MODE MEMORIAL SCHOLARSHIP

One $1000 scholarship for a student with active General Class amateur radio license who is studying at any accredited 4-year college or university. Preference is given to residents of Texas, If no qualified applicant is identified, preference will be given to residents of Arkansas. If no qualified applicant is identified, preference will be given to residents of the ARRL West Gulf (Texas, Oklahoma) or Delta (Arkansas, Louisiana, Mississippi, Tennessee) Divisions. Preference is given to women Amateur Radio operators who are performing at a high academic level. Preference is given to applicants who have made a contact in the AM mode, but is not required.

Award: Scholarship for use in freshman, sophomore, junior, or senior years; not renewable. *Number:* 1. *Amount:* $1000.

Eligibility Requirements: Applicant must be enrolled or expecting to enroll full-time at a four-year institution or university and must have an interest in amateur radio. Available to U.S. citizens.

Application Requirements: Application form. *Deadline:* January 31.

Contact: Ms. Mary Hobart, Secretary
    Phone: 860-594-0397
    E-mail: k1mmh@arrl.org

JACKSON COUNTY ARA SCHOLARSHIP
• *See page 812*

JAMES COTHRAN, KD3NI, SCHOLARSHIP
• *See page 812*

K2TEO MARTIN J. GREEN SR. MEMORIAL SCHOLARSHIP

Available to students with a general amateur license for radio operation. Preference given to students from a ham family. Nonrenewable award for use in undergraduate years.

Award: Scholarship for use in freshman, sophomore, junior, or senior years; not renewable. *Number:* 1. *Amount:* $1000.

Eligibility Requirements: Applicant must be enrolled or expecting to enroll full-time at a four-year institution or university and must have an interest in amateur radio. Available to U.S. citizens.

Application Requirements: Application form. *Deadline:* January 31.

Contact: Ms. Mary Hobart, Secretary
    Phone: 860-594-0397
    E-mail: k1mmh@arrl.org

L.B. CEBIK, W4RNL, AND JEAN CEBIK, N4TZP, MEMORIAL SCHOLARSHIP

One $1000 award is available to a student with a Technician class or higher radio license. Must attend a four-year college or university.

Award: Scholarship for use in freshman, sophomore, junior, or senior years; not renewable. *Number:* 1. *Amount:* $1000.

Eligibility Requirements: Applicant must be enrolled or expecting to enroll full- or part-time at a four-year institution or university and must have an interest in amateur radio. Available to U.S. citizens.

Application Requirements: Application form. *Deadline:* January 31.

Contact: Ms. Mary Hobart, Secretary
    Phone: 860-594-0397
    E-mail: k1mmh@arrl.org

LOUISIANA MEMORIAL SCHOLARSHIP

One $1000 award is available to a student who possesses a technician class or higher amateur radio license and studying international studies. Academic merit, financial need, and interest in promoting Amateur Radio will be taken into consideration. Preference given to an ARRL member who are Baccalaureate or higher degree candidates.

Award: Scholarship for use in freshman, sophomore, junior, senior, graduate, or postgraduate years; not renewable. *Number:* 1. *Amount:* $1000.

Eligibility Requirements: Applicant must be enrolled or expecting to enroll full- or part-time at a four-year institution or university and must have an interest in amateur radio. Available to U.S. citizens.

Application Requirements: Application form, financial need analysis. *Deadline:* January 31.

Contact: Ms. Mary Hobart, Secretary
    Phone: 860-594-0397
    E-mail: k1mmh@arrl.org

MARY LOU BROWN SCHOLARSHIP
• *See page 812*

NEW ENGLAND AMATEUR RADIO FESTIVAL (NEAR–FEST) MEMORIAL SCHOLARSHIP
• *See page 812*

NEW ENGLAND FEMARA SCHOLARSHIP
• *See page 812*

NORMAN E. STROHMEIER, W2VRS, MEMORIAL SCHOLARSHIP
• *See page 812*

OZAUKEE RADIO CLUB, W9CQO, SCHOLARSHIP
• *See page 813*

PEORIA AREA AMATEUR RADIO CLUB SCHOLARSHIP
• *See page 813*

RICHARD W. BENDICKSEN, N7ZL, MEMORIAL SCHOLARSHIP

One $1000 award available to a student with any active amateur radio license attending a four-year college or university.

Award: Scholarship for use in freshman, sophomore, junior, or senior years; not renewable. *Number:* 1. *Amount:* $1000.

Eligibility Requirements: Applicant must be enrolled or expecting to enroll full- or part-time at a four-year institution or university and must have an interest in amateur radio. Available to U.S. citizens.

Application Requirements: Application form. *Deadline:* January 31.

Contact: Ms. Mary Hobart, Secretary
    Phone: 860-594-0397
    E-mail: k1mmh@arrl.org

SCHOLARSHIP OF THE MORRIS RADIO CLUB OF NEW JERSEY

One $1000 award available to a student who possesses a technician class or higher amateur radio license and attends a four-year college or university.

Award: Scholarship for use in freshman, sophomore, junior, or senior years; not renewable. *Number:* 1. *Amount:* $1000.

Eligibility Requirements: Applicant must be enrolled or expecting to enroll full- or part-time at a four-year institution or university and must have an interest in amateur radio. Available to U.S. citizens.

Application Requirements: Application form. *Deadline:* January 31.

Contact: Ms. Mary Hobart, Secretary
    Phone: 860-594-0397
    E-mail: k1mmh@arrl.org

SIX METER CLUB OF CHICAGO SCHOLARSHIP
• *See page 813*

TED, W4VHF, AND ITICE, K4LVV, GOLDTHORPE SCHOLARSHIP
• *See page 599*

THOMAS W. PORTER, W8KYZ, SCHOLARSHIP HONORING MICHAEL DAUGHERTY, W8LSE
• *See page 813*

TOM AND JUDITH COMSTOCK SCHOLARSHIP
• *See page 813*

WAYNE NELSON, KB4UT, MEMORIAL SCHOLARSHIP
• *See page 813*

WILLIAM BENNETT, W7PHO, MEMORIAL SCHOLARSHIP
• *See page 813*

WILLIAM GORDON BUCKNER, W0VZK, MEMORIAL SCHOLARSHIP

One $200 scholarship award for a student with an active Amateur Radio license in any class. Must be attending an accredited 4-year college or university or graduate program. Preference will be given to students performing at a high academic level.

Award: Scholarship for use in freshman, sophomore, junior, senior, or graduate years; not renewable. *Number:* 1. *Amount:* $200.

Eligibility Requirements: Applicant must be enrolled or expecting to enroll full- or part-time at a four-year institution or university and must have an interest in amateur radio. Available to U.S. citizens.

Application Requirements: Application form. *Deadline:* January 31.

Contact: Ms. Mary Hobart, Secretary
Phone: 860-594-0397
E-mail: k1mmh@arrl.org

YANKEE CLIPPER CONTEST CLUB YOUTH SCHOLARSHIP
• *See page 813*

YOU'VE GOT A FRIEND IN PENNSYLVANIA SCHOLARSHIP
• *See page 561*

ZACHARY TAYLOR STEVENS SCHOLARSHIP
• *See page 814*

ARTBA
http://www.artba.org/

ARTBA-TDF LANFORD FAMILY HIGHWAY WORKERS MEMORIAL SCHOLARSHIP PROGRAM
• *See page 599*

ASIAN PACIFIC COMMUNITY FUND
http://www.apcf.org/

ROYAL BUSINESS BANK SCHOLARSHIP PROGRAM
• *See page 600*

ASIAN REPORTER
http://www.arfoundation.net/

ASIAN REPORTER SCHOLARSHIP
• *See page 600*

ASSOCIATION OF ENVIRONMENTAL HEALTH ACADEMIC PROGRAMS (AEHAP)
http://www.aehap.org/

NSF INTERNATIONAL SCHOLAR PROGRAM
• *See page 775*

ASSURED LIFE ASSOCIATION
http://assuredlife.org

ASSURED LIFE ASSOCIATION ENDOWMENT SCHOLARSHIP PROGRAM
• *See page 600*

AUTHOR SERVICES, INC.
http://www.writersofthefuture.com/

L. RON HUBBARD'S ILLUSTRATORS OF THE FUTURE CONTEST
An ongoing competition for new and amateur artists judged by professional artists. Eligible submissions consist of three science fiction or fantasy illustrations. Prize amount ranges from $500 to $5000. Quarterly deadlines: December 31, March 31, June 30 and September 30. All entrants retain rights to artwork.

Award: Prize for use in freshman, sophomore, junior, senior, graduate, or postgraduate years; not renewable. *Number:* 12. *Amount:* $500–$5000.

Eligibility Requirements: Applicant must be enrolled or expecting to enroll full- or part-time at a two-year or four-year or technical institution or university and must have an interest in art. Available to U.S. and non-U.S. citizens.

Application Requirements: *Deadline:* continuous.

Contact: Joni Labaqui, Contest Administrator
Author Services, Inc.
7051 Hollywood Blvd.
Los Angeles, CA 90028
Phone: 323-466-3310
E-mail: contests@authorservicesinc.com

L. RON HUBBARD'S WRITERS OF THE FUTURE CONTEST
An ongoing competition for new and amateur writers judged by professional writers. Eligible submissions are short stories and novelettes of science fiction or fantasy. Deadline varies and prize amount ranges from $500 to $5000.

Award: Prize for use in freshman, sophomore, junior, senior, graduate, or postgraduate years; not renewable. *Number:* 12. *Amount:* $500–$5000.

Eligibility Requirements: Applicant must be enrolled or expecting to enroll full- or part-time at a two-year or four-year or technical institution or university and must have an interest in writing. Available to U.S. and non-U.S. citizens.

Application Requirements: *Deadline:* continuous.

Contact: Joni Labaqui, Contest Administrator
Author Services, Inc.
Author Services, Inc
7051 Hollywood Blvd.
Los Angeles, CA 90028
Phone: 323-466-3310
E-mail: contests@authorservicesinc.com

AUTOMOTIVE HALL OF FAME
http://www.automotivehalloffame.org/

AUTOMOTIVE HALL OF FAME EDUCATIONAL FUNDS
Award for full-time undergraduate and graduate students pursuing studies in automotive and related technologies. Must submit two letters of recommendation supporting automotive interests. Minimum 3.0 cumulative GPA required. Student must study in the United States and either be a United States citizen or on a student visa.

Award: Scholarship for use in freshman, sophomore, junior, senior, or graduate years; renewable. *Number:* 20. *Amount:* $500–$2000.

Eligibility Requirements: Applicant must be enrolled or expecting to enroll full-time at a two-year or four-year or technical institution or university and must have an interest in automotive. Applicant must have 3.0 GPA or higher. Available to U.S. and non-U.S. citizens.

Application Requirements: Application form, essay, financial need analysis, recommendations or references, self-addressed stamped envelope with application, transcript. *Deadline:* June 30.

Contact: Sue Lauster
Automotive Hall of Fame
21400 Oakwood Boulevard
Dearborn, MI 48124-4078
Phone: 313-240-4000
Fax: 313-240-8641

AWEBER COMMUNICATIONS
http://www.aweber.com/

AWEBER DEVELOPING FUTURES SCHOLARSHIP
• *See page 725*

AYN RAND INSTITUTE
https://www.aynrand.org

ATLAS SHRUGGED ESSAY CONTEST
• *See page 600*

BABE RUTH LEAGUE INC.

http://www.baberuthleague.org/

BABE RUTH SCHOLARSHIP PROGRAM

Program to provide assistance to individuals (former Babe Ruth Baseball, Cal Ripken Baseball or Babe Ruth Softball players) who plan on furthering their education beyond high school. Outstanding student athletes will receive $1000 each towards their college tuition.

Award: Scholarship for use in freshman year; not renewable. *Number:* 1–10. *Amount:* $1000.

Eligibility Requirements: Applicant must be high school student; planning to enroll or expecting to enroll full- or part-time at a two-year or four-year institution or university and must have an interest in athletics/sports. Available to U.S. citizens.

Application Requirements: Application form, application form may be submitted online (http://www.baberuthleague.org), recommendations or references, transcript. *Deadline:* September 1.

Contact: Mr. Joseph Smiegocki, Scholarship Committee
Phone: 800-880-3142
Fax: 609-695-2505
E-mail: info@baberuthleague.org

BARONE DEFENSE FIRM

http://baronedefensefirm.com/

BARONE DEFENSE FIRM WIN BACK YOUR LIFE SCHOLARSHIP

• *See page 601*

BILLINGS & BARRETT

https://billingsandbarrett.com/

BILLINGS & BARRETT FIRST IN FAMILY SCHOLARSHIP

• *See page 601*

MATRIX HEALTH GROUP SPRX BLEEDING DISORDERS

https://matrixhealthgroup.com

JOE HOLIBAUGH MEMORIAL SCHOLARSHIP

• *See page 644*

MARK COATS MEMORIAL SCHOLARSHIP

• *See page 644*

MIKE HYLTON MEMORIAL SCHOLARSHIP

• *See page 644*

MILLIE GONZALEZ MEMORIAL SCHOLARSHIP

• *See page 644*

RON NIEDERMAN MEMORIAL SCHOLARSHIP

• *See page 644*

TIM KENNEDY MEMORIAL SCHOLARSHIP

• *See page 645*

BMI FOUNDATION, INC.

http://www.bmifoundation.org/

JOHN LENNON SCHOLARSHIPS

The John Lennon Scholarships are an annual competition open to student songwriters and composers of contemporary musical genres including alternative, pop, rock, indie, electronica, R&B, and experimental. The submitted work must be an original song with lyrics accompanied by whatever instrumentation is chosen by the applicant.

Award: Scholarship for use in freshman, sophomore, junior, senior, graduate, or postgraduate years; not renewable. *Number:* 3–5. *Amount:* $3000–$10,000.

Eligibility Requirements: Applicant must be age 17-24; enrolled or expecting to enroll full- or part-time at a two-year or four-year or technical institution or university and must have an interest in music. Available to U.S. and non-U.S. citizens.

Application Requirements: Application form. *Deadline:* February 1.

Contact: Ms. Samantha Cox, Director
BMI Foundation, Inc.
7 World Trade Center
250 Greenwich Street
New York, NY 10007-0030
Phone: 212-220-3103
E-mail: info@bmifoundation.org

NASHVILLE SONGWRITING SCHOLARSHIP

The Nashville Songwriting Scholarship is an annual competition established in 2015 to encourage and support aspiring country music songwriters nationwide. The award commemorates Broadcast Music, Inc. (BMI)'s 75th Anniversary year and pays homage to musical epicenter and "Songwriting Capital of the World," Nashville, Tennessee. A $5,000 scholarship is awarded for the best original song entry in any of the following genres: Americana, blues, bluegrass, contemporary Christian, country, folk, and roots. GRAMMY-winning recording artist and BMI songwriter Kacey Musgraves has endorsed the competition.

Award: Scholarship for use in freshman, sophomore, junior, senior, graduate, or postgraduate years; not renewable. *Number:* 1. *Amount:* $5000.

Eligibility Requirements: Applicant must be age 17-24; enrolled or expecting to enroll full- or part-time at a two-year or four-year or technical institution or university and must have an interest in music. Available to U.S. and non-U.S. citizens.

Application Requirements: Application form. *Deadline:* February 1.

Contact: Clay Bradley
BMI Foundation, Inc.
7 World Trade Center
250 Greenwich Street
New York, NY 10007
Phone: 212-220-3103
E-mail: info@bmifoundation.org

PEERMUSIC LATIN SCHOLARSHIP

Award for the best song or instrumental work in any Latin genre. The competition is open to songwriters and composers between the ages of 17 and 24 who are current students at colleges and universities in the United States or Puerto Rico. Must submit an original work. Applicants must not have had any musical work commercially recorded or distributed.

Award: Scholarship for use in freshman, sophomore, junior, senior, graduate, or postgraduate years; not renewable. *Number:* 1. *Amount:* $5000.

Eligibility Requirements: Applicant must be age 17-24; enrolled or expecting to enroll full- or part-time at a two-year or four-year or technical institution or university and must have an interest in music. Available to U.S. citizens.

Application Requirements: Application form. *Deadline:* February 1.

Contact: Carolina Arenas, Director
BMI Foundation, Inc.
7 World Trade Center
250 Greenwich Street
New York, NY 10007-0030
Phone: 212-220-3103
E-mail: info@bmifoundation.org

BOETTCHER FOUNDATION

http://www.boettcherfoundation.org/

BOETTCHER FOUNDATION SCHOLARSHIP

• *See page 814*

BOUNCE ENERGY

http://www.bounceenergy.com

BE MORE SCHOLARSHIP
• *See page 601*

BRYAN CAMERON EDUCATION FOUNDATION

http://www.bryancameroneducationfoundation.org/index.php

CAMERON IMPACT SCHOLARSHIP
• *See page 601*

BUY-RITE BEAUTY

https://www.buyritebeauty.com/

BUY-RITES ANNUAL BEAUTY SCHOOL SCHOLARSHIP
• *See page 601*

BY KIDS FOR KIDS, CO.

http://bkfkeducation.com

SALLIE MAE® MAKE COLLEGE HAPPEN CHALLENGE
• *See page 602*

CALIFORNIA COUNCIL OF THE BLIND

http://www.ccbnet.org/

CALIFORNIA COUNCIL OF THE BLIND SCHOLARSHIPS
• *See page 602*

CALIFORNIA INTERSCHOLASTIC FEDERATION

http://www.cifstate.org/

CIF SCHOLAR-ATHLETE OF THE YEAR
• *See page 815*

CIF SPIRIT OF SPORT AWARD
• *See page 815*

CALIFORNIA JUNIOR MISS SCHOLARSHIP PROGRAM

http://www.ajm.org/

CALIFORNIA JUNIOR MISS SCHOLARSHIP PROGRAM
• *See page 815*

CAMP NETWORK

https://www.campnetwork.com/

CAMP COUNSELOR APPRECIATION SCHOLARSHIP
• *See page 603*

CANADA ICELAND FOUNDATION INC. SCHOLARSHIPS

http://www.canadaicelandfoundation.com/

CANADA ICELAND FOUNDATION SCHOLARSHIP PROGRAM

One scholarship of $500, to be awarded annually. To be offered to a university student studying towards a degree in any Canadian university.

Award: Scholarship for use in freshman, sophomore, junior, senior, or graduate years; not renewable. *Number:* 1. *Amount:* $500.

Eligibility Requirements: Applicant must be enrolled or expecting to enroll full-time at an institution or university; studying in Alberta, British Columbia, Manitoba, New Brunswick, Newfoundland, Nova Scotia, Ontario, Quebec, Saskatchewan and must have an interest in leadership. Available to Canadian citizens.

Application Requirements: Application form, community service, recommendations or references, test scores, transcript. *Deadline:* varies.

Contact: Karen Bowman, Administrative Assistant
    Phone: 204-284-5686
    Fax: 204-284-7099
    E-mail: karen@lh-inc.ca

CARDSDIRECT INC.

https://www.cardsdirect.com/

FUTURE DESIGNER SCHOLARSHIP
• *See page 603*

CARING.COM

http://caring.com

CARING.COM STUDENT-CAREGIVER BI-ANNUAL SCHOLARSHIP
• *See page 603*

CEDAR EDUCATION LENDING, LLC

http://www.cedaredlending.com

$500 BECAUSE COLLEGE IS EXPENSIVE SCHOLARSHIP
• *See page 603*

CENTER FOR REINTEGRATION

http://www.reintegration.com

BAER REINTEGRATION SCHOLARSHIP
• *See page 604*

CENTRAL SCHOLARSHIP

http://www.central-scholarship.org

LESSANS FAMILY SCHOLARSHIP
• *See page 604*

STRAUS SCHOLARSHIP PROGRAM FOR UNDERGRADUATE EDUCATION
• *See page 604*

CGTRADER

https://www.cgtrader.com/

ANNUAL CGTRADER SCHOLARSHIP
• *See page 604*

CHARLES E. BOYK LAW OFFICES, LLC

https://www.charlesboyk-law.com/

BOYK LAW VETERAN SCHOLARSHIP
• See page 604

CHRISTIAN COMMUNITY CREDIT UNION

https://www.mycccu.com/

SCHOLARSHIPS FOR SUCCESS
• See page 605

CHRISTIAN RECORD SERVICES INC.

http://www.christianrecord.org

ANNE LOWE SCHOLARSHIPS
• See page 605

CHRISTOPHERS

http://www.christophers.org/

POSTER CONTEST FOR HIGH SCHOOL STUDENTS
Contest invites students in grades nine through twelve to interpret the theme "You can make a difference." Posters must include this statement and illustrate the idea that one person can change the world for the better. Judging is based on overall impact, content, originality, and artistic merit. More information can be found at http://www.christophers.org.

Award: Prize for use in freshman, sophomore, junior, or senior years; not renewable. *Number:* up to 8. *Amount:* $100–$1000.

Eligibility Requirements: Applicant must be high school student; planning to enroll or expecting to enroll full-time at a four-year institution or university and must have an interest in art. Available to U.S. citizens.

Application Requirements: Application form, entry in a contest, poster. *Deadline:* February 13.

Contact: Sarah Holinski, Youth Coordinator
Christophers
5 Hanover Square, 22nd Floor
New York, NY 10004
Phone: 212-759-4050 Ext. 240
Fax: 212-838-5073
E-mail: youth@christophers.org

VIDEO CONTEST FOR COLLEGE STUDENTS
Contest requires college students to use any style or format to express the following theme "One person can make a difference." Entries can be up to 5 minutes in length and must be submitted in standard, full-sized DVD format. Entries will be judged on content, artistic and technical proficiency, and adherence to contest rules. More information is available at http://www.christophers.org.

Award: Prize for use in freshman, sophomore, junior, senior, graduate, or postgraduate years; not renewable. *Number:* 2–6. *Amount:* $1000–$2000.

Eligibility Requirements: Applicant must be enrolled or expecting to enroll full- or part-time at a two-year or four-year or technical institution or university and must have an interest in art. Available to U.S. citizens.

Application Requirements: Application form, DVD, entry in a contest. *Deadline:* February 13.

Contact: Sarah Holinski, Youth Coordinator
Christophers
5 Hanover Square, 22nd Floor
New York, NY 10004
Phone: 212-759-4050 Ext. 240
Fax: 212-838-5073
E-mail: s.holinski@christophers.org

CHURCH HILL CLASSICS

http://www.diplomaframe.com/

FRAME MY FUTURE SCHOLARSHIP CONTEST
• See page 605

CLAGS: CENTER FOR LGBTQ STUDIES

http://www.clags.org/

SYLVIA RIVERA AWARD IN TRANSGENDER STUDIES
This award, which honors the memory of Rivera, a transgender activist, will be given for the best book or article to appear in transgender studies this year (2015). Applications may be submitted by the author of the work or by nomination.

Award: Prize for use in freshman, sophomore, junior, senior, graduate, or postgraduate years; not renewable. *Number:* 1. *Amount:* $1000.

Eligibility Requirements: Applicant must be enrolled or expecting to enroll full- or part-time at a two-year or four-year institution or university and must have an interest in LGBT issues or writing. Available to U.S. and non-U.S. citizens.

Application Requirements: Application form. *Deadline:* June 1.

Contact: Noam Parness, Membership and Fellowships Coordinator
Phone: 212-817-1958
E-mail: clagsfellowships@gmail.com

UNDERGRADUATE STUDENT PAPER AWARD
Each year, CLAGS sponsors a student paper competition open to all undergraduate students enrolled in the CUNY or SUNY system. A cash prize of $250 awarded to the best paper written in a City University of New York or State University of New York undergraduate class on a topic related to gay, lesbian, bisexual, queer, or transgender experiences. Essays should be between 12 and 30 pages, well thought-out, and fully realized.

Award: Prize for use in freshman, sophomore, junior, or senior years; not renewable. *Number:* 1. *Amount:* $250.

Eligibility Requirements: Applicant must be enrolled or expecting to enroll full- or part-time at a four-year institution or university and must have an interest in LGBT issues. Available to U.S. and non-U.S. citizens.

Application Requirements: Essay. *Deadline:* June 1.

Contact: Noam Parness, Membership and Fellowships Coordinator
Phone: 212-817-1958
E-mail: clagsfellowships@gmail.com

CLARA LIONEL FOUNDATION

http://claralionelfoundation.org

CLARA LIONEL FOUNDATION GLOBAL SCHOLARSHIP PROGRAM
• See page 605

CLOTHINGRIC.COM

http://www.clothingric.com

CLOTHINGRIC.COM ANNUAL STUDENT SCHOLARSHIP
• See page 605

CODA INTERNATIONAL

http://www.coda-international.org

MILLIE BROTHER SCHOLARSHIP FOR CHILDREN OF DEAF ADULTS
• See page 605

COGBURN LAW OFFICES

http://cogburnlaw.com/

COGBURN LAW OFFICES ANNUAL SCHOLARSHIP
• See page 606

COLLEGEBOUND FOUNDATION

http://www.collegeboundfoundation.org/

HY ZOLET STUDENT ATHLETE SCHOLARSHIP
• *See page 818*

COLLEGE NOW GREATER CLEVELAND, INC.

http://www.collegenowgc.org/

COLLEGE NOW GREATER CLEVELAND ADULT LEARNER PROGRAM SCHOLARSHIP
• *See page 606*

COLLEGEWEEKLIVE

http://www.collegeweeklive.com/

COLLEGEWEEKLIVE.COM SCHOLARSHIP
$1000 to $5000 scholarship to students for visiting colleges on CollegeWeekLive. Students must submit an online registration and visit 5 schools on the site. For more information, see website http://www.collegeweeklive.com/sign-up?refcode=PAR_PETERSONS_SCHOLARSHIP

Award: Scholarship for use in freshman year; not renewable. *Number:* 1–15. *Amount:* $1000–$5000.

Eligibility Requirements: Applicant must be enrolled or expecting to enroll full- or part-time at a two-year or four-year or technical institution or university and must have an interest in writing. Available to U.S. and non-U.S. citizens.

Application Requirements: Application form, application form may be submitted online (collegeweeklive.com/sign-up?refcode=PAR_PETERSONS_SCHOLARSHIP). *Deadline:* varies.

Contact: Melissa King, Vice President, Marketing
CollegeWeekLive
100 Crescent Road
Needham, MA 02494
Phone: 617-938-6018
E-mail: info@collegeweeklive.com

COLORADO MASONS BENEVOLENT FUND ASSOCIATION

http://www.cmbfa.org/scholarship

COLORADO MASONS BENEVOLENT FUND SCHOLARSHIPS
• *See page 606*

COLUMBUS CITIZENS FOUNDATION

http://www.columbuscitizensfd.org/scholarships/scholarships.html

COLUMBUS CITIZENS FOUNDATION COLLEGE SCHOLARSHIP PROGRAM
• *See page 606*

COMMUNITY BANKERS ASSOCIATION OF ILLINOIS

http://www.cbai.com/

COMMUNITY BANKERS ASSOC OF IL CHILD OF A BANKER SCHOLARSHIP
• *See page 562*

COMMUNITY BANKERS ASSOC. OF IL ESSAY CONTEST
• *See page 607*

CONNECTICUT OFFICE OF HIGHER EDUCATION

http://www.ctohe.org

GOVERNOR'S SCHOLARSHIP PROGRAM—NEED/MERIT SCHOLARSHIP
• *See page 607*

ROBERTA B. WILLIS SCHOLARSHIP PROGRAM—NEED-BASED GRANT
• *See page 607*

CONTEMPORARY RECORD SOCIETY

http://www.crsnews.org/

CONTEMPORARY RECORD SOCIETY NATIONAL COMPETITION FOR PERFORMING ARTISTS
There are no age restrictions to participate. Applicant may submit one performance tape of varied length including music of any period of music with each application. The applicant may use any number of instrumentalists and voices. First prize is a commercial distribution of the winner's recording. Application fee is $50 for each recording submitted. Submit self-addressed stamped envelope with the application for returns. The winning applicant will participate in a CD recording released by CRS. (This prize is not applicable toward tuition.)

Award: Prize for use in freshman, sophomore, junior, senior, graduate, or postgraduate years; not renewable. *Number:* 1. *Amount:* $2000–$6000.

Eligibility Requirements: Applicant must be enrolled or expecting to enroll full- or part-time at a two-year or four-year or technical institution or university and must have an interest in music/singing. Available to U.S. and non-U.S. citizens.

Application Requirements: Application form. *Fee:* $50. *Deadline:* February 29.

Contact: Ms. Caroline Hunt, Administrator
Contemporary Record Society
724 Winchester Rd
Broomall, PA 19008
Phone: 610-2059897
E-mail: crsnews@verizon.net

NATIONAL COMPETITION FOR COMPOSERS' RECORDINGS
First prize is a CD recording grant (not tuition). Limited to nine performers and twenty-five minutes duration. Works with additional performers will be accepted provided there is a release of the original recorded master for CD reproduction. Must submit a musical composition that is non-published and not commercially recorded. Limit of 5 works per applicant.

Award: Prize for use in freshman, sophomore, junior, senior, graduate, or postgraduate years; not renewable. *Number:* 1. *Amount:* $2000–$6000.

Eligibility Requirements: Applicant must be enrolled or expecting to enroll full- or part-time at a two-year or four-year or technical institution or university and must have an interest in music/singing. Available to U.S. and non-U.S. citizens.

Application Requirements: Application form. *Fee:* $50. *Deadline:* February 29.

Contact: Ms. Caroline Hunt, Administrator
Contemporary Record Society
724 Winchester Rd
Broomall, PA 19008
Phone: 610-2059897
E-mail: crsnews@verizon.net

COUNCIL OF CITIZENS WITH LOW VISION INTERNATIONAL C/O AMERICAN COUNCIL OF THE BLIND

http://www.cclvi.org/

FRED SCHEIGERT SCHOLARSHIP
• *See page 607*

COUPONSURF.COM

http://couponsurf.com/

COUPONSURF ENTREPRENEURS SCHOLARSHIP
• See page 607

COURAGE KENNY REHABILITATION INSTITUTE, VOCATIONAL SERVICES DEPARTMENT

http://www.allinahealth.org/couragekenny

SCHOLARSHIP FOR PEOPLE WITH DISABILITIES
• See page 608

CROSLEY LAW FIRM

https://crosleylaw.com

CROSLEY LAW FIRM DISTRACTED DRIVING SCHOLARSHIP
• See page 608

CROSSLITES

http://www.crosslites.com/

CROSSLITES SCHOLARSHIP AWARD

Scholarship contest is open to high school, college and graduate school students. There are no minimum GPA, SAT, ACT, GMAT, GRE, or any other test score requirements.

Award: Prize for use in freshman, sophomore, junior, senior, or graduate years; not renewable. *Number:* 33. *Amount:* $100–$2500.

Eligibility Requirements: Applicant must be enrolled or expecting to enroll full- or part-time at a two-year or four-year or technical institution or university and must have an interest in writing. Available to U.S. and non-U.S. citizens.

Application Requirements: Application form, entry in a contest, essay. *Deadline:* December 15.

Contact: Samuel Certo, Scholarship Committee
CrossLites
1000 Holt Avenue
Winter Park, FL 32789

CSA MEDICAL SUPPLY

https://csamedicalsupply.com

CSA MEDICAL SUPPLY COLLEGE SCHOLARSHIP
• See page 608

THE DALLAS FOUNDATION

http://www.dallasfoundation.org/

THE LANDON RUSNAK SCHOLARSHIP
• See page 822

DANIELS FUND

http://www.danielsfund.org

BOUNDLESS OPPORTUNITY SCHOLARSHIP
• See page 608

DANIELS SCHOLARSHIP PROGRAM
• See page 609

DANLEY'S GARAGE BUILDERS

https://www.danleysgarageworld.com/

DANLEY'S GARAGE BUILDERS SCHOLARSHIP
• See page 609

DAVID S. WYMAN INSTITUTE OF HOLOCAUST STUDIES

http://www.wymaninstitute.org

JOSIAH E. DUBOIS, JR. COLLEGE SCHOLARSHIP ESSAY CONTEST
• See page 609

DEMAS LAW GROUP, P.C.

http://www.injury-attorneys.com/

DEMAS LAW GROUP SCHOLARSHIP
• See page 609

DEMOLAY FOUNDATION INCORPORATED

http://www.demolay.org/

FRANK S. LAND SCHOLARSHIP
• See page 588

DEPARTMENT OF THE ARMY

http://www.goarmy.com/rotc

ARMY ROTC GREEN TO GOLD SCHOLARSHIP PROGRAM FOR TWO-YEAR, THREE-YEAR AND FOUR-YEAR SCHOLARSHIPS, ACTIVE DUTY ENLISTED PERSONNEL
• See page 610

ARMY (ROTC) RESERVE OFFICERS TRAINING CORPS TWO-, THREE-, FOUR-YEAR CAMPUS-BASED SCHOLARSHIPS
• See page 610

U.S. ARMY ROTC FOUR-YEAR COLLEGE SCHOLARSHIP
• See page 610

U.S. ARMY ROTC FOUR-YEAR HISTORICALLY BLACK COLLEGE/UNIVERSITY SCHOLARSHIP
• See page 610

U.S. ARMY ROTC GUARANTEED RESERVE FORCES DUTY (GRFD), (ARNG/USAR) AND DEDICATED ARNG SCHOLARSHIPS
• See page 611

U.S. ARMY ROTC MILITARY JUNIOR COLLEGE (MJC) SCHOLARSHIP
• See page 611

DESERVE MODERN

http://www.DeserveModern.com

DESERVE MODERN SCHOLARSHIP
• See page 611

DESIGN MY COSTUME

http://designmycostume.com/

DESIGN MY COSTUME SCHOLARSHIP
• *See page 611*

DIAMANTE, INC.

http://www.diamanteinc.org/

LATINO DIAMANTE SCHOLARSHIP FUND
• *See page 612*

DIBELLA LAW OFFICES, P.C.

https://www.dibellalawoffice.com/

2018 DIBELLA LAW OFFICES, P.C. SCHOLARSHIP
• *See page 612*

DISABLEDPERSON INC. COLLEGE SCHOLARSHIP

http://www.disabledperson.com/

DISABLEDPERSON INC. NATIONAL COLLEGE SCHOLARSHIP AWARD FOR COLLEGE STUDENTS WITH DISABILITIES
• *See page 612*

DIXIE BOYS BASEBALL

http://www.dixie.org/boys

DIXIE BOYS BASEBALL BERNIE VARNADORE SCHOLARSHIP PROGRAM
• *See page 825*

DIXIE YOUTH SCHOLARSHIP PROGRAM
• *See page 825*

DOLLARS 4 TIC SCHOLARS

http://www.dollars4ticscholars.org/

DOLLARS 4 TIC SCHOLARS TOURETTE SYNDROME SCHOLARSHIP
• *See page 613*

DOLPHIN SCHOLARSHIP FOUNDATION

http://www.dolphinscholarship.org/

DOLPHIN SCHOLARSHIPS
• *See page 613*

DOMNICK CUNNINGHAM AND WHALEN

https://www.dcwlaw.com/

DOMNICK CUNNINGHAM & WHALEN ELDER ABUSE PREVENTION
• *See page 613*

DONALDSON COMPANY

http://www.donaldson.com/

THE DONALDSON COMPANY, INC. SCHOLARSHIP PROGRAM
• *See page 588*

DONTPAYFULL.COM

https://www.dontpayfull.com/

$500 ANNUAL STUDENT SCHOLARSHIP
• *See page 613*

DRONE PILOT GROUND SCHOOL

https://www.dronepilotgroundschool.com

DRONE TECHNOLOGY COLLEGE SCHOLARSHIP
• *See page 613*

EDGAR ALLEN POE LITERARY SOCIETY

http://www.ravens.org/

DISTINGUISHED RAVEN FAC MEMORIAL SCHOLARSHIP
• *See page 614*

EDUCATOR, INC.

https://www.educator.com/

ANNUAL $2,400 STUDENT SCHOLARSHIP
• *See page 614*

ELEARNERS.COM

http://www.elearners.com

ELEARNERS ONLINE STUDENT SCHOLARSHIP
• *See page 614*

ELIE WIESEL FOUNDATION FOR HUMANITY

http://www.eliewieselfoundation.org/

ELIE WIESEL PRIZE IN ETHICS ESSAY CONTEST
Scholarship for full-time junior or senior at a four-year accredited college or university in the United States. Up to five awards are granted.

Award: Prize for use in junior or senior years; not renewable. *Number:* up to 5. *Amount:* $500–$5000.

Eligibility Requirements: Applicant must be enrolled or expecting to enroll full-time at a four-year institution or university and must have an interest in writing. Available to U.S. and non-U.S. citizens.

Application Requirements: Application form, entry in a contest, essay, self-addressed stamped envelope with application, student entry form, faculty sponsor form. *Deadline:* December 3.

Contact: Ms. Chelsea Friedman, Essay Contest Coordinator
Elie Wiesel Foundation for Humanity
555 Madison Avenue, 20th Floor
New York, NY 10022
Phone: 212-490-7788
Fax: 212-490-6006
E-mail: chelsea@eliewieselfoundation.org

ELKS NATIONAL FOUNDATION

http://www.elks.org/enf

ELKS NATIONAL FOUNDATION MOST VALUABLE STUDENT SCHOLARSHIP CONTEST
Five hundred awards, renewable for four years, are allocated nationally by state quota for graduating high school seniors. Based on scholarship, leadership, and financial need. Must be a U.S. citizen pursuing a 4-year degree full-time at an accredited, degree granting U.S. college or university. For more information, visit http://www.elks.org/scholars.

Award: Scholarship for use in freshman, sophomore, junior, or senior years; renewable. *Number:* 500. *Amount:* $4000–$50,000.

Eligibility Requirements: Applicant must be high school student; planning to enroll or expecting to enroll full-time at a four-year institution or university and must have an interest in leadership. Available to U.S. citizens.

Application Requirements: Application form, community service, essay, financial need analysis. *Deadline:* November 27.

Contact: Elks National Foundation Scholarship Office
Elks National Foundation
2750 North Lakeview Avenue
Chicago, IL 60614-2256
Phone: 773-755-4732
E-mail: scholarship@elks.org

ENVIRONMENTAL LITIGATION GROUP P.C.

https://www.elglaw.com/

ENVIRONMENTAL LITIGATION GROUP, P.C. ASBESTOS SCHOLARSHIP
• *See page 615*

EQUALITY SCHOLARSHIP COLLABORATIVE

http://www.equalityscholarship.org

EQUALITY SCHOLARSHIPS FOR COMMUNITY COLLEGE TRANSFER STUDENTS
• *See page 615*

SCHOLARSHIPS FOR HIGH SCHOOL GRADUATES
• *See page 615*

ESSAYHUB

https://essayhub.com/

ESSAY WRITING CONTEST BY ESSAYHUB
• *See page 615*

ESSAYJOLT.COM

http://www.essayjolt.com/

ESSAYJOLT SCHOLARSHIP
• *See page 826*

EVANS SCHOLARS FOUNDATION

http://www.wgaesf.org

CHICK EVANS SCHOLARSHIP FOR CADDIES
• *See page 616*

EVERIPEDIA INC.

https://www.everipedia.com

EVERIPEDIA TECH TITANS DIVERSITY SCHOLARSHIP
• *See page 616*

EXPRESSVPN

https://www.expressvpn.com

EXPRESSVPN FUTURE OF PRIVACY SCHOLARSHIP
• *See page 616*

FEDERAL RESOURCES

http://www.federalresources.com

WARRIOR'S LEGACY SCHOLARSHIP FUND
• *See page 616*

FELDCO WINDOWS, SIDING AND DOORS

http://www.4feldco.com

FELDCO WINDOWS, SIDING AND DOORS SCHOLARSHIP
• *See page 616*

FELDMAN & ROYLE, ATTORNEYS AT LAW

http://www.feldmanroyle.com/

AUTISM SCHOLARSHIPS
• *See page 617*

FELDMAN LAW FIRM PLLC

http://www.afphoenixcriminalattorney.com/

AUTISM SCHOLARSHIP
• *See page 617*

DISABLED VETERANS SCHOLARSHIP
• *See page 617*

FIG TECH INC.

http://www.figloans.com

$1,000 SCHOLARSHIP FOR SOCIAL IMPACT
• *See page 617*

FINALLY SOLD

http://www.finallysold.com

FINALLY SOLD IMPACT MAKER SCHOLARSHIP
• *See page 618*

FINANCE AUTHORITY OF MAINE

http://www.famemaine.com/

TUITION WAIVER PROGRAMS
• *See page 618*

FINANCIAL SERVICE CENTERS OF NEW YORK

http://www.fscny.org

FSCNY YOUNG LEADERS SCHOLARSHIP
• *See page 618*

FIT SMALL BUSINESS

http://www.fitsmallbusiness.com

BUSINESS PLAN SCHOLARSHIP FOR STUDENTS WITH DISABILITIES
• *See page 618*

FLORIDA PTA/PTSA

http://www.floridapta.org/

FLORIDA PTA/PTSA ANNUAL SCHOLARSHIP
• *See page 619*

FLORIDA WOMEN'S STATE GOLF ASSOCIATION

CLUB EMPLOYEES AND DEPENDENTS SCHOLARSHIP
• *See page 829*

FSGA SCHOLARS
• *See page 829*

SARAH E. HUNEYCUTT SCHOLARSHIP
• *See page 829*

FOREST ROBERTS THEATRE

http://www.nmu.edu/

MILDRED AND ALBERT PANOWSKI PLAYWRITING AWARD

Prize designed to encourage and stimulate artistic growth among playwrights. Winner receives a cash prize and a world premiere of their play.

Award: Prize for use in freshman, sophomore, junior, senior, graduate, or postgraduate years; not renewable. *Number:* 1. *Amount:* $2000.

Eligibility Requirements: Applicant must be enrolled or expecting to enroll full- or part-time at a two-year or four-year or technical institution or university and must have an interest in theater or writing. Available to U.S. and non-U.S. citizens.

Application Requirements: Application form, entry in a contest, manuscript in English, self-addressed stamped envelope with application. *Deadline:* October 31.

Contact: Matt Hudson, Playwriting Award Coordinator
Forest Roberts Theatre
Northern Michigan University
1401 Presque Isle Avenue
Marquette, MI 49855-5364
Phone: 906-227-2559
Fax: 906-227-2567

FOUNDATION FOR CHRISTIAN COLLEGE LEADERS

http://www.collegechristianleader.com/

FOUNDATION FOR COLLEGE CHRISTIAN LEADERS SCHOLARSHIP
• *See page 780*

FOUNDATION FOR SIGHT AND SOUND

http://fssny.org

HELP AMERICA HEAR SCHOLARSHIP
• *See page 619*

FOUNDATION OF THE 1ST CAVALRY DIVISION ASSOCIATION

https://www.1cda.org/

FOUNDATION OF THE 1ST CAVALRY DIVISION ASSOCIATION (IA DRANG) SCHOLARSHIP
• *See page 619*

FOUNDATION OF THE 1ST CAVALRY DIVISION ASSOCIATION SCHOLARSHIP
• *See page 619*

FRANCIS OUIMET SCHOLARSHIP FUND

http://www.ouimet.org

FRANCIS OUIMET SCHOLARSHIP
• *See page 830*

FREEDOM ALLIANCE

https://freedomalliance.org

FREEDOM ALLIANCE SCHOLARSHIP FUND
• *See page 620*

FREEDOM FROM RELIGION FOUNDATION

http://www.ffrf.org/

FREEDOM FROM RELIGION FOUNDATION MICHAEL HAKEEM MEMORIAL ONGOING COLLEGE ESSAY COMPETITION
• *See page 780*

FREEDOM FROM RELIGION FOUNDATION WILLIAM J. SCHULZ MEMORIAL COLLEGE-BOUND HIGH SCHOOL SENIOR ESSAY COMPETITION
• *See page 780*

FRIENDS OF COAL LADIES AUXILIARY

friendsofcoalladies.com

FRIENDS OF COAL SCHOLARSHIPS
• *See page 735*

FRIENDS OF THE MINNESOTA ORCHESTRA (FORMERLY WAMSO)

https://friendsofminnesotaorchestra.org/

YOUNG ARTIST COMPETITION
• *See page 620*

FUNNEWJERSEY.COM INC.

http://www.funnewjersey.com

FUNNEWJERSEY.COM SCHOLARSHIP
• *See page 620*

GAY ASIAN PACIFIC ALLIANCE FOUNDATION

http://gapafoundation.org/

GAPA SCHOLARSHIPS

The purpose of the Gay Asian Pacific Alliance (GAPA) Foundation Scholarship is to provide financial assistance to students in high school; undergraduate, graduate or professional school; or trade or vocational school who express activism in the Asian and Pacific Islander (API) and/or lesbian, gay, bisexual, transgender, and queer (LGBTQ) communities.

Award: Scholarship for use in freshman, sophomore, junior, senior, graduate, or postgraduate years; not renewable. *Number:* 3–5. *Amount:* $1000–$3000.

Eligibility Requirements: Applicant must be enrolled or expecting to enroll full- or part-time at a two-year or four-year or technical institution or university and must have an interest in leadership or LGBT issues. Available to U.S. and non-U.S. citizens.

Application Requirements: Application form, essay. *Deadline:* June 30.

Contact: Mr. Drew Ho, Philanthropy Co-Chair
   E-mail: programs@gapafoundation.org

GENERAL BOARD OF HIGHER EDUCATION AND MINISTRY

http://www.gbhem.org

THE REV. DR. KAREN LAYMAN GIFT OF HOPE
• *See page 781*

GEORGIA PRESS EDUCATIONAL FOUNDATION INC.

http://gapress.org/scholarships-internships/

KIRK SUTLIVE SCHOLARSHIP
• *See page 621*

MORRIS NEWSPAPER CORPORATION SCHOLARSHIP
• *See page 621*

GEORGIA STUDENT FINANCE COMMISSION

http://www.GAfutures.org

GEORGIA HERO SCHOLARSHIP
• *See page 621*

GEORGIA PUBLIC SAFETY MEMORIAL GRANT
• *See page 621*

GEORGIA TUITION EQUALIZATION GRANT (GTEG)
• *See page 621*

ZELL MILLER SCHOLARSHIP PROGRAM
• *See page 621*

GERSOWITZ LIBO & KOREK, P.C.

https://www.lawyertime.com

GARDINER FOUNDATION SCHOLARSHIP
• *See page 621*

GIFT BASKETS PLUS

http://www.giftbasketsplus.com

HIGH SCHOOL GRADUATE SCHOLARSHIP CONTEST
• *See page 622*

GLAMOUR

http://www.glamour.com/

TOP 10 COLLEGE WOMEN COMPETITION
Female students with leadership experience on and off campus, excellence in field of study, and inspiring goals can apply for this competition. Winners will be awarded $3000 along with a trip to New York City. Must be a junior studying full-time with a minimum GPA of 3.0. in either the United States or Canada. Non-U.S. citizens may apply if attending U.S. postsecondary institutions.

Award: Prize for use in junior year; not renewable. *Number:* 10. *Amount:* $3000.

Eligibility Requirements: Applicant must be enrolled or expecting to enroll full-time at a four-year institution or university; female and must have an interest in leadership. Applicant must have 3.0 GPA or higher. Available to U.S. and non-U.S. citizens.

Application Requirements: Application form, essay, personal photograph, recommendations or references, transcript. *Deadline:* February 2.

Contact: Lynda Laux-Bachand, Reader Services Editor
   Glamour
   Four Times Square, 16th Floor
   New York, NY 10036-6593
   Phone: 212-286-6667
   Fax: 212-286-6922

GLENN MILLER BIRTHPLACE SOCIETY

http://www.glennmiller.org/

GLENN MILLER INSTRUMENTAL SCHOLARSHIP
One-time awards for high school seniors and college freshmen. Scholarships are awarded as competition prizes and must be used for any education-related expenses. Must submit 10-minute, high-quality audio tape of pieces selected for competition or those of similar style. Applicant is responsible for travel to and lodging during the competition.

Award: Scholarship for use in freshman year; not renewable. *Number:* 3. *Amount:* $1000–$4500.

Eligibility Requirements: Applicant must be high school student; planning to enroll or expecting to enroll full-time at a four-year institution or university and must have an interest in music/singing. Available to U.S. and non-U.S. citizens.

Application Requirements: Application form, entry in a contest, essay, performance tape or CD. *Deadline:* March 15.

Contact: Arlene Leonard, Secretary
   Glenn Miller Birthplace Society
   107 East Main Street, PO Box 61
   Clarinda, IA 51632-0061
   Phone: 712-542-2461
   Fax: 712-542-2461
   E-mail: gmbs@heartland.net

JACK PULLAN MEMORIAL SCHOLARSHIP
One scholarship for a male or female vocalist, awarded as competition prize and, to be used for any education-related expenses. Must submit 10 minute, high-quality audio tape of pieces selected for competition or those of similar style. Applicant is responsible for travel to and lodging during the competition. One-time award for high school seniors and college freshmen. More information on http://www.glennmiller.org/scholar.htm.

Award: Scholarship for use in freshman year; not renewable. *Number:* 1. *Amount:* $1000.

Eligibility Requirements: Applicant must be high school student; planning to enroll or expecting to enroll full-time at a four-year institution or university and must have an interest in music/singing. Available to U.S. and non-U.S. citizens.

Application Requirements: Application form, entry in a contest, essay, performance tape or CD. *Deadline:* March 15.

Contact: Arlene Leonard, Secretary
   Glenn Miller Birthplace Society
   107 East Main Street, PO Box 61
   Clarinda, IA 51632-0061
   Phone: 712-542-2461
   Fax: 712-542-2461
   E-mail: gmbs@heartland.net

RALPH BREWSTER VOCAL SCHOLARSHIP
One scholarship for a male or female vocalist, awarded as competition prize and, to be used for any education-related expenses. Must submit 10 minute, high-quality audio tape of pieces selected for competition or those of similar style. Applicant is responsible for travel to and lodging during the competition. One-time award for high school seniors and college freshmen.

Award: Scholarship for use in freshman year; not renewable. *Number:* 1. *Amount:* $2000.

Eligibility Requirements: Applicant must be high school student; planning to enroll or expecting to enroll full-time at a four-year institution or university and must have an interest in music/singing. Available to U.S. and non-U.S. citizens.

Application Requirements: Application form, entry in a contest, essay, performance tape of competition or concert quality (up to 5 minutes duration). *Deadline:* March 15.

Contact: Arlene Leonard, Secretary
Glenn Miller Birthplace Society
107 East Main Street, PO Box 61
Clarinda, IA 51632-0061
Phone: 712-542-2461
Fax: 712-542-2461
E-mail: gmbs@heartland.net

GLORIA BARRON PRIZE FOR YOUNG HEROES

http://www.barronprize.org/

GLORIA BARRON PRIZE FOR YOUNG HEROES

Award honors young people in North America ages 8 to 18 who have shown leadership and courage in public service to people or to the planet. Award celebrates 25 young heroes each year, with up to 20 top winners each receiving $10,000 to support their service work or higher education. For further information and to apply, visit http://www.barronprize.org.

Award: Prize for use in freshman year; not renewable. *Number:* 15–20. *Amount:* $10,000.

Eligibility Requirements: Applicant must be age 8-18; enrolled or expecting to enroll full- or part-time at a two-year or four-year or technical institution or university and must have an interest in leadership. Available to U.S. and Canadian citizens.

Application Requirements: Application form, community service, essay, personal photograph. *Deadline:* April 15.

Contact: Barbara Ann Richman, Executive Director
Gloria Barron Prize for Young Heroes
PO Box 1470
Boulder, CO 80306
E-mail: director@barronprize.org

GOENNOUNCE, LLC

http://GoEnnounce.com/about

GOENNOUNCE YOURSELF $500 MONTHLY SCHOLARSHIP
• *See page 622*

GOLDSTEIN AND BASHNER

https://www.eglaw.com/

COMBATING CAMPUS ISSUES SCHOLARSHIP
• *See page 622*

GOLF COURSE SUPERINTENDENTS ASSOCIATION OF AMERICA

http://www.eifg.org/

GOLF COURSE SUPERINTENDENTS ASSOCIATION OF AMERICA LEGACY AWARD
• *See page 564*

JOSEPH S. GARSKE COLLEGIATE GRANT PROGRAM
• *See page 564*

GORDON LAW GROUP

https://www.gordonlawltd.com

GORDON LAW GROUP ANNUAL SCHOLARSHIP
• *See page 622*

GREATER GOOD SCIENCE CENTER

https://ggsc.berkeley.edu/

THE PURPOSE CHALLENGE
• *See page 622*

GREATER KANAWHA VALLEY FOUNDATION

http://www.tgkvf.org/

KID'S CHANCE OF WEST VIRGINIA SCHOLARSHIP
• *See page 833*

WEST VIRGINIA GOLF ASSOCIATION FUND
• *See page 834*

GREATER SEATTLE BUSINESS ASSOCIATION

http://thegsba.org/

GSBA SCHOLARSHIP FUND
• *See page 834*

GRUNGO COLARULO

https://gcinjurylaw.com/

GRUNGO COLARULO GIVING BACK TO THE COMMUNITY SCHOLARSHIP
• *See page 623*

HAGAN SCHOLARSHIP FOUNDATION

https://haganscholarships.org/

HAGAN SCHOLARSHIP
• *See page 623*

HANSCOM FEDERAL CREDIT UNION

https://www.hfcu.org/

JOHN F. CONDON MEMORIAL SCHOLARSHIP
• *See page 623*

HARDWICK & PENDERGAST, P.S.

http://www.hardwickpendergast.com/

HARDWICK & PENDERGAST, P.S. SCHOLARSHIP
• *See page 623*

HARNESS HORSE YOUTH FOUNDATION

http://www.hhyf.org/

CURT GREENE MEMORIAL SCHOLARSHIP
• *See page 623*

HARRINGTON FAMILY FOUNDATION

http://harringtonfamilyfoundation.org

OREGON COMMUNITY QUARTERBACK SCHOLARSHIP
• *See page 624*

HAWAII EDUCATION ASSOCIATION

http://www.heaed.com/

HAWAII EDUCATION ASSOCIATION CONTINUING COLLEGE STUDENT SCHOLARSHIP
• *See page 565*

HAWAII EDUCATION ASSOCIATION HIGH SCHOOL STUDENT SCHOLARSHIP
• *See page 565*

HAWAII SCHOOLS FEDERAL CREDIT UNION

http://www.hawaiischoolsfcu.org/

EDWIN KUNIYUKI MEMORIAL SCHOLARSHIP
• *See page 624*

HBCUCONNECT.COM

http://www.hbcuconnect.com/

HBCUCONNECT.COM MINORITY SCHOLARSHIP PROGRAM
• *See page 624*

HEALTH PRODUCTS FOR YOU

https://www.healthproductsforyou.com/

HPFY DISABILITY SCHOLARSHIP
• *See page 737*

HELEN DILLER FAMILY FOUNDATION

http://www.dillerteenawards.org

DILLER TEEN TIKKUN OLAM AWARDS
• *See page 624*

HEMOPHILIA FOUNDATION OF SOUTHERN CALIFORNIA

http://www.hemosocal.org/

CHRISTOPHER MARK PITKIN MEMORIAL SCHOLARSHIP
• *See page 625*

HENKEL CONSUMER ADHESIVES INC.

http://www.ducktapeclub.com/

DUCK BRAND DUCT TAPE "STUCK AT PROM" SCHOLARSHIP CONTEST
• *See page 625*

HERB KOHL EDUCATIONAL FOUNDATION INC.

http://www.kohleducation.org/

HERB KOHL EXCELLENCE SCHOLARSHIP PROGRAM
• *See page 625*

THE HIGGINS FIRM

https://www.thehigginsfirm.com

JUDGE BILL HIGGINS PUBLIC SERVICE SCHOLARSHIP
• *See page 625*

HIGH INCOME PARENTS.COM

http://www.highincomeparents.com

MELISSA READ MEMORIAL SCHOLARSHIP
• *See page 625*

HISPANIC METROPOLITAN CHAMBER SCHOLARSHIPS

http://www.hmccoregon.com/

HISPANIC METROPOLITAN CHAMBER SCHOLARSHIPS
• *See page 626*

THE HIV LEAGUE

http://www.hivleague.org

THE HIV LEAGUE SCHOLARSHIP
• *See page 626*

HOFOSS DEVALL

https://www.hdinjurylaw.com/

HOFFOSS DEVALL LOUISIANA SAFE DRIVER SCHOLARSHIP
• *See page 626*

HOFFOSS DEVALL PROBLEM SOLVING SCHOLARSHIP
• *See page 626*

HOME IMPROVEMENT SOLUTIONS

http://www.myhomeimprovementsolutions.com

HOME IMPROVEMENT SCHOLARSHIP BY HOME IMPROVEMENT SOLUTIONS
• *See page 626*

HOMUS

https://homus.org

HOMUS SCHOLARSHIP PROGRAM
• *See page 627*

HOOVER PRESIDENTIAL FOUNDATION

http://www.hooverpresidentialfoundation.org/travel-grant.php

HERBERT HOOVER UNCOMMON STUDENT AWARD
• *See page 627*

HORIZONS FOUNDATION

http://www.horizonsfoundation.org/

MARKOWSKI-LEACH SCHOLARSHIP
Scholarship of $1250 awarded to a student who attends San Francisco State University, Stanford University, or University of California, and self-identifies as lesbian, gay, bisexual, transgender, or queer. Recipient is chosen based on demonstrated promise for becoming a positive role model for other LGBTQ people. All prospective undergraduate and

graduate students may apply. Students transferring to one of these universities are also encouraged to apply.

Award: Scholarship for use in freshman, sophomore, junior, or senior years; renewable. *Number:* 1. *Amount:* $1250.

Eligibility Requirements: Applicant must be enrolled or expecting to enroll full-time at a two-year or four-year or technical institution or university; studying in California and must have an interest in LGBT issues. Applicant must have 2.5 GPA or higher. Available to U.S. and Canadian citizens.

Application Requirements: Application form, essay, recommendations or references. *Deadline:* April 1.

Contact: Markowski-Leach Scholarship Committee
Horizons Foundation
PO Box 13315, PMB #206
Oakland, CA 94661-0315
E-mail: MLScholarships@gmail.com

HOSTESS COMMITTEE SCHOLARSHIPS/MISS AMERICA PAGEANT

http://www.missamerica.org/

MISS AMERICA COMMUNITY SERVICE SCHOLARSHIPS
• *See page 627*

MISS AMERICA ORGANIZATION COMPETITION SCHOLARSHIPS

Scholarship competition open to 70 contestants, each serving as state representative. Women will be judged in Private Interview, Swimsuit, Evening Wear and Talent competition. Other awards may be based on points assessed by judges during competitions. Upon reaching the National level, award values range from $2000 to $50,000. Additional awards not affecting the competition can be won with values from $1000 to $10,000.

Award: Prize for use in freshman, sophomore, junior, senior, or graduate years; not renewable. *Number:* 70. *Amount:* $2000–$50,000.

Eligibility Requirements: Applicant must be age 17-24; enrolled or expecting to enroll full- or part-time at a two-year or four-year or technical institution or university; female and must have an interest in beauty pageant. Available to U.S. citizens.

Application Requirements: Application form, entry in a contest. *Deadline:* varies.

Contact: Doreen Lindell Gordon, Controller and Scholarship
Administrator
Phone: 609-345-7571 Ext. 27
Fax: 609-347-6079
E-mail: doreen@missamerica.org

MISS AMERICA SCHOLAR AWARD

$1000 award offered to one woman in each state, District of Columbia and U.S. Virgin Islands, competing at the state level, for academic excellence. Competition is opened only to those competing at the state level. Must submit official transcripts of the immediate prior two years (4 semesters) of academic study, along with application.

Award: Scholarship for use in freshman, sophomore, junior, senior, graduate, or postgraduate years; not renewable.

Eligibility Requirements: Applicant must be enrolled or expecting to enroll full- or part-time at a four-year institution or university; female and must have an interest in beauty pageant. Available to U.S. citizens.

Application Requirements: Application form, transcript. *Deadline:* varies.

Contact: Doreen Lindell Gordon, Controller and Scholarship
Administrator
Phone: 609-345-7571 Ext. 27
Fax: 609-347-6079
E-mail: doreen@missamerica.org

HOSTGATOR

https://www.hostgator.com/

HOSTGATOR WEBSITE SCHOLARSHIP
• *See page 627*

HOUSE OF BLUES MUSIC FORWARD FOUNDATION

https://hobmusicforward.org/

LIVE NATION—US CONCERTS SCHOLARSHIP AWARD
• *See page 628*

HOUSTON COMMUNITY SERVICES

AZTECA SCHOLARSHIP
• *See page 628*

HOW TO WIN COLLEGE SCHOLARSHIPS

https://how2winscholarships.com

SAVOR SUMMER COLLEGE SCHOLARSHIP
• *See page 628*

HUBSHOUT

http://hubshout.com/

HUBSHOUT INTERNET MARKETING SCHOLARSHIP
• *See page 628*

HUMANA FOUNDATION

http://www.humanafoundation.org/

HUMANA FOUNDATION SCHOLARSHIP PROGRAM
• *See page 628*

INDIANA LIBRARY FEDERATION

http://www.ilfonline.org/

SUE MARSH WELLER SCHOLARSHIP FUND
• *See page 629*

INSTITUTE OF FOOD TECHNOLOGISTS

http://www.ift.org/

FEEDING TOMORROW UNDERGRADUATE GENERAL EDUCATION SCHOLARSHIPS

Multiple scholarships for college sophomores, juniors, and seniors demonstrating exceptional scholastic achievements, leadership experience and a devotion to the food science and technology profession. Minimum 3.0 GPA required.

Award: Scholarship for use in sophomore, junior, or senior years; not renewable. *Amount:* $1000–$2500.

Eligibility Requirements: Applicant must be enrolled or expecting to enroll full-time at a four-year institution or university. Applicant must have 3.0 GPA or higher. Available to U.S. and non-U.S. citizens.

Application Requirements: Application form. *Deadline:* February 15.

Contact: IFT Foundation Coordinator
Institute of Food Technologists
525 West Van Buren, Suite 1000
Chicago, IL 60607
Phone: 312-782-8424
E-mail: info@ift.org

FEEDING TOMORROW UNDERGRADUATE GENERAL EDUCATION SCHOLARSHIPS

Multiple scholarships for college sophomores, juniors, and seniors demonstrating exceptional scholastic achievements, leadership experience and a devotion to the food science and technology profession. Minimum 3.0 GPA required.

Award: Scholarship for use in sophomore, junior, or senior years; not renewable. *Amount:* $1000–$2500.

Eligibility Requirements: Applicant must be enrolled or expecting to enroll full-time at a four-year institution or university. Applicant must have 3.0 GPA or higher. Available to U.S. and non-U.S. citizens.

Application Requirements: Application form. *Deadline:* February 15.

Contact: IFT Foundation Coordinator
Institute of Food Technologists
525 West Van Buren, Suite 1000
Chicago, IL 60607
Phone: 312-782-8424
E-mail: info@ift.org

INTERNATIONAL COLLEGE COUNSELORS

http://www.internationalcollegecounselors.com

INTERNATIONAL COLLEGE COUNSELORS SCHOLARSHIP
• *See page 629*

INTERNATIONAL DAIRY DELI BAKERY ASSOCIATION

http://www.iddba.org

INTERNATIONAL DAIRY DELI BAKERY ASSOCIATION'S SCHOLARSHIP FOR GROWING THE FUTURE
• *See page 629*

INTERNATIONAL FLIGHT SERVICES ASSOCIATION

http://www.ifsanet.com

AMI SCHOLARSHIP AWARD
• *See page 629*

IOVATE HEALTH SCIENCES INTERNATIONAL INC.

http://www.iovate.com/

SIX STAR PRO NUTRITION SCHOLARSHIP AWARD
• *See page 631*

IOWA STUDENT LOAN

http://www.IowaStudentLoan.org/

COME 2 IOWA (C2IA) SENIOR SCHOLARSHIP
• *See page 631*

IOWA FINANCIAL KNOW-HOW CHALLENGE: SENIOR SCHOLARSHIP
• *See page 631*

ISEECARS.COM

http://www.iseecars.com/

ANNUAL ISEECARS FUTURE ENTREPRENEURS SCHOLARSHIP

iSeeCars.com will award $1,000 to a college student who has a demonstrated interest in entrepreneurship or has plans to become an entrepreneur. The scholarship will be awarded based on the application materials submitted by students.

Award: Scholarship for use in freshman, sophomore, junior, senior, graduate, or postgraduate years; not renewable. *Number:* 1. *Amount:* $1000.

Eligibility Requirements: Applicant must be enrolled or expecting to enroll full-time at a four-year institution or university; studying in Alabama, Alaska, Alberta, Arizona, Arkansas, California, Colorado, Connecticut, Delaware, District of Columbia, Florida, Georgia, Guam, Hawaii, Idaho, Illinois, Indiana, Iowa, Kansas, Kentucky, Louisiana, Maine, Maryland, Massachusetts, Michigan, Minnesota, Mississippi, Missouri, Montana, Nebraska, Nevada, New Hampshire, New Jersey, New Mexico, New York, North Carolina, North Dakota, Ohio, Oklahoma, Oregon, Pennsylvania, Puerto Rico, Rhode Island, South Carolina, South Dakota, Tennessee, Texas, Utah, Vermont, Virginia, Washington, West Virginia, Wisconsin, Wyoming and must have an interest in entrepreneurship. Available to U.S. and non-U.S. citizens.

Application Requirements: Application form, essay, personal photograph. *Deadline:* December 31.

Contact: Scholarship Coordinator
E-mail: team@iseecars.com

JACKIE ROBINSON FOUNDATION

http://www.jackierobinson.org/

JACKIE ROBINSON SCHOLARSHIP
• *See page 631*

JAMES F. BYRNES FOUNDATION

http://www.byrnesscholars.org/

JAMES F. BYRNES SCHOLARSHIP
• *See page 631*

JEANNETTE RANKIN WOMEN'S SCHOLARSHIP FUND

http://www.rankinfoundation.org/

JEANNETTE RANKIN WOMEN'S SCHOLARSHIP FUND
• *See page 632*

JOHN B. FABRIELE, III, LLC

https://www.fabrielelaw.com/

FABRIELE DISABILITY AWARENESS SCHOLARSHIP
• *See page 632*

JOHN F. AND ANNA LEE STACEY SCHOLARSHIP FUND

http://www.nationalcowboymuseum.org/

JOHN F. AND ANNA LEE STACEY SCHOLARSHIP FUND

Scholarships for artists who are high school graduates between the ages of 18 and 35, who are U.S. citizens, and whose work is devoted to the classical or conservative tradition of Western culture. Awards are for drawing or painting only. Must submit no more than six color digital images of work.

Award: Scholarship for use in freshman, sophomore, junior, senior, graduate, or postgraduate years; not renewable. *Number:* 3–5. *Amount:* $1000–$4000.

Eligibility Requirements: Applicant must be age 18-35; enrolled or expecting to enroll full- or part-time at a two-year or four-year or technical institution or university and must have an interest in art. Available to U.S. citizens.

Application Requirements: Application form. *Deadline:* February 1.

Contact: Ms. Melissa Owens, Registrar & Exhibits Coordinator
John F. and Anna Lee Stacey Scholarship Fund
National Cowboy and Western Heritage Museum
1700 NE 63rd Street
Oklahoma City, OK 73111
Phone: 405-478-2250 Ext. 220
Fax: 405-478-4714
E-mail: registrar@nationalcowboymuseum.org

JOHN F. KENNEDY LIBRARY FOUNDATION

http://www.jfklibrary.org/

PROFILE IN COURAGE ESSAY CONTEST
• *See page 632*

JOHNSON ATTORNEYS GROUP

https://californiainjuryaccidentlawyer.com/

NEVER DRINK AND DRIVE SCHOLARSHIP
• *See page 632*

JUNIOR ACHIEVEMENT

http://www.ja.org/

JOE FRANCOMANO SCHOLARSHIP
• *See page 566*

JUNK A CAR

https://www.junkacar.com/

JUNK A CAR 2018 SCHOLARSHIP
• *See page 632*

J. WALTER THOMPSON

https://www.jwt.com/en/

HELEN LANSDOWNE RESOR SCHOLARSHIP
• *See page 633*

KAUFMAN & STIGGER, PLLC

http://www.getthetiger.com/

THE ALBERTA C. KAUFMAN SCHOLARSHIP
• *See page 633*

KELLER LAW OFFICES

http://www.kellerlawoffices.com/

KELLER LAW OFFICES SCHOLARSHIP FOR HIGHER EDUCATION
• *See page 633*

KELLEY & CANTERBURY, LLC

http://kelleyandcanterbury.com/

KELLEY & CANTERBURY, LLC ALASKA CURIOSITY SCHOLARSHIP
• *See page 633*

KELLY LAW TEAM

http://www.jkphoenixpersonalinjuryattorney.com/

AUTISM/ASD SCHOLARSHIP
• *See page 633*

DISABLED VETERAN SCHOLARSHIP
• *See page 634*

DISABLED VETERAN SCHOLARSHIP
• *See page 634*

KEVIN'S REVIEW

http://www.kevinsreview.com

KEVIN'S REVIEW NCLEX ASSISTANCE SCHOLARSHIP
• *See page 634*

KIDGUARD

http://www.kidguard.com/

KIDGUARD FOR EDUCATION ESSAY SCHOLARSHIP FOR HIGH SCHOOL
• *See page 635*

KITCHEN GUIDES

http://www.kitchensguides.com/

SMART KITCHEN IMPROVEMENT SCHOLARSHIP BY KITCHEN GUIDES
• *See page 635*

KNIGHTS OF PYTHIAS

http://www.pythias.org/

KNIGHTS OF PYTHIAS POSTER CONTEST
Poster contest open to all high school students in the U.S. and Canada. Contestants must submit an original drawing. Eight winners are chosen. The winners are not required to attend institution of higher education.

Award: Prize for use in freshman year; not renewable. *Number:* 8. *Amount:* $100–$1000.

Eligibility Requirements: Applicant must be high school student; planning to enroll or expecting to enroll full- or part-time at a four-year institution or university and must have an interest in art. Available to U.S. and Canadian citizens.

Application Requirements: Entry in a contest. *Deadline:* April 30.

Contact: Alfred Saltzman, Supreme Secretary
Phone: 617-472-8800
Fax: 617-376-0363
E-mail: kop@earthlink.net

KOGAN AND DISALVO, P.A.

https://www.kogan-disalvo.com/

KOGAN & DISALVO PERSONAL INJURY LAW AUTONOMOUS VEHICLES SCHOLARSHIP
• *See page 635*

KOPFLER AND HERMANN, ATTORNEYS AT LAW

https://kopflerhermann.com/

KOPFLER & HERMANN OVERCOMING ADVERSITY SCHOLARSHIP
• *See page 635*

LADIES AUXILIARY TO THE VETERANS OF FOREIGN WARS

http://www.ladiesauxvfw.org/

YOUNG AMERICAN CREATIVE PATRIOTIC ART AWARDS PROGRAM
One-time awards for high school students in grades 9 through 12. Must submit an original work of art expressing their patriotism. First place state-level winners go on to national competition. Eight awards of varying amounts. Must reside in same state as sponsoring organization.

Award: Scholarship for use in freshman, sophomore, junior, or senior years; not renewable. *Number:* up to 8. *Amount:* $500–$10,000.

Eligibility Requirements: Applicant must be high school student; planning to enroll or expecting to enroll full-time at a two-year or four-year or technical institution or university; single and must have an interest in art. Available to U.S. citizens.

Application Requirements: Application form, artwork, entry in a contest. *Deadline:* March 31.

Contact: Connie Wahlen, Programs Coordinator
Phone: 816-561-8655
E-mail: cwahlen@ladiesauxvfw.org

LANDSCAPE ARCHITECTURE FOUNDATION

http://www.lafoundation.org

ASLA COUNCIL OF FELLOWS SCHOLARSHIP
• *See page 635*

COURTLAND PAUL SCHOLARSHIP
• *See page 635*

EDSA MINORITY SCHOLARSHIP
• *See page 636*

HAWAII CHAPTER/DAVID T. WOOLSEY SCHOLARSHIP
• *See page 636*

LANDSCAPE FORMS DESIGN FOR PEOPLE SCHOLARSHIP
• *See page 636*

STEVEN G. KING PLAY ENVIRONMENTS SCHOLARSHIP
• *See page 636*

LARSON JEWELERS

http://www.larsonjewelers.com

BAND WITH SUCCESS SCHOLARSHIP
• *See page 636*

LATIN AMERICAN EDUCATIONAL FOUNDATION

http://www.laef.org/

LATIN AMERICAN EDUCATIONAL FOUNDATION SCHOLARSHIPS
• *See page 636*

LA UNIDAD LATINA FOUNDATION

http://www.lulf.org/

LA UNIDAD LATINA FOUNDATION DREAM SCHOLARSHIP
• *See page 636*

LA UNIDAD LATINA FOUNDATION NATIONAL SCHOLARSHIP
• *See page 637*

LAW OFFICE OF DAVID D. WHITE, PLLC

http://www.wm-attorneys.com/

ANNUAL TRAUMATIC BRAIN INJURY SCHOLARSHIPS
• *See page 637*

LAW OFFICE OF DAVID P. SHAPIRO

http://www.davidpshapirolaw.com/about-us/

AUTISM SCHOLARSHIP
• *See page 637*

LAW OFFICE OF HENRY QUEENER

https://queenerlaw.com/

LAW OFFICE OF HENRY QUEENER ANNUAL SCHOLARSHIP
• *See page 637*

LAW OFFICE OF MATTHEW L. SHARP

https://mattsharplaw.com/

LAW OFFICE OF MATTHEW L. SHARP ANNUAL SCHOLARSHIP
• *See page 638*

LAW OFFICE OF MATTHEW SHRUM

http://www.shrumlawoffice.com/

ANNUAL SINGLE MOTHERS SCHOLARSHIP
• *See page 638*

LAW OFFICES OF DAVID A. BLACK

http://www.dbphoenixcriminallawyer.com

SCHOLARSHIP FOR DISABLED VETERANS
• *See page 638*

LAW OFFICES OF DIANNE SAWAYA LLC

https://dlslawfirm.com/

LAW OFFICES OF DIANNE SAWAYA DENVER SAFE DRIVER SCHOLARSHIP
• *See page 638*

LAW OFFICES OF JUDD S. NEMIRO, PLLC

http://www.jnphoenixfamilylawyer.com/

ANNUAL DYSLEXIA SCHOLARSHIP
• *See page 638*

LAW OFFICES OF MARK SHERMAN, LLC

markshermanlaw.com

MARK SHERMAN LAW JUVENILE JUSTICE SCHOLARSHIP
• *See page 639*

LAW OFFICES OF SEAN M. CLEARY

https://www.seanclearypa.com/

LAW OFFICES OF SEAN M. CLEARY SCHOLARSHIP
• *See page 639*

LAW OFFICES OF SHERYL R. RENTZ, P.C.

http://www.srrentzlaw.com/

LAW OFFICES OF SHERYL R. RENTZ 2018 SCHOLARSHIP
• *See page 639*

LAW OFFICES OF TRAGOS, SARTES AND TRAGOS

https://tragoslaw.com/

TRAGOS WRITE YOUR OWN LAW SCHOLARSHIP
• *See page 639*

LEAGUE FOUNDATION

http://www.leaguefoundation.org/

LEAGUE FOUNDATION ACADEMIC SCHOLARSHIP
• *See page 639*

LEE-JACKSON EDUCATIONAL FOUNDATION

http://www.lee-jackson.org/

LEE-JACKSON EDUCATIONAL FOUNDATION SCHOLARSHIP COMPETITION
• *See page 841*

LEMBERG LAW

http://www.lemberglaw.com

LEMBERG LAW AMERICAN DREAM $1,250 UNDERGRADUATE SCHOLARSHIP
• *See page 640*

LEPENDORF & SILVERSTEIN, P.C.

http://www.lependorf.com/

2018 LEPENDORF & SILVERSTEIN, P.C. SCHOLARSHIP
• *See page 640*

LEP FOUNDATION FOR YOUTH EDUCATION

http://www.lepfoundation.org/applications

CURE—CANCER SUPPORT SCHOLARSHIP
• *See page 640*

JOHN LEPPING MEMORIAL SCHOLARSHIP
• *See page 640*

LEVY LAW OFFICES

https://levylawoffices.com/

LEVY LAW OFFICES CINCINNATI SAFE DRIVER SCHOLARSHIP
• *See page 640*

LIBERTY GRAPHICS INC.

http://www.lgtees.com

ANNUAL LIBERTY GRAPHICS ART CONTEST
• *See page 841*

LIFESAVER ESSAYS

https://lifesaveressays.com

LIFE SAVER ESSAYS ESSAY WRITING CONTEST
• *See page 640*

LIGHTHOUSE GUILD

http://www.lighthouseguild.org

LIGHTHOUSE GUILD SCHOLARSHIP PROGRAM
• *See page 689*

THE LINCOLN FORUM

http://www.thelincolnforum.org/

PLATT FAMILY SCHOLARSHIP PRIZE ESSAY CONTEST
The Platt Family Scholarship Prize Essay Contest is designed for students who are full-time students in an American college or university. You do not have to be an American citizen, but you do need to be attending an AMERICAN COLLEGE OR UNIVERSITY during the eligibility period. For details, refer to website http://thelincolnforum.org/scholarship-essay-contest.php

Award: Prize for use in freshman, sophomore, junior, or senior years; not renewable. *Number:* 3. *Amount:* $500–$1500.

Eligibility Requirements: Applicant must be enrolled or expecting to enroll full-time at a two-year or four-year institution or university and must have an interest in writing. Available to U.S. and non-U.S. citizens.

Application Requirements: Entry in a contest, essay. *Deadline:* July 31.

Contact: Don McCue, Director
  Phone: 909-798-7632
  E-mail: archives@akspl.org

LIVE POETS SOCIETY AND JUST POETRY!!! MAGAZINE

http://www.highschoolpoetrycontest.com/

NATIONAL HIGH SCHOOL POETRY CONTEST
• *See page 641*

MAINE STATE SOCIETY FOUNDATION OF WASHINGTON, DC INC.

http://mainestatesociety.org/foundation/

MAINE STATE SOCIETY FOUNDATION SCHOLARSHIP
• *See page 641*

MAINOR WORTH INJURY LAWYERS

https://mainorwirth.com/

MAINOR WIRTH INJURY LAWYERS SCHOLARSHIP
• *See page 641*

MANA DE SAN DIEGO

http://www.manasd.org/

MANA DE SAN DIEGO SYLVIA CHAVEZ MEMORIAL SCHOLARSHIP
• *See page 641*

MARTIN D. ANDREWS SCHOLARSHIP

http://www.mdascholarship.tripod.com/

MARTIN D. ANDREWS MEMORIAL SCHOLARSHIP FUND

One-time award for student seeking undergraduate or graduate degree. Recipient must have been in a Drum Corp for at least three years. Must submit essay and two recommendations. Must be U.S. citizen.

Award: Scholarship for use in freshman, sophomore, junior, senior, or graduate years; not renewable. *Number:* 2–5. *Amount:* $300–$1000.

Eligibility Requirements: Applicant must be enrolled or expecting to enroll full- or part-time at a two-year or four-year institution or university and must have an interest in drum corps. Available to U.S. citizens.

Application Requirements: Application form, essay. *Deadline:* June 1.

Contact: Peter Andrews, Scholarship Committee
Martin D. Andrews Scholarship
2069 Perkins Street
Bristol, CT 06010
Phone: 860-250-4757
E-mail: psandrews@charter.net

MARYLAND ASSOCIATION OF PRIVATE COLLEGES AND CAREER SCHOOLS

http://www.mapccs.org/

MARYLAND ASSOCIATION OF PRIVATE COLLEGES AND CAREER SCHOOLS SCHOLARSHIP
• *See page 642*

MASSACHUSETTS OFFICE OF STUDENT FINANCIAL ASSISTANCE

http://www.osfa.mass.edu/

AGNES M. LINDSAY SCHOLARSHIP
• *See page 642*

CHRISTIAN A. HERTER MEMORIAL SCHOLARSHIP
• *See page 642*

DSS ADOPTED CHILDREN TUITION WAIVER
• *See page 642*

JOHN AND ABIGAIL ADAMS SCHOLARSHIP
• *See page 642*

MASSACHUSETTS ASSISTANCE FOR STUDENT SUCCESS PROGRAM
• *See page 643*

MASSACHUSETTS CASH GRANT PROGRAM
• *See page 643*

MASSACHUSETTS GILBERT MATCHING STUDENT GRANT PROGRAM
• *See page 643*

MASSACHUSETTS PART-TIME GRANT PROGRAM
• *See page 643*

MASSACHUSETTS PUBLIC SERVICE GRANT PROGRAM
• *See page 643*

PAUL TSONGAS SCHOLARSHIP PROGRAM
• *See page 643*

MASSEY AND ASSOCIATES, PC

https://www.masseyattorneys.com/

MASSEY & ASSOCIATES: JUSTICE FOR ALL SCHOLARSHIP
• *See page 643*

MCCURRY FOUNDATION INC.

http://www.mccurryfoundation.org/

MCCURRY FOUNDATION SCHOLARSHIP
• *See page 845*

MEDIGO GMBH

https://www.medigo.com/en

MEDIGO SCHOLARSHIP PROGRAM
• *See page 645*

MENSA FOUNDATION

mensafoundation.org

U.S. SCHOLARSHIP PROGRAM
• *See page 645*

MES FOUNDATION

http://www.mesfoundation.org

RICHARD H. PIERCE MEMORIAL SCHOLARSHIP
• *See page 645*

MINDSUMO

http://www.mindsumo.com

MINDSUMO 15-MINUTE SCHOLARSHIP
• *See page 645*

MINNESOTA MASONIC CHARITIES

http://www.mnmasoniccharities.org

MINNESOTA MASONIC CHARITIES SIGNATURE SCHOLARSHIP
• *See page 645*

MINNESOTA MASONIC CHARITIES UNDERGRADUATE SCHOLARSHIP
• *See page 646*

MITCHELL INSTITUTE

http://www.mitchellinstitute.org/

SENATOR GEORGE J. MITCHELL SCHOLARSHIP RESEARCH INSTITUTE
• *See page 646*

MLD WEALTH MANAGEMENT GROUP

http://mywealthmanagement.ca/

ANNUAL MLD SCHOLASTIC SCHOLARSHIP
• *See page 646*

MUCHGAMES.COM

http://www.muchgames.com

MUCHGAMES.COM STUDENT RESEARCH GRANT OF $1500
• *See page 646*

THE MULLER FIRM, LTD

https://chicagodivorceattys.com/

THE MULLER FIRM, LTD ANNUAL SCHOLARSHIP
• *See page 647*

NATIONAL AIDS MEMORIAL

http://www.aidsmemorial.org

PEDRO ZAMORA YOUNG LEADERS SCHOLARSHIP
• *See page 647*

NATIONAL AMATEUR BASEBALL FEDERATION (NABF)

http://www.nabf.com/

NATIONAL AMATEUR BASEBALL FEDERATION SCHOLARSHIP FUND

Scholarships are awarded to candidates who are enrolled in an accredited college or university. Applicant must be a bona fide participant in a federation event and be sponsored by an NABF-franchised member association. Self-nominated candidates are not eligible for this scholarship award.

Award: Scholarship for use in freshman, sophomore, junior, or senior years; not renewable.

Eligibility Requirements: Applicant must be enrolled or expecting to enroll full-time at a two-year or four-year or technical institution or university and must have an interest in athletics/sports. Available to U.S. citizens.

Application Requirements: Application form, community service, essay, letter of acceptance, recommendations or references, transcript. *Deadline:* November 15.

Contact: Awards Committee Chairman
National Amateur Baseball Federation (NABF)
PO Box 705
Bowie, MD 20718

NATIONAL ASSOCIATION FOR CAMPUS ACTIVITIES

http://www.naca.org/

ALAN DAVIS SCHOLARSHIP
• *See page 647*

JOHN ZAGUNIS STUDENT LEADER SCHOLARSHIP
• *See page 647*

LORI RHETT MEMORIAL SCHOLARSHIP
• *See page 648*

NATIONAL ASSOCIATION FOR CAMPUS ACTIVITIES MID ATLANTIC UNDERGRADUATE SCHOLARSHIP FOR STUDENT LEADERS
• *See page 648*

NATIONAL ASSOCIATION FOR CAMPUS ACTIVITIES SOUTH REGION STUDENT LEADER SCHOLARSHIP
• *See page 648*

TESE CALDARELLI MEMORIAL SCHOLARSHIP
• *See page 648*

NATIONAL ASSOCIATION FOR THE SELF-EMPLOYED

http://www.NASE.org/

NASE SCHOLARSHIPS
• *See page 569*

NATIONAL COLLEGIATE CANCER FOUNDATION

http://collegiatecancer.org/

NATIONAL COLLEGIATE CANCER FOUNDATION SCHOLARSHIPS
• *See page 750*

NATIONAL COSTUMERS ASSOCIATION SCHOLARSHIPS

http://www.costumers.org

NATIONAL COSTUMERS ASSOCIATION SCHOLARSHIPS

The National Costumers Association offers two types of scholarships. The Memorial scholarship is an annual scholarship based on a brief bio and essay and GPA. The Creative scholarship is offered in odd number years is and consists of a hands on project submitted for judging.

Award: Scholarship for use in freshman, sophomore, junior, senior, graduate, or postgraduate years; not renewable. *Number:* 1–5. *Amount:* $250–$1000.

Eligibility Requirements: Applicant must be enrolled or expecting to enroll full-time at a two-year or four-year institution or university and must have an interest in museum/preservation work, sewing, or theater. Applicant must have 2.5 GPA or higher. Available to U.S. and non-U.S. citizens.

Application Requirements: Application form, autobiography, essay, personal photograph. *Deadline:* April 1.

Contact: Linda Adams Foat, Past President
National Costumers Association Scholarships
1321 S Demeter Dr
Freeport, IL 61032
Phone: 815-233-1861
E-mail: ipp@costumers.org

NATIONAL COUNCIL OF JEWISH WOMEN LOS ANGELES (NCJW L LA)

http://ncjwla.org/

THE DODELL WOMEN'S EMPOWERMENT SCHOLARSHIP
• *See page 648*

THE SINGERMAN/NOSSECK MEMORIAL SCHOLARSHIP
• *See page 750*

SOPHIE GREENSTADT SCHOLARSHIP FOR MID-LIFE WOMEN
• *See page 648*

STEPHEN L. TELLER & RICHARD HOTSON TV, CINEMA, AND THEATER SCHOLARSHIP
• *See page 649*

SUSAN SCHULMAN BEGLEY MEMORIAL SCHOLARSHIP
• *See page 649*

NATIONAL FEDERATION OF STATE POETRY SOCIETIES (NFSPS)

http://www.nfsps.com/

NATIONAL FEDERATION OF STATE POETRY SOCIETIES' COLLEGE UNDERGRADUATE POETRY (CUP) COMPETITION
• *See page 649*

NATIONAL FEDERATION OF THE BLIND (NFB)

http://www.nfb.org/scholarships

AAF KENNETH JERNIGAN SCHOLARSHIP FOR $12,000
• *See page 649*

CHARLES AND MELVA T. OWEN SCHOLARSHIP FOR $10,000
• *See page 649*

NATIONAL FFA ORGANIZATION

http://www.ffa.org

NATIONAL FFA COLLEGIATE SCHOLARSHIP PROGRAM
• *See page 570*

NATIONAL INSTITUTE FOR LABOR RELATIONS RESEARCH

http://www.nilrr.org/

NATIONAL INSTITUTE FOR LABOR RELATIONS RESEARCH WILLIAM B. RUGGLES JOURNALISM SCHOLARSHIP
• *See page 650*

NATIONAL MILITARY FAMILY ASSOCIATION

http://www.MilitaryFamily.org

NATIONAL MILITARY FAMILY ASSOCIATION'S MILITARY SPOUSE SCHOLARSHIPS
• *See page 650*

NATIONAL MULTIPLE SCLEROSIS SOCIETY

http://www.nmss.org/

NATIONAL MULTIPLE SCLEROSIS SOCIETY SCHOLARSHIP PROGRAM
• *See page 650*

NATIONAL PRESS FOUNDATION

http://www.nationalpress.org/

EVERT CLARK/SETH PAYNE AWARD
• *See page 650*

NATIONAL SOCIETY FOR HISTOTECHNOLOGY

http://nsh.org/

IRWIN S. LERNER STUDENT SCHOLARSHIPS
• *See page 650*

NATIONAL SOCIETY OF COLLEGIATE SCHOLARS (NSCS)

http://www.nscs.org/

NSCS EXEMPLARY SCHOLAR AWARD
• *See page 571*

NATIONAL SOCIETY OF HIGH SCHOOL SCHOLARS

http://www.nshss.org

CLAES NOBEL ACADEMIC SCHOLARSHIPS
• *See page 571*

NATIONAL SCHOLAR AWARDS FOR NSHSS MEMBERS
• *See page 571*

ROBERT P. SHEPPARD LEADERSHIP AWARD FOR NSHSS MEMBERS
• *See page 572*

NATIONAL SOCIETY OF THE SONS OF THE AMERICAN REVOLUTION

http://www.sar.org/

JOSEPH S. RUMBAUGH HISTORICAL ORATION CONTEST

Prize ranging from $1000 to $3000 is awarded to a sophomore, junior, or senior. The oration must be original and not less than five minutes or more than six minutes in length.

Award: Prize for use in sophomore, junior, or senior years; not renewable. *Number:* 1–3. *Amount:* $1000–$3000.

Eligibility Requirements: Applicant must be enrolled or expecting to enroll full-time at a two-year or four-year or technical institution or university and must have an interest in public speaking. Available to U.S. and non-U.S. citizens.

Application Requirements: Application form, entry in a contest. *Deadline:* June 15.

Contact: Lawrence Mckinley, National Chairman
  National Society of the Sons of the American Revolution
  12158 Holly Knoll Circle
  Great Fall, VA 22066
  E-mail: dustoff@bellatlantic.net

NEBRASKA'S COORDINATING COMMISSION FOR POSTSECONDARY EDUCATION

https://ccpe.nebraska.gov/

NEBRASKA OPPORTUNITY GRANT
• *See page 651*

NEED

http://www.needld.org/

UNMET NEED GRANT PROGRAM
• *See page 651*

NERDIFY

https://gonerdify.com/

NERDY BOT SCHOLARSHIP
• *See page 651*

NEW YORK WOMEN IN COMMUNICATIONS

https://nywici.org/

NEW YORK WOMEN IN COMMUNICATIONS SCHOLARSHIPS
• *See page 652*

NFIB YOUNG ENTREPRENEUR FOUNDATION

http://www.nfib.com/yef

YOUNG ENTREPRENEUR AWARDS

The Young Entrepreneur Awards program was designed to identify and reward students who have demonstrated entrepreneurial spirit and initiative by running their own entrepreneurial venture. Since 2003, YEF has awarded over 2,500 scholarships worth more than $2.5 million to graduating high school seniors. We award students who have demonstrated entrepreneurial talent by owning and/or operating their own business. Young Entrepreneur Awards range from $2,000 to $25,000 and enable students to further their studies in a two-year or four-year institution of higher learning while encouraging them to consider joining the ranks of America's independent business owners. For more information visit http://www.nfib.com/yea.

Award: Scholarship for use in freshman year; not renewable. *Number:* 100. *Amount:* $2000–$25,000.

Eligibility Requirements: Applicant must be high school student; planning to enroll or expecting to enroll full- or part-time at a two-year or four-year or technical institution or university and must have an interest in entrepreneurship. Available to U.S. citizens.

Application Requirements: Application form, essay, interview.

Contact: Molly young, Director, Young Entrepreneur Foundation
NFIB Young Entrepreneur Foundation
1201 F Street NW
Suite 200
Washington, DC 20004
Phone: 202-314-2042
E-mail: yef@nfib.org

NICODEMUS WILDERNESS PROJECT

http://www.wildernessproject.org/

APPRENTICE ECOLOGIST SCHOLARSHIP
• *See page 652*

NIKKO COSMETIC SURGERY CENTER

http://www.drnikko.com/

BREAST CANCER SURVIVOR SCHOLARSHIPS
• *See page 652*

NIMROD INTERNATIONAL JOURNAL

http://www.utulsa.edu/nimrod

THE KATHERINE ANNE PORTER PRIZE FOR FICTION

The Katherine Ann Porter Prize is given for a single extraordinary short story of less than 7,500 words.

Award: Prize for use in freshman, sophomore, junior, senior, graduate, or postgraduate years; not renewable. *Number:* 2. *Amount:* $1000–$2000.

Eligibility Requirements: Applicant must be enrolled or expecting to enroll full- or part-time at a two-year or four-year or technical institution or university and must have an interest in writing. Available to U.S. citizens.

Application Requirements: Application form. *Fee:* $20. *Deadline:* April 30.

Contact: Eilis O'Neal, Editor-in-Chief
Nimrod International Journal
The University of Tulsa, 800 South Tucker Drive
Phone: 918-631-3080
Fax: 918-631-3033
E-mail: nimrod@utulsa.edu

NO BULL SPORTS

http://nobullsports.org/

NO BULL SPORTS SCHOLARSHIP
• *See page 653*

NOPLAG PLAGIARISM CHECKER

http://noplag.com/

NOPLAG SCHOLARSHIP ESSAY CONTEST
• *See page 653*

NORTH CAROLINA ASSOCIATION OF EDUCATORS

http://www.ncae.org/

NORTH CAROLINA ASSOCIATION OF EDUCATORS MARTIN LUTHER KING JR. SCHOLARSHIP
• *See page 653*

NORTH CAROLINA DIVISION OF VOCATIONAL REHABILITATION SERVICES

http://www.dhhs.state.nc.us/

TRAINING SUPPORT FOR YOUTH WITH DISABILITIES
• *See page 653*

NORTH CAROLINA VIETNAM VETERANS, INC.

http://www.ncvvi.org

NC VIETNAM VETERANS, INC., SCHOLARSHIP PROGRAM
• *See page 653*

NORTH DAKOTA UNIVERSITY SYSTEM

http://www.ndus.edu/

NORTH DAKOTA ACADEMIC SCHOLARSHIP
• *See page 654*

NORTH DAKOTA CAREER AND TECHNICAL EDUCATION SCHOLARSHIP
• *See page 654*

NORTH DAKOTA INDIAN SCHOLARSHIP PROGRAM
• *See page 654*

NORTH DAKOTA SCHOLARS PROGRAM
• *See page 654*

NORTH DAKOTA STATE STUDENT INCENTIVE GRANT PROGRAM
• *See page 654*

NORTHWESTERN MUTUAL FOUNDATION

http://www.scholarshipamerica.org

NORTHWESTERN MUTUAL CHILDHOOD CANCER SURVIVOR SCHOLARSHIP
• See page 654

NOVUS BIOLOGICALS, LLC

https://www.novusbio.com

NOVUS BIOLOGICALS SCHOLARSHIP PROGRAM
• See page 753

NURSERECRUITER.COM

https://www.nurserecruiter.com

NURSERECRUITER.COM SCHOLARSHIP
• See page 655

OHIO DEPARTMENT OF HIGHER EDUCATION

http://www.ohiohighered.org

CHOOSE OHIO FIRST SCHOLARSHIP
• See page 655

OHIO COLLEGE OPPORTUNITY GRANT
• See page 655

OHIO SAFETY OFFICERS COLLEGE MEMORIAL FUND
• See page 655

OHIO WAR ORPHANS SCHOLARSHIP
• See page 655

ONE LOVE FOUNDATION

http://www.joinonelove.org

ONE LOVE FOUNDATION PETS VS. PARTNERS SCHOLARSHIP
• See page 656

ONLINEPSYCHOLOGYDEGREES.COM

http://www.onlinepsychologydegrees.com/

ONLINEPSYCHOLOGYDEGREES.COM EDUCATION SCHOLARSHIPS
• See page 656

OPTIMIST INTERNATIONAL FOUNDATION

http://www.optimist.org/

OPTIMIST INTERNATIONAL ESSAY CONTEST

Essay contest for youth under the age of 19 who have not graduated high school or its equivalent. U.S. students attending school on a military installation outside the United States are eligible to enter in their last U.S. home of record. Club winners advance to the District contest to compete for a college scholarship.

Award: Scholarship for use in freshman, sophomore, junior, or senior years; not renewable. *Number:* 40–49. *Amount:* up to $2500.

Eligibility Requirements: Applicant must be enrolled or expecting to enroll full- or part-time at a two-year or four-year or technical institution or university and must have an interest in writing. Available to U.S. and non-U.S. citizens.

Application Requirements: Application form, birth certificate or passport, entry in a contest, essay, self-addressed stamped envelope with application. *Deadline:* varies.

Contact: Danielle Baugher, Director of International Programs
Optimist International Foundation
4494 Lindell Boulevard
St. Louis, MO 63108
Phone: 800-500-8130
Fax: 314-371-6006
E-mail: programs@optimist.org

OPTIMIST INTERNATIONAL ORATORICAL CONTEST

Contest for youth to gain experience in public speaking and to provide them with the opportunity to compete for college scholarships. The contest is open to youth under the age of 19 before graduating high school or the equivalent. Students must first compete at the Club level. Club winners are then entered into the Zone contest and those winners compete in the District contest. District winners are awarded scholarships. District winners will be able to compete in a Regional Contest then be able to compete in the World Championships at St. Louis University in St. Louis, Missouri USA.

Award: Scholarship for use in freshman, sophomore, junior, or senior years; not renewable. *Number:* 90–115. *Amount:* $1000–$2500.

Eligibility Requirements: Applicant must be enrolled or expecting to enroll full- or part-time at a two-year or four-year or technical institution or university and must have an interest in public speaking. Available to U.S. and non-U.S. citizens.

Application Requirements: Application form, birth certificate or passport, speech, entry in a contest, self-addressed stamped envelope with application. *Deadline:* varies.

Contact: Dana Thomas, Director of International Programs
Optimist International Foundation
4494 Lindell Boulevard
St. Louis, MO 63108
Phone: 800-500-8130
Fax: 314-371-6006
E-mail: programs@optimist.org

OREGON COMMUNITY FOUNDATION

http://www.oregoncf.org/

DOROTHY S. CAMPBELL MEMORIAL SCHOLARSHIP FUND

Scholarship for female graduates of Oregon high schools with a strong and continuing interest in the game of golf. For use in the pursuit of a postsecondary education at a four-year college or university in Oregon.

Award: Scholarship for use in freshman, sophomore, junior, or senior years; renewable. *Number:* 9. *Amount:* $1000.

Eligibility Requirements: Applicant must be enrolled or expecting to enroll full-time at a four-year institution or university; female and must have an interest in golf. Available to U.S. citizens.

Application Requirements: Application form, recommendations or references. *Deadline:* March 1.

Contact: Dianne Causey, Program Associate for Scholarships and Grants
Phone: 503-227-6846 Ext. 1418
E-mail: dcausey@oregoncf.org

OREGON STUDENT ASSISTANCE COMMISSION

https://oregonstudentaid.gov/

DOROTHY CAMPBELL MEMORIAL SCHOLARSHIP
• See page 858

ORGANIZATION FOR AUTISM RESEARCH

http://www.researchautism.org

LISA HIGGINS HUSSMAN SCHOLARSHIP
• See page 656

SCHWALLIE FAMILY SCHOLARSHIP
• See page 656

ORGONE BIOPHYSICAL RESEARCH LABORATORY

http://www.orgonelab.org/hochberg.htm

LOU HOCHBERG-UNIVERSITY/COLLEGE ESSAY AWARDS
• See page 656

OUR WORLD UNDERWATER SCHOLARSHIP SOCIETY

http://www.owuscholarship.org/

OUR WORLD UNDERWATER SCHOLARSHIP SOCIETY
• See page 755

OUTRIGGER DUKE KAHANAMOKU FOUNDATION

http://www.dukefoundation.org

ODKF GENERAL SCHOLARSHIP AWARD
• See page 657

PANHELLENIC SCHOLARSHIP FOUNDATION

https://www.panhellenicsf.org/

PANHELLENIC SCHOLARSHIP AWARDS
• See page 657

PAPERCHECK

https://www.papercheck.com/

PAPERCHECK, LLC—CHARLES SHAFAE' SCHOLARSHIP FUND
• See page 657

PARIAN LAW FIRM, LLC

https://westgalawyer.com/

THE EDUCATIONAL JUSTICE SCHOLARSHIP
• See page 658

PEACOCK PRODUCTIONS, INC.

http://amefund.com

AUDRIA M. EDWARDS SCHOLARSHIP FUND
• See page 658

PENGUIN GROUP

http://www.penguin.com/services-academic/essayhome/

SIGNET CLASSIC SCHOLARSHIP ESSAY CONTEST
Open to 11th and 12th grade full-time matriculated students who are attending high schools located in the fifty United States and the District of Columbia, or home-schooled students between the ages of 16 to 18 who are residents of the fifty United States and the District of Columbia. Students should submit four copies of a two- to three-page double-spaced essay answering one of three possible questions on a designated novel. Entries must be submitted by a high school English teacher.

Award: Scholarship for use in freshman year; not renewable. *Number:* 5. *Amount:* $1000.

Eligibility Requirements: Applicant must be high school student; planning to enroll or expecting to enroll full-time at a four-year institution or university and must have an interest in writing. Available to U.S. citizens.

Application Requirements: Entry in a contest, essay, recommendations or references. *Deadline:* April 15.

Contact: Kym Giacoppe, Academic Marketing Assistant
Phone: 212-366-2377
E-mail: academic@penguin.com

PENNSYLVANIA FEDERATION OF DEMOCRATIC WOMEN INC.

http://www.pafedofdemwomen.org

PENNSYLVANIA FEDERATION OF DEMOCRATIC WOMEN INC. ANNUAL SCHOLARSHIP AWARDS
• See page 574

PENNSYLVANIA HIGHER EDUCATION ASSISTANCE AGENCY

http://www.pheaa.org/

BLIND OR DEAF BENEFICIARY GRANT PROGRAM
• See page 658

PET LIFESTYLE AND YOU (P.L.A.Y.)

https://www.petplay.com/

SCHOLARS HELPING COLLARS SCHOLARSHIP
• See page 659

PHI SIGMA PI NATIONAL HONOR FRATERNITY

http://www.phisigmapi.org/

RICHARD CECIL TODD AND CLAUDA PENNOCK TODD TRIPOD SCHOLARSHIP
• See page 575

PHOENIX PRIDE

https://phoenixpride.org/

PHOENIX PRIDE SCHOLARSHIP PROGRAM
• See page 659

PILOT INTERNATIONAL

https://www.pilotinternational.org/

BECKY BURROWS MEMORIAL SCHOLARSHIP
• See page 659

KC INTERNATIONAL SCHOLARSHIP
• See page 659

RUBY NEWHALL MEMORIAL SCHOLARSHIP
• See page 659

PINE CONE FOUNDATION (PCF)

http://pineconefoundation.org/

PINE CONE FOUNDATION SCHOLARSHIP
• See page 660

PLAINTIFF RELIEF

http://plaintiffrelief.com/

PLAINTIFF RELIEF SCHOLARSHIP
• *See page 660*

POLSON AND POLSON, P.C.

https://www.polsonlawfirm.com/

POLSON & POLSON, P.C. CONQUERING ADVERSITY SCHOLARSHIP
• *See page 660*

PONY OF THE AMERICAS CLUB INC.

http://www.poac.org/

POAC NATIONAL SCHOLARSHIP
• *See page 575*

PORTUGUESE AMERICAN LEADERSHIP COUNCIL OF THE UNITED STATES

http://www.palcus.org

PALCUS NATIONAL SCHOLARSHIP PROGRAM
• *See page 660*

POTENTIAL MAGAZINE

http://potentialmagazine.com/

COUNTDOWN TO COLLEGE SCHOLARSHIP
• *See page 661*

"DON'T WAIT TO REACH YOUR POTENTIAL" SCHOLARSHIP
• *See page 661*

PRICE BENOWITZ LLP

http://pricebenowitz.com/

AMATO SANITA BRIGHTER FUTURE SCHOLARSHIP
• *See page 661*

ANGIE DIPIETRO WOMEN IN BUSINESS SCHOLARSHIP
• *See page 661*

KAREN RILEY PORTER GOOD WORKS SCHOLARSHIP
• *See page 661*

KERRI CASTELLINI WOMEN'S LEADERSHIP SCHOLARSHIP
• *See page 661*

KUSH ARORA FEDERAL CRIMINAL JUSTICE REFORM SCHOLARSHIP
• *See page 661*

NATALIA SEGERMEISTER DREAM ACT SCHOLARSHIP
• *See page 662*

PRICE BENOWITZ MAKE A DIFFERENCE SCHOLARSHIP
• *See page 662*

PRICE BENOWITZ SOCIAL JUSTICE SCHOLARSHIP
• *See page 662*

SETH OKIN GOOD DEEDS SCHOLARSHIP
• *See page 662*

STEVE DUCKETT CONSERVATION SCHOLARSHIP
• *See page 757*

THOMAS SOLDAN HEALTHY COMMUNITIES SCHOLARSHIP
• *See page 662*

PRIDE FOUNDATION

http://www.PrideFoundation.org/

PRIDE FOUNDATION SCHOLARSHIP PROGRAM
• *See page 662*

PRO BOWLERS ASSOCIATION

http://www.pba.com/

BILLY WELU BOWLING SCHOLARSHIP
Scholarship awarded annually, recognizing exemplary qualities in male and female college students who compete in the sport of bowling. Winner will receive $1000. Candidates must be amateur bowlers who are currently in college (preceding the application deadline) and maintain at least a 2.5 GPA or equivalent.

Award: Scholarship for use in freshman, sophomore, junior, or senior years; not renewable. *Number:* 1. *Amount:* $1000.

Eligibility Requirements: Applicant must be enrolled or expecting to enroll full-time at a two-year or four-year institution or university and must have an interest in bowling. Applicant must have 2.5 GPA or higher. Available to U.S. citizens.

Application Requirements: Application form, essay, transcript. *Deadline:* May 31.

Contact: Karen Day, Controller
Phone: 206-332-9688
Fax: 206-332-9722
E-mail: karen.day@pba.com

PROMOCODESFORYOU.COM

https://www.promocodesforyou.com

PROMOCODESFORYOU.COM STUDENT SAVINGS SCHOLARSHIP
• *See page 662*

PROMPT

http://prompt.com

PROMPT'S $20,000 SCHOLARSHIP
• *See page 663*

QUALITY FORMATIONS LTD.

https://www.qualitycompanyformations.co.uk/

QUALITY COMPANY FORMATIONS SCHOLARSHIP
• *See page 663*

RAILROAD PASSENGERS ASSOCIATION

https://www.narprail.org/

RAILROAD PASSENGERS ASSOCIATION SCHOLARSHIP
• *See page 663*

REACH HIGHER MONTANA

http://www.ReachHigherMontana.org

REACH HIGHER MONTANA SCHOLARSHIPS
• *See page 663*

REHABCENTER.NET

http://www.rehabcenter.net/

REHABCENTER.NET
• *See page 664*

THE RESERVE OFFICERS ASSOCIATION

http://www.roa.org/

HENRY J. REILLY MEMORIAL SCHOLARSHIP-HIGH SCHOOL SENIORS AND FIRST YEAR FRESHMEN
• *See page 576*

RHINE LAW FIRM, P.C.

https://www.carolinaaccidentattorneys.com/

STRIVE FOR EXCELLENCE SCHOLARSHIP 2018
• *See page 664*

RHODE ISLAND FOUNDATION

http://www.rifoundation.org/

UNITED ITALIAN AMERICAN INC. SCHOLARSHIP
• *See page 864*

RISK MANAGEMENT ASSOCIATION FOUNDATION

http://www.scholarshipamerica.org

THE RISK MANAGEMENT ASSOCIATION FOUNDATION SCHOLARSHIP PROGRAM
• *See page 664*

RJT CRIMINAL DEFENSE

http://www.sandiegocriminallawyerrt.com/

AUTISM SCHOLARSHIP
• *See page 664*

ROBERT H. MOLLOHAN FAMILY CHARITABLE FOUNDATION, INC.

http://www.mollohanfoundation.org/

DR. ROBERTO F. CUNANAN MEMORIAL SCHOLARSHIP
• *See page 864*

RON BROWN SCHOLAR FUND

http://www.ronbrown.org/

RON BROWN SCHOLAR PROGRAM
• *See page 665*

ROVER.COM

https://www.rover.com/

ROVER SITTER SCHOLARSHIP CONTEST
• *See page 665*

ST. ANDREW'S SOCIETY OF WASHINGTON, DC

http://www.saintandrewsociety.org/

ST. ANDREW'S SOCIETY OF WASHINGTON DC FOUNDERS' SCHOLARSHIP
• *See page 665*

ST. ANDREW'S SOCIETY OF WASHINGTON DC SCHOLARSHIPS
• *See page 665*

ST. CLAIRE REGIONAL MEDICAL CENTER

http://www.st-claire.org/

SR. MARY JEANNETTE WESS, S.N.D. SCHOLARSHIP
• *See page 665*

SALUTE TO EDUCATION, INC.

http://www.stescholarships.org/

SALUTE TO EDUCATION SCHOLARSHIP
• *See page 666*

SCHOLAR SERVE

https://www.scholarserve.org

SCHOLAR SERVE AWARDS
• *See page 666*

SCHOLARSHIP AMERICA

https://www.abbvieImmunologyScholarship.com/

ABBVIE IMMUNOLOGY SCHOLARSHIP
• *See page 666*

SCHOLARSHIPOWL.COM

http://www.scholarshipowl.com

YOU DESERVE IT! SCHOLARSHIP
• *See page 865*

SCHOLARSHIP WORKSHOP LLC

http://www.scholarshipworkshop.com/

LEADING THE FUTURE II SCHOLARSHIP
The scholarship is designed to elevate students' consciousness about their future and their role in helping others. Open to high school seniors and college students who are U.S. citizens. Students must visit http://www.scholarshipworkshop.com (see scholarships) to apply. Scholarship is sponsored by Marianne Ragins, $400,000 scholarship winner. Learn more at http://www.scholarshipworkshop.com/movie.

Award: Scholarship for use in freshman, sophomore, junior, or senior years; not renewable. *Number:* 1–3. *Amount:* $100–$300.

Eligibility Requirements: Applicant must be enrolled or expecting to enroll full-time at a four-year institution or university and must have an interest in leadership. Available to U.S. citizens.

Application Requirements: Application form, essay. *Deadline:* March 1.

Contact: Scholarship Coordinator
Phone: 703-579-4245
E-mail: scholars@scholarshipworkshop.com

SELECTBLINDS.COM

http://www.selectblinds.com

SELECTBLINDS.COM $1000 COLLEGE SCHOLARSHIP
• *See page 666*

SEXNER & ASSOCIATES LLC

http://www.sexner.com/personal-injury/

MITCHELL S. SEXNER & ASSOCIATES LLC SCHOLARSHIP
• *See page 667*

SHAWN SUKUMAR ATTORNEY AT LAW

https://www.washingtondccriminallawyer.net/

SHAWN SUKUMAR CRIMINAL JUSTICE REFORM SCHOLARSHIP
• *See page 667*

SHELVING.COM

http://www.shelving.com/

SHELVING.COM BUSINESS SCHOLARSHIP
• *See page 667*

SILICON VALLEY COMMUNITY FOUNDATION

http://www.siliconvalleycf.org

ABBY SOBRATO SCHOLARSHIP
• *See page 667*

BOBETTE BIBO GUGLIOTTA MEMORIAL SCHOLARSHIP FOR CREATIVE WRITING
• *See page 667*

CURRY AWARD FOR GIRLS AND YOUNG WOMEN
• *See page 667*

HAZEL REED BAUMEISTER SCHOLARSHIP PROGRAM
• *See page 668*

HUANG LEADERSHIP DEVELOPMENT SCHOLARSHIP
• *See page 668*

TANG SCHOLARSHIP
• *See page 760*

SIMMONS AND FLETCHER, P.C.

https://www.simmonsandfletcher.com/

SIMMONS AND FLETCHER, P.C., LAW MARKETING SCHOLARSHIP
• *See page 668*

SISTER KENNY REHABILITATION INSTITUTE

http://www.allina.com/ahs/ski.nsf

INTERNATIONAL ART SHOW FOR ARTISTS WITH DISABILITIES
• *See page 693*

SOCIETY FOR APPLIED ANTHROPOLOGY

http://www.sfaa.net/

ANNUAL SFAA STUDENT ENDOWED AWARD
• *See page 668*

SOCIETY OF DAUGHTERS OF THE UNITED STATES ARMY

SOCIETY OF DAUGHTERS OF THE UNITED STATES ARMY SCHOLARSHIPS
• *See page 669*

SOCIETY OF SATELLITE PROFESSIONALS INTERNATIONAL

http://www.sspi.org/

SSPI NORTHEAST CHAPTER SCHOLARSHIP

Students from or studying in the Northeast US region.

Award: Scholarship for use in freshman, sophomore, junior, senior, or graduate years; not renewable. *Number:* 1. *Amount:* $2500.

Eligibility Requirements: Applicant must be enrolled or expecting to enroll full-time at a two-year or four-year institution or university. Available to U.S. and non-U.S. citizens.

Application Requirements: Essay, financial need analysis. *Deadline:* April 15.

Contact: Ms. Tamara Bond-Williams, Membership Director
Society of Satellite Professionals International
250 Park Avenue, 7th Floor
New York, NY 10177
Phone: 212-809-5199 Ext. 103
Fax: 212-825-0075
E-mail: tbond-williams@sspi.org

SONS OF ITALY FOUNDATION

http://www.osia.org/sif

GENERAL STUDY SCHOLARSHIPS
• *See page 669*

HENRY SALVATORI SCHOLARSHIP FOR GENERAL STUDY
• *See page 669*

SOUND MONEY DEFENSE LEAGUE

http://soundmoneydefense.org

MONEY METALS EXCHANGE SCHOLARSHIP PROGRAM
• *See page 669*

SOUTH CAROLINA TUITION GRANTS COMMISSION

http://www.sctuitiongrants.org/

SOUTH CAROLINA TUITION GRANTS PROGRAM
• *See page 669*

SOUTH DAKOTA BOARD OF REGENTS

http://www.sdbor.edu/

SOUTH DAKOTA BOARD OF REGENTS MARLIN R. SCARBOROUGH MEMORIAL SCHOLARSHIP

One-time merit-based award for a student who is a junior at a South Dakota university. Must be nominated by the university and must have community service and leadership experience. Minimum 3.5 GPA required. Application deadline varies.

Award: Scholarship for use in junior year; not renewable. *Number:* 1. *Amount:* $1000.

Eligibility Requirements: Applicant must be enrolled or expecting to enroll full- or part-time at an institution or university; studying in South Dakota and must have an interest in leadership. Applicant must have 3.5 GPA or higher. Available to U.S. citizens.

Application Requirements: Application form, essay.

Contact: Dr. Paul Turman, System Vice President for Research and Economic Development
South Dakota Board of Regents
301 East Capital Avenue, Suite 200
Pierre, SD 57501
Phone: 605-773-3455
Fax: 605-773-2422
E-mail: paul.turman@sdbor.edu

SPINE SURGEON DR. VICTOR HAYES

https://tampabaybackpaindoctor.com/

TAMPA BAY SPINE CENTER ROAD TO RECOVERY SCHOLARSHIP

• *See page 670*

STATE EMPLOYEES ASSOCIATION OF NORTH CAROLINA (SEANC)

http://www.seanc.org/

STATE EMPLOYEES ASSOCIATION OF NORTH CAROLINA (SEANC) SCHOLARSHIPS

• *See page 761*

STEALTHY AND WEALTHY

http://stealthyandwealthy.com

STEALTHY AND WEALTHY STUDENT ENTREPRENEUR GRANT

• *See page 670*

STEINBERG, GOODMAN AND KALISH

https://www.sgklawyers.com/

STEINBERG, GOODMAN AND KALISH SCHOLARSHIP

• *See page 670*

STONEWALL COMMUNITY FOUNDATION

http://www.stonewallfoundation.org/

HARRY BARTEL MEMORIAL SCHOLARSHIP

• *See page 670*

LEVIN-GOFFE SCHOLARSHIP FOR LGBTQI IMMIGRANTS

The Levin-Goffe Scholarship Fund was established to cover up to two years of schooling for immigrants here in New York City who identify as LGBTQI. Scholarships from this fund are intended to provide a measure of economic stability for those who stand at the intersection of marginalization that can be created by being both LGBTQI and an immigrant.

Award: Scholarship for use in sophomore or junior years; not renewable. *Number:* 3. *Amount:* $25,000.

Eligibility Requirements: Applicant must be enrolled or expecting to enroll full-time at a four-year institution or university; studying in New York and must have an interest in LGBT issues. Available to U.S. and non-U.S. citizens.

Application Requirements: Application form.

Contact: Carlie Steen, Program Manager
Stonewall Community Foundation
Stonewall Community Foundation
446 West 33rd Street
New York, NY 10001
Phone: 212-457.1349
E-mail: grants@stonewallfoundation.org

STROLLER DEPOT

https://www.strollerdepot.com/

$1,000 STROLLER DEPOT SCHOLARSHIP

• *See page 670*

STROM & ASSOCIATES

https://stromlawyers.com

STROM & ASSOCIATES ANNUAL SCHOLARSHIP

• *See page 671*

STUDY.COM

study.com

ARMY ROTC STUDY.COM SCHOLARSHIP

• *See page 671*

STUDY.COM CLEP SCHOLARSHIP

• *See page 671*

STUDY.COM SCHOLARSHIP FOR FLORIDA STUDENTS

• *See page 671*

STUDY.COM SCHOLARSHIP FOR TEXAS STUDENTS

• *See page 671*

SUPERCOLLEGE.COM

http://www.supercollege.com/

$1,500 SUPERCOLLEGE.COM SCHOLARSHIP

An award for outstanding high school, college or graduate students. Based on academic and extracurricular achievement, leadership, and integrity. May study any major and attend or plan to attend any accredited college or university in the United States. No paper applications accepted. Applications are only available online at http://www.supercollege.com/scholarship/.

Award: Scholarship for use in freshman, sophomore, junior, senior, or graduate years; not renewable. *Number:* 1–5. *Amount:* $500–$1500.

Eligibility Requirements: Applicant must be enrolled or expecting to enroll full-time at a two-year or four-year or technical institution or university and must have an interest in leadership. Available to U.S. citizens.

Application Requirements: Application form. *Deadline:* continuous.

Contact: Scholarship Coordinator
Phone: 650-618-2221
E-mail: supercollege@supercollege.com

SWISS BENEVOLENT SOCIETY OF NEW YORK

http://www.sbsny.org/

MEDICUS STUDENT EXCHANGE
• *See page 763*

TECHNOSOFT INNOVATIONS, INC.

https://www.technosoftinv.com/

TECHNOSOFT INNOVATIONS SCHOLARSHIP PROGRAM
• *See page 671*

TELEVISION ACADEMY FOUNDATION

http://www.televisionacademy.com/foundation

TELEVISION ACADEMY FOUNDATION
• *See page 671*

TELIOS LAW PLLC

http://telioslaw.com

TELIOS LAW EXCELSIOR SCHOLARSHIP
• *See page 763*

TELIOS LAW SOJOURNER SCHOLARSHIP
• *See page 763*

TENNESSEE STUDENT ASSISTANCE CORPORATION

http://www.tn.gov/collegepays

HELPING HEROES GRANT
• *See page 672*

HOPE ASPIRE AWARD
• *See page 672*

NED MCWHERTER SCHOLARS PROGRAM
• *See page 672*

TELS -HOPE WITH GENERAL ASSEMBLY MERIT SCHOLARSHIP (GAMS)
• *See page 672*

TENNESSEE DUAL ENROLLMENT GRANT
• *See page 672*

TENNESSEE HOPE ACCESS GRANT
• *See page 673*

TENNESSEE HOPE FOSTER CHILD TUITION GRANT
• *See page 673*

TENNESSEE HOPE SCHOLARSHIP
• *See page 673*

TENNESSEE STUDENT ASSISTANCE AWARD
• *See page 673*

TERRY FOUNDATION

http://www.terryfoundation.org/

TERRY FOUNDATION SCHOLARSHIP
• *See page 871*

TERRY FOUNDATION TRANSFER SCHOLARSHIP
• *See page 871*

TETHERBOX

http://www.tetherbox.com/

$1,000 CREATIVE VIDEO CHALLENGE COLLEGE SCHOLARSHIP
• *See page 673*

TEXAS 4-H YOUTH DEVELOPMENT FOUNDATION

http://texas4hfoundation.org/

TEXAS 4-H OPPORTUNITY SCHOLARSHIP
• *See page 871*

TEXAS ASSOCIATION OF DEVELOPING COLLEGES

http://www.txadc.org

THE URBAN SCHOLARSHIPS FUND
• *See page 674*

TEXAS MUTUAL INSURANCE COMPANY

http://www.texasmutual.com/

TEXAS MUTUAL INSURANCE COMPANY SCHOLARSHIP PROGRAM
• *See page 674*

TEXAS OUTDOOR WRITERS ASSOCIATION

http://www.towa.org/

TEXAS OUTDOOR WRITERS ASSOCIATION SCHOLARSHIP
• *See page 872*

TEXAS TENNIS FOUNDATION

http://www.texastennisfoundation.com/

TEXAS TENNIS FOUNDATION SCHOLARSHIPS AND ENDOWMENTS
• *See page 872*

THRIVENT STUDENT RESOURCES

https://www.thriventstudentresources.com/

THRIVENT STUDENT RESOURCES SCHOLARSHIP
• *See page 674*

TKE EDUCATIONAL FOUNDATION

http://www.tke.org/

CHARLES J. TRABOLD SCHOLARSHIP
• *See page 579*

CHARLES R. WALGREEN, JR. LEADERSHIP AWARD
• *See page 580*

CHARLES R. WALGREEN, JR. SCHOLARSHIP AWARD
• *See page 580*

CHRISTOPHER GRASSO SCHOLARSHIP
- *See page 580*

DONALD A. AND JOHN R. FISHER MEMORIAL SCHOLARSHIP
- *See page 580*

DORIS AND ELMER H. SCHMITZ, SR. MEMORIAL SCHOLARSHIP
- *See page 580*

DWAYNE R. WOERPEL MEMORIAL LEADERSHIP SCHOLARSHIP
- *See page 580*

EUGENE C. BEACH MEMORIAL SCHOLARSHIP
- *See page 581*

FATHER TIMOTHY VAKOC MEMORIAL SCHOLARSHIP
- *See page 581*

GABE ANAYA SCHOLARSHIP
- *See page 581*

J.D. WILLIAMS SCHOLARSHIP
- *See page 581*

JOHN A. COURSON SCHOLARSHIP
- *See page 581*

J. RUSSEL SALSBURY MEMORIAL SCHOLARSHIP
- *See page 581*

KENNETH L. DUKE, SR. MEMORIAL SCHOLARSHIP
- *See page 581*

LENWOOD S. COCHRAN SCHOLARSHIP
- *See page 582*

LON G. JUSTICE SCHOLARSHIP
- *See page 582*

MICHAEL CERUSSI LEADERSHIP SCHOLARSHIP
- *See page 582*

MICHAEL J. MORIN MEMORIAL SCHOLARSHIP
- *See page 582*

MILES GRAY MEMORIAL SCHOLARSHIP
- *See page 582*

RONALD REAGAN LEADERSHIP AWARD
- *See page 583*

T.J. SCHMITZ SCHOLARSHIP
- *See page 583*

TKE SERVANT LEADERSHIP SCHOLARSHIP
- *See page 583*

WALLACE MCCAULEY MEMORIAL SCHOLARSHIP
- *See page 583*

WILLIAM V. MUSE SCHOLARSHIP
- *See page 583*

WILLIAM WILSON MEMORIAL SCHOLARSHIP
- *See page 583*

TONALAW

https://www.tonalaw.com/

TONALAW VETERAN'S SCHOLARSHIP
- *See page 674*

TOPPRODUCTS.COM

http://topproducts.com/

TOPPRODUCTS SINGLE MOTHER SCHOLARSHIP
- *See page 675*

TORHOERMAN LAW LLC

http://torhoermanlaw.com

TORHOERMAN LAW DISTRACTED DRIVING ESSAY SCHOLARSHIP
- *See page 675*

TOSHIBA/NSTA

http://www.exploravision.org/

EXPLORAVISION SCIENCE COMPETITION

Competition for students in grades K-12 who enter as small teams by grade level and work on a science project. In each group, first place team members are each awarded a savings bond worth $10,000 at maturity, second place, a $5000 savings bond. Deadline varies.

Award: Prize for use in freshman year; not renewable. *Amount:* $5000–$10,000.

Eligibility Requirements: Applicant must be enrolled or expecting to enroll full- or part-time at a four-year institution or university and must have an interest in science. Available to U.S. citizens.

Application Requirements: Application form, entry in a contest. *Deadline:* varies.

Contact: Paloma Olbes, Media Contact
Phone: 212-388-1400
E-mail: polbes@dba-pr.com

TOURO SYNAGOGUE FOUNDATION

http://www.tourosynagogue.org/

AARON AND RITA SLOM SCHOLARSHIP FUND FOR FREEDOM AND DIVERSITY

Scholarship available for high school seniors who plan to enroll in an institute of higher learning for a minimum of 6 credits. Entries should include an interpretative work focusing on the historic "George Washington Letter to the Congregation" in context with the present time. Text of the letter is available on the website. Submissions may be in the form of an essay, story or poem. Applications, guidelines, resource materials are available on website http://www.tourosynagogue.org

Award: Scholarship for use in freshman year; not renewable. *Number:* 2–4. *Amount:* $500–$1000.

Eligibility Requirements: Applicant must be high school student; planning to enroll or expecting to enroll full- or part-time at a two-year or four-year or technical institution or university and must have an interest in writing. Available to U.S. citizens.

Application Requirements: Application form. *Deadline:* April 20.

Contact: Ms. Meryle Cawley
Touro Synagogue Foundation
85 Touro Street
Newport, RI 02840
Phone: 401-847-4794 Ext. 207
E-mail: tours@tourosynagogue.org

TPA SCHOLARSHIP TRUST FOR THE HEARING IMPAIRED

https://www.tpahq.org/scholarshiptrust/

TPA SCHOLARSHIP TRUST FOR THE HEARING IMPAIRED
- *See page 675*

TRANSFER TIMES

http://www.transfertimes.com

TRANSFER TIMES $6,000 SCHOLARSHIP
- *See page 675*

TRANSTUTORS

http://www.transtutors.com/scholarship

TRANSTUTORS SCHOLARSHIP
- *See page 675*

TRAVELNURSESOURCE.COM

https://www.travelnursesource.com/

FUTURE U.S. NURSE SCHOLARSHIP
- *See page 676*

TROPHYCENTRAL INC.

https://www.trophycentral.com

TROPHYCENTRAL SPORTSMANSHIP AND COMPASSION SCHOLARSHIP AWARD
- *See page 676*

TURBOSQUID

https://www.turbosquid.com/

TURBOSQUID SPRING SCHOLARSHIP
- *See page 676*

ULMAN CANCER FUND FOR YOUNG ADULTS

http://www.ulmanfund.org/scholarships

JACQUELINE SHEARER MEMORIAL SCHOLARSHIP
- *See page 677*

JAMIE L. ROBERTS MEMORIAL SCHOLARSHIP AWARD
- *See page 677*

JEFFREY P. MEYER MEMORIAL SCHOLARSHIP
- *See page 677*

JILL WEAVER STARKMAN SCHOLARSHIP
- *See page 677*

JOHN HANLEY MEMORIAL SCHOLARSHIP
- *See page 678*

LISA HIGGINS-HUSSMAN FOUNDATION SCHOLARSHIP
- *See page 678*

MARILYN YETSO MEMORIAL SCHOLARSHIP
- *See page 678*

OLIVIA M. MARQUART SCHOLARSHIP
- *See page 678*

PERLITA LIWANAG MEMORIAL SCHOLARSHIP
- *See page 678*

SATOLA FAMILY SCHOLARSHIP
- *See page 678*

SEAN SILVER MEMORIAL SCHOLARSHIP AWARD
- *See page 678*

VERA YIP MEMORIAL SCHOLARSHIP
- *See page 679*

VITTORIA DIANNA RICARDO MEMORIAL SCHOLARSHIP
- *See page 679*

UNICO FOUNDATION INC.

http://www.unico.org/

ALPHONSE A. MIELE SCHOLARSHIP
- *See page 679*

BERNARD AND CAROLYN TORRACO MEMORIAL NURSING SCHOLARSHIP PROGRAM
- *See page 679*

DIMATTIO CELLI FAMILY STUDY ABROAD SCHOLARSHIP
- *See page 679*

ELLA T. GRASSO LITERARY SCHOLARSHIP
- *See page 680*

GUGLIELMO MARCONI ENGINEERING SCHOLARSHIP
- *See page 680*

INSERRA SCHOLARSHIPS
- *See page 680*

MAJOR DON S. GENTILE SCHOLARSHIP
- *See page 680*

MARIA AND PAOLO ALESSIO SOUTHERN ITALY SCHOLARSHIP
- *See page 680*

RALPH J. TORRACO SCHOLARSHIP
- *See page 680*

THEODORE MAZZA SCHOLARSHIP
- *See page 681*

WILLIAM C. DAVINI SCHOLARSHIP
- *See page 681*

UNION PLUS SCHOLARSHIP PROGRAM

http://www.unionplus.org/

UNION PLUS EDUCATION FOUNDATION SCHOLARSHIP PROGRAM
- *See page 584*

UNITED STATES BOWLING CONGRESS

http://www.bowl.com/

GIFT FOR LIFE SCHOLARSHIP
- *See page 585*

USBC ALBERTA E. CROWE STAR OF TOMORROW AWARD
• *See page 585*

USBC ANNUAL ZEB SCHOLARSHIP
• *See page 585*

USBC CHUCK HALL STAR OF TOMORROW SCHOLARSHIP
• *See page 586*

USBC EARL ANTHONY MEMORIAL SCHOLARSHIP
• *See page 586*

USBC YOUTH AMBASSADOR OF THE YEAR (M/F)
• *See page 586*

UNITED TRANSPORTATION UNION INSURANCE ASSOCIATION
http://www.utuia.org/

UTUIA SCHOLARSHIP
• *See page 681*

UNIVERSITY CONSORTIUM FOR LIBERIA
http://ucliberia.com/

JOSEPH N. BOAKAI SR. HIGHER EDUCATION SCHOLARSHIP
• *See page 681*

U.S. COAST GUARD
http://www.gocoastguard/cspi

COLLEGE STUDENT PRE-COMMISSIONING INITIATIVE (CSPI)
• *See page 681*

VALUEPENGUIN
http://www.valuepenguin.com

VALUEPENGUIN SCHOLARSHIP
• *See page 682*

VANILLA PILGRIM FOUNDATION
https://www.vanillapilgrim.com/

2018 OPEN ESSAY COMPETITION
• *See page 682*

VETERANAID.ORG
https://www.veteranaid.org

VETERAN BENEFITS SCHOLARSHIP
• *See page 682*

VETERANS OF FOREIGN WARS OF THE UNITED STATES
http://www.vfw.org/

VOICE OF DEMOCRACY PROGRAM
Student must be sponsored by a local VFW Post. Student submits a three to five minute audio essay on a contest theme (changes each year). Open to high school students (9th to 12th grade). Award available for all levels of postsecondary study in an American institution. Open to permanent U.S. residents only. Competition starts at local level. No entries are to be submitted to the National Headquarters. Visit website https://www.vfw.org/VOD/ for more information.

Award: Scholarship for use in freshman, sophomore, junior, senior, graduate, or postgraduate years; not renewable. *Number:* 54. *Amount:* $1000–$30,000.

Eligibility Requirements: Applicant must be high school student; age 14-19; planning to enroll or expecting to enroll full- or part-time at a two-year or four-year or technical institution or university and must have an interest in public speaking or writing. Available to U.S. citizens.

Application Requirements: Application form, essay. *Deadline:* October 31.

Contact: Kris Harmer, Program Coordinator
Veterans of Foreign Wars of the United States
406 West 34th Street
Kansas City, MO 64111
Phone: 816-968-1117
Fax: 816-968-1149
E-mail: kharmer@vfw.org

VETERANS UNITED FOUNDATION
http://www.enhancelives.com

VETERANS UNITED FOUNDATION SCHOLARSHIP
• *See page 682*

VSA
http://www.kennedy-center.org/education/vsa/

VSA PLAYWRIGHT DISCOVERY AWARD
Young writers with disabilities and collaborative groups that include students with disabilities, in U.S. grades 6-12 (or equivalents) or ages 11-18 for non-U.S. students, are invited to explore the disability experience through the art of writing for performance: plays, screenplays, spoken word poetry (for single performer or a group), or music theater. Writers are encouraged to craft short works from their own experiences and observations, create fictional characters and settings, or choose to write metaphorically or abstractly about the disability experience.

Award: Prize for use in freshman year; not renewable. *Number:* 1.

Eligibility Requirements: Applicant must be high school student; planning to enroll or expecting to enroll full- or part-time at an institution or university and must have an interest in theater or writing. Available to U.S. citizens.

Application Requirements: Application form. *Deadline:* February 1.

Contact: Megan Bailey, Administrative Assistant
VSA
2700 F St NW
Washington, DC 20566
Phone: 202-416-8822
E-mail: vsainfo@kennedy-center.org

WALTER W. NAUMBURG FOUNDATION
http://www.naumburg.org/

INTERNATIONAL VIOLONCELLO COMPETITION
Prizes of $2500 to $7500 awarded to violoncellists between the ages of 17 and 31. Application fee is $125.

Award: Prize for use in freshman, sophomore, junior, senior, graduate, or postgraduate years; not renewable. *Number:* 3. *Amount:* $2500–$7500.

Eligibility Requirements: Applicant must be age 17-31; enrolled or expecting to enroll full- or part-time at a two-year or four-year or technical institution or university and must have an interest in music. Available to U.S. and non-U.S. citizens.

Application Requirements: Applicant's audio track (CD) of no less than 30 minutes, application form, entry in a contest, recommendations or references, self-addressed stamped envelope with application. *Fee:* $125. *Deadline:* March 1.

Contact: Lucy Mann, Executive Director
Phone: 212-362-9877
Fax: 212-362-9877
E-mail: luciamann@aol.com

WARD LAW GROUP, PL

http://thecoveragelawyer.com/

WARD LAW GROUP BETTER FUTURE SCHOLARSHIP
• *See page 682*

WESTERN INTERSTATE COMMISSION FOR HIGHER EDUCATION

http://www.wiche.edu/

WICHE'S WESTERN UNDERGRADUATE EXCHANGE (WUE)
• *See page 683*

WHITLEY LAW FIRM

https://whitleylawfirm.com/

WHITLEY LAW FIRM OPIOID CRISIS SCHOLARSHIP
• *See page 683*

WILLIAM G. AND MARIE SELBY FOUNDATION

http://www.selbyfdn.org/

SELBY SCHOLAR PROGRAM
• *See page 877*

WILLIAM RANDOLPH HEARST FOUNDATION

http://www.hearstfdn.org/

UNITED STATES SENATE YOUTH PROGRAM

Scholarship for high school juniors and seniors holding elected student offices. Two students selected from each state. Selection process will vary by state. Contact school principal or state department of education for information. Deadlines: early fall of each year for most states, but specific date will vary by state (see website http://www.ussenateyouth.org). Program is open to citizens of the United States Department of Defense schools overseas and the District of Columbia (not the territories).

Award: Scholarship for use in freshman, sophomore, junior, or senior years; not renewable. *Number:* 104. *Amount:* $10,000.

Eligibility Requirements: Applicant must be high school student; planning to enroll or expecting to enroll full-time at a two-year or four-year institution or university; single; studying in Alabama, Alaska, Arizona, Arkansas, California, Colorado, Connecticut, Delaware, District of Columbia, Florida, Georgia, Hawaii, Idaho, Illinois, Indiana, Iowa, Kansas, Kentucky, Louisiana, Maine, Maryland, Massachusetts, Michigan, Minnesota, Mississippi, Missouri, Montana, Nebraska, Nevada, New Hampshire, New Jersey, New Mexico, New York, North Carolina, North Dakota, Ohio, Oklahoma, Oregon, Pennsylvania, Rhode Island, South Carolina, South Dakota, Tennessee, Texas, Utah, Vermont, Virginia, Washington, West Virginia, Wisconsin, Wyoming and must have an interest in leadership or public speaking. Applicant must have 3.0 GPA or higher. Available to U.S. citizens.

Application Requirements: Application form, essay, interview.

Contact: Lynn DeSmet, Deputy Program Director
William Randolph Hearst Foundation
90 New Montgomery Street
Suite 1212
San Francisco, CA 94105
Phone: 415-908-4540
E-mail: ussyp@hearstfdn.org

WOLTERMAN LAW OFFICE, LPA

https://www.woltermanlaw.com/

WOLTERMAN LAW OFFICE LPA HOPE FOR THE FUTURE SCHOLARSHIP
• *See page 683*

WOMEN MARINES ASSOCIATION

http://www.womenmarines.org

ETHYL AND ARMIN WIEBKE MEMORIAL SCHOLARSHIPS
• *See page 683*

THE LILY H. GRIDLEY MEMORIAL SCHOLARSHIP
• *See page 683*

WMA MEMORIAL SCHOLARSHIPS
• *See page 683*

WOMEN'S BASKETBALL COACHES ASSOCIATION

http://www.wbca.org/

WBCA SCHOLARSHIP AWARD

One-time award for two women's basketball players who have demonstrated outstanding commitment to the sport of women's basketball and to academic excellence. Minimum 3.5 GPA required. Must be nominated by the head coach of women's basketball who is WBCA member.

Award: Scholarship for use in freshman, sophomore, junior, senior, or graduate years; not renewable. *Number:* up to 2. *Amount:* up to $1000.

Eligibility Requirements: Applicant must be enrolled or expecting to enroll full- or part-time at a four-year institution or university; female and must have an interest in athletics/sports. Applicant must have 3.5 GPA or higher. Available to U.S. and non-U.S. citizens.

Application Requirements: Application form, recommendations or references, statistics. *Deadline:* February 15.

Contact: Betty Jaynes, Consultant
Phone: 770-279-8027 Ext. 102
Fax: 770-279-6290
E-mail: bettyj@wbca.org

WOMEN'S JEWELRY ASSOCIATION

http://www.womensjewelryassociation.com

MEMBER GRANTS
• *See page 684*

WOMEN'S JEWELRY ASSOCIATIONS VETERANS GRANT
• *See page 684*

WOMEN'S WESTERN GOLF FOUNDATION

http://www.wwga.org/foundation.htm

WOMEN'S WESTERN GOLF FOUNDATION SCHOLARSHIP

Scholarships for female high school seniors for use at a four-year college or university. Based on academic record, financial need, character, and involvement in golf. Golf skill not a criteria. Must continue to have financial need. Award is $2000 per student per year. Must be 17 to 18 years of age.

Award: Scholarship for use in freshman year; renewable. *Number:* 20–70. *Amount:* $2000.

Eligibility Requirements: Applicant must be high school student; age 17-18; planning to enroll or expecting to enroll full-time at a four-year institution or university; female and must have an interest in golf. Applicant must have 3.0 GPA or higher. Available to U.S. citizens.

Application Requirements: Application form. *Deadline:* March 1.

Contact: David Grady, President
Phone: 817-265-4074
E-mail: grady@orderofomega.org

WRITER'S DIGEST

http://www.writersdigest.com/

WRITER'S DIGEST ANNUAL WRITING COMPETITION

Annual writing competition. Only original, unpublished entries in any of the ten categories accepted. Visit http://www.writersdigest.com/competitions/writers-digest-annual-competition for guidelines and entry form. Application fee.

Award: Prize for use in freshman, sophomore, junior, senior, or graduate years; not renewable. *Number:* 501. *Amount:* $100–$3000.

Eligibility Requirements: Applicant must be enrolled or expecting to enroll full- or part-time at a two-year or four-year or technical institution or university and must have an interest in writing. Available to U.S. and non-U.S. citizens.

Application Requirements: Application form, application form may be submitted online, entry in a contest. *Deadline:* May 1.

Contact: Nicole Howard, Customer Service Representative
Phone: 715-445-4612
Fax: 513-531-0798
E-mail: writing-competitions@fwmedia.com

WRITER'S DIGEST POPULAR FICTION AWARDS

Writing contest accepts as many manuscripts as the applicant likes in each of the following categories: romance, mystery/crime fiction, sci-fi/fantasy, thriller/suspense and horror. Manuscripts must not be more than 4,000 words. http://www.writersdigest.com/popularfictionawards

Award: Prize for use in freshman, sophomore, junior, senior, graduate, or postgraduate years; not renewable. *Number:* 7. *Amount:* $500–$2500.

Eligibility Requirements: Applicant must be enrolled or expecting to enroll full- or part-time at a two-year or four-year or technical institution or university and must have an interest in writing. Available to U.S. and non-U.S. citizens.

Application Requirements: Application form, entry in a contest, manuscript. *Fee:* $20. *Deadline:* September 1.

Contact: Nicole Howard, Customer Service Representative
Phone: 715-445-4612 Ext. 13430
Fax: 513-531-0798
E-mail: writing-competitions@fwmedia.com

WRITER'S DIGEST SELF-PUBLISHED BOOK AWARDS

Awards open to self-published books for which the author has paid full cost. Visit http://www.writersdigest.com/competitions/selfpublished/ for guidelines and entry form. Application fee: $99.

Award: Prize for use in freshman, sophomore, junior, senior, graduate, or postgraduate years; not renewable. *Number:* 45. *Amount:* $1000–$3000.

Eligibility Requirements: Applicant must be enrolled or expecting to enroll full- or part-time at a two-year or four-year or technical institution or university and must have an interest in writing. Available to U.S. and non-U.S. citizens.

Application Requirements: Application form, entry in a contest. *Fee:* $99. *Deadline:* April 1.

Contact: Nicole Howard, Customer Service Representative
Phone: 715-445-4612 Ext. 13430
Fax: 513-531-0798
E-mail: writing-competitions@fwmedia.com

YORKVILLE GOODS LLC

http://yorkvilleblankets.com/

YORKVILLE BLANKETS ASD SCHOLARSHIP
• *See page 684*

ZELUS RECOVERY

http://zelusrecovery.com/

ZELUS RECOVERY $1000 COLLEGE SCHOLARSHIP
• *See page 684*

ZIPRECRUITER

https://www.ziprecruiter.com/

ZIPRECRUITER $3,000 SCHOLARSHIP
• *See page 685*

Miscellaneous Criteria

101ST AIRBORNE DIVISION ASSOCIATION

http://www.screamingeaglefoundation.org/

101ST AIRBORNE DIVISION ASSOCIATION CHAPPIE HALL SCHOLARSHIP PROGRAM

Scholarship to provide financial assistance to students who have the potential to become assets to our nation. The major factors to be considered in the evaluation and rating of applicants are eligibility, career objectives, academic record, financial need, and insight gained from the letter and/or essay requesting consideration, and letters of recommendation. Applicant's parents, grandparents, or spouse, living or deceased must be/had been a regular member with 101st Airborne Division Association in good standing. Dollar amount and total number of awards varies.

Award: Scholarship for use in freshman, sophomore, junior, or senior years; not renewable. *Number:* 15–30. *Amount:* $1000–$2000.

Eligibility Requirements: Applicant must be enrolled or expecting to enroll full-time at a two-year or four-year or technical institution or university. Applicant must have 2.5 GPA or higher. Available to U.S. and non-U.S. citizens.

Application Requirements: Application form, community service, essay, personal photograph. *Deadline:* May 11.

Contact: Mr. Randal Underhill, Executive Director
101st Airborne Division Association
PO Box 929
Fort Campbell, KY 42223-0929
Phone: 931-431-0199 Ext. 35
E-mail: 101exec@comcast.net

1800WHEELCHAIR.COM

http://www.1800wheelchair.com/

1800WHEELCHAIR.COM SCHOLARSHIP

Established in 2006, the 1800wheelchair scholarship fund now bestows two $500 awards each year. We are going to repeat our visual contest. Please submit a 'visual poem', in a style of your choosing, on the theme of overcoming a personal challenge. Limit your 'visual poem' to an 8.5in x 11in piece of paper. You can choose to represent words, images, or both. It can abstract or representational. Please include a personal statement that gives us an idea of who you are and how your poem relates to a challenge you've faced. The poem and essay (combined) should be between 500 and 1,000 words, but feel free to write a little more or less. http://www.1800wheelchair.com/scholarship/

Award: Prize for use in freshman, sophomore, junior, or senior years; renewable. *Number:* 1. *Amount:* $500.

Eligibility Requirements: Applicant must be enrolled or expecting to enroll full-time at a two-year or four-year or technical institution or university. Applicant must have 3.0 GPA or higher. Available to U.S. citizens.

Application Requirements: Essay, personal photograph, portfolio. *Deadline:* May 1.

Contact: Mr. Joseph Piekarski, President
1800Wheelchair.com
320 Roebling Street
Suite 515
Brooklyn, NY 11211
E-mail: scholarship@1800wheelchair.com

365 DATA SCIENCE

https://365datascience.com

ARTIFICIAL INTELLIGENCE & ETHICS SCHOLARSHIP

We are surrounded by artificial intelligence. After all, this is the age of big data and machine learning. Granted, our AIs don't go around on their own; they go around through us–in our pockets, in our cars, in our homes. From the Google search engine, to personal assistants like Siri, Cortana, and Google Assistant, to our own Facebook feed. We not only tolerate artificial intelligence, but we inadvertently depend on it with our studies, work, personal relationships, and consumer decisions. As AI becomes an increasingly indispensable part of human existence, we will be confronted with a looming issue. That of ethics. Artificial Intelligence promises business, technological, and healthcare improvements, but it also paves the way for advanced warfare and countless socio-economic issues. There is a thin line between useful and harmful, if there is even a line at all. Especially considering that an action need not be harmful to have harmful consequences. It seems to us at 365 Data Science that the pillars of the debate about ethics in AI are made up of four concepts: autonomy, trust, power, and accountability. While the phrase "Artificial Intelligence and Ethics" constitutes interesting dinner conversation, the oral debate has its limitations. Given the weight of the topic, we would like you to consider the benefits of the short essay for this discussion: brief, argumentative, and expressive. For the full description, visit our scholarship page: https://365datascience.com/scholarship/. In order to be eligible for the scholarship, you need to 1. submit a 1,000–2,000 word essay on the essay topic set above (word or pdf document), 2. fill out the survey (at the bottom of our scholarship page, 3. email your essay to scholarship@365datascience.com along with the following personal details: full name, country of residence, university (college), area of study. The deadline for submissions is February 28, 2018. Essays sent after the submission deadline will not be considered.

Award: Scholarship for use in freshman, sophomore, junior, senior, graduate, or postgraduate years; not renewable. *Number:* 3. *Amount:* $200–$1000.

Eligibility Requirements: Applicant must be enrolled or expecting to enroll full- or part-time at a two-year or four-year or technical institution or university. Available to U.S. and non-U.S. citizens.

Application Requirements: Essay. *Deadline:* February 28.

Contact: Iliya Valchanov, Co-founder of 365 Data Science
365 Data Science
1, Hristo Belchev str.
Sofia 1000
Phone: 359-889338338
E-mail: iliya.valchanov@365datascience.com

37TH DIVISION VETERANS ASSOCIATION

http://www.37thdva.org/

37TH DIVISION VETERANS ASSOCIATION SCHOLARSHIP GRANT PROGRAM

Must be a current member of the organization in good standing or be the direct lineal descendant (to the third generation) of such a member. Please visit http://www.37thdva.org to see a copy of the application and to determine eligibility. Please note that the 37th Infantry Division was part of the U.S. Army.

Award: Scholarship for use in freshman, sophomore, junior, senior, graduate, or postgraduate years; not renewable.

Eligibility Requirements: Applicant must be enrolled or expecting to enroll full-time at a two-year or four-year or technical institution or university. Available to U.S. citizens.

Application Requirements: Application form, community service, essay. *Deadline:* May 1.

Contact: Mandy Oberyszyn, Executive Director
37th Division Veterans Association
35 East Chestnut Street, Suite 512
Columbus, OH 43215
Phone: 614-228-3788
E-mail: mandy@37thdva.org

A1 GARAGE DOOR SERVICE

http://www.phoenixazgaragedoorrepair.com/

A1 GARAGE DOOR SERVICE COLLEGE SCHOLARSHIP

Ongoing scholarship for $1000, that will be awarded twice annually. Next deadline in July 15, 2015. In addition to the online application, the applicant must submit a an essay (600 words or more) or video which shows a students best idea for a marketing campaign in the service industry. One submission, per student, per semester. Essays/Videos may be features on our website, Facebook page, blog or other social media accounts.

Award: Scholarship for use in freshman, sophomore, junior, or senior years; not renewable. *Number:* 1. *Amount:* $1000.

Eligibility Requirements: Applicant must be enrolled or expecting to enroll full-time at a four-year institution. Applicant must have 2.5 GPA or higher. Available to U.S. citizens.

Application Requirements: Application form, essay. *Deadline:* continuous.

Contact: Tommy Mello
E-mail: tommy.mello.social@gmail.com

ACBL EDUCATIONAL FOUNDATION

https://sites.google.com/site/acbleducationfoundationorg/

KING OR QUEEN OF BRIDGE SCHOLARSHIP

The King or Queen of Bridge Scholarship is a merit program available to a graduating high school senior that is a member of The American Contract Bridge League (ACBL) and who plays and promotes bridge. The ACBL Educational Foundation will present a scholarship up to $2000 to the King or Queen of Bridge. Recent winners have been cited for outstanding tournament performances plus administrative, recreational and promotional activities related to bridge. Application can be found at http://www.acbl.org/kingofbridge

Award: Scholarship for use in freshman year; not renewable. *Number:* 1–2. *Amount:* $1000–$2000.

Eligibility Requirements: Applicant must be high school student and planning to enroll or expecting to enroll full- or part-time at a two-year or four-year or technical institution or university. Available to U.S. and non-U.S. citizens.

Application Requirements: Application form. *Deadline:* May 31.

Contact: Flo Belford, Grant Administrator
E-mail: edfoundation@acbl.org

ACES: THE SOCIETY FOR EDITING

https://aceseditors.org/

ACES EDUCATION FUND SCHOLARSHIPS

Scholarships available to undergraduate students entering their junior or senior year, graduate students, and just-graduating students. Students should be aspiring to be professional editors.

Award: Scholarship for use in junior, senior, or graduate years; not renewable. *Number:* 5. *Amount:* $1500–$2500.

Eligibility Requirements: Applicant must be enrolled or expecting to enroll full-time at a four-year institution or university. Available to U.S. and non-U.S. citizens.

Application Requirements: Application form, essay. *Deadline:* November 15.

Contact: Alex Cruden
E-mail: alex@aceseditors.org

ACTIVIA TRAINING

https://www.activia.co.uk/

ACTIVIA TRAINING US SCHOLARSHIP

Activia Training are pleased to offer a $1,500 annual scholarship for college, university, high school or trade school students in the US. There are two scholarship awards of $750 each year, awarded in November and May, and there is no specific course of study required in order to enter.

Award: Scholarship for use in freshman, sophomore, junior, senior, graduate, or postgraduate years; not renewable. *Number:* 4. *Amount:* $250–$500.

Eligibility Requirements: Applicant must be enrolled or expecting to enroll full- or part-time at a two-year or four-year or technical institution or university. Available to U.S. and non-U.S. citizens.

Application Requirements: Application form. *Deadline:* continuous.

Contact: Ashley Andrews
E-mail: ashleyandrews@activia.co.uk

ACTUALITY MEDIA, LLC

http://www.actualitymedia.org

CHANGEMAKER IN YOUR COMMUNITY DOCUMENTARY COMPETITION

On a Documentary Outreach with Actuality Media, crews work in groups of 3-5 people to research, write, shoot and edit a 10-minute-or-less Documentary Short focused on the work of a local changemaker. Crew members serve as Producer, Director, Editor, Cinematographer or Sound Design. In 2018, our Outreach locations are Guatemala, India, Cambodia and Zambia. The winner of the Changemaker in Your Community Documentary Competition will be able to select any one Outreach location to participate in, to have the full Participation Fee covered by your scholarship.

Award: Scholarship for use in freshman, sophomore, junior, senior, graduate, or postgraduate years; not renewable. *Number:* 1. *Amount:* $3100–$3500.

Eligibility Requirements: Applicant must be enrolled or expecting to enroll part-time at a technical institution. Available to U.S. and non-U.S. citizens.

Application Requirements: Application form. *Deadline:* March 1.

Contact: Mr. Robin Canfield, International Programs Director
Phone: 503-208-5042
E-mail: info@actualitymedia.org

ACUITY TRAINING LIMITED

http://www.acuitytraining.co.uk

ACUITY TRAINING SCHOLARSHIP FOR OUTSTANDING LEADERSHIP AWARD

You have a chance to win a scholarship for $1000. Your video entry should ideally be three to four minutes in length. We want you to include some of the following ideas: A) What is leadership? Why is it valuable and how can it be developed? What is the difference between leadership, management and assertiveness?, B) Examples of how and when you have shown leadership and the benefits that have flowed from that, and C) The importance of leadership qualities in the 21st century workplace? The best submission will be awarded $1000 that can be used to further their education. This award is only available to students that are currently enrolled at a college, university, high school or trade school.

Award: Scholarship for use in freshman, sophomore, junior, senior, graduate, or postgraduate years; not renewable. *Number:* 1. *Amount:* $1000.

Eligibility Requirements: Applicant must be enrolled or expecting to enroll full- or part-time at a two-year or four-year or technical institution or university. Available to U.S. and non-U.S. citizens.

Application Requirements: Application form may be submitted online (http://www.acuitytraining.co.uk/scholarships/), video. *Deadline:* December 31.

Contact: Ben Richardson
Phone: 44-1483688488
E-mail: scholarships@acuitytraining.co.uk

ALFRED G. AND ELMA M. MILOTTE SCHOLARSHIP FUND

http://www.milotte.org/

ALFRED G. AND ELMA M. MILOTTE SCHOLARSHIP

Grant of up to $4000 to high school graduate or students holding the GED. Applicants must have been accepted at a trade school, art school, two-year or four-year college or university for undergraduate or graduate studies.

Award: Scholarship for use in freshman, sophomore, junior, senior, or graduate years; not renewable. *Amount:* up to $4000.

Eligibility Requirements: Applicant must be enrolled or expecting to enroll full- or part-time at a two-year or four-year or technical institution or university. Applicant must have 3.0 GPA or higher. Available to U.S. citizens.

Application Requirements: Application form, recommendations or references, samples of work expressing applicant's observations of the natural world, transcript. *Deadline:* March 1.

Contact: Sean Ferguson, Assistant Vice President
Phone: 800-832-9071
Fax: 800-552-3182
E-mail: info@milotte.org

ALL ABOUT CATS

http://www.allaboutcats.com

A VOICE FOR CATS ESSAY CONTEST SCHOLARSHIP

We at All About Cats are pleased to announce our very first annual A Voice For Cats scholarship contest with a prize of $1000. In our online cat community we strongly believe that enabling access to continuing higher education is very important. We strive to educate and inform our followers, so as to mitigate feline suffering and make the lives of our beloved pets better. Small steps are often necessary to achieve this ideal goal of minimizing pain and distress for our beloved kitties. We at All About Cats will grant a scholarship to one student who will provide the most outstanding essay about any topic, that would give us interesting insight with relation to our community interests. The winning essay will be published on our blog and accredited to the author. There are a growing number of incidents where the mistreatment and suffering of both outdoor and domesticated cats is being overlooked. Help us raise awareness about this issue that is dear to us, by entering the contest and submitting your essay on how to best promote the most humane treatment of felines.

Award: Scholarship for use in freshman, sophomore, junior, senior, graduate, or postgraduate years; not renewable. *Number:* 1. *Amount:* $1000.

Eligibility Requirements: Applicant must be enrolled or expecting to enroll full- or part-time at an institution or university. Available to U.S. and non-U.S. citizens.

Application Requirements: Essay. *Deadline:* April 30.

Contact: Ron Wolff
Phone: 844-873-2876
E-mail: scholarships@wwwallaboutcats.com

ALL-INK.COM PRINTER SUPPLIES ONLINE

ALL-INK.COM COLLEGE SCHOLARSHIP PROGRAM

One-time award for any level of postsecondary education. Minimum 2.5 GPA. Must apply online only at website http://www.all-ink.com. Recipients selected annually.

Award: Scholarship for use in freshman, sophomore, junior, senior, graduate, or postgraduate years; not renewable. *Number:* 5–10. *Amount:* $1000–$5000.

Eligibility Requirements: Applicant must be enrolled or expecting to enroll full-time at a two-year or four-year or technical institution or university. Applicant must have 2.5 GPA or higher. Available to U.S. and non-U.S. citizens.

Application Requirements: Application form, entry in a contest, essay. *Deadline:* December 31.

Contact: Aaron Gale, President
All-Ink.com Printer Supplies Online
1460 North Main Street, Suite 2
Spanish Fork, UT 84660
Phone: 801-794-0123
Fax: 801-794-0124
E-mail: scholarship@all-ink.com

ALPHA KAPPA ALPHA

http://www.akaeaf.org

AKA EDUCATIONAL ADVANCEMENT FOUNDATION, INC. FINANCIAL NEEDS SCHOLARSHIP

Financial needs scholarships are for students who have completed a minimum of one year in a degree-granting institution and have a financial burden that is preventing them from continuing their studies. Students must have a minimum GPA of 2.5 and show evidence of leadership by participating in community or campus activities.

Award: Scholarship for use in sophomore, junior, senior, or graduate years; not renewable.

Eligibility Requirements: Applicant must be enrolled or expecting to enroll full-time at a four-year institution or university. Applicant must have 3.5 GPA or higher. Available to U.S. and non-U.S. citizens.

Application Requirements: Application form, essay, financial need analysis. *Deadline:* continuous.

Contact: Ms. Erika Everett, Executive Director
Alpha Kappa Alpha
5656 South Stony Island
3rd Floor
Chicago, IL 60637
Phone: 773-947-0026
E-mail: eeverett@akaeaf.net

AKA EDUCATIONAL ADVANCEMENT FOUNDATION, INC. MERIT SCHOLARSHIP

Scholarships are for students demonstrating exceptional academic achievements. Applicants must have completed a minimum of one year in a degree-granting institution and will be continuing their program in that institution. Students must have a GPA of 3.0 or higher and show evidence of leadership by participating in community or campus activities.

Award: Scholarship for use in sophomore, junior, senior, or graduate years; not renewable.

Eligibility Requirements: Applicant must be enrolled or expecting to enroll full-time at a four-year institution or university. Applicant must have 3.0 GPA or higher. Available to U.S. and non-U.S. citizens.

Application Requirements: Application form, essay. *Deadline:* continuous.

Contact: Erika Everett, Executive Director
Phone: 773-947-0026
E-mail: akaeaf@akaeaf.net

AKA EDUCATIONAL ADVANCEMENT FOUNDATION, INC. YOUTH PARTNERS ACCESSING CAPITAL SCHOLARSHIP

Youth-PAC awards are for undergraduate members of Alpha Kappa Alpha Sorority, Inc. with at least a sophomore status. Members must have a minimum GPA of 3.0 and participate in leadership, volunteer, civic, or campus activities, as well as demonstrate academic achievements or have a financial need.

Award: Scholarship for use in sophomore, junior, or senior years; not renewable.

Eligibility Requirements: Applicant must be enrolled or expecting to enroll full-time at a four-year institution or university. Applicant must have 3.0 GPA or higher. Available to U.S. and non-U.S. citizens.

Application Requirements: Application form, essay. *Deadline:* April 15.

Contact: Erika Everett, Executive Director
Phone: 773-947-0026
E-mail: akaeaf@akaeaf.net

ALPHA LAMBDA DELTA

http://www.nationalald.org/

JO ANNE J. TROW SCHOLARSHIPS

One-time award for initiated members of Alpha Lambda Delta. Minimum 3.5 GPA required. Must be nominated by chapter.

Award: Scholarship for use in junior year; not renewable. *Number:* 1–36. *Amount:* $1000–$6000.

Eligibility Requirements: Applicant must be enrolled or expecting to enroll full-time at a four-year institution or university. Applicant must have 3.5 GPA or higher. Available to U.S. and non-U.S. citizens.

Application Requirements: Application form, essay. *Deadline:* April 1.

Contact: Eileen Merberg, Executive Director
Alpha Lambda Delta
6800 Pittsford Palmyra Rd
Ste 340
Fairport, NY 14450
Phone: 585-364-0840
E-mail: eileen@nationalald.org

AMBROSIA TREATMENT CENTER

https://www.ambrosiatc.com/?ambTRK=PR

WE DO RECOVER SCHOLARSHIP

Every accomplishment starts with a decision to try. Have you been affected by drug addiction or alcoholism looking to better yourself by continuing your education? Share a positive story of your recovery or the recovery of your loved one. Your story will be featured like the ones above, so use those as an example, but be unique and creative. Then, share on social media! The winner will be selected July 31, 2018, based on the most shares on Facebook or LinkedIn. Please submit the following: a 1,000 word written story, 1-2.5 minute video, and 2+ images of yourself to the survey on our We Do Recover webpage.

Award: Scholarship for use in freshman, sophomore, junior, senior, graduate, or postgraduate years; not renewable. *Number:* 1–3. *Amount:* $500.

Eligibility Requirements: Applicant must be enrolled or expecting to enroll full- or part-time at a two-year or four-year institution or university. Available to U.S. citizens.

Application Requirements: Application form, essay, personal photograph. *Deadline:* July 31.

Contact: Parker Horveath, Digital Marketing Coordinator
E-mail: phorveath@ambrosiatc.com

AMERICAN BULLION, INC.

http://www.americanbullion.com

AMERICAN BULLION SCHOLARSHIP

The American Bullion Scholarship is offered to current college students. Applicants are asked to write a 500-1,000 word essay answering a question regarding precious metals ownership. Winning submissions are selected by a team of executives at American Bullion.

Award: Scholarship for use in freshman, sophomore, junior, senior, graduate, or postgraduate years; not renewable. *Number:* 5. *Amount:* $500.

Eligibility Requirements: Applicant must be enrolled or expecting to enroll full- or part-time at a four-year institution or university. Available to U.S. citizens.

Application Requirements: Application form, application form may be submitted online (https://www.americanbullion.com/scholarship/), essay. *Deadline:* October 31.

Contact: Orkan Ozkan, Chief Executive Officer
American Bullion, Inc.
12301 Wilshire Boulevard, #650
Los Angeles, CA 90025
Phone: 310-689-7720
E-mail: scholarship@americanbullion.com

AMERICAN FIRE SPRINKLER ASSOCIATION

http://www.afsascholarship.org/

AFSA HIGH SCHOOL SCHOLARSHIP CONTEST

One-time award for high school seniors. This scholarship essay contest requires applicants to go online to http://www.afsascholarship.org, and read a short essay about sprinklers and fire safety. After finishing, they complete an eight-question quiz on what they just read. Each correct answer gives the student a chance at winning one of ten $2,000 scholarships (maximum 8 chances per entrant).

Award: Scholarship for use in freshman year; not renewable. *Number:* 10. *Amount:* $2000.

Eligibility Requirements: Applicant must be high school student and planning to enroll or expecting to enroll full-time at a two-year or four-year or technical institution or university. Available to U.S. citizens.

Application Requirements: Application form. *Deadline:* April 1.

Contact: D'Arcy Montalvo, Public Relations Manager
American Fire Sprinkler Association
12750 Merit Drive
Suite 350
Dallas, TX 75251
Phone: 214-349-5965
E-mail: dmontalvo@firesprinkler.org

AFSA SECOND CHANCE SCHOLARSHIP CONTEST

Online entries only. Enter at http://www.afsascholarship.org/ and click on Second Chance Contest; U.S. citizens or legal residents who graduated from U.S. high school may enter. University/trade school/college must be accredited using link provided on Website. No phone calls or emails. Entrants read an online essay and then take online quiz for up to 8 entries into drawing to win.

Award: Scholarship for use in freshman, sophomore, junior, senior, graduate, or postgraduate years; not renewable. *Number:* 5. *Amount:* $1000.

Eligibility Requirements: Applicant must be enrolled or expecting to enroll full-time at a two-year or four-year or technical institution or university. Available to U.S. citizens.

Application Requirements: Application form. *Deadline:* August 30.

Contact: Mrs. D'Arcy Montalvo, PR Manager
American Fire Sprinkler Association
12750 Merit Drive
Suite 350
Dallas, TX 75251
Phone: 214-349-5965
E-mail: dmontalvo@firesprinkler.org

AMERICAN FLORAL ENDOWMENT

http://endowment.org

AFE FLORICULTURE SCHOLARSHIPS

Awarding scholarships for floriculture and horticulture students is a primary function of AFE. We understand the financial burden students face and are doing our part to help! AFE has more than 20 scholarships awarded annually. Online applications and supporting documents are due by May 1 each year.

Award: Scholarship for use in sophomore, junior, senior, graduate, or postgraduate years; not renewable. *Number:* 2–25. *Amount:* $500–$10,000.

Eligibility Requirements: Applicant must be enrolled or expecting to enroll full-time at a two-year or four-year or technical institution or university. Applicant must have 2.5 GPA or higher. Available to U.S. citizens.

Application Requirements: Application form, essay. *Deadline:* May 1.

Contact: Debi Chedester, Executive Director
American Floral Endowment
1001 North Fairfax Street, Suite 201
Alexandria, VA 22324
E-mail: dchedester@afeendowment.org

AMERICAN LEGION AUXILIARY DEPARTMENT OF COLORADO

http://www.alacolorado.com

AMERICAN LEGION AUXILIARY DEPARTMENT OF COLORADO DEPARTMENT PRESIDENT'S SCHOLARSHIP AND SCHOLARSHIP FOR JUNIOR MEMBER

Open to children, spouses, grandchildren, and great-grandchildren of veterans, and veterans who served in the Armed Forces during eligibility dates for membership in the American Legion. Applicants must have been accepted by an accredited school.

Award: Scholarship for use in freshman year; not renewable. *Number:* 2–5. *Amount:* $500–$1000.

Eligibility Requirements: Applicant must be high school student and planning to enroll or expecting to enroll full- or part-time at a two-year or four-year institution or university. Available to U.S. citizens.

Application Requirements: Application form, essay. *Deadline:* March 15.

Contact: Rhonda Larkowski, Department Secretary and Treasurer
American Legion Auxiliary Department of Colorado
7465 East First Avenue, Suite D
Denver, CO 80230
Phone: 303-367-5388
E-mail: www.dept-sec@alacolorado.com

AMERICAN SOCIETY FOR NONDESTRUCTIVE TESTING

http://www.asnt.org

ASNT ROBERT B. OLIVER SCHOLARSHIP

The Robert B. Oliver Scholarship is an incentive to students currently enrolled in course work related to NDT in a program of study leading to an associate degree or post-secondary certificate at a U.S. university, college, technical school or company whose primary purpose is workforce education.

Award: Scholarship for use in freshman, sophomore, junior, or senior years; not renewable. *Number:* 3. *Amount:* $2500.

Eligibility Requirements: Applicant must be enrolled or expecting to enroll full-time at a two-year or technical institution. Available to U.S. citizens.

Application Requirements: Application form, essay. *Deadline:* February 15.

Contact: Jessica Ames, Program Coordinator
American Society for Nondestructive Testing
1711 Arlingate Lane
PO Box 28518
Columbus, OH 43228
E-mail: james@asnt.org

AMERICAN SOCIETY OF MECHANICAL ENGINEERS AUXILIARY INC.

http://www.asme.org/

LUCY AND CHARLES W.E. CLARKE SCHOLARSHIP

Scholarship for high school seniors on a FIRST Robotics Team only.

Award: Scholarship for use in freshman year; not renewable. *Number:* 5–12. *Amount:* $5000.

Eligibility Requirements: Applicant must be high school student and planning to enroll or expecting to enroll full-time at a four-year institution or university.

Contact: RuthAnn Bigley, ASME Auxiliary Staff Coordinator
American Society of Mechanical Engineers Auxiliary Inc.
Two Park Avenue
Mailstop RB
New York, NY 10016
Phone: 212-591-7650
E-mail: bigleyr@asme.org

AMERICAN WELDING SOCIETY

http://www.aws.org/

BARBARA AND RICHARD COUCH HYPERTHERM SCHOLARSHIP

Student pursuing a two or four year degree in an engineering or technical major in the welding or cutting field (applicable areas of mechanical, software, process, electrical engineering). Priority will be given to sons and daughters of Hypertherm associates. Applicant must have a 2.8 minimum overall GPA. Proof of financial need is not required but would be a priority.

Award: Scholarship for use in freshman, sophomore, junior, or senior years; not renewable.

Eligibility Requirements: Applicant must be enrolled or expecting to enroll full- or part-time at a two-year or four-year institution. Applicant must have 2.5 GPA or higher. Available to U.S. and non-U.S. citizens.

Application Requirements: Application form, financial need analysis. *Deadline:* February 15.

Contact: Mr. John Douglass, Associate Director, AWS Foundation
American Welding Society
8669 NW 36 Street, Suite 130
Miami, FL 33166
Phone: 800-443-9353 Ext. 212
E-mail: jdouglass@aws.org

D. FRED AND MARIAN L. BOVIE TECHNICAL SCHOLARSHIP

Awarded to a student pursuing an Associates degree in welding. Applicant must have a minimum 2.8 overall GPA and may be enrolled full or part time. Proof of Financial need is required.

Award: Scholarship for use in freshman or sophomore years; not renewable.

Eligibility Requirements: Applicant must be enrolled or expecting to enroll full- or part-time at a two-year institution. Available to U.S. citizens.

Application Requirements: Application form, financial need analysis. *Deadline:* February 15.

Contact: Mr. John Douglass, Associate Director, AWS Foundation
American Welding Society
8669 NW 36 Street, #130
Miami, FL 33166
Phone: 800-443-9353 Ext. 212
E-mail: jdouglass@aws.org

GLENN W. OYLER MEMORIAL TECHNICAL SCHOLARSHIP

Awarded to a student pursuing a certificate or associates degree in welding or related. The student must be a U.S. citizen with a 2.5 overall GPA, and have proof of financial need. Students in New Mexico and Pennsylvania only.

Award: Scholarship for use in freshman or sophomore years; not renewable.

Eligibility Requirements: Applicant must be enrolled or expecting to enroll full- or part-time at a two-year or technical institution. Applicant must have 2.5 GPA or higher. Available to U.S. citizens.

Application Requirements: Application form, financial need analysis. *Deadline:* February 15.

Contact: Mr. John Douglass, Associate Director, AWS Foundation
American Welding Society
8669 NW 36 Street, Suite 130
Miami, FL 33166
Phone: 800-443-9353 Ext. 212
E-mail: jdouglass@aws.org

JOHN DEERE COMPANY SCHOLARSHIP

Two scholarships, one awarded to a mid-west student pursuing a Bachelor degree in welding engineering, welding engineering technology, manufacturing or mechanical engineering with a welding emphasis. High school attendance or permanent address in states of Iowa, Illinois, Minnesota, Wisconsin or Missouri, with a 3.0 overall GPA and full time. Proof of financial need not required. One scholarship awarded to a female or minority student with the same business degree as above. High school attendance or permanent address in states of Iowa, Illinois, Minnesota, Wisconsin, Missouri, Nebraska, Kansas or North or South Dakota, with a 3.0 overall GPA and full time. Proof of financial need not required.

Award: Scholarship for use in sophomore, junior, or senior years; not renewable.

Eligibility Requirements: Applicant must be enrolled or expecting to enroll full- or part-time at a four-year institution. Applicant must have 3.0 GPA or higher. Available to U.S. citizens.

Application Requirements: Application form, financial need analysis. *Deadline:* February 15.

Contact: Mr. John Douglass, Associate Director, AWS Foundation
American Welding Society
8669 NW 36 Street
Miami, FL 33166
Phone: 800-443-9353 Ext. 212
E-mail: jdouglass@aws.org

ANDY GREEN, ATTORNEY AT LAW, P.C.

http://www.andygreenlaw.com

PERSONS IN OR AFFECTED BY RECOVERY SCHOLARSHIP

The Persons in or Affected by Recovery Scholarship was created to acknowledge the powerful journey that accompanies addiction recovery. As somebody who is personally in recovery, I wanted to make this scholarship available to help those who are working to help themselves. The Persons in or Affected by Recovery Scholarship is open to all qualifying students enrolled in a 2-year, 4-year, graduate level or certification program. Andy Green Law will award one $1,000 scholarship to the student who writes the best response to the following question: Explain your road to recovery (or a loved one's road to recovery), and how it has impacted your desire to pursue your future goals. All entries must be a minimum of 500 and maximum of 1000 words. Diagrams, schematics, illustrations and photographs may be included as supporting documents.

Award: Scholarship for use in freshman, sophomore, junior, senior, or graduate years; not renewable. *Number:* 1. *Amount:* $1000.

Eligibility Requirements: Applicant must be enrolled or expecting to enroll full- or part-time at a two-year or four-year or technical institution or university. Available to U.S. and non-U.S. citizens.

Application Requirements: Application form, essay. *Deadline:* July 1.

Contact: Mr. Andy Green, Attorney
Andy Green, Attorney at Law, P.C.
121 SW Salmon Street, Suite 1100
Portland, OR 97204
Phone: 503-471-1385
E-mail: andygreenlawpdx@gmail.com

APPALACHIAN STUDIES ASSOCIATION

http://www.appalachianstudies.org/

CARL A. ROSS STUDENT PAPER AWARD

All papers must adhere to guidelines for scholarly research. Middle/high school papers should be 8–15 pages in length. Undergraduate/graduate papers should be 15–30 pages in length. Nominations should be submitted by emailing a Microsoft Word copy of the paper to the chair of the selection committee before January 15. Papers submitted to the undergraduate/graduate competition must have been completed during the current or previous academic year. Submissions must include proof of student status during the current or previous academic year; documentation may consist of a copy of a schedule of classes or (unofficial or official) transcript or a letter from a faculty advisor (which should include the faculty advisor's e-mail address, phone number, and mailing address). Students who wish to present their papers at the conference must also submit a proposal for participation by the submission deadline (generally in October). Costs of attending the conference are the winner's responsibility.

Award: Prize for use in freshman, sophomore, junior, senior, or graduate years; not renewable. *Number:* 2. *Amount:* $100.

Eligibility Requirements: Applicant must be enrolled or expecting to enroll full- or part-time at a two-year or four-year institution or university. Available to U.S. and non-U.S. citizens.

Application Requirements: Essay. *Deadline:* January 15.

Contact: Casey LaFrance
E-mail: TC-Lafrance@wiu.edu

APPLYKIT

http://applykit.com

APPLYKIT SCHOLARSHIP $500 NO ESSAY!

The $500 ApplyKit Scholarship is awarded to one user who registers for free at ApplyKit.com. Registration is available at the following website: http://www.applykit.com/user/registration/?partner=petersons. Open to undergraduate students pursuing both full and part-time studies.

Award: Scholarship for use in freshman, sophomore, junior, or senior years; not renewable. *Number:* 1. *Amount:* $500.

Eligibility Requirements: Applicant must be age 15-19 and enrolled or expecting to enroll full- or part-time at a two-year or four-year or technical institution or university. Available to U.S. and non-U.S. citizens.

Application Requirements: Application form may be submitted online (http://www.applykit.com/user/registration/?partner=petersons),. *Deadline:* December 1.

Contact: Alex Hollis, Chief Marketing Officer
ApplyKit
844 Elm Street
Manchester, NH 03101
E-mail: alex@applykit.com

ASM MATERIALS EDUCATION FOUNDATION

http://www.asmfoundation.org/

LADISH CO. FOUNDATION SCHOLARSHIPS

Two scholarships of $2,500 (each). (Student must be a Wisconsin resident and must attend a Wisconsin university to qualify.)

Award: Scholarship for use in junior or senior years; not renewable. *Number:* 1–2. *Amount:* $2500.

Eligibility Requirements: Applicant must be enrolled or expecting to enroll full-time at an institution or university. Available to U.S. and Canadian citizens.

Application Requirements: Essay, financial need analysis, interview, personal photograph. *Deadline:* May 1.

Contact: Jeane Deatherage, Administrator, Foundation Programs
ASM Materials Education Foundation
ASM Materials Education Foundation
9639 Kinsman Road
Materials Park, OH 44073
Phone: 440-338-5151 Ext. 5533
E-mail: scholarshipsUG@asminternational.org

LUCILLE AND CHARLES A. WERT SCHOLARSHIP

One year full tuition of up to $10,000. Established in 2006 through a generous bequest by Dr. and Mrs. Charles Wert.

Award: Scholarship for use in junior or senior years; not renewable. *Number:* 1. *Amount:* $10,000.

Eligibility Requirements: Applicant must be enrolled or expecting to enroll full-time at an institution or university. Available to U.S. and Canadian citizens.

Application Requirements: Essay, financial need analysis, personal photograph. *Deadline:* May 1.

Contact: Jeane Deatherage, Administrator, Foundation Programs
ASM Materials Education Foundation
ASM Materials Education Foundation
9639 Kinsman Road
Materials Park, OH 44073
Phone: 440-338-5151 Ext. 5533
E-mail: scholarshipsUG@asminternational.org

ASSOCIATED MEDICAL SERVICES INC.

http://www.ams-inc.on.ca/

AMS HISTORY OF MEDICINE HANNAH SUMMER STUDENTSHIPS

The Hannah Summer Studentship offers four undergraduate students each summer an opportunity to learn the techniques of historical research and to encourage their serious future study of medical history. The studentships are jointly administered with the Canadian Society for the History of Medicine.

Award: Scholarship for use in freshman, sophomore, junior, senior, or graduate years; not renewable. *Number:* 4. *Amount:* $5500.

Eligibility Requirements: Applicant must be enrolled or expecting to enroll full- or part-time at an institution or university. Available to Canadian citizens.

Application Requirements: Application form.

Contact: Anne Avery, Director of Communications
Associated Medical Services Inc.
#228-162 Cumberland Street
Toronto, ON
Phone: 416-924-3368
Fax: 416-323-3338
E-mail: anne.avery@ams-inc.on.ca

ASSOCIATION OF SIKH PROFESSIONALS

http://www.sikhprofessionals.org/

SIKH EDUCATION AID FUND

This fund has been set up to support financially deserving Sikh students, to recognize Sikh students of outstanding academic abilities, and to support those individuals doing research in the Sikh religion or engaged in Sikh studies. Awards are in the form of scholarships, grants through endowments, and interest-free loans for which repayment is expected after graduation.

Award: Scholarship for use in freshman, sophomore, junior, or senior years. *Amount:* $400–$4000.

Eligibility Requirements: Applicant must be enrolled or expecting to enroll full- or part-time at an institution or university. Available to U.S. citizens.

Application Requirements: *Deadline:* June 1.

BAPTIST JOINT COMMITTEE FOR RELIGIOUS LIBERTY

http://www.BJConline.org

RELIGIOUS LIBERTY ESSAY SCHOLARSHIP CONTEST

To enter, students submit an essay based on the year's topic. All high school juniors and seniors are eligible, and they must have an essay adviser (a teacher or church staff member) to verify that the student's work is his or her own. http://www.BJConline.org/contest.

Award: Scholarship for use in freshman year; not renewable. *Number:* 1–3. *Amount:* $500–$2000.

Eligibility Requirements: Applicant must be high school student and planning to enroll or expecting to enroll full-time at a two-year or four-year or technical institution or university. Available to U.S. citizens.

Application Requirements: Application form, essay. *Deadline:* March 9.

Contact: Charles Watson, Education and Outreach Specialist
Baptist Joint Committee for Religious Liberty
200 Maryland Ave., N.E.
Washington, DC 20002
Phone: 202-544-4226
Fax: 202-544-2094
E-mail: cwatson@BJConline.org

BARBIZON INTERNATIONAL LLC

https://www.barbizonmodeling.com

BARBIZON COLLEGE TUITION SCHOLARSHIP

The Barbizon International scholarship offers $100,000 in college tuition awarded every other year by random drawing. Entry forms are available at high schools throughout the United States. For more details, visit http://www.barbizonmodeling.com/scholarships.

Award: Scholarship for use in freshman, sophomore, junior, or senior years; not renewable. *Number:* 1. *Amount:* $100,000.

Eligibility Requirements: Applicant must be enrolled or expecting to enroll full- or part-time at a two-year or four-year institution or university. Available to U.S. citizens.

Application Requirements: Application form. *Deadline:* December 1.

Contact: Kristina Anderson, Marketing Specialist
Phone: 888-999-9404

BERKSHIRE HATHAWAY HOMESERVICES OF GEORGIA

http://www.bhhsgeorgia.com/

AMERICAN DREAM SCHOLARSHIP

$1000 scholarship for college freshmen. To apply, students must submit a 500-1000 word essay based on one of the three essay questions about their personal experience with homeownership. Send a Word doc attachment to scholarship@bhhsgeorgia.com with essay submission. The file name should be student's full name, state, and date of birth. For example, Chipper-Jones-GA-4-24-1972. All submission emails must contain the student's full name, date of birth, email address, postal address, high school they are currently enrolled in, and a phone number to contact. For more information, visit http://www.bhhsgeorgia.com/american-dream-scholarship.aspx.

Award: Scholarship for use in freshman year; not renewable. *Number:* 1. *Amount:* $1000.

Eligibility Requirements: Applicant must be high school student and planning to enroll or expecting to enroll full-time at a two-year or four-year or technical institution or university. Available to U.S. citizens.

Application Requirements: Essay. *Deadline:* May 30.

Contact: Tony Floyd
Phone: 770-992-4100
E-mail: scholarship@bhhsgeorgia.com

BEST ESSAY EDUCATION COMPANY

https://bestessay.education/

BEST ESSAY SCHOLARSHIP CONTEST

Best Essay Education has created a scholarship essay competition to encourage students to produce their own great essays and have the opportunity to win a sizeable financial award to help with their own educational expenses. To apply, you must be a student at an accredited college, university, community college, oct-tech certificate program, or any graduate or equivalent professional program. High school students who have just enrolled in college, are certainly eligible. Entrants must choose one of the following three prompts: Should students have the right to evaluate their teachers? Why or why not? If so, how should this be done? What new innovations promise to significantly change your life in college? How will they change your life? Of all of the environment threats, which do you see as the most dangerous right now? All eligible essays will be evaluated by a panel of Best Essay Education writers and editors. The following criteria will be used: originality of thought and structure; quality of grammar and composition, including organization, vocabulary, etc.; creativity and depth of thought. The panel shall determine the top three winners, based upon a scored rubric, and will then publish those winner names on its site, and social media pages, as it deems appropriate. Winners will receive notification via email and will be required to reply to those emails. Should a winner fail to respond to the email or, for any reason, refuse the prize award, the award will be provided to the entrant who is next in line.

Award: Scholarship for use in freshman, sophomore, junior, or senior years; not renewable. *Amount:* $400–$1000.

Eligibility Requirements: Applicant must be enrolled or expecting to enroll full- or part-time at a two-year or four-year or technical institution or university. Available to U.S. and non-U.S. citizens.

Application Requirements: Essay. *Deadline:* November 30.

Contact: Lauren Gartner
E-mail: bestessay.education@gmail.com

BLADES OF GREEN

http://bladesofgreen.com

BLADES OF GREEN SCHOLARSHIP

Blades of Green has created a merit-based scholarship fund for individuals seeking undergraduate or graduate level education in environmental studies or related fields. Mark and Brad Leahy have created a $1,000 scholarship for the 2018 academic year. The scholarship will be awarded based on academic excellence, pursuit of further study in environmental education at an accredited college or university, and passion for further study. The scholarship will last for the duration of one year and be paid directly to the winning candidate to use towards tuition and board during the fall semester.

Award: Scholarship for use in freshman, sophomore, junior, senior, or graduate years; not renewable. *Number:* 1. *Amount:* $1000.

Eligibility Requirements: Applicant must be enrolled or expecting to enroll full-time at a four-year institution or university. Available to U.S. citizens.

Application Requirements: Application form, essay. *Deadline:* March 15.

Contact: Angela Hieronimus, HR Manager
Blades of Green
645 Central Avenue East
Edgewater, MD 21037
Phone: 410-867-8873
E-mail: ahieronimus@bladesofgreen.com

BLAKE FAMILY-US METRIC ASSOCIATION AWARD

http://www.us-metric.org

USMA/BLAKE FAMILY METRIC SCHOLARSHIP

The USMA/Blake scholarship is designed to help promote American metrication by providing partial funding for the first year in college to a high school student who has shown an interest in American metrication. Award of the scholarship will be given to a student who submits an application essay showing what they have done to help promote increased usage of the SI Metric System in the United States.

Award: Scholarship for use in freshman year; not renewable. *Number:* 1. *Amount:* $2500.

Eligibility Requirements: Applicant must be high school student and planning to enroll or expecting to enroll full-time at a four-year institution. Available to U.S. and non-U.S. citizens.

Application Requirements: Application form, essay. *Deadline:* March 15.

Contact: Mr. Mark Henschel
Phone: 779-537-5611
E-mail: mw-henschel1@gmail.com

BLINDED VETERANS ASSOCIATION

http://www.bva.org/

KATHERN F. GRUBER SCHOLARSHIP

Award for undergraduate or graduate study is available to dependent children, grandchildren and spouses of legally blind veterans to include Active Duty legally blinded Armed Forces members. The veteran's blindness may be either service or non-service connected. High school seniors may apply. Applicant must be enrolled or accepted for admission as a full-time student in an accredited institution of higher learning, business, secretarial, or vocational school. Six awards of $2000 each are given.

Award: Scholarship for use in freshman, sophomore, junior, senior, or graduate years; not renewable. *Number:* 6. *Amount:* $2000.

Eligibility Requirements: Applicant must be enrolled or expecting to enroll full-time at a two-year or four-year or technical institution or university. Available to U.S. citizens.

Application Requirements: Application form, essay. *Deadline:* April 21.

Contact: Scholarship Coordinator
Blinded Veterans Association
125 N. West St.
Suite 300
Alexandria, VA 22314
Phone: 202-371-8880
E-mail: bva@bva.org

BMI FOUNDATION, INC.

http://www.bmifoundation.org/

BMI FUTURE JAZZ MASTER SCHOLARSHIP

The BMI Future Jazz Master Scholarship competition is open to jazz performers age 17-24 attending colleges and universities nationwide. The $5,000 award was established in 2015 in honor of the National Endowment for the Arts Jazz Masters Fellowship. A panel of Jazz Masters will select the winner based on evidence of talent and potential as a jazz performer. BMI writer and NEA Jazz Master Nancy Wilson lends her support as the honorary spokesperson for this year's competition.

Award: Scholarship for use in freshman, sophomore, junior, senior, graduate, or postgraduate years; not renewable. *Number:* 1. *Amount:* $5000.

Eligibility Requirements: Applicant must be age 17-24 and enrolled or expecting to enroll full- or part-time at a two-year or four-year or technical institution or university. Available to U.S. and non-U.S. citizens.

Application Requirements: Application form. *Deadline:* February 1.

Contact: Pat Cook, Director
BMI Foundation, Inc.
7 World Trade Center
250 Greenwich Street
New York, NY 10007
Phone: 212-220-3103
E-mail: info@bmifoundation.org

BOUNDLESS IMMIGRATION INC.

https://www.boundless.co

BOUNDLESS AMERICAN DREAM SCHOLARSHIP

The Boundless American Dream Scholarship will provide financial support to an exceptionally promising student who fulfills the requirements of Deferred Action for Childhood Arrivals (DACA) or Temporary Protected Status (TPS) and who wants to make the world a better place through technology. Boundless will provide a scholarship of $1,500 to improve this student's ability to design and build technology that solves real problems, based on the student's own vision and needs (including but not limited to support for college/university/graduate studies tuition, attending a coding boot camp, taking an online course, attending a professional conference, or building an early-stage prototype product for a startup idea). The 2018 Boundless American Dream Scholar will be selected for their academic excellence, entrepreneurial spirit, and dedication to community service. Additional details and online application can be found at https://www.boundless.co/boundless-american-dream-scholarship/.

Award: Scholarship for use in freshman, sophomore, junior, senior, graduate, or postgraduate years; not renewable. *Number:* 1. *Amount:* $1500.

Eligibility Requirements: Applicant must be enrolled or expecting to enroll full- or part-time at a two-year or four-year or technical institution or university. Available to Canadian and non-U.S. citizens.

Application Requirements: Application form, essay. *Deadline:* May 31.

Contact: Xiao Wang, CEO
Phone: 855-268-6353
E-mail: help@boundless.co

BRADLEY CORBETT LAW

http://www.bradleycorbettlaw.com/scholarship

LAW OFFICE OF BRADLEY R. CORBETT SCHOLARSHIP

$2000 award for a college or university student in the United States. Scholarship will be awarded to the student who submits the best overall essay; details are available at the website http://www.bradleycorbettlaw.com/scholarship/. Must be a U.S. citizen and submit proof of college enrollment.

Award: Scholarship for use in freshman, sophomore, junior, senior, graduate, or postgraduate years; not renewable. *Number:* 1. *Amount:* $2000.

Eligibility Requirements: Applicant must be enrolled or expecting to enroll full-time at a two-year or four-year or technical institution or university. Available to U.S. citizens.

Application Requirements: Essay, proof of enrollment. *Deadline:* July 15.

Contact: Mr. Cameron Cox, Scholarship Outreach Manager
Bradley Corbett Law
620 South Melrose
Suite 101
Vista, CA 92081
Phone: 619-800-4449
E-mail: ccox@scholarassociation.org

BRIGHT!TAX

https://brighttax.com

BRIGHT!TAX GLOBAL SCHOLAR INITIATIVE

The Bright!Tax Global Scholar Initiative provides assistance with fees for Americans who are or who wish to study abroad.

Award: Scholarship for use in freshman, sophomore, junior, senior, graduate, or postgraduate years; not renewable. *Number:* 2. *Amount:* $1000–$2000.

Eligibility Requirements: Applicant must be enrolled or expecting to enroll full- or part-time at an institution or university. Available to U.S. citizens.

Application Requirements: Application form, essay, personal photograph. *Deadline:* continuous.

Contact: Greg Dewald
E-mail: inquiries@brighttax.com

BRITISH COLUMBIA MINISTRY OF ADVANCED EDUCATION

http://www.studentaidbc.ca/

IRVING K. BARBER BRITISH COLUMBIA SCHOLARSHIP PROGRAM (FOR STUDY IN BRITISH COLUMBIA)

Scholarship to students who, after completing two years at a British Columbia public community college, university college or institute, must transfer to another public postsecondary institution in British Columbia to complete their degree. Students must demonstrate merit as well as exceptional involvement in their institution and community. Must have a GPA of at least 3.5. For more details, visit http://www.aved.gov.bc.ca/studentaidbc/specialprograms/irvingkbarber/bc_scholarship.htm.

Award: Scholarship for use in junior or senior years; not renewable. *Number:* up to 150. *Amount:* up to $5000.

Eligibility Requirements: Applicant must be enrolled or expecting to enroll full-time at a four-year institution or university and studying in British Columbia. Applicant must have 3.5 GPA or higher. Available to Canadian citizens.

Application Requirements: Application form, community service, essay, recommendations or references, test scores, transcript. *Deadline:* March 31.

Contact: Victoria Thibeau, Loan Remission and Management Unit
Phone: 250-387-6100
E-mail: victoria.thibeau@gov.bc.ca

BURGER KING MCLAMORE FOUNDATION

https://bkmclamorefoundation.org/

BURGER KING SCHOLARS PROGRAM

Created in memory of BURGER KING® Co-founder James W. McLamore, the BURGER KING Scholars program has awarded $28.3 million in scholarships to more than 26,800 high school students, BK® employees and their families across the U.S., Canada and Puerto Rico since 2000. In 2016 alone, the Foundation awarded $3 million to more than 2,800 students in North America. Scholarship grants range from $1,000 to $50,000 and are intended to help students offset the cost of attending college or post-secondary vocational/technical school. Recipients are selected based on their grade point average (GPA), work experience, extracurricular activities and community service. Primarily funded by the BURGER KING® system and guests through annual fundraising activities, scholarships are awarded in the spring of each year. Our ultimate goal? To provide one $1,000 scholarship for every BURGER KING® restaurant in North America that's more than $7 million each year! The application period begins on Oct. 15 and closes Dec. 15.

Award: Scholarship for use in freshman year; not renewable. *Amount:* $1000–$5000.

Eligibility Requirements: Applicant must be high school student and planning to enroll or expecting to enroll full-time at a two-year or four-year or technical institution or university. Applicant must have 2.5 GPA or higher. Available to U.S. and Canadian citizens.

Application Requirements: Application form, community service, personal photograph. *Deadline:* December 15.

Contact: Scholarship Management Services
　　　　Phone: 507-931-1682
　　　　E-mail: burgerkingscholars@scholarshipamerica.org

BY KIDS FOR KIDS, CO.

http://bkfkeducation.com

CTIA WIRELESS FOUNDATION DRIVE SMART DIGITAL SHORT CONTEST

Create a digital short to help combat distracted driving. This contest is for legal residents of the United States who are between the ages of 13 and 18. Distracted driving is a serious problem, but you can help. Create a 15-60 second digital short to persuade your peers to not drive distracted, and earn a chance to win $10,000! Scholarships and grants will be awarded to students and teachers. http://drivesmartnow.com

Award: Prize for use in freshman, sophomore, junior, or senior years; not renewable. *Number:* 6. *Amount:* $1000–$10,000.

Eligibility Requirements: Applicant must be age 13-18 and enrolled or expecting to enroll full- or part-time at a two-year or four-year or technical institution or university. Available to U.S. citizens.

Application Requirements: Application form. *Deadline:* December 18.

Contact: Operations & Events Manager
　　　　Phone: 203-321-1226
　　　　E-mail: info@bkfk.com

CALVIN COOLIDGE PRESIDENTIAL FOUNDATION, INC.

http://www.coolidgefoundation.org

COOLIDGE SCHOLARSHIP

The Coolidge Scholarship is a full-ride scholarship that covers a student's tuition, room, board, and expenses for four years of undergraduate study. The Coolidge may be used by recipients at any American university. Anyone of any background, pursuing any academic discipline of study, may apply to this non-partisan, need-blind, program. ONLY current high school juniors are eligible to apply.

Award: Scholarship for use in freshman, sophomore, junior, or senior years; renewable.

Eligibility Requirements: Applicant must be high school student and planning to enroll or expecting to enroll full-time at a four-year institution or university. Available to U.S. citizens.

Application Requirements: Application form, essay.

Contact: Mr. Rob Hammer, Program Manager
　　　　Calvin Coolidge Presidential Foundation, Inc.
　　　　Calvin Coolidge Presidential Foundation, Inc.
　　　　P.O. Box 97
　　　　Plymouth, VT 05056
　　　　Phone: 802-672-3389
　　　　E-mail: coolidgescholars@coolidgefoundation.org

CASUALTY ACTUARIES OF THE SOUTHEAST

http://www.casact.org/community/affiliates/case/

CASUALTY ACTUARIES OF THE SOUTHEAST SCHOLARSHIP PROGRAM

Scholarships available for undergraduate students in the southeastern states for the study of actuarial science. Must be studying in Alabama, Arkansas, Florida, Georgia, Kentucky, Louisiana, Mississippi, North Carolina, South Carolina, Tennessee, or Virginia. Incoming freshmen/first-year students are not eligible for the scholarship. Must have demonstrated strong interest in mathematics or mathematics-related field and high scholastic achievement. Applicants should demonstrate interest in the actuarial profession, mathematical aptitude, and communication skills.

Award: Scholarship for use in sophomore, junior, or senior years; not renewable. *Number:* 2–4. *Amount:* $1000–$1500.

Eligibility Requirements: Applicant must be enrolled or expecting to enroll full-time at a four-year institution or university and studying in Alabama, Arkansas, Florida, Georgia, Kentucky, Louisiana, Mississippi, North Carolina, South Carolina, Tennessee, Virginia. Available to U.S. and Canadian citizens.

Application Requirements: Application form, essay, recommendations or references, transcript. *Deadline:* May 1.

Contact: Karen Jordan
　　　　Casualty Actuaries of the Southeast
　　　　3274 Medlock Bridge Road
　　　　Peachtree Corners, GA 30092
　　　　Phone: 678-684-4877
　　　　E-mail: kjordan@merlinosinc.com

CENTRAL NATIONAL BANK & TRUST COMPANY OF ENID TRUSTEE

http://cnb-ok.com/

MAY T. HENRY SCHOLARSHIP FOUNDATION

A $1000 scholarship renewed annually for four years. Awarded to any student enrolled in an Oklahoma state-supported college, university or tech school. Based on need, scholastic performance and personal traits valued by May T. Henry. Minimum 3.0 GPA required.

Award: Scholarship for use in freshman, sophomore, junior, senior, graduate, or postgraduate years; renewable. *Amount:* $1000.

Eligibility Requirements: Applicant must be enrolled or expecting to enroll full-time at a two-year or four-year or technical institution or university and studying in Oklahoma. Applicant must have 3.0 GPA or higher. Available to U.S. and non-U.S. citizens.

Application Requirements: Application form, essay, financial need analysis, recommendations or references, test scores, transcript. *Deadline:* April 1.

Contact: Trust Department
　　　　Central National Bank & Trust Company of Enid Trustee
　　　　PO Box 3448
　　　　Enid, OK 73702-3448
　　　　Phone: 580-213-1700
　　　　Fax: 580-249-5911
　　　　E-mail: cfelix@cnb-enid.com

CHAMELEONJOHN.COM

http://www.chameleonjohn.com/

$3,000 USA UNIVERSITY STUDENT SCHOLARSHIP

Our mission at ChameleonJohn.com is to help people save money on their online purchases. That is why we get the best coupon codes from hundreds of online stores around the United States. After having saved money for thousands of consumers, we decided to give a hand to students who are struggling financially and thus established an annual University Student Scholarship with which we give away $3,000 every year to one student in the United States.

Award: Scholarship for use in freshman, sophomore, junior, senior, or graduate years; renewable. *Number:* 1. *Amount:* $3000.

Eligibility Requirements: Applicant must be enrolled or expecting to enroll full- or part-time at a two-year or four-year or technical institution or university. Available to U.S. and non-U.S. citizens.

Application Requirements: Essay. *Deadline:* continuous.

Contact: Alan Trapulionis
E-mail: scholarships@chameleonjohn.com

CHEGG

http://www.chegg.com/scholarships

$1,000 MONTHLY SCHOLARSHIP

$1000 monthly scholarship for full-time students planning on attending accredited colleges or universities. Must be a student currently enrolled in a U.S. high school.

Award: Scholarship for use in freshman, sophomore, junior, or senior years; not renewable. *Number:* 1. *Amount:* $1000.

Eligibility Requirements: Applicant must be high school student and planning to enroll or expecting to enroll full-time at a four-year institution or university. Available to U.S. citizens.

Application Requirements: Application form. *Deadline:* continuous.

Contact: Renee Campbell
E-mail: scholarships@chegg.com

CLARICODE

http://www.claricode.com/

CLARICODE MEDICAL SOFTWARE SCHOLARSHIP ESSAY

One awards of $1250 available to full-time undergraduate or graduate students attending a U.S. accredited college or university. Must be at least 18 years old at time of entry and submit a 500 to 1000-word essay on the topic chosen by Claricode (and listed on the website). All majors/concentrations are welcome to apply. For additional information visit website http://www.claricode.com/scholarship.

Award: Scholarship for use in freshman, sophomore, junior, senior, graduate, or postgraduate years; not renewable. *Number:* 1. *Amount:* $1250.

Eligibility Requirements: Applicant must be enrolled or expecting to enroll full-time at a two-year or four-year or technical institution or university. Available to U.S. citizens.

Application Requirements: Application form, application form may be submitted online (http://www.claricode.com/scholarship/), essay. *Deadline:* October 31.

Contact: Chief Executive Officer
E-mail: scholarship@claricode.com

COCA-COLA SCHOLARS FOUNDATION INC.

http://www.coca-colascholars.org/

COCA-COLA SCHOLARS PROGRAM

Renewable scholarship for graduating high school seniors enrolled either full-time or part-time in accredited colleges or universities. Minimum 3.0 GPA required. 252 awards are granted annually.

Award: Scholarship for use in freshman, sophomore, junior, senior, or graduate years; renewable. *Number:* 250. *Amount:* $10,000–$20,000.

Eligibility Requirements: Applicant must be high school student and planning to enroll or expecting to enroll full- or part-time at a two-year or four-year or technical institution or university. Applicant must have 3.0 GPA or higher. Available to U.S. citizens.

Application Requirements: Application form, application form may be submitted online (http://www.coca-colascholars.org), community service, essay, interview, recommendations or references, test scores, transcript. *Deadline:* October 31.

Contact: Mark Davis, President
Coca-Cola Scholars Foundation Inc.
PO Box 442
Atlanta, GA 30301-0442
Phone: 800-306-2653
Fax: 404-733-5439
E-mail: scholars@na.ko.com

COIT SERVICES, INC.

http://www.coit.com/

COIT 2018 CLEAN GIF SCHOLARSHIP CONTEST

This graphic design-centric scholarship challenges you to create a lightly animated GIF that shows us a fast way to get your space cleaned. When you are short on time, what is something unique or clever that makes your place feel or look clean quickly. Your GIF should be designed for posting on social media and can be as many frames as you like, just keep it short and sweet. We will give extra attention to clever submissions with a real sense of humor or brilliant cleaning hack. The most important criterion, though, is fantastic graphic design. The meme should be easy to read and visually appealing- something worth sharing!

Award: Scholarship for use in freshman, sophomore, junior, senior, graduate, or postgraduate years; not renewable. *Number:* 1. *Amount:* $2000.

Eligibility Requirements: Applicant must be enrolled or expecting to enroll full- or part-time at a two-year or four-year or technical institution or university. Available to U.S. and non-U.S. citizens.

Application Requirements: *Deadline:* August 31.

Contact: Tina Youngstein
Phone: 650-697-6190
E-mail: coit.scholarship.2017@gmail.com

COLLEGE INSIDER RESOURCES

http://www.ezcir.com/

COLLEGE INSIDER SCHOLARSHIP PROGRAM

Scholarship offered to undergraduate students with a minimum GPA of 2.5. International students attending college in the United States are also eligible. Refer to website for additional information, http://www.ezcir.com/college_request.asp.

Award: Scholarship for use in freshman, sophomore, junior, or senior years; renewable. *Number:* 1. *Amount:* $1000.

Eligibility Requirements: Applicant must be enrolled or expecting to enroll full-time at a two-year or four-year or technical institution or university. Available to U.S. and non-U.S. citizens.

Application Requirements: Application form. *Deadline:* varies.

Contact: Mr. Cliff deQuilettes, CEO
Phone: 406-652-8900
E-mail: cliff@ezcir.com

COLLEGE JUMPSTART SCHOLARSHIP FUND

http://www.jumpstart-scholarship.net

COLLEGE JUMPSTART SCHOLARSHIP

The College JumpStart Scholarship is an annual, merit-based competition—financial need is not considered—that is open to 10th-12th graders, college students and non-traditional students. The main requirement is that you are committed to going to school and can express your goals for getting a higher education.

Award: Scholarship for use in freshman, sophomore, junior, senior, or graduate years; not renewable. *Number:* 6. *Amount:* $750–$1500.

Eligibility Requirements: Applicant must be high school student and planning to enroll or expecting to enroll full- or part-time at a two-year or four-year or technical institution or university. Available to U.S. citizens.

Application Requirements: Application form, essay. *Deadline:* October 17.

Contact: Scholarship Administrator
E-mail: admin@jumpstart-scholarship.net

COMEDY DEFENSIVE DRIVING

http://comedydefensivedriving.com/

GETTING REAL ABOUT DISTRACTED DRIVING SCHOLARSHIP

At Comedy Defensive Driving, we believe that quality education is too damn expensive for many students and should be obtainable for everyone. If you are up for trying something meaningful to help achieve your goal of a college education, then design an advertisement against distracted driving. You will be judged based on the quality of the content in terms of marketability, and how it effectively convinces drivers to stay focused on the road. To qualify, you must like the Comedy Defensive Driving Facebook fan page, take the pledge to not use your phone while driving, and definitely not to drive while you're buzzed. And definitely don't use your phone if driving. All forms of ads are accepted including PSA, music, billboards, media, graphics, etc. No time restraints, however, keep in mind that you are making an advertisement, not a Ridley Scott movie. Overt profanity, and nudity of any kind will not be allowed. Plagiarism automatically disqualified. There is no GPA requirement, financial requirement, or any other kind of requirement–just knowing you are making the effort to get out of bed and do something positive before noon qualifies. Please submit files (all formats accepted) to scholarships@comedydefensivedriving.com only. We will not be judging based on anything other than the advertisement, so don't sweat over an introductory email; just give us your name, and the best way to reach you if you win. Submission deadline is 4/30/16 and the recipient will be announced by 5/31/16.

Award: Scholarship for use in freshman, sophomore, junior, or senior years; not renewable. *Number:* 1. *Amount:* $1000.

Eligibility Requirements: Applicant must be enrolled or expecting to enroll full- or part-time at a two-year or four-year or technical institution or university. Available to U.S. and Canadian citizens.

Application Requirements: Application form. *Deadline:* May 31.

Contact: Richard Schiller
          Comedy Defensive Driving
          1825 W. Walnut Hill Lane
          Suite 101
          Irving, TX 75038
          E-mail: scholarships@comedydefensivedriving.com

COMMON KNOWLEDGE SCHOLARSHIP FOUNDATION

http://www.cksf.org/

COMMON KNOWLEDGE SCHOLARSHIP

The Common Knowledge Scholarship Foundation (CKSF) is a 501(c)(3) nonprofit organization that creates Internet-based quiz competition for students of all ages. There is no essay, long application, or GPA requirement. A single CKSF registration is good from high school all the way through college and graduate school.

Award: Scholarship for use in freshman, sophomore, junior, senior, graduate, or postgraduate years; renewable. *Number:* 1–15. *Amount:* $250–$1000.

Eligibility Requirements: Applicant must be enrolled or expecting to enroll full- or part-time at a two-year or four-year or technical institution or university. Available to U.S. and non-U.S. citizens.

Application Requirements: Application form may be submitted online (http://www.cksf.org), online registration and quiz competition, portfolio. *Deadline:* continuous.

Contact: Daryl Hulce, President
          Phone: 954-262-8553

COMPARECARDS.COM

http://www.comparecards.com

EDU SCHOLARSHIP AWARD

Each month, CompareCards will award $2500 to any qualifying college (or college bound) student in need who can answer a tricky trivia question. Using their best pop culture and math skills, and probably a bit of help from Professor Google, students should be able to answer a series of questions to arrive at a final answer in no time. After the submission deadline, CompareCards will gather all the correct answers and a tiebreaker question will be emailed with a link to submit the answer. Students who submit the correct tiebreaker answer will be entered into a random drawing and one winner will be selected.

Award: Scholarship for use in freshman, sophomore, junior, senior, graduate, or postgraduate years; not renewable. *Number:* 1–12. *Amount:* $2500.

Eligibility Requirements: Applicant must be enrolled or expecting to enroll full- or part-time at a two-year or four-year or technical institution or university. Available to U.S. citizens.

Application Requirements: Application form may be submitted online (http://www.comparecards.com/scholarship-award). *Deadline:* continuous.

Contact: Sarah Meyer
          E-mail: sarah@comparecards.com

CONCERT ARTISTS GUILD

http://www.concertartists.org/

CONCERT ARTISTS GUILD VICTOR ELMALEH COMPETITION

The Concert Artists Guild Victor Elmaleh Competition is an annual competition open to instrumentalists and chamber ensembles performing classical and non-traditional repertoire.

Award: Prize for use in freshman, sophomore, junior, senior, graduate, or postgraduate years; not renewable.

Eligibility Requirements: Applicant must be enrolled or expecting to enroll at an institution or university. Available to U.S. and non-U.S. citizens.

Application Requirements: Application form. *Fee:* $125. *Deadline:* April 14.

Contact: Jessica Lightfoot, Manager, Programs and Development
          Phone: 212-3335200 Ext. 118
          E-mail: info@concertartists.org

CONNECTHER

http://www.connecther.org/

GIRLS IMPACT THE WORLD SCHOLARSHIP PROGRAM

The Girls Impact the World Film Festival, presented by Connecther, is a film festival and scholarship program in which high school and undergraduate college students submit 3-6 minute short films that focus on a variety of global women's issues, including maternal health, misrepresentation of beauty, athletes against assault of women, violence against women, child-marriage, sex-trafficking, poverty alleviation, environmental issues, etc.

Award: Scholarship for use in freshman, sophomore, junior, or senior years; renewable. *Number:* 12. *Amount:* $1000–$5000.

Eligibility Requirements: Applicant must be age 13-25 and enrolled or expecting to enroll full- or part-time at a two-year or four-year or technical institution or university. Available to U.S. and non-U.S. citizens.

Application Requirements: Application form. *Deadline:* January 20.

Contact: Lila Igram
          Connecther
          12301 Zeller Lane
          Austin, TX 78753
          E-mail: filmfest@connecther.org

CONSTITUTING AMERICA

http://www.constitutingamerica.org

WE THE FUTURE CONTEST

We The Future Contest offers a $1000 scholarship for high school students, $2000 scholarship for college students plus a mentoring trip. Contest information about how to enter, and prizes including scholarships, may be found at http://www.constitutingamerica.org/downloads.php. Entry topics are based on the U.S. Constitution.

Award: Scholarship for use in freshman, sophomore, junior, senior, or graduate years; not renewable. *Number:* 12–12. *Amount:* $1000–$2000.

Eligibility Requirements: Applicant must be enrolled or expecting to enroll full- or part-time at a two-year or four-year institution or university. Available to U.S. citizens.

Application Requirements: Application form may be submitted online (http://www.constitutingamerica.org/docs/WeTheFutureContestPermission.pdf), contest entry form, entry in a contest. *Deadline:* September 17.

Contact: Ms. Amanda Hughes, Outreach Director
Constituting America
PO Box 1988
Colleyville, TX 76034
Phone: 888-937-0917
E-mail: wethepeople917@yahoo.com

CORELLA AND BERTRAM F. BONNER FOUNDATION

http://www.bonner.org

BONNER SCHOLARS PROGRAM

Student apply directly to the colleges and universities sponsoring the program. It is a four year scholarship program, in return students are required to complete 10 hours of community service per week and two summers of service at 300 hours each for which they receive a stipend.

Award: Scholarship for use in freshman, sophomore, junior, or senior years; renewable. *Number:* 325–1300. *Amount:* $5000.

Eligibility Requirements: Applicant must be enrolled or expecting to enroll full-time at a four-year institution or university. Available to U.S. and non-U.S. citizens.

Application Requirements: Application form. *Deadline:* continuous.

Contact: Mr. Robert Hackett, President
Corella and Bertram F. Bonner Foundation
10 Mercer Street
Princeton, NJ 08540
Phone: 609-924-6663
Fax: 609-683-4626
E-mail: rhackett@bonner.org

COUPONCHIEF.COM

https://www.couponchief.com/

COUPONCHIEF.COM SCHOLARSHIP PROGRAM

We at CouponChief.com want to support young leaders that understand frugality and saving money, and how the skills and knowledge of using coupons can contribute to that end. We will award 1 scholarship winner with $1000 to put towards education every year.

Award: Scholarship for use in freshman, sophomore, junior, senior, graduate, or postgraduate years; not renewable. *Number:* 1. *Amount:* $1000.

Eligibility Requirements: Applicant must be enrolled or expecting to enroll full- or part-time at a two-year or four-year or technical institution or university. Available to U.S. citizens.

Application Requirements: *Deadline:* July 31.

Contact: Angela Thompson
CouponChief.com
774 Mays Blvd #10-528
Incline Village, NV 89451
Incline Village, NV 89451
Phone: 858-342-5970
E-mail: angela@couponchief.com

COURAGE TO GROW SCHOLARSHIP PROGRAM

https://couragetogrowscholarship.com/

COURAGE TO GROW SCHOLARSHIP

High school juniors and seniors or college students with a minimum GPA of 2.5 or better are eligible. U.S. citizens only please. An essay of 250 words or less is required. One award of $500 will be given out per month. Applicants can reapply each month throughout the year.

Award: Scholarship for use in freshman, sophomore, junior, senior, graduate, or postgraduate years; not renewable. *Number:* 1–12. *Amount:* $500.

Eligibility Requirements: Applicant must be enrolled or expecting to enroll full- or part-time at a two-year or four-year or technical institution or university. Applicant must have 2.5 GPA or higher. Available to U.S. citizens.

Application Requirements: Application form, essay. *Deadline:* continuous.

Contact: Kimberly Johnson, Founder
Courage to Grow Scholarship Program
PO Box 2507
Chelan, WA 98816
Phone: 509-731-3056
E-mail: support@couragetogrowscholarship.com

COURSE HERO, INC.

http://www.coursehero.com

COURSE HERO $5,000 MONTHLY SCHOLARSHIP

While Course Hero can help you study smarter, we can also help you pay for school with a $5,000 monthly scholarship. It only takes a few minutes to apply! Just sign up for a free account and respond to our creative short-answer question

Award: Scholarship for use in freshman, sophomore, junior, senior, graduate, or postgraduate years; not renewable. *Number:* 1. *Amount:* $1000–$5000.

Eligibility Requirements: Applicant must be enrolled or expecting to enroll full- or part-time at a two-year or four-year institution or university. Available to U.S. citizens.

Application Requirements: *Deadline:* continuous.

Contact: Sura Hussain, Marketing Manager
Course Hero, Inc.
1400B Seaport Boulevard, Floor 2
Redwood City, CA 94063
Phone: 888-634-9397
E-mail: scholarships@coursehero.com

CRESCENT ELECTRIC SUPPLY COMPANY

http://www.cesco.com/

CRESCENT ELECTRIC SUPPLY COMPANY'S ENERGY EFFICIENT SCHOLARSHIP

If you are currently enrolled in college or headed there in 2018 and want to win a $1000 scholarship to help cover expenses, consider entering the Crescent Electric College Scholarship Contest. Crescent Electric Supply Company will award a $1000 scholarship to a highly motivated student who can thoughtfully share a photo of their effort to minimize energy usage on social media.

Award: Scholarship for use in freshman, sophomore, or junior years; not renewable. *Number:* 1. *Amount:* $1000.

Eligibility Requirements: Applicant must be age 16-22 and enrolled or expecting to enroll full-time at a two-year or four-year or technical institution or university. Available to U.S. and Canadian citizens.

Application Requirements: Personal photograph. *Deadline:* August 8.

Contact: Scholarship Director
E-mail: jessie@elitefixtures.com

CSA FRATERNAL LIFE

http://www.csalife.com

CSA FRATERNAL LIFE SCHOLARSHIP

CSA Scholarship Applicants must be a member in good standing of CSA Fraternal Life for a minimum of two (2) continuous years at the time of application. Must also have at least $5,000 face value in permanent life insurance or $1,000 cash value in an annuity with CSA Fraternal Life; be pursuing an undergraduate degree at an accredited junior college, college, or university on a full-time basis (full-time is defined as a minimum 12 credit hours per semester for at least two semesters per academic year). Students planning on attending a technical/vocation school full time are also eligible for an award. Must have a cumulative 3.0 or higher GPA (based on a 4.0 scale) upon graduation from high school. Students already attending college must submit college transcripts which indicate a 3.0 GPA (based on a 4.0 scale). Students applying for a scholarship who have not yet completed a full year of undergraduate studies must submit their high school transcripts indicating a 3.0 or better GPA. ACT or SAT score sheets must be included in your application. Must remain a CSA member in good standing throughout the period covered by the award. Determining factors in qualification include: grade point average (25 points), college test scores (30 points), extracurricular activities including CSA activities (15 points), and essay (30 points). Essays will be evaluated by an independent party. Total points will determine the monetary amount of each award.

Award: Scholarship for use in freshman, sophomore, junior, or senior years; not renewable.

Eligibility Requirements: Applicant must be enrolled or expecting to enroll full-time at a four-year or technical institution or university. Applicant must have 3.0 GPA or higher. Available to U.S. citizens.

Application Requirements: Application form, essay, personal photograph. *Deadline:* March 23.

Contact: Ms. Amanda Lovell, Fraternal Director
CSA Fraternal Life
2050 Finley Road
Suite 70
Lombard, IL 60148
Phone: 630-472-0500 Ext. 4352
Fax: 630-472-1100
E-mail: alovell@csalife.com

CULEARN, LLC

https://www.culearn.org/

CULEARN 2018 SCHOLARSHIP

Paying for college is difficult, especially as college costs continue to rise, and cuLearn is here to help you navigate the confusing world of college finance with our educational resources. In addition, we can help make paying for college a little easier with our 2018 Scholarship drawings. You have the chance to win $2,018 to help cover the costs of college by subscribing to our blog. In 2018, we will be awarding 22 scholarships! Register only once and you will be eligible for each of the 3 drawings in 2018. Drawing dates: May 18, August 18, and November 18, 2018. Earn an additional scholarship entry by submitting a blog post! We want you to share your experience and ideas on how to pay for college while avoiding excessive debt. Your ideas could help others students in planning and paying for college. Submit a qualifying original written blog post and you can earn an extra entry into the scholarship sweepstakes! In fact, you can earn up to 5 extra entries, 1 per submitted blog post. Each blog post must be sent in a separate email. It has to come from the same email address you used in your initial entry. The email's subject line must contain the phrase "cuLearn 2018 Scholarship Entry." The body of the email must contain your first and last name, your school; and an original essay, between approximately 250 and 500 words, containing words of wisdom on how to pay for college while avoiding excessive debt. Final date for submitting blog entries is November 17, 2018. See the official rules for the complete terms to which you will be agreeing.

Award: Scholarship for use in freshman, sophomore, junior, senior, graduate, or postgraduate years; not renewable. *Number:* 22. *Amount:* $2018.

Eligibility Requirements: Applicant must be enrolled or expecting to enroll full- or part-time at a two-year or four-year or technical institution or university. Available to U.S. citizens.

Application Requirements: *Deadline:* November 17.

Contact: Kristy Bertsch, Vice President, Strategic Marketing and
Program Development
cuLearn, LLC
625 Fourth Avenue South
Minneapolis, MN 55415
Phone: 651-485-5502
E-mail: kristy.bertsch@culearn.org

THE DALLAS FOUNDATION

http://www.dallasfoundation.org/

BROOK HOLLOW GOLF CLUB SCHOLARSHIP

Established in 2007 to benefit children or grandchildren of full- or part-time employees of Brook Hollow Golf Club. Applicants must be a child or grandchild of an active employee in good standing of Brook Hollow Golf Club and a graduating high school senior who has been accepted in, or a student already enrolled in, an undergraduate program of study in pursuit of a degree from a public or private, regionally accredited community college, college, university, or vocational or trade institute. Applicants must demonstrate financial need.

Award: Scholarship for use in freshman or sophomore years; renewable. *Amount:* $2000–$4500.

Eligibility Requirements: Applicant must be high school student and planning to enroll or expecting to enroll full-time at a two-year or four-year or technical institution or university.

Application Requirements: Application form, financial need analysis, transcript. *Deadline:* April 1.

Contact: Rachel Lasseter, Program Associate
Phone: 214-741-9898
E-mail: scholarships@dallasfoundation.org

THE HIRSCH FAMILY SCHOLARSHIP

The Hirsch Family Scholarship was established as a scholarship fund in 2009 to benefit dependent children of active employees of Eagle Materials, Performance Chemicals and Ingredients, Martin Fletcher, Hadlock Plastics, Highlander Partners and any of their majority-owned subsidiaries.

Award: Scholarship for use in freshman, sophomore, junior, or senior years; not renewable. *Amount:* $2000–$10,000.

Eligibility Requirements: Applicant must be enrolled or expecting to enroll full-time at a two-year or four-year or technical institution or university.

Application Requirements: Application form, transcript. *Deadline:* March 15.

Contact: Rachel Lasseter, Program Associate
Phone: 214-741-9898
E-mail: scholarships@dallasfoundation.org

KRISTOPHER KASPER MEMORIAL SCHOLARSHIP

Award for a child of a Centex Homes Texas Region employee. Based on the eligibility criteria, one scholarship of at least $1000 will be awarded annually. The scholarship may be used for tuition, fees, or books, and will be paid directly to the school. There will be an opportunity for renewal if renewal requirements are met.

Award: Scholarship for use in freshman, sophomore, junior, or senior years; renewable. *Number:* 1. *Amount:* $1000.

Eligibility Requirements: Applicant must be high school student and planning to enroll or expecting to enroll full-time at a two-year or four-year or technical institution or university. Applicant must have 2.5 GPA or higher.

Application Requirements: Application form, community service, recommendations or references, resume, transcript. *Deadline:* April 15.

Contact: Rachel Lasseter, Program Associate
Phone: 214-741-9898
E-mail: scholarships@dallasfoundation.org

DARIN C. BANKS FOUNDATION

http://www.dcbfoundation.org

DCBF COLLEGE SCHOLARSHIP

DCBF's Annual Scholarship Competition awards (3) $1000 scholarships to high school seniors selected by the DCBF Scholarship Committee. The competition commences November 1, 2018 and closes on January 31, 2019. More details can be found on our website, http://www.dcbfoundation.org or by contacting DCBF@DCBFoundation.org.

Award: Scholarship for use in freshman year; not renewable. *Number:* 3. *Amount:* $1000.

Eligibility Requirements: Applicant must be high school student; age 16-19 and planning to enroll or expecting to enroll full-time at a four-year institution or university. Applicant must have 3.0 GPA or higher. Available to U.S. citizens.

Application Requirements: Application form, community service, interview, portfolio. *Deadline:* January 31.

DAUGHTERS OF THE CINCINNATI

http://www.daughters1894.org/

DAUGHTERS OF THE CINCINNATI SCHOLARSHIP

Need and merit-based award available to graduating high school seniors. Minimum GPA of 3.0 required. Must be daughter of commissioned officer in regular Army, Navy, Coast Guard, Air Force, Marines (active, retired, or deceased). Must submit parent's rank and branch of service. Application can be completed and downloaded from website, http://www.daughters1894.org.

Award: Scholarship for use in freshman year; renewable. *Number:* 4–5. *Amount:* $3000–$5000.

Eligibility Requirements: Applicant must be high school student; planning to enroll or expecting to enroll full-time at a four-year institution or university and female. Applicant must have 3.0 GPA or higher. Available to U.S. citizens.

Application Requirements: Application form, essay, financial need analysis. *Deadline:* March 15.

Contact: Mrs. Evelyn Donatelli, Scholarship Administrator
    Phone: 212-991-9945
    E-mail: scholarships@daughters1894.org

THE DAVID & DOVETTA WILSON SCHOLARSHIP FUND

http://www.wilsonfund.org/

THE DAVID & DOVETTA WILSON SCHOLARSHIP FUND

The purpose of The David and Dovetta Wilson Scholarship Fund (DDWSF) is to provide deserving high school seniors across the nation with financial assistance to pursue their academic goals.

Award: Scholarship for use in freshman year; not renewable. *Number:* 9. *Amount:* $300–$1000.

Eligibility Requirements: Applicant must be enrolled or expecting to enroll full-time at a two-year or four-year institution or university. Available to U.S. citizens.

Application Requirements: Application form, community service, essay, financial need analysis, personal photograph. *Fee:* $20. *Deadline:* March 31.

Contact: Timothy Wilson, Treasurer
    The David & Dovetta Wilson Scholarship Fund
    115-67 237th Street
    Elmont, NY 11003
    Phone: 516-643-5762
    E-mail: ddwsf4@aol.com

DEFENSIVEDRIVING.COM

http://defensivedriving.com

DEFENSIVEDRIVING.COM SCHOLARSHIP

This award will be given to the high school senior or college student who submits the most unique video following the prompt under the Make A Video tab on https://www.defensivedriving.com/scholarship. Applicants are also required to like DefensiveDriving.com's Facebook page to be considered. See detailed instructions here: https://www.defensivedriving.com/scholarship

Award: Scholarship for use in freshman, sophomore, junior, or senior years; not renewable. *Number:* 1. *Amount:* $1000.

Eligibility Requirements: Applicant must be enrolled or expecting to enroll full- or part-time at a two-year or four-year or technical institution or university. Available to U.S. citizens.

Application Requirements: *Deadline:* May 30.

DELETE CYBERBULLYING

http://www.deletecyberbullying.org

DELETE CYBERBULLYING SCHOLARSHIP

The application form is only available online. The purpose of this scholarship is to get students committed to the cause of deleting cyberbullying.

Award: Scholarship for use in freshman, sophomore, junior, senior, or graduate years; not renewable. *Number:* 2. *Amount:* $1500.

Eligibility Requirements: Applicant must be enrolled or expecting to enroll full- or part-time at a two-year or four-year or technical institution or university. Available to U.S. citizens.

Application Requirements: Application form, essay. *Deadline:* June 30.

Contact: Scholarship Coordinator
    E-mail: help@deletecyberbullying.org

DENTAL INSURANCE SHOP

https://www.dentalinsuranceshop.com/index.html

DENTAL INSURANCE SHOP MERIT SCHOLARSHIP

We know saving up for school can be tough. At The Dental Insurance Shop, we believe that scholarships can give ambitious students the opportunity to focus on his or her studies instead of worrying about the cost of books and tuition. With that little extra help, we believe you can achieve greatness. The Dental Insurance Shop is offering a $1,000 non-renewable scholarship to enable one student chosen from all entries to pursue his or her education. All entries must be made by using the application on https://www.dentalinsuranceshop.com/scholarship.html.

Award: Scholarship for use in freshman year; not renewable. *Number:* 1. *Amount:* $1000.

Eligibility Requirements: Applicant must be high school student and planning to enroll or expecting to enroll full-time at a two-year or four-year institution or university. Applicant must have 3.5 GPA or higher. Available to U.S. citizens.

Application Requirements: Application form. *Deadline:* June 30.

Contact: Kevin Knutson
    Dental Insurance Shop
    12280 Nicollet Ave
    Suite #104
    Burnsville, MN 55306
    Phone: 855-871-2242
    E-mail: scholarship@dentalinsuranceshop.com

DIGITAL RESPONSIBILITY

http://www.digitalresponsibility.org

DIGITAL PRIVACY SCHOLARSHIP

The purpose of this scholarship is to help you understand why you should be cautious about what you post on the Internet. You must be a high school freshman, sophomore, junior, or senior or a current or entering college or graduate school student of any level. Home schooled students are also eligible. There is no age limit. Complete the application form including a 140-character message about digital privacy. The top 10 applications will be selected as finalists. The finalists will be asked to write a full length 500- to 1,000-word essay about digital privacy.

Award: Scholarship for use in freshman, sophomore, junior, senior, graduate, or postgraduate years; not renewable. *Number:* up to 2. *Amount:* $500–$1500.

Eligibility Requirements: Applicant must be enrolled or expecting to enroll full- or part-time at a two-year or four-year or technical institution or university. Available to U.S. citizens.

Application Requirements: Application form, application form may be submitted online (http://www.digitalresponsibility.org/digital-privacy-scholarship/), essay. *Deadline:* June 30.

Contact: Scholarship Coordinator
    E-mail: scholarship@digitalresponsibility.org

DON'T TEXT AND DRIVE SCHOLARSHIP

The purpose of this scholarship is to help you understand the risks of texting while driving. You must be a high school freshman, sophomore, junior, or senior or a current or entering college or graduate school student of any level. Home schooled students are also eligible. There is no age limit. Complete the application form including a 140-character message about texting while driving. The top 10 applications will be selected as finalists. The finalists will be asked to write a full length 500- to 1,000-word essay about texting while driving.

Award: Scholarship for use in freshman, sophomore, junior, senior, graduate, or postgraduate years; not renewable. *Number:* up to 2. *Amount:* $500–$1500.

Eligibility Requirements: Applicant must be enrolled or expecting to enroll full- or part-time at a two-year or four-year or technical institution or university. Available to U.S. citizens.

Application Requirements: Application form, application form may be submitted online (http://www.digitalresponsibility.org/dont-text-and-drive-scholarship/), essay. *Deadline:* September 30.

Contact: Scholarship Coordinator
  E-mail: scholarship@digitalresponsibility.org

E-WASTE SCHOLARSHIP

The purpose of this scholarship is to help you understand the impact of e-waste and what can be done to reduce e-waste. You must be a high school freshman, sophomore, junior, or senior or a current or entering college or graduate school student of any level. Home schooled students are also eligible. There is no age limit. Complete the application form below including a 140-character message about e-waste. The top 10 applications will be selected as finalists. The finalists will be asked to write a full length 500- to 1,000-word essay about e-waste.

Award: Scholarship for use in freshman, sophomore, junior, senior, graduate, or postgraduate years; not renewable. *Number:* up to 2. *Amount:* $500–$1500.

Eligibility Requirements: Applicant must be enrolled or expecting to enroll full- or part-time at a two-year or four-year or technical institution or university. Available to U.S. citizens.

Application Requirements: Application form, application form may be submitted online (http://www.digitalresponsibility.org/ewaste-scholarship/), essay. *Deadline:* April 30.

Contact: Scholarship Coordinator
  E-mail: scholarship@digitalresponsibility.org

TECHNOLOGY ADDICTION AWARENESS SCHOLARSHIP

With technology always at the ready at your fingertips, it can be a challenge to unplug. But taking a break from technology is healthy for both the mind and body. The purpose of this scholarship is to help you understand the negative effects of too much screen time. You must be a high school freshman, sophomore, junior, or senior or a current or entering college or graduate school student of any level. Home schooled students are also eligible. There is no age limit. Complete the application form below including a 140-character message about technology addiction. The top 10 applications will be selected as finalists. The finalists will be asked to write a full length 500- to 1,000-word essay about technology addiction.

Award: Scholarship for use in freshman, sophomore, junior, senior, graduate, or postgraduate years; not renewable. *Number:* up to 2. *Amount:* $500–$1500.

Eligibility Requirements: Applicant must be enrolled or expecting to enroll full- or part-time at a two-year or four-year or technical institution or university. Available to U.S. citizens.

Application Requirements: Application form, application form may be submitted online (http://www.digitalresponsibility.org/technology-addiction-awareness-scholarship/), essay. *Deadline:* January 30.

Contact: Scholarship Coordinator
  E-mail: scholarship@digitalresponsibility.org

DISTINGUISHED YOUNG WOMEN

http://www.distinguishedyw.org

DISTINGUISHED YOUNG WOMEN

We are a non-profit organization that offers Life Skills Workshops to prepare young women for life after high school and over $1 billion in college scholarships opportunities. Plus, it is free to participate. Awards are given to participants in the local, state, and national levels of competition. Must be female, high school juniors or seniors, U.S. citizens, and legal residents of the county and state of competition. Participants are evaluated on scholastic achievement, interview, talent, fitness, and public speaking. The number of awards and their amount vary from year to year.

Award: Scholarship for use in freshman, sophomore, junior, senior, or graduate years; not renewable.

Eligibility Requirements: Applicant must be high school student; age 15-19; planning to enroll or expecting to enroll full-time at a two-year or four-year or technical institution or university and single female. Available to U.S. citizens.

Application Requirements: Application form, interview, personal photograph. *Deadline:* continuous.

Contact: Lisa Lawley Burnette, National Field Director
  Distinguished Young Women
  751 Government Street
  Mobile, AL 36602
  Phone: 251-438-3621
  Fax: 251-431-0063
  E-mail: lisa@distinguishedyw.org

DIVERSITYCOMM, INC.

http://www.diversitycomm.net/

DIVERSEABILITY MAGAZINE SCHOLARSHIP

For the 2018 fall semester, DIVERSEability Magazine will be offering a $500 scholarship that is available to disabled undergraduate students. DIVERSEability is a diversity & inclusion magazine featuring individuals with all types of diverse abilities. It's more than just a magazine raising awareness and providing educational, employment and business opportunities–it's a movement celebrating advancements and achievements that inspires the world. We would like you to tell your story in a brief narrative, starting with an introduction about who you are, your interests, and anything else you feel we should know about you. Then, please provide your entry in a 300-500 word essay about your college experience so far, and your future career plans. Graphic or creative presentations are welcome as well. The scholarship will be awarded to the applicant who best demonstrates a genuine desire and goal of using the scholarship to advance in their field, and an overall passion for knowledge. We are now accepting submissions. The deadline for submitting essays is August 15. You may send us your entry either as a link or attachment to your email. Include your name, mobile phone number and contact information in the email.

Award: Scholarship for use in freshman, sophomore, junior, or senior years; renewable. *Number:* 1. *Amount:* $500.

Eligibility Requirements: Applicant must be enrolled or expecting to enroll full- or part-time at a four-year institution or university. Available to U.S. citizens.

Application Requirements: Application form, essay. *Deadline:* August 15.

PROFESSIONAL WOMAN'S MAGAZINE SCHOLARSHIP

For the 2018 Fall Semester, Professional Woman's Magazine will be offering a $500 scholarship that is available to female undergraduate students. We would like you to tell your story in a brief narrative, starting with an introduction about who you are, your interests, and anything else you feel we should know about you. Then, please provide your entry in a 300-500 word essay about your college experience so far, and your future career plans. Graphic or creative presentations are welcome as well.

Award: Scholarship for use in freshman, sophomore, junior, or senior years; renewable. *Number:* 1. *Amount:* $500.

Eligibility Requirements: Applicant must be enrolled or expecting to enroll full- or part-time at a two-year or four-year institution or university and female. Available to U.S. citizens.

Application Requirements: Application form, essay. *Deadline:* August 15.

EASON & TAMBORNINI, A LAW CORPORATION

https://www.capcitylaw.com/

"INJURY TO OPPORTUNITY" SCHOLARSHIP

The "Injury to Opportunity " Scholarship provides a $2,000 benefit to the children of persons who have suffered or perished from a Personal Injury Accident, or a work related injury. Applicants must apply before their 21st birthday; must have had a parent who suffered an injury, resulting in a permanent disability or wrongful death. Application and information are available here: https://www.capcitylaw.com/injury-to-opportunity-scholarship/

Award: Scholarship for use in freshman, sophomore, junior, or senior years; not renewable. *Number:* 1. *Amount:* $2000.

Eligibility Requirements: Applicant must be age 17-20 and enrolled or expecting to enroll full- or part-time at a two-year or four-year or technical institution or university. Available to U.S. and non-U.S. citizens.

Application Requirements: Application form. *Deadline:* continuous.

Contact: Matthew Eason, Partner & Senior Trial Attorney
Eason & Tambornini, A Law Corporation
1234 H St
Suite 200
Sacramento, CA 95814
Phone: 916-438-1819
Fax: 916-438-1820
E-mail: matthew@capcitylaw.com

E-COLLEGEDEGREE.COM

http://www.e-collegedegree.com/

E-COLLEGEDEGREE.COM ONLINE EDUCATION SCHOLARSHIP AWARD

The award is to be used for online education. Application must be submitted online. Visit website for more information and application, http://www.e-collegedegree.com.

Award: Scholarship for use in freshman, sophomore, junior, senior, graduate, or postgraduate years; renewable. *Number:* 1. *Amount:* $1000.

Eligibility Requirements: Applicant must be enrolled or expecting to enroll full- or part-time at a two-year or four-year or technical institution or university. Available to U.S. citizens.

Application Requirements: Application form, entry in a contest, essay. *Deadline:* December 31.

Contact: Chris Lee, Site Manager
e-CollegeDegree.com
9109 West 101st Terrace
Overland Park, KS 66212
Phone: 913-341-6949
E-mail: scholarship@e-collegedegree.com

EDSOUTH

http://www.edsouth.org/

ECAMPUSTOURS SCHOLARSHIP DRAWING

Two $1000 awards are available.

Award: Scholarship for use in freshman, sophomore, junior, senior, or graduate years; not renewable. *Number:* 2. *Amount:* $1000.

Eligibility Requirements: Applicant must be enrolled or expecting to enroll full- or part-time at a two-year or four-year or technical institution or university. Available to U.S. citizens.

Application Requirements: *Deadline:* March 31.

Contact: Director of Communication
E-mail: info-ecampus@edsouth.org

ELEMENTS BEHAVIORAL HEALTH

https://www.elementsbehavioralhealth.com

ELEMENTS BEHAVIORAL HEALTH COLLEGE TUITION SCHOLARSHIP

Write a 500-word essay responding to the following prompt: The new edition of the Associated Press's Stylebook states the word 'addict' should no longer be used as a noun. In short, a person should be identified separate from their disease. Essay Option: Explain why describing someone as addicted rather than nn addict is important to society in combatting addiction. Design Option: If you prefer, feel free to interpret this topic via an infographic or illustration.

Award: Scholarship for use in freshman, sophomore, junior, or senior years; not renewable. *Number:* 3. *Amount:* $1000–$6000.

Eligibility Requirements: Applicant must be enrolled or expecting to enroll full- or part-time at a four-year institution or university. Available to U.S. citizens.

Application Requirements: Application form, essay. *Deadline:* December 31.

EVERIPEDIA INC.

https://www.everipedia.com

INTERNATIONAL WOMEN IN MEDIA SCHOLARSHIP

The International Women in Media Scholarship was established by Everipedia, Inc. in 2017. It aims to increase awareness of women in journalism and the media, along with the challenges they face around the world. Applicants, instead of writing an essay, will create a Wikipedia-style biography page for a woman of their choice. A sample list of women will be provided, but applicants are free to chose their own. Our scholarship offers an award of $500 and is open to all incoming and current college students.

Award: Scholarship for use in freshman, sophomore, junior, senior, graduate, or postgraduate years; renewable. *Number:* 1. *Amount:* $500.

Eligibility Requirements: Applicant must be enrolled or expecting to enroll full- or part-time at a two-year or four-year or technical institution or university. Available to U.S. and non-U.S. citizens.

Application Requirements: Essay. *Deadline:* July 1.

Contact: Mr. Travis Moore, CTO
Everipedia Inc.
972 Hilgard Ave, PH2
Los Angeles, CA 90024
Phone: 702-723-6417
E-mail: scholarships@everipedia.com

EXECUTIVE WOMEN INTERNATIONAL

http://www.ewiconnect.com/

ADULT STUDENTS IN SCHOLASTIC TRANSITION

Scholarship for adult students at transitional points in their lives. Applicants may be single parents, individuals just entering the workforce, or displaced homemakers. Applications are available on the organization's website, http://www.ewiconnect.com.

Award: Scholarship for use in freshman, sophomore, junior, or senior years; not renewable. *Number:* 100–150. *Amount:* $250–$2500.

Eligibility Requirements: Applicant must be enrolled or expecting to enroll full-time at a two-year or four-year or technical institution or university. Available to U.S. and non-U.S. citizens.

Application Requirements: Application form, essay, financial need analysis, interview, personal photograph, recommendations or references, self-addressed stamped envelope with application, tax information, transcript.

EXECUTIVE WOMEN INTERNATIONAL SCHOLARSHIP PROGRAM

Competitive award to high school juniors planning careers in any business or professional field of study which requires a four-year college degree. Award is renewable based on continuing eligibility. All awards are given through local Chapters of the EWI. Applicant must apply through nearest Chapter and live within the Chapter's boundaries. Student must have a sponsoring teacher and school to be considered, and only one applicant per school. For more details visit http://www.ewiconnect.com.

Award: Scholarship for use in freshman, sophomore, junior, or senior years; renewable. *Number:* 75–100. *Amount:* $1000–$10,000.

Eligibility Requirements: Applicant must be high school student; age 15-17 and planning to enroll or expecting to enroll full-time at a four-year institution or university. Available to U.S. and non-U.S. citizens.

Application Requirements: Application form, community service, essay, interview, personal photograph, recommendations or references, self-addressed stamped envelope with application, transcript.

Contact: Mr. James Pollan, Executive Director and Trustee
E-mail: stuhrstudents@earthlink.net

FEDERAL EMPLOYEE EDUCATION AND ASSISTANCE FUND

http://www.feea.org/

FEDERAL EMPLOYEE EDUCATION AND ASSISTANCE FUND SCHOLARSHIP PROGRAM

The FEEA Scholarship Program is for current civilian federal employees and their dependent family members (spouse/child). The applicant or the applicant's sponsoring federal employee must have at least three (3) years of civilian federal service by application deadline. The applicant must be at least a college freshman by the fall semester. All applicants must have at least a 3.0 cumulative grade point average (CGPA) unweighted on a 4.0 scale. All applicants must be current high school seniors or college students working towards an accredited degree or enrolled in a two- or four-year undergraduate, graduate or postgraduate program.

Award: Scholarship for use in freshman, sophomore, junior, senior, graduate, or postgraduate years; not renewable. *Number:* 350–450. *Amount:* $1000.

Eligibility Requirements: Applicant must be enrolled or expecting to enroll full- or part-time at a two-year or four-year or technical institution or university. Applicant must have 3.0 GPA or higher. Available to U.S. citizens.

Application Requirements: Application form, community service, essay. *Deadline:* March 21.

Contact: Niki Gleason, Sr Program and Operations Manager
Federal Employee Education and Assistance Fund
1641 Prince St
Alexandria, VA 22314
Phone: 202-554-0007 Ext. 102
E-mail: ngleason@feea.org

NATIONAL ACTIVE AND RETIRED FEDERAL EMPLOYEE SCHOLARSHIP PROGRAM

Children, grandchildren, great-grandchildren and step-children of all current NARFE members are eligible. Applicant must be a high school senior planning to attend college full time in the fall of the application year. Must have a GPA of at least 3.0 on an unweighted 4.0 scale.

Award: Scholarship for use in freshman year; not renewable. *Amount:* $1000.

Eligibility Requirements: Applicant must be high school student and planning to enroll or expecting to enroll full-time at a two-year or four-year institution or university. Applicant must have 3.0 GPA or higher. Available to U.S. citizens.

Application Requirements: Application form, community service, essay. *Deadline:* March 21.

Contact: Niki Gleason, Sr Program and Operations Manager
Federal Employee Education and Assistance Fund
1641 Prince St
Alexandria, VA 22314
Phone: 202-554-0007 Ext. 102
E-mail: ngleason@feea.org

FIRST CHOICE COLLEGE PLACEMENT LLC

http://www.firstchoicecollege.com/

ADMISSIONHOOK.COM ESSAY CONTEST

This award is part of our ongoing mission to help students get into and pay for the college of their dreams. There are two ways to win the scholarship. First, you can create an account and submit your essay. If your essay is one of the top 5 vote recipients, your essay will be reviewed by a committee and the winner will be notified within 14 days of the close of the scholarship contest. Second, you can create an account and vote on other student's essays (you can also vote on your own). The registered user who votes on the most essays as of the scholarship deadline will receive a $500 scholarship.

Award: Prize for use in freshman, sophomore, junior, or senior years; not renewable. *Number:* 2–4. *Amount:* $500–$1000.

Eligibility Requirements: Applicant must be enrolled or expecting to enroll full-time at a two-year or four-year institution or university. Available to U.S. citizens.

Application Requirements: Application form, essay.

Contact: Mr. James Maroney, Managing Member
First Choice College Placement LLC
50 Cherry Street
Milford, CT 06460
Phone: 203-878-7998
Fax: 203-878-6087
E-mail: james@admissionhook.com

FIRST MARINE DIVISION ASSOCIATION

http://www.1stmarinedivisionassociation.org/

FIRST MARINE DIVISION ASSOCIATION SCHOLARSHIP FUND

Scholarship to assist dependents of deceased or 100 percent permanently disabled veterans of service with the 1st Marine Division in furthering their education towards a bachelor's degree. Awarded to full-time, undergraduate students who are attending an accredited college, university, or higher technical trade school, up to a maximum of four years.

Award: Scholarship for use in freshman, sophomore, junior, or senior years; renewable. *Number:* 15–25. *Amount:* $1750.

Eligibility Requirements: Applicant must be enrolled or expecting to enroll full-time at a two-year or four-year or technical institution or university and single. Available to U.S. citizens.

Application Requirements: Application form, essay. *Deadline:* continuous.

Contact: Col. Len Hayes, Executive Director
Phone: 760-712-7088
E-mail: lenhayes@cox.net

FLORIDA STATE DEPARTMENT OF EDUCATION

http://www.floridastudentfinancialaid.org/

ROSEWOOD FAMILY SCHOLARSHIP FUND

Renewable award for eligible direct descendants of African-American Rosewood families affected by the incident of January 1923. Must not have previously received a baccalaureate degree. For more details, visit the website at http://www.FloridaStudentFinancialAid.org/SSFAD/home/uamain.htm.

Award: Scholarship for use in freshman, sophomore, junior, or senior years; renewable. *Number:* up to 50. *Amount:* up to $6100.

Eligibility Requirements: Applicant must be enrolled or expecting to enroll full- or part-time at a two-year or four-year or technical institution or university and studying in Florida. Available to U.S. citizens.

Application Requirements: Application form, documentation of Rosewood ancestry, financial need analysis. *Deadline:* April 1.

Contact: Florida Department of Education, Office of Student Financial Assistance, Customer Service
Florida State Department of Education
325 West Gaines Street
Tallahassee, FL 32399
Phone: 888-827-2004
E-mail: osfa@fldoe.org

FORECLOSURE.COM

http://www.foreclosure.com/

FORECLOSURE.COM SCHOLARSHIP PROGRAM

The Foreclosure.com Scholarship Program encourages students to offer innovative ideas and solutions to "solve the foreclosure crisis" in the form of an essay. Essay submissions must be between 1000 and 2500 words and all accepted freshman and enrolled under-graduate and graduate-students are eligible to apply. First place prize is $5000 and second through fifth place will be awarded $1,000 each. Checks will be made out to the college or university attended in the form of a non-renewable scholarship grant.

Award: Scholarship for use in freshman, sophomore, junior, or senior years; not renewable. *Number:* 5. *Amount:* $1000–$5000.

Eligibility Requirements: Applicant must be enrolled or expecting to enroll full- or part-time at a two-year or four-year or technical institution or university. Available to U.S. citizens.

Application Requirements: Application form, application form may be submitted online (http://www.foreclosure.com/scholarship), essay. *Deadline:* December 15.

Contact: Mrs. Jacquelyn Marks
Foreclosure.com
1095 Broken Sound Parkway NW
Suite 200
Boca Raton, FL 33435
Phone: 561-988-9669 Ext. 7387

FOSTER CARE TO SUCCESS

http://www.fc2success.org/

FOSTER CARE TO SUCCESS SCHOLARSHIP PROGRAM

Award of up to $6000 to young people under the age of 25 who spent the 12 consecutive months prior to their 18th birthday in foster care or who were adopted or placed into legal guardianship from foster care after their 16th birthday. Scholarships are awarded for the pursuit of postsecondary education, including vocational/technical training, and are renewable for up to five years based on satisfactory progress and financial need.

Award: Scholarship for use in freshman, sophomore, junior, or senior years; not renewable. *Number:* 100. *Amount:* $1000–$6000.

Eligibility Requirements: Applicant must be enrolled or expecting to enroll full- or part-time at a two-year or four-year or technical institution or university. Available to U.S. citizens.

Application Requirements: Application form, essay, financial need analysis. *Deadline:* March 31.

Contact: Dana Brown, Manager, Scholarships and Student Programs
Foster Care to Success
23811 Chagrin Blvd. Suite 210
Cleveland, OH 44122
Phone: 571-203-0270 Ext. 130
E-mail: dana@fc2success.org

FOUNDATION FOR INDEPENDENT HIGHER EDUCATION

http://www.fihe.org/

HSBC FIRST OPPORTUNITY PARTNERS SCHOLARSHIPS

Award targets the students with multiple at-risk factors as identified by financial aid officers in FIHE colleges. For undergraduate students with at least 2.4 GPA after the first semester of the freshman year. Deadline varies.

Award: Scholarship for use in sophomore or junior years; renewable. *Amount:* $5000.

Eligibility Requirements: Applicant must be enrolled or expecting to enroll full-time at a four-year institution or university. Available to U.S. citizens.

Application Requirements: Application form, essay, financial need analysis, transcript. *Deadline:* varies.

Contact: Ms. Jacalyn Cox, Program Manager
E-mail: jcox@fihe.org

UPS SCHOLARSHIP PROGRAM

Scholarship program for undergraduate students attending FIHE-affiliated colleges. Deadline varies.

Award: Scholarship for use in freshman, sophomore, junior, or senior years; not renewable. *Amount:* $2700.

Eligibility Requirements: Applicant must be enrolled or expecting to enroll full- or part-time at a four-year institution or university. Available to U.S. and non-U.S. citizens.

Application Requirements: *Deadline:* varies.

Contact: Dr. Myrvin Christopherson, Acting President
Phone: 202-367-0333
E-mail: info@fihe.org

FOUNDATION FOR OUTDOOR ADVERTISING RESEARCH AND EDUCATION (FOARE)

http://www.oaaa.org/

FOARE SCHOLARSHIP PROGRAM

One-time award of $2000 for 6 students. High school seniors, undergraduates, and graduate students enrolled in or accepted to an accredited institution are eligible to apply. Selections are based on financial need, academic performance, and career goals.

Award: Scholarship for use in freshman, sophomore, junior, senior, or graduate years; not renewable. *Number:* 6. *Amount:* $2000.

Eligibility Requirements: Applicant must be enrolled or expecting to enroll full-time at a four-year institution or university. Available to U.S. citizens.

Application Requirements: Application form, essay, financial need analysis, transcript. *Deadline:* June 15.

Contact: Scholarship Program
Foundation for Outdoor Advertising Research and Education (FOARE)
c/o Thomas M. Smith & Associates
4601 Tilden Street, NW
Washington, DC 20016
Phone: 202-364-7130
E-mail: tmfsmith@starpower.net

THE FRANK M. AND GERTRUDE R. DOYLE FOUNDATION INC.

http://www.frankmdoyle.org/

THE FRANK M. AND GERTRUDE R. DOYLE FOUNDATION, INC.

Eligible applicants for this scholarship must be: Graduating seniors or graduates, (G.E.D. is acceptable), of the Huntington Beach Union High School District, Huntington Beach, California; Washoe County Unified High School District, Reno, Nevada; students or graduates of the Huntington Beach Adult High School; students or graduates of the Washoe County Adult High School; graduates or current/previous students of the following community colleges in Southern California: Orange Coast, Golden West, Coastline, Irvine Valley, Fullerton, Cypress, Santa Ana, Saddleback, or Santiago Canyon. Age is not a factor. Applications may be downloaded from the foundations website, http//http://www.frankmdoyle.org anytime after 1 December. See website for details.

Award: Scholarship for use in freshman, sophomore, junior, senior, graduate, or postgraduate years; not renewable. *Amount:* $500–$30,000.

Eligibility Requirements: Applicant must be age 17-99 and enrolled or expecting to enroll full- or part-time at a two-year or four-year or technical institution or university. Available to U.S. citizens.

Application Requirements: Application form, essay. *Deadline:* February 1.

FRESH PRINTS

https://freshprints.com/

GRAND PLAN SCHOLARSHIP

We want to give back to the young people who have been key to our success by making life a little easier for a student. So we're giving one amazing incoming college freshman or sophomore $1,000 to spend on starting a business, buying books, paying tuition, or whatever other costs come with his or her education.

Award: Scholarship for use in freshman or sophomore years; not renewable. *Number:* 1. *Amount:* $1000.

Eligibility Requirements: Applicant must be enrolled or expecting to enroll full-time at a four-year institution or university. Available to U.S. citizens.

Application Requirements: Application form, essay. *Deadline:* August 18.

Contact: Ben Carey
Phone: 302-382-7825
E-mail: ben@freshprints.com

GERMAN ACADEMIC EXCHANGE SERVICE (DAAD)

http://www.daad.org/

DAAD GROUP STUDY VISITS

Grants are available for an information visit of seven to twelve days to groups of 10 to 15 students, accompanied by a faculty member. They are intended to encourage contact with academic institutions, groups and individuals in Germany, and offer insight into current issues in the academic, scientific, economic, political and cultural realms. All departments/disciplines are eligible, preference is given to groups with a homogeneous academic background and may be drawn from more than one institution. Applications are possible around November, February and May. Groups will not be eligible for funding in successive years.

Award: Grant for use in junior, senior, or graduate years; not renewable.

Eligibility Requirements: Applicant must be enrolled or expecting to enroll full-time at a four-year institution. Available to U.S. and non-U.S. citizens.

Application Requirements: Application form.

Contact: DAAD New York
German Academic Exchange Service (DAAD)
871 UN Plaza
New York, NY 10017
Phone: 212-758-3223
E-mail: daadny@daad.org

DAAD STUDY SCHOLARSHIP

DAAD's flagship competitive scholarship awarded for study at all public universities in Germany. Open to all fields. Study Scholarships are granted for one academic year with the possibility of a one-year extension for students completing a full degree program in Germany (between 10 and 24 months)

Award: Scholarship for use in senior or graduate years; renewable.

Eligibility Requirements: Applicant must be enrolled or expecting to enroll full-time at a four-year institution or university. Available to U.S. and non-U.S. citizens.

Application Requirements: Application form.

Contact: DAAD New York
German Academic Exchange Service (DAAD)
871 UN Plaza
New York, NY 10017
Phone: 212-758-3223
E-mail: daadny@daad.org

GETEDUCATED.COM

https://www.geteducated.com/

$1,000 EXCELLENCE IN ONLINE EDUCATION SCHOLARSHIP

Scholarships for distance education available only to U.S. citizens enrolled in a CHEA-accredited online degree program located in the USA with a minimum cumulative GPA of 3.0. Provide a copy of your most recent grade transcripts, completed application, a copy of your most recent FAFSA or 1040 tax return, and submit a 500-word essay: "What a College Degree Means to Me."

Award: Scholarship for use in freshman, sophomore, junior, senior, or graduate years; not renewable. *Number:* 1–6. *Amount:* $1000.

Eligibility Requirements: Applicant must be enrolled or expecting to enroll full- or part-time at a two-year or four-year institution or university. Applicant must have 3.0 GPA or higher. Available to U.S. citizens.

Application Requirements: Application form, essay, financial need analysis. *Deadline:* March 15.

Contact: Tony Huffman, CEO of GetEducated.com
GetEducated.com
PO Box 458
Monterey, VA 24465
Phone: 802-899-4866
E-mail: thuffman@perdiaeducation.com

GIRLTEREST ONLINE MAGAZINE

http://girlterest.com/

GIRLTEREST SCHOLARSHIP PROGRAM FOR YOUNG WOMEN

Girlterest Online Magazine is offering an annual scholarship to undergraduate and postgraduate female students. As strong advocates for higher learning and women's empowerment, we are proud to give back to aspiring women through the Girlterest Yearly Scholarship. This scholarship is merit based, requires an essay submission, and the winning student will receive $1,000 towards their costs of education. All of the application details and terms, as well as the 2018 essay topics are available on our website at girlterest.com/scholarship/.

Award: Scholarship for use in freshman, sophomore, junior, senior, graduate, or postgraduate years; renewable. *Number:* 1. *Amount:* $1000.

Eligibility Requirements: Applicant must be enrolled or expecting to enroll full- or part-time at a two-year or four-year or technical institution or university and female. Available to U.S. and non-U.S. citizens.

Application Requirements: Essay, personal photograph. *Deadline:* December 30.

Contact: Mrs. Maureen Mizrahi, Co-Founder
Girlterest Online Magazine
33 Burla street 75736
Israel
Rishon leZion
Phone: 66-958570634
E-mail: scholarships@girlterest.com

GOASSIGNMENTHELP

https://www.goassignmenthelp.com.au

GO ASSIGNMENT HELP SCHOLARSHIP

3 Scholarships for $1000 each. Scholarship application is available on website. Scholarship open for all institutions, all majors are eligible. Participant should be at least 13 years of age. For other official rules visit: https://www.goassignmenthelp.com.au/scholarship/official-rules/. Since the essay question pertains to rising students debt, the scholarship is open to students from all majors and across geographies.

Award: Scholarship for use in freshman, sophomore, junior, senior, graduate, or postgraduate years; not renewable. *Number:* 3. *Amount:* $1000.

Eligibility Requirements: Applicant must be age 13-65 and enrolled or expecting to enroll full- or part-time at a two-year or four-year or technical institution or university. Available to U.S. and non-U.S. citizens.

Application Requirements: Essay. *Deadline:* December 15.

Contact: Go-Assignment Scholarship Program
GoAssignmentHelp
187 Wolf Road,
Albany, NY 12205
Phone: 617-933-5480
E-mail: scholarships@goassignmenthelp.com.au

GOLDEN KEY INTERNATIONAL HONOUR SOCIETY

http://www.goldenkey.org/

GOLDEN KEY SERVICE AWARD

One award totaling $500, disbursed as $250 to the recipient and $250 to the charity of the recipient's choice. Undergraduate and graduate members who were enrolled as students during the previous academic year are eligible.

Award: Scholarship for use in sophomore, junior, senior, or graduate years; not renewable. *Number:* 1. *Amount:* $500.

Eligibility Requirements: Applicant must be enrolled or expecting to enroll full- or part-time at a four-year institution or university. Available to Canadian and non-U.S. citizens.

Application Requirements: Application form, community service, cover page from the online registration, statement of project, essay, recommendations or references. *Deadline:* March 3.

Contact: Crystal Hunter, Program Manager
Phone: 800-377-2401
E-mail: awards@goldenkey.org

GOODCALL LLC

http://www.goodcall.com

GOODCALL BEST DECISION SCHOLARSHIP

At GoodCall, we try to help people make smarter decisions by giving them access to important data. We want to know about a great decision you've made in your life. Write an essay between 400 and 500 words detailing one of the most important decisions you've made in your life. What information did you rely on? What decision did you make? How did you know it was the right choice? Please apply through our website; do not email.

Award: Scholarship for use in freshman, sophomore, or senior years; not renewable. *Number:* 1. *Amount:* $2500.

Eligibility Requirements: Applicant must be enrolled or expecting to enroll full-time at a two-year or four-year or technical institution or university. Available to U.S. citizens.

Application Requirements: Essay. *Deadline:* July 31.

GOODSHOP

https://www.goodsearch.com/

GOODSHOP ANNUAL SCHOLARSHIP

Here at Goodshop, we give shoppers instant access to the very best coupons for all their favorite online stores. Simultaneously, we donate a percentage of cashback earned to various charities at no extra cost to our users. This year (and every year) we want to take it one step further by giving money directly to promising students. In keeping with our mission, we're offering a $2000 scholarship towards one talented student every single year. https://www.goodsearch.com/scholarship/

Award: Prize for use in freshman, sophomore, junior, senior, graduate, or postgraduate years; renewable. *Number:* 1. *Amount:* $2000.

Eligibility Requirements: Applicant must be enrolled or expecting to enroll full- or part-time at a two-year or four-year or technical institution or university. Available to U.S. citizens.

Application Requirements: Application form. *Deadline:* December 31.

Contact: Matthew Bienz, Representative
E-mail: matthew.bienz@goodsearch.com

GRAND RAPIDS COMMUNITY FOUNDATION

http://www.grfoundation.org/

FRED AND LENA MEIJER SCHOLARSHIP

Applicants must be an employee of Meijer, Inc. or child of a Meijer, Inc employee who has been employed for at least one year by the application deadline of April 1.Children of Team Members must be full-time students.Team Members may be part or full-time students.

Award: Scholarship for use in freshman, sophomore, junior, or senior years; not renewable. *Number:* 200. *Amount:* $3000.

Eligibility Requirements: Applicant must be enrolled or expecting to enroll full- or part-time at a two-year or four-year or technical institution or university. Applicant must have 2.5 GPA or higher. Available to U.S. citizens.

Application Requirements: Application form, essay, financial need analysis. *Deadline:* April 1.

Contact: Ms. Ruth Bishop, Education Program Officer
Grand Rapids Community Foundation
185 Oakes SW
Grand Rapids, MI 49503
Phone: 616-454-1751 Ext. 103
E-mail: rbishop@grfoundation.org

GUARDIAN DEBT RELIEF

https://www.guardiandebtrelief.com/

GUARDIAN DEBT RELIEF SCHOLARSHIP

Guardian Debt Relief is offering a scholarship for students entering into or already enrolled in college. Guardian Debt Relief realizes the importance of higher education and wants to lend our aid to those who pursue a degree. We want to do our part in lowering the amount of debt with which young adults leave college. We will award five (5) scholarships of $1000 each to impressive college students who qualify. Eligible applicants will be required to submit a 2,000 word essay based on one of the three essay topics listed below. The five (5) most impressive and informative essays will be selected for the awards. The applicants must be enrolled in an accredited 4-year university or college located in the United States. Open to both graduate and undergraduate students. Graduating high school seniors with a GPA of 3.0 or higher are eligible to apply for the scholarship. You must have a cumulative GPA of 3.0 if you are already enrolled in college. You must successfully complete the application form and written essay. The essay must be double spaced and submitted through email. Word Documents and PDF (.doc,.docx,.pdf) formats will be accepted. All other formats will not be considered. All essays must be at least 2000 words in length and must include a heading with your full name and date on the first page. Essays totaling less than 2000 words will not be considered. See website for details, https://www.guardiandebtrelief.com/guardian-debt-relief-scholarship/

Award: Scholarship for use in freshman, sophomore, junior, senior, or graduate years; not renewable. *Number:* 1–5. *Amount:* $1–$1000.

Eligibility Requirements: Applicant must be enrolled or expecting to enroll full- or part-time at a two-year or four-year or technical institution or university. Applicant must have 3.0 GPA or higher. Available to U.S. citizens.

Application Requirements: Application form, essay. *Deadline:* December 31.

Contact: Michael Milington
Phone: 212-5920300
E-mail: scholarships@guardiandebtrelief.com

G.W. NETWORKS INC.

http://mmanuts.com

PRINT IT SCHOLARSHIP FOR ASPIRING CONTENT CREATORS

Please contact us to submit your entry or with any questions you may have by sending an email to scholarships@mmanuts.com with Scholarship Inquiry in the subject line. You may also reach us at our main office at (773) 599-1662.

Award: Scholarship for use in freshman, sophomore, junior, or senior years; not renewable. *Number:* 1. *Amount:* $250.

Eligibility Requirements: Applicant must be age 18-50 and enrolled or expecting to enroll full- or part-time at a two-year or four-year or technical institution or university. Available to U.S. citizens.

Application Requirements: Application form. *Deadline:* March 8.

Contact: Mr. Ingo Weigold, President and Owner
G.W. Networks Inc.
112 E Sunset
Lombard, IL 60148
Phone: 630-379-7673
E-mail: ingo.weigold@mmanuts.com

HARVARD TRAVELLERS CLUB PERMANENT FUND

http://www.travellersfund.org/

HARVARD TRAVELLERS CLUB PERMANENT FUND

From one to three grants made each year to persons with projects that involve intelligent travel and exploration. The travel must be intimately involved with research and/or exploration. Prefer applications from persons working on advanced degrees.

Award: Grant for use in freshman, sophomore, junior, senior, graduate, or postgraduate years; not renewable. *Number:* 1–4. *Amount:* $1000–$4000.

Eligibility Requirements: Applicant must be enrolled or expecting to enroll full- or part-time at a four-year institution or university. Available to U.S. and non-U.S. citizens.

Application Requirements: Application form, financial need analysis. *Deadline:* continuous.

Contact: Mr. Jack Deary, Trustee
Harvard Travellers Club Permanent Fund
170 Hubbard St.
Lenox, MA 01240
E-mail: Jackdeary@harvardtravellersclub.org

HEALTHLINE

http://www.healthline.com/

HEALTHLINE STRONGER SCHOLARSHIP PROGRAM

This year's scholarship is dedicated to the advancement of rare and chronic diseases, either through research, patient advocacy, raising awareness, or community building. Together, we're launching our 2018 scholarship program, which aims to assist and empower college students making a positive impact on rare and/or chronic diseases. If you have demonstrated involvement in the advancement of rare and/or chronic disease(s), either through research, patient advocacy, raising awareness, or community building, tell us about it in your application.

Award: Scholarship for use in junior or senior years; not renewable. *Number:* 4. *Amount:* $5000.

Eligibility Requirements: Applicant must be enrolled or expecting to enroll full-time at a four-year institution or university. Applicant must have 3.0 GPA or higher. Available to U.S. and non-Canadian citizens.

Application Requirements: Application form, essay. *Deadline:* May 1.

Contact: Nicole Lascurain, Marketing Manager
Phone: 415-281-3130

HIGH CLASS VAPE CO.

https://highclassvapeco.com/

HIGH CLASS VAPE CO. SCHOLARSHIP PROGRAM

Two Lucky Students a year will receive a $1000 scholarship by simply applying to our scholarship program. Before applying please read our requirements for our scholarships. Must be an full-time undergrad or graduate student at an accredited college or university (will verify by contacting your school) and maintain at least a 2.5 overall GPA. Submission for the first $1000 scholarship is due by December 30th. The winner will be announced on Jan. 30th, 2018. Submission for the second $1000 scholarship is due by Jun. 1st, 2018. The winner will be announced on Aug. 1st, 2018. All we're looking for is for you to write a compelling paper (maximum 1000 words) on one the following prompts to be considered: How will this money help your educational goals? Tell us about how one particular person changed your life for the better. Everyone has undergone a great deal of adversity in their lives, how have you dealt with an especially difficult scenario and overcome it?

Award: Scholarship for use in freshman, sophomore, junior, senior, or graduate years; renewable. *Number:* 2. *Amount:* $4000.

Eligibility Requirements: Applicant must be enrolled or expecting to enroll full-time at a two-year or four-year or technical institution or university. Applicant must have 2.5 GPA or higher. Available to U.S. and non-U.S. citizens.

Application Requirements: Application form, essay, personal photograph. *Deadline:* December 30.

Contact: Mr. Bill Brink, Marketing Manager
High Class Vape Co.
2322 La Mirada Drive
Vista, CA 92081
Phone: 760-801-0256
E-mail: marketing@highclassvapeco.com

HISPANIC ASSOCIATION OF COLLEGES AND UNIVERSITIES (HACU)

http://www.hacu.net/

HISPANIC ASSOCIATION OF COLLEGES AND UNIVERSITIES SCHOLARSHIP PROGRAMS

The scholarship programs are sponsored by corporate organizations. To be eligible, students must attend a HACU member college or university and meet all additional criteria. Visit website, http//http://www.hacu.net, for details.

Award: Scholarship for use in freshman, sophomore, junior, senior, or graduate years; not renewable. *Number:* up to 200. *Amount:* up to $2000.

Eligibility Requirements: Applicant must be enrolled or expecting to enroll full- or part-time at a two-year or four-year institution or university. Applicant must have 3.0 GPA or higher. Available to U.S. citizens.

Application Requirements: Application form, enrollment certification form, essay, financial need analysis, resume, transcript. *Deadline:* May 27.

Contact: Scholarship Department
Phone: 210-692-3805
Fax: 210-692-0823
E-mail: scholarship@hacu.net

HONOR SOCIETY OF PHI KAPPA PHI

http://www.PhiKappaPhi.org/

STUDY ABROAD GRANT COMPETITION

Grants up to $1000 awarded to undergraduates as support for seeking knowledge and experience by studying abroad. Must have 3.75+ cumulative GPA and attend a school with an Active Phi Kappa Phi chapter. Travel cannot begin prior to May 1.

Award: Grant for use in freshman, sophomore, junior, or senior years; not renewable. *Number:* 50. *Amount:* $1000.

Eligibility Requirements: Applicant must be enrolled or expecting to enroll full-time at a four-year institution or university. Available to U.S. and non-U.S. citizens.

Application Requirements: Application form, community service, essay, letter of acceptance into a study abroad program, recommendations or references, transcript. *Deadline:* April 1.

Contact: Mrs. Kelli Partin, Awards and Benefits Manager
Honor Society of Phi Kappa Phi
7576 Goodwood Boulevard
Baton Rouge, LA 70806
Phone: 225-388-4917 Ext. 35
Fax: 225-388-4900
E-mail: kpartin@phikappaphi.org

HORATIO ALGER ASSOCIATION OF DISTINGUISHED AMERICANS

https://scholars.horatioalger.org/

HORATIO ALGER ASSOCIATION SCHOLARSHIP PROGRAMS

The Association provides financial assistance to high school seniors (U.S citizens only) who have faced adversity, have financial need (family adjusted gross income under $55,000), and are pursuing higher education. Recipients must pursue a bachelor's degree, however, students may start their studies at a 2 year school and then transfer to a 4 year university. Minimum 2.0 GPA required.

Award: Scholarship for use in freshman, sophomore, junior, or senior years; renewable. *Number:* 1009. *Amount:* $7000–$25,000.

Eligibility Requirements: Applicant must be high school student and planning to enroll or expecting to enroll full-time at a four-year institution or university. Available to U.S. and Canadian citizens.

Application Requirements: Application form, community service, essay, financial need analysis. *Deadline:* October 25.

Contact: Ms. Colin Dixon, Educational Programs Assistant
Horatio Alger Association of Distinguished Americans
99 Canal Center Plaza, Suite 320
Alexandria, VA 22314
Phone: 703-684-9444
E-mail: programs@horatioalger.org

HORATIO ALGER NATIONAL CAREER & TECHNICAL SCHOLARSHIP PROGRAM

Must have completed high school or plan to complete high school by spring 2016 with plans to enroll at a non-profit post-secondary institution by fall 2016; exhibit a strong commitment to pursue and complete a career or technical program at an accredited non-profit postsecondary institution in the United States; demonstrated critical financial need (must be eligible to receive the Federal Pell grant as determined by completion of the FAFSA); demonstrated perseverance in overcoming adversity; be involved in community service activities; be younger than 30 years old, and a United States citizen. The application will be open with a rolling deadline until all awards have been given out. Applications will be reviewed monthly.

Award: Scholarship for use in freshman or sophomore years; not renewable. *Number:* 510. *Amount:* $2500.

Eligibility Requirements: Applicant must be high school student and planning to enroll or expecting to enroll full-time at a technical institution. Available to U.S. citizens.

Application Requirements: Application form, essay, financial need analysis. *Deadline:* continuous.

Contact: Mr. Colin Dixon, Educational Programs Administrator
Horatio Alger Association of Distinguished Americans
99 Canal Center Plaza, Suite 320
Alexandria, VA 22314
Phone: 703-684-9444
E-mail: scholarships@horatioalger.org

HOW I DECIDE

http://www.howidecide.org

GM GENIUS

GM Genius is a Fantasy Football college scholarship competition that utilizes an instructional series that teaches participants key decision-making and critical thinking concepts. No minimum GPA, resume or essay required. This program is free and students ages 13-19 are eligible to win. No prior experience with football or fantasy football required!

Award: Scholarship for use in freshman, sophomore, junior, or senior years; not renewable. *Number:* 1–3. *Amount:* $1000–$5000.

Eligibility Requirements: Applicant must be age 13-19 and enrolled or expecting to enroll full- or part-time at a two-year or four-year or technical institution or university. Available to U.S. citizens.

Application Requirements: *Deadline:* continuous.

Contact: Ramin Mohajer
E-mail: Info@gmgenius.com

ILLINOIS DEPARTMENT OF VETERANS' AFFAIRS

https://www.illinois.gov/veterans/Pages/default.aspx

MIA/POW SCHOLARSHIP

Any spouse, natural child, adopted child, or any step child of a veteran. Child must attend school prior to 26th birthday. No age limit for spouse. Veteran must be MIA, POW, died as the result of service connected disability determined by the U.S. Department of Veterans' Affairs or is 100% service connected disabled permanent and total established by the U.S. Department of Veterans' Affairs. Veteran must have been an Illinois resident at time of entry into service or became an Illinois resident within 6 months after entering service. Scholarship is equivalent to four full years of college, including summer terms. Based on a point system with 120 points as the maximum. Applicant has 12 years to utilize scholarship from the date they begin using it.

Award: Scholarship for use in freshman, sophomore, junior, senior, graduate, or postgraduate years; renewable.

Eligibility Requirements: Applicant must be enrolled or expecting to enroll full- or part-time at a two-year or four-year institution or university and studying in Illinois. Available to U.S. and non-U.S. citizens.

Application Requirements: Application form. *Deadline:* continuous.

Contact: Mr. Dan Wellman, Administrator
Illinois Department of Veterans' Affairs
833 South Spring Street
Springfield, IL 62794-9432
Phone: 217-782-7838

IMAGINE AMERICA FOUNDATION

http://www.imagine-america.org

ADULT SKILLS EDUCATION PROGRAM (ASEP)

The Adult Skills Education Program (ASEP) offers scholarships to non-traditional students who decide to pursue career college training. This $1,000 award is available to any qualified adult student for attendance at a participating career college.

Award: Scholarship for use in freshman, sophomore, junior, or senior years; not renewable. *Number:* 10,000. *Amount:* $1000.

Eligibility Requirements: Applicant must be enrolled or expecting to enroll full-time at a two-year or four-year or technical institution. Available to U.S. citizens.

Application Requirements: Application form. *Deadline:* continuous.

Contact: Lee Doubleday, Student Services Representative
Imagine America Foundation
12001 Sunrise Valley Drive, Suite 203
Reston, VA 20191
Phone: 571-267-3015
E-mail: leroyd@imagine-america.org

IMAGINE AMERICA HIGH SCHOOL SCHOLARSHIP

Imagine America, sponsored by the Imagine America Foundation (IAF), is a $1,000 career education award that is available to recent high school graduates who are pursuing postsecondary education at participating career colleges across the United States. Only recent high school graduates who meet the following recommended guidelines should apply: likelihood of successful completion of postsecondary education; high school grade point average of 2.5 or greater; financial need; demonstrated voluntary community service during senior year.

Award: Scholarship for use in freshman, sophomore, junior, or senior years; not renewable. *Number:* 15,000. *Amount:* $1000.

Eligibility Requirements: Applicant must be age 16-19 and enrolled or expecting to enroll full- or part-time at a two-year or four-year or technical institution. Applicant must have 2.5 GPA or higher. Available to U.S. citizens.

Application Requirements: Application form. *Deadline:* December 31.

Contact: Lee Doubleday, Student Services Representative
Imagine America Foundation
12001 Sunrise Valley Drive, Suite 203
Reston, VA 20191
Phone: 571-267-3015
E-mail: leroyd@imagine-america.org

INSUREON

http://www.insureon.com

INSUREON SMALL BUSINESS SCHOLARSHIP

Two $2500 scholarships for undergraduate students attending four-year colleges or universities.

Award: Scholarship for use in freshman, sophomore, junior, or senior years; renewable. *Number:* 2. *Amount:* $2500.

Eligibility Requirements: Applicant must be enrolled or expecting to enroll full-time at a four-year institution. Available to U.S. and non-U.S. citizens.

Application Requirements: Application form. *Deadline:* April 30.

Contact: Mr. Alexander Williamson, Business Analyst
E-mail: alex@insureon.com

INTEREXCHANGE FOUNDATION

http://www.interexchange.org/foundation/

CHRISTIANSON GRANT

The Christianson Grant is awarded to U.S. citizens between 18 and 28 who have arranged their own service project abroad programs. Proposed programs must be at least six months in length and emphasize a work component. The grant program does not support independent research projects or academic study abroad programs. Application deadlines: March 15, July 15, and October 15

Award: Grant for use in freshman, sophomore, junior, senior, graduate, or postgraduate years; not renewable. *Number:* 9. *Amount:* $2500–$10,000.

Eligibility Requirements: Applicant must be age 18-28 and enrolled or expecting to enroll full- or part-time at a two-year or four-year or technical institution or university. Available to U.S. citizens.

Application Requirements: Application form, essay, interview. *Fee:* $50. *Deadline:* continuous.

Contact: Ashley Lulling, Senior Program Coordinator
InterExchange Foundation
100 Wall Street
Suite 301
New York, NY 10005
Phone: 917-305-5404
E-mail: grants@interexchange.org

THE INTERNATIONAL ASSOCIATION OF ASSESSING OFFICERS

http://www.iaao.org

IAAO ACADEMIC PARTNERSHIP PROGRAM

IAAO provides financial support for students to complete research in areas related to property appraisal, assessment administration, and property tax policy. The grant carries with it an obligation to submit a satisfactory report for publication by the editor of any IAAO publication and/or a presentation at an IAAO conference.

Award: Grant for use in junior, senior, graduate, or postgraduate years; not renewable. *Number:* 1–5. *Amount:* $1000–$5000.

Eligibility Requirements: Applicant must be enrolled or expecting to enroll full- or part-time at a four-year institution or university. Available to U.S. and non-U.S. citizens.

Application Requirements: Application form, application form may be submitted online (http://www.iaao.org/APPGrant), essay, recommendations or references. *Deadline:* February 15.

Contact: Tami Knight, Director of Research
The International Association of Assessing Officers
314 West 10th Street
Kansas City, MO 64105
Phone: 816-701-8132
Fax: 816-701-8149
E-mail: knight@iaao.org

INTERNATIONAL FLIGHT SERVICES ASSOCIATION

http://www.ifsanet.com

GOURMET FOODS SCHOLARSHIP AWARD

Individuals are selected to receive the award based on scholastic merit and dedication to an advanced education. Must be an employee of a current IFSA member company in good standing, or a relative of an employee of a current IFSA member company. Please address financial need within essay.

Award: Scholarship for use in freshman, sophomore, junior, or senior years; not renewable. *Number:* 1. *Amount:* $5000.

Eligibility Requirements: Applicant must be enrolled or expecting to enroll full- or part-time at an institution or university. Applicant must have 3.0 GPA or higher. Available to U.S. and non-U.S. citizens.

Application Requirements: Application form, essay, recommendations or references, transcript. *Deadline:* May 14.

Contact: Ms. Kelly McLendon, Programs Manager
International Flight Services Association
1100 Johnson Ferry Road, NE
Suite 300
Atlanta, GA 30342
Phone: 678-303-3042
E-mail: kmclendon@kellencompany.com

HARVEY & LAURA ALPERT SCHOLARSHIP AWARD

Individuals are selected to receive this award based on scholastic merit and dedication to pursuing a career in onboard services operations. Must be an employee of a current IFSA member company in good standing, or a relative of an IFSA member company employee.

Award: Scholarship for use in freshman, sophomore, junior, or senior years; not renewable. *Number:* 1. *Amount:* $5000.

Eligibility Requirements: Applicant must be enrolled or expecting to enroll full-time at an institution or university. Available to U.S. and non-U.S. citizens.

Application Requirements: Application form, essay, recommendations or references, transcript. *Deadline:* May 14.

Contact: Ms. Kelly McLendon, Programs Manager
International Flight Services Association
1100 Johnson Ferry Road, NE
Suite 300
Atlanta, GA 30342
Phone: 678-303-3042
E-mail: kmclendon@kellencompany.com

INTERNATIONAL FRANCHISE ASSOCIATION FRANCHISE EDUCATION AND RESEARCH FOUNDATION

http://www.franchise.org

DON DEBOLT FRANCHISING SCHOLARSHIP PROGRAM

Scholarship award to students with a focus on law, marketing, business and franchise management.

Award: Scholarship for use in junior, senior, graduate, or postgraduate years; not renewable. *Number:* 1. *Amount:* $2500.

Eligibility Requirements: Applicant must be enrolled or expecting to enroll full-time at a two-year or four-year institution or university. Applicant must have 3.0 GPA or higher. Available to U.S. and non-U.S. citizens.

Application Requirements: Application form, essay. *Deadline:* continuous.

Contact: Miriam Brewer, Senior Director
International Franchise Association Franchise Education and
Research Foundation
1900 K Street, NW Suite 700
Washington, DC 20006
Phone: 202-662-0784
E-mail: mbrewer@franchise.org

INTERNATIONAL WATER, SANITATION AND HYGIENE FOUNDATION

http://www.iwsh.org/Pages/default.aspx

IWSH ESSAY SCHOLARSHIP CONTEST

The purpose of this scholarship is to acquaint the uninitiated with the crucial importance the plumbing industry plays in our everyday lives and to introduce students to the global impact of IWSH projects. Must submit an essay based on the following topic: In November 2017, IWSH completed the Community Plumbing Challenge 2017 in Bekasi, West Java, Indonesia. If you had to choose one location within the United States to conduct the next Community Plumbing Challenge (providing safe access to clean water and proper sanitation), which location would you choose and why?

Award: Scholarship for use in freshman, sophomore, junior, senior, graduate, or postgraduate years; not renewable. *Number:* 3. *Amount:* $500–$1000.

Eligibility Requirements: Applicant must be enrolled or expecting to enroll full-time at a two-year or four-year or technical institution or university.

Application Requirements: Essay, personal photograph. *Deadline:* April 30.

Contact: Leticia Gallegos, Executive Assistant
International Water, Sanitation and Hygiene Foundation
4755 East Philadelphia Street
Ontario, CA 91761
Phone: 909-472-4100
E-mail: essay@iwsh.org

JACK KENT COOKE FOUNDATION

http://www.jkcf.org/

COLLEGE SCHOLARSHIP PROGRAM

Scholarships to high-performing high school seniors with financial need who seek to attend and graduate from the nation's best accredited four-year colleges/universities. Candidates are selected based on academic achievement, financial need, persistence, leadership, and desire to help others. Awards vary by individual.

Award: Scholarship for use in freshman, sophomore, junior, or senior years; renewable. *Number:* 40. *Amount:* up to $40,000.

Eligibility Requirements: Applicant must be high school student and planning to enroll or expecting to enroll full-time at a four-year institution or university. Applicant must have 3.5 GPA or higher. Available to U.S. and non-U.S. citizens.

Application Requirements: Application form, application form may be submitted online, essay, financial need analysis, recommendations or references, test scores, transcript.

Contact: Gaby Ruess, Scholarship Committee
Phone: 800-498-6478
Fax: 319-337-1204
E-mail: jkc-g@act.org

JACK KENT COOKE FOUNDATION UNDERGRADUATE TRANSFER SCHOLARSHIP PROGRAM

Scholarships to students and recent alumni from community colleges to complete Bachelor's degrees at accredited four-year colleges/universities in the United States. Candidates are selected based on academic achievement, financial need, persistence, leadership, and desire to help others. Minimum 3.5 GPA required.

Award: Scholarship for use in sophomore, junior, or senior years; renewable. *Number:* 85. *Amount:* up to $40,000.

Eligibility Requirements: Applicant must be enrolled or expecting to enroll full-time at a four-year institution or university. Applicant must have 3.5 GPA or higher. Available to U.S. and non-U.S. citizens.

Application Requirements: Application form, application form may be submitted online (http://www.jkcf.org/scholarship-programs/undergraduate-transfer/), essay, financial need analysis, recommendations or references, resume, transcript.

Contact: Gaby Ruess, Scholarship Committee
Phone: 800-498-6478
Fax: 319-337-1204
E-mail: jkc-g@act.org

JACKSONWHITE ATTORNEYS AT LAW

http://www.jacksonwhitelaw.com/

JACKSONWHITE BI-ANNUAL LABOR LAW SCHOLARSHIP

JacksonWhite seeks to encourage personal and professional growth through higher education. The JacksonWhite Labor Law Bi-Annual Scholarship has been established to support hardworking individuals of any educational background. Education is essential to a successful future and JacksonWhite Law is proud to support determined students.

Award: Scholarship for use in freshman, sophomore, junior, senior, graduate, or postgraduate years; not renewable. *Number:* 1–2. *Amount:* $1000–$2000.

Eligibility Requirements: Applicant must be enrolled or expecting to enroll full-time at a two-year or four-year or technical institution or university. Applicant must have 2.5 GPA or higher. Available to U.S. and non-U.S. citizens.

Application Requirements: Essay. *Deadline:* December 1.

Contact: Miss. Kelsey Misseldine, Client Services Coordinator
JacksonWhite Attorneys at Law
40 North Center Street
Mesa, AZ 85201
Phone: 480-464 1111
E-mail: scholarship@jacksonwhitelaw.com

JACKSONWHITE CRIMINAL LAW BI-ANNUAL SCHOLARSHIP

JacksonWhite understands the financial burden that comes with pursuing your goals in higher education. The JacksonWhite Criminal Law Bi-Annual Scholarship has been established in hopes of contributing to the investment of students and future leaders. Education is essential to a successful future and JacksonWhite Law is proud to support determined students. No application is required to apply for this scholarship.

Award: Scholarship for use in freshman, sophomore, junior, senior, graduate, or postgraduate years; not renewable. *Number:* 1. *Amount:* $1000.

Eligibility Requirements: Applicant must be enrolled or expecting to enroll full-time at a two-year or four-year or technical institution or university. Applicant must have 2.5 GPA or higher. Available to U.S. and non-U.S. citizens.

Application Requirements: Essay. *Deadline:* December 1.

Contact: Ms. Kelsey Misseldine, Client Services Coordinator
JacksonWhite Attorneys at Law
40 North Center Street
Suite 200
Mesa, AZ 85201
E-mail: scholarship@jacksonwhitelaw.com

JACKSONWHITE FAMILY LAW BI-ANNUAL SCHOLARSHIP

Attorney Tim Durkin of JacksonWhite Attorneys at Law is offering the Family Law Bi-Annual Scholarship to honor the importance of higher education. In spite of rising costs to receive a college education, JacksonWhite believes in its value and is proud to support students in their pursuits. Please visit our website for scholarship details.

Award: Scholarship for use in freshman, sophomore, junior, senior, graduate, or postgraduate years; not renewable. *Number:* 1–2. *Amount:* $1000–$2000.

Eligibility Requirements: Applicant must be enrolled or expecting to enroll full-time at a two-year or four-year or technical institution or university. Applicant must have 2.5 GPA or higher. Available to U.S. citizens.

Application Requirements: Essay. *Deadline:* April 30.

Contact: Kelsey Misseldine
JacksonWhite Attorneys at Law
40 North Center Street
Suite 200
Mesa, AZ 85201
Phone: 480-464-1111
E-mail: scholarship@jacksonwhitelaw.com

JACKSONWHITE PERSONAL INJURY BI-ANNUAL SCHOLARSHIP

Aspiring professionals should all have access to higher education. With the increasing costs of universities, this is has become more difficult. JacksonWhite Attorneys at Law believes in the importance of education and is proud to support students in hopes of enriching their future. Please visit our website for scholarship details.

Award: Scholarship for use in freshman, sophomore, junior, senior, graduate, or postgraduate years; not renewable. *Number:* 1–2. *Amount:* $1000–$2000.

Eligibility Requirements: Applicant must be enrolled or expecting to enroll full-time at a two-year or four-year or technical institution or university. Applicant must have 2.5 GPA or higher. Available to U.S. and non-U.S. citizens.

Application Requirements: Essay. *Deadline:* April 30.

Contact: Ms. Kelsey Misseldine, Client Services Coordinator
JacksonWhite Attorneys at Law
40 North Center Street
Suite 200
Mesa, AZ 85201
E-mail: scholarship@jacksonwhitelaw.com

JONATHAN DE ARAUJO REAL ESTATE

http://www.searchmasshomes.com

REAL ESTATE SCHOLARSHIP

Lexington MA Realtor Jonathan de Araujo at Century 21 Commonwealth is committed to continuing efforts to help students who have the ambition and drive to succeed. He is sponsoring an annual scholarship of $1,000 to award one College student with the financial assistance to accomplish their educational goals and prepare for future potential career aspirations related to Real Estate.

Award: Scholarship for use in freshman, sophomore, junior, senior, graduate, or postgraduate years; not renewable. *Number:* 1. *Amount:* $1000.

Eligibility Requirements: Applicant must be enrolled or expecting to enroll full-time at a two-year or four-year institution or university. Applicant must have 2.5 GPA or higher. Available to U.S. citizens.

Application Requirements: Application form, essay. *Deadline:* November 1.

Contact: Jonathan de Araujo, Principal
E-mail: jonathan@searchmasshomes.com

JOURNALISM EDUCATION ASSOCIATION

http://www.jea.org/

NATIONAL HIGH SCHOOL JOURNALIST OF THE YEAR/SISTER RITA JEANNE SCHOLARSHIPS

One-time award recognizes the nation's top high school journalists. Open to graduating high school seniors who have worked at least two years on school media. Applicants must have JEA member as adviser. Minimum 3.0 GPA required. Submit digital portfolio to state contest coordinator by the deadline set by the state organization (usually between Feb. 1 and March 1).

Award: Scholarship for use in freshman year; not renewable. *Number:* 1–7. *Amount:* $850–$3000.

Eligibility Requirements: Applicant must be high school student; age 17-19 and planning to enroll or expecting to enroll full-time at a four-year institution or university. Applicant must have 3.0 GPA or higher. Available to U.S. citizens.

Application Requirements: Application form, essay, personal photograph, portfolio. *Deadline:* March 15.

Contact: Connie Fulkerson, Administrative Assistant
Journalism Education Association
105 Kedzie Hall
828 Mid-Campus Dr S
Manhattan, KS 66506-1500
Phone: 785-532-5532
Fax: 785-532-5563
E-mail: staff@jea.org

JRC INSURANCE GROUP

http://www.jrcinsurancegroup.com/scholarship/

JRC INSURANCE GROUP SCHOLARSHIP

The JRC Insurance Group Scholarship awards one $1,000 prize each semester to the high school senior or college student who best explains why the family breadwinner's income should be protected by life insurance, and the characteristics displayed by those who put their family first. The winner will be the person who best demonstrates the need for life insurance in U.S. households. Two $1,000 cash scholarships will be awarded. One scholarship will be awarded in the fall, and another in the spring. Essays will be reviewed by a selection committee made up of members of the JRC Insurance Group executive team. The winning essay will be selected based on originality and quality of writing. Submission deadlines: February 1, 2018 (spring) and October 15 (fall).

Award: Scholarship for use in freshman, sophomore, junior, senior, or graduate years; not renewable. *Number:* 2. *Amount:* $1000.

Eligibility Requirements: Applicant must be age 18-26 and enrolled or expecting to enroll full-time at a four-year institution or university. Available to U.S. citizens.

Application Requirements: Essay. *Deadline:* October 15.

Contact: Ms. Delia Noto
JRC Insurance Group
3914 Murphy Canyon Road
Suite A236
San Diego, CA 92123
Phone: 855-225-5063
Fax: 858-537-1090
E-mail: info@jrcinsurancegroup.com

KAHN ROVEN, LLP

http://www.kahnroven.com/

KAHN ROVEN, LLP SCHOLARSHIP

What does post-secondary education mean to you? How is it going to help you achieve your future goals? Application needs to be mailed in, but can be found at the following website: http://www.kahnroven.com/scholarship.html

Award: Scholarship for use in freshman year; not renewable. *Number:* 1. *Amount:* $500.

Eligibility Requirements: Applicant must be high school student and planning to enroll or expecting to enroll full-time at a four-year institution or university. Applicant must have 3.0 GPA or higher. Available to U.S. citizens.

Application Requirements: Application form, essay. *Deadline:* April 15.

Contact: Mr. Johnathan Roven
E-mail: kahnroven@gmail.com

KENNEDY FOUNDATION

http://uskennedyfoundation.org/scholarships/kennedy-foundation-scholarship/

KENNEDY FOUNDATION SCHOLARSHIPS

Renewable scholarships for current high school students for up to four years of undergraduate study. Renewal contingent upon academic performance. Must maintain a GPA of 2.5. Send self-addressed stamped envelope for application. See website for details http://www.columbinecorp.com/kennedyfoundation to download an application.

Award: Scholarship for use in freshman year; renewable. *Number:* 8–14. *Amount:* $2000.

Eligibility Requirements: Applicant must be high school student and planning to enroll or expecting to enroll full-time at a two-year or four-year institution or university. Applicant must have 2.5 GPA or higher. Available to U.S. citizens.

Application Requirements: Application form, self-addressed stamped envelope with application, test scores, transcript. *Deadline:* June 30.

Contact: Jonathan Kennedy, Vice President

KIM AND HAROLD LOUIE FAMILY FOUNDATION

http://www.louiefamilyfoundation.org

LOUIE FAMILY FOUNDATION SCHOLARSHIP

Please visit http://www.louiefamilyfoundation.org for scholarship details.

Award: Scholarship for use in freshman year; not renewable. *Number:* 25–35. *Amount:* $1000–$10,000.

Eligibility Requirements: Applicant must be enrolled or expecting to enroll full-time at a two-year or four-year or technical institution or university. Applicant must have 3.0 GPA or higher. Available to U.S. and non-U.S. citizens.

Application Requirements: Application form, essay, personal photograph. *Deadline:* March 31.

Contact: Stan Sze, Director
Kim and Harold Louie Family Foundation
1325 Howard Ave., #949
Burlingame, CA 94010
Phone: 650-491-3434
E-mail: scholarships@louiefamilyfoundation.org

KNOWLEDGE IS KEY, INC.

http://www.knowledgeiskeyinc.org/

KNOWLEDGE IS KEY, INC. SCHOLARSHIP AWARD

The mission of Knowledge Is Key, Inc. (K.I.K) is to educate, encourage and support the general public by providing free educational resources and yearly academic scholarships. Each year, we award a scholarship based on the applicant's academic achievement, writing ability and community involvement. K.I.K's philanthropic efforts focus heavily on enlightening and cultivating communities and thus, scholarship recipients must also demonstrate an active commitment to community elevation. Open to all candidates attending institutions within the U.S. only. The Knowledge Is Key, Inc. Scholarship is available to any individual of any generation who has been accepted to and at time of receipt can prove enrollment in an accredited college, university or trade school.

Award: Scholarship for use in freshman, sophomore, junior, senior, graduate, or postgraduate years; not renewable. *Number:* 1. *Amount:* $1000.

Eligibility Requirements: Applicant must be enrolled or expecting to enroll full- or part-time at a two-year or four-year or technical institution or university. Available to U.S. and non-U.S. citizens.

Application Requirements: Application form, community service, essay. *Deadline:* March 30.

Contact: Candice Chin, Scholarship Committee Chair
Knowledge Is Key, Inc.
29 Marvin Ave.
Uniondale, NY 11553
Phone: 516-610-0214
E-mail: info@knowledgeiskeyinc.org

LA TUTORS

http://www.latutors123.com

INNOVATION IN EDUCATION SCHOLARSHIP

We at LA Tutors are passionate about sparking the creative genius in students and would love to commend those outstanding students who have a made a difference in the lives of others in some innovative or technological fashion. In order to achieve this, we have established a scholarship for students who meet certain criteria.

Award: Scholarship for use in freshman, sophomore, junior, senior, graduate, or postgraduate years; not renewable. *Number:* 1. *Amount:* $500.

Eligibility Requirements: Applicant must be enrolled or expecting to enroll full- or part-time at a two-year or four-year or technical institution or university. Applicant must have 3.0 GPA or higher. Available to U.S. and Canadian citizens.

Application Requirements: Application form, essay, personal photograph.

Contact: Arash Fayz, Director
LA Tutors
9454 Wilshire Blvd. Suite 600
Beverly Hills, CA 90212
Phone: 424-335-0035
Fax: 866-666-9426
E-mail: arash@latutors123.com

LEOPOLD SCHEPP FOUNDATION

http://www.scheppfoundation.org/

LEOPOLD SCHEPP SCHOLARSHIP

Scholarship for undergraduates under 30 years of age and graduate students under 40 years of age at the time of application. Applicants must have a minimum GPA of 3.0. High school seniors are not eligible. All applicants must either be enrolled in college or have completed at least one year of college at the time of issuing the application. Must be citizens or permanent residents of the United States. Deadline varies.

Award: Scholarship for use in sophomore, junior, senior, or graduate years; renewable. *Number:* 1–30. *Amount:* up to $8500.

Eligibility Requirements: Applicant must be enrolled or expecting to enroll full-time at a four-year institution or university. Applicant must have 3.0 GPA or higher. Available to U.S. citizens.

Application Requirements: Application form, financial need analysis, interview, recommendations or references, transcript. *Deadline:* varies.

Contact: Scholarship Committee
Leopold Schepp Foundation
551 Fifth Avenue, Suite 3000
New York, NY 10176
Phone: 212-692-0191

LIFE HAPPENS

http://www.lifehappens.org

LIFE LESSONS SCHOLARSHIP PROGRAM

The Life Lessons Scholarship Program is for college students and college-bound high school seniors who have experienced the death of a parent or legal guardian. To apply students must complete and submit an online application (http://www.lifehappens.org/scholarship), including an essay of no more than 500 words or a 3 minutes video discussing how the death of a parent or guardian affected his or her life financially and emotionally. Applicants must explain how the lack of adequate life insurance coverage (or no coverage at all) impacted their family's financial situation. Please make sure to review the Scholarship Program rules at http://www.lifehappens.org/scholarship-program-rules.

Award: Scholarship for use in freshman, sophomore, junior, senior, or graduate years; not renewable. *Number:* 20–50. *Amount:* $5000–$15,000.

Eligibility Requirements: Applicant must be age 17-24 and enrolled or expecting to enroll full- or part-time at a two-year or four-year or technical institution or university. Available to U.S. citizens.

Application Requirements: Application form, essay. *Deadline:* March 1.

Contact: Julie Holsinger, Manager of Programs
Life Happens
1530 Wison Blvd
Suite 1060
Arlington, VA 22209
Phone: 703-888-5000 Ext. 4446
E-mail: scholarship@lifehappens.org

MALESENSE PRO

https://www.malesensepro.com

MALESENSE PRO INTERNET MARKETING SCHOLARSHIP

We created the MaleSensePro E-Marketing Scholarship for Undergraduate or Postgraduate students with the passion of Internet Marketing to receive a $1000 award.

Award: Scholarship for use in freshman, sophomore, junior, senior, graduate, or postgraduate years; renewable. *Number:* 1–10. *Amount:* $1000–$10,000.

Eligibility Requirements: Applicant must be enrolled or expecting to enroll full- or part-time at a two-year or four-year institution or university. Applicant must have 2.5 GPA or higher. Available to U.S. and non-U.S. citizens.

Application Requirements: *Deadline:* December 31.

Contact: Eric White, Support Team
E-mail: eric@malesensepro.com

MARGARET MCNAMARA EDUCATION GRANTS

http://www.mmeg.org

MARGARET MCNAMARA EDUCATION GRANTS

One-time award for female students from developing countries already enrolled in accredited universities in the USA/Canada and selected universities in Latin America and South Africa (see MMEG.org for details). Candidates must articulate prior and future commitment to improve wellbeing of women and children; plan to return to their countries or a developing country within two years. Must be over 25 years of age. U.S. citizens not eligible.

Award: Grant for use in sophomore, junior, senior, graduate, or postgraduate years; not renewable. *Number:* 27–35. *Amount:* $7000–$15,000.

Eligibility Requirements: Applicant must be enrolled or expecting to enroll full- or part-time at a four-year institution or university and female. Available to citizens of countries other than the U.S. or Canada.

Application Requirements: Application form, essay, financial need analysis, interview, personal photograph. *Deadline:* January 15.

Contact: Chairman, Selection Committee
Washington, DC 20433
E-mail: mmeg@worldbank.org

MCNEELY STEPHENSON

http://www.indianapilaw.com/

COMMUNITY INVOLVEMENT SCHOLARSHIP AWARD

This scholarship is designed to encourage and reward dedication of an exemplary individual who is deeply involved in the community that surrounds them. McNeely Stephenson believes in good citizenship and recognition for those who support their local communities through direct involvement, meaningful commitment and generosity of their time and efforts. Scholarship applicants must submit a detailed report of their community service efforts during their high school careers. This should be submitted in the form of an essay describing the involvement and how they feel this award will further both their college career and their continued dedication to helping others.

Award: Scholarship for use in freshman year; not renewable. *Amount:* $1000.

Eligibility Requirements: Applicant must be high school student and planning to enroll or expecting to enroll full- or part-time at a four-year institution or university. Available to U.S. citizens.

Application Requirements: Application form, essay. *Deadline:* May 1.

Contact: Hallie Huff
Phone: 606-371-8575
E-mail: hallie@gladiatorlawmarketing.com

MICHIGAN CONSUMER CREDIT LAWYERS

http://www.micreditlawyer.com/

MCCL THOUGHT LEADERSHIP SCHOLARSHIP

The scholarship is an essay writing competition. Students are to write on the topic of the student loan debt crisis and what possible solutions there might be to fixing the issue. When the student's application is written and submitted, it is immediately received and reviewed.

Award: Scholarship for use in freshman, sophomore, junior, senior, graduate, or postgraduate years; renewable. *Number:* 1–3. *Amount:* $250–$1000.

Eligibility Requirements: Applicant must be enrolled or expecting to enroll full-time at a four-year institution or university. Applicant must have 2.5 GPA or higher. Available to U.S. citizens.

Application Requirements: Application form may be submitted online (http://www.micreditlawyer.com/mccl-thought-leadership-scholarship/), entry in a contest, essay, transcript. *Deadline:* continuous.

Contact: Philip Rudy, Webmaster
Michigan Consumer Credit Lawyers
211 East 9 Mile Road
Ferndale, MI 48220
Phone: 616-238-3838
E-mail: philip@beshapeless.com

MIE SOLUTIONS

https://www.mie-solutions.com/

MIE SOLUTIONS SCHOLARSHIP

For the 2018 Fall Semester, MIE Solutions will be offering a $500 scholarship to a student who writes a winning essay regarding their future career and educational objectives in computer science and/or computer engineering.

Award: Scholarship for use in freshman, sophomore, junior, or senior years; renewable. *Number:* 1. *Amount:* $500.

Eligibility Requirements: Applicant must be enrolled or expecting to enroll full- or part-time at a four-year institution or university. Available to U.S. citizens.

Application Requirements: *Deadline:* August 15.

MILITARY OFFICERS ASSOCIATION OF AMERICA (MOAA) SCHOLARSHIP FUND

http://www.moaa.org/scholarshipfund

GENERAL JOHN RATAY EDUCATIONAL FUND GRANTS

Grants available to the children of the surviving spouse of retired officers. Must be under 24 years old and the child of a deceased retired officer who was a member of MOAA. For more details and an application go to website http://www.moaa.org/education.

Award: Grant for use in freshman, sophomore, junior, or senior years; renewable. *Number:* 1–5. *Amount:* $4000–$5000.

Eligibility Requirements: Applicant must be enrolled or expecting to enroll full-time at a two-year or four-year institution or university. Applicant must have 3.0 GPA or higher. Available to U.S. citizens.

Application Requirements: Application form, financial need analysis. *Deadline:* March 1.

Contact: Program Director
Phone: 800-234-6622
E-mail: edassist@moaa.org

MOAA AMERICAN PATRIOT SCHOLARSHIP

Students under the age of 24 and who are children of MOAA members and children of active-duty, reserve, National Guard, or enlisted personnel whose military parent has died on active service or whose military parent is severely wounded (as defined as Traumatic SGLI) are eligible to apply. For more information and to access the online application go to website http://www.moaa.org/education.

Award: Grant for use in freshman, sophomore, junior, or senior years; renewable. *Number:* 1–60. *Amount:* $2500–$5000.

Eligibility Requirements: Applicant must be enrolled or expecting to enroll full-time at a two-year or four-year institution or university. Applicant must have 3.0 GPA or higher. Available to U.S. citizens.

Application Requirements: Application form, financial need analysis. *Deadline:* March 1.

Contact: Program Director
Phone: 800-234-6622
E-mail: edassist@moaa.org

MILITARY ORDER OF THE STARS AND BARS

http://www.militaryorderofthestarsandbars.org/

MILITARY ORDER OF THE STARS AND BARS SCHOLARSHIPS

Applicants must be accepted to a degree-granting junior college or four-year college or university or already enrolled in such a facility. Awards shall be made annually, and the total amount of the scholarship money to be awarded each year to each recipient shall not exceed $1000. Applicants must be sponsored by a local MOS&B Chapter or MOS&B State Society. Applicants must be able to prove they are a descendant of a commissioned officer or civil servant of the Confederate States of America. Preference is given to relatives of currently active MOS&B members. All application information is found on the MOS&B website.

Award: Scholarship for use in freshman, sophomore, junior, senior, graduate, or postgraduate years; not renewable. *Number:* 3–6. *Amount:* $1000.

Eligibility Requirements: Applicant must be enrolled or expecting to enroll full-time at a two-year or four-year institution or university. Applicant must have 3.0 GPA or higher. Available to U.S. and non-U.S. citizens.

Application Requirements: Application form, personal photograph. *Deadline:* March 1.

Contact: Ewell Loudermilk, Scholarship Chairman
Military Order of the Stars and Bars
6730 Treece Rd
San Angelo, TX 76905
E-mail: rebelboy264@yahoo.com

MINNESOTA MASONIC CHARITIES
http://www.mnmasoniccharities.org

MINNESOTA MASONIC CHARITIES HERITAGE SCHOLARSHIP
Heritage Scholarships are provided each year to Minnesota high school students with a GPA of 3.0-3.59. Applicants must plan to enroll in a four-year college program.

Award: Scholarship for use in freshman, sophomore, junior, or senior years; renewable. *Number:* 20. *Amount:* $2500.

Eligibility Requirements: Applicant must be high school student and planning to enroll or expecting to enroll full-time at a four-year institution. Applicant must have 3.0 GPA or higher. Available to U.S. citizens.

Application Requirements: Application form, essay. *Deadline:* February 15.

Contact: Ms. Deb Cutsinger, Scholarships Manager
Minnesota Masonic Charities
11501 Masonic Home Drive
Bloomington, MN 55437
Phone: 952-948-6206
E-mail: deb.cutsinger@mnmasonic.org

THE MORRIS K. UDALL AND STEWART L. UDALL FOUNDATION
http://www.udall.gov/

UDALL UNDERGRADUATE SCHOLARSHIP
Fifty one-time scholarships and fifty one-time honorable mention awards to full-time college sophomores or juniors with demonstrated commitment to careers related to the environment, tribal public policy (Native American/Alaska Native students only), or Native American health care (Native American/Alaska Native students only). Students from all fields and disciplines are encouraged to apply. Students must be nominated by their college or university. Visit http://www.udall.gov for additional information.

Award: Scholarship for use in junior or senior years; not renewable. *Number:* 50. *Amount:* $1–$5000.

Eligibility Requirements: Applicant must be enrolled or expecting to enroll full-time at a two-year or four-year institution or university. Available to U.S. and Canadian citizens.

Application Requirements: Application form, application form may be submitted online (http://udall.gov), essay, nomination by campus faculty representative, recommendations or references, transcript. *Deadline:* March 4.

Contact: Paula Randler, Scholarship Program Manager
Phone: 520-901-8564
Fax: 520-901-8570
E-mail: randler@udall.gov

MULLEN & MULLEN LAW FIRM
http://www.mullenandmullen.com

REGIS L. MULLEN $2,500 ACCIDENT INJURY SCHOLARSHIP
Students must apply each year to qualify to compete for that year's award. Only one scholarship will be awarded per year.

Award: Scholarship for use in freshman, sophomore, junior, senior, graduate, or postgraduate years; not renewable. *Number:* 1. *Amount:* $2500.

Eligibility Requirements: Applicant must be enrolled or expecting to enroll full- or part-time at a two-year or four-year institution or university. Applicant must have 3.0 GPA or higher. Available to U.S. citizens.

Application Requirements: Essay. *Deadline:* March 1.
Contact: Shelley Cates, Director of Marketing
Mullen & Mullen Law Firm
1825 Market Center Blvd #200
Dallas, TX 75207
Phone: 214-747-5240
E-mail: scholarships@mullenandmullen.com

NATIONAL ASSOCIATION OF RAILWAY BUSINESS WOMEN
http://www.narbw.org/

NARBW SCHOLARSHIP
Scholarship awarded to the members of NARBW and their relatives. The number of awards varies every year. Applications are judged on scholastic ability, ambition and potential, and financial need.

Award: Scholarship for use in freshman, sophomore, junior, or senior years; not renewable. *Amount:* $500–$1000.

Eligibility Requirements: Applicant must be enrolled or expecting to enroll full-time at a two-year or four-year or technical institution or university and female. Available to U.S. citizens.

Application Requirements: Application form, financial need analysis. *Deadline:* varies.

Contact: Scholarship Chairman
E-mail: narbwinfo@narbw.org

NATIONAL BLACK MBA ASSOCIATION
http://www.nbmbaa.org/

NATIONAL BLACK MBA ASSOCIATION GRADUATE SCHOLARSHIP PROGRAM
Program's mission is to identify and increase the pool of Black talent for business, public, private and non-profit sectors.

Award: Scholarship for use in freshman, sophomore, junior, or senior years; not renewable. *Number:* 10–25. *Amount:* $2500–$15,000.

Eligibility Requirements: Applicant must be enrolled or expecting to enroll full-time at a four-year institution or university. Available to U.S. and non-U.S. citizens.

Application Requirements: Application form, community service, essay, interview, resume, transcript. *Deadline:* April 17.

Contact: Ms. Lori Johnson, Program Administrator, University Relations
National Black MBA Association
180 North Michigan Avenue, Suite 1400
Chicago, IL 60601
Phone: 312-580-8086
E-mail: scholarship@nbmbaa.org

NATIONAL CENTER FOR POLICY ANALYSIS
http://www.ncpa.org

YOUNG PATRIOTS ESSAY CONTEST
The Young Patriots Essay Contest is designed to challenge high school students to creatively solve problems in the realm of economics and public policy through the art of writing. The current prompt is "Drawing on the readings, discuss the relationship between individual freedom and social/economic prosperity. Feel free to incorporate outside research." The short required readings are available for free on the contest main page.

Award: Scholarship for use in freshman year; not renewable. *Number:* 3. *Amount:* $2000–$5000.

Eligibility Requirements: Applicant must be high school student and planning to enroll or expecting to enroll full- or part-time at a two-year or four-year or technical institution or university. Available to U.S. and non-U.S. citizens.

Application Requirements: Application form may be submitted online (http://debate-central.ncpa.org/yp14/), entry in a contest, essay. *Deadline:* January 5.

Contact: Ms. Rachel Stevens, Director of Youth Programs
National Center for Policy Analysis
14180 Dallas Parkway
Suite 350
Dallas, TX 75254
Phone: 972-308-6487
Fax: 972-239-9823
E-mail: Rachel.Stevens@NCPA.org

NATIONAL FOUNDATION FOR WOMEN LEGISLATORS

http://www.womenlegislators.org/

NFWL NRA SCHOLARSHIP

For 20 years now, the National Foundation for Women Legislators and the National Rifle Association have joined forces for the Annual Bill of Rights Essay Scholarship Contest, which provides six female high school juniors or seniors a $3,000 college scholarship, an all-expense-paid trip to NFWL's Annual Conference, and an award that will be presented at the event. To apply for the scholarship, students must write an essay on one of three topics announced each spring, get a letter of recommendation from a currently elected woman (on the state, county, or municipal level), receive a letter of recommendation from a school employee, and submit a resume. The essay topics change each year but always pertain to the constitution. For more information, students should visit https://www.womenlegislators.org/programs/scholarships/.

Award: Scholarship for use in freshman year; not renewable. *Number:* 6. *Amount:* $3000.

Eligibility Requirements: Applicant must be age 13-19; enrolled or expecting to enroll full-time at a two-year or four-year institution or university and female. Available to U.S. citizens.

Application Requirements: Application form, essay. *Deadline:* July 14.

Contact: Jody Thomas, Executive Director
National Foundation for Women Legislators
1727 King Street
Suite 300
Alexandria, VA 22314
Phone: 703-518-7931
E-mail: nfwl@womenlegislators.org

NATIONAL HEMOPHILIA FOUNDATION

http://www.hemophilia.org/

KEVIN CHILD SCHOLARSHIP

Scholarship applicants must be individuals diagnosed with either hemophilia A or B, and a high school senior with aspirations of attending an institute of higher education (college, university or vocational-technical school), a college student already pursuing a post-secondary education, or a student in a graduate-level program. Interested students need to submit an application along with a current official transcript of their grades and one letter of recommendation from a person familiar with their personal and academic achievements (ex. teacher, mentor). The Kevin Child Scholarship recipient will be chosen on the basis of their academic performance, participation in school or community activities and the personal application essay detailing their educational and career goals.

Award: Scholarship for use in freshman, sophomore, junior, senior, or graduate years; not renewable. *Number:* 1. *Amount:* up to $1000.

Eligibility Requirements: Applicant must be enrolled or expecting to enroll full- or part-time at a two-year or four-year or technical institution or university. Available to U.S. citizens.

Application Requirements: Application form, community service, essay, recommendations or references, transcript. *Deadline:* June 3.

Contact: NHF/HANDI
National Hemophilia Foundation
116 West 32nd Street, 11th Floor
New York, NY 10001-3212
Phone: 212-328-3700 Ext. 2
E-mail: handi@hemophilia.org

NATIONAL INSTITUTE OF GENERAL MEDICAL SCIENCES, NATIONAL INSTITUTE OF HEALTH

http://www.nigms.nih.gov

MARC UNDERGRADUATE STUDENT TRAINING IN ACADEMIC RESEARCH (U-STAR) AWARDS

These awards provide support for undergraduate students who are underrepresented in the biomedical sciences to improve their preparation for high-caliber graduate training at the Ph.D. level. Institutions with significant enrollments of college students from underrepresented groups may be eligible to apply. Awards are made to colleges and universities that offer the baccalaureate degree. Only one grant per eligible institution is awarded. MARC institutions select the trainees to be supported. Trainees must be honors students majoring in the biomedical sciences who have expressed interest in pursuing postgraduate education leading to the Ph.D., M.D.-Ph.D. or other combined professional degree-Ph.D. in these fields upon completing their baccalaureate degree. The period of appointment to the MARC U-STAR program is a consecutive 24-month period at the final 2 years of undergraduate training, typically called the junior and senior years.

Award: Grant for use in junior or senior years; renewable.

Eligibility Requirements: Applicant must be enrolled or expecting to enroll at a four-year institution or university. Available to U.S. citizens.

Application Requirements: Application form. *Deadline:* continuous.

Contact: Dr. Sailaja Koduri
National Institute of General Medical Sciences, National
Institute of Health
45 Center Drive, MSC6200
Bethesda, MD 20892
Phone: 301-594-3900
E-mail: sailaja.koduri@nih.gov

NATIONAL JUNIOR ANGUS ASSOCIATION

http://www.angus.org/njaa/

AMERICAN ANGUS AUXILIARY SCHOLARSHIP

Scholarship available to graduating high school senior. May apply only in one state. Any unmarried girl or unmarried boy recommended by a state or regional Auxiliary is eligible.

Award: Scholarship for use in freshman year; not renewable. *Number:* 10. *Amount:* $1000–$14,000.

Eligibility Requirements: Applicant must be high school student; planning to enroll or expecting to enroll full-time at a two-year or four-year or technical institution or university and single. Available to U.S. and Canadian citizens.

Application Requirements: Application form, entry in a contest, personal photograph, recommendations or references, test scores, transcript. *Deadline:* May 1.

Contact: Mrs. Anne Lampe, American Angus Auxiliary Scholarship
Chairman
National Junior Angus Association
5201 East Road 110
Scott City, KS 67871
Phone: 620-872-3915

NATIONAL SOCIETY OF NEWSPAPER COLUMNISTS EDUCATION FOUNDATION

https://columnisteducation.org/

DEAR ABBY COLLEGE COLUMNIST SCHOLARSHIP CONTEST

Undergraduates (including seniors) writing bylined general interest, editorial or specialized (humor, sports, business, arts, culture, etc.) columns appearing in print or online editions of college publications.

Award: Scholarship for use in freshman, sophomore, junior, or senior years; not renewable. *Number:* 3–5. *Amount:* $5000.

Eligibility Requirements: Applicant must be enrolled or expecting to enroll full- or part-time at a two-year or four-year institution or university. Available to U.S. and non-U.S. citizens.

Application Requirements: Application form. *Deadline:* June 29.

Contact: Mike Leonard, Scholarship chair
National Society of Newspaper Columnists Education
Foundation
818 S. Park Ave.
Bloomington, IN 47401
E-mail: leonardbtown@gmail.com

NAVAL SERVICE TRAINING COMMAND/NROTC

http://www.nrotc.navy.mil/

NROTC SCHOLARSHIP PROGRAM

Scholarships are based on merit and are awarded through a highly competitive national selection process. NROTC scholarships pay for college tuition, fees, uniforms, a book stipend, a monthly allowance and other financial benefits. Room and board expenses are not covered. Scholarship nominees must be medically qualified. Upon graduation scholarship recipients have an obligation of eight years commissioned service, five of which must be active duty. For more information, visit our website at https://www.nrotc.navy.mil.

Award: Scholarship for use in freshman, sophomore, junior, or senior years; renewable. *Number:* 2400–2900.

Eligibility Requirements: Applicant must be age 17-23 and enrolled or expecting to enroll full-time at a four-year institution or university. Available to U.S. citizens.

Application Requirements: Application form, essay, interview, recommendations or references, test scores, transcript. *Deadline:* January 31.

Contact: NROTC Scholarship Selection Office (OD2)
Phone: 800-628-7682
E-mail: pnsc_nrotc.scholarship@navy.mil

NAVY-MARINE CORPS RELIEF SOCIETY

http://www.nmcrs.org/education

NMCRS EDUCATION ASSISTANCE PROGRAM

Scholarship and/or zero interest loan for full-time undergraduate students enrolled in accredited colleges or universities. Must be a spouse or child of a Sailor or Marine who is: active duty, retired, or deceased on active duty or after retirement. Must be 23 years of age or younger. Must have minimum 2.0 GPA.

Award: Scholarship for use in freshman, sophomore, junior, or senior years; not renewable. *Number:* 1–300. *Amount:* $500–$3000.

Eligibility Requirements: Applicant must be enrolled or expecting to enroll full-time at a two-year or four-year or technical institution or university. Applicant must have 2.5 GPA or higher. Available to U.S. citizens.

Application Requirements: Application form, financial need analysis. *Deadline:* May 1.

Contact: Mrs. Beverly Langdon, Education, Program Manager
Navy-Marine Corps Relief Society
875 North Randolph Street, Suite 225
Arlington, VA 22203
Phone: 703-696-4960
E-mail: education@nmcrs.org

NEEDHAM AND COMPANY WTC SCHOLARSHIP FUND

http://www.needhamco.com/

NEEDHAM AND COMPANY SEPTEMBER 11TH SCHOLARSHIP FUND

Scholarship going to those individuals who had a pre-September 11th gross income of less than $125,000. Must be currently accepted or attending an accredited university or college. Recipients decided on a case-by-case basis. Fund designed to benefit the children of the victims who lost their lives at the World Trade Center.

Award: Scholarship for use in freshman, sophomore, junior, or senior years; not renewable. *Number:* 8–15. *Amount:* $7000–$10,000.

Eligibility Requirements: Applicant must be enrolled or expecting to enroll full-time at a four-year institution or university. Available to U.S. citizens.

Application Requirements: Application form, financial need analysis. *Deadline:* continuous.

Contact: Joseph Turano, Secretary and Treasurer
Needham and Company WTC Scholarship Fund
445 Park Avenue
New York, NY 10022
Phone: 212-705-0314
E-mail: jturano@needhamco.com

NEW MEXICO COMMISSION ON HIGHER EDUCATION

http://www.hed.state.nm.us/

NEW MEXICO COMPETITIVE SCHOLARSHIP

Scholarships for non-residents or non-citizens of the United States to encourage out-of-state students who have demonstrated high academic achievement in high school to enroll in public four-year universities in New Mexico. Renewable for up to four years. For details visit http://fin.hed.state.nm.us.

Award: Scholarship for use in freshman year; renewable.

Eligibility Requirements: Applicant must be high school student; planning to enroll or expecting to enroll full-time at a four-year institution or university and studying in New Mexico. Available to Canadian and non-U.S. citizens.

Application Requirements: Application form, essay, recommendations or references, test scores. *Deadline:* varies.

Contact: Tashina Moore, Director of Financial Aid
New Mexico Commission on Higher Education
1068 Cerrillos Road
Santa Fe, NM 87505
Phone: 505-476-6549
Fax: 505-476-6511
E-mail: tashina.banks-moore@state.nm.us

NEW YORK STATE HIGHER EDUCATION SERVICES CORPORATION

http://www.hesc.ny.gov

WORLD TRADE CENTER MEMORIAL SCHOLARSHIP

Renewable awards of up to the cost of educational expenses at a State University of New York four-year college. Available to the children, spouses and financial dependents of victims who died or were severely disabled as a result of the September 11, 2001 terrorist attacks on the U.S. and the rescue and recovery efforts.

Award: Scholarship for use in freshman, sophomore, junior, or senior years; renewable.

Eligibility Requirements: Applicant must be enrolled or expecting to enroll full-time at a four-year institution or university and studying in New York. Available to U.S. and non-U.S. citizens.

Application Requirements: Application form, financial need analysis, recommendations or references, transcript. *Deadline:* May 1.

Contact: Scholarship Unit
New York State Higher Education Services Corporation
99 Washington Avenue, Room 1320
Albany, NY 12255
Phone: 888-697-4372

NEXTSTEPU

http://www.nextstepu.com/

WIN FREE COLLEGE TUITION GIVEAWAY

NextStepU.com will award one $2,500 scholarship to one randomly selected winner twice a year. Applicants must enter online at http://www.nextstepu.com/winfreetuition. Winner must be enrolled in college within 3 years of when the prize is awarded. DEADLINE (1): June 30 DEADLINE (2): December 31.

Award: Scholarship for use in freshman, sophomore, junior, senior, or graduate years; not renewable. *Number:* 2. *Amount:* $2500.

Eligibility Requirements: Applicant must be enrolled or expecting to enroll full- or part-time at a two-year or four-year or technical institution or university. Available to U.S. and Canadian citizens.

Application Requirements: Application form. *Deadline:* continuous.

Contact: Web Department
  E-mail: webcopy@nextstepu.com

NICHE

http://www.niche.com

$2,000 NO ESSAY SCHOLARSHIP

Scholarships don't get easier than this. Simply complete the form (found here https://colleges.niche.com/scholarship/no-essay-scholarship/), and you could be the next winner! No GPA, no essay—apply in minutes! The scholarship is awarded monthly, so make sure you apply every month!

Award: Scholarship for use in freshman, sophomore, junior, senior, graduate, or postgraduate years; not renewable. *Number:* 12. *Amount:* $2000.

Eligibility Requirements: Applicant must be enrolled or expecting to enroll full- or part-time at a two-year or four-year or technical institution or university. Available to U.S. citizens.

Application Requirements: Application form. *Deadline:* continuous.

Contact: Karisa Fernandez
  Phone: 4124508840
  E-mail: kfernandez@niche.com

NITRO COLLEGE

https://www.nitrocollege.com/

$2,018 NITRO COLLEGE SCHOLARSHIP

Nitro cares about providing you the resources you need to successfully navigate financing college. That's why we're offering you the opportunity to earn a $2,018 scholarship from Nitro. We know that college is a big step forward in achieving your goals and we want to help you get there using all the tools Nitro has to offer. To apply, complete the scholarship survey questions, participate in our social media activity, and submit the application when completed.

Award: Scholarship for use in freshman, sophomore, junior, senior, or graduate years; not renewable. *Number:* 1. *Amount:* $2018.

Eligibility Requirements: Applicant must be enrolled or expecting to enroll full-time at a two-year or four-year institution or university. Available to U.S. citizens.

Application Requirements: Application form. *Deadline:* continuous.

Contact: Mike Brown
  Nitro College
  1105 North Market Street, Suite 1600
  Wilmington, DE 19801
  E-mail: support@nitrocollege.com

NORTH CAROLINA STATE DEPARTMENT OF HEALTH AND HUMAN SERVICES/DIVISION OF SOCIAL SERVICES

http://www.ncdhhs.gov/dss

NORTH CAROLINA EDUCATION AND TRAINING VOUCHER PROGRAM

Four-year scholarship for NC foster youth and former foster youth. Must have been accepted into or be enrolled in a degree, certificate or other accredited program at a college, university, technical or vocational school and show progress towards a degree or certificate. Must be a U.S. citizen or qualified non-citizen. Applications available at: http://www.statevoucher.org.

Award: Grant for use in freshman, sophomore, junior, or senior years; renewable. *Amount:* $1–$5000.

Eligibility Requirements: Applicant must be age 18-23 and enrolled or expecting to enroll part-time at a two-year or four-year or technical institution or university. Available to U.S. citizens.

Application Requirements: Application form, essay. *Deadline:* continuous.

Contact: Ms. Danielle McConaga, NC DSS LINKS Independent Living Coordinator
  North Carolina State Department of Health and Human Services/Division of Social Services
  820 South Boylan Drive
  Raleigh, NC 27603
  Phone: 919-527-6343
  E-mail: Danielle.McConaga@dhhs.nc.gov

NORTH DAKOTA FARMERS UNION

http://www.ndfu.org

HUBERT K. & JOANN SEYMOUR SCHOLARSHIP

Must be a Farmers Union members to apply. Scholarship is open to high school seniors pursuing a two- or four-year degree in any area of study.

Award: Scholarship for use in freshman year; not renewable. *Number:* 1–2. *Amount:* $1000–$2000.

Eligibility Requirements: Applicant must be high school student and planning to enroll or expecting to enroll full-time at a two-year or four-year institution. Available to U.S. citizens.

Application Requirements: Application form, community service, essay. *Deadline:* April 1.

Contact: Melissa Miller
  North Dakota Farmers Union
  20 F St. NW, Suite 300
  Washington, DC 20001
  Phone: 202-559-9882
  E-mail: melissamiller@nfudc.org

NORTH DAKOTA FARMERS UNION SCHOLARSHIP

Applicants must be pursuing a career important to rural America, but not limited to agribusiness, farm operation or production agriculture. Must be a Farmers Union member to apply.

Award: Scholarship for use in freshman, sophomore, junior, or senior years; not renewable. *Number:* 1–10. *Amount:* $500.

Eligibility Requirements: Applicant must be enrolled or expecting to enroll full-time at a two-year or four-year or technical institution or university. Applicant must have 2.5 GPA or higher. Available to U.S. citizens.

Application Requirements: Application form, financial need analysis. *Deadline:* January 31.

Contact: Pam Musland
  North Dakota Farmers Union
  1415 12th Ave. SE
  Jamestown, ND 58401
  Phone: 800-366-8331

NOVUS BIOLOGICALS, LLC

https://www.novusbio.com

R&D SYSTEMS SCHOLARSHIP

Applicants must have a major declared in a science related field and must be enrolled or accepted for enrollment (Baccalaureate, graduate, associate degree, or diploma) with a declared major in a science related field. Fill out the scholarship application form and submit a transcript of all college/post-secondary coursework (if high school student submit high school transcript). This may be an official or unofficial copy. Submit a written statement addressing the following topics: Submit a 140 character statement/tweet on what you believe is the biggest hurdle for people working in your specific field of interest and why. Write a personal statement of 500 words or less on how you plan to use your degree to further advance science in your field of interest.

Award: Scholarship for use in freshman, sophomore, junior, senior, graduate, or postgraduate years; not renewable. *Number:* 1. *Amount:* $1500.

Eligibility Requirements: Applicant must be high school student and planning to enroll or expecting to enroll full- or part-time at a two-year or four-year institution or university. Available to U.S. and non-U.S. citizens.

Application Requirements: Application form, essay. *Deadline:* July 20.

Contact: Lisa Ikariyama
Novus Biologicals, LLC
8100 Southpark Way
Unit A-8
Littleton, CO 80120
Phone: 303-7301950
E-mail: lisa@novusbio.com

TOCRIS BIOSCIENCE SCHOLARSHIP

Tocris is proud to support students who plan to pursue a science related degree. The Tocris Scholarship Program has been established to award a $1500 scholarship (or international currency equivalent) twice a year for the fall and spring semesters. This scholarship is open worldwide to students accepted/enrolled in a university and plan to pursue a science related degree. The deadline is July 20, 2018 at 11:59 p.m. MST. Winners will be notified by August 3, 2018.

Award: Scholarship for use in freshman, sophomore, junior, senior, graduate, or postgraduate years; not renewable. *Number:* 1. *Amount:* $1500.

Eligibility Requirements: Applicant must be high school student and planning to enroll or expecting to enroll full- or part-time at a two-year or four-year institution or university. Available to U.S. and non-U.S. citizens.

Application Requirements: Application form, essay. *Deadline:* July 20.

Contact: Lisa Ikariyama
Novus Biologicals, LLC
8100 Southpark Way
Unit A-8
Littleton, CO 80120
Phone: 303-730-1950
E-mail: lisa@novusbio.com

OKLAHOMA STATE REGENTS FOR HIGHER EDUCATION

http://www.okhighered.org/

ACADEMIC SCHOLARS PROGRAM

Awards for students of high academic ability to attend institutions in Oklahoma. Renewable up to four years. ACT or SAT scores must fall between 99.5 and 100th percentiles, or applicant must be designated as a National Merit scholar or finalist. Oklahoma public institutions can also select institutional nominees.

Award: Scholarship for use in freshman, sophomore, junior, senior, or graduate years; renewable. *Amount:* $1800–$5500.

Eligibility Requirements: Applicant must be high school student; planning to enroll or expecting to enroll full-time at a two-year or four-year institution or university and studying in Oklahoma. Available to U.S. citizens.

Application Requirements: Application form.

Contact: Scholarship Programs Coordinator
Oklahoma State Regents for Higher Education
PO Box 108850
Oklahoma City, OK 73101-8850
Phone: 800-858-1840
E-mail: studentinfo@osrhe.edu

ONLINECOLLEGEPLANNING.COM

http://onlinecollegeplanning.com

ONLINECOLLEGEPLANNINGSCHOLARSHIP.COM

This scholarship is part of our mission to make college accessible to students. We give two scholarships a year. The scholarship requires a 250 word essay on the biggest influence in making you want to go to college. Value of the scholarship is $1,000. Applications are only accepted online and can be submitted at http://onlinecollegeplanningscholarship.com/

Award: Scholarship for use in freshman year; not renewable. *Number:* 2. *Amount:* $1000.

Eligibility Requirements: Applicant must be high school student; age 13-21 and planning to enroll or expecting to enroll full-time at a four-year institution or university. Applicant must have 2.5 GPA or higher. Available to U.S. citizens.

Application Requirements: Application form, essay. *Deadline:* June 30.

Contact: Mr. James Maroney
OnlineCollegePlanning.com
56 Payne Road
Lebanon, NJ 08833
E-mail: james@onlinecollegeplanningscholarship.com

OPPORTUNITY FINANCIAL, LLC

https://www.opploans.com

OPPU ACHIEVERS SCHOLARSHIP

The OppU Achievers Scholarship celebrates students who transform opportunity into results. It rewards achievement in its many forms and honors those who create opportunity for both themselves and others. Founded in 2016, the scholarship provides $2,500 for current or future education costs. Scholarship selections are made four times a year. Annually, the OppU Achievers Scholarship awards a total of $10,000 to students who have demonstrated outstanding achievement.

Award: Scholarship for use in freshman, sophomore, junior, senior, graduate, or postgraduate years; not renewable. *Number:* 1. *Amount:* $2500.

Eligibility Requirements: Applicant must be enrolled or expecting to enroll full- or part-time at a two-year or four-year or technical institution or university. Applicant must have 3.0 GPA or higher. Available to U.S. and non-U.S. citizens.

Application Requirements: Essay. *Deadline:* continuous.

Contact: Jessica Stevenson, Copywriter
Phone: 800-990-9130
E-mail: JStevenson@opploans.com

OREGON STUDENT ASSISTANCE COMMISSION

https://oregonstudentaid.gov/

ALICE AND MASON WHITE MEMORIAL SCHOLARSHIP

One-time award for graduates of Oregon high schools planning to enroll as college juniors or above for fall term/semester in undergraduate study. Minimum 3.0 GPA and FAFSA required-based on financial need. Evidence in activities chart of at least one extracurricular school activity preferred.

Award: Scholarship for use in junior or senior years; not renewable.

Eligibility Requirements: Applicant must be enrolled or expecting to enroll full-time at a four-year institution or university and studying in Oregon. Applicant must have 3.0 GPA or higher. Available to U.S. citizens.

Application Requirements: Application form, essay, financial need analysis. *Deadline:* March 1.

Contact: Melissa Adams, Scholarship Processing Coordinator
Phone: 541-687-7409
E-mail: melissa.adams@state.or.us

ALLCOTT/HUNT SHARE IT NOW II SCHOLARSHIP, HONORING EMORY S. AND ELIZABETH BURKETT HUNT

Award for first or second generation immigrants to the United States. Eligible applicants must provide an answer to the citizenship status question in Item 4 of the Scholarship Application. Recipients must enroll at least half-time in college in the United States. Financial need may or may not be considered.

Award: Scholarship for use in freshman, sophomore, junior, or senior years; not renewable.

Eligibility Requirements: Applicant must be enrolled or expecting to enroll full- or part-time at a two-year or four-year institution or university. Available to U.S. and non-U.S. citizens.

Application Requirements: Application form, essay. *Deadline:* March 1.

Contact: Melissa Adams, Scholarship Processing Coordinator
Phone: 541-687-7409
E-mail: melissa.adams@state.or.us

BARTOO/MOSHINSKY SCHOLARSHIP

Award is available to dependents of eligible employees of credit unions affiliated with, current clients of, or past clients of Merger Solution

Group, The Watch Reports, and any other division of Bartoo Associates, LLC. Oregon residency is not required. Recipient must enroll at least half-time in a college or university in the United States. Apply/compete annually.

Award: Scholarship for use in freshman, sophomore, junior, or senior years; not renewable.

Eligibility Requirements: Applicant must be enrolled or expecting to enroll full- or part-time at a two-year or four-year institution or university. Available to U.S. citizens.

Application Requirements: Application form. *Deadline:* March 1.

Contact: Melissa Adams, Scholarship Processing Coordinator
Phone: 541-687-7409
E-mail: melissa.adams@state.or.us

BETTER A LIFE SCHOLARSHIP

Scholarship award available to single parents age 17-25. High schools seniors must have at least 3.0 GPA and college students must have at least a 2.5 GPA or GED equivalent. For use at Oregon public and nonprofit colleges and universities. Applicants may not already possess a Bachelor's degree. May reapply for one additional year of funding. Financial need may or may not be considered.

Award: Scholarship for use in freshman, sophomore, junior, or senior years; not renewable.

Eligibility Requirements: Applicant must be age 17-25; enrolled or expecting to enroll full- or part-time at a two-year or four-year institution or university; single and studying in Oregon. Applicant must have 2.5 GPA or higher. Available to U.S. citizens.

Application Requirements: Application form, financial need analysis. *Deadline:* March 1.

Contact: Melissa Adams, Scholarship Processing Coordinator
Phone: 541-687-7409
E-mail: melissa.adams@state.or.us

BRAD AND LISA BAILEY SCHOLARSHIP

Scholarship for Eligible employees of Bend Garbage & Recycling, Deschutes Recycling, Deschutes Transfer, High Country Disposal, and Mid Oregon Recycling. Eligible employees must have been employed by one of these companies for two+ years as of the March scholarship deadline. May enroll less than half time. Financial need may or may not be considered.

Award: Scholarship for use in freshman, sophomore, junior, or senior years; not renewable.

Eligibility Requirements: Applicant must be enrolled or expecting to enroll full- or part-time at a four-year institution or university and studying in Oregon. Available to U.S. citizens.

Application Requirements: Application form. *Deadline:* March 1.

Contact: Melissa Adams, Scholarship Processing Coordinator
Phone: 541-687-7409
E-mail: melissa.adams@state.or.us

BRUCE AND KARIN BAILEY SCHOLARSHIP

Award is for dependents of eligible employees of Bend Garbage & Recycling, Deschutes Recycling, Deschutes Transfer, High Country Disposal, and Mid Oregon Recycling. Eligible employees must have been employed by one of these companies two or more years as of the March scholarship deadline. High school seniors must have at least a 3.25 GPA. Apply/compete annually. Financial need may or may not be considered.

Award: Scholarship for use in freshman, sophomore, junior, or senior years; not renewable.

Eligibility Requirements: Applicant must be enrolled or expecting to enroll full-time at a two-year or four-year institution or university. Applicant must have 3.0 GPA or higher. Available to U.S. citizens.

Application Requirements: Application form, financial need analysis. *Deadline:* March 1.

Contact: Melissa Adams, Scholarship Processing Coordinator
Phone: 541-687-7409
E-mail: melissa.adams@state.or.us

CENTRAL CITY CONCERN SCHOLARSHIP

Scholarship for current employees of Central City Concern who have been employed by the company for two + continuous years as of the March scholarship deadline. Financial need may or may not be considered. Oregon residency is not required. Apply/compete annually.

Award: Scholarship for use in freshman, sophomore, junior, or senior years; not renewable.

Eligibility Requirements: Applicant must be enrolled or expecting to enroll full-time at a four-year institution or university. Available to U.S. and non-U.S. citizens.

Application Requirements: Application form, financial need analysis. *Deadline:* March 1.

Contact: Melissa Adams, Scholarship Processing Coordinator
Phone: 541-687-7409
E-mail: melissa.adams@state.or.us

CHILDREN OF INSITU SCHOLARSHIP

Award available to dependents of eligible employees or former employees of Insitu, Inc. Oregon residency is not required. Recipients must enroll at least half-time in a college or university in the United States. Financial need may or may not be considered.

Award: Scholarship for use in freshman, sophomore, junior, or senior years; not renewable.

Eligibility Requirements: Applicant must be enrolled or expecting to enroll full- or part-time at a four-year institution or university. Available to U.S. citizens.

Application Requirements: Application form, financial need analysis. *Deadline:* March 1.

Contact: Melissa Adams, Scholarship Processing Coordinator
Phone: 541-687-7409
E-mail: melissa.adams@state.or.us

CORNELIA VALENTINE MURPHY MEMORIAL SCHOLARSHIP

Award for undergraduate study to Oregon AFSCME Council #75 members (active, laid-off, retired, or disabled) in good standing, and their dependents, grandchildren, and spouses. Member must have been active in the Oregon Council 1+ year as of the March scholarship deadline or have been a member 1+ year preceding the date of layoff, death, disability, or retirement. Part-time enrollment (minimum six credit hours) will be considered for active members, their spouses (or life partners), or laid-off members. Based on financial aid.

Award: Scholarship for use in freshman, sophomore, junior, or senior years; not renewable.

Eligibility Requirements: Applicant must be enrolled or expecting to enroll full- or part-time at a four-year institution or university. Available to U.S. citizens.

Application Requirements: Application form, essay, financial need analysis. *Deadline:* March 1.

Contact: Melissa Adams, Scholarship Processing Coordinator
Phone: 541-687-7409
E-mail: melissa.adams@state.or.us

DREAM FORMER FOSTER YOUTH SCHOLARSHIP

Award for first-time freshman, undergraduate, or graduate student who meets one of the following criteria: applies for and qualifies for the Chafee Education and Training Grant; or was adopted from foster care between the ages of 14 and 16; or is a former Chafee awardee now over age 23 and currently enrolled in a degree-seeking program, or is a Chafee-eligible youth who did not receive Chafee funds before age 21. Apply/compete annually. Must be enrolled at least half-time. Based on financial need.

Award: Scholarship for use in freshman, sophomore, junior, senior, or graduate years; not renewable.

Eligibility Requirements: Applicant must be enrolled or expecting to enroll full- or part-time at a four-year institution or university. Available to U.S. citizens.

Application Requirements: Application form, financial need analysis. *Deadline:* March 1.

Contact: Melissa Adams, Scholarship Processing Coordinator
Phone: 541-687-7409
E-mail: melissa.adams@state.or.us

ERIK NIELSEN SCHOLARSHIP

Award for at least half-time study at Oregon public and nonprofit colleges. Applicants must have or recently had at least a three-year gap in their education. First preference given to GED recipients, then those with a high school diploma, then undergraduates who have been out of college for at least three years. Not for applicants with an existing Bachelor's degree. Based on financial need.

Award: Scholarship for use in freshman, sophomore, junior, or senior years; not renewable.

Eligibility Requirements: Applicant must be enrolled or expecting to enroll full- or part-time at a two-year or four-year institution or university and studying in Oregon. Available to U.S. citizens.

Application Requirements: Application form, financial need analysis. *Deadline:* March 1.

Contact: Melissa Adams, Scholarship Processing Coordinator
Phone: 541-687-7409
E-mail: melissa.adams@state.or.us

ERNEST ALAN AND BARBARA PARK MEYER SCHOLARSHIP

Award for graduates of Oregon high schools who are transferring or planning to transfer from a community college to a four-year college in Oregon during the same calendar year. Minimum 3.5 GPA. Preference to first-generation college attendees. Apply/compete annually. Based on financial need.

Award: Scholarship for use in freshman, sophomore, junior, or senior years; not renewable.

Eligibility Requirements: Applicant must be enrolled or expecting to enroll full-time at a four-year institution or university and studying in Oregon. Applicant must have 3.5 GPA or higher. Available to U.S. citizens.

Application Requirements: Application form, financial need analysis. *Deadline:* March 1.

Contact: Melissa Adams, Scholarship Processing Coordinator
Phone: 541-687-7409
E-mail: melissa.adams@state.or.us

FORD SONS AND DAUGHTERS OF EMPLOYEES OF ROSEBURG FOREST PRODUCTS COMPANY SCHOLARSHIP

Renewable award for dependents of eligible employees of Roseburg Forest Products Company. Parent must have been a full-time employee a minimum of 18 months prior to the March scholarship application deadline. Must enroll full-time, on campus, in the fall of the application year and be 21 years of age or younger. Not for applicants with existing Bachelor's degrees. May attend any eligible U.S. technical, 2- or 4-year school or college. Must have no felony convictions, or will have satisfied the terms of any felony conviction by August of the application year.

Award: Scholarship for use in freshman, sophomore, junior, or senior years; renewable.

Eligibility Requirements: Applicant must be enrolled or expecting to enroll full-time at a two-year or four-year or technical institution. Available to U.S. citizens.

Application Requirements: Application form, interview. *Deadline:* March 1.

Contact: Scholarship Coordinator
Oregon Student Assistance Commission
44 Club Road, Suite 100
Eugene, OR 97401
Phone: 877-864-2872
E-mail: fordscholarships@tfff.org

GEORGIA HARRIS MEMORIAL SCHOLARSHIP

Award for employees and dependents of eligible employees of Papa's Pizza. Eligible employees must have been employed by Papa's Pizza 1+ year as of the March scholarship deadline. Oregon residency is not required. Must submit essay and apply/compete annually. Financial need may or may not be considered

Award: Scholarship for use in freshman, sophomore, junior, senior, or graduate years; not renewable.

Eligibility Requirements: Applicant must be enrolled or expecting to enroll full-time at a two-year or four-year or technical institution or university. Available to U.S. citizens.

Application Requirements: Application form, essay, financial need analysis. *Deadline:* March 1.

Contact: Melissa Adams, Scholarship Processing Coordinator
Phone: 541-687-7409
E-mail: melissa.adams@state.or.us

GRAY COMMUNITY COLLEGE SCHOLARSHIP

Scholarship available to students attending Oregon community colleges at least half time. Not open to graduating high school seniors. Minimum GPA of 2.5 to 3.5. Scholarship is automatically renewable if renewal criteria met. Based on financial need.

Award: Scholarship for use in freshman or sophomore years; not renewable.

Eligibility Requirements: Applicant must be enrolled or expecting to enroll full- or part-time at a two-year institution and studying in Oregon. Applicant must have 2.5 GPA or higher. Available to U.S. citizens.

Application Requirements: Application form, financial need analysis. *Deadline:* March 1.

Contact: Melissa Adams, Scholarship Processing Coordinator
Phone: 541-687-7409
E-mail: melissa.adams@state.or.us

JEROME B. STEINBACH SCHOLARSHIP

Award for Oregon residents enrolled in Oregon institutions as sophomore or above. Award for undergraduate study only. Must be a U.S. citizen by birth. U.S. Bank employees, their children, or near relatives are not eligible. Based on financial need.

Award: Scholarship for use in sophomore, junior, or senior years; not renewable.

Eligibility Requirements: Applicant must be enrolled or expecting to enroll full-time at a four-year institution or university. Applicant must have 3.5 GPA or higher. Available to U.S. citizens.

Application Requirements: Application form, financial need analysis. *Deadline:* March 1.

Contact: Melissa Adams, Scholarship Processing Coordinator
Phone: 541-687-7409
E-mail: melissa.adams@state.or.us

KONNIE MEMORIAL (DEPENDENTS) SCHOLARSHIP

Scholarship for dependents of eligible employees of Swanson Brothers Lumber Company. Open to graduating high school seniors planning to attend a public college.

Award: Scholarship for use in freshman year; renewable.

Eligibility Requirements: Applicant must be high school student and planning to enroll or expecting to enroll at an institution or university. Available to U.S. citizens.

Application Requirements: Application form. *Deadline:* March 1.

Contact: Melissa Adams, Scholarship Processing Coordinator
Phone: 541-687-7409
E-mail: melissa.adams@state.or.us

MAY TRUCKING COMPANY SCHOLARSHIP

One-time award for dependents of eligible employees of May Trucking Company. Eligible employees must have been employed by May Trucking Company 3+ years as of the March scholarship deadline. Preferred GPA of 3.4 and 1400+ combined SAT scores.

Award: Scholarship for use in freshman, sophomore, junior, or senior years; not renewable.

Eligibility Requirements: Applicant must be enrolled or expecting to enroll full-time at a four-year institution or university. Available to U.S. citizens.

Application Requirements: Application form. *Deadline:* March 1.

Contact: Melissa Adams, Scholarship Processing Coordinator
Phone: 541-687-7409
E-mail: melissa.adams@state.or.us

MIRABELLA EMPLOYEE-YES PROJECT SCHOLARSHIP

One-time award for hourly employees of Mirabella Portland. Oregon residency is not required. May attend school less than half time. Must specify dates of employment. Financial need may or may not be considered.

Award: Scholarship for use in freshman, sophomore, junior, senior, or graduate years; not renewable.

Eligibility Requirements: Applicant must be enrolled or expecting to enroll full- or part-time at a two-year or four-year or technical institution or university. Available to U.S. and non-U.S. citizens.

Application Requirements: Application form, financial need analysis. *Deadline:* March 1.

Contact: Melissa Adams, Scholarship Processing Coordinator
Phone: 541-687-7409
E-mail: melissa.adams@state.or.us

MULTNOMAH COUNTY DEPUTY SHERIFFS ASSOCIATION DEPENDENTS SCHOLARSHIP

Scholarship for children (including stepchildren) of active or deceased members of Multnomah County Deputy Sheriffs' Association (preference to active members).

Award: Scholarship for use in freshman, sophomore, junior, or senior years; not renewable.

Eligibility Requirements: Applicant must be enrolled or expecting to enroll at a four-year institution or university. Available to U.S. citizens.

Application Requirements: Application form. *Deadline:* March 1.

Contact: Melissa Adams, Scholarship Processing Coordinator
Phone: 541-687-7409
E-mail: melissa.adams@state.or.us

MY PATH, OUR FUTURE: HSE SCHOLARS OF OREGON

Annual award for GED graduates or students who will complete their GED. Must enroll at least half time. Oregon residency is preferred. Financial need may or may not be considered.

Award: Scholarship for use in freshman, sophomore, junior, or senior years; not renewable.

Eligibility Requirements: Applicant must be enrolled or expecting to enroll full- or part-time at a four-year institution or university. Available to U.S. citizens.

Application Requirements: Application form. *Deadline:* March 1.

Contact: Melissa Adams, Scholarship Processing Coordinator
Phone: 541-687-7409
E-mail: melissa.adams@state.or.us

NECA OREGON-COLUMBIA CHAPTER SCHOLARSHIP

Award for graduating high school seniors who are either children or grandchildren of members of NECA Oregon-Columbia Chapter, or dependents of employees of NECA Oregon-Columbia Chapter. Scholarship is automatically renewable if renewal criteria met.

Award: Scholarship for use in freshman year; renewable.

Eligibility Requirements: Applicant must be high school student and planning to enroll or expecting to enroll full-time at a two-year or four-year or technical institution or university. Available to U.S. citizens.

Application Requirements: Application form. *Deadline:* March 1.

Contact: Melissa Adams, Scholarship Processing Coordinator
Phone: 541-687-7409
E-mail: melissa.adams@state.or.us

NETTIE HANSELMAN JAYNES MEMORIAL SCHOLARSHIP

Scholarship for elementary or secondary education majors entering senior or fifth-year or graduate students in fifth year for elementary or secondary certificate. Must attend an Oregon public or nonprofit college, Based on financial need.

Award: Scholarship for use in senior or graduate years; not renewable.

Eligibility Requirements: Applicant must be enrolled or expecting to enroll at a four-year institution or university and studying in Oregon. Available to U.S. citizens.

Application Requirements: Application form. *Deadline:* March 1.

Contact: Melissa Adams, Scholarship Processing Coordinator
Phone: 541-687-7409
E-mail: melissa.adams@state.or.us

OREGON DUNGENESS CRAB COMMISSION SCHOLARSHIP

One-time scholarship available to children, stepchildren, or legal dependents of licensed Oregon Dungeness Crab fishermen or crew. Must be 23 years of age or under as of the March scholarship deadline.

Award: Scholarship for use in freshman, sophomore, junior, or senior years; not renewable.

Eligibility Requirements: Applicant must be enrolled or expecting to enroll full-time at a four-year institution or university. Available to U.S. citizens.

Application Requirements: Application form. *Deadline:* March 1.

OREGON MOVING AND STORAGE ASSOCIATION JACK L. STEWART SCHOLARSHIP

Award for eligible members of Oregon Moving and Storage Association and their dependents and grandchildren or dependents and grandchildren of employees of members of Oregon Moving and Storage Association. Apply/compete annually.

Award: Scholarship for use in freshman, sophomore, junior, or senior years; not renewable.

Eligibility Requirements: Applicant must be enrolled or expecting to enroll full-time at a four-year institution or university and studying in Oregon. Available to U.S. citizens.

Application Requirements: Application form. *Deadline:* March 1.

Contact: Melissa Adams, Scholarship Processing Coordinator
Phone: 541-687-7409
E-mail: melissa.adams@state.or.us

OREGON OCCUPATIONAL SAFETY AND HEALTH DIVISION WORKERS MEMORIAL SCHOLARSHIP

One-time award for Oregon high school graduates or GED recipients who are either (1) dependents or spouses of an Oregon worker who has incurred permanent total disability on the job while working for an Oregon employer; or (2) receiving, or have received, fatality benefits as dependents or spouses of an Oregon worker fatally injured on the job while working for an Oregon employer. Requires information about the worker's injury and relationship. Financial need may or may not be considered.

Award: Scholarship for use in freshman, sophomore, junior, or senior years; not renewable.

Eligibility Requirements: Applicant must be enrolled or expecting to enroll full- or part-time at a four-year institution or university. Available to U.S. citizens.

Application Requirements: Application form, essay. *Deadline:* March 1.

Contact: Melissa Adams, Scholarship Processing Coordinator
Phone: 541-687-7409
E-mail: melissa.adams@state.or.us

OREGON SALMON COMMISSION SCOTT BOLEY MEMORIAL SCHOLARSHIP

Award for dependents of licensed commercial Oregon troll salmon permit fishermen and/or captains of the vessels of licensed commercial Oregon troll salmon permit fishermen who have paid assessments to the Oregon Salmon Commission within the past three years. Preference given to graduating high school seniors. Based on financial need.

Award: Scholarship for use in freshman, sophomore, junior, or senior years; not renewable.

Eligibility Requirements: Applicant must be enrolled or expecting to enroll full-time at a four-year institution or university. Available to U.S. citizens.

Application Requirements: Application form, financial need analysis. *Deadline:* March 1.

Contact: Melissa Adams, Scholarship Processing Coordinator
Phone: 541-687-7409
E-mail: melissa.adams@state.or.us

OREGON SCHOLARSHIP FUND COMMUNITY COLLEGE STUDENT AWARD

Scholarship open to students enrolled or planning to enroll at least half time in Oregon community college programs. Recipients may reapply for one additional year. Based on financial need.

Award: Scholarship for use in freshman or sophomore years; renewable.

Eligibility Requirements: Applicant must be enrolled or expecting to enroll full- or part-time at a two-year institution and studying in Oregon. Available to U.S. citizens.

Application Requirements: Application form, financial need analysis. *Deadline:* March 1.

Contact: Melissa Adams, Scholarship Processing Coordinator
Phone: 541-687-7409
E-mail: melissa.adams@state.or.us

OREGON SCHOLARSHIP FUND TRANSFER STUDENT AWARD

Award open to students who are currently enrolled in their second year at a community college and are planning to transfer to a four-year college in Oregon. Must enroll at least half-time. Based on financial need.

Award: Scholarship for use in junior or senior years; renewable.

Eligibility Requirements: Applicant must be enrolled or expecting to enroll full- or part-time at a four-year institution or university and studying in Oregon. Available to U.S. citizens.

Application Requirements: Application form, financial need analysis. *Deadline:* March 1.

Contact: Melissa Adams, Scholarship Processing Coordinator
Phone: 541-687-7409
E-mail: melissa.adams@state.or.us

OREGON TRAWL COMMISSION JOE EASLEY MEMORIAL SCHOLARSHIP

Award for students in any accredited U.S. college or university who are dependents of licensed Oregon Trawl fishermen or crew. Must reapply annually for renewal. Based on financial need.

Award: Scholarship for use in freshman, sophomore, junior, or senior years; not renewable.

Eligibility Requirements: Applicant must be enrolled or expecting to enroll full-time at a four-year institution or university. Available to U.S. citizens.

Application Requirements: Application form, financial need analysis. *Deadline:* March 1.

Contact: Melissa Adams, Scholarship Processing Coordinator
Phone: 541-687-7409
E-mail: melissa.adams@state.or.us

PACIFICSOURCE SCHOLARSHIP

Scholarship for dependents of eligible employees of PacificSource. Eligible employees must have been employed by PacificSource two+ years at no fewer than 20 hours per week as of the March scholarship deadline; PacificSource will recognize previous tenure for employees who were hired as a result of an acquisition/merger. Dependents of PacificSource officers are not eligible to participate. Minimum GPA 3.00 or GED of 2650. For public and nonprofit colleges.

Award: Scholarship for use in freshman, sophomore, junior, or senior years; not renewable.

Eligibility Requirements: Applicant must be enrolled or expecting to enroll at a four-year institution or university. Applicant must have 3.0 GPA or higher. Available to U.S. citizens.

Application Requirements: Application form. *Deadline:* March 1.

Contact: Melissa Adams, Scholarship Processing Coordinator
Phone: 541-687-7409
E-mail: melissa.adams@state.or.us

PETER CONNACHER MEMORIAL SCHOLARSHIP

Renewable award for American prisoners-of-war and their descendants. Written proof of prisoner-of-war status and discharge papers from the U.S. Armed Forces must accompany application. Statement of relationship between applicant and former prisoner-of-war is required. Oregon residency preferred but not required. Financial need may or may not be considered.

Award: Scholarship for use in freshman, sophomore, junior, senior, or graduate years; renewable.

Eligibility Requirements: Applicant must be enrolled or expecting to enroll full-time at a two-year or four-year institution. Available to U.S. citizens.

Application Requirements: Application form, financial need analysis. *Deadline:* March 1.

Contact: Melissa Adams, Scholarship Processing Coordinator
Phone: 541-687-7409
E-mail: melissa.adams@state.or.us

PITB SERVICES SCHOLARSHIP

Scholarship for PITB Services members or dependents of PITB Services members. Must enroll at least half time.

Award: Scholarship for use in freshman, sophomore, junior, or senior years; not renewable.

Eligibility Requirements: Applicant must be enrolled or expecting to enroll full- or part-time at a four-year institution or university. Applicant must have 3.0 GPA or higher. Available to U.S. citizens.

Application Requirements: Application form. *Deadline:* March 1.

Contact: Melissa Adams, Scholarship Processing Coordinator
Phone: 541-687-7409
E-mail: melissa.adams@state.or.us

PITB TRANSPORTATION SCHOLARSHIP

One-time award for high school graduates (including home schooled graduates) who are dependents of PITB Transportation employees or dependents of PITB Transportation members. Must be enrolled in college at least half-time and have a minimum 3.0 GPA.

Award: Scholarship for use in freshman, sophomore, junior, or senior years; not renewable.

Eligibility Requirements: Applicant must be enrolled or expecting to enroll full- or part-time at a four-year institution or university. Applicant must have 3.0 GPA or higher. Available to U.S. citizens.

Application Requirements: Application form. *Deadline:* March 1.

Contact: Melissa Adams, Scholarship Processing Coordinator
Phone: 541-687-7409
E-mail: melissa.adams@state.or.us

PROFESSIONAL LAND SURVEYORS OF OREGON— PETE MARING SCHOLARSHIP

Scholarship for dependents of eligible members of Professional Land Surveyors of Oregon. Career field is other than land surveying. Must be enrolled at an Oregon public or nonprofit college.

Award: Scholarship for use in freshman, sophomore, junior, or senior years; not renewable.

Eligibility Requirements: Applicant must be enrolled or expecting to enroll at a four-year institution or university and studying in Oregon. Available to U.S. citizens.

Application Requirements: Application form, essay. *Deadline:* March 1.

Contact: Melissa Adams, Scholarship Processing Coordinator
Phone: 541-687-7409
E-mail: melissa.adams@state.or.us

REGISTER-GUARD FEDERAL CREDIT UNION SCHOLARSHIP

Award is available to current members of the Register-Guard Federal Credit Union, or those eligible for membership, with preference in the following order: (1) current employees, independent contractors of The Register-Guard including members of their immediate families or households, (2) retired persons as pensioners or annuitants, (3) spouses of persons who died within membership, (4) organizations of such persons, (5) members of the Confederated Tribes of Grande Ronde or their immediate family members, and (6) employees or contracted employees of the law office of Donald Slayton and Alan Seglison or their immediate family members. Minimum 2.5 GPA, or GED of 2500+. Financial need may or may not be considered.

Award: Scholarship for use in freshman, sophomore, junior, senior, or graduate years; not renewable.

Eligibility Requirements: Applicant must be enrolled or expecting to enroll full-time at a two-year or four-year institution or university. Applicant must have 2.5 GPA or higher. Available to U.S. citizens.

Application Requirements: Application form, essay. *Deadline:* March 1.

Contact: Melissa Adams, Scholarship Processing Coordinator
Phone: 541-687-7409
E-mail: melissa.adams@state.or.us

SP FIBER TECHNOLOGIES DEPENDENTS SCHOLARSHIP

Renewable award for dependents of eligible employees of WestRock, formerly SP Fiber Technologies. Eligible employees must have been employed 1+ year as of the March scholarship deadline.

Award: Scholarship for use in freshman, sophomore, junior, or senior years; renewable.

Eligibility Requirements: Applicant must be enrolled or expecting to enroll full-time at a two-year or four-year institution or university. Applicant must have 3.0 GPA or higher. Available to U.S. citizens.

Application Requirements: Application form. *Deadline:* March 1.

Contact: Melissa Adams, Scholarship Processing Coordinator
Phone: 541-687-7409
E-mail: melissa.adams@state.or.us

UNIVERSITY CLUB OF PORTLAND SCHOLARSHIP

Award available to eligible employees and dependents of eligible employees of the University Club of Portland. Eligible employees must be in good standing and must have been employed by University Club of Portland one or more years as of the March scholarship deadline. College applicants must have a minimum 2.5 GPA. Apply/compete annually; prior recipients must be currently enrolled to reapply. Financial need may or may not be considered.

Award: Scholarship for use in freshman, sophomore, junior, senior, or graduate years; not renewable.

Eligibility Requirements: Applicant must be enrolled or expecting to enroll full- or part-time at a four-year institution or university. Available to U.S. citizens.

Application Requirements: Application form. *Deadline:* March 1.

Contact: Melissa Adams, Scholarship Processing Coordinator
Phone: 541-687-7409
E-mail: melissa.adams@state.or.us

WAYNE MORSE LEGACY SCHOLARSHIP

Award for graduates (including GED recipients and home-schooled graduates) of Oregon high schools who are enrolled or planning to enroll at least half-time at Oregon public and nonprofit institutions. Must be a U.S. citizen and have a minimum 2.8 GPA. Can reapply for 1 additional year. Financial need may or may not be considered.

Award: Scholarship for use in freshman, sophomore, junior, senior, or graduate years; not renewable.

Eligibility Requirements: Applicant must be enrolled or expecting to enroll full- or part-time at a two-year or four-year institution or university and studying in Oregon. Applicant must have 2.5 GPA or higher. Available to U.S. citizens.

Application Requirements: Application form, essay. *Deadline:* March 1.

Contact: Melissa Adams, Scholarship Processing Coordinator
Phone: 541-687-7409
E-mail: melissa.adams@state.or.us

OTA GUIDE

http://occupational-therapy-assistant.org/

COTA SCHOLARSHIP FOR OCCUPATIONAL THERAPY ASSISTANTS

The Occupational Therapy profession is experiencing a huge increase in demand. In an effort to encourage more bright students down the path to becoming a COTA to help serve this increase in demand, we created this scholarship for COTA students. Each year we will award one COTA student with a $500 scholarship.

Award: Scholarship for use in freshman, sophomore, junior, senior, graduate, or postgraduate years; not renewable. *Number:* 1–2. *Amount:* $1–$500.

Eligibility Requirements: Applicant must be enrolled or expecting to enroll full- or part-time at a two-year or four-year or technical institution or university. Available to U.S. and non-U.S. citizens.

Application Requirements: Essay. *Deadline:* December 1.

Contact: Kelly Clark
OTA Guide
2801 Oak Crest Avenue
Austin, TX 78704

OWEN SOFTWARE

http://www.pathevo.com/

$2,000 NO ESSAY SCHOLARSHIP

$2,000 "No Essay" Scholarship. Each quarter Pathevo Prep (Owen Software) awards $2,000 to a high school junior or senior upon acceptance in an accredited four year college or university. The award is a random drawing and will be announced to all entrants. The award is given four times a year, renewing quarterly.

Award: Scholarship for use in freshman year; renewable. *Number:* 1. *Amount:* $2000.

Eligibility Requirements: Applicant must be high school student and planning to enroll or expecting to enroll full-time at a four-year institution. Available to U.S. citizens.

Application Requirements: Driver's license. *Deadline:* December 31.

Contact: Susan Hughes
Owen Software
700 King Farm Blvd
#610
Rockville, MD 20850
Phone: 240-453-0030
E-mail: susan.hughes@pathevo.com

PATIENT ADVOCATE FOUNDATION

http://www.patientadvocate.org/

SCHOLARSHIP FOR SURVIVORS

Four years after Patient Advocate Foundation's inception, founder Nancy Davenport-Ennis created Patient Advocate Foundation's Scholarship for Survivors program after witnessing multiple recurring counts of patients whose post-secondary education had been impacted due to their life-threatening, chronic or debilitating illness. Despite their condition, these students excelled academically, served the community, and demonstrated the drive and desire to attend college. The purpose of our scholarship program is to provide support to individuals, under the age of 25, who have been diagnosed with or treated for cancer and/or a chronic/life threatening disease within the past five years.

Award: Scholarship for use in freshman, sophomore, junior, senior, or graduate years; renewable. *Number:* 12. *Amount:* $3000.

Eligibility Requirements: Applicant must be enrolled or expecting to enroll full-time at a two-year or four-year institution or university. Applicant must have 3.0 GPA or higher. Available to U.S. citizens.

Application Requirements: Application form, essay, financial need analysis. *Deadline:* February 25.

Contact: Ms. Shawn Nason, Director, Events, Travel, Admin Services
Patient Advocate Foundation
421 Butler Farm road
Hampton, VA 23666
Phone: 800-532-5274
E-mail: scholarship@patientadvocate.org

PHI BETA SIGMA FRATERNITY INC.

http://www.pbs1914.org/

PHI BETA SIGMA FRATERNITY NATIONAL PROGRAM OF EDUCATION

Scholarships are awarded to both graduate and undergraduate students. Applicants must have minimum 3.0 GPA.

Award: Scholarship for use in freshman, sophomore, junior, senior, or graduate years; not renewable.

Eligibility Requirements: Applicant must be enrolled or expecting to enroll full-time at a four-year institution or university and male. Applicant must have 3.0 GPA or higher. Available to U.S. citizens.

Application Requirements: Application form, essay, personal photograph, recommendations or references, resume, transcript. *Deadline:* June 15.

Contact: Emile Pitre, Chairman
Phi Beta Sigma Fraternity Inc.
2 Belmonte Circle, SW
Atlanta, GA 30311
Phone: 404-759-6827
E-mail: mikewhines@aol.com

POSITIVE COACHING ALLIANCE

https://positivecoach.org/

TRIPLE-IMPACT COMPETITOR SCHOLARSHIP

PCA awards scholarships of $1,000-$2,000 (depending on location) to high school athletes, based on their responses to questions pertaining to how they meet the standard defined in Elevating Your Game: Becoming a Triple-Impact Competitor by PCA Founder Jim Thompson. Eligibility extends to any high school junior residing anywhere in the U.S. and playing for a high school team or in club sports. All details can be found on our website and you may begin an application there as well.

Award: Scholarship for use in freshman year; not renewable. *Number:* 50–150. *Amount:* $1000–$2000.

Eligibility Requirements: Applicant must be high school student and planning to enroll or expecting to enroll full-time at a two-year or four-year institution. Applicant must have 2.5 GPA or higher. Available to U.S. citizens.

Application Requirements: Application form. *Deadline:* May 31.

Contact: Jennie Wulbrun, Program Administrator
Positive Coaching Alliance
1001 N. Rengstorff Ave Ste. 100
Mountain View, CA 94043
Phone: 650-210-0815
E-mail: jennie_wulbrun@positivecoach.org

PRETTY LIGHTROOM PRESETS

https://www.lightroompresets.com/

PRETTY LIGHTROOM PRESETS BI-ANNUAL SCHOLARSHIP

Pretty Lightroom Presets recognizes the importance of higher education and the role it plays in our personal and professional fulfillment. That's why we are so excited to announce the Pretty Presets for Lightroom $500 bi-annual scholarship (awarded twice per year). This ongoing scholarship provides college and university students an opportunity to earn money to further their education and achieve their goals! The deadline for scholarship entries is bi-annually on June 15 and December 15. The winning entry will be published on Pretty Presets Blog. The winner will be notified by e-mail three weeks after the deadline. Scholarship entries will be carefully reviewed by a team of judges at LightroomPresets.com. The scholarship will be paid out in the amount of $500 (U.S.) to each bi-annual winner, in the form of a co-payable check that will be mailed to the college or university attended by the winning student. Carefully research and compose an essay style Adobe Lightroom tutorial of 800 to 1,000 words, with screenshots and photos included to illustrate your points on one of the following topics. You must either own copyright to the images, or have written permission to use the images included in your essay. Use proper grammar and punctuation.Use proper grammar and punctuation. Choose a topic for your tutorial essay: How Lightroom has changed Photography; Lightroom techniques for Fall, Winter, Spring, or Summer photos; How to re-touch skin in Lightroom for photographers; or How to apply a cinematic or film look to photographs using Lightroom. You should presently be a senior in high school, or be transitioning from high school to a college or university; or be already enrolled in a college or university inside the United States or Canada. Employees and their immediate family members of LightroomPresets.com are not eligible to participate. Email your essay in Microsoft Word document or plain text format to scholarship@lightroompresets.com. Please specify your name, contact telephone number, email address and mailing address. Your contact information will be held in confidence and will not be shared. Include the name of the college or university and their mailing address of the financial aid office that you are presently attending or that you'll be attending after high school. Please attach a headshot photo of yourself in.JPG or.PNG format that is at least 300 pixels wide. If we don't receive all requested information by the deadline, your submission may be disqualified.

Award: Scholarship for use in freshman, sophomore, junior, senior, graduate, or postgraduate years; not renewable. *Number:* 2. *Amount:* $500.

Eligibility Requirements: Applicant must be enrolled or expecting to enroll full- or part-time at a two-year or four-year institution or university. Available to U.S. and non-U.S. citizens.

Application Requirements: Essay, personal photograph. *Deadline:* June 15.

Contact: Karlen Kleinkopf
E-mail: scholarship@lightroompresets.com

PRETTY PHOTOSHOP ACTIONS

https://www.photoshopactions.com/

PRETTY PHOTOSHOP ACTIONS BI-ANNUAL SCHOLARSHIP

Pretty Photoshop Actions recognizes the importance of higher education and the role it plays in our personal and professional fulfillment. That's why we are so excited to announce the Pretty Photoshop Actions $500 bi-annual scholarship (awarded twice per year). This ongoing scholarship provides college and university students an opportunity to earn money to further their education and achieve their goals! The deadline for scholarship entries is bi-annually on April 15 and October 15. The winning entry will be published on Pretty Actions Blog. The winner will be notified by e-mail three weeks after the deadline. Scholarship entries will be carefully reviewed by a team of judges at PhotoshopActions.com. The scholarship will be paid out in the amount of $500 (U.S.) to each bi-annual winner, in the form of a co-payable check that will be mailed to the college or university attended by the winning student. Carefully research and compose an essay style Adobe Photoshop tutorial of 800 to 1,000 words, with screenshots and photos included to illustrate your points on one of the following topics. You must either own copyright to the images, or have written permission to use the images included in your essay. Use proper grammar and punctuation. Choose a topic for your tutorial essay: How Photoshop has changed photography; How to re-touch skin in Photoshop for photographers; Favorite tips for enhancing color in Photoshop; Photoshop overlay ideas for adding wow to your portraits. Eligible student entries are as follows: you should presently be a senior in high school, or be transitioning from high school to a college or university; or be already enrolled in a college or university inside the United States or Canada. Employees and their immediate family members of PhotoshopActions.com are not eligible to participate. Email your essay in Microsoft Word document or plain text format to scholarship@photoshopactions.com. Please specify your name, contact telephone number, email address and mailing address. Your contact information will be held in confidence and will not be shared. Include the name of the college or university and their mailing address of the financial aid office that you are presently attending or that you'll be attending after high school. Please attach a headshot photo of yourself in.jpg or.png format that is at least 300 pixels wide. If we do not receive all requested information by the deadline, your submission may be disqualified.

Award: Scholarship for use in freshman, sophomore, junior, senior, graduate, or postgraduate years; not renewable. *Number:* 2. *Amount:* $500.

Eligibility Requirements: Applicant must be enrolled or expecting to enroll full- or part-time at a two-year or four-year institution or university. Available to U.S. and non-U.S. citizens.

Application Requirements: Essay, personal photograph. *Deadline:* April 15.

Contact: Karlen Kleinkopf
E-mail: scholarship@photoshopactions.com

PROOFREADINGSERVICES.COM

http://www.proofreadingservices.com/

HIGH SCHOOL AND UNIVERSITY WRITING SCHOLARSHIPS

Applicants must respond to the following writing prompt: Write about a defining moment in your life in the style of your favorite children's author. Three scholarships will be awarded to high school seniors and three will be awarded to university students. See more at: http://www.proofreadingservices.com/pages/scholarship#sthash.A7Jv5CsH.dpuf.

Award: Scholarship for use in freshman, sophomore, junior, senior, or graduate years; not renewable. *Number:* 6. *Amount:* $100–$500.

Eligibility Requirements: Applicant must be enrolled or expecting to enroll full- or part-time at a two-year or four-year or technical institution or university. Applicant must have 3.0 GPA or higher. Available to U.S. and non-U.S. citizens.

Application Requirements: Application form, essay. *Deadline:* June 1.

Contact: Mr. Luke Palder, CEO
ProofreadingServices.com
1 Broadway
14th Floor
Cambridge, MA 02142
Phone: 800-492-6773
E-mail: scholarship@proofreadingservices.com

PRUDENT PUBLISHING COMPANY INC.

http://www.gallerycollection.com/

10TH ANNUAL CREATE-A-GREETING-CARD $10,000 SCHOLARSHIP CONTEST

Students must submit an original photo, piece of artwork, or computer graphic for the front of a greeting card. The student with the best design will win a $10,000 scholarship and have his or her entry made into an actual greeting card to be sold in The Gallery Collection's line. The winning student's school will also receive a $1000 prize for helping to promote the contest. For complete details visit http://www.gallerycollection.com/greeting-cards-scholarship.htm.

Award: Scholarship for use in freshman, sophomore, junior, senior, or graduate years; not renewable. *Number:* 1. *Amount:* $10,000.

Eligibility Requirements: Applicant must be enrolled or expecting to enroll full- or part-time at a two-year or four-year or technical institution or university. Available to U.S. citizens.

Application Requirements: Application form, entry in a contest, greeting card design. *Deadline:* December 31.

Contact: Scholarship Administrator
Prudent Publishing Company Inc.
Prudent Publishing Company
65 Challenger Road
Ridgefield Park, NJ 07660
Phone: 201-641-7900
E-mail: scholarshipadmin@gallerycollection.com

PUSH FOR EXCELLENCE

http://www.pushexcel.org/

ORA LEE SANDERS SCHOLARSHIP

U.S. citizens who will be freshmen, sophomores, juniors, or seniors are eligible. The scholarship is renewable up to 4 years based upon GPA. Full time study with minimum 2.5 GPA.

Award: Scholarship for use in freshman, sophomore, junior, or senior years; renewable. *Amount:* $1000.

Eligibility Requirements: Applicant must be enrolled or expecting to enroll full-time at a four-year institution or university. Applicant must have 2.5 GPA or higher. Available to U.S. citizens.

Application Requirements: Application form, essay, proof of current enrollment or acceptance in a college or university, recommendations or references, self-addressed stamped envelope with application, transcript. *Deadline:* April 30.

Contact: Scholarship Committee
Push for Excellence
930 East 50th Street
Chicago, IL 60615
Phone: 773-373-3366
E-mail: info@pushexcel.org

RADIO TELEVISION DIGITAL NEWS ASSOCIATION

http://www.rtdna.org

PRESIDENTS SCHOLARSHIP

Two $1,000 awards are given each year to aspiring journalists in honor of former RTDNA Presidents Theodore Koop, Bruce Dennis, James McCulla, John Salisbury, Bruce Palmer, Dick Cheverton, Jim Byron, Ben Chatfield and John Hogan.

Award: Scholarship for use in sophomore, junior, or senior years; not renewable. *Number:* 2. *Amount:* $1000.

Eligibility Requirements: Applicant must be enrolled or expecting to enroll full-time at a four-year institution or university. Available to U.S. and non-U.S. citizens.

Application Requirements: Application form, essay, portfolio. *Deadline:* January 31.

Contact: Ms. Kate McGarrity, Awards and Programs Manager
Radio Television Digital News Association
529 14th Street, NW
Suite 1240
Washington, DC 20045
Phone: 202-662-7254
E-mail: katem@rtdna.org

RATINGLE

http://ratingle.com

RATINGLE SCHOLARSHIP PROGRAM

The Ratingle Scholarship subject is product reviews. Students should choose a unique gadget that made their last year different. The gadget could be of any field (studies/electronics/fun etc.). The video should introduce the product and answer the most important questions others may have before purchasing this product. $1000 prize available.

Award: Prize for use in freshman, sophomore, junior, senior, graduate, or postgraduate years; not renewable.

Eligibility Requirements: Applicant must be enrolled or expecting to enroll full- or part-time at an institution or university. Available to U.S. citizens.

Application Requirements: Essay. *Deadline:* April 18.

Contact: Miss. Hana Renolds, Marketing Manager, Ratingle
Ratingle
8345 NW 66 ST #C7592
MIAMI, FL 33166
Phone: 844-873-2875
E-mail: ratinglereview@gmail.com

RENOVISO

https://renoviso.com

RENOVISO DREAM HOME DESIGN SCHOLARSHIP

The Renoviso Dream Home Design Scholarship enables students to describe their ideal home improvement project. The scholarship will be awarding one student $2,000 to put towards his or her education. From tuition costs to dining and textbooks, the scholarship money can be used to cover any expenses. Eligible students should submit an essay to scholarships@renoviso.com answering the prompt: "If you were a homeowner, what's the one home improvement project you'd choose to complete and why?" This can be a fictional or real example. For instance, would you upgrade your kitchen cabinets and counters because you love entertaining? Would you fix your roof because of your area's harsh winters? Or would you buy a set of new windows for energy-efficiency? Essays will be judged based on the following criteria: content, style, and creativity. One essay per entrant only. Please include your name, mailing, email address, phone number and documentation of your current or upcoming enrollment in an accredited U.S. college or university. The deadline to apply for the scholarship is August 15, 2018. The winner will be featured on Renoviso's blog. We will post his or her name, photo, school they are attending, along with the winning essay. Completed applications must be sent no later than August 15, 2018. Application materials should be emailed to scholarships@renoviso.com. One applicant is awarded a $2,000 scholarship. Renoviso scholarship award recipient will be notified of the selection on or before August 31, 2018.

Award: Scholarship for use in freshman, sophomore, junior, senior, graduate, or postgraduate years; not renewable. *Number:* 1. *Amount:* $2000.

Eligibility Requirements: Applicant must be enrolled or expecting to enroll full- or part-time at a two-year or four-year or technical institution or university. Available to U.S. and non-U.S. citizens.

Application Requirements: Essay. *Deadline:* August 15.

Contact: Paul Buonopane
Renoviso
2 S Market Street
Floor 4
Boston, MA 02109
Phone: 888-867-1660
E-mail: scholarships@renoviso.com

RENTHOP

http://www.renthop.com

RENTHOP COLLEGE AND UNIVERSITY SCHOLARSHIP PROGRAM

To apply, send an essay under 500 words that follows the following prompt: Technology is changing every aspects of our daily lives, from searching for real estate to phones in our pocket that are more powerful than anyone would have imaged a generation prior. In the next 5 years, what do you feel will be the most profound changes that impact college graduates, their careers, and their personal lives? How are your those changes aligned with the RentHop values and those of your school and degree program? Apply today at college-scholarship@renthop.com. You must apply using your school email address.There are two deadlines for the scholarship: April 30th and August 31st. The two deadlines for the scholarship will be available year after year. You must be a current student in an eligible undergraduate program or a graduating high school senior, working towards a Bachelor's degree or associates degree. A total of two students will be chosen as finalists for the $1000 scholarship each year. More scholarships of lesser amounts may be awarded for additional students.

Award: Scholarship for use in freshman, sophomore, junior, or senior years; not renewable. *Number:* 1–2. *Amount:* $1000.

Eligibility Requirements: Applicant must be age 15-26 and enrolled or expecting to enroll full- or part-time at a four-year institution or university. Available to U.S. and non-U.S. citizens.

Application Requirements: Essay. *Deadline:* August 31.

Contact: Faye Chou, Statistical Analyst
RentHop
335 Madison Avenue
4th Floor (GCT Hub)
New York, NY 10017
Phone: 913-982-6682
E-mail: faye@renthop.com

REPLACE MY CONTACTS

http://www.replacemycontacts.com

REPLACE MY CONTACTS ACADEMIC SCHOLARSHIP

$1000 scholarship for college freshmen, sophomores, or juniors or high school seniors. Student must complete survey on sponsor's website and also an essay on a topic listed in order to participate. Only one entry permitted per student. The top eligible essays will be determined by a panel of chosen judges and the public will be encouraged to help select the winner(s) through online visiting. The winning essay(s) will have received the most votes from online voters. Information may be found on the website, http://www.replacemycontacts.com/topics/6276/1000-scholarship-essay-contest.mvc.

Award: Scholarship for use in freshman, sophomore, or junior years; not renewable. *Number:* 1. *Amount:* $1000.

Eligibility Requirements: Applicant must be enrolled or expecting to enroll full-time at a four-year institution or university. Available to U.S. citizens.

Application Requirements: Application form may be submitted online (http://www.replacemycontacts.com/topics/6276/1000-scholarship-essay-contest.mvc), complete website survey, essay. *Deadline:* April 15.

Contact: Todd Messinger, President of Replace My Contacts
Replace My Contacts
4119 Mauch Chunk Road
Coplay, PA 18037
E-mail: scholarship@ReplaceMyContacts.com

RHODE ISLAND FOUNDATION

http://www.rifoundation.org/

BEACON BRIGHTER TOMORROWS SCHOLARSHIP

Scholarship for a dependent child whose parent sustained a work related injury with an employer who had workers compensation insurance with Beacon Mutual Insurance Company. Must have been accepted into an accredited post-secondary institution (including an academic, trade, or vocational program) on a full-time or part-time basis. Must have maintained a grade point average of C or better for the past two years, be a U.S. citizen or legal resident, and demonstrate financial need.

Award: Scholarship for use in freshman, sophomore, junior, or senior years; renewable.

Eligibility Requirements: Applicant must be high school student and planning to enroll or expecting to enroll full- or part-time at a two-year or four-year or technical institution or university. Available to U.S. citizens.

Application Requirements: Application form, copy of student aid report calculated upon completion of the FAFSA , proof of acceptance to an accredited institution, financial need analysis, recommendations or references, transcript. *Deadline:* June 15.

Contact: Libby Monahan, Funds Administrator
Phone: 401-274-4564 Ext. 3117
E-mail: libbym@rifoundation.org

RONALD REAGAN PRESIDENTIAL FOUNDATION AND INSTITUTE

http://www.reaganfoundation.org

GE-REAGAN FOUNDATION SCHOLARSHIP PROGRAM

Honoring the legacy and character of our nation's 40th President, the GE-Reagan Foundation Scholarship Program rewards college-bound students who demonstrate exemplary leadership, drive, integrity, and citizenship with financial assistance to pursue higher education. Each year, the Program selects numerous recipients to receive a $10,000 scholarship renewable for up to an additional three years–up to $40,000 total per recipient. Awards are for undergraduate and graduate study, and may be used for education-related expenses, including tuition, fees, books, supplies, room, and board. In addition, Scholars are invited to participate in a special awards program. To be eligible for this award, applicants must 1. demonstrate at school, at the workplace, and within the community the attributes of leadership, drive, integrity, and citizenship; 2. demonstrate strong academic performance (minimum 3.0 grade point average/4.0 scale or equivalent); 3. be citizens of the United States of America; 4. be current high school seniors attending high school in the United States (students living on U.S. Armed Forces base and home schooled students are also eligible); and 5. plan to enroll in a full-time undergraduate course of study toward a Bachelor's degree at an accredited four-year college or university in the United States for the entire upcoming academic year. In addition, semifinalists must be nominated by an eligible community leader, such as a high school principal, elected official or executive director of a nonprofit organization, and must provide documentation to certify academic performance and financial need. Finalists will be interviewed via Skype or telephone by a member of the selection committee.

Award: Scholarship for use in freshman year; renewable. *Number:* 20. *Amount:* $10,000.

Eligibility Requirements: Applicant must be high school student and planning to enroll or expecting to enroll full-time at a four-year institution or university. Applicant must have 3.0 GPA or higher. Available to U.S. citizens.

Application Requirements: Application form, community service, essay, financial need analysis, interview. *Deadline:* January 4.

Contact: Lynette Idso, Program Manager
Phone: 844-402-0354
E-mail: ge-reagan@scholarshipamerica.org

THE RYAN LAW GROUP

https://theryanlawgroup.com/

THE RYAN LAW GROUP $1,000 COLLEGE SCHOLARSHIP

The Ryan Law Group is awarding one $1,000 scholarship to the student who writes an essay that best demonstrates their aspirations and how it relates to the theme of this year's scholarship, Future Advocates of Justice.

Award: Scholarship for use in freshman, sophomore, junior, or senior years; not renewable. *Number:* 1. *Amount:* $1000.

Eligibility Requirements: Applicant must be enrolled or expecting to enroll full-time at a four-year institution or university. Available to U.S. citizens.

Application Requirements: Essay. *Deadline:* July 31.

Contact: Mr. Frank Eybsen, Marketing Manager
The Ryan Law Group
2101 Rosecrans Ave
Suite 5290
El Segundo, CA 90245
Phone: 310-3214800
E-mail: frank@theryanlawgroup.com

SAMUEL HUNTINGTON FUND

http://www.nationalgridus.com/huntington.asp

SAMUEL HUNTINGTON PUBLIC SERVICE AWARD

Award provides a $15,000 stipend to a graduating college senior to undertake a one-year public service project anywhere in the world immediately following graduation. Written proposals of 1000 words or less are required with application. Project may encompass any activity that furthers the public good. Awards will be based on quality of proposal, academic record, and other personal achievements. Finalists will be interviewed.

Award: Grant for use in senior year; not renewable. *Number:* 1–3. *Amount:* $15,000.

Eligibility Requirements: Applicant must be enrolled or expecting to enroll full-time at a four-year institution or university. Available to U.S. and non-U.S. citizens.

Application Requirements: Application form, essay, financial need analysis. *Deadline:* January 18.

Contact: Amy Stacy, Executive Assistant
Samuel Huntington Fund
National Grid
40 Sylvan Road
Waltham, MA 02451
Phone: 781-907-3358
E-mail: amy.stacy@nationalgrid.com

SCHOLARSHIP AMERICA

http://www.scholarshipamerica.org

BRISTOL-MYERS SQUIBB SCHOLARSHIP FOR CANCER SURVIVORS

The Bristol-Myers Squibb Scholarship for Cancer Survivors program was created to assist cancer survivors who plan to continue their education in college or vocational school programs. Scholarships of up to $10,000 will be awarded to up to 50 qualified students. Applicants must be cancer survivors (diagnosed by a physician as having treatment of cancer and survived), age 25 and under, who are high school seniors or graduates or postsecondary undergraduates. Qualified applicants must plan to enroll in a full-time undergraduate study at an accredited two- or four-year college, university, or vocational-technical school for the entire academic year. They must have a minimum grade point average of 3.5 on a 4.0 scale (or the equivalent). Scholarships will be awarded based on applicant's academic record, demonstrated leadership and participation in school and community activities, honors, work experience, statement of goals and aspirations, personal impact statement and an outside appraisal. Financial need is not considered. Students may reapply to the program each year they meet eligibility requirements.

Award: Scholarship for use in freshman, sophomore, or junior years; not renewable. *Number:* 50. *Amount:* $10,000.

Eligibility Requirements: Applicant must be enrolled or expecting to enroll full-time at a two-year or four-year or technical institution or university. Applicant must have 3.5 GPA or higher. Available to U.S. citizens.

Application Requirements: Application form. *Deadline:* March 31.

SCHOLARSHIP AMERICA DREAM AWARD

Scholarship America's Dream Award is to assist students across the nation entering their second year or higher of education beyond high school. Renewable scholarships are offered for full-time study at an accredited institution of the student's choice with the awards growing in amount each year, allowing students to receive aid throughout their college careers.

Award: Scholarship for use in sophomore, junior, or senior years; renewable. *Number:* 8–10. *Amount:* $5000–$15,000.

Eligibility Requirements: Applicant must be enrolled or expecting to enroll full-time at a two-year or four-year or technical institution or

university. Applicant must have 3.0 GPA or higher. Available to U.S. citizens.

Application Requirements: Application form. *Deadline:* October 15.

SCHOLARSHIP APPLICATION SERVICES LLC

http://celebrityscholarship.com

CELEBRITY SCHOLARSHIP

Are you tired of writing essays? Looking to show off your talents? Applying for financial aid doesn't have to be boring. Unlike traditional scholarships, we're offering something new and creative. Through costume, role-playing, props and self-expression, we are looking for the person who can give us the funniest, quirkiest and most authentic celebrity impersonation. Tell us about your celebrity and why you chose them. Send us your picture or video for a chance to win $500 in scholarship funds. Feel free to use makeup, funky clothing and a smart caption. Remember, if you are impersonating someone, you are paying respect to them. We won't accept submissions that are inappropriate or belittling.

Award: Scholarship for use in freshman, sophomore, junior, senior, graduate, or postgraduate years; not renewable. *Number:* 1. *Amount:* $500.

Eligibility Requirements: Applicant must be enrolled or expecting to enroll full- or part-time at a two-year or four-year or technical institution or university. Available to U.S. citizens.

Application Requirements: Personal photograph. *Deadline:* December 31.

Contact: Eran Blecher, Director
Scholarship Application Services LLC
420 Veneto
Irvine, CA 92614
Phone: 714-627-9252
E-mail: contact@celebrity-scholarship.com

SCHOLARSHIP WORKSHOP LLC

http://www.scholarshipworkshop.com/

RAGINS/BRASWELL NATIONAL SCHOLARSHIP

Scholarship available to high school seniors, undergraduate, and graduate students who attend The Scholarship Workshop presentation or an online class given by Marianne Ragins, $400,000 scholarship winner. Award is based on application, essay, leadership, extracurricular activities, achievements, and community responsibility. Scholarship amounts vary. Learn more at http://www.scholarshipworkshop.com/movie.

Award: Scholarship for use in freshman, sophomore, junior, or senior years; not renewable. *Number:* 1–3. *Amount:* $100–$500.

Eligibility Requirements: Applicant must be enrolled or expecting to enroll full-time at a four-year institution or university. Available to U.S. citizens.

Application Requirements: Application form, essay. *Deadline:* April 30.

Contact: Scholarship Coordinator
Phone: 703-579-4245
E-mail: scholars@scholarshipworkshop.com

SCREEN ACTORS' GUILD FOUNDATION

http://www.sagfoundation.org/

JOHN L. DALES SCHOLARSHIP PROGRAM

Applicant must have ten vested years of pension credits with the SAG AFTRA union or lifetime earnings of $150,000. Must be U.S. citizen. Scholarship amount ranges between $1000 and $5000. Consult office or website for more information.

Award: Scholarship for use in freshman, sophomore, junior, senior, graduate, or postgraduate years; not renewable. *Number:* 1–16. *Amount:* $1000–$5000.

Eligibility Requirements: Applicant must be enrolled or expecting to enroll full- or part-time at a two-year or four-year institution or university. Available to U.S. citizens.

Application Requirements: Application form, community service, essay, financial need analysis, recommendations or references, resume, test scores, transcript. *Deadline:* March 15.

Contact: Davidson Lloyd, Director of Assistance Programs
Screen Actors' Guild Foundation
5757 Wilshire Boulevard
Suite 124
Los Angeles, CA 90036
Phone: 323-549-6649
Fax: 323-549-6710
E-mail: dlloyd@sagfoundation.org

SCREEN ACTORS GUILD FOUNDATION/JOHN L. DALES SCHOLARSHIP FUND (STANDARD)

Applicant must be a member of SAG AFTRA Union or the child of a member of SAG AFTRA Union. Member under the age of twenty-one must have been a member of AFTRA SAG Union for five years and have a lifetime earnings of $30,000. Parent of an applicant must have ten vested years of pension credits OR lifetime earnings of $150,000. Consult office or website for more information. Number and amount of awards vary.

Award: Scholarship for use in freshman, sophomore, junior, senior, graduate, or postgraduate years; not renewable. *Number:* 100–135. *Amount:* $1000–$5000.

Eligibility Requirements: Applicant must be enrolled or expecting to enroll full-time at a two-year or four-year or technical institution or university. Available to U.S. citizens.

Application Requirements: Application form, community service, essay, financial need analysis, recommendations or references, resume, test scores, transcript. *Deadline:* March 15.

Contact: Davidson Lloyd, Director of Assistance Programs
Screen Actors' Guild Foundation
5757 Wilshire Boulevard
Suite 124
Los Angeles, CA 90036
Phone: 323-549-6649
Fax: 323-549-6710
E-mail: dlloyd@sagfoundation.org

SEABEE MEMORIAL SCHOLARSHIP ASSOCIATION, INC.

http://www.seabee.org/

SEABEE MEMORIAL ASSOCIATION SCHOLARSHIP

Award available to children or grandchildren of current or former members of the Naval Construction Force (Seabees) or Naval Civil Engineer Corps. Not available for graduate study or for great-grandchildren of Seabees.

Award: Scholarship for use in freshman, sophomore, junior, or senior years; renewable. *Number:* 127. *Amount:* $3200.

Eligibility Requirements: Applicant must be enrolled or expecting to enroll full-time at a two-year or four-year institution or university. Available to U.S. citizens.

Application Requirements: Application form, essay, financial need analysis. *Deadline:* April 15.

Contact: Sheryl Chiogioji, Administrative Assistant
Seabee Memorial Scholarship Association, Inc.
PO Box 6574
Silver Spring, MD 20916
Phone: 301-570-2850
E-mail: smsa@seabee.org

SEASONS IN MALIBU

https://seasonsmalibu.com

SEASONS IN MALIBU 2018 ANNUAL SCHOLARSHIP

Write an 800-word essay about the importance of mental health and what you hope to do with your career as a mental health professional.

Award: Scholarship for use in freshman, sophomore, junior, senior, graduate, or postgraduate years; not renewable. *Number:* 1. *Amount:* $1500.

Eligibility Requirements: Applicant must be high school student and planning to enroll or expecting to enroll full- or part-time at a two-year or four-year or technical institution or university. Available to U.S. citizens.

Application Requirements: Essay. *Deadline:* March 31.

Contact: Don Varden, CEO
Seasons In Malibu
32223 Pacific Coast Highway Malibu, CA 90265
Malibu, CA 90265
Phone: 424-610-5402
E-mail: seasons.malibu.ca@gmail.com

SECOND MARINE DIVISION ASSOCIATION

http://www.2dmardiv.com/

SECOND MARINE DIVISION ASSOCIATION MEMORIAL SCHOLARSHIP FUND

Renewable award for students who are unmarried, dependent sons, daughters or grandchildren of former or current members of Second Marine Division or attached units. Must submit proof of parent's or grandparent's service. Family adjusted gross income must not exceed $94,000. Award is merit-based. Minimum 2.5 GPA required.

Award: Scholarship for use in freshman, sophomore, junior, or senior years; renewable. *Number:* 35–42. *Amount:* $1200–$1500.

Eligibility Requirements: Applicant must be enrolled or expecting to enroll full-time at a two-year or four-year or technical institution or university and single. Applicant must have 2.5 GPA or higher. Available to U.S. and non-U.S. citizens.

Application Requirements: Application form, essay, financial need analysis, personal photograph. *Deadline:* April 1.

Contact: Mr. Richard Van Horne, Chairman, Board of Trustees, SMDA Memorial Scholarship Fund
Second Marine Division Association
6178 Seven Lakes West
West End, NC 27376
Phone: 910-673-3123
E-mail: rvanhorne@embarqmail.com

SENIORADVISOR.COM

http://www.senioradvisor.com

FUTURE OF ASSISTED LIVING SCHOLARSHIP

Three $2,000 scholarships available to students enrolled in an associate's degree, bachelor's degree or graduate level program at an accredited 2-year college or 4-year university. Each eligible student must submit a 500-750 word essay response to the question: How can your major of study improve the lives of seniors in assisted living facilities in your town? Deadline is December 31. Scholarship award recipients will be announced January 31.

Award: Scholarship for use in freshman, sophomore, junior, senior, or graduate years; not renewable. *Number:* 3. *Amount:* $2000.

Eligibility Requirements: Applicant must be enrolled or expecting to enroll full- or part-time at a two-year or four-year institution or university. Available to U.S. citizens.

Application Requirements: Essay. *Deadline:* December 31.

SGM LAW GROUP PLLC

http://www.immi-usa.com/

SGM LAW GROUP BI-ANNUAL SCHOLARSHIP

This award recognizes outstanding achievements in academics and as a law firm, we seek to reward a passionate and determined student interested in the field of law. As attorneys, we have all benefited from scholarships throughout our academic careers and now we hope to play a small role in helping a deserving student realize his or her academic goals. This scholarship is open to students who are currently enrolled in an accredited university, college or law school within the U.S. Must have a cumulative GPA of 3.0 or higher and must be a full time student enrolled in classes for spring 2018. Students will have the opportunity to earn $1,000 towards their education by submitting a 500–1000 word essay, which can be written on any of the topics listed below. Please be aware that anything over 1000 words will not be considered. Once the winner of this award is chosen, a check for $1,000 will be made to the scholarship recipient's school of choice to help cover education expenses. 1. What hardship did you conquer to achieve your goal of pursuing law studies? 2. Explain your motivation for becoming a lawyer and what about the law inspires you. 3. Discuss the impact of employment immigration on U.S. economy, including the effects of related immigration reforms. 4. What field of law are you interested in and how will you help others with your earned law degree?

Award: Scholarship for use in freshman, sophomore, junior, senior, or graduate years; not renewable. *Number:* 1–2. *Amount:* $1000.

Eligibility Requirements: Applicant must be enrolled or expecting to enroll full- or part-time at a two-year or four-year or technical institution or university. Applicant must have 3.0 GPA or higher. Available to U.S. and non-U.S. citizens.

Application Requirements: Essay. *Deadline:* December 15.

SHOPKO STORES, INC.

http://www.shopko.com/foundation

SHOPKO FOUNDATION TEAMMATE & FAMILY MEMBER SCHOLARSHIP PROGRAM

The Shopko Foundation Teammate and Family Member Scholarship Program, qualified grant winners receive up to $2,500 for a given academic year. The scholarships, awarded through a competitive process, include post-secondary accredited programs: 2- or 4-year colleges and universities, vocational schools, and technical schools. Applicants must be currently enrolled, or planning to enroll, in a full-time course of study for the entire academic year during which the scholarship is awarded. The program is open to full- or part-time Shopko teammates and their dependent children under the age of 24 (as of July 1 of the year scholarships are awarded). Applicants who are children of Shopko teammates must be dependent on a Shopko teammate for over 50% of their cost of living. Shopko teammates must have at least one year of continuous service as of January 1 of the scholarship year.

Award: Scholarship for use in freshman, sophomore, junior, senior, or graduate years; not renewable. *Number:* 30. *Amount:* $2500.

Eligibility Requirements: Applicant must be enrolled or expecting to enroll full-time at a two-year or four-year or technical institution or university. Available to U.S. citizens.

Application Requirements: Application form. *Deadline:* March 1.

SILICON VALLEY COMMUNITY FOUNDATION

http://www.siliconvalleycf.org

BRIGHT FUTURES SCHOLARSHIP

The Bright Futures Scholarship Fund was established in 2010 by Silicon Valley Community Foundation to provide additional scholarship opportunities to the many worthy applicants that seek funding each year. Each year SVCF's scholarship programs receive an average of 600 requests; unfortunately, because the number of scholarships awarded is determined by the amount of funds available, hundreds of bright, promising students are turned down each year. The selection committee looks for students showing academic excellence whose educational opportunities will be increased by financial assistance. In addition, the selection committee will take into consideration the overall quality of the personal statement. Special consideration will be given to working students and those pursuing a teaching or master's degree with an emphasis in the teaching of mathematics.

Award: Scholarship for use in freshman, sophomore, junior, senior, graduate, or postgraduate years; not renewable. *Number:* 20. *Amount:* $1000.

Eligibility Requirements: Applicant must be enrolled or expecting to enroll full-time at a two-year or four-year or technical institution or university. Applicant must have 3.0 GPA or higher. Available to U.S. and non-U.S. citizens.

Application Requirements: Application form. *Deadline:* September 18.

Contact: Scholarships Team
Silicon Valley Community Foundation
2440 West El Camino Real
Suite 300
Mountain View, CA 94040
Phone: 650-450-5487
E-mail: scholarships@siliconvalleycf.org

SABRE PASSPORT TO FREEDOM SURVIVOR SCHOLARSHIP

Inspired by the extraordinary stories of survival shared at the September 2012 Passport to Freedom launch event, Sabre committed to create a scholarship program dedicated to making post-secondary education and vocational training attainable for trafficking survivors. In 2014, Sabre announced the first ever academic scholarship fund created especially for human trafficking survivors. Our vision is to help pave the way for secure and sustainable employment opportunities. With the support of our travel industry and technology partners, the long-term vision is to offer job placement opportunities for scholarship program graduates. Must be a human trafficking survivor. Must be a high school graduate or GED recipient; planning to enroll or enrolled in a two- or four-year college or vocational school on a part-time or full-time basis (as defined by the school of attendance); have a minimum cumulative grade point average of 2.75 on a 4.0 scale, if a current graduating high school senior or college student; and a United States citizen or eligible non-citizen (eligible non-citizens include United States legal residents or T-visa holders).

Award: Scholarship for use in freshman, sophomore, junior, or senior years; not renewable. *Number:* 1–5. *Amount:* $1000–$10,000.

Eligibility Requirements: Applicant must be enrolled or expecting to enroll full- or part-time at a two-year or four-year or technical institution or university. Applicant must have 2.5 GPA or higher. Available to U.S. and non-U.S. citizens.

Application Requirements: Application form, essay, financial need analysis. *Deadline:* May 31.

Contact: Scholarships Team
Silicon Valley Community Foundation
2440 West El Camino Real
Suite 300
Mountain View, CA 94040
Phone: 650-450-5487
E-mail: scholarships@siliconvalleycf.org

SIMON YOUTH FOUNDATION

http://www.sms.scholarshipamerica.org/simonyouth

SIMON YOUTH FOUNDATION COMMUNITY SCHOLARSHIP PROGRAM

Scholarships available to high school seniors attending school and living in close proximity of a Simon Property Mall or Community Center. Recipients should reside within 50 miles of a Simon Mall. Must be planning to enroll in a full-time undergraduate course of study at an accredited two- or four-year college, university, or vocational/technical school.

Award: Scholarship for use in freshman year; not renewable. *Number:* 100–200. *Amount:* $1400–$2500.

Eligibility Requirements: Applicant must be high school student and planning to enroll or expecting to enroll full-time at a two-year or four-year or technical institution or university. Available to U.S. citizens.

Application Requirements: Application form, community service, copy of page 1 of parent's tax Form 1040, financial need analysis, test scores, transcript. *Deadline:* March 1.

Contact: Casey Rubischko, Program Manager
Phone: 507-931-1682

SIMPLILEARN AMERICAS LLC

https://www.simplilearn.com/

SIMPLILEARN STUDENT AMBASSADOR SCHOLARSHIP

Getting a college degree is a huge accomplishment, but it does not necessarily prepare you for the best jobs in today's digital economy. That is where Simplilearn comes in. We provide online training in today's hottest careers–from digital marketing, to cyber security, to cloud computing. As a Simplilearn Ambassador, you can help us spread the word and help your classmates launch their careers. Participation is free. For every visitor you bring to Simplilearn.com, via your unique referral URL, you will get another entry to our $1,000 cash Ambassador Scholarship. Simply fill out the brief form below, select the skills training that you are most interested in, get your unique link to Simplilearn, along with some tips on how to promote us, and start racking up entries to our $1,000 payout. See https://www.simplilearn.com/student-ambassador-scholarship-program for more details.

Award: Scholarship for use in freshman, sophomore, junior, senior, graduate, or postgraduate years; not renewable. *Number:* 1–3. *Amount:* $1000–$3000.

Eligibility Requirements: Applicant must be enrolled or expecting to enroll full- or part-time at a two-year or four-year institution or university. Available to U.S. citizens.

Application Requirements: Application form, personal photograph. *Deadline:* March 17.

Contact: Mr. Nirmal Kumar, Simplilearn Americas LLC
Simplilearn Americas LLC
201 Spear Street
Suite 1100
San Francisco, CA 94105
Phone: 844-532-7688 Ext. 1025
E-mail: scholarship@simplilearn.com

SLOTOZILLA

http://www.slotozilla.com/

INTERNET MARKETING SCHOLARSHIP

Slotozilla is interested in attracting our players as well as helping future marketing experts. Just like ads on the internet, you never know when and where the next marketing genius will pop-out. That is why we created an annual Internet Marketing Scholarship. This scholarship is available for full-time students doing Bachelor or Master course at any accredited college or university. See website for more information, http://www.slotozilla.com/

Award: Scholarship for use in freshman, sophomore, junior, senior, graduate, or postgraduate years; not renewable. *Number:* 1. *Amount:* $500.

Eligibility Requirements: Applicant must be enrolled or expecting to enroll full- or part-time at a two-year or four-year or technical institution or university. Available to U.S. and Canadian citizens.

Application Requirements: Essay. *Deadline:* August 31.

Contact: Vanessa Skadi
E-mail: scholarship@slotozilla.com

SMARTPAPERHELP

http://www.smartpaperhelp.com/

SMART PAPER HELP SCHOLARSHIP

SmartPaperHelp invites students to participate in our Smart Scholarship program. All you have to do is to show off your writing skills and write an essay on one of the given topics: 1. Problems Of Modern Educational System And Their Solutions; 2. Difficulties We Face In College; 3. What Problems Do You See In Your College And How Do They Affect You Personally? Participate and win cash prizes. Full guidelines you can find on the following page: http://www.smartpaperhelp.com/blog/scholarship-program-for-students

Award: Scholarship for use in freshman, sophomore, junior, senior, graduate, or postgraduate years; not renewable. *Number:* 1–3. *Amount:* $400–$1000.

Eligibility Requirements: Applicant must be enrolled or expecting to enroll full- or part-time at a two-year or four-year institution or university. Available to U.S. citizens.

Application Requirements: Application form, essay. *Deadline:* February 29.

Contact: Sheri Aldridge
E-mail: contest@smartpaperhelp.com

SNOW, CARPIO & WEEKLEY, PLC

http://workinjuryaz.com

SCW ACADEMIC SCHOLARSHIP

Video submissions required. High school senior or recent graduate seeking a degree with a 3.0 GPA. To be awarded the fall semester of 2016. Applications must be submitted on our website http://workinjuryaz.com/tucson-workers-compensation-lawyers/#academic See all requirement and info on our website as well.

Award: Scholarship for use in freshman or sophomore years; not renewable. *Number:* 2. *Amount:* $2500.

Eligibility Requirements: Applicant must be enrolled or expecting to enroll full- or part-time at a two-year or four-year or technical institution or university. Applicant must have 3.0 GPA or higher. Available to U.S. citizens.

Application Requirements: Application form. *Deadline:* May 31.

Contact: April Snow
E-mail: snowcarpioaz@gmail.com

SOCIETY FOR APPLIED ANTHROPOLOGY

http://www.sfaa.net/

DEL JONES AWARD

Del Jones was a distinguished member of SfAA and an African American anthropologist who developed perspectives that could assist and transform the lives of oppressed and disadvantaged peoples. Following his death in 1999, close friends and members of the Society established the Del Jones Memorial Fund. This Fund supports a travel grant of $500 for a student to attend the annual meeting of the Society. The Del Jones Travel Award is intended to increase minority participation in SfAA, particularly African American participation, but also to honor the life and work of Del Jones independently of the minority criterion. The winning paper will best reflect the contributions and/or life experiences of Del Jones.

Award: Prize for use in freshman, sophomore, junior, senior, or graduate years; not renewable. *Number:* 2–500.

Eligibility Requirements: Applicant must be enrolled or expecting to enroll full- or part-time at a two-year or four-year institution or university. Available to U.S. and non-U.S. citizens.

Application Requirements: Application form, essay. *Deadline:* December 20.

Contact: Trish Colvin, Office Manager
Society for Applied Anthropology
PO Box 2436
Oklahoma City, OK 73101
Phone: 405-843-5113
Fax: 405-843-8553
E-mail: info@sfaa.net

EDWARD H. AND ROSAMOND B. SPICER TRAVEL AWARDS

The Awards commemorate the lifelong concern of Edward H. and Rosamond B. Spicer in furthering the maturation of students in the social sciences, both intellectually and practically, and their lifelong interest in the nature of community as both cause of, and solution to, problems in the human condition.

Award: Prize for use in freshman, sophomore, junior, senior, or graduate years; not renewable. *Number:* 2. *Amount:* $500.

Eligibility Requirements: Applicant must be enrolled or expecting to enroll full- or part-time at a two-year or four-year institution or university. Available to U.S. and non-U.S. citizens.

Application Requirements: Application form, essay. *Deadline:* December 20.

Contact: Trish Colvin, Office Manager
Society for Applied Anthropology
PO Box 2436
Oklahoma City, OK 73101
Phone: 405-843-5113
Fax: 405-843-8553
E-mail: info@sfaa.net

GIL KUSHNER MEMORIAL TRAVEL AWARD

Scholarship of $500 to attend the SfAA annual meeting. Abstracts (paper or poster) should be concerned with the persistence of cultural groups.

Award: Prize for use in freshman, sophomore, junior, senior, or graduate years; not renewable. *Number:* 2. *Amount:* $500.

Eligibility Requirements: Applicant must be enrolled or expecting to enroll full- or part-time at a two-year or four-year institution or university. Available to U.S. and non-U.S. citizens.

Application Requirements: Essay. *Deadline:* December 20.

Contact: Trish Colvin, Office Manager
Society for Applied Anthropology
PO Box 2436
Oklahoma City, OK 73101
Phone: 405-843-5113
Fax: 405-843-8553
E-mail: info@sfaa.net

HUMAN RIGHTS DEFENDER STUDENT AWARD

The Human Rights Defender Travel Award provides a $500 travel scholarship each year for a student to attend the annual meetings of the Society. This award was made possible by a generous contribution from Michael Cavendish, a Sustaining Member of the Society who is a practicing attorney in Florida and a strong advocate of human rights. As a graduate student, he was first exposed to the link between applied anthropology and disciplines like law, journalism and social work.

Award: Prize for use in freshman, sophomore, junior, senior, or graduate years; not renewable. *Number:* 1. *Amount:* $500.

Eligibility Requirements: Applicant must be enrolled or expecting to enroll full- or part-time at a two-year or four-year institution or university. Available to U.S. and non-U.S. citizens.

Application Requirements: Essay. *Deadline:* December 20.

Contact: Trish Colvin, Office Manager
Society for Applied Anthropology
PO Box 2436
Oklahoma City, OK 73101
Phone: 405-843-5113
Fax: 405-843-8553
E-mail: info@sfaa.net

PETER KONG-MING NEW STUDENT PRIZE

Prize awarded for SFAA's annual student research competition in the applied social and behavioral sciences. The issue of research question should be in the domain of health care or human services (broadly construed). The winner of the competition will receive a cash prize of $3000, a crystal trophy, and travel funds to attend the annual meeting of the SFAA. For more details, see website at http://www.sfaa.net.

Award: Prize for use in freshman, sophomore, junior, senior, or graduate years; not renewable. *Number:* 3. *Amount:* $750–$3350.

Eligibility Requirements: Applicant must be enrolled or expecting to enroll full- or part-time at a two-year or four-year institution or university. Available to U.S. and non-U.S. citizens.

Application Requirements: Essay. *Deadline:* November 30.

Contact: Trish Colvin, Office Manager
Society for Applied Anthropology
PO Box 2436
Oklahoma City, OK 73101
Phone: 405-843-5113
Fax: 405-843-8553
E-mail: info@sfaa.net

VALENE SMITH PRIZE

The posters which are submitted for the Valene Smith Competition will be set up and exhibited with all other posters at the Annual Meeting of the Society for Applied Anthropology and should be concerned in some way with the applied social science of tourism.

Award: Prize for use in freshman, sophomore, junior, senior, or graduate years; not renewable. *Number:* 3. *Amount:* $250–$500.

Eligibility Requirements: Applicant must be enrolled or expecting to enroll full- or part-time at a two-year or four-year institution or university. Available to U.S. and non-U.S. citizens.

Application Requirements: *Deadline:* October 15.

Contact: Trish Colvin, Office Manager
Society for Applied Anthropology
PO Box 2436
Oklahoma City, OK 73101
Phone: 405-843-5113
Fax: 405-843-8553
E-mail: info@sfaa.net

SOCIETY FOR SCIENCE & THE PUBLIC

societyforscience.org

INTEL INTERNATIONAL SCIENCE AND ENGINEERING FAIR

The Intel International Science and Engineering Fair (ISEF) is the culminating event in a series of local, regional, state and international science fairs. Students, grades 9 - 12, who compete successfully at an Intel ISEF-affiliated fair can advance and ultimately participate at the Intel ISEF.

Award: Prize for use in freshman, sophomore, junior, or senior years; not renewable. *Number:* 1–600. *Amount:* $500–$75,000.

Eligibility Requirements: Applicant must be high school student; age 12-20 and planning to enroll or expecting to enroll full- or part-time at a two-year or four-year institution or university. Available to U.S. and non-U.S. citizens.

Application Requirements: Application form, interview. *Deadline:* April 18.

Contact: Lisa Icenroad, Program Manager
Society for Science & the Public
1719 N Street, NW
Washington, DC 20036
Phone: 202-785-2255 Ext. 152
E-mail: licenroad@societyforscience.org

REGENERON SCIENCE TALENT SEARCH

The Regeneron Science Talent Search (STS), a program of Society for Science & the Public, is the nation's most prestigious pre-college science competition. Alumni of STS have made extraordinary contributions to science and hold more than 100 of the world's most distinguished science and math honors, including the Nobel Prize and the National Medal of Science. Each year, 300 Regeneron STS Scholars and their schools are recognized. From the select pool of scholars, 40 student finalists are invited to Washington, DC in March to participate in final judging, display their work to the public, meet with notable scientists, and compete for the top award of $250,000.

Award: Prize for use in freshman, sophomore, junior, senior, or graduate years; not renewable. *Number:* 40. *Amount:* $25,000–$250,000.

Eligibility Requirements: Applicant must be high school student and planning to enroll or expecting to enroll full- or part-time at a two-year or four-year institution or university. Available to U.S. citizens.

Application Requirements: Application form, essay. *Deadline:* November 14.

Contact: Allison Stifel, Regeneron Science Talent Search
Society for Science & the Public
1719 N Street, NW
Washington, DC 20036
Phone: 202-785-2255 Ext. 140
E-mail: astifel@societyforscience.org

SOFT SURROUNDINGS

https://www.softsurroundings.com/

SOFT SURROUNDINGS COLLEGE SCHOLARSHIP

If you are a college student or high school senior interested in fashion design, merchandising, visual presentation, or fashion marketing, Soft Surroundings invites you to apply for this scholarship. To enter, please submit an essay between 500-750 words on the topic of who inspired you to pursue this field of study. Many people working in fashion chose this career path because of the influence of a teacher, family member, or other mentor, and we want to hear your story!

Award: Scholarship for use in freshman, sophomore, junior, senior, or graduate years; renewable. *Number:* 1. *Amount:* $1000.

Eligibility Requirements: Applicant must be enrolled or expecting to enroll full- or part-time at a two-year or four-year institution or university. Available to U.S. citizens.

Application Requirements: Essay. *Deadline:* November 30.

SOROPTIMIST INTERNATIONAL OF THE AMERICAS

http://www.soroptimist.org/

THE SOROPTIMIST LIVE YOUR DREAM: EDUCATION AND TRAINING AWARDS FOR WOMEN

Applicants must be a woman who is the head of her household, the primary financial provider for her family, pursuing a vocational or undergraduate degree and show financial need. To be eligible, applicants must live in one of Soroptimist's 20 member countries. For full eligibility requirements and application instructions go to: http://www.soroptimist.org/awards/eligibility.html

Award: Grant for use in freshman, sophomore, junior, or senior years; not renewable. *Amount:* $500–$15,000.

Eligibility Requirements: Applicant must be enrolled or expecting to enroll full- or part-time at a two-year or four-year or technical institution or university and female. Available to U.S. and non-U.S. citizens.

Application Requirements: Application form, essay, financial need analysis. *Deadline:* November 15.

Contact: Program Assistant
E-mail: lydawards@soroptimist.org

SOUTHWESTERN RUGS DEPOT

https://www.southwesternrugsdepot.com/

SOUTHWESTERN RUGS DEPOT SCHOLARSHIP

Minimum 300 word essay on why decor matters to you. Open to all college students. Deadline Jan. 2nd 2018. Apply here: https://www.southwesternrugsdepot.com/scholarship/

Award: Scholarship for use in freshman, sophomore, junior, senior, or graduate years; not renewable. *Number:* 1. *Amount:* $500.

Eligibility Requirements: Applicant must be enrolled or expecting to enroll full- or part-time at a two-year or four-year or technical institution or university. Available to U.S. and non-U.S. citizens.

Application Requirements: Essay. *Deadline:* January 2.

Contact: Mr. Connor Butterworth
Phone: 770-773-6416
E-mail: contact@southwesternrugsdepot.com

THE SPIKE LAB

https://www.thespikelab.com/english

THE SPIKE LAB COLLEGE SCHOLARSHIP

This year, The Spike Lab is offering its first college scholarship. This award recognizes students in the US and internationally who have developed an awesome project based on their passion (we call this a 'Spike') and want to share it with the world. Your Spike could be anything from writing a novel to starting a small business to spearheading a city-wide street clean up. Really your Spike could be just about anything you have built from the ground up out of sheer passion and determination!

Award: Scholarship for use in freshman year; not renewable. *Number:* 2. *Amount:* $1000–$1500.

Eligibility Requirements: Applicant must be high school student and planning to enroll or expecting to enroll full-time at a two-year or four-year or technical institution or university. Available to U.S. and non-U.S. citizens.

Application Requirements: Application form, interview. *Deadline:* April 15.

Contact: Kim Stewart, Coach and Founding Team
New York, NY 10001
E-mail: kim@thespikelab.com

SR EDUCATION GROUP

http://www.sreducationgroup.org

COMMUNITY COLLEGE SCHOLARSHIP

Community college can be one of the most cost-effective options for people looking to start or change their careers; however, tuition can still be a large burden for many individuals. To help those with high financial need, SR Education Group is awarding $2,500 community college scholarships. To provide our judges with a true understanding of each applicant, he or she must answer two open-ended, personal, and thought-provoking questions. The students whose responses are the most persuasive, compelling, and well-written, as judged by our panel, will be considered finalists.

Award: Scholarship for use in freshman, sophomore, junior, senior, graduate, or postgraduate years; not renewable. *Number:* 2–6. *Amount:* $2500.

Eligibility Requirements: Applicant must be enrolled or expecting to enroll full- or part-time at a two-year or technical institution. Available to U.S. citizens.

Application Requirements: Application form. *Deadline:* continuous.

Contact: SR Education Group
Kirkland, WA 98033
Phone: 425-605-8898
Fax: 425-968-9384
E-mail: scholarships@sreducationgroup.org

SR EDUCATION GROUP $5K SCHOLARSHIPS

SR Education Group is awarding two need-based scholarships of $5,000 each quarter. The scholarships will rotate to help target under-served populations: Military scholarships (two $5,000 winners)–Veterans/active military, their sons, daughters, or spouses; spouses, sons, and daughters of deceased veterans or deceased active duty members are also eligible; children of service members/veterans must be under the age of 21, or if full-time students, under the age of 23. Scholarship for Women (two $5,000 winners): Female students enrolled at a private or public educational institution, and working towards a certificate, diploma, or degree. Scholarship for Minorities (two $5,000 winners)–minority students (Hispanic, African-American, Asian, or Native American ethnicity) enrolled at a private or public educational institution, and working towards a certificate, diploma, or degree. A child is a military dependent through age 21, or through age 23, if enrolled as a full time college student.

Award: Scholarship for use in freshman, sophomore, junior, senior, graduate, or postgraduate years; not renewable. *Number:* 1–2. *Amount:* $5000.

Eligibility Requirements: Applicant must be enrolled or expecting to enroll full- or part-time at a two-year or four-year or technical institution or university. Available to U.S. citizens.

Application Requirements: Application form. *Deadline:* continuous.

Contact: SR Education Group
Kirkland, WA 98033
Phone: 425-605-8898
Fax: 425-968-9384
E-mail: scholarships@sreducationgroup.org

STATE DEPARTMENT FEDERAL CREDIT UNION ANNUAL SCHOLARSHIP PROGRAM

http://www.sdfcu.org/

STATE DEPARTMENT FEDERAL CREDIT UNION ANNUAL SCHOLARSHIP PROGRAM

Scholarships available to members who are currently enrolled in a degree program and have completed 12 credit hours of coursework at an accredited college or university. Must have own account in good standing with SDFCU, have a minimum 2.5 GPA, submit official cumulative transcripts, and describe need for financial assistance to continue their education. Scholarship only open to members of State Department Federal Credit Union.

Award: Scholarship for use in sophomore, junior, senior, or graduate years; not renewable. *Amount:* $2500.

Eligibility Requirements: Applicant must be enrolled or expecting to enroll full-time at a four-year institution or university. Applicant must have 2.5 GPA or higher. Available to U.S. and non-U.S. citizens.

Application Requirements: Application form, financial need analysis. *Deadline:* April 29.

Contact: Scholarship Coordinator
Phone: 703-706-5000
E-mail: sdfcu@sdfcu.org

STRAIGHTFORWARD MEDIA

http://www.straightforwardmedia.com/

DALE E. FRIDELL MEMORIAL SCHOLARSHIP

Scholarships are open to anyone aspiring to attend a university, college, trade school, technical institute, vocational training, or other postsecondary education program. Eligible students may not have already been awarded a full tuition scholarship or waiver from another source. International students are welcome to apply. For more information, visit website http://www.straightforwardmedia.com/fridell/form.php.

Award: Scholarship for use in freshman, sophomore, junior, or senior years; not renewable. *Number:* 2. *Amount:* $1000.

Eligibility Requirements: Applicant must be enrolled or expecting to enroll full- or part-time at a two-year or four-year or technical institution or university. Available to U.S. and non-U.S. citizens.

Application Requirements: Essay. *Deadline:* varies.

Contact: Scholarship Committee
Phone: 605-348-3042

HELPING HAND SCHOLARSHIP

Annual award to help students hampered by debt to continue their studies. Must be attending or planning to attend a college, trade school, technical institute, vocational program or other postsecondary education program. For more information, see web http://www.straightforwardmedia.com/debt2/debt-apply.html.

Award: Scholarship for use in freshman, sophomore, junior, or senior years; not renewable. *Number:* 4. *Amount:* $500.

Eligibility Requirements: Applicant must be enrolled or expecting to enroll full- or part-time at a two-year or four-year or technical institution or university. Available to U.S. and non-U.S. citizens.

Application Requirements: Essay. *Deadline:* varies.

Contact: Scholarship Committee
Phone: 605-348-3042

MESOTHELIOMA MEMORIAL SCHOLARSHIP

Open to all students attending or planning to attend a postsecondary educational program, including 2- or 4-year college or university, vocational school, continuing education, ministry training, and job skills training. Refer to website for details http://www.straightforwardmedia.com/meso/.

Award: Scholarship for use in freshman, sophomore, junior, or senior years; not renewable. *Number:* 4. *Amount:* $500.

Eligibility Requirements: Applicant must be enrolled or expecting to enroll full- or part-time at a two-year or four-year or technical institution or university. Available to U.S. and non-U.S. citizens.

Application Requirements: Essay. *Deadline:* varies.

Contact: Scholarship Committee
Phone: 605-348-3042

STUDENT INSIGHTS

http://www.studentinsights.com

STUDENT-VIEW SCHOLARSHIP PROGRAM

Scholarship available by random drawing from the pool of entrants who respond to an online survey from Student Insights marketing organization. Parental permission to participate required for applicants under age 18.

Award: Scholarship for use in freshman year; not renewable. *Number:* 13. *Amount:* $500–$4000.

Eligibility Requirements: Applicant must be high school student and planning to enroll or expecting to enroll full-time at a two-year or four-year or technical institution or university. Available to U.S. citizens.

Application Requirements: Application form. *Deadline:* April 22.

Contact: Mr. John Becker, Program Coordinator
Student Insights
136 Justice Drive
Valencia, PA 16059
Phone: 724-903-0439
E-mail: contact@studentinsights.com

STUDYPORTALS

http://www.studyportals.eu/

GLOBAL STUDY AWARDS

We want to ultimately encourage young people to study abroad as part of their tertiary studies in order to experience and explore new countries, cultures and languages. The Global Study Awards recognizes studying abroad as a positively life changing experience for many students, opening their minds to alternative ways of personal life and professional career, as well as promoting intercultural understanding and tolerance. The Award prize will be applied toward the cost of tuition fees in the first instance, paid directly to the Higher Education Institution that the successful candidate will attend. If tuition fees are below the maximum individual award fund of €10,000, the remaining funds may be allocated per diem for living costs for a maximum of 52 weeks starting from when the student first registered at the higher education institution.

Award: Scholarship for use in freshman, sophomore, junior, senior, graduate, or postgraduate years; not renewable. *Number:* 1–9. *Amount:* $11,215–$11,215.

Eligibility Requirements: Applicant must be enrolled or expecting to enroll full- or part-time at a two-year or four-year institution or university. Available to U.S. and non-U.S. citizens.

Application Requirements: Application form, application form may be submitted online (http://www.studyportals.com/scholarship), essay, transcript. *Deadline:* varies.

Contact: Ms. Sissy Bottcher, Community Manager
StudyPortals
Torenallee 45 - 4.02
Eindhoven 5617 BA
NLD
Phone: 3-140 218 0238
Fax: 3-140 292 0075
E-mail: students@studyportals.com

SUNTRUST BANK

http://www.suntrusteducation.com/

OFF TO COLLEGE SCHOLARSHIP SWEEPSTAKES AWARD

Award of $1000 to a high school senior planning to attend college in the fall. Must complete an online entry form by accessing the website, http://www.offtocollege.info. Scholarship sweepstakes drawings are random and occur every other week from October 31 to May 15.

Award: Scholarship for use in freshman year; not renewable. *Number:* 15. *Amount:* $1000.

Eligibility Requirements: Applicant must be high school student and planning to enroll or expecting to enroll full- or part-time at a two-year or four-year or technical institution or university. Available to U.S. citizens.

Application Requirements: Application form. *Deadline:* continuous.

Contact: Joy Blauvelt, Scholarship Coordinator
Phone: 800-552-3006

SUPPORT COLLECTORS

https://www.supportcollectors.com/

SUPPORT COLLECTORS SCHOLARSHIP

We want to provide financial assistance to a selected college student who has either been affected by family separation in their own life, or who intends to pursue a career that will have a positive impact on separated families. The selected student will receive an award of $500 for use toward tuition, books, or living expenses. Selection date is January 5.

Award: Scholarship for use in freshman, sophomore, junior, or senior years; not renewable. *Number:* 1. *Amount:* $500.

Eligibility Requirements: Applicant must be enrolled or expecting to enroll full-time at a four-year institution or university. Available to U.S. citizens.

Application Requirements: Application form, essay. *Deadline:* December 15.

TALL CLUBS INTERNATIONAL FOUNDATION, INC.

http://www.tall.org

KAE SUMNER EINFELDT SCHOLARSHIP

Females 5' 10", or males 6' 2" (minimum heights), are eligible to apply for the scholarship. Interested individuals should contact their local Tall Clubs Chapter. Canadian and U.S. winners are selected from finalists submitted by each local chapter.

Award: Scholarship for use in freshman year; not renewable. *Number:* 2–6. *Amount:* $1000.

Eligibility Requirements: Applicant must be age 17-21 and enrolled or expecting to enroll full- or part-time at a two-year or four-year institution or university. Available to U.S. and Canadian citizens.

Application Requirements: Application form, essay, personal photograph, recommendations or references, transcript, verification of height. *Deadline:* March 1.

Contact: Carolyn Goldstein, TCI Foundation Scholarship Contact
  E-mail: tcischolarships@hotmail.com

TECHNICAL ASSOCIATION OF THE PULP & PAPER INDUSTRY (TAPPI)

http://www.tappi.org/

TAPPI PLACE (POLYMERS, LAMINATIONS, ADHESIVES, COATINGS AND EXTRUSIONS) SCHOLARSHIP

Awarded only in even numbered years, the TAPPI PLACE (Polymers, Laminations, Adhesives, Coatings and Extrusions) Scholarship is designed to encourage talented science and engineering students to pursue careers in the packaging industry and to develop awareness of the industry, and of the TAPPI Polymers, Laminations, Adhesives, Coatings, and Extrusions (PLACE) Division. Membership in a TAPPI Student Chapter is required.

Award: Scholarship for use in freshman, sophomore, junior, or senior years; not renewable. *Number:* 1. *Amount:* $4000.

Eligibility Requirements: Applicant must be enrolled or expecting to enroll full-time at a two-year or four-year institution or university. Available to U.S. and non-U.S. citizens.

Application Requirements: Application form. *Deadline:* February 14.

Contact: Mr. Laurence Womack, Director of Standards and Awards
  Technical Association of the Pulp & Paper Industry (TAPPI)
  15 Technology Parkway South
  Suite 115
  Peachtree Corners, GA 30092
  Phone: 770-209-7276
  E-mail: standards@tappi.org

TEXAS FEDERATION OF BUSINESS AND PROFESSIONAL WOMEN'S FOUNDATION

GILDA MURRAY SCHOLARSHIP

Scholarship of $500 awarded to members of BPW/Texas, age 25 or older, to obtain education or training at an accredited college or university, technology institution, or training center. The number of awards varies.

Award: Scholarship for use in freshman, sophomore, junior, or senior years; not renewable. *Amount:* $500.

Eligibility Requirements: Applicant must be enrolled or expecting to enroll full- or part-time at a four-year or technical institution or university. Available to U.S. citizens.

Application Requirements: Application form, essay, recommendations or references, regular attendance at LO meetings, active participation on at least one BPW committee. *Deadline:* May 1.

Contact: Nancy Jackson, Chair
  Phone: 817-283-0862
  E-mail: bpwtx@sbcglobal.net

TEXAS HIGHER EDUCATION COORDINATING BOARD

http://www.collegeforalltexans.com/

GOOD NEIGHBOR SCHOLARSHIP PROGRAM

Provides assistance for tuition to students from other nations of the Western Hemisphere (other than Cuba). Students must have lived for at least five years in the Western Hemisphere, scholastically qualify for admission, and must intend to return to their country upon completion of their program of study. Students that apply for Permanent Resident status or have dual citizenship are not eligible. Renewal awards require student meet the institution's minimum GPA requirement. Contact your institution for more information.

Award: Scholarship for use in freshman, sophomore, junior, senior, or graduate years; not renewable.

Eligibility Requirements: Applicant must be enrolled or expecting to enroll full- or part-time at a two-year or four-year institution or university and studying in Texas. Available to Canadian and non-U.S. citizens.

Application Requirements: Application form.

Contact: Student Financial Aid Office at the institution
  Phone: 888-311-8881

TUITION EQUALIZATION GRANT (TEG) PROGRAM

Renewable award for Texas residents enrolled at least three-quarter time at an independent college or private university in Texas in a degree program that does not lead to ordination or licensure to preach. Awards are based on financial need. Renewal awards also require the student to maintain a minimum overall college GPA of at least 2.5, complete at least 24 SCH's each year (18 SCH's for students in graduate programs), and complete a minimum of 75% of classes attempted each year. Priority deadline to complete the FAFSA is March 15. Must not be receiving athletic scholarship concurrently. Contact college/university financial aid office for application information.

Award: Grant for use in freshman, sophomore, junior, senior, or graduate years; renewable. *Amount:* $1–$5046.

Eligibility Requirements: Applicant must be enrolled or expecting to enroll full- or part-time at a four-year institution or university and studying in Texas. Available to U.S. citizens.

Application Requirements: Financial need analysis.

Contact: Student Financial Aid Programs
  Phone: 888-311-8881

THEPENNYHOARDER.COM

http://www.thepennyhoarder.com/

FRUGAL STUDENT

You just need to tell us in 150 words or less the craziest, funniest, most interesting, unique, or creative way you've ever saved or made extra money.

Award: Scholarship for use in freshman, sophomore, junior, or senior years; renewable. *Number:* 1. *Amount:* $2000.

Eligibility Requirements: Applicant must be enrolled or expecting to enroll full- or part-time at a two-year or four-year institution or university. Available to U.S. citizens.

Application Requirements: Application form, application form may be submitted online (http://www.thepennyhoarder.com/frugal-student-scholarship/), entry in a contest, essay. *Deadline:* December 31.

Contact: Cynthia Moll
  E-mail: scholarships@thepennyhoarder.com

THETA DELTA CHI EDUCATIONAL FOUNDATION INC.

http://www.tdx.org/

THETA DELTA CHI EDUCATIONAL FOUNDATION INC. SCHOLARSHIP

Scholarships for undergraduate or graduate students enrolled in an accredited institution. Awards are based on candidate's history of service to the fraternity, scholastic achievement, and need. See website for

application and additional information
http://www.tdx.org/scholarship/scholarship.html.

Award: Scholarship for use in freshman, sophomore, junior, senior, or graduate years; renewable. *Number:* 15. *Amount:* $1000–$5000.

Eligibility Requirements: Applicant must be enrolled or expecting to enroll full-time at a four-year institution or university. Available to U.S. and non-U.S. citizens.

Application Requirements: Application form, financial need analysis, recommendations or references, transcript. *Deadline:* May 15.

Contact: William McClung, Executive Director
  Phone: 617-742-8886
  Fax: 617-742-8868
  E-mail: execdir@tdx.org

THIRD MARINE DIVISION ASSOCIATION, INC.

http://www.caltrap.com/

THIRD MARINE DIVISION ASSOCIATION MEMORIAL SCHOLARSHIP FUND

Scholarship assistance for children and grandchildren of qualified Third Marine Division Association members (Marine or Navy), or qualified service-connected deceased 3rd Marine Division veterans. For further details visit website http://www.caltrap.com. Total number of awards varies.

Award: Scholarship for use in freshman, sophomore, junior, or senior years; renewable. *Number:* 5–25. *Amount:* $500–$1500.

Eligibility Requirements: Applicant must be age 16-23 and enrolled or expecting to enroll full-time at a two-year or four-year or technical institution or university. Available to U.S. citizens.

Application Requirements: Application form, financial need analysis, personal photograph. *Deadline:* April 15.

Contact: Patrick Conroy, Secretary, Memorial Scholarship Fund
  Third Marine Division Association, Inc.
  3454 Stillwood Blvd.
  Stow, OH 44224-4684
  Phone: 330-322-9952
  E-mail: conroypj11@aol.com

THURGOOD MARSHALL COLLEGE FUND

http://www.tmcf.org/

THURGOOD MARSHALL COLLEGE FUND

Merit & Need-based scholarships for students attending one of the 47 member-schools which are HBCUs (historically black colleges and universities) including 5 member law schools. Must maintain an average GPA of 3.0, demonstrate financial need, and be a U.S. citizen/permanent resident. For further details refer to website, http://www.tmcf.org.

Award: Scholarship for use in freshman, sophomore, junior, senior, or graduate years; renewable. *Amount:* up to $6200.

Eligibility Requirements: Applicant must be enrolled or expecting to enroll full-time at a four-year institution or university. Applicant must have 3.0 GPA or higher. Available to U.S. and Canadian citizens.

Application Requirements: Application form, community service, essay, financial need analysis, interview, personal photograph. *Deadline:* June 1.

Contact: Ms. Deshuandra Walker, Senior Manager of Scholarship
  Programs
  Thurgood Marshall College Fund
  1770 Saint James Place Suite 414
  Houston, TX 77056
  Phone: 713-955-1073
  Fax: 202-448-1017
  E-mail: deshuandra.walker@tmcf.org

TOURISM CARES

http://www.tourismcares.org

ASTA ALASKA AIRLINES SCHOLARSHIP

Scholarship available to a full time or part time student enrolled in the second half of their college career in a travel and tourism or hospitality related program of study at a college or university in the US or Canada.

Award: Scholarship for use in sophomore, junior, or senior years; not renewable. *Number:* 1. *Amount:* $2000.

Eligibility Requirements: Applicant must be enrolled or expecting to enroll full- or part-time at a two-year or four-year institution or university. Applicant must have 3.0 GPA or higher. Available to U.S. and Canadian citizens.

Application Requirements: Application form, essay. *Deadline:* April 1.

Contact: Trish Kelly, Workforce Development Coordinator
  Phone: 781-821-5990 Ext. 214
  E-mail: scholarships@tourismcares.org

TWIN TOWERS ORPHAN FUND

http://www.ttof.org/

TWIN TOWERS ORPHAN FUND

Fund offers assistance to children who lost one or both parents in the terrorist attacks on September 11, 2001. Long-term education program established to provide higher education needs to children until they complete their uninterrupted studies, or reach age of majority. Visit website for additional information http://www.ttof.org.

Award: Scholarship for use in freshman, sophomore, junior, or senior years; not renewable. *Amount:* $1500–$6000.

Eligibility Requirements: Applicant must be enrolled or expecting to enroll full- or part-time at a two-year or four-year or technical institution or university. Available to U.S. citizens.

Application Requirements: Application form, financial need analysis. *Deadline:* continuous.

Contact: Karlene Boss, Case Manager
  Twin Towers Orphan Fund
  1430 Truxtun Ave 5th floor
  Bakersfield 93301
  Phone: 661-633-9076
  Fax: 661-760-8981
  E-mail: ttof2@ttof.org

ULMAN CANCER FUND FOR YOUNG ADULTS

http://www.ulmanfund.org/scholarships

BERNICE MCNAMARA MEMORIAL SCHOLARSHIP

The Ulman Cancer Fund for Young Adults is committed to helping young adults continue their education after being affected by cancer through their own diagnosis or the diagnosis of a loved one. Many scholarships offered by UCF share similar applicant criteria. Applicants need only submit one application, which will be considered for any and all scholarships for which the student applies and is eligible.

Award: Scholarship for use in freshman, sophomore, junior, senior, or graduate years; not renewable. *Number:* 1. *Amount:* $2500.

Eligibility Requirements: Applicant must be age 15-39 and enrolled or expecting to enroll full-time at a two-year or four-year institution or university. Available to U.S. citizens.

Application Requirements: Application form, essay. *Deadline:* March 1.

Contact: Lauriann Parker, Scholarship Coordinator
  Ulman Cancer Fund for Young Adults
  1215 E. Fort Ave.
  Ste. 104
  Baltimore, MD 21230
  Phone: 410-964-0202 Ext. 105
  E-mail: scholarship@ulmanfund.org

UNIGO

https://www.scholarshipexperts.com

ALL ABOUT EDUCATION SCHOLARSHIP

Applicants must complete a profile on the scholarshipexperts.com website, be thirteen years of age or older at the time of application, be legal residents of the 50 United States or the District of Columbia, be currently enrolled (or enroll no later than the fall of 2021) in an accredited post-secondary institution of higher education. Submit an online short written response (250 words or less) for the topic: 'How will a $3,000 scholarship for education make a difference in your life?'

Award: Scholarship for use in freshman, sophomore, junior, senior, graduate, or postgraduate years; not renewable. *Number:* 1. *Amount:* $3000.

Eligibility Requirements: Applicant must be enrolled or expecting to enroll full- or part-time at a two-year or four-year or technical institution or university. Available to U.S. citizens.

Application Requirements: Application form, essay. *Deadline:* April 30.

Contact: Scholarship Committee
Unigo
10751 Deerwood Park Boulevard, #125
Jacksonville, FL 32256
Phone: 904-483-2939
Fax: 904-483-2934
E-mail: info@scholarshipexperts.com

DO-OVER SCHOLARSHIP

Applicants must be thirteen years of age or older at the time of application, be legal residents of the 50 United States or the District of Columbia, be currently enrolled (or enroll no later than the fall of 2021) in an accredited post-secondary institution of higher education. Submit an online short written response (250 words or less) for the question: "If you could get one 'do over' in life, what would it be and why?"

Award: Scholarship for use in freshman, sophomore, junior, senior, graduate, or postgraduate years; not renewable. *Number:* 1. *Amount:* $1500.

Eligibility Requirements: Applicant must be enrolled or expecting to enroll full- or part-time at a two-year or four-year or technical institution or university. Available to U.S. citizens.

Application Requirements: Application form, essay. *Deadline:* June 30.

Contact: Scholarship Committee
Unigo
10751 Deerwood Park Boulevard, #125
Jacksonville, FL 32256
Phone: 904-483-2939
Fax: 904-483-2934
E-mail: info@scholarshipexperts.com

EDUCATION MATTERS SCHOLARSHIP

Applicants must: Complete a profile on the ScholarshipExperts.com website. Be thirteen years of age or older at the time of application. Be legal residents of the fifty United States or the District of Columbia. Be currently enrolled (or enroll no later than the fall of 2021) in an accredited post-secondary institution of higher education. Submit an online short written response (250 words or less) for the question: 'What would you say to someone who thinks education doesn't matter, or that college is a waste of time and money?'

Award: Scholarship for use in freshman, sophomore, junior, senior, graduate, or postgraduate years; not renewable. *Number:* 1. *Amount:* $5000.

Eligibility Requirements: Applicant must be enrolled or expecting to enroll full- or part-time at a two-year or four-year or technical institution or university. Available to U.S. citizens.

Application Requirements: Application form, essay. *Deadline:* November 30.

Contact: Scholarship Committee
Unigo
10751 Deerwood Park Boulevard, #125
Jacksonville, FL 32256
Phone: 904-483-2939
Fax: 904-483-2934
E-mail: info@scholarshipexperts.com

FIFTH MONTH SCHOLARSHIP

Applicants must: Be thirteen years of age or older at the time of application. Be legal residents of the fifty United States or the District of Columbia. Be currently enrolled (or enroll no later than the fall of 2021) in an accredited post-secondary institution of higher education and submit an online short written response (250 words or less) for the topic: 'May is the fifth month of the year. Write a letter to the number five explaining why five is important. Be serious or be funny. Either way, here's a high five to you just for being original.'

Award: Scholarship for use in freshman, sophomore, junior, senior, graduate, or postgraduate years; not renewable. *Number:* 1. *Amount:* $1500.

Eligibility Requirements: Applicant must be enrolled or expecting to enroll full- or part-time at a two-year or four-year or technical institution or university. Available to U.S. citizens.

Application Requirements: Application form, essay. *Deadline:* May 31.

Contact: Scholarship Committee
Unigo
10751 Deerwood Park Boulevard, #125
Jacksonville, FL 32256
Phone: 904-483-2939
Fax: 904-483-2934
E-mail: info@scholarshipexperts.com

I HAVE A DREAM SCHOLARSHIP

Applicants must: Be thirteen years of age or older at the time of application. Be legal residents of the fifty United States or the District of Columbia. Be currently enrolled (or enroll no later than the fall of 2021) in an accredited post-secondary institution of higher education and submit an online short written response (250 words or less) for the topic: 'We want to know, what do you dream about? Whether it's some bizarre dream from last week, or your hopes for the future, share your dreams with us for a chance to win $1,500 for college.'

Award: Scholarship for use in freshman, sophomore, junior, senior, graduate, or postgraduate years; not renewable. *Number:* 1. *Amount:* $1500.

Eligibility Requirements: Applicant must be enrolled or expecting to enroll full- or part-time at a two-year or four-year or technical institution or university. Available to U.S. citizens.

Application Requirements: Application form, essay. *Deadline:* January 31.

Contact: Scholarship Committee
Unigo
10751 Deerwood Park Boulevard, #125
Jacksonville, FL 32256
Phone: 904-483-2939
Fax: 904-483-2934
E-mail: info@scholarshipexperts.com

SHOUT IT OUT SCHOLARSHIP

Applicants must be thirteen years of age or older at the time of application, be legal residents of the 50 United States or the District of Columbia, and be currently enrolled (or enroll no later than the fall of 2021) in an accredited post-secondary institution of higher education and submit an online short written response (250 words or less) for the topic: 'If you could say one thing to the entire world at once, what would it be and why?'

Award: Scholarship for use in freshman, sophomore, junior, senior, graduate, or postgraduate years; not renewable. *Number:* 1. *Amount:* $1500.

Eligibility Requirements: Applicant must be enrolled or expecting to enroll full- or part-time at a two-year or four-year or technical institution or university. Available to U.S. citizens.

Application Requirements: Application form, essay. *Deadline:* September 30.

Contact: Scholarship Committee
Unigo
10751 Deerwood Park Boulevard, #125
Jacksonville, FL 32256
Phone: 904-483-2939
Fax: 904-483-2934
E-mail: info@scholarshipexperts.com

SUPERPOWER SCHOLARSHIP

Applicants must be thirteen years of age or older at the time of application, be legal residents of the 50 United States or the District of Columbia, be currently enrolled (or enroll no later than the fall of 2021) in an accredited post-secondary institution of higher education. Submit an online short written response (250 words or less) for the question: 'Which superhero or villain would you want to changes places with for a day and why?'

Award: Scholarship for use in freshman, sophomore, junior, or senior years; not renewable. *Number:* 1. *Amount:* $2500.

Eligibility Requirements: Applicant must be enrolled or expecting to enroll full- or part-time at a two-year or four-year or technical institution or university. Available to U.S. citizens.

Application Requirements: Application form, essay. *Deadline:* March 31.

Contact: Scholarship Committee
Unigo
10751 Deerwood Park Boulevard, #125
Jacksonville, FL 32256
Phone: 904-483-2939
Fax: 904-483-2934
E-mail: info@scholarshipexperts.com

SWEET & SIMPLE SCHOLARSHIP

Applicants must be thirteen years of age or older at the time of application, be legal residents of the 50 United States or the District of Columbia, and be currently enrolled (or enroll no later than the fall of 2020) in an accredited post-secondary institution of higher education and submit an online short written response (250 words or less) for the topic: "Not every gift has to be expensive or extravagant. In fact, sometimes it's the sweet and simple things that make a real difference in our lives. Think back and tell us about something you received as a gift and why it meant so much to you."

Award: Scholarship for use in freshman, sophomore, junior, senior, graduate, or postgraduate years; not renewable. *Number:* 1. *Amount:* $1500.

Eligibility Requirements: Applicant must be enrolled or expecting to enroll full- or part-time at a two-year or four-year or technical institution or university. Available to U.S. citizens.

Application Requirements: Application form, application form may be submitted online (https://www.scholarshipexperts.com/scholarships/our-scholarships/sweet-and-simple-scholarship), essay. *Deadline:* February 28.

Contact: Scholarship Committee
Unigo
10751 Deerwood Park Boulevard, #125
Jacksonville, FL 32256
Phone: 904-483-2939
Fax: 904-483-2934
E-mail: info@scholarshipexperts.com

TOP TEN LIST SCHOLARSHIP

Applicants must: Be thirteen years of age or older at the time of application. Be legal residents of the fifty United States or the District of Columbia. Be currently enrolled (or enroll no later than the fall of 2021) in an accredited post-secondary institution of higher education. Submit an online short written response (250 words or less) for the topic: 'Create a Top Ten List of the top ten reasons you should get this scholarship.'

Award: Scholarship for use in freshman, sophomore, junior, senior, graduate, or postgraduate years; not renewable. *Number:* 1. *Amount:* $1500.

Eligibility Requirements: Applicant must be enrolled or expecting to enroll full- or part-time at a two-year or four-year or technical institution or university. Available to U.S. citizens.

Application Requirements: Application form, essay. *Deadline:* December 31.

Contact: Scholarship Committee
Unigo
10751 Deerwood Park Boulevard, #125
Jacksonville, FL 32256
Phone: 904-483-2939
Fax: 904-483-2934
E-mail: info@scholarshipexperts.com

UNITED STATES ACHIEVEMENT ACADEMY

http://www.usaa-academy.com/

DR. GEORGE A. STEVENS FOUNDER'S AWARD

One $10,000 scholarship cash grant to enhance the intellectual and personal growth of students who demonstrate a genuine interest in learning. Award must be used for educational purposes. Must maintain a minimum GPA of 3.0.

Award: Grant for use in freshman year; not renewable. *Number:* 1. *Amount:* $10,000.

Eligibility Requirements: Applicant must be high school student and planning to enroll or expecting to enroll full-time at a four-year institution or university. Applicant must have 3.0 GPA or higher. Available to U.S. and non-U.S. citizens.

Application Requirements: Application form.

Contact: Scholarship Committee
Phone: 859-269-5674
Fax: 859-268-9068
E-mail: usaa@usaa-academy.com

NATIONAL SCHOLARSHIP CASH GRANT

The Foundation awards 400 national scholarship cash grants of $1500. All scholarship winners are determined by an independent selection committee. Winners are selected based on GPA, school activities, SAT scores (if applicable), honors and awards. All students in grades 6 to 12 are eligible.

Award: Grant for use in freshman year; not renewable. *Number:* 400. *Amount:* $1500.

Eligibility Requirements: Applicant must be high school student and planning to enroll or expecting to enroll full-time at a four-year institution or university. Applicant must have 3.0 GPA or higher. Available to U.S. and non-U.S. citizens.

Application Requirements: Application form, application form may be submitted online (http://www.fs22.formsite.com/USAA/form23/index.html). *Deadline:* June 1.

Contact: Scholarship Committee
Phone: 859-269-5674
Fax: 859-268-9068
E-mail: usaa@usaa-academy.com

UNITED STATES DEPARTMENT OF STATE

http://www.fulbrightexchanges.org/

FREEMAN AWARDS FOR STUDY IN ASIA

The Freeman-ASIA program is designed to support U.S.-based undergraduates with demonstrated financial need who are planning to study abroad in East or Southeast Asia. The program's goal is to increase the number of U.S. citizens and permanent residents with first-hand exposure to and understanding of Asia and its peoples and cultures. Award recipients are required to share their experiences with their home campuses or communities to encourage study abroad by others and fulfill the program's goal of increasing understanding of Asia in the United States. From its inception in 2001, Freeman-ASIA has made study abroad in East and Southeast Asia possible for over 4,600 U.S. undergraduates from more than 600 institutions.

Award: Scholarship for use in freshman, sophomore, junior, or senior years; not renewable. *Amount:* $3000–$7000.

Eligibility Requirements: Applicant must be enrolled or expecting to enroll full- or part-time at a two-year or four-year institution or university. Available to U.S. citizens.

Application Requirements: Application form, essay, financial need analysis. *Deadline:* continuous.

Contact: Ann Koepke, Outreach Specialist
Phone: 202-314-3537
Fax: 202-479-6806
E-mail: fulbright@grad.usda.gov

GILMAN SCHOLARSHIP

The U.S. Department of State's Benjamin A. Gilman International Scholarship is a grant program that enables students of limited financial means to study or intern abroad, thereby gaining skills critical to our national security and economic competitiveness. The Gilman Scholarship Program broadens the student population that studies and interns abroad by supporting undergraduates who might not otherwise participate due to financial constraints. The program aims to encourage students to study and intern in a diverse array of countries and world regions. The program also encourages students to study languages, especially critical need languages (those deemed important to national security). Veterans of military service are encouraged to apply, and preference is given to veterans when other factors are equivalent. By supporting undergraduate students who have high financial need, the program has been successful in supporting students who have been historically underrepresented in education abroad, including but not limited to first-generation college students, students in STEM fields, ethnic minority students, students with disabilities, students attending HBCUs or other minority-serving institutions, students attending community colleges, and students coming from U.S. states with less study abroad participation.

Award: Scholarship for use in freshman, sophomore, junior, or senior years; not renewable. *Number:* 1000–1100. *Amount:* $1000–$5000.

Eligibility Requirements: Applicant must be enrolled or expecting to enroll full- or part-time at a two-year or four-year or technical institution or university. Available to U.S. citizens.

Application Requirements: Application form, essay, financial need analysis. *Deadline:* continuous.

Contact: Ann Koepke, Outreach Specialist
Phone: 202-314-3537
Fax: 202-479-6806
E-mail: fulbright@grad.usda.gov

UNITED STATES-INDONESIA SOCIETY

http://www.usindo.org/

UNITED STATES-INDONESIA SOCIETY TRAVEL GRANTS

Grants are provided to fund travel to Indonesia or the United States for American and Indonesian students and professors to conduct research, language training or other independent study/research. Must have a minimum 3.0 GPA.

Award: Grant for use in freshman, sophomore, junior, senior, graduate, or postgraduate years; not renewable. *Number:* 1–15. *Amount:* $1000–$2000.

Eligibility Requirements: Applicant must be enrolled or expecting to enroll full- or part-time at a four-year institution or university. Applicant must have 3.0 GPA or higher. Available to U.S. and non-Canadian citizens.

Application Requirements: Application form, basic budget, recommendations or references, resume, transcript. *Deadline:* continuous.

Contact: Thomas Spooner, Educational Officer
Phone: 202-232-1400
Fax: 202-232-7300
E-mail: tspooner@usindo.org

UNPAKT LLC

https://www.unpakt.com/

UNPAKT COLLEGE SCHOLARSHIP

Dream big and tell us where you see yourself moving to start your professional life after college. Dreaming of startups in Redwood City or helping urban development in Buffalo? Focusing on intelligence and politics in Washington, D.C. or educating Bostonian minds? Whether you are planning on moving out of state or staying local, we want to know about it. In no more than 500 words, let us know where you plan to move once you finish your education and why. Winners will be chosen by committee review. Judges will be looking for passion and commitment to the dream. Applicant must be a current college student or recent college graduate (within one year) at time of award announcement on December 31. Apply online. http://www.unpakt.com/scholarship

Award: Prize for use in freshman, sophomore, junior, or senior years; not renewable. *Number:* 1. *Amount:* $1000.

Eligibility Requirements: Applicant must be enrolled or expecting to enroll full-time at a four-year institution or university. Available to U.S. citizens.

Application Requirements: Application form, essay. *Deadline:* December 15.

Contact: Scholarship Coordinator
Phone: 212-677-5333 Ext. 107
E-mail: scholarship@unpakt.com

UPLIFT LEGAL FUNDING

https://upliftlegalfunding.com/

UPLIFT LEGAL FUNDING COLLEGE SCHOLARSHIP PROGRAM

Eligibility is based on the following criteria: United States citizen, accepted to or enrolled in a college or university within the United States. In the spirit of personal injury legal funding, applicants should demonstrate a strong willingness to succeed despite challenges. See more information on our website (upliftlegalfunding.com).

Award: Prize for use in freshman, sophomore, junior, or senior years; not renewable. *Number:* 1. *Amount:* $1500.

Eligibility Requirements: Applicant must be enrolled or expecting to enroll full- or part-time at a two-year or four-year institution or university. Available to U.S. citizens.

Application Requirements: Application form, essay. *Deadline:* continuous.

Contact: Ms. Taylor Williams
Uplift Legal Funding
21515 Hawthorne Blvd
Suite 200, Office 101
Torrance, CA 90503
Phone: 800-385-3660
E-mail: taylor@upliftlegalfunding.com

U.S. BANK INTERNET SCHOLARSHIP PROGRAM

http://www.usbank.com/

U.S. BANK INTERNET SCHOLARSHIP PROGRAM

A high school senior planning to enroll or a current college freshmen, sophomore or junior at an eligible four-year college or university participating in the U.S. Bank No Fee Education Loan Program. Apply online at usbank.com/student banking from October through March. No paper applications accepted.

Award: Scholarship for use in freshman, sophomore, or junior years; not renewable. *Number:* up to 40. *Amount:* up to $1000.

Eligibility Requirements: Applicant must be enrolled or expecting to enroll full- or part-time at a four-year institution or university. Available to U.S. and non-U.S. citizens.

Application Requirements: Application form. *Deadline:* March 31.

Contact: Mary Ennis, Scholarship Coordinator
Phone: 800-242-1200
E-mail: mary.ennis@usbank.com

US PAN ASIAN AMERICAN CHAMBER OF COMMERCE EDUCATION FOUNDATION

http://www.uspaacc.com/

BRUCE LEE SCHOLARSHIP

The applicant should demonstrate academic achievement of 3.3 GPA or higher, leadership in extracurricular activities involvement in community service, and financial need. The amount of the scholarship depends on the sponsors' contributions and varies between $2000 and $5000.

Award: Scholarship for use in freshman year; renewable. *Number:* 1. *Amount:* $2000–$5000.

Eligibility Requirements: Applicant must be high school student and planning to enroll or expecting to enroll full-time at an institution or university. Available to U.S. citizens.

Application Requirements: Application form. *Deadline:* March 17.

Contact: Diana Yee
US Pan Asian American Chamber of Commerce Education
Foundation
1329 18th Street N.W.
Washington D.C. 20036
Phone: 202-378-1121
E-mail: diana@uspaacc.com

VALEANT PHARMACEUTICALS NORTH AMERICA, LLC

http://www.valeant.com

ASPIRE HIGHER SCHOLARSHIP PROGRAM

Valeant Dermatology ASPIRE HIGHER Scholarship Program will award scholarships of up to $10,000 each to nine individual students who will be attending an undergraduate or graduate education program during the following school year. The scholarships recognize students who have been diagnosed and treated for a dermatologic condition and are pursuing a higher education degree. Applicants need not have used a Valeant dermatologic prescription medication to be eligible, and use of a Valeant product will not increase an applicant's chance of being awarded a scholarship. Three scholarships will be awarded in three different categories: Undergraduate Scholar Awards for students pursuing an undergraduate degree, Graduate Scholar Awards for students pursuing a graduate degree and Today's Woman Scholar Awards for students who are mothers pursuing either a graduate or undergraduate degree.

Award: Scholarship for use in freshman, sophomore, junior, senior, or graduate years; not renewable. *Number:* 9. *Amount:* $10,000.

Eligibility Requirements: Applicant must be enrolled or expecting to enroll full- or part-time at a four-year institution or university. Available to U.S. citizens.

Application Requirements: Essay. *Deadline:* April 30.

Contact: Christopher Vancheri
Phone: 973-588-2043
E-mail: cvancheri@coynepr.com

VAPE CRAFT INC.

https://vapecraftinc.com/

VAPE CRAFT SCHOLARSHIP

Please submit to us a completed writing prompt of at least 500 words with one of the writing prompts below and email your finished application to marketing@vapecraftinc.com. What is your major, and why did you decide on said major? Tell us about someone in your life that you consider a hero, and why that is. Many people in this country undergo great adversity, how have you had to deal with adversity, and how did you overcome it?

Award: Scholarship for use in freshman, sophomore, junior, senior, graduate, or postgraduate years; renewable. *Number:* 2. *Amount:* $4000.

Eligibility Requirements: Applicant must be enrolled or expecting to enroll full- or part-time at a two-year or four-year or technical institution or university. Applicant must have 2.5 GPA or higher. Available to U.S. and non-U.S. citizens.

Application Requirements: Essay. *Deadline:* December 30.

Contact: Mr. William Brink, Director of Marketing
Vape Craft Inc.
2322 La Mirada Drive
Vista, CA 92081
Phone: 760-801-0256
E-mail: marketing@vapecraftinc.com

THE VEGETARIAN RESOURCE GROUP

http://www.vrg.org/

THE VEGETARIAN RESOURCE GROUP SCHOLARSHIP

Three scholarships (one $10,000; two $5,000) will be awarded to graduating U.S. high school students who promoted vegetarianism (includes veganism) in their schools and/or communities. Vegetarians do not eat meat, fish, or fowl. Applicants will be judged on a strong commitment to promoting a peaceful world through a vegetarian diet/lifestyle.

Award: Scholarship for use in freshman year; not renewable. *Amount:* $5000–$10,000.

Eligibility Requirements: Applicant must be high school student and planning to enroll or expecting to enroll full- or part-time at a two-year or four-year institution or university. Available to U.S. citizens.

Application Requirements: Application form, essay. *Deadline:* February 20.

Contact: Scholarship Coordinator
Phone: 410-366-8343
Fax: 410-366-8804
E-mail: vrg@vrg.org

VELVETJOBS LLC

http://www.velvetjobs.com

EMPLOYEE MORALE SCHOLARSHIP

Are you an undergraduate or graduate college or university student? VelvetJobs is proud to announce a $1000 scholarship for students studying in the USA or overseas. The "Employee Morale Scholarship" aims to get students thinking about their own potential future management position and how their decisions can affect employee morale. Through our own outplacement services we've dealt with thousands of employers on the issues that affect them most when it comes to retaining employees and keeping them happy. We're looking for students to write about their favorite idea on how to boost and maintain employee morale. Open to U.S. or international students. Entrants must 18 years or older. No GPA requirement. The piece should include a headline of the morale boosting idea and then should include at least 500 words on how to effectively deploy the strategy. Email your essay and the morale boosting idea to scholarship@velvetjobs.com. We will be judging the strategy on both it's uniqueness and it's practicality. That means the idea should stand out from the crowd but also be easily implemented into the workforce. The idea does not have to be overarching to all types of workforce but can be individualized to a specific workforce such as (office based, manufacturing, mobile workers, etc.). The winner will be announced by January 15th. Scholarship funds will be released for the Spring 2018 semester.

Award: Scholarship for use in freshman, sophomore, junior, senior, graduate, or postgraduate years; renewable. *Number:* 1. *Amount:* $1000.

Eligibility Requirements: Applicant must be enrolled or expecting to enroll full- or part-time at a two-year or four-year or technical institution or university. Available to U.S. and non-U.S. citizens.

Application Requirements: Essay. *Deadline:* December 16.

Contact: Christina Murphy, Scholarship Coordinator
VelvetJobs LLC
1400 North Martel Avenue, Suite 108
Los Angeles, CA 90046
Phone: 877-370-7552
E-mail: scholarship@velvetjobs.com

WATERLOGIC

https://www.waterlogic.com/en-us/

WATERLOGIC SCHOLARSHIP

Waterlogic is thrilled to announce this year's scholarship opportunity, open to all current or incoming college students. As a company committed to increasing global access to clean water, we believe this scholarship will foster an increased awareness of issues related to such access, as well as reward a student who has demonstrated a sincere interest in the matter. As such, we look forward to issuing a prize of $1,500 to the student who best outlines their response to the following prompt: Accessible clean water–how can we achieve it? 783 million people worldwide do not have access to safe, clean water. In developing countries, as much as 80% of illnesses are linked to poor water and sanitation conditions. Given the resources of today's technological age, how can the problem of clean water be resolved? Choose one solution and explain how this idea would specifically impact developing countries. The minimum and maximum requirement regarding the length of the essay response is 600-800 words. To be eligible, the applicant must be entering or currently enrolled in an undergraduate degree, be a U.S. citizen, national, or permanent resident, plan on attending an accredited US institution (two- or four-year college), and have a minimum 3.00 GPA. Applications must be sent via the Waterlogic website https://www.waterlogic.com/en-us/scholarship-competition/. The deadline for this scholarship application is May 31, 2018.

Award: Prize for use in freshman, sophomore, junior, or senior years; not renewable. *Number:* 1. *Amount:* $1500.

Eligibility Requirements: Applicant must be high school student and planning to enroll or expecting to enroll full-time at a two-year or four-year or technical institution or university. Applicant must have 3.0 GPA or higher. Available to U.S. citizens.

Application Requirements: Essay. *Deadline:* May 31.

Contact: Mr. Edward Hull, Mr
Waterlogic
77 McCullough Drive, Suite 9
New Castle, DE 19720
Phone: 49-8935856946
E-mail: edward@waterlogic-email.com

WISCONSIN LIBRARY ASSOCIATION

http://wla.wisconsinlibraries.org/awards-scholarships/

WAAL SCHOLARSHIP

The WAAL Professional Development Committee has created three scholarship application forms for individuals wanting to apply for a scholarship to attend the annual WAAL conference.

Award: Scholarship for use in sophomore, junior, senior, or graduate years; not renewable.

Eligibility Requirements: Applicant must be enrolled or expecting to enroll full- or part-time at a four-year institution or university.

Application Requirements: Application form, essay. *Deadline:* March 4.

Contact: Ms. Brigitte Rupp Vacha, WLA Conference Liaison
Wisconsin Library Association
4610 S Biltmore Lane
Suite 100
Madison, WI 53718
Phone: 608-245-3640
Fax: 608-245-3646
E-mail: ruppvacha@wisconsinlibraries.org

WOMEN'S INDEPENDENCE SCHOLARSHIP PROGRAM, INC.

http://www.wispinc.org/

WOMEN'S INDEPENDENCE SCHOLARSHIP PROGRAM

Scholarship for female survivors of intimate partner abuse, separated from their abusive partner a minimum of one year but not more than seven years, and sponsored by a domestic violence service agency they have worked with for a minimum of six months. Funding is available for those attending an accredited course of study at a U.S. institution. The application is only available online and must be submitted electronically.

Award: Scholarship for use in freshman, sophomore, junior, senior, or graduate years; renewable. *Number:* 350–500. *Amount:* $500–$3000.

Eligibility Requirements: Applicant must be enrolled or expecting to enroll full- or part-time at a two-year or four-year or technical institution or university and female. Available to U.S. citizens.

Application Requirements: Application form, essay, financial need analysis. *Deadline:* continuous.

Contact: Ms. Nancy Soward, Executive Director
Women's Independence Scholarship Program, Inc.
4900 Randall Parkway, Suite H
Wilmington, NC 28403
Phone: 910-397-7742 Ext. 101
Fax: 910-397-0023
E-mail: nancy@wispinc.org

WOMEN'S OVERSEAS SERVICE LEAGUE

http://www.wosl.org/

WOMEN'S OVERSEAS SERVICE LEAGUE SCHOLARSHIPS FOR WOMEN

Awarded to women committed to careers in public service who have completed 12 semester or 18 quarter units in any higher education

institution with a 2.5 GPA, are admitted to an institution in a program leading to an Associate's Degree or higher and enrolled for a minimum of 6 semester or 9 quarter hours.

Award: Scholarship for use in sophomore, junior, senior, graduate, or postgraduate years; renewable. *Number:* 10–20. *Amount:* $1000–$2000.

Eligibility Requirements: Applicant must be enrolled or expecting to enroll full- or part-time at a two-year or four-year or technical institution or university and female. Applicant must have 2.5 GPA or higher. Available to U.S. citizens.

Application Requirements: Application form, community service, essay, financial need analysis. *Deadline:* March 1.

Contact: Ms. Ann Kelsey, Scholarship Committee Chair
E-mail: kelsey@openix.com

WOMEN'S SPORTS FOUNDATION

http://www.womenssportsfoundation.org/

LINDA RIDDLE/SGMA ENDOWED SCHOLARSHIP

One $1,500 scholarship to provide female student-athletes of limited financial means the opportunity to continue to pursue their sport in addition to their college studies. If you plan to participate in intercollegiate sports at a Division I school, consult with your college compliance office to determine whether this scholarship will affect your eligibility. Please check website for application procedures.

Award: Scholarship for use in freshman year; not renewable. *Number:* 1. *Amount:* $1500.

Eligibility Requirements: Applicant must be high school student; planning to enroll or expecting to enroll full-time at a two-year or four-year institution and female. Applicant must have 3.5 GPA or higher. Available to U.S. citizens.

Application Requirements: Application form. *Deadline:* May 31.

Contact: Elizabeth Flores
Phone: 516-307-3915
E-mail: LFlores@WomensSportsFoundation.org

WYZANT INC.

WYZANT COLLEGE SCHOLARSHIPS

Each individual who applies (Applicant) will be required to write an essay in English of no more than 300 words answering the question: "Who has been most important tutor, teacher or coach in my life and why?" As part of the application, Applicant may use tools and services provided by WyzAnt to promote the essay to friends and family. Contest runs from October 1 through May 1 each year.

Award: Scholarship for use in freshman, sophomore, junior, or senior years; not renewable.

Eligibility Requirements: Applicant must be enrolled or expecting to enroll full- or part-time at a four-year institution or university. Available to U.S. citizens.

Application Requirements: Essay. *Deadline:* May 1.

YTA.SE

https://yta.se

YTA.SE CLIMATE SCHOLARSHIP

The yta.se Climate Scholarship shall be used to catalyze and bring progress to promising projects and research within real estate sustainability. Anyone who studies on a university-level can apply. Apply by submitting the application form on https://yta.se/blogg/scholarship/ which includes a motivation, description of the project or research and what the scholarship can help achieve in terms of next actions.

Award: Scholarship for use in freshman, sophomore, junior, senior, graduate, or postgraduate years; not renewable. *Number:* 1. *Amount:* $1230.

Eligibility Requirements: Applicant must be enrolled or expecting to enroll full- or part-time at a two-year or four-year or technical institution or university. Available to U.S. and non-U.S. citizens.

Application Requirements: *Deadline:* December 15.

Contact: Mr. Alexander Åquist, Co-Founder
yta.se
Sveavägen 64
Stockholm 111 34
Phone: 46-73-512 59 78
E-mail: alexander@yta.se

ZOOMITA

http://zoomita.com

$1,000 NOT AN ESSAY SCHOLARSHIP

Application essays are hard. Zoomita makes them easier. Create a free account and respond to the mystery question for a chance to win $1,000 toward your college expenses!

Award: Scholarship for use in freshman year; not renewable. *Number:* up to 1. *Amount:* up to $1000.

Eligibility Requirements: Applicant must be high school student; age 15-19 and planning to enroll or expecting to enroll full- or part-time at a four-year or technical institution or university. Available to U.S. and non-U.S. citizens.

Application Requirements: Application form may be submitted online (http://zoomita.com/VGhpc1NIb3VkbEJFSGlkZGVu), response to mystery question. *Deadline:* December 31.

Contact: Sandeep Chauhan
Zoomita
1440 Broadway
Oakland, CA 94612
E-mail: info@edswell.com

INDEXES

Award Name

Al-Ben Scholarship for Scholastic Achievement 193

Alberta Agriculture Food and Rural Development 4-H Scholarship Program 549

Alberta Apprenticeship and Industry Training Scholarships 799

Alberta Barley Commission-Eugene Boyko Memorial Scholarship 105

Alberta Centennial Scholarships-Alberta 720

The Alberta C. Kaufman Scholarship 633

Alberta Pre-Apprenticeship Scholarships 799

Albert E. and Florence W. Newton Nurse Scholarship 487

Albert E. Wischmeyer Memorial Scholarship Award 325

Albert H. Hix, W8AH, Memorial Scholarship 811

Albert M. Lappin Scholarship 554

Albina Fuel Company Scholarship 589

Al Conklin and Bill de Decker Business Aviation Management Scholarship 158

Aldo Freda Legislative Pages Scholarship 863

A Legacy of Hope Scholarships for Survivors of Childhood Cancer 869

Alert1 Student for Seniors Scholarship 593

Alert Scholarship 800

Alexander and Maude Hadden Scholarship 684

The Alexander Foundation Scholarship Program 800

Alexander Rutherford Scholarships for High School Achievement 720

Alexander Scholarship Loan Fund 185

Alfred E. Friend Jr., W4CF, Memorial Scholarship 191

Alfred G. and Elma M. Milotte Scholarship 921

Alfred Steele Engineering Scholarship 312

Alfred "Tup" Holmes Memorial Scholarship 873

AlgaeCal Scholarship 594

Alice and Mason White Memorial Scholarship 951

Alice Glaisyer Warfield Memorial Scholarship 540

Alice L. Haltom Educational Fund 176

Alice T. Schafer Mathematics Prize for Excellence in Mathematics by an Undergraduate Woman 437

All About Education Scholarship 969

Allcott/Hunt Share It Now II Scholarship, Honoring Emory S. and Elizabeth Burkett Hunt 951

Allegheny Mountain Section Air & Waste Management Association Scholarship 336

Allen and Bertha Watson Memorial Scholarship 313

Allen J. Baldwin Scholarship 442

Allied Healthcare Scholarship Program 165

All-Ink.com College Scholarship Program 921

Allison Fisher Scholarship 405

Allogan Slagle Memorial Scholarship 725

Al Neuharth Free Spirit and Journalism Conference Program 402

Alpha Omega Scholarship In Memory Of Peter Agris 215

Alphonse A. Miele Scholarship 679

Alphonso Deal Scholarship Award 243

Alumni Student Assistance Program 727

Alvin E. Heaps Memorial Scholarship 577

Alwin B. Newton Scholarship 281

AMACESP Student Scholarships 150

Amato Sanita Brighter Future Scholarship 661

AMBUCS Scholars-Scholarships for Therapists 148

Amelia Kemp Scholarship 771

American Alpine Club Research Grants 595

American Angus Auxiliary Scholarship 948

American Association for Geodetic Surveying Joseph F. Dracup Scholarship Award 529

American Association of Family & Consumer Sciences National Undergraduate Scholarship 384

American Baptist Home Mission Societies Financial Aid Program 773

American Board of Funeral Service Education Scholarships 361

American Bullion Scholarship 922

American Chemical Society, Rubber Division Undergraduate Scholarship 120

American Chemical Society Scholars Program 187

American Council of Engineering Companies of Oregon Scholarship 210

American Council of the Blind Scholarships 595

American Criminal Justice Association-Lambda Alpha Epsilon National Scholarship 241

American Dental Association Foundation Dental Hygiene Scholarship Program 252

American Dental Association Foundation Dental Student Scholarship Program 252

American Dream Scholarship 926

American Express Scholarship Program 389

American Federation of State, County, and Municipal Employees Oregon Council #75—William Lucy Scholarship 573

American Federation of State, County, and Municipal Employees Oregon Council # 75 Scholarship 573

American Federation of State, County, and Municipal Employees Scholarship Program 549

American Ground Water Trust-AMTROL Inc. Scholarship 259

American Ground Water Trust-Baroid Scholarship 259

American Ground Water Trust-Thomas Stetson Scholarship 259

American Hotel & Lodging Educational Foundation Pepsi Scholarship 244

American Indian Education Fund Scholarship 722

American Indian Nurse Scholarship Program 368

Americanism Essay Contest Scholarship 553

American Jewish League for Israel Scholarship Program 881

American Legion Auxiliary Children of Warriors National Presidents' Scholarship 596

American Legion Auxiliary Department of Alabama Scholarship Program 705

American Legion Auxiliary Department of Arizona Health Care Occupation Scholarships 369

American Legion Auxiliary Department of Arizona Nurses' Scholarships 471

American Legion Auxiliary Department of Arizona Wilma Hoyal-Maxine Chilton Memorial Scholarship 215

American Legion Auxiliary Department of California General Scholarship 705

American Legion Auxiliary Department of California Past Presidents' Parley Nursing Scholarships 471

American Legion Auxiliary Department of Colorado Department President's Scholarship and Scholarship for Junior Member 923

American Legion Auxiliary Department of Colorado Past Presidents' Parley Health Care Professional ScholarshipNurses Scholarship 147

American Legion Auxiliary Department of Connecticut Memorial Educational Grant 550

American Legion Auxiliary Department of Connecticut Past Presidents' Parley Memorial Education Grant 550

American Legion Auxiliary Department of Idaho Nursing Scholarship 471

American Legion Auxiliary Department of Iowa Children of Veterans Merit Award 705

American Legion Auxiliary Department of Iowa Harriet Hoffman Memorial Merit Award for Teacher Training 266

American Legion Auxiliary Department of Iowa M.V. McCrae Memorial Nurses Merit Award 472

American Legion Auxiliary Department of Kentucky Laura Blackburn Memorial Scholarship 700

American Legion Auxiliary Department of Kentucky Mary Barrett Marshall Scholarship 705

American Legion Auxiliary Department of Maine Daniel E. Lambert Memorial Scholarship 706

American Legion Auxiliary Department of Maine Past Presidents' Parley Nurses Scholarship 369

American Legion Auxiliary Department of Massachusetts Department President's Scholarship 595

American Legion Auxiliary Department of Massachusetts Past Presidents' Parley Scholarship 472

American Legion Auxiliary Department of Michigan Medical Career Scholarship 369

American Legion Auxiliary Department of Michigan Memorial Scholarship 706

American Legion Auxiliary Department of Michigan Scholarship for Non-Traditional Student 706

American Legion Auxiliary Department of Minnesota Past Presidents' Parley Health Care Scholarship 370

American Legion Auxiliary Department of Minnesota Scholarships 707

American Legion Auxiliary Department of Missouri Lela Murphy Scholarship 550

American Legion Auxiliary Department of Missouri National President's Scholarship 550

American Legion Auxiliary Department of Missouri Past Presidents' Parley Scholarship 472

American Legion Auxiliary Department of Nebraska Ruby Paul Campaign Fund Scholarship 551

American Legion Auxiliary Department of North Dakota National President's Scholarship 596

American Legion Auxiliary Department of North Dakota Past Presidents' Parley Nurses Scholarship 472

American Legion Auxiliary Department of North Dakota Scholarships 802

American Legion Auxiliary Department of Ohio Continuing Education Fund 707

American Legion Auxiliary Department of Ohio Department President's Scholarship 707

Anthony Munoz Scholarships 598

Anthony Narigi Hospitality Scholarship Fund 391

Antonette Willa Skupa Turner Scholarship 384

AOCS Analytical Division Student Award 190

AOCS Biotechnology Student Excellence Award 105

AOCS Health and Nutrition Division Student Excellence Award 351

AOCS Processing Division Awards 190

A.O. Putnam Memorial Scholarship 319

APEX Scholarship 724

Appaloosa Youth Educational Scholarships 560

Applegate/Jackson/Parks Future Teacher Scholarship 273

ApplyKit Scholarship $500 No Essay! 925

Appraisal Institute Education Trust Education Scholarships 516

Apprentice Ecologist Scholarship 652

AQHF General Scholarship 557

AQHF Journalism or Communications Scholarship 216

AQHF Racing Scholarships 558

AQHF Youth Scholarships 558

Architects Foundation Diversity Advancement Scholarship 131

Architects Foundation Payette Sho-Ping Chin Memorial Academic Scholarship 131

Arc of Washington Trust Fund Stipend Program 599

AREMA Graduate and Undergraduate Scholarships 204

Arizona Don't Text and Drive Scholarship 832

Arizona Hydrological Society Scholarship 259

Arizona Nursery Association Foundation Scholarship 385

Arizona Private School Association Scholarship 810

Arizona Professional Chapter of AISES Scholarship 313

Arizona Quarter Horse Youth Scholarship 558

Arizona Quarter Racing Scholarship 558

Arkansas Academic Challenge Scholarship Program 810

Arkansas Governor's Scholars Program 810

Arkansas Single Parent Scholarship Fund 599

Armed Forces Communications and Electronics Association ROTC Scholarship Program 151

Armenian Relief Society Undergraduate Scholarship 599

Armenian Students Association of America Inc. Scholarships 724

Army Officers Wives Club of the Greater Washington Area Scholarship 701

Army ROTC Green to Gold Scholarship Program for Two-Year, Three-Year and Four-Year Scholarships, Active Duty Enlisted Personnel 610

Army (ROTC) Reserve Officers Training Corps Two-, Three-, Four-Year Campus-Based Scholarships 610

Army ROTC Study.com Scholarship 671

Arne Engebretsen Wisconsin Mathematics Council Scholarship 279

Arrive Alive, Don't Drink & Drive! 2018 Scholarship Contest 814

ARRL Rocky Mountain Division Scholarship 811

Arsham Amirikian Engineering Scholarship 206

ARTBA-TDF Lanford Family Highway Workers Memorial Scholarship Program 599

ARTC Glen Moon Scholarship 268

Arthur and Gladys Cervenka Scholarship Award 325

Arthur E. and Helen Copeland Scholarships 694

Arthur Schramm Scholarship 352

Arthur W. Pense Scholarship 599

Artificial Intelligence & Ethics Scholarship 920

Arts Council of Greater Grand Rapids Minority Scholarship 142

ASABE Foundation Scholarship 311

ASCPA Educational Foundation Scholarship 593

ASCSA Summer Session and Summer Seminars Scholarships 118

Ashby B. Carter Memorial Scholarship Fund Founders Award 568

ASHRAE General Scholarships 294

ASHRAE Legacy Scholarship 295

ASHRAE Region III Boggarm Setty Scholarship 191

ASHRAE Region IV Benny Bootle Scholarship 130

ASHRAE Region VIII Scholarship 295

Asian Reporter Scholarship 600

ASID Foundation Legacy Scholarship for Undergraduates 398

ASLA Council of Fellows Scholarship 635

ASME Auxiliary Undergraduate Scholarship Charles B. Sharp 311

ASNT Engineering Undergraduate Scholarship 290

ASNT Robert B. Oliver Scholarship 923

ASPIRE HIGHER Scholarship Program 972

Associate Degree Nursing Scholarship Program 479

Associated General Contractors NYS Scholarship Program 207

Associated Press Television/Radio Association-Clete Roberts Journalism Scholarship Awards 401

Association for Food and Drug Officials Scholarship Fund 499

Association for Iron and Steel Technology Baltimore Chapter Scholarship 293

Association for Iron and Steel Technology Benjamin F. Fairless Scholarship (AIME) 186

Association for Iron and Steel Technology David H. Samson Canadian Scholarship 187

Association for Iron and Steel Technology Midwest Chapter Betty McKern Scholarship 308

Association for Iron and Steel Technology Midwest Chapter Don Nelson Scholarship 308

Association for Iron and Steel Technology Midwest Chapter Engineering Scholarship 308

Association for Iron and Steel Technology Midwest Chapter Jack Gill Scholarship 309

Association for Iron and Steel Technology Midwest Chapter Mel Nickel Scholarship 309

Association for Iron and Steel Technology Midwest Chapter Non-Engineering Scholarship 309

Association for Iron and Steel Technology Midwest Chapter Western States Scholarship 309

Association for Iron and Steel Technology Northwest Member Chapter Scholarship 309

Association for Iron and Steel Technology Ohio Valley Chapter Scholarship 167

Association for Iron and Steel Technology Pittsburgh Chapter Scholarship 309

Association for Iron and Steel Technology Ronald E. Lincoln Scholarship 280

Association for Iron and Steel Technology Southeast Member Chapter Scholarship 310

Association for Iron and Steel Technology Willy Korf Memorial Scholarship 187

Association for Women in Architecture Foundation Scholarship 131

Association of California Water Agencies Scholarships 123

Association of Energy Service Companies Scholarship Program 569

Association of State Dam Safety Officials (ASDSO) Senior Undergraduate Scholarship 168

Assured Life Association Endowment Scholarship Program 600

ASTA Alaska Airlines Scholarship 968

ASTA Holland America Line Undergraduate Scholarship 542

ASTA Princess Cruises Scholarship 358

Astrid G. Cates and Myrtle Beinhauer Scholarship Funds 578

Astronaut Scholarship Foundation 123

A.T. Anderson Memorial Scholarship Program 121

A.T. Cross Scholarship 591

Atlanta Radio Club Scholarship 811

Atlas Shrugged Essay Contest 600

Attorney Raymond Lahoud Scholar Program 413

Aubrey Lee Brooks Scholarships 854

Audre Lorde Scholarship Fund 771

Audria M. Edwards Scholarship Fund 658

Autism/ASD Scholarship 633

Autism Scholarship 617, 637, 664

Autism Scholarships 617

Automotive Aftermarket Scholarships 177

Automotive Hall of Fame Educational Funds 887

Automotive Recyclers Association Scholarship Foundation Scholarship 561

Automotive Women's Alliance Foundation Scholarships 81

AvaCare Medical Scholarship 115

Aviation Council of Pennsylvania Scholarship Program 151

A. Victor Rosenfeld Scholarship 589

A Voice For Cats Essay Contest Scholarship 921

AWeber Developing Futures Scholarship 725

AWG Ethnic Minority Scholarship 260

AWG Maria Luisa Crawford Field Camp Scholarship 129

AWG Salt Lake Chapter (SLC) Research Scholarship 129

AWG Undergraduate Excellence in Paleontology Award 123

AWRA Richard A. Herbert Memorial Scholarship 458

Azteca Scholarship 628

Babe Ruth Scholarship Program 888

Bachelor of Science Nursing Loan Repayment Program 479

Bachelor of Science Nursing Scholarship Program 480

Bach Organ and Keyboard Music Scholarship 457

Back to School Nursing Scholarship Program 474

BAC Local 3 Sullivan Kraw Scholarship 866

Baer Reintegration Scholarship 604

Baltimore Ravens Scholarship Program 817

DiMattio Celli Family Study Abroad Scholarship *679*

Dimitri J. Ververelli Memorial Scholarship for Architecture and/or Engineering *134*

Director's Scholarship Award *327*

disABLEDperson Inc. National College Scholarship Award for College Students with Disabilities *612*

Disabled Veteran Scholarship *634*

Disabled Veterans Scholarship *617*

Discover Financial Services Scholarship *93*

Displaced Homemaker Scholarship *725*

Distinguished Raven FAC Memorial Scholarship *614*

Distinguished Young Women *934*

DIVERSEability Magazine Scholarship *934*

Diverse Voices in Storytelling Scholarship *227*

Diversity in STEAM Magazine Scholarship *83*

Divorce Prevention Scholarship *848*

Dixie Boys Baseball Bernie Varnadore Scholarship Program *825*

Dixie Youth Scholarship Program *825*

Dr. Ann C. Hollingsworth Student Leadership Scholarship *352*

Dr. Click Cowger Baseball Scholarship *805*

Dr. Dan J. and Patricia S. Pickard Scholarship *731*

Dr. Don and Rose Marie Benton Scholarship *822*

Dr. George A. Stevens Founder's Award *970*

Dr. George M. Smerk Scholarship *539*

Dr. Gerald O'Connor Michigan QHY Scholarship *558*

Dr. Gunnar B. Stickler Scholarship *694*

Dr. Hilda Richards Scholarship *483*

Dr. Ivy M. Parker Memorial Scholarship *197*

Dr. James L. Lawson Memorial Scholarship *216*

Dr. Juan Andrade, Jr. Scholarship *769*

Dr. Juan D. Villarreal/Hispanic Dental Association Foundation *255*

Dr. Lauranne Sams Scholarship *483*

Dr. Lynne Boyle/John Schimpf Undergraduate Scholarship *97*

Dr. Nicholas Padis Memorial Graduate Scholarship *738*

Dr. Pepper Snapple Group Scholarship *766*

Dr. Peter A. Theodos Memorial Graduate Scholarship *374*

Dr. Roberto F. Cunanan Memorial Scholarship *864*

The Dodell Women's Empowerment Scholarship *648*

Dogwood Scholarship *558*

Dollars 4 Tic Scholars Tourette Syndrome Scholarship *613*

Dolphin Scholarships *613*

Domnick Cunningham & Whalen Elder Abuse Prevention *613*

Donald A. and John R. Fisher Memorial Scholarship *580*

Donald and Shirley Hastings Scholarship *312*

Donald A. Williams Scholarship Soil Conservation Scholarship *103*

Donald C. Hyde Essay Program *539*

Donald F. and Mildred Topp Othmer Foundation- National Scholarship Awards *188*

Donald F. Hastings Scholarship *296*

Donald J. Beneteau Scholarship *432*

The Donaldson Company, Inc. Scholarship Program *588*

Don Debolt Franchising Scholarship Program *942*

Don Riebhoff Memorial Scholarship *400*

Don't Mess With Texas Scholarship Program *825*

Don't Text and Drive Scholarship *933*

"Don't Wait to Reach Your Potential" Scholarship *661*

Do-Over Scholarship *969*

Doran/Blair Scholarships *563*

Dorchester Women's Club Music Scholarship *452*

Doris and Elmer H. Schmitz, Sr. Memorial Scholarship *580*

Dorizas Memorial Scholarship *738*

Dorothea Deitz Endowed Memorial Scholarship *279*

Dorothy Campbell Memorial Scholarship *858*

Dorothy Lemke Howarth Memorial Scholarship *197*

Dorothy P. Morris Scholarship *198*

Dorothy S. Campbell Memorial Scholarship Fund *908*

Douglas W. Mummert Scholarship *142*

Douvas Memorial Scholarship *879*

Dow Jones News Fund High School Journalism Workshops Writing, Photography and Multimedia Competition *402*

DREAM Former Foster Youth Scholarship *952*

Drone Technology College Scholarship *613*

Drs. Charlene & Charles Byrd Scholarship *832*

DSS Adopted Children Tuition Waiver *642*

Duane Hanson Scholarship *282*

Duck Brand Duct Tape "Stuck at Prom" Scholarship Contest *625*

Dudley DeBosier Law School Scholarship *414*

Dudley DeBosier Scholarship Program *825*

Duke and Dutchess of Cambridge Scholarship *799*

Dunbar Class of 1958 Scholarship *818*

DuPont Company Scholarship *198*

Durwood McAlister Scholarship *403*

Dutch and Ginger Arver Scholarship *149*

Dwayne R. Woerpel Memorial Leadership Scholarship *580*

Dwight D. Gardner Scholarship *319*

D.W. Simpson Actuarial Science Scholarship *397*

Earl James Fahringer Performing Arts Scholarship *142*

Early Childhood Development Scholarship *840*

Early Childhood Educators Scholarship Program *203*

Eastern Amputee Golf Association Scholarship Fund *687*

Eastern Orthodox Committee on Scouting Scholarships *562*

E. B Miller Memorial Scholarship *460*

eCampusTours Scholarship Drawing *935*

ECA Scholarship *385*

E.C. Hallbeck Scholarship Fund *557*

Eckenfelder Scholarship *169*

Ecolab Scholarship Program *245*

e-CollegeDegree.com Online Education Scholarship Award *935*

E. Craig Brandenburg Graduate Award *781*

Ed Bradley Scholarship *223*

Ed E. and Gladys Hurley Foundation Scholarship *518*

Edith M. Allen Scholarship *270*

Edlong Dairy Technologies Scholarship *353*

Edmond A. Metzger Scholarship *283*

Edmund F. Maxwell Foundation Scholarship *826*

Edna Aimes Scholarship *166*

Edna Blum Scholarship for NYC Residents *766*

Edna Hicks Fund Scholarship *477*

EDSA Minority Scholarship *636*

EDSF Board of Directors Scholarships *364*

Education Achievement Awards *271*

Educational Benefits for Children of Deceased Veterans *609*

The Educational Justice Scholarship *658*

Educational Trust Fund of the CTCPA - Candidate's Scholarship *82*

Education Matters Scholarship *969*

EdU Scholarship Award *930*

Edward D. Hendrickson/SAE Engineering Scholarship *160*

Edward H. and Rosamond B. Spicer Travel Awards *963*

Edward J. and Virginia M. Routhier Nursing Scholarship *487*

Edward J. Brady Memorial Scholarship *296*

Edward J. Dulis Scholarship *314*

Edward J. Nell Memorial Scholarship in Journalism *408*

Edward Leon Duhamel Freemasons Scholarship *577*

Edward M. Nagel Endowed Scholarship *184*

Edward R. Hall Scholarship *103*

Edward S. Roth Manufacturing Engineering Scholarship *327*

Edwards Scholarship *826*

Edward T. Conroy Memorial Scholarship Program *642*

Edward W. Stimpson "Aviation Excellence" Award *154*

Edwin Kuniyuki Memorial Scholarship *624*

E. Eugene Waide, MD Memorial Scholarship *470*

E.H. Marth Food Protection and Food Sciences Scholarship *336*

Eileen J. Garrett Scholarship for Parapsychological Research *523*

Eileen Kraus Scholarship *821*

Elaine B. Hancock Endowed Scholarship *766*

Elaine Chapin Memorial Scholarship Fund *687*

Elaine Rendler-Rene Dosogne-Georgetown Chorale Scholarship *455*

Eleanora G. Wylie Scholarship *478*

eLearners Military Scholarship *696*

eLearners Online Student Scholarship *614*

Elekta Radiation Therapy Scholarship *371*

Elements Behavioral Health College Tuition Scholarship *935*

Elie Wiesel Prize in Ethics Essay Contest *893*

Elizabeth and Sherman Asche Memorial Scholarship Fund *106*

Elizabeth and Wallace Kingsbury Scholarship *584*

Elizabeth Gardner Norweb Summer Environmental Studies Scholarship *107*

The Elizabeth Greenshields Foundation Grant *614*

Elizabeth McLean Memorial Scholarship *211*

Elks Emergency Educational Grants *563*

Elks National Foundation Legacy Awards *563*

Elks National Foundation Most Valuable Student Scholarship Contest *893*

Ella T. Grasso Literary Scholarship *680*

Ellen Hippeli Memorial Scholarship *329*

Elmer S. Imes Scholarship in Physics *507*

Elson T. Killam Memorial Scholarship *210*

EMBARK-Support for the College Journey *843*

Emily Chaison Gold Award Scholarship *564*

Emily M. Hewitt Memorial Scholarship *170*

Fred M. Young Sr./SAE Engineering Scholarship *324*

Fred R. McDaniel Memorial Scholarship *216*

Fred Scheigert Scholarship *607*

Freedom Alliance Scholarship Fund *620*

Freedom From Religion Foundation Michael Hakeem Memorial Ongoing College Essay Competition *780*

Freedom From Religion Foundation William J. Schulz Memorial College-bound High School Senior Essay Competition *780*

Freeman Awards for Study in Asia *735, 970*

French Culinary Institute/Italian Culinary Experience Scholarship *250*

Fresh Start Scholarship *830*

Frieda L. Koontz Scholarship *278*

Friends of 440 Scholarship Fund, Inc. *831*

Friends of Bill Rutherford Education Fund *857*

Friends of Bill Rutherford Education Scholarship *656*

Friends of Coal Scholarships *735*

Frugal Student *967*

Fruits Industries Scholarships *108*

FSCNY Young Leaders Scholarship *618*

FSGA Scholars *829*

Fukunaga Scholarship Foundation *85*

Fulfilling Our Dreams Scholarship Fund *759*

Fulfillment Fund Scholarships *831*

Funk Family Memorial Scholarship *455*

FunNewJersey.com Scholarship *620*

Future Designer Scholarship *603*

Future of Assisted Living Scholarship *961*

Future Teacher Scholarship-Oklahoma *274*

Future U.S. Nurse Scholarship *676*

Gabe Anaya Scholarship *581*

Gabriel A. Hartl Scholarship *150*

GAE GFIE Scholarship for Aspiring Teachers *270*

Gaige Fund Award *167*

Galactic Unite Bytheway Scholarship *202*

Gala Nursing Scholarships *478*

Gamewardens of Vietnam Scholarship *717*

Gannett Foundation/Madelyn P. Jennings Scholarship Award *589*

GAPA Scholarships *895*

Garden Club of America Montine M. Freeman Scholarship in Native Plants *386*

Gardiner Foundation Scholarship *621*

GARMIN-Jerry Smith Memorial Scholarship *149*

GARMIN Scholarship *149*

Gary Wagner, K3OMI, Scholarship *191*

Gateway Press Scholarship *589*

GCA Award in Desert Studies *340*

GCA Awards for Summer Environmental Studies *340*

GCA Summer Scholarship in Field Botany *386*

GCSAA Scholars Competition *387*

GEICO Life Scholarship *564*

GE/LULAC Scholarship *181*

General Electric Women's Network Scholarship *212*

General Federation of Women's Clubs of Massachusetts Nickel for Notes Music Scholarship *620*

General Federation of Women's Clubs of Massachusetts Pennies For Art Scholarship *620*

General Fund Scholarship *885*

General Henry H. Arnold Education Grant Program *695*

General John Ratay Educational Fund Grants *946*

General Scholarship Grants *578*

General Scholarships *278*

General Study Scholarships *669*

General Undergraduate Scholarships *427*

Genevieve Saran Richmond Award *476*

George A. Hall/Harold F. Mayfield Award *118*

George & Susan Carter Scholarship *112*

George and Mary Newton Scholarship *591*

George A. Roberts Scholarship *314*

George Foreman Tribute to Lyndon B. Johnson Scholarship *223*

George Nicholson Student Paper Competition *180*

George W. Woolery Memorial Scholarship *226*

Georgia Engineering Foundation Scholarship Program *318*

Georgia Harris Memorial Scholarship *953*

Georgia HERO Scholarship *621*

Georgia Press Educational Foundation Scholarships *403*

Georgia Public Safety Memorial Grant *621*

Georgia Tuition Equalization Grant (GTEG) *621*

Gerald Boyd/Robin Stone Non-Sustaining Scholarship *405*

Gerald Drake Memorial Scholarship *690*

Geraldo Rivera Scholarship *406*

GE-Reagan Foundation Scholarship Program *959*

Gertrude Botts-Saucier Scholarship *584*

Getting Real About Distracted Driving Scholarship *930*

GGFOA Annual College Scholarship *85*

GIA Publication Pastoral Musician Scholarship *455*

Gift for Life Scholarship *585*

Gilda Murray Scholarship *967*

Gil Kushner Memorial Travel Award *963*

Gilman Scholarship *970*

Girls Impact the World Scholarship Program *930*

Girlterest Scholarship Program for Young Women *938*

Gladys C. Anderson Memorial Scholarship *451*

Glenn Jackson Scholars Scholarships *590*

Glenn Miller Instrumental Scholarship *896*

Glenn W. Oyler Memorial Technical Scholarship *924*

GLHF Individual Class Scholarship *687*

Global Study Awards *966*

Gloria Barron Prize for Young Heroes *897*

GMBS-3rd Place Instrumental Scholarship *453*

GMBS-Bill Baker/Hans Starreveld Scholarship *453*

GMBS-Ray Eberle Vocal Scholarship *453*

GM Genius *941*

GM/LULAC Scholarship *321*

GMP Memorial Scholarship Program *564*

Go Assignment Help Scholarship *938*

GoEnnounce Yourself $500 Monthly Scholarship *622*

Golden Apple Scholars of Illinois *270*

Golden Gate Restaurant Association Scholarship Foundation *246*

Golden Key Service Award *938*

Golden Key Study Abroad Scholarships *564*

Golf Course Superintendents Association of America Legacy Award *564*

GoodCall Best Decision Scholarship *939*

Good Neighbor Scholarship Program *967*

Good Samaritan Foundation Scholarship *478*

Goodshop Annual Scholarship *939*

Goodwin & Scieszka Innovation Scholarship *416*

Gordon Law Group Annual Scholarship *622*

Gordon V. R. Holness Scholarship *282*

Gourmet Foods Scholarship Award *942*

Governor Guinn Millennium Scholarship *850*

Governors' Scholarship for Foster Youth Program *818*

Governor's Scholarship Program—Need/Merit Scholarship *607*

Graduate and Professional Scholarship Program-Maryland *256*

Graduating High School Senior Scholarship *602*

Grand Plan Scholarship *937*

Grant Program for Dependents of Police, Fire, or Correctional Officers *837*

Grants for Disabled Graduate Students in the Sciences *106*

Granville P. Meade Scholarship *876*

Graphic Communications Scholarship Fund of New England *365*

Gray Community College Scholarship *953*

Greater Washington Society of CPAs Scholarship *86*

Great Expectations Award *825*

Great Falls Broadcasters Association Scholarship *544*

Great Lakes Hemophilia Foundation Education Scholarship *688*

Greenhouse Scholars *736*

Green Law Firm Nursing Home & Elderly Care Scholarship *479*

Greenpal Business Scholarship *180*

Green Pest Services Scholarship *861*

Grotto Scholarship *257*

Grungo Colarulo Giving Back to the Community Scholarship *623*

GSBA Scholarship Fund *834*

Guardian Debt Relief Scholarship *939*

Guglielmo Marconi Engineering Scholarship *680*

Guiliano Mazzetti Scholarship Award *328*

Gulf Coast Hurricane Scholarship *196*

Gus Archie Memorial Scholarships *328*

Gustavus B. Capito Fund *478*

Guy M. Wilson Scholarships *708*

Guy P. Gannett Scholarship Fund *404*

Guy Stoops Professional Horsemen's Family Scholarship *559*

Gwinnett Amateur Radio Society Scholarship *812*

Had Richards UDT-SEAL Memorial Scholarship *718*

Hagan Scholarship *623*

Hallie Q. Brown Scholarship *749*

Handicapped Student Grant-Wisconsin *694*

Hansen Scholarship *153*

Hardwick & Pendergast, P.S. Scholarship *623*

Harold and Inge Marcus Scholarship *319*

Harold Johnson Law Enforcement Scholarship *243*

Harold K. Douthit Scholarship *98*

Harold S. Wood Award for Excellence *154*

Harriet A. Simmons Scholarship *274*

Harriet Irsay Scholarship Grant *141*

Harry A. Applegate Scholarship *83*

Harry A. Hodges, W6YOO, Scholarship *812*

Harry Bartel Memorial Scholarship *670*

Harry C. Hamm Family Scholarship *224*

Harry J. Donnelly Memorial Scholarship *93*

Harry J. Morris, Jr. Emergency Services Scholarship *349*

Margaret McNamara Education Grants *945*
Marguerite Ross Barnett Memorial Scholarship *848*
Maria and Paolo Alessio Southern Italy Scholarship *680*
Maria C. Jackson/General George A. White Scholarship *859*
Maria Elena Salinas Scholarship *360*
Marie A. Calderilla Scholarship *866*
Marilyn Yetso Memorial Scholarship *678*
Marine Corps Scholarship Foundation *586*
Marine Corps Tankers Association, John Cornelius/Max English Scholarship *717*
Marion A. and Eva S. Peeples Foundation Trust Scholarship *481*
Marion A. Lindeman Scholarship *376*
Marion Barr Stanfield Art Scholarship *145*
Marion Huber Learning Through Listening Awards *568*
Mark Coats Memorial Scholarship *644*
Markley Scholarship *186*
Markowski-Leach Scholarship *898*
Mark Sherman Law Juvenile Justice Scholarship *639*
Marshall E. McCullough-National Dairy Shrine Scholarships *108*
Martha Ann Stark Memorial Scholarship *279*
Martha R. Dudley LVN/LPN Scholarship *483*
Martin D. Andrews Memorial Scholarship Fund *904*
Martin Duffy Adult Learner Scholarship Award *568*
Martin Luther King, Jr. Memorial Scholarship *269*
Marvin Mundel Memorial Scholarship *320*
Mary Duby Honderich Scholarship *859*
Mary E. Horstkotte Scholarship Fund *857*
Mary Elizabeth Guest Scholarship *526*
Mary Gunther Memorial Scholarship *330*
Maryland Association of Private Colleges and Career Schools Scholarship *642*
Maryland Boys State Scholarship *597*
Maryland SPJ Pro Chapter College Scholarship *409*
Mary Lou Brown Scholarship *812*
Mary Macey Scholarship *112*
Mary Marshall Practical Nursing Scholarship (LPN) *488*
Mary Marshall Registered Nursing Scholarships *488*
Mary McLeod Bethune Scholarship *829*
Mary McMillan Scholarship Award *267*
Mary Morrow-Edna Richards Scholarship *274*
Mary Olive Eddy Jones Art Scholarship *140*
Mary P. Oenslager Scholastic Achievement Awards *568*
Mary Quon Moy Ing Memorial Scholarship Award *217*
Mary Serra Gili Scholarship Award *476*
Mary T. Carothers Summer Environmental Studies Scholarship *340*
Mary V. Munger Memorial Scholarship *199*
Mary York Scholarship Fund *477*
Mas Family Scholarship Award *181*
Masonic Range Science Scholarship *103*
Massachusetts Assistance for Student Success Program *643*
Massachusetts Cash Grant Program *643*
Massachusetts Federation of Polish Women's Clubs Scholarships *744*

Massachusetts Gilbert Matching Student Grant Program *643*
Massachusetts Part-Time Grant Program *643*
Massachusetts Public Service Grant Program *643*
Massey & Associates: Justice For All Scholarship *643*
Master's Scholarship Program *195*
MASWE Scholarship *330*
Materials Processing and Manufacturing Division Scholarship *302*
Math and Science Scholarship *171*
Math, Engineering, Science, Business, Education, Computers Scholarships *178*
Matsuo Bridge Company Ltd. of Japan Scholarship *206*
Maureen L. and Howard N. Blitman, PE Scholarship to Promote Diversity in Engineering *194*
Maynard Jensen American Legion Memorial Scholarship *556*
Mayo Foundations Scholarship *483*
The Mayor's Chesapeake Energy Scholarship *822*
Mayors Educational Assistance Program *849*
Mays Family Scholarship Fund *768*
May T. Henry Scholarship Foundation *928*
May Trucking Company Scholarship *953*
MCCL Thought Leadership Scholarship *946*
McCurry Foundation Scholarship *845*
M.D. "Jack" Murphy Memorial Scholarship *474*
Medical Amateur Radio Council (MARCO) Scholarship *115*
Medical School Scholarship *251*
Medical Scrubs Collection Scholarship *120*
Medicus Student Exchange *763*
Medigo Scholarship Program *645*
Melissa Read Memorial Scholarship *625*
Melville H. Cohee Student Leader Conservation Scholarship *578*
Member Grants *684*
Menominee Indian Tribe Adult Vocational Training Program *747*
Menominee Indian Tribe of Wisconsin Higher Education Grants *747*
Meredith Thoms Memorial Scholarship *306*
Mesothelioma Memorial Scholarship *966*
MIA/POW Scholarship *941*
Michael Cerussi Leadership Scholarship *582*
Michael Jackson Scholarship *227*
Michael J. Morin Memorial Scholarship *582*
Michael J. Powell High School Journalist of the Year *404*
Michael Moody Fitness Scholarship *166*
Michael P. Anderson Scholarship in Space Science *507*
Michael S. Libretti Scholarship *221*
Michele L. McDonald Scholarship *83*
Michigan Competitive Scholarship *846*
Michigan Tuition Grant *846*
Mid-Atlantic Aerospace Scholarship *160*
Mid-Continent Instrument Scholarship *150*
MIE Solutions Scholarship *946*
Mike Hylton Memorial Scholarship *644*
Mike Reynolds Journalism Scholarship *223*
Mike Wallace Memorial Scholarship *220*
Mildred and Albert Panowski Playwriting Award *895*
Miles Gray Memorial Scholarship *582*
Military Award Program (MAP) *696*
Military Dependent's Scholarship Program *709*

Military Order of the Purple Heart Scholarship *712*
Military Order of the Stars and Bars Scholarships *946*
Miljenko "Mike" Grgich's American Dream Scholarship *248*
Miller Electric International World Skills Competition Scholarship *296*
Miller Electric Mfg. Co. Scholarship *297*
Millie Brother Scholarship for Children of Deaf Adults *605*
Millie Gonzalez Memorial Scholarship *644*
Millie Snyder Scholarship *833*
Milton Fisher Scholarship for Innovation and Creativity *862*
MindSumo 15-Minute Scholarship *645*
Minnesota AFL-CIO Scholarships *568*
Minnesota GI Bill Program *846*
Minnesota Indian Scholarship *748*
Minnesota Legionnaires Insurance Trust Scholarship *555*
Minnesota Masonic Charities Heritage Scholarship *947*
Minnesota Masonic Charities Legacy Scholarship *846*
Minnesota Masonic Charities Signature Scholarship *645*
Minnesota Masonic Charities Undergraduate Scholarship *646*
Minnesota Space Grant Consortium Scholarship Program *156*
Minnesota State Grant Program *847*
Minnesota State Veterans' Dependents Assistance Program *847*
Minorities in Government Finance Scholarship *86*
Minority Affairs Committee Award for Outstanding Scholastic Achievement *188*
Minority Scholarship Awards for College Students *189*
Minority Scholarship Awards for Incoming College Freshmen *189*
Minority Scholarship Program *169*
Minority Students in Veterinary Medicine Scholarship *719*
Minority Student Summer Scholarship *130*
Minority Teacher Incentive Grant Program *269*
Minority Teachers of Illinois Scholarship Program *271*
Minority Undergraduate Retention Grant-Wisconsin *771*
Mirabella Employee-YES Project Scholarship *953*
Miriam Schaefer Scholarship *439*
Miss America Community Service Scholarships *627*
Miss America Organization Competition Scholarships *899*
Miss America Scholar Award *899*
Mississippi Association of Broadcasters Scholarship *404*
Mississippi Eminent Scholars Grant *847*
Mississippi Nurses' Association Foundation Scholarship *482*
Mississippi Press Association Education Foundation Scholarship *404*
Mississippi Resident Tuition Assistance Grant *847*
Mississippi Scholarship *122*
Missouri Broadcasters Association Scholarship Program *544*

Missouri Conservation Agents Association Scholarship 848

Missouri Funeral Directors Association Scholarships 361

Missouri Higher Education Academic Scholarship (Bright Flight) 848

Missouri Insurance Education Foundation Scholarship 398

Mitchell S. Sexner & Associates LLC Scholarship 667

MJSA Education Foundation Jewelry Scholarship 144

MOAA American Patriot Scholarship 946

Money Metals Exchange Scholarship Program 669

Montana Society of Certified Public Accountants Scholarship 88

Montana Space Grant Scholarship Program 156

Montana University System Honor Scholarship 848

Monte R. Mitchell Global Scholarship 150

Montesi Scholarship 831

Montgomery GI Bill (Active Duty) Chapter 30 710

Montgomery GI Bill (Selected Reserve) 696

Moody Research Grants 114

Morris Newspaper Corporation Scholarship 621

Morrow & Sheppard College Scholarship 417

Morton B. Duggan, Jr. Memorial Education Recognition Award 371

MO Show-Me Chapter SWCS Scholarship 111

Moss Endowed Scholarship 144

MRCA Foundation Scholarship Program 135

MSCPA Firm Scholarship 84

MTS Student Scholarship 423

MTS Student Scholarship for Graduate and Undergraduate Students 424

MTS Student Scholarship for Graduating High School Seniors 321

MTS Student Scholarship for Two-Year Technical, Engineering and Community College Students 424

Muchgames.com Student Research Grant of $1500 646

MUFG Union Bank Scholarship Program 93

Muggets Scholarship 388

The Muller Firm, LTD Annual Scholarship 647

Multnomah County Deputy Sheriffs Association Dependents Scholarship 954

Music Committee Scholarship 451

MuSonics Scholarship 455

My Path, Our Future: HSE Scholars of Oregon 954

Myrtle and Earl Walker Scholarship Fund 305

NABJ Scholarship 220

NACME Scholars Program 322

NADONA Stephanie Carroll Memorial Scholarship 482

NAHN Scholarships 483

Nancy Curry Scholarship 354

Nancy Gerald Memorial Nursing Scholarship 470

Nancy Lorraine Jensen Memorial Scholarship 202

NANOG Scholarship Program 232

Naqvi Law Scholarship 242

NARBW Scholarship 947

NASA Idaho Space Grant Consortium Scholarship Program 126

NASA Maryland Space Grant Consortium Undergraduate Scholarships 156

NASA Rhode Island Space Grant Consortium Outreach Scholarship for Undergraduate Students 303

NASA Rhode Island Space Grant Consortium Undergraduate Research Scholarship 157

NASA RISGC Science En Espanol Scholarship for Undergraduate Students 157

NASA RISGC Summer Scholarship for Undergraduate Students 157

NASE Scholarships 569

Nashville Songwriting Scholarship 888

NATA Business Scholarship 158

Natalia Segermeister DREAM Act Scholarship 662

National Academy of Television Arts and Sciences Trustees Scholarship 220

National Active and Retired Federal Employee Scholarship Program 936

National Alpha Mu Gamma Scholarships 359

National Amateur Baseball Federation Scholarship Fund 905

National American Arab Nurses Association Scholarships 482

National Asphalt Pavement Association Research and Education Foundation Scholarship Program 209

National Association for Campus Activities Mid Atlantic Higher Education Research Scholarship 186

National Association for Campus Activities Mid Atlantic Undergraduate Scholarship for Student Leaders 648

National Association for Campus Activities Northern Plains Region Student Leadership Scholarship 81

National Association for Campus Activities Scholarships for Student Leaders 186

National Association for Campus Activities South Region Student Leader Scholarship 648

National Association of Black Journalists and Newhouse Foundation Scholarship 405

National Association of Black Journalists Non-Sustaining Scholarship Awards 405

National Association of Broadcasters Grants for Research in Broadcasting 221

National Association of Geoscience Teachers-Far Western Section scholarship 262

National Association of Hispanic Journalists Scholarship 221

National Association of Pastoral Musicians Members' Scholarship 455

National Association of Water Companies-New Jersey Chapter Scholarship 548

National Athletic Trainers' Association Research and Education Foundation Scholarship Program 376

National Beta Club Scholarship 570

National Black MBA Association Graduate Scholarship Program 947

National Black McDonald's Owners Association Hospitality Scholars Program 94

National Board Technical Scholarship 194

National Collegiate Cancer Foundation Scholarships 750

National Community Pharmacist Association Foundation Presidential Scholarship 500

National Competition for Composers' Recordings 891

National Costumers Association Scholarships 905

National Council of State Garden Clubs Inc. Scholarship 108

National Customs Brokers and Forwarders Association of America Scholarship Award 541

National Dairy Shrine/Dairy Marketing Inc. Milk Marketing Scholarships 108

National Dairy Shrine/Iager Dairy Scholarship 109

National Dairy Shrine/Maurice E. Core Scholarship 102

National Defense Transportation Association, Scott Air Force Base-St. Louis Area Chapter Scholarship 849

National Dental Association Foundation Colgate-Palmolive Scholarship Program (Undergraduates) 256

National Don't Text and Drive Scholarship 832

National Environmental Health Association/ American Academy of Sanitarians Scholarship 335

National Express Auto Transport Scholarship 849

National Federation of Paralegal Associates Inc. Thomson Reuters Scholarship 418

National Federation of State Poetry Societies' College Undergraduate Poetry (CUP) Competition 649

National Federation of the Blind of California Merit Scholarships 691

National Federation of the Blind of Missouri Scholarship Program for Legally Blind Students 691

National Federation of the Blind Scholarship for $3,000 690

National Federation of the Blind Scholarship for $7,000 690

National FFA Collegiate Scholarship Program 570

National Foster Parent Association Youth Scholarship 570

National Funeral Directors and Morticians Association Scholarship 361

National Garden Clubs Inc. Scholarship Program 109

National Garden Clubs Scholarship 389

National Guard Scholarship Extension Program 698

National Guard Tuition Supplement Program 699

National High School Journalist of the Year/Sister Rita Jeanne Scholarships 944

National High School Poetry Contest 641

National Honor Society Scholarship Program 570

National Institute for Labor Relations Research William B. Ruggles Journalism Scholarship 650

National Italian American Foundation Category II Scholarship 139

National Italian American Foundation Category I Scholarship 751

National JACL Headquarters Scholarship 107

National Junior Classical League Scholarship 214

National Kidney Foundation of Indiana Scholarship 691

National Latin Exam Scholarship 214

National League for Nursing Ella McKinney Scholarship 486

National Make It With Wool Competition 345

National Military Family Association's Military Spouse Scholarships 650

Sponsor

American Legion Auxiliary Department of Kentucky *700, 705, 801*

American Legion Auxiliary Department of Maine *369, 472, 706, 801*

American Legion Auxiliary Department of Massachusetts *472, 595, 706, 723, 773, 801, 881*

American Legion Auxiliary Department of Michigan *369, 472, 532, 706, 801*

American Legion Auxiliary Department of Minnesota *370, 707, 802*

American Legion Auxiliary Department of Missouri *472, 550, 707, 802*

American Legion Auxiliary Department of Nebraska *551, 707, 802*

American Legion Auxiliary Department of North Dakota *472, 596, 707, 802*

American Legion Auxiliary Department of Ohio *473, 707, 802*

American Legion Auxiliary Department of Oregon *473, 551, 802*

American Legion Auxiliary Department of Pennsylvania *473, 596, 802*

American Legion Auxiliary Department of South Dakota *551, 707, 803*

American Legion Auxiliary Department of Texas *370, 708, 803*

American Legion Auxiliary Department of Utah *552, 708, 803*

American Legion Auxiliary Department of Wisconsin *366, 370, 473, 552, 596, 708, 723, 773, 803, 882*

American Legion Auxiliary National Headquarters *553, 596, 708, 723, 773, 882*

American Legion Baseball *882*

American Legion Department of Arizona *803, 882*

American Legion Department of Arkansas *803, 882*

American Legion Department of Hawaii *803*

American Legion Department of Idaho *553, 708, 804*

American Legion Department of Illinois *553, 804, 882*

American Legion Department of Indiana *553, 804, 882*

American Legion Department of Iowa *554, 804, 882*

American Legion Department of Kansas *451, 497, 554, 805, 882*

American Legion Department of Maine *555, 708, 805*

American Legion Department of Maryland *437, 504, 555, 596, 723, 773, 805, 882*

American Legion Department of Michigan *708, 805, 883*

The American Legion, Department of Minnesota *555, 709, 806, 883*

American Legion Department of Missouri *266, 474, 555, 709, 806*

American Legion Department of Montana *806, 883*

American Legion Department of Nebraska *556, 806, 883*

American Legion Department of New York *807, 883*

American Legion Department of North Carolina *807, 883*

American Legion Department of North Dakota *254, 351, 366, 370, 499, 807, 883*

American Legion Department of Ohio *556, 709*

American Legion Department of Oregon *807, 883*

American Legion Department of Pennsylvania *535, 556, 808, 883*

American Legion Department of South Dakota *808, 883*

American Legion Department of Tennessee *519, 556, 808, 883*

American Legion Department of Texas *808, 883*

American Legion Department of Vermont *556, 597, 808, 883*

American Legion Department of Virginia *809*

American Legion Department of Washington *557, 723, 774, 809, 884*

American Legion Department of West Virginia *557, 588, 709, 723, 809, 884*

American Mathematical Association of Two Year Colleges *437*

American Meteorological Society *448*

American Montessori Society *267*

American Museum of Natural History *884*

American National Cattle Women Inc. *105*

American Nuclear Society *290, 467*

American Occupational Therapy Foundation Inc. *370, 532*

American Oil Chemists' Society *105, 190, 351*

American Optometric Foundation *493*

American Physical Therapy Association *267, 370, 532*

American Physiological Society *114, 167, 337, 370, 422, 462, 466, 527*

American Planning Association *547*

American Postal Workers Union *557, 597*

American Public Power Association *190, 204, 237, 281, 290, 294, 310, 337, 441, 457*

American Public Transportation Foundation *176, 204, 281, 294, 310, 441, 539*

American Quarter Horse Foundation (AQHF) *114, 216, 401, 501, 557, 597, 809, 884*

American Railway Engineering and Maintenance of Way Association *204, 229, 237, 281, 294, 311, 441*

American Respiratory Care Foundation *370, 532*

American Savings Foundation *597, 723, 774, 809, 884*

American-Scandinavian Foundation *421*

American School of Classical Studies at Athens *118, 128, 130, 140, 141, 214, 267, 360, 381, 392, 410, 451, 501, 518, 519, 547, 597, 724, 774, 884*

American Sephardi Foundation *774*

American Sheep Industry Association *345*

American Society for Engineering Education *121, 294, 311, 437, 504*

American Society for Enology and Viticulture *105, 191, 352, 385*

American Society for Information Science and Technology *229, 419*

American Society for Nondestructive Testing *290, 294, 311, 923*

American Society of Agricultural and Biological Engineers *105, 167, 311*

American Society of Agronomy, Crop Science Society of America, Soil Science Society of America *106, 259, 333, 337, 458, 462*

American Society of Certified Engineering Technicians *205, 237, 258, 281, 290, 294, 311, 349, 410, 425, 432, 442, 530, 535, 540*

American Society of Civil Engineers *205*

American Society of Civil Engineers-Maine Section *206*

American Society of Criminology *241, 412, 413, 522*

American Society of Heating, Refrigerating, and Air Conditioning Engineers, Inc. *130, 191, 237, 281, 290, 294, 311, 380, 442, 495, 535*

American Society of Ichthyologists and Herpetologists *167*

American Society of Interior Designers (ASID) Education Foundation Inc. *398*

American Society of Mechanical Engineers Auxiliary Inc. *311, 442, 923*

American Society of Naval Engineers *122, 151, 206, 283, 290, 312, 425, 432, 442, 469, 504*

American Society of Plumbing Engineers *312, 396*

American Society of Safety Engineers (ASSE) Foundation *597, 724, 774, 884*

American Society of Women Accountants *81*

American String Teachers Association *884*

American Traffic Safety Services Foundation *597*

American Water Resources Association *458*

American Water Ski Educational Foundation *560*

American Welding Society *176, 206, 267, 295, 312, 432, 442, 535, 924*

American Wholesale Marketers Association *177*

AMVETS Auxiliary *560, 709*

Anchor Scholarship Foundation *598, 717, 724, 774, 884*

Anderson Sobel Cosmetic Surgery *313*

Andy Green, Attorney at Law, P.C. *924*

Ankin Law *598, 724, 774, 884*

Anthony Munoz Foundation *598, 724, 774, 809, 884*

Appalachian Studies Association *924*

Appaloosa Horse Club-Appaloosa Youth Program *115, 560, 884*

ApplyKit *925*

Appraisal Institute Education Trust *516*

Arab American Scholarship Foundation *216, 509*

Archaeological Institute of America *128*

Architects Foundation *131*

Architectural Precast Association *598, 724, 774, 885*

The Arc New York *366, 371, 474, 524, 526, 532, 599, 724, 774, 810, 885*

ARC of Washington Trust Fund *599, 724, 774, 810*

Arctic Institute of North America *267, 337, 458, 462*

Arizona Business Education Association *267*

Arizona Commission for Postsecondary Education *810*

Arizona Hydrological Society *259, 394, 458, 469, 519*

Arizona Nursery Association *385*

Arizona Private School Association *810*

Arizona Professional Chapter of AISES *313, 371, 458, 504*

Arkansas Department of Higher Education *709, 810*

Arkansas Single Parent Scholarship Fund *599, 724, 774, 811, 885*

Arkansas Student Loan Authority *811*

Armed Forces Communications and Electronics Association, Educational Foundation *122, 151, 229, 283, 298, 313, 432, 437, 450, 504, 528*

Armenian Relief Society of Eastern USA Inc.-Regional Office *599, 724, 774, 885*

Armenian Students Association of America Inc. *724*

Army Officers' Wives Club of Greater Washington Area *701*

Central National Bank & Trust Company of Enid Trustee *928*

Central Scholarship *604, 728, 776, 817, 889*

CGTrader *604, 728, 776, 817, 889*

ChameleonJohn.com *928*

Charles and Lucille King Family Foundation, Inc. *218, 346, 543*

Charles E. Boyk Law Offices, LLC *604, 710, 728, 776, 890*

Charlie Wells Memorial Scholarship Fund *152*

Checks SuperStore *348*

Chegg *929*

Cherokee Nation of Oklahoma *728*

Chicago Area Business Aviation Association *152, 817*

Chicana/Latina Foundation *728, 817*

Chinese American Association of Minnesota *728, 817*

The Chopin Foundation of the United States *452*

Christiana Care Health Systems *372, 474*

Christian Community Credit Union *605, 728, 776, 890*

Christian Record Services Inc. *605, 686, 728, 776, 890*

Christophers *890*

CHS Foundation *100, 106, 385*

Church Hill Classics *605, 728, 776, 890*

Citizen Potawatomi Nation *728*

Civil Air Patrol, USAF Auxiliary *153, 562*

CLAGS: Center for LGBTQ Studies *890*

Clara Lionel Foundation *605, 729, 776, 890*

Claricode *929*

ClothingRIC.com *605, 729, 776, 890*

Club Foundation *390*

The Clunker Junker *299, 316, 396, 540*

Clutch Prep *285, 299, 316, 438, 520*

Coca-Cola Scholars Foundation Inc. *929*

CODA International *605, 729, 776, 890*

Cogburn Law Offices *606, 729, 776, 890*

COIT Services, Inc. *929*

CollegeBound Foundation *729, 817, 891*

College Insider Resources *929*

College JumpStart Scholarship Fund *929*

College Now Greater Cleveland, Inc. *606, 729, 776, 818, 891*

College Photographer of the Year *502*

College Success Foundation *818*

CollegeWeekLive *891*

College Women's Association of Japan *686, 729*

Colorado Commission on Higher Education *819*

Colorado Contractors Association Inc. *238*

Colorado Educational Services and Development Association *819*

Colorado Masons Benevolent Fund Association *606, 729, 776, 819, 891*

Colorado Restaurant Association *356*

Colorado Society of Certified Public Accountants Educational Foundation *82*

Columbus Citizens Foundation *606, 729, 777, 891*

Comcast Leaders and Achievers Scholarship Program *606*

Comedy Defensive Driving *930*

Common Knowledge Scholarship Foundation *930*

Community Bankers Association of Georgia *819*

Community Bankers Association of Illinois *562, 607, 729, 777, 819, 891*

Community Foundation of Western Massachusetts *402, 524, 547, 562, 729, 819*

CompareCards.com *930*

Concert Artists Guild *930*

Congressional Black Caucus Foundation, Inc. *132, 141, 345, 346, 364, 452, 497, 730*

Connecther *930*

Connecticut Army National Guard *702, 821*

Connecticut Association of Latinos in Higher Education (CALAHE) *730, 821*

Connecticut Association of Women Police *242, 412*

Connecticut Building Congress Scholarship Fund, Inc. *132, 208, 238, 299, 316, 411, 443*

Connecticut Chapter of Society of Professional Journalists *218, 402, 502*

Connecticut Chapter of the American Planning Association *547*

Connecticut Community Foundation *821*

Connecticut Education Foundation Inc. *269*

Connecticut Office of Higher Education *269, 607, 730, 777, 821, 891*

Connecticut Society of Certified Public Accountants *82*

Connecticut Women's Hall of Fame *821*

Conservation Federation of Missouri *339, 459, 463*

Console and Hollawell *373, 414*

Constituting America *930*

Contemporary Record Society *891*

Continental Society, Daughters of Indian Wars *242, 255, 270, 352, 367, 373, 384, 475, 489, 492, 493, 494, 500, 512, 525, 526, 533*

Corella and Bertram F. Bonner Foundation *931*

Corporation for Ohio Appalachian Development (COAD) *821*

Costa Rican Vacations *339, 390, 459, 542*

Costume Society of America *138, 140, 141, 381, 384, 451, 497*

Council of Citizens with Low Vision International c/o American Council of the Blind *607, 686, 730, 777, 891*

Couponbirds *106*

CouponChief.com *931*

CouponSurf.com *607, 730, 777, 892*

Courage Kenny Rehabilitation Institute, Vocational Services Department *608, 686, 730, 777, 821, 892*

Courage to Grow Scholarship Program *931*

Course Hero, Inc. *931*

Cozzy.org *730*

Crescent Electric Supply Company *931*

Croatian Scholarship Fund *730*

Crohn's & Colitis Foundation *373*

Crosley Law Firm *608, 731, 777, 892*

CrossLites *892*

Crush The CPA Exam *83*

CSA Fraternal Life *931*

CSA Medical Supply *608, 686, 731, 777, 892*

cuLearn, LLC *932*

The Culinary Trust *246, 352, 356*

Cultural Services of the French Embassy *113, 140, 270, 345, 360, 382, 393, 400, 421, 509, 523*

Cushman Foundation for Foraminiferal Research *170, 423*

Cynthia E. Morgan Scholarship Fund (CEMS) *334, 373, 379, 466, 475, 489, 492, 494, 500, 511, 515, 533*

Cystic Fibrosis Scholarship Foundation *686*

Daedalian Foundation *153*

The Dallas Foundation *133, 208, 316, 411, 438, 443, 505, 514, 731, 821, 892, 932*

Daniel P. Buttafuoco & Associates *777, 822*

Daniels Fund *608, 731, 777, 822, 892*

Danley's Garage Builders *609, 731, 777, 892*

Darin C. Banks Foundation *932*

Daughters of the Cincinnati *933*

The David & Dovetta Wilson Scholarship Fund *933*

David J. Crouse & Associates *822*

Davidson Institute for Talent Development *124, 316, 421, 438, 452, 501, 520*

David S. Wyman Institute of Holocaust Studies *609, 731, 777, 892*

DDSRank *255*

DECA (Distributive Education Clubs of America) *83, 178, 270, 345, 348, 357, 390, 428*

Defense Commissary Agency *710*

DefensiveDriving.com *933*

Delaware Army National Guard *697, 702*

Delaware Community Foundation *475*

Delaware Higher Education Office *316, 339, 609, 710, 823*

Delete Cyberbullying *933*

Delta Omicron Foundation, Inc. *452*

Delta Sigma Pi Leadership Foundation *178*

Demas Law Group, P.C. *609, 731, 777, 892*

DeMolay Foundation Incorporated *588, 610, 731, 778, 824, 892*

Dental Insurance Shop *933*

Denver Foundation *824*

Department of the Army *475, 610, 701, 702, 731, 778, 824, 892*

Department of Veterans Affairs (VA) *696, 697, 701, 702, 704, 710*

Dermatology Nurses' Association *475*

Deserve Modern *611, 731, 778, 892*

Design My Costume *611, 732, 778, 893*

Diamante, Inc. *612, 732, 824, 893*

DiBella Law Offices, P.C. *612, 732, 778, 893*

Digital Responsibility *933*

Digital Third Coast Internet Marketing *96, 178, 428*

Disabled American Veterans *612, 732, 778*

disABLEDperson Inc. College Scholarship *612, 687, 732, 778, 893*

Discipleship Ministries *732, 778*

Distil Networks *124, 170, 192, 208, 231, 264, 285, 291, 299, 316, 339, 348, 423, 426, 433, 438, 443, 449, 459, 463, 466, 469, 490, 500, 505, 520*

Distinguished Young Women *934*

District of Columbia Office of the State Superintendent of Education *824*

DiversityComm, Inc. *83, 125, 141, 153, 165, 231, 238, 261, 264, 285, 291, 300, 316, 339, 346, 348, 349, 352, 363, 364, 420, 421, 423, 426, 433, 438, 443, 449, 452, 463, 466, 469, 490, 505, 520, 528, 696, 698, 701, 702, 704, 710, 717, 732, 934*

Dixie Boys Baseball *825, 893*

Dollars 4 Tic Scholars *613, 732, 778, 893*

Dolphin Scholarship Foundation *613, 732, 778, 893*

Domnick Cunningham and Whalen *613, 732, 778, 893*

Donaldson Company *588, 613, 732, 778, 893*

Don't Mess With Texas *825*

DontPayFull.com *613, 733, 778, 893*

Dotcom-Monitor, Inc. *231, 285, 300, 317*

Dow Jones News Fund *402*

Drone Pilot Ground School *613, 733, 779, 893*

Dudley DeBosier Injury Lawyers *414, 825*

D.W. Simpson & Company *397*

EAA Aviation Foundation, Inc. *153, 170, 317, 505*

Eason & Tambornini, A Law Corporation *934*

East Bay College Fund *825*

Eastern Amputee Golf Association *687*

Eastern Orthodox Committee on Scouting *562, 779*

Greater Salina Community Foundation *382, 510, 514*

Greater Seattle Business Association *834, 897*

Greater Washington Society of CPAs *86*

Greater Washington Urban League *622, 835*

Great Lakes Hemophilia Foundation *687, 835*

Great Minds in STEM *115, 125, 134, 147, 154, 171, 193, 208, 231, 238, 261, 285, 291, 300, 318, 333, 335, 340, 352, 387, 395, 396, 423, 426, 433, 438, 444, 449, 459, 464, 466, 469, 479, 490, 492, 493, 494, 495, 500, 506, 529*

Green Chemistry Institute-American Chemical Society *340*

Greenhouse Scholars *736, 782, 835*

Green Law Firm *479*

Greenpal *180*

Grungo Colarulo *623, 736, 782, 897*

Guardian Debt Relief *939*

G.W. Networks Inc. *939*

Hagan Scholarship Foundation *623, 736, 835, 897*

Hanscom Federal Credit Union *623, 736, 782, 897*

HapCo Music Foundation Inc. *453*

Hardwick & Pendergast, P.S. *623, 736, 782, 897*

Harness Horse Youth Foundation *623, 897*

Harness Tracks of America *624*

Harrington Family Foundation *624, 737, 782, 835, 897*

Harry S. Truman Scholarship Foundation *510, 514*

Hartford Jazz Society Inc. *454*

Harvard Travellers Club Permanent Fund *939*

Hawaiian Lodge, F&AM *86, 119, 134, 208, 231, 255, 271, 367, 374, 379, 382, 423, 426, 438, 444, 469, 479, 489, 490, 500, 513, 520*

Hawaii Association of Broadcasters Inc. *543*

Hawaii Education Association *271, 565, 624, 737, 782, 835, 898*

Hawaii Lodging & Tourism Association *390, 542*

Hawaii Schools Federal Credit Union *624, 737, 782, 835, 898*

Hawaii Society of Certified Public Accountants *86*

Hawaii State Postsecondary Education Commission *835*

HBCUConnect.com *624, 737, 783, 898*

Healthcare Information and Management Systems Society Foundation *367, 374, 379, 520*

Healthline *940*

Health Products For You *737, 783, 898*

Health Professions Education Foundation *165, 255, 374, 479, 500, 511, 515, 525, 533*

Health Research Council of New Zealand *368, 374, 379, 480, 511*

Helen Diller Family Foundation *624, 737, 783, 898*

Hellenic Times Scholarship Fund *737*

Hellenic University Club of New York *737, 835*

Hellenic University Club of Philadelphia *134, 255, 318, 374, 565, 737, 835*

Hemophilia Federation of America *688*

Hemophilia Foundation of Southern California *142, 346, 454, 498, 625, 688, 738, 783, 835, 898*

Henkel Consumer Adhesives Inc. *625, 738, 783, 835, 898*

Herb Kohl Educational Foundation Inc. *625, 738, 783, 836, 898*

Herb Society of America, Western Reserve Unit *101, 107, 171, 341, 387, 411, 464*

Herman O. West Foundation *589*

The Higgins Firm *625, 738, 783, 898*

High Class Vape Co. *940*

High Income Parents.com *625, 738, 783, 898*

Hispanic Annual Salute *626, 738*

Hispanic Association of Colleges and Universities (HACU) *940*

Hispanic Dental Association Foundation *255*

Hispanic Heritage Foundation *738*

Hispanic Metropolitan Chamber Scholarships *626, 739, 783, 836, 898*

Hispanic Scholarship Fund *739*

The HIV League *626, 739, 783, 898*

Hofoss Devall *626, 739, 783, 836, 898*

Holstein Association USA Inc. *101, 180*

Home Improvement Solutions *626, 739, 783, 898*

Homus *627, 688, 739, 783, 898*

Honor Society of Phi Kappa Phi *565, 940*

Hoover Presidential Foundation *627,.739, 783, 836, 898*

Hopi Tribe *739*

Horatio Alger Association of Distinguished Americans *940*

Horizons Foundation *898*

Horticultural Research Institute *101, 333, 387, 411*

Hospital Central Services Inc. *627*

Hostess Committee Scholarships/Miss America Pageant *498, 627, 899*

HostGator *627, 740, 783, 899*

House of Blues Music Forward Foundation *96, 147, 180, 219, 264, 391, 393, 429, 454, 628, 740, 783, 899*

Houston Community Services *628, 740, 783, 836, 899*

Houston Symphony *454*

Houzz *134, 238, 399, 411*

How I Decide *941*

How to Win College Scholarships *628, 740, 783, 899*

HubShout *628, 740, 784, 899*

Humana Foundation *628, 740, 784, 899*

Humane Society of the United States *836*

Idaho Library Association *420*

Idaho Nursery and Landscape Association *388*

Idaho State Board of Education *628, 836*

Idaho State Broadcasters Association *180, 219, 318, 403, 429, 543*

IFDA Educational Foundation *134, 142, 396, 399, 536*

Illinois AMVETS *711, 836*

Illinois Council of the Blind *688, 837*

Illinois Counties Association *837*

Illinois CPA Society/CPA Endowment Fund of Illinois *86*

Illinois Department of Veterans' Affairs *941*

Illinois Nurses Association *480*

Illinois Pilots Association *154*

Illinois PTA *271*

Illinois Real Estate Educational Foundation *516*

Illinois Restaurant Association Educational Foundation *246, 352, 357, 391*

Illinois Society of Professional Engineers *318*

Illinois Student Assistance Commission (ISAC) *271, 526, 698, 703, 711, 837*

Illuminating Engineering Society of North America *135, 300, 318, 399, 498, 543*

Illuminating Engineering Society of North America–Golden Gate Section *135, 285, 346, 399*

Imagine America Foundation *696, 698, 701, 703, 704, 711, 717, 941*

Independent College Fund of New Jersey *480*

Independent Laboratories Institute Scholarship Alliance *171, 193, 208, 261, 285, 301, 318, 341, 349, 434, 444, 506*

Independent Office Products and Furniture Dealers Association *565*

Indiana Broadcasters Association *403, 544*

Indiana Commission for Higher Education *698, 703, 838*

Indiana Department of Veterans Affairs *696, 698, 701, 703, 711, 838*

Indiana Health Care Policy Institute *480*

Indiana Library Federation *629, 740, 784, 838, 899*

Indian American Cultural Association *740, 838*

Indiana Retired Teacher's Association (IRTA) *272*

Indiana Sheriffs' Association *242, 412*

Indiana Wildlife Federation Endowment *341, 459*

Indian Health Services, United States Department of Health and Human Services *125, 165, 171, 375, 481, 493, 500, 511, 523*

Industrial Designers Society of America *396*

Infinity Dental Web *429, 438, 523, 525, 529*

Institute for Humane Studies *219, 264, 382, 393, 416, 421, 510, 523*

Institute for Operations Research and the Management Sciences *180*

Institute of Food Technologists *107, 352, 506, 899*

Institute of Industrial Engineers *319*

Institute of Management Accountants *87, 180*

Insureon *941*

Intellectual Property Owners Education Foundation *838*

Inter-County Energy *838*

InterExchange Foundation *942*

Intermountain Medical Imaging *147, 165, 255, 368, 375, 379, 466, 489, 492, 493, 494, 511, 513, 533*

Internal Audit Foundation *87, 181*

The International Association of Assessing Officers *942*

International Association of Black Actuaries *740*

International Association of Fire Chiefs Foundation *349*

International Association of Fire Fighters *629*

International Brotherhood of Teamsters Scholarship Fund *565*

International Chemical Workers Union *566*

International College Counselors *629, 740, 784, 900*

International Communications Industries Foundation *219, 231, 286, 346*

International Dairy Deli Bakery Association *629, 740, 784, 900*

International Facility Management Association Foundation *135, 238, 301, 320, 399, 547*

International Flight Services Association *629, 740, 784, 900, 942*

International Foodservice Editorial Council *96, 102, 107, 219, 246, 353, 357, 364, 385, 391, 403, 421, 429, 502*

International Food Service Executives Association *357*

International Franchise Association Franchise Education and Research Foundation *942*

International Housewares Association *119*

International Literacy Association *421, 526*

International Order of The King's Daughters and Sons *255, 375, 481, 533, 740*

International Society for Optical Engineering-SPIE *126, 193, 286, 301, 320, 434, 444*

International Society of Automation *301*

Manufacturers Association of Maine *156, 302, 321, 396, 426, 434, 444, 536*

Margaret McNamara Education Grants *945*

Marine Corps Tankers Association Inc. *717*

Marine Technology Society *321, 423, 426, 491*

Marion D. and Eva S. Peeples Foundation Trust Scholarship Program *481*

Martin D. Andrews Scholarship *904*

Maryland Association of Certified Public Accountants Educational Foundation *87*

Maryland Association of Private Colleges and Career Schools *642, 747, 787, 904*

Maryland/Delaware/District of Columbia Press Foundation *404*

Maryland Restaurant Association Education Foundation *249, 354, 357, 391*

Maryland State Higher Education Commission *256, 272, 349, 375, 417, 481, 525, 533, 536, 642, 712, 843*

Massachusetts Association of Land Surveyors and Civil Engineers *321, 341, 531*

Massachusetts Office of Student Financial Assistance *203, 273, 642, 747, 787, 845, 904*

Massey and Associates, PC *643, 747, 787, 904*

Matrix Health Group *644, 685, 726, 775, 888*

McCurry Foundation Inc. *845, 904*

McNeely Stephenson *946*

Medical Scrubs Collection *120, 126, 129, 147, 166, 173, 193, 240, 256, 261, 334, 354, 368, 375, 379, 424, 434, 464, 466, 482, 492, 493, 495, 500, 506, 512, 513, 515, 533*

Medigo GMBH *645, 747, 787, 904*

Menominee Indian Tribe of Wisconsin *747*

Mensa Foundation *645, 747, 787, 904*

Mental Health Association in New York State Inc. *166*

MES Foundation *645, 748, 787, 845, 904*

The Miami Foundation *748, 845*

Michael Moody Fitness *166, 173, 203, 256, 273, 335, 342, 354, 357, 368, 375, 379, 393, 466, 482, 489, 492, 493, 495, 506, 512, 513, 514, 517, 521, 523, 525, 526, 527, 533*

Michigan Association of Broadcasters Foundation *544*

Michigan Association of CPAs *88*

Michigan Consumer Credit Lawyers *946*

Michigan Council of Teachers of Mathematics *439*

Michigan Department of Treasury - Student Financial Services Bureau *845*

Michigan State Horticultural Society *108*

Microsoft Corporation *231*

Midwest Roofing Contractors Association *135, 209, 238, 258, 322, 396, 434, 536*

MIE Solutions *946*

Military Officers Association of America (MOAA) Scholarship Fund *946*

Military Order of the Purple Heart *712*

Military Order of the Stars and Bars *946*

MindSumo *645, 748, 787, 904*

Minerals, Metals, and Materials Society (TMS) *302, 322, 434, 444, 521*

Ministry of Education, Culture, Sports, Science and Technology *360*

Minnesota AFL-CIO *568, 846*

Minnesota Masonic Charities *645, 748, 787, 846, 904, 947*

Minnesota Office of Higher Education *646, 748, 846*

Mississippi Association of Broadcasters *404, 544*

Mississippi Nurses' Association (MNA) *482*

Mississippi Office of Student Financial Aid *646, 847*

Mississippi Press Association Education Foundation *404*

Missouri Broadcasters Association Scholarship Program *544*

Missouri Conservation Agents Association Scholarship *848*

Missouri Department of Higher Education *848*

Missouri Funeral Directors & Embalmers Association *361*

Missouri Insurance Education Foundation *398*

Missouri Travel Council *357, 391, 542*

Mitchell Institute *646, 748, 788, 848, 904*

MLD Wealth Management Group *646, 748, 788, 904*

Modern Law *848*

Montana Broadcasters Association *544*

Montana Federation of Garden Clubs *261, 389, 411, 460*

Montana Society of Certified Public Accountants *88*

Montana University System, Office of Commissioner of Higher Education *848*

Morphisec *231*

The Morris K. Udall and Stewart L. Udall Foundation *947*

Morrow & Sheppard LLP *417*

Mount Sinai Hospital Department of Nursing *482*

Mount Vernon Urban Renewal Agency *849*

Muchgames.com *646, 748, 788, 905*

Mullen & Mullen Law Firm *947*

The Muller Firm, LTD *647, 748, 788, 905*

Mystery Weekly Magazine *748*

NAACP Legal Defense and Educational Fund Inc. *749*

NANA (Northwest Alaska Native Association) Regional Corporation *749*

Naqvi Injury Law *242, 417, 510*

NASA Florida Space Grant Consortium *156, 262, 273, 286, 322, 426, 434, 439, 444, 449, 506*

NASA Idaho Space Grant Consortium *126, 173, 193, 209, 232, 262, 286, 291, 303, 322, 342, 350, 363, 434, 439, 444, 450, 460, 464, 469, 506, 521*

NASA/Maryland Space Grant Consortium *156, 173, 193, 232, 262, 322, 342, 434, 439, 506*

NASA Minnesota Space Grant Consortium *156, 232, 262, 286, 322, 342, 439, 444, 450, 464, 469, 491, 506*

NASA Montana Space Grant Consortium *156, 173, 194, 209, 232, 286, 322, 439, 444*

NASA Rhode Island Space Grant Consortium *157, 273, 303, 322, 439, 450, 521*

NASA's Virginia Space Grant Consortium *126, 157, 173, 194, 232, 239, 258, 286, 303, 322, 342, 396, 434, 439, 445, 506, 521*

NASA Wisconsin Space Grant Consortium *157*

National Academy of Television Arts and Sciences *142, 220, 346, 404, 454, 498, 502, 515, 545*

National Academy of Television Arts and Sciences, Michigan Chapter *97, 220, 346, 405, 498, 545*

National Academy of Television Arts and Sciences-National Capital/Chesapeake Bay Chapter *405, 545*

National Academy of Television Arts & Sciences—Ohio Valley Chapter *220, 346, 404, 544*

National Action Council for Minorities in Engineering-NACME Inc. *322*

National AIDS Memorial *647, 749, 788, 905*

National Air Transportation Foundation *157*

National Alliance of Postal and Federal Employees (NAPFE) *568*

National Amateur Baseball Federation (NABF) *905*

National AMBUCS Inc. *148, 533*

National American Arab Nurses Association *482*

National Asphalt Pavement Association Research and Education Foundation *209, 239*

National Association Directors of Nursing Administration *482*

National Association for Campus Activities *81, 186, 273, 647, 749, 788, 905*

National Association for the Advancement of Colored People *194, 303, 323, 506, 569, 749*

National Association for the Self-Employed *569, 905*

National Association of Black Journalists *220, 405, 502, 545*

National Association of Broadcasters *221, 405, 545*

National Association of Colored Women's Clubs *749*

National Association of Energy Service Companies *569*

National Association of Geoscience Teachers & Far Western Section *262*

National Association of Hispanic Journalists (NAHJ) *221, 360, 364, 406, 502, 545*

National Association of Hispanic Nurses *483*

National Association of Letter Carriers *569*

National Association of Negro Business and Professional Women's Clubs Inc. *264, 406, 749*

National Association of Pastoral Musicians *455, 518*

National Association of Railway Business Women *947*

National Association of Secondary School Principals *570*

National Association of Water Companies-New Jersey Chapter *548*

National Association of Women in Construction *135, 210, 258, 286, 303, 323, 399, 411, 445, 536*

National Athletic Trainers' Association Research and Education Foundation *376, 379, 528, 534*

National Beta Club *570*

National Black MBA Association *947*

National Black Nurses Association Inc. *483*

National Black Police Association *243, 413, 417, 523, 525*

National Board of Boiler and Pressure Vessel Inspectors *194, 286, 445*

National Business Aviation Association Inc. *158*

National Cattlemen's Foundation *102, 108, 221*

National Center for Learning Disabilities, Inc. *689*

National Center for Policy Analysis *947*

National Collegiate Cancer Foundation *750, 788, 905*

National Community Pharmacist Association (NCPA) Foundation *500*

National Construction Education Foundation *239*

National Costumers Association Scholarships *905*

National Council of Jewish Women Los Angeles (NCJW l LA) *273, 484, 648, 750, 788, 849, 905*

National Council of Jewish Women New York Section *689*

National Council of State Garden Clubs Inc. Scholarship *108, 173, 342, 389*

Academic Fields/Career Goals

Child and Family Studies

Civil Engineering

Classics

Communications

National Restaurant Association Educational Foundation Undergraduate Scholarships for College Students *109*
Oregon Wine Brotherhood Scholarship *249*
Peter Kump Memorial Scholarship *248*
Rama Scholarship for the American Dream *245*
Robert Mondavi Winery Memorial Scholarship *248*
Robert W. Hiller Scholarship Fund *250*
South Carolina Tourism and Hospitality Educational Foundation Scholarships *250*
Steven Scher Memorial Scholarship for Aspiring Restauranteurs *248*
StraightForward Media Vocational-Technical School Scholarship *118*
Support Creativity Scholarship *137*
Taste America Scholarships *248*
Technical Training Fund Scholarship *143*
UNCF/Carnival Corporate Scholars Program *184*
WBA Scholarship *250*
W. Price, Jr. Memorial Scholarship *250*

Dental Health/Services
Aboriginal Health Careers Bursary *167*
ADEA/Sigma Phi Alpha Linda DeVore Scholarship *252*
Al & Williamary Viste Scholarship *114*
Allied Healthcare Scholarship Program *165*
American Dental Association Foundation Dental Hygiene Scholarship Program *252*
American Dental Association Foundation Dental Student Scholarship Program *252*
American Legion Auxiliary Department of Colorado Past Presidents' Parley Health Care Professional ScholarshipNurses Scholarship *147*
Annual Healthcare and Life Sciences Scholarship *170*
A.T. Anderson Memorial Scholarship Program *121*
AvaCare Medical Scholarship *115*
BHW Women in STEM Scholarship *124*
Carol Bauhs Benson Scholarship *252*
Carole J. Streeter, KB9JBR, Scholarship *254*
Charles R. Morris Student Research Award *251*
Clark-Phelps Scholarship *256*
Colgate "Bright Smiles, Bright Futures" Minority Scholarship *252*
Continental Society, Daughters of Indian Wars Scholarship *242*
Crest Oral-B Laboratories Dental Hygiene Scholarship *252*
DDSRank Dental Scholarship *255*
Developmental Disabilities Scholastic Achievement Scholarship for College Students who are Lutheran *254*
Dr. Juan D. Villarreal/Hispanic Dental Association Foundation *255*
Elizabeth and Sherman Asche Memorial Scholarship Fund *106*
Graduate and Professional Scholarship Program-Maryland *256*
Grotto Scholarship *257*
Hawaiian Lodge Scholarships *86*
Health Careers Scholarship *255*
Hu-Friedy/Esther Wilkins Instrument Scholarship *253*
Intermountain Medical Imaging Scholarship *147*
Jason Lang Scholarship *251*
Johnson & Johnson Scholarship *253*
Karla Girts Memorial Community Outreach Scholarship *253*
LabRoots STEM Scholarship *116*
Medical Amateur Radio Council (MARCO) Scholarship *115*

Medical School Scholarship *251*
Medical Scrubs Collection Scholarship *120*
Michael Moody Fitness Scholarship *166*
National Dental Association Foundation Colgate-Palmolive Scholarship Program (Undergraduates) *256*
Nicholas S. Hetos, DDS Memorial Graduate Scholarship *255*
Northern Alberta Development Council Bursary *251*
O. Nesheim Memorial Scholarship *254*
Platinum Educational Group Scholarships Program for EMS, Nursing, and Allied Health *117*
Proctor and Gamble Oral Care and HDA Foundation Scholarship *255*
Prosper Shaked Scholarship for Future Medical Professionals *166*
Recovery Village Healthcare Scholarship *256*
Scholarship for Students Pursuing a Business or STEM Degree *91*
Science Ambassador Scholarship *124*
Sigma Phi Alpha Undergraduate Scholarship *253*
Stanley Dentistry Scholarship Fund *257*
StraightForward Media Medical Professions Scholarship *257*
StraightForward Media Vocational-Technical School Scholarship *118*
U. S. Public Health Service-Health Resources and Services Administration, Bureau of Health Professions Scholarships for Disadvantaged Students *257*
Wilma E. Motley Scholarship *253*

Drafting
Community College STEM Scholarships *126*
Kurt H. and Donna M. Schuler Small Grant *205*
MRCA Foundation Scholarship Program *135*
NAWIC Undergraduate Scholarships *135*
OLM Malala Yousafzai Scholarship *143*
Support Creativity Scholarship *137*
Ted G. Wilson Memorial Scholarship Foundation *211*
Vectorworks Design Scholarship *137*

Earth Science
$1,500 STEM Scholarship *120*
AEG Foundation Marliave Fund *258*
Alaska Geological Society Scholarship *259*
American Ground Water Trust-AMTROL Inc. Scholarship *259*
American Ground Water Trust-Baroid Scholarship *259*
American Ground Water Trust-Thomas Stetson Scholarship *259*
Andy Aitkenhead Scholarship *127*
Arizona Hydrological Society Scholarship *259*
Association of State Dam Safety Officials (ASDSO) Senior Undergraduate Scholarship *168*
Astronaut Scholarship Foundation *123*
A.T. Anderson Memorial Scholarship Program *121*
AWG Ethnic Minority Scholarship *260*
AWG Maria Luisa Crawford Field Camp Scholarship *129*
AWG Salt Lake Chapter (SLC) Research Scholarship *129*
AWG Undergraduate Excellence in Paleontology Award *123*
Barry M. Goldwater Scholarship and Excellence in Education Program *123*
BHW Women in STEM Scholarship *124*
B.O.G. Pest Control Scholarship Fund *169*
Carrol C. Hall Memorial Scholarship *128*
Diversity in STEAM Magazine Scholarship *83*
Donald A. Williams Scholarship Soil Conservation Scholarship *103*

Eckenfelder Scholarship *169*
Edward R. Hall Scholarship *103*
Elizabeth and Sherman Asche Memorial Scholarship Fund *106*
Elizabeth Gardner Norweb Summer Environmental Studies Scholarship *107*
Emily M. Hewitt Memorial Scholarship *170*
Environmental Protection Scholarship *172*
Eric D. Dunning Scholarship *235*
Florida Space Research Program *156*
HENAAC Scholarship Program *115*
Independent Laboratories Institute Scholarship Alliance *171*
Janet Cullen Tanaka Geosciences Undergraduate Scholarship *129*
J. Fielding Reed Scholarship *106*
LabRoots STEM Scholarship *116*
Life Member Montana Federation of Garden Clubs Scholarship *261*
Lone Star Rising Career Scholarship *260*
Louise Torraco Memorial Scholarship for Science *174*
Medical Scrubs Collection Scholarship *120*
Minnesota Space Grant Consortium Scholarship Program *156*
Minority Scholarship Program *169*
MO Show-Me Chapter SWCS Scholarship *111*
NASA Idaho Space Grant Consortium Scholarship Program *126*
NASA Maryland Space Grant Consortium Undergraduate Scholarships *156*
National Association of Geoscience Teachers-Far Western Section scholarship *262*
National Garden Clubs Inc. Scholarship Program *109*
National Space Grant Consortium Scholarships *127*
NGWA Foundation's Len Assante Scholarship *262*
Old Man International Sideband Society (OMISS) Scholarship *259*
Osage Chapter Undergraduate Service Scholarship *129*
Rocky Mountain Coal Mining Institute Scholarship *211*
Rogers Family Scholarship *172*
Russell W. Myers Scholarship *172*
Scholarship for Students Pursuing a Business or STEM Degree *91*
Science Ambassador Scholarship *124*
Sehar Saleha Ahmad and Abrahim Ekramullah Zafar Foundation Scholarship *127*
Sigma Xi Grants-In-Aid of Research *110*
Straight North STEM Scholarship *92*
Susan Ekdale Memorial Field Camp Scholarship *260*
Tilford Field Studies Scholarship *258*
Universities Space Research Association Scholarship Award Program *128*
Vermont Space Grant Consortium *104*
Women in Technology Scholarship (WITS) *236*

Economics
280 Group Product Management Scholarship *263*
Actuary of Tomorrow—Stuart A. Robertson Memorial Scholarship *175*
Automotive Women's Alliance Foundation Scholarships *81*
Curtis E. Huntington Memorial Scholarship (Formerly The John Culver Wooddy Scholarship) *263*
Discover Financial Services Scholarship *93*
Diversity in STEAM Magazine Scholarship *83*
Fukunaga Scholarship Foundation *85*
Humane Studies Fellowships *219*

Energy and Power Engineering

Engineering-Related Technologies

Entomology

Hydrology

American Ground Water Trust-AMTROL Inc. Scholarship *259*

American Ground Water Trust-Baroid Scholarship *259*

American Ground Water Trust-Thomas Stetson Scholarship *259*

Arizona Hydrological Society Scholarship *259*

Association of California Water Agencies Scholarships *123*

A.T. Anderson Memorial Scholarship Program *121*

AWG Ethnic Minority Scholarship *260*

AWG Maria Luisa Crawford Field Camp Scholarship *129*

AWG Salt Lake Chapter (SLC) Research Scholarship *129*

Barry M. Goldwater Scholarship and Excellence in Education Program *123*

BHW Women in STEM Scholarship *124*

California Groundwater Association Scholarship *395*

Clair A. Hill Scholarship *123*

Donald A. Williams Scholarship Soil Conservation Scholarship *103*

Eckenfelder Scholarship *169*

Environmental Protection Scholarship *172*

HENAAC Scholarship Program *115*

Janet Cullen Tanaka Geosciences Undergraduate Scholarship *129*

Lone Star Rising Career Scholarship *260*

Minority Scholarship Program *169*

MO Show-Me Chapter SWCS Scholarship *111*

NGWA Foundation's Len Assante Scholarship *262*

Osage Chapter Undergraduate Service Scholarship *129*

Rogers Family Scholarship *172*

Russell W. Myers Scholarship *172*

Sigma Xi Grants-In-Aid of Research *110*

Society of Women Engineers-Rocky Mountain Section Scholarship Program *161*

Straight North STEM Scholarship *92*

Susan Ekdale Memorial Field Camp Scholarship *260*

Industrial Design

Alfred Steele Engineering Scholarship *312*

Association for Iron and Steel Technology Willy Korf Memorial Scholarship *187*

Automotive Women's Alliance Foundation Scholarships *81*

BHW Women in STEM Scholarship *124*

Center for Architecture Design Scholarship *132*

Chapter 198-Downriver Detroit Scholarship *325*

Chapter 67-Phoenix Scholarship *326*

Clunker Junker Cash for Cars and College Scholarship *299*

College and Trade/Technical School Scholarships *154*

Community College STEM Scholarships *126*

Fleming/Blaszcak Scholarship *195*

Fort Wayne Chapter 56 Scholarship *328*

Gulf Coast Hurricane Scholarship *196*

HENAAC Scholarship Program *115*

Industrial Designers Society of America Undergraduate Scholarship *396*

James J. Burns and C. A. Haynes Scholarship *396*

Maine Manufacturing Career and Training Foundation Scholarship *156*

MRCA Foundation Scholarship Program *135*

North Central Region 9 Scholarship *328*

OLM Malala Yousafzai Scholarship *143*

Ruth Clark Furniture Design Scholarship *142*

Safety and Health National Student Design Competition Award for Safety *190*

Simple Solutions Design Competition *305*

Society of Plastics Engineers Scholarship Program *196*

Support Creativity Scholarship *137*

TiMOTION Engineering and Excellence Scholarship *213*

Vectorworks Design Scholarship *137*

Wichita Chapter 52 Scholarship *328*

Insurance and Actuarial Science

Actuarial Diversity Scholarship *397*

Actuary of Tomorrow—Stuart A. Robertson Memorial Scholarship *175*

BHW Women in STEM Scholarship *124*

Curtis E. Huntington Memorial Scholarship (Formerly The John Culver Wooddy Scholarship) *263*

D.W. Simpson Actuarial Science Scholarship *397*

Missouri Insurance Education Foundation Scholarship *398*

New England Employee Benefits Council Scholarship Program *89*

Scholarship for Students Pursuing a Business or STEM Degree *91*

Science Ambassador Scholarship *124*

Spencer Educational Foundation Scholarship *398*

Straight North STEM Scholarship *92*

UNCF/Travelers Insurance Scholarship *185*

Voya Scholars *94*

Interior Design

Alan Lucas Memorial Educational Scholarship *135*

ASID Foundation Legacy Scholarship for Undergraduates *398*

Association for Women in Architecture Foundation Scholarship *131*

Center for Architecture Design Scholarship *132*

Home Builders Foundation Jim Irvine Statewide Scholarship *136*

IFDA Leaders Commemorative Scholarship *399*

IFDA Student Member Scholarship *399*

IFMA Foundation Scholarships *135*

NAWIC Undergraduate Scholarships *135*

OLM Malala Yousafzai Scholarship *143*

Part Time Student Scholarship *399*

Plan New Hampshire Scholarship and Fellowship Program *129*

QualityBath.com Scholarship Program *140*

Residential Design Scholarship *134*

Robert W. Thunen Memorial Scholarships *135*

Ruth Clark Furniture Design Scholarship *142*

Support Creativity Scholarship *137*

Sustainable Residential Design Scholarship *134*

Tricia Levangie Green/Sustainable Scholarship *134*

Vectorworks Design Scholarship *137*

YouthForce 2020 Scholarship Program *137*

International Migration

United Nations Association of Connecticut Scholarship *147*

International Studies

AFIO Undergraduate and Graduate Scholarships *113*

Automotive Women's Alliance Foundation Scholarships *81*

Don Riebhoff Memorial Scholarship *400*

ISF National Scholarship *119*

Mas Family Scholarship Award *181*

Moody Research Grants *114*

National Security Education Program (NSEP) David L. Boren Undergraduate Scholarships *139*

Phi Alpha Theta World History Association Paper Prize *383*

Teaching Assistant Program in France *113*

United Nations Association of Connecticut Scholarship *147*

WIIT Charitable Trust Scholarship Program *401*

Journalism

Allison Fisher Scholarship *405*

Al Neuharth Free Spirit and Journalism Conference Program *402*

Alpha Omega Scholarship In Memory Of Peter Agris *215*

AQHF Journalism or Communications Scholarship *216*

Associated Press Television/Radio Association-Clete Roberts Journalism Scholarship Awards *401*

Bernard Kilgore Memorial Scholarship for the NJ High School Journalist of the Year *407*

Betty Endicott/NTA-NCCB Student Scholarship *405*

Bill Farr Scholarship *409*

BMI Founders Award for Radio Broadcasting *218*

Career Journalism Scholarship *225*

Carl Greenberg Scholarship *409*

Carole Simpson Scholarship *222*

CCNMA Scholarships *218*

CIC/Anna Chennault Scholarship *217*

Connecticut SPJ Bob Eddy Scholarship Program *218*

David J. Clarke Memorial Scholarship *220*

Diverse Voices in Storytelling Scholarship *227*

Dr. Lynne Boyle/John Schimpf Undergraduate Scholarship *97*

Douglas W. Mummert Scholarship *142*

Dow Jones News Fund High School Journalism Workshops Writing, Photography and Multimedia Competition *402*

Durwood McAlister Scholarship *403*

Ed Bradley Scholarship *223*

Edward J. Nell Memorial Scholarship in Journalism *408*

George Foreman Tribute to Lyndon B. Johnson Scholarship *223*

Georgia Press Educational Foundation Scholarships *403*

Gerald Boyd/Robin Stone Non-Sustaining Scholarship *405*

Geraldo Rivera Scholarship *406*

Guy P. Gannett Scholarship Fund *404*

Harold K. Douthit Scholarship *98*

Harriet Irsay Scholarship Grant *141*

Harry C. Hamm Family Scholarship *224*

Helen Johnson Scholarship *409*

Indiana Broadcasters Foundation Scholarship *403*

International Foodservice Editorial Council Communications Scholarship *96*

ISF National Scholarship *119*

Jack Shaheen Mass Communications Scholarship Award *215*

Jackson Foundation Journalism Scholarship *407*

Jackson Foundation Journalism Scholarship Fund *407*

Jake McClain Driver, KC5WXA, Scholarship *229*

Jim McKay Memorial Scholarship *220*

Julianne Malveaux Scholarship *264*

Kathryn Dettman Memorial Journalism Scholarship *402*

Ken Inouye Scholarship *409*

La-Philosophie.com Scholarship *119*
Lee Thornton Scholarship *223*
Leonard M. Perryman Communications Scholarship for Ethnic Minority Students *227*
Lou and Carole Prato Sports Reporting Scholarship *223*
Maria Elena Salinas Scholarship *360*
Marshall E. McCullough-National Dairy Shrine Scholarships *108*
Maryland SPJ Pro Chapter College Scholarship *409*
Mary Quon Moy Ing Memorial Scholarship Award *217*
Mas Family Scholarship Award *181*
Michael J. Powell High School Journalist of the Year *404*
Michael S. Libretti Scholarship *221*
Mike Reynolds Journalism Scholarship *223*
Mike Wallace Memorial Scholarship *220*
Mississippi Association of Broadcasters Scholarship *404*
Mississippi Press Association Education Foundation Scholarship *404*
NABJ Scholarship *220*
National Academy of Television Arts and Sciences Trustees Scholarship *220*
National Association of Black Journalists and Newhouse Foundation Scholarship *405*
National Association of Black Journalists Non-Sustaining Scholarship Awards *405*
National Association of Broadcasters Grants for Research in Broadcasting *221*
National Association of Hispanic Journalists Scholarship *221*
National JACL Headquarters Scholarship *107*
National Press Club Scholarship for Journalism Diversity *406*
National Writers Association Foundation Scholarships *406*
Native American Journalists Association Scholarships *97*
Nebraska Press Association Foundation Scholarship *97*
Newhouse Scholarship Program *364*
Northwest Journalists of Color Scholarship *96*
NSPA Journalism Honor Roll Scholarship *406*
OAB Foundation Scholarship *221*
Ohio News Media Foundation Minority Scholarship *98*
Ohio News Media Foundation University Journalism Scholarship *98*
ONWA Annual Scholarship *98*
Outdoor Writers Association of America - Bodie McDowell Scholarship Award *222*
Overseas Press Club Foundation Scholar Awards *407*
Palm Beach Association of Black Journalists Scholarship *408*
PHD Scholarship *230*
Philadelphia Association of Black Journalists Scholarship *408*
Printing Industry Midwest Education Foundation Scholarship Fund *222*
Randy Falco Scholarship *220*
Robin Roberts/WBCA Sports Communications Scholarship Award *228*
SAJA Journalism Scholarship *410*
Seattle Professional Chapter Of The Association For Women In Communications *402*
Sigma Delta Chi Scholarships *409*
StraightForward Media Media & Communications Scholarship *99*
Tampa Bay Times Fund Career Journalism Scholarships *99*
Texas Gridiron Club Scholarships *226*

Valley Press Club Scholarships, The Republican Scholarship, Channel 22 Scholarship *228*
Vincent Chin Memorial Scholarship *217*
Washington Post Young Journalists Scholarship *406*
Wayne C. Cornils Memorial Scholarship *180*
William C. Rogers Scholarship *403*
William J. (Bill) and Loretta M. O'Neil Scholarship *402*

Landscape Architecture

ASCSA Summer Session and Summer Seminars Scholarships *118*
Association for Women in Architecture Foundation Scholarship *131*
BHW Women in STEM Scholarship *124*
B. Phinizy Spalding, Hubert B. Owens, and The National Society of the Colonial Dames of America in the State of Georgia Academic Scholarships *113*
Bryan A. Champion Memorial Scholarship *101*
Carville M. Akehurst Memorial Scholarship *333*
CBC Scholarship Fund *132*
Center for Architecture Design Scholarship *132*
Center for Architecture, Douglas Haskell Award for Student Journals *132*
Federated Garden Clubs of Connecticut Inc. Scholarships *170*
GCA Award in Desert Studies *340*
Home Builders Foundation Jim Irvine Statewide Scholarship *136*
Horticulture Scholarship from Francis Sylvia Zverina *101*
Horticulture Scholarship of the Western Reserve Herb Society *101*
J. Neel Reid Prize *133*
Katharine M. Grosscup Scholarships in Horticulture *386*
Kurt H. and Donna M. Schuler Small Grant *205*
Life Member Montana Federation of Garden Clubs Scholarship *261*
Muggets Scholarship *388*
National Garden Clubs Inc. Scholarship Program *109*
NAWIC Undergraduate Scholarships *135*
Plan New Hampshire Scholarship and Fellowship Program *129*
QualityBath.com Scholarship Program *140*
Residential Design Scholarship *134*
Robert Lewis Baker Scholarship *386*
Russell W. Myers Scholarship *172*
Spring Meadow Nursery Scholarship *388*
Support Creativity Scholarship *137*
Sustainable Residential Design Scholarship *134*
Ted G. Wilson Memorial Scholarship Foundation *211*
Timothy and Palmer W. Bigelow Jr., Scholarship *101*
Usrey Family Scholarship *333*
Vectorworks Design Scholarship *137*
The Walter J. Travis Memorial Scholarship and The Walter J. Travis-Rudy Zocchi Memorial Scholarship *137*
Whitley Place Scholarship *133*
YouthForce 2020 Scholarship Program *137*

Law Enforcement/Police Administration

AFIO Undergraduate and Graduate Scholarships *113*
Alphonso Deal Scholarship Award *243*
American Society of Criminology Gene Carte Student Paper Competition *241*
Captain James J. Regan Scholarship *412*
Connecticut Association of Women Police Scholarship *242*

Indiana Sheriffs' Association Scholarship Program *242*
ISF National Scholarship *119*
LivSecure Student Scholarship *242*
North Carolina Sheriffs' Association Undergraduate Criminal Justice Scholarships *243*
Oregon Association of Certified Fraud Examiners Scholarship *90*
Sheryl A. Horak Memorial Scholarship *413*
WIFLE Scholarship *244*

Law/Legal Services

Alphonso Deal Scholarship Award *243*
American Society of Criminology Gene Carte Student Paper Competition *241*
Attorney Raymond Lahoud Scholar Program *413*
Automotive Women's Alliance Foundation Scholarships *81*
Benson & Bingham Annual Scholarship *413*
Bernice Pickins Parsons Fund *416*
BESLA Scholarship Legal Writing Competition *414*
Cantor Crane Personal Injury Lawyer $1,000 Scholarship *241*
Council on Approved Student Education's Scholarship Fund *417*
Dudley DeBosier Law School Scholarship *414*
Frank Sarli Memorial Scholarship *417*
Goodwin & Scieszka Innovation Scholarship *416*
Graduate and Professional Scholarship Program-Maryland *256*
Harry J. Donnelly Memorial Scholarship *93*
Humane Studies Fellowships *219*
ISF National Scholarship *119*
Janet L. Hoffmann Loan Assistance Repayment Program *272*
Jason Lang Scholarship *251*
Law Enforcement Family Member Scholarship *415*
Law in Society Award Competition *418*
Law School Scholarship *415*
Law Student Scholarship *415, 416*
Legal College Scholarship Program *414*
LivSecure Student Scholarship *242*
Louthian Law Legal Scholarship *416*
Morrow & Sheppard College Scholarship *417*
Naqvi Law Scholarship *242*
National Federation of Paralegal Associates Inc. Thomson Reuters Scholarship *418*
National JACL Headquarters Scholarship *107*
New England Employee Benefits Council Scholarship Program *89*
Oregon Association of Certified Fraud Examiners Scholarship *90*
Overdose Attorney Scholarship *373*
Robinson & Henry Family Law Scholarship *418*
Robinson & Henry Injury Scholarship *418*
Spence Reese Scholarship *316*
SSPI International Scholarships *160*
Stanfield and D'Orlando Art Scholarship *146*
Student Member Tuition Grant *417*
SUEZ Corporate Scholars Program *94*
Warner Norcross and Judd LLP Scholarship for Students of Color *415*
Washington State Association for Justice American Justice Essay & Video Scholarship *244*
Washington State Association for Justice Past Presidents' Scholarship *419*
WIFLE Scholarship *244*
Williams Law Group Opportunity to Grow Scholarship *139*

TMS/International Symposium on Superalloys
Scholarship Program *302*
TMS/Light Metals Division Scholarship
Program *302*
TMS Outstanding Student Paper Contest–
Undergraduate *303*
TMS/Structural Materials Division
Scholarship *303*
UNCF STEM Scholars Program *175*
Undergraduate STEM Research
Scholarships *127*
Vermont Space Grant Consortium *104*
Victor Technologies Cutting and Welding
Scholarship *297*
W1FDR Scholarship *122*
Wanda Munn Scholarship *201*
William A. and Ann M. Brothers
Scholarship *297*
William A. Rice Family, Women in Welding
Scholarship *298*
William B. Howell Memorial Scholarship *298*
William P. Woodside Founder's Scholarship *314*
Women Forward in Technology Scholarship
Program *124*
Yanmar/SAE Scholarship *305*
YouthForce 2020 Scholarship Program *137*

Mathematics

$1,500 STEM Scholarship *120*
Actuarial Diversity Scholarship *397*
Actuary of Tomorrow—Stuart A. Robertson
Memorial Scholarship *175*
AFCEA STEM Majors Scholarships for
Undergraduate Students *122*
Al & Williamary Viste Scholarship *114*
Alice T. Schafer Mathematics Prize for Excellence
in Mathematics by an Undergraduate
Woman *437*
American Legion Department of Maryland Math-
Science Scholarship *437*
Andy Aitkenhead Scholarship *127*
Armed Forces Communications and Electronics
Association ROTC Scholarship Program *151*
Arne Engebretsen Wisconsin Mathematics Council
Scholarship *279*
A.T. Anderson Memorial Scholarship
Program *121*
Automotive Women's Alliance Foundation
Scholarships *81*
Barry M. Goldwater Scholarship and Excellence in
Education Program *123*
BASF/Alfred Chisholm Endowed Memorial
Scholarship *93*
BHW Women in STEM Scholarship *124*
California Mathematics Council-South Secondary
Education Scholarships *438*
Charles Miller Scholarship *437*
Clutch Prep STEM Scholarship *285*
Community College STEM Scholarships *126*
CTRI/Chris Seeber, KA1GEU, Memorial
Scholarship *268*
Curtis E. Huntington Memorial Scholarship
(Formerly The John Culver Wooddy
Scholarship) *263*
Dan Huettl, WZ7U, Memorial Scholarship *298*
Davidson Fellows Scholarship Program *124*
Davis Scholarship for Women in STEM *202*
Diversity in STEAM Magazine Scholarship *83*
Eric D. Dunning Scholarship *235*
Ethel A. Neijahr Wisconsin Mathematics Council
Scholarship *279*
Florida Space Research Program *156*
Francis J. Flynn Memorial Scholarship *277*
Galactic Unite Bytheway Scholarship *202*
Grants for Disabled Graduate Students in the
Sciences *106*

Hawaiian Lodge Scholarships *86*
HENAAC Scholarship Program *115*
Internet Marketing Scholarship *429*
Kia Motors America STEM/Sustainability
Scholarship *175*
LabRoots STEM Scholarship *116*
Lois Manley, K7LMZ, and Randall Pitchford,
WW7ZZ, Scholarship *206*
Math and Science Scholarship *171*
Minnesota Space Grant Consortium Scholarship
Program *156*
Miriam Schaefer Scholarship *439*
Montana Space Grant Scholarship Program *156*
NASA Idaho Space Grant Consortium Scholarship
Program *126*
NASA Maryland Space Grant Consortium
Undergraduate Scholarships *156*
NASA Rhode Island Space Grant Consortium
Outreach Scholarship for Undergraduate
Students *303*
NASA RISGC Science En Espanol Scholarship for
Undergraduate Students *157*
National Space Grant Consortium
Scholarships *127*
Navajo Generating Station Navajo
Scholarship *324*
Old Man International Sideband Society (OMISS)
Scholarship *259*
Oracle Community Impact Scholarship *235*
Oracle Corporate Scholars Program *184*
Procter & Gamble STEM Scholarship *128*
Prospective Secondary Teacher Course Work
Scholarships *273*
Samsung@First Scholars *233*
Scholarship for Students Pursuing a Business or
STEM Degree *91*
Science Ambassador Scholarship *124*
Science, Mathematics, and Research for
Transformation Defense Scholarship for
Service Program *121*
Sigma Xi Grants-In-Aid of Research *110*
Sister Mary Petronia Van Straten Wisconsin
Mathematics Council Scholarship *279*
Straight North STEM Scholarship *92*
UNCF STEM Scholars Program *175*
Undergraduate STEM Research
Scholarships *127*
Universities Space Research Association
Scholarship Award Program *128*
Vermont Space Grant Consortium *104*
Voya Scholars *94*
W1FDR Scholarship *122*
Whitley Place Scholarship *133*
WIA Foundation Scholarship *162*
William Faulkner-William Wisdom Creative
Writing Competition *440*
Women Forward in Technology Scholarship
Program *124*

Mechanical Engineering

$1,500 STEM Scholarship *120*
AACE International Competitive
Scholarship *130*
Ada I. Pressman Memorial Scholarship *196*
Agnes Malakate Kezios Scholarship *442*
AIAA Foundation Undergraduate
Scholarships *121*
AISI/AIST Foundation Premier Scholarship *280*
AIST William E. Schwabe Memorial
Scholarship *280*
Al-Ben Scholarship for Academic Incentive *193*
Al-Ben Scholarship for Professional Merit *193*
Al-Ben Scholarship for Scholastic
Achievement *193*
Alfred E. Friend Jr., W4CF, Memorial
Scholarship *191*

Allen J. Baldwin Scholarship *442*
Alwin B. Newton Scholarship *281*
American Chemical Society, Rubber Division
Undergraduate Scholarship *120*
American Council of Engineering Companies of
Oregon Scholarship *210*
American Society of Naval Engineers
Scholarship *122*
American Transmission Co. Scholarship *196*
Anne Maureen Whitney Barrow Memorial
Scholarship *196*
Anne Shen Smith Endowed Scholarship *196*
AREMA Graduate and Undergraduate
Scholarships *204*
ASHRAE Region III Boggarm Setty
Scholarship *191*
Association for Iron and Steel Technology
Benjamin F. Fairless Scholarship
(AIME) *186*
Association for Iron and Steel Technology Ronald
E. Lincoln Scholarship *280*
Association for Iron and Steel Technology Willy
Korf Memorial Scholarship *187*
Association of State Dam Safety Officials
(ASDSO) Senior Undergraduate
Scholarship *168*
Astronaut Scholarship Foundation *123*
A.T. Anderson Memorial Scholarship
Program *121*
Automotive Aftermarket Scholarships *177*
Automotive Women's Alliance Foundation
Scholarships *81*
Barry M. Goldwater Scholarship and Excellence in
Education Program *123*
Berna Lou Cartwright Scholarship *442*
Betty Lou Bailey SWE Region F
Scholarship *197*
BHW Women in STEM Scholarship *124*
B.J. Harrod Scholarship *197*
BK Krenzer Memorial Reentry Scholarship *197*
BMW/SAE Engineering Scholarship *160*
Carol Stephens SWE Region F Scholarship *197*
CBC Scholarship Fund *132*
Center for Architecture Design Scholarship *132*
Chapter 198-Downriver Detroit Scholarship *325*
Chapter 4-Lawrence A. Wacker Memorial
Scholarship *326*
Chapter 67-Phoenix Scholarship *326*
College and Trade/Technical School
Scholarships *154*
Community College STEM Scholarships *126*
Cummins Scholarship *197*
Davis Scholarship for Women in STEM *202*
DEED Educational Scholarship *190*
DEED Student Internship *190*
DEED Student Research Grants *204*
DEED Technical Design Project *191*
Delta Air Lines Engineering Scholarship *163*
Delta Faucet Company Scholarship Program *182*
Diversity in STEAM Magazine Scholarship *83*
Dr. Ivy M. Parker Memorial Scholarship *197*
Dorothy Lemke Howarth Memorial
Scholarship *197*
Dorothy P. Morris Scholarship *198*
DuPont Company Scholarship *198*
Eckenfelder Scholarship *169*
Edward D. Hendrickson/SAE Engineering
Scholarship *160*
Environmental Protection Scholarship *172*
Eric J. Gennuso and LeRoy D. (Bud) Loy, Jr.
Scholarship Program *187*
Exelon Scholarship *198*
Florida Space Research Program *156*
Fort Wayne Chapter 56 Scholarship *328*
Frank M. Coda Scholarship *282*
Fred Fields Scholarship *182*

BSN Student Scholarship/Work Repayment Program *482*

Canadian Nurses Foundation Scholarships *474*

Career Mobility Scholarship *475*

Carole J. Streeter, KB9JBR, Scholarship *254*

Caroline Simpson Maheady Scholarship Award *476*

Chester and Helen Luther Scholarship *376*

Clark-Phelps Scholarship *256*

Continental Society, Daughters of Indian Wars Scholarship *242*

C.R. Bard Foundation, Inc. Nursing Scholarship *480*

Cynthia E. Morgan Memorial Scholarship Fund, Inc. *334*

Dr. Hilda Richards Scholarship *483*

Dr. Lauranne Sams Scholarship *483*

Edna Hicks Fund Scholarship *477*

Edward J. and Virginia M. Routhier Nursing Scholarship *487*

E. Eugene Waide, MD Memorial Scholarship *470*

Eleanora G. Wylie Scholarship *478*

Elizabeth and Sherman Asche Memorial Scholarship Fund *106*

Foundation of the National Student Nurses' Association Career Mobility Scholarship *477*

Foundation of the National Student Nurses' Association General Scholarships *478*

Foundation of the National Student Nurses' Association Specialty Scholarship *478*

Frances L. Booth Medical Scholarship sponsored by LAVFW Department of Maine *375*

Franz Stenzel M.D. and Kathryn Stenzel Scholarship *376*

Franz Stenzel M.D. and Kathryn Stenzel Scholarship Fund *376*

Gala Nursing Scholarships *478*

Genevieve Saran Richmond Award *476*

Good Samaritan Foundation Scholarship *478*

Graduate and Professional Scholarship Program-Maryland *256*

Green Law Firm Nursing Home & Elderly Care Scholarship *479*

Gustavus B. Capito Fund *478*

Hawaiian Lodge Scholarships *86*

HCN/Apricity Resources Scholars Program *93*

Health Careers Scholarship *255*

Health Professions Preparatory Scholarship Program *165*

HENAAC Scholarship Program *115*

Indiana Health Care Policy Institute Nursing Scholarship *480*

Inger Lawrence-M.R. Bauer Foundation Nursing Studies Scholarship *484*

Institute for Nursing Scholarship *485*

The Jackson Laboratory College Scholarship Program *126*

James F. Reville Scholarship *366*

Janet L. Hoffmann Loan Assistance Repayment Program *272*

Jill Laura Creedon Scholarship Award *476*

June Gill Nursing Scholarship *485*

The June Miller Nursing Education Scholarship *484*

Kaiser Permanente School of Anesthesia Scholarship *483*

Ketamine Clinics of Los Angeles Scholarship Program *165*

LabRoots STEM Scholarship *116*

Margaret A. Stafford Nursing Scholarship *475*

Marion A. and Eva S. Peeples Foundation Trust Scholarship *481*

Marion A. Lindeman Scholarship *376*

Martha R. Dudley LVN/LPN Scholarship *483*

Mary Marshall Practical Nursing Scholarship (LPN) *488*

Mary Marshall Registered Nursing Scholarships *488*

Mary Serra Gili Scholarship Award *476*

Mary York Scholarship Fund *477*

Mayo Foundations Scholarship *483*

M.D. "Jack" Murphy Memorial Scholarship *474*

Medical Amateur Radio Council (MARCO) Scholarship *115*

Medical School Scholarship *251*

Medical Scrubs Collection Scholarship *120*

Michael Moody Fitness Scholarship *166*

Mississippi Nurses' Association Foundation Scholarship *482*

NADONA Stephanie Carroll Memorial Scholarship *482*

NAHN Scholarships *483*

Nancy Gerald Memorial Nursing Scholarship *470*

National American Arab Nurses Association Scholarships *482*

National League for Nursing Ella McKinney Scholarship *486*

National Society Daughters of the American Revolution Caroline E. Holt Nursing Scholarships *484*

National Society Daughters of the American Revolution Madeline Pickett (Halbert) Cogswell Nursing Scholarship *484*

National Society Daughters of the American Revolution Mildred Nutting Nursing Scholarship *485*

NBNA Board of Directors Scholarship *483*

New York State ENA September 11 Scholarship Fund *485*

NIH Undergraduate Scholarship Program for Students from Disadvantaged Backgrounds *116*

NLN Ella McKinney Scholarship Fund *486*

Nursing Scholarship *475*

Nursing Spectrum Scholarship *484*

Odd Fellows and Rebekahs Ellen F. Washburn Nurses Training Award *485*

ONS Foundation Josh Gottheil Memorial Bone Marrow Transplant Career Development Awards *486*

ONS Foundation/Oncology Nursing Certification Corporation Bachelor's Scholarships *486*

ONS Foundation/Pearl Moore Career Development Awards *486*

Pacific Health Workforce Award *368*

Pacific Mental Health Work Force Award *368*

Peter Gili Scholarship Award *476*

Phoebe Pember Memorial Scholarship *488*

Pilot International Scholarship *377*

Platinum Educational Group Scholarships Program for EMS, Nursing, and Allied Health *117*

Promise of Nursing Scholarship *478*

Prosper Shaked Scholarship for Future Medical Professionals *166*

Rebecca Goldman Scholarship *479*

Recovery Village Healthcare Scholarship *256*

Ruth Finamore Scholarship Fund *477*

Ruth Shaw Junior Board Scholarship *372*

Scholarship for Students Pursuing a Business or STEM Degree *91*

The Society for the Scientific Study of Sexuality Student Research Grant *120*

Society of Pediatric Nurses Educational Scholarship *203*

Sonne Scholarship *480*

StraightForward Media Medical Professions Scholarship *257*

StraightForward Media Nursing School Scholarship *487*

Straight North STEM Scholarship *92*

Tafford Uniforms Nursing Scholarship Program *488*

Tolliver Annual Nursing Scholarship *481*

Touchmark Foundation Nursing Scholarship *488*

Tuition Reduction for Non-Resident Nursing Students *481*

Undine Sams and Friends Scholarship Fund *477*

U.S. Army ROTC Four-Year Nursing Scholarship *475*

U. S. Public Health Service-Health Resources and Services Administration, Bureau of Health Professions Scholarships for Disadvantaged Students *257*

Vocational Nurse & Licensed Vocational Nurse to Associate Degree Nursing Scholarship Program *480*

Walter C. and Marie C. Schmidt Scholarship *486*

Walter Reed Smith Scholarship *184*

Willard & Marjorie Scheibe Nursing Scholarship *487*

WOCN Accredited Nursing Education Program Scholarship *489*

Occupational Safety and Health

A.T. Anderson Memorial Scholarship Program *121*

BHW Women in STEM Scholarship *124*

Campus Safety, Health and Environmental Management Association Scholarship Award Program *342*

Conditional Grant Program *212*

Continental Society, Daughters of Indian Wars Scholarship *242*

Cynthia E. Morgan Memorial Scholarship Fund, Inc. *334*

Hawaiian Lodge Scholarships *86*

Intermountain Medical Imaging Scholarship *147*

Michael Moody Fitness Scholarship *166*

Prosper Shaked Scholarship for Future Medical Professionals *166*

Recovery Village Healthcare Scholarship *256*

StraightForward Media Medical Professions Scholarship *257*

Straight North STEM Scholarship *92*

William and Dorothy Ferrell Scholarship *268*

Oceanography

$1,500 STEM Scholarship *120*

A.T. Anderson Memorial Scholarship Program *121*

AWG Ethnic Minority Scholarship *260*

AWG Maria Luisa Crawford Field Camp Scholarship *129*

AWG Salt Lake Chapter (SLC) Research Scholarship *129*

Barry M. Goldwater Scholarship and Excellence in Education Program *123*

BHW Women in STEM Scholarship *124*

Charles H. Bussman Undergraduate Scholarship *423*

Diversity in STEAM Magazine Scholarship *83*

Eckenfelder Scholarship *169*

Emily M. Hewitt Memorial Scholarship *170*

Financial Support for Marine or Maritime Studies *425*

Hawaiian Lodge Scholarships *86*

HENAAC Scholarship Program *115*

Janet Cullen Tanaka Geosciences Undergraduate Scholarship *129*

John C. Bajus Scholarship *423*

LabRoots STEM Scholarship *116*

Lone Star Rising Career Scholarship *260*

Minnesota Space Grant Consortium Scholarship Program *156*

Minority Scholarship Program *169*

MTS Student Scholarship *423*

Norm Manly—YMTA Maritime Educational
Scholarships *425*
Osage Chapter Undergraduate Service
Scholarship *129*
Paros-Digiquartz Scholarship *424*
Rockefeller State Wildlife Scholarship *172*
Rogers Family Scholarship *172*
ROV Scholarship *424*
Russell W. Myers Scholarship *172*
Scholarship for Students Pursuing a Business or
STEM Degree *91*
Science Ambassador Scholarship *124*
Susan Ekdale Memorial Field Camp
Scholarship *260*
Women Forward in Technology Scholarship
Program *124*

Oncology

$1,500 STEM Scholarship *120*
American Legion Auxiliary Department of
Colorado Past Presidents' Parley Health Care
Professional ScholarshipNurses
Scholarship *147*
Annual Healthcare and Life Sciences
Scholarship *170*
A.T. Anderson Memorial Scholarship
Program *121*
AvaCare Medical Scholarship *115*
BHW Women in STEM Scholarship *124*
Carole J. Streeter, KB9JBR, Scholarship *254*
Continental Society, Daughters of Indian Wars
Scholarship *242*
Cynthia E. Morgan Memorial Scholarship Fund,
Inc. *334*
HENAAC Scholarship Program *115*
Intermountain Medical Imaging Scholarship *147*
Jerman-Cahoon Student Scholarship *371*
LabRoots STEM Scholarship *116*
Medical Scrubs Collection Scholarship *120*
Michael Moody Fitness Scholarship *166*
ONS Foundation/Oncology Nursing Certification
Corporation Bachelor's Scholarships *486*
ONS Foundation/Pearl Moore Career
Development Awards *486*
Professional Advancement Scholarship *367*
Prosper Shaked Scholarship for Future Medical
Professionals *166*
Scholarship for Students Pursuing a Business or
STEM Degree *91*
Science Ambassador Scholarship *124*
Siemens Clinical Advancement Scholarship *372*
StraightForward Media Medical Professions
Scholarship *257*
Straight North STEM Scholarship *92*
Varian Radiation Therapy Advancement
Scholarship *372*

Optometry

$1,500 STEM Scholarship *120*
American Legion Auxiliary Department of
Colorado Past Presidents' Parley Health Care
Professional ScholarshipNurses
Scholarship *147*
Annual Healthcare and Life Sciences
Scholarship *170*
A.T. Anderson Memorial Scholarship
Program *121*
AvaCare Medical Scholarship *115*
BHW Women in STEM Scholarship *124*
Carole J. Streeter, KB9JBR, Scholarship *254*
Continental Society, Daughters of Indian Wars
Scholarship *242*
Health Professions Preparatory Scholarship
Program *165*
HENAAC Scholarship Program *115*
Intermountain Medical Imaging Scholarship *147*

Ketamine Clinics of Los Angeles Scholarship
Program *165*
LabRoots STEM Scholarship *116*
Medical Scrubs Collection Scholarship *120*
Michael Moody Fitness Scholarship *166*
Prosper Shaked Scholarship for Future Medical
Professionals *166*
Scholarship for Students Pursuing a Business or
STEM Degree *91*
Science Ambassador Scholarship *124*
StraightForward Media Medical Professions
Scholarship *257*
Straight North STEM Scholarship *92*
Vistakon Award of Excellence in Contact Lens
Patient Care *493*

Osteopathy

$1,500 STEM Scholarship *120*
American Legion Auxiliary Department of
Colorado Past Presidents' Parley Health Care
Professional ScholarshipNurses
Scholarship *147*
A.T. Anderson Memorial Scholarship
Program *121*
AvaCare Medical Scholarship *115*
BHW Women in STEM Scholarship *124*
Carole J. Streeter, KB9JBR, Scholarship *254*
Continental Society, Daughters of Indian Wars
Scholarship *242*
Cynthia E. Morgan Memorial Scholarship Fund,
Inc. *334*
HENAAC Scholarship Program *115*
Intermountain Medical Imaging Scholarship *147*
LabRoots STEM Scholarship *116*
Maine Osteopathic Association Scholarship *375*
Medical Scrubs Collection Scholarship *120*
Michael Moody Fitness Scholarship *166*
Prosper Shaked Scholarship for Future Medical
Professionals *166*
Scholarship for Students Pursuing a Business or
STEM Degree *91*
Science Ambassador Scholarship *124*
StraightForward Media Medical Professions
Scholarship *257*
Straight North STEM Scholarship *92*

Paper and Pulp Engineering

$1,500 STEM Scholarship *120*
Ada I. Pressman Memorial Scholarship *196*
Alfred E. Friend Jr., W4CF, Memorial
Scholarship *191*
American Chemical Society Scholars
Program *187*
American Transmission Co. Scholarship *196*
Anne Maureen Whitney Barrow Memorial
Scholarship *196*
Anne Shen Smith Endowed Scholarship *196*
ASHRAE Region III Boggarm Setty
Scholarship *191*
A.T. Anderson Memorial Scholarship
Program *121*
Betty Lou Bailey SWE Region F
Scholarship *197*
BHW Women in STEM Scholarship *124*
B.J. Harrod Scholarship *197*
BK Krenzer Memorial Reentry Scholarship *197*
Carol Stephens SWE Region F Scholarship *197*
Coating and Graphic Arts Division
Scholarship *365*
Corrugated Packaging Division
Scholarships *307*
Dr. Ivy M. Parker Memorial Scholarship *197*
Dorothy Lemke Howarth Memorial
Scholarship *197*
Dorothy P. Morris Scholarship *198*
Eckenfelder Scholarship *169*

Engineering Division Scholarship *496*
Environmental Working Group Scholarship *344*
Exelon Scholarship *198*
Gary Wagner, K3OMI, Scholarship *191*
HENAAC Scholarship Program *115*
IBM Linda Sanford Women's Technical
Advancement Scholarship *198*
Lillian Moller Gilbreth Memorial
Scholarship *198*
Mary V. Munger Memorial Scholarship *199*
Minority Scholarship Program *169*
Olive Lynn Salembier Memorial Reentry
Scholarship *199*
Paper and Board Division Scholarships *331*
Roberta Banaszak Gleiter Engineering Endeavor
Scholarship *199*
Science Ambassador Scholarship *124*
Steven Engineering Scholarship *192*
StraightForward Media Engineering
Scholarship *202*
Straight North STEM Scholarship *92*
Susan Miszkowicz September 11 Memorial
Scholarship *199*
SWE Baltimore-Washington Section
Scholarship *199*
SWE Central New Mexico Pioneers
Scholarship *200*
SWE Central New Mexico Reentry
Scholarship *200*
SWE Mid-Hudson Section Scholarship *200*
SWE Phoenix Section Scholarship *200*
SWE Region E Scholarship *200*
SWE Region G Judy Simmons Memorial
Scholarship *200*
SWE Region H Scholarships *201*
SWE Region J Scholarship *201*
TAPPI Process Control Scholarship *497*
TE Connectivity Excellence in Engineering
Scholarship *201*
Turner Construction Scholarship *201*
W1FDR Scholarship *122*
Wanda Munn Scholarship *201*
William L. Cullison Scholarship *461*

Peace and Conflict Studies

AFIO Undergraduate and Graduate
Scholarships *113*
National Security Education Program (NSEP)
David L. Boren Undergraduate
Scholarships *139*
United Nations Association of Connecticut
Scholarship *147*
Veterans for Peace Scholarship *497*
Washington State Association for Justice
American Justice Essay & Video
Scholarship *244*

Performing Arts

Adele Filene Student Presenter Grant *138*
CBC Spouses Heineken USA Performing Arts
Scholarship *452*
Charlotte Plummer Owen Memorial
Scholarship *279*
Dr. Lynne Boyle/John Schimpf Undergraduate
Scholarship *97*
Dorchester Women's Club Music
Scholarship *452*
Douglas W. Mummert Scholarship *142*
Earl James Fahringer Performing Arts
Scholarship *142*
Eugenia Vellner Fischer Award for Performing
Arts *498*
Herb Smith/Eunice Fleming Scholarship *453*
Jim McKay Memorial Scholarship *220*
John Lennon Endowed Scholarship Program *227*
Martha Ann Stark Memorial Scholarship *279*

Mike Wallace Memorial Scholarship *220*
Music Committee Scholarship *451*
National Academy of Television Arts and Sciences Trustees Scholarship *220*
NOA Vocal Competition/Legacy Award Program *143*
OLM Malala Yousafzai Scholarship *143*
Ossie Davis Endowment Scholarship Program *146*
Polish Arts Club of Buffalo Scholarship Foundation Trust *144*
Polly Holliday Scholarship *145*
Princess Grace Awards in Dance, Theater, and Film *347*
QualityBath.com Scholarship Program *140*
Randy Falco Scholarship *220*
Robert W. Thunen Memorial Scholarships *135*
SEIU Moe Foner Scholarship Program for Visual and Performing Arts *144*
Stella Blum Student Research Grant *138*
Volkwein Memorial Scholarship *279*
VSA International Young Soloists Award *457*

Pharmacy

$1,500 STEM Scholarship *120*
Al & Williamary Viste Scholarship *114*
Allied Healthcare Scholarship Program *165*
American Legion Auxiliary Department of Colorado Past Presidents' Parley Health Care Professional ScholarshipNurses Scholarship *147*
Association for Food and Drug Officials Scholarship Fund *499*
A.T. Anderson Memorial Scholarship Program *121*
AvaCare Medical Scholarship *115*
Barry M. Goldwater Scholarship and Excellence in Education Program *123*
BHW Women in STEM Scholarship *124*
Continental Society, Daughters of Indian Wars Scholarship *242*
CVS Pharmacy, Inc. Pharmacy Scholarship *501*
Cynthia E. Morgan Memorial Scholarship Fund, Inc. *334*
Hawaiian Lodge Scholarships *86*
Health Professions Preparatory Scholarship Program *165*
HENAAC Scholarship Program *115*
The Jackson Laboratory College Scholarship Program *126*
Jason Lang Scholarship *251*
Medical Amateur Radio Council (MARCO) Scholarship *115*
Medical Scrubs Collection Scholarship *120*
National Community Pharmacist Association Foundation Presidential Scholarship *500*
Nicholas and Mary Agnes Trivillian Memorial Scholarship Fund *374*
O. Nesheim Memorial Scholarship *254*
Platinum Educational Group Scholarships Program for EMS, Nursing, and Allied Health *117*
Prosper Shaked Scholarship for Future Medical Professionals *166*
Scholarship for Students Pursuing a Business or STEM Degree *91*
StraightForward Media Medical Professions Scholarship *257*
StraightForward Media Vocational-Technical School Scholarship *118*
Women Forward in Technology Scholarship Program *124*

Philosophy

ASCSA Summer Session and Summer Seminars Scholarships *118*
Davidson Fellows Scholarship Program *124*
La-Philosophie.com Scholarship *119*

StraightForward Media Liberal Arts Scholarship *139*
UNCF/Koch Scholars Program for Undergraduates *94*

Photojournalism/Photography

AQHF Journalism or Communications Scholarship *216*
Career Journalism Scholarship *225*
Carole Simpson Scholarship *222*
CCNMA Scholarships *218*
CIC/Anna Chennault Scholarship *217*
College Photographer of the Year Competition *502*
Connecticut SPJ Bob Eddy Scholarship Program *218*
Douglas W. Mummert Scholarship *142*
Ed Bradley Scholarship *223*
George Foreman Tribute to Lyndon B. Johnson Scholarship *223*
International Foodservice Editorial Council Communications Scholarship *96*
Jim McKay Memorial Scholarship *220*
Kerdragon Scholarship *143*
Leonard M. Perryman Communications Scholarship for Ethnic Minority Students *227*
Lou and Carole Prato Sports Reporting Scholarship *223*
Mary Quon Moy Ing Memorial Scholarship Award *217*
Mike Reynolds Journalism Scholarship *223*
Mike Wallace Memorial Scholarship *220*
National Academy of Television Arts and Sciences Trustees Scholarship *220*
National Association of Black Journalists Non-Sustaining Scholarship Awards *405*
National Association of Hispanic Journalists Scholarship *221*
Native American Journalists Association Scholarships *97*
Nebraska Press Association Foundation Scholarship *97*
Newhouse Scholarship Program *364*
Northwest Journalists of Color Scholarship *96*
Outdoor Writers Association of America - Bodie McDowell Scholarship Award *222*
Palm Beach Association of Black Journalists Scholarship *408*
Pauly D'Orlando Memorial Art Scholarship *146*
Printing Industry Midwest Education Foundation Scholarship Fund *222*
QualityBath.com Scholarship Program *140*
Randy Falco Scholarship *220*
Raymond Davis Scholarship *305*
StraightForward Media Media & Communications Scholarship *99*
Support Creativity Scholarship *137*
Tampa Bay Times Fund Career Journalism Scholarships *99*
Texas Gridiron Club Scholarships *226*
Valley Press Club Scholarships, The Republican Scholarship, Channel 22 Scholarship *228*
Vincent Chin Memorial Scholarship *217*
Visual Task Force Scholarship *502*

Physical Sciences

$1,500 STEM Scholarship *120*
AFCEA STEM Majors Scholarships for Undergraduate Students *122*
AIAA Foundation Undergraduate Scholarships *121*
Al & Williamary Viste Scholarship *114*
Al-Ben Scholarship for Academic Incentive *193*
Al-Ben Scholarship for Professional Merit *193*
Al-Ben Scholarship for Scholastic Achievement *193*

American Legion Department of Maryland Math-Science Scholarship *437*
American Physical Society Corporate-Sponsored Scholarship for Minority Undergraduate Students Who Major in Physics *506*
American Society of Naval Engineers Scholarship *122*
Andy Aitkenhead Scholarship *127*
Arizona Professional Chapter of AISES Scholarship *313*
Armed Forces Communications and Electronics Association ROTC Scholarship Program *151*
Association for Iron and Steel Technology Ohio Valley Chapter Scholarship *167*
A.T. Anderson Memorial Scholarship Program *121*
AWG Ethnic Minority Scholarship *260*
AWG Maria Luisa Crawford Field Camp Scholarship *129*
AWG Salt Lake Chapter (SLC) Research Scholarship *129*
Barbara Lotze Scholarships for Future Teachers *504*
Barry M. Goldwater Scholarship and Excellence in Education Program *123*
BASF/Alfred Chisholm Endowed Memorial Scholarship *93*
BHW Women in STEM Scholarship *124*
Carrol C. Hall Memorial Scholarship *128*
Charles S. Brown Scholarship in Physics *507*
Coastal Plains Chapter of the Air and Waste Management Association Environmental Steward Scholarship *337*
CTRI/Chris Seeber, KA1GEU, Memorial Scholarship *268*
Dan Huettl, WZ7U, Memorial Scholarship *298*
Diversity in STEAM Magazine Scholarship *83*
Elizabeth and Sherman Asche Memorial Scholarship Fund *106*
Elmer S. Imes Scholarship in Physics *507*
Eric D. Dunning Scholarship *235*
Florida Space Research Program *156*
Grants for Disabled Graduate Students in the Sciences *106*
Harvey Washington Banks Scholarship in Astronomy *507*
HENAAC Scholarship Program *115*
H.H. Dow Memorial Student Achievement Award of the Industrial Electrolysis and Electrochemical Engineering Division of the Electrochemical Society Inc . *125*
High Technology Scholars Program *173*
Hubertus W.V. Wellems Scholarship for Male Students *194*
Independent Laboratories Institute Scholarship Alliance *171*
Janet Cullen Tanaka Geosciences Undergraduate Scholarship *129*
Kia Motors America STEM/Sustainability Scholarship *175*
LabRoots STEM Scholarship *116*
Leatrice Gregory Pendray Scholarship *121*
Lois Manley, K7LMZ, and Randall Pitchford, WW7ZZ, Scholarship *206*
Lone Star Rising Career Scholarship *260*
Louise Torraco Memorial Scholarship for Science *174*
Math and Science Scholarship *171*
Math, Engineering, Science, Business, Education, Computers Scholarships *178*
Medical Scrubs Collection Scholarship *120*
Michael Moody Fitness Scholarship *166*
Michael P. Anderson Scholarship in Space Science *507*
Minnesota Space Grant Consortium Scholarship Program *156*

Special Education

Sports-Related/Exercise Science

Statistics

Surveying, Surveying Technology, Cartography, or Geographic Information Science

Therapy/Rehabilitation

Trade/Technical Specialties

Urban and Regional Planning

Women's Studies

Civic, Professional, Social, or Union Affiliation

AFL-CIO
Martin Duffy Adult Learner Scholarship
Award 568
Minnesota AFL-CIO Scholarships 568
Project BEST Scholarship 575
Ronald Lorah Memorial Scholarship 538
Ted Bricker Scholarship 525
Texas AFL-CIO Scholarship Program 579
Union Plus Education Foundation Scholarship
Program 584

Airline Pilots Association
Airline Pilots Association Scholarship
Program 549

Alpha Mu Gamma
National Alpha Mu Gamma Scholarships 359

American Angus Association
Angus Foundation Scholarships 570

American Congress on Surveying and Mapping
ACSM Fellows Scholarship 529
ACSM Lowell H. and Dorothy Loving
Undergraduate Scholarship 529
American Association for Geodetic Surveying
Joseph F. Dracup Scholarship Award 529
Berntsen International Scholarship in
Surveying 529
Berntsen International Scholarship in Surveying
Technology 530
Cady McDonnell Memorial Scholarship 530
Nettie Dracup Memorial Scholarship 530
Schonstedt Scholarship in Surveying 530
Tri-State Surveying and Photogrammetry Kris
M. Kunze Memorial Scholarship 176

American Criminal Justice Association
American Criminal Justice Association-Lambda
Alpha Epsilon National Scholarship 241

American Dental Assistants Association
Juliette A. Southard Scholarship 549

American Dental Hygienist's Association
Colgate "Bright Smiles, Bright Futures" Minority
Scholarship 252
Crest Oral-B Laboratories Dental Hygiene
Scholarship 252
Sigma Phi Alpha Undergraduate
Scholarship 253

American Dietetic Association
Academy of Nutrition and Dietetics Foundation
Scholarship Program 351

American Federation of State, County, and Municipal Employees
AFSCME: American Federation of State,
County, and Municipal Employees Local
2067 Scholarship 573
American Federation of State, County, and
Municipal Employees Oregon Council # 75
Scholarship 573

American Federation of State, County, and
Municipal Employees Scholarship
Program 549
Jerry Clark Memorial Scholarship 509
Union Plus Credit Card Scholarship
Program 550

American Federation of Teachers
Robert G. Porter Scholars Program-American
Federation of Teachers Dependents 550

American Health Information Management Association
AHIMA Foundation Student Merit
Scholarship 378

American Institute of Aeronautics and Astronautics
AIAA Foundation Undergraduate
Scholarships 121
Leatrice Gregory Pendray Scholarship 121

American Legion or Auxiliary
Albert M. Lappin Scholarship 554
Americanism Essay Contest Scholarship 553
American Legion Auxiliary Department of
Connecticut Memorial Educational
Grant 550
American Legion Auxiliary Department of
Connecticut Past Presidents' Parley
Memorial Education Grant 550
American Legion Auxiliary Department of Iowa
M.V. McCrae Memorial Nurses Merit
Award 472
American Legion Auxiliary Department of
Minnesota Past Presidents' Parley Health
Care Scholarship 370
American Legion Auxiliary Department of
Missouri Lela Murphy Scholarship 550
American Legion Auxiliary Department of
Missouri National President's
Scholarship 550
American Legion Auxiliary Department of
Missouri Past Presidents' Parley
Scholarship 472
American Legion Auxiliary Department of
Nebraska Ruby Paul Campaign Fund
Scholarship 551
American Legion Auxiliary Department of North
Dakota Past Presidents' Parley Nurses
Scholarship 472
American Legion Auxiliary Department of
Oregon Spirit of Youth Scholarship 551
American Legion Auxiliary Department of South
Dakota College Scholarships 551
American Legion Auxiliary Department of South
Dakota Senior Scholarship 551
American Legion Auxiliary Department of South
Dakota Thelma Foster Scholarship for Senior
Auxiliary Members 551
American Legion Auxiliary Department of Utah
National President's Scholarship 552
American Legion Auxiliary Department of
Wisconsin Della Van Deuren Memorial
Scholarship 552

American Legion Auxiliary Department of
Wisconsin H.S. and Angeline Lewis
Scholarships 552
American Legion Auxiliary Department of
Wisconsin Merit and Memorial
Scholarships 552
American Legion Auxiliary Department of
Wisconsin Past Presidents' Parley Health
Career Scholarships 366
American Legion Auxiliary Department of
Wisconsin Past Presidents' Parley Registered
Nurse Scholarship 473
American Legion Auxiliary Department of
Wisconsin President's Scholarships 552
American Legion Auxiliary Non-Traditional
Students Scholarships 553
American Legion Auxiliary Spirit of Youth
Scholarships for Junior Members 553
American Legion Department of Idaho
Scholarship 553
American Legion Department of Maryland
General Scholarship Fund 555
American Legion Department of Maryland
Math-Science Scholarship 437
American Legion Department of Minnesota
Memorial Scholarship 555
American Legion Department of Washington
Children and Youth Scholarships 557
American Legion Family Scholarship 553
Charles L. Bacon Memorial Scholarship 555
Charles W. and Annette Hill Scholarship 554
Hugh A. Smith Scholarship Fund 554
James V. Day Scholarship 555
Joseph P. Gavenonis College Scholarship (Plan
I) 556
Marine Corps Scholarship Foundation 586
Maynard Jensen American Legion Memorial
Scholarship 556
Minnesota Legionnaires Insurance Trust
Scholarship 555
Ohio American Legion Scholarships 556
Rosedale Post 346 Scholarship 554
Sons of the American Legion William F. "Bill"
Johnson Memorial Scholarship 557
Ted and Nora Anderson Scholarships 554

American Occupational Therapy Association
Carlotta Welles Scholarship 370

American Postal Workers Union
E.C. Hallbeck Scholarship Fund 557
Vocational Scholarship Program 557

American Quarter Horse Association
AQHF General Scholarship 557
AQHF Journalism or Communications
Scholarship 216
AQHF Racing Scholarships 558
AQHF Youth Scholarships 558
Arizona Quarter Horse Youth Scholarship 558
Arizona Quarter Racing Scholarship 558
Boon San Kitty Scholarship 558
Christopher Lawrence Junker Nebraska
Scholarship 558

Kaiser Permanente School of Anesthesia
Scholarship 483
Martha R. Dudley LVN/LPN Scholarship 483
Mayo Foundations Scholarship 483
NBNA Board of Directors Scholarship 483
Nursing Spectrum Scholarship 484

National Board of Boiler and Pressure Vessel Inspectors
National Board Technical Scholarship 194

National Federation of Press Women
Frank Sarli Memorial Scholarship 417

National Foster Parent Association
National Foster Parent Association Youth
Scholarship 570

National Honor Society
National Honor Society Scholarship
Program 570

National Junior Red Angus Association
4 RAAA/Junior Red Angus Scholarship 576
Dee Sonstegard Memorial Scholarship 576
Farm and Ranch Connection Scholarship 576
Leonard A. Lorenzen Memorial
Scholarship 576

National Military Intelligence Association
National Military Intelligence Association
Scholarship 450

National Society of Accountants
Stanley H. Stearman Scholarship 88

National Society of Collegiate Scholars
NSCS Exemplary Scholar Award 571
NSCS Merit Award 571
NSCS Scholar Abroad Scholarship 571

National Society of High School Scholars
Claes Nobel Academic Scholarships 571
National Scholar Awards for NSHSS
Members 571
Robert P. Sheppard Leadership Award for
NSHSS Members 572

National Society of Professional Engineers
Paul H. Robbins Honorary Scholarship 194

Native American Journalists Association
Native American Journalists Association
Scholarships 97

New England Water Works Association
Elson T. Killam Memorial Scholarship 210
Francis X. Crowley Scholarship 182
Joseph Murphy Scholarship 210

New Jersey Association of Realtors
New Jersey Association of Realtors Educational
Foundation Scholarship Program 516

Northeastern Loggers Association
Northeastern Loggers' Association
Scholarships 572

North East Roofing Contractors Association
North East Roofing Educational Foundation
Scholarship 572

Northwest Automatic Vending Association
Northwest Automatic Vending Association
Scholarship 574

Office and Professional Employees International Union
Office and Professional Employees International
Union Howard Coughlin Memorial
Scholarship Fund 572

Ohio Farmers Union
Joseph Fitcher Scholarship Contest 110
Virgil Thompson Memorial Scholarship
Contest 103

Oregon State Fiscal Association
Oregon State Fiscal Association
Scholarship 574

Other Student Academic Clubs
ASABE Foundation Scholarship 311
Berna Lou Cartwright Scholarship 442
Mary Morrow-Edna Richards Scholarship 274
Phi Alpha Theta World History Association Paper
Prize 383
Sylvia W. Farny Scholarship 442
William J. Adams, Jr. and Marijane E. Adams
Scholarship 105

Parent-Teacher Association/Organization
Continuing Education-PTA Volunteers
Scholarship 561
Frieda L. Koontz Scholarship 278
General Scholarships 278
S. John Davis Scholarship 278

Phi Alpha Theta
Phi Alpha Theta Paper Prizes 382
Phi Alpha Theta Undergraduate Student
Scholarship 383
Phi Alpha Theta/Western Front Association
Paper Prize 383
Phi Alpha Theta World History Association Paper
Prize 383

Phi Delta Kappa International
Phi Delta Kappa International Prospective
Educator Scholarships 275

Phi Kappa Phi
Literacy Grant Competition 565

Philipino-American Association
PAMAS Restricted Scholarship Award 574

Phi Sigma Kappa
Wenderoth Undergraduate Scholarship 575
Zeta Scholarship 575

Pony of the Americas Club
POAC National Scholarship 575

Professional Horsemen Association
Guy Stoops Professional Horsemen's Family
Scholarship 559
Professional Horsemen's Scholarship Fund 575

Reserve Officers Association
Henry J. Reilly Memorial Scholarship-High
School Seniors and First Year
Freshmen 576
Henry J. Reilly Memorial Undergraduate
Scholarship Program for College
Attendees 577

Retail, Wholesale and Department Store Union
Alvin E. Heaps Memorial Scholarship 577

Service Employees International Union
SEIU Jesse Jackson Scholarship Program 577
SEIU John Geagan Scholarship 577
SEIU Moe Foner Scholarship Program for Visual
and Performing Arts 144

SEIU Nora Piore Scholarship Program 577
SEIU Scholarship Program 577

Sigma Alpha Mu Foundation
Undergraduate Achievement Awards 578
Young Scholars Program 578

Sigma Chi Fraternity
General Scholarship Grants 578

Slovenian Women's Union of America
Slovenian Women's Union of America
Scholarship Foundation 578

Society for Human Resource Management
SHRM Foundation Student Scholarships 394

Society of Architectural Historians
Richland/Lexington SCSEA Scholarship 579

Society of Automotive Engineers
Ralph K. Hillquist Honorary SAE
Scholarship 305
SAE Long Term Member Sponsored
Scholarship 325

Society of Motion Picture and Television Engineers
Louis F. Wolf Jr. Memorial Scholarship 224
Student Paper Award 224

Society of Pediatric Nurses
Society of Pediatric Nurses Educational
Scholarship 203

Society of Physics Students
Society of Physics Students Leadership
Scholarships 508
Society of Physics Students Outstanding Student
in Research 508
Society of Physics Students Peggy Dixon Two-
Year College Scholarship 508

Society of Women Engineers
Bechtel Corporation Scholarship 329
Betty Lou Bailey SWE Region F
Scholarship 197
Carol Stephens SWE Region F Scholarship 197
Honeywell Scholarship 198
Invenergy Women's Network Scholarship 212
Judith Resnick Memorial Scholarship 330
Mary V. Munger Memorial Scholarship 199
Roberta Banaszak Gleiter Engineering Endeavor
Scholarship 199
Rochelle Nicolette Perry Memorial
Scholarship 306
SWE Baltimore-Washington Section
Scholarship 199
SWE Central New Mexico Pioneers
Scholarship 200
SWE Central New Mexico Reentry
Scholarship 200
SWE Phoenix Section Scholarship 200
SWE Region E Scholarship 200
SWE Region G Judy Simmons Memorial
Scholarship 200
SWE Region H Scholarships 201
SWE Region J Scholarship 201
Turner Construction Scholarship 201
Virginia Counts/Betty Irish SWE for Life
Scholarship 447

Soil and Water Conservation Society
Donald A. Williams Scholarship Soil
Conservation Scholarship 103
Melville H. Cohee Student Leader Conservation
Scholarship 578
Walt Bartram Memorial Education Award 328

Corporate Affiliation

Employment/Volunteer Experience

Impairment

IMPAIRMENT

Nationality or Ethnic Heritage

Kentucky

AbbVie Immunology Scholarship *666*
AG Bell College Scholarship Program *594*
American Legion Auxiliary Department of
  Kentucky Mary Barrett Marshall
  Scholarship *705*
Annual CGTrader Scholarship *604*
Annual iSeeCars Future Entrepreneurs
  Scholarship *900*
Anthony Munoz Scholarships *598*
Army ROTC Green to Gold Scholarship Program
  for Two-Year, Three-Year and Four-Year
  Scholarships, Active Duty Enlisted
  Personnel *610*
Army (ROTC) Reserve Officers Training Corps
  Two-, Three-, Four-Year Campus-Based
  Scholarships *610*
Benson & Bingham Annual Scholarship *413*
Casualty Actuaries of the Southeast Scholarship
  Program *928*
CBC Spouses Education Scholarship *730*
CBC Spouses Heineken USA Performing Arts
  Scholarship *452*
CBC Spouses Visual Arts Scholarship *132*
Christian A. Herter Memorial Scholarship *642*
Classic Scholarships *874*
Clunker Junker Cash for Cars and College
  Scholarship *299*
Clutch Prep STEM Scholarship *285*
College Access Program (CAP) Grant *743*
Early Childhood Development Scholarship *840*
Environmental Protection Scholarship *172*
Finally Sold Impact Maker Scholarship *618*
Frank S. Land Scholarship *588*
Greenhouse Scholars *736*
Hagan Scholarship *623*
HENAAC Scholarship Program *115*
Indiana Health Care Policy Institute Nursing
  Scholarship *480*
John Zagunis Student Leader Scholarship *647*
Jules Cohen Scholarship *284*
Kelley & Canterbury, LLC Alaska Curiosity
  Scholarship *633*
Kentucky National Guard Tuition Award *699*
Kentucky Society of Certified Public Accountants
  College Scholarship *87*
Kentucky Transportation Cabinet Civil
  Engineering Scholarship Program *209*
Kentucky Tuition Grant (KTG) *841*
Korean-American Scholarship Foundation Eastern
  Region Scholarships *743*
Levy Law Offices Cincinnati Safe Driver
  Scholarship *640*
Milton Fisher Scholarship for Innovation and
  Creativity *862*
Minority Students in Veterinary Medicine
  Scholarship *719*
Morrow & Sheppard College Scholarship *417*
National Association for Campus Activities
  Scholarships for Student Leaders *186*
National Institute for Labor Relations Research
  William B. Ruggles Journalism
  Scholarship *650*
National Make It With Wool Competition *345*
National Restaurant Association Educational
  Foundation Undergraduate Scholarships for
  College Students *109*
Pedro Zamora Young Leaders Scholarship *647*
Polly Holliday Scholarship *145*
Residential Construction Management
  Scholarship *238*
Residential Design Scholarship *134*
Social Entrepreneurship Scholarship *233*
Sustainable Residential Design Scholarship *134*

SWE Region G Judy Simmons Memorial
  Scholarship *200*
Tese Caldarelli Memorial Scholarship *648*
Tolliver Annual Nursing Scholarship *481*
Two Ten Footwear Foundation Scholarship *676*
Two Ten Foundation Footwear Design
  Scholarship *874*
Union Plus Education Foundation Scholarship
  Program *584*
United States Senate Youth Program *918*
U.S. Army ROTC Four-Year College
  Scholarship *610*
U.S. Army ROTC Four-Year Historically Black
  College/University Scholarship *610*
U.S. Army ROTC Four-Year Nursing
  Scholarship *475*
U.S. Army ROTC Guaranteed Reserve Forces
  Duty (GRFD), (ARNG/USAR) and Dedicated
  ARNG Scholarships *611*
U.S. Army ROTC Military Junior College (MJC)
  Scholarship *611*
ValuePenguin Scholarship *682*
Women in Architecture Scholarship *134*
Women in Rural Electrification (WIRE)
  Scholarships *840*
You Deserve It! Scholarship *865*

Louisiana

AbbVie Immunology Scholarship *666*
AG Bell College Scholarship Program *594*
Annual CGTrader Scholarship *604*
Annual iSeeCars Future Entrepreneurs
  Scholarship *900*
Army ROTC Green to Gold Scholarship Program
  for Two-Year, Three-Year and Four-Year
  Scholarships, Active Duty Enlisted
  Personnel *610*
Army (ROTC) Reserve Officers Training Corps
  Two-, Three-, Four-Year Campus-Based
  Scholarships *610*
ASHRAE Region VIII Scholarship *295*
Benson & Bingham Annual Scholarship *413*
Broadcast Scholarship Program *544*
Casualty Actuaries of the Southeast Scholarship
  Program *928*
CBC Spouses Education Scholarship *730*
CBC Spouses Heineken USA Performing Arts
  Scholarship *452*
CBC Spouses Visual Arts Scholarship *132*
Christian A. Herter Memorial Scholarship *642*
Classic Scholarships *874*
Clunker Junker Cash for Cars and College
  Scholarship *299*
Clutch Prep STEM Scholarship *285*
Finally Sold Impact Maker Scholarship *618*
Frank S. Land Scholarship *588*
Greenhouse Scholars *736*
Gulf Coast Hurricane Scholarship *196*
Hagan Scholarship *623*
HENAAC Scholarship Program *115*
Hoffoss Devall Louisiana Safe Driver
  Scholarship *626*
Jackson County ARA Scholarship *812*
Jules Cohen Scholarship *284*
Kelley & Canterbury, LLC Alaska Curiosity
  Scholarship *633*
Korean-American Scholarship Foundation
  Southern Region Scholarships *744*
Louisiana Department of Veterans Affairs State
  Educational Aid Program *712*
Louisiana National Guard State Tuition Exemption
  Program *699*
Markley Scholarship *186*
Milton Fisher Scholarship for Innovation and
  Creativity *862*

Minority Students in Veterinary Medicine
  Scholarship *719*
Morrow & Sheppard College Scholarship *417*
National Association for Campus Activities
  Scholarships for Student Leaders *186*
National Institute for Labor Relations Research
  William B. Ruggles Journalism
  Scholarship *650*
National Make It With Wool Competition *345*
National Restaurant Association Educational
  Foundation Undergraduate Scholarships for
  College Students *109*
Pedro Zamora Young Leaders Scholarship *647*
Residential Construction Management
  Scholarship *238*
Residential Design Scholarship *134*
Rockefeller State Wildlife Scholarship *172*
Society of Louisiana CPAs Scholarships *91*
Sustainable Residential Design Scholarship *134*
Taylor Opportunity Program for Students Honors
  Level *842*
Taylor Opportunity Program for Students
  Opportunity Level *842*
Taylor Opportunity Program for Students
  Performance Level *842*
Taylor Opportunity Program for Students Tech
  Level *843*
Two Ten Footwear Foundation Scholarship *676*
Two Ten Foundation Footwear Design
  Scholarship *874*
Union Plus Education Foundation Scholarship
  Program *584*
United States Senate Youth Program *918*
U.S. Army ROTC Four-Year College
  Scholarship *610*
U.S. Army ROTC Four-Year Historically Black
  College/University Scholarship *610*
U.S. Army ROTC Four-Year Nursing
  Scholarship *475*
U.S. Army ROTC Guaranteed Reserve Forces
  Duty (GRFD), (ARNG/USAR) and Dedicated
  ARNG Scholarships *611*
U.S. Army ROTC Military Junior College (MJC)
  Scholarship *611*
ValuePenguin Scholarship *682*
Women in Architecture Scholarship *134*
You Deserve It! Scholarship *865*

Maine

AbbVie Immunology Scholarship *666*
AG Bell College Scholarship Program *594*
Annual CGTrader Scholarship *604*
Annual iSeeCars Future Entrepreneurs
  Scholarship *900*
Army ROTC Green to Gold Scholarship Program
  for Two-Year, Three-Year and Four-Year
  Scholarships, Active Duty Enlisted
  Personnel *610*
Army (ROTC) Reserve Officers Training Corps
  Two-, Three-, Four-Year Campus-Based
  Scholarships *610*
Benson & Bingham Annual Scholarship *413*
CBC Spouses Education Scholarship *730*
CBC Spouses Heineken USA Performing Arts
  Scholarship *452*
CBC Spouses Visual Arts Scholarship *132*
Christian A. Herter Memorial Scholarship *642*
Classic Scholarships *874*
Clunker Junker Cash for Cars and College
  Scholarship *299*
Clutch Prep STEM Scholarship *285*
Dr. James L. Lawson Memorial Scholarship *216*
EMBARK-Support for the College Journey *843*
Finally Sold Impact Maker Scholarship *618*
Frank S. Land Scholarship *588*
Greenhouse Scholars *736*

Two Ten Foundation Footwear Design
Scholarship *874*
Union Plus Education Foundation Scholarship
Program *584*
United States Senate Youth Program *918*
U.S. Army ROTC Four-Year College
Scholarship *610*
U.S. Army ROTC Four-Year Historically Black
College/University Scholarship *610*
U.S. Army ROTC Four-Year Nursing
Scholarship *475*
U.S. Army ROTC Guaranteed Reserve Forces
Duty (GRFD), (ARNG/USAR) and Dedicated
ARNG Scholarships *611*
U.S. Army ROTC Military Junior College (MJC)
Scholarship *611*
ValuePenguin Scholarship *682*
Women in Architecture Scholarship *134*
World Trade Center Memorial Scholarship *949*
You Deserve It! Scholarship *865*
YouthForce 2020 Scholarship Program *137*

North Carolina
AbbVie Immunology Scholarship *666*
AG Bell College Scholarship Program *594*
Annual CGTrader Scholarship *604*
Annual iSeeCars Future Entrepreneurs
Scholarship *900*
Army ROTC Green to Gold Scholarship Program
for Two-Year, Three-Year and Four-Year
Scholarships, Active Duty Enlisted
Personnel *610*
Army (ROTC) Reserve Officers Training Corps
Two-, Three-, Four-Year Campus-Based
Scholarships *610*
ASHRAE Region IV Benny Bootle
Scholarship *130*
Aubrey Lee Brooks Scholarships *854*
Benson & Bingham Annual Scholarship *413*
Casualty Actuaries of the Southeast Scholarship
Program *928*
CBC Spouses Education Scholarship *730*
CBC Spouses Heineken USA Performing Arts
Scholarship *452*
CBC Spouses Visual Arts Scholarship *132*
Classic Scholarships *874*
Clunker Junker Cash for Cars and College
Scholarship *299*
Clutch Prep STEM Scholarship *285*
Finally Sold Impact Maker Scholarship *618*
Frank S. Land Scholarship *588*
Greenhouse Scholars *736*
Hagan Scholarship *623*
HENAAC Scholarship Program *115*
Jagannathan Scholarship *855*
Jules Cohen Scholarship *284*
Kelley & Canterbury, LLC Alaska Curiosity
Scholarship *633*
Korean-American Scholarship Foundation Eastern
Region Scholarships *743*
Korean-American Scholarship Foundation
Southern Region Scholarships *744*
Latino Diamante Scholarship Fund *612*
L. Phil and Alice J. Wicker Scholarship *217*
Mary Morrow-Edna Richards Scholarship *274*
Milton Fisher Scholarship for Innovation and
Creativity *862*
Minority Students in Veterinary Medicine
Scholarship *719*
Morrow & Sheppard College Scholarship *417*
National Association for Campus Activities
Scholarships for Student Leaders *186*
National Association for Campus Activities South
Region Student Leader Scholarship *648*

National Institute for Labor Relations Research
William B. Ruggles Journalism
Scholarship *650*
National Make It With Wool Competition *345*
National Restaurant Association Educational
Foundation Undergraduate Scholarships for
College Students *109*
NCAB Scholarship *545*
North Carolina Association of CPAs Foundation
Scholarships *88*
North Carolina Community College Grant
Program *855*
North Carolina National Guard Tuition Assistance
Program *700*
North Carolina Sheriffs' Association
Undergraduate Criminal Justice
Scholarships *243*
North Carolina Veterans Scholarships Class I-
A *714*
North Carolina Veterans Scholarships Class I-
B *714*
North Carolina Veterans Scholarships Class
II *714*
North Carolina Veterans Scholarships Class
III *715*
North Carolina Veterans Scholarships Class
IV *715*
Pedro Zamora Young Leaders Scholarship *647*
Polly Holliday Scholarship *145*
Residential Construction Management
Scholarship *238*
Residential Design Scholarship *134*
Stanley Dentistry Scholarship Fund *257*
Sustainable Residential Design Scholarship *134*
Tailor Made Lawns Scholarship Fund *111*
Ted G. Wilson Memorial Scholarship
Foundation *211*
Triangle Pest Control Scholarship *93*
Two Ten Footwear Foundation Scholarship *676*
Two Ten Foundation Footwear Design
Scholarship *874*
Union Plus Education Foundation Scholarship
Program *584*
United States Senate Youth Program *918*
University of North Carolina Need-Based
Grant *855*
U.S. Army ROTC Four-Year College
Scholarship *610*
U.S. Army ROTC Four-Year Historically Black
College/University Scholarship *610*
U.S. Army ROTC Four-Year Nursing
Scholarship *475*
U.S. Army ROTC Guaranteed Reserve Forces
Duty (GRFD), (ARNG/USAR) and Dedicated
ARNG Scholarships *611*
U.S. Army ROTC Military Junior College (MJC)
Scholarship *611*
ValuePenguin Scholarship *682*
Wachovia Technical Scholarship Program *536*
Women in Architecture Scholarship *134*
You Deserve It! Scholarship *865*

North Dakota
AbbVie Immunology Scholarship *666*
AG Bell College Scholarship Program *594*
American Legion Auxiliary Department of North
Dakota National President's Scholarship *596*
American Legion Auxiliary Department of North
Dakota Past Presidents' Parley Nurses
Scholarship *472*
American Legion Auxiliary Department of North
Dakota Scholarships *802*
American Legion Department of Minnesota
Memorial Scholarship *555*
American Legion Department of North Dakota
National High School Oratorical Contest *807*

Annual CGTrader Scholarship *604*
Annual iSeeCars Future Entrepreneurs
Scholarship *900*
Army ROTC Green to Gold Scholarship Program
for Two-Year, Three-Year and Four-Year
Scholarships, Active Duty Enlisted
Personnel *610*
Army (ROTC) Reserve Officers Training Corps
Two-, Three-, Four-Year Campus-Based
Scholarships *610*
Benson & Bingham Annual Scholarship *413*
CBC Spouses Education Scholarship *730*
CBC Spouses Heineken USA Performing Arts
Scholarship *452*
CBC Spouses Visual Arts Scholarship *132*
Classic Scholarships *874*
Clunker Junker Cash for Cars and College
Scholarship *299*
Clutch Prep STEM Scholarship *285*
Finally Sold Impact Maker Scholarship *618*
Frank S. Land Scholarship *588*
Greenhouse Scholars *736*
Hagan Scholarship *623*
Hattie Tedrow Memorial Fund Scholarship *807*
HENAAC Scholarship Program *115*
Jules Cohen Scholarship *284*
Kelley & Canterbury, LLC Alaska Curiosity
Scholarship *633*
Milton Fisher Scholarship for Innovation and
Creativity *862*
Minnesota Legionnaires Insurance Trust
Scholarship *555*
Minority Students in Veterinary Medicine
Scholarship *719*
Morrow & Sheppard College Scholarship *417*
National Association for Campus Activities
Scholarships for Student Leaders *186*
National Defense Transportation Association,
Scott Air Force Base-St. Louis Area Chapter
Scholarship *849*
National Institute for Labor Relations Research
William B. Ruggles Journalism
Scholarship *650*
National Make It With Wool Competition *345*
National Restaurant Association Educational
Foundation Undergraduate Scholarships for
College Students *109*
North Central Region 9 Scholarship *328*
North Dakota Academic Scholarship *654*
North Dakota Career and Technical Education
Scholarship *654*
North Dakota Indian Scholarship Program *654*
North Dakota Scholars Program *654*
North Dakota State Student Incentive Grant
Program *654*
O. Nesheim Memorial Scholarship *254*
Pedro Zamora Young Leaders Scholarship *647*
PFund Foundation Scholarship Program *861*
Residential Construction Management
Scholarship *238*
Residential Design Scholarship *134*
Sustainable Residential Design Scholarship *134*
SWE Region H Scholarships *201*
Touchmark Foundation Nursing Scholarship *488*
Two Ten Footwear Foundation Scholarship *676*
Two Ten Foundation Footwear Design
Scholarship *874*
Union Plus Education Foundation Scholarship
Program *584*
United States Senate Youth Program *918*
U.S. Army ROTC Four-Year College
Scholarship *610*
U.S. Army ROTC Four-Year Historically Black
College/University Scholarship *610*
U.S. Army ROTC Four-Year Nursing
Scholarship *475*

Pedro Zamora Young Leaders Scholarship *647*
Postsecondary Education Gratuity Program *700*
Ready to Succeed Scholarship Program *860*
Residential Construction Management
  Scholarship *238*
Residential Design Scholarship *134*
Robert W. Valimont Endowment Fund Scholarship
  (Part II) *535*
Roothbert Fund Inc. Scholarship *864*
Seol Bong Scholarship *693*
Sustainable Residential Design Scholarship *134*
SWE Region E Scholarship *200*
SWE Region G Judy Simmons Memorial
  Scholarship *200*
Tese Caldarelli Memorial Scholarship *648*
Two Ten Footwear Foundation Scholarship *676*
Two Ten Foundation Footwear Design
  Scholarship *874*
Union Plus Education Foundation Scholarship
  Program *584*
United States Senate Youth Program *918*
U.S. Army ROTC Four-Year College
  Scholarship *610*
U.S. Army ROTC Four-Year Historically Black
  College/University Scholarship *610*
U.S. Army ROTC Four-Year Nursing
  Scholarship *475*
U.S. Army ROTC Guaranteed Reserve Forces
  Duty (GRFD), (ARNG/USAR) and Dedicated
  ARNG Scholarships *611*
U.S. Army ROTC Military Junior College (MJC)
  Scholarship *611*
ValuePenguin Scholarship *682*
West Virginia Higher Education Grant
  Program *877*
Women in Architecture Scholarship *134*
You Deserve It! Scholarship *865*

Puerto Rico

AG Bell College Scholarship Program *594*
Annual CGTrader Scholarship *604*
Annual iSeeCars Future Entrepreneurs
  Scholarship *900*
Army ROTC Green to Gold Scholarship Program
  for Two-Year, Three-Year and Four-Year
  Scholarships, Active Duty Enlisted
  Personnel *610*
Army (ROTC) Reserve Officers Training Corps
  Two-, Three-, Four-Year Campus-Based
  Scholarships *610*
Benson & Bingham Annual Scholarship *413*
CBC Spouses Education Scholarship *730*
CBC Spouses Heineken USA Performing Arts
  Scholarship *452*
CBC Spouses Visual Arts Scholarship *132*
Classic Scholarships *874*
Clunker Junker Cash for Cars and College
  Scholarship *299*
HENAAC Scholarship Program *115*
Jules Cohen Scholarship *284*
National Institute for Labor Relations Research
  William B. Ruggles Journalism
  Scholarship *650*
National Restaurant Association Educational
  Foundation Undergraduate Scholarships for
  College Students *109*
Pedro Zamora Young Leaders Scholarship *647*
Residential Design Scholarship *134*
Simmons and Fletcher, P.C., Law Marketing
  Scholarship *668*
Sustainable Residential Design Scholarship *134*
Two Ten Footwear Foundation Scholarship *676*
Two Ten Foundation Footwear Design
  Scholarship *874*
U.S. Army ROTC Four-Year College
  Scholarship *610*

U.S. Army ROTC Four-Year Historically Black
  College/University Scholarship *610*
U.S. Army ROTC Four-Year Nursing
  Scholarship *475*
U.S. Army ROTC Guaranteed Reserve Forces
  Duty (GRFD), (ARNG/USAR) and Dedicated
  ARNG Scholarships *611*
U.S. Army ROTC Military Junior College (MJC)
  Scholarship *611*
ValuePenguin Scholarship *682*
You Deserve It! Scholarship *865*

Rhode Island

AbbVie Immunology Scholarship *666*
AG Bell College Scholarship Program *594*
Annual CGTrader Scholarship *604*
Annual iSeeCars Future Entrepreneurs
  Scholarship *900*
Army ROTC Green to Gold Scholarship Program
  for Two-Year, Three-Year and Four-Year
  Scholarships, Active Duty Enlisted
  Personnel *610*
Army (ROTC) Reserve Officers Training Corps
  Two-, Three-, Four-Year Campus-Based
  Scholarships *610*
Benson & Bingham Annual Scholarship *413*
Bruce and Marjorie Sundlun Scholarship *863*
CBC Spouses Education Scholarship *730*
CBC Spouses Heineken USA Performing Arts
  Scholarship *452*
CBC Spouses Visual Arts Scholarship *132*
Classic Scholarships *874*
Clunker Junker Cash for Cars and College
  Scholarship *299*
Clutch Prep STEM Scholarship *285*
Dr. James L. Lawson Memorial Scholarship *216*
Edward J. and Virginia M. Routhier Nursing
  Scholarship *487*
Finally Sold Impact Maker Scholarship *618*
Frank S. Land Scholarship *588*
Greenhouse Scholars *736*
HENAAC Scholarship Program *115*
Jules Cohen Scholarship *284*
Kelley & Canterbury, LLC Alaska Curiosity
  Scholarship *633*
Korean-American Scholarship Foundation
  Northeastern Region Scholarships *744*
Lily and Catello Sorrentino Memorial
  Scholarship *863*
Milton Fisher Scholarship for Innovation and
  Creativity *862*
Minority Students in Veterinary Medicine
  Scholarship *719*
Morrow & Sheppard College Scholarship *417*
NASA Rhode Island Space Grant Consortium
  Outreach Scholarship for Undergraduate
  Students *303*
NASA Rhode Island Space Grant Consortium
  Undergraduate Research Scholarship *157*
NASA RISGC Science En Espanol Scholarship for
  Undergraduate Students *157*
NASA RISGC Summer Scholarship for
  Undergraduate Students *157*
National Association for Campus Activities
  Scholarships for Student Leaders *186*
National Institute for Labor Relations Research
  William B. Ruggles Journalism
  Scholarship *650*
National Make It With Wool Competition *345*
National Restaurant Association Educational
  Foundation Undergraduate Scholarships for
  College Students *109*
New England Employee Benefits Council
  Scholarship Program *89*
New England Regional Student Program-Tuition
  Break *850*

Norton E. Salk Scholarship *136*
Patricia W. Edwards Memorial Art
  Scholarship *144*
Pedro Zamora Young Leaders Scholarship *647*
Residential Construction Management
  Scholarship *238*
Residential Design Scholarship *134*
Roothbert Fund Inc. Scholarship *864*
Seol Bong Scholarship *693*
State of Maine Grant Program *827*
Sustainable Residential Design Scholarship *134*
Two Ten Footwear Foundation Scholarship *676*
Two Ten Foundation Footwear Design
  Scholarship *874*
Union Plus Education Foundation Scholarship
  Program *584*
United States Senate Youth Program *918*
U.S. Army ROTC Four-Year College
  Scholarship *610*
U.S. Army ROTC Four-Year Historically Black
  College/University Scholarship *610*
U.S. Army ROTC Four-Year Nursing
  Scholarship *475*
U.S. Army ROTC Guaranteed Reserve Forces
  Duty (GRFD), (ARNG/USAR) and Dedicated
  ARNG Scholarships *611*
U.S. Army ROTC Military Junior College (MJC)
  Scholarship *611*
ValuePenguin Scholarship *682*
Women in Architecture Scholarship *134*

South Carolina

AbbVie Immunology Scholarship *666*
AG Bell College Scholarship Program *594*
Annual CGTrader Scholarship *604*
Annual iSeeCars Future Entrepreneurs
  Scholarship *900*
Army ROTC Green to Gold Scholarship Program
  for Two-Year, Three-Year and Four-Year
  Scholarships, Active Duty Enlisted
  Personnel *610*
Army (ROTC) Reserve Officers Training Corps
  Two-, Three-, Four-Year Campus-Based
  Scholarships *610*
ASHRAE Region IV Benny Bootle
  Scholarship *130*
Benson & Bingham Annual Scholarship *413*
Casualty Actuaries of the Southeast Scholarship
  Program *928*
CBC Spouses Education Scholarship *730*
CBC Spouses Heineken USA Performing Arts
  Scholarship *452*
CBC Spouses Visual Arts Scholarship *132*
Classic Scholarships *874*
Clunker Junker Cash for Cars and College
  Scholarship *299*
Clutch Prep STEM Scholarship *285*
Finally Sold Impact Maker Scholarship *618*
Frank S. Land Scholarship *588*
Greenhouse Scholars *736*
Hagan Scholarship *623*
HENAAC Scholarship Program *115*
Jules Cohen Scholarship *284*
Kelley & Canterbury, LLC Alaska Curiosity
  Scholarship *633*
Korean-American Scholarship Foundation
  Southern Region Scholarships *744*
L. Phil and Alice J. Wicker Scholarship *217*
Milton Fisher Scholarship for Innovation and
  Creativity *862*
Minority Students in Veterinary Medicine
  Scholarship *719*
Morrow & Sheppard College Scholarship *417*
National Association for Campus Activities
  Scholarships for Student Leaders *186*

National Association for Campus Activities South Region Student Leader Scholarship *648*

National Institute for Labor Relations Research William B. Ruggles Journalism Scholarship *650*

National Make It With Wool Competition *345*

National Restaurant Association Educational Foundation Undergraduate Scholarships for College Students *109*

Palmetto Fellows Scholarship Program *868*

Pedro Zamora Young Leaders Scholarship *647*

Polly Holliday Scholarship *145*

Residential Construction Management Scholarship *238*

Residential Design Scholarship *134*

SCACPA Educational Fund Scholarships *92*

South Carolina HOPE Scholarship *868*

South Carolina Need-Based Grants Program *868*

South Carolina Tourism and Hospitality Educational Foundation Scholarships *250*

South Carolina Tuition Grants Program *669*

Sustainable Residential Design Scholarship *134*

Ted G. Wilson Memorial Scholarship Foundation *211*

Triangle Pest Control Scholarship *93*

Tuition Assistance for Certain War Veterans' Children *716*

Two Ten Footwear Foundation Scholarship *676*

Two Ten Foundation Footwear Design Scholarship *874*

Union Plus Education Foundation Scholarship Program *584*

United States Senate Youth Program *918*

U.S. Army ROTC Four-Year College Scholarship *610*

U.S. Army ROTC Four-Year Historically Black College/University Scholarship *610*

U.S. Army ROTC Four-Year Nursing Scholarship *475*

U.S. Army ROTC Guaranteed Reserve Forces Duty (GRFD), (ARNG/USAR) and Dedicated ARNG Scholarships *611*

U.S. Army ROTC Military Junior College (MJC) Scholarship *611*

ValuePenguin Scholarship *682*

Women in Architecture Scholarship *134*

You Deserve It! Scholarship *865*

South Dakota

AbbVie Immunology Scholarship *666*

AG Bell College Scholarship Program *594*

American Legion Department of Minnesota Memorial Scholarship *555*

Annual CGTrader Scholarship *604*

Annual iSeeCars Future Entrepreneurs Scholarship *900*

Army ROTC Green to Gold Scholarship Program for Two-Year, Three-Year and Four-Year Scholarships, Active Duty Enlisted Personnel *610*

Army (ROTC) Reserve Officers Training Corps Two-, Three-, Four-Year Campus-Based Scholarships *610*

Benson & Bingham Annual Scholarship *413*

CBC Spouses Education Scholarship *730*

CBC Spouses Heineken USA Performing Arts Scholarship *452*

CBC Spouses Visual Arts Scholarship *132*

Classic Scholarships *874*

Clunker Junker Cash for Cars and College Scholarship *299*

Clutch Prep STEM Scholarship *285*

Excellence in Accounting Scholarship *92*

Finally Sold Impact Maker Scholarship *618*

Frank S. Land Scholarship *588*

Greenhouse Scholars *736*

Hagan Scholarship *623*

HENAAC Scholarship Program *115*

Jules Cohen Scholarship *284*

Kelley & Canterbury, LLC Alaska Curiosity Scholarship *633*

Milton Fisher Scholarship for Innovation and Creativity *862*

Minnesota Legionnaires Insurance Trust Scholarship *555*

Minority Students in Veterinary Medicine Scholarship *719*

Morrow & Sheppard College Scholarship *417*

National Association for Campus Activities Scholarships for Student Leaders *186*

National Defense Transportation Association, Scott Air Force Base-St. Louis Area Chapter Scholarship *849*

National Institute for Labor Relations Research William B. Ruggles Journalism Scholarship *650*

National Make It With Wool Competition *345*

National Restaurant Association Educational Foundation Undergraduate Scholarships for College Students *109*

North Central Region 9 Scholarship *328*

Pedro Zamora Young Leaders Scholarship *647*

PFund Foundation Scholarship Program *861*

Residential Construction Management Scholarship *238*

Residential Design Scholarship *134*

South Dakota Board of Regents Annis I. Fowler/Kaden Scholarship *276*

South Dakota Board of Regents Marlin R. Scarborough Memorial Scholarship *913*

South Dakota Opportunity Scholarship *869*

Sustainable Residential Design Scholarship *134*

SWE Region H Scholarships *201*

Touchmark Foundation Nursing Scholarship *488*

Two Ten Footwear Foundation Scholarship *676*

Two Ten Foundation Footwear Design Scholarship *874*

Union Plus Education Foundation Scholarship Program *584*

United States Senate Youth Program *918*

U.S. Army ROTC Four-Year College Scholarship *610*

U.S. Army ROTC Four-Year Historically Black College/University Scholarship *610*

U.S. Army ROTC Four-Year Nursing Scholarship *475*

U.S. Army ROTC Guaranteed Reserve Forces Duty (GRFD), (ARNG/USAR) and Dedicated ARNG Scholarships *611*

U.S. Army ROTC Military Junior College (MJC) Scholarship *611*

ValuePenguin Scholarship *682*

WICHE's Western Undergraduate Exchange (WUE) *683*

Women in Architecture Scholarship *134*

You Deserve It! Scholarship *865*

Tennessee

AbbVie Immunology Scholarship *666*

AG Bell College Scholarship Program *594*

American Legion Department of Tennessee Eagle Scout of the Year *556*

Annual CGTrader Scholarship *604*

Annual iSeeCars Future Entrepreneurs Scholarship *900*

Army ROTC Green to Gold Scholarship Program for Two-Year, Three-Year and Four-Year Scholarships, Active Duty Enlisted Personnel *610*

Army (ROTC) Reserve Officers Training Corps Two-, Three-, Four-Year Campus-Based Scholarships *610*

Benson & Bingham Annual Scholarship *413*

Casualty Actuaries of the Southeast Scholarship Program *928*

CBC Spouses Education Scholarship *730*

CBC Spouses Heineken.USA Performing Arts Scholarship *452*

CBC Spouses Visual Arts Scholarship *132*

Classic Scholarships *874*

Clunker Junker Cash for Cars and College Scholarship *299*

Clutch Prep STEM Scholarship *285*

Dependent Children Scholarship Program *672*

Finally Sold Impact Maker Scholarship *618*

Frank S. Land Scholarship *588*

Greenhouse Scholars *736*

Hagan Scholarship *623*

Helping Heroes Grant *672*

HENAAC Scholarship Program *115*

HOPE Aspire Award *672*

JROTC Scholarship *519*

Jules Cohen Scholarship *284*

Kelley & Canterbury, LLC Alaska Curiosity Scholarship *633*

Korean-American Scholarship Foundation Southern Region Scholarships *744*

Milton Fisher Scholarship for Innovation and Creativity *862*

Minority Students in Veterinary Medicine Scholarship *719*

Morrow & Sheppard College Scholarship *417*

National Association for Campus Activities Scholarships for Student Leaders *186*

National Association for Campus Activities South Region Student Leader Scholarship *648*

National Institute for Labor Relations Research William B. Ruggles Journalism Scholarship *650*

National Make It With Wool Competition *345*

National Restaurant Association Educational Foundation Undergraduate Scholarships for College Students *109*

Ned McWherter Scholars Program *672*

Pedro Zamora Young Leaders Scholarship *647*

Polly Holliday Scholarship *145*

Promise of Nursing Scholarship *478*

Reduction in Force Tuition Assistance Benefit *870*

Residential Construction Management Scholarship *238*

Residential Design Scholarship *134*

Sustainable Residential Design Scholarship *134*

TEA Don Sahli-Kathy Woodall Future Teachers of America Scholarship *276*

TEA Don Sahli-Kathy Woodall Minority Scholarship *276*

TEA Don Sahli-Kathy Woodall Sons and Daughters Scholarship *277*

TEA Don Sahli-Kathy Woodall STEA Scholarship *277*

TELS -HOPE with General Assembly Merit Scholarship (GAMS) *672*

Tennessee Dual Enrollment Grant *672*

Tennessee HOPE Access Grant *673*

Tennessee HOPE Foster Child Tuition Grant *673*

Tennessee HOPE Scholarship *673*

Tennessee HOPE Scholarship for Nontraditional Students *870*

Tennessee Reconnect Grant *871*

Tennessee Student Assistance Award *673*

Two Ten Footwear Foundation Scholarship *676*

Two Ten Foundation Footwear Design Scholarship *874*

Union Plus Education Foundation Scholarship Program *584*

United States Senate Youth Program *918*

West Virginia

Wisconsin

E.H. Marth Food Protection and Food Sciences Scholarship *336*

Ethel A. Neijahr Wisconsin Mathematics Council Scholarship *279*

Finally Sold Impact Maker Scholarship *618*

Frank S. Land Scholarship *588*

Greenhouse Scholars *736*

Hagan Scholarship *623*

HENAAC Scholarship Program *115*

Jules Cohen Scholarship *284*

Kelley & Canterbury, LLC Alaska Curiosity Scholarship *633*

Milton Fisher Scholarship for Innovation and Creativity *862*

Minnesota Legionnaires Insurance Trust Scholarship *555*

Minority Students in Veterinary Medicine Scholarship *719*

Minority Undergraduate Retention Grant-Wisconsin *771*

Morrow & Sheppard College Scholarship *417*

National Association for Campus Activities Northern Plains Region Student Leadership Scholarship *81*

National Association for Campus Activities Scholarships for Student Leaders *186*

National Defense Transportation Association, Scott Air Force Base-St. Louis Area Chapter Scholarship *849*

National Institute for Labor Relations Research William B. Ruggles Journalism Scholarship *650*

National Make It With Wool Competition *345*

National Restaurant Association Educational Foundation Undergraduate Scholarships for College Students *109*

North Central Region 9 Scholarship *328*

Pedro Zamora Young Leaders Scholarship *647*

PFund Foundation Scholarship Program *861*

Residential Construction Management Scholarship *238*

Residential Design Scholarship *134*

Sister Mary Petronia Van Straten Wisconsin Mathematics Council Scholarship *279*

Sustainable Residential Design Scholarship *134*

SWE Region H Scholarships *201*

Talent Incentive Program Grant *878*

Touchmark Foundation Nursing Scholarship *488*

Two Ten Footwear Foundation Scholarship *676*

Two Ten Foundation Footwear Design Scholarship *874*

Union Plus Education Foundation Scholarship Program *584*

United States Senate Youth Program *918*

U.S. Army ROTC Four-Year College Scholarship *610*

U.S. Army ROTC Four-Year Historically Black College/University Scholarship *610*

U.S. Army ROTC Four-Year Nursing Scholarship *475*

U.S. Army ROTC Guaranteed Reserve Forces Duty (GRFD), (ARNG/USAR) and Dedicated ARNG Scholarships *611*

U.S. Army ROTC Military Junior College (MJC) Scholarship *611*

ValuePenguin Scholarship *682*

Veterans Education (VetEd) Reimbursement Grant *694*

Virchow, Krause and Company Scholarship *95*

Wisconsin Academic Excellence Scholarship *878*

Wisconsin Broadcasters Association Foundation Scholarship *228*

Wisconsin Higher Education Grants (WHEG) *878*

Wisconsin Native American/Indian Student Assistance Grant *771*

Wisconsin Space Grant Consortium Undergraduate Scholarship Program *157*

Women in Architecture Scholarship *134*

You Deserve It! Scholarship *865*

Wyoming

AbbVie Immunology Scholarship *666*

AG Bell College Scholarship Program *594*

Annual CGTrader Scholarship *604*

Annual iSeeCars Future Entrepreneurs Scholarship *900*

Army ROTC Green to Gold Scholarship Program for Two-Year, Three-Year and Four-Year Scholarships, Active Duty Enlisted Personnel *610*

Army (ROTC) Reserve Officers Training Corps Two-, Three-, Four-Year Campus-Based Scholarships *610*

Benson & Bingham Annual Scholarship *413*

Boundless Opportunity Scholarship *608*

CBC Spouses Education Scholarship *730*

CBC Spouses Heineken USA Performing Arts Scholarship *452*

CBC Spouses Visual Arts Scholarship *132*

Classic Scholarships *874*

Clunker Junker Cash for Cars and College Scholarship *299*

Clutch Prep STEM Scholarship *285*

Douvas Memorial Scholarship *879*

Finally Sold Impact Maker Scholarship *618*

Frank S. Land Scholarship *588*

Greenhouse Scholars *736*

Hagan Scholarship *623*

Hathaway Scholarship *879*

HENAAC Scholarship Program *115*

Jules Cohen Scholarship *284*

Kelley & Canterbury, LLC Alaska Curiosity Scholarship *633*

Korean-American Scholarship Foundation Western Region Scholarships *744*

Livingston Family - H.J. King Memorial Scholarship *587*

Milton Fisher Scholarship for Innovation and Creativity *862*

Minority Students in Veterinary Medicine Scholarship *719*

Morrow & Sheppard College Scholarship *417*

National Association for Campus Activities Scholarships for Student Leaders *186*

National Defense Transportation Association, Scott Air Force Base-St. Louis Area Chapter Scholarship *849*

National Institute for Labor Relations Research William B. Ruggles Journalism Scholarship *650*

National Make It With Wool Competition *345*

National Restaurant Association Educational Foundation Undergraduate Scholarships for College Students *109*

Pedro Zamora Young Leaders Scholarship *647*

Residential Construction Management Scholarship *238*

Residential Design Scholarship *134*

Superior Student in Education Scholarship-Wyoming *278*

Sustainable Residential Design Scholarship *134*

Two Ten Footwear Foundation Scholarship *676*

Two Ten Foundation Footwear Design Scholarship *874*

Union Plus Education Foundation Scholarship Program *584*

United States Senate Youth Program *918*

U.S. Army ROTC Four-Year College Scholarship *610*

U.S. Army ROTC Four-Year Historically Black College/University Scholarship *610*

U.S. Army ROTC Four-Year Nursing Scholarship *475*

U.S. Army ROTC Guaranteed Reserve Forces Duty (GRFD), (ARNG/USAR) and Dedicated ARNG Scholarships *611*

U.S. Army ROTC Military Junior College (MJC) Scholarship *611*

ValuePenguin Scholarship *682*

WICHE's Western Undergraduate Exchange (WUE) *683*

Women in Architecture Scholarship *134*

Wyoming Farm Bureau Continuing Education Scholarships *587*

Wyoming Farm Bureau Federation Scholarships *588*

Wyoming Trucking Association Scholarship Trust Fund *95*

You Deserve It! Scholarship *865*

CANADA

Alberta

AG Bell College Scholarship Program *594*

Alberta Pre-Apprenticeship Scholarships *799*

Annual CGTrader Scholarship *604*

Annual iSeeCars Future Entrepreneurs Scholarship *900*

Belcourt Brosseau Metis Awards *733*

Benson & Bingham Annual Scholarship *413*

Bill Mason Scholarship Fund *275*

Canada Iceland Foundation Scholarship Program *889*

Charles S. Noble Junior Football Scholarships *720*

Charles S. Noble Junior Hockey Scholarships *720*

Clunker Junker Cash for Cars and College Scholarship *299*

International Education Awards-Ukraine *720*

Jason Lang Scholarship *251*

Jimmie Condon Athletic Scholarships *720*

Keyera Energy-Peter J. Renton Memorial Scholarship *721*

Languages in Teacher Education Scholarships *265*

Laurence Decore Awards for Student Leadership *721*

Leo J. Krysa Undergraduate Scholarship *138*

National Association for Campus Activities Northern Plains Region Student Leadership Scholarship *81*

National Association for Campus Activities Scholarships for Student Leaders *186*

National Restaurant Association Educational Foundation Undergraduate Scholarships for College Students *109*

Northern Alberta Development Council Bursary *251*

Persons Case Scholarships *721*

Prairie Baseball Academy Scholarships *800*

Simmons and Fletcher, P.C., Law Marketing Scholarship *668*

Terry Fox Humanitarian Award *673*

Touchmark Foundation Nursing Scholarship *488*

You Deserve It! Scholarship *865*

British Columbia

AG Bell College Scholarship Program *594*

Annual CGTrader Scholarship *604*

Belcourt Brosseau Metis Awards *733*

Benson & Bingham Annual Scholarship *413*

Bill Mason Scholarship Fund *275*

Canada Iceland Foundation Scholarship Program *889*

Military Service

Marine Corps

Navy

Nationality or Ethnic Heritage

African

American Meteorological Society Minority Scholarships 448

Black EOE Journal Scholarship 732

CANFIT Nutrition, Physical Education and Culinary Arts Scholarship 245

Lemberg Law American Dream $1,250 Undergraduate Scholarship 640

Northwest Journalists of Color Scholarship 96

OLM Malala Yousafzai Scholarship 143

Albanian

Lemberg Law American Dream $1,250 Undergraduate Scholarship 640

OLM Malala Yousafzai Scholarship 143

American Indian/Alaska Native

2018 PDFelement $1000 Scholarship 684

5 Strong Scholars Scholarship 719

Aboriginal Health Careers Bursary 167

AcadGild Merit-Based Scholarships 593

Accenture American Indian Scholarship 722

Actuarial Diversity Scholarship 397

Adolph Van Pelt Special Fund for Indian Scholarships 725

AFSCME/UNCF Union Scholars Program 113

Agnes Jones Jackson Scholarship 569

AIET Minorities and Women Educational Scholarship 516

AIFS DiversityAbroad.com Scholarship 723

Al-Ben Scholarship for Academic Incentive 193

Al-Ben Scholarship for Professional Merit 193

Al-Ben Scholarship for Scholastic Achievement 193

Allogan Slagle Memorial Scholarship 725

Alumni Student Assistance Program 727

Amelia Kemp Scholarship 771

American Chemical Society Scholars Program 187

American Indian Education Fund Scholarship 722

American Indian Nurse Scholarship Program 368

American Meteorological Society Minority Scholarships 448

American Physical Society Corporate-Sponsored Scholarship for Minority Undergraduate Students Who Major in Physics 506

Amy Hunter-Wilson, MD Scholarship 378

APEX Scholarship 724

Architects Foundation Diversity Advancement Scholarship 131

Arizona Professional Chapter of AISES Scholarship 313

Arts Council of Greater Grand Rapids Minority Scholarship 142

A.T. Anderson Memorial Scholarship Program 121

Audre Lorde Scholarship Fund 771

AWG Ethnic Minority Scholarship 260

Beatrice Medicine Awards 760

BIA Higher Education Grant 739

Blackfeet Nation Higher Education Grant 726

Breakthrough to Nursing Scholarships for Racial/Ethnic Minorities 477

Bureau of Indian Education Grant Program 726

CANFIT Nutrition, Physical Education and Culinary Arts Scholarship 245

Carole Simpson Scholarship 222

Catherine W. Pierce Scholarship 140

Cherokee Nation Higher Education Scholarship 728

Chief Manuelito Scholarship Program 754

CIC/Anna Chennault Scholarship 217

Citizen Potawatomi Nation Tribal Scholarship 728

ClothingRIC.com Annual Student Scholarship 605

Colgate "Bright Smiles, Bright Futures" Minority Scholarship 252

College Student Assistance Program 727

College Student Pre-Commissioning Initiative (CSPI) 681

Continental Society, Daughters of Indian Wars Scholarship 242

David Risling Emergency Aid Scholarship 725

Dell Corporate Scholars Program 213

Displaced Homemaker Scholarship 725

Ed Bradley Scholarship 223

EDSA Minority Scholarship 636

Elizabeth and Sherman Asche Memorial Scholarship Fund 106

Epsilon Sigma Alpha Foundation Scholarships 733

Essay Writing Contest by EssayHub 615

GE/LULAC Scholarship 181

GM/LULAC Scholarship 321

HBCUConnect.com Minority Scholarship Program 624

Health Professions Preparatory Scholarship Program 165

Help to Save Scholarship 106

Higher Education Supplemental Scholarship Isleta Pueblo Higher Education Department 576

Home Improvement Scholarship by Home Improvement Solutions 626

Homus Scholarship Program 627

Hopi Education Award 739

Hubertus W.V. Wellems Scholarship for Male Students 194

Hyatt Hotels Fund for Minority Lodging Management 245

Indian Health Service Health Professions Pre-graduate Scholarships 125

International Order of the King's Daughters and Sons North American Indian Scholarship 740

Jackie Robinson Scholarship 631

Jim Bourque Scholarship 267

Judith McManus Price Scholarship 547

Kansas Ethnic Minority Scholarship 742

Ken Inouye Scholarship 409

LAGRANT Foundation Scholarship for Graduates 97

LAGRANT Foundation Scholarship for Undergraduates 97

Leonard M. Perryman Communications Scholarship for Ethnic Minority Students 227

Mae Lassley Osage Scholarship 758

Martin Luther King, Jr. Memorial Scholarship 269

Master's Scholarship Program 195

Math, Engineering, Science, Business, Education, Computers Scholarships 178

Maureen L. and Howard N. Blitman, PE Scholarship to Promote Diversity in Engineering 194

Menominee Indian Tribe Adult Vocational Training Program 747

Menominee Indian Tribe of Wisconsin Higher Education Grants 747

Minnesota Indian Scholarship 748

Minorities in Government Finance Scholarship 86

Minority Affairs Committee Award for Outstanding Scholastic Achievement 188

Minority Scholarship Awards for College Students 189

Minority Scholarship Awards for Incoming College Freshmen 189

Minority Scholarship Program 169

Minority Students in Veterinary Medicine Scholarship 719

Minority Student Summer Scholarship 130

Minority Teacher Incentive Grant Program 269

Minority Teachers of Illinois Scholarship Program 271

Minority Undergraduate Retention Grant-Wisconsin 771

NACME Scholars Program 322

National Dental Association Foundation Colgate-Palmolive Scholarship Program (Undergraduates) 256

National Press Club Scholarship for Journalism Diversity 406

National Society Daughters of the American Revolution American Indian Scholarship 751

National Society Daughters of the American Revolution Frances Crawford Marvin American Indian Scholarship 751

Native American Journalists Association Scholarships 97

Native American Leadership in Education (NALE) 178

Native American Natural Resource Research Scholarship 459

Native American Supplemental Grant 757

NativeVision 751

Navajo Generating Station Navajo Scholarship 324

New York State Aid to Native Americans 752

North Dakota Indian Scholarship Program 654

Northern Cheyenne Tribal Education Department 753

Northwest Journalists of Color Scholarship 96

Nurture for Nature Scholarship 692

Ohio News Media Foundation Minority Scholarship 98

Ohkay Owingeh Tribal Scholarship of the Pueblo of San Juan 663

OLM Malala Yousafzai Scholarship 143

Oneida Higher Education Scholarship Program 754

Oregon Native American Chamber of Commerce Scholarship 754

Osage Nation Higher Education Scholarship 657

Owanah Anderson Scholarship 725

Peter Doctor Memorial Indian Scholarship Foundation Inc. 756

Pine Cone Foundation Scholarship 660

PoP'ay Scholarship 663

Public Relations Society of America Multicultural Affairs Scholarship 98

Rama Scholarship for the American Dream 245

RDW Group Inc. Minority Scholarship for Communications 224

Richard S. Smith Scholarship 732

Guglielmo Marconi Engineering Scholarship *680*
Henry Salvatori Scholarship for General Study *669*
Inserra Scholarships *680*
Italian-American Chamber of Commerce of Chicago Scholarship *741*
Italian Language Scholarship *215*
Lemberg Law American Dream $1,250 Undergraduate Scholarship *640*
Major Don S. Gentile Scholarship *680*
Maria and Paolo Alessio Southern Italy Scholarship *680*
National Italian American Foundation Category I Scholarship *751*
OLM Malala Yousafzai Scholarship *143*
Sons of Italy Foundation's National Leadership Grant Competition *761*
Sons of Italy National Leadership Grants Competition/ Henry Salvatori Scholarship *761*
Sons of Italy National Leadership Grants Competition Language Scholarship *361*

Japanese
American Meteorological Society Minority Scholarships *448*
CANFIT Nutrition, Physical Education and Culinary Arts Scholarship *245*
Lemberg Law American Dream $1,250 Undergraduate Scholarship *640*
National JACL Headquarters Scholarship *107*
Northwest Journalists of Color Scholarship *96*
OLM Malala Yousafzai Scholarship *143*
Scholarship for the Visually Impaired to Study Abroad *686*
Scholarship for the Visually Impaired to Study in Japan *686*
Teri and Art Iwasaki Scholarship *741*

Jewish
Diller Teen Tikkun Olam Awards *624*
Jewish Federation of Metropolitan Chicago Academic Scholarship Program *742*
JVS Scholarship Program *741*
Lemberg Law American Dream $1,250 Undergraduate Scholarship *640*
Lessans Family Scholarship *604*
OLM Malala Yousafzai Scholarship *143*
Sara and Max Goldsammler Scholarship Fund *754*

Korean
American Meteorological Society Minority Scholarships *448*
Kimbo Foundation Scholarship *743*
Korean-American Scholarship Foundation Eastern Region Scholarships *743*
Korean-American Scholarship Foundation Northeastern Region Scholarships *744*
Korean-American Scholarship Foundation Southern Region Scholarships *744*
Korean-American Scholarship Foundation Western Region Scholarships *744*
Lemberg Law American Dream $1,250 Undergraduate Scholarship *640*
Northwest Journalists of Color Scholarship *96*
OLM Malala Yousafzai Scholarship *143*
Seol Bong Scholarship *693*

Lao/Hmong
Distinguished Raven FAC Memorial Scholarship *614*
Lemberg Law American Dream $1,250 Undergraduate Scholarship *640*

Nisei Student Relocation Commemorative Fund *652*
Northwest Journalists of Color Scholarship *96*
OLM Malala Yousafzai Scholarship *143*

Latin American/Caribbean
Automotive Women's Alliance Foundation Scholarships *81*
CCNMA Scholarships *218*
Clara Lionel Foundation Global Scholarship Program *605*
Fulfilling Our Dreams Scholarship Fund *759*
La Unidad Latina Foundation Dream Scholarship *636*
La Unidad Latina Foundation National Scholarship *637*
Lemberg Law American Dream $1,250 Undergraduate Scholarship *640*
Mas Family Scholarship Award *181*
Northwest Journalists of Color Scholarship *96*
OLM Malala Yousafzai Scholarship *143*

Latvian
Lemberg Law American Dream $1,250 Undergraduate Scholarship *640*
OLM Malala Yousafzai Scholarship *143*

Lebanese
Lemberg Law American Dream $1,250 Undergraduate Scholarship *640*
Northwest Journalists of Color Scholarship *96*
OLM Malala Yousafzai Scholarship *143*

Lithuanian
Alpha Omega Scholarship In Memory Of Peter Agris *215*
Lemberg Law American Dream $1,250 Undergraduate Scholarship *640*
OLM Malala Yousafzai Scholarship *143*

Mexican
American Meteorological Society Minority Scholarships *448*
Automotive Women's Alliance Foundation Scholarships *81*
Fleming/Blaszcak Scholarship *195*
Latinos in Technology Scholarship *760*
La Unidad Latina Foundation Dream Scholarship *636*
La Unidad Latina Foundation National Scholarship *637*
Lemberg Law American Dream $1,250 Undergraduate Scholarship *640*
Minority Students in Veterinary Medicine Scholarship *719*
Northwest Journalists of Color Scholarship *96*
OLM Malala Yousafzai Scholarship *143*
Our World Underwater Scholarship Society *755*
Transportation Clubs International Ginger and Fred Deines Mexico Scholarship *541*

Mongolian
Lemberg Law American Dream $1,250 Undergraduate Scholarship *640*
Northwest Journalists of Color Scholarship *96*
OLM Malala Yousafzai Scholarship *143*

New Zealander
Lemberg Law American Dream $1,250 Undergraduate Scholarship *640*
OLM Malala Yousafzai Scholarship *143*
Our World Underwater Scholarship Society *755*
Pacific Health Workforce Award *368*
Pacific Mental Health Work Force Award *368*

Nicaraguan
La Unidad Latina Foundation Dream Scholarship *636*

La Unidad Latina Foundation National Scholarship *637*
Lemberg Law American Dream $1,250 Undergraduate Scholarship *640*
OLM Malala Yousafzai Scholarship *143*

Norwegian
King Olav V Norwegian-American Heritage Fund *139*
Lemberg Law American Dream $1,250 Undergraduate Scholarship *640*
Nancy Lorraine Jensen Memorial Scholarship *202*
OLM Malala Yousafzai Scholarship *143*

Polish
Lemberg Law American Dream $1,250 Undergraduate Scholarship *640*
Massachusetts Federation of Polish Women's Clubs Scholarships *744*
OLM Malala Yousafzai Scholarship *143*
Polish American Club of North Jersey Scholarships *744*
Polish Arts Club of Buffalo Scholarship Foundation Trust *144*
Polish Heritage Scholarship *756*
Polish National Alliance of Brooklyn USA Inc. Scholarships *744*
Polish Women's Alliance Academic College Undergraduate Scholarships *756*
Tomaszkiewicz-Florio Scholarship *745*

Portuguese
Cabrillo Civic Clubs of California Scholarship *727*
Lemberg Law American Dream $1,250 Undergraduate Scholarship *640*
OLM Malala Yousafzai Scholarship *143*
PALCUS National Scholarship Program *660*

Rumanian
Lemberg Law American Dream $1,250 Undergraduate Scholarship *640*
OLM Malala Yousafzai Scholarship *143*

Russian
Lemberg Law American Dream $1,250 Undergraduate Scholarship *640*
OLM Malala Yousafzai Scholarship *143*

Scandinavian
Lemberg Law American Dream $1,250 Undergraduate Scholarship *640*
OLM Malala Yousafzai Scholarship *143*

Scottish
Lemberg Law American Dream $1,250 Undergraduate Scholarship *640*
OLM Malala Yousafzai Scholarship *143*
Our World Underwater Scholarship Society *755*
St. Andrews Scholarship *758*
St. Andrew's Society of Washington DC Founders' Scholarship *665*
St. Andrew's Society of Washington DC Scholarships *665*

Slavic/Czech
First Catholic Slovak Ladies Association Fraternal Scholarship Award *734*
Lemberg Law American Dream $1,250 Undergraduate Scholarship *640*
OLM Malala Yousafzai Scholarship *143*

Spanish
Lemberg Law American Dream $1,250 Undergraduate Scholarship *640*
OLM Malala Yousafzai Scholarship *143*
Our World Underwater Scholarship Society *755*

Sub-Saharan African

Lemberg Law American Dream $1,250 Undergraduate Scholarship *640*

Northwest Journalists of Color Scholarship *96*

OLM Malala Yousafzai Scholarship *143*

Swedish

Lemberg Law American Dream $1,250 Undergraduate Scholarship *640*

OLM Malala Yousafzai Scholarship *143*

Our World Underwater Scholarship Society *755*

Swiss

Lemberg Law American Dream $1,250 Undergraduate Scholarship *640*

Medicus Student Exchange *763*

OLM Malala Yousafzai Scholarship *143*

Our World Underwater Scholarship Society *755*

Pellegrini Scholarship Grants *763*

Swiss Benevolent Society of Chicago Scholarships *762*

Swiss Benevolent Society of San Francisco Scholarships *762*

Syrian

Lemberg Law American Dream $1,250 Undergraduate Scholarship *640*

Northwest Journalists of Color Scholarship *96*

OLM Malala Yousafzai Scholarship *143*

Turkish

Lemberg Law American Dream $1,250 Undergraduate Scholarship *640*

Northwest Journalists of Color Scholarship *96*

OLM Malala Yousafzai Scholarship *143*

Ukrainian

International Education Awards-Ukraine *720*

Lemberg Law American Dream $1,250 Undergraduate Scholarship *640*

OLM Malala Yousafzai Scholarship *143*

Vietnamese

Lemberg Law American Dream $1,250 Undergraduate Scholarship *640*

Nisei Student Relocation Commemorative Fund *652*

Northwest Journalists of Color Scholarship *96*

OLM Malala Yousafzai Scholarship *143*

Welsh

Lemberg Law American Dream $1,250 Undergraduate Scholarship *640*

OLM Malala Yousafzai Scholarship *143*

Yemeni

Lemberg Law American Dream $1,250 Undergraduate Scholarship *640*

National American Arab Nurses Association Scholarships *482*

Northwest Journalists of Color Scholarship *96*

OLM Malala Yousafzai Scholarship *143*

Religious Affiliation

Baha'i Faith
OLM Malala Yousafzai Scholarship *143*

Baptist
ABCNJ Leadership Impact Scholarship *765*
American Baptist Home Mission Societies
Financial Aid Program *773*
OLM Malala Yousafzai Scholarship *143*
Texas Black Baptist Scholarship *764*

Brethren
OLM Malala Yousafzai Scholarship *143*

Buddhist Faith
OLM Malala Yousafzai Scholarship *143*

Christian
Cynthia H. Kuo Scholarship *759*
Foundation For College Christian Leaders
Scholarship *780*
OLM Malala Yousafzai Scholarship *143*
Scholarships for Success *605*
Young Christian Leaders Scholarship *777*

Disciple of Christ
Help to Save Scholarship *106*
OLM Malala Yousafzai Scholarship *143*

Eastern Orthodox
Alpha Omega Scholarship In Memory Of Peter
Agris *215*
Eastern Orthodox Committee on Scouting
Scholarships *562*
OLM Malala Yousafzai Scholarship *143*

Episcopalian
OLM Malala Yousafzai Scholarship *143*
Stuart & Lucille Armstrong Scholarship *782*

Friends
OLM Malala Yousafzai Scholarship *143*

Hindu Faith
OLM Malala Yousafzai Scholarship *143*

Jewish
Ben Selling Scholarship *518*
Broome and Allen Boys Camp and Scholarship
Fund *774*
Diller Teen Tikkun Olam Awards *624*
Jewish Federation of Metropolitan Chicago
Academic Scholarship Program *742*
JVS Scholarship Program *741*
Lessans Family Scholarship *604*
OLM Malala Yousafzai Scholarship *143*
Sara and Max Goldsammler Scholarship
Fund *754*

Latter-Day Saints
OLM Malala Yousafzai Scholarship *143*

Lutheran
Amelia Kemp Scholarship *771*
Belmer/Flora Prince Scholarship *797*
Developmental Disabilities Scholastic
Achievement Scholarship for College Students
who are Lutheran *254*
OLM Malala Yousafzai Scholarship *143*

Methodist
Bishop Joseph B. Bethea Scholarship *735*
David W. Self Scholarship *778*
E. Craig Brandenburg Graduate Award *781*
Edith M. Allen Scholarship *270*
Helen and Allen Brown Scholarship *781*
Leonard M. Perryman Communications
Scholarship for Ethnic Minority Students *227*
OLM Malala Yousafzai Scholarship *143*
The Rev. Dr. Karen Layman Gift of Hope *781*
Richard S. Smith Scholarship *732*

Muslim Faith
Annual Award Program *779*
ISF National Scholarship *119*
OLM Malala Yousafzai Scholarship *143*

Pentecostal
OLM Malala Yousafzai Scholarship *143*

Presbyterian
National Presbyterian College Scholarship *791*
Native American Supplemental Grant *757*
OLM Malala Yousafzai Scholarship *143*
Samuel Robinson Award *791*
Student Opportunity Scholarship *275*

Protestant
Ed E. and Gladys Hurley Foundation
Scholarship *518*
OLM Malala Yousafzai Scholarship *143*

Roman Catholic
Fourth Degree Pro Deo and Pro Patria
(Canada) *567*
Fourth Degree Pro Deo and Pro Patria
Scholarships *567*
Francis P. Matthews and John E. Swift Educational
Trust Scholarships *567*
Italian Catholic Federation First Year
Scholarship *566*
John W. McDevitt (Fourth Degree)
Scholarships *567*
Mae Lassley Osage Scholarship *758*
OLM Malala Yousafzai Scholarship *143*
Percy J. Johnson Endowed Scholarships *567*
Post High School Tuition Scholarships *776*

Seventh-Day Adventist
OLM Malala Yousafzai Scholarship *143*

Unitarian Universalist
Children of Unitarian Universalist Ministers *796*
Joseph Sumner Smith Scholarship *796*
Marion Barr Stanfield Art Scholarship *145*
OLM Malala Yousafzai Scholarship *143*
Pauly D'Orlando Memorial Art Scholarship *146*
Roy H. Pollack Scholarship *519*
Stanfield and D'Orlando Art Scholarship *146*

Residence

Georgia

Guam

Indiana

Army (ROTC) Reserve Officers Training Corps Two-, Three-, Four-Year Campus-Based Scholarships *610*

Benson & Bingham Annual Scholarship *413*

Blue Grass Energy Academic Scholarship *814*

Classic Scholarships *874*

Clunker Junker Cash for Cars and College Scholarship *299*

Clutch Prep STEM Scholarship *285*

College Access Program (CAP) Grant *743*

Department of Veterans Affairs Tuition Waiver-KY KRS 164-507 *840*

Duck Brand Duct Tape "Stuck at Prom" Scholarship Contest *625*

Early Childhood Development Scholarship *840*

Environmental Protection Scholarship *172*

Finally Sold Impact Maker Scholarship *618*

Frank S. Land Scholarship *588*

Hagan Scholarship *623*

Health Professions Preparatory Scholarship Program *165*

Indian Health Service Health Professions Pre-graduate Scholarships *125*

Inter-County Energy Scholarship *838*

IP Video Contest *838*

Jackson Energy Scholarship Essay Contest *839*

Katharine M. Grosscup Scholarships in Horticulture *386*

Kentucky Educational Excellence Scholarship (KEES) *840*

Kentucky National Guard Tuition Award *699*

Kentucky Society of Certified Public Accountants College Scholarship *87*

Kentucky Transportation Cabinet Civil Engineering Scholarship Program *209*

Kentucky Tuition Grant (KTG) *841*

Levy Law Offices Cincinnati Safe Driver Scholarship *640*

Logan Telephone Cooperative Scholarship *841*

Milton Fisher Scholarship for Innovation and Creativity *862*

Minority Students in Veterinary Medicine Scholarship *719*

Moss Endowed Scholarship *144*

National Don't Text and Drive Scholarship *832*

National Institute for Labor Relations Research William B. Ruggles Journalism Scholarship *650*

National Make It With Wool Competition *345*

National Restaurant Association Educational Foundation Undergraduate Scholarships for College Students *109*

NTA Pat and Jim Host Scholarship *392*

OnlinePsychologyDegrees.com Education Scholarships *656*

Polly Holliday Scholarship *145*

RehabCenter.net *664*

Salt River Electric Scholarship Program *865*

Shelby Energy Cooperative Scholarships *865*

Sidney B. Meadows Scholarship Endowment Fund *389*

Sr. Mary Jeannette Wess, S.N.D. Scholarship *665*

Thrivent Student Resources Scholarship *674*

Tolliver Annual Nursing Scholarship *481*

Two Ten Footwear Foundation Scholarship *676*

Two Ten Foundation Footwear Design Scholarship *874*

U.S. Army ROTC Four-Year College Scholarship *610*

U.S. Army ROTC Four-Year Historically Black College/University Scholarship *610*

U.S. Army ROTC Four-Year Nursing Scholarship *475*

U.S. Army ROTC Guaranteed Reserve Forces Duty (GRFD), (ARNG/USAR) and Dedicated ARNG Scholarships *611*

U.S. Army ROTC Military Junior College (MJC) Scholarship *611*

U.S. Bates Scholarship Program *566*

Women in Rural Electrification (WIRE) Scholarships *840*

You Deserve It! Scholarship *865*

Louisiana

180 Medical College Scholarship Program *797*

2018 Open Essay Competition *682*

AG Bell College Scholarship Program *594*

Annual CGTrader Scholarship *604*

Army ROTC Green to Gold Scholarship Program for Two-Year, Three-Year and Four-Year Scholarships, Active Duty Enlisted Personnel *610*

Army (ROTC) Reserve Officers Training Corps Two-, Three-, Four-Year Campus-Based Scholarships *610*

Benson & Bingham Annual Scholarship *413*

Broadcast Scholarship Program *544*

Classic Scholarships *874*

Clunker Junker Cash for Cars and College Scholarship *299*

Clutch Prep STEM Scholarship *285*

Dixie Boys Baseball Bernie Varnadore Scholarship Program *825*

Dixie Youth Scholarship Program *825*

Duck Brand Duct Tape "Stuck at Prom" Scholarship Contest *625*

Dudley DeBosier Scholarship Program *825*

Ed E. and Gladys Hurley Foundation Scholarship *518*

Finally Sold Impact Maker Scholarship *618*

Frank S. Land Scholarship *588*

Fred R. McDaniel Memorial Scholarship *216*

Gertrude Botts-Saucier Scholarship *584*

Gulf Coast Hurricane Scholarship *196*

Hagan Scholarship *623*

Health Professions Preparatory Scholarship Program *165*

Hoffoss Devall Louisiana Safe Driver Scholarship *626*

Indian Health Service Health Professions Pre-graduate Scholarships *125*

IP Video Contest *838*

Jackson County ARA Scholarship *812*

Jake McClain Driver, KC5WXA, Scholarship *229*

Louisiana Department of Veterans Affairs State Educational Aid Program *712*

Louisiana National Guard State Tuition Exemption Program *699*

Milton Fisher Scholarship for Innovation and Creativity *862*

Minority Students in Veterinary Medicine Scholarship *719*

Moss Endowed Scholarship *144*

National Don't Text and Drive Scholarship *832*

National Institute for Labor Relations Research William B. Ruggles Journalism Scholarship *650*

National Restaurant Association Educational Foundation Undergraduate Scholarships for College Students *109*

OnlinePsychologyDegrees.com Education Scholarships *656*

RehabCenter.net *664*

Rockefeller State Wildlife Scholarship *172*

Sidney B. Meadows Scholarship Endowment Fund *389*

Society of Louisiana CPAs Scholarships *91*

Swayze Woodruff Memorial Mid-South Scholarship *560*

Taylor Opportunity Program for Students Honors Level *842*

Taylor Opportunity Program for Students Opportunity Level *842*

Taylor Opportunity Program for Students Performance Level *842*

Taylor Opportunity Program for Students Tech Level *843*

Thrivent Student Resources Scholarship *674*

Two Ten Footwear Foundation Scholarship *676*

Two Ten Foundation Footwear Design Scholarship *874*

U.S. Army ROTC Four-Year College Scholarship *610*

U.S. Army ROTC Four-Year Historically Black College/University Scholarship *610*

U.S. Army ROTC Four-Year Nursing Scholarship *475*

U.S. Army ROTC Guaranteed Reserve Forces Duty (GRFD), (ARNG/USAR) and Dedicated ARNG Scholarships *611*

U.S. Army ROTC Military Junior College (MJC) Scholarship *611*

U.S. Bates Scholarship Program *566*

Western Fraternal Life National Scholarship *587*

You Deserve It! Scholarship *865*

Maine

180 Medical College Scholarship Program *797*

2018 Open Essay Competition *682*

AG Bell College Scholarship Program *594*

American Legion Auxiliary Department of Maine Daniel E. Lambert Memorial Scholarship *706*

American Legion Auxiliary Department of Maine Past Presidents' Parley Nurses Scholarship *369*

American Legion Department of Maine Children and Youth Scholarship *708*

American Society of Civil Engineers-Maine High School Scholarship *206*

Androscoggin Amateur Radio Club Scholarship *229*

Annual CGTrader Scholarship *604*

Annual Liberty Graphics Art Contest *841*

Army ROTC Green to Gold Scholarship Program for Two-Year, Three-Year and Four-Year Scholarships, Active Duty Enlisted Personnel *610*

Army (ROTC) Reserve Officers Training Corps Two-, Three-, Four-Year Campus-Based Scholarships *610*

Benson & Bingham Annual Scholarship *413*

Blessed Leon of Our Lady of the Rosary Award *756*

Byron Blanchard, N1EKV, Memorial Scholarship *811*

Classic Scholarships *874*

Clunker Junker Cash for Cars and College Scholarship *299*

Clutch Prep STEM Scholarship *285*

CTRI/Chris Seeber, KA1GEU, Memorial Scholarship *268*

Daniel E. Lambert Memorial Scholarship *708*

Dr. James L. Lawson Memorial Scholarship *216*

Duck Brand Duct Tape "Stuck at Prom" Scholarship Contest *625*

EMBARK-Support for the College Journey *843*

Finally Sold Impact Maker Scholarship *618*

Foundation for Seacoast Health Scholarships *373*

Frances L. Booth Medical Scholarship sponsored by LAVFW Department of Maine *375*

Frank S. Land Scholarship *588*

Oregon

180 Medical College Scholarship Program 797
2018 Open Essay Competition 682
AG Bell College Scholarship Program 594
Alert Scholarship 800
American Legion Auxiliary Department of Oregon Department Grants 802
American Legion Auxiliary Department of Oregon National President's Scholarship 802
American Legion Auxiliary Department of Oregon Nurses Scholarship 473
American Legion Auxiliary Department of Oregon Spirit of Youth Scholarship 551
American Legion Department of Oregon High School Oratorical Contest 807
ANDEO Scholarship 857
Annual CGTrader Scholarship 604
Army ROTC Green to Gold Scholarship Program for Two-Year, Three-Year and Four-Year Scholarships, Active Duty Enlisted Personnel 610
Army (ROTC) Reserve Officers Training Corps Two-, Three-, Four-Year Campus-Based Scholarships 610
Asian Reporter Scholarship 600
Audria M. Edwards Scholarship Fund 658
A. Victor Rosenfeld Scholarship 589
Bank of the Cascades Scholarship 857
Benjamin Franklin/Edith Green Scholarship 857
Benson & Bingham Annual Scholarship 413
Blue Wolfe Scholarship 857
Cady McDonnell Memorial Scholarship 530
Chapter 63-Portland James E. Morrow Scholarship 326
Chapter 63-Portland Uncle Bud Smith Scholarship 326
Charles Patrick Scholarship 335
Chester and Helen Luther Scholarship 376
Clark-Phelps Scholarship 256
Classic Scholarships 874
Clunker Junker Cash for Cars and College Scholarship 299
Clutch Prep STEM Scholarship 285
Dorothy Campbell Memorial Scholarship 858
Duck Brand Duct Tape "Stuck at Prom" Scholarship Contest 625
Ernest Alan and Barbara Park Meyer Scholarship Fund 857
Finally Sold Impact Maker Scholarship 618
Ford Opportunity Program 830, 858
Ford ReStart Program 830
Ford Restart Program 858
Ford Scholars Program 830, 858
Frank S. Land Scholarship 588
Franz Stenzel M.D. and Kathryn Stenzel II Scholarship 858
Franz Stenzel M.D. and Kathryn Stenzel Scholarship 376
Franz Stenzel M.D. and Kathryn Stenzel Scholarship Fund 376
Friends of Bill Rutherford Education Fund 857
Glenn Jackson Scholars Scholarships 590
Hagan Scholarship 623
Harry Ludwig Memorial Scholarship 692
HB Design Scholarship 365
Health Professions Preparatory Scholarship Program 165
Hispanic Metropolitan Chamber Scholarships 626
Huffstutter Family Stylist Scholarship 241
Ida M. Crawford Scholarship 858
Indian Health Service Health Professions Pre-graduate Scholarships 125
IP Video Contest 838
Jackson Foundation Journalism Scholarship 407

Jackson Foundation Journalism Scholarship Fund 407
James Carlson Memorial Scholarship 274
Jeffrey Alan Scoggins Memorial Scholarship 323
Jim and Dianna Murphy Scholarship 537
John Mark Turetzky Scholarship 376
Kerdragon Scholarship 143
Law Enforcement and Criminal Justice College Scholarship Program 243
Lois Manley, K7LMZ, and Randall Pitchford, WW7ZZ, Scholarship 206
Lynda Pilger Memorial Scholarship 858
Maria C. Jackson/General George A. White Scholarship 859
Mary Duby Honderich Scholarship 859
Mary E. Horstkotte Scholarship Fund 857
Mary Elizabeth Guest Scholarship 526
Mary Lou Brown Scholarship 812
Milton Fisher Scholarship for Innovation and Creativity 862
Minority Students in Veterinary Medicine Scholarship 719
Moss Endowed Scholarship 144
National Don't Text and Drive Scholarship 832
National Institute for Labor Relations Research William B. Ruggles Journalism Scholarship 650
National League for Nursing Ella McKinney Scholarship 486
National Make It With Wool Competition 345
National Restaurant Association Educational Foundation Undergraduate Scholarships for College Students 109
NLN Ella McKinney Scholarship Fund 486
Northwest Danish Association Scholarship 753
NWFEDA—Northwest Fire Equipment Dealers Association Scholarship 350
OAB Foundation Scholarship 221
OAIA Scholarship 90
OnlinePsychologyDegrees.com Education Scholarships 656
Oregon Albacore Commission Scholarship 859
Oregon Community Quarterback Scholarship 624
Oregon Head Start Association—Frank Roberts Scholarship 859
Oregon Sheep Growers Association Memorial Scholarship 110
Oregon State Fiscal Association Scholarship 574
Oregon Student Access Commission Employee and Dependents Scholarship 859
Oregon Wine Brotherhood Scholarship 249
Pacific NW Federal Credit Union Scholarship 859
Peter Crossley Memorial Scholarship 859
Pride Foundation Scholarship Program 662
RehabCenter.net 664
Royden M. Bodley Scholarship 343
Rube and Minah Leslie Educational Fund 857
Salem Electric Cooperative Scholarship 859
Salem Foundation Ansel & Marie Solie Scholarship 692
Sehar Saleha Ahmad and Abrahim Ekramullah Zafar Foundation Scholarship 127
SEIU Local 503/OPEU Student Financial Aid Scholarship 860
Society of American Military Engineers Portland Post Scholarship 195
Teacher Education Scholarship 274
Technical Training Fund Scholarship 143
Thrivent Student Resources Scholarship 674
Two Ten Footwear Foundation Scholarship 676
Two Ten Foundation Footwear Design Scholarship 874

U.S. Army ROTC Four-Year College Scholarship 610
U.S. Army ROTC Four-Year Historically Black College/University Scholarship 610
U.S. Army ROTC Four-Year Nursing Scholarship 475
U.S. Army ROTC Guaranteed Reserve Forces Duty (GRFD), (ARNG/USAR) and Dedicated ARNG Scholarships 611
U.S. Army ROTC Military Junior College (MJC) Scholarship 611
U.S. Bates Scholarship Program 566
Walter C. and Marie C. Schmidt Scholarship 486
W.C. and Pearl Campbell Scholarship 860
Western Association of State Highway and Transportation Officials Scholarship 541
Western Fraternal Life National Scholarship 587
WICHE's Western Undergraduate Exchange (WUE) 683
William Bennett, W7PHO, Memorial Scholarship 813
William E. Keene Memorial Scholarship 335
Wilse Morgan, WX7P, Memorial ARRL Northwestern Division Scholarship 177
You Deserve It! Scholarship 865

Pennsylvania

180 Medical College Scholarship Program 797
2018 Open Essay Competition 682
AG Bell College Scholarship Program 594
Allegheny Mountain Section Air & Waste Management Association Scholarship 336
Alphonse A. Miele Scholarship 679
American Legion Auxiliary Department of Pennsylvania Past Department Presidents' Memorial Scholarship 473
American Legion Auxiliary Department of Pennsylvania Scholarship for Dependents of Disabled or Deceased Veterans 802
American Legion Auxiliary Department of Pennsylvania Scholarship for Dependents of Living Veterans 596
American Legion Department of Pennsylvania High School Oratorical Contest 808
Annual CGTrader Scholarship 604
Army ROTC Green to Gold Scholarship Program for Two-Year, Three-Year and Four-Year Scholarships, Active Duty Enlisted Personnel 610
Army (ROTC) Reserve Officers Training Corps Two-, Three-, Four-Year Campus-Based Scholarships 610
Benson & Bingham Annual Scholarship 413
Bernard and Carolyn Torraco Memorial Nursing Scholarship Program 679
Beulah Frey Environmental Scholarship 338
Blind or Deaf Beneficiary Grant Program 658
Careers Through Culinary Arts Program Cooking Competition for Scholarships 246
Christopher Demetris Scholarship 737
Classic Scholarships 874
Clunker Junker Cash for Cars and College Scholarship 299
Clutch Prep STEM Scholarship 285
DiMattio Celli Family Study Abroad Scholarship 679
Dimitri J. Ververelli Memorial Scholarship for Architecture and/or Engineering 134
Dr. Nicholas Padis Memorial Graduate Scholarship 738
Dr. Peter A. Theodos Memorial Graduate Scholarship 374
Dorizas Memorial Scholarship 738
Duck Brand Duct Tape "Stuck at Prom" Scholarship Contest 625
Ella T. Grasso Literary Scholarship 680

Patty & Melvin Alperin First Generation Scholarship *863*

Pierre H. Guillemette Scholarship *532*

Ravenscroft Family Award *756*

RDW Group Inc. Minority Scholarship for Communications *224*

RehabCenter.net *664*

Rhode Island Association of Former Legislators Scholarship *863*

Rhode Island Commission on Women/Freda Goldman Education Award *863*

Rhode Island Pilots Association Scholarship *159*

Rhode Island Society of Certified Public Accountants Scholarship *91*

Roothbert Fund Inc. Scholarship *864*

Seol Bong Scholarship *693*

Shaw-Worth Memorial Scholarship *836*

Stephen Phillips Memorial Scholarship Fund, Inc. *869*

Timothy and Palmer W. Bigelow Jr., Scholarship *101*

Two Ten Footwear Foundation Scholarship *676*

Two Ten Foundation Footwear Design Scholarship *874*

United Italian American Inc. Scholarship *864*

U.S. Army ROTC Four-Year College Scholarship *610*

U.S. Army ROTC Four-Year Historically Black College/University Scholarship *610*

U.S. Army ROTC Four-Year Nursing Scholarship *475*

U.S. Army ROTC Guaranteed Reserve Forces Duty (GRFD), (ARNG/USAR) and Dedicated ARNG Scholarships *611*

U.S. Army ROTC Military Junior College (MJC) Scholarship *611*

U.S. Bates Scholarship Program *566*

Willard & Marjorie Scheibe Nursing Scholarship *487*

Yankee Clipper Contest Club Youth Scholarship *813*

South Carolina

180 Medical College Scholarship Program *797*

2018 Open Essay Competition *682*

AG Bell College Scholarship Program *594*

Annual CGTrader Scholarship *604*

Army ROTC Green to Gold Scholarship Program for Two-Year, Three-Year and Four-Year Scholarships, Active Duty Enlisted Personnel *610*

Army (ROTC) Reserve Officers Training Corps Two-, Three-, Four-Year Campus-Based Scholarships *610*

Benson & Bingham Annual Scholarship *413*

Classic Scholarships *874*

Clunker Junker Cash for Cars and College Scholarship *299*

Clutch Prep STEM Scholarship *285*

Dixie Boys Baseball Bernie Varnadore Scholarship Program *825*

Dixie Youth Scholarship Program *825*

Duck Brand Duct Tape "Stuck at Prom" Scholarship Contest *625*

Finally Sold Impact Maker Scholarship *618*

Frank S. Land Scholarship *588*

Hagan Scholarship *623*

Health Professions Preparatory Scholarship Program *165*

Helen James Brewer Scholarship *383*

Indian Health Service Health Professions Pre-graduate Scholarships *125*

IP Video Contest *838*

James Cothran, KD3NI, Scholarship *812*

James F. Byrnes Scholarship *631*

Milton Fisher Scholarship for Innovation and Creativity *862*

Minority Students in Veterinary Medicine Scholarship *719*

Moss Endowed Scholarship *144*

National Don't Text and Drive Scholarship *832*

National Institute for Labor Relations Research William B. Ruggles Journalism Scholarship *650*

National Restaurant Association Educational Foundation Undergraduate Scholarships for College Students *109*

OnlinePsychologyDegrees.com Education Scholarships *656*

Palmetto Fellows Scholarship Program *868*

Polly Holliday Scholarship *145*

RehabCenter.net *664*

Richland/Lexington SCSEA Scholarship *579*

SCACPA Educational Fund Scholarships *92*

Sidney B. Meadows Scholarship Endowment Fund *389*

South Carolina HOPE Scholarship *868*

South Carolina Need-Based Grants Program *868*

South Carolina Tourism and Hospitality Educational Foundation Scholarships *250*

South Carolina Tuition Grants Program *669*

Ted G. Wilson Memorial Scholarship Foundation *211*

Thrivent Student Resources Scholarship *674*

Tuition Assistance for Certain War Veterans' Children *716*

Two Ten Footwear Foundation Scholarship *676*

Two Ten Foundation Footwear Design Scholarship *874*

U.S. Army ROTC Four-Year College Scholarship *610*

U.S. Army ROTC Four-Year Historically Black College/University Scholarship *610*

U.S. Army ROTC Four-Year Nursing Scholarship *475*

U.S. Army ROTC Guaranteed Reserve Forces Duty (GRFD), (ARNG/USAR) and Dedicated ARNG Scholarships *611*

U.S. Army ROTC Military Junior College (MJC) Scholarship *611*

U.S. Bates Scholarship Program *566*

Watson-Brown Foundation Scholarship *877*

You Deserve It! Scholarship *865*

South Dakota

180 Medical College Scholarship Program *797*

2018 Open Essay Competition *682*

AG Bell College Scholarship Program *594*

Alert Scholarship *800*

American Legion Auxiliary Department of South Dakota College Scholarships *551*

American Legion Auxiliary Department of South Dakota Senior Scholarship *551*

American Legion Department of South Dakota High School Oratorical Contest *808*

Annual CGTrader Scholarship *604*

Army ROTC Green to Gold Scholarship Program for Two-Year, Three-Year and Four-Year Scholarships, Active Duty Enlisted Personnel *610*

Army (ROTC) Reserve Officers Training Corps Two-, Three-, Four-Year Campus-Based Scholarships *610*

Benson & Bingham Annual Scholarship *413*

Carol Bauhs Benson Scholarship *252*

Classic Scholarships *874*

Clunker Junker Cash for Cars and College Scholarship *299*

Clutch Prep STEM Scholarship *285*

Come 2 Iowa (C2IA) Senior Scholarship *631*

Duck Brand Duct Tape "Stuck at Prom" Scholarship Contest *625*

Finally Sold Impact Maker Scholarship *618*

Frank S. Land Scholarship *588*

Hagan Scholarship *623*

Health Professions Preparatory Scholarship Program *165*

Indian Health Service Health Professions Pre-graduate Scholarships *125*

IP Video Contest *838*

L. Phil and Alice J. Wicker Scholarship *217*

Milton Fisher Scholarship for Innovation and Creativity *862*

Minority Students in Veterinary Medicine Scholarship *719*

Moss Endowed Scholarship *144*

National Don't Text and Drive Scholarship *832*

National Institute for Labor Relations Research William B. Ruggles Journalism Scholarship *650*

National Make It With Wool Competition *345*

National Restaurant Association Educational Foundation Undergraduate Scholarships for College Students *109*

OnlinePsychologyDegrees.com Education Scholarships *656*

PFund Foundation Scholarship Program *861*

Printing Industry Midwest Education Foundation Scholarship Fund *222*

RehabCenter.net *664*

South Dakota Board of Regents Annis I. Fowler/Kaden Scholarship *276*

South Dakota Board of Regents Bjugstad Scholarship *104*

South Dakota Opportunity Scholarship *869*

Stanley Moore FUI Foundation Regional Scholarship *855*

Thrivent Student Resources Scholarship *674*

Two Ten Footwear Foundation Scholarship *676*

Two Ten Foundation Footwear Design Scholarship *874*

U.S. Army ROTC Four-Year College Scholarship *610*

U.S. Army ROTC Four-Year Historically Black College/University Scholarship *610*

U.S. Army ROTC Four-Year Nursing Scholarship *475*

U.S. Army ROTC Guaranteed Reserve Forces Duty (GRFD), (ARNG/USAR) and Dedicated ARNG Scholarships *611*

U.S. Army ROTC Military Junior College (MJC) Scholarship *611*

U.S. Bates Scholarship Program *566*

Western Fraternal Life National Scholarship *587*

WICHE's Western Undergraduate Exchange (WUE) *683*

You Deserve It! Scholarship *865*

Tennessee

180 Medical College Scholarship Program *797*

2018 Open Essay Competition *682*

AG Bell College Scholarship Program *594*

Alphonse A. Miele Scholarship *679*

American Legion Department of Tennessee Eagle Scout of the Year *556*

American Legion Department of Tennessee High School Oratorical Contest *808*

Annual CGTrader Scholarship *604*

Army ROTC Green to Gold Scholarship Program for Two-Year, Three-Year and Four-Year Scholarships, Active Duty Enlisted Personnel *610*

Army (ROTC) Reserve Officers Training Corps Two-, Three-, Four-Year Campus-Based Scholarships *610*

Benson & Bingham Annual Scholarship *413*

Washington

Wyoming

CANADA

Alberta

National Restaurant Association Educational
Foundation Undergraduate Scholarships for
College Students *109*
Northern Alberta Development Council
Bursary *251*
Persons Case Scholarships *721*
Prairie Baseball Academy Scholarships *800*
Queen Elizabeth II Golden Jubilee Citizenship
Medal *721*
Registered Apprenticeship Program/Career and
Technologies Studies (RAPS/CTS)
Scholarships *535*
RehabCenter.net *664*
Rutherford Scholars *721*
Simmons and Fletcher, P.C., Law Marketing
Scholarship *668*
TAC Foundation Scholarships *213*
Teletoon Animation Scholarship *145*
Terry Fox Humanitarian Award *673*
Tiessen Foundation Broadcast Scholarship *542*
Winspear Fund *452*
You Deserve It! Scholarship *865*

British Columbia
AG Bell College Scholarship Program *594*
Annual CGTrader Scholarship *604*
Benson & Bingham Annual Scholarship *413*
Bill Mason Scholarship Fund *275*
Canadian Bates Scholarship Program *566*
Clunker Junker Cash for Cars and College
Scholarship *299*
Duck Brand Duct Tape "Stuck at Prom"
Scholarship Contest *625*
Jim Bourque Scholarship *267*
Leo J. Krysa Undergraduate Scholarship *138*
National Restaurant Association Educational
Foundation Undergraduate Scholarships for
College Students *109*
Simmons and Fletcher, P.C., Law Marketing
Scholarship · *668*
TAC Foundation Scholarships *213*
Teletoon Animation Scholarship *145*
Terry Fox Humanitarian Award *673*
You Deserve It! Scholarship *865*

Manitoba
180 Medical College Scholarship Program *797*
AG Bell College Scholarship Program *594*
Annual CGTrader Scholarship *604*
Benson & Bingham Annual Scholarship *413*
Bill Mason Scholarship Fund *275*
Canadian Bates Scholarship Program *566*
Clunker Junker Cash for Cars and College
Scholarship *299*
Duck Brand Duct Tape "Stuck at Prom"
Scholarship Contest *625*
Jim Bourque Scholarship *267*
Leo J. Krysa Undergraduate Scholarship *138*
National Restaurant Association Educational
Foundation Undergraduate Scholarships for
College Students *109*
OnlinePsychologyDegrees.com Education
Scholarships *656*
RehabCenter.net *664*
Simmons and Fletcher, P.C., Law Marketing
Scholarship *668*
TAC Foundation Scholarships *213*
Teletoon Animation Scholarship *145*
Terry Fox Humanitarian Award *673*
You Deserve It! Scholarship *865*

New Brunswick
AG Bell College Scholarship Program *594*
Annual CGTrader Scholarship *604*
Benson & Bingham Annual Scholarship *413*
Bill Mason Scholarship Fund *275*
Canadian Bates Scholarship Program *566*

Clunker Junker Cash for Cars and College
Scholarship *299*
Duck Brand Duct Tape "Stuck at Prom"
Scholarship Contest *625*
Jim Bourque Scholarship *267*
Leo J. Krysa Undergraduate Scholarship *138*
National Restaurant Association Educational
Foundation Undergraduate Scholarships for
College Students *109*
RehabCenter.net *664*
Simmons and Fletcher, P.C., Law Marketing
Scholarship *668*
TAC Foundation Scholarships *213*
Teletoon Animation Scholarship *145*
Terry Fox Humanitarian Award *673*
You Deserve It! Scholarship *865*

Newfoundland
AG Bell College Scholarship Program *594*
Annual CGTrader Scholarship *604*
Benson & Bingham Annual Scholarship *413*
Bill Mason Scholarship Fund *275*
Canadian Bates Scholarship Program *566*
Clunker Junker Cash for Cars and College
Scholarship *299*
Duck Brand Duct Tape "Stuck at Prom"
Scholarship Contest *625*
Jim Bourque Scholarship *267*
Leo J. Krysa Undergraduate Scholarship *138*
National Restaurant Association Educational
Foundation Undergraduate Scholarships for
College Students *109*
RehabCenter.net *664*
Simmons and Fletcher, P.C., Law Marketing
Scholarship *668*
TAC Foundation Scholarships *213*
Teletoon Animation Scholarship *145*
Terry Fox Humanitarian Award *673*
You Deserve It! Scholarship *865*

Northwest Territories
AG Bell College Scholarship Program *594*
Annual CGTrader Scholarship *604*
Benson & Bingham Annual Scholarship *413*
Bill Mason Scholarship Fund *275*
Canadian Bates Scholarship Program *566*
Clunker Junker Cash for Cars and College
Scholarship *299*
Duck Brand Duct Tape "Stuck at Prom"
Scholarship Contest *625*
Jim Bourque Scholarship *267*
Leo J. Krysa Undergraduate Scholarship *138*
National Restaurant Association Educational
Foundation Undergraduate Scholarships for
College Students *109*
OnlinePsychologyDegrees.com Education
Scholarships *656*
Simmons and Fletcher, P.C., Law Marketing
Scholarship *668*
TAC Foundation Scholarships *213*
Teletoon Animation Scholarship *145*
Terry Fox Humanitarian Award *673*
You Deserve It! Scholarship *865*

Nova Scotia
AG Bell College Scholarship Program *594*
Annual CGTrader Scholarship *604*
Benson & Bingham Annual Scholarship *413*
Bill Mason Scholarship Fund *275*
Canadian Bates Scholarship Program *566*
Clunker Junker Cash for Cars and College
Scholarship *299*
Duck Brand Duct Tape "Stuck at Prom"
Scholarship Contest *625*
Jim Bourque Scholarship *267*
Leo J. Krysa Undergraduate Scholarship *138*

National Restaurant Association Educational
Foundation Undergraduate Scholarships for
College Students *109*
Simmons and Fletcher, P.C., Law Marketing
Scholarship *668*
TAC Foundation Scholarships *213*
Teletoon Animation Scholarship *145*
Terry Fox Humanitarian Award *673*
You Deserve It! Scholarship *865*

Ontario
AG Bell College Scholarship Program *594*
Annual CGTrader Scholarship *604*
Army ROTC Green to Gold Scholarship Program
for Two-Year, Three-Year and Four-Year
Scholarships, Active Duty Enlisted
Personnel *610*
Army (ROTC) Reserve Officers Training Corps
Two-, Three-, Four-Year Campus-Based
Scholarships *610*
Benson & Bingham Annual Scholarship *413*
Bill Mason Scholarship Fund *275*
Clunker Junker Cash for Cars and College
Scholarship *299*
Duck Brand Duct Tape "Stuck at Prom"
Scholarship Contest *625*
Jim Bourque Scholarship *267*
Leo J. Krysa Undergraduate Scholarship *138*
National Restaurant Association Educational
Foundation Undergraduate Scholarships for
College Students *109*
OnlinePsychologyDegrees.com Education
Scholarships *656*
Simmons and Fletcher, P.C., Law Marketing
Scholarship *668*
TAC Foundation Scholarships *213*
Teletoon Animation Scholarship *145*
Terry Fox Humanitarian Award *673*
Two Ten Footwear Foundation Scholarship *676*
U.S. Army ROTC Four-Year Historically Black
College/University Scholarship *610*
U.S. Army ROTC Four-Year Nursing
Scholarship *475*
You Deserve It! Scholarship *865*

Prince Edward Island
AG Bell College Scholarship Program *594*
Annual CGTrader Scholarship *604*
Benson & Bingham Annual Scholarship *413*
Bill Mason Scholarship Fund *275*
Canadian Bates Scholarship Program *566*
Clunker Junker Cash for Cars and College
Scholarship *299*
Duck Brand Duct Tape "Stuck at Prom"
Scholarship Contest *625*
Jim Bourque Scholarship *267*
Leo J. Krysa Undergraduate Scholarship *138*
National Restaurant Association Educational
Foundation Undergraduate Scholarships for
College Students *109*
RehabCenter.net *664*
Simmons and Fletcher, P.C., Law Marketing
Scholarship *668*
TAC Foundation Scholarships *213*
Teletoon Animation Scholarship *145*
Terry Fox Humanitarian Award *673*
You Deserve It! Scholarship *865*

Quebec
AG Bell College Scholarship Program *594*
Annual CGTrader Scholarship *604*
Benson & Bingham Annual Scholarship *413*
Bill Mason Scholarship Fund *275*
Canadian Bates Scholarship Program *566*
Clunker Junker Cash for Cars and College
Scholarship *299*
Jim Bourque Scholarship *267*

Talent/Interest Area

NOTES

NOTES

NOTES

NOTES

NOTES

NOTES

NOTES